HOW TO USE THIS BOOK

1. If you know the name of your plant, the problem it has, or the insect that is bothering it, look up that name in the index beginning on **PAGE 17**.

2. If you don't know the name of your plant, turn to one of these sections:

3. If you have a household pest and don't know its name, turn to **PAGE 799**.

4. If you want to know more about a problem, turn to one of these pages:

5. For a complete description of ORTHO products and a list of the problems each solves, turn to **PAGE 921**.

THE ORTHO PROBLEM SOLVER

THE ORTHO PROBLEM SOLVER

Edited by Michael D. Smith

Ortho Information Services
San Francisco, California

Associate Editor
Julia W. Hall

Researcher/writers
Clare A. Binko
Gene Joyner
Deni W. Stein
Lauren B. Swezey

Writer, houseplant section
Robert D. Raabe

Designers
John A. Williams
Barbara Ziller

Photographic Editor
Michael D. McKinley

Production Manager
Laurie S. Blackman

Indexer
Elinor Lindheimer

Copy Editors
Jessie Wood
Scott Lowe
Nancy Cooney

Research Assistant
Ann Tweed

Editorial Assistants
Wade F. Anderson
Alice E. Mace
William F. Yusavage

Typographer
George Lithograph

Color Separation
Color Tech

Publisher
Robert L. Iacopi

Editorial Director
Min S. Yee

Chevron Chemical Company
575 Market Street, San Francisco, CA 94105

To the members of the Cooperative Extension Service, who have been solving America's garden problems since 1914.

PREFACE

We at Ortho, as publishers of gardening books and as manufacturers of a leading line of garden chemicals, have been very aware of the difficulty experienced by home gardeners in finding information about plant problems. This book is an attempt to make that information conveniently accessible to every gardener.

Our goal in writing *The Ortho Problem Solver* has been to help the reader:

1. Diagnose a problem correctly.
2. Understand what is causing it.
3. Find a solution.

We have avoided using terms that are known only to horticulturists or experienced gardeners, but if you want to know these terms, there is a glossary on page 216. We have tried to give you only the information that you need to solve your specific problem, but if you want to know more about it, we refer you to pages that give more information.

Our first step in writing *The Ortho Problem Solver* was to gather plant lists from more than 200 horticulturists in all parts of the country. These lists represented nearly all of the plants grown in the homes and gardens of each state. From this information, we compiled a list of the most popular house and garden plants.

Then we sent this list to professionals in the fields of plant problem-solving — entomologists, plant pathologists, and Cooperative Extension agents — and asked them to tell us about the most serious problems these plants had in their part of the country. From this information we compiled the plant problems included in *The Ortho Problem Solver*.

We gave the task of writing the houseplant section to an expert — Dr. Robert Raabe, Extension Plant Pathologist at the University of California, Berkeley, and a specialist in the problems of houseplants.

Information about problems of garden plants and their solutions come from our own scientists at Ortho and from the Cooperative Extension services of each of the states. We consulted the Cooperative Extension because Extension scientists have had the opportunity to study the most severe problems in their state. Also, since Extension literature is constantly updated, we knew the information would be current.

Some of the most difficult information to locate concerned the range of each problem — the information on the small maps that accompany each problem. Although we feel it is important for a reader to know whether a certain problem is serious in his area, the range of most of these problems is tenuous and constantly changing. A problem may be severe in one county and nonexistent in the next. At best, these maps represent a generalization and an approximization. If a map needs to be adjusted for your area, please let us know. We will refine the maps in future editions so they reflect as accurately as possible constantly changing situations.

A word of explanation is needed about the solutions we offer. The "Solution" section of each problem assumes that you have seen the problem at the time when the symptoms first become obvious. Our solution begins by telling you what you can do right now to alleviate that problem. Then it tells you what changes you can make in the environment or in your gardening practices to prevent the return of that problem. In

many cases, this involves a chemical spray as an immediate solution, and a cultural change or a resistant variety as a long-range solution.

We offer several solutions for most of the problems in this book. We leave it to your judgment to choose those most appropriate to your situation. For example, we tell you that you can protect your sycamore tree from anthracnose by spraying it with a fungicide in the spring. If your sycamore is six feet high, you might choose to spray it next spring. But if it is 40 feet high, you will find that hiring an arborist to spray it will be expensive. From our description of the problem, you know that anthracnose seldom does permanent harm to the tree, so you may choose to do nothing.

We recommend Ortho products by brand name in this book because we are a part of Chevron Chemical Company, which manufactures these products, and we can vouch for their quality and consistency. If Ortho does not make a product to solve a problem, we recommend chemical solutions by their generic names — the common name of the active ingredient. When we recommend chemicals by the names of their active ingredients, we say to apply a product "that contains" the active ingredient. This wording alerts you to the fact that you may not find a product by that name, but must look on the list of active ingredients on the product labels. Ask your garden center professional to help you select a product.

When we recommend an Ortho product, we know that it will do the job for which we recommend it, and that it will not harm your plant if you use it according to label directions. But when choosing products by a generic name — even if these are Ortho products — read the label carefully. Although all *malathion* is the same, all products containing it are not. Even though we know *malathion* will solve a particular problem and tell you so, some products that contain *malathion* may be manufactured for a different purpose, and may injure your plant. Be sure that the plant you wish to spray is listed on the product label.

Also, since we can't know the individual circumstances of your problem, the solutions we offer are not guaranteed. We offer the best general proposals we know for helping to solve common garden problems, but we do not and cannot assume liability for failure of our recommendations to solve any particular problem or for any injury that comes as a result of following these instructions. Always read pesticide labels carefully and follow the label directions to the letter.

Since you are the ultimate judge of how successful we have been in helping you to solve your garden problems, we invite you to tell us of any inaccuracy or omission you find in *The Ortho Problem Solver*. We hope, with your help, to make the book ever more useful to the home gardener. Please send your comments to:

The Ortho Problem Solver
Ortho Information Services
Chevron Chemical Company
P.O. Box 3744
San Francisco, CA 94119

CONSULTANTS

This has been a vast project and we have received help from hundreds of people — members of the Cooperative Extension Service, horticulturists, nursery professionals, and knowledgeable amateur gardeners. The following names are those of major consultants — people who spent many hours checking manuscripts for accuracy and who patiently answered our questions about fine points of obscure garden problems. The accuracy and validity of this book are due to their careful work.

Dr. James Beutel
Extension Pomologist
University of California, Davis

Bartow H. Bridges, Jr.
Landscape Architect and
    Horticulturist
Virginia Beach, VA

Dr. G. Douglas Crater
Extension Horticulturist,
    Floriculture
University of Georgia

Dr. T. E. Crocker
Professor of Fruit Crops
University of Florida

Dr. J. A. Crozier
Chevron Chemical Company
San Francisco, CA

Dr. Spencer H. Davis, Jr.
Horticultural Consultant
Milltown, NJ

Dr. Clyde Elmore
Extension Weed Scientist
University of California, Davis

Dr. James R. Feucht
Extension Professor,
    Department of Horticulture
Colorado State University

Dr. Ralph Garren, Jr.
Small Fruit Specialist
Cooperative Extension Service
Oregon State University

Duane Hatch
Cooperative Extension Service
Utah State University

Dr. Sammy Helmers
Area Extension Horticulturist
Stevenville, TX

Kermit Hildahl
Cooperative Extension
University of Missouri

Everett E. Janne
Landscape Horticulturist
Texas Agricultural Extension Service
College Station, TX

Dr. Ron Jones
Department of Plant Pathology
North Carolina State University

Dr. Charles Marr
Extension Horticulturist
Kansas State University

Bernard Moore
Extension Plant Diagnostician, Retired
Oregon State University

Dr. Norman F. Oebker
Vegetables Specialist
Cooperative Extension Service
University of Arizona

Dr. Howard Ohr
Plant Pathologist
Cooperative Extension Service
University of California, Riverside

PREFACE

Dr. Albert O. Paulus
Plant Pathologist
University of California, Riverside

Dr. Charles C. Powell, Jr.
Department of Plant Pathology
Ohio State University

Dr. Charles Sacamano
Professor of Horticulture
University of Arizona

Professor Donald Schuder
Extension Entomologist
Purdue University

Dr. Arden Sherf
Professor, Department of Pathology
Cornell University

Dr. Walter Stevenson
Associate Professor of
  Plant Pathology
University of Wisconsin

William Titus
County Coordinator
Cooperative Extension Service
Plainview, NY

Dr. John Tomkins
Associate Professor of Pomology
Cornell University

Carl A. Totemeier
Director
Old Westbury Gardens
Old Westbury, NY

John White
County Extension Agent —
  Horticulture
El Paso, TX

Dr. Gayle Worf
Extension Plant Pathologist
University of Wisconsin

SPECIAL CONSULTANTS

Many other gardening professionals and gifted amateurs have shared their experience and wisdom with us. The people on the following list are specialists in particular problems. They have often been able to supply answers when nobody else could, and we are deeply indebted to them for their contribution to *The Ortho Problem Solver*.

Dr. Eugene Brady
Professor of Entomology
University of Georgia

Dr. Maynard Cummings
Extension Wildlife Specialist
University of California, Davis

Dr. August De Hertogh
Department of Horticultural Science
North Carolina State University

Dr. M. Ali Harivandi
Cooperative Extension Service
University of California, Berkeley

Phil Horne
Mosley Nurseries
Lake Worth, FL

Joseph R. Konwinski
Turfgrass Consultant
Lake Worth, FL

Dr. Lloyd A. Lider
Professor of Viticulture
University of California, Davis

John Pehrson
Extension Agent
Parlier, CA

Warren G. Roberts
U.C. Davis Arboretum Superintendent
University of California, Davis

Donald Rosedale
Cooperative Extension Service
University of California, Riverside

Dr. Terrel P. Salmon
Extension Wildlife Specialist
University of California, Davis

Ross R. Sanborn
University of California
Farm Advisor
Contra Costa County, California

Joseph Savage
Entomologist
Cooperative Extension Service
Cornell University

Arthur Slater
Senior Environmental Health and
  Safety Technologist
University of California, Berkeley

Richard Tassan
Staff Research Assistant
University of California, Berkeley

Dr. O. Clifton Taylor
Statewide Air Pollution Research Center
University of California, Riverside

PHOTOGRAPHERS

In order to make *The Ortho Problem Solver* as useful as possible, we have published a color photograph of every problem in the book. Gathering this many photographs was a tremendous task. We relied extensively on college professors and county extension agents for photographic contributions. Many of the photographs were taken originally for use in teaching students or the public about plant problems. We wish to thank the following photographers for their invaluable assistance in supplying these photographs.

After each photographer's name, we have listed the pages on which their photographs appear. The letter that follows the page number shows the position of the photograph on the page, from left to right. A lower-case letter "i" refers to an insert photograph.

American Phytopathological
Society: 256B
  K. Hickey: 615C (also on cover)
  Kirby: 723B
  A.A. MacNab: 735Bi, 742Ai
  J.R. McGrew: 748A
  A.F. Sherf: 727B, 733B, 736B
  T.B. Sutton: 662C
  K. Yoder: 657B

Ralph J. Adkins: 450C, 459A, 478B, 481B, 489B, 496C, 512C, 516A, 541C, 556C, 572C, 583B, 594A, 604A, 609B, 621B, 699Ai, 699Bi, 715Ai, 716B, 725A, 740B, 747B, 766B, 782C, 787A, 794B, 828C, 829C, 835C, 839A, 842C, 849B, 852C, 878C

Airrigation Engineering
Co., Inc.: 459C

William W. Allen: 634A, 634B, 670C

Arthur L. Antonelli: 587A

William C. Aplin: 318B

Max E. Badgley: 229A, 619C, 635C (also on cover), 643C, 643Ci, 644A, 666Bi, 679, 745A, 790A, 801B, 802A, 808B, 812B, 815B, 816C, 878B, 880A, 881B, 883C, 884C, 885A, 885C, 887Ai

J.R. Baker: 492A, 534B, 570B

D.R. Bienz: 866A, 866C

Ray R. Bingham: 625C, 634C, 699C, 744A

John Blaustein: 902A, 917A, 919C

Allen Boger: 255B, 294B, 295B, 298B, 302B, 314B, 317A, 326A, 327B, 350C, 351B, 440B, 445C, 451B, 453A, 454C, 461A, 465C, 466C, 467C, 468C, 469B, 471B, 479A, 480C, 487A, 499C, 502A, 504A, 504Ai, 513A, 516C, 518A, 522C, 539B, 545C, 565C, 585B, 594B, 598B, 604B, 614B, 618A, 618C, 622A, 681A, 682B, 682C, 683B, 684B, 686C, 687B, 688A, 699B, 700B, 702B, 702C, 704A, 706B, 710B, 714A, 731C, 743A, 743C, 749B, 762B, 778C, 779A, 786A, 786B, 792Ci, 793B, 860B, 860C, 873B, 892A, 898C, 900B, 901B, 903C, 912C

R. Harper Brame: 462C, 477B, 501B, 521C, 537A, 566C (also on cover), 572Ci, 573B, 582C, 593B, 610B, 668B, 688C, 699A, 702Ai, 729A, 740A, 788C, 790B

Bartow H. Bridges, Jr.: 305B, 312C, 440C, 454A, 460A, 467A, 489A, 490A, 491C, 511C, 528B, 528C, 540C, 558B, 864B, 904A, 919A

Jackie D. Butler: 300A, 307B, 311C

Ralph S. Byther: 238B, 269C, 290C, 299A, 335B, 350A, 410C, 411A, 429C, 430A, 445B, 470B, 470C, 474C, 483Ai, 492C, 495A, 501C, 506C, 507C, 509C, 523C, 527C, 555B, 556A, 559B, 560B, 565A, 565Ai, 571B, 575A, 586B, 589B, 600B, 619Bi, 626A, 628C, 629C, 633B, 639C, 651C, 656A, 662A, 669A, 672A, 675B, 675C, 675Ci, 688B, 701C, 708A, 708B, 709C, 710A, 711C, 712A, 712B, 719C, 720A, 722C, 732C, 738A, 738B, 751B, 756C, 759B, 759C, 760A, 770B, 777A, 778B, 779B, 780B, 780C, 788B, 862B, 865C, 917C

PREFACE

Kristie Callan: 234B, 237A, 240B, 240C, 241B, 243A, 245B, 246C, 247C, 250B, 253B, 262A, 266A, 270B, 272C, 275B, 282C, 283A, 283C, 291C, 334C, 336C, 339A, 345B, 346A, 346B, 347B, 348B, 349B, 350B, 351A, 352B, 353A, 353B, 353C, 356A, 358A, 358B, 359A, 359C, 360A, 360C, 361A, 361B, 361C, 362B, 363B, 363C, 364A, 364C, 365B, 366B, 366C, 367A, 368A, 368B, 369B, 370A, 370B, 371A, 371B, 371C, 372C, 373C, 374A, 374C, 375A, 375B, 375C, 376A, 377A, 378A, 378C, 379A, 379C, 380A, 380B, 380C, 381B, 382A, 382B, 382C, 383C, 384A, 384B, 384C, 385A, 385B, 385C, 386A, 386B (also on cover), 387A, 387B, 387C, 388A, 389A, 389B, 389C, 390A, 390C, 391A, 391C, 392A, 392B, 392C, 393A, 393C, 394A, 394B, 394C, 396C, 397A, 397B, 397C, 398A, 399A, 400A, 400B, 400C, 401A, 401C, 402A, 404B, 404C, 405A, 405C, 406A, 407A, 407C, 408A, 409A, 410A, 410B, 411C, 413B, 415A, 417A, 417B, 417C, 418B, 419A, 419B, 420A, 420B, 420C, 421A, 421C, 422A, 422C, 423A, 423B, 423C, 424A (also on cover), 424C, 425C, 426C, 427A, 427C, 428B, 428C, 429A, 429B, 430B, 430C, 431A, 431B, 432A, 432C, 433A, 433B, 433C, 434A, 435B, 482B, 497C, 526C, 625A, 719B (also on cover), 750A, 750B, 750C, 758B, 781A, 899C, 911C

T.D. Canerday: 884A

Chevron Chemical Company: 307C, 320A, 525C, 552B, 587C, 597A, 658A, 691C, 824A, 850C, 899A, 906B, 907A, 907B, 908C, 912A, 915B

Jack K. Clark: 328B, 367B, 462A, 621C, 645Ci, 647B, 650B, 673B, 673Bi, 674B, 745B, 747Ci, 769Ci, 800C, 804C, 807C, 814C, 815A, 816A, 882C, 887A, 889, 893A, 893C

Jack K. Clark, BIO-TEC Images: 409C, 746B, 807B

Clemson University: 728C, 803B

James S. Coartney: 228A, 509A, 585A, 613, 628B

Josephine Coatsworth: 901C, 909B, 916C

Sharon J. Collman: 303C, 312A, 330C, 343, 349A, 356C, 395B, 425B, 437, 443B, 444C, 446B, 446C, 448B, 451C, 452B, 452C, 455C, 457A, 457B, 458A, 462B, 466B, 469C, 475B, 481C, 482A, 483A, 502C, 508A, 508C, 510C, 512B, 513C, 514C, 517A, 518B, 535A, 535Ai, 536B, 537B, 543A, 543B, 562A, 562C, 567C, 568A, 568Ai, 569B, 569Bi, 583C (also on cover), 586C, 587B, 589A, 590B, 591C, 593A, 595B, 602C, 609A, 616B, 640B, 693C, 759A, 784A, 785C, 789C, 826A, 832C, 888, 900A, 909A, 916B

David M. Coppert: 426B, 685C

Samuel Cotner: 363A, 692B, 713C, 714C, 716C, 717A, 721B, 721Bi, 724C, 727A, 734B, 735C, 740C, 741B, 751A, 768Ci, 770C, 774C, 775B, 782B, 793A

David J. Cross: 209, 235C, 247B, 258C, 268B, 334B, 813C, 919B

J.A. Crozier: 233C, 234A, 235B, 239B, 311Ai, 313A, 315B, 315C, 317B, 319A, 320C, 324C, 331A, 331B, 331Bi, 331C, 332A, 332B, 332C, 333A, 347C, 362C, 416A, 416B, 445A, 509B, 519A, 526B, 536C, 564B, 592A, 609Ai, 615B (also on cover), 691B, 692A, 715A, 715B, 725B, 728B, 732A, 761C, 771A, 771C, 793C, 795C, 827C, 834B, 835B, 838B, 841B, 851A, 851B, 859A

Maynard W. Cummings: 309C, 616C, 617A, 649A, 747A, 804A, 804B, 805A, 805B, 807A, 890A, 890Ai, 890B, 890C, 891A, 891C, 895A

Margery Daughtrey: 415B, 532C

The Davey Tree Expert Company: 308B, 457C, 478C, 486A, 569C, 569Ci, 575B, 576A, 600C, 864A

Spencer H. Davis, Jr.: 225B, 242A, 254A, 260A, 280B, 336A, 338A, 408C, 456C, 467B, 469A, 473B, 480A, 496B, 498C, 500A, 502B, 508B, 527A, 528A, 535B, 536A, 556B, 557Bi, 557Ci, 559A, 580C, 581C, 582B, 583A, 600A

Jim DeFilippis: 442C (also on cover), 515C, 530A, 530B, 547C (also on cover), 590Bi, 620B, 644B, 876B

James F. Dill: 434C, 463A, 474B, 498B, 534C, 553C, 555C, 560A, 561A, 576C, 595C, 618B, 630B, 683C, 693A, 698A, 698Ai, 700A, 708C, 711A, 725C, 729Ai, 734A, 735B, 742B, 751Ci, 769A, 769B, 772B, 777B, 789A, 789B, 808C, 811A, 812C, 813B, 818A, 837A, 877C, 880B, 886C, 892C

Michael A. Dirr: 325B, 441B, 517B, 542B, 549C, 553A, 564C, 584B, 606A, 610C, 611B, 849A, 868C, 869B, 869C, 911B

Walter Ebeling: 802B, 809A, 810A, 811Ai, 811B, 815C, 817A

C.L. Elmore: 313C, 315A, 826C, 827A, 828A, 837B, 840A, 840B, 841A, 842A, 843A, 843C, 844A, 844B, 844C, 846A, 846B, 847B, 848B

Barbara H. Emerson: 319C, 823B, 823C, 824C, 825A, 826B, 827B, 828B, 836A, 838A (also on cover), 839B, 839C, 847C, 849C, 850A, 851C

Frank Emerson: 910A

Arthur W. Engelhard: 393B, 857C

Entomological Society of America — Ries Memorial Slide Library: 475Ai, 477A, 801A, 877A, 881C, 882A

James Feucht: 305Ci, 308C, 405B, 413A, 448C, 459B, 464A, 471A, 475A, 506B, 511A, 554Ci, 559C, 567B, 568B, 579A, 597B, 602B, 607B, 623A, 630Ci, 868A, 900C

Charles Marden Fitch: 228B, 228C, 232C, 241C, 263A (also on cover), 267A, 270C, 276A, 276B, 276C, 278B, 280C, 286A, 323, 329A, 358C, 365C, 383B, 402B, 404A, 442A, 442B, 484A, 491B, 515A, 577C, 579B, 591B, 592B, 639B, 694B, 735Ai, 748C (also on cover), 786C, 793Ai, 805C, 813A, 831A, 859C, 865A, 871, 874B (also on cover), 876A, 877B, 895B, 918C

W.E. Fletcher: 226A, 255C, 489C

Paul F. Frese: 412C

Raymond J. Gill: 229B, 234C, 235A, 247A, 265B, 484B

A.S. Greathead: 696C

Nelson Groffman: 892B, 894C

Dennis H. Hall: 697C, 706A, 726A, 736C, 736Ci, 756A, 775A, 781C, 782A, 785A, 791B, 794A

M. Ali Harivandi: 295C, 301A, 303B, 313B, 825C, 836B, 838C, 840C, 841C, 842B, 845B, 845C

Raymond F. Hasek: 230Ai, 239C, 262C, 290A

Duane L. Hatch: 494C, 503B, 655B, 655Bi, 681C, 689C, 692C, 693B, 710C, 714B, 718C, 722A, 754C, 772C

George R. Hawkes: 614C, 622B, 622C, 646A, 681B, 867C, 904C, 905A

Richard W. Henley: 257A, 257C, 258A, 258B, 265C, 267B, 268C, 271A, 271C, 277B, 283B, 522A

W. Richard Hildreth: 517C

R.K. Horst: 275C, 281A, 287C, 373A, 379B, 406C, 415C, 491A, 640A, 683A

Tony Howarth: 914A

Angus J. Howitt: 627A, 627Ai, 631C, 637C

Robert L. Iacopi: 493C

E.E. Janne: 300C, 552A, 808A, 830B, 833B, 869A

R.A. Jaynes: 535C

A.L. Jones: 624A, 624B, 627C, 632C, 633A, 641A, 655A (also on cover), 655C, 657C, 658C, 659C, 662Bi, 668C, 669B, 671C, 858C

R.K. Jones: 257B, 414A, 414B, 490C, 666A, 779C

Gene Joyner: 303A, 303Ai, 306C (also on cover), 321B, 476A, 476B, 482C, 485A, 485B, 487B, 487C, 488A, 488B, 495C, 512A, 520A, 521B, 525A, 529B, 529C, 531A, 532A, 539A, 548B, 549B, 550B, 551A, 551B, 551C, 563C, 566B, 598C, 636A, 636B, 636Bi, 636C, 641C, 642A, 642C, 643A, 645A, 646C, 648B, 649C, 653B, 653C, 653Ci, 654A, 745C, 829B, 835A

M. Keith Kennedy: 230A, 242B, 260B, 269B, 272B, 278A, 299B, 306A, 328C, 336B, 338C, 352C, 362A, 381A, 395C, 444A, 461C, 477C, 486Ci, 505C, 506A, 507A, 515B, 545B, 546C, 554A, 555A, 555Ai, 592C, 596B, 638B, 661C, 674C, 690A, 790C, 879B

R.R. Kriner: 301C, 540B, 542C, 561C, 596A, 623B, 626C, 627Bi, 628A, 629A, 629B, 638A, 654C, 656B, 656C, 657A, 658B, 659A, 661A, 671B, 672C, 707A, 707B, 709A, 715C, 720B, 730A, 743B, 765A, 774Ai, 776B, 783A, 802C

F. Laemmlen: 359B, 468A, 468B, 733C, 763A

Susan M. Lammers: 399B

Michael Lamotte: 612, 921–983

Michael Landis: 292, 798, 896, 906A, 907C, 908B, 909C, 911A, 917B, 918A, 918B

PREFACE

James H. LaRue: 637A, 667C, 669C, 670B

Peter Lindtner: 355C, 539C, 602A, 617B, 619A, 633C, 738C, 834C, 847A

Don Linzy: 303Ci

Kenneth Lorenzen: 813Ai

Fred Lyon: 294C

Robert E. Lyons: 229C, 237C

J.D. MacDonald: 337B, 337Bi

Phil Mayer: 806A

Arthur H. McCain: 335C, 403B, 500C

Charles A. McClurg: 726B, 729C, 862A

J.R. McGrew: 744B, 744C, 747C

Michael McKinley: 220, 222, 223, 249A, 287B, 325A, 325C, 326B, 326C, 327C, 328A, 342, 426A, 441A, 451A, 452A, 455A, 460C, 461B, 540A, 684A, 824B, 883B, 899B, 903A, 913A, 916A

J.A. Menge: 647C

Richard W. Merritt: 814A, 814B

Richard L. Miller: 523A, 546B, 568C, 593C, 764A, 764B, 774A, 775C, 803C, 809C, 811C, 875B, 894B

Cooperative Extension Association of Nassau County, New York: 291B, 298C, 298Ci, 305C, 316C, 470A, 473A, 513B, 524B, 562B, 604C, 606B, 608C, 609C

Jean R. Natter: 226C, 227C, 321A (also on cover), 321C, 460B, 549A, 695A, 801C, 852A, 856C, 861C (also on cover), 865B, 867A, 876C

New York State Turfgrass Association: 298A, 299Ci, 302C, 311A, 314A, 314Ai, 314C, 316A, 316B, 318C, 320B

Lester P. Nichols: 231B, 256A, 269A, 279C, 496A, 499B, 514A, 537C, 541A, 610A

R.A. Norton: 615A, 616A, 620A, 661B, 663B, 670A

Howard D. Ohr: 308A

Oregon State University — Department of Entomology: 776C

Oregon State University — Ken Gray Collection: 299Bi, 301Ci, 302Ci, 411B, 441C, 494B, 596C, 596Ci, 601B, 608B, 651A, 651B, 660C, 662B, 663A, 673C, 720C, 722B, 728A, 728Ai, 730B, 739A, 755A, 760B, 780A, 872C, 885B, 885Bi

J. Parker: 870

John W. Parrish: 309A, 521A

Jerry M. Parsons: 697B, 732B, 753B, 753C, 757A, 783C, 794C, 861A

John Pehrson: 643B, 647A

Sandra Perry: 253C, 264C, 368C, 544C

Robert G. Platt: 648A

D.K. Pollet: 538C, 566A, 578B, 652B, 652C, 664B, 664C, 665A, 665B, 671A

C.C. Powell: 221, 237B, 263B, 285C, 304A, 327A, 330B, 333C, 338B, 340C, 369A, 369C, 377B, 378B, 407B, 414C, 450B, 479B, 479C, 480B, 497A, 511B, 544B, 545A, 557C, 572B, 574C, 585C, 689A, 698B, 857B, 893B

R.P. Puck: 695C (also on cover), 696A, 696B, 696Bi

Purdue University: 627B

Cecil B. Quirino: 245A, 357A, 519B, 799, 800B, 803A (also on cover), 816B, 817B, 817C, 834A, 884B, 914B, 914C, 915A

Robert D. Raabe: 230C, 231A, 231C, 232A, 232B, 233A, 233B, 236A, 236B, 236C, 238A, 238C, 239A, 242C, 243B, 243C, 244A, 244B, 244C, 246A, 246B, 248A, 248C, 249C, 250A, 250C, 251B, 251C, 252A, 252B, 254Ai, 254B, 255A, 256C, 259B, 259C, 260C, 260Ci, 261A, 261B, 262B, 264A, 265A, 267C, 270A, 271B, 272A, 273A, 273C, 274A, 274B, 274C, 277C, 278C, 279B, 281B, 281C, 282B, 284A, 284B, 285A, 286B, 286C, 287A, 288A, 288B, 288C, 289A, 289C, 291A, 333B, 337A, 345C, 349C, 351C, 372B, 377C, 381C, 383A, 388B, 391B, 396A, 403C, 422B, 435A, 446A, 466A, 493A, 493B, 519C, 525B, 530C, 533A, 533B, 550A, 572A, 582A, 590A, 594C, 624C, 632A, 642A, 650A, 674A, 680C, 746A, 771B, 787B, 792B, 855, 857A

Ann F. Rhoads: 251A, 352A, 455B, 463C, 486B, 588C, 757C (also on cover), 862C

Paul A. Rogers: 339B, 550C, 550Ci, 577A, 580A, 906B

Barbara Rothenberger: 339C, 355B, 365A, 376B, 552C, 603B, 645B, 703C

Ray Rothenberger: 354B, 431C

Alvin D. Rutledge: 705C, 712C, 733A

Anita Sabarese: 222, 223, 280A, 314Bi, 354A, 355A, 355Ci, 356B (also on cover), 412B, 443C, 447A, 449A (also on cover), 449B, 449C, 453B, 524C, 554B, 571A, 605B, 619B, 685A, 686B, 689B, 741A, 761A, 768C, 784C, 794Ai, 811Bi, 829A, 830A, 830C (also on cover), 831B, 831C, 832A, 833A, 833C, 837C, 843B, 845A, 850B, 852B, 853C, 873A, 874C, 875A, 878A, 879C, 886B, 894A

Joseph Savage: 481A

D.F. Schoeneweiss: 340B, 374B 458C, 497B, 503A, 505B, 576B, 581A, 599C, 607C, 902B

Donald L. Schuder: 310B, 499A, 502Bi, 523B, 524A, 561B, 569A, 575C, 577B, 608A, 608Ai, 635A, 638C, 640C, 879A

Carl H. Shanks: 711B, 778A, 780Ai, 846C

Emroy L. Shannon: 554C, 666C, 761B, 859B

A.F. Sherf: 579C, 630C, 660B, 682A, 684C, 687C, 690B, 694C, 700C, 701A, 701B, 702A, 703A, 705A, 705B, 716A, 717B, 717C, 718A, 718B, 721A, 723A, 723C, 726C, 727C, 734C, 735C, 736A, 737B, 741C, 742A, 746C, 752A, 752B, 755B, 755C, 756B, 762C, 763B, 763C, 765B, 765C, 766C, 767A, 767B, 767C, 768A, 768B, 769C, 770A, 773A, 787C, 788A, 791A, 791C, 792A, 792C, 795A, 856B, 858A, 858B, 860A, 868B, 886A, 891B, 902C

G.S. Sibbett: 666B, 676A

James Lee Sikkema: 295A, 300B, 310C, 318A, 346C, 348A, 398B, 418A, 428A, 444B, 472C, 504B, 560C, 620C, 621A, 764C, 866B, 901A, 908A

Richard W. Smiley: 297A, 297B, 297C, 297Ci, 301B, 307A, 307Ai, 310A

Michael D. Smith: 223, 227B, 289B, 296A, 296B, 296C, 304B, 317C, 347A, 425A, 443A, 447B, 447C, 447Ci, 453C, 454B, 456A, 456B, 458B, 463B, 464B, 464C, 465A, 465B, 471C, 472A, 472B, 483C, 498A, 520C, 547B, 584C, 586A, 586Ai, 603A, 632B, 639A, 645C, 646B, 667B, 676Bi, 685B, 686A, 687A, 690C, 691A, 694A, 703B, 737A, 739C, 796B, 812A, 821, 825B, 832B, 836C, 848A, 848C, 853A, 853B, 861B, 863C, 867B, 873C, 873Ci, 874A, 883A, 904B, 905B, 910B, 910C, 915C

K.A. Sorensen: 707C

Leon Stacey: 605C, 704C, 729B, 753A, 796A

Arvil R. Stark: 293, 299C, 304C, 306B, 311B, 312B

Deni Weider Stein: 309B, 403A, 589C, 591A, 611C

Lauren Bonar Swezey: 225C, 226B, 227A, 245C, 264B, 266B, 273B, 290B, 302A, 305A, 324B, 329B, 334A, 335A, 340A, 357C, 366A, 450A, 483B, 490B, 494A, 495B, 500B, 503C, 505A, 510B, 514B, 520B, 532B, 547A, 563B, 573C, 598A, 599A, 676B

George Taloumis: 903B, 912B

Sherman V. Thomson: 357B, 479Ci, 486C, 546A, 556Bi, 563A, 563Ai, 565B, 597C, 617C, 630A, 660A, 864C

Tom Tracy: 913B

USDA: 724B, 730C

USDA Forest Service, Southern Forest Experiment Station: 809B, 810B, 810C

University of California: 319B, 580B, 623C, 631A, 644C, 663C, 767Ai, 818B, 880C

University of California, Berkeley, Cooperative Extension: 337C, 478A, 510A, 531C, 531Ci, 533C, 533Ci, 534A, 543C, 548A, 558A, 558C, 573A, 578A, 578C, 675A, 777C, 881A

University of California, Riverside, Cooperative Extension: 751C, 773C

University of California, Riverside, Statewide Air Pollution Research Center: 863A, 863B

University of Illinois, Champaign-Urbana: 285B, 396B, 430Ai, 601A

Van Waters & Rogers: 749C, 806B, 806C

R. Webb: 590C

John A. Weidhaas, Jr.: 252C, 266C, 398C, 475C, 484C, 484Ci, 529A, 538B, 548C, 584A, 588A, 606C

Kenneth Whitam: 481Bi, 542A

Steve Whiteley: 882B

John A. Wott: 348C, 354C, 448A, 557B

Frank T. Yoshikawa: 649B

David F. Young, Jr.: 665C, 704Ai, 875C

HOW TO USE THIS BOOK

1. If you know the name of your plant, the problem it has, or the insect that is bothering it, look up that name in the index beginning on **PAGE 17**.

2. If you don't know the name of your plant, turn to one of these sections:

Houseplants **PAGE 221**

Lawns **PAGE 293**

Groundcovers **PAGE 323**

Annuals, Perennials, and Bulbs **PAGE 343**

Trees, Shrubs, and Vines **PAGE 437**

Fruit and Nut Trees **PAGE 613**

Vegetables, Berries, and Grapes **PAGE 679**

3. If you have a household pest and don't know its name, turn to **PAGE 799**.

4. If you want to know more about a problem, turn to one of these pages:

Weeds **PAGE 821**

Plant Diseases **PAGE 855**

Insects **PAGE 871**

Animal Pests **PAGE 889**

Soil, Cultural, and Climate Problems **PAGE 897**

5. For a complete description of ORTHO products and a list of the problems each solves, turn to **PAGE 921**.

TABLE OF CONTENTS

A

A-20 grass. *See* Bluegrass
A-34 grass. *See* Bluegrass
Aaron's beard. *See*
 Hypericum
Abelia
 as crown gall resistant, 998
 bees attracted by, 996
 fungus diseases on,
  susceptibility to, 1000
Abelmoschus esculentus.
 See Okra
Abies (Fir)
 A. concolor (Colorado fir)
  as armillaria root rot
   resistant, 1001
 bird damage to
  sapsuckers, 999
 branches on
  brittle
   balsam woolly aphids,
   475
  dirty white crust on
   balsam woolly aphids,
   475
  dying
   spruce budworms, 474
  reddish
   balsam woolly aphids,
   475
  reddish brown ends on
   spruce budworms, 474
  swellings on tips of
   balsam woolly aphids,
   475
  white waxy egg masses in
   bark on
   balsam twig aphids, 474
  white woolly masses on
   balsam woolly aphids,
   475
 culture, 474
 diseases on
  verticillium wilt, 995
 Douglas fir. *See*
  Pseudotsuga
 dying
  Douglas fir tussock moths,
  475
  spruce budworms, 474
  spruce spider mites, 475
 fertilizing, 474, 924, 927
 fungus diseases on
  susceptibility to, 1000,
  1001
  verticillium wilt, 995
 honeydew on plants below
  balsam twig aphids, 474
 insects on
  balsam twig aphids, 474
  balsam woolly aphids, 475
  Douglas fir tussock moths,
  475, 554
  gypsy moths, 1000

Japanese beetles, 997
 spruce budworms, 474,
 553
 spruce spider mites, 475
needles on
 caterpillars on
  Douglas fir tussock
  moths, 475
  spruce budworms, 474
 chewed
  spruce budworms, 474
 curled
  balsam twig aphids, 474
 dirty
  spruce spider mites, 475
 dirty white crust on
  balsam woolly aphids,
  475
 dropping
  balsam woolly aphids,
  475
  spruce spider mites, 475
 dying
  balsam twig aphids, 474
 eaten
  Douglas fir tussock
  moths, 475
 silken webbing on
  spruce spider mites, 475
 stippled
  spruce spider mites, 475
 turning brown
  spruce spider mites, 475
 twisted
  balsam twig aphids, 474
 webbed together
  spruce budworms, 474
 white woolly masses on
  balsam woolly aphids,
  475
 yellowing
  balsam woolly aphids,
  475
  spruce spider mites, 475
planting locations for, 474
pruning, 474
sapsucker damage to, 999
shoots on
 black sooty mold on
  balsam twig aphids, 474
 honeydew on
  balsam twig aphids, 474
 shiny, sticky substance on
  balsam twig aphids, 474
 tiny, waxy, bluish gray or
  pale green insects on
  balsam twig aphids, 474
soil pH for, 474
tan pellets on ground under
 Douglas fir tussock moths,
 475
trunk of
 dirty white crust on
  balsam woolly aphids,
  475
 white waxy egg masses in
  bark on
  balsam twig aphids, 474
 white woolly masses on
  balsam woolly aphids,

475
twigs on
 rough bark on
  balsam twig aphids, 474
 swollen, knobby ends on
  balsam woolly aphids,
  475
 twisted
  balsam twig aphids, 474
 white waxy egg masses in
  bark on
  balsam twig aphids, 474
 watering, 474
 white waxy egg masses in
  bark on
  balsam twig aphids, 474
Abscission, defined, 216
Acacia
 bees attracted by, 996
 culture, 476
 diseases on
  armillaria root rot, 476
  varieties resistant to, 476,
  1001
  mushroom root rot, 476
  powdery mildew, 995
  susceptibility to, 1000
  thornbugs on, 476
Acalymma species. *See*
 Cucumber beetles,
 striped
Acaricide, defined, 216
Acephate
 as ingredient
  in ORTHO Orthenex
  Insect & Disease Control,
  956
  in ORTHO Systemic Rose
  & Floral Spray, 965
 for *Abies*
  Douglas fir tussock moths
  on, 475
 for aphids
  cooley spruce gall
   on *Pseudotsuga*, 571
  on flowers, 356
 for barberry loopers
  on *Mahonia*, 543
 for beetles
  on flowers, 355
 for boxwood psyllids, 489
 for caterpillars
  on flowers, 356
 for cooley spruce gall
  aphids
  on *Pseudotsuga*, 571
 for cotoneaster webworms,
 503
 for Douglas fir tussock
  moths
  on *Abies*, 475
  on *Picea*, 554
 for flowers
  aphids on, 356
  beetles on, 355
  caterpillars on, 356
  greenhouse whiteflies on,
  357
  Japanese beetles on, 355

leafminers on, 352
 for greenhouse whiteflies
  on flowers, 357
 on groundcovers, 328
 for Japanese beetles
  on flowers, 355
 for *Jasminum*
  whiteflies on, 530
 for leafminers
  on flowers, 352
 for *Mahonia*
  barberry loopers on, 543
 for *Mesembryanthemum*
  scales on, 337
 for *Picea*
  Douglas fir tussock moths
  on, 554
 for *Pseudotsuga*
  cooley spruce gall aphids
  on, 571
 for psyllids
  boxwood, 489
 for scales
  on *Mesembryanthemum*,
  337
 for webworms
  cotoneaster, 503
 for whiteflies
  on *Jasminum*, 530
Acer (Maple; Boxelder)
 A. campestre (Hedge
  maple)
  for limited space, 996
 A. circinatum (Vine maple)
  as shade tolerant, 997
 A. ginnala (Amur maple)
  for limited space, 996
 A. macrophyllum (Big-leaf
  maple)
  as armillaria root rot
   resistant, 1001
  conks on, 446
 A. negundo (Boxelder)
  insects on
   boxelder bugs, 803
   Japanese beetles, 997
  soil pH for, 1003
 A. palmatum (Japanese
  maple)
  as armillaria root rot
   resistant, 1001
  as shade tolerant, 997
  fertilizer for, 924
  for limited space, 996
 A. platanoides (Norway
  maple)
  anthracnose on, 479
  as smog tolerant, 996
 A. rubrum (Red maple)
  as wet soil tolerant, 997
  Japanese beetles on, 997
 A. saccharinum (Silver
  maple)
  Japanese beetles on, 997
 A. saccharum (Sugar
  maple)
  as smog tolerant, 996
 A. tataricum (Tatarian
  maple)
  as low-growing tree, 998

black bugs with reddish
 lines near
 boxelder bugs, 477
branches on
 bark sloughing off of
  borers, 477
 dark streaks under bark on
  verticillium wilt, 479
 dying back
  borers, 477
  cottony scales and
   mealybugs, 478
 holes in
  borers, 477
 sap or sawdust around
  holes in
  borers, 477
 tunnels in
  borers, 477
 weak
  borers, 477
conks on, 446
culture, 476
diseases on
 anthracnose, 479
 Botryosphaeria ribis, 1002
 fungal leaf spot, 478
 maple anthracnose, 479
 powdery mildew, 995
 verticillium wilt, 479
dying
 verticillium wilt, 479
fertilizing, 476, 927
flowers on
 discolored or distorted
  boxelder bugs, 477
frost crack susceptible, 457
honeydew on plants and
  objects under
 aphids, 477
insects on
 ants
  aphids and, 477
 aphids, 477
 bladder gall mites, 478
 borers, 477
 boxelder bugs, 477, 803
 cottony scales and
  mealybugs, 478
 Japanese beetles, 997
 spindle gall mites, 478
leaf scorch on, 479
leaves on
 black sooty mold on
  aphids, 477
 cottony scales and
  mealybugs, 478
 bladderlike growths on
  gall mites, 478
 blotches on
  fungal leaf spot, 478
 brown
  summer leaf scorch, 479
  verticillium wilt, 479
 brown spots on
  anthracnose, 479
  fungal leaf spot, 478
 dark dots under
  anthracnose, 479
 discolored

aphids, 477
 boxelder bugs, 477
distorted
 boxelder bugs, 477
 gall mites, 478
dropping
 aphids, 477
 cottony scales and
  mealybugs, 478
 fungal leaf spot, 478
 gall mites, 478
 summer leaf scorch, 479
drying
 verticillium wilt, 479
dying
 anthracnose, 479
 fungal leaf spot, 478
 summer leaf scorch, 479
galls on
 gall mites, 478
gray spots on
 fungal leaf spot, 478
honeydew on
 aphids, 477
 cottony scales and
  mealybugs, 478
irregular growths on
 gall mites, 478
red bugs with dark heads
  on
 boxelder bugs, 477
red spots on
 fungal leaf spot, 478
scorched
 anthracnose, 479
shiny, sticky substance on
 aphids, 477
 cottony scales and
  mealybugs, 478
small
 aphids, 477
sparse
 borers, 477
spherical growths on
 gall mites, 478
spots on
 fungal leaf spot, 478
stunted
 verticillium wilt, 479
tan spots on
 fungal leaf spot, 478
tiny insects under
 aphids, 477
white cottony masses on
 cottony scales and
  mealybugs, 478
wilting
 summer leaf scorch, 479
 verticillium wilt, 479
wrinkled
 aphids, 477
yellow spots on
 fungal leaf spot, 478
yellowing
 cottony scales and
  mealybugs, 478
 fungal leaf spot, 478
 gall mites, 478
 verticillium wilt, 479
low-growing, 998

planting locations for, 476
 limited space, 996
 shade tolerance, 997
 smog tolerance, 996
pollution tolerant, 996
seeds on
 discolored or distorted
  boxelder bugs, 477
shade tolerant varieties of,
 997
shoots on
 discolored or distorted
  boxelder bugs, 477
smog tolerant varieties of,
 996
SO2 tolerant, 996
street trees
 low-growing varieties, 998
 pollution tolerant varieties,
  996
summer leaf scorch on, 479
transplants
 summer leaf scorch and,
  479
twigs on
 dying
  anthracnose, 479
  borers, 477
  cottony scales and
   mealybugs, 478
 reddish oval areas on
  anthracnose, 479
 sunken cankers on
  anthracnose, 479
watering, 476
 summer leaf scorch and,
  479
weedlike
 herbicides for, 970
wilting
 verticillium wilt, 479
Aceria species
 A. fraxinivorus (Ash flower
  gall mite), 517
 A. neocynodonis
  (Bermudagrass mite), 307
Acheta domesticus (House
 crickets), 801
Achillea (Yarrow)
 as weed
  in lawns
   herbicides for, 971, 978
 bees attracted by, 996
 culture, 360
 diseases on
  powdery mildew, 360, 995
 fertilizing, 360
 flowering times for, 992
 germination of, 992
 in lawns
  herbicides for, 971, 978
 leaves on
  powdery patches on
   powdery mildew, 360
  yellowing and dying
   powdery mildew, 360
 planting locations for, 360
 planting times for, 992
 stems on

powdery patches on
  powdery mildew, 360
 watering, 360
Achimenes
 See also African violet
  family
 culture, 230
 water spots on, 230
Acid soil, 902
 See also Soil pH
 correcting, 902
 defined, 216
 lawns in
  nitrogen and, 306
  liming, 306
  nitrogen utilization and,
   306
Acid-Gro Fertilizer, 936
 for iron deficiency
  in *Tolmiea,* 289
Acid-loving plants
 correcting soil pH for, 923
 fertilizers for, 923, 924,
  926, 936
 iron deficiency in, 902
 peat moss for, 918
 soil pH for, 902
Acolorrhaphe wrightii.
  See Palm family,
  outdoors
Acrobasis species
 A. nuxvorella (Pecan nut
  casebearer), 665
 A. vaccinii (Cranberry
  fruitworm), 707
Aculops lycopersici (Tomato
 russet mite), 790
Aculus species
 A. fockeui (Plum rust mite)
  on fruit and nut trees, 623
  on plum, 669
 A. ligustri (Privet rust
  mite), 538
Acyrthosiphon pisum (Pea
 aphid), 760
Adelges species
 A. abietis (Eastern spruce
  gall aphid), 554
 A. cooleyi (Cooley spruce
  gall aphid)
  on *Picea,* 554
  on *Pseudotsuga,* 571
 A. laricis (Woolly larch
  aphid), 537
 A. piceae (Balsam woolly
  aphid), 475
Adventitious, defined, 216
Aeration
 defined, 216
 for compacted soil, 900
 in lawns, 305, 900
Aerators, for groundcovers,
 325
Aeschynanthus (Lipstick
 plant)
 culture, 231
 water spots on, 231

Aesculus (Buckeye; Horse chestnut)
  A. californica (California buckeye)
    as summer-deciduous, 480
    as frost crack susceptible, 457
    culture, 480
    diseases on
      leaf blotch, 480
      powdery mildew, 995
    insects on
      gypsy moths, 1000
      summer leaf scorch on, 480
African violet family
  See also Achimenes; Episcia; Saintpaulia; Sinningia; Streptocarpus
  fertilizers for, 928, 931, 932
  insects on
    cyclamen mites, 778
    insecticides for, 948, 951, 969
  water spots on, 230, 288
Agapanthus (Lily of the Nile)
  as smog tolerant, 996
  diseases on
    verticillium wilt, 995
Ageratum (Floss flower)
  culture, 361, 992
  diseases on
    gray mold, 361
    root and stem rot, 361
    southern blight, 996
  fertilizing, 361
  flower buds
    holes in
      corn earworms, 361
      tobacco budworms, 361
  flowering times for, 992
  flowers on
    gray mold on, 361
  germination of, 992
  insects on
    corn earworms, 361
    greenhouse whiteflies, 362
    insecticides for, 948
    tobacco budworms, 361
  leaves on
    brown blotches on
      gray mold, 361
    brown spots on
      gray mold, 361
    dying
      root and stem rot, 361
    fuzzy brown or grayish mold on
      gray mold, 361
    holes in
      corn earworms, 361
      tobacco budworms, 361
    mottled
      greenhouse whiteflies, 362
    rotting
      gray mold, 361

root and stem rot, 361
soft
  gray mold, 361
tiny winged insects on
  greenhouse whiteflies, 362
white waxy substance under
  greenhouse whiteflies, 362
wilting
  root and stem rot, 361
yellowing
  greenhouse whiteflies, 362
planting locations for, 361
planting times for, 992
roots of
  dark
    root and stem rot, 361
  rotted
    root and stem rot, 361
stems on
  brown or grayish mold on
    gray mold, 361
  brown spots or blotches on
    gray mold, 361
  dying
    root and stem rot, 361
  rotted
    gray mold, 361
    root and stem rot, 361
  soft
    gray mold, 361
striped green, brown, or yellow caterpillars on
  corn earworms, 361
  tobacco budworms, 361
stunted growth in
  root and stem rot, 361
watering, 361
  gray mold and, 361
  root and stem rot and, 361
wilting
  root and stem rot, 361
Aglaonema (Chinese evergreen)
  culture, 231
  growing locations for
    light and, 990
  mealybugs on, 231
  root and stem rot on, 231
Agrilus species
  A. angelicus (Oak twig girdler), 577
  A. anxius (Bronze birch borer), 486
  A. difficilis (Honeylocust borer), 524
Agrobacterium species
  A. rubi
    on brambles, 711
  A. tumefaciens
    galls from, 860, 869
    on brambles, 711
    on *Euonymus*, 513
    on fruit and nut trees, 624
    on persimmon, 667
    on *Rosa*, 594

on trees, 446, 624, 860
Agropyron repens (Quackgrass), 826
  in lawns, 312
Agrostis species. *See* Bentgrass
Agrotis ipsilon (Black cutworm), 729
Ailanthus (Tree-of-heaven)
  as disease and insect resistant, 998, 1001
  as paving tolerant, 469
  diseases on
    armillaria root rot
      resistance to, 1001
    crown gall
      resistance to, 998
    verticillium wilt, 480
Air pollution damage
  from nitrogen dioxide, 863
  from ozone, 862
  from PAN, 863
  from sulfur dioxide, 863
  industrial pollution (SO2)
    plants tolerant of, 996
    to beans, 687
    to flowers, 352
    to *Petunia*, 417
    to *Pinus*, 559
    to trees, 463
    to vegetables, 687
Airplant. *See Kalanchoe*
Ajuga (Carpet bugle)
  as shade tolerant, 305, 318, 325, 326, 991
  culture, 330
  diseases on
    crown rot, 330
    powdery mildew, 995
  leaves on
    crisp, shriveling, falling off
      scorch, 330
    light brown
      scorch, 330
    yellowing
      crown rot, 330
  pulls up easily
    crown rot, 330
  scorch on, 330
  watering
    scorch and, 330
  white cobwebby strands on and around
    crown rot, 330
  wilting and dying suddenly
    crown rot, 330
  yellow-brown and white pellets in soil around
    crown rot, 330
Albizia (Mimosa; Silk tree)
  A. julibrissin (Silk tree)
    as drought tolerant, 997
    planting locations for, 481, 996, 997
  A. palmatum (Japanese maple)
    for lawns, 997

as weed
  in lawns
    herbicides for, 977
  crown dieback on
    mimosa wilt, 481
  culture, 481
  diseases on
    crown gall
      resistance to, 998
    mimosa wilt, 481
  insects on
    mimosa webworms, 481
  soil pH for, 1003
Albugo occidentalis
  on spinach, 775
Alcea (Hollyhock)
  bees attracted by, 996
  culture, 362
  diseases on
    powdery mildew, 995
    rust, 362
    southern blight, 996
    verticillium wilt, 995
  fertilizing, 362
  flower buds on
    webbing on
      two-spotted spider mites, 362
  flowering times for, 992
  germination of, 992
  insects on
    two-spotted spider mites, 362
  planting locations for, 362
  planting times for, 992
Alder. *See Alnus*
Alder flea beetle (*Altica ambiens*), 482
Aldrin
  for subterranean termites, 808
Alfalfa, leafcutter bees and, 592
Alfilaria (*Erodium cicutarium*), 835
Algae
  Cephaleuros virescens
    on *Magnolia*, 542
  defined, 216
  on trees, 447
  Oscillatoria species
    on lawns, 321
  Symploca species
    on lawns, 321
Algal spot
  on *Magnolia*, 542
Alkali soils, 901, 903
Alkaline soil, 902
  defined, 902
  manure and, 918
All About Annuals (ORTHO), 984
All About Bulbs (ORTHO), 984
All About Fertilizers, Soils & Water (ORTHO), 984
  on compost, 918

on raised beds, 900

All About Ground Covers (ORTHO), 984

All About Growing Fruits and Berries (ORTHO), 984

All About Houseplants (ORTHO), 984

All About Landscaping (ORTHO), 985

All About Lawns (ORTHO), 985

All About Perennials (ORTHO), 985

All About Pruning (ORTHO), 985

All About Roses (ORTHO), 985

All About Shade Gardening (ORTHO), 985

All About Tomatoes (ORTHO), 986

All About Trees (ORTHO), 440, 441, 986

All About Vegetables (ORTHO), 986

Allethrin
as ingredient
in ORTHO Hi-Power Household Insect Fogger, 947
for carpet beetles, 802
for clothes moths, 802
for clover mites, 803

Allium, as flower
culture, 363
flowering times for, 992
planting times for, 992
thrips on, 363

Allium, as vegetable. *See* Onion family

Allium, as weed
A. canadense (Wild onion), 831
in lawns
herbicides for, 971, 978
A. vineale (Wild garlic), 831
in lawns, 314
herbicides for, 971, 978
in pastures 314
in wheat, 314

Almond
branches on
cocoons in crotches of
peach twig borers, 625
culture, 625
diseases on
bacterial blight, 1000
coryneum blight, 626
peach blight, 626
shothole fungus, 626
fertilizing, 625, 927
flowering. *See Prunus*
flowers on

gummy exudate at base of
shothole fungus, 626
turning brown
shothole fungus, 626
fruit on
poor yield of
shothole fungus, 626
harvesting, 625
insects on
filbertworms, 651
peach twig borers, 625
leaf buds on
dying
peach twig borers, 625
leaves on
dying and dropping
shothole fungus, 626
holes in
shothole fungus, 626
spots on
shothole fungus, 626
nuts on
dropping
shothole fungus, 626
harvesting, 625
pollination for, 625
reddish brown caterpillars inside
peach twig borers, 625
spots on
shothole fungus, 626
planting locations for, 625
pollination for, 625
pruning, 625
shoots on
reddish brown caterpillars inside
peach twig borers, 625
soil pH for, 625
twigs on
wilting and dying
peach twig borers, 625
watering, 625

Alnus (Alder)
culture, 482
diseases on
powdery mildew, 995
honeydew on plants and objects under
aphids, 481
insects on
alder flea beetles, 482
aphids, 481
woolly aphids, 481
leaves on
black sooty mold on
aphids, 481
dark brown larvae with black heads on
alder flea beetles, 482
discolored
aphids, 481
eaten
alder flea beetles, 482
honeydew on
aphids, 481
shiny, sticky substance on
aphids, 481
small
aphids, 481

tiny green or gray insects under
aphids, 481
planting locations for, 482, 997
shiny blue to greenish blue beetles on
alder flea beetles, 482
twigs on
tiny green or gray insects on
aphids, 481

Alphitobius species (Mealworms), 817

Alternaria blight
on *Zinnia*, 435

Alternaria fruit rot
controlling, 968

Alternaria leaf spot
controlling, 954, 957, 959, 967, 968
on *Brassaia*, 599
on cabbage family, 717
on cucurbits, 735
on lawns
controlling, 954
on *Pelargonium*, 415

Alternaria species
A. cucumerina
on cucurbits, 735
A. dauci
on carrots, 721
A. porri
on onion family, 756
A. solani
on potatoes, 770
tomatoes, 793
A. tenuis
on *Pelargonium*, 415
A. zinniae
on *Brassaia*, 599
on cabbage family, 717
on *Zinnia*, 435

Altica species
A. ambiens (Alder flea beetle), 482
A. chalybea (Grape flea beetle), 744

Aluminum
in acid soil, 902

Aluminum plant (*Pilea*)
insecticide for, 969

Aluminum Sulfate. *See* ORTHO Aluminum Sulfate

Alumroot. *See Heuchera*

Alyssum
diseases on
verticillium wilt, 995
sweet. *See Lobularia*

Amaranthus (Amaranth)
diseases on
cotton root rot, 994
powdery mildew, 995
flowering times for, 992
germination of, 992
pigweeds, 847

planting times for, 992

Amaryllis. *See Hippeastrum*

Amber (*Hypericum perforatum*), 833

Ambrosia species. *See* Ragweed

Amelanchier (Serviceberry)
as crown gall resistant, 998
as fireblight susceptible, 1001
as quince rust susceptible, 1000
as shade tolerant, 997
as wet soil tolerant, 997
insects on
gypsy moths, 1000
pear leaf blister mites, 504, 600
woolly aphids, 608
planting locations for, 997
soil pH for, 1003

American cockroach (*Periplaneta americana*), 816

Aminotriazole
for bitter nightshade, 850
for black nightshade, 850
for common cattail, 832
for hairy nightshade, 850
for Japanese honeysuckle, 850
for milkweed, 847
for mugwort, 847
for Virginia peppergrass, 833

Ammonia, as nitrogen source, 904

Ammoniacal nitrogen, 904

Ammoniated sawdust, for heavy soils, 898

Ammonium
as nitrogen source, 904

Ammonium sulfamate (AMS)
as ingredient
in ORTHO Brush Killer A, 970

Ammonium sulfate
ferrous
for mosses and liverworts in lawns, 833
for blueberries, 706
for fruit and nut trees
correcting soil pH for, 624
for *Juniperus*
correcting soil pH for, 533
for lawns
liverworts on, 833
mosses in, 321, 833
Ophiobolus patch on, 299
for pecan
root rot on, 666
for trees
for correcting soil pH for, 466

Amsinckia douglasiana

(Douglas fiddleneck), 851

Anagasta kuehniella (Flour moths), 817

Anarsia lineatella. See Peach twig borer

Anasa tristis (Squash bugs), 734

Anastrepha suspense (Caribbean fruit fly) on citrus, 643

Ancylis comptana fragariae (Strawberry leafroller), 777

Andromeda. *See Pieris*

Andromeda lacebug (*Stephanitis takeyai*), 556

Anemone (Windflower)
culture, 363
diseases on
aster yellows, 994
leaf spot, 363
Southern blight, 363
tuber rot, 363
verticillium wilt, 995
dying
tuber rot, 363
failure to bloom in,
tuber rot, 363
fertilizing, 363
flowering times for, 992
flowers on
fail to bloom
tuber rot, 363
malformed
aphids, 364
streaked
aphids, 364
tiny green insects on
aphids, 364
insects on
ants, 364
aphids, 364
leaves on, 363
curled
aphids, 364
decaying at base
tuber rot, 363
distorted
aphids, 364
dying
leaf spot, 363
fail to grow
tuber rot, 363
gray mold on
leaf spot, 363
honeydew on
aphids, 364
shiny, sticky substance on
aphids, 364
spots or blotches on
. leaf spot, 363
tiny green insects on
aphids, 364
wilting
tuber rot, 363
yellowing
leaf spot, 363
tuber rot, 363

planting directions for
tuber rot and, 363
planting locations for, 363
planting times for, 992
roots of
rotting
tuber rot, 363
stems on
brown, pinhead-sized
pellets on
tuber rot, 363
tiny green insects on
aphids, 364
white matted strands on
tuber rot, 363
tubers
fail to grow
tuber rot, 363
rotting
tuber rot, 363
watering, 363
white matted strands at
bases of
tuber rot, 363

Angoumois grain moths, 817

Angular leaf spot
controlling, 957
on cucurbits, 736

Anilazine
for alternaria leaf spot
on cucurbits, 735

Animal pests
bark-feeding, 455
in fruit and nut trees, 617
in trees, 455
birds, 893
in brambles, 709
in lawns, 310
See also Bird damage
cats, 892
deer, 455, 617, 891
dogs, 892
earthworms, 892
groundhogs, 895
in avocado, 636
in fig, 649
in flowers
deer, 891
mice, 890
tree squirrels, 893
woodchucks, 895
in fruit and nut trees, 616,
617
bark-feeding, 617
birds, 616, 893
deer, 617
ground squirrels, 617, 894
mice, 617
rabbits, 617, 894
raccoons, 616, 894
skunks, 895
tree squirrels, 616, 893
in grapes, 747
in lawns
birds, 310
moles, 890
pocket gophers, 309
in trees, 455

bark-feeding, 455
deer, 455, 891
mice, 455, 890
rabbits, 455
sapsuckers, 454, 893
squirrels, 455
tree, 458, 893
voles, 455
woodchucks, 895
in vegetables
birds, 893
deer, 891
ground squirrels, 894
mice, 890
rabbits, 894
raccoons, 894
skunks, 895
woodchucks, 895
mice, 455, 617, 804, 890
moles, 890
pocket gophers
in lawns, 309
rabbits, 455, 617, 894
raccoons, 616, 894
in *Ranunculus,* 421
rats, 805
sapsuckers, 893
in trees, 454
skunks, 895
squirrels, 455
ground, 617, 894
tree, 458, 616, 806, 893
traps for, 891
house mice, 804
rats, 805
tree squirrels, 806
voles, 455
in *Wisteria,* 611
woodchucks, 895

Annual aster. *See Callistephus*

Annual bluegrass. *See* Bluegrass, annual

Annual morning glory. *See* Morning glory

Annual plant, defined, 216

Annual speargrass. *See* Bluegrass, annual

Annuals. *See* Flowers

Ant, Roach & Spider Killer. *See* ORTHO Ant, Roach & Spider Killer

Anthemis cotula (Mayweed), 837

Anthracnose
and twig blight
on *Ligustrum,* 539
controlling, 954, 957, 959,
967, 968
foxglove, 392
maple, 479
oak, 575
on brambles, 712
resistance to, 1008
on cucurbits, 736
on grapes, 745
on lawns, 297

controlling, 954
on *Ligustrum,* 539
on mango, 653
on peppers, 763
on tomato, 787
spot
on *Cornus,* 501
walnut, 675

Anthurium
culture, 232
diseases on
root rot, 232
fertilizers for, 931
insects on
mealybugs, 232
spider mites, 232
leaves on
polishes for, 952

Antirrhinum (Snapdragon)
culture, 364
diseases on
aster yellows, 994
cotton root rot, 994
fungicides for, 946
fusarium wilt, 994
powdery mildew, 995
root and stem rot, 365
rust, 364, 1008
dying
root and stem rot, 365
rust, 364
fertilizing, 364
iron deficiency and, 929
flower buds on
webbing on
two-spotted spider mites,
365
flowering times for, 992
germination of, 992
in containers
watering, 364
insects on
cyclamen mites, 778
insecticides for, 948
two-spotted spider mites,
365
iron deficiency in, 929
leaves on
dirty
two-spotted spider mites,
365
dropping
two-spotted spider mites,
365
drying out
rust, 364
two-spotted spider mites,
365
reddish brown pustules
under
rust, 364
stippled
two-spotted spider mites,
365
webbing between or
under
two-spotted spider mites,
365
wilting

root and stem rot, 365
yellow spots on
rust, 364
yellowing
root and stem rot, 365
two-spotted spider mites,
365
planting directions for
root and stem rot and, 365
rust and, 364
planting locations for, 364
planting times for, 364, 992
roots of
decayed
root and stem rot, 365
soil pH for, 364
stems on
decaying
root and stem rot, 365
lesions on
root and stem rot, 365
reddish brown pustules on
rust, 364
stunted growth in
root and stem rot, 365
rust, 364
watering, 364
root and stem rot and, 365
rust and, 364
wilting
root and stem rot, 365

Ants, 883
aphids and, 883
on *Acer*, 477
on *Anemone*, 364
on apple, 628
on *Aquilegia*, 366
on *Astilbe*, 367
on *Bambusa*, 484
on beans, 699
on *Betula*, 486
on cabbage family, 716
on *Camellia*, 494
on *Centaurea*, 376
on *Chrysanthemum*, 381
on citrus, 644
on *Cosmos*, 385
on *Crataegus*, 506
on currants; gooseberries,
738
on *Daphne*, 510
on *Digitalis*, 392
on eggplant, 741
on *Fagus*, 513
on *Fatshedera*, 514
on flowers, 356
on *Fraxinus*, 517
on *Freesia*, 393
on fruit and nut trees, 620,
621
on *Fuchsia*, 519
on *Gardenia*, 521
on *Gerbera*, 394
on grapes, 744
on groundcovers, 329
on *Hemerocallis*, 398
on *Hibiscus*, 525
on *Ixora*, 530
on *Juniperus*, 534
on *Laburnum*, 536

on *Lagerstroemia*, 536
on *Lilium*, 407
on *Liriodendron*, 540
on peas, 760
on *Philadelphus*, 552
on *Pinus*, 560
on *Pittosporum*, 563
on *Platanus*, 566
on trees, 444, 462
on *Tropaeolum*, 426
on *Tulipa*, 430
on vegetables, 692
on walnut, 674
bean aphids and
on *Tropaeolum*, 426
carpenter (*Camponotus*
species)
in households, 811
cotton and cowpea aphids
and
on *Hibiscus*, 525
cottony cushion scales and
on citrus, 644
cottony scales and
on *Bambusa*, 484
cowpea and bean aphids
and
on *Laburnum*, 536
crapemyrtle aphids and,
536
fire (*Solenopsis* species),
884
insecticides for, 941, 943,
952, 956
on lawns, 310
giant bark aphids and
on *Quercus*, 578
on *Salix*, 596
harvester
on lawns, 310
honeydew and
on fruit and nut trees, 620,
621
on trees, 454
in households, 803
carpenter (*Camponotus*
species), 811
insecticides for, 938, 940
insecticides for, 938, 941–
945, 948–950, 952, 954,
958, 964
mealybugs and, 883
on cactus family, 492
on citrus, 644
on *Coleus*, 383
on flowers, 356
on fruit and nut trees, 620,
621
on *Acer*
aphids and, 477
on *Anemone*
aphids and, 364
on apple
aphids and, 628
on *Aquilegia*
aphids and, 366
on *Astilbe*
aphids and, 367
on *Bambusa*
aphids and, 484

cottony scales and
mealybugs and, 484
on *Bauhinia*
snow scales and, 485
on beans
aphids and, 699
on *Betula*
aphids and, 486
on cactus family
mealybugs and, 492
on *Camellia*
aphids and, 494
scales and, 494
on *Centaurea*
aphids and, 376
on *Chrysanthemum*
aphids and, 381
on citrus
aphids and, 644
mealybugs and
cottonycushion scales
and, 644
on *Coleus*
mealybugs and, 383
on *Cosmos*
aphids and, 385
on *Crataegus*
aphids and, 506
on currants; gooseberries
aphids and, 738
on *Daphne*
aphids and, 510
on *Digitalis*
aphids and, 392
on eggplant
aphids and, 741
on *Fagus*
aphids and, 513
on *Fatshedera*
aphids and, 514
on flowers, 356
on *Fraxinus*
aphids and, 517
on *Freesia*
aphids and, 393
on fruit and nut trees, 620
honeydew and, 620, 621
on *Fuchsia*
aphids and, 519
on *Gardenia*
aphids and, 521
on *Gerbera*
aphids and, 394
on groundcovers
aphids and, 329
on *Hedera*
scales and, 336
on *Hemerocallis*
aphids and, 398
on *Hibiscus*
aphids and, 525
on *Ixora*
aphids and, 530
on *Juniperus*
aphids and, 534
on *Laburnum*
cowpea and bean aphids
and, 536
on *Lagerstroemia*
crapemyrtle aphids and,

536
on lawns, 310
insecticides for, 942
on *Lilium*
aphids and, 407
on *Liriodendron*
tuliptree aphids and, 540
on mango
scales and, 654
on peas
pea aphids and, 760
on *Philadelphus*
aphids and, 552
on *Pinus*
aphids and, 560
on *Pittosporum*
aphids and, 563
on *Platanus*
aphids and, 566
on *Quercus*
giant bark aphids and,
578
on *Rhododendron*
rhododendron aphids and,
587
on *Rosa*
rose aphids and, 591
on *Salix*
giant bark aphids and,
596
on trees
aphids and, 444, 462
honeydew and, 454
on *Tropaeolum*
aphids and, 426
on *Tulipa*
aphids and, 430
on vegetables
aphids and, 692
on walnut
aphids and, 674
pea aphids and, 760
rhododendron aphids and,
587
rose aphids and, 591
scales and, 883
on *Camellia*, 494
on flowers, 356
on fruit and nut trees, 620
on *Hedera*, 336
on mango, 654
snow scales and
on *Bauhinia*, 485
tuliptree aphids and, 540
whiteflies and, 883
on flowers, 356
on fruit and nut trees, 620,
621

Aphanomyces raphani
on radishes, 773
Aphelandra (Zebra plant)
culture, 233
mealybugs on, 233
salt damage to, 233, 990
sunburn on, 233
Aphelenchoides species
A. fragariae
on *Asplenium*, 263
A. olesistus

on *Begonia*, 369
A. ritzema-bosi
 on *Chrysanthemum*, 378
Aphid lions, 887
Aphids, 877
 ants and, 883
 on apple, 628
 on flowers, 356
 on fruit and nut trees, 620
 apple, 628
 insecticides for, 954, 964
 woolly (*Eriosoma lanigerum*)
  on *Crataegus*, 506
 ash-gray snowball
  (*Neoceruraphis viburnicola*)
  on *Viburnum*, 610
 balsam twig (*Mindarus abietinus*)
  on *Abies*, 474
 balsam woolly (*Adelges piceae*)
  on *Abies*, 475
 bamboo (*Takecallis* species)
  on *Bambusa*, 484
 bean (*Aphis fabae*)
  on *Laburnum*, 536
  on *Tropaeolum*, 426
 bean mosaic virus and, 703
 black citrus (*Toxoptera aurantii*)
  on *Camellia*, 494
 black pecan (*Tinocallis caryaefoliae*), 666
 brown arborvitae (*Cinara tujafilina*)
  on cypress family, 509
 Cinara species
  on *Juniperus*, 534
  on *Pinus*, 560
 Cooley spruce gall
  (*Adelges cooleyi*)
  on *Picea*, 554
  on *Pseudotsuga*, 571
 cotton (*Aphis gossypii*)
  on *Hibiscus*, 525
 cowpea (*Aphis craccivora*)
  on *Hibiscus*, 525
  on *Laburnum*, 536
 crapemyrtle (*Tinocallis kahawaluokalani*), 536
 curly dwarf and
  on globe artichoke, 696
 diseases and, 880
 Drepanaphis species
  on *Acer*, 477
 Eastern spruce gall
  (*Adelges abietis*)
  on *Picea*, 554
 Eulachnus species
  on *Pinus*, 560
 European dusky-veined
  walnut (*Panaphis juglandis*), 674
 galls from, 869
 giant bark (*Longistigma caryae*)

on *Platanus*, 566
on *Quercus*, 578
on *Salix*, 596
green peach (*Myzus persicae*)
 insecticides for, 967
 on lettuce, 749
 on potatoes
  leaf roll virus and, 771
green spruce (*Cinara fornacula*)
 on *Picea*, 555
greenbugs (*Schizaphis graminum*)
 on lawns, 304
insecticides for, 941, 944,
 946–948, 951, 954–956,
 961, 962, 964–967, 969
lacewings and, 887
leaf curl
 on *Fraxinus*, 517
leaf gall (*Tamalia coweni*)
 on *Arctostaphylos*, 483
leaf gall
 witch-hazel (*hormaphis hamamelidis*), 524
leaf roll virus and
 on potatoes, 771
linden (*Myzocallis tiliae*), 605
maize dwarf mosaic and
 on corn, 727
mosaic virus and
 on beans, 703
 on *Chrysanthemum*, 380
 on cucurbits, 736
 on *Cymbidium*, 386
 on *Dahlia*, 388
 on *Iris*, 403
 on peppers, 765
 on *Ranunculus*, 422
oleander (*Aphis nerii*), 547
on *Acer*, 477
 Drepanaphis species, 477
 Periphyllus species, 477
on *Alnus*, 481
on *Anemone*, 364
on apple, 628
on *Aquilegia*, 366
on *Astilbe*, 367
on beans, 699
 bean mosaic virus and, 703
on *Betula*, 486
on cabbage family, 716
on *Camellia*, 494
on *Capsicum*, 243
on *Centaurea*, 376
on *Chrysanthemum*, 381
 mosaic virus and, 380
on *Cineraria*, 245
on citrus, 644
 insecticides for, 940
on corn
 maize dwarf mosaic and, 727
on *Cosmos*, 385
on *Crataegus*, 506
on *Crocus*, 385
on cucurbits

mosaic virus and, 736
on currants; gooseberries, 738
on *Cymbidium*
 mosaic virus and, 386
on cypress family, 509
on *Dahlia*
 mosaic virus and, 388
on *Daphne*, 510
on *Digitalis*, 392
on eggplant, 741
on *Fagus*, 513
on *Fatshedera*, 514
on flowers, 356
 ants and, 356
 virus diseases and, 352, 861
on *Fraxinus*, 517
on *Freesia*, 393
on fruit and nut trees, 620
 ants and, 620
 honeydew and, 620, 621
 sooty mold and, 621
 virus diseases and, 861
on *Fuchsia*, 519
on *Gardenia*, 521
 sooty mold and, 521
on *Gerbera*, 394
on *Gladiolus*
 viruses and, 395
on globe artichoke
 curly dwarf and, 696
on grapes, 744
on groundcovers, 329
on *Gynura*, 267
on *Hemerocallis*, 398
on *Hibiscus*, 525
on houseplants, 228
 Capsicum, 243
 Gynura, 267
 Hoya, 270
 insecticides for, 950, 969
on *Hoya*, 270
on *Iris*
 mosaic and, 403
on *Ixora*, 530
on *Jasminum*
 sooty mold and, 531
on *Juniperus*, 534
 Cinara species, 534
on *Laburnum*, 536
on *Lagerstroemia*, 536
on lettuce, 749
on *Lilium*, 407
on *Liriodendron*, 540
 sooty mold and, 539
on *Lonicera*, 540
 woolly honeysuckle
  (*Prociphilus xylosteri*), 540
on *Nerium*, 547
 sooty mold and, 547
on pecan, 666
on peppers
 mosaic virus and, 765
on *Philadelphus*, 552
on *Pinus*, 560
on *Pittosporum*, 563
on *Platanus*, 566
on plum, 670

on *Podocarpus*, 566
on potatoes
 leaf roll virus and, 771
 viruses and, 767, 771
on *Pyracantha*, 573
 sooty mold and, 573
on *Ranunculus*
 ranunculus mosaic and, 422
on spinach, 692
on swiss chard, 783
on *Tolmiea*, 289
 viruses and, 289
on tomato, 790
 viruses and, 794
on trees, 444, 448, 462
 honeydew from, 454
 sooty mold and, 445
on *Tropaeolum*, 426
on *Tulipa*, 430
on vegetables, 692
 viruses and, 861
on *Viburnum*, 610
on walnut, 674
pea (*Acyrthosiphon pisum*), 760
Periphyllus species
 on *Acer*, 477
Prociphilus species
 on *Fraxinus*, 517
 P. xylosteri (Wooly
  honeysuckle aphids), 540
ranunculus mosaic and, 422
rhododendron
 (*Macrosiphum rhododendri*), 587
rose (*Macrosiphum rosae*), 591
sooty mold and
 on *Gardenia*, 521
 on *Jasminum*, 531
 on *Liriodendron*, 539
 on *Nerium*, 547
 on *Pyracantha*, 573
spirea (*Aphis spiraecola*), 601
spruce
 Elatobium abietinum
  on *Picea*, 555
 green (*Cinara fornacula*)
  on *Picea*, 555
tuliptree (*Macrosiphum liriodendri*), 540
twig
 balsam (*Mindarus abietinus*)
  on *Abies*, 474
virus diseases and, 861
 see also specific viruses
 on flowers, 352, 861
 on fruit and nut trees, 861
 on *Gladiolus*, 395
 on *Tolmiea*, 289
 on tomato, 794
 on vegetables, 861
walnut (*Chromaphis juglandicola*), 674
witch-hazel leaf gall
 (*Hormaphis*

Arbutus (Madrone)
  A. menziesii (Madrone)
    as armillaria root rot
      resistant, 1001
  A. unedo (Strawberry tree)
    as drought tolerant, 997
    planting locations for, 997
  canker and dieback on, 483
Arceuthobium species. *See*
  Dwarf mistletoe
Archips species
  A. argyrospilus. See Fruit
    tree leafroller
  A. rosanus. (European
    leafroller; Filbert
    leafroller), 651
Arctostaphylos (Bearberry;
  Manzanita)
  A. densiflora
    "Harmony"
    leaf gall aphids on, 483
  A. uva-ursi (Bearberry;
    Kinnikinnick)
    as drought resistant, 991
  fungus diseases on
    susceptibility to, 1000
    leaf gall aphids on, 483
  aphids on
    leaf gall, 483
  bees attracted by, 996
  culture, 483
  diseases on
    susceptibility to, 1000
    verticillium wilt, 995
  insects on
    leaf gall aphids, 483
  leaves on
    distorted or reddish
      leaf gall aphid, 483
    green or reddish galls on
      leaf gall aphid, 483
  soil pH for, 1003
Arctotheca
  A. calendula
    saline soils and, 999
Argyresthia species
  (Leafminers; Tip moths)
  on *Juniperus*, 533
Argyrotaenia velutinana
  (Redbanded leafroller)
  on grapes, 743
Armillaria mellea
  on *Acacia*, 476
  on fruit and nut trees, 624
  on grapes, 746
  on *Juniperus*, 533
  on *Quercus*, 580
  on strawberries, 780
  on trees, 446, 466, 858
Armillaria root rot, 858
  See also Honey mushroom;
    Mushroom root rot; Oak
    root fungus; Shoestring
    fungus
  on grapes, 746
  on strawberries, 780
  on trees, 446, 858
  plants resistant to, 1001

resistance to, 1001
Armored scales, 879
Armyworms
  beet
    insecticides for, 951
  fall
    insecticides for, 947, 954,
      956, 964
  insecticides for, 940–943,
    946, 956, 963, 965
  on corn, 724
    poor pollination and, 725
  on lawns
    insecticides for, 952
  on *Petunia*, 417
Aronia (Chokeberry)
  as quince rust susceptible,
    1000
Arrowwood. *See Viburnum*
Artemisia vulgaris
  (Mugwort), 847
Artichoke plume moth
  (*Platyptilia
    carduidactyla*)
  on globe artichoke, 696
Artichokes. *See* Globe
  artichoke; Jerusalem
  artichoke
Asclepias syriaca. See
  Milkweed
Ascochyta blight
  controlling, 968
  on peas, 759
Ash. *See* Fraxinus
  mountain. *See* Sorbus
Ash flower gall mite
  (*Aceria fraxinivorus*),
    517
Ash hornworms
  insecticides for, 956
Ash plant bugs
  insecticides for, 951
Ash sawflies, blackheaded
  insecticides for, 951
Ash-gray snowball aphid
  (*Neoceruraphis
    viburnicola*)
  on *Viburnum*, 610
Ashes. *See* Wood ashes
Asiatic chestnut. *See*
  *Castanea crenata;
    Castanea molissima*
Asparagus (Asparagus fern)
  bending toward light
    insufficient light, 235
  culture, 235
  dying
    mealybugs, 236
  growing locations for
    light and, 235
    sunburn and, 235
  honeydew on surfaces
    below
    mealybugs, 236
    scales, 235
  insects on

insecticides for, 969
  mealybugs, 236
  scales, 235
leaves on
  brown crusty bumps on
    scales, 235
  deformed
    mealybugs, 236
  dropping
    insufficient light, 235
    scales, 235
  dying
    mealybugs, 236
  honeydew on
    mealybugs, 236
    scales, 235
  oval white insects in white
    cottony masses on
    mealybugs, 236
  pale green
    insufficient light, 235
  shiny or sticky substance
    on
    mealybugs, 236
    scales, 235
  spots on
    mealybugs, 236
  white cottony masses on
    mealybugs, 236
    scales, 235
  withering
    mealybugs, 236
  yellowing
    insufficient light, 235
    scales, 235
light requirements for, 235
slow growth in
  insufficient light, 235
stems on
  bending toward light
    insufficient light, 235
  brown crusty bumps on
    scales, 235
  dying
    insufficient light, 235
  elongated
    insufficient light, 235
  oval white insects in white
    cottony masses on
    mealybugs, 236
  shiny, sticky substance on
    scales, 235
  turning tan or brown
    insufficient light, 235
  weak
    insufficient light, 235
  white cottony masses on
    mealybugs, 236
    scales, 235
sunburn on
  watering and, 235
weak
  insufficient light, 235
withering
  mealybugs, 236
Asparagus (edible)
  as fusarium wilt
    susceptible, 1009
  California 500
    as rust resistant, 698

culture, 697
diseases on
  cotton root rot, 994
  fusarium wilt, 697
    susceptibility to, 1009
  rust, 698
  verticillium wilt, 995
dying
  fusarium wilt, 697
ferns on
  beetles or grubs on
    asparagus beetles, 698
  chewed, 698
    asparagus beetles, 698
  reddish brown, orange, or
    black blisters on
    rust, 698
fertilizing, 697, 934, 936
  small spears and, 697
germination of, 1009
harvesting, 697
  small spears and, 697
insects on
  asparagus beetles, 698
leaf scales on
  white or pink cottonlike
    strands under
    fusarium wilt, 697
Martha Washington
  as rust resistant, 698
Mary Washington
  as rust resistant, 698
planting dates for, 1009
planting directions for, 697
  fusarium wilt and, 697
planting locations for, 697
  fusarium wilt and, 697
  small spears and, 697
roots of
  reddish
    fusarium wilt, 697
rust-resistant varieties of,
  698
seeds
  germination of, 1009
snails and slugs on
  baits for, 938
soil pH for, 697, 1002
spears
  beetles or grubs on
    asparagus beetles, 698
  maturing early
    rust, 698
  shiny black specks on
    asparagus beetles, 698
skinny
  immature plants, 697
  overharvesting, 697
  poor soil, 697
small
  immature plants, 697
  overharvesting, 697
  poor soil, 697
sparse
  rust, 698
tips chewed and scarred
  asparagus beetles, 698
turning brown
  fusarium wilt, 697
wilting

fusarium wilt, 697
yellowing
   fusarium wilt, 697
stems on
   beetles or grubs on
      asparagus beetles, 698
   reddish brown, orange, or
      black blisters on
      rust, 698
tops on
   dying back
      rust, 698
   turning brown or yellow
      rust, 698
   Waltham Washington
      as rust resistant, 698
   watering, 697
   rust and, 698
Asparagus beetle (*Crioceris
   asparagi; C.
   duodecimpunctata*), 698
   controlling, 961
Asparagus fern. *See
   Asparagus*
Aspen. *See* Populus
Aspidistra (Cast iron plant)
   light requirements for, 990
   salt damage to, 990
Asplenium (Bird's nest fern)
See also Ferns
   nematodes on, 263
   salt damage to, 990
Aspon
   as ingredient
      in ORTHO Chinch Bug &
      Sod Webworm Control,
      939
Aster leafhopper
   (*Macrosteles fascifrons*)
See also Six-spotted
   leafhopper
   insecticides for, 963
   on *Coreopsis*, 384
   on flowers, 357
   on lettuce, 750
   on vegetables, 691
Aster yellows, 861
   on *Callistephus*, 373
   on carrots, 721
   on celery, 723
   on *Chrysanthemum*, 380
   on *Coreopsis*
      leafhoppers and, 384
   on flowers
      leafhoppers and, 357
   on *Gladiolus*, 396
   on lettuce, 752
      leafhoppers and, 750
   on vegetables
      leafhoppers and, 691
   plants susceptible to, 994
Aster
   annual. *See Callistephus*
   China. *See Callistephus*
   diseases on
      aster yellows, 994
      fungicides for, 946
      leaf spot, 366

powdery mildew, 367, 995
   rust, 560
flowering times for, 992
germination of, 992
insects on
   celery leaftiers, 722
   Japanese beetles, 997
   leaftiers, 722
leaves on
   dying
      leaf spot, 366
      powdery mildew, 367
   grayish white powdery
      patches on
      powdery mildew, 367
   spots or blotches on
      leaf spot, 366
   yellowing
      leaf spot, 366
      powdery mildew, 367
planting times for, 992
stems on
   grayish white powdery
      patches on
      powdery mildew, 367
Asterolecanium species (Pit
   scales)
   on *Quercus*, 578
Astilbe
   diseases on
      fusarium wilt, 994
   flowering times for, 992
   flowers on
      malformed
         aphids, 367
   germination of, 992
   insects on
      ants, 367
      aphids, 367
   leaves on
      curled and distorted
         aphids, 367
      shiny, sticky substance on
         aphids, 367
      yellowing
         aphids, 367
   planting times for, 992
Atrazine
   for henbit
      in lawns, 317
Aucuba (Gold-dust plant)
   as shade tolerant, 997
   culture, 483
   fertilizing, 923, 924
   sunburn on, 483
Automeris io (Io caterpillar)
   on *Rosa*, 592
Avena fatua (Wild oats), 830
Avocado plant, indoors
   culture, 236
   greenhouse whiteflies on,
      236
   salt damage to, 990
Avocado tree, outdoors
   animal damage to, 636
   Bacon
      as California variety, 1001
   bird damage to, 636

branches on
   dying
      phytophthora root rot,
      637
   oval white insects in white
      cottony masses on
      mealybugs, 236
Brogdon
   as Florida variety, 1001
California varieties of, 1001
Choquette
   as Florida variety, 1001
culture, 635
diseases on
   armillaria root rot, 1001
   bacterial blight, 1000
   Botryosphaeria ribis, 1002
   cercospora leaf spot, 636
   fruit scab, 636
   phytophthora root rot, 637
   southern blight, 996
   susceptibility to, 1000
dying
   mealybugs, 236
   phytophthora root rot, 637
fertilizing, 635, 925, 936
Florida varieties of, 1001
fruit on
   deformed
      fruit scab, 636
   distorted
      omnivorous loopers, 635
   eaten
      animal damage, 636
   harvesting, 635
   holes in
      animal damage, 636
   rotting
      cercospora leaf spot, 636
   scabby areas on
      fruit scab, 636
   scarred
      omnivorous loopers, 635
   slow growth in
      cercospora leaf spot, 636
   small
      fruit scab, 636
      phytophthora root rot,
      637
   spots on
      cercospora leaf spot, 636
Fuerte
   as California variety, 1001
   hardiness of, 1001
   harvesting, 635
Hass
   as California variety, 1001
   honeydew on surfaces
      below
      mealybugs, 236
   insects on
      insecticides for, 968
      mealybugs, 236
      Mediterranean fruit flies,
      1002
      omnivorous loopers, 635
   leaves on
      angular brown spots on
      cercospora leaf spot, 636
      chewed

omnivorous loopers, 635
deformed
   mealybugs, 236
dropping
   cercospora leaf spot, 636
   phytophthora root rot,
   637
dying
   mealybugs, 236
eaten
   omnivorous loopers, 635
grayish tufts on spots on
   cercospora leaf spot, 636
holes in
   cercospora leaf spot, 636
honeydew on
   mealybugs, 236
oval white insects in white
   cottony masses on
   mealybugs, 236
small
   phytophthora root rot,
   637
sparse
   phytophthora root rot,
   637
spots on
   mealybugs, 236
sticky material on
   mealybugs, 236
striped yellow to pale
   green worms on
   omnivorous loopers, 635
stripped to membrane
   omnivorous loopers, 635
webbed together
   omnivorous loopers, 635
white cottony masses on
   mealybugs, 236
wilting
   mealybugs, 236
   phytophthora root rot,
   637
yellowing
   phytophthora root rot,
   637
planting locations for, 635
Pollock
   as Florida variety, 1001
pruning, 635
snails and slugs on
   baits for, 938
soil pH for, 635
stems on
   oval white insects in white
      cottony masses on
      mealybugs, 236
Tonnage
   as Florida variety, 1001
trunk of
   darkened bark on
      phytophthora root rot,
      637
   discolorations under bark
      on
      phytophthora root rot,
      637
watering, 635
weak
   cercospora leaf spot, 636

Balsam woolly aphid
  (*Adelges piceae*)
  on *Abies*, 475
Bamboo. *See Bambusa*
Bambusa (Bamboo)
  creeping
    as invasive, 484
  culture, 484
  diseases on
    verticillium wilt, 995
  insects on
    ants
      aphids and, 484
    bamboo aphids, 484
    bamboo scales, 484
    planting directions for
      invasiveness and, 484
    watering, 484
Bamboo aphids (*Takecallis*
  species), 484
Barberry. *See Berberis*
Barberry looper (*Coryphista*
  meadii)
  on *Mahonia*, 543
Bare-root plants
  choosing, 916
  defined, 216
Bark beetles
  elm
    on *Ulmus*, 607, 609
      Dutch elm disease and,
      607
  European
    on *Ulmus*, 609
  fruit tree
    insecticides for, 953
  hickory (*Scolytus*
    quadrispinosus), 652
  insecticides for, 953
  ips engraver beetles (*Ips*
    species)
    on *Pinus*, 558
  native
    on *Ulmus*, 609
  on *Pinus*, 558
    insecticides for, 953
  on *Quercus*
    oak wilt and, 579
  on trees, 468
Bark shedding, 456
Bark wounds, 911
Bark-feeding animals. *See*
  Animal pests
Bark
  as mulch, 918
  as soil amendment, 918
  wounds on, 911
Barley, wild
  herbicides for, 974
Barnaby's thistle (Yellow
  starthistle), 844
Barnyardgrass
  (*Echinochloa crus-galli*),
  829
  herbicides for, 966, 973
  on lawns, 313
Baron grass

as mildew resistant, 308
Basal rot
  fusarium
    on onion family, 755
Basal stalk rot
  controlling, 968
Basic copper sulfate
  for algal spot
    on *Magnolia*, 542
  for alternaria leaf spot
    on *Pelargonium*, outdoors,
    415
  for *Anemone*
    leaf spot on, 363
  for angular leaf spot
    on cucurbits, 736
  for anthracnose
    oak, 575
    on mango, 653
  for apple
    fireblight on, 630
  for apricot
    bacterial leaf spot on, 632
  for avocado, outdoors
    cercospora leaf spot on,
    636
    fruit scab on, 636
  for bacterial blast
    on cherry, 639
    on plum, 672
  for bacterial blight
    on *Morus*, 546
    on *Syringa*, 602
  for bacterial canker
    on cherry, 639
    on peach; nectarine, 658
    on plum, 672
  for bacterial diseases, 859
  for bacterial gummosis
    on cherry, 639
    on plum, 672
  for bacterial leaf spot
    on apricot, 632
    on *Begonia*, outdoors, 368
    on peach; nectarine, 655
    on plum, 668
  for bacterial leaf spot and
    stem canker
    on *Hedera*, 335
  for bacterial speck
    on tomato, 787
  for bacterial spot
    on peppers, 763
    on tomato, 787
  for *Begonia*, outdoors,
    bacterial leaf spot on, 368
  for brown rot gummosis
    on citrus, 647
  for bud rot
    on palms, outdoors, 550
  for *Campanula*
    leaf spot on, 373
  for cercospora leaf spot
    on avocado, 636
  for cherry
    bacterial blast on, 639
    bacterial canker on, 639
    bacterial gummosis on,
    639

for citrus
  brown rot gummosis on,
  647
  collar rot on, 647
  foot rot on, 647
  greasy spot on, 646
for collar rot
  on citrus, 647
for *Cotoneaster*
  fireblight in, 503
for *Crataegus*
  fireblight on, 505
for crown rot
  on rhubarb, 773
for cucurbits
  angular leaf spot on, 736
for cypress family
  twig and needle blight on,
  507
for didymellina leaf spot
  on *Iris*, 403
for *Eriobotrya*
  fireblight on, 512
for fig
  rust on, 649
for fireblight
  on apple, 630
  on *Cotoneaster*, 503
  on *Crataegus*, 505
  on *Eriobotrya*, 512
  on pear, 660
  on *Pyracantha*, 572
  on *Sorbus*, 599
  on trees, 466
for foot rot
  on citrus, 647
for fruit scab
  on avocado, outdoors, 636
for greasy spot
  on citrus, 646
for *Hedera*
  bacterial leaf spot and
    stem canker on, 335
for *Helianthemum*
  leaf spot on, 397
for *Hemerocallis*
  leaf spot on, 398
for *Heuchera*
  leaf spot on, 399
for *Iris*
  didymellina leaf spot on,
  403
for leaf blister
  oak, 576
for leaf scorch
  on strawberries, 779
for leaf spot
  alternaria
    on *Pelargonium*,
    outdoors, 415
  bacterial
    on *Begonia*, outdoors,
    368
    on plum, 668
  cercospora
    on avocado, 636
  on *Anemone*, 363
  on *Campanula*, 373
  on *Helianthemum*, 397
  on *Hemerocallis*, 398

on *Heuchera*, 399
on *Iris*, 403
on *Primula*, 420
on strawberries, 778
on *Tagetes*, 424
on *Tropaeolum*, 426
on *Vinca*, 340
for *Magnolia*
  algal spot on, 542
for mango
  anthracnose on, 653
  scab on, 653
for *Morus*
  bacterial blight on, 546
for *Narcissus*
  smoulder on, 410
for oak anthracnose, 575
for oak leaf blister, 576
for palms, outdoors
  bud rot on, 550
for peach; nectarine
  bacterial canker on, 658
  bacterial leaf spot on, 655
  shothole fungus on, 655
for pear
  fireblight on, 660
for *Pelargonium*, outdoors
  alternaria leaf spot on, 415
for peppers
  bacterial spot on, 763
for plum
  bacterial blast on, 672
  bacterial canker on, 672
  bacterial gummosis on,
  672
  bacterial leaf spot on, 668
for *Primula*
  leaf spot on, 420
for *Pyracantha*
  fireblight on, 572
for *Quercus*
  oak anthracnose on, 575
  oak leaf blister on, 576
for rhubarb
  crown rot on, 773
  root rot on, 773
for rust
  on fig, 649
for scab
  fruit
    on avocado, 636
    on mango, 653
for shothole fungus
  on peach; nectarine, 655
for smoulder
  on *Narcissus*, 410
for *Sorbus*
  fireblight on, 599
for strawberries
  leaf scorch on, 779
  leaf spot on, 778
for *Syringa*
  bacterial blight on, 602
for *Tagetes*
  leaf spot on, 424
for tomato
  bacterial speck on, 787
  bacterial spot on, 787
for trees
  fireblight on, 466

poor yield of
  bean mosaic, 703
  failure to harvest, 700
  high temperatures, 700
  hopperburn, 702
  root rot, 703
  soil moisture and, 700
rabbits in, 694
roots of
  red spots or streaks on
    root rot, 703
  white grubs on
    bean leaf beetles, 699
seedlings
  collapsing
    seed corn maggots, 704
  dying
    bean anthracnose, 700
    seed corn maggots, 704
  first leaves spotted on
    bean anthracnose, 700
  stems rotting on
    bean anthracnose, 700
  weak
    seed corn maggots, 704
  wilting
    seed corn maggots, 704
seeds
  cream-colored maggots on
    seed corn maggots, 704
  fail to sprout
    seed corn maggots, 704
  shriveled in pods
    bean mosaic, 703
  germination of, 1009
  slow growth in
    root rot, 703
snails and slugs on
  baits for, 938
snap
  harvesting time for, 698
  planting dates for, 1009
  soil pH for, 698
soybeans
  harvesting time for, 698
stems on
  black, hard, seedlike
    structures in mold on
    white mold, 701
  brown or black streaks on
    root rot, 703
  elongated reddish brown
    spots on
    bean anthracnose, 700
  red spots or streaks on
    root rot, 703
  reddish lesions around
    bacterial blight, 701
  rust-colored spots on
    rust, 701
  soft, watery spots on
    white mold, 701
  tiny pale green to black
    insects on
    aphids, 699
white grubs on
  bean leaf beetles, 699
white mold in spots on
  white mold, 701
stunted growth in

bean mosaic, 703
root rot, 703
watering, 698
  bacterial blights and, 701
  failure to set pods and, 700
  root rot and, 703
  rust and, 701
  white mold and, 701
wax bush
  bean-mosaic-resistant
    varieties of, 1010
wilting
  bean leaf beetles, 699
  root rot, 703
wounds on
  hail damage, 689
yellowing
  bean leaf beetles, 699
  curly top, 703
Bear bind. *See* **Field
  bindweed**
Bearberry. *See*
  ***Arctostaphylos uva
  ursi***
Beargrass. *See* **Sandbur**
Bedbugs (*Cimex lectularius*),
  809
  insecticides for, 963
Bedding plants
  fertilizers for, 926
Bedding, pests in
  bedbugs, 809
  brown recluse spiders, 815
  clover mites, 803
  earwigs, 801
Bedstraw
  in lawns
    herbicides for, 971
Bee nettle. *See* **Henbit**
Beech. *See* ***Fagus***
Beefwood. *See* ***Casuarina***
Bees
  attracting, 996
  carpenter (*Xylocopa
    virginica*)
    in households, 811
  fireblight and
    on *Crataegus*, 505
    on *Eriobotrya*, 512
    on *Pyracantha*, 572
    on *Sorbus*, 599
    on trees, 466
  fuchsia mites and, 519
  honeydew and
    on fruit trees, 621
    on trees, 454
  leafcutter (*Megachile*
    species)
    on *Rosa*, 592
  mites and
    on *Fuchsia*, 519
  on *Crataegus*
    fireblight and, 505
  on cucurbits
    pollination by, 731
  on *Eriobotrya*
    fireblight and, 512
  on fruit trees

honeydew and, 621
pollination and, 614
on *Fuchsia*
  fuchsia mites and, 519
on nut trees
  pollination and, 614
on *Pyracantha*
  fireblight and, 572
on *Sorbus*
  fireblight and, 599
on trees
  fireblight and, 466
  honeydew and, 454
plants attractive to, 996
pollination by
  of cucurbits, 731
  of fruit and nut trees, 614
See also Honeybees
Beet armyworms
  insecticides for, 951
Beet leafhopper (*Circulifer
  tenellus*)
  on beans
    curly top and, 703
  on beets
    curly top and, 706
  on cucurbits, 733
  on tomato
    curly top and, 794
Beet leafminer (*Pegomya
  hyoscyami*), 705
Beetles, 872
  See also Borers; Curculios;
    Leafminers; Weevils
  Asiatic
    on lawns, 299
  asparagus (*Crioceris
    asparagi; C.
    duodecimpunctata*), 698
    insecticides for, 961
  bark. *See* Bark beetles
  bean
    insecticides for, 941
    Mexican (*Epilachna
      varivestis*), 699
    insecticides for, 946, 963,
      967
  bean leaf (*Cerotoma
    trifurcata*), 699
    insecticides for, 963
  black carpet
    insecticides for, 947
  blister (*Epicauta* species)
    grasshoppers and, 740
    insecticides for, 947, 954,
      964, 967
    on eggplant, 740
    on potatoes, 769
  borers. *See* Borers
  carpet
    black
      insecticides for, 947
    insecticides for, 949
  cigarette (*Lasioderma
    serricorne*)
    in households, 818
  click
    on potatoes, 767
    See also Wireworms

Colorado potato
  (*Leptinotarsa
    decemlineata*)
    insecticides for, 946, 963,
      967
    on eggplant, 740
    on potatoes, 768
cottonwood leaf
  insecticides for, 951
cucumber. *See* Cucumber
  beetles
described, 355, 358
diabrotica. *See* Cucumber
  beetles, spotted
diseases and, 880
dried fruit
  insecticides for, 946
drugstore (*Stegobium
  paniceum*)
  in households, 818
elm leaf
  insecticides for, 947, 951,
    954, 964
flea. *See* Flea beetles
flour (*Tribolium* and
  Oryzaephilus species)
  in households, 817
fruit tree bark (*Scalytus
  rugulosus*)
  on cherry, 639
grain
  sawtoothed
    in households, 817
  insecticides for, 947
ips engraver (*Ips* species)
  on *Pinus*, 558
Japanese (*Popillia
  japonica*)
  on trees, 442
Japanese. *See* Japanese
  beetle
June
  on lawns, 299
lady, 886
ladybird, 886
larvae of. *See* Leafminers
leaf (*Chrysomela* species)
  elm (*Pyrrhalta luteola*),
    609
  insecticides for, 951
  on *Populus*, 568
  on *Salix*, 595
strawberry
  insecticides for, 948
willow
  insecticides for, 951
masked chafer
  on lawns, 299
May
  on lawns, 299
Mexican bean (*Epilachna
  varivestis*), 699
  insecticides for, 946, 963,
    967
nocturnal
  on vegetables, 689
on beans
  bean leaf (*Cerotoma
    trifurcata*), 699
  Mexican bean (*Epilachna*

varivestis), 699
insecticides for, 946, 963,
   967
on flowers, 355, 358
on *Rosa*, 593
on trees, 441, 449
on vegetables, 689
potato
   Colorado (*Leptinotarsa
      decemlineata*)
   insecticides for, 946, 963,
      967
   on eggplant, 740
   on potatoes, 768
powderpost
   in households, 809
sap-feeding
   insecticides for, 963
   on *Platanus*
      canker stain disease and,
         565
   on *Quercus*
      oak wilt and, 579
sawtoothed grain
   in households, 817
   insecticides for, 947
   snout, 873
   See also Curculios; Root
      weevils; Weevils
spotted cucumber. *See*
   Cucumber beetles,
   spotted
strawberry leaf
   insecticides for, 948
striped cucumber. *See*
   Cucumber beetles,
   striped
twelve-spotted
   insecticides for, 961
willow
   insecticides for, 951
wood-boring
   on *Quercus,* 577
Beets
as smog tolerant, 996
as verticillium wilt
   susceptible, 1009
boron deficiency in, 705
culture, 704
diseases on
   cercospora leaf spot, 705
   curly top, 703, 706
   damping-off, 706
   leaf spot, 705
   powdery mildew, 995
   root rot
      boron deficiency and,
         705
   scab, 766
   southern blight, 996
   verticillium wilt
      susceptibility to, 1009
dying
   curly top, 706
   flea beetles, 704
fertilizing, 704, 934, 936
   boron deficiency and, 705
   damping-off and, 706
germination of, 1009

greenish yellow insects on
   beet leafhoppers, 706
harvesting, 704
in containers
   fertilizing, 704
insects on
   beet leafhoppers
      curly top and, 706
   beet leafminers, 705
   celery leaftiers, 722
   flea beetles, 704
   millipedes, 693
   seed corn maggots, 704
   wireworms, 730
leaves on
   blisters or tunnels in
      beet leafminers, 705
   blotches on
      beet leafminers, 705
      leaf spot, 705
   brittle
      curly top, 706
   brown areas peeling apart
      in
      beet leafminers, 705
   brown edges on
      boron deficiency, 705
   cream-colored maggots in
      beet leafminers, 705
   dead areas on
      leaf spot, 705
   drying out
      flea beetles, 704
   dying
      boron deficiency, 705
      flea beetles, 704
      leaf spot, 705
   gray mold on
      leaf spot, 705
   holes in
      flea beetles, 704
   puckering along veins
      under
      curly top, 706
   rolled margins on
      curly top, 706
   rough-feeling under
      curly top, 706
   small, dark-bordered spots
      on
      leaf spot, 705
   stunted
      curly top, 706
   tiny black beetles on
      flea beetles, 704
   tiny black specks inside
      tunnels in
      beet leafminers, 705
   turning reddish purple
      boron deficiency, 705
   white eggs under
      beet leafminers, 705
   yellowing
      leaf spot, 705
millipedes on, 693
planting directions for
   damping-off and, 706
planting locations for, 704
planting times for, 1009
   beet leafminers and, 705

damping-off and, 706
roots of
   black areas on or inside
      boron deficiency, 705
   cracked
      boron deficiency, 705
   stunted
      curly top, 706
   wrinkled
      boron deficiency, 705
seedlings
   discolored stems on
      damping-off, 706
   falling over
      damping-off, 706
   soft and thin stem bases on
      damping-off, 706
   water-soaked stems on
      damping-off, 706
   wilting
      flea beetles, 704
seeds
   fail to sprout
      damping-off, 706
   germination of, 1009
snails and slugs on
   baits for, 938
soil pH for, 704, 1002
   boron deficiency and, 705
stunted growth in
   boron deficiency, 705
watering, 704
   damping-off and, 706
   leafspot and, 705
wilting
   flea beetles, 704
yellowing
   curly top, 706
Beggarweed, creeping
herbicide for, 974
***Begonia,* indoors**
angelwing
   insecticide for, 969
bending toward light
   insufficient light, 237
culture, 237
diseases on
   powdery mildew, 237
dying
   mealybugs, 237
flower buds on
   webbing on
      spider mites, 238
flowers on
   fail to grow
      insufficient light, 237
   white powdery patches on
      powdery mildew, 237
heat requirements for
   powdery mildew and, 237
honeydew on surfaces
   below
   mealybugs, 237
insects on
   cyclamen mites, 285
   greenhouse whiteflies,
      238
   insecticides for, 948
   mealybugs, 237

spider mites, 238
leaves on
   deformed
      mealybugs, 237
   dirty
      spider mites, 238
   dropping
      insufficient light, 237
      powdery mildew, 237
      spider mites, 238
   drying out
      spider mites, 238
   dying
      mealybugs, 237
   honeydew on
      greenhouse whiteflies,
         238
      mealybugs, 237
   mottled
      greenhouse whiteflies,
         238
   oval white insects in white
      cottony masses on
      mealybugs, 237
   pale
      insufficient light, 237
   spots on
      mealybugs, 237
   sticky material on
      mealybugs, 237
   stippled
      spider mites, 238
   tiny winged insects under
      greenhouse whiteflies,
         238
   turning brown
      powdery mildew, 237
   webbing between or
      under
      spider mites, 238
   white cottony masses on
      mealybugs, 237
   white powdery patches on
      powdery mildew, 237
   white waxy powder on
      insects on
      greenhouse whiteflies,
         238
   withering
      mealybugs, 237
   yellowing
      greenhouse whiteflies,
         238
      insufficient light, 237
      powdery mildew, 237
      spider mites, 238
light requirements for
   insufficient light and, 237
   powdery mildew and, 237
slow growth in
   insufficient light, 237
stems on
   elongated and weak
      insufficient light, 237
   oval white insects in
      cottony masses on
      mealybugs, 237
   white powdery patches on
      powdery mildew, 237
sunburn on

watering and, 237
tiny insects fluttering
  around
  greenhouse whiteflies,
  238
weak
  insufficient light, 237
withering
  mealybugs, 237
Begonia, outdoors
  collapsing
    bacterial leaf spot, 368
    root and stem rot, 369
  culture, 367
  diseases on
    bacterial leaf spot, 368
    fungal leaf spot, 368
    gray mold, 368
    powdery mildew, 369, 995
    root and stem rot, 369
    verticillium wilt, 995
  dying
    root and stem rot, 369
  fertilizing, 367, 928, 932
  fibrous
    culture, 367
  flowering times for, 367,
    992
  flowers on
    gray mold and spots on
      gray mold, 368
  germination of, 992
  honeydew on
    mealybugs, 370
  in containers
    watering, 367
  insects on
    insecticide for, 948
    leaf nematodes, 369
    mealybugs, 370
  leaf buds
    fail to develop
      leaf nematodes, 369
  leaves on
    blotches on
      bacterial leaf spot, 368
      fungal leaf spot, 368
      gray mold, 368
      leaf nematodes, 369
    brown spots with yellow,
      translucent margins on
      bacterial leaf spot, 368
    curling upward
      leaf nematodes, 369
    deformed
      mealybugs, 370
    dropping
      bacterial leaf spot, 368
      leaf nematodes, 369
    dying
      bacterial leaf spot, 368
      fungal leaf spot, 368
      powdery mildew, 369
    fuzzy mold on
      gray mold, 368
    grayish powdery spots on
      powdery mildew, 369
    oval white insects in
      cottony masses on
      mealybugs, 370

powdery spots and
  patches on
  powdery mildew, 369
rotting
  gray mold, 368
  root and stem rot, 369
shiny and sticky
  mealybugs, 370
slimy ooze on
  bacterial leaf spot, 368
small blisterlike spots on
  bacterial leaf spot, 368
soft
  gray mold, 368
spots on
  bacterial leaf spot, 368
  fungal leaf spot, 368
  gray mold, 368
  powdery mildew, 369
  white cottony masses on
    mealybugs, 370
withering
  leaf nematodes, 369
  mealybugs, 370
yellowing
  fungal leaf spot, 368
  powdery mildew, 369
planting locations for, 367
  root and stem rot and, 369
planting times for, 367, 992
roots of
  dark
    root and stem rot, 369
  rotted
    root and stem rot, 369
soil pH for, 367
stems on
  brown spots and blotches
    on
    gray mold, 368
  cobwebby strands on
    root and stem rot, 369
  discolored, water-soaked
    areas on
    root and stem rot, 369
  fuzzy mold on
    gray mold, 368
  oval white insects in
    cottony masses on
    mealybugs, 370
  powdery spots and
    patches on
    powdery mildew, 369
  rotted
    gray mold, 368
  soft
    gray mold, 368
  white cottony masses on
    mealybugs, 370
strawberry
  insecticide for, 969
stunted growth in
  leaf nematodes, 369
  root and stem rot, 369
tuberous
  fertilizing, 367, 924, 928,
    932
  flowering times for, 367
  planting locations for, 367
  planting time for, 367

watering, 367
  bacterial leaf spot and,
    368
  gray mold and, 368
  leaf nematodes and, 369
wilting
  root and stem rot, 369
Bellflower. *See Campanula*
Bellis
  B. perennis (English daisy)
    as verticillium wilt
    resistant, 995
Beneficial insects
  bees. *See* Bees; Honeybees
  cinnabar moth
    tansy ragwort eaten by,
    846
  crickets as, 881
  earwigs as, 693
  lacewings, 887
  lady beetles, 886
  leafcutter bees
    on *Rosa,* 592
  parasitic wasps
    on hornworms, 740
  praying mantids, 886
  Trichogramma species
    for omnivorous loopers
    on avocado, 635
Benlate
  for ash anthracnose, 516
  for bulb rot
    on *Lilium,* 406
  for camellia flower blight,
    493
  for dieback
    on *Rosa,* 594
  for diplodia tip blight
    on *Pinus,* 557
  for *Euonymus*
    powdery mildew on, 512
  for *Fraxinus*
    ash anthracnose on, 516
  for fungal leaf spot
    on *Photinia,* 553
    on *Rhododendron,* 583
  for *Lilium*
    root and bulb rot on, 406
  for petal blight
    on *Rhododendron,* 581
  for *Photinia*
    fungal leaf spot on, 553
  for *Pinus*
    diplodia tip blight on, 557
  for powdery mildew
    on *Euonymus,* 512
    on *Platanus,* 564
  for *Rhododendron*
    fungal leaf spot on, 583
    petal blight on, 581
  for root and bulb rot
    on *Lilium,* 406
  for stem cankers and
    dieback
    on *Rosa,* 594
Benomyl
  for anthracnose
    on lawns, 297
    walnut, 675

for apple
  powdery mildew on, 630
for apricot
  scab on, 633
for *Araucaria*
  needle blight on, 482
for beans
  watery soft rot on, 701
  white mold on, 701
for *Begonia*
  fungal leaf spot on, 368
  gray mold on, 368
for black knot
  on plum, 671
for blueberries
  stem and blossom blight
    on, 708
for botrytis blight
  on *Tulipa,* 430
for brambles
  powdery mildew on, 712
for brown rot
  on plum, 669
for bulb and stem rot
  on *Tulipa,* 429
for canker and dieback
  on *Vinca,* 340
for canker wilt
  on *Gleditsia,* 524
for celery
  early blight on, 723
  late blight on, 722
for *Chrysanthemum*
  leaf spot on, 378
for *Cineraria*
  powdery mildew on, 382
for citrus
  greasy spot on, 646
for *Cornus*
  flower and leaf blight on,
    501
for *Cosmos*
  powdery mildew on, 384
for cucurbits
  powdery mildew on, 737
for *Delphinium*
  powdery mildew on, 389
for didymellina leaf spot
  on *Iris,* 403
for early blight
  on celery, 723
for flower and leaf blight
  on *Cornus,* 501
for fruit and nut trees
  powdery mildew on, 621
for fungal leaf spot
  on *Begonia,* outdoors, 368
  on *Kalmia,* 535
  on trees, 450
for fungus diseases
  on trees, 450
for fusarium blight
  on lawns, 298
for fusarium bulb rot
  on *Narcissus,* 411
for fusarium patch
  on lawns, 297
for *Gleditsia*
  canker wilt on, 524
for gliocladium rot

on palms, indoors, 278
for gray mold
on *Begonia*, outdoors, 368
on *Paeonia*, 412
on *Pelargonium*, outdoors, 414
on *Salvia*, 423
for greasy spot
on citrus, 646
for groundcovers
powdery mildew on, 328
for *Hydrangea*
powdery mildew on, 527
for *Impatiens*
leaf spot on, 402
for *Iris*
leaf spot on, 403
for *Juniperus*
twig blight and, 532
for *Kalmia*
fungal leaf spot on, 535
for late blight
on celery, 722
for *Lathyrus*
powdery mildew on, 405
for lawns
anthracnose on, 297
fusarium blight on, 298
fusarium patch on, 297
powdery mildew on, 308
stripe smut on, 307
for leaf blight
flower blight and
on *Cornus*, 501
for leaf scorch
on strawberries, 779
for leaf spot
on *Chrysanthemum*, 378
on *Impatiens*, 402
on *Iris*, 403
on *Phlox*, 419
on *Primula*, 420
on strawberries, 778
on *Tagetes*, 424
for *Lonicera*
powdery mildew on, 541
for *Narcissus*
fusarium bulb rot on, 411
for needle blight
on *Araucaria*, 482
for *Paeonia*
gray mold on, 412
for palms, indoors
gliocladium rot on, 278
for pecan
scab on, 666
for *Pelargonium*, outdoors
gray mold on, 414
for *Phlox*
leaf spot on, 419
for plum
black knot on, 671
brown rot on, 669
for powdery mildew
on apple, 630
on brambles, 712
on *Cineraria*, 382
on *Cosmos*, 384
on cucurbits, 737
on *Delphinium*, 389

on fruit and nut trees, 621
on groundcovers, 328
on *Hydrangea*, 527
on *Lathyrus*, 405
on lawns, 308
on *Lonicera*, 541
on sunflower, 784
on trees, 445
on vegetables, 688
on *Viburnum*, 610
on *Zinnia*, 434
for *Primula*
leaf spot on, 420
for *Pyracantha*
scab on, 572
for *Salvia*
gray mold on, 423
for scab
on apricot, 633
on pecan, 666
on *Pyracantha*, 572
for stem and blossom blight
on blueberries, 708
for stem blight
blossom blight and
on blueberries, 708
for strawberries
leaf scorch on, 779
leaf spot on, 778
for stripe smut
on lawns, 307
for sunflower
powdery mildew on, 784
for *Tagetes*
leaf spot on, 424
for trees
fungal leaf spot on, 450
fungus diseases on, 450
powdery mildew on, 445
for *Tulipa*
botrytis blight on, 430
bulb and stem rot on, 429
for twig blight
on *Juniperus*, 532
for vegetables
powdery mildew on, 688
for *Viburnum*
powdery mildew on, 610
for *Vinca*
canker and dieback on, 340
for walnut anthracnose, 675
for watery soft rot
on beans, 701
for white mold
on beans, 701
for *Zinnia*
powdery mildew on, 434
ORTHO Pruning Seal and
for *Platanus*
canker stain disease on, 565
Bensulide
for *Dichondra*
annual bluegrass in, 332
crabgrass in, 332
Bentgrass (*Agrostis* species)
See also Lawns
Arlington

as dollar spot resistant, 990
as cool season grass, 300, 301
as drought tolerant, 304
as shade tolerant, 991
as turf, 311
as weed
herbicides for, 974
in lawns, 311
characteristics of, 991
diseases on
dollar spot, 298
varieties resistant to, 990
fusarium blight, 298
Ophiobolus patch, 299
germination times for, 991
herbicides for, 974
mowing heights for, 294
Pennpar
as dollar spot resistant, 990
planting times for, 300, 301
planting zone for, 991
weeds in
herbicide for, 973
Berberis (Barberry)
as crown gall resistant, 998
B. polyantha
as armillaria root rot resistant, 1001
bees attracted by, 996
Japanese barberry
soil pH for, 1003
Bermuda mites. *See* Bermudagrass mites
Bermudagrass (*Cynodon dactylon*)
See also Lawns
as drought tolerant, 304, 991
as warm season grass, 300, 301
as weed, 826
in *Dichondra*, 332
in lawns, 302, 311
herbicides for, 972, 974, 976, 977
brown patches on
Bermudagrass mites, 307
characteristics of, 304, 311, 991
cool weather grasses and, 302
dead patches on
Bermudagrass mites, 307
diseases on
dollar spot, 298
powdery mildew, 308
dormancy in, 302
fertilizing
Bermudagrass mites and, 307
germination times for, 991
insects on
Bermudagrass mites, 307
mole crickets, 303
"knots" or rosettes on
Bermudagrass mites, 307

mowing heights for, 294
planting directions for, 991
planting times for, 300, 301
planting zone for, 991
weeds in
herbicides for, 972, 977
yellow patches on
Bermudagrass mites, 307
Bermudagrass mite (*Aceria neocynodonis*), 307
insecticides for, 940, 942
Berries. *See* Blueberries; Brambles; Strawberries; Vegetables, berries, and grapes
Berry moths, grape (*Endopiza viteana*), 743
Beta vulgaris. *See* Beets
Beta vulgaris cicla. *See* Swiss chard
Betony, Florida (*Stachys floridana*), 850
in lawns
herbicides for, 977
Betula (Birch)
as crown gall resistant, 998
B. alba (White birch)
bark shedding on, 456
birch leafminers on, 486
B. alleghentiensis (Yellow birch)
gypsy moths on, 1000
B. nigra (River birch)
as wet soil tolerant, 997
planting locations for, 997
B. papyrifera (Paper birch)
birch leafminers on, 486
gypsy moths on, 1000
B. pendula (European white birch)
as smog tolerant, 996
B. populifolia (Gray birch)
birch leafminers on, 486
B. pumila (Swamp birch)
as armillaria root rot resistant, 1001
bird damage to, 999
branches on
D-shaped holes and ridges on
bronze birch borers, 486
dying back
aphids, 486
bronze birch borers, 486
dieback, 487
swollen, sawdust-filled ridges on
bronze birch borers, 486
culture, 485, 486
diseases on
crown gall
resistance to, 998
dieback, 487
verticillium wilt, 995
drought stress on
dieback and, 487
dying

bronze birch borers, 486
fertilizing, 485, 486, 927
fill injury to, 999
honeydew on plants or
objects below
aphids, 486
insects on
ants
aphids and, 486
aphids, 486
witch-hazel leaf gall, 524
birch leafminers, 486
bronze birch borers, 486
dieback and, 487
witch-hazel leaf gall
aphids, 524
leaves on
brown blisters in
birch leafminers, 486
brown blotches on
birch leafminers, 486
dropping
dieback, 487
honeydew on
aphids, 486
increased on lower
branches
bronze birch borers, 486
puckered
aphids, 486
shiny, sticky substance on
aphids, 486
sparse at top
bronze birch borers, 486
tiny yellow, green, or
blackish insects under
aphids, 486
turning brown
bronze birch borers, 486
twisted
aphids, 486
yellowing
aphids, 486
bronze birch borers, 486
dieback, 487
lightning injury to, 999
planting locations for, 485,
486
pruning, 485
sapsucker damage to, 999
stems on
tiny yellow, green, or
blackish insects on
aphids, 486
stunted growth in
dieback, 487
trunk on
D-shaped holes and ridges
on
bronze birch borers, 486
swollen, sawdust-filled
ridges on
bronze birch borers, 486
twigs on
dying back
aphids, 486
bronze birch borers, 486
watering, 485, 486
dieback and, 487
Bidens bipinnata

(Spanishneedles), 834
Biennial plant, defined,
216
Billbugs (*Sphenophorus*
species)
insecticides for, 940–942
on lawns, 302
Bindweed. *See* Field
bindweed
Birch. *See Betula*
Birch leafminer (*Fenusa
pusilla*), 486
insecticides for, 951, 966
Birch sawflies, dusky
insecticides for, 951
Bird damage, 893
See also Animal pests
by sapsuckers, 893
to trees, 454
diseases, 804
in households, 804
to avocado, outdoors, 636
to brambles
protection from, 709
to corn, 725
by starlings, 725
to fig, 649
to fruit and nut trees, 616
to grapes, 747
to lawns, 310
to *Ranunculus*, 421
to trees, 454
to vegetables, 683
to *Wisteria*, 611
Bird's eye rot
on grapes, 745
Bird's nest fern. *See
Asplenium*
Bird's nest plant. *See* Wild
carrot
Bird's pepper (*Lepidium
virginicum*), 833
Birdgrass. *See* Prostrate
knotweed
Birdseed. *See* Groundsel
Birka grass
as mildew resistant, 308
Bischofia
culture, 487
false oleander scales on,
487
Biting flies
in households, 814
insecticides for, 948
Biting midges
near households, 814
Bitter nightshade
(*Solanum dulcamara*),
850
Bitter rot
controlling, 948, 957
on apple, 627
resistance to, 1005
Bittercress, herbicides for,
974

Bittersweet. *See Celastrus*
Bitterweed (*Ambrosia
artemisiifolia*). *See*
Ragweed
Bitterweed (*Conyza
canadensis*), 846
aster yellows harbored by,
994
Black carpet beetles
insecticides for, 947
Black citrus aphids
(*Toxoptera* aurantii)
on *Camellia*, 494
Black clover. *See* Black
medic
Black flies
in households, 814
Black gnats
near households, 814
Black gum. *See Nyssa*
Black haw. *See Viburnum*
Black heart
on celery, 723
Black knot
on plum, 671
Black leg
on cabbage family, 718
Black locust. *See Robinia*
Black medic (*Medicago
lupulina*), 840
herbicides for, 971, 974,
977, 978
in lawns, 315
Black mold
controlling, 968
Black nightshade (*Solanum
nigrum*), 850
Black olive. *See Bucida*
Black pecan aphid
(*Tinocallis caryaefoliae*),
666
Black plastic mulch, 918
Black pox
controlling, 948
Black root rot
on radishes, 773
on spinach, 779
Black rot
controlling, 948
on cabbage family, 715
cabbage maggots and, 716
on grapes, 743
varieties resistant to, 1007
on sweet potato, 782
Black scale (*Saissetia oleae*)
on citrus, 644
insecticides for, 940
on *Nerium*, 548
Black spot
controlling, 942, 944, 946,
956, 957, 959, 961, 962
on *Rosa*, 589
stem cankers and, 594
tolerance to, 993
Black swallowtail

butterfly
on parsley, 757
Black vine weevil
(*Otiorhynchus sulcatus*)
See also Taxus weevil
insecticides for, 951, 956
on *Rhododendron*, 586
on strawberries, 780
on *Taxus*, 604
Black widow spiders
(*Latrodectus* species)
in households, 801, 815
Black-eyed Susan
aster yellows and, 861
Blackbirds
in corn, 725
Blackeye peas. *See* Peas,
southern or blackeye
Blackheaded ash sawflies
insecticides for, 951
Blackjacks. *See Plantain*
Blackleg
on *Pelargonium*, outdoors,
415
Blackline
on walnut, 676
Blackseed plantain
herbicides for, 974
Blackspot
controlling, 958, 965, 968
Blackweed. *See* Ragweed
Bladder gall mite (*Vasates
quadripedes*)
on *Acer*, 478
Blanket flower. *See
Gaillardia*
Blast. *See* Bacterial blast
Blatella germanica. See
Cockroaches, German
Blatta orientalis. See
Cockroaches, oriental
Bleaching
on houseplants, 226
Blind nettle. *See Henbit*
Blissus species. *See* Chinch
bugs
Blister beetles (*Epicauta*
species)
insecticides for, 947, 954,
964, 967
on eggplant, 740
on peppers, 769
Blister mite
(*Eriophyes buceras*)
on *Bucida*, 488
insecticides for, 958
on pear
insecticides for, 942
pear leaf (*Eriophyes pyri*)
on *Sorbus*, 600
pear leaf (*Phytoptus pyri*)
on *Cotoneaster*, 504
on pear, 662
Blister rust
white pine

on currants; gooseberries,
738
Blood leaf. *See Iresine*
Blood Meal. *See* ORTHO
Blood Meal
Blood stanch (*Conyza
canadensis*), 846
aster yellows harbored by,
994
Blossom blight, 857
See also Botrytis blight;
Gray mold
controlling, 968
stem blight, and
on blueberries, 708
Blossom drop
on peppers, 762
Blossom-end rot
on cucurbits, 732
on peppers, 763
on tomato, 786
Blotch
cercospora
controlling, 957
Blow ball. *See* Dandelion
Blue daisy. *See* Chicory
Blue mold
on spinach, 775
See also Downy mildew
Blue sailors. *See* Chicory
Blue toadflax
herbicides for, 974
Bluebell of Scotland. *See
Campanula*
Blueberries
berries on
caterpillars in
fruitworms, 707
dropping before ripening
mummy berry, 708
gray, shriveled, and hard
mummy berry, 708
reddish buff or tan
mummy berry, 708
sawdustlike material
inside
fruitworms, 707
shriveled
fruitworms, 707
webbed together with silk
fruitworms, 707
blossoms on
brown or grayish mold on
stem and blossom blight,
708
brown spots and blotches
on
stem and blossom blight,
708
turning brown and
withering
mummy berry, 708
branches on
dying
scales, 709
culture, 706
diseases on

mummy berry, 708
powdery mildew, 995
stem and blossom blight,
708
susceptibility and
resistance to, 1000
fertilizing, 706, 936
fruit on
circular indentations in
plum curculios, 707
dropping
plum curculios, 707
harvesting, 706
plum curculios, 707
hollow
plum curculios, 707
leaking juice
blueberry maggots, 707
ripening early
plum curculios, 707
shriveled
plum curculios, 707
soft and mushy
blueberry maggots, 707
white, tapered maggots in
blueberry maggots, 707
yellowish white grubs in
plum curculios, 707
harvesting, 706
highbush
disease susceptibility in,
1000
planting locations for,
1003
insects on
blueberry fruitflies, 707
blueberry maggots, 707
cherry fruitworms, 707
cranberry fruitworms, 707
cutworms, 689
leafrollers and leaftiers,
708
plum curculios, 707
scales, 709
leaves on
black centers on
mummy berry, 708
black sawdust and silk
threads inside
leafrollers and leaftiers,
708
caterpillars inside
leafrollers and leaftiers,
708
crusty or scaly bumps on
scales, 709
dropping
scales, 709
dying
mummy berry, 708
rolled or tied together
leafrollers and leaftiers,
708
soft and rotted
stem and blossom blight,
708
white cottony masses on
scales, 709
wilting
mummy berry, 708

yellowing
scales, 709
nodes on
crusty or scaly bumps on
scales, 709
white cottony masses on
scales, 709
planting directions for, 706
planting locations for, 706,
1003
varieties and, 1003
rabbiteye
disease resistance in, 1000
planting locations for,
1003
shoots on
dying
mummy berry, 708
wilting at tips
mummy berry, 708
soil pH for, 706, 1002
stems on
brown or grayish mold on
stem and blossom blight,
708
brown spots and blotches
on
stem and blossom blight,
708
crusty or scaly bumps on
scales, 709
soft and rotted
stem and blossom blight,
708
white cottony masses on
scales, 709
watering, 706
stem and blossom blight
and, 708
Blueberry fruitfly. *See*
Blueberry maggot
Blueberry maggot
(*Rhagoletis mendax*), 707
insecticides for, 946
Bluegrass
A-20
as dollar spot resistant,
990
as fusarium blight
resistant, 990
as helminthosporium leaf
spot resistant, 990
as mildew resistant, 308
as rust resistant, 990
as septoria leaf spot
tolerant, 307
as stripe smut resistant,
990
A-34
as mildew resistant, 308
as red thread resistant,
990
as rust resistant, 990
as septoria leaf spot
tolerant, 307
as stripe smut resistant,
990
Adelphi
as dollar spot resistant,

990
as fusarium blight
resistant, 990
as fusarium patch
resistant, 990
as helminthosporium leaf
spot resistant, 990
as red thread resistant,
990
as septoria leaf spot
tolerant, 307
as stripe smut resistant,
990
annual (*Poa annua*), 825
herbicides for, 966, 970,
973, 974, 976
on *Dichondra*, 332
on lawns, 311
dead patches of, 296
Aquila
as stripe smut resistant,
990
Arboretum
as fusarium blight
susceptible, 990
as cool season grass, 300–
302
as shade tolerant, 305
Baron
as helminthosporium leaf
spot resistant, 990
Belturf
as fusarium blight
susceptible, 990
Birka
as helminthosporium leaf
spot resistant, 990
as red thread resistant,
990
as septoria leaf spot
tolerant, 307
as stripe smut resistant,
990
Bonnieblue
as dollar spot resistant,
990
as fusarium blight
resistant, 990
as fusarium patch
resistant, 990
as helminthosporium leaf
spot resistant, 990
as red thread resistant,
990
as rust resistant, 990
as septoria leaf spot
tolerant, 307
as stripe smut resistant,
990
Bristol
as dollar spot resistant,
990
as helminthosporium leaf
spot resistant, 990
Brunswick
as fusarium blight
susceptible, 990
as helminthosporium leaf
spot resistant, 990
as stripe smut resistant,

Bronze birch borer (*Agrilus anxius*), 486
  dieback and, 487
Brooks fruit spot
  controlling, 948
Broom. *See Cytisus*
Browallia
  diseases on
    fusarium wilt, 994
    verticillium wilt, 995
  flowering times for, 992
  germination of, 992
  greenhouse whiteflies on, 370
  planting times for, 992
Brown arborvitae aphid (*Cinara tujafilina*)
  on cypress family, 509
Brown dog ticks. *See* Ticks
Brown mildew
  on *Quercus*, 576
Brown patch
  controlling, 954, 957
  on lawns, 298
Brown recluse spiders (*Loxosceles reclusa*)
  in households, 801, 815
Brown rot
  controlling, 944, 948, 957
  on apricot, 632
    resistance to, 1005
  on cherry, 640
  on citrus, 642
  on grapes
    varieties resistant to, 1007
  on peach; nectarine, 657
  on plum, 669
Brown rot gummosis
  on citrus, 647
Brown soft scale
  on citrus, 644
Brown-banded cockroach (*Supella longipalpa*), 816
Brownseed paspalum
  herbicide for, 974
Bruchus pisorum (Pea weevil), 760
Bryobia praetiosa. See Clover mites
B.T. *See Bacillus thuringiensis*
Bucida (Black olive)
  blister mites on, 488
  culture, 488
  leaf drop in, 488
Buckeye. *See Aesculus*
Buckhorn plantain (*Plantago lanceolata*), 843
  herbicides for, 971, 974, 978
  See also Plantain
Buckthorn
  Amsinckia douglasiana, 851
  Rhamnus

as diseases and insect resistant, 998
  powdery mildew on, 995
Bud, defined, 216
Bud and flower blight, 857
  See also Blossom blight; Botrytis blight; Gray mold
Bud rot
  on *Canna*, 374
  on palms, 550
Budworms
  insecticides for, 951, 956, 965
  on flowers, 416
  on herbs, 748
  on *Pelargonium*, outdoors, 416
  on *Petunia*, 417
  on vegetables, 690
  See also Caterpillars
  spruce (*Choristoneura* species)
    on *Abies*, 474
    on *Picea*, 553
  tobacco (*Heliothis* species)
    on *Ageratum*, 361
Buffalo gnats, 814
Bug-Geta Snail & Slug Pellets. *See* ORTHO Bug-Geta Snail & Slug Pellets
Bugle. *See Ajuga*
Bugs
  described, 355
  leaf, 876
  lygus, 876
  on flowers, 355
  plant, 876
Buildings
  See also Household pests
  dry rot in, 812
  pests in
    ants, 803, 883
    baits for, 943, 959
    birds, 804
    biting flies, 814
    black widow spiders, 815
    borers
      roundheaded, 810
    boxelder bugs, 477
    brown recluse spiders, 815
    carpenter ants, 811
    carpenter bees, 811
    centipedes, 884
    cockroaches, 816
    daddy longlegs, 801
    drywood termites, 810
    fire ants
      insecticides for, 943
    honeybees, 813
    house mice, 804
    insecticides for, 940–942, 952, 955, 957
    pillbugs, 885
    powderpost beetles, 809
    raccoons, 805, 894
    rats, 805

    roundheaded borers, 810
    scorpions, 816
    sowbugs, 885
    spiders, 801
      black widow, 815
      brown recluse, 815
    termites, 808, 957
    ticks, 807
    tree squirrels, 806
    woodwasps, 811
    yellowjackets, 812
  pests near
    birds, 804
    biting flies, 814
    biting midges, 814
    skunks, 807
  pests under
    ants, 803
    daddy longlegs, 801
    ground squirrels, 894
    skunks, 807
  pets in
    repellents for, 962
  weeds near
    herbicides for, 972, 974–976
Bulb and root rot
  on *Tulipa*, 429
Bulb flies
  narcissus (*Merodon equestris*), 411
Bulb rot
  fusarium
    on *Narcissus*, 411
  root rot and
    on *Lilium*, 406
    on *Tulipa*, 429
Bulbs. *See* Flowers
Bull nettle. *See* Horsenettle
Bull thistle
  herbicides for, 971, 974
Bullgrass
  herbicides for, 976
Bulrush (*Scirpus* species), 831
Bunk. *See* Chicory
Bunya-bunya. *See Araucaria*
Burclover
  herbicides for, 974
Burdock
  in lawns
    herbicides for, 971, 978
Burgrass (*Cenchrus* species), 829
Burnut, ground (*Tribulus terrestris*), 835
Burweed (*Amsinckia douglasiana*), 851
Bush red pepper. *See Capsicum*
Butia capitata. See Palm family
Buttercups

  in lawns
    herbicides for, 971
  Persian. *See Ranunculus*
Butterflies
  See also Caterpillars
  black swallowtail
    on parsley, 757
  cabbage, 715
Butternut
  diseases on
    walnut anthracnose, 675
Buxus (Boxwood)
  as crown gall resistant, 998
  as shade tolerant, 997
  branches on
    dying back
      nematodes, 490
      winter injury, 489
    lack of new growth on
      boxwood psyllids, 489
  buds on
    dying
      boxwood psyllids, 489
  culture, 488
  diseases on
    armillaria root rot
      resistance to, 1001
    crown gall
      resistance to, 998
    phytophthora root rot, 490
    root rot, 490
    verticillium wilt, 995
  dying
    nematodes, 490
    root rot, 490
  fertilizing, 488
  insects on
    boxwood leafminers, 489
    boxwood psyllids, 489
    nematodes, 490
    spider mites, 490
  leaves on
    "off-color"
      root rot, 490
    brown and yellow flecks on
      boxwood leafminers, 489
    brownish pupae in
      boxwood leafminers, 489
    cupped
      boxwood psyllids, 489
    dead but still attached
      root rot, 490
    dirty
      spider mites, 490
    distorted
      spider mites, 490
    dropping
      boxwood leafminers, 489
    drying out
      winter injury, 489
    maggots in
      boxwood leafminers, 489
    red or rust brown
      winter injury, 489
    silken webbing under
      spider mites, 490
    small, transparent-winged flies on

cabbage worms, 715
diamondback moths, 715
flea beetles, 716
insects clustered under
aphids, 716
pellets between
cabbage worms, 715
watery soft rot, 718
silken cocoons under
diamondback moths, 715
sticky substance on
aphids, 716
tiny black beetles on
flea beetles, 716
transparent windows in
diamondback moths, 715
white to black pea-sized
pellets between
watery soft rot, 718
wilting
black leg, 718
black rot, 717
watery soft rot, 718
yellow or black veins on
black rot, 717
yellow spots on
alternaria leaf spot, 717
yellowing
aphids, 716
black rot, 717
clubroot, 718
downy mildew, 717
pH for, 718
planting locations for, 713
alternaria leaf spot and,
717
planting times for
bolting and, 714
growth cracks and, 713
roots of
brown grooves in
cabbage maggots, 716
maggots in, 716
misshapen
clubroot, 718
rotting
black leg, 718
clubroot, 718
slimy channels in
cabbage maggots, 716
swollen
clubroot, 718
seedlings
chewed
cutworms, 715
cut off near ground
cutworms, 715
dark spots on stems of
alternaria leaf spot, 717
dying
downy mildew, 717
flea beetles, 716
gray, brown, or black
worms in soil near
cutworms, 715
stunted growth in
alternaria leaf spot, 717
wilting
flea beetles, 716
yellowing

downy mildew, 717
seeds
germination of, 1009
soil pH for, 713, 718, 1002
stems on
black specks in spots on
black leg, 718
brown, gray-centered
spots on
black leg, 718
insects clustered on
aphids, 716
maggots in, 716
turning black
black leg, 718
water soaked areas on
watery soft rot, 718
sticky substance on
aphids, 716
storing
in refrigerator, 713
stunted growth in
black leg, 718
transplanting, 713
watering, 713
black leg and, 718
downy mildew and, 717
growth cracks and, 713
watery soft rot and, 718
wilting
black leg, 718
cabbage maggots, 716
clubroot, 718
flea beetles, 716
yellowing
black leg, 718
black rot, 717
cabbage maggots, 716
Cabbage looper
(*Trichoplusia ni*), 690
insecticides for, 951, 956,
963
on cabbage family, 715
on *Calendula*, 371
on lettuce, 750
on turnips, 796
Cabbage maggot (*Hylemya
brassicae*)
See also Root maggots
on cabbage family, 716
Cabbage palm. *See
Cordyline*
Cabbage worms
insecticides for, 961
Cabbageworms, imported
(*Pieris rapae*)
insecticides for, 946, 963
on cabbage family, 715
on turnips, 796
Cabling trees, 910
Cacti, indoors
as ornamentals. *See* Cacti,
outdoors
book about
*The World of Cactus &
Succulents* (ORTHO),
987
branches on

oval white insects in white
cottony masses on
mealybugs, 242
culture, 241
diseases on
bacterial soft rot, 241
scab, 242
dying
bacterial soft rot, 241
mealybugs, 242
overwatering, 241
failure to grow in
overwatering, 241
flowering times for, 241
growing locations for, 241
bacterial soft rot and, 241
honeydew on surfaces
below
mealybugs, 242
mealybugs on, 242
roots of
brown and dying
overwatering, 241
fail to grow
overwatering, 241
scab on, 242
soil for, 241
stems on
brown, corky, or leathery
areas on
scab, 242
deformed
scab, 242
dying
bacterial soft rot, 241
oval white insects in white
cottony masses on
mealybugs, 242
rotting
bacterial soft rot, 241
soft, mushy, circular areas
on
bacterial soft rot, 241
sunken areas on
bacterial soft rot, 241
scab, 242
water-soaked tissue
around cavities in
bacterial soft rot, 241
white cottony masses on
mealybugs, 242
watering, 241
bacterial soft rot and, 241
excessive, 241
withering
mealybugs, 242
Cacti, outdoors
as houseplants. *See* Cacti,
indoors
cold injury to
soft rot and, 491
collapsed areas on
soft rot, 491
culture, 491
book about
*The World of Cactus &
Succulents* (ORTHO),
987
discolored areas on
soft rot, 491

diseases on
gray mold, 491
soft rot, 491
verticillium wilt, 995
dying
cactus scales, 491
gray and crusty
appearance to
cactus scales, 491
gray bumps on
cactus scales, 491
grayish mold on
soft rot, 491
honeydew on
mealybugs, 492
insects on
ants
mealybugs and, 492
cactus scales, 491
mealybugs, 492
oval, white insects
clustered on
mealybugs, 492
planting locations for
soft rot and, 491
prickly pear
soft rot on, 491
slimy or rotted areas on
soft rot, 491
sticky substance on
mealybugs, 492
sunburn on, 491
turning brown
sunburn, 491
watering
soft rot and, 491
weak
mealybugs, 492
white cottony masses on
mealybugs, 492
white scaly bumps on
cactus scales, 491
yellowing
cactus scales, 491
mealybugs, 492
sunburn, 491
Cactus scale (*Diaspis
echinocacti*)
on cacti, outdoors, 491
Caladium
fertilizing, 923, 924
Calathea (Zebra plant)
as salt sensitive, 990
insecticide for, 969
Calceolaria
cotton root rot on, 994
Calcium deficiency
acid soils and, 902
in celery
black heart and, 723
in cucurbits
blossom-end rot and, 732
Calcium sulfate. *See
Gypsum*
Calendula (Pot marigold)
culture, 370, 371
diseases on
aster yellows, 994

fungicides for, 946
leaf spot, 371
powdery mildew, 371, 995
southern blight, 996
verticillium wilt, 995
dying
powdery mildew, 371
fertilizing, 370
flower buds on
chewed
cabbage loopers, 371
flowering times for, 992
germination of, 992
in containers
watering, 370
insects on
cabbage loopers, 371
leaves on
chewed
cabbage loopers, 371
dropping
leaf spot, 371
dying
leaf spot, 371
powdery mildew, 371
gray mold on
leaf spot, 371
green caterpillars with
white stripes on
cabbage loopers, 371
holes in
cabbage loopers, 371
papery texture to
leaf spot, 371
ragged edges on
cabbage loopers, 371
spots or blotches on
leaf spot, 371
powdery mildew, 371
withering
powdery mildew, 371
yellowing
powdery mildew, 371
planting locations for, 370
planting times for, 370, 992
soil pH for, 370
stems on
spots and patches on
powdery mildew, 371
verticillium wilt
resistance to, 995
watering, 370
withering
powdery mildew, 371
California buckeye. *See
Aesculus californica*
California oakworm. *See*
Oak moth
California poppy. *See
Eschscholzia*
California red scale
on citrus, 644
Caliroa cerasi. See
Pearslug
Calla. *See Zantedeschia*
Calliopsis. *See Coreopsis*
Callistemon (Bottlebrush)
bees attracted by, 996

C. viminalis (Weeping
bottlebrush)
saline soils and, 999
Callistephus (Annual aster;
China aster)
culture, 372
diseases on
aster yellows, 373, 994
fusarium wilt, 994
rust, 372
wilt disease, 372
fertilizing, 372
flowering times for, 372,
992
flowers on
distorted
aster yellows, 373
drooping
wilt disease, 372
turning green
aster yellows, 373
germination of, 992
in containers
watering, 372
insects on
leafhoppers
aster yellows and, 373
leaves on
dying
wilt disease, 372
orange-red pustules under
rust, 372
pale veins on
aster yellows, 373
wilting
rust, 372
wilt disease, 372
yellowing
aster yellows, 373
rust, 372
wilt disease, 372
planting locations for, 372
planting times for, 372, 992
roots of
decaying
wilt disease, 372
stems on
dark streaks and
discolorations on or in
wilt disease, 372
pink spore mass on
wilt disease, 372
thin
aster yellows, 373
stunted growth in
aster yellows, 373
wilt disease, 372
watering, 372
rust and, 372
weeds in
aster yellows and, 373
Calluna (Heather)
as acid tolerant, 327
as crown gall resistant, 998
bees attracted by, 996
fertilizing, 924
fungus diseases on
susceptibility to, 1000
soil pH for, 1003

correcting, 944
Callus, defined, 216
Calocedrus. See
Libocedrus
C. decurrens (Incense
cedar)
as armillaria root rot
resistant, 1001
Caloptilia syringella. See
Lilac leafminer
Caltrop (*Tribulus terrestris*),
835
Calycanthus (Sweet shrub)
as shade tolerant, 997
Cambium, defined, 216
Camellia
as shade tolerant, 997
branches on
white cottony masses on
cottony scales and
mealybugs, 494
buds on
bumps on
scales, 494
malformed
aphids, 494
white cottony masses on
cottony scales and
mealybugs, 494
C. japonica (Common
camellia)
flowering times for, 492
fungus diseases on
susceptibility to, 1000
C. sasanqua (Sasanqua
camellia)
flowering times for, 492
fungus diseases on
resistance to, 1000
culture, 492
diseases on
camellia flower blight, 493
camellia leaf gall, 492
camellia yellow mottle leaf
virus, 493
leaf gall, 492
sooty mold, 495
fertilizing, 492, 923, 924,
928, 932, 935, 936
iron deficiency and, 495,
929
flowering times for, 492
flowers on
buds of malformed
aphids, 494
dark brown to black
resting structures in base
on
camellia flower blight,
493
spots or blotches on
camellia flower blight,
493
yellow mottle leaf virus,
493
turning brown
camellia flower blight,
493

galls on
camellia leaf gall, 492
honeydew on
aphids, 494
scales, 494
sooty mold and, 495
insects on
ants
aphids and, 494
cottony scales and
mealybugs and, 494
scales and, 494
aphids, 494
black citrus, 494
sooty mold and, 495
cottony scales and
mealybugs, 494
insecticides for, 948
scales, 494
sooty mold and, 495
whiteflies
sooty mold and, 495
iron deficiency in, 495, 929
leaves on
black sooty mold on,
sooty mold, 495
aphids, 494
cottony scales and
mealybugs, 494
scales, 494
brown and dying
sunscald, 493
bumps on
scales, 494
cupped, twisted
aphids, 494
dropping
scales, 494
honeydew on
cottony scales and
mealybugs, 494
pale green to yellow
iron deficiency, 495
shiny, sticky substance on
aphids, 494
cottony scales and
mealybugs, 494
scales, 494
thickened, fleshy, and
enlarged
camellia leaf gall, 492
white and peeling
underneath
camellia leaf gall, 492
white cottony masses
under
cottony scales and
mealybugs, 494
yellow splotches on
yellow mottle leaf virus,
493
yellowing
aphids, 494
cottony scales and
mealybugs, 494
iron deficiency, 495
scales, 494
yellow mottle leaf virus,
493
yellowish or bronze

centers on
  sunscald, 493
new shoots on
  thickened, fleshy, and
    enlarged
    camellia leaf gall, 492
    leaf gall, 492
nodes on
  bumps on
    scales, 494
planting locations for, 492
  camellia leaf gall and, 492
  shade tolerance and, 997
  sunscald and, 493
pruning, 492
soil pH for, 492, 1002,
  1003
  correcting, 923, 944, 958
  iron deficiency and, 495
stems on
  bumps on
    scales, 494
stunted growth in
  cottony scales and
    mealybugs, 494
  iron deficiency, 495
  sunscald on, 493
twigs on
  black sooty mold on
    sooty mold, 495
  dying back
    scales, 494
watering, 492
  sunscald and, 493
weak
  cottony scales and
    mealybugs, 494
  yellow mottle leaf virus,
    493
Campanula (Bellflower;
  Canterbury bells)
bees attracted by, 996
culture, 373
diseases on
  crown rot, 374
  fusarium wilt, 994
  leaf spot, 373
  southern blight, 996
fertilizing, 373
flowering times for, 373,
  992
germination of, 992
in containers, 373
  watering, 373
leaves on
  decaying
    crown rot, 374
  dying
    leaf spot, 373
  spots or blotches on
    leaf spot, 373
  wilting
    crown rot, 374
  yellowing
    crown rot, 374
    leaf spot, 373
planting directions for
  crown rot and, 374
planting times for, 373, 992
pulls up easily

crown rot, 374
roots of
  decayed
    crown rot, 374
stems on
  brown or black pellets on
    crown rot, 374
  white fungal strands on
    crown rot, 374
  wilting and decaying
    crown rot, 374
  yellowing
    crown rot, 374
Camphor tree. *See*
  Cinnamomum
Camponotus species
  (Carpenter ants)
in households, 811
Canada thistle (*Cirsium
  arvense*), 843
  herbicides for, 974, 978
Candytuft. *See Iberis*
Cane and crown gall
  on brambles, 711
Cane blight
  controlling, 942, 958
  on brambles, 711
Canker and dieback
  on *Arbutus*, 483
  on *Carpinus*, 496
  on *Fagus*, 514
  on *Fraxinus*, 518
  on *Picea*, 556
  on *Populus*, 569
  on *Salix*, 597
  on *Sorbus*, 601
  on *Vinca*, 340
Canker disease
  bacterial
    on *Betula*, 487
    on cherry, 639
      resistance to, 1008
    on plum, 672
  crown
    on *Cornus*, 502
  cytospora
    on apricot, 633
  dieback and
    on *Arbutus*, 483
    on *Betula*, 487
    on *Carpinus*, 496
    on *Fagus*, 514
    on *Fraxinus*, 518
    on *Picea*, 556
    on *Populus*, 569
    on *Salix*, 597
    on *Sorbus*, 601
    on *Vinca*, 340
    on *Cercis*, 499
    on *Elaeagnus*, 511
  perennial
    on apricot, 633
Canker rot
  on trees
    breakage and, 473
Canker stain disease
  on *Platanus*, 565
Canker wilt

on *Gleditsia*, 524
Cankers, 868
  defined, 216
  from bacterial diseases,
    859
  on apple
    from fireblight, 630
  on apricot, 633
  on *Betula*
    dieback and, 487
  on cherry, 639
  on fruit and nut trees, 618
  on trees, 451, 456, 465
    wilting and, 451
    breakage and, 473
    oozing sap and, 453
    removing, 911
Cankerworms, fall
  insecticides for, 948, 951,
    956
Cankerwort. *See*
  Dandelion
Canna
  culture, 374
  diseases on
    bud rot, 374
    cotton root rot, 994
    southern blight, 996
  insects on
    corn earworms, 374
  planting times for, 992
Canterbury bells. *See*
  Campanula
Cape jasmine. *See*
  Gardenia
Cape marigold. *See*
  Dimorphotheca
Capsella bursa-pastoris.
  See Shepherds purse
Capsicum (Ornamental
  pepper), indoors
  bending toward light
    insufficient light, 242
  buds on
    tiny green insects on
      aphids, 243
  culture, 243
  flowers on
    dropping prematurely
      insufficient light, 242
    fail to grow
      insufficient light, 242
  fruits on
    fail to grow
      insufficient light, 242
  honeydew on furniture
    under
    aphids, 243
  insects on
    aphids, 243
    greenhouse whiteflies,
      243
  leaves on
    discolored or curled
      aphids, 243
    dropping
      insufficient light, 242
  honeydew on

aphids, 243
  greenhouse whiteflies,
    243
  mottled
    greenhouse whiteflies,
      243
  shiny, sticky substance on
    aphids, 243
  small
    aphids, 243
  tiny green insects on
    aphids, 243
  tiny winged insects under
    greenhouse whiteflies,
      243
  white waxy powder on
    insects on
    greenhouse whiteflies,
      243
  yellowing
    greenhouse whiteflies,
      243
  insufficient light, 242
light requirements for, 242
poor growth in
  insufficient light, 242
stems on
  elongated
    insufficient light, 242
  tiny green insects on
    aphids, 243
  weak
    insufficient light, 242
tiny insects fluttering
  around
  greenhouse whiteflies,
    243
watering, 243
  light and, 242
  sunburn and, 242
weak
  insufficient light, 242
Capsicum (Ornamental
  pepper), outdoors
  culture, 375
  flowering times for, 375
  germination of, 992
  planting times for, 992
  verticillium wilt on, 375
Capsicum annuum. *See*
  Peppers
Captan
  as damping-off preventive,
    917
  for beets, 706
  for flowers, 358, 359
  for *Iberis*, 401
  for tomato, 795
  for vegetables, 682, 683
  as ingredient
    in ORTHO Home Orchard
      Spray, 948
    in ORTHO Orthocide
      Garden Fungicide, 963
    in ORTHO Tomato
      Vegetable Dust, 967
  for almond
    coryneum blight on, 626
    peach blight on, 626

shothole fungus on, 626
for anthracnose
on brambles, 712
spot
on *Cornus,* 501
for apple scab
on *Malus,* 544
for apricot
coryneum blight on, 633
peach blight on, 633
scab on, 633
shothole fungus on, 633
for ash anthracnose, 516
for beans
root rot on, 703
for beets
as damping-off preventive, 706
for black knot
on plum, 671
for blueberries
stem and blossom blight on, 708
for brambles
anthracnose on, 712
for brown rot
on plum, 669
for bulbs
storing, 917
for *Cornus*
spot anthracnose on, 501
for coryneum blight
on almond, 626
on apricot, 633
for crown and root rot
on *Petunia,* 418
for crown rot
on rhubarb, 773
for *Dimorphotheca*
gray mold on, 393
for downy mildew
on grapes, 748
for fabraea leaf spot
on pear, 662
for flowers
as damping-off preventive, 358, 359
for *Fraxinus*
ash anthracnose on, 516
for grapes
downy mildew on, 748
for gray mold
on *Dimorphotheca,* 393
for *Iberis*
damping-off on, 401
for *Impatiens*
leaf spot on, 402
for leaf and stem blight
on *Pachysandra,* 338
for leaf blight
pear, 662
for leaf spot
on *Impatiens,* 402
on vegetables, 688
for *Malus*
apple scab on, 544
for mushrooms
on lawns, 321
for onion family
smut on, 756

for *Pachysandra*
leaf and stem blight on, 338
volutella blight on, 338
for peach blight
on almond, 626
on apricot, 633
for peach; nectarine
shothole fungus on, 655
for pear
fabraea leaf spot on, 662
pear leaf blight on, 662
for *Petunia*
crown and root rot on, 418
for plum
black knot on, 671
brown rot on, 669
for rhubarb
crown rot on, 773
foot rot on, 773
for root rot
on beans, 703
on *Petunia,* 418
on rhubarb, 773
for scab
apple
on *Malus,* 544
on apricot, 633
for shothole fungus
on almond, 626
on apricot, 633
on peach; nectarine, 655
for smut
on onion family, 756
for spot anthracnose
on *Cornus,* 501
for stem and blossom blight
on blueberries, 708
for tomato
as damping-off preventive, 795
for vegetables
as damping-off preventive, 682, 683
leaf spot on, 688
for volutella blight
on *Pachysandra,* 338
Carbaryl
as ingredient
in ORTHO Gypsy Moth & Japanese Beetle Killer, 947
in ORTHO Liquid Sevin, 954
in ORTHO Rose & Floral Dust, 961
in ORTHO Rose & Flower Jet Duster, 962
in ORTHO Sevin 5 Dust, 963
in ORTHO Sevin Garden Dust, 963
in ORTHO Sevin Garden Spray, 964
for *Abies*
Douglas fir tussock moths on, 475
for *Alnus*
alder flea beetles on, 482
for andromeda lacebugs

on *Pieris,* 556
for aphids
cowpea and bean
on *Laburnum,* 536
on flowers, 356
on fruit and nut trees, 620
for artichoke plume moths
on globe artichoke, 696
for aster leafhoppers
on flowers, 357
on vegetables, 691
for barberry loopers
on *Mahonia,* 543
for beetles
on trees, 441
for *Begonia,* outdoors
mealybugs on, 370
for blueberries
blueberry fruitflies on, 707
blueberry maggots on, 707
cherry fruitworms on, 707
cranberry fruitworms on, 707
leafrollers and leaftiers on, 708
plum curculios on, 707
for borers, 873
common stalk
on corn, 729
on *Iris,* 404
for budworms
spruce, 553
for cactus scales, 491
for carpenter bees
in households, 811
for caterpillars
on flowers, 356
on *Pelargonium,* outdoors, 416
on vegetables, 690
for cherry fruitworms
on blueberries, 707
for cicadas, 882
for codling moths
on quince, 672
for *Coreopsis*
leafhoppers on, 384
spotted cucumber beetles on, 383
for corn
common stalk borers on, 729
grasshoppers on, 728
for cowpea and bean
aphids
on *Laburnum,* 536
for cranberry fruitworms
on blueberries, 707
for cucumber beetles
on vegetables, 690
spotted
on *Coreopsis,* 383
on vegetables, 690
striped
on vegetables, 690
for cutworms
on *Nicotiana,* 411
for Douglas fir tussock moths
on *Abies,* 475

on *Picea,* 554
for earwigs
on vegetables, 683
for filbert leafrollers, 651
for filbertworms, 651
for flea beetles
alder, 482
on radish, 772
on vegetables, 691
for flowers
aphids on, 356
aster leafhoppers on, 357
caterpillars on, 356
Japanese beetles on, 355
mealybugs on, 356
scales on, 356
six-spotted leafhoppers on, 357
whiteflies on, 356
for fruit and nut trees
aphids on, 620
leafhoppers on, 620
mealybugs on, 620
scales on, 620
whiteflies on, 620
for fruitflies
blueberry, 707
for fruitworms
on blueberries, 707
for *Gleditsia*
plantbug-leafhopper complex on, 523
for globe artichoke
artichoke plume moths on, 696
for grapes
grape leaf skeletonizers on, 744
for grasshoppers, 881
on corn, 728
on vegetables, 683
for *Hedera,* outdoors
scales on, 336
for hickory
hickory bark beetles on, 652
for *Iris*
iris borers on, 404
for Japanese beetles
on flowers, 355
on vegetables, 690
for *Jasminum*
scales on, 530
for *Juniperus*
juniper webworms on, 535
for *Laburnum*
cowpea and bean aphids on, 536
for leafhopper-plantbug complex
on *Gleditsia,* 523
for leafhoppers
aster
on vegetables, 691
on *Coreopsis,* 384
on fruit and nut trees, 620
on vegetables, 691
for leafrollers
on blueberries, 708
on filbert, 651

for leaftiers
  on blueberries, 708
for maggots
  on blueberries, 707
for *Mahonia*
  barberry loopers on, 543
for mealybugs
  on *Begonia*, outdoors, 370
  on flowers, 356
  on fruit and nut trees, 620
for moths
  codling
    on quince, 672
  Douglas fir tussock
    on *Abies*, 475
    on *Picea*, 554
for *Nicotiana*
  cutworms on, 411
for *Pachysandra*
  scales on, 338
for palms, outdoors
  palm leaf skeletonizers on, 551
for pear
  pearslugs on, 663
for pecan
  pecan weevils on, 664
for *Pelargonium*, outdoors
  caterpillars on, 416
for *Picea*
  Douglas fir tussock moths on, 554
  spruce budworms on, 553
for *Pieris*
  andromeda lacebugs on, 556
for *Pinus*
  pine webworms on, 561
for plantbug-leafhopper
    complex
  on *Gleditsia*, 523
for plum curculios
  on blueberries, 707
for quince
  codling moths on, 672
for radish
  flea beetles on, 772
for *Sassafras*
  sassafras weevils on, 598
for scales
  cactus
    on cacti, outdoors, 491
  on flowers, 356
  on fruit and nut trees, 620
  on *Hedera*, 336
  on *Jasminum*, 530
  on *Pachysandra*, 338
for six-spotted leafhoppers
  on flowers, 357
for snout beetles, 873
  on ornamentals, 873
  on vegetables, 873
for sowbugs and pillbugs
  on vegetables, 692
for spotted cucumber
    beetles
  on *Coreopsis*, 383
  on vegetables, 690
for spruce budworms
  on *Picea*, 553

for striped cucumber
    beetles
  on vegetables, 690
for trees
  beetles on, 441
  weevils on, 873
for vegetables
  caterpillars on, 690
  cucumber beetles on, 690
  earwigs on, 683
  flea beetles on, 691
  grasshoppers on, 683
  Japanese beetles on, 690
  leafhoppers on, 691
  snout beetles on, 873
  sowbugs and pillbugs on, 692
  weevils on, 873
for webworms
  pine, 561
for weevils, 873
  on ornamentals, 873
  on vegetables, 873
  sassafras, 598
for whiteflies
  on flowers, 356
  on fruit and nut trees, 620
Cardaria draba (Whitetop)
  herbicide for, 905
Cardinal flower. *See Lobelia*
Carelessweed. *See Amaranthus*
Caribbean fruit fly
    (*Anastrepha suspensa*)
  on citrus, 643
Carissa
  C. grandiflora (Natal plum)
    saline soils and, 999
  culture, 495
  root rot on, 495
Carnation. *See Dianthus*
Carob. *See Ceratonia*
Carolina nettle. *See Horsenettle*
Carpenter ants
    (*Camponotus* species)
  in households, 811
Carpenter bees (*Xylocopa virginica*), 811
Carpet beetles, 802
  insecticides for, 947, 949
Carpet bugle. *See Ajuga*
Carpetgrass
  characteristics of, 991
  mowing heights for, 294
Carpetweed (*Mollugo verticillata*), 851
  herbicides for, 966, 970, 973, 978
Carpinus (Hornbeam)
  as crown gall resistant, 998
  as disease and insect resistant, 998
  as drought tolerant, 997
  culture, 496
  diseases on

canker and dieback, 496
  crown gall
    resistance to, 998
  verticillium wilt, 995
  planting locations for, 496, 997
Carpobrotus (Ice plant)
  as drought resistant, 991
  for sunny areas, 991
Carrot rust fly (*Psila rosae*), 720
  insecticide for, 942
Carrot weevil (*Listronotus oregonensis*), 720
Carrots
  Ace
    as leaf blight resistant, 721
    burned appearance to leaf blights, 721
  Chantenay
    for heavy soil, 719
  culture, 719
    misshapen roots and, 719
  Denver 126
    as leaf blight resistant, 721
  diseases on
    aster yellows, 721, 994
    fungicides for, 968
    leaf blights, 721
    scab, 766
    southern blight, 996
    verticillium wilt, 995
  fertilizing, 719, 928, 932, 934, 936
  for leaf blight resistance, 721
    misshapen roots and, 719
  germination of, 1009
  harvesting, 719
  Imperator 408
    as leaf blight resistant, 721
  Imperator 58
    as leaf blight resistant, 721
  in heavy soil
    misshapen roots and, 719
    varieties for, 719
  insects on
    carrot rust flies, 720
    carrot weevils, 720
    insecticides for, 963
    Japanese beetles, 997
    millipedes, 693
    nematodes, 719, 720
    wireworms, 730
  leaf-blight-resistant
    varieties of, 721
  leaves on
    dying
      carrot rust flies, 720
      leaf blights, 721
    in tight bunches
      aster yellows, 721
    rusty red to reddish purple
      aster yellows, 721
    spots or blotches on
      leaf blights, 721
    stunted
      aster yellows, 721
      carrot rust flies, 720

yellowing
    aster yellows, 721
    carrot rust flies, 720
  millipedes on, 693
  Nantes
    for heavy soil, 719
  Oxhart
    for heavy soil, 719
  planting dates for, 1009
  planting locations for, 719
  roots on
    beads or knots on
      nematodes, 720
    bitter tasting
      aster yellows, 721
    burrows with red
      sawdustlike material in
      carrot rust flies, 720
    green tops on
      sun exposure, 719
    misshapen, 719
      aster yellows, 721
      nematodes, 720
    scarred
      carrot weevils, 720
    scars on
      carrot rust flies, 720
    strong flavor to tops on
      sun exposure, 719
    stunted
      aster yellows, 721
    tiny hairlike roots on
      aster yellows, 721
    tiny leaves growing at top
        of
      aster yellows, 721
    white grubs in
      carrot weevils, 720
    zigzag tunnels in
      carrot weevils, 720
  seedlings
    overcrowded, 719
  thinning
    misshapen roots and, 719
  seeds
    germination of, 1009
  Short 'n Sweet
    for heavy soil, 719
  short varieties of, 719
  snails and slugs on
    baits for, 938
  soil pH for, 719
  Spartan Bonus
    as leaf blight resistant, 721
  stems on
    shriveling and dying
      leaf blights, 721
    spots or blotches on
      leaf blights, 721
  stored
    rotting
      carrot rust flies, 720
  stunted growth in, 720
    nematodes, 720
  watering, 719
    green root tops and, 719
    leaf blight and, 721
  wild. *See* Wild carrot
  yellowing
    nematodes, 720

49

blanching, 721
calcium deficiency in
  black heart and, 723
culture, 721
  black heart and, 723
diseases on
  aster yellows, 723, 752,
    994
    varieties resistant to, 723
  black heart, 723
  cotton root rot, 994
  early blight, 723
    varieties resistant to, 723
  fungicides for, 968
  fusarium wilt
    susceptibility to, 1009
  late blight, 722
    varieties resistant to, 722
  verticillium wilt, 995
fertilizing, 721, 934, 936
  black heart and, 723
  tough, stringy, and bitter
    stalks and, 722
harvesting, 721
  tough, stringy, and bitter
    stalks and, 722
heart of
  black and rotting
    black heart, 723
insects on
  carrot rust flies, 720
  celery leaftiers, 722
  celeryworms, 757
  leafhoppers
    aster yellows and, 723
  parsleyworms, 757
leaves on
  brittle
    aster yellows, 723
  caterpillars inside webs on
    celery leaftiers, 722
  dying
    early blight, 723
    late blight, 722
  spots on
    early blight, 723
    late blight, 722
  thickened
    aster yellows, 723
  velvety growth on spots on
    early blight, 723
  white silken threads on
    celery leaftiers, 722
  white webs on
    celery leaftiers, 722
  yellowing
    black heart, 723
nitrogen excess in
  black heart and, 723
planting directions for, 721
planting locations for, 721
planting times for
  tough, stringy, and bitter
    stalks and, 722
seedstalks on
  premature, 722
seeds
  late blight spores on, 722
soil pH for, 721
  black heart and, 723

stalks on
  brittle
    aster yellows, 723
  curled
    aster yellows, 723
  dying
    late blight, 722
  spots on
    early blight, 723
    late blight, 722
  tough, stringy, and bitter,
    722
  twisted
    aster yellows, 723
  velvety growth on spots on
    early blight, 723
  stunted growth in
    aster yellows, 723
transplanting, 721
watering, 721
  black heart and, 723
  tough, stringy, and bitter
    stalks and, 722
  yellowing
    aster yellows, 723
Celery leaftier (*Udea*
  rubigalis), 722
Celeryworm (*Papilio*
  polyxenes asterius)
  on parsley, 757
Celosia (Cockscomb)
  culture, 375
  diseases on
    aster yellows, 994
    leaf spot, 375
  flowering times for, 992
  germination of, 992
  insects on
    Japanese beetles, 997
    two-spotted spider mites,
      375
  planting times for, 992
Celtis (Hackberry)
  as cotton root rot resistant,
    994
  C. australis (European
    hackberry)
  as armillaria root rot
    resistant, 1001
  as disease and insect
    resistant, 998
  C. occidentalis (common or
    American hackberry)
  as armillaria root rot
    resistant, 1001
  witch's broom on, 498
culture, 498
diseases on
  powdery mildew
    witch's broom and, 498
insects on
  gall mites
    witch's broom and, 498
  gypsy moths, 1000
  hackberry leaf gall
    psyllids, 499
soil pH for, 1003
witch's broom on, 498
Cenchrus species. **See**

Sandbur
Centaurea (Bachelor's
  button; Basket flower)
  C. solstitialis. See Yellow
    starthistle
  culture, 376
  diseases on
    aster yellows, 994
    fusarium wilt, 994
    powdery mildew, 995
    root and stem rot, 376
  fertilizing, 376
  insects on
    ants, 376
    aphids, 376
Centipedegrass
  as warm season grass, 300,
    301
  characteristics of, 991
  herbicides for, 974, 977
  insects on
    mole crickets, 303
  mowing heights for, 294
  nutsedge in, 314
  planting times for, 300, 301
  weeds in
    herbicides for, 974, 977
    nutsedge, 314
Centipedes, 884
  baits for, 943, 959
  garden. *See* Garden
    symphylans
  insecticides for, 944, 945,
    947, 948, 950, 958
  millipedes compared to,
    884
Centruroides species
  (Scorpions), 816
Cephaleuros virescens
  on *Magnolia*, 542
Cerastium vulgatum. **See**
  Mouseear chickweed
Ceratocystis species
  C. fagacearum
    on *Quercus*, 579
  C. fimbriata f. platani
    on *Platanus*, 565
  C. fimbriata
    on sweet potato, 782
  C. ulmi
    on *Ulmus*, 607
Ceratomia catalpae. **See**
  Catalpa sphinx
Ceratonia
  C. siliqua (Carob)
    as armillaria root rot
      resistant, 1001
Cercidiphyllum
  C. japonicum (Katsura
    tree)
    as disease and insect
      resistant, 998
Cercis (Redbud)
  as drought tolerant, 997
  as low-growing tree, 998
  as shade tolerant, 997
  as street tree, 998
  C. canadensis (Eastern

redbud)
  for lawns, 997
  C. occidentalis (California
    redbud)
    as armillaria root rot
      resistant, 1001
  C. siliquastrum (Judas tree)
    as armillaria root rot
      resistant, 1001
culture, 499
diseases on
  Botryosphaeria ribis, 1002
  canker, 499
  crown gall
    resistance to, 998
  verticillium wilt, 499
Japanese beetles on, 997
Cercocarpus (Mountain
  mahogany)
  as drought tolerant, 997
  planting locations for, 997
  soil pH for, 1002, 1003
Cercospora leaf spot
  See also Cercospora spot or
    blotch
  controlling, 967, 968
  on avocado, 636
  on peppers, 765
Cercospora species
  C. apii
    on celery, 723
  C. beticola
    on beets, 705
  C. calendulae
    on *Calendula*, 371
  C. capsici
    on peppers, 765
  C. carotae
    on carrots, 721
  C. citri-grisea
    on citrus, 646
  C. purpurea
    on avocado, 636
Cercospora spot or blotch
  See also Cercospora leaf
    spot
  controlling, 957, 967
Ceriman. *See Monstera*
Cerotelium fici
  on fig, 649
Cerotoma trifurcata. **See**
  Bean leaf beetle
Chaenomeles (Flowering
  quince)
  C. lagenaria (Japanese
    quince)
    as armillaria root rot
      resistant, 1001
  diseases on
    fireblight
      susceptibility to, 1001
    rust, 500
  insecticide for, 948
Chaff scales
  on citrus
    insecticides for, 940
Chamaecyparis (False
  cypress). *See Cypress*

family
Chamaedorea (Parlor palm)
salt damage to, 990
Chamaerops
C. *humilis* (European fan
palm)
saline soils and, 999
Charlock (*Brassica kaber*),
834
Cheat. *See* Downy brome
Cheatgrass. *See* Downy
brome
Cheeses. *See* Mallow
Cheeseweed. *See* Mallow
Cheiranthus (Wallflower)
as verticillium wilt
resistant, 995
bees attracted by, 996
Chelating agents
in fertilizers, 905
Chemical damage
to *Chlorophytum*, 245
to *Spathiphyllum*, 287
Chenopodium album
(Common lambsquarters),
848
Cherry
blossoms on
decaying
brown rot, 640
gray spores on
brown rot, 640
hanging on tree
brown rot, 640
turning brown
bacterial canker, 639
brown rot, 640
wilting
bacterial canker, 639
brown rot, 640
branches on
abnormal patterns of
oriental fruit moths, 638
amber, sour-smelling ooze
bacterial canker, 639
brownish black beetles on
shothole borers, 639
cocoons on
oriental fruit moths, 638
crusty bumps on
San Jose scales, 640
dying
bacterial canker, 639
peachtree borers, 639
San Jose scales, 640
shothole borers, 639
pinkish white grubs in
shothole borers, 639
sawdust-filled tunnels in
shothole borers, 639
small holes in
shothole borers, 639
sticky
shothole borers, 639
sunken, elliptical lesions
on
bacterial canker, 639

weak
San Jose scales, 640
wilting
peachtree borers, 639
brush. *See Syzygium
paniculatum*
buds on
dying
shothole borers, 639
Catalina. *See Prunus,*
evergreen forms of
clear-winged moths on
peachtree borers, 639
cornelian. *See Cornus mas*
culture, 637
diseases on
bacterial blast, 639
bacterial blight, 1000
bacterial canker, 639,
1008
varieties resistant and
susceptible to, 1008
bacterial gummosis, 639
brown rot, 640
cherry leafspot, 641
varieties resistant to, 641,
1008
fruit rot, 640
fungicides for, 948
resistance to, 1008
susceptibility to, 1000
yellow leaf spot, 641
dying
peachtree borers, 639
fertilizing, 637, 927
flowering. *See Prunus*
fruit on
crescent-shaped scars on
plum curculios, 638
dark, sunken lesions in
bacterial canker, 639
dropping prematurely
brown rot, 640
cherry fruit flies, 637
plum curculios, 638
drying out
brown rot, 640
gray spores on
brown rot, 640
harvesting, 637
holes in
cherry fruit flies, 637
oriental fruit moths, 638
plum curculios, 638
malformed
cherry fruit flies, 637
poor quality
cherry leafspot, 641
pearslugs, 638
poor yield of
cherry leafspot, 641
pearslugs, 638
pulpy
cherry fruit flies, 637
rotting
brown rot, 640
cherry fruit flies, 637
rotting and hanging on
tree
brown rot, 640

shriveled and shrunken
cherry fruit flies, 637
shriveled, blackened, and
soft
plum curculios, 638
soft and watery
cherry leafspot, 641
specks on
San Jose scales, 640
spots on
brown rot, 640
cherry leafspot, 641
turning brown
brown rot, 640
worms in
cherry fruit flies, 637
oriental fruit moths, 638
yellow-gray grubs in
plum curculios, 638
harvesting, 637
hollyleaf. *See Prunus,*
evergreen forms of
insects on
fruit flies, 1008
cherry, 637
Mediterranean, 1002
fruit tree bark beetle, 639
gypsy moths, 1000
insecticides for, 948
oriental fruit moths, 638
peachtree borers, 639
pearslugs, 638, 663
plum curculios, 638
San Jose scales, 640
shothole borers, 639
leaves on
angular holes in
bacterial canker, 639
chewed between veins
pearslugs, 638
cream-colored spores
under
cherry leafspot, 641
dark green to orange
sluglike worms on
pearslugs, 638
decaying
brown rot, 640
dropping
pearslugs, 638
San Jose scales, 640
dying
cherry leafspot, 641
oriental fruit moths, 638
fail to grow
bacterial canker, 639
pale green
San Jose scales, 640
purple spots on
cherry leafspot, 641
remaining in winter
San Jose scales, 640
turning brown
brown rot, 640
San Jose scales, 640
shothole borers, 639
wilting
brown rot, 640
peachtree borers, 639
San Jose scales, 640

shothole borers, 639
withering
San Jose scales, 640
yellowing
cherry leafspot, 641
San Jose scales, 640
moths with clear wings on
peachtree borers, 639
planting locations for, 637,
1008
pollinators for, 1008
pruning, 637
snails and slugs on
baits for, 938
soil pH for, 637
sour
as self-fruitful, 1008
disease resistance in, 1008
planting locations for,
1008
sweet
disease resistance in, 1008
planting locations for,
1008
pollinators for, 1008
trunk of
amber, sour-smelling gum
oozing from
bacterial canker, 639
holes in
peachtree borers, 639
sawdust around holes in
peachtree borers, 639
small holes in
shothole borers, 639
sticky gum oozing from
shothole borers, 639
sunken, elliptical lesions
on
bacterial canker, 639
thick ooze from holes in
peachtree borers, 639
twigs on
brown sunken cankers on
brown rot, 640
dying
brown rot, 640
oriental fruit moths, 638
peachtree borers, 639
shothole borers, 639
gray spores on
brown rot, 640
gummy ooze from lesions
on
brown rot, 640
small holes in
shothole borers, 639
sticky gum oozing from
shothole borers, 639
sunken lesions on
brown rot, 640
wilting
oriental fruit moths, 638
peachtree borers, 639
worms in
oriental fruit moths, 638
varieties of
disease resistance in, 641,
1008
planting locations for,

1008
pollinators for, 1008
watering, 637
Cherry fruit flies
insecticides for, 946
Cherry fruitworm
(*Grapholitha packardii*)
insecticides for, 946
on blueberries, 707
Cherry laurel leaftiers
insecticides for, 956
Cherry leafspot, 641
controlling, 957
resistance to, 1008
Cherry-laurel. *See* Prunus,
evergreen forms of
Chestnut. *See* Castanea
horse. *See* Aesculus
Chicken mites
insecticides for, 963
**Chickweed & Clover
Control.** *See* ORTHO
Chickweed & Clover
Control
**Chickweed, Spurge &
Oxalis Killer D.** *See*
ORTHO Chickweed,
Spurge & Oxalis Killer
D
Chickweed
common (*Stellaria media*),
837
in lawns, 316
herbicides for, 971, 973,
978
herbicides for, 966, 970,
971, 974, 976, 978
Indian. *See* Carpetweed
mouseear (*Cerastium
vulgatum*), 839
in lawns, 316
herbicides for, 971, 974,
978
whorled. *See* Carpetweed
Chicory (*Cichorium
intybus*), 844
aster yellows and, 861
in lawns
herbicides for, 971
Chiggers
in households, 808
insecticides for, 941–943,
949
Chilling injury. *See* Cold
damage; Winter injury
China aster. *See*
Callistephus
Chinamans greens. *See*
Amaranthus species
**Chinch Bug & Sod
Webworm Control.** *See*
ORTHO Chinch Bug &
Sod Webworm Control
Chinch Bug Killer. *See*
ORTHO Chinch Bug
Killer

Chinch bugs (*Blissus
species*)
insecticides for, 939, 941–
943, 952, 965
on lawns, 301
Chinese evergreen. *See*
Aglaonema
Chinese flame tree. *See*
Koelreuteria
Chinese pistache. *See*
Pistacia
Chinese scholar tree. *See*
Sophora
Chionanthus (Fringe tree)
as crown gall resistant, 998
for lawns, 997
Chionaspis pinifoliae. *See*
Pine needle scale
Chlordane
for subterranean termites,
808
**Chlorine, as minor
nutrient, 905**
Chloroneb
as damping-off preventive
for flowers, 358, 359
for tomato, 795
for vegetables, 682
for pythium blight
on lawns, 300
Chlorophyll, defined, 216
Chlorophytum (Spider
plant)
dead leaf tips on
insufficient water, 245
salt damage, 245
toxic salts, 245
insecticide for, 969
salt damage to, 245, 990
Chlorosis, defined, 216
Chlorothalonil
as ingredient
in ORTHO Liquid Lawn
Disease Control, 954
in ORTHO Vegetable
Disease Control, 968
for *Aesculus*
leaf blotch on, 480
for alternaria leaf spot
on cucurbits, 735
for anthracnose
on lawns, 297
for cucurbits
alternaria leaf spot on, 735
for dieback
stem cankers and
on *Rosa*, 594
for downy mildew
on *Lobularia*, 408
for *Dracaena*
fusarium leaf spot on, 257
for gray mold
on *Salvia*, 423
for lawns
anthracnose on, 297
septoria leaf spot on, 307
for leaf blotch

on *Aesculus*, 480
for *Lobularia*
downy mildew on, 408
for *Pinus*
needle cast on, 557
for *Rosa*
stem cankers and dieback
on, 594
for *Salvia*
gray mold on, 423
for septoria leaf spot
on lawns, 307
for stem cankers and
dieback
on *Rosa*, 594
Chlorothal
for goosegrass
in lawns, 312
Chlorpyrifos
as ingredient, 943
in ORTHO Lawn Insect
Spray, 952
in ORTHO Fire Ant
Control, 943
Choisya (Mexican orange)
culture, 500
spider mites on, 500
Chokeberry (*Aronia*), 1000
Choristoneura species. *See*
Spruce budworm
C. rosaceana. *See*
Oblique-banded
leafroller
Christmas rose. *See*
Helleborus
Chromaphis juglandicola
(Walnut aphid), 674
Chryptorhynchus lapathi
(Mottled willow borer),
597
Chrysanthemum (Daisies;
Marguerites; Mums),
outdoors
bushy
mosaic, 380
culture, 376, 377
diseases on
aster yellows, 380, 994
bacterial blight, 380
fungicides for, 968
fusarium wilt, 994
leaf spot, 378
mosaic, 380
powdery mildew, 377, 995
rust, 372, 377
varieties resistant to, 992
southern blight, 996
verticillium wilt, 379
dying
nematodes, 379
rust, 377
English lawn daisy (*Bellis
perennis*), 317
falling over
leggy growth, 377
fertilizing, 376
iron deficiency and, 929
field daisy

aster yellows and, 861
flower buds on
tiny brown or
straw-colored insects
inside
thrips, 378
flowering times for, 992
flowers on
brown streaks on
mosaic, 380
brown
thrips, 378
distorted
aphids, 381
aster yellows, 380
mosaic, 380
thrips, 378
silvery streaks or flecks on
thrips, 378
small
aster yellows, 380
mosaic, 380
sparse
leggy growth, 377
verticillium wilt, 379
turning green
aster yellows, 380
webbing over
spider mites, 379
germination of, 992
in containers
watering, 376
insects on
ants, 381
aphids, 381
mosaic virus and, 380
chrysanthemum
leafminers, 381
insecticides for, 948
Japanese beetles, 997
leaf nematodes, 378
nematodes, 379
spider mites, 379
thrips, 378
two-spotted spider mites,
379
iron deficiency in, 929
leaves on
brown edges on
aster yellows, 380
brown pustules under
rust, 377
brown
leaf nematodes, 378
curled
aphids, 381
dirty
spider mites, 379
distorted
mosaic, 380
thrips, 378
dropping
leaf spot, 378
rust, 377
spider mites, 379
drying out
chryanthemum leafminer,
381
spider mites, 379
dying

leathery
  mites, 645
light-brown spots on rind of
  brown rot, 642
pitted
  greasy spot, 646
  snails and slugs, 645
poor yield of
  brown rot gummosis, 647
  tristeza, 647
raised corky areas on
  citrus scab, 642
rind splitting on, 642
rotten spots on
  Caribbean fruit flies, 643
scarred
  snails and slugs, 645
shiny, sticky substance on
  aphids, 644
silvery
  citrus thrips, 643
  mites, 645
streaked
  citrus thrips, 643
white maggots under
  rotten spots on
  Caribbean fruit flies, 643
white mold on rind of
  brown rot, 642
grafting
  psorosis and, 647
grapefruit
  cold hardiness of, 1003
  diseases on
    citrus scab, 642
    psorosis, 647
  fertilizing, 925
  rootstocks for
    tristeza and, 647
harvesting, 641
honeydew on plants and
  objects under
  aphids, 644
insects fluttering rapidly
  around
  citrus whiteflies, 643
insects on
  ants
    aphids and, 644
    cottony cushion scales
      and, 644
    mealybugs and, 644
  aphids, 644, 940
  tristeza and, 647
  black scales, 644, 940
  brown soft scales, 644
  California red scales, 644
  Caribbean fruit flies, 643
  chaff scales, 940
  citrus bud mites, 645
  citrus red mites, 645, 940
  citrus rust mites, 645, 940
  citrus snow scales, 644
  citrus thrips, 643
  citrus whiteflies, 643
  cottonycushion scales, 644
  Florida red scales, 644, 940
  Glover scales, 940

insecticides for, 940, 955, 958, 968, 969
mealybugs, 644
Mediterranean fruit flies, 1002
mites, 645
rust, 958
orangedog caterpillars, 645
purple mites, 645
purple scales, 940
rust mites, 958
scales, 644, 940
snow scales, 940
Texas citrus mites, 940
whiteflies, 940
yellow scales, 940
iron deficiency in, 646
kumquat
  cold hardiness of, 1003
leaf buds on
  turning brown and
    shriveling
    citrus thrips, 643
leaves on
  ash-colored
    tristeza, 647
  black mold on
    aphids, 644
    citrus whiteflies, 643
    cottonycushion scales, 644
    mealybugs, 644
  bronze
    tristeza, 647
  brown scablike lesions on
    citrus scab, 642
  caterpillars on
    orangedog caterpillars, 645
  chewed
    orangedog caterpillars, 645
    snails and slugs, 645
  crusty, waxy, or smooth
    bumps on
    scales, 644
  cupped
    aphids, 644
  curled
    aphids, 644
    citrus thrips, 643
    tristeza, 647
  dirty
    aphids, 644
  disagreeable odor from
    caterpillars on
    orangedog caterpillars, 645
  distorted
    citrus scab, 642
    citrus thrips, 643
  dropping
    citrus scab, 642
    cottonycushion scales, 644
    greasy spot, 646
    mealybugs, 644
    nitrogen deficiency, 646
    scales, 644

dying
  brown rot gummosis, 647
  brown rot, 642
eaten
  orangedog caterpillars, 645
greasy black or brown
  spots under
  greasy spot, 646
greenish yellow or clear
  flecks or streaks on
  psorosis, 647
holes in
  snails and slugs, 645
honeydew on
  aphids, 644
  citrus whiteflies, 643
  cottony cushion scales, 644
  mealybugs, 644
  scales, 644
leathery
  citrus thrips, 643
orange spots under
  greasy spot, 646
pale blotches on
  psorosis, 647
pale
  iron deficiency, 646
  nitrogen deficiency, 646
scratched
  mites, 645
shiny, sticky substance on
  aphids, 644
  cottony cushion scales, 644
  mealybugs, 644
  scales, 644
silvery gray
  citrus thrips, 643
stippled
  mites, 645
stunted
  iron deficiency, 646
sunken spots or rings on
  psorosis, 647
thickened
  aphids, 644
tiny green or black insects
  on
  aphids, 644
tiny winged insects under
  citrus whiteflies, 643
webbing between or
  under
  mites, 645
white cottony masses on
  cottonycushion scales, 644
  mealybugs, 644
white
  iron deficiency, 646
withering
  cottonycushion scales, 644
  mealybugs, 644
yellowing
  brown rot gummosis, 647
  cottonycushion scales, 644

iron deficiency, 646
mealybugs, 644
mites, 645
nitrogen deficiency, 646
scales, 644
tristeza, 647
yellowish blistered spots
  under
  greasy spot, 646
lemon
  citrus scab, 642
  cold hardiness of, 1003
  fertilizing, 925
lime
  cold hardiness of, 1003
  fertilizing, 925
  Rangpur rootstock
    as tristeza tolerant, 647
Mandarin orange
  cold hardiness of, 1003
  rootstock
    as tristeza tolerant, 647
minor nutrient deficiency
  in, 646, 905
nitrogen deficiency in, 646
orange
  cold hardiness of, 1003
  diseases on
    citrus scab, 642
    psorosis, 647
  fertilizing, 925
  rootstocks for
    pythophthora and, 647
    tristeza and, 647
  sour
    citrus scab on, 642
    tristeza and, 647
phytophthora-resistant
  varieties of, 647
planting directions for
  psorosis and, 647
planting locations for, 641
  cold hardiness and, 1003
  nitrogen deficiency and, 646
pruning, 641
rootstocks
  phytophthora-resistant
    varieties of, 647
  tristeza-tolerant varieties
    of, 647
Satsumas
  citrus scab on, 642
snails and slugs on, 645
  baits for, 938
soil pH for, 641
  iron deficiency and, 646
  nitrogen deficiency and, 646
sour orange rootstocks
  as tristeza susceptible, 647
sparse growth on
  tristeza, 647
stems on
  black mold on
    citrus whiteflies, 643
  crusty, waxy, or smooth
    bumps on
    scales, 644
  tiny green or black insects

Capitan
  as leaf blight resistant, 727
  as MDM tolerant, 727
Cherokee
  as bacterial wilt tolerant,
    726
Comanche
  as bacterial wilt tolerant,
    726
  as corn smut tolerant, 725
  as leaf blight resistant, 727
Comet
  as leaf blight resistant, 727
Commander
  as leaf blight resistant, 727
culture, 724
Deep Gold
  as corn smut tolerant, 725
diseases on
  bacterial wilt, 726
    flea beetles and, 727
  corn smut, 725
  fungicides for, 968
  leaf blights, 727
  maize dwarf mosaic
    (MDM), 727
  northern leaf blight, 727
  root, stalk, and ear rot, 726
  smut, 725
  southern leaf blight, 727
  Stewart's wilt, 726
  verticillium wilt, 995
drought-stressed
  corn rootworms and, 728
dwarfed
  corn rootworms, 730
  maize dwarf mosaic, 727
dying
  bacterial wilt, 726
  flea beetles, 727
  root, stalk, and ear rot, 726
early yellow
  as bacterial wilt tolerant,
    726
ears on
  absent
    common stalk borers, 729
  chewed
    grasshoppers, 728
  dropping
    European corn borers,
      728
  eaten
    wildlife, 694
  galls on
    corn smut, 725
  holes pecked in
    birds, 725
  kernels missing from
    birds, 725
  malformed
    corn rootworms, 728
  moldy kernels in
    root, stalk, and ear rot,
      726
  partially developed
    kernels in
    corn rootworms, 728
    grasshoppers, 728
  partially filled

poor pollination, 725
pink to brown kernels in
  root, stalk, and ear rot,
    726
poor yield of
  bacterial wilt, 726
  close planting, 726
  common stalk borers, 729
  lesser corn stalk borers,
    729
  nematodes, 726
  nutrient deficiency, 726
  poor irrigation, 726
  poor soil drainage, 726
poorly developed
  corn smut, 725
  European corn borers,
    728
puffballs on
  corn smut, 725
tan to dark brown
  caterpillars with yellow,
  orange, or brown stripes
  on
  armyworms, 724
worms on
  armyworms, 724
  corn earworms, 724
falling over easily
  corn rootworms, 730
feather duster appearance
  to
  maize dwarf mosaic, 727
fertilizing, 724, 934, 936
  bacterial wilt and, 726
  corn smut and, 725
  root, stalk, and ear rot and,
    726
  seed corn maggots and,
    730
germination of, 1009
Golden Beauty
  as corn smut tolerant, 725
greenish yellow to brown
  jumping insects on
  grasshoppers, 728
Guardian
  as MDM tolerant, 727
Gusto
  as corn smut tolerant, 725
harvesting, 724
insects on
  aphids
    maize dwarf mosaic and,
      727
  armyworms, 724
    poor pollination and, 725
  click beetles, 730
  common stalk borers, 729
  corn earworms, 724, 788
    poor pollination and, 725
  corn rootworms, 728, 730
    poor pollination and, 725
  cotton bollworms, 788
  cutworms, 729
  European corn borers, 728
  flea beetles, 727
    bacterial wilt and, 727
  grasshoppers, 728
    poor pollination and, 725

insecticides for, 942, 963
  lesser corn stalk borers,
    729
  nematodes
    poor yield and, 726
    stunted growth and, 726
  poor pollination and, 725
  seed corn maggots, 730
  stalk borers, 729
  tomato fruitworms, 788
  wireworms, 730
jumping insects on
  grasshoppers, 728
leaves on
  beetles on
    corn rootworms, 730
    flea beetles, 727
  black specks on velvety
    growths on
    leaf blights, 727
  brown, dry streaks on
    bacterial wilt, 726
  caterpillars, armyworms,
    724
  chewed
    armyworms, 724
    common stalk borers, 729
    corn earworms, 724
    corn rootworms, 728
    lesser corn stalk borers,
      729
  drying out
    flea beetles, 727
  dying
    flea beetles, 727
  eaten
    armyworms, 724
  galls on
    corn smut, 725
  greenish yellow to grayish
    tan spots on
    leaf blights, 727
  holes in
    European corn borers,
      728
    flea beetles, 727
    grasshoppers, 728
  puffballs on
    corn smut, 725
  ragged
    common stalk borers, 729
    corn earworms, 724
    lesser corn stalk borers,
      729
  reddish brown or
    yellow-margined spots on
    leaf blights, 727
  streaks on
    bacterial wilt, 726
  striped yellow and green
    maize dwarf mosaic, 727
  white eggs under
    European corn borer, 728
  wilting
    flea beetles, 727
  yellow-green with red
    blotches or streaks
    maize dwarf mosaic, 727
  yellowing
    close planting, 726

nematodes, 726
nutrient deficiency, 726
poor irrigation, 726
poor soil drainage, 726
manure for
  corn smut and, 725
  seed corn maggots and,
    730
Merit
  as bacterial wilt tolerant,
    726
  as corn smut tolerant, 725
  as MDM tolerant, 727
Midway
  as corn smut tolerant, 725
nitrogen deficiency in
  poor yield and, 726
  stunted growth and, 726
NK 199
  as bacterial wilt tolerant,
    726
nutrient deficiency in
  poor yield and, 726
  root, stalk, and ear rot and,
    726
  stunted growth and, 726
phosphorus deficiency in,
  681
planting directions for
  lesser corn stalk borers
    and, 729
  pollination and, 725
  poor yield and, 726
  stunted growth and, 726
planting locations for, 724
  corn rootworms, 728
  poor yield and, 726
  stunted growth and, 726
planting times for
  corn rootworms and, 728
pollinating, 725
poor pollination in, 725
Quicksilver
  as MDM tolerant, 727
raccoons in, 694, 894
roots of
  worms on
    corn rootworms, 730
    wireworms, 730
seedlings
  chewed
    cutworms, 729
  coiling worms in soil near
    cutworms, 729
  cut off near ground
    cutworms, 729
  dying
    bacterial wilt, 726
    root, stalk, and ear rot,
      726
  gray, brown, or black
    worms in soil near
    cutworms, 729
  leafless
    seed corn maggots, 730
  weak
    seed corn maggots, 730
  wilting
    bacterial wilt, 726
seeds

resistance to, 1009
powdery mildew, 737, 995
scab, 733
verticillium wilt
　susceptibility to, 1009
wild
　mosaic virus harbored
　　by, 736, 752
dying
　anthracnose, 736
　cucumber beetles, 734
　downy mildew, 737
　powdery mildew, 737
fertilizing, 731, 934, 936
　bitter taste and, 732
　blossom-end rot and, 732
for corn
　repelling raccoons from,
　　694
fruit on
　bitter tasting, 732
　anthracnose, 736
　low fertility, 732
　mosaic virus, 736
brown to black spots on
　blossom-end rot, 732
cracked white spots on
　angular leaf spot, 736
cracked
　scab, 733
dark green velvety growth
　on spots on
　scab, 733
darkened
　anthracnose, 736
decaying
　scab, 733
dry corky spots on
　scab, 733
dying
　anthracnose, 736
green and white blotches
　on
　mosaic virus, 736
harvesting, 731
large seeds in
　overmaturity, 732
light green worms with
　black dots on
　pickleworms, 733
misshapen, 732
moldy spots on
　blossom-end rot, 732
mottled
　mosaic virus, 736
pinkish ooze from spots on
　anthracnose, 736
poor yield of
　pickleworms, 733
　poor pollination, 731
poor-flavored
　downy mildew, 737
　overmaturity, 732
rotting
　anthracnose, 736
shriveled
　anthracnose, 736
　bacterial wilt, 735
small
　downy mildew, 737

smooth, white skin on
　mosaic virus, 736
spots or blotches on
　angular leaf spot, 732
　anthracnose, 736
　blossom-end rot, 732
　mosaic virus, 736
　scab, 733
sticky substance oozing
　from spots on
　scab, 733
storing, 731
sunken, dark brown spots
　on
　anthracnose, 736
tough
　overmaturity, 732
warts on
　mosaic virus, 736
water-soaked, sunken
　spots on blossom ends of
　blossom-end rot, 732
white powdery growth on
　powdery mildew, 737
white spots on
　angular leaf spot, 736
germination of, 1009
gourds
　harvesting, 731
　insects on
　　squash vine borer, 735
harvesting, 731
　lack of flavor and, 732
　large seeds and, 732
　toughness and, 732
honeydew melon
　see also melon
　as verticillium wilt
　　susceptible, 1009
insects on
　aphids
　　mosaic virus and, 736
　bees
　　pollination and, 731
　beet leafhoppers, 733
　cucumber beetles, 734
　　angular leaf spot and,
　　　736
　　anthracnose and, 736
　　bacterial wilt and, 735
　　mosaic virus and, 736
　Japanese beetles, 997
　Mediterranean fruit flies,
　　1002
　pickleworms, 733
　spider mites, 734
　spotted cucumber beetles,
　　734
　squash bugs, 734
　squash vine borers, 735
　striped cucumber beetles,
　　734
leaves on
　black and crisp
　　squash bugs, 734
　brick-red egg clusters on
　　squash bugs, 734
　brittle
　　beet leafhoppers, 733
　brown, dry spots on

anthracnose, 736
chewed
　bacterial wilt, 735
circular water-soaked
　spots on
　alternaria leaf spot, 735
curled
　beet leafhoppers, 733
　mosaic virus, 736
dark concentric circles in
　spots on
　alternaria leaf spot, 735
dirty
　spider mites, 734
distorted
　mosaic virus, 736
dropping
　alternaria leaf spot, 735
　spider mites, 734
dry blotches on
　alternaria leaf spot, 735
dry
　bacterial wilt, 735
　powdery mildew, 737
　spider mites, 734
dying
　anthracnose, 736
　bacterial wilt, 735
　downy mildew, 737
　powdery mildew, 737
gray or tan spots on
　angular leaf spot, 736
green, gray, brown bugs
　on
　squash bugs, 734
holes in
　angular leaf spot, 736
　cucumber beetles, 734
　scab, 733
mottled yellow and green
　mosaic virus, 736
puckered
　beet leafhoppers, 733
ragged holes in
　angular leaf spot, 736
　scab, 733
spots or blotches on
　alternaria leaf spot, 735
　angular leaf spot, 736
　anthracnose, 736
　scab, 733
spots with ragged holes on
　anthracnose, 736
stippled
　beet leafhoppers, 733
　spider mites, 734
stunted
　mosaic virus, 736
tearlike droplets on spots
　on
　angular leaf spot, 736
turning brown
　downy mildew, 737
　powdery mildew, 737
water-soaked, irregular
　spots on
　angular leaf spot, 736
webbing between or
　under
　spider mites, 734

white or gray spots on
　scab, 733
white powdery growth on
　powdery mildew, 737
white residue on spots on
　angular leaf spot, 736
white, purple, or black
　hairy growth under
　downy mildew, 737
wilting, and recovering at
　night
　bacterial wilt, 735
wilting
　bacterial wilt, 735
　powdery mildew, 737
　squash bugs, 734
yellow, water-soaked spots
　on
　anthracnose, 736
yellow-green
　black-striped or spotted
　　beetles on
　cucumber beetles, 734
yellowing
　downy mildew, 737
　powdery mildew, 737
　spider mites, 734
melon
　see also specific melons
　diseases on
　　anthracnose, 736
　　cotton root rot, 994
　　curly top, 706
　　fusarium wilt, 1009
　　Mediterranean fruit flies,
　　　1002
　　pickleworms, 733
　　powdery mildew, 995
　　southern blight, 996
　　verticillium wilt, 1009
　fertilizers for, 934, 936
　germination of, 1009
　insects on
　　insecticides for, 941, 942,
　　　963
　　Japanese beetles, 997
　　Mediterranean fruit flies,
　　　1002
　　pickleworms, 733
　　spider mites, 734
　planting dates for, 1009
　poor yield of
　　poor pollination, 731
　snails and slugs on
　　baits for, 938
metallic green moth on
　squash vine borers, 735
muskmelon
　see also melon
　diseases on
　　alternaria leaf spot, 735
　　anthracnose, 736
　　bacterial wilt, 735
　　downy mildew, 737
　　mosaic virus, 736
　　scab, 733
　　verticillium wilt, 1009
　harvesting, 731
　insects on
　　Mediterranean fruit flies,

leafminers and tip moths, 508
yellowing
scales, 510
spider mites, 509
winter injury, 508
yellowish scaly bumps on scales, 510
physiological leaf browning and shedding on, 508
planting locations for, 507
shade tolerance and, 997
twig and needle blight and, 507
winter injury and, 508
shade-tolerant varieties of, 997
stems on
brownish crusty or yellowish scaly bumps on scales, 510
white cottony masses on scales, 510
stunted growth in
aphids, 509
Thuja species (Arborvitae)
as shade tolerant, 997
as smog tolerant, 996
as wet soil tolerant, 997
disease resistance in, 1000
fertilizers for, 926, 927, 936
insects on
Japanese beetles, 997
leafminers and tip moths, 508
spider mites, 509
planting locations for, 507, 997
watering, 507
trunk of
red-brown tissue under bark on
cypress root rot, 509
twigs on
dying
twig and needle blight, 507
winter injury, 508
tiny green or brown insects on
aphids, 509
turning brown
twig and needle blight, 507
watering, 507
winter injury and, 508
weak
aphids, 509
winter injury to, 508
Cypress root rot
on cypress family, 509
Cytisus (Broom)
bees attracted by, 996
Heather. *See Calluna*
soil pH for, 1002, 1003
Cytospora canker
on apricot, 633

Cytospora species
C. cincta
on apricot, 633
C. kunzei
on *Picea*, 556
C. leucostoma
on apricot, 633

D

Daddy longlegs
in households, 801
Daffodil. *See Narcissus*
Dahlia
bushy growth in mosaic, 388
culture, 386, 992
diseases on
fungicides for, 946
fusarium wilt, 387, 994
mosaic, 388
powdery mildew, 388, 995
root and stem rot, 387
southern blight, 996
tuber rot, 387
verticillium wilt, 387
wilt disease, 387
dying
root and stem rot, 387
tuber rot, 387
fertilizing, 386
flowering times for, 386, 992
flowers on
drooping
wilt disease, 387
germination of, 992
insects on
aphids
mosaic virus and, 388
celery leaftiers, 722
cyclamen mites, 778
leaftiers, 722
leaves on
distorted
mosaic, 388
dying
root and stem rot, 387
wilt disease, 387
fail to grow
tuber rot, 387
grayish white powdery spots and patches on
powdery mildew, 388
mottled
mosaic, 388
pale green veins in
mosaic, 388
wilting
powdery mildew, 388
root and stem rot, 387
tuber rot, 387
wilt disease, 387
yellowing
mosaic, 388

powdery mildew, 388
root and stem rot, 387
tuber rot, 387
wilt disease, 387
planting locations for, 386
planting times for, 992
roots of
black
root and stem rot, 387
moldy
tuber rot, 387
rotted
root and stem rot, 387
tuber rot, 387
wilt disease, 387
soil pH for, 386
stems on
dark streaks and discolorations on or inside
wilt disease, 387
dying
root and stem rot, 387
small black fungal bodies inside
root and stem rot, 387
white fungal strands at bases of
root and stem rot, 387
wilting
root and stem rot, 387
stunted growth in
mosaic, 388
tubers, stored
dark brown, dry, firm areas on
tuber rot, 387
dark brown, soft, mushy areas on
tuber rot, 387
pink and yellow mold on
tuber rot, 387
tubers
moldy or rotted
tuber rot, 387
watering, 386
wilting
root and stem rot, 387
Daisies. *See Chrysanthemum*
English lawn (*Bellis perennis*), 317
Transvaal. *See Gerbera*
Dalapon
for common cattail, 832
for *Dichondra* Bermudagrass in, 332
for wild iris, 830
Dallisgrass (*Paspalum dilatatum*), 827
herbicides for, 972, 973
in lawns, 313, 823
Damping-off, 857, 858
See also Collar rots; Crown rots; Root rots
controlling, 957
cylindrocladium controlling, 959
on beets, 706

on flowers, 358, 359
on *Iberis*, 401
on lawns, 300
on newly seeded lawns, 300
on tomato, 795
on vegetables, 682, 683
Dandelion (*Taraxacum officinale*), 845
aster yellows and, 861, 994
on flowers, 357
carrots near
aster leafhoppers and, 701
false
herbicides for, 974
herbicides for, 974, 976
in lawns, 319
herbicides for, 319, 971, 972, 978
near flowers
aster yellows and, 357
leafhoppers and, 357
near potatoes
potato leafhoppers and, 769
near trees
aster yellows and, 861
near vegetables
aster yellows and, 861
leafhoppers and, 691
Daphne
as shade tolerant, 997
culture, 510
D. cneorum (Rock daphne)
fungus diseases on resistance to, 1000
diseases on
crown rot, 510
southern blight, 996
susceptibility to, 1000
insects on
ants, 510
aphids, 510
insecticides for, 948
planting locations for
crown rot and, 510
shade tolerance, 997
Dasineura species
D. gleditschiae (honeylocust pod gall midge), 523
R. rhodophaga (Rose midge), 590
Datana integerrima. See Walnut caterpillar
Daucus carota. See Wild Carrot
David viburnum. *See Viburnum davidii*
Dawn redwood. *See Metasequoia glyptostroboides*
Daylily. *See Hemerocallis*
DCPA
for annual bluegrass in lawns, 311
for barnyardgrass in lawns, 313

Eastern spruce gall
on *Picea*, 554
on corn, 727
on *Dahlia*, 388
on flowers, 356
on fruit and nut trees, 620
on swiss chard, 783
on *Tropaeolum*, 426
on vegetables, 692
woolly
on *Sorbus*, 600
for armyworms
on corn, 724
for aster leafhoppers
on flowers, 357
for bean aphids
on *Tropaeolum*, 426
for beans
seed corn maggots on, 704
for beetles
on flowers, 355
for beets
leafminers on, 705
for *Betula*
witch-hazel leaf gall
aphids on, 524
for borers
on corn, 729
peach twig
on almond, 625
for boxelder bugs
in households, 803
for brambles
raspberry crown borers
on, 710
raspberry fruitworms on,
709
for *Bromeliads*
mealybugs on, 240
for *Callistephus*
leafhoppers on, 373
for caterpillars
on flowers, 356
on vegetables, 690
for cherry
cherry fruit flies on, 637
for *Chrysanthemum*
leafhoppers on, 380
for *Clivia*
mealybugs on, 247
for *Columnea*
mealybugs on, 251
for common stalk borers
on corn, 729
for cooley spruce gall
aphids
on *Picea*, 554
on *Pseudotsuga*, 571
for *Coreopsis*
leafhoppers on, 384
spotted cucumber beetles
on, 383
for corn
aphids on, 727
armyworms on, 724
common stalk borers on,
729
grasshoppers on, 728
lesser corn stalk borers on,
729

seed corn maggot on, 730
for *Cotoneaster*
webworms on, 503
for cottony scales and
mealybugs
on *Morus*, 546
for cucumber beetles
on vegetables, 690
for cutworms
on flowers, 360
on *Nicotiana*, 411
on *Tagetes*, 425
for cypress family
leafminers and tip moths
on, 508
for *Dahlia*
aphids on, 388
for Eastern spruce gall
aphids
on *Picea*, 554
for *Episcia*
mealybugs on, 258
for filbert
leafrollers on, 651
for *Fittonia*
mealybugs on, 265
for flowers
aphids on, 356
aster leafhoppers on, 357
beetles on, 355
caterpillars on, 356
cutworms on, 360
greenhouse whiteflies on,
357
leafminers on, 352
mealybugs on, 356
scales on, 356
six-spotted leafhoppers
on, 357
whiteflies on, 356
for fruit and nut trees
aphids on, 620
leafhoppers on, 620
mealybugs on, 620
scales on, 620
whiteflies on, 620
for fruit flies
cherry, 637
for fruitworms
raspberry, 709
for *Gladiolus*
leafhoppers on, 396
for *Gleditsia*
plantbug-leafhopper
complex on, 523
for grasshoppers
on corn, 728
on vegetables, 683, 691
for greenhouse whiteflies
See also Diazinon, for
whiteflies
on flowers, 357
for Japanese beetles
on vegetables, 690
for *Juniperus*
juniper webworms on, 535
for leafhopper-plantbug
complex
on *Gleditsia*, 523
for leafhoppers

on *Callistephus*, 373
on *Chrysanthemum*, 380
on *Coreopsis*, 384
on flowers, 357
on fruit and nut trees, 620
on *Gladiolus*, 396
for leafminers and tip
moths
on cypress family, 508
for leafminers
on beets, 705
on cypress family, 508
on flowers, 352
on vegetables, 688
for leafrollers
filbert, 651
for lesser corn stalk borers
on corn, 729
for *Ligustrum*
privet rust mite and privet
mite on, 538
for mealybugs
on *Anthurium*, 232
on *Bromeliads*, 240
on *Clivia*, 247
on *Columnea*, 251
on *Episcia*, 258
on *Fittonia*, 265
on flowers, 356
on fruit and nut trees, 620
on *Morus*, 546
on orchids, 276
on *Streptocarpus*, 289
for *Morus*
cottony scales and
mealybugs on, 546
for *Narcissus*
thrips on, 409
for *Nicotiana*
cutworms on, 411
for orchids
mealybugs on, 276
for peach twig borers
on almond, 625
for *Picea*
cooley spruce gall aphids
on, 554
Eastern spruce gall aphids
on, 554
for plantbug-leafhopper
complex
on *Gleditsia*, 523
for privet rust mite and
privet mite, 538
for *Pseudotsuga*
cooley spruce gall aphids
on, 571
for raspberry crown borers
on brambles, 710
for raspberry fruitworms
on brambles, 709
for scales
on flowers, 356
on fruit and nut trees, 620
for scorpions
in households, 816
for seed corn maggots
on beans, 704
on corn, 730
for six-spotted leafhoppers

on flowers, 357
for *Sorbus*
woolly aphids on, 600
for sowbugs and pillbugs
on vegetables, 692
for spotted cucumber
beetles
on *Coreopsis*, 383
on vegetables, 690
for spruce gall aphids
cooley
on *Picea*, 554
Eastern
on *Picea*, 554
for *Streptocarpus*
mealybugs on, 289
for striped cucumber
beetles
on vegetables, 690
for swiss chard
aphids on, 783
for symphylans
on vegetables, 885
for *Tagetes*
cutworms on, 425
for thornbugs
on *Acacia*, 476
for thrips
on *Narcissus*, 409
for tip moths
on cypress family, 508
for *Tropaeolum*
aphids on, 426
for vegetables
aphids on, 692
caterpillars on, 690
cucumber beetles on, 690
grasshoppers on, 683, 691
Japanese beetles on, 690
leafminers on, 688
sowbugs and pillbugs on,
692
symphylans on, 885
whiteflies on, 692, 879
for webworms
cotoneaster, 503
for whiteflies
See also Diazinon, for
greenhouse whiteflies
on flowers, 356
on fruit and nut trees, 620
on vegetables, 692, 879
for witch-hazel leaf gall
aphids, 524
on *Betula*, 524
for woolly aphids
on *Sorbus*, 600
on *Ligustrum*, 538
Diazinon Granules. *See*
ORTHO Diazinon
Granules
Diazinon Insect Spray. *See*
ORTHO Diazinon
Insect Spray
**Diazinon Soil & Foliage
Dust.** *See* ORTHO
Diazinon Soil &
Foliage Dust
Diazinon Soil & Turf

Insect Control. *See*
ORTHO Diazinon Soil
& Turf Insect Control

Dibotryon morbosum
on plum, 671

Dicamba
as ingredient
in ORTHO Chickweed,
Spurge & Oxalis Killer D,
971
for cudweed, 836
for English lawn daisy
in lawns, 317
for Japanese honeysuckle,
850
for tansy ragwort, 846

Dichlobenil
as ingredient
in ORTHO Casoron
Granules, 970
for Florida betony, 850
for horsetail, 832
for puncturevine, 835
for red sorrel, 845
for sowthistle, 845
for yellow starthistle, 844

Dichomeris marginella
(Juniper webworm), 535

Dichondra (*Dichondra
repens*)
See also Lawns
as weed
herbicides for, 971, 977,
978
brown areas on, from edges
toward center
flea beetles, 331
culture, 331
cut off near ground
cutworms, 331
diseases on
fungicides for, 954
fertilizing, 930
tools for, 979
gray, brown, or black
nocturnal worms on
cutworms, 331
insects on
baits for, 964
cutworms, 331
flea beetles, 331
insecticides for, 942, 952
applying, 979
leaves on
chewed along edges
cutworms, 331
holes in
flea beetles, 331
snails and slugs, 331
sheared off
cutworms, 331
snails and slugs, 331
planting
tools for, 979
powdery material on
slime molds, 308
silvery trails on
snails and slugs, 331
slime molds on, 308

snails and slugs on, 331
baits for, 964
weeds in
annual bluegrass, 332
Bermudagrass, 332
cloverlike
oxalis, 333
crabgrass, 332
devilgrass, 332
herbicides for, 973
oxalis, 333
wiregrass, 332
yellow woodsorrel, 333

Dichondra flea beetles
insecticides for, 941, 952

Dicofol
as ingredient
in ORTHO Isotox Insect
Killer, 951
in ORTHO Orthenex
Insect & Disease Control,
956
in ORTHO Rose & Floral
Dust, 961
in ORTHO Rose & Flower
Jet Duster, 962
for *Acer*
bladder and spindle gall
mites on, 478
for *Alcea*
two-spotted spider mites
on, 362
for ash flower gall mites
on *Fraxinus*, 517
for beans
spider mites on, 700
for bladder gall mites
on *Acer*, 478
for brambles
spider mites on, 711
for *Bucida*
blister mites on, 488
for *Celosia*
two-spotted spider mites
on, 375
for *Choisya*
spider mites on, 500
for *Chrysanthemum*,
outdoors
two-spotted spider mites
on, 379
for citrus, outdoors
mites on, 645
for *Coleus*, outdoors
mites on, 382
for *Cotoneaster*
pear leaf blister mites on,
504
for cyclamen mites
on *Cyclamen*, 253
on *Saintpaulia*, 285
on strawberries, 778
for flowers
spider mites on, 353
for *Fragaria*
spider mites on, 334
for fruit and nut trees
mites on, 623, 886
for *Fuchsia*

fuchsia mites on, 519
for gall mites
ash flower, 517
for grapes
spider mites on, 745
for houseplants
spider mites on, 228
for *Lathyrus*
two-spotted spider mites
on, 406
for *Ligustrum*
privet rust mites and privet
mites on, 538
for mites
ash flower gall, 517
blister
on *Bucida*, 488
cyclamen
on *Cyclamen*, 253
on *Saintpaulia*, 285
on strawberries, 778
fuchsia, 519
oak, 575
on citrus, outdoors, 645
on *Coleus*, outdoors, 382
on fruit and nut trees, 623,
886
on peach; nectarine, 658
on pear, 661
on plum, 669
on vegetables, 686, 886
pear rust
on fruit and nut trees, 623
on pear, 661
plum rust
on fruit and nut trees, 623
on plum, 669
two-spotted spider
on fruit and nut trees, 623
for oak mites, 575
for peach; nectarine
mites on, 658
for pear leaf blister mites
on *Cotoneaster*, 504
for pear rust mites, 623
on fruit and nut trees, 623
on pear, 661
for pear
mites on, 661
for plum rust mites
on fruit and nut trees, 623
on plum, 669
for plum
mites on, 669
for privet rust mites and
privet mites, 538
for *Quercus*
oak mites on, 575
for russet mites
on tomato, 790
for rust mites
pear or plum
on fruit and nut trees, 623
for *Saintpaulia*
cyclamen mites on, 285
for spider mites, 379
on beans, 700
on *Choisya*, 500
on *Chrysanthemum*,
outdoors, 379

on flowers, 353
on fruit and nut trees, 886
on grapes, 745
on houseplants, 228
on strawberries, 777
on vegetables, 886
on walnut, 675
two-spotted
on *Alcea*, 362
on *Celosia*, 375
on *Chrysanthemum*,
outdoors, 379
on fruit and nut trees, 623
on *Lathyrus*, 406
on pear, 661
on plum, 669
on tomato, 790
on *Verbena*, 431
for spindle gall mites
on *Acer* 478
for strawberries
cyclamen mites on, 778
spider mites on, 777
for tomato
tomato russet mites on, 790
two-spotted spider mites
on, 790
for two-spotted spider
mites; *see* for spider
mites, two-spotted
for vegetables
mites on, 686, 886
for *Verbena*
two-spotted spider mites
on, 431
for walnut
spider mites on, 675

Didymellina leaf spot
controlling, 959
on *Iris*, 403

Didymellina macrospora
on *Iris*, 403

Dieback
canker and
on *Arbutus*, 483
on *Carpinus*, 496
on *Fagus*, 514
on *Fraxinus*, 518
on *Picea*, 556
on *Populus*, 569
on *Salix*, 597
on *Sorbus*, 601
on *Vinca*, 340
diagnosing, 1008
from cold damage, 866
on *Betula*, 487
on *Rhododendron*, 585
on *Rosa*, 594
stem cankers and
on *Rosa*, 594

Dieffenbachia (Dumbcane)
bending toward light
insufficient light, 255
culture, 254
diseases on
bacterial leaf spot, 256
bacterial stem blight, 256
dying
mealybugs, 255

transplanting, 739
watering, 739
wilting
verticillium wilt, 741
Egyptiangrass. *See*
Johnsongrass
Elaeagnus
as drought tolerant, 997
culture, 511
diseases on
canker, 511
verticillium wilt, 511
E. angustifolia (Oleaster;
Russian olive)
as armillaria root rot
resistant, 1001
soil pH for, 1002, 1003
planting locations for, 997
soil pH for, 1002
Elasmopalpus lignosellus
(Lesser corn stalk borer),
729
Elatobium abietinum
(Spruce aphids), 555
Elder; Elderberry. *See*
Sambucus
Eleagnus. See Elaeagnus
Electric wires, damage to
rats, 805
Eleusine indica. See
Goosegrass
Elm. *See Ulmus*
Elm bark beetles, 607, 609
Elm bark scales, 609
Elm beetles
pruning and, 607
Elm leaf beetle (*Pyrrhalta
luteola*), 609
insecticides for, 947, 951,
954, 956, 964
Elsinoe species
E. ampelina
on grapes, 745
E. corni
on *Cornus*, 501
E. fawcetti
on citrus, 642
E. mangiferae
on mango, 653
E. veneta
on brambles, 712
Emerald ripple. *See*
Peperomia
Empoasca fabae. See
Potato leafhopper
Endive
diseases on
aster yellows, 994
fertilizers for, 934, 936
Endopiza viteana. See
Grape berry moths
Endothia parasitica
on *Castanea*, 496
English daisy. *See Bellis
perennis*

English ivy. *See Hedera*
English laurel. *See
Prunus*, evergreen
forms of
English lawn daisy (*Bellis
perennis*), 317
Environmental stress
to trees
oozing sap and, 453
Eolaweed. *See Hypericum
perforatum*
Epicauta species. *See*
Blister beetles
Epilachna varivestis. See
Mexican bean beetle
Epimedium
as acid tolerant, 327
as shade tolerant, 325, 326,
991
Episcia (Flame violet)
See also African violet
family
mealybugs on, 258
water spots on, 258
Epitrimerus pyri. See Pear
rust mite
Eptam
for downy brome, 830
for Florida betony, 850
for morning glory, 849
for mugwort, 847
for nutsedges, 831
for quackgrass, 826
for sandbur, 829
for wild oats, 830
Equipment. *See* Tools and
equipment
Equisetum species. *See*
Horsetail
Erect palm lilly. *See
Cordyline*
Erica (Heath)
as acid tolerant, 327
culture, 511
diseases on
powdery mildew, 995
root rot, 511
susceptibility to, 1000
E. arborea (Tree heath)
as armillaria root rot
resistant, 1001
soil pH for, 1002, 1003
Erigeron. See Horseweed
Eriobotrya (Loquat)
bees attracted by, 996
bird damage to, 999
diseases on
fireblight, 512
susceptibility to, 1001
insects on
fireblight and, 512
Mediterranean fruit flies,
1002
Eriophyes species
E. buceras.

See Blister mite
E. fici.
See Fig mites
E. pyri. See Pear leaf
blister mite
gall mites
on *Celtis*
witch's broom and, 498
Eriosoma species. *See*
Wooly aphids
E. lanigerum. See Woolly
apple aphid
Erodium cicutarium
(Redstem filaree), 835
Erosion, 899
Erwinia species
E. amylovora
on apple, 630
on *Cotoneaster*, 503
on *Crataegus*, 505
on *Eriobotrya*, 512
on *Malus*, 544
on pear, 660
on *Pyracantha*, 572
on *Sorbus*, 599
on trees, 466
E. carotovora
on *Hyacinth*, 400
on *Iris*, 404
on *Zantedeschia*, 434
var. *aroideae*
on potatoes, 771
var. *atroseptica*
on potatoes, 770
E. chrysanthemi
on *Chrysanthemum*, 380
on *Dieffenbachia*, 256
on *Syngonium*, 287
E. nimipressuralis
on *Morus*, 545
on *Populus*, 567
on *Salix*, 597
on trees, 454
on *Ulmus*, 610
on cacti, 241
Erysiphe powdery mildew
controlling, 968
Erysiphe species
E. cichoracearum
on *Achillea*, 360
on *Aster*, 367
on *Begonia*, 237, 369
on *Calendula*, 371
on *Chrysanthemum*, 377
on *Cineraria*, 382
on *Cosmos*, 384
on cucurbits, 737
on *Dahlia*, 388
on *Phlox*, 419
on sunflower, 784
on *Verbena*, 430
on *Zinnia*, 434
plants infected by, 995
E. lagerstroemiae
on *Lagerstroemia*, 537
E. polygoni
on *Hydrangea*, 527
on *Iberis*, 400

on *Lathyrus*, 405
on *Lonicera*, 541
on peas, 759
plants infected by, 995
E. stewartii
on corn, 726
E. tracheiphila
on cucurbits, 735
Erythroneura species
(Grape leafhopper), 745
insecticide for, 955
Escallonia
bees attracted by, 996
Eschscholzia (California
poppy)
as smog tolerant, 996
diseases on
cotton root rot, 994
powdery mildew, 995
Espalier, defined, 216
Ethazole
for lawns
pythium blight on, 300
Ethion
as ingredient
in ORTHO Citrus Insect
Spray, 940
Ethyl hexanediol
to repel chiggers, 808
Ethyl thiophanate
for lawns
stripe smut on, 307
Etradiazole
for *Brassaia*
root rot on, 239
Euborellia annulipes
(Ringlegged earwig)
in households, 801
Eucalyptus
diseases on
armillaria root rot
varieties resistant to,
1001
powdery mildew, 995
susceptibility to, 1000
verticillium wilt, 995
Eucommia
E. ulmoides (Hardy rubber
tree)
as disease and insect
resistant, 998
Eugenia
as armillaria root rot
resistant, 1001
Eulachnus species. *See*
Aphids
Euonymus
branches on
dying
crown gall, 513
Euonymus scales, 512
corky galls at base of
crown gall, 513
culture, 513
diseases on

Fall panicum (*Panicum dichotomiflorum*), 828
Fall webworm (*Hyphantria cunea*)
  insecticides for, 951, 956
  on fruit and nut trees, 620
  on trees, 443
False aralia. *See Dizygotheca*
False cypress. *See* Cypress family
False guineagrass (*Sorgum halepense*). *See* Johnsongrass
False oleander scale (*Pseudaulacaspis cockerelli*)
  on *Bischofia*, 487
  on *Nerium*, 548
False powderpost beetles
  in households, 809
Fannia canicularis (Little house fly), 800
Fasciation, 216, 869
  defined, 216
Fat hen (*Chenopodium album*), 848
Fatshedera
  as salt sensitive, 990
  culture, 514
  insects on
    ants, 514
    aphids, 514
    insecticides for, 948
Fatsia (Aralia), indoors
  as salt sensitive, 990
  culture, 234
  false aralia. *see Dizygotheca*
  insecticides for, 969
  insects on
    insecticides for, 969
    mealybugs, 234
Fatsia (Aralia), outdoors
  culture, 514
  fungus diseases on
    susceptibility to, 1000
  spider mites on, 514
Felt plant. *See Kalanchoe*
Feltia ducens (Dingy cutworm), 729
Fences
  weeds near
    herbicides for, 972, 974–977
    poison ivy, 975, 976
    poison oak, 976
Fennel
  dog. *See* Mayweed
  herbicides for, 974, 978
Fenusa pusilla (Birch leafminer), 486
Ferbam
  for anthracnose and twig blight
    on *Ligustrum*, 539

for anthracnose
  foxglove, 392
    on *Digitalis*, 392
  on brambles, 712
  on grapes, 745
for apple
  cedar-apple rust on, 630
for brambles
  anthracnose on, 712
  cane blight on, 711
for cedar-apple rust
  on apple, 630
  on *Juniperus*, 535
  on *Malus*, 545
for *Chaenomeles*
  rust on, 500
for *Crataegus*
  hawthorn rust on, 505
for *Digitalis*
  foxglove anthracnose on, 392
for fabraea leaf spot
  on pear, 662
for fungal leaf or stem gall
  on trees, 446
for fungal leaf spots
  on *Kalmia*, 535
  on *Photinia*, 553
for grapes
  anthracnose on, 745
for hawthorn rust
  on *Crataegus*, 505
for *Helianthemum*
  leaf spot on, 397
for *Hippeastrum*
  leaf scorch on, 270
for *Ilex*
  leaf spot on, 528
for *Iris*
  rust on, 403
for *Juniperus*
  cedar-apple rust on, 535
for *Kalmia*
  fungal leaf spots on, 535
for leaf and stem rusts
  on trees, 445
for leaf blight
  on pear, 662
for leaf or stem gall
  on trees, 446
for leaf rusts
  on trees, 461
for leaf scorch
  on *Hippeastrum*, 270
for leaf spot
  fabraea
    on pear, 662
  on *Helianthemum*, 397
  on *Ilex*, 528
  on *Leucothoe*, 537
for *Leucothoe*
  leaf spot on, 537
for *Ligustrum*
  anthracnose and twig blight on, 539
for *Malus*
  cedar-apple rust on, 545
for needle cast
  on *Pinus*, 557
for needle rust

on *Pinus*, 560
for peach; nectarine
  shothole fungus on, 655
for pear
  fabraea leaf spot on, 662
  pear leaf blight on, 662
for *Photinia*
  fungal leaf spots on, 553
for *Pinus*
  needle cast on, 557
  needle rust on, 560
for *Pyracantha*
  scab on, 572
for rust
  hawthorn
    on *Crataegus*, 505
  leaf
    on trees, 461
  leaf and stem
    on trees, 445
  needle
    on *Pinus*, 560
  on *Chaenomeles*, 500
  on *Iris*, 403
  on *Pinus*, 560
  on *Sorbus*, 600
for scab
  on *Pyracantha*, 572
for shothole fungus
  on peach; nectarine, 655
for *Sorbus*
  rust on, 600
for trees
  fungal leaf or stem gall on, 446
  leaf and stem rusts on, 445
  leaf rusts on, 461
for twig blight
  on *Ligustrum*, 539
Fern & Ivy Food. *See* ORTHO Fern & Ivy Food
Fern pine. *See Podocarpus*
Ferns, indoors
  asparagus. *See Asparagus*
  bird's-nest. *See Asplenium*
  Boston
    insecticides for, 951, 969
    culture, 261
    fertilizing, 261, 927, 928, 936
    salt damage and, 262
  fronds on
    leaflets dropping off of, 515
  growing locations for, 261
  humidity and, 262
  holly
    insecticides for, 969
  insecticides for, 969
  root rot on, 262
  salt damage to, 261, 262, 990
  scales on, 263
  soil mixture for, 261
    humidity and, 262
    root rot and, 262
  sprengeri
    insecticides for, 969

table
  insecticides for, 969
  watering, 261
  root rot and, 262
  salt damage and, 261, 262
Ferns, outdoors
  as acid tolerant, 327
  as cotton root rot susceptible, 994
  culture, 515
  fertilizers for, 924, 928, 936
  insects on
    cottony scales and mealybugs, 515
    scales, 515
Ferrous sulfate
  for correcting soil pH, 868, 902
  for trees, 465
Fertilization, excessive
  of lawns
    thatch and, 304
Fertilizer burn
  in flowers
    wilting and, 353
Fertilizer labels
  how to read, 905
Fertilizers
  See also specific fertilizers
  ammonium sulfate. *See* Ammonium sulfate
  applying, 980, 984
  books about
    All About Fertilizers, Soils & Water, (ORTHO), 984
  calculating area for, 982, 983
  defined, 216
  for groundcovers, 326
  for lawns. *See* Lawns
  frost damage and, 448
  grade of, 326
  labels on
    how to read, 905
  mixing, 980
  N-P-K ratio in, 326
  nutrients in, 326
  role of, 1008
  salt damage and, 864
  selecting, 984
  tools for
    ORTHO Broadcast Spreader, 979
    ORTHO Drop Spreader, 979
    ORTHO Lawn and Garden Sprayer, 980
    ORTHO Lawn Sprayer, 960
    ORTHO Tractor Pull Spreader, 982
    ORTHO Whirlybird Spreader, 983
Fescue
  as cool season grass, 300
  as shade tolerant, 305
  diseases on

fireblight and
on *Eriobotrya*, 512
on *Sorbus*, 599
fruit. *See* Fruit flies
honeydew and
on fruit and nut trees, 621
on trees, 454
house (*Musca domestica*)
in households, 800
insecticides for, 948
insecticides for, 941, 945, 947, 949, 950, 958
larvae of. *See* Leafminers
leaf-mining. *See* Leafminers
little house (*Fannia canicularis*)
in households, 800
narcissus bulb (*Merodon equestris*), 411
on *Eriobotrya*
fireblight and, 512
on fruit and nut trees
honeydew and, 621
on *Sorbus*
fireblight and, 599
on trees
fireblight and, 466
honeydew and, 454
rust
carrot (*Psila rosae*)
on carrots, 720
sand. *See* Biting midges
vinegar
insecticides for, 942, 946
walnut husk (*Rhagoletis* species), 673
Florida betony (*Stachys floridana*), 850
in lawns
herbicides for, 977
Florida purslane. *See* Florida pusley
Florida pusley (*Richardia scabra*), 838
herbicides for, 966, 971, 973, 974, 976
in lawns
herbicides for, 977, 978
Florida red scales
on citrus, 644
insecticides for, 940
Floss flower. *See Ageratum*
Flotox Garden Sulfur. *See* ORTHO Flotox Garden Sulfur
Flour beetles (*Tribolium* and *Oryzaephilus* species)
in households, 817
Flour moths
Angoumois grain moths
in households, 817
Indian meal moth (*Plodia interpunctella*)
in households, 817
Mediterranean (*Anagasta kuehniella*)
in households, 817

Flower and leaf blight
on *Cornus*, 501
Flower blight, botrytis
controlling, 957
Flower spot
on flowers, 350
Flower thrips (*Frankliniella* species), 883
insecticides for, 956, 965
on *Rosa*, 588
Flowering almond. *See Prunus*
Flowering cherry. *See Prunus*
Flowering onion. *See Allium*
Flowering peach. *See Prunus*
Flowering plum. *See Prunus*
Flowering quince. *See Chaenomeles*
Flowering tobacco. *See Nicotiana*
Flowers
See also Landscaped beds; *specific flowers*
air pollution damage on, 352
animal pests in
deer, 891
mice, 890
tree squirrels, 893
woodchucks, 895
annuals
book about
All About Annuals (ORTHO), 984
culture, 984
fertilizers for, 924, 935
in shallow soils, 899
weeds near, 823
books about
All About Annuals (ORTHO), 984
All About Bulbs (ORTHO), 984
All About Perennials (ORTHO), 985
All About Roses (ORTHO), 985
Gardening with Color (ORTHO), 987
brown droppings near
rodents, 354
bulbs
as verticillium wilt resistant, 995
books about
All About Bulbs (ORTHO), 984
choosing, 916
culture, 984
digging up, 917
fertilizing, 925, 933, 937
phosphorus deficiency in
correcting, 925
planting directions for,

925
precooling, 917
purchasing, 916
storing, 917
undersize
failure to bloom and, 345
cold damage to
protecting from, 912
corms
undersize
failure to bloom and, 345
cultivating
mechanical injury and, 354
culture, 984, 985, 992
books about
All About Annuals (ORTHO), 984
All About Bulbs (ORTHO), 984
All About Perennials (ORTHO), 985
All About Roses (ORTHO), 985
diagnosing problems in, 1008
diseases on
aphids and, 356
aster leafhoppers and, 357
aster yellows
susceptibility to, 994
bacterial leaf spot, 350
bacterial soft rot, 860
bacterial wilt, 860
blossom blight, 857
botrytis blight, 857
bud and flower blight, 857
cotton root rot
resistance to, 994
crown rot, 859
damping-off, 358, 359
fungal leaf spot, 350
fungicides for, 944, 946, 956, 957, 959, 961, 962, 965, 968
applying, 983
fusarium wilt, 858
susceptibility to, 994
gray mold, 857
leaf and stem rusts, 445
leaf spot, 350
mosaic viruses, 352, 861
poor flowering and, 346
powdery mildew, 351
ring-spot viruses, 352, 861
root rot, 353, 859
rust, 351
sclerotium root rot, 859
slow or no growth and, 348
southern blight, 859
susceptibility to, 996
southern wilt, 859
stem and root rot, 353
stunts viruses, 861
verticillium wilt, 858
resistance to, 995
virus diseases, 352, 861
water molds, 857
yellows, 352

dormancy in
slow or no growth and, 348
dried
yarrow used for, 836
dying
dormancy, 348
nematodes, 348, 353
nitrogen deficiency, 350
failure to bloom in, 345
failure to grow in, 347, 348
acid soil and, 348
phosphorus deficiency and, 348
fertilizers for, 924, 935
fertilizing, 925, 926, 928, 932, 933, 935, 937, 966
damping-off and, 358
failure to bloom and, 345
fertilizer burn and, 353
iron deficiency and, 929
nitrogen deficiency and, 350
poor flowering and, 346
slow or no growth and, 348
flower buds on
dropping
transplant shock, 346
dying
thrips, 347
fail to open
beetles, 355
holes in
caterpillars, 356
sheared off
caterpillars, 356
turning brown
thrips, 347
webbing on
spider mites, 353
flower spots on, 350
flowering times for, 992
flowers on
distorted
aphids, 356
spray damage, 350
thrips, 347
viruses, 352
dropping
transplant shock, 346
dying
spray damage, 350
eaten
chewing insects, 355
Japanese beetles, 355
nocturnal insects, 355, 358
fail to bloom
immature plants, 345
insufficient light, 345
nitrogen excess, 345
undersize bulbs, 345
undersize corms, 345
unseasonable cool spell, 345
wrong season, 345
holes in
beetles, 355
chewing insects, 355

insecticide for, 946
on apple, 629
on pear, 663
Fruiting body, defined, 216
Fruitworms
cherry (*Grapholitha packardii*)
insecticide for, 946
on blueberries, 707
cranberry (*Acrobasis vaccinii*)
insecticide for, 946
on blueberries, 707
insecticides for, 947, 954, 964
on blueberries, 707
cherry (*Grapholitha packardii*), 707
cranberry (*Acrobasis vaccinii*), 707
raspberry (*Byturus* species)
insecticides for, 946, 967
on brambles, 709
tomato (*Heliothis zea*)
insecticides for, 963, 967
on tomato, 788
See also Corn earworm; Cotton bollworm
Fuchsia
birds on
fuchsia mites and, 519
culture, 518
fertilizing, 518, 928, 932
flowering times for, 518
in containers
fertilizing, 518
watering, 518
insects on
ants, 519
aphids, 519
bees, 519
fuchsia mites, 519
greenhouse whiteflies, 519
insecticide for, 969
whiteflies, 519
planting locations for, 518
pruning, 518
Fuchsia mites (*Aculops fuchsiae*), 519
Fungal leaf or stem gall
on trees, 446
Fungal leaf spot
on *Begonia*, 368
on flowers, 350
on *Hedera*, 335
on *Kalmia*, 535
on *Photinia*, 553
on *Rhododendron*, 583
Fungal wilt
on *Matthiola*, 408
See also Fusarium wilt; Phytophthora wilt; Sclerotium wilt; Wilt
Fungi, 856
See also Mushrooms
Albugo occidentalis

on spinach, 775
Alternaria species
A. cucumerina
on cucurbits, 735
A. dauci
on carrots, 721
A. mellea
on *Acacia*, 476
on fruit and nut trees, 624
on grapes, 746
on *Juniperus*, 533
on *Quercus*, 580
on strawberries, 780
on trees, 446, 466, 858
A. porri
on onion family, 756
A. raphani
on radishes, 773
A. solani
on potato, 770
on tomato, 793
A. tenuis
on *Pelargonium*, 415
A. zinniae, 435
on *Zinnia*, 435
on *Brassaia*, 599
on cabbage family, 717
Botryosphaeria ribis
on *Cercis*, 499
Botrytis species, 857
B. cinerea
on *Begonia*, outdoors, 368
on blueberries, 708
on brambles, 710
on cacti, outdoors, 491
on *Cornus*, 501
on *Cymbidium*, 386
on *Dimorphotheca*, 393
on *Euphorbia*, 260
on *Gerbera*, 394
on *Paeonia*, 412
on *Pelargonium*, outdoors, 414
on strawberry, 777
on *Zinnia*, 435
B. paeoniae
on *Paeonia*, 412
B. tulipa
on *Tulipa*, 430
on *Ageratum*, 361
on *Dahlia*, 387
on houseplants, 227
on *Petunia*, 417
on *Verbena*, 431
Ceratocystis species
C. fagacearum
on *Quercus*, 579
C. fimbriata
on sweet potato, 782
C. ulmi
on *Ulmus*, 607
Cercospora species
C. apii
on celery, 723
C. beticola
on beets, 705
C. calendulae
on *Calendula*, 371
C. capsici

on peppers, 765
C. carotae
on carrots, 721
C. citri-grisea
on citrus, 646
C. purpurea
on avocado, outdoors, 636
Cerotelium fici
on fig, 649
Cladosporium species
C. carpophilum
on apricot, 633
on peach; nectarine, 655
C. cucumerinum
on cucurbits, 733
Clitocybe species
C. tabescens
on *Acacia*, 476
on fruit and nut trees, 624
on *Quercus*, 580
on shrubs, 858
on trees, 858
Coccomyce hiemalis
on cherry, 641
Coleosporium species
C. solidaginis
on *Callistephus*, 372
on *Pinus*, 560
Colletotrichum species
C. coccodes
on tomato, 787
C. fuscum
on *Digitalis*, 392
C. gloeosporioides
on mango, 653
C. lagenarium
on cucurbits, 736
C. lindemuthianum
on beans, 700
Coryneum species
C. beijerinckii
on almond, 626
on apricot, 633
C. carpophilum
on peach; nectarine, 655
Cronartium species
C. harknessii
on *Pinus*, 562
C. quercuum
on *Pinus*, 562
C. ribicola
on currants; gooseberries, 738
on *Pinus*, 559
Cylindrocarpon species
on *Lilium*, 406
Cytospora species
C. cincta
on apricot, 633
C. kunzei
on *Picea*, 556
C. leucostoma
on apricot, 633
Dibotryon morbosum
on plum, 671
Didymellina macrospora
on *Iris*, 403
Diplocarpon species
D. earliana

on strawerries, 779
D. rosae
on *Rosa*, 589
Diplodia pinea
on *Pinus*, 557
Elsinoe species
E. ampelina
on grapes, 745
E. corni
on *Cornus*, 501
E. fawcetti
on citrus, 642
E. mangiferae
on mango, 653
E. veneta
on brambles, 712
Endothia parasitica
on *Castanea*, 496
Erysiphe species
E. cichoracearum
on *Achillea*, 360
on *Aster*, 367
on *Begonia*, indoors, 237
on *Begonia*, outdoors, 369
on *Calendula*, 371
on *Chrysanthemum*, outdoors, 377
on *Cineraria*, 382
on *Cosmos*, 384
on cucurbits, 737
on *Dahlia*, 388
on *Phlox*, 419
on sunflower, 784
on *Verbena*, 430
on *Zinnia*, 434
plants infected by, 995
E. lagerstroemiae
on *Lagerstroemia*, 537
E. polygoni
on *Hydrangea*, 527
on *Iberis*, 400
on *Lathyrus*, 405
on *Lonicera*, 541
on peas, 759
plants infected by, 995
Exobasidium species
E. camelliae
on *Camellia*, 492
E. vaccinii
on *Rhododendron*, 582
Fabraea maculata
on pear, 662
Frommea obtusa
on *Duchesnea*, 333
Fusarium species, 858
F. moniliforme
on corn, 726
on *Dracaena*, 257
F. nivale
on lawns, 297
F. oxysporum
vegetables susceptible to, 1009
F. oxysporum f. callistephi
on *Callistephus*, 372
F. oxysporum f. lycopersici
on tomato, 791

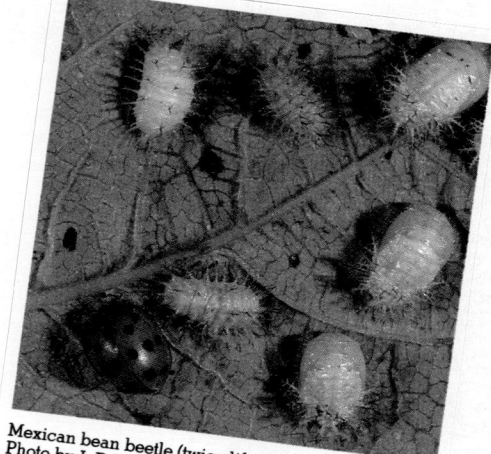

Mexican bean beetle (twice life size).
Photo by J. Dill.

The beetle shown in the far left column on page 699 of The Ortho Problem Solver is incorrectly identified as a Mexican bean beetle. Correct this error by mounting the above photograph of Mexican bean beetles directly on the page.

Pyrenochaeta terrestris
  on onion family, 755
Pythium species, 422, 857, 858
  on *Aglaonema*, 231
  on *Anthurium*, 232
  on beans, 703
  on *Brassaia*, 239
  on *Cyclamen*, 254
  on *Dahlia*, 387
  on *Euphorbia*, 260
  on lawns, 300
    newly seeded, 300
  on *Lilium*, 406
  on *Pelargonium*, indoors, 280
  on *Peperomia*, 281
  on *Philodendron*, 282
  on *Primula*, 420
  on *Ranunculas*, 422
  on *Rhododendron*, 585
  on *Zygocactus*, 291
  P. mamillatum
    on *Ageratum*, 361
Ramularia primulae
  on *Primula*, 420
Rhizoctonia species, 858
  on *Coleus*, 249
  on lawns, 300
    newly seeded, 300
  on *Lilium*, 406
  on *Philodendron*, 282
  on *Primula*, 420
  on *Tulipa*, 429
  R. solani
    on *Ageratum*, 361
    on *Aglaonema*, 231
    on *Anthurium*, 232
    on beans, 703
    on *Dianthus*, 391
    on *Gazania*, 334
    on *Hedera*, 336
    on lettuce, 751
    on *Peperomia*, 281
Rhizopus nigricans
  on brambles, 710
Sclerotinia species
  S. camelliae
    on *Camellia*, 493
  S. narcissicola
    on *Narcissus*, 410
  S. rolfsii
    on *Iris*, 404
  S. sclerotiorum
    on *Aquilegia*, 366
    on beans, 701
    on cabbage family, 718
    on *Campanula*, 374
    on *Dahlia*, 387
    on lettuce, 751
Sclerotium species, 858
  on *Ajuga*, 330
  on *Daphne*, 510
  on *Tulipa*, 429
  S. delphinii
    on *Delphinium*, 390
    on *Helleborus*, 398
  S. rolfsii, 363, 859
    on *Anemone*, 363
    on *Campanula*, 374

on *Delphinium*, 390
on peanuts, 761
on *Sedum*, 423
plants susceptible to, 996
Septoria species
  on lawns, 307
  S. apiicola
    on celery, 722
  S. lycopersici
    on tomato, 793
slime molds
  on lawns, 308
soil-inhabiting
  Plasmodiophora brassicae, 718
  Sphaceloma perseae
    on avocado, 636
  Sphaeropsis tumefaciens
    on *Nerium*, 549
  Sphaerotheca species
    on *Tolmiea*, 290
    plants infected by, 995
  S. fuliginea
    on cucurbits, 737
    plants infected by, 995
  S. humuli var. *fuliginea*
    on *Kalanchoe*, 272
  S. humuli
    on brambles, 712
    on *Phlox*, 419
  S. lanestris
    on *Quercus*, 576
  S. mors-uvae
    on currants; gooseberries, 738
  S. pannosa var. *rosae*
    on *Rosa*, 589
  S. phytophila
    on *Celtis*
      witch's broom and, 498
Stagonospora curtisii
  on *Hippeastrum*, 270
Streptomyces scabies
  on potato, 766
Stromatinia gladioli
  on *Gladiolus*, 397
Taphrina species
  T. caerulescens
    on *Quercus*, 576
  T. deformans
    on peach; nectarine, 656
Thielaviopsis basicola
  on *Euphorbia*, 260
Thyronectria austro-americana
  on *Gleditsia*, 524
Uncinula necator
  on grapes, 746
Urocystis cepulae
  on onion family, 756
Uromyces phaseoli
  on beans, 701
Ustilago species
  U. maydis
    on corn, 725
  U. striiformis
    on lawns, 307
Venturia species
  V. inaequalis
    on apple, 629

on *Malus*, 544
  V. pyrina
    on pear, 659
Verticillium species, 858
  on *Acer*, 479
  on *Ailanthus*, 480
  on *Catalpa*, 497
  on *Cercis*, 499
  on *Chrysanthemum*, outdoors, 379
  on *Cotinus*, 503
  on *Elaeagnus*, 511
  on *Lathyrus*, 405
  on *Matthiola*, 408
  on *Papaver*, 413
  on *Pistacia*, 563
  on *Rosa*, 594
  on *Rudbeckia*, 422
  on *Salvia*, 423
  V. albo-atrum
    on brambles, 710
    on *Callistephus*, 372
    on *Helianthus*, 397
    on *Rhus*, 581
    on tomato, 792
  V. dahliae
    on *Capsicum*, 375
    on *Cinnamomum*, 500
    on *Dahlia*, 387
    on strawberries, 779
  Volutella pachysandrae
    on *Pachysandra*, 338
Fungicide, defined, 216
Fungicides. *See* ORTHO fungicides
Funginex Rose Disease Control. *See* ORTHO **Funginex Rose Disease Control**
Fungus diseases, 856–859
  alternaria blight
    on *Zinnia*, 435
  alternaria leaf spot
    on *Brassaia*, 599
    on cabbage family, 717
    on cucurbits, 735
    on *Pelargonium*, outdoors, 415
  anthracnose
    ash, 516
    foxglove, 392
    on *Digitalis*, 392
    maple, 479
    oak, 575
    on *Acer*, 479
    on brambles, 712
    on cucurbits, 736
    on grapes, 745
    on lawns, 297
    on mango, 653
    on peppers, 763
    on tomato, 787
    on walnut, 675
    spot
      on *Cornus*, 501
  anthracnose and twig blight
    on *Ligustrum*, 539
  anthurium root rot

on *Anthurium*, 232
apple scab
  on *Malus*, 544
armillaria root rot
  on grapes, 746
  on *Quercus*, 580
  on strawberries, 780
  on trees, 446, 858
ascochyta blight
  on peas, 759
ash anthracnose
  on *Fraxinus*, 516
Azalea petal blight, 581
basal rot
  on onion family, 755
bean anthracnose
  on beans, 700
bird's eye rot
  on grapes, 745
bitter rot
  on apple, 627
black knot
  on plum, 671
black leg
  on cabbage family, 718
black root rot
  on radishes, 773
  on spinach, 779
black rot
  on grapes, 743
  on sweet potato, 782
black spot
  on *Rosa*, 589
blister rust
  white pine
    on currants; gooseberries, 738
blossom blight, 857
  stem blight and
    on blueberries, 708
botrytis
  on *Cyclamen*, 254
  on *Euphorbia*, 260
botrytis blight, 857
  on *Tulipa*, 430
botrytis gray mold
  on houseplants, 227
bottom rot
  on lettuce, 751
brown patch
  on lawns, 298
brown rot
  on apricot, 632
  on cherry, 640
  on citrus, 642
  on plum, 669
brown rot gummosis
  on citrus, 647
bud and flower blight, 857
bud rot
  on palm family, outdoors, 550
bulb rot
  root rot and
    on *Lilium*, 406
    on *Tulipa*, 429
cacti, indoors
  soft rot on, 491
camellia flower blight, 493
camellia leaf gall, 492

cane blight
  on brambles, 711
canker
  and dieback
    on *Arbutus*, 483
    on *Carpinus*, 496
    on *Fagus*, 514
    on *Fraxinus*, 518
    on *Picea*, 556
    on *Populus*, 569
    on *Salix*, 597
    on *Sorbus*, 601
    on *Vinca*, 340
  crown
    on *Cornus*, 502
    on *Cercis*, 499
    on *Elaegnus*, 511
    on fruit and nut trees, 618
    on trees, 456
cankers and, 868
canker stain disease
  on *Platanus*, 565
canker wilt
  on *Gleditsia*, 524
cedar-apple rust, 630, 856
  on apple, 630
  on *Juniperus*, 535
  on *Malus*, 545
cercospora leaf spot
  on avocado, 636
  on beets, 705
  on peppers, 765
cherry leaf spot, 641
chestnut blight, 496
citrus scab, 642
clubroot, 714
  on cabbage family, 718
collar rot, 857
  on citrus, 647
common scab
  on potato, 766
corm rot
  penicillium
    on *Gladiolus*, 396
corn smut, 725
coryneum blight
  on almond, 626
  on apricot, 633
  on peach; nectarine, 655
cotton root rot, 859
  on fruit and nut trees, 624
  on *Hedera*, 336
  on *Juniperus*, 533
  on pecan, 666
  on trees, 466
  plants resistant to, 994
crown and root rot
  on *Delphinium*, 390
  on *Petunia*, 418
crown canker
  on *Cornus*, 502
crown rot and decline
  on *Quercus*, 580
crown rot or wilt
  on *Aquilegia*, 366
crown rot, 857, 859
  decline and
    on *Quercus*, 580
  on *Ajuga*, 330
  on *Aquilegia*, 366

on *Campanula*, 374
on *Ceanothus*, 498
on *Daphne*, 510
on *Delphinium*, 390
on fruit and nut trees, 624
on *Gazania*, 334
on *Helleborus*, 398
on *Iris*, 404
on *Juniperus*, 533
on *Quercus*, 580
on rhubarb, 773
on *Saintpaulia*, 286
on trees, 466
on walnut, 676
root rot and
  on *Ceanothus*, 498
  on *Delphinium*, 390
  on fruit and nut trees, 624
  on *Juniperus*, 533
  on *Petunia*, 418
  on *Saintpaulia*, 286
  on trees, 466
wilt and
  on *Aquilegia*, 366
cypress root rot
  on cypress family, 509
cytospora canker
  on apricot, 633
damping-off, 857, 858
  on beets, 706
  on flowers, 358, 359
  on *Iberis*, 401
  on lawns, 300
  on tomato, 795
  on vegetables, 682, 683
decline
  crown rot and
    on *Quercus*, 580
  diagnosing, 1008
didymellina leaf spot
  on *Iris*, 403
dieback
  canker and
    on *Arbutus*, 483
    on *Carpinus*, 496
    on *Fagus*, 514
    on *Fraxinus*, 518
    on *Picea*, 556
    on *Populus*, 569
    on *Salix*, 597
    on *Sorbus*, 601
    on *Vinca*, 340
  on *Betula*, 487
  on *Rhododendron*, 585
  on *Rosa*, 594
  stem cankers and
    on *Rosa*, 594
diplodia tip blight
  on *Pinus*, 557
dollar spot
  on lawns, 298
downy mildew
  on cabbage family, 717
  on cucurbits, 737
  on grapes, 748
  on *Lobularia*, 408
  on onion family, 756
  on spinach, 775
dry rot, 812
  on *Gladiolus*, 397

Dutch elm disease
  on *Ulmus*, 607
  elm bark beetles and, 609
ear rot
  root and stalk rot and
    on corn, 726
early blight
  on celery, 723
  on potato, 770
  on tomato, 793
eastern gall rust
  on *Pinus*, 562
fabraea leaf spot
  on pear, 662
flower and leaf blight
  on *Cornus*, 501
flower blight
  leaf blight and
    on *Cornus*, 501
fly speck
  on apple, 628
foot rot
  on citrus, 647
  on *Gerbera*, 394
  on rhubarb, 773
foxglove anthracnose, 392
frog-eye leaf spot
  on peppers, 765
fruit rot
  on brambles, 710
  on cherry, 640
  on eggplant, 742
fruit scab
  on avocado, 636
fungal leaf or stem gall
  on trees, 446
fungal leaf spot
  on *Acer*, 478
  on *Begonia*, 368
  on flowers, 350
  on *Kalmia*, 535
  on *Photinia*, 553
  on *Rhododendron*, 583
fungal wilt
  on *Matthiola*, 408
  see also fusarium wilt;
    phytophthora wilt;
    sclerotium wilt; wilt
    disease
fusarium basal rot
  on onion family, 755
fusarium blight
  on lawns, 298
fusarium bulb rot
  on *Narcissus*, 411
fusarium leaf spot
  on *Dracaena*, 257
fusarium patch
  on lawns, 297
fusarium wilt, 858, 1009
  on asparagus, 697
  on *Dianthus*, 390
  on tomato, 684, 791
  vegetables susceptible to,
    1009
gall rust
  eastern
    on *Pinus*, 562
  western
    on *Pinus*, 562

galls from, 869
gliocladium rot
  on palms, indoors, 278
gray mold, 857
  See also Soft rot
  botrytis
    on houseplants, 227
  on *Ageratum*, 361
  on *Begonia*, outdoors, 368
  on *Cymbidium*, 386
  on *Dimorphotheca*, 393
  on *Gerbera*, 394
  on *Pelargonium*, outdoors,
    414
  on *Petunia*, 417
  on strawberries, 777
  on *Verbena*, 431
  on *Zinnia* 435
greasy spot
  on citrus, 646
gummosis
  on fruit and nut trees, 617
hawthorn rust
  on *Crataegus*, 505
honey mushroom
  on trees, 858
late blight
  on celery, 722
  on potato, 770
  on tomato, 792
leaf and stem blight
  on *Pachysandra*, 338
leaf and stem rusts
  on trees, 445
leaf blight
  flower blight and
    on *Cornus*, 501
  on carrots, 721
  on corn, 727
  pear, 662
leaf blister
  oak, 576
leaf blotch
  on *Aesculus*, 480
leaf curl
  on peach; nectarine, 656
leaf gall
  on *Camellia*, 492
  on *Rhododendron*, 582
  on trees, 446
leaf rusts
  on trees, 445, 461
leaf scorch
  on *Hippeastrum*, 270
  on strawberries, 779
leaf spot
  alternaria
    on cabbage family, 717
    on *Pelargonium*,
      outdoors, 415
  cercospora
    on avocado, 636
    on peppers, 765
  fabraea
    on pear, 662
  frog-eye
    on peppers, 765
  fruit rot and
    on eggplant, 742
  on *Anemone*, 363

on *Dracaena*
  fusarium leaf spot, 257
on eggplant
  leaf spot and fruit rot, 742
  phomopsis leaf spot, 742
  verticillium wilt on, 741
on *Elaeagnus*
  canker, 511
  verticillium wilt, 511
on *Erica*
  root rot, 511
on *Euonymus*
  powdery mildew, 512
on *Euphorbia*
  botrytis, 260
  root and stem rot, 393
on *Fagus*
  canker and dieback, 514
on ferns
  root rot, 262
on fig
  rust, 649
  souring, 649
on flowers
  blossom blight, 857
  botrytis blight, 857
  bud and flower blight, 857
  collar rots, 857
  crown rot, 857, 859
  damping-off, 358, 359
  fungal leaf spot, 350
  fusarium wilt, 858
  gray mold, 857
  powdery mildew, 351
  rust, 351
  sclerotium root rot, 859
  slow or no growth and, 348
  southern blight, 859
  southern wilt, 859
  stem and root rot, 353
  verticillium wilt, 858
  water molds, 857
on *Fragaria*
  leaf spot, 333
  root rot, 334
on *Fraxinus*
  ash anthracnose, 516
  canker and dieback, 518
on fruit and nut trees
  blossom blight, 857
  botrytis blight, 857
  bud and flower blight, 857
  cankers, 618
  cotton root rot, 624
  gray mold, 857
  gummosis, 617
  mushroom root rot, 624
  oak root fungus, 624
  powdery mildew, 621
  root and crown rots, 624
  shoestring root rot, 624
  Texas root rot, 624
  verticillium wilt, 858
on *Gardenia*
  sooty mold, 521
on *Gazania*
  crown rot, 334
on *Gerbera*
  foot rot, 394

gray mold, 394
on *Gladiolus*
  dry rot, 397
  penicillium corm rot, 396
on *Gleditsia*
  canker wilt, 524
on grapes
  anthracnose, 745
  armillaria root rot, 746
  bird's eye rot, 745
  black rot, 743
  downy mildew, 748
  powdery mildew, 746
on groundcovers
  powdery mildew, 328
on *Hedera*
  leaf spot, 335
on *Helianthemum*
  leaf spot, 419
on *Helianthus*
  verticillium wilt, 397
on *Helleborus*
  crown rot, 398
on *Hemerocallis*
  leaf spot, 398
on *Heuchera*
  leaf spot, 399
on *Hippeastrum*
  leaf scorch, 270
on houseplants
  botrytis gray mold, 227
on *Hydrangea*
  powdery mildew, 527
on *Hypericum*
  leaf spot, 336
  rust, 337
on *Iberis*
  damping-off, 401
  powdery mildew on, 400
on *Ilex*
  leaf spot, 528
on *Impatiens*
  leaf spot, 402
on *Iris*
  crown rot, 404
  leaf spots, 403
  rust, 403
on *Jasminum*
  sooty mold, 531
on *Juniperus*
  cedar-apple rust, 535
  root and crown rots, 533
  twig blight, 532
on *Kalanchoe*
  powdery mildew, 272
on *Kalmia*
  leaf spots, 535
on *Lagerstroemia*
  powdery mildew, 537
on *Lathyrus*
  powdery mildew, 405
  wilt disease, 405
on lawns
  anthracnose, 297
  brown patch, 298
  collar rots, 857
  crown rots, 857
  damping-off, 300
  dollar spot, 298
  fusarium blight, 298

fusarium patch, 297
Helminthosporium leaf
  spot, 305
leaf spot, 305
melting out, 305
Ophiobolus patch, 299
pink snow mold, 297
powdery mildew, 308
pythium blight, 300
rust, 308
septoria leaf spot, 307
stripe smut, 307
tip burn, 307
water molds, 857
on lettuce
  bottom rot, 751
  watery soft rot, 751
  white mold, 751
on *Leucothoe*
  leaf spot, 537
on *Ligustrum*
  anthracnose and twig
    blight, 539
on *Lilium*
  root and bulb rot, 406
on *Liriodendron*
  sooty mold, 539
on *Lobularia*
  downy mildew, 408
  root and stem rot, 407
on *Lonicera*
  powdery mildew, 541
on *Mahonia*
  rust, 543
on *Malus*
  apple scab, 544
  cedar-apple rust, 545
on mango
  anthracnose, 653
  scab, 653
on *Matthiola*
  fungal wilt, 408
on *Mesembryanthemum*
  root rot, 337
on *Narcissus*
  fusarium bulb rot, 411
  smoulder, 410
on *Nerium*
  witch's broom, 549
on onion family
  basal rot, 755
  downy mildew, 756
  fusarium basal rot, 755
  pink root, 755
  purple blotch, 756
  smut, 756
on *Pachysandra*
  leaf and stem blight, 338
  volutella blight, 338
on *Paeonia*
  phytophthora blight, 413
on palm family, outdoors
  bud rot, 550
on palms, indoors
  gliocladium rot, 278
on *Papaver*
  verticillium wilt, 413
on peach; nectarine
  brown rot, 657
  coryneum blight, 655

leaf curl, 656
peach blight, 655
scab, 655
shothole fungus, 655
on peanuts
  southern blight, 761
  southern stem rot, 761
  stem rot, 761
on pear
  fabraea leaf spot, 662
  pear leaf blight, 662
  scab, 659
on peas
  ascochyta blight, 759
  powdery mildew, 759
on pecan
  cotton root rot, 666
  scab, 666
  Texas root rot, 666
on *Pelargonium*, indoors·
  root and stem rot, 280
on *Pelargonium*, outdoors, 415
  alternaria leaf spot, 415
  blackleg, 415
  gray mold, 414
  rust, 414
on peppers
  anthracnose, 763
  cercospora leaf spot, 765
  frog-eye leaf spot, 765
on *Petunia*
  gray mold, 417
on *Philodendron*
  root rot, 282
on *Phlox*
  leaf spot, 419
  powdery mildew, 419
on *Photinia*
  fungal leaf spots, 553
on *Pinus*
  diplodia tip blight, 557
  needle cast, 557
  needle rust, 560
  western and eastern gall
    rust, 562
on *Pistacia*
  verticillium wilt, 563
on *Platanus*
  canker stain disease, 565
  powdery mildew, 564
  sycamore anthracnose, 565
on plum
  black knot, 671
  brown rot, 669
on *Populus*
  canker and dieback, 569
on potatoes
  common scab, 766
  early blight, 770
  late blight, 770
  scab, 766
on *Potentilla*
  leaf spot, 339
  rust, 339
on *Primula*, 420
  leaf spot, 420
on *Prunus*, evergreen
  forms of

on *Hedera*, 336
on pecan, 666
on trees, 466
plants resistant to, 994
crown rot and
on *Ceanothus*, 498
on *Delphinium*, 390
on fruit and nut trees, 624
on *Juniperus*, 533
on *Petunia*, 418
on *Saintpaulia*, 286
on trees, 466
cypress
on cypress family, 509
mushroom
on *Acacia*, 476
on trees, 466
on *Ageratum*, 361
on *Aglaonema*, 231
on *Antirrhinum*, 365
on beans, 703
on *Brassaia*, 239
on *Buxus*, 490
on *Carissa*, 495
on *Ceanothus*, 498
on *Centaurea*, 376
on *Coleus*, 249
on corn, 726
on *Cosmos*, 384
on *Cyclamen*, 254
on *Dahlia*, 387
on *Delphinium*, 390
on *Erica*, 511
on *Euphorbia*, 260, 393
on *Fragaria*, 334
on *Hedera*, 336
on houseplants
too much water or poor
drainage and, 226
on *Juniperus*, 533
on *Lilium*, 406
on *Lobularia*, 407
on *Mesembryanthemum*,
337
on *Pelargonium*, 280
on *Peperomia*, 281
on *Philodendron*, 282
on *Primula*, 420
on *Ranunculus*, 422
on *Rhododendron*, 585
on rhubarb, 773
on *Saintpaulia*, 286
on *Sedum*, 423
on *Taxus*, 604
on trees, 446, 466, 472
on *Tulipa*, 429
on vegetables, 684, 685
on *Vinca*, 340
on *Viola*, 433
on *Zygocactus*, 291
phytophthora
on avocado, 637
on *Buxus*, 490
sclerotium, 859
shoestring
on grapes, 746
on *Quercus*, 580
on strawberries, 780
on trees, 466
stem rot and

on *Ageratum*, 361
on *Aglaonema*, 231
on *Antirrhinum*, 365
on *Begonia*, outdoors,
369
on *Centaurea*, 376
on *Cosmos*, 384
on *Dahlia*, 387
on *Euphorbia*, 393
on flowers, 353
on *Hedera*, 336
on *Lobularia*, 407
on *Pelargonium*,
outdoors, 280
on *Peperomia*, 281
on *Primula*, 420
on *Sedum*, 423
on vegetables, 684
on *Vinca*, 340
on *Viola*, 433
on *Zygocactus*, 291
Texas
on *Hedera*, 336
on pecan, 666
on trees, 466
root, stalk, and ear rot
on corn, 726
rust, 856
cedar-apple, 856
on *Juniperus*, 535
eastern gall
on *Pinus*, 562
gall
on *Pinus*, 562
hawthorn
on *Crataegus*, 505
leaf and stem
on trees, 445
leaf
on trees, 461
needle
on *Pinus*, 560
on *Alcea*, 362
on *Antirrhinum*, 364
on beans, 701
on brambles, 712
on *Callistephus*, 372
on *Chaenomeles*, 500
on *Duchesnea*, 333
on fig, 649
on flowers, 351
on *Hypericum*, 337
on *Iris*, 403
on lawns, 308
on *Mahonia*, 543
on *Pelargonium*, outdoors,
414
on *Pinus*, 560
on *Potentilla*, 339
on *Rhododendron*, 583
on *Rosa*, 589
on *Sorbus*, 600
on sunflower, 785
on trees, 446
orange
on brambles, 712
western gall
on *Pinus*, 562
white pine blister
on currants; gooseberries,

738
white
on spinach, 775
scab
citrus
on citrus, 642
on apple, 629
on apricot, 633
on cucurbits, 733
on mango, 653
on peach; nectarine, 655
on pear, 659
on pecan, 666
on potato, 766
on *Pyracantha*, 572
sclerotium root rot, 859
scurf
on sweet potato, 782
septoria leaf spot
on lawns, 307
on tomato, 793
shoestring fungus
on trees, 446, 858
shoestring root rot
on fruit and nut trees, 624
on grapes, 746
on *Juniperus*, 533
on *Quercus*, 580
on strawberries, 780
on trees, 466
shothole fungus
on almond, 626
on apricot, 633
on peach; nectarine, 655
slow or no growth and
on flowers, 348
smoulder
on *Narcissus*, 410
smut
on corn, 725
on onion family, 756
soft rot
on cacti, outdoors, 491
watery
on cabbage family, 718
soil pasteurization for, 919
sooty blotch and fly speck
on apple, 628
sooty mold
on *Camellia*, 495
on *Gardenia*, 521
on *Jasminium*, 531
on *Liriodendron*, 539
on *Pyracantha*, 573
souring
on fig, 649
southern blight, 859
on *Anemone*, 363
on peanuts, 761
southern leaf blight
on corn, 727
southern stem rot
on peanuts, 761
southern wilt, 859
spot anthracnose
on *Cornus*, 501
stalk rot
root and ear rot and
on corn, 726
stem blight

blossom blight and
on blueberries, 708
stem and blossom blight
on blueberries, 708
stem and root rot
see also root and stem rot
on flowers, 353
on *Sedum*, 423
on *Viola*, 433
stem cankers
dieback and
on *Rosa*, 594
stem gall
on trees, 446
stem rot
on *Dianthus*, 391
on peanuts, 761
root rot and
on *Ageratum*, 361
on *Aglaonema*, 231
on *Antirrhinum*, 365
on *Begonia*, outdoors,
369
on *Centaurea*, 376
on *Cosmos*, 384
on *Dahlia*, 387
on *Euphorbia*, 393
on flowers, 353
on *Hedera*, outdoors, 336
on *Lobularia*, 407
on *Pelargonium*, indoors,
280
on *Peperomia*, 281
on *Primula*, 420
on *Sedum*, 423
on vegetables, 684
on *Vinca*, 340
on *Viola*, 433
on *Zygocactus*, 291
southern
on peanuts, 761
stem rust
leaf rust and
on trees, 445
stripe smut
on lawns, 307
sycamore anthracnose
on *Platanus*, 565
Texas root rot, 859
on *Hedera*, outdoors, 336
on *Juniperus*, 533
on pecan, 666
on trees, 466
tip burn
on lawns, 307
tuber rot
on *Anemone*, 363
on *Dahlia*, 387
twig blight
on *Juniperus*, 532
on *Ligustrum*, 539
twig and needle blight
on cypress family, 507
verticillium wilt, 408, 858
on *Acer*, 479
on *Ailanthus*, 480
on *Capsicum*, 375
on *Catalpa*, 497
on *Cercis*, 499
on *Chrysanthemum*,

outdoors, 379
on *Cinnamomum,* 500
on *Cotinus,* 503
on eggplant, 741
on *Elaeagnus,* 511
on *Helianthus,* 397
on *Papaver,* 413
on *Pistacia,* 563
on *Rosa,* 594
on *Rudbeckia,* 422
on *Salvia,* 423
on strawberries, 779
on tomato, 792
on vegetables
susceptibility to, 1009
volutella blight
on *Pachysandra,* 338
walnut anthracnose, 675
water molds, 857
watery soft rot
on cabbage family, 718
on lettuce, 751
western gall rust
on *Pinus,* 562
white mold
on beans, 701
on lettuce, 751
white pine blister rust
on currants; gooseberries,
738
white rust
on spinach, 775
wilt and root rot
on *Rhododendron,* 585
wilt disease
see also fusarium wilt;
verticillium wilt
crown rot and
on *Aquilegia,* 366
on *Callistephus,* 372
on *Dahlia,* 387
on *Lathyrus,* 405
on *Rhus,* 581
on tomato, 684
wilting and
on flowers, 353
witch's broom
on *Nerium,* 549
yellow leafspot
on cherry, 641
Fungus gnats
on houseplants, 230
Furnishings, pests in
bedbugs, 809
boxelder bugs, 803
brown recluse spiders, 815
carpet beetles, 802
clover mites, 803
crickets, 801
fleas, 806
house mice, 804
powderpost beetles, 809
rats, 805
spiders
brown recluse, 815
woodwasps, 811
Furrow irrigation, 906
Fusarium basal rot
on onion family, 755

Fusarium blight
on lawns, 298
resistance and
susceptibility to, 990
Fusarium bulb rot
on *Narcissus,* 411
Fusarium leaf spot
on *Dracaena,* 257
Fusarium patch
on lawns, 297
varieties resistant to, 990
Fusarium **species,** 405, 858
F. moniliforme
on corn, 726
on *Dracaena,* 257
F. nivale
on lawns, 297
F. oxysporum
on vegetables
susceptibility to, 1009
on *Zygocactus,* 291
F. oxysporum f. *callistephi*
on *Callistephus,* 372
F. oxysporum f.
lycopersici
on tomato, 791
F. oxysporum f.
perniciosum, 481
on *Albizia,* 481
F. oxysporum f. *rhois*
on *Rhus,* 581
F. oxysporum var. *dianthi*
on *Dianthus,* 390
F. oxysporum var. *narcissi*
on *Narcissus,* 411
on asparagus, 697
on beans, 703
on *Dahlia,* 387
on *Lathyrus,* 405
on *Lilium,* 406
on *Matthiola,* 408
on onion family, 755
on tomato, 684
on *Tulipa,* 429
Fusarium wilt, 858
flowers susceptible to, 994
on asparagus, 697
on *Dianthus,* 390
on flowers
susceptibility to, 994
on tomato, 684, 791
resistance to, 1010
sunscald and, 786
on vegetables
susceptibility to, 1009
See also Wilt disease
Fusicladium **species**
F. effusum
on pecan, 666
F. pyracanthae
on *Pyracantha,* 572

G

Gaillardia (Blanket flower)
diseases on
aster yellows, 994
powdery mildew, 995
verticillium wilt, 995
flowering times for, 992
germination of, 992
planting times for, 992
Galinsoga
in lawns
herbicides for, 971
Gall aphids
cooley spruce (*Adelges
cooleyi*)
on *Picea,* 554
Eastern spruce (*Adelges
abietis*)
on *Picea,* 554
Gall midges
on grapes, 747
Gall mites
ash flower (*Aceria
fraxinivorus*)
on *Fraxinus,* 517
Eriophyes species
witch's broom and
on *Celtis,* 498
Gall wasps
on grapes, 747
on *Quercus,* 579
Gallex
for *Olea*
olive knot on, 555
Gallflies
on *Quercus,* 579
Galls, 869
defined, 302
from bacterial diseases,
859
on *Nerium,* 549
on brambles
from cane and crown gall,
711
on *Celtis*
from hackberry leaf gall
psyllids, 499
on grapes, 747
See also Crown gall
Gambusia affinis
(Mosquitofish), 815
Garbage cans
pests around
raccoons, 805
Garden centipedes. *See*
Garden symphylans
Garden fleahoppers, 876
Garden spurge
herbicides for, 974
Garden symphylans
(*Scutigerella
immaculata*), 885

on strawberries, 781
on vegetables, 693
Gardenia (Cape jasmine),
indoors
cold damage to, 266
culture, 266
iron deficiency in, 266
polishes for, 952, 953
Gardenia (Cape jasmine),
outdoors
branches on
dying back
nematodes, 522
buds on
distorted
aphids, 521
yellowish green insects on
aphids, 521
creeping, as acid tolerant
groundcover, 327
culture, 521
disease on
sooty mold, 521
fertilizing, 923, 924, 926,
935, 936
iron deficiency and, 520,
929
honeydew on, 521
insects on
ants, 521
aphids, 521
greenhouse whiteflies,
521
insecticide for, 968
mealybugs
sooty mold and, 521
nematodes, 522
scales
sooty mold and, 521
spider mites, 520
iron deficiency in, 520, 929
leaves on
black sooty mold on, 521
curled or distorted
aphids, 521
spider mites, 520
dropping
soil moisture change, 520
temperature change, 520
drying out
greenhouse whiteflies,
521
honeydew on
aphids, 521
greenhouse whiteflies,
521
sooty mold and, 521
mottled yellow
nematodes, 522
pale green to yellow
iron deficiency, 520
silken webbing under
spider mites, 520
sticky substance on
aphids, 521
stippled
spider mites, 520
tiny insects under
aphids, 521

greenhouse whiteflies, 521
wilting during days
  nematodes, 522
wrinkled
  aphids, 521
yellowing
  aphids, 521
  greenhouse whiteflies, 521
  iron deficiency, 520
  soil moisture change, 520
  sooty mold, 521
  spider mites, 520
  temperature change, 520
planting directions for
  iron deficiency and, 520
  nematodes and, 522
roots of
  bushy, dark, and stunted
    nematodes, 522
  tiny galls on
    nematodes, 522
soil pH for, 1002, 1003
  correcting, 923
  iron deficiency and, 520
stems on
  yellowish green insects on
    aphids, 521
stunted growth in
  nematodes, 522
tiny winged insects
  fluttering around
    greenhouse whiteflies, 521
twigs on
  black sooty mold on, 521
watering
  leaf drop and, 520
weak
  nematodes, 522
Gardening with Color
  (ORTHO), 987
Gardens. *See* Landscaping
Garlic. *See* Onion family;
  Wild garlic
Gas lines, damage to
  near trees, 471
  rats, 805
Gaultheria
  as acid tolerant, 327
Gazania
  crown rot on, 334
  culture, 334
  planting locations for, 334, 991
    crown rot and, 334
  saline soils and, 999
General Purpose Plant
  Food. *See* ORTHO
  General Purpose Plant
  Food
Geranium
  as houseplant. *See*
    Pelargonium, indoors
  as shrub. *See Pelargonium*,
    outdoors
  ivy

insecticides for, 969
strawberry. *See Saxifraga*
wild
  herbicides for, 974
  in lawns
    herbicides for, 978
Gerbera (Transvaal daisy)
  culture, 394, 992
  diseases on
    foot rot, 394
    gray mold, 394
    powdery mildew, 995
  fertilizing, 394
  flowering times for, 992
  germination of, 992
  insects on
    ants, 394
    aphids, 394
  planting directions for
    gray mold and, 394
  planting locations for, 394
  planting times for, 992
German cockroach
  (*Blattella germanica*).
  See Cockroaches
German velvetgrass
  (*Holcus mollis*), 826
Germination, defined, 302
Geum
  verticillium wilt on, 995
Giant bark aphid
  (*Longistigma caryae*)
  on *Platanus*, 566
  on *Quercus*, 578
  on *Salix*, 596
Gill-over-the-ground. *See*
  Ground ivy
Gingko (Maidenhair tree)
  as disease and insect
    resistant, 998
    armillaria root rot, 1001
    crown gall, 998
    Japanese beetles, 997
  as drought tolerant, 997
  planting locations for, 997
Girdle, defined, 302
Glade grass
  as mildew resistant, 308
  as shade tolerant, 305
  See also Bluegrass
Gladiolus
  corms, stored
    dry rot and, 397
    penicillium corm rot and, 396
  corms
    brown and corky
      gladiolus thrips, 395
    corky, reddish brown,
      sunken lesions on
      penicillium corm rot, 396
    dark sunken lesions on
      dry rot, 397
      scab, 396
    dry and corky
      dry rot, 397
    fail to grow
      penicillium corm rot, 396

moldy
  penicillium corm rot, 396
raised, brittle rims on
  lesions on
    scab, 396
rotted
  penicillium corm rot, 396
shiny, varnishlike spots on
  scab, 396
sunken lesions on scab, 396
viruses in, 395
culture, 395, 992
diseases on
  aster yellows, 396
  corm rot, 396
  dry rot, 397
  penicillium corm rot, 396
  scab, 396
  southern blight, 996
  verticillium wilt, 995
  virus, 395
dying at top
  aster yellows, 396
dying
  scab, 396
failure to grow in
  penicillium corm rot, 396
fertilizing, 395
  iron deficiency and, 929
flower stalks on
  distorted
    aster yellows, 396
flowering times for, 992
flowers on
  blackish brown, slender,
    winged insects in
    gladiolus thrips, 395
  blooming prematurely
    virus, 395
  deformed and discolored
    gladiolus thrips, 395
  green
    aster yellows, 396
  silvery white streaks on
    gladiolus thrips, 395
  streaked, spotted, or
    mottled
    virus, 395
insects on
  aphids
    viruses and, 395
  gladiolus thrips, 395
  leafhoppers
    aster yellows and, 396
iron deficiency in, 929
leaves on
  black fungal pellets on
    decayed bases of
    dry rot, 397
  blackish brown, slender,
    winged insects on
    gladiolus thrips, 395
  dying
    dry rot, 397
    gladiolus thrips, 395
    penicillium corm rot, 396
  elongated dead spots on
    scab, 396
  falling over

scab, 396
raised, reddish brown
  specks on
    scab, 396
rotted bases on
  dry rot, 397
shiny ooze on
  scab, 396
shredded appearance to
  dry rot, 397
silvery white streaks on
  gladiolus thrips, 395
stiff
  virus, 395
streaked, spotted, or
  mottled
  virus, 395
thin
  aster yellows, 396
turning brown
  gladiolus thrips, 395
weak
  aster yellows, 396
wilting
  penicillium corm rot, 396
yellowing
  aster yellows, 396
  dry rot, 397
  penicillium corm rot, 396
  virus, 395
planting directions for
  dry rot and, 397
  penicillium corm rot and, 396
planting locations for, 395
  scab and, 396
  viruses and, 395
planting times for, 395, 992
soil pH for, 395
spindly
  aster yellows, 396
stems on
  soft, watery rot at bases of
    scab, 396
stunted growth in
  aster yellows, 396
  gladiolus thrips, 395
  virus, 395
watering, 395
Gladiolus thrips
  insecticides for, 956
Glaucomys species. *See*
  Tree squirrels
Glechoma hederacea. See
  Ground ivy
Gleditsia (Honey locust)
  as verticillium wilt
    resistant, 995
  bees attracted by, 996
  branches on
    dying back
      honey locust borers, 524
      honey locust pod gall
        midges, 523
    dying
      canker wilt, 524
    gummy ooze from
      canker wilt, 524
      honey locust borers, 524

reddish streaks on bark of
canker wilt, 524
small tan to black
depressed areas girdling
canker wilt, 524
varnishlike coating on
honey locust borers, 524
weak
honey locust borers, 524
culture, 522
diseases on
canker wilt, 524
verticillium wilt, 995
dying
canker wilt, 524
fertilizing, 522
G. triacanthos forma
inermis 'Shademaster'
(Shademaster locust)
as armillaria root rot
resistant, 1001
insects on
honey locust borers, 524
honey locust pod gall
midges, 523
honey locust spider mites,
523
mimosa webworms, 522
plantbug-leafhopper
complex, 523
leaflets on
dropping
honey locust pod gall
midges, 523
galls on
honey locust pod gall
midges, 523
whitish larvae inside galls
on
honey locust pod gall
midge, 523
leaves on
caterpillars on
mimosa webworms, 522
deformed
plantbug-leafhopper
complex, 523
dirty
honey locust spider mites,
523
discolored
canker wilt, 524
dropping
canker wilt, 524
honey locust spider mites,
523
mimosa webworms, 522
plantbug-leafhopper
complex, 523
dying
mimosa webworms, 522
fire-scorched look to
mimosa webworms, 522
mottled yellow
plantbug-leafhopper
complex, 523
silk threads tying clumps
of
mimosa webworms, 522
silken webbing under

honey locust spider mites,
523
skeletonized
mimosa webworms, 522
stippled yellow or whitish
honey locust spider mites,
523
turning brown
honey locust spider mites,
523
mimosa webworms, 522
wedge- or shield-shaped
insects on
plantbug-leafhopper
complex, 523
wilting
canker wilt, 524
yellowing
honey locust borers, 524
honey locust spider mites,
523
planting locations for, 522
pruning, 522
trunk of
gummy ooze from
honey locust borers, 524
small tan to black
depressed areas girdling
canker wilt, 524
varnishlike coating on
honey locust borers, 524
twigs on
dying back
honey locust pod gall
midges, 523
plantbug-leafhopper
complex, 523
watering, 522
Gliocladium rot
on palms, indoors, 278
Gliocladium vermoeseni
on palms, indoors, 278
Globe artichoke
culture, 695
diseases on
curly dwarf, 696
southern blight, 996
verticillium wilt
susceptibility to, 1009
harvesting, 695
insects on
aphids or leafhoppers
curly dwarf and, 696
artichoke plume moths,
696
weeds near
milk thistle
curly dwarf and, 696
thistles
artichoke plume moths
and, 696
Gloeodoes pomigena
on apple, 628
Gloeosporium species
G. apocryptum
on Acer, 479
G. aridum
on Fraxinus, 516
G. piperatum

on peppers, 763
Glomerella cingulata
on apple, 627
Glory-bower
greenhouse whiteflies on,
247
Glover scales
on citrus
insecticide for, 940
Gloxinia. See Sinningia
Glyphosate
for barnyardgrass, 829
for bracken, 832
for dallisgrass, 827
for fall panicum, 828
for Florida betony, 850
for German velvetgrass,
826
for horsenettle, 848
for Japanese honeysuckle,
850
for lippia, 839
for pineappleweed, 836
for wild garlic, 831
for wild onion, 831
Gnaphalium species. See
Cudweed
Gnats
fungus
on houseplants, 230
in households, 814
insecticides for, 945, 948,
950, 958
Gnomonia species
G. leptostyla
on walnut, 675
G. platani
on Platanus, 565
G. species
on Quercus, 575
Goatweed (Hypericum
perforatum), 833
Gold dust plant. See
Aucuba
Golden-rain-tree. See
Koelreuteria
Goldenrod
rust on, 560
Goldfish
for mosquitoes
near households, 815
Golf course greens
fertilizing
iron deficiency and, 929
Gooseberries. See
Currants; Gooseberries
Goosefoot
herbicides for, 966
white. See Common
lambsquarters
Goosegrass (Eleusine
indica), 828
herbicides for, 966, 973,
974, 976
in lawns, 312
Gophers. See Rodents

Grackles
in corn, 725
Grade change
trees and, 470
Graft, defined, 302
Grafting
on citrus
psorosis and, 647
Grain weevil (Sitophilus
species)
in households, 818
Grains, pest in. See Food
products, pests in
Granadilla (Passiflora)
as powdery mildew
susceptible, 995
Granary weevil. See Grain
weevil
Grape berry moth
(Endopiza viteana)
insecticides for, 946, 948
on grapes, 743
Grape flea beetle (Altica
chalybea), 744
Grape ivy. See Cissus
Grape leaf skeletonizer
(Harrisina species), 744
Grape leaf-folders
insecticide for, 946
Grape leafhopper
(Erythroneura species),
745
insecticides for, 955
Grape phylloxera, 747
Grapes
See also Vegetables,
berries, and grapes
bird damage to, 747
branches on
dying
armillaria root rot, 746
holes in
twig and branch borers,
746
sap flowing from
twig and branch borers,
746
buds on
chewed
grape flea beetles, 744
metallic beetles on
grape flea beetles, 744
canes on
green to red swellings on
gall wasps or gall
midges, 747
grubs inside galls on, 747
sunken purple to black
lesions on
black rot, 743
culture, 742
diseases on
anthracnose, 745
armillaria root rot, 746
bird's eye rot, 745
black rot, 743
varieties resistant to,

1007
cotton root rot, 994
downy mildew, 748
  varieties resistant to, 1007
fungicides for, 948
oak root fungus, 746
powdery mildew, 746
  varieties resistant to, 1007
shoestring root rot, 746
dying
  armillaria root rot, 746
  grape phylloxera, 747
fertilizing, 742
fruit on
  black droppings on
    grape leafhoppers, 745
  black sooty fungus on
    aphids, 744
  black
    black rot, 743
  brown
    downy mildew, 748
  caterpillars inside
    webbing on
      leafrollers, 743
  dark green to purple
    worms in
      grape berry moths, 743
  disappearing
    birds, 747
  dropping
    aphids, 744
    leafrollers, 743
  drying out
    black rot, 743
  dying
    downy mildew, 748
  harvesting, 742
  holes in
    leafrollers, 743
  misshapen
    anthracnose, 745
  poor yield of
    armillaria root rot, 746
    grape flea beetles, 744
    grape phylloxera, 747
  red
    downy mildew, 748
  ripening slowly
    downy mildew, 748
    grape leafhoppers, 745
    powdery mildew, 746
  rotting and remaining on
    stem
      black rot, 743
  rusty
    powdery mildew, 746
  scaly
    powdery mildew, 746
  shriveled
    black rot, 743
    downy mildew, 748
    leafrollers, 743
  spots on
    anthracnose, 745
    black rot, 743
  sunscald on
    downy mildew and, 748

webbing on
  grape berry moths, 743
  leafrollers, 743
white cottony growth on
  downy mildew, 748
white powdery growth on
  powdery mildew, 746
yellow
  downy mildew, 748
galls on, 747
harvesting, 742
insects on
  ants, 744
  aphids, 744
  cutworms, 689
  gall midges, 747
  gall wasps, 747
  grape berry moths, 743
  grape flea beetles, 744
  grape leaf skeletonizers, 744
  grape leafhoppers, 745
  grape phylloxera, 747
  insecticides for, 948
  Japanese beetles, 690
  leafrollers, 743
  Mediterranean fruit flies, 1002
  omnivorous leafrollers, 743
  redbanded leafrollers, 743
  spider mites, 745
  twig and branch borers, 746
leaves on
  black sooty fungus on
    aphids, 744
  brittle
    downy mildew, 748
  brown
    downy mildew, 748
    grape flea beetles, 744
    grape leafhoppers, 745
    powdery mildew, 746
  caterpillars inside
    webbing on
      leafrollers, 743
  caterpillars on
    grape leaf skeletonizers, 744
  chewed
    grape leaf skeletonizers, 744
  curled
    anthracnose, 745
    aphids, 744
    leafrollers, 743
  dirty
    spider mites, 745
  distorted
    aphids, 744
    downy mildew, 748
  dropping
    downy mildew, 748
    grape leafhoppers, 745
    powdery mildew, 746
    spider mites, 745
    twig and branch borers, 746
  drying out

spider mites, 745
dying
  armillaria root rot, 746
  powdery mildew, 746
eaten between veins
  grape leaf skeletonizers, 744
galls on
  gall midges or gall
    wasps, 747
  grape phylloxera, 747
grubs in galls on
  gall midges or gall
    wasps, 747
grubs on
  grape flea beetles, 744
holes in
  leafrollers, 743
honeydew on
  aphids, 744
insects under
  aphids, 744
  grape leafhoppers, 745
metallic beetles on
  grape flea beetles, 744
pea-shaped galls on
  grape phylloxera, 747
puckered
  aphids, 744
red
  armillaria root rot, 746
shiny, sticky substance on
  aphids, 744
spots on
  black rot, 743
  downy mildew, 748
  grape leafhoppers, 745
stippled
  grape leafhoppers, 745
  spider mites, 745
swellings on
  gall midges or gall
    wasps, 747
  grape leafhoppers, 745
webbing on, under, or
  between
    grape berry moths, 743
    leafrollers, 743
    spider mites, 745
white cocoons on
  grape berry moths, 743
white cottony growth
  under
    downy mildew, 748
white powdery growth on
  powdery mildew, 746
white
  grape leafhoppers, 745
yellowing
  armillaria root rot, 746
  grape leafhoppers, 745
  powdery mildew, 746
  spider mites, 745
mushrooms at base of
  armillaria root rot, 746
pesticide burn on, 687
planting directions for, 742
planting locations for, 742, 1007

twig and branch borers

and, 746
planting time for, 742
roots of
  black rootlike strands
    growing in
      armillaria root rot, 746
  decaying
    armillaria root rot, 746
  tubers or swelling on
    grape phylloxera, 747
  white fan-shaped growth
    under bark on
      armillaria root rot, 746
shoots on
  breaking
    twig and branch borers, 746
  brittle
    downy mildew, 748
  brown
    downy mildew, 748
  distorted
    downy mildew, 748
  dying
    anthracnose, 745
    twig and branch borers, 746
  holes in wood below
    twig and branch borers, 746
  holes in
    twig and branch borers, 746
  sap flowing from
    twig and branch borers, 746
  spots on
    anthracnose, 745
  weak
    twig and branch borers, 746
  white flaky material on
    wood below
      twig and branch borers, 746
  white grubs in
    twig and branch borers, 746
  wilting
    twig and branch borers, 746
snails and slugs on
  baits for, 938
soil pH for, 742, 1002
stems on
  dark bordered spots on
    anthracnose, 745
  purple, brown or green
    insects on
      aphids, 744
  sunken purple to black
    lesions on
      black rot, 743
  sunken spots with light
    gray centers on
      anthracnose, 745
  white powdery growth on
    powdery mildew, 746
stunted growth in
  armillaria root rot, 746

downy mildew, 748
grape flea beetles, 744
grape leafhoppers, 745
grape phylloxera, 747
tendrils on
brittle
downy mildew, 748
brown
downy mildew, 748
distorted
downy mildew, 748
green to red swellings on
gall midges or gall
wasps, 747
grubs inside galls on
gall midges or gall
wasps, 747
sunken purple to black
lesions on
black rot, 743
trunks of
mushrooms at bases of,
746
armillaria root rot, 746
white fan-shaped growth
under bark on
armillaria root rot, 746
watering, 742
weak
anthracnose, 745
powdery mildew, 746
Grapholitha species
G. *molesta. See* Oriental
fruit moth
G. *packardii. See* Cherry
fruitworm
Grass seed. *See* **Lawns, seed
for**
Grass webworms, tropical
insecticides for, 952
Grasses. *See* **Lawns;
Pastures**
Grasshoppers, 881
blister beetles and, 740
diseases and, 880
insecticides for, 943, 946,
952, 954, 956, 964
on corn, 728
poor pollination and, 725
on flowers, 355
on lawns
insecticides for, 952
on vegetables, 683, 691
Grasslike weeds. *See*
Weeds, grasslike
Gravel
as mulch, 918
Gray leaf spot
controlling, 954, 957, 968
on lawns, 954
Gray mold, 856, 857
See also Blossom blight;
Soft rot
botrytis
controlling, 968
on houseplants, 227
on *Ageratum*, 361
on *Begonia*, 368

on *Cymbidium*, 386
on *Dimorphotheca*, 393
on *Gerbera*, 394
on *Paeonia*, 412
on *Pelargonium*, 414
on *Petunia*, 417
on *Salvia*, 423
on strawberries, 777
on *Verbena*, 431
on *Zinnia*, 435
Grease spot
on lawns, 300
Greasy spot
on citrus, 646
Green foxtail. *See* **Foxtails**
Green peach aphid (*Myzus
persicae*)
insecticide for, 967
on lettuce, 749
Green scurf
on *Magnolia*, 542
Green spruce aphid (*Cinara
fornacula*)
on *Picea*, 555
**Green striped
mapleworms**
insecticide for, 956
Green vine. *See* **Wild
morning glory**
Greenbug (*Schizaphis
graminum*)
insecticide for, 956
on lawns, 304
Greenhouse whitefly
(*Trialeurodes
vaporariorum*)
on *Ageratum*, 362
on avocado, indoors, 236
on *Begonia*, indoors, 238
on *Browallia*, 370
on *Capsicum*, 243
on *Chrysanthemum*,
indoors, 244
on *Clerondendron*, 247
on *Coleus*, indoors, 250
on *Coleus*, outdoors, 383
on eggplant, 741
on flowers, 357
on *Fuchsia*, 519
on *Gardenia*, 521
on groundcovers, 328
on *Hibiscus*, 525
on houseplants, 229
on *Lantana*, 405
on *Pelargonium*, indoors,
280
on *Pelargonium*, outdoors,
416
on *Poinsettia*, 261
on tomato, 790
on *Verbena*, 432
Greenhouses
insects in
insecticides for, 968, 969
snails and slugs in
baits for, 938
Greenol Liquid Iron. *See*

ORTHO Greenol
Liquid Iron
Grevillea (Silk oak)
as disease and insect
resistant, 998
sapsucker damage to, 999
Grimsel. *See* **Groundsel**
Ground bark
as soil amendment, 918
Ground burnut (*Tribulus
terrestris*), 835
Ground ivy (*Glechoma
hederacea*), 841
in lawns, 841
herbicides for, 971, 978
Ground squirrels. *See*
Squirrels
Groundcovers, 324, 340
*See also specific
groundcovers*
acid-tolerant varieties of,
327
bare areas in
compacted soil, 325
drought, 325
excess water, 326
insufficient light, 325
weeds, 324
book about
All About Ground Covers
(ORTHO), 984
diseases on
compacted soil and, 325
powdery mildew, 328
drought on, 325
drought resistant, 991
dying
compacted soil, 325
fertilizing, 326
scorch and, 327
tools for, 983
flower buds on
webbing on
spider mites, 328
for erosion control, 899
for shady areas, 991
for sunny areas, 991
heat scorch on, 327
insects on
ants, 329
aphids, 329
baits for, 964
greenhouse whiteflies,
328
Japanese beetles
resistance to, 997
spider mites, 328
invading other areas, 324
iron deficiency in, 327
lack of nutrients in, 326
lawn pennywort as, 841
leaves on
black mold on
greenhouse whiteflies,
328
brown edges on
drought, 325
scorch, 327

brown tips on
scorch, 327
chewed
snails and slugs, 329
crisp edges on
drought, 325
curled
aphids, 329
dark green
insufficient light, 325,
326
dead tips and edges on
scorch, 327
dirty
spider mites, 328
distorted
aphids, 329
dropping
drought, 325
insufficient light, 325,
326
powdery mildew, 328
scorch, 327
spider mites, 328
drying out
spider mites, 328
dying
powdery mildew, 328
eaten
snails and slugs, 329
grayish white powdery
patches on
powdery mildew, 328
honeydew on
aphids, 329
greenhouse whiteflies,
328
mottled
greenhouse whiteflies,
328
pale
acid soil, 327
iron deficiency, 327
shiny, sticky substance on
aphids, 329
stippled
spider mites, 328
stunted
compacted soil, 325
iron deficiency, 327
tiny pale green to black
insects under
aphids, 329
tiny winged insects on
greenhouse whiteflies,
328
turning brown
scorch, 327
webbing between or
under
spider mites, 328
white, waxy powder on
insects on
greenhouse whiteflies,
328
white
iron deficiency, 327
withering
scorch, 327
yellowing

Hopperburn
from leafhoppers, 880
on beans, 702
Hormaphis hamamelidis
(Witch-hazel leaf gall
aphid), 524
Hornbeam. *See* Carpinus
hop. *See* Ostrya
Hornet & Wasp Killer. *See*
ORTHO Hornet &
Wasp Killer
Hornets
insecticides for, 949, 958
Horntails (Woodwasps)
in households, 811
Hornworms
See also Caterpillars
ash
insecticides for, 956
insecticides for, 947, 954,
956, 964, 967
on herbs, 748
on *Pelargonium*, outdoors,
416
on *Petunia*, 417
on vegetables, 690
tobacco (*Manduca sexta*)
on eggplant, 740
on peppers, 764
on tomato, 789
tomato (*Manduca
quinquemaculata*)
insecticides for, 963
on eggplant, 740
on peppers, 764
on tomato, 789
Horse chestnut. *See*
Aesculus
Horse flies. *See* Flies,
biting
Horse thistle (*Lactuca
serriola*), 842
Horsenettle (*Solanum
carolinense*), 848
near potato
viruses and, 771
near tomato
viruses and, 794
Horsetail (*Equisetum*
species), 832
herbicides for, 970
Horseweed (*Conyza
canadensis*), 846
aster yellows harbored by,
994
Host, defined, 302
Hosta (Plantain lily)
as acid tolerant, 327
as shade tolerant, 325, 326
flowering times for, 992
germination of, 992
leaves on
holes in
snails and slugs, 399
planting times for, 992
snails and slugs on, 399
House crickets (*Acheta*

domesticus), 801
House flies, 800
diseases spread by, 800
insecticides for, 948
little (*Fannia canicularis*),
800
Musca domestica, 800
House mice (*Mus musculus*),
804
See also Rodents
House Plant Food. *See*
ORTHO House Plant
Food
Houseflies, 800
insecticides for, 955
Household pests
ants, 803, 883
baits for, 943, 955, 959
bedbugs (*Cimex
lectularius*), 809
bees (*Apis mellifera*), 813
beetles
carpet, 802
cigarette, 818
drugstore, 818
flour, 817
powderpost, 809
birds, 804
biting flies, 814
biting midges, 814
black flies, 814
black widow spiders
(*Latrodectus* species),
815
borers
new house, 810
old house, 810
roundheaded, 810
boxelder bugs, 477, 803
brown recluse spiders
(*Loxosceles reclusa*), 815
carpenter ants
(*Camponotus* species),
811
carpenter bees (*Xylocopa
virginica*), 811
carpet beetles, 802
centipedes, 884
chiggers, 808
cigarette beetles, 818
clothes moths, 802
clover mites, 803
cockroaches, 816
insecticides for, 945
crickets, 801, 881
drugstore beetles, 818
drywood termites, 810
earwigs, 801, 884
fire ants
insecticides for, 943
firebrats, 802
fleas, 806
insecticides for, 944, 945
flies
biting, 814
black, 814
fruit, 800
insecticides for, 945
vinegar, 800

flour beetles, 817
flour moths, 817
fruit flies, 800
gnats
insecticides for, 945
grain weevils, 818
grasshoppers, 881
honeybees (*Apis mellifera*),
813
horntails, 811
house flies, 800
house mice, 804
houseflies, 800
insecticides for, 938, 940–
942, 945, 947–950, 952
mealworms, 817
mice, 804
midges, biting, 814
millipedes, 885
mosquitoes, 815
insecticides for, 945
moths, clothes, 802
new house borers, 810
old house borers, 810
paper wasps, 813
pillbugs, 885
powderpost beetles, 809
raccoons (*Procyon lotor*),
805, 894
rats, 805
red bugs, 808
roundheaded borers, 810
scorpions, 816
silverfish and firebrats, 802
skunks, 807
solitary wasps, 813
sowbugs, 885
spiders, 801
black widow (*Latrodectus*
species), 815
brown recluse (*Loxosceles
reclusa*), 815
insecticides for, 945
termites, 810
drywood, 810
subterranean, 808
ticks, 807
tree squirrels, 806
vinegar flies, 800
wasps
insecticides for, 945
paper, 813
solitary, 813
yellowjackets, 812
woodwasps, 811
yellowjackets, 812
Houseplants
See also Containers, plants
in; *specific houseplants*
bending toward light
insufficient light, 227
bleaching on, 226
book about
All About Houseplants
(ORTHO), 984
buds on
tiny green insects on
aphids, 228
cottony appearance to
mealybugs, 229

cottony masses on
mealybugs, 229
culture
book about
All About Houseplants
(ORTHO), 984
diagnosing problems in,
990
diseases on
botrytis gray mold, 227
root rot
drainage and, 226
rooting cuttings and, 914
watering and, 226
drainage for, 226
excessive watering and,
226
dying
mealybugs, 229
too little water, 225
too much water or poor
drainage, 226
failure to bloom in
insufficient light, 227
failure to grow in
insufficient light, 227
too little water, 225
too much water or poor
drainage, 226
fertilizing, 927, 928, 930,
932, 936, 937
salt damage and, 225
flower buds on
webbing on
spider mites, 228
flowers on
fail to grow
insufficient light, 227
fuzzy gray or brown
growth on
botrytis gray mold, 227
intensified color on
botrytis gray mold, 227
spots on
botrytis gray mold, 227
growing locations for, 226
bleaching and, 226
diagnosing problems
from, 990
light and, 227, 914, 990
sunburn and, 226
honeydew on plants and
objects under, 228, 229
greenhouse whiteflies,
229
scales, 228
insects fluttering rapidly
around
greenhouse whiteflies,
229
insects on
aphids, 228
boxelder bugs, 803
fungus gnats, 230
greenhouse whiteflies,
229
insecticides for, 948, 950,
951, 968, 969
applying, 915
mealybugs, 229

caterpillars inside
webbing on
juniper webworms, 535
brown
alkaline soils, 532
aphids, 534
dog urine, 532
drought, 532
juniper webworms, 535
leafminers and tip moths,
533
natural leaf browning
and shedding, 532
overfertilized soils, 532
poor drainage, 532
root and crown rots, 533
runoff from roads, 532
salt burn, 532
spider mites, 534
twig blight, 532
winter injury, 532
chewed
bagworms, 443
dirty
spider mites, 534
dropping
aphids, 534
natural leaf browning
and shedding, 532
spider mites, 534
dull
root and crown rots, 533
dying from tips back
twig blight, 532
eaten
bagworms, 443
gray
twig blight, 532
honeydew on
aphids, 534
juniper scales, 534
juniper scales, 534
orange jellylike "horns" on
brown galls on
cedar-apple rust, 535
reddish
drought, 532
wind damage, 532
winter injury, 532
reddish brown
twig blight, 532
scaly bumps
juniper scales, 534
shiny or sticky substance
on
aphids, 534
juniper scales, 534
small greenish caterpillars
inside
leafminers and tip moths,
533
stippled yellow or grayish
spider mites, 534
webbing on
juniper webworms, 535
wilting
root and crown rots, 533
yellowing, 534
juniper scales, 534
dog urine, 532

drought, 532
leafminers and tip moths,
533
root and crown rots, 533
salt burn, 532
winter injury, 532
no new growth on
juniper scales, 534
planting directions for
root and crown rots and,
533
planting locations for, 531,
997
cedar-apple rust and, 535
hawthorn rust and, 505
rust and, 500, 600
salt burn and, 532
twig blight and, 532
winter injury and, 532
pruning, 531
quince rust
Chaenomeles and, 500
roots of
brownish and decayed
root and crown rots, 533
fan-shaped white strands
under bark of
root and crown rots, 533
fine woolly brown strands
on
root and crown rots, 533
salt damage to, 532
soil pH for
root and crown rots and,
533
salt burn and, 532
stems on
black sooty mold on
aphids, 534
brownish and decayed
root and crown rots, 533
fan-shaped white strands
under bark of
root and crown rots, 533
shiny or sticky substance
on
aphids, 534
tiny black or brown insects
on
aphids, 534
stunted growth in
aphids, 534
bagworms, 443
turning brown
dog urine, 532
drought, 532
natural leaf browning and
shedding, 532
salt burn, 532
winter injury, 532
twigs on
black dots on
twig blight, 532
dying back
rust, 500
twig blight, 532
dying
cedar-apple rust, 535
gray
twig blight, 532

light to reddish brown
twig blight, 532
swellings on
rust, 500
tiny black or brown insects
on
aphids, 534
watering, 531
dog urine damage and,
532
drought damage and, 532
root and crown rots and,
533
salt burn and, 532
twig blight and, 532
wind damage and, 532
winter injury and, 532
weak
root and crown rots, 533
white powdery spores on
soil around
root and crown rots, 533
wilting
root and crown rots, 533
winter injury to, 532
Juvenile, defined, 302

K

Kaffir lily. See Clivia
Kalanchoe (Maternity plant)
culture, 272
insects on
cyclamen mites, 285
insecticide for, 969
mealybugs, 272
powdery mildew, 272
Kalmia (Mountain laurel)
as shade tolerant, 997
culture, 535
diseases on
crown gall
resistance to, 998
fungal leaf spots, 535
fertilizing, 535
iron deficiency and, 536
insects on
gypsy moths, 1000
Japanese beetles, 997
iron deficiency on, 536
leaves on
dying and dropping
fungal leaf spots, 535
pale
iron deficiency, 536
spots or blotches on
fungal leaf spots, 535
yellowing
fungal leaf spots, 535
iron deficiency, 536
planting directions, 536
planting locations for
fungal leaf spots and, 535
shade tolerance, and, 997
soil pH for, 1002, 1003

iron deficiency and, 536
Kalopanax
K. pictus (Castor-aralia)
as disease and insect
resistant, 998
Kangaroo ivy. See *Cissus*
Karathane
for *Platanus*
powdery mildew on, 564
Katsura tree
(*Cercidiphyllum
japonicum*)
as disease and insect
resistant, 998
Kedlock (*Brassica kaber*),
834
Kentia palm (*Howea*)
salt damage to, 990
Kentucky coffee-tree
(*Gymnocladus dioica*)
as disease and insect
resistant, 998
Kerria (Japanese rose)
as disease and insect
resistant, 998
soil pH for, 1002, 1003
Kinnick; Kinnikinnick.
See *Arctostaphylos
uva-ursi*
Klamath weed (*Hypericum
perforatum*), 833
Kleenup Ready-to-Use
Weed & Grass Killer.
See ORTHO Kleenup
Ready- to-Use Weed &
Grass Killer
Kleenup Systemic Weed &
Grass Killer. See
ORTHO Kleenup
Systemic Weed &
Grass Killer
Knotgrass. See Knotweed,
prostrate; Quackgrass
Knotweed
herbicides for, 966, 970–
972, 974, 978
prostrate (*Polygonum
aviculare*), 837
herbicides for, 974
in lawns, 314
Kochia
herbicides for, 966
Koelreuteria (Chinese flame
tree; Golden-rain tree)
as crown gall resistant, 998
as drought tolerant, 997
as lawn tree, 997
K. paniculata (Varnish
tree)
as disease and insect
resistant, 998
as low-growing tree, 998
as street tree, 998
planting locations for, 997
Kohlrabi
See also Cabbage family

clubroot on, 718

L

Labidura riparia (striped earwig)
in households, 801
Laburnum (Bean tree; Golden- chain tree)
as crown gall resistant, 998
as disease and insect resistant, 998
culture, 536
insects on
ants, 536
cowpea and bean aphids, 536
Lace fern
insecticide for, 969
Lacebugs, 877
(*Stephanitis* species)
on *Rhododendron*, 582
andromeda (*Stephanitis takeyai*)
on *Pieris*, 556
hawthorn (*Corythucha cydoniae*)
on *Cotoneaster*, 504
on *Crataegus*, 505
on *Pyracantha*, 572
insecticides for, 941, 951, 956, 961–963, 965, 966, 968
oak (*Corythucha arcuata*), 576
on trees, 450, 463
leaf spots and, 450
sycamore (*Corythucha* species), 564
Lacewings, 887
Lactuca sativa. See Lettuce
Lactuca serriola (Prickly lettuce), 842
Lady beetle, 886
Lady's purse. See Shepherd's purse
Ladybird beetle, 886
Ladybug, 886
Ladysthumb (*Polygonum persicaria*), 842
herbicides for, 970, 974
Lagerstroemia (Crape myrtle)
as lawn tree, 997
culture, 536
diseases on
fungicides for, 946
powdery mildew, 537, 995
fertilizing, 924
insects on
ant, 536
crapemyrtle aphids, 536

L. indica
as low-growing tree, 998
as street tree, 998
soil pH for, 1002, 1003
Lakes, weeds near. See Water, weeds near
Lamb's tongue. See Plantain
Lamb's-quarters
common (*Chenopodium album*), 848
herbicides for, 966, 970, 971, 973, 974, 976, 978
Lamium amplexicaule. See Henbit
Lampranthus (Ice plant; Trailing iceplant)
as drought resistant, 991
for sunny areas, 991
saline soils and, 999
Landscaped beds
See also Landscaping
calculating area of, 982, 983
fertilizing
tools for, 982, 983
insecticides for
tools for applying, 982
weeds in
black medic, 840
dallisgrass, 827
dichondra, 840
Florida betony, 850
Johnsongrass, 828
lippia, 839
sowthistle, 845
Virginia peppergrass, 833
wild carrot, 835
yellow starthistle, 844
Landscaping
See also Landscaped beds
books about
All About Landscaping (ORTHO), 985
All About Shade Gardening (ORTHO), 985
Award-Winning Small-Space Gardens (ORTHO), 986
Easy Maintenance Gardening (ORTHO), 986
Gardening with Color (ORTHO), 987
choosing plants, 916
color in
book about
Gardening with Color (ORTHO), 987
diagnosing problems in, 1008
for low maintenance
book about
Easy Maintenance Gardening, 986
for shady areas
book about

All About Shade Gardening (ORTHO), 985
for small spaces
books about
Award-Winning Small-Space Gardens (ORTHO), 986
insects and
diagnosing, 1008
lawn trees, 997
low-growing trees for, 998
street trees, 998
tools for, 987
See also Tools and equipment
with containers
book about
Award-Winning Small-Space Gardens (ORTHO), 986
with herbs, 986
Lantana
bees attracted by, 996
creeping
herbicides for, 974
culture, 405, 992
diseases on
fusarium wilt, 994
verticillium wilt
resistance to, 995
greenhouse whiteflies on, 405
Larch. See *Larix*
Larch aphids
woolly (*Adelges laricis; A. lariciatus*), 537
Large brown patch
on lawns
controlling, 954
Large crabgrass. See Crabgrass
Larix (Larch)
as crown gall resistant, 998
as verticillium wilt resistant, 995
bird damage to, 999
culture, 537
fertilizers for, 926, 936
fungus diseases on
susceptibility to, 1000
insects on
Douglas fir tussock moths, 475, 554
spruce budworms, 474, 553
woolly larch aphids, 537
needles on
yellowing, with white, woolly masses on
woolly larch aphids, 537
sapsucker damage to, 999
snow-covered appearance to
woolly larch aphids, 537
Larkspur. See *Delphinium*
Larva, defined, 302
Lasioderma serricorne

(Cigarette beetle)
in households, 818
Laspeyresia species
L. caryana. See Hickory shuckworm
L. pomonella. See Codling moth
Late blight
controlling, 967, 968
on celery, 722
on potato, 770
on tomato, 792
sunscald and, 786
Lateral bud, defined, 302
Lath houses
snails and slugs in
baits for, 938
Lathyrus (Sweet pea)
culture, 405, 992
diseases on
powdery mildew, 405, 995
southern blight, 996
wilt disease, 405
fertilizing, 405
flower buds on
webbing on
two-spotted spider mites, 406
flowering times for, 992
flowers on
drooping
wilt disease, 405
germination of, 992
insects on
Japanese beetles, 997
two-spotted spider mites, 406
leaves on
drying out and dropping
two-spotted spider mites, 406
dying
wilt disease, 405
grayish white powdery spots and patches on
powdery mildew, 405
mealy and stippled
two-spotted spider mites, 406
webbing between or under
two-spotted spider mites, 406
wilting
powdery mildew, 405
wilt disease, 405
yellowing
powdery mildew, 405
two-spotted spider mites, 406
wilt disease, 405
planting locations for, 405
planting times for, 992
stems on
discolored inside bases
wilt disease, 405
watering, 405
Latrodectus species (Black widow spiders)

wind damage to
  fusarium blight and, 298
worms on, at night or after
    rain
  earthworms, 310
yellowing
  Bermudagrass mites, 307
  chinch bugs, 301
  dull lawn mower, 302
  from nitrogen deficiency,
    306
  fusarium patch, 297
  nematodes, 306
  septoria leaf spot, 307
  stripe smut, 307
yellowing with pink edges
  fusarium patch, 297
Layered soils, 901
Leaching, defined, 302
Leader, defined, 302
Leaf and flower spots
  on flowers, 350
Leaf and stem blight
  bacterial
    on houseplants
      Geranium; Pelargonium,
      280
  on Pachysandra, 338
Leaf and stem rusts
  on trees, 445
Leaf beetles (*Chrysomela*
    species)
  bean
    insecticides for, 963
  cottonwood
    insecticides for, 951
  elm (*Pyrrhalta luteola*)
    insecticides for, 951
    on *Ulmus,* 609
  insecticides for, 947
  on *Populus,* 568
  on *Salix,* 595
  strawberry
    insecticides for, 948
  willow
    insecticides for, 951
Leaf blight
  bacterial, stem and
    on *Pelargonium,* indoors,
    280
  controlling, 968
  flower blight and
    on *Cornus,* 501
  helminthosporium
    controlling, 968
  on carrots, 721
  on corn, 727
  on pear, 662
Leaf blister, oak, 576
Leaf blotch
  on *Aesculus,* 480
Leaf bugs, 876
  fourlined
    insecticides for, 955
Leaf burn, 865
  See also Summer leaf
    scorch

Leaf curl
  on peach; nectarine, 656
Leaf curl aphids
  on *Fraxinus,* 517
Leaf drop
  on *Bucida,* 488
  on *Euphorbia,* 259
  on *Gardenia,* outdoors, 520
  on *Hibiscus,* 525
Leaf gall, camellia, 492
  on *Rhododendron,* 582
Leaf gall aphid (*Tamalia
    coweni*)
  on *Arctostaphylos,* 483
Leaf gall psyllids
  hackberry (*Pachypsylla*
    species), 499
  on *Celtis,* 499
Leaf galls
  from psyllids, 880
  on fruit and nut trees, 880
  on trees, 880
  on vegetables, 880
Leaf margins, defined, 302
Leaf nematodes
  (*Aphelenchoides* species)
  on *Begonia,* 369
  on *Chrysanthemum,* 378
Leaf Polish. *See* ORTHO
    Leaf Polish (Aerosol);
    ORTHO Leaf Polish
    (Pump)
Leaf roll
  on potato, 771
    discolored tubers and, 767
  on tomato, 793
    sunscald and, 786
Leaf rusts
  on trees, 445, 461
Leaf scar, defined, 302
Leaf scorch, 865
  on *Ajuga,* 330
  on fruit and nut trees, 622
  on *Hedera,* 335
  on *Hippeastrum,* 270
  on strawberries, 779
  on trees, 461
  summer
    on *Acer,* 479
    on *Aesculus,* 480
    on *Catalpa,* 497
    on *Cornus,* 502
    on *Euonymus,* 513
    on *Magnolia,* 541
    on *Platanus,* 565
    on *Quercus,* 574
Leaf spot
  alternaria
    controlling, 954, 957, 959
    on *Brassaia,* 599
    on cabbage family, 717
    on cucurbits, 735
    on lawns
      controlling, 954
    on *Pelargonium,* outdoors,
      415
  angular

controlling, 957
  on cucurbits, 736
bacterial, 859
  on *Begonia,* outdoors, 368
  on *Dieffenbachia,* 256
  on flowers, 350
  on *Hedera,* outdoors, 335
  on *Pelargonium,* outdoors,
    415
  on *Philodendron,* 283
  on plum, 668
  peach; nectarine, 1006
cercospora
  controlling, 968
  on avocado, outdoors, 636
  on beets, 705
  cherry, 641
  controlling, 957
  varieties resistant to, 1008
  controlling, 942, 954, 957,
    958, 961, 962, 968
curvularia
  on lawns
    controlling, 954
didymellina
  controlling, 959
  on *Iris,* 403
fabraea
  on pear, 662
fruit rot and
  on eggplant, 742
fungal
  on flowers, 350
  on *Hedera,* outdoors, 335
  on *Kalmia,* 535
  on *Photinia,* 553
fusarium
  on *Dracaena,* 257
gray
  controlling, 954, 957, 968
  on lawns
    controlling, 954
helminthosporium
  on bluegrass
    varieties resistant and
    susceptible to, 990
  on *Anemone,* 363
  on *Aster,* 366
  on beets, 705
  on brambles
    varieties resistant to, 1008
  on *Calendula,* 371
  on *Campanula,* 373
  on *Ceanothus,* 497
  on *Celosia,* 375
  on *Chrysanthemum,*
    outdoors, 378
  on *Delphinium,* 389
  on flowers, 350
  on *Fragaria,* 333
  on *Hedera,* outdoors, 335
  on *Helianthemum,* 397
  on *Hemerocallis,* 398
  on *Heuchera,* 399
  on *Hypericum,* 336
  on *Ilex,* 528
  on *Impatiens,* 402
  on *Iris,* 403
  on lawns
    controlling, 954

on *Leucothoe,* 537
on peanuts, 761
on *Pelargonium,* outdoors,
  415
on *Phlox,* 419
on *Photinia,* 553
on *Potentilla,* 339
on *Primula,* 420
on *Prunus,* evergreen
  forms of, 571
on strawberries, 688, 778
  varieties resistant to, 1007
on *Tagetes,* 424
on *Tropaeolum,* 426
on vegetables, 688
on *Vinca,* 340
on *Viola,* 433
phomopsis
  on eggplant, 742
septoria
  controlling, 957, 959
  on lawns, 307
  on tomato, 793
    sunscald and, 786
yellow
  on cherry, 641
Leaf spot and fruit rot
  on eggplant, 742
Leaf-feeding caterpillars
  See also Gypsy moth
  on *Populus,* 567
  on *Quercus,* 577
  on *Salix,* 595
  on *Tilia,* 605
  on trees, 443
Leaf-folders, grape
  insecticides for, 946
Leafbeetles
  elm
    insecticides for, 956
  willow
    insecticides for, 956
Leafcutter bees (*Megachile*
    species)
  on *Rosa,* 592
**Leafhopper-plantbug
    complex**
  on *Gleditsia,* 523
Leafhoppers, 880
  ants and, 883
  on fruit and nut trees, 620
  aster (*Macrosteles
    fascifrons*)
  on *Coreopsis,* 384
  on flowers, 357
  on lettuce, 750
  on vegetables, 691
  aster yellows and, 861
    in carrots, 721
  on *Callistephus,* 373
  on celery, 723
  on *Chrysanthemum,*
    outdoors, 380
  on *Gladiolus,* 396
  on lettuce, 752
  on trees, 861
  on vegetables, 861
  on weeds, 861

leaves on
  bitter taste to
    aster yellows, 752
  bolting, 749
  brown
    aster leafhoppers, 750
    bottom rot, 751
  brown margins on
    tip burn, 751
  brown or green pellets
    between
    cabbage loopers, 750
  brown spots on
    tip burn, 751
  curled
    aphids, 749
    mosaic virus, 752
  distorted
    aphids, 749
  drooping and dying
    watery soft rot, 751
  green, yellow, or purple
    insects under
    aphids, 749
  holes in
    cabbage loopers, 750
  mottled green and yellow
    mosaic virus, 752
  pale veins on
    mosaic virus, 752
  pink to tan latex deposits
    on
    aster yellows, 752
  puckered
    aphids, 749
  ruffled
    mosaic virus, 752
  rust-colored spots on
    bottom rot, 751
  short and thick
    aster yellows, 752
  slimy
    bottom rot, 751
    tip burn, 751
  stippled
    aster leafhoppers, 750
  tip burn on, 751
  white, gray, or black
    pellets between
    watery soft rot, 751
  withering
    watery soft rot, 751
  yellow to white heart on
    aster yellows, 752
  yellowing
    aphids, 749
    mosaic virus, 752
loose-leaf
  bolt-resistant varieties of,
    749
  harvesting, 749
pale green insects hopping
  or flying around
  aster leafhoppers, 750
pink to tan latex deposits in
  heart of
  aster yellows, 752
planting directions for, 749
  bottom rot and, 751
planting locations for, 749

bottom rot and, 751
watery soft rot and, 751
planting times for, 1009
  bolting and, 749
prickly (*Lactuca serriola*),
  842
  herbicides for, 974
  in lawns
    herbicides for, 971
rabbits in, 694
seed stalk emerging from
  bolting, 749
seeds
  diseases carried by
    mosaic virus, 752
  germination of, 1009
snails and slugs on
  baits for, 938
soil pH for, 749
stems on
  water-soaked areas near
    soil on
    watery soft rot, 751
stunted growth in
  aster yellows, 752
  mosaic virus, 752
tip burn on, 751
transplanting, 749
virus diseases on
  mosaic virus, 752
watering, 749
  tip burn and, 751
  watery soft rot and, 751
weeds in
  aster yellows and, 752
  leafhoppers and, 752
  mosaic virus and, 752
wild. *See* Lettuce, prickly
Leucothoe
  as shade tolerant, 997
  culture, 537
  diseases on
    crown gall
      resistance to, 998
    leaf spot, 537
  soil pH for, 537, 1002,
    1003
Libocedrus (Incense cedar)
  as disease and insect
    resistant, 998, 1001
  branches on
    swellings on
      from rust, 500
    witch's broom on
      from rust, 500
  diseases on
    quince rust, 1000
    rust, 500
      Chaenomeles and, 500
      Sorbus and, 600
      witch's broom and, 500
      susceptibility to, 1000
  insects on
    juniper scales, 534
    witch's broom on
      from rust, 500
Lice
  on poultry
    insecticides for, 963

plant. *See* Aphids
  jumping. *See* Psyllids
Lichens
  on trees, 447
Lighting, supplementary,
  914
Lightning injury
  to palm family, outdoors,
    551
  to trees, 456
  susceptility to, 999
Ligustrum (Privet)
  as pollution tolerant, 996
  as shade tolerant, 997
  bees attracted by, 996
  branches on
    bark splitting open on
      anthracnose and twig
        blight, 539
    dying back
      anthracnose and twig
        blight, 539
    scales, 538
    sunken oval areas with
      pink pustules at base of
      anthracnose and twig
        blight, 539
  culture, 538
  diseases on
    anthracnose and twig
      blight, 539
    powdery mildew, 995
  fertilizing, 538, 923, 924,
    926, 927, 936
  iron deficiency and, 929
  insects on
    lilac leafminers, 602
    privet rust mites and privet
      mites, 538
    scales, 538
  iron deficiency in, 929
  L. amurense (Amur privet)
    as anthracnose and twig
      blight resistant, 539
  L. ibota (Ibota privet)
    as anthracnose and twig
      blight resistant, 539
  L. lucidum (Glossy privet)
    as disease and insect
      resistant, 998
  L. obtusifolium var.
    regelianum (Regal privet)
    as anthracnose and twig
      blight resistant, 539
  L. ovalifolium (California
    privet)
    as anthracnose and twig
      blight resistant, 539
  L. tschonskii
    as armillaria root rot
      resistant, 1001
  leaves on
    black sooty mold on
      scales, 538
    brown
      anthracnose and twig
        blight, 539
      privet rust mites and
        privet mites, 538

bumps on
  scales, 538
cupped
  privet rust mites and
    privet mites, 538
dropping
  privet rust mites and
    privet mites, 538
  scales, 538
drying out
  anthracnose and twig
    blight, 539
dull green
  privet rust mites and
    privet mites, 538
shiny, sticky substance on
  scales, 538
yellowing
  privet rust mites and
    privet mites, 538
  scales, 538
planting locations for, 538
shade tolerance, 997
stunted growth in
  privet rust mites and privet
    mites, 538
twigs on
  bark splitting open on
    anthracnose and twig
      blight, 539
  dying back
    anthracnose and twig
      blight, 539
  sunken oval areas with
    pink pustules at base of
    anthracnose and twig
      blight, 539
wax leaf
  fertilizing, 926
weak
  privet rust mite and privet
    mite, 538
Lilac. *See Syringa*
Lilac borers (*Podoseia
  syringae*)
  insecticides for, 953
Lilac leafminers (*Caloptilia
  syringella*)
  insecticides for, 951
Lilium (Lily)
  as smog tolerant, 996
  bulbs
    fail to grow
      root and bulb rot, 406
  culture, 406, 992
  diseases on
    fleck, 407
    mosaic virus, 407
      aphids and, 407
      resistance and
        susceptibility to, 993
    root and bulb rot, 406
    southern blight, 996
    virus, 407
  disfigured
    viruses, 407
  fertilizing, 406
  flower buds on
    fail to open

root and bulb rot, 406
withering
root and bulb rot, 406
flowering times for, 992
flowers on
dying
root and bulb rot, 406
malformed
aphids, 407
partially open
virus, 407
small
virus, 407
streaked
virus, 407
in containers
watering, 406
insects on
ants, 407
aphids, 407
viruses and, 407
leaves on
brown edges on
root and bulb rot, 406
curled
aphids, 407
virus, 407
dead tips on
root and bulb rot, 406
distorted
aphids, 407
viruses, 407
dying
root and bulb rot, 406
virus, 407
mottled light and dark
green
virus, 407
sticky, shiny substance on
aphids, 407
streaked or flecked
virus, 407
yellowing
aphids, 407
root and bulb rot, 406
stems on
tiny pale green to black
insects on
aphids, 407
stunted growth in
root and bulb rot, 406
virus, 407
wilting
root and bulb rot, 406
Lily. *See Lilium*
Lily of the Nile. *See
Agapanthus*
Lily-of-the-valley. *See
Convallaria*
Lily-of-the-valley shrub.
See Pieris
Lima beans. *See* Beans,
lima
Limb breakage
on fruit and nut trees, 618
Lime
applying, 1002, 1003
dolomitic limestone, 902

for groundcovers, 327
for growing transplants,
917
for *Hydrangea*, 526
pink flowers on, 526
for lawns, 295
for *Syringa*, 601
ground
for correcting soil pH,
1002
Lime-sulfur
as ingredient
in ORTHO Dormant
Disease Control, 942
in Orthorix, 958
dormant strength
for *Lagerstroemia*
powdery mildew on, 537
for *Acer*
cottony scales and
mealybugs on, 478
for anthracnose
on brambles, 712
on grapes, 745
for aphids
cooley spruce gall
on *Picea*, 554
for apple scab
on *Malus*, 544
for blister mites
pear leaf
on *Cotoneaster*, 504
on *Sorbus*, 600
for brambles
anthracnose on, 712
spider mites on, 711
for cooley spruce gall
aphids
on *Picea*, 554
for *Cotoneaster*
pear leaf blister mites on,
504
for cottony maple leaf
scales
on *Nyssa*, 549
for cottony scales and
mealybugs
on *Acer*, 478
on *Morus*, 546
for currants; gooseberries
powdery mildew on, 738
for dieback
stem cankers and
on *Rosa*, 594
for grapes
anthracnose on, 745
for *Malus*
apple scab on, 544
for mites
oak
on *Quercus*, 575
on pear, 661
pear leaf blister
on *Cotoneaster*, 504
on *Sorbus*, 600
for *Morus*
cottony scales and
mealybugs on, 546
for *Nyssa*
cottony maple leaf scales

on, 549
for oak mites, 575
for pear leaf blister mites
on *Cotoneaster*, 504
on *Sorbus*, 600
for pear rust mites, 661
for pear
mites on, 661
for *Picea*
cooley spruce gall aphids
on, 554
pine needle scales on, 555
for pine needle scales
on *Picea*, 555
on *Pinus*, 560
for powdery mildew
on currants; gooseberries,
738
for *Quercus*
oak mites on, 575
for *Rosa*
stem cankers and dieback
on, 594
for scab
apple
on *Malus*, 544
for scales
cottony maple leaf
on *Nyssa*, 549
pine needle
on *Picea*, 555
on *Pinus*, 560
for *Sorbus*
pear leaf blister mites on,
600
for spider mites
on brambles, 711
two-spotted
on pear, 661
for spruce gall aphids
on *Picea*, 554
for stem cankers and
dieback
on *Rosa*, 594
for two-spotted spider mites
on pear, 661
Lindane
as ingredient
in ORTHO Lindane Borer
& Leaf Miner Spray, 953
for aphids
cooley spruce gall
on *Pseudotsuga*, 571
for apricot
peachtree borers on, 634
for beetles
powderpost
in households, 809
for *Betula*
bronze birch borers on,
486
for borers
bronze birch, 486
honeylocust, 524
on *Crataegus*, 507
on fruit and nut trees, 619
on trees, 455
peachtree
on apricot, 634
on plum, 671

for cherry
peachtree borers on, 639
shothole borers on, 639
for cooley spruce gall
aphids
on *Pseudotsuga*, 571
for *Crataegus*
borers on, 507
for flowers
snout beetles on, 873
weevils on, 873
for fruit and nut trees
borers on, 619
for *Gleditsia*
honeylocust borers on, 524
honeylocust pod gall
midges on, 523
for peachtree borers
on apricot, 634
on cherry, 639
on plum, 671
for pecan
pecan phylloxeras on, 665
for plum
peachtree borers on, 671
for pod gall midges
honeylocust, 523
for powderpost beetles
in households, 809
for *Pseudotsuga*
cooley spruce gall aphids
on, 571
for shothole borers
on cherry, 639
for snout beetles, 873
on ornamentals, 873
on vegetables, 873
for symphylans, 885
on ornamentals, 885
for trees
borers on, 455
snout beetles on, 873
weevils on, 873
for vegetables
snout beetles on, 873
weevils on, 873
for weevils, 873
on ornamentals, 873
on vegetables, 873
**Lindane Borer & Leaf
Miner Spray.** *See*
ORTHO Lindane Borer
& Leaf Miner Spray
Linden. *See Tilia*
Linden aphid (*Myzocallis
tiliae*), 605
Linuron,
for Virginia peppergrass,
833
Lion's tooth. *See*
Dandelion
Lippia (*Phyla nodiflora*), 839
as groundcover, 839
as lawn, 839
as weed, 839
herbicide for, 978
saline salts and, 999
Lipstick plant. *See*

M

Macronoctua onusta. See Iris borers

Macronutrients, defined, 302

Macrosiphum species
  M. liriodendri (Tuliptree aphid), 540
  M. rhododendri (Rhododendron aphid), 587
  M. rosae (Rose aphid), 591

Macrosteles fascifrons. See Aster leafhopper; Six-spotted leafhopper

Madrone. *See* Arbutus

Maggots
  apple, 627
    insecticides for, 946, 947, 964
  blueberry (*Rhagoletis mendax*)
    insecticides for, 946
    on blueberries, 707
  cherry fruitworms
    insecticides for, 946
  onion (*Hylemya antiqua*)
    on onion family, 755
  root (*Hylemya* species). *See* Root maggots
  seed corn (*Hylemya platura*)
    on beans, 704
    on corn, 730
    on radish, 772

Magicicada septendecim (Periodical cicada), 882
  insecticides for, 947, 954, 964

Magnesium deficiency
  acid soils and, 902

Magnolia
  bird damage to, 999
  branches on
    dying
      magnolia scales, 542
  culture, 541
  diseases on
    algal spot, 542
    crown gall
      resistance to, 998
    green scurf, 542
    powdery mildew, 995
    varieties resistant to, 998
  dying
    magnolia scales, 542
  fertilizing, 541, 923, 924, 926, 936
  iron deficiency and, 542
  flowering times for, 541
  in lawns
    varieties for, 997
  insects on

gypsy moths, 1000
Japanese beetles, 997
magnolia scales, 542
tuliptree scales, 540
varieties resistant to, 998
iron deficiency in, 542
leaves on
  black sooty mold on
    magnolia scales, 542
  brown
    summer leaf scorch, 541
  dying and dropping
    summer leaf scorch, 541
  greenish brown spots on
    algal spot, 542
  pale
    iron deficiency, 542
  reddish brown velvety patches on
    algal spot, 542
  shiny, sticky substance on
    magnolia scales, 542
  small
    iron deficiency, 542
    magnolia scales, 542
  withering
    summer leaf scorch, 541
  yellow edges on
    iron deficiency, 542
  yellowing
    magnolia scales, 542
M. acuminata
  as disease and insect resistant, 998
M. grandiflora (Southern magnolia)
  as armillaria root rot resistant, 1001
M. Kobus borealis
  as disease and insect resistant, 998
M. salicifolia (Anise magnolia)
  as disease and insect resistant, 998
M. soulangiana (Saucer magnolia)
  as lawn tree, 997
M. stellata (Star magnolia)
  as disease and insect resistant, 998
  as lawn tree, 997
planting locations for, 541
  summer leaf scorch and, 541
pruning, 541
sapsucker damage to, 999
soil pH for, 541, 1002
  iron deficiency and, 542
stems on
  enlarged
    magnolia scales, 542
  powdery white or shiny brown bumps on
    magnolia scales, 542
  purple or white appearance to
    magnolia scales, 542
summer leaf scorch on, 541
twigs on

dying back, 542
  algal spot, 542
greenish brown spots or reddish velvety patches on
  algal spot, 542
masses of purple insects on
  magnolia scales, 542
powdery white or shiny brown bumps on
  magnolia scales, 542
stunted growth in
  algal spot, 542
watering, 541
  summer leaf scorch and, 541

Magnolia scale (*Neolecanium cornuparvum*), 542

Mahogany, Mountain. *See* Cercocarpus

Mahonia (Holly grape; Oregon grape)
  as shade tolerant, 997
  culture, 543
  diseases on
    armillaria root rot
      resistance to, 1001
    crown gall
      resistance to, 998
    rust, 543
  fertilizing, 543, 924
    winter injury and, 543
  insects on
    barberry loopers, 543
    mahonia loopers, 543
  planting locations for, 543
    shade tolerance and, 997
    winter injury and, 543
  winter injury to, 543

Mahonia looper (Barberry looper), 543

Maiden cane
  herbicides for, 974

Maidenhair tree. *See* Ginkgo

Maize dwarf mosaic (MDM)
  on corn, 727

Malacosoma species. *See* Tent caterpillar

Malathion 50 Insect Spray. *See* ORTHO Malathion 50 Insect Spray

Malathion
  as ingredient
    in ORTHO Home Orchard Spray, 948
    in ORTHO Rose & Floral Dust, 961
    in ORTHO Rose & Flower Jet Duster, 962
  for *Abies*
    spruce budworms on, 474
  for aphids
    bean
      on *Tropaeolum*, 426

cooley spruce gall
  on *Picea*, 554
cotton and cowpea
  on *Hibiscus*, 525
cowpea and bean
  on *Laburnum*, 536
Eastern spruce gall
  on *Picea*, 554
on *Centaurea*, 376
on currants; gooseberries, 738
on *Daphne*, 510
on *Dianthus*, 391
on *Digitalis*, 392
on *Fagus*, 513
on flowers, 356
on *Freesia*, 393
on fruit and nut trees, 620
on *Gerbera*, 394
on *Hemerocallis*, 398
on *Hibiscus*, 525
on *Iris*, 403
on *Ixora*, 530
on *Laburnum*, 536
on *Lilium*, 407
on *Liriodendron*, 540
on swiss chard, 783
on *Tropaeolum*, 426
on vegetables, 692
tuliptree, 540
woolly
  on *Sorbus*, 600
woolly honeysuckle, 540
woolly larch, 537
for apricot
  peachtree borers on, 634
for *Aquilegia*
  columbine leafminers on, 365
for *Araucaria*
  mealybugs on, 235
  scales on, 234
for aster leafhoppers
  on flowers, 357
  on vegetables, 691
for avocado, indoors
  mealybugs on, 236
for bean aphids
  on *Tropaeolum*, 426
for bedbugs, 809
  in households, 809
for beet leafhoppers
  on beets, 706
  on tomato, 794
for beet leafminers, 705
for beetles
  cigarette
    in households, 818
  drugstore
    in households, 818
  flour
    in households, 817
  on flowers, 355
  sawtoothed grain
    in households, 817
for beets
  beet leafhoppers on, 706
  beet leafminers on, 705
for *Begonia*, indoors
  mealybugs on, 237

for *Begonia,* outdoors
  leaf nematodes on, 369
  mealybugs on, 370
for blueberries
  blueberry fruitflies on, 707
  blueberry maggots on, 707
  cherry fruitworms on, 707
  cranberry fruitworms on,
    707
  leafrollers and leaftiers on,
    708
  plum curculios on, 707
for borers
  on *Iris,* 404
  peachtree
    on apricot, 634
    on plum, 671
for boxelder bugs
  in households, 803
for *Browallia*
  greenhouse whiteflies on,
    370
for budworms, spruce, 553
for cacti, indoors
  mealybugs on, 242
for cacti, outdoors
  cactus scales on, 491
  mealybugs on, 492
for *Callistephus*
  leafhoppers on, 373
for caterpillars
  on *Tropaeolum,* 426
for celery
  celery leaftiers on, 722
  leafhoppers on, 723
for *Centaurea*
  aphids on, 376
for cherry fruitworms
  on blueberries, 707
for cherry
  peachtree borers on, 639
for *Chrysanthemum,*
  outdoors
  leaf nematode in, 378
  leafhoppers on, 380
for cigarette beetles
  in households, 818
for citrus
  cottonycushion scales on,
    644
  mealybugs on, 644
for clover mites
  in households, 803
for *Coleus,* outdoors
  greenhouse whiteflies on,
    383
  mealybugs on, 383
for columbine leafminers,
  365
for cooley spruce gall
  aphids
  on *Picea,* 554
for cotton and cowpea
  aphids
  on *Hibiscus,* 525
for cottony scales and
  mealybugs
  on ferns, 515
  on *Morus,* 546
for cottonycushion scales

on citrus, 644
for cowpea and bean
  aphids
  on *Laburnum,* 536
for cranberry fruitworms
  on blueberries, 707
for currants; gooseberries
  aphids on, 738
for *Cycas*
  scales on, 252
for cypress family
  leafminers and tip moths
    on, 508
for *Daphne*
  aphids on, 510
for *Dianthus*
  aphids on, 391
for *Digitalis*
  aphids on, 392
for drugstore beetles
  in households, 818
for Eastern spruce gall
  aphids
  on *Picea,* 554
for eggplant
  spider mites on, 742
for *Fagus*
  aphids on, 513
for ferns
  cottony scales and
    mealybugs on, 515
  scales on, 515
for fig
  scales on, 650
for flea beetles
  on vegetables, 691
for flies
  walnut husk, 673
for flour beetles, 817
for flowers
  aphids on, 356
  aster leafhoppers on, 357
  beetles on, 355
  greenhouse whiteflies on,
    357
  Japanese beetles on, 355
  leafminers on, 352
  mealybugs on, 356
  scales on, 356
  six-spotted leafhoppers
    on, 357
  snout beetles on, 873
  spittlebugs on, 357
  weevils on, 873
  whiteflies on, 356, 357
for *Freesia*
  aphids on, 393
for fruit and nut trees
  aphids on, 620
  leafhoppers on, 620
  mealybugs on, 620
  psyllids on, 880
  scales on, 619, 620
  whiteflies on, 620
for fruitflies, blueberry, 707
for fruitworms
  on blueberries, 707
for gall aphids
  cooley spruce
    on *Picea,* 554

Eastern spruce
  on *Picea,* 554
for *Gerbera*
  aphids on, 394
for *Gladiolus*
  leafhoppers on, 396
  thrips on, 395
for grain weevils, 818
for granary weevils, 818
for grasshoppers, 881
  on vegetables, 683
for greenhouse whiteflies
  see also for whiteflies
  on *Browallia,* 370
  on *Coleus,* outdoors, 383
  on flowers, 357
  on groundcovers, 328
  on *Verbena,* 432
for groundcovers
  greenhouse whiteflies on,
    328
for *Hedera,* outdoors
  scales on, 336
for *Hemerocallis*
  aphids on, 398
for *Hibiscus*
  cotton and cowpea aphids
    on, 525
for *Iris*
  aphids in, 403
  iris borers on, 404
for *Ixora*
  aphids on, 530
for Japanese beetles
  on flowers, 355
for *Jasminum*
  scales on, 530
for *Laburnum*
  cowpea and bean aphids
    on, 536
for *Larix*
  woolly larch aphids on,
    537
for leaf nematodes
  on *Begonia,* outdoors, 369
  on *Chrysanthemum,*
    outdoors, 378
for leafhoppers
  aster
    on vegetables, 691
  beet
    on beets, 706
    on tomato, 794
  on *Callistephus,* 373
  on celery, 723
  on *Chrysanthemum,*
    outdoors, 380
  on fruit and nut trees, 620
  on *Gladiolus,* 396
  on *Parthenocissus,* 552
  on vegetables, 691
for leafminers
  columbine, 365
  on beets, 705
  on cypress family, 508
  on flowers, 352
  spinach
    on swiss chard, 784
for leafrollers, 875
  on blueberries, 708

for leaftiers, 875
  celery, 722
  on blueberries, 708
for *Lilium*
  aphids on, 407
for *Liriodendron*
  tuliptree aphids on, 540
  tuliptree scales on, 540
for *Lonicera*
  woolly honeysuckle
    aphids on, 540
for maggots
  blueberry, 707
for mealybugs
  on *Araucaria,* 235
  on avocado, indoors, 236
  on *Begonia,* indoors, 237
  on *Begonia,* outdoors, 370
  on cacti, indoors, 242
  on cacti, outdoors, 492
  on citrus, 644
  on *Coleus,* outdoors, 383
  on ferns, 515
  on flowers, 356
  on fruit and nut trees, 620
  on *Morus,* 546
  on orchids, 276
for *Mesembryanthemum*
  scales on, 337
for mites, clover
  in households, 803
for *Morus*
  cottony scales and
    mealybugs on, 546
for orchids
  mealybugs on, 276
  scales on, 276
for ornamentals
  snout beetles on, 873
  weevils on, 873
for *Pachysandra*
  scales on, 338
for parsley
  celeryworms on, 757
  parsleyworms on, 757
for *Parthenocissus*
  leafhoppers on, 552
for peachtree borers
  on apricot, 634
  on cherry, 639
  on plum, 671
for pear
  pearslugs on, 663
for pecan
  pecan phylloxeras on, 665
  spittlebugs on, 665
for *Picea*
  cooley spruce gall aphids
    on, 554
  Eastern spruce gall aphids
    on, 554
  spruce budworms on, 553
for plum
  peachtree borers on, 671
for plum curculios
  on blueberries, 707
for psyllids
  on fruit and nut trees, 880
  on vegetables, 880
for rice weevils

in households, 818
for sawtoothed grain
 beetles
 in households, 817
for scales
 cactus
  on cacti, outdoors, 491
 cottonycushion
  on citrus, 644
 on *Araucaria*, 234
 on *Cycas*, 252
 on ferns, 515
 on fig, 650
 on flowers, 356
 on fruit and nut trees, 619,
  620
 on *Hedera*, outdoors, 336
 on *Jasminum*, 530
 on *Mesembryanthemum*,
  337
 on orchids, 276
 on *Pachysandra*, 338
 tuliptree, 540
for six-spotted leafhoppers
 on flowers, 357
for snout beetles, 873
for *Sorbus*
 woolly aphids on, 600
for sowbugs and pillbugs
 on vegetables, 692
for spinach leafminers
 on swiss chard, 784
for spittlebugs, 881
 on flowers, 357
 on food crops, 881
 on pecan, 665
for spruce budworms
 on *Abies*, 474
 on *Picea*, 553
for spruce gall aphids
 cooley
  on *Picea*, 554
 Eastern
  on *Picea*, 554
for swiss chard
 aphids on, 783
 spinach leafminers on,
  784
for symphylans, 885
for thrips
 on *Gladiolus*, 395
for tip moths
 on cypress family, 508
for tomato
 beet leafhoppers on, 794
for trees
 snout beetles on, 873
 weevils on, 873
for *Tropaeolum*
 aphids on, 426
 caterpillars on, 426
for tuliptree aphids, 540
for tuliptree scales, 540
for vegetables
 aphids on, 692
 flea beetles on, 691
 grasshoppers on, 683
 leafhoppers on, 691
 leafrollers on, 875
 leaftiers on, 875

psyllids on, 880
snout beetles on, 873
sowbugs and pillbugs on,
 692
weevils on, 873
whiteflies on, 692
for *Verbena*
 greenhouse whiteflies on,
  432
for walnut
 walnut husk flies on, 673
for weevils, 873
 grain
  in households, 818
 granary
  in households, 818
 on ornamentals, 873
 on vegetables, 873
 rice
  in households, 818
for whiteflies
 see also for greenhouse
  whiteflies
 on flowers, 356
 on fruit and nut trees, 620
 on vegetables, 692
for woolly aphids
 on *Sorbus*, 600
for woolly honeysuckle
 aphids, 540
for woolly larch aphids, 537
Mallow (*Malva* species), 841
 herbicides for, 971, 974,
  978
 in lawns, 320
 rust harbored by, 362
Malus (Crabapple)
 See also Apple
 as low-growing tree, 998
 as street tree, 998
 bird damage to, 999
 branches on
  brown ooze on bark of
   fireblight, 544
  dark sunken areas on
   fireblight, 544
 culture, 544
 diseases on
  armillaria root rot, 1001
  cedar-apple rust, 545
   varieties susceptible to,
    1000
  fireblight, 466, 544
   susceptibility to, 1001
   varieties tolerant of, 1001
  powdery mildew, 995
  scab, 544
   varieties resistant to,
    1001
  verticillium wilt
   resistance to, 995
 flowers on
  scorched appearance to
   fireblight, 544
  wilting and turning black
   fireblight, 544
 fruit on
  corky black spots on
   apple scab, 544

deformed
 apple scab, 544
 cedar-apple rust, 545
dropping prematurely
 cedar-apple rust, 545
spots on
 apple scab, 544
 cedar-apple rust, 545
insects on
 gypsy moths, 1000
 scales, 545
leaves on
 black sooty mold on
  scales, 545
 black
  fireblight, 544
 crusty, scaly, or waxy
  bumps on
  scales, 545
 curled
  fireblight, 544
 dropping
  apple scab, 544
  cedar-apple rust, 545
  scales, 545
 hanging downward
  fireblight, 544
 olive-colored, velvety
  spots on
  apple scab, 544
 orange, black-dotted spots
  on
  cedar-apple rust, 545
 pale yellow spots on
  cedar-apple rust, 545
 puckered tissue around
  spots on
  apple scab, 544
 scorched appearance to
  fireblight, 544
 shiny, sticky substance on
  scales, 545
 small cups with fringed
  edges under
  cedar-apple rust, 545
 wilting
  fireblight, 544
 yellowing
  apple scab, 544
  scales, 545
M. floribunda (Japanese
 flowering crab)
 as armillaria root rot
  resistant, 1001
M. pumila. See Apple
M. sargentii (Sargent
 crabapple)
 soil pH for, 1002, 1003
planting locations for, 544
 cedar-apple rust and, 545
sapsucker damage to, 999
stems on
 crusty, waxy, or scaly
  bumps on
  scales, 545
twigs on
 brown ooze on bark of
  fireblight, 544
 corky black spots on
  apple scab, 544

cracks on sunken areas on
 fireblight, 544
dark, sunken, and dry
 bases on
 fireblight, 544
rough-surfaced,
 olive-green spots on
 apple scab, 544
water-soaked bark at
 bases of
 fireblight, 544
Malva species. *See* Mallow
Mancozeb
for *Acer*
 fungal leaf spot on, 478
for *Aesculus*
 leaf blotch on, 480
for *Ageratum*
 gray mold on, 361
for algae
 on lawns, 321
for anthracnose
 spot
  on *Cornus*, 501
for apple scab
 on *Malus*, 544
for *Aster*
 leaf spot on, 366
for blossom blight, 857
for botrytis blight, 857
 on *Tulipa*, 430
for brambles
 botrytis blight on, 857
for bud and flower blight,
 857
for *Chaenomeles*
 rust on, 500
for *Chrysanthemum*,
 outdoors
 rust in, 377
for *Cornus*
 flower and leaf blight on,
  501
 spot anthracnose on, 501
for *Delphinium*
 leaf spot on, 389
for dieback
 stem cankers and
  on *Rosa*, 594
for flower and leaf blight
 on *Cornus*, 501
for flowers
 botrytis blight on, 857
 fungal leaf spot on, 350
for *Fragaria*
 leaf spot on, 333
for fruit and nut trees
 botrytis blight on, 857
for fungal leaf or stem gall
 on trees, 446
for fungal leaf spot
 see also for leaf spot
 on *Acer*, 478
 on flowers, 350
 on *Rhododendron*, 583
 on trees, 450
for *Gerbera*
 gray mold on, 394
for gray mold, 857

insecticides for, 969
spraying, 915
on *Hoya*, 271
on *Jasminum*
sooty mold and, 531
on *Kalanchoe*, 272
on *Liriodendron*
sooty mold and, 539
on *Maranta*, 273
on *Monstera*, 274
on *Morus*, 546
on *Nerium*
bacterial gall and, 549
sooty mold and, 547
on orchids, 276
on palms, indoors, 278
on *Peperomia*, 281
on *Philodendron*, 283
on *Pittosporum*, 563
on *Plectranthus*, 284
on *Populus*, 568
on *Pyracantha*
sooty mold and, 573
on *Saintpaulia*, 286
on *Streptocarpus*, 289
on *Syngonium*, 288
on trees, 444, 448
honeydew from, 454
sooty mold and, 445
Planococcus citri
on citrus, 644
sooty mold and
on *Gardenia*, outdoors, 521
on *Jasminum*, 531
on *Liriodendron*, 539
on *Nerium*, 547
on *Pyracantha*, 573
spreader-stickers for, 915
Mean's grass. See Johnsongrass
Mechanical injury
diagnosing, 1008
leaf burn and, 865
leaf scorch and, 865
to flowers
wilting and, 354
to trees, 465
from fill, 999
oozing sap and, 453
wilting and, 451
Mecoprop
for English lawn daisy
in lawns, 317
for Japanese honeysuckle, 850
Medflies. See Mediterranean fruit flies
Medic, black. See Black medic
Medicago lupulina. See **Black medic**
Medic
black
in lawns
herbicides for, 971
Mediterranean flour moth

(*Anagasta kuehniella*).
See Flour moths
Mediterranean fruit flies, 882
plants infested by, 1002
Megachile species
(Leafcutter bees)
on *Rosa*, 592
Megacyllene robiniae
(Locust borer)
on *Rohnia*, 587
Melanconis species
on *Betula*, 487
Melanose
controlling, 959
Melissopus latiferreanus
(Filbertworm), 651
Melittia satyrininformis.
See Squash vine borer
Melons. See Cucurbits
diseases on
curly top, 703
Melonworms
insecticides for, 947, 954, 963, 964, 967
Melting out
See also Helminthosporium
leaf spot
controlling, 954, 957
Merodon equestris
(Narcissus bulb fly), 411
Mescal bean. See Sophora
Mesembryanthemum (Ice plant)
as drought resistant, 991
for sunny areas, 991
root rot on, 337
scales on, 337
Mesospora hypericorum
on *Hypericum*, 337
Metaldehyde
for snails and slugs
on artichoke, 696
Metamorphosis, defined, 302
Metasequoia
M. glyptostroboides (Dawn redwood)
as armillaria root rot resistant, 1001
as disease and insect resistant, 998
Meteor cherry. See Cherry
Methidathion
for scales
on walnut, 675
Methiocarb
as ingredient
in ORTHO Slug-Geta Snail & Slug Bait, 964
Methoxychlor
as ingredient
in ORTHO Home Orchard Spray, 948
in ORTHO Tomato

Vegetable Dust, 967
for angoumois grain moths
in households, 817
for aphids
on vegetables, 692
for aster leafhoppers
on vegetables, 691
for beets
flea beetles on, 704
for carpet beetles, 802
for caterpillars
on vegetables, 690
for clothes moths, 802
for curculios, plum
on pear, 661
for elm bark beetles
on *Ulmus*, 607
for flea beetles
on beets, 704
on radish, 772
on sweet potato, 783
on turnip, 796
for flour moths
in households, 817
for flowers
spittlebugs on, 357
for hickory bark beetles, 652
for Indian meal moths
in households, 817
for leafhoppers
aster
on vegetables, 691
for Mediterranean flour moths
in households, 817
for moths
angoumois grain
in households, 817
clothes, 802
flour
in households, 817
Indian meal
in households, 817
for pear
plum curculios on, 661
for radish
flea beetles on, 772
for sowbugs and pillbugs
on vegetables, 692
for spittlebugs
on flowers, 357
for sweet potato
flea beetles on, 783
for turnips
flea beetles on, 796
for *Ulmus*
elm bark beetles on, 607
for vegetables
aphids on, 692
caterpillars on, 690
leafhoppers on, 691
sowbugs and pillbugs on, 692
Methyl bromide
as soil fumigant, 919
Methyl thiophanate
for lawns
fusarium patch on, 297

Mexican bean beetle
(*Epilachna varivestis*), 699
insecticides for, 946, 963, 967
Mexican breadfruit. See Monstera
Mexican clover. See Florida pusley
Mexican mealybugs
insecticides for, 951
Mexican orange. See Choisya
Mice, 890
See also Rodents
in fruit and nut trees, 617
in households, 804
in trees, 455
in tulips, 428
in vegetables, 694
Michelmas daisy. See Aster
Microclimate, defined, 302
Micronutrients, 905
See also Minor nutrient deficiency
defined, 302
Microsphaera species
M. alni
on *Euonymus*, 512
on *Platanus*, 564
on *Syringa*, 602
on *Viburnum*, 610
plants infected by, 995
plants infected by, 995
Microthyriella rubi
on apple, 628
Midges
biting
near households, 814
galls from, 869
gall
on grapes, 747
honeylocust pod gall
(*Dasineura gleditschiae*), 523
rose (*Dasineura rhodophaga*), 590
insecticides for, 965
Mildew
brown
on *Quercus*, 576
downy. *See* Downy mildew
Milfoil. See Achillea
Military grass (*Bromus tectorum*), 830
Milk purslane. See Spotted spurge
Milk thistle (*Silybum marianum*)
near globe artichoke
curly dwarf and, 696
Milkweed (*Asclepias syriaca*), 847
near curcurbits
mosaic virus and, 736

Milletgrass. *See*
   Johnsongrass
Millipedes, 885
   baits for, 943, 959, 964
   centipedes compared to,
      884
   insecticides for, 940–943,
      949
   on vegetables, 693
Mimosa. *See Albizia*
Mimosa webworm
   (*Homadaula anisocentra*),
   481
   insecticides for, 951, 956,
      966
   on *Gleditsia*, 522
Mimosa wilt, 481
Mimulus (Monkey flower)
   as verticillium wilt
      resistant, 995
Mindarus abietinus
   (Balsam twig aphid)
   on *Abies*, 474
Miners
   leaf. *See* Leafminers
   spruce needle (*Taniva
      albolineana*)
      on *Picea*, 555
Minor nutrient deficiency,
   868
   See also specific nutrients
   in citrus, 646
   in *Primula*, 421
   in trees, 465
Minor nutrients, 905
   on fertilizer labels, 905
Mirror plant (*Coprosma
   repens*)
   as saline soil tolerant, 999
Mistletoe
   dwarf (*Arceuthobium*
      species), 863
      on trees, 447
      witch's broom and, 869
   leafy (*Phoradendron*
      species), 864
      on *Quercus*, 579
      on trees, 447
Mites, 886
   ash flower gall (*Aceria
      fraxinivorus*), 517
   Bermudagrass (*Aceria
      neocynodonis*), 307
   insecticides for, 940–942
   bladder gall (*Vasates
      quadripedes*)
      on *Acer*, 478
   blister
      Eriophyes buceras
         on *Bucida*, 488
      pearleaf (*Phytoptus pyri*),
         662
      insecticide for, 942
      on *Cotoneaster*, 504
      on pear, 662
      on *Sorbus*, 600
   citrus bud, 645

citrus red, 645
   insecticides for, 940
citrus rust, 645
   insecticides for, 940
clover (*Bryobia praetiosa*)
   in households, 803
   insecticides for, 940–943,
      949, 955
cyclamen
   (*Steneotarsonemus
      pallidus*)
   on *Cyclamen*, 253
   on *Saintpaulia*, 285
defined, 302
diseases and, 880
fig (*Eriophyes fici*)
   on fig, 650
fuchsia (*Aculops fuchsiae*),
   519
gall
   ash flower (*Aceria
      fraxinivorus*), 517
   Eriophyes species
      on *Celtis*, 498
      galls from, 869
   hemlock rust (*Nalepella
      tsugifoliae*)
      on *Tsuga*, 606
   insecticides for, 941, 946
northern fowl
   on poultry
      insecticides for, 963
oak (*Oligonychus bicolor*),
   575
Oligonychus species
   on *Pinus*, 558
   on citrus, 645
      insecticides for, 940
   on *Coleus*, outdoors, 382
   on fruit and nut trees, 623
   on peach; nectarine, 658
   on pear, 661
   on *Picea*, 556
   on *Pinus*, 558
   on plum, 669
   on poultry
      insecticides for, 963
   on *Tagetes*, 425
   on trees, 441, 448, 450
      leaf spots and, 450
   on vegetables, 686
pear rust (*Epitrimerus pyri*)
   on fruit and nut trees, 623
   on pear, 661
pearleaf blister (*Phytoptus
   pyri*)
   insecticide for, 942
   on *Cotoneaster*, 504
   on pear, 662
   on *Sorbus*, 600
plum rust (*Aculus fockeui*)
   on fruit and nut trees, 623
   on plum, 669
privet (*Brevipalpus
   obovatus*), 538
privet rust (*Aculus ligustri*),
   538
purple
   on citrus, 645
red spider

insecticide for, 955
russet
   insecticide for, 944
   on tomato
      insecticide for, 944
rust
   hemlock (*Nalepella
      tsugifoliae*), 606
   insecticides for, 958
   pear (*Epitrimerus pyri*)
      on fruit and nut trees, 623
   plum (*Aculus fockeui*)
      on fruit and nut trees, 623
   southern red (*Oligonychus
      ilicis*)
      insecticide for, 965
      on *Ilex*, 528
   spider. *See* Spider mites
   spindle gall (*Vasates
      quadripedes*)
      on *Acer*, 478
   spruce
      insecticide for, 951, 955
   spruce spider (*Oligonychus
      ununguis*)
      on *Abies*, 475
   Texas citrus
      insecticide for, 940
   two-spotted spider. *See*
      Spider mites
Mock orange. *See*
   *Philadelphus;
   Pittosporum*
Mock strawberry. *See*
   Duchesnea
Modesto ash. *See Fraxinus
   velutina* var. *glabra*
   ('Modesto')
Moisture deficiency. *See*
   Drought injury
   in lawns
      dollar spot and, 298
      fusarium blight and, 298
      rust and, 308
Moisture excess
   in lawns
      diseases encouraged by
         pythium blight, 300
Molds
   on lawns
      powdery mildew. 308
      slime molds, 308
Mold
   gray. *See* Gray mold
   sooty. *See* Sooty mold
   white. *See* White mold
Mole Cricket Bait. *See*
   ORTHO Mole Cricket
   Bait
Mole crickets (*Scapteriscus*
   species)
   bait for, 955
   insecticide for, 942
   on lawns, 303
Moles
   See also Animal pests
   on lawns, 309
   on vegetables, 694

Mollugo verticillata
   (Carpetweed), 851
Molybdenum
   as minor nutrient, 905
Monarthropalpus buxi
   (Boxwood leafminer), 489
Monellia species (Yellow
   aphid)
   on pecan, 666
Moneywort. *See* Creeping
   charlie
Monilinia species
   M. fructicola
      on apricot, 5086, 632
      on brambles, 710
      on cherry, 640
      on peach; nectarine, 657
      on plum, 669
   M. laxa
      on apricot, 632
      on cherry, 640
      on peach; nectarine, 657
      on plum, 669
   M. vaccinii-corymbosi
      on blueberries, 708
Monilochaetes infuscans
   on sweet potatoes, 782
Monkey puzzle tree. *See*
   Araucaria
Monocots
   as verticillium wilt
      resistant, 995
Monstera (Mexican
   breadfruit; Split-leaf
   philodendron)
   culture, 274
   insufficient light for, 274
   mealybugs on, 274
   salt damage to, 274, 990
   sunburn on
   watering and, 274
Monuron
   for oxalis
      in *Dichondra*, 333
Morning glory (*Ipomoea*
   species), 849
   herbicides for, 971, 978
   wild (*Convolvulus
      arvensis*), 849
   herbicides for, 974
   in lawns, 320
   in unplanted areas
      herbicides for, 977
   sweet potato weevils and,
      782
Morocco millet. *See*
   Johnsongrass
Morus (Mulberry)
   as paving tolerant, 469
   black sooty mold on
      scales, 546
   branches on
      black sooty mold on
         scales, 546
      crusty or scaly bumps on
         scales, 546
   dying back

Neodiprion species
(Sawflies)
on *Pinus*, 561
Neolecanium
cornuparvum (Magnolia scale), 542
Nephthytis
insecticide for, 969
Nerium (Oleander)
as toxic plant, 549
bees attracted by, 996
branches on
abnormal clusters of new shoots on
witch's broom, 549
brownish or black crusty bumps on
black scales, 548
dying
false oleander scales, 548
tiny soft-bodied insects on
oleander aphids, 547
wartlike spongy growths on
bacterial gall, 549
buds on
tiny soft-bodied insects on
oleander aphids, 547
culture, 549
diseases on
bacterial blight, 1000
bacterial gall, 549
sooty mold, 547
verticillium wilt, 995
witch's broom, 549
fertilizing, 549
insects on
black scales, 548
false oleander scales, 548
mealybugs
bacterial gall and, 549
sooty mold and, 547
oleander aphids, 547
sooty mold and, 547
oleander caterpillars, 548
scales
bacterial gall and, 549
black, 548
false oleander, 548
sooty mold and, 547
whiteflies
sooty mold and, 547
leaves on
black sooty mold on
black scales, 548
sooty mold, 547
brownish or black crusty bumps on
black scales, 548
brown
black scales, 548
chewed
oleander caterpillars, 548
distorted
bacterial gall, 549
oleander aphids, 547
dropping
black scales, 548
false oleander scales, 548

eaten
oleander caterpillars, 548
honeydew on
black scales, 548
false oleander scales, 548
sooty mold on, 547
ooze dripping from veins on
bacterial gall, 549
orange caterpillars with short black hairs on
oleander caterpillars, 548
shiny, sticky substance on
black scales, 548
false oleander scales, 548
slow-growing
oleander aphids, 547
swellings on
bacterial gall, 549
tiny soft-bodied insects on
oleander aphids, 547
white to light brown bumps on
false oleander scales, 548
yellow to greenish yellow spots on
false oleander scales, 548
yellowing
bacterial gall, 549
false oleander scales, 548
oleander aphids, 547
sooty mold, 547
planting locations for, 549
saline soils and, 999
shoots on
abnormal clusters of witch's broom, 549
brown or dying clusters of witch's broom, 549
longitudinal swellings on
bacterial gall, 549
stems on
white to light brown bumps on
false oleander scales, 548
yellow to greenish yellow spots on
false oleander scales, 548
twigs on
black sooty mold on
sooty mold, 547
brownish or black crusty bumps on
black scales, 548
dying back
black scales, 548
watering, 549
Nettle
bee. *See* Henbit
bull. *See* Horsenettle
Carolina. *See* Horsenettle
dead. *See* Henbit
red dead
herbicides for, 974
stinging (*Urtica dioica*), 848
herbicides for, 966
Neutroleum alpha
for skunk odors, 807, 895

New house borers
(*Arhopalus productus*), 810
New Zealand spinach
as aster yellows susceptible, 994
as bolt-resistant spinach substitute, 774
as verticillium wilt susceptible, 1009
Nicotiana (Flowering tobacco)
bees attracted by, 996
culture, 411
cutworms on, 411
powdery mildew on, 995
Nierembergia (Cupflower)
as verticillium wilt resistant, 995
Nightshades (*Solanum* species)
bitter (*S. dulcamara*), 850
black (*S. nigrum*), 850
hairy (*S. sarachoides*), 850
Nimbleweed. *See* Nimblewill
Nimblewill (*Muhlenbergia schreberi*), 827
herbicides for, 974, 976
Nitrate fertilizers, 904
Nitrogen (N), 904
ground bark or sawdust and, 918
on fertilizer label, 905
role of, 904
for groundcovers, 326
Nitrogen deficiency, 867
acid soils and, 902
dollar spot and
in lawns, 298
in citrus, indoors, 246
in citrus, outdoors, 646
in fruit and nut trees, 622
in lawns, 306
dollar spot and, 298
rust and, 308
in *Plectranthus*, 284
in vegetables, 685
weeds and
red sorrel, 845
Nitrogen dioxide injury.
See Air pollution damage
Nitrogen excess
in celery
black heart and, 723
in lawns, 306
brown patch and, 298
fusarium blight and, 298
helminthosporium leaf spot and, 305
in trees
failure to bloom and, 440
No-see-ums (Biting midges)
near households, 814
Nocturnal insects
on flowers

beetles, 355
on trees, 449
on vegetables, 689
pillbugs, 885
sowbugs, 885
Nodding spurge
herbicides for, 973
Node, defined, 302
Nonesuch. *See* Black medic
Norfolk Island pine. *See* *Araucaria*
Norse fire plant. *See* *Columnea*
Northern fowl mites
on poultry
insecticides for, 963
Northstar cherry. *See* Cherry
Nugget grass
as mildew resistant, 308
Nut trees. *See* Fruit and nut trees
Nutgrass. *See* Nutsedge
Nutrient deficiencies
in acid-loving plants
correcting, 936
Nutsedge (*Cyperus* species), 831
herbicides for, 972–974, 976
in lawns, 314
purple (*C. rotundus*), 831
yellow (*C. esculentus*), 831
Nymph, defined, 302
Nyssa (Black gum; Sourgum; Tupelo)
as *Botryosphaeria ribis* susceptible, 1002
as crown gall resistant, 998
as disease and insect resistant, 998
cottony maple leaf scales on, 549
gypsy moths on, 1000

O

Oak anthracnose, 575
Oak lacebug (*Corythucha arcuata*), 576
Oak leaf blister, 576
Oak leafminers, 575
Oak mite (*Oligonychus bicolor*), 575
Oak moth (*Phryganidia californica*), 578
insecticide for, 968
Oak root fungus, 858
See also Armillaria root rot; Mushroom root rot;

on *Acer*, 477
on *Chrysanthemum*,
  outdoors, 380
on flowers, 381
on *Gladiolus*, 395
on grapes, 744
on peppers, 765
on potato, 771
on *Rhododendron*, 587
on strawberries, 778
spruce
  on *Picea*, 555
woolly apple, 628
  on apple, 628
for apple
  fruit tree leafrollers on,
    629
  woolly apple aphids on,
    628
for avocado, indoors,
  greenhouse whiteflies on,
    236
for Bermudagrass
  Bermudagrass mites on,
    307
for billbugs
  on lawns, 302
for *Buxus*
  boxwood leafminers on,
    489
  spider mites on, 490
for cabbage family
  cabbage worms on, 715
for *Capsicum*
  greenhouse whiteflies on,
    243
for *Chrysanthemum*,
  indoors
  greenhouse whiteflies on,
    244
  mealybugs on, 244
for *Chrysanthemum*,
  outdoors
  aphids on, 380
  chrysanthemum
    leafminers on, 381
for *Cineraria*
  chrysanthemum
    leafminers on, 381
for *Clerodendron*
  greenhouse whiteflies on,
    247
for *Coleus*, indoors
  greenhouse whiteflies on,
    250
for cottony scales
  on *Acer*, 478
  on fruit and nut trees, 878
for cucurbits
  cucumber beetles on, 734,
    735
for cutworms, 875
  on *Dichondra*, 331
  on flowers, 875
for *Dichondra*
  cutworms on, 331
  flea beetles on, 331
for *Euphorbia*
  greenhouse whiteflies on,
    261

for fleas
  in yards, 806
for flowers
  ants on, 356
  aphids on, 381
  cutworms on, 875
for fruit and nut trees
  cottony scales on, 878
  mites on, 886
  spider mites on, 886
for fruit tree leafrollers
  on apple, 629
for fungus gnats
  on houseplants, 230
for giant bark aphids
  on *Salix*, 596
for *Gladiolus*
  aphids on, 395
  gladiolus thrips on, 395
for gnats
  fungus
    on houseplants, 230
for grapes
  aphids on, 744
for green spruce aphids
  on *Picea*, 555
for greenhouse whiteflies
  on avocado, indoors, 236
  on *Capsicum*, 243
  on *Chrysanthemum*,
    indoors, 244
  on *Clerodendron*, 247
  on *Coleus*, indoors, 250
  on *Euphorbia*, 261
  on houseplants, 229
  on *Pelargonium*, indoors,
    280
for holly leafminers, 527
for houseplants
  fungus gnats on, 230
  greenhouse whiteflies on,
    229
  scales on, 228
for *Ilex*
  holly leafminers on, 527
for lawns, 310
  Bermudagrass mites on,
    307
  billbugs on, 302
for leafhoppers, 861, 880
  on trees, 462, 861
  on vegetables, 861
  on weeds, 861
for leafminers, 874
  chrysanthemum
    on *Chrysantheum*,
      outdoors, 381
    on *Cineraria*, 381
  on *Buxus*, 489
  on ornamentals, 874
  on trees, 449
  on vegetables, 874
for leafrollers
  on strawberries, 777
for mealybugs
  on *Acer*, 478
  on *Aglaonema*, 231
  on *Plectranthus*, 284
for millipedes, 885
for mites

on fruit and nut trees, 886
on vegetables, 886
for *Pelargonium*, indoors
  greenhouse whiteflies on,
    280
for peppers
  aphids on, 765
for *Picea*
  spruce aphids and green
    spruce aphids on, 555
for pine needle scales
  on *Picea*, 555
for *Plectranthus*
  mealybugs on, 284
for potato
  aphids on, 771
for *Rhododendron*
  rhododendron aphids on,
    587
  rhododendron whiteflies
    on, 587
  spider mites on, 582
for *Salix*
  giant bark aphids on, 596
for scales
  on houseplants, 228
  pine needle
    on *Picea*, 555
for spider mites
  on *Buxus*, 490
  on fruit and nut trees, 886
  on *Rhododendron*, 582
  on strawberries, 777
  on vegetables, 886
for spruce aphids and
  green spruce aphids
  on *Picea*, 555
for strawberries
  aphids on, 778
  spider mites on, 777
  strawberry leafrollers on,
    777
for thrips
  on *Gladiolus*, 395
for trees
  leafhoppers on, 462, 861
  leafminers on, 449
for vegetables
  leafhoppers on, 861
  leafminers on, 874
  mites on, 886
  spider mites on, 886
for weeds
  leafhoppers on, 861
for whiteflies
  greenhouse; *see* for
    greenhouse whiteflies
  rhododendron, 587
for woolly apple aphids
  on apple, 628
**ORTHO Diazinon Soil &
  Foliage Dust**, 941
for aphids
  on beans, 699
  on cabbage family, 716
for cabbage family
  aphids on, 716
  cabbage maggots on, 716
  cutworms on, 715
  diamondback moth larvae

on, 715
for cabbage loopers
  on lettuce, 750
for cabbage maggots
  on cabbage family, 716
for cabbage root maggots
  on radish, 772
for corn
  cutworms on, 729
  wireworms on, 730
for cutworms, 875
  on cabbage family, 715
  on corn, 729
  on lawns, 875
  on lettuce, 750
  on peppers, 765
  on *Petunia*, 418
  on tomato, 794
  on vegetables, 875
for cyclamen mites
  on strawberries, 778
for diamondback moth
  larvae
  on cabbage family, 715
for garden centipedes
  on strawberries, 781
  on vegetables, 693
for garden symphylans
  on strawberries, 781
  on vegetables, 693
for lawns, 875
  cutworms on, 875
for lettuce
  cabbage loopers on, 750
  cutworms on, 750
for mites
  on strawberries, 778
for onion family
  onion maggots on, 755
  onion thrips on, 757
for peppers
  cutworms on, 765
for *Petunia*
  cutworms on, 418
for potato
  wireworms on, 767
for radish
  root maggots on, 772
  seed corn root maggots on,
    772
for strawberries
  cyclamen mites on, 778
  garden centipedes on, 781
  garden symphylans on,
    781
for thrips
  on onion family, 757
for tomato
  cutworms on, 794
for vegetables
  cutworms on, 875
  garden centipedes on, 693
  garden symphylans on,
    693
for wireworms
  on corn, 730
  on potato, 767
**ORTHO Diazinon Soil &
  Turf Insect Control**,
  942

for Chinch Bug Killer, 939
for Kleenup Systemic Weed
& Grass Killer, 974
for Liquid Lawn Disease
Control, 954
for Orthene Systemic Insect
Control, 956
for Orthenex Insect &
Disease Control, 956
for Ortho-Klor 44
Chlordane Spray, 957
for Vegetable Disease
Control, 968
ORTHO Lawn Green, 930
**ORTHO Lawn Insect
Spray, 952**
for chinch bugs, 301
for *Dichondra*
cutworms on, 331
flea beetles on, 331
for grubs, 299
on lawns, 309
for lawns, 310
grubs in, 309
mole control for, 309
for mosquitoes
near households, 815
for sod webworms, 299
ORTHO Lawn Sprayer, 960
for Azalea & Camelea
Food, 923
for Chinch Bug Killer, 939
for Evergreen & Azalea
Food, 926
for Fire Ant Control, 943
for Greenol Liquid Iron,
929
for Lawn Green, 930
for Lawn Insect Spray, 952
for liquid fertilizers, 899
for Orchid Food, 931
for Ortho-Klor 44
Chlordane Spray, 957
for Orthorix Spray, 958
for Sevin Garden Spray,
964
for Sob Webworm Control,
965
**ORTHO Leaf Polish
(Aerosol), 952**
**ORTHO Leaf Polish
(Pump), 953**
ORTHO leaf polishes
Leaf Polish (Aerosol), 952
Leaf Polish (Pump), 953
Volck Oil Spray, 968
**ORTHO Lindane Borer &
Leaf Miner Spray, 953**
for *Acer*
borers on, 477
for apple
flatheaded borers on, 631
for beetles
bark
on trees, 468
ips engraver
on *Pinus*, 558
for birch leafminers, 486

for borers, 873
dogwood, 502
flatheaded
on apple, 631
lilac, 603
locust
on *Robinia*, 587
mottled willow, 597
on *Acer*, 477
on *Fraxinus*, 517
on *Rhododendron*, 584
peachtree
on peach; nectarine, 659
poplar and willow
on *Populus*, 569
on *Salix*, 597
for *Cornus*
dogwood borers on, 502
for flatheaded borers
on apple, 631
for *Fraxinus*
borers on, 517
for ips engraver beetles
on *Pinus*, 558
for juniper twig girdlers,
531
for juniper twig girdler
on *Juniperus*, 531
for leafminers
birch, 486
locust
on *Robinia*, 588
for lilac borers, 603
for locust borers
on *Robinia*, 587
for locust leafminers
on *Robinia*, 588
for mottled willow borers
on *Salix*, 597
for peach; nectarine
peachtree borers *on*, 659
for *Pinus*
ips engraver beetles on,
558
white pine weevils on, 562
for *Populus*
poplar and willow borers
on, 569
for rhododendron borers,
584
for *Robinia*
locust borers on, 587
locust leafminers on, 588
for *Salix*
mottled willow borers on,
597
poplar and willow borers
on, 597
for *Syringa*
lilac borers on, 603
for trees
bark beetles on, 468
for white pine weevils
on *Pinus*, 562
**ORTHO Liquid African
Violet Food, 931**
for *Saintpaulia*, 284
**ORTHO Liquid Fence &
Grass Edger, 975**

for paved areas and
walkways, 825
**ORTHO Liquid Lawn
Disease Control, 954**
for brown patch, 298
for dollar spot, 298
for helminthosporium leaf
spot, 305
for rust, 308
ORTHO Liquid Sevin, 954
for *Ageratum*
corn earworms on, 361
tobacco budworms on, 361
for *Allium*
thrips on, 363
for *Alnus*
aphids on, 481
woolly aphids on, 481
for *Anemone*
aphids on, 364
for aphids
on *Alnus*, 481
on *Anemone*, 364
on *Aquilegia*, 366
on *Astilbe*, 367
on *Cosmos*, 385
on *Crocus*, 385
on *Fagus*, 513
on *Fatshedera*, 514
on flowers, 381
on *Fuchsia*, 519
on *Gardenia*, outdoors,
521
on *Gerbera*, 394
on groundcovers, 329
on *Platanus*, 566
woolly
on *Alnus*, 481
on *Crataegus*, 506
woolly apple
on *Crataegus*, 506
for apples
apple maggots on, 627
for *Aquilegia*
aphids on, 366
for *Astilbe*
aphids on, 367
for bagworms
on *Juniperus*, 443
for *Bambusa*
scales on, 484
for *Bauhinia*
snow scales on, 485
for beetles
on *Rosa*, 593
on trees, 442
for borers
European corn
on peppers, 764
peachtree
on peach; nectarine, 659
for *Canna*
corn earworms on, 374
for caterpillars, 874
leaf-feeding
on trees, 443
oleander, 548
on *Rosa*, 592
tent

on trees, 443
for cherry
oriental fruit moths on, 638
for *Chrysanthemum*,
outdoors
thrips on, 378
for corn borers
European
on peppers, 764
for corn earworms
on *Ageratum*, 361
on *Canna*, 374
for *Cosmos*
aphids on, 385
for cottony maple leaf
scales
on *Nyssa*, 549
for *Crataegus*
scales on, 506
woolly aphids on, 506
woolly apple aphids on,
506
for *Crocus*
aphids on, 385
for cucurbits
pickleworms on, 733
for European corn borers
on peppers, 764
for *Fagus*
aphids on, 513
for fall webworms
on trees, 443
for *Fatshedera*
aphids on, 514
for flowers
aphids on, 381
for *Forsythia*
fourlined plant bugs on,
516
for fruit and nut trees
leafrollers on, 875
leaftiers on, 875
for fruit tree leafrollers
on pear, 663
for fruitworms
tomato, 788
for *Fuchsia*
aphids on, 519
for *Gardenia*, outdoors
aphids on, 521
for *Gerbera*
aphids on, 394
for giant bark aphids
on *Platanus*, 566
for groundcovers
aphids on, 329
for gypsy moths
on trees, 442, 876
for Japanese beetles, 873
on trees, 442
for *Juniperus*
bagworms on, 443
juniper scales on, 534
for leaf-feeding caterpillars
on trees, 443
for leafminers
on trees, 449
for leafrollers, 875
fruit tree
on pear, 663

on trees, 449
for leaftiers, 875
for *Ligustrum*
scales on, 538
for *Liriodendron*
tuliptree scales on, 540
for *Magnolia*
magnolia scales on, 542
for *Malus*
scales on, 545
for *Nerium*
oleander caterpillars on, 548
for *Nyssa*
cottony maple leaf scales on, 549
for oriental fruit moths
on cherry, 638
for peach; nectarine
peachtree borers on, 659
for pear
fruit tree leafrollers on, 663
for peppers
European corn borers on, 764
for pickleworms
on cucurbits, 733
for *Platanus*
giant bark aphids on, 566
for *Podocarpus*
scales on, 566
for *Populus*
scales on, 568
for *Rosa*
beetles on, 593
caterpillars on, 592
roseslugs on, 593
for scales
cottony maple leaf
on *Nyssa*, 549
magnolia
on *Magnolia*, 542
on *Bambusa*, 484
on *Crataegus*, 506
on *Ligustrum*, 538
on *Malus*, 545
on *Podocarpus*, 566
on *Populus*, 568
on *Tsuga*, 606
on *Ulmus*, 609
snow
on *Bauhinia*, 485
tuliptree, 540
for snow scales
on *Bauhinia*, 485
for tent caterpillars
on trees, 443
for thrips, 883
on *Allium*, 363
on *Chrysanthemum*,
outdoors, 378
on ornamentals, 883
for tobacco budworms
on *Ageratum*, 361
for tomato
tomato fruitworms on, 788
for trees
fall webworms on, 443
gypsy moths on, 442, 876

Japanese beetles on, 442
leaf-feeding caterpillars
on, 443
leafminers on, 449
leafrollers on, 449
tent caterpillars on, 443
for *Tsuga*
scales on, 606
for tuliptree scales, 540
for *Ulmus*
scales on, 609
for woolly aphids
on *Alnus*, 481
on *Crataegus*, 506
for woolly apple aphids
on *Crataegus*, 506
**ORTHO Malathion 50
Insect Spray, 955**
for *Abies*
balsam twig aphids on, 474
balsam woolly aphids on, 475
spruce spider mites on, 475
for *Acer*
boxelder bugs on, 477
for aphids, 877
green peach
on lettuce, 749
on apple, 628
on *Bambusa*, 484
on beans, 699, 703
on cabbage family, 716
on *Camellia*, 494
on *Chrysanthemum*,
outdoors, 380
on *citrus*, outdoors, 644
on cypress family, 509
on food crops, 877
on grapes, 744
on houseplants, 228
on *Juniperus*, 534
on lettuce, 749, 752
on *Pinus*, 560
on potato, 767, 771
on strawberries, 778
on tomato, 790, 794
on trees, 444, 462
pea
on peas, 760
woolly, 877
on fruit and nut trees, 619
on *Pinus*, 559
for apple
aphids on, 628
plum curculios on, 627
San Jose scales on, 629
for apricot
plum curculios on, 631
San Jose scales on, 635
for *Araucaria*
spider mites on, 482
for aster leafhoppers
on lettuce, 750
for avocado, indoors,
greenhouse whiteflies on, 236
for balsam twig aphids
on *Abies*, 474

for balsam woolly aphids
on *Abies*, 475
for *Bambusa*
bamboo aphids on, 484
cottony scales and
mealybugs on, 484
for beans
aphids on, 699, 703
potato leafhoppers on, 702
spider mites on, 700
for boxelder bugs
on *Acer*, 477
for bugs
leaf, 876
lygus, 876
plant, 876
for *Buxus*
spider mites on, 490
for cabbage family
aphids on, 716
for *Camellia*
aphids on, 494
cottony scales and
mealybugs on, 494
for *Capsicum*
greenhouse whiteflies on, 243
for caterpillars, 874
orangedog
on citrus, outdoors, 645
for cherry
plum curculios on, 638
San Jose scales on, 640
for *Chrysanthemum*,
indoors
greenhouse whiteflies on, 244
for *Chrysanthemum*,
outdoors
aphids on, 380
spider mites on, 379
thrips on, 378
two-spotted spider mites
on, 379
for citrus
aphids on, 644
citrus thrips on, 643
citrus whiteflies on, 643
orangedog caterpillars on, 645
scales on, 247, 644
for *Clerodendron*
greenhouse whiteflies on, 247
for *Coleus*, indoors
greenhouse whiteflies on, 250
for cottony scales
on *Bambusa* 484
on *Camellia*, 494
on fruit and nut trees, 619
for curculios
plum
on apple, 627
on apricot, 631
on cherry, 638
on peach; nectarine, 654
on plum, 668
for cypress family
aphids on, 509

for *Euphorbia*
greenhouse whiteflies on, 261
for fleahoppers
garden, 876
for fleas
in yards, 806
for flower thrips, 883
on fruit and nut trees, 883
on vegetables, 883
for *Forsythia*
fourlined plant bugs, 516
for fruit and nut trees
cottony scales, mealybugs,
and woolly aphids on, 619
flower thrips on, 883
leafrollers on, 875
leaftiers on, 875
mealybugs on, 619
mites on, 886
soft scales on, 879
spider mites on, 886
for garden fleahoppers, 876
for *Gardenia*, indoors
scales on, 266
for grapes
aphids on, 744
grape leafhoppers on, 745
leafrollers on, 743
spider mites on, 745
for green peach aphids
on lettuce, 749
for greenhouse whiteflies, 879
see also for whiteflies
Clerodendron, 247
on avocado, indoors, 236
on *Capsicum*, 243
on *Chrysanthemum*,
indoors, 244
on *Coleus*, indoors, 250
on *Euphorbia*, 261
on houseplants, 229
on *Pelargonium*, indoors, 280
on tomato, 790
for houseplants
aphids on, 228
greenhouse whiteflies on, 229
for Japanese beetles, 873
on trees, 442
for *Juniperus*
aphids on, 534
for leaf bugs, 876
for leafhoppers, 880
on lettuce, 750, 752
potato
on beans, 702
on potato, 769
for leafrollers, 875
omnivorous
on grapes, 743
redbanded
on grapes, 743
for leaftiers, 875
for lettuce
aphids on, 749, 752
green peach aphids on,

for *Celtis*
  hackberry leaf gall
    psyllids on, 499
  psyllids on, 499
for *Codiaeum*
  mealybugs on, 248
for cottony scales, 878
  on *Camellia*, 494
  on trees, 444, 878
for *Crataegus*
  aphids on, 506
for Cuban laurel thrips
  on *Ficus*, 515
for cypress family
  scales on, 510
for *Dieffenbachia*
  mealybugs on, 255
for *Dizygotheca*
  mealybugs on, 257
for elm leaf beetles, 609
for euonymus scales
  Euonymus, 512
  on *Celastrus*, 498
for fall webworms
  on fruit and nut trees, 620
  on trees, 443
for *Ficus*
  Cuban laurel thrips on,
    515
for flower thrips, 883
  on grasses, 883
  on ornamentals, 883
  on *Rosa*, 588
for flowers
  thrips on, 347, 883
for fruit and nut trees
  fall webworms on, 620
  tent caterpillars on, 620
for *Gardenia*, indoors
  scales on, 266
for *Gardenia*, outdoors
  greenhouse whiteflies on,
    521
for giant bark aphids
  on *Quercus*, 578
for *Gleditsia*
  mimosa webworm on, 522
for grasses
  flower thrips on, 883
for greenbugs
  on lawns, 304
for greenhouse whiteflies,
  879
  on *Ageratum*, 362
  on *Gardenia*, outdoors,
    521
  on *Lantana*, 405
for grubs
  on trees, 472
for gypsy moths
  on trees, 442, 876
for hackberry leaf gall
  psyllids, 499
for hawthorn lacebugs
  on *Pyracantha*, 572
for *Hedera*, indoors
  mealybugs on, 270
for honeylocust spider
  mites, 523
for *Ilex*

scales on, 529
for *Juniperus*
  bagworms on, 443
for lacebugs, 877
  hawthorn
    on *Pyracantha*, 572
  on ornamentals, 877
  on *Rhododendron*, 582
  on trees, 463
  sycamore
    on *Platanus*, 564
for *Lantana*
  greenhouse whiteflies on,
    405
for lawns
  greenbugs on, 304
for leaf beetles
  elm, 609
  on *Salix*, 595
for leaf-feeding
  caterpillars, 595
  on *Salix*, 595
  on trees, 443
for leafhoppers
  on trees, 462
for leafminers, 874
  birch, 486
  oak, 575
  on ornamentals, 874
  on trees, 449
for leafrollers, 875
  on *Rosa*, 591
  on trees, 449
for leaftiers, 875
for *Magnolia*
  magnolia scales on, 542
for mealybugs
  on *Brassaia*, 239
  on *Camellia*, 494
  on *Codiaeum*, 248
  on *Dieffenbachia*, 255
  on *Dizygotheca*, 257
  on *Hedera*, indoors, 270
  on *Philodendron*, 283
  on *Syngonium*, 288
  on trees, 444
for midges
  rose, 590
for mimosa webworms, 481
  on *Gleditsia*, 522
for miners
  spruce needle
    on *Picea*, 555
for *Morus*
  scales on, 546
for *Nerium*
  black scales on, 548
for oak lacebugs, 576
for oak leafminers, 575
for *Philadelphus*
  aphids on, 552
for *Philodendron*
  mealybugs on, 283
for *Picea*
  spruce needle miners on,
    555
for *Pinus*
  pine needle scales on, 560
  pine tip or shoot moths on,
    562

sawflies on, 561
for pit scales
  on *Quercus*, 578
for *Pittosporum*
  aphids on, 563
for *Platanus*
  sycamore lacebugs on,
    564
for *Podocarpus*
  scales on, 566
for psyllids
  hackberry leaf gall, 499
  on trees, 880
for *Pyracantha*
  aphids on, 573
  hawthorn lacebugs on,
    572
  scales on, 573
for *Quercus*
  giant bark aphids on, 578
  oak lacebugs on, 576
  oak leafminers on, 575
  pit scales on, 578
for *Rhododendron*
  lacebugs on, 582
  root weevils on, 586
for root weevils
  on *Rhododendron*, 586
  on trees, 472, 874
for *Rosa*
  caterpillars on, 592
  flower thrips on, 588
  leafrollers on, 591
  rose aphids on, 591
  rose midges on, 590
  scales on, 593
for *Salix*
  leaf beetles on, 595
  leaf-feeding caterpillars
    on, 595
  scales on, 596
for sawflies
  on *Pinus*, 561
for scales
  armored, 879
  black
    on *Nerium*, 548
  euonymus, 512
  magnolia, 542
  on *Begonia*, indoors, 238
  on *Camellia*, 494
  on cypress family, 510
  on *Gardenia*, indoors, 266
  on *Ilex*, 529
  on *Morus*, 546
  on *Podocarpus*, 566
  on *Pyracantha*, 573
  on *Rosa*, 593
  on *Salix*, 596
  on *Syringa*, 603
  on trees, 444
  on *Tsuga*, 606
  on *Ulmus*, 609
  pine needle
    on *Pinus*, 560
  pit
    on *Quercus*, 578
  soft
    on trees, 879
  wax, 878

for shoot moths
  on *Pinus*, 562
for soft scales
  on trees, 879
for *Spiraea*
  spirea aphids on, 601
for sycamore lacebugs
  on *Platanus*, 564
for *Syngonium*
  mealybugs on, 288
for *Syringa*
  scales on, 603
for *Taxus*
  taxus weevils on, 604
for tent caterpillars
  on fruit and nut trees, 620
  on trees, 443
for thrips
  flower, 883
    on grasses, 883
    on ornamentals, 883
    on *Rosa*, 588
    on flowers, 347, 883
  on trees, 463
for tip moths
  pine, 562
for trees
  aphids on, 444, 462
    woolly, 444
  cottony scales on, 444,
    878
  fall webworms on, 443
  flower thrips on, 883
  grubs on, 472
  gypsy moths on, 442, 876
  lacebugs on, 463
  leaf-feeding caterpillars
    on, 443
  leafhoppers on, 462
  leafminers on, 449
  leafrollers on, 444
  mealybugs on, 444
  psyllids on, 880
  root weevils on, 472, 874
  scales on, 444
  soft scales on, 879
  tent caterpillars on, 443
  thrips on, 463
  woolly aphids on, 444
for *Tsuga*
  scales on, 606
for *Tulipa*
  aphids on, 430
for *Ulmus*
  elm leaf beetles on, 609
  scales on, 609
for *Viburnum*
  aphids on, 610
for wax scales, 878
for webworms
  fall
    on fruit and nut trees, 620
    on trees, 443
  mimosa, 481
for weevils
  black vine
    on *Taxus*, 604
  root
    on trees, 472, 874
  taxus, 604

for *Saintpaulia*
mealybugs on, 286
for scales
on *Begonia*, indoors, 238
on ferns, indoors, 263
on *Ficus*, 265
on *Hedera*, indoors, 269
on palms, indoors, 278
for spider mites
on *Brassaia*, 239
on *Dieffenbachia*, 256
on *Dracaena*, 258
on *Hedera*, indoors, 269
on *Hoya*, 271
on *Maranta*, 273
on palms, indoors, 277
on *Philodendron*, 283
on *Tolmiea*, 256
for *Syngonium*, 288
mealybugs on, 288
for *Tolmiea*
spider mites on, 256
from scales
on *Asparagus*, 235
Ortho-Gro Liquid Plant
Food. See ORTHO
Ortho-Gro Liquid
Plant Food
Orthocide Garden
Fungicide. See ORTHO
Orthocide Garden
Fungicide
Orthorix Spray. See
ORTHO Orthorix
Spray
Oryzaephilus species. See
Flour beetles
Oscillatoria species. See
Algae
Ostrinia nubilalis. See
European corn borer
Ostrya (Hop hornbeam)
as disease and insect
resistant, 998
Otiorhynchus species
O. ovatus (Strawberry root
weevil), 780
O. rugosostriatus (Rough
strawberry root weevil),
780
O. sulcatus (Black vine
weevil; Taxus weevil)
on strawberries, 780
on *Taxus*, 604
Otiorhynchus sulcatus.
See Black vine weevil
Outdoor Insect Fogger. See
ORTHO Outdoor
Insect Fogger
Overwatering. See
Watering, excessive
Ovulinia azaleae, 581
on *Rhododendron*, 581
Oxalis (*Oxalis corniculata*;
O. europa; *Oxalis
stricta*), 840
in *Dichondra*, 333

herbicides for, 971, 974,
976–978
in lawns, 315
Oxydendrum (Sourwood)
as crown gall resistant, 998
Oxytetracycline
for palm family, outdoors
lethal yellowing on, 550
Oystershell scale
(*Lepidosaphes ulmi*)
on *Fraxinus*, 518
on *Malus*, 545
on walnut, 675
Ozone
damage from. See Air
pollution damage
defined, 302

P

Pachypsylla species
(Hackberry leaf gall
psyllids), 499
Pachysandra (Japanese
spurge)
as acid tolerant, 327
as shade tolerant, 305, 318,
325, 326, 991
diseases on
leaf and stem blight, 338
volutella blight, 338
insects on
ants, 338
Japanese beetles, 997
oystershell scales, 338
scales, 338
iron deficiency in, 327
nutrient deficiency in, 326
scorch on, 338
winter injury to, 338
Pacific poison oak (*Rhus
diversiloba*). See Poison
oak
Paeonia (Peony)
culture, 412
diseases on
fusarium wilt
susceptibility to, 994
gray mold, 412
phytophthora blight, 413
failure to bloom in, 412
insecticides for, 948
Pagoda tree, Japanese. See
Sophora japonica
Painted daisy. See
Chrysanthemum
Painted tongue. See
Salpiglossis
Palisade cells, defined, 302
Palm leaf skeletonizer
(*Homaledra sabalella*)
on palms, outdoors, 551

Palms, indoors
See also Palms, outdoors
culture, 277
fertilizing, 277
salt damage and, 277
gliocladium rot on, 278
growing locations for, 277
insects on
insecticides for, 968, 969
mealybugs, 278
scales, 278
spider mites, 277
parlor (*Chamaedorea*)
as salt sensitive, 990
sago. See *Cycas*
salt damage to, 277, 990
soil for, 277
watering, 277
salt damage and, 277
Palms, outdoors
See also Palms, indoors
bird damage to, 999
culture, 551
diseases on
armillaria root rot, 1001
bud rot, 550
cotton root rot, 994
lethal yellowing, 550
varieties susceptible to,
999
verticillium wilt
resistance to, 995
fertilizing, 551, 927
frizzle top on, 551
varieties susceptible to,
551
insects on
leafhoppers
lethal yellowing and, 550
palm leaf skeletonizers,
551, 999
lightning damage to, 551
manganese deficiency in
frizzle top and, 551
planting locations for, 551
lightning and, 551
salt-sensitive varieties of,
990
sapsucker damage to, 999
soil pH for, 1002, 1003
watering, 551
Pampas grass (*Cortaderia
selloana*)
saline soils and, 999
PAN (peroxyacetyl nitrate)
damage from. See Air
pollution damage
defined, 302
Panaphis juglandis
(European dusky-veined
walnut aphid), 674
Panda plant. See
Kalanchoe
Pandanus (Screw pine)
as salt sensitive, 990
Panicgrass. See
Barnyardgrass
Panicum

dichotomiflorum (Fall
panicum), 828
Panicum, Texas
herbicides for, 966
Pansy. See *Viola*
Papaipema nebris
(Common stalk borer)
on corn, 729
Papaver (Poppy)
California poppy. See
Eschscholzia
culture, 413
diseases on
cotton root rot, 994
powdery mildew, 995
verticillium wilt, 413
insects on
Japanese beetles, 997
Paper products, pests in
cigarette beetles, 818
cockroaches, 816
crickets, 801
drugstore beetles, 818
firebrats, 802
silverfish, 802
Paper wasps (*Polistes*
species)
in households, 813
Papilio cresphontes
(Orangedog caterpillar)
on citrus, outdoors, 645
Papilio polyxenes asterius
(Celeryworm;
Parsleyworm), 757
Paradichlorobenzene
crystals
for carpet beetles, 802
for clothes moths, 802
Paraquat
for wild garlic, 831
for wild onion, 831
Parasite, defined, 302
Parasitic plants
dwarf mistletoe
on conifers, 863
leafy mistletoe
on *Quercus*, 579
on trees, 864
Parking areas. See Paved
areas
Parlor palm (*Chamaedorea*)
as salt sensitive, 990
Parlor palm (Kentia palm)
as salt sensitive, 990
insecticide for, 969
Parrotia
P. persica (Persian
parrotia)
as disease and insect
resistant, 998
Parsleyworm (*Papilio
polyxenes asterius*), 757
Parsley
as aster yellows
susceptible, 994
culture, 757

on tomato, 792
P. lateralis
 plants susceptible and
  resistant to, 1000
P. palmivora
 on *Hedera*, outdoors, 336
 on palms, outdoors, 550
P. parasitica
 on *Peperomia*, 281
 on *Saintpaulia*, 286
Phytoptus species
 P. avellanae. See Filbert
  bud mite
 P. pyri. See Pearleaf
  blister mite
Picea (Spruce)
 as crown gall resistant, 998
 as verticillium wilt
  resistant, 995
 bare appearance to
  spruce aphids and green
  spruce aphids, 555
 bird damage to, 999
 branches on
  amber-colored ooze on
   canker and dieback, 556
  black spore-producing
   bodies under bark on
   canker and dieback, 556
  breaking
   Eastern spruce gall
   aphids, 554
  dying
   canker and dieback, 556
   spruce budworms, 553
  galls on
   Cooley spruce gall
   aphids, 554
   Eastern spruce gall
   aphids, 554
  reddish brown ends on
   spruce budworms, 553
  stunted
   Cooley spruce gall
   aphids, 554
   Eastern spruce gall
   aphids, 554
  white patches on
   canker and dieback, 556
 culture, 553
 diseases on
  canker and dieback, 556
  susceptibility to, 1000
 dying
  Douglas fir tussock moths,
   554
  pine needle scales, 555
  spruce budworms, 553
 fertilizing, 553, 924, 926,
  927, 936
 fill injury to, 999
 insects on
  bark beetles
   Douglas fir tussock moths
   and, 554
  Cooley spruce gall aphids,
   554, 571
  Douglas fir tussock moths,
   475, 554

Eastern spruce gall
  aphids, 554
 green spruce aphids, 555
 Japanese beetles, 997
 mites, 556
 pine needle scales, 555
 spruce aphids, 555
 spruce budworms, 474,
  553
 spruce needle miners, 555
 spruce spider mites, 556,
  606
 woolly aphids, 559
 woolly larch aphids, 537
lightning injury to, 999
needles on
 brown
  canker and dieback, 556
  pine needle scales, 555
  spruce aphids and green
   spruce aphids, 555
  spruce needle miners,
   555
  spruce spider mites, 556
 caterpillars on
  Douglas fir tussock
   moths, 554
  spruce budworms, 553
 chewed
  spruce budworms, 553
 dropping
  canker and dieback, 556
  pine needle scales, 555
  spruce aphids and green
   spruce aphids, 555
  spruce spider mites, 556
 drying out
  canker and dieback, 556
 eaten
  Douglas fir tussock
   moths, 554
 flattened white scaly
  bumps on
  pine needle scales, 555
 greenish brown larva
  inside
  spruce needle miners,
   555
 hanging along branches
  canker and dieback, 556
 sawdustlike material
  around webbing on
  spruce needle miners,
   555
 stippled yellow and dirty
  spruce spider mites, 556
 tiny green insects on
  spruce aphids and green
   spruce aphids, 555
 webbing on
  spruce budworms, 553
  spruce needle miners,
   555
  spruce spider mites, 556
 white appearance to
  pine needle scales, 555
P. abies (Norway spruce)
 as smog tolerant, 996
 canker and dieback on,
  556

Eastern spruce gall aphids
  on, 554
P. pungens (Colorado blue
  spruce)
 as smog tolerant, 996
 canker and dieback on,
  556
 planting locations for, 553
 pruning, 553
 sapsucker damage to, 999
 sickly appearance to
  spruce aphids and green
  spruce aphids, 555
 smog tolerant varieties of,
  996
 soil pH for, 1002, 1003
 tan-colored pellets on
  ground around
  Douglas fir tussock moths,
   554
 twigs on
  silken webbing on
   spruce spider mites, 556
 watering, 553
 weak
  Eastern spruce gall
   aphids, 554
Pickleworms (*Diaphania
  nitidalis*)
 insecticides for, 947, 954,
  963, 964, 967
 on cucurbits, 733
Pickpurse. *See* Shepherds
  purse
Picnic areas
 insecticide for, 958
Pieris (Andromeda;
  Lily-of-the-valley shrub)
 andromeda lacebugs on,
  556
 as crown gall resistant, 998
 as shade tolerant, 997
 fungus diseases on
  susceptibility to, 1000
 soil pH for, 1002, 1003
Pieris rapae. See Imported
  cabbageworm
Pigeongrass. *See* Foxtails
Piggyback plant. *See
  Tolmiea*
Pigweed (*Amaranthus*
  species), 847
 herbicides for, 966, 970,
  973
 in lawns (*Amaranthus*
  species)
  herbicides for, 971, 977,
   978
 prostrate (*Amaranthus*
  species)
  herbicides for, 974
 redroot (*Amaranthus*
  species)
  herbicides for, 966, 974
 spiny (*Amaranthus* species)
  herbicides for, 966
Pigweed, white (Common
  lamb's-quarters), 848

Pilea (Aluminum plant)
 insecticide for, 969
Pillbugs, 885
 baits for, 943, 959
 insecticides for, 947
 on vegetables, 692
Pinching plants, 919
Pincushion flower. *See
  Scabiosa*
Pine bark beetles
 insecticide for, 953
Pine needle scale
  (*Chionaspis pinifoliae*)
 on *Picea*, 555
 on *Pinus*, 560
Pine sawflies
 European
  insecticide for, 951
 redheaded
  insecticide for, 951
Pine spittlebug
  (*Aphrophora parellela*),
  561
Pine tip moths (*Rhyacionia*
  species), 562
 insecticides for, 966
Pine webworm (*Tetralopha
  robustella*), 561
Pine. *See Pinus*
 screw (*Pandanus*)
  as salt sensitive, 990
 umbrella (*Sciadopitys
   verticillata*)
  as disease and insect
  resistant, 998
Pineappleweed (*Matricaria
  matricarioides*), 836
 herbicide for, 970
Pineus species. *See* Woolly
  aphids
Pink root
 on onion family, 755
Pink snow mold
 on lawns, 297
Pinks. *See Dianthus*
Pinkweed. *See* Prostrate
  knotweed
Pinus (Pine)
 air pollution damage to,
  559
 bird damage to, 999
 blue stain fungus on
  ips engraver beetles, 558
 branches on
  black sooty mold on
   aphids, 560
   pine and Saratoga
   spittlebugs, 561
  brown nests on ends of
   pine webworms, 561
  brown tips on
   pine tip or shoot moths,
   562
  distorted
   western or eastern gall
   rust, 562

dry tips on
pine tip or shoot moths,
562
dying
air pollution damage, 559
diplodia tip blight, 557
needle cast, 557
pine and Saratoga
spittlebugs, 561
pine tip or shoot moths,
562
root nematodes, 558
spruce spider mites, 558
white pine blister rust,
559
honeydew on
aphids, 560
light brown caterpillars
inside nests on
pine webworms, 561
off-color
western or eastern gall
rust, 562
orange or yellow swellings
on
western or eastern gall
rust, 562
pitch flowing from swollen
areas on
white pine blister rust,
559
red tips on
air pollution damage, 559
rough, elongated, swollen
areas on
white pine blister rust,
559
rough, spherical swellings
on
western or eastern gall
rust, 562
shiny, sticky substance on
aphids, 560
stunted growth on
western or eastern gall
rust, 562
weak
western or eastern gall
rust, 562
witch's brooms on
western or eastern gall
rust, 562
yellow or orange swellings
on
western or eastern gall
rust, 562
white pine blister rust,
559
yellow tips on
pine tip or shoot moths,
562
yellow to brownish spots
on
white pine blister rust,
559
brown new growth on
diplodia tip blight, 557
buds on
remaining dead on tree
diplodia tip blight, 557

bushy appearance to
pine tip or shoot moths,
562
crooked appearance to
pine tip or shoot moths,
562
culture, 557
dense, stunted growth
beyond galls on
western or eastern gall
rust, 562
diseases on
armillaria root rot
varieties resistant to,
1001
blue stain fungus
ips engraver beetles and,
558
diplodia tip blight, 557,
998
needle cast, 557
needle rust, 560
susceptibility to, 998,
1000
verticillium wilt
resistance to, 995
western gall rust and
eastern gall rust, 562
white pine blister rust, 559,
738
distorted
pine tip or shoot moths,
562
dying
air pollution damage, 559
aphids, 560
pine and Saratoga
spittlebugs, 561
pine needle scales, 560
root nematodes, 558
white pine blister rust, 559
fertilizing, 557, 924, 927,
936
air pollution damage and,
559
diplodia tip blight and,
557
fill injury to, 999
forked appearance to
white pine weevils, 562
honeydew on plants and
objects below
aphids, 560
insects on
ants, 560
aphids, 560
woolly, 559
bark beetles, 558
ips engraver beetles, 558
Douglas fir tussock moths,
475, 554
gypsy moths, 1000
ips engraver beetles, 558
Japanese beetles, 997
mites, 558
pine and Saratoga
spittlebugs, 561
pine needle scales, 560
pine tip or shoot moths,
562

pine webworms, 561
root nematodes, 558
sawflies, 561
spruce budworms, **474,**
553
spruce spider mites, 558
white pine weevils, 562
woolly aphids, 559
jack pine
Saratoga spittlebugs on,
561
lightning injury to, 999
needles on
black sooty mold on
aphids, 560
bright orange spores on
pustules on
needle rust, 560
brown
needle cast, 557
pine needle scales, 560
spruce spider mites, 558
chewed
sawflies, 561
cream-colored to reddish
brown worms at tips or
bases of
pine tip or shoot moths,
562
cream-colored, baglike
pustules on
needle rust, 560
deformed
aphids, 560
dirty
spruce spider mites, 558
discolored
air pollution damage, 559
aphids, 560
needle cast, 557
pine and Saratoga
spittlebugs, 561
pine needle scales, 560
spruce spider mites, 558
white pine blister rust,
559
woolly aphids, 559
dropping
air pollution damage, 559
aphids, 560
needle cast, 557
needle rust, 560
pine and Saratoga
spittlebugs, 561
pine needle scales, 560
spruce spider mites, 558
dwarfed
air pollution injury, 559
dying
pine tip or shoot moths,
562
woolly aphids, 559
eaten
pine webworms, 561
sawflies, 561
flattened white bumps on
pine needle scales, 560
gray-green, tan, or black
caterpillarlike larvae on
sawflies, 561

honeydew on
aphids, 560
pitch on
pine tip or shoot moths,
562
red
air pollution damage, 559
reddish brown
white pine blister rust,
559
remaining dead on tree
diplodia tip blight, 557
shiny, sticky substance on
aphids, 560
silken webbing on
spruce spider mites, 558
small green, brown, or
black insects on
aphids, 560
stippled yellow
spruce spider mites, 558
swollen, cracked, black
structures on
needle cast, 557
tiny, black, elongated
structures on midribs of
needle cast, 557
white appearance to
pine needle scales, 560
white woolly masses on
woolly aphids, 559
yellow flecks on
air pollution injury, 559
yellowing
air pollution damage, 559
pine and Saratoga
spittlebugs, 561
woolly aphids, 559
Norfolk Island pine. *See
Araucaria*
P. canariensis (Canary
Island pine)
as armillaria root rot
resistant, 1001
P. edulis (Pinon pine)
as drought tolerant, 997
planting locations for, 997
P. halepensis (Alleppo
pine)
saline soils and, 999
P. mugo (Mugho pine)
as diplodia tip blight
susceptible, 998
as drought tolerant, 997
disease resistance in, 1000
planting locations for, 997
P. nigra (Austrian pine)
as armillaria root rot
resistant, 1001
as diplodia tip blight
susceptible, 998
P. ponderosa (Ponderosa
pine)
as diplodia tip blight
susceptible, 998
P. radiata (Monterey pine)
as armillaria root rot
resistant, 1001
spruce spider mites on,
558

insecticide for, 955
on beans
hopperburn and, 702
on potato, 769
Potentilla (Cinquefoil)
as drought tolerant, 997
as verticillium wilt
resistant, 995
culture, 339
diseases on
leaf spot, 339
powdery mildew, 995
rust, 339
in lawns
herbicides for, 978
P. fructicosa (Bush
cinquefoil)
soil pH for, 1002, 1003
Pothos. *See Scindapsus*
Potted plants. *See*
Containers, plants in
Potter wasps, 813
Poultry
insecticide for, 963
Powderpost beetles
in households, 809
Powdery mildew, 856, 995
controlling, 942, 944, 946,
956, 957, 959, 961, 962,
965, 968
on *Achillea*, 360
on apple, 630
resistance to, 1005
on *Aster*, 367
on *Begonia*, indoors, 237
on *Begonia*, outdoors, 369
on brambles, 712
resistance to, 1008
on *Calendula*, 371
on *Cineraria*, 382
on *Cosmos*, 384
on cucumber, 688
on cucurbits, 737
on currants; gooseberries,
738
on *Dahlia*, 388
on *Delphinium*, 389
on *Euonymus*, 512
on flowers, 351
on grapes, 746
varieties resistant to, 1007
on groundcovers, 328
on *Hydrangea*, 527
on *Iberis*, 400
on *Kalanchoe*, 272
on *Lagerstroemia*, 537
on *Lathyrus*, 405
on lawns, 308
on *Lonicera*, 541
on peas, 759
on *Phlox*, 419
on *Platanus*, 564
on *Quercus*, 576
on *Rosa*, 589
tolerance to, 993
on strawberries
resistance to, 1007
on sunflower, 784
on *Syringa*, 602
on *Tolmiea*, 290

on trees, 445
on vegetables, 688
on *Verbena*, 430
on *Viburnum*, 610
on *Zinnia*, 434
Prayer plant. *See Maranta*
Praying mantids, 886
Prickly glass wort. *See*
Russian thistle
Prickly lettuce (*Lactuca
serriola*), 842
herbicide for, 974
Primrose. *See Primula*
evening (*Oenothera*)
as verticillium wilt
resistant, 995
Primula (Primrose)
as cotton root rot resistant,
994
as verticillium wilt
resistant, 995
culture, 419, 992
diseases on
leaf spot, 420
root and stem rot, 420
dying
root and stem rot, 420
evening primrose
(*Oenothera*)
herbicides for, 974, 977
fertilizing, 419, 932
flowering times for, 992
germination of, 992
in containers
watering, 419
leaves on
dying
leaf spot, 420
root and stem rot, 420
pale green or white
minor nutrient
deficiency, 421
small
minor nutrient
deficiency, 421
soft and rotted bases on
root and stem rot, 420
spots and blotches on
leaf spot, 420
wilting
root and stem rot, 420
yellowing
leaf spot, 420
minor nutrient
deficiency, 421
root and stem rot, 420
minor nutrient deficiency
in, 421
planting locations for, 419
planting times for, 419, 992
pulls up easily
root and stem rot, 420
soil pH for, 419
minor nutrient deficiency
and, 421
stems on
decaying
root and stem rot, 420
watering, 419

leaf spot and, 420
Prince's feather. *See
Amaranthus*
Privet. *See Ligustrum*
Privet mite (*Brevipalpus
obovatus*), 538
Privet rust mite (*Aculus
ligustri*), 538
Prociphilus species
on *Fraxinus*, 517
P. xylosteri. (Woolly
honeysuckle aphids), 540
Procyon lotor. See
Raccoons
Propagating plants, 914
Propoxur
as ingredient
in ORTHO Ant, Roach &
Spider Killer, 938
in ORTHO Earwig, Roach
& Sowbug Bait, 943
in ORTHO Hornet & Wasp
Killer, 949
in ORTHO Mole Cricket
Bait, 955
in ORTHO Pest-B-Gon
Roach Bait, 959
for household pests
clover mites, 803
grain weevils, 818
granary weevils, 818
rice weevils, 818
scorpions, 816
Prostrate knotweed
(*Polygonum aviculare*),
837
See also Knotweed
herbicides for, 974
in lawns, 314
Prostrate pigweed
herbicide for, 974
Pruning Seal. *See* ORTHO
Pruning Seal
Pruning Sealer. *See*
ORTHO Pruning
Sealer
Pruning
Abies, 474
after transplanting, 916
almond, 625
apple, 626
apricot, 631
avocado trees, 635
Betula, 485
book about
All About Pruning, 985
Camellia, 492
cherry, 637
citrus, 641
cold damage and, 866
Coleus, indoors, 249
Cornus, 501
Crataegus, 504
diagnosing problems from,
1008
Dieffenbachia, 254
dressings for
ORTHO Pruning Seal, 960

ORTHO Pruning Sealer,
960
Euphorbia, 259
fig, 648
filbert, 650
flowers
perennial, 985
Fraxinus, 516
fruit and nut trees
after neglect, 625
cankers and, 618
diagnosing problems
from, 1008
limb breakage and, 618
small fruit and, 616
sunscald and, 618
Fuchsia, 518
Gleditsia, 522
Hedera, indoors, 268
hickory, 652
Hydrangea, 526
Ilex, 527
Ixora
cold damage and, 529
Juniperus, 531
Ligustrum, 538
Magnolia, 541
mango, 653
peach; nectarine, 654
flowering, 570
pear, 659
flowering, 574
pecan, 664
persimmon, 667
Picea, 553
Pinus, 557
Platanus, 564
plum, 668
Populus, 567
Prunus, 570
Pyracantha, 571
Pyrus, 574
Quercus, 574
quince, 672
Rhododendron, 581
Rosa, 588
Salix, 595
shrubs, 985
Syringa, 601
trees, 985
borers and, 451
broken branches on, 910
failure to bloom and, 440
oozing sap and, 453
sunscald and, 457, 866
transplant shock and, 453
wounds and, 451
Ulmus, 607
vines, 985
walnut, 673
Wisteria, 611
Prunus (Flowering almond;
Flowering cherry;
Flowering peach;
Flowering plum)
as fireblight susceptible,
1001
as frost crack susceptible,
457
as lawn tree, 997

as low-growing tree, 998
as street tree, 998
citrus whiteflies on, 570
culture, 570
P. armeniaca. See Apricot
P. avium. See Cherry
P. domestica. See Plum
P. dulcis. See Almond
P. ersica. See Peach;
Nectarine
P. salicina. See Plum
problems or, 570
Prunus, evergreen forms
of (Catalina cherry;
Cherry laurel; English
laurel; Hollyleaf cherry)
citrus whiteflies on, 570
culture, 570
diseases on
leaf spot, 571
powdery mildew, 995
fertilizing, 570, 924, 927
flowering times for, 570
planting locations for, 570
leaf spot and, 571
Pseudaulacaspis species
P. caroliniana (American
cherry laurel)
as armillaria root rot
resistant,
P. cockerelli. See False
oleander scale
P. ilicifolia (Hollyleaf
cherry)
as armillaria root rot
resistant,
P. pentagona (White peach
scale), 658
Pseudomonas species
on *Pelargonium,* outdoors,
415
P. caryophylli
on *Dianthus,* 391
P. lachrymans
on cucurbits, 736
P. marginata
on *Gladiolus,* 396
P. phaseolicola
on beans, 701
P. primulae
on *Primula,* 420
P. solanacearum
on *Tropaeolum,* 427
on *Verbena,* 431
P. syringae
on cherry, 639
on peach; nectarine, 658
on plum, 672
on *Syringa,* 602
on tomato, 787
P. syringae mori
on *Morus,* 546
P. syringae sevastanoi
on *Olea,* 555
P. syringae tonelliana
on *Nerium,* 549
plants susceptible to, 1000
Pseudoperonospora
cubensis

on cucurbits, 737
Pseudotsuga (Douglas fir)
as smog tolerant, 996
bird damage to, 999
fertilizers for, 926, 936
fungus diseases on
susceptibility to, 1000
insects on
cooley spruce gall aphids,
554, 571
Douglas fir tussock moths,
475, 554
spruce budworms, 474,
553
Psila rosae (Carrot rust fly),
720
Psorosis
on citrus, 647
Psylla buxi (Boxwood
psyllid), 489
Psyllids, 880
boxwood (*Psylla buxi*), 489
hackberry leaf gall
(*Pachypsylla* species),
499
insecticides for, 951, 956
on fruit and nut trees, 880
on trees, 880
honeydew from, 454
on vegetables, 880
pear (*Psylla pyricola*)
insecticides for, 946, 955
on pear, 662
Pteridium species
(Bracken), 832
insecticide for, 951
Puccinia species
on *Iris,* 403
P. antirrhini
on *Antirrhinum,* 364
P. asparagi
on asparagus (edible), 698
P. chrysanthemi, 377
on *Chrysanthemum,*
outdoors, 377
P. helianthi
on sunflower, 785
P. malva cearum
on *Alcea,* 362
P. pelargonii-zonalis
on *Pelargonium,* outdoors,
414
Puffballs, 852
as weeds, 852
in lawns, 321
Pulex irritans (Human flea)
in households, 806
Pulvinaria species
P. acericola (Cottony
maple leaf scale)
on *Nyssa,* 549
P. delottoi
on *Mesembryanthemum,*
337
Pulvinariella
mesembryanthemi
on *Mesembryanthemum,*
337

Puncturevine (*Tribulus
terrestris*), 835
herbicides for, 966, 974
Purple blotch
on onion family, 756
Purple leaf plum. *See
Prunus*
Purple passion vine. *See
Gynura*
Purple scales
on citrus
insecticide for, 940
Purslane (*Portulaca
oleracea*), 839
Florida. *See* Florida pusley
herbicides for, 966, 970,
973, 974
in lawns, 317
herbicides for, 971, 972,
977, 978
milk. *See* Spotted spurge
Pursley. *See* Purslane
Pusley, Florida (*Richardia
scabra*), 838
herbicides for, 966, 971,
973, 974, 976
in lawns
herbicides for, 977, 978
Pyracantha (Firethorn)
as crown gall resistant, 998
as verticillium wilt
resistant, 995
bees attracted by, 996
branches on
white woolly material on
woolly apple aphids, 573
woody growths on
woolly apple aphids, 573
culture, 571
diseases on
Botryosphaeria ribis, 1002
fireblight, 572
varieties tolerant of, 1001
powdery mildew, 995
scab, 572
varieties resistant to,
1001
sooty mold, 573
varieties resistant to, 1001
dying
fireblight, 572
fertilizing, 571, 923, 924,
926, 936
flowering time for, 571
flowers on
turning black and wilting
fireblight, 572
fruit on
corky and black spots on
scab, 572
deformed
scab, 572
dying
scab, 572
rough-surfaced,
olive-green spots on
scab, 572
scabby lesions on

scab, 572
insects on
aphids, 573
woolly apple, 573
bees
fireblight and, 572
hawthorn lacebugs, 572
insecticide for, 948
lacebugs, 572
Mediterranean fruit flies,
1002
scales, 573
sooty mold and, 573
woolly apple aphids, 573
woolly hawthorn aphids,
573
leaves on
black
fireblight, 572
black, shiny, hard droplets
under
hawthorn lacebugs, 572
black sooty mold on
scales, 573
sooty mold, 573
woolly apple aphids, 573
brown
scab, 572
brownish insects with
clear lacy wings under
hawthorn lacebugs, 572
crusty, scaly, or waxy
bumps under
scales, 573
dark blotches on
scab, 572
dropping
scab, 572
scales, 573
hanging downward
fireblight, 572
honeydew on
scales, 573
sooty mold and, 573
woolly apple aphids, 573
mottled or speckled gray
and green
hawthorn lacebugs, 572
scabby lesions on
scab, 572
shiny or sticky substance
on
scales, 573
woolly apple aphids, 573
spiny, wingless insects
under
hawthorn lacebugs, 572
wilting
fireblight, 572
yellowing
scab, 572
scales, 573
sooty mold, 573
woolly apple aphids, 573
planting locations for, 571
pruning, 571
saline soils and, 999
soil pH for, 571
stems on
crusty, scaly, or waxy

422
  root rot and, 422
  planting times for, 421, 992
  roots of
    dark and rotted
      root rot, 422
  seedlings
    eaten
      bird damage, 421
  soil pH for, 421
  stems on
    dark brown and limp
      root rot, 422
  stunted growth in
    ranunculus mosaic, 422
  tubers
    dark and rotted
      root rot, 422
  watering, 421, 422
Ranunculus mosaic, 422
Raphanus sativus. See
  Radish
Raphiolepis (India
    hawthorn)
  as powdery mildew
    susceptible, 995
  bees attracted by, 996
  R. umbellata (Yedda
    hawthorn)
    as armillaria root rot
      resistant, 1001
Raspberries. *See* Brambles
Raspberry crown borer
    (*Pennitsetia marginata*)
  on brambles, 710
Raspberry fruitworm
    (*Byturus* species)
  insecticides for, 946, 967
  on brambles, 709
Raspberry root borer
    (*Pennitsetia marginata*)
  on brambles, 710
Raspberry sawflies
  insecticide for, 946
Rats
  See also Rodents
  on avocado, 636
Rattlesnakeweed. *See*
  Florida betony
Rattus species. *See* Rats
Rayless chamomille
    (*Matricaria
    matricarioides*), 836
Red berry trouble
  controlling, 958
Red bugs. *See* Chiggers
Red cedar. *See Juniperus
  virginiana*
Red dead nettle
  herbicides for, 974
Red flour beetle. *See* Flour
  beetles
Red mite, southern. *See*
  Southern red mite
Red root. *See Amaranthus*
Red shanks (*Polygonum*

persicaria), 842
Red sorrel (*Rumex
    acetosella*), 845
  in lawns, 319
    herbicides for, 971, 978
Red spider mites
  insecticides for, 944, 948,
    951, 955, 958, 968, 969,
    978
  on houseplants
    insecticide for, 950
  on tomato
    insecticide for, 944
Red stele
  on strawberries, 780
    resistance to, 1007
Red thread
  on lawns,
    controlling, 954
    varieties resistant to, 990
Red-banded leafrollers
  insecticides for, 955
Red-breasted sapsucker
    (*Sphyrapicus varius
    ruber*), 893
Redbanded leafroller
    (*Argyrotaenia velutinana*)
  on grapes, 743
Redbud. *See Cercis*
Redheaded pine sawflies
  insecticide for, 951
Redroot pigweed
  herbicide for, 974
Redstem filaree (*Erodium
    cicutarium*), 835
Redweed (*Rumex acetosella*),
    845
Redwood
  dawn. *See Metasequoia
    glyptostroboides*
Resmethrin
  as ingredient, 944, 945
  in ORTHO Home &
    Garden Insect Killer, 948
  in ORTHO House Plant
    Insect Spray, 950
  in ORTHO Household
    Insect Killer, 950
  in ORTHO Systemic Rose
    & Floral Spray, 965
  in ORTHO Whitefly &
    Mealybug Killer, 969
  for clover mites
    in households, 803
  for *Fuchsia*
    greenhouse whiteflies on,
    519
  for *Hibiscus*
    greenhouse whiteflies on,
    525
Rhagoletis species
  cherry fruit flies, 637
    insecticide for, 946
  R. mendax. (Blueberry
    maggot), 707
    insecticide for, 946
  walnut husk fly, 673

Rhamnus (Buckthorn)
  as disease and insect
    resistant, 998
  as powdery mildew
    susceptible, 995
Rheum rhabarbarum. See
  Rhubarb
Rhizoctonia fruit rot
  controlling, 968
Rhizoctonia solani
  on beans, 703
  on *Dianthus*, 391
  on lawns, 298
  on lettuce, 751
Rhizoctonia species, 858
  on *Coleus*, indoors, 249
  on lawns, 300
    newly seeded, 300
  on *Lilium*, 406
  on *Philodendron*, 282
  on *Primula*, 420
  on *Tulipa*, 429
  R. solani, 232
    on *Ageratum*, 361
    on *Aglaonema*, 231
    on *Anthurium*, 231
    on *Gazania*, 334
    on *Hedera*, outdoors, 336
    on *Peperomia*, 281
Rhizoctonia stem rot
  on *Dianthus*, 391
Rhizopus nigricans
  on brambles, 710
Rhododendron (Azalea;
    Rhododendron)
  as shade tolerant, 997
  branches on
    bark flaking off of
      rhododendron borers,
      584
    dark discoloration under
      bark of
        wilt and root rot, 585
    dying back
      dieback, 585
      scales, 586
    scales on, 586
    shallow tunnels, ridges,
      and holes in bark on
        rhododendron borers,
        584
    sunken dead areas at
      bases of
        dieback, 585
    wilting ends on
      dieback, 585
  buds on
    tiny green or pink insects
      on
        rhododendron aphids,
        587
  culture, 581
  diseases on
    Botryosphaeria ribis, 1002
    dieback, 585
    fungal leaf spot, 583
    leaf gall, 582
    petal blight, 581

phytophthora root rot, 585
  variety resistant to, 1000
powdery mildew, 995
pythium root rot, 585
rust, 583
susceptibility to, 1000
wilt and root rot, 585
  variety resistant to, 1000
dying
  wilt and root rot, 585
fertilizing, 581, 923, 924,
  926, 928, 932, 935, 936
iron deficiency and, 929
salt burn and, 584
flower buds on
  deformed
    rhododendron aphids,
    587
flowers on
  slimy and dying
    petal blight, 581
  spots on
    petal blight, 581
insects on
  ants
    rhododendron aphids
      and, 587
  azalea whiteflies, 587
  cyclamen mites, 285
  insecticides for, 948, 953
  Japanese beetles, 997
  lacebugs, 582
  rhododendron aphids, 587
  rhododendron borers, 584
  rhododendron whiteflies,
    587
  root weevils, 586
  scales, 586
  spider mites, 582
iron deficiency in, 583, 929
leaf gall on, 582
leaves on
  black or grayish
    long-snouted insects on
      root weevils, 586
  black sooty mold on
    rhododendron aphids,
    587
    rhododendron whiteflies,
    587
  bleached tan or off-white
    sunscald, 584
  blotches on
    fungal leaf spot, 583
  brown
    windburn, 585
    winter injury, 585
  brown spots on
    fungal leaf spot, 583
  brown, dead edges on
    salt burn, 584
  brownish insects with lacy
    wings under
      lacebugs, 582
  curled or rolled
    dieback, 585
    rhododendron aphids,
    587
    rhododendron whiteflies,
    587

root weevils, 586
wilt and root rot, 585
dirty
spider mites, 582
distorted
leaf gall, 582
spider mites, 582
drooping and curling
root weevils, 586
dropping
rust, 583
salt burn, 584
scales, 586
drying out
windburn, 585
winter injury, 585
dying
dieback, 585
fungal leaf spot, 583
wilt and root rot, 585
fleshy
leaf gall, 582
gray spots on
fungal leaf spot, 583
hard, black, shiny droplets
under
lacebugs, 582
honeydew on
rhododendron aphids,
587
rhododendron whiteflies,
587
mottled
lacebugs, 582
rhododendron whiteflies,
587
notched or scalloped
margins on
root weevils, 586
off-white
sunscald, 584
pale
iron deficiency, 583
salt burn, 584
powdery appearance to
leaf gall, 582
red spots on
fungal leaf spot, 583
reddish brown
dieback, 585
scales on, 586
shiny, sticky substance on
rhododendron aphids,
587
rhododendron whiteflies,
587
silken webbing under
spider mites, 582
spiny wingless insects
under
lacebugs, 582
spots on
dieback, 585
fungal leaf spot, 583
rhododendron borers,
584
rust, 583
stippled yellow or bronze
spider mites, 582
stunted

root weevil larvae, 586
tan
sunscald, 584
tan spots on
fungal leaf spot, 583
thickened
leaf gall, 582
tiny green or pink insects
on
rhododendron aphids,
587
tiny white winged insects
under
rhododendron whiteflies,
587
water-soaked spots on
dieback, 585
wilting
dieback, 585
rhododendron borers,
584
wilt and root rot, 585
yellow spots on
fungal leaf spot, 583
rust, 583
yellow to orange-red
powdery material on
rust, 583
yellowing
fungal leaf spot, 583
iron deficiency, 583
rhododendron whiteflies,
587
root weevils, 586
scales, 586
wilt and root rot, 585
main stem on
bark chewed on
root weevil larvae, 586
bark flaking off of
rhododendron borers,
584
shallow tunnels, ridges,
and holes in bark on
rhododendron borers,
584
white grubs on
root weevil larvae, 586
petal blight on, 581
pinching, 930
planting locations for, 581
fungal leaf spot and, 583
lacebugs and, 582
leaf gall and, 582
shade tolerance and, 997
sunscald and, 584
windburn and, 585
winter injury and, 585
pruning, 581
R. mucronatum (Evergreen
snow azalea)
azalea whiteflies on, 587
R. obtusum (Hiryu azalea)
as *Phytophthora* resistant,
1000
roots of
chewed
root weevil larvae, 586
salt burn on, 584
shoots on

wilting
rhododendron borers,
584
soil drainage for
salt burn and, 584
wilt and root rot and, 585
soil pH for, 581, 583, 1002,
1003
correcting, 923, 944, 958
stunted growth in
iron deficiency, 583
lacebugs, 582
sunscald on, 584
tiny white insects fluttering
around
rhododendron whiteflies,
587
twigs on
sunken dead areas on
dieback, 585
watering, 581
salt burn and, 584
weak
rust, 583
wilting
wilt and root rot, 585
windburn on, 585
winter injury to, 585
Rhododendron aphid
(*Macrosiphum
rhododendri*), 587
Rhododendron borer
(*Synanthedon
rhododendri*), 584
insecticide for, 953
Rhododendron whitefly
(*Dialeurodes
chittendeni*), 587
Rhubarb
culture, 773
diseases on
crown rot, 773
foot rot, 773
root rot, 773
southern blight
susceptibility to, 996
verticillium wilt
susceptibility to, 1009
dying
crown rot, 773
insects on
rhubarb curculios, 774
leaves on
brown, sunken, water-
soaked spots at bases of
crown rot, 773
wilting, yellowing, and
dying
crown rot, 773
roots of
rotting
crown rot, 773
stalks on
black weevils on
rhubarb curculios, 774
collapsing
crown rot, 773
rusty-yellow powder on
rhubarb curculios, 774

small black spots on
rhubarb curculios, 774
watering, 773
crown rot and, 773
weeds near
rhubarb curculios and,
774
Rhubarb curculio (*Lixus
concavus*), 774
Rhus (Sumac)
as crown gall resistant, 998
diseases on
powdery mildew
susceptibility to, 995
wilt, 581
R. aromatica (Fragrant
sumac)
as armillaria root rot
resistant, 1001
Rhus diversiloba (Pacific
poison oak), 853
Rhus radicans (Poison ivy),
852
Rhus toxcidendron (Poison
oak), 853
Rhyacionia species (Pine tip
or shoot moths), 562
Rhynchopacha triatomaea
(Cotoneaster webworm),
503
Ribbon plant
insecticides for, 969
Ribes species. *See*
Currants; Gooseberries
Ribgrass. *See* **Plantain**
Rice fields
weeds in
bulrush, 831
Rice weevils
in households, 818
insecticide for, 947
Richardia scabra (Florida
pusley), 838
herbicides for, 973, 974,
976–978
Ring rot
on potato, 768
Ring-spot viruses, 861
controlling, 968
on flowers, 352
Ringlegged earwig
(*Euborellia annulipes*)
in households, 801
Roaches. *See* **Cockroaches**
Roadsides
weeds on
chicory, 844
common groundsel, 844
common yarrow, 836
cudweed, 836
Douglas fiddleneck, 851
field bindweed, 849
foxtails, 829
full panicum, 828
German velvetgrass, 826
horsetail, 832

red, green, or brownish
  beetles on
    beetles, 593
red, orange, or black
  powdery material in spots
  under
    rust, 589
rolled
  leafrollers, 591
shiny, sticky substance on
  rose aphids, 591
  scales, 593
spots on
  stem cankers and
  dieback, 594
stippled
  rose leafhoppers, 590
  spider mites, 590
stunted
  verticillium wilt, 594
tiny green or pink insects
  on
    rose aphids, 591
webbing on or under
  leafrollers, 591
  spider mites, 590
white cottony masses on
  scales, 593
wilting
  stem cankers, 594
  verticillium wilt, 594
worms on
  caterpillars, 592
  roseslugs, 593
yellow flecks on
  flower thrips, 588
yellow margins on
  verticillium wilt, 594
yellow to brown spots or
  blotches on
    rust, 589
    viruses, 591
yellowing
  black spot, 589
  crown gall, 594
  powdery mildew, 589
  scales, 593
  stem cankers, 594
  verticillium wilt, 594
miniature
  light for, 914
phosphorus deficiency in
  correcting, 925
planting locations for, 588
pollination of
  leafcutter bees and, 592
pruning, 588
  dressings for, 960
roots of
  large corky galls on
  crown gall, 594
shoots on
  dying
    rose midges, 590
stems on
  chewed tips on
    beetles, 593
  crusty or scaly bumps on
    scales, 593
  dead tips on

rose midges, 590
dying
  leafcutter bees, 592
  scales, 593
  stem cankers, 594
large corky galls on
  crown gall, 594
nests on ends of
  leafcutter bees, 592
tiny green or pink insects
  on
    rose aphids, 591
tiny whitish maggots on
  tips of
    rose midges, 590
tunnels in
  leafcutter bees, 592
white cottony masses on
  scales, 593
stunted growth in
  crown gall, 594
  powdery mildew, 589
  viruses, 591
twigs on
  black dots on powdery
    material on
    powdery mildew, 589
  broken or cut ends on
    leafcutter bees, 592
  dying back
    leafcutter bees, 592
  grayish white powdery
    material on
    powdery mildew, 589
watering, 588
  black spot and, 589
weak
  crown gall, 594
  spider mites, 590
weeds near
  herbicides for, 966, 970
whitish insects flying
  around
    rose leafhoppers, 590
wilting
  verticillium wilt, 594
Rose and Floral Dust. See
  ORTHO Rose and
  Floral Dust
Rose aphid (*Macrosiphum
  rosae*), 591
Rose chafers
  insecticides for, 948, 961,
  962
Rose leafhopper
  (*Edwardsiana rosae*), 590
  insecticides for, 955, 961,
  962
Rose mallow. See Hibiscus
Rose midge (*Dasineura
  rhodophaga*), 590
  insecticides for, 956, 965
Rose, moss. See Portulaca
Rose-of-Sharon. See
  Hibiscus
Rose. See Rosa
  Christmas. *See Helleborus*
  Japanese. *See Kerria*

moss. *See Portulaca*
rosin. *See Hypericum*
sun. *See Helianthemum*
Rosea iceplant
  (*Drosanthemum*)
  saline soils and, 999
Rosemary. See
  Rosmarinus
Roseslugs
  insecticides for, 947, 954,
  961, 962, 964
  on *Rosa*, 593
Rosin rose. See Hypericum
Rosmarinus (Rosemary)
  as drought tolerant, 997
  bees attracted by, 996
  planting locations for, 991,
  997
  R. lockwoodii
    saline soils and, 999
  R. officinalis 'Prostratus'
    (Dwarf rosemary)
    as groundcover
    for sunny areas, 991
Rotenone
  as ingredient
    in ORTHO Rotenone Dust
    or Spray, 961
    in ORTHO Tomato &
    Vegetable Insect Spray,
    967
    in ORTHO Tomato
    Vegetable Dust, 967
  for household pests
    boxelder bugs, 803
    cigarette beetles, 818
    drugstore beetles, 818
  for vegetables
    cucumber beetles on, 690
    flea beetles on, 691
Rotenone Dust or Spray.
  See ORTHO Rotenone
  Dust or Spray
**Rough strawberry root
  weevil** (*Otiorhynchus
  rugosostriatus*), 780
Round worms. See
  Nematodes
Roundheaded borers, 810
  insecticide for, 953
Rubber plant. See Ficus,
  indoors
Rubber tree, hardy
  (*Eucomia ulmoides*)
  as disease and insect
  resistant, 998
Rubus species. *See*
  Brambles; Wild
  blackberry
Rudbeckia (Black-eyed
  Susan; Coneflower)
  culture, 422, 992
  diseases on
    powdery mildew, 995
    southern blight, 996
    verticillium wilt, 422
Rugby grass

as mildew resistant, 308
Rumex species
  R. acetosella. See Red
    sorrel
  R. crispus. See Curly dock
Rush nut. See Nutsedge
Russet mites
  tomato (*Aculops
    lycopersici*), 790
  insecticide for, 944
Russian cactus. See
  Russian thistle
Russian olive. See
  Elaeagnus
Russian thistle (*Salsola kali*
  var. *tenuifolia*), 834
  beet leafhoppers harbored
    by, 834, 856
  herbicides for, 966
Rust, 856
  cedar-apple, 630, 856
    on apple, 630
    varieties susceptible and
      resistant to, 1005
    on *Juniperus*, 535
    on *Malus*, 545
    plants susceptible to, 1000
  chrysanthemum
    resistance to, 377, 992
  controlling, 942, 946, 956,
    957, 959, 965, 968
  eastern gall
    on *Pinus*, 562
  hawthorn
    on *Crataegus*, 505
  leaf
    on trees, 461
  leaf and stem
    on trees, 445
  needle
    on *Pinus*, 560
  on *Alcea*, 362
  on *Antirrhinum*, 364
  on *Asparagus*, 698
  on beans, 701
  on bluegrass
    varieties resistant to, 990
  on brambles, 712
  on *Callistephus*, 372
  on *Chaenomeles*, 500
  on *Chrysanthemum*, 377
  on *Duchesnea*, 333
  on fig, 649
  on flowers, 351
  on *Hypericum*, 337
  on incense cedar
    Chaenomeles and, 500
  on *Iris*, 403
  on *Juniperus*, 535
    Chaenomeles and, 500
  on lawns
    varieties resistant to, 990
  on *Mahonia*, 543
  on mallow, 362
  on *Pelargonium*, outdoors,
    414
  on *Pinus*, 560
  on *Potentilla*, 339

nightshade), 850
S. sarachoides (Hairy
nightshade), 850
S. tuberosum. See Potato
Soldierweed. *See*
Amaranthus
Soleirolia
S. soleirolii (Baby's tears)
for shady areas, 991
Solenopsis species. *See* Fire
ants
Solitary wasps, 813
Sonchus species. *See*
Sowthistle
Sooty blotch
fly speck and
on apple, 628
Sooty mold
controlling, 968, 969
on *Camellia*, 495
on fruit and nut trees, 621
on *Gardenia*, 521
on *Jasminum*, 531
on *Liriodendron*, 539
on *Nerium*, 547
on *Pyracantha*, 573
on trees, 445
Sophora
S. japonica (Japanese
pagoda tree)
as armillaria root rot
resistant, 1001
as disease and insect
resistant, 998
soil pH for, 1002, 1003
Sorbus (Ash; Mountain ash)
berries on
deformed
pearleaf blister mites,
600
branches on
cracks or sunken areas on
canker and dieback, 601
discolored bark on
canker and dieback, 601
dying
canker and dieback, 601
liquid oozing from
canker and dieback, 601
purplish brown insects
under white cottony
masses on
woolly aphids, 600
culture, 599
diseases on
canker and dieback, 601
fireblight, 599
susceptibility to, 1001
quince rust, 1000
rust, 600
dying
fireblight, 599
fertilizing, 599, 936
flowering times for, 599
flowers on
wilting and turning black
fireblight, 599
insects on

bees
fireblight and, 599
flies
fireblight and, 599
gypsy moths, 1000
pearleaf blister mites, 504,
600
woolly aphids, 600
woolly apple aphids, 600
leaves on
black
fireblight, 599
black sooty mold on
woolly aphids, 600
brown
canker and dieback, 601
curled
fireblight, 599
dropping
pearleaf blister mites,
600
rust, 600
dying
canker and dieback, 601
hanging dead on tree
fireblight, 599
mottled brown or blackish
pearleaf blister mites,
600
orange cups under
rust, 600
reddish or brownish
blisters under
pearleaf blister mites,
600
sticky substance on
woolly aphids, 600
wilting
fireblight, 599
yellow, thickened spots on
rust, 600
yellowing
woolly aphids, 600
planting locations for, 599
rust and, 600
roots of
marblelike knots on
woolly aphids, 600
stunted
woolly aphids, 600
S. aucuparia (European
mountain ash)
as verticillium wilt
resistant, 995
soil pH for, 1002, 1003
stems on
black sooty mold on
woolly aphids, 600
sticky substance on
woolly aphids, 600
stunted growth in
woolly aphids, 600
trunk of
black sooty mold on
woolly aphids, 600
cracks or sunken areas on
canker and dieback, 601
discolored bark on
canker and dieback, 601
liquid oozing from

canker and dieback, 601
purplish brown insects
under white cottony
masses on
woolly aphids, 600
sticky substance on
woolly aphids, 600
twigs on
brown ooze on
fireblight, 599
cracks on
fireblight, 599
dark, sunken, and dry
bark on
fireblight, 599
purplish brown insects
under white cottony
masses on
woolly aphids, 600
water-soaked bark on
bases of
fireblight, 599
yellowing
woolly aphids, 600
watering, 599
weak
woolly aphids, 600
Sorghum halepense. See
Johnsongrass
Sorrel
field. *See* Sorrel, red
French
dehydration of, 684
red (*Rumex acetosella*),
845
in lawns, 319
herbicides for, 971, 978
sheep. *See* Sorrel, red
Sour dock. *See* Curly dock
Sour grass. *See* Red sorrel
Sourgrass. *See* Oxalis
Sourgum. *See Nyssa*
Souring
on fig, 649
Sourwood (*Oxydendrum*)
as crown gall resistant, 998
Southern blight, 859
on *Anemone*, 363
on peanuts, 761
plants susceptible to, 996
See also Sclerotium root rot;
Crown rot; Southern wilt
Southern corn rootworm
(*Diabrotica* species)
on *Coreopsis*, 383
Southern peas. *See* Peas,
southern or blackeye
Southern red mite
(*Oligonychus ilicis*)
insecticide for, 965
on *Ilex*, 528
on *Rhododendron*, 582
Southern stem rot
on peanuts, 761
Southern wilt, 859
See also Sclerotium root rot;
Crown rot; Southern

blight
Sowbugs, 885
baits for, 943, 959, 964
in households
insecticides for, 938, 940
insecticides for, 938, 941–
945, 948–950, 952, 958
on vegetables, 692
Sowthistle (*Sonchus*
species), 845
herbicides for, 974
in lawns
herbicides for, 977, 978
Spanishneedles (*Bidens
bipinnata*), 834
Spathe flower. *See*
Spathiphyllum
Spathiphyllum (Spathe
flower; White flag)
as salt sensitive, 287
culture, 287
dead leaf tips on, 287
light requirements for, 990
watering
salt damage and, 287
Speargrass. *See* Bluegrass,
annual
Speedwell (*Veronica
filiformis*), 838
in lawns, 318
herbicides for, 971, 978
Sphaceloma perseae
on avocado, 636
Sphaeropsis tumefaciens
on *Nerium*, 549
Sphaerotheca species
on *Tolmiea*, 290
plants infected by, 995
plants susceptible to, 995
S. fuliginea
on cucurbits, 737
plants infected by, 995
S. humuli var. *fuliginea*
on *Kalanchoe*, 272
S. humuli
on brambles, 712
on *Phlox*, 419
S. lanesris
on *Quercus*, 576
S. mors-uvae
on currants; gooseberries,
738
S. pannosa var. *rosae*
on *Rosa*, 589
S. phytophila
on *Celtis*
witch's broom and, 498
Sphagnum moss, 833
Sphenophorus species. *See*
Billbugs
Sphyrapicus species
(Sapsuckers), 893
Spices. *See* Herbs
Spider flower. *See* Cleome
Spider mites, 886
See also Mites

Syzygium
  S. paniculatum (Brush
    cherry)
    saline soils and, 999

T

Tackweed (*Tribulus
  terrestris*), 835
Tagetes (Marigold)
  cultivating
    cutworms and, 425
  culture, 424, 992
  diseases on
    aster yellows, 994
    fusarium wilt, 994
    leaf spot, 424
    southern blight, 996
  fertilizing, 424
  flower buds on
    webbing over
      mites, 425
  flowering times for, 992
  germination of, 992
  in containers
    watering, 424
  insects on
    cutworms, 425
    insecticides for, 948, 969
    mites, 425
  leaves on
    dirty, dry, and dropping
      mites, 425
    dying
      leaf spot, 424
    sheared off
      cutworms, 425
    spots or blotches on
      leaf spot, 424
    stippled
      mites, 425
    twisted
      leaf spot, 424
    webbing on or under
      mites, 425
    yellowing
      leaf spot, 424
      mites, 425
  planting directions for
    cutworms and, 425
  planting locations for, 424
  planting times for, 424, 992
  seedlings
    chewed or sheared off
      cutworms, 425
    gray, brown, or black
      worms in soil near
      cutworms, 425
  stems on
    webbing on
      mites, 425
  transplanting
    cutworms and, 425
  watering, 424
    leaf spot and, 424

Takecallis species (Bamboo
  aphid), 484
Tall fescue
  herbicides for, 974, 976
Tall thistle
  herbicides for, 974
Tamalia coweni (Leaf gall
  aphid)
  on *Arctostaphylos*, 483
Tamarix (Tamarisk)
  as crown gall resistant, 998
  as disease and insect
    resistant, 998
  gypsy moths on, 1000
Taniva albolineana (Spruce
  needle miner), 555
Tansy, wild. *See* Ragweed
Tansy mustard
  in lawns
    herbicide for, 971
Tansy ragwort (*Senecio
  jacobaea*), 846
Taphrina species
  T. caerulescens
    on *Quercus*, 576
  T. deformans
    on peach; nectarine, 656
Taraxacum officinale. *See*
  Dandelion
Tarnished plant bug
  (*Lygus lineolaris*)
  insecticides for, 955, 963
  on peach; nectarine, 657
Taxodium (Bald cypress)
  as armillaria root rot
    resistant, 1001
  as disease and insect
    resistant, 998
  as wet soil tolerant, 997
  fungus diseases on
    susceptible to, 1000
  planting locations for, 997
Taxus (Yew)
  as shade tolerant, 997
  culture, 603
  diseases on
    root rot, 604
    susceptibility to, 1000
  fertilizing, 603, 926, 936
  insects on
    black vine weevils, 604
    taxus weevils, 604
  planting locations for, 603
    poor soil and, 604
    root rot and, 604
    shade tolerance, 997
  poor soil and, 604
  soil pH for
    importance of, 604
  watering, 603
    root rot and, 604
Taxus weevil (*Otiorhynchus
  sulcatus*), 604
**Temperatures, average
  minimum,** 1004
Tenebrio species

(Mealworms)
  in households, 817
Tent caterpillars
  (*Malacosoma* species)
  insecticides for, 947, 948,
    951, 954–956, 964
  on fruit and nut trees, 620
  on trees, 443
Tentiform leafminers
  insecticide for, 946
Tentmakers
  poplar
    insecticide for, 951
Termites
  drywood, 810
  insecticide for, 957
  subterranean, 808
Ternstroemia
  T. sylvatica (Mexican
    ternstroemia)
    as armillaria root rot
      resistant, 1001
Tetralopha robustella
  (Pine webworm), 561
**Tetramethylthiuram
  disulfide**
  for deer
    in trees, 891
Tetranychus species. *See*
  Spider mites
  T. urticae. *See*
    Two-spotted spider mite
Texas citrus mites
  insecticides for, 940
Texas mountain laurel.
  See Sophora
Texas panicum
  herbicides for, 966
Texas root rot, 859
  on fruit and nut trees, 624
  on *Hedera*, outdoors, 336
  on *Juniperus*, 533
  on pecan, 666
  on trees, 466
  plants resistant to, 994
Thatch
  on lawns, 295, 304
    fusarium blight and, 298
    Helminthosporium leaf
      spot and, 305
Thermobia species. *See*
  Firebrats
Thielaviopsis basicola
  on *Euphorbia*, 260
Thiram
  as damping-off preventive,
    917
    for beets, 706, 917
    for flowers, 358, 359
    for tomato, 795
    for vegetables, 682, 683
  for *Malus*
    cedar-apple rust on, 545
  for onion family
    smut on, 756

for vegetables
  as damping-off preventive,
    683
Thistles
  See also Sowthistle;
    Starthistle
  aster yellows and, 861, 994
  on flowers, 357
  Barnaby's (Yellow
    starthistle), 844
  Cirsium species
    artichoke plume moths
      and, 696
    C. arvense (Canada
      thistle), 843
  field
    herbicide for, 974
  milk (*Silybum marianum*)
    curly dwarf and
      on globe artichoke, 696
  near flowers
    aster yellows and, 357
    leafhoppers and, 357
  near globe artichokes
    artichoke plume moths
      and, 696
    curly dwarf and, 696
  near potato
    potato leafhoppers and,
      769
  near trees
    aster yellows and, 861
  near vegetables
    aster yellows and, 861
    leafhoppers and, 691
  Russian (*Salsola kali* var.
    tenuifolia), 834
    leafhoppers and
      beet, 834
    on flowers, 357
Thorn. *See Crataegus*
Thornbug (*Umbonia
  crassicornis*)
  on *Acacia*, 476
Thousand-legged worms.
  See Millipedes
Thrips, 883
  citrus (*Scirtothrips citri*),
    643
  Cuban laurel
    (*Gynaikothrips ficorum*)
    on *Ficus*, outdoors, 515
  flower (*Frankliniella*
    species), 883
  F. tritici
    on *Rosa*, 588
  on *Chrysanthemum*, 378
  gladiolus (*Thrips simplex*),
    395
  on *Allium*, 363
  on *Ficus*
    Cuban laurel
      (*Gynaikothrips ficorum*),
      515
  on flowers, 347
  on houseplants
    insecticides for, 950
  on *Narcissus*, 409
  on trees, 441, 448, 450,

cutworms, 689
earwigs, 689
nocturnal pests, 689
weevils, 689
cut off near ground
beetles, 689
caterpillars, 689
cutworms, 689
earwigs, 689
nocturnal pests, 689
weevils, 689
discolored bases on
damping-off, 683
dying
dehydration, 682
flea beetles, 691
eaten
birds, 683
grasshoppers, 683
millipedes, 693
rabbits, 683
snails and slugs, 683
fail to grow
crusted soil, 682
damping-off, 682
excess water, 682
incorrect planting depth,
682
lack of water, 682
slow germination, 682
soil temperature, 682
falling over
damping-off, 683
silvery winding trails
around
snails and slugs, 683,
689
soft and thin bases on
damping-off, 683
thinning, 917
water-soaked bases on
damping-off, 683
wilting
dehydration, 682
flea beetles, 691
seeds
eaten
millipedes, 693
fail to sprout
crusted soil, 682
damping-off, 682
excess water, 682
incorrect planting depth,
682
lack of water, 682
slow germination, 682
soil temperature, 682
germination of, 1009
starting outdoors, 917
watering, 917
shade tolerant, 681
silvery trails around
snails and slugs, 683, 689
smog-tolerant varieties of,
996
snails and slugs on, 683,
689
bait for, 938
soil loosened around
moles, 694

soil mounds near
pocket gophers, 695
soil pH for, 1002, 1003
iron deficiency and, 686
nutrient availability and,
681
sowbugs and pillbugs on,
692
stalks on
knocked over
wildlife, 694
stems on
chewed
beetles, 689
caterpillars, 689
cucumber beetles, 690
cutworms, 689
earwigs, 689
nocturnal pests, 689
weevils, 689
gouges on
hail damage, 689
holes in
cucumber beetles, 690
wounds on
hail damage, 689
storing
botrytis blight and, 857
stripped of leaves
hail damage, 689
stunted growth in
aphids, 692
cool weather, 681
cucumber beetles, 690
dehydration, 684
excess water, 681
garden symphylans, 693
incorrect pH, 681
insufficient light, 681
nematodes, 685
nitrogen deficiency, 685
phosphorus deficiency,
681
poor soil and cool weather,
681
root rot, 685
salt damage, 686
weeds and, 824
watering, 906
dehydration and, 684
guidelines for, 906
nitrogen deficiency and,
685
root and stem rot and, 684
root rot and, 681, 685
salt damage and, 686
seed germination and, 682
seedlings, 682
stunted growth and, 681
timing for, 907
types of, 906
weeds and, 824
weak
aphids, 692
leafhoppers, 691
weeds near
annual bluegrass, 825
aster yellows and, 861
bitter nightshade, 850
black nightshade, 850

chickweed
common, 837
mouseear, 839
crabgrass, 827
field bindweed, 849
goosegrass, 828
hairy nightshade, 850
herbicides for, 824, 973
lamb's-quarters, common,
848
leafhoppers and, 691
milkweed, 847
mouseear chickweed, 839
nimblewill, 827
pigweeds, 847
prostrate knotweed, 837
purslane, 839
stinging nettles, 848
yarrow, common, 836
white multilegged pests in
soil around
garden symphylans, 693
wildlife eating; *see* animal
pests in
wilting
dehydration, 684
flea beetles, 691
moles, 694
nematodes, 685
pocket gophers, 695
root and stem rot, 684
woodchucks in, 694, 895
worms on
caterpillars, 690
yellowing
nematodes, 685
Velvet leaf
in lawns
herbicides for, 971
Velvet plant. *See Gynura*
Velvetbean caterpillars
insecticide for, 963
Velvetgrass, German
(*Holcus mollis*), 826
herbicide for, 976
Velvetweed
herbicide for, 974
***Venturia* species**
V. inaequalis
on apple, 629
on *Malus*, 544
V. pyrina
on pear, 659
Verbena
as verticillium wilt
resistant, 995
cultivating
bacterial wilt and, 431
diseases on
bacterial wilt, 431
gray mold, 431
powdery mildew, 430, 995
dying
bacterial wilt, 431
flowers on
rotting
gray mold, 431
spots on

gray mold, 431
insects on
greenhouse whiteflies,
432
two-spotted spider mites,
431
leaves on
brown spots or blotches on
gray mold, 431
dirty, drying out, and
dropping
two-spotted spider mites,
431
dying
powdery mildew, 430
honeydew on
greenhouse whiteflies,
432
mold on
gray mold, 431
greenhouse whiteflies,
432
mottled
greenhouse whiteflies,
432
soft and rotting
gray mold, 431
stippled
two-spotted spider mites,
431
tiny, winged insects on
greenhouse whiteflies,
432
webbing between or
under
two-spotted spider mites,
431
white powdery material on
powdery mildew, 430
white waxy powder on
insects under
greenhouse whiteflies,
432
withering
powdery mildew, 430
yellowing
greenhouse whiteflies,
432
powdery mildew, 430
two-spotted spider mites,
431
planting locations for, 431
stems on
brown or grayish mold on
gray mold, 431
brown spots or blotches on
gray mold, 431
discolored tissue inside
bacterial wilt, 431
grayish white powdery
material on
powdery mildew, 430
soft and rotting
bacterial wilt, 431
soft
gray mold, 431
watering
gray mold and, 431
wilting
bacterial wilt, 431

dark sunken areas on
walnut anthracnose, 675
walnut blight, 674
decayed areas on husks of
walnut husk flies, 673
decayed kernels in
walnut blight, 674
dropping prematurely
codling moths, 673
walnut anthracnose, 675
harvesting, 673
holes in
codling moths, 673
husks of sticking to shells
walnut husk flies, 673
poor yield of
aphids, 674
walnut anthracnose, 675
walnut blight, 674
sawdustlike material on
codling moths, 673
shiny black fluid on
walnut blight, 674
shriveled kernels in
walnut anthracnose, 675
walnut blight, 674
walnut husk flies, 673
small
walnut anthracnose, 675
stained shells on
codling moths, 673
walnut blight, 674
walnut husk flies, 673
worms in
codling moths, 673
yellow maggots inside
husks of
walnut husk flies, 673
planting locations for, 673
pruning, 673
shiny ooze exuding from
walnut blight, 674
shoots on
brown sunken lesions on
walnut anthracnose, 675
dead sunken lesions on
walnut blight, 674
dying
blackline, 676
sprouting from rootstock
blackline, 676
soil pH for, 673
sparse growth in
blackline, 676
stems on
crusty, waxy, or scaly
bumps on
scales, 675
tiny yellow insects on
aphids, 674
stunted growth in
crown rot, 676
trunk of
caterpillars on
walnut caterpillars, 674
darkened around soil line
crown rot, 676
discolorations under bark
of
crown rot, 676

sap oozing from
crown rot, 676
twigs on
lesions on
walnut blight, 674
watering, 673
weak
blackline, 676
walnut anthracnose, 675
Walnut anthracnose, 675
Walnut aphid (*Chromaphis
juglandicola*), 674
Walnut blight, 674
Walnut caterpillar (*Datana
integerrima*), 674
insecticide for, 946
Walnut husk fly (*Rhagoletis
species*), 673
Walnut wilt
on tomato, 791
Wandering Jew. *See
Tradescantia*
Warrens A-34 grass
as shade tolerant, 305
Washingtonia (Washington
palm). *See* Palms,
outdoors
Wasps
digger
insecticides for, 940, 942
galls from, 869
gall
on grapes, 747
in households, 813
insecticides for, 945, 947–
950, 958
Water
pests in
grasshoppers, 881
weeds near
bulrush, 831
common cattail, 832
horsetail, 832
mugwort, 847
stinging nettle, 848
wild iris, 830
Water molds, 857
See also Crown rots;
Damping-off; Root rot
Water spots
on *Achimenes*, 230
on *Aeschynanthus*, 231
on *Columnea*, 251
on *Episcia*, 258
on *Saintpaulia*, 285
on *Sinningia*, 287
on *Streptocarpus*, 288
Water, lack of. *See
Drought; Moisture
deficiency*
Waterbugs. *See
Cockroaches*
Watergrass. *See
Barnyardgrass*
Watering, 906
amount of, 906

basin irrigation, 906
book about
*All About Fertilizers, Soils
& Water* (ORTHO), 984
by hand, 906
by sprinklers, 906
chemical damage and, 287
cold damage and, 912
container plants, 913
drainage problems and,
907
drip irrigation, 906
sandy soils and, 899
troubleshooting, 908
excessive, 865
for flowers, 349
for lawns
thatch and, 304
oedema and, 868
root rot and, 865
furrow irrigation, 906
guidelines for, 906
heat damage and, 912
importance of, 864
for houseplants, 225
in sandy soils, 899
in shallow soils, 899
lawns, 906
excessive, 304
leaf burn and, 865
leaf scorch and 865
measuring amount of, 906
mechanism of, 907
newly planted trees, 916
problems from
diagnosing, 1008
salt damage and, 864
seeds, 917
timing for, 907
water movement, 907
Watery soft rot
on beans, 701
on cabbage family, 718
on lettuce, 751
Wax plant. *See Hoya*
Wax scales, 878
Webworms
cotoneaster (*Rhynchopacha
triatomaea*), 503
fall (*Hyphantria cunea*)
insecticides for, 951, 956
on fruit and nut trees, 620
on trees, 443
insecticides for, 966
juniper (*Dichomeris
marginella*), 535
mimosa (*Homadaula
anisocentra*), 481
insecticides for, 951, 956,
966
on *Gleditsia*, 522
oak
insecticides for, 951, 956
pine (*Tetralopha
robustella*), 561
sod
insecticides for, 939–943,
952, 954, 956, 964, 965
tropical grass

insecticides for, 952
Weed killers. *See*
Herbicides
Weed-B-Gon for Southern
Grasses. *See* ORTHO
Weed-B-Gon for
Southern Grasses
Weed-B-Gon Lawn Weed
Killer. *See* ORTHO
Weed-B-Gon Lawn
Weed Killer
Weeds
See also specific weeds
annual bluegrass (*Poa
annua*), 825
in lawns, 311
annual speargrass, 825
aster-yellows-susceptible
varieties of, 861
Barnaby's thistle, 844
barnyardgrass
(*Echinochloa crus-galli*),
829
bee nettle, 851
bentgrass
in lawns, 311
Bermudagrass (*Cynodon
dactylon*), 826
in lawns, 311
betony, Florida (*Stachys
floridana*), 850
bindweed, field
(*Convolvulus arvensis*),
849
in lawns, 320
bird's nest plant, 835
bird's pepper, 833
black clover, 840
black medic (*Medicago
lupulina*), 840
in lawns, 315
black-eyed Susan
as aster yellows
susceptible, 861
blackberry, wild (*Rubus
species*), 834, 853
bluegrass
annual (*Poa annua*), 825
bracken (*Pteridium
species*), 832
brake fern, 832
bristlegrass, 829
broadleaf plantain
(*Plantago major*), 843
broadleaf
bee nettle, 851
in lawns, 317
bindweed, field, 849
in lawns, 320
black clover, 840
in lawns, 315
black medic, 840
in lawns, 315
chickweed
common (*Stellaria
media*), 316, 837
in lawns, 316
Indian, 851
mouseear, (*Cerastium*

aster yellows and, 861
wild garlic (*Allium vineale*), 831
  in lawns, 314
wild iris (*Iris* species), 830
wild lettuce, 842
wild morning glory; *see* morning glory
wild mustard (*Brassica kaber*), 834
wild oats (*Avena fatua*), 830
wild onion (*Allium canadense*), 831
wild portulaca, 839
wild tansy, 843
wiregrass; *see* Bermudagrass; prostrate knotweed
witchgrass, 826
  smooth, 828
  spreading, 828
woodsorrel, yellow; *See* Oxalis
wormwood, 847
yardgrass, 828
yarrow, common (*Achillea millefolium*), 836
yellow dock, 842
yellow starthistle (*Centaurea solstitialis*), 844
yellow woodsorrel; *See* Oxalis
Weeping Chinese banyan. *See* Ficus, indoors,
Weeping fig. *See* Ficus, indoors
Weeping mulberry. *See* Morus
Weevils, 873
  black vine (*Otiorhynchus sulcatus*)
    insecticides for, 951, 956
    on *Rhododendron*, 586
    on strawberries, 780
    on *Taxus*, 604
  carrot (*Listronotus oregonensis*)
    on carrots, 720
  described, 358
  grain (*Sitophilus* species)
    in households, 818
  granary
    in households, 818
  hyperodes
    insecticides for, 942
  nocturnal
    on vegetables, 689
  obscure root
    insecticides for, 951, 956
  on flowers, 358
  on trees, 449
  on vegetables, 689
  pea (*Bruchus pisorum*), 760
    insecticides for, 961
    on peas, 760
  pecan (*Curculio caryae*), 664

rice
  in households, 818
  insecticides for, 947
root, 873, 874
  obscure
    insecticides for, 951, 956
    on *Rhododendron*, 586
    on trees, 472
  rough strawberry root (*Otiorhynchus rugosostriatus*)
    insecticides for, 780, 948, 963
  sassafras (*Odontopus calceatus*), 598
  strawberry root (*Otiorhynchus sulcatus*), 780
    insecticides for, 948, 963
  sweet potato (*Cylas formicarius elegantulus*), 782
  taxus (*Otiorhynchus sulcatus*), 604
    insecticide for, 953
  white pine (*Pissodes strobi*), 562
    insecticides for, 953
Western bean cutworms
  insecticide for, 963
Western poison oak. *See* Poison oak
Wet or marshy areas. *See* Water, weeds near
Wettable sulfur. *See* Sulfur
Wetting agent
  for dry root ball
    on trees, 452
  for houseplants, 225
Wetwood
  on *Morus*, 545
  on *Populus*, 567
  on *Salix*, 597
  on trees, 454
  on *Ulmus*, 610
Wheat oats. *See* Wild oats
Wheatgrass. *See* Quackgrass
Wheat
  rust on, 543
  wild garlic in, 314
Whirly Duster. *See* ORTHO Whirly Duster
Whirlybird Spreader. *See* ORTHO Whirlybird Spreader
White cedar. *See* Cypress family, *Chamaecyparis*
White clover. *See* Clover
White flag. *See* Spathiphyllum
White goosefoot (Common lamb's quarters), 848
White grubs. *See* Grubs
White iceplant

('*Delosperma* Alba')
  saline soils and, 999
White man's foot. *See* Plantain
White mold
  on beans, 701
  on lettuce, 751
White peach scale (*Pseudaulacaspis pentagona*)
  on peach; nectarine, 658
White pigweed (Common lamb's quarters), 848
White pine blight, 559
  See also Air pollution damage
White pine blister rust
  on currants; gooseberries, 559, 738
  on *Pinus*, 559
White pine weevil (*Pissodes strobi*), 562
  insecticides for, 953
White rust
  on spinach, 775
White-marked tussock moths
  insecticide for, 956
Whitebanded elm leafhopper (*Scaphoideus luteolus*), 608
Whiteflies, 454, 879
  ants and, 883
    on flowers, 356
    on fruit and nut trees, 620
  azalea (*Pealius azaleae*)
    on *Rhododendron*, 587
  citrus (*Dialeurodes citri*)
    on citrus, outdoors, 643
    insecticide for, 940
    on *Prunus*, 570
  diseases and, 880
  greenhouse. *See* Greenhouse whitefly
  insecticides for, 941, 946, 948, 951, 955, 956, 965–969
    on citrus, outdoors, 643
    insecticide for, 940
    on eggplant, 741
    on flowers
      ants and, 356
    on fruit and nut trees
      ants and, 620
      honeydew and, 621
      sooty mold and, 621
    on *Gardenia*, outdoors
      sooty mold and, 521
    on houseplants
      insecticides for, 950, 969
    on *Jasminum*, 530
      sooty mold and, 531
    on *Liriodendron*
      sooty mold and, 539
    on *Nerium*
      sooty mold and, 547
    on *Pyracantha*

sooty mold and, 573
  on trees, 448
    honeydew from, 454
    sooty mold and, 445
  on vegetables, 692
  rhododendron (*Dialeurodes chittendeni*), 587
  sooty mold and
    on *Gardenia*, outdoors, 521
    on *Jasminum*, 531
    on *Liriodendron*, 539
    on *Nerium*, 547
    on *Pyracantha*, 573
Whitefly & Mealybug Killer. *See* ORTHO Whitefly & Mealybug Killer
Whitetop (*Cardaria draba*)
  herbicides for, 974
Whorled chickweed, 851
Wild barley
  herbicides for, 974
Wild blackberry (*Rubus* species), 834
  herbicide for, 974
Wild carrot (*Daucus carota*), 835
  aster yellows and, 861
  herbicides for, 971, 974, 978
Wild chicory
  aster yellows and, 861
Wild garlic (*Allium vineale*)
  as weed, 831
  in lawns, 314
    herbicides for, 971, 978
  in pastures, 314
  in wheat, 314
Wild geranium
  herbicides for, 974, 977, 978
Wild iris (*Iris* species), 830
Wild lettuce. *See* Prickly lettuce
Wild lilac. *See* Ceanothus
Wild morning glory (*Convolvulus arvensis*), 849
  herbicides for, 974
  in lawns, 320
  in unplanted areas
    herbicides for, 977
  near sweet potato
    sweet potato weevils and, 782
Wild mustard (*Brassica kaber*), 834
Wild oats (*Avena fatua*), 830
  herbicide for, 976
Wild onion (*Allium canadense*)
  as weed, 831
  in lawns
    herbicides for, 971, 978
Wild opium. *See* Prickly

SOLVING PLANT PROBLEMS

Diagnosing problems in landscape plants requires careful observation of the problem plants and their environment. The key to an accurate diagnosis is knowing *how* to look for clues to a problem and the *type* of clues to look for. The checklist on the next page gives a step-by-step procedure for gathering clues and diagnosing the problem. It will help you to develop a case history, eliminate unlikely causes of the problem, and find the real cause.

HOW TO OBSERVE

Begin your observations by examining the plant from a distance. Note its general condition. Is the entire plant affected, or only a few stems, branches, or leaves? If the entire plant shows symptoms, this indicates that the cause will probably be found on the trunk or roots, or in the soil. Look for patterns and relationships with other plants. Is the problem confined to the sunny side of the plant? Is only the young growth affected? Are there many sick plants in one spot? Locate a part of the plant that shows obvious symptoms and take a closer look. Mottled or discolored leaves may indicate an insect or disease problem. A 5 to 15-power hand lens will allow you to see insects or fungus spores that are not easily visible to the naked eye.

If the initial inspection does not reveal any obvious reason for the symptoms, developing a case history for the plant may lead you to a less conspicuous cause of the problem. What has the weather been like recently? Has the temperature been fluctuating drastically? What kind of winter was it? An unusually dry, cold winter can cause dieback on trees and shrubs that may not become apparent until new growth begins in spring. Study the recent care of the plant. Has it been watered or fertilized regularly? All plants require fertilizer. Without regular feeding, their leaves turn yellow and growth is poor. (For information about fertilizers, see page 905.) When you are observing the area around the plant, be aware of changes in the environment. Construction around established plants can be very damaging, although symptoms of decline may not appear for several years. Drastic changes in light, such as moving a houseplant from a sunny window to a dark corner, or pruning a fruit tree heavily, may cause problems that appear many days later.

It may be necessary to dig into the plant or the soil to find the cause of the problem. If there is a hole in a stem, cut into it. Or slice a piece of bark off a wilting branch to determine whether the wood is discolored or healthy. The only way to learn about the roots of a sick plant is to dig up a small plant, or to carefully dig a hole to examine the roots of a large plant. The key to a root problem may be the soil. Investigate the drainage

This five-power hand lens is an important tool in diagnosing plant problems.

(see page 901), probe the soil with a soil auger to determine the soil depth and the type of soil, or test the pH of the soil with a pH kit. (For more information about testing the soil, see page 903.) Look at all sides of the question and explore each clue.

Particular types of plants are susceptible to typical problems at certain times of the year. For instance, cherries are usually plagued with fruit flies in the spring when the fruit is ripening, and snapdragons are likely to be infected with rust in spring and summer when the temperature is mild and moisture is present.

PUTTING IT ALL TOGETHER

When you're reading about a plant problem in *The Ortho Problem Solver*, read carefully. Every word and phrase is important for understanding the nature of the problem. "May" means that the symptom develops only sometimes. And certain phrases offer you clues about the problem, such as the time of year to expect it ("In spring to midsummer . . .") and where to look for the symptom (". . . on the undersides of the leaves").

Unfortunately, plants frequently develop more than one problem at a time. Plants have natural defenses against diseases and insects. But when the plant is weakened by one problem, its defenses are lowered and other problems are able to infect it. For instance, borers are often responsible for a tree's decline, but borers seldom are a serious problem on healthy trees. A borer problem may indicate another problem, such as a recent severe winter, or root rot.

When using *The Ortho Problem Solver*, look for the cause of your plant's problem under the listing for that plant, and under the general problem headings that begin each section. If you are not able to find the problem here, look through some of the Galleries near the end of the book; you may pick up a clue here that will indicate the general nature of your problem.

THE CHECKLIST

Use this checklist to develop a case history for the problem and to identify symptoms that will lead to an accurate diagnosis. Answer each question that pertains to your plant carefully and thoroughly. When looking for symptoms and answering questions about the condition of the plant, begin with the leaves, flowers, or fruit (unless it is apparent that the problem is elsewhere), because they are the easiest to examine. Once you've eliminated those possibilities, move down the plant to the stems, or branches and trunk. Inspect the roots after all other possibilities have been rejected.

INFORMATION ABOUT THE PLANT

LOOK AT THIS	WHAT TO LOOK FOR	LOOK AT THIS	WHAT TO LOOK FOR
Kind of plant	☐ What type of plant is it? ☐ Does it prefer moist or dry conditions? ☐ Can it tolerate cold or does it grow best in a warm climate? ☐ Does the plant grow best in acid or alkaline soil?	Condition of plant	☐ Are there any abnormal growths, discolorations, or injuries on the branches, stems, or trunk? ☐ Is there anything wrapped around and girdling the plant or nailed into the wood? ☐ Does the trunk have a normal flare at the base, or is it constricted or entering the ground straight like a pole?
Age	☐ Is the plant young and tender, or old and in a state of decline?		☐ If the entire plant is affected, what do the roots look like? Are they white and healthy, or are they discolored? (Use a trowel to dig around the roots of large plants; pull up small, sick plants to investigate the roots; and examine roots of container plants by removing the container. For instructions on examining roots of container plants, see page 914.) Is the bark brown and decayed?
Size	☐ Is the plant abnormally small for its age? ☐ How much has the plant grown in the last few years? ☐ Is the size of the trunk or stem in proportion to the number of branches?		
Time in present site	☐ Was the plant recently transplanted? ☐ Has it had time to become established, or is it still in a state of shock from transplanting? ☐ Is the plant much older than the housing development or buildings nearby?		☐ Have the roots remained in the soil ball, or have they grown into the surrounding soil? (For information about balled roots, see page 470.) ☐ Are there insects on the plant, or is there evidence of insects, such as holes, droppings, sap, or sawdustlike material?
Symptom development	☐ When were the symptoms first noticed? ☐ Have symptoms been developing for a long period of time, or have they appeared suddenly?		☐ What other symptoms are visible on the plant? ☐ Has the problem appeared in past years?
Condition of plant	☐ Is the entire plant affected, is the problem found on only one side of the plant, or are symptoms scattered throughout the plant? ☐ What part or parts of the plant are affected? ☐ Are all of the leaves affected, or only the leaves on a few branches? ☐ Are the leaves abnormal in size, color, shape, or texture? ☐ Do the flowers and fruit show symptoms?		

PLANT ENVIRONMENT

LOOK AT THIS	WHAT TO LOOK FOR	LOOK AT THIS	WHAT TO LOOK FOR
Location of property	☐ Is the property near a large body of fresh or salt water? ☐ Is the property located downwind from a factory, or is it in a large polluted urban area? ☐ Is the property part of a new housing development that was built on land fill?		about drainage, see page 901.) Does the soil have a sour smell? ☐ Is the soil hard and compacted? (For information about compaction, see page 900.) ☐ Has the soil eroded away from around the roots? (For information about erosion, see page 899.)
Location of plant	☐ Is the plant growing next to a building? If so, is the location sunny or shady? Is the wall of the building light in color? How intense is the reflected light? ☐ Has there been any construction, trenching, or grade change nearby within the past several years? ☐ Have there been any natural disturbances? ☐ How close is the plant to a road? Is the road de-iced in the winter? ☐ Is the plant growing over or near a gas, water, or sewer line, or next to power lines? ☐ Is the ground sloping or level?	Soil coverings	☐ Is there asphalt, cement, or other solid surface covering the soil around the plant? (For information about paving over roots, see page 469.) How close is it to the base of the plant? How long has it been there? ☐ Has the soil surface been mulched or covered with crushed rock? ☐ Was the mulch obtained from a reputable dealer? ☐ Are weeds or grass growing around the base of the plant? How thickly?
Relationship to other plants	☐ Are there large shade trees overhead? ☐ Is the plant growing in a lawn or groundcover? ☐ Are there plants growing nearby that are also affected? Do the same species show similar symptoms? Are unrelated plants affected? How close by are they?	Recent care	☐ Has the plant or surrounding plants been fertilized or watered recently? (For information about fertilizers and watering, see pages 904 and 906.) ☐ If fertilizer was used, was it applied according to label directions? (For information on how to read a fertilizer label, see page 905.) ☐ Has the plant or the area been treated with a fungicide or insecticide? (For information about how to spray and dust, see page 915.) ☐ Was the treatment for this problem or another one? ☐ Was the pesticide registered for use on the plant (is the plant listed on the product label)? ☐ Was the pesticide applied according to label directions? ☐ Did it rain right after spraying, so the spray was washed off? ☐ Did you repeat the spray if the label suggested it? ☐ Have weed killers (herbicides) or lawn weed and feeds been used in the area in the past year? How close by? (For information about applying herbicides, see page 915.) ☐ Did you spray on a windy day? ☐ Has the plant been pruned heavily, exposing shaded areas to full sun? ☐ Were stumps left after pruning, or was the bark damaged during the pruning process? (For information about pruning, see ORTHO's book *All About Pruning*.)
Weather	☐ Have you had unusual weather conditions recently (cold, hot, dry, wet, windy, snowy, etc.), or in the past few years?		
Microclimate	☐ What are the weather conditions in the immediate vicinity of the plant? ☐ Is the plant growing under something that prevents it from receiving moisture? ☐ How windy is the location? ☐ How much light is the plant receiving? Is it the optimum amount for the type of plant? (For information about supplying extra light to houseplants, see page 914.)		
Soil conditions	☐ What kind of soil is the plant growing in? Is it clayey, sandy, or loamy? (For information about heavy, sandy, and rocky soil, see pages 898 to 900.) ☐ How deep is the soil? (For information about shallow soil, see page 899.) Is there a layer of rock or hardpan beneath the topsoil? (For information about hardpan, see page 900.) ☐ What is the pH of the soil? (For information about testing the soil for pH, see page 903.) ☐ Does the soil drain well, or does the water remain on the surface after a heavy rain or irrigation? (For information		

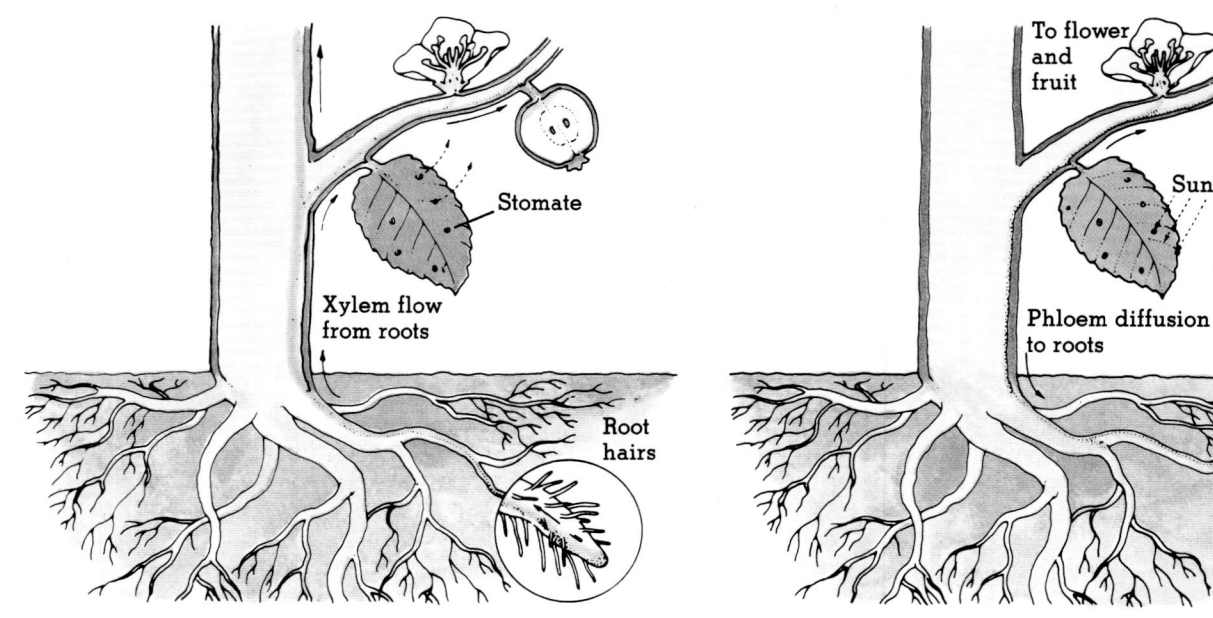

TRANSPORT

The transport system of a plant does many of the same jobs that the circulatory system does in a human being, but it is not called circulation because it does not go in a circle, as the human blood stream does. Plants have two transport systems, one carrying water and dissolved minerals from the roots to the top of the plant, and the other carrying sugars and other manufactured material from the leaves to all other parts of the plant.

Xylem flow: The part of a plant's transport system that carries water upward flows through a system of microscopic tubes called the *xylem* (pronounced ZYE-lem). In woody plants, the xylem is the outermost layer of wood. This wood, which is just under the bark, contains the xylem tubes. These tubes extend into the leaves and, through the leaf veins, into every part of the leaf. The xylem tubes end in the leaf tissue. Water leaves the xylem in the leaf tissue and evaporates through microscopic pores called *stomates* in the leaf surface.

Transpiration: This evaporation out of the stomates is called *transpiration*. Transpiration not only provides the power that moves water and nutrients into the top of the plant, but it also cools the leaf, just as evaporation cools a wet towel. Although the principles are different, you can think of transpiration as pulling water from the roots to the leaves just as soda is sucked through a drinking straw. Since plants can only transport nutrients that are dissolved in water, insoluble materials are not available to them.

Three main factors reduce xylem flow: dry soil, a sick root system, or a plugged or cut xylem system. Any of several diseases or injuries can cause these problems. If the xylem flow is reduced below a certain point, the leaves receive less nutrients than they need to sustain good health, and begin to show symptoms of nutrient deficiencies, usually by turning pale green or yellow, with the veins remaining green. If the xylem flow is reduced when the water demand is high — during hot weather — the leaves may wilt or scorch. This happens because the leaves lose water faster than it can be replaced.

Stomate control: Plants control transpiration by opening and closing their stomates. The stomates are shut at night. They open in the morning, but may shut down partially if the light is dim. Stomates also close if a leaf runs out of water. This usually happens before any sign of wilting is seen. If the weather is hot when the leaf runs out of water, and if the leaf is in the sun, it is very likely to overheat and burn. This is called *sunburn* or *scorch*, depending on the pattern of the burning.

Phloem flow: The part of the transport system that carries sugars and other manufactured material from the leaves to other parts of the plant is called the phloem (FLO-em). This system of tubes lies inside the bark. If you peel off some bark in the spring, the phloem is visible as the white part of the bark. Flow in the phloem is by diffusion, and is much slower than xylem flow. Sugars and other material manufactured in the leaves diffuse through the phloem to growing shoots, flowers, fruit, and roots. Since the roots are so large, most of the phloem flow in the trunk of a tree is downward.

PHOTOSYNTHESIS

Photosynthesis is a chemical reaction that locks up the sun's energy in the form of a chemical so that it can be used to support life. This reaction takes carbon dioxide from the air and combines it with water from the soil to make sugars. Photosynthesis takes place in the green parts of plants. The green pigment is called *chlorophyll*. It is chlorophyll that collects and focuses the energy in light to make sugar. Most photosynthesis takes place in leaves, in a layer of cells, called the *palisade layer*, near the upper surface of the leaf. Carbon dioxide enters the leaf through the stomates in the lower surface and enters the palisade cells, where it is combined with water to make sugar. As a by-product of this reaction, oxygen is released to the air. The sugars are then transported through the phloem to all parts of the plant, where they are burned to release their energy. All animals and humans depend on both the sugars and the oxygen produced by plants, so all life on earth depends on photosynthesis.

Light: Light is the source of energy that combines carbon dioxide and water to make sugar. The more light a plant receives, the more sugar it makes, the faster it grows, and the more flowers and fruit it produces. In dim light, a plant makes barely enough sugar to maintain its life. But in bright light, it makes a surplus that it uses for growth and reproduction.

Water stress: Carbon dioxide enters the leaves through the stomates. Since most plants can't store carbon dioxide, photosynthesis can take place only when the stomates are open. If a plant does not have enough water, it closes its stomates to avoid losing water it can't afford to lose. But when the stomates are closed, photosynthesis stops. One of the first effects of water stress is that photosynthesis — and growth — stops.

TOP GROWTH

Unlike human growth, which takes place in all parts of the body, plant growth occurs in only a few places, called the *growing points*. The growing points in a plant are in the tips of the roots and shoots, and just under the bark in woody plants.

Tip growth: The growing points in the tips of shoots and roots are composed of tiny bunches of cells that divide repeatedly, building the specialized organs of the plant but always remaining at the tip of the new growth. The new plant parts are tiny while they are in the growing point, but they are complete, with all the cells they will ever have. As the growing point moves beyond them, the new parts fill with water and swell, as a rubber raft does when it is blown up, until they reach their full size. But all the time they are expanding, no new cell division is taking place.

Buds: The growing point moves ahead, but a bud is left at the base of each leaf. A bud is a growing point that is, for the moment, dormant. On some plants, such as tomatoes, these *axillary buds* begin growing as soon as they are formed. Others, such as those on apple trees, remain dormant until the following spring. Then they all begin growing at once. Some of the buds never open by themselves, but can be made to open and begin growing by pinching off the growing point at the end of the branch they are on.

Stem growth: The other place a woody plant grows is under the bark. A sheet of cells, called the *cambium*, lies between the wood and the bark. These cells divide repeatedly just as those in the shoot and root tips do. As they divide, they produce xylem cells toward the center of the stem, and phloem cells toward the outside. When growth is fastest, in the spring, large xylem cells are made; as growth slows in the summer, smaller cells are made. The difference in the size of these cells makes up the annual rings visible in most wood.

Flowers and fruit: Flowers are produced by the growing point just as the leaves and stem are. Flowers begin as buds, which in some plants open immediately, and in others wait for the following spring. At the base of each flower is an *ovary*, an organ that will contain the seed, and in some plants, becomes the fruit.

ROOT GROWTH

TRUNK GROWTH

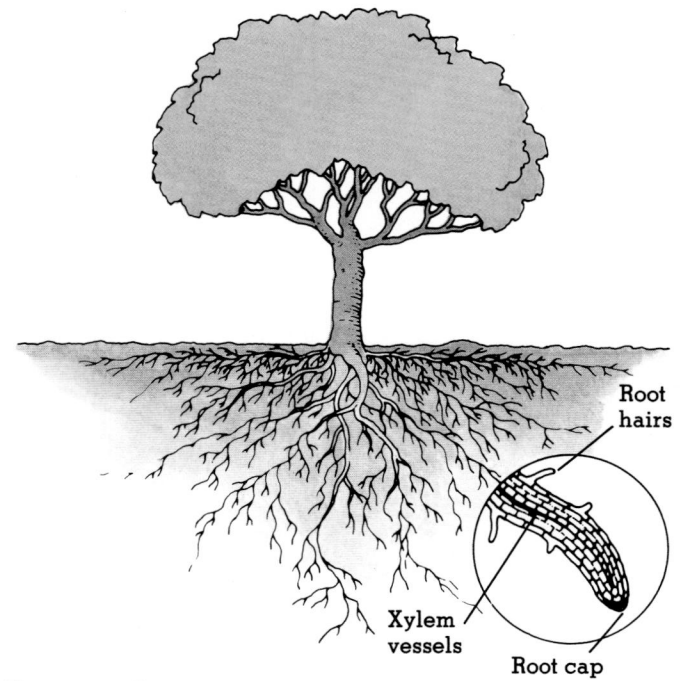

Root
hairs

Xylem
vessels

Root cap

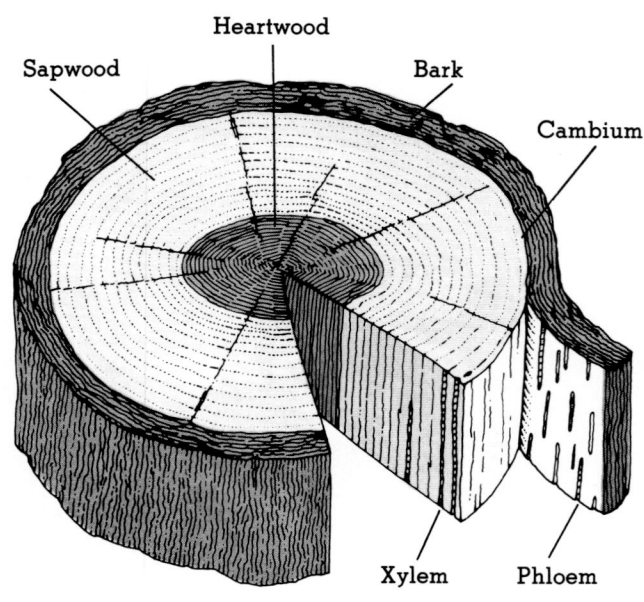

Heartwood

Sapwood

Bark

Cambium

Xylem

Phloem

ROOT GROWTH

Plants live in two distinctly different environments: the air and the soil. The root system of a plant "mines" the soil for water and nutrients, the raw materials used by the plant. These raw materials are transported through the stems to the leaves, where they are combined with carbon dioxide to make sugars and complex chemicals. These processed chemicals are then transported through the stems back to the roots, where they are used for growth.

Root tips: As the growing point at the end of the root moves through the soil it leaves behind a soft, white, threadlike root tip. Downy *root hairs* grow from the tip. Most of the absorbing of water and nutrients is done by the root tips. As the root ages it becomes yellow, then brown, and the root hairs disintegrate. By the time the root turns brown, it no longer absorbs very much water from the soil.

The root system: Roots need three things for vigorous growth: oxygen, water, and nutrients. Of these three, oxygen is the one most frequently in short supply. Because plants cannot transport oxygen, each part of the plant must absorb it directly from the air. Oxygen diffuses through the spaces between soil particles to reach the roots. Where roots find an abundance of these three necessities, they proliferate.

The root system of a plant is often thought of as extending through the soil about as far as the top growth does above the ground. But plants vary greatly in the extent of their root systems. Trees may have roots that extend dozens or even hundreds of feet beyond their top growth, especially if the soil is frequently dry. Also, the root system is often not symmetrical, but is more dense on the side that more frequently receives food or water.

Although some plants have very deep root systems, garden plants get most of their nutrients from the top foot of soil. For this reason, plants are sensitive to the condition of the surface of the soil. If it is paved over, or becomes compacted, the roots near the surface receive less oxygen and water, and may die.

TRUNK GROWTH

Growth of tree trunks and expansion of the stems of woody plants take place in the *cambium*, a layer of dividing cells just under the bark. As each cell in the cambium divides, one of the two new cells becomes either a xylem cell or a phloem cell, and the other remains a cambium cell and divides again.

Wood: As the newest xylem cells expand, they push the cambium layer a little farther away from the center of the tree. The new cells live for only a year or two; then they die and only their woody cell wall remains. This cell wall continues to function as a xylem tube for another year or two, then it becomes plugged with the detritus of life and ceases to function. By this time, the cell is deep in the wood of the tree, and is heavily packed with a rigid material called *lignin*, the material that gives stiffness and rigidity to wood.

Bark: The phloem cells that form in the cambium are pushed to the outside of the tree by their expansion and the expansion of the new xylem cells. Like the xylem cells, they transport nutrients for a couple of years, then die and dry out to become the bark of the tree. However, the green bark on young stems is composed of a living layer of cells called the *epidermis*. As the twig ages and expands, this living bark is replaced by the dead phloem cells.

Girdling: If the phloem and xylem are cut through in a ring around the trunk of a tree, the flow of water to the top of the tree is stopped, the leaves wilt, and the top of the plant dies. The roots may die, or they may resprout and grow a new top. If only the bark is cut through — by root weevils, for instance — water can still reach the top of the tree, and it does not wilt. But the flow of sugars and nutrients from the leaves to the roots has been stopped, and the roots slowly starve. As they cease functioning, the top also starves, inevitably killing the tree.

Bark wounds: Any wound in the bark of a tree trunk interrupts the flow of water and nutrients through the tree. If a spot is repeatedly wounded, as frequently happens when a lawn tree is hit with a lawnmower, the growth of the plant is slowed and it becomes stunted.

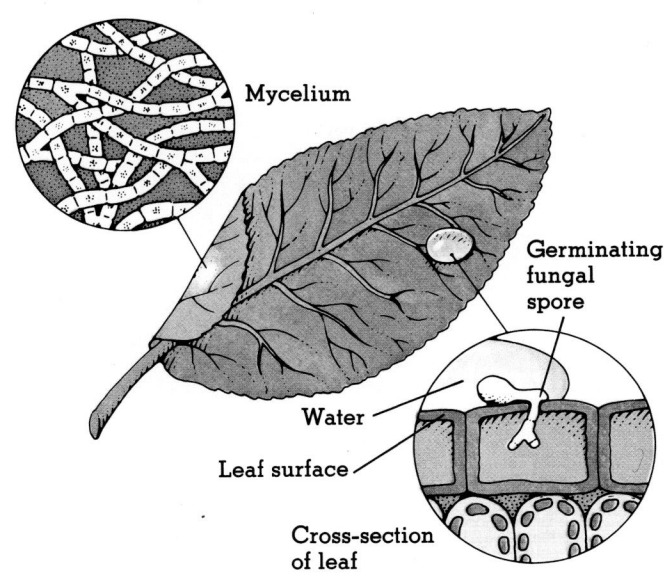

Mycelium

Germinating fungal spore

Water

Leaf surface

Cross-section of leaf

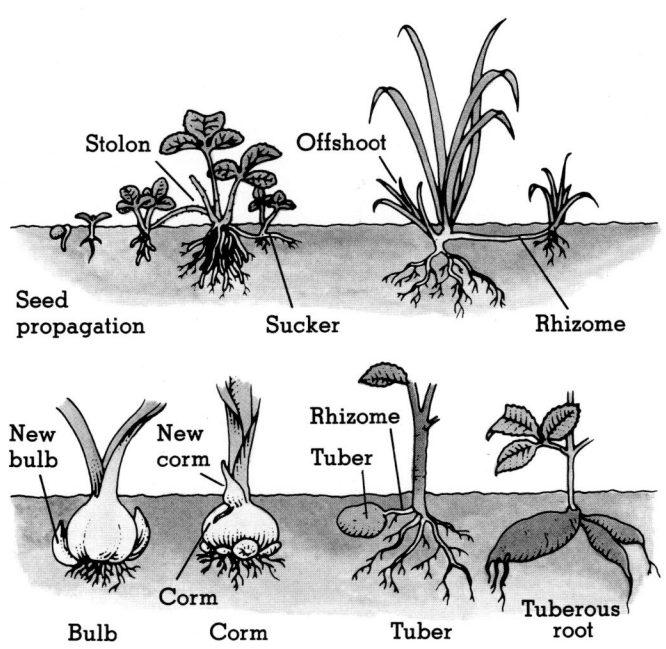

Stolon   Offshoot

Seed propagation   Sucker   Rhizome

New bulb   New corm   Rhizome   Tuber

Corm

Bulb   Corm   Tuber   Tuberous root

FUNGI

Fungi are primitive plants that do not contain chlorophyll and cannot make their own sugars as green plants do. Their structure is simple; most fungi are composed of a network of threads, which are sometimes bundled into cords. These threads and cords are called the *mycelium* (my-SEE-lee-um), and make up the body of the fungus. They are most easily seen as the fragile white threads that form under rotting leaves. Most fungi decompose dead plant matter into simpler chemicals. They are responsible for most of the decay of plant material in nature. But some fungi cause plant diseases by invading living plants. Fungus diseases spread in several ways, but three of these ways are most common: through the soil, by splashing water, and by the wind.

Soil-spread fungi: Fungi that live in the soil and attack plant roots are most commonly spread by moving soil or infected plants from one place to another. Soil-borne fungi are often brought to the garden initially on the roots of a transplant, then spread from one end of the garden to the other by irrigation water or cultivation.

Water-spread fungi: Other fungi depend on splashing water to spread their spores. Many of the fungi that cause leaf spots on trees and shrubs spend the winter as spores on the bark or on fallen leaves, then in the spring are washed to new leaves by splashing rain.

Wind-spread fungi: The third common way fungi spread is by dustlike spores that are carried by the wind to other plants. Many of these spores live for only a few hours or days after they are released into the air, so they must find suitable conditions for germination soon. For almost all such fungi, "suitable conditions" means a drop of water on a leaf surface. It takes a fungus spore from 4 to 8 hours to germinate and penetrate a leaf. If the drop of water in which it is growing dries out during this time, the spore dies. The notable exception to this need for a drop of water in which to germinate is powdery mildew (see page 445), the spores of which can germinate on a dry leaf. But even powdery mildew is more active in wet conditions.

HOW PLANTS SPREAD

Plants have two ways of propagating themselves: by seed, and by growing new plants from parts of the old one.

Seed propagation: Most plants make seeds, and some make vast numbers of them. Annual plants (those that live for only one growing season) depend on seeds to continue their species. They often put all their energy into ripening a crop of seeds. Annual weeds, such as crabgrass, usually make thousands of seeds per plant. It is important to kill these weeds before they make their seeds, or you will have the same job to do all over again the following year.

Offshoots: All other methods of propagation involve some form of growing new plants from parts of the old one. Offshoots are new plants that arise from the base of the old one. If allowed to continue, this will eventually lead to a dense bunch of plants. Offshoots can usually be broken or cut off and planted to make new plants.

Rhizomes and stolons: These horizontal stems form new plants at a distance from the mother plant. *Rhizomes* travel underground and form new plants where they near the surface. *Stolons* travel aboveground, and make new plants where they come in contact with the ground.

Suckers: The word *sucker* has two different but similar meanings. It refers to a stem that arises from the base of the trunk. It also refers to a plant that arises from the roots of the parent plant, often at some distance from the trunk. Plants that sucker freely, if left to their own devices, will form a thicket in a couple of years. The type of sucker that arises from a root is a whole plant, and can be removed and planted elsewhere.

Bulbs: Plants form a wide variety of underground food storage organs. Most of these organs remain dormant for part of the year, and then, because of the large amount of food stored in them, burst into vigorous growth. If the storage organ is formed from fleshy leaves, it is called a *bulb*. If it is formed from a vertical stem, it is called a *corm*. If it is formed from a rhizome, it is called a *tuber*. If it is formed from a root, it is called a *tuberous root*. When they are dormant, these organs can be moved to new locations, or stored before being replanted.

GLOSSARY

Abscission: A natural dropping of leaves, flowers, and other plant parts.

Acaricide: A chemical that kills spider mites and other types of mites. Acaricides are also known as miticides.

Acid soil: Soils with a pH below 7.0. Acid soils can cause problems when their pH is below 5.5. For more information about acid soils, see page 902.

Adventitious: Plant parts that form in unusual locations. For example, roots that grow from leaves or aboveground stems.

Aeration: To increase the amount of air space in the soil by tilling or otherwise loosening the soil.

Algae: Simple plants without visible structure that grow in wet locations. Some types of algae form a slippery black or green scum on wet soil, plants, walkways, and other surfaces.

Alkaline soil: Soil with a pH above 7.0. Alkaline soils slow the growth of many plants when their pH is above 8.0. For more information about alkaline soils, see page 902.

Annual plant: A plant that grows, flowers, produces seeds or fruit, and dies in a year or less. Many herbaceous flowers and vegetables are annual plants.

Axil: The location on a stem between the upper surface of a leaf or leafstalk and the stem from which is it growing.

Axillary buds: Buds that form in leaf axils.

Balled and burlapped plants: Trees and shrubs that are dug out of the ground with the intact soil ball surrounding the roots; the soil ball is then wrapped in burlap or plastic.

Bare-root plants: Trees and shrubs that are dug out of the ground and sold with their roots bare of soil. Roses and fruit trees are commonly sold in this manner. Bare-root plants are available in the winter.

Biennial plant: A plant that grows, flowers, produces seeds or fruit, and dies in two years. Some herbaceous flowers and vegetables are biennial. Most biennial plants produce foliage the first year and bloom the second year.

Bolting: Rapid development of flowers and seedheads in vegetables. Premature bolting may be stimulated by hot weather, drought, or lack of nutrients.

Bract: A modified leaf that is sometimes brightly colored, resembling a petal.

Bud: A condensed shoot consisting mainly of undeveloped tissue. Buds are often covered with scales, and develop into leaves, flowers, or both.

Callus: A mass of cells, often barklike in appearance, that forms over wounded plant tissue.

Cambium: A thin ring of tissue within the stem, branch, and trunk that continually forms nutrient and water-conducting vessels.

Canker: A discolored lesion that forms in stems, branches, or trunks as a result of infection. Cankers are often sunken, and may exude a thick sap. For more information about cankers, see page 868.

Chlorophyll: The green plant pigment that is necessary for photosynthesis.

Chlorosis: Yellowing of foliage due to a loss or breakdown of chlorophyll. Chlorosis may result from disease or infestation, poor growing conditions, or lack of nutrients.

Cold frame: A protective structure that uses the sun's energy to provide heat for plants. Plants may be grown in cold frames early in the spring before all danger of freezing is past.

Complete fertilizer: A fertilizer containing nitrogen, phosphorus, and potassium, the three nutrients in which plants are most commonly deficient.

Compost: Partially decomposed organic matter used to amend the soil. Compost is often made from grass clippings, leaves, and manure.

Conifers: Woody trees and shrubs that produce cones. Common conifers include pines, firs, spruces, junipers, redwood, and hemlocks.

Conks: Mushroomlike fruiting bodies of several different kinds of tree-decaying fungi.

Corm: A short, solid, enlarged, underground stem from which roots grow. Corms are food-storage organs. They contain one bud that will produce a new plant.

Dead-heading: The removal of old blossoms to encourage continued bloom or to improve the appearance of the plant.

Deciduous: Plants that shed all of their leaves annually, usually in the fall.

Defoliation: Leaf drop that often results from infection, infestation, or adverse environmental conditions.

Desiccation: Dehydration or loss of water.

Dormant: A state of rest and reduced metabolic activity in which plant tissues remain alive but do not grow.

Dormant oil: Oil sprayed on deciduous trees while they are dormant. Dormant oils are used to kill overwintering insects or insect eggs on plant bark.

Espalier: To train a plant (usually a tree or vine) along a railing or trellis so that the branches grow flat against the rail or trellis that supports them.

Evergreen: A plant that retains all or most of its foliage throughout the year.

Fasciation: An abnormal fusion of stems, leaves, or flowers, or the production of distorted growth. For more information about fasciation, see page 869.

Fertilizers: These substances contain plant nutrients. Fertilizers may be liquid or dry, and may be formulated in many different ways. For more information about fertilizers, see page 905.

Formulation: The form in which a compound may be produced. For example, a pesticide may be powdered, liquid, granular, or in an oil solution.

Frass: Sawdustlike insect excrement.

Fruiting body: A fungal structure that produces spores.

Fungicide: A chemical that kills fungi or prevents them from infecting healthy plant tissue.

Galls: Abnormal growths that form on plant roots, shoots, and leaves. Galls often result from infection or insect infestation. For more information about galls, see page 869.

Germination: The sprouting of seeds.

Girdle: Encircling of plant roots, stems, trunks, or branches resulting in a constriction of the plant part, or a reduction of water and nutrient flow through the girdled plant part.

Graft: To unite a stem or bud of one plant to a stem or root of another plant.

Gummosis: Oozing of plant sap, often from a plant wound or canker. Gummosis may occur as a result of infection or insect infestation.

Hardiness: The ability of a plant to withstand cold temperatures.

Hardening off: The process of plant adjustment to cold temperatures.

Heartwood: The inner core of wood inside a woody stem or trunk.

Herbaceous: Plants that are mainly soft and succulent, forming little or no woody tissue.

Herbicide: A chemical that kills or retards plant growth. Herbicides may kill the entire plant; or they may kill only the aboveground plant parts, leaving the roots alive.

Host: An organism that is parasitized by another organism, such as a plant that is infected by a fungus, or infested by an aphid.

Humidity: The amount of water vapor (moisture) in the air.

Hybrid: The offspring of two distinct plant species; a plant obtained by crossing two or more different species, subspecies, or varieties of plant. Hybrids are often made to produce a plant that has the best qualities of each parent.

Immune: A plant that is not susceptible to a disease or insect.

Infiltration (soil): The process by which water moves into the soil.

Insecticide: A chemical that kills insects.

Internode: The section of stem between two nodes.

Interveinal: Between the (leaf) veins. Interveinal yellowing, or *chlorosis*, refers to a discoloration occurring between the leaf veins.

Juvenile: An early growth phase differentiated from later growth by a distinctly different leaf shape, habit of growth, or other characteristics.

Larva: An immature stage through which some types of insects must pass before developing into adults. Caterpillars are the larvae of moths and butterflies, and grubs are the larvae of beetles. Larvae are typically wormlike in appearance.

Lateral bud: A bud forming along the side of a stem or branch rather than at the end.

Leaching: The removal of salts and soluble minerals from the soil by flushing the soil with water.

Leader: The main stems or trunk of a tree or shrub from which side stems or branches are produced.

Leaf margins: The edges of a leaf. Variations in the shape of leaf margins are used to help identify many plants and differentiate among them.

Leaf scar: The tiny scar left on a twig or stem after a leaf or leafstalk (petiole) drops off.

Leafstalk: A stalk that attaches a leaf to the stem; a petiole.

Lesion: A wound, discoloration, or scar caused by disease or injury.

Macronutrients: Nutrients required by plants for normal growth. Macronutrients such as nitrogen, phosphorus, and potassium are needed in large quantities by most plants.

Metamorphosis: Changes in body shape undergone by many insects as they develop from eggs into adults.

Microclimate: The environment immediately surrounding a plant; very localized climate conditions. Many different microclimates may occur at the same time in different areas of a garden.

Micronutrients: Nutrients required by plants for normal growth. Micronutrients (also called minor nutrients) such as iron, zinc, and manganese are needed in small quantities by most plants.

Mites: A group of tiny animals related to spiders, many of which feed on plants.

Mulch: A layer of organic or inorganic material on the soil surface. Mulches help to moderate the temperature of the soil surface, reduce loss of moisture from the soil, suppress weed growth, and reduce run-off. For more information about mulches, see page 918.

Mycelium: Microscopic fungal strands that form the major part of a fungal growth.

Nematode: Microscopic worms that live in the soil and feed on plant roots. Some nematodes feed on plant stems and leaves. For more information about nematodes, see page 862.

Node: The part of a stem where leaves and buds are attached.

Nymph: An immature stage through which some types of insects must pass before developing into adults. Nymphs usually resemble the adult form, but lack wings and cannot reproduce.

Oedema: Watery blisters or swellings that form on many herbaceous plants. These swellings may burst open, forming rust-colored lesions.

Organic matter: A substance derived from plant or animal material. For more information about organic matter, see page 918.

Ozone: A common air pollutant that may cause plant injury. For more information about ozone, see page 862.

Palisade cells: A layer of columnar cells located just beneath the upper surface of a leaf.

PAN (peroxyacetyl nitrate): A common air pollutant that may cause plant injury. For more information about PAN, see page 863.

Parasite: An organism that obtains its food from another living organism. Parasites live on or in their host.

Pathogen: An organism (such as a fungus, bacterium, or virus) capable of causing a disease.

Peat: Partially degraded vegetable matter found in marshy areas. Peat is commonly used as a soil amendment.

Perennial plant: A plant that lives for more than 2 years, often living for many years. Almost all woody plants and many herbaceous plants are perennials.

Permanent wilting point: The point of soil dryness at which plants can no longer obtain water from the soil. Once plants have reached the permanent wilting point they do not recover, even if they are supplied with water.

Pesticide: A chemical used to kill an organism considered a pest.

Petiole: A stalk that attaches the leaf to the stem; a leafstalk.

pH: A measure of the acidity or alkalinity of a substance; a measure of the relative concentration of hydrogen ions and hydroxyl ions. For more information about pH, see page 902.

Phloem: Nutrient-conducting vessels found throughout the plant. Phloem vessels transport nutrients produced in the foliage down through the stems, branches, or trunk to the roots.

Photosynthesis: The process by which plants use the sun's light to produce food (carbohydrates).

Plant disease: Any condition that impairs the normal functioning and metabolism of a plant. A plant disease may be caused by a fungus, bacterium, or virus, or by an environmental factor such as lack of nutrients or sunburn.

Propagation: Means of reproducing plants, such as by seeds, cuttings, budding, or grafting.

Protectant: A chemical that protects a plant from infection or infestation.

Pupa: An immature resting stage through which some types of insects must pass before becoming adults.

Resistant plant: A plant that can overcome the effects of a disease or insect infestation, or a plant that is not very susceptible to attack by a pathogen.

Rhizome: An underground stem from which roots grow. Rhizomes function as storage organs, and may be divided to produce new plants.

Rootstock: 1. The roots and crown, or roots, crown, and trunk of a plant upon which another plant is grafted. 2. The crown and roots of some types of perennial herbaceous plants, also known as *rhizomes*.

Root zone: The volume of soil that contains the roots of a plant.

Runners: Aboveground, trailing stems that form roots at their nodes when they make contact with moist soil.

Sapwood: The outer cylinder of wood in a trunk between the heartwood and the bark.

Saturated soil: Soil that is so wet that all the air pores in the soil are filled with water.

Sclerotium: A compact mass of fungal strands (mycelium) that functions as a resting stage for a fungus. Sclerotia are usually brown or black, and can usually withstand adverse conditions.

Slow-release fertilizers: Fertilizers that release their nutrients into the soil slowly and evenly, over a long period of time.

Soil heaving: Expansion and contraction of soil during periods of freezing and thawing. Plant roots may be sheared off, or plants may be lifted out of the ground during soil heaving.

Solubility: The degree to which a compound will dissolve in water. Compounds with high solubility will dissolve in water more readily than compounds with low solubility.

Soluble fertilizers: Fertilizers that dissolve easily in water and are immediately available for plant use.

Spore: A microscopic structure produced by fungi, mosses, and ferns that can germinate to form a new plant or a different stage of the same plant.

Spur: A short lateral branch bearing buds that will develop into flowers and then into fruit.

Stomates: Tiny pores located mainly on the undersides of leaves. Oxygen, carbon dioxide, water vapor, and other gasses move in and out of the leaf through these pores.

Sucker: A shoot or stem that grows from an underground plant part.

Surfactant: A substance added to a spray that increases its wetting and spreading properties. Surfactants are also called *wetting agents* or *spreader-stickers*.

Systemic pesticide: A pesticide that is absorbed into part or all of the plant tissue.

Tender plant: A plant that cannot tolerate freezing temperatures.

Terminal bud: A bud at the end of a stem or branch.

Toxin: A poisonous substance produced by a plant or an animal.

Translocation: The movement of a compound from one location in a plant to another.

Transpiration: Evaporation of water from plant tissue to the atmosphere. Transpiration occurs mainly through the stomates in the leaves.

Vascular system: The system of tissues (phloem and xylem) that conducts nutrients and water throughout the plant.

Vein clearing: A lightening or total loss of color of leaf veins. Vein clearing often results from plant infection or nutrient deficiency.

Vernalization: A cooling period required by many plants in order to germinate, grow, or flower properly.

Vigor: The health of a plant. A vigorous plant grows rapidly and produces healthy, normal amounts of foliage and flowers. A nonvigorous plant grows slowly, if at all, and produces stunted, sparse growth.

Wetting agent: A substance that changes the surface tension of water or other liquid, causing it to wet a repellent surface more thoroughly. Wetting agents are often used when spraying pesticides on waxy or fuzzy foliage.

Xylem: Water-conducting vessels found throughout the plant. Xylem vessels transport water and minerals from the roots upward through the plant.

THE
ORTHO
PROBLEM
SOLVER

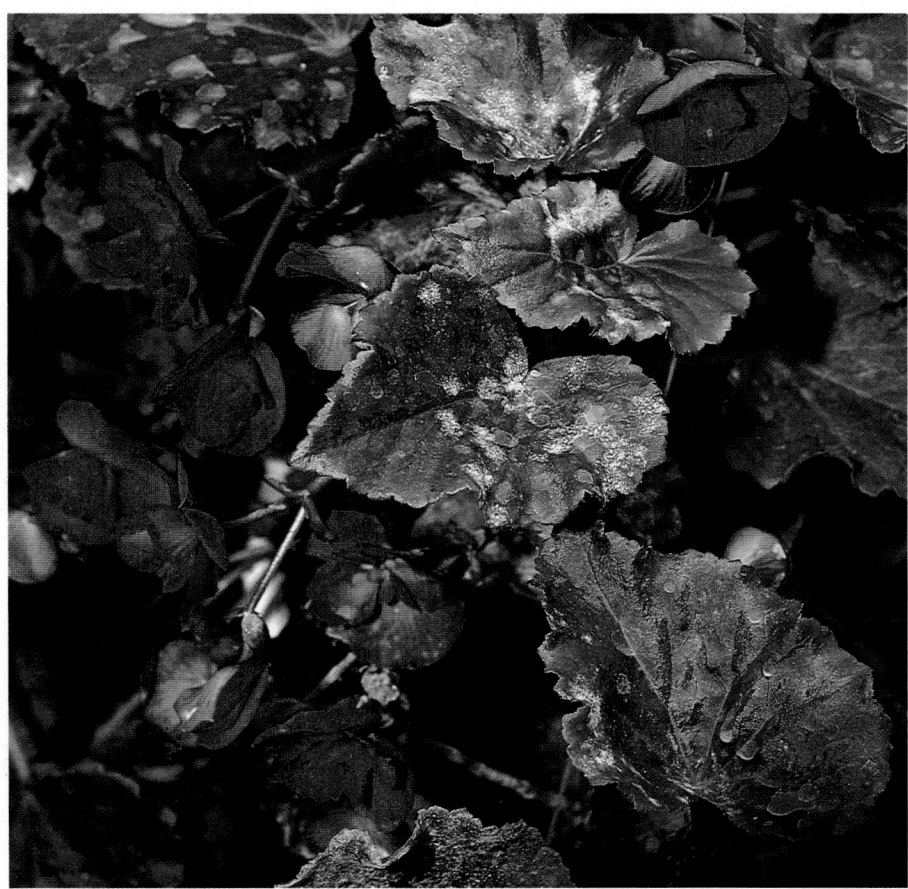

On the next 9 pages, you will find some of the most common problems of any houseplant. Look for your plant's problem on these pages. If you don't find it there, look up your plant in the alphabetical section beginning on page 230, where you will find some of the most common problems of specific houseplants. If you don't know the name of your houseplant, find it in the Houseplant Identifier on the next page.

PLANTS IN THE HOME

To us, our homes may be comfortable and inviting, but to our plants, they constitute harsh and uncomfortable environments. The pots we use to contain our plants limit root space. We often underwater and underfertilize — or overwater and over-fertilize. And the light levels in our home vary from full sunlight to very dim light. A plant in the wrong place can burn from too much light or starve for lack of light. All these inhospitable conditions put stress on plants. Nevertheless, house-plants can be easy to grow; all you need is an understanding of these stress factors and the ability to minimize them or compensate for them.

Most problems with houseplants are probably caused by the fact that they are confined to containers. In nature, plant roots are free to range over a wide and deep area. If the surface layers of soil dry out, deep roots can still supply water to the plant. But plants in containers are at the mercy of their caretakers. If some-body doesn't water them, the plants may suffer frequently from lack of water.

Knowing when and how to water houseplants is a skill — an easily learned skill, but one that must be learned. For instructions for watering plants in containers, see page 913.

The second environmental stress suffered frequently by houseplants is caused by low levels of light. Each species of plant is adapted to a certain level of light. Most houseplants are adapted to tropical forests, where the light level is low, so they are able to tolerate the dim (for a plant) light in our homes. But most of the locations in our homes are too dim for any plant. Picking the right location in your house for each plant is part of the skill of raising houseplants. In general, plants raised for their foliage tolerate lower levels of light than plants raised for their flowers or fruit, and foliage plants with green leaves need less light than those with brightly colored leaves.

If the light is too bright for a plant, its leaves bleach to a gray or yellow color, and may burn. If the light is too dim, the plant grows very slowly, doesn't flower, and may lean toward the light. Move your plants around until you find the location that suits them best.

Although our houses create difficult environments for plants, they also protect them from extremes of weather and many of the diseases and insects that prey on outdoor plants. In the following pages, you will see that a few insects or diseases are repeated over and over. This is because insect and disease problems of houseplants are less varied and less severe than with outdoor plants — although you may not think so if you are fighting off an invasion of mealybugs. If you learn to recognize insect, disease, and environmental stress problems as soon as they appear, and deal with them immediately, your houseplants will reward you with beauty and health.

Above: Powdery mildew on a begonia. See page 237.
Left: A healthy episcia. See page 258.

HOUSEPLANT IDENTIFIER

Chamaedorea 277 Bamboo palm	*Chamaedorea* 277 Parlor palm	*Chrysalidocarpus* 277 Areca palm	*Howea* 277 Kentia palm	*Rhapis* 277 Lady palm	*Cycas* 252 Sago palm
Dizygotheca 257 False aralia	*Asparagus* 235 Asparagus fern	*Nephrolepis* 261 Boston fern	*Pellaea* 261 Button fern	*Hedera* 268 Ivy	*Cissus* 245 Grape ivy
Ficus 263 Creeping fig	*Ficus* 263 Mistletoe fig	*Fittonia* 265 Nerve plant	*Cyclamen* 253 Cyclamen	*Peperomia* 281 Watermelon peperomia	*Peperomia* 281 'Emerald-Ripple'
Episcia 258 Flame violet	*Maranta* 273 Red-veined prayer plant	*Maranta* 273 Prayer plant	*Iresine* 272 Bloodleaf	*Begonia* 237 Rex begonia	*Begonia* 237 Rex begonia
Syngonium 287 Nephthytis	*Philodendron* 282 Philodendron	*Plectranthus* 284 Swedish ivy	*Hoya* 271 Wax plant	*Tolmiea* 289 Piggyback plant	*Cineraria* 245 Cineraria
Pelargonium 279 Geranium	*Aeschynanthus* 231 Lipstick plant	*Columnea* 251 Column flower	*Gynura* 267 Purple passion vine	*Coleus* 249 Coleus	*Tradescantia* 291 Wandering Jew

Achimenes 230 Rainbow flower	*Saintpaulia* 284 African violet	*Streptocarpus* 288 Cape primrose	*Sinningia* 286 Gloxinia	*Dracaena* 257 Dracaena	*Fatsia* 234 Aralia
Ficus lyrata 263 Fiddle-leaf fig	*Ficus elastica* 263 Rubber plant	*Brassaia* 239 Schefflera	*Monstera* 274 Split-leaf philodendron	*Asplenium* 261 Bird's-nest fern	*Spathiphyllum* 287 Spathe flower
Anthurium 232 Anthurium	*Aglaonema* 231 Chinese evergreen	*Dieffenbachia* 254 Dumb cane	*Billbergia* 240 Bromeliad	*Aphelandra* 233 Zebra plant	*Codiaeum* 248 Croton
Polypodium 261 Rabbit's-foot fern	*Platycerium* 261 Staghorn fern	*Ficus* 263 Weeping fig	*Araucaria* 234 Norfolk Island pine	*Kalanchoe* 272 Kalanchoe	*Zygocactus* 291 Christmas cactus
Opuntia 241 Cactus	*Haworthia* 267 Haworthia	*Chlorophytum* 245 Spider plant	*Chrysanthemum* 243 Chrysanthemum	*Euphorbia* 259 Poinsettia	*Cordyline* 251 Ti plant
Clerodendrum 247 Glory-bower	*Gardenia* 266 Gardenia	*Hippeastrum* 270 Amaryllis	*Paphiopedilum* 275 Orchid	*Capsicum* 242 Ornamental pepper	*Clivia* 247 Kaffir lily

PROBLEMS COMMON TO MANY HOUSEPLANTS

Dry poinsettia.

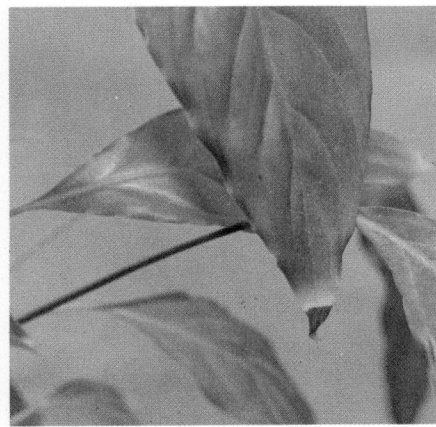

Salt damage to a spathiphyllum.

PROBLEM: Leaves are small, and plants fail to grow well and may be stunted. Plant parts or whole plants wilt. Margins of leaves or tips of leaves of narrowleafed plants may dry and become brittle but still retain a dull green color. Bleached areas may occur between the veins. Such tissues may die and remain bleached, or turn tan or brown. Plants may die.

ANALYSIS: Too little water
Plants need water in order to grow. Besides making up most of the plant tissue, water is also the medium that carries nutrients into the plant, so a plant that is frequently short of water is also short of nutrients. Water also cools the leaves as it evaporates from them. If a leaf has no water to evaporate, it may overheat in the sun and burn. If plants wilt and then are given water, sometimes the margins or tips of the leaves will have completely wilted and will not recover. If this occurs, the margins or tips will die and become dry and brittle, but will retain a dull green color.

SOLUTION: Water plants immediately and thoroughly. If the soil is completely dry, add a bit of wetting agent (available at garden centers) or soak the entire pot in water for a couple of hours. Follow the watering guidelines given on page 913.

PROBLEM: The leaf margins of plants with broad leaves or the leaf tips of plants with long, narrow leaves turn brown and die. This browning occurs on the older leaves first, but when the condition is severe, new leaves may also be affected. On some plants, the older leaves may yellow and die.

ANALYSIS: Salt damage
Salt damage is a common problem on container-grown plants. Soluble salts are picked up by the roots and accumulate in the margins and tips of the leaves. When concentrations become high enough, the tissues are killed. Salts can accumulate from water or from the use of fertilizers; or they may be present in the soil used in potting. Salts accumulate faster and do more harm if plants are not watered thoroughly. Water that is high in lime does not cause as much salt damage as water that is high in other salts.

SOLUTION: Leach excess salts from the soil by flushing with water. Water thoroughly at least three times in a row, letting the water drain from the pot each time. This is most easily done if the pot is placed in the bathtub, a basin, or outside in the shade to drain. If you use a saucer to catch the water, empty the saucer after each watering. If the plant is too large to lift, empty the saucer with a turkey baster. Never let a plant stand in the drainage water. To prevent further salt accumulation, follow the watering instructions on page 913. For a list of plants sensitive to salts, see page 990.

PROBLEMS COMMON TO MANY HOUSEPLANTS

Sunburn on dieffenbachia.

Overwatering damage to schefflera.

Nitrogen-deficient Swedish ivy.

PROBLEM: Dead tan or brown patches develop on leaves that are exposed to direct sunlight. Or leaf tissue may lighten or turn gray. In some cases, the plant remains green but growth is stunted. Damage is most severe when the plant is allowed to dry out.

ANALYSIS: Sunburn or bleaching
Sunburn or bleaching occurs when a plant is exposed to more intense sunlight than it can tolerate. Plants vary widely in their ability to tolerate direct sunlight; some plants can tolerate full sunlight, while others will burn or bleach if exposed to any direct sun. Bleaching occurs when light and heat break down chlorophyll (green plant pigment), causing a lightening or graying of the damaged leaf tissue. On more sensitive plants, or when light and heat increase in intensity, damage is more severe, and plant tissues die. Sometimes tissue inside the leaf is damaged, but outer symptoms do not develop. Instead, growth is stunted. Plants are more susceptible to bleaching and sunburn when they are allowed to dry out, because the normal cooling effect that results when water evaporates from leaves is reduced. Plants that are grown in low light conditions burn very easily if they are suddenly moved to a sunny location.

SOLUTION: Move plants that cannot tolerate direct sun to a shaded spot. Or cut down the light intensity by closing the curtains when the plant is exposed to direct sun. Prune off badly damaged leaves, or trim away damaged leaf areas to improve the plant's appearance. Keep plants well watered. For more information about watering, see page 913.

PROBLEM: Plants fail to grow and may wilt. Leaves lose their glossiness and may become light green or yellow. The roots are brown and soft, and do not have white tips. (For instructions on examining the rootball, see page 914.) The soil in the bottom of the pot may be very wet and have a foul odor. Plants may die.

ANALYSIS: Too much water or poor drainage
Although plants need water to live, the roots also need air. If the soil is kept too wet, the air spaces are filled with water, and the roots are weakened and may die. Weakened plants are more susceptible to root-rotting fungi, which wet soils favor. Plants with diseased roots do not absorb as much water as they did when they were healthy, so the soil remains wet. If roots are damaged or diseased, they cannot pick up water and nutrients needed for plant growth.

SOLUTION: Discard severely wilted plants and those without white root tips. Do not water less severely affected plants until the soil is barely moist. Then follow the instructions on watering given on page 913. Prevent the problem by using a light soil with good drainage.

PROBLEM: The oldest leaves — usually the lower leaves — turn yellow and may drop. Yellowing starts at the leaf margins and progresses inward without producing a distinct pattern. The yellowing may progress upward until only the newest leaves remain green. Growth is slow, new leaves are small, and the whole plant may be stunted.

ANALYSIS: Nitrogen deficiency
Nitrogen is a nutrient that is used by the plant in many ways, including the production of chlorophyll (the green pigment in leaves and stems). Nitrogen is used in large amounts by the plant. When there is not enough nitrogen for the entire plant, it is taken from the older leaves for use in new growth. Nitrogen is easily leached from soil during regular watering. Of all the plant nutrients, it is the one most likely to be lacking in the soil.

SOLUTION: Spray the leaves with Ra-Pid-Gro Plant Food for a quick response. Fertilize houseplants with ORTHO House Plant Food 5–10–5, ORTHO Fish Emulsion Fertilizer 5–1–1, or ORTHO Ortho-Gro Liquid Plant Food 12–6–6. Add the fertilizer at regular intervals, as recommended on the label.

Iron-deficient piggyback plant.

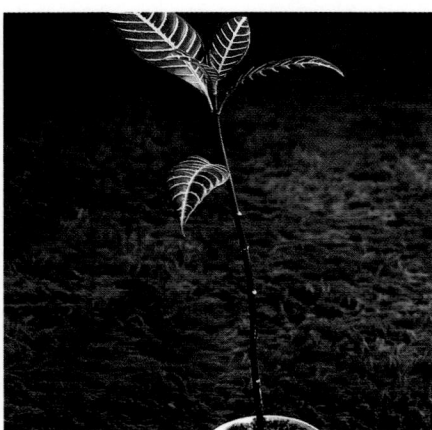

Leaf drop on zebra plant.

Botrytis on fuchsia.

PROBLEM: Newer leaves turn yellow at the margins. The yellowing progresses inward, so that in the advanced stages the last tissues to lose their green color are those immediately surrounding the veins. This condition may gradually work down the plant a short distance, but only rarely is the whole plant affected. The plant may be stunted.

ANALYSIS: Iron deficiency
This is a common problem with acid-loving plants, which grow best in soil with a pH between 5.5 and 6.5. (For more information on soil acidity, see page 902.) The yellowing is due to a deficiency of iron in the plant. The soil is seldom deficient in iron. However, when the soil pH is 7.0 or higher, iron is found in a less soluble form that is not available to some plants. Plants use iron in the formation of the green pigment (chlorophyll) in the leaves. When it is lacking, the new leaves become yellow.

SOLUTION: Spray the foliage with ORTHO Greenol Liquid Iron 6.13% and apply it to the soil in the pot to correct iron deficiency. Use acid-forming fertilizers, such as ORTHO Azalea, Camellia & Rhododendron Food 5–10–10. When planting or transplanting acid-loving plants, use an acidic soil mix that contains at least 50 percent peat moss. Use a minimum amount of lime or dolomite in the soil mix.

PROBLEM: Plants fail to grow well. Leaves may be lighter green and smaller than normal. Lobes and splits that are normal in leaves may fail to develop. Lower leaves may yellow and drop. Stems and leaf stalks may elongate and be spindly and weak. Plants grow toward a light source. Flowering plants fail to produce flowers, and plants with colorful foliage become pale. Variegated plants may lose their variegation and become green.

ANALYSIS: Insufficient light
Plants use light as a source of energy, and grow slowly in light that is too dim for their needs. If most of the available light is coming from one direction, stems and leaves bend in that direction. If the light is much too dim, plants grow poorly. Although foliage plants generally need less light than plants grown for their flowers or fruit, plants with colorful foliage need abundant light.

SOLUTION: Move the plant to a brighter location. The brightest spots in most homes are the sills of windows that face east, west, or south, or locations as close to a window as possible. To avoid sunburn on sensitive plants, close lightweight curtains when the sun shines directly on the plant. If not enough light is available, supply extra light. (For information about supplemental light for plant growth, see page 914.) Move plants from one location to another until you find a place where they grow well. For a list of plants that tolerate dim light, see page 990.

PROBLEM: Brown spots and blotches appear on the leaves and possibly on the stems. Spots on flowers may be white, tan, brown, or purple, or the natural color of the flower may be intensified. If stems are infected they may rot, causing the top part of the plant to topple and die. Under humid conditions, the infected portions may be covered with a fuzzy gray or brown growth.

ANALYSIS: Botrytis gray mold
This disease is caused by any of several fungi (*Botrytis* species) that are common on dead or decaying matter. Spores cannot infect healthy, active tissues but invade only weakened, dead, or inactive tissues. Once the fungus is established, it can move into healthy tissues, rotting them. The fungus is favored by high humidity and cool temperatures (below 65°F). Under these conditions, the infected tissues may be covered with the vegetative strands and spores of the fungus, giving them a gray or brown, fuzzy appearance.

SOLUTION: Remove all diseased plant material. Remove dead plant material, particularly old flowers. Avoid getting water on the foliage and flowers, and avoid growing plants under crowded conditions. Provide good air circulation around plants. If the problem remains, grow plants in warmer areas.

PROBLEMS COMMON TO MANY HOUSEPLANTS

Spider mite damage to prayer plant.

Brown scale on fern stalk (twice life size).

Aphids on ivy (half life size).

PROBLEM: Leaves are stippled, yellowing, and dirty. Leaves may dry out and drop. There may be webbing over flower buds, between leaves, or on the lower surfaces of the leaves. To determine if a plant is infested wth mites, hold a sheet of white paper underneath an affected leaf and tap the leaf sharply. Minute green, red, or yellow specks the size of pepper grains will drop to the paper and begin to crawl around. The pests are easily seen against the white background.

ANALYSIS: Spider mites
These mites, related to spiders, are major pests of many garden, greenhouse, and houseplants. They cause damage by sucking sap from the undersides of the leaves. As a result of feeding, the green pigment disappears, producing the stippled appearance. Under warm, dry conditions, which favor mites, they can build up to tremendous numbers.

SOLUTION: Spray infested plants with ORTHO Houseplant Insect Control or ORTHO Whitefly & Mealybug Killer. (For instructions on spraying houseplants, see page 915.) Plants need to be sprayed weekly for several weeks to kill the mites as they hatch from the eggs. To avoid introducing mites into your house, inspect newly purchased plants carefully.

PROBLEM: Nodes, stems, and leaves are covered with white, cottony, cushion-like masses or brown crusty bumps or clusters of somewhat flattened reddish, gray, or brown scaly bumps. The bumps can be scraped or picked off easily. Leaves turn yellow and may drop. A shiny or sticky material may cover the leaves.

ANALYSIS: Scale insects
Several different types of scale insects attack houseplants. Some types can infest many different plants. Scales hatch from eggs. The young, called *crawlers*, are small (about $\frac{1}{10}$ inch), soft-bodied, and move about on the plant and to other plants. After moving about for a short time, they insert their mouthparts into the plant, withdrawing the sap. The legs usually atrophy, and the scales remain in the same area for the rest of their lives. Some develop a soft covering over their bodies, while others develop a hard covering. Some species of scales are unable to digest fully all the sugar in the plant sap, and excrete the excess in a fluid called honeydew, which may cover the leaves or drip onto surfaces below.

SOLUTION: Spray with ORTHO Whitefly & Mealybug Killer or ORTHO House Plant Insect Control. Spraying is more effective against the crawlers than against adults. Repeated applications may be necessary.

PROBLEM: Leaves are curling, discolored, and reduced in size. A shiny or sticky substance may coat the leaves. Tiny ($\frac{1}{8}$ inch) nonwinged, green soft-bodied insects cluster on the buds, young stems, and leaves.

ANALYSIS: Aphids
Aphids do little damage in small numbers. However, they are extremely prolific and populations can rapidly build up to damaging numbers on houseplants. Damage occurs when the aphid sucks the juices from the leaves. The aphid is unable to digest fully all the sugar in the plant sap and excretes the excess in a fluid called honeydew, which often drops onto leaves below. Any furniture below the plants may be coated with honeydew.

SOLUTION: Use ORTHO Indoor Plant Insect Spray, ORTHO House Plant Insect Control, or ORTHO Whitefly & Mealybug Killer. Check the labels for directions and for plants on which these products can be used. Spray houseplants according to directions given on page 915.

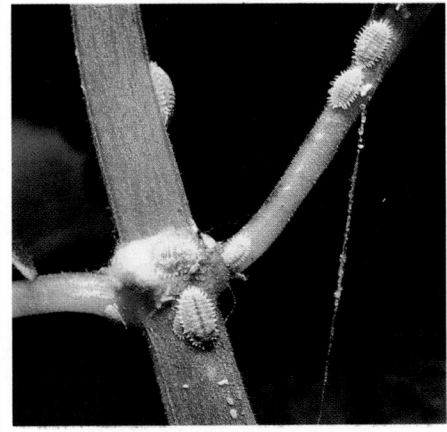

Citrus mealybugs on coleus (twice life size).

Longtailed mealybugs (twice life size).

Greenhouse whiteflies (twice life size).

PROBLEM: White cottony or waxy insects are on the undersides of the leaves, on the stems, and particularly in the crotches or where leaves are attached. The insects tend to congregate, giving a cottony appearance. Cottony masses that contain eggs of the insects may also be present. A sticky substance may cover the leaves or drop onto surfaces below the plant. Infested plants are unsightly, do not grow well, and may die if severely infested.

ANALYSIS: Mealybugs

Mealybugs are one of the more serious problems of houseplants. There are many different types of mealybugs and virtually all houseplants are attacked by one or more of these insects. Female mealybugs have soft bodies that appear to have segments, and are covered with waxy secretions, giving them a cottony appearance. The female may produce live young or may deposit hundreds of yellow to orange eggs in white cottony egg sacs. The young insects, called *nymphs*, crawl about the same plant or to nearby plants. Males do no damage because they do not feed and are short-lived. Female mealybugs feed by sucking sap from the plant. They take in more than they can use, and excrete the excess in a sugary fluid called honeydew, which coats the leaves and may drop to surfaces below the plant. This fluid may mar finished furniture.

SOLUTION: Control of mealybugs on houseplants is difficult. Spray with ORTHO Whitefly and Mealybug Killer or ORTHO House Plant Insect Control. Make sure your plant is listed on the product label. For information on spraying houseplants, see page 915. Repeat applications at intervals of two weeks and continue for a little while after it appears that the mealybugs have been controlled. The waxy coverings on the insects and on the egg sacs, and the tendency of the insects to group together, protect them from insecticides. If only a few mealybugs are present, wipe them off with a damp cloth, or use cotton swabs dipped in rubbing alcohol. Carefully check all parts of the plant to make sure all insects are removed. Search for egg sacs under the rims or bottoms of pots, in cracks or on the undersides of shelves, and on brackets or hangers. Wipe off any sacs; they are a constant source of new insects. Discard severely infested plants, and avoid taking cuttings from such plants. The growing area should be thoroughly cleaned with soapy water before starting new plants. Be on a constant vigil for mealybugs, and start control measures immediately if they appear. Inspect new plants thoroughly before putting them in the house.

PROBLEM: Tiny, winged insects $1/12$ inch long feed mainly on the undersides of the leaves. The insects are covered with white waxy powder. When the plant is touched, insects flutter rapidly around it. Leaves may be mottled and yellow.

ANALYSIS: Greenhouse whitefly (*Trialeurodes vaporariorum*)

This insect is a common pest of many houseplants. The 4-winged adult lays eggs on the undersides of leaves. The larvae are the size of a pinhead, flat, oval, and semitransparent, with white waxy filaments radiating from the body. They feed for about a month before changing to the adult form. Both the larval and adult forms suck sap from the leaves. The larvae are more damaging because they feed more heavily. Adults and larvae cannot fully digest all the sugar in the sap, and excrete the excess in a fluid called honeydew, which coats the leaves and may drop from the plant.

SOLUTION: Spray with ORTHO Whitefly & Mealybug Killer or ORTHO House Plant Insect Control. Make sure your plant is listed on the product label. For instructions on spraying houseplants, see page 915. Spray weekly as long as the problem continues. Remove heavily infested leaves.

Fungus gnat and larva (10 times life size).

PROBLEMS OF INDIVIDUAL HOUSEPLANTS

PROBLEM: Small (up to ⅛ inch), slender, dark insects fly around when plants are disturbed. They frequently run across the foliage and soil, and may also be found on windows. Roots may be damaged, and seedlings may die.

ANALYSIS: Fungus gnats
These insects are small flies that do little damage but are unpleasant if present in large numbers. They lay their eggs in soil that contains organic material. After a week the eggs hatch, and the larvae crawl through the upper layer of the soil. The larvae are white, ¼ inch long, and have black heads. They feed on fungi that grow on organic matter. The larvae usually do not damage plants but, when present in large numbers, may feed on the roots of some plants, killing very young seedlings. The larvae feed for about two weeks before maturing into adults. There can be many generations in one year.

SOLUTION: Spray with an insecticide containing *diazinon* according to the instructions on page 915. Repeated applications may be necessary. Keep doors and windows closed to keep fungus gnats out.

This section is arranged alphabetically by the botanical name of each plant. If you are not familiar with the botanical name of your plant, check the index on page 224.

Water spots.

PROBLEM: Small, light tan to reddish brown, somewhat angular spots appear on the upper surfaces of the leaves. These spots are scattered, and are found most frequently on the older leaves.

ANALYSIS: Water spots
Members of the African violet family, including achimenes, are very sensitive to rapid temperature changes. This most commonly occurs when cold tap water contacts the leaves during watering. If chilling occurs in the presence of light, the chlorophyll (the green pigment in plants) is broken down. In this plant family, all of the chlorophyll is found in a single layer of cells near the upper leaf surface. If the chlorophyll is broken down, the green color disappears. In achimenes, the leaf tissue of different varieties varies in color, but these colors are masked by the green chlorophyll. When the chlorophyll disappears, the underlying color of the tissue becomes apparent.

SOLUTION: Avoid wetting the leaves when watering achimenes. Or use tepid water, which will not spot the leaves.

Achimenes cultural information
Light: Needs bright light
Water: When the soil surface is moist but not wet

AESCHYNANTHUS (LIPSTICK PLANT) — AGLAONEMA (CHINESE EVERGREEN)

Water spots.

Root rot.

Mealybugs (half life size).

PROBLEM: Small tan to brown spots appear on the upper surfaces of the leaves. Spots are not found on the newest leaves.

ANALYSIS: Water spots
Members of the African violet family, including lipstick plant, are very sensitive to rapid temperature changes. Water spots occur most commonly when cold water is splashed on the leaves while the plant is being watered. If this happens in the presence of light, the green pigment (chlorophyll) is destroyed. In this plant family, all of the chlorophyll in the leaves is found in a single layer of cells near the upper surface. If the chlorophyll in that layer is broken down, the green color disappears and the color of the underlying leaf tissue is exposed.

SOLUTION: The spots cannot be removed. Pick off unsightly leaves. Prevent new spots by being careful not to splash water on the leaves when watering. Or use tepid water, which will not spot the leaves.

Aeschynanthus cultural information
Light: Needs bright light
Water: When the soil is moist but not wet

PROBLEM: Plants fail to grow, and the lower leaves may turn yellow, wilt, and die. An area of dead tissue may be found on the main stem just at the soil line. Many of the roots are brown, mushy, and easily detached. For information on inspecting roots, see page 914. Infected plants may die.

ANALYSIS: Root and stem rot
This plant disease is caused by any of several soil-dwelling fungi. *Rhizoctonia solani* may attack portions of the main stem and form brown, sunken areas. The fungus may girdle the stem, causing the portion above to die. *Rhizoctonia* and *Pythium* species may attack the roots, turning them brown and mushy, with dark tips. If the roots are severely damaged or killed, they cannot supply the plant with moisture and nutrients.

SOLUTION: Grow plants in a well-drained soil mix. For information on soil mixes, see page 913. Give adequate water, as described on page 913, but do not overwater. If stem or root rot occurs and the top of the plant is still vigorous, cut it off above the diseased area and root it according to the instructions on page 914. Discard the roots of diseased plants, and the soil in which they grew. Wash pots thoroughly, and soak them in a mixture of 1 part household bleach to 9 parts water for 30 minutes. Rinse with plain water and dry thoroughly before reusing.

PROBLEM: Oval, white insects up to ¼ inch long cluster in white, cottony masses on leaves, stems, and in the crotches where branches or leaves are attached. A sticky material may coat the leaves. Leaves may be spotted or deformed. When the condition is severe, leaves and plants may wither and die.

ANALYSIS: Mealybugs
Several species of this common insect feed on Chinese evergreen. Mealybugs damage plants by sucking sap, causing leaf distortion and death. The adult female mealybug may produce live young, or may lay eggs in a white fluffy mass of wax. The immature mealybugs, called *nymphs*, crawl all over the plant and onto nearby plants. Soon after they begin to feed, they produce white waxy filaments that cover their bodies, giving them a cottony appearance. As they mature, they become less mobile. Mealybugs cannot digest all the sugar in the sap and excrete the excess in a fluid called honeydew, which coats the leaves and may drop onto furniture below the plant.

SOLUTION: Spray infested plants with an insecticide containing *diazinon*. For instructions on spraying houseplants, see page 915. Where practical, wipe mealybugs off the plant with a damp cloth or with cotton swabs dipped in alcohol. Avoid bringing mealybugs into the house by carefully inspecting new plants. For additional information on mealybugs, see page 229.

Aglaonema cultural information
Light: Tolerates dim light
Water: When the soil just below the surface is barely moist

ANTHURIUM

Mealybugs (twice life size).

Spider mites (life size).

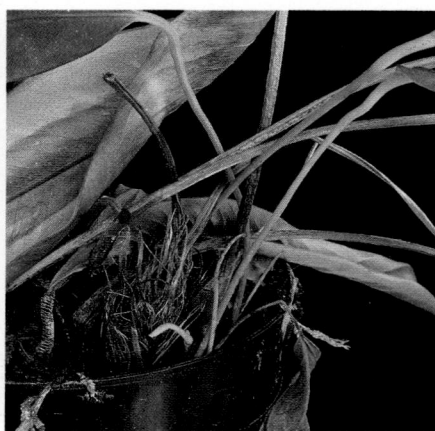

Root rot.

PROBLEM: Oval, white insects up to ¼ inch long cluster in white, cottony masses on leaves, stems, and in the crotches where the leaves are attached. A sticky material may coat the leaves. Leaves may be spotted or deformed. When the condition is severe, leaves and plants may wither and die.

ANALYSIS: Mealybugs
Several species of this common insect feed on anthurium. Mealybugs damage plants by sucking sap, causing leaf distortion and death. The adult female mealybug may produce live young, or may lay eggs in a white fluffy mass of wax. The immature mealybugs, called *nymphs*, crawl all over the plant and onto nearby plants. Soon after they begin to feed, they produce white waxy filaments that cover their bodies, giving them a cottony appearance. As they mature, they become less mobile. Mealybugs cannot digest all the sugar in the sap and excrete the excess in a fluid called honeydew, which coats the leaves and may drop onto furniture below the plant.

SOLUTION: Spray infested plants with an insecticide containing *diazinon*. (For instructions on spraying houseplants, see page 915.) Where practical, wipe mealybugs off the plant with a damp cloth or with cotton swabs dipped in alcohol. Inspect the pot, including the bottom, for mealybug egg masses. Wipe these off. Avoid bringing mealybugs into the house by carefully inspecting new plants. For additional information on mealybugs, see page 229.

PROBLEM: Leaves are stippled, yellow, and dirty; they may dry out and drop. There may be webbing between leaves or on the lower surfaces of the leaves. To determine if a plant is infested with mites, hold a sheet of white paper underneath an affected plant and tap the leaves sharply. Minute green, red, or yellow specks the size of pepper grains will drop to the paper and begin to crawl around. The pests are easily seen against the white background.

ANALYSIS: Spider mites
These mites, related to spiders, are major pests of many garden and houseplants, including anthurium. They cause damage by sucking sap from the undersides of the leaves. As a result of this feeding the green pigment (chlorophyll) disappears, causing the stippled appearance. Under warm, dry conditions, which favor mites, they can build up to tremendous numbers.

SOLUTION: Spray infested plants with ORTHO House Plant Insect Spray. (For instructions on spraying houseplants, see page 915.) Plants need to be sprayed weekly for several weeks to kill the mites as they hatch. To avoid introducing mites, inspect new plants carefully.

Anthurium cultural information
Light: Needs bright light
Water: When the soil surface is moist but not wet

PROBLEM: Plants fail to grow. Leaves or the whole plant may wilt and die. Examination of the rootball (as described in page 914) shows the roots are brown and mushy. When the disease is severe, all of the roots are rotted, and the plant can be lifted easily from the soil.

ANALYSIS: Root rot
This disease is caused by soil-dwelling fungi (*Pythium* species or *Rhizoctonia solani*) that are favored by wet, poorly drained soils. Anthuriums grow best with excellent drainage; although they need lots of water, the soil mix should drain quickly.

SOLUTION: Grow anthuriums in potting mixes that drain quickly. For information on soil mixes, see page 913. Do not keep the soil too wet, and never let plants stand in drainage water. Fertilize plants regularly while they are actively growing. Discard dead plants and the soil in which they grew.

APHELANDRA (ZEBRA PLANT)

Sunburn.

Salt damage.

Mealybugs (half life size).

PROBLEM: Leaves that are exposed to sunlight become yellow between the veins, and may die and turn brown. The brown areas may have a silver cast. If the condition is severe, the dead areas may coalesce and large areas may be affected.

ANALYSIS: Sunburn
Sunburn on aphelandra is caused by exposure to too much light. As a result, the tissues lose their green color between the veins, and may die and turn brown. Plants that are allowed to dry out are more susceptible to sunburn than those that are given adequate water.

SOLUTION: Avoid growing aphelandra in direct sunlight. Do not allow the soil to dry out.

Aphelandra cultural information
Light: Needs bright light
Water: When the soil surface is moist but not wet

PROBLEM: Margins of older leaves die and turn brown. The brown tissues are brittle. When the condition is severe, all leaves may have dead margins. Tissue adjacent to the dead margins of older leaves may turn yellow.

ANALYSIS: Salt damage
Aphelandra is sensitive to excess salts. Soluble salts are picked up by the roots and accumulate in the leaf margins, where concentrations may be high enough to kill the tissue. Salts can accumulate from water or from the use of fertilizers, or they may be present in the soil used in potting. Salts accumulate more rapidly and do more harm if the plant is not watered thoroughly.

SOLUTION: Leach excess salts from the soil by flushing with water. Water the plant at least 3 times, letting the water drain each time. This is done most easily in a bathtub or laundry sink, or outside. Always water aphelandra from the top of the pot. Enough water should be added at each watering that some of the water drains through the pot. Empty the saucer after the pot has finished draining. If the plant is too large to handle easily, use a turkey baster to remove the drainage water. For additional watering instructions, see page 913.

PROBLEM: Oval, white insects up to ¼ inch long cluster in white, cottony masses on leaves, stems, and in the crotches where the leaves are attached. A sticky material may coat the leaves. Leaves may be spotted or deformed. When the condition is severe, leaves and plants may wither and die.

ANALYSIS: Mealybugs
Several species of this common insect feed on zebra plants. Mealybugs damage plants by sucking sap, causing leaf distortion and death. The adult female mealybug may produce live young, or may lay eggs in a white fluffy mass of wax. The immature mealybugs, called *nymphs,* crawl all over the plant and onto nearby plants. Soon after they begin to feed, they produce white waxy filaments that cover their bodies, giving them a cottony appearance. As they mature, they become less mobile. Mealybugs cannot digest all the sugar in the sap and excrete the excess in a fluid called honeydew, which coats the leaves and may drop onto furniture below the plant.

SOLUTION: Spray infested plants with ORTHO Whitefly & Mealybug Killer or ORTHO House Plant Insect Control. (For instructions on spraying houseplants, see page 915.) Where practical, wipe mealybugs off the plant with a damp cloth or with cotton swabs dipped in alcohol. Inspect the pot, including the bottom, for mealybug masses. Wipe these off. Avoid bringing mealybugs into the house by carefully inspecting new plants. For additional information on mealybugs, see page 229.

ARALIA (FATSIA)

Scale (half life size).

PROBLEM: Stems and leaves are covered with white, cottony, cushionlike masses or brown crusty bumps. The bumps can be scraped or picked off easily. Leaves turn yellow and may drop. A shiny or sticky material may cover leaves and stems.

ANALYSIS: Scale insects
Several different types of scale insects attack aralia. Some types can infest many different plants. Scales hatch from eggs. The young, called *crawlers*, are small (about 1/10 inch), soft-bodied, and move about on the plant and onto other plants. After moving about for a short time, they insert their mouthparts into the plant, feeding on the sap. The legs disappear, and the scales remain in the same place for the rest of their lives. Some develop a soft covering, others a hard covering. Some species of scales are unable to digest fully all the sugar in the plant sap and excrete the excess in a fluid called honeydew, which may cover the leaves or drip onto surfaces below.

SOLUTION: Spray infested plants indoors with ORTHO Whitefly & Mealybug Killer or ORTHO House Plant Insect Control; or take the plants outside and spray them with ORTHO Isotox Insect Killer according to the directions on the label. Spraying is more effective against the crawlers than against the adults. Repeated applications may be necessary. For additional information on spraying houseplants, see page 915.

Aralia cultural information
Light: Needs medium light
Water: When the soil just below the surface is barely moist

Mealybugs (half life size).

PROBLEM: Oval, white insects up to 1/4 inch long cluster in white, cottony masses on leaves, stems, and in the crotches where branches or leaves are attached. A sticky material may coat the leaves. Leaves may be spotted or deformed. When the condition is severe, leaves and plants may wither and die.

ANALYSIS: Mealybugs
Several species of this common insect feed on aralia. Mealybugs damage plants by sucking sap, causing leaf distortion and death. The adult female mealybug may produce live young, or may lay eggs in a white fluffy mass of wax. The immature mealybugs, called *nymphs*, crawl all over the plant and onto nearby plants. Soon after they begin to feed, they produce white waxy filaments that cover their bodies, giving them a cottony appearance. As they mature, they become less mobile. Mealybugs cannot digest all the sugar in the sap and excrete the excess in a fluid called honeydew, which coats the leaves and may drop onto furniture below the plant.

SOLUTION: Spray infested plants indoors with ORTHO Whitefly & Mealybug Killer or ORTHO House Plant Insect Control; or take the plants outside and spray them with ORTHO Isotox Insect Killer. (For instructions on spraying houseplants, see page 915.) Where practical, wipe mealybugs off the plant with a damp cloth or with cotton swabs dipped in alcohol. Inspect the pot, including the bottom, for mealybug egg masses. Wipe these off. Avoid bringing mealybugs into the house by carefully inspecting new plants. For additional information on mealybugs, see page 229.

ARAUCARIA (NORFOLK ISLAND PINE)

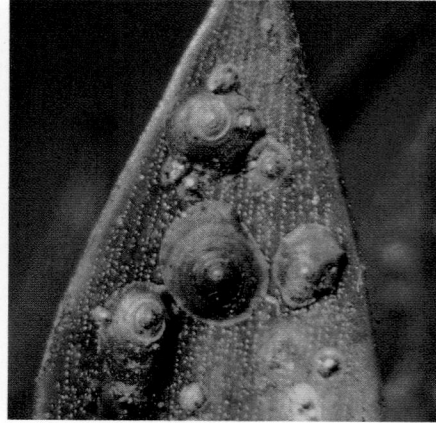

Scale (4 times life size).

PROBLEM: Stems and needles are covered with white, cottony, cushionlike masses or brown crusty bumps. The bumps can be scraped or picked off easily. Needles turn yellow and may drop. A shiny or sticky material may cover leaves and stems.

ANALYSIS: Scale insects
Several different types of scale insects attack Norfolk Island pine. Some types can infest many different plants. Scales hatch from eggs. The young, called *crawlers*, are small (about 1/10 inch), soft-bodied, and move about on the plant and onto other plants. After moving about for a short time, they insert their mouthparts into the plant, feeding on the sap. The legs disappear, and the scales remain in the same place for the rest of their lives. Some develop a soft covering, others a hard covering. Some species of scales are unable to digest fully all the sugar in the plant sap and excrete the excess in a fluid called honeydew, which may cover the leaves or drip onto surfaces below.

SOLUTION: Spray infested plants with an insecticide containing *malathion*. Spraying is more effective against the crawlers than against the adults. Repeated applications may be necessary. For additional information on spraying houseplants, see page 915.

Araucaria cultural information
Light: Tolerates dim light
Water: When the soil just below the surface is barely moist

ASPARAGUS (ASPARAGUS FERN)

Mealybug (twice life size).

Weak stems.

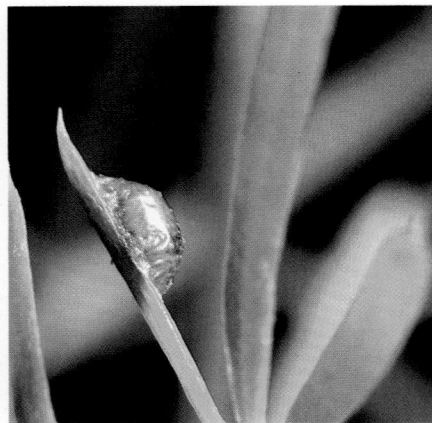

Scale (3 times life size).

PROBLEM: Oval, white insects up to ¼ inch long cluster in white, cottony masses on needles, stems, and in the crotches where the branches are attached. A sticky material may coat the needles. Growth may be deformed. When the condition is severe, plants may die.

ANALYSIS: Mealybugs
Several species of this common insect feed on Norfolk Island pine. Mealybugs damage plants by sucking sap, causing leaf distortion and death. The adult female mealybug may produce live young, or may lay eggs in a white fluffy mass of wax. The immature mealybugs, called *nymphs*, crawl all over the plant and onto nearby plants. Soon after they begin to feed, they produce white waxy filaments that cover their bodies, giving them a cottony appearance. As they mature, they become less mobile. Mealybugs cannot digest all the sugar in the plant sap and excrete the excess in a fluid called honeydew, which coats the plant and may drop onto furniture below.

SOLUTION: Spray infested plants with an insecticide containing *malathion*. (For instructions on spraying houseplants, see page 915.) Where practical, wipe mealybugs off the plant with a damp cloth or with cotton swabs dipped in alcohol. Inspect the pot, including the bottom, for mealybug egg masses. Wipe these off. Avoid bringing mealybugs into the house by carefully inspecting new plants. For additional information on mealybugs, see page 229.

PROBLEM: Leaves (which in asparagus are needlelike) turn pale green or yellow, beginning with the older leaves and progressing toward the tip of the stem. Yellow leaves may drop. Stems may be elongated and weak; sometimes they bend toward the light. Stems in the center of the plant may die and turn tan or brown.

ANALYSIS: Insufficient light
Plants use light as a source of energy, and grow slowly in light that is too dim for their needs. If most of the available light comes from one direction, the stems and leaves bend in that direction. If the light is much too dim, the plant has little energy and grows poorly. Although foliage plants generally need less light than plants grown for their flowers or fruit, asparagus fern has a relatively high need for light.

SOLUTION: Move the plant to a brighter location. Asparagus fern will tolerate direct sun if it is kept well watered. But if it is allowed to become dry while in direct sunlight, it will sunburn. (For more information on sunburn, see page 226.) If a brighter location is not available, provide supplemental lighting as described on page 914. If you wish to grow a houseplant in a dim location, select a plant that is tolerant of dim light from the list on page 990.

PROBLEM: Stems and leaves are covered with white, cottony, cushionlike masses or brown crusty bumps. The bumps can be scraped or picked off easily. Leaves turn yellow and may drop. A shiny or sticky material may cover leaves and stems.

ANALYSIS: Scale insects
Several different types of scale insects attack asparagus fern. Some types can infest many different plants. Scales hatch from eggs. The young, called *crawlers*, are small (about ¹⁄₁₀ inch), soft-bodied, and move about on the plant and onto other plants. After moving about for a short time, they insert their mouthparts into the plant, feeding on the sap. The legs disappear, and the scales remain in the same place for the rest of their lives. Some develop a soft covering, others a hard covering. Some species of scales are unable to digest fully all the sugar in the plant sap and excrete the excess in a fluid called honeydew, which may cover the leaves or drip onto surfaces below.

SOLUTION: Spray with ORTHO Whitefly & Mealybug Killer or ORTHO House Plant Insect Control. Spraying is more effective against the crawlers than against the adults. Repeated applications may be necessary. For additional information on spraying houseplants, see page 915.

Asparagus cultural information
Light: Needs bright light
Water: When the soil just below the surface is dry

AVOCADO

Mealybugs (life size).

Greenhouse whiteflies (life size).

Mealybugs (half life size).

PROBLEM: Oval, white insects up to ¼ inch long cluster in white, cottony masses on leaves, stems, and in the crotches where the leaves are attached. A sticky material may coat the leaves. Leaves may be spotted or deformed. When the condition is severe, leaves and plants may wither and die.

ANALYSIS: Mealybugs
Several species of this common insect feed on asparagus fern. Mealybugs damage plants by sucking sap, causing leaf distortion and death. The adult female mealybug may produce live young, or may lay eggs in a white fluffy mass of wax. The immature mealybugs, called *nymphs*, crawl all over the plant and onto nearby plants. Soon after they begin to feed, they produce white waxy filaments that cover their bodies, giving them a cottony appearance. As they mature, they become less mobile. Mealybugs cannot digest all the sugar in the sap and excrete the excess in a fluid called honeydew, which coats the leaves and may drop onto furniture below the plant.

SOLUTION: Spray infested plants with ORTHO Whitefly & Mealybug Killer or ORTHO House Plant Insect Control. (For instructions on spraying houseplants, see page 915.) Where practical, wipe mealybugs off the plant with a damp cloth or with cotton swabs dipped in alcohol. Inspect the pot, including the bottom, for mealybug egg masses. Wipe these off. Avoid bringing mealybugs into the house by carefully inspecting new plants. For additional information on mealybugs, see page 229.

PROBLEM: Tiny, winged insects 1/12 inch long feed on the undersides of the leaves. The insects are covered with white waxy powder. When the plant is touched, insects flutter rapidly around it. Leaves may be mottled and yellowing.

ANALYSIS: Greenhouse whitefly (*Trialeurodes vaporariorum*)
This insect is a common pest of avocado. The 4-winged adult lays eggs on the undersides of leaves. The larvae are the size of a pinhead, flat, oval, immobile, and semitransparent, with radiating white waxy filaments. In about a month, they change to the winged adult form. The larvae are more damaging because they suck more sap from the plants than do the adults. They cannot digest all the sugar in the sap they remove, and excrete the excess in a sugary material called honeydew, which coats the leaves and may drop from the plant onto furniture below.

SOLUTION: Spray with ORTHO House Plant Insect Spray. Spray weekly as long as the problem continues. Remove heavily infested leaves. If only a few leaves are infested, wipe off larvae with a damp cloth.

PROBLEM: Oval, white insects up to ¼ inch long cluster in white, cottony masses on leaves, stems, and in the crotches where branches or leaves are attached. A sticky material may coat the leaves. Leaves may be spotted or deformed. When the condition is severe, leaves and plants may wither and die.

ANALYSIS: Mealybugs
Several species of this common insect feed on avocado plants. Mealybugs damage plants by sucking sap, causing leaf distortion and death. The adult female mealybug may produce live young, or may lay eggs in a white fluffy mass of wax. The immature mealybugs, called *nymphs*, crawl all over the plant and onto nearby plants. Soon after they begin to feed, they produce white waxy filaments that cover their bodies, giving them a cottony appearance. As they mature, they become less mobile. Mealybugs cannot digest all the sugar in the sap and excrete the excess in a fluid called honeydew, which coats the leaves and may drop onto furniture below the plant.

SOLUTION: Spray infested plants with an insecticide containing *malathion*. Where practical, wipe mealybugs off the plant with a damp cloth or with cotton swabs dipped in alcohol. Inspect the pot, including the bottom, for mealybug egg masses. Wipe these off. Avoid bringing mealybugs into the house by carefully inspecting new plants. For additional information on mealybugs, see page 229.

Avocado cultural information
Light: Needs bright light
Water: When the soil just below the surface is barely moist

BEGONIA

Sparse growth.

Powdery mildew.

Mealybugs (half life size).

PROBLEM: Leaves fade to light green. In variegated varieties, the colors in the leaves become lighter and less intense. Stems become elongated and weak. Lower leaves may yellow and drop. Flowering varieties stop producing flowers.

ANALYSIS: Insufficient light
Plants use light as a source of energy, and grow slowly in light that is too dim for their needs. If most of the available light is coming from one direction, the stems and leaves bend in that direction. If the light is much too dim, the plant has little energy and grows poorly. Plants grown for their brightly colored leaves — or for their flowers — have a relatively high need for light.

SOLUTION: Move the plant to a brighter location, such as a lightly curtained sunny window. If a brighter location is not available, provide supplemental lighting as described on page 914. If you wish to grow a houseplant in a dim location, select a plant that is tolerant of dim light from the list on page 990.

PROBLEM: White powdery patches appear on the leaves, stems, and flowers. Leaves may be covered with the powdery growth. This material usually appears first on older leaves and on the upper surfaces of the leaves. Tissue under the powdery growth may turn yellow or brown. Sometimes such leaves drop from the plant.

ANALYSIS: Powdery mildew
Powdery mildew on begonia is caused by a fungus (*Erysiphe cichoracearum*). The powdery patches on begonia are composed of fungus strands and spores. These spores are carried by air currents and are capable of infecting leaves, stems, and flowers of the same or nearby plants. The disease is favored by dim light and warm days with cool nights. Older leaves are more susceptible than new leaves. Plants in dry soil are more susceptible. Severe infections cause yellowing, browning, and leaf drop.

SOLUTION: Spray with a fungicide containing *dinocap*, *cycloheximide*, or *wettable sulfur*. For instructions on spraying houseplants, see page 915. Remove infected leaves. Move plants to locations with more light. Keep plants out of cool drafts and in rooms with temperatures as even as possible.

Begonia cultural information
Light: Needs bright light
Water: When the soil just below the surface is barely moist

PROBLEM: Oval, white insects up to $\frac{1}{4}$ inch long cluster in white, cottony masses on leaves, stems, and in the crotches where the leaves are attached. A sticky material may coat the leaves. Leaves may be spotted or deformed. When the condition is severe, leaves and plants may wither and die.

ANALYSIS: Mealybugs
Several species of this common insect feed on begonias. Mealybugs damage plants by sucking sap, causing leaf distortion and death. The adult female mealybug may produce live young, or may lay eggs in a white fluffy mass of wax. The immature mealybugs, called *nymphs*, crawl all over the plant and onto nearby plants. Soon after they begin to feed, they produce white waxy filaments that cover their bodies, giving them a cottony appearance. As they mature, they become less mobile. Mealybugs cannot digest all the sugar in the sap and excrete the excess in a fluid called honeydew, which coats the leaves and may drop onto furniture below the plant.

SOLUTION: Spray infested plants with ORTHO Whitefly & Mealybug Killer. Where practical, wipe mealybugs off the plant with a damp cloth or with cotton swabs dipped in alcohol. Inspect the pot, including the bottom, for mealybug egg masses. Wipe these off. Avoid bringing mealybugs into the house by carefully inspecting new plants. For additional information on mealybugs, see page 229.

BEGONIA

Spider mite damage.

Scales (three times life size).

Whiteflies (life size).

PROBLEM: Leaves are stippled, yellow, and dirty; they may dry out and drop. There may be webbing over flower buds, between leaves, or on the lower surfaces of the leaves. To determine if a plant is infested with mites, hold a sheet of white paper underneath an affected plant and tap the leaves sharply. Minute green, red, or yellow specks the size of pepper grains will drop to the paper and begin to crawl around. The pests are easily seen against the white background.

ANALYSIS: Spider mites
These mites, related to spiders, are major pests of many garden and houseplants, including begonias. They cause damage by sucking sap from the undersides of the leaves. As a result of this feeding the green pigment (chlorophyll) disappears, causing the stippled appearance. Under warm, dry conditions, which favor mites, they can build up to tremendous numbers.

SOLUTION: Spray infested plants with ORTHO Whitefly & Mealybug Killer or ORTHO House Plant Insect Spray. (For instructions on spraying houseplants, see page 915.) Plants need to be sprayed weekly for several weeks to kill the mites as they hatch. To avoid introducing mites, inspect new plants carefully.

PROBLEM: Stems and leaves are covered with white, cottony, cushionlike masses or brown crusty bumps. The bumps can be scraped or picked off easily. Leaves turn yellow and may drop. A shiny or sticky material may cover leaves and stems.

ANALYSIS: Scale insects
Several different types of scale insects attack begonias. Some types can infest many different plants. Scales hatch from eggs. The young, called *crawlers*, are small (about $\frac{1}{10}$ inch), soft-bodied, and move about on the plant and onto other plants. After moving about for a short time, they insert their mouthparts into the plant, feeding on the sap. The legs disappear, and the scales remain in the same place for the rest of their lives. Some develop a soft covering, others a hard covering. Some species of scales are unable to digest fully all the sugar in the plant sap and excrete the excess in a fluid called honeydew, which may cover the leaves or drip onto surfaces below.

SOLUTION: Spray infested plants indoors with ORTHO Whitefly & Mealybug Killer, or take the plant outdoors and spray with ORTHO Orthene Systemic Insect Control. Spraying is more effective against the crawlers than against the adults. Repeated applications may be necessary. For additional information on spraying houseplants, see page 915.

PROBLEM: Tiny, winged insects $\frac{1}{12}$ inch long feed on the undersides of the leaves. The insects are covered with white waxy powder. When the plant is touched, insects flutter rapidly around it. Leaves may be mottled and yellowing.

ANALYSIS: Greenhouse whitefly
(*Trialeurodes vaporariorum*)
This insect is a common pest of begonia. The 4-winged adult lays eggs on the undersides of leaves. The larvae are the size of a pinhead, flat, oval, immobile, and semitransparent, with white waxy filaments radiating from the body. They feed for about a month before changing to the adult form. The larvae are more damaging because they suck more sap from the plants than do the adults. They cannot digest all the sugar in the sap they remove, and excrete the excess in a sugary material called honeydew, which coats the leaves and may drop from the plant.

SOLUTION: Spray with ORTHO Whitefly & Mealybug Killer. For instructions on spraying houseplants, see page 915. Spray weekly as long as the problem continues. Remove heavily infested leaves.

BRASSAIA (SCHEFFLERA)

Root rot.

Mealybugs (life size).

Spider mite damage.

PROBLEM: Plants fail to grow. Lower leaves may turn yellow and drop. The roots are brown, soft, and mushy. The roots do not have white tips. When the condition is severe, no roots are found on the outside of the rootball, and plants may wilt and die. For information about examining the roots, see page 914.

ANALYSIS: Root rot
This plant disease is caused by any of several fungi (*Pythium* species) that are favored by wet soil. The disease is usually an indication that the plant has been watered too frequently or that the soil mix is too heavy and does not drain well. The fungi are common in garden soils, but pasteurized soil or soilless potting mixes are free of them unless they are introduced on a plant or dirty pot, or transferred from another pot on dirty fingers. Root rot spreads quickly through a root system if the soil remains wet.

SOLUTION: If most of the plant has wilted, or if there are no white tips remaining on the root system, the plant is probably too far gone to save. Discard it and the soil in which it grew. Wash the pot thoroughly before reusing it. Disinfect clay pots by soaking for 10 minutes in a solution of 1 part household bleach to 9 parts water. If only part of the plant is affected, or if white root tips are still visible on the rootball, drench with a fungicide containing *etradiazole*; or dry the plant out as described on page 857. Prevent recurrence by planting in a mix that drains well, and by letting the soil dry slightly between waterings. For more information, see page 913.

PROBLEM: Oval, white insects up to ¼ inch long cluster in white, cottony masses on leaves, stems, and in the crotches where branches or leaves are attached. A sticky material may coat the leaves. Leaves may be spotted or deformed. When the condition is severe, leaves and plants may wither and die.

ANALYSIS: Mealybugs
Several species of this common insect feed on schefflera. Mealybugs damage plants by sucking sap, causing leaf distortion and death. The adult female mealybug may produce live young, or may lay eggs in a white fluffy mass of wax. The immature mealybugs, called *nymphs*, crawl all over the plant and onto nearby plants. Soon after they begin to feed, they produce white waxy filaments that cover their bodies, giving them a cottony appearance. As they mature, they become less mobile. Mealybugs cannot digest all the sugar in the sap and excrete the excess in a fluid called honeydew, which coats the leaves and may drop onto furniture below the plant.

SOLUTION: Spray infested plants indoors with ORTHO Whitefly & Mealybug Killer or ORTHO House Plant Insect Control; or take the plants outside and spray them with ORTHO Orthene Systemic Insect Control or ORTHO Isotox Insect Killer. (For instructions on spraying houseplants, see page 915.) Where practical, wipe mealybugs off the plant with a damp cloth or with cotton swabs dipped in alcohol. Inspect the pot, including the bottom, for mealybug egg masses. Wipe these off. Avoid bringing mealybugs into the house by carefully inspecting new plants. For additional information on mealybugs, see page 229.

PROBLEM: Leaves are stippled, yellow, and dirty; they may dry out and drop. There may be webbing between leaves or on the lower surfaces of the leaves. To determine if a plant is infested with mites, hold a sheet of white paper underneath an affected plant and tap the leaves sharply. Minute green, red, or yellow specks the size of pepper grains will drop to the paper and begin to crawl around. The pests are easily seen against the white background.

ANALYSIS: Spider mites
These mites, related to spiders, are major pests of many garden and houseplants, including schefflera. They cause damage by sucking sap from the undersides of the leaves. As a result of this feeding the green pigment (chlorophyll) disappears, causing the stippled appearance. Under warm, dry conditions, which favor mites, they can build up to tremendous numbers.

SOLUTION: Spray infested plants with ORTHO House Plant Insect Control, ORTHO Isotox Insect Killer, or ORTHO Whitefly & Mealybug Killer. (For instructions on spraying houseplants, see page 915.) Plants need to be sprayed weekly for several weeks to kill the mites as they hatch. To avoid introducing mites, inspect new plants carefully.

Brassaia cultural information
Light: Needs bright light
Water: When the soil just below the surface is dry

Overwatering damage.

Mealybugs (⅓ life size).

BROMELIADS

LIGHT: Bromeliads will tolerate considerable variation in light exposure. Because they are flowering plants, most do better in bright light. Some will tolerate dim light, and will flower under such conditions.

SOIL MIX: Plant in osmunda fiber, shredded fir bark, coarse sphagnum, or any of these mixed with an equal amount of coarse sand.

FERTILIZER: Fertilize with ORTHO House Plant Food 5–10–5 or ORTHO Ortho-Gro Liquid Plant Food 12–6–6 once every three months. Fertilize plants growing in reduced light less frequently.

WATER:
How much: Add enough water so that some drains out the bottom of the pot. Most bromeliads have cupped leaves that form a vase and hold water. It is important to keep this vase filled. Flush out old water with fresh water.
How often: Water when the planting medium is dry. Do not let the pot stand in drainage water.

PROBLEM: Plants fail to grow. Root development is poor and roots may rot. The whole plant can be lifted easily from the soil. The plant may die.

ANALYSIS: Heavy soil and overwatering
Most bromeliads that are grown as houseplants are epiphytes (plants that grow on other plants instead of in the ground). Because of this, their roots are usually exposed to the air and can't tolerate wet conditions for very long. If planted in heavy soil, or in soil that is too wet, water fills the spaces between the soil particles so that the roots can't get enough air and die.

SOLUTION: Grow bromeliads only in planting mixes that have exceptional drainage, such as coarse bark, lava rock, or osmunda fiber. Water the plants every day until the roots are established. After that, plants should be watered 1 or 2 times a week.

PROBLEM: Oval, white insects up to ¼ inch long cluster in white, cottony masses on leaves, stems, and in the crotches where the leaves are attached. A sticky material may coat the leaves. Leaves may be spotted or deformed. When the condition is severe, leaves and plants may wither and die.

ANALYSIS: Mealybugs
Several species of this common insect feed on bromeliads. Mealybugs damage plants by sucking sap, causing leaf distortion and death. The adult female mealybug may produce live young, or may lay eggs in a white fluffy mass of wax. The immature mealybugs, called *nymphs*, crawl all over the plant and onto nearby plants. Soon after they begin to feed, they produce white waxy filaments that cover their bodies, giving them a cottony appearance. As they mature, they become less mobile. Mealybugs cannot digest all the sugar in the sap and excrete the excess in a fluid called honeydew, which coats the leaves and may drop onto furniture below the plant.

SOLUTION: Spray infested plants with an insecticide containing *diazinon*. (For instructions on spraying houseplants, see page 915.) Where practical, wipe mealybugs off the plant with a damp cloth or with cotton swabs dipped in alcohol. Inspect the pot, including the bottom, for mealybug egg masses. Wipe these off. Avoid bringing mealybugs into the house by carefully inspecting new plants. For additional information on mealybugs, see page 229.

CACTUS

Stem rot.

Bacterial soft rot.

CACTUS

FLOWERING TIME: Summer.

LIGHT: Most cacti thrive in bright sunny conditions. They should be grown in south or west-facing windows.

SOIL: Cacti should be planted in a sandy mix for good aeration and drainage. Use half regular potting mix and half semicoarse to coarse builder's sand. For more information on potting mixes, see page 913.

FERTILIZER: Fertilize once every three months during the growing season with ORTHO House Plant Food 5-10-5, ORTHO Fish Emulsion Fertilizer 5-1-1 or ORTHO Ortho-Gro Liquid Plant Food 12-6-6.

WATER:
How much: Add enough water so that some drains out of the bottom of the pot. Empty the saucer when the water has finished draining.
How often: Water when the surface soil is dry. In winter, the plants do not need to be watered as frequently as they do in the spring and early summer. For additional information on watering, see page 913.

TEMPERATURE: Place cacti in the warmest areas of the house during spring and summer.

PROBLEM: Plants fail to grow well, and may die. Roots fail to grow, and may be dead and brown.

ANALYSIS: Overwatering
Most cacti are native to areas that are hot and dry, with very sandy soils. Such soils have large spaces between the particles and therefore have little ability to retain moisture. Because cacti need a lot of air around the roots, they do well in sandy soils. If deprived of air, the roots decay, and the plants fail to grow or die.

SOLUTION: Grow cacti in a very sandy or loose mix. (For a discussion of soil mixes, see page 913.) Cacti should be watered thoroughly and then allowed to dry out before watering again. But do not leave them completely dry in containers for very long, or they will die.

PROBLEM: Soft, mushy, circular areas appear in the stems. As these areas enlarge, they become sunken and the tissues die. These cavities are frequently surrounded by tissue that appears to be water soaked. The whole stem may rot, and the plant may die.

ANALYSIS: Bacterial soft rot
This plant disease is caused by any of several bacteria (*Erwinia* species) that enter the cactus through a wound under wet conditions. Once established, the bacteria produce materials that dissolve the layers between the cells. As the cells die liquids are released from them, producing a soft, mushy rot. At high temperatures, the bacteria move through the tissue rapidly. The dead tissue dries, producing sunken cavities. The bacteria may invade the whole stem and kill the plant.

SOLUTION: Cut out the diseased area with a knife. Remove at least ½ inch of apparently healthy tissue around the diseased spot. The operation disfigures the plant, but the cactus may live and produce new portions that can be used to propagate more plants. Avoid wounding plants, and avoid getting water on them. Keep them separated enough so that good air circulation keeps them dry.

CACTUS

Scab.

CAPSICUM (ORNAMENTAL PEPPER)

Mealybugs (life size).

Insufficient light.

PROBLEM: Irregular brown, corky, or leathery areas develop on the stems. These areas continue to enlarge until much of the plant may be covered. When these areas develop on younger tissue, they may cause sunken areas and deformities on the stem.

ANALYSIS: Scab
The cause of scab is unknown. It seems to be most prevalent on plants subjected to high humidity and low light. But sometimes it appears to spread, which suggests that it may be infectious.

SOLUTION: Grow cacti under conditions that are as close to ideal as possible: adequate light, and dry air and soil. Discard severely affected plants, and do not propagate from them. Isolate mildly affected plants from those not affected.

PROBLEM: Oval, white insects up to ¼ inch long cluster in white, cottony masses on stems and in the crotches where the stems or branches are attached. A sticky material may coat the plant. When the condition is severe, plants may wither and die.

ANALYSIS: Mealybugs
Several species of this common insect feed on cacti. Mealybugs damage plants by sucking sap, causing plant distortion and death. The adult female mealybug may produce live young, or may lay eggs in a white fluffy mass of wax. The immature mealybugs, called *nymphs*, crawl all over the plant and onto nearby plants. Soon after they begin to feed, they produce white waxy filaments that cover their bodies, giving them a cottony appearance. As they mature, they become less mobile. Mealybugs cannot digest all the sugar in the sap and excrete the excess in a fluid called honeydew, which coats the stems and may drop onto furniture below the plant.

SOLUTION: Spray infested plants with an insecticide containing *malathion*. Some varieties of cactus are sensitive; test the spray on a small area before spraying the entire plant. (For instructions on spraying houseplants, see page 915.) Where practical, wipe mealybugs off the plant with a damp cloth or with cotton swabs dipped in alcohol. Inspect the pot, including the bottom, for mealybug egg masses. Wipe these off. Avoid bringing mealybugs into the house by carefully inspecting new plants. For additional information on mealybugs, see page 229.

PROBLEM: Plants stop producing flowers and fruit. Flowers may drop from the plant. Plants lose their deep green color and bushy habit. Older leaves may yellow and drop. Stems elongate and are weak.

ANALYSIS: Insufficient light
Plants use light as a source of energy, and grow slowly in light that is too dim for their needs. If most of the available light is coming from one direction, the stems and leaves bend in that direction. If the light is much too dim, the plant has little energy and grows poorly. Plants grown for their flowers or fruit, such as ornamental pepper, have a relatively high need for light.

SOLUTION: Move the plant to a brighter location. Ornamental pepper will tolerate direct sun if it is kept well watered. But if it is allowed to become dry while in direct sunlight, it will sunburn. (For more information on sunburn, see page 226.) If a brighter location is not available, provide supplemental lighting as described on page 914. If you wish to grow a houseplant in a dim location, select a plant that is tolerant of dim light from the list on page 990.

─────── CHRYSANTHEMUM ───────

Aphids (half life size).

Whiteflies (twice life size).

Weak growth.

PROBLEM: New leaves are curled, discolored, and reduced in size. A shiny or sticky substance may coat the leaves. Tiny (⅛ inch), nonwinged, green, soft-bodied insects cluster on the buds, young stems, and leaves.

ANALYSIS: Aphids
Aphids do little damage in small numbers. However, they are extremely prolific and populations can rapidly build up to damaging numbers on ornamental peppers. Damage results when the aphids suck sap from the leaves and stems. Aphids are unable to digest fully all the sugar in the plant sap and excrete the excess in a fluid called honeydew, which often drops onto leaves or furniture below the plant.

SOLUTION: Use ORTHO House Plant Insect Spray. For additional information on spraying houseplants, see page 915.

───────────

Capsicum cultural information
Light: Needs bright light
Water: When the soil just below the surface is dry

───────────

PROBLEM: Tiny, winged insects ¹/₁₂ inch long feed on the undersides of the leaves. The insects are covered with white waxy powder. When the plant is touched, insects flutter rapidly around it. Leaves may be mottled and yellowing.

ANALYSIS: Greenhouse whitefly
(*Trialeurodes vaporariorum*)
This insect is a common pest of ornamental pepper. The 4-winged adult lays eggs on the undersides of leaves. The larvae are the size of a pinhead, flat, oval, immobile, and semitransparent, with radiating white waxy filaments. In about a month, they change to the winged adult form. The larvae are more damaging because they suck more sap from the plants than do the adults. They cannot digest all the sugar in the sap they remove, and excrete the excess in a sugary material called honeydew, which coats the leaves and may drop from the plant onto furniture below.

SOLUTION: Spray with ORTHO House Plant Insect Spray. For instructions on spraying houseplants, see page 915. Spray weekly as long as the problem continues. Remove heavily infested leaves.

PROBLEM: Soon after potted plants are brought inside, their leaves turn yellow, wilt, and fall off. The plants are located in dim light.

ANALYSIS: Insufficient light
Chrysanthemums are outdoor plants that need full sun, but they will tolerate household conditions for a few weeks if they are kept in a bright place and are well watered. Flowering mums from a florist have been grown in bright sun, and will not remain healthy in a location that does not allow them full sun for at least part of the day.

SOLUTION: Move the plants to a brighter location. However, if the leaves are very yellow they will not be able to tolerate direct sun until they become accustomed to higher light levels. Put the plants in a lightly curtained window for a week before exposing them to full sun. It is difficult to get satisfactory flowers from a forced mum a second time the same season. As soon as possible after the blossoms die, cut the flower stalks to the ground and plant the mums in the garden. They may not bloom that fall, but will probably bloom the following year.

CHRYSANTHEMUM

Mealybugs (half life size).

Spider mite damage.

Whiteflies (life size).

PROBLEM: Oval, white insects up to ¼ inch long cluster in white, cottony masses on leaves, stems, and in the crotches where the leaves are attached. A sticky material may coat the leaves. Leaves may be spotted or deformed. When the condition is severe, leaves and plants may wither and die.

ANALYSIS: Mealybugs
Several species of this common insect feed on chrysanthemums. Mealybugs damage plants by sucking sap, causing leaf distortion and death. The adult female mealybug may produce live young, or may lay eggs in a white fluffy mass of wax. The immature mealybugs, called *nymphs*, crawl all over the plant and onto nearby plants. Soon after they begin to feed, they produce white waxy filaments that cover their bodies, giving them a cottony appearance. As they mature, they become less mobile. Mealybugs cannot digest all the sugar in the sap and excrete the excess in a fluid called honeydew, which coats the leaves and may drop onto furniture below the plant.

SOLUTION: Spray infested plants indoors with ORTHO House Plant Insect Control, or take plants outside and spray them with ORTHO Diazinon Insect Spray. (For instructions on spraying houseplants, see page 915.) Where practical, wipe mealybugs off the plant with a damp cloth or with cotton swabs dipped in alcohol. Inspect the pot, including the bottom, for mealybug egg masses. Wipe these off. Avoid bringing mealybugs into the house by carefully inspecting new plants. For additional information on mealybugs, see page 229.

PROBLEM: Leaves are stippled, yellow, and dirty; they may dry out and drop. There may be webbing over flower buds, between leaves, or on the lower surfaces of the leaves. To determine if a plant is infested with mites, hold a sheet of white paper underneath an affected plant and tap the leaves sharply. Minute green, red, or yellow specks the size of pepper grains will drop to the paper and begin to crawl around. The pests are easily seen against the white background.

ANALYSIS: Spider mites
These mites, related to spiders, are major pests of many garden and houseplants, including chrysanthemums. They cause damage by sucking sap from the undersides of the leaves. As a result of feeding the green pigment (chlorophyll) disappears, causing the stippled appearance. Under warm, dry conditions, which favor mites, they can build up to tremendous numbers.

SOLUTION: Spray infested plants with ORTHO House Plant Insect Control. (For instructions on spraying houseplants, see page 915.) Plants need to be sprayed weekly for several weeks to kill the mites as they hatch. To avoid introducing mites, inspect new plants carefully.

Chrysanthemum cultural information
Light: Needs bright light
Water: When the soil surface is moist but not wet

PROBLEM: Tiny, winged insects ¹⁄₁₂ inch long feed on the undersides of the leaves. The insects are covered with white waxy powder. When the plant is touched, insects flutter rapidly around it. Leaves may be mottled and yellowing.

ANALYSIS: Greenhouse whitefly (*Trialeurodes vaporariorum*)
This insect is a common pest of chrysanthemum. The 4-winged adult lays eggs on the undersides of leaves. The larvae are the size of a pinhead, flat, oval, immobile, and semitransparent, with radiating white waxy filaments. In about a month, they change to the winged adult form. The larvae are more damaging because they suck more sap from the plants than do the adults. They cannot digest all the sugar in the sap they remove, and excrete the excess in a sugary material called honeydew, which coats the leaves and may drop from the plant onto furniture below.

SOLUTION: Spray with ORTHO House Plant Insect Spray or ORTHO Malathion 50 Insect Spray. For instructions on spraying houseplants, see page 915. Spray weekly as long as the problem continues. Remove heavily infested leaves.

CHLOROPHYTUM (SPIDER PLANT)

Dead leaf tips.

PROBLEM: Tips of leaves turn brown or tan. The damaged area spreads slowly along the leaf. Older leaves are most severely affected.

ANALYSIS: Dead leaf tips
There are several reasons why spider plant leaf tips die. Frequently the problem is a combination of causes.
1. *Salt damage:* Salts accumulate in the soil from irrigation water or fertilizer. Excess salts are carried to the leaves and deposited in the tips of pointed leaves like those of spider plants. When enough salts accumulate there, the leaf tip dies. Salts accumulate most rapidly when the soil is dry.
2. *Too dry:* The leaf tip, being farthest from the roots, is the first part of the leaf to die when the plant is not getting enough water.
3. *Toxic salts:* Some chemicals, usually in the form of soluble salts, are damaging in very small amounts. They accumulate in leaf tips as other salts do, killing the tissue there. The most common of these chemicals are chloride and borate.

SOLUTION: Remove the dead tips by trimming the leaves to a point with a pair of scissors.
1. Flush the salts from the soil with several thorough waterings, discarding the drainage water each time. In the future, add enough water at each watering so that some drains through the pot. Empty the saucer when the pot has finished draining.
2. Water the plant regularly, following the directions on page 913.
3. There isn't much you can do about traces of toxic chemicals in the water, other than find another source of water. Distilled or deionized water is always free of chemicals.

CINERARIA

Aphids (life size).

PROBLEM: New leaves are curled, discolored, and reduced in size. A shiny or sticky substance may coat the leaves. Tiny (1/8 inch), nonwinged, green, soft-bodied insects cluster on the buds, young stems, and leaves.

ANALYSIS: Aphids
Aphids do little damage in small numbers. However, they are extremely prolific and populations can rapidly build up to damaging numbers on cineraria. Damage results when the aphids suck sap from the leaves and stems. Aphids are unable to digest fully all the sugar in the plant sap and excrete the excess in a fluid called honeydew, which often drops onto leaves or furniture below the plant.

SOLUTION: Use ORTHO House Plant Insect Spray. For additional information on spraying houseplants, see page 915.

Cineraria cultural information
Light: Needs bright light
Water: When the soil surface is moist but not wet

CISSUS (GRAPE IVY)

Salt damage.

PROBLEM: Margins of older leaves die and turn brown and brittle. In severe cases, all leaves may have dead margins. Tissues adjacent to the dead margins of older leaves may turn yellow. New leaves may be distorted.

ANALYSIS: Salt damage
Grape ivy and kangaroo ivy are sensitive to excess salts. Soluble salts are picked up by the roots and accumulate in the leaf margins, where concentrations may become high enough to kill the tissues. Salts can accumulate from water or the use of fertilizers; or they may be present in the soils used in potting. Salts accumulate more rapidly and do more harm if the plant is not watered thoroughly.

SOLUTION: If symptoms of salt damage occur, leach excess salts from the soil by flushing with water. Water the plant at least 3 times, letting the water drain each time. This is done most easily in a bathtub or laundry sink or outside. Always water grape ivy and kangaroo ivy from the top of the pot. Enough water should be added at each watering so that some drains through the pot. Empty the saucer after the pot has finished draining. If the plant is too large to handle easily, use a turkey baster to remove the drainage water. (For additional watering instructions, see page 913.) Do not overfertilize.

Cissus cultural information
Light: Needs medium light
Water: When the soil just below the surface is dry

CISSUS (GRAPE IVY) ——————

CITRUS ——————————

Mealybug (twice life size).

Iron-deficient leaves.

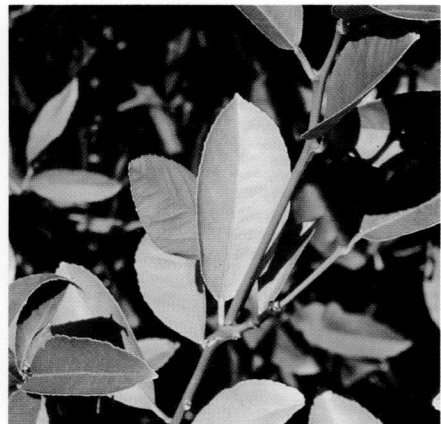

Yellowing caused by nitrogen deficiency.

PROBLEM: Oval, white insects up to ¼ inch long cluster in white, cottony masses on leaves, stems, and in the crotches where the leaves are attached. A sticky material may coat the leaves. Leaves may be spotted or deformed. When the condition is severe, leaves and plants may wither and die.

ANALYSIS: Mealybugs
Several species of this common insect feed on grape ivy. Mealybugs damage plants by sucking sap, causing leaf distortion and death. The adult female mealybug may produce live young, or may lay eggs in a white fluffy mass of wax. The immature mealybugs, called *nymphs*, crawl all over the plant and onto nearby plants. Soon after they begin to feed, they produce white waxy filaments that cover their bodies, giving them a cottony appearance. As they mature, they become less mobile. Mealybugs cannot digest all the sugar in the sap and excrete the excess in a fluid called honeydew, which coats the leaves and may drop onto furniture below the plant.

SOLUTION: Spray infested plants with ORTHO House Plant Insect Control. (For instructions on spraying houseplants, see page 915.) Where practical, wipe mealybugs off the plant with a damp cloth or with cotton swabs dipped in alcohol. Inspect the pot, including the bottom, for mealybug egg masses. Wipe these off. Avoid bringing mealybugs into the house by carefully inspecting new plants. For additional information on mealybugs, see page 229.

PROBLEM: Older (lower) leaves start turning yellow at the margins; yellowing progresses inward on the leaves, and upward on the plant. Older leaves may drop, and the plant may wilt. Or yellowing may start on new growth, with the leaf margins losing their green color first and the areas surrounding the veins losing their color last.

ANALYSIS: Yellowing of leaves
Yellow leaves on citrus may be caused by any of several factors:

1. If the older leaves turn yellow but the new leaves remain green, the problem is probably nitrogen deficiency. Nitrogen is an essential plant nutrient. If it is deficient, the plant will withdraw nitrogen from the old leaves for the sake of the new growth. For more information about nitrogen deficiency, see page 226.

2. Yellowing of older leaves may be associated with root rot. Examine the root system as explained on page 914. If the roots are brown, dead, and soft, without white tips, root rot is the problem. Rotted roots are unable to absorb nutrients and water needed by the plant.

3. If only the new leaves are yellow, the plant is probably deficient in iron. This condition is caused by alkaline soil. In alkaline soil, iron is less available to the plant, and some plants cannot absorb all the iron they need. For information on acid and alkaline soils, see page 902.

SOLUTION: The numbered solutions below correspond to the numbers in the analysis.

1. For a quick response, spray the leaves with Ra-Pid-Gro Plant Food. Feed citrus plants regularly with ORTHO House Plant Food 5–10–5.

2. Avoid excess watering of soil in which citrus is growing. For instructions on watering container plants, see page 913. Plant citrus in a well-drained soil mix.

3. Fertilize citrus with ORTHO Greenol Liquid Iron 6.13%. Treat the soil with *ferrous sulfate* to increase acidity.

CLERODENDRUM (GLORY-BOWER) ____ CLIVIA

Scale (3 times life size).

Greenhouse whiteflies (twice life size).

Mealybugs (¼ life size).

PROBLEM: Stems and leaves are covered with white, cottony, cushionlike masses or brown crusty bumps. The bumps can be scraped or picked off easily. Leaves turn yellow and drop. A shiny or sticky material may cover leaves and stems.

ANALYSIS: Scale insects
Several different types of scale insects attack citrus plants. Some types can infest many different plants. Scales hatch from eggs. The young, called *crawlers*, are small (about ¹⁄₁₀ inch), soft-bodied, and move about on the plant and onto other plants. After moving about for a short time, they insert their mouthparts into the plant, feeding on the sap. The legs disappear, and the scales remain in the same place for the rest of their lives. Some develop a soft covering, others a hard covering. Some species of scales are unable to digest fully all the sugar in the plant sap and excrete the excess in a fluid called honeydew, which may cover the leaves or drip onto surfaces below.

SOLUTION: Take the infested plant outside and spray it with ORTHO Malathion 50 Insect Spray or ORTHO Citrus Insect Spray. Spraying is more effective against the crawlers than against the adults. Repeated applications may be necessary. For additional information on spraying houseplants, see page 915.

Citrus cultural information
Light: Needs bright light
Water: When the soil just below the surface is dry

PROBLEM: Tiny, winged insects ¹⁄₁₂ inch long feed on the undersides of the leaves. The insects are covered with white waxy powder. When the plant is touched, insects flutter rapidly around it. Leaves may be mottled and yellowing.

ANALYSIS: Greenhouse whitefly
(*Trialeurodes vaporariorum*)
This insect is a common pest of clerodendron. The 4-winged adult lays eggs on the undersides of leaves. The larvae are the size of a pinhead, flat, oval, immobile, and semitransparent, with radiating white waxy filaments. In about a month, they change to the winged adult form. The larvae are more damaging because they suck more sap from the plants than do the adults. They cannot digest all the sugar in the sap they remove, and excrete the excess in a sugary material called honeydew, which coats the leaves and may drop from the plant onto furniture below.

SOLUTION: Spray with ORTHO House Plant Insect Spray. Spray weekly as long as the problem continues. Remove heavily infested leaves.

Clerodendrum cultural information
Light: Needs bright light
Water: When the soil is moist but not wet

PROBLEM: Oval, white insects up to ¼ inch long cluster in white, cottony masses on leaves and in the crotches where the leaves are attached. A sticky material may coat the leaves. Leaves may be spotted or deformed. When the condition is severe, leaves and plants may wither and die.

ANALYSIS: Mealybugs
Several species of this common insect feed on clivia. Mealybugs damage plants by sucking sap, causing leaf distortion and death. The adult female mealybug may produce live young, or may lay eggs in a white fluffy mass of wax. The immature mealybugs, called *nymphs*, crawl all over the plant and onto nearby plants. Soon after they begin to feed, they produce white waxy filaments that cover their bodies, giving them a cottony appearance. As they mature, they become less mobile. Mealybugs cannot digest all the sugar in the sap and excrete the excess in a fluid called honeydew, which coats the leaves and may drop onto furniture below the plant.

SOLUTION: Spray infested plants with an insecticide containing *diazinon*. (For instructions on spraying houseplants, see page 915.) Where practical, wipe mealybugs off the plant with a damp cloth or with cotton swabs dipped in alcohol. Inspect the pot, including the bottom, for mealybug egg masses. Wipe these off. Avoid bringing mealybugs into the house by carefully inspecting new plants. For additional information on mealybugs, see page 229.

CODIAEUM (CROTON)

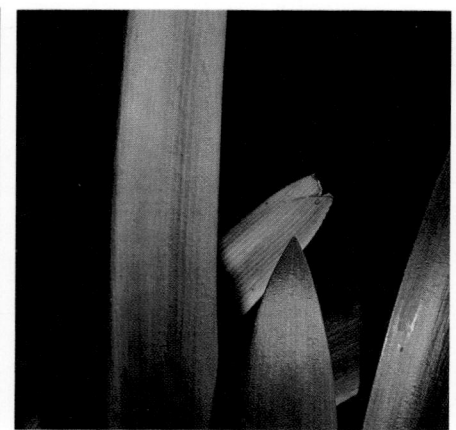
Leaf bleaching from too much light.

PROBLEM: Plants fail to flower. Or yellow areas appear on leaves. Brown spots may appear in the yellow areas.

ANALYSIS: Incorrect light
Clivia is a sensitive plant regarding light. It needs abundant light to produce flowers. But because it is native to shady areas, it does not like direct sunlight, and if it is given too much the green pigment (chlorophyll) will disappear on exposed portions of leaves. If this situation continues, tissues will die and turn brown in the affected areas.

SOLUTION: Grow clivia in an east-facing window or in a curtained south or west-facing window. During the summer, clivia can be grown outside in semishade.

Clivia cultural information
Light: Needs bright light
Water: When the soil just below the surface is barely moist

CODIAEUM

LIGHT: Grow crotons in bright light to maintain the brilliant leaf colors. If new leaves are green, move the plants to a brighter spot.

SOIL: Crotons can be grown in any of the standard soil mixes for houseplants. For more information about soil mixes, see page 913.

FERTILIZER: Feed once a month with ORTHO Fish Emulsion Fertilizer 5–1–1 or ORTHO Ortho-Gro Liquid Plant Food 12–6–6.

WATER:
How much: Add enough water so that some drains out of the bottom of the pot. Empty the saucer when the water has finished draining.
How often: Water when the top inch of soil is barely moist. For additional information on watering houseplants, see page 913.

TEMPERATURE: Average house temperatures of 68° to 70°F are adequate.

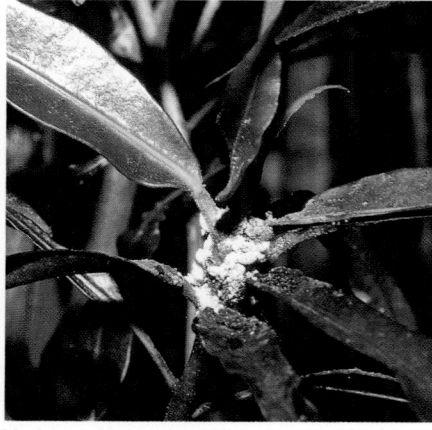
Mealybugs (3 times life size).

PROBLEM: Oval, white insects up to ¼ inch long cluster in white, cottony masses on leaves, stems, and in the crotches where branches or leaves are attached. A sticky material may coat the leaves. Leaves may be spotted or deformed.

ANALYSIS: Mealybugs
Several species of this common insect feed on croton. Mealybugs damage plants by sucking sap, causing leaf distortion and death. The adult female mealybug may produce live young, or may lay eggs in a white fluffy mass of wax. The immature mealybugs, called *nymphs,* crawl all over the plant and onto nearby plants. Soon after they begin to feed, they produce white waxy filaments that cover their bodies, giving them a cottony appearance. As they mature, they become less mobile. Mealybugs cannot digest all the sugar in the sap and excrete the excess in a fluid called honeydew, which coats the leaves and may drop onto furniture below the plant.

SOLUTION: Spray infested plants indoors with ORTHO House Plant Insect Control; or take the plants outside and spray them with ORTHO Orthene Systemic Insect Control. (For instructions on spraying houseplants, see page 915.) Where practical, wipe mealybugs off the plant with a damp cloth or with cotton swabs dipped in alcohol. Inspect the pot, including the bottom, for mealybug egg masses. Wipe these off. For additional information on mealybugs, see page 229.

COLEUS

New leaves are green.

Root rot.

PROBLEM: New leaves are green, instead of brightly colored. Stems may be thin and bend toward a light source. The lower leaves may drop.

ANALYSIS: Insufficient light
Plants use light as a source of energy, and grow slowly in light that is too dim for their needs. If most of the available light is coming from one direction, the stems and leaves bend in that direction. Although foliage plants generally need less light than plants grown for their flowers or fruit, brightly colored plants like croton need fairly bright light in order to produce the pigments that color their leaves.

SOLUTION: Move the plant to a brighter location. A lightly curtained sunny window is ideal. If a brighter location is not available, provide supplemental lighting as described on page 914. Crotons may be grown outside in the summer. When moving them from indoors to outdoors, place the plants in light shade for at least two days before putting them in full sun. If you wish to grow a houseplant in a dim location, select a plant that is tolerant of dim light from the list on page 990.

COLEUS

FLOWERING TIME: Although coleus are not grown for their flowers, they frequently produce flowers. Flowering depends on the size of the plant; larger plants flower any time.

LIGHT: Grow coleus in as much light as possible to maintain the brilliant colors. If colors fade and stems elongate, move to a brighter spot.

SOIL: Coleus can be grown in any of the soil mixes for general houseplants. For additional information on soil mixes, see page 913.

FERTILIZER: Feed once a month with ORTHO Fish Emulsion Fertilizer 5-1-1, ORTHO House Plant Food 5-10-5, or ORTHO Ortho-Gro Liquid Plant Food 12-6-6.

WATER:
How much: Add enough water so that some drains out of the bottom of the pot.
How often: Water when the top inch of soil is barely moist. For additional information on watering houseplants, see page 913.

TEMPERATURE: Average house temperatures of 68° to 70°F are adequate for coleus.

SPECIAL CONDITIONS: Pinch stems to encourage branching. Cut off flower stems as they appear. Plants may be grown outside in partial shade in the summer.

PROBLEM: Lower leaves wilt or all of the leaves wilt. The plant may be stunted, and leaf colors fade. The lower portion of the main stem above the soil line may be darkened. Examination of the roots, as described on page 914, shows them to be brown, dead, and mushy, with no white tips. Severely infected plants may die.

ANALYSIS: Root rot
Root rot of coleus is caused by a fungus (*Phytophthora* species or *Rhizoctonia* species). These soil-borne fungi are favored by excessively wet soil and poor drainage. Plants weakened by poor light, inadequate fertilization, excess salts, or other adverse factors are more susceptible to root rot fungi. Damaged roots are unable to pick up water and nutrients. *Phytophthora* frequently moves into the main stem, girdling it and killing the plant.

SOLUTION: Once coleus plants are infected, little can be done to help. A tip cutting can be taken from the plant and rooted. (For instructions, see page 914.) The diseased plant and the soil in which it was growing should be discarded. Soak the pot in a solution of one part chlorine bleach to nine parts water for 30 minutes before reuse. To prevent the disease, use a well-drained soil mix, as described on page 913.

COLEUS

Insufficient light.

Mealybugs (half life size).

Greenhouse whiteflies (life size).

PROBLEM: Leaves fade and look bleached. Stems are long, with large spaces between the leaves. Young stems may be weak and unable to support themselves. Young stems tend to grow toward the light source. Brown patches may appear in the faded area.

ANALYSIS: Insufficient light
Plants use light as a source of energy, and grow slowly in light that is too dim for their needs. If most of the available light is coming from one direction, the stems and leaves bend in that direction. If the light is much too dim, the plant has little energy and grows poorly. Although foliage plants generally need less light than plants grown for their flowers or fruit, coleus has a relatively high need for light.

SOLUTION: Move the plant to a brighter location, such as a lightly curtained sunny window. If a brighter location is not available, provide supplemental lighting as described on page 914. If you wish to grow a houseplant in a dim location, select a plant that is tolerant of dim light from the list on page 990.

PROBLEM: Oval, white insects up to ¼ inch long cluster in white, cottony masses on leaves, stems, and in the crotches where the leaves are attached. A sticky material may coat the leaves. Leaves may be spotted or deformed. When the condition is severe, leaves and plants may wither and die.

ANALYSIS: Mealybugs
Several species of this common insect feed on coleus. Mealybugs damage plants by sucking sap, causing leaf distortion and death. The adult female mealybug may produce live young, or may lay eggs in a white fluffy mass of wax. The immature mealybugs, called *nymphs*, crawl all over the plant and onto nearby plants. Soon after they begin to feed, they produce white waxy filaments that cover their bodies, giving them a cottony appearance. As they mature, they become less mobile. Mealybugs cannot digest all the sugar in the sap and excrete the excess in a fluid called honeydew, which coats the leaves and may drop onto furniture below the plant.

SOLUTION: Spray infested plants with ORTHO Whitefly & Mealybug Killer, ORTHO Orthene Systemic Insect Control, or ORTHO House Plant Insect Control. (For instructions on spraying houseplants, see page 915.) Where practical, wipe mealybugs off the plant with a damp cloth or with cotton swabs dipped in alcohol. Inspect the pot, including the bottom, for mealybug egg masses. Wipe these off. Avoid bringing mealybugs into the house by carefully inspecting new plants. For additional information on mealybugs, see page 229.

PROBLEM: Tiny, winged insects ¹/₁₂ inch long feed on the undersides of the leaves. The insects are covered with white waxy powder. When the plant is touched, insects flutter rapidly around it. Leaves may be mottled and yellowing.

ANALYSIS: Greenhouse whitefly
(*Trialeurodes vaporariorum*)
This insect is a common pest of coleus. The 4-winged adult lays eggs on the undersides of leaves. The larvae are the size of a pinhead, flat, oval, immobile, and semitransparent, with radiating white waxy filaments. In about a month, they change to the winged adult form. The larvae are more damaging because they suck more sap from the plants than do the adults. They cannot digest all the sugar in the sap they remove, and excrete the excess in a sugary material called honeydew, which coats the leaves and may drop from the plant onto furniture below.

SOLUTION: Spray with ORTHO Whitefly & Mealybug Killer or ORTHO House Plant Insect Control. For instructions on spraying houseplants, see page 915. Spray weekly as long as the problem continues. Remove heavily infested leaves.

COLUMNEA _____

CORDYLINE (TI PLANT) _____

Water spots.

Mealybugs (half life size).

Salt damage.

PROBLEM: Small, sunken white to tan spots are scattered on the upper surfaces of the leaves.

ANALYSIS: Water spots
Columnea water spots result from a rapid temperature change in the presence of light. This usually occurs when cold water is dropped on the foliage during watering. The green pigment (chlorophyll) in columnea leaves is found in a layer of cells near the upper surface of the leaf. A rapid temperature change in the presence of light destroys the chlorophyll, causing the loss of green color and allowing the color of the underlying tissue to show through.

SOLUTION: The spots are permanent. Remove unsightly leaves. When watering columnea plants, be careful not to get water on the foliage, or use tepid water.

_____

Columnea cultural information
Light: Needs bright light
Water: When the soil just below the surface is barely moist

_____

PROBLEM: Oval, white insects up to ¼ inch long cluster in white, cottony masses on leaves, stems, and in the crotches where the leaves are attached. A sticky material may coat the leaves. Leaves may be spotted or deformed. When the condition is severe, leaves and plants may wither and die.

ANALYSIS: Mealybugs
Several species of this common insect feed on columnea. Mealybugs damage plants by sucking sap, causing leaf distortion and death. The adult female mealybug may produce live young, or may lay eggs in a white fluffy mass of wax. The immature mealybugs, called *nymphs,* crawl all over the plant and onto nearby plants. Soon after they begin to feed, they produce white waxy filaments that cover their bodies, giving them a cottony appearance. As they mature, they become less mobile. Mealybugs cannot digest all the sugar in the sap and excrete the excess in a fluid called honeydew, which coats the leaves and may drop onto furniture below the plant.

SOLUTION: Spray infested plants with an insecticide containing *diazinon.* (For instructions on spraying houseplants, see page 915.) Where practical, wipe mealybugs off the plant with a damp cloth or with cotton swabs dipped in alcohol. Inspect the pot, including the bottom, for mealybug egg masses. Wipe these off. Avoid bringing mealybugs into the house by carefully inspecting new plants. For additional information on mealybugs, see page 229.

PROBLEM: Tips of older leaves die and turn brown and brittle. This condition progresses down the margins of the leaves. In severe cases, all leaves may have dead tips and margins. Tissues adjacent to the dead margins may turn yellow.

ANALYSIS: Salt damage
Cordylines are very sensitive to excess salts. Soluble salts are picked up by the roots and accumulate in the leaf tips, where concentrations may become high enough to kill the tissues. Salts can accumulate from water or the use of fertilizers; or they may be present in the soil used in potting. Salts accumulate more rapidly and do more harm if the plant is not watered thoroughly.

SOLUTION: If symptoms of salt damage occur, leach excess salts from the soil by flushing with water. Water the plant at least 3 times, letting the water drain through each time. This is done most easily in a bathtub or laundry sink or outside. Always water cordylines from the top of the pot. Enough water should be added at each watering so that some drains through the pot. Empty the saucer after the pot has finished draining. If the plant is too large to handle easily, use a turkey baster to remove the drainage water. (For additional watering instructions, see page 913.) Do not overfertilize. Dead tips can be trimmed off with scissors. If the leaves are trimmed to a point, the damage is less noticeable.

CORDYLINE (TI PLANT)

Spider mite damage.

PROBLEM: Leaves are stippled, yellow, and dirty; they may dry out and drop. There may be webbing between leaves or on the lower surfaces of the leaves. To determine if a plant is infested with mites, hold a sheet of white paper underneath an affected plant and tap the leaves sharply. Minute green, red, or yellow specks the size of pepper grains will drop to the paper and begin to crawl around. The pests are easily seen against the white background.

ANALYSIS: Spider mites
These mites, related to spiders, are major pests of many garden and houseplants, including ti plants. They cause damage by sucking sap from the undersides of the leaves. As a result of feeding, the green pigment (chlorophyll) disappears, causing the stippled appearance. Under warm, dry conditions, which favor mites, they can build up to tremendous numbers.

SOLUTION: Spray infested plants with ORTHO House Plant Insect Spray. (For instructions on spraying houseplants, see page 915.) Plants need to be sprayed weekly for several weeks to kill the mites as they hatch. To avoid introducing mites, inspect new plants carefully.

CYCAS (SAGO PALM)

Salt damage.

PROBLEM: Margins of older leaves die and turn brown, beginning at the base of the fronds and progressing outward. In severe cases, all fronds may have dead margins. Tissues adjacent to dead margins of older fronds may turn yellow.

ANALYSIS: Salt damage
Sago palms are sensitive to excess salts. Soluble salts are picked up by the roots and accumulate in the leaf margins, where concentrations may become high enough to kill the tissues. Salts can accumulate from water or the use of fertilizers; or they may be present in the soil used in potting. Salts accumulate more rapidly and do more harm if the plant is not watered thoroughly.

SOLUTION: If symptoms of salt damage occur, leach excess salts from the soil by flushing with water. Water the plant at least 3 times, letting the water drain each time. This is done most easily in a bathtub, or laundry sink or outside. Always water sago palms from the top of the pot. Enough water should be added at each watering so that some drains through the pot. Empty the saucer after the pot has finished draining. If the plant is too large to handle easily, use a turkey baster to remove the drainage water. (For additional watering instructions, see page 913.) Do not overfertilize.

Cycas cultural information
Light: Needs bright light
Water: When the soil just below the surface is barely moist

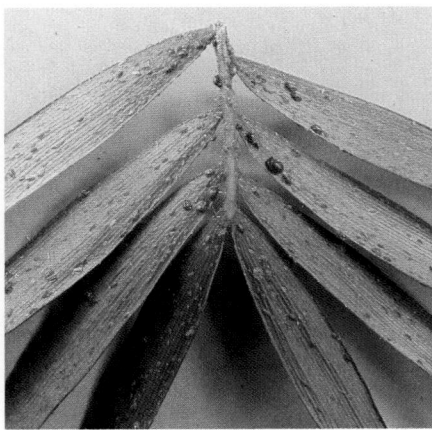

Scale (life size).

PROBLEM: Fronds and leaflets are covered with white, cottony, cushionlike masses or brown crusty bumps. The bumps can be scraped or picked off easily. Fronds turn yellow and may drop. A shiny or sticky material may cover the fronds.

ANALYSIS: Scale insects
Several different types of scale insects attack cycas. Some types can infest many different plants. Scales hatch from eggs. The young, called *crawlers*, are small (about 1/10 inch), soft-bodied, and move about on the plant and onto other plants. After moving about for a short time, they insert their mouthparts into the plant, feeding on the sap. The legs disappear, and the scales remain in the same place for the rest of their lives. Some develop a soft covering, others a hard covering. Some species of scales are unable to digest fully all the sugar in the plant sap and excrete the excess in a fluid called honeydew, which may cover the fronds or drip onto surfaces below.

SOLUTION: Spray with an insecticide containing *malathion*. Spraying is more effective against the crawlers than against the adults. Repeated applications may be necessary. For additional information on spraying houseplants, see page 915.

CYCLAMEN ——

High temperature damage.

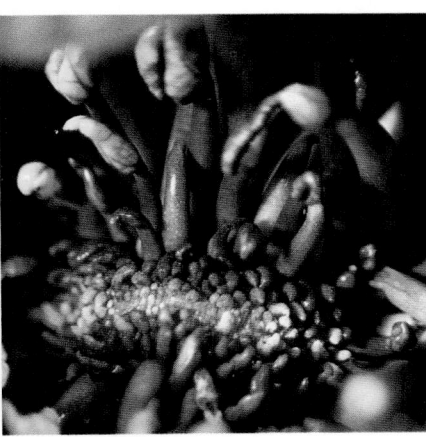
Cyclamen mite damage.

CYCLAMEN ————————

LIGHT: Flowering plants need more light than foliage plants. To keep cyclamen plants in flower, place them in a south-facing window.

SOIL: Grow cyclamens in a loose, well-drained soil mix. For more information about soil mixes, see page 913.

FERTILIZER: Fertilize monthly with ORTHO Ortho-Gro Liquid Plant Food 12–6–6 or ORTHO Evergreen & Azalea Food 10–8–7 according to directions on the label.

WATER:
How much: Add enough water to the pot so that a little water drains from the bottom.
How often: Water whenever the top inch of soil is slightly moist. Do not let the soil get dry.

TEMPERATURE: Cyclamens will continue to flower when daytime temperatures are warm and nighttime temperatures are cool. In mild climates, put the plant outside at night. In areas with extremely cold winters, put the plant in a cool area but do not allow it to freeze. When days and nights are warm, the leaves will yellow and the plant will stop flowering.

SPECIAL CONDITIONS: Do not allow cyclamens to become dry. In bright light, plants that are dry will sunburn. Avoid overwatering. Cyclamens are very susceptible to root rots.

PROBLEM: Outer leaves turn yellow. Leaves may die and turn brown, and their stems become soft. Plants stop flowering.

ANALYSIS: High temperatures
Although cyclamen are cool weather plants, they will tolerate warm days as long as they have cool nights (below 55°F). Cool temperatures initiate flower buds. Constant high temperatures inhibit flower buds, and plants stop flowering. High temperatures also prevent the plant from growing well, causing leaves to lose their green color and die.

SOLUTION: Grow cyclamen plants in a cool room with as much light as possible. If a cool room is not available, put them near a window at night. If temperatures are not below freezing, put the plants outside at night. Under alternating temperatures, they will flower for long periods. Keep plants adequately watered and fertilized.

PROBLEM: Leaves become curled, wrinkled, and cupped in scattered areas. New leaves may be more severely affected, remain very small, have a bronze discoloration, and be severely misshapen. Flower buds are distorted, and may drop or fail to open.

ANALYSIS: Cyclamen mite
(*Steneotarsonemus pallidus*)
Cyclamen mite is a very small mite related to spiders. These mites attack a number of houseplants, and can be very damaging on cyclamen. Their feeding injures the plant tissues, causing the leaves and flower buds to be malformed and stunted. They infest the new growth most heavily, but will crawl to other parts of the plant or to other plants. Cyclamen mites reproduce rapidly.

SOLUTION: Spray plants with *dicofol* at intervals of 2 weeks until new growth is no longer affected. Discard severely infested plants. Spray plants according to instructions given on page 915. Houseplants showing cyclamen mite damage should be isolated from other plants until the mites are under control. Nearby plants should be observed closely so that if symptoms appear, they can be sprayed. Avoid touching leaves of infested plants and then touching leaves of other plants.

Botrytis. *Insert:* Spotted petals.

Root rot.

PROBLEM: Leaves in the center of the plant turn yellow, wilt, and die. Leaf and flower stems in the center of the plant develop a soft rot near their base and collapse. Plants stop flowering. Much of the center of the plant may die. Plant tissues there may be covered with a gray to brown powdery fungal growth. Flower petals of colored varieties may have spots of deeper color.

ANALYSIS: Botrytis
This disease is caused by a fungus (*Botrytis* species) that is commonly found on dead and decaying plant materials. The spores of the fungus can invade dead or weak tissues and flowers, but not healthy stems and leaves. However, leaves and stems in contact with infected tissue can be invaded. The fungus is favored by moist conditions and temperatures below 65°F. Under very humid conditions, the infected tissues may be covered with a fuzzy gray or brown growth composed of the strands and spores of the fungus. The spores are spread by air currents and, in the presence of water, will invade dead leaves on old flowers in the center of cyclamen plants. On cyclamen flowers of colored varieties, the fungus may cause spots of deeper color.

SOLUTION: No chemical control is presently available for home use. Remove any dead plant materials, especially old flowers and leaves in the center of the plant. Avoid getting foliage and flowers wet when watering. Do not mist plants. Increase air circulation to keep humidity low.

PROBLEM: Older leaves turn yellow and may curl up at the margins. The leaf stems and flower stems may wilt. The plant may be stunted. All of the leaves may wilt, die, and turn brown. The roots are brown, dead, and soft, with no white tips. (For instructions on examining plant roots, see page 914.) All of the roots may be rotted, and the bulb may be lifted easily from the soil.

ANALYSIS: Root rot
Root rot in cyclamen is caused by a soil-dwelling fungus (*Pythium* species) that infects the roots of many other plants as well. This fungus is favored by constantly wet soil. Plants weakened by other factors are more susceptible to attack by the fungus, which invades the roots and kills them, causing the plant to wilt. The fungus may invade so much of the root system that the plant dies.

SOLUTION: If the roots of a cyclamen are severely rotted, take the bulb from the soil and remove all of the rotted roots. Allow the bulb to air dry for several days before replanting. Prevent root rot by planting in a well-drained potting mix. For more information about potting mixes, see page 913.

DIEFFENBACHIA

LIGHT: Dieffenbachia will tolerate considerable variations in light, and will grow in full sun to medium light, as in a north-facing window.

SOIL: Any standard potting mix. For information on potting mixes, see page 913.

FERTILIZER: Fertilize once a month during spring and summer with ORTHO Fish Emulsion Fertilizer 5–1–1, ORTHO House Plant Food 5–10–5, or ORTHO Ortho-Gro Liquid Plant Food 12–6–6.

WATER:
How much: Add enough water so that some drains out of the bottom of the pot. Empty the saucer when the water has finished draining.
How often: Water when the top inch of soil is barely moist. For additional information on watering houseplants, see page 913.

TEMPERATURE: Average house temperatures are adequate.

SPECIAL CONDITIONS: Plants may grow too tall and need to be cut back. This will force multiple stems and make the plant more attractive. For information on rooting the tops, see page 914. Because they are adaptable to low light conditions, dieffenbachia are sometimes grown in inadequate light, where they grow poorly. Variegated varieties with very white blotches may sunburn if grown in direct sunlight.

Mealybugs (half life size).

Spindly growth.

Sunburn.

PROBLEM: Oval, white insects up to ¼ inch long cluster in white, cottony masses on leaves, stems, and in the crotches where the leaves are attached. A sticky material may coat the leaves. Leaves may be spotted or deformed. When the condition is severe, leaves and plants may wither and die.

ANALYSIS: Mealybugs
Several species of this common insect feed on dieffenbachia. Mealybugs damage plants by sucking sap, causing leaf distortion and death. The adult female mealybug may produce live young, or may lay eggs in a white fluffy mass of wax. The immature mealybugs, called *nymphs*, crawl all over the plant and onto nearby plants. Soon after they begin to feed, they produce white waxy filaments that cover their bodies, giving them a cottony appearance. As they mature, they become less mobile. Mealybugs cannot digest all the sugar in the sap and excrete the excess in a fluid called honeydew, which coats the leaves and may drop onto furniture below the plant.

SOLUTION: Spray infested plants indoors with ORTHO Whitefly & Mealybug Killer or ORTHO House Plant Insect Control; or take the plants outside and spray them with ORTHO Orthene Systemic Insect Control. (For instructions on spraying houseplants, see page 915.) Where practical, wipe mealybugs off the plant with a damp cloth or with cotton swabs dipped in alcohol. Inspect the pot, including the bottom, for mealybug egg masses. Wipe these off. Avoid bringing mealybugs into the house by carefully inspecting new plants. For additional information on mealybugs, see page 229.

PROBLEM: Lower leaves turn yellow, starting at the margins. These leaves may wilt, die, and turn light brown. Dead leaves hang down and remain attached to the stem. This condition may progress up the stem until only a few green leaves are left at the top of the plant. Plants may become weak, and the remaining leaves may face toward the light.

ANALYSIS: Insufficient light
Plants use light as a source of energy, and grow slowly in light that is too dim for their needs. If most of the available light comes from one direction, the stems and leaves bend in that direction. If the light is much too dim, the plant has little energy and grows poorly. Although foliage plants generally need less light than plants grown for their flowers or fruit, dieffenbachia has a relatively high need for light.

SOLUTION: Move the plant to a brighter location. If it is allowed to become dry while in direct sunlight, it will sunburn. (For more information on sunburn, see page 226.) If a brighter location is not available, provide supplemental lighting as described on page 914. If you wish to grow a houseplant in a dim location, select a plant that is tolerant of dim light from the list on page 990. If your dieffenbachia has lost most of its lower leaves, reroot the top as described on page 914, cutting the stem back to two nodes. The stem will resprout.

PROBLEM: Areas between the veins near the margins of older leaves turn yellow, and then tan or light brown. Very light green or white tissues of variegated varieties turn brown between the veins.

ANALYSIS: Sunburn
Dieffenbachia is adaptable to varying amounts of light from bright to relatively dim. Leaf tissue that is deficient in green pigment (chlorophyll) is very susceptible to sunburn, so if variegated dieffenbachias are grown in very bright light, they may sunburn. Leaves on plants that dry out are also susceptible to sunburn. Older leaves are the first to be affected by sunburn when a plant dries out.

SOLUTION: Grow variegated dieffenbachias that have white areas in filtered light. Avoid letting dieffenbachias dry out. Follow watering directions as given on page 913. Avoid moving plants directly from very dim light to very bright light.

DIEFFENBACHIA (DUMB CANE)

Bacterial stem blight.

Bacterial leaf spot.

Spider mite damage.

PROBLEM: Soft sunken areas with water-soaked margins appear on the stems. Cracks sometimes appear in the affected areas. Lower leaves may turn yellow and become severely wilted. They tend to hang on the stem even when collapsed. If the condition is severe, the stem may rot clear through so that the top of the plant breaks off. Brown streaks occur inside infected stems.

ANALYSIS: Bacterial stem blight
This plant disease is caused by a bacterium (*Erwinia chrysanthemi*). Under wet conditions, the bacteria gain entrance through wounds on the stem. Propagation pieces from infected plants may be infected. Inside the stems, the bacteria cause a soft rot of the tissue, resulting in sunken areas or complete collapse of the stem. Inner stem tissue is discolored brown. Cuttings from infected stems frequently produce infected plants; or they may not root.

SOLUTION: There is no cure for this disease. Do not use any stem material for propagation if it has brown streaks in it.

PROBLEM: Small yellow spots with translucent centers appear on the leaves. The spots may enlarge to ¼ inch in diameter, and may become orange with clear centers. Under humid conditions, glistening mounds of bacteria may appear, first on the undersides and then on the upper sides of the spots. The spots may merge, causing larger areas to be affected. The spots are sometimes angular because they are bounded by the veins. If the spots are numerous, leaves have a speckled appearance. Infected leaves may turn yellow, wilt, and die.

ANALYSIS: Bacterial leaf spot
This disease is caused by a bacterium (*Xanthomonas dieffenbachiae*). Under humid conditions, the bacteria gain entrance through wounds or natural openings in the leaves of dieffenbachia. Inside the leaf the bacteria rot the tissue, causing the spots. Under very humid conditions, so many bacteria may be produced that they ooze out of the tissue in a mass. If many infections occur the leaf dies.

SOLUTION: Once leaves are infected, nothing can be done to control the spots already formed. Prevent the spread of the disease to other portions of the leaf or to other plants by keeping the leaves dry. Do not mist the plants. Keep the plants in a room where condensation does not form on the leaves. Remove and destroy severely infected leaves.

PROBLEM: Leaves are stippled, yellow, and dirty; they may dry out and drop. There may be webbing between leaves or on the lower surfaces of the leaves. To determine if a plant is infested with mites, hold a sheet of white paper underneath an affected plant and tap the leaves sharply. Minute green, red, or yellow specks the size of pepper grains will drop to the paper and begin to crawl around. The pests are easily seen against the white background.

ANALYSIS: Spider mites
These mites, related to spiders, are major pests of many garden and houseplants, including dieffenbachia. They cause damage by sucking sap from the undersides of the leaves. As a result of this feeding the green pigment (chlorophyll) disappears, causing the stippled appearance. Under warm, dry conditions, which favor mites, they can build up to tremendous numbers.

SOLUTION: Spray infested plants with ORTHO House Plant Insect Control or ORTHO Whitefly & Mealybug Killer. (For instructions on spraying houseplants, see page 915.) Plants need to be sprayed weekly for several weeks to kill the mites as they hatch. To avoid introducing mites, inspect new plants carefully.

DIZYGOTHECA (FALSE ARALIA) ——— DRACAENA

Mealybugs (⅓ life size).

Fusarium leaf spot.

Salt damage.

PROBLEM: Oval, white insects up to ¼ inch long cluster in white, cottony masses on leaves, stems, and in the crotches where branches or leaves are attached. A sticky material may coat the leaves.

ANALYSIS: Mealybugs
Several species of this common insect feed on false aralia. Mealybugs damage plants by sucking sap. The adult female mealybug may produce live young, or may lay eggs in a white fluffy mass of wax. The immature mealybugs, called *nymphs*, crawl all over the plant and onto nearby plants. Soon after they begin to feed, they produce white waxy filaments that cover their bodies, giving them a cottony appearance. Mealybugs cannot digest all the sugar in the sap and excrete the excess in a fluid called honeydew, which coats the leaves and may drop onto furniture below the plant.

SOLUTION: Spray infested plants indoors with ORTHO Whitefly & Mealybug Killer or ORTHO House Plant Insect Control; or take the plants outside and spray them with ORTHO Orthene Systemic Insect Control or ORTHO Isotox Insect Killer. (For instructions on spraying houseplants, see page 915.) Where practical, wipe mealybugs off the plant with a damp cloth or with cotton swabs dipped in alcohol. Inspect the pot, including the bottom, for mealybug egg masses. Wipe these off. For additional information on mealybugs, see page 229.

Dizygotheca cultural information
Light: Needs bright light
Water: When the soil just below the surface is barely moist

PROBLEM: Circular, reddish brown spots appear on the leaves. The spots are surrounded by a yellow margin. Several spots may join to form blotches. Badly spotted leaves may turn yellow and die.

ANALYSIS: Fusarium leaf spot
This plant disease is caused by a fungus (*Fusarium moniliforme*). Fungal spores are spread from plant to plant by splashing water. The spores germinate on a wet leaf surface within a matter of hours, causing a new spot. In most cases, spotting is unsightly but not harmful. However, if spotting is severe the leaf may weaken and die.

SOLUTION: Clip off badly spotted leaves. Keep the foliage dry to prevent the spread of the fungus. If spotting continues, spray the plant with a fungicide containing *chlorothalonil*.

PROBLEM: Tips of older leaves die and turn brown and brittle. In severe cases, tips of new leaves may be dead and brown. Tissues adjacent to the dead tips on older leaves may be yellow.

ANALYSIS: Salt damage
Dracaena is very sensitive to excess salts. Soluble salts are picked up by the roots and accumulate in the leaf tips, where concentrations become high enough to kill the tissues. Salts can accumulate from water or the use of fertilizers; or they may be present in the soil used in potting. Salts accumulate more rapidly and do more harm if the plant is not watered thoroughly.

SOLUTION: Leach excess salts from the soil by flushing with water. Water the plant at least 3 times, letting the water drain each time. This is done most easily in a bathtub or laundry sink or outside. Always water dracaena from the top of the pot. Enough water should be added at each watering so that some drains through the pot. Empty the saucer after the pot has finished draining. If the plant is too large to handle easily, use a turkey baster to remove the drainage water. (For additional watering instructions, see page 913.) Trim the dead tips to a point with a pair of scissors. Do not overfertilize.

Dracaena cultural information
Light: Tolerates dim light
Water: When the soil just below the surface is dry

EPISCIA

Spider mite damage.

Water spots.

Mealybugs (half life size).

PROBLEM: Leaves are stippled, yellow, and dirty; they may dry out and drop. There may be webbing between leaves or on the lower surfaces of the leaves. To determine if a plant is infested with mites, hold a sheet of white paper underneath an affected plant and tap the leaves sharply. Minute green, red, or yellow specks the size of pepper grains will drop to the paper and begin to crawl around. The pests are easily seen against the white background.

ANALYSIS: Spider mites
These mites, related to spiders, are major pests of many garden and houseplants, including dracaena. They cause damage by sucking sap from the undersides of the leaves. As a result of this feeding the green pigment (chlorophyll) disappears, causing the stippled appearance. Under warm, dry conditions, which favor mites, they can build up to tremendous numbers.

SOLUTION: Spray infested plants indoors with ORTHO Whitefly & Mealybug Killer or ORTHO House Plant Insect Control; or take the plants outdoors and spray them with ORTHO Isotox Insect Killer. (For instructions on spraying houseplants, see page 915.) Plants need to be sprayed weekly for several weeks to kill the mites as they hatch. To avoid introducing mites, inspect new plants carefully.

PROBLEM: Small pale yellow to brown spots appear on the upper surfaces of the leaves. Older leaves are affected more than young leaves.

ANALYSIS: Water spots
Members of the African violet family — including episcia — are very sensitive to rapid temperature changes. Water spots most commonly occur when cold water used in watering is allowed to get on the foliage. If the rapid temperature change occurs in the presence of light, the chlorophyll (green pigment) in the leaves is broken down. In the members of this plant family, all of the chlorophyll in the leaf is found in a single layer of cells near the upper surface. If the chlorophyll in that layer is broken down, the green color disappears, and the underlying leaf color shows through.

SOLUTION: Avoid getting cold water on the foliage when watering episcia plants. Or use water at room temperature. Spotted leaves will not recover. Pick off unsightly leaves.

Episcia cultural information
Light: Needs bright light
Water: When the soil surface is moist but not wet

PROBLEM: Oval, white insects up to $\frac{1}{4}$ inch long cluster in white, cottony masses on leaves, stems, and in the crotches where leaves are attached. A sticky material may coat the leaves. Leaves may be spotted or deformed. When the condition is severe, leaves and plants may wither and die.

ANALYSIS: Mealybugs
Several species of this common insect feed on episcia. Mealybugs damage plants by sucking sap, causing leaf distortion and death. The adult female mealybug may produce live young, or may lay eggs in a white fluffy mass of wax. The immature mealybugs, called *nymphs*, crawl all over the plant and onto nearby plants. Soon after they begin to feed, they produce white waxy filaments that cover their bodies, giving them a cottony appearance. As they mature, they become less mobile. Mealybugs cannot digest all the sugar in the sap and excrete the excess in a fluid called honeydew, which coats the leaves and may drop onto furniture below the plant.

SOLUTION: Spray infested plants indoors with an insecticide containing *diazinon*. (For instructions on spraying houseplants, see page 915.) Where practical, wipe mealybugs off the plant with a damp cloth or with cotton swabs dipped in alcohol. Inspect the pot, including the bottom, for mealybug egg masses. Wipe these off. Avoid bringing mealybugs into the house by carefully inspecting new plants. For additional information on mealybugs, see page 229.

EUPHORBIA (POINSETTIA)

EUPHORBIA

LIGHT: Poinsettias need abundant light to grow well and flower; grow them in a south-facing window. They also need short days to set flower buds. Put plants in a closet for 13 hours a day for a period of 7 weeks starting around the middle of September, and no later than October 1. They can be brought into bloom any time of the year by giving the short-day treatment 10 weeks before flowering is desired.

SOIL: Any standard houseplant mix. For information on soil mixes, see page 913.

FERTILIZER: Fertilize monthly during the spring, summer, and fall with ORTHO Ortho-Gro Liquid Plant Food 12–6–6 or ORTHO House Plant Food 5–10–5.

WATER:
How much: Add enough water so that some drains out of the bottom of the pot. Empty the saucer as soon as the water drains.
How often: Water when the top soil is barely moist. If allowed to dry out, poinsettias drop their leaves. For additional information on watering houseplants, see page 913.

TEMPERATURE: Poinsettias grow best at warm temperatures. Grow in warm rooms where the temperature does not fall below 60°F at night.

SPECIAL CONDITIONS: Poinsettias will get spindly if not pruned. Pinch regularly to shape plant until August. Do not prune after short-day treatment begins, or flower buds will be removed.

Sporadic flowering.

PROBLEM: Plants continue to produce new leaves, but fail to produce flower heads.

ANALYSIS: Failure to bloom
Poinsettias set flower buds in the fall when the days are less than 12 hours long. In order for flower buds to be produced, they need to be kept in total darkness for at least 13 hours a day for 7 weeks. If this does not occur, they will continue to grow and produce new leaves but not flower heads.

SOLUTION: Poinsettias should be put in a dark closet in the evening and left there 13 hours. This should be done each day for 7 weeks, or until buds begin to appear. No light should hit the plants during this period in the dark, or they will not flower. During the day, the plants should be placed in the brightest light available. To get flowers by Christmas, the periods of darkness should start about September 15, and no later than October 1. If the poinsettia stems are long and weak, prune them back in July or August. Grow poinsettias in as bright light as possible. During the summer, they can be grown outside. Plants grown inside cannot be moved directly to full sunshine or they will sunburn. Plants should be placed in a shady area for at least two days before being moved into full sun.

Leaf drop.

PROBLEM: Lower leaves turn yellow and drop. The leaf dropping progresses up the stem until only the colored bracts may be left on the plant.

ANALYSIS: Leaf drop
Leaf drop in poinsettia may be caused by any of several factors.
1. Root rot, which kills the roots, preventing the top from getting water.
2. Inadequate or irregular watering.
3. Too much water. Even in the absence of disease-producing organisms, too much water will result in lack of air to the roots, causing leaf drop.
4. Insufficient light.

SOLUTION: The numbered solutions below correspond to the numbers in the analysis.
1. Root rot is discussed on page 260.
2. and **3.** Keep plants adequately watered, as discussed on page 913.
4. Give poinsettia plants as much light as possible. Grow them in a sunny window. Supplemental light, as described on page 914, may be desirable.

EUPHORBIA (POINSETTIA)

Root rot of poinsettia.

Botrytis on poinsettia.

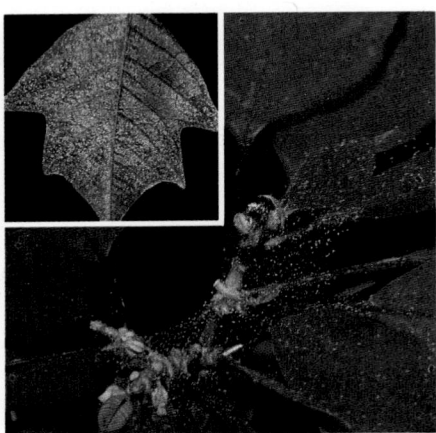

Spider mites and webs (life size). *Insert:* Damage.

PROBLEM: Starting at the bottom, leaves turn yellow and drop off. Other leaves may wilt. Eventually the stem has only the colored bracts at the top. Examination of the root system (as described on page 914) reveals dead roots that are brown and soft without white tips.

ANALYSIS: Root rot
Root rot in poinsettia is caused by any of several soil-dwelling fungi (*Pythium* species and *Thielaviopsis basicola*). These fungi invade the small roots, killing them. When the condition is extensive, the plant can no longer obtain water or nutrients, and the leaves drop. Poinsettia plants retain their colored bracts for a long time after the roots have been killed.

SOLUTION: If only a few leaves are yellowing, be careful not to keep the soil too wet. Allow the plants to dry, as discussed on page 857. If the plant is severely affected, discard it. To prevent root rot, grow plants in soil mixes that have excellent drainage. (For information about soil mixes, see page 913.) Give poinsettias abundant light.

PROBLEM: Dark brown to purple spots appear on the petallike leaves (bracts) of the red varieties of poinsettia. Tan to brown spots appear on the bracts of the white or pink varieties. In all varieties, the spots tend to appear first at the margins of the bracts, but may appear anywhere on them. The spots may enlarge until a whole bract is destroyed. The flowers (the tiny upright structures in the center of the bracts) die and are covered with a gray to brown, powdery growth. A brown, slightly sunken, soft area may be found on the stem. If this girdles the stem, the portion above it dies.

ANALYSIS: Botrytis
This disease is caused by a fungus (*Botrytis cinerea*). The fungus is unable to directly attack actively growing plant material, but can attack weakened, dead, or inactive tissues. Flowers and bracts are inactive tissues. During periods of high moisture and low temperatures, botrytis will infect such tissues. Once they are invaded, the fungus can then grow into any adjacent healthy plant tissue, such as the stem or leaves. During periods of high humidity, the fungus produces many gray to brown spores borne on dark brown stalks. These spores are carried by air currents, and in the presence of moisture will invade susceptible tissues on the same or other plants.

SOLUTION: It is not necessary to spray to control this disease. Avoid getting water on the bracts or flowers. Keep poinsettia plants in a warm room (above 65°F). Remove and destroy infected parts. Do not keep poinsettias in an environment where the humidity is high.

PROBLEM: Leaves are stippled, yellow, and dirty; they may dry out and drop. There may be webbing between leaves or on the lower surfaces of the leaves. To determine if a plant is infested with mites, hold a sheet of white paper underneath an affected plant and tap the leaves sharply. Minute green, red, or yellow specks the size of pepper grains will drop to the paper and begin to crawl around. The pests are easily seen against the white background.

ANALYSIS: Spider mites
These mites, related to spiders, are major pests of many garden and houseplants, including poinsettia. They cause damage by sucking sap from the undersides of the leaves. As a result of feeding, the green pigment (chlorophyll) disappears, causing the stippled appearance. Under warm, dry conditions mites can build up to tremendous numbers.

SOLUTION: Spray infested plants indoors with ORTHO House Plant Insect Spray or ORTHO House Plant Insect Control; or take the plants outside and spray them with ORTHO Isotox Insect Killer. (For instructions on spraying houseplants, see page 915.) Plants need to be sprayed weekly for several weeks to kill the mites as they hatch. To avoid introducing mites, inspect new plants carefully.

Whiteflies (twice life size).

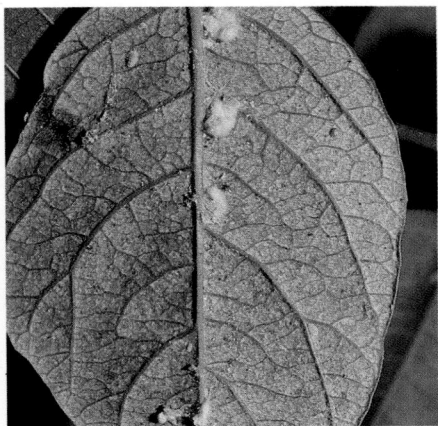

Mealybugs (life size).

FERNS

PROBLEM: Tiny, winged insects 1/12 inch long feed on the undersides of the leaves. The insects are covered with white waxy powder. When the plant is touched, insects flutter rapidly around it. Leaves may be mottled and yellowing.

ANALYSIS: Greenhouse whitefly
(*Trialeurodes vaporariorum*)
This insect is a common pest of poinsettia. The 4-winged adult lays eggs on the undersides of leaves. The larvae are the size of a pinhead, flat, oval, immobile, and semitransparent, with radiating white waxy filaments. In about a month, they change to the winged adult form. The larvae are more damaging because they suck more sap from the plants than do the adults. They cannot digest all the sugar in the sap they remove, and excrete the excess in a sugary material called honeydew, which coats the leaves and may drop from the plant onto furniture below.

SOLUTION: Spray with ORTHO House Plant Insect Control or ORTHO Isotox Insect Killer. For instructions on spraying houseplants, see page 915. Spray weekly as long as the problem continues. Remove heavily infested leaves.

PROBLEM: Oval, white insects up to 1/4 inch long cluster in white, cottony masses on leaves, stems, and in the crotches where stems or leaves are attached. A sticky material may coat the leaves. Leaves may be spotted or deformed. When the condition is severe, leaves and plants may wither and die.

ANALYSIS: Mealybugs
Several species of this common insect feed on euphorbia. Mealybugs damage plants by sucking sap, causing leaf distortion and death. The adult female mealybug may produce live young, or may lay eggs in a white fluffy mass of wax. The immature mealybugs, called *nymphs*, crawl all over the plant and onto nearby plants. Soon after they begin to feed, they produce white waxy filaments that cover their bodies, giving them a cottony appearance. As they mature, they become less mobile. Mealybugs cannot digest all the sugar in the sap and excrete the excess in a fluid called honeydew, which coats the leaves and may drop onto furniture below the plant.

SOLUTION: Spray infested plants indoors with ORTHO House Plant Insect Control; or take the plants outside and spray them with ORTHO Isotox Insect Killer. (For instructions on spraying houseplants, see page 915.) Where practical, wipe mealybugs off the plant with a damp cloth or with cotton swabs dipped in alcohol. Inspect the pot, including the bottom, for mealybug egg masses. Wipe these off. Avoid bringing mealybugs into the house by carefully inspecting new plants. For additional information on mealybugs, see page 229.

FERNS

LIGHT: Ferns are adaptable regarding light, and will grow in any filtered light including light from a north-facing window.

SOIL: Use a standard potting mix and add an equal amount of peat moss. For information on potting mixes, see page 913.

FERTILIZER: Fertilize once a month during the growing season (early spring through late summer) with ORTHO Fish Emulsion Fertilizer 5–1–1 or ORTHO Fern & Ivy Food 10–8–7.

WATER:
How much: Add enough water so that 10 percent of the water drains through the pot.
How often: Water when the top inch of soil is still moist, but not wet. For additional information on watering houseplants, see page 913.

TEMPERATURE: Ferns will do well in average house temperatures.

SPECIAL CONDITIONS: Ferns are sensitive to salts, and salts must be flushed from the soil with extra water. Do not let ferns stand in drainage water.

FERNS

Dieback caused by low humidity.

Salt damage.

Root rot.

PROBLEM: Leaves turn yellow and eventually die. Fronds may die from the tips down. The center parts of the plant are more severely affected than are the outer portions.

ANALYSIS: Low humidity
Most ferns need higher humidity than homes provide. The ferns used as houseplants are adapted to forest floors and creeksides, where the air is usually moist. In the winter, when homes are heated, the air can become as dry as desert air. Air is particularly dry near heater vents or radiators. The problem is made more severe if the soil in which the fern is growing is allowed to dry out.

SOLUTION: Move the fern to a more humid location, such as a well-lit bathroom. Misting does not help relieve stress on the fern. The mist only dampens the fronds for a few minutes at a time. Placing the plant in a tray of gravel in which some water is kept raises the humidity around the plant only if the damp air is not allowed to escape. If there is free movement of air around the plant, the practice is of little value. A portable humidifier will raise the humidity in the immediate vicinity while it is operating. Plant ferns in a potting mix that contains a high proportion of organic material, such as peat moss or ground bark, and which drains quickly. Never allow the potting mix to dry out.

PROBLEM: Margins of older leaves die and turn brown, beginning at the base of the fronds and progressing outward. In severe cases, all fronds may have dead margins. Tissues adjacent to the dead margins of older fronds may turn yellow.

ANALYSIS: Salt damage
Ferns are sensitive to excess salts. Soluble salts are picked up by the roots and accumulate in the leaf margins, where concentrations may become high enough to kill the tissues. Salts accumulate from water or the use of fertilizers; or they may be present in the soil used in potting. Salts accumulate more rapidly and do more harm if the plant is not watered thoroughly.

SOLUTION: If symptoms of salt damage occur, leach excess salts from the soil by flushing with water. Water the plant at least 3 times, letting the water drain each time. This is done most easily in a bathtub or laundry sink or outside. Always water ferns from the top of the pot. Enough water should be added at each watering so that some drains through the pot. Empty the saucer after the pot has finished draining. If the plant is too large to handle easily, use a turkey baster to remove the drainage water. (For additional watering instructions, see page 913.) Do not overfertilize.

PROBLEM: Plants fail to grow and are stunted. Roots are soft and decayed. The outer portion of the roots slips off easily from the central portion. (For instructions on examining roots, see page 914.) The top of the plant may fall over or be lifted easily out of the soil. Infected plants may die.

ANALYSIS: Root rot
This plant disease is caused by soil-dwelling fungi (*Pythium* species). These fungi attack and rot the roots of many plants, including ferns. The fungi may invade only the smaller rootlets, stunting the plant; or they may invade the main root system and cause severe rotting. Fern roots are dark, so inspecting them may be difficult. Infected roots are unable to pick up enough moisture and nutrients to support the plant. The leaves of ferns are so stiff that they wilt only slightly. Plants in soil that is too dry or too wet are more susceptible. If root rot is severe, the plant can be lifted easily from the soil.

SOLUTION: Do not let the soil stay too wet or too dry. (For instructions on watering houseplants, see page 913.) When planting, use a soil mix that allows excellent drainage. (For information on soil mixes, see page 913.) Discard severely infected plants.

Scale (twice life size).

Foliar nematode damage to bird's-nest fern.

PROBLEM: Stems and fronds are covered with white, cottony, cushionlike masses or brown crusty bumps. The bumps can be scraped or picked off easily. Fronds turn yellow and may drop. A shiny or sticky material may cover fronds and stems.

ANALYSIS: Scale insects
Several different types of scale insects attack ferns. Some types can infest many different plants. Scales hatch from eggs. The young, called *crawlers*, are small (about $^1/_{10}$ inch), soft-bodied, and move about on the plant and onto other plants. After moving about for a short time, they insert their mouthparts into the plant, feeding on the sap. The legs disappear, and the scales remain in the same place for the rest of their lives. Some develop a soft covering, others a hard covering. Some species of scales are unable to digest fully all the sugar in the plant sap and excrete the excess in a fluid called honeydew, which may cover the fronds or drip onto surfaces below.

SOLUTION: Spray infested plants with ORTHO Whitefly & Mealybug Killer or ORTHO House Plant Insect Control. Spraying is more effective against the crawlers than against the adults. Repeated applications may be necessary. For additional information on spraying houseplants, see page 915.

PROBLEM: Brown spots appear first near the central vein at the bases of the leaves. The spots spread outward between the parallel veins forming brown bands. Much of the leaf may become infected. Severely infected leaves or entire plants may die.

ANALYSIS: Foliar nematode
(*Aphelenchoides fragariae*)
This disease is caused by a nematode that infests the leaves. Nematodes are microscopic, clear worms that usually infect the roots of plants. This nematode, however, infects the foliage of a large number of plants, including bird's-nest fern. The nematodes enter the leaves through the breathing pores. Inside the leaves, they feed on the tissues, killing them, then spread into healthy tissue, extending the damage. The veins in the leaves act as barriers, resulting in the parallel bands. The nematodes reproduce rapidly in the infected leaves. They spread outside the leaves when the leaves are wet by swimming through the film of water. They may be splashed to other leaves or plants. When the condition is severe, leaves or plants may be killed.

SOLUTION: Cut off and destroy infested leaves. If plants are severely infested, destroy them. Avoid getting the leaves wet when watering. Do not spray or mist the foliage of bird's-nest fern. Keep plants in rooms warm enough so that dew does not form and the leaves do not exude water at their margins.

FICUS (ORNAMENTAL FIGS)

LIGHT: Most figs should be grown in the best light available. Fiddle leaf fig can tolerate somewhat lower light.

SOIL: Any standard houseplant mix. For information on soil mixes, see page 913.

FERTILIZER: Fertilize once a month with ORTHO Fish Emulsion Fertilizer 5–1–1, ORTHO House Plant Food 5–10–5, or ORTHO Ortho-Gro Liquid Plant Food 12–6–6. Plants in reduced light should be fertilized once every two months.

WATER:
How much: Add enough water so that some drains out of the bottom of the pot.
How often: Water when the soil under the surface is moist but not wet. *Ficus* must not be allowed to dry out. For additional information on watering houseplants, see page 913.

TEMPERATURE: Keep *Ficus* as warm as possible under house conditions.

SPECIAL CONDITIONS: Avoid moving *Ficus* to areas where light levels are different. Abrupt changes in light cause leaf yellowing and dropping on some species. If moving plants to different light intensities, move them several times so that the change in light is gradual.

FICUS (ORNAMENTAL FIGS)

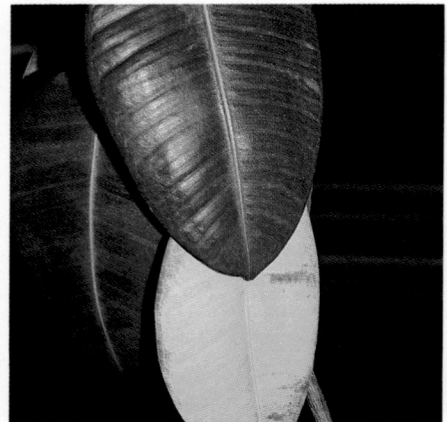

Leaf yellowing on rubber plant.

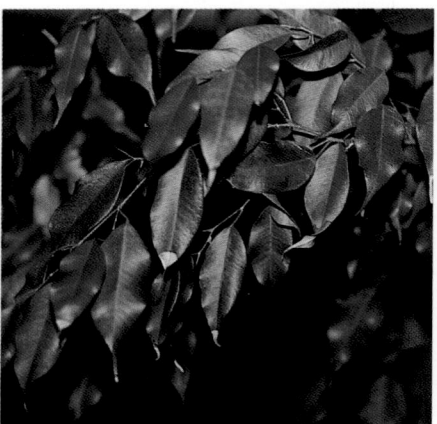

Salt damage to Java fig.

Oedema on fiddleleaf fig.

PROBLEM: Older leaves begin to yellow at the margins. This condition progresses inward until the whole leaf is yellow. Yellow leaves usually drop from the plant. Sometimes only a few leaves are left on a plant. New leaves are small, and may be light green.

ANALYSIS: Insufficient light
Plants use light as a source of energy, and grow slowly in light that is too dim for their needs. If the light is much too dim, the plant has little energy and grows poorly. Although foliage plants generally need less light than plants grown for their flowers or fruit, *Ficus* has a relatively high need for light.

SOLUTION: Move the plant to a brighter location. *Ficus* will tolerate direct sun if it is kept well watered. But if it is allowed to become dry while in direct sunlight, it will sunburn. (For more information on sunburn, see page 226.) If a brighter location is not available, provide supplemental lighting as described on page 914. If you wish to grow a houseplant in a dim location, select a plant that is tolerant of dim light from the list on page 990.

PROBLEM: Margins of older leaves die and turn brown and brittle. In severe cases, all leaves may have dead margins. Tissues adjacent to the dead margins of older leaves may turn yellow.

ANALYSIS: Salt damage
Ficus is sensitive to excess salts. Soluble salts are picked up by the roots and accumulate in the leaf margins, where concentrations may become high enough to kill the tissues. Salts can accumulate from water or the use of fertilizers; or they may be present in the soil used in potting. Salts accumulate more rapidly and do more harm if the plant is not watered thoroughly.

SOLUTION: If symptoms of salt damage occur, leach excess salts from the soil by flushing with water. Water the plant at least 3 times, letting the water drain each time. This is done most easily in a bathtub or laundry sink or outside. Always water *Ficus* from the top of the pot. Enough water should be added at each watering so that some drains through the pot. Empty the saucer after the pot has finished draining. If the plant is too large to handle, use a turkey baster to remove the drainage water. (For additional watering instructions, see page 913.) Do not overfertilize.

PROBLEM: Small (up to $\frac{3}{16}$ inch) yellow or brown spots appear on the upper surfaces of older leaves. On the undersides of the spots and sometimes on the veins are small, raised, corky areas, which may be lighter green or tan. These spots may have a dark brown center, and may be surrounded by a water-soaked area. If many spots occur, the lower leaves may turn yellow and drop.

ANALYSIS: Oedema
Oedema is a disease found on many plants. It is not caused by infection, but results from environmental factors. The exact cause of oedema is unknown. It is believed to be caused by excessive watering during periods of high humidity, but it also develops sometimes in plants that are kept dry and in low humidity. In *Ficus*, a milky juice may leak out of the corky spots. When this juice dries, it leaves a brown spot on the raised area.

SOLUTION: Give *Ficus* adequate light and adequate moisture. Avoid keeping the soil too wet, especially during periods of cloudy, damp weather. Avoid letting plants dry out.

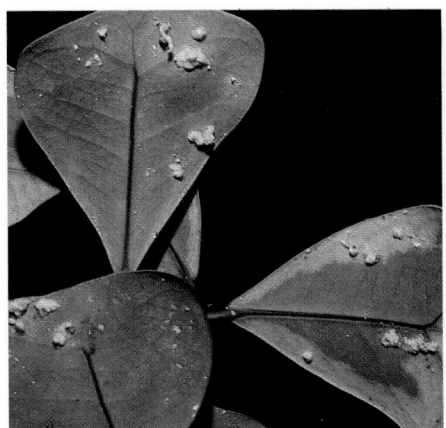

Mealybugs on mistletoe fig (life size).

Florida wax scale (twice life size).

Mealybugs (half life size).

PROBLEM: Oval, white insects up to ¼ inch long cluster in white, cottony masses on leaves, stems, and in the crotches where branches or leaves are attached. A sticky material may coat the leaves. Leaves may be spotted or deformed. When the condition is severe, leaves and plants may wither and die.

ANALYSIS: Mealybugs
Several species of this common insect feed on *Ficus*. Mealybugs damage plants by sucking sap, causing leaf distortion and death. The adult female mealybug may produce live young, or may lay eggs in a white fluffy mass of wax. The immature mealybugs, called *nymphs*, crawl all over the plant and onto nearby plants. Soon after they begin to feed, they produce white waxy filaments that cover their bodies, giving them a cottony appearance. As they mature, they become less mobile. Mealybugs cannot digest all the sugar in the sap and excrete the excess in a fluid called honeydew, which coats the leaves and may drop onto furniture below the plant.

SOLUTION: Spray infested plants with ORTHO Whitefly & Mealybug Killer or ORTHO House Plant Insect Control. (For instructions on spraying houseplants, see page 915.) Where practical, wipe mealybugs off the plant with a damp cloth or with cotton swabs dipped in alcohol. Inspect the pot, including the bottom, for mealybug egg masses. Wipe these off. Avoid bringing mealybugs into the house by carefully inspecting new plants. For additional information on mealybugs, see page 229.

PROBLEM: Stems and leaves are covered with white, cottony, cushionlike masses or brown crusty bumps. The bumps can be scraped or picked off easily. Leaves turn yellow and may drop. A shiny or sticky material may cover leaves and stems.

ANALYSIS: Scale insects
Several different types of scale insects attack *Ficus*. Some types can infest many different plants. Scales hatch from eggs. The young, called *crawlers*, are small (about ¹⁄₁₀ inch), soft-bodied, and move about on the plant and onto other plants. After moving about for a short time, they insert their mouthparts into the plant, feeding on the sap. The legs disappear, and the scales remain in the same place for the rest of their lives. Some develop a soft covering, others a hard covering. Some species of scales are unable to digest fully all the sugar in the plant sap and excrete the excess in a fluid called honeydew, which may cover the leaves or drip onto surfaces below.

SOLUTION: Spray infested plants with ORTHO Whitefly & Mealybug Killer or ORTHO House Plant Insect Control. Spraying is more effective against the crawlers than against the adults. Repeated applications may be necessary. For additional information on spraying houseplants, see page 915.

PROBLEM: Oval, white insects up to ¼ inch long cluster in white, cottony masses on leaves, stems, and in the crotches where the leaves are attached. A sticky material may coat the leaves. Leaves may be spotted or deformed. When the condition is severe, leaves and plants may wither and die.

ANALYSIS: Mealybugs
Several species of this common insect feed on nerve plant. Mealybugs damage plants by sucking sap, causing leaf distortion and death. The adult female mealybug may produce live young, or may lay eggs in a white fluffy mass of wax. The immature mealybugs, called *nymphs*, crawl all over the plant and onto nearby plants. Soon after they begin to feed, they produce white waxy filaments that cover their bodies, giving them a cottony appearance. As they mature, they become less mobile. Mealybugs cannot digest all the sugar in the sap and excrete the excess in a fluid called honeydew, which coats the leaves and may drop onto furniture below the plant.

SOLUTION: Spray infested plants with an insecticide containing *diazinon*. (For instructions on spraying houseplants, see page 915.) Where practical, wipe mealybugs off the plant with a damp cloth or with cotton swabs dipped in alcohol. Inspect the pot, including the bottom, for mealybug egg masses. Wipe these off. Avoid bringing mealybugs into the house by carefully inspecting new plants. For additional information on mealybugs, see page 229.

GARDENIA

Cold damage.

Iron deficiency.

Brown soft scale (twice life size).

PROBLEM: Plants fail to produce flowers. If buds are produced, they drop from the plant without opening. Foliage may be light green; plants may be stunted.

ANALYSIS: Too cold
Gardenia plants are native to warm areas. If they do not receive enough heat, they cannot manufacture enough food to grow well, and they stop producing flowers. If too cold, the plants will be stunted and not as much green pigment (chlorophyll) will be produced.

SOLUTION: Grow gardenia plants in the warmest location with the most light possible. If the room is cool at night, move the plant to a warm room. In the summer, the plant can be grown outside in light shade.

Gardenia cultural information
Light: Needs bright light
Water: When the soil just below the surface is barely moist

PROBLEM: The newest leaves turn yellow at the margins. As the leaves become more yellow, the veins remain green. In severe cases, the entire leaf is yellow and small. The plant may be stunted.

ANALYSIS: Iron deficiency
This is a common problem with acid-loving plants like gardenia, which grow best in soil with a pH between 5.5 and 6.5. (For more information on soil acidity, see page 902.) The leaf yellowing is due to a deficiency of iron and other minor nutrients in the plant. The soil is seldom deficient in iron. However, iron is often found in an insoluble form that is not available to gardenias, especially when the soil pH is too high. Plants use iron in the formation of the green pigment (chlorophyll) in the leaves.

SOLUTION: Spray the foliage with ORTHO Greenol Liquid Iron 6.13%, and apply it to the soil in the pot to correct iron deficiency. Use only acid-forming fertilizers like ORTHO Azalea, Camellia & Rhododendron Food 5–10–10. When potting or transplanting gardenias, use an acidic soil mix that has about 50 percent peat moss. Use a minimum amount of lime or dolomite in the soil mix.

PROBLEM: Stems and leaves are covered with white, cottony, cushionlike masses or brown crusty bumps. The bumps can be scraped or picked off easily. Leaves turn yellow and may drop. A shiny or sticky material may cover leaves and stems.

ANALYSIS: Scale insects
Several different types of scale insects attack gardenias. Some types can infest many different plants. Scales hatch from eggs. The young, called *crawlers*, are small (about 1/10 inch), soft-bodied, and move about on the plant and onto other plants. After moving about for a short time, they insert their mouthparts into the plant, feeding on the sap. The legs disappear, and the scales remain in the same place for the rest of their lives. Some develop a soft covering, others a hard covering. Some species of scales are unable to digest fully all the sugar in the plant sap and excrete the excess in a fluid called honeydew, which may cover the leaves or drip onto surfaces below.

SOLUTION: Spray infested plants indoors with ORTHO House Plant Insect Control; or take the plants outside and spray them with ORTHO Malathion 50 Insect Spray, ORTHO Orthene Systemic Insect Control, or ORTHO Isotox Insect Killer, according to the directions on the label. Spraying is more effective against the crawlers than against the adults. Repeated applications may be necessary. For additional information on spraying houseplants, see page 915.

GYNURA (PURPLE PASSION VINE)

Aphids (life size).

PROBLEM: New leaves are curled, discolored, and reduced in size. A shiny or sticky substance may coat the leaves. Tiny (⅛ inch), nonwinged, green, soft-bodied insects cluster on the buds, young stems, and leaves.

ANALYSIS: Aphids
Aphids do little damage in small numbers. However, they are extremely prolific and populations can rapidly build up to damaging numbers on purple passion vines. Damage results when the aphids suck sap from the leaves and stems. Aphids are unable to digest fully all the sugar in the plant sap and excrete the excess in a fluid called honeydew, which often drops onto leaves or furniture below the plant.

SOLUTION: Use ORTHO House Plant Insect Control, ORTHO House Plant Insect Spray, or ORTHO Whitefly & Mealybug Killer. For additional information on spraying houseplants, see page 915.

Gynura cultural information
Light: Needs bright light
Water: When the soil just below the surface is barely moist

PROBLEM: Oval, white insects up to ¼ inch long cluster in white, cottony masses on leaves, stems, and in the crotches where the leaves are attached. A sticky material may coat the leaves. Leaves may be spotted or deformed. When the condition is severe, leaves and plants may wither and die.

ANALYSIS: Mealybugs
Several species of this common insect feed on purple passion vine. Mealybugs damage plants by sucking sap, causing leaf distortion and death. The adult female mealybug may produce live young, or may lay eggs in a white fluffy mass of wax. The immature mealybugs, called *nymphs*, crawl all over the plant and onto nearby plants. Soon after they begin to feed, they produce white waxy filaments that cover their bodies, giving them a cottony appearance. As they mature, they become less mobile. Mealybugs cannot digest all the sugar in the sap and excrete the excess in a fluid called honeydew, which coats the leaves and may drop onto furniture below the plant.

SOLUTION: Spray infested plants indoors with ORTHO Whitefly & Mealybug Killer or ORTHO House Plant Insect Control. Or take the plants outside and spray them with ORTHO Isotox Insect Killer. (For instructions on spraying houseplants, see page 915.) Where practical, wipe mealybugs off the plant with a damp cloth or with cotton swabs dipped in alcohol. Inspect the pot, including the bottom, for mealybug egg masses. Wipe these off. Avoid bringing mealybugs into the house by carefully inspecting new plants. For additional information on mealybugs, see page 229.

HAWORTHIA

Salt damage.

PROBLEM: Tips of older leaves die and turn brown. In severe cases, the tips of all leaves may be dead.

ANALYSIS: Salt damage
Haworthia is sensitive to excess salts. Soluble salts are picked up by the roots and accumulate in the leaf tips, where concentrations may become high enough to kill the tissues. Salts can accumulate from water or the use of fertilizers; or they may be present in the soil used in potting. Salts accumulate more rapidly and do more harm if the plant is not watered thoroughly.

SOLUTION: If symptoms of salt damage occur, leach excess salts from the soil by flushing with water. Water the plant at least 3 times, letting the water drain each time. This is done most easily in a bathtub or laundry sink or outside. Always water haworthia from the top of the pot. Enough water should be added at each watering so that some drains through the pot. Empty the saucer after the pot has finished draining. (For additional watering instructions, see page 913.) Do not overfertilize.

Haworthia cultural information
Light: Needs bright light
Water: When the soil just below the surface is dry

HEDERA (IVY)

Sunburn.

Salt damage.

HEDERA (IVY)

LIGHT: Ivy is adaptable regarding light. It will grow in bright light, but will also grow in low light, as in a north-facing window.

SOIL: Use any of the standard potting mixes. For information on soil mixes, see page 913.

FERTILIZER: For best growth, fertilize once a month with ORTHO Fish Emulsion Fertilizer 5-1-1 or ORTHO Fern & Ivy Food 10-8-7. If less growth is desired, fertilize every other month.

WATER:
How much: Add enough water so that some drains through the pot.
How often: Water when the top layer of soil begins to get dry. Ivy is very tolerant of dry conditions. For additional information on watering houseplants, see page 913.

TEMPERATURE: Average house temperatures are suitable.

SPECIAL CONDITIONS: Do not let ivy plants stand in drainage water. Excessive moisture will favor oedema (see page 269). Fertilizing and watering less frequently will result in slower growth and more compact plants. Plants can be cut back to induce compactness.

PROBLEM: Pale green to yellow blotches appear between the leaf veins. These blotches may become bleached white or tan as the tissue between the veins dies. Whole sections between veins may be affected. Spots may merge, affecting larger areas.

ANALYSIS: Sunburn
Excessive sunlight causes the green pigment (chlorophyll) to disappear in ivy leaves. This happens most easily if the plant is allowed to dry out. Once the tissues have lost their chlorophyll, the sunlight kills the tissues between the veins. The underlying color of different ivy species determines the color of the dead tissues. Plants moved from inside to direct sunlight will sunburn very severely.

SOLUTION: Keep ivy plants well watered so they do not dry out, particularly if they are in direct sunlight. If you are moving plants from inside to outside, place them in the shade for several days before putting them in direct sunlight.

PROBLEM: Margins of older leaves die and turn brown and brittle. In severe cases, all leaves may have dead margins. Tissues adjacent to the dead margins of older leaves may turn yellow.

ANALYSIS: Salt damage
Ivy is sensitive to excess salts. Soluble salts are picked up by the roots and accumulate in the leaf margins, where concentrations may become high enough to kill the tissues. Salts can accumulate from water or the use of fertilizers; or they may be present in the soil used in potting. Salts accumulate more rapidly and do more harm if the plant is not watered thoroughly.

SOLUTION: If symptoms of salt damage occur, leach excess salts from the soil by flushing with water. Water the plant at least 3 times, letting the water drain each time. This is done most easily in a bathtub or laundry sink or outside. Always water ivy from the top of the pot. Enough water should be added at each watering so that some drains through the pot. Empty the saucer after the pot has finished draining. If the plant is too large to handle easily, use a turkey baster to remove the drainage water. (For additional watering instructions, see page 913.) Do not overfertilize.

Oedema.

Brown soft scale (twice life size).

Spider mites (twice life size) and webs.

PROBLEM: Small (3/16 inch), red to black spots appear on the upper surfaces of the leaves. On the undersides of these spots are raised corky areas that first appear light green and water-soaked. Eventually they become dark brown or black. In severe cases, leaves may become yellow.

ANALYSIS: Oedema
Oedema is a disease found on many plants. It is not infectious but results from unfavorable environmental factors. The exact cause of oedema is unknown. It is believed to be due to excessive watering during periods of high humidity. However, it occasionally occurs with low humidity and on ivy plants that have been kept dry.

SOLUTION: Grow ivy with adequate moisture and fertilizer. Avoid keeping soil too wet or too dry. To give adequate light, grow ivy in a window that faces east, south, or west. Avoid overcrowding plants.

PROBLEM: Stems and leaves are covered with white, cottony, cushion-like masses or brown crusty bumps or clusters of somewhat flattened, reddish, gray or brown scaly bumps. The bumps can be scraped off or picked off easily. Leaves turn yellow and may drop. A shiny or sticky material may cover leaves and stems.

ANALYSIS: Scale insects
Several different types of scale insects attack ivy. Some types can infest many different plants. Scales hatch from eggs. The young, called *crawlers*, are small (about 1/10 inch), soft-bodied, and move about on the plant and onto other plants. After moving about for a short time, they insert their mouthparts into the plant, feeding on the sap. The legs atrophy, and the scales remain in the same place for the rest of their lives. Some develop a soft covering, others a hard covering. Some species of scales are unable to digest fully all the sugar in the plant sap and excrete the excess in a fluid called honeydew, which may cover the leaves or drip onto surfaces below.

SOLUTION: Spray infested plants with ORTHO Whitefly & Mealybug Killer or ORTHO House Plant Insect Control according to the directions on the label. Spraying is more effective against the crawlers than against the adults. Repeated applications may be necessary. For additional information on spraying houseplants, see page 915.

PROBLEM: Leaves are stippled, yellow, and dirty; they may dry out and drop. There may be webbing between leaves or on the lower surfaces of the leaves. To determine if a plant is infested with mites, hold a sheet of white paper underneath an affected plant and tap the leaves sharply. Minute green, red, or yellow specks the size of pepper grains will drop to the paper and begin to crawl around. The pests are easily seen against the white background.

ANALYSIS: Spider mites
These mites, related to spiders, are major pests of many garden and houseplants, including ivy. They cause damage by sucking sap from the undersides of the leaves. As a result of this feeding, the green pigment (chlorophyll) disappears, causing the stippled appearance. Under warm, dry conditions, which favor mites, they can build up to tremendous numbers.

SOLUTION: Spray infested plants with ORTHO House Plant Insect Control or ORTHO Whitefly & Mealybug Killer. (For instructions on spraying houseplants, see page 915.) Plants need to be sprayed weekly for several weeks to kill the mites as they hatch. To avoid introducing mites, inspect new plants carefully.

HEDERA (ENGLISH IVY) ————

Mealybugs (life size).

PROBLEM: Oval, white insects up to ¼ inch long cluster in white, cottony masses on leaves, stems, and in the crotches where the leaves are attached. A sticky material may coat the leaves. Leaves may be spotted or deformed. When the condition is severe, leaves and plants may wither and die.

ANALYSIS: Mealybugs
Several species of this common insect feed on ivy. Mealybugs damage plants by sucking sap, causing leaf distortion and death. The adult female mealybug may produce live young, or may lay eggs in a white fluffy mass of wax. The immature mealybugs, called *nymphs*, crawl all over the plant and onto nearby plants. Soon after they begin to feed, they produce white waxy filaments that cover their bodies, giving them a cottony appearance. As they mature, they become less mobile. Mealybugs cannot digest all the sugar in the sap and excrete the excess in a fluid called honeydew, which coats the leaves and may drop onto furniture below the plant.

SOLUTION: Spray infested plants indoors with ORTHO Whitefly & Mealybug Killer; or take the plants outside and spray them with ORTHO Orthene Systemic Insect Control or ORTHO Isotox Insect Killer. (For instructions on spraying houseplants, see page 915.) Where practical, wipe mealybugs off the plant with a damp cloth or with cotton swabs dipped in alcohol. Inspect the pot, including the bottom, for mealybug egg masses. Wipe these off. Avoid bringing mealybugs into the house by carefully inspecting new plants. For additional information on mealybugs, see page 229.

HIPPEASTRUM (AMARYLLIS) ————

Leaf scorch.

PROBLEM: Red spots and lesions appear on the flower stalk, leaves, and petals. The spots may elongate to several inches in length. Reddish brown, sunken lesions (cankers) with bright red borders may develop on the flower stalks. Flower stalks may be stunted, distorted, and growing at an angle. Severely infected flower stalks fail to bloom.

ANALYSIS: Leaf scorch
This plant disease is caused by a fungus (*Stagonospora curtisii*) that attacks both growing plants and bulbs in storage. Soon after infected bulbs produce growth, fungal spores are splashed and blown to the stems and leaves. The spores germinate and infect the tissue, causing spots and cankers to form. The disease is spread by contaminated bulbs, and is most severe in moist conditions.

SOLUTION: Discard severely infected plants. Infection may be controlled on mildly infected plants by keeping them in a dry location and spraying with a fungicide containing *ferbam* or *zineb* every 2 weeks until they bloom. Check all bulbs before planting, and discard infected bulbs.

Hippeastrum cultural information
Light: Needs bright light
Water: When the soil surface is moist but not wet

HOYA (WAX PLANT) ————

Aphids (twice life size).

PROBLEM: New leaves are curled, discolored, and reduced in size. A shiny or sticky substance may coat the leaves. Tiny (⅛ inch), nonwinged, green, soft-bodied insects cluster on the buds, young stems, and leaves.

ANALYSIS: Aphids
Aphids do little damage in small numbers. However, they are extremely prolific and populations can rapidly build up to damaging numbers on hoya. Damage results when the aphids suck sap from the leaves and stems. Aphids are unable to digest fully all the sugar in the plant sap and excrete the excess in a fluid called honeydew, which often drops onto leaves or furniture below the plant.

SOLUTION: Use ORTHO House Plant Insect Spray. For additional information on spraying houseplants, see page 915.

Hoya cultural information
Light: Needs bright light
Water: When the soil just below the surface is barely moist

Spider mite damage.

Failure to flower.

Mealybugs (half life size).

PROBLEM: Leaves are stippled, yellow, and dirty; they may dry out and drop. There may be webbing over flower buds, between leaves, or on the lower surfaces of the leaves. To determine if a plant is infested with mites, hold a sheet of white paper underneath an affected plant and tap the leaves sharply. Minute green, red, or yellow specks the size of pepper grains will drop to the paper and begin to crawl around. The pests are easily seen against the white background.

ANALYSIS: Spider mites
These mites, related to spiders, are major pests of many garden and houseplants, including wax plant. They cause damage by sucking sap from the undersides of the leaves. As a result of this feeding, the green pigment (chlorophyll) disappears, causing the stippled appearance. Under warm, dry conditions, which favor mites, they can build up to tremendous numbers.

SOLUTION: Spray infested plants with ORTHO Whitefly & Mealybug Killer. (For instructions on spraying houseplants, see page 915.) Plants need to be sprayed weekly for several weeks to kill the mites as they hatch. To avoid introducing mites, inspect new plants carefully.

PROBLEM: Plants fail to flower. Vines tend to grow toward a light source. Leaves are produced far apart on the stems.

ANALYSIS: Insufficient light
Plants use light as a source of energy. If there is only enough light for leaf and vine growth, hoya will not bloom. It must have bright light in order to make flowers. If the light is too dim for optimum growth, the plant not only will not bloom, but growth is slowed, and the vines grow toward a light source. Leaves will be small and far apart on the vines.

SOLUTION: Move the plant to a brighter location. Hoya will tolerate direct sun if it is kept well watered. But if it is allowed to become dry while in direct sunlight, it will sunburn. (For more information on sunburn, see page 226.) If a brighter location is not available, provide supplemental lighting as described on page 914. If you wish to grow a houseplant in a dim location, select a plant that is tolerant of dim light from the list on page 990.

PROBLEM: Oval, white insects up to ¼ inch long cluster in white, cottony masses on leaves, stems, and in the crotches where the leaves are attached. A sticky material may coat the leaves. Leaves may be spotted or deformed. When the condition is severe, leaves and plants may wither and die.

ANALYSIS: Mealybugs
Several species of this common insect feed on wax plant. Mealybugs damage plants by sucking sap, causing leaf distortion and death. The adult female mealybug may produce live young, or may lay eggs in a white fluffy mass of wax. The immature mealybugs, called *nymphs*, crawl all over the plant and onto nearby plants. Soon after they begin to feed, they produce white waxy filaments that cover their bodies, giving them a cottony appearance. As they mature, they become less mobile. Mealybugs cannot digest all the sugar in the sap and excrete the excess in a fluid called honeydew, which coats the leaves and may drop onto furniture below the plant.

SOLUTION: Spray infested plants indoors with ORTHO Whitefly & Mealybug Killer. (For instructions on spraying houseplants, see page 915.) Where practical, wipe mealybugs off the plant with a damp cloth or with cotton swabs dipped in alcohol. Inspect the pot, including the bottom, for mealybug egg masses. Wipe these off. Avoid bringing mealybugs into the house by carefully inspecting new plants. For additional information on mealybugs, see page 229.

IRESINE (BLOOD LEAF) ————— ## KALANCHOE —————

Weak stems.

Powdery mildew.

Mealybugs (¼ life size).

PROBLEM: Leaves fade from deep red to very light red. Stems elongate, and leaves are produced farther apart on the stems. Stems become weak.

ANALYSIS: Insufficient light
Plants use light as a source of energy, and grow slowly in light that is too dim for their needs. If most of the available light comes from one direction, the stems and leaves bend in that direction. If the light is much too dim for them, the plant has little energy and grows poorly. Plants with brightly colored leaves, such as blood leaf, need bright light to develop the color fully.

SOLUTION: Move the plant to a brighter location, such as a lightly curtained sunny window. If a brighter location is not available, provide supplemental lighting as described on page 914. If you wish to grow a houseplant in a dim location, select a plant that is tolerant of dim light from the list on page 990.

Iresine cultural information
Light: Needs bright light
Water: When the soil just below the surface is barely moist

PROBLEM: White to light tan powdery patches appear on the leaves and stems. Severely infected leaves may turn yellow, wither, and fall.

ANALYSIS: Powdery mildew
On kalanchoe, powdery mildew is caused by a fungus (*Sphaerotheca humuli* var. *fuliginea*). It grows on the surface of the leaves and stems, producing white strands and spores that make powdery patches. The spores are carried by air currents to other plants. If the fungus is abundant, leaves are weakened, turn yellow, and die. Powdery mildew is favored by reduced light.

SOLUTION: Spray with a fungicide containing *dinocap* or *cycloheximide*. (For instructions on spraying houseplants, see page 915.) Remove severely infected leaves. Move any infected kalanchoe plants away from healthy ones. Grow kalanchoe in a sunny window.

Kalanchoe cultural information
Light: Needs bright light
Water: When the soil just below the surface is dry

PROBLEM: Oval, white insects up to ¼ inch long cluster in white, cottony masses on leaves, stems, and in the crotches where the leaves are attached. A sticky material may coat the leaves. Leaves may be spotted or deformed. When the condition is severe, leaves and plants may wither and die.

ANALYSIS: Mealybugs
Several species of this common insect feed on kalanchoe. Mealybugs damage plants by sucking sap, causing leaf distortion and death. The adult female mealybug may produce live young, or may lay eggs in a white fluffy mass of wax. The immature mealybugs, called *nymphs*, crawl all over the plant and onto nearby plants. Soon after they begin to feed, they produce white waxy filaments that cover their bodies, giving them a cottony appearance. As they mature, they become less mobile. Mealybugs cannot digest all the sugar in the sap and excrete the excess in a fluid called honeydew, which coats the leaves and may drop onto furniture below the plant.

SOLUTION: Spray infested plants indoors with ORTHO Whitefly & Mealybug Killer or ORTHO House Plant Insect Control; or take the plants outside and spray them with ORTHO Isotox Insect Killer. (For instructions on spraying houseplants, see page 915.) Where practical, wipe mealybugs off the plant with a damp cloth or with cotton swabs dipped in alcohol. Inspect the pot, including the bottom, for mealybug egg masses. Wipe these off. Avoid bringing mealybugs into the house by carefully inspecting new plants. For additional information on mealybugs, see page 229.

MARANTA (PRAYER PLANT)

Salt damage.

Spider mite damage.

Mealybugs (life size).

PROBLEM: Margins of older leaves die and turn brown and brittle. In severe cases, all leaves may have dead margins. Tissues adjacent to the dead margins of older leaves may turn yellow.

ANALYSIS: Salt damage
Prayer plant is very sensitive to excess salts. Soluble salts are picked up by the roots and accumulate in the leaf margins, where concentrations may become high enough to kill the tissues. Salts can accumulate from water or the use of fertilizers; or they may be present in the soil used in potting. Salts accumulate more rapidly and do more harm if the plant is not watered thoroughly.

SOLUTION: If symptoms of salt damage occur, leach excess salts from the soil by flushing with water. Water the plant at least 3 times, letting the water drain each time. This is done most easily in a bathtub or laundry sink or outside. Always water prayer plant from the top of the pot. Enough water should be added at each watering so that some drains through the pot. Empty the saucer after the pot has finished draining. If the plant is too large to handle easily, use a turkey baster to remove the drainage water. (For additional watering instructions, see page 913.) Do not overfertilize.

Maranta cultural information
Light: Needs medium light
Water: When the soil just below the surface is barely moist

PROBLEM: Leaves are stippled, yellow, and dirty; they may dry out and drop. There may be webbing between leaves or on the lower surfaces of the leaves. To determine if a plant is infested with mites, hold a sheet of white paper underneath an affected plant and tap the leaves sharply. Minute green, red, or yellow specks the size of pepper grains will drop to the paper and begin to crawl around. The pests are easily seen against the white background.

ANALYSIS: Spider mites
These mites, related to spiders, are major pests of many garden and houseplants, including prayer plants. They cause damage by sucking sap from the undersides of the leaves. As a result of this feeding, the green pigment (chlorophyll) disappears, causing the stippled appearance. Under warm, dry conditions, which favor mites, they can build up to tremendous numbers.

SOLUTION: Spray infested plants indoors with ORTHO House Plant Insect Control or ORTHO Whitefly & Mealybug Killer; or take the plants outside and spray them with ORTHO Isotox Insect Spray. (For instructions on spraying houseplants, see page 915.) Plants need to be sprayed weekly for several weeks to kill the mites as they hatch. To avoid introducing mites, inspect new plants carefully.

PROBLEM: Oval, white insects up to ¼ inch long cluster in white, cottony masses on leaves, stems, and in the crotches where the leaves are attached. A sticky material may coat the leaves. Leaves may be spotted or deformed. When the condition is severe, leaves and plants may wither and die.

ANALYSIS: Mealybugs
Several species of this common insect feed on prayer plants. Mealybugs damage plants by sucking sap, causing leaf distortion and death. The adult female mealybug may produce live young, or may lay eggs in a white fluffy mass of wax. The immature mealybugs, called *nymphs*, crawl all over the plant and onto nearby plants. Soon after they begin to feed, they produce white waxy filaments that cover their bodies, giving them a cottony appearance. As they mature, they become less mobile. Mealybugs cannot digest all the sugar in the sap and excrete the excess in a fluid called honeydew, which coats the leaves and may drop onto furniture below the plant.

SOLUTION: Spray infested plants indoors with ORTHO Whitefly & Mealybug Killer or ORTHO House Plant Insect Control; or take the plants outside and spray them with ORTHO Isotox Insect Killer. (For instructions on spraying houseplants, see page 915.) Where practical, wipe mealybugs off the plant with a damp cloth or with cotton swabs dipped in alcohol. Inspect the pot, including the bottom, for mealybug egg masses. Wipe these off. Avoid bringing mealybugs into the house by carefully inspecting new plants. For additional information on mealybugs, see page 229.

MONSTERA (SPLIT-LEAF PHILODENDRON)

Failure to split.

Salt damage.

Mealybug (life size).

PROBLEM: New leaves do not grow as large as older leaves. New leaves are darker green, and have fewer or no splits in them. The stem is elongated, with more space between the new leaves. The leaves turn toward the light. Older leaves may turn yellow.

ANALYSIS: Insufficient light
Split-leaf philodendrons need a lot of light to grow correctly. In the absence of enough light, the leaves become smaller and darker green with no splits, so that the plant can use all the light available to manufacture food.

SOLUTION: Give split-leaf philodendrons enough light so that normal splitting of the leaves occurs. If leaves do not split, move the plant to a brighter area. Although they will tolerate somewhat reduced levels of light, split-leaf philodendrons grow best in a curtained south, east, or west-facing window.

Monstera cultural information
Light: Needs medium light
Water: When the soil just below the surface is barely moist

PROBLEM: Margins of older leaves die and turn brown and brittle. In severe cases, all leaves may have dead margins. Tissues adjacent to the dead margins of older leaves may turn yellow.

ANALYSIS: Salt damage
Split-leaf philodendron is sensitive to excess salts. Soluble salts are picked up by the roots and accumulate in the leaf margins, where concentrations may become high enough to kill the tissues. Salts can accumulate from water or the use of fertilizers; or they may be present in the soil used in potting. Salts accumulate more rapidly and do more harm if the plant is not watered thoroughly.

SOLUTION: If symptoms of salt damage occur, leach excess salts from the soil by flushing with water. Water the plant at least 3 times, letting the water drain each time. This is done most easily in a bathtub or laundry sink or outside. Always water split-leaf philodendron from the top of the pot. Enough water should be added at each watering so that some drains through the pot. Empty the saucer after the pot has finished draining. If the plant is too large to handle easily, use a turkey baster to remove the drainage water. (For additional watering instructions, see page 913.) Do not overfertilize.

PROBLEM: Oval, white insects up to ¼ inch long cluster in white, cottony masses on leaves, stems, and in the crotches where the leaves are attached. A sticky material may coat the leaves. Leaves may be spotted or deformed.

ANALYSIS: Mealybugs
Several species of this common insect feed on split-leaf philodendron. Mealybugs damage plants by sucking sap, causing leaf distortion and death. The adult female mealybug may produce live young, or may lay eggs in a white fluffy mass of wax. The immature mealybugs, called *nymphs,* crawl all over the plant and onto nearby plants. Soon after they begin to feed, they produce white waxy filaments that cover their bodies, giving them a cottony appearance. As they mature, they become less mobile. Mealybugs cannot digest all the sugar in the sap and excrete the excess in a fluid called honeydew, which coats the leaves and may drop onto furniture below the plant.

SOLUTION: Spray infested plants with ORTHO Whitefly & Mealybug Killer. Where practical, wipe mealybugs off the plant with a damp cloth or with cotton swabs dipped in alcohol. Inspect the pot, including the bottom, for mealybug egg masses. Wipe these off. Avoid bringing mealybugs into the house by carefully inspecting new plants. For additional information on mealybugs, see page 229.

ORCHIDS _____

Failure to bloom.

Virus.

ORCHIDS _____

LIGHT: Many orchids like abundant light, and grow best in bright light. Some may need filtered light during the hottest part of the day, and some may need filtered light all day.

FERTILIZER: Fertilize with half-strength ORTHO Ortho-Gro Liquid Plant Food 12–6–6 once every two weeks during the growing and blooming season. The rest of the year, fertilize every other month.

WATER:
How much: Orchids should be watered until water runs out the bottom of the pot.
How often: Orchids in osmunda fiber, shredded tree fern, or fir bark should be watered once a week during the growing and blooming season, and less often during the winter months. Orchids in soil mixes should be watered when the soil at the top is barely moist.

SOIL MIX: Epiphytic orchids (*Cattleya, Laelia, Miltonia, Oncidium, Phalaenopsis, Vanda*) should be grown in osmunda fiber, shredded tree fern, or fir bark. If using bark, orchids with large roots should be planted in coarse bark; those with smaller roots should be planted in medium-sized bark; those with small roots should be planted in fine bark. Epiphytic orchids may also be grown on pieces of tree fern to which sphagnum moss has been tied. *Cymbidium, Epidendrum, and Paphiopedilum* should be grown in an orchid mix or a mix containing 5 parts fine fir bark to 1 part standard orchid mix.

PROBLEM: Plants do not bloom. The leaves are a deep green.

ANALYSIS: Insufficient light
Plants use light as a source of energy, and will not bloom unless they have enough light to fulfill their needs for growth, and some surplus. Although orchids are adapted to blooming in shaded locations, they still need relatively bright light, compared to houseplants that are grown for their foliage.

SOLUTION: Move the plants to a brighter location, but do not put them in direct sun. If the light is too bright, the leaves will turn yellow and burn. A lightly curtained window that receives more than four hours of sun a day is an ideal location for orchids. If a brighter location is not available, provide supplementary lighting as described on page 914. For a list of plants that will tolerate dim light, see page 990.

PROBLEM: Leaves are mottled with yellow blotches. Or they have yellow streaks or flecks that later turn dark brown or black. Leaves may have partial, complete, or concentric rings of dark-colored tissue. New leaves may be stunted and cupped. Flowers may be mottled and the colors broken. They may be moderately or severely distorted, and may have brown flecks or streaks in them. Affected flowers do not last long.

ANALYSIS: Viruses
Several viruses infect orchids. Some infect many different types of orchids, and others infect only a few. Viruses cause a plant to manufacture new viruses from its protein. In the process, the metabolism of the plant is upset. Different symptoms appear, depending upon the orchid and the virus present. Viruses are easily transmitted on tools used in cutting orchid plants.

SOLUTION: Observe the effects of viruses on the plants. If flowers are badly malformed or discolored, discard the plants. Keep plants that are virus-free separate from those showing virus symptoms, because the viruses are easily transmitted. Sterilize cutting tools by dipping them in rubbing alcohol when moving from one plant to another. Do not purchase plants that show such symptoms.

ORCHIDS

Spider mite damage.

Orchid scale (half life size).

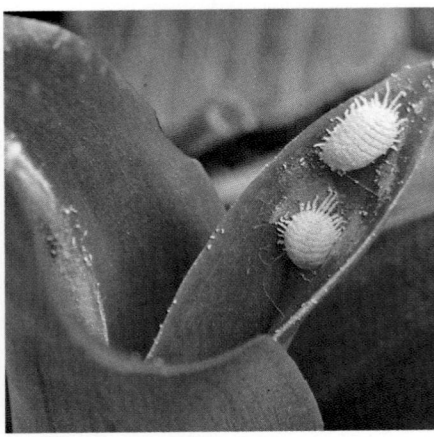

Mealybugs (twice life size).

PROBLEM: Leaves are stippled, yellow, and dirty; they may dry out and drop. There may be webbing over flower buds, between leaves, or on the lower surfaces of the leaves. To determine if a plant is infested with mites, hold a sheet of white paper underneath an affected plant and tap the leaves sharply. Minute green, red, or yellow specks the size of pepper grains will drop to the paper and begin to crawl around. The pests are easily seen against the white background.

ANALYSIS: Spider mites
These mites, related to spiders, are major pests of many garden and houseplants, including orchids. They cause damage by sucking sap from the undersides of the leaves. As a result of feeding, the green pigment (chlorophyll) disappears, causing the stippled appearance. Under warm, dry conditions, which favor mites, they can build up to tremendous numbers.

SOLUTION: Spray infested plants with ORTHO House Plant Insect Spray or take them outdoors and spray with ORTHO Orthene Systemic Insect Control. (For instructions on spraying houseplants, see page 915.) Plants need to be sprayed weekly for several weeks to kill the mites as they hatch. To avoid introducing mites, inspect new plants carefully.

PROBLEM: Stems and leaves are covered with white, cottony, cushionlike masses or brown crusty bumps. The bumps can be scraped or picked off easily. Leaves turn yellow and may drop. A shiny or sticky material may cover leaves and stems.

ANALYSIS: Scale insects
Several different types of scale insects attack orchids. Some types can infest many different plants. Scales hatch from eggs. The young, called *crawlers*, are small (about $\frac{1}{10}$ inch), soft-bodied, and move about on the plant and onto other plants. After moving about for a short time, they insert their mouthparts into the plant, feeding on the sap. The legs disappear, and the scales remain in the same place for the rest of their lives. Some develop a soft covering, others a hard covering. Some species of scales are unable to digest fully all the sugar in the plant sap and excrete the excess in a fluid called honeydew, which may cover the leaves or drip onto surfaces below.

SOLUTION: Spray infested plants with an insecticide containing *malathion*. Spraying is more effective against the crawlers than against the adults. Repeated applications may be necessary. For additional information on spraying houseplants, see page 915.

PROBLEM: Oval, white insects up to $\frac{1}{4}$ inch long cluster in white, cottony masses on leaves, stems, and in the crotches where the leaves are attached. A sticky material may coat the leaves. Leaves may be spotted or deformed. When the condition is severe, leaves and plants may wither and die.

ANALYSIS: Mealybugs
Several species of this common insect feed on orchids. Mealybugs damage plants by sucking sap, causing leaf distortion and death. The adult female mealybug may produce live young, or may lay eggs in a white fluffy mass of wax. The immature mealybugs, called *nymphs*, crawl all over the plant and onto nearby plants. Soon after they begin to feed, they produce white waxy filaments that cover their bodies, giving them a cottony appearance. As they mature, they become less mobile. Mealybugs cannot digest all the sugar in the sap and excrete the excess in a fluid called honeydew, which coats the leaves and may drop onto furniture below the plant.

SOLUTION: Spray infested plants with an insecticide containing *malathion* or *diazinon*. For rare or unusual varieties, test the spray on a few leaves before spraying the entire plant. (For instructions on spraying houseplants, see page 915.) Where practical, wipe mealybugs off the plant with a damp cloth or with cotton swabs dipped in alcohol. Inspect the pot, including the bottom, for mealybug egg masses. Wipe these off. Avoid bringing mealybugs into the house by carefully inspecting new plants. For additional information on mealybugs, see page 229.

PALMS

PALMS

LIGHT: Most palms will grow better in full light, but many are adaptable to somewhat reduced light. Grow in an east-facing or curtained south or west-facing window, or in a room with light from a number of windows.

SOIL: Any of the standard houseplant soil mixes. For information on soil mixes, see page 913.

FERTILIZER: Fertilize once a month during early spring and summer when the plant is growing actively. Fertilizing is not necessary during the winter. Use ORTHO Fish Emulsion Fertilizer 5-1-1, ORTHO House Plant Food 5-10-5, or ORTHO Ortho-Gro Liquid Plant Food 12-6-6.

WATER:
How much: Add enough water so that some drains through the pot. Empty the saucer after draining is through.
How often: Water when the top soil is barely moist. For additional information on watering, see page 913.

TEMPERATURE: Most palms will grow better when warm, but will tolerate a wide range of temperatures. They will not do well when grown below 60°F.

Spider mites (half life size), webs, and damage.

PROBLEM: Fronds or leaflets are stippled, yellow, and dirty; they may dry out and drop. There may be webbing between leaflets or on the lower surfaces of the leaflets. To determine if a plant is infested with mites, hold a sheet of white paper underneath an affected plant and tap the frond sharply. Minute green, red, or yellow specks the size of pepper grains will drop to the paper and begin to crawl around. The pests are easily seen against the white background.

ANALYSIS: Spider mites
These mites, related to spiders, are major pests of many garden and houseplants, including palms. They cause damage by sucking sap from the undersides of the leaflets. As a result of this feeding, the green pigment (chlorophyll) disappears, causing the stippled appearance. Under warm, dry conditions mites can build up to tremendous numbers.

SOLUTION: Spray infested plants with ORTHO Whitefly & Mealybug Killer or ORTHO House Plant Insect Control. (For instructions on spraying houeplants, see page 915.) Plants need to be sprayed weekly for several weeks to kill the mites as they hatch. To avoid introducing mites, inspect new plants carefully.

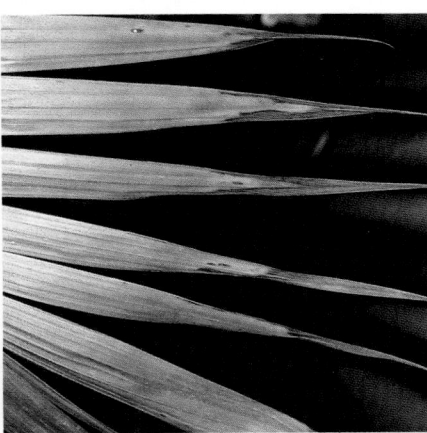

Salt damage.

PROBLEM: Margins of the older leaves die and turn brown, beginning at the base of the fronds and progressing outward. In severe cases, all fronds may have dead margins. Tissues adjacent to the dead margins of older fronds may turn yellow.

ANALYSIS: Salt damage
Palms are sensitive to excess salts. Soluble salts are picked up by the roots and accumulate in the leaf margins, where concentrations may become high enough to kill the tissues. Salts can accumulate from water or the use of fertilizers; or they may be present in the soil used in potting. Salts accumulate more rapidly and do more harm if the plant is not watered thoroughly.

SOLUTION: If symptoms of salt damage occur, leach excess salts from the soil by flushing with water. Water the plant at least 3 times, letting the water drain each time. This is done most easily in a bathtub or laundry sink or outside. Always water palms from the top of the pot. Enough water should be added at each watering so that some drains through the pot. Empty the saucer after the pot has finished draining. If the plant is too large to handle easily, use a turkey baster to remove the drainage water. (For additional watering instructions, see page 913.) Do not overfertilize. If practical, trim the damaged leaf tips to a point with a pair of scissors.

Mealybugs (half life size).

Scale (life size).

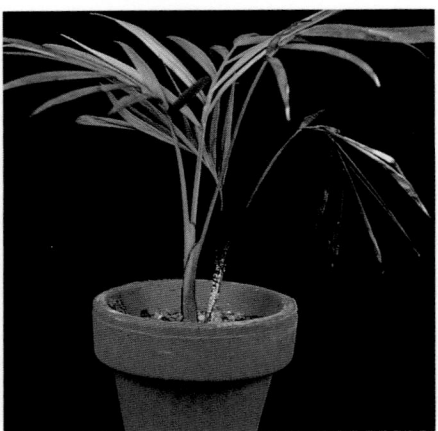

Gliocladium rot.

PROBLEM: Oval, white insects up to ¼ inch long cluster in white, cottony masses on fronds, leaflets, or stems, and in the crotches where fronds are attached. A sticky material may coat the leaflets. Leaflets may be spotted or deformed. When the condition is severe, leaves and plants may wither and die.

ANALYSIS: Mealybugs
Several species of this common insect feed on palms. Mealybugs damage plants by sucking sap, causing leaf distortion and death. The adult female mealybug may produce live young, or may lay eggs in a white fluffy mass of wax. The immature mealybugs, called *nymphs*, crawl all over the plant and onto nearby plants. Soon after they begin to feed, they produce white waxy filaments that cover their bodies, giving them a cottony appearance. As they mature, they become less mobile. Mealybugs cannot digest all the sugar in the sap and excrete the excess in a fluid called honeydew, which coats the leaflets and may drop onto furniture below the plant.

SOLUTION: Spray infested plants with ORTHO Whitefly & Mealybug Killer or ORTHO House Plant Insect Control. (For instructions on spraying houseplants, see page 915.) Where practical, wipe mealybugs off the plant with a damp cloth or with cotton swabs dipped in alcohol. Inspect the pot, including the bottom, for mealybug egg masses. Wipe these off. Avoid bringing mealybugs into the house by carefully inspecting new plants. For additional information on mealybugs, see page 229.

PROBLEM: Stems and fronds are covered with white, cottony, cushionlike masses or brown crusty bumps. The bumps can be scraped or picked off easily. Fronds turn yellow and may drop. A shiny or sticky material may cover fronds and stems.

ANALYSIS: Scale insects
Several different types of scale insects attack palms. Some types can infest many different plants. Scales hatch from eggs. The young, called *crawlers*, are small (about ¹⁄₁₀ inch), soft-bodied, and move about on the plant and onto other plants. After moving about for a short time, they insert their mouthparts into the plant, feeding on the sap. The legs disappear, and the scales remain in the same place for the rest of their lives. Some develop a soft covering, others a hard covering. Some species of scales are unable to digest fully all the sugar in the plant sap and excrete the excess in a fluid called honeydew, which may cover the fronds or drip onto surfaces below.

SOLUTION: Spray infested plants with ORTHO Whitefly & Mealybug Killer or ORTHO House Plant Insect Control. Spraying is more effective against the crawlers than against the adults. Repeated applications may be necessary. For additional information on spraying houseplants, see page 915.

PROBLEM: Brown spots appear on leaf stems. Leaflets turn yellowish brown on one side of the leaf stalk. The fronds die starting at the bottom, leaving only several alive at the top of the plant. When the condition is severe, the whole plant dies. A pinkish brown mold appears on the leaf bases. Sometimes the central bud area will rot, and the inner portions will be covered with a pinkish brown mass of fungal growth.

ANALYSIS: Gliocladium rot
This disease is caused by a fungus (*Gliocladium vermoeseni*) that infects parlor palm (*Chamaedorea*) and some other palms. The fungus produces large numbers of pink spores on infected leaf bases and in infected bud area. These spores are carried by air currents, and will infect other palms if the leaves are wet. The fungus kills the leaves, and may invade the central bud and kill it too. Gliocladium rot is favored by low temperatures.

SOLUTION: Remove any leaves that have symptoms. Avoid getting water on the fronds. Keep plants in warm rooms, and give them adequate light, water, and fertilizer. Plant sprays containing the fungicide *benomyl* may help. For information on spraying houseplants, see page 915.

PELARGONIUM (GERANIUM)

PELARGONIUM

FLOWERING TIME: Summer, but will flower all year if given enough light.

LIGHT: Flowering plants need more light than foliage plants. Give geraniums as much light as possible. Grow in south-facing windows. Geraniums grown for foliage do not need as much light as flowering types.

SOIL: Any of the standard mixes for houseplants. For information on soil mixes, see page 913.

FERTILIZER: Fertilize once a month during spring and summer with ORTHO House Plant Food 5–10–5 or ORTHO Ortho-Gro Liquid Plant Food 12–6–6.

WATER:
How much: Add enough water so that some drains out of the bottom of the pot.
How often: Water when the surface soil is dry. Avoid keeping the soil too wet or too dry because these conditions favor oedema. For more information on watering houseplants, see page 913.

TEMPERATURE: Average house temperatures are adequate for geraniums.

Spindly growth.

PROBLEM: Lower leaves turn yellow and may drop. New leaves are pale green. Plants fail to produce flower buds. Stems become elongated and lean toward the light.

ANALYSIS: Insufficient light
Plants use light as a source of energy, and grow slowly in light that is too dim for their needs. If most of the available light comes from one direction, the stems and leaves bend in that direction. If the light is much too dim, the plant has little energy and grows poorly. Plants grown for their flowers, such as geranium and pelargonium, have a relatively high need for light.

SOLUTION: Move the plant to a brighter location. Geranium and pelargonium need direct sun. But if they are allowed to become dry while in direct sunlight, they will sunburn. (For more information on sunburn, see page 226.) If a brighter location is not available, provide supplemental lighting as described on page 914. If you wish to grow a houseplant in a dim location, select a plant that is tolerant of dim light from the list on page 990. Geranium and pelargonium can be grown outside in full sun. When moving them from inside to outside, put them in a semishady area for several days before moving them to direct sunlight. This will prevent them from sunburning.

Oedema.

PROBLEM: Small spots appear on the undersides of the leaves. These spots are raised, corky, and water-soaked. Spots appear more frequently on older leaves, and rarely on new leaves. In old tissues, spots may become tan. When the condition is severe, leaves may yellow and drop. Corky streaks may appear on stems.

ANALYSIS: Oedema
Oedema is a disease found on many plants. It is not caused by infection, but results from environmental factors. The exact cause of oedema is unknown. It is believed to be caused by excessive watering during periods of high humidity, but it sometimes occurs on geraniums that have been kept dry and grown under low humidity.

SOLUTION: Give geraniums bright light (see page 279) and enough water, and fertilize regularly. Avoid growing plants too close together. Do not keep the soil too wet during periods of damp, cloudy weather.

PELARGONIUM (GERANIUM)

Whiteflies (life size).

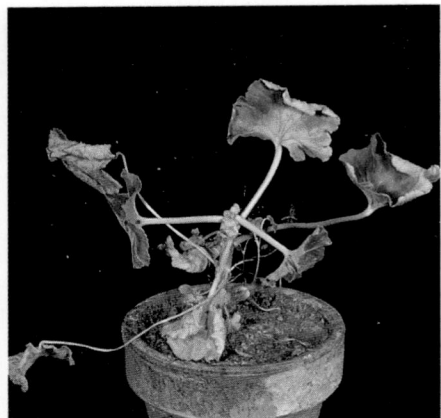

Bacterial leaf and stem blight.

Root and stem rot.

PROBLEM: Tiny, winged insects ¹⁄₁₂ inch long feed on the undersides of the leaves. The insects are covered with white waxy powder. When the plant is touched, insects flutter rapidly around it. Leaves may be mottled and yellowing.

ANALYSIS: Greenhouse whitefly (*Trialeurodes vaporariorum*)
This insect is a common pest of geranium. The 4-winged adult lays eggs on the undersides of leaves. The larvae are the size of a pinhead, flat, oval, immobile, and semitransparent, with radiating white waxy filaments. In about a month, they change to the winged adult form. The larvae are more damaging because they suck more sap from the plants than do the adults. They cannot digest all the sugar in the sap they remove, and excrete the excess in a sugary material called honeydew, which coats the leaves and may drop from the plant onto furniture below.

SOLUTION: Spray with ORTHO House Plant Insect Control, ORTHO Whitefly & Mealybug Killer, or ORTHO Isotox Insect Killer. For instructions on spraying houseplants, see page 915. Spray weekly as long as the problem continues. Remove heavily infested leaves.

PROBLEM: Small dark spots may appear on the undersides of geranium or ivy geranium leaves. These spots enlarge, and are soon visible on both surfaces of the leaves. Spots turn brown or black, and usually have a water-soaked area around them. Large areas of the leaf may die in angular patterns surrounded by the veins. Affected leaves turn yellow and may drop. The stems and leaf stems turn black and shrivel. Roots may also turn black. Plants may die.

ANALYSIS: Bacterial leaf and stem blight
This disease is caused by a bacterium (*Xanthomonas pelargonii*) that infects leaves through wounds and natural openings. Once inside, it kills the tissues rapidly. The bacteria spread down the leaf stems into the main stem, killing tissue as they move. They may even spread into the roots. Martha Washington geranium (pelargonium) is not affected.

SOLUTION: Destroy infected plants. Avoid getting water on the foliage of geraniums. Do not touch the foliage of diseased plants and then the foliage of healthy plants. Make cuttings only from uninfected plants. Discard soil from diseased plants. Any tools used for trimming plants should be cleaned with rubbing alcohol before using on geraniums and pelargoniums.

PROBLEM: Lower leaves turn yellow or red and may drop from the plant. Plants are stunted. A black discoloration appears in the stem at the soil line and progresses upward. Upper leaves may wilt. The whole plant may die and be easily lifted from the soil. The rootball has many dead roots, which are brown, soft, and without white tips. For instructions on examining the rootball, see page 914.

ANALYSIS: Root and stem rot
This disease is caused by a soil-dwelling fungus (*Pythium* species) that invades the root system through the small roots. It moves rapidly through the root system and up the stem, killing the roots. Infected plants are unable to obtain water and nutrients, resulting in stunting and wilting.

SOLUTION: Avoid keeping the soil too wet when growing geranium and pelargonium plants. If the disease occurs, take tip cuttings and root them to produce new plants, following the directions on page 914. Discard dead plants. Pasteurize soil before using again as described on page 913. Thoroughly wash pots and soak them for 20 minutes in 1 part household bleach to 9 parts water. Allow the pots to dry before using. When planting, use a light soil mix. For instructions on soil mixes, see page 913.

PEPEROMIA

Root and stem rot.

Oedema.

Mealybugs (life size).

PROBLEM: Plants fail to grow, and are stunted. Roots are brown and soft, without white tips. (For information on examining roots, see page 914.) The stem may have brown, sunken areas at or below the soil line. Leaves may die and turn black. Plants may wilt and die.

ANALYSIS: Root and stem rot
Root rot is caused by any of several fungi (*Pythium* species, *Phytophthora parasitica*, or *Rhizoctonia solani*). These soil-dwelling fungi infect the roots of many plants. They invade the small roots and spread through the root system, killing it. Infected root systems are unable to pick up enough nutrients and water to supply the plant. The fungi are favored by wet soil. Also, peperomia plants are weakened by wet soil, and become more susceptible to root rot. *Phytophthora* and *Rhizoctonia* can also infect the crown and lower stem, causing the tissues to collapse.

SOLUTION: Discard infected plants and the soil in which they grew. To prevent root rot in peperomias, plant them in a soil mix that drains well. (For information on soil mixes, see page 913.) Wait until the top of the soil is just beginning to dry before watering. Soak pot for 30 minutes in a mixture of 1 part household bleach to 9 parts of water before reusing.

PROBLEM: Small corky spots appear on the undersides of the leaves. When first formed these spots are clear or water-soaked, but later become tan or brown. If leaves are severely affected, they may turn yellow.

ANALYSIS: Oedema
Oedema is a disease found on many plants. It is not caused by infection, but results from unfavorable environmental conditions. The exact cause of oedema is unknown. It is believed to be caused by excessive watering during periods of high humidity, but it also develops occasionally on plants that are kept dry and in low humidity.

SOLUTION: Grow peperomia under as favorable conditions as possible. Give adequate light, water, and fertilizer. Avoid keeping the soil too wet.

Peperomia cultural information
Light: Needs medium light
Water: When the soil just below the surface is dry

PROBLEM: Oval, white insects up to ¼ inch long cluster in white, cottony masses on leaves, stems, and in the crotches where the leaves are attached. A sticky material may coat the leaves. Leaves may be spotted or deformed. When the condition is severe, leaves and plants may wither and die.

ANALYSIS: Mealybugs
Several species of this common insect feed on peperomia. Mealybugs damage plants by sucking sap, causing leaf distortion and death. The adult female mealybug may produce live young, or may lay eggs in a white fluffy mass of wax. The immature mealybugs, called *nymphs*, crawl all over the plant and onto nearby plants. Soon after they begin to feed, they produce white waxy filaments that cover their bodies, giving them a cottony appearance. As they mature, they become less mobile. Mealybugs cannot digest all the sugar in the sap and excrete the excess in a fluid called honeydew, which coats the leaves and may drop onto furniture below the plant.

SOLUTION: Spray infested plants with ORTHO Whitefly & Mealybug Killer or ORTHO House Plant Insect Control. (For instructions on spraying houseplants, see page 915.) Where practical, wipe mealybugs off the plant with a damp cloth or with cotton swabs dipped in alcohol. Inspect the pot, including the bottom, for mealybug egg masses. Wipe these off. Avoid bringing mealybugs into the house by carefully inspecting new plants. For additional information on mealybugs, see page 229.

PHILODENDRON ────────────────────────

Salt damage.

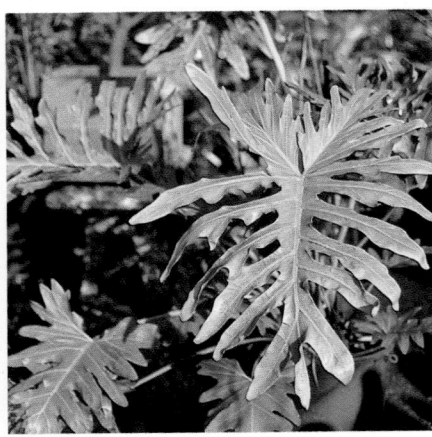

Root rot.

PHILODENDRON ──────────

LIGHT: Most philodendrons will tolerate a variety of light conditions, from filtered sunlight to that coming through a north window.

SOIL: Any standard houseplant soil mix. For information on soil mixes, see page 913.

FERTILIZER: Fertilize monthly with ORTHO Fish Emulsion Fertilizer 5-1-1, ORTHO House Plant Food 5-10-5, or ORTHO Ortho-Gro Liquid Plant Food 12-6-6.

WATER:
How much: Add enough water so that some drains through the pot. Discard any water that drains through the pot.
How often: Water when the top soil is barely moist. For additional information on watering houseplants, see page 913.

TEMPERATURE: Average house temperatures are adequate.

SPECIAL CONDITIONS: Philodendrons may be climbers or nonclimbers. Climbers need support, and may eventually get so large they have to be cut back severely. Climbing types produce aerial roots, which need to be attached to the support or removed.

PROBLEM: Margins of older leaves die and turn brown and brittle. In severe cases, all leaves may have dead margins. Tissues adjacent to the dead margins of older leaves may turn yellow.

ANALYSIS: Salt damage
Philodendron is sensitive to excess salts. Soluble salts are picked up by the roots and accumulate in the leaf margins, where concentrations may become high enough to kill the tissues. Salts can accumulate from water or the use of fertilizers; or they may be present in the soil used in potting. Salts accumulate more rapidly and do more harm if the plant is not watered thoroughly.

SOLUTION: If symptoms of salt damage occur, leach excess salts from the soil by flushing with water. Water the plants at least 3 times, letting the water drain each time. This is done most easily in a bathtub or laundry sink, or outside. Always water philodendron from the top of the pot. Enough water should be added at each watering so that some drains through the pot. Empty the saucer after the pot has finished draining. If the plant is too large to handle easily, use a turkey baster to remove the drainage water. (For additional watering instructions, see page 913.) Do not overfertilize.

PROBLEM: The lower leaves turn yellow. Leaves may drop from the plant. Plants may be stunted. Roots may be soft and dead, with no white tips. For information on examining roots, see page 914.

ANALYSIS: Root rot
This plant disease is caused by any of several fungi (*Pythium* and *Rhizoctonia* species) that are favored by wet soil. The disease is usually an indication that the plant has been watered too frequently or that the soil mix is too heavy and does not drain well. The fungi are common in garden soils, but pasteurized soil or soilless potting mixes are free of them unless they are introduced on a plant, a dirty pot, or transferred from another pot on dirty fingers. Root rot spreads quickly through a root system if the soil remains wet.

SOLUTION: If most of the plant has wilted, or if there are no white tips remaining on the root system, the plant is probably too far gone to save. Discard it and the soil in which it grew. Wash the pot thoroughly before reusing it. Disinfect clay pots by soaking for 10 minutes in a solution of 1 part household bleach to 9 parts water. If only part of the plant is affected, or if white root tips are still visible on the rootball, dry the plant out as described on page 857. There are no fungicides presently available that adequately control this disease. Prevent recurrence by planting in a mix that drains well, and by letting the soil dry slightly between waterings. For more information on watering container plants, see page 913.

Erwinia leaf spot.

Spider mite damage.

Mealybugs (half life size).

PROBLEM: Small water-soaked spots appear on the leaves. These spots enlarge to irregular blotches, surrounded by yellow margins. The infected tissue turns brown or black. Severely infected leaves turn yellow, die, and drop from the plant.

ANALYSIS: Bacterial leaf spot
This disease is caused by bacteria that also attack dieffenbachia and other foliage plants. Under humid conditions, the bacteria gain entrance through wounds or natural openings in the leaves. Inside the leaf, the bacteria rot the tissue, causing the spots. Under very humid conditions large numbers of bacteria may be produced, and may ooze out of the tissues in a mass. If infection is severe, so much wilting results that the leaf dies.

SOLUTION: Once leaves are infected, no measures will control the spots already formed. To keep the disease from spreading to other plants, keep the leaves dry. Don't mist the plants. Keep plants in rooms where condensation does not form on the leaves. Remove and destroy infected leaves. Avoid touching diseased leaves and then touching uninfected leaves.

PROBLEM: Leaves are stippled, yellow, and dirty; they may dry out and drop. There may be webbing between leaves or on the lower surfaces of the leaves. To determine if a plant is infested with mites, hold a sheet of white paper underneath an affected plant and tap the leaves sharply. Minute green, red, or yellow specks the size of pepper grains will drop to the paper and begin to crawl around. The pests are easily seen against the white background.

ANALYSIS: Spider mites
These mites, related to spiders, are major pests of many garden and houseplants, including philodendron. They cause damage by sucking sap from the undersides of the leaves. As a result of this feeding, the green pigment (chlorophyll) disappears, causing the stippled appearance. Under warm, dry conditions, which favor mites, they can build up to tremendous numbers.

SOLUTION: Spray infested plants indoors with ORTHO Whitefly & Mealybug Killer or ORTHO House Plant Insect Control; or take the plants outside and spray them with ORTHO Isotox Insect Killer. (For instructions on spraying houseplants, see page 915.) Plants need to be sprayed weekly for several weeks to kill the mites as they hatch. To avoid introducing mites, inspect new plants carefully.

PROBLEM: Oval, white insects up to ¼ inch long cluster in white, cottony masses on leaves, stems, and in the crotches where branches or leaves are attached. A sticky material may coat the leaves. Leaves may be spotted or deformed. When the condition is severe, leaves and plants may wither and die.

ANALYSIS: Mealybugs
Several species of this common insect feed on philodendron. Mealybugs damage plants by sucking sap, causing leaf distortion and death. The adult female mealybug may produce live young, or may lay eggs in a white fluffy mass of wax. The immature mealybugs, called *nymphs*, crawl over the plant and onto nearby plants. Soon after they begin to feed, they produce white waxy filaments that cover their bodies, giving them a cottony appearance. As they mature, they become less mobile. Mealybugs cannot digest all the sugar in the sap and excrete the excess in a fluid called honeydew, which coats the leaves and may drop onto furniture below the plant.

SOLUTION: Spray infested plants indoors with ORTHO Whitefly & Mealybug Killer; or take the plants outside and spray them with ORTHO Orthene Systemic Insect Control or ORTHO Isotox Insect Killer. (For instructions on spraying houseplants, see page 915.) Where practical, wipe mealybugs off the plant with a damp cloth or with cotton swabs dipped in alcohol. Inspect the pot, including the bottom, for mealybug egg masses. Wipe these off. Avoid bringing mealybugs into the house by carefully inspecting new plants. For additional information on mealybugs, see page 229.

PLECTRANTHUS (SWEDISH IVY)

Nitrogen deficiency.

PROBLEM: The oldest leaves — usually the lower leaves — turn yellow and may drop. Yellowing starts at the leaf margins and progresses inward without producing a distinct pattern. The yellowing may progress upward until only the newest leaves remain green. Growth is slow, new leaves are small, and the whole plant may be stunted.

ANALYSIS: Nitrogen deficiency
Nitrogen is a nutrient that is used by the plant in many ways, including the production of chlorophyll (the green pigment in leaves and stems). Nitrogen is used in large amounts by the plant. When there is not enough nitrogen for the entire plant, it is taken from the older leaves for use in new growth. Nitrogen is easily leached from the soil during regular watering. Of all the plant nutrients, it is the one most likely to be lacking in the soil.

SOLUTION: Take the plant outdoors and spray the leaves with Ra-Pid-Gro Plant Food for a quick response, or fertilize houseplants with ORTHO House Plant Food 5–10–5, ORTHO Fish Emulsion Fertilizer 5–1–1, or ORTHO Fern & Ivy Food 10–8–7. Add the fertilizer at regular intervals, as recommended on the label.

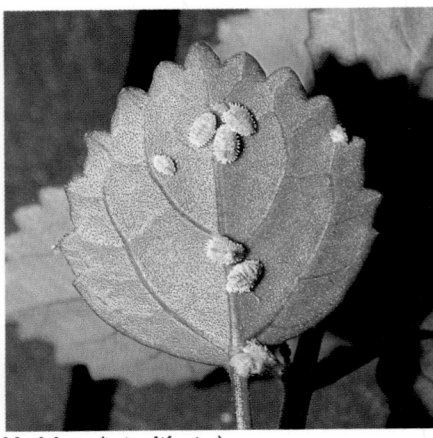

Mealybugs (twice life size).

PROBLEM: Oval, white insects up to ¼ inch long cluster in white, cottony masses on the stems and leaves. They tend to congregate in the crotches where the leaves or branches are attached. Leaves may be spotted, deformed, and withered. Infested leaves may be shiny and sticky. Severely infested plants may die.

ANALYSIS: Mealybugs
Several species of this common insect feed on Swedish ivy. Mealybugs damage plants by sucking sap, causing leaf distortion and death. The adult female mealybug may produce live young, or may deposit her eggs in a white, fluffy mass of wax. The immature mealybugs, called *nymphs*, crawl all over the plant and onto nearby plants. Soon after they begin to feed, they produce filaments of white wax that cover their bodies, giving them a cottony appearance. As they mature, they become less mobile. Mealybugs cannot digest fully all the sugar in the sap and excrete the excess in a fluid called honeydew, which coats the leaves and may drop onto other leaves or furniture below the plant.

SOLUTION: Spray infested plants with ORTHO Whitefly & Mealybug Killer or ORTHO House Plant Insect Control. Follow the directions on the label. Applications should be repeated every 7 to 10 days until the insects are controlled. Wash the mealybugs off the plant with a strong stream of water, or wipe them off with a cotton swab dipped in alcohol. For additional information on spraying houseplants, see page 915. For additional information on mealybugs, see page 229.

SAINTPAULIA (AFRICAN VIOLET)

SAINTPAULIA

LIGHT: African violets need abundant light to produce flowers. Grow them in bright light, but not in direct sunlight.

SOIL: Any standard houseplant mix. For information on potting mixes, see page 913.

FERTILIZER: Fertilize monthly with ORTHO House Plant Food 5–10–5 or ORTHO Liquid African Violet Food 6–9–5.

WATER:
How much: Add enough water so that some drains out of the bottom of the pot.
How often: Water plants when the soil just under the surface is moist but not wet. For additional information on watering houseplants, see page 913.

TEMPERATURE: Average house temperatures are adequate, but do not leave African violets in rooms where the temperature falls below 60°F at night.

SPECIAL CONDITIONS: Avoid getting cold water on the leaves when watering, and don't let the plant sit in drainage water. Do not expose plants to cold drafts.

Failure to flower.

Water spots.

Cyclamen mite damage.

PROBLEM: Although the plant seems healthy, it does not bloom.

ANALYSIS: Insufficient light
Violets, like other flowering plants, won't bloom unless they are properly fed and watered. But if the plant is a good green color and is growing well but not blooming, it is probably not receiving enough light. Plants use light as a source of energy, and will not bloom unless they can afford the energy to do so. African violets will bloom at lower levels of light than will require most other plants, but they do require a fairly bright location to bloom well.

SOLUTION: Move the plant to a brighter location. The ideal light level for African violets is as bright as possible without being direct sun. If the light is coming through a window that is exposed to the sun, the window should be curtained so that the sunlight coming through is not quite bright enough to make shadows. If the light is too bright, the leaves will lose their bright green color and become pale, with an orange or yellow cast. If the light is both bright and hot, the leaves will burn. If you don't have a location in your house bright enough, give the plants supplemental light as explained on page 914. Use fluorescent fixtures, and place them as close to the top of the plants as possible.

PROBLEM: White to light yellow blotches in various patterns, including circles, occur on the older leaves. Small islands of green may be separated by the discolored areas. Brown spots sometimes appear in the colored areas.

ANALYSIS: Water spots
Members of the African violet family are very sensitive to rapid temperature changes. Water spots occur most commonly when cold water is splashed on the leaves while the plant is being watered. If this happens in light, the chlorophyll (green pigment) is destroyed. In this plant family, all of the chlorophyll in the leaves is found in a single layer of cells near the upper surface. If the chlorophyll in that layer is broken down, the green color disappears, and the color of the underlying leaf tissue is exposed.

SOLUTION: Avoid getting cold water on African violet leaves when watering. Or use tepid water, which will not cause spotting if it touches the leaves. Spotted leaves will not recover. Pick them off if they are unsightly.

PROBLEM: Leaves in the center of the plant are severely stunted, and may be curled downward. These leaves may be bronze, gray, or tan. The hairs on these leaves are matted. Flower buds fail to open.

ANALYSIS: Cyclamen mite
(*Steneotarsonemus pallidus*)
Cyclamen mites infest a number of plants, including azaleas, begonias, cyclamen, gloxinia, ivy, kalanchoe, schefflera, and African violet. This very small mite (it can not be seen with the naked eye) feeds on the new growth, causing it to be stunted and curled. Buds fail to open. The female mite lays her eggs on the leaf surfaces. The young crawl about the same plant or other plants, where they feed and cause damage. These mites are favored by high humidity.

SOLUTION: Spray with *dicofol*. (For instructions on spraying houseplants, see page 915.) Isolate mildly infested plants from uninfested plants. Soak pots from which infested plants were removed for 30 minutes in a mixture of 1 part household bleach to 9 parts water. Wash the area where pots were sitting with the same dilution of household bleach.

SAINTPAULIA (AFRICAN VIOLET)

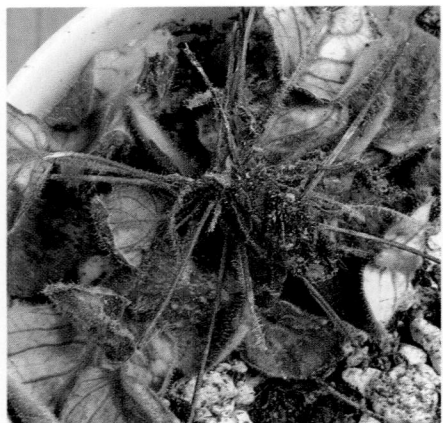

Root and crown rot.

PROBLEM: Leaves appear dull. Those in the center of the plant turn dark green and then black. This darkening rapidly progresses outward until the whole top of the plant is dead. The roots are dead and rotted. For instructions on examining plant roots, see page 914.

ANALYSIS: Root and crown rot
This plant disease is caused by a soil-dwelling fungus (*Phytophthora parasitica*) that attacks the roots of African violet plants. The disease spreads rapidly through the root system and crown of the plant into the leaves, eventually killing the plant. The fungus is active over a wide range of soil moisture conditions. It is spread by using contaminated soil or pots, or it may be carried from one pot to another on the fingers when testing the soil for moisture. It may also be spread from pot to pot if pans are used to subirrigate plants.

SOLUTION: There is no available chemical for controlling this fungus. Discard diseased plants. Discard the soil in which diseased plants grew. Soak pots for 30 minutes in a mixture of 1 part household bleach to 9 parts water. Do not check the moisture level in pots by touching the soil.

Mealybugs (twice life size).

PROBLEM: Oval, white insects up to ¼ inch long cluster in white, cottony masses on leaves, stems, and in the crotches where the leaves are attached. A sticky material may coat the leaves. Leaves may be spotted or deformed. When the condition is severe, leaves and plants may wither and die.

ANALYSIS: Mealybugs
Several species of this common insect feed on African violet. Mealybugs damage plants by sucking sap, causing leaf distortion and death. The adult female mealybug may produce live young, or may lay eggs in a white fluffy mass of wax. The immature mealybugs, called *nymphs*, crawl all over the plant and onto nearby plants. Soon after they begin to feed, they produce white waxy filaments that cover their bodies, giving them a cottony appearance. As they mature, they become less mobile. Mealybugs cannot digest all the sugar in the sap and excrete the excess in a fluid called honeydew, which coats the leaves and may drop onto furniture below the plant.

SOLUTION: Spray infested plants with ORTHO Whitefly & Mealybug Killer. (For instructions on spraying houseplants, see page 915.) Where practical, wipe mealybugs off the plant with a damp cloth or with cotton swabs dipped in alcohol. Inspect the pot, including the bottom, for mealybug egg masses. Wipe these off. Avoid bringing mealybugs into the house by carefully inspecting new plants. For additional information on mealybugs, see page 229.

SINNINGIA (GLOXINIA)

Elongated leaf stalks.

PROBLEM: Leaves turn a deep green. Plants stop flowering. Leaves and flowers are borne on elongated stems rather than on top of the fleshy root. Buds that are formed fail to open.

ANALYSIS: Insufficient light
Plants use light as a source of energy, and grow slowly in light that is too dim for their needs. They produce few flowers. If most of the available light is coming from one direction, the stems and leaves bend in that direction. If the light is much too dim the plant elongates, resulting in leaves and buds being produced in pairs along the stem rather than from a basal rosette. Plants grown for their flowers, such as gloxinia, need abundant light.

SOLUTION: Move the plant to a brighter location. Gloxinia will tolerate direct sun if it is kept well watered. But if it is allowed to become dry while in direct sunlight, it will sunburn. (For more information on sunburn, see page 226.) If a brighter location is not available, provide supplemental lighting as described on page 914. If you wish to grow a houseplant in a dim location, select a plant that is tolerant of dim light from the list on page 990.

SPATHIPHYLLUM (SPATHE FLOWER) — **SYNGONIUM (NEPHTHYTIS)** —

Water spots.

Dead leaf tips.

Bacterial leaf spot.

PROBLEM: Pale green to light yellow rings or blotches appear on the upper surfaces of the leaves — usually the older leaves. These spots may be abundant and cover much of a leaf, or they may be small and scattered.

ANALYSIS: Water spots
Members of the African violet family — including gloxinia — are very sensitive to rapid temperature changes. Water spots occur most commonly when cold water is splashed on the leaves while the plant is being watered. If this happens in light, the chlorophyll (green pigment) is destroyed. In this plant family, all of the chlorophyll in the leaves is found in a single layer of cells near the upper surface. If the chlorophyll in that layer is broken down, the green disappears, and the color of the underlying leaf tissue is exposed.

SOLUTION: Avoid getting cold water on the foliage of gloxinia when watering. Or use tepid water, which will not cause spotting if it touches the leaves. Spotted leaves will not recover. Pick off unsightly leaves.

Sinningia cultural information
Light: Needs bright light
Water: When the soil just below the surface is barely moist

PROBLEM: Tips of leaves turn brown or tan. The damaged area spreads slowly along the leaf. Older leaves are most severely affected.

ANALYSIS: Dead leaf tips
There are several reasons why spathe flower leaf tips die. Frequently the problem is a combination of causes.
1. *Salt damage:* Salts accumulate in the soil from irrigation water or fertilizer. Excess salts are carried to the leaves and deposited in the tips of pointed leaves like those of spathe flower plants. When enough salts accumulate there, the leaf tip dies.
2. *Too dry:* The leaf tip, being farthest from the roots, is the first part of the leaf to die when the plant is not getting enough water.
3. *Toxic salts:* Some chemicals, usually in the form of soluble salts, are damaging in very small amounts. They accumulate in leaf tips as other salts do, killing the tissue there. The most common of these chemicals are chloride and borate.

SOLUTION: Remove dead tips by trimming leaves to a point with scissors.
1. Flush the salts from the soil with several thorough waterings, discarding the drainage water each time.
2. Water the plant regularly, following the directions on page 913.
3. There isn't much you can do about traces of toxic chemicals in the water. Distilled or deionized water is always free of chemicals.

Spathiphyllum cultural information
Light: Tolerates dim light
Water: When the soil surface is moist but not wet

PROBLEM: Irregular, oblong spots appear scattered on the leaves. New spots are very small but rapidly enlarge so that much of the leaf may be covered. Spots at first may be dark green, but eventually become dark brown or black as the tissue dies. Tissues around the dead areas look water-soaked, and have a yellow margin. Shiny drops may be found on the undersides of the spots. As these dry, they may become white or dark brown. Leaves may be killed.

ANALYSIS: Bacterial leaf spot
This disease is caused by either of two bacteria (*Erwinia chrysanthemi* or *Xanthomonas vitians*). The bacteria may be carried internally in the stems of syngonium, or may be on the leaf surfaces. High temperatures and high humidity favor infection and disease development. When conditions are favorable, the bacteria rapidly invade the leaf tissues, killing them as they progress.

SOLUTION: Break off and discard the infected leaves. Avoid getting water on the foliage. Space plants so that air can circulate around the leaves to keep them dry. Discard severely infected plants. Before using the pot again, wash it, and then soak it for 30 minutes in a solution of 1 part of household bleach to 9 parts of water.

Syngonium cultural information
Light: Tolerates dim light
Water: When the soil just below the surface is barely moist

SYNGONIUM (NEPHTHYTIS) ———

STREPTOCARPUS ———

Mealybugs (life size).

Failure to flower.

Water spots.

PROBLEM: Oval, white insects up to ¼ inch long cluster in white, cottony masses on leaves, stems, and in the crotches where the leaves are attached. A sticky material may coat the leaves. Leaves may be spotted or deformed. When the condition is severe, leaves and plants may wither and die.

ANALYSIS: Mealybugs
Several species of this common insect feed on nephthytis. Mealybugs damage plants by sucking sap, causing leaf distortion and death. The adult female mealybug may produce live young, or may lay eggs in a white fluffy mass of wax. The immature mealybugs, called *nymphs*, crawl all over the plant and onto nearby plants. Soon after they begin to feed, they produce white waxy filaments that cover their bodies, giving them a cottony appearance. As they mature, they become less mobile. Mealybugs cannot digest all the sugar in the sap and excrete the excess in a fluid called honeydew, which coats the leaves and may drop onto furniture below the plant.

SOLUTION: Spray infested plants indoors with ORTHO Whitefly & Mealybug Killer or ORTHO House Plant Insect Control; or take the plants outside and spray them with ORTHO Orthene Systemic Insect Control. (For instructions on spraying houseplants, see page 915.) Where practical, wipe mealybugs off the plant with a damp cloth or with cotton swabs dipped in alcohol. Inspect the pot, including the bottom, for mealybug egg masses. Wipe these off. Avoid bringing mealybugs into the house by carefully inspecting new plants. For additional information on mealybugs, see page 229.

PROBLEM: Plants fail to produce flowers; or, if they are flowering, they fail to produce new flower stems and buds. Lower leaves may become lighter green.

ANALYSIS: Insufficient light
Plants use light as a source of energy, and grow slowly in light that is too dim for their needs. If most of the available light is coming from one direction, the leaves bend in that direction. If the light is much too dim, the plant will stop producing flowers. Plants that are grown for their flowers, such as streptocarpus, need bright light.

SOLUTION: Move the plant to a brighter location. Streptocarpus will tolerate direct sun if it is kept well watered. But if it is allowed to become dry while in direct sunlight, it will sunburn. (For more information on sunburn, see page 226.) If a brighter location is not available, provide supplemental lighting as described on page 914. If you wish to grow a houseplant in a dim location, select a plant that is tolerant of dim light from the list on page 990.

PROBLEM: Small, angular, white to light tan spots appear on the upper surfaces of the leaves — usually the older leaves.

ANALYSIS: Water spots
Members of the African violet family — including streptocarpus — are very sensitive to rapid temperature changes. Water spots occur most commonly when cold water is splashed on the leaves while the plant is being watered. If this happens in light, the chlorophyll (green pigment) is destroyed. In this plant family, all of the chlorophyll in the leaves is found in a single layer of cells near the upper surface of the leaf. If the chlorophyll in that layer is broken down, the green color disappears, and the color of the underlying tissue is exposed.

SOLUTION: Avoid getting cold water on the foliage of streptocarpus when watering. Or use tepid water, which will not cause spotting if it touches the leaves. Spots will not disappear. Pick off unsightly leaves.

———

Streptocarpus cultural information
Light: Needs bright light
Water: When the soil just below the surface is barely moist

TOLMIEA (PIGGYBACK PLANT)

Mealybugs (half life size).

Iron deficiency.

Virus.

PROBLEM: Oval, white insects up to ¼ inch long cluster in white, cottony masses on leaves, stems, and in the crotches where the leaves are attached. A sticky material may coat the leaves. Leaves may be spotted or deformed. When the condition is severe, leaves and plants may wither and die.

ANALYSIS: Mealybugs
Several species of this common insect feed on streptocarpus. Mealybugs damage plants by sucking sap, causing leaf distortion and death. The adult female mealybug may produce live young, or may lay eggs in a white fluffy mass of wax. The immature mealybugs, called *nymphs*, crawl all over the plant and onto nearby plants. Soon after they begin to feed, they produce white waxy filaments that cover their bodies, giving them a cottony appearance. As they mature, they become less mobile. Mealybugs cannot digest all the sugar in the sap and excrete the excess in a fluid called honeydew, which coats the leaves and may drop onto furniture below the plant.

SOLUTION: Spray infested plants with an insecticide containing *diazinon*. (For instructions on spraying houseplants, see page 915.) Where practical, wipe mealybugs off the plant with a damp cloth or with cotton swabs dipped in alcohol. Inspect the pot, including the bottom, for mealybug egg masses. Wipe these off. Avoid bringing mealybugs into the house by carefully inspecting new plants. For additional information on mealybugs, see page 229.

PROBLEM: The newest leaves turn yellow at the margins. The veins usually remain green. In severe cases, the entire leaf is yellow and small. The plant may be stunted.

ANALYSIS: Iron deficiency
This is a common problem with acid-loving plants like piggyback, which grow best in soil with a pH between 5.5 and 6.5. (For more information on soil acidity, see page 902.) The leaf yellowing is due to a deficiency of iron and other minor nutrients in the plant. Plants use iron in the formation of the green pigment (chlorophyll) in the leaves. The soil is seldom deficient in iron. However, iron is often found in an insoluble form that is not available to piggyback plants, especially when the soil pH is too high.

SOLUTION: To correct iron deficiency, spray the foliage with ORTHO Ortho-Gro Liquid Plant Food 12–6–6, and apply it to the soil in the pot. Use acid-forming fertilizers such as Acid-Gro Fertilizer 30–12–11. When potting or transplanting piggybacks, use an acid soil mix that contains about 50 percent peat moss. Use a minimum amount of lime or dolomite in the soil mix.

PROBLEM: All leaves have blotches of various shades of yellow and green. Plants showing color blotches fail to grow as rapidly as green plants of the same type. Infected plants are of a variegated variety.

ANALYSIS: Virus
Several viruses have been found in variegated piggyback plants. The most common is cucumber mosaic virus. Viruses disrupt the normal functioning of the cells and, as a result, not as much chlorophyll is produced. This causes different shades of green and yellow to appear in the leaves. Insects transmit the virus from one plant to another. Although viruses have been shown to be present in variegated piggyback plants, it has not been proven that viruses are the cause of the variegation.

SOLUTION: Keep variegated piggyback plants isolated from other plants. Aphids can transmit the virus to other susceptible plants. Control aphids as described on page 228.

TOLMIEA (PIGGYBACK PLANT)

Salt damage.

Spider mite damage.

Powdery mildew.

PROBLEM: Margins of older leaves die and turn brown and brittle. In severe cases, all leaves may have dead margins. Tissues adjacent to the dead margins of older leaves may turn yellow.

ANALYSIS: Salt damage
Piggyback is sensitive to excess salts. Soluble salts are picked up by the roots and accumulate in the leaf margins, where concentrations may become high enough to kill the tissues. Salts can accumulate from water or the use of fertilizers; or they may be present in the soil used in potting. Salts accumulate more rapidly and do more harm if the plant is not watered thoroughly.

SOLUTION: Leach excess salts from the soil by flushing with water. Water the plant at least 3 times, letting the water drain each time. This is done most easily in a bathtub or laundry sink or outside. Always water piggyback from the top of the pot. Enough water should be added at each watering so that some drains through the pot. Empty the saucer after the pot has finished draining. If the plant is too large to handle easily, use a turkey baster to remove the drainage water. (For additional watering instructions, see page 913.) Avoid overfertilizing.

Tolmiea cultural information
Light: Needs bright light
Water: When the soil surface is moist but not wet

PROBLEM: Leaves are stippled, yellow, and dirty; they may dry out and drop. There may be webbing between leaves or on the lower surfaces of the leaves. To determine if a plant is infested with mites, hold a sheet of white paper underneath an affected plant and tap the leaves sharply. Minute green, red, or yellow specks the size of pepper grains will drop to the paper and begin to crawl around. The pests are easily seen against the white background.

ANALYSIS: Spider mites
These mites, related to spiders, are major pests of many garden and houseplants, including piggyback plants. They cause damage by sucking sap from the undersides of the leaves. As a result of this feeding the green pigment (chlorophyll) disappears, causing the stippled appearance. Under warm, dry conditions, which favor mites, they can build up to tremendous numbers.

SOLUTION: Spray infested plants with ORTHO House Plant Insect Control or ORTHO Whitefly & Mealybug Killer. (For instructions on spraying houseplants, see page 915.) Plants need to be sprayed weekly for several weeks to kill the mites as they hatch. To avoid introducing mites, inspect new plants carefully.

PROBLEM: White powdery patches appear on the upper surfaces of the older leaves. The leaf tissue under the patches may show yellow or brown flecks. Whole leaves may die, become dry, and drop from the plant.

ANALYSIS: Powdery mildew
Powdery mildew on piggyback is caused by a fungus (*Sphaerotheca* species) that grows on the surfaces of the leaves. The powdery patches consist of fungal strands and spores. The spores are spread by air currents to uninfected plants. The fungus takes nutrients from the plant, causing yellowing or browning of tissues. When the condition is severe, the leaf may die. Powdery mildews are favored by reduced light, warm days, and cool nights.

SOLUTION: Spray with a fungicide containing *dinocap* or *cycloheximide*. (For information on spraying houseplants, see page 915.) Grow piggyback plants in bright light and in rooms where the temperature does not fluctuate much from day to night. Remove infected leaves as they appear.

TRADESCANTIA (WANDERING JEW) —— ZYGOCACTUS (CHRISTMAS CACTUS) ——

Dieback.

Stem rot.

Weak growth.

PROBLEM: Tips of older leaves turn yellow, then die and turn brown. This condition occurs more frequently on long stems than on short stems. The longer the stem, the more tip burn is found.

ANALYSIS: Dieback
The cause of dieback is unknown. It looks like salt damage (see page 225), but often occurs on plants that have been leached regularly. As wandering Jew stems grow long, the plant does not support the old leaves, and they turn yellow and die starting at the tips.

SOLUTION: Remove dead leaves as they appear. Keep pinching the tips of the stems so they do not become too long. This will force new buds to grow farther back on the stems. New leaves will not show this problem. Plants may occasionally need to be cut back severely so that only several inches are left on each stem. After cutting back, reduce the amount of water and fertilizer given until the plant is actively growing again.

Tradescantia cultural information
Light: Needs medium light
Water: When the soil is just barely moist

PROBLEM: Stems wilt, and turn lighter green and dull. Plants stop flowering, are stunted, and may die. Large brown, circular, sunken areas may appear on the main stem at or just below the soil line.

ANALYSIS: Root and stem rot
Root rot in zygocactus is caused by fungi (*Phythium* species or *Phytophthora* species). These soil-inhabiting fungi invade the small roots and spread through the root system, killing it. As a result, plants are unable to obtain water or nutrients to maintain growth. Root rot may be so severe that the plant dies. Stems of plants weakened by these root-rotting fungi are susceptible to attack by the stem-rotting fungus *Fusarium oxysporum*. This soil-borne fungus invades the stems of plants weakened by root rot. The fungus causes large brown, sunken areas on the main stems at or below the soil line. If it girdles the stem, the plant will die.

SOLUTION: Discard severely infected plants. If the plant is not severely affected, dry it out as described on page 857. There are no fungicides available that adequately control these disease organisms. To prevent the disease, water zygocactus infrequently, when the top inch of soil is slightly moist. Water thoroughly so that some water drains through the pot. Discard any water that drains through. For more information on watering, see page 913.

PROBLEM: Stems are slightly elongated, and are lighter green than normal. Plants do not produce any flowers.

ANALYSIS: Insufficient light
Plants use light as a source of energy, and grow slowly in light that is too dim for their needs. If the light is much too dim, the plant has little energy, and grows poorly. Although it may grow and look healthy in relatively low light, it will not bloom. Zygocactus needs higher levels of light to flower well.

SOLUTION: Move the plant to a brighter location. Zygocactus will tolerate direct sun if it is kept well watered. But if it is allowed to become dry while in direct sunlight, it will sunburn. (For more information on sunburn, see page 226.) If a brighter location is not available, provide supplemental lighting as described on page 914. Because long hours of light will prevent zygocactus from flowering, avoid giving more than 10 hours of light per day. Zygocactus can spend the summer in light shade outside, and be brought indoors when night temperatures drop to 50°F. If you wish to grow a houseplant in a dim location, select a plant that is tolerant of dim light from the list on page 990.

Zygocactus cultural information
Light: Needs bright light
Water: When the soil is just barely moist

On the next two pages, you will find some general guidelines for the care of lawns. Following that, lawn problems are grouped according to the general appearance of the problem. Find the description in the list below that most nearly describes your problem.

LAWNS

A lawn is made up of thousands of individual grass plants. Turfgrasses are adapted to growing in dense stands, and are fiercely competitive. If we give them conditions to their liking, they will grow so vigorously that few problems will be able to gain a toehold. You will find some basic guidelines for lawn care on the next two pages. If you follow these guidelines, most of the effort you expend on your lawn will be to keep it growing vigorously, rather than to fight weeds, diseases, and insects.

This is especially true of weeds. All weeds begin as seedlings in your lawn, and a vigorous turf will smother seedlings. Once weeds are established, however, they may be able to hold their own against the lawn. The two basic rules of lawn weed control are to keep the lawn growing vigorously, and to stop weeds before they gain a toehold. If you follow these rules, the only weeding you will ever have to do will be to kill an occasional interloper before it goes to seed. For more information about weed control, see page 823.

All the diseases that attack lawns are caused by fungi. Fungi are simple plants that prefer moist conditions, and are usually controlled by keeping leaves or soil dry. But this cannot be done with lawns. Because of their shallow root system, they must be watered frequently, and because they are packed so closely together and are so close to the soil, the air around the grass blades is usually humid.

So the most frequently repeated disease preventative measure you will see in the next few pages is to regulate the amount of nitrogen the grass receives. Grass is greedy for nitrogen. If given large amounts when it can't grow fast enough to use it all, it hoards it in its tissues. This wealth of nutrients makes the grass an inviting target for fungi. But if the lawn is weakened from too *little* fertilizer, its defenses are lowered and it is unable to fight off diseases. So proper nitrogen fertilization is a key to preventing lawn diseases.

Lawn insects are often local problems, and their severity fluctuates from year to year. In some parts of the country, insects are minor lawn problems, but in others, lawns may be destroyed by them. The key to solving insect problems is often to understand the life cycle of the insect, and to apply the proper measures at the right time.

You will find a little more information about lawn care on page 908, where methods for repairing the ravages of some disease and insect problems are described.

Above: Thatch. See page 304. Left: A healthy lawn. By keeping the lawn vigorous, many problems can be prevented. See page 294.

CULTURAL GUIDELINES FOR LAWNS

Sprinkler irrigation.

Mowing.

Proper watering is essential in maintaining a healthy, vigorous lawn. Follow these guidelines for proper watering:

■ Water deeply and infrequently. Apply 1 to 2 inches of water each irrigation. Water every 3 days (in hot, dry areas) to 10 days if it does not rain. If the lawn wilts (see page 304), water immediately.

■ Light and frequent watering promotes disease and encourages shallow roots. A lawn with shallow roots is more subject to drought damage than a lawn with deep roots.

■ The lawn will use more water in hotter areas, or where there are tree roots near the surface.

■ Water less often during cloudy and cool weather, and more often during hot and windy weather.

■ Measure the amount of water you apply with several straight-sided cans scattered under the sprinkler.

■ Check to see if you are applying enough water by digging a hole with a trowel a couple of hours after watering. The water should penetrate at least 8 inches.

■ Apply the water slowly enough that it does not run off. If you cannot change sprinkler heads, turn off the sprinklers for 30 minutes whenever runoff occurs. Continue this cycle until you have applied enough water. Aerating (see page 305) will improve penetration.

A well-groomed lawn — one that is mowed at the right height when it needs it — is better able to resist insects, diseases, and weeds. Follow these guidelines for proper mowing:

■ Mow when the grass grows $1/3$ to $1/2$ times over the recommended height. For example, if the lawn's recommended mowing height is 2 inches, cut it when it is 3 inches high.

■ Suggested mowing heights:

Bahiagrass	2 to 3 inches
Bentgrass	$3/8$ to $3/4$ inches
Bermudagrass	$1/2$ to $1^1/2$ inches
Bluegrass	2 to 3 inches
Carpetgrass	1 to 2 inches
Centipedegrass	1 to 2 inches
Fine fescue	1 to $2^1/2$ inches
Ryegrass	1 to $2^1/2$ inches
St. Augustine	$1^1/2$ to 3 inches
Tall fescue	3 to 4 inches
Zoysia	$1/2$ to $1^1/2$ inches

■ Sharpen mower blades frequently so they do not tear the grass blades. Torn blades give the lawn a whitish cast.

■ Never cut off more than half of the grass blade at a mowing. Mowing too short exposes the shaded lower stems to sunlight, causing them to burn and turn brown. If the grass is much too high, reduce its height a little at a time.

■ It is not necessary to remove grass clippings if the clippings are able to drop into the lawn out of sight. Clippings do not contribute to thatch. But if your lawn is maintained very short, or if the clippings sit on top of the grass, remove them to avoid smothering the grass.

■ Mow the lawn when the grass is dry.

Uneven fertilization.

Dethatched lawn. The piles are thatch.

Seedlings emerging in new lawn.

Fertilizers supply the nutrients a lawn needs to grow well and remain healthy. Follow these guidelines for proper fertilizing.

■ Use a fertilizer that supplies all three major nutrients: nitrogen, phosphate, and potash. For a discussion of plant nutrients, see page 867.

■ Too much fertilizer during periods of stress causes lawn diseases. Avoid heavy fertilization during stress periods. Warm season grasses are under stress during the cool part of the year; cool season grasses are under stress during hot weather.

■ Spread the fertilizer evenly over the lawn with a dropper spreader or a broadcast spreader.

■ Apply fertilizer to moist soil, and water thoroughly immediately after application. This dilutes the dissolved fertilizer and prevents it from burning the lawn.

■ Some general guidelines for feeding grasses: If you live in Zone A (see map on page 991), feed in midspring, early fall, and late fall. If you live in Zone C, fertilize when the grass turns green in the spring and repeat every 6 weeks until cool weather. If you live in Zone B and your lawn turns brown every winter, follow the directions for Zone C. If the lawn remains green during the winter, feed in early spring, late spring, early fall, and late fall.

Thatch is an accumulation of partially decomposed grass stems and roots that accumulates between the live grass and the soil. Check the thickness of a thatch layer by cutting a triangular plug from the lawn with a knife. A thatch layer from 1/4 to 1/2 inch thick is normal; when it exceeds 1/2 inch it becomes harmful to the lawn.

Thatch interferes with the flow of nutrients, water, and air to the roots. Lawns with excess thatch dry out quickly and are difficult to water without runoff. Insects and plant diseases live in a thick thatch layer. The thatch also interferes with the action of insecticides and fungicides, making control difficult.

Thatch accumulation gives the lawn a spongy texture. This causes the lawn mowers to bounce, scalping the lawn in spots.

Thatch builds up when the lawn is overfertilized, overwatered, or when the soil is too acid. Grass clippings from mowing do not contribute to thatch.

Thatch accumulates over many years, and should not be removed all at once. Remove thatch with a dethatching machine (often called a verticutter) (see page 304). These are available from rental agencies, or hire a contractor to do the job for you. Dethatch annually until the condition is corrected. The best time to dethatch is just before a period of fast growth: late spring for warm season grasses, early fall for cool season grasses.

Test the pH of the thatch layer according to the instructions on page 903. If the pH is below 6.0, correct it with periodic applications of lime. Twice a year, spread 25 pounds of lime per 1000 square feet of lawn and water well.

Avoid problems with new lawns by following these guidelines.

Getting ready
■ The best time to plant a new lawn is just before a period of rapid growth for the type of grass you are planting.

■ Kill old lawns or weeds with ORTHO Kleenup Systemic Weed & Grass Killer. You can plant 1 week after treatment.

■ Improve the soil with organic amendments (page 901). Rototill, spade, or rake deeply to loosen the soil.

■ Rake out any clods or rocks from the top 2 inches of soil. Level the ground, water it, roll with a garden roller to settle the soil, then level again. Repeat until the ground remains level after watering and rolling.

Seeding
■ Spread seed with a dropper spreader or a broadcast spreader. Rake lightly to mix the seed into the top 1/4 inch of soil. Roll with a light roller to press the seed firmly into the soil. In dry weather, spread 1/8 to 1/4 inch of mulch (sawdust or straw — don't use peat moss) to keep the seeds moist. Sprinkle lightly by hand whenever the mulch begins to dry out.

Laying sod
■ Lay sod as soon as possible after it is cut. Fit the edges tightly together. Don't stretch the sod. Keep the sod moist until it is established — about 2 weeks. Test by tugging gently at a corner. When you feel resistance, it is established.

DEAD PATCHES

Dog urine spots.

Burn caused by a fertilizer spill.

Dead annual bluegrass.

PROBLEM: Circular spots, straw brown in color, 8 to 10 inches in diameter, appear in the lawn. A ring of deep green grass may surround each patch. There are no spots or webbing on the grass blades and the grass does not mat down. Dogs have been in the area.

ANALYSIS: Dog urine injury
Dog urine burns grass. The salts in the urine cause varying stages of damage, from slight discoloration to killing it outright. The nitrogen in the urine may encourage the immediately surrounding grass to grow rapidly, resulting in a dark green ring. Lawns suffer the most damage in hot, dry weather.

SOLUTION: Water the affected areas thoroughly to wash away the urine. This reduces but does not eradicate the brown discoloration. Surrounding grass eventually fills in the affected areas. For quick repair, spot sod as on page 908. If possible, keep dogs off the lawn.

PROBLEM: Grass dies and turns yellow in irregular patches or definite regular stripes or curves. Grass bordering the areas is a healthy green color. Yellow areas do not spread or enlarge. They appear within 2 to 5 days after fertilizing or after a chemical is spilled on the lawn.

ANALYSIS: Chemical or fertilizer burn
Chemicals such as pesticides, fertilizers, gasoline, and hydrated lime may burn the grass if applied improperly or accidentally spilled. When excessive amounts of these materials contact grass plants, they cause the blades to dry out and die.

SOLUTION: Damage can be prevented or minimized by picking up the spilled material, then washing the chemical from the soil immediately. If the substance is water-soluble, water the area thoroughly — 3 to 5 times longer than usual. If the substance is not soluble in water, such as gasoline or weed oil, flood the area with a solution of dish soap diluted to about the same strength as used for washing dishes. Then water as indicated above. Some substances, such as pre-emergence herbicides, cannot be washed from the soil. Replace the top foot of soil in the spill area. Prevent further damage by filling gas tanks, spreaders, and sprayers on an unplanted surface, such as a driveway. Apply chemicals according to the label instructions. Apply fertilizers when the grass blades are dry and the soil is moist. Water thoroughly afterward to dilute the fertilizer and wash it into the soil. Keep dropper spreaders closed when stopped or turning. Follow the directions on page 979.

PROBLEM: Areas of grass that were once lush and green die and turn straw brown. Irregular patches appear with the onset of hot summer weather in places where the grass had a whitish appearance in late spring.

ANALYSIS: Annual bluegrass (*Poa annua*)
Annual bluegrass is one of the most troublesome but least noticed weeds in the lawn. This member of the bluegrass family is lighter green, more shallow-rooted, and less drought and heat tolerant than Kentucky bluegrass. Annual bluegrass, as its name suggests, lives for only one year, although some areas also have perennial strains. The seed germinates in cool weather from late summer to late fall. Annual bluegrass grows rapidly in the spring, especially if the lawn is fertilized then. Seed heads appear in mid- to late spring, the same height that the grass is cut. The seed heads give the lawn a whitish appearance. When hot, dry weather arrives, the plants die. The seeds fall to the soil and wait for cooler weather to germinate. Annual bluegrass is most serious where the soil is compacted.

SOLUTION: Weedkillers are only partially effective in controlling annual bluegrass. Prevent seeds from germinating by applying an herbicide containing *DCPA* in early to mid-fall. Do not use *DCPA* if you plan to reseed the lawn in the fall. Replace the dead areas with sod. Do not cut the lawn too short. Lawns more than 2½ inches tall have very little annual bluegrass. Core the lawn in compacted areas (see page 305). For more information on annual bluegrass, see page 825.

Dead crabgrass.

Anthracnose on bluegrass.

Fusarium patch. *Insert:* Closeup.

PROBLEM: Brown patches develop in the lawn with the first frost in the fall. Close examination of the dead spots reveals that it is not the lawn grass that has died, but a weed.

ANALYSIS: Crabgrass dying out
Crabgrass (*Digitaria* species) is an annual grassy weed in lawns. It forms large flat clumps, smothering the lawn grass as it spreads. Crabgrass dies with the first killing frost in the fall, or with the onset of cold weather, leaving dead patches in the lawn. Crabgrass sprouts from seeds in early spring. It is a prolific seed producer; a single plant can make thousands of seeds during the course of the summer.

SOLUTION: Treat with an herbicide containing *DCPA* or *siduron* in the early spring 2 weeks before the last expected frost, or about the time the forsythia bloom. These pre-emergence weed killers kill the seed as it germinates. Kill actively growing crabgrass with ORTHO Crab Grass Killer or ORTHO Crab Grass & Dandelion Killer. Maturing plants are harder to kill, so repeat the treatment 2 more times, 4 to 7 days apart, if necessary. Control crabgrass growing in cracks in sidewalks and driveways with ORTHO Kleenup Ready-To-Use Weed & Grass Killer. To keep your lawn healthy and vigorous, follow the guidelines on pages 294 and 295. A thick lawn has very little crabgrass. For more information on crabgrass, see page 312.

PROBLEM: In the summer and fall, irregular areas of reddish brown to light tan grass appear in the lawn. These areas may range from 2 inches to 10 to 20 feet in diameter. Small, oval, reddish purple spots occur on the blades. A fine webbing may cover the spots, or tiny black specks may be seen in the spots.

ANALYSIS: Anthracnose
This lawn disease is caused by a fungus (*Colletotrichum graminicola*) that attacks lawns under stress, especially those that are poorly fertilized or underwatered. The disease is active in warm (80° to 85°F), humid weather, and results in root decay and stem rot. When weather conditions are favorable for the disease, grass may be killed within 2 days.

SOLUTION: Treat the infected lawn with a fungicide containing *benomyl*, *zineb*, or *chlorothalonil* at the first sign of the disease. Repeat the treatment 3 more times at intervals of 7 to 10 days. Reduce potential damage from anthracnose by fertilizing and watering as suggested on page 294.

PROBLEM: Pale yellow areas, 2 inches to 1 foot in diameter and pink along the edges, occur in the lawn in the late winter and early spring. Blades are light tan and stick together. A white cottony growth may cover the blades.

ANALYSIS: Fusarium patch
This grass disease is caused by a fungus (*Fusarium nivale*) that may attack lawns in the fall, winter, or spring when the turf remains wet from snow, rain, or poor surface drainage. The disease, also called *pink snow mold*, is most severe on bentgrass, but also occurs on other grasses. It is most prevalent in cool (daytime temperatures below 65°F), humid weather, or when snow falls on unfrozen soil. The fungus often grows beneath the snow or as it melts. Usually, only the grass blades are affected, but when the snow mold is severe, the crowns also are attacked, killing the plants.

SOLUTION: Treat the lawn in early spring at the first sign of the disease with a fungicide containing *benomyl*, *iprodione*, or *methyl thiophanate*. Repeat the treatment in 10 to 14 days. Treat the lawn again in mid to late fall when the daytime temperatures remain below 60°F and the weather is wet. Make 2 applications, 10 to 14 days apart. To discourage snow mold, avoid applying fertilizers that are high in nitrogen late in the fall. To prevent matting, keep mowing the lawn until the grass stops growing in the fall. Reduce the thatch layer if necessary. For more information on lawn maintenance practices, see pages 294 and 295.

DEAD PATCHES

Fusarium blight.

Brown patch.

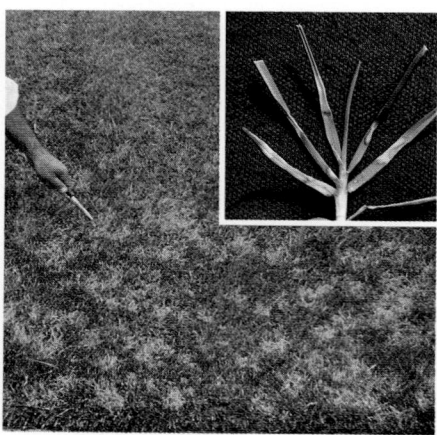

Dollar spot damage. *Insert:* Close-up.

PROBLEM: Patches of grass turn light green, then straw-colored from June through August. "Hot spots" in the yard along driveways, sidewalks, and buildings usually discolor first. These circular, crescent, or streaked areas range from a few inches to several feet in size. Often the center patch remains green, resulting in a "frog-eye" pattern. Irregular tan lesions extend the full width of the blade. The basal portions of dead stems dry out and turn brown or black.

ANALYSIS: Fusarium blight
This lawn disease is caused by a fungus (*Fusarium roseum*) that is active during hot (75° to 100°F) summer weather, primarily attacking bentgrass and Kentucky bluegrass. Lawns under stress from lack of moisture, hot dry winds, low pH (pH 6.0 or less), thick thatch, and close mowing are most susceptible to the disease. Lush, dense growth from excessive nitrogen fertilization is readily attacked. In cool fall weather, new grass fills in the dead areas, but the disease may recur there the following year.

SOLUTION: Rake out the dead grass and follow the cultural practices outlined on pages 294 and 295. Reseed with resistant varieties. A mixture of 15 percent or more perennial ryegrass and 85 percent or less bluegrass greatly reduces the occurrence of fusarium blight. Next year, before the disease occurs, treat with a fungicide containing *benomyl* or *iprodione* in late May, followed by 2 applications 10 to 14 days apart. Water thoroughly the day before; water again afterwards. Complete control is difficult to achieve. For a list of resistant and susceptible varieties of bluegrass, see page 990.

PROBLEM: Circular patches of dead grass a few inches to a few feet in diameter appear in the lawn during periods of high humidity and warm (75° to 85°F) temperatures. Brown areas are sometimes surrounded by dark, purplish smoky rings. Filmy white tufts cover blades in the early morning before the dew dries. Grass blades pull out easily from the base of the plant. After 2 to 3 weeks, the center brown grass may recover and turn green, giving brown areas a doughnut shape.

ANALYSIS: Brown patch
Brown patch is caused by a fungus (*Rhizoctonia solani*). It is one of the most prevalent diseases in warm, humid areas, attacking all turfgrasses. Lush, tender growth from excessive nitrogen fertilization is the most susceptible to attack. Sometimes only the blades are affected and the grass recovers in 2 to 3 weeks. When the infection is severe and warm weather continues, the disease attacks plant crowns and kills the grass.

SOLUTION: Control brown patch with ORTHO Liquid Lawn Disease Control. Spray when the disease is first noticed, and at least 3 more times at 7 to 10 day intervals. Continue to repeat the treatments as long as warm, humid weather continues. To reduce recurring infections, follow the cultural practices described on pages 294 and 295.

Resistant varieties of ryegrass: Birdie, Citation, Derby, Diplomat, Omega, Pennfine, Yorktown II.

PROBLEM: The grass turns light brown to straw-colored in circular areas from the size of a silver dollar to 6 inches in diameter during the warm, wet weather of May and June and September and October. The small dead areas may merge to form large irregular patches. Small, light brown blotches with reddish brown borders appear on the leaf blades. These spots extend across the entire width of the blade. In the early morning before the dew dries, a white cobwebby growth may cover the infected blades.

ANALYSIS: Dollar spot
This lawn disease, also called *small brown patch*, is caused by a fungus (*Sclerotinia homoeocarpa*). It is most active during warm (60° to 85°F) moist days and cool nights. It attacks many kinds of lawn grasses, but is most severe on bentgrass, Bermudagrass, and Kentucky bluegrass. Lawns troubled by dollar spot are usually under stress from lack of moisture and nitrogen. An infection seldom causes permanent damage, although it takes the lawn several weeks or months to recover. The disease spreads on shoes, hoses, mowers, and other equipment.

SOLUTION: Control dollar spot with ORTHO Liquid Lawn Disease Control. Make 2 applications, 7 to 10 days apart, beginning when the disease is first evident. The grass recovers quickly if treated promptly. Maintain the cultural practices outlined on page 294. For a list of resistant varieties, see page 990.

Ophiobolus patch.

Sod webworm (twice life size).

Damaged lawn. *Insert:* White grub (twice life size).

PROBLEM: In midsummer, primarily in the Pacific Northwest, the grass thins, turns light brown, and dies in doughnut-shaped rings or arcs. These areas, 2 to 36 inches in diameter, turn dull gray in winter. The centers are invaded by weeds and annual bluegrass. When the condition is severe the affected areas merge, forming large irregular patches.

ANALYSIS: Ophiobolus patch
This lawn disease is caused by a fungus (*Ophiobolus graminis*) that becomes active in cool, wet weather, but the symptoms develop in dry summer weather. The disease is especially common on bentgrass. Both roots and shoots are severely attacked. Affected areas do not recover for several months.

SOLUTION: Ophiobolus patch is difficult to control with fungicides. Spray with *wettable sulfur*, making 2 applications of 1.25 pounds per 1000 square feet, 1 month apart in early spring. Apply 7½ pounds of *ammonium sulfate* per 1000 square feet in March, May, June, and early September. Water thoroughly afterwards to prevent burning. Apply 7 pounds of 0–10–10 fertilizer per 1000 square feet in March and June. When the disease has disappeared, use a balanced lawn fertilizer for normal fertilization.

PROBLEM: From mid-May to October the grass turns brown in patches the size of a saucer in the hottest and driest areas of the lawn. These areas may expand to form large irregular patches. Grass blades are chewed off at the soil level. Silky white tubes are found nestled in the root area. Inside are light brown or gray worms with black spots, from ¼ to ¾ inch long. White or gray moths fly in a zigzag pattern over the lawn in the evening. When the moth lands it folds its wings along the body, rather than letting them spread like most moths.

ANALYSIS: Sod webworms
Several different moths with similar habits are called sod webworms or *lawn moths*. The moths that fly in the evening are the adults of this pest. They do not damage the lawn, but drop eggs into the grass as they fly. The eggs hatch into worms that feed on grass blades at night or on cloudy, rainy days. In the daytime the worm hides in white silky tubes in the soil. Sometimes an entire lawn is killed in a few days.

SOLUTION: Control sod webworms with ORTHO Lawn Insect Spray (liquid), ORTHO Sod Webworm Control (liquid), or ORTHO Chinch Bug & Sod Webworm Control (granular) when large numbers of moths are noticed at dusk, or at the first sign of damage. First rake out all the dead grass and mow the lawn. Water thoroughly before spraying. For best results, apply the insecticide in the late afternoon or evening when the worms are most active. Do not cut or water the lawn for 1 to 3 days afterwards. To avoid recurring damage, treat the lawn again every 2 months beginning in late spring or early summer. Damaged lawns may recover rapidly if the insects are controlled early.

PROBLEM: In August and September the grass turns brown in large irregular patches. Brown areas of grass roll up easily like a carpet. Milky white grubs from ⅛ to 1 inch long, with brown heads and 3 pairs of legs, lie curled in the soil.

ANALYSIS: Grubs
Grubs are the larvae of different kinds of beetles, including May and June beetles (also called *white grubs*), Asiatic, Japanese, and masked chafer beetles. The grubs feed on turf roots and may kill the entire lawn. The adult beetles do not damage the lawn, but lay eggs in the soil. May and June beetles lay eggs in the spring and summer. The Asiatic, Japanese, and masked chafer beetles lay eggs in mid to late summer. The eggs hatch and the grubs feed on roots 1 to 3 inches deep in the soil. In late fall they move deep in the soil to overwinter, and resume feeding in the spring.

SOLUTION: The younger the grubs are, the easier they are to kill. Apply ORTHO Lawn Insect Spray (liquid), ORTHO Diazinon Insect Spray (liquid), or ORTHO Diazinon Soil & Turf Insect Control (granular) when you first notice damage and grubs. For preventive control, apply the insecticide just after eggs are laid. Contact your county agent (page 1011) for the correct time in your area. Water the lawn thoroughly within 1 hour after application to help carry the insecticide into the root zone where the grubs are feeding. Soil insecticides take time to be effective, so the grubs may be active for up to 35 days. Some grubs appear to be resistant to pesticides, so retreatments may be necessary. To save areas just beginning to fade, keep the soil moist but not wet.

DEAD PATCHES

Pythium blight on seedlings.

Bare spots.

Poor seed germination.

PROBLEM: In hot weather from April to October the grass wilts, shrivels, and turns light brown in irregular spots ½ to 4 inches in diameter. Spots enlarge rapidly, forming streaks a foot or more wide, or patches 1 to 10 feet in diameter. Infected blades mat together when walked on. Blades are often meshed together by white, cobwebby threads in the early morning before the dew dries. Grass sometimes dies within 24 hours.

ANALYSIS: Pythium blight
This lawn disease, also called *grease spot* and *cottony blight*, is caused by a fungus (*Pythium* species). It attacks lawns under stress from heat (85° to 95°F), poorly drained soil, and excessive moisture. Dense, lush grass is the most susceptible. All turfgrasses are affected, ryegrasses the most severely. The fungus spores spread easily in free-flowing water, on lawn mower wheels, and in footsteps. The disease is hard to control because it spreads so rapidly, killing large areas in hours. Pythium blight is common in the fall on topseeded ryegrass.

SOLUTION: Treat the lawn with a fungicide containing *chloroneb* or *ethazole* as soon as the disease is noticed. Repeat treatments every 5 to 10 days either until the disease stops, or until cooler weather resumes. Keep traffic off the diseased area to avoid spreading spores. To prevent recurring infections, follow the cultural practices outlined on pages 294 and 295. Severely infected areas often do not recover, so reseed or resod to reestablish the lawn. Treat next year during hot, humid weather.

PROBLEM: Seeds in newly planted lawns sprout slowly or not at all. Or seedlings rot and fall over at the soil line.

ANALYSIS: Seeds fail to grow
There are several reasons why lawn seeds may not grow.

1. *Lack of water:* Once the seed germinates and breaks its seed coat, the soil must stay evenly moist. If the soil around the seedling dries out, the seedling will die.

2. *Temperature:* Seeds planted at the wrong time of year take longer or fail to sprout. If planted at the proper time, seeds should sprout within 3 weeks. For seed germination times at optimum temperatures, see page 991.

3. *Old seeds:* Seeds left over from last year will sprout if they've been stored in a cool, dry place. Seeds older than 1 year, or that have not been stored properly, sprout poorly if at all.

4. *Seeds planted too deep:* Seeds planted deeper than ¼ inch to ½ inch usually don't sprout.

5. *Unprepared soil:* Seeds must be in direct contact with the soil to sprout. Seeds that sprout in a thatch layer or directly on top of the soil are subject to drying out.

6. *Damping-off:* This fungus disease is caused by fungi (*Pythium* and *Rhizoctonia* species). Damping-off kills seedlings either before or after emergence if the soil is kept too wet and is rich in nitrogen. For more information on damping-off, see page 858.

SOLUTION: The numbered solutions below correspond to the numbers in the analysis.

1. Sprinkle a newly planted lawn frequently enough that only the very surface is allowed to dry out. To help conserve moisture, mulch the seed bed lightly with a ¼ inch layer of straw or sawdust.

2. Plant warm season grasses (Bermudagrass, centipedegrass, and bahiagrass) in spring or early summer as the weather warms. Plant cool season grasses (rye, fescue, bentgrass, and bluegrass) in early to mid-fall or early spring.

3. Use seed produced for sale this year. Check the seed testing date on the box before purchasing.

4. After sowing the seed, gently rake the soil to mix the seed into the top ¼ inch.

5. Till or rake the soil surface before planting. Don't throw seed on top of thatch or unprepared soil.

6. When reseeding blank spots or the entire lawn, spray the seed bed with ORTHO Orthocide Garden Fungicide. Fill in any low spots where water may puddle. Water less often. Let the soil surface dry slightly between waterings until the seedlings are 1 inch high. Then reduce the frequency of watering to allow the top ¼ inch to dry between waterings. Don't add nitrogen fertilizer until the seedlings are 3 inches high.

Sod not rooted.

Dying patches of sod.

Adult chinch bug (15 times life size).

PROBLEM: Newly sodded areas turn yellow, then brown. Sod rolls up easily like a carpet. No roots are visible on the bottom of the sod.

ANALYSIS: Sod fails to establish
Sod should establish in 2 to 3 weeks. Test by gently tugging a corner. If it resists, then the roots have grown into the soil. Sod can fail to establish for a number of reasons:

1. *Sod dried out:* Until the roots grow into the soil, sod is very susceptible to drying out.

2. *Unprepared soil:* If the sod is laid directly on thatch it dries out quickly. If it is laid on hard soil, the roots have difficulty growing into the soil.

3. *Old sod:* Old sod has many yellow blades among the green blades. It may be weak from water or heat stress, and will establish poorly or not at all. Sod may be damaged by remaining rolled up for only 2 days in hot weather. In cool weather it can remain rolled for over a week without damage.

4. *Time of year:* Sod can be installed almost any time of the year, but it will establish slowly if it is laid when the grass is not actively growing.

SOLUTION: The numbered solutions below correspond to the numbers in the analysis.

1. Water frequently enough to keep the sod and the soil under it moist.

2. Before laying sod, the soil should be tilled or thoroughly raked. Remove all dead grass and debris, and level the grade.

3. Choose uniformly green sod that is not turning yellow or pale green. Lay the sod as soon as possible. Don't leave it rolled and stacked for more than a day in hot weather. However, it can be stored rolled for 2 to 3 days in a cool, shady area. Keep the soil on the outer pieces moist.

4. Lay cool season grass sod (bluegrass or bentgrass) in late summer to early fall or early spring. Avoid midsummer. Lay warm season grass sod (Bermudagrass, St. Augustine grass, bahiagrass, or centipedegrass) in the late spring and early summer.

PROBLEM: The grass turns yellowish brown, dries out, and dies in sunny areas and and along sidewalks and driveways. To check for chinch bugs, select a sunny spot on the edge of an affected area where yellow grass borders healthy green grass. Cut out both ends of a tin can. Push one end of the can 2 to 3 inches into the soil. Keep it filled with water for 10 minutes. Black to brown insects with white wings, 1/8 to 1/4 inch long, float to the surface in 5 to 10 minutes. Pink to brick red nymphs with a white stripe around the body may also be numerous.

ANALYSIS: Chinch bugs
(*Blissus* species)
These insects feed on many kinds of lawn grasses, but St. Augustine grass is a favorite. Both the adults and the nymphs suck the juices out of the blades. At the same time, they inject a poison that causes the blades to turn brown and die. Heavy infestations may completely kill the grass. These sun- and heat-loving insects seldom attack shady lawns. They can move rapidly across an entire lawn in several days.

SOLUTION: Control chinch bugs with ORTHO Lawn Insect Spray (liquid), ORTHO Chinch Bug Killer (liquid), or ORTHO Chinch Bug & Sod Webworm Control (granular) as soon as you see damage. Water the lawn before spraying, applying 1/2 to 1 inch of water to bring the insects to the surface. To prevent recurring damage from newly hatched nymphs, treat every 2 months until frost. In southern Florida, repeat the applications the year around.

DEAD PATCHES

Scalped spot.

Dormant Bermudagrass.

Billbug damage. *Insert:* Close-up.

PROBLEM: Grass has yellow patches after mowing. A few days later, patches may turn tan or brown and die.

ANALYSIS: Improper mowing
Too much grass was removed from the damaged places when the lawn was mowed. This can happen in two ways:
1. *Scalping*, or mowing near the soil level, occurs when the mower cuts too low in some areas. This can happen if the lawn is bumpy, in which case the high spots get scalped, or when the lawn is spongy, causing the mower to bounce. Where the grass has been cut too short, the lower parts of the blades are exposed to sunlight, which burns them. If the base of the grass plant was damaged by the scalping, the grass may die. Otherwise, it will probably recover in a week or so.
2. *Grass has grown too tall* between mowings. If the mower is cutting at the proper height, but the grass has grown too long between mowings, the lower parts of the grass blades are exposed and burned. The grass is seldom killed from being mowed when it is too long, but it remains unsightly for a week or two.

SOLUTION: The damaged spots need no special care. To prevent further damage:
1. If the lawn surface is uneven, level the high spots with the procedure described on page 908. If the lawn is spongy from an accumulation of thatch, follow the procedure described on page 295. Raise the mower blade to the height suggested on page 294.
2. Mow frequently enough so that you don't remove more than half of the blade. If the grass is very tall when you mow, raise the blade to half the grass height, and lower it gradually over the next few mowings.

PROBLEM: Brown patches of irregular shape and size develop with the first frost in the fall. The leaf and stem structure of the dead grass look different from the living grass. There are no signs of insect or disease damage.

ANALYSIS: Warm weather grasses becoming dormant
Warm weather perennial grasses become dormant with the onset of cold weather. The tops die back, but the perennial roots live over the winter and resprout in the spring. Two of the most common invading warm weather grasses are zoysia and Bermudagrass. When these grasses invade cool weather (bluegrass) lawns, the warm weather grasses turn brown in the fall, while the cool weather grasses remain green through the winter.

SOLUTION: It is very difficult to eradicate these grasses from the lawn. Once the grass turns brown, it is too late to treat. Next year, spot treat the undesirable grasses with ORTHO Kleenup Systemic Weed & Grass Killer or ORTHO Kleenup Ready-To-Use Weed & Grass Killer. Wait 1 week, and reseed. The grass will still be green, but the roots will die in a week or two and will not resprout. If new plants emerge in the spring, spot treat with the same herbicide or let the two kinds of grass grow together. If your lawn is in full sun, consider growing only warm season grass. As the warm season grass becomes dormant in the fall, camouflage the brown with a seeding of ryegrass or spray it with a green dye. For more information on Bermudagrass, see page 311.

PROBLEM: The grass turns brown and dies in expanding patches from mid-June to late August. When pulled, the grass lifts easily. Lying in the soil are fat, humpbacked white grubs with brown heads, without legs, and from ¼ to ½ inch long. Black, slow-moving snouted weevils ¼ to ½ inch long occasionally walk on sidewalks and driveways in May and October.

ANALYSIS: Billbugs
(*Sphenophorus* species)
The larvae of this pest damage lawns by hollowing out the grass stems and chewing off the roots. They can destroy an entire lawn. In May, the adults lay eggs in holes they chew in grass stems. The newly hatched larvae feed inside the stems, hollowing out the stem and crown, leaving very fine sandlike excrement. Large larvae feed on roots. Once the larvae move down to the roots and inside the plant's crown, chemical control can't reach them.

SOLUTION: Control billbugs with ORTHO Diazinon Soil & Turf Insect Control (granular) or ORTHO Diazinon Insect Spray (liquid). Young larvae can be controlled if treated while still feeding on the grass blades. If the larvae have already moved down to the roots, then water and fertilize the lawn to stimulate new growth. Repeated treatments are not usually necessary unless the billbugs are migrating from your neighbors' yards. Small damaged areas usually recover if the larvae are killed. Reseed or resod large areas. Next year, treat in early May to kill the adults as they lay eggs.

Damaged lawn. *Insert:* Mole cricket (¾ life size).

Dead patches caused by salt accumulation.

Crane fly grub (half life size).

PROBLEM: Small mounds of soil are scattered on the soil surface. The lawn feels spongy underfoot. Large areas of grass turn brown and die. To determine if the lawn is infested with mole crickets, make a solution of 1 ounce of liquid dishwashing detergent in 2 gallons of water. Drench the mixture into 4 square feet of turf. Mole crickets, greenish gray to brown insects, 1½ inches long, with short front legs and shovellike feet, will come to the surface within 3 minutes.

ANALYSIS: Mole crickets
(*Scapteriscus* species)
Several species of mole crickets attack lawns. They prefer bahia and Bermudagrass, but also feed on St. Augustine, zoysia, and centipedegrass. They damage lawns by tunneling through the top 1 to 2 inches of soil, loosening it and uprooting plants, causing them to dry out. They also feed on grass roots, weakening the plants. They feed at night, and may tunnel as much as 10 to 20 feet a night. In the daytime, they return to their underground burrows. Adults migrate from their burrows to new areas twice a year, in the spring from March to July, and again from November to December.

SOLUTION: In July, after the eggs hatch and before the young nymphs cause much damage, treat the lawn with ORTHO Mole Cricket Bait or ORTHO Diazinon Insect Spray. Mow grass and water before applying, since mole crickets are not active in dry soil. Do not water for 36 hours after application. If damage continues, treat again in late summer to early fall. Keep the lawn watered to encourage new root growth. For instructions on watering lawns, see page 294.

PROBLEM: Grass slowly dies, especially in the lowest areas of the lawn. A white or dark crust may be present on the soil.

ANALYSIS: Salt damage
Salt damage occurs when salt accumulates in the soil to damaging levels. This can happen in two ways: either the lawn is not receiving enough water from rainfall or irrigation to wash the salts from the soil, or the drainage is so poor that water does not pass through the soil. In either case, as water evaporates from the soil and grass blades, the salts that were dissolved in the water accumulate near the surface of the soil. In some cases, a white or dark brown crust of salts forms on the surface of the soil. Salts can originate in the soil, in the irrigation water, or in applied fertilizers.

SOLUTION: The only way to eliminate salt problems is to wash the salts through the soil with water. If the damage is only at a low spot in the lawn, fill in the spot to level the lawn. If the entire lawn drains poorly, improve drainage by aerating according to the directions on page 305; or improve the soil as described on page 901. If the soil drains well, increase the amount of water applied at each watering by 50 percent or more, so that excess water will leach salts below the root zone of the grass. Fertilize according to the instructions on page 295.

PROBLEM: Grass blades are eaten in patches, often beginning at the edges of the lawn. The patches may spread until most of the lawn is affected. A brownish paste covers the ground in heavily infested areas. Legless, brownish gray grubs, about an inch long, may be found just under the surface of the soil. Late last summer, many long-legged, mosquitolike insects were present around the house.

ANALYSIS: European crane fly
(*Tipula paludosa*)
The adult form of this insect looks like a large mosquito with very long legs that break off easily. They often swarm around houses in large numbers in late summer. Their numbers are alarming, but adult crane flies do not sting or do any other damage. They lay eggs in lawns, pastures, or fields in late summer. The grubs that hatch from the eggs feed on grass blades and clover during the fall, spend the winter buried in the soil, and resume feeding in the spring. The most severe damage is done in March and April. Feeding stops by mid-May. The adults emerge in late August and September. The grass is usually not killed in the damaged areas, and recovers after feeding stops.

SOLUTION: Spray the lawn with ORTHO Diazinon Insect Spray when damage first appears. Treatment is most effective between April 1 and April 15.

DEAD PATCHES

Greenbugs (3 times life size).

PROBLEM: Patches of grass under trees turn rust-colored, then brown, and die. Discolored areas then spread outward into sunny areas of the lawn. Yellow to rust-colored spots with dark centers occur on the blades.

ANALYSIS: Greenbug
(*Schizaphis graminum*)
The greenbug is a small aphid that feeds on grains such as wheat, corn, and sorghum. It has recently become a serious pest of Kentucky bluegrass lawns in some areas of the Midwest. The greenbug seldom attacks other kinds of turfgrass. Damage occurs as the greenbug pierces the leaf tissue, sucks the sap, and injects a toxin into the blades. This feeding weakens both the roots and aboveground plant parts. If uncontrolled, greenbugs can kill the turf. Greenbugs prefer well-maintained and managed lawns. However, underwatered lawns that are attacked also suffer severe damage. Overuse of fertilizers may predispose the lawn to attack. Greenbugs are most numerous after mild winters and cool springs.

SOLUTION: Spray the infested lawn with ORTHO Orthene Systemic Insect Control at the first sign of damage. Repeat if the damage and infestation continue. Prevent water stress by watering as suggested on page 294. Apply fertilizers as suggested on page 295.

GRASS THIN

Lawn damaged by drought.

PROBLEM: Footprints in the lawn make a long-lasting imprint instead of bouncing right back. The grass blades turn a bluish green or slate gray color and wilt. In the cool evening, the grass recovers and looks all right until the sun and heat of the following day make it darken and wilt. Areas begin to thin out, and after a few days the lawn begins to look and feel like straw and dies.

ANALYSIS: Drought
A lawn suffers from drought damage when water evaporates from the lawn faster than it is absorbed. Drought damage occurs first in the hottest and driest areas of the lawn — along sidewalks, driveways, south or west-facing slopes, south sides of reflecting buildings, and areas with sandy soil. Grass blades don't wilt like broadleafed plants do. They don't droop, but roll or fold up lengthwise.

SOLUTION: Water the lawn immediately, following the guidelines on page 294. If the grass has turned yellow, it will take several weeks for the affected areas to recover. If you are not very conscientious about watering your lawn, consider planting a drought tolerant turfgrass.

Drought tolerant turfgrasses: Bahia, Bermudagrass, Red fescue, Tall fescue, Zoysia.

Thatch.

PROBLEM: Grass thins out in sunny or shady areas of the lawn. Weeds invade the sparse areas. Grass may suddenly die in large patches during summer heat and drought. Cut and lift several plugs of grass 2 to 3 inches deep. Look to see if the stringy, feltlike material between the grass and soil surface is thicker than ¼ inch.

ANALYSIS: Thatch
Thatch is a tightly intermingled layer of partially decomposed stems and roots of grass, which develops between the actively growing grass and the soil surface. Thatch slows grass growth by restricting the movement of water, air, and nutrients in the soil. Thatch is normal in the lawn, but when it is thicker than ¼ inch, the lawn begins to suffer. As the layer accumulates, the grass roots grow in the thatch instead of down into the soil. Thatch is similar to peat moss — it dries out quickly and is very difficult to rewet. Thatch accumulation is encouraged by overly vigorous grass growth from excessive fertilization and frequent watering. Grass clippings do not contribute to thatch. For more information on thatch, see page 295.

SOLUTION: To reduce the thatch and increase the lawn's vigor, power rake or dethatch the lawn. Dethatch cool season grasses in the fall, and warm season grasses in the early spring before new growth begins. The machines for the job can be rented, or hire a contractor. Dethatchers have vertical rotating blades that slice through the turf, cutting out thatch. First, mow the lawn as short as possible. With the machine, go over the lawn 1 to 3 times as you would with a lawn mower. Take up the debris, fertilize, and water to hasten the lawn's recovery.

Lawn damaged by soil compaction.

Lawn damaged by shade.

Lawn thinned by leaf spot. *Insert:* Spotted blades.

PROBLEM: In heavily traveled areas, the grass becomes thin and develops bare spots. Water runs off quickly.

ANALYSIS: Compacted soil
Soil is easily compacted, or pressed together, in areas where there is frequent foot or vehicular traffic. Clay soils are more likely to become compacted than loamy or sandy soils. Soil that has been compacted has few air spaces. Compaction prevents air, water, and nutrients from penetrating into the soil and reaching the grass roots. This results in a shallow root system, and frequent water and nutrient stress.

SOLUTION: Water daily during hot periods, and fertilize frequently to keep the grass alive until you can relieve the compacted soil. Aerate the compacted soil with a coring machine. These machines can be rented, or hire a contractor to do the job for you. Coring machines remove cores of soil, allowing water and nutrients to pass into the soil. Water the lawn a few days before aerating, so the soil is moist. Do not aerate dry or wet soil. After aerating, allow the removed soil cores to dry a few days in the sun, then rake them up or break them by dragging a heavy flat board over them. In a few weeks the grass begins to fill in the holes in the lawn. Hand coring tools are available for aerating small areas. Aerate heavily trafficked areas annually. Reduce foot traffic in the area by installing a walk or patio, erecting a fence, or planting a hedge to divert traffic.

PROBLEM: Grass becomes thin under trees. Blades are thin and dark green. Moss and algae sometimes grow on the soil.

ANALYSIS: Shade
Planting and maintaining a good lawn under shade trees is difficult. Shallow-rooted trees like maples, pines, and beeches absorb much of the nutrients and water that are applied and intended for the grass. Trees that cast dense shade block out the sun that the grass needs to grow. It is especially difficult to grow grass under pines and other conifers. Some lawn diseases, such as powdery mildew, are more active in the shade, where they thrive in the higher humidity.

SOLUTION: Prune some of the branches from the trees to let more light to the grass. When seeding shady areas, select shade tolerant grasses: in the North, fescues and some bluegrasses such as Glade, Warrens A-34, and Nugget; in the South, St. Augustine grass. Seed in the fall so the seedlings have a chance to establish before the tree leafs out in the spring. Rake up fallen leaves every 4 or 5 days in the fall so they do not suffocate the grass. Mow the grass in the shade higher than in the full sun. Water and fertilize more heavily under trees so there is enough for both the lawn and the tree.

If you have trouble keeping a lawn healthy under a tree, try one of these shade-loving groundcovers: ajuga, English ivy, pachysandra, periwinkle.

PROBLEM: The grass turns brown and thins out in irregular patches 2 or more feet in diameter from spring until fall. Both the green and brown grass blades have small oval spots with strawcolored centers and dark maroon borders.

ANALYSIS: Helminthosporium leaf spot
This lawn disease, also called *melting out*, is caused by a fungus (*Helminthosporium* species). It is one of the most destructive lawn diseases, especially on Kentucky bluegrass. In cool spring and fall weather, *Helminthosporium* causes spots on grass blades, but does not kill them. In warm summer weather the fungus can kill the grass blades, spread to the base on the plant, and kill entire plants. Lawns that are excessively lush from high nitrogen fertilization or are under stress from short mowing, thick thatch, and light, frequent watering, are the most susceptible to attack.

SOLUTION: Spray the lawn with ORTHO Liquid Lawn Disease Control when leaf spotting is first noticed. Make at least 3 more applications, 7 to 10 days apart. Keep your lawn healthy and vigorous by following the guidelines for good lawn care on pages 294 and 295. Be particularly careful to use a balanced lawn fertilizer, reduce the thatch layer, and water thoroughly and infrequently. For a list of resistant and susceptible varieties of bluegrass, see page 990.

GRASS THIN

Nematode damage.

PROBLEM: The grass grows slowly, thins out, and turns pale green to yellow. In hot weather the blades may wilt. Main roots are short with few side roots, or many roots may grow from one point.

ANALYSIS: Nematodes
Nematodes are microscopic worms that live in the soil. They are not related to earthworms. Nematodes feed on grass roots, damaging and stunting them. The damaged roots can't supply sufficient water and nutrients to the leaf blades, and the grass is stunted or slowly dies. Nematodes are found throughout the United States, but are most severe in the South. They prefer moist, sandy loam soils. They can move only a few inches each year on their own, but they may be carried long distances by soil, water, tools, or infested plants. Testing roots and soil is the only positive method for confirming the presence of nematodes. Contact your local Cooperative Extension Office (see page 1011) for sampling instructions and addresses of testing laboratories. Soil and root problems such as poor soil structure, drought stress, nutrient deficiency, and root rots can also produce symptoms of decline similar to those caused by nematodes. These problems should be eliminated as causes before sending soil and root samples for testing. For information on soil problems and root rots, see pages 901 and 856.

SOLUTION: There are no chemicals available to homeowners to kill nematodes in planted soil. However, they can be controlled before planting a new lawn by soil fumigation. For information on fumigating soil, see page 919.

LAWN PALE OR YELLOW

Unfertilized lawn with green clover.

PROBLEM: Grass is pale green to yellow and grows more slowly than usual. If the condition persists, the grass will become sparse and weeds will invade.

ANALYSIS: Nitrogen deficiency
Nitrogen is a key element in maintaining a healthy lawn with few insect and disease problems. It is best to maintain a level of nitrogen in the soil that: (1) avoids excessive leaf growth, which needs more frequent mowing; (2) doesn't encourage shoot growth at the expense of root growth; and (3) varies according to the cultural and environmental conditions present. Because heavy rains and watering leach nitrogen from the soil, periodic feedings are necessary throughout the growing season. Acid soil may cause nitrogen to be unavailable to the grass.

SOLUTION: Fertilize the lawn with a lawn fertilizer according to the instructions on the label. To prevent burning and to move the nutrients into the soil, water thoroughly after application. Grass begins using the nitrogen in the fertilizer within 15 to 24 hours. (For more information on fertilizing, see page 294.) If the soil is acid, below pH 5.5, liming is necessary for good nitrogen utilization. For more information on pH and liming, see pages 902 and 1002.

Grass blades damaged by a dull lawn mower.

PROBLEM: When viewed from a distance, the lawn has a white or gray cast. The leaf ends are ragged and dead at the tip. White hairs may protrude from the cut tips.

ANALYSIS: Dull lawn mower
If a reel or rotary lawn mower is dull, it tears the tip off the grass blade rather than cutting it cleanly. Perennial ryegrass and tall fescues have fibers running the length of the blade that do not cut easily. If the blade tip is torn, these fibers usually remain protruding from the torn end. It is particularly important to keep the mower sharp when cutting these grasses.

SOLUTION: Reel mowers should be sharpened two or three times during the growing season. Rotary mowers should be sharpened after every few mowings. Reel mowers may be sharpened at a hardware store that offers this service. Rotary mower blades can be removed and sharpened with a file. For more information on mower care and sharpening, see the ORTHO book *How To Select, Use & Maintain Garden Equipment.*

Stripe smut. *Insert:* Infected blades.

Bermudagrass mite damage.

Septoria leaf spot.

PROBLEM: Grass turns pale green to yellow in cool spring and fall weather. First, long yellowish streaks appear on the blades. These streaks turn gray to black. The blades then curl, wither, and shred in thin strips from the tip downward. Affected plants occur singly or in spots from a few inches to more than a foot in diameter. These areas grow more slowly and are shorter than surrounding healthy grass.

ANALYSIS: Stripe smut
This grass disease is caused by a fungus (*Ustilago striiformis*) that attacks many kinds of turfgrasses, but is most prevalent on Merion Kentucky bluegrass. The disease is most active in cool (50° to 60°F) weather. The diseased plants then die during the next hot weather. The spores infect the plant's crown and adjoining underground stems. The fungus then grows throughout the plant's tissues. Stripe smut is favored by high soil fertility and excessive watering.

SOLUTION: Stripe smut is difficult to eliminate completely, but its severity can be lessened. Treat the lawn with *benomyl* or *ethyl thiophanate* in October or early March with 2 applications 14 to 21 days apart. Water thoroughly afterwards to carry the fungicide to the roots so it can be absorbed into the plant. Follow the guidelines for good lawn care on pages 294 and 295. For a list of resistant varieties of bluegrass, see page 990.

PROBLEM: Bermudagrass plants grow in a tight "knot" or rosette, turn yellow, then brown and die. To determine if the grass is infested with mites, shake one of these rosettes over a sheet of dark paper. Minute, creamy white specks the size of pepper grains will drop to the paper and begin to crawl around. These pests are easily seen against the dark background.

ANALYSIS: Bermudagrass mite (*Aceria neocynodonis*)
These mites, related to spiders, are major pests of Bermudagrass, but do not attack other grasses. They damage the grass by sucking sap from the base of leaves, and from under leaf sheaths and stems. Their feeding results in very short internodes (distance between leaves) so that the plants form tight rosettes or "knots." When the mite population is large, there is no new green growth. These pests are most numerous in warm (75°F and above) humid weather on well-fertilized lawns. They reproduce rapidly, and by midsummer build up to tremendous numbers.

SOLUTION: Treat the infested lawn with ORTHO Diazinon Insect Spray or ORTHO Diazinon Soil & Turf Insect Control when the grass greens in the spring. Repeat whenever damage appears. Water and fertilize the lawn as discussed on pages 294 and 295 to keep it healthy and vigorous. Although fertilizer may increase the mite population, it also hastens the lawn's recovery.

PROBLEM: In the spring and fall, the lawn has a gray cast. The tips of the blades are pale yellow to gray, with red or yellow margins. Pale areas may be ⅛ to 1 inch long. Tiny black dots are scattered in the diseased spots on the blades.

ANALYSIS: Septoria leaf spot
This lawn disease, also called *tip burn*, is caused by a fungus (*Septoria* species) that infects most northern grass species and Bermudagrass. It is most prevalent in the cool, wet weather of spring and fall. Unfertilized lawns are most susceptible. The disease usually attacks in the spring, declines during the hot summer months, and returns in the fall. Because the disease infects the leaf tips first, frequent mowing removes much of the diseased part of the blades.

SOLUTION: Treat the infected lawn with a fungicide containing *maneb, chlorothalonil,* or *iprodione* as soon as the discoloration appears. Repeat the treatment 3 more times, 7 to 10 days apart, or as long as weather favorable for the disease continues. Keep the lawn healthy and vigorous by following the guidelines for good lawn care on pages 294 and 295. Mow the lawn regularly. Since no variety is completely resistant, plant a blend of two or three disease-tolerant varieties.

Tolerant bluegrass varieties: A-20, A-34, Adelphi, Birka, Bonnieblue, Glade, Ruby, Sydsport, Touchdown, and Victa.

POWDERY MATERIAL ON GRASS

Rust.

Powdery mildew.

Slime mold.

PROBLEM: Grass turns light green or yellow and begins to thin out. An orange powder coats the grass blades and rubs off on fingers, shoes, and clothing. Reddish brown lesions under the powder do not rub off.

ANALYSIS: Rust
This lawn disease is caused by a fungus (*Puccinia* species) that occurs most frequently on Merion Kentucky bluegrass, ryegrass, and zoysia. It is most active during moist, warm (70° to 75°F) weather, but can be active all winter in mild winter areas. Heavy dew favors its development. Grasses under stress from nitrogen deficiency, lack of moisture, and close mowing are most susceptible to attack. Rust is also more severe in the shade. The orange powder is composed of millions of microscopic spores which spread easily in the wind. Lawns attacked severely by rust are more likely to suffer winter damage.

SOLUTION: Rust develops slowly, often more slowly than the grass grows. Fertilize with a high-nitrogen fertilizer to maintain rapid growth. Mow frequently, removing the clippings. If the disease is severe, treat with ORTHO Liquid Lawn Disease Control. Repeat the application every 7 to 14 days until the lawn improves. For a list of rust-resistant varieties of bluegrass, see page 990. A blend of 2 or more of these varieties is more resistant than a single variety.

PROBLEM: Whitish gray mold develops on the upper surfaces of grass blades during cool rainy weather. The lawn looks as if it has been dusted with flour. The leaf tissue under the mold turns yellow and then tan or brown. Severely infected plants wither and die.

ANALYSIS: Powdery mildew
This lawn disease is caused by a fungus (*Erysiphe graminis*) which occurs when the nights are cool (65° to 70°F) and damp, and the days warm and humid. It is most severe on Merion Kentucky bluegrass, but also attacks other varieties of bluegrass, fescue, and Bermudagrass. Lawns growing in the shade are the most affected. Powdery mildew slows the growth of leaves, roots, and underground stems, causing gradual deterioration of the grass and making it more susceptible to other problems. Lawns growing rapidly from excessive nitrogen fertilization are very susceptible to attack from this fungus. The fine white mildew on the blades develops into powdery spores that spread easily in the wind. The spores can infect a grass plant in 2 to 4 hours.

SOLUTION: Treat the lawn with *benomyl* when the mildew is first seen. Repeat the application every 7 to 10 days until the mildew is no longer seen. Reduce the shade and improve air circulation by pruning surrounding trees and shrubs. Follow the guidelines on pages 294 and 295 for a healthy, vigorous lawn.

Mildew resistant varieties of Kentucky bluegrass: A-20, A-34, Aquila, Baron, Birka, Glade, Nugget, Rugby, Sydsport, Touchdown.

PROBLEM: Bluish gray, black, or yellow pinhead-size balls cover grass blades in the spring, summer, and fall following heavy rains or watering. Balls feel powdery when rubbed between the fingers. Affected areas range in size from a few inches to several feet.

ANALYSIS: Slime molds
These fungi feed on decaying organic matter in the soil. They do not feed on green plants. When the powdery covering is heavy, it may damage the grass by shading the blades from sunlight, causing them to turn yellow. Slime molds occur on dichondra, all turfgrasses, and some weeds. While slime molds are feeding on decaying organic matter in the soil, they are white, gray, or yellow slimy masses on the soil. When they are ready to reproduce, they extend up onto grass blades and form powdery balls containing spores. This phase of the life cycle is more noticeable than is the slimy mass phase.

SOLUTION: In most cases control is not necessary. Although slime molds are unsightly, they do not permanently damage the lawn. Remove the molds from the grass by hosing with a strong stream of water, or sweeping with a broom.

DARK GREEN AREAS

Fairy ring.

PROBLEM: Circles or arcs of dark green grass occur in the lawn. The circles may be as small as 1 foot or as large as hundreds of feet in diameter. The grass just inside the darker area may be lighter green than the rest of the lawn. Mushrooms may grow in the dark green area.

ANALYSIS: Fairy ring
This condition is caused by one of several fungi that grow on organic matter in the soil. These fungi do not harm the grass directly, but may inhibit water flow into the soil. The ring of darker green grass is caused by nutrients released as the fungus breaks down organic matter. If the lawn is low in nutrients, the darker area will be more pronounced in contrast to the paler grass around it. The fungus begins growth at a central point and grows outward at a rate of a foot or two a year, forming the circle. Mushrooms, which are the fruiting bodies of the fungus, appear when weather conditions are right for them.

SOLUTION: Fairy ring is not a turfgrass disease, and does not harm the lawn. It is very difficult to control, but its effects can be masked by fertilizing the lawn well so that all the grass will be dark green. If there is a region of pale green or yellow grass within the ring, aerate the lawn and water thoroughly so that water penetrates the soil surface. For information on aerating and watering, see pages 305 and 294.

DIGGING IN LAWN

Soil mounds from pocket gophers.

PROBLEM: Mounds of soil appear on the lawn. Usually crescent-shaped, these mounds open outward from a hole in the soil. There are no ridges on the surface of the lawn.

ANALYSIS: Pocket gophers
The pocket gopher lives and feeds almost entirely underground, coming to the surface only to bring up soil from its burrows, look for new territory, or feed close to its hole. Pocket gophers eat plant roots and occasionally whole plants. If they are active in your lawn, they are probably attracted by clover, which they love. This rodent has fur-lined pouches on each side of its mouth. It has small eyes and ears, a sparsely haired tail, long sharp claws, and a blunt head. Pocket gophers form their typical crescent-shaped mounds by pushing soil from their tunnels.

SOLUTION: Trapping is the quickest and surest way to eliminate pocket gophers from your yard. There are two types of traps — the wire trap and the box trap. Find the main runway by probing with a sharp rod about a foot deep a short distance on each side of a fresh mound. Dig a hole to intersect the run and insert two traps in the run, one facing in each direction. With cord or soft wire tie the traps together or to a stake above ground. To keep soil from falling on the traps, cover the hole with sod or a board, and sprinkle with soil to block out all light. Check and move the traps daily. For more information on pocket gophers, see page 890.

Ridges in lawn caused by mole tunnels.

PROBLEM: Raised ridges, 3 to 5 inches wide, crisscross the lawn. These ridges sometimes turn brown.

ANALYSIS: Moles
Moles are small rodents that live underground. They feed on grubs, earthworms, and other insects. Moles are 4 to 6 inches long, with velvety fur and small hidden eyes. Their strong forelegs, with broad, trowellike claws, are used to dig and push the soil as they move through the ground. As they mine their way through the soil, they sever the grass roots and raise the sod. These raised and loosened areas dry out quickly. Moles are also objectionable because their ridges give the lawn an uneven surface that can result in scalping when mowed.

SOLUTION: The best way to rid your lawn of moles is to control the insects they feed on. Their main diet is grubs. Treat the lawn with ORTHO Lawn Insect Spray (liquid), ORTHO Diazinon Insect Spray (liquid), or ORTHO Diazinon Soil & Turf Insect Control (granular). (For further information on grubs, see page 299.) Once their food supply is gone, moles will leave the area within a few weeks. If a few remain behind, traps are effective. Set the traps on active tunnels. To determine which tunnels are active, roll or tamp down the ridges in the early morning. Those that are raised by the afternoon are still active. Several kinds of mole traps are available in hardware and rental stores. Poison baits are not always effective, and should be used with caution around children and pets.

DIGGING IN LAWN

Bird damage.

Earthworm (life size).

Ant hill.

PROBLEM: Many birds are pecking in the lawn.

ANALYSIS: Birds tearing lawn
Birds pecking in the lawn indicate an insect problem in the lawn. Starlings, crows, sparrows, grackles, and robins are commonly found feeding on grubs, chinch bugs, and sod webworms. If left untended, the insects will probably do more damage than the birds, which disturb the lawn's root system only slightly by tearing and pulling the roots while searching for insects.

SOLUTION: The best way to keep birds from digging in your lawn is to rid it of insects. The following ORTHO products control the lawn insects that birds feed on. Select the most appropriate product and follow the label directions. ORTHO Lawn Insect Spray (liquid), ORTHO Diazinon Insect Spray (liquid), ORTHO Chinch Bug Killer (liquid), ORTHO Sod Webworm Control (liquid), ORTHO Chinch Bug & Sod Webworm Control (granular). Not all of the above products are sold in every region of the United States. For more information on controlling lawn insects, see page 299 for grubs and sod webworms, and page 301 for chinch bugs.

PROBLEM: Small mounds or clumps of granular soil appear scattered throughout the lawn. Earthworms may be seen at night or after a heavy rain.

ANALYSIS: Earthworms
Earthworms feed on dead roots and stems, and are usually an indication of fertile soil. They prefer moist, medium to fine-textured soil that is high in organic matter. They are seldom found in dry, sandy soil. Although the earthworm castings — small piles of soil — may mar the appearance of the lawn, and the earthworms may damage new seedlings, their activity improves the soil in several ways. Their movement from the surface to underlying soil helps mix the organic matter on the top with the soil below, and reduces thatch accumulation. Their channels in the soil improve air and water movement through the soil. The castings also help improve the soil structure.

SOLUTION: Earthworms are beneficial to the soil, so control measures are not required. Break up the mounds of soil with a rake.

PROBLEM: Small mounds or hills of soil occur in the lawn. Each mound has a hole in the center. Black, brown, or red ants scurry about.

ANALYSIS: Ants
Ants live underground in hot, dry areas of the lawn. They do not feed on grass, but when numerous may damage the plants in several ways. The mounds of soil in their hills smother and kill grass plants. As the ants tunnel among grass roots the soil may dry out, killing the plants. Ants also feed on newly planted grass seeds and sometimes store the seeds in their nests. Some ants, especially fire ants and harvester ants, bite people and animals. Most ants become a nuisance when they travel from their mounds and invade homes.

SOLUTION: Treat ant hills with ORTHO Diazinon Granules, ORTHO Diazinon Soil & Turf Insect Control, or ORTHO Diazinon Insect Spray. Water lightly after the treatment. Repeat the application as new mounds appear and as long as the ants are active. Once the ants have disappeared, reseed any bare or dead spots.

GRASSLIKE WEEDS

Seed heads. *Insert:* Annual bluegrass plant.

Bentgrass invading a bluegrass lawn.

Bermudagrass.

PROBLEM: In midspring, the grass has a whitish appearance. Pale green grasslike plants grow among desirable grasses.

ANALYSIS: Annual bluegrass
(*Poa annua*)
Annual bluegrass is one of the most troublesome but least noticed weeds in the lawn. This member of the bluegrass family is lighter green, more shallow-rooted, and less drought tolerant than Kentucky bluegrass. As its name suggests, most annual bluegrass lives for only one year, although some areas also have perennial strains. The seed germinates in cool weather from late summer to late fall. Annual bluegrass grows rapidly in the spring, especially if the lawn is fertilized then. Seed heads appear in mid- to late spring, the same height that the grass is cut. The seed heads give the lawn a whitish appearance. When hot, dry weather arrives, the plants die. The seeds fall to the soil and wait for cooler weather to germinate. Annual bluegrass is most serious where the soil is compacted.

SOLUTION: Weedkillers are only partially effective in controlling annual bluegrass. Prevent seeds from germinating by applying an herbicide containing *DCPA* or *bensulide* as a pre-emergence treatment in early to mid-fall. Do not use if you plan to reseed the lawn in the fall. Replace the dead areas in the summer with sod. Do not cut the lawn too short. Lawns more than 2½ inches tall have very little annual bluegrass. Aerate the lawn in compacted areas (see page 305). For more information on annual bluegrass, see page 825.

PROBLEM: Patches of soft, matted grass develop in the lawn. Sometimes the grass looks dead, with long straggly stems. In the spring, it greens up more slowly than the surrounding grass.

ANALYSIS: Bentgrass
(*Agrostis* species)
There are several kinds of bentgrass. It is most commonly grown on golf course putting greens, where the grass is cut very short, from ¼ inch to ½ inch. Bentgrass needs to be cut short to be attractive. The invasive nature of bentgrass makes it a weed in bluegrass and ryegrass lawns, which are cut 1½ to 2 inches tall. At this height, bentgrass becomes matted and straggly. Bentgrass is very invasive, and will crowd out other grasses. It is introduced into a lawn in several ways: seeds in the soil, lawn equipment, seed mixtures and sod, or from nearby unmowed areas.

SOLUTION: Kill bentgrass patches with ORTHO Kleenup Systemic Weed & Grass Killer while it is actively growing from early summer to early fall. Omit a regular mowing before treating to allow for enough leaf tissue to absorb the chemical. Spray enough to wet the foliage. Kleenup will also kill any desirable grasses it contacts. One week after spraying, mow the bentgrass close and reseed the area. The bentgrass will still be green when it is mowed, but the roots will die and not resprout.

PROBLEM: In southern areas of the United States, patches of fine-textured grass grow in the lawn. The slightly hairy, gray-green stems creep along the soil, with erect shoots 6 to 18 inches tall. Leaf blades are ⅛ inch wide. This grass turns brown in the winter if subjected to temperatures below 50°F.

ANALYSIS: Bermudagrass
(*Cynodon dactylon*)
Bermudagrass is one of the most widely used lawn grasses in the South. It has a very deep root system and is drought and heat tolerant. The leaves are not cold tolerant, and turn brown when the temperature approaches freezing. Its vigorous, creeping growth habit makes it a weed that invades non-Bermudagrass lawns and flower beds.

SOLUTION: Spot treat the Bermudagrass with ORTHO Kleenup Weed & Grass Killer anytime the grass is actively growing, up to 2 to 4 weeks before the first killing frost. After 1 week, mow the treated grass as closely as possible, and reseed. The grass will still be green when it is mowed, but roots will die in 3 or 4 weeks and will not resprout. If regrowth occurs in the spring, spot treat with the same herbicide. To prevent Bermudagrass from invading your lawn from other lawns, mow higher than 1½ inches, spot treat as needed each summer, and water the lawn adequately during the summer. Fertilize more heavily in the fall than at any other time of year. In the South, Bermudagrass makes a nice lawn if mowed short (½ to 1 inch), grown in full sunlight, and given nitrogen throughout the growing season. For more information on Bermudagrass, see page 302.

GRASSLIKE WEEDS

Quackgrass.

Crabgrass.

Goosegrass.

PROBLEM: A grassy weed with hollow stems grows in a newly seeded lawn. Wheatlike spikes grow at the tips of the stems. The narrow leaf blades are bluish green and rough on the upper surface. A pair of "claws" occurs at the junction of the blade and the stem. Rings of root hairs grow every ¾ to 1 inch along the underground stems.

ANALYSIS: Quackgrass
(*Agropyron repens*)
This cool season perennial, also called *couchgrass* or *witchgrass*, spreads extensively through the lawn by long white underground stems. It reproduces by seeds and these underground stems. Quackgrass is found most frequently in fertile, newly seeded lawns. It grows much more rapidly than grass seedlings, often crowding them out.

SOLUTION: Kill clumps of actively growing quackgrass with ORTHO Kleenup Ready-to-Use Weed & Grass Killer. To kill germinating quackgrass seedlings, apply a weed killer containing *DCPA* in the early spring, 2 weeks before the last expected frost, or about the time the forsythia bloom.

PROBLEM: A grassy weed forms broad, flat clumps in thin areas of the lawn. It grows rapidly through the summer, rooting easily at the stem joints. The pale green blades are 2 to 5 inches long and ⅓ inch wide. Seed heads 2 to 6 inches tall grow from the center of the plant.

ANALYSIS: Crabgrass
(*Digitaria* species)
Crabgrass sprouts from seeds in the early spring, growing rapidly and producing seeds all summer until the first killing frost in the fall. Then the plants turn brown and die. The seeds lie dormant over the winter and sprout in the spring. When a lawn begins to thin out from insects, disease, or poor maintenance, crabgrass is one of the first weeds to invade the area.

SOLUTION: Kill actively growing crabgrass with ORTHO Crab Grass Killer or ORTHO Crab Grass & Dandelion Killer. Older plants are harder to kill; repeat the treatment 2 more times, at 4 to 7 day intervals. To kill crabgrass seeds as they germinate, apply the weedkiller *DCPA* in the early spring, 2 weeks before the last expected frost, or about the time the forsythia bloom. Follow the guidelines on pages 294 and 295 for a healthy, vigorous lawn. A thick lawn has very little crabgrass.

PROBLEM: A smooth, flat-stemmed, grassy weed forms in the lawn resembling the spokes of a wheel. Blades, ⅛ inch wide and 2 to 10 inches long, are slightly hairy near the base. Stems do not root at their joints. Seedstalks 2 to 6 inches tall grow from the tops of stems.

ANALYSIS: Goosegrass
(*Eleusine indica*)
This warm season annual weed, also known as *silver crabgrass*, resembles crabgrass, but is darker green, germinates later in the spring, and doesn't root at the stem joints. This weed reproduces by seeds and grows an extensive root system that is difficult to pull up. Goosegrass invades thin areas of the lawn where the soil is compacted and infertile.

SOLUTION: Kill clumps of actively growing goosegrass with ORTHO Kleenup Ready-to-Use Weed & Grass Killer. After 7 days remove the weed. It will still be green, but the roots have been killed and will not resprout. Reduce the soil compaction, if necessary, as instructed on page 305. Then reseed or resod. To kill goosegrass seedlings as they germinate, apply a weed killer containing *chlorothal* in late spring or early summer. Maintain a healthy, dense lawn by following the guidelines on pages 294 and 295.

Dallisgrass.

PROBLEM: A bunch-type, grassy weed with coarse-textured leaves grows in the lawn. The leaves are ½ inch wide and 4 to 10 inches long. Stems 2 to 6 inches long radiate from the center of the plant in a star pattern. Seed stalks with 3 to 5 fingerlike segments may grow from the top of the stems. The seeds are covered with fine, silken hairs.

ANALYSIS: Dallisgrass
(*Paspalum dilatatum*)
This warm season grassy weed is one of the most troublesome in the southern United States. It begins growth in very early spring and prefers warm, moist areas and high-cut lawns. However, once established in low-cut lawns it spreads rapidly. It is a perennial plant with deep roots that reproduces by seeds and underground stems.

SOLUTION: Treat bunches of actively growing dallisgrass in early spring or summer with ORTHO Crab Grass Killer or ORTHO Kleenup Ready-To-Use Weed & Grass Killer. Repeat the treatment 2 more times at intervals of 7 days.

Tall fescue.

PROBLEM: Clumps of very coarse, tough grass invade thin areas of the lawn. The medium-dark green blades, ½ inch wide, are ribbed on the top surface, and smooth on the bottom. In the spring and fall, the lower parts of the stems turn reddish purple. The blades tend to shred when mowed.

ANALYSIS: Tall fescue
(*Festuca arundinacea*)
This cool season, perennial, bunch-type grass is very durable. It is commonly used on athletic fields because it holds up well under hard wear. Tall fescue makes an attractive turf when grown by itself. However, when it is seeded with, or invades, bluegrass, Bermudagrass, or ryegrass lawns, it is considered a weed. It becomes very clumpy and makes an uneven turf. When insects and diseases attack the desirable grasses in the lawn, the tall fescue is usually not affected. It resists diseases and grubs, and sod webworms attack it only if they've eaten everything else. It is also heat tolerant, and its deep roots help it survive periods of heavy moisture and drought.

SOLUTION: Kill clumps of tall fescue with ORTHO Kleenup Systemic Weed & Grass Killer while it is actively growing from early summer to early fall. Omit 1 regular mowing before treating to allow for enough leaf tissue to absorb the chemical. Kleenup will also kill any desirable grasses it contacts. One week after spraying, mow the tall fescue and reseed the area. The tall fescue may still be green when it is removed, but the roots will die in 3 or 4 weeks and will not resprout.

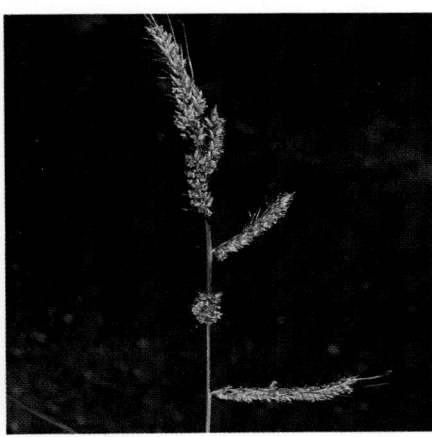

Barnyardgrass.

PROBLEM: In summer and fall, a low-growing grassy weed with reddish purple stems 1 to 3 feet long grows in the lawn. The smooth leaves are ¼ to ½ inch wide, with a prominent midrib.

ANALYSIS: Barnyardgrass
(*Echinochloa crus-galli*)
Barnyardgrass, also called *watergrass*, is a warm season annual weed that is usually found in poorly managed lawns of low fertility. It reproduces by seeds, and develops into a plant with a shallow root system. Although the natural growth habit of barnyardgrass is upright, when mowed regularly it forms ground-hugging mats.

SOLUTION: Kill mats of actively growing barnyardgrass with an herbicide containing *DSMA*. Repeat the treatment 2 more times, at intervals of 7 to 10 days, until the plants die. *DSMA* may discolor the turf for 2 to 3 weeks. Improve soil fertility and maintain a dense, healthy lawn by following the guidelines on pages 294 and 295. To kill barnyardgrass seedlings as they sprout, apply a weed killer containing *DCPA* in the early spring 2 weeks before the last expected frost, or about the time the forsythia bloom.

Nutsedge. *Insert:* Underground stems and tubers.

Wild garlic. *Insert:* Aerial bulblets.

Prostrate knotweed.

PROBLEM: In the summer, this weed grows more rapidly than the grass and stands above the turf. The erect, single, triangular stem has narrow, grasslike, yellow-green leaves arranged in threes from the base of the plant. Seed heads are yellow-brown.

ANALYSIS: Nutsedge
(*Cyperus* species)
Nutsedge, commonly called *nutgrass*, is a hard-to-kill perennial weed. It reproduces by underground stems, seeds, and tubers. The tubers, the size of popcorn kernels, sprout in late spring and early summer. The plant tops die back in the fall, leaving new tubers in the soil to repeat the cycle the following year. The tubers and underground stems are firmly anchored in the ground. When a plant is pulled up, some of the tubers and underground stems are left behind to resprout into new plants.

SOLUTION: Nutsedge is difficult to control. Treat with ORTHO Crab Grass Killer or ORTHO Crab Grass & Dandelion Killer when the plants first become active in the spring. Repeat 2 or 3 more times, 10 to 14 days apart. If you miss a treatment, the weeds recover and take longer to control. Treat again the following spring to kill any persistent tubers. These herbicides may temporarily (2 to 4 weeks) discolor desirable grasses. On centipedegrass and St. Augustine grass lawns, use the weed killer *atrazine* in January, February, or March, before the weeds germinate.

PROBLEM: An onion-like weed with a characteristic garlic odor grows in the lawn. The leaves are slender, hollow, and round. The leaves join together at the lower half of the main stem, just above where it emerges from the base of an underground bulb. Greenish purple flowers bloom at the same height as the leaves.

ANALYSIS: Wild garlic
(*Allium vineale*)
Wild garlic is also commonly called *wild onion*. This perennial weed reproduces mostly by bulbs and bulblets formed under and above ground. Both soft and hard bulblets are formed underground. The soft bulblets germinate in the fall. The hard bulblets remain dormant over the winter, germinating the following spring, or a year or two later. Wild garlic also produces bulblets at the tips of some of its leaves. As they mature, they fall to the soil and sprout into new plants. Wild garlic spreads rapidly through the lawn and is very difficult to control.

SOLUTION: Treat the lawn with ORTHO Weed-B-Gon Lawn Weed Killer or ORTHO Weed-B-Gon Jet Weeder as the leaves emerge in the spring. Repeat the application in 2 weeks. Because the plants can regrow from the bulbs, and the bulbs sprout at different times of the year, repeat the treatments annually for the next 2 or 3 years.

If wild garlic grows in pastures where milk cows feed, it makes the milk less appetizing by giving it a garlic flavor. Also, when this weed is harvested with wheat, the milled flour has a garlic odor.

PROBLEM: A very low-growing weed with oval, bluish green leaves grows in the thin and trampled areas of the lawn. The smooth leaves are 1 inch long and ¼ inch wide, and attach to the wiry stems at prominent "knots" or joints. This weed forms mats up to 2 feet in diameter. Very tiny greenish white flowers bloom at the leaf and stem joints from June to November.

ANALYSIS: Prostrate knotweed
(*Polygonum aviculare*)
Prostrate knotweed, sometimes called *wiregrass*, is an annual plant that reproduces from its numerous seeds, which germinate in the spring as the soil warms. Prostrate knotweed in a lawn is an indication of low fertility and compacted soil. It frequently grows in the compacted soils along driveways, and in paths cut through lawns. Sometimes it is also found in newly established lawns. Knotweed cannot get started in a vigorous, dense turf.

SOLUTION: Treat the lawn with ORTHO Weed-B-Gon Lawn Weed Killer or ORTHO Weed-B-Gon Jet Weeder in early spring when the seedlings are still young. Repeated treatments may be needed. Divert the traffic trampling the grass and loosen compacted soil (see page 305). Follow the guidelines on pages 294 and 295 for a healthy, vigorous lawn.

Clover.

Black medic.

Oxalis.

PROBLEM: A weed with leaves composed of 3 round leaflets at the top of a hairy leaf stalk 2 to 4 inches tall grows in the lawn. The leaf stalks sprout from the base of the plant. White or pink-tinged flowers, 1/2 inch in size, bloom from June to September. They often attract bees.

ANALYSIS: Clover
(*Trifolium* species)
Clover is a common perennial weed in lawns throughout the United States. Although some people like it in a lawn, others consider it messy, or they don't like the bees that are attracted to the flowers. Clover reproduces by seeds and above-ground rooting stems. The seeds can live in the soil for 20 years or more. The plant, which has a creeping, prostrate habit, suffocates lawn grasses, resulting in large patches of clover. When buying a box of grass seed, be sure to read the label carefully. Clover seeds are sometimes contained in seed mixtures. Since clover produces its own nitrogen, it thrives in lawns that are low in this plant nutrient.

SOLUTION: Treat the lawn with ORTHO Chickweed & Clover Control or ORTHO Weed-B-Gon Weed Killer in the spring and early fall. Repeated treatments are often necessary.

PROBLEM: A low-growing, trailing weed forms dense mats in the lawn. The stems are slightly hairy, and the three-leaflet cloverlike leaves are slightly toothed at the tips. Small, bright yellow flowers bloom in May and June, followed by black kidney-shaped pods.

ANALYSIS: Black medic
(*Medicago lupulina*)
This annual weed is also called *black clover* because of its cloverlike leaves and black seeds. It is common in lawns throughout the United States in June, July, and August. Black medic reproduces by seed and has a shallow taproot. It usually invades lawns with poor, sterile soil where lawn grasses don't grow, or grow poorly. If not controlled, a single black medic plant enlarges into a thick mat that crowds out lawn grasses.

SOLUTION: Treat the lawn with ORTHO Chickweed, Spurge & Oxalis Killer D, ORTHO Weed-B-Gon Lawn Weed Killer, or ORTHO Weed-B-Gon For Southern Grasses from late spring to early summer, or early to midfall, when the weeds are growing actively, and preferably before seeds form. Don't water for 24 hours after treating. Improve soil fertility by following the fertilizing guidelines on page 294.

PROBLEM: A weed with pale green leaves divided into three heart-shaped leaflets invades thin areas of the lawn. The leaves are 1/4 to 3/4 inch wide, and are similar to clover. The stems root at the lower joints and are often thinly covered with fine hairs. Small, bright yellow flowers are 1/2 inch long with 5 petals. Cucumber-shaped light green seed pods develop from the fading flowers. Plants grow prostrate to erect 4 to 12 inches high.

ANALYSIS: Oxalis
(*Oxalis stricta*)
Oxalis, also called *yellow woodsorrel*, is a perennial plant that thrives in dry, open places. It invades lawns that are begining to thin from insect, disease, or maintenance problems. Oxalis reproduces from the seeds formed in the seed pods. When the pods dry, a light touch causes them to explode, shooting their seeds several feet in all directions. Oxalis leaves contain oxalic acid, which gives them a sour taste.

SOLUTION: Control oxalis with ORTHO Weed-B-Gon Lawn Weed Killer or ORTHO Weed-B-Gon For Southern Grasses. The most effective time to spray is when the weeds are actively growing in the spring or late summer to fall. Oxalis is not easy to kill; several treatments are usually needed. Check the soil pH level (see page 903), and follow the guidelines on pages 294 and 295 for a healthy, vigorous lawn. A healthy lawn helps smother the oxalis.

BROADLEAF WEEDS

Mouseear chickweed.

Spotted spurge.

Common chickweed.

PROBLEM: A weed with extremely hairy, ½ inch-long lance-shaped leaves grows in sunny areas of the lawn. The leaves are attached directly to the stems without a leaf stalk. Starlike white flowers bloom from April to October. The stems root easily at their joints.

ANALYSIS: Mouseear chickweed (*Cerastium vulgatum*)
Mouseear chickweed is a troublesome perennial weed found throughout the United States. It grows in full sunlight on infertile and heavily watered soil. Mouseear chickweed invades lawns that thin out due to insects, disease, or mechanical damage. It reproduces by seeds and by the stems that root easily at their joints wherever they touch the soil. It has a low, prostrate growing habit, and forms a dense mat that crowds out the grass.

SOLUTION: Treat the lawn with ORTHO Chickweed & Clover Control or ORTHO Weed-B-Gon Lawn Weed Killer when the plant is growing actively in the early spring or late fall. Repeated applications may be needed. Don't water for 2 days after applying.

PROBLEM: A low-growing weed with oval pale to dark green leaves ¼ to ¾ inch long appears in the lawn. Each leaf has a purple spot. Stems ooze milky white sap when broken. The leaves are slightly hairy on the underside and smooth on top. Tiny pinkish white flowers bloom in midsummer. The numerous pale green stems fan out on the soil surface and over the top of the grass, forming mats up to 2 feet in diameter.

ANALYSIS: Spotted spurge (*Euphorbia maculata*)
Spotted spurge, also called *milk purslane*, invades thin areas of the lawn, smothering the grass. Spurge sprouts from seeds in the spring, and dies with the first frost. This weed commonly invades lawns that are dry and infertile, but it can also be found in well-maintained lawns.

SOLUTION: Treat the lawn with ORTHO Weed-B-Gon Lawn Weed Killer or ORTHO Weed-B-Gon For Southern Grasses or spot treat with ORTHO Weed-B-Gon Jet Weeder in the late spring or early summer. Keep the lawn well watered (see page 294) to discourage spurge from invading dry areas.

PROBLEM: A weed with small (½ inch long) heart-shaped leaves and starlike white flowers grows in thin spaces in the lawn. A row of hairs appears on the leaf stalk attaching the leaves to the stems. The stems root easily at their joints.

ANALYSIS: Common chickweed (*Stellaria media*)
This weed grows from seeds that sprout in the fall and live for less than a year. It grows primarily in damp shady areas under trees and shrubs, and on the north side of buildings. Common chickweed invades home lawns when they begin to thin out from insects, disease, mechanical damage, or shade. It reproduces by seeds and by the creeping stems that root at their joints wherever they touch the soil. It has a low prostrate growing habit, forming a dense mat that crowds out the grass.

SOLUTION: Treat the lawn with ORTHO Chickweed & Clover Control or ORTHO Weed-B-Gon Lawn Weed Killer when it is growing actively in the early spring or late fall. Repeated applications may be necessary. Do not water for 2 days after applying.

Henbit.

English lawn daisy.

Purslane.

PROBLEM: A weed with rounded, toothed leaves, ³/₄ inch wide, grows in the lawn. The lower leaves are attached to the square (4-sided) upright stems by short leaf stalks; upper leaves attach directly to the stems. Stems root easily at lower joints. Lavender, ½ inch flowers appear from April to June and again in September.

ANALYSIS: Henbit
(*Lamium amplexicaule*)
This weed, also known as *dead nettle* or *bee nettle*, is found in lawns and flower and vegetable gardens across the country. It is a winter annual that sprouts from seeds in September and grows rapidly in the fall and the following spring. Henbit also reproduces by stems that root easily wherever the stem joints touch the soil. Henbit most frequently invades thin areas in lawns with rich soil.

SOLUTION: Treat the lawn with ORTHO Chickweed, Spurge & Oxalis Killer D in early spring when henbit is growing most rapidly. In the South, use a weed killer containing *atrazine*. Do not water for 24 hours after treating. A few small plants can be hand pulled.

PROBLEM: A weed with slightly hairy, elongated oval leaves forms a tight rosette in the lawn. White to pink flowers with yellow centers, up to 2 inches across, appear from April to June and again from September to November.

ANALYSIS: English lawn daisy
(*Bellis perennis*)
As its name suggests, English lawn daisy came originally from Europe and was chiefly grown as an ornamental garden plant. Although it is a welcome member of the perennial garden, it often escapes cultivation and becomes a weed in the lawn. This perennial plant reproduces by seeds, and thrives in moist, cool soil. When growing in the lawn, English lawn daisy may indicate low soil fertility.

SOLUTION: Treat the lawn with an herbicide containing *dicamba* or *mecoprop* before July 1. Repeat the treatment around September 15 to control any regrowth. Do not use *dicamba* around trees and shrubs since it may seep into the soil and harm the roots. Improve soil fertility by following the guidelines outlined on page 295.

PROBLEM: A low-growing weed with reddish brown, thick, succulent stems is found in thin areas or newly seeded lawns. The leaves are thick, fleshy, and wedge-shaped. Small yellow flowers sometimes bloom in the leaf and stem joints. Stems root where they touch the soil.

ANALYSIS: Purslane
(*Portulaca oleracea*)
Purslane, a summer annual weed that thrives in hot, dry weather, is seldom found in the spring when the lawn is being treated for other weeds. Purslane grows vigorously, forming a thick mat. The small yellow flowers open only in the full sunlight. Purslane primarily invades bare spots in lawns or thin lawns that have not been watered properly. Purslane stores water in its thick fleshy stems and leaves, and therefore survives longer than grass during dry weather.

SOLUTION: Spray the lawn with ORTHO Weed-B-Gon Lawn Weed Killer or ORTHO Weed-B-Gon Jet Weeder when the weed is actively growing. If the lawn has just been reseeded, do not treat until the seedlings have been mowed 3 times. Wait 3 to 4 weeks before seeding bare areas. On St. Augustine grass, use ORTHO Weed-B-Gon For Southern Grasses.

BROADLEAF WEEDS

Ground ivy.

Creeping charlie.

Speedwell.

PROBLEM: A low-growing, creeping weed with rounded, scalloped leaves grows in shady areas of the lawn. The nickel- to quarter-size leaves grow at the end of a long leaf stalk. The stalks are paired opposite each other along the square stem. Light blue to purple flowers, ½ to ¾ inch long, bloom from April to July.

ANALYSIS: Ground ivy
(*Glechoma hederacea*)
Ground ivy, also called *creeping ivy*, is a perennial that was originally planted in some areas as a groundcover. It has now become a major weed in the northern United States. Ground ivy reproduces by seeds and creeping stems that root wherever they touch the soil. This plant has shallow roots and forms a dense mat throughout the lawn, crowding out grasses. Although it is found primarily in shaded areas, ground ivy also survives in the sunlight.

SOLUTION: Treat the lawn with ORTHO Weed-B-Gon Lawn Weed Killer or ORTHO Weed-B-Gon Jet Weeder in the spring or fall when the plants are growing actively. A spring treatment gives the best result by killing the plants before the leaves mature. Where the ground ivy has formed a dense mat, it may be necessary to apply the herbicide for several years in a row. Hand pulling is not a good way to control ground ivy. Since the roots are perennial, they can resprout into new plants. The ground ivy may be telling you that the area is too shady to grow a lawn.

PROBLEM: A ground-hugging weed with creeping stems grows in moist, shady areas of the lawn. The leaves are oval to round and up to 1 inch long. Yellow flowers, ¾ inch in diameter, appear from May to September.

ANALYSIS: Creeping charlie
(*Lysimachia nummularia*)
Also called *moneywort* or *creeping jenny*, this weed invades areas of the lawn where grass won't grow because of shade and constantly moist soil. It is a perennial weed that reproduces by creeping stems that root easily at their joints wherever they touch the soil. It also reproduces by seeds. Creeping charlie is sometimes planted as a groundcover in shaded, moist rock gardens.

SOLUTION: Treat the weeds with ORTHO Kleenup Ready-to-Use Weed & Grass Killer in early spring or fall. Kleenup may kill some surrounding grass, so reseed 7 to 10 days after treating. Improve the soil drainage as outlined on page 901.

PROBLEM: A weed with roundish-oval bright green leaves grows in shady, moist areas of the lawn. The scallop-edged leaves are paired, growing opposite each other. Tiny white flowers with blue edges bloom on stalks taller than the leaves. On the stems below the flowers are characteristic heart-shaped seed pods.

ANALYSIS: Speedwell
(*Veronica filiformis*)
Speedwell, also called *creeping veronica*, was originally used as a rock garden plant. Over the years it has become a weed, invading lawns and flower beds. This perennial plant reproduces by creeping stems that root easily at their nodes wherever they touch the soil. The seeds in the heart-shaped seed pods seldom mature, so the plant does not reproduce from seeds. Speedwell thrives in moist, shady areas, but will grow in the sunlight if the soil remains moist. This ground-hugging plant spreads quickly. In a few years it can spread from a few patches to cover the entire lawn. However, it does not completely crowd out the desirable grass. Areas that are well fertilized, well drained, and get lots of sunlight are not invaded by speedwell.

SOLUTION: This weed is difficult to control. When the plant is flowering or actively growing, spray with ORTHO Weed-B-Gon Lawn Weed Killer. Several applications may be required.

Curly dock.

Dandelion.

Sheep sorrel.

PROBLEM: A weed forming a rosette with large smooth leaves, 6 to 12 inches long, grows in thin areas of the lawn. The leaves are reddish green, with curly and wavy margins.

ANALYSIS: Curly dock
(*Rumex crispus*)
Curly dock is a persistent perennial weed that grows from a large, deep, brownish yellow taproot. It reproduces by seed and invades thin areas of the lawn. Because frequent mowing cuts off the flower stalk, curly dock seldom flowers when growing in the lawn.

SOLUTION: In mid to late spring, or early to late fall, treat curly dock with ORTHO Weed-B-Gon Lawn Weed Killer. Treat again if plants resprout. Hand digging and removal is not only time consuming and tedious, but also impractical, since pieces of root that are left behind will sprout into new plants.

PROBLEM: From spring to fall, a weed with bright yellow flowers blooms in the lawn. Flower stems grow 2 to 10 inches above the plants. The medium green leaves, 3 to 10 inches long, are lobed along the sides. The plant has a deep, fleshy taproot.

ANALYSIS: Dandelion
(*Taraxacum officinale*)
This perennial is the most common and easily identified weed in the United States. It reproduces by seeds and from shoots that grow from the fleshy taproot. This taproot grows 2 to 3 feet deep in the soil, surviving even the severest of winters. Dandelions grow in any soil, and are most numerous in full sunlight. In the early spring, new sprouts emerge from the taproot. As the yellow flowers mature and ripen, they form white "puff balls" containing seeds. The wind carries the seed for miles to other lawns. The tops die back in late fall and the taproot overwinters to start the cycle again in the spring. Dandelions prefer wet soil, and are often a sign of overwatering.

SOLUTION: Treat the lawn with ORTHO Weed-B-Gon Lawn Weed Killer or ORTHO Weed-B-Gon Jet Weeder for spot treatment. For best results make 2 applications, first in the early summer and again in the early fall. Do not water or mow for 2 days afterwards. Hand digging and removal is not only time consuming and tedious, but also impractical, since pieces of root that are broken off and left in the soil will sprout into new plants.

PROBLEM: Arrow-shaped leaves, 1 to 4 inches long, with 2 lobes at the base of each leaf, form a dense rosette. Erect, upright stems grow 4 to 14 inches tall. Two types of flowers appear in midspring; one is reddish green, the other yellowish green.

ANALYSIS: Sheep sorrel
(*Rumex acetosella*)
This cool-season perennial is also called *red sorrel* or *sour grass* because of its sour taste. It grows in dry, sterile, sandy or gravelly soil and is usually an indication of acid soil or low nitrogen fertility. Sheep sorrel reproduces by seeds and red underground rootstalks. The root system is shallow but extensive, and is not easily removed.

SOLUTION: In spring or fall treat with ORTHO Weed-B-Gon Lawn Weed Killer or ORTHO Chickweed, Spurge & Oxalis Killer D. In the South, use ORTHO Weed-B-Gon For Southern Grasses. Don't mow for 5 days before treating, or for 2 days after. Sheep sorrel is difficult to control, so several treatments may be necessary. To discourage sheep sorrel, test the soil pH as outlined on page 903 and correct to between 6.0 and 7.0 if necessary. Improve the soil fertility by following the fertilization guidelines on page 294. Improve sandy soil by adding organic matter as instructed on page 901.

BROADLEAF WEEDS

Mallow.

Buckhorn plantain.

Morning glory.

PROBLEM: A weed with hairy stems, 4 to 12 inches long, spreads over the lawn. The stem tips turn upward. Round, heart-shaped, hairy leaves, ½ to 3 inches wide and slightly lobed along the edges, are attached to the stems by a long leaf stalk. White to lilac flowers, 2 ½ inches in diameter with 5 petals, bloom singly or in clusters at the leaf and stem junction.

ANALYSIS: Mallow (*Malva* species)
Mallow, also called *cheeseweed*, is found throughout the United States in lawns, fields, and along roadways. It is an annual, or sometimes a biennial, and reproduces by seeds. It has a straight, nearly white taproot that is difficult to pull from the soil. Mallow is most commonly found in poorly managed lawns and in soils high in manure content.

SOLUTION: Treat the lawn with ORTHO Weed-B-Gon Lawn Weed Killer or ORTHO Chickweed, Spurge & Oxalis Killer D from midspring to early summer. Don't water for 5 days before treating, or 2 days after. Maintain a thick, healthy lawn by following the guidelines on pages 294 and 295.

PROBLEM: A weed forming a rosette with lance-shaped leaves 4 to 12 inches long grows in the lawn. The leaves have 3 to 5 nearly parallel, prominent veins. Erect white flower spikes, 4 to 12 inches tall, appear from May to October. A similar weed has egg-shaped leaves attached to 1-inch leaf stalks, which are in turn attached to the center of a rosette. These leaves are 2 to 10 inches long, with 5 to 7 prominent veins. Erect greenish white flower spikes, 2 to 10 inches tall, bloom from May to September. The leaves of both plants lie flat on the soil.

ANALYSIS: Plantain (*Plantago* species)
Both buckhorn plantain (*P. lanceolata*), with lance-shaped leaves, and broadleaf plantain (*P. major*), with egg-shaped leaves, are perennial weeds that resprout from their roots each year. They reproduce from seeds formed on the flower spikes, and from new shoots from the roots. As thin areas develop in the lawn from insect, disease, or maintenance problems, one or both of these weeds can move in. As the plants grow larger and lie flat on the soil, they suffocate the surrounding grass.

SOLUTION: Spray the lawn with ORTHO Weed-B-Gon Lawn Weed Killer, ORTHO Weed-B-Gon Jet Weeder or ORTHO Weed-B-Gon For Southern Grasses in the spring or fall when the plants are actively growing. Repeated applications are often necessary. An application in September gives the best results by reducing the infestation next year. Do not mow 5 days before or 2 days after spraying.

PROBLEM: A plant with long twining stems grows across the lawn. The leaves are arrow-shaped and up to 2 inches long. White to pink funnel-shaped flowers, about 1 inch across, appear from May to September.

ANALYSIS: Wild morning glory (*Convolvulus arvensis*)
This deep-rooted perennial weed, also known as *field bindweed*, is found throughout most of the United States in lawns, gardens, fields, and along roadways. It is one of the most troublesome and difficult weeds to eliminate because of its extensive root system. The roots may grow 15 to 20 feet deep. Roots or pieces of roots left behind from hand pulling or spading easily resprout. Morning glory reproduces by seeds and roots and twines and climbs over shrubs and fences, and up into trees. It prefers rich, sandy, or gravelly soil, but will grow in almost any garden soil.

SOLUTION: Treat plants from late spring through early summer, or early to late fall, with ORTHO Weed-B-Gon Lawn Weed Killer or ORTHO Chickweed, Spurge & Oxalis Killer D. In the South use ORTHO Weed-B-Gon For Southern Grasses. Because of the deep roots, another treatment may be necessary. Treat again whenever new growth appears. Or spot treat with ORTHO Kleenup Systemic Weed & Grass Killer and reseed.

Mushrooms.

Algae.

Moss.

PROBLEM: Mushrooms sprout up in the lawn after wet weather. They may be growing in circles of dark green grass. When the weather gets colder or the soil dries out they disappear.

ANALYSIS: Mushrooms
Mushrooms, also called *toadstools* and *puffballs*, live on organic matter buried in the soil. The mushroom is the above-ground fruiting or reproducing structure of a fungus that lives on and helps to decay the organic matter. The organic matter may include buried logs, lumber, roots, or stumps. Most mushrooms do not damage the lawn, but are objectionable because they are unsightly. Mushrooms growing in circles of dark green grass, called fairy rings, may make the soil impervious to water and injure the grass. For more information on fairy rings, see page 309.

SOLUTION: There is no practical or permanent way to eliminate mushrooms. When the buried wood is completely decayed, the mushrooms will disappear. The easiest and most practical solution, although it is only temporary, is to break the mushrooms with a rake or lawn mower.

PROBLEM: A green to black slimy scum covers bare soil and crowns of grass plants. When dry, it becomes crusty, cracks, and peels easily.

ANALYSIS: Algae (*Symploca* species and *Oscillatoria* species)
Algae are fresh water plants that invade shady, wet areas of the lawn. They injure grass by smothering or shading it as they grow over the crowns of the plants. Invaded areas become slippery. Algae live in compacted soil and soil that is high in nitrogen and organic matter. They need constantly or frequently wet conditions to survive. Organic fertilizers encourage algae, especially in the cool seasons. Algae may be carried from place to place by animals, equipment, people, and birds. Water taken from ponds, lakes, and streams and used for irrigation usually contains algae.

SOLUTION: Patches of algae may be sprayed with *maneb*, *mancozeb*, or *wettable sulfur* 2 times, 1 month apart, in early spring. This is only a temporary solution. Algae will soon return if the conditions promoting them are not corrected. Reduce soil compaction as instructed on page 305. Improve drainage, as outlined on page 901, and prune nearby trees to reduce shading. Avoid high nitrogen fertilizers in late fall and winter. Maintain a healthy, vigorous lawn according to the lawn maintenance guidelines on pages 294 and 295.

PROBLEM: Green, velvety, low-growing plants cover bare soil in shady areas of the lawn.

ANALYSIS: Moss
Moss invades thin or bare areas of the lawn. It does not grow in a vigorous lawn. Moss is encouraged by poor fertility, poor drainage, compacted soil, shade, and high acidity. Moss plants sprout from spores and fill in bare or thin areas.

SOLUTION: Remove moss by hand or by power raking. Reduce shade by pruning nearby trees. Correct soil compaction as outlined on page 305, and improve drainage as suggested on page 901. Test the soil pH as instructed on page 903, and correct if necessary. Follow the lawn maintenance guidelines on pages 294 and 295 for a healthy, vigorous lawn. Large patches of moss not easily removed by raking may be "burned" with *ammonium sulfate*. Apply to damp moss in early spring. Do not water after the application. Surrounding lawn grass may darken for about a week.

Some of the problems common to all groundcovers are described on the next 6 pages. If you don't find your problem there, look up your ground-cover in the index on page 330. Only plants that are known primarily as groundcovers are listed here. If your groundcover is a dwarf form of a plant more commonly seen as a shrub, see page 437. If it is a perennial flower, see page 343.

GROUNDCOVERS

We often assume that the worst problem of groundcovers is weeds. Once weeds have invaded a groundcover, they are very difficult to control; the groundcover is too dense for a hoe, and it is often difficult or impossible to find an herbicide that will kill the weeds without killing the groundcover. So the weeds must be removed by hand pulling — the slowest and most tedious method of weeding.

But the weeds are often only a symptom of some other problem. If a ground-cover is dense and growing vigorously, it will smother any weed seedlings that germinate in it, and keep itself essentially weed-free. Weeds invade spots that are bare or getting thin from some other problem.

The most critical period in the life of a groundcover is the first couple of years after it is planted. If you can keep it free of weeds until it covers the ground completely, your groundcover will keep itself pretty much free of weeds from then on.

A related problem occurs when a groundcover itself becomes a weed, and invades adjacent areas. This happens when the groundcover chosen for the location is too vigorous.

Another common problem in ground-covers is that of traffic. Unlike most planting areas, groundcovers are neither clearly made for walking on nor clearly prohibit it. As a result, they are often trampled through, breaking the plants and compacting the soil. Sometimes the solution is to erect barriers or put paths across the groundcover, but often the best thing to do is to select a different groundcover. Groundcovers that are knee-deep discourage traffic. Indeed, a deep groundcover can be used to divert traffic from other areas without cutting up the landscape with fences and hedges.

Above: Aphids on an ivy stem. See page 329. Left: A healthy ajuga groundcover under a Japanese aralia. Ajuga looks best in the shade.

PROBLEMS COMMON TO MANY GROUNDCOVERS

Weeds invading ivy planting.

PROBLEM: Weeds are growing in the ground-cover.

ANALYSIS: Weed invasion
A dense groundcover chokes out weeds and remains trouble-free. However, if the planting is new, or if bare spots are developing, weed control can be a difficult problem.

SOLUTION: If there are only a few weeds, pull them by hand. If the weeds are growing in bare spots in the ground-cover, or if the weeds are projecting above the groundcover, treat them with ORTHO Kleenup Ready-To-Use Weed & Grass Killer. Be careful not to drip the solution on desirable plants. To prevent reinfestation, apply ORTHO Casoron Granules around woody groundcovers, or ORTHO Garden Weed Preventer around nonwoody groundcovers. Apply according to label instructions. Replant bare areas immediately. Feed and water the groundcover well to keep it dense. To keep weeds out of new plantings, apply ORTHO Garden Weed Preventer after planting. If the groundcover is not one that spreads by rooting, apply a mulch of black plastic or an organic material from 3 to 5 inches deep between plants. As is true of weed control anywhere in the garden, it is best to remove weeds as soon as they are seen. Weeds are far more difficult to control once they are well established. For more information on weed control in groundcovers, see page 324. Also see the entry for your groundcover in the alphabetical listing following this section.

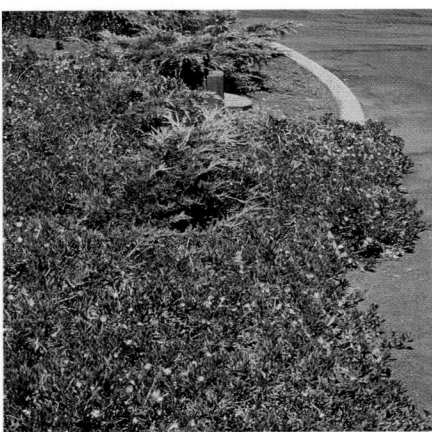

African daisy groundcover invading landscaped area.

PROBLEM: Groundcover plants spread into surrounding lawns, shrubs, and flower beds.

ANALYSIS: Invading other areas
Some groundcovers are too vigorous for their location. In order to keep them from invading other garden areas, you must cut them back frequently. These plants are more suited to large areas where they receive little care. Some of these very vigorous groundcovers are Japanese honeysuckle, polygonum, African daisy, and crown vetch.

SOLUTION: Kill the existing planting with ORTHO Kleenup Systemic Weed & Grass Killer. After 1 week, cut off the old groundcover and replant. The plants may still be green when they are removed, but the roots will die in a couple of weeks and will not resprout. Kleenup is inactivated in the soil, so the new plants will not be affected. Consult your local nurseryman, County Extension Agent (see page 1011), or neighbors to learn which groundcovers grow well in your area and in the space you have selected. A plastic or metal strip or edging installed around the border helps restrict the plants. For more information on the many kinds of groundcovers and their care, see the ORTHO book *All About Groundcovers.*

BARE SPOTS

Irish moss in a dark location.

Compacted area in vinca.

Polygonum dying from lack of water.

PROBLEM: The planting is thin, with bare spots. Plants are spindly and leggy, with leaves that are darker green than usual. Leaves may drop, beginning with the lowest leaves and progressing upward.

ANALYSIS: Insufficient light
Plants use light to manufacture the food they need to survive. Without enough light they become weak, stunted, and susceptible to attack from insects and disease. The plants that suffer most in low light areas are those that require full sun. Shade-loving plants will tolerate varying degrees of shade.

SOLUTION: If a tree is shading the planting, consider pruning some of the branches to let more light pass through to the groundcover. If there is a group of trees, consider removing one or more of them. Or plant a groundcover that tolerates shade, such as ajuga, English ivy, epimedium, hosta, pachysandra, or vinca.

PROBLEM: Leaves turn yellow and do not grow as large as usual. Plants are stunted and die in some areas, leaving bare spots. There are no signs of insect or disease damage.

ANALYSIS: Compacted soil
Soil compacts easily in areas where foot or vehicular traffic is heavy. This is especially a problem where a groundcover has been planted in an area that used to be a lawn or path. Compaction prevents air and water from penetrating into the soil and to the roots. Air in the soil is necessary for healthy root growth. Plants growing in compacted soil are more subject to disease, primarily root and crown rots, because the soil doesn't drain properly. Water often puddles on compacted soil.

SOLUTION: If the soil is dry, use a soil penetrant to increase the wetting capacity of the soil. Poke holes around the plants with a lawn aerator to allow air and water to penetrate the soil. The holes must be at least 3 inches deep, and no more than 3 inches apart. Cultivate the bare spots, add organic matter as outlined on page 918, and replant. Consider stepping stones or mulch paths to keep traffic off the groundcover.

PROBLEM: Bare spots appear in the groundcover. Plants are pale green or yellow and grow slowly. The edges of the leaves turn brown and crisp. The soil is frequently dry.

ANALYSIS: Drought
The plants are not receiving enough water. This may be due to one of several problems.
1. Not enough water is applied at each watering. This frequently happens with hand watering. Although the ground is moist, or even muddy after watering, the water may not have penetrated to the plant roots.
2. Water is applied too infrequently. If rainfall is not supplemented by irrigation during drought periods, or if irrigation is too infrequent, the plants use up all the water in the soil and suffer stress before more water is applied.
3. Water is running off on the surface instead of entering the soil. This occurs when the soil is dense or compacted, or when water is applied faster than the soil can absorb it.

SOLUTION: Follow these guidelines to prevent drought damage.
1. Apply at least an inch of water at each watering. Set tin cans under the sprinkler, and water until an inch of water has accumulated in each can.
2. Water whenever the soil an inch or so deep feels just barely moist.
3. If water is running off the groundcover, irrigate with a sprinkler head that applies water more slowly. Or water until runoff begins, stop for half an hour to let the soil absorb the water, then continue until 1 inch has been applied. If the soil is compacted, improve water penetration by aerating the soil with a lawn aerator. See page 305 for instructions.

Bare spots from excess water.

Spindly growth.

Underfertilized ajuga.

PROBLEM: Leaves turn yellow, starting with the older, lower leaves and progressing to the younger leaves. Plants grow very little. The roots are shallow, and may be rotted. The soil is very moist.

ANALYSIS: Excess water
Excess moisture in the soil can result from watering too frequently or from too much rainfall. Water replaces air in the spaces between soil particles. Roots, which need air to grow, are restricted to the surface by the lack of air. These shallow-rooted plants are smaller than usual and more susceptible to drought. Many root and crown rotting fungi thrive in wet soil, killing plants. Groundcovers growing in wet soil seldom spread out to fill in the planted area.

SOLUTION: Allow the soil to partially dry out between waterings. The soil an inch or so beneath the surface should be as dry as a well-wrung-out sponge before you water again. Of course, there is nothing you can do about the weather; but if you replant the area, improve drainage according to the instructions on page 901 before replanting. If the soil drains quickly, excess water seldom damages plants.

PROBLEM: Plants are spindly and leggy, with leaves that are darker green than usual. Leaves may drop, beginning with the lowest leaves and progressing upward.

ANALYSIS: Insufficient light
Plants use light to manufacture the food they need to survive. Without enough light they become spindly, stunted, and susceptible to attack from insects and diseases. The plants that suffer most in low-light areas are those that require full sun. Shade-loving plants will tolerate varying degrees of shade.

SOLUTION: If a tree is shading the planting, consider pruning some of the branches to let more light pass through to the groundcover. If there is a group of trees, consider removing one or more of them. Or plant a groundcover that tolerates shade, such as ajuga, English ivy, epimedium, hosta, pachysandra, or vinca.

PROBLEM: Leaves are smaller than usual and turn pale green to yellow. Plants grow very little.

ANALYSIS: Lack of nutrients
Fertilizer supplies the nutrients plants need to stay vigorous and healthy; adequate fertilizing may result in fewer insect and disease problems. The 3 essential nutrients that plants require in the largest amounts are nitrogen (N), phosphorus (P), and potassium (K). *Nitrogen* gives the leaves their green color and encourages rapid growth. Without nitrogen, plants turn pale green to yellow. *Phosphorus* encourages flowering and fruiting, and helps build a strong root system. *Potassium* increases the plants' resistance to disease and aids in overall growth. Most garden fertilizers contain all 3 nutrients. On the bag are 3 numbers, called the N–P–K ratio or fertilizer grade, which state the nutrient content. For example, a fertilizer bag reading 5–10–10 has, by weight, 5 percent nitrogen, 10 percent phosphate (phosphorus), and 10 percent potash (potassium). Many fertilizers also supply trace, or minor, nutrients that plants need in minute amounts, which may be lacking in the soil.

SOLUTION: Fertilize your groundcover at regular intervals. Use a fertilizer that contains the 3 major nutrients unless you live in an arid region. In arid regions, the soil probably contains sufficient phosphate and potassium, so you only need to add nitrogen. Follow label instructions for amounts and timing of fertilizing. Water well after fertilizing to dilute the fertilizer and wash it into the soil.

Iron deficiency in pachysandra.

Leaf yellowing on vinca caused by acid soil.

Scorched ivy leaves.

PROBLEM: Leaves turn pale green or yellow. The newest leaves (those at the tips of the stems) are most severely affected. Except in extreme cases, the veins of affected leaves remain green. In extreme cases, the newest leaves are small and all-white or yellow. Older leaves may remain green.

ANALYSIS: Iron deficiency
Plants frequently suffer from deficiencies of iron and other minor nutrients such as manganese and zinc, elements essential to normal plant growth and development. Deficiencies can occur when one or more of these elements are depleted in the soil. Often, minor nutrients are present in the soil, but alkaline (pH 7.5 and higher) or wet soil conditions cause them to form compounds that cannot be used by the plant. An alkaline condition can result from overliming, or from lime leached from cement or brick. Regions where soil is derived from limestone, and those with low rainfall, usually have alkaline soils.

SOLUTION: Spray the foliage with ORTHO Greenol Liquid Iron 6.13%, and apply it to the soil around the plants to correct the deficiency of minor nutrients. Check the soil pH (see the instructions on page 903). Correct the pH of the soil by treating it with *ferrous sulfate* and watering it in well. Maintain an acid pH by fertilizing with ORTHO Azalea, Camellia & Rhododendron Food 5–10–10.

PROBLEM: Plants grow slowly and the leaves turn pale green to yellow. Plants don't improve very much when fertilized. A soil test shows a pH below 6.0.

ANALYSIS: Acid soil
Soils with a pH of less than 6.0 are common in areas of heavy rainfall. Heavy rains leach lime from the soil, making it more acid. The amounts and types of nutrients available to plants are limited in acid soils. Below a pH of 5.5, the availability of nitrogen, phosphorus, potassium, calcium, and other nutrients decreases. These nutrients are essential for healthy plants. Plants vary in their tolerance for acid soils. Most plants grow best with a soil pH between 6.0 and 7.5. For more information about soil pH, see page 902.

SOLUTION: Test your soil pH with an inexpensive test kit available in garden centers. Many County Extension Offices (see page 1011 for a list) also test soil pH. To make a soil less acid, apply lime. See page 1002 for instructions, or follow the directions given with the soil testing kit. Soil acidity corrections are only temporary. Add lime to your soil every year or two if you live in an acid-soil area.

Acid tolerant groundcovers: Epimedium, ferns, creeping gardenia, gaultheria, heaths and heathers, pachysandra, hosta, sarcococca, vancouveria, tiarella.

PROBLEM: Tips and edges of the leaves are brown and dead. Leaves may fall.

ANALYSIS: Scorch
Leaf scorch may be caused by any of a number of conditions.
1. *Heat scorch:* In hot weather, water evaporates rapidly from the leaves. If the roots can't absorb and convey water fast enough to replenish this loss, the leaves turn brown and wither. This condition is often seen when shade-loving plants receive too much sun.
2. *Winter injury* occurs on plants growing in full sun. On a clear winter day, the sun heats the leaf surface, increasing the need for water. If the ground is frozen, or if it has been a dry fall and winter, the roots can't absorb enough water.
3. *Salt injury* results from excess salts in the soil. These salts can come from irrigation water, de-icing salts, or fertilizers. This condition is worse in poorly drained soils, where salts can't be easily leached.

SOLUTION: Follow these guidelines to prevent scorching.
1. Keep groundcovers well watered during hot weather. For a list of sun and shade tolerant groundcovers, see page 991.
2. To prevent winter scorch, be sure that the soil is moist before the ground freezes. Provide shade during clear, cold weather.
3. Leach the salts from the soil with very heavy waterings. If your irrigation water is salty, leach regularly to keep salt from accumulating in the soil. When you fertilize, apply only the amounts recommended on the label, and water thoroughly afterward.

PROBLEMS COMMON TO MANY GROUNDCOVERS — INSECTS

Powdery mildew on euonymus.

PROBLEM: Leaves and stems are partially or entirely covered with grayish white powdery patches. Leaves die and may drop off. The patches occur primarily on the upper surfaces of the leaves.

ANALYSIS: Powdery mildew
This common plant disease is caused by several fungi that thrive in both humid and dry weather. The powdery patches consist of fungal strands and spores. The spores are spread by the wind to healthy plants. The fungus saps plant nutrients, causing yellowing and sometimes death of the leaf. A severe infection may kill the plant. Since powdery mildews attack many different kinds of plants, the fungus from a diseased plant may infect other types of plants in the garden. See page 995 for a list of powdery mildews and the plants they attack. Under favorable conditions, powdery mildew can spread through a closely spaced planting in a matter of days or weeks.

SOLUTION: Spray with a fungicide containing *benomyl*, *triforine*, or *folpet*. These fungicides do not kill the fungus on leaves that are already diseased. They do, however, protect healthy leaves by killing the mildew spores as they germinate on the leaf. Follow label directions regarding frequency of application. Clean infected leaves and debris from the garden.

Spider mite (50 times life size).

PROBLEM: Leaves are stippled, yellowing, and dirty. Leaves may dry out and drop. There may be webbing over flower buds, between leaves, or on the lower surfaces of the leaves. To determine if the plant is infested with mites, hold a sheet of white paper underneath an affected branch and tap the branch sharply. Minute green, red, or yellow specks the size of pepper grains will drop to the paper and begin to crawl around. The pests are easily seen against the white background.

ANALYSIS: Spider mites
Mites, related to spiders, are major pests of many garden and greenhouse plants. They cause damage by sucking sap from the underside of the leaves. As a result of feeding, the green leaf pigment disappears, producing the stippled appearance. Some mites are active throughout the growing season, but are favored by hot, dry weather (70°F and up). By midsummer, they build up to tremendous numbers. Other mites are most prolific in cooler weather. They feed and reproduce primarily during spring and, in some cases, fall. At the onset of hot weather (70°F and up), the mites have caused their maximum damage.

SOLUTION: Treat infested plants with ORTHO Isotox Insect Killer or ORTHO Diazinon Insect Spray when the mites first appear. Repeat the treatment 2 more times 7 to 10 days apart. Continue the treatments if the mites reappear.

Greenhouse whiteflies (10 times life size).

PROBLEM: Tiny, winged insects $1/12$ inch long are found mainly on the undersides of the leaves. The insects are covered with white, waxy powder. When the plant is touched, insects flutter rapidly around it. Leaves may be mottled and yellowing. In warm winter areas, black mold may cover the leaves.

ANALYSIS: Greenhouse whitefly
(*Trialeurodes vaporariorum*)
Greenhouse whitefly is a common insect pest of many garden and greenhouse plants. The four-winged adult lays eggs on the undersides of leaves. The larvae are the size of a pinhead, and look quite different from the adult. The larvae are flat, oval-shaped, and semitransparent, with white waxy filaments radiating from the body. They feed for about a month before changing to the adult form. Both the larval and adult forms suck sap from the leaves. The larvae are more damaging because they feed more heavily. Adults and larvae cannot fully digest all the sugar in the plant sap and excrete the excess in a fluid called honeydew, which coats the leaves. Sooty mold, a black moldy fungus, grows on the honeydew. In warm winter areas, the insect can be active year-round with eggs, larvae, and adults present at the same time. The whitefly is unable to live through freezing winters. Spring reinfestations in freezing winter areas come from migrating whiteflies and infested greenhouse-grown plants placed in the garden.

SOLUTION: Control whiteflies by spraying with an insecticide containing either *diazinon*, *malathion*, or *acephate* every 7 to 10 days as necessary. Spray the foliage thoroughly, covering both the upper and lower surfaces of the leaves.

Aphids on ivy (twice life size).

Snail and slug damage to ivy.

PROBLEM: The leaves are curled, distorted, and yellow. A shiny, sticky substance may coat the leaves. Tiny (⅛ inch) pale green to black soft-bodied insects cluster under leaves and stems. Ants may be present. If the infestation continues, plants may become stunted.

ANALYSIS: Aphids
Aphids do little damage in small numbers. However, they are extremely prolific and populations can rapidly build up to damaging numbers during the growing season. Damage occurs when the aphid sucks the juices from the leaves of the groundcover. The aphid is unable to digest fully all the sugar in the plant sap and excretes the excess in a fluid called honeydew. Ants feed on honeydew and are often present where there is an aphid infestation.

SOLUTION: Spray with ORTHO Orthene Systemic Insect Control or ORTHO Isotox Insect Killer as soon as the insects appear. Repeat the spray if the plant becomes reinfested.

PROBLEM: Stems and leaves may be sheared off and eaten. Silvery trails wind around on the plants and soil nearby. Snails or slugs may be seen moving around or feeding on the plants, especially at night. Inspect the garden for them at night by flashlight.

ANALYSIS: Snails and slugs
These pests are mollusks, and are related to clams, oysters, and other shellfish. They feed on a wide variety of garden plants. Like other mollusks, snails and slugs need to be moist all the time. For this reason, they avoid direct sun and dry spots, and hide during the day in damp places, such as under flower pots or in thick groundcover. They emerge at night or on cloudy days to feed. Snails and slugs are similar, except that the snail has a hard shell into which it withdraws when disturbed. Slugs lay masses of white eggs encased in a slimy mass in protected places. Snails bury their eggs in the soil, also in a slimy mass. The young look like miniature versions of their parents.

SOLUTION: Scatter ORTHO Slug-Geta Snail & Slug Bait granules or ORTHO Bug-Geta Snail & Slug Pellets in bands around the areas you wish to protect. Also scatter the bait in areas where snails or slugs might be hiding, such as in dense groundcover, weedy areas, compost piles, or pot storage areas. Before spreading the bait, wet down the areas to be treated to encourage snail and slug activity that night. Repeat the application every 2 weeks as long as snails and slugs are active.

INDEX TO GROUNDCOVERS

Crown rot.

Scorch.

PROBLEM: Lower leaves turn yellow. White cob-webby strands may cover stems and spread over the soil. Large patches suddenly wilt and die during the first few warm, humid days of spring. Plants pull up easily, with most of the roots and crown rotted away. Tiny, hard, yellow-brown and white pellets are found in the soil.

ANALYSIS: Crown rot
This disease is caused by a fungus (*Sclerotium* species) that occurs mostly in wet, poorly drained soil. The fungus attacks many kinds of plants, and causes the only serious disease of ajuga. The fungus enters the plant through the roots and crown and spreads into the stem, rotting it and causing the plant to wilt and die. In mild infections, new growth sometimes sprouts from buds that have not been killed. The tiny fungal pellets found in the soil survive winters and other unfavorable conditions to infect other plants. The fungus most frequently enters the garden originally in infested soil or plants, and lives for years in the soil.

SOLUTION: Remove and destroy all infected plants. Do not replant in the area until the infected soil has either been removed, or drenched with a fungicide containing *PCNB*. To prevent crown rot, plant ajuga in well-drained soil. For instructions on improving soil drainage, see page 901.

Ajuga cultural information
Light: Light shade
Water: Do not allow to dry out
Soil: Rich, loamy, well drained
Fertilizer: Medium

PROBLEM: Leaves turn light brown along the edges and then toward the center. Leaves feel crisp and then shrivel, sometimes falling off. Plants grow in full sun and are not watered regularly.

ANALYSIS: Scorch
Leaf scorch is caused by excessive evaporation of moisture from the leaves. In hot weather, water evaporates rapidly from the leaves. If the roots can't absorb and convey water fast enough to replenish this loss, the leaves turn brown and wither. Browning usually occurs first along the leaf edges and the top of the plant — those areas farthest from the roots and the water source. Unless it receives water, the plant dies. With small plants like ajuga, this process can happen within a few days. Leaf scorch can also occur in moist soil, if the weather is exceptionally hot and dry.

SOLUTION: Ajuga grows best in shade, but will tolerate the sun if the weather is not too hot. If you have a tendency to water irregularly or to neglect your landscape, plant ajuga in the shade. This low-maintenance groundcover requires well-drained soil that is not allowed to dry out.

DICHONDRA

Cutworms (life size).

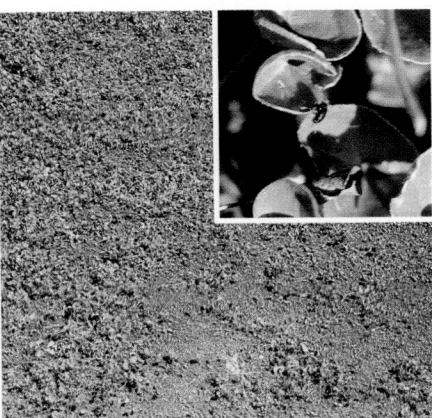

Flea beetle damage. *Insert:* Flea beetle (life size).

Slug on dichondra (life size).

PROBLEM: Leaves are chewed along the edges. Young plants may be chewed or cut off near the ground. By using a flashlight at night, gray, brown, or black worms, 1½ to 2 inches long, may be seen feeding on the dichondra. The worms coil when disturbed.

ANALYSIS: Cutworms
Several species of cutworms attack plants in the garden. The most likely pests of dichondra plantings are the surface-feeding cutworms. For information on the climbing cutworms that may attack other plants in the garden, see page 689. Cutworms hide in the soil during the day, and feed only at night. Adult cutworms are dark, night-flying moths with bands or stripes on their forewings.

SOLUTION: Control cutworms in dichondra with ORTHO Diazinon Soil & Turf Insect Control, ORTHO Diazinon Insect Spray, or ORTHO Lawn Insect Spray. Apply at the first sign of cutworms or damage. Since cutworms are most active at night, treat in the evening. Repeat if damage continues.

Dichondra cultural information
Light: Sun or light shade
Water: While soil is still moist
Soil: Heavy or light
Fertilizer: Medium to heavy

PROBLEM: From May to October, dichondra leaves turn brown, first along the edges of the lawn, then progressing toward the center. Small round holes like shotholes are chewed in the upper surfaces of the leaves. To determine if this is an insect problem, spread a white handkerchief on the border between a damaged area and a healthy area. Black insects, about ¹⁄₂₅ inch long, will hop onto the white cloth, where they are easily seen.

ANALYSIS: Flea beetles
The adult flea beetle is the most damaging pest of dichondra. Although it hops like a flea, it is a true beetle. The adult spends the winter in garden trash and weeds, emerging with the warm spring weather to begin feeding and laying eggs. Damage is spotty at first because the beetles are so small. In a short time, however, they can destroy a lawn. The discoloration of the leaves is often mistaken for drought damage or fertilizer burn.

SOLUTION: Spray the infested dichondra with ORTHO Diazinon Insect Spray or ORTHO Lawn Insect Spray at the first sign of damage. Water the area first, then apply the insecticide according to the label directions. Repeat once a month throughout the growing season. A healthy planting of dichondra is more resistant to attack from flea beetles than an unhealthy one, and recovers more quickly if it does become infested. Fertilize once a month from March to September.

PROBLEM: Holes are chewed in the leaves. Leaves may be sheared off entirely. Silvery trails wind around on the plants and nearby soil. If you inspect the lawn with a flashlight after dark, you will discover snails — slimy creatures with shells — or slugs — slimy creatures without shells — feeding on the dichondra.

ANALYSIS: Snails and slugs
Snails and slugs are not insects, but are related to mollusks — clams, oysters, and other shellfish. They feed on a wide variety of plants, including vegetables, flowers, and groundcovers. Snails feed mostly at night, but may also be active on cloudy, wet days. When not feeding, both snails and slugs hide in cool, dark places, such as in groundcovers, and under rocks, logs, and garbage cans.

SOLUTION: Control snails and slugs in dichondra with ORTHO Slug-Geta Snail and Slug Bait or ORTHO Bug-Geta Snail & Slug Pellets. First water the areas to be treated. Sprinkle lightly afterwards to wash the pellets off the leaves and onto the soil. Repeat every 2 weeks if further damage is seen.

DICHONDRA

Annual bluegrass.

Bermudagrass.

Crabgrass.

PROBLEM: Clumps of pale green grass with whitish seed heads grow in the dichondra.

ANALYSIS: Annual bluegrass
(*Poa annua*)
Annual bluegrass is one of the most troublesome and difficult weeds to control in lawns and dichondra. This member of the bluegrass family is lighter green, more shallow-rooted, and less drought tolerant than the bluegrass used for lawns. As its name suggests, annual bluegrass lives only one year. The seeds germinate in cool weather from late summer to late fall. Annual bluegrass grows rapidly in the spring, especially if the lawn is fertilized then. In mid to late spring, seed heads appear that give the grass a whitish appearance. When hot weather arrives, the annual bluegrass dies.

SOLUTION: Weed killers are only partially effective in controlling annual bluegrass. Prevent seeds from germinating by applying weed killer containing *bensulide* in late summer. Water 10 to 15 minutes after application to wash the weed killer off the leaves and into the soil. Keep children and pets off the lawn until the weed killer has been washed into the soil and the leaves have dried. Keep your dichondra lawn healthy to help it resist invasion by annual bluegrass.

PROBLEM: Patches of a fine-textured grass grow in dichondra lawns. The slightly hairy, gray-green stems creep along the soil. The erect shoots are 6 to 8 inches tall, and the leaf blades are ⅛ inch wide. This grass turns brown in the winter if temperatures drop below 50°F.

ANALYSIS: Bermudagrass
(*Cynodon dactylon*)
Bermudagrass, also called *devilgrass* and *wiregrass*, is widely used as a lawn grass in the southern and western United States. Its deep root system makes it very drought tolerant, but its vigorous creeping habit makes it a weed in dichondra lawns, gardens, and other planted areas. This grass reproduces from seeds, roots, and stem segments.

SOLUTION: Control Bermudagrass in dichondra lawns with a weed killer containing *dalapon* in late spring and summer. If the dichondra has not been recently fertilized, fertilize 5 to 7 days before treating with the weed killer. Water thoroughly 1 to 2 days before the weed killer treatment. Use the weed killer according to the directions, or the dichondra will turn yellow and the leaf edges will burn. Do not water after applying the weed killer until the dichondra shows signs of drought stress. Control of Bermudagrass is slow; retreatment will probably be necessary. Keep dichondra lawns thick and healthy by fertilizing once a month from March to September. If only a few patches exist, spot-treat with ORTHO Kleenup Systemic Weed & Grass Killer or ORTHO Kleenup Ready-To-Use Weed & Grass Killer, and replant after 7 days.

PROBLEM: A narrow-leaf weed forming broad, flat clumps invades thin areas of a dichondra lawn. The weed grows rapidly throughout the summer, rooting at the stem joints. The pale green blades are 2 to 5 inches long and ½ inch wide. Spikes 2 to 6 inches tall grow from the center of the plant.

ANALYSIS: Crabgrass
(*Digitaria* species)
Crabgrass, one of the most common annual weeds, completes its life cycle in 1 year. It sprouts in the early spring and produces seeds all summer, until the first killing frost in the fall when the plants turn brown and die. The seeds sprout the following spring. When dichondra begins to thin out from insect damage, disease, or poor maintenance, crabgrass is one of the first weeds to invade the area.

SOLUTION: Apply a pre-emergence weed killer containing *bensulide* from mid-January to the end of February. Water after application for 10 to 15 minutes to wash the herbicide off the leaves and into the soil. If crabgrass is already in the planting, apply ORTHO Crab Grass Killer. Repeated applications may be required. Keep your dichondra lawn healthy to help it resist invasion by crabgrass.

DUCHESNEA

FRAGARIA (WILD STRAWBERRY)

Oxalis.

Rust.

Leaf spot.

PROBLEM: A weed with pale green leaves divided into 3 heart-shaped leaflets invades thin areas of dichondra. The ¼- to ¾-inch-wide leaves are similar to clover. The stems root at the lower joints and are often thinly covered with fine hairs. The small, bright yellow flowers are ½ inch long, with 5 petals. Plants grow prostrate to erect, 4 to 12 inches high.

ANALYSIS: Oxalis
(*Oxalis stricta*)
Oxalis, commonly called *yellow woodsorrel*, is a perennial plant that thrives in dry, open places. When an area begins to thin from insect damage, disease, or drought, oxalis quickly moves in. Oxalis reproduces from seeds formed in cucumber-shaped seed pods. When the pods dry, a light touch causes them to explode, shooting their seeds several feet in all directions. Oxalis leaves contain oxalic acid, which gives them a distinctive sour taste.

SOLUTION: Apply a pre-emergent weed killer containing *monuron* in the spring before the oxalis germinates. Follow the directions carefully; over-application will injure the dichondra. Water immediately to prevent chemical leaf burn. Keep your dichondra lawn healthy and able to resist invasion by oxalis by following the cultural instructions on page 331.

PROBLEM: Bright orange spots appear on the undersides of the leaves. Only the older leaves are affected; younger leaves show no spotting. Leaves yellow, and if severely infected, dry and drop. Severely infected plants may die.

ANALYSIS: Rust
This plant disease is caused by a fungus (*Frommea obtusa*) that causes extensive damage on duchesnea. Infection starts in the early spring, attacking only the older leaves. Rust spores are spread from plant to plant by the wind. The plant must be wet for 6 to 8 hours before the fungus infects the leaf. Rust fungi survive only on living plant tissue and as spores on seeds. They do not remain active on dead plant parts or in the soil. The fungus is most active in moist conditions, with cool nights and warm days. Temperatures of 90°F and higher kill the spores.

SOLUTION: No control measures for this rust fungus have been discovered. Since the fungus requires moisture on the leaves in order to infect them, avoid overhead watering. Instead, use a soaker hose that waters the plants along the soil surface. Water in the morning to allow the soil to dry as much as possible by nightfall. Pick off any infected leaves as soon as you notice them.

Duchesnea cultural information
Light: Light shade
Water: While soil is still moist
Soil: Sandy, well drained
Fertilizer: Medium

PROBLEM: Spots and blotches appear on the leaves. The spots may be yellow, red, tan, gray, or brown, ranging in size from barely visible to ¼ inch in diameter. Several spots may join to form blotches. Leaves often turn yellow, die, and fall off. Leaf spotting is most severe in warm, humid weather. In damp conditions, a fine gray mold sometimes covers the infected leaf tissue.

ANALYSIS: Leaf spot
Several different fungi cause leaf spots on wild strawberry. Some of these fungi eventually kill the plant. Others merely spot the leaves, and are unsightly but not harmful. The fungi are spread from plant to plant by splashing water, wind, and contaminated tools. They survive the winter on diseased plant debris not cleaned out of the garden. Most of the leaf spot fungi do their greatest damage in humid conditions and mild weather (temperatures between 50° and 85°F).

SOLUTION: Spray the infected planting with a fungicide containing *maneb*, *zineb*, or *mancozeb* every 3 to 10 days. Because leaf spot fungi are most active during warm, humid weather, spray more frequently during those weather conditions. These fungicides protect the new healthy foliage, but do not kill the fungus on leaves that are already infected.

Fragaria cultural information
Light: Full sun
Water: While soil is still moist
Soil: Sandy, well drained
Fertilizer: Medium

FRAGARIA (WILD STRAWBERRY)

Root rot.

PROBLEM: Leaves turn yellow, starting with the older lower ones and moving up the stem to the younger ones. Plants grow very little. When they are pulled up, the roots are found to be black, soft, and rotted. The soil is very moist.

ANALYSIS: Root rot
This disease is caused by a number of different fungi that persist indefinitely in the soil. They thrive in waterlogged, heavy soils. Waterlogged soil may result from overwatering or from poor soil drainage. Infection causes the roots to decay, resulting in wilting, yellowing leaves, and the death of the plant. These fungi are generally spread by infected soil and transplants, contaminated equipment, and moving water.

SOLUTION: Allow the soil around the plant to dry out. (For more information on this technique, see page 857.) Remove and discard severely infected plants. Avoid future root rot problems by planting in well-drained soil. For information on improving soil drainage, see page 901. For more information on root rots, see page 856.

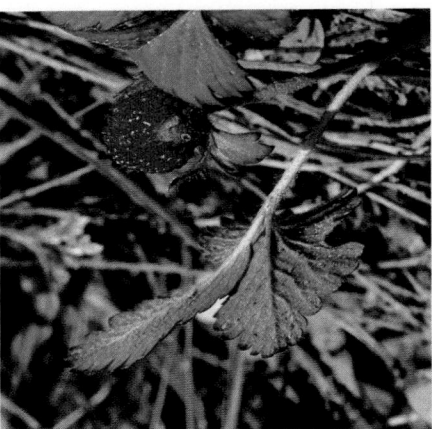

Spider mites (40 times life size).

PROBLEM: Leaves are speckled or spotted, yellow, and dirty. Leaves may dry out and fall. Often there is webbing over flower buds, between leaves, or on the lower surfaces of the leaves. Discoloration is most severe during hot, dry weather. To determine if the plant is infested with mites, hold a sheet of white paper underneath a few stippled leaves and tap the leaves sharply. Minute green, red, or yellow specks the size of pepper grains will drop to the paper and begin to crawl around. The mites are easily seen against the white background.

ANALYSIS: Spider mites
Spider mites, related to spiders, are major pests of many garden plants. They cause damage by sucking sap from the undersides of leaves. As a result of feeding, the green leaf pigment disappears, producing the stippled appearance. Mites are active throughout the growing season but are favored by hot, dry weather (70°F and up). By midsummer they build up to tremendous numbers.

SOLUTION: Spray with a miticide containing *dicofol* when damage is first noticed. Cover all the leaves thoroughly and direct sprays to the undersides of the leaves. Repeat applications 3 more times at intervals of 7 days. Hose down plants frequently to knock off webs and mites.

GAZANIA

Crown rot.

PROBLEM: Lower leaves turn yellow. Tan cobwebby strands may cover stems and spread over the soil. Large patches suddenly wilt and die during the first warm days of spring. Plants pull up easily with most of the roots and crown rotted away.

ANALYSIS: Crown rot
This fungus (*Rhizoctonia solani*) occurs mostly in heavy, poorly drained soil. Although this fungus attacks many kinds of plants, it is the cause of the only serious disease of gazania. The fungus rots the roots and crown, causing the plant to wilt and die. In mild infections, new growth sometimes sprouts from buds that have not been completely killed. The fungus lives indefinitely in the soil and is spread from plant to plant on contaminated tools and by splashing water.

SOLUTION: Remove and destroy all infected plants immediately. Do not replant in the same area until the infected soil has either been carefully removed, or drenched with a fungicide containing *PCNB*. Let the soil dry out between waterings (see page 857). Before replanting the area, improve the drainage. For instructions on improving drainage, see page 901.

Gazania cultural information
Light: Full sun
Water: Allow to dry between waterings
Soil: Loamy, well drained
Fertilizer: Light

HEDERA (IVY)

Heat scorch.

PROBLEM: Dead brown spots appear on the leaves. The spots are always on the part of the leaf that is exposed most directly to the sun. Plants grow in direct sun.

ANALYSIS: Scorch
Ivy can suffer from two kinds of scorch: heat and winter burn. Leaf scorch is caused by excessive evaporation from the leaves. In hot weather, water evaporates rapidly from the leaves. If the roots can't absorb and convey water fast enough to replenish this loss, then leaf tissue is killed. Ivy growing on a sunny wall is particularly affected by scorch because the wall radiates the sun's heat onto the plants. Winter injury occurs on plants growing in the full sun of a southern or western exposure. On a very sunny, clear winter day, the sun heats the leaf surface, increasing the plant's water requirement. If the ground is frozen, or if it has been a dry fall and winter, the ivy roots can't absorb the needed water. The leaf then turns brown and dries out.

SOLUTION: Keep ivy amply watered during hot weather. Pick off scorched leaves to improve the appearance of the planting. Fertilize heavily to encourage quick regrowth. In areas with hot summers, ivy does best in shady locations. To reduce the chance of winter scorch, be sure the soil is moist before the ground freezes.

Fungal leaf spot.

PROBLEM: Large tan to brown spots appear on the leaves. These oval or circular areas occur on both the upper and the lower surfaces of the leaves. Spots often enlarge to cover most of the leaf surface. Small black specks may be seen scattered over the surface of the spots. The leaves may turn brownish red, die, and fall.

ANALYSIS: Leaf spot
A number of different fungi cause leaf spotting on ivy. Some of these fungi may kill tender stems. Others merely spot the leaves and are unsightly. The fungi are spread from plant to plant by wind, splashing water, insects, and contaminated tools. They spend the winter on diseased plant debris left in the garden. Leaf spots affect a wide variety of plants including flowers, vegetables, and groundcovers. Most of the leaf spot fungi do their greatest damage in temperatures between 50° and 85°F.

SOLUTION: Spray the infected planting every 3 to 10 days with a fungicide containing *maneb* or *folpet*. Because leaf spots are most active during warm, humid weather, be sure to spray more frequently during those weather conditions. *Maneb* and *folpet* protect the new healthy foliage, but do not kill the fungus on leaves that are already infected. Leaves that are spotted over more than half their surface should be removed and thrown away to reduce the spread of the infection to less severely affected plants. Don't work in the diseased plants when the leaves are wet, or you will help spread the fungi.

Bacterial leaf spot.

PROBLEM: Pale green angular areas spot the leaves. As the spots enlarge, they turn brown and black with red margins. They eventually dry out and crack. Leaf stems turn black and shrivel. A black decay begins on the stems and spreads to the older wood. Brown-black lesions form on the stems. During warm, humid weather, an ooze flows from the infected stems.

ANALYSIS: Bacterial leaf spot and stem canker
This disease, caused by a bacterium (*Xanthomonas hederae*), occurs frequently on English ivy growing in humid areas. Leaves kept constantly moist are particularly susceptible to invasion by these bacteria. It spreads from plant to plant in splashing rain, on insects such as ants, bees, and flies, and on contaminated equipment. People also spread the bacteria when they work around wet, infected plants. Other organisms often enter the dying tissue and stem lesions, causing further decay.

SOLUTION: When the foliage is dry, pick and remove infected leaves and plants. Spray the entire planting once a week with a fungicide containing *basic copper sulfate*, as long as the disease is present. Avoid planting English ivy in hot, humid areas. Water early in the day to allow the foliage to dry quickly.

Hedera cultural information
Light: Light shade to heavy shade
Water: While soil is still moist
Soil: Most soils
Fertilizer: Light to medium

HEDERA (IVY)

Stem rot.

PROBLEM: Leaves turn dark green, wilt and then turn dark brown and cling to the stems. The stems become soft, sunken, and reddish brown. When the dying plants are dug up, many of the roots are found to be soft and rotting. There many be fine brown strands on the roots, and mats, 2 to 12 inches in diameter, of white powdery spores on the soil.

ANALYSIS: Root and stem rots
Root and stem rots on ivy are caused by several fungi that attack the roots, stems, and lower leaves, killing the plants rapidly. *Rhizoctonia solani* and *Phytophthora palmivora* cause wilting and root decay. *Phymatotrichum omnivorum*, a severe problem in the Southwest, causes a disease known as *cotton* or *Texas root rot*. It wilts the plant and also forms brown strands on the roots and powdery mats on the soil. These fungi live in the soil and on living roots, and are easily spread by contaminated tools, splashing water, and fungal strands in the soil. Plants growing in heavy alkaline soils are the most susceptible to attack.

SOLUTION: Once the plants wilt, nothing can be done. To reduce the spread of *Rhizoctonia* and *Phytophthora*, let the soil dry out between waterings according to the directions on page 857. Cotton root rot is more virulent in alkaline soil. Increase the acidity of the soil by spreading *ferrous sulfate* and watering it in well according to the directions on page 902. When planting new beds, improve the drainage with the methods described on page 901.

Brown soft scale (twice life size).

PROBLEM: The stems or the undersides of leaves are covered with raised tan to reddish black crusty or waxy bumps. The bumps can be picked off; the undersides are usually soft. Leaves may turn yellow and fall. In some cases, a sticky substance coats the leaves. A black sooty mold often grows on the sticky material. Ants may be present.

ANALYSIS: Scales
Scales are insects that spend the winter on the trunk and twigs of the plants. They lay eggs in spring and in early summer (late spring in the South); the young scales, called *crawlers*, settle on leaves and twigs. The small (1/10 inch), soft-bodied young feed by inserting their mouthparts and sucking sap from the plant. The legs usually atrophy and a hard crusty or waxy shell develops over the body. The mature female scales lay their eggs underneath the shell. Some species of scales that infest English ivy are unable to digest all the sugar in the plant sap and excrete the excess in a fluid called honeydew. A black sooty mold fungus may develop on the honeydew. Ants feed on the sticky substance and are often present where scales cluster. An uncontrolled infestation of scales may kill the vines after 1 or 2 seasons.

SOLUTION: Spray with an insecticide containing *malathion* or *carbaryl* in early summer (late spring in the South), when the young are active. The following early spring, before new growth begins, spray the vines with a *dormant oil spray* to control overwintering insects. For more information about scales, see page 878.

HYPERICUM (ST. JOHN'S WORT)

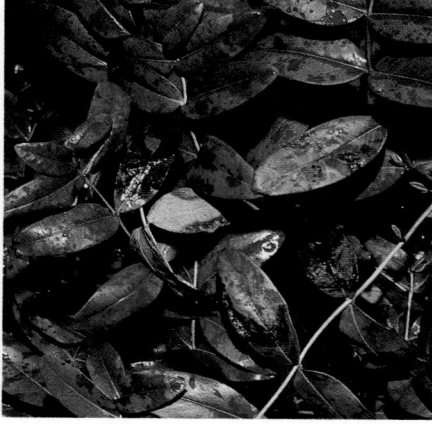

Leaf spot.

PROBLEM: Spots and blotches appear on the leaves. The spots may be yellow, red, tan, gray or brown. They range in size from barely visible to 1/4 inch in diameter. Several spots may join to form blotches. Leaves often turn yellow, die, and fall. Leaf spotting is most severe in warm, humid weather. In damp conditions, a fine gray mold sometimes covers the infected leaf tissue.

ANALYSIS: Leaf spot
A number of different fungi cause leaf spotting on plants. Those that occur on hypericum spot the leaves and are unsightly, but not harmful. The fungi are spread from plant to plant by wind, splashing water, insects, and contaminated tools. They survive the winter on diseased plant debris left in the garden. Most of the leaf spot fungi do their greatest damage in temperatures between 50° and 85°F.

SOLUTION: Leaf spots on hypericum are not critical and won't kill the plant. If you don't like the unsightly leaves, a fungicide containing *maneb* or *folpet* can be sprayed every 3 to 10 days. Because leaf spots are most active during warm, humid weather, spray more frequently during those weather conditions. *Maneb* and *folpet* protect new healthy foliage, but do not kill the fungus on leaves that are already infected.

Hypericum cultural information
Light: Sun or partial shade
Water: While soil is still moist
Soil: Sandy or loamy
Fertilizer: Light to medium

MESEMBRYANTHEMUM (ICE PLANT)

Rust.

Root rot. *Insert:* Closeup.

Mesembryanthemum scales (twice life size).

PROBLEM: Very small orange spots appear on the undersides of the leaves. On the upper surfaces, these areas are light yellow. Infected leaves may drop. Long orange areas appear on the stems.

ANALYSIS: Rust
This disease is caused by a fungus (*Mesospora hypericorum*) that attacks several plants beside hypericum. Infection starts in the early spring, at the same time that new plant growth begins. Rust spores are spread from plant to plant by wind and splashing water. The plant must be wet for 6 to 8 hours before the fungus infects the leaf. Rust survives only on living plant tissue and as spores on seeds. It does not remain active on dead plant parts or in the soil. The disease is most active in moist conditions, with cool nights and warm days. Temperatures of 90°F and higher kill the spores.

SOLUTION: Spray infected plants with a fungicide containing *zineb* once a week throughout the growing season. It is important to thoroughly spray both the upper and lower surfaces of the leaves. For even spray coverage, use a spreader-sticker according to the directions on page 915. *Zineb* protects the new, healthy foliage; it does not kill the fungus on leaves that are already diseased. Water in the morning rather than the late afternoon or evening to allow foliage time to dry. Remove and destroy all infected plants in the fall to reduce the chance of new infection next year.

PROBLEM: Leaves turn yellow, starting with the older, lower leaves and progressing to the younger ones. Plants grow very little. When they are pulled up, the roots are black, soft, and rotted. The soil is very moist.

ANALYSIS: Root rot
This disease is caused by a number of different fungi that are present in moist soils. These fungi normally do little damage, but can cause root rot in waterlogged soils. Waterlogged soil may result from overwatering or poor soil drainage. Infection causes the roots to decay, resulting in wilting, yellowing leaves, and the death of the plant.

SOLUTION: Ice plant is a drought tolerant plant that needs very little watering. Allow the soil around the plants to dry out between waterings. For more information on this technique, see page 857. Remove and discard severely infected plants. Avoid future root rot problems by planting in well-drained soil. For information on improving soil drainage, see page 901. For more information on root rots, see page 856.

PROBLEM: White sacs appear on the new growth, stems, and undersides of the leaves in early spring and late summer to midfall. Lime green and yellow flecks, almost the same color as the plant, are on the stems and leaves. Plants may turn reddish purple.

ANALYSIS: Scales (*Pulvinaria delottoi, Pulvinariella mesembryanthemi*)
The two insects that attack ice plant are a serious problem in home gardens and in highway plantings along the California coast. They damage and kill plants by sucking the sap from the leaves and stems. Both scales feed actively year-round, but cause much less damage in the winter. The females mature and lay their eggs in white sacs from February to May and August to October. The eggs are spread from plant to plant by the wind. The fall generation causes the most damage because the plants are already under stress from the summer heat and dryness.

SOLUTION: These pests are very difficult to control. Once the plants have turned reddish purple, it is too late to spray. Discard them and plant new ones. For mildly infested plants, treat with *malathion* or *acephate*, mixed with a summer oil spray. Do not spray when the white sacs are first present, because the eggs are protected. Spray shortly afterward, when the young crawlers have hatched and begin feeding. For best control, spray both the upper and lower surfaces of the plants. Extensive studies are under way on the natural predators of these pests. Beetles and wasps have been very successful in keeping the scales under control on highway plantings.

PACHYSANDRA (JAPANESE SPURGE)

Scorch.

PROBLEM: Irregular blotches, light to dark brown, spot the leaves. Leaves are crisp, shrivel up, and sometimes fall off. Plants may be growing in the full sun.

ANALYSIS: Scorch
Pachysandra can suffer from two kinds of scorch: heat and winter burn. Leaf scorch is caused by excessive evaporation of moisture from the leaves. In hot weather, water evaporates rapidly from the leaves. If the roots can't absorb and convey water fast enough to replenish this loss, then the leaves turn brown and wither. In very hot weather, scorch may occur even though the soil is moist. Winter injury occurs on plants growing in the full sun of a southern or western exposure. Although the pachysandra may be in the shade during the spring and summer, in the winter after a sheltering tree has dropped its leaves, it is in the full sun. On a clear winter day, the sun heats the leaf surface, increasing the plant's water requirement. If the ground is frozen, or if it has been a dry fall and winter, the pachysandra roots can't absorb the needed water.

SOLUTION: Keep the soil moist. If scorch persists, consider growing a groundcover that is more resistant to drought in that area. To prevent winter scorch, keep the soil moist until the ground is frozen.

Leaf and stem blight.

PROBLEM: Irregular brown and black blotches appear on the leaves and spread to cover almost the entire leaf. Leaves are soft and water soaked. Areas on the stem turn black, soft, and sunken. In wet weather, pinkish spore masses appear along the stem.

ANALYSIS: Leaf and stem blight
This disease is caused by a fungus (*Volutella pachysandrae*). Plants are more susceptible to attack from this fungus if they are weak from spider mites or winter injury; if they are too crowded; if planted in the full sun; or if the area stays too moist from tree leaves falling into the bed. The fungus is most active in rainy, cool spring weather, and spreads from plant to plant on splashing water and contaminated tools. The spores survive the winter on infected stems and leaves that are left in the garden. If not controlled, this blight can kill an entire planting of pachysandra in 1 or 2 seasons.

SOLUTION: Pull out and discard all diseased plants. Although this may seem like an endless job, you will get much better control of this difficult-to-control disease. Then spray the cleaned bed with a fungicide containing *captan* or *mancozeb* 3 times, at intervals of 1 week, beginning when the disease is discovered or when new growth starts in the spring. Thin and shear the beds periodically to improve air circulation. Rake out fallen leaves in the fall to reduce the chance of the disease occurring in the spring. Keep pachysandra healthy by controlling scale and reducing winter scorch.

Oystershell scale (life size).

PROBLEM: The stems and the undersides of leaves are covered with gray, reddish brown, yellow, or white flecks or bumps. These bumps or flecks are round, pear-shaped, or narrow, and rub off easily. Leaves turn yellow and often fall. Plants seldom grow new leaves, and eventually die.

ANALYSIS: Scales
Scales are insects that spend the winter on the trunk and twigs of the plants. They lay eggs in spring and in early summer (late spring in the South); the young scales, called *crawlers,* settle on leaves and twigs. These small (1/10 inch), soft-bodied young feed by inserting their mouthparts and sucking sap from the plant. The legs usually atrophy and a hard crusty or waxy shell develops over the body. The mature female scales lay their eggs underneath the shell. Some species of scales that infest pachysandra are unable to digest all the sugar in the plant sap and excrete the excess in a fluid called honeydew. A black sooty mold fungus may develop on the honeydew. Ants feed on the sticky substance, and are often present where scales cluster. An uncontrolled infestation of scales may kill the vines after 2 or 3 seasons.

SOLUTION: Spray with an insecticide containing *malathion* or *carbaryl* in early summer (late spring in the South), when the young are active. The following early spring, before new growth begins, spray the vines with a *dormant oil spray* to control overwintering insects. For more information about scales, see page 878.

POTENTILLA (CINQUEFOIL)

Leaf spot.

PROBLEM: Small reddish purple and brown spots with darker margins appear on the leaves. These oval to round spots occur on both the top and bottom surfaces of the leaves. Spots often enlarge to cover most of the leaf surface. Small black specks may be seen scattered over the surface of the spots. The leaves often turn yellow, die, and fall.

ANALYSIS: Leaf spot
A number of different fungi cause leaf spotting on potentilla. Some of these fungi may kill the plant. Others merely spot the leaves and are unsightly, but not too harmful. The fungi are spread from plant to plant by wind, splashing water, insects, and contaminated tools. They survive the winter on diseased plant debris left in the garden. Most of the leaf spot fungi do their greatest damage in temperatures between 50° and 85°F.

SOLUTION: Spray the infected planting every 3 to 10 days with a fungicide containing *zineb* or *mancozeb*. Because leaf spot fungi are most active during warm, humid weather, spray more frequently during those weather conditions. These fungicides protect the new healthy foliage, but do not kill the fungus on leaves that are already infected. Leaves that are spotted over more than half their surface should be removed and destroyed to reduce the spread of the fungus to less severely affected plants. Don't touch the diseased plants when the leaves are wet, or you will help spread the fungus.

TRACHELOSPERMUM (STAR JASMINE)

Rust.

PROBLEM: Very small orange spots appear on the undersides of the leaves. On the upper surfaces, these areas are light yellow. Long orange areas appear on the stems. Plants wilt and drop their infected leaves.

ANALYSIS: Rust
A number of fungi (*Phragmidium* species) attack members of the rose family, including potentilla. Rust spores are spread from plant to plant by wind and splashing water. The plant must be wet for at least 4 hours before the fungus infects the leaf. Rust survives only on living plant tissue and as spores on seeds. It does not remain active on dead plant parts or in the soil. The disease is most severe in moist conditions, with cool nights and warm days.

SOLUTION: Spray infected plants with a fungicide containing *zineb* or *maneb* once a week throughout the growing season. It is important to wet both the lower and upper surfaces of the leaves. For even spray coverage, use a spreader-sticker according to the directions on page 915. *Zineb* and *maneb* protect the new, healthy foliage by killing the rust spores as they germinate on the leaf; they do not kill the fungus on diseased leaves. Water in the morning rather than the late afternoon or evening, to allow wet leaves time to dry. Remove and destroy all infected plants in the fall to reduce the chances of new infections next year.

Potentilla cultural information
Light: Full sun to partial shade
Water: While soil is still moist
Soil: Well drained, loamy
Fertilizer: Medium

Iron deficiency.

PROBLEM: Yellowing starts along the edges of the leaves and progresses inward. Eventually the areas between the veins are yellow, with the veins remaining bright green. The plant grows slowly, forming leaves that are smaller than usual.

ANALYSIS: Iron deficiency
Leaf yellowing in star jasmine is due to a deficiency of iron in the plant. The soil is seldom deficient in iron. However, the iron is often in an insoluble form and not available to the plant, especially in soil of pH 7.0 and above. Overliming the soil or lime leached from cement or brick will raise the soil pH. In addition, regions with low rainfall generally have high-pH soils. Iron is necessary for the formation of the green pigment in the leaf. Without it, the leaves yellow.

SOLUTION: Spray the leaves and the soil around the plants with ORTHO Greenol Liquid Iron 6.13%. If the soil has a pH of over 7.0, treat it with *ferrous sulfate*. (For instructions, see page 902.) Do not lime soils with a pH of over 7.0.

Trachelospermum cultural information
Light: Sun or shade
Water: While soil is still moist
Soil: Loam
Fertilizer: Medium

VINCA (PERIWINKLE)

Root and stem rot.

Dieback.

Leaf spot.

PROBLEM: Shoot tips wilt and die. There are no black specks on the affected stems. Plants pull up easily, with most of the roots and lower stem soft and rotted away. Individual plants are affected first, and within several weeks entire clumps wilt and die.

ANALYSIS: Root and stem rot
This plant disease is caused by a fungus (*Pellicularia filamentosa*). It is the most serious disease affecting periwinkle. It occurs mostly in heavy, poorly drained soil, and during periods of wet weather. It can be found throughout the growing season in most periwinkle plantings. The fungus enters the plant through the roots and crown and rots the cells, causing the plant to wilt and die. The fungus persists indefinitely in the soil, and spreads from plant to plant on contaminated tools and splashing water.

SOLUTION: Remove and destroy badly infected plants. Allow the soil to dry between waterings according to the method described on page 857 until the spread of the disease is halted. If the area is replanted, improve the drainage by one of the methods described on page 901. To prevent recurrence of the disease, allow the soil to dry between waterings until it is barely moist.

Vinca cultural information
Light: Light shade
Water: While soil is still moist
Soil: Well drained
Fertilizer: Medium

PROBLEM: Shoot tips wilt, turn brown, and die. The infection progresses down the stem to the soil surface, killing the plant. Affected stems turn black. Tiny black specks are often seen on the diseased stems. Dark brown spots sometimes develop on leaves, which then die and fall. Individual plants are affected first, and within several weeks entire clumps wilt and die.

ANALYSIS: Canker and dieback
This disease is caused by two fungi (*Phomopsis livella* and *Phoma exigua*) that attack periwinkle in the spring soon after the new growth begins. This disease is most prevalent during very rainy seasons. The fungal spores spread from plant to plant on splashing water and contaminated tools. This disease can be devastating, killing an entire planting in a few weeks.

SOLUTION: Thoroughly soak stems and soil with a fungicide containing *benomyl*. Apply 2 or 3 times, at intervals of 1 month, beginning in early spring. Prune and remove plants that are more than half affected. This helps reduce the chance of the fungus spreading. Drench soil and stems with *benomyl* when planting a new bed of periwinkle. Once the plants are established, these treatments may be reduced or eliminated unless the disease returns. To reduce the chances of new infections, water early in the day, rather than late afternoon or evening, so the leaves have time to dry out before nightfall.

PROBLEM: Spots and blotches appear on the leaves. The spots may be yellow, red, tan, gray, or brown. They range in size from barely visible to ¼ inch in diameter. Several spots may join to form blotches. Leaves may yellow and die. Leaf spotting is most severe in warm, humid weather. In damp conditions, a fine gray mold may cover the infected leaf tissue.

ANALYSIS: Leaf spot
A number of different fungi cause leaf spots. Some of these fungi may eventually kill the plant, or weaken it so that it becomes susceptible to attack by other organisms. Others merely cause spotting that is unsightly but not harmful. These fungi are spread by splashing water, wind, insects, and tools. They generally survive the winter in diseased plant debris. Most of these fungi do their greatest damage in mild weather (50° to 85°F).

SOLUTION: Spray the infected planting every 3 to 10 days with a fungicide containing *basic copper sulfate*. Rake out infected fallen leaves.

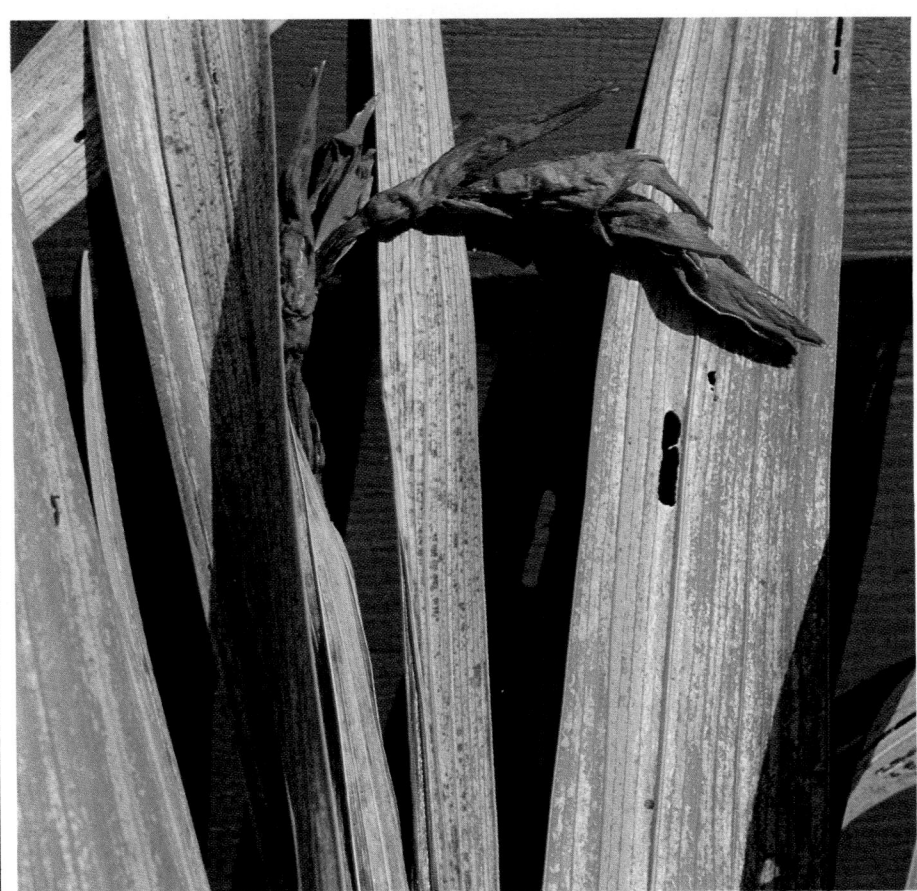

Some of the problems common to many flowers and perennial ornamentals are discussed in the next 17 pages. If you don't find your problem here, look up your plant in the index to flowers on the next page.

PROBLEMS COMMON TO MANY FLOWERS	PAGE
Poor flowering	345
Slow growth	347
Discolored or spotted leaves	349
Wilting plants	353
Insects	355
Leaves and flowers chewed	358
Seedlings die	358

ANNUALS, PERENNIALS, AND BULBS

Annuals, perennials, and bulbs (include the soft-bodied ornamentals in this group) are the princesses of the garden. They are usually raised for their beauty alone, and serve no other function, such as diverting traffic or giving shade. So the measure of how well they perform their function is in their beauty.

Annuals are grown anew each year from seeds or transplants. They grow rapidly to the flowering stage, then bloom abundantly for the rest of the growing season. But ideal growing conditions are needed to keep them vigorous. They are most successful if they are treated like vegetables — their bed should be cultivated and fertilized before planting, fertilizer should be added at regular intervals throughout their growing season, and they should be watered regularly.

Because annuals only last for a single season, one solution to their problems is to throw the plants away and begin with new ones instead of treating specific problems. Because annuals usually accumulate problems as they age, there is often a point toward the end of the season when the gardener decides that the annual bed is no longer attractive and cleans it out.

Perennials, on the other hand, are long-term investments. Because they are meant to last for many years, it is important that they be adapted to their environment. This means selecting the right types for your climate, and finding the right place in your yard for each plant. It is sometimes necessary to move a plant several times before finding just the right combination of shade, soil type, and pro-

tection from the elements. But finding that location is often the key to having trouble-free perennials.

Bulbs can be treated either as annuals or perennials. All bulbs are perennials, but those not adapted to your climate will not naturalize and multiply their numbers each year. Tulips, for instance, make smaller and fewer blooms each year, and are usually most satisfactory if new bulbs are purchased each fall. But other bulbs, such as daffodils, are adapted to much of the United States, and will increase in number each year with a minimum of effort. If you wish to keep bulbs as perennials, feed and water the foliage after the blooming period is past, because it is during this period that energy is being stored in the bulb for next year's flower.

Above: Damage caused by gladiolus thrips. See page 395. Left: A healthy perennial border, with lilies blooming in front of a snake plant.

INDEX TO ANNUALS, PERENNIALS, AND BULBS ───────────────────

INDEX TO ANNUALS, PERENNIALS, AND BULBS

PROBLEMS COMMON TO MANY FLOWERS

Lobelia without flowers.

Flowerless geranium.

PROBLEM: The plant produces no flowers. The foliage is healthy, and there are no signs of insects or disease.

ANALYSIS: No flowers on a healthy plant
Healthy plants may fail to bloom for several reasons.

1. *Wrong season:* Most plants bloom only during a specific season. Often, plants have particular seasonal light and temperature requirements that must be met before they will flower.

2. *Unseasonable cool spell:* If the weather is unseasonably cool or cloudy, many plants adapted to hot, sunny weather stop flowering.

3. *Insufficient light:* Plants differ in the amount of light they require to flower properly. Generally, flowers that thrive in sunny conditions bloom poorly or fail to bloom in shaded locations.

4. *Too much nitrogen:* All plants need nitrogen and several other nutrients to grow and flower properly. However, if they receive an excessive amount of nitrogen, some plants will grow lush, succulent foliage at the expense of flower production.

5. *Immature plants:* Biennials (plants that live for 2 years) and perennials (plants that live for many years) usually do not bloom during their first year of growth, even during their normal flowering season. They need to attain a minimum size or age before they will flower.

6. *Undersize bulbs:* Plants grown from bulbs or corms (such as daffodils, tulips, and gladioli) will not produce flowers if they are planted from undersize bulbs or corms.

SOLUTION: The numbered solutions below correspond to the numbers in the analysis.

1. Find out the flowering season of your plants. For a list of common flowers and their blooming seasons, see page 992.

2. Plants will start to flower again when the weather warms up.

3. Look up your specific plant in the alphabetical section beginning on page 360 to determine its light requirement. If your plant is not receiving enough light, transplant it to a sunnier location.

4. Fertilize your flowers with ORTHO Bloom Builder 0–10–10 according to label directions.

5. Check to see if your plant is either a biennial or a perennial (see page 992). If it is, you can expect it to flower next year.

6. Purchase only large, healthy bulbs and corms. After a year or two, plants grown from undersize bulbs and corms will eventually flower as the bulbs and corms increase in size.

PROBLEMS COMMON TO MANY FLOWERS — POOR FLOWERING

Transplant shock on cineraria.

Poor flowering on gazanias.

Small petunia blossoms.

PROBLEM: Recently transplanted flowers drop their flower buds before they open. Often, blossoms and leaves also drop prematurely. The plant may wilt during the hot part of the day even if the soil is moist.

ANALYSIS: Transplant shock
Even under ideal conditions, many plants drop some of their buds, flowers, and leaves when they are transplanted. Bud and leaf drop result from root damage that occurs during transplanting. Tiny hairlike rootlets that grow at the periphery of the root system absorb most of the water the plant uses. When these rootlets are damaged during transplanting, the amount of water that can be supplied to the foliage and flowers is decreased. Flower buds, flowers, and leaves fall off, and the plant wilts. The more the roots are damaged during transplanting, the greater will be the leaf and bud drop. Also, because plants lose water rapidly during hot, dry, windy periods, transplanting then will cause plants to undergo greater shock. They will not recover as quickly. As the root system regrows, new flower buds will form.

SOLUTION: Transplant when the weather is cool, in the early morning, late afternoon, and on cloudy days. When transplanting, disturb the soil around the roots as little as possible. Preserve as much of the root system as possible. If the roots have been disturbed, or if the plant is large or old, pinch off about a third of the growth, to reduce the amount of foliage needing water. Water immediately after transplanting with ORTHO Upstart Root Stimulator 5–15–5. For more information about transplanting, see page 916.

PROBLEM: There are few blooms, and the flowers may be small.

ANALYSIS: Poor flowering
Lack of flowers can result from any of several causes.

1. *Insufficient light:* Many plants require full or part day sun to flower properly. Even plants that flower well in filtered light will not produce many blossoms when planted in deep shade. Plants receiving inadequate light are often leggy or spindly.

2. *Diseased plants:* Frequently, plants that have been attacked by disease or insect pests do not flower well. Mottled, discolored, or dying foliage or chewed leaves usually indicate the presence of a diseased organism or plant pest.

3. *Old flowers left on plant:* Many plants slow down their flower production when the older blossoms are allowed to fade and form seeds. The plant diverts its energy into producing seeds rather than flowers.

4. *Overcrowding:* Plants that are overcrowded must compete for light, nutrients, and water. When supplies of nutrients are inadequate, overall plant growth, including flowering, decreases.

5. *Too much nitrogen:* Plants require a balanced diet of nutrients (nitrogen, phosphorous, potassium) to grow and bloom properly. Excessive nitrogen from high-nitrogen fertilizers throws off the balance of nutrients and encourages lush, green leaf growth at the expense of flower production.

SOLUTION: The numbered solutions below correspond to the numbers in the analysis.

1. Check the light requirements of your plants. (For a list of common flowers and their light requirements, see page 992.) If plants are not receiving enough light, move them to a sunnier location.

2. Look up your plant in the alphabetical section beginning on page 360 to find what diseases may affect it. Treat accordingly.

3. Remove flowers as they start to fade.

4. Thin out overcrowded plantings.

5. Fertilize your plants with ORTHO Bloom Builder 0–10–10. The phosphorous and potassium in the fertilizer will promote flowering.

Thrips damage to morning glory.

PROBLEM: Flower buds turn brown and die before they open. There are often silvery white streaks on the leaves. Flowers that have opened are often streaked and distorted. If the flower buds are peeled open, tiny (1/20 inch) insects resembling brown or straw-colored wood slivers can be seen moving around at the base of the petals.

ANALYSIS: Thrips
Several species of this common insect pest attack garden flowers. Thrips are found in protected parts of the plant, such as the insides of flower buds, where they feed by rasping the soft plant tissue, then suck the released plant sap. The injured tissue dies and turns white or brown, causing the characteristic streaking of the leaves and flowers. Because thrips migrate long distances on wind currents, they can quickly infest widespread areas. In cold climates, thrips feed and reproduce from spring until fall. With the onset of freezing weather, they find sheltered areas such as grass clumps and hibernate through the winter. In warm weather climates, thrips feed and reproduce all year. These pests reach their population peak in late spring to midsummer. They are especially troublesome during prolonged dry spells.

SOLUTION: Thrips cannot be eliminated completely, but they can be kept under control. Spray infested plants with ORTHO Orthene Systemic Insect Control or ORTHO Isotox Insect Killer. Spray 2 or 3 times at intervals of 10 days as soon as damage is noticed. Make sure your plant is listed on the product label. Repeat the spray if reinfestation occurs. Pick off and destroy old, infested flowers.

Mums that weren't disbudded.

PROBLEM: The plant produces many small flowers rather than a few large, showy flowers. The leaves are healthy.

ANALYSIS: Many small flowers
Large, showy flowers will not be produced on certain plants, such as chrysanthemums and carnations, unless most of the flower buds are removed. Generally, these plants produce long stems with a terminal flower bud at the end and secondary flower buds at the base of each leaf on the flower stem. The plant has only a limited amount of nutrients with which to nourish each bud. If there are many buds, each bud will receive only a small amount of nutrients, and will develop into a small flower.

SOLUTION: Pinch off the side flower buds as soon as they are large enough to be handled. The earlier they are removed, the larger the terminal flower will be.

Geraniums in low light.

PROBLEM: The plant grows slowly or not at all, and is located in a shaded area. Growth is weak and leggy, and flowering is poor. The leaves may be dark green and larger than normal. The oldest leaves may drop off. There are no signs of disease or insect pests.

ANALYSIS: Insufficient light
Plants contain a green pigment, chlorophyll, which uses sunlight to produce energy. This energy is used to make food for plant growth and development. Plants differ in the amount of light they need to grow properly. Some plants need many hours of direct sunlight daily, while others thrive in shaded locations. Any plant that receives less light than it requires cannot produce as much food as it needs. It grows slowly and is weak and leggy.

SOLUTION: Look in the alphabetical section that begins on page 360 to determine the light requirement of your flower. If your plant is not receiving enough light, transplant it to a sunnier location. Replace it with plants that will tolerate low-light conditions. For a list of shade-tolerant plants, see page 992.

PROBLEMS COMMON TO MANY FLOWERS — SLOW GROWTH

Zinnias planted too late.

Phosphorus-deficient columbine.

Slow-growing zinnias.

PROBLEM: The plant fails to grow, or grows very slowly. There are no signs of insects or diseases.

ANALYSIS: Poor growth
There are many reasons why a plant might grow slowly.

1. *Improper planting time:* Many plants require warm temperatures and long hours of sunlight to grow well. If transplants that need warm weather are set out too early in the spring, or too late in the fall when temperatures are cool, they will not grow.

2. *Unseasonable cool spell:* If the weather is unseasonably cool or cloudy, most plants will slow down their growth rate, even those adapted to cool temperatures.

3. *Natural dormancy:* Many perennials and all bulbs undergo a period of no growth, which usually occurs soon after they have flowered. Although it may seem that the plant is inactive during this period, it is actually developing roots, bulbs, or rhizomes for next year's growth. The foliage of many perennials and bulbs eventually dies back completely, and the plant becomes entirely dormant.

4. *Phosphorus deficiency:* Phosphorus is a plant nutrient essential to normal plant growth and development. Many garden soils are deficient in phosphorus. When plants do not receive enough phosphorus they usually grow very slowly, or stop growing altogether. Sometimes their foliage also turns dark green, or may redden slightly.

SOLUTION: The numbered solutions below correspond to the numbers in the analysis.

1. Check page 992 for a list of common flowers and their growing seasons. As the weather warms up, the plants will start to grow.

2. Plants will start to grow again when unseasonable cool spells have passed. If the weather is especially cloudy and moist, check for signs of disease. Fungal and bacterial infections are especially troublesome during periods of moist weather. For information about plant diseases, see pages 856 and 859.

3. Check the list of common flowers on page 992 to see if your plant is a bulb or perennial with a natural dormancy period.

4. For a quick response, spray the leaves with Ra-Pid-Gro Plant Food. Fertilize plants with ORTHO Superphosphate 0–20–0 according to label directions.

PROBLEM: Plants grow slowly, are stunted, and the leaves often turn pale green to yellow. Plants don't improve when fertilized. The pH of the soil is below 5.5.

ANALYSIS: Acid soil
Soils that have a pH of 5.5 or lower are too acid for most plants. Acid soils are commonly found in the Pacific Northwest and along the East Coast. The heavy rains in these areas leach the salts from the soils, leaving them acidic. The amounts and types of nutrients available to plants are limited in acid soils. Below a pH of 5.5, the amount of available nitrogen, phosphorus, potassium, calcium, magnesium, and other nutrients decreases. These nutrients are essential for healthy plants. Most plants grow best with a pH of 6.0 to 8.0.

SOLUTION: To make a soil less acidic, apply dolomitic limestone. This type of ground limestone contains calcium and magnesium, nutrients in which acid soils are usually deficient. The amount of lime you need to apply depends on the soil texture, how acid the soil is, and how much organic matter it contains. (For a chart of liming requirements, see page 1002.) Soil acidity corrections are only temporary because heavy rains leach the lime from the soil. Test your soil every 2 to 3 years, and correct accordingly.

DISCOLORED OR SPOTTED LEAVES

Discolored iris leaves caused by lack of water.

Dried-out crocus.

Overwatering damage on primrose.

PROBLEM: Leaves turn pale green to yellow. The plant may be stunted. In many cases, leaf edges turn brown and crisp, and some of the leaves shrivel and die. There are no signs of disease or pests. Unlike nitrogen deficiency, the leaves do not discolor from the base of the plant upward. For information on nitrogen deficiency, see page 350.

ANALYSIS: Leaves discolored
There are several reasons why leaves discolor.

1. *Frequent stress:* Plants require at least a minimal supply of water to remain healthy and grow properly. When they are allowed to dry out once or twice, they usually survive. However, plants that suffer from frequent drought stress undergo changes in their metabolism that result in leaf discoloration, stunting, and lack of growth. If the soil is allowed to dry out completely, the plant will die.

2. *Salt buildup in the soil:* Leaf discoloration and browning occur when excess salts dissolved in the soil water are taken up into the plant and accumulate in the leaf tissue. Soil salts build up to damaging levels in soils that are not occasionally flushed. Salt buildup commonly occurs in arid regions of the country.

3. *Sunburn:* Shade-loving plants placed in a sunny location will develop discolored leaves. Sunburned leaves often develop a whitish or yellow bleached appearance. Leaves that are not directly exposed to the sun usually remain green and uninjured.

SOLUTION: The numbered solutions below correspond to the numbers in the analysis.

1. Do not let your plants wilt between waterings. Consult the alphabetical section beginning on page 360 for the moisture needs of your plant. Provide plants with adequate water. For more information about proper watering, see page 906.

2. Flush out soil salts periodically by watering deeply and thoroughly.

3. Check to see whether your plant is adapted to sun or to shade. Consult the alphabetical section beginning on page 360 for the light needs of your plant. Transplant shade-loving plants to a shaded location.

PROBLEM: Leaves turn light green or yellow. Leaf edges may turn brown, and some of the leaves may die. In many cases the plant is stunted. Flowering is poor. If the plant is pulled out of the ground, the roots are found to be soft and rotted. The soil is frequently or constantly wet.

ANALYSIS: Overwatering
Overwatering is a serious and common problem that often results in the decay and death of the plant roots. Roots require oxygen to function normally. Oxygen is contained in tiny air spaces (pores) in the soil. When water is applied to the soil, the air is pushed out of the soil pores and replaced with water. If this water cannot drain properly, or is constantly reapplied, the soil pores will remain filled with water. The roots cannot absorb the oxygen they need in such saturated conditions, and they begin to decay. As the roots continue to rot, they are less able to supply the plant with nutrients and water, resulting in the decline and eventual death of the plant.

SOLUTION: Allow the soil to dry out slightly between waterings. For more information on watering see page 906. If your soil is poorly drained, improve the soil drainage. For information about improving soil drainage, see page 901.

PROBLEMS COMMON TO MANY FLOWERS — DISCOLORED OR SPOTTED LEAVES

Nitrogen-deficient impatiens.

Fungal leaf spot on impatiens.

Leaf spot.

PROBLEM: Leaves turn pale green, then yellow beginning with the older leaves. Growth is slowed. Older leaves may drop. New leaves are small. Severely affected plants may die.

ANALYSIS: Lack of nitrogen
Garden soils are frequently deficient in nitrogen, the most important nutrient for plant growth. Nitrogen is essential in the formation of plant protein, chlorophyll (green leaf pigment), and many other compounds. When a plant becomes deficient in nitrogen, it breaks down proteins and chlorophyll in the oldest leaves to recover nitrogen to be recycled for new growth. This loss of chlorophyll causes the older leaves to turn yellow. A continuing shortage of nitrogen results in overall yellowing. Because nitrogen is leached from the soil more readily than are other plant nutrients, and because it is needed in larger quantities than are other nutrients, it must be added to almost all garden soils, and for all flowers. Nitrogen leaches from sandy soil more readily than from clay soil, and it leaches more quickly when rainfall or irrigation is heavy.

SOLUTION: Spray the leaves with Ra-Pid-Gro Plant Food for a quick response. Fertilize with ORTHO Ortho-Gro Liquid Plant Food 12–6–6 or ORTHO General Purpose Plant Food 8–8–8. Repeat applications according to directions. Fertilize more frequently in sandy soils or where rainfall is heavy. For more information about fertilizers, see page 904.

PROBLEM: Spots and blotches appear on the leaves and flowers.

ANALYSIS: Leaf and flower spots
Several disease and environmental factors contribute to spotting and blotching of leaves and flowers.

1. *Fungal leaf spots:* Spots caused by fungi are usually small, circular, and may be found on all of the leaves. The spots range in size from barely visible to ¼ inch in diameter. They may be yellow, red, tan, gray, brown, or black. Often the leaves are yellow and dying. Infection is usually most severe during moist, mild weather (50° to 85°F).

2. *Bacterial leaf spots:* Spots caused by bacteria are usually tiny and angular in shape. They are usually dark-colored and are sometimes accompanied by rotting and oozing from infected areas. Bacterial spots may be found on all parts of the plant, and are most often favored by warm, moist conditions.

3. *Sunburn:* Shade-loving plants placed in a sunny location will develop spots and blotches. Sun-loving plants may also develop sunburn symptoms if they are allowed to dry out. Initially, sunburned leaves develop a whitish or yellowish bleached appearance. Large, dark, angular blotches form on the damaged tissue. Leaves that are not directly exposed to the sun remain green and uninjured.

4. *Spray damage:* Spotting of foliage and flowers may also be caused by insecticide, fungicide, and herbicide spray damage. Spots are usually irregular in shape, and vary in the patterns they form on the leaf. Spray injury often includes distortion, browning, and death of flowers and young leaves. Sprays may drift in from other areas to damage plants.

SOLUTION: The numbered solutions below correspond to the numbers in the analysis.

1. Generally, picking off the diseased leaves gives adequate control. Clean up plant debris. Spray plants with *maneb*, *mancozeb*, or *zineb* if plants are severely infected. Make sure your plant is listed on the fungicide label before spraying.

2. If practical, pick off and destroy spotted leaves. If the plant is severely infected, discard it. Clean up plant debris. Avoid overhead watering. Dip contaminated tools in rubbing alcohol.

3. Pick off the injured leaves and plant parts. Check to see whether your plant is adapted to sun or shade. Transplant shade-loving plants to a shaded location, or provide shade. Provide plants with adequate water, especially during hot, sunny, or windy days. For a discussion of proper watering, see page 906.

4. Once damage has occurred, there is nothing you can do. Read and follow directions carefully when spraying. Avoid spraying on windy days when the spray can drift onto the wrong plants. If spray drifts onto the wrong plant, rinse off the leaves immediately. Pick off dead or badly injured plant parts.

Iron-deficient chrysanthemum.

Powdery mildew.

Rust on hypericum.

PROBLEM: Leaves turn pale green or yellow. The newest leaves — those at the tips of the stem — are most severely affected. Except in extreme cases, the veins of affected leaves remain green. In extreme cases, the newest leaves are small and all-white or yellow. Older leaves may remain green.

ANALYSIS: Iron deficiency
Plants frequently suffer from deficiencies of iron and other minor nutrients such as manganese and zinc, elements essential to normal plant growth and development. Deficiencies can occur when one or more of these elements are depleted in the soil. Often these minor nutrients are present in the soil, but alkaline (pH 7.5 or higher) or wet soil conditions cause them to form compounds that cannot be used by the plant. An alkaline condition can result from overliming, or from lime leached from cement or brick. Regions where soil is derived from limestone, and those with low rainfall, usually have alkaline soils.

SOLUTION: Spray the foliage with ORTHO Greenol Liquid Iron 6.13%, and apply it to the soil around the plants to correct the deficiency of minor nutrients. Check the soil pH according to the instructions on page 903. Correct the pH of the soil according to the instructions on page 902. Maintain an acid pH by fertilizing with ORTHO Azalea, Camellia & Rhododendron Food 5–10–10.

PROBLEM: Leaves and stems are covered with grayish white powdery spots and patches. In many cases, these patches occur primarily on the upper surfaces of the leaves. The infected leaves eventually turn yellow and wither.

ANALYSIS: Powdery mildew
This common plant disease is caused by a number of closely related fungi that thrive in both humid and dry weather. The powdery patches consist of fungal strands and spores. The spores are spread by the wind to healthy plants. The fungus saps the plant nutrients, causing the leaves to turn yellow and sometimes to die. A severe infection may kill the plant. Since some powdery mildews attack many different kinds of plants, the fungus from a diseased plant may infect other types of plants in the garden. (For a list of powdery mildews and the plants they attack, see page 995.) Under favorable conditions, powdery mildew can spread through a closely spaced planting in a matter of days or weeks. In the late summer and fall, the fungus forms small, black, spore-producing bodies, which are dormant during the winter, but which can infect more plants the following spring. Powdery mildew is generally most severe in the late summer.

SOLUTION: There are a number of different fungicides that may be used to treat powdery mildew. Look up your specific plant in the alphabetical listing beginning on page 360 to determine which fungicide should be used. Spray at regular intervals of 10 to 12 days, or as often as necessary to protect new growth. Remove and destroy severely infected plants. Where practical, pick off diseased leaves. Clean up and destroy plant debris.

PROBLEM: Yellow or orange spots appear on the upper surfaces of the leaves. Yellowish orange, rust, or chocolate-colored pustules of spores develop on the undersides of the leaves. Infected leaves usually wilt and either hang down along the stem or drop prematurely. The plant may be stunted.

ANALYSIS: Rust
This plant disease is caused by any of a number of related fungi. Most rust fungi spend the winter as spores on living plant tissue and, in some cases, in plant debris. Some rust fungi also infect various weeds and woody trees and shrubs during part of their life cycle. Flower infection usually starts in the early spring as soon as conditions are favorable for plant growth. The spores are spread to healthy plants by splashing water and wind. Some rust fungi cannot infect the flower host unless the foliage is wet for 6 to 8 hours. Rust is favored by moist weather, cool nights, and warm days.

SOLUTION: Several different fungicides are used to control rust. Look up your specific plant in the alphabetical listing beginning on page 360 to determine which fungicide to use. Spray infected plants thoroughly, covering both the upper and lower surfaces of the leaves. Some plants are so susceptible to rust that you may need to spray at weekly intervals throughout the summer. Water in the morning rather than the late afternoon or evening. This will allow wet foliage to dry out more quickly. Remove and destroy all infected plants in the fall to prevent them from infecting new plantings. Plant rust-resistant varieties, if available. For a list of resistant flower varieties, see page 992.

PROBLEMS COMMON TO MANY FLOWERS — DISCOLORED OR SPOTTED LEAVES

Nasturtiums damaged by ozone.

Leafminer damage to dahlia.

Virus-damaged gladiolus.

PROBLEM: The upper surfaces of the leaves may be bleached, with white flecks or reddish brown spots. Sometimes the leaves are distorted. Older leaves are more affected than younger ones.

ANALYSIS: Air pollution
Some gases released into the atmosphere from cars and factories damage plants. The most common type of pollution is *smog*. Air pollution damage is most commonly a problem in urban areas, but also occurs in rural areas where gardens are located downwind from factories. Some plants are severely affected, and may even die. Flower production is reduced on pollution-damaged plants. For information on the three most common pollutants, *ozone*, *PAN*, and *sulfur dioxide*, see page 862. Many different environmental factors affect a plant's susceptibility to air pollution. Research is presently being conducted throughout the country to better understand these factors and to find ways to protect plants from air pollutants.

SOLUTION: Air pollution injury is usually a localized problem. Check with your neighbors to see if the same kinds of plants in their gardens have been affected the same way. Because injury from air pollutants is similar in appearance to injury from nutrient deficiencies, insects, diseases, and mites, these problems should be eliminated as causes before attributing the damage to air pollution. Nothing can be done about air pollutants. If you live in a smoggy area, select plants that are smog resistant from the list on page 996.

PROBLEM: Light-colored irregular trails wind through the leaves. Blotches may eventually appear on infested leaves. Some of the trails and blotches are filled with black matter. Severely infested leaves may dry up and die.

ANALYSIS: Leafminers
Most of the insects that cause this type of damage belong to the family of leafmining flies. The tiny adult flies lay their eggs on the undersides of the leaves. The maggots that hatch from these eggs penetrate the leaf and live between the upper and lower surfaces. They feed on the inner leaf tissue, creating winding trails and blotches. Their dark excrement may dot or partially fill sections of the trails. Generally, the larvae emerge from the leaves to pupate. Leafminers are continually present from the spring until the fall. The last generation of maggots pupates in the soil or plant debris through the winter, to emerge as adult flies the following spring.

SOLUTION: Spray infested plants with ORTHO Orthene Systemic Insect Control. Make sure that your plant is listed on the product label. Pick off and destroy infested leaves. Remove and destroy all plant remains in the fall.

PROBLEM: Leaves may be mottled yellow-green, or may be uniformly yellowing. In some cases, the foliage develops yellow rings, or the veins may turn yellow. Flowers and leaves may be smaller than normal, and distorted. The plant is usually stunted, and flowering is generally poor.

ANALYSIS: Viruses
Several different viruses infect flowering plants. These viruses include *mosaics*, *yellows*, and *ring-spots*. The severity of virus infections depends on the plant and on the strain of virus. In some cases, symptoms of infection may not show up unless several viruses are present in the plant at the same time. Virus infections do not generally kill the plant, but may greatly reduce its overall vigor and beauty. Many viruses are spread by aphids, which feed on diseased plants and transfer the virus to healthy plants. If diseased plants are touched or pruned, some viruses can be transferred to healthy plants on hands and equipment contaminated by plant sap. Viruses usually persist in the plant indefinitely. Cuttings or divisions made from diseased plants will also be infected.

SOLUTION: There are no chemicals that control or eliminate virus diseases. Remove weak, infected, and stunted plants. Wash your hands thoroughly and dip pruning shears in rubbing alcohol after working on infected plants. Purchase only healthy plants. (For more information on selecting healthy plants, see page 916.) Keep the aphid population under control. For more information about disease-carrying aphids and their control, see page 880.

—— **WILTING PLANTS** ——

Mite damage to columbine.

Wilting snapdragons.

Wilting pincushion flowers.

PROBLEM: Leaves are stippled, yellowish, bronze, or reddish, and are often dirty. There may be webbing over flower buds, between leaves, or on the lower surfaces of the leaves. To determine if the plant is infested with mites, hold a sheet of white paper underneath an affected plant and tap the plant sharply. Minute green, red, or yellow specks the size of pepper grains will drop to the paper and begin to crawl around. These pests are easily seen against the white background.

ANALYSIS: Spider mites
These common pests of many garden and greenhouse plants are related to spiders. They cause damage by sucking sap from the undersides of the leaves. As a result of feeding, the green leaf pigment disappears, producing the stippled, discolored appearance. Mites are active throughout the growing season, but are favored by hot, dry weather (70°F and up). By midsummer, they build up to tremendous numbers. During cold weather, spider mites hibernate in the soil, on weeds and plants retaining foliage, and on tree bark.

SOLUTION: Spray infested plants with a pesticide containing *dicofol*. Make sure that your plant is listed on the product label. Spray plants thoroughly, being sure to cover both the upper and lower surfaces of the leaves. Repeat the spray at least 2 more times at intervals of 5 to 7 days.

PROBLEM: The plant is wilting. The leaves are discolored yellow or brown, and may be dying. The soil may be moist or dry.

ANALYSIS: Root problems
These symptoms are caused by one of several root problems:

1. *Stem and root rot diseases:* Many fungi and bacteria decay plant roots and stems. In addition to leaf wilting and discoloration, there are frequently spots and lesions on the leaves and stems. The infected tissue may be soft and rotted, and the plant pulls out of the ground easily to reveal rotted roots. Most of these disease-causing organisms thrive in wet soil.

2. *Fertilizer burn:* Excessive amounts of fertilizer cause plants to wilt. The leaves wilt and become dull and brown. Later they become dark brown or black and dry up. When too much fertilizer is applied and not watered in well, a concentrated solution of fertilizer salts is formed in the soil. This concentrated solution makes it difficult for plants to absorb the water they need and may even draw water out of the plant.

3. *Nematodes:* These microscopic worms (which are not related to earthworms) live in the soil and feed on plant roots. While feeding, they inject a toxin into the roots. The damaged roots can't supply adequate water and nutrients to the aboveground plant parts, so the plant slowly dies. Infested plants are weak, slow-growing, often turn bronze or yellowish, and wilt on hot, dry days, even when the soil is wet. If the plant is pulled up, the roots are seen to be stunted and often dark and stubby. There may be nodules on the roots.

SOLUTION: The numbered solutions below correspond to the numbers in the analysis.

1. Look up your plant in the alphabetical section beginning on page 360 to determine which root and stem rot diseases may affect it. Treat accordingly. Also see page 856 for more information about important fungal and bacterial plant diseases.

2. Dilute the fertilizer in the soil and leach it below the root zone by watering the plant heavily. Soak the affected area thoroughly with plain water, let it drain, then soak again. Repeat 3 to 4 times. Cut off dead plant parts. Follow directions carefully when fertilizing.

3. If you have a chronic problem with wilting, yellowing plants that slowly die, and you've eliminated all other possibilities, test for nematodes. Testing roots and soil is the only positive method for confirming their presence. Contact your local Cooperative Extension Office (see page 1011 for a list of offices) for sampling instructions, addresses of testing laboratories, and control procedures for your area. For instructions for controlling nematodes, see page 862.

PROBLEMS COMMON TO MANY FLOWERS — WILTING PLANTS

Wilting hosta.

Transplant shock — begonias.

Intense heat — impatiens.

PROBLEM: The plant wilts frequently, and the soil is frequently or always dry. The leaves turn brown, shrivel, and may be crisp.

ANALYSIS: Lack of water

The most common cause of plant wilting is dry soil. Water in the soil is taken up by the plant roots. It moves up into the stems and leaves, and evaporates into the air through microscopic breathing pores in the surface of the leaf. Water pressure in the plant cells keeps the cell walls rigid and prevents the plant from collapsing. When the soil is dry, the roots are unable to furnish the leaves and stems with water, the water pressure in the cells drops, and the plant wilts. Most plants will recover if they have not wilted severely. However, frequent or severe wilting will curb a plant's growth and eventually kill it.

SOLUTION: Water the plant thoroughly, applying enough water to wet the soil to the bottom of the root zone. If the soil is crusted or compacted, cultivate the soil around the plant before watering. To help conserve soil moisture, apply a mulch around the plant. (For more information about proper watering, see page 906.) Do not allow the plant to wilt between waterings. Look up your plant in the alphabetical section to determine its moisture requirement.

PROBLEM: The plant is wilting, but the foliage looks healthy. There are no signs of disease or insects. The soil is moist.

ANALYSIS: Heat or acute root damage

If a plant wilts in moist soil, but the leaves look healthy, the problem has probably occurred recently:

1. *Intense heat or wind:* During hot, windy periods, plants may wilt even though the soil is wet. Wind and heat cause water to evaporate very quickly from the leaves. The roots can't take in water as fast as it is lost.

2. *Transplant shock:* Plants frequently wilt soon after being transplanted. Although called transplant "shock," this is not the same condition as shock in a human being, but refers to wilt resulting from injured roots. Roots are usually broken or injured to some degree during transplanting. Damaged roots are unable to supply the plant with enough water, even when the soil is wet. As the root system restores itself, its water-absorbing capacity increases. Unless they are severely injured, the plants will soon recover.

3. *Rodents:* The roots, underground stems, and bulbs of many plants are often disturbed or fed upon by various rodents, including pocket gophers and field mice. Root, bulb, and stem damage result in rapid wilting and sometimes death of the plant.

4. *Mechanical injury:* Cultivating, digging, hoeing, thinning, weeding, and any other kind of activity that damages plant roots can cause wilting and sometimes death.

SOLUTION: The numbered solutions below correspond to the numbers in the analysis.

1. As long as the soil is kept moist during periods of intense heat and wind, the plants will probably recover without harm when the temperature drops or the wind dies down. Recovery may be hastened by shading the plants and by sprinkling them with water to cool off the foliage and reduce the rate of water evaporation from the leaves.

2. Preserve the root system as much as possible when transplanting. Keep as much of the soil around the roots as possible. Transplant when the weather is cool, in the early morning, late afternoon, or on cloudy days. If the roots have been disturbed, or if the plant is large and old, prune off about a third of the growth. This reduces the amount of water needed. Water immediately after transplanting with ORTHO Upstart Root Stimulator 5–15–5. If possible, transplant when the plant is dormant. For more information about transplanting, see page 916.

3. Rodents may be trapped or baited. For details about rodent control, see page 891.

4. Prevent mechanical injury to plants by working very carefully around them.

INSECTS

Damaged leaves.

Cucumber beetle feeding on zinnia (half life size).

Damaged zinnias. *Insert:* Japanese beetle (life size).

PROBLEM: Holes appear in the leaves and flowers. Some of the leaves, stems, and flowers may be chewed off. Insects are feeding on the plants.

ANALYSIS: Chewing insects
Many kinds of insects feed on plants during the day, including beetles, grasshoppers, and caterpillars. Beetles are hard-bodied insects with tough, leathery wing covers. The wing covers meet in the middle of the back, forming a straight line. Caterpillars are smooth or hairy soft-bodied worms.

SOLUTION: Control these insects by spraying with insecticides. For more information about controlling chewing insects, look up beetles on page 872; grasshoppers on page 881; and caterpillars on page 874.

PROBLEM: Insects are chewing holes in leaves and flowers. Their hard wing covers are folded across their backs, meeting in a straight line down the center of the back. They are frequently shiny and brightly colored.

ANALYSIS: Beetles
Many different species of beetles infest flowers. In the spring or summer, beetles fly to garden plants and feed on flowers, buds, and leaves. Punctured flower buds usually fail to open, and fully open flowers are often eaten. Because many beetles feed at night, only their damage may be noticed, not the insects. Female beetles lay their eggs in the soil or in the flowers in late summer or fall. The emerging larvae crawl down into the soil to spend the winter, or they mature and pass the winter in plant debris. The larvae of some beetles feed on plant roots before maturing in the fall or spring.

SOLUTION: Spray infested plants with an insecticide containing *carbaryl, diazinon, acephate,* or *malathion.* Make sure your plant is listed on the product label.

PROBLEM: The leaf tissue has been eaten between the veins, making the leaves lacy. Flowers are eaten. Metallic green and bronze, winged beetles, ½ inch long, are feeding in clusters on the flowers and foliage.

ANALYSIS: Japanese beetles
(*Popillia japonica*)
As their name suggests, these beetles are native to Japan. They were first seen in New Jersey in 1916 and have since become a major pest in the eastern United States. They feed on hundreds of different species of plants. The adult beetles are present from June to October. They feed only in the daytime, and are most active on warm, sunny days. The female beetles live for 30 to 45 days. Just before they die, they lay their eggs just under the soil surface in lawns. The grayish white grubs that hatch from these eggs feed on grass roots. As the weather turns cold in the late fall, the grubs burrow 8 to 10 inches into the soil, where they hibernate. When the soil warms up in the spring, the grubs migrate back to the surface and resume feeding. They pupate and re-emerge as adult beetles in late May or June.

SOLUTION: Spray infested plants with an insecticide containing *acephate, carbaryl,* or *malathion.* Make sure that your plant is listed on the product label. Japanese beetle traps may also be used.

PROBLEMS COMMON TO MANY FLOWERS — INSECTS

Caterpillar (life size).

Ants on euphorbia (half life size).

Aphids on poppy (⅓ life size).

PROBLEM: Holes appear in the leaves and buds. Leaves, buds, and flowers may be entirely sheared off. Caterpillars are feeding on the plants.

ANALYSIS: Caterpillars
Numerous species of these moth or butterfly larvae feed on garden plants. Usually the adult moths or butterflies begin laying eggs on garden plants with the onset of warm spring weather. The larvae that emerge from these eggs feed on the leaves, flowers, and buds for 2 to 6 weeks, depending on the weather conditions and the species. Mature caterpillars pupate in cocoons either buried in the soil or attached to leaves, tree bark, or buildings. Some caterpillar species have only one generation a year. With these species, all the caterpillars hatch, grow, and pupate at the same time. Other species have numerous generations, so caterpillars of various sizes may be present throughout the growing season. The last generation of caterpillars in the fall survives the winter as pupae. The adult moths and butterflies emerge the following spring.

SOLUTION: Spray infested plants with an insecticide containing *acephate, carbaryl,* or *diazinon.* Make sure that your plant is listed on the product label. Small numbers of caterpillars may be removed by hand.

PROBLEM: Ants are crawling on the plants and soil. In many cases, these plants are infested with aphids, scales, mealybugs, or whiteflies.

ANALYSIS: Ants
These insects, familiar to gardeners throughout the country, do not directly damage plants. Ants may be present for any of several reasons. Many ants feed on honeydew, a sweet, sticky substance excreted by several species of insects, including aphids, scales, mealybugs, and whiteflies. Ants are attracted to plants infested with these pests. In order to insure an ample supply of honeydew, ants may actually carry or "herd" aphids to healthy plants. Aphid infestations are frequently spread in this manner. Ants may also feed on flower seeds and nectar. Although they do not feed on healthy plants, ants may eat decayed or rotted plant tissue. Ants generally live in underground colonies or nests. Certain species may form colonies in trees or in building foundations.

SOLUTION: Destroy ant nests by treating anthills with ORTHO Diazinon Granules or spraying the nest and surrounding soil with ORTHO Diazinon Insect Spray. Control aphids, scales, mealybugs, and whiteflies by spraying the infested plants with *malathion, carbaryl,* or *diazinon.* Make sure that your plant is listed on the product label.

PROBLEM: Leaves are curled, distorted, and yellowing. Often the flowers are malformed. Tiny (⅛ inch) yellow, green, or dark-colored soft-bodied insects are clustered on the leaves, stems, and flowers. A shiny, sticky substance may coat the leaves. Ants are sometimes present.

ANALYSIS: Aphids
These common insects do little damage in small numbers. However, they are extremely prolific and populations can rapidly build up to damaging numbers during the growing season. Damage occurs when the aphid sucks the juices from the leaves and buds. The aphid is unable to digest fully all the sugar in the sap and excretes the excess in a fluid called honeydew, which often drops onto the leaves below. A sooty mold fungus may develop on the honeydew, causing the leaves to appear black and dirty. Ants feed on this sticky substance, and are often present where there is an aphid infestation. In warm areas, aphids are active year-round. In cooler climates, where winter temperatures drop below freezing, the adults cannot survive. However, the eggs they lay in the fall on tree bark, old leaves, and plant debris can survive the winter to cause reinfestation in the spring. Aphids transmit plant diseases such as mosaics and viral yellows.

SOLUTION: Spray with an insecticide containing *acephate, diazinon,* or *malathion.* Make sure that your plant is listed on the product label. Clean up plant debris in the fall. For more information about disease-carrying insects, see page 880.

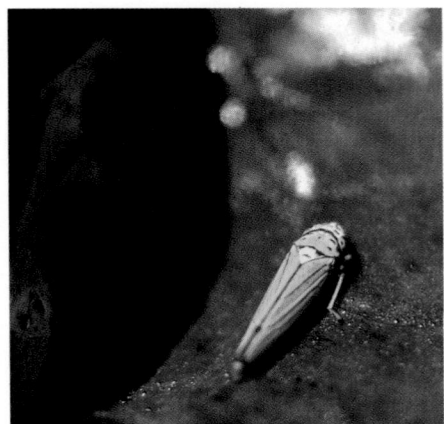
Aster leafhopper (4 times life size).

Whiteflies on fuchsia (twice life size).

Spittlebug froth.

PROBLEM: Spotted, pale green insects up to ⅛ inch long hop or fly away quickly when the plant is touched. The leaves are stippled and may be yellowing.

ANALYSIS: Aster leafhopper (*Macrosteles fascifrons*)
This insect, also known as the *six-spotted leafhopper*, feeds on many vegetable and ornamental plants. It generally feeds on the undersides of leaves, sucking the sap, which causes stippling. This leafhopper transmits *aster yellows*, a plant disease that can be quite damaging. (For more information, see page 861.) Leafhoppers at all stages of maturity are active during the growing season. They hatch in the spring from eggs laid on perennial weeds and ornamental plants. Even areas where the winters are so cold that the eggs cannot survive are not free from infestation because leafhoppers migrate in the spring from warmer regions.

SOLUTION: Spray plants with an insecticide containing *diazinon, carbaryl,* or *malathion.* Check to make sure that your plant is listed on the product label. Eradicate nearby weeds that may harbor leafhopper eggs and aster yellows, especially thistles, plantains, and dandelions. For more information about controlling disease-carrying insects, see page 880.

PROBLEM: Tiny, winged insects ¹/₁₂ inch long feed on the undersides of the leaves. The insects are covered with white waxy powder. When the plant is touched, insects flutter rapidly around it. Leaves may be mottled and yellowing. In warm winter areas, black mold may cover the leaves.

ANALYSIS: Greenhouse whitefly (*Trialeurodes vaporariorum*)
This insect is a common pest of many garden and greenhouse plants. The four-winged adult lays eggs on the undersides of leaves. The larvae are the size of a pinhead, flat, oval-shaped, and semi-transparent, with white waxy filaments radiating from the body. They feed for about a month before changing to the adult form. Both the larval and adult forms suck sap from the leaves. The larvae are more damaging because they feed more heavily. Adults and larvae cannot fully digest all the sugar in the plant sap and excrete the excess in a fluid called honeydew, which often drops onto the leaves below. A sooty mold fungus may develop on the honeydew. In warm winter areas these insects can be active year-round, with eggs, larvae, and adults present at the same time. Whiteflies are unable to live through freezing winters. Spring reinfestations in freezing winter areas come from migrating whiteflies and from infested greenhouse-grown plants placed in the garden.

SOLUTION: Spray infested plants with an insecticide containing *acephate, diazinon,* or *malathion.* Make sure that your plant is listed on the product label. When spraying, be sure to cover both the upper and lower surfaces of the leaves.

PROBLEM: Masses of white, frothy foam are clustered between the leaves and stems. If the froth is removed, small, green, soft-bodied insects can be seen feeding on the plant tissue. The plant may be stunted.

ANALYSIS: Spittlebugs
These insects, also known as *froghoppers,* appear in the spring. Spittlebug eggs, laid in the fall, survive the winter to hatch when the weather warms in the spring. The young spittlebugs, called *nymphs,* produce a foamy froth that protects them from sun and predators. This froth envelops the nymphs completely while they suck sap from the tender stems and leaves. The adult spittlebugs are not as damaging as the nymphs. The adults are ¼ inch long, pale yellow to dark brown, and winged. They hop or fly away quickly when disturbed. Spittlebugs seldom harm plants, but if the infestation is very heavy, the plant may be stunted. Their presence is usually objectionable only for cosmetic reasons.

SOLUTION: Wash spittlebugs from plants with a garden hose. If plants are heavily infested, spray with an insecticide containing *malathion* or *methoxychlor.* Make sure that the plant is listed on the product label. Repeated treatments are not usually necessary.

357

PROBLEMS COMMON TO MANY FLOWERS — LEAVES, FLOWERS CHEWED ———— SEEDLINGS DIE ————

Cineraria damaged by nocturnal insects.

Snails feeding on hosta (¼ life size).

Damping-off of marigold seedlings.

PROBLEM: Holes appear in the leaves and flowers. Some of the leaves, stems, and flowers may be sheared off. There are no insects to be seen feeding on the plants during the day. When the affected plants are inspected at night with a flashlight, insects may be seen feeding on the foliage and flowers.

ANALYSIS: Nocturnal insects
Several kinds of insects feed on plants only at night, including some beetles, weevils, and caterpillars, and all earwigs and cutworms. Beetles are hard-bodied insects with tough, leathery wing covers. The wing covers meet in the middle of the back, forming a straight line. Weevils look like beetles, except that they have elongated snouts. Earwigs are reddish brown, flat, elongated insects up to 1 inch long with pincers projecting from the rear of the body. Caterpillars and cutworms are smooth or hairy soft-bodied worms. These insects usually hide in the soil, in debris, or in other protected locations during the day.

SOLUTION: Control these insects by spraying with insecticides. For more information about controlling nocturnal insects, look up beetles on page 872; weevils on page 873; earwigs on page 884; caterpillars on page 874; and cutworms on page 875.

PROBLEM: Holes are chewed in the leaves, or entire leaves may be sheared from the stems. Flowers are partially eaten. Silvery trails wind around on the plants and soil nearby. Snails or slugs may be seen moving around or feeding on the plants, especially at night. Check for them by inspecting the garden at night by flashlight.

ANALYSIS: Snails and slugs
These pests are mollusks, and are related to clams, oysters, and other shellfish. They feed on a wide variety of garden plants. Like other mollusks, snails and slugs need to be moist all the time. For this reason, they avoid direct sun and dry places, and hide during the day in damp places, such as under flower pots or in thick groundcover. They emerge at night or on cloudy days to feed. Snails and slugs are similar in appearance, except that the snail has a hard shell, into which it withdraws when disturbed. Slugs lay masses of white eggs encased in a slimy mass in protected places. Snails bury their eggs in the soil, also in a slimy mass. The young look like miniature versions of their parents.

SOLUTION: Scatter ORTHO Slug-Geta Snail & Slug Bait or ORTHO Bug-Geta Snail & Slug Pellets in bands around the areas you wish to protect. Also scatter the bait in areas where snails or slugs might be hiding, such as in dense groundcovers, weedy areas, compost piles, or pot storage areas. Before spreading the bait, wet down the treated areas to encourage snail and slug activity that night. Repeat the application every 2 weeks as long as snails and slugs are active.

PROBLEM: Seedlings die soon after emerging from the soil, and are found lying on the ground.

ANALYSIS: Wilted seedlings
Seedlings may wilt and die from lack of water or from disease:
1. *Dehydration:* Seedlings are succulent, and have shallow roots. If the soil dries out even an inch or so below the surface, they may die.
2. *Damping-off:* Young seedlings are very susceptible to damping-off, a plant disease caused by fungi. Damping-off is favored by wet soil with a high nitrogen level. Damping-off can be a problem when the weather remains cold, or cloudy and wet while seeds are germinating, or if seedlings are too heavily shaded.

SOLUTION: The numbered solutions below correspond to the numbers in the analysis.
1. Do not allow the soil to dry out completely. Water when the soil surface starts to dry slightly. During warm or windy weather, you may need to water several times a day.
2. Allow the soil surface to dry slightly between waterings. Do not start seeds in soil that is rich in nitrogen. Add nitrogen fertilizers after the seedlings have produced their first true leaves. Protect seeds during germination by coating them with a fungicide containing *captan*, *thiram*, or *chloroneb*. Add a pinch of fungicide to a packet of seeds (or ½ teaspoon per pound), and shake well to coat the seeds with the fungicide. For more information about damping-off, see page 858. For more information about starting seeds, see page 917.

Damping-off on petunia.

Damping-off on snapdragon.

Seedlings sheared off by snails.

PROBLEM: Seedlings fail to emerge.

ANALYSIS: Germination problems
Seeds may fail to emerge for several reasons:

1. *Dehydration:* Once the seeds have started to grow, even before they have emerged from the soil, they will die easily if allowed to dry out.

2. *Damping-off:* Germinating seedlings are very susceptible to damping-off, a plant disease caused by fungi. These fungi inhabit most soils, decaying the young seedlings as they emerge from the seed. Damping-off is favored by wet, rich soil.

3. *Slow germination:* Seeds of different kinds of plants vary considerably in the amount of time they require to germinate.

4. *Poor seed viability:* Seeds that are old, diseased, or of inferior quality may fail to germinate.

5. *Wrong planting depth:* Seeds of different kinds of flowers vary in their planting depth requirements. If planted too deeply or shallowly, the seeds may fail to germinate.

6. *Seeds washed away:* If a seedbed is flooded or watered with a forceful spray, the seeds may wash away. Heavy rains can also wash seeds away.

7. *Cold weather:* Cold weather may delay seed germination considerably, or prevent germination entirely.

SOLUTION: The numbered solutions below correspond to the numbers in the analysis.

1. Do not allow the soil to dry out completely. Check the seedbed and seed flats at least once a day. Water when the soil surface starts to dry slightly.

2. Allow the soil surface to dry slightly between waterings. Do not start seeds in soil that is high in nitrogen. Add nitrogen fertilizers after the seedlings have produced their first true leaves. For more information on starting seeds, see page 917.

3. Check the list of flower germination periods on page 992 to see if your seeds germinate slowly.

4. Purchase seeds from a reputable nursery or seed company. Plant seeds packed for the current year.

5. Plant seeds at the proper depth. For a list of seed planting depths, see page 992.

6. Water seedbeds gently. Do not allow the water to puddle and run off. Use a watering can or hose nozzle that delivers a gentle spray.

7. Even though germination may be delayed, many of the seeds will probably sprout when the weather warms up. Next year, plant seeds later in the season, after the soil has warmed up. For a list of common flowers and their ideal germination temperatures and planting times, see page 992.

PROBLEM: Seedlings are sheared off and eaten, with only the stems emerging from the ground. Silvery trails wind around on the plants and soil nearby. Snails or slugs may be seen moving around or feeding on the plants, especially at night. Check for them by inspecting the garden after dark with a flashlight.

ANALYSIS: Snails and slugs
These pests are mollusks, and are related to clams, oysters, and other shellfish. They feed on a wide variety of garden plants. Like other mollusks, snails and slugs need to be moist all the time. For this reason, they avoid direct sun and dry places, and hide during the day in damp places, such as under flower pots or in thick groundcover. They emerge at night or on cloudy days to feed. Snails and slugs are similar in appearance, except that the snail has a hard shell into which it withdraws when disturbed. Slugs lay masses of white eggs encased in a slimy mass in protected places. Snails bury their eggs in the soil, also in a slimy mass. The young look like miniature versions of their parents.

SOLUTION: Scatter ORTHO Slug-Geta Snail & Slug Bait or ORTHO Bug-Geta Snail & Slug Pellets in bands around the areas you wish to protect. Also scatter the bait in areas where snails or slugs might be hiding, such as in dense groundcovers, weedy areas, compost piles, or pot storage areas. Before spreading the bait, wet down the treated areas to encourage snail and slug activity that night. Repeat the application every 2 weeks as long as snails and slugs are active.

SEEDLINGS DIE

SEEDLINGS DIE _____

Cutworm damage to petunia seedlings.

PROBLEM: Seedlings are chewed or cut off near the ground. Gray, brown, or black worms, 1½ to 2 inches long, may be found about 2 inches deep in the soil near the base of the damaged plants. The worms coil when disturbed.

ANALYSIS: Cutworms
Several species of cutworms attack plants in the vegetable garden. The most likely pests of seedlings planted early in the season are the surface-feeding cutworms. A single surface-feeding cutworm can sever the stems of many young plants in one night. Cutworms hide in the soil during the day, and feed only at night. Adult cutworms are dark, night-flying moths with bands or stripes on their forewings. In the South, cutworms may also attack fall-planted seedlings.

SOLUTION: Apply *diazinon* dust or granules around the base of undamaged plants when stem cutting is observed. Since cutworms are difficult to control, it may be necessary to repeat applications at weekly intervals. Before transplanting in the same area, apply a preventive treatment of *diazinon* and work it into the soil. Cultivate the soil thoroughly in late summer and fall to expose and destroy eggs, larvae, and pupae. Further reduce damage with "cutworm collars" around the stem of each plant. These collars can be made of stiff paper, aluminum foil, tin cans, or milk cartons. They should be at least 2 inches high and pressed firmly into the soil. For more information about cutworms, see page 875.

PROBLEMS OF INDIVIDUAL ANNUALS, PERENNIALS, AND BULBS

This section is arranged alphabetically by the botanical name of each plant. If you are not familiar with the botanical name of your plant, check the index on page 344.

ACHILLEA (YARROW) _____

Powdery mildew.

PROBLEM: Leaves and stems are partially or entirely covered with grayish white powdery patches. The patches occur primarily on the upper surfaces of the leaves. The leaves may turn yellow and die.

ANALYSIS: Powdery mildew
This common plant disease is caused by a fungus (*Erysiphe cichoracearum*) that thrives in both humid and dry weather. The powdery patches consist of fungal strands and spores. The spores are spread by the wind to healthy plants. The fungus saps plant nutrients, causing yellowing and sometimes death of the leaf. Under favorable conditions, powdery mildew can spread through a closely spaced planting in a matter of days or weeks.

SOLUTION: Spray with a fungicide containing *dinocap* to stop the spread of the disease. *Dinocap* protects the new healthy foliage, but will not eradicate the fungus on leaves that are already infected. Spray at regular intervals of 10 to 12 days, or as often as necessary to protect new growth. Use a spreader-sticker when spraying. (For information on spreader-stickers, see page 915.) Space plants far enough apart to allow good air circulation. Avoid watering in the late afternoon or evening. Clean up infected leaves and debris.

Achillea cultural information
Light: Full sun
Water: Allow to dry between waterings
Soil: Any kind
Fertilizer: Medium

AGERATUM (FLOSS FLOWER)

Gray mold.

Root and stem rot.

Corn earworms (⅛ life size).

PROBLEM: Brown spots and blotches appear on the leaves and possibly on the stems. As the disease progresses, a fuzzy brown or grayish mold forms on the infected tissue. Gray mold and spots may appear on the flower, especially during periods of cool, wet weather. The leaves and stems may be soft and rotted.

ANALYSIS: Gray mold
This widespread plant disease is caused by a fungus (*Botrytis* species). The fungus initially attacks foliage and flowers that are weak or dead, causing spotting and mold. The fuzzy mold that develops is composed of millions of microscopic spores. Once gray mold has become established on plant debris and weak or dying leaves and flowers, it can invade healthy plant tissue. Splashing water spreads the fungus, as can bits of infected plant debris that land on the leaves. Crowded plantings, rain, and overhead watering enhance the spread of the disease. Cool temperatures and high humidity favor gray mold growth. In warm winter areas where freezing is rare, gray mold can be a year-round problem.

SOLUTION: Spray infected plants once every 10 to 14 days with a fungicide containing *maneb* or *mancozeb*. Continue spraying as long as mold is visible. Clean up plant debris, and remove old flowers and dying or infected leaves and stems. Avoid wetting the foliage when watering.

Ageratum cultural information
Light: Sun
Water: While the soil is still moist
Soil: Rich, well drained
Fertilizer: Medium to heavy

PROBLEM: Wilting may start on the lower leaves and progress up the plant until all the leaves are wilted; or it may occur very rapidly. Lower leaves and stems often rot. When the plant is pulled out of the ground, the roots are found to be very dark and sometimes badly rotted.

ANALYSIS: Root and stem rot
This disease is caused by fungi (*Rhizoctonia solani* and *Pythium mamillatum*) that are present in most soils. *Rhizoctonia* is a problem all over the country; *Pythium* is more common in the West. These fungi can live for several years on organic matter in the soil. They thrive in moist, fertile conditions. *Pythium* prefers heavy, poorly aerated soils, while *Rhizoctonia* favors aerated, well-drained soils. The fungi initially attack the main stem at the soil line or the root system, stunting the plant and causing it to wilt. They then move into the stems and lower leaves, causing rot and eventual death. They also attack seedlings and cause damping-off. For information about damping-off, see page 858.

SOLUTION: If all the foliage is wilted, it is best to replace the plants. Try to save plants not so severely affected by letting the soil dry out between waterings. (For further information on this technique, see page 857.) This drying out process also helps prevent further spread of the disease to healthy plants. Plant in well-drained soil. For information about improving soil drainage, see page 901.

PROBLEM: Striped green, brown, or yellow caterpillars are chewing holes in leaves and buds. The caterpillars range in size from ¼ inch to 2 inches.

ANALYSIS: Corn earworm
(*Heliothis zea*)
This caterpillar is the larval stage of a night-flying moth. In addition to feeding on many different ornamental plants, the caterpillar is a major agricultural pest. It is considered to be one of the most destructive pests of corn in the United States. The moths survive the winter as pupae in the soil, emerging in the spring to lay their light yellow eggs singly on the undersides of leaves. The caterpillars hatch in 2 to 8 days and feed for several weeks on leaves and buds, then crawl into the soil and pupate. One to three weeks later the new adults emerge to begin the cycle again, laying eggs in the evenings and on warm, overcast days. In cooler areas of the country, the caterpillars are present from early spring to the first frost. In warmer areas, the feeding caterpillars are present year-round.

SOLUTION: Control corn earworms with ORTHO Orthene Systemic Insect Control or ORTHO Liquid Sevin, applied when the caterpillars first appear. Repeat every 10 to 14 days as needed. Deep cultivating in the fall and winter will help destroy some of the overwintering pupae.

AGERATUM (FLOSS FLOWER)

ALCEA (HOLLYHOCK)

Whiteflies (half life size).

Rust.

Spider mites and webbing.

PROBLEM: Tiny, winged insects $1/12$ inch long are found mainly on the lower surfaces of leaves. The insects are covered with white, waxy powder. When the plant is touched, insects flutter rapidly around it. Leaves may be mottled and yellowing.

ANALYSIS: Greenhouse whitefly
(*Trialeurodes vaporariorum*)
Greenhouse whitefly is a common insect pest of many garden and greenhouse plants. The 4-winged adult lays eggs on the undersides of leaves. The larvae are the size of a pinhead and look quite different from the adult. The larvae are flat, oval-shaped, and semitransparent, with white waxy filaments radiating from the body. They remain attached to the underside of a leaf for about a month before changing to the adult form. Both the larval and adult forms suck sap from the leaves. The larvae are more damaging because they feed more heavily. In warm winter areas, the insect can be active year-round, with eggs, larvae, and adults present at the same time. The whitefly is unable to live through freezing winters. Spring reinfestations in freezing winter areas come from migrating whiteflies and infested greenhouse-grown plants placed in the garden.

SOLUTION: Control whiteflies by spraying with ORTHO Orthene Systemic Insect Control or ORTHO Isotox Insect Killer every 7 to 10 days as necessary, being careful to cover both the upper and lower surfaces of the leaves.

PROBLEM: Yellow or orange spots appear on the upper surfaces of the leaves in the early spring. Reddish brown pustules develop on the undersides of the leaves and possibly on the stems. These pustules may turn dark brown as the growing season progresses. Severely infected leaves shrivel, turn gray or tan, and hang down along the stem.

ANALYSIS: Rust
This fungus (*Puccinia malvacearum*) causes the most serious and widespread disease of hollyhock. The fungus spends the winter as spores on living plant tissue and plant debris. Infection starts in the early spring as soon as conditions are favorable for plant growth. The spores are spread to healthy plants by splashing water and air currents. A number of weeds known as cheeseweeds or mallows (*Malva* species) are frequently infected with rust, and are a source of spores. Rust is favored by wet conditions.

SOLUTION: Spray with a fungicide containing *maneb* or *zineb* in the spring as soon as the first signs of infection are noticed. Spray the foliage thoroughly, being sure to cover both the upper and lower surfaces of the leaves. These fungicides protect the new, healthy foliage, but do not eradicate the fungus on diseased leaves. Spray once every 7 to 10 days, or as often as necessary to protect new growth until the end of the growing season. Remove and destroy all infected foliage in the fall when the plant has stopped growing, and again in early spring just as the new foliage starts to grow. Pick off and destroy infected plant parts during the growing season. Remove and destroy any nearby cheeseweed plants that may harbor rust.

PROBLEM: Leaves are stippled, yellowing, and dirty. Leaves may dry out and drop. There may be webbing over flower buds, between leaves, or on the lower surfaces of the leaves. To determine if the plant is infested with mites, hold a sheet of white paper underneath an affected leaf and tap the leaf sharply. Minute green, red, or yellow specks the size of pepper grains will drop to the paper and begin to crawl around. These pest are easily seen against the white background.

ANALYSIS: Two-spotted spider mite
(*Tetranychus urticae*)
These mites, related to spiders, are major pests of many garden and greenhouse plants. They cause damage by sucking sap from the underside of the leaves. As a result the green leaf pigment disappears, producing the stippled appearance. Mites are active throughout the growing season, but are favored by hot, dry weather (70°F and up). By midsummer, they build up to tremendous numbers.

SOLUTION: Spray with a pesticide containing *dicofol* when damage is first noticed. Spray the foliage thoroughly, covering both the upper and lower surfaces of the leaves. Repeat the spraying 3 more times at 7 day intervals. Remove severely infested leaves.

Alcea cultural information
Light: Full sun
Water: Do not allow to dry out
Soil: Rich, loamy
Fertilizer: Heavy

ALLIUM (ORNAMENTAL ONION) ——— ANEMONE (WINDFLOWER) ———

Onion thrips (life size).

Tuber rot.

Leaf spot.

PROBLEM: Silvery white streaks appear on the leaves, and the leaf tips may be brown and distorted. The leaves may eventually wither and die. If the affected leaves are peeled away from the stem, tiny (1/25 inch) insects resembling brown or straw-colored wood slivers can be seen moving around.

ANALYSIS: Thrips
Several species of this common insect pest attack alliums, including the onion thrips (*Thrips tabaci*). Thrips are usually found in the protected area between the base of the leaves and the stem, where they feed by rasping the soft plant tissue, then sucking the released sap. In cold climates, thrips feed and reproduce from spring until fall. With the onset of freezing weather, they find sheltered areas such as grass clumps and hibernate through the winter. In warm winter climates, thrips feed and reproduce all year. These pests reach their population peak in late spring to midsummer. They are especially troublesome during prolonged dry spells.

SOLUTION: Thrips can be kept under control, although not eliminated entirely. Spray plants with an insecticide containing *acephate* or *carbaryl* 2 or 3 times at weekly intervals. Repeat the spray if reinfestation occurs. Pick off and destroy old infested leaves and flowers.

Allium cultural information
Light: Sun
Water: While soil is still moist
Soil: Well drained
Fertilizer: Light

PROBLEM: Flowers fail to develop. Leaves decay at the base, yellow, wilt, and collapse, and the plant dies. The base of the plant and the lower stems are covered with white matted strands that eventually develop small brown pellets the size of pinheads. The tubers and roots are partially or entirely rotted. The diseased tubers may develop a soft rot. Tubers may fail to produce foliage at all in the spring.

ANALYSIS: Tuber rot
This disease, also known as *southern blight*, is caused by a fungus (*Sclerotium rolfsii*) that lives in the soil. It is widespread and attacks many different plants. Tuber rot may infect and decay tubers in the ground that have not yet produced foliage. It generally attacks plant stems at the soil level and then moves down into the tuber and roots, causing rot and plant death. The fungus can grow over the soil to attack adjacent plants. Tuber rot is spread by diseased tubers and transplants, seeds, moving water, infested soil, and contaminated tools. This fungus can persist in the soil for many years. It is favored by warm (70°F and up), moist conditions.

SOLUTION: Chemical controls are not effective on diseased plants. Remove and destroy all infected plants and surrounding soil for 6 inches beyond the diseased area. Drench the area where the infected plants were growing with a fungicide containing *PCNB*. To help prevent infection next year, spread a *PCNB* fungicide onto uninfested soil and dig it in to a depth of 6 inches before planting healthy tubers.

PROBLEM: Spots and blotches appear on the leaves. The spots may be yellow, red, tan, gray, or brown. They range in size from barely visible to 1/4 inch in diameter. Several spots may join to form blotches. Leaves may be yellow and dying. Leaf spotting is most severe in warm, humid weather. In some cases, a fine gray mold covers the infected leaf tissue in damp conditions.

ANALYSIS: Leaf spot
Several different fungi cause leaf spots. Some of these fungi may eventually kill the plant, or weaken it so that it becomes susceptible to attack by other organisms. Others merely cause spotting that is unsightly but not harmful. These fungi are spread by splashing water, wind, insects, and tools. They generally survive the winter in diseased plant debris. Some of the leaf spot organisms affect a large number of plants. Most of these fungi do their greatest damage during mild weather (50° to 85°F).

SOLUTION: Spray with a fungicide containing *basic copper sulfate* at intervals of 3 to 10 days. Because leaf spots are favored by warm, humid conditions, it is important to spray frequently during these periods. *Basic copper sulfate* protects the new healthy foliage but will not eradicate the fungus on leaves that are already infected. Pick off infected leaves, and clean up plant debris.

Anemone cultural information
Light: Sun to partial shade
Water: Do not allow to dry out
Soil: Rich, well drained
Fertilizer: Medium

ANEMONE (WINDFLOWER) ———— ANTIRRHINUM (SNAPDRAGON) ————

Aphids (life size).

PROBLEM: Flowers are streaked and malformed. Young leaves are curled and distorted. A shiny, sticky substance may coat the leaves. Tiny (⅛ inch) green, soft-bodied insects cluster on the buds, leaves, and stems. Ants may be present.

ANALYSIS: Aphids
Aphids do little damage in small numbers. However, they are extremely prolific and populations can rapidly build up to damaging numbers during the growing season. Damage occurs when the aphid sucks the juices from the anemone leaves and flower buds. The aphid is unable to digest fully all the sugar in the plant sap, and excretes the excess in a fluid called honeydew, which often drops onto the leaves below. Ants feed on this sticky substance, and are often present where there is an aphid infestation.

SOLUTION: Spray with ORTHO Liquid Sevin as soon as the insects appear. Repeat the spray if the plant becomes reinfested.

ANTIRRHINUM ————

ADAPTATION: Throughout the United States.

FLOWERING TIME: Fall through late spring in zones 9 and 10. Spring through midsummer in colder areas. To determine your zone, see the map on page 1004.

LIGHT: Full sun.

PLANTING TIME: Plant in the fall in zones 9 and 10. In colder areas, plant in the spring when all danger of frost is past. To determine your zone, see the map on page 1004.

SOIL: Any good garden soil. pH 6.0 to 8.0

FERTILIZER: Fertilize with ORTHO Rose & Flower Food 8-12-4 or ORTHO General Purpose Plant Food 8-8-8 according to label directions.

WATER:
 How much: Apply enough water to wet the soil to 12 inches deep.
 Containers: Apply enough water so that 10 percent of the water drains from the bottom of the container.
 How often: Water when the soil one inch below the surface is just barely moist.

HANDLING: For bushy plants, pinch off growing tips when the plants have 4 to 6 sets of leaves. Cut back the fading flower spikes to stimulate continued bloom.

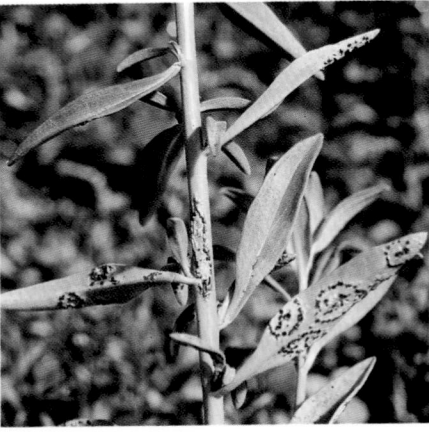

Rust.

PROBLEM: Pale yellow spots appear on the upper surfaces of the leaves. Reddish brown pustules of spores develop on the undersides of the leaves. Often these pustules form concentric circles. There may be spores on the stems. Severely infected leaves dry up. The plant is stunted in growth, and may die prematurely.

ANALYSIS: Rust
This common disease of snapdragons is caused by a fungus (*Puccinia antirrhini*). Fungal spores are spread by wind and splashing water. Rust can survive only on living plant tissue and as spores on seed. It does not persist on dead plant parts. Plants must be wet for 6 to 8 hours before the fungus can infect the leaf surface. The disease is favored by moist conditions, cool nights (50° to 55°F), and warm days (70° to 75°F). Temperatures in the 90°F range and higher kill the spores.

SOLUTION: Spray infected plants with a fungicide containing *maneb* or *zineb* at intervals of 5 to 18 days. Avoid wetting the foliage. Water in the morning rather than the late afternoon or evening to give foliage a chance to dry out. Pick off and destroy infected plant parts during the growing season. Remove all snapdragon plants at the end of the growing season to prevent infected plants from reinfecting new plantings. Space plants far enough apart to allow good air circulation.

Root and stem rot.

Spider mites and their damage.

Leafminer damage.

PROBLEM: The plant may suddenly wilt and die, or it may die slowly from the top down. The leaves turn yellow, and overall growth is stunted. There may be lesions on the stems. The roots are decayed.

ANALYSIS: Root and stem rot
This disease is caused by a number of different fungi that live in the soil. They thrive in waterlogged, heavy soils. The fungi can attack the plant stems and roots directly or enter them through wounds. Infection causes the stems and roots to decay, resulting in wilting, yellowing leaves, and plant death. These fungi are generally spread by infested soil and transplants, contaminated equipment, and moving water. Many of these organisms also cause *damping-off* of seedlings (see page 858).

SOLUTION: Let the soil dry out between irrigations. (For more information on this technique, see page 857.) Improve soil drainage. For more information about soil drainage, see page 901. Before planting next year, apply *PCNB* to the soil and work it in to a depth of 6 inches.

PROBLEM: Leaves are stippled, yellowing, and dirty. Leaves may dry out and drop. There may be webbing over flower buds, between leaves, or on the lower surfaces of leaves. To determine if the plant is infested with mites, hold a sheet of white paper underneath an affected plant and tap the stalk sharply. Minute green, red, or yellow specks the size of pepper grains will drop to the paper and begin to crawl around. These pests are easily seen against the white background.

ANALYSIS: Two-spotted spider mite
(*Tetranychus urticae*)
These mites, related to spiders, are major pests of many garden and greenhouse plants. They cause damage by sucking sap from the underside of the leaves. As a result, the green leaf pigment disappears, producing the stippled appearance. Mites are active throughout the growing season, but are favored by hot, dry weather (70°F and up). By midsummer, they can build up to tremendous numbers.

SOLUTION: Spray with ORTHO Isotox Insect Killer when damage is first noticed. Spray the foliage thoroughly, covering both the upper and lower surfaces of the leaves.

PROBLEM: White or light green winding trails and blotches appear in the leaves. Some of the trails are filled with black matter. The infested leaves may turn white and die.

ANALYSIS: Columbine leafminer
(*Phytomyza* species)
This insect belongs to the family of leaf-mining flies. The pale brown adult fly lays its eggs on the undersides of leaves. The eggs hatch and the larvae that emerge penetrate the leaf and live between the upper and lower surfaces of the leaf. They feed on the inner leaf tissue, creating winding trails. Their dark excrement may dot or partially fill sections of the trails. The larvae may be continually present from spring until fall.

SOLUTION: Spray with an insecticide containing *malathion* and a spreader-sticker. (For information on spreader-stickers, see page 915.) Respray at the first sign of further infestation. Pick off and destroy infected leaves. Remove and destroy all plant remains in the fall.

AQUILEGIA (COLUMBINE)

Aphids.

PROBLEM: Tiny (⅛ inch) green, cream-colored, or brown soft-bodied insects cluster on the buds, leaves, and stems. Young leaves are curled and distorted. There may be a shiny, sticky substance coating the leaves. Ants may be present.

ANALYSIS: Aphids
Aphids do little damage in small numbers. However, they are extremely prolific and populations can rapidly build up to damaging numbers during the growing season. Damage occurs when the aphid sucks the juices from the columbine leaves and flower buds. The aphid is unable to digest fully all the sugar in the plant sap and excretes the excess in a fluid called honeydew. The honeydew often drops onto the leaves below. Ants feed on this sticky material and are often present where there is an aphid infestation.

SOLUTION: Spray with ORTHO Liquid Sevin or an insecticide containing *malathion* as soon as the insects appear. Repeat the spray if the plant is reinfested. Use a spreader-sticker when spraying. (For information on spreader-stickers, see page 915.)

Aquilegia cultural information
Light: Shade, filtered sun
Water: While the soil is still moist
Soil: Moist, well drained
Fertilizer: Medium

Crown rot.

PROBLEM: Leaves and stems are wilting. The diseased branches slowly dry out and finally die. White fungal strands may grow on the stems of severely infected plants. When sliced open, an infected stem may be filled with white fungal threads and small black fungal pellets. The soil around the plant may be filled with white fungal strands and brown spherical pellets the size of a pinhead.

ANALYSIS: Crown rot or wilt
This disease is caused by a fungus (*Sclerotinia sclerotiorum*) that lives in the soil. The fungus survives the winter as fungal strands and dormant pellets in plant debris, or in the soil. It is favored by high humidity and moist soils, and attacks plant roots. *Sclerotinia* produces wind-blown spores in the spring and summer that may also infect the foliage. As the fungus spreads in the plant, wilting and eventual death occur. *Sclerotinia* can persist in the soil for 3 years or more, and is spread by infested soil and transplants.

SOLUTION: Let the soil dry out between waterings. (For more information on this technique, see page 857.) Cultivate the soil around the crown of the plant to help it dry out more quickly. Remove and destroy diseased plants and the soil immediately around them. Before planting columbine in an area that is known to be infested, broadcast a fungicide containing *PCNB* onto the soil and dig it in to a depth of 6 inches.

ASTER

Leaf spot.

PROBLEM: Spots and blotches appear on the leaves. The spots may be yellow, red, tan, gray, brown, or black. They range in size from barely visible to ¼ inch in diameter. Several spots may join to form blotches. Leaves may be yellowing and dying. Leaf spotting is most severe in warm, humid weather.

ANALYSIS: Leaf spot
Asters are susceptible to several fungi that cause leaf spots. Some of these fungi may eventually kill the plant, or weaken it so that it becomes susceptible to attack by other organisms. Others merely cause spotting that is unsightly but not harmful. These fungi are spread by splashing water, wind, insects, tools, and infected seed. They generally survive the winter in diseased plant debris. Most of these fungi do their greatest damage during mild weather (50° to 85°F). Infection is favored by moist conditions.

SOLUTION: Spray at 7 to 10 day intervals with a fungicide containing *zineb* or *mancozeb*. Because leaf spots are favored by warm, humid conditions, it is important to spray frequently during these periods. These fungicides protect the new healthy foliage but will not eradicate the fungus on leaves that are already infected. Clean up infected leaves and debris.

ASTILBE

Powdery mildew.

PROBLEM: Leaves and stems are partially or entirely covered with grayish white powdery patches. The patches occur primarily on the upper surfaces of leaves. The leaves may be yellowing and dying.

ANALYSIS: Powdery mildew
This common plant disease is caused by a fungus (*Erysiphe cichoracearum*) that thrives in both humid and dry weather. The powdery patches consist of fungal strands and spores. The spores are spread by the wind to healthy plants. The fungus saps the plant nutrients, causing yellowing and sometimes death of the leaf. Since this mildew attacks many different kinds of plants, the fungus from a diseased plant may infect other types of plants in the garden. (See page 995 for a list of susceptible plants.) Under favorable conditions, powdery mildew can spread through a closely spaced planting in a matter of days or weeks.

SOLUTION: Spray with fungicide containing *phaltan* to stop the spread of the disease. This fungicide protects the new healthy foliage, but will not eradicate the fungus on leaves that are already infected. Spray at regular intervals of 10 to 12 days, or as often as necessary to protect new growth. Space plants far enough apart to allow good air circulation. Clean up infected leaves and debris.

BEGONIA

Aphid (10 times life size).

PROBLEM: Young leaves are curled, distorted, and yellowing. The flowers may be malformed. There may be a sticky or shiny substance coating the leaves. Tiny (1/8 inch), pale green to black, soft-bodied insects are clustered on the leaves and stems. Ants may be present.

ANALYSIS: Aphids
Aphids do little damage in small numbers. However, they are extremely prolific and populations can rapidly build up to damaging numbers during the growing season. Damage occurs when the aphid sucks the juices from the leaves and flower buds. The aphid is unable to digest fully all the sugar in the plant sap and excretes the excess in a fluid called honeydew. The honeydew often drops onto the leaves below. Ants feed on this sticky substance, and are often present where there is an aphid infestation.

SOLUTION: Spray with ORTHO Liquid Sevin as soon as the insects appear. Repeat the spray if the plant is reinfested.

BEGONIA

ADAPTATION: Throughout the United States.

FLOWERING TIME:
Tuberous: Early to late summer.
Fibrous: Spring to late fall.

LIGHT:
Tuberous: Filtered light to full shade.
Fibrous: Full shade to half-day sun. Dark-colored plants can tolerate full-day sun.

PLANTING TIME:
Tuberous: Start indoors in the spring in zones 1 through 9. To determine your zone, see the map on page 1004. You may start them outdoors in zone 10.
Fibrous: Start all year round in zones 9 and 10. Start in spring through summer in zones 2 through 8.

SOIL: Well drained, rich in organic matter. pH 6.0 to 7.0

FERTILIZER:
Tuberous: Fertilize with ORTHO Rose & Flower Food 8–12–4 every 2 weeks at half the recommended rate. Stop fertilizing about 6 weeks before the first fall frost.
Fibrous: Fertilize with ORTHO Rose & Flower Food 8–12–4 or ORTHO General Purpose Plant Food 8–8–8.

WATER:
How much: Apply enough water to wet the soil 6 to 8 inches deep.
Containers: Apply enough water so that 10 percent of the water drains from the bottom of the container.
How often: Water when the soil 1 inch below the surface is moist but not wet.

BEGONIA

Gray mold.

Leaf spot.

Bacterial leaf spot.

PROBLEM: Brown spots and blotches appear on the leaves and possibly on the stems. As the disease progresses, a fuzzy brown or grayish mold forms on the infected tissue. Gray mold and spots often appear on the flowers, especially during periods of cool, wet weather. The leaves and stems may be soft and rotted.

ANALYSIS: Gray mold
This widespread plant disease is caused by a fungus (*Botrytis cinerea*) that is found on most dead plant tissue. The fungus initially attacks foliage and flowers that are weak or dead, causing spotting and mold. The fuzzy mold that develops is composed of millions of microscopic dark spores. Once gray mold has become established on plant debris and weak or dying leaves and flowers, it can invade healthy plant tissue. Splashing water spreads the fungus, as can bits of infected plant debris that land on the leaves. Cool temperatures and high humidity favor the growth of gray mold. Crowded plantings, rain, and overhead watering also enhance the spread of the disease. Infection is a greater problem in spring and fall when temperatures are lower. In warm winter areas where freezing is rare, gray mold can be a year-round problem.

SOLUTION: Control gray mold with a fungicide containing *benomyl*. Spray every 1 to 2 weeks as long as the mold is visible. Clean up plant debris, and remove dying or infected leaves, stems, and flowers. Provide enough space between plants to allow good air circulation. Try to avoid wetting the foliage when watering.

PROBLEM: Spots and blotches appear on the leaves. The spots may be yellow, red, tan, gray, or brown. They range in size from barely visible to ¼ inch in diameter. Several spots may join together to form blotches. Leaves may be yellowing and dying. Leaf spotting is most severe in warm, humid weather.

ANALYSIS: Fungal leaf spot
Begonias are susceptible to several fungi that cause leaf spots. Some of these fungi may eventually kill the plant, or weaken it so that it becomes susceptible to attack by other organisms. Others merely cause spotting that is unsightly but not harmful. These fungi are spread by splashing water, wind, insects, tools, and infected transplants and seed. They survive the winter in diseased plant debris. Some of the leaf spot organisms affect a large number of plants. Most of these fungi do their greatest damage during mild weather (50° to 85°F). Infection is favored by moist conditions.

SOLUTION: Spray with a fungicide containing *zineb* or *benomyl* at intervals of 7 to 10 days. Because leaf spots are favored by warm, humid conditions, it is important to spray frequently during these periods. These fungicides protect the new healthy foliage. In addition, *benomyl* will eradicate the fungus on leaves that are already infected. Clean up infected leaves and debris.

PROBLEM: Small, blister-like spots appear on the leaves. The spots are translucent and turn brown with yellow, translucent margins. The spots enlarge and run together, giving the leaf a blotched appearance. Sometimes a slimy substance oozes from the infected areas, turning light brown as it dries. Infected leaves often die prematurely. If the stems become infected, the entire plant may collapse.

ANALYSIS: Bacterial leaf spot
This disease is caused by bacteria (*Xanthomonas begoniae*) that infect tuberous and fibrous begonias. The slimy substance that oozes from infected lesions is composed of bacterial cells, which can live for 3 months or more. The bacteria are spread by splashing water, contaminated equipment, and infected transplants. Infection is favored by high humidity. Localized leaf infection causes early leaf drop. If the plant's water-conducting tissue is infected, the whole plant will soften and collapse.

SOLUTION: Spray with *basic copper sulfate* or *streptomycin* at intervals of 7 to 10 days to prevent the spread of the disease. Infected tissue will not recover, but new growth and healthy leaves will be protected. Cut off and discard infected plant parts. After working with diseased plants, disinfect tools by dipping them in rubbing alcohol. Remove and destroy severely infected plants and the soil immediately surrounding them. Avoid wetting or splashing the leaves. Space plants far enough apart to allow good air circulation.

Powdery mildew.

PROBLEM: The leaves and stems are covered with grayish white powdery spots and patches that occur primarily on the upper surfaces of the leaves. Older spots and patches often turn brown. The leaves may be yellow and dying.

ANALYSIS: Powdery mildew
This common plant disease is caused by either of two fungi (*Erysiphe cichoracearum* or *Oidium begoniae*) that thrive in both humid and dry weather. The powdery patches consist of fungal strands and spores. The spores are spread by the wind to healthy plants. The fungi sap plant nutrients, causing yellowing and sometimes death of the leaf. A severe infection may kill the plant. Since these powdery mildews attack many different kinds of plants, the fungus from a diseased plant may infect other types of plants in the garden. (See page 995 for a list of powdery mildews and the plants they attack.) Under favorable conditions, powdery mildew can spread through a closely spaced planting in a matter of days or weeks.

SOLUTION: Spray ORTHO Orthocide Garden Fungicide or ORTHO Funginex Rose Disease Control, which protect the new, healthy leaves by preventing powdery mildew spores from entering them. Space plants far enough apart to allow good air circulation. Clean up infected leaves and debris.

Root and stem rot on tuberous begonia.

PROBLEM: Growth slows or stops. The roots are dark and rotted. The plant may wilt, topple over, and die. There may be discolored, water-soaked spots on the stems at the soil level. Leaves may be yellow, and the lower leaves and stems may rot. Cobwebby strands may appear on lower portions of the stems in wet weather.

ANALYSIS: Root and stem rot
This disease is caused by a number of different fungi that persist indefinitely in the soil. They thrive in waterlogged, heavy soils. Some of these fungi primarily attack the plant stems at the soil level, while others attack the roots. Infection causes the roots and stems to decay, resulting in wilting, yellowing leaves, and the death of the plant. These fungi are generally spread by infested soil and transplants, contaminated equipment, and moving water. Many of these organisms also cause damping-off of seedlings. For more information about damping-off, see page 858.

SOLUTION: Allow the soil around the plants to dry out. For more information on this technique, see page 857. Remove and discard severely infected plants. Avoid future root rot problems by planting in well-drained soil. For information on improving soil drainage, see page 901. For more information on root and stem rot, see page 856.

Leaf nematode damage.

PROBLEM: Angular brown leaf blotches develop on the lower leaves first, then on the upper leaves. The blotches enlarge and eventually the leaves curl up, wither, and drop off. The plant is stunted, and new leaf buds may not develop.

ANALYSIS: Leaf nematode
(*Aphelenchoides olesistus*)
This plant condition is caused by nematodes — microscopic worms that live and feed inside the leaf tissue. Infestation occurs when the foliage is wet. Nematodes migrate in the thin film of water on the outside of the leaf to infect healthy tissue, and are spread from plant to plant by splashing water. They are most severe in warm, humid areas. Leaf nematodes can survive for 3 or more years in plant debris and in the soil.

SOLUTION: Remove and destroy severely infested plants. Pick off and destroy all the infested leaves and the next two leaves directly above them. As much as possible, avoid wetting the foliage. Inspect new plants carefully to be sure they are not diseased, and do not plant in infested soil. Spray weekly with an insecticide containing *malathion* or *dimethoate* using a spreader-sticker, until the symptoms stop spreading. For information on spreader-stickers, see page 915.

369

BEGONIA

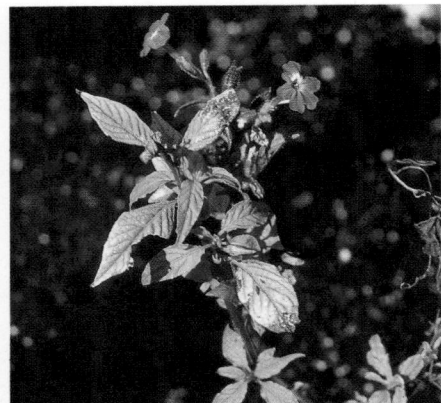

Mealybugs (half life size).

PROBLEM: Oval, white insects up to ¼ inch long cluster in white cottony masses on stems and leaves. Leaves may be deformed and withered. The infested leaves are often shiny and sticky.

ANALYSIS: Mealybugs
Several species of this common insect feed on begonias. Mealybugs damage plants by sucking sap, causing leaf distortion and death. The adult female mealybug may produce live young, or may deposit her eggs in white, fluffy masses of wax. The immature mealybugs, called *nymphs*, are very active and crawl all over the plant. Soon after the nymphs begin to feed, they exude filaments of white wax that cover their bodies, giving them a cottony appearance. As they mature, their mobility decreases. Mealybugs cannot fully digest all the sugar in the sap and excrete the excess in a fluid called honeydew. Mealybugs can be spread when they are brushed onto uninfested plants, or when young, active nymphs crawl to nearby plants. They may also be spread by the wind, which can blow egg masses and nymphs from plant to plant. Mealybug eggs and some adults can survive through the winter in warm climates. Spring reinfestations in colder areas come from infested new plants placed in the garden.

SOLUTION: Spray infested plants with an insecticide containing *malathion* or *carbaryl* and a spreader-sticker (see page 915). Spray at intervals of 7 to 10 days until the mealybugs are gone. Gently hose down plants to wash off honeydew. Remove and destroy severely infested leaves and plants.

BROWALLIA

Whitefly damage.

PROBLEM: Tiny, winged insects ¹⁄₁₂ inch long are feeding on the undersides of the leaves. The insects are covered with white, waxy powder. When the plant is touched, insects flutter rapidly around it. Leaves may be mottled and yellowing. In warm winter areas, black mold may cover the leaves.

ANALYSIS: Greenhouse whitefly
(*Trialeurodes vaporariorum*)
This insect is a common pest of many garden and greenhouse plants. The four-winged adult lays eggs on the undersides of leaves. The larvae are the size of a pinhead, flat, oval-shaped, and semi-transparent, with white waxy filaments radiating from the body. They feed for about a month before changing to the adult form. Both the larval and adult forms suck sap from the leaves. The larvae are more damaging because they feed more heavily. Adults and larvae cannot fully digest all the sugar in the plant sap and excrete the excess in a fluid called honeydew. A black sooty mold fungus may develop on the honeydew. In warm winter areas the insect can be active year-round, with eggs, larvae, and adults present at the same time. The whitefly is unable to live through freezing winters. Spring reinfestations in freezing winter areas come from migrating whiteflies and from infested greenhouse-grown plants placed in the garden.

SOLUTION: Control whiteflies by spraying with an insecticide containing *malathion* every 7 to 10 days as necessary. Spray the foliage thoroughly, being sure to cover both the upper and lower surfaces of the leaves.

CALENDULA

CALENDULA

ADAPTATION: Throughout the United States.

FLOWERING TIME: Fall through late spring in zones 9 and 10. Spring through midsummer in colder areas. To determine your zone, see the map on page 1004.

LIGHT: Full sun.

PLANTING TIME: In zones 3 through 8, plant in the spring when all danger of frost is past. Calendulas can also be planted in the fall in zones 9 and 10.

SOIL: Any good well-drained garden soil. pH 6.0 to 8.0

FERTILIZER: Fertilize with ORTHO Rose & Flower Food 8–12–4 or ORTHO General Purpose Plant Food 8–8–8 according to label directions.

WATER:
How much: Apply enough water to plants in the ground to wet the soil 6 to 8 inches deep.
Containers: Apply enough water so that 10 percent of the water drains from the bottom of the container.
How often: Water when the soil 1 inch below the surface is just barely moist.

HANDLING: Pinch off fading flowers to encourage continued bloom. Calendulas reseed themselves readily.

Powdery mildew.

Leaf spot.

Cabbage loopers (⅓ life size).

PROBLEM: Stems and the upper surface of leaves are covered with grayish white powdery spots and patches. Older spots and patches may turn brown. Severely infected plants wither and die.

ANALYSIS: Powdery mildew
This common plant disease is caused by a fungus (*Erysiphe cichoracearum*) that thrives in both humid and dry weather. The powdery patches consist of fungal strands and spores. The spores are spread by the wind to healthy plants. The fungus saps plant nutrients, causing yellowing and sometimes death of the leaf. A severe infection may kill the plant. Since some powdery mildews attack many different kinds of plants, the fungus from a diseased plant may infect other types of plants in the garden. (For a list of susceptible plants, see page 995.) Under favorable conditions, powdery mildew can spread through a closely spaced planting in a matter of days or weeks.

SOLUTION: Spray with ORTHO Funginex Rose Disease Control as soon as the disease is noticed and at intervals of 7 to 10 days thereafter. Pick off yellowed, withered leaves. Space plants far enough apart to allow good air circulation. Clean up infected leaves and debris.

PROBLEM: Small reddish or yellowish spots on the leaves may run together to form blotches. The infected leaf tissue turns ashy gray and has a dry, papery texture. Leaves may die and fall off. Leaf spotting is most severe in warm, humid weather. Fine gray mold may cover infected leaf tissue in damp conditions.

ANALYSIS: Leaf spot
This disease of calendula is primarily caused by the fungus *Cercospora calendulae*, although several other leaf spotting fungi occasionally attack calendula. Some of these fungi may eventually kill the plant, or weaken it so that it becomes susceptible to attack by other organisms. Others merely cause spotting that is unsightly but not harmful. These fungi are spread by splashing water, wind, insects, and tools. Leaf spot organisms are favored by moist conditions and high temperatures. They are most common during the summer months and in warm climates. The fungus survives the winter in or on seeds and in plant debris.

SOLUTION: Spray with a fungicide containing *maneb* at intervals of 7 to 10 days. Because leaf spots are favored by warm, humid conditions, it is important to spray frequently during these periods. *Maneb* protects the new, healthy foliage but will not eradicate the fungus on leaves that are already infected. Remove and destroy plant debris in the fall to help prevent reinfection next spring.

PROBLEM: Foliage and flower buds are chewed. Leaves have ragged edges and irregular or round holes. Green caterpillars up to 1½ inches long with white stripes feed on the leaves.

ANALYSIS: Cabbage looper
(*Trichoplusia ni*)
These destructive caterpillars feed on many garden ornamentals and vegetables. With the warm weather of spring, the brownish adult moth lays its tiny, pale green eggs at night on the upper surfaces of leaves. The eggs hatch into active green larvae, which feed extensively on buds and foliage for 2 to 4 weeks. Looper damage can occur from early spring through late fall. The caterpillars spend the winter as pupae attached to plant leaves.

SOLUTION: Spray with ORTHO Isotox Insect Killer when the caterpillars first appear. Repeat 10 to 14 days later if reinfestation occurs. In the fall, remove plant debris and weeds that may harbor pupae. *Bacillus thuringiensis*, a biological control, is effective when sprayed on young loopers.

CALLISTEPHUS (CHINA ASTER)

CALLISTEPHUS

ADAPTATION: Throughout the United States.

FLOWERING TIME: Summer to fall.

LIGHT: Full sun.

PLANTING TIME: Spring, after all danger of frost is past.

SOIL: Any good well-drained garden soil.

FERTILIZER: Fertilize with ORTHO Rose & Flower Food 8–12–4 or ORTHO General Purpose Plant Food 8–8–8 according to label directions.

WATER:
How much: Apply enough water to wet the soil 8 to 10 inches deep.
Containers: Apply enough water so that 10 percent of the water drains from the bottom of the container.
How often: Water when the soil 1 inch below the surface is just barely moist.

Rust.

PROBLEM: Orange-red pustules appear on the undersides of the leaves. Severely infected leaves turn yellow and wither.

ANALYSIS: Rust
This plant disease is caused by a fungus (*Coleosporium solidaginis*) that infects china asters and several flowers in the daisy family. The fungus, which may spend part of its life cycle on pine trees, infects asters in the spring. Rust spores are spread from plant to plant by wind and splashing water. The foliage must be wet for at least 6 hours before the fungus can infect the leaf surfaces. Rust can survive only on living plant tissue or as spores on seed. It does not remain infectious on dead plant parts or in the soil. The disease is favored by moist conditions, cool nights, and warm days.

SOLUTION: Spray infected plants thoroughly with ORTHO Funginex Rose Disease Control or ORTHO Orthenex Insect & Disease Control. Pick off severely infected and dying leaves. Water in the morning rather than the late afternoon or evening to allow wet foliage to dry out more quickly. Remove and destroy all infected plants in the fall to prevent them from surviving the winter and reinfecting new plantings.

Fusarium wilt.

PROBLEM: The lower leaves turn yellow, then wilt and die; or all of the foliage may turn yellow and then wither. Older plants may be stunted. Yellowing and wilting often affect only one side of the plant. The flower heads droop. Dark brown areas may appear on the infected stem. When the stem is sliced open near the base of the plant, dark streaks and discolorations are seen on the inner stem tissue. The root system may be partially or entirely decayed. There may be a pink spore mass on the main stem at or below the soil line.

ANALYSIS: Wilt disease
This disease affects many ornamental plants. In *Callistephus* it is caused by either of two soil-inhabiting fungi (*Verticillium albo-atrum* and *Fusarium oxysporum* f. *callistephi*) that live on plant debris or in the soil. The disease is spread by contaminated seeds, plants, soil, and equipment. The fungus enters the plant through the roots and spreads up into the stems through the water-conducting vessels. The vessels become discolored and plugged. This plugging cuts off the flow of water to the leaves, which results in leaf yellowing, wilting, and death.

SOLUTION: No chemical control is available. It is best to destroy infected plants. The fungi can be removed from the soil only by fumigation techniques. (For more information about soil fumigation, see page 919.) However, the best solution is usually to use plants that are resistant to wilt diseases. For a list of wilt-resistant plants, see pages 994 and 995.

CAMPANULA (BELLFLOWER)

Aster yellows.

PROBLEM: The leaf veins pale and may lose all their color. Part or all of the foliage yellows. The flowers are distorted and may turn green. The plant may grow many thin stems bearing pale, spindly leaves. The plant is usually dwarfed.

ANALYSIS: Aster yellows
This plant disease is caused by mycoplasmas, microscopic organisms similar to bacteria. The mycoplasmas are transmitted from plant to plant by leafhoppers. (For further information about leafhoppers, see page 880.) The symptoms of aster yellows are more severe and appear more quickly in warm weather. Although the disease may be present in the plant, aster yellows may not manifest its symptoms in temperatures of 55°F or less. The disease also infects many ornamental plants, vegetables, and weeds. For a list of plants susceptible to aster yellows, see page 994.

SOLUTION: Aster yellows cannot be eliminated entirely, but can be kept under control. Remove and destroy infected China asters. To remove sources of infection, eradicate nearby weeds that may harbor aster yellows and leafhopper eggs. Spray leafhopper-infested plants with an insecticide containing *diazinon* or *malathion*. Repeat the spray whenever leafhoppers are seen.

CAMPANULA

ADAPTATION: Throughout the United States.

FLOWERING TIME: Spring through fall, depending upon the species.

LIGHT: Filtered sun to shade.

PLANTING TIME: Spring, when all danger of frost is past. Campanula can also be planted in fall in zones 9 and 10. To determine your zone, see the map on page 1004.

SOIL: Any good garden soil. pH 5.5 to 7.5

FERTILIZER: Fertilize with ORTHO Rose & Flower Food 8–12–4 or ORTHO General Purpose Plant Food 8–8–8 according to label directions.

WATER:
How much: Apply enough water to wet the soil 6 to 8 inches deep.
Containers: Apply enough water so that 10 percent of the water drains from the bottom of the container.
How often: Water when the soil 1 inch below the surface is moist but not wet.

Leaf spot.

PROBLEM: Spots and blotches appear on the leaves. The spots may be yellow, red, tan, gray, or brown. They range in size from barely visible to ¼ inch in diameter. Several spots may join to form blotches. Leaves may be yellow and dying. Leaf spotting is most severe in warm, humid weather. In damp conditions, a fine gray mold sometimes covers the infected leaf tissue.

ANALYSIS: Leaf spot
Several different fungi cause leaf spots. These fungi usually just cause spotting, which is unsightly but not harmful. They are spread by splashing water, wind, insects, and tools. They generally survive the winter in diseased plant debris. Most of the leaf spot organisms do their greatest damage in mild weather (50° to 85°F).

SOLUTION: Spray the diseased plants with a *basic copper sulfate* fungicide at intervals of 5 to 10 days. Pick off severely infected leaves. Because leaf spots are favored by warm, humid conditions, it is important to spray frequently during these periods. *Basic copper sulfate* protects the new healthy foliage but will not eradicate the fungus on leaves that are already infected.

CAMPANULA (BELLFLOWER) ———— CANNA ——————

Crown rot.

Bud rot.

Corn earworms (⅓ life size).

PROBLEM: The leaves and stems turn yellow, wilt, and decay. The base of the plant and lower stems are covered with white matted fungal strands, which may develop small brown or black pellets the size of pinheads or black, irregular structures about ¼ inch in diameter. The decaying stems may be filled with thin, elongated black pellets. The plant pulls easily out of the ground to reveal decayed roots.

ANALYSIS: Crown rot
This disease is caused by two fungi (*Sclerotium rolfsii*, also known as *southern blight*, and *Sclerotinia sclerotiorum*), that live in the soil. These fungi usually attack the plant stems at or just below the soil level. Both of these fungi thrive in high humidity and moist soils. The southern blight fungus, in particular, is favored by warm temperatures (80° to 90°F), and is very damaging in this temperature range. Both fungi survive the winter as fungal strands and pellets in plant debris and as fungal pellets in the soil. They are spread by infested soil, seeds and transplants, moving water, and contaminated equipment. *Sclerotium* can also grow through the soil to attack adjacent plants.

SOLUTION: Let the soil dry out between waterings and improve soil drainage. (For further details on these techniques, see pages 857 and 901.) Remove and destroy all infected plants and surrounding soil for 6 inches beyond the diseased plant. Drench the area where the infected plants were growing with a fungicide containing *PCNB*. To help prevent infection next year, broadcast a *PCNB* fungicide onto uninfested soil and dig it in to a depth of 6 inches before replanting.

PROBLEM: The newly opened young leaves may be partially or entirely blackened, or they may be covered with tiny white spots. The older leaves may be distorted. Often they are covered with yellow or brown spots and streaks. In many cases, the flower buds turn black and die before they open. Entire stalks are often decayed. A sticky substance may coat infected leaf tissue.

ANALYSIS: Bud rot
This plant disease is caused by bacteria (*Xanthomonas* species) that usually attack the young canna leaves and flowers while they are still curled in the buds. The bacteria can spread down from the leaves and flowers into the stems, causing plant decay and death. Some of the infected tissue may exude a sticky ooze, which is filled with millions of bacteria. The bacteria are spread by splashing water and rain, and by direct contact with equipment, hands, and insects. Wet conditions enhance the rapid spread of the disease. Bud rot survives through the winter in diseased rhizomes, contaminated soil, and infected plant debris to reinfect young plants the following spring.

SOLUTION: There are no effective chemical controls for this disease. In order to control bud rot, it is important to reduce excess moisture around the plants. Water in the morning to give the foliage a chance to dry out during the day. Try to avoid wetting the foliage when watering. Space plants far enough apart to allow good air circulation. Pick off infected leaves and flowers. Remove severely diseased plants and the soil immediately surrounding them. Clean up plant debris. Plant only healthy plants and rhizomes. For information on choosing healthy plants, see page 916.

PROBLEM: The leaves are filled with holes and are often ragged. The flowers may not appear, or may be distorted. Striped green, brown, or yellow caterpillars are chewing on the leaves and inside the rolled leaf buds. The caterpillars range in size from ¼ inch to 2 inches.

ANALYSIS: Corn earworm
(*Heliothis zea*)
This caterpillar is the larva of a night-flying moth. In addition to feeding on many different ornamental plants, the corn earworm is one of the most destructive pests of corn in the United States. The moths lay their light yellow eggs singly on the undersides of leaves. The caterpillars hatch in 2 to 8 days and feed for several weeks on leaves and buds, then crawl into the soil and pupate. One to three weeks later the new adults emerge to begin the cycle again, laying eggs in the evenings and on warm, overcast days. In cooler areas of the country, the caterpillars are present from early spring to the first frost. In warmer areas, the feeding caterpillars are present year-round.

SOLUTION: Control corn earworms with ORTHO Liquid Sevin, applied when the caterpillars first appear. Repeat every 10 to 14 days as needed. Deep cultivation in the fall and winter will help destroy some of the overwintering pupae.

———————————

Canna cultural information
Light: Sun
Water: While the soil is still moist
Soil: Rich
Fertilizer: Medium

CAPSICUM (ORNAMENTAL PEPPER) ——— CELOSIA (COCKSCOMB) ———

Verticillium wilt.

Leaf spot.

Spider mite webbing.

PROBLEM: The leaves and tender stems wilt, turn yellow, then brown, and finally die. The plant may be stunted in growth and often drops many of its leaves. Some of the leaves may curl inward. When an infected stem is sliced open, dark streaks can be seen in the inner stem tissue. Flowering and fruiting are poor.

ANALYSIS: Verticillium wilt
This wilt disease affects many ornamental plants. It is caused by a soil-inhabiting fungus (*Verticillium dahliae*) that lives on plant debris or in the soil. The disease is spread by contaminated seeds, plants, soil, and equipment. The fungus enters the plant through the roots and spreads up into the stems and leaves through the water-conducting vessels in the stems. The vessels become discolored and plugged. This plugging cuts off the flow of water to the leaves, causing leaf yellowing and wilting.

SOLUTION: No chemical control is available. It is best to destroy infected plants. Verticillium can be removed from the soil only by fumigation techniques. (For more information about soil fumigation, see page 919.) However, the best solution is usually to use plants that are resistant to verticillium. For a list of wilt-resistant plants, see page 995.

Capsicum cultural information
Light: Sun
Water: When soil is just barely moist
Soil: Well drained
Fertilizer: Medium

PROBLEM: Yellow or brown spots appear on the leaves. The spots may run together to form blotches. The leaves may be yellowing and dying. Leaf spotting is most severe in humid weather.

ANALYSIS: Leaf spot
Several different fungi cause leaf spots on cockscomb. Some of these fungi may eventually kill the plant, or weaken it so that it becomes susceptible to attack by other organisms. Others merely cause spotting that is unsightly but not harmful. These fungi are spread by splashing water, wind, insects, and tools. They survive the winter in diseased plant debris. Some leaf spot organisms can affect a large number of plants. Most of these fungi do their greatest damage during mild weather (50° to 85°F).

SOLUTION: Spray with a fungicide containing *zineb* at intervals of 3 to 10 days. Because leaf spots are favored by humid conditions, it is important to spray frequently during these periods. *Zineb* protects the new healthy foliage but will not eradicate the fungus on leaves that are already infected. Clean up infected leaves and debris.

PROBLEM: Leaves are stippled, yellowing, and dirty. Leaves may dry out and drop. There may be webbing over flower buds, between leaves, or on the lower surfaces of leaves. To determine if the plant is infested with mites, hold a sheet of white paper underneath an affected plant and tap the stalk sharply. Minute green, red, or yellow specks the size of pepper grains will drop to the paper and begin to crawl around. These pests are easily seen against the white background.

ANALYSIS: Two-spotted spider mite (*Tetranychus urticae*)
These mites, related to spiders, are major pests of many garden and greenhouse plants. They cause damage by sucking sap from the underside of the leaves. As a result of feeding, the green leaf pigment disappears, producing the stippled appearance. Mites are active throughout the growing season, but are favored by hot, dry weather (70°F and up). By mid-summer, they build up to tremendous numbers.

SOLUTION: Spray with a pesticide containing *dicofol* when damage is first noticed. Spray the foliage thoroughly, making sure to cover both the upper and lower surfaces of the leaves. Repeat the spray 3 more times at intervals of 7 days.

Celosia cultural information
Light: Sun
Water: Do not allow to dry out
Soil: Rich
Fertilizer: Medium

CENTAUREA (BACHELOR BUTTONS, DUSTY MILLER) _____

Aphids on bachelor buttons (life size).

PROBLEM: Tiny (⅛ inch) pale green to black soft-bodied insects are clustered on the leaves. Leaves may be curled, distorted, and yellowing. Flowers may be malformed. Overall growth is often stunted. A shiny, sticky substance may coat the leaves. Ants are often present.

ANALYSIS: Aphids
Several different species of aphids infest centaurea plants. Aphids do little damage in small numbers. However, they are extremely prolific and populations can rapidly build up to damaging numbers during the growing season. Damage occurs when the aphid sucks the juices from the leaves and flower buds. The aphid is unable to digest fully all the sugar in the plant sap and excretes the excess in a fluid called honeydew, which often drops onto the leaves below. Ants feed on this sticky substance, and are often present where there is an aphid infestation.

SOLUTION: Spray the infested plants with an insecticide containing *malathion*. Repeat the spray if the plant becomes reinfested.

Centaurea cultural information
Light: Full sun
Water: Allow the soil to dry between waterings
Soil: Light, well drained
Fertilizer: Average

Root and stem rot on dusty miller.

PROBLEM: Leaves turn yellow, wilt, and eventually die. The roots and lower stems may be soft and rotten. There may be white fungal strands on infected stems and around the base of the plant.

ANALYSIS: Root and stem rot
This disease is caused by any of a number of different fungi that persist indefinitely in the soil. They thrive in waterlogged, heavy soil. Some of these fungi attack the plant stems at the soil level, while others attack the roots. Infection causes the roots and stems to decay. This results in wilting, then yellowing leaves, and eventually the death of the plant. These fungi are generally spread by infested soil and transplants, contaminated equipment, and splashing or running water. Many of these organisms also cause damping-off of seedlings. For more information, about damping-off, see page 858.

SOLUTION: Allow the soil around the plant to dry out. (For more information on this technique, see page 857.) Remove and discard severely infected plants. Avoid future root rot problems by planting in well-drained soil. For information on improving soil drainage, see page 901. For more information on root and stem rots, see page 856.

CHRYSANTHEMUM (SHASTA DAISY,

CHRYSANTHEMUM _____

ADAPTATION: Throughout the United States.

FLOWERING TIME:
Chrysanthemums: Late summer to late fall.
Shasta daisies: Late spring to late summer.
Marguerites: Spring to fall.

LIGHT: Full sun.

SOIL: Any good garden soil. pH 6.0 to 8.0

FERTILIZER: Fertilize with ORTHO Rose & Flower Food 8–12–4 or ORTHO General Purpose Plant Food 8–8–8 according to label directions.

WATER:
How much: Apply enough water to plants in the ground to wet the soil 8 to 12 inches deep.
How often: Water when the soil 1 inch below the surface is just barely moist.

HANDLING:
Chrysanthemums: Pinch plants frequently during the spring to encourage bushy growth. For more information, see page 377.
Shasta daisies: Divide clumps every 2 or 3 years. Pinch off old flowers to encourage continued bloom.
Marguerites: Replace plants every 3 years. Do not cut them back; they will not resprout.

MARGUERITE, MUM)

Weak, leggy growth.

Powdery mildew.

Rust.

PROBLEM: Mums are leggy, and many of the stems are thin and spindly. Some plants topple and may need to be tied.

ANALYSIS: Leggy growth
Legginess in mums can be caused by two things:
1. *Natural growth pattern:* Most mum varieties grow tall and leggy naturally.
2. *Too much shade:* Mums are sun-loving plants. Chrysanthemums planted in a shaded area produce thin, leggy growth even when pinched back. Under shaded conditions, the plants may not flower well.

SOLUTION: To prevent leggy growth, follow these guidelines:
1. Plants that are leggy may be pinched back to encourage bushier growth as long as they have not yet formed flower buds. Next year, when your new plants are 6 to 8 inches tall, carefully pinch or nip off the young growing tips just above a leaf. The tiny side bud that is located between this leaf and the stem will grow into a new branch. Every two weeks, pinch back all the new growing points that have formed as a result of the previous weeks' pinching. Stop pinching the plant by August. For more information about pinching, see page 919. Purchase short-growing mum varieties.
2. Move or transplant your chrysanthemums to a location that receives at least 4 or 5 hours of direct sun daily. For more information about transplanting, see page 916.

PROBLEM: The leaves and stems are covered with grayish white powdery spots and patches that occur primarily on the upper surfaces of the leaves. The leaves eventually yellow and wither.

ANALYSIS: Powdery mildew
This common plant disease is caused by a fungus (*Erysiphe cichoracearum*) that thrives in both humid and dry weather. The powdery patches consist of fungal strands and spores. The spores are spread by the wind to healthy plants. The fungus saps plant nutrients causing leaf yellowing and sometimes death of the leaf. Since this powdery mildew attacks many different kinds of plants, the fungus from a diseased plant may infect other types of plants in the garden. (See page 995 for a list of susceptible plants.) Under favorable conditions, powdery mildew can spread through a closely spaced planting in a matter of days or weeks.

SOLUTION: Spray infected plants with ORTHO Phaltan Rose & Garden Fungicide or ORTHO Funginex Rose Disease Control to stop the spread of the disease. Spray at regular intervals of 7 to 10 days, or as often as necessary to protect new growth. Space plants far enough apart to allow good air circulation. Clean up infected leaves and debris.

Chrysanthemum cultural information
Light: Sun
Water: While soil is still moist
Soil: Well drained
Fertilizer: Medium to heavy

PROBLEM: Pale spots appear on the upper surfaces of the leaves. Chocolate brown pustules of spores form on the undersides of the leaves and on the stems. Infected leaves may wither and fall prematurely. The plant is stunted and may die.

ANALYSIS: Rust
This common disease of chrysanthemums is caused by a fungus (*Puccinia chrysanthemi*). The fungal spores are spread by wind and splashing water. Rust can survive only on living plant tissue and as spores on seed; it does not persist on dead plant parts. Plants must remain wet for 6 to 8 hours before the fungus can infect the leaf surface. The disease is favored by moist conditions, cool nights, and warm days. Temperatures of 90°F and higher will kill the spores. Rust can survive the winter on old infected plants.

SOLUTION: Spray infected plants with a fungicide containing *zineb* or *mancozeb* at weekly intervals as soon as the disease is noticed; continue spraying throughout the growing season. Water in the morning rather than the late afternoon or evening, to allow wet foliage to dry out more quickly. Pick off and destroy infected plant parts during the growing season. Space plants far enough apart to allow good air circulation. Remove and destroy all infected plants in the fall to keep them from reinfecting new plantings. Next year, grow only rust-resistant varieties. For a list of rust-resistant chrysanthemums, see page 992.

CHRYSANTHEMUM (SHASTA DAISY, MARGUERITE, MUM)

Leaf spot.

Foliar nematode damage.

Thrips damage on chrysanthemum.

PROBLEM: Spots and blotches appear on the leaves. The spots may be yellow, tan, brown, or black. They range in size from barely visible to more than 1 inch in diameter. Several spots may join to form blotches. Leaves may turn yellow and drop, or wither and hang down along the stem.

ANALYSIS: Leaf spot
Several different fungi cause leaf spots on chrysanthemums. Some of these fungi may eventually kill the plant, or weaken it so that it becomes susceptible to attack by other organisms. Others merely cause spotting that is unsightly but not harmful. These fungi are spread by splashing water or by the wind. They generally survive the winter in diseased plant debris. Most of these fungi do their greatest damage in moist, mild (50° to 85°F) weather.

SOLUTION: Where practical, pick off infected leaves. Spray the plants with ORTHO Phaltan Rose & Garden Fungicide, or with a fungicide containing *maneb*, *folpet*, or *benomyl*. Spray weekly throughout the growing season.

PROBLEM: Fan-shaped or angular yellow-brown to gray leaf blotches develop progressively upward from the lower leaves. The blotches join together and the leaf turns brown or black. The leaf then withers, dies, and hangs down along the stem. The plant is stunted and new leaf buds do not develop. In the spring, young, succulent, leafy growth becomes thickened, distorted, and brittle.

ANALYSIS: Leaf nematode
(*Aphelenchoides ritzema-bosi*)
The cause of this damage is a microscopic worm (*nematode*) that lives and feeds inside the leaf tissue. The nematode is restricted in its movement by larger leaf veins. This confined feeding range creates the angular shape of the blotch. When the foliage is wet, the nematode migrates in the thin film of water on the outside of the leaf to infect healthy tissue. This pest is spread from plant to plant by splashing water. It penetrates the plant tissue by entering through small breathing pores on the underside of the leaf. Leaf nematodes are most damaging in the wet-summer, warmer regions of the country. They can survive for 3 years or more in plant debris and in the soil.

SOLUTION: Remove and destroy severely infested plants. Pick off and destroy all of the infested leaves and the next 2 leaves directly above them. Avoid wetting the foliage as much as possible. Check new plants carefully to be sure they are not diseased, and do not replant them in infected soil. Spray with an insecticide containing *malathion*, using a spreader-sticker (see page 915). Spray weekly until the symptoms stop spreading.

PROBLEM: Silvery white streaks and flecks appear on the leaves and flowers. The leaves and flowers may be distorted and brown. If the flower buds are peeled open, tiny (1/20 to 1/16 inch) insects resembling brown or straw-colored wood slivers can be seen moving around at the base of the petals.

ANALYSIS: Thrips
Several species of this common insect attack chrysanthemums, daisies, and many other garden plants. Thrips are generally found in protected locations such as the insides of the leaf and flower buds, where they feed by rasping the soft plant tissue, then sucking the released plant sap. The injured tissue dies and turns white, causing the characteristic streaking of the leaves and flowers. Because thrips migrate long distances on wind currents, they can quickly infest widespread areas. In cold climates, thrips feed and reproduce from spring until fall. With the onset of freezing weather, they find sheltered areas such as grass clumps and hibernate through the winter. In warm winter climates, thrips feed and reproduce all year. These pests reach their population peak in late spring to midsummer. They are especially troublesome during prolonged dry spells.

SOLUTION: Thrips can be kept under control, although not eliminated entirely. Spray plants before they bloom with ORTHO Liquid Sevin or ORTHO Malathion 50 Insect Spray 2 to 3 times at regular intervals of 1 week. Repeat the spray if reinfestation occurs. Pick off and destroy old infested leaves and flowers.

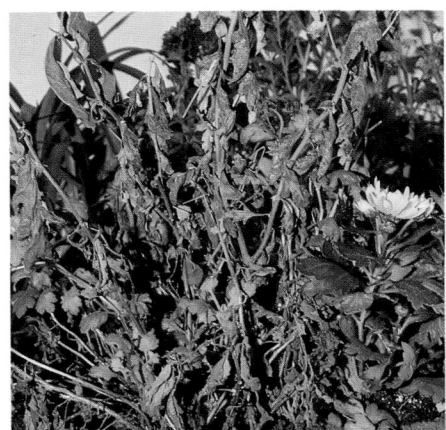

Verticillium wilt.

PROBLEM: Leaves yellow, wilt, and die, starting with the lower leaves and progressing up the plant. Older plants may be stunted. Leaf wilting and death often affect only one side of the plant. Flowering is poor. There may be dark brown areas on the infected stems. When the stem is sliced open near the base of the plant, dark streaks and discolorations of the inner stem tissue are revealed.

ANALYSIS: Verticillium wilt
This wilt disease affects many ornamental plants. It is caused by a soil-inhabiting fungus (*Verticillium* species) that persists indefinitely on plant debris or in the soil. The disease is spread by contaminated seeds, plants, soil, equipment, and ground water. The fungus enters the plant through the roots and spreads up into the stems and leaves through the water-conducting vessels in the stems. These vessels become discolored and plugged. This plugging cuts off the flow of water to the leaves, causing leaf yellowing and wilting.

SOLUTION: No chemical control is available. It is best to destroy infected plants. Verticillium can be removed from the soil only by fumigation techniques. (For more information about soil fumigation, see page 919.) However, the best solution is usually to plant flowers that are resistant to verticillium. For a list of verticillium-resistant plants, see page 995.

Nematode damage on chrysanthemum.

PROBLEM: Leaves turn bronze to yellow. On hot, dry days they may wilt, then recover at night. Plants are weak and grow slowly. Roots are stunted, often bushy and dark, and may have round nodules attached to them.

ANALYSIS: Nematodes
Nematodes are microscopic worms that live in the soil. They are not related to earthworms. Nematodes feed on plant roots, damaging and stunting them. The damaged roots can't supply sufficient water and nutrients to the aboveground plant parts, and the plant is stunted or slowly dies. Nematodes are found throughout the United States, but are most severe in the South. They prefer moist, sandy loam soils. Nematodes can move only a few inches each year on their own, but they may be carried long distances by soil, water, tools, or infested plants. Testing roots and soil is the only positive method for confirming the presence of nematodes. Contact your local Cooperative Extension Office (see page 1011) for sampling instructions and addresses of testing laboratories. Soil and root problems such as poor soil structure, drought stress, nutrient deficiency, and root rots can also produce symptoms of decline similar to those caused by nematodes. These problems should be eliminated as causes before sending soil and root samples for testing. For information on soil problems and root rots, see pages 901 and 857.

SOLUTION: There are no chemicals available to homeowners to kill nematodes in planted soil. However, they can be controlled before planting by soil fumigation. For information on fumigating soil, see page 919.

Two-spotted spider mite damage.

PROBLEM: Leaves are stippled, yellowing, and dirty. Leaves may dry out and drop. There may be webbing over flower buds, between leaves, or on the lower surfaces of leaves. To determine if the plant is infested with mites, hold a sheet of white paper underneath an affected leaf and tap the leaf sharply. Minute green, red, or yellow specks the size of pepper grains will drop to the paper and begin to crawl around. These pests are easily seen against the white background.

ANALYSIS: Two-spotted spider mite
(*Tetranychus urticae*)
These mites, related to spiders, are major pests of many garden and greenhouse plants. They cause damage by sucking sap from the underside of the leaves. As a result of feeding, the green leaf pigment disappears, producing the stippled appearance. Mites are active throughout the growing season, but are favored by hot, dry weather (70°F and up). By midsummer, they build up to tremendous numbers.

SOLUTION: Spray with ORTHO Malathion 50 Insect Spray or a pesticide containing *dicofol* when damage is first noticed. Spray the foliage thoroughly, making sure to cover both the upper and lower surfaces of the leaves. Repeat the spray 3 more times at intervals of 7 days.

CHRYSANTHEMUM (SHASTA DAISY, MARGUERITE, MUM)

Bacterial blight.

Mosaic.

Aster yellows.

PROBLEM: Gray lesions with a water-soaked appearance occur on the stems. Stem portions above these lesions decay, turn brown or black, and fall over. Decay may progress downward to the base of the stems.

ANALYSIS: Bacterial blight
This disease, which is caused by a bacterium (*Erwinia chrysanthemi*), occurs most frequently in warm (80° to 90°F), humid areas. The bacteria enter the plant through stem wounds or through the root system. The infected stem is unable to transport water to the top of the plant, which wilts and dies. The rotted tissue contains millions of bacteria, which are spread to other plants through handling, and by contaminated tools and soil. The bacteria can live for several months in the soil and plant debris.

SOLUTION: There is no chemical control for this disease. Remove and destroy all infected plants. Clean up plant debris. After handling diseased plants, wash your hands before handling healthy plants. Disinfect tools by dipping them in rubbing alcohol. To avoid reinfection from contaminated soil, do not replant chrysanthemums in the same area for at least 6 months.

PROBLEM: Leaves are mottled, and the leaf veins may turn pale. Plants may be dwarfed and bushy. Flowers are small and may have brown streaks. Leaves, stems, and flowers may be deformed.

ANALYSIS: Mosaic
This plant disease is caused by several different viruses. Mosaic is primarily transmitted from plant to plant by aphids. The symptoms of mosaic virus can vary considerably in their severity depending on the type of virus, plant species, and variety. Viruses can be transmitted to chrysanthemums from many weeds and ornamental plants. Some plants may be infected with mosaic virus without showing the typical symptoms.

SOLUTION: Infected plants cannot be cured. They should be removed and destroyed. Spray aphid-infested plants in the area with ORTHO Diazinon Insect Spray or ORTHO Malathion 50 Insect Spray. Repeat the spray at intervals of 7 days as often as necessary to keep the aphids under control. To reduce the numbers of plants that may harbor viruses, keep your garden free of weeds. For more information about controlling disease-carrying insects, see page 880.

PROBLEM: The leaf veins pale and may lose all their color. Part or all of the foliage turns yellow. Leaf edges may turn brown. The flowers are dwarfed, distorted, and may turn green. The plant may grow many thin stems bearing pale, spindly leaves. The plant is generally stunted.

ANALYSIS: Aster yellows
This plant disease is caused by mycoplasmas, microscopic organisms similar to bacteria. The mycoplasmas are transmitted from plant to plant primarily by leafhoppers. (For more information about leafhoppers, see page 880.) The symptoms of aster yellows are more severe and appear more quickly in warm weather. Although the disease may be present in the plant, aster yellows may not manifest its symptoms in temperatures of 55°F or less. The disease also infects many ornamental plants, vegetables, and weeds. For a list of plants susceptible to aster yellows, see page 994.

SOLUTION: Aster yellows cannot be eliminated entirely, but can be kept under control. Remove and destroy infected plants. To remove sources of infection, eradicate nearby weeds that may harbor aster yellows and leafhopper eggs. Spray leafhopper-infested plants with an insecticide containing *diazinon* or *malathion*. Repeat the spray whenever leafhoppers are seen. For more information about controlling disease-carrying insects, see page 880.

Leafminer trails in chrysanthemum leaf.

Aphids (life size).

Chrysanthemum leafminer damage.

PROBLEM: Light-colored, irregular, winding trails or tunnels appear in the leaves. Some of the trails are filled with black matter. Severely infested leaves dry up and hang down along the stems.

ANALYSIS: Chrysanthemum leafminer (*Phytomyza syngenesiae*) This insect belongs to the family of leaf-mining flies. The minute adult fly lays its eggs on the undersides of leaves. The eggs hatch and the larvae that emerge penetrate the leaf and live between the upper and lower surfaces of the leaves. They feed on the inner leaf tissue, creating winding trails. Their dark excrement may dot or partially fill sections of the trails. The larvae are continually present from the spring until the fall.

SOLUTION: Spray with ORTHO Diazinon Insect Spray. Respray at the first sign of further infestation. Pick off and destroy infected leaves. Remove and destroy all plant remains in the fall.

PROBLEM: Young leaves are curled, stunted, and yellowing. The flowers may be malformed. There may be a sticky or shiny substance coating the leaves. Tiny (1/8 inch), soft-bodied insects that may range in color from pale green to dark brown or black are clustered on the leaves and stems. Ants may be present.

ANALYSIS: Aphids
Aphids do little damage in small numbers. However, they are extremely prolific and populations can rapidly build up to damaging numbers during the growing season. Damage occurs when the aphid sucks the juices from the chrysanthemum leaves and flower buds. The aphid is unable to digest fully all the sugar in the plant sap and excretes the excess in a fluid called honeydew. The honeydew often drops onto the leaves below. Ants feed on this sticky substance, and are often present where there is an aphid infestation.

SOLUTION: Spray with ORTHO Liquid Sevin, ORTHO Diazinon Insect Spray or ORTHO Malathion 50 Insect Spray as soon as the insects appear. Repeat the spray if the plant is reinfested.

PROBLEM: Light-colored, irregular, winding trails or tunnels appear in the leaves. Some of the trails are filled with black matter. Severely infested leaves dry up and hang down along the stems.

ANALYSIS: Chrysanthemum leafminer (*Phytomyza syngenesiae*) This insect, which is a serious pest of chrysanthemum as well as cineraria, belongs to the family of leaf-mining flies. The minute adult fly lays its eggs on the undersides of leaves. The eggs hatch and the larvae that emerge penetrate the leaves and live between the upper and lower surfaces of the leaves. They feed on the inner leaf tissue, creating winding trails. Their dark excrement can dot or partially fill sections of the trails. The larvae are continually present from the spring until the fall.

SOLUTION: Spray with ORTHO Diazinon Insect Spray and a spreader-sticker (see page 915). Respray at the first sign of further infestation. Pick off and destroy infested leaves. Remove and destroy all plant remains in the fall.

Cineraria cultural information
Light: Shade
Water: While the soil is still moist
Soil: Loamy, well drained
Fertilizer: Medium

CINERARIA

Powdery mildew.

PROBLEM: Grayish white, powdery spots and patches cover the upper surfaces of the leaves, the stems, and possibly the flower buds. The infected plant parts are dwarfed and stunted. The leaves may eventually turn yellow and wither.

ANALYSIS: Powdery mildew
This common plant disease is caused by a fungus (*Erysiphe cichoracearum*) that thrives in both humid and dry weather. The powdery patches consist of fungal strands and spores. The spores are spread by the wind to healthy plants. The fungus saps plant nutrients, causing leaf yellowing and sometimes death of the leaf. A severe infection may kill the plant. Since this powdery mildew attacks many different kinds of plants, the fungus from a diseased plant may infect other types of plants in the garden. (See page 995 for a list of susceptible plants.) Under favorable conditions, powdery mildew can spread through a closely spaced planting in a matter of days or weeks. The disease is generally most severe late in the growing season.

SOLUTION: Spray infected plants with a fungicide containing *benomyl* to stop the spread of the disease. *Benomyl* protects the new, healthy foliage by killing the powdery mildew spores as they germinate on the leaf. It will also eradicate the fungus on leaves that are already infected. Spray at regular intervals of 7 to 10 days, or as often as necessary to protect new growth. Space plants far enough apart to allow good air circulation. Clean up infected leaves and debris.

CLIVIA

Sunburn.

PROBLEM: Leaves are pale green to yellowish white in color; they may turn brown and brittle. There is very little new growth. Plants are exposed to at least several hours of direct sun during the day. Only the leaves exposed to the sun are affected. There are no signs of plant pests or diseases.

ANALYSIS: Sunburn
Clivias are adapted to shady conditions, and will not tolerate more than a few hours of direct sun, especially hot afternoon sunlight. Even if they receive only one or two hours of direct sunlight, they may discolor slightly, turning yellow-green. The bright light and intense heat break down the chlorophyll (green plant pigment), and eventually the plant tissue dies.

SOLUTION: Transplant your clivias to a shaded or partially shaded location. Do not place them in a western or southwestern exposure. Replace them with plants that are adapted to a sunny location.

Clivia cultural information
Light: Shade
Water: When the soil is just barely moist
Soil: Tolerates a wide variety
Fertilizer: Medium

COLEUS

Spider mites.

PROBLEM: Leaves are stippled, yellowing, and dirty. Leaves may dry out and die. There may be webbing over flower buds, between leaves and stems, or on the lower surfaces of leaves. To determine if the plant is infested with mites, hold a sheet of white paper underneath an affected leaf and tap the leaf sharply. Minute green, red, or yellow specks the size of pepper grains will drop to the paper and begin to crawl around. These pests are easily seen against the white background.

ANALYSIS: Mites
Mites, related to spiders, are major pests of many garden and greenhouse plants. They cause damage by sucking sap from the undersides of the leaves. As a result of feeding, the green leaf pigment disappears, producing the stippled appearance. Mites are active throughout the growing season, but are favored by hot, dry weather (70°F and up). By midsummer, they build up to tremendous numbers.

SOLUTION: Spray with a pesticide containing *dicofol* when damage is first noticed. Spray the foliage thoroughly, making sure to cover both the upper and lower surfaces of the leaves. Repeat the spray 3 more times at intervals of 7 days.

Coleus cultural information
Light: Shade
Water: While the soil is still moist
Soil: Loamy, well drained
Fertilizer: Medium

![Greenhouse whiteflies (life size).]

Greenhouse whiteflies (life size).

![Mealybugs (twice life size).]

Mealybugs (twice life size).

Spotted cucumber beetles.

PROBLEM: Tiny, winged insects ¹⁄₁₂ inch long are found mainly on the undersides of the leaves. The insects are covered with white, waxy powder. When the plant is touched, insects flutter rapidly around it. Leaves may be mottled and yellowing. In warm winter areas, black mold may cover the leaves.

ANALYSIS: Greenhouse whitefly
(*Trialeurodes vaporariorum*)
Greenhouse whitefly is a common insect pest of many garden and greenhouse plants. The 4-winged adult lays eggs on the undersides of leaves. The larvae are the size of a pinhead and look quite different from the adult. The larvae are flat, oval-shaped, and semitransparent, with white waxy filaments radiating from the body. They remain attached to the underside of a leaf for about a month before changing to the adult form. Both the larval and adult forms suck sap from the leaves. The larvae are more damaging because they feed more heavily. Whiteflies cannot fully digest all the sugar in the sap, and excrete the excess in a fluid called honeydew, which coats the leaves. A sooty mold fungus may develop on the honeydew, causing the coleus leaves to appear black and dirty. In warm winter areas, the insect can be active year-round with eggs, larvae, and adults present at the same time. The whitefly is unable to live through freezing winters. Spring reinfestations in freezing winter areas come from migrating whiteflies and infested greenhouse-grown plants placed in the garden.

SOLUTION: Control whiteflies by spraying with an insecticide containing *malathion* every 7 to 10 days as necessary. Spray both the upper and lower surfaces of the leaves.

PROBLEM: Oval, white insects up to ¹⁄₄ inch long cluster in white, cottony masses on the stems and leaves. Leaves may be deformed and withered. The infested leaves are often shiny and sticky. Ants may be present.

ANALYSIS: Mealybugs
Several species of this common insect feed on coleus. Mealybugs damage plants by sucking sap, causing leaf distortion and death. The adult female mealybug may produce live young, or may deposit her eggs in white, fluffy masses of wax. The immature mealybugs, called *nymphs*, are very active and crawl all over the plant. Soon after the nymphs begin to feed, they exude filaments of white wax that cover their bodies, giving them a cottony appearance. As they mature, their mobility decreases. Mealybugs cannot fully digest all the sugar in the sap, and excrete the excess in a fluid called honeydew, which coats the leaves. Ants may feed on the honeydew. Mealybugs are spread by the wind, which may blow egg masses and nymphs from plant to plant. Ants may also move them, or young, active nymphs can crawl to nearby plants. Mealybug eggs and some adults can survive through the winter in warm climates. Spring reinfestations in colder areas come from infested new plants placed in the garden.

SOLUTION: Spray infested plants with an insecticide containing *malathion* and a spreader-sticker (see page 915). Spray at intervals of 7 to 10 days until the mealybugs are gone. Gently hose down plants to knock off mealybugs and wash off honeydew. Remove and destroy severely infested leaves and plants.

PROBLEM: Yellow-green, winged beetles ¹⁄₄ inch long, with black spots, are chewing small holes in the leaves and flower petals.

ANALYSIS: Spotted cucumber beetle
(*Diabrotica* species)
Several closely related spotted cucumber beetles (one of which is also known as the *southern corn rootworm*) feed on many different vegetable and ornamental plants. The adult beetle hibernates in weeds and perennials. When temperatures reach 70°F in the spring, the adult resumes feeding on leaves and flowers. The female beetle lays eggs in or on the soil around the base of the plants. The wormlike yellowish white larvae feed on the plant roots and are very damaging to many vegetable crops such as corn, cucumbers, melons, and squash. The larvae pupate in midsummer and emerge as adult beetles, which feed exclusively on foliage and flowers. They are especially attracted to light-colored, late summer flowers like coreopsis.

SOLUTION: Spray plants with an insecticide containing *carbaryl* or *diazinon*. Repeat the spray when plants are reinfested, allowing at least 7 days between applications. To kill the larvae, thoroughly cultivate the soil as soon as temperatures reach 70°F in the spring. Reduce the number of hibernating beetles by cleaning up weeds in the fall.

Coreopsis cultural information
Light: Sun
Water: When almost dry
Soil: Well drained
Fertilizer: Medium

COREOPSIS

Aster leafhopper damage.

PROBLEM: Pale green, winged insects up to ⅛ inch long, usually feed on the undersides of the leaves. They hop away quickly when the plant is touched. The leaves may be stippled.

ANALYSIS: Aster leafhopper (*Macrosteles fascifrons*)
This insect, also known as the *six-spotted leafhopper*, feeds on many different ornamental and vegetable plants. It generally feeds on the undersides of the leaves, sucking the plant sap, which causes the stippling. This leafhopper can infect plants with the disease *aster yellows* (see page 861). Leafhoppers at all stages of maturity are active throughout the growing season. Adult leafhoppers cannot overwinter where the temperatures approach freezing. However, the eggs they lay in the fall survive on perennial weeds and ornamental plants. The eggs hatch and the emerging insects reinfest plants when the weather warms up in the spring. Even areas that have winters so cold that the eggs cannot survive are not free from infestation, because leafhoppers can migrate in the spring from warmer regions.

SOLUTION: It is important to keep leafhoppers under control because, in addition to the damage their feeding causes, they can infect plants with aster yellows. Spray infested plants with an insecticide containing *diazinon* or *carbaryl*, making sure to cover the lower surfaces of the leaves. Repeat the spray as often as necessary to keep the insects under control, allowing at least 10 days to pass between applications. Eradicate nearby weeds that may harbor leafhopper eggs and aster yellows. (For more information about controlling disease-carrying insects see page 880.)

COSMOS

Powdery mildew.

PROBLEM: The leaves and stems are covered with grayish white powdery spots and patches that occur primarily on the upper leaf surfaces. The leaves eventually turn yellow.

ANALYSIS: Powdery mildew
This common plant disease is caused by a fungus (*Erysiphe cichoracearum*) that thrives in both humid and dry weather. The powdery patches consist of fungal strands and spores. The spores are spread by the wind to healthy plants. The fungus saps plant nutrients, causing yellowing and sometimes death of the leaf. Since this powdery mildew attacks many different kinds of plants, the fungus from a diseased plant may infect other types of plants in the garden. (See page 995 for a list of susceptible plants.) Under favorable conditions, powdery mildew can spread through a closely spaced planting in a matter of days or weeks. Generally the disease is most severe in late summer and early fall.

SOLUTION: Spray infected plants with a fungicide containing either *folpet* or *benomyl* to stop the spread of the disease. These fungicides protect the new healthy foliage, but will not eradicate the fungus on leaves that are already infected. These may be picked off. Spray at regular intervals of 10 to 12 days, or as often as necessary to protect new growth. Space plants far enough apart to allow good air circulation.

Cosmos cultural information
Light: Sun
Water: When the soil is almost dry
Soil: Any good garden soil
Fertilizer: Medium

Root and stem rot.

PROBLEM: The plant suddenly wilts and dies; or it may die slowly from the top down. The leaves may yellow, and overall growth may be stunted. Small black fungal pellets may appear on the lower stems and roots. The stem may be soft and mushy at the soil level. The roots may be decayed.

ANALYSIS: Root and stem rot
This disease is caused by a number of different fungi that persist indefinitely in the soil. They thrive in waterlogged, heavy soils. Some of these fungi primarily attack the plant stems at the soil level, while others attack the roots. Infection causes the roots, stems, or both to decay, resulting in wilting, yellowing leaves and plant death. These fungi are generally spread by infested soil and transplants, contaminated equipment, and moving water. Many of these organisms also cause damping-off of seedlings. For more information about damping off, see page 858.

SOLUTION: Allow the soil around the plants to dry out. For more information on this technique, see page 857. Remove and discard severely infected plants. Avoid future root rot problems by planting in well-drained soil. For information on improving soil drainage, see page 901. For more information on root and stem rot, see page 856.

Spider mite damage.

Aphids (life size).

Aphids (life size).

PROBLEM: Leaves are stippled, yellowing, and dirty. Leaves may dry out and drop. There may be webbing over flower buds, between leaves and stems, or on the lower surfaces of the leaves. To determine if the plant is infested with mites, hold a sheet of white paper underneath an affected leaf and tap the leaf sharply. Minute green, red, or yellow specks the size of pepper grains will drop to the paper and begin to crawl around. These pests are easily seen against the white background.

ANALYSIS: Two-spotted spider mite (*Tetranychus urticae*)
These mites, related to spiders, are major pests of many garden and greenhouse plants. They cause damage by sucking sap from the underside of the leaves. As a result of feeding, the green leaf pigment disappears, producing the stippled appearance. Mites are active throughout the growing season, but are favored by hot, dry weather (70°F and up). By midsummer, they build up to tremendous numbers.

SOLUTION: Spray with ORTHO Isotox Insect Killer when damage is first noticed. Spray the foliage thoroughly, making sure to cover both the upper and lower surfaces of the leaves.

PROBLEM: Leaves may be curled, distorted, and yellowing. The flowers may be malformed. Tiny (⅛ inch) pale green to black, soft-bodied insects are clustered on the leaves and stems. A sticky, shiny substance may coat the leaves. Ants may be present.

ANALYSIS: Aphids
Aphids do little damage in small numbers. However, they are extremely prolific and populations can rapidly build up to damaging numbers during the growing season. Damage occurs when the aphid sucks the juices from the cosmos leaves and flower buds. The aphid is unable to fully digest all the sugar in the plant sap and excretes the excess in a fluid called honeydew. The honeydew often drops onto the leaves below. Ants feed on this sticky substance, and are often present where there is an aphid infestation.

SOLUTION: Spray with ORTHO Isotox Insect Killer or ORTHO Liquid Sevin as soon as the insects appear. Repeat the spray if the plant is reinfested.

PROBLEM: Leaves may be curled, distorted, and yellowing. The flowers may be malformed. Tiny (⅛ inch) yellow-green to black, soft-bodied insects are clustered on the undersides of the leaves and the base of the plant. A sticky, shiny substance may coat the leaves.

ANALYSIS: Aphids
Aphids do little damage in small numbers. However, they are extremely prolific and populations can rapidly build up to damaging numbers during the growing season. Damage occurs when the aphid sucks the juices from the crocus leaves and flower buds. The aphid is unable to digest fully all the sugar in the plant sap and excretes the excess in a fluid called honeydew. The honeydew often drops onto the leaves below.

SOLUTION: Spray with ORTHO Liquid Sevin as soon as the insects appear. Repeat the spray if the plant becomes reinfested.

CYMBIDIUM

Mosaic.

Gray mold.

PROBLEM: Leaves are mottled or streaked. Pale rings may develop on the foliage. As the leaves grow older, black or brown stripes develop along the leaf veins, and irregular, sunken blotches may form. The flowers may be marred with dark green or light-colored rings or streaks.

ANALYSIS: Mosaic
This plant disease is caused by a number of closely related viruses. The symptoms of mosaic infections vary in their severity depending on the strain of virus and the cymbidium variety. Virus infections generally do not kill the plant, but may greatly reduce its overall vigor and beauty. Mosaic persists in the plant indefinitely. Cuttings or divisions made from the diseased plant will also be infected. If diseased plants are touched or pruned, the virus can be transferred to healthy plants on contaminated hands, knives, and other pruning equipment. Aphids and other insects may also transmit these viruses.

SOLUTION: There are no chemicals that control or eliminate virus diseases. Discard weak or severely infected plants. Wash your hands and dip pruning shears into rubbing alcohol after working on infected plants. Purchase only healthy plants. For information on selecting healthy plants, see page 916. Keep aphids under control. For more information about disease-carrying aphids and their control, see page 880.

PROBLEM: Tiny brown spots appear on the blossoms. Spotting increases as the flower ages. If wet conditions continue, gray mold develops on the infected flower parts when the flower starts to die back naturally.

ANALYSIS: Gray mold
This widespread plant disease is caused by a fungus (*Botrytis cinerea*) that is found on most dead plant tissue. The fungus attacks the flowers, causing spotting and sometimes mold. The fuzzy gray mold that may develop is composed of millions of microscopic spores. The fungus is spread by the wind, splashing water, or by infected pieces of plant tissue contacting healthy tissue. Cool temperatures and high humidity favor gray mold growth. Infection is more of a problem in spring and fall, when temperatures are lower. In warm winter areas, where freezing is rare, gray mold can be a year-round problem.

SOLUTION: No chemicals are currently available that will control gray mold on cymbidium. Adequate sanitation controls this fungus satisfactorily. Clean up plant debris, and remove dying or moldy flowers. Provide enough space between plants to allow good air circulation. Try to avoid wetting the foliage and flowers when watering.

DAHLIA

DAHLIA

ADAPTATION: Throughout the United States.

FLOWERING TIME: Summer to midfall.

LIGHT: Full sun.

PLANTING TIME: In the spring when all danger of frost is past.

SOIL: High in organic matter. pH 6.0 to 8.0

FERTILIZER: Fertilize with ORTHO Rose & Flower Food 8–12–4 or ORTHO General Purpose Plant Food 8–8–8 according to label directions.

WATER:
How much: Apply enough water to plants in the ground to wet the soil to 1 to 1½ feet. For plants in containers, apply enough water so that 10 percent of the water drains from the bottom of the container.
How often: Water when the soil is moist but not wet. Dahlias cannot tolerate drying out. Mulch plants to help maintain soil moisture.

HANDLING: Dig up and divide tuberous roots in the fall. Store them in a perforated plastic bag packed in vermiculite or peat moss. Keep them in a dark, cool (35° to 45°F) location.

Tuber rot.

Stem and root rot.

Wilt disease.

PROBLEM: Tuberous roots in storage develop dark brown, sunken areas that are usually dry and firm, but are sometimes soft and mushy. Tufts of pink and yellow mold may cover part or all of the roots. Tubers that have been planted may not produce any foliage. If they do, the foliage turns yellow and wilts. When dug up, the tubers and roots are rotted and moldy.

ANALYSIS: Tuber rot
This disease is caused primarily by two common soil-inhabiting fungi (*Fusarium* species and *Botrytis* species). The fungi generally don't infect the tubers unless they are wounded. If the roots are damaged when they are dug out of the ground, the fungi will penetrate the wounds and rot the tissue. The tubers rot rapidly when they are stored in warm, humid conditions. If tubers suffer frost damage while they are in storage, they will also be susceptible to fungal invasion. Sometimes tuberous roots in storage are contaminated but the fungal decay has not progressed far enough to be noticed. When they are planted the following spring, they may not produce foliage. If they do produce foliage, the fungus causes wilting, yellowing, and eventually death of the plant. For more information about fusarium wilt, see page 858.

SOLUTION: Infected roots cannot be saved. To prevent tuber rot next year, dig up the roots carefully after they have matured fully. Discard any roots that show decay. Handle them carefully to prevent injuries. Store the roots in peat moss in a cool, dark place that is safe from frost. For more information about bulbs and roots, see page 917.

PROBLEM: Leaves and stems are wilted and dying. White fungal strands may be growing on the main stem at the base of the plant. When sliced open, infected stems may be found to be filled with small black fungal bodies. In many cases, the roots are black and rotted.

ANALYSIS: Root and stem rot
This disease is caused by a number of different fungi (including *Sclerotinia*, *Pythium*, and *Pellicularia* species) that persist indefinitely in the soil. They thrive in waterlogged, heavy soil. The fungi infect the plant roots and stems, causing them to decay. This results in wilting, then yellowing leaves, and eventually the death of the plant. These fungi are generally spread by infested soil and transplants, contaminated equipment, and splashing or running water. Many of these organisms also cause damping-off of seedlings. For more information about damping-off, see page 858.

SOLUTION: Allow the soil around the plants to dry out. (For more information on this technique, see page 857.) Remove and discard severely infected plants. Avoid future root rot problems by planting in well-drained soil. For information on improving soil drainage, see page 901. For more information on stem rots, see page 856.

PROBLEM: The lower leaves turn yellow, wilt and die; or all of the foliage may turn yellow and then wither. Older plants may be stunted. Yellowing and wilting often affect only one side of the plant. The flower heads droop. There may be dark brown areas on the infected stem. When the stem is sliced open near the base of the plant, dark streaks and discolorations are seen on the inner stem tissue. The root system may be partially or entirely decayed.

ANALYSIS: Wilt disease
Wilt disease affects many ornamental plants. It is caused by either of two soil-inhabiting fungi (*Verticillium dahliae* and *Fusarium* species) that persist indefinitely on plant debris or in the soil. The disease is spread by contaminated seeds, plants, soil, and equipment. The fungus enters the plant through the roots and spreads up into the stems through the water-conducting vessels. The vessels become discolored and plugged. This plugging cuts off the flow of water to the leaves, causing leaf yellowing and wilting.

SOLUTION: No chemical control is available. It is best to destroy infected plants. Verticillium and fusarium can be removed from the soil only by fumigation techniques. (For more information about soil fumigation, see page 919.) However, the best solution is usually to use plants that are resistant to verticillium and fusarium. For a list of wilt-resistant plants, see pages 994 and 995.

DAHLIA

Powdery mildew.

PROBLEM: The leaves and stems are covered with grayish white powdery spots and patches that occur primarily on the upper surfaces of the leaves. The leaves eventually yellow and wither.

ANALYSIS: Powdery mildew
This common plant disease is caused by a fungus (*Erysiphe cichoracearum*) that thrives in both humid and dry weather. The powdery patches consist of fungal strands and spores. The spores are spread by the wind to healthy plants. The fungus saps the plant nutrients, causing yellowing and sometimes death of the leaf. Since this powdery mildew attacks many different kinds of plants, the fungus from a diseased plant may infect other types of plants in the garden. (See page 995 for a list of susceptible plants.) Under favorable conditions, powdery mildew can spread through a closely spaced planting in a matter of days or weeks. It is generally most severe in the late summer.

SOLUTION: Spray infected plants with ORTHO Funginex Rose Disease Control to stop the spread of the disease. Funginex protects the new, healthy foliage, but will not eradicate the fungus on leaves that are already infected. These leaves may be picked off. Spray every 10 to 12 days, or as often as necessary to protect new growth. Space plants far enough apart to allow good air circulation. Remove and destroy severely infected plants. Clean up plant debris.

DELPHINIUM

Mosaic.

PROBLEM: The leaf veins and leaf tissue next to the veins turn pale green, or the leaves may be mildly to severely mottled. The leaves are often distorted or yellowing. The plant may be stunted and bushy.

ANALYSIS: Mosaic
This plant disease is caused by a virus that is transmitted from plant to plant by aphids. The symptoms of mosaic virus vary considerably in their severity, depending on the plant variety. Severely affected plants will not die from mosaic, but their overall vigor and beauty are greatly reduced. In contrast, some plants infected with mosaic don't show any symptoms at all. The virus survives the winter in the roots of perennial ornamental plants and weeds.

SOLUTION: Control mosaic virus by eliminating the virus-carrying aphids. Spray aphid-infested plants with ORTHO Isotox Insect Killer. Repeat the spray as often as necessary to keep the aphids under control, allowing 7 days to pass between sprays. Remove and destroy infected plants and nearby weeds that may harbor the virus.

DELPHINIUM

ADAPTATION: Throughout the United States.

FLOWERING TIME: Late spring to fall.

LIGHT: Full sun.

PLANTING TIME: Plant in the fall for bloom next spring to summer, or plant in the spring for bloom in late summer and spring of the following year.

SOIL: Well drained, high in organic matter. pH 6.0 to 8.0

FERTILIZER: When planting, add a small handful of ORTHO Bone Meal 0–12–0 or ORTHO Superphosphate 0–20–0 to the bottom of the planting hole. During the growing season, fertilize with ORTHO Rose & Flower Food 8–12–4 or ORTHO General Purpose Plant Food 8–8–8 according to label directions.

WATER:
  How much: Apply enough water to wet the soil to 1½ feet deep.
  How often: Water when the soil 1 inch below the surface is just barely moist.

HANDLING: When planting, do not bury the crown of the plant. Cut back old flower stalks to promote further bloom. When new shoots are 6 to 8 inches high, cut back old stems to ground. Stake tall varieties.

Snail and slug damage.

Leaf spot.

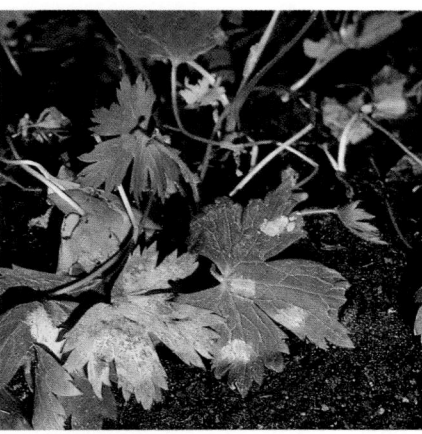

Powdery mildew.

PROBLEM: Holes are chewed in the leaves, or entire leaves may be sheared from the stems. Silvery trails wind around on the plants and soil nearby. Snails or slugs may be seen moving around or feeding on the plants, especially at night. Check for them by inspecting the garden at night by flashlight.

ANALYSIS: Snails and slugs
These pests are mollusks, and are related to clams, oysters, and other shellfish. They feed on a wide variety of garden plants. Like other mollusks, snails and slugs need to be moist all the time. For this reason, they avoid direct sun and dry places, and hide during the day in damp places, such as under flower pots or in thick groundcover. They emerge at night or on cloudy days to feed. Snails and slugs are similar in appearance, except that the snail has a hard shell, into which it withdraws when disturbed. Slugs lay masses of white eggs encased in a slimy mass in protected places. Snails bury their eggs in the soil, also in a slimy mass. The young look like miniature versions of their parents.

SOLUTION: Scatter ORTHO Slug-Geta Snail & Slug Bait in bands around the areas you wish to protect. Also scatter the bait in areas where snails or slugs might be hiding, such as in dense groundcovers, weedy areas, compost piles, or pot storage areas. Before spreading the bait, wet down the treated areas to encourage snail and slug activity that night. Repeat the application every 2 weeks as long as snails and slugs are active.

PROBLEM: Spots and blotches appear on the leaves. The spots may be yellow, red, tan, gray, or brown. They range in size from barely visible to ¼ inch in diameter. Several spots may join to form blotches. Leaves may be yellow and dying. Leaf spotting is most severe in warm, humid weather. In damp conditions, a fine gray mold sometimes covers the infected leaf tissue.

ANALYSIS: Leaf spot
Several different fungi cause leaf spots. Some of these fungi may eventually kill the plant, or weaken it so that it becomes susceptible to attack by other organisms. Others merely cause spotting that is unsightly but not harmful. These fungi are spread by splashing water, wind, insects, and tools. They generally survive the winter in diseased plant debris. Most of the leaf spot organisms do their greatest damage in mild weather (50° to 85°F).

SOLUTION: Spray with a fungicide containing *maneb* or *mancozeb* at intervals of 3 to 10 days. Because leaf spots are favored by warm, humid conditions, it is important to spray frequently during these periods. These fungicides protect the new healthy foliage but will not eradicate the fungus on leaves that are already infected. These leaves may be picked off. Clean up plant debris during the growing season and in the fall.

PROBLEM: Leaves and stems are covered with grayish white powdery spots and patches, which occur primarily on the upper surfaces of the leaves. Severely infected young leaves become curled and distorted. The infected foliage eventually turns yellow and withers.

ANALYSIS: Powdery mildew
This common plant disease is caused by a fungus that thrives in both humid and dry weather. The powdery patches consist of fungal strands and spores. The spores are spread by the wind to healthy plants. The fungus saps the plant nutrients, causing leaf yellowing and often death of the leaf. A severe infection may kill the plant. Since some powdery mildews attack many different kinds of plants, the fungus from a diseased plant may infect other types of plants in the garden. (See page 995 for a list of powdery mildews and the plants they attack.) Under favorable conditions, powdery mildew can spread through a closely spaced planting in a matter of days or weeks. It is generally most severe in the late summer.

SOLUTION: Spray infected plants with a fungicide containing *benomyl* to stop the spread of the disease. *Benomyl* protects the new, healthy foliage by killing the powdery mildew spores as they germinate on the leaf. It will not eradicate the fungus on diseased leaves. These leaves may be picked off. Spray at regular intervals of 10 to 12 days or as often as necessary to protect new growth. Space plants far enough apart to allow good air circulation. Remove and destroy severely infected plants. Clean up plant debris.

DELPHINIUM

Crown and root rot.

PROBLEM: The lower leaves turn yellow and the plant wilts and dies, sometimes in a matter of a few days. The plant pulls up easily to reveal rotted dark-brown or black roots and lower stems. There may be white fungal strands on infected stems and around the base of the plant. Small tan to reddish brown pellets the size of pinheads or larger form on the infected plant tissue and on the soil surrounding the plant.

ANALYSIS: Crown and root rot
This plant disease is caused by either of 2 closely related fungi (*Sclerotium delphinii* and *Sclerotium rolfsii*), which infect many kinds of vegetable and ornamental plants. These fungi initially attack the root system and then move upward into the base of the plant. They decay the roots and clog the water-conducting tissue in the lower stems and base of the plant, causing wilting and death of the plant. Crown and root rots are most severe in poorly drained soil and during periods of warm, moist weather. Fungal pellets form which survive in dry soil and extremes of temperature to reinfect plants when conditions are suitable for plant growth. These pellets can persist in the soil or plant debris indefinitely. Both fungal strands and pellets are spread by moving water and contaminated soil and equipment.

SOLUTION: Remove and destroy infected plants and the soil immediately around them. Improve soil drainage and let the soil dry out between waterings. (For further information about these techniques see pages 857 and 901.) Do not put susceptible plants in areas that have been contaminated with these fungi. For a list of plants susceptible to sclerotium, see page 996.

DIANTHUS (CARNATION, PINK, SWEET WILLIAM)

DIANTHUS

ADAPTATION: Throughout the United States. Carnations may be grown as annuals in zones 3 to 8, but may need winter protection to be grown as perennials in these areas. They do not need protection in zones 9 and 10. To determine your climate zone, see the map on page 1004.

FLOWERING TIME: Late spring and summer.

LIGHT: Full sun.

PLANTING TIME: Spring, after all danger of frost is past.

SOIL: Well drained, pH 6.5 to 8.0

FERTILIZER: Fertilize with ORTHO Rose & Flower Food 8–12–4 or ORTHO General Purpose Plant Food 8–8–8 according to label directions.

WATER:
How much: Apply enough water to wet the soil to the bottom of the root zone. For pinks and sweet william, wet the soil 4 to 6 inches deep. For carnations, wet the soil 8 to 10 inches deep.
Containers: Apply enough water to container plants so that about 10 percent of the water drains from the bottom of the container.
How often: Water when the soil is just barely moist.

Fusarium wilt.

PROBLEM: Leaves and stems turn gray-green, then pale yellow, and wilt. Yellowing and wilting often affect only one side of the plant. Plant shoots may be curled and distorted. The stems are soft and can be easily crushed. When a stem is split open, dark streaks and discolorations of the inner stem tissue are revealed. The roots are generally healthy.

ANALYSIS: Fusarium wilt
This wilt disease affects many ornamental plants. It is caused by a soil-inhabiting fungus (*Fusarium oxysporum* var. *dianthi*) that persists indefinitely on plant debris or in the soil. The disease is spread by contaminated seeds, plants, soil, and equipment. The fungus enters the plant through the roots and spreads up into the stems and leaves through the water-conducting vessels in the stems. The vessels become discolored and plugged. This plugging cuts off the flow of water to the leaves, causing leaf yellowing and wilting.

SOLUTION: No chemical control is available. It is best to destroy infected plants. Fusarium can be removed from the soil only by fumigation techniques. (For more information about soil fumigation, see page 919.) However, the best solution is usually to use plants that are resistant to fusarium.

Bacterial wilt.

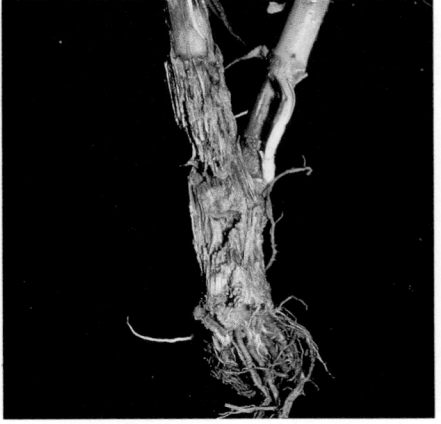

Rhizoctonia stem rot on carnation.

Virus.

PROBLEM: Stems wilt or the entire plant may wilt. The leaves dry, turn yellow, and die. The roots are often rotted. Cracks may appear around the base of the stem, with yellow streaks extending up the length of the stem. When the stems are sliced open, yellowish to brownish discolorations of the stem tissue are revealed. The infected interior portions of the stem are sticky.

ANALYSIS: Bacterial wilt
This disease of carnations and pinks is caused by a bacterium (*Pseudomonas caryophylli*) that lives in the soil. The bacteria penetrate the plant stems through wounds or cuts in the roots or the base of the stem. Once inside, the wilt organisms multiply and clog the water-conducting stem tissue, causing the plant to wilt and die. The bacteria can also move down into the root system, causing decay. A sticky fluid, which coats infected stems and roots, contains millions of bacteria. The bacteria are spread to other plants by water, handling, contaminated soil, plant debris, and contaminated equipment. Bacterial wilt damage increases as the temperature grows warmer.

SOLUTION: Once a plant is infected, it cannot be cured. It is best to remove and destroy all infected plants. Clean up plant debris. If you've been handling infected plants, wash your hands thoroughly with soap and hot water and dip any contaminated tools in rubbing alcohol before working on healthy plants. Do not replant healthy carnations or pinks in contaminated soil. Avoid damage to plants when cultivating.

PROBLEM: The leaves turn pale and wilt, sometimes very suddenly. The lower leaves are rotted. The stem is slimy and decayed, and minute black pellets may be just barely visible around the base of the plant.

ANALYSIS: Stem rot
This plant disease is caused by a fungus (*Rhizoctonia solani*) that is found in almost all soils. It penetrates the plant at or just below the soil level, rotting through the outer stem bark into the inner stem tissue. Unlike the soft, outer stem rot, the inner stem tissue becomes dry and corky when it is infected. As the rot progresses up the stem, the lower leaves rot, the foliage pales and withers, and the plant may die. *Rhizoctonia* thrives in warm, moist conditions.

SOLUTION: If all the foliage is wilted, it is best to replace the plants. Plants not so severely affected can be saved. An effective cultural method to help control the disease is to let the soil dry out between waterings. (For further information on this technique, see page 857.) Next year before planting, spray or dust the soil with a fungicide containing *PCNB*.

PROBLEM: The leaves are mottled or have yellow to reddish spots, rings, or streaks parallel to the leaf veins. The lower leaves may turn yellow. Sometimes there are blotches on the leaves. The flowers may be streaked or blotched with light or dark colors, or coloring may be uneven.

ANALYSIS: Virus
Several different viruses infect carnations. Generally, virus infections are not very harmful to the plant. In fact, symptoms of infection may not show up unless several viruses are present in the plant at the same time. However, in severe infections, viruses can cause the lower leaves to turn yellow by suppressing the development of the green pigment (chlorophyll) in the leaf tissue. As a result, the leaves produce less food, causing the plant to be weakened. Certain viruses are spread by aphids, which feed on diseased plants and transfer the virus to healthy plants. Other viruses can be spread when the plants are pruned or handled. If diseased plants are touched or pruned, the virus can be transferred to healthy plants on contaminated hands or equipment.

SOLUTION: Once the plant is infected, there is no chemical that will control the virus. Remove weak and stunted plants. Wash your hands thoroughly and dip pruning shears into rubbing alcohol after working on infected plants. Keep the aphid population low by spraying infested plants with an insecticide containing *malathion*. Purchase only healthy plants. For further information on selecting healthy plants, see page 916.

DIGITALIS (FOXGLOVE)

Aphid damage.

PROBLEM: Tiny (⅛ inch) pale green to black, soft-bodied insects cluster on the leaves and stems. The leaves may be curled, distorted, spotted, and yellowing. The flowers may be malformed. A sticky, shiny substance may coat the leaves. Ants are often present.

ANALYSIS: Aphids
Aphids do little damage in small numbers. However, they are extremely prolific and populations can rapidly build up to damaging numbers during the growing season. Damage occurs when the aphid sucks the juices from the foxglove leaves and flower buds. The aphid is unable to digest fully all the sugar in the plant sap and excretes it in a fluid called honeydew. The honeydew often drops onto the leaves below. Ants feed on this sticky substance, and are often present where there is an aphid infestation.

SOLUTION: Spray with an insecticide containing *malathion* as soon as the insects appear. Repeat the spray if the plant becomes reinfested.

Digitalis cultural information
Light: Sun
Water: When the soil is just barely moist
Soil: Any good garden soil
Fertilizer: Medium

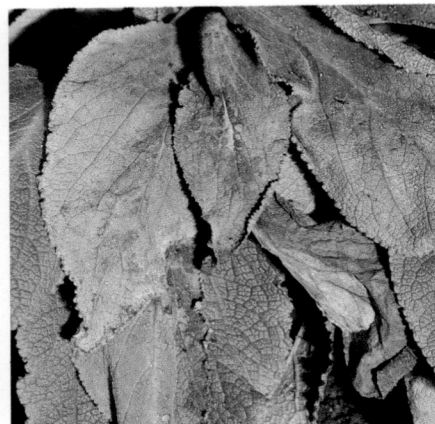

Foxglove anthracnose.

PROBLEM: Light or purplish brown spots up to ⅛ inch in diameter appear on the leaves. The spots are circular or angular, and have purplish margins. Often, black, rough areas develop in the centers of the leaf spots. There may be sunken lesions on the leaf veins and stems, and severely infected leaves turn yellow, wither, and drop off. Often the plants are stunted and die, especially during periods of warm, moist weather. Seedlings may wilt and die.

ANALYSIS: Foxglove anthracnose
This plant disease is caused by a fungus (*Colletotrichum fuscum*) that infects only foxgloves. The fungal spores are spread from plant to plant by splashing water or rain, insects, animals, and contaminated tools. If the leaves are wet, the spores germinate and infect the leaf tissue, creating spots and lesions. Anthracnose is favored by warm temperatures and moist conditions. The fungus survives the winter in diseased plant debris and infected seed. This fungus also causes damping-off of foxglove seedlings. For further information on damping-off, see page 858.

SOLUTION: Spray diseased plants with a fungicide containing *ferbam* or *ziram*. Repeat the spray throughout the growing season at intervals of 7 to 10 days. Remove and destroy plant debris in the fall. If practical, infected leaves may be picked off. Water in the morning so the foliage will have a chance to dry out. Try to avoid wetting the foliage when watering.

DIMORPHOTHECA (AFRICAN DAISY)

Wilt.

PROBLEM: The lower leaves turn yellow, then wilt and die; or all of the foliage may turn yellow and then wither. The flower heads may droop. Often, the plant is affected only on one side. When the stem is sliced open near the base of the plant, dark streaks and discolorations of the inner stem tissue are revealed. The root system may be partially or entirely rotted.

ANALYSIS: Wilt disease
Wilt disease affects many ornamental plants. It is caused by either of 2 soil-inhabiting fungi (*Verticillium albo-atrum* or *Fusarium* species) that persist indefinitely on plant debris or in the soil. The disease is spread by contaminated seeds, plants, soil, and equipment. The fungus enters the plant through the roots and spreads up into the stems and leaves through the water-conducting vessels in the stems. The vessels become discolored and plugged. This plugging cuts off the flow of water to the leaves, causing leaf yellowing and wilting.

SOLUTION: No chemical control is available. It is best to destroy infected plants. Verticillium and fusarium can be removed from the soil only by fumigation techniques. (For more information about soil fumigation, see page 919.)

Dimorphotheca cultural information
Light: Sun
Water: Allow to dry between waterings
Soil: Any good garden soil
Fertilizer: Medium

EUPHORBIA (POINSETTIA) ———— FREESIA

Gray mold.

Root and stem rot.

Aphids (life size).

PROBLEM: Brown spots and blotches appear on the leaves and possibly on the stems. As the disease progresses, a fuzzy brown or grayish mold forms on the infected tissue. Gray mold and spots often appear on the flowers, especially during periods of cool, wet weather. The leaves and stems may be soft and rotted.

ANALYSIS: Gray mold
This widespread plant disease is caused by a fungus (*Botrytis cinerea*) that is found on most dead plant tissue. The fungus initially attacks foliage and flowers that are weak or dead, causing spotting and mold. The fuzzy mold that develops is composed of millions of microscopic spores. Once gray mold has been established on plant debris and weak or dying leaves and flowers, it can invade healthy plant tissue. Crowded plantings, rain, and overhead watering enhance the spread of the disease. Cool temperatures and high humidity favor gray mold growth. Infection is more of a problem in spring and fall when temperatures are lower. In warm winter areas where freezing is rare, gray mold can be a year-round problem.

SOLUTION: Spray infected plants once every 10 to 14 days with a fungicide containing *captan* or *zineb*. Continue spraying as long as the mold is visible. Clean up plant debris, and remove dying or infected leaves, stems, and flowers. Provide enough space between plants to allow good air circulation. Try to avoid wetting the foliage when watering.

PROBLEM: Leaves turn yellow, wilt and die. Stems may be soft and rotted, and the plant may be easily pulled out of the ground. The roots are dark and rotted.

ANALYSIS: Root and stem rot
This disease is caused by any of several different fungi and bacteria that live in the soil. They thrive in waterlogged, heavy soil. Some of these fungi and bacteria attack the plant stems at the soil level, while others attack the roots. Infection causes the roots and stems to decay. This results in wilting, then yellowing leaves, and eventually the death of the plant. These fungi and bacteria are generally spread by infested soil and transplants, contaminated equipment, and splashing or running water.

SOLUTION: Allow the soil around the plants to dry out. (For more information on this technique, see page 857.) Remove and discard severely infected plants. Avoid future root rot problems by planting in well-drained soil. For information on improving soil drainage, see page 901. For more information on root and stem rots, see page 857.

Euphorbia cultural information
Light: Full sun
Water: When the soil is just barely moist
Soil: Any good, well-drained garden soil
Fertilizer: Medium

PROBLEM: Tiny (⅛ inch) pale green to black, soft-bodied insects are clustered on the leaves. The leaves may be curled, distorted, and yellowing. The flowers may be malformed. A shiny, sticky substance coats the leaves. Ants are often present.

ANALYSIS: Aphids
Aphids do little damage in small numbers. However, they are extremely prolific and populations can rapidly build up to damaging numbers during the growing season. Damage occurs when the aphid sucks the juices from the freesia leaves and flower buds. The aphid is unable to digest fully all the sugar in the plant sap and excretes the excess in a fluid called honeydew. The honeydew often drops onto the leaves below. Ants feed on this sticky substance and are often present where there is an aphid infestation.

SOLUTION: Spray with an insecticide containing *malathion* as soon as the insects appear. Repeat the spray if the plant becomes reinfested.

Freesia cultural information
Light: Sun
Water: When soil is just barely moist
Soil: Any good garden soil
Fertilizer: Medium

GERBERA (TRANSVAAL DAISY)

Foot rot.

Gray mold.

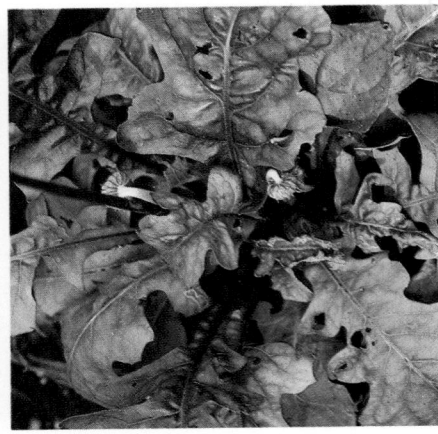

Aphid damage.

PROBLEM: Leaves wilt, turn reddish, and eventually die. The *crown* (where the leaves meet the roots) and roots are soft, water-soaked, and blackish brown.

ANALYSIS: Foot rot
This plant disease is caused by a soil-dwelling fungus (*Phytophthora* species) that penetrates the crown of the plant, then moves down into the roots. Infection causes the crown and roots to decay, resulting in wilting, reddened leaves, and eventually the death of the plant. Foot rot is most severe in heavy, poorly drained soil and generally moist conditions. The fungus is spread by contaminated soil, transplants, tools, and running water.

SOLUTION: Destroy all severely infected plants; they usually will not recover. Allow the soil around the plants to dry out. (For more information on this technique, see page 857.) Do not replant gerberas in infested soil for several years. Avoid future foot rot problems by planting in well-drained soil. For information on improving soil drainage, see page 901. For more information on root and stem rots, see page 856.

PROBLEM: Brown spots and blotches appear on the leaves and possibly on the stems. As the disease progresses, a fuzzy brown or grayish mold forms on the infected tissue. Gray mold and spots often appear on the flowers, especially during periods of cool, wet weather. The leaves and stems may be soft and rotted.

ANALYSIS: Gray mold
This widespread plant disease is caused by a fungus (*Botrytis cinerea*) that is found on most dead plant tissue. The fungus initially attacks foliage and flowers that are weak or dead, causing spotting and mold. The fuzzy mold that develops is composed of millions of microscopic spores. Once gray mold has become established on plant debris and weak or dying leaves and flowers, it can invade healthy plant tissue. The fungus is spread by splashing water, or by infected pieces of plant tissue contacting healthy tissue. Cool temperatures and high humidity favor gray mold growth. Crowded plantings, rain, and overhead watering also enhance the spread of the disease. Infection is more of a problem in spring and fall, when temperatures are lower. In warm winter areas where freezing is rare, gray mold can be a year-round problem.

SOLUTION: Spray infected plants once every 10 to 14 days with a fungicide containing *maneb* or *mancozeb*. Continue spraying as long as the mold is visible. Clean up plant debris, and remove dying or infected leaves, stems, and flowers. Provide enough space between plants to allow good air circulation. Try to avoid wetting the foliage when watering.

PROBLEM: The leaves may be curled, distorted, and yellowing. Often, the flowers are malformed. Tiny (1/8 inch) yellow to pale green soft-bodied insects cluster on the leaves, stems, and flowers. A shiny, sticky substance may coat the leaves. Ants are sometimes present.

ANALYSIS: Aphids
Aphids do little damage in small numbers. However, they are extremely prolific and populations can rapidly build up to damaging numbers during the growing season. Damage occurs when the aphid sucks the juices from the gerbera leaves and flower buds. The aphid is unable to digest fully all the sugar in the plant sap and excretes the excess in a fluid called honeydew. The honeydew often drops onto the leaves below. Ants feed on this sticky substance and are often present where there is an aphid infestation.

SOLUTION: Spray with ORTHO Liquid Sevin or an insecticide containing *malathion* as soon as the insects appear. Repeat the spray if the plant becomes reinfested.

Gerbera cultural information
Light: Sun
Water: When the soil is just barely moist
Soil: Well drained
Fertilizer: Medium

GLADIOLUS

Gladiolus thrips damage.

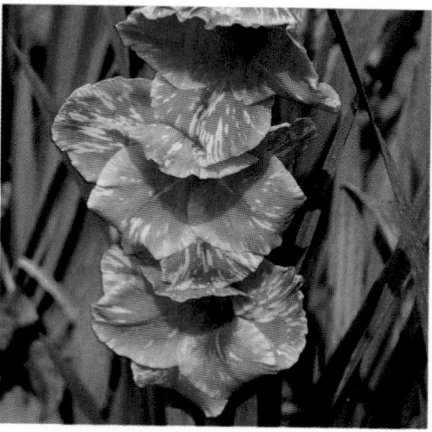
Streaking of gladiolus flowers caused by virus.

GLADIOLUS

ADAPTATION: Throughout the United States.

FLOWERING TIME: Summer to fall.

LIGHT: Full sun.

PLANTING TIME: From late winter or spring, when all danger of frost is past, to midsummer.

SOIL: Any good garden soil. pH 5.5 to 7.5

FERTILIZER: Fertilize with ORTHO Rose & Flower Food 8–12–4 or ORTHO General Purpose Plant Food 8–8–8 according to label directions.

WATER:
How much: Apply enough water to wet the soil 6 to 8 inches deep.
How often: Water when the soil 1 inch below the surface is just barely moist.

HANDLING: For continuous summer bloom, make successive plantings at 2 week intervals from mid-April to mid-July. For cut flowers, harvest when the bottom flower is open. When cutting flowers, allow at least four leaves to remain on the plant.

PROBLEM: Silvery white streaks appear on flowers and foliage. The leaves turn brown and die. Flowers may be deformed and discolored. In the early morning, late afternoon, or on overcast days, blackish brown, slender, winged insects $\frac{1}{16}$ inch long can be seen on the foliage and flower petals. On warm, sunny days these insects hide between leaves and in flower buds. They can be detected only by pulling apart a flower bud or 2 overlapping leaves.

ANALYSIS: Gladiolus thrips
(*Thrips simplex*)
This insect, one of the most common pests of gladiolus plants, also feeds on many other garden ornamentals. Both the immature and adult thrips feed on plant sap by rasping the plant tissue. The injured tissue turns white, causing the characteristic streaking and silvering of the leaves and flowers. The adult female thrips inserts her eggs into growing plant tissue; the emerging young mature within 2 to 4 weeks. Thrips actively feed and reproduce from spring until the first frost of fall. They cannot survive freezing temperatures. In warm winter climates, the adult thrips hibernate in the soil until spring. In cold winter climates, they overwinter by hibernating on gladiolus corms in storage. Corms infested by thrips turn brown and corky and may fail to grow, or produce only stunted, poor quality flowers and foliage.

SOLUTION: Spray infested plants with ORTHO Isotox Insect Killer or ORTHO Diazinon Insect Spray. Repeat the spray at intervals of no less than 10 days if reinfestation occurs. Dust corms with an insecticide containing *malathion* before storing. Discard brown or corky corms.

PROBLEM: Leaves and flowers are streaked, spotted, or mottled. The leaves may also be yellowing, stiff, or thickened. Often the plant blooms prematurely, and the flowers only partially open and then fade rapidly. The entire plant may be dwarfed, although sometimes only the flower spike is stunted.

ANALYSIS: Virus
There are a number of different viruses that infect gladiolus plants. Depending on weather conditions and plant variety, the symptoms of infection can vary from barely noticeable to quite severe. Viral infections rarely cause a plant to die, but can weaken it seriously. The virus increases in the corms (the "bulbs" of the gladiolus plant) year after year. Successive plantings from diseased corms provide flowers of poor quality. Viruses are spread by aphids. These insects feed on diseased plants and transfer the virus to healthy plants at subsequent feedings.

SOLUTION: Once the plant is infected, there is no chemical that will control the virus. To prevent the spread of the disease to healthy plants, remove and destroy infected plants. Keep the aphid population under control by spraying infested plants with ORTHO Diazinon Insect Spray. Because 2 of the viruses that infect gladioli are very common on vegetables in the bean and cucumber families, where practical, avoid planting gladioli near beans, clover, cucumbers, squash, melons, or tomatoes. For more information about controlling disease-carrying insects, see page 880.

GLADIOLUS

Aster yellows.

Scab.

Penicillium corm rot.

PROBLEM: There are many thin, weak leaves, which may turn yellowish green. The flower spikes are twisted and distorted. The flowers often remain green. The plant is generally small and spindly, and frequently the top of the plant is killed.

ANALYSIS: Aster yellows
This plant disease is caused by mycoplasmas, microscopic organisms similar to bacteria. The mycoplasmas are transmitted from plant to plant primarily by leafhoppers. (For more information about leafhoppers, see page 880.) The symptoms of aster yellows are more severe and appear more quickly in warm weather. Even when the disease is present in the plant, aster yellows may not manifest its symptoms in temperatures of 55°F or less. The disease also infects many ornamental plants, vegetables, and weeds. For a list of plants susceptible to aster yellows, see page 994.

SOLUTION: Aster yellows cannot be eliminated entirely, but can be kept under control. Remove and destroy infected plants. To remove sources of infection, eradicate nearby weeds that may harbor aster yellows and leafhopper eggs. Spray leafhopper-infested plants with an insecticide containing *diazinon* or *malathion*. Repeat the spray whenever leafhoppers are seen. For more information about controlling disease-carrying insects, see page 880.

PROBLEM: Sunken black lesions on the corm (the "bulb" of the gladiolus plant) are covered with a shiny, varnishlike material and are encircled by raised, brittle rims. Later in the season, after the corms have been planted, many tiny, raised, reddish brown specks develop on the bases of the emerging leaves. These specks become soft, elongated dead spots, which may be covered with and surrounded by a shiny, oozing material in wet weather. The leaves usually fall over.

ANALYSIS: Scab
This disease, caused by bacteria (*Pseudomonas marginata*), earns its name from the scablike lesions it produces on the gladiolus corms. The bacteria penetrate the corm tissue and then move up into the stem base, producing a soft, watery rot. This decay causes the leaves to fall over. The shiny, varnishlike spots that form on the leaves and corms contain millions of bacteria. Wet, heavy soil and warm temperatures favor the rapid development of this disease. The bacteria can live for several years in infected corms and plant debris. The bacteria are spread by splashing water, and by contaminated corms, soil, tools, and insects. Severely infected plants may die.

SOLUTION: There is no chemical control for this disease. Destroy infected corms. Remove and destroy infected plants. Plant healthy corms in well-drained soil where diseased gladioli have not grown.

PROBLEM: Corky, reddish brown, sunken lesions ½ inch or larger in diameter appear on the corm (the "bulb" of the gladiolus plant). In cool, moist conditions, the rotted areas of the corm become covered with a blue-green mold. Infected corms that have been planted may not produce any foliage. Foliage that is produced turns yellow and wilts. The corms are rotted and moldy.

ANALYSIS: Penicillium corm rot
This disease is caused by a common fungus (*Penicillium gladioli*) that is most often noticed on corms in storage. The fungi infect the corm through wounds or abrasions that usually occur when the corm is dug out of the ground to be put into storage. After the initial infection, the rot spreads throughout the corm and up into the stem tissue. The corms rot rapidly when they are stored in warm, humid conditions. The fungus forms masses of blue-green spores and tiny brown fungal pellets that can survive through dry conditions and extremes of temperatures to invade healthy corms. If mildly infected corms are planted, they may or may not produce foliage, depending upon how severely their infection has progressed. Eventually, any foliage produced will turn yellow and die.

SOLUTION: Destroy all corms showing decay. Store corms in a dry, cool (40° to 45°F) location. Dig them up carefully only when the gladiolus leaves have turned entirely yellow in the fall. Handle the corms carefully to prevent injuries. Dip them in a solution of ORTHO Phaltan Rose and Garden Fungicide before storing, and again before planting them.

HELIANTHEMUM (SUNROSE)

HELIANTHUS (SUNFLOWER)

Dry rot.

Leaf spot.

Verticillium wilt.

PROBLEM: Foliage turns yellow and dies prematurely. Leaf bases are rotted and may be shredded. Black fungal pellets the size of pepper grains may cover the decayed leaf bases and husks of the corms (the "bulbs" of the gladiolus plant). There are dark brown to black sunken lesions on the corms. These lesions are dry and corky. They may enlarge and join together, destroying the entire corm.

ANALYSIS: Dry rot
This plant disease is caused by a fungus (*Stromatinia gladioli*) that attacks corms either in storage or in the soil. After the initial infection, the decay spreads up into the leaf bases, killing the leaves prematurely. Corms that are planted in cold, wet soil or stored in moist conditions are most susceptible to dry rot. The fungus is spread by contaminated soil and corms. The tiny black fungal pellets that form on infected tissue can survive for 10 years or more in the soil.

SOLUTION: Discard infected corms and plants. Plant in well-drained soil. Dig corms before the onset of cold, wet weather and store them in a dry place. If you wish to replant in areas where infected corms have been growing, fumigate the soil. For information about soil fumigation, see page 919.

PROBLEM: Spots and blotches appear on the leaves, ranging in size from barely visible to 1/4 inch in diameter. Several spots may join to form blotches. Leaves may be yellow and dying. Leaf spotting is most severe in warm, humid weather.

ANALYSIS: Leaf spot
Several different fungi cause leaf spots. Some of these fungi may cause leaf yellowing and death, while others merely cause spotting, which is unsightly but not harmful. These fungi are spread by splashing water, wind, insects, and tools. They survive the winter in diseased plant debris. Most of these leaf spot organisms do their greatest damage in mild weather (50° to 85°F).

SOLUTION: Spray at weekly intervals with a fungicide containing *basic copper sulfate, mancozeb,* or *ferbam.* Because leaf spots are favored by warm, humid conditions, it is important to spray conscientiously during these periods. These fungicides protect the new healthy foliage but will not eradicate the fungus on leaves that are already infected. Pick off severely infected leaves.

Helianthemum cultural information
Light: Sun
Water: Allow to dry between waterings
Soil: Well drained
Fertilizer: Light

PROBLEM: Mottling, yellowing, and wilting start on the lower leaves and progress slowly upward. Diseased leaves soon wither. Dark brown areas may appear on the infected stems. When a stem is sliced open near the base of the plant, dark streaks and discolorations of the inner stem tissue are revealed. Although sunflowers may be infected while they are young, they generally do not show symptoms until they flower.

ANALYSIS: Verticillium wilt
This wilt disease affects many ornamental plants. It is caused by a a soil-inhabiting fungus (*Verticillium albo-atrum*). The disease is spread by contaminated seeds, plants, soil, and equipment. The fungus enters the plant through the roots and spreads up into the stems and leaves through the water-conducting vessels in the stems. The vessels become discolored and plugged. This plugging cuts off the flow of water to the leaves, causing leaf yellowing and wilting.

SOLUTION: No chemical control is available. It is best to destroy infected plants. Verticillium can be removed from the soil only by fumigation techniques. (For more information about soil fumigation, see page 919.) However, the best solution is usually to use plants that are resistant to verticillium. See page 995 for a list of wilt-resistant plants.

Helianthus cultural information
Light: Sun
Water: When soil is just barely moist
Soil: Any good garden soil
Fertilizer: Medium to heavy

HELLEBORUS

Crown rot.

HEMEROCALLIS (DAYLILY)

Leaf spot.

Aphids (¼ life size).

PROBLEM: The leaves turn yellow, wilt, and collapse and the plant finally dies. The base of the plant and the lower stems and leaves are covered with white matted strands. Reddish brown to black pellets the size of pinheads or larger form on the infected plant tissue and soil surrounding the base of the plant.

ANALYSIS: Crown rot
This disease is caused by a soil-inhabiting fungus (*Sclerotium delphinii*). It is widespread and attacks many kinds of plants. The fungus penetrates the stems at or just below the soil level, causing decay and death of the root and stem tissue. The fungus can grow through the soil to attack adjacent plants. The crown rot fungus is spread by moving water, diseased transplants, infested soil, air currents, and contaminated tools. The fungal pellets that form can survive in plant debris and dry soil to reinfect healthy plants when conditions are suitable. Crown rot is most severe in moist soil during warm (70°F and up), moist weather.

SOLUTION: Remove and destroy all infected plants and surrounding soil to 6 inches beyond the diseased area. Drench the area where the infected plants were growing with a fungicide containing *PCNB*. To help prevent infection next year, broadcast a *PCNB* fungicide onto uninfested soil and dig it in to a depth of 6 inches before planting.

Helleborus cultural information
Light: Part to full shade
Water: While soil is still moist
Soil: Well drained
Fertilizer: Medium

PROBLEM: Spots and blotches appear on the leaves, ranging in size from barely visible to ¼ inch in diameter. Several spots may join to form blotches. Leaves may be yellow and dying. Leaf spotting is most severe in warm, humid weather.

ANALYSIS: Leaf spot
There are several different fungi that cause leaf spots. Some of these fungi may eventually kill the plant, or weaken it so that it becomes susceptible to attack by other organisms. Others merely cause spotting that is unsightly but not harmful. These fungi are spread by splashing water, wind, insects, and contaminated tools. They generally survive the winter in diseased plant debris. Most of these fungi do their greatest damage in mild weather (50° to 85°F).

SOLUTION: Spray at weekly intervals with a fungicide containing *basic copper sulfate* or *maneb*. Because leaf spots are favored by warm, humid conditions, it is important to spray conscientiously during these periods. These fungicides protect the new, healthy foliage but will not eradicate the fungus on leaves that are already infected. Pick off severely infected leaves.

Hemerocallis cultural information
Light: Sun or partial shade
Water: While soil is still moist
Soil: Any good garden soil
Fertilizer: Medium

PROBLEM: Tiny (⅛ inch) pale green to brown soft-bodied insects are clustered on the leaves. Leaves may be curled, distorted, and yellowing. Flowers may be malformed. A sticky, shiny substance may coat the leaves. Ants are often present.

ANALYSIS: Aphids
Aphids do little damage in small numbers. However, they are extremely prolific and populations can rapidly build up to damaging numbers during the growing season. Damage occurs when the aphid sucks the juices from the daylily leaves. The aphid is unable to digest fully all the sugar in the plant sap and excretes the excess in a fluid called honeydew, which often drops onto the leaves below. Ants feed on this sticky substance, and are often present where there is an aphid infestation.

SOLUTION: Spray the infested plants with an insecticide containing *malathion*. Repeat the spray if the plant becomes reinfested.

HEUCHERA (CORAL BELLS)

Leaf spots.

PROBLEM: Spots and blotches appear on the leaves. The spots may be yellow or brown. They range in size from barely visible to ¼ inch in diameter. Several spots may join to form blotches. Leaves may be yellow and dying. Leaf spotting is most severe in warm, humid weather. In damp conditions, a fine gray mold sometimes covers the infected leaf tissue.

ANALYSIS: Leaf spot
There are a number of different fungi that cause leaf spots. Some of these fungi may eventually kill the plant, or weaken it so that it becomes susceptible to attack by other organisms. Others merely cause spotting that is unsightly but not harmful. These fungi are spread by splashing water, wind, insects, and contaminated tools. They generally survive the winter in diseased plant debris. Most of the leaf spot organisms do their greatest damage in mild weather (50° to 85°F).

SOLUTION: Where practical, pick off the diseased leaves. Spray with a fungicide containing *basic copper sulfate* or *maneb* every 7 to 10 days, or frequently enough to protect the new foliage as it grows. These fungicides protect the new healthy foliage but will not eradicate the fungus on leaves that are already infected. Because leaf spots are favored by humid conditions, it is important to spray frequently during these periods.

Heuchera cultural information
Light: Shade or partial shade
Water: Do not allow to dry out
Soil: Any good garden soil
Fertilizer: Medium

HOSTA (PLANTAIN LILY)

Snail damage.

PROBLEM: Irregularly shaped holes with smooth edges are chewed in the leaves. Leaves and stems may be chewed off entirely. Silvery trails wind around on the plants and nearby soil. Snails and slugs may be seen moving around or feeding on the plants, especially at night. Check for them by inspecting the garden at night by flashlight.

ANALYSIS: Snails and slugs
These pests are mollusks, and are related to clams, oysters, and other shellfish. They feed on a wide variety of garden plants. Like other mollusks, snails and slugs need to be moist all the time. For this reason, they avoid direct sun and dry places, and hide during the day in damp places, such as under flower pots or in thick groundcover. They emerge at night or on cloudy days to feed. The young look like miniature versions of their parents.

SOLUTION: Scatter ORTHO Bug-Geta Snail & Slug Pellets or ORTHO Slug-Geta Snail & Slug Bait granules around the areas you wish to protect. Also scatter the bait in areas where snails or slugs might be hiding, such as in dense groundcover, weedy areas, compost piles, or pot storage areas. Before spreading the bait, wet down the treated areas to encourage snail and slug activity that night. Repeat the application every 2 weeks as long as snails and slugs are active.

Hosta cultural information
Light: Partial to full shade
Water: Do not allow to dry out
Soil: Well drained
Fertilizer: Medium

HYACINTHUS (HYACINTH)

HYACINTHUS

ADAPTATION: Zones 4 through 8. Hyacinths may be grown in zones 9 and 10 if they are precooled (see below). To determine your zone, see the map on page 1004.

FLOWERING TIME: Spring.

LIGHT: Full sun to half-day sun.

PLANTING TIME: Fall.

SOIL: Well drained. pH 6.0 to 8.0

FERTILIZER: When planting, mix 1 teaspoon of ORTHO Bone Meal 0–12–0 or ORTHO Superphosphate 0–20–0 into the soil at the bottom of the planting hole. During the growing season, fertilize with ORTHO General Purpose Plant Food 8–8–8 according to label directions.

WATER:
How much: Apply enough water to wet the soil 1 to 1½ feet deep.
How often: Water when the soil an inch below the surface is just barely moist. Stop watering the bulbs when the foliage turns yellow.

HANDLING: Continue to water and fertilize plants regularly until the foliage turns yellow. Remove foliage after it has turned yellow. In zones 9 and 10, precool bulbs for 6 weeks before planting by storing them in paper bags in the refrigerator crisper.

HYACINTHUS (HYACINTH)

Short stems.

PROBLEM: Flower stems are very short, and the flowers may be smaller than normal. Sometimes only the tip of the flower stalk emerges and blooms at ground level. There are no signs of insects or disease, and the foliage appears healthy.

ANALYSIS: Short stems
This condition is the result of warm spring temperatures, lack of adequate chilling, or a combination of both. Hyacinth bulbs contain embryonic flowers and stems. A minimum of 6 weeks exposure to cool temperatures (45° to 50°F) during the winter stimulates the stem cells to elongate, causing the immature hyacinth to emerge from the ground. During cool spring weather (50° to 55°F) the stems continue to elongate to their full length, at which point the flowers mature and open. In warm winter areas, the hyacinth stems often fail to elongate properly due to inadequate chilling. Also, during unseasonal spring hot spells (when air temperature reaches 70°F or higher) the hyacinth flowers are stimulated by the heat to mature and open before the stems have entirely emerged from the ground.

SOLUTION: There is nothing you can do to increase the length of the hyacinth stem once the flower has matured. If warm spring temperatures are common in your area, plant hyacinths in locations where they will receive either filtered light, or direct sun only in the morning or late afternoon. The lower air and soil temperatures in such areas will help to increase stem lengths. If you live in a warm winter area, place hyacinth bulbs in paper bags in the fall, and chill them in the crisper section of the refrigerator for 6 weeks before planting.

Diseased bulb on left.

PROBLEM: Bulbs that have been planted may not produce any foliage; or if foliage is produced the flower stalk may not form. Sometimes the flower stalk develops, but the flowers open irregularly and rot off. The entire stalk may rot at the base and fall over. If pulled gently, the leaves and flower stalk may lift entirely off the bulb, which is soft, rotted, and filled with a white, thick, foul-smelling ooze.

ANALYSIS: Bacterial soft rot
This plant disease is caused by bacteria (*Erwinia carotovora*) that infect hyacinth bulbs both in storage and when planted in the ground. The bacteria initially penetrate and decay the upper portion of the bulb. The disease then progresses upward into the leaves and flower stalks, and down through the bulb and roots. The thick ooze that accompanies the decay is filled with millions of bacteria. Bulbs that are infected before they are planted will produce little, if any, growth. Even well-established, healthy plants may decay quite rapidly after they are infected, sometimes within 3 to 5 days. The bacteria survive in infected plant debris and bulbs, and are spread by contaminated insects and tools, and diseased bulbs and plants. Soft rot is favored by moist conditions. If bulbs freeze while they are in storage, they are especially susceptible to infection.

SOLUTION: There is no cure for this disease. Remove and destroy all bulbs and plants showing signs of decay. Store bulbs in a dry, cool (40° to 45°F) location. Plant only healthy bulbs in well-drained soil. Do not overwater. For instructions on proper watering, see page 906.

IBERIS (CANDYTUFT)

Powdery mildew.

PROBLEM: The leaves and stems are covered with grayish white powdery spots and patches that occur primarily on the surfaces of the leaves. Leaves eventually turn yellow.

ANALYSIS: Powdery mildew
This common plant disease is caused by a fungus (*Erysiphe polygoni*) that thrives in both humid and dry weather. The powdery patches consist of fungal strands and spores. The spores are spread by the wind to healthy plants. A severe infection may kill the plant. Since this powdery mildew attacks several different kinds of plants, the fungus from a diseased plant may infect other types of plants in the garden. For a list of susceptible plants, see page 995. Under favorable conditions, powdery mildew can spread through a closely spaced planting in a matter of days or weeks.

SOLUTION: Spray infected plants with a fungicide containing *folpet* or *cycloheximide* to stop the spread of the disease. These fungicides protect the new, healthy foliage by killing the powdery mildew spores as they germinate on the leaves. They will not eradicate the fungus on leaves that are already infected. Severely infected plants should be removed. Spray at regular intervals of 7 to 10 days, or as often as necessary to protect new growth. Space plants far enough apart to allow good air circulation. Clean up plant debris.

Iberis cultural information
Light: Sun
Water: When the soil is just barely moist
Soil: Any good garden soil
Fertilizer: Medium

IMPATIENS (BALSAM)

Damping-off.

PROBLEM: Seeds don't sprout, or seedlings fall over soon after they emerge. Areas on the stem at the soil line are water-soaked and discolored. The base is soft and thin.

ANALYSIS: Damping-off
The fungi that cause damping-off are favored by wet soil with a high nitrogen level. Under these conditions, the fungi are more active, and the seedlings are more succulent and susceptible to attack. Damping-off often affects flowers that are planted too early in the spring, before the soil has had a chance to dry and warm sufficiently for quick seed germination. Damping-off can also be a problem when the weather remains cloudy and wet while seeds are germinating, or if seedlings are too heavily shaded.

SOLUTION: To prevent damping-off, take these precautions:
1. Allow the surface of the soil to dry slightly between waterings.
2. Do not start seeds in soil that has a high nitrogen level. Add nitrogen fertilizers after the seedlings have produced their first true leaves.
3. Plant seeds after the soil has reached the temperature needed for quick germination. For ideal germination temperatures, see page 992.
4. Protect seeds during germination by coating them with fungicides containing *captan* or *PCNB*. Add a pinch of fungicide to a packet of seeds (or ½ teaspoon per pound), and shake well to coat the seeds with the fungicide. For more information on starting seeds, see page 917.

IMPATIENS

ADAPTATION: Throughout the United States.

FLOWERING TIME: Spring to fall.

LIGHT: Filtered sun to deep shade. Impatiens may be planted in direct sun if they are not allowed to dry out.

PLANTING TIME: Spring, after all danger of frost is past.

SOIL: Any good garden soil that is rich in organic matter. pH 6.0 to 8.0

FERTILIZER: Fertilize with ORTHO Rose & Flower Food 8–12–4 or ORTHO General Purpose Plant Food 8–8–8 according to label directions.

WATER:
How much: Apply enough water to plants in the ground to wet the soil 8 to 10 inches deep.
Containers: Apply enough water so that 10 percent of the water drains from the bottom of the container.
How often: Water when the soil 1 inch below the surface is moist but not wet.

Sunburn.

PROBLEM: Leaves are light and faded, often turning pale green to yellowish white. Some of the leaves may turn brown and brittle, and drop. There is very little new growth. The plants are exposed to at least several hours of direct sun during the day. There are no signs of plant pests or diseases.

ANALYSIS: Sunburn
Impatiens are adapted to shady conditions, and will not tolerate more than a few hours of direct sun, especially intense afternoon sun. Even if they receive only one or two hours of direct sunlight, they may drop leaves and discolor slightly, turning yellow-green. The excess light breaks down the plant tissue, causing the chlorophyll (green plant pigment) to disappear. Impatiens are most sensitive to sunburn when they are allowed to dry out.

SOLUTION: Transplant your impatiens to a shaded or partially shaded location, or to a location where they will receive morning sun. Avoid placing them in an area where they are exposed to afternoon sun. Replace them with plants that are adapted to a sunny location.

IMPATIENS (BALSAM)

Leaf spot.

PROBLEM: The leaves are spotted or blotched with brown spots that may range in size from barely visible to ¼ inch in diameter. Several spots may join to form blotches. The leaves may turn yellow and die. Leaf spotting is most severe in wet weather.

ANALYSIS: Leaf spot
There are a number of different fungi that cause leaf spots. Some of these fungi will eventually kill the plant, while others merely cause spotting that is unsightly but not harmful. These fungi are spread by splashing water, wind, insects, and contaminated tools. Fungal strands or spores survive the winter in plant debris. Most of the leaf spot organisms do their greatest damage in humid conditions and temperatures of 50° to 85°F.

SOLUTION: Spray infected plants with a fungicide containing *captan*, *benomyl*, or *folpet* at intervals of 7 to 10 days. Make sure your plant is listed on the product label. Because leaf spots are favored by warm, wet conditions, it is important to spray conscientiously during these periods. Pick off spotted, diseased leaves and clean up plant debris.

Spider mite damage.

PROBLEM: Leaves are stippled, yellowing, and dirty. Leaves may dry out and drop. There may be webbing over flower buds, between leaves, or on the lower surfaces of the leaves. To determine if the plant is infested with mites, hold a sheet of white paper underneath an affected plant and tap the plant sharply. Minute green, red, or yellow specks the size of pepper grains will drop to the paper and begin to crawl around. These pests are easily seen against the white background.

ANALYSIS: Two-spotted spider mite (*Tetranychus urticae*)
These mites, related to spiders, are major pests of many garden and greenhouse plants. They cause damage by sucking sap from the undersides of the leaves. As a result of feeding, the green leaf pigment disappears, producing the stippled appearance. Mites are active throughout the growing season, but are favored by hot, dry weather (70°F and up). By midsummer, they build up to tremendous numbers.

SOLUTION: Spray the infested plants with ORTHO Isotox Insect Killer. Repeat the spray 2 more times at regular intervals 7 to 10 days.

IRIS

IRIS

ADAPTATION:
Rhizomatous: Zones 5 through 10.
Bulbous: Zones 7 through 10.
Irises may be grown in colder areas if heavily mulched. To determine your zone, see the map on page 1004.

FLOWERING TIME:
Rhizomatous: Early summer.
Bulbous: Late spring through early summer.

LIGHT: Full sun.

PLANTING TIME:
Rhizomatous: Summer.
Bulbous: Fall.

SOIL: Well drained. pH 6.0 to 8.0

FERTILIZER: Fertilize with ORTHO Rose & Flower Food 8-12-4 or ORTHO General Purpose Plant Food 8-8-8 according to label directions.

WATER:
How much: Apply enough water to wet the soil to 1½ feet deep.
How often: Water when the soil 1 inch below the surface is just barely moist.

HANDLING: Mulch irises after the first hard fall frost. Divide rhizomatous iris clumps every 3 to 5 years.

Didymellina leaf spot.

Mosaic on Dutch iris.

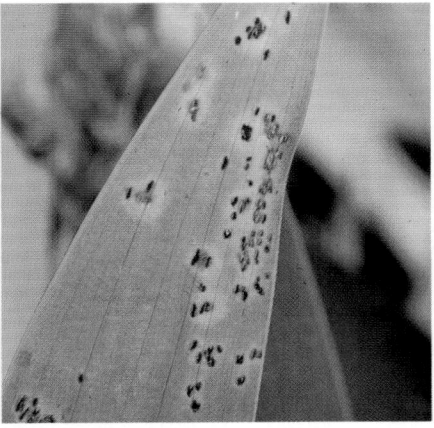

Rust.

PROBLEM: Tiny brown spots from ⅛ to ¼ inch in diameter appear on the leaves. The spots have distinct reddish borders and may be surrounded by water-soaked margins that later turn yellow. After the plant has flowered, the spots enlarge rapidly and may join together to form blotches. Spotting is most severe in wet weather. The leaves die prematurely.

ANALYSIS: Leaf spots
This disease is caused by a fungus (*Didymellina macrospora*) that infects only irises and a few other closely related plants. This fungus attacks the leaves, and occasionally the flower stalks and buds. It will not affect iris roots, bulbs, or rhizomes. Although the fungus does not directly kill the plant, several years of repeated infection results in premature leaf death each summer, greatly reducing rhizome and bulb vigor. Some varieties of iris suffer leaf dieback even when they are only lightly spotted, while other varieties can be covered with spots before they start to die. When the leaves are wet, or during periods of high humidity, the fungal spots produce spores that are spread to other plants by wind or splashing water. The fungus spends the winters in old infected leaves and debris.

SOLUTION: Spray plants with a fungicide containing *zineb, basic copper sulfate,* or *benomyl.* Repeat the spray every 7 to 10 days until the foliage starts to die back. Clean up plant debris and clip off diseased foliage in the fall. Spray again when new growth appears, and repeat the spray 4 to 6 more times at intervals of 7 to 10 days. Use a spreader-sticker when spraying (see page 915).

PROBLEM: Leaves are mottled light and dark green. Foliage may be streaked or stippled yellow. Young leaves are most severely affected. The plant may be stunted, and often the flowers are smaller than normal. There may be dark teardrop or feathery markings on the flowers.

ANALYSIS: Mosaic
This plant disease is caused by a virus. Depending upon the species or variety of iris, symptoms of infection can vary from barely noticeable to quite severe. Iris grown from bulbs (such as Dutch iris) are most severely affected by this virus. Mosaic rarely causes a plant to die, but can weaken or disfigure it extensively. The virus increases in the bulbs and rhizomes year after year. Successive plantings of diseased bulbs and rhizomes provide only poor quality flowers and foliage. Mosaic is spread by aphids. These insects feed on diseased plants and transfer the virus to healthy plants at later feedings.

SOLUTION: Once the plant is infected, there are no chemicals that will control the virus. Remove and destroy severely infected, weakened plants. Keep the aphid population under control by spraying infested plants with an insecticide containing *malathion.* Repeat the spray if reinfestation occurs. For more information about controlling disease-carrying insects, see page 880.

PROBLEM: Rust-colored, powdery pustules appear on both sides of the leaves. Later in the season, these pustules turn dark brown. Severely infected leaves may die prematurely.

ANALYSIS: Rust
This plant disease is caused by a number of closely related fungi (*Puccinia* species). The rust-colored pustules are composed of millions of microscopic spores. Some of the rust spores spend the winter on iris leaves that have not died back entirely, while others overwinter on other kinds of plants. Infection usually starts in the spring as soon as conditions are favorable for plant growth. The spores are spread to healthy plants by splashing water and wind. Because iris varieties vary greatly in their susceptibility to rust, some may be killed prematurely, while others may not be affected. Rust is greatly favored by wet weather.

SOLUTION: Spray infected plants with a fungicide containing *mancozeb, ferbam,* or *zineb.* Repeat the spray 2 or 3 more times at intervals of 7 to 10 days. Remove and destroy old and dying iris leaves in the fall. Water in the morning to allow the foliage a chance to dry out before nightfall. Plant rust-resistant varieties, if available.

Rust-resistant Dutch iris: Early Blue, Gold and Silver, Golden West, Imperator, Lemon Queen, and Texas Gold.

IRIS

Iris borer damage.

Crown rot.

Bacterial soft rot.

PROBLEM: Dark streaks, water-soaked spots, and possibly slits develop in new leaves in the spring to early summer. The leaf edges may be chewed and ragged. By midsummer, the foliage is wilting and discolored. The leaf bases are loose and rotted. The rhizomes are often filled with holes and may be soft and rotted. Pink caterpillars, from 1 to 2 inches long, are feeding inside the rhizomes.

ANALYSIS: Iris borer
(*Macronoctua onusta*)
The larva of this night-flying moth is the most destructive insect pest of iris. In the fall, the adult moth lays eggs in old leaf and flower stalks. The eggs hatch in late April or early May. The emerging larvae initially feed on the leaf surface, producing ragged leaf edges and watery feeding scars. They then bore into the inner leaf tissue, and gradually mine their way down into the rhizome, on which they feed throughout the summer. The damaged rhizome is very susceptible to bacterial soft rot. The larvae leave the rhizome, pupate in the soil, and emerge as adult moths in the fall.

SOLUTION: Clean up plant debris by April to eliminate overwintering borer eggs. Apply an insecticide dust containing *carbaryl*, *dimethoate*, or *malathion* weekly from the time first growth starts until the beginning of June. In May and June, squeeze the leaves in the vicinity of feeding damage to kill feeding borers inside. Destroy heavily infested plants and rhizomes. To kill the borers in lightly infested rhizomes, poke a wire into borer holes.

PROBLEM: The leaves of irises grown from rhizomes (such as bearded iris) die, starting with the leaftips and progressing downward, eventually killing the plant. The leaf bases and possibly the rhizomes are dry, brown, and rotted. The leaves of irises grown from bulbs (such as Dutch iris) are stunted, turn yellow, and die prematurely. The leaves and stems at the soil level are rotted and the bulbs are soft and crumbly. White, matted, fungal strands cover the crowns and soil surrounding both rhizomatous and bulbous irises. Small, tan to reddish brown pellets the size of mustard seeds form on the infected plant tissue and soil.

ANALYSIS: Crown rot
This disease is caused by a widespread fungus (*Sclerotium rolfsii*) that initially penetrates the stems at the soil level. It decays and kills the leaf and stem bases, bulbs, and often part or all of the rhizomes. The fungus can grow over the soil to attack nearby plants. Crown rot is spread by moving water, diseased transplants, infested soil, and contaminated tools. The fungal pellets can survive for many years in dry soil and extremes of temperature to reinfect healthy plants when conditions are suitable. Crown rot is most severe in overcrowded plantings and during periods of warm temperatures (70°F and up) and moist conditions.

SOLUTION: Remove and destroy infected plants, bulbs, rhizomes, and the soil immediately surrounding them to 6 inches beyond the diseased area. Drench the area with a fungicide containing *PCNB*. Next year, repeat the soil drench at planting time and again when new growth is showing. Plant in well-drained soil, and thin out overcrowded plantings.

PROBLEM: Leaves turn yellow, wilt, and eventually die. Dieback often starts at the leaf tips and progresses downward. The entire leaf cluster (fan) may be found lying on the ground. If pulled gently, the leaf fan sometimes lifts off the rhizome (the elongated, jointed, underground stem). Leaf bases and rhizomes are often rotted and foul-smelling.

ANALYSIS: Bacterial soft rot
This plant disease is caused by a bacterium (*Erwinia carotovora*). It is a serious and common disease of bearded and other rhizomatous irises. The bacteria enter the plant through wounds in the leaves and rhizomes, which are frequently made by iris borers. As the infection develops, the plant tissue decays into a soft, foul-smelling mass. Finally, the plant dies and the inner rhizome tissue disintegrates. Infection and rapid decay are favored by moist, dark conditions. These bacteria live in the soil and in plant debris. They are spread by contaminated plants and rhizomes, soil, insects, and tools.

SOLUTION: Remove and destroy all diseased plants; they cannot be cured. Discard diseased rhizomes before planting. If only a small portion of the rhizome is infected, it may possibly be saved by cutting off the diseased portion. Avoid wounding the rhizomes when digging them up. After dividing rhizomes, let the wounds heal for a few days before replanting. Plant irises in a sunny, well-drained location. Plant the rhizome shallowly, so the upper portion is exposed. Clean up plant debris in the fall. Control iris borers.

LANTANA

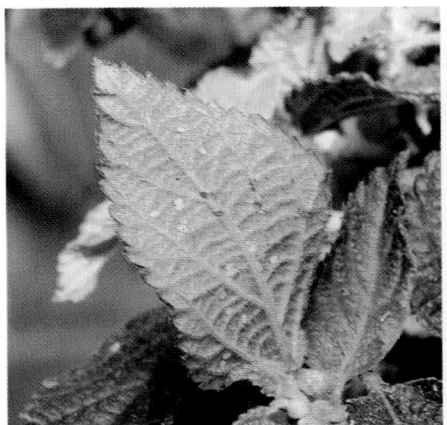
Greenhouse whiteflies (twice life size).

PROBLEM: Tiny, winged insects $1/12$ inch long are found on the leaves. The insects are covered with white, waxy powder. When the plant is touched, insects flutter rapidly around it. The leaves may be mottled and yellowing.

ANALYSIS: Greenhouse whitefly (*Trialeurodes vaporariorum*)
This insect is a common pest of many garden ornamentals and greenhouse plants. The 4-winged adult lays eggs on the undersides of leaves. The larvae are the size of a pinhead, flat, oval-shaped, and semitransparent, with white, waxy filaments radiating from the body. They feed for about a month before changing to the adult form. Both the larval and adult forms suck sap from the leaves. The larvae are more damaging because they feed more heavily. In warm winter areas, the insect can be active year-round. The whitefly is unable to live through freezing winters. Spring reinfestations in such areas come from migrating whiteflies and from infested greenhouse-grown plants placed in the garden.

SOLUTION: Control whiteflies by spraying with ORTHO Orthene Systemic Insect Control, allowing at least 7 days to pass between applications.

Lantana cultural information
Light: Sun
Water: Let the soil dry out between waterings
Soil: Any good garden soil
Fertilizer: Light

LATHYRUS (SWEET PEA)

Powdery mildew.

PROBLEM: The leaves and stems are covered with grayish white powdery spots and patches that occur primarily on the upper surfaces of the older leaves. Leaves eventually turn yellow and wither.

ANALYSIS: Powdery mildew
This common plant disease is caused by a fungus (*Erysiphe polygoni*) that can be severe on sweet peas. Powdery mildew thrives in both humid and dry weather. The powdery patches consist of fungal strands and spores. The spores are spread by the wind to healthy plants. The fungus saps plant nutrients, causing yellowing and sometimes death of the leaves, especially the older ones. A severe infection may occasionally kill the plant. Since this powdery mildew attacks many different kinds of plants, the fungus from a diseased plant may infect other types of plants in the garden. For a list of susceptible plants, see page 995. Under favorable conditions, powdery mildew can spread through a closely spaced planting in a matter of days or weeks.

SOLUTION: Spray infected plants with a fungicide containing *benomyl*, or dust them with *sulfur*. These fungicides protect the new, healthy foliage by killing the powdery mildew spores as they germinate on the leaves. They will not eradicate the fungus on leaves that are already infected. If practical, these may be picked off. Severely infected plants should be removed. Spray or dust at regular intervals of 7 to 10 days, or as often as necessary to protect new growth. Clean up plant debris.

Wilt.

PROBLEM: Lower leaves turn yellow, then wilt and die; or all of the foliage may turn yellow and then wither. Flower heads may droop. When the stem is sliced open near the base of the plant, dark streaks and discolorations of the inner stem tissue are revealed.

ANALYSIS: Wilt disease
This widespread plant disease is caused by either of 2 fungi (*Verticillium* species or *Fusarium* species). These fungi live indefinitely on plant debris and in the soil. The disease is spread by contaminated seeds, plants, soil, and equipment. The fungus enters the plant through the roots and spreads up into the stems and leaves through the water-conducting vessels in the stems. The vessels become discolored and plugged. This plugging cuts off the flow of water to the leaves, causing leaf yellowing and wilting.

SOLUTION: No chemical control is available. It is best to destroy infected plants. These fungi can be removed from the soil only by fumigation techniques. (For more information about soil fumigation, see page 919.) However, the best solution is usually to use plants that are resistant to verticillium and fusarium.

Lathyrus cultural information
Light: Sun
Water: Keep the soil moist
Soil: Any good garden soil
Fertilizer: Medium to heavy

405

LATHYRUS (SWEET PEA)

Two-spotted spider mite damage.

PROBLEM: Leaves are stippled, yellowing, and mealy. Leaves may dry out and drop. There may be webbing over flower buds, between leaves, or on the lower surfaces of the leaves. To determine if the plant is infested with mites, hold a sheet of white paper underneath an affected leaf and tap the leaf sharply. Minute green, red, or yellow specks the size of pepper grains will drop to the paper and begin to crawl around. The pests are easily seen against the white background.

ANALYSIS: Two-spotted spider mite
(*Tetranychus urticae*)
These mites, related to spiders, are major pests of sweet peas and many other garden and greenhouse plants. Mites cause damage by sucking sap from the undersides of the leaves. As a result of feeding, the green leaf pigment disappears, producing the stippled appearance. Mites are active throughout the growing season, but are favored by hot, dry weather (70°F and up). By midsummer, they build up to tremendous numbers.

SOLUTION: Spray the infested plants with a pesticide containing *dicofol*. Repeat the spray 2 more times at regular intervals of 5 to 7 days.

LILIUM (LILY)

LILIUM

ADAPTATION: Throughout the United States.

FLOWERING TIME: Depending upon the species, late spring to late summer.

LIGHT: Full sun to part shade, depending on the variety.

PLANTING TIME: When bulbs are available (fall through spring).

SOIL: Well drained, high in organic matter. ph 6.0 to 7.5

FERTILIZER: When planting, mix 1 teaspoon of ORTHO Bone Meal 0–12–0 into the soil at the bottom of the planting hole. During the growing season, fertilize with ORTHO Rose & Flower Food 8–12–4 or ORTHO General Purpose Plant Food 8–8–8 according to label directions.

WATER:
  How much: Apply enough water to wet the soil 8 to 12 inches deep.
  Containers: Apply enough water so that 10 percent of the water drains from the bottom of the container.
  How often: Water when the soil 1 inch below the surface is just barely moist.

HANDLING: After the plants have bloomed, allow them to die back, then cut them off at ground level.

Root and bulb rot. Diseased plant on right.

PROBLEM: Plants are stunted and wilting, and the lower leaves turn yellow. The tips of the lower leaves may be dying, and brown, dead patches may appear along the leaf edges. The flower buds may wither and fail to open. The bulbs and roots are rotted.

ANALYSIS: Root and bulb rots
Rot problems are common with lilies. These plant diseases are caused by various fungi (*Rhizoctonia, Phytophthora, Pythium, Fusarium, Cylindrocarpon*). These fungi attack and decay the bulbs and roots, causing stunting, wilting, and eventually the death of the foliage and flowers. These bulb and root rot organisms live in the soil and stored bulbs, and are favored by wet soil. Sometimes bulbs in storage are lightly infected but the fungal decay hasn't progressed far enough to be easily noticed. When planted, these bulbs may rot so quickly that they do not produce any foliage.

SOLUTION: Remove and destroy infected plants. Check all bulbs carefully and discard any that are moldy, rotted, or dry and crumbly. Before planting, dip clean, healthy bulbs in a fungicide solution containing *truban* or *benomyl*. Plant in well-drained soil. Store bulbs in a cool (40° to 45°F), dry location.

Aphids (life size).

Virus.

Root and stem rot.

PROBLEM: Leaves may be curled, distorted, and yellowing. Flowers are sometimes malformed. Tiny (⅛ inch) pale green to black soft-bodied insects are clustered on the leaves and stems. A sticky, shiny substance may coat the leaves. Ants are often present.

ANALYSIS: Aphids
There are a number of different species of this common insect that feed on lilies. Aphids cause their damage by sucking plant sap; this feeding produces leaf curling, yellowing, and distortion. In the process of feeding, certain aphids can infect lilies with mosaic virus disease. The aphid is unable to digest fully all the sugar in the plant sap and excretes the excess in a fluid called honeydew. The honeydew often drops onto the leaves below. Ants feed on this sticky substance, and are often present where there is an aphid infestation.

SOLUTION: Spray infested plants with an insecticide containing *malathion*. Repeat the spray if reinfestation occurs, allowing at least a week to pass between applications. In the fall, clean up plant debris that might harbor aphid eggs.

PROBLEM: The leaves are mottled and streaked light and dark green, and the plant may be stunted and dying. The leaves may be spotted with tiny yellow, brown, or gray flecks. These flecks are elongated and run parallel to the leaf veins. Plants with these flecks are often stunted and have small, streaked flowers that do not open fully. Their leaves may be twisted or curled, and frequently die prematurely, starting from the bottom of the plant.

ANALYSIS: Virus
There are several virus diseases of lilies that cause mottling or flecking of the foliage. *Mosaic viruses* produce leaf mottling and discoloration. Depending on the species or variety, the symptoms of infection can be mild or severe. *Fleck* is produced if a plant is simultaneously infected by the *symptomless lily virus* and the *cucumber mosaic virus* (which may or may not produce mottling by itself). Leaf flecking is usually accompanied by stunting and poor quality flowers and foliage. The plant is generally disfigured. Viruses remain in infected bulbs year after year, so successive plantings of diseased bulbs will produce only poor quality flowers and foliage. All of these viruses are spread by aphids, which pick up the virus while feeding on diseased plants and then transmit it to healthy plants at later feedings.

SOLUTION: There is no chemical control for viruses. Remove and destroy infected plants. Control aphids by spraying infested plants with an insecticide containing *malathion*. Respray if reinfestation occurs. Plant mosaic-resistant or immune lilies, a list of which can be found on page 993.

PROBLEM: Leaves and stems turn yellow, wilt, and die. The lower leaves and stems may be soft and rotted. White fungal strands may grow around the base of the plants.

ANALYSIS: Root and stem rot
This disease is caused by any of a number of different fungi that persist indefinitely in the soil. They thrive in waterlogged, heavy soil. Some of these fungi attack the plant stems at the soil level, while others attack the roots. Infection causes the roots and stems to decay. This results in wilting, then yellowing leaves, and eventually the death of the plant. These fungi are generally spread by infested soil and transplants, contaminated equipment, and splashing or running water. Many of these organisms also cause damping-off of seedlings. For more information about damping-off, see page 858.

SOLUTION: Allow the soil around the plants to dry out. (For more information on this technique, see page 857.) Remove and discard severely infected plants. Avoid future root rot problems by planting in well-drained soil. For information on improving soil drainage, see page 901. For more information on root and stem rots, see page 856.

Lobularia cultural information
Light: Part to full sun
Water: When the soil is almost dry
Soil: Well drained
Fertilizer: Light

LOBULARIA (SWEET ALYSSUM) ———

Downy mildew.

PROBLEM: Pale green to yellow spots develop on the leaves. A white, downy growth may be present on the upper and especially on the lower surfaces of the leaves. Infected leaves turn yellow, and the plant eventually dies.

ANALYSIS: Downy mildew
This plant disease is caused by a fungus (*Peronospora parasitica*) that infects flowers and vegetables in the cabbage family. The characteristic downy mold that develops on infected plants is composed of many microscopic spores. These spores may be blown or splashed to healthy plants, and germinate on wet stems and leaves. Downy mildew is favored by cool days and nights, and moist or humid weather conditions. The fungus survives the winter in plant debris or in perennial plants or roots.

SOLUTION: This fungus is difficult to eliminate entirely during cool, moist weather. However, you can control it by spraying infected plants with a fungicide containing *chlorothalonil*. Repeat at intervals of 7 to 10 days. Water early in the day to allow the plants to dry out before nightfall. Remove and destroy plant debris.

MATTHIOLA (STOCK) ———

MATTHIOLA ———

ADAPTATION: Throughout the United States.

FLOWERING TIME: Spring through early summer. In zones 9 and 10, late winter through early summer. To determine your zone, see the map on page 1004.

LIGHT: Full sun.

PLANTING TIME: Spring, after all danger of frost is past. In zones 9 and 10, plant in early fall.

SOIL: Any good well-drained garden soil.

FERTILIZER: Fertilize with ORTHO Rose & Flower Food 8–12–4 or ORTHO General Purpose Plant Food 8–8–8 according to label directions.

WATER:
How much: Apply enough water to plants in the ground to wet the soil 6 to 8 inches deep.
Containers: Apply enough water so that about 10 percent of the water drains from the bottom of the container.
How often: Water when the soil 1 inch below the surface is just barely moist.

Verticillium wilt.

PROBLEM: Leaves turn yellow and die, starting at the base of the plant. The plant is stunted. When the stem near the base of the plant is sliced open, dark streaks and discolorations are seen in the inner stem tissue.

ANALYSIS: Fungal wilt
This widespread plant disease is caused by either of two fungi (*Verticillium or Fusarium*) that persist indefinitely on plant debris or in the soil. The disease is spread by contaminated seeds, plants, soil, and equipment. The fungus enters the plant through the roots and spreads up into the stems and leaves through the water-conducting vessels in the stems. The vessels become discolored and plugged. This plugging cuts off the flow of water to the leaves, causing leaf yellowing and wilting.

SOLUTION: No chemical controls are available. It is best to destroy infected plants. Verticillium and fusarium can be removed from the soil only by fumigation techniques. (For more information about soil fumigation, see page 919.) However, the best solution is usually to use plants that are resistant to verticillium and fusarium.

NARCISSUS (DAFFODIL, JONQUIL)

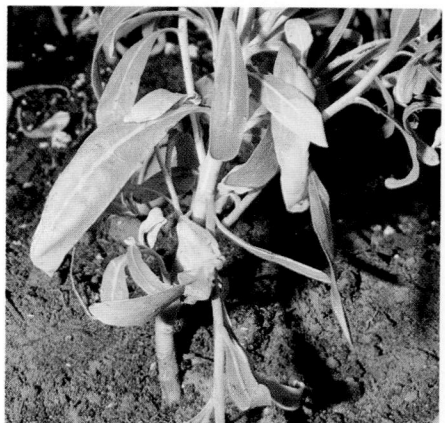

Bacterial wilt.

PROBLEM: Young plants (2 to 4 inches tall) wilt and collapse. The main stems are soft and yellowish, and have a water-soaked appearance. There may be dark green or brown lines along the stems. The lower leaves of older plants turn yellow and die. The scars on the stems where the leaves have fallen off have a water-soaked appearance and are darkened. When the stem is sliced open, a thick yellow fluid oozes out.

ANALYSIS: Bacterial wilt
This plant disease is caused by a bacterium (*Xanthomonas incanae*) that infects both young and mature plants. Because the bacteria are sometimes carried in the seed, infection may begin at germination. These bacteria usually penetrate older plants through leaf scars on the stems, or through wounds on the stems and roots. Once inside, they multiply and break down the inner stem tissue. This results in plant wilting, stunting, poor growth, and eventually death. The sticky yellowish fluid inside the stems is filled with millions of bacteria. These wilt organisms are spread to other plants by moving water, contaminated soil, plant debris, and tools. They can live in plant debris and the soil for up to 2 years, and are favored by cool, wet weather.

SOLUTION: Infected plants cannot be cured. It is best to remove and destroy them. Clean up plant debris. Wash your hands thoroughly with soap and hot water after handling infected plants. Dip contaminated tools in rubbing alcohol before working on healthy plants. Don't replant healthy stocks in contaminated soil for 3 years.

NARCISSUS

ADAPTATION: Throughout the United States.

FLOWERING TIME: Spring.

LIGHT: Full sun is best. Daffodils will tolerate light shade, but may stop blooming after several years.

PLANTING TIME: Fall.

SOIL: Any good well-drained garden soil. pH 6.0 to 8.0

FERTILIZER: When planting, mix 1 teaspoon of ORTHO Bone Meal 0–12–0 or ORTHO Superphosphate 0–20–0 into the soil at the bottom of the planting hole. During the growing season, fertilize with ORTHO Rose & Flower Food 8–12–4 or ORTHO General Purpose Plant Food 8–8–8 according to label directions.

WATER:
How much: Apply enough water to wet the soil 1½ feet deep.
How often: Water when the soil 1 inch below the surface is just barely moist. Stop watering the bulbs after the foliage has turned yellow.

HANDLING: Continue to water and fertilize plants regularly until the foliage turns yellow, then remove the dead leaves.

Flower thrips (8 times life size).

PROBLEM: Silvery white streaks and flecks appear on the leaves and especially on the flowers. The leaves may turn brown. If the flowers or overlapping leaves are peeled open, slender, dark brown to straw-colored insects ranging in size from ¹/₂₀ to ¹/₁₆ inch can be seen moving around.

ANALYSIS: Thrips
This common insect pest attacks daffodils and many other garden plants. Thrips are found in protected parts of the plant like the insides of flower buds, where they feed by rasping the soft plant tissue, then sucking the released plant sap. The injured tissue turns white, causing the characteristic streaking of the leaves and flowers. Because thrips migrate long distances on wind currents, they can quickly infest widespread areas. In cold climates, thrips feed and reproduce from spring until fall. With the onset of freezing weather, they find sheltered areas such as grass clumps and hibernate through the winter. In warm weather climates, thrips feed and reproduce all year. These pests reach their population peak in late spring to midsummer. They are especially troublesome during prolonged dry spells.

SOLUTION: Thrips cannot be eliminated completely, but they can be kept under control. Spray with an insecticide containing *diazinon* as soon as damage is noticed. Repeat the spray if reinfestation occurs, allowing at least 10 days to pass between applications. Pick off and destroy infested flowers.

NARCISSUS (DAFFODIL, JONQUIL)

Failure to bloom.

Weak growth — no flowers.

Smoulder.

PROBLEM: Foliage is healthy, but may be sparse. Few or no flowers are produced. Flowers that are produced may be smaller than normal.

ANALYSIS: Failure to bloom
There are several cultural reasons why daffodils fail to flower:

1. *Overcrowding:* The bulbs multiply each year, producing larger clumps of flowers and foliage the following spring. If the bulbs are not dug out of the soil, divided, and transplanted every few years, they become overcrowded.

2. *Too much shade:* Daffodils planted in a shaded spot will usually bloom well the first year. However, they require a sunny location for continued flowering over a long period of time. The leaves use light to manufacture food, which is stored in the bulbs for next year's growth and flowering. Inadequate light reduces the amount of stored food in the bulbs, resulting in few or no flowers.

3. *Overheating:* If bulbs are stored at high temperatures (80°F and up), the flower embryo inside the bulb is killed. Leaves will grow in the spring, but flowers will not be produced.

4. *Undersized bulbs:* If flower bulbs are much smaller than normal, they may produce only foliage for the first 1 or 2 years. Undersized bulbs don't store enough food to produce both leaves and blossoms. But the bulbs will grow larger, until finally they produce flowers.

5. *Foliage removed too soon:* After a daffodil flowers, the remaining foliage continues to use the sun's rays to manufacture food for new bulbs and next year's flowers. If the foliage is removed before it has a chance to die back naturally, the new bulbs may not have enough food stored to produce a flower.

SOLUTION: The numbered solutions below correspond to the numbers in the analysis.

1. Bulbs should be divided when flower production drops off. As a general rule, divide bulbs every 3 to 4 years.

2. Grow daffodils in a location where they will receive 4 or more hours of full sun. Plants in the shade can be transplanted to a sunny location any time after the flowering period. Try to keep the soil and root immediately surrounding the bulb intact when transplanting.

3. Store bulbs at a cool temperature (55° to 60°F) and in a well-ventilated location.

4. Purchase only large, healthy bulbs.

5. Let the foliage turn yellow before removing it.

PROBLEM: Stored bulbs are yellow brown and rotted. Black crusty fungal mats may grow on the infected bulbs. When infected bulbs are planted, leaves that emerge from the soil are distorted and crumpled. They may be stuck together. Brown streaks develop on the leaf tips or edges. Black crusty fungal pellets appear on the streaked foliage. During cold, wet weather, a gray-brown fuzzy mold may appear on the infected tissues. Flowers may be spotted.

ANALYSIS: Smoulder
This plant disease is caused by a fungus (*Sclerotinia narcissicola*) that infects bulbs both in storage and in the ground, causing bulb rot and flower and foliage decay. When infected bulbs start to grow, the fungus spreads up into the foliage, causing leaf distortion and streaking. Smoulder is favored by wet, poorly drained soil. The fungus forms black pellets on the bulbs and leaves. These pellets can survive through dry conditions and extremes of temperature to invade healthy bulbs. The disease is spread by contaminated soil and bulbs.

SOLUTION: Remove and destroy infected plants and bulbs. During wet weather, spray plants weekly with a fungicide containing *basic copper sulfate*. Plant bulbs in well-drained soil. Avoid planting bulbs in soil where infected plants have grown previously.

Fusarium bulb rot.

Narcissus bulb fly larva (life size).

Cutworm (¼ life size).

PROBLEM: Leaves turn yellow, and the plant is stunted and dies prematurely. If the bulb is unearthed, there may be few or no roots. Bulbs in storage develop a chocolate or purple-brown, spongy decay that is especially noticeable when the outer fleshy bulb scales are pulled away. There may be white fungal strands growing on the bulbs.

ANALYSIS: Fusarium bulb rot
This disease is caused by a fungus (*Fusarium oxysporum* var. *narcissi*) that attacks both growing plants and bulbs in storage. Growing plants are infected through their roots, while stored bulbs may be infected through wounds or abrasions in the bulb tissue. Infected bulbs that are planted continue to decay in the ground and produce few or no roots and stunted, yellowing foliage. The fungus persists in the soil indefinitely, and is spread by contaminated bulbs, soil, and tools. Generally, bulb rot is most destructive when soil temperatures reach 60° to 75°F. The disease is most common in warm climates where temperatures rarely drop below freezing, and in daffodils that are forced for indoor winter use.

SOLUTION: Discard all diseased plants and bulbs and the surrounding soil for 6 inches around the bulb. Dig bulbs up carefully to prevent wounds. Store them in a cool (55° to 60°F), well-ventilated place. Soak clean, healthy bulbs in a warm (80° to 85°F) bath of a fungicide containing *benomyl* (2 tablespoons per gallon) for 15 to 30 minutes. Do not replant healthy bulbs in an area where diseased plants have previously grown.

PROBLEM: Narcissus and daffodil bulbs feel soft and spongy, and produce little or no growth after they are planted. Foliage that does emerge is yellow, stunted, and looks grassy. No flowers are produced. In the spring, when the daffodils start to bloom, flying insects that resemble small bumblebees (½ to ¾ inch long), can be seen hovering around the plants. These black, hairy insects have bands of yellow, buff, or orange around their bodies.

ANALYSIS: Narcissus bulb fly
(*Merodon equestris*)
This insect, a member of the fly family, is a common pest of many ornamental bulb plants. In the spring, the adult fly lays its eggs on the leaf bases and soil immediately surrounding the plant. The emerging larvae tunnel through the soil to the bulb, and feed on the bulb tissue throughout the summer, making it soft and pulpy. The larvae spend the winter in the bulb as wrinkled, plump, grayish white to yellow maggots ½ to ¾ inches long. In the spring, they either remain in the bulb or move out into the surrounding soil to pupate. After 1 to 2½ months, the adult bulb fly emerges and starts the egg-laying cycle again.

SOLUTION: Check all bulbs carefully before planting. If they are soft or spongy, discard them. Dust the remaining bulbs with an insecticide containing *trichlorfon* before planting them, and again after they've been planted but before they're covered with soil. In May, drench the foliage and surrounding soil with a solution containing *trichlorfon* to kill the adults and emerging larvae. Make sure that daffodils are listed on the pesticide label.

PROBLEM: Young plants are chewed or cut off near the ground. Gray, brown, or black worms, 1½ to 2 inches long, may be found about 2 inches deep in the soil near the base of the damaged plants. The worms coil when disturbed.

ANALYSIS: Cutworms
Several species of cutworms attack plants in the flower garden. The most likely pests of young nicotiana plants are the surface-feeding cutworms. A single surface-feeding cutworm can sever the stems of many young plants in one night. Cutworms hide in the soil during the day, and feed only at night. Adult cutworms are dark, night-flying moths with bands or stripes on their forewings. Cutworm damage is most severe on young plants in the spring.

SOLUTION: Apply an insecticide dust containing either *carbaryl* or *diazinon* around the bases of plants when damage is first noticed. Since cutworms are difficult to control, it may be necessary to repeat dusting at weekly intervals. Cultivate thoroughly in late summer and fall to expose and destroy eggs, pupae, and larvae. Further reduce damage with "cutworm collars" around the stem of each plant. These collars can be made of stiff paper or aluminum foil. They should be at least 2 inches high, and pressed firmly into the soil.

Nicotiana cultural information
Light: Sun
Water: When the soil is almost dry
Soil: Any good garden soil
Fertilizer: Medium

PAEONIA (PEONY)

PAEONIA

ADAPTATION:
Herbaceous peonies: Zones 3 through 7.
Tree peonies: Zones 3 through 9. To determine your zone, see the map on page 1004.

FLOWERING TIME: Spring.

LIGHT: Full sun, or half-day sun in hot, dry areas.

PLANTING METHOD: Plant peonies in the fall, placing the eyes of the tubers 2 inches below the soil surface.

SOIL: Well drained, high in organic matter. pH 6.0 to 7.5

FERTILIZER: When planting, mix a half cup of ORTHO Superphosphate 0–20–0 into the soil for each plant. During the growing season, fertilize with ORTHO Rose & Flower Food 8–12–4 or ORTHO General Purpose Plant Food 8–8–8 according to label directions.

WATER:
How much: Apply enough water to wet the soil 1½ to 2 feet deep.
How often: Water when the soil 1 inch below the surface is just barely moist.

HANDLING: Divide herbaceous peony clumps every 6 to 10 years. When cutting flowers, leave 3 or 4 leaves on the stems. To insure good bloom next year, pick only a third of this year's blooms for cut flowers.

Failure to bloom.

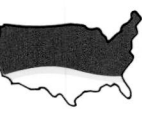

PROBLEM: Peonies fail to produce flower buds, or produce buds that fail to develop into flowers.

ANALYSIS: Failure to bloom
There are several reasons that peonies may fail to bloom:
1. *Roots buried at wrong depth:* Peonies that are planted too deeply or shallowly often fail to bloom.
2. *Immature transplants:* Peony roots that have been divided and transplanted usually fail to flower for at least 2 years. If the divisions were extremely small, the plants may not flower for as long as 5 years.
3. *Crowded plantings:* Old, established peony clumps eventually become overcrowded and stop producing flowers.
4. *Too much shade:* Peonies stop blooming when they are heavily shaded by trees, tall shrubs, or buildings.
5. *Lack of fertilization:* Peonies that are not being fed enough will fail to bloom. Sometimes they will form buds, but the buds will not develop.

SOLUTION: The numbers below correspond to the numbered sections in the analysis.
1. Carefully dig up and reset the roots so that the eyes are 1½ to 2 inches below the soil surface.
2. With time, the young plants will mature and start flowering.
3. Peonies usually need to be divided after 6 to 10 years, or any time after that when flower production starts to drop off. Dig up and divide old clumps into divisions containing 3 to 5 eyes. These young divisions may be replanted.
4. Transplant peonies to a sunny location.
5. Apply a handful of ORTHO General Purpose Plant Food 8–8–8 in early spring and work it in lightly around each plant.

Gray mold.

PROBLEM: New shoots wilt and die. The bases of the wilted stems are brownish black and rotted. Young flower buds turn black and wither. Older buds and open flowers turn soft and brown, and develop a gray or brown fuzzy covering in wet weather. This fuzzy growth, which may develop on all infected plant parts, is very distinctive. Its presence can be used to help distinguish this disease from *Phytophthora* (see the next column), with which it is often confused. Irregular brown lesions or patches form on the leaves. In severe cases, the plant base and roots may decay.

ANALYSIS: Gray mold
This common disease of peonies is caused by a fungus (*Botrytis paeoniae* or *B. cinerea*). Gray mold is most serious in the wet, cool conditions of early spring. Fungal growth on the stems, leaves, and flowers causes spotting, blackening, and decay. The fuzzy growth that forms on infected tissue is composed of millions of tiny spores. This fungus is spread by wind, splashing rain or water, or contaminated plants, soil, and tools. The fungus forms small black pellets that survive in plant debris and in the soil for many years.

SOLUTION: Remove and destroy all decayed or wilting plant parts. Clean up plant debris during the growing season and again in the fall. In the spring, spray emerging shoots with a fungicide containing *mancozeb, zineb,* or *benomyl.* Repeat the spray 2 more times at intervals of 5 to 10 days. Respray if the infection recurs. If available, *mancozeb* or *zineb* is preferable because they also control *Phytophthora.*

PAPAVER (POPPY)

PELARGONIUM (GERANIUM)

Peonies infected with phytophthora blight.

Verticillium wilt.

PROBLEM: New shoots wilt and turn black. Flowers, buds, leaves, and stems shrivel and turn dark brown and leathery. Black lesions several inches long often appear on the lower sections of the stem. The plant pulls up easily. Roots are black and rotted. The fuzzy mold that is characteristic of gray mold (see previous column) does not occur in this disease.

ANALYSIS: Phytophthora blight
This disease of peonies and many other plants is caused by a fungus (*Phytophthora cactorum*) that is common in most soils. Like gray mold, this fungus is favored by the cool, wet conditions of early spring. It can survive in the soil and in plant debris for many years in the form of tiny fungal pellets. Initially the fungus attacks either the roots or the developing shoots at the soil level, causing shoot wilting and a dark decay of the stem tissue. Wherever the fungus is splashed onto the plant, it may cause lesions, spots, and a typical brown, leathery decay. This disease is spread by splashing rain or water, and by contaminated plants, soil, and tools. It is most serious in heavy, poorly drained soils.

SOLUTION: Remove and destroy plants with decayed roots. Pick off and destroy infected plant parts. Clean up plant debris. Spray the foliage and drench the base of the plant with a fungicide containing *zineb*, *mancozeb*, or *maneb*. Spray 3 times at intervals of 5 to 10 days. Reapply the spray if infection recurs. Thin out overcrowded plants. Plant peonies in well-drained soil.

PROBLEM: Leaves turn yellow, wilt, and die, starting with the lower leaves and progressing up the plant. Older plants may be stunted. Leaf wilting and death may affect only one side of the plant. Flowering is poor. There may be dark brown areas on the infected leaf stems.

ANALYSIS: Verticillium wilt
This wilt disease affects many ornamental plants. It is caused by a fungus (*Verticillium* species) that persists indefinitely on plant debris or in the soil. The disease is spread by contaminated seeds, plants, soil, and equipment. The fungus enters the plant through the roots and spreads up into the stems and leaves through the water-conducting vessels in the stems. These vessels become discolored and plugged. This plugging cuts off the flow of water to the leaves, causing leaf yellowing and wilting.

SOLUTION: No chemical control is available. It is best to destroy infected plants. Verticillium can be removed from the soil only by fumigation techniques. (For more information about soil fumigation, see page 919.) However, the best solution is usually to use plants that are resistant to verticillium. For a list of verticillium resistant plants, see page 995.

Papaver cultural information
Light: Full sun
Water: Let the soil dry between waterings
Soil: Any good garden soil
Fertilizer: Medium

PELARGONIUM

ADAPTATION: Throughout the United States.

FLOWERING TIME: Spring and summer. In zones 9 and 10, some pelargoniums bloom throughout the year. To determine your zone, see the map on page 1004.

LIGHT: Full sun or light shade.

PLANTING TIME: Spring, when all danger of frost is past; or any time of year in zones 9 and 10.

SOIL: Well drained. pH 6.0 to 8.0

FERTILIZER: Fertilize with ORTHO Rose & Flower Food 8–12–4 or ORTHO General Purpose Plant Food 8–8–8 according to label directions.

WATER:
How much: Apply enough water to plants in the ground to wet the soil 8 to 10 inches deep.
Containers: Apply enough water so that 10 percent of the water drains from the bottom of the container.
How often: Water when the soil 1 inch below the surface is just barely moist.

HANDLING: Remove old flower clusters to encourage continuing bloom.

PELARGONIUM (GERANIUM)

Gray mold.

Oedema on ivy geranium.

Rust.

PROBLEM: Brown spots and blotches form on the leaves and possibly on the stems. As the disease progresses, a fuzzy brown or grayish mold forms on the infected tissue. Gray mold and spots often appear on the flowers, especially during periods of cool, wet weather. The leaves and stems may be soft and rotted.

ANALYSIS: Gray mold
This widespread plant disease is caused by a fungus (*Botrytis cinerea*) that is found on most dead plant tissue. The fungus initially attacks foliage and flowers that are weak or dead, causing spotting and mold. The fuzzy mold that develops is composed of millions of microscopic spores. Once gray mold has become established on plant debris and weak or dying leaves and flowers, it can invade healthy plant tissue. The fungus is spread by water, or by bits of infected plant debris that land on the leaves. Cool temperatures and high humidity favor gray mold growth. Crowded plantings, rain, and overhead watering enhance the spread of the disease. Infection is more of a problem in spring and fall when temperatures are lower. In warm winter areas where freezing is rare, gray mold can be a year-round problem.

SOLUTION: Clean up plant debris, and remove dying or infected leaves, stems, and flowers. Spray infected plants once every 10 to 14 days with a fungicide containing *benomyl* or *zineb*. Continue spraying as long as the mold is visible. Provide enough space between plants to allow good air circulation. Try to avoid wetting the foliage when watering.

PROBLEM: Water-soaked spots appear on the leaves. Eventually, these spots turn brown and corky. Affected leaves may turn yellow and drop off. Corky ridges may form on the stems and leaf stalks. In most cases, the soil is moist and the air is cool and humid.

ANALYSIS: Oedema
Oedema is not caused by a pest, but results from an accumulation of water in the plant. Oedema often develops when the soil is moist or wet, and the atmosphere is humid and cool. Under these conditions, water is absorbed rapidly from the soil and lost slowly from the leaves, resulting in an excess amount of water in the plant. This excess water causes cells to burst. The ruptured cells eventually form spots and ridges. Oedema occurs most frequently in late winter and early spring during cloudy weather.

SOLUTION: Plant geraniums in soil that drains well, and avoid overwatering them. For information on proper watering, see page 906.

PROBLEM: Yellow spots up to ¼ inch in diameter appear on the leaves and stems. Reddish brown spore pustules develop on the undersides of the leaves. These pustules may be arranged in concentric circles. Severely infected leaves may turn yellow and drop prematurely.

ANALYSIS: Rust
This plant disease is caused by a fungus (*Puccinia pelargonii-zonalis*). Rust spores are spread by the wind and splashing water to healthy plants. After the leaf has been wet for 5 hours the spores germinate, forming a spot, and later a pustule. Rust generally does not kill the plant, but heavily infected plants may drop some leaves. The fungus survives only on living plant tissue. Wet conditions favor the development and spread of this disease.

SOLUTION: Spray with a fungicide containing *maneb*, *zineb*, or *mancozeb* at intervals of 10 days. Spray the foliage thoroughly, making sure to cover both the upper and lower surfaces of the leaves. These fungicides will protect the new, healthy foliage from infection, but they will not eradicate the fungus on diseased leaves, which should be picked off. If possible, avoid wetting the foliage. Water early in the day to allow foliage to dry out quickly.

Alternaria leaf spot.

Bacterial leaf spot.

Blackleg.

PROBLEM: Dark brown, irregularly shaped spots appear on the leaves. The spots range in size from barely visible to ⅓ inch in diameter. They are frequently surrounded by dark or yellow concentric circles. Spotting occurs mostly on the older leaves, although new growth may also be affected. Severely infected leaves shrivel, turn black, and fall off.

ANALYSIS: Alternaria leaf spot
This disease of geraniums is caused by a fungus (*Alternaria tenuis*) that is favored by prolonged cool, moist conditions. Infection rarely kills the plant, but can weaken and disfigure it. The fungus forms spores on the diseased leaves; these spores are readily blown or splashed to healthy leaves. Wherever the spores land, fungal strands grow, decay, and spot the plant tissue. The fungus survives on plant debris, and is spread by the wind and splashing water.

SOLUTION: Pick off and destroy infected leaves and clean up plant debris. If infection is severe and persistent, spray the plants with a fungicide containing *zineb* or *basic copper sulfate*. Spray every 7 to 10 days until the spotting has diminished.

PROBLEM: Dark, circular, sunken spots up to ¼ inch in diameter, or larger, angular dead areas appear on the leaves. The leaves wilt and die. They either fall off the plant immediately, or hang down along the stem for several weeks. Many or all of the stems shrivel and turn brown or black. The roots are black but not rotted. When an infected stem is sliced open, a thick yellow fluid may ooze from the cut surface. Older diseased plants may retain only a few tufts of leaves at the stem tips.

ANALYSIS: Bacterial stem rot and leaf spot
This very common and widespread disease of geraniums is caused by bacteria (*Xanthomonas pelargonii* or *Pseudomonas* species). The disease develops most rapidly when the plants are growing vigorously and during periods of warm, moist weather. The bacteria decay the leaf tissue, causing the small spots and lesions, then may penetrate throughout the entire plant, causing wilting and rotting. The thick fluid that oozes from cut stems is filled with millions of bacteria. Infection is spread to healthy plants when bacteria are splashed onto the leaves, or when they make contact with contaminated tools. The bacteria can live in plant debris and in the soil for 3 months or more. Not all plants are killed by this disease. However, they often remain weak, stunted, and disfigured.

SOLUTION: Remove and destroy infected plants. Clean up plant debris. Avoid overhead watering. Sterilize contaminated tools by dipping them in rubbing alcohol. Wash your hands thoroughly after handling infected plants. Purchase only healthy plants. For information on plant selection, see page 916.

PROBLEM: Dark lesions form at the bases of the stems. These lesions enlarge and turn black and shiny. The blackening progresses up the stem. The leaves wilt and drop, and the plant may eventually die.

ANALYSIS: Blackleg
This common disease of geraniums is caused by a fungus (*Pythium* species) that lives in the soil. Blackleg is favored by wet, poorly drained soil. The fungus attacks the stems at the soil level, then spreads upward. The stems decay and the foliage wilts, shrivels, and eventually dies. Blackleg is spread by contaminated soil, transplants, and tools.

SOLUTION: Remove and destroy infected plants. If they have been growing in containers, throw out the soil in which they grew. Wash contaminated tools and pots, then dip them in a solution of 1 part chlorine bleach to 9 parts warm water for 1 minute or more. Plant healthy geraniums in well-drained soil and let them dry out between waterings. For further information on this technique, see page 857.

PELARGONIUM (GERANIUM)

Greenhouse whiteflies (life size).

PROBLEM: Tiny, winged insects 1/12 inch long are found mainly on the undersides of the leaves. The insects are covered with white, waxy powder. When the plant is touched, insects flutter rapidly around it. Leaves may be mottled and yellowing. In warm winter areas, black mold may cover the leaves.

ANALYSIS: Greenhouse whitefly (*Trialeurodes vaporariorum*)
Greenhouse whitefly is a common insect pest of many garden and greenhouse plants. The 4-winged adult lays eggs on the undersides of leaves. The larvae are the size of a pinhead, flat, oval-shaped, and semitransparent, with white waxy filaments radiating from the body. They feed for about a month before changing to the adult form. Both the larval and adult forms suck sap from the leaves. The larvae are more damaging because they feed more heavily. Adults and larvae cannot fully digest all the sugar in the sap, and excrete the excess in a fluid called honeydew, which often drops onto the leaves below. A sooty mold fungus may develop on the honeydew, causing the geranium leaves to appear black and dirty. In warm winter areas, the insect can be active year-round, with eggs, larvae, and adults present at the same time. The whitefly is unable to live through freezing winters. Spring reinfestations in freezing winter areas come from migrating whiteflies and from infested greenhouse-grown plants placed in the garden.

SOLUTION: Control whiteflies by spraying with ORTHO Isotox Insect Killer. Be sure to cover both the upper and lower surfaces of the leaves.

Geranium budworm (twice life size).

PROBLEM: Irregular or round holes appear in the leaves and buds. Leaves, buds, and flowers may be entirely chewed off. Worms or caterpillars are feeding on the plants.

ANALYSIS: Caterpillars
Many species of these moth or butterfly larvae feed on geraniums and other garden plants. Some common caterpillars include budworms, hornworms, and loopers. Usually, the adult moths or butterflies begin to lay their eggs on garden plants with the onset of warm spring weather. The larvae that emerge from these eggs feed on the leaves, flowers, and buds for 2 to 6 weeks, depending on weather conditions and species. Mature caterpillars pupate in cocoons attached to leaves or buildings, or buried in the soil. There may be one to several overlapping generations during the growing season. The last generation of caterpillars in the fall survives the winter as pupae. The adult moths and butterflies emerge the following spring.

SOLUTION: Spray infested plants with ORTHO Isotox Insect Killer. Repeat the spray if reinfestation occurs, allowing at least 7 to 10 days to pass between applications. The bacterial insecticide *Bacillus thuringiensis* may also be used.

PETUNIA

PETUNIA

ADAPTATION: Throughout the United States.

FLOWERING TIME: Summer and fall.

LIGHT: Full sun.

PLANTING TIME: Spring, when all danger of frost is past.

SOIL: Well drained.

FERTILIZER: Fertilize with ORTHO Rose & Flower Food 8–12–4 or ORTHO General Purpose Plant Food 8–8–8 according to label directions.

WATER:
How much: Apply enough water to plants in the ground to wet the soil 6 to 8 inches deep.
Containers: Apply enough water so that about 10 percent of the water drains from the bottom of the container.
How often: Water when the soil 1 inch below the surface is just barely moist.

HANDLING: If plants become rangy, pinch back about half of the growth to force additional bushy growth.

Gray mold.

Smog damage.

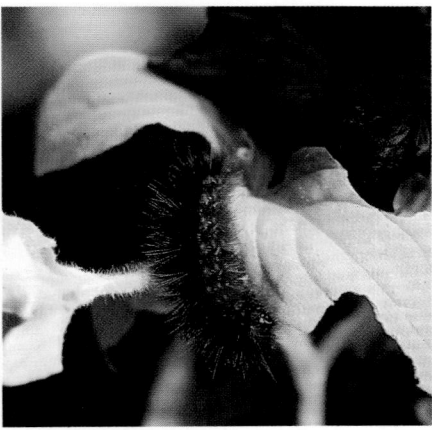
Caterpillar (life size).

PROBLEM: Gray or brown spots appear on the flowers, especially during periods of wet weather. Brown spots and blotches may appear on the leaves and stems. As the disease progresses, a fuzzy brown or grayish mold may form on the infected tissue.

ANALYSIS: Gray mold
This widespread plant disease is caused by a fungus (*Botrytis* species) that is found on most dead plant tissue. The fungus initially attacks foliage and flowers that are weak or dead, causing spotting and sometimes mold. The fuzzy mold that may develop is composed of millions of microscopic spores. Once gray mold has become established on plant debris and weak or dying leaves and flowers, it can invade healthy plant tissue. The fungus is spread by the wind, splashing water, or infected pieces of plant tissue contacting healthy tissue. Cool temperatures and high humidity favor gray mold growth. Crowded plantings, rain, and overhead watering also enhance the spread of the disease. Infection is more of a problem in the spring and fall when temperatures are lower. In warm winter areas, where freezing is rare, gray mold can be a year-round problem.

SOLUTION: Spray infected plants once every 10 to 14 days with a fungicide containing *maneb* or *mancozeb*. Continue spraying as long as the mold is visible. Remove infected flowers and leaves, and clean up plant debris. Try to avoid wetting the flowers when watering.

PROBLEM: Bands of bleached, dead tissue appear on the upper and lower surfaces of the leaves. Usually, the youngest leaves are the most severely affected, but in severe cases all of the leaves may be damaged. The leaf edges are pinched or twisted where damage has occurred. The plants are located in or near an urban area.

ANALYSIS: Smog damage
Petunias, especially white or light-colored varieties, are very sensitive to smog. PAN (peroxyacetyl nitrate) and ozone are two major components of smog that damage petunias and many other plants. PAN and ozone form as the result of chemical reactions between sunlight and products of petroleum combustion such as automobile exhaust. These compounds enter the plant through tiny breathing pores on the undersides of the leaves. Once inside the plant, PAN and ozone kill the leaf cells. Generally, injury first develops at the tips of young leaves and becomes more widespread as the leaves mature. The leaf edges become pinched or twisted where damage has occurred because the dead tissue is unable to expand with the rest of the growing leaf. Warm temperatures, high humidity, high light intensity, and moist soil stimulate leaf pores to open. When these conditions prevail, smog compounds can easily enter and damage the leaves.

SOLUTION: There is nothing you can do once damage has occurred. Pinch off severely damaged leaves. Do not plant white or light-colored petunias in smoggy areas. Shade plants on hot, smoggy days. Plant PAN and ozone tolerant flowers. For a list, see page 996.

PROBLEM: Irregular or round holes appear in the leaves and buds. Leaves, buds, and flowers may be entirely chewed off. Smooth or hairy caterpillars, up to 4 inches in length, are feeding on the plants.

ANALYSIS: Caterpillars
Numerous species of these moth or butterfly larvae feed on petunias and many other garden plants. Some common caterpillars include budworms, armyworms, hornworms, and loopers. As a rule, the adult moths or butterflies start to lay eggs on garden plants with the onset of warm weather in spring. The larvae that emerge feed on the leaves, flowers, and buds for 2 to 6 weeks, depending on weather conditions and species. Mature caterpillars pupate in cocoons attached to leaves and structures, or in the soil. There may be one to several overlapping generations during the growing season. The last generation of caterpillars in the fall survives the winter as pupae. The adult moths and butterflies emerge the following spring.

SOLUTION: Spray infested plants with ORTHO Isotox Insect Killer. Repeat the spray if reinfestation occurs, allowing at least 7 to 10 days to pass between applications.

PETUNIA

Cutworm damage.

PROBLEM: Young plants are chewed or cut off near the ground. Many leaves may be sheared from the stems. Gray, brown, or black worms, 1½ to 2 inches long, may be found about 2 inches deep in the soil near the base of the damaged plants. The worms coil when disturbed.

ANALYSIS: Cutworms
Several species of cutworms attack petunias and many other flowers and vegetable plants. The most likely pests of young petunia plants set out early in the season are the surface-feeding cutworms and climbing cutworms. A single surface-feeding cutworm can sever the stems of many young plants in one night. Climbing cutworms shear the leaves off of older plants. Cutworms hide in the soil during the day, and feed only at night. Adult cutworms are dark, night-flying moths with bands or stripes on their forewings.

SOLUTION: Apply ORTHO Diazinon Soil & Turf Insect Control or ORTHO Diazinon Soil & Foliage Dust around the base of undamaged plants when stem cutting is observed. Since cutworms are difficult to control, it may be necessary to repeat the dusting at weekly intervals. Before transplanting into the area, apply a preventive treatment of ORTHO Diazinon Soil & Turf Insect Control and work it into the soil. Cultivate the soil thoroughly in late summer and fall to expose and destroy eggs, larvae, and pupae. Further reduce damage with "cutworm collars" around the stem of each plant. These collars can be made of stiff paper or aluminum foil. They should be at least 2 inches high, and pressed firmly into the soil.

Crown and root rot.

PROBLEM: There is a dark discoloration and dry rot of the lower stems and the base of the plant. Part or all of the foliage turns pale, wilts, and dies. The root system is small and the plant pulls up easily.

ANALYSIS: Crown and root rot
This disease is caused by a fungus (*Phytophthora* species) that lives in the soil. The fungus initially attacks the roots or stem at or just below the soil level. The dark, dry decay of the lower stem tissue and the roots eventually reduces the water flow to the leaves and flowers, causing the plant to wilt and finally die. Crown and root rot is most severe in heavy, poorly drained soils and wet conditions. The fungus is spread by contaminated soil, transplants, and tools.

SOLUTION: Remove and destroy the infected plants and the soil within 6 inches of their roots. If possible, improve the soil drainage (see page 901 for instructions). Replant with healthy plants. (For information on selecting healthy plants, see page 916.) Drench the entire bed with a solution containing *captan* in a concentration of 2 tablespoons per gallon of water. Repeat the drench at monthly intervals during the growing season. Let the soil dry out between waterings, as described on page 857.

PHLOX

PHLOX

ADAPTATION: Throughout the United States.

FLOWERING TIME: Early summer to fall.

LIGHT: Full sun.

PLANTING TIME: Spring or fall in zones 8 through 10. To determine your zone, see the map on page 1004. In colder areas, plant in spring, when all danger of frost is past.

SOIL: Any good garden soil.

FERTILIZER: Fertilize with ORTHO Rose & Flower Food 8–12–4 or ORTHO General Purpose Plant Food 8–8–8 according to label directions.

WATER:
How much: Apply enough water to plants in the ground to wet the soil 6 inches deep.
Containers: Apply enough water so that about 10 percent of the water drains from the bottom of the container.
How often: Water when the soil 1 inch below the surface is just barely moist.

PRIMULA (PRIMROSE)

Leaf spot.

PROBLEM: Spots and blotches appear on the leaves. The spots may be yellow, red, tan, gray, or brown. They range in size from barely visible to ¼ inch in diameter. Several spots may join to form blotches. The leaves may be yellow and dying. Leaf spotting is most severe in warm, humid weather. In some cases the infected leaf tissue turns ash gray and has a dry, papery texture.

ANALYSIS: Leaf spots
There are a number of different fungi that cause leaf spots. Some of these fungi may eventually kill the plant, or weaken it so that it becomes susceptible to attack by other organisms. Others merely cause spotting that is unsightly but not harmful. These fungi are spread by splashing water or wind. They generally survive the winter in diseased plant debris. Most of the leaf spot fungi do their greatest damage in mild weather (50° to 85°F).

SOLUTION: Spray with a fungicide containing *maneb* or *benomyl* (or a combination) at intervals of 7 to 10 days. Because leaf spots are favored by humid conditions, it is important to spray frequently during these periods. Pick off severely infected leaves, and clean up plant debris.

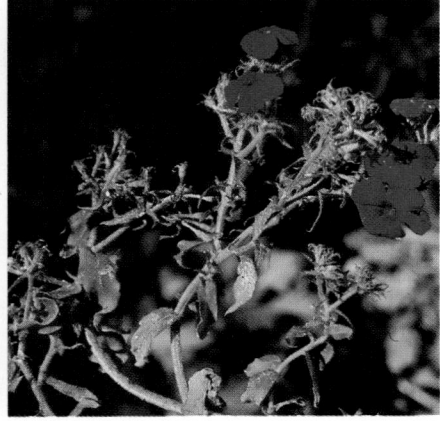

Powdery mildew.

PROBLEM: Leaves and stems are covered with grayish white powdery spots and patches. The patches occur primarily on the upper surfaces of the older leaves. The leaves eventually turn yellow and wither.

ANALYSIS: Powdery mildew
This common plant disease can be caused by either of two closely related fungi (*Erysiphe cichoracearum* and *Sphaerotheca humuli*) that thrive in both humid and dry weather. The powdery patches consist of fungal strands and spores. The spores are spread by the wind to healthy plants. The fungus saps plant nutrients, causing yellowing and sometimes death of the leaves. A severe infection may kill the plant. Since these powdery mildews attack many different kinds of plants, the fungus from a diseased plant may infect other types of plants in the garden. (For a list of susceptible plants, see page 995.) Under favorable conditions, powdery mildew can spread through a planting in a matter of days or weeks.

SOLUTION: Spray infected plants with ORTHO Funginex Rose Disease Control. This fungicide protects the new, healthy foliage. Damaged leaves may be picked off. Severely infected plants should be removed. Spray at regular intervals of 7 to 10 days or as often as necessary to protect new growth. Space plants far enough apart to allow good air circulation. Clean up plant debris.

PRIMULA

ADAPTATION: Throughout the United States.

FLOWERING TIME: In zones 9 and 10, winter through spring. In colder areas, most primroses bloom in early spring. To determine your zone, see the map on page 1004.

LIGHT: Deep shade or filtered sun.

PLANTING TIME: Fall in zones 9 and 10. In colder areas, spring, when all danger of frost is past.

SOIL: Any good garden soil that is rich in organic matter. pH 5.5 to 7.5

FERTILIZER: Fertilize with ORTHO Rose & Flower Food 8-12-4 or ORTHO General Purpose Plant Food 8-8-8 according to label directions.

WATER:
How much: Apply enough water to plants in the ground to wet the soil 6 inches deep.
Containers: Apply enough water so that 10 percent of the water drains from the bottom of the container.
How often: Water when the soil 1 inch below the surface is moist but not wet.

HANDLING: Divide every 3 or 4 years just after the plants have finished blooming.

PRIMULA (PRIMROSE)

Leaf spots.

Root and stem rot.

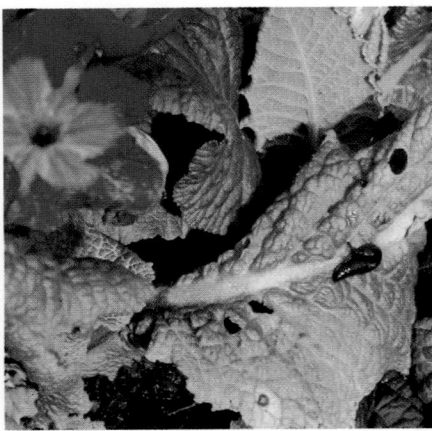

Slug (⅓ life size).

PROBLEM: Spots and blotches appear on the leaves. The spots range in size from ⅛ to ¼ inch, and are especially numerous on the lower leaves. The spots may be circular or irregular in shape, and are often brown with hazy yellow borders. They may also be yellow with ash-colored centers. Often, several spots join to form blotches. Severely infected leaves usually turn yellow and die.

ANALYSIS: Leaf spots
Primroses may be spotted by any of several different fungi (including *Ramularia primulae* and *Phyllosticta primulicola*). The spotting is unsightly but not harmful to the plant. However, the infected leaf tissue becomes susceptible to further attack by bacteria (*Pseudomonas primulae*), which cause dark brown spots with yellow borders. If bacterial infection becomes severe, many of the infected leaves will die. Both bacteria and fungi survive the winter in infected plant debris. They are spread by splashing water, contaminated tools, and transplants. In addition, some of the fungi form spores, which may be spread by the wind. Most of the leaf spot organisms do their greatest damage in mild weather (temperatures of 50° to 85°F).

SOLUTION: Remove and discard badly spotted leaves and all plant debris. Try to avoid splashing water on the foliage when watering. If spotting and blotching are persistent and severe, spray plants with a fungicide containing *benomyl*, *mancozeb*, or *basic copper sulfate* every 10 to 14 days.

PROBLEM: Older leaves turn yellow, wilt, and die. The leaf bases may be soft and rotted, and the plant may pull out of the ground easily. The roots are dark and rotted.

ANALYSIS: Root and stem rot
This disease is caused by any of a number of different fungi (including *Pythium* and *Rhizoctonia* species) that persist indefinitely in the soil. They thrive in waterlogged, heavy soil. Some of these fungi attack the plant stems at the soil level, while others attack the roots. Infection causes the roots and stems to decay. This results in wilting, then yellowing leaves, and eventually the death of the plant. These fungi are generally spread by infested soil and transplants, contaminated equipment, and splashing or running water. Many of these organisms also cause damping-off of seedlings. For more information about damping-off, see page 858.

SOLUTION: Allow the soil around the plants to dry out. (For more information on this technique, see page 857.) Remove and discard severely infected plants. Avoid future root rot problems by planting in well-drained soil. For information on improving soil drainage, see page 901. For more information on root and stem rots, see page 856.

PROBLEM: Irregular holes with smooth edges are chewed in the leaves. Leaves may be sheared off entirely. Silvery trails wind around on the plants and soil nearby. Snails or slugs may be seen moving around or feeding on the plants, especially at night. Check for them by inspecting the garden at night by flashlight.

ANALYSIS: Snails and slugs
These pests are mollusks, and are related to clams, oysters, and other shellfish. They feed on a wide variety of garden plants. Like other mollusks, snails and slugs need to be moist all the time. For this reason, they avoid direct sun and dry places, and hide during the day in damp places, such as under flower pots or in thick groundcover. They emerge at night or on cloudy days to feed. Snails and slugs are similar in appearance, except that the snail has a hard shell, into which it withdraws when disturbed. Slugs lay masses of white eggs encased in a slimy mass in protected places. Snails bury their eggs in the soil, also in a slimy mass. The young look like miniature versions of their parents.

SOLUTION: Scatter ORTHO Bug-Geta Snail & Slug Pellets or ORTHO Slug-Geta Snail & Slug Bait granules around the areas you wish to protect. Also scatter the bait in areas where snails or slugs might be hiding, such as in dense groundcovers, weedy areas, compost piles, or pot storage areas. Before spreading the bait, wet down the treated areas to encourage snail and slug activity that night. Repeat the application every 2 weeks as long as snails and slugs are active.

RANUNCULUS

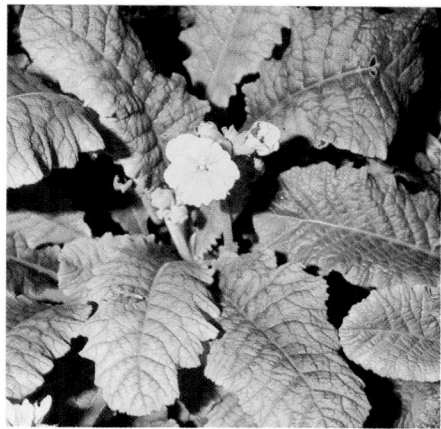

Iron deficiency.

PROBLEM: Leaves turn pale green or yellow. The newest leaves (those at the tips of the stem) are most severely affected. Except in extreme cases, the veins of affected leaves remain green. In extreme cases, the newest leaves are small and all-white or yellow. Older leaves may remain green.

ANALYSIS: Iron deficiency
Plants frequently suffer from deficiencies of iron and other minor nutrients, such as manganese and zinc, elements essential to normal plant growth and development. Deficiencies can occur when one or more of these elements are depleted in the soil. Often, minor nutrients are present in the soil, but alkaline (pH 7.5 and higher) or wet soil conditions cause them to form compounds that cannot be used by primroses. An alkaline condition can result from overliming, or from lime leached from cement or brick. Regions where soil is derived from limestone, and those with low rainfall, usually have alkaline soils.

SOLUTION: To correct the deficiency of minor nutrients spray the foliage with ORTHO Greenol Liquid Iron 6.13%, and apply it to the soil around the plants. Correct the pH of the soil by treating it with *ferrous sulfate* and watering it in well. Maintain an acid pH by fertilizing with ORTHO Azalea, Camellia & Rhododendron Food 5–10–10. If wet soil is a problem, improve the soil drainage. For information on improving soil drainage, see page 901.

RANUNCULUS

ADAPTATION: Throughout the United States. Ranunculus will overwinter in zones 8 through 10. To determine your zone, see the map on page 1004.

FLOWERING TIME: Summer.

LIGHT: Full sun.

PLANTING TIME: Plant tuberous roots in the fall in zones 8 through 10. In colder areas, start tuberous roots indoors in the fall or late winter, or plant them outside in the spring when all danger of frost is past.

SOIL: Well drained. pH 6.0 to 8.0

FERTILIZER: Fertilize with ORTHO Rose & Flower Food 8–12–4 or ORTHO General Purpose Plant Food 8–8–8 according to label directions.

WATER:
How much: Apply enough water to plants in the ground to wet the soil 6 to 8 inches deep.
Containers: Apply enough water so that 10 percent of the water drains from the bottom of the container.
How often: Water when the soil 1 inch below the surface is just barely moist.

HANDLING: Plant tuberous roots with the "toes" down. After the foliage dies in the late summer, dig up the tuberous roots and store them in a dry location.

Bird damage.

PROBLEM: Tender young leaves are torn. Seedlings may be entirely eaten. Birds may be seen feeding in the garden, or their tracks may be noticed around the damaged plants.

ANALYSIS: Bird damage
Birds are fond of ranunculus and frequently eat the tender parts of the plants. Individual birds may develop the habit of feeding on ranunculus, and visit the plants every day.

SOLUTION: Protect emerging shoots and young transplants with cages or coverings made of 1″ chicken wire. Cages about 10″x10″x24″ are self-supporting. Larger cages may need to be reinforced with heavy wire. Cheesecloth cages supported with stakes, wire, or string may also be used. For more information about birds, see page 893.

RANUNCULUS

Root rot.

PROBLEM: The plant is wilting. The leaves and stems are dark brown, limp, and have a water-soaked appearance. Roots and tubers are dark and rotted.

ANALYSIS: Root rot
This disease is caused by several fungi that persist indefinitely in the soil. They thrive in waterlogged, heavy soils. Some of these fungi attack the plant stems at the soil level, while others attack the roots. Infection causes the roots, tubers, and stems to decay. This results in wilting, then yellowing leaves, and eventually the death of the plant. These fungi are generally spread by infested soil and contaminated transplants, equipment, and splashing or running water.

SOLUTION: Remove and discard infected plants and the soil immediately surrounding them. Let the soil dry out between waterings. (For more information on this technique, see page 857.) Plant ranunculas in well-drained soil. For information on soil drainage, see page 901.

Ranunculus mosaic.

PROBLEM: Leaves are mottled yellow-green. Plants may be stunted, and flowers may be smaller than normal. In some cases, the petals are streaked.

ANALYSIS: Ranunculus mosaic
This virus disease infects ranunculus plants and tubers. The severity of infection varies from plant to plant. Mosaic does not kill ranunculus, but greatly reduces their overall vigor and beauty. The virus is spread by aphids that feed on diseased plants, then transmit the virus to healthy plants when they feed again. Mosaic persists in the plant indefinitely. Tubers obtained from diseased plants are also infected.

SOLUTION: There are no chemicals that control virus diseases. Discard infected plants. Prevent the spread of the virus by keeping the aphid population under control. For more information about disease-carrying aphids and their control, see page 880.

RUDBECKIA (GLORIOSA DAISY)

Verticillium wilt.

PROBLEM: Leaves yellow, wilt, and die, beginning with the lower leaves and progressing up the plant. Older plants may be stunted. Yellowing and wilting often affect only one side of the plant. Flowering is poor. There may be dark brown areas on the infected stems. When the stem is sliced open near the base of the plant, dark streaks and discolorations of the inner stem tissue are seen.

ANALYSIS: Verticillium wilt
This wilt disease affects many ornamental plants. It is caused by a soil-inhabiting fungus (*Verticillium* species) that persists indefinitely on plant debris or in the soil. The disease is spread by contaminated seeds, plants, soil, and equipment. The fungus enters the plant through the roots and spreads up into the stems and leaves through the water-conducting vessels in the stems. The vessels become discolored and plugged. This plugging cuts off the flow of water to the leaves, causing leaf yellowing and wilting.

SOLUTION: No chemical control is available. It is best to destroy infected plants. Verticillium can be removed from the soil only by fumigation techniques. (For more information about soil fumigation, see page 919.) However, the best solution is usually to use plants that are resistant to verticillium. For a list of verticillium-resistant plants, see page 995.

Rudbeckia cultural information
Light: Sun
Water: When the soil is just barely moist
Soil: Well drained
Fertilizer: Medium

SALVIA (SAGE)

Gray mold.

PROBLEM: Brown spots and blotches appear on the leaves and possibly on the stems. As the disease progresses, a fuzzy brown or grayish mold forms on the infected tissue. Gray mold and spots often appear on the flowers, especially during periods of cool, wet weather. The leaves and stems may be soft and rotted.

ANALYSIS: Gray mold
This widespread plant disease is caused by a fungus (*Botrytis* species) that is found on most dead plant tissue. The fungus initially attacks foliage and flowers that are weak or dead, causing spotting and mold. The fuzzy mold that develops is composed of millions of microscopic spores. Once gray mold has become established on plant debris and weak or dying leaves and flowers, it can invade healthy plant tissue. The fungus is spread by splashing water, or by bits of infected plant debris that land on the leaves. Cool temperatures and high humidity favor gray mold growth. Crowded plantings, rain, and overhead watering enhance the spread of the disease. Infection is more of a problem in spring and fall, when temperatures are lower. In warm winter areas where freezing is rare, gray mold can be a year-round problem.

SOLUTION: Spray infected plants every 10 to 14 days with a fungicide containing *chlorothalonil* or *benomyl*. Continue spraying as long as the mold is visible. Clean up plant debris, and remove dying or infected leaves, stems, and flowers. Provide enough space between plants to allow good air circulation. Try to avoid wetting the foliage when watering.

Verticillium wilt. Diseased plant on right.

PROBLEM: Leaves yellow, wilt, and die, starting with the lower leaves and progressing up the plant. Older plants may be stunted. Yellowing and wilting often affect only one side of the plant. Flowering is poor. There may be dark brown areas on the infected stems. When the stem is sliced open near the base of the plant, dark streaks and discolorations of the inner stem tissue are seen.

ANALYSIS: Verticillium wilt
This wilt disease affects many ornamental plants. It is caused by a soil-inhabiting fungus (*Verticillium* species) that persists indefinitely on plant debris or in the soil. The disease is spread by contaminated seeds, plants, soil, and equipment. The fungus enters the plant through the roots and spreads up into the stems and leaves through the water-conducting vessels in the stems. The vessels become discolored and plugged. This plugging cuts off the flow of water to the leaves, causing leaf yellowing and wilting.

SOLUTION: No chemical control is available. It is best to destroy infected plants. Verticillium can be removed from the soil only by fumigation techniques. (For more information about soil fumigation, see page 919.) However, the best solution is usually to use plants that are resistant to verticillium. For a list of verticillium-resistant plants, see page 995.

Salvia cultural information
Light: Sun
Water: When soil is just barely moist
Soil: Well drained
Fertilizer: Light

SEDUM

Stem and root rot.

PROBLEM: The leaves and stems may be dark, soft, and rotted, or they may turn dull gray, then yellow. Finally, they shrivel and drop off. Sometimes the base of the plant and the lower stems are covered with white matted strands. These strands eventually develop small black or brown pellets the size of a pinhead.

ANALYSIS: Stem and root rot
This disease is caused by several different fungi (including *Sclerotium rolfsii*). These fungi may persist indefinitely in the soil. They thrive in waterlogged, heavy soil. Some of these fungi attack the roots directly, while others penetrate either the roots or stems. Infection causes the roots and stems to decay, resulting in wilting, rotting leaves, and finally the death of the plant. These fungi are generally spread by infested soil and contaminated transplants, equipment, and moving water. Some of these fungi may survive the winter in the form of fungal pellets and strands in the soil and plant debris.

SOLUTION: Let the soil dry out between waterings. (For information on this technique, see page 857.) Remove and destroy all infected plants and debris. Improve soil drainage by adding organic matter. For information on correcting soil drainage, see page 901.

Sedum cultural information
Light: Sun to shade
Water: Let soil dry between waterings
Soil: Any good garden soil
Fertilizer: Light

SEDUM

TAGETES (MARIGOLD)

Snail (half life size).

PROBLEM: Stems and leaves may be sheared off and eaten. Silvery trails wind around on the plants and soil nearby. Snails or slugs may be seen moving around or feeding on the plants, especially at night. Check for them by inspecting the garden at night by flashlight.

ANALYSIS: Snails and slugs
These pests are mollusks, and are related to clams, oysters, and other shellfish. They feed on a wide variety of garden plants. Like other mollusks, snails and slugs need to be moist all the time. For this reason, they avoid direct sun and dry places, and hide during the day in damp places, such as under flower pots or in thick groundcovers. They emerge at night or on cloudy days to feed. Snails and slugs are similar in appearance, except that the snail has a hard shell, into which it withdraws when disturbed. Slugs lay masses of white eggs encased in a slimy mass in protected places. Snails bury their eggs in the soil, also in a slimy mass. The young look like miniature versions of their parents.

SOLUTION: Scatter ORTHO Bug-Geta Snail & Slug Pellets or ORTHO Slug-Geta Snail & Slug Bait granules around the areas you wish to protect. Also scatter the bait in areas where snails or slugs might be hiding, such as in dense groundcovers, weedy areas, compost piles, or pot storage areas. Before spreading the bait, wet down the treated areas to encourage snail and slug activity that night. Repeat the application every 2 weeks as long as snails and slugs are active.

TAGETES

ADAPTATION: Throughout the United States.

FLOWERING TIME: Summer to fall.

LIGHT: Full sun.

PLANTING TIME: Spring, after all danger of frost is past.

SOIL: Any good garden soil.

FERTILIZER: Fertilize with ORTHO Rose & Flower Food 8–12–4 or ORTHO General Purpose Plant Food 8–8–8 according to label directions.

WATER:
   How much: Apply enough water to plants in the ground to wet the soil 10 to 12 inches deep.
   Containers: Apply enough water so that 10 percent of the water drains from the bottom of the container.
   How often: Water when the soil 1 inch below the surface is just barely moist.

HANDLING: Pinch off fading blooms to promote continuous flowering.

Leaf spot.

PROBLEM: Spots and blotches appear on the leaves. The spots may be yellow, reddish, brown, gray, or black. They range in size from barely visible to ¼ inch in diameter. Several spots may join to form blotches. Leaves and leaflets may be twisted or yellowing and dying. Leaf spotting is most severe in warm, humid weather.

ANALYSIS: Leaf spot
There are several different fungi that cause leaf spots. Some of these fungi may eventually kill the plant. Most of them merely cause spotting, which is unsightly but not harmful to the plant. These fungi are spread by splashing water or wind. They generally survive the winter in diseased plant debris. Most of these fungi do their greatest damage in mild weather (50° to 85°F).

SOLUTION: Remove and destroy badly spotted leaves and all plants. Try to avoid splashing water on the foliage when watering. Spray plants every 10 to 14 days with a fungicide containing *benomyl* or *basic copper sulfate*.

Mite damage.

Leafminer damage.

Cutworm (¼ life size).

PROBLEM: Leaves are stippled, yellowing, and dirty. Leaves may dry out and drop. There may be webbing over flower buds, between leaves and stems, or on the lower surfaces of the leaves. To determine if the plant is infested with mites, hold a sheet of white paper underneath an affected leaf and tap the plant sharply. Minute green, red, or yellow specks the size of pepper grains will drop to the paper and begin to crawl around. These pests are easily seen against the white background.

ANALYSIS: Mites
These major pests of many garden and greenhouse plants are related to spiders. They cause damage by sucking sap from the underside of the leaves. As a result of feeding, the green leaf pigment disappears, producing the stippled appearance. Mites are active throughout the growing season, but are favored by hot, dry weather (70°F and up). By midsummer, they can build up to tremendous numbers.

SOLUTION: Spray with ORTHO Isotox Insect Killer according to label directions when damage is first noticed. Spray the foliage thoroughly, being sure to cover both the upper and lower surfaces of the leaves.

PROBLEM: Light-colored winding trails appear in the leaves. Blotches may eventually develop. Severely infested leaves may dry up and die.

ANALYSIS: Leafminers
Several species of leaf-mining flies cause this type of damage to marigolds and many other flowers. The minute adult flies lay their eggs on the undersides of the leaves. The larvae that emerge from these eggs penetrate the leaf and live between the upper and lower surfaces. They feed on the inner leaf tissue, creating winding trails and blotches. Their dark excrement dots or partially fills sections of the trails. The larvae usually emerge from the leaves to pupate. Leafminers are continually present from spring until fall. The last generation of larvae pupates in the soil or plant debris through the winter and emerges as adult flies the following spring.

SOLUTION: Spray infested plants with ORTHO Isotox Insect Killer or ORTHO Orthene Systemic Insect Control according to label directions. Pick off and destroy infested leaves. Remove and destroy all plant remains in the fall.

PROBLEM: Young plants are chewed or cut off near the ground. Many leaves may be sheared from their stems. Gray, brown, or black worms, 1½ to 2 inches long, may be found in the top 2 inches of soil near the base of the damaged plants. The worms coil when disturbed.

ANALYSIS: Cutworms
Several species of cutworms attack marigolds and many other flower and vegetable plants. The most likely pests of young marigold plants early in the season are surface-feeding and climbing cutworms. A single surface-feeding cutworm can sever the stems of many young plants in one night. Climbing cutworms may shear the leaves off older plants. Cutworms hide in the soil during the day, and feed only at night. The adult forms of cutworms are dark, night-flying moths with bands or stripes on their forewings.

SOLUTION: Apply an insecticidal dust or spray containing *diazinon* around the base of undamaged plants when stem cutting is observed. Since cutworms are difficult to control, it may be necessary to repeat the treatment at weekly intervals. Before transplanting into the area, apply a preventive treatment of insecticide and work it into the soil. Cultivate the soil thoroughly in late summer and fall to expose and destroy eggs, larvae, and pupae. Further reduce damage with cutworm "collars" around the stem of each plant. These collars can be made of stiff paper or aluminum foil. They should be at least 2 inches high, and pressed firmly into the soil.

TROPAEOLUM (NASTURTIUM)

Leaf spots.

Aphids (twice life size).

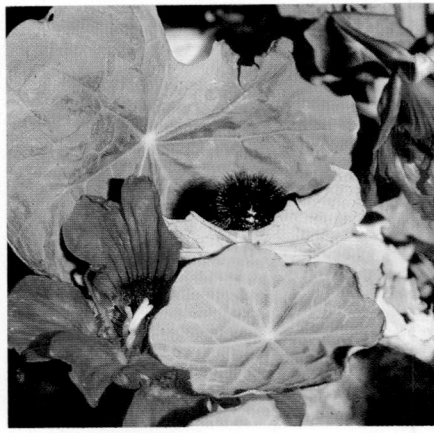

Caterpillars (half life size).

PROBLEM: Spots and blotches appear on the leaves. The spots may be yellow, red, tan, gray, or black. They range in size from barely visible to ¼ inch in diameter. Several spots may join together to form blotches. Some of the leaves may be yellow and dying. Leaf spotting is most severe in warm, humid weather.

ANALYSIS: Leaf spot
Nasturtiums are susceptible to several fungi that cause leaf spots. Some of these fungi may eventually kill the plant or weaken it so that it becomes susceptible to attack by other organisms. Others merely cause spotting that is unsightly but not harmful. These fungi are spread by splashing water, wind, insects, tools, and infected transplants and seed. They survive the winter in diseased plant debris. Most of these fungi do their greatest damage during mild weather (50° to 85°F). Infection is favored by moist conditions.

SOLUTION: Picking off the diseased leaves generally gives adequate control. If infection is severe, spray with a copper-containing fungicide, such as *basic copper sulfate*. Clean up debris.

PROBLEM: Tiny (⅛ inch) pale green to dark green or black soft-bodied insects are clustered on the leaves. Leaves may be curled, distorted, and yellowing. Flowers may be malformed. A shiny, sticky substance may coat the leaves. Ants are often present.

ANALYSIS: Aphids
Several species of aphids infest nasturtiums, including the *bean aphid* (*Aphis fabae*). Aphids do little damage in small numbers. However, they are extremely prolific and populations can rapidly build up to damaging numbers during the growing season. Damage occurs when the aphid sucks the juices from the nasturtium leaves. The aphid is unable to digest fully all the sugar in the plant sap and excretes the excess in a fluid called honeydew, which often coats the leaves. Ants feed on this sticky substance, and are often present where there is an aphid infestation.

SOLUTION: Spray the plant with an insecticide containing *malathion*, *diazinon*, or *dimethoate*. Repeat the spray if the plant becomes reinfested. Hose off the foliage to remove the honeydew.

PROBLEM: Holes appear in the leaves and buds. Leaves, buds, and flowers may be entirely chewed off. Worms or caterpillars are feeding on the plants.

ANALYSIS: Caterpillars
Many species of these moth or butterfly larvae feed on nasturtiums and other garden plants. The adult moths or butterflies of most species start to lay their eggs on garden plants with the onset of warm spring weather. The larvae that emerge from these eggs feed on the leaves, flowers, and buds for 2 to 6 weeks, then pupate in cocoons either attached to leaves or structures or buried in the soil. The adult moths and butterflies emerge the following spring.

SOLUTION: Spray infested plants with an insecticide containing *malathion*. Repeat the spray if reinfestation occurs, allowing at least 7 to 10 days to pass between applications. You may also control caterpillars with a spray containing *Bacillus thuringiensis*. This bacterial insecticide is most effective while the caterpillars are small.

Tropaeolum cultural information
Light: Sun to partial shade
Water: When the soil is just barely moist
Soil: Any good garden soil
Fertilizer: Light

TULIPA (TULIP)

Bacterial wilt.

PROBLEM: The leaves wilt, turn yellow, and die. The stems have a water-soaked appearance and are soft and rotten. When sliced open, the stems are found to be discolored, and a thick gray fluid oozes out. The roots may be black and decayed.

ANALYSIS: Bacterial wilt
This disease is caused by a bacterium (*Pseudomonas solanacearum*) that is common in warm, humid climates. It attacks many different ornamentals and vegetables in the tomato family. The bacteria enter the plant through wounds or cuts in the roots. Once inside the roots, they move up into the stem and cause clogging and decay of the water-conducting stem tissue, resulting in wilting and death. The thick gray fluid that oozes from decayed or wounded tissue contains millions of bacteria. The bacteria are spread to other plants by water, contaminated soil, debris, and equipment. They can live for 6 years or more in the soil. Bacterial wilt is most damaging in warm areas (75° to 95°F) and moist conditions.

SOLUTION: There are no chemical controls for this disease. Remove and destroy all diseased plants. To avoid reinfection from contaminated soil, do not replant nasturtiums in the same area. When cultivating the soil, avoid damaging the stems, roots, and tubers. If bacterial wilt is prevalent in your garden, do not plant nasturtiums near vegetables like tomatoes, eggplants, peppers, and potatoes, which are also susceptible to this disease.

TULIPA

ADAPTATION: Throughout the United States. In zones 9 and 10, bulbs must be prechilled (see below for details).

FLOWERING TIME: Spring.

LIGHT: Full sun to filtered light.

PLANTING TIME: Fall.

SOIL: Well-drained soil, pH 6.0 to 8.0

FERTILIZER: When planting, add 1 teaspoon of ORTHO Bone Meal 12–0–0 or ORTHO Superphosphate 0–20–0 to the bottom of the planting hole and mix it into the soil. During the growing season, fertilize with ORTHO Rose & Flower Food 8–12–4 or ORTHO General Purpose Plant Food 8–8–8 according to label directions.

WATER:
How much: Apply enough water to wet the soil 1 to 1½ feet deep.
How often: Water when the soil an inch below the surface is just barely moist.

HANDLING: In zones 9 and 10, precool bulbs for 6 to 8 weeks before planting. Store bulbs in paper bags in the refrigerator crisper. Tulips usually do not flower as well the second or third year after planting. Either replace them, or dig, separate, precool if necessary and replant.

Short stems.

PROBLEM: Flower stems are very short, and the flowers may be smaller than normal. Sometimes the flowers bloom at ground level. The foliage appears healthy.

ANALYSIS: Short stems
This condition is the result of warm spring temperatures, a lack of adequate winter cooling, or a combination of both. Tulip bulbs contain embryonic flowers and stems. A minimum of 6 weeks exposure to cool temperatures (40° to 50°F) stimulates the stem cells to elongate, causing the immature tulip to emerge from the ground. During cool spring weather (40° to 50°F), the stems continue to elongate to their full length and then the flowers mature and open. In warm winter areas, stems often fail to elongate properly. Also, during unseasonable spring hot spells (when air temperatures reach 60°F and higher), the tulip flower is stimulated by the heat to mature and open before the stems have grown to their full potential.

SOLUTION: There is nothing you can do to increase the length of the tulip stem once the flower has matured. If warm spring temperatures are common in your area, plant tulips where they will receive either filtered light, or direct sun only in the early morning. Plant single-flowered, long-stemmed tulips such as the Darwin, Darwin hybrids, cottage, and lily-flowered tulips. If you live in a warm winter area, place tulip bulbs in paper bags in the fall, and chill them in the crisper section of the refrigerator for 6 weeks before planting; or buy precooled bulbs. In zones 9 and 10, delay planting tulips until mid-December.

TULIPA (TULIP)

Old planting.

Undersized bulbs.

Rodent damage.

PROBLEM: Tulip bulbs produce healthy foliage, but fail to bloom.

ANALYSIS: Failure to bloom
Healthy tulips may fail to bloom for several reasons:

1. *Lack of cooling:* Tulip bulbs require a minimum exposure of 6 weeks to cool temperatures (40° to 50°F) in the fall in order to flower properly. Cooling stimulates the embryonic flower stem within the bulb to elongate and emerge from the ground.

2. *Foliage removed too soon:* After a tulip flowers, the remaining foliage continues to manufacture food for new bulbs and next year's flowers.

3. *Lack of fertilization:* When tulips are grown in infertile soil for more than one season, they form small, poor quality bulbs. Such bulbs produce only sparse foliage and few, if any, flowers.

4. *Undersized bulbs:* Bulbs smaller than 2½ inches in circumference may not contain an embryonic flower. They will produce only foliage for 1 or 2 years, increasing in size and weight until they enlarge enough to produce a flower.

5. *Old plantings:* Tulip flowers are largest and most prolific the first spring after newly purchased bulbs have been planted. After flowering, the original bulb usually disintegrates and several small "daughter bulbs" form. Often these daughter bulbs are too small to provide many flowers. Depending on the variety, a planting of tulips generally continues to flower for only 2 to 4 years, each year producing fewer flowers. Tulips are especially short-lived in warm winter areas (zones 9 and 10; see page 1004 for zone map).

SOLUTION: The numbered solutions below correspond to the numbers in the analysis.

1. In warm winter areas (zones 9 and 10), precool bulbs before planting, or buy precooled bulbs. For details on cooling bulbs, see page 427. Postpone planting until mid-December.

2. Let foliage turn yellow before removing it.

3. Fertilize bulbs when planting, after the new leaves emerge in the spring, and after they bloom. For details on fertilizing, see page 427.

4. Purchase only large, healthy bulbs from a reputable nursery or mail-order company.

5. Replace old tulips with fresh bulbs. You may also dig up, separate, and replant old bulbs. However, it will often be at least one year before they will flower again. Unless your soil and climate conditions are ideal for growing tulips, the bulbs and flowers will never be as large and prolific as they were the first year. You can prolong the flowering life of a tulip planting by planting the bulbs deeper than usual. Place them 12 inches deep in the soil rather than the usual 6 inches. It is essential that the soil be well drained, because water buildup around the bulbs will cause them to rot.

PROBLEM: Tulips do not emerge in the spring. Bulbs have been partially or completely eaten. Tulip stems may be chewed off. The entire plant sometimes disappears. There may be crescent-shaped mounds of soil clustered in the yard. There may also be tiny holes in the soil and small, dry, rectangular, brown pellets on the ground.

ANALYSIS: Rodents
Pocket gophers and field mice are rodents that feed extensively on tulip bulbs. *Pocket gophers*, found primarily in the West, are tan, furry, rodents, 6 inches long, that live almost entirely underground. They form crescent-shaped mounds of dirt. *Field mice* live both above ground in protective vegetation and below ground in shallow tunnels and burrows. Signs of field mice include clusters of tiny droppings, and small holes in the soil, which are entrances to their underground tunnels. Both of these animals feed on bulbs throughout the year.

SOLUTION: Prevent gopher damage by lining the inside of the planting bed with ½ inch mesh chicken wire along the bottom and up the sides. To prevent mouse damage, lay ¼ inch mesh hardware cloth on the top of the planted area, burying the edges several inches under the soil surface. Remove the hardware cloth before shoots emerge in the spring. For more information about rodents and their control, see pages 894 and 890.

Poor growth.

Diseased plants.

Bulb rot.

PROBLEM: Tulip bulbs do not produce any growth in the spring.

ANALYSIS: Failure to grow
Improper cultural techniques, diseases, animal pests, and natural decline can all contribute to lack of growth in tulips.

1. *Lack of cooling:* Tulip bulbs require a period of cooling to develop properly. They need to spend at least 6 weeks below 50°F in order to perform ideally. If newly purchased bulbs are not precooled, or soil temperatures remain at 55°F or above during the winter, root formation, flower emergence, and the production of new daughter bulbs for future flowering will be inhibited.

2. *Foliage removed too soon:* After a tulip flowers, the remaining foliage continues to use the sun's rays to manufacture food for the developing new bulbs and next year's flowers. If the foliage is removed before it has a chance to turn yellow naturally, the new bulbs will either be very small or will not form at all.

3. *Lack of fertilization:* After the first year, tulips will not continue to perform well when planted in infertile soil. They form only weak, small bulbs and flowers. After several years, they will stop producing growth.

4. *Root rot:* Infected tulip bulbs planted in heavy, poorly drained soil frequently decay.

5. *Rodents:* Mice, pocket gophers, and other rodents may feed on tulip bulbs. Dig in the area where the bulbs were planted and check for underground tunnels and half-eaten bulbs, both of which indicate rodent damage. For more information on rodents, see page 428.

SOLUTION: The numbered solutions below correspond to the numbers in the analysis.

1. In warm winter areas (zones 9 and 10; see page 1004 for zone map), refrigerate newly purchased bulbs for 6 weeks. For details, see page 427.

2. Allow foliage to turn yellow before removing it.

3. Add ORTHO Bone Meal 0–12–0 when planting bulbs. Fertilize emerging tulips in the spring with ORTHO Rose & Flower Food 8–12–4 and refertilize once a month after the plants have flowered until the foliage dies back.

4. Before planting, discard discolored, spongy, or moldy bulbs. Plant in well-drained soil. For information on improving soil drainage, see page 901.

5. The most effective method of protecting tulips is to plant them in baskets made of ¼ inch wire mesh. Traps or baits may also be used. For further information on rodent control, see page 428.

PROBLEM: Foliage is sparse and stunted. Often the leaves turn red, wilt, and die. When the plant is dug up, rotted bulbs are revealed. The bulbs may be either mushy or firm and chalky. Usually they are covered with a white, pink, or gray mold. There may be reddish brown to black pinhead-sized pellets on the bulb husks, leaf bases, and in the soil immediately surrounding the plant.

ANALYSIS: Root and bulb rot
This disease of tulips is caused by several different soil-inhabiting fungi that attack and decay the bulbs and roots. The fungi form tiny pellets on the bulbs and in the soil. These pellets survive through dry conditions and extremes of temperature. Bulbs and root rots are favored by wet, poorly drained soils. Bulbs injured during digging or storing are especially susceptible to infection. Sometimes bulbs in storage are lightly infected, but the fungal decay hasn't progressed far enough to be easily noticed. When planted, these bulbs may rot so quickly that they don't produce any foliage.

SOLUTION: Remove and destroy infected plants and the soil immediately surrounding them. Check and discard infected bulbs before planting. Avoid wounding bulbs when cultivating around them or handling them. Dip clean, healthy bulbs in a warm (80° to 85°F) solution of *benomyl* before storing, and again before planting them. Plant in a well-drained location. Do not replant tulips in infested soil for at least 3 years.

TULIPA (TULIP)

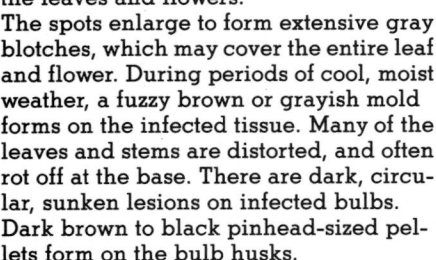

Botrytis blight. *Insert:* Infected bulbs.

PROBLEM: Light to dark-colored spots appear on the leaves and flowers. The spots enlarge to form extensive gray blotches, which may cover the entire leaf and flower. During periods of cool, moist weather, a fuzzy brown or grayish mold forms on the infected tissue. Many of the leaves and stems are distorted, and often rot off at the base. There are dark, circular, sunken lesions on infected bulbs. Dark brown to black pinhead-sized pellets form on the bulb husks.

ANALYSIS: Botrytis blight
This common disease of tulips is caused by a fungus (*Botrytis tulipae*). The fungus persists through the winter and hot, dry periods as tiny fungal pellets in the soil, plant debris, and bulbs. In the spring, these pellets produce spores that attack foliage and flowers, causing spotting, decay, and mold. Wounded, weak, and dead plant tissues are especially susceptible to infection. The fungus is spread by splashing water. Botrytis blight is most serious during periods of cool, moist weather. Tulip bulbs that are injured when they are dug up to be stored are especially vulnerable to infection.

SOLUTION: Remove and destroy diseased plants, leaves, flowers, and debris. Before planting tulip bulbs, check them for signs of infection, and discard diseased bulbs. Start spraying emerging plants when they are 4 inches tall with a fungicide containing *zineb*, *mancozeb*, or *benomyl*. Use a spreader-sticker when spraying (see page 915). Spray plants every 5 to 7 days until the flowers bloom. Remove tulip flowers just as they start to fade, and cut off the foliage at ground level when it turns yellow. Rotate plants to a new location next year.

Aphids (half life size).

PROBLEM: Leaves are curled, distorted, and yellowing. Flowers may be malformed. Tiny (⅛ inch) yellow-green to gray soft-bodied insects are clustered on the leaves. A sticky, shiny substance may coat the leaves. Ants may be present.

ANALYSIS: Aphids
Aphids do little damage in small numbers. However, they are extremely prolific and populations can rapidly build up to damaging numbers during the growing season. Damage occurs when the aphid sucks the juices from the tulip leaves and flower buds. The aphid is unable to digest fully all the sugar in the plant sap and excretes the excess in a fluid called honeydew, which coats the leaves. Ants feed on the honeydew, and are often present where there is an aphid infestation. Aphids can also transmit virus diseases to tulips while feeding.

SOLUTION: Spray infested plants with ORTHO Orthene Systemic Insect Control. Repeat the spray if the plant is reinfested. Use a spreader-sticker when spraying. For information on spreader-stickers, see page 915.

VERBENA

Powdery mildew.

PROBLEM: Leaves and stems are covered with grayish white powdery spots and patches. These patches occur on the upper surfaces of the leaves. The infected leaves eventually turn yellow and wither.

ANALYSIS: Powdery mildew
This common plant disease is caused by a fungus (*Erysiphe cichoracearum*) that thrives in both humid and dry weather. The powdery patches consist of fungal strands and spores. The spores are spread by the wind to healthy plants. The fungus saps plant nutrients, causing yellowing and sometimes death of the leaves. A severe infection may kill whole plants. Since this powdery mildew attacks many different kinds of plants, the fungus from a diseased plant may infect other types of plants in the garden. (For a list of susceptible plants, see page 995.) Under favorable conditions, powdery mildew can spread through a planting in a matter of days.

SOLUTION: Spray infected plants with a fungicide containing *folpet*, *dinocap*, or *cycloheximide*. Spray at regular intervals of 10 to 12 days or as often as necessary to protect new growth. Remove and destroy severely infected plants. Where practical, pick off diseased leaves. Clean up and destroy plant debris.

Gray mold.

Bacterial wilt.

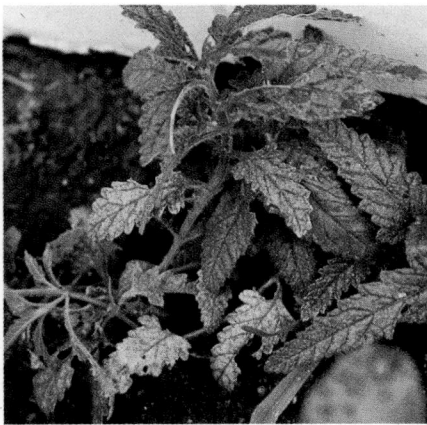

Mite damage.

PROBLEM: Brown spots and blotches appear on the leaves and possibly on the stems. As the disease progresses, a fuzzy brown or grayish mold forms on the infected tissue. Gray mold and spots often appear on the flowers, especially during periods of cool, wet weather. The leaves and stems may be soft and rotted.

ANALYSIS: Gray mold
This widespread plant disease is caused by a fungus (*Botrytis* species) that is found on most dead plant tissue. The fungus initially attacks foliage and flowers that are weak or dead, causing spotting and mold. The fuzzy mold that develops is composed of millions of microscopic spores. Once gray mold has become established on plant debris and weak or dying leaves and flowers, it can invade healthy plant tissue. The fungus is spread by splashing water or by bits of infected plant tissue contacting healthy tissue. Cool temperatures and high humidity favor gray mold growth. Crowded plantings, rain, and overhead watering also encourage the spread of the disease. Infection is more of a problem in spring and fall when temperatures are lower. In warm winter areas where freezing is rare, gray mold can be a year-round problem.

SOLUTION: Spray infected plants every 10 to 14 days with a fungicide containing *maneb* or *mancozeb*. Continue spraying as long as the mold is visible. Clean up plant debris, and remove dying or infected leaves, stems, and flowers. Provide enough space between plants to allow good air circulation. Try to avoid wetting the foliage when watering.

PROBLEM: The plant wilts, turns yellow, and dies. When sliced open, the stem is found to be streaked and discolored. The lower stems near the soil may be soft and rotten.

ANALYSIS: Bacterial wilt
This disease is caused by a bacterium (*Pseudomonas solanacearum*) that is especially common in warm, humid climates. It attacks many different ornamental and vegetable plants. The bacteria enter the plant through wounds or cuts in the roots. Once inside the roots, they move up into the stem and cause clogging and decay of the water-conducting stem tissue, resulting in plant wilting and death. The infected tissue contains millions of bacteria, which are spread to other plants by water, contaminated soil, debris, and equipment. The bacteria may live for 6 years or more in the soil. They thrive and are most damaging in warm areas (75° to 95°F) and moist conditions.

SOLUTION: There are no chemical controls for this disease. Remove and destroy all wilted plants. To avoid reinfection from contaminated soils, do not replant verbenas in the same area next year. When cultivating the soil, avoid damaging the stems and roots. Plant in well-drained soil.

PROBLEM: Leaves are stippled, yellowing, and dirty. Leaves may dry out and drop. There may be webbing between the leaves or on the lower surfaces of the leaves. To determine if the plant is infested with mites, hold a sheet of white paper underneath an affected leaf and tap the leaf sharply. Minute green, red, or yellow specks the size of pepper grains will drop to the paper and begin to crawl around. These pests are easily seen against the white background.

ANALYSIS: Two-spotted spider mite (*Tetranychus urticae*)
These mites, related to spiders, are major pests of many garden and greenhouse plants. They cause damage by sucking sap from the undersides of the leaves. As a result of feeding, the green leaf pigment disappears, producing the stippled appearance. Mites are active throughout the growing season, but are favored by hot, dry weather (70°F and up). By midsummer, they build up to tremendous numbers.

SOLUTION: Spray the infested plants with a pesticide containing *dicofol*. Repeat the spray 2 more times at regular intervals of 5 to 7 days.

VERBENA

VIOLA (PANSY, VIOLET)

Greenhouse whiteflies (life size).

PROBLEM: Tiny, winged insects ¹/₁₂ inch long are found mainly on the undersides of the leaves. The insects are covered with white waxy powder. When the plant is touched, insects flutter rapidly around it. Leaves may be mottled and yellowing. Black mold may cover the leaves.

ANALYSIS: Greenhouse whitefly (*Trialeurodes vaporariorum*)
This insect is a common pest of many garden and greenhouse plants. The 4-winged adult lays eggs on the undersides of leaves. The larvae are the size of a pinhead, flat, oval-shaped, and semi-transparent, with white waxy filaments radiating from the body. They feed for about a month before changing to the adult form. Both the larval and adult forms suck sap from the leaves. The larvae are more damaging because they feed more heavily. Adults and larvae cannot fully digest all the sugar in the plant sap, and excrete the excess in a fluid called honeydew, which often drops onto the leaves below. A sooty black mold fungus may develop on the honeydew, causing the verbena leaves to appear black and dirty. In warm winter areas the insect can be active year-round, with eggs, larvae, and adults present at the same time. The whitefly is unable to live through freezing winters. Spring reinfestations in freezing areas come from migrating whiteflies and from infested greenhouse-grown plants placed in the garden.

SOLUTION: Control whiteflies by spraying infested plants every 7 to 10 days with an insecticide containing *malathion*. Spray the foliage thoroughly, being sure to cover both the upper and lower surfaces of the leaves.

VIOLA

ADAPTATION: Throughout the United States.

FLOWERING TIME:
Violets: Spring and summer.
Pansies and violas: Fall, winter, and spring in zones 8 through 10. Spring and summer in colder areas. To determine your zone, see the map on page 1004.

LIGHT:
Violets: Half-day sun to full shade.
Pansies and violas: Full sun or filtered light.

PLANTING TIME: In zones 3 through 7, plant in spring when all danger of frost is past. In zones 8 through 10, plant fall through spring.

SOIL: Well drained and high in organic matter.

FERTILIZER: Fertilize with ORTHO Rose & Flower Food 8–12–4 or ORTHO General Purpose Plant Food 8–8–8 according to label directions.

WATER:
How much: Apply enough water to plants in the ground to wet the soil 6 inches deep.
Containers: Apply enough water so that about 10 percent of the water drains from the bottom of the container.
How often: Water when the soil 1 inch below the surface is moist but not wet.

HANDLING: Pinch off fading flowers to encourage continuous bloom. Pinch back weak, rangy growth.

Spindly growth and poor flowering.

PROBLEM: Leaves are small and thin, and stems are long and spindly. Flowering is poor, and flowers are small.

ANALYSIS: Spindly growth and poor flowering
There are several cultural problems that may contribute to spindly growth.
1. *Failure to remove old flowers:* If the fading flowers remain on the plant, only a few small new flowers will be produced. When the old flowers are allowed to remain, the plant uses its energy in seed development instead of producing new flowers.
2. *Inadequate light:* Pansies and violas grow lanky and flower poorly when planted in deep shade. They require at least strong filtered light to grow compactly, and will flower most profusely in full sun during mild weather.
3. *Old age:* Pansies and violas are perennials, and theoretically will last from year to year. In cold winter climates, they are killed by freezing temperatures. In warm winter areas, they will often last for a year or more, but usually start to produce lanky, unattractive growth after the first growing season.

SOLUTION: The numbers below correspond to the numbers in analysis.
1. Pinch off flowers when they start to fade. For a discussion of pinching, see page 919.
2. Grow plants in full sun, part day sun, or strong filtered light.
3. Treat pansies and violas as annuals. Plant them in the spring (or fall in zones 9 and 10) and replace them when they start to decline in the summer. Rangy plants may be rejuvenated if the spindly stems are pinched back to ¹/₃ of their height.

Leaf spot on viola.

PROBLEM: Leaves and stems are spotted or blotched. The spots may be grayish white, yellow, tan, or brown, ranging in size from barely visible to ¼ inch in diameter. Sometimes these spots are bordered with black margins. Often, they join together to form blotches. The petals may be distorted and disfigured with brown lesions. The leaves may turn yellow and die. Sometimes elongated, sunken lesions also develop on the stems and flower stalks. Severely infected plants may die.

ANALYSIS: Leaf spot
Several different fungi cause leaf spots on pansies, violas, and violets. Some of these fungi will eventually kill the plant, while others merely cause spotting that is unsightly but not harmful. These fungi are spread by splashing water and wind. Fungal strands or spores survive the winter in plant debris and sometimes in infected seed. Most of the leaf spot organisms do their greatest damage in humid conditions and mild weather (50° to 85°F).

SOLUTION: Remove dying plants. Where practical, pick off infected leaves and clean up plant debris. Spray plants with a fungicide containing *zineb*, *maneb*, or *mancozeb* at weekly intervals. When spraying, use a spreader-sticker. For information about spreader-stickers, see page 915.

Root and stem rot.

PROBLEM: Leaves turn yellow, wilt, and die. The roots and lower stems are soft and rotten. There may be white fungal strands on infected stems and around the base of the plant.

ANALYSIS: Root and stem rot
This disease is caused by a number of different fungi that persist indefinitely in the soil. They thrive in waterlogged, heavy soils. Infection causes the stem and roots to decay, resulting in wilting, yellowing leaves, and the death of the plant. These fungi are generally spread by infested soil and transplants, contaminated equipment, and splashing or running water.

SOLUTION: Remove dead and dying plants. It is important to allow the soil to dry between irrigations; root and stem rots are encouraged by waterlogged conditions. (For more information on this technique, see page 857.) Improve soil drainage. For more information about soil drainage, see page 901.

Slug damage.

PROBLEM: Irregular holes with smooth edges are chewed in the leaves. Leaves, stems, and flowers may be chewed off entirely. Silvery trails wind around on the plants and soil nearby. Snails and slugs may be seen moving around or feeding on the plants, especially at night. Check for them by inspecting the garden at night by flashlight.

ANALYSIS: Snails and slugs
These pests are mollusks, and are related to clams, oysters, and other shellfish. They feed on a wide variety of garden plants. Like other mollusks, snails and slugs need to be moist all the time. For this reason, they avoid direct sun and dry places, and hide during the day in damp places, such as under flower pots or in thick groundcover. They emerge at night or on cloudy days to feed. Snails and slugs are similar in appearance, except that the snail has a hard shell, into which it withdraws when disturbed. Slugs lay masses of white eggs encased in a slimy mass in protected places. Snails bury their eggs in the soil, also in a slimy mass. The young look like miniature versions of their parents.

SOLUTION: Scatter ORTHO Bug-Geta Snail & Slug Pellets or ORTHO Slug-Geta Snail & Slug Bait granules around the areas you wish to protect. Also scatter the bait in areas where snails or slugs might be hiding such as in dense groundcovers, weedy areas, compost piles, or pot storage areas. Before spreading the bait, wet down the treated areas to encourage snail and slug activity that night. Repeat the application every 2 weeks as long as snails and slugs are active.

ZANTEDESCHIA (CALLA LILY)

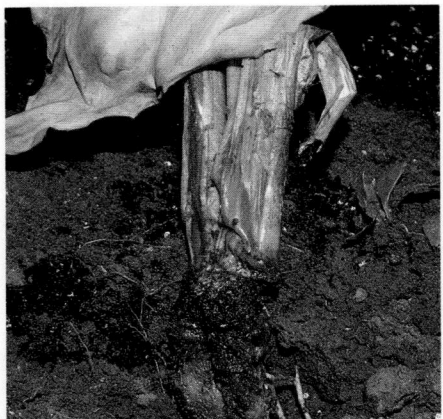

Soft rot.

PROBLEM: Leaf bases and rhizomes (elongated underground stems) are soft and slimy. The edges of the leaves may appear as if they are soaked with water or oil, and are soft and slimy. In some cases, the leaves wilt, turn yellow, and die. Foliage and flower stalks rot off at the soil surface. The entire plant may wilt suddenly and die.

ANALYSIS: Soft rot
This plant disease is caused by a bacterium (*Erwinia carotovora*). The bacteria penetrate calla rhizomes and leaf bases through wounds. Leaf bases and rhizomes decay, turning soft and slimy. Sometimes the infection spreads up into the leaf tissue and down into the roots. Soft rot is favored by moist conditions and wet soils. The bacteria live in the soil and plant debris. They are spread by infected rhizomes, transplants, and contaminated soil and tools.

SOLUTION: Discard all diseased plants and the soil immediately surrounding them. Inspect all rhizomes before planting them, and discard those that are severely rotted. If only a small portion is decayed, cut out the diseased portion, then wash and dry the rhizome before planting. Plant in well-drained soil. Do not bury rhizomes deeper than 2 inches when planting.

ZINNIA

ADAPTATION: Throughout the United States.

FLOWERING TIME: Summer and fall.

LIGHT: Full sun.

PLANTING TIME: Spring, after all danger of frost is past.

SOIL: Any good garden soil.

FERTILIZER: Fertilize with ORTHO Rose & Flower Food 8–12–4 or ORTHO General Purpose Plant Food 8–8–8 according to label directions.

WATER:
How much: Apply enough water to plants in the ground to wet the soil 8 to 10 inches deep.
Containers: Apply enough water so that 10 percent of the water drains from the bottom of the container.
How often: Water when the soil 1 inch below the surface is just barely moist.

HANDLING: Zinnias thrive in hot weather. They will grow more quickly and will be less susceptible to disease if they are planted out after the days and nights have warmed up in the spring or early summer.

ZINNIA

Powdery mildew.

PROBLEM: Leaves and stems are covered with grayish white powdery spots and patches. These patches occur primarily on the upper surfaces of the leaves. The leaves eventually turn yellow and wither.

ANALYSIS: Powdery mildew
This common plant disease is caused by a fungus (*Erysiphe cichoracearum*) that thrives in both humid and dry weather. The powdery patches consist of fungal strands and spores. The spores are spread by the wind to healthy plants. The fungus saps plant nutrients, causing yellowing and sometimes death of the leaf. A severe infection may kill the plant. Since this powdery mildew attacks many different kinds of plants, the fungus from a diseased plant may infect other types of plants in the garden. (For a list of susceptible plants, see page 995). Under favorable conditions, powdery mildew can spread through a closely spaced planting in a matter of days or weeks.

SOLUTION: Spray infected plants with ORTHO Funginex Rose Disease Control or ORTHO Orthenex Insect & Disease Control at regular intervals of 7 to 10 days, or as often as necessary to protect the new growth. The fungicide protects the new, healthy foliage, but may not eradicate the fungus on leaves that are already infected. Pick off severely infected leaves. Space plants far enough apart to allow good air circulation. Clean up plant debris.

Alternaria blight.

Gray mold.

PROBLEM: Reddish brown circular or irregular spots up to ½ inch in diameter appear on the leaves. The centers of the spots may turn grayish white. The blossoms are also often spotted. Severely infected leaves, stems, and flowers turn brown and die. There may be dark, sunken lesions at the base of the stems. The entire plant frequently wilts and dies.

ANALYSIS: Alternaria blight
This common and widespread disease of zinnias is caused by a fungus (*Alternaria zinniae*). The disease is favored by moist conditions. The fungal spores are spread from plant to plant by wind and splashing water. The fungus survives on infected debris in the soil and in contaminated seed. This fungus also causes damping-off of seedlings. For more information about damping-off, see page 858.

SOLUTION: Remove dying plants. Spray infected plants with ORTHO Phaltan Rose & Garden Fungicide. Pick off infected leaves and flowers. Clean up plant debris. Avoid overhead watering.

PROBLEM: Brown spots and blotches appear on the leaves and possibly on the stems. As the disease progresses, a fuzzy brown or grayish mold forms on the infected tissue. Gray mold and spots often appear on the flowers, especially during periods of cool, wet weather. The leaves and stems may be soft and rotted.

ANALYSIS: Gray mold
This widespread plant disease is caused by a fungus (*Botrytis cinerea*) that is found on most dead plant tissue. The fungus initially attacks foliage and flowers that are weak or dead, causing spotting and mold. The fuzzy mold that develops is composed of millions of microscopic spores. Once gray mold has become established on plant debris and weak or dying leaves and flowers, it can invade healthy plant tissue. The fungus is spread by splashing water, or by infected pieces of plant tissue contacting healthy tissue. Cool temperatures and high humidity favor gray mold growth. Crowded plantings, rain, and overhead watering also enhance the spread of the disease. Infection is more of a problem in spring and fall, when temperatures are lower. In warm winter areas, where freezing is rare, gray mold can be a year-round problem. For more information about gray mold, see page 857.

SOLUTION: Spray infected plants with a fungicide containing *maneb* or *mancozeb* every 10 to 14 days. Continue spraying as long as the mold is visible. Clean up plant debris, and remove dying or infected leaves, stems, and flowers. Provide enough space between plants to allow good air circulation. Try to avoid wetting the foliage when watering.

Some of the problems common to all woody ornamentals are listed on the next 33 pages. If you don't find your problem here, locate your tree, shrub, or vine in the index on the next page.

TREES, SHRUBS, AND VINES

Trees, shrubs, and vines — the woody ornamentals — usually represent the greatest investment of all the plants in the garden. Not in dollars, perhaps, but in the years of care and waiting for them to reach maturity, and in their contribution to the landscape.

Shade trees are particularly valuable. The death of a single shade tree can drastically alter the nature of a garden, as well as lower the value of a home. As a result, this group of plants is probably better studied than other ornamental groups, and its problems are better understood.

But in spite of being more thoroughly studied than other groups of plants, the problems of woody ornamentals — and particularly of shade trees — are not easy to solve. The size of the plants is a major factor in their treatment. Many homeowners will decide to tolerate a leaf spot disease rather than spend hundreds of dollars a year to have their tree sprayed.

Also, because of the size of plants in this group, problems develop slowly and may be firmly entrenched before they are noticed. Root damage to a tree made during the installation of a new driveway may not cause any symptoms for a year or two, but may cause the death of the tree in eight or ten years.

Because of their permanence, woody ornamentals should be adapted to the spot in which they will grow. It is worth the time it takes to find out what species thrive in your area before buying. If a plant is adapted to the area and is properly fed, watered, and pruned, it is able to fight off many of the diseases and insects that might otherwise plague it.

One of the most serious problems of trees is internal decay, or heart rot. This disease occurs everywhere, and is one of the most common causes of tree death. It can be caused by many different fungi, all of which enter through breaks in the bark. A vigorous tree can wall off the diseased wood, stopping the spread of the rot. But as a tree grows older, or if it is weakened by some other condition, it loses its ability to wall off the fungus, and its wood slowly rots, often causing it to become hollow. Rotten or hollow trees are not only likely to die, they are also dangerous. When limbs break or entire trees fall, the cause is usually heart rot. For more information, see page 473.

Above: Powdery mildew on a rose. See page 589.
Left: Leaf spots on maple. See page 478.

PROBLEMS COMMON TO MANY TREES, SHRUBS, AND VINES

Flowerless dogwood in dark location.

Flower buds pruned off crapemyrtle.

PROBLEM: Plants fail to bloom, or bloom only sparsely and sporadically.

ANALYSIS: Few or no flowers
Plants produce few or no buds or flowers for any of several reasons.

1. *Juvenility:* Plants, like people, must reach a certain age or size before they are able to reproduce. They will not develop flowers or fruit until this time.

2. *Inadequate winter cooling:* In order to produce flowers, many plants must undergo a period of cooling during the winter. The plant must be exposed for a certain number of hours to temperatures between 30° and 45°F. The number of hours needed is different for different plant species. If the cooling requirement is not satisfied, flowering will be delayed and reduced, and flower buds may drop off. This is a common problem when plants adapted to cold climates are grown in the warmer southern climates.

3. *Improper pruning:* If a plant is pruned improperly or too severely, flower and fruit production can be reduced or, in some cases, prevented. Drastic pruning, especially on young plants, stimulates a flush of green growth, which inhibits flowering. Flowering will also be reduced if flower buds are pruned off.

4. *Nutrient imbalance:* Plants overfertilized with nitrogen tend to produce a flush of green growth. Some plants will not make flowers while they are growing vigorously.

5. *Shade:* Flowering plants require a certain amount of light to produce flowers. If these plants are grown in inadequate light, they produce few or no flowers.

SOLUTION: The numbered solutions below correspond to the numbers in the analysis.

1. Plants will eventually begin to flower if they are otherwise healthy and adapted to the area. The juvenile stage in some trees and vines may last 10 to 15 years.

2. Plant trees and shrubs that are adapted to your area. Consult your local garden center, Cooperative Extension Office (for a list, see page 1011), or a book on plant selection, such as ORTHO's book *How to Select & Care for Shrubs & Hedges or All About Trees*.

3. For instructions on proper pruning techniques, see ORTHO's book *All About Pruning*.

4. Do not overfertilize plants or make a heavy application of nitrogen before flowering. For more information about fertilizers, see page 904.

5. Thin out shading trees, or move plants to a sunnier area. For more information about transplanting, see page 916. For a list of shade loving plants, see page 997.

INSECTS

Drought.

Bud drop caused by cold injury.

Long-horned beetle (twice life size).

PROBLEM: Many or all of the buds or flowers die or drop off.

ANALYSIS: Buds die or drop
Buds may die or drop for any of several reasons.

1. *Transplant shock:* Whenever a tree or shrub is transplanted, it goes through a period of shock. Dormant plants usually recover more quickly and are injured less than growing plants. However, even when transplanted properly, dormant plants may still lose some of their buds. Plants that have begun growth or are in bloom often drop many of their flower buds or flowers shortly after transplanting. Some buds may remain on the plant but not open.

2. *Cold or frost injury:* Flower buds or flowers may be killed by cold or freezing temperatures. Many or all of them either fail to open or drop off. Cold injury occurs during the winter when temperatures drop below the lowest point that can be tolerated by buds of that particular plant species. Frost injury is caused by an unseasonal cold snap, in either fall or spring, which damages buds, developing flowers, and tender shoots of growing plants.

3. *Drought:* Flowers or flower buds dry and drop off when there is a temporary lack of moisture in the plant. This may be due to dry soil, minor root injuries, or anything else that disrupts water movement to the top of the plant.

4. *Insects:* Certain insects, such as thrips and mites, feed on flower buds. When infestations are heavy, their feeding kills flower buds, causing them to dry and drop off. Some infested buds may open, but are distorted.

SOLUTION: The numbered solutions below correspond to the numbers in the analysis.

1. Whenever possible, transplant trees and shrubs during the dormant season. (For more information about transplanting, see page 916.) Avoid wounding the roots when planting, and do not let the plant dry out. (For more information about watering, see page 906.)

2. Plant trees and shrubs adapted to your area. Consult your local garden center, Cooperative Extension Office (see page 1011), or a book on plant selection, such as ORTHO's books *How to Select & Care for Shrubs & Hedges* or *The World of Trees.* Protect shrubs and small trees from early or late cold snaps by covering them with burlap or a plastic tent. Placing a light underneath the covering will offer additional protection.

3. Water trees and shrubs regularly. (For more information about watering, see page 906.) Most plants will recover from minor root injuries. Frequent shallow waterings and light fertilization (see page 904) may speed the recovery process. Avoid wounding plants.

4. Insects can be controlled with various chemicals. For more information about thrips and mites and their controls, look under your specific plant or on pages 463 and 462.

PROBLEM: Shiny or dull, hard-bodied insects with tough, leathery wing covers appear on the plant. The wing covers meet in the middle of the back, forming a straight line down the insect's body. Leaf tissue is chewed, notched, or eaten between the veins, giving the leaves a lacy appearance. The bark may be chewed, or flowers may be eaten. Holes may be found in branches or in the trunk.

ANALYSIS: Beetles
Many different types of beetles feed on ornamental trees and shrubs. In most cases, both larvae (grubs) and adults feed on the plants, so damage is often severe. The insects spend the winter as grubs inside the plant or in the soil, or as adults in bark crevices or in hiding places on the ground. Adult beetles lay eggs on the plant during the growing season. Depending on the species, the grubs may feed on foliage, mine inside the leaves, bore into stems or branches, or feed on roots. Beetle damage to leaves rarely kills the plant. Grubs feeding inside the wood or underground are much more damaging, and often kill branches or the whole plant.

SOLUTION: Grubs feeding in the soil or inside the plant are difficult to detect and control. Control measures are often aimed at the adults. Several different insecticides, including ones containing *carbaryl,* may be used to control these pests. Make sure your plant is listed on the label. Certain beetles are covered in this book. Look under your specific plant in the alphabetical section beginning on page 474. For more information about beetles, see page 872.

PROBLEMS COMMON TO MANY TREES, SHRUBS, AND VINES — INSECTS

Gypsy moth larvae (life size).

Gypsy moth and egg masses (life size).

Japanese beetle (life size).

PROBLEM: Leaves are chewed; the entire tree is often defoliated by early summer. Large (up to 2½ inches long), hairy, blackish caterpillars with rows of red and blue spots on their backs are feeding on the leaves, hiding under leaves or bark, or crawling on buildings, cars, or other objects outdoors. Insect droppings accumulate underneath the infested tree. Trees defoliated for several consecutive years may be killed, especially weak trees.

ANALYSIS: Gypsy moth (*Lymantria dispar*)
The gypsy moth is a general feeder, devouring over 450 species of plants. Gypsy moth populations fluctuate from year to year. When the moths' numbers are low, oaks are the preferred host. When their numbers increase, entire forests may be defoliated and the moths spread to other trees and shrubs. Repeated, severe defoliation weakens trees and reduces plant growth. Defoliated trees are rarely killed unless already in a weakened condition. However, they are more susceptible to attack by other insects and diseases, which may kill them. Gypsy moths are also an extreme nuisance in urban areas and in parks and campgrounds. The overwintering masses of eggs, covered with yellow hairs, are attached to almost any object outdoors. The eggs hatch from April to May. The tiny larvae crawl to trees where they feed, or drop on silken threads to be carried by the wind to other plants. As the caterpillars mature, they feed at night and rest during the day. The larvae may completely cover sides of houses or other objects during these resting periods. When population levels are high, the insects feed continually on the tree and large amounts of excrement accumulate beneath it. The larval hairs may cause allergies. The larvae pupate in sheltered places, and dark brown male or white wingless female moths emerge in July.

SOLUTION: If the insects are bothersome or trees are weak or unhealthy either from last year's gypsy moth feeding or from drought, mechanical damage, or other insects and diseases, treatment with insecticides is required. Insecticides should be applied before larvae are 1 inch long, and the tree must be covered thoroughly. It is best to contact a professional arborist for large trees. Spray smaller trees with ORTHO Gypsy Moth & Japanese Beetle Killer, ORTHO Isotox Insect Killer, ORTHO Orthene Systemic Insect Control, or ORTHO Liquid Sevin when tiny larvae are first noticed. Repeat the sprays at weekly intervals if damage continues. Homeowners can reduce infestations by destroying egg masses during the winter months. During the spring when larvae are feeding, place burlap bands on trees, leaving the bottom edge unattached. Larvae will crawl under these flaps to hide during the day. Collect and destroy them. Keep trees healthy. Fertilize regularly and water during periods of drought. (For information about fertilizing and watering see pages 904 and 906.) When planting trees in the yard, choose species that are less favored by the gypsy moth. (For a list of these plants, and of plants favored by the gypsy moth, see page 1000.) Trees less favored by the insects are damaged only slightly by larval feeding. In addition, they may reduce damage to more favored hosts when interplanted by preventing a large buildup of insects in the area. Do not transport items that may have eggs or larvae attached to them.

PROBLEM: The leaf tissue is chewed between the veins, giving the leaves a lacy appearance. If the plant is flowering, the flowers are also eaten. The entire plant may be defoliated. Metallic green and bronze winged beetles, ½ inch long, are feeding in clusters on the plant.

ANALYSIS: Japanese beetles (*Popillia japonica*)
As their name suggests, these beetles are native to Japan. They were first seen in New Jersey in 1916 and have since become a major pest in the eastern United States. They feed on hundreds of different species of plants. The adult beetles are present from June to October. They feed only in the daytime, and are most active on warm, sunny days. The female beetles live for 30 to 45 days. Just before they die, they lay their eggs just under the soil surface in lawns. Grayish white grubs soon hatch and feed on grass roots. As the weather turns cold in the late fall, the grubs move 8 to 10 inches down into the soil, where they remain dormant for the winter. When the soil warms up in the spring, the grubs move back up near the soil surface and resume feeding on roots. They soon pupate and reemerge as adult beetles in late May or June.

SOLUTION: Control the adults with ORTHO Isotox Insect Killer, ORTHO Gypsy Moth & Japanese Beetle Killer, ORTHO Liquid Sevin, or ORTHO Malathion 50 Insect Spray in late May or June. Make sure your plant is listed on the product label. Repeat the spray 10 days later if damage continues. For a list of plants rarely fed upon by adult beetles, see page 997.

Looper (twice life size).

Western tent caterpillars (¼ life size).

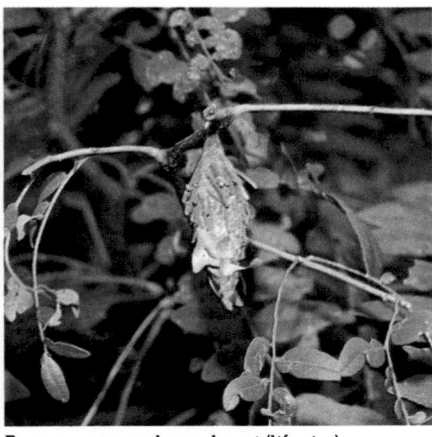

Bagworm case on honey locust (life size).

PROBLEM: Caterpillars are clustered or feeding singly on the leaves. The surface of the leaf is eaten, giving the remaining tissue a lacy appearance; or the whole leaf is chewed. Sometimes the leaves are webbed. The tree may be completely defoliated. Damage appears any time between spring and fall. Repeated heavy infestations may weaken or kill plants.

ANALYSIS: Leaf-feeding caterpillars
Many different species of caterpillars feed on the leaves of trees and shrubs. Depending on the species, the moths lay their eggs from early spring to midsummer. The larvae that hatch from these eggs feed singly or in groups on buds, on one leaf surface (skeletonizers), or on the entire leaf. Certain caterpillars web leaves together as they feed. In some years, damage is minimal due to unfavorable environmental conditions or control by predators and parasites. However, when conditions are favorable, entire plants may be defoliated by late summer. Defoliation weakens them because there are no leaves left to produce food. When heavy infestations occur several years in a row, branches or entire plants may be killed.

SOLUTION: Spray with ORTHO Isotox Insect Killer, ORTHO Orthene Systemic Insect Control, or ORTHO Liquid Sevin when damage is first noticed. Spray the leaves thoroughly. Repeat the spray if the plant becomes reinfested. Make sure your plant is listed on the product label.

PROBLEM: In the spring or summer, silk nests appear in the branch crotches or on the ends of branches. Leaves are chewed; branches or the entire tree may be defoliated. Groups of caterpillars are feeding in or around the nests.

ANALYSIS: Tent caterpillars and fall webworm (*Malacosoma* species and *Hyphantria cunea*)
These insects feed on many ornamental trees. In the summer, *tent caterpillars* lay masses of eggs in a cementing substance around twigs. They hatch in early spring as the leaves unfold, and the young caterpillars construct their nests. On warm, sunny days, they emerge from the nests to devour the surrounding foliage. In mid to late summer, brownish or reddish moths appear. The *fall webworm* lays many eggs on the undersides of leaves in the spring. In early summer, the young caterpillars make nests over the ends of branches, inside which they feed. As the leaves are devoured, the caterpillars extend the nests over more foliage. Eventually the entire branch may be enclosed with this unsightly webbing. The caterpillars drop to the soil to pupate. Up to four generations occur between June and September. Damage is most severe in the late summer.

SOLUTION: Spray with ORTHO Isotox Insect Killer, ORTHO Orthene Systemic Insect Control, ORTHO Liquid Sevin, or the bacterial insecticide *Bacillus thuringiensis*. Make sure your plant is listed on the product label. The bacterial insecticide is most effective against small caterpillars. Remove egg masses found in winter.

PROBLEM: Leaves are chewed; branches or the entire tree may be defoliated. Carrot-shaped cases or "bags," from 1 to 3 inches long, hang from the branches. The bags are constructed from interwoven bits of dead foliage, twigs, and silk. When a bag is cut open, a tan or blackish caterpillar or a yellowish grub-like insect may be found inside. A heavy attack by bagworms may stunt deciduous trees or kill evergreens.

ANALYSIS: Bagworm (*Thyridopteryx ephemeraeformis*)
Bagworms eat the leaves of many trees and shrubs. The larvae hatch in late May or early June and immediately begin feeding. Each larva constructs a bag that covers its entire body, and to which it adds as it develops. The worm partially emerges from its bag to feed. When all the leaves are eaten off the branch, the bagworm moves to the next branch, dragging its bag along. By late August the larva spins silken bands around a twig, attaches a bag permanently, and pupates. In the fall, the winged male moth emerges from his case, flies to a bag containing a female, mates, and dies. The female bagworm spends her entire life inside her bag. After mating, she lays 500 to 1000 eggs and dies. The eggs spend the winter in the mother's bag.

SOLUTION: Spray with ORTHO Orthene Systemic Insect Control, ORTHO Isotox Insect Killer, or ORTHO Liquid Sevin between late May and mid-July. Older bagworms are more difficult to control. Repeat the spray after 10 days if leaf damage is still occurring. Handpick and destroy bags in winter to reduce the number of eggs.

PROBLEMS COMMON TO MANY TREES, SHRUBS, AND VINES — SCALES OR POWDER ON PLANT

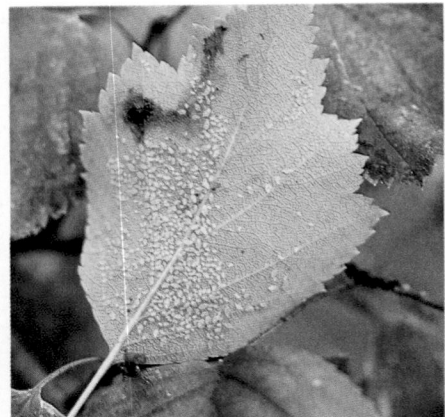

Aphids on hawthorn (life size).

Lecanium scale on redbud (life size).

Pine bark aphid on white pine (¼ life size).

PROBLEM: Tiny (⅛ inch) green, yellow, black, brownish, or gray soft-bodied insects cluster on the bark, leaves, or buds. Some species are covered with white, fluffy wax. The insects may have wings. Leaves are discolored, and may be curled and distorted. They sometimes drop off. A shiny or sticky substance may coat the leaves. A black sooty mold often grows on the sticky substance. Plants may lack vigor, and branches sometimes die. Ants may be present.

ANALYSIS: Aphids
Many different aphids infest ornamental trees and shrubs. They do little damage in small numbers. However, they are extremely prolific, and populations can rapidly build up to damaging numbers during the growing season. Damage occurs when the aphid sucks the juices from the plant. Sap removal often results in scorched, discolored, or curled leaves and reduced plant growth. A severe infestation of bark aphids may cause branches to die. Aphids are unable to digest fully all the sugar in the plant sap, and excrete the excess in a fluid called honeydew, which drops onto the leaves and contaminates anything beneath the tree or shrub. A sooty mold fungus may develop on the honeydew, causing the leaves to appear black and dirty. Ants feed on this sticky substance, and are often present where there is an aphid infestation.

SOLUTION: Spray with ORTHO Isotox Insect Killer, ORTHO Orthene Systemic Insect Control, or ORTHO Malathion 50 Insect Spray when damage is first noticed. Make sure your plant is listed on the product label. Repeat the spray if the plant becomes reinfested.

PROBLEM: Leaves, stems, branches, or trunk are covered with crusty or waxy bumps, or clusters of somewhat flattened scaly bumps. The bumps can be scraped or picked off; the undersides are usually soft. Leaves turn yellow and may drop. In some cases, a shiny or sticky substance coats the leaves. A black sooty mold often grows on the sticky substance.

ANALYSIS: Scales
Many types of scales infest trees and shrubs. They lay their eggs on leaves or bark, and in spring to midsummer the young scales, called *crawlers*, settle on leaves, branches, or the trunk. The small (¹⁄₁₀ inch), soft-bodied young feed by sucking sap from the plant. The legs usually atrophy, and a hard crusty or waxy shell develops over the body. The female scales lay their eggs underneath their shell. Some species of scales are unable to digest fully all the sugar in the plant sap, and excrete the excess in a fluid called honeydew. A sooty mold fungus may develop on the honeydew, causing the leaves to appear black and dirty. An uncontrolled infestation of scales may kill a plant after 2 or 3 seasons.

SOLUTION: Spray with ORTHO Isotox Insect Killer or ORTHO Orthene Systemic Insect Control when the young are active. Contact your local Cooperative Extension Office (see page 1011) to determine the best time to spray for scales in your area. The following early spring, before new growth begins, spray the trunk and branches with a *dormant oil spray* to control overwintering insects. Make sure your plant is listed on the product label. For more information on scales, see page 878.

PROBLEM: The undersides of the leaves and stems, branch crotches, or trunk are covered with white, cottony masses. Leaves may be curled, distorted, and yellowing. Knotlike galls may form on the stems or trunk. Sometimes a shiny or sticky substance coats the leaves. A black sooty mold may be growing on the sticky substance. Twigs and branches may die.

ANALYSIS: Cottony scales, mealybugs, and woolly aphids
Cottony scales, mealybugs, and woolly aphids all produce white, waxy secretions that cover their bodies. This visual similarity makes separate identification difficult for the home gardener. Young insects are usually inconspicuous on the host plant. Their bodies range in color from yellowish green to brown, blending in with the leaves or bark. As the insects mature, they exude filaments of white wax, giving them a cottony appearance. Mealybugs and scales generally deposit their eggs in the white, fluffy masses. Damage is caused by the withdrawal of plant sap from the leaves, branches, or trunk. Because the insects are unable to digest fully all the sugar in the plant sap, they excrete the excess in a fluid called honeydew, which often drops onto the leaves or plants below. A sooty mold fungus may develop on the honeydew, causing the leaves and twigs to appear black and dirty.

SOLUTION: Spray with ORTHO Isotox Insect Killer or ORTHO Orthene Systemic Insect Control. Make sure your plant is listed on the product label. Add a spreader-sticker to the spray to improve coverage. (For more information about spreader-stickers, see page 915.)

Powdery mildew on London plane tree.

Rust on Oregon grape.

Sooty mold on tuliptree.

PROBLEM: Leaves, flowers, and young stems are covered with a thin layer or irregular patches of a grayish white powdery material. Infected leaves may turn yellowish or reddish and drop. Some leaves or branches may be distorted. In late fall, tiny black dots (spore-producing bodies) are scattered over the white patches like ground pepper.

ANALYSIS: Powdery mildew
This common plant disease is caused by any of several fungi that thrive in both humid and dry weather. Plants growing in shady areas are often severely infected. The powdery patches consist of fungal strands and spores. The spores are spread by the wind to healthy plants. The fungus saps the plant nutrients, causing discoloring and sometimes the death of the leaf. Certain powdery mildews also cause leaf or branch distortion. Since these powdery mildews often attack many different kinds of plants, the fungus from a diseased plant may infect other plants in the garden. For a list of powdery mildews and the plants they attack, see page 995.

SOLUTION: Several different fungicides, including those containing *triforine*, *benomyl*, *dinocap*, and *cycloheximide*, are used to control powdery mildew. For control suggestions, look under your specific plant in the alphabetical section beginning on page 474.

PROBLEM: Yellow, orange, red, or black powdery pustules appear on the upper or lower surfaces of the leaves, or occasionally on the bark. The powdery material can be scraped or rubbed off. Leaves are discolored or mottled yellow to brown. In some cases, leaves become twisted, distorted, and dry, and drop off. Infected stems may be swollen, blistered, or develop oblong or hornlike galls, up to 2 inches long.

ANALYSIS: Leaf and stem rusts
Many different species of rust fungi infect trees and shrubs. Some rusts produce spore pustules on leaves or stems, and others produce galls or hornlike structures on various parts of the plant. Most rusts attack only one species or a few related species of plants. However, some rusts require two different plant species to complete their life cycles. Part of the life cycle is spent on the tree or shrub and part is spent on various weeds, flowers, or other woody trees and shrubs. In most cases, the symptoms produced on the two hosts are very different. Rust spores are spread to healthy plants by wind and splashing water. When conditions are favorable (moisture and moderate temperatures, 54° to 74°F), the spores germinate and infect the tissue.

SOLUTION: Several fungicides, including *triforine*, *ferbam*, *maneb*, *zineb*, *mancozeb*, and *cycloheximide*, may be used to control rust. Look under the entry for your plant in the alphabetical section of the book beginning on page 474 to determine which fungicide is appropriate. Some rust fungi are fairly harmless to the plant and do not require control measures. Rake up and destroy leaves in the fall.

PROBLEM: A black sooty mold is growing on the leaves and twigs. It can be completely wiped off the surfaces. Cool, moist weather hastens the growth of the mold.

ANALYSIS: Sooty mold
These common black molds are found on a wide variety of plants in the garden. They are caused by any of several fungi that grow on the sugary material left on plants by aphids, scales, mealybugs, whiteflies, and other insects that suck sap from the plant. The insects are unable to digest all the sugar in the sap, and excrete the excess in a fluid called honeydew, which drops onto the leaves below. The honeydew may also drop out of infested trees and shrubs onto plants growing beneath them. The sooty mold fungi develop on the honeydew, causing the leaves to appear black and dirty. Sooty molds are unsightly, but are fairly harmless because they do not attack the leaf directly. Extremely heavy infestations prevent light from reaching the leaf, so that the leaf produces fewer nutrients and may turn yellow. The presence of sooty molds indicates that the plant or a nearby plant is infested with insects.

SOLUTION: Sooty molds can be wiped from the leaves with a wet rag, or they will eventually be washed off by rain. Prevent more sooty mold by controlling the insect that is producing the honeydew. Inspect the leaves and twigs above the sooty mold to find what type of insect is present. See the following pages for control instructions: for aphids, page 877; for scales and mealybugs, page 878; for whiteflies, page 879.

PROBLEMS COMMON TO MANY TREES, SHRUBS, AND VINES — GALLS OR GROWTH

Gall rust on pine.

Leaf galls on willow.

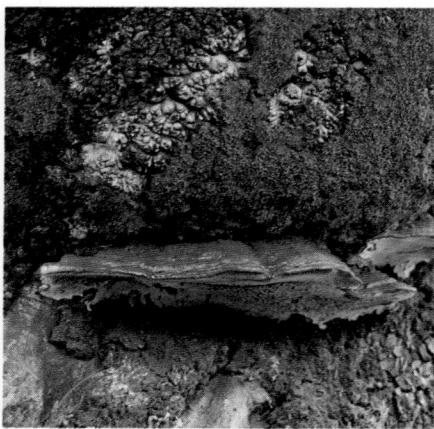

A conk on the trunk of a bigleaf maple.

PROBLEM: Swellings, thickenings, and growths develop on the leaves, shoots, branches, or trunk. Plants with numerous galls on branches or the trunk may be weak, and leaves may be yellowing. Branches may die.

ANALYSIS: Galls or growths on leaves, branches, or trunk
These growths can be caused by 3 factors.

1. *Fungal leaf or stem gall:* Several different fungi, including rust fungi, cause enlargement and thickening of leaves and shoots. Affected plant parts are usually many times larger than normal, and are often discolored and succulent. Some leaf or stem galls turn brown and hard with age. The galls are unsightly but rarely harmful to the plant. Fungal galls are most severe when spring weather is wet.

2. *Bacterial crown gall:* This plant disease is caused by a soil-inhabiting bacterium (*Agrobacterium tumefaciens*) that infects many ornamentals, fruits, and nuts in the garden. The bacteria enter the plant through wounds in the roots or the base of the trunk (the crown). The galls disrupt the flow of water and nutrients up the roots, stems, and trunk, weakening and stunting the top growth. Galls do not usually kill the plant. For more information on crown gall, see page 860.

3. *Insect galls:* Many different types of insects cause galls by feeding on plant tissue or by injecting a toxin into the tissue during feeding. As a result of this irritation, blisters or growths of various shapes form on leaves, swellings develop on roots or stems, and buds and flowers grow abnormally. Most gall-forming insects cause minor damage to the plant, but the galls may be unsightly.

SOLUTION: The numbered solutions below correspond to the numbers in the analysis.

1. Pick off and destroy affected parts as soon as they appear. If galls are a problem this year, spray next spring with a fungicide containing *ferbam*, *zineb*, *mancozeb*, or *maneb* just before the buds open. Add a spreader-sticker to the spray. (For more information about spreader-stickers, see page 915.) Repeat the spray 2 weeks later.

2. Infected plants cannot be cured. However, they often survive for many years. To improve the appearance of shrubs with stem galls, prune out and destroy affected stems below the galled area. Sterilize pruning shears with rubbing alcohol after each cut. Destroy severely infected shrubs. Consult a professional horticulturist to remove galls from valued trees. The bacteria will remain in the soil for at least 2 to 3 years. If you replace a tree or shrub, plant a resistant species. For a list of plants resistant to crown gall, see page 998.

3. Many gall-forming insects require no controls. However, if you feel the galls are unsightly or if galls are causing dieback, control measures may be necessary. For recommended control measures, look under the entry for your plant in the alphabetical section beginning on page 474.

PROBLEM: Mushrooms appear around the base of the tree. Or white, yellow, gray, or brownish growths that are usually hard and woody protrude from the trunk. The plant may appear unhealthy.

ANALYSIS: Mushrooms and conks
Mushrooms and conks are the reproductive bodies of fungi. Most mushroom fungi live on decaying matter. When conditions are favorable, the fungi produce mushrooms and conks (hard, woody growths that protrude from tree trunks) containing spores, which are spread by the wind. A number of different mushroom fungi decay live trees. Most of these grow only in older wood, which they enter through wounds. Mushrooms or conks usually appear annually in the dead portions of the trees. Some conks may remain attached to the wood for years. *Armillaria mellea*, a fungus that causes a disease called *mushroom root rot*, *oak root fungus*, or *shoestring root rot*, invades healthy roots. In the fall or winter, mushrooms appear around the base of the plant, growing on the infected roots.

SOLUTION: By the time conks or mushrooms appear on the trunk, it is too late to do anything about the wood rot. Inspect the tree to determine the extent of decay (contact a professional arborist if necessary). Trees or branches with extensive decay should be removed. Keep plants vigorous by fertilizing and watering regularly. (For more information about fertilizers and watering, see pages 904 and 906.) The spread of armillaria root rot may be inhibited if it is found in only part of the roots. For more information about this root rot, see page 466.

Lichen.

Leafy mistletoe.

Dwarf mistletoe. *Insert:* Seeds.

PROBLEM: Brown, gray, green, or yellow crusty, soft, or leaflike growths develop on trees in moist forested areas. The growths are usually found on the lower or shaded part of trunks and branches.

ANALYSIS: Algae, lichens, and mosses
Algae, lichens, and mosses are sometimes mistaken for diseases, especially the tree they are attached to appears unhealthy. However, they do not harm the plant. Most algae grow where moisture is abundant, on the lower, shady side of the trunk. They appear only as a green color that is not very noticeable on the bark. Lichens are a combination of green algae and fungi. They range in color from brown to green and appear crusty or leaflike. They are sensitive to air pollution, and are found only in areas where the air is clean. Unlike algae and mosses, lichens can withstand both heat and drought. True mosses are small green plants with tiny leaves and stems growing in a mat. They are abundant in moist areas, and are much more apparent than algae. Spanish moss is a flowering plant (in the pineapple family) that is very noticeable hanging from branches of Southern trees.

SOLUTION: Algae, lichen, and mosses do not harm the plant. No controls are necessary.

PROBLEM: Leafy olive-green plants up to 4 feet across are attached to the branches. The tufts are most noticeable during the winter on trees without their leaves. Affected branches are often swollen. Some may break from the weight of the plants. Branches beyond the growth occasionally die.

ANALYSIS: Leafy mistletoe
(*Phoradendron* species)
Leafy mistletoes are semiparasitic plants that manufacture their own food but depend on their host plant for water and minerals. The plant produces sticky seeds that are spread by birds from one tree to another, or by falling from higher to lower branches. The seeds germinate almost anywhere, but penetrate only young, thin bark. The rootlike attachment organs of the plant penetrate the tree's water-conducting vessels, which they tap for mineral nutrients and water. At the point of attachment, the branch or trunk swells, sometimes to 2 or 3 times its normal size. Growth of mistletoe is slow at first, but after 6 or 8 years, plants may be 3 feet across. Trees heavily infested with mistletoe may be weakened, and sometimes die.

SOLUTION: Prune off limbs 18 inches below the point of mistletoe attachment. The rootlike attachment organs may spread through host tissue up to 1½ feet from the swollen area. They must be removed or the mistletoe will resprout. To prevent the spread of seeds, remove tufts before seeds form in the spring. If it is impractical to prune the tree limbs, remove the mistletoe and wrap the infected areas with black plastic to kill the resprouting mistletoe.

PROBLEM: Twigs and small branches of conifers are swollen and cankered. Witch's brooms (many small tufts of branches) usually form on infested branches. As swellings or witch's brooms increase in size, the tree loses vigor. Foliage becomes sparse and yellowish, and dieback develops in the upper part of the tree. Short, succulent, leafless, yellow, brown, or olive-green shoots develop in the bark of affected branches. Over a period of years the tree may die.

ANALYSIS: Dwarf mistletoe
This parasitic plant infests many conifers. Dwarf mistletoe lacks a normal root system and true leaves. It relies on its host plant to supply most of the nutrients it requires. In this respect it is different from leafy mistletoe (see page 447), which depends on its host plant only for water and minerals. In midsummer, dwarf mistletoe spreads by sticky seeds that are explosively discharged for distances up to 50 feet. Seeds land on needles and then slide down to the bark when the needles are moistened. When seeds germinate, usually the following spring, rootlike structures penetrate the bark. The structures form a network in the branches, causing swellings and the formation of cankers. Dwarf mistletoe weakens the tree as it saps nutrients and water, and distorts the growth of branches. Within 1 to 3 years after infection, aerial shoots are produced that are from ½ to 4 inches long, depending on the species.

SOLUTION: Remove dying trees. Prune off branches of less severely infested trees, making the cuts at the trunk. Remove new infestations as they appear.

PROBLEMS COMMON TO MANY TREES, SHRUBS, AND VINES — DISTORTED GROWTH

Witch's broom on hackberry.

Leaf distortion on ash caused by aphids.

Herbicide damage on forsythia.

PROBLEM: A dense tuft of small, weak twigs develops on a branch. Leaves on the tuft may be smaller than normal and off-color. The branches are weak and unhealthy.

ANALYSIS: Witch's broom
A witch's broom is a dense proliferation of twig growth, usually caused by an insect, plant disease, or mistletoe (see page 447). The witch's broom looks messy, but is not harmful to the plant. The insect or disease that caused it, however, may be.

SOLUTION: If the witch's broom affects the appearance of the plant, prune it off. It may be difficult for the home gardener to identify the cause of brooming. If witch's brooms continue to develop, contact a professional arborist or your local Cooperative Extension Office. For a list of Cooperative Extension Offices, see page 1011.

PROBLEM: Leaves are distorted or curled; new growth may also be deformed. Insects are sometimes found on distorted leaves, and affected leaves are often discolored.

ANALYSIS: Leaves distorted or curled
Leaves may be distorted by herbicides, insects, or cold:

1. *Herbicide damage:* Phenoxy herbicides, such as 2,4-D, cause new growth on trees or shrubs to be deformed. Leaves and stem tips may be distorted and gnarled. Leaves are often discolored, but may remain green. Distorted new growth often continues to appear throughout the growing season. In severe cases, the plant is killed. Herbicide damage may be caused by misapplication of weedkillers, spray drift from neighbors, and spray equipment used for other purposes not cleaned after an herbicide application.

2. *Insects:* Many types of insects cause leaf distortion and curling. Thrips, certain caterpillars, and sucking insects, including aphids, scales, mealybugs, leafhoppers, mites, and whiteflies may cause leaf distortion or curling as a result of their feeding on plant tissue. These insects are usually found on the lower surfaces of the leaves or inside curled leaves during spring or summer. Leaves are often discolored, and plant growth is slowed.

3. *Frost injury:* Leaves become distorted, crinkled, and discolored, and shoot tips on evergreens curl downward when they are exposed to cold temperatures. The injury is caused by low temperatures after growth starts in the spring, or by sudden cold periods, which damage young, tender tissue before plants are dormant in the fall. Buds and flowers may die, and bark may crack.

SOLUTION: The numbered solutions below correspond to the numbers in the analysis.

1. Damaged plants usually survive. Prune off injured parts and water the plant thoroughly. If a granular herbicide was applied, flush the soil with water several times. To avoid future damage, do not spray on windy days. Wash herbicides from sprayers thoroughly before spraying desirable plants, or keep a second sprayer for herbicides.

2. Various insecticides are used to control these insects. For more information about the insects and their controls, check under your specific plant in the alphabetical section of the book beginning on page 474.

3. Where practical, remove injured parts. If cold temperatures are expected in spring or fall when plants are growing, cover them with burlap. Do not apply fertilizer late in the growing season. This encourages tender new growth, which may be damaged. Plant trees and shrubs adapted to your area.

HOLES OR TRAILS IN LEAVES

Leafroller on linden.

Leafminer damage to holly.

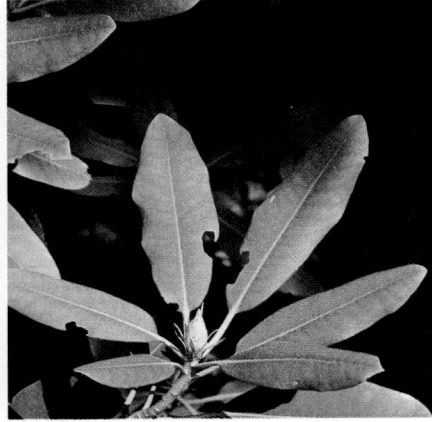

Root weevil notches in rhododendron leaves.

PROBLEM: Leaves are rolled, usually lengthwise, and tied together with webbing. The rolled leaves are chewed. When a rolled leaf is opened a green caterpillar, ½ to ¾ inch long, may be found feeding inside. Flower buds may also be chewed.

ANALYSIS: Leafrollers
Several different leafrollers feed on the leaves and buds of woody ornamentals. Some species feed on only one plant. Others feed on many plants in the garden. Leafrollers are the larvae of small (up to ¾ inch) brownish moths. The insects spend the winter as eggs or larvae on the plant. In the spring the larvae feed on the young foliage, sometimes tunneling into and mining the leaf first. They roll one or more leaves around themselves, tying the leaves together with a silken webbing, then feed within the rolled leaves. This provides protection from weather, parasites, and chemical sprays. Some leafrollers mature in summer and have several generations each year. Other leafrollers have only one generation. In the fall, the larvae either mature into moths and lay the overwintering eggs, or they spend the winter inside the rolled leaf.

SOLUTION: Spray with ORTHO Isotox Insect Killer, ORTHO Orthene Systemic Insect Control, or ORTHO Liquid Sevin in the spring when leaf damage is first noticed. Make sure your plant is listed on the product label. For the insecticides to be most effective, they should be applied before the larvae are protected inside the rolled leaves. Check the plant periodically in the spring for the first sign of an infestation.

PROBLEM: Green or whitish translucent winding trails, blisters, or blotches develop on the leaves. The trails, blisters, or blotches later turn brown. If an infested leaf is torn open, one to several small green, yellowish, or whitish insects may be found between the upper and lower surfaces of the leaves.

ANALYSIS: Leafminers
Leafminers are the larvae of flies, moths, beetles, or sawflies. The larvae feed between the upper and lower surfaces of the leaves. The adult female moths lay their eggs on or inside the leaves, usually in early to late spring. The emerging larvae feed between the leaf surfaces, producing blisters, blotches, or trails. The infested tissue stands out prominently against the normal green foliage as it turns whitish or light green to brown. The insects pupate inside the leaves or in the soil and emerge as adults. Some adults also feed on the leaves, chewing holes or notches in them.

SOLUTION: Control of leafminers is difficult because they spend most of their lives protected inside the leaves. Insecticides are usually aimed at the adults. Once leafminers are noticed in the leaves, inspect the foliage periodically; or check with your local Cooperative Extension Office (see page 1011) to determine when the adults emerge. Then spray with ORTHO Orthene Systemic Insect Control, ORTHO Isotox Insect Killer, ORTHO Liquid Sevin, or ORTHO Diazinon Insect Spray. Make sure your plant is listed on the product label.

PROBLEM: Holes or notches appear in leaves and flowers. Some of the leaves, stems, and flowers may be sheared off. Severely infested plants may be stripped of foliage. No insects are visible on the plants during the day. When the affected plants are inspected at night with a flashlight, insects may be seen feeding on the foliage and flowers.

ANALYSIS: Nocturnal insects
Several types of insects feed on plants only at night, including beetles, weevils, and caterpillars. Beetles are hard-bodied insects with tough, leathery wing covers. The wing covers meet in the middle of the back, forming a straight line. Weevils look like beetles with elongated snouts. Caterpillars are smooth or hairy, soft-bodied worms. Nocturnal insects usually hide in the soil, debris, or other protected places during the day.

SOLUTION: Control these insects with insecticides. For more information about nocturnal insects and the specific insecticides that control them, look up beetles on page 872; weevils on page 873; and caterpillars on page 874.

PROBLEMS COMMON TO MANY TREES, SHRUBS, AND VINES — SPOTS ON LEAVES

Snail damage to aucuba.

Leaf spots on catalpa.

Leaf spots on liquidambar.

PROBLEM: Irregular holes with smooth edges are chewed in the leaves. Leaves may be sheared off entirely. Silvery trails wind around the plants and soil nearby. Snails and slugs may be seen moving around or feeding on the leaves, especially at night. Check for them by inspecting the garden at night by flashlight.

ANALYSIS: Snails and slugs
These pests are mollusks, and are related to clams, oysters, and other shellfish. They feed on a wide variety of plants, including ornamentals and vegetables. Like other mollusks, snails and slugs need to be moist all the time. For this reason, they avoid direct sun and dry places, and hide during the day in damp places, such as under flower pots or in thick groundcover. They emerge at night or on rainy days to feed. Snails and slugs are similar, except that the snail has a hard shell, into which it withdraws when disturbed. Slugs lay masses of white eggs encased in a slimy mass in protected places. Snails bury their eggs in the soil, also in a slimy mass. The young look like miniature versions of their parents.

SOLUTION: Scatter ORTHO Bug-Geta Snail & Slug Pellets, or ORTHO Slug-Geta Snail & Slug Bait granules around the trees and shrubs you wish to protect. Also scatter the bait in areas where snails or slugs might be hiding, such as in dense groundcovers, weedy areas, compost piles, or pot storage areas. Before spreading the bait, wet down the treated areas to encourage snail and slug activity that night. Repeat the application every 2 weeks as long as snails and slugs are active.

PROBLEM: Spots and blotches appear on the leaves and flowers.

ANALYSIS: Spots on leaves
Several diseases, insects, and environmental factors cause spots and blotches on leaves and flowers.

1. *Fungal leaf spot:* Spots caused by fungi are often small and circular, and may be found on all the leaves. Sometimes only the older or younger leaves are affected. The spots range in size from barely visible to ¾ inch in diameter. They may be yellow, red, tan, gray, brown, or black, and often have a definite margin. Spots sometimes join together to form blotches. Often the leaves turn yellow and die. Infection is usually most severe during moist, mild weather (50° to 85°F).

2. *Insects:* Several different types of insects, including lacebugs, leafhoppers, mites, plantbugs, and thrips, cause spotting of leaves. Leaves may be spotted brownish, yellow, or white, or they may be completely discolored. Sometimes the insects are visible, feeding on the lower or upper surfaces of the leaves. For more information about these insects, look in the encyclopedia section starting on page 872.

3. *Sunburn:* Shade loving plants placed in a sunny location will develop spots and blotches on the leaves most directly exposed to the sun. Sun loving plants will also develop sunburn symptoms if they are allowed to dry out. Initially, sunburned leaves develop a whitish or yellowish bleached appearance between the veins. Large, dark blotches form on the damaged tissue. Leaves not directly exposed to the sun remain green and uninjured.

SOLUTION: The numbered solutions below correspond to the numbers in the analysis.

1. Spray plants with a fungicide containing *benomyl, maneb, mancozeb,* or *zineb* when new growth begins. Repeat at intervals of 2 weeks for as long as the weather remains favorable for infection. Make sure your plant is listed on the product label. Raking and destroying leaves in the fall may help control the fungus.

2. These insects can be controlled with various types of insecticides. For effective chemicals, look under the entry for your plant in the alphabetical section beginning on page 474.

3. Where practical, pick off the injured leaves and plant parts. Check to see whether your plant is adapted to sun or shade. (For a list of common shade plants, see page 997.) Provide shade, or transplant shade loving plants. (For more information about transplanting, see page 916.) Water plants regularly, especially on hot, sunny, or windy days. (For watering instructions, see page 906.)

WILTING

Wilting philadelphus.

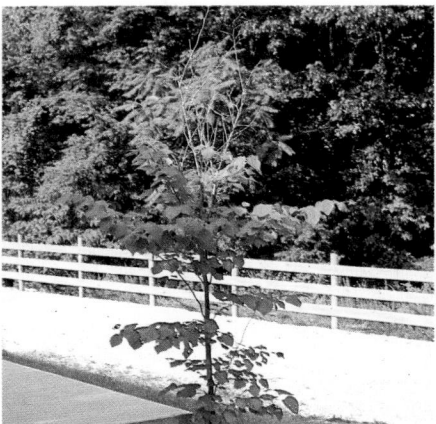

Leaf drop on dogwood due to borer infestation.

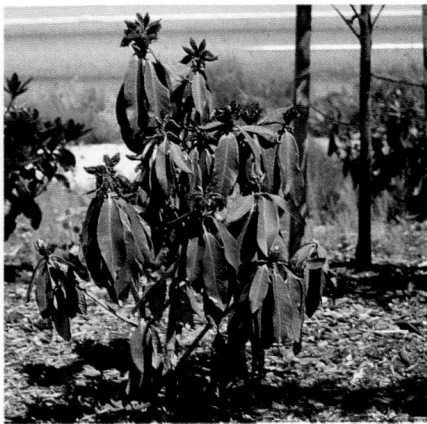

Wilting rhododendron.

PROBLEM: The plant wilts often, and the soil is frequently or always dry. The leaves or leaf edges may turn brown and shrivel.

ANALYSIS: Lack of water
Water in the soil is taken up by the plant roots. It moves up into the stems and leaves, and evaporates into the air through tiny breathing pores in the surfaces of the leaves. Water pressure within plant cells keeps the cell walls rigid, and prevents the leaves and stems from collapsing. When the soil is dry, the roots are unable to furnish the leaves and stems with water, the water pressure in the cells drops, and the plant wilts. Most plants will recover if they have not wilted severely. However, frequent or severe wilting will curb a plant's growth and may eventually kill it.

SOLUTION: Water the plant immediately. To prevent future wilting, follow the cultural instructions for your plant in the alphabetical section beginning on page 474. For more information about watering, see page 906.

PROBLEM: All or part of the plant is wilting, and the leaves may turn yellow, then brown, and die. There are wounds or sunken lesions on the plant; or there are holes in the branches or trunk, surrounded by sap or sawdust.

ANALYSIS: Damaged trunk or stem
Damage to the wood or bark disrupts water and nutrient movement through the plant, causing wilting.

1. *Wounds:* Any kind of mechanical injury that breaks roots, stems, or bark causes the plant to wilt. Plants may be accidentally wounded by motor vehicles, animals, or foot traffic; or their roots may be damaged by cultivation, construction injuries, or other soil disturbance. In severe cases, the plants die.

2. *Cankers:* Cankers are sunken, dark-colored lesions that develop as a result of infection by fungi or bacteria. Cankers on small or young plants often cause the portion of the plant above the canker to wilt. Branches or the entire plant may eventually die.

3. *Borers:* Most borers are the larvae of beetles or moths. Many kinds of borers infest stems, branches, or trunks. The larvae feed by tunneling through the bark, sapwood, and heartwood, stopping the flow of nutrients and water in that area. Large trees and shrubs usually turn yellow and brown rather than wilting.

SOLUTION: The numbered solutions below correspond to the numbers in the analysis.

1. Thin out some of the branches and keep the plant well watered. During hot weather, provide shade to reduce evaporation from the leaves. Prevent mechanical injuries to plants by being careful when working around the roots and stems. If necessary, place barriers around plants to prevent damage from vehicles, animals, and foot traffic.

2. Prune off dying branches. Avoid wounding plants. For more information about cankers and their controls, see page 456.

3. Prune out stems with borers. Keep plant well watered and fertilized. For more information about borers and their controls, see page 455.

PROBLEMS COMMON TO MANY TREES, SHRUBS, AND VINES — WILTING

Wilting dogwood.

Arborvitae planted too shallow.

Dry rootball.

PROBLEM: The plant is wilting, but the foliage usually looks healthy. There are no signs of insects or disease, and the soil is moist. Wilting is most common on shrubs or plants with limited root systems.

ANALYSIS: Extreme heat or wind
During hot, windy periods small or young plants may wilt, even though the soil is wet. Wind and heat cause water to evaporate very quickly from the leaves. If the roots can't absorb and convey water fast enough to replenish this loss, the leaves wilt. For information about scorched leaves due to extreme heat and wind, see page 461.

SOLUTION: Keep the plant well watered during hot spells, and sprinkle it with water to cool off the foliage. The plant will usually recover when the temperature drops or the wind dies down. Provide shade during hot weather, and temporary windbreaks for protection from wind. Plant shrubs adapted to your area.

PROBLEM: A recently planted tree or shrub wilts frequently. Roots or the rootball may be exposed.

ANALYSIS: Planted too shallow
Newly planted trees and shrubs may wilt frequently if they are planted too shallow. Plants that have been set in the ground at a higher level than they were originally growing wilt because the exposed soil ball dries out quickly. This may kill the surface roots, especially if the soil washes away, exposing them.

SOLUTION: Remove the plant, along with its soil ball, and replant it more deeply. The plant should be set at the same level as when it was growing in the pot or the ground. Water the plant thoroughly so the entire soil ball is moistened. Keep the plant well watered until it becomes established. For more information about planting, see page 916.

PROBLEM: The entire plant is wilting. The soil surrounding the plant is moist, but the rootball is dry.

ANALYSIS: Dry rootball
Plants that are sold in the nursery balled and burlapped are grown in fields. When the plants reach a size suitable for selling, they are dug up with a ball of soil around their roots. Sometimes the soil in which they are grown is extremely heavy. When the heavy soil is balled and burlapped, it sometimes shrinks as it dries or is compacted, and the ball becomes impermeable to water. After planting, water runs off the outside of the ball rather than moistening the soil, causing the roots to dry out. Rootballs of balled and burlapped plants or of container plants may also dry out if the soil in which the plant is set is much lighter or heavier than the soil in the rootball. The water runs into the lighter soil instead of moistening the soil around the roots; or the surrounding heavy clay soil draws out the water from the light soil in the rootball, causing the rootball to dry out.

SOLUTION: To wet the rootball, build a basin around the plant the diameter of the rootball. Keep water in the basin for 3 hours. Add a wetting agent (which can be purchased at your local nursery) to the water initially. Continue watering in the basin for 6 weeks. Water whenever the rootball (not the surrounding soil) is moist but not wet 1 inch below the surface. Water or soak the rootball before planting. If soil textures are very different, provide a transition zone, using 50-50 light and heavy soil as backfill. Build a basin and water as above for 6 weeks.

FLUID ON BARK OR LEAVES

Leaf drop on linden due to transplant shock.

Oozing sap on cherry.

Oozing sap on Coulter pine.

PROBLEM: The plant is wilting, but the foliage usually looks healthy. There are no signs of insects or disease, and the soil is moist. The plant was recently transplanted.

ANALYSIS: Transplant shock
Plants frequently wilt or stop growing for a while after being transplanted. Transplant "shock" is not related to shock in humans, but is the result of roots being cut or injured during transplanting. Wilting occurs when the roots are unable to supply the plant with enough water, even when the soil is wet.

SOLUTION: To reduce the water requirement of the plant, prune off ¼ to ⅓ of the branches. Water the plant well until it becomes established. (For more information about watering, see page 906.) If necessary, provide shade during hot weather. In the future, transplant when the tree or shrub is dormant if possible, and when the weather is cool, in early morning, late afternoon, or on a cloudy day. For more information about transplanting, see page 916.

PROBLEM: Beads of amber-colored or whitish, sticky sap appear on healthy bark. Or sap oozes from patches of bark, cankers, wounds, or pruning cuts.

ANALYSIS: Oozing sap
Oozing sap, also called *gummosis*, occurs in all trees and shrubs to a greater or lesser degree. It is caused by one or a combination of the following factors.

1. *Natural tendency:* Certain species of plants have a tendency to ooze sap. Frequently, small beads of sap form on healthy bark of these plants.

2. *Environmental stress:* Plants that are stressed because they are growing in wet soil may produce large quantities of sap, even though they are not diseased. Also, many plants respond to changes in weather conditions or soil moisture by oozing profusely.

3. *Mechanical injury:* Almost all plants ooze sap when the bark is wounded. This is especially noticeable on maple and birch. If these trees are injured during the fall, they will ooze a large amount of sap the following spring.

4. *Disease:* Plants respond to certain fungal and bacterial infections by forming cankers, dark, sunken areas that gum profusely. Gummosis or oozing sap is often one of the initial signs of infection.

5. *Borer damage:* Many different insects bore holes into bark. Sap oozes from these holes. The tunnels these insects bore in the wood often become infected by decay organisms.

SOLUTION: The numbered solutions below correspond to the numbers in the analysis.

1. As long as the bark appears healthy, there is nothing to worry about.

2. If your plant is growing in wet, poorly drained soil, allow the soil to dry out between waterings. Provide for drainage away from trunks and roots. If oozing sap occurs as a result of rapid changes in weather and soil moisture, reduce the effects of stress on the plant by keeping it healthy. Maintain health and vigor of the plant by fertilizing and watering regularly. For more information about fertilizers and watering, see pages 904 and 906.

3. Avoid mechanical injuries to the plant. Stake, tie, and prune properly. See page 911 for more information about pruning and treating wounds.

4. Remove badly infected branches and cut out cankers. For details about canker removal and treatment, see page 911. Keep the plant in a vigorous growing condition by fertilizing and watering regularly.

5. Borers are difficult to control once they have burrowed into the wood. For more information about borers and their controls, see page 455.

PROBLEMS COMMON TO MANY TREES — FLUIDS PRESENT

HOLES OR CRACKS IN BARK

Slime flux on poplar.

Honeydew on maple.

Sapsucker holes.

PROBLEM: Sour-smelling sap oozes from wounds, cracks, and branch crotches, mainly during the growing season. The sap drips down the bark and dries, causing unsightly gray streaks. There may be some wilting on affected branches. Insects are attracted to the sour-smelling ooze.

ANALYSIS: Slime flux
Slime flux, also called *wetwood*, is caused by a bacterium (*Erwinia nimipressuralis*). The bacteria infect the heartwood, producing abnormally high sap pressure. This pressure is caused by bacterial fermentation, and forces the fermented sap, or flux, out of wounds, cracks, or crotches in the tree. Flux is especially copious when the tree is growing rapidly. Large areas of the bark may be coated with the smelly, bacteria-laden sap, which dries to a grayish-white color. In addition, wounds do not heal and the bark is unsightly. A tree with this problem is often under water stress, which may cause drought damage (wilting and scorched leaves) to the branches. The problem may persist for years.

SOLUTION: There are no chemical controls for this condition. Bore a slightly slanted drainage hole through the wood below each oozing wound. Insert a ½-inch-diameter plastic tube just until it stays firmly in place. If the tube penetrates the water-soaked wood inside the tree, it will interfere with drainage. The tube will carry the dripping sap away from the trunk. Disinfect tools with rubbing alcohol after pruning infected trees.

PROBLEM: A shiny or sticky substance coats the leaves and sometimes the twigs. Insects may be found on the leaves directly above, and ants, flies, or bees may be present. A black sooty mold is often growing on the sticky substance.

ANALYSIS: Honeydew
Honeydew is a sweet, sticky substance that is secreted by aphids, mealybugs, psyllids, whiteflies, and certain scales. These sucking insects cannot fully digest all the sugar in the plant sap, and excrete the excess in a fluid called honeydew, which drops onto the leaves directly below and adheres to anything beneath the tree or shrub. Lawn furniture or cars under infested plants may be stained. Ants and certain flies and bees feed on honeydew, and may be found around the plant. A sooty mold fungus often develops on the sticky substance, causing the leaves and twigs to appear black and dirty. The fungus does not infect the leaf, but grows superficially on the honeydew. Extremely heavy fungus infestations may prevent light from reaching the leaf, reducing food production.

SOLUTION: Honeydew can be wiped off the leaves with a wet rag; or it will eventually be washed off by rain. Prevent more honeydew by controlling the insect that is producing it. Inspect the leaves and twigs above the honeydew to find what type of insect is present. See the following pages for control instructions: for aphids, page 877; for scales, page 878; for whiteflies, page 879; for mealybugs, page 878.

PROBLEM: Rows of parallel holes, ¼ inch in diameter, appear on trunks. Sap often oozes from the holes, and portions of the surrounding bark may fall off. When damage is severe, part or all of the tree is killed. Yellow-bellied or red-breasted birds may be seen pecking on the tree.

ANALYSIS: Sapsuckers
Two different species of sapsuckers, members of the woodpecker family, feed on tree bark and sap. The red-breasted sapsucker is found in the Pacific Northwest. The yellow-bellied sapsucker is common throughout much of the United States. Sapsuckers peck into many trees before finding a suitable one that has sap with a high sugar content. Once the birds find a favorite tree, they visit it many times a day and feed on it year after year. Portions of the bark often fall off after sapsuckers have pecked many holes. If the trunk is girdled, the tree above the damaged area dies. Sometimes disease organisms enter the holes and damage or kill the tree.

SOLUTION: It is difficult to prevent sapsucker damage to trees. Wrapping the damaged trunk with burlap or smearing a sticky material, such as the latex used for ant control, above and below the holes may inhibit new pecking damage. For a list of trees most commonly attacked by sapsuckers, see page 999.

Borer emergence holes.

Rodent damage to crabapple.

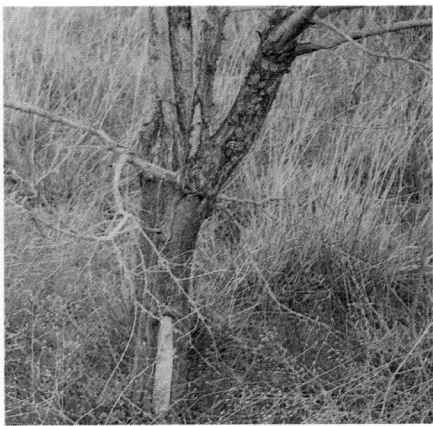

Porcupine damage to elm.

PROBLEM: Foliage on a branch or at the top of the tree is sparse; eventually the twigs and branches die. Holes or tunnels are apparent in the trunk or branches. Sap or sawdust usually surrounds the holes. The bark may die over the tunnels and slough off, or there may be knotlike swellings on the trunk and limbs. Weakened branches break during wind or snow storms. Weak, young, or newly transplanted trees may be killed.

ANALYSIS: Borers
Borers are the larvae of beetles or moths. Many kinds of borers attack trees and shrubs. Females lay their eggs in bark crevices throughout the summer. The larvae feed by tunneling through the bark, sapwood, and heartwood. This stops the flow of nutrients and water in that area by cutting the conducting vessels; branch and twig dieback result. Sap flow acts as a defense against borers if the plant is healthy. When the insect burrows into the wood, tree sap fills the hole and drowns the insect. Factors that weaken the tree, such as mechanical injuries, transplanting, damage by leaf-feeding insects, and poor growing conditions make it more attractive to egg-laying females.

SOLUTION: Cut out and destroy all dead and dying branches. Severely infested young plants should be removed. Spray or paint the trunk and branches with an insecticide containing *lindane*. Contact your local Cooperative Extension Office (see page 1011) for the best time to spray in your area. Repeat 3 more times at intervals of 2 weeks. Maintain plant health and vigor by watering and fertilizing regularly.

PROBLEM: Bark has been chewed or gnawed from the trunk and lower branches. In some cases, the trunk is entirely girdled. Deer, rabbits, mice, or squirrels may have been seen in the yard, or their tracks may be evident on the ground or snow. Damage is usually most severe during the winter, when other food sources are scarce.

ANALYSIS: Bark-feeding animals
Several animals chew on tree bark.
1. Deer feed on leaves, shoots, buds, and bark. They feed by pulling and twisting the bark or twig tissue, leaving ragged or twisted twig ends or patches of bark. Generally they feed on the lower branches and upper trunk. The males may also damage plants by rubbing their antlers on the trunk and branches.
2. Rabbits chew on the bark at the base of the trunk. They chew bark and twigs off cleanly, leaving a sharp break. The damaged trunk is often scarred with paired gouges left by the rabbit's front teeth. Rabbits generally feed no more than 2 feet above the ground or snow level. They damage small or young plants more severely.
3. Field mice, or *voles*, damage plants by chewing off the bark at the base of the trunk just at or slightly above or below ground or snow level. They may girdle the trunk, often killing the plant. Mice leave tiny scratches in the exposed wood. Some species of mice feed on plant roots, causing the slow decline and death of the plant.
4. Squirrels damage trees and shrubs by wounding the bark. Red squirrels feed on maple sap in the spring. The resulting bark wounds are V-shaped. Canker disease fungi sometimes invade the wounds, weakening or killing the tree. Some squirrels feed on bark when food is scarce in the winter. Other species of squirrels use bark and twigs for building nests.

SOLUTION: There are various methods that may be used to exclude or control deer, rabbits, mice and voles, and squirrels in the garden. These methods usually involve protecting the plants with fencing and tree guards, or controlling the animals with traps. For more information about the animals and their controls, see page 891 for deer, page 894 for rabbits and ground squirrels, and page 893 for tree squirrels.

PROBLEMS COMMON TO MANY TREES, SHRUBS, AND VINES — HOLES OR CRACKS IN BARK

Canker on ceanothus.

Bark shedding on madrone.

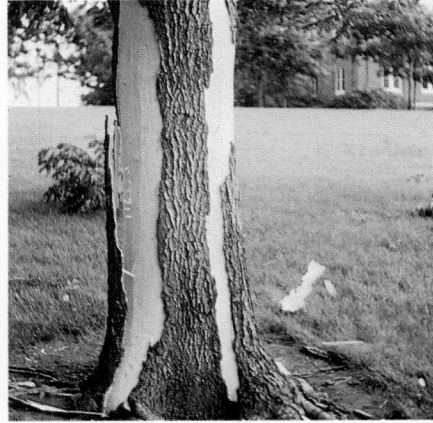

Lightning-damaged tree.

PROBLEM: Sunken, oval, or elongated dark-colored lesions (cankers) develop on the trunk or branches. The bark at the edge of the canker may thicken and roll inward. In some cases, sticky, amber-colored sap oozes from the canker. Foliage on infected plants may be stunted and yellowing. Some of the leaves may turn brown and drop off. Twigs and branches may gradually die, and the plant may eventually be killed.

ANALYSIS: Cankers
Many different species of fungi and bacteria cause cankers and dieback. Infection usually occurs through injured or wounded tissue. Bark that has been damaged by sunscald, cold, pruning wounds, or mechanical injury is especially susceptible. Some decay organisms infect the leaves first, then spread down into healthy twigs. Cankers form as the decay progresses. Some plants produce a sticky sap that oozes from the cankers. The portion of the branch or stem above the canker may die from the clogging of the water and nutrient-conducting vessels in the branch. Cankers that form on the trunk are the most serious, and may kill the tree. The plant may halt the development of a canker by producing callus tissue, a growth of barklike cells, to wall off the decay.

SOLUTION: Remove badly infected branches and cut out cankers. For details about canker removal and treatment, see page 911. Avoid wounding the plant. Keep the plant vigorous by fertilizing and watering regularly. For instructions, see pages 904 and 906.

PROBLEM: Bark is cracking or peeling, usually on the older branches and trunk.

ANALYSIS: Bark shedding
The shedding or cracking of bark is often noticeable and may be of concern to people not familiar with this natural process. The outer bark changes over the lifetime of a tree. The bark of young trees is live tissue, usually smooth and relatively soft. As the trees mature, the bark dies and hardens, sometimes becoming rough. Trunks and branches increase in diameter with age. The increase in girth causes the outer bark of many plants to crack in a variety of patterns. With some tree species, such as white birch, cracking develops to such an extent that the bark peels and falls off. Newly exposed bark is often smooth and lighter in color than the bark that was shed. Some trees, such as sycamore and shagbark hickory, characteristically have loose outer bark. The bark is constantly in the process of peeling and shedding.

SOLUTION: This process is normal. No controls are necessary.

PROBLEM: Part or all of the tree suddenly turns brown and dies. There may be no external signs of damage, or a strip of bark may be burned or stripped from the entire length of the trunk. In less severe cases, trees survive for several years or recover completely. Sometimes tops of trees or branches explode, leaving a jagged stub. There has been a lightning storm recently.

ANALYSIS: Lightning damage
Tall trees, trees growing in open locations, and trees growing in moist soil or along river banks are susceptible to damage by lightning. Lightning damage is variable. Some trees die suddenly from internal damage or burned roots without any external sign that lightning has struck. Other trees burst into flames or explode when struck. Sometimes only a strip of bark is burned or stripped from the trunk and the tree recovers. Some species of trees are more resistant to lightning bolts than others. (For a list of trees resistant and susceptible to lightning injury, see page 999.) Some scientists believe that trees high in starch, deep-rooted species, and decaying trees are more susceptible to damage than trees high in oils, shallow-rooted species, or healthy trees.

SOLUTION: Remove all loose and injured bark. To reduce or prevent damage, water trees during dry spells. Remove severely damaged trees. Valuable old trees can be protected with lightning conductors. Contact a professional arborist.

Sunscald on laburnum.

Sunscald on dogwood.

Frost cracks.

PROBLEM: Patches of bark die, crack, and later develop into cankers. The dead bark eventually sloughs off, exposing undamaged wood. The affected bark area is always on the southwest side of the tree. Trees with dark bark may be more severely affected. The cracks and cankers develop in either summer or winter.

ANALYSIS: Sunscald
When a tree growing in a deeply shaded location is suddenly exposed to intense sunlight, or when a tree is heavily pruned, the southwest side of newly exposed bark is injured by the rapid change in temperature. This may develop when a forested area is excessively thinned, or when a tree is moved from a shaded nursery to an open area, such as a lawn.
1. *Summer sunscald:* With intense summer heat, exposed bark is killed and a canker develops, usually revealing the undamaged wood beneath the bark. Within several seasons, the tree may break at the cankered area and topple. Summer sunscald is most severe when the soil is dry.
2. *Winter sunscald:* Bark injury develops when there are rapid changes in bark temperature between cold nights and sunny winter days. Exposed bark, usually on the southwest side of the tree, becomes much warmer than the air during the day, but cools rapidly after sunset. This rapid temperature change often results in bark cracking and, later, cankering. Trees with thin, dark bark are most severely affected.

SOLUTION: Once the bark is injured, there is nothing you can do. Wrap the trunks of recently exposed or newly transplanted trees with tree-wrapping paper, available in nurseries. White interior latex or whitewash is also effective. The wrap or paint should be left on for at least two years. Reapply the paint the second season if it has washed off. Trees will eventually adapt to increased exposure by producing thicker bark. Give trees adequate water in the summer and, if necessary, in the fall, especially recently transplanted trees. Water transplants when the top 2 inches of the rootball are dry. For more information about watering, see page 906.

PROBLEM: Longitudinal cracks develop on the trunk, usually on the south and west sides. The cracks generally close during the growing season.

ANALYSIS: Frost cracks
Frost cracks develop from the expansion and shrinkage of bark and wood during periods of wide temperature fluctuations. This causes internal mechanical stress, splitting the bark and outer wood. The sudden break is often accompanied by a loud noise. Cracks usually heal over during the growing season, but they may remain partially open after the weather warms, or reopen during the next winter.

SOLUTION: If a large crack fails to heal, a rod or bolt may be installed to hold it together. Consult a professional arborist. Plant trees adapted to your climate. Protect young susceptible trees by wrapping the trunks with tree-wrapping paper in late fall, or by painting the trunk with whitewash.

Trees that are most susceptible to frost cracks:

Botanical name	Common name
Acer	Maple
Aesculus	Horse chestnut
Liriodendron tulipifera	Tuliptree
Malus	Crabapple
Platanus acerifolia	London plane tree
Prunus	Flowering peach and cherry
Quercus	Oak
Salix	Willow
Tilia	Linden
Ulmus	Elm

TREES, SHRUBS, AND VINES

Tree squirrel.

Limb breakage caused by weak fork.

Limb breakage caused by snow load.

PROBLEM: Many small twigs with healthy leaves attached are lying under the tree or shrub. Squirrels may be seen in the area.

ANALYSIS: Tree squirrels

Tree squirrels may damage trees by shearing off small twigs, which they use for building nests. Twigs appear to have been cut off with a dull knife or shears. The squirrels gather the twigs up and carry them to their nests, but they usually leave many behind. They normally clip 2 or 3 times more twigs than they need. Trees heavily pruned by squirrels may be bushier than normal.

SOLUTION: Squirrels usually do not harm the tree by clipping twigs. However, if they are altering the shape of the tree, protect it with tree guards wrapped around the trunk, or control the squirrels by using live traps. For more information about tree squirrels, see page 893.

PROBLEM: Branches break and fall, usually during storms or high winds. Some may drop in the middle of the day during a hot spell.

ANALYSIS: Limb breakage

Several different environmental factors cause limb breakage.

Weak fork: The angle between a branch and the trunk, called the *fork*, is normally greater than 45°. If the angle is much less than this, bark is sometimes trapped between the branch and the trunk, preventing the wood from growing together at that point. This weakens the branch. As the branch and trunk increase in length, the additional weight causes the fork to split at the weak junction. A large portion of the tree may fall. Some trees that develop weak forks break more readily than others because of their growth habits and brittle wood.

Wind: Branches may fall during high winds, especially in areas where there are tornadoes, hurricanes, and other forms of extreme winds. Moderate winds often hasten the dropping of limbs weakened by injury, insects, or disease.

Sudden limb drop: Large limbs sometimes drop during the middle of the day for no apparent reason. This usually occurs on hot, calm days. The cause is not known.

Snow and ice: Plants heavily coated with snow or ice may lose large limbs due to the additional weight. Evergreen trees, or deciduous trees with leaves still attached, are most susceptible because of the greater surface to which the snow or ice can adhere.

SOLUTION: If the break is a split, or if a third of the bark at the break is intact, it can be bolted back in place. (For more information about bracing and cabling, see page 910.) If less than a third of the bark is intact, or if the branch has fallen off the tree, prune off the remaining branch stub. (For more information about pruning off broken branches, see page 910.) To prevent further damage, brace or cable trees, and knock off snow and ice constantly to prevent buildup. In areas with high winds, prune back some of the branches to reduce the wind load. In the future, do not plant trees with brittle wood that breaks easily. For a list of trees with weak forks and brittle wood, see page 999.

Twig girdler (twice life size).

Heart rot.

Roots plugging sewer.

PROBLEM: Small, cleanly cut twigs, ¼ inch to 2 inches in diameter, are lying under the tree in the fall. The tree is often abnormally bushy. Small (up to 1 inch), whitish larvae may be found inside the fallen twigs.

ANALYSIS: Twig pruners and twig girdlers
Several species of wood-boring beetles cause unsightly damage to trees by altering their natural form. In midsummer to fall, the wood-boring beetles lay their eggs in the wood of small twigs. The *twig pruner* larvae tunnel toward the base of the twigs, eating all but the outer bark. In the fall, they back into the hollowed-out twigs. High winds cause the nearly severed twigs containing the larvae to break and drop to the ground. Adult *twig girdlers* lay eggs in twigs, then chew a circle arond the outside of the twigs. The girdled twigs die and break off. The eggs in the fallen twig are able to develop without being hindered by the flow of sap through the twig. Both twig pruner and twig girdler larvae mature in the twigs on the ground. The damage to the tree is the result of excessive pruning on the branch tips. Several new side shoots develop where the twigs break off, causing abnormal bushiness and an unnatural shape.

SOLUTION: Spray with an insecticide containing *lindane* after the first leaves are fully expanded in spring. Make a second application 30 days later. Gather and destroy all severed twigs in the late fall, when the insects are inside them.

PROBLEM: Branches break and fall, usually during storms. The wood in the area of breakage is discolored and often spongy. Soft or woody mushroom-like growths may be found on the wood.

ANALYSIS: Heart rot
Heart rot is caused mainly by fungi. Decay organisms rot dead wood (such as fallen trees) as part of nature's recycling process. A number of them may also invade live trees through wounds. Healthy, vigorous trees may stop the spread of decay by producing cells that wall off the invaded area. Old trees with many wounds often have little resistance to microorganisms, and decay spreads through the wood. The decay does not usually kill the living tissue of the tree, so branches and leaves are kept alive. But internal decay reduces the strength of affected limbs. During a storm, weakened branches fall. Some of the decay organisms develop yellowish to brown, mushroomlike growths, called *conks*, on the outside wood in areas where decay is present. For more information about mushrooms and conks, see page 446.

SOLUTION: Cut off the remaining branch stub so it's flush against the larger branch or tree trunk (see page 910). Inspect the rest of the tree to determine the extent of decay (it may be necessary to contact a professional arborist). Branches or the entire plant should be removed if decay is extensive. As much as possible, avoid wounding plants. Keep them in a vigorous growing condition by fertilizing and watering regularly. For more information about fertilizers and watering, see pages 904 and 906.

PROBLEM: Sewer drains are backed up. Trees or large shrubs are growing on the property.

ANALYSIS: Roots plugging sewer
The roots of trees and large shrubs plug up sewer lines. Roots cannot invade pipes by puncturing them. Unsealed pipe joints and cracks are common entrance points. Once inside, the invading root has a constant source of nutrients and moisture and grows rapidly. As the root expands it forces the crack open. Inside, the root branches and grows until it plugs the pipe, causing the drains to back up.

SOLUTION: Plugged drains must be cleared by a plumber. To prevent further plugging, pour 1 pound of *copper sulfate crystals* into the lowest entry point to the sewer line (a toilet or basement drain) before bedtime, when drains and sewer lines are not in use. Flush the toilet or wash the crystals into the pipes with a bucket of water. The copper sulfate crystals collect in the mass of roots and kill them. Copper sulfate is not absorbed by roots, so the rest of the plant is not harmed. The dead roots rot in a few weeks. Repeat the treatment every 6 months.

PROBLEMS COMMON TO MANY TREES, SHRUBS, AND VINES — ROOTS **DISCOLORED LEAVES**

Roots cracking pavement.

Surface roots in a lawn.

Salt burn on philadelphus.

PROBLEM: Roots are exposed on the surface of the soil, or are making bumps by growing just beneath it. Or roots are cracking and raising the pavement. Exposed roots may be lumpy and galled.

ANALYSIS: Surface roots
Several factors can cause roots near the surface to expand:

1. *Surface roots in lawns:* If plants receive only light irrigations on the soil surface, roots in this upper zone will expand, pushing above the surface. Plants growing in lawns that receive light irrigations often have shallow roots.

2. *Waterlogged soil:* Roots need oxygen to grow and develop. Waterlogged soil has very little oxygen available for root growth because the soil pores are filled with water. The only available oxygen is near the soil surface, so the surface roots develop most.

3. *Natural tendency:* Some plant species are more likely than others to develop surface roots.

4. *Compacted soil:* Trees and shrubs growing in compacted soil develop surface roots.

5. *Confined roots:* Plants growing in areas with limited root space, such as in containers, often have roots growing on the soil surface.

6. *Planting strips:* Trees growing in planting strips adjacent to lawns frequently crack the sidewalks that separate them from the lawns. All of the available water and food is beyond the walk, in the lawns. The roots that extend under the walk into the lawn expand rapidly, cracking the walk.

SOLUTION: The numbered solutions below correspond to the numbers in the analysis.

1. In addition to lawn watering, deep-water trees in lawns every 2 weeks, to a depth of 3 to 4 feet. Cover the roots by slowly raising the level of the lawn (1 inch per year) with soil topdressing.

2. If the soil is waterlogged from over-watering, cut back on watering. (For information about watering, see pages 906 and 907.) If necessary, improve drainage around the plant (see page 901). Cover the exposed roots with 2 to 4 inches of soil. Before planting new trees and shrubs, make sure drainage is adequate.

3. For a list of plants likely to develop surface roots, see page 998.

4. Cover exposed roots with 2 to 4 inches of soil and loosen compacted soil with a crowbar. Before planting in compacted soil, loosen the soil (see page 918).

5. Plant shrubs or small trees that are adapted to growing in confined root areas (see page 996).

6. Sever small roots that are pushing up pavement. If possible, avoid cutting large roots. In the future, plant large trees on the lawn side of the sidewalk, and use shrubs in planting strips.

PROBLEM: Edges of older leaves turn brown or black, and die. The rest of the leaf may be lighter green than normal. The browning or blackening develops in dry or wet soil, but it is more severe in dry soil. In the worst cases, leaves drop from the plant.

ANALYSIS: Salt burn
This problem is common in areas of low rainfall. It also occurs in soils with poor drainage, in areas where salt has been used to melt snow and ice, and where too much fertilizer has been applied. Excess salts dissolved in the soil water accumulate in the leaf edges, where they kill the tissue. These salts also interfere with water uptake by the plant. This problem is rare in areas of high rainfall, where the soluble salts are leached from most soils. Poorly drained soils also accumulate salts because they do not leach well; much of the applied water runs off instead of washing through the soil. Fertilizers, which are soluble salts, also cause salt burn if too much is applied or if it is not diluted with a thorough watering after application.

SOLUTION: In areas with low rainfall, leach accumulated salts from the soil with an occasional heavy watering (about once a month). If possible, improve the drainage around the plants. (For instructions on improving drainage, see page 901.) If plants are severely damaged, replace them with healthy plants. Follow package directions when using fertilizers; several light applications are better than one heavy application. Water thoroughly afterward. Avoid the use of bagged steer manure, which contains large amounts of salt.

Leaf scorch on maple.

Leaf scorch on birch.

Cedar-apple rust on hawthorn.

PROBLEM: Leaf edges and the tissues between the veins turn tan or brown. Leaves are scorched and have a dry appearance. Brown areas often increase in size until little green is left except around the center vein. Dead leaves may remain attached to the plant, or they may drop. Leaf scorch is most severe in the upper branches, and when the soil is dry.

ANALYSIS: Leaf scorch
Scorch is caused by a lack of water in the leaves. This lack can result from any of several causes.

1. *Extreme heat and wind:* Leaf scorch is caused by excessive evaporation of moisture from the leaves. In hot or windy weather, water evaporates rapidly from the leaves. If the roots can't absorb and convey water fast enough to replenish this loss, the leaves turn brown and wither. This usually occurs in dry soil, but leaves can also scorch when the soil is moist and temperatures are near 100°F for extended periods. Young plants with limited root systems are most susceptible.

2. *Winter burn:* Winter burn is similar to scorch from intense heat or wind except that it occurs during warm, windy days in late winter. In colder climates, water cannot be replaced by the roots because the soil is frozen, resulting in leaf desiccation. Conifers are most susceptible, especially those planted in exposed areas. The symptoms may not appear until spring.

3. *Damaged roots:* Trees and shrubs may develop scorched and yellow leaves, early fall color, and dieback after the roots have been injured.

4. *Underwatering:* Many plants that are regularly underwatered will survive. They do not function normally, however, and the leaves frequently burn and wilt over the entire plant.

SOLUTION: The numbered solutions below correspond to the numbers in the analysis.

1. To prevent further scorch, deep-water plants during periods of hot weather to wet down the entire root space. Because of their limited root systems, recently transplanted trees and shrubs should be watered more often than established plants. Water them when the root ball is dry 2 inches below the surface. If the leaves scorched when the soil was moist, provide shade during periods of hot weather and screens for protection from wind; or transplant to a protected area.

2. Provide windbreaks and shelter for plants growing in cold, windy regions. Covering smaller plants with burlap helps prevent leaf drying. If necessary, water in late fall or winter to insure adequate soil moisture. Mulch plants after they are dormant to reduce the depth of frost penetration into the soil.

3. For more information about damaged roots, see pages 469 and 470.

4. Do not let the soil dry out to the point where leaves scorch. Check the moisture needs of your plant under its cultural information.

PROBLEM: Leaves are discolored or mottled yellow to brown. Yellow, orange, red, or blackish powdery pustules appear on the leaves. The powdery material can be scraped off. Leaves may become twisted, distorted, and dry, and drop off. Twigs may also be infected. Plants are often stunted.

ANALYSIS: Leaf rusts
Many different species of leaf rust fungi infect trees and shrubs. Most rusts attack only one or a few related plants. However, some rusts require two different plant species to complete their life cycles. Part of the life cycle is spent on the tree or shrub and part is spent on various weeds, flowers, or other woody trees or shrubs. Rust fungi survive the winter as spores on or in living plant tissue or in plant debris. The spores are spread to healthy plants by wind and splashing water. When conditions are favorable (moisture on the leaf in the form of rain, dew, or fog, and moderate temperatures, 54° to 74°F), the spores germinate and infect the tissue. Leaf discoloration and mottling develop as the fungus saps the plant nutrients. Some rust fungi produce spores in spots or patches, while others develop into hornlike structures.

SOLUTION: Several fungicides, including those containing *triforine, ferbam, maneb, zineb,* and *cycloheximide,* may be used to control rust. Look under the entry for your plant in the alphabetical section of the book beginning on page 474 to determine which fungicide is appropriate. Some rust fungi are fairly harmless to the plant and do not require control measures. Where practical, remove and destroy infected leaves as they appear. Rake up and destroy leaves in the fall.

PROBLEMS COMMON TO MANY TREES, SHRUBS, AND VINES — DISCOLORED LEAVES

Spirea aphids (4 times life size).

Leafhopper damage to dogwood.

Spider mite damage to boxwood.

PROBLEM: The newest leaves are discolored. Leaves and twigs may be curled and distorted. Many leaves may drop from the plant, and branches sometimes die. A shiny or sticky substance often coats the leaves. A black sooty mold may grow on the sticky substance. Tiny (⅛ inch) green, yellow, black, brownish, or gray soft-bodied insects cluster on the leaves, stem tips, bark, or buds. The insects may have wings. Ants are sometimes present.

ANALYSIS: Aphids
Many different aphids infest ornamental trees and shrubs. They do little damage in small numbers. However, they are extremely prolific, and populations can rapidly build up to damaging numbers during the growing season. Damage occurs when the aphid sucks the juices from the leaves. Sap removal often results in scorched, discolored, or curled leaves and reduced plant growth. A severe infestation of bark aphids may cause branches to die. The aphid is unable to digest fully all the sugar in the plant sap, and excretes the excess in a fluid called honeydew, which drops onto the leaves and contaminates anything beneath the tree or shrub. A sooty mold fungus may develop on the honeydew, causing the leaves to appear black and dirty. Ants feed on the sticky substance, and are often present where there is an aphid infestation.

SOLUTION: Spray with ORTHO Isotox Insect Killer, ORTHO Orthene Systemic Insect Control, or ORTHO Malathion 50 Insect Spray when damage is first noticed. Make sure your plant is listed on the product label. Repeat the spray if the plant becomes reinfested.

PROBLEM: Leaves are stippled white, yellow, or light green, and leaves and stems may be distorted. Sometimes the plant has a burned appearance. Infested leaves may drop prematurely. When infestations are severe, twigs and small branches sometimes die. Whitish or green wedge-shaped insects, up to ½ inch long, hop and fly away quickly when the plant is touched.

ANALYSIS: Leafhoppers
Many species of leafhoppers infest ornamental trees and shrubs. Some leafhoppers cause only minor damage to the leaves, while other species severely retard plant growth. Leafhoppers usually spend the winter as eggs in bark slits made by the females, although some may overwinter in the South and migrate north in the spring. Injury to the bark from egg laying may kill twigs. When the weather warms in the spring, the young leafhoppers emerge and settle on the undersides of the leaves, where they suck out the plant sap, causing the stippling and distortion. Severely infested leaves often drop in midsummer. Some leafhoppers cause a condition known as "hopperburn." Insect feeding causes distortion, and gives the leaves a burned appearance. There may be several generations of leafhoppers each year.

SOLUTION: Spray with ORTHO Isotox Insect Killer, ORTHO Orthene Insect Spray, or ORTHO Diazinon Insect Spray when damage is first noticed. Cover the lower surfaces of the leaves thoroughly. Make sure your plant is listed on the product label.

PROBLEM: Leaves are stippled yellow, white, or bronze and dirty. Sometimes there is a silken webbing on the leaves or stems. New growth may be distorted, and the plant may be weak and stunted. To determine if the plant is infested with mites, hold a sheet of white paper underneath an affected leaf or branch and tap it sharply. Minute green, red, or yellow specks the size of pepper grains will drop to the paper and begin to crawl around.

ANALYSIS: Spider mites
Spider mites, related to spiders, are major pests of many plants. They cause damage by sucking sap from the undersides of the leaves and buds. As a result of feeding, the green leaf pigment disappears, producing the stippled appearance. Many mites produce a fine webbing over the foliage as they feed, which collects dust and dirt. Some mites are active throughout the growing season, and are especially favored by hot, dry weather (70°F and up). Other mites, especially those infesting conifers, are most prolific in cooler weather. They are most active in the spring and sometimes fall, and during warm periods in winter in mild climates. At the onset of hot weather, these mites have usually caused their maximum damage.

SOLUTION: Spray with ORTHO Isotox Insect Killer, ORTHO Orthenex Insect & Disease Control, or ORTHO Orthene Systemic Insect Control when damage is first noticed. Repeat the spray 2 more times at intervals of 7 to 10 days. Make sure your plant is listed on the product label.

Lacebug and droppings (4 times life size).

Greenhouse thrips damage to coffee.

Air pollution damage.

PROBLEM: The upper surfaces of the leaves are mottled or speckled yellow, gray, or white and green. The mottling is distinguished from other insect damage — such as that caused by mites or leafhoppers — by the shiny, hard, black droplets found on the undersides of damaged leaves. Small (⅛ inch), light or dark, spiny, wingless insects or brownish insects with clear lacy wings may be visible around the droplets. The plant is usually stunted. Damage occurs in spring and summer.

ANALYSIS: Lacebugs
Many species of lacebugs feed on trees and shrubs. Each species usually infests only one type of plant. Depending on species, lacebugs spend the winter as adults in protected areas on the plant, or as eggs in leaf veins, or cemented in the black droplets on the lower surfaces of the leaf. Both the spiny, wingless, immature insects and the lacewing adults suck sap from the undersides of the leaves. The green leaf pigment disappears, resulting in the characteristic speckling or mottling. As the lacebugs feed, droplets of brown excrement accumulate around them. Damage is unsightly and food production by the leaf is reduced, resulting in loss of plant vigor.

SOLUTION: Spray with ORTHO Isotox Insect Killer or ORTHO Orthene Systemic Insect Control when damage first appears in the spring. Make sure your plant is listed on the product label. Cover the undersides of the leaves thoroughly. Repeat the spray 7 to 10 days later. A third application may be necessary if the plant becomes reinfested in midsummer.

PROBLEM: Young leaves are severely curled and distorted. Parts of the leaf may die and turn black, or the entire leaf may drop from the plant. Or leaves are flecked and appear bleached or silvery, often becoming papery and wilted. Shiny black spots may cover the surfaces. Flowers and buds may also be affected. They either fail to open properly or are brown and distorted. Minute (1/25 inch), white or yellow, spindle-shaped insects and black or brown winged insects are barely visible either inside the distorted leaves and flowers or on the undersides of the leaves. Heavily infested plants may be stunted.

ANALYSIS: Thrips
Thrips are a common pest of many garden and greenhouse plants. Some species cause leaf or flower distortion; others cause a flecking of the leaves, producing a bleached appearance. Thrips feed by rasping the soft plant tissue, then sucking the released plant sap. Some leaf thrips leave unsightly, black, varnishlike spots of excrement around the areas where they feed. The black or brown adults have wings. They can spread rapidly by flying to new plants; or they may be blown long distances by the wind. They lay their eggs either on the plant or in surrounding weeds. The young are yellow or white and spindle-shaped.

SOLUTION: Spray the leaves or buds and flowers with ORTHO Isotox Insect Killer, ORTHO Orthene Systemic Insect Control, or ORTHO Malathion 50 Insect Spray. Make sure your plant is listed on the product label. Remove and destroy infested buds and flowers.

PROBLEM: Upper surfaces of leaves are stippled or flecked black, purple, or white. Dark spots soon fade to tan or brown. Or the tissue between the veins turns gray-green to light brown and bleaches to a light tan after several days. Leaves may curl, and many may drop off the plant. Growth is often slowed, and the plant is weak.

ANALYSIS: Air pollution
The breakdown products of some gases released into the atmosphere by cars and factories damage plants. The most common types of pollution affecting trees and shrubs are ozone and sulfur dioxide. (For more information, see page 862.) Air pollution damage is most commonly a problem in urban areas, but also can occur in rural areas where plants are located downwind from factories. Many different environmental and genetic factors affect a plant's susceptibility to air pollution, causing trees and shrubs to react differently. One plant may show leaf stippling and curling, while an identical plant growing next to it shows no symptoms. Research is presently being conducted throughout the country to better understand these factors, and to find ways to protect plants from air pollutants.

SOLUTION: Air pollution injury is usually a localized problem. Check with your neighbors to see if the same kinds of plants in their gardens have been affected the same way. Because injury from air pollutants is similar in appearance to injury from nutrient deficiencies, insects, diseases, and mites, these problems should be eliminated as causes before attributing the damage to air pollution. If you live in a polluted area, select plants that are tolerant from the list on page 996.

PROBLEMS COMMON TO MANY TREES, SHRUBS, AND VINES — DISCOLORED LEAVES

Overwatering damage to viburnums.

Nitrogen-deficient fuchsia.

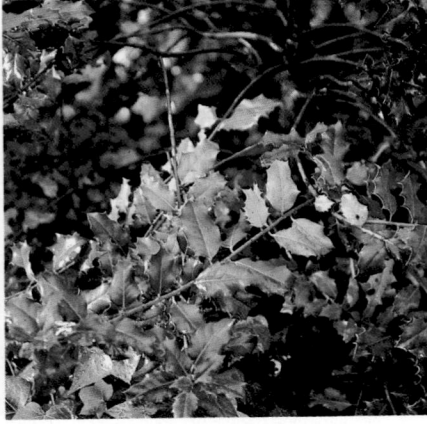

Seasonal leaf drop on holly.

PROBLEM: Leaves turn light green to yellow and may drop. The edges of the leaves may be brown. In many cases, the plant grows very little. It may pull out of the ground easily, because the roots are soft and rotted. The soil is frequently or constantly wet.

ANALYSIS: Overwatering or poor drainage
Overwatering and poor drainage are serious common problems that often kill plants. Roots require air to function normally. Air is contained in tiny pores in the soil. When the soil is watered, air is forced out of the soil pores and replaced with water. If water cannot drain out of the soil, or if it is constantly reapplied, the soil pores remain filled with water. The roots cannot absorb the oxygen they need in such saturated conditions, and they die. As the roots rot, the root system is less able to supply the plant with nutrients and water, resulting in starvation and eventually the death of the plant.

SOLUTION: Do not apply water so frequently that the soil is constantly wet. Depending on the particular requirements of your tree or shrub (see cultural information for your specific plant in the alphabetical section beginning on page 474), allow the soil to dry partially or completely between waterings. (For more information on this technique, see page 857.) If your soil drains poorly, improve drainage as described on page 901.

PROBLEM: Leaves turn yellow and may drop, beginning with the older leaves. New leaves are small, and growth is slow.

ANALYSIS: Lack of nitrogen
Nitrogen, one of the most important nutrients for plant growth, is deficient in most soils. Nitrogen is essential in the formation of green leaf pigment, and in many other compounds necessary for plant growth. When they are short on nitrogen, plants take nitrogen from their older leaves for new growth. Poorly drained, over-watered, compacted, and cold soils are often infertile. Plants growing in these soils often show symptoms of nitrogen deficiency. Various soil problems and other nutrient deficiencies also cause leaf discoloration. Study the symptoms carefully.

SOLUTION: For a quick response, spray the leaves and the soil beneath the plant with Ra-Pid-Gro Plant Food. Fertilize plants regularly with ORTHO Evergreen Tree & Shrub Food 12–6–6, ORTHO General Purpose Plant Food 8–8–8, or a fertilizer for a specific type of plant, such as ORTHO Rose Food 8–12–4. (For more information about fertilizers, see page 905.) ORTHO Dried Blood Meal 12–0–0, which contains nitrogen in a long-lasting, slow-release form, can be used to supplement regular feeding. Add organic amendments to compacted soils and those low in organic matter, and improve drainage in poorly drained soils. (For more information about organic matter and drainage, see pages 918 and 901.) Do not keep the soil constantly wet. (For more information about watering, see page 906.)

PROBLEM: Older needles or the leaves nearest the trunk or main stem turn yellow, reddish, or brown and drop. Or all the leaves drop off the plant. This condition may develop over a few days or several weeks.

ANALYSIS: Seasonal leaf drop
1. *Evergreen plants:*
This is a natural process similar to the dropping of leaves by deciduous plants. Evergreen leaves normally have a life span of 2 to 4 years. Leaf drop may occur every year, or only every second or third year. When growing conditions have been favorable the previous season, leaf shedding occurs over several weeks and is less noticeable. However, if the plant has been exposed to unfavorable conditions during the growing season, such as drying, or a spider mite or insect infestation, leaf drop develops within a few days. Some plants, such as arborvitae, drop their foliage in the fall. Holly leaf drop occurs in late winter. Many western trees drop old leaves in the spring, as new leaves are formed. Pines drop their needles at various times of the year, depending on the species. Leaf drop is also caused by new growth shading older, interior growth.
2. *Deciduous plants:*
In autumn, many trees and shrubs drop all their leaves as they become dormant before winter arrives. The leaves often turn beautiful colors before falling. If the plant is weak from poor growing conditions, diseases, or pests, leaf fall may develop prematurely, often in midsummer. A few plants, such as California buckeye, normally drop their leaves in midsummer.

SOLUTION: No control measures are necessary.

BRANCHES DIE

Iron-deficient azalea.

Dog urine damage to boxwood.

Canker on sycamore.

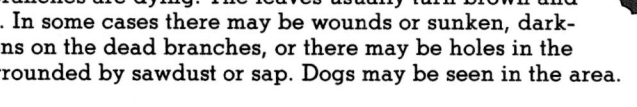

PROBLEM: Leaves turn pale green or yellow. The newest leaves (those at the tips of the stems) are most severely affected. Except in extreme cases, the veins of affected leaves remain green. Older leaves may remain green. The plant may be stunted.

ANALYSIS: Iron deficiency
Plants frequently suffer from deficiencies of iron and other minor nutrients, such as manganese and zinc, elements essential to normal plant growth and development. Deficiencies can occur when one or more of these elements are depleted in the soil. Often these minor nutrients are present in the soil, but alkaline (pH 7.5 or higher) or wet soil conditions cause them to form compounds that cannot be used by the plant. An alkaline condition can result from overliming, or from lime leached from cement or brick. Regions where soil is derived from limestone, and those with low rainfall, usually have alkaline soils.

SOLUTION: To correct the nutrient deficiency, spray the foliage with ORTHO Greenol Liquid Iron 6.13%, and apply it to the soil around the plants. Apply ORTHO Orthorix Spray to correct the pH. (For more information about pH, see page 902.) Treating the soil with *ferrous sulfate* may also correct the pH of the soil. Place it in holes (6 inches deep for shrubs and 2 feet deep for trees) around the tree under the branches, and water it in well. Maintain an acid pH by fertilizing with ORTHO Azalea, Camellia & Rhododendron Food 5-10-10. When planting in an area with alkaline soil, add a handful of *soil sulfur*; or add at least 50 percent peat moss to the soil and mix it in well.

PROBLEM: Branches are dying. The leaves usually turn brown and may drop off. In some cases there may be wounds or sunken, dark-colored lesions on the dead branches, or there may be holes in the branches surrounded by sawdust or sap. Dogs may be seen in the area.

ANALYSIS: Twig or branch dieback
Dieback can result from any of several causes:

1. *Mechanical injury:* Any type of injury that causes a wound may kill branches. Branches on shrubs or trees may be wounded by motor vehicles, animals, wires, nails, or tools. If the wound girdles the branch, nutrients and water can't reach the leaves and the branch dies. Wounds are also entrance points for many diseases and pests.

2. *Cankers:* Cankers are sunken dark-colored lesions that are caused by fungi and bacteria. They kill the living tissue underneath the bark, inhibiting the movement of nutrients and water through the tree. If a canker covers as much as half the circumference of a branch, the branch often dies.

3. *Borers:* Borers are the larvae of beetles or moths. The larvae feed by tunneling through bark, sapwood, and heartwood. This cuts the flow of nutrients and water in that area, killing the branch beyond the tunneling.

4. *Dog urine:* The leaves on branches near the ground turn brown and die when dogs urinate on them. The salts in the urine burn the leaves. Dogs repeat their visits to certain shrubs or hedges, eventually killing branches.

SOLUTION: The numbered solutions below correspond to the numbers in the analysis.

1. Dying limbs with large wounds that almost girdle the branch should be removed. Repair small wounds by removing ragged edges and dead bark. (For more information about bark wounds, see page 911.) Avoid wounding plants. Do not use bare wire on branches, and do not nail anything to trees. If necessary, place protective barriers around plants to prevent damage. Do not plant trees and shrubs in areas where they are likely to be hit by vehicles or trampled.

2. For more information about cankers and their controls, see page 456.

3. For more information about borers and their controls, see page 455.

4. If a dog has recently urinated on a plant, wash the urine off the leaves and soak the ground around the plant to dilute the salts in the urine. Twigs and branches already damaged may recover. Prune off any dead wood. Protect plants from new damage with ORTHO Scram Dog & Cat Repellent; or erect barriers around the plants.

PROBLEMS COMMON TO MANY TREES, SHRUBS, AND VINES — BRANCHES DIE

Root rot of juniper.

Crown rot of madrone.

Fireblight on crabapple.

PROBLEM: The normal leaf color dulls, and the plant loses vigor. Leaves may wilt or turn yellow or light brown. Major branches or the entire plant may die. The roots and lower stems are brownish, and the roots are often decayed. Fine woolly brown strands may form on the roots, and white powdery spores form on the soil surface. Or fan-shaped plaques of white strands may appear between the bark and wood of the roots and lower stems.

ANALYSIS: Root and crown rots
Root and crown rots are caused by any of several different fungi that live in the soil and on roots.

SOLUTION: The numbered solutions below correspond to the numbers in the analysis.

1. *Phytophthora* species: These fungi cause browning and decaying on the roots and browning of the lower stems. The plant usually dies slowly; however, young plants may wilt and die rapidly. The disease is most prevalent in heavy, waterlogged soils. For more information about *Phytophthora*, see page 857.

1. Remove dead and dying plants. When replanting, use plants that are resistant to *Phytophthora*. (For a list of resistant trees and shrubs, see page 1000.) Improve soil drainage (see page 901). Avoid overwatering plants.

2. *Phymatotrichum omnivorum:* This fungus causes the disease commonly known as *cotton root rot* or *Texas root rot.* It is a serious problem on many plants in the Southwest. The plant may suddenly wilt and die. Brown strands form on the roots, and white powdery spores form on the soil. The disease is most severe in heavy, alkaline soils. For more information about *Phymatotrichum*, see page 859.

2. Remove dead and dying plants. When replanting, buy only resistant plants. (For a list of resistant trees and shrubs, see page 994.) Before planting, increase the soil acidity by adding 1 pound of *ammonium sulfate* for every 10 square feet of soil. Make a circular ridge around the planting area and fill the basin with 4 inches of water. Repeat the treatment in 5 to 10 days.

3. *Armillaria mellea:* This fungus causes a disease that is commonly known as *shoestring root rot, mushroom root rot,* or *oak root fungus. Armillaria* is identified by the presence of fan-shaped plaques of white fungal strands between the bark and the wood of the roots and lower stems. This fungus grows rapidly under wet conditions. Honey-colored mushrooms appear at the base of the plant in the fall. For more information about *Armillaria*, see page 858.

3. Remove dead and dying plants. The life of a newly infected plant may be prolonged if the disease has not reached the lower stems. Expose the base of the plant to air for several months by removing 3 to 4 inches of soil. Prune off diseased roots. Use a fertilizer to stimulate growth. (For more information about fertilizing trees and shrubs, see page 904.) When replanting, use only resistant plants. (For a list of plants resistant to *Armillaria*, see page 1001.) Avoid overwatering plants (see page 857).

PROBLEM: Blossoms and leaves of some twigs suddenly wilt and turn black as if scorched by fire. Leaves curl and hang downward. The bark at the base of the blighted twig becomes water-soaked, then dark, sunken, and dry; cracks may develop at the edge of the sunken area. In warm, moist spring weather drops of brown ooze appear on the sunken bark.

ANALYSIS: Fireblight
This disease is caused by a bacterium (*Erwinia amylovora*) that is very destructive to many trees and shrubs. (For a list of susceptible plants, see page 1001.) The bacteria spend the winter in the sunken areas (cankers) on the branches. In the spring, the bacteria ooze out of the cankers and are carried by insects to the plant blossoms. Flies and other insects are attracted to the sweet, sticky ooze and become smeared with it. When the insects visit a flower for nectar, they infect it with the bacteria. The bacteria spread rapidly through the plant tissue in warm (65°F or higher), humid weather. Bees visiting these infected blossoms carry bacteria-laden nectar to healthy blossoms. Rain, wind, and tools may also spread the bacteria.

SOLUTION: During spring and summer, prune out infected branches 12 to 15 inches beyond any visible discoloration and destroy. Sterilize the pruning tools with rubbing alcohol after each cut. A protective spray of a pesticide containing *basic copper sulfate* or *streptomycin* applied before bud break in the spring will help prevent infection. Repeat at intervals of 5 to 7 days until the end of bloom. In summer or fall, after the disease stops spreading, prune out infected branches.

WEAK OR DYING PLANT

Lawn mower blight on oak.

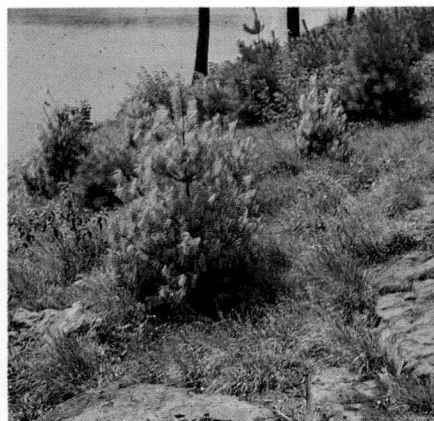

Pines growing in shallow soil.

Stunted ash growing in compacted soil.

PROBLEM: Leaves are small and discolored, and often drop prematurely. Twigs may die. The plant is stunted and in a general state of decline. Bark at the base of the trunk is wounded. The tree is planted in a lawn.

ANALYSIS: Lawn mower blight
Trees growing in lawns may be severely injured by slight but repeated injuries to the bark from lawn mowers. Lawn mower blades may also slice through the bark into the wood. Nutrients and water cannot pass through the damaged part of the trunk to reach the top of the tree. In severe cases, young trees are killed. Lawn mower wounds are often entry points for diseases, which may also kill the tree. For more information about bark wounds, see page 468.

SOLUTION: Prune off dying twigs and branches, and fertilize with ORTHO Evergreen, Tree & Shrub Food 12–6–6 or ORTHO General Purpose Plant Food 8–8–8. To prevent additional damage to the trunk, remove all grass from around the base of the tree or install a tree guard to eliminate the need for edging and trimming grass around the trunk.

PROBLEM: Leaves are small and discolored, and often drop prematurely. Eventually twigs and then larger branches die. The plant is stunted and in a general state of decline. The tree is planted in soil that is less than 2 feet deep and underlaid with rock or rocklike soil.

ANALYSIS: Shallow soil or hardpan
Large plants growing in shallow soil with rock or hardpan (a rocklike layer of soil) beneath them are stunted and show symptoms of decline. Shallow soils usually do not provide adequate root space for large plants. As plants increase in size, they run out of food and water frequently. These soils usually do not drain during wet weather, so trees planted in them suffer from lack of air in the soil. Because the root system is shallow, the tree is liable to blow over in a storm.

SOLUTION: If possible, move the plant to an area with deeper soil and replace it with shallow-rooted plants. If the plant can't be moved, increase plant vigor by fertilizing and watering regularly. (For more information about fertilizers and watering, see pages 904 and 906.) Prune off any dead and dying branches. Avoid overwatering plants growing over an impervious soil layer. Guy or stake the tree to secure it in storms. If you wish to plant more trees in shallow soil, take one of these precautions. If the underlayment is hardpan, break holes in it as described on page 900. If it is bedrock, add at least 2 feet of soil and plant a tree or shrub that does not grow large. For a list of small trees for areas with restricted root space, see page 996.

PROBLEM: Leaves are small and discolored, and often drop prematurely. Eventually twigs and then larger branches die. The plant is stunted and in a general state of decline. The soil under the tree is hard and dense, probably from heavy traffic.

ANALYSIS: Compacted soil
Constant vehicle or foot traffic in an area compacts soil. Compacted soil is too dense to admit air. Plant roots, which need air, stop growing or die. Water also enters the soil very slowly, so the tree or shrub suffers frequently from drought. Soil compaction is most common along roads or paths where traffic is heavy. Compacted soil is hard and difficult to probe when digging with a hand trowel or shovel.

SOLUTION: Divert traffic away from plants. If necessary, erect barriers to keep traffic out, using fences, walls, or dense or thorny shrubbery. Remove severely affected plants. Relieve the compaction to a depth of 4 to 6 inches with a soil aerator. Prevent further compaction by planting deep groundcovers, or by covering the compacted area with 2 to 4 inches of stone, crushed rock, or bark mulch. For more information about compaction, see page 900.

TREES, SHRUBS, AND VINES

PROBLEMS COMMON TO MANY TREES, SHRUBS, AND VINES — WEAK OR DYING PLANT

Girdling roots.

Ash trunk injured by wire.

Bark beetle damage.

PROBLEM: Leaves are small and discolored, and often drop prematurely. Eventually twigs and then larger branches die. The plant is stunted and in a general state of decline. A root is wrapped around the trunk of a tree, at or just below the surface of the soil. It completely encircles the trunk, and is imbedded in it.

ANALYSIS: Girdling roots
A girdling root is a root that wraps itself around the main root system or the trunk. As the trunk enlarges, it is strangled by its own root, slowly reducing the flow of nutrients and water to the top of the tree. The girdling root may be visible above ground, or it may develop underground and remain undetected until the tree is in a severe state of decline. Trees with girdling roots often do not have a normal flare where the trunk enters the soil, but plunge directly into the soil like a telephone pole. The trunk may even be slightly constricted. Girdling roots usually develop when a containerized tree is planted or transplanted. If the roots that normally circle the inside of a container are not trimmed, they may eventually girdle the tree. Girdling roots occasionally develop spontaneously in field-grown or wild trees also. The trunk is weakened if it is severely constricted, and may break in a high wind.

SOLUTION: Remove the part of the root that is girdling the trunk. If the girdling root is large (more than a quarter of the diameter of the trunk), prune the tree to compensate for the roots that were lost. If the trunk is severely constricted, guy or stake the tree for a few years to prevent breakage at the narrow point.

PROBLEM: Leaves are small and discolored, and often drop prematurely. Eventually twigs and then larger branches die. The plant is stunted and in a general state of decline. A large patch of bark is damaged, or a wire circles the trunk and is deeply imbedded in it.

ANALYSIS: Injury to trunk
Anything that slows the flow of water and nutrients through the trunk harms the tree. Since the nutrient and water circulation system of the tree is immediately under the bark, damage to the bark usually interrupts circulation between the tree and its roots. Damage most commonly occurs from a large wound on the trunk. If the wound covers over half the circumference of the trunk, it is major damage and threatens the life of the tree. Wires or cables wrapped around the trunk grow tighter as the trunk expands, cutting into the wood and slowly reducing circulation.

SOLUTION: Remove loose discolored bark splinters and wood from the wound according to the directions given on page 911. Remove any girdling wires and dead or dying branches. Fertilize and water well according to the directions on pages 904 and 906. Do not wrap bare wires around trees. Use 3 to 4-inch-wide nylon strapping around the trunk with wire connected through grommets in the ends of the strap.

PROBLEM: Leaves are small and discolored, and often drop prematurely. Eventually twigs and larger branches die. The plant is stunted and in a general state of decline. There are many small holes in the bark. Sap, pitch, or sawdust may be coming out of the holes.

ANALYSIS: Bark beetles
Bark beetles may seriously damage older, mature conifers growing in the home garden. They usually infest only weakened trees, but trees under stress from drought and healthy trees growing near stressed trees may also be attacked. In the spring, adults fly in search of weak or susceptible trees. When suitable trees are located, the beetles tunnel through the bark, making egg-laying galleries between the bark and the wood. They produce a chemical substance (pheromone) that attracts more beetles; the beetles mate and lay eggs in the galleries. The whitish larvae form tunnels that radiate from the egg gallery and cut off the flow of nutrients and water through the trunk. The larvae mature and may emerge that season to produce a new generation of beetles. Some beetles also transmit diseases.

SOLUTION: Cut down dead trees and those trees in which 50 percent of the foliage is yellowing. Do not leave infested wood in the area. Burn the wood immediately, or strip off and burn the bark before storing the stripped wood. Spray less severely infested trees with ORTHO Lindane Borer & Leaf Miner Spray. Make sure your tree is listed on the product label. Repeat the spray one month later. Water trees during periods of drought and fertilize weakened trees with ORTHO Evergreen, Tree & Shrub Food 12–6–6.

Damage to maple roots.

Root nematode damage.

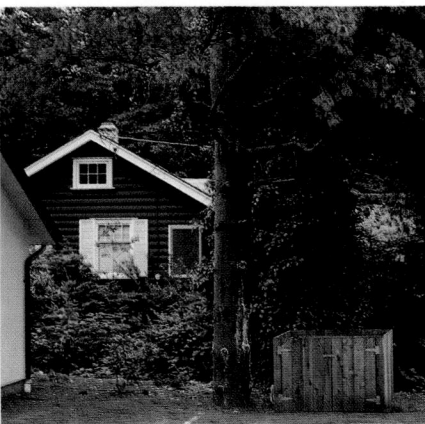

Paving over roots.

PROBLEM: Leaves turn yellow and then brown. Branches die. The tree declines, usually over a period of several years, and may die. Trenching or construction has occurred under the tree within the past two years.

ANALYSIS: Mechanical injuries to roots
Roots may be severed during excavation for building, trenching for cables and pipes, when soil is tilled, or when there is any other type of activity around a tree that disturbs its roots. Root injuries may be difficult to detect or diagnose. Check the area for overturned soil, patched lawn, or fresh patches of asphalt. If the tree is growing very near a recent construction site and is showing decline symptoms, it is likely that its roots were damaged and then covered with soil. Excavate the soil around the declining tree with a hand trowel to determine if the roots are injured, and the extent of the injury.

SOLUTION: Remove the tree if it is in a severe state of decline. If it is only mildly affected, thin out the branches so the top of the tree is in proportion to the remaining roots. (If 20 percent of the roots are damaged, prune off 20 percent of the branches.) If the roots are uncovered, refill the hole as soon as possible. Water during dry periods. In the future, avoid excavating or trenching around plants. If it is unavoidable, cut as few roots as possible. Dig the trench or hole as far away from the trunk as possible. If the trench must pass near the tree, fewer roots will be damaged if you tunnel under the tree rather than trench next to it.

PROBLEM: Leaves are small and discolored, and often drop prematurely. Eventually twigs and then larger branches die. The plant is stunted and in a general state of decline.

ANALYSIS: Root nematodes
Root nematodes are microscopic worms that live in the soil. They feed on plant roots, damaging and stunting them, or causing them to become enlarged. The damaged roots can't supply sufficient water and nutrients to the aboveground plant parts, and the plant is stunted or slowly dies. Nematodes are found throughout the United States, especially in areas with moist, sandy loam soils. They can move only a few inches each year on their own, but they may be carried long distances by soil, water, tools, or infested plants. Laboratory testing of roots and soil is the only positive method for confirming the presence of nematodes. Contact your local Cooperative Extension Office (see page 1011) for sampling instructions and addresses of testing laboratories. Soil and root problems such as poor soil structure, drought stress, overwatering, nutrient deficiency, and root rots can also produce symptoms of decline similar to those caused by nematodes. These problems should be eliminated as causes before sending soil and root samples for testing.

SOLUTION: There are no chemicals available to homeowners to kill nematodes in planted soil. However, they can be controlled before planting by soil fumigation. For information on fumigating soil, see page 919.

PROBLEM: Leaves turn yellow and then brown. Branches die back. The tree declines, usually over a period of several years, and may die. A large part of the soil under the tree has been recently paved.

ANALYSIS: Paving over roots
Impervious soil coverings, such as cement and asphalt, placed over the roots of an established tree may kill the tree. The greater the coverage of roots, the more likely it is that the tree will die. The supply of water and air to the roots is blocked, stopping their growth and eventually killing them. Some species of trees are more resistant than others, and young trees are more resistant than established trees. In areas where the water table is high, some trees may survive. Soil sterilants, often used by paving companies to kill weeds, will increase the probability of the tree dying.

SOLUTION: Remove the tree if it is in a severe state of decline. If the tree shows only mild symptoms and it is a valuable specimen, it may be saved by removing the pavement. Before laying pavement in the future, protect trees by installing a system of tile pipes in gravel, which allows for the passage of water and air. If it is necessary to kill weeds, use a weed killer rather than a soil sterilant.

Some trees that can tolerate paving over their roots are: *Ailanthus altissima* (tree of heaven), *Ficus retusa* (laurel fig), *Fraxinus* species (ash), *Morus* species (mulberry), and *Ulmus parvifolia* (Chinese elm).

PROBLEMS COMMON TO MANY TREES, SHRUBS, AND VINES — WEAK OR DYING PLANT

Balled roots.

Tree death caused by grade change.

Tree decline due to construction and grade change.

PROBLEM: Leaves are small and discolored, and often drop prematurely. Eventually twigs and then larger branches die. The plant is stunted and in a general state of decline. The plant is not firmly rooted, but may be rocked back and forth in the soil or pulled out easily.

ANALYSIS: Balled roots
Balled roots develop when the roots remain in the original soil ball instead of growing into the surrounding soil. This occurs when the planting hole is improperly prepared or when pot-bound plants are set in the ground without having their roots trimmed. Container plants are usually grown in a light soil mix. If they are placed in soil that is heavy, poorly aerated, or soggy, the roots may not grow into it. Instead, the roots twine around the original soil until they form a hard, tangled mass and can no longer supply adequate moisture. Container plants that sit in a nursery for a long time before they are sold become pot-bound. If roots are not trimmed, they will continue to grow in the original soil ball rather than growing out into the soil of the planting site. A plant with balled roots will become stunted and decline. It may blow over in a storm.

SOLUTION: If the planting hole was improperly prepared, remove the plant and add soil amendments to lighten the surrounding soil. (For more information about preparing a planting hole, see page 916.) Before replanting, untangle and prune the balled roots so they will grow into the surrounding soil. When planting container plants, trim roots to encourage new growth out of the soil ball. Keep the plant well watered until it becomes established.

PROBLEM: Leaves turn yellow and may drop. Branches die. The tree declines, usually over a period of several years, and may die. The soil level under the tree was recently changed, either raised or lowered.

ANALYSIS: Grade change
Raising or lowering the level of the soil (the grade) around trees can be very damaging. If the grade has been raised, the tree emerges from the soil in a straight line (no flare at the base of the trunk). If the grade has been lowered, roots are exposed.

1. *Grade raised:* A large quantity of soil dumped around a tree usually suffocates the roots by cutting off their supply of air and water. The extent of damage depends on the kind of tree, its age and condition, the type and depth of fill, and how much of the root system is covered. Young, healthy trees are much more tolerant than old trees, and soil containing gravel or sand causes less severe injury than heavy clay soil. If only a portion of the root system is covered, or if the fill is relatively shallow (less than 3 inches of porous soil or less than 1 to 2 inches of clay soil), the tree will be weakened, but it does not usually die. Severe decline symptoms (progressive dieback from the top down) often do not occur for several years. Insects or diseases may kill the weakened plant sooner than it would have been killed otherwise.

2. *Grade lowered:* Many roots may be severed when soil is removed from around a tree, and exposed roots will dry out. The number and size of the roots severed determines the extent of damage. Cutting large roots close to the trunk is more likely to kill the tree than cutting the ends of roots. The plant is often unstable, and may blow down in a strong wind.

SOLUTION: Once the decline symptoms develop, considerable damage has already occurred.

1. By the time symptoms caused by raising the grade are noticed, it is usually too late to do anything. If possible, remove the fill if there are no symptoms and it has been around the tree for less than one growing season. If the tree is in a severe state of decline, remove it. If decline symptoms are not severe and fill is less than 12 inches deep, therapeutic treatments may save the tree. Remove all dead and dying branches and remove the soil from around the base of the trunk. Dig holes to the original soil level every few feet over the entire root area (under the branches) and place 6-inch bell tiles in the holes. In the future, valuable trees to be filled over should be protected by installing tile pipes in a thick bed of gravel covered with a minimum amount of fill. For a list of trees that are severely, moderately, or rarely damaged by fill, see page 999.

2. Remove the tree if it is in a severe state of decline caused by lowering the grade. Unstable trees should be cabled to a stable object or removed. For trees with symptoms, prune off damaged roots and torn bark. Cut back the top growth so it is in balance with the remaining roots (if 20 percent of the roots are damaged, cut off 20 percent of the branches). Water trees during dry periods.

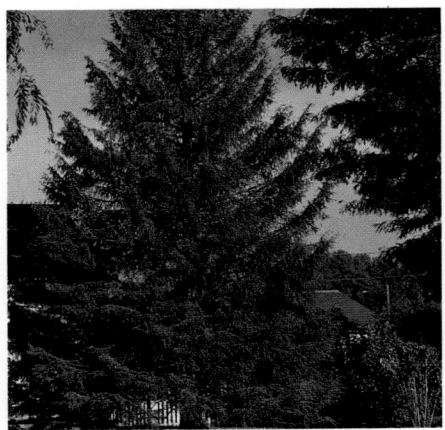

Spruce killed by gas leak.

Tree decline caused by poor drainage.

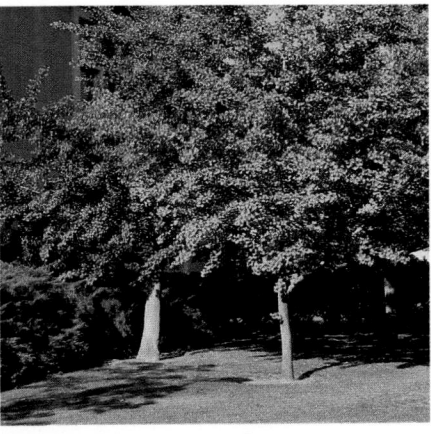

Stunted ginkgo growing in a lawn.

PROBLEM: The plant slowly or suddenly turns brown and dies. Lawn and flowers surrounding the plant usually die, and nearby trees and shrubs may turn yellow or slowly die. Soil removed from around the roots of the dying plant is very dark and smells like rotten eggs. An underground gas line runs within 100 feet of the plant.

ANALYSIS: Gas leak
Major leaks from underground natural gas pipes can cause severe injury or sudden death to nearby plants. Natural gas is not toxic to plants, but it forces the air out of the soil. Oxygen in the soil is necessary for plant growth. Methane-consuming bacteria use up any remaining oxygen. When oxygen is unavailable, roots die and the tree starves. In addition, other toxic compounds may be formed. A rotten egg smell may be noticed in the area, caused by bacteria that release sulfur compounds. Plants near the leak often die quickly, and plants further away decline slowly. Gas injury can also occur where plantings are made over or within several hundred feet of a landfill in which organic materials have been planted. The organic materials produce gas as they decompose. Sometimes utility companies will send manufactured gas (produced from coal or coke) through lines during peak loads when there is not enough natural gas. If there is a leak, manufactured gas will kill plants quickly.

SOLUTION: If you suspect a gas leak, contact your local utility company. Remove dead plants. The soil beneath the plant should be aerated to flush out the gas. Contact a professional arborist to aerate the soil.

PROBLEM: Leaves are small and discolored, and often drop prematurely. Eventually twigs and then larger branches die. The plant is stunted and in a general state of decline. The soil is constantly wet, either from frequent watering or because the soil drains slowly.

ANALYSIS: Overwatering
Many trees and shrubs do not grow well in soil that is constantly wet. This condition is most common around lawns, especially when the soil drains slowly. Lawns need much more water than do most trees and shrubs. When the soil is constantly wet, the roots cannot absorb the oxygen they need to function normally, they begin to decay, and the plant slowly declines. This problem is very common in areas of low rainfall when lawns are planted around established plants or native trees that cannot tolerate the increased soil moisture.

SOLUTION: Do not continually apply water so that the soil is constantly wet. Depending on the requirements of your tree or shrub (see cultural information for your specific plant), allow the soil to dry partially or fully between waterings. If possible, move the tree or shrub to a new location with better drainage. (For more information about transplanting, see page 916.) Replace it with a plant that tolerates poor drainage (for a list, see page 997), or improve the drainage (see page 901). If the plant cannot be moved, water it less frequently. Cover the area under the tree with a mulch, or with a groundcover that requires little water.

PROBLEM: The tree or shrub is growing very slowly. Leaves may turn yellow, and twigs may die. The plant is growing in a lawn.

ANALYSIS: Lawn competition
The growth of plants can be retarded by grass growing over their roots. A lawn requires large amounts of fertilizer. Lawns will deplete the soil of nutrients that are necessary for vigorous growth of a tree or large shrub planted in it.

SOLUTION: If lawn is growing around a recently planted tree, remove an area of lawn at least 30 inches in diameter from around the trunk (18 to 24 inches is adequate for shrubs). Fertilize with ORTHO Evergreen, Tree & Shrub Food 12–6–6 or ORTHO General Purpose Plant Food 8–8–8. This area can be mulched, or planted with flowers. As the plant grows, enlarge the cleared area. If you wish to keep a lawn under the tree or shrub, fertilize the plant as growth starts each spring with ORTHO Evergreen, Tree & Shrub Food 12–6–6, placed in holes 4 feet apart under the drip line (tips of outer branches). Make holes 2 feet deep with a crowbar or soil auger and pour in the fertilizer, using a total of 2 cups for each 1 inch diameter of tree trunk. For young trees — 1 to 2 inches in diameter — use 1 cup of fertilizer; use ½ cup for trees under 1 inch in diameter. For shrubs, apply ½ cup of plant food for each 3 feet of height. Water the plant well after fertilizing. Plant trees adapted to growing in a lawn; for a list, see page 997.

PROBLEMS COMMON TO MANY TREES, SHRUBS, AND VINES — TREE FALLS OVER

Root weevil damage to azalea.

Shallow roots.

Tree blown over by wind.

PROBLEM: Leaves are small and discolored, and often drop prematurely. Eventually twigs and then larger branches die. The plant is stunted and in a general state of decline. If soil is removed from around the base of the plant, exposing some roots, small rootlets or bark on the roots are seen to be chewed. White grubs may be found in the soil around the roots.

ANALYSIS: Root weevil larvae
Root weevil larvae, called *grubs*, infest the roots of many ornamental plants. The damage caused by the white, legless grubs is often so gradual that the insects are well established before injury is apparent. If the grubs remain undetected, the plant may die abruptly with the onset of hot, dry weather. Female weevils lay eggs at the soil line near the stem during the summer months. The emerging grubs burrow into the soil. They feed on the roots in the fall, and then spend the winter in the soil. Most root weevils cause their major damage in the spring. Their feeding girdles the roots and stems, disrupting the flow of nutrients and water through the plant and causing the roots and the top of the plant to die.

SOLUTION: Discard dying plants. To prevent the next generation of weevils from causing damage, eliminate the adults. Spray the foliage and the ground under the plant with ORTHO Orthene Systemic Insect Control or ORTHO Isotox Insect Killer. Contact your Cooperative Extension Office (see page 1011) for the time of weevil emergence in your area. Before spraying, make sure that your plant is listed on the product label. Repeat the spray 2 more times 3 weeks apart.

PROBLEM: The entire plant falls over with part or all of the roots attached.

ANALYSIS: Tree falls over
Anything that drastically affects the size or strength of the roots may decrease the stability of the tree.

1. *Root rot:* A number of different soil fungi and bacteria cause the roots to rot. When the roots decay, they lose their ability to support the plant. The plant may fall when the foliage still appears healthy, or it may turn brown first. Only a few of the roots may be attached when the plant falls.

2. *Severed roots:* Roots may be severed during construction where trenching and earthmoving equipment is used. The number and size of the roots severed determines the probability of the plant falling.

3. *Wet soil:* Plants growing in excessively wet soil may fall, especially after a long period of rain, when the soil is saturated and no longer gives good support. A leaning tree, or one pushed by strong winds, can pull loose. Plants with shallow root systems are most susceptible.

4. *Shallow roots:* Plants with a shallow root system may fall during strong winds. Those growing in compacted, shallow, or soggy soil, or where surface watering has been practiced, generally have shallow root systems.

5. *Undeveloped root system:* Young plants, or plants with girdled or balled roots, have root systems that may not support the rest of the plant. During a storm with high winds, the plant may blow over. The attached roots appear bunched or twisted.

SOLUTION: If the plant is only leaning slightly, saturate the soil and force the plant upright. Stake or wire it in place.

1. Once the plant has fallen, nothing can be done. In the future, avoid wounding roots, a common entrance point for root rot organisms. Do not overwater plants (see page 906), and keep them in a vigorous growing condition. For more information about root rots, see page 857.

2. Avoid severing roots during construction activities, especially large supporting roots. If damaging many of the roots is unavoidable, either remove the plant or brace it. For more information about bracing, see page 910.

3. Do not keep the soil constantly wet. If you live in an area that receives heavy rains, cable or brace the plant (see page 910), or provide additional drainage, such as tile drains. For more information about improving soil drainage, see page 901.

4. For ways to encourage deeper root systems, see page 460.

5. Stake young trees (see page 911). Prevent girdled and balled roots by using proper planting techniques (see page 916). For more information about girdled and balled roots and their remedies, see page 468.

Broken trunk.

Internal decay.

PROBLEM: The plant bends over or the trunk breaks at or above the soil line.

ANALYSIS: Broken trunk
Plants may break and fall over because of any of several conditions.

SOLUTION: The numbered solutions below correspond to the numbers in the analysis.

1. *Internal decay:* This condition is caused by fungi that enter the tree through wounds. Healthy and vigorous trees may stop the spread of decay by walling off the invaded area. Old trees with many wounds often have little resistance against microorganisms, and decay spreads through the wood. There is usually enough healthy tissue left to keep the branches and leaves alive. But when a storm occurs, or sometimes on a calm day, the entire tree may crack in the decayed area and fall over. This condition can also develop on single branches.

1. If only part of the plant has fallen, inspect the rest of it to determine the extent of decay. It may be necessary to contact a professional arborist. The entire plant should be removed if decay is extensive. Avoid wounding plants, and keep them in a vigorous growing condition by fertilizing and watering regularly. (For more information about fertilizers and watering, see pages 904 and 906.)

2. *Cankers and canker rots: Cankers* are localized dead areas on the bark and wood that begin at a wound. They are caused by disease, mechanical injury, or sunscald, or develop where branches have been cut off. (For more information about cankers, see page 456.) Microorganisms inhibit the normal healing process, preventing wounds from closing. The tissue appears sunken, and is often surrounded by callus tissue, a barklike growth of cells. These cankered areas lose the normal flexibility of wood. When a strong wind occurs, the plant cracks at the canker and falls. *Canker rots* develop when microorganisms attack healthy wood adjacent to and beneath a canker. Tree trunks or branches with this condition are more likely to fall because both the canker and wood decay are weakening the tree.

2. Once the plant has fallen, there is nothing that can be done. In the future, avoid wounding plants. If you notice a large canker on the trunk, check to see if it is surrounded by callus tissue. If it is, the wound is healing properly and is less likely to become a canker rot. If little or no callus tissue surrounds the canker, and the canker appears sunken, decay may be starting. Consult a professional arborist to determine the possibility of the plant falling. To encourage wound healing, fertilize and water the plant regularly.

ABIES

ADAPTATION: Zones 4 through 7. (To determine your zone, see the map on page 1004.) Not adapted to hot, dry areas.

LIGHT: Full sun.

SOIL: Grows best in well-drained, non-alkaline (below pH 7.0) soils.

FERTILIZER: Fertilize with ORTHO Evergreen, Tree & Shrub Food 12–6–6 according to label directions.

WATER:
How much: Apply enough water to wet the soil 3 to 4 feet deep. To determine the proper amount of water for your soil type, see page 906.
How often: Firs grow best in moist soils. Water when the soil is moist but not wet 4 inches below the surface. For more information about watering, see page 906.

PRUNING: Plant firs in open areas where they have room to spread. Do not prune off branches unless necessary. New side growth can be sheared to develop a dense, bushy tree. New growth will not usually develop on the lower trunk if a limb is removed. To avoid altering the pyramidal growth of the tree, do not prune off the top.

Spruce budworm (twice life size).

PROBLEM: Needles on the ends of branches are chewed and webbed together. In mid-July the branch ends often turn reddish brown. Branches or the entire tree may die after 3 to 5 years of defoliation. Reddish brown caterpillars, 1¼ inches long, with yellow or white raised spots, are feeding on the needles.

ANALYSIS: Spruce budworms
(*Choristoneura* species)
Spruce budworms are very destructive to ornamental spruce, fir, and Douglas fir, and may infest pine, larch, and hemlock. The budworm is cyclical. It comes and goes in epidemics 10 or more years apart. The moths are small (½ inch long) and grayish, with bands and spots of brown. The females lay pale green eggs in clusters on the needles in late July and August. The larvae that hatch from these eggs crawl to hiding places in the bark or in lichen mats; or they are blown by the wind to other trees, where they hide. The tiny larvae spin a silken case and hibernate until spring. In May, when the weather warms, the caterpillars tunnel into needles. As they grow, they feed on opening buds; later they chew off needles and web them together. The larvae feed for about 5 weeks, pupate on twigs, and emerge as adults.

SOLUTION: Spray with an insecticide containing *malathion* or the bacterial insecticide *Bacillus thuringiensis* when the buds begin to grow in late May. If the trees are sprayed too early, the larvae are protected inside the needles and will not be killed.

Balsam twig aphid damage.

PROBLEM: The youngest needles are curled and twisted, with their lighter underside turned upward. Some needles are killed. Young twigs are twisted and bark is roughened. Shoots may become saturated with a shiny, sticky secretion called honeydew so that needles adhere to one another. A black sooty mold may grow on the honeydew. Tiny (⅛ inch) waxy bluish gray adult or pale green immature, soft-bodied insects cluster on the shoots.

ANALYSIS: Balsam twig aphid
(*Mindarus abietinus*)
The twig aphid does little damage in small numbers. However, aphids are extremely prolific and populations can rapidly build up to damaging numbers during the growing season. Damage occurs when the aphid sucks the juices from the fir shoots. The aphid is unable to digest fully all the sugar in the sap and excretes the excess in a fluid called honeydew. The honeydew often drops onto the shoots or other plants below. A sooty mold fungus may develop on the honeydew, causing the fir leaves to appear black and dirty. Late in the summer, females lay several large (¹⁄₁₀ inch) eggs, covered with tiny rods of white wax, in bark crevices. The eggs are conspicuous and are a useful index of the amount of injury that may occur during the next year.

SOLUTION: Control with ORTHO Orthene Systemic Insect Control or ORTHO Malathion 50 Insect Spray in late April or early May to kill aphids when they first appear. Repeat spray in mid-May if the tree becomes reinfested.

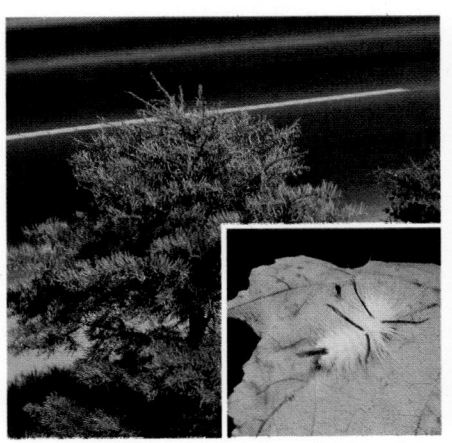

Tussock moth damage. *Insert:* Larva (¼ life size).

Balsam woolly aphid damage.

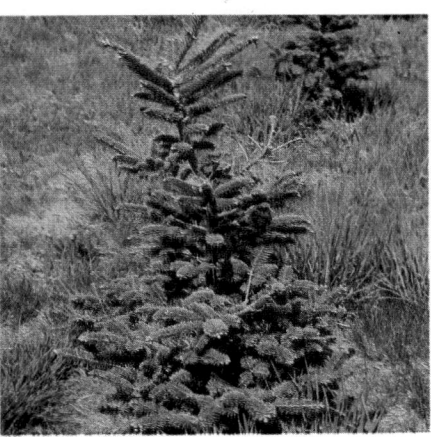

Spider mite damage.

PROBLEM: Much of the foliage is eaten, starting at the top of the tree and progressing downward. The entire tree may be defoliated in one season. Trees that lose most of their needles a second year are usually killed. Inch-long, hairy, gray or light brown caterpillars with tufts of orange hairs on their backs may be feeding on the needles. When populations are high, many tan-colored pellets drop from the tree and litter the ground.

ANALYSIS: Douglas fir tussock moth (*Orgyia pseudotsugata*)
Douglas fir tussock moth populations are cyclical. Every 7 to 10 years, forest populations build up to epidemic proportions. When this occurs, true firs, Douglas fir, spruce, pine, and larch may be completely defoliated. In cities, damaging numbers may be found every year. In mid to late summer the hairy, wingless female moths lay their eggs in a frothy substance covered with a layer of hair-like scales. When the eggs hatch the following spring, the caterpillars begin feeding on the new needles at the top of the tree. As the younger foliage is devoured the caterpillars move downward, feeding on older needles. Large numbers of tan excrement pellets accumulate around the base of the tree. Since conifers do not replace their old needles, defoliated trees are often killed after two seasons. Less severely damaged trees may be killed later by bark beetles. In August, the caterpillars pupate to emerge as adults.

SOLUTION: Spray with an insecticide containing *acephate*, *carbaryl*, or the bacteria *Bacillus thuringiensis* when caterpillars or damage are first noticed in May or early June. Repeat the spray 2 weeks later if damage continues.

PROBLEM: The ends of twigs swell, forming knobs. The trunk, limbs, and needles may be covered by white, woolly masses or a dirty white crust. Young needles gradually turn yellow from the tip down and drop off. No new growth is evident. More susceptible species, such as balsam fir or subalpine fir, may be killed before swelling on terminal growth occurs.

ANALYSIS: Balsam woolly aphid (*Adelges piceae*)
This small, soft-bodied insect is a pest only of true firs. The adult is covered by dense, white, woolly material. When this substance is removed, the minute wingless insect appears purplish to black. The adult lays eggs on the bark of fir trees in early spring. These eggs hatch into tiny spiderlike "crawlers" that are blown long distances by the wind. Once the aphid has found a suitable tree it sucks the juices from the needles. A growth-promoting substance is injected into the tree at the same time, causing the swelling of the branch tips. The wood becomes reddish and brittle. As the insect matures it becomes immobile, the legs atrophy, and it secretes white filaments of wax that eventually cover its body.

SOLUTION: Spray with ORTHO Orthene Systemic Insect Control or ORTHO Malathion 50 Insect Spray when woolly tufts first appear in early spring. The insects will be killed but the woolly material will remain on the tree. Thorough coverage is necessary to achieve adequate control. To penetrate the waxy filaments, high-pressure equipment should be used. A fall spray may help control overwintering insects on the tree.

PROBLEM: The needles are stippled yellow and dirty. Sometimes there is a silken webbing on the shoots. Needles may turn brown and fall off. Hot, dry weather favors this problem. To determine if the tree is infested with mites, hold a sheet of white paper underneath some stippled needles and tap the foliage sharply. Tiny dark green or black specks about the size of a pepper grain will drop to the paper and begin to crawl around. The pests are easily seen against the white background.

ANALYSIS: Spruce spider mite (*Oligonychus ununguis*)
The spruce spider mite is one of the most important pests of firs and many other conifers. It sucks sap from the underside of the needles, causing the stippled appearance. This symptom can be confused with certain types of air pollution damage (see page 862). Spider mites first appear in April or May, hatching from eggs laid at the base of fir needles the previous October. A complete generation may be produced in only 17 days, so mites can rapidly build up to tremendous numbers during the growing season. Young fir trees may die the first season. If mites are left uncontrolled over a period of years, older trees die progressively from the lower branches upward.

SOLUTION: Control with ORTHO Orthene Insect Spray, ORTHO Isotox Insect Killer, or ORTHO Malathion 50 Insect Spray in early spring to kill young mites of the first generation. Spraying must be repeated 3 more times, 7 to 10 days apart, to kill young mites as they hatch from eggs. Additional sprays may be needed in early fall if the tree becomes reinfested.

ACACIA

Thornbugs (half life size).

PROBLEM: Groups of ½-inch greenish sucking insects with red or brown markings and sharp spines on their backs are feeding on the tree. Small twigs and branches turn yellow and die.

ANALYSIS: Thornbug
(*Umbonia crassicornis*)
Thornbugs feed by sucking sap from the branches of several types of trees and shrubs, but seem to prefer earleaf acacia (*Acacia auriculiformis*). Large numbers of thornbugs of all sizes may often be found feeding together. Adults are strong fliers, and can travel long distances to find host plants. When large numbers of thornbugs are present, many small branches may be killed. Several generations of thornbugs are produced in a year. The greatest numbers occur during the winter and spring.

SOLUTION: Spray infested trees with an insecticide containing *diazinon* as soon as thornbugs are discovered. Repeat the treatment if the tree becomes reinfested.

Acacia cultural information
Light: Full sun
Water: Drought tolerant once established
Soil: Tolerates many types of soil
Fertilizer: Medium

Mushroom root rot.

PROBLEM: Leaves turn light green, then yellow, and finally brown, and then fall off. Sometimes only one portion of the tree may be affected, but gradually the entire tree dies. Clusters of tan mushrooms may be seen at the base of infected trees. When the tree bark is cut open near the soil line, a white layer of fungal growth can be seen just beneath the outer bark on the surface of the wood.

ANALYSIS: Mushroom root rot
Mushroom root rot affects certain species of acacia, including the earleaf acacia (*Acacia auriculiformis*) and the Sydney acacia (*A. floribunda*). This disease is caused by either of two closely related soil-dwelling fungi (*Clitocybe tabescens* and *Armillaria mellea*). *Armillaria* occurs throughout the United States, but is most severe in the West. *Clitocybe* occurs mainly in the Southeast. The fungi invade the root system, and slowly spread through the tree roots. When they enter the main stem, they girdle the stem and kill the tree. Death can occur in a few weeks in small trees, or may take months in large trees.

SOLUTION: There is no practical cure for this disease. By the time symptoms appear, the fungus is too far advanced to stop. In areas where diseased trees have been growing, use only plants that are resistant to mushroom root rot. (For a list of plants resistant to *armillaria*, see page 1001.) The fungi can be eradicated from the soil by fumigation techniques. For information, see page 919.

Some acacias resistant to *armillaria* are *Acacia longifolia*, *A. mearnsii*, and *A. verticillata*.

ACER (MAPLE, BOX ELDER)

ACER

ADAPTATION: Throughout the United States.

LIGHT: Full sun to part shade.

SOIL AND PLANTING: Any good, deep, well-drained garden soil. When choosing a planting site, pick an area that will handle the ultimate spread and height of the tree.

FERTILIZER: Fertilize with ORTHO Evergreen, Tree & Shrub Food 12–6–6 according to label directions.

WATER:
How much: Apply enough water to wet the soil 3 to 4 feet deep. To determine the proper amount of water for your soil type, see page 906.
How often: Maples prefer moist soil. Water when the soil is moist but no longer wet 4 inches below the surface. For more information about watering, see page 906.

Boxelder bugs (3 times life size).

Aphids on maple leaves.

Borer droppings.

PROBLEM: New leaves are discolored and distorted. Flowers, seeds, and tender new shoots may also be affected. Small (½ inch) bright red bugs with dark heads may be found on the leaves throughout the summer. Black bugs with reddish lines on their backs may be seen in large numbers around buildings or in homes.

ANALYSIS: Boxelder bugs
(*Leptocoris* species)
Two species of plant bugs feed on boxelder trees, especially the female (seed-bearing) trees. They may also feed on other trees and plants around the home. The red, immature boxelder bugs suck sap from leaves and other plant parts, but they are rarely harmful to the tree. Boxelder bugs are mainly a problem because the black adults are a nuisance around homes. (For more information on boxelder bugs as household pests, see page 803.) Large numbers of adults hibernate inside homes or in the walls of buildings. In the spring, they fly to boxelder trees and lay their eggs in crevices in the bark. The larvae that hatch from these eggs feed until fall, mature, and then migrate back to buildings to spend the winter. In warmer areas of the country there may be two generations of bugs a year.

SOLUTION: Spray infested trees with ORTHO Malathion 50 Insect Spray during the summer when insects are first noticed. Wet the tree thoroughly. This will reduce the number of migrating bugs in the fall, although it may not completely eliminate bugs around the home since they can migrate from plants not in the immediate area. Repeat the spray if the tree becomes reinfested.

PROBLEM: The newest leaves are wrinkled, discolored, and reduced in size. Leaves may drop off. Silver and Norway maples may be nearly defoliated. A shiny, sticky substance may coat the leaves. A black sooty mold often grows on the sticky substance. Tiny (⅛ inch) green and black, or reddish, soft-bodied insects cluster on the undersides of leaves. Ants may be present.

ANALYSIS: Aphids
(*Periphyllus* and *Drepanaphis* species) Aphids do little damage in small numbers. However, they are extremely prolific and populations can rapidly build up to damaging numbers during the growing season. Damage occurs when the aphid sucks the juices from the maple leaves. The aphid is unable to fully digest all the sugar in the plant sap and excretes the excess in a fluid called honeydew, which often drops onto the leaves below. Plants or objects beneath the tree may also be coated with honeydew. A sooty mold fungus may develop on the honeydew, causing the maple leaves to appear black and dirty; or rain may wash the honeydew off before the fungus has a chance to grow. Ants feed on this sticky substance, and are often present where there is an aphid infestation.

SOLUTION: Control with ORTHO Orthene Systemic Insect Control or ORTHO Diazinon Insect Spray or ORTHO Isotox Insect Spray when aphids first appear. Direct the spray to the undersides of the leaves. Repeat the spray if the tree becomes reinfested.

PROBLEM: The foliage is sparse on a branch or at the top of the tree; eventually the twigs and branches die back. Holes or tunnels are apparent in the trunk or branches. The bark may die over the tunnels and slough off, revealing trails. Sap or sawdust sometimes surrounds the holes. Weakened branches may break during wind or snow storms. Weak, young, or newly transplanted trees are most susceptible to injury, and may be killed.

ANALYSIS: Borers
Borers are the larvae of beetles or moths. Many kinds of borers attack maples. Throughout the summer, females lay eggs in bark crevices. The larvae feed by burrowing into the tree and tunneling through the bark, sapwood, or heartwood. This stops the flow of nutrients and water in that area by cutting the conducting vessels; branch and twig dieback result. Sap flow acts as a defense against borers. When the borer burrows into the wood, tree sap fills the hole and drowns the insect. Young or weakened trees are attractive to borers and may not produce enough sap to drown all the borers that invade them.

SOLUTION: Borers are difficult to control once they have burrowed into the wood. Cut out and destroy all dead and dying branches. Young trees that are severely infested should be removed. In spring, spray or paint the trunk and branches with ORTHO Lindane Borer & Leaf Miner Spray to kill young larvae before they burrow into the wood. Repeat 2 more times at intervals of 2 weeks. Maintain plant health and vigor by watering and fertilizing regularly.

ACER (MAPLE, BOX ELDER)

Cottony maple scale (¼ life size).

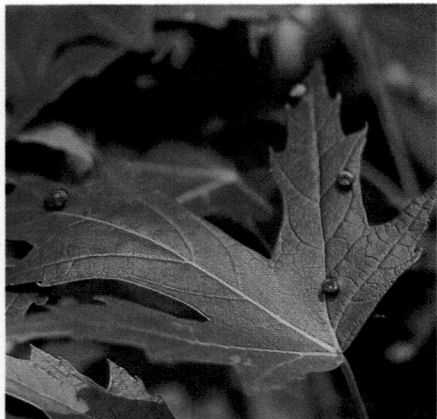

Galls caused by bladder gall mites.

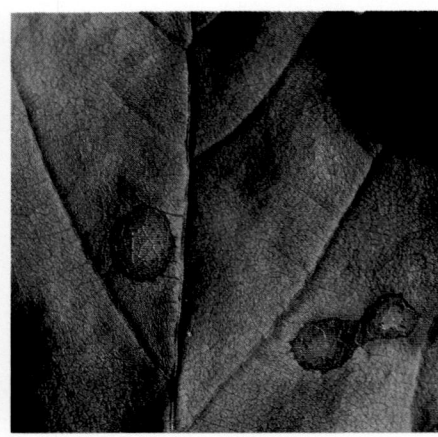

Phyllosticta leaf spot.

PROBLEM: The undersides of leaves, stems, or branch crotches are covered with white, cottony, cushionlike masses. Leaves turn yellow and may drop prematurely. Sometimes there is a shiny or sticky substance coating the leaves. A black sooty mold often grows on the sticky substance. Numerous side shoots sometimes grow out of an infested crotch area. Twigs and branches may die back.

ANALYSIS: Cottony scales and mealybugs
Cottony scales and mealybugs are common on maples throughout the United States. The similarities in appearance of these insects make separate identification difficult. They are very conspicuous in late spring and summer because the females are covered with a white, cottony egg sac, containing up to 2500 eggs. The young insects that hatch from these eggs are yellowish brown to green. They feed throughout the summer on the stems and undersides of the leaves. Damage is caused by the withdrawal of plant sap from leaves and branches. The insects are unable to digest fully all the sugar in the sap and they excrete the excess in a fluid called honeydew. The honeydew often drops onto leaves or plants below. A sooty mold fungus may develop in the honeydew, causing the maple leaves and other plants to appear black and dirty. If the insects are not controlled, heavily infested branches may die after several seasons.

SOLUTION: Apply ORTHO Diazinon Insect Spray in midsummer when the young are active. The following spring, when trees are dormant, spray with *lime sulfur* to control insects on the bark.

PROBLEM: In early spring, maple leaf tissue develops irregular, spherical, or bladderlike growths, known as galls, on the upper surfaces of the leaves. Leaves next to the trunk and on large branches are most affected. The galls are yellowish green at first but later turn pinkish to red and finally black. If the galls are numerous, leaves become deformed, and some turn yellow and drop prematurely.

ANALYSIS: Bladder gall mite and spindle gall mite
(*Vasates quadripedes* and *Vasates aceris-crumena*)
Bladder and spindle gall are caused by tiny mites, too small to be seen with the naked eye. Each gall contains one mite. The mites congregate on buds just before they open in the spring. As the buds open, each mite punctures and enters a leaf on the underside, injecting a growth-promoting substance that causes abnormal tissue formation. A gall encloses the mite, with an opening remaining on the underside. The mites feed and females lay eggs inside their galls. The eggs hatch, and as they mature, the young mites crawl out through the opening and infest new leaves. In July, mite activity stops and they migrate to the bark to spend the winter.

SOLUTION: Control measures are not necessary because galls generally cause no serious injury. However, if you wish to prevent unsightly leaves next year, spray buds, branches, and trunk with a *dormant oil spray* or an insecticide containing *dicofol* before the buds start to open in spring.

PROBLEM: Spots and blotches appear on the leaves. The spots may be yellow, red, tan, gray, or brown. They range in size from being barely visible to ¾ inch in diameter. Several spots may join to form blotches. Leaves may be yellow and dying. Some leaves may drop. Leaf spotting is most severe in warm, humid weather.

ANALYSIS: Fungal leaf spot
There are many different fungi that cause leaf spots. These spots are unsightly but rarely harmful to the tree. The fungi are spread by wind and splashing water. Spots develop where the fungi enter the tissue. If wet or humid weather persists, the fungi is spread through the tissue and blotches form. The fungi survive the winter on twigs and fallen leaves. Most leaf spot organisms do their greatest damage in mild weather (between 50° and 85°F).

SOLUTION: Fungal leaf spots on maples are usually not harmful and do not require control measures. To protect valued specimens, spray with a fungicide containing *zineb* or *mancozeb*. Repeat 3 more times at intervals of 2 weeks. To thoroughly cover leaves on tall branches, use high-pressure equipment. To reduce recurrence next year, rake up and destroy the leaves in the fall.

Leaf scorch.

Anthracnose on Norway maple.

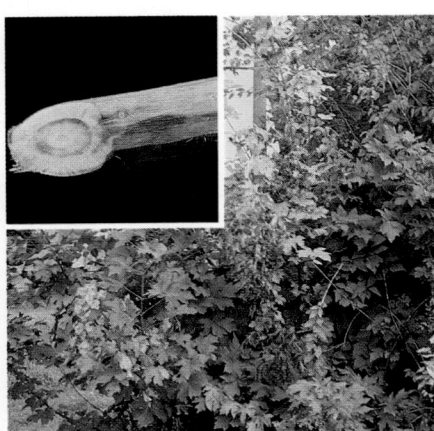

Verticillium wilt. *Insert:* Infected stem.

PROBLEM: During hot weather, usually in July or August, leaves turn brown on the edges between the veins. Sometimes the whole leaf dies. Many leaves may drop during late summer. This problem is most severe on the youngest branches. Trees do not generally die.

ANALYSIS: Summer leaf scorch
Leaf scorch is caused by excessive loss of moisture from the leaves due to evaporation. In hot weather, water evaporates rapidly from the leaves. If the roots can't absorb and convey water fast enough to replenish this loss, then the leaves turn brown and wither. This usually occurs in dry soil, but leaves can also scorch when the soil is moist. Drying winds, severed roots, limited soil area, or low temperatures can also cause scorch. For more information about scorch, see page 865.

SOLUTION: To prevent further scorch, deep-water trees during periods of hot weather to wet down the entire root space. (For more information about watering trees, see page 906.) Newly transplanted trees should be watered whenever the rootball is dry 1 inch below the surface. There are no controls for scorch occurring on trees in moist soil. Plant trees adapted to your climate.

PROBLEM: Irregular, light brown spots of dead tissue appear on the leaf from late May to August. They develop during or just following wet, humid weather. Many spots occur along the veins. They may enlarge and run together, causing the death of the entire leaf. Leaves partially killed appear as if sunscorched. This disease is distinguished from sunscorch by the presence of dark dots (spore-producing structures) barely visible on the underside of the leaf. The spore-producing structures develop while the leaves are still on the tree. Sunken reddish oval areas often develop on the infected twigs.

ANALYSIS: Maple anthracnose
This plant disease is caused by a fungus (*Gloeosporium apocryptum*) that spends the winter on fallen leaves or in sunken cankers on twigs in the tree. During rainy weather, spores are blown and splashed onto young leaves. Dead spots develop on the leaf where the fungus enters the tissue. The spots expand and the fungus can kill the leaf in rainy seasons, causing defoliation. The tree will grow new leaves if defoliation takes place in spring or early summer. When the tree is severely affected for successive years, the fungus will enter and kill branches.

SOLUTION: Trees affected by this disease for a single year do not require a chemical control. Rake and burn old leaves and prune out dead twigs below the canker on the bark. This reduces the amount of disease next year. If the following spring is wet and humid, spray valuable specimens with a fungicide containing *zineb* or *maneb* when the leaves uncurl. Repeat the treatment 2 more times at 14 day intervals.

PROBLEM: The leaves on a branch turn yellow at the margins, then brown and dry. During hot weather, the leaves may wilt. New leaves may be stunted and yellowish. The infected tree may die slowly, branch by branch, over several seasons. Or the whole tree may wilt and die within a few months. Some trees may recover. The tissue under the bark on the dying side shows dark streaks which may be very apparent or barely visible when exposed. To examine for streaks, peel back the bark at the bottom of the dying branch.

ANALYSIS: Verticillium wilt
This wilt disease affects many ornamental trees and shrubs. It is caused by a soil-inhabiting fungus (*Verticillium* species) that persists indefinitely on plant debris or in the soil. The disease is spread by contaminated seeds, plants, soil, equipment, and ground water. The fungus enters the tree through the roots and spreads up into the branches through the water-conducting vessels in the trunk. The vessels become discolored and plugged. This plugging cuts off the flow of water and nutrients to the branches, causing the leaf discoloration and wilting.

SOLUTION: No chemical control is available. Fertilize and water the affected tree to stimulate vigorous growth. Remove all dead wood. Do not remove branches on which leaves have recently wilted. These branches may produce new leaves in 3 to 4 weeks or next spring. Remove dead trees. If replanting in the same area, plant trees and shrubs that are resistant to verticillium. For a list of resistant trees and shrubs, see page 995. For more information about verticillium wilt, see page 858.

AESCULUS (HORSE CHESTNUT, BUCKEYE)

Leaf blotch.

Summer leaf scorch.

PROBLEM: Reddish brown blotches with bright yellow margins appear on the leaf. Spots may be as small as ¼ inch, or may nearly cover the leaf. When the whole leaf is infected, it becomes dry and brittle; many leaves may drop from the tree. The first infection occurs in spring, but blotches may not appear until July. Blotching is most severe in very wet springs. This problem is sometimes confused with leaf scorch caused by hot summer weather. It can be distinguished from scorch by the black specks in the center of the blotch.

ANALYSIS: Leaf blotch
This plant disease is caused by a fungus (*Guignardia aesculi*). In the spring, spores that develop on dead leaves on the ground are blown and splashed by rain onto young leaves. Water-soaked blotches appear in early summer, but are not usually noticed until they turn brown. In midsummer, numerous pinpoint black spore-producing structures develop in the blotches.

SOLUTION: Leaf blotch cannot be controlled once infection has occurred. When the first leaves appear the following spring, if the season is wet and there is danger of infection, spray with a fungicide containing *zineb*, *mancozeb*, or *chlorothalonil*. Repeat 2 more times at intervals of 10 days. Rake up and destroy leaves in the fall.

Aesculus cultural information
Light: Full sun
Water: While soil is still moist
Soil: Tolerates many types of soil
Fertilizer: Light

PROBLEM: During hot weather, usually in July or August, leaves turn brown around the edges and between the veins. Sometimes the whole leaf dies. Many leaves may drop during late summer. This problem is most severe on the youngest branches. Trees do not generally die.

ANALYSIS: Summer leaf scorch
In hot weather, water evaporates rapidly from the leaves. If the roots can't absorb and convey water fast enough to replenish this loss, the leaves turn brown and wither. This usually occurs in dry soil, but leaves can also scorch when the soil is moist. Chestnut trees vary in their susceptibility; one may be very susceptible while the tree next to it may show no sign of scorch. Drying winds, severed roots, limited soil area, or low temperatures can also cause scorch. For more information about scorch, see page 865.

SOLUTION: To prevent further scorch, deep-water trees during periods of hot weather to wet down the entire root space. (For more information about watering trees, see page 906.) Newly transplanted trees should be watered whenever the rootball is dry 1 inch below the surface. There are no controls for scorch on trees in moist soil. Plant trees adapted to your climate.

The California buckeye (*Aesculus californica*) is summer-deciduous. Every spring, about May or June, its leaves begin to show scorch symptoms that progress until all the leaves have dropped off. This is normal and cannot be prevented.

AILANTHUS (TREE-OF-HEAVEN)

Verticillium wilt.

PROBLEM: The leaves on a branch turn yellow at the margins, then brown and dry. During hot weather, the leaves may wilt. New leaves may be stunted and yellowish. The infected tree may die slowly, branch by branch, over several seasons. Or the whole tree may wilt and die within a few months. Some trees may recover. The tissue under the bark on the dying side shows dark streaks when cut. To examine for streaks, peel back the bark at the bottom of the dying branch. The dark discoloration may be very apparent or barely visible in the area just underneath the bark.

ANALYSIS: Verticillium wilt
This wilt disease affects many ornamental trees and shrubs. It is caused by a soil-inhabiting fungus (*Verticillium* species) that persists indefinitely on plant debris or in the soil. The disease is spread by contaminated seeds, plants, soil, equipment, and ground water. The fungus enters the tree through the roots and spreads up into the branches through the water-conducting vessels in the trunk. The vessels become discolored and plugged. This plugging cuts off the flow of water and nutrients to the branches, causing the leaf discoloration and wilting.

SOLUTION: No chemical control is available. Fertilize and water the affected tree to stimulate vigorous growth. Prune off all dead wood. Remove dead trees. If replanting in the same area, plant trees or shrubs that are resistant to verticillium. For a list of resistant trees and shrubs, see page 995. For more information about verticillium, see page 858.

ALBIZIA (MIMOSA, SILK TREE)

Mimosa webworm damage.

PROBLEM: Small clumps of leaves tied together with silk threads are scattered over the tree. The upper surfaces of the leaves are skeletonized. The leaves turn brown and die, causing infested trees to appear as if scorched by fire. Small (up to 1 inch), pale gray or brown caterpillars with 5 white stripes feed inside the silken nests. Damage appears from June to August or September. Small trees may be completely defoliated in late summer. Trees are not killed, but repeated defoliations can seriously weaken them.

ANALYSIS: Mimosa webworm
(*Homadaula anisocentra*)
The mimosa webworm is the larval stage of a small moth that feeds only on mimosa and honey locust trees. The webworm passes the winter as a pupa in a white silken cocoon. The moth emerges in spring and lays eggs on leaf stems or on old silk from previous infestations. The eggs hatch and the larvae feed on the leaflets for several weeks, webbing the leaflets together for protection against predators and weather. In August a second generation of webworms appears. The larvae of this second generation are the most damaging because they are usually so numerous. In cooler areas of the country 2 generations occur each year between June and August. In warmer areas there is a third generation in September.

SOLUTION: Spray with ORTHO Orthene Systemic Insect Control when webbing first appears in early June. Repeat in August. Use high-pressure equipment to penetrate the webs and thoroughly cover the tree. In the fall, rake and destroy debris under infested trees, or turn over the soil and bury the leaves.

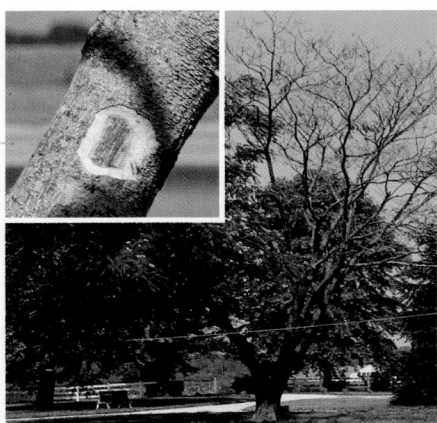
Crown dieback. *Insert:* Discoloration under bark.

PROBLEM: The leaves wilt, usually in the upper portion of the crown. The wilted leaves turn yellow, then brown, and finally die, although they may remain green or yellowish for weeks. Eventually the leaves drop, often leaving the leaf stalk attached, and the branch dies. The tree may die very rapidly, in only a few months after the first symptoms appear, or it may live for a year or two. The tissue under the bark on the wilting branch shows brownish streaks when cut. To examine for discoloration, peel back the bark at the bottom of the dying branch. The streaks are very apparent in the area just underneath the bark.

ANALYSIS: Mimosa wilt
Mimosa wilt is a highly destructive disease that attacks only the mimosa tree. It is caused by a soil-inhabiting fungus (*Fusarium oxysporum f. perniciosum*). The fungus enters the tree through wounded roots, then spreads up into the branches through the water-conducting vessels in the trunk. These vessels become discolored and plugged, cutting off water to the branches. This causes the leaves and branches to wilt and eventually die.

SOLUTION: No controls are available. Cut down and destroy dead and dying trees to prevent spreading of the fungus. Do not plant another mimosa where a tree has died of wilt disease.

Albizia cultural information
Light: Full sun
Water: Water while soil is still moist
Soil: Well drained, tolerates alkaline soil
Fertilizer: Light

ALNUS (ALDER)

Aphids (twice life size).

PROBLEM: Leaves may be discolored and reduced in size. A shiny or sticky substance usually coats the leaves. A black sooty mold may grow on the sticky substance. Tiny (⅛ inch), green, soft-bodied insects or gray insects coated with white, woolly, or waxy strands cluster on the undersides of the leaves or on the twigs.

ANALYSIS: Aphids
Several different types of aphids infest alder. Some are called *woolly aphids* because the waxy covering over their bodies looks like wool; others are green and have no woolly covering. Aphids do little damage in small numbers. However, they are extremely prolific and populations can rapidly build up to damaging numbers during the growing season. Damage occurs when the aphid sucks the juices from the alder leaves and twigs. The aphid is unable to digest fully all the sugar in the sap and excretes the excess in a fluid called honeydew, which often drops onto the leaves below. Plants or objects beneath the tree may also be coated with honeydew. A sooty mold fungus may develop on the sticky substance, causing the alder leaves to appear black and dirty.

SOLUTION: Spray with ORTHO Orthene Systemic Insect Control when aphids are noticed. Direct the spray to the branches and the undersides of the leaves. Repeat the spray if the tree becomes reinfested.

ALNUS (ALDER)

Alder flea beetles (life size).

PROBLEM: The leaf tissue is eaten between the veins. When infestations are severe, the tree may be completely defoliated. Small (⅛ inch) shiny blue to greenish blue beetles, with many fine punctures on their backs, may be seen on the tree or on the ground; or small (¼ inch) dark brown larvae with black heads may be found on the leaves.

ANALYSIS: Alder flea beetle
(*Altica ambiens*)
Alder flea beetles are not normally found in large numbers. However, they periodically build up to epidemic proportions and devour alder leaves. The shiny blue or greenish beetles spend the winter in protected places, such as in litter on the ground and under wood. In the spring, the females lay orange eggs on the leaves. The brown larvae that hatch from these eggs eat the leaves between the veins throughout July and August. When mature, the larvae drop to the ground and pupate. In warm climates, there may be a second generation of beetles.

SOLUTION: Spray the leaves with an insecticide containing *carbaryl* when damage is first noticed in the spring. Repeat the spray at intervals of 7 to 10 days if the tree becomes reinfested.

Alnus cultural information
Light: Full sun
Water: Grows best in moist soil
Soil: Tolerates many types
Fertilizer: Medium

ARAUCARIA (NORFOLK ISLAND PINE)

Needle blight.

PROBLEM: Needles at branch tips turn yellowish, then reddish brown, and die. Branch tips may also die, and the condition usually begins on the branch tips and progresses back toward the main trunk. The problem can occur at any level on the tree, but is more severe on the middle and lower portions.

ANALYSIS: Needle blight
This plant disease is caused by any of several fungi that invade needles and twigs. Trees are infected by airborne spores from nearby plants. Infection is favored by warm, moist conditions. Large areas of severely infected trees may be killed, and small trees may be completely killed by needle blight.

SOLUTION: Spray infected trees with a fungicide containing *manzate* or *benomyl*. Repeat treatments as needed according to label directions. Keep tree foliage as dry as possible to reduce the chance of infection.

Araucaria cultural information
Light: Full sun
Water: Drought-tolerant once established
Soil: Tolerates many types
Fertilizer: Light to medium

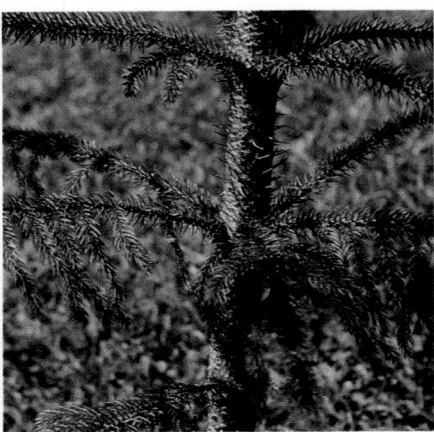

Spider mite damage.

PROBLEM: Needles turn light green, then yellow, and finally brown. Damage almost always appears on the inside of the tree next to the trunk and then spreads upward and outward along the branches. Lower portions of the tree are usually affected first, and damage is most severe during periods of hot, dry weather. To check for pests, hold a piece of white paper beneath a dying area and tap the needles sharply. Minute red or yellow specks the size of a pepper grain will drop to the paper and begin to crawl around. They are easily seen against the white background.

ANALYSIS: Spider mites
(*Oligonychus* species)
This spider relative damages plants by sucking the juices from the leaves and stems. This feeding results in the discoloration and sometimes death of the needles. Damage is often severe enough to kill small trees. Mite levels increase rapidly in hot, dry weather (70°F and higher). Mites are most active during late spring and early summer, but some mite activity occurs throughout the year in warm regions.

SOLUTION: Apply ORTHO Isotox Insect Killer or ORTHO Malathion 50 Insect Spray when browning needles are first noticed. Repeat sprays at intervals of 7 to 10 days according to label directions until the mites are controlled. Mites in missed areas continue to reproduce and rapidly reinfest treated areas.

ARBUTUS (MADRONE)

Twig dieback on madrone. *Insert:* Canker.

PROBLEM: Leaves on infected trees are stunted and lighter green than normal. Some leaves turn brown and drop. Twigs may die back. There are sunken, brownish, water-soaked areas on branches or near the base of the trunk. The sunken areas have a definite margin. Sometimes a black liquid substance is exuded from the canker. The tree may be killed.

ANALYSIS: Canker and dieback
Several different fungi cause canker and dieback on madrone. The fungi are spread by wind, rain, soil, tools, and equipment. They enter the tree at a wound, killing the surrounding healthy tissue. A sunken canker develops and expands through the wood in all directions. Tree sap containing the fungus may ooze from the wound. The canker cuts off the flow of nutrients and water to the branch. The tree may stop the spreading disease by producing callus tissue, a rapid growth of barklike cells, to wall off the fungus. If the expanding canker is stopped before it covers half the diameter of the trunk, the tree usually survives. However, the fungus may grow faster than the callus, or the tree may not produce a callus, resulting in the death of the branch or the whole tree.

SOLUTION: Prune off dead twigs and small cankered branches, cutting at least 4 inches below the canker. Cankers on larger branches can be excised with a knife and chisel. Remove all discolored bark and wood, and a 1-inch border of apparently healthy bark around the wound. After each cut, sterilize the knife and chisel with rubbing alcohol. Clean the wound with the alcohol. To prevent the development of new cankers, avoid wounding trees.

ARCTOSTAPHYLOS (MANZANITA)

Leaf gall.

PROBLEM: Green or reddish galls appear at the edges or tips of the newest leaves. The leaves are twisted and distorted. When the gall is torn open, a small (1/8 inch), dark green to black insect or insect excrement is seen. On kinnikinnick (*Arctostaphylos uva-ursi*), the entire leaf may be thickened and reddish. Leaf galls appear in early summer.

ANALYSIS: Leaf gall aphid
(*Tamalia coweni*)
This leaf gall aphid is only a pest of *Arctostaphylos* species. Damage occurs when the aphid sucks the juices from the leaf and rolls a third of the leaf around itself. A growth-promoting substance is injected into the leaf at the same time, causing the thickening of the leaf. The aphid begins feeding in spring but the gall does not form until early summer. On most species of *Arctostaphylos*, the galls are more disfiguring than damaging. However, on kinnikinnick, all new leaves may be disfigured, preventing growth and spread of the groundcover.

SOLUTION: Once the gall has formed around the aphid, this insect is difficult to control. Pick off and destroy disfigured leaves. The following spring, spray with a systemic insecticide to protect new foliage.

Arctostaphylos cultural information
Light: Full sun to partial shade
Water: Allow the soil to dry between waterings
Soil: Well drained, loose
Fertilizer: Light

AUCUBA

Sunburn.

PROBLEM: Dark brown or black patches develop on leaves exposed to direct sunlight. The entire leaf or shoot may turn black.

ANALYSIS: Sunburn
Aucuba plants are shade-loving; they cannot tolerate direct sun, especially intense afternoon sun. The sunlight burns the leaves, causing them to turn brown or black. Sunburn is most severe when the soil is dry. Some pests and diseases may cause symptoms similar to those of sunburn. For more information, see page 865.

SOLUTION: There is nothing you can do once the foliage has been damaged. Prune off dead leaves and shoots. Prevent further sunburn by transplanting plants to a shady location, or providing shade around the plants. Keep plants well watered.

Aucuba cultural information
Light: Part shade to full shade
Water: Moist or dry conditions
Soil: Tolerates many types
Fertilizer: Light

483

BAMBOO

Invasive bamboo.

Aphids (twice life size).

Bamboo scale (life size). *Insert:* Close-up.

PROBLEM: Bamboo is invading parts of the garden where it is not wanted.

ANALYSIS: Invasive bamboo
Creeping types of bamboo can be very invasive. Unlike the slower-spreading clumping bamboos, creeping bamboos form underground rootstocks that spread quickly. The rootstocks grow through the soil and send up shoots every couple of feet. The large types of creeping bamboo are especially vigorous, and are very difficult to control. Removal of the shoot is ineffective because the rootstocks will resprout.

SOLUTION: Locate the rootstock where it leaves the original planting. It is usually 2 to 4 inches below the soil surface in a direct line between the invasive shoot and the parent planting. Cut the rootstock and pull it up, with all the shoots attached to it. Prevent reinvasion by surrounding the bamboo planting with an underground barrier. Sink lengths of an impregnable material such as copper or galvanized iron sheeting 12 to 18 inches deep into the soil. Or dig a trench to the same depth and fill it with concrete.

PROBLEM: Young leaves are curled and yellowing. There may be a shiny or sticky substance coating the leaves. A black sooty mold often grows on the sticky substance. Tiny (⅛ inch), pale yellow, soft-bodied insects with black markings cluster on the undersides of leaves. Ants may be present. The plant is often weak and stunted.

ANALYSIS: Bamboo aphids
(*Takecallis* species)
Aphids do little damage in small numbers. However, they are extremely prolific and populations can rapidly build up to damaging numbers during the growing season. Damage occurs when the aphid sucks the juices from the bamboo leaves. The aphid is unable to digest fully all the sugar in the sap and excretes the excess in a fluid called honeydew. The honeydew often drops onto the leaves below. A sooty mold fungus may develop on the honeydew causing the bamboo leaves to appear black and dirty; or rain may wash the honeydew off before the fungus has a chance to grow. Ants feed on honeydew and are often present where there is an aphid infestation.

SOLUTION: Spray with ORTHO Malathion 50 Insect Spray when aphids first appear. Direct the spray to the undersides of the leaves. Repeat the spray in summer if the plant becomes reinfested.

Bamboo cultural information
Light: Full sun
Water: Drought tolerant once established
Soil: Tolerates many types
Fertilizer: Light to medium

PROBLEM: Stems or leaves are covered with brownish crusty bumps or thick, white, waxy bumps, or clusters of somewhat flattened yellowish scaly bumps. The bumps can be scraped or picked off; the undersides are usually soft. Leaves turn yellow and may drop. In some cases, a shiny or sticky substance coats the leaves. A black sooty mold often grows on the sticky substance.

ANALYSIS: Scales
Several different types of scales infest bamboo. In spring to midsummer the young scales, called *crawlers*, settle on leaves and stems. The small (¹⁄₁₀ inch), soft-bodied young feed by inserting their mouthparts and sucking sap from the plant. The legs usually atrophy and a hard crusty or waxy shell develops over the body. The mature female scales lay their eggs underneath their shell. Some species of scales that infest bamboo are unable to digest fully all the sugar in the plant sap, and excrete the excess in a fluid called honeydew, which often drops onto the leaves below. A sooty mold fungus may develop on the honeydew, causing the bamboo leaves and stems to appear black and dirty. An uncontrolled infestation of scales may kill the plant after 2 or 3 seasons.

SOLUTION: Spray with ORTHO Liquid Sevin in late spring when the young are active. Contact your local Cooperative Extension Office (see page 1011) to determine the best time to spray for scales in your area. Or spray with a *summer oil* to kill the adults, and hose down the plants the next day. For more information about scales, see page 878.

BAUHINIA (ORCHID TREE)

Snow scale (life size).

PROBLEM: Branches are infested with minute (¹⁄₃₂ to ¹⁄₁₆ inch) insects with white shells. Twigs and limbs that are heavily infested usually die, and small trees may be killed. Infested limbs have few, if any, leaves.

ANALYSIS: Snow scale
(*Unaspis citri*)
Snow scale gets its name from the color and appearance of the male scales. Female snow scales are brown to blackish, and are hard to see against the tree bark. Scales feed by sucking the plant sap. Often they are unable to digest fully all the sugar in the sap, and excrete the excess as a sugary fluid called honeydew. A sooty mold fungus may develop on the honeydew, causing the bauhinia leaves to appear black and dirty. Ants also feed on the honeydew, and are often present where scales are feeding. Scale infestations are most serious between spring and late fall.

SOLUTION: Spray infested trees with ORTHO Liquid Sevin. Repeat sprayings as needed according to label directions. Prune out dead branches on severely infested trees, and apply frequent, light applications of fertilizer to speed up recovery.

Bauhinia cultural information
Light: Full sun to part shade
Water: Keep the soil moist
Soil: Tolerates many types
Fertilizer: Medium

Iron deficiency.

PROBLEM: Some leaves turn pale green to yellow. The newest leaves (those at the tips of the branches) may be completely yellow, with only the veins remaining green. Only the leaf edges of older leaves may be yellowing. The plant may be stunted.

ANALYSIS: Iron deficiency
This is a common problem in acid-loving trees like bauhinia. Bauhinia grows best in soil with a pH between 5.5 and 6.5. (For more information on soil acidity, see page 902.) The yellowing is due to a deficiency of iron and other minor nutrients in the tree. The soil is seldom deficient in iron. However, iron is often found in an insoluble form that is not available to the plant, especially in soil with a pH of 7.0 or higher. An alkaline soil can result from overliming, or from lime leached from cement or brick. Regions where soil is derived from limestone also have high-pH soils. Plants use iron in the formation of the green pigment in the leaves. When iron is lacking, new leaves are yellow.

SOLUTION: Spray the foliage with ORTHO Greenol Liquid Iron 6.13%, and apply it to the soil around the tree to correct the deficiency of minor nutrients. Correct the pH of the soil by treating it with *ferrous sulfate*. Maintain an acid pH by fertilizing with ORTHO Azalea, Camellia & Rhododendron Food 5–10–10. When planting orchid trees, add peat moss, acid topsoil, or other materials to help acidify the planting soil.

BETULA (BIRCH)

BETULA

ADAPTATION: Zones 1 through 9. (To determine your zone, see the map on page 1004.) Most birches are not adapted to desert areas.

LIGHT: Full sun. Partial shade in warm areas.

SOIL: Birches tolerate a wide variety of soil types.

FERTILIZER: Fertilize with ORTHO Evergreen, Tree & Shrub Food 12–6–6 according to label directions.

WATER:
How much: Apply enough water to wet the soil 3 to 4 feet deep. To determine the proper amount of water for your soil type, see page 906.
How often: Birches grow best in moist soil. Water when the soil is moist but not wet 4 inches below the surface. For more information about watering, see page 906.

PRUNING: Birches usually bleed heavily when pruned in winter or spring, so it is best to prune at other times of the year. Prune to maintain shape.

BETULA (BIRCH)

Aphids (half life size).

Leafminer damage.

Dieback. *Insert:* Adult borer (half life size).

PROBLEM: Young leaves are puckered, twisted, and yellowing. There may be a shiny or sticky substance dripping from the trees and coating the leaves. Sometimes twigs or branches die back. Tiny (⅛ inch) yellow, green, or blackish soft-bodied insects cluster on the undersides of leaves or on the stems.

ANALYSIS: Aphids
Aphids do little damage in small numbers. However, they are extremely prolific and populations can rapidly build up to damaging numbers during the growing season. Damage occurs when the aphid sucks the juices from birch leaves or stems. Some aphid species attacking birch are unable to digest fully all the sugar in the sap and they excrete the excess in a fluid called honeydew. The honeydew often drops onto the leaves below. Plants or objects beneath the tree may also be coated with honeydew. Ants feed on honeydew and are often present where there is an aphid infestation.

SOLUTION: Control with ORTHO Orthene Systemic Insect Control or ORTHO Isotox Insect Killer when aphids first appear. Direct the spray to the undersides of the leaves or at the bark, depending on where the aphids are feeding. Repeat the spray in summer if the tree becomes reinfested.

PROBLEM: Brown blisters appear in the new leaves. Eventually the blisters run together, forming a large blotch. The top of the tree is generally most severely affected, but in some areas the entire tree is infested and brown. A small (up to ¼ inch), whitish larva may be found inside the blister.

ANALYSIS: Birch leafminer
(*Fenusa pusilla*)
This sawfly is a common pest of gray birch (*Betula populifolia*), paper birch (*B. papyrifera*), white birch (*B. alba*), and cut leaf birch. It rarely attacks black (*B. lenta*), yellow (*B. alleghéniensis*), European white (*B. pendula*), or river birch (*B. nigra*). When the first birch leaves are half grown in spring, the fly hovers around the trees and lays eggs on the leaves. When the eggs hatch, the larvae feed between the upper and lower surfaces of the leaves, causing blisters. The mature larva chews its way out of the leaf and drops to the ground to pupate. The adult fly emerges and the cycle repeats itself 2 or more times during the growing season. The adult lays eggs only on young leaves, so later in the season only terminal growth and sprout growth are affected.

SOLUTION: Larvae are difficult to control once they are protected inside the leaf. If blotches are noticed in spring, spray with ORTHO Orthene Systemic Insect Control, ORTHO Isotox Insect Killer, or ORTHO Lindane Borer & Leaf Miner Spray in early July to control young larvae of the second generation. Repeat in mid-July. The following spring, spray as the leaves are unfolding (early May) to prevent leafminer damage. Repeat 2 more times, 10 days apart.

PROBLEM: Leaves are yellowing and the foliage is sparse at the top of the tree. There is increased side growth on the lower branches. Twigs and branches may die. The leaves on these branches turn brown but don't drop. There are D-shaped holes and ridges on the trunk and branches. Swollen ridges are packed with sawdust. Weak, young, or newly transplanted trees may be killed.

ANALYSIS: Bronze birch borer
(*Agrilus anxius*)
The birch borer is the larva of an olive-brown beetle about ½ inch long. For about 6 weeks in summer, adult beetles lay eggs in bark crevices, usually around a wound. They also feed on the leaves during egg laying. The larvae that hatch from these eggs are white and have flat heads. They bore into the wood just beneath the bark. The feeding and tunneling of the larvae stop the flow of nutrients and water in that area by cutting the conducting vessels; branch and twig dieback result. If the tree is healthy, sap flow acts as a defense against borers; when the insect burrows into the wood, tree sap fills the hole and drowns the insect. Factors that weaken the tree such as poor growing conditions, transplanting, and mechanical injuries make it more attractive to female beetles.

SOLUTION: Cut out and destroy all dead and dying branches. Severely infested young trees should be removed. In spring, spray or paint the trunk and branches with an insecticide containing *lindane* to kill young larvae before they burrow into the wood. Repeat 3 more times at intervals of 2 weeks. Maintain tree vigor by watering and fertilizing regularly.

BISCHOFIA ———— **BOUGAINVILLEA** ————

Dieback.

False oleander scale (twice life size).

Bougainvillea caterpillar (¼ life size).

PROBLEM: Leaves on the ends of branches turn yellow and drop. The upper branches die from the tips back. The tree is weak and stunted.

ANALYSIS: Dieback
Dieback on birch is caused by any of several different species of fungi (*Melanconis* species) that attack trees weakened by drought. The fungus enters a branch and, if the tree is weak, produces a dark discoloration in the wood. Healthy trees can resist the attack of this weak fungus and show few symptoms. Upper branches progressively die as the fungus grows through the wood. Several other fungi that produce cankers on the branches or trunk of birches may also cause dieback. The bronze birch borer (see page 486) may cause similar dieback symptoms, and often invades trees weakened by dieback. In addition, birch trees under drought stress may show some twig dieback.

SOLUTION: No chemicals are known to control this fungus. Prune off affected branches well below the diseased area. Fertilize and water the tree regularly to promote vigorous growth. For more information about fertilizers and watering, see pages 904 and 906.

PROBLEM: Yellow to greenish yellow spots develop on the leaves. Tiny, white to light brown raised bumps are often seen in the discolored areas. The bumps can be scraped or picked off; the undersides are usually soft. Leaves turn yellow and may drop. Sometimes a shiny or sticky substance coats the leaves.

ANALYSIS: False oleander scale
(*Pseudaulacaspis cockerelli*)
This insect feeds on many garden plants, and is capable of rapid reproduction. The female scale deposits large masses of eggs under her wax shell. After hatching, the young scales, called *crawlers*, move about the host plant until they locate a feeding site. They begin to feed and then develop the protective scale cover. Several generations of scales are produced each year. Scales feed by sucking the plant juices from tender leaves and stems. Some scales are unable to digest fully all the sugar in the plant sap, and excrete the excess in a fluid called honeydew, which often drops onto the leaves below. A sooty mold may develop on the honeydew, causing the leaves to appear black and dirty.

SOLUTION: Apply ORTHO Isotox Insect Killer thoroughly to infested trees. Repeat sprays at intervals of 7 to 10 days until scales are controlled. Dead scales remain on the plant but are dry and contain no fluids when scraped off and examined.

Bischofia cultural information
Light: Full sun
Water: Drought tolerant once established
Soil: Tolerates many types
Fertilizer: Medium

PROBLEM: Leaves have holes chewed in them, or they may be missing completely. New leaves are most severely affected, and the problem occurs most during warm weather from spring to fall. Green caterpillars ¾ inch long may be present on the damaged leaves.

ANALYSIS: Bougainvillea caterpillars
(*Macalla thrysisalis*)
These caterpillars are the larval stage of a tiny moth that lays its eggs on bougainvillea leaves. After hatching, the caterpillars feed on the leaves and complete their development into the adult stage in 4 to 5 weeks. Several generations are produced during the year, with the greatest infestations occurring in the late spring.

SOLUTION: Apply ORTHO Liquid Sevin according to label directions. Repeat the sprayings at weekly intervals as long as caterpillars are present.

Bougainvillea cultural information
Light: Full sun to part shade
Water: Infrequent, deep watering
Soil: Loose, well drained
Fertilizer: Light to medium

BUCIDA (BLACK OLIVE)

Blister mite damage.

PROBLEM: Leaves are deformed and have brown bumps of varying sizes. Severely infested leaves may drop. The problem is most severe in the spring and summer.

ANALYSIS: Blister mite
(*Eriophyes buceras*)
This tiny, pale white spider relative sucks fluids from the leaves to cause the brown blisterlike areas that may resemble leaf spots. Mite development is very rapid. They take only 5 to 7 days to reach the adult stage under ideal conditions, and many generations are produced each year. Mite activity is greatest during the spring and summer. These mites are difficult to see without magnification, and their damage is often blamed on other pests.

SOLUTION: Spray the tree with a pesticide containing *dicofol*. Repeat the spray every 1 to 2 weeks until mites are controlled. Be sure that the spray reaches all parts of the tree; otherwise, mites in missed areas quickly reinfest treated ones.

Bucida cultural information
Light: Full sun
Water: Drought tolerant once established
Soil: Tolerates many types
Fertilizer: Low to medium

Red leaves.

PROBLEM: Many leaves of all ages and sizes suddenly turn red or orange and fall off. No insects or diseases are observed on the fallen leaves. The problem may occur at any time, but is most severe during the winter and early spring. Trees usually replace the fallen leaves within a few weeks.

ANALYSIS: Leaf drop
Leaf drop on black olive may be sudden and dramatic. It is usually caused by abrupt changes in temperature or in soil moisture. Winter leaf drop is often caused by cold wind or by drought. Individual trees vary in the ease with which they drop leaves.

SOLUTION: No treatment is necessary once the leaves have fallen. Future leaf drop can be made less severe by keeping the tree in good condition. Apply ORTHO General Purpose Plant Food 8–8–8 every 6 to 8 weeks during the growing season. Do not let the soil dry out.

BUXUS (BOXWOOD)

BUXUS

ADAPTATION: Zones 5 through 10. (To determine your zone, see the map on page 1004.) Protect from drying winds.

LIGHT: Full sun or partial shade, especially in hot climates.

SOIL: Well drained, rich in organic matter.

FERTILIZER: Fertilize with ORTHO Evergreen, Tree & Shrub Food 12–6–6 or ORTHO General Purpose Plant Food 8–8–8 according to label directions.

WATER:
 How much: Apply enough water to wet the soil 1 to 2 feet deep. To determine the proper amount of water for your soil type, see page 906.
 How often: Boxwood will not tolerate drought. Water when the soil is moist but not wet 2 inches below the surface. For more information about watering, see page 906.

Boxwood psyllid damage.

Boxwood leafminer larvae (twice life size).

Winter injury on Japanese boxwood.

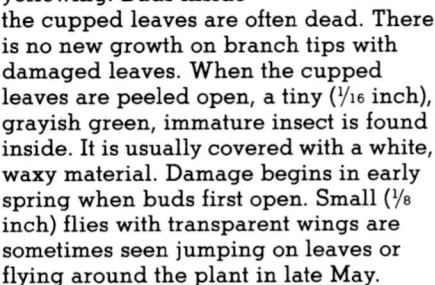

PROBLEM: Terminal leaves are cupped and yellowing. Buds inside the cupped leaves are often dead. There is no new growth on branch tips with damaged leaves. When the cupped leaves are peeled open, a tiny ($\frac{1}{16}$ inch), grayish green, immature insect is found inside. It is usually covered with a white, waxy material. Damage begins in early spring when buds first open. Small ($\frac{1}{8}$ inch) flies with transparent wings are sometimes seen jumping on leaves or flying around the plant in late May.

ANALYSIS: Boxwood psyllid
(*Psylla buxi*)
The boxwood psyllid is prevalent in temperate regions of the country where boxwood is grown. American boxwood is more severely attacked than English boxwood. The immature psyllid feeds by sucking the juices from growing leaves, resulting in the yellowing and cupping. As it feeds it secretes a white, waxy material that protects it from parasites and chemical sprays. The insect matures in early summer, and the female fly lays her eggs in the base of buds, where they remain until the following spring.

SOLUTION: Control with an insecticide containing *acephate* when damage is first noticed in early spring; repeat 2 weeks later. Spray the plant thoroughly to penetrate the waxy secretions and leaf buds.

PROBLEM: The leaves are puckered or blistered. The lower surface of the leaf is spotted yellow; the upper surface is green at first and then flecked brown and yellow. Leaves may drop prematurely. Growth is poor and the plant is rangy. Twigs may die back if the plant is infested more than one year. When the leaf is torn open, 2 or more small ($\frac{1}{8}$ inch), yellowish maggots or brownish pupae may be found between the upper and lower surfaces of the leaf.

ANALYSIS: Boxwood leafminer
(*Monarthropalpus buxi*)
The boxwood leafminer is one of the most serious pests of boxwood. The larvae spend the winter in the leaf. When the weather warms in spring, they feed on the tissue between the leaf surfaces. In late April or May a tiny ($\frac{1}{10}$ inch), gnat-like, orange fly emerges from the pupal case inside the leaf. The emerging flies swarm around the plant in early morning, mating and laying eggs in the leaves. New blisters develop in midsummer from feeding by this next generation of larvae. When the weather turns cold, the larvae become inactive until the following spring.

SOLUTION: Leafminer control depends on applying insecticides just before eggs are laid in late spring. Larvae already in the leaf may not be killed if the spray is applied late. Control with ORTHO Diazinon Insect Spray in late April or early May. If eggs are laid before a control is applied, an insecticide containing *dimethoate* applied in late June may kill young miners.

PROBLEM: Leaves are rusty brown to red, and dry. Twigs and branches may die back. The shrub is growing in an area where cold, dry, windy days are common or where plants may be exposed to late fall or early spring freezes.

ANALYSIS: Winter injury
Boxwood is severely damaged by cold, drying winter winds, especially if temperatures are below freezing and the weather is clear. The leaves lose their moisture more rapidly than it can be replaced by the root system. Cells in the leaf dry out and die. This condition is most pronounced when water is unavailable because the soil is frozen. Leaves, along with twigs and branches, also die during early fall or late spring freezes, when the plant is growing. Young succulent growth cannot withstand the cold temperatures.

SOLUTION: No cure is available once plants have been injured. Pick off damaged leaves where practical, and prune out dead twigs and branches. Provide shelter and windbreaks for plants growing in cold regions. Covering boxwoods with burlap bags helps prevent leaf drying. To avoid succulent growth in the fall, do not fertilize or prune late in the season. Water in late fall or winter, if necessary, to insure adequate soil moisture. Mulch plants after they become dormant to reduce the depth of frost penetration into the soil.

BUXUS (BOXWOOD)

Dieback caused by phytophthora root rot.

Spider mite damage.

Nematode damage.

PROBLEM: The young leaves are yellowish or "off-color" and wilting. Eventually part or all of the plant wilts and dies, even though the soil is sufficiently moist. Dead leaves remain attached to the plant. Heavy, poorly drained soil favors disease development. When cut, the tissue under the bark close to ground level shows a dark discoloration. To look for discoloration, peel back the bark at the bottom of the plant. There is a distinct margin between white healthy wood and dark diseased wood. If the plant is pulled up, examination of young roots reveals browning, decaying, and an absence of white rootlets. Healthy roots are firm and white.

ANALYSIS: Root rot
This plant disease is caused by a soil-inhabiting fungus (*Phytophthora cinnamomi*) that attacks more than 100 kinds of ornamental plants. The fungus is carried in infected plants, infested soil, or soil water. It enters the roots and works its way up the plant, blocking the upward flow of water and nutrients. Plants in overwatered or poorly drained soils are more susceptible to attack.

SOLUTION: No chemical control is available. Once the fungus becomes established in the soil, it will remain indefinitely. Remove diseased plants; do not replant the same area with susceptible plants. For a list of resistant trees and shrubs, see page 1000. However, if replanting is necessary because the shrub is part of a hedge, replacing the soil in that area will reduce the chance of root rot. Remove as much soil as possible in the area where the old roots have penetrated and replace with uninfected soil. Avoid overwatering.

PROBLEM: Leaves are stippled yellow or whitish and dirty. There may be a silken webbing on the lower surfaces of the leaves. New leaves may be distorted. To determine if the plant is infested with mites, hold a sheet of white paper underneath a branch that has stippled leaves and tap the branch sharply. Minute reddish or green specks the size of a pepper grain will drop to the paper and begin to crawl around. These pests are easily seen against the white background.

ANALYSIS: Spider mites
Spider mites, related to spiders, are major pests of many garden plants. They cause damage by sucking sap from the undersides of leaves. As a result of feeding, green leaf pigment disappears producing the stippled appearance. Mites infesting boxwood are most prolific in cooler weather. They are most active in the spring and occasionally, in the fall. At the onset of hot weather (70°F and up), the mites have caused their maximum damage.

SOLUTION: Control with ORTHO Diazinon Insect Spray or ORTHO Malathion 50 Insect Spray when stippling is first noticed in spring. Wet the undersides of the leaves thoroughly. Repeat 3 more times at 7 to 10 day intervals to kill young mites as they hatch from eggs. To prevent unsightly injury to foliage, it is important to apply control measures early in the season when damage first appears. Injured leaves remain on the plant for more than one growing season. Hose down plants frequently to knock off webs and mites.

PROBLEM: The leaves are bronze to yellow. They may wilt on hot, dry days but recover at night. The plant lacks vigor. After several years, plants are noticeably stunted and branches may die back. The roots are stunted and often bushy and dark. There may be knots on the roots.

ANALYSIS: Nematodes
Nematodes are microscopic worms that live in the soil. They feed on plant roots, damaging and stunting them. The damaged roots can't supply sufficient water and nutrients to the aboveground plant parts, and the plant is stunted or slowly dies. Nematodes prefer moist, sandy loam soils. They can move only a few inches each year on their own, but they may be carried long distances by soil, water, tools, or infested plants. Testing roots and soil is the only positive method for confirming the presence of nematodes. Contact your local Cooperative Extension Office (see page 1011) for sampling instructions and addresses of testing laboratories. Soil and root problems such as poor soil structure, drought stress, nutrient deficiency, and root rots can also produce symptoms similar to those caused by nematodes. These problems should be eliminated as causes before sending soil and root samples for testing. For information on soil problems and root rots, see pages 901 and 856.

SOLUTION: There are no chemicals available to homeowners to kill nematodes in planted soil. However, they can be controlled before planting by soil fumigation. For information on fumigating soil, see page 919.

CACTUS

Soft rot on prickly pear cactus.

Sunburn.

Cactus scale (twice life size).

PROBLEM: Areas of the plant are discolored, and the upper surface eventually rots and collapses. The collapsed tissue disintegrates and becomes slimy. When conditions are moist, a grayish mold develops on the infected tissue.

ANALYSIS: Soft rot
This plant disease, also called *gray mold*, is caused by a fungus (*Botrytis cinerea*) that infects many flowers, fruits, and vegetables in the garden. Cacti that are overwatered, planted in moist shady areas, or damaged by cold weather are most susceptible. The fungus infects weakened tissue when conditions are moist or humid, causing the tissue to disintegrate. When the weather turns dry, the fungus stops spreading to healthy tissue. However, if wet or humid conditions persist, a grayish mold consisting of fungal strands and spores develops on the infected tissued.

SOLUTION: Remove infected parts, cutting well into healthy green tissue. Avoid overwatering. Move plants that are growing in moist, shady locations to areas with better air circulation and more light.

PROBLEM: During sunny weather, a section of the plant facing the sun turns yellow. Severely affected areas may turn brown later. The plant has been moved recently, from shade or low light to full sun.

ANALYSIS: Sunburn
Cacti are sun-loving plants. When growing in full sun, they produce thick cell walls that can withstand high light intensity and heat. However, plants may be burned by the sun if they are suddenly moved from a protected area (such as indoors) to an area that receives full sun. The cell walls cannot withstand high levels of ultraviolet light, and are damaged or killed.

SOLUTION: When moving plants out of the house or from areas of winter protection where light intensity has been low, place them in partial shade first (early morning, late afternoon, or filtered light) so they can adjust to the higher light intensity. In 1 to 2 weeks, cactus species that are adapted to full sun can be moved from partial shade into direct sunlight.

PROBLEM: The plant is covered with clusters of somewhat flattened, circular, gray bumps, or with slender, white, scaly bumps. The bumps can be scraped or picked off; the undersides are soft. The plant may be yellowed.

ANALYSIS: Cactus scale
(*Diaspis echinocacti*)
This scale is common on cactus both outdoors and indoors. The infestation may be so heavy that the entire surface appears gray and crusty. The scale lays eggs in the spring. In late spring the young scales, called *crawlers*, settle on other parts of the plant. The tiny ($\frac{1}{30}$ inch), soft-bodied young feed by inserting their mouthparts and sucking sap from the plant. The legs atrophy and a hard, crusty, gray shell develops over the bodies of the females. The males are white and remain soft. The mature female scales lay their eggs underneath their shell. An uncontrolled infestation may kill the cactus after 2 or 3 seasons. Several other species of scales may also infest cactus.

SOLUTION: Spray with an insecticide containing *malathion* or *carbaryl* in late spring when the young are active. Some cacti are sensitive to malathion and may be injured. Test spray a small section of the plant and wait 24 hours to see if a burned area develops. Use a stiff brush to remove adult scales.

Cactus cultural information
Light: Full sun
Water: Allow to dry between waterings; reduce watering in fall
Soil: Sandy, loose, well drained
Fertilizer: Medium

CACTUS

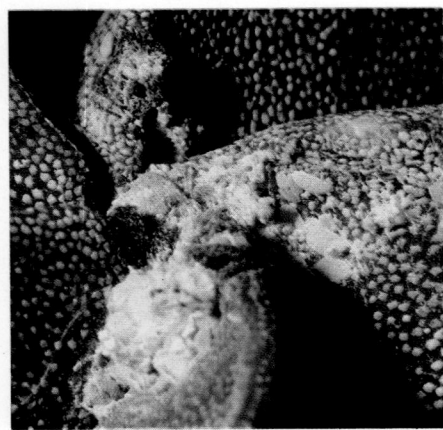

Mealybugs (twice life size).

PROBLEM: Oval, white insects up to ¼ inch long cluster in white, cottony masses on the plant. The plant is yellowing and lacks vigor. A sticky substance may coat the plant. Ants may be present.

ANALYSIS: Mealybugs
Several species of mealybugs are among the worst pests of cacti. Mealybugs damage plants by sucking the plant sap. The adult female mealybugs may produce live young, or may deposit her eggs in white, fluffy masses of wax. The immature mealybugs, called *nymphs*, are very active and crawl all over the plant. Soon after the nymphs begin to feed, they exude filaments of white wax that cover their bodies, giving them a cottony appearance. As they mature, their mobility decreases. Mealybugs cannot fully digest all the sugar in the sap, and excrete the excess in a fluid called honeydew, which coats the plant. Ants may feed on the honeydew. Mealybugs can be spread when they are brushed onto uninfested plants, or when the young, active nymphs crawl to nearby plants. Mealybugs may also be spread by the wind, which can blow egg masses and nymphs from plant to plant.

SOLUTION: Spray infested plants with an insecticide containing *malathion*. Spray at intervals of 7 to 10 days until mealybugs are gone. Some cacti are sensitive to *malathion*, and may be injured. Test spray a small section of the plant and wait 24 hours to see if a burned area develops.

CAMELLIA

CAMELLIA

ADAPTATION: Zones 7 through 10. Not adapted to desert areas.

FLOWERING TIME:
Common camellia (*C. japonica*): October to April.
Sasanqua camellia (*C. sasanqua*): September to December.

LIGHT: Protect from hot sun.

SOIL: Well drained, rich in organic matter, acid (pH 5.5 to 6.5). Mulch the soil to prevent drying.

FERTILIZER: Fertilize with ORTHO Azalea, Camellia & Rhododendron Food 5–10–10 according to label directions.

WATER:
How much: Apply enough water to wet the soil 2 to 3 feet deep. To determine the proper amount of water for your soil type, see page 906.
How often: Camellias prefer moist soil. Water when the soil is moist but not wet under the mulch.

PRUNING: Prune just after flowering. Remove dead or weak wood and thin out overly dense growth. To encourage bushiness, cut back top growth, leaving 1 inch of new growth.

Leaf gall.

PROBLEM: Developing leaves and new shoots are thickened, fleshy, and enlarged. Diseased leaves can be up to 10 times thicker than normal leaves. The upper surface of the leaf is green, but the underside is white and peeling. There are usually no more than a few diseased shoots on a plant. This problem is most common in periods of warm, moist weather.

ANALYSIS: Camellia leaf gall
This plant disease is caused by a fungus (*Exobasidium camelliae*); it is found on camellias only in the Southeast. The disease is more common on sasanqua varieties than on japonica. As the buds open in spring, fungal spores blown by wind to the plant or overwintering on the bark enter the tissue. The spores need moisture to germinate. Plants grown in areas of poor air movement, or in deep shade where moisture levels are high, are more likely to be infected.

SOLUTION: Sprays to control leaf gall must be applied before infection occurs. Once the galls develop, the best control is to remove them when they are first noticed. Search carefully to remove all galls. If they are not removed and destroyed, the disease will be more severe the following year. To prevent new infection next spring, spray with a fungicide containing *zineb* before new leaves open. Repeat at intervals of 2 weeks until new leaves are fully grown. If practical, move the plant to an area with better air circulation and avoid planting shrubs in areas of deep shade.

Camellia flower blight.

Virus.

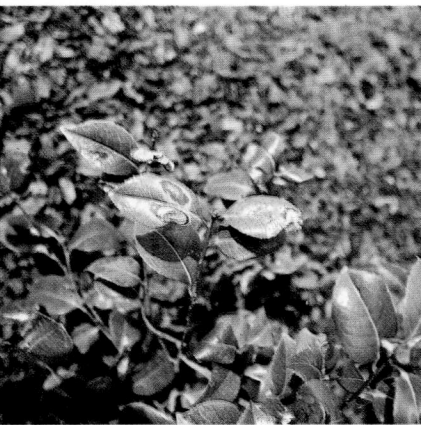

Sunburn.

PROBLEM: Tan or brown spots or blotches spread across the flower. Infection takes place any time after the camellia buds begin to show color. The whole flower may turn brown. This disease is distinguished from frost, sunscald, or wind damage by a pattern of darkened veins, which give a netted effect in the spots. Dark brown to black resting structures an inch or more in diameter form in the base of the flower.

ANALYSIS: Camellia flower blight
This serious and widespread plant disease is caused by a fungus (*Sclerotinia camelliae*) that attacks only the flowers of camellias. In late winter to early spring, black fungal resting structures in the soil produce spores that are carried by the wind to new flowers. If moisture is present, the spores germinate and cause infection. The flowers may turn completely brown within 48 hours. The fungus continues to grow in the flower, eventually producing black resting structures that drop from the shrub with the flower. These resting structures can persist in the soil for at least 5 years.

SOLUTION: Remove and destroy infected flowers to eliminate the source of new infections the following spring. Many spores are produced in one infected flower. All diseased flowers must be carefully collected. Rake up and destroy old leaves, flowers, and plant debris. A soil spray with a fungicide containing *PCNB* will inhibit spore production. Begin spray in December and repeat every 3 to 4 weeks throughout the blooming season. If this disease is a problem in your area, protect the flowers with a spray containing *benlate* as soon as they begin to show color. Repeat every 3 days to protect new flowers.

PROBLEM: Irregular yellow splotches of various sizes and shapes appear on the leaves. Some leaves may be entirely yellow. The uninfected portions remain dark green. Colored flowers may have irregular white blotches. White flowers show no symptoms. Some camellia varieties with extensive leaf yellowing may be weak and stunted.

ANALYSIS: Camellia yellow mottle leaf virus
The virus is transmitted by propagating from an infected plant or by grafting from an infected plant to a healthy one. This generally occurs in the nursery where the plant was grown. Sometimes the virus disease is intentionally transmitted to get variegated flowers. The disease is usually fairly harmless unless there is extensive leaf yellowing. Yellowing results from the suppression of green pigment (chlorophyll) development by the virus. The leaves produce less food, causing the plant to be weakened.

SOLUTION: Once the plant is infected there is no chemical that will control the virus. Remove excessively weak camellias. Buy only healthy plants. For further information on selecting healthy plants, see page 916.

PROBLEM: During warm sunny weather, the center portion of the leaf turns yellowish or bronze. Severely affected areas turn brown and die. The spots usually appear between the veins. The shrub is planted in direct sun or against a south- or west-facing wall.

ANALYSIS: Sunscald
Camellias are shade-loving plants. Their leaves are sensitive to the heat of direct sun, which kills the leaf tissue. Scalding occurs when the shrub is planted in full sun or against a south- or west-facing wall. It takes only one hot summer day for damage to appear. The injury is unsightly but is not damaging to the plant. However, weakened leaves are more susceptible to invasion by fungi and bacteria. Plants deficient in water are more susceptible to sunscald.

SOLUTION: Once leaves are scalded, they will not recover. Remove affected leaves where practical. Move injured plants to a shaded location or provide some shade where they are now planted. For more information about transplanting, see page 916.

CAMELLIA

Black citrus aphid (life size).

Cottony scales (life size).

Camellia scales (twice life size).

PROBLEM: Young leaves are cupped, twisted, and may be yellowing. Flower buds are malformed. A shiny, sticky substance may coat the leaves. A black sooty mold often grows on the sticky substance. Tiny (¹⁄₁₆ to ⅛ inch) black, yellow, or green soft-bodied insects cluster on the buds, stems, and undersides of leaves. Ants may be present.

ANALYSIS: Aphids
The most common aphid infesting camellias is the black citrus aphid (*Toxoptera aurantii*), which causes leaf cupping and malformed buds. Several other aphids may also attack camellias. Aphids do little damage in small numbers. However, they are extremely prolific and populations can rapidly build up to damaging numbers during the growing season. Damage occurs when the aphid sucks the juices from the camellia leaves and stems. Some aphid species attacking camellias are unable to digest fully all the sugar in the plant sap and excrete the excess in a fluid called honeydew. The black citrus aphid produces large quantities of honeydew, which often drops onto the leaves below. Plants beneath the shrub may also be coated with honeydew. A black sooty mold fungus may develop on the honeydew, or rain may wash it off before the fungus has a chance to grow. Ants feed on the sticky substance, and are often present where there is an aphid infestation.

SOLUTION: Control with ORTHO Isotox Insect Killer or ORTHO Malathion 50 Insect Spray when aphids first appear. Direct the spray to the undersides of the leaves. Repeat the spray in midsummer if the plant becomes reinfested.

PROBLEM: Buds, young branches, or the undersides of leaves are covered with white, cottony, cushionlike masses. The leaves are yellowing and the plant may be weak and stunted. A shiny, sticky substance may coat the leaves. A black sooty mold often grows on this sticky substance. Ants may be present.

ANALYSIS: Cottony scales and mealybugs
Cottony scales and mealybugs are common on camellias. The visual similarities between these two insects make separate identification difficult. They are very conspicuous in late spring and summer because the females are covered with a white, cottony egg sac, containing up to 2500 eggs. Females lay their egg masses on leaves or branches. The young insects that hatch from these eggs are yellowish brown to green and inconspicuous. They feed throughout the summer on the stems and leaves. Damage is caused by the withdrawal of plant sap from the leaves and young branches. Some species of scales and mealybugs that infest camellias are unable to digest fully all the sugar in the plant sap and excrete the excess in a fluid called honeydew. A sooty mold fungus may develop on the sticky substance, causing the camellia leaves to appear black and dirty. Plants infested for more than 1 year are weakened and may be stunted.

SOLUTION: Control with ORTHO Orthene Systemic Insect Control, ORTHO Malathion 50 Insect Spray, or ORTHO Isotox Insect Killer in midsummer when the young are active. Repeat if plants become reinfested. To control scales early or late in the season, spray with ORTHO Volck Oil Spray in spring after blooming or in fall prior to blooming.

PROBLEM: Nodes, stems, buds, and leaves are covered with brown or black crusty bumps or thick, white, waxy bumps. The bumps can be scraped or picked off; the undersides are usually soft. Leaves may turn yellow and drop off, and twigs may die back. In some cases, a shiny, sticky substance coats the leaves. A black sooty mold often grows on the sticky substance. Ants are sometimes present.

ANALYSIS: Scales
Many species of scales infest camellias. They lay their eggs on leaves or bark, and in spring to midsummer the young scales, called *crawlers*, settle on the various parts of the shrub. These small (¹⁄₁₀ inch), soft-bodied young feed by sucking sap from the plant. The legs usually atrophy and a hard crusty or waxy shell develops over the body. The mature female scales lay their eggs underneath the shell. Some species of scales that infest camellias are unable to digest all the sugar in the plant sap, and excrete the excess in a fluid called honeydew. A sooty mold fungus may develop on the honeydew. An uncontrolled infestation of scales may kill the plant after 2 or 3 seasons.

SOLUTION: Control with ORTHO Isotox Insect Killer or ORTHO Orthene Systemic Insect Control when the young are active. Contact your local Cooperative Extension Office (see page 1011) to determine the best time to spray for scales in your area. To control scales early or late in the season, spray with ORTHO Volck Oil Spray in the spring after blooming, or in the fall prior to blooming. For more information about scales, see page 878.

CARISSA (NATAL PLUM)

Sooty mold.

Iron deficiency.

Root rot.

PROBLEM: A black sooty mold is growing on leaves and twigs. It can be completely wiped off the surfaces.

ANALYSIS: Sooty mold
This common black mold is caused by several species of fungi that grow on the sugary material left on plants by aphids, scales, mealybugs, whiteflies, and other insects that suck sap from the plant. The insects are unable to digest all the sugar in the sap and excrete the excess in a fluid called honeydew, which drops onto the leaves below. The honeydew may also drop out of infested trees and shrubs onto camellias growing beneath them. Sooty mold is unsightly, but it is fairly harmless because it does not attack the leaf directly. Extremely heavy infestations prevent light from reaching the leaf, so that the leaf produces fewer nutrients and may turn yellow. The presence of sooty mold indicates that the camellia or another plant near it is infested with insects.

SOLUTION: Sooty mold can be wiped from the leaves with a wet rag, or it will eventually be washed off by rain. Prevent more sooty mold by controlling the insect that is producing the honeydew. Inspect the leaves and twigs above the sooty mold to find what type of insect is present. For control instructions, see the following pages: for aphids, scales, and mealybugs, page 494; for whiteflies, page 879.

PROBLEM: Some of the leaves are pale green to yellow. The newest leaves may be completely yellow with only the veins remaining green. On older leaves, only the leaf edges may be yellowing. The plant may be stunted.

ANALYSIS: Iron deficiency
This is a common problem in acid-loving plants like camellia. The plant prefers soil with a pH between 5.5 and 6.5. (For more information on soil acidity, see page 902.) The yellowing is due to a deficiency of iron and other minor nutrients in the plant. The soil is seldom deficient in iron. However, iron is often found in an insoluble form that is not available to the plant, especially in soil with a pH of 7.0 or higher. A high soil pH can result from overliming, or from lime leached from cement or brick. Regions where soil is derived from limestone, and those with low rainfall, also have high-pH soils. Plants use iron in the formation of the green pigment in the leaves. When it is lacking, new leaves are yellow.

SOLUTION: Spray the foliage with ORTHO Greenol Liquid Iron 6.13%, and apply it to the soil around the plants to correct the iron deficiency. Correct the pH of the soil by treating it with ORTHO Aluminum Sulfate and watering it in well. Maintain an acid pH by fertilizing with ORTHO Azalea, Camellia & Rhododendron Food 5–10–10. When planting camellia, add at least 50 percent peat moss to the soil if you live in an area where the soil is alkaline or has poor drainage. Never lime the soil around camellia.

PROBLEM: Small twigs and branches or entire plants turn brown and die. The leaves on affected branches may turn yellow before turning brown. No pests are seen on the dying plants, and plants of any age may be affected.

ANALYSIS: Root rot
This plant disease is caused by any of a number of different fungi that live in the soil. These fungi thrive in waterlogged, heavy soil. Some of these fungi attack the plant stems at the soil level, while others attack the roots. Infection causes the roots and stems to decay. This results in wilting, then yellowing leaves, and eventually the death of the plant. These fungi are generally spread by infested soil, contaminated equipment, and splashing or running water.

SOLUTION: Allow the soil around the plants to dry out. (For more information on this technique, see page 857.) Remove and discard severely infected plants. Avoid future root rot problems by planting in well-drained soil. For information on improving soil drainage, see page 901. For more information on root and stem rots, see page 856.

Carissa cultural information
Light: Full sun to part shade
Water: When the soil is almost dry
Soil: Loose, well drained
Fertilizer: Medium

CARPINUS (HORNBEAM)

Canker.

PROBLEM: Leaves on affected branches are stunted and lighter green than normal. Some leaves turn brown and drop. Twigs may die back. There are sunken, brownish, water-soaked areas on the branches. A liquid may exude from the canker. The tree may be killed.

ANALYSIS: Canker and dieback
A number of different fungi cause canker and dieback on hornbeam. They enter the tree at a wound, killing the surrounding healthy tissue. A sunken canker develops; tree sap containing the fungus may ooze from the wound. The canker cuts off the flow of nutrients and water through the vessels, causing the leaves to turn yellow. The tree may stop the spreading disease by producing callus tissue, a rapid growth of barklike cells that walls off the fungus. If the expanding canker is stopped before it covers half the branch, the branch usually survives. However, the fungus may grow faster than the callus, or the tree may not produce it.

SOLUTION: Prune off dead twigs and small cankered branches. Cankers on larger branches can be excised with a knife or chisel. Remove all discolored bark and wood, and a 1-inch border of apparently healthy bark around the wound. After each cut, sterilize the knife or chisel with rubbing alcohol. To prevent the development of new cankers, avoid wounding trees. Do not overwater.

Carpinus cultural information:
Light: Full sun
Water: Moist or dry conditions
Soil: Tolerates many types
Fertilizer: Light

CASTANEA (CHESTNUT)

Chestnut blight canker.

PROBLEM: Leaves on 1 or more branches are yellow or brown and dry. Dead leaves hang on diseased branches long after normal leaf fall. On young wood, there are swollen, yellow-brown areas. On older wood, the areas are reddish and often split longitudinally. Trees usually die within 3 or 4 years.

ANALYSIS: Chestnut blight
This plant disease is caused by a fungus (*Endothia parasitica*). It is one of the most destructive plant diseases in North America. It was first discovered in New York in 1904, and within 30 years every stand of chestnut trees in the eastern half of the United States had been infected or killed. Almost all of the native chestnut trees are gone. The blight does not kill the roots, but leaves old sprouting stumps to harbor the fungus. New sprouts may grow for several years before they are killed. Trees planted on the West Coast or in the Midwest, outside the natural range of the chestnut, may grow to maturity. The spores enter the tree at a wound; a swollen canker develops and expands through the wood. The canker cuts off the flow of nutrients and water through the vessels, causing dieback of the parts beyond the affected area. Cankers develop throughout the tree, eventually killing it.

SOLUTION: There is no effective control for chestnut blight. Remove diseased trees, including the stump. Asiatic chestnuts are resistant to the disease.

Castanea cultural information
Light: Full sun
Water: Occasional deep watering
Soil: Well drained, nonalkaline
Fertilizer: Light

CATALPA

Catalpa sphinx caterpillars (half life size).

PROBLEM: Small holes are chewed in the upper surfaces of the leaves. Large yellow and black striped caterpillars with a sharp "horn" at the tail end feed in groups on young leaves. As the caterpillars develop (to a length of 1 to 3 inches), they spread throughout the tree and feed singly on leaf edges. The tree may be completely defoliated. Damage occurs from May to August.

ANALYSIS: Catalpa sphinx
(*Ceratomia catalpae*)
The caterpillar is the larval stage of a large night-flying moth that is seldom seen. The moth passes the winter as a pupa in the ground. In spring, the moth emerges and the female lays her eggs on young catalpa leaves. The eggs hatch and the larvae feed for several weeks. If the larvae are left uncontrolled they develop into moths, producing a second generation of caterpillars that may completely defoliate the tree by mid to late summer.

SOLUTION: Control with ORTHO Orthene Systemic Insect Control or ORTHO Isotox Insect Killer when damage is first noticed in spring. Repeat in midsummer if the tree becomes reinfested. In fall, clean up debris beneath the tree to reduce the number of overwintering pupae.

The catalpa sphinx caterpillar is good fishing bait. Control the insects by hand-picking them off the tree and then go fishing.

CEANOTHUS (WILD LILAC)

Scorched leaves.

Verticillium wilt.

Leaf spot.

PROBLEM: During hot weather, usually in July or August, leaves turn brown around the edges and between the veins. Sometimes the whole leaf dies. Many leaves may drop during late summer. This problem is most severe on the youngest branches. Trees do not generally die. Browning and withering can develop whether the soil around the roots is moist or dry.

ANALYSIS: Summer leaf scorch
Leaf scorch is caused by excessive evaporation of moisture from the leaves. In hot weather, water evaporates rapidly from the leaves. If the roots can't absorb and convey water fast enough to replenish this loss, then the leaves turn brown and wither. This usually occurs in dry soil, but leaves also can scorch when the soil is moist. Drying winds, severed roots, limited soil area or low temperatures can also cause scorch. For more information about leaf scorch, see page 865.

SOLUTION: To prevent further scorch, deep-water trees during periods of hot weather to wet down the entire root space (see page 906 for more information about watering trees). Newly transplanted trees should be watered whenever the rootball is dry 2 inches below the surface. There are no controls for scorch on trees in moist soil. Plant trees adapted to your climate.

Catalpa cultural information
Light: Full sun
Water: Occasional deep watering
Soil: Tolerates many types
Fertilizer: Light

PROBLEM: The leaves on a branch turn yellow at the margins, then brown and dry. During hot weather, the leaves may wilt. New leaves are stunted and yellow. The leaves on uninfected portions remain green. The infected tree may die slowly, branch by branch, over several seasons. Or the whole tree may wilt and die within a few months. Some trees may recover. The tissue under the bark on the dying side shows brownish streaks when cut. To examine for streaks, peel back the bark at the bottom of the dying branch. The brown discoloration may be very apparent or barely visible in the cut area.

ANALYSIS: Verticillium wilt
This wilt disease affects many ornamental trees and shrubs. It is caused by a soil-inhabiting fungus (*Verticillium* species). The disease is spread by contaminated seeds, plants, soil, equipment, and ground water. The fungus enters the tree through the roots and spreads up into the branches through the water-conducting vessels in the trunk. The vessels become discolored and plugged. The plugging cuts off the flow of water and nutrients to the branches, causing the leaf discoloration and branch wilting.

SOLUTION: No chemical control is available. Fertilize and water the affected tree to stimulate vigorous growth. Remove all dead wood. Do not remove branches on which leaves have recently wilted. These branches may produce new leaves in 3 to 4 weeks or next spring. Remove dead trees. If replanting in the same area, plant trees and shrubs that are resistant to verticillium (see page 995).

PROBLEM: Spots and blotches appear on the leaves. The spots may be yellow, red, tan, gray, or brown. They range in size from barely visible to ¼ inch in diameter. Several spots may join to form blotches. Leaves may yellow and die. Some leaves may drop. Leaf spotting is most severe in moist, humid weather.

ANALYSIS: Leaf spot
Several different fungi cause leaf spots on ceanothus. These spots are unsightly but rarely harmful to the plant. Plants weakened by low temperatures and wind exposure are most susceptible to invasion by leaf spot fungi. The fungi are spread by wind and splashing water. Spots develop where the fungi enter the tissue. If wet or humid weather persists, the fungi spread through the tissue and blotches form. They survive the winter on the leaves and twigs. Most leaf organisms do their greatest damage in mild weather (between 50° and 85°F).

SOLUTION: Once leaves become spotted they will remain so. Where practical, remove infected leaves from the plant. Collect and destroy any fallen leaves. To reduce unsightly damage, spray with a fungicide containing *zineb* when new growth begins in spring. Repeat 2 more times at intervals of 2 weeks, or for as long as the weather remains favorable for infection. Add a spreader-sticker to the spray. For more information on spreader-stickers, see page 915.

Ceanothus cultural information
Light: Full sun
Water: Grows best in dry soil
Soil: Tolerates many types
Fertilizer: Light

CEANOTHUS (WILD LILAC)

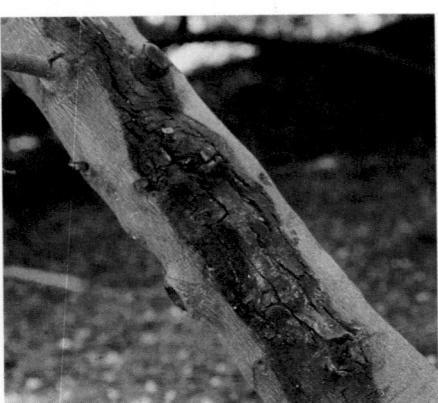

Canker on ceanothus.

PROBLEM: The young leaves are yellowish or off-color. Many of the leaves wilt and fall off, and overall plant growth is sparse. Eventually the whole plant dies. The roots are dark and rotted. There may be a dark, sunken canker on the stem near the soil line.

ANALYSIS: Root and crown rot
This disease is caused by any of a number of different fungi that thrive in waterlogged, heavy soils. Some of these fungi attack the plant stems at the soil level, while others attack the roots. Infection causes the roots and stems to decay, resulting in wilting, then yellowing leaves, and eventually the death of the plant. These fungi are spread by infested soil and transplants.

SOLUTION: Remove dead and dying plants. Allow the soil around the plants to dry out. (For more information on this technique, see page 857.) Avoid future root rot problems by planting in well-drained soil. For information on improving soil drainage, see page 901.

CELASTRUS (BITTERSWEET)

Euonymus scale (4 times life size).

PROBLEM: Yellow or whitish spots appear on the upper surfaces of the leaves. Leaves may drop, and the plant may become bare by midsummer. In severe cases, stems die back. The stems and the undersides of the leaves are covered with dark brown, oystershell-shaped, crusty bumps or soft, white, elongated scales. The bumps and scales can be scraped off.

ANALYSIS: Euonymus scale
(*Unaspis euonymi*)
This scale, a serious pest of bittersweet and many other ornamental shrubs, is found throughout the United States. The scales spend the winter on the twigs and branches of bittersweet, laying their eggs in spring. In late spring to early summer the young scales, called *crawlers*, settle on leaves or stems. The small ($\frac{1}{10}$ inch), soft-bodied young feed by inserting their mouthparts and sucking sap from the plant. The legs atrophy and a crusty or waxy shell develops over the body. The males are white and very noticeable on the leaves and stems. The mature female scales are brown and shaped like an oystershell. They lay their eggs underneath the shell. The cycle may be repeated up to 3 times during the growing season. An uncontrolled infestation of these scales may kill the plant after 2 or 3 years. Several other species of scale also infest bittersweet. For more information about scales, see page 878.

SOLUTION: Spray with ORTHO Isotox Insect Killer or ORTHO Orthene Systemic Insect Control in early summer (late spring in the South), when the young are active. The following spring, before new growth begins, spray the trunk and branches with a *dormant oil spray* to control overwintering insects.

CELTIS (HACKBERRY)

Witch's broom.

PROBLEM: There are broomlike growths of twigs throughout the tree. The clusters of twigs are most noticeable after leaf fall. Affected branches are weakened and break easily during windstorms.

ANALYSIS: Witch's broom
Witch's broom is most severe on common or American hackberry (*Celtis occidentalis*). The cause of this problem is not definitely known. However, a powdery mildew fungus (*Sphaerotheca phytophila*) and a gall mite (*Eriophyes* species) are usually associated with witch's broom. Gall mites cause proliferation of tissue in many plants. In spring, affected buds are larger and more open than normal. Microscopic mites and black spore-producing bodies from the fungus may be found inside. Branches from the affected buds become dwarfed and clustered, giving the witch's broom effect. Although the damage is unsightly, trees with this problem are not seriously harmed.

SOLUTION: There is no effective chemical control for this problem. If the brooms are unsightly, prune them off. For more information about pruning, see ORTHO's book *All About Pruning*.

Celtis cultural information
Light: Full sun
Water: Drought tolerant once established
Soil: Tolerates many types
Fertilizer: Light

CERCIS (REDBUD)

Galls caused by leaf gall psyllids.

Canker.

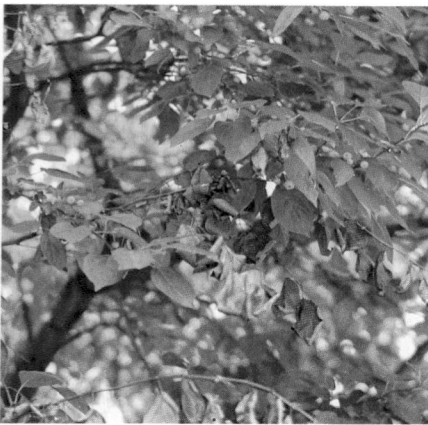
Verticillium wilt.

PROBLEM: The lower surfaces of the leaves are covered with cylindrical nipple- or crater-shaped or blisterlike growths. The upper surface of the leaf is spotted and yellowing. If the growth is broken open during the summer, a tiny (1/10 inch) yellowish orange insect is found inside. In late August or September, houses are invaded and windows and screens are covered with dark-colored flying insects, 1/8 inch long.

ANALYSIS: Hackberry leaf gall psyllids (*Pachypsylla* species)
The hackberry psyllid adults are considered more a nuisance than a destructive tree pest. The growth and vigor of the tree are not noticeably affected by the insects. Adult psyllids spend the winter in protected places such as buildings, trash, and bark crevices. In spring, just as the hackberry buds swell, the adults emerge from hibernation and fly or crawl around the ends of twigs. Eggs are deposited on the undersides of unfolded leaves; when they hatch, the immature insects feed by sucking the sap. This feeding stimulates abnormal leaf growth, producing the galls that enclose the insects and protect them from predators. The adults emerge in early fall, invading homes and buildings around hackberry trees.

SOLUTION: Once the protective galls have formed around the insects, there is no way to kill them. If adult psyllids invade the home, reduce the infestation by vacuuming them up. Destroy the sweeper bag contents. Spray trees with ORTHO Orthene Systemic Insect Control as leaves are unfolding in the spring to control overwintering adults and newly hatched immature psyllids before galls are formed.

PROBLEM: The leaves on a branch wilt and turn brown. Eventually they drop. Twigs or branches are often dead or dying. There are sunken oval areas, with black centers and cracks along the edges, at the base of the affected twigs or branches.

ANALYSIS: Canker
This plant disease, caused by a fungus (*Botryosphaeria ribis*), is the most destructive disease of redbud. It also affects more than 50 woody plants in the eastern half of the country. (For a list of susceptible plants, see page 1002.) Spores, produced in the sunken areas during wet periods in spring and summer, are spread to healthy branches by splashing rain and wind. The fungus enters the tree through wounds or dead and dying twigs, and a sunken canker develops. The fungus slowly spreads through the wood in all directions, cutting off the flow of nutrients and water to the affected branch. The leaves wilt and die, and branches above the cankered area are usually killed.

SOLUTION: There is no effective chemical control available. Prune out and destroy dead twigs and branches, cutting at least 3 inches below the cankered area. Sterilize pruning shears after each cut with rubbing alcohol. Paint the cuts with ORTHO Pruning Seal. Remove dying trees. To help prevent infection, avoid wounding trees.

Cercis cultural information
Light: Full sun to shade
Water: Generally grows best in moist soil
Soil: Tolerates many types
Fertilizer: Light

PROBLEM: The leaves on a branch turn yellow at the margins, then brown and dry. During hot weather, the leaves may wilt. New leaves may be stunted and yellowish. The infected tree may die slowly, branch by branch, over several seasons. Or the whole tree may wilt and die within a few months. Some trees may recover. The tissue under the bark on the dying side shows dark streaks when cut. To examine for streaks, peel back the bark at the bottom of the dying branch. The dark discoloration may be very apparent or barely visible in the area just underneath the bark.

ANALYSIS: Verticillium wilt
This wilt disease attacks many ornamental trees and shrubs. It is caused by a soil-inhabiting fungus (*Verticillium* species). The disease is spread by contaminated seeds, plants, soil, equipment, and ground water. The fungus enters the tree through the roots and spreads up into the branches through the water-conducting vessels in the trunk. The vessels become discolored and plugged. The plugging cuts off the flow of water and nutrients to the branches, causing leaf discoloration and wilting.

SOLUTION: No chemical control is available. Fertilize and water the affected tree to stimulate vigorous growth. Remove all dead wood. Do not remove branches on which leaves have recently wilted. These branches may produce new leaves in 3 to 4 weeks or next spring. Remove dead trees. If replanting in the same area, plant trees that are resistant to verticillium (see page 995).

499

CHAENOMELES (FLOWERING QUINCE) . CHOISYA _____ CINNAMOMUM (CAMPHOR TREE) _____

Rust.

Spider mite damage.

Verticillium wilt.

PROBLEM: Yellow or orange spots appear on young leaves and twigs. Heavy infection causes spotted leaves to fall prematurely. The plant may be weak and stunted.

ANALYSIS: Rust
This disease is caused by two species of fungi (*Gymnosporangium clavipes* and *G. libocedri*). These fungi require both quince and certain junipers or incense cedar to complete their life cycles. Rust spores on quince cannot infect another quince, but must alternate between quince and one of the evergreens. Windborne spores from the evergreen plant infect quince in spring. With warm, wet weather, the spores germinate and infect the leaves and twigs, causing the spotting. In August, spores are released during dry weather and carried by wind back to the evergreen plant. Rust (*G. clavipes*) on junipers causes swellings and possibly dieback on twigs. The main trunk has rough black patches or rings around the bark. Swellings and witch's broom (a dense bushy growth on the branches) develop from rust infection on incense cedars.

SOLUTION: To prevent infection from incense cedar and junipers, spray with a fungicide containing *ferbam*, *zineb*, or *mancozeb* as soon as new leaves appear. Repeat the spray 2 more times at weekly intervals. Do not plant flowering quince within several hundred yards of incense cedars and junipers. For a list of plants susceptible to quince rust, see page 1000.

PROBLEM: Leaves are stippled yellow and dirty. Sometimes there is a silken webbing on the lower surfaces of the leaves. New leaves may be distorted. To determine if the plant is infested with mites, hold a sheet of white paper underneath an affected leaf and tap the leaf sharply. Minute green, red, or yellow specks the size of pepper grains will drop to the paper and begin to crawl around. The pests are easily seen against the white background.

ANALYSIS: Spider mites
Spider mites, related to spiders, are major pests of many garden plants. They cause damage by sucking sap from the undersides of leaves. As a result of feeding, the green leaf pigment disappears, producing the stippled appearance. Mites are active throughout the growing season, but most are favored by hot, dry weather (70°F and up). By midsummer, they build up to tremendous numbers.

SOLUTION: Spray with a pesticide containing *dicofol* to control mites. Repeat spray 3 more times, 5 to 7 days apart.

_____

Choisya cultural information
Light: Full sun to part shade
Water: Occasional deep watering
Soil: Loose, well drained, nonalkaline
Fertilizer: Medium

PROBLEM: The leaves on a branch turn yellow at the margins, then brown and dry. During hot weather, the leaves may wilt. New leaves may be stunted and yellowish. The infected tree may die slowly, branch by branch, over several seasons. Or the whole tree may wilt and die within a few months. The tissue under the bark on the dying side shows dark streaks when cut. To examine for streaks, peel back the bark at the bottom of the dying branch.

ANALYSIS: Verticillium wilt
This wilt disease is caused by a soil-inhabiting fungus (*Verticillium dahliae*) that lives in the soil. The fungus enters the tree through the roots and spreads up into the branches through the water-conducting vessels in the trunk. The vessels become discolored and plugged. The plugging cuts off the flow of water and nutrients to the branches, causing the leaf discoloration and wilting.

SOLUTION: No chemical control is available. Fertilize and water the affected tree to stimulate vigorous growth. Remove all dead wood. If replanting in the same area, plant trees and shrubs that are resistant to verticillium. For a list of resistant trees and shrubs, see page 995. For more information about verticillium, see page 858.

_____

Cinnamomum cultural information
Light: Full sun
Water: Occasional deep watering
Soil: Loose, well drained, nonalkaline
Fertilizer: Light

CORNUS (DOGWOOD)

CORNUS

ADAPTATION: Throughout the United States except in desert areas.

FLOWERING TIME: February to July. Colors range from white to red. Clusters of reddish berries develop in fall that often persist after the leaves have fallen.

LIGHT: Partial shade to full sun.

SOIL: Well drained, rich in organic matter, acid (pH 5.5 to 6.5).

FERTILIZER: Fertilize with ORTHO Azalea, Camellia & Rhododendron Food 5–10–10 according to label directions.

WATER:
How much: Apply enough water to wet the soil 2 to 3 feet deep. To determine the proper amount of water for your soil type, see page 906.
How often: Most dogwoods prefer moist soil. Water when the soil is moist but not wet 4 inches below the soil surface. For more information about watering, see page 906.

PRUNING: Shrubs grown for their colorful bark should be given a vigorous pruning in the spring every few years to force new, colorful growth. Shrubs grown as dense screens should be cut back at the base every spring.

Spot anthracnose.

PROBLEM: Small (up to ⅛ inch) circular or elongated reddish purple spots appear on the flower petals (bracts). If spotting is severe, the flowers are malformed. The centers of the spots eventually dry and may drop out, leaving a small round hole. The leaves are infected after blooming, showing dark purple, circular spots or blotches. Young shoots and berries are also infected. Severely infected shoots die. The disease is worst in wet weather.

ANALYSIS: Spot anthracnose
This plant disease is caused by a fungus (*Elsinoë corni*). The fungus survives the winter on infected plant tissue. During wet weather in early spring, the fungus is splashed onto the dogwood blooms. Spots develop where the fungus enters the tissue. If wet weather continues, it spreads to the leaves and twigs.

SOLUTION: If spots are noticed on dogwood blooms in spring, spray with a fungicide containing *captan* or *mancozeb* at petal fall. Repeat 4 weeks later and again in September after flower buds form. The following spring, begin spraying when flower buds start to open. Prune out and destroy infected twigs. Rake up and destroy leaves in the fall.

Flower and leaf blight.

PROBLEM: In rainy seasons, irregular, brown, wrinkled patches appear on the bracts (leaves that look like flower petals) at the end of their bloom period. If the weather remains wet or humid, gray mold develops on the patches. When the bracts fall, young leaves they touch often become infected and shrivel. The infected leaves usually drop.

ANALYSIS: Flower and leaf blight
This plant disease is caused by a fungus (*Botrytis cinerea*) that infects many flowers, fruits, and vegetables in the garden. The fungus is spread to aging flowers by wind and splashing rain. Brown patches develop where the fungus enters the tissue. If the weather turns dry, the fungus stops spreading, and symptoms disappear when the flowers fall. However, if wet or humid weather continues throughout the spring, a grayish mold consisting of fungal strands and spores develops on the diseased flowers. As the bracts fall on young leaves, the fungal strands penetrate the leaf tissue and the leaves become blighted.

SOLUTION: Once the flowers and leaves are infected, it is too late to spray. Pick off all fading flowers and blighted leaves. Sprays must be applied early in the flowering period. If the weather is extremely wet or humid during early bloom the following spring, spray with a fungicide containing *benomyl*, *zineb*, *maneb*, or *mancozeb* at midbloom.

CORNUS (DOGWOOD)

Summer leaf scorch.

Dogwood borer. *Insert:* Adult (life size).

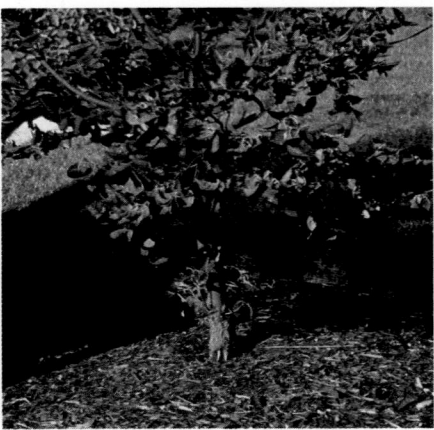

Crown canker.

PROBLEM: During hot weather, usually in July or August, leaves turn brown at the edges and between the veins. Sometimes the whole leaf dies. Many leaves may drop during late summer. This problem is most severe on the youngest branches. Trees do not generally die. Browning and withering can develop whether the soil around the roots is moist or dry.

ANALYSIS: Summer leaf scorch
Leaf scorch is caused by excessive evaporation of moisture from the leaves. In hot weather, water evaporates rapidly from the leaves. If the roots can't absorb and convey water fast enough to replenish this loss, the leaves turn brown and wither. For optimum growth, dogwoods require moist soil. Leaf scorch is most severe when water is unavailable because the soil is dry. However, scorch may also develop when the soil is moist if the weather is extremely hot. Drying winds, severed roots, and limited soil area can also cause scorch. For more information about scorch, see page 865.

SOLUTION: To prevent further scorch, deep-water trees during periods of hot weather to wet down the entire root space. (For more information about watering trees, see page 906.) Newly transplanted trees should be watered whenever the rootball is dry 2 inches below the surface. There are no controls for scorch on trees in moist soil. Plant trees adapted to your climate. In hot summer areas, plant dogwoods in partial shade.

PROBLEM: In midsummer, the leaves turn red and drop prematurely; eventually twigs or branches die back. Bark sloughs off around holes in a swollen area on the trunk or at the base of branches. Late in the summer, a fine sawdust may drop from the holes. Young trees are usually killed.

ANALYSIS: Dogwood borer
(*Synanthedon scitula*)
The dogwood borer, also known in the South as the *pecan borer*, is the larva of a brownish, clear-wing moth, ½-inch long. The borer infects flowering dogwood, pecan, and many other ornamental and fruit trees. The moths are active from late May until September. They may be seen flying around trees during the summer. The moth lays its eggs on the bark, usually near a wound or old borer injury. After the eggs hatch, the ½-inch-long white larvae with brown heads wander around until they find an opening in the bark. They feed in the wood just under the bark, girdling the branches and causing the dieback. The larvae spend the winter inside the tree. Several other borers also infest dogwood. For more information about borers, see page 873.

SOLUTION: Spray or paint the trunk and branches with ORTHO Lindane Borer & Leaf Miner Spray, beginning in April or May. Repeat 4 more times at monthly intervals. Water and fertilize the tree regularly to maintain vigor. (For a guide to watering and fertilizers for trees and shrubs, see pages 906 and 904.) To prevent borer entrance, avoid wounding the trunks and branches. You can also reduce the amount of borer damage by inserting a fine wire up the entry hole to kill the larva.

PROBLEM: The leaves on one or more branches at the top of the tree are small and pale green. They turn prematurely red in mid or late summer. Twigs and branches die back and sometimes the whole tree dies. The symptoms usually develop over several years. At the base of the tree dark-colored sap may ooze from one point. As the disease progresses, a sunken area develops around the oozing sap and the bark crumbles, leaving wood exposed. The exposed wood in the sunken area is dark and discolored.

ANALYSIS: Crown canker
This plant disease, also known as *collar-rot*, is caused by a soil-inhabiting fungus (*Phytophthora cactorum*). The fungus is carried in affected plants or in infested soil or soil water. It is often a problem following periods when flooding has resulted in standing water around the base of trees. It enters the root crown through wounds and slowly kills the tissue, causing a sunken canker. The above-ground symptoms are caused by the blockage of water and nutrients through the trunk. When the canker encircles the trunk, the tree dies.

SOLUTION: Small cankers can be removed surgically with some success if all discolored bark and wood, including a 1-inch border area of apparently healthy bark and wood, is removed. Remove an elliptical piece of wood from the tree with a sharp knife, sterilizing the knife with rubbing alcohol after each cut. Clean the wound with alcohol and cover with ORTHO Pruning Seal. If the tree dies, do not plant another dogwood in the same area for 3 to 5 years. Avoid wounding and watering the base of the tree.

COTINUS (SMOKE TREE) _____   **COTONEASTER** _____

Verticillium wilt.

Cotoneaster webworm damage.

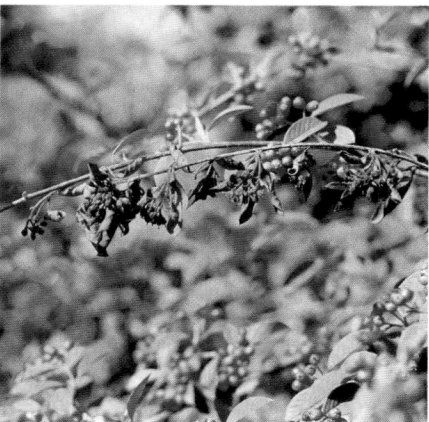

Fireblight.

PROBLEM: The leaves on a branch turn reddish purple at the margins, then brown, and curl inward. During hot weather, the leaves may wilt. Generally, the leaves drop prematurely. The infected plant may die slowly, branch by branch, over several seasons. Or the whole plant may wilt and die within a few months. Some shrubs may recover. The tissue under the bark on the dying side shows brownish streaks when cut. To examine for streaks, peel back the bark at the bottom of the dying branch. The brown discoloration may be very apparent or barely visible in the area just underneath the bark.

ANALYSIS: Verticillium wilt
This wilt disease attacks many ornamental trees and shrubs. It is caused by a soil-inhabiting fungus (*Verticillium* species) that persists indefinitely on plant debris or in the soil. The disease is spread by contaminated seeds, plants, soil, equipment, and ground water. The fungus enters the tree through the roots and spreads up into the branches through the water-conducting vessels in the trunk. The vessels become discolored and plugged. The plugging cuts off the flow of water and nutrients to the branches, causing leaf discoloration and wilting.

SOLUTION: No chemical control is available. Fertilize and water the affected tree to stimulate vigorous growth. Remove all dead wood. Do not remove branches on which leaves have recently wilted. These branches may produce new leaves in 3 to 4 weeks or next spring. Remove dead shrubs. If replanting in the same area, plant trees and shrubs that are resistant to verticillium. For a list of resistant trees and shrubs, see page 995; for more information about verticillium, see page 858.

PROBLEM: Clumps of leaves tied together with silk threads are scattered all over the bush. The leaves are skeletonized and brown. Small (up to ½ inch) yellow to dark brown caterpillars are feeding inside the dense silken webbing. Small plants may die.

ANALYSIS: Cotoneaster webworn
(*Rhynchopacha triatomaea*)
This webworn is the larval stage of a grayish black night-flying moth that is seldom seen. The webworm spends the winter in a large silken nest in a branch junction. It pupates in the spring, and the emerging moth lays eggs on the leaf stems. The larvae that hatch from these eggs feed throughout the summer on the leaflets, webbing them together for protection against predators and weather.

SOLUTION: Spray with an insecticide containing *acephate* or *diazinon* when webbing first appears. Repeat the spray in 2 weeks if damage continues.

_____

Cotoneaster cultural information
Light: Full sun
Water: Drought tolerant once established
Soil: Tolerates many types
Fertilizer: Light
_____

PROBLEM: New shoots suddenly wilt in spring and turn black as if scorched by fire. The bark at the base of the blighted shoots becomes water soaked, then dark, sunken, and dry; cracks may develop at the edge of the sunken area. In warm, moist spring weather, drops of brown ooze appear on the sunken bark. Young plants may die.

ANALYSIS: Fireblight
This plant disease is caused by a bacterium (*Erwinia amylovora*) that is very destructive to many trees and shrubs. For a list of susceptible plants, see page 1001. The bacteria spend the winter in sunken cankers on the branches. In spring, the bacteria ooze out of the cankers. Bees, flies, and other insects are attracted to the sweet, sticky ooze and become smeared with it. When the insects visit a cotoneaster flower for nectar, they infect it with the bacteria. The bacteria spread rapidly through the plant tissue in warm (65°F or higher), humid weather. Insects visiting these infected blossoms later carry bacteria-laden nectar to healthy blossoms. Rain, wind, and tools may also spread the bacteria. Tender or damaged leaves may be infected in midsummer.

SOLUTION: During spring and summer, prune out infected branches 12 to 15 inches beyond any visible discoloration and destroy them. A protective spray of a pesticide containing *basic copper sulfate* or *streptomycin*, applied before bud break in spring, will help prevent infection. Repeat at intervals of 5 to 7 days until the end of bloom. In the fall, prune out infected branches. Sterilize pruning shears with rubbing alcohol after each cut.

COTONEASTER ———————————————— **CRATAEGUS (HAWTHORN)** ——————

Damaged leaves. *Insert:* Lacebugs (⅓ life size).

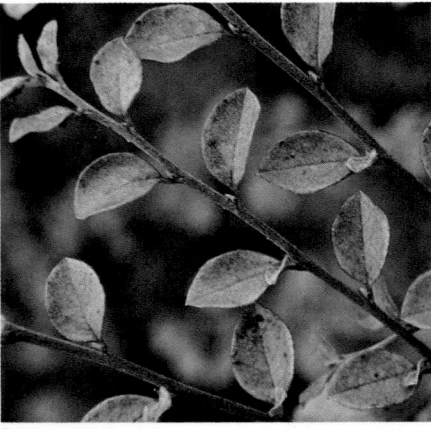

Spider mite damage.

CRATAEGUS (HAWTHORN) —

PROBLEM: The upper surfaces of the leaves are mottled yellow and green. The mottling may be confused with mite or leafhopper damage, but can be distinguished from other insect damage by the hard, black, shiny droplets found on the undersides of damaged leaves. Small (⅛ inch), light or dark spiny wingless insects or brownish insects with clear lace wings may be visible around the droplets and next to the midrib. The plant may be stunted. Damage occurs in spring and summer.

ANALYSIS: Hawthorn lacebug
(*Corythucha cydoniae*)
The hawthorn lacebug is found throughout the United States on cotoneaster, hawthorn, pyracantha, and fruiting quince. It overwinters as an adult on the plant in bark crevices, branch crotches, or other protected areas on the shrub. Both the spiny, wingless, immature insects and the lacewinged adults suck sap from the undersides of leaves throughout the growing season. As a result of feeding, the green leaf pigment disappears, causing the characteristic yellowing. Droplets of black excrement accumulate around the insects while they feed. Damage is unsightly and food production by the leaf is reduced, resulting in a loss of plant vigor.

SOLUTION: Spray with ORTHO Isotox Insect Killer or ORTHO Orthene Systemic Insect Control when damage first appears in spring. Thoroughly cover the undersurfaces of the leaves where insects feed. Repeat 7 to 10 days later. A third application may be necessary if the plant becomes reinfested in the summer.

PROBLEM: Reddish or brownish blisters, ⅛ inch across, develop on the undersides of the leaves. The blisters may be massed together to almost cover the leaf. The upper surface of the leaf is mottled brown or blackish. Berries may be deformed.

ANALYSIS: Pear leaf blister mite
(*Phytoptus pyri*)
This microscopic pinkish or white mite is found wherever cotoneaster is grown. It also infests pear, apple, mountain ash, and service berry. Adults spend the winter in bud scales, often hundreds in a single bud. As the buds swell in spring, the mites lay their eggs; the young feed and burrow into the undersides of unfolding leaves. New generations of mites are produced inside the blisters throughout the summer. As cold weather approaches, the mites migrate back to the bud scales to overwinter.

SOLUTION: Once the mite has entered the underside of the leaf it is difficult to control. Spray the undersides of the leaves with a miticide containing *dicofol* when damage is first noticed. Repeat 10 days later. The following early spring, just before growth starts, spray with ORTHO Volck Oil Spray or with ORTHO Orthorix Spray. As the leaves emerge, spray with a miticide containing *dicofol*. Repeat 10 days later.

ADAPTATION: Primarily zones 4 through 9. (To determine your climate zone, see the map on page 1004.) Not adapted to low desert areas.

FLOWERING TIME: Late spring.

LIGHT: Full sun.

SOIL: Hawthorns will thrive in almost any type of garden soil. However, most prefer a soil pH below 7.8.

FERTILIZER: Fertilize with ORTHO Evergreen, Tree & Shrub Food 12–6–6 according to label directions.

WATER:
How much: Apply enough water to wet the soil 2 to 3 feet deep. To determine the proper amount of water for your soil type, see page 906.
How often: Keep hawthorns on the dry side. Water when the soil is dry 4 inches below the surface. For more information about watering, see page 906.

PRUNING: Cut off any blighted or dead branches. Some shrubs may be sheared to form a dense hedge.

Fireblight.

Hawthorn rust.

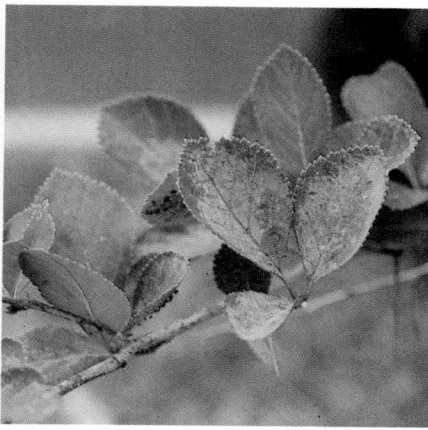

Lacebug damage.

PROBLEM: Blossoms and leaves of infected twigs suddenly wilt and turn black as if scorched by fire. Brown or blackened leaves cling to the branches. The bark at the base of the blighted twig becomes water-soaked, then dark, sunken, and dry; cracks may develop at the edge of the sunken area. In warm, moist spring weather, drops of brown ooze appear on the sunken bark. Young trees may die.

ANALYSIS: Fireblight
This disease is caused by a bacterium (*Erwinia amylovora*) that is very destructive to hawthorn and many other related plants. (For a list of susceptible plants, see page 1001.) The bacteria spend the winter in the sunken cankers on the branches. In spring, the bacteria ooze out of the cankers and attract bees and other insects. When the insects visit a hawthorn flower for nectar, they infect it with the bacteria. The bacteria spread rapidly through the plant tissue in warm (65°F or higher), humid weather. Insects visiting these infected blossoms later carry bacteria-laden nectar to healthy blossoms. Rain, wind, and tools may also spread the bacteria.

SOLUTION: During spring and summer, prune out infected branches 12 to 15 inches beyond any visible discoloration and destroy them. A protective spray of a pesticide containing *basic copper sulfate* or *streptomycin*, applied before bud break in spring, will help prevent infection. Repeat at intervals of 5 to 7 days until the end of bloom. In the fall, prune out infected branches. Sterilize pruning shears with rubbing alcohol after each cut. When planting new trees, use resistant varieties. For a list of hawthorns resistant to fireblight, see page 1001.

PROBLEM: In the summer, orange, red, gray, or brown spots develop on the upper surfaces of the leaves. Leaves are often distorted, and many may drop. Infected twigs and fruit are also deformed. Tiny whitish tubes may develop on the fruit and twigs, or brownish, horn-shaped bodies may develop in the fruit and on the undersides of leaves.

ANALYSIS: Hawthorn rust
This plant disease is caused by any of several species of fungi (*Gymnosporangium* species) that infect both hawthorns and red cedars or other species of junipers. The fungi cannot spread from hawthorn to hawthorn, but must alternate between junipers and hawthorns. In the spring, orange spores from junipers are carried by the wind to hawthorns. With warm, wet weather, the spores germinate and infect the leaves, twigs, and fruit. Depending on the species of rust, leaves become spotted, or the leaves, twigs, and fruit become deformed. Fruiting bodies develop on infected parts, which produce spores that are blown back to junipers. Some species of rust cause very little damage, while others may cause severe defoliation.

SOLUTION: If practical, eliminate junipers within a mile of hawthorns. If rust is a problem on your hawthorns, spray trees with a fungicide containing *maneb*, *zineb*, or *ferbam*, beginning just as the flower buds open. Repeat the spray 2 or 3 more times at intervals of 7 to 10 days.

PROBLEM: The upper surfaces of the leaves are mottled yellow and green. The mottling may be confused with mite or leafhopper damage, but can be distinguished from other insect damage by the hard, black, shiny droplets found on the undersides of damaged leaves. Small (⅛ inch) light or dark spiny wingless insects or brownish insects with clear lace wings may be visible around the droplets and next to the midrib. The plant may be stunted. Damage occurs in spring and summer.

ANALYSIS: Hawthorn lacebug
(*Corythucha cydoniae*)
The hawthorn lacebug is found throughout the United States on hawthorn, cotoneaster, pyracantha, and fruiting quince. It survives the winter as an adult on the plant in bark crevices, branch crotches, or other protected areas on the tree. Both the spiny, wingless, immature insects and the lace-wing adults suck sap from the undersides of leaves throughout the growing season. As a result of feeding, the green leaf pigment disappears, causing the characteristic yellowing. Droplets of black excrement accumulate around the insects while they feed. Damage is unsightly and food production by the leaf is reduced, resulting in a loss of plant vigor.

SOLUTION: Spray with ORTHO Isotox Insect Killer when damage first appears in spring. Thoroughly cover the undersides of the leaves where insects feed. Repeat 7 to 10 days later. A third application may be necessary if the plant becomes reinfested in the summer.

CRATAEGUS (HAWTHORN)

Aphids (half life size).

Woolly aphids (half life size).

Cottony cushion scales (twice life size).

PROBLEM: Young leaves are tightly curled, stunted, and yellowing. New growth may stop completely. A shiny, sticky substance may coat the leaves and drip onto plants and other objects, such as cars parked beneath the tree. A black sooty mold often grows on the sticky substance. Tiny (⅛ inch) green, pinkish, yellow, or black soft-bodied insects cluster on branch tips and the undersides of leaves. Ants may be present.

ANALYSIS: Aphids
Aphids do little damage in small numbers. However, they are extremely prolific and populations can rapidly build up to damaging numbers during the growing season. Damage occurs when the aphid sucks the juices from hawthorn leaves and stems. Some aphid species that attack hawthorn are unable to digest fully all the sugar in the sap and excrete the excess in a fluid called honeydew. The honeydew often drops onto the leaves or plants below. A sooty mold fungus may develop on the honeydew, causing the hawthorn leaves to appear black and dirty. Ants feed on this sticky substance, and are often present where there is an aphid infestation.

SOLUTION: Control aphids with ORTHO Isotox Insect Killer or ORTHO Orthene Systemic Insect Control when insects or damage are first noticed in late spring. Repeat at intervals of 2 weeks if damage continues.

PROBLEM: The twigs, branches, and sometimes the trunk are covered with white, cottony masses. The leaves and twigs are yellowing and the tree may be stunted. A sticky substance may coat the leaves, stems, and trunk. A black sooty mold may grow on the sticky substance.

ANALYSIS: Woolly aphids
(*Eriosoma* species)
Several species of woolly aphids attack hawthorn. They do little damage in small numbers. However, they are extremely prolific and populations can rapidly build up to damaging numbers during the growing season. Damage occurs when the woolly aphid sucks the juices from the hawthorn twigs, branches, or trunk. It is unable to digest fully all the sugar in the plant sap and excretes the excess in a fluid called honeydew. The honeydew often drops onto leaves or plants below. A sooty mold fungus may develop on the sticky substance, causing the hawthorn leaves to appear black and dirty. The woolly apple aphid (*Eriosoma lanigerum*) may also cause damage by burrowing down into the soil and feeding on the roots. The feeding causes marble-like knots to form and results in stunted roots and a weak tree.

SOLUTION: Control with ORTHO Isotox Insect Killer or ORTHO Liquid Sevin when damage is first noticed. Repeat at intervals of 2 weeks if the plant becomes reinfested. If you suspect a root infestation, carefully dig away the soil from around some roots and check for aphids or galls. If aphids or galls are present, apply ORTHO Systemic Rose & Flower Care 8–12–4 to the soil around the tree and water it in thoroughly.

PROBLEM: The leaves or bark are covered with white, cottony masses; brown or whitish crusty bumps; or clusters of somewhat flattened brown or white scaly bumps. The bumps can be scraped or picked off. Leaves turn yellow and may drop. Sometimes a shiny, sticky substance coats the leaves. A black sooty mold often grows on the sticky substance. Branches are killed by heavy infestations.

ANALYSIS: Scales
Many species of scales infest hawthorn. They lay their eggs on leaves or bark and in spring to midsummer the young scales, called *crawlers*, settle around them. The small (¹⁄₁₀ inch), soft-bodied young feed by sucking sap from the plant. The legs usually atrophy and, with some types, a shell develops over the body. The types of scales that do not develop shells are very conspicuous. The females are covered with a white, cottony egg sac, containing up to 2500 eggs. Scales covered with a shell are less noticeable. The shell often blends in with the plant, and the eggs are inconspicuous beneath the covering. Some species of scales are unable to digest fully all the sugar in the plant sap, and excrete the excess in a fluid called honeydew. A sooty mold fungus may develop on the honeydew, causing the hawthorn leaves to appear black and dirty.

SOLUTION: Control with ORTHO Isotox Insect Killer or ORTHO Liquid Sevin when the young are active. Contact your local Cooperative Extension Office (see page 1011) to determine the best time to spray for scales in your area. To control scales during the dormant season, spray with ORTHO Volck Oil Spray. For more information about scales, see page 878.

CYPRESS FAMILY (ARBORVITAE, CHAMAECYPARIS, INCENSE CEDAR)

Borer hole.

PROBLEM: Foliage is sparse on a branch or at the top of the tree; eventually the twigs and branch die. Holes or tunnels are apparent in the trunk or branches. The bark may die over the tunnels and slough off, revealing trails. Sap or sawdust usually surrounds the holes. Weakened branches break during wind or snow storms. Weak, young, or newly transplanted trees are most susceptible to injury, and may be killed.

ANALYSIS: Borers
The borers that attack hawthorn are the larvae of several different types of beetles that also infest a wide variety of other trees and shrubs. Throughout the summer, females lay eggs in bark crevices. The larvae feed by tunneling through the bark, sapwood, or heartwood. This stops the flow of nutrients and water in that area by cutting the conducting vessels; branch and twig dieback result. Sap flow acts as a defense against borers if the tree is healthy. When the borer burrows into the wood, tree sap fills the hole and drowns the insect. Factors that weaken the tree, such as mechanical injuries, damage by leaf-feeding insects, poor growing conditions, and transplanting make it more attractive to female beetles.

SOLUTION: Cut out and destroy all dead and dying branches. Reduce the amount of borer damage by inserting a fine wire into the entry hole and pushing it up the feeding channel to kill the larva. Insecticides containing *lindane* may help if damage is not too severe. Spray the trunk and branches at monthly intervals from May through July. Maintain plant health and vigor by watering and fertilizing regularly.

CYPRESS FAMILY

ADAPTATION:
Chamaecyparis species: Zones 4 through 9. Plants should be protected from hot, dry winds.
Cupressocyparis and *Cupressus* species: Zones 5 through 10.
Thuja species: Zones 2 through 9. (To determine your climate zone, see the map on page 1004.)

LIGHT: Full sun.

SOIL:
Chamaecyparis species: Needs good drainage.
Cupressocyparis and *Cupressus* species: Tolerate a wide variety of soils.
Thuja species: Any good garden soil.

FERTILIZER: Fertilize with ORTHO Evergreen, Tree & Shrub Food 12–6–6 according to label directions.

WATER:
How much: Apply enough water to wet the soil 3 to 4 feet deep. To determine the proper amount of water for your soil type, see page 906.
How often:
Chamaecyparis species: Grows best in moist soil, but will tolerate some drought. Water when the soil is moist but no longer wet 4 inches below the surface.
Cupressocyparis species: Water when the soil is barely moist 4 inches below the surface.
Cupressus species: Grows best if kept on the dry side. Water when the soil is dry 4 inches below the surface.
Thuja species: Will tolerate wet soil, but does best in moist soil. Water when the soil is moist but not wet 4 inches below the surface. For more information about watering, see page 906.

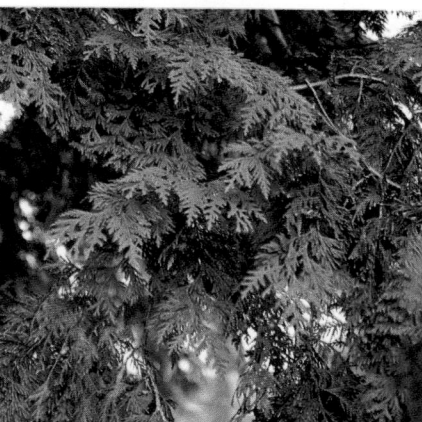

Twig and needle blight damage on western red cedar.

PROBLEM: Needles, twigs, and branches turn brown. In some cases, the upper branches die from the tips back; in other cases, the lower two-thirds of the plant dies. The needles often drop in late summer, starting at the tips and leaving the infected branches bare. Sometimes minute black dots appear on the dead needles and stems. This disease is most serious in wet weather or in shady locations. Plants may be killed.

ANALYSIS: Twig and needle blight
A number of different fungi cause twig and needle blight on plants in the cypress family. During wet weather, spores germinate on twigs and spread into the needles and twigs above and below the point of entrance, killing them. Reinfection may continue until the whole plant dies, or the plant may persist for many years in an unsightly condition. With some fungi, black spore-producing bodies develop and spend the winter on dead needles.

SOLUTION: Prune out and destroy infected branches below the line between diseased and healthy tissue, making the cut into live tissue. Valuable specimens can be sprayed with a fungicide containing *basic copper sulfate* at weekly intervals throughout the growing season. Plant trees in areas with good air circulation and full sun.

CYPRESS FAMILY (ARBORVITAE, CHAMAECYPARIS, INCENSE CEDAR)

Leaf browning on cedar.

Leafminer damage to arborvitae.

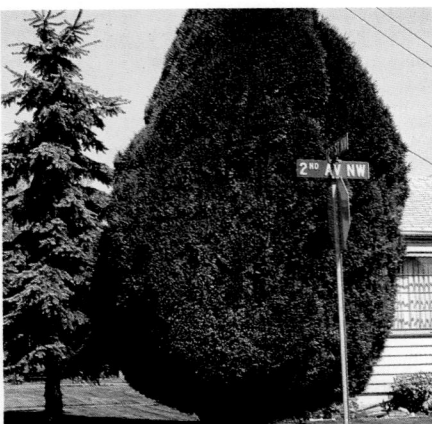

Winter injury to arborvitae.

PROBLEM: The older leaves, on the inside of the tree nearest the trunk, turn brown and drop. This condition may develop in a few days or over several weeks, in either spring or fall.

ANALYSIS: Leaf browning and shedding
Leaf browning and shedding is a natural process similar to the dropping of leaves of deciduous trees. It is usually more pronounced on arborvitae (*Thuja*) than on other plants in the cypress family. Sometimes it takes place every year; in other cases, it occurs every second or third year. When growing conditions have been favorable the previous season, leaf shedding occurs over several weeks and is less noticeable. However, if the plant has been exposed to unfavorable conditions such as drying, or a spider mite or insect infestation, during the growing season, leaf drop develops within a few days. Leaf drop is also caused by new growth shading older interior growth.

SOLUTION: No chemical controls are necessary. Fertilize and water plants regularly. Provide full sun. Check plants for insects and mites during the growing season.

PROBLEM: Leaf tips turn yellow, then brown and dry, contrasting sharply with the healthy green foliage. Damage is most severe in plants growing in shady areas. When a yellow leaf is torn open, a small (⅕ inch long) greenish caterpillar with a dark head may be found inside. Gray or brownish moths with a ⅓-inch wingspread may be seen flying around the plant in April, May, or June.

ANALYSIS: Leafminers and tip moths (*Argyresthia* species)
Several species of insects, known as leafminers in the eastern United States and tip moths on the West Coast, infest arborvitae, cypress, and juniper. Damage is unsightly, but plants may lose over half of their foliage and still survive. The larvae spend the winter inside the leaf tips. When the weather warms in late spring, adult moths emerge and lay eggs on the leaves. The eggs hatch and the larvae tunnel into the leaf tips, devouring the green tissue. The tips above the point of entry yellow and die. The larvae feed until late fall, or through the winter until early spring.

SOLUTION: Spray with an insecticide containing *diazinon* or *malathion* when eggs are hatching in June or July (mid-August in the far northeastern states). Trim and destroy infested leaves in fall and spring.

PROBLEM: Leaves turn yellow at first, then rusty brown and dry. Twigs and branches may die back. The tree is growing in a climate where cold, dry, windy days are common or where plants may be exposed to late fall or early spring freezes. The soil may be frozen.

ANALYSIS: Winter injury
Arborvitae are damaged by cold, drying winter winds, especially if temperatures are below freezing. These trees are commonly planted as windbreaks and in exposed areas where growing conditions may be unfavorable. Moisture is lost from the leaves more rapidly than it can be replaced by the root system. Cells in the leaves dry out and die. This condition is most pronounced when water is unavailable because the soil is dry or frozen. Leaves, along with twigs and branches, also die during early fall or late spring freezes when the plant is growing. Young succulent growth cannot withstand freezing temperatures.

SOLUTION: Prune out dead twigs and branches. Provide shelter for plants growing in extremely cold areas. To avoid succulent growth in fall, do not fertilize late in the season. During a dry fall, irrigate plants thoroughly to reduce winter injury.

Aphid damage to cypress.

Spider mite webs on Italian cypress.

Root rot on Port Orford cedar.

PROBLEM: Needles turn brown on twigs and branches; branches may die back. The plant is often weak and stunted. A white cottony material or a sticky substance may coat the needles. Small (⅙ inch) green or brown soft-bodied insects cluster on twigs and branches. Ants may be present.

ANALYSIS: Aphids
Aphids do little damage in small numbers. However, they are extremely prolific and populations can rapidly build up to damaging numbers during the growing season. Damage occurs when the aphid sucks the juices from the twigs and branches. The brown arborvitae aphid (*Cinara tujafilina*) excretes a white, cottony material as it feeds. Other aphids that attack plants in the cypress family are unable to digest all the sugar in the plant sap and excrete the excess in a fluid called honeydew. The honeydew often drops onto the leaves below. Ants feed on this sticky substance, and are often present where there is an aphid infestation.

SOLUTION: Spray with ORTHO Isotox Insect Killer or ORTHO Malathion 50 Insect Spray when insects or damage are first noticed. Repeat at intervals of 2 weeks if damage continues.

PROBLEM: The needles are stippled, yellowing, and dirty. Sometimes there is a silken webbing on the needles and stems. Needles may turn brown and fall off. To determine if the tree is infested with mites, hold a sheet of white paper underneath some stippled needles and tap the foliage sharply. Minute dark green, black, or red specks about the size of pepper grains will drop to the paper and begin to crawl around. The pests are easily seen against the white background.

ANALYSIS: Spider mites
Spider mites, especially the spruce spider mite (*Oligonychus ununguis*), are among the most destructive pests of evergreen trees. In the cypress family, they attack mainly arborvitae (*Thuja* species) and *Chamaecyparis*. They cause damage by sucking sap from the underside of the needles. As a result of feeding, the green leaf pigment disappears, producing the stippled appearance. This symptom can be confused with certain types of air pollution damage. Mites are active throughout the growing season but are favored by hot, dry weather (70°F and up). By midsummer, they build up to tremendous numbers. Young plants may die the first season. If mites are left uncontrolled over a period of years, older trees die progressively from the lower branches upward.

SOLUTION: Control with ORTHO Isotox Insect Killer or ORTHO Orthene Insect Spray in mid to late May to kill young mites of the first generation. Repeat the spray 2 more times, at intervals of 7 to 10 days. Additional spraying may be needed later in the season if the plant becomes reinfested.

PROBLEM: Foliage turns off-color, starting from the bottom branches and progressing upward. Trees with green foliage fade to tan or light brown. Varieties of plants with blue foliage turn greenish at first, then fade to tan or light brown. The brownish foliage is crisp and dry, and eventually drops. By the time the trees turn brownish, they are dead. If bark is removed on the lower trunk, a sharp line is usually seen between healthy white tissue and infected red-brown tissue.

ANALYSIS: Root rot
This plant disease is caused by soil-inhabiting fungi (*Phytophthora* species) that infect many different plants. (For a list of susceptible plants, see page 1000.) The fungi are carried in plants, soil, or soil water. They invade and kill the roots and then spread into the main trunk, cutting off the flow of nutrients and water through the tree. The foliage turns brown, and the tree dies.

SOLUTION: There are no effective chemical controls. Once the fungus becomes established in the soil, it will remain indefinitely. Replace the trees with resistant plants. For a list of resistant plants, see page 1000.

CYPRESS FAMILY

Cypress bark scale (half life size).

PROBLEM: Needles and stems are covered with white, cottony masses or brownish, crusty bumps. The bumps can be scraped or picked off. Needles turn yellow and new growth slows. In severe cases, branches die back. A shiny, sticky substance may coat the leaves. A black sooty mold often grows on the sticky substance.

ANALYSIS: Scales
Several species of scales infest plants in the cypress family. They lay their eggs on the needles or bark and in spring to midsummer the young scales, called *crawlers*, settle on needles and twigs. The small (1/10 inch), soft-bodied young feed by sucking sap from the plant. The legs usually atrophy and, with some types, a shell develops over the body. The types of scales that do not develop shells are very conspicuous. The females are covered with a white, cottony egg sac, containing up to 2500 eggs. Scales covered with a shell are less noticeable. The shell often blends in with the plant and the eggs are inconspicuous beneath the covering. Some species of scales are unable to digest fully all the sugar in the plant sap, and excrete the excess in a fluid called honeydew. A sooty mold fungus may develop on the honeydew, causing the leaves to appear black and dirty.

SOLUTION: Control with ORTHO Isotox Insect Killer or ORTHO Orthene Systemic Insect Control when the young are active. Contact your local Cooperative Extension Office (see page 1011) to determine the best time to spray for scales in your area. Repeat if the plant becomes reinfested. During the winter, spray with ORTHO Volck Oil Spray. For more information about scales, see page 878.

DAPHNE

Crown rot.

PROBLEM: Leaves turn yellow and wither. Diseased branches slowly dry out and die. White fungal strands, or brown irregular-shaped or round pellets may be found at the base of the plant or on the ground nearby. If the plant is pulled up, the roots appear black and decayed.

ANALYSIS: Crown rot
This disease is caused by fungi (*Sclerotium* species) that live in the soil and attack many different shrubs and flowers in the garden. The fungi penetrate the stems at or below the soil level. They move down into the roots and up into the base of the plant, causing death of the root system and stem tissue. Crown rot is spread by moving water, infested soil, and contaminated tools. The fungus can also grow over the soil to attack adjacent plants. The brown fungal pellets that form can survive in dry soil and extremes of temperatures to reinfect healthy plants when conditions are suitable. These pellets can live in the soil or in plant debris for many years. Crown rot is most severe during periods of warm (70°F and up), moist soil and weather conditions.

SOLUTION: Once the plant is infected, there is no chemical that will control the fungus. Remove and destroy the infected plant and the surrounding soil to 6 inches beyond the area of the plant. Removing the soil will help eliminate the fungus. Drench the remaining soil in the region of the diseased plant with a fungicide containing *PCNB* prior to planting more daphne. Plant in well-drained soil.

Aphids (half life size).

PROBLEM: Young leaves are curled, stunted, and yellowing. Buds and shoots are distorted and there may be little new growth. A shiny, sticky substance may coat the leaves. A black sooty mold may grow on the sticky substance. Tiny (1/8 inch) greenish soft-bodied insects cluster on the undersides of leaves or on the stems. Ants may be present.

ANALYSIS: Aphids
Aphids do little damage in small numbers. However, they are extremely prolific and populations can rapidly build up to damaging numbers during the growing season. Damage occurs when the aphid sucks the juices from the daphne leaves or stems. The aphid is unable to digest fully all the sugar in the sap and excretes the excess in a fluid called honeydew. The honeydew often drops onto the leaves below. A sooty mold fungus may develop on the honeydew, causing the daphne leaves to appear black and dirty. Ants feed on this sticky substance, and are often present where there is an aphid infestation.

SOLUTION: Control with an insecticide containing *malathion* when damage or insects are first noticed in late spring. Repeat at intervals of 2 weeks if damage continues.

Daphne cultural information
Light: Full sun or part shade
Water: Keep the soil moist
Soil: Very well drained, neutral
Fertilizer: Medium

ELEAGNUS (RUSSIAN OLIVE, SILVERBERRY)

Verticillium wilt.

PROBLEM: The leaves on a branch turn yellow at the margins, then brown and dry. During hot weather, the leaves may wilt. New leaves may be stunted and yellowish. The infected tree may die slowly, branch by branch, over several seasons. Or the whole tree may wilt and die within a few months. Some plants may recover. The tissue under the bark on the dying side may show dark streaks when cut. To examine for streaks, peel back the bark at the bottom of the dying branch. The dark discoloration may be very apparent or barely visible in the area just underneath the bark.

ANALYSIS: Verticillium wilt
This wilt disease attacks many ornamental trees and shrubs. It is caused by a soil-inhabiting fungus (*Verticillium* species) that persists indefinitely on plant debris or in the soil. The fungal strands and spores are spread by contaminated seeds, plants, soil, equipment, and ground water. The fungus enters the tree through the roots and spreads up into the branches through the water-conducting vessels in the trunk. The vessels become discolored and plugged. The plugging cuts off water to the branches, causing the leaf discoloration and wilting.

SOLUTION: No chemical control is available. Fertilize and water the affected tree to stimulate vigorous growth. Remove all dead wood. Do not remove branches on which leaves have recently wilted. These branches may produce new leaves in 3 to 4 weeks or next spring. Remove dead plants. If replanting in the same area, plant trees and shrubs that are resistant to verticillium (see page 995).

Stem canker.

PROBLEM: The leaves on a branch, or the entire tree, wilt and turn brown. Eventually they drop. Twigs and branches are often dead and dying. Sunken or swollen brownish or reddish areas appear on the branches or trunk.

ANALYSIS: Canker and dieback
A number of different fungi cause canker and dieback on Russian olive. The fungi are spread by wind, rain, soil, tools, and equipment. They usually enter the tree at a wound, killing the surrounding healthy tissue. A sunken or swollen canker develops and expands through the wood in all directions. Tree sap containing the fungus may ooze from the wound. As a result of the canker, the flow of nutrients and water through the vessels is cut off, causing the leaves to wilt and die. The tree may stop the spread of the fungus by producing callus tissue. If the expanding canker is stopped before it covers half the diameter of the branch or trunk, the branch or tree usually survives. However, the fungus may grow faster than the callus, or the tree may not produce it, resulting in the death of the branch or the entire tree (if the canker is on the main trunk).

SOLUTION: No chemical control is available. Avoid wounding trees. Avoid overwatering. Prune out and destroy dead branches below the cankered area. Sterilize pruning shears with rubbing alcohol after each cut. Remove dying trees.

Eleagnus cultural information
Light: Full sun to part shade
Water: Drought tolerant
Soil: Tolerates many types
Fertilizer: Light

ERICA (HEATH AND HEATHER)

Root rot.

PROBLEM: One or more branches fade, turn yellow, and die. The plant is stunted. Eventually the whole plant wilts and dies, even though the soil may be sufficiently moist. The problem is more common where the soil is heavy and poorly drained. The tissue under the bark close to ground level shows a dark discoloration when cut. To look for discoloration, peel back the bark at the bottom of the plant. There is a distinct margin between white healthy wood and dark infected wood. If the plant is pulled up, young roots are brown and decaying.

ANALYSIS: Root rot
This plant disease is caused by a soil-inhabiting fungus (*Phytophthora cinnamomi*) that is carried in affected plants or in infested soil or soil water. It enters the roots and works its way up into the plant. Water and nutrient uptake are blocked, causing the aboveground symptoms. Plants in overwatered or poorly drained soils, or those weakened from recent transplanting, are more susceptible to attack.

SOLUTION: Once the fungus becomes established in the soil, it will remain indefinitely. Remove diseased plants. Do not replant susceptible plants in the same area. (For a list of resistant trees and shrubs, see page 1000.) Buy only healthy plants, and plant them in well-drained soil or raised beds.

Erica cultural information
Light: Full sun
Water: Grows best in moist soil
Soil: Light, very well drained, acid
Fertilizer: Light

ERIOBOTRYA (LOQUAT) — — — — —

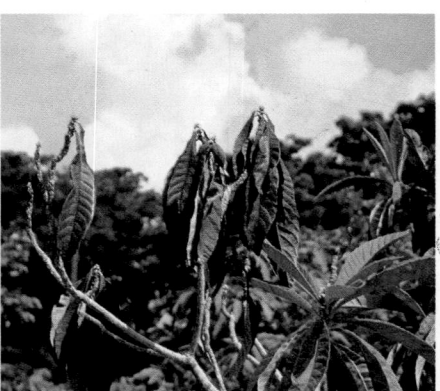

Fireblight.

PROBLEM: Blossoms and leaves of infected twigs suddenly wilt and turn black as if scorched by fire. Leaves curl and hang downward. The bark at the base of the blighted twigs becomes water-soaked, then dark, sunken, and dry; cracks may develop at the edge of the sunken area. In warm, wet fall weather, drops of brown ooze appear on the sunken bark. Young plants may die.

ANALYSIS: Fireblight
This plant disease is caused by a bacterium (*Erwinia amylovora*) that is very destructive to loquat and many other closely related plant species. Blackened, dying branches are very noticeable in the fall and winter, and greatly detract from the beauty of the tree. The bacteria live in sunken cankers on the branches. In the fall, the bacteria ooze out of the cankers. Bees, flies, and other insects are attracted to the sticky ooze and become smeared with it. When the insects visit a flower for nectar, they infect it with the bacteria. The disease spreads rapidly through the plant tissue in warm (70° to 85°F), humid weather. Insects visiting these infected blossoms carry bacteria-laden nectar to healthy blossoms. Rain and wind may also spread the bacteria, infecting tender or damaged leaves in the winter.

SOLUTION: Prune out and destroy infected branches 12 to 15 inches beyond any visible discoloration. Sterilize pruning shears with rubbing alcohol after each cut. A protective spray of a pesticide containing *basic copper sulfate* or *streptomycin* applied before bud break in the fall will help prevent infection. Repeat at intervals of 5 to 7 days until the end of bloom.

EUONYMUS — — — — —

Powdery mildew.

PROBLEM: The surfaces of the leaves are covered with a thin layer or irregular patches of a grayish white powdery mildew. Infected leaves are yellow and may drop prematurely. In late summer, tiny black dots (spore-producing bodies) are scattered over the white patches like ground pepper.

ANALYSIS: Powdery mildew
This plant disease is caused by 2 species of fungi (*Oidium euonymi japonici* and *Microsphaera alni*) that thrive in both humid and dry weather. The powdery patches or thin powdery layer consist of fungal strands and spores. The spores are spread by wind to healthy plants. The fungus saps plant nutrients, causing leaf yellowing and sometimes death of the leaf. In late summer and fall, the fungus forms small black spore-producing bodies that are dormant during the winter, but produce spores to reinfect new plants the following spring. The fungus is especially devastating in low-light situations, and is generally most severe in late summer and fall. Since *Microsphaera alni* attacks many different kinds of plants, the fungus from a diseased plant may infect other types of plants in the garden. For a list of powdery mildews and the plants they attack, see page 995.

SOLUTION: Spray with ORTHO Funginex Rose Disease Control or ORTHO Orthenex Insect & Disease Control when mildew is first noticed. Clean up plant debris in late summer.

Euonymus scale (twice life size).

PROBLEM: Yellow or whitish spots appear on the leaves. Almost all the leaves may drop by midsummer. Branches often die, and heavy infestations may kill the plant. Stems and lower surfaces of the leaves are covered with somewhat flattened, white, scaly bumps and dark brown oystershell-shaped bumps. In severe cases, the whole plant appears white.

ANALYSIS: Euonymus scale (*Unaspis euonymi*)
Many species of scales infest euonymus, but the most common and destructive is euonymus scale. It is especially damaging to evergreen euonymus. The dark brown females spend the winter on the plant and lay their eggs in the spring. In late spring to early summer the young scales, called *crawlers*, settle on the leaves and twigs, or are blown by the wind to other susceptible plants. The small (1/10 inch), soft-bodied young suck sap from the plant. The legs atrophy and a shell develops, brown over the females and white over the males. The females lay their eggs underneath their shell.

SOLUTION: Euonymus scale may be hard to detect until after it has caused serious damage. Check the plant periodically for yellow spotting and scales. Spray with ORTHO Isotox Insect Killer, ORTHO Orthene Systemic Insect Control, or ORTHO Volck Oil Spray in early June and mid-July. In the South, a third application may be necessary in early September. To control scales during the dormant season, spray with ORTHO Volck Oil Spray. For very heavy infestations, cut plants to the ground and spray new growth in June. For more information on scales, see page 878.

FAGUS (BEECH)

Leaf scorch.

Crown gall.

Aphids.

PROBLEM: During hot weather, usually in July or August, leaves turn brown on the edges and between the veins. Sometimes the whole leaf dies. Many leaves may drop during late summer. This problem is most severe on the youngest branches. Plants do not usually die.

ANALYSIS: Summer leaf scorch
Leaf scorch is caused by excessive evaporation of moisture from the leaves. In hot weather, water evaporates rapidly from the leaves. If the roots can't absorb and convey water fast enough to replenish this loss, the leaves turn brown and wither. This usually occurs in dry soil, but leaves can also scorch when the soil is moist. Drying winds, severed roots, or limited soil area can also cause scorch. For more information about scorch, see page 865.

SOLUTION: To prevent further scorch, deep-water plants during periods of hot weather to moisten the entire root space. Recently transplanted shrubs should be watered more often than established plants because of their limited root systems. Water them when the soil in the rootball is still moist, but no longer wet. If possible, shade the shrub during very hot weather. Hosing down the leaves may help cool the shrub and slow evaporation. Plant shrubs adapted to your climate.

Euonymus cultural information
Light: Full sun to part shade
Water: Moist or dry soils
Soil: Tolerates many types
Fertilizer: Light

PROBLEM: Large, corky galls up to several inches in diameter appear at the base of the plant and on the stems and roots. The galls are rounded, with a rough, irregular surface. Plants with numerous galls are weak; growth is slowed and leaves turn yellow. Branches may die back.

ANALYSIS: Crown gall
This plant disease is caused by soil-inhabiting bacteria (*Agrobacterium tumefaciens*) that infect many ornamentals, fruits, and vegetables in the garden. The bacteria are often brought to a garden initially on the roots of an infected plant, and are spread with the soil and by contaminated pruning tools. The bacteria enter the shrub through wounds in the roots or at the base of the stem (the crown). They produce a substance that stimulates rapid cell growth in the plant, causing gall formation on the roots, crown, and sometimes branches. The galls disrupt the flow of water and nutrients up the roots and stems, weakening and stunting the top of the plant. Galls do not usually cause the shrub to die.

SOLUTION: Crown gall cannot be eliminated from the shrub. However, infected plants may survive many years. To improve the appearance of the plant, prune out and destroy affected stems below the galled area. Sterilize pruning shears after each cut with rubbing alcohol. Destroy severely infected shrubs. The bacteria will remain in the soil for 2 to 3 years. If you wish to replace the shrub soon, plant only resistant species. For a list of plants resistant to crown gall, see page 998. For more information about crown gall, see page 860.

PROBLEM: Young leaves are curled, stunted, and yellowing. New growth may stop completely. A shiny, sticky substance may coat the leaves and drip onto plants and other objects, such as cars parked beneath the tree. A black sooty mold often grows on the sticky substance. Tiny (⅛ inch) green, whitish, or black soft-bodied insects cluster on the undersides of leaves and on stems. Ants are sometimes present.

ANALYSIS: Aphids
Aphids do little damage in small numbers. However, they are extremely prolific and populations can rapidly build up to damaging numbers during the growing season. Damage occurs when the aphid sucks the juices from beech leaves and stems. Some aphid species that attack beech are unable to digest fully all the sugar in the plant sap and excrete the excess in a fluid called honeydew. The honeydew often drops onto the leaves or other plants and objects below. A sooty mold fungus may develop on the honeydew, causing the beech leaves to appear black and dirty. Ants feed on this sticky substance, and are often present where there is an aphid infestation. Certain aphids that infest beech, called *woolly aphids*, excrete a white, cottony material while they feed. During heavy infestations, stems and the undersides of leaves may be covered with this secretion.

SOLUTION: Spray with ORTHO Liquid Sevin or with an insecticide containing *malathion* when insects or damage are first noticed. Repeat at weekly intervals if the plant becomes reinfested.

FAGUS (BEECH)

Canker.

PROBLEM: Leaves on affected branches are stunted and lighter green than normal. Some leaves turn brown and drop. Twigs may die back. There are sunken, brownish, water-soaked areas on branches or near the base of the trunk. The sunken areas have a definite margin. Sometimes a brown or reddish liquid is exuded from the canker. The tree may be killed.

ANALYSIS: Canker and dieback
A number of different fungi cause canker and dieback on beech. The fungi enter the tree at a wound, killing the surrounding healthy tissue. A sunken canker develops; tree sap containing the fungus may ooze from the wound. The canker cuts off the flow of nutrients and water to the branch, causing the leaves to turn yellow. Leaf drop and twig dieback follow if infection continues. The tree may wall off the spreading fungus by producing callus tissue, a rapid growth of barklike cells. If the expanding canker is stopped before it covers half the diameter of the trunk or branch, the tree or branch usually survives. However, the fungus may grow faster than the callus, or the tree may not produce a callus, resulting in the death of the branch or the whole tree.

SOLUTION: Prune off dead twigs and small cankered branches, cutting at least 4 inches below the canker. Cankers on larger branches can be excised with a knife and chisel. Remove all discolored bark and wood, and a 1-inch border of apparently healthy bark around the wound. After each cut, sterilize the knife and chisel with rubbing alcohol, and clean the wound with alcohol. To prevent the development of new cankers, avoid wounding trees.

FATSHEDERA

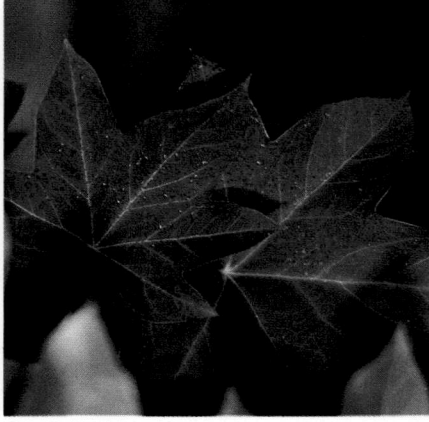

Aphids (⅛ life size).

PROBLEM: Young leaves are curled, distorted, and yellowing. New growth may stop completely. A shiny or sticky substance may coat the leaves. A black sooty mold often grows on the sticky substance. Tiny (⅛ inch) greenish or black soft-bodied insects cluster on the leaves. Ants may be present.

ANALYSIS: Aphids
Aphids do little damage in small numbers. However, they are extremely prolific and populations can rapidly build up to damaging numbers during the growing season. Damage occurs when the aphid sucks the juices from fatshedera leaves and stems. Some aphid species attacking fatshedera are unable to digest fully all the sugar in the plant sap and excrete the excess in a fluid called honeydew. The honeydew often drops onto the leaves below. A sooty mold fungus may develop on the honeydew, causing the fatshedera leaves to appear black and dirty. Ants feed on this sticky substance, and are often present where there is an aphid infestation.

SOLUTION: Spray with ORTHO Liquid Sevin when insects or damage are first noticed. Repeat at weekly intervals if damage continues.

Fatshedera cultural information
Light: Part shade to shade
Water: Keep the soil moist
Soil: Loose, well drained
Fertilizer: Medium

FATSIA (ARALIA)

Spider mite webbing.

PROBLEM: Leaves are stippled, yellowing, and dirty. Sometimes there is a silken webbing on the lower surfaces of the leaves. New leaves may be distorted. To determine if the plant is infested with mites, hold a sheet of white paper underneath an affected leaf and tap the leaf sharply. Minute green, red, or yellow specks the size of pepper grains will drop to the paper and begin to crawl around. These pests are easily seen against the white background.

ANALYSIS: Spider mites
These mites, related to spiders, are major pest of many garden and greenhouse plants. They cause damage by sucking sap from buds and the undersides of leaves. As a result of feeding, the green leaf pigment disappears, producing the stippled appearance. Mites are active during the growing season, but are favored by hot, dry weather (70°F and up). By midsummer, they build up to tremendous numbers.

SOLUTION: Spray with ORTHO Isotox Insect Killer when damage is first noticed. Wet the undersides of the leaves thoroughly. Repeat the application if the plant becomes reinfested. Hose down plants frequently to knock off webs and mites.

Fatsia cultural information
Light: Part shade to shade
Water: Grows best in moist soil
Soil: Tolerates many types
Fertilizer: Heavy

FERNS

Brown scale (twice life size).

PROBLEM: The fronds are covered with brown crusty bumps or thick, white, waxy bumps or clusters of somewhat flattened yellow or whitish scaly bumps. The bumps can be scraped or picked off. Fronds may turn yellow and leaflets may drop. In some cases, a shiny, sticky substance coats the fronds. Scales are sometimes mistaken for reproductive spores produced by the fern. The round, flat, sometimes hairy spores are found only on the undersides of fronds, spaced at regular intervals. They are difficult to pick or scrape off.

ANALYSIS: Scales
Many different types of scales infest ferns. They lay their eggs on the fronds, and in spring to midsummer the young scales, called *crawlers*, settle down to feed. These small (1/10 inch), soft-bodied young feed by sucking sap from the plant. The legs usually atrophy and a hard crusty or waxy shell develops over the body. The mature female scales lay their eggs underneath the shell. Some species of scale that infest ferns are unable to digest fully all the sugar in the plant sap, and excrete the excess in a fluid called honeydew, which coats the fronds.

SOLUTION: Spray with an insecticide containing *malathion* when the young are active. Contact your local Cooperative Extension Office (see page 1011) to determine the best time to spray for scales in your area. Some ferns may be damaged by this chemical. Test the spray on a frond before spraying the entire plant. Wait a few days to see if the area turns brown. Cut off infested fronds on plants that are sensitive to sprays. Discard severely infested plants.

FERNS

Mealybugs (1/3 life size).

PROBLEM: Leaflets or stems are covered with white, cottony, cushion-like masses. Leaflets turn yellow and may drop; fronds may die.

ANALYSIS: Cottony scales and mealybugs
Cottony scales and mealybugs infest many plants in the garden. Mealybugs are usually found outdoors only in the warmer climates. The visual similarities between these insects make separate identification difficult. They are very conspicuous in late spring and summer because the females are covered with a white, cottony egg sac, containing up to 2500 eggs. Females lay their egg masses on leaves and stems. The young insects that hatch from these eggs are yellowish brown to green. They feed throughout the summer, causing damage by withdrawing plant sap from the ferns. Some species of scales and mealybugs are unable to digest fully all the sugar in the plant sap and excrete the excess in a fluid called honeydew. A sooty mold fungus may grow on the honeydew, causing the leaves to appear black and dirty.

SOLUTION: Spray with an insecticide containing *malathion* when insects are first noticed. Some ferns may be damaged by this chemical. Test the spray on a small portion of the plant before using. Wait a few days to see if the area turns brown. Cut off infested stems on plants that are sensitive to sprays. Discard severely infested plants.

Fern cultural information
Light: Part shade to shade
Water: Keep the soil moist
Soil: Loose, rich, well drained
Fertilizer: Medium

FICUS (ORNAMENTAL FIGS)

Cuban laurel thrips damage.

PROBLEM: Young, expanding leaves are curled and distorted, with purplish red spots on the undersides. The leaves soon turn yellow and drop. Minute (1/25 inch) black insects are feeding and laying tiny white eggs on the inside of the rolled leaves.

ANALYSIS: Cuban laurel thrips
(*Gynaikothrips ficorum*)
Ficus retusa (Cuban laurel), especially the variety *nitida*, may be severely infested with this thrips in California, Florida, and Texas. Other species of *Ficus* are attacked only if there are not enough Cuban laurel leaves to feed on when the insects are abundant. Thrips feed on plant sap by shredding and rasping the plant tissue, resulting in distortion and spotting. Damage is unsightly, but the feeding does not cause permanent injury to the plant. On hot days the adults fly around the plant and infest new leaves. Breeding is almost continuous, but populations are highest between October and December.

SOLUTION: Spray with ORTHO Isotox Insect Killer or ORTHO Orthene Systemic Insect Control when damage is first noticed. Repeat 3 more times at intervals of 7 to 10 days.

Ficus cultural information
Light: Full sun to part shade
Water: Grows best in moist soil
Soil: Loose, well drained
Fertilizer: Medium

FORSYTHIA ————— **FRAXINUS (ASH)** —————

Fourlined plant bug (3 times life size).

PROBLEM: Tan to reddish brown spots, 1/16 inch in diameter, develop on young forsythia leaves. Spots may join together to form a blotch; leaves may be distorted. Yellowish green bugs, 1/4 inch long, with four black stripes, may be found feeding on the leaves. Damage occurs during May and June.

ANALYSIS: Fourlined plant bug
(*Poecilocapsus lineatus*)
This plant bug is a pest on forsythia and many other ornamental and vegetable plants in the northern United States. A small number of bugs can cause many unsightly leaves. Eggs are laid inside the stems in slits cut by the adult females in early summer. The eggs spend the winter there, hatching in spring when the forsythia leaves unfold. The plant bugs feed for about 6 weeks. Their sharp mouthparts pierce the leaf tissue, injecting a toxic secretion at the same time. As a result of feeding, the green pigment disappears. Spots develop where the tissue is killed.

SOLUTION: Spray with ORTHO Malathion 50 Insect Spray or with an insecticide containing *carbaryl* when damage is first noticed in spring. Repeat the spray at intervals of 7 to 10 days if damage continues.

Forsythia cultural information
Light: Full sun
Water: When the soil is almost dry
Soil: Tolerates many types
Fertilizer: Medium

FRAXINUS (ASH) —————

ADAPTATION: Throughout the United States. Some species are not adapted to windy areas, or develop winter injury due to temperature fluctuations.

FLOWERING TIME: Several species of ash (especially the flowering ash *F. ornus*) produce conspicuous fragrant white flowers in late spring.

LIGHT: Full sun.

SOIL: Ashes are adapted to a wide variety of soils, and some will tolerate soil that is soggy and poorly drained. Many are deep-rooted, making them good lawn trees.

FERTILIZER: Fertilize with ORTHO Evergreen, Tree & Shrub Food 12–6–6 according to label directions.

WATER:
How much: Apply enough water to wet the soil 3 to 4 feet deep. To determine the proper amount of water for your soil type, see page 906.
How often: Some species of ashes are drought tolerant; others prefer periodic deep waterings.

PRUNING: Some species of ash, such as Modesto ash, develop narrow crotch angles (angles at which the branches attach to the tree). If a narrow-angled, small branch is removed, a dormant bud below it will grow, producing a branch with a wider angle.

Ash anthracnose.

PROBLEM: During wet or humid weather, irregular light brown spots of dead tissue appear on the leaves from late May to August. Sunken reddish areas develop and run together, killing the leaf. Partially killed leaves look as if they have been sunscorched. Anthracnose is distinguished from sunscorch by brown dots (spore-producing bodies) that are barely visible on the undersides of the leaves. There may be severe defoliation and twig dieback.

ANALYSIS: Ash anthracnose
This plant disease is caused by a fungus (*Gloeosporium aridum*). It may be very serious on Modesto ash (*Fraxinus velutina*) in California and the northeastern states. The fungus spends the winter on infected leaves and twigs. During rainy weather, spots develop where spores are blown and splashed onto young leaves. The spots expand and can kill the leaf in rainy seasons, causing defoliation. If defoliation takes place in the spring or early summer, the tree will grow new leaves. If the tree is severely affected for 2 or 3 successive years, the fungus may enter and kill entire branches.

SOLUTION: Trees affected by this disease for a single year do not require chemical control. Rake and destroy old leaves and, where practical, prune out dead twigs below the sunken reddish canker on the bark. Fertilize early in the growing season to stimulate vigorous growth. If the following spring is wet, spray with a fungicide containing *benlate* or *captan* when the leaves uncurl. Repeat the treatment 2 more times at intervals of 14 days.

Aphid damage.

Ash flower galls.

Borer damage.

PROBLEM: Young leaves are curled and yellowing. Sometimes they are tightly folded into a mass. In other cases the undersides are covered with white cottony masses. A shiny, sticky substance usually coats the leaves. A black sooty mold may develop on the sticky substance. Inside the folded leaf or underneath the cottony masses are tiny (⅛ inch) green or purplish soft-bodied insects. Ants may be present.

ANALYSIS: Aphids
(*Prociphilus* species)
Several closely related species of aphids attack ash. Woolly aphids produce a white cottony mass over their bodies, which makes them very conspicuous. Leaf curl aphids cause the ash leaves to curl and fold tightly around themselves. Leaf curl aphids are mainly a problem on white, green, red, and Modesto ash. Neither of these aphids does much harm to the tree. However, when many leaves are tightly curled or covered with the woolly masses, they make the tree unsightly. Damage occurs when the aphids suck the juices from the ash leaves, causing them to curl and yellow. The aphids are unable to digest fully all the sugar in the plant sap and excrete the excess in a fluid called honeydew, which often drops onto the leaves or plants below. A sooty mold fungus may develop on the honeydew, causing the ash leaves to appear black and dirty. Ants feed on this sticky substance, and are often present where there is an aphid infestation.

SOLUTION: Spray with ORTHO Isotox Insect Killer when aphids or damage are first noticed. Spray trees infested with woolly aphids thoroughly to penetrate the wool.

PROBLEM: Irregular galls, from ¼ to ¾ inch in diameter, form on flowers. The clusters of galls dry out and remain on the tree. They are very conspicuous throughout the winter.

ANALYSIS: Ash flower gall mite
(*Aceria fraxinivorus*)
Ash flower galls are caused by tiny mites, too small to be seen with the naked eye. The mites attack the male flowers of white ash (*Fraxinus americana*) and green ash (*F. pennsylvanica lanceolata*). As the buds open in the spring, the mites puncture the tissue, injecting a growth-promoting substance into it. The flowers develop abnormally and form clusters of galls. The galls are unsightly, but are rarely harmful to the tree.

SOLUTION: Once the galls form there is nothing you can do. Next spring, spray valuable specimens with a pesticide containing *dicofol* after buds swell and before new growth emerges.

PROBLEM: Foliage is sparse on a branch or at the top of the tree; eventually the twigs and branches die back. Holes or tunnels are apparent in the trunk or branches. Sap or sawdust usually surrounds the holes. The bark may die over the tunnels and slough off, or there may be knotlike swellings on the trunk and limbs. Weakened branches break during wind or snow storms. Weak, young, or newly transplanted trees may be killed.

ANALYSIS: Borers
Borers are the larvae of beetles or moths. There are many kinds of borers that attack ash trees. Throughout the summer, females lay eggs in bark crevices. The borer larvae feed by tunneling through the bark, sapwood, or heartwood. This stops the flow of nutrients and water in that area by cutting the conducting vessels; branch and twig dieback result. If the tree is healthy, sap flow acts as a defense against borers. When the insect burrows into the wood, tree sap fills the hole and drowns the insect. Factors that weaken the tree, such as mechanical injuries, transplanting, damage by leaf-feeding insects, and poor growing conditions make it more attractive to egg-laying females.

SOLUTION: Cut out and destroy all dead and dying branches. Severely infested young trees should be removed. In the spring, spray or paint the trunk with ORTHO Lindane Borer & Leaf Miner Spray to kill young larvae before they burrow into the wood. Repeat 3 more times at intervals of 2 weeks. Maintain plant health and vigor by watering and fertilizing regularly.

FRAXINUS (ASH)

Canker.

PROBLEM: Leaves of affected trees are stunted and lighter green than normal. Some leaves turn brown and drop. Twigs may die back. There are brownish, water-soaked, or cracked areas on branches or near the base of the trunk. The sunken areas have a distinct margin. A black liquid may ooze from the canker. The tree may be killed.

ANALYSIS: Canker and dieback
A number of different fungi cause canker and dieback on ash. The fungi are spread by wind, rain, soil, and equipment. They enter the tree at a wound, killing the surrounding healthy tissue. A canker develops; tree sap containing the fungus may ooze from the wound. The canker cuts off the flow of nutrients and water to the branch, causing the leaves to turn yellow. Leaf drop and twig dieback follow if infection continues. The tree may wall off the spreading fungus by producing callus tissue, a rapid growth of barklike cells. If the expanding canker is stopped before it covers half the diameter of the trunk or branch, the tree or branch usually survives. However, the fungus may grow faster than the callus, or the tree may not produce a callus, resulting in the death of the branch or the whole tree.

SOLUTION: Prune off dead twigs and small cankered branches, cutting at least 4 inches below the canker. Cankers on larger branches can be excised with a knife and chisel. Remove all discolored bark and wood, and a 1-inch border of apparently healthy bark around the wound. After each cut, sterilize the knife and chisel with rubbing alcohol, and clean the wound with alcohol. To prevent the development of new cankers, avoid wounding trees.

Oystershell scale (half life size).

PROBLEM: Leaves on one or more branches turn yellow, and eventually drop. Affected branches often die. Large portions of the tree may be killed. The twigs, branches, or trunk are covered with small (1/8 inch by 1/16 inch), gray, crusty bumps that look like tiny oystershells.

ANALYSIS: Oystershell scale
(*Lepidosaphes ulmi*)
Oystershell scale is a common pest of many deciduous trees and shrubs. The scales lay their eggs in late summer, and the eggs hatch the following spring around late May or early June. The young scales, called *crawlers*, move around the bark, and then settle on twigs or branches. These small (1/10 inch) soft-bodied young feed by sucking sap from the plant. The legs atrophy and a crusty shell develops over the body. The mature female scales lay their eggs underneath their shell. Many other types of scales may infest ash.

SOLUTION: Remove dead and heavily encrusted, dying branches. Spray with ORTHO Isotox Insect Killer in late May or early June when the young are active. The following early spring, before new growth begins, spray the trunk and branches with ORTHO Volck Oil Spray to control overwintering insects. For more information about scales, see page 878.

FUCHSIA

FUCHSIA

ADAPTATION: Zones 9 and 10. (To determine your zone, see the map on page 1004.) Protect in dry, windy areas. Roots are hardy with mulching in zone 8, but tops die back with hard frosts.

FLOWERING TIME: Summer until first frost. To promote continuous blooming, remove old flowers before berries form.

LIGHT: Partial shade. Full sun in foggy summer areas.

SOIL: Fast-draining soil high in organic matter. Mulch the base of the plant.

FERTILIZER: Fertilize with ORTHO Rose & Flower Food 8–12–4 or ORTHO Ortho-Gro Liquid Plant Food 12–6–6.

WATER:
   How much: Apply enough water to wet the soil 1 to 1½ feet deep. To determine the proper amount of water for your soil type, see page 906.
   Containers: Apply enough water so that 10 percent of the water drains from the bottom of the container.
   How often: Water when the soil is moist but not wet 2 inches below the surface.

PRUNING: Pinch the growing tips frequently in the spring. In frost-free areas, prune in the early spring by removing the same amount of wood as was formed the previous season. In cold winter areas, prune off twiggy growth in the fall. In the spring, cut back into live wood, leaving at least two healthy buds.

Whiteflies (twice life size).

Aphids (3 times life size).

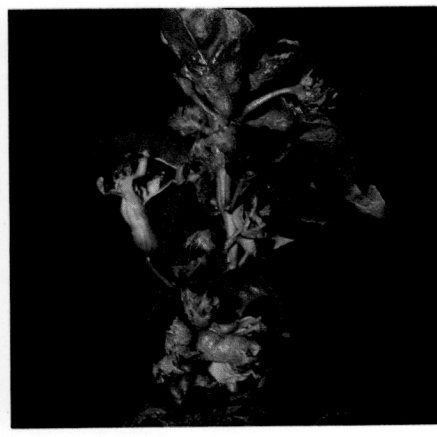

Fuchsia mite damage.

PROBLEM: Tiny, winged insects, 1/12 inch long, are found on the undersides of the leaves. The insects are covered with white waxy powder. When the plant is touched, the insects flutter rapidly around it. Leaves turn yellow and dry, and may be distorted. A black sooty mold may cover the foliage.

ANALYSIS: Greenhouse whitefly (*Trialeurodes vaporariorum*)
This insect is one of the most serious pests of greenhouse-grown fuchsias and fuchsias growing in warm winter areas. The 4-winged adult lays eggs on the undersides of leaves. The larvae are the size of a pinhead, flat, oval, and semitransparent, with white waxy filaments radiating from the body. They feed for about a month before changing to the adult form. Both the larval and adult forms suck sap from the leaves. The larvae are more damaging because they feed more heavily. Adults and larvae cannot fully digest all the sugar in the plant sap and excrete the excess in a fluid called honeydew. A black sooty mold fungus may develop on the honeydew. In warm winter areas the insects can be active year-round, with eggs, larvae, and adults present at the same time. Whiteflies are unable to live through freezing winters. Spring reinfestations in freezing winter areas come from migrating whiteflies and from infested greenhouse-grown plants placed in the garden.

SOLUTION: Spray with ORTHO Isotox Insect Killer or with an insecticide containing *resmethrin* when insects are first noticed. Spray the foliage thoroughly, being sure to cover both the upper and lower surfaces of the leaves.

PROBLEM: Young leaves are curled, wrinkled, and yellowing. A shiny or sticky substance may coat the leaves. Tiny (1/8 inch) green, yellow, or pinkish soft-bodied insects cluster on the undersides of leaves or on the stems. Ants may be present.

ANALYSIS: Aphids
Aphids do little damage in small numbers. However, they are extremely prolific and populations can rapidly build up to damaging numbers during the growing season. Damage occurs when the aphid sucks the juices from fuchsia leaves. Some aphids that attack fuchsia are unable to digest fully all the sugar in the plant sap and excrete the excess in a fluid called honeydew. The honeydew often drops onto the leaves below. Ants feed on this sticky substance, and are often present where there is an aphid infestation.

SOLUTION: Control with ORTHO Isotox Insect Killer or ORTHO Whitefly & Mealybug Killer when insects or damage are first noticed. Repeat the spray if the plant becomes reinfested.

PROBLEM: New growth is severely curled, gnarled, and thickened, and flowers and flower buds are distorted. The plant is growing poorly, and may be weak.

ANALYSIS: Fuchsia mite (*Aculops fuchsiae*)
The fuchsia mite is a microscopic wormlike mite that infests only fuchsia. It is a recent arrival in California, probably arriving from Brazil, where it is native. Unlike spider mites, fuchsia mites do not cause leaf stippling. Instead, they damage the plant by causing distortion and thickening that may be due to hormonelike materials secreted into the plant as they feed. Fuchsia mites are probably present all year long. They are spread from plant to plant by the wind, and probably by hummingbirds and bees as they visit plants.

SOLUTION: Pick off and destroy distorted growth. Spray with a pesticide containing *dicofol* 3 times at intervals of 7 to 10 days.

GARDENIA

Yellow leaves.

Iron deficiency.

Spider mite damage.

PROBLEM: Many older leaves turn yellow and fall off. No insects or diseases are observed on the fallen leaves, and the remaining leaves are a healthy green color. The problem may occur at any time, but is most often noticed during the winter and spring.

ANALYSIS: Leaf drop
Abrupt changes in soil moisture levels or air temperatures account for most yellowing leaves. A normal loss of foliage occurs in early spring just as bloom buds begin to appear and, in the Southeast, at the end of the rainy season. Yellowing and dropping of leaves at other times are almost always related to changes in weather or soil moisture levels. Gardenia varieties differ in the severity of leaf loss, but healthier plants generally have less leaf drop.

SOLUTION: Apply ORTHO Azalea, Camellia & Rhododendron Food 5–10–10 or ORTHO Evergreen & Azalea Food 10–8–7 every 4 to 6 weeks to keep plants in good health. Avoid letting plants dry out excessively between waterings.

PROBLEM: Some of the leaves turn pale green to yellow. The newest leaves may be completely yellow, with only the veins and the tissue near the veins remaining green. On older leaves, only the leaf edges may be yellowing. The plant may be stunted.

ANALYSIS: Iron deficiency
This is a common problem with acid-loving plants like gardenias. These plants prefer soil with a pH between 5.0 and 6.0. (For more information on soil acidity, see page 902.) The yellowing is due to a deficiency of iron and other minor nutrients in the plant. The soil is seldom deficient in iron. However, iron is often found in an insoluble form that is not available to the plant, especially in soil with a pH of 7.0 or higher. A high soil pH can result from overliming, or from lime leached from cement or brick. Regions where soil is derived from limestone, and those with low rainfall, also have high-pH soils. Plants use iron in the formation of the green pigment in the leaves. When it is lacking, new leaves are yellow.

SOLUTION: Spray the foliage with ORTHO Greenol Liquid Iron 6.13%, and apply it to the soil around the plants to correct the iron deficiency. Correct the pH of the soil by treating it with *ferrous sulfate* and watering it in well. Maintain an acid pH by fertilizing with ORTHO Azalea, Camellia & Rhododendron Food 5–10–10. If you live in an area where the soil is alkaline or has poor drainage, add at least 50 percent peat moss to the soil when planting gardenias. Never lime the soil around gardenias.

PROBLEM: Leaves are stippled, yellowing, and dirty. Sometimes a silken webbing appears on the lower surfaces of the leaves. New leaves may be distorted. To determine if the plant is infested with mites, hold a sheet of white paper underneath an affected leaf and tap the leaf sharply. Minute green, red, or yellow specks the size of pepper grains will drop to the paper and begin to crawl around. The pests are easily seen against the white background.

ANALYSIS: Spider mites
These mites, which are related to spiders, are major pests of many garden and greenhouse plants. They cause damage by sucking sap from buds and the undersides of the leaves. As a result of feeding, the green leaf pigment disappears, producing the stippled appearance. Mites are active throughout the growing season, but are favored by hot, dry weather (70°F and up). By midsummer, they increase to tremendous numbers.

SOLUTION: Spray with ORTHO Isotox Insect Killer when damage is first noticed. Wet the undersides of the leaves thoroughly. Repeat the application 2 more times at intervals of 7 to 10 days. Hose down plants frequently to knock off webs and mites.

Whiteflies (life size).

Aphids (twice life size).

Sooty mold.

PROBLEM: Tiny, winged insects, $1/12$ inch long, feed on the undersides of the leaves. The insects are covered with white waxy powder. When the plant is touched, insects flutter rapidly around it. Leaves may be yellow and dry. A black sooty mold may cover the leaves.

ANALYSIS: Greenhouse whitefly (*Trialeurodes vaporariorum*)
This insect is a common pest of many garden and greenhouse plants. The 4-winged adult lays eggs on the undersides of leaves. The larvae are the size of a pinhead, flat, oval-shaped, and semi-transparent, with white waxy filaments radiating from the body. They feed for about a month before changing to the adult form. Both the larval and adult forms suck sap from the leaves. The larvae are more damaging because they feed more heavily. Adults and larvae cannot fully digest all the sugar in the plant sap, and excrete the excess in a fluid called honeydew, which often drops onto the leaves below. A sooty mold fungus may develop on the honeydew, causing the gardenia leaves to appear black and dirty. In warm winter areas the insect can be active year-round, with eggs, larvae, and adults present at the same time.

SOLUTION: Spray with ORTHO Isotox Insect Killer or ORTHO Orthene Systemic Insect Control when the insects are first noticed, being sure to cover both the upper and lower surfaces of the leaves. Repeat 3 more times at intervals of 5 to 7 days.

PROBLEM: Young leaves are curled, wrinkled, and yellowing. Buds may be distorted. Often, a sticky substance coats the leaves. A black sooty mold may grow on the sticky substance. Tiny ($1/8$ inch) yellowish green soft-bodied insects cluster on the undersides of the leaves, stems, or buds. Ants may be present.

ANALYSIS: Aphids
Aphids do little damage in small numbers. However, they are extremely prolific and populations can rapidly build up to damaging numbers during the growing season. Damage occurs when the aphid sucks the juices from the gardenia leaves. Some aphids that attack gardenia are unable to digest fully all the sugar in the plant sap and excrete the excess in a fluid called honeydew. The honeydew often drops onto the leaves below. A sooty mold fungus may develop on the honeydew, causing the gardenia leaves to appear black and dirty. Ants feed on the honeydew, and are often present where there is an aphid infestation.

SOLUTION: Spray with ORTHO Isotox Insect Killer or with ORTHO Liquid Sevin when insects or damage are first noticed. Repeat the spray if the plant becomes reinfested. Or spray with a combination of ORTHO Malathion 50 Insect Spray and ORTHO Volck Oil Spray, which will control the aphids and help to remove sooty mold.

Gardenia cultural information
Light: Full sun to part shade
Water: Keep the soil moist
Soil: Loose, rich, well drained, nonalkaline
Fertilizer: Heavy

PROBLEM: A black sooty mold grows on the leaves and twigs. It can be completely wiped off the surfaces. Cool, moist weather hastens the growth of this substance.

ANALYSIS: Sooty mold
This common black mold is found on a wide variety of plants in the garden. It is caused by several species of fungi that grow on the sugary material left on plants by aphids, scales, mealybugs, whiteflies, and other insects that suck sap from the plant. The insects are unable to digest all the sugar in the plant sap and excrete the excess in a fluid called honeydew, which drops onto the leaves below. The honeydew may also drop out of infested trees and shrubs onto gardenias growing beneath them. The sooty mold fungus develops on the honeydew, causing the gardenia leaves to appear black and dirty. Sooty mold is unsightly, but it is fairly harmless because it does not attack the leaf directly. Extremely heavy infestations prevent light from reaching the leaf, so that the leaf produces fewer nutrients and may turn yellow. The presence of sooty mold indicates that the gardenia or another plant near it is infested with insects.

SOLUTION: Sooty mold can be wiped from the leaves with a wet rag, or it will eventually be washed off by rain. Prevent more sooty mold by controlling the insect that is producing the honeydew. Inspect the leaves and twigs above the sooty mold to find what type of insect is present. See the following pages for control instructions: for aphids, see page 877; for scales, see page 878; for whiteflies, see page 879; for mealybugs, see page 878.

GARDENIA

Nematode-damaged roots.

PROBLEM: Leaves are mottled yellow. They may wilt on hot, dry days but recover at night. The plant lacks vigor. After several years, plants are noticeably stunted and branches may die back. The roots are stunted, and often bushy and dark. Sometimes tiny galls are found on the roots.

ANALYSIS: Nematodes
Nematodes are microscopic worms that live in the soil. They feed on plant roots, damaging and stunting them. The damaged roots can't supply sufficient water and nutrients to the above-ground plant parts, and the plant is stunted or slowly dies. Nematodes prefer moist, sandy loam soils. They can move only a few inches each year on their own, but they may be carried long distances by soil, water, tools, or infested plants. Testing roots and soil is the only positive method for confirming the presence of nematodes. Contact your local Cooperative Extension Office (see page 1011) for sampling instructions and addresses of testing laboratories. Soil and root problems such as poor soil structure, drought stress, nutrient deficiency, and root rots can also produce symptoms similar to those caused by nematodes. These problems should be eliminated as causes before sending soil and root samples for testing. For information on soil problems and root rots, see pages 901 and 856.

SOLUTION: There are no chemicals available to homeowners to kill nematodes in planted soil. However, they can be controlled before planting by soil fumigation. For information on fumigating soil, see page 919.

GLEDITSIA (HONEYLOCUST)

GLEDITSIA (HONEYLOCUST)

ADAPTATION: Zones 4 through 10. (To determine your zone, see the map on page 1004.) Adapted to cold, hot, windy, or polluted areas.

LIGHT: Full sun.

SOIL: Tolerates a wide variety of soils.

FERTILIZER: Fertilize with ORTHO Evergreen, Tree & Shrub Food 12-6-6 according to label directions.

WATER:
How much: Apply enough water to wet the soil 3 to 4 feet deep. To determine the proper amount of water for your soil type, see page 906.
How often: Honeylocust will tolerate some drought, but grows best when given periodic deep waterings. Water when the soil is barely moist 4 inches below the surface.

PRUNING: Prune off excessively long, weepy new growth in midsummer. Cut off about half of the new growth. Old trees in low vigor should be pruned severely every 2 to 4 years during the dormant season.

GLEDITSIA (HONEYLOCUST)

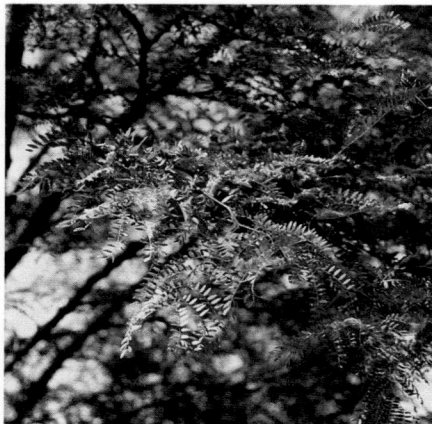

Mimosa webworm damage on honeylocust.

PROBLEM: Small clumps of leaves tied together with silk threads are scattered over the tree. The upper surfaces of the leaves are skeletonized. The leaves turn brown and die, causing infested trees to look as if they have been scorched by fire. Small (up to 1 inch), pale gray or brown caterpillars with 5 white stripes are feeding inside the silken nests. Small trees or the Sunburst variety of thornless honeylocust may be completely defoliated by late summer. Trees are not killed, but repeated defoliations can seriously weaken them.

ANALYSIS: Mimosa webworm
(*Homadaula anisocentra*)
The mimosa webworm is the larval stage of a small moth. It feeds only on honeylocust and mimosa trees. The webworm passes the winter as a pupa in a white silken cocoon. The cocoon is found in sheltered places such as crevices in the bark of the infested tree, or in soil and plant refuse beneath the tree. The moth emerges in the spring and lays her eggs. When the eggs hatch the larvae feed on the leaflets for several weeks. A second generation of webworms hatches in August. The larvae of this second generation are the most damaging because they are usually so numerous. In warmer areas, a third generation hatches in September.

SOLUTION: Spray with ORTHO Orthene Systemic Insect Control when webbing first appears. Repeat in August. Use high pressures to penetrate the webs and cover the tree thoroughly. In the fall, rake up and burn debris under infested trees, or turn over the soil and bury the leaves.

Plantbug-leafhopper damage.

PROBLEM: In early spring, the new expanding leaves become deformed, curled, and mottled yellow. Leaves drop and twigs die back in severe cases. When the leaves are disturbed, small (1/4 inch) green or brownish wedge-shaped or shield-shaped insects hop or fly around the plant.

ANALYSIS: Plantbug-leafhopper complex
Several plantbugs and a leafhopper may be found on the same tree, feeding on the leaflets. The damage they cause is similar, making it difficult to distinguish the injury caused by each type of insect. Eggs, laid the previous summer near the buds and on small twigs, hatch as the leaves unfold. The young insects suck the sap from the leaves and may inject toxins, causing the mottling and distortion. Plantbugs and leafhoppers feed until the middle of summer. When infestations are heavy, twigs die back.

SOLUTION: Spray with an insecticide containing *diazinon* or *carbaryl* when damage is first noticed in spring. Spray the foliage thoroughly, making sure to cover both the upper and lower surfaces of the leaves. To prevent damage next year, spray before the buds open in the spring.

Spider mite damage on honeylocust.

PROBLEM: The leaves are stippled yellow or whitish and dirty. By midsummer, all of the foliage may turn yellow or brownish and drop. Sometimes there is a silken webbing on the lower surfaces of the leaves. The tree may be weak and stunted. To determine if the plant is infested with mites, hold a sheet of white paper underneath a branch that has stippled leaves and tap the branch sharply. Minute reddish or green specks the size of pepper grains will drop to the paper and begin to crawl around.

ANALYSIS: Honeylocust spider mite (*Platytetranychus multidigituli*)
These mites infest only honeylocust trees. They are a serious pest in the eastern half of the United States. The mites cause damage by sucking sap from the undersides of leaves. As as result of feeding, the green leaf pigment disappears, producing the stippled appearance. Hot, dry weather (70°F and up) favors rapid development of these mites, so by midsummer they may build up to tremendous numbers. If the injury is severe enough, the leaflets turn yellow or brown and drop in midsummer, and most of the mites die due to lack of food. The trees usually leaf out again in late summer, with conspicuous green leaves appearing on the branch tips. Trees infested for more than one year are weakened and may be stunted.

SOLUTION: Spray with ORTHO Orthene Insect Spray or ORTHO Isotox Insect Killer. Direct the spray to the undersides of the leaves. Repeat 2 more times at intervals of 7 to 10 days to kill mites as they hatch from eggs. Apply control measures early in the season to prevent unsightly injury to foliage.

Pod gall midge damage.

PROBLEM: Green, globular, podlike galls, 1/8 inch in diameter, develop on new leaflets in spring and early summer. The galls turn reddish, then brown, and many of the infested leaflets drop. Twigs or branches sometimes die back after several years of infestation. One to several whitish larvae, 1/4 inch long, are feeding inside the gall.

ANALYSIS: Honeylocust pod gall midge (*Dasineura gleditschiae*)
The larvae stage of this tiny black fly causes unsightly galls on honeylocust trees, especially the thornless varieties. The adult female midge begins laying eggs on new leaflets in the spring. When the eggs hatch the larvae feed on the tissue, causing the leaflet to fold over them and form a pod gall. As the larvae develop inside, the galls turn brown. The flies emerge to lay more eggs. Honeylocust produces new leaves over a long period, so the cycle may repeat itself up to 7 times annually. The galls are not usually damaging to the tree. However, the ornamental value of the tree is reduced when the galled leaflets dry up and drop prematurely. Twigs sometimes die back after repeated attack, but new shoots normally form at the base of the dead twigs.

SOLUTION: Prune off dead twigs. Spray with an insecticide containing *lindane* in late May and again in late July.

GLEDITSIA (HONEYLOCUST)

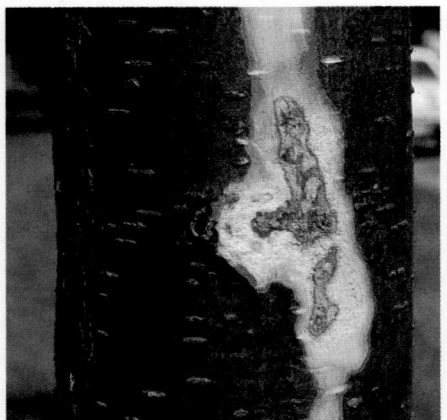

Honeylocust borer damage.

PROBLEM: Large quantities of wet, gummy sap ooze from holes in the trunk and branches. The sap dries to a varnishlike material. The leaves on a branch with oozing sap are often yellowing, and the branch may die back. Weakened branches break during wind or snow storms. Weak, young, or newly transplanted trees are most susceptible to injury, and may be killed.

ANALYSIS: Honeylocust borer (*Agrilus difficilis*)
This white, flat-headed borer is the larva of a metallic black beetle, ½ inch long. The adult lays eggs on the bark in June. The eggs hatch and the larvae feed by tunneling in the sapwood beneath the bark. This stops the flow of nutrients and water in that area by cutting the conducting vessels; twig and branch dieback may result. Feeding also weakens the tree structurally, causing limbs to break during storms. Sap flow through the tree acts as a defense against the borers. When the insect burrows into the wood, the tree sap fills the hole and drowns the insect. Young trees or those weakened by other factors are attractive to borers. Factors that weaken the trees, such as transplanting, storm injuries, defoliation by leaf-eating insects, and especially drought, predispose them to attack by borers.

SOLUTION: Cut out and destroy all dead and dying branches. Severely infested young trees should be removed. In the spring, spray or paint the trunk and branches with an insecticide containing *lindane*. Spray to kill young larvae before they burrow into the wood. Repeat 3 more times at intervals of 2 weeks. Maintain tree health and vigor by watering and fertilizing regularly.

Cankers.

PROBLEM: Leaves on an infected branch or throughout the tree are discolored and wilting. Eventually the leaves drop, and the branch or the entire tree dies. Small (up to ½ inch), slightly depressed, tan to black cankers on the affected area may grow together and enlarge to girdle the trunk or branch. The wood under the bark surrounding the canker is streaked reddish brown. Gummy sap may ooze from the canker.

ANALYSIS: Canker wilt
Canker wilt of honeylocust is caused by a fungus (*Thyronectria austro-americana*) that is spread by wind and splashing rain. The fungus enters the wood through wounds, killing the surrounding healthy tissue. A canker forms that ranges in size from a pinhead to ½ inch in diameter. The cankers often enlarge and grow together, cutting off the flow of nutrients and water through the branch or trunk. The leaves wilt, and the area above the canker dies. If cankers develop on the trunk, the entire tree may die. Several other fungi also cause cankers on honeylocust.

SOLUTION: There are no effective chemical controls. Prune off dying branches well below the cankered areas. Fertilize and water the tree regularly to promote vigorous growth. (For more information about fertilizing and watering, see pages 904 and 906.) Avoid wounding the tree. A fungicide containing *benomyl* applied as a paste to wounds may help prevent or slow down infection.

HAMAMELIS (WITCH HAZEL)

Galls caused by witch-hazel leaf gall aphid.

PROBLEM: The upper surfaces of the leaves are covered with ½ inch long green cone-shaped galls with red tips. The galls develop in the spring but remain on the leaves throughout the summer. Underneath each gall on the lower surface of the leaf is a small opening. If the gall is broken open before late May, one or more tiny (1/12 inch), whitish insects are found inside.

ANALYSIS: Witch-hazel leaf gall aphid (*Hormaphis hamamelidis*)
Galls on witch hazel are unsightly but not damaging to the plant. The aphid is more injurious to birch (*Betula*), where it feeds on the leaves during the summer. No galls are produced on birch leaves. Gall aphids spend the winter as eggs on the twigs of witch hazel. In early spring, as the leaves unfold, the eggs hatch and the young crawl to the leaves. Each aphid initiates the formation of one gall by feeding on the leaf. The feeding activity stimulates abnormal leaf growth, producing galls that enclose the insects. The female aphid produces many young which fill the interior of the gall. When the aphids mature in late spring or early summer they develop wings, emerge through the opening in the lower surface of the leaf, and fly to birch leaves. Several generations are produced on birch. In the fall, the aphids fly back to witch hazel and lay eggs on the twigs.

SOLUTION: If the infested birch tree is in the area, spray it in summer with ORTHO Isotox Insect Killer. This will prevent migration of the aphids back to witch hazel in the fall and prevent further damage to the birch tree. To control aphids on witch hazel, spray with a *dormant oil* before the buds open in spring.

HIBISCUS (ROSE-OF-SHARON)

Yellow leaves.

Greenhouse whiteflies (twice life size).

Aphids (half life size).

PROBLEM: Many older leaves turn yellow and fall off. No insects or diseases are observed on the fallen leaves, and the remaining leaves are a healthy green color. The problem may occur at any time but is most often noticed during the early fall and spring.

ANALYSIS: Leaf drop
Abrupt changes in soil moisture levels or air temperatures account for most yellowing leaves. A normal loss of older foliage occurs in early spring and at the end of the summer rainy seasons. Yellowing and dropping of leaves at other times is almost always related to changes in weather or soil moisture levels. Hibiscus varieties differ in the severity of leaf loss, but healthier plants generally have less leaf drop.

SOLUTION: Apply ORTHO Azalea, Camellia & Rhododendron Food 5–10–10 every 4 to 6 weeks to keep plants in good health. Avoid letting plants dry out excessively between waterings.

Hibiscus cultural information
Light: Full sun to part shade
Water: Frequent, deep watering (deciduous shrubs take some drought)
Soil: Loose, very well drained
Fertilizer: Heavy (medium for deciduous)

PROBLEM: Tiny, winged insects, $\frac{1}{12}$ inch long, are found mainly on the lower surfaces of the leaves. The insects are covered with white waxy powder. When the plant is touched, insects flutter rapidly around it. The leaves may be mottled and yellowing. In warm winter areas, a black sooty mold may cover the foliage.

ANALYSIS: Greenhouse whitefly
(*Trialeurodes vaporariorum*)
This insect is a common pest of many garden and greenhouse plants. The 4-winged adult lays eggs on the undersides of leaves. The larvae are the size of a pinhead, flat, oval-shaped, and semitransparent, with white waxy filaments radiating from the body. They feed for about a month before changing to the adult form. Both the larval and adult forms suck sap from the leaves. The larvae are more damaging because they feed more heavily. Adults and larvae digest all the sugar in the plant sap and excrete the excess in a fluid called honeydew, which often drops onto the leaves below. A sooty mold fungus may develop on the honeydew causing the hibiscus leaves to appear black and dirty. In warm winter areas the insects can be active year-round, with eggs, larvae, and adults present at the same time. Whiteflies are unable to live through freezing winters. Spring reinfestations in freezing winter areas come from migrating whiteflies and from infested greenhouse-grown plants placed in the garden.

SOLUTION: Control with an insecticide containing *resmethrin* when whiteflies are first noticed. Repeat the spray 3 more times at intervals of 2 weeks to control the young as they hatch.

PROBLEM: Flowers and the newest leaves are wrinkled, distorted, and yellowing. On hot days the leaves may wilt, and eventually drop off. A shiny, sticky substance often coats the leaves. A black sooty mold sometimes grows on the sticky substance. Tiny ($\frac{1}{8}$ inch) yellowish green or black soft-bodied insects cluster on the branch tips and the leaves. Ants may be present.

ANALYSIS: Cotton aphid and cowpea aphid
(*Aphis gossypii* and *A. craccivora*)
Both of these aphids feed on many ornamentals in the garden. They do little damage in small numbers. However, they are extremely prolific and populations can rapidly build up to damaging numbers during the growing season. Damage occurs when the aphid sucks the juices from the hibiscus leaves. The aphid is unable to digest fully all the sugar in the plant sap and excretes the excess in a fluid called honeydew. The honeydew often drops onto the leaves below. A sooty mold fungus may develop on the honeydew, causing the hibiscus leaves to appear black and dirty. Ants feed on honeydew, and are often present where there is an aphid infestation.

SOLUTION: Spray with an insecticide containing *malathion* when aphids are first noticed. Repeat the spray if the plant becomes reinfested.

HYDRANGEA

HYDRANGEA

ADAPTATION: Zones 6 through 10. To determine your zone, see the map on page 1004.

FLOWERING TIME: Late spring to fall.

LIGHT: Partial shade (full sun in cool coastal areas).

SOIL: Rich, well drained, high in organic matter. Soil acidity affects the uptake of aluminum in the plant, which determines whether the flowers will be pink or blue. Blue flowers result from a pH of 5.0 to 5.5, and pink flowers occur in soils with a pH of 6.0 to 6.5 or higher. (For more information about pH, see page 902.) White hydrangeas are not affected by soil acidity.

FERTILIZER: Fertilize with ORTHO Azalea, Camellia & Rhododendron Food 5–10–10 or ORTHO General Purpose Plant Food 8–8–8 according to label directions. For blue flowers, apply ORTHO Aluminum Sulfate to the soil to increase soil acidity and provide aluminum; for pink flowers, apply lime to decrease the soil acidity. Apply aluminum or lime in the spring to change the color of next spring's flowers.

WATER:
How much: Apply enough water to wet the soil 1½ to 2 feet deep. To determine the proper amount of water for your soil type, see page 906.
How often: Hydrangeas prefer moist soil. Water when the soil is moist but not wet 4 inches below the surface. For more information about watering, see page 906.

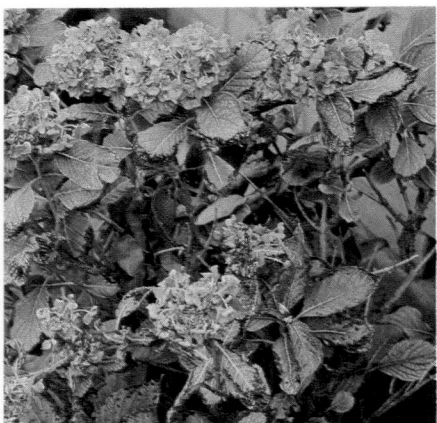
Sunburn.

PROBLEM: During warm, sunny weather, leaves on the outside of the plant turn yellowish or brown in the center of the leaf tissue. Some leaves may drop.

ANALYSIS: Sunburn
Hydrangeas are shade plants; their leaves are sensitive to the heat of the sun. The outside leaves facing the light turn yellow or brown when the shrub is planted in full sun. The injury is unsightly, but is not damaging to the plant. Plants are more susceptible to sunburn when the soil in which they are planted is dry. Hydrangea leaves may also scorch (die and turn brown at the edges) during hot weather. For more information, see pages 460 and 461.

SOLUTION: Move the injured plant to a shaded location or provide some shade where it is now growing. (For more information about transplanting, see page 916.) Keep plants adequately watered. For more information about watering, see page 906.

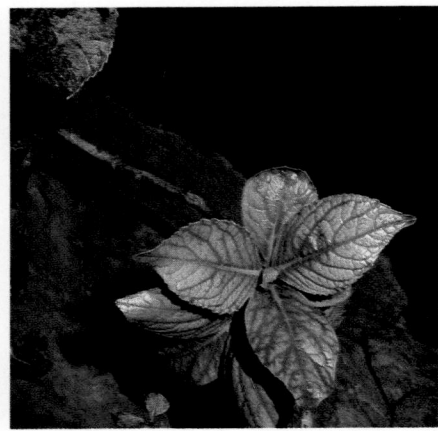
Iron deficiency.

PROBLEM: Some of the leaves turn pale green to yellow. The newest leaves may be completely yellow, with only the veins remaining green. On older leaves, only the leaf edges may be yellowing. The plant may be stunted.

ANALYSIS: Iron deficiency
This is a common problem with acid-loving plants like hydrangea. The plant prefers soil with a pH between 5.5 and 6.5. (For more information on soil acidity, see page 902.) The yellowing is due to a deficiency of iron and other minor nutrients in the plant. The soil is seldom deficient in iron. However, iron is often found in an insoluble form that is not available to the plant, especially in soil with a pH of 7.0 or higher. A high soil pH can result from overliming, or from lime leached from cement or brick. Regions where soil is derived from limestone, and those with low rainfall, also have high-pH soils. Plants use iron in the formation of the green pigment in the leaves. When it is lacking, new leaves are yellow.

SOLUTION: Spray the foliage with ORTHO Greenol Liquid Iron 6.13%, and apply it to the soil around the plants to correct the iron deficiency. Correct the pH of the soil by treating it with ORTHO Aluminum Sulfate and watering it in well. Maintain an acid pH by fertilizing with ORTHO Azalea, Camellia & Rhododendron Food 5–10–10. When planting hydrangea, add at least 50 percent peat moss to the soil. This is especially important if you live in an area where the soil is alkaline or has poor drainage.

HYDRANGEA _____   **ILEX (HOLLY)** _____

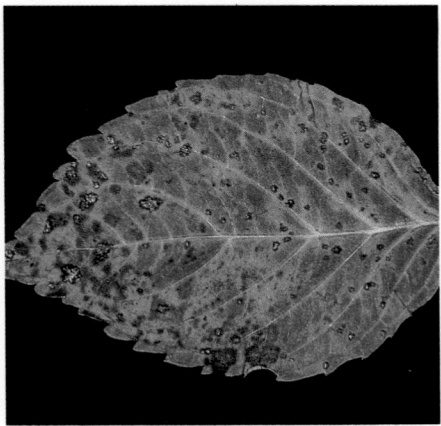

Powdery mildew.

PROBLEM: Leaves, branch tips, buds, and flower stalks are covered with a thin layer or irregular patches of a grayish white powdery material. Infected leaves may turn purplish brown, and they usually drop prematurely. The buds and the blooms may be deformed or die.

ANALYSIS: Powdery mildew
This common plant disease is caused by a fungus (*Erysiphe polygoni*) that thrives in both humid and dry weather. The powdery patches consist of fungal strands and spores. The spores are spread by the wind to healthy plants. The fungus saps the plant nutrients, causing leaf browning, bud deformation, and occasionally the death of the leaf. Since this mildew attacks many different kinds of plants, the fungus from a diseased plant may infect other types of plants in the garden. For a list of susceptible plants, see page 995.

SOLUTION: Spray the upper and lower surfaces of the leaves with a fungicide containing *benomyl* or *dinocap* when the plants show the first signs of mildew.

ILEX (HOLLY) _____

ADAPTATION: Zones 3 through 10. (To determine your climate zone, see the map on page 1004.)

BERRIES: Many species of holly are grown for their berries, which are showy in fall and winter. Most holly plants are either male or female, and both must be present in your neighborhood for female plants to develop berries. Male plants do not produce berries.

LIGHT: Full sun to shade. Berry production is greatest in full sun.

SOIL: Well drained and slightly acid (pH around 6.5).

FERTILIZER: Fertilize with ORTHO Azalea, Camellia & Rhododendron Food 5–10–10 according to label directions.

WATER:
How much: Apply enough water to wet the soil 2 to 3 feet deep. To determine the amount of water for your soil type, see page 906.
How often: Holly grows best with ample water. Water when the soil is moist but no longer wet 4 inches below the surface.

PRUNING: Some varieties may be sheared for hedges.

Leafminer damage on holly.

PROBLEM: Yellowish or brown winding trails or blotches appear in the leaves. The leaves may also be distorted and flecked with tiny brown dots. In severe cases, all the leaves are affected and most of them may drop from the plant. When the blotch is torn open, a small (1/6 inch), yellowish white maggot is found between the upper and lower surfaces of the leaf.

ANALYSIS: Holly leafminers
(*Phytomyza* species)
The damage caused by these leafminers is unsightly and ruins the value of those types of holly used as winter holiday decorations. Both the larva and adult cause damage. The insect spends the winter as a larva or pupa inside a fallen leaf or a leaf still attached to the plant. When new growth begins in spring, a tiny black fly emerges. The female deposits eggs inside the leaf by making a slit in the lower surfaces of the leaf. The flies (only the females in some species) feed on the sap by stabbing through the leaf surface. This feeding causes the brown flecking and distortion. The eggs deposited inside the leaves hatch into maggots that feed on the inner leaf tissue, producing the mines or trails. In a heavy infestation, the plant may drop almost all its leaves and will remain bare until the following spring.

SOLUTION: Control with ORTHO Isotox Insect Killer or ORTHO Diazinon Insect Spray as new leaves emerge in spring. Repeat the spray in 2 or 3 weeks. Rake up and destroy fallen leaves.

ILEX (HOLLY)

Leaf spots.

Iron deficiency.

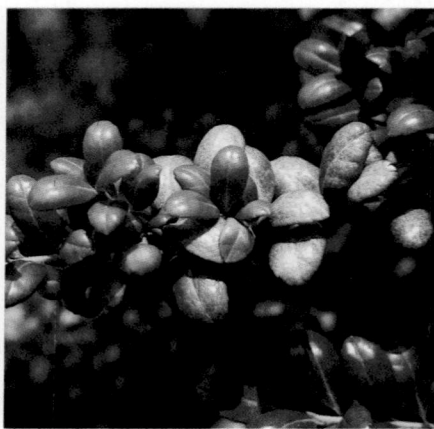
Southern red mite damage on Japanese holly.

PROBLEM: Spots and blotches appear on the leaves. The spots may be yellow, red, tan, gray, or brown. They range in size from barely visible to ½ inch in diameter. Several spots may join to form blotches. Leaves may turn yellow and die. Some leaves may drop. Leaf spotting is most severe in warm, humid weather.

ANALYSIS: Leaf spot
Several different fungi cause leaf spots on holly. These spots are unsightly but rarely harmful to the plant. The fungi are spread by splashing water and wind. Spots develop where the fungi enter the tissue. If wet or humid weather persists, the fungi spread through the tissue and blotches form. They survive the winter on the leaves and twigs. Most leaf spot organisms do their greatest damage in mild weather (between 50° and 85°F). Egg depositing sites of holly leafminers also cause leaf spotting. For more information, see page 527.

SOLUTION: Where practical, remove infected leaves from the plant. On valuable specimens, spray with a fungicide containing *ferbam* or *maneb* when new growth begins in the spring. Repeat at intervals of 2 weeks for as long as the weather remains favorable for infection.

Small, pinhead-size gray spots with purple halos may be confused with fungal leaf spots. These spots, known as *spine spots*, are caused by the spines of adjacent leaves puncturing the tissue. Examination with a magnifying glass will reveal tiny holes in the center of the spot.

PROBLEM: Some of the leaves turn pale green to yellow. The newest leaves may be completely yellow with only the veins remaining green. On older leaves, only the leaf edges may be yellowing. The plant may be stunted.

ANALYSIS: Iron deficiency
This is a common problem with acid-loving plants like holly. The plant prefers soil with a pH between 6.0 and 6.5. (For more information on soil acidity, see page 902.) The yellowing is due to a deficiency of iron and other minor nutrients in the plant. The soil is seldom deficient in iron. However, iron is often found in an insoluble form that is not available to the plant, especially in soil with a pH of 7.0 or higher. A high soil pH can result from overliming, or from lime leached from cement or brick. Regions where soil is derived from limestone, and those with low rainfall, also have high-pH soils. Plants use iron in the formation of the green pigment in the leaves. When it is lacking, new leaves are yellow.

SOLUTION: Spray the foliage with ORTHO Greenol Liquid Iron 6.13%, and apply it to the soil around the plants to correct the iron deficiency. Correct the pH of the soil by treating it with *ferrous sulfate* and watering it in well. Maintain an acid pH by fertilizing with ORTHO Azalea, Camellia & Rhododendron Food 5–10–10. When planting holly, add at least 50 percent peat moss to the soil if you live in an area where the soil is alkaline or has poor drainage. Never lime the soil around holly.

PROBLEM: Leaves are stippled yellow or grayish green and dirty, and are often smaller than normal. There may be a silken webbing on the lower surfaces of the leaves. To determine if the plant is infested with mites, hold a sheet of white paper underneath a branch that has stippled leaves and tap the branch sharply. Minute reddish specks the size of pepper grains will drop to the paper and begin to crawl around. The pests are easily seen against the white background.

ANALYSIS: Southern red mite (*Oligonychus ilicis*)
The southern red mite, also known as *red spider*, is a major pest of many evergreen plants in the eastern half of the United States. The mites cause damage by sucking sap from both the top and undersides of leaves. As a result of feeding, the green leaf pigment disappears, producing the stippled appearance. These mites are most prolific in cooler weather. They feed and reproduce primarily during spring and, in some cases, fall. At the onset of hot weather (70°F and up), the mites have caused their maximum damage.

SOLUTION: Control with ORTHO Orthene Insect Spray or ORTHO Isotox Insect Killer when stippling is first noticed in spring. Cover the leaves thoroughly. Repeat the spray 3 more times at intervals of 7 to 10 days to kill young mites as they hatch from eggs. It is important to apply control measures early in the season when damage first appears to prevent unsightly injury to foliage. Injured leaves remain on the plant for more than one growing season. Hose down plants frequently to knock off webs and mites.

IXORA

Chinese wax scale (¼ life size).

Cold damage.

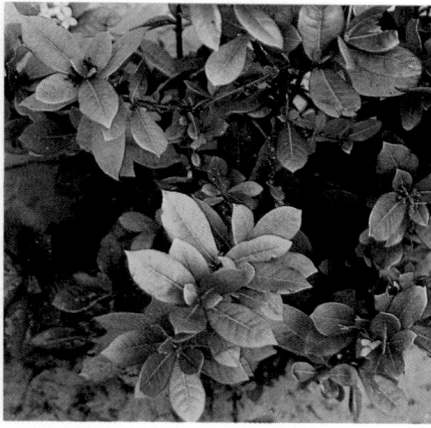

Iron deficiency.

PROBLEM: The leaves, stems, or berries are covered with brown or black crusty bumps; or thick, white, waxy bumps; or clusters of somewhat flattened scaly bumps. The bumps can be scraped or picked off; the undersides are usually soft. Leaves may turn yellow and drop, and branches may die. In some cases, a shiny, sticky substance coats the leaves. A black sooty mold often grows on the sticky substance.

ANALYSIS: Scales
Many different species of scales infest holly. They lay their eggs on the leaves or bark in the spring, and in midsummer the young scales, called *crawlers*, settle on the various parts of the tree or shrub. The small (⅒ inch) soft-bodied young feed by sucking sap from the plant. The legs usually atrophy and a hard crusty or waxy shell develops over the body. The mature female scales lay their eggs underneath their shell. Some species of scales infesting holly are unable to digest fully all the sugar in the plant sap, and excrete the excess in a fluid called honeydew. A black sooty mold fungus may develop on the honeydew. An uncontrolled infestation of scales may kill the plant after 2 or 3 seasons.

SOLUTION: Spray with ORTHO Isotox Insect Killer or ORTHO Orthene Systemic Insect Control when the young are active. Contact your local Cooperative Extension Office (see page 1011) to determine the best time to spray for scales in your area. The following spring, before new growth begins, spray the trunk and branches with a *dormant oil spray*. For more information about scales, see page 878.

PROBLEM: Many of the leaves have brown edges and tips. More than half of the leaf may be affected. Newer leaves show more symptoms that older ones. Shoot tips may be discolored or dead, and smaller branches may be killed. The problem occurs from December to March, following cold weather.

ANALYSIS: Cold damage
Ixora is a tropical plant, and is frequently injured by freezing temperatures in some growing areas. Mild damage results in leaf injury and discoloration. Severe injury can cause leaf and twig death or even kill plants back to the soil line.

SOLUTION: Delay pruning until spring, or until all danger of additional damage has passed. Fertilize injured plants lightly but frequently to speed recovery. Keep plants healthy to minimize damage. Cover and protect exposed plants on nights when freezing temperatures are expected. If possible, plant only in protected locations away from chilling winds. To reduce damage, water plants thoroughly the day before freezing temperatures are expected.

Ixora cultural information
Light: Full sun
Water: Occasional deep watering
Soil: Acid, well drained
Fertilizer: Medium to heavy

PROBLEM: Some leaves turn pale green to yellow. The newest leaves (those at the tips of the branches) may be completely yellow, with only the veins remaining green. Only the leaf edges of older leaves may be yellowing. The plant may be stunted.

ANALYSIS: Iron deficiency
This is a common problem in acid-loving plants like ixora. Ixora grows best in soil with a pH between 5.5 and 6.5. (For more information on soil acidity, see page 902.) The yellowing is due to a deficiency of iron and other minor nutrients in the plant. The soil is seldom deficient in iron. However, iron is often found in an insoluble form that is not available to the plant, especially in soil with a pH of 7.0 or higher. An alkaline soil can result from overliming, or from lime leached from cement or brick. Regions where soil is derived from limestone also have high-pH soils. Plants use iron in the formation of the green pigment in the leaves. When iron is lacking, new leaves are yellow.

SOLUTION: Spray the foliage with ORTHO Greenol Liquid Iron 6.13%, and apply it to the soil around the plants to correct the deficiency of minor nutrients. Correct the pH of the soil by treating it with *ferrous sulfate* and watering it in well. Maintain an acid pH by fertilizing with ORTHO Azalea, Camellia & Rhododendron Food 5–10–10. When planting ixora, add peat moss, acid soil, or other materials to help acidify the planting soil.

Ixora

Jasminum (Jasmine)

Aphids (twice life size).

Soft scale (twice life size).

Whiteflies (3 times life size).

PROBLEM: Leaves are yellow, curled, and often distorted. Soft-bodied insects, about 1/8 inch long, cluster on the undersides of the leaves and on new growth. They may be green, black, or orange. A shiny or sticky substance may coat some of the leaves.

ANALYSIS: Aphids
Aphids do little damage in small numbers. However, they are extremely prolific and populations can rapidly build up to damaging numbers during the growing season. Damage occurs when the aphid sucks the juices from the ixora leaves. The aphid is unable to digest fully all the sugar in the plant sap and excretes the excess in a sugary fluid called honeydew, which often drops onto the leaves below. A sooty mold fungus may develop on the honeydew, causing the ixora leaves to appear black and dirty. Ants feed on the honeydew, and are often present where there is an aphid infestation.

SOLUTION: Apply an insecticide containing *malathion* according to label directions. Repeat sprayings as needed. Make sure that ixora is listed on the product label.

PROBLEM: The undersides of the leaves are covered with brownish or black crusty bumps or thick, white, waxy bumps or clusters of tan, yellowish, brown, or reddish scaly bumps. The bumps can be scraped or picked off; the undersides are usually soft. Leaves turn yellow and may drop; small branches may die back. In some cases, a sticky substance coats the leaves. A black sooty mold often grows on the sticky substance.

ANALYSIS: Scales
Many types of scales infest jasmine shrubs and vines. They lay their eggs on the leaves or bark, and in spring to midsummer the young scales, called *crawlers,* settle on leaves and twigs. The small (1/10 inch), soft-bodied young feed by sucking sap from the plant. The legs usually atrophy and a hard crusty or waxy shell develops over the body. The mature female scales lay their eggs underneath the shell. Some species of scales that infest jasmine are unable to digest fully all the sugar in the plant sap, and excrete the excess in a fluid called honeydew. A sooty mold fungus may develop on the honeydew, causing the jasmine leaves to appear black and dirty.

SOLUTION: Spray with an insecticide containing *malathion* or *carbaryl* when the young are active. Contact your local Cooperative Extension Office (see page 1011) to determine the best time to spray for scales in your area. The following early spring before new growth begins, spray the plant with a *dormant oil spray* to control overwintering insects. For more information about scales, see page 878.

PROBLEM: Tiny, winged insects 1/12 inch long feed on the undersides of the leaves. The insects are covered with a white waxy powder. When the plant is touched, insects flutter rapidly around it. Leaves may be mottled and yellowing.

ANALYSIS: Whitefly
This insect is a common pest of many garden and greenhouse plants. The 4-winged adult lays eggs on the undersides of leaves. The larvae are flat, oval-shaped, and semitransparent. They feed for about a month before changing to the adult form. Both the larval and adult forms suck sap from the leaves. The larvae are more damaging because they feed more heavily. Adults and larvae cannot fully digest all the sugar in the plant sap, and excrete the excess in a fluid called honeydew, which often drops onto the leaves below. A sooty mold fungus may develop on the honeydew. In warm winter areas these insects can be active year-round.

SOLUTION: Spray with an insecticide containing *acephate.* Make sure your plant is listed on the product label.

Jasminum cultural information
Light: Full sun to part shade
Water: Drought-tolerant once established
Soil: Tolerates many types
Fertilizer: Medium

JUNIPERUS (JUNIPER)

Sooty mold.

PROBLEM: A black sooty mold is growing on the leaves and twigs. It can be completely wiped off the surfaces. Cool, moist weather hastens the growth of this substance.

ANALYSIS: Sooty mold
This common black mold is found on a wide variety of plants in the garden. It is caused by any of several species of fungi that grow on the sugary material left on plants by aphids, scales, mealybugs, whiteflies, and other insects that suck sap from the plant. The insects cannot fully digest all the sugar in the sap and excrete the excess in a fluid called honeydew, which drops onto the leaves below. The sooty mold fungus develops on the honeydew, causing the jasmine leaves to appear black and dirty. Sooty mold is unsightly, but it is fairly harmless because it does not attack the leaf directly. Extremely heavy infestations prevent light from reaching the leaf, so that the leaf produces fewer nutrients and may turn yellow. The presence of sooty mold indicates that the jasmine is infested with insects.

SOLUTION: Sooty mold can be wiped from the leaves with a wet rag; or it will eventually be washed off by rain. Inspect the leaves and twigs above the sooty mold to find what type of insect is present. For information on controlling the insect, see the following pages: for aphids, page 877; for scales and mealybugs, page 878; and for whiteflies, page 879.

JUNIPERUS (JUNIPER)

ADAPTATION: Throughout the United States.

LIGHT: Full sun (or partial shade in hot climates).

SOIL: Junipers prefer sandy, well-drained soil but they will thrive in almost any type of garden soil.

FERTILIZER: Fertilize with ORTHO Evergreen, Tree & Shrub Food 12–6–6 or ORTHO General Purpose Plant Food 8–8–8 according to label directions.

WATER:
How much: Apply enough water to wet the soil 1 to 3 feet deep, depending on the size of the juniper. To determine the proper amount of water for your soil type, see page 906.
How often: Young junipers should be watered when the soil 4 inches below the surface is just barely moist. Established plants are drought resistant and require summer watering only in the hottest climates. Water when the soil 4 inches below the surface is dry. Do not plant junipers where they will receive water meant for a lawn.

PRUNING: Some junipers grow tall (to 90 feet) or spread up to 15 feet. It is best to use a variety that will fit the area to be planted rather than depending on pruning. Older junipers will not sprout new growth from older wood, so never remove all the foliage from a branch. If a shrub is to be sheared, begin when the plant is young, and shear lightly and regularly.

Dieback. *Insert:* Girdler tunnels.

PROBLEM: One or more branches turn yellow. Eventually they turn brown and dry. Plants do not usually die. If the bark is peeled back at the base of the affected branch, holes or tunnels are found in the wood. There may be a small (¼ inch long) cream-colored larva with a brown head feeding inside the tunnel.

ANALYSIS: Juniper twig girdler
(Periploca nigra)
The juniper twig girdler is found in the eastern half of the United States and in California, but it is damaging to junipers only in California. All species of junipers are attacked. The low-growing, thin-stemmed varieties are the most seriously damaged. The twig girdler is the larva of a tiny black moth. In Southern California, the female lays eggs on woody stems from March to May. In Northern California, the moth lays eggs from May to July. When the eggs hatch, the larvae tunnel into the stems beneath the bark. The plant may be infested for 2 or 3 years before damage becomes noticeable. Feeding by the larvae cuts off the flow of nutrients and water through the stems, so that the branches turn yellow and may die. If the stem is not entirely eaten or girdled, the branch may survive for several years.

SOLUTION: Control of this insect depends on applying insecticides before the larvae have tunneled into the stem. Spray with ORTHO Lindane Borer & Leaf Miner Spray in April and again in May in Southern California. In Northern California, spray in early June and again in late June or early July. Drench the woody stems thoroughly. Prune out and destroy dead branches.

JUNIPERUS (JUNIPER)

Drought damage.

Salt burn.

Twig blight.

PROBLEM: Needles turn yellow and then brown and dry, either on the outer, lower branches; on the inside of the plant nearest the trunk; from the top of the plant down; or from the tips back. Sometimes only a branch or one side of the plant is affected. In other cases, the whole plant turns brown.

ANALYSIS: Needle browning
Any of a number of different conditions may cause the needles to turn brown on junipers.

SOLUTION: The numbered solutions below correspond to the numbers in the analysis.

1. *Dog urine:* When dogs urinate on it, the foliage on the outer, lower branches turns yellow, then brown, as if scorched. The salts in the urine burn the foliage.

1. Wash the foliage and thoroughly soak the ground around the plant to dilute the salts in the urine if it is suspected that a dog has recently urinated on it.

2. *Natural leaf browning and shedding:* The older needles, on the inside of the plant nearest the trunk, turn brown and drop off in spring or fall. This is a natural process similar to the dropping of leaves of deciduous plants.

2. No controls are necessary.

3. *Drought or winter injury:* When the plant is damaged by drought or winter injury, needles gradually turn yellow, then brown or reddish from the top of the plant down and from the tips of the branches back. This may happen when the soil is dry and the plant is not getting enough water, or when the soil is frozen in the winter.

3. Prune out dead twigs and branches. Provide adequate water during periods of extended drought and shelter plants growing in windy locations. Water in late fall or early winter, if necessary, to insure adequate soil moisture during the winter. Mulch plants after they are dormant to reduce the depth of frost penetration into the soil. Do not plant junipers in areas where they are not adapted.

4. *Salt burn:* Needles turn brown from the tips back. This condition may develop on one side of the plant only, or the whole plant may be affected. Salt burn is common in alkaline soils found in areas of low rainfall, when water has a high salt content, in soils with poor drainage, in overfertilized soils, or along roadsides where winter runoff contains road salts. The salts in the soil inhibit water and nutrient uptake, causing the needles to turn brown. Similar symptoms can occur in ocean-front plantings from wind-borne salt mist.

4. Prune off badly damaged areas. Avoid new injury by giving plants a heavy irrigation once during the growing season to leach out excess salts from the root zone. If you suspect that your water contains salts, have it analyzed through your Cooperative Extension Office (see page 1011) or local water department. Do not overfertilize plants; follow package directions. Avoid planting in areas where road or sea salt may be a problem. Occasionally hose down ocean-front plantings to remove salt accumulations on the foliage.

PROBLEM: Needles, twigs, and smaller branches turn light brown to reddish brown, then gray, gradually dying from the tips back. Plants less than 5 years old are often killed. Minute black dots may appear on the needles and stems when the needles have dried and turned grayish. The disease is most serious during wet weather or in shady, moist locations. This problem sometimes resembles drought damage. However, the border between healthy tissue and dead tissue is sharp with this disease but gradual with drought. In addition, the disease is found only on isolated branches rather than uniformly throughout the plant, as with drought.

ANALYSIS: Twig blight
This plant disease is caused by a fungus (*Phomopsis juniperovora*). It is highly destructive to junipers, cryptomeria, chamaecyparis, and arborvitae throughout most of the country. The spores are spread by splashing rain, overhead watering, insects, and tools. The fungus enters through wounds or healthy tissue, killing the stem and needles above and below the point of entrance. Black spore-producing structures develop and overwinter on dead needles.

SOLUTION: Spray with *benomyl* when symptoms first appear around May. Repeat 3 or 4 more times at weekly intervals. Prune out and destroy infected branches below the line between diseased and healthy tissue, making the cut into live tissue. Plant trees in areas with good air circulation and full sun.

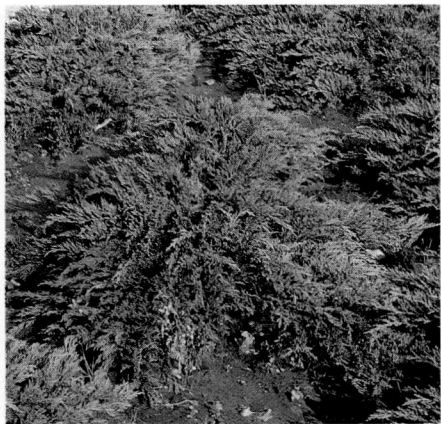

Dieback caused by phytophthora root rot.

Stem browning.

Cypress tip moth and cocoon (life size).

PROBLEM: The normal foliage color dulls, and the plant loses vigor. The foliage may wilt, or it may turn yellow or light brown. Major branches or the entire plant may die. The plant sometimes lives for many months in a weakened condition, or it may die quickly. The roots and lower stems are brownish and the roots are often decayed. There may be fine woolly brown strands on the roots and white powdery spores on the soil surface; or there may be fan-shaped plaques of white strands between the bark and wood of the roots and lower stems. Mushrooms may appear at the base of the plant in the fall.

ANALYSIS: Root and crown rots
Root and crown rots on junipers are caused by several different fungi. The fungi live in the soil and on living roots.

SOLUTION: The numbered solutions below correspond to the numbers in the analysis.

1. *Phytophthora* species: These fungi cause browning and decay on the roots, and browning of the lower stems. The plants usually dies slowly, but young plants may wilt and die rapidly. The disease is most prevalent in heavy, water-logged soils. For more information about *Phytophthora*, see page 857.

1. Remove dead and dying plants. When replanting, use plants that are resistant to *Phytophthora*. (For a list of resistant trees and shrubs, see page 1000.) Improve soil drainage (see page 901). Avoid overwatering junipers.

2. *Phymatotrichum omnivorum:* This fungus, also known as *cotton root rot* or *Texas root rot*, is a severe problem on many plants in the Southwest. The plant often wilts and dies suddenly. Older plants may die more slowly, showing general decline and dieback symptoms. Brown strands form on the roots and white powdery spores form on the soil. The disease is most severe in heavy, alkaline soils. For more information about *Phymatotrichum*, see page 859.

2. Remove dead and dying plants. When replanting, buy only resistant varieties. (For a list of resistant trees and shrubs, see page 994.) Before planting, increase the soil acidity by adding 1 pound of *ammonium sulfate* for every 10 square feet of soil. Make a circular ridge around the planting area and fill the basin with 4 inches of water. Repeat the treatment in 5 to 10 days. Improve drainage. For more information about soil drainage, see page 901.

3. *Armillaria mellea:* This disease is also known as *shoestring root rot*, *mushroom root rot*, or *oak root fungus*. *Armillaria* is identified by the presence of fan-shaped plaques of white fungal strands between the bark and the wood of the roots and lower stems. This fungus grows rapidly under wet conditions. Honey-colored mushrooms appear at the base of the plant in the fall. For more information about *Armillaria*, see page 858.

3. Remove dead plants. The life of a newly infected plant may be prolonged if the disease has not reached the lower stems. Expose the base of the plant to air for several months by removing several inches of soil. Prune off diseased roots. When replanting, use only resistant varieties. (For a list of plants resistant to *Armillaria*, see page 1001.) Avoid overwatering junipers (see page 857).

PROBLEM: Leaf tips turn yellow at first, then brown and dry. They contrast sharply with the healthy green foliage. Damage is most severe in plants growing in shady areas. When the yellow leaf is torn open, a small (1/8 inch long), greenish caterpillar with a dark head may be found inside. Gray or brownish moths with a 1/3 -inch wingspread may be seen flying around the plant in April, May, or June.

ANALYSIS: Leafminers and tip moths (*Argyresthia* species)
Several species of insects, known as *leafminers* in the eastern United States and *tip moths* on the West Coast, infest junipers, arborvitae, and cypress. Damage is unsightly, but plants may lose over half their foliage and still survive. The larvae spend the winter inside the leaf tips. When the weather warms in late spring, the larvae pupate, then emerge as adult moths to lay eggs on the leaves. The larvae that hatch from these eggs tunnel into the leaf tips, devouring the green tissue. The tips above the point of entry yellow and die. The larvae feed until late fall or through the winter until early spring.

SOLUTION: Spray with ORTHO Isotox Insect Killer when eggs are hatching in June or July (mid-August in the far northeastern states). Trim and destroy infested leaves in fall and spring.

JUNIPERUS (JUNIPER)

Spider mite damage (on left).

Aphids (4 times life size).

Juniper scale (4 times life size).

PROBLEM: The needles are stippled yellow or grayish and dirty. There may be a silken webbing on the twigs. Needles may turn brown and fall off. To determine if the plant is infested with mites, hold a sheet of white paper underneath some stippled needles and tap the foliage sharply. Minute green, red, yellow, or black specks the size of pepper grains will drop to the paper and begin to crawl around. The pests are easily seen against the white background.

ANALYSIS: Spruce spider mite (*Oligonychus ununguis*) **and two-spotted mite** (*Tetranychus urticae*) Spider mites, related to spiders, are among the most important pests of junipers and other evergreen trees and shrubs. They cause damage by sucking sap from the needles. As a result of feeding, the green leaf pigment disappears, producing the stippled appearance. *Spruce spider mites* are more prolific in cooler weather. They feed and reproduce primarily during spring and, in some cases, fall. At the onset of hot weather (70°F and up), the mites have caused their maximum damage. *Two-spotted mites* develop rapidly in hot, dry weather (70°F and up), so by midsummer they build up to tremendous numbers.

SOLUTION: Spray with ORTHO Isotox Insect Killer or ORTHO Orthene Insect Spray when damage is first noticed. Repeat the application 3 more times at intervals of 7 days. Hose down plants frequently to knock off webs and mites.

PROBLEM: Needles turn brown and eventually drop from the plant. When infestations are heavy, branches die back and the plant is stunted. A shiny, sticky substance may coat the needles and stems. A black sooty mold often grows on the sticky substance. Tiny (⅛ inch) black or brown soft-bodied insects with long spiderlike legs cluster on the twigs and stems. Ants may be present.

ANALYSIS: Aphids
Aphids do little damage in small numbers. However, they are extremely prolific and populations can rapidly build up to damaging numbers during the growing season. Damage occurs when the aphid sucks the juices from the juniper bark, causing needle browning and branch dieback. The aphid is unable to digest fully all the sugar in the plant sap and excretes the excess in a fluid called honeydew. The honeydew often drops onto needles and plants below. A black sooty mold fungus may develop on the honeydew, or rain may wash it off before the fungus has a chance to grow. Ants feed on this sticky substance, and are often present where there is an aphid infestation.

SOLUTION: Control with ORTHO Isotox Insect Killer or ORTHO Malathion 50 Insect Spray when aphids are first noticed. Cover the twigs and stems thoroughly. Repeat the spray if the plant becomes reinfested.

PROBLEM: The tree or shrub looks gray and off-color and there is no new growth. Eventually the needles turn yellow. Branches and possibly the whole plant may die back. The foliage is covered with clusters of tiny (⅛ inch), somewhat flattened yellow and white scaly bumps. A shiny, sticky substance may coat the leaves. A black sooty mold often grows on the sticky substance.

ANALYSIS: Juniper scale (*Carulaspis juniperi*)
This scale is found throughout the United States on many types of junipers and also on cypress (*Cupressus* species only) and incense cedar. The female scales spend the winter on the plant. They lay their eggs in spring, and in midsummer (late spring in the South) the new generation, called *crawlers*, settles on the needles. These small (1/10 inch), soft-bodied young feed by sucking sap from the plant. The legs atrophy and a crusty shell develops over the body. The mature female scales lay their eggs underneath the shell. Juniper scales are unable to digest fully all the sugar in the plant sap and excrete the excess in a fluid called honeydew. A sooty mold fungus may develop on the honeydew. An uncontrolled infestation of scales may kill the plant in 2 or 3 seasons.

SOLUTION: Spray with ORTHO Isotox Insect Killer or ORTHO Liquid Sevin in midsummer (late spring in the South) when the young are active. The following early spring, before new growth begins, spray the trunk and branches with a *dormant oil spray* to control overwintering insects. For more information about scales, see page 878.

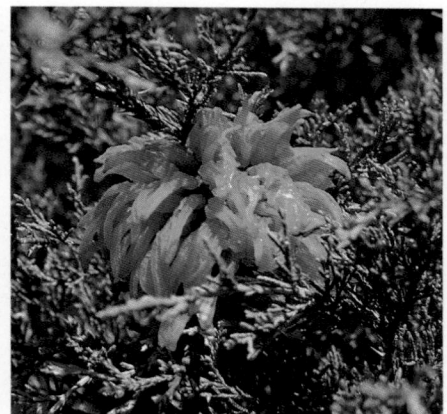

Damaged plant. *Insert:* Juniper webworm (life size).

Cedar-apple rust.

Fungal leaf spots.

PROBLEM: The needles on a branch or throughout the entire plant turn brown. Branches with extensive browning are usually heavily and tightly webbed. Brownish striped caterpillars, up to ½ inch long, are feeding on needles inside the webbing.

ANALYSIS: Juniper webworm (*Dichomeris marginella*)
This webworm feeds only on junipers. The damage caused by the caterpillars often goes unnoticed until the plant is heavily infested. The young larvae usually inhabit the inner parts of the plant first, which, on the bushier junipers, are well concealed. The small brown and gray female moths lay their eggs in May or June in the crotches of the needles. When the eggs hatch, the larvae burrow into the needles. As the larvae grow, they feed on other foliage but use their initial hollowed-out needles as "retreat cells." In late summer, the caterpillars web the foliage together as they feed and then spend the winter inside it. As the weather warms in spring, the caterpillars become active again and continue to produce large amounts of webbing until they pupate and mature into moths.

SOLUTION: Spray with an insecticide containing *diazinon* or *carbaryl* when damage is first noticed to kill young larvae. If the foliage is heavily webbed, use high pressure spray equipment for penetration and thorough coverage. A fall or early spring spray is effective against inactive caterpillars.

PROBLEM: In spring or early summer, brownish green swellings appear on the upper surface of the needles. The galls enlarge until, by fall, they range in size from 1 to 2 inches in diameter. The galls turn chocolate brown and are covered with small circular depressions. The following spring, during warm, rainy weather, the small depressions swell and produce orange, jellylike "horns" up to ¾ inch long. The galls eventually die, but remain attached to the tree for a year or more. Infected twigs usually die.

ANALYSIS: Cedar-apple rust
This disease is caused by a fungus (*Gymnosporangium juniperi-virginianae*) that infects both juniper and apple trees. It cannot spread from juniper to juniper or apple to apple, but must alternate between the two. Wind-borne spores from apple leaves infect juniper needles in the summer. The fungus grows very little until the following spring, when the galls begin to form. The second spring after infection, spores from the orange "horns" are carried by the wind to apple trees and infect the leaves and fruit. By midsummer, orange spots appear on the apples and upper surfaces of the leaves. (For more information about cedar-apple rust on apples, see page 630.) In August, spores are released and carried by the wind back to junipers. The entire cycle takes 18 to 20 months on juniper plus 4 to 6 months on apple. For a list of susceptible plants, see page 1000.

SOLUTION: Remove galls by hand and destroy. When practical, do not plant junipers and apple trees within several hundred yards of one another. Spraying junipers with *ferbam* in August may help prevent new infections from apple trees.

PROBLEM: Spots and blotches appear on the leaves. The spots may be yellow, red, tan, gray, or brown. They range in size from barely visible to ½ inch in diameter. Several spots may join to form blotches. Leaves may be yellow and dying. Some leaves may drop. Leaf spotting is most severe in moist, humid weather.

ANALYSIS: Fungal leaf spots
There are many different fungi that cause leaf spots on mountain laurel. These spots are unsightly but rarely harmful to the plant. Plants weakened by low temperatures and wind exposure may be more susceptible to invasion by leaf spot fungi. The fungi are spread by splashing water and wind. Spots develop where the fungi enter the tissue. If wet or humid weather persists, the fungi spread through the tissue and blotches form. They survive the winter on the leaves and twigs. Most leaf spot organisms do their greatest damage in mild weather (between 50° and 85°F).

SOLUTION: Where practical, remove infected leaves from the plant. Collect and destroy any fallen leaves. On valuable specimens, spray with fungicide containing *ferbam* or *benomyl* when new growth begins in spring. Repeat 2 more times at intervals of 2 weeks for as long as the weather remains favorable for infection.

Kalmia cultural information
Light: Part shade
Water: When the soil is almost dry
Soil: Loose, rich, well drained, acid
Fertilizer: Medium

KALMIA (MOUNTAIN LAUREL)

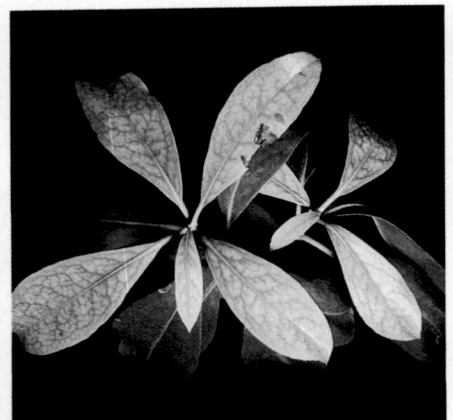

Iron deficiency.

PROBLEM: Some of the leaves turn pale green to yellow. The newest leaves may be completely yellow with only the veins remaining green. On older leaves, only the leaf edges may be yellowing. The plant may be stunted.

ANALYSIS: Iron deficiency
This is a common problem with acid-loving plants like kalmia. The plant prefers soil with a pH between 5.5 and 6.5. (For more information on soil acidity, see page 902.) The yellowing is due to a deficiency of iron or other minor nutrients in the plant. The soil is seldom deficient in iron. However, iron is often found in an insoluble form that is not available to the plant, especially in soil with a pH of 7.0 or higher. A high soil pH can result from overliming, or from lime leached from cement or brick. Regions where soil is derived from limestone, and those with low rainfall, also have high-pH soils. Plants use iron in the formation of the green pigment in the leaves. When it is lacking, new leaves are yellow.

SOLUTION: Spray the foliage with ORTHO Greenol Liquid Iron 6.13%, and apply it to the soil around the plants to correct the iron deficiency. Correct the pH of the soil by treating it with *ferrous sulfate* and watering it in well. Maintain an acid pH by fertilizing with ORTHO Azalea, Camellia & Rhododendron Food 5–10–10. When planting mountain laurel, add at least 50 percent peat moss to the soil. This is especially important if you live in an area where the soil is alkaline or has poor drainage. Never lime the soil around mountain laurel.

LABURNUM (GOLDENCHAIN TREE)

Aphids (half life size).

PROBLEM: The leaves may turn pale green or yellow. Sometimes they wilt and have a scorched appearance. A shiny, sticky substance coats the leaves. A black sooty mold may grow on this sticky substance. Tiny (1/8 inch) black or dark green soft-bodied insects cluster on the branch tips and leaf stalks. Ants may be present.

ANALYSIS: Cowpea aphid and bean aphid (*Aphis craccivora* and *A. fabae*)
Both of these aphids feed on many ornamental garden plants. They do little damage in small numbers. However, they are extremely prolific and populations can rapidly build up to damaging numbers during the growing season. The leaves often scorch and wilt because the aphids extract so much plant sap. The aphids are unable to digest fully all the sugar in the sap and excretes the excess in a fluid called honeydew. The honeydew often drops onto leaves below. Plants or objects beneath the tree may also be coated with honeydew. A black sooty mold fungus may develop on the honeydew, or rain may wash it off before the fungus has a chance to grow. Ants feed on this sticky substance, and are often present where there is an aphid infestation.

SOLUTION: Spray with an insecticide containing *carbaryl* or *malathion* when aphids are first noticed. Repeat the spray if the plant becomes reinfested.

Laburnum cultural information
Light: Full sun to part shade
Water: Grows best in moist soil
Soil: Well drained, nonalkaline
Fertilizer: Light

LAGERSTROEMIA (CRAPEMYRTLE)

Honeydew coated leaves.

PROBLEM: Irregular yellow blotches appear on the leaves. Eventually the yellow areas turn brown. The leaves may drop prematurely. A shiny, sticky substance often coats the leaves. A black sooty mold may be growing on the sticky substance. Tiny (1/8 inch) soft-bodied insects are clustered on twigs and the upper and lower surfaces of the leaves.

ANALYSIS: Crapemyrtle aphid
(*Tinocallis kahawaluokalani*)
This aphid species attacks only crapemyrtle. It is usually abundant wherever the tree is grown. The aphids do little damage in small numbers. However, they are extremely prolific and populations can rapidly build up to damaging numbers during the growing season. Damage occurs when the aphid sucks the juices from the crapemyrtle leaves. The aphid is unable to digest fully all the sugar in the plant sap and excretes the excess in a fluid called honeydew. The honeydew often drops onto the leaves below. Plants or objects beneath the tree may also be coated with honeydew. A black sooty mold fungus may develop on this sticky substance. Ants feed on honeydew, and are often present where there is an aphid infestation.

SOLUTION: Control with ORTHO Isotox Insect Killer when aphids first appear. Spray the foliage thoroughly, being sure to cover the twigs and both the upper and lower surfaces of the leaves.

Lagerstroemia cultural information
Light: Full sun
Water: Infrequent, deep watering
Soil: Well drained, nonalkaline
Fertilizer: Light

LARIX (LARCH)

LEUCOTHOE

Powdery mildew.

Woolly larch aphids (¼ life size).

Leaf spots.

PROBLEM: Leaves, shoots, and flower buds are covered with a thin layer or irregular patches of a grayish white powdery material. The leaves and shoots are distorted and stunted, and the flower buds usually fail to open. Infected leaves may look reddish beneath the mildew; the leaves often drop prematurely.

ANALYSIS: Powdery mildew
This common plant disease is usually caused by a fungus (*Erysiphe lagerstroemiae*) that thrives in both humid and dry weather. The powdery patches consist of fungal strands and spores. The spores are spread by the wind to healthy plants. The fungus saps the plant nutrients, causing leaf and shoot distortion and bud failure. This particular powdery mildew infects only crapemyrtle. Several other species of powdery mildew that commonly infect other trees and shrubs occasionally infect this plant.

SOLUTION: Spray the upper and lower surfaces of the leaves with ORTHO Funginex Rose Disease Control when the plant shows the first signs of mildew. In the spring, before buds open, spray with a dormant *lime sulfur* spray.

PROBLEM: Needles are covered with white, woolly masses. If the infestation is heavy, the tree appears to be covered with snow in midsummer. The needles may turn yellow, and the tree may be stunted.

ANALYSIS: Woolly larch aphids
(*Adelges laricis* and *A. lariciatus*)
Woolly larch aphids are small, soft-bodied insects. The adults infesting larch are always covered by a dense, white, woolly material. The larch aphids spend the winter on spruce trees. The females lay their eggs in the spring, and the newly hatched young feed at the base of the spruce buds, causing small pineapple-shaped galls to form. Within the galls are chambers, each containing several young larch aphids. The galls crack open in late spring, and the winged adults fly to larch trees, where the females lay their eggs. The next generation of aphids secretes white filaments of wax that eventually cover their bodies. The woolly material may completely cover the needles by midsummer. Generally, the tree is not injured unless it is infested for several consecutive seasons. In late summer, another generation of larch aphids with wings is produced that flies back to spruce to spend the winter.

SOLUTION: Next May when the aphids first appear, spray with an insecticide containing *malathion*.

Larix cultural information
Light: Full sun
Water: Moist or dry conditions
Soil: Tolerates many types
Fertilizer: Light

PROBLEM: Spots and blotches appear on the leaves. The spots may be yellow, red, tan, gray, or brown. They range in size from barely visible to ½ inch in diameter. Several spots may join together to form blotches. Leaves may turn yellow and die. Some leaves may drop. Leaf spotting is most severe in warm, humid weather.

ANALYSIS: Leaf spots
There are many different fungi that cause leaf spots. These spots are unsightly but rarely harmful to the plant. Plants weakened by low temperatures and wind exposure are more susceptible to invasion by leaf spot fungi. The fungi are spread by splashing water and wind. Spots develop where the fungi enter the tissue. If wet or humid weather persists, the fungi spread through the tissue and blotches form. They survive the winter on the leaves and twigs. Most leaf spot organisms do their greatest damage in mild weather (between 50° and 85°F).

SOLUTION: Once leaves become infected they will remain so. Where practical, remove infected leaves from the plant. In areas where spotting is severe every year, spray with a fungicide containing *ferbam* when the leaves appear in early spring. Repeat 3 more times at intervals of 2 weeks.

Leucothoe cultural information
Light: Part shade to shade
Water: Keep the soil moist
Soil: Loose, rich, well drained, acid
Fertilizer: Medium

LIGUSTRUM (PRIVET)

LIGUSTRUM (PRIVET)

ADAPTATION: Throughout the United States.

FLOWERING TIME: Late spring to early summer.

LIGHT: Full sun to part shade.

SOIL: Must be well drained.

FERTILIZER: Fertilize with ORTHO Evergreen, Tree & Shrub Food 12–6–6 or ORTHO General Purpose Plant Food 8–8–8 according to label directions.

WATER:
How much: Apply enough water to wet the soil 2 to 3 feet deep. To determine the proper amount of water for your soil type, see page 906.
How often: Privets grow best when well watered, but they will tolerate drought. Water when the soil is barely moist 4 inches below the surface.

PRUNING: Prune to maintain shape or to hedge. If flowers are desired, prune after blooming. Otherwise, prune any time.

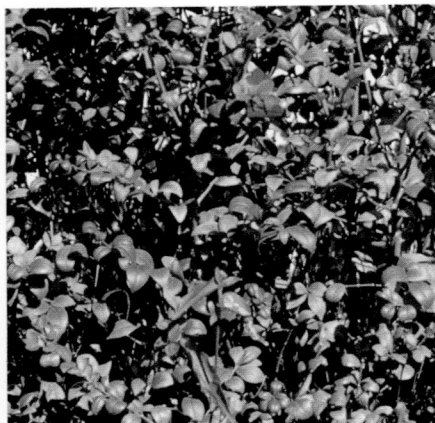

Privet rust mite damage.

PROBLEM: The leaves are dull green and severely cupped. They may turn bronze, brown, or yellow and drop; or they may drop off the plant while still green. The plant is weak and often stunted.

ANALYSIS: Privet rust mite and privet mite (*Aculus ligustri* and *Brevipalpus obovatus*)
Both of these mites are extremely small, and generally cannot be seen without magnification. They cause damage by sucking sap from the leaf tissue. As a result of feeding, the leaf cups or curls under, and often drops from the plant. The privet rust mite may feed only on the cells in the surface of the leaf, causing a bronze russeting or browning. The green leaf pigment is unaffected. Or it may feed deeper in the tissue, resulting in leaf yellowing caused by the disappearance of the green pigment. Some types of privet drop their leaves before discarding develops. The rust mite is most prolific during cool weather. It feeds and reproduces primarily during spring and fall. The privet mite is usually active throughout the growing season. By midsummer it may build up to tremendous numbers.

SOLUTION: Spray with a pesticide containing *dicofol* or *diazinon* when damage is first noticed. Spray the foliage thoroughly, being sure to cover both the upper and lower surfaces of the leaves. Repeat the application 3 more times at intervals of 7 days.

Scales (life size).

PROBLEM: The undersides of the leaves, trunk, or the branches are covered with brownish crusty bumps, or clusters of somewhat flattened yellowish, brown, reddish, gray, or white scaly bumps. The bumps can be scraped or picked off. Leaves turn yellow and may drop, and twigs or branches may die back. A shiny, sticky substance often coats the leaves. A black sooty mold may grow on the sticky substance.

ANALYSIS: Scales
Many different types of scales infest privet. They lay their eggs on the leaves or bark, and in spring to midsummer the young scales, called *crawlers*, settle on leaves, twigs, or the trunk. These small (1/10 inch), soft-bodied young feed by sucking sap from the plant. The legs usually atrophy and a hard crusty shell develops over the body. The mature female scales lay their eggs underneath the shell. Some species of scales that infest privet are unable to digest fully all the sugar in the plant sap, and excrete the excess in a fluid called honeydew. A sooty mold fungus may develop on the honeydew, causing the privet leaves to appear black and dirty. An uncontrolled infestation of scales may kill twigs or branches after 2 or 3 seasons.

SOLUTION: Spray with ORTHO Isotox Insect Killer or with ORTHO Liquid Sevin when the young are active. Contact your local Cooperative Extension Office (see page 1011) to determine the best time to spray for scales in your area. The following early spring, before new growth begins, spray the trunk and branches with ORTHO Volck Oil Spray to control overwintering insects. For more information about scales, see page 878.

LIRIODENDRON (TULIPTREE)

Anthracnose.

Summer leaf yellowing.

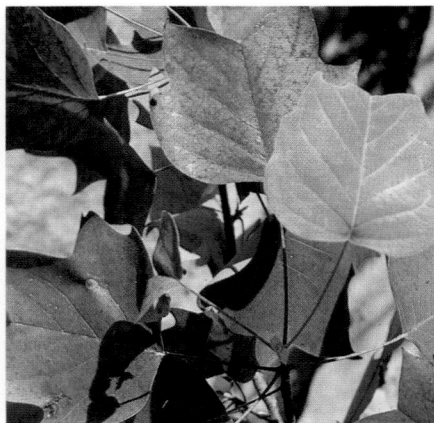
Sooty mold.

PROBLEM: Following warm, humid weather, leaves turn brown and dry and cling to the stem. Sunken oval areas, spotted with pink pustules, develop at the base of twigs and branches. The bark over the sunken areas turns brown and splits open, exposing the wood. Twigs and branches may die back.

ANALYSIS: Anthracnose and twig blight
This plant disease is caused by a fungus (*Glomerella cingulata*) that infects many ornamentals and fruit trees in the garden. It is most severe in plants weakened by such factors as drought, nutrient deficiency, and low temperatures. The fungus spends the winter on infected twigs and stems on the plant. During warm, humid weather, spores are blown and splashed onto healthy stems. The spores enter the tissue, and the fungus grows through the wood in all directions. The cells collapse and a sunken area (canker) develops. The canker cuts off the flow of water and nutrients to the branch, causing the leaves to turn brown and dry. If the canker encircles the wood completely, the stem above it dies.

SOLUTION: Prune twigs and stems well below the infected area. Spray with a fungicide containing *zineb* or *ferbam* at weekly intervals as long as the weather remains favorable for infection.

Privets resistant to anthracnose and twig blight: Amur privet (*Ligustrum amurense*); California privet (*L. ovalifolium*); Ibota privet (*L. ibota*); and Regal privet (*L. obtusifolium* var. *regelianum*).

PROBLEM: Starting in mid to late summer, the older leaves turn yellow and drop prematurely. Small brownish specks may appear between the veins before the leaves drop. Leaf drop develops during or just following hot, dry periods. It is most common in young or recently transplanted trees.

ANALYSIS: Summer leaf yellowing
Tuliptrees are sensitive to hot, dry summer weather, especially when the soil around the roots is allowed to dry out. The older leaves turn yellow and drop before the normal period of leaf drop in fall. Young or newly transplanted trees with limited root systems are particularly susceptible. Root injuries, soil level changes, and insects may also cause premature yellowing and leaf drop.

SOLUTION: Supply water during hot, dry periods. Newly transplanted trees require more water than established trees. Water when the top 2 inches of soil in the rootball are dry. (For more information about watering, see page 906.) Fertilize plants regularly to keep them vigorous and inspect them periodically for insects.

PROBLEM: A black sooty mold is growing on the leaves and twigs. It can be completely wiped off the surfaces. Cool, moist weather hastens the growth of this substance.

ANALYSIS: Sooty mold
This common black mold is found on a wide variety of plants in the garden. It is caused by any of several species of fungi that grow on the sugary material left on plants by aphids, scales, mealybugs, whiteflies, and other insects that suck sap from the plant. The insects are unable to digest all the sugar in the sap and excrete the excess in a fluid called honeydew, which drops onto the leaves below. The sooty mold fungus develops on the honeydew. Sooty mold is unsightly, but it is fairly harmless because it does not attack the leaf directly. The presence of sooty mold indicates that the plant or another plant near it is infested with insects.

SOLUTION: Sooty mold will eventually be washed off by rain. Prevent more sooty mold by controlling the insect that is producing the honeydew. Inspect the leaves and twigs above the sooty mold to find what type of insect is present. See the following pages for control instructions: for aphids, page 877; for scales, page 878; for whiteflies, page 879; for mealybugs, page 878.

Liriodendron cultural information
Light: Full sun
Water: Grows best in moist soil
Soil: Loose, rich, well drained, nonalkaline
Fertilizer: Light

LIRIODENDRON (TULIPTREE)

Aphids (half life size).

LONICERA (HONEYSUCKLE)

Witch's broom.

Tuliptree scale (¾ life size).

PROBLEM: The newest leaves turn yellow and may be small and distorted. A shiny, sticky substance coats the leaves and drips onto plants or objects below. A black sooty mold often grows on the sticky substance. Tiny (⅛ inch) greenish yellow soft-bodied insects cluster on the undersides of leaves. Ants may be present.

ANALYSIS: Tuliptree aphid
(*Macrosiphum liriodendri*)
This aphid infests the tuliptree wherever it is grown, and may be present from spring through fall. The aphids do not seriously harm the tree. However, they are extremely prolific and the population can rapidly build up and produce much unsightly damage. Damage occurs when the aphid sucks the juices from the tuliptree leaves. The aphid is unable to digest fully all the sugar in the plant sap and excretes copious quantities of the sugary material in a fluid called honeydew. The honeydew drops onto the leaves below. Plants or objects beneath the tree are also coated with it. A sooty mold fungus may develop on the honeydew, causing the tuliptree leaves and other coated plants to appear black and dirty. Ants feed on this sticky substance, and are often present where there is an aphid infestation.

SOLUTION: Spray with an insecticide containing *malathion* when aphids are first noticed. Direct the spray to the undersides of the leaves. Repeat the spray if the tree becomes reinfested.

PROBLEM: The twigs and branches are covered with brown, turtle-shaped, crusty bumps, ⅓ inch in diameter. Leaves turn yellow and may drop. A shiny, sticky substance coats the leaves. A black sooty mold often grows on the sticky substance. If the infestation is heavy, branches die back, starting at the bottom of the tree. The tree may be killed by severe infestations.

ANALYSIS: Tuliptree scale
(*Toumeyella liriodendri*)
The tuliptree scale is a serious pest of tuliptrees, magnolias, and lindens. The immature insect spends the winter on the twigs and branches of the tree. Starting in spring, it feeds by inserting its mouthparts and sucking the sap and nutrients from the bark tissue. The scale is unable to digest fully all the sugar in the plant sap, and excretes the excess in a fluid called honeydew, which drops onto leaves or other plants below. A sooty mold fungus may develop on the honeydew, causing the tuliptree leaves and other coated plants to appear black and dirty. The scale matures in August, and the female lays eggs underneath its brown shell. A single female lays up to 3000 eggs. In the fall the young scales, called *crawlers*, settle on the twigs to spend the winter. Repeated heavy infestations kill branches and possibly the whole tree. Several other types of scales also infest tuliptree. For more information about scales, see page 878.

SOLUTION: Spray with ORTHO Liquid Sevin or an insecticide containing *malathion* in mid-August when the young are active. The following early spring, before new growth begins, spray the trunk and branches with a *dormant oil spray* to control overwintering insects.

PROBLEM: The leaves are covered with white, cottony masses. Beneath the white masses are clusters of small (⅛ inch) yellow and black soft-bodied insects. The leaves curl and may turn yellow. Witch's brooms may occur. A shiny, sticky substance usually coats the leaves and stems. A black sooty mold may grow on the sticky substance.

ANALYSIS: Woolly honeysuckle aphid
(*Prociphilus xylostei*)
Honeysuckle is not seriously harmed by this aphid, but the woolly material and curled leaves are unsightly. The honeysuckle aphid does little damage in small numbers. However, it is extremely prolific and populations can rapidly build up to damaging numbers during the growing season. Leaf curling develops when the aphid sucks the juices from the honeysuckle leaves. While it is feeding, the aphid secretes masses of white, waxy filaments that cover its body and look like cotton. The aphid is unable to digest fully all the sugar in the plant sap and excretes the excess in a fluid called honeydew. The honeydew often drops onto leaves and other plants below. A sooty mold fungus may develop on the honeydew, causing the leaves and other coated plants to appear black and dirty.

SOLUTION: Spray with an insecticide containing *malathion*. Once the honeysuckle leaves curl, the woolly aphids are protected inside them. For the best control, the spray should be applied early in the season, before the leaves curl.

MAGNOLIA

Powdery mildew.

PROBLEM: The leaves, branch tips, and buds are covered with a thin layer or irregular patches of grayish white powdery material. Infected leaves may turn yellow and drop. The buds may be deformed or die. In fall, black dots (spore-producing bodies) are scattered over the powdery material like ground pepper.

ANALYSIS: Powdery mildew
This common plant disease is caused by two fungi (*Microsphaera alni* and *Erysiphe polygoni*) that thrive in both humid and dry weather. The powdery patches consist of fungal strands and spores. The spores are spread by the wind to healthy plants. The fungus saps the plant nutrients, causing leaf yellowing and bud deformation, and sometimes the death of the leaf and bud. Since these mildews attack many different kinds of plants, the fungus from a diseased plant may infect other types of plants in the garden. For a list of susceptible plants, see page 995.

SOLUTION: Spray both the upper and lower surfaces of the leaves with a fungicide containing *benomyl*, *dinocap*, or *cycloheximide* when the plants show the first sign of mildew. Repeat every 2 weeks as long as new mildew appears.

Lonicera cultural information
Light: Full sun to part shade
Water: When the soil is almost dry (some are drought tolerant)
Soil: Loose, well drained (some tolerate poor drainage)
Fertilizer: Medium

MAGNOLIA

ADAPTATION: Zones 5 through 9. To determine your zone, see the map on page 1004.

FLOWERING TIME: Late winter to fall, depending on the species.

LIGHT: Full sun (partial shade in desert areas).

SOIL: Well drained, rich in organic matter, neutral or slightly acid (pH 6.5 to 7.0). Magnolias will not tolerate salts in the soil or compacted soil. Avoid digging around their roots.

FERTILIZER: Fertilize with ORTHO Azalea, Camellia & Rhododendron Food 5–10–10 according to label directions.

WATER:
How much: Apply enough water to wet the soil 3 to 4 feet deep. To determine the proper amount of water for your soil type, see page 906.
How often: Magnolias prefer moist growing conditions. Water when the soil is moist but not wet 4 inches below the surface. For more information about watering, see page 906.

PRUNING: Magnolias do not require pruning, except to remove dead wood. When planting, allow enough room for growth.

Leaf scorch.

PROBLEM: During hot weather, usually in July or August, leaves turn brown around the edges and between the veins. Sometimes the whole leaf dies. Many leaves may drop during late summer. This problem is most severe on the youngest branches. Trees do not generally die.

ANALYSIS: Summer leaf scorch
Leaf scorch is caused by excessive evaporation from the leaves. In hot weather, water evaporates rapidly from the leaves. If the roots can't absorb and convey water fast enough to replenish this loss, the leaves turn brown and wither. For optimum growth, magnolias require moist soil. Leaf scorch is most severe when water is unavailable because the soil is dry. However, if the weather is extremely hot, scorch may also develop when the soil is moist. Drying winds, severed roots, limited soil area, or low temperatures can also cause scorch. For more information about scorch, see page 865.

SOLUTION: To prevent further scorch, deep-water trees during periods of hot weather to wet down the entire root space. (For more information about watering trees, see page 906.) Newly transplanted trees should be watered whenever the rootball is dry 2 inches below the surface. If possible, shade trees during very hot weather. Plant trees adapted to your climate.

MAGNOLIA

Algal spot.

Iron deficiency.

Magnolia scale (half life size).

PROBLEM: Leaves and twigs are covered with reddish brown velvety patches or greenish brown spots. Twigs may be stunted or die back.

ANALYSIS: Algal spot
Algal spot, also called *green scurf*, is caused by algae (*Cephaleuros virescens*) that are common on magnolias and other ornamentals in the southern parts of the country. During moist weather, cells of the algae enter the leaves or the other tissue of twigs and spread rapidly. The invaded twig tissue may swell and crack. If the crack encircles the twig, the twig dies. The infected magnolia leaves turn greenish brown at first. If the algae develop spore-producing bodies (tiny round heads on fine, dense reddish hairs) the patches appear reddish brown and velvety or cushiony. The algae spread rapidly when rains are frequent and heavy. Trees weakened by drought or poor growing conditions are most susceptible to algal spot.

SOLUTION: Control measures are not usually necessary. If trees are weak, improve growing conditions by watering and fertilizing regularly. Prune dead twigs. If algal spot is severe, spray with a fungicide containing *basic copper sulfate*, plus an oil or a spreader-sticker, in December and January and at the start of the rainy season. Repeat one month later. For more information about spreader-stickers, see page 915.

PROBLEM: Some of the leaves turn pale green to yellow. The newest leaves may be completely yellow with only the veins remaining green. On older leaves, only the leaf edges may be yellowing. The plant may be stunted.

ANALYSIS: Iron deficiency
This is a common problem with acid-loving plants like magnolia, which grow best in soil with a pH between 5.5 and 6.5. (For more information on soil acidity, see page 902.) The yellowing is due to a deficiency of iron and other minor nutrients in the plant. The soil is seldom deficient in iron. However, iron is often found in an insoluable form that is not available to the plant, especially in soil with a pH of 7.0 or higher. A high soil pH can result from overliming, or from lime leached from cement or brick. Regions where soil is derived from limestone, and those with low rainfall, also have high-pH soils. Plants use iron in the formation of the green pigment in the leaves. When it is lacking, new leaves are yellow.

SOLUTION: Spray the foliage with ORTHO Greenol Liquid Iron 6.13%, and apply it to the soil around the plants to correct the iron deficiency. Correct the pH of the soil by treating it with *ferrous sulfate* and watering it in well. Maintain an acid pH by fertilizing with ORTHO Azalea, Camellia & Rhododendron Food 5–10–10.

PROBLEM: Twigs and stems are covered with powdery white or shiny brown crusty bumps, ½ inch in diameter, or soft masses of purple insects. Stems that are normally light green may appear enlarged and purple or whitish. The crusty bumps can be scraped or picked off; the undersides are soft. Leaves may be yellowing and smaller than normal; trees may be weakened or killed. A shiny, sticky substance usually coats the leaves. A black sooty mold often grows on the sticky substance.

ANALYSIS: Magnolia scale
(*Neolecanium cornuparvum*)
This is the largest scale insect found in the United States. The immature purple insect spends the winter on the twigs and branches of the tree. Starting in spring, it feeds by inserting its mouthparts and sucking the sap and nutrients from the bark tissue. The scale is unable to digest fully all the sugar in the plant sap, and excretes the excess in a fluid called honeydew. A sooty mold fungus may develop on the honeydew. The scales mature in August and the female lays her eggs beneath her powdery white or shiny brown shell. In the fall the young scales, called *crawlers*, settle on the twigs to spend the winter. Repeated heavy infestations kill branches and possibly the whole tree. Several other types of scales also infest magnolia. For more information about scales, see page 878.

SOLUTION: Spray with ORTHO Orthene Systemic Insect Control or ORTHO Liquid Sevin in September when the young are active. The following early spring, before new growth begins, spray with a *dormant oil spray* to control overwintering insects.

MAHONIA (OREGON GRAPE)

Winter injury to Oregon grape.

Rust.

Barberry looper (half life size).

PROBLEM: The leaves are rusty brown to red, and dry. Twigs may die. The shrub is growing in a climate where cold, dry, windy days are common in winter or where plants may be exposed to late fall or early spring freezes. The soil may be frozen.

ANALYSIS: Winter injury
Oregon grape is damaged by cold, drying winter wind, especially if temperatures are below freezing and the weather is clear and sunny. The leaves lose their moisture more rapidly than it can be replaced by the root system. Cells in the leaves dry out and die. This condition is most pronounced when water is unavailable because the soil is frozen. Leaves and twigs may also die during early fall or late spring freezes when the plant is growing. Young, succulent growth cannot withstand the cold temperatures.

SOLUTION: No cure is available once plants have been injured. Where practical, pick off damaged leaves and prune out dead twigs. Provide shelter and windbreaks for plants growing in cold regions. Covering Oregon grape with burlap bags in winter helps prevent leaf drying. To avoid succulent growth in the fall, do not fertilize or prune late in the season. Water in late fall or winter, if necessary, to insure adequate soil moisture. Mulch plants after they are dormant to reduce the depth of frost penetration into the soil.

PROBLEM: Yellow spots appear on the upper surfaces of the leaves during the growing season. Corresponding to these spots, on the undersides of the leaves, are spots or pustules containing a powdery yellowish material. The powdery material can be rubbed or scraped off easily. Heavily infested plants usually lack vigor.

ANALYSIS: Rust
Rust on Oregon grape is caused by any of several different fungi. Some of these rust fungi spend their entire life on Oregon grape. Others must spend part of their life on another plant (weeds or wheat) before they can reinfect Oregon grape. The wind spreads spores to the leaves. With moisture (rain, dew, or fog) and moderate temperatures (55° to 75°F), the spores enter the tissue on the undersides of the leaves. Spots usually develop directly above on the upper surface of the leaf as the fungus saps the plant nutrients.

SOLUTION: No chemicals are available to control rust on Oregon grape. Prune off and destroy heavily infested stems.

Mahonia cultural information
Light: Full sun to shade
Water: Keep the soil moist
Soil: Loose, rich, nonalkaline
Fertilizer: Medium

PROBLEM: Patches of tissue are eaten from one surface of the leaf; the corresponding upper or lower surface turns brown and appears lacy. Later, the entire leaf surface is eaten. By midsummer, the plant may be defoliated. Large (up to 1-inch long), brownish caterpillars with light and dark stripes may be found on the undersides of the leaves. The caterpillars crawl in a looping motion.

ANALYSIS: Barberry looper
(*Coryphista meadii*)
Barberry loopers, also called *mahonia loopers*, are the larvae of brownish gray moths with black bands across their wings. In the spring, the females lay their eggs on Oregon grape leaves. The emerging larvae feed as skeletonizers first, eating only one surface of the leaf. As the loopers mature, they feed on the entire leaf. When fully grown, the caterpillars drop to the ground and pupate in the soil. There may be as many as 3 generations of loopers during a growing season.

SOLUTION: Spray with an insecticide containing *carbaryl* or *acephate* when insects are first noticed in the spring. Make sure your plant is listed on the product label. Repeat the spray if the plant becomes reinfested.

MALUS (CRABAPPLE)

Fireblight.

Scab.

MALUS (CRABAPPLE)

ADAPTATION: Zones 2 to 10 (to determine your zone, see the map on page 1004). Most are not adapted to mild winter or desert areas.

FLOWERING TIME: Spring.

LIGHT: Full sun.

SOIL: Adapted to a wide variety of soils, but grows best in rich, well-drained garden soil.

FERTILIZER: Fertilize with ORTHO Evergreen, Tree & Shrub Food 12–6–6 according to label directions.

WATER:
How much: Apply enough water to wet the soil 3 to 4 feet deep. To determine the proper amount of water for your soil type, see page 906.
How often: Water when the soil is barely moist 4 inches below the surface. For more information about watering, see page 906.

INSECTS AND DISEASES: Problems of crabapple are very similar to those of apple. For more information about plant problems on crabapple, see insects and diseases of apples in the section starting on page 626.

PROBLEM: The blossoms and leaves of infected twigs suddenly wilt and turn black as if scorched by fire. The leaves curl and hang downward. The bark at the base of the blighted twig becomes water-soaked, then dark, sunken, and dry; cracks may develop at the edge of the sunken area. In warm, moist spring weather, drops of brown ooze appear on the sunken bark. Young trees may die.

ANALYSIS: Fireblight
This disease is caused by a bacterium (*Erwinia amylovora*) that is very destructive to many trees and shrubs. (For a list of susceptible plants, see page 1001.) The bacteria spend the winter in the sunken areas (cankers) on the branches. In the spring, the bacteria ooze out of the cankers. Insects that are attracted to this ooze become smeared with it, and when the insects visit a flower for nectar, they infect it with the bacteria. The bacteria spread rapidly through the plant tissue in warm (65°F or higher), humid weather. Insects visiting these infected blossoms later carry bacteria-laden nectar to healthy blossoms. Rain, wind, and tools may also spread the bacteria. Tender or damaged leaves may be infected in midsummer.

SOLUTION: Prune out infected branches 12 to 15 inches beyond any visible discoloration and destroy them. Sterilize pruning shears with rubbing alcohol after each cut. A protective spray of a pesticide containing *fixed copper* or *streptomycin*, applied before bud break in spring, will help prevent infection. Repeat at intervals of 5 to 7 days until the end of bloom. For a list of crabapples resistant to fireblight, see page 1001.

PROBLEM: Olive-colored, velvety spots, ¼ inch or more in diameter, appear on the leaves. The tissue around the spots may be puckered. The leaves often turn yellow and drop. In a wet year, the tree may lose all of its leaves by midsummer. The fruit and twigs develop circular, rough-surfaced, olive-green spots, which eventually turn corky and black. The fruit is usually deformed.

ANALYSIS: Apple scab
This plant disease is caused by a fungus (*Venturia inaequalis*). It is a serious problem on crabapples and apples in areas where spring weather is humid and mild (60° to 70°F). The fungus spends the winter in infected fallen leaves. In the spring, spore-producing structures in the dead leaves continuously discharge spores into the air. The spores are blown by the wind to new leaves and fruit buds. If there is water on the tissue surfaces, the fungus infects them and a spot develops. More spores are produced from these spots, and from twig infections from the previous year. The spores are splashed by the rain to infect new leaf and fruit surfaces. As temperatures increase during the summer, the fungus becomes less active.

SOLUTION: To obtain adequate control of scab, protective sprays must be applied starting as soon as bud growth begins in spring. Spray with a fungicide containing *captan*, *lime sulfur*, or *mancozeb*. Repeat 5 to 8 times at intervals of 7 to 10 days. Rake up and destroy infected leaves and fruit in the fall. When planting new trees, use resistant varieties. For a list of crabapples resistant to scab, see page 1001.

Cedar-apple rust.

Oystershell scale (twice life size).

Slime flux.

PROBLEM: Pale yellow spots appear on the leaves and fruit in mid to late spring. These spots gradually enlarge, turn orange, and develop minute black dots. Small (1/16 inch) cups with fringed edges form on the lower surfaces of the leaves. Infected leaves and fruit may drop prematurely; the fruit are often deformed.

ANALYSIS: Cedar-apple rust
This plant disease is caused by a fungus (*Gymnosporangium juniperi-virginianae*) that affects both crabapples and certain species of juniper and red cedar. This disease cannot spread from crabapple to crabapple, or from juniper to juniper, but must alternate between the two. In the spring, spores from brown and orange galls on juniper or cedar are blown up to 3 miles to crabapple trees. During mild, wet weather, the spores germinate and infect the leaves and fruit, causing spotting and premature leaf and fruit drop. During the summer, spores are produced in small cups on the undersides of the leaves. These spores are blown back to junipers and cedars, causing new infections. For more information about cedar-apple rust on junipers, see page 535.

SOLUTION: Cedar-apple rust cannot be controlled on this season's foliage and fruit. Next spring, spray trees with a fungicide containing *ferbam, maneb,* or *thiram* when the flower buds turn pink, again when 75 percent of the petals have fallen from the blossoms, and once more 10 days later. If possible, do not plant crabapples within several hundred yards of junipers or red cedar.

PROBLEM: Stems or leaves are covered with brownish crusty bumps or thick, white, waxy bumps, or clusters of somewhat flattened yellowish scaly bumps. The bumps can be scraped or picked off; the undersides are usually soft. Leaves turn yellow and may drop. In some cases, a shiny or sticky substance coats the leaves. A black sooty mold often grows on the sticky substance.

ANALYSIS: Scales
Several different types of scales infest crabapples. They lay their eggs on leaves or bark, and in spring to midsummer the young scales, called *crawlers*, settle on leaves and twigs. The small (1/10 inch), soft-bodied young feed by inserting their mouthparts and sucking sap from the plant. The legs usually atrophy and a hard crusty or waxy shell develops over the body. The mature female scales lay their eggs underneath their shell. Some species of scales that infest crabapples are unable to digest fully all the sugar in the plant sap and excrete the excess in a fluid called honeydew, which often drops onto the leaves below. A sooty mold fungus may develop on the honeydew, causing the crabapple leaves to appear black and dirty. An uncontrolled infestation of scales may kill the plant after 2 or 3 seasons.

SOLUTION: Spray with ORTHO Liquid Sevin in late spring when the young are active. Contact your local Cooperative Extension Office (see page 1011) to determine the best time to spray for scales in your area. The following early spring, before new growth begins, spray the trunk and branches with a *dormant oil spray* to control overwintering insects. For more information about scales, see page 878.

PROBLEM: Sour-smelling sap oozes from wounds, cracks, and branch crotches, mainly during the growing season. The sap drips down the bark and dries, causing unsightly gray or black streaks. Leaves may wilt on affected branches. Insects are attracted to the sour-smelling ooze.

ANALYSIS: Slime flux
Slime flux of mulberries, also called *wetwood*, is caused by bacteria (*Erwinia nimipressuralis*). The bacteria affect the heartwood, producing abnormally high sap pressure. This pressure is caused by bacterial fermentation, and forces the fermented sap, or flux, out of wounds, cracks, or crotches in the tree. Flux is especially copious when the tree is growing rapidly. Large areas of the bark may be coated with the smelly, bacteria-laden sap, which dries to a grayish white color. In addition, wounds do not heal and the bark is unsightly. A tree with this problem is often under water stress, which may cause drought damage (wilting and scorched leaves) to the branches. The problem may persist for years.

SOLUTION: There are no chemical controls for this condition. Bore a slightly slanted drainage hole through the wood below each oozing wound. Insert a 1/2-inch-diameter plastic tube just until it stays firmly in place. If the tube penetrates the water-soaked wood inside the tree, it will interfere with drainage. The tube will carry the dripping sap away from the trunk. Disinfect tools with rubbing alcohol after pruning infected trees.

Bacterial blight.

Scale (3 times life size).

Cottony scale (3 times life size).

PROBLEM: Brown, water-soaked spots appear on the leaves and shoots. In wet weather, the spots enlarge rapidly, eventually becoming black and sunken. The leaves at the tips of the infected twigs are distorted; later they wilt and dry up. There are black streaks underneath the bark of infected twigs. The streaks extend downward from the blackened areas on the shoots. Infected shoots may exude an ooze in wet weather. Twigs often die, and the tree may be stunted.

ANALYSIS: Bacterial blight
This blight is caused by a bacterium (*Pseudomonas syringae mori*) that is common on both black and white mulberry. The bacteria spend the winter in the infected areas on the tree. During wet spring weather bacteria ooze out and are splashed by the rain to young leaves and twigs and nearby trees. Where the bacteria enter the tissue, a water-soaked spot develops. If rainy weather continues, the bacteria spread and twigs may die.

SOLUTION: In the fall, prune out infected branches well below the blighted area and destroy them. A protective spray used after pruning may help control the bacteria. Spray with a pesticide containing *basic copper sulfate* or *streptomycin*. Do not plant young mulberry trees near older infected trees.

Morus cultural information
Light: Full sun
Water: Occasional deep watering, tolerates some drought
Soil: Tolerates many types
Fertilizer: Light

PROBLEM: The leaves, stems, or branches are covered with brownish purple crusty bumps or clusters of somewhat flattened brown, gray, or yellow scaly bumps. The bumps can be scraped or picked off; the undersides are usually soft. Leaves turn yellow and may drop. In some cases, a shiny, sticky substance coats the leaves. A black sooty mold often grows on the sticky substance.

ANALYSIS: Scales
Many different types of scales infest mulberry. They lay their eggs on leaves or bark, and in spring to midsummer the young scales, called *crawlers*, settle on leaves, twigs, and branches. These small (1/10 inch), soft-bodied young feed by sucking sap from the plant. The legs usually atrophy and a hard crusty shell develops over the body. The mature female scales lay their eggs underneath the shell. Some species of scales that infest mulberry are unable to digest fully all the sugar in the plant sap, and excrete the excess in a fluid called honeydew, which often drops onto the leaves or plants below. A sooty mold fungus may develop on the honeydew, causing the mulberry leaves or other plants to appear black and dirty. An uncontrolled infestation of scales may kill branches after 2 or 3 years.

SOLUTION: Spray with ORTHO Orthene Systemic Insect Control when the young are active. Contact your local Cooperative Extension Office (see page 1011) to determine the best time to spray for scales in your area. To control scales during the dormant season, spray the trunk and branches with ORTHO Volck Oil Spray. For more information about scales, see page 878.

PROBLEM: The undersides of the leaves, stems, branch crotches, and/or trunk are covered with white, cottony masses. Leaves may turn yellow and drop. A shiny, sticky substance may coat the leaves. A black sooty mold often grows on the sticky substance. Numerous side shoots sometimes grow out of an infested crotch area. Twigs and branches may die.

ANALYSIS: Cottony scales and mealybugs
Cottony scales and mealybugs are common on mulberry wherever it is grown. The visual similarities between these insects make separate identification difficult. They are very conspicuous in late spring and summer because the females are covered with a white, cottony egg sac, containing up to 2500 eggs. Females lay their egg masses on leaves or branches. The young insects that hatch from these eggs are yellowish brown to green. Damage is caused by the withdrawal of plant sap from the leaves and branches. The insects are unable to digest fully all the sugar in the plant sap and excrete the excess in a fluid called honeydew, which often drops onto the leaves or plants below. A sooty mold fungus may develop on the honeydew, causing the mulberry leaves and other plants to appear black and dirty. Leaf drop and twig dieback occur when the white masses completely cover the leaves and branches.

SOLUTION: Spray with an insecticide containing *diazinon* or *malathion* in midsummer when the young are active. The following spring, when the tree is dormant, spray with *lime sulfur* to control overwintering insects on the bark.

NANDINA (HEAVENLY BAMBOO)

Iron deficiency.

PROBLEM: Some of the leaves are pale green (or pale red) to yellow. The newest leaves may be completely yellow, with only the veins remaining green. On older leaves, only the leaf edges may be yellowing. The plant may be stunted.

ANALYSIS: Iron deficiency
This is a common problem in plants, such as nandina, that do not tolerate alkaline soils. Nandina grows best in soil with a pH between 5.5 and 6.5. (For more information about soil acidity, see page 902.) The yellowing is due to a deficiency of iron and other minor nutrients in the plant. The soil is seldom deficient in iron. However, iron is often found in an insoluble form that is not available to the plant, especially in soil with a pH of 7.0 or higher. A high soil pH can result from overliming, or from lime leached from cement or brick. Regions where soil is derived from limestone, and those with low rainfall, also have high-pH soils.

SOLUTION: Spray the foliage with ORTHO Greenol Liquid Iron 6.13%, and apply it to the soil around the plants to correct the iron deficiency. Correct the pH of the soil by treating it with *ferrous sulfate* and watering it in well. Maintain an acid pH by fertilizing with ORTHO Azalea, Camellia & Rhododendron Food 5–10–10.

Nandina cultural information
Light: Full sun to shade
Water: Grows best in moist soil
Soil: Loose, rich, well drained, nonalkaline
Fertilizer: Medium

NERIUM (OLEANDER)

Sooty mold.

PROBLEM: A black sooty mold is growing on leaves and twigs. It can be completely wiped off the surfaces. Cool, moist weather hastens the growth of the mold.

ANALYSIS: Sooty mold
This common black mold is found on a wide variety of plants in the garden. It is caused by several species of fungi that grow on the sugary material left on plants by aphids, scales, mealybugs, whiteflies, and other insects that suck sap from the plant. The insects are unable to digest all the sugar in the sap and excrete the excess in a fluid called honeydew, which drops onto the leaves below. The honeydew may also drop out of infested trees and shrubs onto oleanders growing beneath them. The sooty mold fungus develops on the honeydew, causing the oleander leaves to appear black and dirty. Sooty mold is unsightly, but it is fairly harmless because it does not attack the leaf directly. Extremely heavy infestations prevent light from reaching the leaf, so that the leaf produces fewer nutrients and may turn yellow. The presence of sooty mold indicates that the oleander or another plant near it is infested with insects.

SOLUTION: Sooty mold can be wiped from the leaves with a wet rag; or it will eventually be washed off by rain. Prevent more sooty mold by controlling the insect that is producing the honeydew. Inspect the leaves and twigs above the sooty mold to find what type of insect is present. For control instructions, see the following pages: for aphids, page 877; for scales, page 878; for whiteflies, page 879; for mealybugs, page 878.

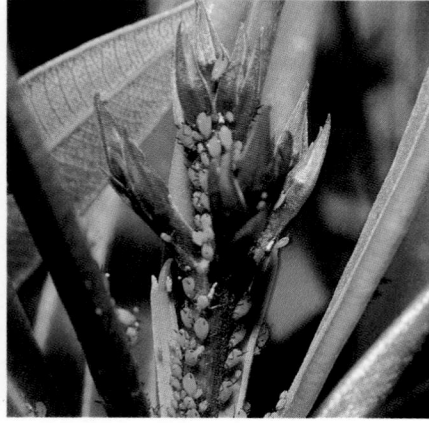

Oleander aphids (life size).

PROBLEM: Huge colonies of tiny (1/8 inch), soft-bodied insects cluster on the leaves, branch tips, and buds. The infested leaves may turn yellow, and new growth may be slowed and distorted.

ANALYSIS: Oleander aphid
(*Aphis nerii*)
This aphid heavily infests oleander in the southwestern states. The aphids appear in early spring. They are extremely prolific and populations rapidly build up to huge numbers during the early part of the growing season. The aphids suck the juices from the oleander leaves, but oleander is such a vigorous plant that the insect usually causes little damage. There may be some leaf yellowing and distortion on the ends of the branches. In early summer to midsummer, when temperatures increase and natural enemies, such as wasps and lady beetles, are abundant, the aphid population declines. Several other aphid species also infest oleander.

SOLUTION: If aphids are abundant and causing damage to the plant, spray the leaves and branch tips thoroughly with ORTHO Isotox Insect Spray. Repeat the spray if the plant becomes reinfested.

NERIUM (OLEANDER)

Black scale (twice life size).

False oleander scale (twice life size).

Oleander caterpillar (half life size).

PROBLEM: The leaves, twigs, and branches are covered with brownish or black crusty bumps, ⅕ inch in diameter. On the surface of the bumps, ridges form the letter H. Leaves turn brown in patches and may drop; twigs may die. A shiny sticky substance may coat the leaves. A black sooty mold often grows on the sticky substance.

ANALYSIS: Black scale
(*Saissetia oleae*)
Black scale is a serious pest of many trees and shrubs in the South. It may also infest greenhouse-grown plants in colder climates. The scales spend the winter on the trunk and twigs of oleander. They lay their eggs in the spring, and in late spring the young scales, called *crawlers*, settle on leaves, twigs, and branches. The small (¹⁄₁₀ inch), soft-bodied young feed by sucking sap from the plant. The legs atrophy and a hard shell develops over their body. The mature female scales lay their eggs underneath the shell. These scales are unable to digest fully all the sugar in the plant sap and excrete the excess in a fluid called honeydew. A sooty mold fungus may develop on the honeydew, causing the oleander leaves to appear black and dirty. An uncontrolled infestation of scales may kill branches or the entire plant after several seasons. Many other scales also infest oleander. For more information about scales, see page 878.

SOLUTION: Spray with ORTHO Isotox Insect Killer or ORTHO Orthene Systemic Insect Control in late spring when the young are active. The following early spring, spray the trunk and branches with a *dormant oil spray* to control overwintering insects.

PROBLEM: Yellow to greenish yellow spots develop on the leaves. Tiny white to light brown raised bumps are often seen in the discolored areas. The bumps can be scraped or picked off; the undersides are usually soft. Stems may also be infested. Leaves turn yellow and drop. Small branches may be killed when infestations are heavy.

ANALYSIS: False oleander scale
(*Pseudaulacaspis cockerelli*)
This insect feeds on many garden plants, and is capable of rapid reproduction. The female scale deposits large masses of eggs under her wax shell. After hatching, the young scales, called *crawlers*, move about the host plant until they locate a feeding site. They then begin to feed and develop the protective scale cover. Several generations of scales are produced each year. Scales feed by sucking the plant juices from tender leaves and stems. Some scales are unable to digest fully all the sugar in the plant sap, and excrete the excess in a fluid called honeydew, which often drops onto the leaves below. A sooty mold may develop on the honeydew, causing the oleander leaves to appear black and dirty.

SOLUTION: Apply ORTHO Isotox Insect Killer thoroughly to infested plants. Repeat sprays at intervals of 7 to 10 days until scales are controlled. Dead scales remain on the plant but are dry and contain no fluids when scraped off and examined.

PROBLEM: Leaves are badly chewed or missing. Orange caterpillars up to 2 inches long with many short black hairs may be feeding on the damaged plants.

ANALYSIS: Oleander caterpillar
(*Syntomedia epilais juncundissima*)
This chewing pest is the larval stage of a colorful, purple, 2-inch moth with white markings on greenish black wings. The caterpillars hatch from eggs laid on the leaves. Development is rapid; the adult stage is reached in about a month. This rapid maturation enables several generations of caterpillars to be produced during the year. They cause their greatest damage from early spring until fall.

SOLUTION: Apply ORTHO Orthene Systemic Insect Control or ORTHO Liquid Sevin. Repeat treatments as needed according to label directions. Severely infested plants that have lost most of their leaves usually grow new leaves within a few weeks after caterpillars are controlled. Applying a light amount of a complete fertilizer will also help plants recover more quickly.

Bacterial gall.

Witch's broom.

Cottony maple leaf scale (twice life size).

PROBLEM: There are wartlike spongy growths on older branches, and longitudinal swellings on young green shoots. Leaves are distorted and yellowing, and may develop swellings. Ooze may drip from the leaf veins.

ANALYSIS: Bacterial gall
This plant disease is caused by a bacterium (*Pseudomonas syringae tonelliana*) that infects all of the aboveground parts of oleander. The bacteria enter through wounds, possibly those caused by sucking insects such as scales and mealybugs. On young shoots, cankers develop; on older woody stems, the bacteria initiate the development of wartlike galls. Growth above these galls is often scraggly. Large quantities of ooze that contains bacteria may be exuded from leaf veins.

SOLUTION: Prune out and destroy infected stems well below the galls. Sterilize pruning shears with rubbing alcohol after each cut.

All parts of the oleander plant are highly toxic, and contact with leaves can produce dermatitis. Smoke from burning plant parts can cause severe skin and respiratory irritations.

PROBLEM: Abnormal clusters of new shoots appear just below the branch tips. These shoots grow only a few inches, and then turn brown and die. On heavily infected plants, large areas may be killed.

ANALYSIS: Witch's broom
These abnormal growths on oleander are caused by a fungus (*Sphaeropsis tumefaciens*) that infects branch tips during the fall and winter. Witch's broom symptoms do not usually appear until spring, after additional growth has taken place and the infected tissue is several inches below the growing tip. Multiple shoots grow from the infected area, producing the witch's broom effect. Wind and insects spread the disease. Most oleanders are easily infected.

SOLUTION: No practical controls are available at present. Prune out affected areas as soon as symptoms are noticed, making cuts at least 6 inches below the witch's broom. Sterilize pruning tools in rubbing alcohol after pruning.

Nerium cultural information
Light: Full sun
Water: Drought tolerant once established
Soil: Tolerates many types
Fertilizer: Light

PROBLEM: The undersides of the leaves are covered with white, cottony, cushionlike masses. Leaves may turn yellow and drop. Sometimes a shiny, sticky substance coats the leaves. A black sooty mold often grows on the sticky substance. Twigs and branches may die back.

ANALYSIS: Cottony maple leaf scale (*Pulvinaria acericola*)
The cottony maple leaf scale is a pest of sour gum in the eastern part of the country. The immature scales spend the winter on the twigs and branches. Damage is caused when the insects suck plant sap from the leaves and branches. The scales feed in the spring, mate, and then the females migrate to the leaves to lay their eggs. The females are very conspicuous because they are covered with a white, cottony egg sac, containing up to 2500 eggs. The young scales that hatch from these eggs move to new leaves to feed, settling along the larger veins. The pale green insects are inconspicuous against the green leaves. In fall, the immature scales migrate back to the bark. The insects are unable to digest fully all the sugar in the plant sap, and excrete the excess in a fluid called honeydew, which often drops onto the leaves or plants below. A sooty mold fungus may develop on the honeydew, causing the black gum leaves and other plants to appear black and dirty. With repeated heavy infestations, twigs and branches die after several years.

SOLUTION: Spray with ORTHO Liquid Sevin in midsummer when the young are active. The following spring, while the tree is still dormant, spray with *lime sulfur* to control overwintering insects on the bark.

OLEA (OLIVE)

Olive knot.

PROBLEM: Twigs, branches, leaves, and sometimes the fruit develop knotty swellings, up to several inches across. As the swellings enlarge the surfaces become rough, and irregular fissures form. Growth above these swellings slows, and shoots or the entire tree may die.

ANALYSIS: Olive knot
Olive knot is caused by a bacterium (*Pseudomonas syringae sevastanoi*) that lives and multiplies inside the knots. During rainy weather, between October and May, the bacteria ooze out of the knots and are washed and blown by rain and wind to the twigs, branches, and leaves. When new growth begins in spring, small swellings develop. The swellings enlarge, eventually becoming knotty and hard; growth above these knots is slowed. Trees grown for their fruit may produce few olives.

SOLUTION: Where practical, prune off the knots from the tree during the summer, sterilizing pruning shears after each cut with rubbing alcohol. Painting the knots with the bactericide Gallex* may help control the spread of the bacteria. Keep the tree in a vigorous growing condition by fertilizing and watering regularly to prevent large losses of leaves. Avoid wounding the tree. If branches on the tree require pruning, do so during the dry season to avoid new infections.

Olea cultural information
Light: Full sun
Water: Moist or dry soil
Soil: Rich, well drained, but tolerates many types
Fertilizer: Light

PALMS

Lethal yellowing.

PROBLEM: Many palm fronds turn yellow and die, beginning with the lower fronds and progressing upward. On coconut palm (*Cocos nucifera*), fronds yellow, and all the nuts usually drop. The nuts are black where they were attached to the flower stalk. New flower stalks are blackened, and do not set any fruit. Dead fronds tend to cling to the tree instead of falling off, and after 3 to 6 months, all the fronds and the bud have been killed. Shortly thereafter the entire palm top falls off, leaving only the bare trunk. No insects can be recognized on the dying fronds.

ANALYSIS: Lethal yellowing
This serious palm disease is caused by bacterialike organisms called *mycoplasmas*, which are carried from palm to palm by leafhoppers, tiny sucking insects. Leafhoppers feed on fronds, especially the newly emerging ones, and are difficult to detect and control. For more information about leafhoppers, see page 880.

SOLUTION: There is no cure for lethal yellowing. To suppress the disease and prolong the life of palms showing lethal yellowing symptoms, inject them every 4 months with the antibiotic *oxytetracycline*. Avoid planting susceptible palms. (For a list, see page 999.) Remove infected palms to avoid spreading the disease.

Bud rot. *Insert:* Close-up.

PROBLEM: The palm stops producing new fronds and the last new frond to appear turns yellow, then brown, and dies. The entire bud can be pulled out; it appears rotten, and may have a foul odor. One by one the fronds next to the bud turn yellow, then brown, and die. Eventually the entire top of the palm falls away, leaving the bare trunk standing. Palms of all ages and sizes are affected, and most damage follows periods of cold weather and high rainfall.

ANALYSIS: Bud rot
This often fatal palm disease is caused by a fungus (*Phytophthora palmivora*) that enters the palm through wounds or other openings. The spores can also be washed down into the palm bud by heavy rains. Once infected, palms may die within a short time. Most severe bud rot occurs from spring to fall.

SOLUTION: Spray the entire top of the palm with a fungicide containing *basic copper sulfate*. Be sure the bud area is thoroughly covered with the fungicide. Use a spreader-sticker with the fungicide to enable it to coat plant parts more effectively. (For more information on spreader-stickers, see page 915.) Repeat treatments as needed, following the label directions. Give a light application of fertilizer to speed the palm's recovery. Remove palms that die from bud rot as soon as possible to prevent infection of nearby healthy palms.

Palm leaf skeletonizer damage.

Frizzle top.

Lightning damage.

PROBLEM: Palm fronds become ragged and develop brown splotched areas covered with unsightly masses of webbing and excrement. Yellowish white caterpillars ⅝ inch long with several reddish brown stripes running the length of their bodies are feeding on the fronds. Fronds are rarely completely eaten.

ANALYSIS: Palm leaf skeletonizer (*Homaledra sabalella*)
This caterpillar is the larva of a small brownish moth that lays eggs in clusters on the underside of the husk that surrounds new leaflets. Caterpillars feed on the fronds for 25 to 30 days after hatching, and then pupate in the webbing on the frond. Several generations of caterpillars are produced each year, primarily during the spring and summer.

SOLUTION: Apply an insecticide containing *carbaryl* according to label directions. Repeat sprays are often required. For a list of palms most frequently attacked, see page 999.

Palm cultural information
Light: Full sun to partial shade
Water: When the soil is almost dry
Soil: Tolerates many types
Fertilizer: Medium

PROBLEM: Newly emerging fronds fail to grow to their normal length. Often they are light yellow to brown, and have a frizzled look. In severe cases, fronds turn dark brown to black, and the palm bud may die, resulting in the death of the tree.

ANALYSIS: Frizzle top
This problem in certain palms results from a lack of manganese, a minor nutrient. It occurs only where palms have been planted in infertile soil or soil that is subject to serious leaching of nutrient materials. A lack of regular fertilizing in home landscapes often greatly contributes to frizzle top.

SOLUTION: Apply *manganese sulfate* or a special palm fertilizer containing *manganese sulfate* according to label instructions. Severely affected palms may take 6 months or more to recover completely. Repeat fertilizer treatments at recommended intervals to prevent frizzle top from reappearing.

Palms most susceptible to frizzle top:
Date palm (*Phoenix*), royal palm (*Roystonea*), and queen palm (*Arecastrum*).

PROBLEM: Palm fronds suddenly begin to droop around the trunk, beginning with the lower ones. Frond color may be green at first, but changes rapidly to yellow and then to brown. After about two weeks most of the fronds have drooped down or fallen off, and the central bud area wilts and bends over. Sometimes a reddish fluid bleeds along the trunk. No pests or signs of diseases are seen on dying fronds, and the problem occurs shortly after a severe electrical storm.

ANALYSIS: Lightning damage
Severe electrical shock often kills palms very quickly, and each year hundreds are lost to lightning strikes in areas that have frequent thunderstorms.

SOLUTION: Usually nothing can save a palm that has suffered a severe lightning strike; however, some palms may recover. Regular applications of fertilizer to trees not killed outright will help them to recover. Dead palms should be removed so that they do not become a safety hazard. Do not plant tall-growing palms in open, exposed areas.

PARTHENOCISSUS (BOSTON IVY) ———

Leafhopper damage.

PROBLEM: Leaves are stippled with white specks; the entire plant may be whitened. When the infestation is heavy, many leaves turn brown and drop from the plant. Small (⅛ inch), wedge-shaped yellow insects with red, yellow, or black markings are found on the undersides of the leaves. When the plant is touched, the insects run, hop, or fly away.

ANALYSIS: Leafhoppers
(*Erythroneura* species)
Many different species of leafhoppers feed on *Parthenocissus*. This group also feeds on several types of fruit trees and small fruits. The leafhoppers spend the winter as adults in protected areas, usually under fallen leaves or in weeds. When the weather warms in the spring, they fly to plants and feed on the undersides of the developing leaves. The leafhoppers suck the fluids from the plant cells, causing the stippled appearance. The adult females insert their eggs into the leaf tissue. The eggs hatch in 2 weeks and the wingless young leafhoppers feed and develop on the lower surfaces of the leaves. They mature in 3 to 5 weeks. There may be as many as 3 generations a year.

SOLUTION: Spray with ORTHO Isotox Insect Killer or with an insecticide containing *malathion* when the damage is first noticed. Direct the spray to the undersides of the leaves.

Parthenocissus cultural information
Light: Full sun
Water: Grows best in moist soil
Soil: Loose, well drained
Fertilizer: Medium

PHILADELPHUS (MOCK ORANGE) ———

Black bean aphids (life size).

PROBLEM: The newest leaves are wrinkled and yellowing. Leaves may drop off and new growth may be slowed. A shiny, sticky substance may coat the leaves. A black sooty mold often grows on this sticky substance. Tiny (⅛ inch) greenish yellow or dark green soft-bodied insects cluster on the underside of leaves and on the branch tips. Ants may be present.

ANALYSIS: Aphids
Aphids do little damage in small numbers. However, they are extremely prolific and populations can rapidly build up to damaging numbers during the growing season. Damage occurs when the aphid sucks the juices from the mock orange leaves. The aphid is unable to digest fully all the sugar in the sap and excretes the excess in a fluid called honeydew, which often drops onto the leaves below. A sooty mold fungus may develop on the honeydew, causing the mock orange leaves to appear black and dirty. Ants feed on honeydew and are often present where there is an aphid infestation.

SOLUTION: Control with ORTHO Orthene Systemic Insect Control when aphids first appear. Direct the spray to the undersides of the leaves. Repeat the spray if the plant becomes reinfested.

Philadelphus cultural information
Light: Full sun
Water: Allow the soil to dry between waterings
Soil: Loose, well drained
Fertilizer: Medium

Iron deficiency.

PROBLEM: Some of the leaves turn pale green to yellow. The newest leaves may be completely yellow, with only the veins remaining green. On older leaves, only the edges may be yellowing. The plant may be stunted.

ANALYSIS: Iron deficiency
This is a common problem in plants such as mock orange that do not tolerate highly alkaline soils. The plant grows best in soil with a pH between 6.0 and 6.5. (For more information about soil acidity, see page 902.) The yellowing is due to a deficiency of iron and other minor nutrients in the plant. The soil is seldom deficient in iron. However, iron is often found in an insoluble form that is not available to the plant, especially in soil with a pH of 7.5 or higher. A high soil pH can result from overliming, or from lime leached from cement or brick. Regions where soil is derived from limestone, and those with low rainfall, also have high-pH soils. Plants use iron in the formation of the green pigment in the leaves. When it is lacking, new leaves are yellow.

SOLUTION: Spray the foliage with ORTHO Greenol Liquid Iron 6.13%, and apply it to the soil around the plants to correct the iron deficiency. Correct the pH of the soil by treating it with *ferrous sulfate* and watering it in well. Maintain an acid pH by fertilizing with ORTHO Azalea, Camellia & Rhododendron Food 5–10–10. Never lime the soil around mock orange.

PICEA (SPRUCE)

Fungal leaf spots.

PROBLEM: Spots or blotches appear on the leaves. The spots are usually purple at first, then gray to brown with purple margins. They range in size from barely visible to ¾ inch in diameter. Several spots may join to form blotches. Leaves may be yellow, and many may fall to the ground. Leaf spotting is most severe in moist, humid weather.

ANALYSIS: Fungal leaf spots
Several different fungi cause leaf spots on photinia. These spots are unsightly but rarely harmful to the plant. Plants weakened by low temperatures and wind exposure may be more susceptible to invasion by leaf spot fungi. The fungi are spread by splashing water and wind. Spots develop where the fungi enter the tissue. If wet or humid weather persists, the fungi spread through the tissue and blotches form. They survive the winter on the leaves and twigs. Most leaf spot organisms do their greatest damage in mild weather (between 50° and 85°F).

SOLUTION: Once leaves become spotted they will remain so. Where practical, remove infected leaves from the plant. Collect and destroy any fallen leaves. On valuable specimens, spray with a fungicide containing *ferbam*, *benomyl*, or *copper* when new growth begins in spring. Repeat at intervals of 2 weeks, or for as long as the weather remains favorable for infection.

Photinia cultural information
Light: Full sun
Water: Moist or dry conditions
Soil: Any good garden soil
Fertilizer: Medium

PICEA

ADAPTATION: Zones 2 to 8 (to determine your zone, see the map on page 1004). Not adapted to desert areas.

LIGHT: Full sun to partial shade.

SOIL: Tolerates a wide variety of soils.

FERTILIZER: Fertilize with ORTHO Evergreen, Tree & Shrub Food 12–6–6 or ORTHO Azalea, Camellia & Rhododendron Food 5–10–10 according to label directions.

WATER:
How much: Apply enough water to wet the soil 3 to 4 feet deep. To determine the proper amount of water for your soil type, see page 906.
How often: Water when the soil is just barely moist 4 inches below the surface. For more information about watering, see page 906.

PRUNING: Prune to maintain shape. If two leaders (tops) develop, remove one. For dense, bushy growth, remove a third of each year's new growth. When planting, allow enough room for spread and height — some spruce grow to 150 feet.

Spruce budworm larva (twice life size).

PROBLEM: Needles on the ends of branches are chewed and webbed together. In mid-July the branch ends often turn reddish brown. Branches or the entire tree may die after 3 to 5 years of defoliation. Reddish brown caterpillars, 1¼ inches long, with yellow or white raised spots, are feeding on the needles.

ANALYSIS: Spruce budworm
(*Choristoneura* species)
Spruce budworms are very destructive to ornamental spruce, fir, and Douglas fir, and may infest pine, larch, and hemlock. The budworm is cyclical. It comes and goes in epidemics 10 or more years apart. The moths are small (½ inch long) and grayish, with bands and spots of brown. The females lay pale green eggs in clusters on the needles in late July and August. The larvae that hatch from these eggs crawl to hiding places in the bark or in lichen mats; or they are blown by the wind to other trees, where they hide. The tiny larvae spin a silken case and hibernate there until spring. In May, when the weather warms, the caterpillars tunnel into needles. As they grow, they feed on opening buds; later they chew off needles and web them together. The larvae feed for about 5 weeks, pupate on twigs, and emerge as adults.

SOLUTION: Spray with ORTHO Orthene Systemic Insect Control when the buds begin to grow in late May.

PICEA (SPRUCE)

Galls.

Stem gall.

Damaged tree. *Insert:* Cocoons (⅓ life size).

PROBLEM: The ends of branches develop green, pineapple-shaped galls in the spring; in late summer, they turn brown and dry. Growth continues beyond the galls, but the branch may be severely stunted. Galled stems are weak and may break during storms. When large numbers of galls are formed, the tree may be less vigorous.

ANALYSIS: Eastern spruce gall aphid (*Adelges abietis*)
This gall aphid is most damaging to Norway spruce, but may occasionally infest white, black, and red spruce. The insect spends the winter at the base of a terminal bud. When buds begin to grow in the spring, the aphids lay clusters of several hundred eggs that are covered with white, waxy threads. The young that hatch from these eggs feed on developing needles. They suck the juices from the needles, inducing the formation of galls that enclose them. The aphids live and feed in chambers inside the galls. In mid to late summer, the galls turn brown and crack open. Aphids that emerge lay eggs near the tip of the needles. The young that hatch from these eggs spend the winter at the base of the buds.

SOLUTION: Spray with an insecticide containing *malathion* or *diazinon* in the spring just before growth begins, and again in the fall after the galls turn brown and crack open, around late September.

PROBLEM: Green or purplish sausage-shaped galls, 2½ inches long, appear on the ends of side branches. The branches may be severely stunted. The galls turn brown and are very noticeable in late summer.

ANALYSIS: Cooley spruce gall aphid (*Adelges cooleyi*)
The cooley spruce gall aphid requires two years to complete its life cycle, and may spend part of its life on both spruce and Douglas fir. In late spring the insect feeds, matures, and lays several hundred eggs at the base of needles near the branch tips. When the eggs hatch, the young insects move to growing needles. They suck the juices from the needles, inducing the formation of galls that enclose them. The aphids live and feed in chambers inside the galls. In July, the insects mature and emerge through openings in the dried galls. These aphids develop wings and migrate to Douglas fir or another spruce. The aphids on Douglas fir lay eggs, producing a generation of woolly aphids. (For more information about the spruce gall aphid on Douglas fir, see page 571.) Some of these aphids develop wings and migrate back to spruce to produce the overwintering insects. Others are wingless and remain on Douglas fir. Aphids that do not migrate to Douglas fir lay eggs on spruce after emerging from the galls.

SOLUTION: Where practical, remove galls before they open in midsummer. Spray with *lime sulfur* or with an insecticide containing *malathion* or *diazinon* just before buds break in the spring (early April). If using *malathion* or *diazinon*, repeat the spray after the galls open in late summer.

PROBLEM: Much of the foliage is eaten, starting at the top of the tree and progressing downward. The entire tree may be defoliated in one season. Inch-long, hairy, gray or light brown caterpillars, with tufts of orange hairs on their backs, may be found feeding on the needles. When populations are high, many tan-colored pellets drop from the tree and litter the ground.

ANALYSIS: Douglas fir tussock moth (*Orgyia pseudotsugata*)
Douglas fir tussock moth populations are cyclical. Every 7 to 10 years, moth populations in forested areas build up to epidemic proportions. When this occurs, spruce, Douglas firs, true firs, pine, and larch may be completely defoliated. In cities, damaging numbers may be found every year. In mid to late summer, hairy, wingless female moths lay their eggs in a frothy substance covered with a layer of hairlike scales. When the eggs hatch the following spring, the caterpillars begin feeding on the new needles at the top of the tree. As the younger foliage is devoured the caterpillars move downward, feeding on older needles. Large quantities of tan excrement pellets accumulate around the base of the tree. Since conifers do not replace their old needles, defoliated trees are often killed after two seasons. Less severely damaged trees may be killed later by bark beetles. In August the caterpillars pupate, to emerge later as adults.

SOLUTION: Spray with an insecticide containing *acephate*, *carbaryl*, or the bacteria *Bacillus thuringiensis* when caterpillars or damage are first noticed in May or early June. Repeat the spray 2 weeks later if damage continues.

Damaged needles. *Insert:* Larva (life size).

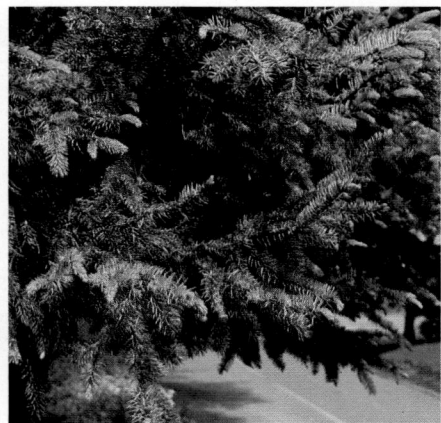

Spruce aphid damage to blue spruce.

Pine needle scale (4 times life size).

PROBLEM: Groups of brown needles are webbed together, usually near the inside of the lower branches. There is a sawdustlike material around the webbing. The entire tree may be severely infested, giving it an unsightly appearance. If a partially brown needle is broken open, a small (up to ¼ inch), greenish brown larva may be seen feeding inside.

ANALYSIS: Spruce needle miner
(*Taniva albolineana*)
The spruce needle miner is the larva of a small (½ inch) dark brown moth. The moth lays eggs in late spring to early summer on the undersides of old needles. The larvae that hatch from these eggs bore into the base of the needles, feeding on the interior. When the interior is consumed, the caterpillars cut off the needles at their base and web them together, forming a nest. The needle miners feed until the first frost and then enter a hollow needle, where they spend the winter. When the weather warms in spring, the larvae continue feeding until April or May. They pupate inside the webbed nest of needles and emerge as adults to lay more eggs. Several other types of needle miners may cause similar damage to spruce trees.

SOLUTION: Wash out infested needles with a strong stream of water and destroy them. Spray with ORTHO Orthene Systemic Insect Control in late June. Repeat the treatment in 7 to 10 days.

PROBLEM: Many of the older needles turn brown and drop. Only the newest needles remain green. The tree looks bare and sickly. Tiny (⅛ inch) green soft-bodied insects may be seen feeding on the needles.

ANALYSIS: Spruce aphid and green spruce aphid (*Elatobium abietinum* and *Cinara fornacula*)
These aphids may be very destructive to spruce in the North. The aphids appear in early spring, around February. They are extremely prolific and populations can rapidly build up to damaging numbers during March and April. Damage occurs when the aphids suck the juices from the spruce needles. They usually remain on a single needle until it is almost ready to drop. By the time the needles turn brown and the damage is noticeable, the insect population has declined. It may take a heavily damaged tree several years to recover and replace its lost foliage.

SOLUTION: By the time the damage is noticed, it is usually too late to treat the tree this year. Spray with ORTHO Isotox Insect Killer or ORTHO Diazinon Insect Spray the following February or March. Repeat the spray 10 days later.

PROBLEM: Needles are covered with clusters of somewhat flattened, white, scaly bumps. When heavily infested, the foliage may appear completely white. The bumps can be scraped or picked off; the undersides are usually soft. Needles turn brown and eventually drop. Repeated severe infestations may kill young trees or weaken older trees.

ANALYSIS: Pine needle scale
(*Chionaspis pinifoliae*)
These scale insects may seriously damage spruce and pine trees and may infest fir, hemlock, and cedar. The scales survive the winter on the spruce needles as eggs beneath the dead mother scales. The eggs hatch in late spring and the young scales, called *crawlers*, move to new green needles. The small (1/10 inch) soft-bodied young feed by inserting their mouthparts and sucking sap from the plant. The legs atrophy and a crusty white shell develops over the body. The mature female scales lay their eggs underneath their shell in June or July. This next generation feeds throughout late summer and matures in fall. Females of this generation lay the overwintering eggs.

SOLUTION: Spray young trees with ORTHO Isotox Insect Killer or ORTHO Diazinon Insect Spray in late spring when the young are active. The following early spring, before new growth begins and when the danger of frost is past, spray with a pesticide containing *lime sulfur* to kill the overwintering eggs. Inspect ornamental spruce twice a year for evidence of infestation. Older trees seldom require controls.

PICEA (SPRUCE)

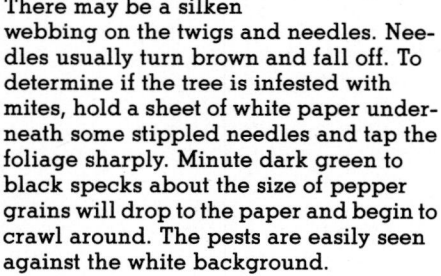

Spruce spider mite damage.

PROBLEM: Needles are stippled yellow and dirty. There may be a silken webbing on the twigs and needles. Needles usually turn brown and fall off. To determine if the tree is infested with mites, hold a sheet of white paper underneath some stippled needles and tap the foliage sharply. Minute dark green to black specks about the size of pepper grains will drop to the paper and begin to crawl around. The pests are easily seen against the white background.

ANALYSIS: Spruce spider mite
(Oligonychus ununguis)
The spruce spider mite is one of the most damaging pests of spruces and many other conifers. These mites suck sap from the undersides of the needles. As a result of feeding the green pigment disappears, causing the stippled appearance. This symptom may be mistaken for certain types of air pollution damage (see page 862). Spider mites first appear between April and June, hatching from eggs laid at the base of spruce needles the previous October. In subtropical areas, mites may be active during warm periods in winter. A complete generation may be produced in only 17 days, so mites can rapidly build up to tremendous numbers during the growing season. Young spruce trees may die the first season. If left uncontrolled for several years, older trees may die, with symptoms progressing from the lower branches upward. Several other kinds of mites may infest spruce trees.

SOLUTION: Control with ORTHO Orthene Insect Spray or ORTHO Isotox Insect Killer. Repeat the spray 2 more times, 7 to 10 days apart. Additional sprays may be needed in early fall or spring if the tree becomes reinfested.

Dieback. *Insert:* White pitch on bark.

PROBLEM: The needles on the branches nearest the ground turn brown and dry. Occasionally this condition develops first in the upper branches. The needles may drop immediately, or they may remain attached for a year. Eventually the entire branch dies back. Amber-colored pitch usually oozes from the infected area, becoming white as it dries. The infection may spread to the higher branches. To determine if the tree is infected, slice off the bark on a dead branch in the area where the diseased tissue and healthy tissue meet. Small black spore-producing bodies are found beneath the bark.

ANALYSIS: Canker and dieback
This plant disease is caused by fungus *(Cytospora kunzei)* that is very destructive to Norway and Colorado blue spruce. The fungus enters the tree at a wound, killing the surrounding healthy tissue. A canker develops and expands through the wood in all directions. When the canker encircles a branch, the branch dies and the needles turn brown. Sap oozes from the dying branch. Eventually small black spore-producing bodies develop in the bark. Older (over 15 years), weak, or injured trees are most susceptible to the disease.

SOLUTION: Prune off and destroy dead or dying branches well below the infected area, or where the branch meets the trunk. After each cut, sterilize the pruning shears with rubbing alcohol. Do not prune during wet weather. Avoid wounding trees with lawnmowers, tools, and other equipment. Keep trees vigorous by watering during dry spells and fertilizing every few years.

PIERIS (ANDROMEDA)

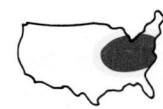

Lacebug damage.

PROBLEM: The upper sides of the leaves are mottled or speckled yellow or gray and green. The mottling may be confused with mite or leafhopper damage, but it can be distinguished from damage caused by other insects by the hard, black, shiny droplets found on the undersides of damaged leaves. Small (1/8 inch) light or dark spiny, wingless insects or brownish insects with clear lacy wings may be visible around the droplets. The plant may be stunted. Damage occurs in spring and summer.

ANALYSIS: Andromeda lacebug
(Stephanitis takeyai)
The andromeda lacebug is found throughout the Northeast on *Pieris japonica* and leucothoe. The lacebugs spend the winter as eggs in the leaf vein or cemented in the black droplets on the lower surface of the leaves. The eggs hatch in May. The spiny, wingless, immature insects and later the brown lacy-winged adults suck sap from the undersides of the leaves. The green leaf pigment disappears, resulting in the characteristic yellow or gray mottling. As the lacebugs feed, droplets of black excrement accumulate around them. Damage is unsightly and food production by the leaf is reduced, resulting in loss of plant vigor.

SOLUTION: Spray with ORTHO Isotox Insect Killer or with an insecticide containing *carbaryl* when damage first appears in spring. Cover the undersides of the leaves thoroughly. Repeat 7 to 10 days later. A third application may be necessary if the plant becomes reinfested in the summer. It is important to spray early, preventing as much damage as possible. Damaged leaves will be unsightly for more than a year.

PINUS (PINE)

BRANCHES DISCOLOR AND DIE

PINUS (PINE)

ADAPTATION: Throughout the United States.

LIGHT: Full sun.

SOIL: Tolerates a wide variety of soils, but the soil should be well drained.

FERTILIZER: To avoid rank growth, do not fertilize pines heavily. When fertilizing, use ORTHO Evergreen, Tree & Shrub Food 12–6–6 or ORTHO Azalea, Camellia & Rhododendron Food 5–10–10 according to label directions.

WATER: Once established, pines require very little supplemental watering. Water young plants and potted plants when the soil is barely moist 2 inches below the surface. Established plants may require additional water during periods of extended drought, especially when growing in areas that normally receive water. For more information about watering, see page 906.

PRUNING: Prune to maintain shape. To slow growth or increase bushiness, cut back the candles (new growth before needles begin to emerge) at least halfway. When planting, allow large species enough room for growth. Pines often drop many needles annually. This is a natural process of growth, not a cause for concern.

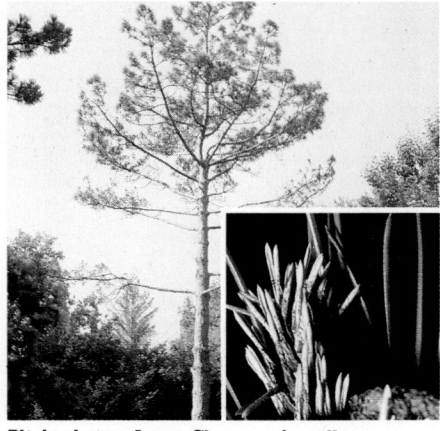

Blighted pine. *Insert:* Close-up of needles.

PROBLEM: New growth is stunted and brown. Dead buds and needles remain on the tree for several years, glued in place by resin (sap). With repeated infections, limbs die back and tree growth is stunted. The lowest branches are affected first. This disease may be mistaken for damage caused by insects or other diseases. Insect damage is recognized by the presence of larvae or tunnels and sawdustlike material in the shoot. No other disease causes resin production and the retention of needles.

ANALYSIS: Diplodia tip blight
This plant disease is causd by a fungus (*Diplodia pinea*) that may severely damage or kill Austrian pine. Several other types of pines may also be infected. (For a list, see page 998.) Trees 25 to 30 years old are most susceptible. The fungus is commonly found on the decaying tissue of almost all pine trees that have died from other problems. The fungus from these and other infected trees spreads to living tissue when growing conditions are poor and trees are weakened. During moist weather in spring, spores ooze from black spore-producing bodies on dead tissue. The spores are carried by wind and rain to young needles and buds. The fungus enters and kills the tissue. Within a year, the fungus produces more spores.

SOLUTION: Spray the entire tree top with a fungicide containing *benlate* or *fixed copper* just before the buds begin to grow. Repeat 2 more times at intervals of 10 days. When the weather is dry, prune off dead branch tips. Keep trees vigorous by watering during dry periods and fertilizing every 3 to 5 years. For watering and fertilizing instructions, see pages 906 and 904.

Needle cast. *Insert:* Fruiting structures.

PROBLEM: The tips of the needles on last year's growth turn brown in winter. By spring, the infected needles are completely discolored, giving the tree a scorched appearance. Many needles may drop from the tree, leaving only the new green growth. Tiny, black, elongated structures develop on the midrib of dead needles. The black structures may be swollen, with cracks down the middle. In severe cases, branch tips die back. Shaded parts of the tree are more frequently infected.

ANALYSIS: Needle cast
This plant disease is caused by either of two species of fungi (*Hypoderma lethale* and *Lophodermium pinastri*). It is most severe on young pine trees, but older trees may be infected on the lower branches. In the summer, spores are released during wet weather from the elongated black fruiting structures on infected needles. Splashing rain and wind may carry the spores several hundred feet. The fungus enters the tissue but the symptoms do not appear until early the following spring. Brown spots with yellow margins develop on the needles in March or April. The fungus grows through the tissue, and by late April or May the needles are completely brown. The needles drop, and the spores from these infections continue the cycle.

SOLUTION: If needle cast was serious in the spring, spray valuable specimens with a fungicide containing *ferbam*, *maneb*, or *chlorothalonil* starting in late July. Repeat the spray at intervals of 10 to 14 days through September. If trees are shaded, remove any shade-producing structures or plants, where practical.

PINUS (PINE) — BRANCHES DISCOLOR AND DIE

Monterey pines killed by ips engraver beetles.

Nematode damage to Japanese black pine.

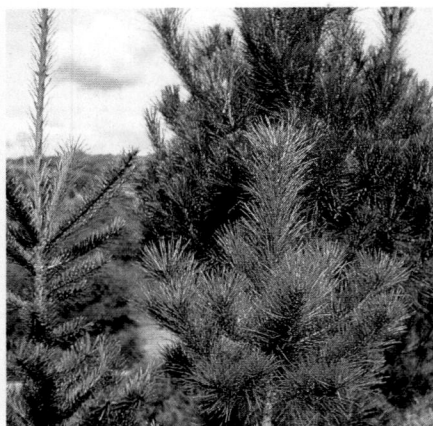

Monterey pine damaged by spruce spider mite.

PROBLEM: The newest growth at the top of the tree turns yellow, then reddish brown. Within 4 to 6 weeks the whole tree may turn completely brown. There are numerous tiny (⅛ inch) holes in the main trunk. A sawdustlike material usually surrounds them. If the bark is peeled back around these holes, Y- or H-shaped engravings may be seen on the wood. Shiny black beetles, ³⁄₁₆ inch long, with scooped-out rear ends, may be feeding in the wood.

ANALYSIS: Ips engraver beetles
(*Ips* species)
In some areas, ips beetles are serious pests of pines. Like other bark beetles, engraver beetles usually infest only weakened trees. However, trees under stress from drought, and healthy pines growing near stressed trees, are also susceptible to attack. In the spring, adults tunnel into the bark on either the upper or the lower part of the tree, depending on the species of ips beetle. A chemical substance is produced that attracts more beetles, which mate and lay their eggs in the tunnels. After the eggs hatch, the white grubs burrow under the bark, girdling the wood and cutting off the flow of nutrients and water through the trunk. The beetles also cause damage by introducing a blue stain fungus, which interrupts sap flow and hastens the death of the tree. A number of other bark beetles also infest pines (see page 468).

SOLUTION: Cut down dead trees and those trees where over 50 percent of the foliage is yellowed. Burn the wood, strip off the bark, or remove it from the area. Spray less severely infested trees with ORTHO Lindane Borer & Leaf Miner Spray. Water trees during droughts.

PROBLEM: The tree is yellowing and growing poorly. Branches die, or the entire tree turns brown and dies.

ANALYSIS: Root nematodes
Many different types of root nematodes infect pines. Nematodes are microscopic worms that live in the soil. They are not related to earthworms. Root nematodes feed on plant roots, damaging and stunting them. The damaged roots can't supply sufficient water and nutrients to the aboveground parts, and the plant is stunted or slowly dies. Root nematodes prefer moist, sandy loam soils. They can move only a few inches each year on their own, but they may be carried long distances by soil, water, tools, or infested plants. Testing roots and soil is the only positive method for confirming the presence of nematodes. Contact your local Cooperative Extension Office (see page 1011) for sampling instructions and addresses of testing laboratories. Soil and root problems such as poor soil structure, drought stress, nutrient deficiency, and root rots can also produce symptoms of decline similar to those caused by nematodes. These problems should be eliminated as causes before sending soil and root samples for testing. (For information on soil problems and root rots, see pages 901 and 856.) Another type of nematode that lives inside the conducting vessels causes similar aboveground symptoms.

SOLUTION: There are no chemicals available to homeowners to kill nematodes in planted soil. However, they can be controlled before planting by soil fumigation. For more information on fumigating soil, see page 919.

PROBLEM: Needles are stippled yellow, and dirty. Sometimes there is a silken webbing on the twigs and needles. To determine if the tree is infested with mites, hold a sheet of white paper underneath some stippled needles and tap the foliage sharply. Minute dark green or black specks the size of pepper grains will drop to the paper and begin to crawl around. The pests are easily seen against the white background.

ANALYSIS: Spruce spider mite
(*Oligonychus ununguis*)
The spruce spider mite is one of the most damaging pests of evergreen trees. These mites suck sap from the undersides of the needles. As a result of feeding, the green leaf pigment disappears, producing the stippled appearance. This symptom may be mistaken for certain types of air pollution damage (see page 862). Spider mites first appear between April and June, hatching from eggs laid at the base of pine needles the previous October. Mites can rapidly build up to tremendous numbers during the growing season. Young pine trees may die the first season. If left uncontrolled for several years, older trees sometimes die, with symptoms progressing from the lower branches upward. Several other species of *Oligonychus* infest pines on the West Coast. Some of these mites are most numerous in the spring, while others are found throughout the summer and fall.

SOLUTION: Spray with ORTHO Isotox Insect Killer or ORTHO Orthene Insect Spray. Repeat the application 2 more times at intervals of 7 to 10 days. Additional sprays may be needed later in the season or in spring if the tree becomes reinfested.

INSECTS OR POWDERY MATERIAL ON TREE

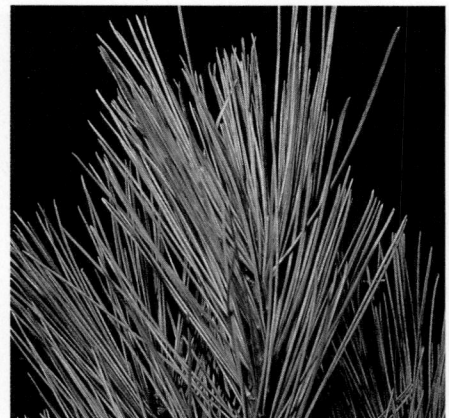

Air pollution damage to white pine needles.

White pine blister rust.

Woolly aphids on Austrian pine (life size).

PROBLEM: The newest needles are flecked yellow, and the tips of the branches may turn red and die. The previous year's needles are deep yellow and dwarfed; many needles may drop from the branches. Repeated injury may cause the death of the tree. This problem is most noticeable in October. Air pollution damage is difficult to diagnose correctly. Damage due to fungi, insects, root injuries, and salts should be eliminated first as causes of these symptoms.

ANALYSIS: Air pollution injury
Air pollution injury, also called *white pine blight* because it was first noticed on Eastern white pine (*Pinus strobus*), is caused by ozone, a component of automobile exhaust, and sulfur dioxide, from the combustion of fossil fuels. (For more information about ozone and sulfur dioxide pollution, see page 862.) The optimum conditions of temperature, humidity, wind direction, and cloud cover, as well as of plant tissue development, are necessary for injury to occur. Therefore, air pollution damage may be more severe in certain years than in others. Injury develops as a flecking or reddening on young needles, then a yellowing and dropping of one- or two-year-old needles. Healthy pines also lose their older needles, but generally not until the third year.

SOLUTION: There are no controls for air pollution injury. Remove dead trees. Trees in a vigorous condition are less susceptible to severe damage. Water the trees during dry spells and fertilize regularly. For more information about watering and fertilizing trees, see pages 906 and 904.

PROBLEM: Branches or the main stem develop rough, elongated, slightly swollen areas. The infected areas are usually yellowish orange. Pitch may flow from the swollen areas. Branches or the entire tree often die. Dead foliage appears reddish brown, and may be very apparent if surrounded by green trees.

ANALYSIS: White pine blister rust
This plant disease is caused by a fungus (*Cronartium ribicola*) that alternately infects pines and either currants or gooseberries (*Ribes* species). Wind-blown spores from *Ribes* leaves infect pine needles in later summer. From there, the fungus grows into nearby branches. Small yellow to brownish spots develop. In one or two seasons, the bark develops swollen yellowish orange cankers. The canker grows, and the following season white blisters containing orange-yellow spores push through the bark. The spores are carried by the wind back to currants or gooseberies. (For more information about rust on *Ribes*, see page 738.) The pine bark in the cankered area dries out and cracks, resulting in the death of the underlying wood. The branches and foliage above this area die and turn reddish brown.

SOLUTION: Remove all gooseberry and currant bushes, including the root systems — which are capable of resprouting — for at least 1,000 feet from white pines. Cut off and destroy infected pine branches. Cankers on the trunk can be removed surgically with some success if all discolored bark and wood is destroyed, including a border of apparently healthy bark and wood. Use a sharp knife sterilized with rubbing alcohol after each cut. Spray the wound with a fungicide containing *cycloheximide*.

PROBLEM: The needles or trunk are covered with white, woolly masses. If the infestation is heavy, the tree appears to be covered with snow. Infested shoots may droop; the needles turn yellow and may die. Trees heavily infested for several years are usually stunted.

ANALYSIS: Woolly aphids
(*Pineus* species)
These small (⅛ inch), soft-bodied insects are not true aphids, but they are closely related. The adults are always covered with dense white filaments of wax. When this substance is removed, the insects appear purplish or green. Some species of these woolly "aphids" spend part of their life on other types of evergreens, usually spruce, often producing galls on the branches. In early summer, the insects migrate to pines and suck sap from the needles. Other species spend their entire life on pines, feeding and reproducing on the trunks. Those species that spend the winter on other plants produce a generation in the fall that flies to the winter host.

SOLUTION: Control with ORTHO Isotox Insect Killer or ORTHO Malathion 50 Insect Spray. Spray pines with infested trunks in late April; spray pines with infested needles in late June. Cover the tree thoroughly. Repeat the spray if the plant becomes reinfested.

PINUS (PINE) — INSECTS OR POWDERY MATERIAL ON TREE

Pine needle scale (life size).

Needle rust.

Aphids on white pine (life size).

PROBLEM: Needles are covered with clusters of somewhat flattened, white scaly bumps. When heavily infested, the foliage may appear completely white. The bumps can be scraped or picked off; the undersides are usually soft. Needles turn brown and eventually drop. Repeated severe infestations may kill young trees or weaken older trees.

ANALYSIS: Pine needle scale
(*Chionaspis pinifoliae*)
These scale insects may seriously damage pine and spruce trees and may infest fir, hemlock, and cedar. The scales survive the winter on the pine needles as eggs beneath the dead mother scales. The eggs hatch in late spring and the young scales, called *crawlers*, move to new green needles. The small ($\frac{1}{10}$ inch) soft-bodied young feed by inserting their mouthparts and sucking sap from the plant. The legs atrophy and a crusty white shell develops over the body. The mature female scales lay their eggs underneath their shell in July. This next generation feeds throughout late summer and matures in fall. Females of this generation lay the overwintering eggs.

SOLUTION: Spray young trees with ORTHO Isotox Insect Killer or ORTHO Orthene Systemic Insect Control in late spring when the young are active. The following early spring, before new growth begins and when the danger of frost is past, spray with a pesticide containing *lime sulfur* to kill the overwintering eggs. Inspect ornamental pines twice a year for evidence of infestation. Older trees seldom require controls.

PROBLEM: Cream-colored, baglike pustules, $\frac{1}{16}$ to $\frac{1}{8}$ inch long, develop on the needles in the spring. The pustules rupture, releasing bright orange spores. Trees with heavy infestations often drop many needles. Young trees may be stunted.

ANALYSIS: Needle rust
This plant disease is caused by any of several different fungi (*Coleosporium* species) that infect pine trees, goldenrods, and asters. The fungi cannot spread from pine tree to pine tree, but must alternate between pines and goldenrods or asters. Wind-borne spores from goldenrods or asters infect pine needles in summer and fall. The following spring, cream-colored pustules (blisters) develop, and needles may drop. The pustules rupture, and orange spores are blown to goldenrods and asters, where bright orange-yellow pustules develop on the undersides of the leaves.

SOLUTION: Spray young or valuable pine trees with a fungicide containing *ferbam* or *zineb*. Where practical, remove goldenrods and asters around pines.

PROBLEM: Needles are discolored and may be deformed; many may drop from the tree. New growth is often slowed, and twigs may die. A shiny, sticky substance often coats the needles and/or branches. A black sooty mold may grow on the sticky substance. Small (up to $\frac{1}{6}$ inch), green, brown, or black soft-bodied insects cluster on the needles, twigs, or main stems of small trees. An uncontrolled infestation may kill young trees.

ANALYSIS: Aphids
(*Cinara* species and *Eulachnus* species)
Several different aphids infest the needles or bark of pines. Aphids do little damage in small numbers. However, they are extremely prolific and populations can rapidly build up to damaging numbers during the growing season. Damage occurs when the aphid sucks the juices from the pine needles, growing tips, or bark. The aphid is unable to digest fully all the sugar in the sap and excretes the excess in a fluid called honeydew, which often drops onto the needles and bark below. Plants or objects beneath the tree may also be coated with honeydew. A sooty mold fungus may develop on the honeydew, causing the pine needles, bark, or other coated plants to appear black and dirty. Ants feed on this sticky substance, and are often present where there is an aphid infestation.

SOLUTION: Control with ORTHO Isotox Insect Killer or ORTHO Malathion 50 Insect Spray when aphids first appear. Repeat the spray if the tree becomes reinfested in mid or late summer.

Pine spittlebug (3 times life size).

Pine webworm.

Sawfly larvae (life size).

PROBLEM: A frothy mass of bubbles appears on the twigs at the base of the needles. A small (¼ inch) tan or green wingless insect may be found inside the mass. Needles may turn yellow and drop off; black sooty mold may grow on surrounding branches. Continuous heavy infestations of insects kill branches or cause the death of young or weak trees.

ANALYSIS: Pine and Saratoga spittlebugs
(*Aphrophora parellela* and *A. saratogensis*)
The pine spittlebug may cause serious injury to Scotch and white pines. The Saratoga spittlebug kills branches of jack and red pines. The pine spittlebug adults are grayish brown, wedge-shaped insects, ½ inch long. The females lay their eggs at the base of buds in late summer. The eggs hatch the following May, and the young insects suck the sap from twigs and the main trunk. Drops of undigested sap mixed with air are excreted by the bug, producing the frothy "spittle" that surrounds its body. Some of the excreted sap drops onto lower branches, which may be colonized by a black sooty mold fungus. The life cycle of the Saratoga spittlebug is similar, but the tan females lay their eggs on plants beneath the tree. The adults migrate to trees in late June, feed until late fall, and then return to the low-growing plants to lay their eggs.

SOLUTION: Spray with ORTHO Isotox Insect Killer when insects are first noticed — in late May and again in July for the pine spittlebug, and in late June or early July for the Saratoga spittlebug. Use high pressures.

PROBLEM: Brown, globular nests made of silk, brown needles, and a sawdustlike material appear on the ends of branches in early or midsummer. The branches are often stripped of most of their foliage, and tree growth is slowed. Light brown caterpillars, up to ¾ inch long, may be feeding inside the nests.

ANALYSIS: Pine webworm
(*Tetralopha robustella*)
This webworm is found throughout the eastern United States on many different pines. The nests are unsightly only; rarely are trees seriously injured. The gray moths lay their eggs on pine needles between May and September. When the eggs hatch, the larvae feed within the needles until they are too large. Then they construct nests made of silk, dead needles, and brown excrement, which they wrap around twigs. Each nest may contain from 1 to 75 or more worms. When mature, the insects drop to the ground and pupate below the soil surface. In the South, moths may emerge to repeat the cycle one more time. The webworms spend the winter in the soil.

SOLUTION: Cut out and destroy the nests. Or spray with an insecticide containing *carbaryl*, or the bacterial insecticide *Bacillus thuringiensis* when the larvae are small and before the needles are webbed in mid-June. Repeat the spray in early August if the tree becomes reinfested.

PROBLEM: The needles are partially chewed, or the entire branch may be defoliated. In some cases, only the younger needles are eaten. Usually, however, the older needles are preferred. Gray-green, tan, or black caterpillarlike larvae, up to an inch long, are clustered on the needles. The larvae have many legs (prolegs) on their abdomens.

ANALYSIS: Sawflies
(*Neodiprion* species and *Diprion* species)
Many species of sawflies infest pines. The dark, clear-winged adults are nonstinging wasps. The females insert rows of eggs in the needles with sawlike egg-laying organs. The larvae that hatch from these eggs feed in groups on the outer part of the needles. As the larvae grow, they feed on a larger portion of the foliage; eventually, entire needles are devoured. Small trees may be completely defoliated. The larvae then move to adjacent trees to feed. Some species of sawflies feed only in the spring or summer. Others are present throughout the growing season, producing 5 or 6 generations a year. When the larvae mature, they drop to the ground and spin cocoons. Most sawflies spend the winter in the soil, although several species overwinter as eggs on the needles.

SOLUTION: Spray the needles with ORTHO Orthene Systemic Insect Control or ORTHO Isotox Insect Killer when damage or the insects are first noticed. Inspect the trees periodically during the growing season to detect infestations before severe defoliation occurs.

PINUS (PINE) — INSECTS ———— DISTORTED GROWTH ————

European pine shoot moth damage.

White pine weevil damage.

Western gall rust on Monterey pine.

PROBLEM: Branch tips turn yellow, then brown and dry. The dead branches contrast sharply with healthy green foliage. In the summer, pitch accumulates around the dead needles. Trees may appear bushier than normal, or they may be crooked and distorted. Vigorous trees may recover. At the base of needles or inside a brown, resin-coated tip, cream-colored to reddish brown worms, up to ¾ inch long, may be found feeding on the tissue.

ANALYSIS: Pine tip or shoot moths (*Rhyacionia* species)
Seven species of tip moths infest various pines in different parts of the country. The adult is a reddish brown and gray moth, up to an inch long. The moths fly at night, but they may be seen during the day if a branch is disturbed. The moths lay their eggs in mid to late spring at the ends of branches. The larvae that hatch from these eggs bore into needles and buds. Some species of tip moths feed for several weeks, pupate inside the buds, and emerge as moths. The females lay their eggs, and the cycle is repeated 3 or 4 times during the growing season. Other species have only one cycle, and feed until fall.

SOLUTION: If practical, prune out and destroy infested twigs in May or early June. Spray with ORTHO Orthene Systemic Insect Control or ORTHO Isotox Insect Killer in mid-April or early May. Repeat the spray in mid-May. If the tree becomes reinfested, spray again in mid-summer.

PROBLEM: The main shoot at the top of the tree stops growing and turns yellow in midsummer. The shoot tip usually droops, producing a "shepherd's crook." Several new shoots may develop from below the dying shoot so that the top of the tree is forked. In fall and winter the drooping shoot appears brown and dry. There is a white resin on the bark, and small holes in the dead shoot.

ANALYSIS: White pine weevil (*Pissodes strobi*)
The white pine weevil attacks the leaders of both pines and spruce. This small (⅕ inch), brown, snouted beetle with white patches spends the winter in dead plant material at the base of the tree. In the spring, just before new growth begins, it moves to the top of the tree to feed on the inner bark tissue. Eggs are then laid in small punctures in the bark. Resin droplets ooze from the punctures, which later dry and turn white. The ¼-inch larvae that hatch from these eggs bore into the wood. The feeding cuts off the flow of water and nutrients through the stem, causing the shoot to droop and die. Several new shoots often develop from below the dead shoot, destroying the natural shape of the tree. In late summer, the larvae mature and return to the ground to spend the winter.

SOLUTION: Control the adults with ORTHO Lindane Borer & Leaf Miner Spray in late April when the buds begin to swell. Spray the top of the tree thoroughly. It is usually impractical to spray large trees. Prune out and destroy infested twigs in early June before the beetles emerge. Train one side branch to replace the dead leader by pruning off all but one of the new shoots.

PROBLEM: Rough, spherical swellings develop on branches or on the main trunk. In the spring, the swellings appear orange or yellow. Growth beyond the galls is often stunted, distorted, and off-color.

ANALYSIS: Western gall rust and eastern gall rust
These plant diseases are caused by two species of fungi (*Cronartium harknessii* and *C. quercuum*). Western gall rust requires only one host to complete its life cycle; spores from one pine can infect another. Eastern gall rust requires both pine and oak to complete its life cycle. In early spring, orange or yellow spores are produced over the ruptured surfaces of the swellings (galls). The spores are blown and carried by wind and insects to susceptible trees. When moisture and temperatures are optimum, western gall rust spores infect pine tissue, causing an increase in the number and size of plant cells. Within 6 months to a year, swellings develop. The galls enlarge and produce spores after one to two years. Eastern gall rust spores infect only oak. Spores produced on the oak trees reinfect pines. The galls caused by both fungi interrupt the sap movement in the tree. They also stimulate witch's brooms, dense stunted growth beyond the galls. If many of these develop the tree becomes unsightly and weak, and limbs break during storms.

SOLUTION: Where practical, prune off galled branches before the galls produce spores in early spring.

PISTACIA (PISTACHE)

Verticillium wilt. *Insert:* Infected stem.

PROBLEM: The leaves on a branch turn yellow at the margins, then brown and dry. During hot weather, the leaves may wilt. New leaves may be stunted and yellowish. The infected tree may die slowly, branch by branch, over several seasons. Some trees may recover. The tissue under the bark on the dying side shows dark streaks when cut. To examine for streaks, peel back the bark at the bottom of the dying branch.

ANALYSIS: Verticillium wilt
This wilt disease affects many ornamental trees and shrubs. It is caused by a soil-inhabiting fungus (*Verticillium* species). The disease is spread by contaminated seeds, plants, soil, equipment, and ground water. The fungus enters the tree through the roots and spreads up into the branches through the water-conducting vessels in the stems. The vessels become discolored and plugged. This plugging cuts off the flow of water and nutrients to the branches, causing the leaf discoloration and wilting.

SOLUTION: No chemical control is available. Fertilize and water the affected plant to stimulate vigorous growth. Prune off all dead wood. Remove dead plants. If replanting in the same area, plant trees or shrubs that are resistant to verticillium. For more information about verticillium, see page 858.

Pistacia cultural information
Light: Full sun
Water: Moist or dry soil
Soil: Well drained
Fertilizer: Light

PITTOSPORUM

Aphid damage.

PROBLEM: The newest leaves are wrinkled and yellowing. Leaves may drop off, and new growth may be slowed. A shiny, sticky substance often coats the leaves. A black sooty mold may grow on the sticky substance. Tiny (⅛ inch) greenish yellow soft-bodied insects cluster on the underside of leaves and on branch tips. Ants may be present.

ANALYSIS: Aphids
Aphids do little damage in small numbers. However, they are extremely prolific and populations can rapidly build up to damaging numbers during the growing season. Damage occurs when the aphid sucks the juices from the pittosporum leaves. The aphid is unable to digest fully all the sugar in the plant sap and excretes the excess in a fluid called honeydew, which often drops onto the leaves below. A sooty mold fungus may develop on the honeydew, causing the pittosporum leaves to appear black and dirty. Ants feed on this sticky substance, and are often present where there is an aphid infestation.

SOLUTION: Control with ORTHO Orthene Insect Spray or ORTHO Isotox Insect Killer when aphids first appear. Direct the spray to the undersides of the leaves. Repeat the spray if the plant becomes reinfested.

Pittosporum cultural information
Light: Full sun to part shade
Water: Allow the soil to dry between waterings
Soil: Loose, well drained
Fertilizer: Medium

Cottony cushion scale (twice life size).

PROBLEM: The undersides of the leaves, stems, branch crotches, and trunk are covered with white, cottony, cushionlike masses. Leaves may turn yellow and drop. A shiny, sticky substance may coat the leaves. A black sooty mold often grows on the sticky substance. Numerous side shoots may grow out of an infested crotch area. Twigs and branches may die back.

ANALYSIS: Cottony scales and mealybugs
Cottony scales and mealybugs are common on pittosporum wherever it is grown. The similarity in appearance between these insects makes separate identification difficult. They are very conspicuous in late spring and summer because the females are covered with a white, cottony egg sac, containing up to 2500 eggs. Females lay their egg masses on leaves or branches. The young insects that hatch from these eggs are yellowish brown to green. They feed throughout the summer on the trunk, stems, and leaves. Damage is caused by the withdrawal of plant sap from the leaves and branches. The insects are unable to digest fully all the sugar in the plant sap and excrete the excess in a fluid called honeydew, which often drops onto the leaves below. A sooty mold fungus may develop on the honeydew, causing the pittosporum leaves to appear black and dirty. Leaf drop and twig dieback occur when the white masses completely cover the leaves and branches.

SOLUTION: Spray with ORTHO Isotox Insect Killer in midsummer when the young are active. The following spring, when the tree is dormant, spray with ORTHO Volck Oil Spray to control overwintering insects on the bark.

PLATANUS (SYCAMORE, PLANE TREE)

PLATANUS

ADAPTATION: Zones 4 through 9. (To determine your zone, see the map on page 1004.) Adapted to harsh city conditions.

LIGHT: Full sun.

SOIL: Tolerates a wide variety of soils. pH 5.5 to 7.5

FERTILIZER: Fertilize with ORTHO Evergreen, Tree & Shrub Food 12–6–6 according to label directions.

WATER: Once established, plane trees require very little supplemental watering. Water newly transplanted and young trees when the soil is barely moist 2 inches below the surface. For more information about watering, see page 906.

PRUNING: Prune to maintain shape. Plane trees can also be pollarded (branches cut back to the same spot every year), producing a dense, ball-shaped growth habit. When planting, allow enough room for the height and large trunk of these trees.

Powdery mildew.

PROBLEM: Young leaves and twigs are covered with a thin layer or irregular patches of grayish white powdery material. Infected leaves are distorted, and many may turn yellow and drop off. New growth is often stunted. In late summer, tiny black dots (spore-producing bodies) are scattered over the white patches like ground pepper. The problem is often more serious on heavily pruned trees.

ANALYSIS: Powdery mildew
This common plant disease is caused by a fungus (*Microsphaera alni*) that thrives in both humid and dry weather. The powdery patches consist of fungal strands and spores. The spores are spread by the wind to healthy plants. The fungus saps the plant nutrients, causing distortion, yellowing, and sometimes death of the leaf. Since this mildew attacks many different kinds of trees, the fungus from a diseased tree may infect other trees in the garden. For a list of susceptible plants, see page 995.

SOLUTION: Spray young trees with a fungicide containing *benlate* or *karathane* when the trees show the first sign of mildew. It is seldom practical to spray large trees. When planting new trees, plant the resistant variety Yarwood if it is adapted to your climate.

Sycamore lacebug damage.

PROBLEM: The upper surfaces of the leaves are mottled or speckled white and green. The mottling may be confused with mite or leafhopper damage. However, it can be distinguished from damage caused by other insects by the shiny, hard, brown droplets found on the undersides of damaged leaves. Small (⅛ inch), light or dark, spiny, wingless insects, or brownish insects with clear lacy wings, may be visible around the droplets. Foliage on severely infested trees may be completely white, then turn brown by mid-August.

ANALYSIS: Sycamore lacebug
(*Corythucha* species)
Two species of lacebugs infest sycamores and London plane trees. They survive the winter as adults in bark crevices or in other protected areas on the tree. When the buds begin to open in the spring, the adults attach their eggs to the undersides of the leaves with a brown, sticky substance. The eggs hatch and the spiny, wingless, immature insects, and later the brown lacy-winged adults, suck sap from the undersides of the leaves. The green leaf pigment disappears, resulting in the characteristic white and green mottling. As the lacebugs feed, droplets of brown excrement accumulate around them.

SOLUTION: Spray young trees with ORTHO Isotox Insect Killer or ORTHO Orthene Systemic Insect Control when damage first appears in spring. Cover the undersurfaces of the leaves thoroughly. Repeat 7 to 10 days later. It is important to spray early, preventing as much damage as possible. It is usually impractical to spray large trees.

Anthracnose. *Insert:* Spore-producing bodies.

Summer leaf scorch.

Cankers.

PROBLEM: In the spring, buds or expanding shoots turn brown and die. Dead areas appear along the veins of young leaves. As the leaves mature, the spots may expand and cover them entirely. Most infected leaves drop from the tree. Later in the season, twigs and older leaves may be infected. Infected twigs hang on the tree or drop to the ground with the leaves. Larger limbs may die. Dark brown spore-producing bodies appear on the bark and dead leaves. The tree is often stunted and bushy.

ANALYSIS: Sycamore anthracnose
This plant disease is caused by a fungus (*Gnomonia platani*) that is the most serious problem of sycamore (*P. oxidentalis*) and causes minor damage to the London plane tree (*P. acerfolia*). The fungus survives the winter on fallen leaves and twigs, and in swollen cankers in the tree. During cool (below 55°F), wet weather, spores are blown and splashed onto buds, expanding shoots, and young leaves. The fungus enters the tissue and kills it, causing the buds and shoots to die back. The fungus moves down onto the twigs, and spores develop. The spores may infect mature leaves or any new growth on the tree, causing a sunscorched appearance. Swollen, cracked cankers develop on infected twigs and branches. When the cankers encircle the wood, the limbs die.

SOLUTION: Prune off and destroy infected twigs and dead branches. In areas where spring is cool and moist, spray trees with a fungicide containing *zineb* or *maneb* when buds begin to grow in the spring. Repeat when leaves reach full size, and again 2 weeks later.

PROBLEM: During hot weather, usually in July or August, leaves turn brown around the edges and between the veins. Sometimes the whole leaf dies. Many leaves may drop during late summer. This problem is most severe on the youngest branches. Trees do not usually die. This problem may be mistaken for damage caused by anthracnose or lacebugs. However, the brown areas caused by anthracnose cross over the veins and often cover the entire leaf. Lacebugs leave brown droplets of excrement on the lower surfaces of the leaves.

ANALYSIS: Summer leaf scorch
Leaf scorch is caused by excessive evaporation of moisture from the leaves. In hot weather, water evaporates rapidly from the leaves. If the roots can't absorb and convey water fast enough to replenish this loss, the leaves turn brown and wither. This usually occurs in dry soil, but leaves can also scorch when the soil is moist. Drying winds, severed roots, limited soil area or salts in the soil also cause scorch. For more information about scorch, see page 865.

SOLUTION: To prevent further scorch, deep-water trees during periods of hot weather to wet the entire root space. (For more information about watering trees, see page 906.) Newly transplanted trees should be watered whenever the rootball is dry 2 inches below the surface. There are no controls for scorch occurring on trees in moist soil. Plant trees adapted to your climate.

PROBLEM: The leaves are small and yellow on part or all of the tree, and the foliage is sparse. Dark, elongated, sunken areas appear on the trunk or larger branches. If an affected branch is cut off, bluish black or reddish discoloration is seen running toward the center of the wood.

ANALYSIS: Canker stain disease
This plant disease, caused by a fungus (*Ceratocystis fimbriata* f. *platani*), is very destructive to the London plane tree (*Platanus acerifolia*). Other sycamores may also be affected. The fungus is very contagious. It enters the tree through a wound, or may be spread by pruning tools, ladders, contaminated wound dressings, or sap-feeding beetles. The surrounding healthy tissue is killed and a sunken canker develops. The vessels become discolored and plugged as the fungus spreads through the wood. This plugging cuts off the flow of water and nutrients, causing leaf yellowing and the death of the branch or tree.

SOLUTION: Avoid all unnecessary cutting, and avoid injuring trees. Prune trees in winter when the fungus is less active. Disinfect tools after each use with rubbing alcohol. Remove and destroy infected trees. In areas where the disease is present, mix ½ teaspoon *benomyl* with 1 gallon of ORTHO Pruning Seal and apply to pruning cuts.

PLATANUS

Giant bark aphids (life size).

PROBLEM: Small (¼ inch) black and beige soft-bodied insects with long black legs cluster on twigs and the undersides of limbs. Twigs may be completely covered with a mat of black eggs. When populations are large, twigs and branches die back. A shiny, sticky substance may coat the limbs. A black sooty mold often grows on the sticky substance. Ants may be present.

ANALYSIS: Giant bark aphid
(*Longistigma caryae*)
The giant bark aphid is the largest species of aphid known. Because of its long legs, it appears much larger than its actual size of ¼ inch. The aphids do little damage in small numbers. However, they are extremely prolific and populations can rapidly build up to damaging numbers during the late summer. When populations are large, black eggs are matted all over the bark of infested limbs. Damage occurs when the aphid sucks the juices from the twigs and branches. The aphid is unable to digest fully all the sugar in the sap, and excretes the excess in large quantities in a fluid called honeydew, which often coats plants or objects beneath the tree. A sooty mold fungus may develop on the honeydew, causing the bark to appear black and dirty. Ants feed on the sticky substance, and are often present where there is an aphid infestation. Several other species of aphids may infest sycamore leaves and twigs.

SOLUTION: Spray with ORTHO Isotox Insect Killer or ORTHO Liquid Sevin when aphids first appear. Spray the bark thoroughly. Repeat the spray if the tree becomes reinfested.

PODOCARPUS

Aphids (twice life size).

PROBLEM: Leaves near branch tips may be curled and are sometimes covered with a shiny or sticky substance. Gray-blue, ⅛-inch, soft-bodied insects cluster on the stems and undersides of the leaves, especially on new growth.

ANALYSIS: Aphids
Aphids do little damage in small numbers. However, they are extremely prolific and populations can rapidly build up to damaging numbers during the growing season. Damage occurs when the aphid sucks the juices from the podocarpus leaves. The aphid is unable to digest fully all the sugar in the plant sap and excretes the excess in a sugary material called honeydew, which often drops onto the leaves below. A sooty mold fungus may develop on the honeydew, causing the podocarpus leaves to appear black and dirty. Ants feed on the honeydew, and are often present where there is an aphid infestation.

SOLUTION: Apply ORTHO Isotox Insect Killer at recommended rates. Repeat sprayings as needed according to label directions to keep aphids from reinfesting the plant.

Podocarpus cultural information
Light: Full sun to part shade
Water: When the soil is almost dry
Soil: Loose, well drained
Fertilizer: Light to medium

Wax scale (life size).

PROBLEM: The stems or the undersides of the leaves are covered with somewhat flattened yellowish, brown, or white scaly bumps. The bumps can be scraped or picked off; the undersides are usually soft. Leaves turn yellow and may drop, and twigs and branches may die.

ANALYSIS: Scales
Several different types of scales infest podocarpus. They lay their eggs on the trunk and twigs, and in spring to early summer the young scales, called *crawlers*, settle on leaves and twigs. The small (¹⁄₁₀ inch), soft-bodied young feed by inserting their mouthparts and sucking sap from the plant. The legs usually atrophy and a crusty shell develops over the body. The mature female scales lay their eggs underneath their shell. An uncontrolled infestation of scales may kill the plant after 2 or 3 seasons.

SOLUTION: Spray with ORTHO Isotox Insect Killer, ORTHO Orthene Systemic Insect Control, or ORTHO Liquid Sevin when the young are active. Contact your local Cooperative Extension Office (see page 1011) to determine the best time to spray for scales in your area. The following winter or spring, spray the trunk and branches with a *dormant oil spray* to control overwintering insects. For more information about scales, see page 878.

POPULUS (POPLAR, ASPEN, COTTONWOOD)

Slime flux.

Satin moth caterpillars (life size).

POPULUS

ADAPTATION: Throughout the United States.

LIGHT: Full sun.

SOIL: Tolerates a wide variety of soils. Roots are invasive.

FERTILIZER: Fertilize with ORTHO Evergreen, Tree & Shrub Food 12–6–6 according to label directions.

WATER:
How much: Apply enough water to wet the soil 3 to 4 feet deep. To determine the proper amount of water for your soil type, see page 906.
How often: Some poplars are drought tolerant once established. However, most poplars prefer moist soils, and some even tolerate soils that are soggy or flooded.

PRUNING: Prune off suckers and broken branches, and prune to maintain shape.

PROBLEM: Sour-smelling sap oozes from wounds, cracks, and branch crotches, mainly during the growing season. The sap drips down the bark and dries, causing unsightly gray streaks. There may be some wilting on affected branches. Insects are attracted to the sour-smelling ooze.

ANALYSIS: Slime flux
Slime flux of poplars, also called *wetwood*, is caused by a bacterium (*Erwinia nimipressuralis*). The bacteria affect the heartwood, producing abnormally high sap pressure. The pressure is caused by bacterial fermentation, and forces the fermented sap, or flux, out of the wounds, cracks, or crotches in the tree. Flux is especially copious when the tree is growing rapidly. Large areas of the bark may be coated with the smelly, bacteria-laden sap, which dries to a grayish white color. In addition, wounds do not heal and the bark is unsightly. A tree with this problem is often under water stress, which may cause drought damage (wilting and scorched leaves) to the branches. The problem may persist for many years.

SOLUTION: There are no chemical controls for this condition. Bore a slightly slanted drainage hole through the wood below each oozing wound. Insert a ½-inch-diameter plastic tube, just until it holds firmly in place. If the tube penetrates the water-soaked wood inside the tree, it will interfere with drainage. The tube will carry the dripping sap away from the trunk. Disinfect tools with rubbing alcohol after pruning infected trees.

PROBLEM: The surface of the leaf is eaten, giving the remaining tissue a lacy appearance, or the whole leaf is chewed. Sometimes leaves or branches are webbed. The tree may be completely defoliated. Damage appears any time between spring and fall. Caterpillars are feeding on the leaves. Repeated heavy infestations may weaken or kill trees.

ANALYSIS: Leaf-feeding caterpillars
Many different species of caterpillars feed on poplar leaves wherever the trees are grown. Depending on the species, the moths lay their eggs from early spring to midsummer. The larvae that hatch from these eggs feed singly or in groups on buds, on one leaf surface (skeletonizers), or on the entire leaf. Certain caterpillars web leaves together, or web a branch as they feed. In some years, damage is minimal due to unfavorable environmental conditions or control by predators and parasites. However, when conditions are favorable, entire trees may be defoliated by late summer. Defoliation weakens trees because there are no leaves left to produce food. When heavy infestations occur several years in a row, branches or entire trees may be killed.

SOLUTION: Spray with ORTHO Isotox Insect Killer, ORTHO Liquid Sevin, or with the bacterial insecticide *Bacillus thuringiensis* (*B.t.*) when damage is first noticed. Cover the leaves thoroughly. *B.t.* must be applied when caterpillars are small. Repeat the spray if the tree becomes reinfested.

POPULUS (POPLAR, ASPEN, COTTONWOOD)

Damaged leaves. *Insert:* Leaf beetles (half life size).

Oystershell scales (¼ life size).

Poplar scales (life size).

PROBLEM: The leaf tissue is eaten between the veins, giving the leaves a lacy appearance. Sometimes only the major veins remain. The bark of young trees may be chewed. Small blackish larvae or ¼-inch-long yellow beetles with round or oblong black spots are feeding on the leaves. Clusters of yellow eggs may be found on the lower sufaces of the leaves. With repeated infestations, young trees may die.

ANALYSIS: Leaf beetles
(*Chrysomela* species)
Several species of leaf beetles may seriously damage poplars, especially in urban plantings. They spend the winter as adults under the bark in plant debris on the ground, or in homes. When new growth begins in the spring, the beetles fly to trees to feed on the leaves and twigs. The females lay groups of yellow eggs on the undersides of the leaves. The clusters of larvae that hatch from these eggs feed on the leaf tissue between the veins, skeletonizing the leaf. There are 4 or more generations of leaf beetles each year, so larvae and adults may be present throughout the growing season.

SOLUTION: Spray with ORTHO Isotox Insect Killer when damage is first noticed in spring. If necessary, repeat the spray in mid-July.

PROBLEM: The trunk, stems, or the undersides of the leaves are covered with brown, black, or red-orange crusty bumps or somewhat flattened brownish, white, or grayish scaly bumps. The bumps can be scraped or picked off; the undersides are usually soft. Leaves turn yellow and may drop. In some cases, a shiny, sticky substance coats the leaves. A black sooty mold often grows on the sticky substance. Large portions of the tree may be killed if infestations are heavy.

ANALYSIS: Scales
Many different types of scales infest poplar. They lay their eggs on leaves or bark, and in spring to midsummer the young scales, called *crawlers*, settle on leaves, twigs, and the trunk. The small (¹⁄₁₀ inch), soft-bodied young feed by sucking sap from the plant. The legs usually atrophy and a hard crusty shell develops over the body. The mature female scales lay their eggs underneath the shell. Some species of scales that infest poplar are unable to digest fully all the sugar in the plant sap, and excrete the excess in a fluid called honeydew. A sooty mold fungus may develop on the honeydew, causing the poplar leaves to appear black and dirty. An uncontrolled infestation of scales may kill the tree after 2 or 3 seasons.

SOLUTION: Spray with ORTHO Isotox Insect Killer or ORTHO Liquid Sevin when the young are active. Contact your local Cooperative Extension Office (see page 1011) to determine the best time to spray for scales in your area. To control overwintering insects, spray with ORTHO Volck Oil Spray before growth begins in the spring. For more information about scales, see page 878.

PROBLEM: The undersides of the leaves, stems, branch crotches, and/or trunk are covered with white, cottony masses. Leaves may turn yellow and drop. A shiny, sticky substance may coat the leaves. A black sooty mold often grows on the sticky substance. Numerous side shoots sometimes grow out of an infested crotch area. Twigs and branches may die back.

ANALYSIS: Cottony scales and mealybugs
Cottony scales and mealybugs are common on poplar wherever it is grown. The visual similarity between these insects makes separate identification difficult. They are very conspicuous in late spring and summer because the females are covered with a white, cottony egg sac, containing up to 2500 eggs. Females lay their egg masses on leaves or branches. The young insects that hatch from these eggs are yellowish brown to green. They feed throughout the summer on leaves, stems, and trunk. Damage is caused by the withdrawal of plant sap from the leaves and branches. The insects are unable to digest fully all the sugar in the plant sap and excrete the excess in a fluid called honeydew, which often drops onto the leaves or plants below. A sooty mold fungus may develop on the honeydew, causing the poplar leaves and other plants to appear black and dirty. Leaf drop and twig dieback occur when the white masses completely cover the leaves and branches.

SOLUTION: Spray with ORTHO Isotox Insect Killer in midsummer when the young are active. The following spring, when the tree is dormant, spray with *lime sulfur* to control overwintering insects on the bark.

Poplar borer (half life size).

Damaged tree. *Insert:* Adult borer (half life size).

Dieback. *Insert:* Canker.

PROBLEM: Swollen areas with holes in their centers develop on twigs, branches, or the trunk. Many side shoots may grow from below the swellings, destroying the tree's natural form. The leaves on infested twigs and branches turn yellow and may be chewed on the edges. There is usually a sawdustlike material and many broken twigs beneath the tree.

ANALYSIS: Poplar borers
(*Saperda* species)
At least five species of beetles feed on poplars, causing galls to form. The inch-long, striped and spotted, brownish or gray beetles with long antennae appear in late spring or early summer. The females lay eggs in small holes gnawed in the bark of twigs and branches that are more than 1/2 inch in diameter. As the legless, whitish grubs hatch from these eggs, they tunnel into the wood. Excess tissue grows around the wound, resulting in a swollen area or gall. When infestations are severe, nearly all twigs and branches more than 1/2 inch in diameter have one or more galls. The galls weaken the twigs and branches, causing them to break and litter the ground during stormy weather. The grubs remain in the wood for 1 or 2 years before maturing.

SOLUTION: Remove and destroy severely damaged trees. Spray the bark of less severely damaged trees with ORTHO Lindane Borer & Leaf Miner Spray in late May or early June. Repeat the treatment 2 weeks later.

PROBLEM: The leaves turn yellow and there are holes in the twigs. Large quantities of sawdustlike material cling to the bark just below the holes. Sap often oozes from the holes. Young trees may be killed and older trees may lose their natural form due to the production of numerous side shoots. Small (3/8 inch) black or dark brown weevils, with pale yellow spots and long snouts, may be seen around the tree from midsummer until fall.

ANALYSIS: Poplar and willow borer
(*Cryptorhynchus lapathi*)
Most species of poplar and all willow trees may be attacked by this weevil. The adult weevils cause minor injury by chewing holes in the bark of twigs. The major damage is caused by the white, C-shaped larvae. During mid to late summer, the larvae hatch from eggs laid in holes chewed by the female weevils. The larvae burrow into and feed on the inner bark. In the spring, large quantities of frass (sawdust and excrement) are expelled from the holes as the larvae tunnel into the center of the twigs to pupate. The feeding and tunneling cause branches to break easily and disrupt nutrient and water movement through the tree. The leaves yellow and the tree often becomes bushy from the growth of numerous side shoots. The larvae pupate in June, and emerge as adults in midsummer. Several other types of borers may also infest the trunk and branches of poplars.

SOLUTION: Remove and destroy severely infested trees or branches before early summer. Spray the bark of trees with ORTHO Lindane Borer & Leaf Miner Spray in late July or early August.

PROBLEM: Dark sunken areas appear on the twigs, branches, or trunk. Leaves on infected branches may be spotted, or they may be stunted and lighter green than normal. Twigs and branches are often killed. Young or weakened trees are most susceptible.

ANALYSIS: Canker and dieback
Several different fungi cause canker and dieback on poplars. Lombardy poplars are especially vulnerable. The fungi enter the tree through a wound or, in some cases, through the leaves, killing the surrounding healthy tissue. A dark sunken canker develops in the wood and expands through it in all directions. If the fungus infects the leaves first, it grows down through the leaf stems and forms cankers on the twigs. The canker cuts off the flow of nutrients and water to the twigs or branch, causing the leaves to turn yellow. Twig or branch dieback follow if the canker girdles the wood. The tree may wall off the spreading fungus by producing callus tissue, a rapid growth of barklike cells. If the expanding canker is stopped before it covers half the diameter of the trunk, the tree usually survives. However, the fungus may grow faster than the callus, or the tree may not produce a callus, resulting in the death of the branch or the whole tree.

SOLUTION: Prune off dead twigs and small cankered branches, cutting well below the canker. Remove and destroy severely infected trees. To prevent the development of new cankers, avoid wounding trees. Keep trees vigorous by fertilizing and watering. For information on fertilizers and watering, see pages 904 and 906.

PRUNUS (FLOWERING CHERRY)

PRUNUS (EVERGREEN FORMS)

Citrus whitefly (5 times life size).

PRUNUS

ADAPTATION: Zones 3 to 9 (to determine your zone, see the map on page 1004).

FLOWERING TIME: Spring.

LIGHT: Full sun.

SOIL: Any good, fast-draining garden soil.

FERTILIZER: Fertilize with ORTHO Evergreen, Tree & Shrub Food 12–6–6 according to label directions.

WATER:
How much: Apply enough water to wet the soil 3 to 4 feet deep. To determine the proper amount of water for your soil type, see page 906.
How often: Water when the soil is barely moist 4 inches below the surface. For more information about watering, see page 906.

PRUNING: Most species require only maintenance pruning. Remove dead or broken branches. The flowering peaches and nectarines produce a better show of flowers if cut back severely every year immediately after flowering.

INSECTS AND DISEASES: Problems of flowering fruit trees are very similar to those of trees that produce fruit. For more information about plant problems on flowering fruit trees, see page 625 for almond; page 637 for cherry; page 654 for peach; and page 668 for plum.

PROBLEM: Tiny, winged insects, $\frac{1}{12}$ inch long, feed on the leaf surfaces. The insects are covered with white waxy powder. When the plant is touched, insects flutter rapidly around it. Leaves may be mottled and yellowing. In warm winter areas, a black sooty mold may cover the leaves.

ANALYSIS: Citrus whitefly
(*Dialeurodes citri*)
This insect is a common pest of many garden plants. The adult lays her eggs on the undersides of leaves. The larvae are the size of a pinhead, flat, oval-shaped, and semitransparent, with white waxy filaments radiating from the body. They feed for about a month before changing to the adult form. Both the larval and adult forms suck sap from the leaves. The larvae are more damaging because they feed more heavily. Adults and larvae cannot fully digest all the sugar in the plant sap, and excrete the excess in a fluid called honeydew, which often drops onto the leaves below. A sooty mold fungus may develop on the honeydew, causing the laurel leaves to appear black and dirty. In warm winter areas the insects can be active year-round, with eggs, larvae, and adults present at the same time. Whiteflies are unable to live through freezing winters. Spring reinfestations in freezing winter areas come from migrating whiteflies.

SOLUTION: Control with ORTHO Isotox Insect Killer if the whiteflies are noticeably damaging the leaves. Repeat the spray at least 2 more times at intervals of 2 weeks to control the young as they hatch.

PRUNUS (EVERGREEN)

ADAPTATION: Zones 7 through 10. To determine your zone, see the map on page 1004.

FLOWERING TIME: Spring or summer.

LIGHT: Full sun (some species prefer partial shade in hot summer areas).

SOIL: Any good, well-drained garden soil.

FERTILIZER: Fertilize with ORTHO Azalea, Camellia & Rhododendron Food 5–10–10 or ORTHO Evergreen, Tree & Shrub Food 12–6–6 according to label directions.

WATER:
How much: Apply enough water to wet the soil 2 to 3 feet deep. To determine the proper amount of water for your soil type, see page 906.
How often: Most cherry laurels are drought tolerant once established, but they grow best with periodic deep watering. Water when the soil is dry 4 inches below the surface. For more information about watering, see page 906.

PRUNING:
Tree forms: Prune to a single trunk.
Shrubs: Prune to maintain shape. Cut back overly long growth. Some species can be pruned to form a hedge.

Leaf spot.

PROBLEM: Spots and blotches appear on the leaves. The spots may be yellow, purple, red, tan, gray, or brown. They range in size from barely visible to ³/₄ inch in diameter. Several spots may join to form blotches. The infected tissue sometimes dries up and falls out, causing a shothole appearance. Leaves may turn yellow and drop off. Leaf spotting is most severe in warm, humid weather.

ANALYSIS: Leaf spot
Several different fungi and bacteria cause leaf spot. These spots are unsightly but rarely harmful to the plant. Plants weakened by low temperatures and wind exposure may be more susceptible to invasion by leaf spotting organisms. The fungi and bacteria are spread by splashing water and wind. Spots develop where the organisms enter the tissue. If wet or humid weather persists, the disease spreads through the tissue and blotches form. Most leaf spot organisms do their greatest damage in mild weather (between 50° and 85°F).

SOLUTION: Once leaves become spotted they will remain so. Where practical, remove infected leaves from the plant. Collect and destroy any fallen leaves. To reduce plant susceptibility, provide windbreaks and protection from low temperatures.

Cooley spruce gall aphid (3 times life size).

PROBLEM: White, cottony tufts appear on the undersides of needles in midsummer. Small (¹/₈ inch) blackish insects may be found underneath the cottony material. The needles are spotted yellow and distorted; many may drop from the tree prematurely.

ANALYSIS: Cooley spruce gall aphid (*Adelges cooleyi*)
The cooley spruce gall aphid requires both Douglas fir and spruce to complete its 2-year life cycle. The aphids spend the winter on spruce. The following spring, the females lay their eggs around the new needles. The emerging young feed there, inducing the formation of galls that enclose them (see page 554). In midsummer, the galls open and the mature aphids migrate to Douglas fir, where the females lay their eggs on the needles. The young aphids cover themselves with a white cottony or woolly material. They suck sap from the needles, causing yellowing and distortion. When infestations are heavy, many needles drop off. The next spring, winged aphids develop; some fly back to spruce, while others may remain on Douglas fir.

SOLUTION: Spray with an insecticide containing *acephate*, *diazinon*, or *lindane* when new growth is expanding to control the young insects as they hatch.

PYRACANTHA

ADAPTATION: Zones 5 through 10. To determine your zone, see the map on page 1004.

FLOWERING TIME: Small white flowers, usually in the spring. Yellow, orange, or red berries in the fall, sometimes lasting through the winter.

LIGHT: Full sun to partial shade.

SOIL: Any good, well-drained, slightly acid (pH 5.5 to 6.5) garden soil.

FERTILIZER: Fertilize with ORTHO Azalea, Camellia & Rhododendron Food 5–10–10 according to label directions.

WATER:
How much: Apply enough water to wet the soil 1 to 2 feet deep. To determine the proper amount of water for your soil type, see page 906.
How often: Do not keep the soil constantly wet or plant pyracantha near sprinkler systems. Water when the soil is dry 4 inches below the surface. For more information about watering, see page 906.

PRUNING: Give pyracantha plenty of room to spread. To maintain shape, pinch off young growth or prune back long branches just before growth starts. Pyracantha is often used as an espalier (a plant trained to grow flat against a wall or fence). For more information about this technique, see ORTHO's book *All About Pruning*.

PYRACANTHA

Fireblight.

Scab.

Hawthorn lacebugs (half life size).

PROBLEM: Blossoms and leaves of infected twigs suddenly wilt and turn black as if scorched by fire. The leaves curl and hang downward. The bark at the base of the blighted twigs becomes water-soaked, then dark, sunken, and dry; cracks may develop at the edge of the sunken area. In warm, moist spring weather, drops of brown ooze appear on the sunken bark. Young plants may die.

ANALYSIS: Fireblight
This disease is caused by a bacterium (*Erwinia amylovora*) that is very destructive to many trees and shrubs. (For a list of susceptible plants, see page 1001.) The bacteria spend the winter in the sunken areas (cankers) on the branches. In the spring, the bacteria ooze out of the canker. Bees, flies, and other insects are attracted to the sweet, sticky ooze and become smeared with it. When the insects visit a flower for nectar, they infect it with the bacteria. The bacteria spread rapidly through the plant tissue in warm (65°F or higher), humid weather. Insects visiting these infected blossoms later carry bacteria-laden nectar to healthy blossoms. Tender or damaged leaves may be infected in midsummer.

SOLUTION: During spring and mid to late summer, prune out infected branches 12 to 15 inches beyond any visible discoloration and destroy. A protective spray of a bactericide containing *basic copper sulfate* or *streptomycin*, applied before bud break in spring, will help prevent infection. Repeat at intervals of 5 to 7 days until the end of bloom. In the fall, prune out infected branches. Sterilize pruning shears after each cut with rubbing alcohol. For a list of pyracantha varieties resistant to fireblight, see page 1001.

PROBLEM: Dark blotches, with fringed edges, ¼ inch or more in diameter, appear on the leaves. The leaves turn yellow, then brown, and drop from the plant. Berries and twigs develop circular, rough-surfaced, olive-green spots that eventually turn corky and black. The infected berries die.

ANALYSIS: Scab
This plant disease is caused by a fungus (*Fusicladium pyracanthae*) that produces scabby lesions on pyracantha leaves and berries similar to those caused by scab fungi on apple and other fruit trees. Scab may be a serious problem in areas where winter or spring weather is humid and mild (60° to 70°F). In the spring, spores are blown by the wind to new leaves and flower buds. If the leaves and buds are wet, the fungus infects them and a spot develops. More spores are produced from these spots. These spores are splashed by rain to infect new leaf, twig, and berry surfaces. The spots on the berries and twigs turn corky and black and the berries become deformed during development. As the temperature increases in summer, the fungus becomes less active.

SOLUTION: To obtain adequate control of scab, protective sprays must be started as soon as bud growth begins in spring. Spray with a fungicide containing *ferbam*, *maneb*, or *benomyl*. Repeat 3 more times at intervals of 10 days. Plant scab-resistant varieties (see page 1001).

PROBLEM: The upper surfaces of the leaves are mottled or speckled gray and green. The mottling may be confused with mite or leafhopper damage. It can be distinguished from other insect damage by the black, shiny, hard droplets found on the undersides of damaged leaves. Small (⅛ inch), light or dark, spiny, wingless insects or brownish insects with clear, lacy wings may be visible around the droplets and next to the midrib. The plant is usually stunted. Damage occurs in spring and summer.

ANALYSIS: Hawthorn lacebug (*Corythucha cydoniae*)
The hawthorn lacebug is found throughout the United States on pyracantha, hawthorn, cotoneaster, and fruiting quince. It spends the winter as an adult on the plant in bark crevices, branch crotches, or other protected areas on the host. When growth begins in spring, the adults attach their eggs to the undersides of the leaves with a brown, sticky substance. The eggs hatch and the spiny, wingless, immature insects, and later the brown lacy-winged adults, suck sap from the undersides of the leaves. The green leaf pigment disappears, resulting in the characteristic gray and green mottling. As the lacebugs feed, droplets of brown excrement accumulate around them. Damage is unsightly and food production by the leaf is reduced, resulting in a loss of plant vigor.

SOLUTION: Spray with ORTHO Isotox Insect Killer or ORTHO Orthene Systemic Insect Control when damage first appears in spring. Thoroughly cover the undersides of the leaves where insects feed. Repeat 7 to 10 days later. A third application may be necessary if the plant becomes reinfested in the summer.

Kuno scales (twice life size) and honeydew drops.

Woolly apple aphids (twice life size).

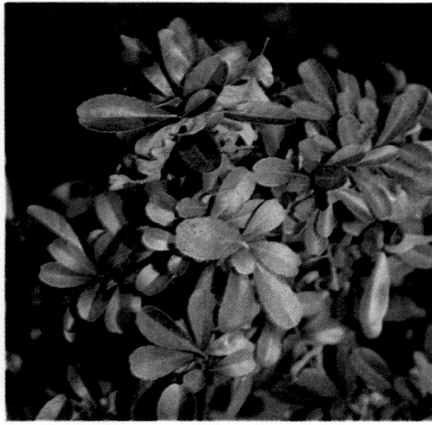

Sooty mold.

PROBLEM: The stems or the undersides of the leaves are covered with white and brown crusty bumps or thick, white, waxy bumps or clusters of somewhat flattened scaly bumps. The bumps can be scraped or picked off; the undersides are usually soft. Leaves turn yellow and may drop, and the plant may be stunted. A sticky substance may coat the leaves. A black sooty mold often grows on the sticky substance.

ANALYSIS: Scales
Many different types of scales infest pyracantha. In spring to midsummer the young scales, called *crawlers*, settle on leaves and twigs. The small (1/10 inch), soft-bodied young feed by sucking sap from the plant. The legs usually atrophy and a hard crusty or waxy shell develops over the body. The mature female scales lay their eggs underneath the shell. Some species of scales that infest pyracantha are unable to digest fully all the sugar in the plant sap, and excrete the excess in a fluid called honeydew. A sooty mold fungus may develop on the honeydew, causing the pyracantha leaves to appear black and dirty. An uncontrolled infestation of scales may kill the plant after 2 or 3 seasons.

SOLUTION: Spray with ORTHO Isotox Insect Killer or ORTHO Orthene Systemic Insect Control when the young are active. Contact your local Cooperative Extension Office (see page 1011) to determine the best time to spray for scales in your area. To control overwintering insects, spray the trunk and branches with ORTHO Volck Oil Spray in spring. For more information about scales, see page 878.

PROBLEM: Woody growths and a white, woolly material form on the twigs and branches in summer. The plant has an unthrifty appearance, with yellowing leaves and possibly some twig dieback. A shiny, sticky substance often coats the leaves. A black sooty mold may grow on the sticky substance.

ANALYSIS: Woolly apple aphid (*Eriosoma lanigerum*)
The woolly apple aphid causes woody growths or galls to form on the twigs, branches, and roots of pyracantha, apple trees, and flowering fruit trees. The aphids spend the winter on elm trees or, in the West, on pyracantha or fruit trees. In the summer, they migrate to the plant and cluster on the stems, twigs, and around old pruning wounds. They also crawl down to the roots. Damage occurs when the aphids suck the juices from the wood. Their feeding induces galls to form, weakening the plant. A white, woolly material covers the aphids as they feed, making them very conspicuous on the shrub. The aphids are unable to digest fully all the sugar in the plant sap and excrete the excess in a fluid called honeydew, which often drops onto the leaves below. A sooty mold fungus may develop on the honeydew, causing the pyracantha leaves to appear black and dirty. The woolly hawthorn aphid and several leaf-feeding aphids may also infest pyracantha.

SOLUTION: Spray with ORTHO Orthene Systemic Insect Control or ORTHO Isotox Insect Killer in summer when aphids or their damage are first noticed.

PROBLEM: A black sooty mold is growing on the leaves and twigs. It can be completely wiped off the surfaces. Cool, moist weather hastens the growth of this substance.

ANALYSIS: Sooty mold
This common black mold is found on a wide variety of plants in the garden. It is caused by any of several species of fungi that grow on the sugary material left on plants by aphids, scales, mealybugs, whiteflies, and other insects that suck sap from the plant. The insects are unable to digest all the sugar in the sap and excrete the excess in a fluid called honeydew, which drops onto the leaves below. The honeydew may also drop out of infested trees and shrubs onto pyracantha growing beneath them. The sooty mold fungus develops on the honeydew, causing the pyracantha leaves to appear black and dirty. Sooty mold is unsightly, but it is fairly harmless because it does not attack the leaf directly. Extremely heavy infestations prevent light from reaching the leaf, so that the leaf produces less food and may turn yellow. The presence of sooty mold indicates that the pyracantha or another plant near it is infested with insects.

SOLUTION: Sooty mold can be wiped from the leaves with a wet rag, or it will eventually be washed off by rain. Prevent more sooty mold by controlling the insect that is producing the honeydew. Inspect the leaves and twigs above the sooty mold to find what type of insect is present. See the following pages for control instructions: for aphids, page 877; for scales, page 878; for whiteflies, page 879; for mealybugs, page 878.

PYRUS (ORNAMENTAL PEAR)

PYRUS

ADAPTATION: Zones 4 to 10 (to determine your zone, see the map on page 1004). Tolerant of harsh city conditions.

FLOWERING TIME: Late winter to early spring.

LIGHT: Full sun.

SOIL: Tolerates a wide variety of soils.

FERTILIZER: Fertilize with ORTHO Evergreen, Tree & Shrub Food 12–6–6 according to label directions.

WATER: Drought-resistant once established, but will also tolerate moist soil. Water during periods of extended drought.

PRUNING: Heavily pruned trees seldom flower. Prune only to maintain shape. Evergreen pears need to be pruned to a single trunk to obtain a tree form.

INSECTS AND DISEASES: Problems of flowering pear are very similar to those found on pears that produce fruit. For information about plant problems on flowering pear, see the section starting on page 659.

QUERCUS (OAK)

QUERCUS

ADAPTATION: Throughout the United States. There are oaks for all climates and conditions, including salt air, heat, wind, and moist areas.

LIGHT: Full sun.

SOIL: Any good, deep, well-drained garden soil. Some oaks do not tolerate alkaline soils (pH 7.0 and above).

FERTILIZER: Some oaks benefit from periodic feedings under the outer branches. Fertilize with ORTHO Evergreen, Tree & Shrub Food 12–6–6 according to label directions.

WATER: Some oaks grow best with ample water and will thrive in lawns. Others, such as the western native oaks, prefer drier conditions. They will decline and eventually die if overwatered. For a list of oaks and their water requirements, see page 998.
  How much: Apply enough water to wet the soil 4 to 5 feet deep. To determine the proper amount of water for your soil type, see page 906.
  How often: Water young trees when the soil is barely moist 4 inches below the surface. *Oaks requiring ample water:* established trees should be watered when the soil is barely moist 4 inches below the surface. *Oaks preferring dry conditions:* never water around the trunk. Most of these oaks need no supplemental water once established.

PRUNING: Prune to maintain shape and to remove dead wood. When planting, allow room for growth.

LEAVES DISCOLORED

Summer leaf scorch.

PROBLEM: During hot weather, usually in July or August, leaves turn brown around the edges and between the veins. Sometimes the whole leaf dies. Many leaves may drop during late summer. This problem is most severe on the youngest branches. Trees do not generally die.

ANALYSIS: Summer leaf scorch
Leaf scorch is caused by excessive evaporation of moisture from the leaves. In hot weather, water evaporates rapidly from the leaves. If the roots can't absorb and convey water fast enough to replenish this loss, the leaves turn brown and wither. This usually occurs in dry soil, but leaves can also scorch when the soil is moist. Drying winds, severed roots, limited soil area, or soil with a high salt concentration contribute to scorch. For more information about scorch, see page 865.

SOLUTION: To prevent further scorch, deep-water trees during periods of hot weather to wet down the entire root space. For more information about watering trees, see page 906. Newly transplanted trees should be watered whenever the rootball is dry 1 inch below the surface. There are no controls for scorch on trees in moist soil. Plant trees adapted to your climate.

Oak anthracnose.

Oak leafminer damage.

Oak mite damage.

PROBLEM: Brown, dead spots appear along the veins in the spring, and expand outward to the leaf edges. Leaves become curled, puckered, and twisted. In wet seasons, many leaves may fall. Leaves on the lower branches are generally more severely infected. Small sunken areas may form on twigs; the twigs may die.

ANALYSIS: Oak anthracnose
This plant disease is caused by fungi (*Gnomonia* species) that infect the leaves of white oaks and, in California, several other oaks. The fungi spend the winter on fallen leaves or in sunken cankers on twigs in the tree. During rainy weather, spores are blown and splashed onto young leaves. Dead spots develop where the fungi enter the tissue. The spots enlarge and the leaves become puckered and twisted. When moist weather continues into summer, the fungi may kill the leaves, causing severe defoliation. The fungi may also enter twigs, causing canker and twig dieback.

SOLUTION: There is nothing you can do to control anthracnose this year. If next spring is wet, spray young trees and valuable specimens with a fungicide containing *zineb* or *basic copper sulfate* when the buds are opening.

PROBLEM: Brown patches or trails appear on the leaves, starting in the spring. By August, the leaves may be completely brown and drop from the tree. When a brown spot is torn open, one to several small green or whitish caterpillars may be found inside.

ANALYSIS: Oak leafminers
The larvae of several species of moths mine the leaves of oak. The insects spend the winter as pupae inside dried, fallen leaves. In the spring, the moths emerge and lay their eggs on the newly developed green leaves. The larvae that hatch from these eggs burrow into the leaf and feed on the tissue between the upper and lower surfaces of the leaves. The outer tissue turns brown, producing patches or trails. The larvae mature, pupate, and emerge as moths to repeat the cycle up to five times during the growing season. When infestations are heavy, the trails run together, covering the entire leaf surface, and nearly all the leaves are affected. When this occurs the leaves drop prematurely, reducing the ornamental value of the tree.

SOLUTION: Spray young trees or heavily infested valuable specimens with ORTHO Orthene Systemic Insect Control when damage is first noticed in late spring or early summer. Spray the leaves thoroughly. Repeat the spray if new mines are noticed in July. Rake up and destroy the fallen leaves in autumn.

PROBLEM: Leaves are stippled yellow or bronze and dirty. Sometimes there is a silken webbing on the leaf surfaces. New leaves may be slightly distorted. To determine if the plant is infested with mites, hold a sheet of white paper underneath a stippled leaf and tap the leaf sharply. Minute yellow, brown, or red specks the size of pepper grains will drop to the paper and begin to crawl around. The pests are easily seen against the white background.

ANALYSIS: Oak mite
(*Oligonychus bicolor*)
Mites, related to spiders, are major pests of many garden plants. The oak mite causes damage by sucking sap from the upper surfaces of the leaves. As a result of feeding, the green pigment disappears, producing the stippled appearance. Mites infesting oak are most prolific in warm weather, and are most active in midsummer. Mite damage is usually not noticeable until much of the foliage is stippled. This damage seldom seriously injures oak trees, but it is unsightly.

SOLUTION: Control with ORTHO Orthene Insect Spray or with an insecticide containing *dicofol* when damage is first noticed in the summer. Wet the upper surfaces of the leaves thoroughly. Repeat the spray 2 weeks later. A *dormant oil* or *lime sulfur* spray may be applied before growth starts in early spring to control the overwintering mites.

QUERCUS (OAK) — LEAVES DISCOLORED

INSECTS

Oak leaf blister.

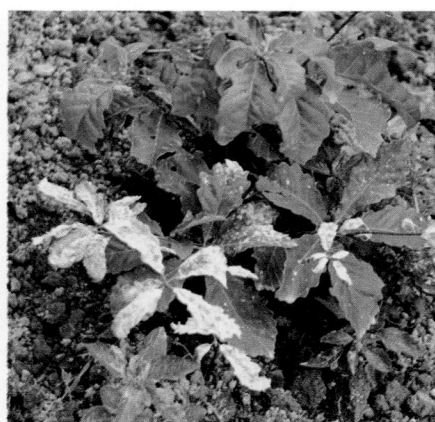

Powdery mildew on bur oak.

Lacebugs (3 times life size).

PROBLEM: Puckered, circular areas, up to ½ inch in diameter, appear on the leaves in the spring. The blisterlike spots are yellowish green at first, and later die and turn brown. The leaves usually remain attached to the tree.

ANALYSIS: Oak leaf blister
Leaf blister is caused by a fungus (*Taphrina caerulescens*) that is unsightly but rarely harmful to the tree. It is a problem on various species of oaks, particularly red, black, scarlet, and live oaks. The fungus spends the winter in the bud scales on the tree. During cool, wet springs, it enters the developing leaves. Green blisters form where the fungus enters the tissue. The infected tissue eventually dies and turns brown. In the fall, the fungus produces the overwintering spores. If the following spring is cool and wet, the cycle begins again.

SOLUTION: If leaf blister was a problem the previous year and the weather this spring is cool and wet, spray the tree with a fungicide containing *zineb*, *maneb*, *mancozeb*, or *basic copper sulfate* 1 or 2 weeks before the leaves appear. Wet the entire tree thoroughly.

PROBLEM: The leaf surfaces and the new shoots are covered with a dense layer of grayish white powdery material, which later becomes tan, then brown. Affected new shoots are usually swollen, fleshy, and shortened. The leaves on these shoots may be small and yellow; eventually they turn brown and shrivel. Many side shoots may develop from the infected branch, producing a "witch's broom."

ANALYSIS: Powdery mildew
This common plant disease is caused by a fungus (*Sphaerotheca lanestris*) that thrives in both humid and dry weather. It is sometimes called *brown mildew* because the fungus changes in color from grayish white to brown with age. It is most destructive to coast live oak (*Quercus agrifolia*) in California, but is also found on white, southern red, holly, bur, and post oaks in the southern and western states. The powdery layer consists of fungal strands and spores. The spores are spread by the wind to healthy plants. The fungus saps the plant nutrients, causing stunted, yellow leaves and swollen, distorted branches, which often develop into a witch's broom. Several other common powdery mildews that do not cause witch's brooms also infect oaks.

SOLUTION: Where practical, remove the witch's brooms during the winter to reduce the amount of fungus. Succulent summer growth is most susceptible. Avoid causing new growth by excessive pruning, fertilization, and irrigation during this period.

PROBLEM: The upper surfaces of the leaves are mottled or speckled white and green. The mottling may be mistaken for damage caused by mites or leafhoppers. However, it can be distinguished from other insect damage by the shiny, hard, brown droplets found on the undersides of damaged leaves. Small (⅛ inch), light or dark, spiny, wingless insects, or brownish insects with clear lacy wings, may be visible around the droplets. Foliage on severely infested trees may curl, turn brown, and drop prematurely.

ANALYSIS: Oak lacebug
(*Corythucha arcuata*)
The oak lacebug may be found feeding in great numbers on the undersides of oak leaves. The lacebugs spend the winter as adults in bark crevices or in other protected areas on the tree. When the buds begin to open in spring, the adults attach their eggs to the undersides of the leaves with a brown, sticky substance. When the eggs hatch, the spiny, wingless immature insects, and later the brown lacy-winged adults, suck sap from the leaves. The green leaf pigment disappears, resulting in the characteristic white and green mottling. As the lacebugs feed, droplets of brown excrement accumulate around them. The damage is unsightly, and food production by the leaf is reduced, resulting in a loss of plant vigor.

SOLUTION: Spray with ORTHO Orthene Systemic Insect Control or ORTHO Isotox Insect Killer when damage first appears in the spring. Cover the undersides of the leaves thoroughly. It is important to spray early, to prevent as much damage as possible.

Oak twig girdler damage.

Oak twig pruner (life size).

Gypsy moth caterpillars (half life size).

PROBLEM: Patches of dead leaves appear throughout the tree, contrasting sharply with healthy green foliage. To determine if the tree is infested with this insect, prune off an affected twig with dead leaves. Peel back the bark between the healthy green and brown foliage. A winding trail filled with a brown sawdustlike material and possibly a ¾-inch flattened, legless, white larva may be seen just underneath the bark.

ANALYSIS: Oak twig girdler
(*Agrilus angelicus*)
The twig girdler is the larva of a ¼-inch brownish bronze beetle. The adults feed on leaves, then lay their eggs on twigs in early summer. When the eggs hatch, the larvae burrow into the wood. They tunnel through the twig, just underneath the bark, in the direction of the trunk. As the larvae tunnel, they fill their trails with brown frass — excrement mixed with sawdust. The tunneling cuts off the flow of nutrients and water in that area, causing the leaves on the ends of the twigs to turn brown and die. More leaves die as the larvae continue to tunnel. After two years of feeding, the insect burrows back into the dead twig, pupates, and emerges as an adult.

SOLUTION: When practical, prune out and destroy infested twigs in midsummer. Keep oaks vigorous by giving them optimum growing conditions (see cultural information on page 574).

PROBLEM: Small, cleanly cut twigs, ¼ inch to 2 inches in diameter, are lying under the tree in the fall. The tree is often abnormally bushy. There may be small (up to 1 inch) whitish larvae inside the fallen twigs.

ANALYSIS: Twig pruners and twig girdlers
Several species of wood-boring beetles cause unsightly damage to oaks by altering the natural form of the tree. In midsummer to fall, these wood-boring beetles lay their eggs in the wood of small twigs. The twig pruner larvae tunnel toward the base of the twigs, eating all but the outer bark. In the fall, they back into the hollowed-out twig. High winds cause the nearly severed twigs containing the larvae to break and drop to the ground. With twig girdlers, it is the adults that cause the damage to the twigs. After laying their eggs, the adults chew a circle around the outside of the twigs. Girdled twigs die and break off. The eggs in the fallen twig are then able to develop without being hindered by the flow of tree sap through the twig. Both twig pruner and twig girdler larvae mature in the twigs on the ground. The damage to the tree is the result of excessive pruning on the branch tips. Several new side shoots develop where the twigs break off, causing abnormal bushiness and an unnatural shape.

SOLUTION: Gather and destroy all severed twigs in late fall when the insects are inside.

PROBLEM: The surface of the leaf is eaten, giving the remaining tissue a lacy appearance, or the whole leaf is chewed. Sometimes the leaves are webbed together. The tree may be completely defoliated. Damage appears any time between spring and fall. Caterpillars are feeding on the leaves. Repeated heavy infestations may weaken or kill trees.

ANALYSIS: Leaf-feeding caterpillars
Many different species of caterpillars feed on oak leaves wherever the trees are grown. Depending on the species, the moths lay their eggs from early spring to midsummer. The larvae that hatch from these eggs feed singly or in groups on buds, on one leaf surface (skeletonizers), or on the entire leaf. Certain caterpillars web the leaves together as they feed. In some years, damage is minimal due to unfavorable environmental conditions or control by predators and parasites. However, when conditions are favorable, entire trees may be defoliated by late summer. Defoliation weakens trees because there are no leaves left to produce food. When heavy infestations occur several years in a row, branches or entire trees may be killed.

SOLUTION: Spray with ORTHO Isotox Insect Killer or ORTHO Gypsy Moth & Japanese Beetle Killer when damage is first noticed. Spray the leaves thoroughly. Repeat the spray if the tree becomes reinfested.

QUERCUS (OAK) — INSECTS

Oak moth larva (twice life size).

Giant bark aphids (life size).

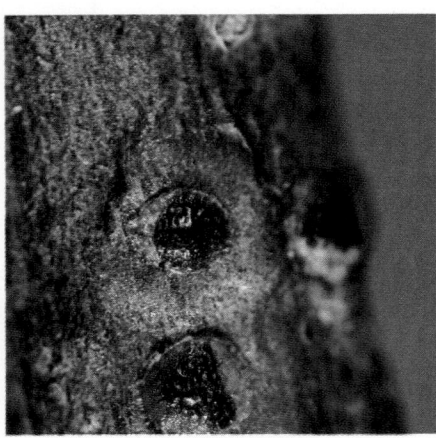

Oak pit scales (3 times life size).

PROBLEM: Dead brown patches appear on the leaves in the spring. One of the leaf surfaces inside these patches has been eaten. Later, the whole leaf is chewed and the tree may be completely defoliated. Large (up to 1¼ inches) olive-green caterpillars with black and yellow stripes and a brownish head are feeding on the leaves.

ANALYSIS: Oak moth
(*Phryganidia californica*)
This insect, also called the *California oakworm*, may completely defoliate oaks in California. Defoliated trees are not usually killed, but it may take them years to recover. Defoliation two years in a row can kill the tree. In addition, falling excrement and young larvae hanging from silken threads may be a nuisance around homes. The oak moth spends the winter as an egg or young larva on the leaves of evergreen oaks. When temperatures warm in the spring, the caterpillars begin feeding on one surface of the leaf. The leaf surface opposite this chewed area turns brown. When the caterpillars are half grown, they feed on the entire leaf. In May or June, the mature larvae pupate, emerge as pale brown moths, mate, and lay eggs. The larvae that hatch from these eggs feed on leaves until fall. Deciduous oaks are attacked only by this second generation.

SOLUTION: Spray evergreen oaks with ORTHO Orthene Systemic Insect Control when insects are first noticed, or with the bacteria *Bacillus thuringiensis* in the spring as soon as the larvae begin eating through the entire leaf. In the summer, spray deciduous oaks or reinfested evergreen oaks when damage is first noticed.

PROBLEM: Small (¼ inch) black and beige soft-bodied insects with long black legs cluster on twigs and the undersides of limbs. Twigs may be completely covered with a mat of black eggs. When populations are large, twigs and branches die. A shiny, sticky substance may coat the limbs. A black sooty mold often grows on the sticky substance. Ants may be present.

ANALYSIS: Giant bark aphid
(*Longistigma caryae*)
The giant bark aphid is the largest species of aphid known. Because of its long legs, it appears much larger than its ¼-inch size. The aphids do little damage in small numbers. However, they are extremely prolific and populations can rapidly build up to damaging numbers during the late summer. When populations are large, black eggs are matted all over the bark of infested limbs. Damage occurs when the aphid sucks the juices from the twigs and branches. The aphid is unable to digest fully all the sugar in the sap, and excretes large quantities in a fluid called honeydew, which may coat plants or objects beneath the tree. A sooty mold fungus may develop on the honeydew, causing the bark to appear black and dirty. Ants feed on the sticky substance, and are often present where there is an aphid infestation. Several other species of aphids may also infest oak leaves.

SOLUTION: Spray with ORTHO Isotox Insect Killer or ORTHO Orthene Systemic Insect Control when aphids first appear. Wet the bark thoroughly. Repeat the spray if the tree becomes reinfested.

PROBLEM: During the summer or early fall, leaves turn brown and twigs or branches die back. Dead leaves usually remain attached to the branches throughout the winter. In the spring, new leaves may appear 3 weeks late on infested deciduous oaks. Repeated heavy infestations often kill young trees. Small (1/12 inch), somewhat flattened, green, golden, or brown scaly bumps cluster on the twigs and branches. The bark is pitted where these insects cluster.

ANALYSIS: Pit scales
(*Asterolecanium* species)
Several species of pit scales may seriously damage oaks. The scales lay their eggs in spring and summer. The young scales, called *crawlers*, that hatch from these eggs settle on new growth and last year's branches, not far from the parent. The small (1/16 inch), soft-bodied young feed by inserting their mouthparts and sucking sap from the plant. Pits develop where the scales feed. The legs atrophy and a hard, crusty shell develops over the body. The mature female scales lay eggs underneath their shells. Several other types of scales also infest oak. For more information about scales, see page 878.

SOLUTION: Spray with ORTHO Isotox Insect Killer or ORTHO Orthene Systemic Insect Control in mid-May to June when the young are active. To control overwintering insects, spray with ORTHO Volck Oil Spray in winter or spring. Cover the tree thoroughly.

GROWTHS ON TREE

Gall caused by gall wasps.

PROBLEM: Round balls grow on twigs, or abnormal growths in a wide variety of shapes, sizes, and colors develop on the leaves, twigs, or branches. Infected leaves may be discolored or distorted and drop prematurely. In some cases, infected twigs and branches die.

ANALYSIS: Oak galls
Tiny insects, called *gall wasps* or *gallflies*, cause hundreds of different types of growths (galls) to develop on oak trees. The galls may be round, spiny, star-shaped, flattened, or elongated. Each species of insect (either a fly or a nonstinging wasp) causes its own specific gall to form. The galls are thought to be caused by a chemical that the insect injects into the plant tissue. The mature female lays her eggs on the various parts of the plant. The eggs hatch into legless grubs that cause the gall to form around them. The insects feed and develop inside the galls, mature, and either spend the winter inside them or emerge to produce another generation. Most galls do not harm the tree. However, some leaf galls inhibit food production, and several types of twig galls disrupt water and nutrient movement through the wood, causing twig dieback.

SOLUTION: If galled branches are distorted and unsightly, cut them off and destroy them before the adults emerge from the galls in spring.

Leafy mistletoe.

PROBLEM: Leafy, olive-green tufts of plants up to 3 feet across are attached to the branches. The plants may be covered with white, pink, or red berries. The tufts are most noticeable during the winter when there are no leaves on the tree. In severe cases, twigs may die or affected branches may be swollen where the tufts are attached.

ANALYSIS: Leafy mistletoe
(*Phoradendron* species)
Mistletoes are semi-parasitic plants that manufacture their own food but depend on their host plant for water and minerals. Those infecting oak are unsightly, but are rarely harmful to the tree. The plant produces sticky seeds that are spread by birds from one tree to another. The seeds germinate almost anywhere, but penetrate only young, thin bark. The attachment organs of the plant penetrate the tree's water-conducting vessels, from which they obtain their water and minerals. Growth of the mistletoe is slow at first, but in 6 to 8 years plants may be 3 feet across.

SOLUTION: If control is desired, prune off limbs 12 to 18 inches below the point of mistletoe attachment. The rootlike attachment organs may spread through the host tissue up to a foot from the place of original infection. They must be removed from the wood or the mistletoe will resprout. To prevent the spread of seeds, remove tufts before seeds form in spring. If it is not practical to prune a branch, cut off the mistletoe flush with the bark and wrap the area with several layers of black plastic, taped firmly to the tree. Since the mistletoe needs light to grow, the new sprouts will be killed by the darkness under the plastic.

TREE DYING

Oak wilt.

PROBLEM: The leaves on one or more branches wilt, turn bronze, and then fall prematurely. Infected trees of the red oak group may die within a few weeks. Infected trees of the white oak group may die within a few weeks or may die slowly over a period of 2 to 3 years. If an affected branch is cut off, a brown discoloration or ring is seen in the wood just beneath the bark. In the spring, the bark around the infected area may rupture, exposing mats of fungus.

ANALYSIS: Oak wilt
This plant disease is caused by a fungus (*Ceratocystis fagacearum*) that is spread from tree to tree by insects, grafted (intertwined) roots, and tools. Sap-feeding beetles and other insects become coated with the sticky spores that are formed under ruptured bark, and carry them to healthy trees. The fungus spreads through the water-conducting vessels in the wood, causing the discoloration and plugging. The leaves wilt, and the branches — or the entire tree — die. Bark-feeding beetles, which feed on dying trees, may spread the disease long distances. Closely planted trees (50 feet or less between trees) of the same species may pass the fungus through grafted roots.

SOLUTION: Remove infected trees. If the wood is saved, peel off the bark and split the wood immediately. To prevent the spread of the disease through root grafts of closely planted infected and healthy trees, cut a trench midway between the trees, 2 feet deep and extending beyond the spread of the branches. Prune trees in November when the fungus is less active, sterilizing tools after each cut with rubbing alcohol.

QUERCUS (OAK) — TREE DYING

Cankers.

Fungal mats.

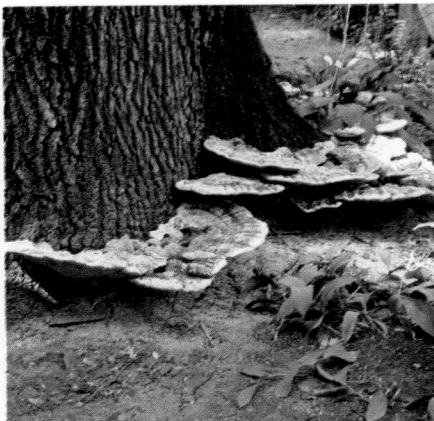

Polyporos rot.

PROBLEM: Leaves are stunted and yellow, and the foliage throughout the tree may be sparse. Branches eventually die. Weakened trees are most severely infected. Occasionally, trees die suddenly without showing symptoms; but in most cases trees die slowly over a period of several years. Honey-colored mushrooms, 2 to 5 inches in diameter, may grow singly or in clusters during the fall or winter on the lower trunk or on the ground near infected roots. If the soil is removed from around the base of the tree black rootlike strands, about the diameter of pencil lead, are seen attached to the larger roots. A white fan-shaped growth occurs between the bark and wood of these larger roots and on the trunk just below the soil surface. The infected tissue has a mushroom odor.

ANALYSIS: Armillaria root rot
This plant disease, also called *oak root fungus* or *shoestring root rot*, is caused by a fungus (*Armillaria mellea*) that rots the roots of many woody and nonwoody plants. Oaks are often lightly infected with this fungus for years with no damage. However, when the trees are under stress from drought, overwatering, physical injuries, insects, or diseases, they often succumb to *Armillaria*. The fungus is spread short distances (under a foot) through the soil by the rootlike fungal strands. When they contact susceptible plant roots, the strands penetrate the host if conditions are favorable. Once the fungus enters the bark tissue it produces a white fan-shaped mat of fungal strands that invade and decay the tissue of the roots and lower trunk. The fungus spreads rapidly if the oak tree is in a weakened state. Water and nutrient uptake by the roots is inhibited, causing the foliage and branches to die. In the fall, mushrooms — the reproductive bodies of the fungus — often appear around infected trees. A closely related fungus (*Clitocybe tabescens*) found in the Southeast produces symptoms on oak very similar to armillaria root rot.

SOLUTION: Remove and destroy infected trees, including the stump and the root system. The fungus can live on the stumps and roots for many years, infecting susceptible plants nearby. Healthy-appearing plants growing adjacent to diseased trees may already be infected. Check around the roots and lower stems for signs of the fungus. The life of a tree may be prolonged if it is not severely infected. Remove the soil from around the rotted parts of the roots and trunk. Cut out the diseased tissue down to healthy wood and allow them to air dry through the summer. Do not water the tree. Cover the exposed parts before temperatures drop below freezing. When replacing trees that have been infected with *Armillaria*, use resistant plants. (For a list, see page 1001.) Avoid planting susceptible species in recently cleared forest lands where armillaria root rot is common. To inhibit disease development in an established oak tree, provide optimum growing conditions, avoid injuring the tree, and control pests and diseases.

PROBLEM: The leaves are yellowing and the foliage is sparse on a branch or on one section of the tree; the tree slowly dies. Large branches may break off. The tree is planted in a lawn or in an area that receives summer watering; or the soil has been raised around the base of the trunk.

ANALYSIS: Crown rot and decline
This plant disease is a common and serious problem of oaks, especially native oaks growing in urban parts of California. It is the result of too much moisture around the base of the tree in summer. Many oaks prefer dry soil. Planting in a lawn or in an area that receives summer watering weakens the tree. These conditions are favorable to the development of soil fungi (especially *Phytophthora* species) that enter weakened roots and slowly destroy them. The flow of nutrients and water is cut off to the top of the tree, causing the foliage to yellow and drop. The fungi may also move up into the trunk and destroy the wood. Entire branches eventually die. The diseased branches can no longer support their weight and they crack and fall. A raised soil level also weakens a tree by keeping the base of the tree too moist, leaving it susceptible to attack by soil fungi.

SOLUTION: Stop all watering of the soil beneath the tree. Remove all plants and lawn that require summer watering from around the trunk. Prune off dead or dying branches. Do not raise the soil around the trunk. If the base of the trunk is covered, remove the soil down to its original level. For more information about raised soil level under trees, see page 470.

RHUS (SUMAC)

Verticillium wilt.

PROBLEM: The leaves on a branch turn yellow at first, and then redden prematurely. During hot weather, the leaves may wilt. New leaves may be stunted and yellow. The infected plant may die slowly, branch by branch, over several seasons. Or the whole plant may wilt and die within a few months. Some plants may recover. The tissue under the bark on the dying side shows dark streaks when cut. To examine for streaks, peel back the bark at the bottom of the dying branch. The dark discoloration may be very apparent or barely visible in the area just underneath the bark.

ANALYSIS: Wilt
This disease affects many ornamental plants. It is caused by either of two soil-inhabiting fungi (*Verticillium albo-atrum* or *Fusarium oxysporum* f. *rhois*) that live on plant debris or in the soil. The disease is spread by contaminated seeds, plants, soil, equipment, and groundwater. The fungus enters the plant through the roots and spreads up into the branches through the water-conducting vessels in the main stem. The vessels become discolored and plugged. This plugging cuts off the flow of water and nutrients to the branches, causing the leaf discoloration and wilting.

SOLUTION: No chemical control is available. Fertilize and water the affected plant to stimulate vigorous growth. Prune off all dead wood. Do not remove branches on which leaves have recently wilted. These branches may produce new leaves in 3 to 4 weeks or next spring. Remove dead plants.

RHODODENDRON (AZALEA)

RHODODENDRON (AZALEA)

ADAPTATION: Zones 4 through 10 except in desert areas. (To determine your zone, see the map on page 1004.) Azaleas are more tolerant of warm, dry climates than rhododendrons.

FLOWERING TIME: Late winter to early summer.

LIGHT: Partial shade (full sun in cool summer areas). Plants don't bloom well in deep shade.

SOIL: Rich, well-drained, acid (pH 4.5 to 6.5) soil, high in organic matter and low in salts. (For more information about pH, see page 902.) When planting, add at least 50 percent peat moss to the soil, and always keep 2 inches of mulch around the base of the plant.

FERTILIZER: Fertilize with ORTHO Azalea, Camellia & Rhododendron Food 5–10–10 according to label directions.

WATER:
How much: Apply enough water to wet the soil 1 to 2½ feet deep. To determine the proper amount of water for your soil type, see page 906.
How often: Water when the soil is moist but not wet under the mulch. For more information about watering, see page 906.

PRUNING: Prune just after flowering.
Azaleas: For a bushier plant, pinch off growing tips.
Rhododendrons: Remove dead flower trusses. Be careful not to break the new buds. To renew old, lanky plants, reduce the height of the plant by a third for three successive years.

FLOWERS DYING

Azalea petal blight.

PROBLEM: Circular spots the size of pinheads form on the flower petals. The spots are pale or whitish on colored flowers, and rust-colored on white flowers. Spots quickly enlarge to form irregular blotches until the entire flower collapses. The petals feel slimy when rubbed between the fingers. Diseased flowers dry up and cling to the plant. Leaves and stems are not injured.

ANALYSIS: Azalea petal blight
Petal blight is very destructive to azaleas and rhododendrons in humid coastal regions. It is caused by a fungus (*Ovulinia azaleae*). In early spring, the fungus infects early-flowering azaleas. With favorable weather conditions, the disease spreads rapidly, turning the flowers to mush within a day. Spores from early-flowering azaleas infect later-flowering varieties. Small hard black "resting structures," composed of fungal strands, form on dead flowers if the weather stays wet. Many of these resting structures drop to the ground and remain in the litter. The following season, they produce spores that cause the initial infection on the early-flowering varieties.

SOLUTION: Spray the flowers with a fungicide containing *zineb* or *benomyl* when the disease is first noticed. Repeat every 3 to 4 days until flowering ends. To prevent infection the following year, begin spraying as the first color begins to show. Clean up litter around the base of the plants and pick off diseased flowers to reduce spore production in early spring. Reduce spore production by spraying the ground under the shrub before flowering begins with a fungicide containing *PCNB*.

RHODODENDRON (AZALEA)

Spider mite damage on azalea.

PROBLEM: Leaves are stippled yellow or bronze and dirty. There may be a silken webbing on the lower surfaces of the leaves. New leaves may be distorted. To determine if the plant is infested with mites, hold a sheet of white paper underneath an affected leaf or branch and tap sharply. Minute green, red, or yellow specks the size of pepper grains will drop to the paper and begin to crawl around. The pests are easily seen against the white background.

ANALYSIS: Spider mites
Spider mites, related to spiders, are major pests of many garden plants. They cause damage by sucking sap from buds and the undersides of leaves. As a result of feeding, the green leaf pigment disappears, producing the stippled appearance. The southern red mite (*Oligonychus ilicis*), found in the Northeast, Southeast, and Great Lakes states, is most prolific in cooler weather. It feeds and reproduces primarily during spring and fall. Other spider mites found on rhododendrons develop rapidly in hot, dry weather (70°F and up); by midsummer they build up to tremendous numbers.

SOLUTION: Spray with ORTHO Isotox Insect Killer or ORTHO Diazinon Insect Spray when damage first appears. Direct sprays to the undersides of the leaves. Repeat application if plant becomes reinfested. To prevent unsightly injury to foliage, it is important to apply control measures early in the season when damage first appears. Injured leaves remain on the plant for more than one growing season. Hose down plants frequently to knock off webs and mites.

GROWTH ON LEAVES

Leaf gall on azalea.

PROBLEM: Developing leaves and flowers are thickened, fleshy, and distorted. Initially the thickenings are whitish or light green. As the thickenings enlarge they become white or pink, with a powdery appearance. Later in the growing season, the distorted leaves turn dark and hard. This problem is most severe in spring, during cool moist weather, and where plants are growing in areas of poor air circulation or in full shade.

ANALYSIS: Leaf gall
This plant disease is caused by a fungus (*Exobasidium vaccinii*). It is most common on azaleas but sometimes occurs on rhododendrons. As the buds open in spring, fungal spores blown by wind to the plant or washed by rain from the bark enter the tissue. The spores need moisture to germinate. Plants grown in areas of poor air movement or in deep shade, where moisture levels are high, will usually have more galls than will other plants. After infection takes place, a growth-promoting substance is triggered in the plant, causing the thickening and distortion. By midsummer the white powdery fungal spores cover the distorted leaves.

SOLUTION: Sprays to control leaf gall must be applied before infection occurs. Once the galls develop, the best control is to remove them when they are first noticed. If the galls are not removed and destroyed, the disease will be more severe the following year. To reduce new infection next spring, spray with a fungicide containing *tribasic copper sulfate* or *zineb* before buds open. Repeat at intervals of 2 weeks until new leaves are fully grown. Provide air circulation and avoid planting shrubs in areas of deep shade.

DISCOLORED OR SPOTTED LEAVES

Lacebug damage on rhododendron.

PROBLEM: The upper sides of the leaves are mottled or speckled yellow and green. The mottling may be confused with mite or leafhopper damage. It can be distinguished from other insect damage by hard, black, shiny droplets that are found on the undersides of damaged leaves. Small (⅛ inch) spiny wingless insects or brownish insects with clear lacy wings may be seen around the droplets. The plant is usually stunted. Damage occurs in spring and summer.

ANALYSIS: Lacebugs
(*Stephanitis* species)
Populations of lacebugs are highest when rhododendrons and azaleas are grown in sunny rather than shady locations. The wingless, immature insects and the lacy-winged adults suck sap from the undersides of leaves. As they feed, droplets of black excrement accumulate around them. Damage is unsightly and food production by the leaf is reduced, making the plant less vigorous.

SOLUTION: Spray with ORTHO Orthene Systemic Insect Control or ORTHO Isotox Insect Killer when damage first appears. Cover the undersurfaces of the leaves thoroughly. Repeat 7 to 10 days later. A third application may be necessary if plants become reinfested in summer. It is important to spray early to prevent as much damage as possible.

Rust on rhododendron.

Iron deficiency on rhododendron.

Leaf spots on azalea.

PROBLEM: Yellow spots, up to ¼ inch in diameter, may appear on the upper surfaces of the leaves during the growing season. Directly under the spots, on the undersides of the leaves, are spots or blisters containing a yellow to orange-red powdery material. The powdery material can be rubbed or scraped off easily. Infected leaves may drop off the plant prematurely. Heavily infected plants usually lack vigor.

ANALYSIS: Rust
Several different fungi cause rust on rhododendrons and azaleas. The yellow to orange-red spores are spread by the wind to the leaves. With moisture (rain, dew, or fog) and moderate temperatures (55° to 75°F), the spores enter the tissue on the undersides of the leaves. Spots usually develop directly above — on the upper surfaces — as the fungus saps the plant nutrients.

SOLUTION: No chemicals are available to control rust on rhododendrons and azaleas. Where practical, pick off infected leaves.

PROBLEM: The leaves are pale green to yellow. The newest leaves may be completely yellow with only the veins, and the tissue right next to the veins, remaining green. With progressively older leaves, only the leaf edges may be yellowing. The plant may be stunted.

ANALYSIS: Iron deficiency
This is a common problem in acid-loving plants like azaleas and rhododendrons. These plants prefer soil with a pH between 5.0 and 6.0. (For more information on soil acidity, see page 902.) The yellowing is due to a deficiency of iron in the plant. The soil is seldom deficient in iron. However, iron is often found in an insoluble form that is not available to the plant, especially in soil with a pH of 7.0 or higher. A high soil pH can result from overliming, or from lime leached from cement or brick. Regions where soil is derived from limestone and those with low rainfall also have high pH soils. Plants use iron in the formation of the green pigment in the leaves. When it is lacking, new leaves are yellow.

SOLUTION: Spray the foliage with ORTHO Greenol Liquid Iron 6.13%, and apply it to the soil around the plants to correct the iron deficiency. Correct the pH of the soil by treating it with ORTHO Aluminum Sulfate and watering it in well. Maintain an acid pH by fertilizing with ORTHO Azalea, Camellia & Rhododendron Food 5–10–10. When planting azaleas or rhododendrons, add at least 50 percent peat moss to the soil. This is especially important if you live in an area where the soil is alkaline or has poor drainage. Never lime the soil around azaleas or rhododendrons.

PROBLEM: Spots and blotches appear on the leaves. The spots may be yellow, red, tan, gray, or brown. They range in size from barely visible to ¾ inch in diameter. Several spots may join to form blotches. Leaves may be yellow and dying. Some leaves may drop. Leaf spotting is most severe in warm, humid weather.

ANALYSIS: Fungal leaf spot
There are a number of different fungi that cause leaf spots. These spots are unsightly but rarely harmful to the plant. Plants weakened by low temperatures and wind exposure are most susceptible to invasion by leaf spot fungi. The fungi are spread by splashing water and wind. Spots develop where the fungi enter the tissue. If wet or humid weather persists, the fungi spread through the tissue and blotches form. They survive the winter on the leaves and twigs. Most leaf spot organisms do their greatest damage in mild weather (between 50° and 85°F).

SOLUTION: Once leaves become spotted they will remain so. Where practical, remove infected leaves from the plant. Collect and destroy any fallen leaves. Spray with a fungicide containing *mancozeb*, *benlate*, or *zineb* when new growth begins in the spring. Repeat 2 more times at intervals of 2 weeks, or for as long as the weather remains favorable for infection. Add a spreader-sticker to the spray. (For more information about spreader-stickers, see page 915.) To reduce plant susceptibility, provide windbreaks and protection from low temperatures.

RHODODENDRON (AZALEA) — LEAVES OR BRANCHES DIE

Rhododendron borer damage.

Salt burn.

Sunburn on azalea.

PROBLEM: Crisp, round spots, the size of a dime or nickel, are scattered like polka dots on the leaves. Leaves and shoots on the outer edge of the plant may wilt. The bark on the main stem and lower branches flakes off easily. Underneath this area shallow tunnels, ridges, and holes are seen.

ANALYSIS: Rhododendron borer (*Synanthedon rhododendri*)
The larva of this clear-winged moth is a serious pest of rhododendrons in the Atlantic coast states. The small (up to ½ inch), yellowish white caterpillar with brown legs and head causes severe wounds by tunneling into the bark and wood of the trunk and branches. The borer is seldom seen because the larva develops inside the wood. In early summer, it emerges as an adult moth, lays its eggs on the bark, and dies. The eggs hatch in June and the larvae burrow into the wood to feed.

SOLUTION: The rhododendron borer is difficult to control once it has burrowed into the wood. In fall, winter, or early spring (before May), cut out and destroy all dead and dying branches. Severely bored sections should be sacrificed. In early May, spray or paint the trunk and branches with ORTHO Lindane Borer & Leaf Miner Spray to kill young larvae before they burrow. Repeat 3 more times at intervals of 2 weeks. Maintain plant health and vigor by watering and fertilizing regularly.

PROBLEM: Leaf edges are brown and dead. Browning usually occurs on older leaves first. This distinguishes the problem from wind burn, which develops on young, exposed leaves first. Leaves may be lighter green than normal. In a severe case, leaves drop off.

ANALYSIS: Salt burn
This problem is most common in areas of low rainfall. It also occurs in soils with poor drainage, and where too much fertilizer has been applied. Excess salts dissolved in the soil water accumulate in the leaf edges, where they kill the tissue. These salts also interfere with water uptake by the plant. This problem is rare in areas of high rainfall, where the soluble salts are leached from most soils. Poorly drained soils do not leach well; much of the applied water runs off the surface instead of washing through the soil. Fertilizers, which are soluble salts, also cause salt burn if too much is applied or if they are not diluted with a thorough watering after application.

SOLUTION: Salt burn damage does not disappear from the leaves, but injury can be avoided in the future. In areas of low rainfall, leach accumulated salts from the soil with an occasional heavy irrigation (about once a month). If possible, improve the drainage around the plants by removing them and adding soil amendments. For instructions on improving drainage, see page 901. If plants are severely damaged, replace them with healthy plants. Follow package directions when using commercial fertilizers; water thoroughly after application. Avoid the use of bagged steer manure, which contains large amounts of salt, on azaleas and rhododendrons.

PROBLEM: During warm, sunny weather, the center portion of the leaf bleaches to a tan or off-white color. Once the initial damage has occurred, the spot does not usually increase in size. Injury is generally more severe on plants with light-colored flowers.

ANALYSIS: Sunburn
Rhododendrons and azaleas are generally classified as shade plants. Their leaves are sensitive to the heat of direct sun, which kills the leaf tissue. Scalding occurs when the shrub is planted in full sun. The intense reflection from a light-colored, south-facing wall can also scald leaves. It takes only one hot summer day for damage to appear. The injury is unsightly but is not damaging to the plant. However, weakened leaves are more susceptible to invasion by fungi and bacteria. Plants that do not receive enough water are more susceptible to sunscald.

SOLUTION: Move the injured plant to a shaded location, or provide some shade where it is now planted. (For more information about transplanting, see page 916.) Once leaves are scalded, they will not recover. Where practical, remove affected leaves. Don't let plants dry out during hot weather.

Winter injury on rhododendron.

Dieback on rhododendron.

Phytophthora root rot.

PROBLEM: Young and exposed leaves are brown and dry, especially around the leaf margins and near the tips. The shrub is planted in a windy location, or is growing in a cold climate where cold, dry, windy days are common. The soil may be frozen or dry.

ANALYSIS: Windburn and winter injury
Windburn and winter injury on rhododendron and azalea leaves are common on plants growing in wind-swept locations. In cold climates, where temperatures commonly fall below freezing, strong winds cause leaves to lose their moisture more rapidly than it can be replaced by the root system. The leaf edges dry out and die. This is most pronounced when water is unavailable because the soil is frozen. Leaf burning also occurs on exceptionally windy, dry days in summer.

SOLUTION: Once the leaf edges have been damaged, the injury remains. Where practical, pick off damaged leaves. To prevent winter injury and windburn, plant shrubs in locations protected from wind; or provide windbreaks. Plants should be watered and fertilized regularly to maintain health and vigor. Water in late fall or winter, if necessary, to ensure adequate soil moisture. Mulch plants after they are dormant to reduce the depth of frost penetration into the soil.

PROBLEM: The leaves and terminal portion of a branch are permanently wilted, and dying. Leaves may turn reddish brown and remain attached to the plant. Or the leaves may be rolled and have spots that look water-soaked. There are often sunken, brownish, dead areas at the base of the wilted branch. Generally it is the older branches that are affected. In hot weather, the entire plant may die.

ANALYSIS: Dieback
Dieback is caused by several different fungi. The fungi are spread by splashing water, rain, and infected soil and tools. They enter the plant through wounds, through dead and dying twigs, and through the leaves. A sunken dead area or canker usually develops on the twigs or branches, cutting off the flow of nutrients and water on that side of the plant. The leaves and stems above the canker wilt and die. With some fungi, no canker develops. Instead, the fungus is carried through the water-conducting tissue, producing toxins and plugging the tissue, which causes the leaves and branch tips to wilt and die back. Plants under stress from hot weather die more rapidly.

SOLUTION: Once the branch is wilted and dying, there is no chemical that will control the disease. Prune out and destroy all wilted or cankered branches by cutting into healthy tissue a few inches below the canker. Those plants in which infection started at the leaves with water-soaked spots can be protected with a spray the following year. Spray with a *basic copper* fungicide after blooming. Repeat 2 more times at intervals of 14 days.

PROBLEM: The young leaves are yellowish and wilting. Eventually the whole plant wilts and dies, even though the soil is moist. Dead leaves remain attached to the plant and are rolled along the midrib. The symptoms may develop over a few weeks, or may take many months. Heavy, poorly drained soil favors disease development. The tissue under the bark close to ground level shows a dark discoloration when cut. To check for discoloration, peel back the bark at the bottom of the plant. There is a distinct margin between white healthy wood and dark diseased wood.

ANALYSIS: Wilt and root rot
This plant disease is caused by several different soil-inhabiting fungi (*Phytophthora* and *Pythium* species) that attack a wide variety of ornamental plants. The fungi destroy the roots, and may work their way up the stem. If they girdle the stem, the plant wilts and dies. Very wet conditions favor the fungi, which are most common in heavy, poorly drained soils. Although azaleas and rhododendrons need constant moisture, they must also have good drainage.

SOLUTION: No chemical control is available. Dry the plant out, following the technique on page 857. Improve the drainage of the soil before replanting azaleas or rhododendrons in the same location. For methods of improving soil drainage, see page 901. If drainage cannot be improved, plant in beds raised a foot or more above grade. Or plant shrubs that are resistant to wilt and root rot. See page 1000 for a list.

RHODODENDRON — PLANT DIES _____ **INSECTS** _____

Damaged azalea. *Insert:* Grub (twice life size).

PROBLEM: The leaves on a branch or the entire plant may be yellowing and stunted, or the leaves may droop and curl, especially with the onset of hot weather. The leaf margins may be notched. To determine if the plant is infested with these insects, wash the soil away to expose the base of the stem and a few inches of the main roots. Inspect the bark for signs of chewing. Look for small (¼ to ½ inch), legless grubs in the soil.

ANALYSIS: Root weevil larvae
Several species of root weevils infest rhododendrons and azaleas. The larval stage of the insect (the grub) causes the most damage by feeding on roots and the base of the stem. If the grubs remain undetected, the plant may die abruptly with the onset of hot weather. Female weevils lay eggs at the soil line near the stem during the summer months. The emerging grubs burrow into the soil. They feed on the roots in fall, and then spend the winter in the soil. Most root weevils cause their major damage when they resume feeding in spring. Their feeding girdles the roots and stems, disrupting the flow of nutrients and water through the plant and causing the roots and the top of the plant to die. Minor damage may be caused by the night-feeding adults notching the foliage.

SOLUTION: Discard severely wilted plants. To prevent the next generation of weevils from causing damage, eliminate the adults. Spray the foliage and the ground under the plant with ORTHO Orthene Systemic Insect Control when notching first appears in May or June. Repeat the spray 2 more times at intervals of 3 weeks.

Notching caused by root weevils.

PROBLEM: The leaf margins are scalloped or notched. The leaves may be green and healthy, or they may be yellowing and curled. To determine if the plant is infested with this insect, inspect the foliage after dark, using a flashlight. Black or grayish insects, ⅕ to ⅖ inches long, with elephantlike snouts and with rows of tiny round depressions on their backs, are feeding on the leaf edges. These insects are present from May or June to as late as September.

ANALYSIS: Root weevil adults
Root weevils are common pests of many garden plants. The adult weevils feed at night, notching leaf margins. This feeding detracts from the appearance of the plant, but usually does not cause serious injury. Severe damage and death of the plant may result from larvae feeding on roots, if the weevils are left uncontrolled. The grubs feed unseen on the roots in spring, and from mid or late summer into fall.

SOLUTION: To control adults, spray with ORTHO Orthene Systemic Insect Control or ORTHO Isotox Insect Killer when notching first appears in May or June. Thoroughly cover the foliage and the soil beneath the plant. Repeat 2 more times at intervals of 3 weeks.

Check for the presence of these weevils with a pitfall trap. Sink a tin can in the soil so the rim is flush with the surface. Pour a few inches of soapy water in the bottom. Inspect the trap daily and replenish the water as necessary. When adults are trapped, begin spraying.

Azalea bark scale (life size).

PROBLEM: The undersides of the leaves, the young branches, or the branch crotches, are covered with clusters of somewhat flattened white, yellowish, brown, reddish, or gray scaly bumps. The bumps can be scraped or picked off; the undersides are usually soft. Leaves may turn yellow and drop off, and branches may die back. The plant is killed when infestations are heavy.

ANALYSIS: Scales
Many species of scales infest rhododendrons and azaleas throughout the country. Scales spend the winter on the trunk and twigs of the plant. They lay eggs in spring and in midsummer; the young scales, called *crawlers*, settle on the various parts of the shrub. The small (¹⁄₁₀ inch), soft-bodied young feed by inserting their mouthparts and sucking sap from the plant. The legs usually atrophy and a scaly or crusty shell develops over the body. The mature female scales lay their eggs underneath the shell. Leaf drop and twig dieback occur when scales completely cover the leaves and branches. An uncontrolled infestation may kill a plant after 2 or 3 seasons.

SOLUTION: Spray with ORTHO Isotox Insect Killer or ORTHO Orthene Systemic Insect Control in midsummer (late spring in the South), when the young are active. The following early spring, before new growth begins, spray the branches and trunk with a *dormant oil spray* to control overwintering insects. For more information about scales, see page 878.

—■ ROBINIA (LOCUST) ————

Aphids (¼ life size).

Whiteflies on rhododendron (life size).

Locust borers (life size).

PROBLEM: Tiny (⅛ inch) green or pink soft-bodied insects cluster on the leaves and developing buds. The flower buds may be deformed, and the leaves often have curled edges. A shiny or sticky substance usually coats the leaves. A black sooty mold may grow on the sticky substance. Ants may be present.

ANALYSIS: Rhododendron aphid (*Macrosiphum rhododendri*)
Rhododendron aphids do little damage in small numbers, and plants can tolerate large numbers without much effect. However, aphids are extremely prolific and populations can rapidly build up to damaging numbers during the growing season. Damage occurs when the aphid sucks the juices from the rhododendron leaves and buds. The aphid is unable to digest fully all the sugar in the plant sap and excretes the excess in a fluid called honeydew. The honeydew often drops onto the leaves below. A sooty mold fungus may develop on the honeydew, causing the rhododendron leaves to appear black and dirty. Ants feed on the sticky substance, and are often present where there is an aphid infestation.

SOLUTION: Spray with ORTHO Isotox Insect Killer or ORTHO Diazinon Insect Spray when aphids are noticed. Spray the plant thoroughly. Repeat the spray if the plant becomes reinfested.

PROBLEM: Tiny, white, winged insects ¹⁄₁₂ inch long are found mainly on the undersides of the leaves. When the plant is touched, the insects flutter rapidly around it. The upper surfaces of new leaves may be mottled and yellow; sometimes the leaf edges curl. A shiny or sticky substance usually coats the leaves. A black sooty mold may grow on the sticky substance.

ANALYSIS: Rhododendron whitefly (*Dialeurodes chittendeni*)
This whitefly attacks only rhododendrons. The 4-winged adult lays eggs on the undersides of leaves. The larvae are the size of a pinhead, flat, greenish, oval, and semitransparent. They feed for about a month before changing to the adult form. Both the larvae and adults suck sap from the leaves. The larvae are more damaging because they feed more heavily. Adults and larvae cannot fully digest all the sugar in the plant sap, and excrete the excess in a fluid called honeydew, which drops onto leaves below. A sooty mold fungus may develop on the honeydew, causing the rhododendron leaves to appear black and dirty. Only rhododendrons that have leaves with smooth undersurfaces are infested. A similar whitefly, called the azalea whitefly (*Pealius azaleae*), infests the hairy-leaved, evergreen snow azalea (*Rhododendron mucronatum*).

SOLUTION: Spray with ORTHO Isotox Insect Killer or ORTHO Diazinon Insect Spray when insects are first noticed. Repeat the spray 2 more times at intervals of 7 to 10 days. Thoroughly spray both the upper and lower surfaces of the leaves.

PROBLEM: Foliage is yellow and stunted, and may be sparse. Swellings form on the branches and trunk. The bark cracks, and scars develop at the cracks. Sawdust is often found around the scars. Branches may break off.

ANALYSIS: Locust borer (*Megacyllene robiniae*)
The locust borer is found wherever black locust is grown, but its damage is more severe in the eastern half of the country. Trees more than 4 years old are most heavily damaged. The female beetles lay their eggs from August to October in bark crevices and around wounds. The white, legless larvae that hatch from these eggs bore through to the inner bark and spend the winter there. In spring, the larvae tunnel into the sapwood and, eventually, the heartwood. The tunneling stops the flow of nutrients and water in that area by cutting the conducting vessels. The leaves yellow, branches and the trunk are weakened and scarred, and they often break. In late summer, the larvae pupate in the tunnel and emerge as adults to lay eggs. Several other borers may also infest black locust.

SOLUTION: Spray the trunk and larger branches with ORTHO Lindane Borer & Leaf Miner Spray in the middle of August. Repeat the spray during the first week of September.

Robinia cultural information
Light: Full sun
Water: Drought tolerant once established
Soil: Tolerates many types
Fertilizer: Light

ROBINIA (LOCUST)

Locust leafminers (half life size).

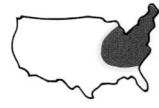

PROBLEM: Yellow to brown patches or trails appear on the leaves in late spring. Some of the leaves may also be chewed. The patches or trails enlarge to form blotches. If a blotch is torn open, whitish larvae with black heads may be found inside. During midsummer, the lower surfaces of the leaves are eaten, giving the leaves a lacy appearance. Small (¼ inch) orange-yellow beetles with a broad black stripe may be seen on the leaves. Many or all of the leaves may turn brown and drop off.

ANALYSIS: Locust leafminer
(*Odontota dorsalis*)
The locust leafminer is destructive in both the larval and adult stages. In the spring, adult beetles feed on the developing locust leaves. After a short time, the females deposit eggs in brown fecal matter on the undersides of the leaves. The emerging larvae burrow into the leaf tissue and feed, making a single trail between the upper and lower surfaces of the leaf. As they increase in size, the larvae feed in separate mines. They pupate, and the beetles emerge from the leaf in midsummer. The beetles skeletonize the leaves by feeding on their lower surfaces. The leaves turn brown, and many or all of them drop off the tree. If the tree grows another set of leaves, a second generation of leafminers often destroys all of them. Infested trees are unsightly, and with repeated infestations they may die.

SOLUTION: Spray with ORTHO Lindane Borer & Leaf Miner Spray as the leaves are developing and again in early July. If you notice damage late in the season, begin spraying the following spring.

ROSA (ROSE)

ROSA

ADAPTATION: Throughout the United States.

FLOWERING TIME: Spring and summer (through fall in the south).

LIGHT: Full sun. Plant in areas with good air circulation.

SOIL: Any good, well-drained garden soil.

FERTILIZER: Fertilize with ORTHO Rose Food 8–12–4 or ORTHO Rose & Flower Food 8–12–4 according to label directions.

WATER:
How much: Apply enough water to wet the soil 1½ to 2 feet deep. To determine the proper amount of water for your soil type, see page 906.
How often: Roses need plenty of water. Water when the soil is moist but not wet 4 inches deep. For more information about watering, see page 906.

PRUNING: Remove dead or unhealthy wood. Remove branches that cross through the center of the plant. Prune off at least a third to half of last year's growth. For more information about pruning and care of roses, see ORTHO's book *All About Roses.*

FLOWERS DAMAGED

Flower thrips damage.

PROBLEM: Young leaves are distorted and foliage may be flecked with yellow. Flower buds are deformed, and usually fail to open. The petals of open blossoms, especially those of white or light-colored varieties, are often covered with brown streaks and spots. If a deformed or streaked flower is pulled apart and shaken over white paper, tiny yellow or brown insects fall out and are easily seen against the white background.

ANALYSIS: Flower thrips
(*Frankliniella tritici*)
Flower thrips are the most abundant and widely distributed thrips in the United States. They live inside the buds and flowers of many garden plants. Both the immature and the adult thrips feed on plant sap by rasping the tissue. The injured petal tissue turns brown and the young expanding leaves become deformed. Injured flower buds usually fail to open. Thrips initially breed on grasses and weeds. When these plants begin to dry up or are harvested, the insects migrate to succulent green ornamental plants. The adults lay their eggs by inserting them into the plant tissue. A complete life cycle may occur in 2 weeks, so populations can build up rapidly. Most damage to roses occurs in early summer.

SOLUTION: Thrips are difficult to control because they continuously migrate to roses from other plants. Immediately remove and destroy infested buds and blooms. Spray with ORTHO Orthene Systemic Insect Control, ORTHO Isotox Insect Killer, or ORTHO Orthenex Insect & Disease Control, 3 times at intervals of 7 to 10 days.

LEAVES DISCOLORED OR SPOTTED

Black spot.

Powdery mildew.

Rust.

PROBLEM: Circular black spots with fringed margins appear on the upper surfaces of the leaves in the spring. The tissue around the spots or the entire leaf may turn yellow, and the infected leaves may drop prematurely. Severely infected plants may lose all of their leaves by midsummer. Flower production is often reduced and quality is poor.

ANALYSIS: Black spot
Black spot is caused by a fungus (*Diplocarpon rosae*) that is a severe problem in areas where high humidity or rain is common in spring and summer. The fungus spends the winter on infected leaves and canes. The spores are spread from plant to plant by splashing water and rain. The fungus enters the tissue, forming spots the size of a pinhead. The black spots enlarge, up to ¾ inch in diameter, as the fungus spreads; spots may join to form blotches. Twigs may also be infected. Plants are often killed by repeated severe infections. Roses differ in their susceptibility to black spot. For a list of tolerant and susceptible varieties, see page 993.

SOLUTION: Spray or dust with ORTHO Funginex Rose Disease Control, ORTHO Orthenex Insect & Disease Control, or ORTHO Rose & Floral Dust. Repeat the treatment at intervals of 7 to 10 days for as long as the weather remains wet. Sprays may be omitted during hot, dry spells in summer. Prune off infected canes. Avoid overhead watering. In the fall, rake up and destroy the fallen leaves. After pruning plants during the dormant season, spray with ORTHO Orthorix Spray. The following spring, when new growth starts, begin the spray program again.

PROBLEM: The young leaves, young twigs, and flower buds are covered with a thin layer of grayish white powdery material. Infected leaves may be distorted and curled and many may turn yellow or purplish and drop off. New growth is often stunted, and young canes may be killed. Badly infected flower buds do not open properly. In late summer, tiny black dots (spore-producing bodies) may be scattered over the powdery covering like ground pepper.

ANALYSIS: Powdery mildew
This common plant disease is caused by a fungus (*Sphaerotheca pannosa* var. *rosae*). It is one of the most widespread and serious diseases of rose. The powdery covering consists of fungal strands and spores. The spores are spread by the wind to healthy plants. The fungus saps the plant nutrients, causing distortion, discoloring, and often death of the leaves and canes. Powdery mildew may occur on roses any time during the growing season when rainfall is low or absent, temperatures are between 70° and 80°F, nighttime relative humidity is high, and daytime relative humidity is low. In areas where there is high rainfall in spring and summer, control may not be needed until the drier months of late summer. Rose varieties differ in their susceptibility to powdery mildew. For a list of roses tolerant of and susceptible to powdery mildew, see page 993.

SOLUTION: Apply ORTHO Funginex Rose Disease Control or ORTHO Orthenex Insect & Disease Control at the first sign of mildew. Repeat the spray at intervals of 7 to 10 days if mildew reappears. Rake up and destroy leaves in the fall.

PROBLEM: Yellow to brown spots, up to ¼ inch in diameter, appear on the upper surfaces of the leaves, starting in the spring or late fall. The lower leaves are affected first. On the undersides of the leaves are spots or blotches containing a red, orange, or black powdery material that can be scraped off. Infected leaves may become twisted and dry, and drop off the plant, or they may remain attached. Twigs may also be infected. Severely infected plants lack vigor.

ANALYSIS: Rust
Rose rust is caused by any of several species of fungi (*Phragmidium* species) that infest only rose plants. The orange fungal spores are spread by wind to rose leaves. With moisture (rain, dew, or fog) and moderate temperatures (55° to 75°F), the spores enter the tissue on the undersides of the leaves. Spots develop directly above, on the upper surfaces. Rose varieties differ in their susceptiblity to rust. For a list of roses that are tolerant of and susceptible to rust, see page 993. In the fall, black spores develop in the spots. These spores can survive the winter on dead leaves. In spring, the fungus produces the spores that cause new infections. Rust may also infect and damage young twigs.

SOLUTION: At the first sign of rust, spray with ORTHO Funginex Rose Disease Control or ORTHO Orthenex Insect & Disease Control. Repeat at intervals of 7 to 14 days for as long as conditions remain favorable for infection. Rake up and destroy infected leaves in the fall. Prune off infected twigs. Apply ORTHO Orthorix Spray as a dormant application.

589

ROSA (ROSE) — LEAVES MOTTLED

Spider mite damage.

Damaged leaf. *Insert:* Leafhopper (twice life size).

Rose midge damage.

PROBLEM: Leaves are stippled, bronzed, and dirty. There may be a silken webbing on the lower surfaces of the leaves or on the new growth. Infested leaves often turn brown, curl, and drop off. New leaves may be distorted. Plants are usually weak and appear unthrifty. To determine if the plant is infested with mites, hold a sheet of white paper underneath an affected leaf and tap the leaf sharply. Minute green, red, or yellow specks the size of pepper grains will drop to the paper and begin to crawl around. The pests are easily seen against the white background.

ANALYSIS: Spider mites
These mites, related to spiders, are major pests of many garden and greenhouse plants. They cause damage by sucking sap from the undersides of the leaves. As a result of feeding, the green leaf pigment disappears, producing the stippled appearance. Many leaves may drop off. Severely infested plants produce few flowers. Mites are active throughout the growing season, but are favored by hot, dry weather (70°F and up). By midsummer, they build up to tremendous numbers.

SOLUTION: Spray with ORTHO Orthenex Insect & Disease Control or ORTHO Isotox Insect Killer when damage is first noticed. Cover the undersides of the leaves thoroughly. Repeat the application 2 more times at intervals of 7 to 10 days.

PROBLEM: Whitish insects, up to ½ inch long, hop and fly away quickly when the plant is touched. The leaves are stippled white. Severely infested plants may be killed.

ANALYSIS: Rose leafhopper
(*Edwardsiana rosae*)
The rose leafhopper is a serious pest of roses and apples, and infests a number of ornamental trees as well. It spends the winter as an egg, usually in pimplelike spots on rose canes or on apple bark. When the weather warms in the spring, the young leafhoppers emerge and settle on the undersides of the leaves. They feed by sucking out the plant sap, which causes the stippling of the leaves. The insects mature, and the females produce a second generation of leafhoppers. Eggs may be deposited in the leaf veins or leaf stems of the rose; or the leafhopper may fly to another woody plant to lay her eggs. This second generation of leafhoppers feeds until fall. The damage caused by their feeding on the leaves, and by egg-laying in the rose canes, may kill the plant.

SOLUTION: Spray with ORTHO Isotox Insect Killer or ORTHO Orthenex Insect & Disease Control, or dust with ORTHO Rose & Floral Dust when damage is first noticed. Cover the lower surfaces of the leaves thoroughly. Repeat the spray if the plant becomes reinfested.

PROBLEM: The buds are deformed, or black and crisp, and the stem tips are dead. Tiny whitish maggots may be seen feeding at the base of buds or on the stem tips.

ANALYSIS: Rose midge
(*Dasineura rhodophaga*)
The rose midge is the larva of a tiny (¹⁄₂₀ inch) yellowish fly that appears in mid or late summer. The females lay their eggs in the growing tips, flower buds, and unfolding leaves, often 20 or 30 eggs to a bud. The eggs hatch in about 2 days and the maggots feed, causing the tissue and buds to become distorted and blackened. When mature, the larvae drop to the ground to pupate. New adults appear in 5 to 7 days to lay more eggs. When infestations are severe, most or all of the buds and new shoots in an entire rose garden are killed.

SOLUTION: Cut out and destroy infested stem tips and buds, and spray with ORTHO Orthene Systemic Insect Control. Repeat the spray if the plant becomes reinfested.

INSECTS

Virus disease.

Rose aphids (life size).

Rolled leaves.

PROBLEM: Yellow or brown rings, or yellow splotches of various sizes, appear on the leaves. The uninfected portions remain dark green. New leaves may be puckered and curling; flower buds may be malformed. Sometimes there are brown rings on the canes. The plants are usually stunted.

ANALYSIS: Mosaic and streak viruses
A number of viruses infect roses. The viruses are transmitted when an infected plant is grafted or budded to a healthy one. This generally occurs in the nursery where the plant was grown. Some plants may show symptoms in only a few leaves. However, the virus is throughout the plant, and further symptoms may appear later. Most rose viruses are fairly harmless unless there is extensive yellowing or browning. The virus suppresses the development of the green pigment (chlorophyll), causing the splotches or rings. Food production is reduced, which may result in stunted plant growth.

SOLUTION: No cure is available for virus-infected plants. There is little natural spread of rose viruses; therefore only weak plants need to be removed. When purchasing rose bushes, buy only healthy plants from a reputable dealer. For further information on selecting healthy plants, see page 916.

PROBLEM: Tiny (⅛ inch) green or pink soft-bodied insects cluster on leaves, stems, and developing buds. When insects are numerous, flower buds are usually deformed and may fail to open properly. A shiny, sticky substance often coats the leaves. A black sooty mold may grow on the sticky substance. Ants may be present.

ANALYSIS: Rose aphid
(*Macrosiphum rosae*)
Rose aphids do little damage in small numbers. Plants can tolerate fairly high populations without much effect. However, the aphids are extremely prolific, and populations can rapidly build up to damaging numbers during the growing season. Damage occurs when the aphid sucks the juices from the rose stems and buds. The aphid is unable to digest fully all the sugar in the plant sap and excretes the excess in a fluid called honeydew, which often drops onto the leaves below. A sooty mold fungus may develop on the honeydew, causing the rose plants to appear black and dirty. Ants feed on the sticky substance, and are often present where there is an aphid infestation. When aphid populations are high, flower quality and quantity are reduced.

SOLUTION: Spray with ORTHO Isotox Insect Killer, ORTHO Orthenex Insect & Disease Control, or ORTHO Orthene Systemic Insect Control, or dust with ORTHO Rose & Floral Dust when clusters of aphids are noticed. Repeat the spray if the plant becomes reinfested.

PROBLEM: Leaves are rolled, usually lengthwise, and tied together with webbing. The rolled leaves are chewed and the plant may be defoliated. When a rolled leaf is opened, a green caterpillar, ½ to ¾ inch long may be found inside, surrounded by silky webbing. Flower buds also may be chewed.

ANALYSIS: Leafrollers
Several different leafrollers feed on rose leaves and buds. They may also feed on many other plants in the garden. Leafrollers are the larvae of small (up to ¾ inch) brownish moths. The larvae feed on the young foliage in the spring, sometimes tunneling into and mining the leaf first. They roll one to several leaves around themselves, tying the leaves together with silken webbing. The leafrollers feed very little once the leaves are rolled. The rolled leaves provide protection from weather, parasites, and chemical sprays. Some leafrollers mature in summer and have several generations during the growing season. Other leafrollers have only one generation a year.

SOLUTION: Spray with ORTHO Isotox Insect Killer or ORTHO Orthene Systemic Insect Control in the spring when leaf damage is first noticed. For the insecticide to be most effective, it should be applied before the larvae are protected inside the rolled leaves. Check the plant periodically in spring for the first sign of an infestation.

ROSA (ROSE) — INSECTS

Leafcutter bee damage.

Caterpillar (life size).

Io caterpillar (life size).

PROBLEM: Small, precise ovals or circles are cut from the leaves. Rose twigs with broken or cut ends may die back for several inches. Hairy, black or metallic blue, green, or purple bees are sometimes seen flying around the plant.

ANALYSIS: Leafcutter bees
(*Megachile* species)
The leafcutter bees are important pollinators of plants such as alfalfa, clover, and forage crops. The females cut circular pieces of leaf tissue from rose plants to line their nests and plug their egg cells. The nests are made in dead twigs and in the ends of rose stems or other plant stems that have been cut. Damage to rose plants is minor. However, tunneled stems containing eggs may die back for several inches.

SOLUTION: Cut out infested, dying stems. To prevent egg-laying in stems, push carpet tacks into the ends of all cut stems after pruning. Since leafcutter bees are pollinators, no chemical controls should be used.

PROBLEM: Holes appear in the leaves and buds. Leaves, buds, and flowers may be entirely chewed off. Worms or caterpillars are feeding on the plants.

ANALYSIS: Caterpillars
Many species of these moth or butterfly larvae feed on roses and other garden plants. The adult moths or butterflies of most species start to lay their eggs on garden plants with the onset of warm spring weather. The larvae that emerge from these eggs feed on the leaves, flowers, and buds for 2 to 6 weeks, then pupate in cocoons attached to leaves or structures, or buried in the soil. The adult moths and butterflies emerge the following spring.

SOLUTION: Spray infested plants with ORTHO Household Insect Control, ORTHO Orthene Systemic Insect Control, or ORTHO Liquid Sevin according to label directions. You may also control caterpillars with a spray containing *Bacillus thuringiensis*. This bacterial insecticide is most effective while the caterpillars are small.

PROBLEM: Round or irregular holes appear in the leaves and buds. Leaves, buds, and flowers may be entirely chewed off. Two-inch, greenish caterpillars covered with short green spines and with a red and white stripe running the length of the body are found on the plants. Caterpillars are most active at night, and can occur in large numbers.

ANALYSIS: Io caterpillar
(*Automeris io*)
This caterpillar is the larva of a 3-inch, yellowish brown moth that lays its eggs on the rose leaves. After hatching, caterpillars eat leaves and flowers, and develop into adults within a few weeks. Several generations of caterpillars are produced each year, primarily between early spring and late fall. Their spines give a painful sting.

SOLUTION: Spray infested plants with ORTHO Isotox Insect Killer or the bacterial insecticide *Bacillus thuringiensis*. If additional caterpillars are found, allow at least 7 days to pass between spray applications.

Roseslug (life size).

Japanese beetle (life size).

Rose scale (life size).

PROBLEM: The upper or lower surfaces of the leaves are eaten between the veins, leaving a lacy, translucent layer of tissue that turns brown. Later, large holes or the entire leaf, except the main vein, may be chewed. Pale green to metallic green sluglike worms, up to ¾ inch long, with large brown heads, may be found feeding on the leaves. Some have hairs covering their bodies, and others appear wet and slimy.

ANALYSIS: Roseslugs
Roseslugs are the larvae of black and yellow wasps called *sawflies*. The adult flies appear in spring. They lay their eggs between the upper and lower surfaces of the leaves along the leaf edges, with a sawlike egg-laying organ. Depending on the species of roseslug, some of the larvae that emerge exude a slimy substance, giving them a sluglike appearance. Others are hairy. The roseslugs begin feeding on one surface of the leaf tissue, skeletonizing it. Later, several species of these slugs chew holes in the leaf or devour it entirely. When they are mature, the larvae drop to the ground, burrow into the soil, and construct cells in which to pass the winter. Some roseslugs pupate, emerge, and repeat the cycle 2 to 6 times during the growing season. Severely infested roses may be greatly weakened, and produce fewer blooms.

SOLUTION: Dust with ORTHO Rose & Floral Dust or spray with ORTHO Liquid Sevin when damage is first noticed.

PROBLEM: Holes appear in the flowers and flower buds; open flowers may be entirely eaten. Affected buds often fail to open, or they open deformed. The stem tips may be chewed, or the leaves may be notched or riddled with holes. Red, green spotted, brownish, or metallic green beetles up to ½ inch long are sometimes seen on the flowers or foliage.

ANALYSIS: Beetles
A number of different beetles infest roses. They may destroy the ornamental value of the plant by seriously damaging the flowers and foliage. The insects usually spend the winter as larvae in the soil or as adults in plant debris on the ground. In late spring or summer, mature beetles fly to roses and feed on the flowers, buds, and sometimes the leaves. Punctured flower buds usually fail to open, and open flowers are often devoured. Many beetles feed at night, so their damage may be all that is noticed. The female beetles lay their eggs in the soil or in the flowers in late summer or fall. The emerging larvae crawl down into the soil to spend the winter, or mature and pass the winter as adults. The larvae of some beetles feed on plant roots before maturing in fall or spring.

SOLUTION: Spray with ORTHO Gypsy Moth & Japanese Beetle Killer, ORTHO Isotox Insect Killer or ORTHO Liquid Sevin, or dust with the combination insecticide-fungicide ORTHO Rose & Floral Dust.

PROBLEM: Stems and leaves are covered with white, cottony masses, or brown or black crusty bumps, or clusters or somewhat flattened white, yellowish, or brown scaly bumps. The bumps can be scraped or picked off. Leaves turn yellow and may drop. In some cases, a shiny, sticky substance coats the leaves. A black sooty mold often grows on the sticky substance. Stems are killed by heavy infestations.

ANALYSIS: Scales
Many different types of scale insects infest roses. They lay their eggs on the leaves or canes, and in spring to midsummer the young scales, called *crawlers*, settle on the leaves and twigs. These small (1/10 inch), soft-bodied young feed by sucking sap from the plant. The legs usually atrophy and with some types, a shell develops over the body. The types of scale that do not develop shells are very conspicuous. The females of the cottony cushion scale are covered with a white, cottony egg sac, containing up to 2500 eggs. Scales covered with a shell are less noticeable. The shell often blends in with the plant, and the eggs are inconspicuous beneath their covering. Some species of scales are unable to digest fully all the sugar in the plant sap, and excrete the excess in a fluid called honeydew.

SOLUTION: Control with ORTHO Isotox Insect Killer or ORTHO Orthene Systemic Insect Control when the young are active. Contact your local Cooperative Extension Office (see page 1011) to determine the best time to spray in your area. To control overwintering insects, spray with ORTHO Volck Oil in spring. For more information about scales, see page 878.

ROSA (ROSE) — BUMPS ON STEM ___ BRANCH DIES ___

Crown gall.

Stem cankers.

Verticillium wilt.

PROBLEM: Large, corky galls, up to several inches in diameter, appear at the base of the plant and on the stems and roots. The galls are rounded, with rough, irregular surfaces, and may be dark and cracked. Plants with numerous galls are weak; growth is slowed and leaves turn yellow. Branches or the entire plant may die back.

ANALYSIS: Crown gall
This plant disease is caused by a soil-inhabiting bacterium (*Agrobacterium tumefaciens*) that infects many ornamentals and fruits in the garden. The bacteria are spread with the soil and contaminated pruning tools, and are often brought to a garden initially on the roots of an infected plant. The bacteria enter the shrub through wounds in the roots or the base of the stem. They produce a compound that stimulates rapid cell growth in the plant, causing gall formation on the roots, crown, and sometimes the branches. The galls disrupt the flow of water and nutrients up the roots and stems, weakening and stunting the top of the plant. Galls do not usually cause the death of the shrub.

SOLUTION: Crown gall cannot be eliminated from the shrub. However, infected plants may survive for many years. To improve the appearance of the plant, prune out and destroy galled stems. Sterilize pruning shears after each cut with rubbing alcohol. Destroy severely infected shrubs. The bacteria will remain in the soil for 2 to 3 years. If you wish to replace the shrub soon, plant resistant species. For a list of plants resistant to crown gall, see page 998. For more information about crown gall, see page 860.

PROBLEM: Yellowish, reddish, or brown sunken areas develop on the canes. The sunken areas may have a purple margin, or they may be cracked. The leaves on affected canes are sometimes spotted, yellow, or wilting. Stems may die back.

ANALYSIS: Stem cankers and dieback
A number of different fungi cause stem cankers on roses. During wet or humid weather the fungi enter the plant at a wound caused by the thorns, or at a cut stem. A sunken canker develops and expands through the tissue in all directions. The fungus may cut off the flow of nutrients and water through the stem, causing the leaves to wilt or yellow, and twigs to die back. Rose plants that are infected with black spot (see page 589) or in a weakened condition are more susceptible to invasion by stem canker fungi.

SOLUTION: Cut out and destroy cankered canes at least 5 inches below the infected area. Sterilize pruning tools after each cut with rubbing alcohol. After pruning, spray the canes with a fungicide containing *lime sulfur*. Sprays aimed at controlling black spot will help control canker. Or spray with a fungicide containing *maneb, mancozeb, benlate, chlorothalonil,* or *folpet* starting in the spring. Repeat every 10 to 14 days for as long as the weather is wet or humid.

PROBLEM: The leaves on a branch turn yellow at the margins, then brown and dry. During hot weather, the leaves may wilt. New leaves may be stunted and yellowish. The infected plant may die slowly, branch by branch, over several seasons. Or the whole plant may wilt and die within a few months. Some plants may recover. Infected rose canes frequently turn purple at the base. The tissue under the bark on dying canes shows dark streaks when cut. To examine for streaks, peel back the bark at the bottom of the dying branch.

ANALYSIS: Verticillium wilt
This wilt disease affects many ornamental trees and shrubs. It is caused by a soil-inhabiting fungus (*Verticillium* species) that persists indefinitely on plant debris or in the soil. The fungus is spread by contaminated seeds, plants, soil, equipment, and ground water. The fungus enters the rose plant through the roots and spreads up into the branches through the water-conducting vessels in the main stem. The vessels become discolored and plugged. This plugging cuts off the flow of water and nutrients to the branches, causing the leaf discoloration and wilting.

SOLUTION: No chemical control is available. Fertilize and water the affected plant to stimulate vigorous growth. Prune off all dead wood. Do not remove branches on which leaves have recently wilted. These branches may produce new leaves in 3 to 4 weeks. Remove dead shrubs. If replanting in the same area, plant trees and shrubs that are resistant to verticillium (see page 995). For more information about verticillium, see page 858.

SALIX (WILLOW)

Willow hornworm (half life size).

Leaf beetle larva (8 times life size).

SALIX (WILLOW)

ADAPTATION: Throughout the United States.

LIGHT: Full sun.

SOIL: Tolerates a wide variety of soils, including those that are wet. Roots are shallow, invasive, and fiercely competitive.

FERTILIZER: Fertilize with ORTHO Evergreen, Tree & Shrub Food 12–6–6 according to label directions.

WATER:

How much: Apply enough water to wet the soil 3 to 4 feet deep. To determine the proper amount of water for your soil type, see page 906.

How often: Willows require ample water. Water when the soil is moist but not wet 4 inches below the surface. For more information about watering, see page 906.

PRUNING: Willows are fast-growing, short-lived trees with brittle wood. Prune to maintain the shape and to remove dead or broken branches. If you wish to be able to walk under weeping willows, prune so that the lowest branches are at least 10 feet above the ground.

PROBLEM: The surface of the leaf is eaten, giving the remaining tissue a lacy appearance, or the whole leaf is chewed. Sometimes the leaves are webbed together. The tree may be completely defoliated. Damage appears any time between spring and fall. Caterpillars are clustered or feeding singly on the leaves. Repeated heavy infestations may weaken or kill trees.

ANALYSIS: Leaf-feeding caterpillars
Many different species of caterpillars feed on willow leaves wherever the trees are grown. Depending on the species, the moths lay their eggs any time between early spring and midsummer. The larvae that hatch from these eggs feed on buds, on one surface of the leaf (skeletonizers), or on the entire leaf. Certain caterpillars web the leaves together as they feed. In some years, damage is miminal due to unfavorable environmental conditions or control by predators and parasites. However, when conditions are favorable, entire trees may be defoliated by late summer. Defoliation weakens trees because there are no leaves left to produce food. When heavy infestations occur several years in a row, branches or entire trees may be killed.

SOLUTION: Spray with ORTHO Orthene Systemic Insect Control when damage is first noticed. Spray the leaves thoroughly. Repeat the spray if the tree becomes reinfested.

PROBLEM: Leaf tissue is eaten between the veins, giving the leaves a lacy appearance; or circular holes are chewed out of the leaves. The foliage may turn brown and dry. Twigs may die. With severe infestations, the tree may lose most of its leaves. Small blackish or white larvae, or brown, yellowish, or metallic green or blue beetles may be found feeding on the leaves.

ANALYSIS: Leaf beetles
A number of different beetles feed on willow leaves. In late spring or summer, the beetles fly to willow trees. Some feed on the willow leaves for a number of weeks, while others lay eggs soon after arriving. The females lay groups of eggs on the undersides of the leaves. The emerging larvae feed on the leaf tissue between the veins, or on one surface of the leaf.

SOLUTION: Spray valuable specimens with ORTHO Isotox Insect Killer or ORTHO Orthene Systemic Insect Control when damage is first noticed in spring. Repeat the spray if the tree becomes reinfested.

SALIX (WILLOW)

Giant bark aphids (twice life size).

Scurfy scale (life size).

Damaged stem. *Insert:* Adult (3 times life size).

PROBLEM: Small (¼ inch) black and beige soft-bodied insects with long black legs cluster on twigs and the undersides of limbs. They usually persist after leaf fall until freezing weather. Twigs may be completely covered with a mat of black eggs. When populations are large, twigs and branches die. A shiny, sticky substance may coat the limbs. A black sooty mold often grows on the sticky substance. Ants may be present.

ANALYSIS: Giant bark aphid
(*Longistigma caryae*)
The giant bark aphid is the largest species of aphid known. Because of its long legs, it appears much larger than its ¼ inch size. The aphids do little damage in small numbers. However, they are extremely prolific and populations can rapidly build up to damaging numbers during the late summer. When populations are large, black eggs are matted all over the bark of infested limbs. Damage occurs when the aphid sucks the juices from the twigs and branches. The aphid is unable to digest fully all the sugar in the sap, and excretes large quantities in a fluid called honeydew, which may coat plants and objects beneath the tree. A sooty mold fungus may develop on the honeydew, causing the bark to appear black and dirty. Ants feed on the sticky substances, and are often present where there is an aphid infestation. Several other species of aphids may also infest willow leaves and twigs.

SOLUTION: Spray with ORTHO Isotox Insect Killer or ORTHO Diazinon Insect Spray when aphids first appear. Spray the bark thoroughly. Repeat the spray if the tree becomes reinfested.

PROBLEM: Stems and leaves are covered with white, cottony masses or brownish, crusty bumps or clusters of somewhat flattened yellow, brown, gray, or white scaly bumps. The bumps can be scraped or picked off. Leaves turn yellow and may drop. In some cases a shiny, sticky substance coats the leaves. A black sooty mold often grows on the sticky substance. Branches are killed by heavy infestations.

ANALYSIS: Scales
Many different types of scale insects infest willow. They lay their eggs on leaves or bark. In spring to midsummer the young scales, called *crawlers,* settle on leaves and twigs. The small (1/10 inch), soft-bodied young feed by sucking sap from the plant. The legs usually atrophy and, with some types, a shell develops over the body. The types of scales that do not develop shells are very conspicuous. The females are covered with a white, cottony egg sac, containing up to 2500 eggs. Scales covered with a shell are less noticeable. The shell often blends in with the plant, and the eggs are inconspicuous beneath their covering. Some species of scales are unable to digest fully all the sugar in the plant sap, and excrete the excess in a fluid called honeydew. A sooty mold fungus may develop on the sticky substance, causing the willow leaves to appear black and dirty.

SOLUTION: Spray with ORTHO Isotox Insect Killer or ORTHO Orthene Systemic Insect Control when the young are active. Contact your local Cooperative Extension Office (see page 1011) to determine the best time to spray for scales in your area. For more information about scales, see page 878.

PROBLEM: Swollen areas with holes in their centers develop on twigs, branches, or the trunk. Many side shoots may grow from below the swellings, destroying the tree's natural form. The leaves on infested twigs and branches turn yellow and may be chewed on the edges. Sawdust and many broken twigs are often found beneath the tree.

ANALYSIS: Willow borers
(*Saperda* species)
At least five species of this beetle feed on willows, causing galls, or swollen areas, to form. The 1-inch, striped and spotted, brownish or gray beetles with long antennae appear in late spring or early summer. The females lay their eggs in small holes that they gnaw in the bark of twigs and branches that are more than ½ inch in diameter. The emerging legless, whitish grubs tunnel into the wood. Excess tissue accumulates around the wound, resulting in a gall. When infestations are severe, nearly all twigs and branches more than ½ inch in diameter have one or more galls. The galls weaken the twigs, causing them to break and litter the ground during stormy weather. The grubs remain in the wood 1 to 2 years before maturing into adults.

SOLUTION: Remove and destroy severely damaged trees. Spray the bark of less severely damaged trees with ORTHO Lindane Borer & Leaf Miner Spray in late May or early June. Repeat the spray 2 weeks later.

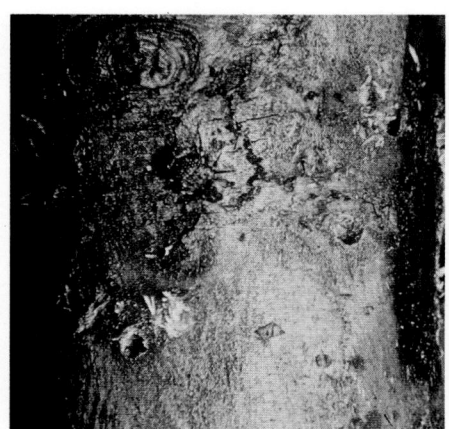

Mottled willow borer (half life size).

Dieback.

Slime flux.

PROBLEM: Leaves turn yellow and holes appear in the twigs. Large quantities of sawdust cling to the bark just below the holes. Sap often oozes from the holes. Young trees may be killed, and older trees may lose their natural form due to the production of numerous side shoots. Small (⅜ inch) black or dark brown weevils with pale yellow spots and long snouts may be seen around the tree from midsummer until fall.

ANALYSIS: Mottled willow borer (*Cryptorhynchus lapathi*)
All willows and most species of poplars may be attacked by this weevil, also called the *poplar and willow borer*. The adult weevils cause minor injury by chewing holes in the bark of twigs. The major damage is caused by the C-shaped larvae, which are white with brown heads. During mid to late summer, the larvae hatch from eggs laid in holes chewed by the female weevils. The larvae burrow into and feed on the inner bark. In the spring, large quantities of frass (sawdust and excrement) are expelled from the holes as the larvae tunnel into the center of the twigs to pupate. The feeding and tunneling cause branches to break easily and disrupt nutrient and water movement through the tree. The leaves turn yellow, and the tree often becomes bushy from the growth of numerous side shoots. The larvae pupate in June and emerge as adults in midsummer. Several other borers may also infest the trunk and branches of willows.

SOLUTION: Remove and destroy severely infested trees or branches before early summer. Spray the bark of trees with ORTHO Lindane Borer & Leaf Miner Spray in late July or early August.

PROBLEM: Dark sunken areas appear on the twigs, branches, or trunk.
Leaves on infected branches may be spotted, or they may be stunted and lighter green than normal. Twigs and branches are often killed. Young or less vigorous trees are most susceptible.

ANALYSIS: Canker and dieback
Several different fungi cause canker and dieback on willows. The fungi enter the tree through a wound or, in some cases, the leaves, killing the surrounding healthy tissue. A dark sunken canker develops in the wood. If the fungus infects the leaves first, it grows down through the leaf stems and forms cankers on twigs. The canker cuts off the flow of nutrients and water to the twigs or branch, causing the leaves to turn yellowish. Twig or branch dieback follows if the canker girdles the wood. The tree may stop the spreading canker by producing callus tissue, a rapid growth of barklike cells, to wall off the fungus. If the expanding canker is stopped before it covers half the diameter of the branch or trunk, the tree usually survives.

SOLUTION: Prune off twigs and small cankered branches, cutting at least 4 inches below the canker. Cankers on larger branches can be excised with a knife and chisel. Remove all discolored bark and wood, and a 1-inch border of apparently healthy bark around the wound. After each cut, sterilize the tools with rubbing alcohol. Remove and destroy severely infected trees. To prevent the development of new cankers, avoid wounding trees. Keep trees vigorous by fertilizing and watering (see pages 904 and 906).

PROBLEM: Sour-smelling sap oozes from wounds, cracks, and branch crotches, mainly during the growing season. The sap drips down the bark and dries, causing unsightly gray streaks. There may be some wilting on affected branches. Insects are attracted to the sour-smelling ooze.

ANALYSIS: Slime flux
Slime flux, also called *wetwood*, is caused by a bacterium (*Erwinia nimpressuralis*). The bacteria infect the heartwood, producing abnormally high sap pressure. This pressure is caused by bacterial fermentation, and forces the fermented sap, or flux, out of wounds, cracks, or crotches in the tree. Flux is especially copious when the tree is growing rapidly. Large areas of the bark may be coated with the smelly, bacteria-laden sap, which dries to a grayish-white color. In addition, wounds do not heal and the bark is unsightly. A tree with this problem is often under water stress, which may cause drought damage (wilting and scorched leaves) to the branches. The problem may persist for years.

SOLUTION: There are no chemical controls for this condition. Bore a slightly slanted drainage hole through the wood below each oozing wound. Insert a ½-inch-diameter plastic tube just until it stays firmly in place. If the tube penetrates the water-soaked wood inside the tree, it will interfere with drainage. The tube will carry the dripping sap away from the trunk. Disinfect tools with rubbing alcohol after pruning infected trees.

SARCOCOCCA

Sunburned foliage.

PROBLEM: During warm, sunny weather the leaves turn yellowish; or the center portions of the leaves bleach out to a tan color. Once the initial damage has occurred, the yellowing does not usually increase in size.

ANALYSIS: Sunburn
Sarcococca is a shade plant. It can't tolerate the heat of direct sunlight. Burning occurs on hot days if the shrub is exposed to direct sunlight or to sunlight reflected from a light-colored, south-facing wall. It takes only one hot day for damage to appear. The injury is unsightly but does not seriously injure the plant. However, weakened leaves are more susceptible to invasion by fungi and bacteria. Plants in dry soil are much more susceptible to sunscald.

SOLUTION: Move the injured plant to a shaded location; or provide shade where it is now planted. (For more information about transplanting, see page 916.) Once leaves are scalded they will not recover. Where practical, remove affected leaves.

Sarcococca cultural information
Light: Part shade to deep shade; sun in cool summer areas
Water: Keep the soil moist
Soil: Loose, rich, well drained, nonalkaline
Fertilizer: Medium

SASSAFRAS

Sassafras weevil damage.

PROBLEM: Holes appear in the leaves in spring; buds may also be eaten. Brown blotches develop at or near the leaf tips in early summer. Small ($\frac{1}{12}$ inch) black weevils with long snouts may be found feeding on the foliage in spring and midsummer.

ANALYSIS: Sassafras weevil
(*Odontopus calceatus*)
Both the larva and adult of the sassafras weevil, also called the *yellow poplar weevil* or *magnolia leafminer*, feed on sassafras leaves. The adults survive the winter in leaf litter beneath the plant. When the weather warms in early spring, the beetles fly to the trees and feed on the buds and developing leaves. In late spring, the females lay their eggs on the undersides of the leaves. The emerging white, legless larvae burrow into the leaf tips, between the upper and lower surfaces of the leaves, causing brown blotches to form. The larvae pupate inside the leaves and emerge as adults. The beetles feed, usually until July, and then drop to the ground to spend the winter. Japanese beetles may also seriously damage sassafras. For information on Japanese beetles, see page 873.

SOLUTION: Spray with an insecticide containing *carbaryl* when damage is first noticed in the spring.

Sassafras cultural information
Light: Full sun to part shade
Water: Keep the soil moist
Soil: Sandy, well drained
Fertilizer: Light

SCHEFFLERA

Leafminer trails.

PROBLEM: Light-colored, irregular, winding trails appear in the leaves. Some of the trails are filled with black matter. Severely infested leaves may die or drop prematurely. Infested leaves are usually discolored.

ANALYSIS: Leafminer
Most of the insects that cause this type of damage belong to the family of leaf-mining flies. The minute adult flies lay their eggs on the undersides of the leaves. The larvae (maggots) that emerge from these eggs penetrate the leaf, and live between the upper and lower surfaces. They feed on the inner leaf tissue, creating winding trails. Their dark excrement can dot or partially fill sections of the trails. The larvae generally emerge from the leaves to pupate. Leafminers cause damage continually from spring until fall. The last generation of maggots pupates in the soil or plant debris throughout the winter to emerge as adult flies the following spring.

SOLUTION: Apply ORTHO Isotox Insect Killer to infested plants according to label directions. Repeat sprayings as needed according to label directions. Remove and discard unsightly infested leaves.

SORBUS (MOUNTAIN ASH)

Alternaria leaf spot.

PROBLEM: Leaves have dark brown to black, water-soaked spots, often with a yellow halo. Spots range in size from a pinpoint to 2 inches or more, and may be found on branches and leaf stems as well as on leaves. Leaves drop off. Severely infected plants may lose many leaves.

ANALYSIS: Alternaria leaf spot
This leaf spot disease, caused by a fungus (*Alternaria* species), can be severe when plants are kept too moist. Alternaria fungus is found throughout the year, but is most prevalent during wet, warm weather. Once infected, plants rapidly develop symptoms. Spores from developing lesions are carried by the wind or splashing water to other parts of the plant or to nearby plants.

SOLUTION: Spray with a fungicide containing *manzate*. Repeat sprays at the intervals recommended on the label until no new spots are seen. Keep the leaves as dry as possible to reduce the danger of infection.

Schefflera cultural information
Light: Full sun to part shade
Water: When the soil is almost dry
Soil: Tolerates many types
Fertilizer: Medium

SORBUS (MOUNTAIN ASH)

ADAPTATION: Zones 2 through 8. To determine your zone, see the map on page 1004.

FLOWERING TIME: White flowers in late spring. Bright orange-red berries develop in midsummer and usually last until the following spring.

LIGHT: Full sun to partial shade.

SOIL: Any good, well-drained garden soil.

FERTILIZER: Fertilize with ORTHO Evergreen, Tree & Shrub Food 12–6–6 according to label directions.

WATER:
How much: Apply enough water to wet the soil 2 to 3 feet deep. To determine the proper amount of water for your soil type, see page 906.
How often: Water when the soil is just barely moist 4 inches below the surface. For more information about watering, see page 906.

Fireblight.

PROBLEM: The blossoms and leaves of infected twigs suddenly wilt and turn black as if scorched by fire. The leaves curl and hang downward. The bark at the base of the blighted twig becomes water-soaked, then dark, sunken, and dry; cracks may develop at the edge of the sunken area. In warm, moist spring weather drops of brown ooze appear on the sunken bark. Young trees may die.

ANALYSIS: Fireblight
This plant disease is caused by a bacterium (*Erwinia amylovora*) that is very destructive to many trees and shrubs. (For a list of susceptible plants, see page 1001.) The bacteria spend the winter in the sunken cankers on the branches. In the spring, the bacteria ooze out of the cankers. Bees, flies, and other insects are attracted to the sticky ooze and become smeared with it. When the insects visit a mountain ash flower for nectar, they infect it with the bacteria. The bacteria spread rapidly through the plant tissue in warm (65°F or higher), humid weather. Insects visiting these infected blossoms later carry bacteria-laden nectar to healthy blossoms. Rain, wind, and tools may also spread the bacteria. Tender or damaged leaves may be infected in midsummer.

SOLUTION: Prune out infected branches 12 to 15 inches beyond any visible discoloration and destroy them. Sterilize pruning shears with rubbing alcohol after each cut. A protective spray of a pesticide containing *basic copper sulfate* or *streptomycin*, applied before bud break in the spring, will help prevent infection. Repeat at intervals of 5 to 7 days until the end of bloom.

SORBUS (MOUNTAIN ASH)

Rust.

Pearleaf blister mite damage.

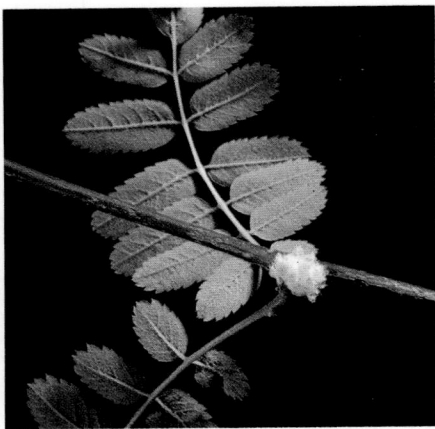

Woolly apple aphid (¼ life size).

PROBLEM: Light yellow, thickened, circular spots appear on the leaves in summer. Later in the season, orange cups develop on the lower surfaces of the leaves, directly below the thickened spots. Spotted leaves may drop.

ANALYSIS: Rust
This plant disease is caused by any of a number of different fungi (*Gymnosporangium* species). These fungi require both mountain ash and certain junipers or incense cedar to complete their life cycles. Rust spores on mountain ash cannot infect another mountain ash, but can infect only one of the evergreens. Wind-borne spores from the evergreen plant infect mountain ash in the spring. The spores germinate during warm, wet weather and infect the leaves, causing spotting. In late summer, spores are released during dry weather and carried by the wind back to the evergreen plant. Rust on junipers and incense cedar causes swellings, dieback, and excessive branching.

SOLUTION: Protect valuable specimens with a fungicide containing *ferbam* at the first sign of spotting. The spray will not eradicate the fungus on leaves that are already infected, but will protect uninfected leaves. Repeat the spray at weekly intervals throughout the spring. If possible, do not plant junipers or incense cedars within several hundred yards of mountain ash.

PROBLEM: Reddish or brownish blisters, ⅛ inch across, appear on the undersides of the leaves. The blisters may be massed together to nearly cover the leaf. The upper surface is mottled brown or blackish. Affected leaves may drop off, and berries may be deformed.

ANALYSIS: Pearleaf blister mite
(*Phytoptus pyri*)
This microscopic, elongated, pinkish or white mite is generally found throughout the country wherever mountain ash is grown. It also infests pear, apple, cotoneaster, and serviceberry. The adults spend the winter in bud scales, often hundreds in a single bud. As the buds swell in the spring, the mites lay their eggs. The young burrow into the undersides of unfolding leaves, forming blisters. New generations of mites are produced inside the blisters throughout the summer. As cold weather approaches, the mites migrate back to the buds to spend the winter.

SOLUTION: Once the mites have entered the undersides of the leaves, they are difficult to control. Spray the undersides of the leaves with *lime sulfur* or a *dormant oil spray* in late fall or early spring.

PROBLEM: Twigs, branches, and possibly the trunk are covered with white, cottony masses. Underneath the white masses are clusters of small (⅛ inch), purplish brown, soft-bodied insects. Leaves and twigs are yellowing, and the tree may be stunted. A sticky substance may coat the leaves, stems, and trunk. A black sooty mold may develop on the sticky substance.

ANALYSIS: Woolly aphids
(*Eriosoma* species)
Several species of woolly aphids attack mountain ash. They do little damage in small numbers. However, they are extremely prolific and populations can rapidly build up to damaging numbers during the growing season. Damage occurs when the woolly aphid sucks the juices from twigs, branches, or the trunk. It is unable to digest fully all the sugar in the plant sap and excretes the excess in a fluid called honeydew, which often drops onto the leaves below. A sooty mold fungus may develop on the sticky substance, causing the mountain ash leaves to appear black and dirty. The woolly apple aphid (*Eriosoma lanigerum*) may also cause damage by burrowing down into the soil and feeding on roots. This feeding causes marblelike knots to form, and results in stunted roots. The tree is weakened and growth is poor.

SOLUTION: Control with an insecticide containing *malathion* or *diazinon* when damage is first noticed. Aphids protected with the white, woolly material are more difficult to control. Spray the tree thoroughly. Repeat the spray if the tree becomes reinfested.

SPIRAEA ——— SYRINGA (LILAC) ———

Canker.

Spirea aphids (twice life size).

PROBLEM: Vertical cracks or sunken areas appear on the branches or trunk. The bark is discolored, and a liquid may ooze from the sunken areas. The leaves and twigs above these areas turn brown and die. Young trees, wounded trees, or trees of low vigor are most susceptible, and are usually killed.

ANALYSIS: Canker and dieback
Several different fungi cause canker and dieback on mountain ash. The fungi are spread by rain, wind, soil, tools, and equipment. They enter the tree through a wound, killing the surrounding healthy tissue. A sunken canker or crack develops as the fungi grow through the wood. Tree sap containing the fungus may ooze from the wound. The canker cuts off the flow of nutrients and water to the branch, causing the leaves to turn brown and the branch to die. This process may take several years. After one or more branches begin to turn brown, the tree usually dies within a year.

SOLUTION: The tree usually will not survive once the branches start dying, so it is best to remove and destroy the tree. Prevention is the only control. Avoid wounding trees. Do not use a lawn mower near the base of the tree. Keep the tree in optimum health by watering and fertilizing regularly (see pages 906 and 904), and by controlling insects, especially borers (see page 455).

PROBLEM: Tiny (⅛ inch), dark green, soft-bodied insects cluster on the flowers, undersides of the leaves, and young shoots. Leaves are curled, yellowing, and stunted, and growth of the plant is slowed. A shiny or sticky substance may coat the leaves. A black sooty mold often grows on the sticky substance.

ANALYSIS: Spirea aphid
(*Aphis spiraecola*)
These aphids do little damage in small numbers. However, they are extremely prolific in the early summer, and populations can rapidly build up to damaging numbers by late June. Damage occurs when the aphid sucks the juices from the spirea leaves. The aphid is unable to digest fully all the sugar in the plant sap and excretes the excess in a fluid called honeydew, which often drops onto the leaves below. A sooty mold fungus may develop on the honeydew, causing the spirea leaves to appear black and dirty.

SOLUTION: Control with ORTHO Isotox Insect Killer or ORTHO Orthene Systemic Insect Control when damage is first noticed. Spray the plant thoroughly. Repeat the spray if the plant becomes reinfested.

Spiraea cultural information
Light: Full sun to part shade
Water: Keep the soil moist
Soil: Tolerates many types
Fertilizer: Light

SYRINGA (LILAC)

ADAPTATION: Zones 3 through 7. (To determine your zone, see the map on page 1004.) Generally not adapted to warm climates, but some species grow in zones 8 and 9.

FLOWERING TIME: May or June.

LIGHT: Full sun.

SOIL: Any good garden soil high in organic matter with a neutral pH (approximately 6.5 to 8.0). For more information about pH, see page 902.

FERTILIZER: Fertilize with ORTHO General Purpose Plant Food 8-8-8 according to label directions. Add lime to acid soils (pH 4.5 to 5.5). For more information about adding lime to the soil, see page 1002.

WATER:
How much: Apply enough water to wet the soil 2 to 3 feet deep. To determine the proper amount of water for your soil type, see page 906.
How often: Water when the soil is barely moist 4 inches below the surface. For more information about watering, see page 906.

PRUNING: To shape young plants, pinch off growing tips. Remove dead flowers immediately after blooming and prune out dead and weak wood. To renew old plants, cut a few of the oldest stems to the ground each year after flowering; or cut the entire plant almost to the ground.

SYRINGA (LILAC)

Powdery mildew.

Bacterial blight.

Lilac leafminer damage.

PROBLEM: The leaves are covered with a thin layer or irregular patches of a grayish white powdery material. Infected leaves may turn yellow and drop off. New growth is often stunted. In late summer, tiny black dots (spore-producing bodies) are scattered over the white patches like ground pepper.

ANALYSIS: Powdery mildew
This common plant disease is caused by a fungus (*Microsphaera alni*) that thrives in both humid and dry weather. The powdery patches consist of fungal strands and spores. The fungus saps plant nutrients, causing yellowing and sometimes the death of the leaf. Since this mildew attacks many different kinds of trees and shrubs, the fungus from a diseased plant may infect other plants in the garden. For a list of susceptible species, see page 995.

SOLUTION: Spray plants with ORTHO Funginex Rose Disease Control when the plant shows the first sign of mildew. Cover the upper and lower surfaces of the leaves thoroughly. Repeat the treatment at intervals of 7 to 10 days until mildew disappears.

PROBLEM: Brown spots, surrounded by large areas of yellow, appear on the leaves in early spring. On older leaves, spots slowly increase in size during rainy periods. The leaves are usually distorted. Immature leaves turn black and die. Infected young stems bend over at the lesion, wither and die. Mature stems develop spots that enlarge along the length of the stem. The leaves die within the infected area. Flowers often become limp, turn dark brown, and die.

ANALYSIS: Bacterial blight
This plant disease is caused by a bacterium (*Pseudomonas syringae*) that may seriously damage lilacs during cool, wet weather. The bacteria overwinter in lilac buds, infected twigs and plant debris, and on other hosts. (For a list, see page 1000.) They are spread by wind, rain, and splashing water. The bacteria cause spots on leaves that are olive-green at first, later turning brown, surrounded by yellow. If wet weather persists, the bacteria spread through the tissue, forming blotches. Young plant parts are more severely affected. Leaves and young shoots blacken rapidly and die. Leaves die on older stems, usually only within the infected area. When the flowers open, they often become limp and blighted. White-flowered lilacs are usually most susceptible to bacterial blight.

SOLUTION: Prune out and destroy blighted shoots immediately, cutting well below the infected tissue. Sterilize pruning tools after each cut with rubbing alcohol. If the disease has been serious, spray with a fungicide containing *basic copper sulfate* early the following spring. Repeat the spray at intervals of 7 to 10 days for as long as the weather remains wet.

PROBLEM: Light green blotches appear on the leaves in early summer; the blotches turn brown and are often wrinkled. Later, the leaf tips are curled and tied together with silken webbing. The upper surfaces of the rolled leaves appear eaten. If a blotch is torn open, a tiny green worm may be found inside. The rolled leaf tips may contain a thin white cocoon or a pale yellow worm, up to 1/3 inch long. When an infestation is heavy, nearly every leaf turns brown, giving the plant a burned appearance.

ANALYSIS: Lilac leafminer
(*Caloptilia syringella*)
The lilac leafminer is the larva of a small brown moth that infests both lilac and privet. In late spring, moths emerge and deposit their eggs on the lower surfaces of the leaves. The emerging larvae enter the leaves and mine within the tissue between the upper and lower surfaces. Blotches, or mines, develop as the larvae increase in size. About the time the mines turn brown, the worms crawl to the leaf tips and curl the leaves around themselves. They feed for several weeks inside the leaves and then drop to the ground to pupate. The adults that emerge in late summer lay the eggs of a second generation, which survives the winter as pupae in plant litter.

SOLUTION: If the infestation is heavy, spray with ORTHO Isotox Insect Killer when green mines are first noticed (before the leaves are rolled), or when adults are laying eggs in June and August. If the infestation is light, pick off and destroy both mined and curled leaves. This should be done before the larvae drop to the ground to pupate.

TAXUS (YEW)

Scales (¼ life size).

Borer damage.

PROBLEM: The trunk and branches are covered with clusters of somewhat flattened grayish, brownish, or white scaly bumps that can be scraped or picked off; the undersides of the bumps are usually soft. Leaves are dwarfed and yellow, and may drop; plant growth is poor. Twigs and branches may die.

ANALYSIS: Scales
Several species of scales infest lilacs. They lay their eggs on the bark, and in early to late spring the young scales, called *crawlers*, settle on the trunk, branches, and twigs. The small (¹⁄₁₀ inch), soft-bodied young feed by sucking sap from the plant. The legs usually atrophy and a hard, crusty shell develops over the body. The mature female scales lay their eggs underneath their shell. In warmer climates, there may be several generations a year. An uncontrolled infestation of scales may kill the plant after 2 or 3 seasons.

SOLUTION: Spray with ORTHO Isotox Insect Killer or ORTHO Orthene Systemic Insect Control in early to late spring when the young are active. Spray the trunk and the branches thoroughly. Repeat the spray if the plant becomes reinfested. Early the following spring, spray the trunk and branches with ORTHO Volck Oil Spray to control the overwintering insects. For more information about scales, see page 878.

PROBLEM: Branch tips wilt in late summer, especially during warm, dry periods. Affected branches may die or break off. The stems near the ground are swollen and cracked. Sawdust is often found around holes in the stems and on the ground below infested stems.

ANALYSIS: Lilac borer
(*Podosesia syringae*)
The lilac borer is the larva of a 1-inch, brownish, clear-winged moth that resembles a wasp. Moths may be seen flying around the plant in late spring. The moths lay their eggs in cracks or bark wounds at the base of the stems. The cream-colored larvae bore into the wood and feed on the sapwood and heartwood. The stems become swollen and may break where the larvae are feeding. Their feeding also cuts off the flow of nutrients and water through the stems, causing the shoots to wilt and die. The larvae spend the winter in the stems. In the spring, they feed for a few weeks before maturing into moths. Several other borers may infest lilac.

SOLUTION: Before the moths emerge in the spring (April to May), cut out infested stems to ground level and destroy them. In late April, spray or paint the trunks and stems with ORTHO Lindane Borer & Leaf Miner Spray. Repeat the treatment 2 more times at intervals of 7 to 10 days. Borers can also be destroyed by injecting liquid insecticides into the holes with an oil can. Holes should then be plugged with putty or a caulking compound. Or kill borers by inserting a flexible wire into the borer hole in early summer.

TAXUS

ADAPTATION: Zones 4 through 8.

LIGHT: Sun or shade. Plant in shade in hot, dry climates and protect from wind.

SOIL: Any good, very well-drained garden soil. Plants will be stunted and sickly in heavy, wet soil.

FERTILIZER: Fertilize with ORTHO Evergreen, Tree & Shrub Food 12–6–6 according to label directions.

WATER:
How much: Apply enough water to wet the soil 2 to 3 feet deep. To determine the proper amount of water for your soil type, see page 906.
How often: Yews are drought tolerant once established, but they grow best in moist soil as long as it is well drained. Water when the soil is barely moist 3 to 6 inches below the surface. Hose the foliage frequently during the driest periods. For more information about watering, see page 906.

TAXUS (YEW)

Yew in poorly drained soil.

Root rot.

Needles notched by taxus weevils.

PROBLEM: Young leaves turn yellow. Eventually the entire plant may turn yellow, wilt, and die. The plant is growing in heavy, poorly drained, acid or alkaline soil.

ANALYSIS: Poor soil
Yews are particularly sensitive to improper growing conditions. When they are planted in soil that is heavy, poorly drained, very acid (between pH 4.5 and 5.5) or very alkaline (above pH 7.5), the plants do not usually survive. The bark on the roots decays and sloughs off, and the roots die. The roots can no longer supply sufficient amounts of nutrients and water to the leaves, resulting in leaf yellowing and wilting. The plant usually dies within several months.

SOLUTION: Improve the soil drainage (see page 901) or, if the plant is small, move it to an area with better drainage. Check the acidity of your soil (see page 903). If the pH is below 6.0, add ground limestone around the base of the plant. Add ORTHO Aluminum Sulfate to the soil if the pH is above 7.0. The optimum pH for yews is between 6.0 and 6.5. Do not water yews heavily.

PROBLEM: The young leaves are yellowish or off-color and wilting. Eventually the whole plant wilts and dies, even though the soil is sufficiently moist. Dead, brown leaves remain attached to the plant. The symptoms may develop over a few weeks, or may take many months. Heavy, poorly drained soil favors disease development. When cut, the tissue under the bark close to ground level shows a dark discoloration. To look for discoloration, peel back the bark at the bottom of the plant. There is usually a distinct margin between white, healthy wood and dark, diseased wood. If the plant is pulled up, examination of young roots reveals browning, decaying, and an absence of white rootlets. Healthy roots are firm and white.

ANALYSIS: Root rot
This plant disease is caused by a soil-inhabiting fungus (*Phytophthora cinnamomi*) that attacks more than 100 kinds of ornamental plants. The fungus is carried in plants, soil, or soil water. It enters the roots and works its way up the plant, blocking the upward flow of water and nutrients. Plants in overwatered or poorly drained soils are more susceptible to attack.

SOLUTION: No chemical control is available. Once the fungus becomes established in the soil, it will remain indefinitely. Remove diseased plants. Do not replant the same area with susceptible plants. (For a list of resistant trees and shrubs, see page 1000.) However, if replacement is necessary because the shrub is part of a hedge, remove as much soil as possible in the area where the old roots have penetrated and replace with light, clean soil before planting. Avoid overwatering.

PROBLEM: Needles turn yellow and often wilt in hot weather. The edges of some needles may be notched. The plant is growing poorly, and branches or the entire plant may die. To determine if the plant is infested with this insect, in mid to late June inspect the foliage after dark, using a flashlight. Black weevils, 3/8 inch long, with elephantlike snouts and rows of tiny round depressions on their backs, are feeding on the needle edges, especially near the trunk.

ANALYSIS: Taxus weevil
(*Otiorhynchus sulcatus*)
This root weevil, also known as the *black vine weevil*, is a serious pest of yews and many other plants in the garden. The weevil spends the winter either as an adult, in trash and weeds, or as a larva, on the roots of plants. The adult emerges from its hiding place in June. It feeds on the needle edges during the night, and hides during the day. Its feeding does not usually cause serious injury, but many notched needles usually indicates a high larval population on the roots. During the summer, the weevil lays eggs for a month or more. The white larvae feed on roots from midsummer until fall, and again in spring. When infestations are heavy, the plant no longer receives enough nutrients and water, and dies.

SOLUTION: Inspect the center of the plant every year for insects and recently notched needles (notched needles from a previous year may still be on the plant). To control the adults, spray the foliage and soil beneath the plant with ORTHO Isotox Insect Killer or ORTHO Orthene Systemic Insect Control, starting in mid-June. Repeat the spray 3 more times at intervals of 3 weeks.

TILIA (LINDEN)

TILIA (LINDEN)

ADAPTATION: Zones 4 through 10. (To determine your zone, see the map on page 1004.) Good street or lawn tree.

FLOWERING TIME: Summer.

LIGHT: Full sun.

SOIL: Tolerates a wide variety of soils, but grows best in deep, rich soils.

FERTILIZER: Fertilize with ORTHO Evergreen, Tree & Shrub Food 12–6–6 according to label directions.

WATER:
How much: Apply enough water to wet the soil 3 to 4 feet deep. To determine the proper amount of water for your soil type, see page 906.
How often: Lindens are somewhat drought tolerant, but they grow best in moist soils. Water when the soil is barely moist 4 inches below the surface. For more information about watering, see page 906.

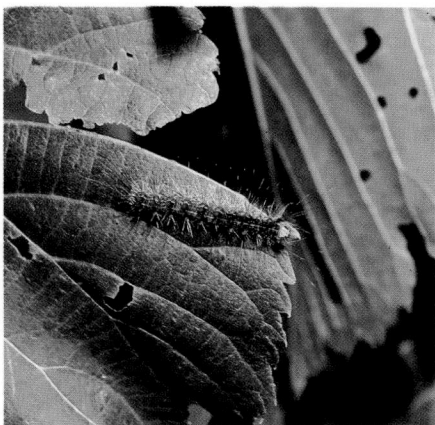

Gypsy moth caterpillars (half life size).

PROBLEM: The surface of the leaf is eaten, giving the remaining tissue a lacy appearance; or the whole leaf is chewed. Sometimes the leaves and branches are webbed. The tree may be completely defoliated. Damage appears any time between spring and fall. Caterpillars are clustered or feeding singly on the leaves. Repeated heavy infestations may weaken or kill trees.

ANALYSIS: Leaf-feeding caterpillars
Many different species of caterpillars feed on linden leaves wherever the trees are grown. Depending on the species, the moths lay their eggs in early spring to midsummer. The larvae that hatch from these eggs feed singly or in groups on buds, on one leaf surface (skeletonizers), or on the entire leaf. Certain caterpillars web the branches or leaves as they feed. In some years, damage is minimal due to unfavorable environmental conditions or control by predators and parasites. However, when conditions are favorable, entire trees may be defoliated by late summer. Defoliation weakens trees because there are no leaves left to produce food. When heavy infestations occur several years in a row, branches or entire trees may be killed.

SOLUTION: Spray with ORTHO Gypsy Moth & Japanese Beetle Killer or ORTHO Isotox Insect Killer when damage is first noticed. Spray the leaves thoroughly. Repeat the spray if the tree becomes reinfested.

Aphids (twice life size).

PROBLEM: Leaves are curling, discolored, and reduced in size. A shiny or sticky substance may coat the leaves. A black sooty mold often grows on the sticky substance. Tiny (1/8 inch), winged, green, soft-bodied insects with black stripes cluster on the leaves. Ants may be present.

ANALYSIS: Linden aphid
(*Myzocallis tiliae*)
Aphids do little damage in small numbers. However, they are extremely prolific and populations can rapidly build up to damaging numbers during the growing season. Damage occurs when the aphid sucks the juices from the linden leaves. The aphid is unable to digest fully all the sugar in the plant sap and excretes the excess in a fluid called honeydew, which often drops onto the leaves below. Plants or objects beneath the tree may also be coated with honeydew. A sooty mold fungus may develop on the sticky substance, causing the linden leaves to appear black and dirty. Ants feed on honeydew, and are often present where there is an aphid infestation.

SOLUTION: Spray with ORTHO Isotox Insect Killer when aphids appear. Direct the spray to the undersides of the leaves. Repeat the spray if the plant becomes reinfested.

TSUGA (HEMLOCK)

Sunscorch and drought injury.

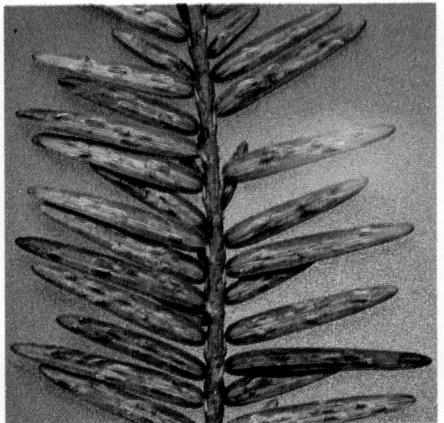

Fiorinia hemlock scale (life size).

Spruce spider mite damage.

PROBLEM: During hot weather (95°F and over), usually in July or August, the ends of the branches die. The top of the tree appears brown and scorched. Browning can develop whether the soil around the roots is moist or dry. During prolonged periods of drought, the tree may die.

ANALYSIS: Scorch
Hemlocks are very sensitive to hot weather, which scorches the needles. In hot weather, water evaporates rapidly from the needles. If the roots can't absorb and convey water fast enough to replenish this loss, the needles turn brown and the branch tips die. This usually occurs in dry soil, but needles can also scorch when the soil is moist and temperatures are near 100°F for extended periods. Hemlocks growing in shallow, rocky soil or on sites with southern exposure are especially susceptible to scorch, and sometimes the entire tree turns brown and dies.

SOLUTION: To prevent further scorch, water trees deeply during periods of hot weather and prolonged drought. Wet the entire root space. (For more information about watering trees, see page 906.) Newly transplanted trees should be watered whenever the rootball is dry 2 inches below the surface. There are no controls for scorch on trees in moist soil. Plant trees adapted to your climate.

PROBLEM: The stems and undersides of the needles are covered with thick, white, waxy bumps or clusters of somewhat flattened grayish, white, or brown scaly bumps. The bumps can be scraped or picked off; the undersides are usually soft. Needles turn yellow and may drop.

ANALYSIS: Scales
Several species of scales infest hemlock. They lay their eggs on the leaves or bark, and in spring to midsummer the young scales, called *crawlers*, settle on the needles and twigs. These small (¹⁄₁₀ inch), soft-bodied young feed by sucking sap from the plant. The legs usually atrophy and a hard crusty or waxy shell develops over the body. The mature female scales lay their eggs underneath their shell. An uncontrolled infestation of scales may kill branches after 2 or 3 seasons.

SOLUTION: Spray with ORTHO Isotox Insect Killer, ORTHO Orthene Systemic Insect Control, ORTHO Volck Oil Spray, or ORTHO Liquid Sevin when the young are active. Contact your local Cooperative Extension Office (see page 1011) to determine the best time to spray for scales in your area. The following spring, before new growth begins, spray the trunk and branches with a *dormant oil spray* to control the overwintering insects. For more information about scales, see page 878.

Tsuga cultural information
Light: Full sun to part shade
Water: Keep the soil moist
Soil: Loose, rich, deep, acid
Fertilizer: Light

PROBLEM: Needles are stippled, gray, and dirty. When the infestation is heavy, the tree may appear totally gray. There is usually a silken webbing between the needles. Young trees may die the first season; older trees die progressively from the lower branches upward, over a period of years. To determine if the plant is infested with mites, hold a sheet of white paper underneath an affected branch and tap the branch sharply. Minute dark green to black specks the size of pepper grains will drop to the paper and begin to crawl around. The pests are easily seen against the white background.

ANALYSIS: Spruce spider mite
(*Oligonychus ununguis*)
This mite is a major pest of conifers throughout the country. It attacks hemlocks, spruce, junipers, and several other trees. The mites cause damage by sucking sap from the needles. As a result of feeding, the green pigment disappears, producing the stippled appearance. The spruce spider mite is most prolific in cooler weather. It is active in the spring and fall. At the onset of hot weather (70°F and up), the mite goes dormant and usually has caused its maximum damage. Several other mites infest hemlock. The microscopic hemlock rust mite (*Nalepella tsugifoliae*) causes needles to turn bluish, then to yellow and drop off.

SOLUTION: Spray the needles thoroughly with ORTHO Orthene Insect Spray or ORTHO Malathion 50 Insect Spray when damage is first noticed. Repeat 2 more times at intervals of 7 to 10 days to kill young mites as they hatch. To control insects during the dormant season, apply ORTHO Volck Oil Spray.

ULMUS (ELM)

Dutch elm disease.

Diseased stem on left.

ULMUS (ELM)

ADAPTATION: Zones 3 to 10 (to determine your zone, see the map on page 1004). Not adapted to desert areas.

LIGHT: Full sun.

SOIL: Tolerates a wide variety of soils.

FERTILIZER: Fertilize with ORTHO Evergreen, Tree & Shrub Food 12–6–6 according to label directions.

WATER: Water during periods of extended drought. (For more information about watering, see page 906.)

PRUNING: Prune off dead wood and destroy or strip off the bark to eliminate breeding sites for elm beetles (see page 609), which transmit Dutch elm disease.

PROBLEM: Leaves wilt, curl, and turn yellow on one or more branches in the top of the tree; many leaves drop off. Trees may die slowly over a period of a year or longer. Or trees wilt and die within a few weeks, often in the spring soon after they have leafed out. Cross sections of infected branches may show a ring of brown dots in the wood, just underneath the bark. Small holes may be found in the bark of infected branches.

ANALYSIS: Dutch elm disease

Dutch elm disease is caused by a fungus (*Ceratocystis ulmi*) that invades and plugs the water-conducting vessels in the tree. The fungus enters the wood through feeding wounds made by elm bark beetles (see page 609). In the spring, the adult beetles emerge from holes in the bark of elm trees where they have spent the winter. If the trees are infected with the Dutch elm fungus, the beetles have sticky spores of the fungus on and inside their bodies. The beetles disperse to healthy elm trees, where they feed in crotches of small twigs, usually high in the tree, and deposit the fungus spores in the wounds. The fungus then spreads through the tree. The infected elm usually develops the disease that summer. The fungus produces a toxin that interferes with the water-conducting vessels in the wood, reducing the amount of water available to the leaves. The foliage on the infected branch wilts, turns yellow, and drops. Surrounding branches, and eventually the entire tree, become infected and the tree dies. When elms are closely planted (50 feet or less between trees), the fungus may spread through natural root grafts between trees. Trees infected through the roots generally wilt and die rapidly, often when growth begins in spring. These trees do not show browning in the wood when the branches are cut.

SOLUTION: Curing a tree of Dutch elm disease is usually not possible. Disease development may be delayed on lightly infected trees (less than 5 percent of the crown is infected) that were initially infected by bark beetles rather than by root grafts. Removal of early infections by tree surgery may save a tree for a number of years. Remove yellowing branches at least 10 feet below the point where brown streaks are visible in the wood. Sterilize pruning tools with rubbing alcohol after each cut. Spray the wound with an insecticide containing *methoxychlor*. Systemic fungicides (fungicides that are carried throughout the tree) injected into the tree by a trained arborist may increase the life span of a lightly infected tree. Contact an arborist when yellowing is first noticed. Prevention involves three different measures that should be carried out on a communitywide basis. (1) A good sanitation program will slow the spread of the fungus. Since bark beetles carrying the fungus breed in dead or dying elm wood, all dead or dying trees, damaged limbs, and prunings should be removed and burned or buried. The bark of all stumps should be peeled to just below ground level. (2) Controlling bark beetles with insecticides is practical only on valuable specimens, when used in conjunction with a sanitation program. Spray with an insecticide containing *methoxychlor* in early spring before leaves come out. Use high-pressure spray equipment, and cover the entire tree thoroughly. (3) To prevent transmission of the fungus through the roots of closely planted trees, grafted roots should be severed either by mechanical trenching or by soil injection of a chemical. This is especially important if there is a diseased tree nearby. Contact a professional arborist.

ULMUS (ELM)

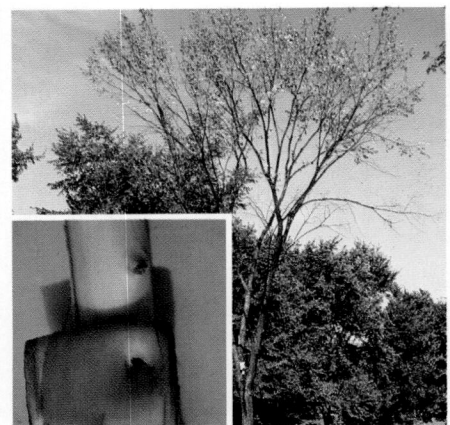

Phloem necrosis. *Insert:* Diseased stem.

Whitebanded elm leafhopper damage.

Woolly aphids (¼ life size).

PROBLEM: Leaves on the entire tree droop, curl, and turn bright yellow; eventually they turn brown and fall. Trees infected during spring or early summer may live over the winter, produce a thin crop of leaves, and die the next summer. Trees infected in midsummer may wilt and die within 3 to 4 weeks. If the bark on the roots or lower trunk is peeled back, the inner layers will be found to be a butterscotch color and will have a faint odor of wintergreen.

ANALYSIS: Phloem necrosis
This destructive plant disease of American elms is caused by mycoplasmas, microscopic organisms similar to bacteria. They are transmitted from tree to tree by leafhoppers. The organisms are introduced into plant sap as the leafhoppers feed on the undersides of the leaves. The nutrient-conducting vessels (phloem) are destroyed, first in the roots, then in the lower portions of the tree. The bark loosens and falls away, and the tree wilts. American elms may be attacked at any age.

SOLUTION: There is no cure for this disease. Infected trees should be removed and burned. To prevent phloem necrosis, control leafhoppers with ORTHO Isotox Insect Killer in late May or early June. A second application may be necessary if a flush of new growth occurs during July or August. For more information about controlling disease-carrying insects, see page 880.

PROBLEM: Leaves are stippled white, and small twigs may be killed. Grayish-brown insects up to ½ inch long hop and fly away quickly when the leaves are touched.

ANALYSIS: Whitebanded elm leafhopper (*Scaphoideus luteolus*)
Elm leafhoppers by themselves cause only minor damage to elms. However, they carry mycoplasmas (microscopic organisms similar to bacteria) within their bodies that cause the very serious disease *phloem necrosis.* The leafhoppers spend the winter as eggs in the bark of twigs. Slits made by the egg-laying organ of the female leafhopper may injure or kill twigs. When the weather warms in spring, the young leafhoppers emerge and settle on the undersides of the leaves. They suck the plant sap, causing stippling. The leafhoppers that are carrying phloem necrosis transmit it as they feed. Infected trees often die. Several other leafhoppers that infest elms may also transmit phloem necrosis.

SOLUTION: Control leafhoppers with ORTHO Isotox Insect Killer in late May or early June. A second application may be necessary if a flush of new growth occurs during July or August. Insects carrying the phloem necrosis organism are difficult to control because it takes only one to infect the tree. For more information about controlling disease-carrying insects, see page 880.

PROBLEM: Leaves are covered with white, cottony masses. Underneath the white masses are clusters of small (⅛ inch), purplish brown, soft-bodied insects. The leaves are curled, distorted, and yellowing, and the tree is often weak and growing poorly.

ANALYSIS: Woolly aphids (*Eriosoma* species)
Several species of woolly aphids attack elm throughout the country. When present in large numbers, they are both unsightly and severely damaging to the leaves. The aphids overwinter as eggs in bark crevices. The eggs hatch in spring as the elm leaves unfold. The aphids crawl to the undersides of the leaves to feed on plant sap. They cover themselves with a white, cottony mass as they feed. At the end of June, a generation of winged aphids may develop. They often leave the elm tree and fly to one of their summer hosts, such as apple, serviceberry, pyracantha, hawthorn, or mountain ash. In the fall, these aphids return to elms and lay the overwintering eggs.

SOLUTION: Spray with ORTHO Isotox Insect Killer when insects are first noticed in the spring. Cover the undersides of the leaves thoroughly. Repeat the spray 7 to 10 days later if damage continues.

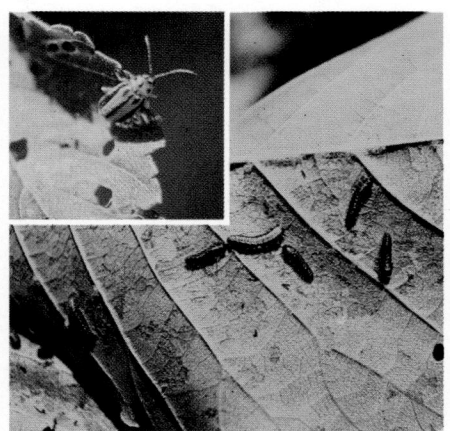

Larvae (¾ life size). *Insert:* Beetle (life size).

Galleries of elm bark beetles (¼ life size).

Elm bark scale (life size).

PROBLEM: The lower surface of the leaf is eaten between the veins, giving the leaves a lacy appearance. There may also be small holes in the leaves. Severely infested leaves turn brown; the entire tree may appear scorched. Many leaves drop off by midsummer. Small (½ inch) yellow and black insects, or ¼-inch yellowish green and black striped beetles, may be found on the undersides of the leaves.

ANALYSIS: Elm leaf beetle
(*Pyrrhalta luteola*)
All species of elm are attacked by the leaf beetle, but the beetles may have local preferences. The beetles spend the winter as adults in buildings or in protected places outside. In the fall, when the beetles are looking for shelter, they often become a nuisance inside homes. The adults fly back to elm trees in the spring. They eat small holes in the developing leaves, mate, and lay their eggs. The emerging black larvae feed on the lower surface of the leaf between the veins. As the larvae mature, they turn a dull yellow with black stripes. After feeding for several weeks, the larvae pupate. Bright yellow pupae may be seen around the base of the tree in late June or early July. Adults emerge, and there may be one or two more generations. Trees that lose many of their leaves early in the season may grow new ones, which also may be eaten.

SOLUTION: Spray with ORTHO Isotox Insect Killer, ORTHO Orthene Systemic Insect Control, or ORTHO Liquid Sevin when damage is first noticed. To prevent severe leaf damage, sprays should be applied just as the leaves grow to full size. Repeat the spray if the tree becomes reinfested.

PROBLEM: Small (⅛ inch), shiny, dark reddish brown beetles or dull brown beetles with a rough body surface may be found feeding in the crotches of twigs around the middle of May. The bark is chewed and appears rough. Small holes may be found in the bark of weak or dying trees.

ANALYSIS: Elm bark beetles
These bark beetles by themselves cause very little injury to elm trees. However, they can be extremely damaging because they often carry the destructive Dutch elm fungus (see page 607). The fungus is carried on the bodies of the beetles as they move from infected breeding sites. The shiny reddish brown European bark beetle is generally a more important carrier than the dull brown native species because it usually outnumbers the native beetles. Spore-bearing beetles infect a healthy tree with the fungus as they feed on small twigs. The beetles then seek breeding sites under the bark of weakened, dead, or recently cut elm trees up to several miles away. The female beetles tunnel galleries in the wood under the bark, where they lay their eggs. The white larvae mine the wood at right angles to the gallery, producing many radiating tunnels. If these dead or dying trees are infected with the Dutch elm fungus, the larvae become covered with fungal spores. They emerge as adults in the spring and fly to healthy trees. These trees then become infected with Dutch elm fungus, which spreads through the whole tree.

SOLUTION: For information about controlling bark beetles and preventive and control measures for Dutch elm disease, see page 607.

PROBLEM: The leaves, branches, or trunk are covered with white, cottony, cushionlike masses, or brownish or whitish crusty bumps. The bumps can be scraped or picked off. Leaves turn yellow and may drop. In some cases, a shiny or sticky substance coats the leaves. A black sooty mold often grows on the sticky substance. Branches are killed by heavy infestations.

ANALYSIS: Scales
Many different types of scales infest elm. They lay their eggs on leaves and bark, and in spring to midsummer the young scales, called *crawlers*, settle on leaves, twigs, and branches. These small (¹⁄₁₀ inch), soft-bodied young feed by sucking sap from the plant. The legs usually atrophy and, with some types, a shell develops over the body. The types of scale that do not develop shells are very conspicuous. The females are covered with a white, cottony egg sac, containing up to 2500 eggs. Scales covered with a shell may be less noticeable. The shell often blends in with the plant, and the eggs are inconspicuous beneath their covering. Some species of scales are unable to digest fully all the sugar in the plant sap, and excrete the excess in a fluid called honeydew. A sooty mold fungus may develop on the honeydew, causing the elm leaves to appear black and dirty.

SOLUTION: Spray with ORTHO Orthene Systemic Insect Control, ORTHO Volck Oil Spray, or ORTHO Liquid Sevin when the young are active. Contact your local Cooperative Extension Office (see page 1011) for the best time to spray for scales in your area. Control scales during the dormant season with ORTHO Volck Oil Spray. For more information about scales, see page 878.

ULMUS (ELM)

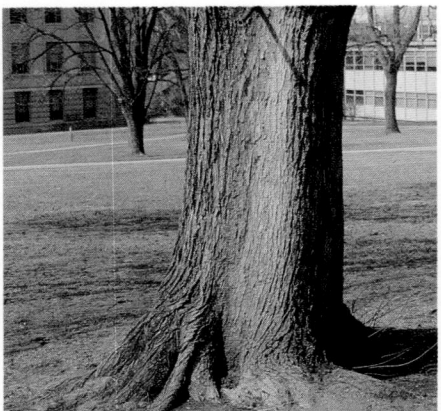

Slime flux.

PROBLEM: Sour-smelling sap oozes from wounds, cracks, and branch crotches, mainly during the growing season. The sap drips down the bark and dries, causing unsightly gray streaks. There may be some wilting on affected branches. Insects are attracted to the sour-smelling ooze.

ANALYSIS: Slime flux
Slime flux of elms, also called *wetwood*, is caused by a bacterium (*Erwinia nimipressuralis*). The bacteria infect the heartwood, producing abnormally high sap pressure. This pressure is caused by bacterial fermentation, and forces the fermented sap, or flux, out of wounds, cracks, or crotches in the tree. Flux is especially copious when the tree is growing rapidly. Large areas of the bark may be coated with the smelly, bacteria-laden sap, which dries to a grayish-white color. In addition, wounds do not heal and the bark is unsightly. A tree with this problem is often under water stress, which may cause drought damage (wilting and scorched leaves) to the branches. The problem may persist for years.

SOLUTION: There are no chemical controls for this condition. Bore a slightly slanted drainage hole through the wood below each oozing wound. Insert a ½-inch-diameter plastic tube just until it stays firmly in place. If the tube penetrates the water-soaked wood inside the tree, it will interfere with drainage. The tube will carry the dripping sap away from the trunk. Disinfect tools with rubbing alcohol after pruning infected trees.

VIBURNUM

Aphids (life size).

PROBLEM: Tiny (⅛ inch), ash-gray, reddish brown, or dark green soft-bodied insects cluster on the leaves and stem tips. Leaves are discolored, and may be extremely curled and distorted. Leaves sometimes drop off. A shiny or sticky substance may coat the leaves. A black sooty mold often grows on the sticky substance.

ANALYSIS: Aphids
Several different kinds of aphids infest viburnum. They do little damage in small numbers. However, they are extremely prolific and populations can rapidly build up to damaging numbers during the growing season. Damage occurs when the aphid sucks the juices from the viburnum leaves. The aphid is unable to digest fully all the sugar in the plant sap and excretes the excess in a fluid called honeydew, which often drops onto the leaves below. A sooty mold fungus may develop on the honeydew, causing the viburnum leaves to appear black and dirty. The ash-gray snowball aphid (*Neoceruraphis viburnicola*) causes severe curling and distortion of the leaves and leaf stems of the snowball viburnum (*Viburnum opulus*). Other species of viburnum are usually immune. The other species of aphids that infest viburnum do not cause leaf curling.

SOLUTION: Spray with ORTHO Isotox Insect Killer or ORTHO Orthene Systemic Insect Control when aphids first appear. Direct the spray to the undersides of the leaves. Repeat the spray if the plant becomes reinfested.

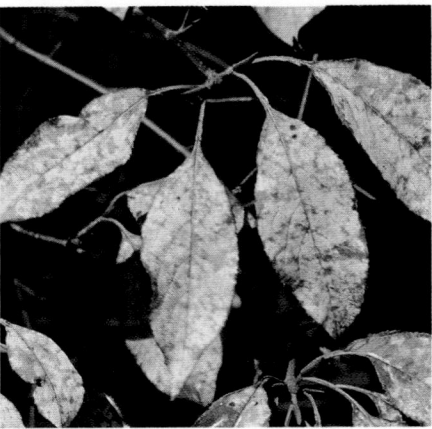

Powdery mildew.

PROBLEM: Leaves are covered with a thin layer or irregular patches of a grayish white powdery material. Infected leaves may turn yellow and drop. In late fall, tiny black dots (spore-producing bodies) are scattered over the white patches like ground pepper.

ANALYSIS: Powdery mildew
This common plant disease is caused by a fungus (*Microsphaera alni*) that thrives in both humid and dry weather. Plants growing in shady areas are often severely infected in the fall. The powdery patches consist of fungal strands and spores. The spores are spread by the wind to healthy plants. The fungus saps the plant nutrients, causing yellowing and sometimes death of the leaf. Since this powdery mildew attacks many different kinds of woody plants, the fungus from a diseased plant may infect other woody plants in the garden. (For a list of susceptible plants, see page 995.)

SOLUTION: Spray the surfaces of the leaves with a fungicide containing *benomyl* or *dinocap* when the plants show the first sign of mildew. Repeat the spray at intervals of 7 to 10 days until mildew disappears.

Viburnum cultural information
Light: Full sun or part shade
Water: When soil is moist but not wet
Soil: Heavy loam
Fertilizer: Heavy

WISTERIA

WISTERIA

ADAPTATION: Throughout the United States (protect in zones below zone 5). To determine your zone, see the map on page 1004.

FLOWERING TIME: April and May.

LIGHT: Full sun to partial shade (Japanese wisteria blooms best in full sun).

SOIL: Any good, well-drained garden soil.

FERTILIZER: Fertilize with ORTHO General Purpose Plant Food 8–8–8 according to label directions.

WATER:
How much: Apply enough water to wet the soil 2 to 3 feet deep. To determine the proper amount of water for your soil type, see page 906.
How often: Young wisteria needs ample water. Water when the soil is moist but not wet 4 inches below the surface. Established plants flower best with less water. Water established plants when the soil is barely moist 4 inches below the surface. For more information about watering, see page 906.

PRUNING: Establish a framework on newly planted wisterias. Pinch off long streamers and rub off buds that develop on the trunk. Prune older plants during the dormant season. Thin out or cut back side shoots and shorten the flower-producing spurs (short shoots containing fat flower buds that grow from the side shoots) to 2 or 3 buds. In the summer, cut back some of the streamers.

Failure to bloom.

PROBLEM: No flowers appear in the spring, but the vine is healthy and vigorous.

ANALYSIS: Not blooming
Most wisterias purchased from nurseries bloom well after 2 or 3 years. These plants are usually asexually propagated (plants started from cuttings or by some method other than from seed). Vines started from seed often do not bloom for 10 to 15 years or longer. Wisterias also may fail to bloom because of improper growing conditions, poor pruning practices, or freeze damage. Young plants should be well fed and watered. Plants old enough to bloom flower best with less food and water. Too much nitrogen fertilizer during the growing season causes lush, overly vigorous, green growth and poor flower bud production (flower buds for next season's bloom are produced in early summer). Heavy pruning also may produce lush, overly vigorous growth, or flower buds may be mistakenly removed.

SOLUTION: Do not grow wisteria from seed. Buy nursery-grown vines. If your old wisteria did not bloom in spring and is lush and growing vigorously, do not use nitrogen fertilizer for an entire season. Fertilize in early summer with ORTHO Bloom Builder 0–10–10 to promote flower bud formation for next season. Prune back vigorous shoots in summer. In winter, cut back or thin out side shoots from the main stems. Spurs (short fat stems bearing flower buds) develop on these side shoots. Cut back spurs to 2 to 3 buds. Do not drastically prune the side shoots. Drastic pruning will eliminate all the spurs so no flowers are produced.

Bird injury.

PROBLEM: Flower buds disappear from the clusters. This becomes most noticeable when the remaining buds open; long, bare stalks protrude from the plant, with blossoms only at the base. Birds may be seen around the plant.

ANALYSIS: Birds
Birds are pests of many berries and soft, sweet fruits in the garden. Some birds also feed on blossoms, especially when other food is limited. In early spring, when wisteria flowers are developing, birds may devour many of the buds, leaving long bare stalks. The damage does not harm the plant, but flowering may be drastically reduced.

SOLUTION: Once most of the buds have disappeared, there is nothing you can do. If you notice birds around the plant before many buds have been eaten, protect the vines with netting. For more information about bird control, see page 893.

Some of the problems common to all fruit and nut trees are listed on the next 12 pages. If you don't find your problem there, look up your specific fruit or nut tree in the index below. Several problems that occur in all trees may also be found in the section discussing problems common to trees, shrubs, and vines, on page 440.

FRUIT AND NUT TREES

Although fruit and nut trees are increasingly valued for their ornamental contribution to the landscape, they are primarily raised for food. The measure of success with these trees lies in the quality and quantity of their fruit. And, since the production of fruit and nuts takes energy over and above the energy needed for simple growth, fruit and nut trees are seldom satisfactory if they just barely survive.

The production of large crops of tasty fruit or nuts requires more time and skill than does the successful raising of ornamentals, or even vegetables. In addition to the soil preparation, regular feeding, and watering that most garden plants require to flourish, fruit and nut trees need proper pruning and pest control.

All fruit trees need some pruning, at least while they are young. Some, such as citrus, need very little when mature. But others, such as peach, need fairly heavy,

skillful pruning to remain fruitful and problem-free. Proper pruning requires an understanding of the growth and bearing habits of each type of fruit or nut tree. It is an easy skill to learn, but some study must be given to master it. If you don't have a skilled friend to teach you, you can learn from a book, such as Ortho's book, *All About Growing Fruits and Berries*.

In the course of evolution, the trees that we raise for their fruit and nuts developed a large seed (in the case of nuts) or seed package (in the case of fruit) in order to be attractive to animals and birds. The animals and birds then dispersed their seeds over a far larger area than could be accomplished by gravity or the wind. But in developing fruit that was attractive to animals and birds, they also developed fruit that was attractive to insects and diseases.

Most fruit trees need regular spraying to produce a large crop that is free of holes and blemishes. Commercial orchardists spray many times each season to produce the superior fruit we have become accustomed to in modern supermarkets. Most home gardeners are willing to tolerate a few more wormy apples than supermarket buyers, but still usually find it necessary to follow some sort of spray schedule.

Because these schedules are different in different parts of the country, depending on local problems and climate, we are unable to offer spray schedules in this book. But spray schedules are available from local Cooperative Extension offices. See page 1011.

Fruit and nut trees may be more trouble than ornamentals, but the rewards are also greater. Fresh, sweet fruit right off the tree is a reward worth a great deal of effort.

Above: Aphids on an apple leaf. See page 628.
Left: A bountiful harvest is the reward for solving fruit tree problems.

PROBLEMS COMMON TO MANY FRUIT AND NUT TREES

Poor fruiting on almond.

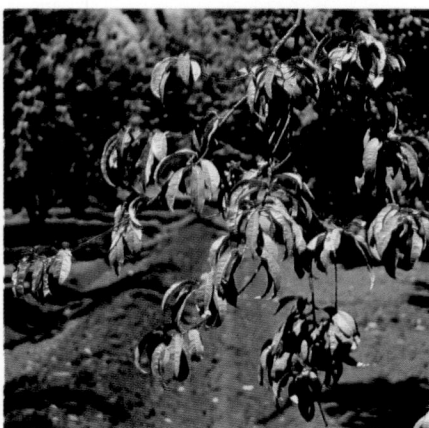

Failure to fruit on peach.

PROBLEM: Trees produce few or no fruits. The tree appears healthy, and is growing vigorously. There are no signs of insect pests or diseases.

ANALYSIS: Few or no fruits
Fruit trees may fail to bear fruit for any of several reasons.

1. *Lack of pollination:* In order to produce fruit, many varieties of fruit trees must be cross-pollinated (pollinated with pollen from a different variety). If a cross-pollinating variety is not present in the garden or nearby neighborhood, the tree may bloom profusely, but produce few or no fruits.

2. *Lack of pollinators:* Most fruit trees are pollinated by bees. If, due to rain or cold weather, bees are not present when the tree is flowering, or if they are killed by tree-spraying, pollination and fruit set will not occur.

3. *Cold damage:* Flowers may be killed when temperatures drop below freezing. Some fruit tree flowers can tolerate temperatures in the 20°F range, but flower hardiness varies considerably with the species and variety.

4. *Biennial bearing:* Certain types of fruit trees, especially apples, pears, and some citrus varieties, tend to bear a heavy crop of fruit one year, and few or no fruits the following year. The production of large quantities of fruit inhibits the formation of next year's flowers. Then the lack of fruit stimulates the production of many flowers for the following year.

5. *Improper pruning:* If the fruit-bearing wood is pruned off during the dormant season, the tree will fail to flower and fruit.

SOLUTION: The numbered solutions below correspond to the numbers in the analysis.

1. Check the list of common fruit tree varieties on page 1005 to determine whether your tree requires a pollinator.

2. There is nothing you can do about lack of bee activity due to rain or cold weather. If your trees bloom early in the season when inclement weather is more likely, plant late-blooming varieties.

3. Once flowers have been killed or damaged by an unseasonal cold spell, there is nothing you can do. If you expect temperatures to drop during the night, you can protect your trees in several ways (see page 912). Plant late-blooming varieties to avoid cold damage.

4. To help even out fruit production from year to year, thin fruits about 4 to 6 weeks after the trees have bloomed. For information about thinning fruits, look up your tree in the alphabetical section beginning on page 625.

5. To determine where the fruit is produced, look up your fruit tree in the alphabetical section. Avoid pruning off large amounts of fruit-bearing wood.

Premature drop of cherries.

Poor-quality pear.

Poor-quality apples.

PROBLEM: Fruit drops prematurely. The tree appears to be healthy; there are no signs of insect pests or diseases.

ANALYSIS: Premature fruit drop
Premature fruit drop has several causes:
1. *Natural thinning:* Most fruit trees initially produce more fruit than they can mature. Premature fruit drop is a natural means of thinning out the excess fruit. Such fruit may be as small as a fraction of an inch in diameter.
2. *Stress:* Large quantities of fruit may drop when the tree is under stress. Stress may be caused by conditions such as excessive heat, drought, cold, or overwatering, and by rapid changes in soil moisture and air temperature.
3. *Freeze damage:* Unseasonal spring frosts often freeze and kill developing young fruits, causing them to drop off.
4. *Lack of pollination:* If the flowers are not pollinated, they may develop into pea-sized fruits, then fall off.

SOLUTION: The numbers below correspond to the numbers in the analysis.
1. As long as your tree appears healthy, there is nothing to worry about.
2. Help reduce stress to the tree by watering and fertilizing it properly. For cultural information, look up your tree in the alphabetical section beginning on page 625.
3. Once fruits are damaged by frost, there is nothing you can do. For information on how to protect your trees from frost damage, see page 912. Plant trees that are hardy in your area. For a list of common fruit and nut trees and their hardiness, see page 1005.
4. Check the lists on page 1005 to determine if your tree requires a pollinator.

PROBLEM: Fruits and nuts are not flavorful. Fruits may be dry, watery, pulpy, or grainy, and may taste sour or tart.

ANALYSIS: Poor-tasting fruit and nuts
Fruits and nuts may be poor in flavor for a number of reasons.

1. *Lack of nutrients:* Trees planted in infertile soil grow poorly and often produce small crops of inferior-tasting fruits and nuts.

2. *Environmental stress:* Trees may be stressed by too much or too little soil moisture, excessively high or low temperatures, or rapid, unseasonable weather changes. Under environmental stress, many types of trees may fail to ripen fruits or nuts properly, producing dry, pulpy, or otherwise poor-tasting fruits and nuts.

3. *Disease or insect damage:* Diseases and pests often slow root, shoot, and leaf growth, and prevent fruits and nuts from ripening properly. Fruits and nuts themselves may also be infected or infested, resulting in poor flavor.

4. *Untimely harvest:* When fruits are prematurely harvested, they may taste tart, flavorless, dry, or starchy. But pears taste gritty or mealy if they are allowed to ripen on the tree. For more information about harvesting pears, see page 661.

5. *Fruit naturally unflavorful:* Tree varieties vary considerably in the quality of their fruits and nuts. No matter how healthy and vigorous your tree is, the variety may just naturally produce a flavorless crop. Seedling trees often produce insipid fruit.

SOLUTION: The numbered solutions below correspond to the numbers in the analysis.

1. Fertilize trees regularly according to label directions with ORTHO Evergreen, Tree & Shrub Food 12–6–6.

2. To reduce stress caused by too much or too little soil moisture, avoid overwatering or underwatering your tree. (For details on proper watering, see page 906.) Minimize tree stress resulting from weather and temperature fluctuations by maintaining the tree in good health. For specific cultural information, look up your tree in the alphabetical section starting on page 625.

3. To help ensure high-quality fruit and nut crops, keep your trees as free of insect pests and diseases as possible. To determine what is infecting or infesting your tree, look up your tree in the alphabetical section.

4. As a general rule, fruits are ripe when they are fully colored, slightly soft, and easy to separate from the branch when gently lifted. For details on harvesting, look up your specific tree.

5. If your tree appears to be healthy, but has continued to produce poor-quality fruits over several years, plant a variety that bears more flavorful fruits. Check with your local Cooperative Extension Office (see page 1011) for a list of flavorful fruit and nut trees that are adapted to your area.

PROBLEMS COMMON TO MANY FRUIT AND NUT TREES — ANIMAL DAMAGE

Small cherries.

Bird-damaged apple.

Squirrel eating green cherry.

PROBLEM: The tree is healthy, and produces many small fruits. There are no signs of pests or diseases.

ANALYSIS: Fruit too small
Certain fruit trees, including peaches, nectarines, Japanese plums, and apples, tend to produce large quantities of small fruit when the trees are not pruned or thinned adequately. If the fruit-bearing wood is not pruned during the dormant season, the tree will set many more fruits than can grow to full size. Even when properly pruned, certain fruit trees have a tendency to overbear. A tree has only a limited amount of nutrients that can be supplied to the fruits. When a tree overbears, it distributes smaller quantities of nutrients to each maturing fruit, resulting in large numbers of small fruits.

SOLUTION: Prune your tree properly during the dormant season, and thin the young fruits when they are thumbnail size (4 to 8 weeks after bloom). For pruning and thinning details, look up your fruit tree in the alphabetical section beginning on page 625.

PROBLEM: Ripened fruits and nuts have holes in them and may be partially eaten. Fruits and nuts may disappear from the tree, or may have been knocked to the ground. Birds, tree squirrels, or raccoons may be seen feeding in the trees.

ANALYSIS: Animals eating fruit and nuts
Some birds and animals, especially tree squirrels and raccoons, feed on tree fruits and nuts.

1. Birds are notorious pests of many tree fruits, especially cherries, figs, persimmons, and other soft, sweet fruits. They peck at the ripening fruit, leaving holes in the flesh. The wounded fruits may decay, becoming inedible. Some birds also feed on the fruit blossoms and tiny developing fruits, greatly reducing the overall fruit yield.

2. Tree squirrels feed on a large variety of foods, including bark, leaves, insects, and eggs. However, they prefer maturing nuts and fruits. They can strip entire trees of nuts, many of which they store for later use. They often leave partially eaten nuts on the ground around the tree. Tree squirrels are especially fond of filberts.

3. Raccoons are usually found in wooded areas near a source of water. They feed on a wide variety of foods, including ripening fruits and nuts. Raccoons may strip off fruits and nuts and carry them away, or feed on them in the tree. In the process of feeding, they often knock many fruits and nuts to the ground.

SOLUTION: The numbered solutions below correspond to the numbers in the analysis.

1. The most effective way of controlling birds is to throw nets over the trees, securing the nets tightly around the trunk. Birds are most likely to damage ripening fruits. Check the trees every morning, and harvest fruits and nuts that have ripened. Bright, shiny objects hung in trees frighten birds, and will repel them for a while.

2. Prevent tree squirrels from climbing fruit and nut trees by wrapping 2-foot-wide bands of metal (made from materials like aluminum roof flashing) snugly around tree trunks at least 6 feet above the ground level. Prune trees so that all their branches are at least 6 feet above the ground and 6 feet away from other trees and structures. If necessary, dwarf trees or shrubs can be completely enclosed in a chicken-wire cage. If permissible in your area, you can also trap tree squirrels. For more information about trapping, see page 891.

3. Raccoons are intelligent, inquisitive animals that can be very difficult to control. To discourage raccoons from climbing between trees, or from a building to a tree, keep the limbs pruned so that they do not touch each other, and do not make contact with the roof. Wrap metal guards at least 18 inches wide around tree trunks at least 3 feet above the ground. For more information about controlling raccoons, see page 894.

BARK OR WOOD PROBLEMS

Ground squirrel damage to almond trees.

Gummosis on peach.

Gummosis on apricot.

PROBLEM: Leaves and buds or shoots are chewed from the trees.
Bark may be chewed or gnawed from the trunk or lower branches. In some cases, the trunk is entirely girdled. Deer, rabbits, or mice may be seen in the yard, or their tracks may be seen on the ground or snow. Damage is usually most severe during the winter months.

ANALYSIS: Bark-feeding animals
Several animals chew on tree bark.
1. Deer damage trees by feeding on leaves, shoots, buds, and bark. They feed by pulling or twisting the bark or twigs, leaving ragged or twisted twig ends or patches of bark. The males may also damage trees by rubbing their antlers on the trunk and branches.
2. Rabbits damage fruit trees by chewing on the bark at the base of the trunk, and clipping off tender shoots. They chew bark and twigs off cleanly, leaving a sharp break. The damaged trunk is often marked with paired gouges where the rabbits have fed. They generally feed no more than 2 feet above the ground or snow level. Rabbits damage young or dwarf trees most severely.
3. Field or meadow mice damage fruit trees by chewing off the bark at the base of the trunk, just at or slightly above or below ground or snow level. They may girdle the trunk, killing the tree. Mice leave tiny scratches in the exposed wood.

SOLUTION: Various methods may be used to control deer, rabbits, and mice. For more information, see page 891 for deer control; page 894 for rabbit control; and page 890 for mouse control.

PROBLEM: Beads of sticky, amber-colored sap appear on healthy bark, cankers (sunken lesions), wounds, or pruning cuts.

ANALYSIS: Gummosis
Oozing sap (gummosis), which occurs in all trees to a greater or lesser extent, is caused by one or several of the following factors.

1. *Natural tendency:* Certain species of fruit trees, especially cherries, apricots, peaches, and plums, have a natural tendency to ooze sap. Small beads of sap often form on the bark of these trees.

2. *Environmental stress:* Trees that are under stress because they are growing in wet, poorly drained, or very dry soil may produce large quantities of sap, even though they are not diseased. Also, many fruit trees respond to rapid changes in weather conditions or soil moisture by gumming profusely.

3. *Mechanical injury:* Almost all trees ooze sap when the bark or wood is wounded. Wounding results from limb breakage; lawnmower injury; pruning; improper staking, tying, or guying techniques; and other practices that damage the bark and wood.

4. *Disease:* Fruit trees respond to certain fungal and bacterial infections by forming cankers that gum profusely. Gummosis is often one of the initial signs of infection.

5. *Insect damage:* Several species of insects bore into tree bark, causing sap to ooze from the damaged areas. The larvae of certain beetles and moths are the most damaging types of boring insects. The tunnels they form in the wood often become infected with decay organisms.

SOLUTION: The numbered solutions below correspond to the numbers in the analysis.

1. As long as the bark appears healthy, there is nothing to worry about.

2. If your tree is growing in wet, poorly drained soil, allow the soil to dry out between waterings. Provide for drainage of water away from tree trunks and roots. To help prevent crown rot, carefully remove enough soil around the base of the trunk to expose the first major roots.

3. Avoid unnecessary mechanical injuries to the tree. Stake, tie, and prune properly. For more information, see ORTHO's book *All About Pruning.* For instructions on staking and tying, see page 911.

4. Remove badly infected branches and cut out cankers. For details about canker removal and treatment, see page 911. Keep the tree healthy. For cultural information, look up your tree in the alphabetical section beginning on page 625.

5. Borers are difficult to control once they have burrowed into the wood. For instructions on borer control, see page 619.

FRUIT AND NUT TREES

PROBLEMS COMMON TO MANY FRUIT AND NUT TREES — BARK OR WOOD PROBLEMS

Fruit overload on apple branch.

Cytospora canker on peach.

Sunscald.

PROBLEM: Branches laden with large quantities of ripening fruit break off.

ANALYSIS: Limb breakage
Trees that produce large fruit, such as peaches, nectarines, apples, and pears, have problems with limbs breaking as the fruit reaches full size. Branches that have not been pruned or thinned properly are most likely to break. Trees that produce fruit on thin, year-old wood, like peaches and nectarines, are most susceptible to limb breakage.

SOLUTION: Prune off stubs where branches have broken. (For information about pruning stubs, see page 910.) Prop up any branches that are bent or appear ready to break. Cut a notch at one end of a board and place the board about a third of the way inward from the tip of the sagging branch. Set the branch into the notch, and then push the board into the ground. If the soil is not soft, you may need to dig a hole in the ground first. The board should be pushed in at a slight angle (20°), leaning toward the center of the tree. During the dormant season prune the tree properly, and thin young fruit. For pruning and thinning details, look up your fruit tree in the alphabetical section beginning on page 625.

PROBLEM: Sunken, oval, or elongated dark lesions (cankers) develop on the trunk or branches. The bark at the edge of the canker may thicken and roll inward. Sticky, amber-colored sap may ooze from the canker. The foliage on infected branches may be stunted and yellowing; some of the leaves may turn brown and drop off. Twigs and branches may die back, and the tree may eventually die.

ANALYSIS: Cankers
Several different species of fungi and bacteria cause cankers on fruit and nut trees. These organisms may be spread by wind, splashing water, or contaminated tools. Infection usually occurs through injured or wounded tissue. Bark that has been damaged by sunscald, cold, pruning wounds, or mechanical injury is especially susceptible. The decay organisms sometimes infect the leaves directly, then spread down into healthy twigs. Cankers form as the decay progresses. Many fruit trees produce a sticky sap that oozes from the cankers. The portion of the branch or stem above the canker may die from decay or from clogging of the water and nutrient-conducting vessels in the branch. Cankers that form on the trunk are the most serious, and may kill the tree. The tree may halt the development of a canker by producing callus tissue, a growth of barklike cells, to wall off the infection.

SOLUTION: Remove badly infected branches and cut out cankers. For details about canker removal and treatment, see page 911. Avoid wounding the tree, and keep it healthy. For cultural information, see the alphabetical section beginning on page 625.

PROBLEM: Patches of bark on the trunk or branches darken and die. Often, these patches appear on the southwest side of the tree. Cracks and sunken lesions (cankers) may eventually develop in the dead bark. Damaged trees have been recently transplanted or heavily pruned.

ANALYSIS: Sunscald
When a tree is shaded by other trees or structures, or is covered with dense foliage, the bark on the trunk and branches remains relatively thin. If the tree is suddenly exposed to intense sunlight, the newly exposed bark and the wood just beneath the bark may be injured by the sun's heat. This frequently happens when young trees are moved from a shaded nursery to an open area, and when trees are heavily pruned during periods of intense sunlight. The problem also occurs on cold, clear days in winter, as cold bark is quickly warmed by the sun. The damaged bark usually splits open, forming long cracks or cankers. Decay fungi may invade the exposed wood. Sunscald is most severe when the soil is dry. Young trees may die from sunscald.

SOLUTION: Unless the tree is very young, or extremely damaged, it will usually recover with proper care. Water and fertilize the tree to stimulate new growth. To prevent further damage, wrap the trunks and main branches of recently pruned or newly transplanted trees with tree-wrapping paper. Or paint the exposed bark with a white interior latex or whitewash. The tree will eventually adapt to increased exposure by growing more foliage and producing thicker bark.

INSECTS

Borer holes.

Cherry scale. *Insert:* Lecanium scale (life size).

Citrus mealybugs.

PROBLEM: Foliage on a branch or at the top of the tree is sparse; eventually the twigs and branches die. Holes or tunnels are apparent in the trunk or branches. Sap or sawdust may be present near the holes. The bark over the tunnels may die or slough off, or there may be knotlike swellings on the trunk and limbs. Weakened branches break during wind or snow storms. Weak, young, or newly transplanted trees may be killed.

ANALYSIS: Borers
Borers are the larvae of beetles or moths. Many kinds of borers attack fruit and nut trees. Females lay their eggs in bark crevices throughout the summer. The larvae feed by tunneling through the bark or wood. Borer tunnels stop the flow of nutrients and water through the area by damaging the conducting vessels; branch and twig dieback result. Sap flow may act as a defense against borers if the tree is healthy. When the borer burrows into the wood, tree sap fills the hole and drowns the insect. Trees that are weakened by mechanical injuries, disease, poor growing conditions, or insect infestation are more susceptible to borer attack.

SOLUTION: Cut out and destroy all dead and dying branches. Severely infested young trees should be removed. Spray or paint the trunk and branches with an insecticide containing *lindane* to kill young larvae before they burrow into the wood. Contact your local Cooperative Extension Office (see page 1011) to determine the appropriate time to apply the insecticide in your area. Make sure that your tree is listed on the product label. Maintain tree health and vigor by watering and fertilizing regularly.

PROBLEM: The stems or undersides of the leaves are covered with crusty bumps or thick, white, waxy bumps or clusters of somewhat flattened scaly bumps. The bumps can be scraped or picked off; the undersides are usually soft. Leaves turn yellow and may drop. In some cases, a shiny or sticky substance coats the leaves.

ANALYSIS: Scales
Several different types of scales infest fruit trees. They lay their eggs on leaves or bark, and in spring to midsummer the young scales, called *crawlers*, settle on leaves and twigs. The small (1/10 inch), soft-bodied young feed by sucking sap from the plant. The legs usually atrophy and a hard crusty or waxy shell develops over the body. The mature female scales lay their eggs underneath their shell. Some species of scales are unable to digest all the sugar in the plant sap, and excrete the excess in a fluid called honeydew. An uncontrolled infestation of scales may kill the plant after 2 or 3 seasons.

SOLUTION: Spray with an insecticide containing *malathion* when the young are active. Make sure that your fruit tree is listed on the product label. Contact your local Cooperative Extension Office (see page 1011) to determine the best time to spray for scales in your area. Early the following spring, before new growth begins, spray the trunk and branches with a *dormant oil spray* to control overwintering insects. For more information about scales, see page 878.

PROBLEM: The undersides of the leaves, stems, branch crotches, or trunk are covered with white, cottony masses. Leaves may be curled, distorted, and yellowing, and knotlike galls may form on the stems or trunk. Sometimes a shiny or sticky substance coats the leaves. Twigs and branches may die.

ANALYSIS: Cottony scales, mealybugs, and woolly aphids
Cottony scales, mealybugs, and woolly aphids produce white, waxy secretions that cover their bodies. Their similarity makes separate identification difficult. When the insects are young, they are usually inconspicuous on the host plant. Their bodies range in color from yellowish green to brown, blending in with the leaves or bark. As the insects mature, they exude filaments of white wax, giving them a cottony appearance. Mealybugs and scales generally deposit their eggs in white, fluffy masses. Damage is caused by the withdrawal of plant sap from the leaves, branches, or trunk. The insects are unable to digest fully all the sugar in the plant sap and excrete the excess in a fluid called honeydew, which often drops onto the leaves or plants below.

SOLUTION: Spray the branches, trunk, and foliage with ORTHO Fruit & Vegetable Insect Control or ORTHO Malathion 50 Insect Spray. Make sure that your fruit tree is listed on the product label. During the dormant season, spray the trunk and branches with ORTHO Volck Supreme Oil Spray.

PROBLEMS COMMON TO MANY FRUIT AND NUT TREES — INSECTS

Aphids (life size).

Ants feeding on mango (half life size).

Tent caterpillar nest (life size).

PROBLEM: The youngest leaves are curled, twisted, discolored, and stunted. Leaves may drop, and in severe cases the tree may defoliate. The developing fruits may be small and misshapen. A shiny or sticky substance may coat the leaves. A black sooty mold often grows on the sticky substance. Tiny (⅛ inch) yellow, green, purplish, or black soft-bodied insects cluster on the young shoots and undersides of the leaves.

ANALYSIS: Aphids
Many species of these insects infest fruit trees. Aphids do little damage in small numbers. However, they are extremely prolific and populations can rapidly build up during the growing season. Damage occurs when the aphid sucks the juices from the leaves and immature fruit. The aphid is unable to digest fully all the sugar in the sap and excretes the excess in a fluid called honeydew, which often drops onto the leaves below. A sooty mold fungus may develop on the honeydew, causing the leaves to appear black and dirty. At harvest time, the fruit may be small, misshapen, and pitted due to aphid damage earlier in the season.

SOLUTION: Spray with an insecticide containing *malathion*. Make sure that your fruit is listed on the product label. Repeat the spray if the tree becomes reinfested.

PROBLEM: Ants are crawling on the trunk, branches, and fruit. In many cases, the trees are also infested with aphids, scales, and leafhoppers.

ANALYSIS: Ants
Most ants do not directly damage plants. They may be present for any of several reasons. Many ants feed on honeydew, a sweet, sticky substance excreted by several species of insects, including aphids, scales, mealybugs, whiteflies, and leafhoppers. Ants are attracted to plants infested with these pests. In order to supply them with food, ants may carry aphids to an uninfested tree. Ants may also feed on flower nectar, fruit, or tree exudate, or on fruit that has had its skin broken or is rotting. Ants usually live in underground nests. Some species make colonies in trees and building foundations.

SOLUTION: Destroy ant nests by treating anthills with ORTHO Diazinon Granules, or by spraying the nest and surrounding soil with ORTHO Diazinon Insect Spray. Control aphids, scales, mealybugs, and whiteflies by spraying the infested plants with an insecticide containing *carbaryl*, *malathion*, or *diazinon*. Make sure that your fruit tree is listed on the product label. To prevent ants from crawling up the trunk, apply a ring of sticky latex ant deterrent to the trunk. For more information about ants, see page 883.

PROBLEM: In the spring or summer, silk nests appear in the branch crotches or on the ends of branches. The leaves are chewed; branches or the entire tree may be defoliated. Groups of bluish, black, tan, or greenish hairy caterpillars, with spots or stripes, are feeding in or around the nests.

ANALYSIS: Tent caterpillars and fall webworm (*Malacosoma* species and *Hyphantria cunea*)
These insects feed on many fruit and ornamental trees. The fall webworm and several species of tent caterpillars are distributed throughout the United States. In the summer, adult tent caterpillar moths lay masses of eggs in a cementing substance around twigs. The eggs hatch in early spring as the leaves unfold, and the young caterpillars immediately begin to construct their nests. On warm, sunny days, they devour the surrounding foliage. In mid to late summer, brownish or reddish adult moths appear. The fall webworm moth lays many eggs on the undersides of leaves in the spring. In early summer, the young caterpillars begin feeding and surrounding themselves with silk nests. The caterpillars drop to the soil to pupate. Up to 4 generations occur between June and September.

SOLUTION: Spray with ORTHO Fruit & Vegetable Insect Control, ORTHO Home Orchard Spray, or with the bacterial insecticide *Bacillus thuringiensis*. Make sure your plant is listed on the product label. For best results, use *Bacillus thuringiensis* while the caterpillars are small. Remove egg masses found in the winter.

POWDERY MATERIAL ON LEAVES

Yellowjacket feeding on honeydew.

Powdery mildew.

Sooty mold on citrus.

PROBLEM: A shiny or sticky substance coats the leaves, fruit, and sometimes twigs. A black sooty mold often grows on the sticky substance. Insects may be found on the leaves, and ants, flies, or bees may be present.

ANALYSIS: Honeydew
Honeydew is a sweet, sticky substance that is secreted by aphids, mealybugs, whiteflies, and some scales. These sucking insects cannot digest all the sugar in the plant sap, and excrete the excess in this sticky fluid. The honeydew drops onto the leaves directly below and onto anything beneath the tree. Ants, flies, and bees feed on honeydew, and may be found around the plant. A sooty mold fungus often develops on the sticky substance, causing the leaves, fruit, and twigs to appear black and dirty. The fungus does not infect the leaf but grows on the honeydew. Extremely heavy infestations may prevent light from reaching the leaf, reducing food production.

SOLUTION: Honeydew will eventually be washed off by rain, or may be hosed off. Prevent more honeydew by controlling the insect that is producing it. Inspect the foliage to determine what type of insect is present. See the following pages for control instructions: for aphids, page 877; for scales, page 878; for whiteflies, page 879; for mealybugs, page 878.

PROBLEM: Gray-white powdery patches appear on the leaves. New growth is often stunted, curled, and distorted. Infected buds may be shriveled and open later than usual, and infected leaves often turn brittle and die. The fruit is sometimes small and misshapen, and may be russet-colored or covered with white powdery patches.

ANALYSIS: Powdery mildew
This common plant disease is caused by a fungus that thrives in both humid and dry weather. The fungus spends the winter in leaf and flower buds. In the spring, spores are blown to the new leaves, which are very susceptible to infection. The fungus saps the plant nutrients, causing distortion and often death of the tender foliage. Fruit yield may be greatly reduced. Powdery mildew is favored by warm days and cool nights.

SOLUTION: Spray infected trees with a fungicide containing *benomyl*, *dinocap*, or *sulfur*. (Do not use *sulfur* on apricots.) Make sure that your fruit tree is listed on the spray label. Most fruit trees should be sprayed at regular intervals of 10 to 14 days until 3 to 4 weeks after the petals have fallen from the blossoms. Resume spraying whenever the mildew recurs. For more details about spraying, check your specific fruit tree in the alphabetical section beginning on page 625.

PROBLEM: A black sooty mold is growing on the leaves, fruit, and twigs. It can be completely wiped off the surfaces of the leaves. Cool, moist weather hastens the growth of this substance.

ANALYSIS: Sooty mold
This common black mold is found on a wide variety of plants in the garden. It is caused by any of several species of fungi that grow on the sugary material left on plants by aphids, scales, mealybugs, whiteflies, and other insects that suck sap from the plant. The insects are unable to digest fully all the sugar in the sap, and excrete the excess in a fluid called honeydew, which drops onto the leaves and fruit below. The sooty mold fungus develops on the honeydew, causing the leaves to appear black and dirty. Sooty mold is unsightly, but it is fairly harmless because it does not attack the leaf directly. Extremely heavy infestations prevent light from reaching the leaf, so that the leaf produces fewer nutrients and may turn yellow. The presence of sooty mold indicates that the tree is infested with insects.

SOLUTION: Sooty mold will eventually be washed off by rain. Prevent more sooty mold by controlling the insect that is producing the honeydew. Inspect the foliage to determine what type of insect is present. See the following pages for control instructions: for aphids, page 877; for scales, page 878; for whiteflies, page 879; for mealybugs, page 878.

PROBLEMS COMMON TO MANY FRUIT AND NUT TREES — LEAVES DISCOLORED OR MOTTLED

Leaf scorch on hickory.

Nitrogen-deficient peach.

Nitrogen-deficient citrus.

PROBLEM: During hot weather, usually in July or August, leaves turn brown around the edges and between the veins. Sometimes the whole leaf dies. Many leaves may drop during late summer. This problem is most severe on the youngest branches. Trees do not generally die.

ANALYSIS: Leaf scorch
Leaf scorch is caused when water evaporates from the leaves faster than it can be supplied. In hot weather, water evaporates rapidly from the leaves. If the roots can't absorb and convey water fast enough to replenish this loss, the leaves turn brown and wither. This usually occurs in dry soil, but leaves can also scorch when the soil is moist and temperatures are very high for extended periods. Drying winds, severed roots, limited soil area, salt buildup, or low temperatures can also cause scorch. For more information about leaf scorch, see page 865.

SOLUTION: To prevent further scorch, deep-water trees during periods of hot weather to wet down the entire root space. (For more information about watering trees, see page 906.) Newly transplanted trees should be watered whenever the rootball is dry 2 inches below the surface. There are no controls for scorch on trees in moist soil. Plant trees adapted to your climate.

PROBLEM: The older leaves turn yellow. Eventually, the rest of the leaves turn yellow-green, and then yellow. Yellow leaves usually die and drop off. New leaves are small, and growth is slow. Fruit production is poor.

ANALYSIS: Nitrogen deficiency
Nitrogen, the most important nutrient for plant growth and development, is deficient or unavailable in almost all soils. Nitrogen is essential in the formation of plant tissue, green leaf pigment, and many other compounds necessary for plant growth. When not enough nitrogen is available in the soil, the tree utilizes nitrogen from its older leaves for new growth. The older leaves become deficient in nitrogen, and turn yellow. A continuing shortage of nitrogen causes overall yellowing, stunting, and death of the older leaves, and a reduced fruit yield. Fast-growing, young fruit trees usually require large amounts of nitrogen. If it is not supplied, the foliage turns yellow and grows poorly. Nitrogen naturally present in the soil is made available to trees as organic matter decomposes. Soils that are low in organic matter, such as sandy and readily leached soils, are often infertile. Also, nitrogen leaches more quickly when rainfall or irrigation is heavy. Poorly drained, overwatered, and compacted soils lack oxygen that is necessary for the utilization of nitrogen. Trees growing in these soils often exhibit symptoms of nitrogen deficiency. In addition, trees growing in cold (50°F and below), hot (90°F and up), acid (pH 5.5 and lower), or alkaline (pH 7.8 and higher) soils are often low in nitrogen.

SOLUTION: Fertilize trees regularly with ORTHO Evergreen, Tree & Shrub Food 12–6–6 or ORTHO General Purpose Plant Food 8–8–8. (For more information about fertilizers, see page 904.) ORTHO Dried Blood Meal 12–0–0, which contains nitrogen in a long-lasting, slow-release form, can be used to supplement a regular feeding program. Add organic matter to compacted soils and those low in organic substances. Improve soil drainage in poorly drained soils. (For more information about improving soil drainage, see page 901.) Do not keep the soil constantly wet. (For more information about watering, see page 906.) Raise or lower soil pH in soils that are acid or alkaline. For more information about pH, see page 902.

Iron-deficient apple leaves.

Spider mites (6 times life size).

Root knot nematode damage.

PROBLEM: Leaves turn pale green or yellow. The newest leaves (those at the tips of the branches) are most severely affected. Except in extreme cases, the veins of affected leaves remain green. Older leaves may remain green. Fruit production may be reduced, and fruit flavor may be poor.

ANALYSIS: Iron deficiency
Plants frequently suffer from deficiencies of iron and other minor nutrients, such as manganese and zinc, elements essential to normal tree growth and development. Deficiencies can occur when one or more of these elements are depleted in the soil. Often, these minor nutrients are present in the soil but alkaline (pH 7.5 or higher) or wet soil conditions cause them to form compounds that cannot be used by the tree. An alkaline condition can result from overliming, or from lime leached from cement or brick. Regions where soil is derived from limestone, and those with low rainfall, usually have alkaline soils.

SOLUTION: To correct the deficiency of nutrients, apply ORTHO-Gro Liquid Plant Food 12–6–6 to the soil around the plants. Check the soil pH. (For information on pH, see page 902.) Correct the pH of the soil by treating it with *ferrous sulfate* and watering it in well.

PROBLEM: Leaves are stippled, yellowing, silvered, or bronzed. There may be webbing over flower buds, between leaves, or on the lower surfaces of the leaves. The fruit may be roughened or russet-colored. To determine if the tree is infested with certain species of mites, hold a sheet of white paper underneath an affected leaf and tap the leaf sharply. Minute green, red, or yellow specks the size of pepper grains will drop to the paper and begin to crawl around.

ANALYSIS: Mites
These pests, related to spiders, commonly attack fruit trees and other garden plants. Certain mites, like the two-spotted spider mite, are large enough to be detected as described above. Smaller mites, like the plum and pear rust mites, are microscopic, and cannot be seen without the aid of a strong hand lens or microscope. Mites cause damage by sucking sap from the fruit surface and the undersides of the leaves. As a result of feeding, the green leaf pigment disappears, producing the stippled or silvered appearance. Mites are active throughout the growing season, but are favored by hot, dry weather (70°F and up). By midsummer, they build up to tremendous numbers.

SOLUTION: Spray infested trees with ORTHO Fruit & Vegetable Insect Control, or with a pesticide containing *dicofol*. Repeat the spray at least 2 more times at intervals of 7 to 10 days. Make sure that your tree is listed on the spray label. If you are not sure whether your tree is infested with microscopic mites, bring an infested shoot or twig to your local County Extension Office (see page 1011) for confirmation.

PROBLEM: Leaves are bronzed and yellowing. They may wilt on hot, dry days, but recover at night. The tree is generally weak. After several years, the tree is noticeably stunted, and branches may die.

ANALYSIS: Nematodes
Nematodes are microscopic worms that live in the soil. They are not related to earthworms. Nematodes feed on tree roots, damaging and stunting them. The damaged roots can't supply sufficient water and nutrients to the branches and leaves, and the tree is stunted or slowly dies. Nematodes are found throughout the United States, but are most severe in the South. They prefer moist, sandy loam soils. Nematodes can move only a few inches each year on their own, but they may be carried long distances by soil, water, tools, or infested plants. Testing roots and soil is the only positive method for confirming the presence of nematodes. Contact your local Cooperative Extension Office (see page 1011) for sampling instructions and addresses of testing laboratories. Soil and root problems such as poor soil structure, drought stress, nutrient deficiency, and root rots can also produce symptoms of decline similar to those caused by nematodes. These problems should be eliminated as causes before sending soil and root samples for testing. For information on soil problems and root rots, see pages 901 and 856.

SOLUTION: There are no chemicals available to kill nematodes in planted soil. However, they can be controlled before planting by soil fumigation. For information on fumigating soil, see page 919.

PROBLEMS COMMON TO MANY FRUIT AND NUT TREES — TREE STUNTED OR DECLINING

Crown rot on cherry.

Phytophthora rot on apple.

Crown gall on cherry.

PROBLEM: The normal leaf color dulls, and the plant loses vigor. Leaves may wilt, or turn yellow or light brown. Major branches or the entire tree may die. The tree sometimes lives for many months in a weakened condition, or it may die quickly. The roots and lower trunk are brownish, and the roots may be decayed. Fine woolly brown strands may form on the roots, and white powdery spores form on the soil surface. Or fan-shaped plaques of white strands may appear between the bark and wood of the roots and lower stems. Mushrooms may appear at the base of the plant in the fall.

PROBLEM: Large corky galls, up to several inches in diameter, appear at the base of the tree and on the roots. The galls are rounded, with a rough, irregular surface. Trees with numerous galls are weak; growth may be slowed, and the foliage may turn yellow.

ANALYSIS: Root and crown rots
Root and crown rots are caused by any of several different fungi that live in the soil and on roots. They are spread by water, soil, and transplants.

SOLUTION: The numbered solutions below correspond to the numbers in the analysis.

1. *Phytophthora* species. These fungi cause browning and decay of the roots and browning of the lower trunk. The tree usually dies slowly, but young trees may wilt and die rapidly. The disease is most prevalent in heavy, waterlogged soils. For more information about phytophthora, see page 857.

1. Remove dead and dying trees. When replanting, use plants that are resistant to phytophthora. (For a list, see page 1000.) Improve soil drainage. (For more information, see page 901.) Avoid overwatering plants, as discussed on page 857.

2. *Phymatotrichum omnivorum.* This fungus, commonly known as *cotton root rot* or *Texas root rot*, is a serious problem on many plants in the Southwest. Young trees may suddenly wilt and die. Brown strands form on the roots, and white powdery spores form on the soil. The disease is most severe in heavy, alkaline soils. For more information about phymatotrichum, see page 859.

2. Remove dead and dying trees. When replanting, use only resistant varieties. (For a list, see page 994.) Before planting, increase the soil acidity by adding 1 pound of *ammonium sulfate* for every 10 square feet of soil. Make a circular ridge around the planting area, and fill the basin with 4 inches of water. Repeat the treatment in 5 to 10 days. Improve soil drainage. For more information, see page 901.

3. *Armillaria mellea.* This disease is commonly known as *shoestring root rot*, *mushroom root rot*, or *oak root fungus*. It is identified by the presence of fan-shaped plaques of white fungal strands between the bark and the wood of the roots and lower trunk. Honey-colored mushrooms appear at the base of the plant in the fall. For more information about armillaria, see page 858.

3. Remove dead trees. The life of a newly infected plant may be prolonged if the disease has not reached the lower trunk. Expose the base of the plant to air for several months by removing 3 to 4 inches of soil. Prune off diseased roots. Use a fertilizer to stimulate growth. (For more information, see page 904.) When replanting, use only resistant plants. (For a list, see page 1001.) Avoid overwatering plants, as discussed on page 857.

ANALYSIS: Crown gall
This plant disease is caused by a soil-inhabiting bacterium (*Agrobacterium tumefaciens*) that infects many ornamentals, fruits, and vegetables in the garden. The bacteria are spread in the soil, and are often brought to a garden initially on the roots of an infected plant. The bacteria enter the tree through wounds in the roots or the base of the trunk (the crown). They produce a substance that stimulates rapid cell growth in the plant, causing gall formation. The galls disrupt the flow of water and nutrients up the roots and trunk, weakening and stunting the top growth. They do not usually cause the tree to die.

SOLUTION: Infected trees cannot be cured. However, they often survive for many years. Although the disease cannot be eliminated from the tree, individual galls can be removed by professionals. If you wish to remove galls from valued trees, consult a professional horticulturist or landscape contractor. The bacteria will remain in the soil for as long as 3 years after an infected tree has been removed. Replant with one of the resistant trees from the list on page 998. For more information about crown gall, see page 860.

_____ **ALMOND** _____

Neglected fruit tree.

PROBLEM: Overall
growth is slow. Foliage
may be sparse, discol-
ored, or stunted. Branches are dense and
intertwined. Twigs and branches may be
dying or dead, and fruit is small and of
poor quality. The tree may be diseased or
infested with insects.

ANALYSIS: Tree neglect
Most fruit trees will decline in vigor and
fruitfulness if they are neglected for several years. Fruit trees are susceptible to a
number of fungal and bacterial diseases
that can affect the roots, crown, branches,
foliage, and fruits. Many insect pests also
weaken fruit trees by feeding, boring
into, or otherwise damaging them. Most
fruit trees need to be pruned annually in
order to stimulate the production of new
fruiting wood, or eliminate excess or old
fruiting wood. In addition, proper watering and fertilizing is important in maintaining tree health and fruitfulness.

SOLUTION: Control pests and diseases.
To determine what types of insects and
diseases are affecting your tree and how
to control them, look up your tree in the
alphabetical section beginning on this
page. Thin out weak, diseased, intertwined, and dying twigs and branches. If
the tree needs to be heavily pruned, or
restructured, gradually prune it into
proper shape over a period of 3 years.
Remove all invasive growth (grass,
groundcover) from around the base of the
tree. Water and fertilize the tree properly. For specific details on pruning, watering, and fertilizing, look up your tree in
the alphabetical section. For general information on pruning, see ORTHO's
book *All About Pruning*. For more information on fertilizers and watering, see
pages 904 and 906.

ALMOND _____

ADAPTATION: Zones 8 through 10.

POLLINATION: Cross-pollinate with
another variety.

SOIL: Any good, deep, well-drained
soil. pH 5.5 to 8.0

FERTILIZER: Fertilize with ORTHO Evergreen, Tree & Shrub Food 12–6–6 according to label directions.

WATER:
How much: Apply enough water to
wet the soil 3 to 4 feet deep. To determine the proper amount of water for
your soil type, see page 906.
How often: Water when the soil 6
inches below the surface is just barely
moist.

PRUNING: Almonds bear on short
fruiting branches (spurs) on 2 to 5-
year-old wood. Thin out weak, crossing, or dead twigs and branches. The
maturing almonds themselves do not
need to be thinned.

HARVEST: Harvest almonds when most
of the hulls have split open. Pick them
off, or knock them off of the tree by
striking the branches with a rubber
mallet or cloth-covered stick. After removing the hulls, pile the almonds 1 to
2 inches deep in the sun to dry them.
Drying usually takes several days to a
week.

Peach twig borer (life size).

PROBLEM: New growth at
the tips of the twigs wilts
and dies. When new
shoots or maturing nuts are cut open,
reddish brown caterpillars, about ½ inch
long, may be visible inside. There may
be silken cocoons in the crotches of the
branches.

ANALYSIS: Peach twig borer
(*Anarsia lineatella*)
This borer, the larva of a gray night-
flying moth, infests peaches, apricots,
nectarines, and plums, as well as almonds. The young larvae hibernate during the winter in silk-lined cavities
under loose bark or in the crotches of the
branches. In the spring they emerge and
bore into new twigs and buds, usually
killing them. When fully grown, they pupate in silken cocoons on the branches.
About 2 weeks later they emerge as
moths and lay eggs on twigs and nuts.
This second generation burrows into and
feeds almost entirely on the nuts.

SOLUTION: Once the borers have infest-
ed the nuts, they cannot be killed. Next
spring, spray with ORTHO Fruit & Vegetable Insect Control just before the flower
buds open. Repeat when 90 percent of
the petals have dropped from the blossoms, and spray a third time when the
late portions of the blossoms split from
the small developing almond fruit. Don't
spray during full bloom, or you will kill
the bees that are pollinating the almond
flowers.

ALMOND

Shothole fungus.

PROBLEM: Small pur- plish spots appear on the leaves in early spring. The spots turn brown and enlarge to ¼ inch in diameter. The centers of the spots die and drop out, leaving a small round hole. The blossoms may turn brown and have a gummy exudate at the base. The almond yield may be reduced, and corky spots may appear on the hulls. In severe cases, the tree may drop all its leaves.

ANALYSIS: Shothole fungus
This disease is also called *coryneum blight* and *peach blight*. It is caused by a fungus (*Coryneum beijerinckii*) that attacks almonds and stone fruits. The fungus spends the winter in lesions on the twigs and buds. The spores are spread by spring rains and infect the new leaves. Infection causes the leaf tissue to produce a layer of cells that wall off the damaged area. The center of the spot then drops out. Severe infection may defoliate the tree, produce smaller almonds, and cause some almonds to drop. The disease is favored by wet spring weather.

SOLUTION: There is no adequate control during the growing season. Next spring, spray the tree with a fungicide containing *captan* when the petals have emerged from the bud, but before they are fully opened. Spray again when the petals have fallen from the flowers, and once more 5 weeks later.

APPLE

ADAPTATION AND POLLINATION: See variety chart on page 1005.

SOIL: Any good, deep, well-drained soil. pH 5.5 to 8.0

FERTILIZER: Fertilize with ORTHO Evergreen, Tree & Shrub Food 12–6–6 according to label directions.

WATER:
How much: Apply enough water to wet the soil 3 to 4 feet deep. To determine the proper amount of water for your soil type, see page 906.
How often: Water when the soil 6 inches below the surface is just barely moist.

PRUNING: Apples are borne on short fruiting branches (spurs) that grow on year-old wood. The spurs continue to fruit for about 10 years. Prune lightly, since the removal of many spurs will reduce the apple yield. Thin out weak, crossing, or dead twigs and branches. When apples are thumbnail size, thin them to 6 inches apart, with one fruit per spur.

HARVEST: Apples are ripe when their seeds turn dark brown to black, the flesh turns creamy white, and the apple stem separates easily from the spur when the fruit is gently lifted. Harvest earlier if you prefer tart apples.

APPLE

Codling moth larva (life size).

PROBLEM: The fruit is blemished by small holes surrounded by dead tissue. A brown, crumbly material resembling sawdust may surround the holes. Brown-headed, pinkish white worms up to 1 inch long may be found in the fruit. The interior of the fruit is often dark and rotted. Many apples drop prematurely.

ANALYSIS: Codling moth
(*Laspeyresia pomonella*)
This worm, the larva of a small gray-brown moth, is one of the most serious apple pests in the United States. This insect attacks pears, quinces, and several other fruit and nut trees in addition to apples. The moths appear in the spring when the apple trees are blooming. They lay their eggs on the leaves, twigs, and developing fruit. When the eggs hatch, the larvae tunnel into the fruit. They feed for several weeks, then emerge from the fruit, often leaving a mass of dark excrement on the skin and inside the fruit. After pupating in sheltered locations on or around the tree, another generation of moths emerge in midsummer. Apples may be damaged by worms continuously throughout the summer. In the fall, mature larvae spin cocoons in protected places, such as under loose bark or in tree crevices. They spend the winter in these cocoons, emerging as moths in the spring.

SOLUTION: Once the worms have penetrated the apples, it is impossible to kill them. To protect uninfested apples, spray with ORTHO Home Orchard Spray or ORTHO Fruit & Vegetable Insect Control at intervals of 10 days, as directed on the label. Remove and destroy all fallen apples, and clean up debris. Next spring, spray according to label direction when the new growth appears.

Apple maggot (4 times life size). *Insert:* Adult.

Plum curculio (3 times life size).

Bitter rot.

PROBLEM: The fruit may be dimpled and pitted, with brown trails winding through the flesh. White, tapered, legless maggots about ⅜ inch long may be present in the fruit. Severely infested apples are brown and pulpy inside. Frequently, many apples drop prematurely.

ANALYSIS: Apple maggot
(*Rhagoletis pomonella*)
These worms, also known as *railroad worms* and *apple fruit flies*, are the larvae of flies that resemble the common housefly. Apple maggots infest plums, cherries, and pears in addition to apples. The adult flies emerge from pupae between late June and the beginning of September. They lay eggs in the fruit through holes they puncture in the skin. The maggots that emerge from the eggs make brown trails through the flesh as they feed. Infested apples usually drop to the ground. The mature maggots emerge from the apple and burrow in the soil to pupate. They remain in the soil throughout the winter, and emerge as adult flies the following June.

SOLUTION: There is no way to kill the maggots after apples are infested. Protect healthy apples from the adult flies by spraying at intervals of 7 to 10 days from the end of June until the beginning of September with ORTHO Fruit & Vegetable Insect Control, ORTHO Liquid Sevin or ORTHO Home Orchard Spray. Pick up and destroy fallen apples every week throughout the summer.

PROBLEM: The ripening fruit is misshapen, rotten, and often drops prematurely. Holes about ⅛ inch in diameter and deep, crescent-shaped scars appear on the fruit. When cut open, such fruits may be found to contain crescent-shaped, yellow-gray grubs with brown heads.

ANALYSIS: Plum curculio
(*Contrachelus nenuphar*)
These insects, found east of the Rocky Mountains, attack stone fruits and pears, as well as apples. The adult insects are brown beetles with long, curved snouts. They hibernate in debris and other protected places during the winter. The beetles emerge in the spring when new growth starts and begin feeding on young leaves, blossoms, and developing fruit. After 5 to 6 weeks, the female beetles start to lay eggs in the young fruit. The grubs that hatch from the eggs feed for several weeks in the fruit. The infested apples usually drop to the ground. The grubs eventually leave the apples and bore into the soil, where they pupate. The emerging beetles feed on fruit for a few weeks, then go into hibernation. Or, in the South, they lay eggs, producing a second generation of grubs in the late summer.

SOLUTION: Once the fruit is infested, there is no way to kill the grubs inside the fruit. Spray with ORTHO Home Orchard Spray or ORTHO Malathion 50 Insect Spray to kill beetles that may be feeding on fruit, or laying eggs. Pick up and destroy all fallen fruit. Next spring, spray the trees when the petals are falling from the blossoms; repeat applications according to the directions on the label.

PROBLEM: Sunken, light brown, circular spots appear on the half-grown fruit. These spots gradually enlarge to 1 inch in diameter. Concentric rings and sticky pink masses of spores may appear on the spotted areas during moist weather. The rotted apple flesh tastes bitter. Sunken lesions may form on the branches.

ANALYSIS: Bitter rot
This plant disease, which also affects pears, is caused by a fungus (*Glomerella cingulata*). The fungus spends the winter in rotted apples left in the tree and on the ground, and in sunken lesions on the branches. Spores are spread by splashing rain to healthy apples in the spring. Infection can occur throughout the fruiting season. In areas where hot, humid conditions last for long periods of time, bitter rot can quickly destroy an entire apple crop. This disease primarily attacks the fruit, and does not severely damage the health of the tree.

SOLUTION: Spray infested trees with ORTHO Home Orchard Spray or Orthocide Garden Fungicide, according to label directions. To prevent recurrence next year, prune out branches with lesions, and remove and destroy rotted apples from the tree. Next spring, spray the trees with ORTHO Home Orchard Spray or Orthocide Garden Fungicide just before the blossoms start to open. Continue spraying according to label directions.

Apples that are fairly resistant to bitter rot: Delicious, Rome Beauty, Stayman, Winesap, York Imperial.

APPLE

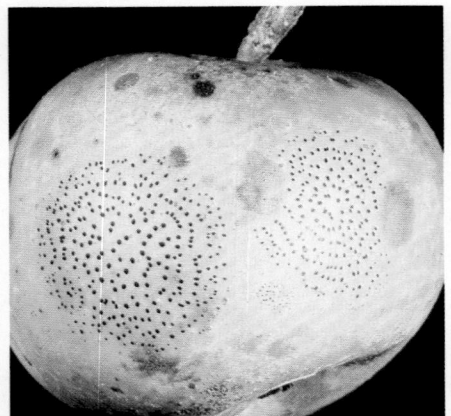

Sooty blotch and fly speck.

Aphid damage.

Woolly apple aphids (twice life size).

PROBLEM: Clusters of 10 to 30 or more raised, shiny, black specks appear on the apple skins. There are indefinite dark brown to olive-green smudges on the surface of the fruit.

ANALYSIS: Sooty blotch and fly speck
Although these two plant diseases are not caused by the same fungus, they are so commonly found in association that they are usually described together. Sooty blotch is caused by the fungus *Gloeodoes pomigena*, and fly speck is caused by the fungus *Microthyriella rubi*. These fungi spend the winter on the twigs of apples and many other woody plants. During mild, wet weather in spring, the fungi produce spores that are blown to and infect the developing apples. About a month after the initial infection, specks and blotches appear on the maturing fruit. Although these diseases are unsightly, they are external and do not generally affect the taste of the apples. Spores are not produced when temperatures rise above 85°F, so infection generally occurs during the spring and late summer or fall, but rarely in midsummer.

SOLUTION: To prevent the possible infection of healthy fruit, spray with ORTHO Home Orchard Spray. Infected apples are edible; rub them vigorously to remove the specks and blotches. Next spring, spray with ORTHO Home Orchard Spray according to label directions when the new growth appears.

PROBLEM: The newest leaves are curled, twisted, discolored, and stunted. Leaves may drop off, and in severe cases the tree may defoliate. The developing apples are often small and misshapen. A shiny, sticky substance may coat the leaves. A black sooty mold often grows on this sticky substance. Tiny (⅛ inch) green, red, purplish, or rosy brown soft-bodied insects cluster on the young shoots and undersides of the leaves. Ants may be present.

ANALYSIS: Aphids
Aphids do little damage in small numbers. However, they are extremely prolific and populations can rapidly build up to damaging numbers during the growing season. Damage occurs when the aphid sucks the juices from the leaves and immature fruit. The aphid is unable to digest fully all the sugar in the sap and excretes the excess in a fluid called honeydew. The honeydew often drops onto the leaves below. Plants or objects beneath the tree may also be coated with honeydew. A sooty mold fungus may develop on the honeydew, causing the leaves to appear black and dirty. Ants feed on this sticky substance, and are often present where there is an aphid infestation. At harvest time, apples may be small, misshapen, and pitted due to aphid damage earlier in the season.

SOLUTION: Control with ORTHO Home Orchard Spray, ORTHO Malathion 50 Insect Spray, or ORTHO Fruit & Vegetable Insect Control as soon as the insects appear. Repeat according to label directions if the tree becomes reinfested.

PROBLEM: Twigs, branches, leaves, and possibly the trunk of the tree are covered with white, cottony masses. There may be galls on the infested limbs. Beneath the white masses are clusters of small (⅛ inch), purplish brown, soft-bodied insects. The leaves are yellowing. Young trees are often stunted, and may die.

ANALYSIS: Woolly apple aphid
(*Erisosoma lanigerum*)
These insects may be found wherever apples are grown. Woolly apple aphids usually suck sap from the twigs and branches, but cause their most serious damage when some of the aphids burrow into the soil and feed on the roots. This feeding causes root galls to form, inhibiting the flow of water and nutrients up into the tree. In addition to forming galls and nodules, the roots also become fibrous and stunted. Young trees often die from root infestations.

SOLUTION: Spray the tree trunk, branches, and foliage with ORTHO Fruit & Vegetable Insect Control or ORTHO Diazinon Insect Spray as soon as the pests are noticed. Repeat the spray as directed on the label. If you suspect root infestation, carefully dig away the soil from around the crown and check the roots for aphids and galls. Although it is not possible to rid the roots of aphids, you can usually control them by keeping the trunk, branches, and foliage free of aphids. In addition to spraying, hose off clusters of aphids on the tree between sprays. Remove dying trees.

San Jose scale (half life size).

Fruit tree leafrollers (life size).

Scab.

PROBLEM: Some of the leaves are pale green to yellow and may drop prematurely from weakened limbs. The bark is encrusted with small (¹/₁₆ inch) hard, circular, slightly raised bumps with dull yellow centers. If the hard cover is scraped off, the insect underneath is yellow or olive-colored. There may be severe limb dieback, and entire branches may be killed. Red spots with white centers mar the apple skins.

ANALYSIS: San Jose scale
(*Quadraspidiotus perniciosus*)
These insects infest the bark, leaves, and fruit of many fruit trees. The scales bear live young in the spring. In late spring to midsummer the young scales, called *crawlers*, settle on leaves and twigs. The soft-bodied young feed by inserting their mouthparts and sucking sap from the plant. The legs atrophy and a hard, crusty shell develops over the body. An uncontrolled infestation of San Jose scales may kill large branches after 2 or 3 seasons.

SOLUTION: During the dormant season, spray the trunk and branches with ORTHO Volck Supreme Oil Spray. Spray with ORTHO Fruit & Vegetable Insect Control or ORTHO Malathion 50 Insect Spray, to kill the crawlers. For further information about scales, see page 878.

PROBLEM: Irregular holes appear in the leaves and fruit. Some of the leaves are rolled and held together with a web. Inside these rolled leaves are pale green worms with brown heads, up to ¾ inch long. The maturing apples are scarred and misshapen.

ANALYSIS: Fruit tree leafroller
(*Archips argyrospilus*)
These worms, the larvae of brown moths, are common pests of many fruit and ornamental trees. The moths lay their eggs on branches or twigs in June or July. The eggs hatch the following spring, and the emerging larvae feed on the blossoms and developing fruit and foliage. Leafrollers often wrap leaves around ripening fruit, then feed on the fruit inside. After about a month, the mature larvae pupate within rolled leaves, to emerge as moths in June or July.

SOLUTION: If practical, pick off and destroy rolled leaves to reduce the numbers of moths that will emerge later in the season. Next spring, spray the tree with ORTHO Home Orchard Spray or ORTHO Fruit & Vegetable Insect Control when 75 percent of the petals have fallen from the blossoms. Repeat the spray according to the directions on the label.

PROBLEM: Olive-brown velvety spots, ¼ inch or more in diameter, appear on the leaves and young fruit. As the infected apples mature, the spots develop into light to dark brown corky lesions. The fruit is often cracked and malformed, and may drop prematurely. Severely infected trees may completely defoliate.

ANALYSIS: Scab
This plant disease is caused by a fungus (*Venturia inaequalis*). It is one of the most serious diseases of apples in areas where spring weather is mild (60° to 70°F) and wet. The fungus spends the winter in infected leaf debris. In the spring, spores are produced and blown by the wind to developing leaves, flowers, and young apples. If there is adequate moisture on the foliage and fruit, the fungus infects them, and spots develop. The infected tissues produce more spores, which are splashed and blown to new leaf and fruit surfaces, where further spotting and decay occur. As the temperature increases, the fungus becomes less active. However, late summer rains initiate additional spore production, and apples that are infected when they are almost ready to be harvested will develop scab lesions after they are picked.

SOLUTION: Unless severely infected, the apples are edible. To prevent recurrence of the disease next year, remove and destroy leaf debris and infected fruit in the fall. Next spring, spray with ORTHO Home Orchard Spray or ORTHO Orthocide Garden Fungicide, according to label directions.

Apple varieties resistant to scab: Prima, Priscilla, Sir Prize.

APPLE

Powdery mildew.

Cedar-apple rust.

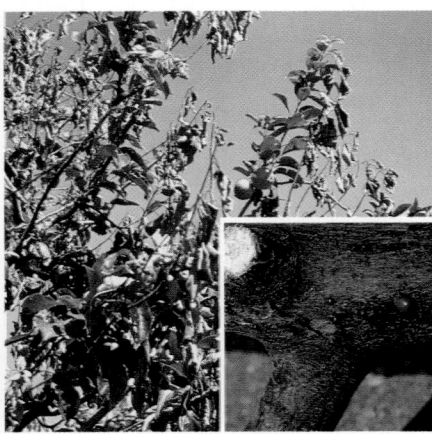

Twig dieback. *Insert:* Bacterial ooze.

PROBLEM: Gray-white powdery patches appear on the leaves. The new growth is often stunted, curled, and distorted. Infected buds may be shriveled and open later than usual, and infected leaves often turn brittle and die. The fruit may turn russet colored and be dwarfed.

ANALYSIS: Powdery mildew
This plant disease is caused by a fungus (*Podosphaera leucotricha*) that thrives in both humid and dry weather. The fungus spends the winter in leaf and flower buds. In the spring, spores are blown to the emerging young leaves, which are very susceptible to infection. The fungus saps plant nutrients, causing distortion and often death of the tender foliage. The fruit yield may be greatly reduced, since the infected blossoms do not set fruit. Young, developing apples that are attacked become dwarfed and turn russet colored. However, the fruit can be eaten if peeled. Powdery mildew is favored by warm spring days and cool nights.

SOLUTION: Spray infected trees with a fungicide containing *benomyl* and continue spraying at intervals of 10 to 14 days until 3 to 4 weeks after the petals have fallen from the blossoms. Resume spraying whenever the mildew recurs.

Apple varieties particularly susceptible to mildew: Cortland, Gravenstein, Idared, Jonathan, Rome Beauty.

PROBLEM: Pale yellow spots appear on the leaves and fruit in mid to late spring. These spots gradually enlarge, turn orange, and develop minute black dots. Small (⅙ inch) cups with fringed edges form on the lower surfaces of the leaves. Infected leaves and fruit may drop prematurely; the fruit is often small and deformed.

ANALYSIS: Cedar-apple rust
This plant disease is caused by a fungus (*Gymnosporangium juniperi-virginianae*) that affects both apples and certain species of juniper and red cedar. This disease cannot spread from apple to apple, or juniper to juniper, but must alternate between the two. In the spring, spores from brown and orange galls on juniper or cedar are blown up to 3 miles to apple trees. During mild, wet weather, the spores germinate and infect the leaves and fruit, causing spotting, and eventually premature leaf and apple drop. During the summer, spores are produced in the small cups on the underside of the leaves. These spores are blown back to junipers and cedars, causing new infections and starting the cycle over again. For more information about cedar-apple rust on junipers, see page 535.

SOLUTION: Cedar-apple rust cannot be controlled on this season's apples and leaves. Next spring, spray apple trees with a fungicide containing *zineb* or *ferbam* when the flower buds turn pink, again when 75 percent of the petals have fallen from the blossoms, and once more 10 days later. When practical, do not plant apples within several hundred yards of junipers or red cedar.

PROBLEM: Blossoms turn brown and die. Young, leafy twigs wilt from the tips down, turn brown, and die. A bend often develops at the tips of the twigs. On the branches, and at the base of the blighted twigs, the bark becomes water-soaked in appearance, then dark, sunken, and dry. In warm, moist spring weather, drops of brown ooze appear on the surface of these lesions. During the summer, shoots or branches may wilt and turn dark brown.

ANALYSIS: Fireblight
This plant disease is caused by a bacterium (*Erwinia amylovora*) that commonly affects apples, pears, and several ornamental plants. (For a list of susceptible plants, see page 1001.) The bacteria spend the winter in sunken lesions (cankers) on the branches and twigs. In the spring the bacteria ooze out of the canker and are carried by insects to the apple blossoms. Splashing rain, honeybees, and other insects continue to spread the bacteria to healthy blossoms. Bacterial decay causes cankers to develop on the twigs and branches, often resulting in conspicuous branch and twig dieback. Wounded leaves, twigs, and suckers are also susceptible to infection. For more information about fireblight, see page 660.

SOLUTION: Prune and destroy infected twigs and branches at least 12 inches beyond visible decay. Sterilize pruning shears with rubbing alcohol after each cut. A protective spray of *basic copper sulfate* or *streptomycin* applied before the blossoms open next spring will help prevent infection. Repeat at intervals of 5 to 7 days until the end of the blooming period. For a list of resistant apple varieties, see page 1005.

--- APRICOT ---

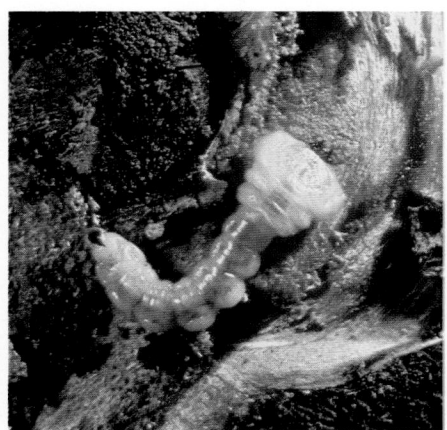

Pacific flatheaded borer (twice life size).

PROBLEM: Leaves wilt and turn brown. Patches of bark on the trunk are sunken, discolored, and may be soaked with sap. There may be holes about ⅜ inch in diameter in the affected bark. Sawdust-filled tunnels in the wood may contain yellowish white, flat-headed grubs about ¾ inch long. In late spring to midsummer, bronze or copper-colored beetles ½ to ¾ inch long may be seen feeding on the foliage. Newly planted or weak trees are most severely affected.

ANALYSIS: Flatheaded borers
(*Chrysobothris* species)
In addition to damaging apples, these insects attack many other trees and shrubs. In late spring to midsummer, the females begin to lay eggs in crevices in the bark. The emerging larvae bore through the bark into the outer layer of wood, creating winding tunnels. These tunnels damage the nutrient and water-conducting vessels in the tree, causing twig and branch dieback and sometimes killing the tree. The mature larvae bore deep into the heartwood to pupate; adult beetles emerge the following spring. Newly transplanted, weakened, and diseased trees are most susceptible to borer infestation.

SOLUTION: Apply ORTHO Lindane Borer & Leaf Miner Spray according to label directions. Keep your tree healthy and vigorous by watering, fertilizing, and pruning it properly. For more cultural information, see page 626. Discourage borer infestation by wrapping the trunk soon after bloom with tree wrapping paper or burlap. Prune out and destroy infested branches.

APRICOT

ADAPTATION AND POLLINATION: See variety chart on page 1005.

SOIL: Any good, deep, well-drained garden soil. pH 5.5 to 8.0

FERTILIZER: Fertilize with ORTHO Evergreen, Tree & Shrub Food 12–6–6 according to label directions.

WATER:
How much: Apply enough water to wet the soil 3 to 4 feet deep. To determine the proper amount of water for your soil type, see page 906.
How often: Water when the soil 6 inches below the surface is just barely moist.

PRUNING: Apricots are borne on short fruiting branches (spurs), which grow on 2-year-old wood. The spurs continue to fruit for 2 to 4 years. Prune back last year's growth to half its length, and thin out spurred branches that have stopped fruiting (4 years or older). Thin out weak, crossing, or dead twigs and branches. For large apricots, thin fruits when they are large enough to handle to 3 to 5 inches apart, with no more than 2 fruits per spur.

HARVEST: Harvest when the fruits are fully colored and slightly soft. When they are ripe, the apricot stem separates easily from the spur when the fruit is gently lifted.

Plum curculio (5 times life size).

PROBLEM: The ripening fruit is misshapen, rotten, and often drops prematurely. There are holes about ⅛ inch in diameter and deep, crescent-shaped scars on the fruit. When cut open, the damaged fruit may contain crescent-shaped yellow-gray grubs with brown heads.

ANALYSIS: Plum curculio
(*Conotrachelus nenuphar*)
These insects, found east of the Rockies, attack other stone fruits, apples, and pears, as well as apricots. The adult insects are brown beetles with long curved snouts. They hibernate in debris and other protected places during the winter. The beetles emerge in the spring when new growth starts and begin feeding on young leaves, blossoms, and developing fruit. After 5 to 6 weeks, the female beetles start to lay eggs in the young fruit. The grubs that hatch from the eggs feed for several weeks in the fruit. Usually the infested apricots drop to the ground. The grubs eventually leave the fruit and bore into the soil, where they pupate. The emerging beetles feed on fruit for a few weeks, then go into hibernation. Or, in the South, they will lay eggs, producing a second generation of grubs in the late summer.

SOLUTION: Once the fruit is infested, there is no way to kill the grubs inside the fruit. Spray with ORTHO Home Orchard Spray or ORTHO Malathion 50 Insect Spray to kill beetles that may be feeding on fruit, or laying eggs. Pick up and destroy all fallen fruit. Next spring, spray the trees when the petals are falling from the blossoms; repeat applications according to directions on the label.

APRICOT

Twig blight.

Fruit rot.

Bacterial leaf spot.

PROBLEM: The blossoms and young leaves decay, wilt, and turn brown during the first 2 weeks of the bloom period. Often the decayed blossoms fail to drop and hang on the tree throughout the growing season. In humid conditions, masses of gray spores may appear on the infected flower parts. There is often extensive twig dieback. Sunken lesions (cankers) may develop on the twigs and branches as the season progresses; a thick gummy material often oozes from these cankers.

PROBLEM: Small circular brown spots appear on the young apricots. Later in the season, as the apricots start to mature, these spots may enlarge to rot part or all of the fruit. During moist weather, the rotted apricots are covered with tufts of gray spores. When the infected fruit is sliced open, the flesh inside is seen to be brown, firm, and fairly dry. Infected apricots either drop prematurely or dry out, turn dark brown, and remain on the tree past the normal harvest period. Many twigs die. There are sunken lesions (cankers) on some of these twigs. A thick, gummy material often oozes from these cankers.

PROBLEM: Water-soaked spots on the undersides of the leaves turn brown or black; often the centers of the spots fall out. The tips of the leaves may die, and eventually the leaves will drop. When the fruit sets, the surface may be dotted with spots that later turn into deep sunken brown pits, often surrounded by yellow rings. Sunken lesions can often be seen at the joints of the twigs.

ANALYSIS: Bacterial leaf spot
This disease is caused by a bacterium (*Xanthomonas pruni*) that also attacks peach, nectarine, and plum. The disease is common east of the Rocky Mountains, and is one of the more destructive stone fruit diseases. The bacteria spend the winter in the lesions on the twigs, oozing out in the spring to be carried by splashing raindrops to the young leaves and shoots, which they infect and decay. Periods of frequent rainfall favor the infection.

ANALYSIS: Brown rot
This plant disease, caused by either of two closely related fungi (*Monolinia laxa* or *M. fructicola*), is very destructive to apricots and to all of the stone fruits. The fungi spend the winter in twig cankers or in rotted apricots (mummies) in the tree or on the ground. In the spring, spores are blown or splashed from cankers or mummies to the healthy flower buds. After penetrating and decaying the flowers, the fungus grows down into the twigs, producing brown, sunken cankers. During moist weather a thick, gummy sap oozes from the lesions, and tufts of gray spores may form on the infected areas. Spores from cankers and infected blossoms or mummies are splashed and blown to the maturing fruit. Young apricots are fairly resistant to infection, but maturing apricots are vulnerable. Brown rot develops most rapidly in mild, moist conditions.

SOLUTION: There is no adequate control for this disease. Spraying with *basic copper sulfate* when the buds open may help suppress the disease, but will not eliminate it.

SOLUTION: If there are still uninfected blossoms left on your tree, spray with ORTHO Home Orchard Spray to protect them from further infection. Spray twice at 10-day intervals. Next spring, spray trees at early bloom with ORTHO Home Orchard Spray and continue to spray according to label directions. To protect maturing apricots from infection, spray them with ORTHO Home Orchard Spray about 3 weeks before they are to be harvested. Remove and destroy all infected apricots and mummies. Prune out cankers and blighted twigs. Clean up and destroy all debris around the tree. Plant resistant varieties.

Apricot resistance to brown rot:
  Most susceptible: Blenheim, Derby Royal, Royal
  Fairly resistant: Tilton

Scab.

Shothole fungus.

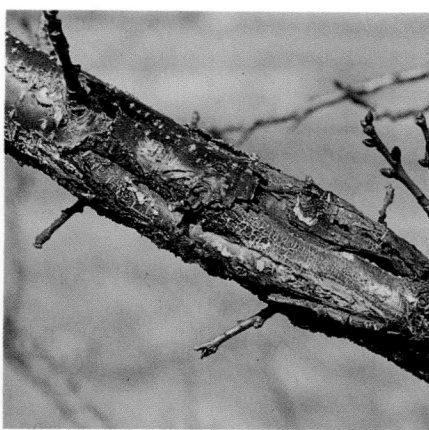

Cytospora canker.

PROBLEM: Small, olive-green spots appear on the half-grown fruit. These spots are usually centered around the stem end of the apricot. The spots eventually turn brown and velvety. The fruit is often dwarfed, deformed, or cracked. There may be small brown spots and holes in the leaves, and many twigs die back.

ANALYSIS: Scab
This plant disease is caused by a fungus (*Cladosporium carpophilum*), that attacks peaches, nectarines, cherries, and plums as well as apricots. The fungus spends the winter on twig lesions. In the spring, spores are splashed and blown to the developing foliage and fruit. The young fruit do not show scab lesions for at least a month after they are initially infected. Spores produced on the infected leaves, twigs, and fruit will continue to infect healthy apricots throughout the growing season.

SOLUTION: It's too late to do anything about the spots on this year's fruit, but they are edible if peeled. Next year, spray a fungicide containing *captan* or *benomyl* on the tree when the petals have fallen from the blossoms. If scab is serious in your area, continue to spray at intervals of 10 to 14 days about a month before the apricots are harvested.

PROBLEM: Small purplish spots appear on the leaves and developing fruit in early spring. There may be small round holes in the infected leaves. Infected leaf buds and leaves often die. The spots on the maturing apricots turn scablike, drop off, and leave rough, corky lesions.

ANALYSIS: Shothole fungus
This plant disease, also called *coryneum blight* and *peach blight*, is caused by a fungus (*Coryneum beijerinckii*) that attacks almonds and some of the stone fruits. The fungus spends the winter in lesions on the twigs and buds. In the spring, the spores are splashed by rain to the developing blossoms, leaves, and fruit, causing spotting and tissue death. Infection causes the leaf tissue to produce a layer of cells that walls off the damaged area. The center of the spot then drops out. Severe infection may defoliate the tree and reduce the apricot yield. The disease is favored by wet spring weather.

SOLUTION: There is no adequate control during the growing season. To prevent twig and leaf bud infection, spray the tree this fall with a fungicide containing *captan* soon after the leaves have fallen. Spray again in the spring when the petals have fallen from the flowers.

PROBLEM: Oval or oblong sunken lesions on the bark enlarge gradually. A sticky gum may ooze from the lesion, sometimes followed by the emergence of curly orange threads. Later, small black freckles appear on the bark along the edge of the lesions. Leaves on the affected branches may turn brown and die, or the entire branch may die.

ANALYSIS: Cytospora canker
This plant disease, also known as *perennial canker*, is caused by 2 related fungi (*Cytospora cincta* and *C. leucostoma*) that also attack peach, plum, and cherry. The fungi spend the winter in sunken lesions (cankers) or on dead wood. In the spring, black fungal bodies develop in the bark, and curly orange fungal chains form. These chains release spores that are spread by wind and splashing rain to healthy trees. Infection usually occurs through injured tissues. Bark that is damaged by sunscald, cold, pruning wounds, or mechanical injury is especially susceptible. Fungal decay causes the formation of depressed lesions (cankers). A sticky gum may ooze from the cankers. The branch or stem above the canker may die due to decay or clogging of the water-conducting tissue in the branch. Mild, wet weather (70° to 85°F) enhances the development of this disease.

SOLUTION: No fully adequate control is available; a combination of procedures must be used. Remove badly infected branches and cut out cankers. For more information about canker removal and treatment, see page 911. Avoid mechanical injuries to the tree and paint the trunk with white latex paint to protect against cold injury and sunburn.

APRICOT

Peachtree borer (twice life size).

Peach twig borer (twice life size).

Oriental fruit moth larva (twice life size).

PROBLEM: Holes appear in the lower part of the trunk or in the upper trunk and lower crotches. A thick gummy substance may ooze from these holes. There may be sawdust around the holes or base of the tree. In mid to late summer, empty pupa skins may protrude from these holes. During the spring and summer, some of the leaves and branches may wilt. Severely affected trees may die.

ANALYSIS: Peachtree borers
(*Synanthedon* species)
These moth larvae are most damaging to peaches, but also attack other stone fruits and some ornamental trees. The clear-winged moths (which resemble wasps) lay their eggs in mid to late summer. The larvae that emerge bore into the bark. Their tunnels interfere with the circulation of water and nutrients, causing twig and branch wilting and dieback. The borers feed throughout the winter and into the spring. A gummy sap often oozes from the borer tunnels. This sap is often mixed with sawdustlike particles, the product of larval feeding. The borers pupate in early to midsummer. Their cocoons are located at the base of the tree or just inside their tunnels. The moths emerge several weeks later.

SOLUTION: Apply a spray containing *lindane* to the trunk and lower branches. Do not spray the fruit or foliage. Next year, in late May or early June, kill the egg-laying moths by spraying the trunk and crotches with an insecticide containing *malathion*. Continue spraying at intervals of 3 weeks until early August. Individual borers may be killed by inserting a wire into the borer holes.

PROBLEM: New growth at the tips of the twigs wilts and dies. When the affected twigs are sliced open lengthwise, worms about 1/2 inch long are found inside. The reddish brown color of these worm distinguishes them from Oriental fruit moth worms, which cause similar damage. Later in the season, some of the maturing fruit when cut open are also found to contain these worms. During the summer, there may be cocoons attached to the branches or tree crotches.

ANALYSIS: Peach twig borer
(*Anarsia lineatella*)
This borer attacks all of the stone fruits, and is particularly damaging along the Pacific Coast. The young larvae hibernate during the winter in burrows under loose bark or in other protected places on the tree. When the tree blooms in the spring, the larvae emerge and bore into the young buds, shoots, and tender twigs, causing twig and leaf death. When mature, they leave the twigs and pupate in cocoons attached to branches. After several weeks, gray moths emerge and lay eggs on the twigs, leaves, and fruit. Egg laying and larval damage can occur all through the growing season. Later in the summer, larvae feed almost exclusively on the maturing fruit. In addition to ruining the fruit, these pests may cause abnormal branching patterns on young trees.

SOLUTION: Worms in the twigs and fruit cannot be killed with pesticides. To prevent future worm damage, kill the moths by spraying infested trees with ORTHO Fruit & Vegetable Insect Control according to label directions. Next spring, spray again just before the blossoms open. Repeat the treatment 2 more times at intervals of 10 to 14 days.

PROBLEM: New growth at the tips of the twigs wilts and dies. When the affected twigs are sliced open lengthwise, worms about 1/2 inch long are found inside. The pinkish white color of these worms distinguishes them from peach twig borers, which cause similar damage. Later in the season, some of the maturing fruit when cut open are also found to contain these worms. Often there are holes filled with a sticky gum in the apricots.

ANALYSIS: Oriental fruit moth
(*Grapholitha molesta*)
The larvae of these night-flying moths damage stone fruits, apples, and pears. In the spring brown adult moths lay eggs on the young apricot twigs and leaves. The larvae emerge and bore into the young buds, shoots, and tender twigs, causing twig and leaf death. Egg laying and larval damage can occur all through the growing season. Late in the summer, larvae feed almost exclusively on the maturing fruit. They leave gum-filled holes in the apricots when they exit to pupate. In addition to ruining fruit, these pests may cause abnormal branching patterns on young trees when large numbers of twigs are infested.

SOLUTION: Worms in the twigs and fruit cannot be killed with pesticides. To prevent future worm damage, kill the moths by spraying infested trees with ORTHO Fruit & Vegetable Insect Control according to label directions. Next spring, spray again when the petals start to fall from the blossoms. Repeat the treatment 2 more times at intervals of 10 to 14 days.

_____ AVOCADO _____

San Jose scale (twice life size).

PROBLEM: The leaves are pale green to yellow, and may drop prematurely from weakened limbs. The bark is encrusted with small (¹/₁₀ inch or smaller) hard, circular, slightly raised bumps with dull yellow centers. If the hard cover is scraped off, the insect underneath is found to be yellow or olive. There may be severe limb dieback, and entire branches may be killed. Fruit may be marred by red-purple specks.

ANALYSIS: San Jose scale
(*Quadraspidiotus perniciosus*)
These insects infest the bark, leaves, and fruit of many fruit trees. The scales bear live young in the spring. In late spring to midsummer the young scales, called *crawlers*, settle on leaves and twigs. The small (¹/₁₆ inch), soft-bodied young feed by inserting their mouthparts and sucking sap from the plant. The legs usually atrophy and a hard, crusty shell develops over the body. An uncontrolled infestation of San Jose scale may kill large branches after 2 or 3 seasons.

SOLUTION: During the dormant season, spray the trunk and branches with ORTHO Volck Supreme Oil Spray. The crawlers may be killed with ORTHO Malathion 50 Insect Spray or ORTHO Fruit & Vegetable Insect Control, applied in the late spring. For further information about scales, see page 878.

AVOCADO _____

ADAPTATION: See the variety chart on page 1001.

SOIL: Any good, deep, very well-drained soil. pH 6.0 to 8.0

FERTILIZER: Fertilize with ORTHO Citrus & Avocado Food 12–6–10 according to label directions.

WATER:
How much: Apply enough water to wet the soil 3 to 4 feet deep. To determine the proper amount of water for your soil type, see page 906.
How often: Water when the soil 6 inches below the surface is just barely moist.

PRUNING: During the summer, prune lightly to shape the tree. Remove weak, diseased, or dead twigs and branches. Thin the fruits only if there is danger of branch breakage from excessive weight.

HARVEST: Avocados do not soften on the tree, so it is difficult to tell when the fruit is ripe. Purple or dark varieties are usually mature when the fruit starts to turn from green to dark. When fruits of green varieties begin to mature, the bright green color diminishes, a yellow tinge appears on the skin and stem, the fruit becomes smoother, and small corky areas may appear on the skin. The seed coat will turn brown and papery. When picking, cut the stem as close to the fruit as possible without injury.

Omnivorous looper (twice life size).

PROBLEM: The upper surfaces of the leaves may be stripped away, leaving a thin brown membrane; or the leaves may be entirely chewed between the veins. The fruit may be distorted or scarred. Striped yellow to pale green worms up to 2½ inches long are eating the leaves. These worms may be seen on the leaf edges, or in between two leaves that are webbed together. Severely infested trees may be partially defoliated.

ANALYSIS: Omnivorous looper
(*Sabulodes caberata*)
This worm, the larva of a brown night-flying moth, attacks avocados and other trees and shrubs. The moths lay eggs on the undersides of the leaves. The larvae that hatch from these eggs feed on the foliage and developing fruit for about 6 weeks. Then they pupate inside leaves that they web together. Larval damage occurs all year, but is most severe during the spring and summer.

SOLUTION: There are several natural predators that keep this pest under control, including tiny wasps (*Trichogramma* species), flies, viruses, and fungi. If infestation is severe, spray with *Bacillus thuringiensis*, a bacterial insecticide. *Bacillus thuringiensis* is most effective when the loopers are small.

AVOCADO

Fruit scab.

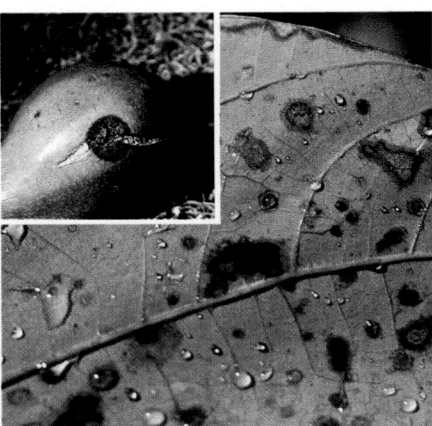

Cercospora leaf spot. *Insert:* Infected fruit.

Animal damage.

PROBLEM: Fruit develop raised, dark brown to purplish brown, scablike areas. Spots may be scattered, or they may grow together to form large scabby areas that cover the entire surface of the fruit. Heavily infected fruit may be deformed or dwarfed. Fruit of all sizes can be affected. The disease does not affect the eating quality of the mature fruit. However, other decay organisms may gain entrance into the fruit through scab lesions.

ANALYSIS: Fruit scab
This disfiguring disease is caused by a fungus (*Sphaceloma perseae*) that is carried over from one season to the next on stem and leaf lesions. Young fruit are usually infected just after the petals fall from the flowers. As fruit ages, it becomes more resistant to infection, but does not acquire immunity until it is more than half grown.

SOLUTION: Spray the entire tree with a fungicide containing *basic copper sulfate*. Use a spreader-sticker with the fungicide to enable it to coat plant parts more effectively. (For more information on spreader-stickers, see page 915.) Apply sprays at the following times:
1. Late January to mid-February, when flower buds swell.
2. Mid-February to mid-March, at fruit set.
3. Three to four weeks after second spray.
4. May 1 to May 15 (all varieties).
5. June 1 to June 15 (midseason and late varieties).
6. July 15 (late varieties only).

PROBLEM: Leaves are covered with angular brown spots, about $1/16$ inch in diameter, that often penetrate completely through the leaf. Individual spots may grow together to form large spots. During moist periods throughout the year, spores are produced in grayish tufts on either surface of the spot. Severely infected leaves often drop.

ANALYSIS: Cercospora leaf spot
This plant disease is caused by a fungus (*Cercospora purpurea*) that infects avocado leaves and fruit. Old leaf infections are the usual source of spores. In some years, much leaf loss can occur, weakening the tree and slowing fruit development. When the fungus attacks the fruit, the spots often provide convenient entryways for other fungi that rot the fruit.

SOLUTION: Spray the tree with a fungicide containing *basic copper sulfate*. Use a spreader-sticker with the fungicide to enable it to coat plant parts more effectively. (For more information on spreader-stickers, see page 915.) Apply sprays at the following times:
1. Late January to mid-February, when flower buds begin to swell.
2. Mid-February to mid-March, at fruit set.
3. Three to four weeks after second spray.
4. May 1 to May 15 (all varieties).
5. June 1 to June 15 (midseason and late varieties).
6. July 15 (late varieties only).

PROBLEM: Fruit has large holes chewed in it. In some cases, the entire fruit except for the seed may be eaten. Fruit loss is heaviest during the ripening season, but some losses may occur earlier. No insects or similar pests can be found doing the damage.

ANALYSIS: Animal damage
Birds, squirrels, and rats are fond of avocados, and can destroy large quantities of fruit. Birds attack immature fruit; rats and squirrels tend to attack mature or nearly mature fruit.

SOLUTION: When the problem becomes too severe on mature fruit, pick all remaining fruit. Traps may be used to catch squirrels and rats, but birds cannot usually be discouraged easily. Netting may have to be placed over fruit to protect them. Scare devices are sometimes effective in controlling most animal pests. Physical barriers to prevent trees from being climbed are much more effective. For more information, see page 616.

CHERRY

Phytophthora root rot.

PROBLEM: Leaves are smaller than normal, yellowish, and may wilt and drop. The foliage is sparse, and there is little new growth. Entire branches may die, and the fruit is often small. Eventually the entire tree may wilt and die, even though the soil is sufficiently moist. The bark on part or all of the trunk just above or below the soil line may be darkened. When the diseased bark is scraped away, the underlying sapwood is discolored tan to black.

ANALYSIS: Phytophthora root rot
This plant disease is caused by a soil-inhabiting fungus (*Phytophthora cinnamomi*) that infects many fruit, nut, and ornamental trees and shrubs. It penetrates the roots and crown of the tree. As the fungus decays the sapwood, the flow of water and nutrients is blocked, eventually resulting in the death of the tree. The fungus is spread by infected plants, and by infested soil and soil water. Phytophthora root rot is greatly favored by wet or poorly drained soil. Trees planted in lawns, flower beds, or other moist or poorly drained areas are highly susceptible to this disease.

SOLUTION: No chemical control is available. Once the fungus becomes established in the soil, it will remain indefinitely. The lives of mildly infected trees may be prolonged. Remove the soil from around the crown of the tree, exposing the major roots. Always keep this area dry by providing drainage away from the tree. Avoid overwatering. Remove severely diseased and dying trees. Do not replant susceptible plants in the same area. For a list of resistant trees and shrubs, see page 1000.

CHERRY

ADAPTATION AND POLLINATION: See the variety chart on page 1008.

SOIL: Any good, deep, well-drained garden soil. pH 5.5 to 8.0.

FERTILIZER: Fertilize with ORTHO Evergreen, Tree & Shrub Food 12–6–6 according to label directions.

WATER:
How much: Apply enough water to wet the soil 3 to 4 feet deep. To determine the proper amount of water for your soil type, see page 906.
How often: Water when the soil 6 inches below the surface is just barely moist.

PRUNING: Cherries are borne on short fruiting branches (spurs) that grow on 2-year-old wood. The spurs are very long-lived and often continue to bear for 10 years or more. Prune lightly, thinning out weak, crossing, or dead twigs and branches.

HARVEST: Harvest when the cherries are fully colored. With ripe cherries, the stem will easily separate from the spur when the fruit is gently lifted or pulled. When picking cherries, avoid damaging the spurs.

Cherry fruit fly maggots (3 times life size).

PROBLEM: The fruit is malformed, shrunken, or shriveled. Often the cherries are rotten and pulpy; there may be holes in the fruit. Tapered, yellow-white, legless worms up to ¼ inch long may be found in the cherries. Many cherries drop prematurely.

ANALYSIS: Cherry fruit flies
(*Rhagoletis* species)
These worms are the larvae of several closely related flies. The adult flies, about half the size of the common house fly, appear in the late spring for a period of about a month. They lay eggs in the cherries through holes they puncture in the skin. After several days the eggs hatch into maggots that tunnel through the cherry flesh. Infested cherries usually drop to the ground, and the mature maggots burrow into the soil to pupate. They remain in the soil throughout the winter, and emerge as adults next spring.

SOLUTION: You cannot control the worms in this year's fruit, but you can probably prevent the recurrence of the problem next year. Look for the adult flies in late spring as the fruit is forming. As soon as fruit flies appear, spray with ORTHO Fruit & Vegetable Insect Control. Repeat the application 2 more times at intervals of 14 days.

CHERRY

Plum curculio (4 times life size).

Pearslug larva (twice life size).

Oriental fruit moth damage.

PROBLEM: The fruit is shriveled, blackened, and soft, and often drops prematurely. There are holes about ⅛ inch in diameter and deep, crescent-shaped scars on the fruit. When damaged fruit is cut open, crescent-shaped yellow-gray grubs with brown heads may be found.

ANALYSIS: Plum curculio
(*Conotrachelus nenuphar*)
These insects, found east of the Rocky Mountains, attack other stone fruits, apples, and pears as well as cherries. The adult insects are brown beetles with long curved snouts. They hibernate in debris and other protected places during the winter. The beetles emerge in the spring when new growth starts and feed on young leaves, blossoms, and developing fruit. After 5 to 6 weeks, the female beetles lay eggs in the young cherries. During this process, they cut distinctive crescent-shaped slits into the fruit. The young grubs that hatch from the eggs feed for several weeks in the fruit. Usually the infested cherries drop to the ground. The grubs eventually leave the fruit and bore into the soil, where they pupate. The emerging beetles feed on fruit for a few weeks, then go into hibernation. Or, in the South, they lay eggs, producing a second generation of grubs in the late summer.

SOLUTION: Once the fruit is infested, there is no way to kill the grubs inside the fruit. Spray with ORTHO Home Orchard Spray or ORTHO Malathion 50 Insect Spray to kill beetles that may be feeding on fruit, or laying eggs. Pick up and destroy all fallen cherries. Next spring, spray all trees when the petals are falling from the blossoms; repeat applications according to label directions.

PROBLEM: The upper surfaces of the leaves are chewed between the veins, leaving a lacy, translucent layer of tissue that turns brown. Dark green to orange, wet, sluglike worms up to ½ inch long may be feeding on the leaves. Severely infested trees may be defoliated.

ANALYSIS: Pearslug
(*Caliroa cerasi*)
Although pearslugs closely resemble slugs, they are actually the larvae of black and yellow flies that infest pears, plums, and some ornamental trees in addition to cherries. The adult flies, which appear in the late spring, lay their eggs in the leaves. The young larvae that hatch from these eggs exude a slimy, olive-green substance, giving them a sluglike appearance. They feed on the foliage for about a month, then drop to the ground, burrow into the soil, and pupate. Young trees that are severely infested by pearslugs may be greatly weakened and will produce fewer, poor quality cherries.

SOLUTION: Spray the infested tree with ORTHO Home Orchard Spray. Repeat the spray if infestation recurs.

PROBLEM: New growth at the tips of the twigs wilts and dies. When the affected twigs are sliced open lengthwise, pinkish white worms up to ½ inch long are found inside. Later in the season, some of the maturing fruit when cut open may also be found to contain these worms.

ANALYSIS: Oriental fruit moth
(*Grapholitha molesta*)
The larvae of these night-flying moths damage stone fruits, apples, and pears. The larvae hibernate in cocoons on the tree bark, or in branch crotches. In the spring they pupate, emerge as brown adult moths, and lay eggs on the young cherry twigs and leaves. The larvae bore into the young buds, shoots, and tender twigs, causing twig and leaf death. When mature they leave the twigs, spin cocoons, and pupate in the tree or in debris on the ground. After several weeks, moths emerge to lay their eggs. Egg laying and larval damage can occur all through the growing season. Later in the summer, larvae feed almost exclusively on the maturing cherries. They leave gum-filled holes in the cherries when they exit to pupate. In addition to ruining the fruit, these pests may cause abnormal branching patterns on young trees when large numbers of twigs are infested.

SOLUTION: Worms in the twigs and fruit cannot be killed with pesticides. To prevent future worm damage, kill the moths by spraying infested trees with ORTHO Fruit & Vegetable Insect Control or ORTHO Liquid Sevin. Apply as directed on the label.

Shothole borer beetle (life size).

Sap oozing from borer hole.

Bacterial canker.

PROBLEM: Many small holes (1/16 to 1/8 inch in diameter) are bored in the twigs, branches, and sometimes trunk of the tree. A sticky gum often oozes from the holes. The holes may be plugged with the bodies of dead insects. When sliced open, the branches reveal sawdust-filled tunnels in the wood. Pinkish white, slightly curved grubs may be found in the tunnels. Brownish black beetles 1/10 inch long are often present on the bark. The foliage on damaged branches sometimes wilts and turns brown. Twigs and buds may be killed, and entire branches may die.

ANALYSIS: Shothole borer
(*Scolytus rugulosus*)
This beetle, sometimes known as the *fruit tree bark beetle*, also attacks other stone fruits and many ornamental trees. The adult beetles that emerge in the late spring or early summer feed at the base of buds and small twigs, often killing them. The female beetles bore into the wood, creating tunnels in which they lay their eggs. The grubs that hatch from the eggs bore into the inner wood, creating sawdust-filled burrows 2 to 4 inches long. The grubs pupate just under the bark, then emerge as adult beetles. The last generation of grubs spends the winter in the tunnels, emerging the following spring. Weakened, diseased, and dying trees and branches are most susceptible to borer infestation.

SOLUTION: Apply a spray containing *lindane* to the lower part of the trunk, wetting the bark thoroughly. Avoid spraying the fruit and foliage. During the dormant season, remove and destroy infested branches. Keep the tree healthy by watering and fertilizing it properly. For cultural information, see page 637.

PROBLEM: Holes appear in the lower part of the trunk or in the upper trunk and lower crotches. A thick, gummy substance may ooze from these holes. There may be sawdust around the holes or the base of the tree. In mid to late summer, empty pupa skins may protrude from these holes. During the spring and summer, some of the leaves and branches may wilt. Severely affected trees may die.

ANALYSIS: Peachtree borers
(*Synanthedon species*)
The larvae of these moths are damaging to stone fruits and some ornamental trees. The clear-winged moths (which resemble wasps) lay their eggs in mid to late summer. The larvae that emerge bore into the bark either just above or just below the ground level, or in the upper trunk and main crotches. Their tunnels interfere with the circulation of water and nutrients, causing twig and branch wilting and dieback throughout the growing season. The borers feed throughout the winter and into the spring in their tunnels. A gummy sap may ooze from the borer tunnels. This sap is often mixed with sawdustlike particles, the product of larval feeding. The borers pupate in early to midsummer; their cocoons are located at the base of the tree or just inside their tunnels. The moths emerge several weeks later.

SOLUTION: Apply a spray containing *lindane* to the trunk and lower branches. Do not spray the fruit or foliage. Next year, in late May or June, kill the egg-laying moths by spraying the trunk and crotches with a pesticide containing *malathion*. Continue spraying at intervals of 3 weeks until early August. Individual borers may be killed by inserting a wire into the borer holes.

PROBLEM: Sunken, elliptical lesions appear on the trunk or branches. Throughout the fall, winter, and spring, thick, amber, sour-smelling gum oozes from these lesions. In the spring, especially when the weather is very wet and cold, blossoms may turn brown and wither. Individual branches may fail to produce foliage, or, as the season progresses, entire branches may die back. There may be angular holes in the leaves. Sometimes dark, sunken lesions appear in the fruit.

ANALYSIS: Bacterial canker
This plant disease, also known as *bacterial gummosis* or *bacterial blast*, attacks various fruit and nut trees, but is most severe on cherries. This disease is caused by bacteria (*Pseudomonas syringae*). During the fall, winter, and early spring, large quantities of bacteria-containing gum ooze from the cankers. Splashing rain spreads the bacteria to dormant buds, twigs, and branches. Infection occurs through wounds in the twigs and branches, and bacterial decay causes cankers to form. Bacterial activity decreases in summer. However, slowly developing cankers may encircle a branch, and by midsummer, the affected branches and limbs start to die back. With the onset of cool, wet, fall weather, bacterial activity increases again. This disease is most serious on young trees.

SOLUTION: Bacterial canker is difficult to control. Prune out diseased branches. After each cut, sterilize pruning shears with rubbing alcohol. In the fall, spray with a fungicide containing *basic copper sulfate*. Keep the tree healthy. For care of cherries, see page 637. For a list of resistant cherries, see page 1008.

CHERRY

Fruit rot.

Cankers.

San Jose scales (life size).

PROBLEM: Blossoms and young leaves decay, wilt, and turn brown during the first 2 weeks of the bloom period. The decayed blossoms may fail to drop and hang on the tree through the growing season. In humid conditions, masses of gray spores may appear on the infected flower parts. There is often extensive twig dieback. Sunken lesions sometimes develop on the twigs and branches as the season progresses. These lesions may exude a sticky ooze.

ANALYSIS: Brown rot
This plant disease, caused by either of 2 closely related fungi (*Monilinia laxa* or *M. fructicola*), is very destructive to all of the stone fruits. The fungi spend the winter in twin cankers or in rotted cherries (mummies) in the tree or on the ground. In the spring, spores are blown or splashed from cankers or mummies to the healthy flower buds. After penetrating and decaying the flowers, the fungus grows down into the twigs, producing brown, sunken cankers. During moist weather a thick, gummy sap oozes from the lesions, and tufts of gray spores may form on the infected areas. Spores from cankers and infected blossoms or mummies are splashed and blown to the maturing cherries. Young cherries are fairly resistant to infection, but maturing cherries are vulnerable. Brown rot develops most rapidly in mild, moist conditions.

SOLUTION: If there are still uninfected blossoms left on the tree, spray with ORTHO Home Orchard Spray or ORTHO Orthocide Garden Fungicide to protect them from further infection. Spray twice at intervals of 10 days. To protect maturing cherries from infection, spray again about 3 weeks before they are to be harvested. Remove and destroy all infected fruits and mummies. Prune out cankers and blighted twigs. Clean up and destroy all debris around the tree. Next spring, spray trees at early and full bloom with ORTHO Home Orchard Spray or ORTHO Orthocide Garden Fungicide.

PROBLEM: Small, circular brown spots appear on the young cherries. Later in the season, as the fruit begins to mature, these spots may enlarge to rot part or all of the cherries. During moist weather, the rotten fruit is covered with tufts of gray spores. Infected cherries either drop prematurely or dry out, turn dark brown, and remain on the tree past the normal harvest period. Many twigs die. There are sunken lesions (cankers) on some of these twigs. A thick, gummy material often oozes from these cankers.

PROBLEM: Some of the leaves are pale green to yellow and may drop prematurely from weakened limbs. Or they may turn brown and wither, and remain attached to the tree into the winter. The bark is encrusted with small (1/10 inch) hard, circular, slightly raised bumps with dull yellow centers. If the hard cover is scraped off, the insect underneath is yellow or olive. There may be severe limb dieback and entire branches may be killed. The fruit may be marred by specks.

ANALYSIS: San Jose scale
(*Quadraspidiotus perniciosus*)
These insects infest the bark, leaves, and fruit of many fruit trees. The scales bear live young in the spring. In late spring to midsummer the young scales, called *crawlers*, settle on leaves and twigs. The small (1/16 inch), soft-bodied young feed by inserting their mouthparts and sucking sap from the plant. The legs atrophy and a hard, crusty shell develops over the body. An uncontrolled infestation of San Jose scale may kill large branches after 2 or 3 seasons.

SOLUTION: During the dormant season, spray the trunk and branches with ORTHO Volck Supreme Oil Spray. The crawlers may be killed with ORTHO Malathion 50 Insect Spray or ORTHO Fruit & Vegetable Insect Control, applied in the late spring. For further information about scale, see page 878.

CITRUS

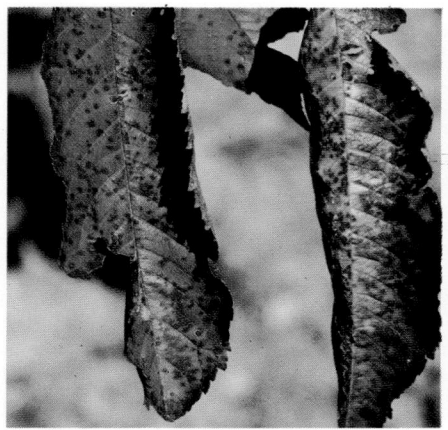

Cherry leafspot.

PROBLEM: Purple spots appear on the upper surfaces of the leaves. The centers of the spots may fall out, leaving holes in the leaves. Many of the spotted leaves are yellow and dying. The undersides of the leaves may be dotted with cream-colored masses of spores. In severe cases, the fruit is also spotted. The tree defoliates prematurely, and the cherry yield is reduced and of poor quality. The fruit is often soft and watery.

ANALYSIS: Cherry leafspot
This plant disease, also known as *yellow leafspot*, is caused by a fungus (*Coccomyces hiemalis*). The fungus spends the winter in fallen leaves. About the time the cherry trees are finished blooming, large numbers of spores are splashed and blown from the ground to the emerging leaves. The infection and premature death of the leaves greatly reduces the amount of food the tree can make and store. This results in weakened trees and reduced, poor quality fruit yields. Such trees are much more susceptible to cold injury during the following winter. Cherry leafspot is most severe during mild (60° to 70°F), wet weather.

SOLUTION: Spray with ORTHO Orthocide Garden Fungicide or ORTHO Home Orchard Spray according to label directions. In the fall, remove and destroy all leaf debris around the trees. Next spring, spray with ORTHO Orthocide Garden Fungicide or ORTHO Home Orchard Spray when the petals fall from the tree; repeat the spray at least 2 more times at intervals of 10 to 14 days. If the problem is severe, continue spraying until 7 days before harvest. Meteor and Northstar cherries are resistant to cherry leafspot.

CITRUS

ADAPTATION: See the variety chart on page 1003.

SOIL: Any good, well-drained soil. pH 5.5 to 8.0

FERTILIZER: Fertilize with ORTHO Citrus & Avocado Food 12–6–10 according to label directions.

WATER:
How much: Apply enough water to wet the soil 3 to 4 feet deep. To determine the proper amount of water for your soil type, see page 906. To avoid wetting the trunk and crown of the plant, water into a basin that keeps the water at least 12 inches out from the trunk.
How often: Water when the soil 6 to 12 inches below the surface is just barely moist.

PRUNING: Prune only to shape the tree, and to remove suckers and dead twigs and branches. Lightly thin the inside of the tree if the growth is dense.

HARVEST: When the fruits are fully colored, taste one to determine if it is ripe. If the flavor is not yet sweet enough for the variety, allow the fruits to ripen for another few weeks, then try again. To harvest, clip fruits off with pruning shears rather than pulling them off.

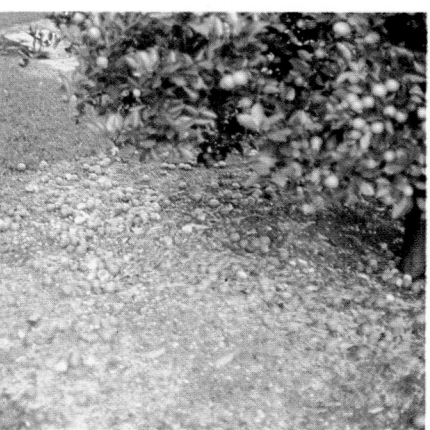

Fruit drop.

PROBLEM: Large amounts of young, newly formed fruit drop from the tree. Fruit drop continues until the fruit has grown to about ½ inch in diameter. The tree appears healthy otherwise.

ANALYSIS: Fruit drop
Some fruit normally drops every year. This is a natural thinning process, and does not mean the tree is diseased or injured. If more fruit seems to be dropping than usual, the tree is being watered too little or too often. Or the supply of nitrogen may be inadequate. For more information about excessive fruit drop, see page 615.

SOLUTION: The only control you have over the amount of fruit that is lost this way is to see that the tree is maintained in healthy condition. There will still be natural thinning, but it will not be excessive. Be sure the tree has the amounts of water and fertilizer it needs while it is setting fruit. If the weather has been warmer or more windy than usual, water deeply and more frequently.

CITRUS

Split grapefruit.

Brown rot on lemon.

Citrus scab.

PROBLEM: The rind splits as the fruit ripens. The split may be short and shallow, or it may be deep and wide, exposing the fruit segments.

ANALYSIS: Fruit splitting
Fruit splitting usually results from fluctuations in temperature, humidity, soil moisture, and possibly fertilizer levels. This condition may be a result of several of these factors rather than any one cause. The amount of split fruit varies from year to year. Usually, only a small portion of fruit on each tree is affected. Fruit splitting is most serious on thin-skinned citrus varieties.

SOLUTION: There is no chemical control. Avoid extreme fluctuations in soil moisture and fertilization levels. For more information about citrus culture, see page 641.

PROBLEM: Firm light-brown spots appear on the rind. These spots may cover a large part or all of the fruit. During periods of high humidity, a white mold often appears on the infected rind. Diseased fruit usually drops. Sometimes leaves and twigs die. Dark lesions that exude a sticky ooze may appear on the trunk near the base of the tree.

ANALYSIS: Brown rot
This plant disease is caused by any of several closely related soil-inhabiting fungi (*Phytophthora* species), some of which may also cause a debilitating canker and gummosis disease of citrus. (For more information about *brown rot gummosis*, see page 647.) These fungi thrive in heavy wet soil, and are most damaging during periods of wet weather. Spores are spread by splashing rain or irrigation water to the maturing fruit, blossoms, and tender shoots on the lower portion of the tree. The fungi that attack and decay the fruit produce spores that are splashed to additional fruit higher in the tree. During periods of rainy weather, an entire crop may be infected.

SOLUTION: Spray the ground and the bottom 3 to 4 feet of the foliage with ORTHO Orthocide Garden Fungicide. To prevent recurrence of the disease, spray again just before seasonal rains begin. Remove and destroy infected fruit and blighted twigs. Prune off branches that touch the ground.

PROBLEM: Fruit has raised, corky areas. Leaves may be deformed and twisted, with brown scablike lesions. Heavily infected fruit fail to develop normally, and infected leaves may fall prematurely.

ANALYSIS: Citrus scab
This plant disease is caused by a fungus (*Elsinoë fawcetti*) that attacks the new leaves, fruit, and stems of many types of citrus, especially sour orange, lemons, Temple and Murcott honey orange, grapefruit, and Satsumas. Leaves and fruit are infected in early spring from spores released from old scab lesions. Once infection has taken place, scablike, corky, brown areas develop on leaves and fruit. Scab is more severe following a rainy spring or overwatering.

SOLUTION: Spray trees at least twice with ORTHO Phaltan Rose & Garden Fungicide. Apply the first spray in late winter prior to spring growth, and the second spray just after the petals have fallen from the blossoms, before the new fruits are larger than a large pea. To discourage infection, keep foliage as dry as possible during the spring growth period.

Caribbean fruit fly larvae (3 times life size).

Citrus thrips damage.

Citrus whiteflies (3 times life size).

PROBLEM: Many ripe fruit fall from trees. Each fallen fruit has a small rotten spot and a tiny hole in the skin. Small white maggots are found in the flesh just beneath the rotten areas.

ANALYSIS: Caribbean fruit fly (*Anastrepha suspensa*)
Female flies deposit their eggs in ripe fruit just beneath the skin, where they hatch in 2 to 3 days into tiny maggots. The larvae feed inside the fruit for 7 to 10 days; during this period the fruit usually drops to the ground. The larvae enter the soil to pupate, emerging 14 to 18 days later as adult flies. The adults, which are seldom seen, are brown with brown markings on their wings and are about ½ inch long.

SOLUTION: No chemical is available for controlling flies on home citrus trees. Because adult flies are attracted to mature and overripe fruit, pick fruit as soon as it matures. Pick up any fallen fruit and dispose of it so that fly larvae do not have a chance to mature.

PROBLEM: Leaf buds shrivel and turn brown. Some of the leaves are silvery gray, leathery, curled, and distorted. The fruit may be silvery, scabbed, streaked, and deformed. To determine if the plant is infested with these insects, hold a sheet of white paper underneath an affected shoot and tap the stem sharply. Minute yellow-brown insects, resembling wood slivers, will drop to the paper and begin to crawl around.

ANALYSIS: Citrus thrips (*Scirtothrips citri*)
These insects are pests of citrus and various ornamental trees. Thrips cause their damage by rasping the tissue of young leaves and immature fruits. They feed on the plant sap that exudes from the injured tissue. Adult thrips lay their eggs in leaves and stems in the fall. The following spring, the young thrips that emerge from these eggs begin feeding on the new growth. These pests are often found in protected areas like the insides of leaf buds. Thrip damage occurs throughout the growing season, and is especially severe during hot, dry weather.

SOLUTION: Spray infested plants with ORTHO Fruit & Vegetable Insect Control or ORTHO Malathion 50 Insect Spray. Use a spreader-sticker when spraying. (For more information about spreader-stickers, see page 915.) Follow directions carefully, and repeat at regular intervals of 7 to 10 days as long as new damage is seen.

PROBLEM: Tiny, winged insects ¹⁄₁₂ inch long feed mainly on the undersides of the leaves. The insects are covered with a white waxy powder. When the plant is touched, insects flutter rapidly around it. A black film or mold may cover the leaves and stems.

ANALYSIS: Citrus whitefly (*Dialeurodes citri*)
This tiny sucking insect lays eggs on the undersides of leaves, where they hatch into flat, oval-shaped semitransparent larvae. The larvae feed by sucking the plant juices from the leaves. Citrus whiteflies cannot fully digest all the sugar in the plant sap, and the excess is excreted in a fluid called honeydew, which often drops onto the leaves below. A sooty mold fungus may develop on the honeydew, causing the leaves to appear black and dirty. There are several generations of citrus whiteflies each year, with peaks of activity in March-April, June-July, and September-October.

SOLUTION: Apply ORTHO Malathion 50 Insect Spray or ORTHO Citrus Insect Spray as directed on the label for the specific type of citrus involved. Thorough coverage of both the upper and lower surfaces of the leaves is very important to get adequate control. Complete control of adult whiteflies is difficult, but spraying will usually control the immature stages and lessen the problem of sooty mold.

Aphids (life size).

Cottonycushion scale (twice life size).

Brown soft scale (twice life size).

PROBLEM: The newest leaves are curled, cupped, and thickened. Leaves and fruit directly under the curled leaves may be coated with a shiny, sticky substance. A black sooty mold may grow on this sticky substance. Tiny (1/8 inch) green or black, soft-bodied insects cluster on the stems and leaves. Blossoms may be deformed. Ants may be present.

ANALYSIS: Aphids
Aphids do little damage in small numbers. However, they are extremely prolific and populations can rapidly build up to damaging numbers during the growing season. Damage occurs when the aphid sucks the juices from the citrus leaves. The aphid is unable to digest fully all the sugar in the sap and excretes the excess in a fluid called honeydew. The honeydew often drops onto the leaves and fruit below. Plants or objects beneath the tree may also be coated with honeydew. A sooty mold fungus may develop on the honeydew, causing the leaves and fruit to appear black and dirty. Ants feed on this sticky substance and are often present where there is an aphid infestation. Repeated aphid attacks may greatly slow the growth and development of young citrus trees.

SOLUTION: Apply ORTHO Citrus Insect Spray, ORTHO Malathion 50 Insect Spray, or ORTHO Fruit & Vegetable Insect Control as soon as the insects appear.

PROBLEM: White, cottony masses cluster on the leaves, stems, branches, and possibly the trunk. Some of the foliage may wither and turn yellow; leaves and fruit may drop. A shiny or sticky substance often coats the leaves. A black, sooty mold may grow on the sticky substance.

ANALYSIS: Mealybugs (*Planococcus citri*) and cottonycushion scale (*Icerya purchasi*)
These insects, frequently found together on citrus plants, look so much alike that separate identification is difficult. In late spring and summer, the females are covered with white, cottony masses containing up to 2500 eggs. Females lay their conspicuous egg masses on leaves, twigs, and branches. The inconspicuous young insects that hatch from these eggs are yellowish brown to green. They feed by sucking sap from the plant tissues. They are unable to digest fully all the sugar in the plant sap, and excrete the excess in a fluid called honeydew. A sooty mold fungus may develop on the honeydew, causing the citrus leaves to appear black and dirty. Mealybugs and scales can be spread in any of several ways. The wind can blow egg masses and insects from plant to plant. Ants can carry them to new locations on the plant. Or the active young insects can crawl to new locations by themselves.

SOLUTION: Spray infested trees with an insecticide containing *malathion* or *diazinon*, covering both surfaces of the leaves. Repeat the spray 5 to 7 days later. Use a spreader-sticker when spraying. For information about spreader-stickers, see page 915. Do not spray when the plant is in full bloom. Do not apply within 7 days of harvest.

PROBLEM: Crusty, waxy, or smooth bumps, up to 1/4 inch in diameter, are found on the trunk, stems, foliage, and sometimes fruit. Often the leaves turn yellow and drop. Fruit may also drop. In some cases, a shiny or sticky substance coats the leaves.

ANALYSIS: Scales
Many species of these insects attack citrus. Some of the most damaging are California red scale, Florida red scale, brown soft scale, black scale, and citrus snow scale. Scales spend the winter on the trunk and twigs of the tree. They lay eggs or bear live young in late spring to midsummer. The young scales, called *crawlers*, settle on the leaves, twigs, and sometimes developing fruit. The small (1/10 inch), soft-bodied young resemble small aphids. They feed by sucking sap from the plant. The legs usually atrophy, and a hard crusty or waxy shell develops over the body. Some species of scale are unable to digest fully all the sugar in the plant sap and excrete the excess in a fluid called honeydew. An uncontrolled infestation of scales may seriously damage or even kill limbs after 2 or 3 seasons.

SOLUTION: Spray with ORTHO Citrus Insect Spray, ORTHO Fruit & Vegetable Insect Control, or ORTHO Malathion 50 Insect Spray according to label directions in the spring after the bloom period. In late summer or fall, spray with ORTHO Volck Supreme Oil Spray. Do not apply products containing petroleum oil during hot (90°F) or freezing weather.

Orangedog caterpillar larva (half life size).

Snail (half life size).

Damaged leaves. *Insert:* Mite (12 times life size).

PROBLEM: Leaves are chewed or entirely eaten. Large, brown 1½ to 2-inch caterpillars with yellow or white patches are found on damaged leaves. When disturbed, the caterpillars push out two red, hornlike projections from skin folds just behind the head; the projections give off a strong, disagreeable odor.

ANALYSIS: Orangedog caterpillar
(*Papilio cresphontes*)
This caterpillar is the immature stage of a beautiful black and yellow butterfly. The butterfly lays tiny orange eggs on the new citrus leaves. The caterpillars that hatch from these eggs resemble bird droppings and have few natural enemies, so they feed almost unmolested. Most damage occurs during the spring and summer. Young trees can be defoliated in only a few days, but they usually grow new leaves within a short time, and no permanent damage results.

SOLUTION: When practical, pick off and destroy caterpillars. Spraying is not needed unless large numbers of trees are involved, or trees are so large that it is too difficult to reach caterpillars. Sprays such as ORTHO Malathion 50 Insect Spray will kill these caterpillars.

PROBLEM: Holes are chewed in the leaves, and the fruit may be pitted or scarred. Silvery trails wind around on the trunk, branches, and nearby soil. Snails or slugs may be seen moving around or feeding on the tree. They often cluster on the trunk or under leaf debris that accumulates around the tree. Check for them by lifting up the lower branches and removing the leaf debris, or by inspecting the damaged tree at night by flashlight.

ANALYSIS: Snails and slugs
These pests are related to mollusks such as clams and oysters, and are widespread and very troublesome to many garden plants. They hide or feed in shaded, cool locations during the day, venturing out to feed in exposed locations at night, or during cloudy, wet days. They prefer cool, dark, moist conditions, and may frequently be found under rocks, leaves, in groundcovers, and under logs or garbage cans. Because citrus trees are often surrounded by leaf debris and have low-hanging branches, they provide a protected environment ideal for snails and slugs.

SOLUTION: Clean up leaf debris under citrus trees, and remove low-hanging branches to eliminate snail and slug hiding places. Scatter ORTHO Bug-Geta Snail & Slug Pellets in bands around the infested trees and around other daytime hiding places. Wet down the treated areas to encourage snail and slug activity that night; they will be more likely to feed on fresh pellets. Snails and slugs that are visible on the tree can be removed by hand.

PROBLEM: Leaves are stippled, yellowing, or scratched in appearance. There may be webbing over flower buds, between leaves, or on the lower surfaces of the leaves. The fruit is often brown or russet colored, leathery, or silvery, and may drop prematurely. To determine if the plant is infested with mites, hold a sheet of white paper underneath an affected branch and tap the branch sharply. Minute green, red, or yellow specks will drop to the paper and begin to crawl around. In some cases, you will need to inspect the leaves with a 10-power magnifying glass to see the mites.

ANALYSIS: Mites
These pests, related to spiders, are very damaging to all types of citrus. There are several species of mites that attack citrus, including citrus red mites, citrus bud mites, purple mites, and citrus rust mites. Mites cause damage by sucking sap from the leaves and young fruit. As a result of feeding, the green leaf pigment disappears, producing a yellowed, stippled appearance. Feeding damage also causes tissue death, resulting in the browning and silvering of the fruit and foliage. Mites are active throughout the growing season, but are favored by hot, dry weather (70°F and up). By midsummer, they build up to tremendous numbers. A severe mite infestation greatly weakens the plant, and can seriously reduce the size and quality of the fruit.

SOLUTION: Spray infested trees with ORTHO Citrus Insect Spray, or a pesticide containing *dicofol*. Be sure to cover both the upper and lower surfaces of the leaves. Repeat the spray at least 2 more times at intervals of 7 days.

Nitrogen-deficient citrus leaves.

Iron deficiency on orange leaves.

Greasy spot.

PROBLEM: Foliage turns pale green, and the older leaves gradually turn yellow and often fall off. Overall growth is stunted. The tree may flower profusely, but usually fails to set much fruit.

ANALYSIS: Lack of nitrogen
Nitrogen, the most important nutrient for plant growth and development, is deficient in almost all soils. Nitrogen is essential in the formation of plant protein, fiber, enzymes, chlorophyll (green leaf pigment), and many other compounds. When a plant becomes deficient in nitrogen, it breaks down chlorophyll and other compounds in its older leaves to recover nitrogen, which it reuses for new growth. This loss of chlorophyll causes the older leaves to turn yellow. Soils that are low in organic matter, and sandy, readily leached soils are frequently deficient in nitrogen. These kinds of soils, in particular, need to be supplemented with fertilizers. Poor drainage, cold (50°F and below), and acidity or alkalinity can also cause soil nitrogen to become less available for plant use.

SOLUTION: Spray the foliage with Ra-Pid-Gro Plant Food for a quick response. Fertilize plants with ORTHO Citrus & Avocado Food 12–6–10 as directed on the label. For more information about fertilizers, see page 904.

PROBLEM: Some of the leaves turn pale green or yellow. The newest leaves (those at the tips of the branches) are most severely affected. Except in extreme cases, the veins of affected leaves remain green. In extreme cases, the newest leaves are small and all-white or yellow. Older leaves may remain green.

ANALYSIS: Iron deficiency
Citrus trees frequently suffer from deficiencies of iron and other minor nutrients such as manganese and zinc, elements essential to normal plant growth and development. Deficiencies can occur when one or more of these elements are depleted in the soil. Often these minor nutrients are present in the soil but alkaline (pH 7.5 and higher) or wet soil conditions cause them to form compounds that cannot be used by the tree. An alkaline condition can result from overliming, or from lime leached from cement or brick. Regions where soil is derived from limestone, and those with low rainfall, usually have alkaline soils. Some citrus trees turn yellow naturally in cold weather. However, if iron is available the foliage will turn green again when the weather warms.

SOLUTION: Apply ORTHO Citrus & Avocado Food 12–6–10 to the soil around the plants to correct the deficiency of minor nutrients. Improve soil drainage (see page 901).

PROBLEM: Yellowish blistered spots develop on the undersides of leaves. These spots become orange and finally a greasy black or brown. Heavily infected leaves fall from the tree prematurely, especially in the fall and winter. On fruit, tiny pitted areas may develop between the oil glands in the peel, causing an unsightly blemish, but fruit quality is not affected.

ANALYSIS: Greasy spot
This disease is caused by a fungus (*Cercospora citri-grisea*) that attacks many types of citrus. Fungi that have spent the winter in fallen, infected leaves begin releasing spores in the spring. The spores infect the lower surface of the leaves; infection peaks in June and July. Fungus spores also invade fruit skin, causing pitting between the oil glands.

SOLUTION: Pick up and remove fallen leaves to reduce sources of new spores. Apply a fungicide containing *basic copper sulfate* or *benomyl* in June or July. A second spray may have to be applied in August or September to protect late summer growth. To slow down infection, keep trees as dry as possible, especially in early summer.

Tristeza.

Psorosis.

Brown rot gummosis.

PROBLEM: Leaves are ash-colored, bronze, or yellowing, and often curl upward around the midrib. New growth is sparse. Growth has been slow, and some twigs and branches die. Or the tree may suddenly die within several weeks or months, leaving the foliage attached. The upper portion of the bud union often bulges over the lower rootstock portion. When small patches of bark along the rootstock area of the bud union are removed, tiny pinholes can frequently be seen with the aid of a hand lens dotting the inner surface of the patches.

ANALYSIS: Tristeza
This plant disease, also known as *quick decline*, is caused by a virus that affects the rootstocks of citrus plants. Aphids spread the virus to trees grafted onto susceptible rootstocks. Orange and grapefruit trees grafted onto *sour orange* rootstocks are especially susceptible to this disease. The virus attacks the food-conducting vessels in the rootstock bark, impeding the flow of nutrients, causing the starvation and death of the root system. Trees often live for several years after they have been infected, although continuing to decline in vigor and fruit yield. Sometimes trees die rapidly after infection, especially during periods of drought.

SOLUTION: There is no cure for this disease. Remove severely infected trees. Purchase plants with rootstocks tolerant to tristeza.

Rootstock varieties tolerant to tristeza: Mandarin Orange, Rangpur Lime, Sweet Orange, and Trifoliate Orange.

PROBLEM: Rough flaky or scaly lesions develop on the trunk or main branches of mature trees. Gummy deposits may form on the bark as the disease progresses. Greenish yellow or clear flecks or streaks usually appear on the young leaves. Severely infected fruit and foliage may have pale blotches or sunken, circular spots or rings.

ANALYSIS: Psorosis
This plant disease, which is caused by a virus, is also known in California as *scaly bark*, a name that, in Florida, is used for a different disease. Psorosis is a serious problem on orange, grapefruit, and tangerine, and can affect all citrus trees. This virus is spread by grafting infected citrus plant tissue (budwood) to healthy plants. As the disease develops the tree weakens, and twigs and limbs may die.

SOLUTION: No cure is known. Prune out diseased branches. If the lesions on the trunk are still small (not more than 3 to 4 inches across), scrape deeply enough to remove all diseased bark and wood layers. Also scrape clean an area of outer bark to about 5 inches out from the lesion. Wipe the treated area with rubbing alcohol, and seal with ORTHO Pruning Sealer. Disinfect tools with rubbing alcohol. If you are planting new trees, ask for stock registered as being free of the disease.

PROBLEM: Firm brownish patches of bark appear at the base of the trunk. Often a thick amber gum oozes from the infected area. The bark eventually dries, cracks, and weathers away, leaving a dark sunken canker. Some of the maturing fruit may be brown and decaying. The foliage may turn yellow and die.

ANALYSIS: Brown rot gummosis
This plant disease, also known as *foot rot* or *collar rot*, is caused by a soil-inhabiting fungus (*Phytophthora* species). The fungus thrives in heavy, wet soils. Infection occurs when spores are splashed to the trunk, penetrating the bark either directly or through wounds. As the canker develops, the branches above the infected trunk may start to die. Fruit infection can occur when spores are splashed to the developing fruit. (For information about *brown rot*, see page 642.) Sometimes cankers heal over by themselves, but often they continue to spread, causing a loss in vigor and fruit production, and eventually killing the tree.

SOLUTION: Do not let water settle around the base of the tree. Gently remove the soil from around the trunk until the main lateral roots are just barely covered. Small trunk lesions may be removed by cutting away the diseased bark plus an additional surrounding ½ inch of the healthy bark. Spray around the base of the trunk with a fungicide containing *basic copper sulfate*. When planting new trees, purchase plants that are grafted onto phytophthora-resistant rootstocks such as *Trifoliate orange* and *Troyer citrange*.

CITRUS

Cold-damaged Valencia oranges.

Cold damage.

PROBLEM: The tree has been exposed to freezing temperatures. Tender shoots may blacken and die; older foliage often turns yellowish brown, leathery, and eventually withers and falls. The fruit rind may be scarred with brown or green sunken lesions. Or, even though the fruit rind appears normal, when the fruit is cut open, the flesh is dry. Severely damaged trees suffer twig and branch dieback. The bark along the branches or trunk may split open.

ANALYSIS: Cold damage
Citrus plants are frost-tender, and are easily damaged by temperatures below 32°F. Although many citrus plants can recover from a light frost, they cannot tolerate periods of freezing weather. Damage to fruit occurs when the juice-filled cells freeze and rupture. The released fluid evaporates through the rind, leaving the flesh dry and pulpy. In addition to causing leaf and twig dieback, temperatures of 20°F and lower promote bark splitting, which may not become apparent for several weeks or months.

SOLUTION: Don't prune back damaged branches immediately. If there is still danger of frost, drive four stakes into the ground around the tree, and cover the tree with fabric, cardboard, or plastic. Remove this cover when the weather warms up. The trunks and main limbs of young trees may be protected by wrapping them with corn stalks, palm fronds, or fiberglass building insulation. Do not shade the foliage. Keep the soil moist during a freeze but be careful not to overwater. Limit fertilizer to a minimum. Damaged fruit can be removed immediately following the freeze. Always wait for new growth to appear before pruning. As soon as the danger of frost is past, you can prune blackened shoots and withered foliage. If the tree has suffered serious injury, it may take as long as 6 months before you will be able to determine the extent of the damage to the trunk and main limbs. You can then prune out the dead wood. For more information on pruning, see ORTHO's book *All About Pruning*.

FIG

FIG

ADAPTATION: See the variety chart on page 1003.

SOIL: Any good, deep, well-drained soil. pH 5.5 to 8.0

FERTILIZER: Fertilize with ORTHO Evergreen, Tree & Shrub Food 12–6–6 according to label directions.

WATER:
How much: Apply enough water to wet the soil 3 to 4 feet deep. To determine the proper amount of water for your soil type, see page 906.
How often: Water when the soil 6 inches below the surface is just barely moist.

PRUNING: Lightly thin out branches, and head back long shoots to maintain tree vigor and shape during the dormant season. Remove weak, diseased, dead, or crossing twigs and branches.

HARVEST: Harvest figs when they have fully ripened. They are ripe when the fruits bend over at the neck, and the flesh is soft. Remove the fruit with the stem still attached. If you find the milky sap irritating, wear gloves and protective clothing when picking figs.

Bird damage to mission fig.

Souring.

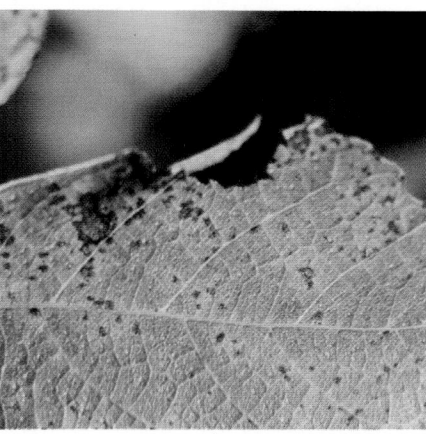

Rust.

PROBLEM: Ripened figs have holes in them and may be partially eaten. They may have been knocked to the ground. Birds may be seen feeding on ripening figs.

ANALYSIS: Bird damage
Some birds feed heavily on ripening figs. When the fruit is fully ripe, birds peck at the soft flesh, leaving holes in the fruit. The wounded figs may decay, becoming inedible.

SOLUTION: You can save many of your figs by harvesting daily. Check the tree every morning, and harvest those figs that have ripened. Nets thrown over the tree are also effective in reducing bird damage. Nets may be purchased at your local nursery or hardware store. For more information about birds, see page 893.

PROBLEM: A pink, sticky fluid may drip from the tiny hole ("eye") at the end of the ripening fig. The fruit is soft and mushy. When cut open, an infected fig has a strong fermented or alcoholic odor.

ANALYSIS: Souring
This plant disease is caused by various types of yeast. The yeasts that cause souring are spread by insects (including the dried fruit beetle and the vinegar fly). The insects enter the fig through the eye. If the fig is infected, the insects become contaminated with yeast cells while crawling around inside the fig. They can then infect healthy figs. The dark, moist conditions inside the ripening fig provide an ideal environment for the rapid decay and fermentation of the fruit.

SOLUTION: There is no chemical control for this disease. Pick off and destroy infected figs. Plant closed-eye fig varieties.

Fig varieties with small or closed eyes: Brown Turkey, Celeste, Green Ischia, and Mission.

PROBLEM: Rust-colored, raised spots appear on the undersides of the leaves. Opposite these spots, on the upper surfaces of the leaves, are dark brown, smooth spots. Infected leaves turn yellow and die prematurely. Fruit yields may be reduced.

ANALYSIS: Rust
This plant disease is caused by a fungus (*Cerotelium fici*) that infects figs and several other closely related plants. The fungi spend the winter as spores on the bark or in plant debris. Infection starts in the spring as soon as the tree begins growing. The spores are spread to healthy leaves by wind and splashing water. They germinate on wet foliage, causing spotting and eventually premature leaf drop. Although rust infects the leaves rather than the fruit, premature leaf drop may weaken the tree after several years, causing a reduction in fruit yields.

SOLUTION: Spray the tree with a fungicide containing *basic copper sulfate*. Repeat the spray every 3 to 4 weeks throughout the growing season. Spray thoroughly, covering both the upper and lower surfaces of the leaves.

Fig mosaic.

Fig scale (twice life size).

PROBLEM: Leaves are mottled yellow, and may have translucent areas. Often, the fruit is spotted yellow. The leaves may be stunted, and the foliage and fruit may drop prematurely.

ANALYSIS: Fig mosaic
This plant disease is caused by a virus. Mosaic rarely causes a plant to die, but can weaken it extensively, greatly reducing the fruit yield. The virus may be spread by microscopic fig mites (*Eriophyes fici*), which feed on diseased figs and transfer the virus to healthy trees at later feedings. The virus is also spread by infected cuttings.

SOLUTION: The virus cannot be chemically controlled. Reduce the numbers of fig mites by applying a *dormant oil spray* in the winter. If you are planting new trees, select healthy stock from a reliable nursery. For information on selecting healthy nursery plants, see page 916.

PROBLEM: The stems or undersides of the leaves are covered with brownish crusty bumps or thick, white, waxy bumps, or clusters of somewhat flattened yellowish, gray, or brownish scaly bumps. The bumps can be scraped or picked off; the undersides are usually soft. Leaves turn yellow and may drop. In some cases, a shiny or sticky substance coats the leaves. A black sooty mold often grows on the sticky substance.

ANALYSIS: Scales
Several different types of scale insects infest figs. They lay their eggs on leaves or bark, and in spring to midsummer the young scales, called *crawlers*, settle on leaves and twigs. These small ($\frac{1}{10}$ inch), soft-bodied young feed by sucking sap from the plant. The legs usually atrophy, and a hard, crusty or waxy shell develops over the body. The mature female scales lay their eggs underneath their shell. Some species of scales infesting figs are unable to digest fully all the sugar in the plant sap and excrete the excess in a fluid called honeydew, which often drops onto the leaves below. A sooty mold fungus may develop on the honeydew, causing the fig leaves to appear black and dirty.

SOLUTION: Spray with an insecticide containing *malathion* in early to midsummer when the young crawlers are active. The following late winter or early spring, before new growth begins, spray the trunk and branches with ORTHO Volck Supreme Oil Spray to control overwintering insects. For more information about scales, see page 878.

ADAPTATION AND POLLINATION: Filberts grow well in the Pacific Northwest, the East, and the Southeast. Plant at least 2 different cultivars to ensure good nut production.

SOIL: Any good, deep, well-drained soil. pH 5.5 to 7.5

FERTILIZER: Fertilize with ORTHO Evergreen, Tree & Shrub Food 12–6–6 according to label directions.

WATER:
  How much: Apply enough water to wet the soil 3 to 4 feet deep. To determine the proper amount of water for your soil type, see page 906.
  How often: Water when the soil 6 inches below the surface is just barely moist.

PRUNING: Filberts form on the current season's growth. Prune lightly, removing weak, diseased, or dead twigs and branches. To encourage heavy nut production, prune off half of the new growth every second or third year.

HARVEST: In the fall, the husks will open up, and the nuts will fall to the ground. Remove nuts from the ground as soon as possible, or squirrels and other animals will remove them first.

Filbertworm hole.

Filbert leafroller larvae (twice life size).

Bacterial blight.

PROBLEM: The kernel of the nut is blackened and destroyed. There may be a hole in the shell, and winding trails at the flattened base of the nut. Or amber-headed white worms, up to ½ inch long, may be feeding in the nuts.

ANALYSIS: Filbertworm
(*Melissopus latiferreanus*)
The larvae of these reddish brown moths infest many different types of nut trees, including chestnuts, beechnuts, and almonds, but they are most damaging to filberts. The adult moths lay their eggs on or near the developing nuts during the spring and summer. The larvae that hatch from these eggs crawl down between the shell and the husk, then tunnel into the husk until they reach the base of the nut. They then bore up into the developing kernel, where they feed for several weeks. After maturing, the larvae exit through holes they make in the shells. They drop to the ground, spin cocoons, and pupate. Adult moths may either emerge later in the summer or remain in the cocoons until the following spring or summer.

SOLUTION: Spray the trees with an insecticide containing *carbaryl* when the moths emerge in the spring. Repeat the spray 2 weeks later. Contact your County Extension Office to find out the dates of moth emergence in your area. (For a list of Extension Offices, see page 1011.) In the fall, clean up debris around the trees to reduce the number of overwintering cocoons.

PROBLEM: Irregular holes appear in the leaves and buds. Some of the leaves are rolled and held together with a web. Young buds and nuts are often enclosed within the rolled leaves. When these rolled leaves are peeled open, pale green worms up to ¾ inch long with brown heads are found inside. Some of the maturing nuts may be damaged.

ANALYSIS: Filbert leafroller
(*Archips rosanys*)
These worms, also known as *European leafrollers*, are the larvae of brown moths. They infest many different ornamental trees. The moths lay their eggs on branches or twigs in June or July. The eggs hatch the following spring, and the emerging larvae feed on the buds and developing foliage. Leafrollers often wrap leaves around ripening nuts and tender buds, then feed inside. After about a month, the mature larvae pupate within rolled leaves to emerge later as moths that lay the eggs for a second generation of leafrollers that summer. Heavy leafroller infestations may cause tree stunting and sometimes defoliation.

SOLUTION: If practical, pick off and destroy rolled leaves to reduce the numbers of moths that will emerge later in the season. Next spring, kill the young larvae by spraying with an insecticide containing either *diazinon* or *carbaryl* when the filbert leaves are about ¾ to 1 inch long.

PROBLEM: Small angular or irregular spots develop on the leaves. Initially these spots are yellow-green, and appear water-soaked. They later turn reddish brown. Dark green lesions on the stems eventually turn reddish brown. Stems and twigs may die back. Often the leaves wither, die, and cling to the dead stems. There may be sunken lesions (cankers) on the branches and trunk. Young trees (up to 4 years old) may die.

ANALYSIS: Bacterial blight
This plant disease is caused by a bacterium (*Xanthomonas corylina*) that is common on filberts in the Northwest. The bacteria are spread by splashing rain and contaminated pruning tools. They may attack leaves and buds directly, or penetrate twigs and stems through wounds. As the infection progresses down into the branches and trunk, cankers may form that encircle and kill the branches and trunks of young trees. Trees weakened by sunburn, winter injury, and poor growing conditions are most susceptible to infection. Bacterial blight is most severe after heavy fall rains.

SOLUTION: Spray trees with *tribasic copper sulfate* in the fall before rains begin. In late winter, prune out infected twigs and branches, sterilizing pruning tools with rubbing alcohol between cuts.

HICKORY

HICKORY

ADAPTATION AND POLLINATION:
Hickories grow throughout the eastern half of the United States. Plant several varieties to assure nut production.

SOIL: Any good, deep, well-drained soil. pH 5.5 to 8.0

FERTILIZER: Fertilize with ORTHO Evergreen, Tree & Shrub Food 12–6–6 according to label directions.

WATER:
How much: Apply enough water to wet the soil 5 to 6 feet deep. To determine the proper amount of water for your soil type, see page 906.
How often: Water when the soil 6 inches below the surface is just barely moist.

PRUNING: Nuts form on the current season's growth. Prune hickories lightly, removing weak, diseased, or dead twigs and branches.

HARVEST: Harvest the nuts in the fall by gently knocking the tree with a rubber mallet or cloth-covered pole.

Hickory shuckworm (life size).

PROBLEM: Cream-colored worms up to ⅜ inch long are feeding in the immature nuts, many of which fall to the ground prematurely. Later in the season, after the shells have hardened, the worms may be found in the green shucks.

ANALYSIS: Hickory shuckworm
(*Laspeyresia caryana*)
These worms, the larvae of small brown moths, are also known as *pecan shuckworms*. They are pests of hickory and pecan trees wherever they are grown. The larvae spend the winter in shucks on the ground or in the tree. The shuckworms pupate and emerge as adult moths in the spring to lay their eggs on hickory leaves and nuts. The larvae that hatch from these eggs tunnel into the soft green hickory nut shells and feed on the developing kernels. Infested nuts usually drop. Later in the season, after the nut shells have hardened, the larvae tunnel into the shucks. Their feeding damage interferes with the proper development of the kernels. Shuckworm damage may occur throughout the spring and summer.

SOLUTION: Chemical controls are not practical for the home gardener. Clean up and destroy all dropped nuts and shucks to eliminate many of the overwintering larvae. If infestations are severe, contact a professional tree spraying company.

Bark beetles and larvae (twice life size).

PROBLEM: Leaves turn brown and wilt, and some of the twigs and branches may die. Severely infested trees sometimes defoliate prematurely. Dark brown beetles ⅛ to ¼ inch long may be seen on the buds, leaf stalks, and bark. When sliced open, an infested branch reveals tunnels running through the sapwood. There may be slightly curved, white grubs, up to ¼ inch long, in the tunnels. There are usually small perforations in the bark of the branches and trunk.

ANALYSIS: Hickory bark beetle
(*Scolytus quadrispinosus*)
These beetles are pests of all the hickory species, including pecans. The adult beetles that appear in early summer feed at the bases of tender buds, leaf stalks, and sometimes the developing nuts. The female beetles bore down through the twigs into the branches, forming tunnels in which they lay their eggs. The grubs that hatch from these eggs tunnel into the inner wood. These tunnels interfere with the flow of water and nutrients through the tree, and may result in branch or tree death. The grubs pupate in their tunnels, then exit through the bark as adult beetles either later in the summer or the following spring. Weakened, diseased, and dying trees and branches are most susceptible to beetle infestation.

SOLUTION: Spray infested trees with an insecticide containing *carbaryl* or *methoxychlor* to kill the exposed beetles. During the dormant season, remove and destroy infested branches. Keep the tree healthy by watering and fertilizing it properly.

MANGO ——————————————————————————

Scab.

Anthracnose. *Insert:* Infected fruit.

MANGO ————————

ADAPTATION: Zone 10. To determine your climate zone, see the map on page 1004.

SOIL: Any good, deep, well-drained soil. pH 5.5 to 7.5

FERTILIZER: Fertilize with ORTHO Evergreen, Tree & Shrub Food 12–6–6 according to label directions.

WATER:
How much: Apply enough water to wet the soil 2 to 3 feet deep. To determine the proper amount of water for your soil, see page 906.
How often: Water when the soil 6 inches below the surface is just barely moist.

PRUNING: Mangoes grow on shoots that form on last year's wood. Prune trees lightly, removing weak, diseased, or dead twigs and branches.

HARVEST: Harvest when the fruits have turned yellow or reddish, and the flesh yields slightly when squeezed. Pick the fruit by twisting it sideways or upward sharply to snap the stem, or clip the fruit off with pruning shears, leaving a small piece of stem attached to the fruit. The milky mango stem sap can cause dermatitis in some people.

PROBLEM: Fruits have grayish to grayish brown spots that become covered with cracked, fissured, corky tissue as the spots and fruit enlarge. Velvety, grayish brown spore masses are present on fruit lesions during moist periods. Small (1/16 inch), brown to black angular spots may be present on the leaves, causing crinkling and distortion on new leaves and shotholes on mature leaves.

ANALYSIS: Scab
This plant disease is caused by a fungus (*Elsinoë mangiferae*) that infects young fruit, twigs, leaves, and blossom spikes. During the bloom period and throughout the warmer months, infection takes place from spores on previously infected areas. Spores may be produced on fruit until it reaches maturity.

SOLUTION: Spray the tree with a fungicide containing *basic copper sulfate*. Use a spreader-sticker with the fungicide to enable it to coat plant parts more effectively. (For more information on spreader-stickers, see page 915.) Apply sprays at the following times:
1. Weekly from the first appearance of flower spikes until all fruit have set.
2. Monthly from the time fruit sets until mid-May for early varieties and mid-June for late varieties.

PROBLEM: Minute black or brown angular or irregular spots appear on the leaves, flowers, and fruit. As the spots enlarge, dead areas are formed on leaves, flowers may be killed, and fruit may have large infected areas with surface cracks extending into the flesh. Affected areas decay rapidly. The most serious problems occur in the late winter to summer on leaves, late winter to spring on flowers, and near or at the time of maturity on fruit.

ANALYSIS: Anthracnose
This plant disease is caused by a fungus (*Colletotrichum gloeosporioides*) that attacks mango leaves, flowers, and fruit. Spores from infections on older leaves infect flowers, new leaves, and fruit. Periods of wet, rainy weather favor disease development. On fruit, the highest fungus activity occurs when the fruit begins to soften near maturity.

SOLUTION: Spray the tree with a fungicide containing *basic copper sulfate*. Use a spreader-sticker with the fungicide to enable it to coat plant parts more effectively. (For more information on spreader-stickers, see page 915.) Apply sprays at the following times:
1. Weekly from the first appearance of flower spikes until all fruit have set.
2. Monthly from the time fruit sets until mid-May for early varieties and mid-June for late varieties.

MANGO

False oleander scale (life size).

PROBLEM: Stems and leaves are covered with brownish crusty bumps or clusters of somewhat flattened reddish, white, or brownish scaly bumps. The bumps can be scraped or picked off; the undersides are usually soft. Leaves turn yellow and may drop. A shiny or sticky substance may coat the leaves. A black sooty mold often grows on the sticky substance. Ants may be present. Branches are killed by heavy infestations.

ANALYSIS: Scales
Members of this diverse group of insects are damaging to many trees. Scales lay their eggs in spring to midsummer. The young scales, called *crawlers*, settle on leaves and twigs. The small (¹⁄₁₀ inch), soft-bodied young feed by sucking sap from the plant. The legs usually atrophy and a shell develops over the body. Some species of scales are unable to digest fully all the sugar in the plant sap, and excrete the excess in a fluid called honeydew. A sooty mold fungus may develop on the honeydew, causing the mango leaves to appear black and dirty. Ants feed on this sticky substance, and are often present where scales cluster.

SOLUTION: Spray trees with a combination of ORTHO Volck Oil Spray and ORTHO Malathion 50 Insect Spray at the rate of 1 tablespoon of each per gallon of water. Repeat sprays as needed up to 2 days before harvest.

PEACH AND NECTARINE

PEACH AND NECTARINE

ADAPTATION AND POLLINATION: See the variety chart on page 1006.

SOIL: Any good, deep, well-drained soil. pH 5.5 to 7.5

FERTILIZER: Fertilize with ORTHO Evergreen, Tree & Shrub Food 12–6–6 according to label directions.

WATER:
How much: Apply enough water to wet the soil 3 to 4 feet deep. To determine the proper amount of water for your soil type, see page 906.
How often: Water when the soil 6 inches below the surface is just barely moist.

PRUNING: Peaches and nectarines bear on 1-year-old wood. Prune half of last year's growth annually. Thin out weak, crossing, or dead twigs and branches. Thin fruits to 6 inches apart when they are thumbnail size.

HARVEST: Harvest when the fruits are fully colored and slightly soft. With a ripe peach or nectarine, the stem will easily separate from the branch when the fruit is gently lifted.

Plum curculio and larva (4 times life size).

PROBLEM: The ripening fruit is misshapen and rotten, and often drops prematurely. Holes about ⅛ inch in diameter and deep, crescent-shaped scars appear on the fruit. When cut open, damaged fruits may be found to contain crescent-shaped yellow-gray grubs with brown heads.

ANALYSIS: Plum curculio
(*Conotrachelus nenuphar*)
These insects, found east of the Rocky Mountains, attack stone fruits, apples, and pears. The adults are brown beetles with long, curved snouts. They hibernate in debris and other protected places during the winter. The beetles emerge in the spring when new growth starts, and begin feeding on young leaves, blossoms, and developing fruit. After 5 to 6 weeks, the female beetles start to lay their eggs in the young fruit, cutting distinctive, crescent-shaped slits into the peaches and nectarines. The grubs that hatch from the eggs feed for several weeks in the fruit. The infested fruits usually drop to the ground. The grubs eventually leave the fruit and bore into the soil, where they pupate. The emerging beetles feed on fruit for a few weeks, and then go into hibernation. In the South, they lay eggs, producing a second generation of grubs in late summer.

SOLUTION: There is nothing you can do to kill the grubs inside the fruit. Spray with ORTHO Home Orchard Spray or ORTHO Malathion 50 Insect Spray to kill beetles that are feeding on fruit or laying eggs. Pick up and destroy all fallen fruit. Next spring, spray the trees when the petals are falling from the blossoms. Repeat applications according to directions on the label.

Scab.

Shothole fungus. *Insert: Infected fruit.*

Bacterial leaf spot.

PROBLEM: Small, olive-green spots appear on the half-grown fruit. These spots are generally centered around the stem end of the peach or nectarine. The spots eventually turn brown and velvety. The fruit is often dwarfed, deformed, or cracked. There are usually small brown spots and holes in the leaves, and many twigs die.

ANALYSIS: Scab
This plant disease is caused by a fungus (*Cladosporium carpophilum*) that attacks all the stone fruits. In the spring, spores are splashed and blown from lesions on the twigs to the developing foliage and fruit. The young fruit do not show scab lesions for at least a month after they are initially infected. Spores that are produced on the infected leaves, twigs, and fruit will continue to infect healthy peaches and nectarines throughout the growing season.

SOLUTION: It's too late to do anything about the spots on this year's fruit, but they are edible if peeled. Next year, spray with ORTHO Orthocide Garden Fungicide or ORTHO Home Orchard Spray when the petals have fallen from the blossoms. If scab is a serious problem in your area, continue to spray at intervals of 10 to 14 days until about a month before the fruits are harvested.

PROBLEM: Small purplish spots appear on the young twigs, leaves, and developing fruit in early spring, and eventually turn brown. These leaf spots often drop out, leaving shotholes in the leaf. Infected buds, shoots, and leaves may die. The spots on the maturing peaches turn scablike, drop off, and leave rough, corky lesions.

ANALYSIS: Shothole fungus
This plant disease, also called *coryneum blight* and *peach blight*, is caused by a fungus (*Coryneum carpophilum*) that attacks peaches, nectarines, apricots, and almonds. The fungus spends the winter in lesions on the twigs and buds. In the spring, the spores are splashed by rain to the developing buds, leaves, and fruit, causing spotting and tissue death. Infection causes the leaf tissue to produce a layer of cells, which walls off the damaged area. The center of the spot then drops out. Severe infection may cause extensive twig and bud blighting, and possibly premature defoliation, reducing the peach and nectarine yield. The disease is favored by wet spring weather.

SOLUTION: There is no adequate control during the growing season. To prevent twig and leaf bud infection, spray the trees with ORTHO Orthorix Spray or ORTHO Dormant Disease Control in the fall immediately after the leaves have dropped.

PROBLEM: Brown or black angular spots appear on leaves. The centers of the spots often fall out. The tips of the leaves may die, and eventually the leaves turn yellow and drop. The surface of the fruit may be dotted with brown to black spots, and become pitted and cracked. Sunken lesions may form on the twigs. Severely infected trees may drop all their leaves.

ANALYSIS: Bacterial leaf spot
This plant disease is caused by a bacterium (*Xanthomonas pruni*) that also attacks apricots and plums. This is one of the more destructive diseases of stone fruit east of the Rocky Mountains. In the spring, bacteria ooze from lesions on the twigs, to be carried by splashing rain to the young leaves, shoots, and developing fruits. Frequent rainfall favors the infection. Trees that defoliate early in the summer are weakened, and produce small crops of peaches and nectarines of poor quality.

SOLUTION: There is no adequate control for this disease. Spraying with *basic copper sulfate* when the flower buds open in the spring may help suppress the disease, but will not eliminate it. When planting new trees, use resistant varieties.

Peach varieties resistant to bacterial leaf spot:
   Susceptible: Blake, Elberta, and Rio-Oso-Gem.
   Fairly resistant: Lizzie, Redhaven, Redskin, and Sunhaven.
   Resistant: Belle of Georgia, Early-Free-Red, and Hiley.

PEACH AND NECTARINE

Leaf curl on peach.

Peach twig borer (life size).

Oriental fruit moth larva (twice life size).

PROBLEM: Leaves are puckered, thickened, and curled from the time they first appear in the spring. Emerging shoots are swollen and stunted. Initially the infected foliage is red or orange, but it later turns pale green to yellow. As the season progresses, a grayish white powdery material develops on the leaves. Eventually these leaves shrivel and drop. Fruiting is poor, and the fruit that is present may be covered with raised, wrinkled, irregular lesions.

ANALYSIS: Leaf curl
This plant disease is caused by a fungus (*Taphrina deformans*) that attacks peaches and nectarines wherever they are grown. Infection occurs as soon as the buds begin to open in the spring. Fungal spores are splashed from the bark to the buds by spring rains. Later in the season, the infected leaves develop a grayish white covering of spores that are blown onto the bark. Infected trees are greatly weakened by the premature loss of foliage in early summer. Leaf curl is most severe when spring weather is cool and wet.

SOLUTION: Infected leaves cannot be cured. To prevent the recurrence of the disease next year, spray the trees with ORTHO Orthorix Spray or ORTHO Dormant Disease Control in the fall immediately after the leaves have dropped or in the spring just as the buds begin to swell, but before they open. If the disease has been severe, spray in both fall and spring.

PROBLEM: New growth at the tips of the twigs wilts and dies. When affected twigs are sliced open lengthwise, worms about ½ inch long are discovered inside. The reddish brown color of these worms distinguishes them from oriental fruit moth worms, which cause similar damage. Later in the season, some of the maturing fruits also contain these worms. During the summer, cocoons may be attached to the branches or tree crotches.

ANALYSIS: Peach twig borer
(*Anarsia lineatella*)
This borer attacks all of the stone fruits, and is particularly damaging on the Pacific Coast. The young larvae hibernate during the winter in silk-lined burrows under loose bark or in other protected places on the tree. When the tree starts to bloom in the spring, the larvae bore into young buds and shoots. They feed on the tender twigs, killing twigs and leaves. When mature, they leave the twigs and pupate in cocoons attached to branches. After several weeks, gray moths emerge and lay their eggs on the twigs, leaves, and fruit. Egg laying and larval damage can occur all through the growing season. Later in the summer, larvae feed almost exclusively on the maturing fruit. In addition to ruining the fruit, peach twig borers may cause abnormal branching patterns on young trees when large numbers of twigs are infested.

SOLUTION: Worms in the twigs and fruit cannot be killed with pesticides. To prevent future worm damage, kill the moths by spraying infested trees with ORTHO Fruit & Vegetable Insect Control or ORTHO Home Orchard Spray. Next spring, spray again just before the blossoms open. Repeat the treatment 2 more times at intervals of 10 to 14 days.

PROBLEM: New growth at the tips of the twigs wilts and dies. When affected twigs are sliced open lengthwise, worms about ½ inch long are found inside. The pinkish white color of these worms distinguishes them from peach twig borers, which cause similar damage. Later in the season, some of the maturing fruit also contain these worms. Often the peaches and nectarines have holes filled with a sticky gum.

ANALYSIS: Oriental fruit moth
(*Grapholitha molesta*)
The larvae of these night-flying moths damage stone fruits, apples, and pears. The larvae hibernate in cocoons on the tree bark or buried in crotches. In the spring they pupate, emerge as brown adult moths, and lay eggs on the young twigs, leaves, and fruit. The larvae bore into the young buds and shoots, killing twigs and leaves. When mature, they leave the twigs, spin cocoons, and pupate in the tree or in debris on the ground. After several weeks, moths emerge and lay eggs. Larval damage can occur all through the growing season. Later in the summer, the larvae feed almost exclusively on the maturing fruit. They leave gum-filled holes in the peaches and nectarines when they exit to pupate.

SOLUTION: Worms in the twigs and fruit cannot be killed with pesticides. To prevent future worm damage, kill the moths by spraying infested trees with ORTHO Home Orchard Spray or ORTHO Fruit & Vegetable Insect Control. Next spring, spray again when the petals start to fall from the blossoms. Repeat the treatment 2 more times at intervals of 10 to 14 days.

Catfacing on peach.

Blighted shoots.

Fruit rot.

PROBLEM: Sunken, corky areas mar the fruit surface. Blossoms may drop without setting fruit. Many of the young fruits drop prematurely. Some of the developing leaves and twigs are deformed. Brown, green, or rust-colored bugs ¼ to ½ inch long may be seen feeding on the buds and fruit.

ANALYSIS: Catfacing
The sunken, corky "catface" disfigurations that appear on the fruit are usually caused by the tarnished plant bug (*Lygus lineolaris*) and various species of stinkbugs. The insects hibernate in vetch or other broadleafed weeds during the winter. When the trees start to bloom in the spring, these bugs feed on the young buds, blooms, and fruits, causing bud and fruit drop, twig malformation, and catfacing. Most of the damage occurs early in the season, although the bugs may occasionally feed on the fruits up until harvest. Hail or cold weather may also damage the tender blooms and fruit surfaces, causing catface injuries.

SOLUTION: To control plant bugs, spray with ORTHO Home Orchard Spray or ORTHO Malathion 50 Insect Spray when the buds turn pink. Repeat the spray when the petals have dropped from most of the blossoms and whenever bugs are seen in the trees. Next fall, clean up weeds and plant debris to eliminate hibernating locations for the overwintering bugs.

PROBLEM: Small circular brown spots appear on the young fruits. Later in the season, as the peaches or nectarines start to mature, these spots may enlarge to rot part or all of the fruit. During moist weather, the rotted fruits are covered with tufts of gray spores. When the infected peaches or nectarines are sliced open the flesh inside is found to be brown, firm, and fairly dry. Infected fruits either drop prematurely or dry out, turn dark brown, and remain on the tree past the normal harvest period. Healthy fruits may rot when they contact infected fruits in storage.

ANALYSIS: Brown rot
This plant disease, caused by either of two closely related fungi (*Monilinia laxa* or *M. fructicola*), is very destructive to all of the stone fruits. The fungi spend the winter in twig cankers or in rotted fruits (mummies) in the tree or on the ground. In the spring, spores are blown or splashed from cankers or mummies to the healthy flower buds. After penetrating and decaying the flowers, the fungus grows down into the twigs, producing brown, sunken cankers. During moist weather, a thick, gummy sap oozes from the lesions, and tufts of gray spores may form on the infected areas. Spores from cankers and infected blossoms or mummies are splashed and blown to the maturing fruit. Young peaches and nectarines are fairly resistant to infection, but maturing fruits are vulnerable. Brown rot develops most rapidly in mild, moist conditions.

SOLUTION: If there are still uninfected blossoms left on your tree, spray with ORTHO Home Orchard Spray or ORTHO Orthocide Garden Fungicide to protect them from further infection. Repeat the spray 10 days later. To protect maturing peaches and nectarines from infection, spray them about 3 weeks before they are to be harvested. Remove and destroy all infected fruits and mummies. Prune out cankers and blighted twigs. Clean up and destroy all debris around the tree. Next spring, spray trees as the first flowers begin to open, and continue to spray according to label directions.

PROBLEM: Blossoms and young leaves decay, wilt, and turn brown during the first 2 weeks of the bloom period. The decayed blossoms may fail to drop, and hang on the tree throughout the growing season. In humid conditions, masses of gray spores may appear on the infected flower parts. There is often extensive twig dieback. Sunken lesions develop on the twigs and branches as the season progresses. These lesions usually exude a sticky ooze.

PEACH AND NECTARINE

Spider mite damage.

Terrapin scale (4 times life size).

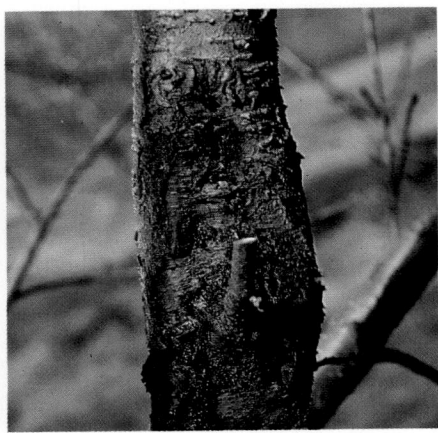

Bacterial canker on peach.

PROBLEM: Leaves are stippled, yellowing, and dirty. Leaves may dry out and drop. There may be webbing between leaves or on the lower surfaces of the leaves. To determine if the plant is infested with mites, hold a sheet of white paper underneath an affected leaf and tap the leaf sharply. Minute green, red, or yellow specks the size of pepper grains will drop to the paper and begin to crawl around. The pests are easily seen against the white background.

ANALYSIS: Mites
These pests, related to spiders, attack many garden and greenhouse plants. They cause damage by sucking sap from the undersides of the leaves. As a result of feeding, the green leaf pigment disappears, producing the stippled appearance. Mites are active throughout the growing season, but are favored by hot, dry weather (70°F and up). By midsummer, they build up to tremendous numbers. Severely infested trees may produce small, poor-quality fruits.

SOLUTION: Spray infested trees with ORTHO Home Orchard Spray or ORTHO Fruit & Vegetable Insect Control. Repeat the spray 2 more times at intervals of 7 to 10 days. Do not apply pesticides within 3 weeks of harvest.

PROBLEM: Some of the leaves are pale green to yellow and may drop prematurely. The bark is encrusted with small (1/16 inch), hard, raised bumps that are often light gray to white, or dark brown with raised yellow centers. There may be severe limb dieback. The fruit may be mottled or spotted.

ANALYSIS: Scales
Although peaches and nectarines are attacked by many different species of scale insects, the two most common are San Jose scale (*Quadraspidiotus perniciosus*) and white peach scale (*Pseudaulacaspis pentagona*). The scales lay their eggs or bear live young in the spring. In late spring to midsummer the young scales, called *crawlers*, settle on leaves and twigs. These small (1/16 inch), soft-bodied young feed by sucking sap from the plant. Their legs usually atrophy, and a hard, crusty shell develops over the body. An uncontrolled infestation of scales may kill large branches after 2 or 3 seasons.

SOLUTION: During the dormant season, spray the trunk and branches with ORTHO Volck Supreme Oil Spray. The crawlers may be killed with ORTHO Malathion 50 Insect Spray or ORTHO Fruit & Vegetable Insect Control applied in the late spring. For further information about scales, see page 878.

PROBLEM: Sunken elliptical lesions appear on the trunk or branches. Throughout the fall, winter, and spring a thick, sour-smelling, amber gum oozes from these lesions. In the spring, especially when the weather is excessively wet and cold, blossoms may turn brown and wither, and some of the leaf and flower buds die and become covered with gum. Individual branches may fail to produce foliage; or, as the season progresses, entire branches may die back. There may be angular holes in the leaves. Often, many shoots sprout from the rootstock.

ANALYSIS: Bacterial canker
This plant disease, also known as *bacterial gummosis* or *bacterial blast*, is caused by a bacterium (*Pseudomonas syringae*). During the fall, winter, and early spring, large quantities of bacteria-containing gum ooze from the cankers. Splashing rain spreads the bacteria to dormant buds, twigs, and branches. Infection occurs through wounds in the twigs and branches, and bacterial decay causes cankers to form. Slowly developing cankers may encircle a branch, and by midsummer the affected branches and limbs die back. With the onset of cool fall weather, bacterial activity increases. This disease is most serious on young trees.

SOLUTION: Prune out diseased branches. After each cut, sterilize the pruning shears by dipping them in rubbing alcohol. In the fall, spray with a fungicide containing *basic copper sulfate* to obtain partial control. Keep the tree healthy by fertilizing and watering properly. For cultural information, see page 654.

_____ PEAR _____

Peachtree borer larva and pupa (life size).

PROBLEM: Holes appear in the lower part of the trunk or in the upper trunk and lower crotches. A thick, gummy substance often oozes from these holes. Sawdust may surround the holes or collect at the base of the tree. In mid to late summer, empty pupa skins may protrude from the holes. During the spring and summer, some of the leaves and branches may wilt. Severely affected trees may die.

ANALYSIS: Peachtree borers
(*Synanthedon* species)
These moth larvae are very damaging to peaches and nectarines. The clear-winged moths, which resemble wasps, lay their eggs in mid to late summer. The larvae that emerge bore into the bark. Their tunnels interfere with the circulation of water and nutrients, causing twigs and branches to wilt and die. These borers feed throughout the winter and into the spring. A gummy sap — often mixed with sawdustlike particles — may ooze from the tunnels. The borers pupate in early to midsummer in cocoons located at the base of the tree or just inside their tunnels. The moths emerge several weeks later.

SOLUTION: Spray the trunk and lower branches with ORTHO Lindane Borer & Leaf Miner Spray. Next year, in late May or early June, kill the egg-laying moths by spraying the trunk and crotches with ORTHO Liquid Sevin. Spray at intervals of 3 weeks until early August. Contact your local Cooperative Extension Office (see page 1011) for peachtree borer emergence dates in your area. Individual borers may be killed by inserting a wire into their holes.

PEAR _____

ADAPTATION AND POLLINATION: See the variety chart on page 1006.

SOIL: Any good, deep, well-drained soil. pH 5.5 to 8.0

FERTILIZER: Fertilize with ORTHO Evergreen, Tree & Shrub Food 12–6–6 according to label directions.

WATER:
   How much: Apply enough water to wet the soil 3 to 4 feet deep. To determine the proper amount of water for your soil type, see page 906.
   How often: Water when the soil 6 inches below the surface is just barely moist.

PRUNING: Pears are borne on short fruiting branches (spurs) that grow on 1-year-old wood. The spurs continue to fruit for 5 to 8 years. Prune lightly, because removal of many spurs will reduce the pear yield. Thin out weak, crossing, or dead twigs and branches.

HARVEST: Unlike most other fruit, pears should not be allowed to ripen on the tree. Pick them when they have reached their mature size and are starting to lose their green color. Do not allow them to soften or turn entirely yellow before harvesting. As a general rule, most pears may be safely harvested during September. Contact your local Cooperative Extension Office (see page 1011) for specific harvest dates and for your location and pear varieties. After harvesting, place the pears in a plastic bag, and refrigerate them for at least 2 weeks. To ripen them, remove them from the refrigerator and keep at room temperature. After 5 to 10 days, they should be fully ripe.

Scab.

PROBLEM: Olive-brown velvety spots, 1/4 inch or more in diameter, appear on the leaves and young fruit. As the infected pears mature, the spots develop into light to dark brown corky lesions. The fruit is often cracked and malformed, and may drop prematurely. There are small, blisterlike pustules on many of the twigs.

ANALYSIS: Scab
This plant disease is caused by a fungus (*Venturia pyrina*) that commonly infects pears. The fungus spends the winter in infected plant debris and twig lesions. In the spring, spores are produced and discharged into the air. They are blown to the developing leaves, flowers, twigs, and young pears. If the leaves and fruit are wet the fungus infects them, and spots develop. The infected tissues produce more spores, which further spread the disease. As temperatures increase in the summer, the fungus becomes less active.

SOLUTION: Unless they are severely infected, the pears are edible if the scabby areas are removed. To prevent recurrence of the disease next year, remove and destroy leaf debris and infected fruit in the fall. Next spring, spray with ORTHO Home Orchard Spray or ORTHO Orthocide Garden Fungicide according to label directions.

PEAR

Infected blossoms.

Blighted twig.

Codling moth larva (¾ life size).

PROBLEM: Blossoms turn black and die. Young leafy twigs wilt from the tips down, turn black, and die. A bend often develops at the tips of the infected twigs. On the branches, and at the base of the blighted twigs, the bark becomes water-soaked in appearance, then dark, sunken, and dry. Cracks may develop at the edge of the sunken area. In warm, moist spring weather, drops of brown ooze appear on the surface of these lesions. During the summer, shoots or branches may wilt and turn dark brown to black. Infected fruit shrivels, turns black, and remains on the tree.

ANALYSIS: Fireblight
This plant disease is caused by a bacterium (*Erwinia amylovora*) that is very severe on pears, and also affects apples and several ornamental plants in the rose family. (For a list of susceptible plants, see page 1001.) The bacteria spend the winter in sunken lesions (cankers) on the branches and twigs. In the spring, the bacteria ooze out of the cankers and are carried by insects to the pear blossoms. Once a few of the blossoms have been contaminated, splashing rain, honeybees, and other insects continue to spread the bacteria to healthy blossoms. The bacteria spread down through the flowers into the twigs and branches, where cankers develop. Often, developing cankers will encircle a shoot or branch by midsummer, causing conspicuous branch and twig dieback. Although fireblight is spread primarily through flower infection, leaves and twigs damaged by hail or wounded in some other manner are also susceptible to infection. Tender, succulent shoots and sprouts are also vulnerable to infection. Although severely diseased trees may be killed, more commonly only the fruiting stems (spears) are killed, resulting in greatly reduced fruit yields. Fireblight is most severe during warm (65° to 85°F), wet weather.

SOLUTION: After the infection has stopped spreading in the summer or fall, prune out and destroy infected twigs and branches at least 18 inches beyond visible decay. Sterilize pruning shears after each cut with rubbing alcohol. A protective spray of *basic copper sulfate* or *streptomycin* applied before the blossoms open next spring will help prevent infection. Repeat at intervals of 5 to 7 days until the end of the blooming period. Avoid fertilizing with high-nitrogen fertilizers to prevent excess growth of shoots and suckers. Plant varieties that are less susceptible to fireblight.

Pear varieties resistant and susceptible to fireblight:
  Susceptible: Barlett, Bosc, and Clapp.
  Fairly Resistant: Baldwin, Dutchess, Garber, Moonglow, Orient, Seckel, and Starking Delicious.

PROBLEM: Fruit is blemished by small holes surrounded by dead tissue. A brown, crumbly material that resembles sawdust may surround the holes. Brown-headed, pinkish white worms up to 1 inch long may be found in the fruit. The interior of the fruit may be dark and rotted. Many pears drop prematurely.

ANALYSIS: Codling moth
(*Laspeyresia pomonella*)
This worm, the larva of a small gray-brown moth, attacks apples, quinces, and several other fruit and nut trees in addition to pears. The moths appear in the spring, and lay their eggs on the leaves, twigs, and developing fruit. The eggs soon hatch, and the larvae that emerge tunnel into the fruit. They feed for several weeks, then emerge from the pears, often leaving a mass of dark excrement on the skin and inside the fruit. After pupating in sheltered locations on or around the tree, another generation of moths emerges in midsummer. Pears may be damaged by worms continuously throughout the summer. In the fall the mature larvae spin cocoons in protected places, such as under loose bark or in tree crevices. They spend the winter in these cocoons and, with the warming temperatures of spring, pupate and emerge as moths.

SOLUTION: Once the worms have penetrated the pears, it is impossible to kill them. To protect uninfested pears, spray with ORTHO Home Orchard Spray or ORTHO Fruit & Vegetable Insect Control at intervals of 10 to 14 days as directed on the label. Remove and destroy all fallen pears, and clean up debris around the trees. Next spring, spray 10 to 14 days after petals have fallen from the blossoms, according to label directions.

Plum curculio larva (life size).

Overripe pear.

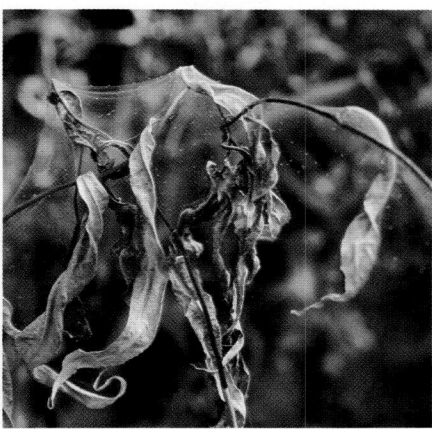

Spider mite damage.

PROBLEM: The ripening fruit is misshapen, rotten, and often drops prematurely. Holes about ⅛ inch in diameter and deep, crescent-shaped scars appear on the fruit. When cut open, such fruit may be found to contain crescent-shaped yellow-gray grubs with brown heads.

ANALYSIS: Plum curculio
(*Conotrachelus nenuphar*)
These insects, found east of the Rocky Mountains, commonly attack stone fruits, apples, and pears. The adult insects are brown beetles with long curved snouts. They hibernate in debris and other protected places during the winter. The beetles emerge in the spring when new growth starts and begin feeding on young leaves, blossoms, and developing fruit. After 5 to 6 weeks, the female beetles start to lay eggs in the young fruit. During this process they cut distinctive crescent-shaped slits into the pears. The grubs that hatch from the eggs feed for several weeks in the fruit. Usually the infested pears drop to the ground. The grubs eventually leave the fruit and bore into the soil, where they pupate. The emerging beetles feed on fruit for a few weeks, then go into hibernation. Or, in the South, they lay eggs, producing a second generation of grubs in the late summer.

SOLUTION: There is no way to kill the grubs inside the fruit. Spray with ORTHO Malathion 50 Insect Spray or an insecticide containing *methoxychlor* to kill beetles that may be feeding on fruit or laying eggs. Pick up and destroy all fallen fruit. Next spring, spray the trees when the petals are falling from the blossoms; repeat applications according to the directions on the label.

PROBLEM: The fruit tastes mealy, mushy, or gritty. The flavor is poor, and the inner flesh may be soft and discolored. The fruit was picked when it had softened or turned yellow on the tree.

ANALYSIS: Fruit harvested too late
Unlike most other fruits, pears must be harvested before they are fully ripe. When left to ripen on the tree, they turn mealy, develop clusters of hard cells (stone cells), and lose their flavor and succulence.

SOLUTION: Most pear varieties should be picked when they have reached their mature size and are starting to lose their green color. Do not allow them to soften or turn entirely yellow before harvesting. As a general rule, most pears may be safely picked during September. Contact your local Cooperative Extension Office (see page 1011) for specific harvest dates for your location and pear varieties. After harvesting, place the pears in a closed plastic bag and refrigerate them for at least two weeks. To soften them, remove them from the bag, and keep them at room temperature. After 5 to 10 days, they should be fully ripe.

PROBLEM: Leaves are stippled, yellowing, or bronzed. There may be webbing over flower buds, between leaves, or on the lower surfaces of the leaves. Fruit may be russeted. To determine if the tree is infested with certain species of mites, hold a sheet of white paper underneath an affected leaf and tap the leaf sharply. Minute green, red, or yellow specks the size of pepper grains will drop to the paper and begin to crawl around.

ANALYSIS: Mites
Several species of mites, including the two-spotted spider mite (*Tetranychus urticae*) and the pear rust mite (*Epitrimerus pyri*) attack pears. Two-spotted spider mites, which cause leaf stippling and webbing, may be detected as described above. Pear rust mites, which cause fruit russeting and leaf stippling and bronzing, cannot be seen without the aid of a microscope or strong hand lens. These pests, related to spiders, cause damage by sucking plant sap. As a result of feeding, the green leaf pigment disappears, producing the stippled or bronzed appearance. Mites are active throughout the growing season, but are favored by hot, dry weather (70°F and up).

SOLUTION: Spray infested trees with ORTHO Fruit & Vegetable Insect Control or ORTHO Malathion 50 Insect Spray. Repeat the spray 2 more times at intervals of 7 to 10 days. After the leaves have dropped next fall, spray the tree with a *lime sulfur* solution and a *dormant oil*. If you are not sure whether your trees are infested with pear rust mites, bring an infested fruit spur to your local County Extension Office (see page 1011) for confirmation.

PEAR

Pearleaf blister mite damage.

Pear psylla damage (4 times life size).

Fabraea leaf spot.

PROBLEM: Yellow to green blisters about 1/8 inch across appear on the undersides of the leaves. These blisters turn red, then black. Buds are deformed and may not set fruit, so the fruit yield is often reduced. Many of the pears that do mature are russet-colored and deformed. They may crack open. If one of the leaf blisters is opened and inspected with a strong hand lens, tiny pinkish white mites may be seen.

ANALYSIS: Pearleaf blister mite
(*Phytoptus pyri*)
These microscopic mites are related to spiders. They attack pears, apples, and several other ornamental trees and shrubs. The mites spend the winter under leaf and flower bud scales. They lay eggs in the spring when the buds begin to swell. The young mites that hatch from these eggs burrow into the emerging leaves, causing blisters to form. Blister mite damage may continue throughout the growing season. With the onset of cold weather, the adult mites move back under the bud scales.

SOLUTION: There is no control for damage on the fruit this year. To help prevent blister mite damage next year, spray the infested tree with ORTHO Orthorix Spray in the fall and again the following spring as directed on the label. Early next spring, before the buds open, spray with a *dormant oil spray*.

PROBLEM: Leaves and fruit are covered with a shiny or sticky substance called honeydew. A black mold usually grows on the honeydew. Tiny (1/10 inch) reddish brown winged insects may be seen feeding on the foliage. Some of the leaves may turn yellow and drop. Severely infested trees may defoliate prematurely.

ANALYSIS: Pear psylla
(*Psylla pyricola*)
These insects are related to aphids. The adults overwinter in crevices in the tree trunks, in groundcover, or in other protected places. In the late winter or early spring the females lay eggs on the bark, and later on the emerging foliage. The young psyllas feed on the leaves and developing pears, causing damage by sucking the plant sap. The psyllas are unable to digest fully all the sugar in the plant sap, and excrete the excess in a fluid called honeydew, which drops onto the leaves and fruit. A sooty mold fungus may develop on the honeydew, causing the pear leaves and fruit to appear black and dirty. Psylla damage may occur throughout the growing season.

SOLUTION: These pests are very hard to kill during the growing season. To control them next year, kill the overwintering adults and eggs by spraying the tree with a *dormant oil spray* in the early spring.

PROBLEM: Tiny purplish black spots appear on the leaves and shoots. These spots enlarge up to 1/4 inch in diameter and turn dark brown. Spots on shoots may join together, forming twig cankers. Infected leaves turn yellow and drop. Small red spots develop on the fruit, eventually turning into dark, sunken lesions. Diseased pears may be cracked and misshapen, with rough skins. Severely infected trees may defoliate prematurely.

ANALYSIS: Fabraea leaf spot
This plant disease, also known as *pearleaf blight*, is caused by a fungus (*Farbraea maculata*) that attacks pears and quinces. The fungus spends the winter in twig cankers and leaf debris. In the spring, spores are splashed to the leaves, shoots, and young fruit. Spots develop where the fungus penetrates the plant tissue. Infection may continue throughout the growing season. The premature death of the infected foliage greatly reduces the amount of food the tree can make and store. This results in weakened trees, lower yields, and poor quality fruit.

SOLUTION: To protect leaves and fruit that have not yet been infected, spray with a fungicide containing *captan* or *ferbam*. Remove and destroy all leaf debris around the trees. Next spring, spray just before the trees bloom, and again after the petals fall from the tree.

Fruit tree leafroller (twice life size).

Pearslug (twice life size).

San Jose scales (life size).

PROBLEM: Irregular holes appear in the leaves and fruit. Some of the leaves are rolled and held together with a web. One or several young fruit may be enclosed within the rolled leaves. When these rolled leaves are peeled open, pale green worms up to ¾ inch long with brown heads are found inside. The maturing pears are scarred and misshapen.

ANALYSIS: Fruit tree leafroller
(*Archips argyrospilus*)
These worms, the larvae of brown moths, are common pests of many fruit and ornamental trees. In June or July, the moths lay eggs on twigs and branches. When the eggs hatch the following spring, the larvae feed on the blossoms and developing fruit and foliage. Leafrollers often wrap leaves around ripening fruit, then feed on the fruit inside, causing much damage to the pears. After about a month, the mature larvae pupate inside rolled leaves.

SOLUTION: If practical, pick off and destroy rolled leaves to reduce the number of moths that will emerge later in the season. Next spring, spray the tree with ORTHO Home Orchard Spray, ORTHO Liquid Sevin, or ORTHO Fruit & Vegetable Insect Control when 75 percent of the petals have fallen from the blossoms. Repeat the spray according to the directions on the label.

PROBLEM: The upper surfaces of the leaves are chewed between the veins, leaving a lacy, translucent layer of tissue that turns brown. Dark green to orange, wet, sluglike worms up to ½ inch long may be feeding on the leaves. Severely infested trees may be defoliated.

ANALYSIS: Pearslug
(*Caliroa cerasi*)
Although pearslugs resemble slugs, they are actually the larvae of black and yellow flies that infest pears, cherries, plums, and some ornamental trees. The adult flies appear in the late spring and lay their eggs in the leaves. The larvae that hatch from these eggs exude a slimy, olive-green substance, giving them a sluglike appearance. They feed on the foliage for about a month, then drop to the ground, burrow into the soil, and pupate. The second generation of larvae spends the winter in cocoons buried in the soil. Young trees that are severely infested with pearslugs may be greatly weakened, producing pears of poor quality.

SOLUTION: Spray the infested tree with an insecticide containing *malathion* or *carbaryl*. Repeat the spray if reinfestation recurs.

PROBLEM: Some of the leaves are pale green to yellow, and may drop prematurely on weakened limbs. The bark is encrusted with small (¹⁄₁₆ inch), hard, circular, slightly raised bumps with dull yellow centers. If the hard cover is scraped off, the insect underneath is yellow or olive. Entire branches may be killed. Red-purple spots mar some of the infested fruits and shoots.

ANALYSIS: San Jose scale
(*Quadraspidiotus perniciosus*)
These insects infest the bark, leaves, and fruit of many fruit trees. The scales bear live young in the spring. In late spring to midsummer the young scales, called *crawlers*, settle on leaves, twigs, and fruit. The small (¹⁄₁₆ inch), soft-bodied young feed by inserting their mouthparts and sucking sap from the plant. The legs usually atrophy and a hard, crusty shell develops over the body. An uncontrolled infestation of San Jose scales may kill large branches after 2 or 3 seasons.

SOLUTION: During the dormant season, spray the trunk and branches with ORTHO Volck Supreme Oil Spray. The crawlers may be killed with ORTHO Malathion 50 Insect Control applied in the late spring. For further information about scales, see page 878.

PECAN

PECAN

ADAPTATION AND POLLINATION: See the variety chart on page 1003.

SOIL: Any good, deep, well-drained soil. pH 5.5 to 8.0

FERTILIZER: Fertilize with ORTHO Evergreen, Tree & Shrub Food 12–6–6 according to label directions.

WATER:
How much: Apply enough water to wet the soil 3 to 4 feet deep. To determine the proper amount of water for your soil type, see page 906.
How often: Water when the soil 6 inches below the surface is just barely moist.

PRUNING: Nuts form on the current season's growth. Prune pecans lightly, removing weak, diseased, or dead twigs and branches.

HARVEST: Harvest the nuts in the fall by gently knocking the tree with a rubber mallet or cloth-covered pole when the shucks have split and the nuts are exposed.

Pecan weevil (twice life size).

PROBLEM: Immature pecans that drop to the ground during August are marked with dark patches and tobaccolike stains. Later in the season, there are ⅛-inch holes in some of the ripe nuts. When cut open, the kernels are found to be destroyed, and may contain creamy-white curved grubs up to ½ inch long. Reddish brown to gray long-beaked beetles, ½ inch long, may be seen in the tree. If the limbs are shaken, these beetles will drop to the ground.

ANALYSIS: Pecan weevil
(*Curculio caryae*)
This insect is very damaging to pecans and hickories in both its immature and adult stages. The adult weevils appear in late summer and feed on the immature pecans. The injured nuts drop from the tree. As soon as the kernels harden, the female weevils drill holes through the shucks and shells, and lay their eggs in the kernels. The grubs that hatch from these eggs feed on the kernels for several weeks, then leave the nut, drop to the ground, and burrow into the soil. They will emerge after 2 to 3 years as adult weevils.

SOLUTION: Spray severely infested trees with an insecticide containing *carbaryl*. Spray at intervals of 10 to 14 days until the shucks split from the shells. Weevils may also be partially controlled by shaking them from lightly infested trees. Place sheets under the tree, then lightly jar the limbs. Collect and kill the dislodged weevils that fall onto the sheet. Repeat every 2 weeks until the weevils are no longer present.

Hickory shuckworm (twice life size).

PROBLEM: Cream-colored worms up to ⅜ inch long, are feeding in the immature nuts, many of which fall to the ground prematurely. Later in the season, after the shells have hardened, the worms may be found in the green shucks.

ANALYSIS: Hickory shuckworm
(*Laspeyresia caryana*)
These worms, the larvae of small brown moths, are also known as *pecan shuckworms*. They are pests of pecan and hickory trees wherever they are grown. The larvae spend the winter in shucks on the ground or in the tree. The shuckworms pupate and emerge as adult moths in the spring to lay their eggs on pecan leaves and nuts. The young larvae that hatch from these eggs tunnel into the soft green pecan shells and feed on the developing kernels. Infested nuts usually drop. Later in the season, after the nut shells have hardened, the larvae tunnel into the shucks. Their feeding damage interferes with the development of the kernels. Shuckworm damage may occur throughout the spring and summer.

SOLUTION: Chemical controls are not practical for the home gardener. Clean up and destroy all dropped nuts and shucks to eliminate many of the overwintering larvae.

Pecan phylloxeras (life size).

Pecan nut casebearer damage.

Spittlebugs.

PROBLEM: Green to yellow-green swellings (galls) appear on the leaves, shoots, and nuts. These galls, which range in size from ⅛ to 1 inch in diameter, split open in the late spring. Shoots with galls on them may be weak and dying. When the galls are cut open, tiny soft-bodied insects resembling aphids may be seen inside.

ANALYSIS: Pecan phylloxera
(*Phylloxera* species)
These insects, closely related to aphids, are common pests of pecan and hickory trees. Phylloxera eggs, laid in the fall, survive the winter on twigs and branches. The eggs hatch when the leaf buds open in the spring. The emerging insects feed on the new spring growth by sucking the plant sap. They inject a substance into the plant while feeding that causes the plant tissue to swell, forming galls. Eventually the galls envelop the feeding insects. After the phylloxeras mature, they lay their eggs and die. When this second generation of winged insects matures, the galls split open, releasing them. Although these pests are present throughout the summer, they are most damaging to the new spring growth.

SOLUTION: Once the galls have formed, the insects cannot be killed. During the dormant season, spray the tree with a *dormant oil spray* to kill the overwintering eggs. Next spring when the buds start to open, spray with an insecticide containing either *malathion* or *lindane*.

PROBLEM: Olive-green worms up to ½ inch long with yellow-brown heads are feeding on the twigs, foliage, and developing nuts. Some of the young shoots are wilting. Nut clusters may be webbed together. There are holes in some of the nuts, and many of the kernels have been destroyed. Many nuts drop prematurely. Some of the nuts may contain worms or pupae, either in the kernel or in the shuck.

ANALYSIS: Pecan nut casebearer
(*Acrobasis nuxvorella*)
These worms, the larvae of small, dark gray moths, are very damaging to pecans. The larvae come out of hibernation when the buds open in the spring. They feed on the developing buds for a short time, then tunnel into the new shoots to pupate. The adult moths emerge just as the nuts start to form, and lay their eggs on the young pecans. This second generation of worms webs clusters of nuts together, then bores into and feeds on them. This generation of casebearers usually damages many pecans because each worm eats 3 or 4 of the immature nuts during its larval stage. After reaching their mature size, the larvae pupate inside the nuts and become moths. Larval damage continues throughout the summer, but lessens in severity as the nuts enlarge.

SOLUTION: Spray with ORTHO Fruit & Vegetable Insect Control. Next spring, contact your local County Extension Office (see page 1011) to determine when moths are laying eggs in your area. Spray during this period and again 6 weeks later. Destroy all infested nuts that fall to the ground.

PROBLEM: Masses of white, frothy foam cluster on the twigs, buds, and nuts. If the froth is washed off, small, green, soft-bodied insects can be seen feeding on the plant tissue. Young, tender shoots sometimes die, and the nut yield may be reduced.

ANALYSIS: Spittlebugs
(*Clastoptera achatina* and *C. obtusa*)
These insects, also known as *froghoppers*, appear in the spring and again in the midsummer. Spittlebug eggs are laid in the fall and survive the winter in cracks in the bark. The young spittlebugs — called *nymphs* — emerge soon after the pecan nuts have set. The foamy froth they produce completely envelops them while they suck the sap from the tender buds, twigs, and nuts. The adult spittlebugs are not as damaging as the nymphs. The adults are ¼ inch long, yellow to reddish brown, and winged. They hop or fly away quickly when disturbed. Large numbers of spittlebugs can kill many young shoots, resulting in a reduced nut yield.

SOLUTION: Spray infested trees with an insecticide containing *malathion*. Repeat the spray if reinfestation occurs.

PECAN

Scab.

Black-bordered pecan aphid (4 times life size).

Cotton root rot.

PROBLEM: Olive-colored spots up to ¼ inch across appear on the twigs and the undersides of the leaves. Large areas of the leaves may turn black. The tree may defoliate prematurely. Tiny black dots that develop on the shucks usually enlarge to form black sunken lesions. Infected nuts drop prematurely.

ANALYSIS: Scab
This plant disease is caused by a fungus (*Fusicladium effusum*). It is the most serious disease of pecans. The fungus spends the winter on twigs and old leaves and shucks on the tree and ground. In the spring, fungal spores are splashed and blown to the developing new growth. If there is adequate moisture, the spores infect the plant tissue, causing spotting and blighting. The infected tissue produces additional spores, which spread to the young nuts. As the pecan leaves mature they become resistant to scab infection. However, the shucks are susceptible to fungal attack as long as they continue to grow and develop.

SOLUTION: If there are some healthy nuts left on the tree, spray with a fungicide containing *benomyl*. Remove and destroy old shucks and plant debris. Next spring, spray again when the buds open, and spray 3 more times at intervals of 2 to 3 weeks. Do not spray after the shucks begin to split open.

Pecan resistance to scab:
Susceptible: Burkett, Mahan, Schley, Success, and Western.
Fairly resistant: Curtis, Dependable, Elliot, Gloria Grande, and Shawnee.
Resistant: Cheyenne, Desirable, Kiowa, and Mohawk.

PROBLEM: Small (⅟₁₆ to ⅛ inch) yellow, light to dark green, or black soft-bodied insects are feeding on the foliage. Rectangular yellow areas about ¼ inch long may appear on the leaves. These yellow areas turn brown, and the affected leaves drop. In some cases, the youngest leaves are curled, twisted, and dying. A shiny or sticky substance may coat the leaves. A black sooty mold may grow on this sticky substance. The pecan yield is often reduced. Severely infested trees may defoliate prematurely.

ANALYSIS: Aphids
Several species of aphids infest pecans, including the black pecan aphid (*Tinocallis caryaefoliae*) and yellow aphid (*Monellia* species). Aphids do little damage in small numbers. However, they are extremely prolific and populations can rapidly build up to damaging numbers during the growing season. Damage occurs when the aphid sucks the juices from the pecan leaves. The aphid is unable to digest fully all the sugar in the plant sap and excretes the excess in a fluid called honeydew, which often drops onto the leaves below. A sooty mold fungus may develop on the honeydew, causing the pecan leaves to appear black and dirty. Black pecan aphids are especially damaging to pecans. They are responsible for the yellow-spotted, dying leaves of many pecans in the Southeast.

SOLUTION: Spray infested trees with ORTHO Fruit & Vegetable Insect Control. If reinfestation occurs, repeat the spray as directed on the label.

PROBLEM: During the summer, the foliage turns yellow, wilts, and dies. The dead leaves may remain attached to the tree. Cottony white or powdery tan mats of spores 2 to 12 inches in diameter may appear on the soil near the affected tree. If the soil around the base of the tree is loosened and removed to expose some of the roots, the bark of the roots is usually found to be brownish, rotted, and soft. There may be light to dark brown spherical fungal pellets the size of pinheads on the infected roots.

ANALYSIS: Cotton root rot
This plant disease, also known as *Texas root rot*, is caused by a fungus (*Phymatotrichum omnivorum*). Cotton root rot, a serious problem in the Southwest, infects many kinds of flowers, trees, and shrubs. The fungus becomes active as the soil warms in the spring. Fungal strands grow through the soil to penetrate and decay the roots, eventually killing the tree. The fungal strands may spread up to 30 feet in one year. Cotton root rot is often brought into a garden initially in infected transplants or contaminated soil and tools. The fungus thrives in heavy, moist, alkaline soils. It may persist in the soil for 5 years or more.

SOLUTION: There is no practical chemical control. Mildly affected trees may be saved by fertilizing with *ammonium sulfate*. For more information about this technique, see page 859. It is best to replace dying trees with plants that are resistant to cotton root rot. For a list of resistant plants, see page 994.

PERSIMMON ──

Fruit drop.

Sunburn.

PERSIMMON ──────────────

ADAPTATION: Oriental persimmons can be grown in zones 7 through 10. Native persimmons can be grown in zones 4 through 10. To determine your climate zone, see the map on page 1004.

SOIL: Any good, deep, well-drained soil. pH 5.5 to 8.0

FERTILIZER: Fertilize with ORTHO Evergreen, Tree & Shrub Food 12–6–6 according to label directions.

WATER:
How much: Apply enough water to wet the soil 3 to 4 feet deep. To determine the proper amount of water for your soil type, see page 906.
How often: Water when the soil 6 inches below the surface is just barely moist.

PRUNING: Prune lightly. Remove weak or lank growth and crossed, diseased, and broken limbs.

HARVEST: Allow astringent persimmons to become soft and fully colored before harvesting. Nonastringent varieties may be harvested and eaten before they have softened. Clip fruit off rather than pulling them off.

PROBLEM: Fruit drops prematurely. The tree appears to be healthy; there are no signs of insects, pests, or diseases.

ANALYSIS: Fruit drop
Persimmons have a natural tendency to drop their fruit prematurely. Large quantities of fruit may drop when the tree is under stress. Stress may be caused by conditions such as excessive heat, drought, cold, or overwatering. Excessive fruit drop may also occur on trees that are growing vigorously due to heavy nitrogen fertilization.

SOLUTION: Although fruit drop cannot be eliminated, it can be reduced. Avoid overfertilizing and overwatering or underwatering the tree. For more information about the proper culture of persimmons, see page 667.

PROBLEM: During hot weather, usually in August or September, dark brown or black patches appear on the developing fruit. Leaves may turn brown around the edges and between the veins.

ANALYSIS: Sunburn
Sunburn is caused by excessive evaporation of moisture from the leaves and fruit. In hot weather, water evaporates rapidly from the fruit and foliage. If the roots can't absorb and convey water fast enough to replenish this loss, the fruit surfaces exposed to the sun overheat and burn; in severe cases, the leaves turn brown and wither. This usually occurs in dry soil, but fruit and leaves can also burn when the soil is moist and temperatures are around 100°F. Drying winds, severed roots, and limited soil area can also cause sunburn. For more information about leafscorch, see page 865.

SOLUTION: There is nothing you can do once the fruit has been damaged, but it is still edible. To help prevent further sunburn, deep-water plants during periods of hot weather to wet down the entire root space. (For more information about watering, see page 906.) Newly transplanted trees should be watered whenever the rootball is dry 2 inches below the surface.

PLUM

PLUM

ADAPTATION AND POLLINATION: See the variety chart on page 1006.

SOIL: Any good, deep, well-drained soil. pH 5.5 to 8.0

FERTILIZER: Fertilize with ORTHO Evergreen, Tree & Shrub Food 12–6–6 according to label directions.

WATER:
How much: Apply enough water to wet the soil 3 to 4 feet deep. To determine the proper amount of water for your soil type, see page 906.
How often: Water when the soil 6 inches below the surface is just barely moist.

PRUNING: European and American plums are borne on short fruiting branches (spurs) that continue to fruit for many years. Prune lightly, because removal of many spurs will reduce the plum yield. Thin out weak, crossing, and dead twigs and branches. Japanese plums are borne on 1-year-old wood and on spurs that grow on 2-year-old wood. The spurs continue to fruit for 2 to 4 years. Prune back last year's growth to half its length, and thin out spurred branches that have stopped fruiting. Thin out weak, crossing, or dead twigs and branches. For large plums, thin fruit to 4 to 6 inches apart.

HARVEST: Harvest when the fruit are fully colored and slightly soft. When they are ripe, the plum stem will easily separate from the spur or branch when the fruit is gently lifted.

Plum curculio damage.

PROBLEM: Ripening fruit is misshapen, rotten, and often drops prematurely. Holes about ⅛ inch in diameter and deep, crescent-shaped scars appear on the fruit. When cut open, such fruit may be found to contain crescent-shaped, yellow-gray grubs with brown heads.

ANALYSIS: Plum curculio
(*Conotrachelus nenuphar*)
These insects, found east of the Rocky Mountains, commonly attack other stone fruits, apples, and pears, as well as plums. The adult insects are brown beetles with long curved snouts. They hibernate in debris and other protected places during the winter. The beetles emerge in the spring when new growth starts and begin feeding on young leaves, blossoms, and developing fruit. After 5 to 6 weeks, the female beetles start to lay eggs in the young fruit. During this process they cut distinctive crescent-shaped slits into the plums. The grubs that hatch from the eggs feed for several weeks in the fruit. The infested plums usually drop to the ground. The grubs eventually leave the fruit and bore into the soil, where they pupate. The emerging beetles feed on fruit for a few weeks, then go into hibernation. Or, in the South, they lay eggs, producing a second generation of grubs in the late summer.

SOLUTION: Once the fruit is infested, there is no way to kill the grubs inside the fruit. Spray with ORTHO Home Orchard Spray or ORTHO Malathion 50 Insect Spray to kill beetles that may be feeding on fruit or laying eggs. Pick up and destroy all fallen fruit. Next spring, spray the trees when the petals are falling from the blossoms; repeat applications according to the directions on the label.

Bacterial leaf spot on Stanley prunes.

PROBLEM: Brown or black angular spots develop on the leaves. The centers of the spots often fall out. The tips of the leaves may die, and severely infected leaves turn yellow and drop. When the fruit sets, the surface may be dotted with brown to black spots. The surface of the fruit becomes pitted and cracked. Sunken lesions may form on the twigs. Severely infected trees may defoliate.

ANALYSIS: Bacterial leaf spot
This plant disease, caused by bacteria (*Xanthomonas pruni*), also attacks apricots and peaches. The disease is common east of the Rocky Mountains. The bacteria spend the winter in lesions on the twigs, oozing out in the spring to be carried by splashing rain to young leaves, shoots, and developing fruit. Periods of frequent rainfall favor the infection. Trees that defoliate early in the summer become weakened, and produce few plums of poor quality.

SOLUTION: There is no adequate control for this disease. Spraying when the flower buds open in the spring with *basic copper sulfate* may help suppress the disease, but will not eliminate it.

Blossom blight.

Fruit rot.

Spider mite damage.

PROBLEM: Blossoms and young leaves decay, wilt, and turn brown during the first two weeks of the bloom period. Often the decayed blossoms fail to drop, and hang on the tree through the growing season. In humid conditions, masses of gray spores may appear on the infected flower parts. There is often extensive twig dieback. Sunken lesions sometimes develop on the twigs and branches as the season progresses. These lesions usually exude a sticky ooze.

ANALYSIS: Brown rot
This plant disease, caused by either of two closely related fungi (*Monilinia laxa* or *M. fructicola*), is very destructive to all the stone fruits. The fungi spend the winter in twig cankers or in rotted fruits (mummies) in the tree or on the ground. In the spring, spores are blown or splashed from cankers or mummies to the healthy flower buds. After penetrating and decaying the flowers, the fungus grows down into the twigs, producing brown, sunken cankers. During moist weather a thick, gummy sap oozes from the lesions, and tufts of gray spores may form on the infected areas. Spores from cankers and infected blossoms or mummies are splashed and blown to the maturing fruit. Young fruits are fairly resistant to infection, but maturing fruits are vulnerable. Brown rot develops most rapidly in mild, moist conditions.

SOLUTION: If there are still uninfected blossoms left on the tree, spray with ORTHO Home Orchard Spray, or with a fungicide containing *captan* or *benomyl* to protect them from further infection. Spray twice at intervals of 10 days. To protect maturing plums and nectarines from infection, spray them with ORTHO Home Orchard Spray or with a fungicide containing *captan* or *benomyl* about 3 weeks before they are to be harvested. Remove and destroy all infected fruits and mummies. Prune out cankers and blighted twigs. Clean up and destroy all debris around the tree. Next spring, spray trees at early bloom. Continue to spray according to label directions.

PROBLEM: Small circular brown spots appear on the young fruits. Later in the season, as the plums start to mature, these spots may enlarge to rot part or all of the fruit. During moist weather the rotted fruits are covered with tufts of gray spores. When the infected plums are sliced open, the flesh inside is brown, usually firm, and fairly dry. Infected fruits either drop prematurely or dry out, turn dark brown, and remain on the tree past the normal harvest period. Many twigs die. There are sunken lesions (cankers) on some of these twigs. A thick, gummy material often oozes from these cankers.

PROBLEM: Leaves are stippled, yellowing, or silvery and curling. There may be webbing over flower buds, between leaves, or on the lower surfaces of the leaves. Fruit may be roughened or russeted. To determine if the tree is infested with certain species of mites, hold a sheet of white paper underneath an affected leaf and tap the leaf sharply. Minute green, red, or yellow specks the size of pepper grains will drop to the paper and begin to crawl around.

ANALYSIS: Mites
Several species of mites attack plums, including the two-spotted spider mite (*Tetranychus urticae*) and the plum rust mite (*Aculus fockeui*). Two-spotted spider mites, which cause leaf stippling and webbing, may be detected as described above. Plum rust mites, which cause leaf silvering and curling and fruit russeting, are microscopic, and cannot be seen without the aid of a microscope or strong hand lens. These pests, related to spiders, cause damage by sucking sap from the fruit surface and the undersides of the leaves. As a result of feeding, the green leaf pigment disappears, producing the stippled or silvered appearance. Mites are active throughout the growing season, but are favored by hot, dry weather (70°F and up). By midsummer, they build up to tremendous numbers.

SOLUTION: Spray infested trees with ORTHO Home Orchard Spray. Repeat the spray 2 more times at intervals of 7 to 10 days. If you are not sure whether your tree is infested with plum rust mites, bring an infested fruit spur to your local Cooperative Extension Office (see page 1011) for confirmation.

Aphids (twice life size).

Peach twig borer (life size).

Oriental fruit moth damage.

PROBLEM: The youngest leaves are curled, twisted, discolored, and stunted. Leaves may drop off; in severe cases, the tree may defoliate. The developing plums may be small and misshapen. A shiny or sticky substance may coat the leaves. A black sooty mold often grows on the sticky substance. Tiny (⅛ inch) green, yellow, purplish, or black soft-bodied insects cluster on the young shoots and undersides of the leaves.

ANALYSIS: Aphids
Several species of these insects infest plums. Aphids do little damage in small numbers. However, they are extremely prolific and populations can rapidly build up to damaging numbers during the growing season. Damage occurs when the aphid sucks the juices from the plum leaves. The aphid is unable to digest fully all the sugar in the plant sap and excretes the excess in a fluid called honeydew, which often drops onto the leaves and fruit below. A sooty mold fungus may develop on the honeydew, causing the plum leaves to appear black and dirty.

SOLUTION: Spray with ORTHO Home Orchard Spray or ORTHO Fruit & Vegetable Insect Control as soon as the insects appear. Repeat according to label directions if the tree becomes reinfested. To kill overwintering insects or eggs, spray with ORTHO Volck Oil Spray in the spring while the tree is still dormant.

PROBLEM: New growth at the tips of the twigs wilts and dies. When the affected twigs are sliced open lengthwise, worms about ½ inch long are found inside. The reddish brown color of these worms distinguishes them from *oriental fruit moth worms*, which cause similar damage. Later in the season, some of the maturing fruit also contain these worms.

ANALYSIS: Peach twig borer
(*Anarsia lineatella*)
This borer attacks all of the stone fruits, and is particularly damaging on the Pacific Coast. The young larvae hibernate during the winter in silk-lined burrows under loose bark or in other protected places on the tree. When the tree blooms in the spring, the larvae emerge and bore into young buds and shoots, causing twig and leaf death. When mature, they leave the twigs and pupate in cocoons attached to branches. After several weeks, gray moths emerge and lay eggs on the twigs, leaves, and fruit. Egg laying and larval damage can occur throughout the growing season. Later in the summer, larvae feed almost exclusively on the maturing fruit. These pests may cause abnormal branching on young trees.

SOLUTION: Worms in the twigs and fruit cannot be killed with pesticides. To prevent future worm damage, kill the moths by spraying infested trees with ORTHO Fruit & Vegetable Insect Control or ORTHO Home Orchard Spray according to label directions. Next spring, spray again just after the petals fall from the blossoms. Repeat the treatment 2 more times at intervals of 10 to 14 days.

PROBLEM: New growth at the tips of the twigs wilts and dies. When the affected twigs are sliced open lengthwise, worms about ½ inch long are found inside. The pinkish white color of these worms distinguishes them from *peach twig borers*, which cause similar damage. Later in the season, some of the maturing fruits also contain these worms. Often there are holes filled with a sticky gum in the plums.

ANALYSIS: Oriental fruit moth
(*Grapholitha molesta*)
The larvae of these night-flying moths damage stone fruits, apples, and pears. The larvae hibernate in cocoons on the tree bark or buried in crotches. In the spring they pupate, emerge as brown adult moths, and lay eggs on the young plum twigs and leaves. The larvae bore into the young buds, shoots, and tender twigs, causing twig and leaf death. When mature they leave the twigs, spin cocoons, and pupate in the tree or in debris on the ground. After several weeks, moths emerge to lay eggs. Egg laying and larval damage continues throughout the growing season. Later in the summer, the larvae feed mainly on the maturing fruit. They leave gum-filled holes in the plums when they exit to pupate. In addition to ruining the fruit, these pests may cause abnormal branching on young trees.

SOLUTION: Worms in the twigs and fruit cannot be killed with pesticides. To prevent future worm damage, kill the moths by spraying infested trees with ORTHO Fruit & Vegetable Insect Control according to label directions. Next spring, spray again when the petals start to fall from the blossoms. Repeat the treatment 2 more times at intervals of 10 to 14 days.

Terrapin scale (twice life size).

Peachtree borer (twice life size).

Black knot.

PROBLEM: Stems, small branches, or the undersides of the leaves are covered with brownish crusty bumps or thick, white, waxy bumps, or clusters of flattened yellowish, gray, or brownish scaly bumps. The bumps can be scraped or picked off; the undersides are usually soft. Leaves turn yellow and may drop. In some cases, a shiny or sticky substance coats the leaves. A black sooty mold often grows on the sticky substance.

ANALYSIS: Scales
Several different types of scales infest plum trees. They lay their eggs on leaves or bark, and in spring to midsummer the young scales, called *crawlers*, settle on leaves and twigs. The small (1/10 inch), soft-bodied young feed by inserting their mouthparts and sucking sap from the plant. The legs usually atrophy and a hard crusty or waxy shell develops over the body. The mature female scales bear live young or lay their eggs underneath their shell. Some species of scales are unable to digest fully all the sugar in the plant sap, and excrete the excess in a fluid called honeydew, which often drops onto the leaves below. A sooty mold fungus may develop on the honeydew, causing the plum leaves to appear black and dirty.

SOLUTION: Spray with ORTHO Fruit & Vegetable Insect Control in midsummer when the crawlers are active. The following early spring, while the tree is still dormant, spray the trunk and branches with ORTHO Volck Supreme Oil Spray to control overwintering insects. For more information about scales, see page 878.

PROBLEM: Holes appear in the lower part of the trunk or in the upper trunk and lower crotches. A thick, gummy substance may ooze from these holes. There may be sawdust around the holes or base of the tree. In mid to late summer, empty pupa skins may protrude from these holes. During the spring and summer, some of the leaves and branches may wilt. Severely affected trees may die.

ANALYSIS: Peachtree borers
(*Synanthedon* species)
The larvae of these moths are most damaging to stone fruits, but also attack other ornamental trees. The clear-winged moths (which resemble wasps) lay their eggs in mid to late summer. The larvae that emerge bore into the bark. Their tunnels interfere with the circulation of water and nutrients, causing twigs and branches to wilt and die. These borers feed throughout the winter and into the spring. A gummy sap may ooze from the borer tunnels. This sap is often mixed with sawdustlike particles, the product of larval feeding. The borers pupate in early to midsummer. Their cocoons are located at the base of the tree or just inside their tunnels. The moths emerge several weeks later.

SOLUTION: Apply a spray containing *lindane* to the trunk and lower branches. Do not spray the fruit or foliage. Next year, in late May or early June, kill the egg-laying moths by spraying the trunk and crotches with an insecticide containing *malathion*. Continue spraying at intervals of 3 weeks until early August. Individual borers may be killed by inserting a wire into the borer holes.

PROBLEM: Soft greenish knots or elongated swellings form on twigs and branches. These knots develop into black, corky, cylindrical galls that may range from 1/2 to 1 1/2 inches in diameter and be more than 12 inches in length. Twigs and branches beyond the galls are usually stunted, and eventually die.

ANALYSIS: Black knot
This plant disease is caused by a fungus (*Dibotryon morbosum*) that is severe on plums, and occasionally attacks cherries. Fungal spores form during wet weather in the spring. Galls appear 6 months to a year after infection. The galls slowly enlarge and elongate. They eventually cut off the flow of water and nutrients to the branches, causing stunting, wilting, and dieback. Black knot spreads most rapidly during warm (55° to 75°F), wet spring weather.

SOLUTION: Prune out and destroy infected twigs and branches during the fall and winter. When pruning, cut at least 4 inches below visible signs of infection. Cut out knots on the trunk or large limbs down to the wood, and at least 1/2 inch outward past the diseased tissue. Next spring, spray the tree with a fungicide containing *captan* or *benomyl* just before the buds open. Repeat the spray 2 more times at intervals of 7 to 10 days. Plant resistant varieties.

Plum resistance to black knot:
Very susceptible: Bluefre, Damson, Shropshire, and Stanley.
Moderately resistant: Bradshaw, Early Italian, Fellenberg, Formosa, Methley, Milton, Santa Rosa, and Shiro.
Resistant: President.

PLUM

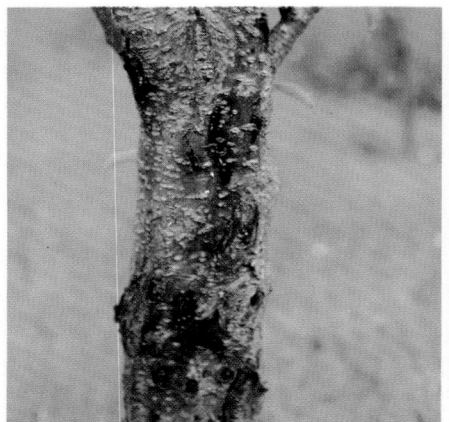

Bacterial canker on Santa Rosa plum.

PROBLEM: Sunken, elliptical lesions (cankers) appear on the trunk or branches. Throughout the fall, winter, and spring a thick, amber, sour-smelling gum may ooze from these cankers. In the spring, especially during wet, cold weather, blossoms may turn brown and wither. Some of the leaf and flower buds die and become covered with gum. Entire branches may die. There may be angular holes in the leaves, and sometimes there are dark, sunken lesions in the fruit.

ANALYSIS: Bacterial canker
This plant disease is also known as *bacterial gummosis* or *bacterial blast*, and is caused by a bacterium (*Pseudomonas syringae*). During the fall, winter, and early spring, bacteria-containing gum that oozes from the cankers is spread by splashing rain to dormant buds, twigs, and branches. Infection occurs through wounds in the twigs and branches, and bacterial decay causes cankers to form. Bacterial activity decreases as the weather warms up. However, slowly developing cankers may encircle a branch, and by midsummer the affected branches and limbs start to die. With the onset of cool, wet, fall weather, bacterial activity increases. This disease is most severe on young trees.

SOLUTION: Although this disease cannot be entirely controlled, partial control may be obtained by spraying with a fungicide containing *basic copper sulfate* in the fall just after the leaves have dropped. Prune out diseased branches. After each pruning cut, sterilize pruning shears by dipping in rubbing alcohol. Keep the tree healthy by fertilizing and watering properly. For cultural information, see page 668.

QUINCE

QUINCE

ADAPTATION: Zones 4 through 10. To determine your climate zone, see the map on page 1004.

SOIL: Any good garden soil. pH 5.5 to 8.0

FERTILIZER: Fertilize with ORTHO Evergreen, Tree & Shrub Food 12–6–6 according to label directions.

WATER:
How much: Apply enough water to wet the soil 3 to 4 feet deep. To determine the proper amount of water for your soil type, see page 906.
How often: Water when the soil 4 inches below the surface is just barely moist.

PRUNING: The fruit is borne on the branch tips of the current year's growth. Prune to shape the plant as a tree rather than as a shrub. Remove diseased, dead, or crossing twigs and branches, and suckers and twigs along the trunk.

HARVEST: Harvest fruits in the fall when they are fully colored.

Codling moth damage.

PROBLEM: The fruit is blemished with small holes surrounded by dead tissue. Brown, crumbly material resembling sawdust may surround the holes. Brown-headed, pinkish white worms up to 1 inch long may be found in the fruit. The interior of the fruit is often dark and rotted. Many quinces drop prematurely.

ANALYSIS: Codling moth
(*Laspeyresia pomonella*)
This worm, a serious pest of apples, attacks several other fruit and nut trees in addition to quinces. The gray-brown moths appear in the spring when the quince trees are blooming. They lay their eggs on the leaves, twigs, and developing fruit. The larvae feed for several weeks, then emerge from the fruit, often leaving a mass of dark excrement on the skin and inside the fruit. After pupating in sheltered locations on or around the tree, another generation of moths emerges in midsummer. Quinces may be damaged by worms continuously throughout the summer. In the fall, the mature larvae spin cocoons in protected places, such as under loose bark or in tree crevices. They spend the winter in these cocoons, emerging as moths in the spring.

SOLUTION: Once the worms have penetrated the quinces, it is impossible to kill them. To protect uninfested quinces, spray with an insecticide containing *carbaryl* at intervals of 3 weeks. Remove and destroy all fallen quinces, and clean up debris around the trees. To control infestation next spring, spray quinces with *carbaryl* 2 weeks after the petals fall from the blossoms, then spray again 3 weeks later.

WALNUT

WALNUT

ADAPTATION AND POLLINATION:
Zones 4 through 8. To determine your climate zone, see the map on page 1004.

SOIL: Any good, deep, well-drained soil. pH 5.5 to 8.0

FERTILIZER: Fertilize with ORTHO Evergreen, Tree & Shrub Food 12–6–6 according to label directions.

WATER:
How much: Apply enough water to wet the soil 5 to 6 feet deep. To determine the proper amount of water for your soil, see page 906. Avoid wetting the trunk and crown of the tree by watering into a basin that keeps the water at least 4 feet away from the trunk.
How often: Water when the soil 6 inches below the surface is just barely moist.

PRUNING: Walnuts form on the current season's growth. Prune trees lightly, removing weak, diseased, or dead twigs and branches. Thin the inside of the tree if the growth is dense.

HARVEST: In the fall, the nuts drop to the ground. You may hasten nut drop by striking the branches with a rubber mallet or cloth-covered stick. After removing the husks, spread the nuts one layer deep in a shaded, well-ventilated location to dry.

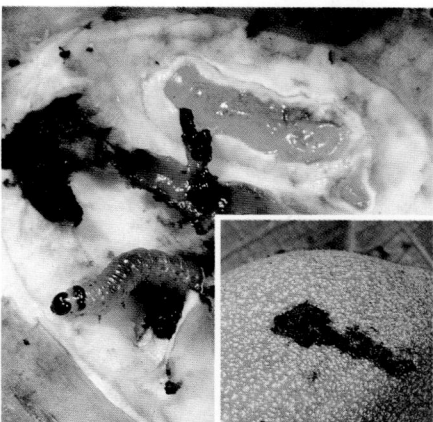

Larvae (¾ life size). *Insert:* Frass on husk.

PROBLEM: Nut shells are stained, and there may be holes at the base of the nuts. A brown, crumbly material that resembles sawdust (frass) may surround the holes. Brown-headed, pinkish white worms up to 1 inch long may be found in the nuts. Infested nuts usually drop prematurely.

ANALYSIS: Codling moth
(*Laspeyresia pomonella*)
The larva of this small gray brown moth is a very serious pest of apples and pears, in addition to attacking walnuts and several other fruit and nut trees. The moths appear in the spring when the young nuts are forming. They lay their eggs on the leaves, twigs, and developing walnuts. The larvae that emerge from these eggs tunnel into the nuts. They feed for several weeks, then leave the nut, often leaving a mass of dark excrement on the husks and inside the nuts. After pupating in sheltered locations on or around the tree, another generation of moths emerges in midsummer. Walnuts may be damaged by worms throughout the summer. The larvae spend the winter in cocoons in protected places, such as under loose bark or in tree crevices. Early blooming walnut varieties are most susceptible to codling moth damage.

SOLUTION: Once the worms have penetrated the nuts, it is impossible to kill them. Next spring, spray trees with ORTHO Fruit & Vegetable Insect Control when the developing nuts are ⅜ to ½ inch in diameter. Repeat the spray 6 to 8 weeks later. Remove and destroy all fallen nuts, and clean up debris around the trees. Plant late-blooming varieties such as Hartley and Vina.

Walnut husk fly damage.

PROBLEM: Soft, blackened, decayed areas cover part or all of the walnut husk. Cream to yellow-colored maggots up to ⅜ inch long are feeding inside the husk. The walnut shells are stained dirty black; sometimes the husks stick to the shells. The kernels are often stained, and may be shriveled.

ANALYSIS: Walnut husk fly
(*Rhagoletis* species)
These maggots are the larvae of several closely related flies. The adult flies, slightly smaller than a housefly, are yellow-brown with banded wings. The flies begin laying their eggs in the developing walnut husks in late July and early August. The maggots that hatch from these eggs feed in the husks for about a month, then drop to the ground and pupate in the soil until the following summer. As a result of maggot feeding, the husks become black and decayed, and the shells and kernels are stained. The maggots never feed on the kernels, and although the walnut meats may be shriveled or discolored, they usually taste normal.

SOLUTION: Walnut husk flies are very difficult to control. Partial control may be obtained by killing the adult flies before they lay their eggs. Spray with an insecticide containing *malathion*, covering all of the foliage thoroughly. Respray 2 weeks later. Contact your local County Extension Office (see page 1011) for information regarding husk fly emergence dates in your area.

WALNUT

Walnut blight.

Walnut aphid (12 times life size).

Walnut caterpillars (half life size).

PROBLEM: Buds turn dark brown to black, and die. There are brown spots on the leaves and dead, sunken lesions on the shoots. Some of the leaves may be deformed. Black, sunken, hard areas develop on the nuts. A shiny black fluid may exude from these lesions. Infected nuts have stained shells or shriveled kernels. Nut yield may be reduced.

ANALYSIS: Walnut blight
This plant disease is caused by a bacterium (*Xanthomonas juglandis*) that is common on walnuts. The bacteria spend the winter in diseased buds, twig lesions, and old infected nuts attached to the tree. A thick, shiny fluid containing millions of bacteria exudes from the infected plant parts in the spring. Spring rains splash the bacteria to the buds, shoots, flowers, and developing nuts, starting new infections. Bacterial infection reduces nut set and can continue to spread to healthy nuts and foliage throughout the summer during periods of wet weather. If the nuts are infected before their shells harden (when the nuts are ¾ grown), the bacteria may spread into and decay the kernels. Because the wet, rainy conditions of spring favor the rapid spread of walnut blight, early-blooming walnut varieties are most susceptible to this disease.

SOLUTION: Next spring, spray with a pesticide containing *basic copper sulfate* when catkins start to shed pollen, then spray again when the small nutlets start to appear. If the weather remains wet, spray once more after 2 weeks. Plant late-blooming varieties such as Vina and Hartley.

PROBLEM: Tiny (¹⁄₁₆ inch) soft-bodied yellow insects are clustered on the leaves and stems. The youngest leaves may be curled, thickened, and discolored. A shiny or sticky substance coats the leaves. A black sooty mold may grow on the sticky substance. Ants are sometimes present. Severely infested trees may suffer a reduction in nut yield.

ANALYSIS: Aphids
Several species of aphids infest walnuts, including the walnut aphid (*Chromaphis juglandicola*) and the European dusky-veined walnut aphid (*Panaphis juglandis*). These insects do little damage in small numbers. However, they are extremely prolific and populations can rapidly build up to damaging numbers during the growing season. Damage occurs when the aphid sucks the juices from the walnut leaves. The aphid is unable to digest fully all the sugar in the plant sap and excretes the excess in a fluid called honeydew, which often drops onto the leaves below. A sooty mold may develop on the honeydew, causing the walnut leaves to appear black and dirty. Ants feed on the honeydew, and are often present where there is an aphid infestation.

SOLUTION: Moderate numbers of aphids do little harm. If there are more than 15 or 20 aphids per leaflet, spray with ORTHO Fruit & Vegetable Insect Control. Repeat as directed on the label.

PROBLEM: Reddish brown to black hairy caterpillars with pale yellow to gray stripes running lengthwise along their bodies are feeding on walnut leaves. These caterpillars, which range in size up to 2 inches, feed in clusters. The leaves are chewed, and severely infested trees may be completely defoliated.

ANALYSIS: Walnut caterpillar
(*Datana integerrima*)
These caterpillars, the larvae of brown moths, are common pests of walnut, pecan, and several other nut trees. The adult moths emerge in the spring to lay their eggs on the young leaves. The larvae that hatch from these eggs feed on the foliage, often clustered together. Caterpillars group together on the trunk and molt (shed their skins) several times during their life cycle. When mature, they drop to the ground and pupate in the soil, emerging as adult moths either later in the season or the following spring. Caterpillar damage may occur throughout the growing season. These pests can be very destructive. Severely infested trees may be defoliated within 24 hours.

SOLUTION: Spray infested trees with ORTHO Fruit & Vegetable Insect Control. Repeat as directed on the label. Pick off and kill caterpillars when they are clustered on the trunk while molting.

Oystershell scales (life size).

Walnut blister mite damage.

Anthracnose. *Insert:* Infected nut.

PROBLEM: The undersides of the leaves, stems, or small branches are covered with brownish crusty bumps or thick, white, waxy bumps, or clusters of flattened yellowish, gray, or brownish scaly bumps. The bumps can be scraped or picked off; the undersides are usually soft. Leaves turn yellow and may drop. In some cases, a shiny or sticky substance coats the leaves. A black sooty mold often grows on the sticky substance.

ANALYSIS: Scales
Several different types of scale insects infest walnut trees. They lay their eggs on leaves or bark, and in spring to midsummer the young scales, called *crawlers*, settle on leaves and twigs. The small (1/10 inch), soft-bodied young feed by sucking sap from the plant. The legs usually atrophy and a hard crusty or waxy shell develops over the body. The mature female scales lay their eggs underneath their shell. Some species of scales that infest walnuts are unable to digest fully all the sugar in the plant sap, and excrete the excess in a fluid called honeydew, which often drops onto the leaves below. A black sooty mold fungus may grow on the honeydew.

SOLUTION: Spray with ORTHO Fruit & Vegetable Insect Control in midsummer when the crawlers are active. Contact your local Cooperative Extension Office (see page 1011) to determine the best time to spray for scales in your area. The following early spring, before new growth begins, spray the trunk and branches with an insecticide containing *methidathion* to control overwintering insects. For more information about scales, see page 878.

PROBLEM: Leaves are stippled, yellowing, or bronzed; they may dry out and drop. There may be webbing between the leaves or on the lower surfaces of the leaves. Severely infested trees may drop all their leaves. To determine if the tree is infested with mites, hold a sheet of white paper underneath an affected leaf and tap the leaf sharply. Minute green, red, or yellow specks the size of pepper grains will drop to the paper and begin to crawl around. These pests are easily seen against the white background.

ANALYSIS: Spider mites
These mites, related to spiders, are major pests of many trees, shrubs, and flowers. They cause damage by sucking sap from the undersides of the leaves. As a result of feeding, the green leaf pigment disappears, producing the stippled, bronzed appearance. Mites are active throughout the growing season, but are favored by hot, dry weather (70°F and up). By midsummer, they build up to tremendous numbers.

SOLUTION: Spray the infested tree with ORTHO Fruit & Vegetable Insect Control or a pesticide containing *dicofol*. To kill overwintering mites on the branches, spray the tree with *dormant oil* early next spring just before the buds open.

PROBLEM: Circular reddish to grayish brown spots up to 3/4 inch in diameter appear on the leaves from May to the end of the summer. Oval or irregular brown sunken lesions may develop on the green shoots. Tiny, dark, sunken spots may appear on the walnut husks. Infected nuts often drop prematurely. The kernels of harvested nuts may be dark and shriveled. Infected leaves usually drop, and the tree may defoliate by midsummer.

ANALYSIS: Walnut anthracnose
This plant disease is caused by a fungus (*Gnomonia leptostyla*) that attacks walnuts and butternuts. The fungus spends the winter in twig lesions and on plant debris on the ground. In the spring, spores are discharged during rainy weather and blown to the new growth. If the surfaces of the leaves are wet, the spores can infect the leaves and shoots. The fungus can continue to infect healthy leaf, nut, and shoot tissue throughout the growing season, especially during periods of wet and humid weather. Trees that defoliate prematurely become weakened, and frequently suffer a large reduction in nut yield and size.

SOLUTION: If you notice the problem early in the summer, spray the infected tree with a fungicide containing *benomyl, maneb,* or *zineb.* Repeat the spray 2 more times at intervals of two weeks. Remove and destroy all plant debris. Next spring, spray the tree when the leaves are half their mature size. Spray again 2 more times at intervals of 2 weeks.

WALNUT

Crown rot.

Blackline. *Insert:* Closeup.

PROBLEM: The bark on part or all of the trunk just above or below the soil line is darkened. Sap may ooze from the affected bark. When the diseased bark is scraped away, the underlying sapwood is found to be discolored tan to black. Foliage may be sparse and yellowing. There is little new growth, and the tree may be stunted.

ANALYSIS: Crown rot
This plant disease is caused by soil-inhabiting fungi (*Phytophthora* species) that infect many trees and shrubs. The fungi penetrate the bark of the lower trunk or upper roots, forming lesions. As the fungi progress inward, they decay the nutrient-conducting tissue under the bark, interfering with the flow of nutrients to the roots. If left unchecked, the fungi will encircle and decay the entire trunk, eventually causing the death of the tree. Crown rot is greatly favored by wet soil. Trees planted in lawns, flower beds, or other moist areas are highly susceptible.

SOLUTION: If the rot has not completely encircled the tree, it can probably be saved. To let the crown dry out, remove the soil within 4 feet of the base of the tree, exposing the major roots. Keep this area dry. During the rainy season, slope the remaining soil away from the hole to keep it from filling with water. After the tree shows signs of recovering (look for healthy new growth), replace the soil around the base of the tree. Or, if possible, fill the hole with stones instead of soil to help keep the roots dry. Avoid planting flowers, shrubs, or other vegetation immediately around the tree.

PROBLEM: Growth is weak and sparse, and many of the leaves are drooping and yellow. Foliage may drop prematurely. Many of the shoots die. Eventually the upper part of the tree dies. Numerous shoots sprout from the root stock. Small holes and cracks may be seen on the graft union between the rootstock and the upper part of the tree. When patches of bark along the graft union are removed, a dark brown or black line of corky tissue up to $\frac{1}{4}$ inch wide is exposed.

ANALYSIS: Blackline
This plant disease is caused by a virus that infects English walnuts grafted onto black walnut rootstock. Blackline usually affects trees 5 years of age or older. The virus is spread in the pollen of English walnuts to healthy trees. Infected trees develop a layer of black, corky cells at the graft union. This layer initially forms in small portions of the union. As it increases in size and encircles the entire graft union, the flow of water and nutrients between the rootstock and the top is reduced and finally cut off entirely, killing the upper part of the tree.

SOLUTION: Infected trees cannot be cured. They will need to be replaced eventually. If desired, the black walnut rootstock may be saved. To do so, remove the dead top growth, then prune out most of the sprouts, leaving a few of the most vigorous ones to develop into a new top.

Some of the problems common to many vegetables, berries, and grapes are described on the next 15 pages. If you don't find your problem here, look up your plant in the index on the next page.

VEGETABLES, BERRIES, AND GRAPES

The secret to growing food crops that are both delicious and prolific is to grow them quickly. If growth continues at its maximum rate from the time the seedling emerges until harvest, the plant not only grows bigger and makes more fruit*, but it has less time to store the chemicals that give strong or bitter flavors.

The way to grow plants quickly is to give them ideal growing conditions. In the vegetable garden, this usually means selecting the right location, preparing the soil properly, feeding and watering as the plants need it, and keeping the garden free of weeds and pests.

But rich soil and ideal growing conditions are ideal for weeds, too. Weeds slow the growth of vegetables by competing with them for light, water, and food. But studies are revealing that many weeds also inhibit the growth of plants with which they share garden space.

It's easy to think of our garden problems as mostly dealing with weeds, insects, or disease. But often problems are encouraged by our habitual garden practices. We can seldom eliminate a disease or insect problem by changing our garden practices, but by adopting

garden practices that minimize our problems, we can often turn a catastrophe into a mere nuisance.

The most effective solution for disease and insect problems on vegetables is usually to select plant varieties that are resistant to a particular pest or disease. For many years, plant breeders have been concentrating on breeding vegetables that are resistant to the major problems that plague that plant. Some of their successes have been astonishing, and have done a great deal to help vegetable gardeners.

Above: Aphids on a tomato. See page 790.
Left: Healthy vegetables can be decorative as well as delicious.

*Throughout this section, we use the word "fruit" in the botanical sense, to mean the part of the plant associated with the seeds. In the kitchen, a "tomato" is a vegetable, but in the garden, a "tomato" is a tomato plant; the part we eat is the tomato fruit.

INDEX TO VEGETABLES, BERRIES, AND GRAPES

PROBLEMS COMMON TO MANY VEGETABLES, BERRIES, AND GRAPES

Poor-quality tomatoes.

PROBLEM: Fruit have poor or strong flavor and are smaller than normal. Fruit yield is low.

ANALYSIS: Poor-quality produce
Vegetables and berries may yield poor-quality produce for many reasons.
1. *Hot weather* affects the flavor of some fruit, especially cool season crops such as lettuce and members of the cabbage family. Their taste becomes strong and bitter.
2. *Fluctuations in soil moisture* affect the flavor of many fruits, especially cucumbers. Sweet and white potato tubers crack and appear unappetizing. Alternating wet and dry soil results in erratic growth with poor-quality fruit and reduced yields.
3. *Poor soil fertility* causes plants to grow poorly and yield few if any fruit. Those fruits produced are frequently off-flavor and may not develop fully.
4. *Overmature fruit* deteriorate rapidly and lose their flavor. Allowing fruit to overripen on the plant reduces future yields by using energy the plant could have used to produce more fruit.

SOLUTION: Follow these guidelines for better-quality produce. (For more information on each of these recommendations, see the entry for your plant in the alphabetical section beginning on page 695.)
1. Plant vegetables and small fruits at the times of year suggested on page 1009.
2. Follow the irrigation guidelines for your vegetable.
3. Fertilize your plants as instructed.
4. Pick fruit as they mature, so more fruit will be produced. Follow the harvesting guidelines specific to your plant.

Slow growth caused by insufficient light.

Phosphorus deficiency on corn.

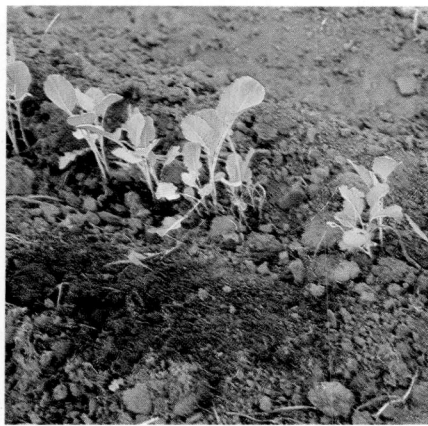

Slow growth from too acid soil.

PROBLEM: Plants grow slowly or not at all. Leaves are light green, and few or no flowers or fruit are produced. Plants are shaded for much of the day. Lower leaves may turn yellow and drop.

ANALYSIS: Insufficient light
Plants need sunlight to manufacture food and produce fruit. Without adequate sunlight they grow slowly. Vegetable and berry plants that yield fruit, such as tomatoes, brambles, strawberries, beans, and peppers, require at least 6 hours of sunlight a day. Some leafy and root vegetables, however, will tolerate light shade. These vegetables include beets, cabbage, carrots, chives, kale, leeks, lettuce, mustard, green onions, parsley, radishes, Swiss chard, and turnips.

SOLUTION: Prune any surrounding trees to allow more sunlight. Plant vegetables that require less sunlight in somewhat shady areas of the garden. If possible, move your garden site, or grow vegetables in containers on a sunny patio or porch.

PROBLEM: Plants grow slowly. Leaves are pale green to yellow, or darker than normal, and dull. Few flowers and fruit are produced. Fruit that are produced mature slowly. Plants pulled from the soil may have small, black, and rotted root systems. Plants may die.

ANALYSIS: Poor soil or cool weather
Vegetables and small fruits may grow slowly and produce few fruit for any of several reasons.

1. *Excess water:* If the soil is constantly wet, either from frequent watering or poor drainage, roots become shallow, stunting the plant. Wet soil also encourages root rotting fungi, which destroy the root system and kill the plant.

2. *Phosphorus deficiency:* Phosphorus is a major nutrient needed by plants for root formation, flower and fruit production, and overall cell growth. Phosphorus-deficient plants grow slowly, and have dark leaves that may be tinted with purple or have purple veins. This nutrient may be lacking either because it is not present in the soil, or because it is in a form that is unavailable to plants.

3. *Incorrect pH:* The soil pH limits the amounts and kinds of nutrients available to plants. Vegetables grow best with a pH of 6.0 to 8.0. Required nutrients are usually available in adequate amounts at this range. For more information on pH, see page 902.

4. *Cool weather:* Warm-season vegetables such as tomatoes, beans, and okra require temperatures over 70°F for best growth and fruit production. If they are planted too early in the season, the cool weather slows their growth. Affected plants may take several months to recover from this setback, and still may not produce abundantly.

SOLUTION: The numbered solutions below correspond to the numbers under analysis.

1. Allow the soil around plants to dry out. (For more information on this technique, see page 857.) Remove and discard any plants with rotting roots. Avoid future root rot problems by planting in well-drained soil. For information on improving soil drainage, see page 901.

2. Spray the leaves with Ra-Pid-Gro Plant Food for a quick response. Fertilize with a balanced fertilizer such as ORTHO Vegetable Garden Food 5–10–10 or ORTHO General Purpose Plant Food 8–8–8. Follow the rates on the package, or those given for each vegetable on the following pages.

3. Test the soil pH and correct to 6.0 to 8.0 according to the instructions on page 903.

4. Plant vegetables at the correct time of year. For planting times for your area, see page 1009. Discard warm-season vegetable plants that have been set back by cool temperatures. Replant with healthy transplants.

PROBLEMS COMMON TO MANY VEGETABLES, BERRIES, AND GRAPES — SEEDLING PROBLEMS

Dehydration.

Crusted soil.

Wilted broccoli.

PROBLEM: Seedlings don't emerge through the soil.

ANALYSIS: Seedlings don't emerge
Seedlings may fail to sprout for any of several reasons.

1. *Lack of water:* Seeds need water to soften and break the seed coat. Seeds planted in dry soil will not germinate.

2. *Seeds washed away:* Heavy rains or watering may wash seeds from the planting site or deeper into the soil than they were planted.

3. *Slow germination:* Some seeds require a longer time to germinate than others.

4. *Soil temperature:* Warm-season vegetables (tomatoes, beans, peppers) germinate best at soil temperatures between 60° and 85°F. If temperatures fall below this range, the inside of the seed is damaged. Cool-season vegetables (cabbage, peas, lettuce) germinate best at soil temperatures below 75°F, and become dormant at higher temperatures.

5. *Incorrect planting depth:* Seeds need oxygen for good germination. If planted too deep, they suffocate. If planted too shallow, they dry out.

6. *Crusted soil:* Seedlings are unable to push their way up through crusted soil.

7. *Damping-off:* This disease is caused by soil-inhabiting fungi, which attack seeds as they germinate, killing them before they emerge. For more information on damping-off, see page 858.

SOLUTION: The numbered solutions correspond to the numbers under analysis.

1. Keep the soil moist, letting the surface dry slightly between waterings.

2. Water carefully with a spray or mist or cover the seed row with burlap or cheesecloth to keep the soil and seeds from washing away.

3. Read the seed packet for information on special germinating conditions.

4. Plant seeds at the correct time of year. For planting times for your area, see page 1009. If starting seeds indoors, improve the germination rate by providing bottom heat with soil heating cables or placing the seeded containers in a warm place, such as the top of a refrigerator.

5. Plant seeds according to the depth stated on the packet.

6. Plant seeds in loose, crumbly soil, or cover the seed row with vermiculite, sand, or burlap to keep the soil from crusting. For more information on starting seeds, see page 917.

7. Protect seeds during germination by coating them with a fungicide containing *captan*, *thiram*, or *chloroneb*. Add a pinch of fungicide to a packet of seeds (or ½ teaspoon per pound), and shake well to coat the seeds with the fungicide.

PROBLEM: Seedlings wilt and die. The soil is dry.

ANALYSIS: Dehydration
Seedlings need a continuous supply of water. Seedlings growing in sandy soil are especially susceptible to drying out, because sandy soil does not hold much water. Seedling roots may penetrate only the top inch of soil. If that top inch dries out, the seedling has no moisture on which to draw. The young roots are tender and very susceptible to drying. Seedlings are so small that if they wilt, they seldom recover as do older plants. If they do recover, it may take some time for them to resume their normal growth.

SOLUTION: Water seedlings whenever the surface of the soil dries. In hot weather, you may have to water more than once a day. To reduce their need for water, shade seedlings with a layer of cheesecloth during hot weather. By the time the young plants have formed their first true leaves (the leaves that look like those on a mature plant), their root systems are a few inches deep, and they are no longer as susceptible to drying out.

Damping-off of radish seedlings.

Peas eaten by rabbits.

Bean seedlings eaten by slugs.

PROBLEM: Seedlings fall over soon after they emerge. Areas on the stem at the soil line are water-soaked and discolored. The base of the stem is soft and thin.

ANALYSIS: Damping-off
Damping-off is a common problem in wet soil with a high nitrogen level. Wet, rich soil promotes damping-off in two ways: the fungi that cause it are more active under these conditions, and the seedlings are more susceptible to attack. Damping-off is often a problem when the weather remains cloudy and wet, and when seedlings are heavily shaded or crowded. Seedlings started indoors in a wet, unsterilized medium are also susceptible.

SOLUTION: To prevent fungi from attacking your seedlings, take these precautions:
1. Allow the surface of the soil to dry slightly between waterings.
2. Do not start seeds in soil that has a high nitrogen level. Add nitrogen fertilizers after the seedlings have produced their first true leaves.
3. Protect the seeds during germination with a fungicide containing *captan* or *thiram*. Add a pinch of fungicide to a packet of seeds (or ½ teaspoon per pound) and shake well to coat the seeds.
4. Use a sterilized medium for starting seeds indoors, such as a sterilized potting soil or a mixture of peat moss, perlite, and vermiculite.
5. Thin seedlings to allow good air circulation through the planting.

PROBLEM: Seedling leaves are chewed ragged. Seedlings may completely disappear, or short stubs of the stems may remain.

ANALYSIS: Seedlings eaten
Several animal and insect pests feed on seedlings.

1. Many kinds of *birds*, especially grackles, blackbirds, and crows eat entire seedlings. The plants are most susceptible to bird attack when they have just emerged.

2. *Snails and slugs* feed at night and on cloudy days, chewing holes in leaves or devouring entire seedlings. Silvery winding trails are evidence of their presence. During the day they hide in damp places under rocks, flower pots, or debris.

3. *Earwigs* are dark brown insects with pinchers on their tail end. They feed at night, and chew holes in leaves and stems.

4. *Rabbits* may eat an entire seedling, or leave only a short stub of the stem standing in the soil.

5. *Grasshoppers* are present throughout the growing season, and migrate from area to area as their food source is depleted. They eat entire seedlings. Grasshoppers are prevalent in hot, dry weather.

SOLUTION: The numbered solutions below correspond to the numbers in the analysis.

1. Cover seedlings with a tent made of cheesecloth or netting stretched over a wooden frame. Scarecrows and dangling aluminum pie plates may help to deter birds.

2. Control snails and slugs with ORTHO Bug-Geta Snail & Slug Pellets. Sprinkle lightly after application to activate the pellets. The moisture will also attract snails and slugs. Treat along the seeded rows, and in hiding places such as rocks, boards, flower pots, or compost piles. For more information on snails and slugs, see page 689.

3. To control earwigs, treat with an insecticide containing *carbaryl* along the seeded rows and in hiding places under stones, rocks, and debris. For more information on earwigs, see page 693.

4. Keep rabbits out of the garden by erecting a 1-foot-high fence of small-gauge fencing wire around the garden. Anchor the bottom of the fence with boards 1 to 2 inches deep in the soil to prevent the rabbits from digging underneath. For more information on rabbits, see page 894.

5. Control grasshoppers and protect uneaten seedlings with an insecticide containing *carbaryl*, *diazinon*, or *malathion*. Repeat at weekly intervals as long as grasshoppers are present. For more information on grasshoppers, see page 691.

PROBLEMS COMMON TO MANY VEGETABLES, BERRIES, AND GRAPES — WILTING

Wilting French sorrel.

PROBLEM: Plants wilt. Soil is dry. Plants may recover when watered.

ANALYSIS: Dehydration
Plants need water for both root and leaf growth. Plants growing in sandy soil are very susceptible to drying out because the soil does not retain much water. Plants usually recover in a short time after being watered. Repeated wilting will stunt plants, reducing their yield and the quality of their produce. Ripening fruit on repeatedly wilted plants do not mature fully, sometimes crack, and are frequently flavorless. Some members of the cabbage family wilt on hot days even though the soil is moist. This is normal and does not harm the plant.

SOLUTION: Water immediately and thoroughly. Follow the watering guidelines for your plant found in the alphabetical section beginning on page 695. To reduce the need for watering, use mulches as discussed on page 918.

Root rot on broccoli.

PROBLEM: Leaves wilt and turn yellow. Lower leaves are affected first, then the upper ones. Few or no fruit are produced. Plants do not recover when watered, and usually die.

ANALYSIS: Root and stem rot
This disease is caused by any of a number of different fungi that live in the soil. They thrive in waterlogged, heavy soils. The fungi attack the plant roots or the stems at the soil level. Infection causes the roots and stems to decay, resulting in wilting, then yellowing leaves, and eventually the death of the plant. Many of these fungi also cause *damping-off* of seedlings. For more information about damping-off, see page 683.

SOLUTION: Allow the soil around the plants to dry out. (For more information on this technique, see page 857.) Remove and discard severely infected plants. Avoid future root rot problems by planting in well-drained soil. (For information on improving soil drainage, see page 901.) Avoid overwatering by following the watering guidelines for your plant found in the alphabetical section beginning on page 695.

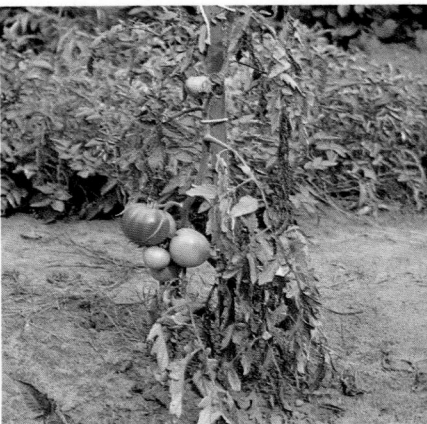

Fusarium wilt on tomato.

PROBLEM: Leaves wilt, turn yellow, and may turn brown. Few or no fruit are produced. Growth slows and plants may be stunted. When the stem is sliced open lengthwise, the tissue just under the bark may be brown.

ANALYSIS: Wilt diseases
Wilt diseases infect many vegetables and berries. They may be caused by any of several fungi that live in the soil. The fungi are spread by contaminated plants, soil, and equipment. They enter the plant through the roots and spread through the water-conducting vessels in the stems. The vessels become discolored and plugged. This plugging cuts off the flow of water and nutrients to the leaves, resulting in leaf yellowing and wilting. The plugging also results in a reduced yield and poor quality fruit. Severely infected plants die.

SOLUTION: No chemical controls are available. Wilt fungi can be removed from the soil only by fumigation techniques. (For more information about soil fumigation, see page 919.) However, the best solution is usually to avoid plants that are susceptible to wilt diseases. For a list of vegetables and berries that are susceptible to wilt diseases, see page 1009.

LEAVES DISCOLORED OR MOTTLED

Nematode damage on beans.

Nitrogen-deficient tomato.

Root rot on bush beans.

PROBLEM: Plants wilt in hot, dry weather and re-cover at night. They are stunted and yellow. Round and elongated nodules may occur on the roots. Plants may die.

ANALYSIS: Nematodes
Nematodes are microscopic worms that live in the soil. They are not related to earthworms. Nematodes feed on plant roots, damaging and stunting them. The damaged roots can't supply sufficient water and nutrients to the aboveground plant parts, and the plant is stunted or slowly dies. Nematodes are found throughout the United States, but are most severe in the South. They prefer moist, sandy loam soils. Nematodes can move only a few inches each year on their own, but they may be carried long distances by soil, water, tools, or infested plants. Testing roots and soil is the only positive method for confirming the presence of nematodes. Contact your local Cooperative Extension Office (see page 1011) for sampling instructions and addresses of testing laboratories. Soil and root problems such as poor soil structure, drought stress, nutrient deficiency, and root rots can also produce symptoms of decline similar to those caused by nematodes. These problems should be eliminated as causes before sending soil and root samples for testing. For information on soil problems and root rots, see pages 901 and 684.

SOLUTION: No chemicals are available to homeowners to kill nematodes in planted soil. However, they can be controlled before planting by soil fumigation. For information on fumigating soil, see page 919.

PROBLEM: The bottom leaves turn light green to pale yellow, and may die or drop. Growth slows, and new leaves are small. Flowers turn yellow and drop. Fruit are small, and may be distorted and discolored.

ANALYSIS: Nitrogen deficiency
Plants need nitrogen for making chlorophyll, the green pigment in their leaves, and for overall healthy growth and high-quality fruit production. When plants lack nitrogen, growth slows, blossoms drop, and fruit yield is reduced. Nitrogen may either be lacking in the soil, or be present in a form that is not available to the plant. In cool, rainy, early spring weather, little or no nitrogen is available. Later in the season, as vegetables are growing rapidly and maturing, the plants may deplete the supply of nitrogen in the soil. During a drought, nitrogen is carried to the soil surface as the water it is dissolved in evaporates. Once the nitrogen is above the plant's root zone, the roots are unable to absorb it. Rain or irrigation water carries the nitrogen back to the root zone where it is available to the plant.

SOLUTION: For a quick response, spray the foliage with ORTHO-Gro Liquid Plant Food 12–6–6 or Ra-Pid-Gro Plant Food. Water the plant with the same solution. Remove any fruit from severely affected plants to allow them time to resume normal growth. Fertilize according to the recommendations for your plant in the alphabetical section beginning on page 695. For more information about nitrogen deficiency, see page 867.

PROBLEM: Leaves turn yellow, starting with the older, lower leaves and progressing to the younger ones. Plants grow very little. Flowers yellow and drop. Fruit shrivel and do not ripen. When the plant is pulled up, the roots are black, soft, and rotted. The soil has frequently been very moist.

ANALYSIS: Root rot
This plant disease is caused by any of a number of different fungi that are present in most soil. These fungi normally do little damage, but can cause root rot in wet or waterlogged soils. Waterlogged soil may result from overwatering or poor soil drainage. Infection causes the roots to decay, resulting in wilting, yellowing leaves, flower and fruit drop, reduced fruit yield, and eventually the death of the plant.

SOLUTION: To avoid root rot problems, do not overwater. Follow the watering guidelines under the entry for your plant in the alphabetical section beginning on page 695. Remove and discard severely infected plants. Avoid future root rot problems by planting in well-drained soil. For information on improving soil drainage, see page 901. For more information on root rots, see page 856.

PROBLEMS COMMON TO MANY VEGETABLES, BERRIES, AND GRAPES — LEAVES DISCOLORED OR MOTTLED

Iron-deficient beans.

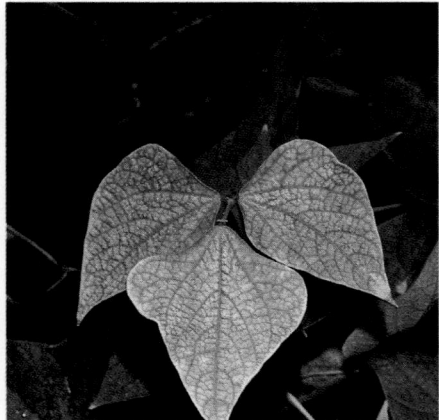

Spider mite damage on string beans.

Salt damage on radishes.

PROBLEM: Leaves turn pale green or yellow. The newest leaves (those at the tips of the stems) are most severely affected. Except in extreme cases, the veins of affected leaves remain green. In extreme cases, the newest leaves are small and all-white or yellow. Older leaves may remain green.

ANALYSIS: Iron deficiency
Plants frequently suffer from deficiencies of iron and other minor nutrients, such as manganese and zinc, elements essential to normal plant growth and development. Deficiencies can occur when one or more of these elements are depleted in the soil. Often, these minor nutrients are present in the soil, but alkaline (pH 7.5 and higher) or wet soil conditions cause them to form compounds that cannot be used by the plant. An alkaline condition can result from overliming, or from lime leached from cement or brick. Regions where soil is derived from limestone, and those with low rainfall, usually have alkaline soils.

SOLUTION: Feed the plants with a fertilizer containing *chelated iron*. Check the soil pH. Correct to the recommended level for your plant as given in the alphabetical section beginning on page 695. Make alkaline soil more acid with *ferrous sulfate*.

PROBLEM: Leaves are stippled, yellowing, and dirty. Leaves may dry out and drop. There may be webbing over flower buds between leaves, or on the lower surfaces of the leaves. To determine if the plant is infested with mites, hold a sheet of white paper underneath an affected leaf or stem and tap the leaf or stem sharply. Minute green, red, or yellow specks the size of pepper grains will drop to the paper and begin to crawl around. The pests are easily seen against the white background.

ANALYSIS: Mites
Mites, related to spiders, are major pests of many garden and greenhouse plants. They cause damage by sucking sap from the undersides of the leaves. As a result of feeding, the green leaf pigment disappears, producing the stippled appearance. Although mites do not attack the fruit directly, they do cause leaf drop, which weakens the plant and reduces fruit yield. If the plants are severely infected, flowers do not form or do not bloom, resulting in no fruit. Mites are active throughout the growing season, but are favored by hot, dry weather (70°F and up). By midsummer, they may build up to tremendous numbers.

SOLUTION: Treat infested plants with *diazinon* or *dicofol* at the first sign of damage. Repeat at weekly intervals until no further damage occurs. Make sure that your vegetable or small berry is listed on the label. Hose plants frequently with a strong stream of water to wash off mites and webs.

PROBLEM: Leaf edges and areas between the veins turn dark brown and die. Burned leaves may drop. Growth slows or stops. A white or dark crust may be on the soil.

ANALYSIS: Salt damage
Salt damage occurs when salt accumulates in the soil to damaging levels. This can happen in either of two ways: the garden is not receiving enough water from rainfall or irrigation to wash the salts from the soil, or the drainage is so poor that water does not pass through the soil. In either case, as water evaporates from the soil and plant leaves, the salts that were dissolved in the water accumulate near the soil surface. In some cases, a white or dark brown crust of salts forms on the surface. Salts can originate in the soil, in the irrigation water, or in applied fertilizers.

SOLUTION: The only way to eliminate salt problems is to wash the salts through the soil with water. If the damage is only at a low spot in the garden, fill in the spot to level the area. If the entire garden drains poorly, improve the drainage according to the directions on page 901. If the soil drains well, increase the amount of water applied at each watering by 50 percent or more, so that excess water will leach salts below the root zone of the plants. Fertilize according to instructions for your plant in the alphabetical section beginning on page 695.

Potassium-deficient tomato.

Grapes with spray injury.

Air pollution damage to bean.

PROBLEM: Plants grow slowly. Small brown spots appear along the leaf margins. Leaf edges turn yellow, then bronze and finally brown, curl downward, and die. The discoloration may then spread from the leaf edges to areas between the veins. Few fruit are produced, and those that are produced ripen poorly and may be distorted.

ANALYSIS: Potassium deficiency
Potassium is a major nutrient that plants need for overall growth and to help move food manufactured in the leaves to stems, roots, and other parts. Without this movement of food, plants are unable to produce new growth. Plants require larger amounts of potassium as their fruit matures. Fruit yields are reduced in plants deficient in potassium, and such plants are more susceptible to attack from some diseases. Sandy soils, and soils in regions of high rainfall, are often deficient in potassium.

SOLUTION: Spray the foliage with Ra-Pid-Gro Plant Food or ORTHO Ortho-Gro Liquid Plant Food 12–6–6. Water the plant with the same solution. Fertilize with ORTHO Vegetable Garden Food 5–10–10, or follow the fertilization guidelines for your plant in the alphabetical section beginning on page 695.

PROBLEM: Irregular spots occur on leaves. Young leaves and blossoms may be distorted and brown. Plants may have been recently sprayed with pesticides.

ANALYSIS: Pesticide burn
Insecticides, fungicides, and herbicides damage plants when used improperly. Damage usually occurs within 24 hours of the time the plants were sprayed. Pesticides may drift from other areas on windy days and damage plants. Pesticides may burn plants when the temperature is above 90°F at the time of spraying, or if it rises above 90°F within a few hours of spraying. Pesticides not mixed and applied according to the label directions also burn plants. Pesticides used in tanks that were once used for herbicides may be contaminated, since traces of herbicides are difficult to remove from sprayers.

SOLUTION: Once plants are damaged, there is nothing to do. Keep the plants healthy with regular watering and fertilizing. In the future, do not spray when temperatures are above 90°F. Avoid spraying on windy days, when sprays may drift. Mix according to the label directions. Do not increase the dosage. When mixing two or more chemicals, be sure they are compatible. Always keep the solution well mixed by shaking the tank periodically while spraying. This is especially important when using wettable powder formulations. Purchase fresh pesticides each year. Wash herbicides thoroughly from sprayers before filling with other pesticides or fertilizer. Or keep a separate sprayer for herbicides.

PROBLEM: The upper surfaces of the younger leaves are stippled yellow, tan, or bronze. The entire leaf may be stippled, giving the leaf a yellowish or pale green appearance.

ANALYSIS: Air pollution
Some gases released into the atmosphere from cars and factories damage plants. The most common type of pollution is *smog.* Air pollution damage is most commonly a problem in urban areas, but also occurs in rural areas where gardens are located downwind from factories or large urban centers. Some plants are severely affected, and may even die. Fruit and vegetable production is reduced on pollution-damaged plants. For information on the three most common pollutants, *ozone, PAN,* and *sulfur dioxide,* see page 862. Many different environmental factors affect a plant's susceptibility to air pollution. Research is presently being conducted throughout the country to better understand these factors and to find ways to protect plants from air pollutants.

SOLUTION: Air pollution injury is usually a localized problem. Check with your neighbors to see if the same kinds of plants in their gardens have been affected the same way. Because injury from air pollutants is similar in appearance to injury from nutrient deficiencies, insects, diseases, and mites, these problems should be eliminated as causes before attributing the damage to air pollution. Nothing can be done about air pollution damage. If you live in a smoggy area, select plants that are smog resistant from the list on page 996.

PROBLEMS COMMON TO MANY VEGETABLES, BERRIES, AND GRAPES — LEAVES DISCOLORED OR MOTTLED

Leaf spot on strawberry.

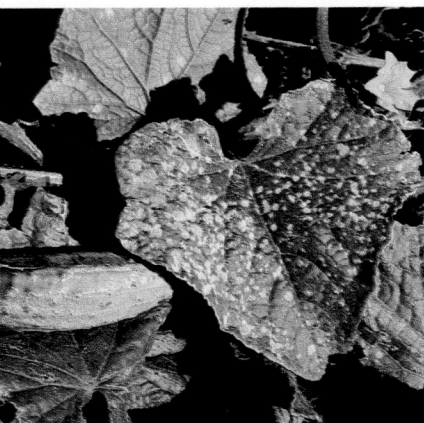

Powdery mildew on a cucumber.

Leafminer trails on tomato.

PROBLEM: Spots and blotches appear on the leaves. The spots may be yellow, red, tan, gray, or brown. They range in size from barely visible to ¼ inch in diameter. Several spots may join to form blotches. Leaves may be yellow and dying. Leaf spotting is most severe in warm, humid weather. Fruit may be spotted like the leaves, or be discolored brown or yellow. A fine gray or white mold sometimes covers the infected leaf or fruit tissue in damp conditions.

ANALYSIS: Leaf spot
Several different fungi cause leaf spots. Some of these fungi may eventually kill the plant, or weaken it so that it becomes susceptible to attack by other organisms. Others merely cause spotting that is unsightly but not harmful. Infected fruit are less appetizing, some are inedible, and the yield is reduced. Fruit infected only slightly are still edible if the discolored tissue is cut away. Leaf spotting fungi are spread by splashing water or wind. They generally survive the winter in diseased plant debris. Most of the fungi do their greatest damage in mild weather (50° to 85°F).

SOLUTION: Treat infected plants with a fungicide containing *captan*, *maneb*, or *zineb* at the first sign of the disease. Repeat the treatment at intervals of 7 to 10 days until weather conditions favorable to the spread of the disease no longer occur. Make sure that your plant is listed on the product label. Remove all plant debris from the garden after harvest to reduce the amount of overwintering spores.

PROBLEM: The upper surfaces of the leaves are covered with a white powdery growth. Areas of the leaves turn brown and dry. Older leaves are affected first, progressing to younger leaves. Fruit may also be covered with the white powdery growth.

ANALYSIS: Powdery mildew
This common plant disease is caused by fungi that thrive in both humid and dry weather. The powdery patches consist of fungal strands and spores. The spores are spread by the wind to healthy plants. The fungus saps the plant nutrients, causing yellowing and sometimes death of the leaf. Fruit yield may also be reduced. A severe infection may kill the plant. Since powdery mildews attack many different kinds of plants, the fungus from a diseased plant may infect other types of plants in the garden. For a list of powdery mildews and the plants they attack, see page 995. Under favorable conditions, powdery mildew can spread through a closely spaced planting in a matter of days or weeks.

SOLUTION: Control powdery mildew on vegetable and berry plants with ORTHO Vegetable Disease Control at the first sign of the disease. Don't use sulfur on squash, pumpkins, or cucumbers. Continue at intervals of 7 days as long as the disease is a problem. Make sure that your plant is listed on the fungicide label. Remove all plant debris from the garden after harvest. When available, grow varieties of vegetables and small fruits that are resistant to powdery mildews.

PROBLEM: Light-colored, irregular blotches, blisters, or tunnels appear on the leaves. The tan areas peel apart easily like facial tissue. Tiny black specks are found inside the tunnels.

ANALYSIS: Leafminers
These insect pests belong to a family of leaf-mining flies. The tiny black or yellow adult fly lays its white eggs on the undersides of leaves, or in the leaves. The maggots that hatch from these eggs tunnel between the upper and lower surfaces of the leaves, feeding on the inner tissue. The tunnels and blotches are called *mines*. The black specks inside are the maggots' droppings. Damaged portions of leaves are no longer edible. The yield is usually not affected on fruit-producing vegetables and berries unless many of the leaves are damaged. Several overlapping generations occur during the growing season, so larvae are present continually from spring until fall.

SOLUTION: Control leafminers with ORTHO Fruit & Vegetable Insect Control when the egg clusters are first seen under the leaves. Repeat 2 more times at weekly intervals to control succeeding generations. Once the leafminers enter the leaves, the sprays are ineffective. Spraying after the mines first appear will control only those leafminers that attack after the application. Make sure that your plant is listed on the insecticide label. Clean all plant debris from the garden after harvest to reduce overwintering spots for the pupae.

INSECTS ON THE PLANT

Hail damage to tomato.

Cabbage plants damaged by nocturnal pests.

Slug damage.

PROBLEM: Leaves are shredded or entirely stripped from the plant during a hail storm. Wounds or deep gouges appear on the fruit and stems; scars form several days after the storm. Young, tender plants may be knocked to the ground.

ANALYSIS: Hail damage
Hail storms often occur from July through September in the midwestern and northeastern United States. Beans, tomatoes, eggplants, peppers, and other maturing vegetables may be stripped of their leaves. The developing fruits are often wounded; usually the wounds heal and the fruit is still edible. However, the wounds may form unsightly scars, and fruit growth may be distorted. Hail-damaged fruit is sometimes mistakenly thought to be diseased or infested.

SOLUTION: Prune off dead and dying shoots and decaying fruit. Fertilize plants with ORTHO Vegetable Garden Food 5-10-10, ORTHO General Purpose Plant Food 8-8-8, or ORTHO Tomato & Vegetable Food 6-18-6 to stimulate new growth. Plants will produce new leaves and fruit if the damage has occurred early enough in the growing season. When hail storms are expected, protect plants by covering them with burlap or plastic tarp suspended over stakes.

PROBLEM: Young plants are chewed or cut off near the ground. Some of the leaves, stems, flowers, and fruit are chewed. When the affected plants are inspected at night with a flashlight, insects may be seen feeding on the plants.

ANALYSIS: Nocturnal pests
Several kinds of insects feed on plants only at night, including some beetles, weevils, caterpillars, and all earwigs and cutworms. Beetles are hard-bodied insects with tough, leathery wing covers. Weevils look like beetles, except that they have elongated snouts. Earwigs are reddish brown, flat, elongated insects up to 1 inch long with pincers projecting from the rear of the body. Caterpillars and cutworms are smooth or hairy, soft-bodied worms. There are two types of cutworms, surface-feeding and climbing. Surface-feeding cutworms are the most likely pests of young vegetable plants set out early in the season. A single surface-feeding cutworm can sever the stems of many young plants in one night. The cutworm eats through the stems of young plants just above ground level. Climbing cutworms climb up the stem or trunk of grapes, blueberries, and tomatoes to feed on young leaves, buds, and fruit. All of these nocturnal pests usually hide in the soil, in debris, or in other protected locations during the day.

SOLUTION: Control nocturnal pests by treating with insecticides. For more information about these pests and control measures, see beetles on page 872, weevils on page 873, earwigs on page 884, caterpillars on page 874, and cutworms on page 875.

PROBLEM: Irregular holes with smooth edges are chewed in the leaves. Some leaves may be sheared off entirely. Silvery trails wind around the plants and soil nearby. At night, check with a flashlight for slimy creatures with or without hard brown shells feeding on the leaves.

ANALYSIS: Snails and slugs
These pests are mollusks, and are related to clams, oysters, and other shellfish. They feed on the leaves of a wide variety of garden plants, and may completely devour a young seedling. Ripe and unripe fruit lying on the ground may be attacked by snails and slugs. This is especially true when the fruit are shaded by the foliage, as with strawberries and unstaked tomatoes. Like other mollusks, snails and slugs need to be moist all the time. For this reason, they avoid direct sun and dry places, and hide during the day in damp places, such as under flower pots or in thick groundcovers. They emerge at night or on cloudy days to feed. Slugs lay masses of white eggs encased in a slimy mass in protected places. Snails bury their eggs in the soil, also in a slimy mass. The young look like miniature versions of their parents.

SOLUTION: Scatter ORTHO Bug-Geta Snail & Slug Pellets in bands around the areas you wish to protect. Also scatter the pellets in areas where snails and slugs might be hiding, such as in dense groundcovers, weedy areas, compost piles, or pot storage areas. Wet down the treated areas to encourage snail and slug activity that night. Repeat every 2 weeks as needed.

PROBLEMS COMMON TO MANY VEGETABLES, BERRIES, AND GRAPES — INSECTS ON THE PLANT

Cabbage looper (twice life size).

Japanese beetles on grape (⅓ life size).

Spotted cucumber beetle (life size).

PROBLEM: Irregular or round holes appear in the leaves and buds. Leaves, buds, and flowers may be entirely chewed off. Worms or caterpillars are feeding on the plants.

ANALYSIS: Caterpillars
Several species of these moth or butterfly larvae feed on many vegetable and berry plants. Some common caterpillars are budworms, hornworms, and loopers. Most moths or butterflies start to lay their eggs on garden plants with the onset of warm weather in the spring. The larvae that emerge from these eggs feed on the leaves, flowers, and buds for 2 to 6 weeks, depending on weather conditions and species. Mature caterpillars pupate in cocoons attached to leaves or structures, or buried in the soil. There may be one generation a year, or overlapping generations during the growing season. The last generation of caterpillars in the fall survives the winter as pupae. Moths and butterflies emerge from the pupae the following spring.

SOLUTION: Spray infested plants with an insecticide containing *carbaryl, diazinon,* or *methoxychlor.* The bacterium *Bacillus thuringiensis* is effective against the early stages of some caterpillars. Make sure that your plant is listed on the product label. Repeat the treatment if reinfestation occurs, allowing at least 7 days to pass between applications.

PROBLEM: The leaf tissue has been chewed between the veins, giving the leaf a lacy appearance. Metallic green and bronze, winged beetles, ½ inch long, are feeding in clusters on the foliage, especially on the tender new leaves.

ANALYSIS: Japanese beetles
(*Popillia japonica*)
As their name suggests, these beetles are native to Japan. They were first seen in New Jersey in 1916 and have since become a major pest in the eastern United States. They feed on hundreds of different plant species. The adult beetles are present from June to October. They feed only in the daytime, rapidly defoliating plants. Leaves exposed to direct sun are the most severely attacked. Badly damaged leaves drop. Any reduction in leaf tissue ultimately affects the overall vigor and production of fruit. Japanese beetles can fly up to 5 miles, and travel from yard to yard. Consequently, repeated sprays are necessary to control them. (For a list of plants rarely attacked by the adult beetle, see page 997.) The larva of the Japanese beetle, a white grub, feeds on grass roots, frequently killing entire lawns.

SOLUTION: Spray infested plants with an insecticide containing *carbaryl* or *diazinon.* Repeat as needed at intervals of 10 days. Make sure that your plants are listed on the product label. Treat for grubs in the lawn as outlined on page 299.

PROBLEM: Holes are chewed in the leaves, leaf stalks, and stems by yellow-green beetles with black spots or stripes.

ANALYSIS: Cucumber beetles
Both *striped cucumber beetles* (*Acalymma* species) and *spotted cucumber beetles* (*Diabrotica* species) are common pests of vegetable plants. It is important to control these beetles because they may infect plants with two serious diseases that damage and may kill cucurbits (squash, melons, and cucumbers): *squash mosaic* (page 736) and *bacterial wilt* (page 735). Adult beetles survive the winter in plant debris and weeds. As soon as vegetable plants are set in the garden in the spring, the beetles attack the leaves and stems, and may totally destroy the plants. Adults lay their yellow-orange eggs in the soil at the base of the plants. The grubs that hatch from these eggs eat the roots and the stems below the soil line, causing the plants to be stunted or to die prematurely. Severely infested plants produce few fruit. The slender white grubs feed for several weeks, pupate in the soil, and emerge as adults to repeat the cycle. There is one generation a year in the North and two or more in the South.

SOLUTION: Treat the plants with an insecticide containing *carbaryl, diazinon,* or *rotenone* at the first sign of the beetles. Repeat at weekly intervals if the plants become reinfested. Make sure that your plant is listed on the product label.

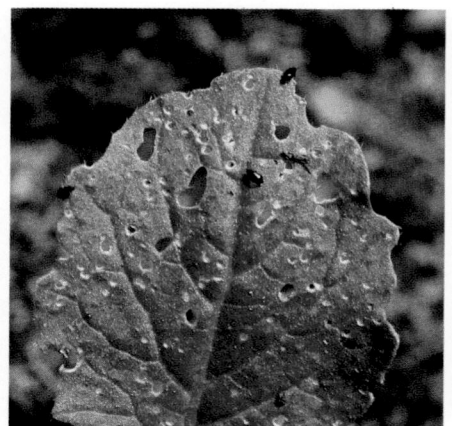

Flea beetle on turnip leaf (twice life size).

Grasshopper injury to corn silk.

Leafhopper (3 times life size).

PROBLEM: Leaves are riddled with shotholes about ⅛ inch in diameter. Tiny (1/16 inch) black beetles jump like fleas when disturbed. Leaves of seedlings and eventually whole plants may wilt and die.

ANALYSIS: Flea beetles
These beetles jump like fleas, but are not related to them. Both adult and immature flea beetles feed on a wide variety of garden vegetables and berries. The immature beetle, a legless gray grub, injures plants by feeding on the roots and the lower surfaces of leaves. Adults chew holes in leaves. Flea beetles are most damaging to seedlings and young plants. Leaves of seedlings riddled with holes dry out quickly and die. Adult beetles survive the winter in soil and garden debris. They emerge in early spring to feed on weeds until vegetables sprout or plants are set in the garden. Grubs hatch from eggs laid in the soil and feed for 2 to 3 weeks. After pupating in the soil, they emerge as adults to repeat the cycle. There are 1 to 4 generations a year. Adults may feed for up to 2 months.

SOLUTION: Control flea beetles on vegetable and small fruit plants with an insecticide containing *carbaryl, malathion,* or *diazinon* when the leaves first show damage. Watch new growth for evidence of further damage, and repeat the treatment at weekly intervals as needed. Make sure that your plant is listed on the insecticide label. Remove all plant debris from the garden after harvest to reduce the number of overwintering spots for adult beetles.

PROBLEM: Large holes are chewed in the margins of the leaves. Greenish yellow to brown jumping insects, ½ to 1½ inches long, with long hind legs are eating the plants. Some fruit and corn ears may be chewed.

ANALYSIS: Grasshoppers
Grasshoppers attack a wide variety of plants. They eat leaves and occasionally fruit, migrating as they deplete their food sources. They are most numerous in the rows near weedy areas. In late summer, adult grasshoppers lay their eggs in pods in the soil. The adults continue feeding until cold weather kills them. The eggs hatch the following spring. Grasshopper problems are most severe during hot, dry weather. Grasshoppers migrate into green gardens and yards as surrounding areas dry up in the summer heat. Periods of cool, wet weather help keep their numbers under control.

SOLUTION: Treat the plants with ORTHO Fruit & Vegetable Insect Control as soon as grasshoppers appear. Repeat at weekly intervals if the plants become reinfested. Make sure that your plant is listed on the product label.

PROBLEM: Spotted, pale green insects up to ⅛ inch long hop, move sideways, or fly away quickly when a plant is touched. The leaves are stippled.

ANALYSIS: Leafhoppers
Leafhoppers feed on many vegetables and small fruits. They generally feed on the undersides of leaves, sucking the sap, which causes stippling. Severely infested vegetable and small fruit plants may become weak and produce few edible fruit. One leafhopper, the *aster leafhopper* (*Macrosteles fascifrons*), transmits *aster yellows*, a plant disease that can be quite damaging. For further details see page 861. Leafhoppers at all stages of maturity are active during the growing season. They hatch in the spring from eggs laid on perennial weeds and ornamental plants. Even areas where the winters are so cold that the eggs cannot survive are not free from infestation because leafhoppers migrate in the spring from warmer regions.

SOLUTION: Spray infested plants with an insecticide containing *carbaryl, malathion, diazinon,* or *methoxychlor.* Be sure to cover the lower surfaces of the leaves. Repeat the spray as often as necessary to keep the insects under control. Allow at least 10 days between applications. Make sure that your plants are listed on the product label. Eradicate nearby weeds, especially thistles, plantains, and dandelions, which may harbor leafhopper eggs. For more information about controlling disease-carrying insects, see page 880.

VEGETABLES, BERRIES, AND GRAPES

PROBLEMS COMMON TO MANY VEGETABLES, BERRIES, AND GRAPES _____

INSECTS IN THE SOIL _____

Whiteflies (life size).

Aphids on spinach (half life size).

Sowbugs (life size).

PROBLEM: Tiny, winged insects ¹/₁₂ inch long feed on the undersides of the leaves. The insects are covered with white waxy powder. When the plant is touched, insects flutter rapidly around it. Leaves may be mottled and yellowing. In warm winter areas, black mold may cover the leaves.

ANALYSIS: Whitefly
This insect is a common pest of many garden and greenhouse plants. The 4-winged adult lays eggs on the undersides of leaves. The larvae are the size of a pinhead, flat, oval, and semitransparent, with white waxy filaments radiating from the body. They feed for about a month before changing to the adult form. Both the larval and adult forms suck sap from the leaves. The larvae are more damaging because they feed more heavily. Adults and larvae cannot fully digest all the sugar in the plant sap, and excrete the excess in a fluid called honeydew, which often drops onto the lower leaves. A sooty mold fungus may develop on the honeydew, causing the leaves to appear black and dirty. In warm winter areas these insects can be active year-round, with eggs, larvae, and adults present at the same time. Whiteflies are unable to live through freezing winters. Spring reinfestations in freezing winter areas come from migrating whiteflies and infested greenhouse-grown plants placed in the garden.

SOLUTION: Control whiteflies by spraying with an insecticide containing *malathion* or *diazinon* every 7 to 10 days as necessary. Spray the foliage thoroughly, being sure to cover both the upper and lower surfaces of the leaves.

PROBLEM: Pale green, yellow, purple, or black soft-bodied insects cluster on the undersides of the leaves. Leaves turn yellow, and may be curled, distorted, and puckered. Plants may be stunted and produce few fruit.

ANALYSIS: Aphids
Aphids are one of the most common pests in the garden. They do little damage in small numbers, but are extremely prolific and populations can rapidly build up to damaging numbers during the growing season. Damage occurs when the aphids suck the juices from vegetable or small fruit leaves and flower buds. Aphids usually prefer young tender leaves. Severely infested plants may be stunted and weak, producing few fruit. Fruit yield is also reduced when the aphids spread plant virus diseases. Aphids feed on nearly every plant in the garden, and are spread from plant to plant by the wind, water, and people. Aphids are unable to digest fully all the sugar in the plant sap and excrete the excess in a fluid called honeydew, which often drops onto lower leaves. Ants feed on this sticky substance, and are often present where there is an aphid infestation.

SOLUTION: Control aphids on vegetables and berries with an insecticide containing *malathion, diazinon, pyrethrin,* or *methoxychlor* as soon as the insects appear. Repeat the spray if the plants become reinfested. Make sure that your plant is listed on the product label. For more information on controlling disease-carrying insects, see page 880.

PROBLEM: Flat, oval, brown or gray creatures up to ½ inch long are found on and in the soil. These crusty pests have 7 pairs of legs, and may roll up into a ball when disturbed.

ANALYSIS: Sowbugs and pillbugs
These soil-inhabiting pests are not insects, but are related to crabs. They live in damp protected places and feed on decaying plant parts. They are frequently found in manure, and may be brought into the garden in a fresh load. Although found in many gardens, sowbugs and pillbugs are a minor pest of vegetables unless populations are high. They may feed on seedling roots and underground stems, and occasionally may feed on tender new growth. They may eat lettuce leaves and heads, tomatoes, and other soft fruit and leaves that are in contact with the soil.

SOLUTION: Since sowbugs and pillbugs are more of a nuisance than a destructive pest, insecticide treatments are seldom needed in the home vegetable garden. However, if they are numerous and troublesome, treat the soil and hiding places with an insecticide containing *carbaryl, diazinon, malathion,* or *methoxychlor.* Make sure that your plants are listed on the product label.

692

Earwig (twice life size).

Symphylans (3 times life size).

Millipedes (half life size).

PROBLEM: Dark, reddish brown insects up to ¾ inch long, with pincers projecting from the rear of the body, are found under objects in the garden. They scurry for cover when disturbed. Holes may be chewed in leaves and blossoms.

ANALYSIS: Earwigs
Although seen in most gardens, earwigs are only minor pests of vegetables and berries, unless populations are high, when they can become major pests. They feed predominantly on decaying plant material and other insects. Earwigs feed at night and hide under stones, debris, and bark in the daytime. They have wings but seldom fly, preferring to run instead. Adult earwigs lay eggs in the soil in late winter to early spring. The young that hatch from these eggs may feed on green shoots and eat holes in leaves. As the earwigs mature, they feed occasionally on blossoms and ripening fruit. Earwigs are beneficial when they feed on other insect larvae and on snails. They sometimes invade homes.

SOLUTION: Because earwigs typically cause only minor damage, insecticide sprays are seldom needed in the vegetable garden. However, if they are numerous and troublesome, treat the soil with an insecticide containing ORTHO Diazinon Soil & Turf Insect Control. Since earwigs are most active at night, treat in the late afternoon or evening. Make sure that your plant is listed on the product label. Pick fruit as it ripens. For information on controlling earwigs indoors, see page 801.

PROBLEM: Slender white pests about ¼ inch long with 6 to 12 pairs of legs and long antennae are present in the soil. Plants may be stunted.

ANALYSIS: Garden symphylans
(*Scutigerella immaculata*)
These soil-inhabiting pests, also called *garden centipedes*, are a problem in both outdoor plantings and greenhouses. They thrive in damp soil that is high in organic matter, and avoid sunlight. Symphylans damage plants by feeding on the fine roots and root hairs, which reduces the amount of water the plant absorbs. They also tunnel through underground stems, stunting and sometimes killing plants. These weakened plants produce few fruit, if any at all. Symphylans are most active in the spring, but egg-laying occurs from spring through summer. They lay their white eggs in clusters one foot deep in the soil. The young have short antennae and 6 pairs of legs, but these develop to long antennae and 12 pairs as they mature into adults. Symphylans may live 4 to 5 years, so symphylans of all ages are found in the soil at one time.

SOLUTION: Treat the soil around vegetable plants with an insecticide containing *diazinon* at the first sign of symphylans. Repeat the treatment as needed to control these pests. Make sure that your plant is listed on the insecticide label.

PROBLEM: Hard-shelled, cylindrical worms up to an inch long are found in the soil, frequently coiled like a watch spring. They are brown to pinkish brown, with 2 pairs of legs on each body segment.

ANALYSIS: Millipedes
Millipedes may have from 30 to 400 legs, but not as many as 1000, as their name suggests. They prefer soils high in organic matter. These scavengers feed on decaying vegetable matter and manure. They may also feed on seedlings or small roots, and sometimes eat bean, pea, or corn seeds. They frequently tunnel into root crops such as carrots, potatoes, parsnips, beets, and turnips, and into ripening fruit that is in contact with damp soil.

SOLUTION: Treat infested soil with an insecticide containing *carbaryl* or ORTHO Diazinon Soil & Turf Insect Control. Repeat the treatment as needed. Make sure that your plant is listed on the insecticide label. Place straw or newspapers under ripening fruit. Pick fruit as it ripens.

PROBLEMS COMMON TO MANY VEGETABLES, BERRIES, AND GRAPES — ANIMAL PESTS

Mole.

Raccoon.

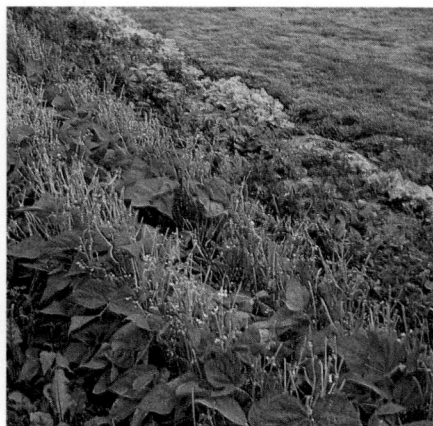

Snapbeans eaten by rabbits.

PROBLEM: Raised ridges, 3 to 5 inches wide, crisscross the garden. Plants may be disturbed. Mounds of soil with no holes appear in the garden.

ANALYSIS: Moles
Moles are small animals that live underground and feed on earthworms and insects. They are 4 to 6 inches long, with velvety fur and tiny, hidden eyes. They use their strong forelegs with broad, trowellike claws to dig and push the soil as they move through the ground. Although they seldom eat plants, they often loosen the soil around plant roots as they search for earthworms and grubs. This loosened soil dries out quickly, causing the plants to wilt.

SOLUTION: Tamp down the soil around wilted plants, water them thoroughly, and shade them until they recover. Because moles seldom eat the roots, the damage is usually not permanent. In the East, trap moles by setting spear-type traps over active surface runs. Locate active runs by tamping down the ridges in a few spots. Spots that are raised again the next day are active runs. Western moles are not easily caught in surface traps. Locate a main run, usually 6 to 10 inches deep, by probing around a fresh pile of soil. Dig down to the run and set a scissors-type trap according to package directions. Poison baits are not very effective with moles. Poison gas is dangerous and difficult to use properly. For more information about moles, see page 890.

PROBLEM: Plants are chewed or completely eaten. Ripening fruit, pods, and ears are partially or completely eaten. Deer, raccoons, squirrels, rabbits, woodchucks, or mice may be seen in the garden.

ANALYSIS: Wildlife
Various forms of wildlife feed in the garden.

1. *Deer* feed on leaves and fruit. They are most active at dawn and dusk.

2. *Raccoons* knock over cornstalks to feed on maturing ears. They may also feed on other ripening fruit. Raccoons feed at night.

3. *Squirrels* feed on ripening fruit and climb cornstalks to feed on maturing ears.

4. *Rabbits* feed on young bean, pea, lettuce, and cabbage plants, eating the young leaves and frequently leaving short stubs of stems standing in the soil.

5. *Woodchucks*, also called *groundhogs*, feed in the afternoons and avoid tomatoes, eggplants, red and green peppers, chives, and onions.

6. *Mice* may bite into ripening tomatoes, cucumbers, and beans that are close to the ground to eat the seeds inside. Mice frequently travel underground in mole tunnels.

SOLUTION: There are several ways to exclude or repel wildlife from your garden.

1. The only sure way to exclude deer is with a woven wire fence 8 feet tall. Cotton drawstring bags filled with bloodmeal fertilizer or human hair and suspended on stakes in the garden sometimes repel them. For more information on deer, see page 891.

2. Exclude raccoons with a 5 to 6-foot-tall fence. Electric fencing above the wire fence may also be needed. Protect corn by interplanting with members of the cucurbit family. Raccoons will not walk on the prickly vines. Sprinkle ripening corn with cayenne pepper. For more information on raccoons, see page 894.

3. Protect ears of corn from squirrels by sprinkling corn silks with cayenne pepper. For more information on squirrels, see page 893.

4. To exclude rabbits, erect a fence 18 inches tall and anchor it by burying the edges 5 to 6 inches deep in the soil. For more information on rabbits, see page 894.

5. Deter woodchucks with a wire fence that is buried 1 foot deep and extended horizontally underground 10 to 12 inches. For more information on woodchucks, see page 895.

6. Stake, trellis, or cage plants to keep fruit off the ground, and away from mice. For more information on mice, see page 890.

ARTICHOKES

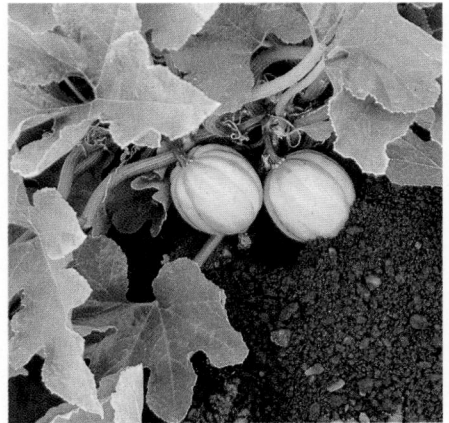

Pocket gopher hole.

PROBLEM: Plants wilt suddenly or disappear. Mounds of soil are clustered in the garden. These mounds are usually crescent shaped, and open outward from a hole in the soil. There are no ridges on the soil surface.

ANALYSIS: Pocket gophers
Pocket gophers live and feed almost entirely underground. They come to the surface only to bring up soil from their burrows, to look for new territory, or to feed within a few inches of their holes. Gophers feed on plant roots. This rodent has fur-lined pouches on each side of its mouth. It has small eyes and ears, a sparsely haired tail, long sharp claws, and a blunt head. Gophers are solitary, and only one inhabits a burrow at a time. The mounds of soil are formed as gophers push soil out of their holes to enlarge their burrow system. Gophers may be present without mounding soil.

SOLUTION: Trapping is the quickest and surest way to eliminate a pocket gopher from your yard. Find the main runway (which runs in both directions) by probing with a sharp rod about a foot deep near a fresh mound or an eaten plant. Dig a hole to intersect the run and insert two traps in the run, one facing in each direction. Tie the traps together or to a stake above ground. To keep soil from falling on the traps, and to keep animals and children away from the trap, cover the hole with sod or a board. Sprinkle the board with soil to block out all light. Check and move the traps daily. Although only one gopher occupies a burrow system at a time, migrating gophers will move into an abandoned burrow. Level all the mounds and watch for signs that the burrow has been reoccupied.

GLOBE ARTICHOKE

ADAPTATION: Frost-free areas with cool, humid summers.

PLANTING TIME: Early to midspring.

PLANTING METHOD: Set crown or root pieces 6 to 8 inches deep, and 4 to 6 feet apart. Set containerized plants so that the top of their rootball is even with the garden soil. Space 4 to 6 feet apart. Or, start seeds indoors 4 to 6 weeks before planting outdoors. Store seeds in the refrigerator in moist peat moss for 2 weeks before planting.

SOIL: Any good garden soil that is rich in organic matter. pH 6.0 to 6.5

FERTILIZER: Feed twice a year, in the spring and fall, with ½ pound of ORTHO General Purpose Plant Food 8–8–8 per plant.

WATER:
How much: Apply enough water at each irrigation to wet the soil 1 to 1½ feet deep.
How often: Water when the soil 1 inch deep is dry.

HARVEST: Cut artichokes with 1 inch of stem, while the buds are still tight. Overmature artichokes have loose scales that point outward with purple flowers in between. The bud scales of the Creole variety, commonly grown in southern Louisiana, naturally point outward. Smaller artichokes will be produced along the stalk after the first one is cut. Remove the entire stalk after it stops producing.

Cold damage.

PROBLEM: White blisters or dark streaks and patches appear on artichoke leaves (bud scales). Discoloration appears soon after temperatures have dropped to freezing.

ANALYSIS: Cold damage
Artichokes are tender perennials; they are easily injured by freezing temperatures. Damage is most likely to occur in the late summer or early fall after a frosty night. The damage may not be noticed in the early morning following the frost, but as the temperature warms throughout the day the discoloration appears.

SOLUTION: Discolored artichokes are still edible; in most cases damage is only cosmetic. Discard artichokes so badly damaged that they are entirely shriveled and brown. If you anticipate freezing temperatures, protect plants by covering them with newspaper or burlap.

ARTICHOKES

Slug damage.

Damaged artichoke. *Insert:* Larva (half life size).

Curly dwarf.

PROBLEM: Artichoke buds (heads), stems, and leaves are disfigured with white or tan scars. Silvery trails wind around on the plants and soil nearby. Snails or slugs may be seen moving around or feeding on the plants, especially at night. Inspect the garden for them at night by flashlight.

ANALYSIS: Snails and slugs
These pests are mollusks, and are related to clams, oysters, and other shellfish. They feed on a wide variety of garden plants. Like other mollusks, snails and slugs need to be moist all the time. For this reason, they avoid direct sun and dry places, and hide during the day in damp places, such as under flower pots or in thick groundcover. They emerge at night or on cloudy days to feed. Snails and slugs are similar except that the snail has a hard shell, into which it withdraws when disturbed. Slugs lay masses of white eggs encased in a slimy mass in protected places. Snails bury their eggs in the soil, also in a slimy mass. The young look like miniature versions of their parents.

SOLUTION: Scatter a snail and slug bait containing *metaldehyde* on the ground around the artichoke plants. Also scatter the bait in areas where snails or slugs might be hiding, such as in dense groundcovers, weedy areas, compost piles, or pot storage areas. Before spreading the bait, wet down the areas to be treated to encourage snail and slug activity that night. Repeat the application every 2 weeks as long as snails and slugs are active. Do not apply bait to the plant itself.

PROBLEM: Irregular holes appear in the artichoke bud scales (the "leaves" of the artichoke bud), in the stem, and in the new foliage. Small worms may be seen feeding on new foliage and beneath the bud scales. Brown moths with plumed wings, about 1 inch across, fly near the plant in the evening.

ANALYSIS: Artichoke plume moth (*Platyptilia carduidactyla*)
The larvae of this moth feed on the tender parts of the artichoke plant. The adult moth lays eggs on the underside of the foliage or on the stem below the bud. The larvae bore into the artichoke, blemishing the bud scales and tunneling the heart. Insect damage may occur all year around, but is particularly severe in the spring. This insect also lives on thistles (*Cirsium* species).

SOLUTION: Apply an insecticide containing *carbaryl* to the foliage, buds, and stems, when the worms first appear or when the plant shows damage. Repeat the dusting weekly as long as new damage appears. Pick and destroy all wormy artichoke buds and foliage. In the fall, remove or bury all plant debris. Also remove all nearby thistles that may harbor the insect.

PROBLEM: The plant is stunted. The foliage may be curled, and the artichokes are misshapen and small. The plant eventually dies.

ANALYSIS: Curly dwarf
This plant disease is caused by a virus transmitted by sucking insects such as aphids and leafhoppers. The most common — and often the only — symptom of virus infection is stunting. Curly dwarf virus is transmitted from infected artichokes or, on the Pacific Coast, from milk thistle (*Silybum marianum*), a common weed.

SOLUTION: There are no chemical controls for virus diseases in plants. Remove and destroy the infected plants. To prevent reintroducing the virus, use a virus-free root stock. Also protect your artichokes by removing milk thistle and other weeds from the area. For more information about controlling disease-carrying insects, see page 880.

ASPARAGUS _____

ASPARAGUS _____

ADAPTATION: Throughout the United States, except in the Southeast.

PLANTING TIME: See page 1009.

PLANTING METHOD: Set crowns, buds upward, in a trench 6 to 8 inches deep, and 12 inches apart. As the plants grow, gradually fill in the trench with soil until even with the surrounding soil. Or, sow seeds 1 inch deep and 3 inches apart.

SOIL: Any good garden soil. pH 6.5 to 8.0

FERTILIZER: At planting time, use 4 pounds of ORTHO Vegetable Garden Food 5–10–10 per 100 square feet. Side-dress in late July to early August with 1.2 pounds per 100-foot row. After the first year, fertilize twice a year, once in the spring before the shoots emerge, and again just after harvest.

WATER:
How much: Apply enough water at each irrigation to wet the soil 1 to 1½ feet deep.
How often: Water when the soil is just barely moist.

HARVEST: Plants must grow for 2 years before harvesting to build strong roots to insure crops for at least 10 years. In the spring of the third year, pick when the spears are 7 to 10 inches tall with tight heads. To avoid wounding the crown, snap the spears, do not tear or cut them. Harvest for 2 weeks. The fourth year, pick for 4 weeks, and the fifth and following years for 8 weeks. In California, harvest for 4, 8, and 12 weeks respectively.

Small spears.

PROBLEM: Spears are small and skinny.

ANALYSIS: Small spears
Asparagus spears may be small for any of several reasons:
1. *Poor fertility:* Underfertilized plants cannot produce adequate fern growth and food for next year's crop.
2. *Immature plants:* Asparagus crowns produce small spears for the first 2 or 3 years following planting.
3. *Poor drainage:* Asparagus plants do not produce well in poorly drained soil.
4. *Overharvested plants:* When harvest continues late in the season, the plants are unable to produce enough foliage and do not store enough food for next year's crop.

SOLUTION: Follow the growing and harvesting guidelines on this page. Improve the soil drainage and aeration as outlined on page 901.

Fusarium wilt.

PROBLEM: The growing shoot turns yellow to dingy brown and wilts. During wet weather, white or pink cottonlike strands often appear under the leaf scales. Wilting is most severe among full-grown plants during the months of July and August. When the infected plant is dug up, all or part of the root system is seen to be a reddish color. The plant eventually dies.

ANALYSIS: Fusarium wilt
This wilt disease is caused by a fungus (*Fusarium* species). Asparagus plants under stress from poor growing conditions (drought, poor drainage, insect or disease injury, etc.) are more severely affected. The fungus lives on organic matter in the soil. The disease is spread by contaminated seeds, plants, soil, and equipment; it often enters a garden on the roots of a transplant. The fungus enters the plant through the roots and spreads up into the stems and leaves through the water-conducting vessels in the stems. The vessels become discolored and plugged, cutting off the flow of water to the leaves. Because fusarium is favored by wet weather and warm temperatures (70° to 85°F), the fungi build up in warm soils.

SOLUTION: No chemical control is available. It is best to destroy infected plants. Next year, plant healthy crowns where asparagus has not been planted for 2 to 4 years. If you plant in infected soil, fumigate the soil about 3 weeks before planting. For more information about soil fumigation, see page 919. For more information about fusarium wilt, see page 858.

ASPARAGUS

Larvae. *Insert:* Adults (twice life size).

PROBLEM: The tips of young asparagus spears are chewed and scarred. Later, when the spears develop into asparagus ferns, they are also chewed. Small (¼ inch) metallic blue or black beetles with yellow markings and a narrow red head may feed on the tips of the spears, and later on the ferns and stems. Reddish orange beetles with black spots may be present. Shiny black specks are found on the spear tips. Humpbacked orange or slate-gray grubs may also be seen.

ANALYSIS: Asparagus beetle (*Crioceris asparagi*) and spotted asparagus beetle (*Crioceris duodecimpunctata*)
These two beetles injure asparagus plants throughout the growing season. The blue-black *asparagus beetle* is found throughout the United States. The orange and black *spotted asparagus beetle* is found east of the Mississippi River. The beetles are particularly a problem when young asparagus shoots emerge in the spring. Both adults and grubs injure the plants by feeding on shoots, ferns, and stems. This feeding robs the root system of food manufactured in the foliage and necessary for healthy growth next year.

SOLUTION: Apply ORTHO Rotenone Dust or Spray when the beetles are first noticed. Repeat the applications as long as the beetles or grubs are feeding. Also treat the fern growth in late summer or early fall to prevent adults from overwintering on the ferns and reinfesting next year's crop.

Rust.

PROBLEM: Tops turn yellow, then brown, and die back in early to midsummer. Reddish brown, orange, or black blisters appear on the ferns and stems. Spears mature earlier than usual.

ANALYSIS: Rust
This plant disease is caused by a fungus (*Puccinia asparagi*). This year's rust weakens the plant by reducing the amount of food manufactured in the leaves to be stored in the roots. Since this stored food supplies the energy for next year's crop, fewer shoots are produced the following year. Damage is most severe when the tops are attacked several years in a row. In severe cases, the plants die. Warm temperatures and high humidity from fog, heavy dew, or overhead watering favor rust infection. Damage is worst during very wet seasons. Rust spores from diseased tops that have been left in the garden infect new shoots as they emerge in the spring. The wind spreads the spores from plant to plant.

SOLUTION: After the harvest, spray the ferns and stems with a fungicide containing *maneb* or *zineb*. Repeat the treatment at intervals of 10 days when weather conditions favor rust infection. Do not spray while spears are still being harvested. Cut the tops down close to the ground after they die in the fall, and destroy them. Don't add them to the compost pile or leave them lying around the garden. If you plant more asparagus, select rust-resistant varieties.

Rust-resistant asparagus varieties: California 500, Martha Washington, Mary Washington, and Waltham Washington.

BEANS

ADAPTATION: Throughout the United States.

PLANTING TIME: See page 1009.

PLANTING METHOD: Sow seeds 1 to 1½ inches deep and 1 to 2 inches apart. Thin to 2 to 4 inches apart when the seedlings have their first set of leaves.

SOIL: Any good garden soil, somewhat friable for easy seedling emergence. pH 6.0 to 8.0

FERTILIZER: At planting time, use 3 pounds of ORTHO Vegetable Garden Food 5–10–10 per 100 square feet, or 1 pound per 25-foot row. Side-dress every 3 to 4 weeks with 1 pound per 25-foot row.

WATER:
How much: Apply enough water to wet the soil 8 to 10 inches deep.
How often: Water when the soil is just barely moist.

HARVEST: Break the beans from the vines, being careful not to jerk or tear the vine. Pick beans when they are ready. If over-mature beans remain on the vines, production is greatly reduced. Cool beans in the refrigerator until use.
Harvesting times:
Snap (green) beans: When the seed in the pod begins to swell.
Lima Beans: When the pods are well-filled, but still bright green.

Mexican bean beetle and larva (twice life size).

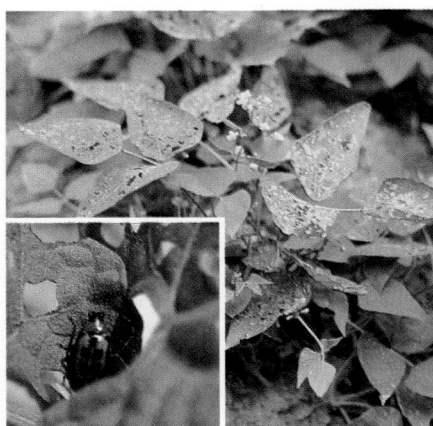

Bean leaf beetle (twice life size).

Bean aphids (half life size).

PROBLEM: The tissue between the leaf veins is eaten, giving the leaves a lacelike appearance. Copper-colored beetles about ¼ inch long feed on the undersides of the skeletonized leaves. The beetles have 16 black spots on their backs. Orange to yellow soft-bodied grubs about ⅓ inch long with black-tipped spines on their backs may also be present. Leaves dry up, and the plant may die.

ANALYSIS: Mexican bean beetle
(*Epilachna varivestis*)
This beetle is found throughout the United States. It prefers lima beans, but also feeds on pole and bush beans and cowpeas. Feeding damage by both adults and larvae can reduce pod production. The adult beetles spend the winter in plant debris in the garden, to emerge in late spring and early summer. They lay yellow eggs on the undersides of the leaves. Larvae that hatch from these eggs, in early to midsummer, are green at first, gradually turning yellow. There are 1 to 4 generations per year. Frequently, all stages of beetles appear at the same time throughout the season. Hot, dry summers and cold winters reduce the beetle population.

SOLUTION: Apply Ortho Sevin Garden Dust or ORTHO Fruit & Vegetable Insect Control when the adults first appear. Be sure to spray the undersides of the leaves where the insects feed. Early treatments to control the adults may save extra applications later to control the larvae, which are more damaging and harder to control. Remove and destroy all plant debris after the harvest to reduce overwintering spots for adults.

PROBLEM: Holes are chewed in the leaves. Yellow to red beetles with black spots and a black band around the outer edge of the body are feeding on the undersides of the leaves. The plant may later turn yellow and wilt. If you pull the plant up you may see slender white grubs up to ⅓ inch long feeding on the roots and stem.

ANALYSIS: Bean leaf beetle
(*Cerotoma trifurcata*)
This widely distributed insect attacks all beans, as well as peas. Adult beetles feed on the undersides of leaves, blossoms, and pods throughout the growing season. Grubs feed on the roots and stems below the soil line. Females lay clusters of orange eggs on the soil at the base of plants. The grubs that hatch from these eggs attack the plant below the soil, feeding on the roots and sometimes girdling the stem at the soil level. This feeding can kill the plant. Both adults and grubs cause serious damage to young plants. There are 1 to 3 generations per year.

SOLUTION: Apply ORTHO Sevin Garden Dust at the first sign of damage. Be sure to spray the undersides of the leaves where the beetles feed. Repeat at intervals of 7 to 10 days whenever damage occurs. Clean all debris from the garden at the end of the season to eliminate overwintering spots for adults.

PROBLEM: Young leaves are curled, distorted, and yellow. Tiny (⅛ inch) pale green to black, soft-bodied insects cluster on leaves and stems. There may be a shiny, sticky substance coating the leaves. Ants may be present.

ANALYSIS: Aphids
Aphids do little damage in small numbers. However, they are extremely prolific and populations can rapidly build up to tremendous numbers during the growing season. Damage occurs when the aphid sucks the juices from the bean leaves. The aphid is unable to digest fully all the sugar in the plant sap and excretes the excess in a fluid called honeydew. The honeydew often drops onto the leaves below. Ants feed on the sticky substance and are often present where there is an aphid infestation.

SOLUTION: Spray with ORTHO Fruit & Vegetable Insect Control, ORTHO Malathion 50 Insect Spray, or ORTHO Diazinon Soil & Foliage Dust as soon as the insects appear. Repeat at intervals of 1 week if the plant is reinfested.

Two-spotted spider mite damage.

Failure to set pods.

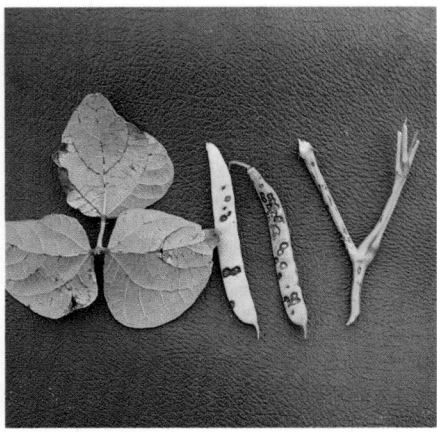

Anthracnose spots.

PROBLEM: Leaves are stippled, yellowing, and dirty. Leaves may dry out and drop. There may be webbing between leaves or on the lower surfaces of the leaves. To determine if the plant is infested with mites, hold a sheet of white paper underneath an affected leaf and tap the leaf sharply. Minute green, red, or yellow specks the size of pepper grains will drop to the paper and begin to crawl around. The pests are easily seen against the white background.

ANALYSIS: Two-spotted spider mite (*Tetranychus urticae*)
These mites, related to spiders, are major pests of many garden and greenhouse plants. They cause damage by sucking sap from the undersides of the leaves. As a result of feeding, the green leaf pigment disappears, producing the stippled appearance. Mites are active throughout the growing season, but are favored by hot, dry weather (70°F and up). By midsummer, they build up to tremendous numbers.

SOLUTION: Apply ORTHO Malathion 50 Insect Spray or a pesticide containing *dicofol* when the damage is first seen. Spray thoroughly, being sure to cover both the upper and lower surfaces of the leaves. Mites are difficult to control because they reproduce so rapidly. Repeated applications are necessary, especially during hot, dry weather, at intervals of 7 to 10 days. Hose down plants every few days to knock off webs and mites.

PROBLEM: The plants look healthy but there are only a few fully formed pods.

ANALYSIS: Failure to set pods
Failure to set pods may result from any of several factors.
1. *High temperatures:* Maturing bean plants prefer temperatures between 70° and 80°F. If the maximum temperature is consistently over 85°F, as it often is in the summer, flowers often drop off without setting pods — a condition known as *blossom drop.* Heat can also cause the blossoms to deteriorate on the plant without actually dropping off. This condition is known as *blossom blast.* Hot, dry winds also contribute to both blossom drop and blast.
2. *Extremes in soil moisture:* Plants growing in soil that is either too wet or too dry are stressed by a lack of oxygen and water. Irregular watering contributes to this problem. Weakened plants produce few pods.
3. *Overmature pods:* Leaving mature pods on the vine forces the plant to put its energy into seed formation in the pod, rather than to forming new pods.

SOLUTION: The numbers below correspond to the numbers in the analysis.
1. In areas where very hot summers or hot, dry winds are common, plant beans for late spring harvest and again for fall harvest.
2. Water regularly, allowing the soil surface to dry out between waterings. To conserve moisture during hot, dry weather, use a 3 to 4 inch mulch of straw or chopped leaves.
3. Pick the pods regularly when they are young and tender and before large seeds develop inside. Do not allow any pods to mature.

PROBLEM: Small brown specks on pods enlarge to black, circular, sunken spots. In wet weather, a salmon-colored ooze appears in the infected spots. Elongated dark reddish brown spots appear on the stems and veins on the underside of the leaves. If seedlings are attached, the stems may rot, or the first young leaves may be spotted. In either case, the seedlings die.

ANALYSIS: Bean anthracnose
This bean disease is caused by a fungus (*Colletotrichum lindemuthianum*) that affects all kinds of beans, but is most destructive on lima beans. It occurs in the eastern and central states, rarely west of the Rocky Mountains. The fungus thrives in cool, wet weather. The salmon-colored ooze that often appears in the infected spots during wet weather consists of slime spores. The spores are carried by splashing water, animals, people, or tools to healthy plants. The fungus lives on diseased bean seeds and on plant debris that has been left in the garden.

SOLUTION: Apply a fungicide containing *maneb* or *zineb* at flowering and repeat 3 more times at intervals of 7 to 10 days. Continue treatments whenever wet weather occurs. Remove and destroy any diseased plants. The disease spreads rapidly on moist foliage, so do not work in the garden when the plants are wet. To avoid reintroducing this fungus into your garden, purchase seeds from a reputable seed company. Do not plant beans in the infected area for 2 or 3 years. Rotate your bean planting site every year.

Halo blight.

Rust.

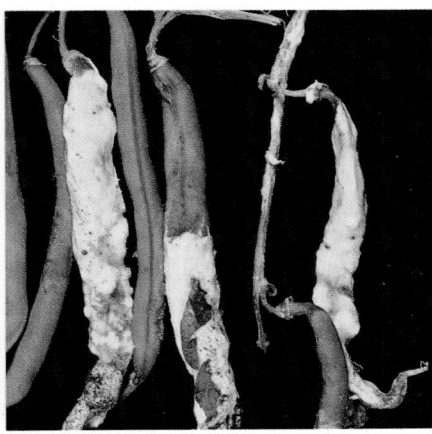

White mold.

PROBLEM: Small, water-soaked spots appear on the leaves. These spots enlarge, turn brown, and may kill the leaf. In cool weather, narrow greenish yellow halos may border the infected spots. The leaves either turn yellow and die slowly or turn brown rapidly and drop off. Long reddish lesions may girdle the stem. In moist conditions, a tan or yellow ooze is produced in spots on pods.

ANALYSIS: Bacterial blights
Two widespread bacterial blights on beans are *common blight* (caused by *Xanthomonas phaseoli*) and *halo blight* (caused by *Pseudomonas phaseolicola*). These bacteria attack all kinds of beans. Common blight is more severe in warm, moist weather; halo blight is favored by cool temperatures. The bacteria are usually introduced into a garden on infected seed, and can live on infected plant debris in the soil for as long as 2 years. They are spread by rain, splashing water, and contaminated tools. The bacteria multiply rapidly in humid weather. If the water-conducting tissue is invaded, bacteria and dead cells eventually clog the veins, causing leaf discoloration. Often bacteria ooze from infected spots in a yellow or cream-colored mass.

SOLUTION: There are no chemical controls for bacterial blights. Avoid overhead watering. Do not work with the beans when the plants are wet. Do not plant beans in the same area more often than every third year. Purchase new seed each year from a reputable company.

PROBLEM: Rust-colored spots form, mostly on the undersides of the leaves. Severely infected leaves turn yellow, wilt, dry up, and fall off. Stems and pods may also have spots.

ANALYSIS: Bean rust
This plant disease is caused by a fungus (*Uromyces phaseoli*) that affects only bean plants. It is most common on mature plants, and most damaging to pole beans and lima beans. Scarlet runner beans are sometimes mildly affected. Each rust spot develops thousands of spores that are spread by wind and splashing water. The disease develops rapidly during periods of cool nights and warm days. High humidity from rain, dew, or watering also encourages rust. Heavy vine growth, which shades the ground and prevents air circulation, produces ideal conditions for the disease. At the end of the summer when the nights are longer, the fungus produces another type of spore. This thick-walled black spore spends the winter on infected bean plant debris.

SOLUTION: Apply ORTHO Vegetable Disease Control to snap beans at the first sign of the disease. Weekly applications may be necessary if conditions favorable to the disease continue. Avoid overhead irrigation. Water in the morning rather than evening to allow wet foliage to dry quickly. Thin seedlings and space plants far enough apart to allow air to circulate freely. In the fall, remove and destroy all infected plants to prevent the fungus from surviving and reinfecting in the spring. Do not plant beans in the same area more often than every third year.

PROBLEM: Soft, watery spots appear on stems, leaves, and pods. Under moist conditions these spots enlarge rapidly. A white mold grows in the infected spots. Often there are small, black, hard, seedlike structures in the mold. The leaves may turn yellow, wilt, and die. Rotted pods are soft and mushy.

ANALYSIS: White mold
This plant disease, also called *watery soft rot*, is caused by a fungus (*Sclerotinia sclerotiorum*), that attacks many vegetables. The fungus needs abundant moisture and moderate temperatures (60° to 75°F), and thrives during periods of heavy dew or continuous light rains. Infection occurs on blossoms, leaves, stems, and pods. The disease spreads when infected tissue contacts healthy tissue. If moist conditions continue, the entire plant may die. A plant attacked early in the season seldom sets pods.

SOLUTION: Control of this disease can be difficult. Once the disease is established in the planting, or pods are formed, sprays are ineffective. Remove all diseased plants as soon as symptoms are noticed. Water in the morning rather than the evening to allow wet foliage time to dry. Next year plant in well-drained soil, and thin seedlings to allow good air circulation among the plants. Avoid excessive nitrogen fertilization, which encourages highly susceptible, succulent leaf growth. If possible, plant beans in the same area only once every 3 to 4 years, rotating them with nonsusceptible plants such as corn, beets, Swiss chard, or spinach. Spray the foliage with a fungicide containing *benomyl* when approximately 25 percent of the buds are open, and again about 7 days later.

BEANS

Hopperburn. *Insert:* Leafhopper (3 times life size).

Snakehead.

Baldhead.

PROBLEM: Leaves are stippled. Some are scorched, with a green midrib and brown edges curled under. Spotted, pale green, winged insects up to ⅛ inch long hop, run, or fly away quickly when the plant is touched.

ANALYSIS: Hopperburn
Hopperburn is caused by the potato leafhopper (*Empoasca fabae*), which injects a toxin into the leaves as it feeds. Bean yields may be drastically reduced from hopperburn. Leafhoppers are active throughout the growing season. They hatch in the spring from eggs laid on perennial weeds and ornamental plants. Even areas that have winters so cold that the eggs cannot survive are not free from infestation, because leafhoppers migrate in the spring from warmer regions.

SOLUTION: Treat infested plants with ORTHO Malathion 50 Insect Spray or ORTHO Sevin Garden Dust at the first sign of damage. Be sure to cover the lower surfaces of the leaves, where the leafhoppers feed. Repeat the spray as often as necessary to keep the insects under control. Allow at least 10 days between applications.

PROBLEM: Seedlings have no leaves or only one leaf. The young plants may sprout late and are often stunted. A normal seedling pushes its way through the soil with a curved stem. The stem then straightens and unfolds two seed leaves.

ANALYSIS: Snakehead and baldhead
Snakeheads are seedlings whose seed leaves have been broken or injured. *Baldheads* are seedlings with no true leaves or stem tip above the seed leaves. They may be caused by:

1. *Seed damage:* In the seed, the tiny plant is connected to the seed leaves by slender threads. Despite careful handling by seed companies, seeds can be damaged during harvesting or handling.

2. *Soil texture and planting depth:* Bean sprouts push their large seed up and out of the soil. During that struggle the seeds may be damaged, particularly in clay soils, when the soil surface is crusted.

3. *Snails, slugs, birds, or insects:* The succulent young leaves may be eaten by animal or insect pests before or after emergence. The seed corn maggot (see page 704) is sometimes responsible.

SOLUTION: Pull out damaged seedlings; they rarely grow into normal plants.

1. Buy seed from a reputable garden company. Handle carefully before and during planting.

2. Plant new seeds in loose soil 1 to 1½ inches deep. Cover with a layer of sand, vermiculite, or some other loose material to prevent the soil from crusting. Do not use peat moss — it dries out quickly.

3. For protection from birds, cover the seedbed with cheesecloth. Remove once the seedlings emerge through the soil. Discourage soil-inhabiting pests with ORTHO Diazinon Soil & Foliage Dust at planting; for slugs and snails use ORTHO Bug-Geta Snail & Slug Pellets.

Fusarium root rot.

Bean yellow mosaic.

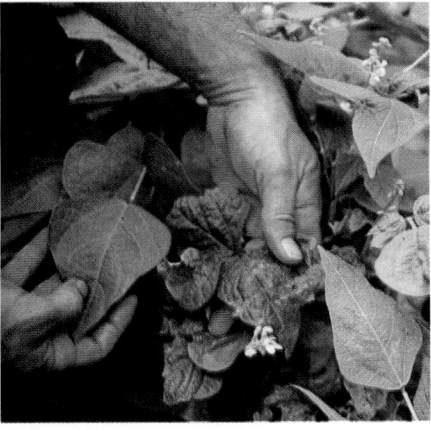

Curly top.

PROBLEM: Leaves turn yellow. Overall growth is slow, and the plant may be dwarfed. In hot, dry weather the plant suddenly wilts and sometimes dies. Few pods are produced. Red spots or streaks may be seen on stems and roots. Underground stems may be streaked dark brown or black.

ANALYSIS: Root rot
This plant disease is caused by several soil-inhabiting fungi (*Fusarium* species, *Pythium* species, and *Rhizoctonia solani*) that attack beans and many other vegetables. The fungi live in the soil, invading the plant through the roots and underground stem. As the disease progresses, the roots decay and shrivel. The leaves turn yellow, and growth slows. The plant becomes dwarfed, wilts, and sometimes dies. Under favorable growing conditions, the bean plants may grow new side roots to replace the rotted ones. These plants will survive, but the yield will be reduced. Root rots develop most rapidly at soil temperatures between 60° and 85°F.

SOLUTION: There is no completely effective chemical control for this problem. Pull out and discard wilted plants. Rotate your bean planting site yearly. If this is not practical, sprinkle with a fungicide containing *captan* or *PCNB* in the row at planting time (1 teaspoon per 20 foot row). Plant in well-drained soil and let the soil surface dry out between waterings.

PROBLEM: Leaves are mottled yellow and green, and may be longer and narrower than usual, and puckered. Raised dark areas develop along the central vein, and the leaf margins curl downward. The whole plant is stunted. Pods on the affected plants may be faded, rough, and few in number. The seeds inside are shriveled and small. The damage is most noticeable when the temperature is between 60° and 75°F.

ANALYSIS: Bean mosaic
Bean common mosaic and bean yellow mosaic are widespread virus diseases. Common mosaic virus affects only French and snap beans; yellow mosaic virus affects lima beans, peas, summer squash, clover, gladiolus, and other perennial flowers. Both diseases are spread by aphids, which transmit the virus as they feed. (For more information on aphids, see page 692.) In warmer parts of the country with large aphid populations, the disease spreads rapidly. Common bean mosaic is also spread in infected seed. If the infection occurs early in the season when the plants are young, the plants may not bear pods. Infection later in the season does not affect pod production as severely. For more information on virus diseases, see page 861.

SOLUTION: There are no chemical controls for plant viruses. To reduce the aphid population and the spread of disease, apply ORTHO Malathion 50 Insect Spray or ORTHO Fruit & Vegetable Insect Control as soon as the first insects appear. Remove all infected plants and all clover plants in the vicinity of the garden. Plant virus resistant varieties of beans listed on page 1010.

PROBLEM: Leaves are pale green, puckered, and curl downward, and are thick and brittle. The plant is dwarfed and bushy, stops growing, and may die. Bean pods are stunted.

ANALYSIS: Curly top
This virus disease affects many vegetables, including beans, beets, tomatoes, squash, and melons. The virus is transmitted from plant to plant by the beet leafhopper (*Circulifer tenellus*), so the disease is common only in the West, where this insect lives. The pale greenish yellow leafhopper feeds from early May through June. It sucks the sap and virus from the infected leaves, and then injects the virus into healthy plants at its next feeding stop. Curly top symptoms vary in their severity, depending on the variety and age of the plant. Young infected plants usually die. Older plants may turn yellow and die.

SOLUTION: There are no chemical controls for this virus. Remove and destroy all infected plants. To reduce the chances of infection in your garden, control the beet leafhopper with ORTHO Sevin Garden Dust, ORTHO Fruit & Vegetable Insect Control, or ORTHO Tomato Vegetable Dust. For more information about controlling disease-carrying insects, see page 880. Begin when the insect swarms first appear in early May. Beans planted after the insect stops feeding in June are not infected.

BEANS

Weak seedlings. *Insert:* Seedcorn maggot (life size).

PROBLEM: Seeds may not sprout. If they do, the weak plants wilt and collapse shortly after emerging. Cream-colored, legless maggots about ¼ inch long are feeding on the seeds.

ANALYSIS: Seedcorn maggot
(*Hylemya platura*)
The seedcorn maggot feeds on many vegetables including beets, beans, peas, onions, cucumbers, and cabbage. It damages seeds and germinating seedlings by tunneling into them and feeding on the tissue. If the seed is only partially destroyed, the plants that sprout are weak, sickly, and soon die. These pests can be responsible for snakeheads (see page 702). The seedcorn maggot is favored by cold, wet soil with a high manure content. It spends the winter as a larva or a pupa in soil, plant debris, or manure, and becomes active in the early spring. Small adult flies emerge from May to July, and lay eggs in the rich soil or on seeds or seedlings. The overwintering maggots cause the most damage. Those of later generations are of less importance. There are 3 to 5 generations a year.

SOLUTION: Remove any damaged seeds and sickly plants. Replant with insecticide-treated seeds. To treat the seed yourself, mix one packet of seed with ¼ teaspoon of an insecticide powder that contains *diazinon*. Shake carefully in a jar until the seeds are thoroughly coated. Or work the *diazinon* into the soil at planting time, or spray over the row. Plant seeds when the soil has warmed above 55°F in the spring so they germinate quickly. Shallow-planted seeds germinate more quickly. Use only moderate amounts of manure and till it in thoroughly.

BEETS

BEETS

ADAPTATION: Throughout the United States.

PLANTING TIME: See page 1009.

PLANTING METHOD: Sow seeds ½ to 1 inch deep. Thin seedlings to stand 2 to 4 inches apart when they have 2 to 3 leaves. Thinnings can be eaten in salads.

SOIL: Any good garden soil. pH 6.0 to 7.0

FERTILIZER: At planting time, use 3 to 4 pounds of ORTHO Vegetable Garden Food 5–10–10 per 100 square feet, or 1 pound per 25-foot row. Side-dress every 3 to 4 weeks with 1 pound per 25-foot row.
   Containers: Water thoroughly every 2 to 3 weeks with a solution of ORTHO Tomato & Vegetable Food 6–18–6.

WATER:
   How much: Apply enough water at each watering to wet the soil 8 to 10 inches deep.
   How often: Water when the soil 1 inch deep is just slightly moist.

HARVEST: Beets are edible at different stages of maturity, but smaller ones are more colorful and less tough and stringy than larger ones. Pull beets from the ground when they reach the size listed on the seed packet. Leave 1 to 2 inches of the leaf stalk attached to the beet. Beet greens are also edible, and should be harvested when 4 to 6 inches tall.

Flea beetle (5 times life size).

PROBLEM: Leaves are riddled with shotholes about ⅛ inch in diameter. Tiny (1/16 inch) black beetles jump like fleas when disturbed. Leaves of seedlings and eventually whole plants may wilt and die.

ANALYSIS: Flea beetles
These beetles jump like fleas, but are not related to them. Both adult and immature flea beetles feed on a wide variety of garden vegetables. The immature beetle, a legless gray grub, injures plants by feeding on the roots and the lower surface of leaves. Adults chew holes in leaves. Flea beetles are most damaging to seedlings and young plants. Leaves of seedlings riddled with holes dry out quickly and die. Adult beetles spend the winter in soil and garden debris. They emerge in early spring to feed on weeds until vegetables sprout or plants are set in the garden. Grubs hatch from eggs laid in the soil and feed for 2 to 3 weeks. After pupating in the soil, they emerge as adults to repeat the cycle. There are 1 to 4 generations a year. Adults may feed for up to 2 months.

SOLUTION: Control flea beetles with an insecticide containing *carbaryl* or *methoxychlor* when the leaves first show damage. Watch new growth for further evidence of feeding, and repeat treatments at weekly intervals as needed. Remove all plant debris from the garden after the harvest to eliminate overwintering areas for the adult beetle.

Leafminer damage.

Cercospora leaf spot.

Boron-deficient beet.

PROBLEM: Light colored, irregular blotches, blisters, or tunnels appear in the leaves. Brown areas peel apart easily like facial tissue. Tiny black specks are found inside the tunnels.

ANALYSIS: Beet leafminer
(*Pegomya hyoscyami*)
This insect pest belongs to a family of leaf-mining flies. The tiny black or yellow adult fly lays its white eggs on the underside of leaves. When the eggs hatch, the cream-colored maggots bore into the leaf. They tunnel between the upper and lower surfaces of the leaf, feeding on the inner tissue. The tunnels and blotches are called *mines*. The black specks inside are the maggot's droppings. The beet leaves are no longer edible, but the root is. Several overlapping generations occur during the growing season, so larvae are present continually from spring until fall.

SOLUTION: Spray with an insecticide containing *malathion* or *diazinon* when the white egg clusters are first seen under the leaves. Repeat 2 more times at weekly intervals to control succeeding generations. Once the miners enter the leaves, the sprays are ineffective. Spraying after the mines first appear will control only those leafminers that attack after the application. Leafminers are not active in the fall and winter, so if beets will grow in your area at this time of year, you can avoid most of the damage from this pest.

PROBLEM: The leaves have small, circular, distinct spots with dark borders. These spots may run together to form blotches or dead areas. The leaves often turn yellow and die. Leaf spotting is most severe in warm, humid weather, when a fine gray mold may cover the infected tissue. Older leaves are more severely affected than younger ones.

ANALYSIS: Leaf spot
This common, destructive fungus (*Cercospora beticola*) attacks beets, spinach, and Swiss chard. The fungus invades the leaves but not the beet root. However, severe infection damages many leaves and hinders the development of the root. The spotting makes the leaves unappetizing. The fungus is spread by wind, contaminated tools, and splashing water, and is favored by moist conditions and high temperatures. Leaf spot is most common during the summer months and in warm areas. This fungus survives the winter on plant debris not cleaned out of the garden.

SOLUTION: Picking off and destroying the first spotted leaves retards the spread of leaf spot. Leaf spots on beets seldom cause enough damage to warrant fungicide sprays. If your planting is large or the disease becomes very severe, you may spray with a fungicide containing *zineb* at weekly intervals. Do not work among wet plants. If possible, avoid overhead watering; use drip or furrow irrigation instead. Use a mulch to reduce the need for watering. Clean all plant debris from the garden after the harvest to reduce the number of overwintering spores.

PROBLEM: Black areas occur on the outer skin and inside the beet root. The root may be wrinkled and cracked. Plants are stunted and the leaves brown along the edges. The lower surfaces of the leaves turn reddish purple. Bottom leaves die.

ANALYSIS: Boron deficiency
Boron is plant nutrient that is present in most soils. All vegetables require boron, but some require a greater amount than others. Boron is used by the plant to manufacture food and to move the food from one part of the plant to another. Plants suffer from a boron deficiency when boron is either lacking in the soil, or is in a form the plants can't use. Boron deficiency is most common during dry weather and in alkaline soil. Boron may be lacking in any type of soil, but most frequently in sandy soil. Beets are affected when they are more than 1 inch in diameter. The roots are still edible if the discolored areas are cut away. Root rotting fungi and bacteria may invade cracked roots.

SOLUTION: Treat plants as soon as damage is noticed with a solution of 1 tablespoon of household borax dissolved in 12 quarts of water. Apply this solution to a 100-foot row. Next year, treat the soil soon after planting. Repeat the treatment in 2 to 3 weeks. Test the soil pH as instructed on page 903, and correct if necessary to maintain a pH between 6.0 and 7.0. Add organic matter to sandy soil as outlined on page 918. Maintain even soil moisture, so that the soil never dries out.

Curly top.

Damping-off.

PROBLEM: The leaf margins roll upward and feel brittle. The undersides of the leaves are rough, with puckering along the veins. The leaves and roots are stunted; the plant may die.

ANALYSIS: Curly top
This virus disease affects many vegetables, including beets, beans, tomatoes, squash, and melons. The virus is transmitted from plant to plant by the beet leafhopper (*Circulifer tenellus*), and is common only in the West, where this insect lives. The beet leafhopper is a pale greenish yellow insect about 1/8 inch long that feeds from early May through June. It sucks the sap and virus from the infested leaves, and then injects the virus into healthy plants at its next feeding stop. (For more information about leafhoppers, see page 880.) Curly top symptoms vary in their severity, depending on the variety and the age of the plant. Young infected plants usually die. Older plants may turn yellow and die.

SOLUTION: There is no direct control for curly top. To reduce the chance of infection, control the beet leafhopper with an insecticide containing *malathion*, beginning when the insect swarms first appear. For information about controlling disease-carrying insects, see page 880. Destroy infected plants. A light screening of cheesecloth over the plants keeps leafhoppers from landing on the plants.

PROBLEM: Seeds don't sprout, or seedlings fall over soon after they emerge. Areas on the stem at the soil line are water-soaked and discolored. The base of the stem is soft and thin.

ANALYSIS: Damping-off
Damping-off is a common problem in wet soil with a high nitrogen level. Wet, rich soil promotes damping-off in two ways: the fungi are more active under these conditions, and the seedlings are more succulent and susceptible to attack. Damping-off is often a problem with crops that are planted too early in the spring, before the soil has had a chance to dry and warm sufficiently for quick seed germination. Damping-off can also be a problem when the weather remains cloudy and wet while seeds are germinating, or if seedlings are too heavily shaded.

SOLUTION: To prevent damping-off, take these precautions:
1. Allow the surface of the soil to dry slightly between waterings.
2. Do not start seeds in soil that has a high nitrogen level. Add nitrogen fertilizers after the seedlings have produced their first true leaves.
3. Plant seeds after the soil has reached the temperature needed for quick germination, at least 60°F.
4. Protect seeds during germination by coating them with a fungicide containing *captan* or *thiram*. Add a pinch of fungicide to a packet of seeds (or 1/2 teaspoon per pound), and shake well to coat the seeds with the fungicide. For more information on starting seeds, see page 917.

BLUEBERRIES _____

ADAPTATION: Throughout the United States. For varietal adaptations, see page 1003.

PLANTING TIME:
Cold winter areas: Spring.
Mild winter areas: Fall or spring.

PLANTING METHOD: For best fruit set, plant at least three different varieties. Select dormant 2 to 3-year-old plants that are 12 to 36 inches tall. Prune back to 3 or 4 strong shoots. Set plants so the top of their rootball is 1 to 2 inches deeper than the surrounding garden soil. Mulch with a 4 to 6-inch layer of sawdust, pine bark, or leaf mold.

SOIL: Light, acid soil that is high in organic matter. pH 4.0 to 5.2

FERTILIZER: As soon as the bushes begin to grow after planting, feed with ORTHO General Purpose Plant Food 8-8-8, 1 1/2 ounces per plant. For the next 2 years, feed with 3 ounces per plant just as the buds break in the spring. Thereafter, feed with 3 to 8 ounces of *ammonium sulfate* per plant. *Ammonium sulfate* not only fertilizes the bushes, but also helps maintain an acid soil.

WATER:
How much: Apply enough water to wet the soil 1 foot deep at each irrigation.
How often: Water when the soil under the mulch is just barely moist.

HARVEST: Pick blueberries when they are solid blue with a light whitish bloom. Pull them gently from the cluster.

Cranberry fruitworms (¾ life size).

Blueberry maggots and adult (twice life size).

Plum curculio (twice life size).

PROBLEM: Clusters of berries are webbed together with silk. Berries may be shriveled and full of sawdustlike material. Inside the berries are smooth pink-red or pale yellow-green caterpillars about ⅜ to 1 inch long.

ANALYSIS: Cherry fruitworm (*Grapholitha packardii*) or cranberry fruitworm (*Acrobasis vaccinii*)
These 2 fruitworms are serious pests of blueberries and cranberries. They also attack cherries and apples. Each caterpillar destroys 2 to 6 berries. They do not damage the leaves. In midspring, adult moths lay eggs on developing berries and leaves. The caterpillars that hatch from these eggs bore into the berries at the junction of the stem and berry. When they are about half grown, the fruitworms move to another berry, usually one touching the infested berry. This way the fruitworm can move to a new food source without exposing itself. About mid-June, when the caterpillar is full grown, it crawls to the soil, garden debris, or a pruning stub, where it remains through the remainder of the growing season and the winter. Adult moths emerge in midspring to start the cycle again.

SOLUTION: Once the fruit is infested there is no way to kill the worms inside. Handpick and destroy all infested fruit. If your planting is large, or if the fruitworm infestation this year was severe, spray the plants immediately after bloom, before the berries are ¼ inch in diameter, with an insecticide containing *carbaryl*, *diazinon*, or *malathion*. Repeat once 10 days later.

PROBLEM: Ripening blueberries leak juice and are soft and mushy. White, tapered maggots about ⅜ inch long are feeding inside the berries.

ANALYSIS: Blueberry maggot (*Rhagoletis mendax*)
This insect, also called the *blueberry fruitfly*, is the most important pest of blueberries in the Midwest and on the East Coast. Maggots attack both green and ripe fruit, and often ruin an entire crop. They are most severe after unusually cold winters and when the weather is very wet at harvest time, and frequent pickings are not possible. The maggots spend the winter as pupae in the soil. From late June through August, the adult flies lay eggs just under the skin of the fruit. The maggots that hatch from the eggs feed in the berry for about 20 days, then drop to the soil where they pupate for 1 to 2 years. There is only one generation a year.

SOLUTION: Harvest frequently, destroying any infested berries. Next year, beginning in early July, treat the plants with an insecticide containing *carbaryl*, *diazinon*, or *malathion*. Repeat the treatment at intervals of 10 days through the harvest. Treatments the following year may be necessary to control any pupae that mature after two years.

PROBLEM: Fruit ripens earlier than usual. Shriveled, hollow berries lie on the soil beneath the plants. Berries still on the plants have small circular indentations in them. Inside are smooth, legless, yellowish white grubs with brown heads.

ANALYSIS: Plum curculio (*Conotrachelus nenaphar*)
This insect prefers plums and peaches, but also damages blueberries, apples, and cherries. The adult weevil is ¼ inch long, with an elongated snout and brown warty body with gray or white patches. In midspring, it lays 1 egg in a small circular indentation in each berry. Each female weevil lays about 150 eggs. When the eggs hatch, the grubs bore into the center of the fruit, where they feed for several weeks. The infested berries stop growing and fall to the ground. When the grubs are fully grown, the berries are completely hollow. The larvae burrow into the soil to pupate. Several weeks later the adult emerges. If green berries are still on the bushes, the adult lays eggs, starting the cycle again.

SOLUTION: Once the fruit is infested there is no way to kill the grubs inside. Pick and destroy the infested fruit. Next spring, spray the plants with an insecticide containing *carbaryl* or *malathion* immediately after bloom, before the fruits are ¼ inch in diameter. Repeat 2 more times, 7 to 10 days apart.

BLUEBERRIES

Mummy berry.

Botrytis blossom blight.

Red banded leafroller larva and pupa (life size).

PROBLEM: As the berries ripen, they become reddish buff or tan in color. Many fall off before they ripen. Mature berries are gray, shriveled, and hard. Blossoms turn brown and wither. The centers of new leaves are black. Eventually the entire leaf and/or shoot tips wilt and die.

ANALYSIS: Mummy berry
This plant disease is caused by a fungus (*Monilinia vaccinii-corymbosi*) that occurs irregularly, and may be severe some years and nonexistent other years. This is due primarily to the spring weather. Cold, wet weather favors the fungus. The disease spores spend the winter on infected fruit mummies on the ground and on twigs. The spores infect leaves, shoots, and flowers shortly after they begin growing in the spring. The spores infect young fruit through the flower. In order for the disease to develop, spores must land on very young tissue before a natural waxy layer covers the plant surfaces.

SOLUTION: This disease is very difficult to control. Once the berries have mummied, it is too late to do anything this year. Discard all mummies on the twigs and the ground. Next spring, apply the fungicide *triforine* 3 times, 7 to 10 days apart, beginning at bud break. Cultivate around the plants in early spring to bury any remaining mummies. Add 2 inches of sawdust mulch to keep the spores from reaching the new growth.

PROBLEM: Brown spots and blotches appear on the flowers and stems. As the disease progresses, a fuzzy brown or grayish mold forms on the infected tissue. Gray mold often appears on the flowers, especially during periods of cool, wet weather. The leaves and stems may be soft and rotted.

ANALYSIS: Stem and blossom blight
This plant disease is caused by a fungus (*Botrytis cinerea*) that is found on most dead plant tissue. The fungus initially attacks flowers that are weak or dead, causing spotting and mold. The fuzzy mold that develops is composed of fungus strands and millions of microscopic spores. Once gray mold has become established on plant debris and weak or dying flowers, it can invade healthy plant tissue. The fungus is spread by splashing water, or by infected pieces of tissue contacting healthy tissue. Cool temperatures and high humidity favor gray mold growth. Crowded plantings, rain, and overhead watering also enhance the spread of the fungus. Infection is more of a problem in spring and fall, when temperatures are lower. In mild winter areas, where freezing is rare, gray mold can be a year-round problem.

SOLUTION: Spray plants with a fungicide containing *captan* or *benomyl* at the first sign of the disease. Continue spraying at intervals of 10 to 14 days as long as wet weather continues. Clean up plant debris and infected parts. Provide enough space between plants to allow good air circulation. Try to avoid wetting the foliage when watering.

PROBLEM: Leaves are rolled or tied together. Inside the rolled leaves is a tubelike shelter made of black sawdust and silk threads. A yellowish white or purple-brown caterpillar may be found in the tube. The caterpillar may have red stripes.

ANALYSIS: Leafrollers and leaftiers
Leafrollers are caterpillars that roll up leaves and feed inside. Leaftiers tie leaves together with silk threads and feed inside. Several kinds of leafrollers and tiers attack blueberries. Although they may slightly weaken the plant, they do not significantly reduce berry production. Adult moths lay eggs in early spring. From April to September the larvae feed on leaves near the stem tips. They roll the leaves together, and feed on the upper leaf tissue within the tied leaves. This area becomes somewhat discolored on the outside of the leaf. They may also feed on the tips of the tied leaves. After feeding, they move to another set of leaves, roll or tie them, and feed again.

SOLUTION: Spray the plants with an insecticide containing *carbaryl* or *malathion* as soon as the problem is discovered or immediately after bloom. Repeat at intervals of 7 to 10 days as the rolling continues. If only a few stem tips are affected, pick them off and squash the caterpillar inside.

BRAMBLES (BLACKBERRIES, RASPBERRIES)

Putnam scale (4 times life size).

PROBLEM: Nodes, stems, and leaves are covered with white, cottony, cushionlike masses or brownish, crusty bumps or clusters of somewhat flattened reddish, gray, or brownish scaly bumps. The bumps can be picked off. Leaves turn yellow and may drop. Branches are killed by heavy infestations.

ANALYSIS: Scales
These insects are damaging to many plants in the garden. They damage blueberries by reducing berry production and weakening the plant. The scales lay their eggs on leaves or bark, and in spring to midsummer the young scales, called *crawlers*, settle on leaves and twigs. The small (1/10 inch), soft-bodied young feed by inserting their mouthparts and sucking sap from the plant. The legs usually atrophy and, with some types, a shell develops over the body. The types of scale that do not develop shells are very conspicuous. The females are covered with a white, cottony egg sac containing up to 2500 eggs. Scales covered with a shell are less noticeable. The shell often blends in with the plant and the eggs are inconspicuous beneath the covering.

SOLUTION: Control scales with ORTHO Fruit & Vegetable Insect Control when the young are active. Contact your local Cooperative Extension Office (see page 1011) to determine the best time to spray for scales in your area. Repeat if the plants become reinfested. Next spring, just before the new leaves emerge, spray the plants with a *dormant oil*. For more information about scales, see page 878.

BRAMBLES

ADAPTATION: Throughout the United States. For varietal adaptions, see page 1008.

PLANTING TIME: Late fall or early spring.

PLANTING METHOD: Select 1-year-old dormant plants that are 12 to 24 inches tall. Set plants 3 to 6 feet apart, and deep enough so that the top of their rootball is 1 inch deeper than the surrounding garden soil. Prune canes back to 6 to 12-inch stubs.

SOIL: Any good garden soil that is high in organic matter. pH 5.5 to 6.8

FERTILIZER: At planting time, use 1 pound of ORTHO General Purpose Plant Food 8-8-8 per 20-foot row. Thereafter, apply 2 pounds per 20-foot row once a year in early spring before new growth begins.

WATER:
How much: Apply enough water at each irrigation to wet the soil 1 to 2 feet deep.
How often: Water when the soil 2 inches deep is barely moist.

HARVEST: Berries are ripe when they are a deep, rich color and slightly soft. Ripe fruit are easily removed when pulled gently. When picked, only raspberries pull free of their central core. All other bramble fruits have a central core. Pick every 2 to 3 days. Protect ripening fruit from birds with netting available in your garden center or through mail-order garden supply companies. Store berries in the refrigerator until use.

Raspberry fruitworm (twice life size).

PROBLEM: Berries drop or decay before they are fully ripe. Inside the fruit are light yellow worms, 1/4 inch long, with brown markings. Holes are chewed in the leaves.

ANALYSIS: Raspberry fruitworm
(*Byturus* species)
Raspberries and loganberries in the northern part of the country are attacked by these pests. Early red raspberries are the most severely damaged. Both the adults and larvae feed on buds, blossoms, leaves, and fruit. Feeding damage to the blossoms and developing fruit reduces fruit set and yield. When infestations are large, many leaves are eaten. Light brown adult beetles 1/8 inch long emerge from the soil in early spring as the new leaves are unfolding. They feed on these leaves and buds, and the females lay their white eggs in the blossoms and fruit. The larvae that hatch then feed in the fruit. After feeding, they drop to the soil, where they pupate, and emerge the following spring as adults. There is only one generation a year.

SOLUTION: Once the fruit is infested, sprays are ineffective. Remove and destroy all infested berries. Next year, treat the plants with ORTHO Fruit & Vegetable Insect Control. Spray first when the blossom buds first appear, and again just before the blossoms open.

BRAMBLES (BLACKBERRIES, RASPBERRIES)

Fruit rot on blackberries.

Verticillium wilt of raspberry.

Raspberry crown borer (life size).

PROBLEM: Ripening berries are covered with tufts of gray, green, white, or black cottony growths. A smelly, watery liquid may ooze from berries.

ANALYSIS: Fruit rot
Several different fungi (*Botrytis cinerea, Monilinia fructicola,* and *Rhizopus nigricans*) cause fruit rot on raspberries and blackberries. These diseases are widespread and develop fastest on overripe and bruised raspberries. Warm, wet weather, especially during harvest, favors these fungi. They can infect the fruit before or after harvest.

SOLUTION: Fungicide sprays help reduce fruit rot, but good harvest practices are a must. Pick ripening berries frequently to avoid an accumulation of overripe fruit. Harvest in the cool early morning, and handle the fruit carefully to avoid bruising. Cool the picked berries in the refrigerator immediately. To reduce fruit rot, spray the plants with a fungicide containing *captan*. Repeat at intervals of 7 to 10 days during the harvest.

PROBLEM: In mid to late summer the leaves turn yellow, wilt, dry, and fall off. Yellowing starts on the lower leaves and moves up the stems. Canes may turn bluish black from the soil line upward. Fruit withers, or is small and tasteless. Plants may die the following year.

ANALYSIS: Verticillium wilt
This wilt disease affects many garden plants. It is caused by a soil-inhabiting fungus (*Verticillium albo-atrum*) that persists indefinitely on plant debris or in the soil. The disease is spread by contaminated seeds, plants, soil, and equipment. The fungus enters the plant through the roots and spreads into the canes and leaves through the water-conducting vessels in the stems. The vessels become discolored and plugged. This plugging cuts off the flow of water and nutrients to the leaves, causing leaf yellowing and wilting. Plants under stress from hot, dry midsummer weather are most susceptible.

SOLUTION: No chemical control is available. It is best to destroy infected plants. Verticillium can be removed from the soil by fumigation techniques. For more information about soil fumigation, see page 919. However, the best solution is usually to use varieties that are resistant to verticillium wilt.

Blackberry varieties resistant to verticillium wilt: Evergreen and Himalaya. Ollalieberry and loganberry are also resistant.

PROBLEM: In early summer, canes wilt and begin dying. Some canes are spindly, lack vigor, and grow very little. Canes often break off easily at ground level. There may be white grubs, $\frac{1}{4}$ to $1\frac{1}{4}$ inches long inside some of the canes.

ANALYSIS: Raspberry crown borer (*Pennitsetia marginata*)
This insect pest, also called the *raspberry root borer,* attacks brambles in the northern United States. The borer damages plants by feeding on the roots and crown (base) of the plant. Root feeding weakens all cane fruits, but often kills raspberries. The crown borer has a 2-year life cycle. In late summer, the adult moth lays a total of about 100 eggs on the undersides of several leaves. The eggs hatch in early fall, and the larvae move to the soil near the plant crown, where they spend the winter. As the weather warms in the spring, the larvae enter the plant and begin hollowing out the crown. This feeding causes the canes to swell and eventually die. The larvae continue feeding throughout the year, spend the winter in the canes, and feed again the spring. They mature and emerge from the canes as adults in late summer. One and two year old larvae may be present at the same time.

SOLUTION: In early spring, drench the crown and lower 2 feet of the canes with an insecticide containing *diazinon*. Repeat controls annually for at least 2 years because of this insect's 2-year life cycle. Cut out and destroy canes when pruning.

Cane blight on raspberries.

Spider mite damage.

Crown gall on blackberry.

PROBLEM: Branches wilt and die in midsummer. Brownish purple areas occur on pruned ends or wounded areas of canes and extend downward, sometimes encircling the stem. Infected canes turn gray in late summer.

ANALYSIS: Cane blight
This plant disease is caused by a fungus (*Leptosphaeria coniothyrium*). It is more prevalent on black raspberries than on red and purple raspberries and blackberries. The fungus spends the winter on diseased canes. The spores are spread from plant to plant by the wind. In wet weather in late spring and early summer, the spores enter canes through cracks in the bark, broken fruit stems, and wounds from pruning and insects. The spores don't infect young tissue directly. Canes weakened from cane blight are more subject to winter injury.

SOLUTION: Apply ORTHO Dormant Disease Control in late fall and early spring. Follow with 2 applications of a fungicide containing *ferbam* or *folpet*: one just before bloom, when the new canes are 1½ to 2 feet tall; and the other just after harvest. Remove infected canes before growth starts in the spring. Prune in dry weather at least 3 days before rain, just above a bud so the wounds have time to dry up.

PROBLEM: Leaves are stippled, yellowing, and dirty. Leaves may dry out and drop. There may be webbing between leaves, or on the young stems and lower surfaces of the leaves. To determine if the plant is infested with mites, hold a sheet of white paper underneath an affected leaf and tap the leaf sharply. Minute green, red, or yellow specks the size of pepper grains will drop to the paper and begin to crawl around. These pests are easily seen against the white background.

ANALYSIS: Spider mites
These mites, related to spiders, are major pests of many garden plants, including brambles. They cause damage by sucking sap from the underside of the leaves. As a result of feeding, the green leaf pigment disappears, producing the stippled appearance. Mites are active throughout the growing season, but are favored by hot, dry weather (70°F and up). By midsummer, they build up to tremendous numbers.

SOLUTION: Spray with ORTHO Fruit & Vegetable Insect Control when damage is first noticed. Spray the leaves thoroughly, being sure to cover the undersides of the leaves. Repeat the treatment 3 more times at intervals of 7 days. Hose down the plants frequently to knock off webs and mites. Next spring, spray the plants with *lime sulfur* when the leaves are just beginning to emerge.

PROBLEM: Plants are stunted, break and fall over easily, and produce dry, seedy berries. Irregular, wartlike growths (galls) may appear on canes. The canes may dry out and crack. Galls also occur just below the soil level on the roots and crown. They range from pinhead-sized to several inches in diameter, and are white or grayish brown.

ANALYSIS: Cane and crown gall
These diseases are caused by bacteria (*Agrobacterium rubi* and *A. tumefaciens*) that occur on blackberries, raspberries, boysenberries, loganberries, and youngberries throughout the United States. The plants become weak and produce fewer berries. The bacteria are often brought to a garden initially on the roots of an infected plant, and are spread with the soil and by contaminated pruning tools. The bacteria enter the plant through wounds in the roots or the base of the stem (the crown). They produce a substance that stimulates rapid cell growth in the plant, causing gall formation on the roots, crown, and canes. The galls disrupt the flow of water and nutrients up the roots and stems, weakening and stunting the top of the plant. Galls do not usually cause the plant to die.

SOLUTION: Crown gall cannot be eliminated from the plant. Although infected plants may survive for many years, they will produce few berries. Dig up and discard diseased plants and the soil within 6 inches of a gall. Wait at least 3 years before replanting brambles in areas where the disease has occurred. Plant gall-free plants in clean soil. Prune and cultivate carefully to avoid wounding plants. For more information on crown gall, see page 860.

BRAMBLES (BLACKBERRIES, RASPBERRIES)

Anthracnose spots on raspberry.

Powdery mildew on raspberry.

Orange rust on blackberry.

PROBLEM: Stem tips die. Oval spots with purple edges and light gray centers appear on the canes. Spots enlarge, sometimes circling the entire stem. Canes may dry and crack. Most of the spots occur on the inside of the canes toward the center of the plant, and from 6 to 30 inches up from the ground. The leaves may have small yellow spots with purple margins. The centers of the spots often drop out, leaving a hole.

ANALYSIS: Anthracnose
This disease, caused by a fungus (*Elsinoe veneta*), is one of the most important diseases of black and purple raspberries. Although the disease is common on red raspberries, they are not seriously affected by it. Overgrown, unpruned bushes are very susceptible to anthracnose. The disease is most serious when heavy rains continue late in the spring and into the summer. The fungus survives the winter in infected canes, and infects new growth in the early spring. Canes weakened by anthracnose are more susceptible to winter injury.

SOLUTION: Apply a fungicide containing *lime sulfur* in early spring when the leaf buds swell and expose from ½ to ¾ inch of the new leaves. This is the most important and effective time to spray. Follow with 3 applications of a fungicide containing *ferbam* or *captan*: (1) when the new canes are 6 to 8 inches tall; (2) when they are 12 to 15 inches tall; and (3) just before bloom. After harvest, prune out old infected canes.

PROBLEM: A whitish gray powder covers the leaves, fruit, and young growing tips of the canes. Canes may be dwarfed or distorted. Fruit may wither and die.

ANALYSIS: Powdery mildew
This common plant disease seriously affects red raspberries and occasionally attacks purple and black raspberries and blackberries. It is caused by a fungus (*Sphaerotheca humuli*) that thrives in both humid and dry weather. The powdery patches consist of fungal strands and spores. The spores are spread by the wind to healthy plants. The fungus saps plant nutrients, causing yellowing and sometimes the death of the leaf. A severe infection may kill the plant. Since this powdery mildew attacks many different kinds of plants, the fungus from a diseased plant may infect other types of plants in the garden. (For a list of susceptible plants, see page 995.) Under favorable conditions, powdery mildew can spread through a row of berries in a matter of days or weeks.

SOLUTION: Spray the plants with a fungicide containing *benomyl* when the blossoms first open. Repeat at weekly intervals if the plants become reinfected. Next fall, and again in the spring as the buds begin to swell, spray the plants with ORTHO Orthorix Spray. Space the plants far enough apart to allow good air circulation so they can dry rapidly after rain or watering.

Red raspberry varieties resistant to powdery mildew: Meeker, Sumner, and Willamette.

PROBLEM: Leaves are dwarfed, misshapen, and yellowish. Blisterlike pustules and bright orange dust cover the undersides of the leaves.

ANALYSIS: Orange rust
This plant disease is caused by a fungus (*Gymnoconia peckiana*). It is severe on wild and cultivated blackberries and dewberries. It sometimes attacks black raspberries, but doesn't affect red and purple raspberries. The disease spreads throughout the entire plant. Infected plants never recover and never bloom. Spores are produced on the plant each year after it is infected. The fungus spreads from plant to plant on the wind. In the spring, orange spores land on leaves. After infecting them, the fungus spreads throughout the plant into the canes, crown, and roots. The disease spreads into new shoots as the plant grows.

SOLUTION: Fungicide sprays and pruning are not effective. Remove and destroy infected plants as soon as they are noticed. Remove any wild blackberries growing nearby. Thin the plants for good air circulation. Pull out all weeds. Grow rust-resistant varieties.

Blackberry varieties resistant to rust: Boysenberry, Ebony King, Eldorado, Lawton, Orange Evergreen, and Youngberry. Leucretia is a rust-resistant dewberry.

CABBAGE FAMILY

CABBAGE FAMILY

ADAPTATION: Throughout the United States.

PLANTING TIME: See page 1009.

PLANTING METHOD: Set transplants so the top of their rootball is even with the garden soil.

Spacing: Cabbage, cauliflower, and broccoli — 15 to 24 inches apart; Brussels sprouts — 30 to 36 inches apart; kohlrabi — 4 to 6 inches apart; kale and collards — 8 to 12 inches apart. Or, sow seeds ½ to 1 inch deep and 1 inch apart. Thin according to the spacings listed above when the seedlings have 2 or 3 leaves.

SOIL: Any good garden soil. pH 6.0 to 7.0

FERTILIZER: At planting time use 2 to 4 pounds of ORTHO Vegetable Garden Food 5–10–10 per 100 square feet, or 1 pound per 25-foot row. Side-dress every 3 to 4 weeks with 1 pound per 25-foot row, or 1 to 2 tablespoons per plant.

Containers: Water thoroughly every 2 to 3 weeks with a solution of ORTHO Tomato & Vegetable Food 6–18–6.

WATER:

How much: Apply enough water at each irrigation to wet the soil 8 to 10 inches deep.

How often: Water when the soil 1 inch deep is barely moist.

HARVEST:

Broccoli: When the buds are still tight, before they open into yellow flowers. Smaller heads will grow along the stem after the first head is harvested.

Brussels sprouts: Pick sprouts from the bottom up when they are about 1 inch in diameter and still tight. Remove the leaves as you pick.

Cabbage: Cut just below the head when firm and before it cracks.

Chinese cabbage: Cut the entire head when it is 12 to 16 inches tall.

Cauliflower: Cut when the heads are 6 to 8 inches in diameter with tight curds. For information on blanching, see page 714.

Collards and kale: Pick the leaves when plant is 1 foot tall. Or the entire plant may be harvested. Kale flavor improves after a freeze.

Kohlrabi: Harvest when the bulb is 2 to 3 inches in diameter.

Growth cracks.

PROBLEM: The head of the cabbage plant cracks open soon after it reaches picking size.

ANALYSIS: Growth cracks
A cabbage head may crack if not harvested soon after it matures. Splitting results from the pressure of water taken up into the head after it is solid and mature. Tomatoes, carrots, potatoes, and sweet potatoes are also susceptible to growth cracking. Cracked vegetables are still edible.

SOLUTION: Harvest cabbage heads as soon as they feel firm. Stagger planting times so that all the heads don't mature at the same time. Or select several varieties that will ripen at different times. There are 3 ways to delay harvest by reducing the water supply to mature heads: (1) When the heads are firm, give the plants less water at each watering; (2) Break off some of the roots by lifting and twisting the cabbage plant; (3) Cut the roots on 2 sides of the plant by pushing a spade into the soil 6 to 8 inches deep. Surplus cabbage heads can be stored in the crisper section of your refrigerator.

CABBAGE FAMILY — PROBLEMS WITH THE HEAD

Bolting cabbage.

Small broccoli head.

Discolored cauliflower head.

PROBLEM: In hot weather, an elongated stalk with flowers grows from the main stem of broccoli, cauliflower, and Brussels sprouts plants. On cabbage, the head splits open, and the stalk emerges from within.

ANALYSIS: Bolting
Bolting, or seed stalk formation, results from exposure of the plants to cold temperatures early in their lives. Once a plant has matured to the point where its leaves are about 2 inches wide, exposure to cold (40° to 50°F) temperatures for several days in a row causes flower buds to form within the growing point. These buds remain dormant until hot weather arrives. With the arrival of hot weather, the buds develop into tall flower stalks. As the plant bolts, its flavor deteriorates and bitterness develops.

SOLUTION: Discard plants that have bolted. Avoid setting out plants too early in the winter or spring. If cabbage plants are set out in the fall or winter, harvest them before hot weather causes them to bolt. Cutting the flower stalk will not prevent poor flavor from developing.

PROBLEM: Broccoli plants form small heads or none at all. Plant may be slightly wilted, yellow, or flowering.

ANALYSIS: Poor heading
Broccoli plants may develop small or no heads for any of several reasons. Small heads are of low quality, with either a bitter taste or little flavor.
1. *Planted too close:* Roots compete with each other for water and nutrients.
2. *Dry soil:* Broccoli needs constant moisture throughout the growing season.
3. *Root maggots:* These pests feed on roots and weaken the plants.
4. *Nematodes:* These soil-inhabiting microscopic worms also weaken plants.
5. *Clubroot:* This fungal root disease weakens and kills plants.
6. *Bolting:* Plants go to seed in hot weather.
7. *Poor soil fertility:* Broccoli plants are heavy feeders, and need additional nutrients throughout the season.

SOLUTION: Follow these steps to produce large broccoli heads.
1. Set plants 15 to 24 inches apart in rows 24 to 36 inches apart.
2. For watering instructions, see page 713.
3. To control root maggots, see the recommendations on page 716.
4. For information on nematodes, see page 685.
5. For information on clubroot, see page 718.
6. To prevent bolting, see the recommendations on this page.
7. Follow the fertilizing instructions on page 713.
If possible, rotate your cabbage family planting site every year.

PROBLEM: Yellow, green, or purple discolorations mar cauliflower heads. The leaves are healthy and green.

ANALYSIS: Discolored head
Developing cauliflower heads need to be protected from the sunlight to remain white. Exposure to light causes yellow, green, or purple pigment to form. The resulting discoloration not only affects the appearance, but also causes a stronger flavor. Brown or black spots, up to 1 inch in diameter, on the head may be caused by the disease *downy mildew*, as described on page 717.

SOLUTION: Prevent further discoloration by tying the lower leaves up over the developing heads. To avoid possible head rotting, wait until the head is 2½ inches in diameter. Be sure the heads are dry, then tie the leaves loosely, giving the head room to grow. Secure the leaves with soft twine or a wide elastic band. This "blanching" or whitening process takes one to two weeks, depending on the weather and the variety of cauliflower. Check under the protective canopy occasionally for hiding pests. The head is ready for harvest when it is firm and shows no signs of splitting.

To avoid the need for blanching, plant the variety "Self Blanch," which does what its name implies — its leaves naturally curl over the head without assistance. The "Purple Head" variety doesn't need blanching either. Its head is a purple color that turns green when cooked.

INSECTS

Imported cabbageworm. *Insert:* Adult (life size).

Diamondback moth larvae (life size).

Cutworm (twice life size).

PROBLEM: Round or irregular holes appear in leaves. Green worms with light stripes down their backs, up to 1½ inches long, feed on the leaves or heads. Masses of green or brown pellets may be found between the leaves. Cabbage and cauliflower heads may be tunnelled.

ANALYSIS: Cabbage worms
These destructive worms are either the *cabbage looper* (*Trichoplusia ni*) or the *imported cabbageworm* (*Pieris rapae*). Both worms attack all members of the cabbage family, as well as lettuce. Adults lay eggs throughout the growing season. Adults of the imported cabbageworm attach yellow, bullet-shaped eggs to the undersides of leaves. These white butterflies are frequently seen around cabbage plants in the daytime. The brownish cabbage looper moth lays pale green eggs on the upper surfaces of leaves in the evening. Worms may be present from early spring until late fall. In the South, they may be present all year. Worms spend the winter as pupae attached to a plant or nearby object.

SOLUTION: Control cabbage worms with ORTHO Sevin Garden Dust, ORTHO Diazinon Insect Spray, or ORTHO Rotenone Dust or Spray as soon as damage is seen. Cabbage worms can also be killed with *Bacillus thuringiensis*, a biological control, while they are small. Repeat treatments weekly as long as worms are found, but stop 3 days before harvest. Remove plant debris after harvest to destroy the pupae.

The cabbage looper is named for its habit of arching its back and moving in a looping motion.

PROBLEM: Small holes and transparent holes appear in the leaves. Small (¼ inch) green worms feed on the undersides of the leaves. When disturbed, the worms wriggle rapidly and often drop from the plant on a silk thread.

ANALYSIS: Diamondback moth (*Plutella xylostella*)
These worms are the larvae of gray or brown moths that fly in the evening. The adults don't damage plants. The larvae feed on the undersides of leaves of members of the cabbage family, chewing holes and eating the lower surfaces of the leaves. After feeding for about 2 weeks, the larvae pupate in transparent silken cocoons attached to the undersides of leaves. Adult moths spend the winter hidden under plant debris. There are 2 to 7 generations a year that damage both spring and fall plantings.

SOLUTION: Apply ORTHO Diazinon Soil & Foliage Dust or ORTHO Diazinon Insect Spray to the foliage when the young worms first appear, or when the leaves show feeding damage. The dust must reach the undersides of the leaves in order to be most effective. Repeat the dusting each week as long as the caterpillars are found. Clean up plant debris in the fall and cultivate the soil thoroughly to expose and destroy overwintering moths.

PROBLEM: Seedlings and young transplants are chewed or cut off near the ground. If you dig near the freshly damaged plant you may find dull gray, brown, or black worms about 2 inches deep. They have spots or stripes on their smooth bodies, are about 1½ to 2 inches long, and coil when they are disturbed.

ANALYSIS: Cutworms
Several species of these moth larvae are pests in the vegetable garden. The most likely pests of young cabbage plants set out early in the season are the surface-feeding cutworms. Cutworms spend the days hidden in the soil, and feed only at night. A cutworm can sever the stems of several young plants in a single night. All adult cutworms are dark, night-flying moths with bands or stripes on their forewings. In the South, cutworms may also attack fall-planted cabbage.

SOLUTION: Apply ORTHO Diazinon Soil & Turf Insect Control or ORTHO Diazinon Soil & Foliage Dust around the base of the plants when stem cutting is observed. Since cutworms are difficult to control, it may be necessay to repeat dusting at weekly intervals. Before transplanting in the same area of planting in an area previously full of weeds, apply a preventive treatment of ORTHO Diazinon Soil & Turf Insect Control and work it into the soil. Further reduce damage with "cutworm collars" around the stem of each plant. These collars can be made of stiff paper or aluminum foil. They should be at least 1 inch high and be pressed firmly into the soil. Cultivate the soil thoroughly in late summer and fall to expose and destroy eggs, pupae, and larvae.

Cabbage root maggot (life size).

Flea beetles (twice life size).

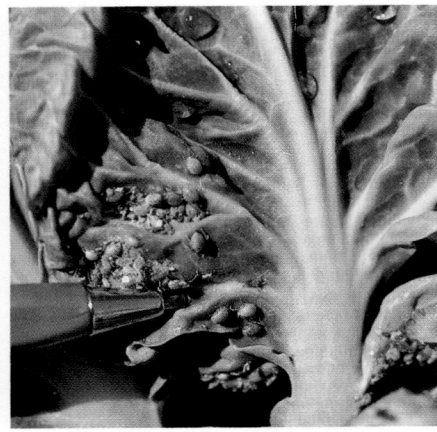

Aphids on cabbage (twice life size).

PROBLEM: Young plants wilt in the heat of the day. They may later turn yellow and die. Soft-bodied, white maggots about 1/3 inch long, are feeding in the roots. The roots are honeycombed with slimy channels and scarred by brown grooves. Damage is particularly severe during cool, moist weather in spring, early summer, and fall.

ANALYSIS: Cabbage maggot
(*Hylemya brassicae*)
The cabbage maggot is an important pest in the northern United States. Early maggots attack the roots and stems of cabbage, cauliflower, broccoli, radishes, and turnips in the spring and early summer. Later insects injure late cabbage, turnips, and radishes in the fall. The adult is a gray fly, somewhat smaller than a housefly, with black stripes and bristles down its back. It lays eggs on stems and nearby soil. The maggots hatch in 2 to 3 days and tunnel into the stems and roots of plants, sometimes to a depth of 6 inches. Not only does the cabbage maggot cause feeding damage, but it spreads black rot bacteria (see 717).

SOLUTION: Once the growing plant wilts and turns yellow, nothing can be done. To control maggots in the next planting, mix ORTHO Diazinon Soil & Turf Insect Control (granules) or ORTHO Diazinon Soil & Foliage Dust 4 to 6 inches into the soil before seeding or transplanting. Control lasts about 1 month. Since control depends on the maggots coming into direct contact with the insecticide, correct timing and thorough mixing are important. To prevent egg laying, screen flies from the seedbed with a cheesecloth cover.

PROBLEM: Leaves are riddled with shotholes, about 1/8 inch in diameter. Tiny (1/16 inch) black beetles jump like fleas when disturbed. Leaves of seedlings and eventually whole plants may wilt and die.

ANALYSIS: Flea beetles
These beetles jump like fleas, but are not related to them. Both adult and immature flea beetles feed on a wide variety of garden vegetables. The immature beetle, a legless grey grub, injures plants by feeding on the roots and the lower surface of leaves. Adults chew holes in leaves. Flea beetles are most damaging to seedlings and young plants. Leaves of seedlings riddled with holes dry out quickly and die. Adult beetles spend the winter in soil and garden debris. They emerge in early spring to feed on weeds until vegetables sprout or plants are set in the garden. Grubs hatch from eggs laid in the soil and feed for 2 to 3 weeks. After pupating in the soil, they emerge as adults to repeat the cycle. There are 1 to 4 generations a year. Adults may feed up to 2 months.

SOLUTION: Control flea beetles with ORTHO Sevin Garden Dust or ORTHO Rotenone Dust or Spray when the leaves first show damage. Watch new growth for evidence of further damage, and repeat the treatment at weekly intervals as needed. Clean all debris from the garden after harvest to eliminate overwintering spots for adult beetles.

PROBLEM: Some leaves are yellowed and cupped downward. Tiny (1/8 inch) pale green or gray soft-bodied insects cluster under leaves, on stems, and on heads. There may be a shiny, sticky substance coating the leaves. Ants may be present.

ANALYSIS: Aphids
Aphids do little damage in small numbers. However, they are extremely prolific and populations can rapidly build up to damaging numbers during the growing season. Damage occurs when the aphid sucks the juices from the plant. The aphid is unable to digest fully all the sugar in the plant sap and excretes the excess in a fluid called honeydew. The honeydew often drops onto the leaves below. Ants feed on the sticky substance, and are often present where there is an aphid infestation. The most common aphid attacking the cabbage family is the *cabbage aphid (Brevicoryne brassicae)*. The cabbage aphid spends the winter as eggs on plant debris in the garden. In the South, they are active year-round.

SOLUTION: Spray with ORTHO Malathion 50 Insect Spray or ORTHO Diazinon Soil & Foliage Dust as soon as the insects appear. Repeat at intervals of 1 week if the plant is reinfected. Clean all plant debris from the garden after harvest to reduce the number of overwintering eggs.

DISCOLORED LEAVES

Downy mildew on broccoli.

Alternaria leaf spot on Chinese cabbage.

Black rot.

PROBLEM: Small irregular tannish purple to dark brown spots appear on the lowest leaves. Later, these spots enlarge, turn yellow, dry, and the leaves drop off. In moist weather a downy white mold appears on the undersides of the leaves opposite the leaf spot. There may be sunken black spots up to 1 inch in diameter on cabbage heads, and a similar blackening on cauliflower curds and broccoli. Seedlings turn yellow and die in a few days.

ANALYSIS: Downy mildew
This plant disease is caused by a fungus (*Peronospora parasitica*) that affects all members of the cabbage family at any stage in their growth. It is most devastating to seedlings, which can die in only a few days. Moisture and temperature are important to the spread, growth, and development of the fungus. The downy growth consists of fungus spores that are spread by splashing water and wind to other leaves or plants. The disease develops most rapidly when night temperatures range from 45° to 60°F for 4 nights in a row, and day temperatures do not go above 75°F. Affected heads and leaves are edible but unappetizing.

SOLUTION: Apply ORTHO Vegetable Disease Control when the young plants are first set out. Repeat at weekly intervals as long as cool, moist conditions prevail. To discourage furthur infection, take steps to reduce the excess moisture in the garden. Allow enough space between maturing plants for air to circulate freely. Avoid overhead watering.

PROBLEM: Small, circular, yellow spots appear on the older leaves. As the spots enlarge to 2 to 3 inches in diameter, they develop brown concentric rings. The spots may be covered with a black growth. Seedlings may be stunted and have dark spots on the stems. Cauliflower and broccoli heads turn brown along the margins.

ANALYSIS: Alternaria leaf spot
This plant disease is caused by fungi (*Alternaria* species) that attack members of the cabbage family that are low in vigor, poorly fertilized or under environmental stress. When spotting is severe, the size and flavor of the yield may be reduced. The fungi are most active in hot (75° to 85°F), wet weather, when rain or dew keeps the leaves wet for more than 9 hours. These fungi are spread by splashing water or wind. They generally survive the winter in plant debris, and may be introduced into the garden on contaminated seeds or plants.

SOLUTION: Treat infected plants at the first sign of the disease with ORTHO Vegetable Disease Control or a fungicide containing *maneb* or *zineb*. Repeat the treatment at intervals of 7 to 10 days until the weather is no longer favorable to the spread of the disease. To reduce the amount of overwintering spores, remove all plant debris from the garden after harvest. Rotate the cabbage family planting site every year. Keep plants healthy by following the cultural guidelines on page 713.

PROBLEM: Young plants turn yellow, then brown, and die. On older plants, yellow areas develop along the leaf margins, then progress into the leaf in a V-shape; these areas later turn brown and die. Lower (older) leaves wilt and drop off. The veins running from the infected leaf margins to the center stem are black. When the stem is cut across, a black ring and sometimes yellow ooze are seen in the cross-section.

ANALYSIS: Black rot
This plant disease is caused by a bacterium (*Xanthomonas campestris*) that affects all members of the cabbage family at any stage in their growth. The bacteria live in or on seed or in infected plant debris for as long as 2 years. Insects, splashing water, and garden tools carry bacteria to other leaves and plants. They enter the plant through natural openings or wounds and spread in the water- and nutrient-conducting vessels of the plant. The infected tissue may form pockets where dead cells and bacteria accumulate as a yellow ooze. Warm, humid weather favors the spread and development of the bacteria. Black rot can kill seedlings rapidly. The diseased heads are edible but unappetizing.

SOLUTION: There are no chemical controls for black rot. Discard infected plants. To avoid further infection, plant only disease-free seed and healthy plants. Place plants far enough apart to allow good air circulation. Avoid overhead irrigation. Plant in soil that has not grown cabbage for at least 2 years.

Cabbage varieties resistant to black rot: Defender and Guardian.

CABBAGE FAMILY — DISCOLORED LEAVES

Watery soft rot.

Black leg on cabbage.

Clubroot on kohlrabi.

PROBLEM: A water-soaked area develops on the stem near the soil line. As it extends upward leaves die, wither, and droop to the ground. The head becomes wet and slimy. In moist weather, a thick, white, cottony mold covers the head. White to black pellets about the size of a pea are found in the mold and between dead leaves.

ANALYSIS: Watery soft rot
This plant disease is caused by a fungus (*Sclerotinia sclerotiorum*) that attacks cabbage and Chinese cabbage. All parts of the plant may become infected. The infection starts on the stem and spreads downward, rotting the roots. As it spreads upward, the leaves die and the head rots. The fungus is most active in moderate (55° to 75°F), wet weather. Water on the leaves from rain, fog, dew, and irrigation provide the moisture necessary for infection. The fungus survives the winter inside the pellets in the soil and on infected plant debris.

SOLUTION: There are no chemical controls for this disease. Remove and destroy all infected plants when symptoms are first observed. Avoid overhead watering by using drip or furrow irrigation. Clean all plant debris from the garden after harvest to reduce the amount of overwintering spores. Rotate the cabbage planting site every year.

PROBLEM: Brown spots with gray centers appear on the lower stems and leaves. Tiny black specks appear in the spots. Stems turn black. Plants become stunted, yellow, wilt, and may die. Wilted leaves remain attached to the stem.

ANALYSIS: Black leg
This plant disease is caused by a fungus (*Phoma lingam*) that is prevalent in wet weather, especially in early summer. All parts of the plant may be infected. Infections on the stem spread downward, rotting the roots. Plants usually die, but when the soil is moist they may grow new roots. The fungal spores live in the soil and on plant debris for up to 3 years, and may be introduced into the garden on infected seeds or plants. The spores spread to healthy plants in splashing water. The leaves must be wet from rain, dew, or irrigation for infection to occur.

SOLUTION: There are no chemical controls for this disease. Remove and destroy all infected plants. Do not work among wet plants. Avoid overhead watering by using drip or furrow irrigation. Remove all plant debris from the garden after harvest to reduce the number of overwintering spores. Rotate the cabbage family planting site every year. Purchase treated seeds and healthy plants from a reputable nursery. Before planting, seeds may be immersed in hot (122°F) water for 25 minutes to kill any spores that may be on them.

PROBLEM: The plant wilts on hot, sunny days and recovers at night. The older (outer) leaves turn yellow and drop. The roots are swollen and misshapen. The largest swellings are just below the soil surface. Growth slows, and the plant eventually dies.

ANALYSIS: Clubroot
This plant disease is caused by a soil-inhabiting fungus (*Plasmodiophora brassicae*) that persists in the soil for many years. Warm, moist weather conditions, together with an acid soil favor the infection. The fungus causes cells to grow and divide within the root tissue. This causes swelling and a general weakening of the plant, allowing other fungi and bacteria to invade the roots and cause root rot. As the roots decompose, they liberate millions of spores into the soil, where they are spread by shoes, tools, or in drainage water. Most members of the cabbage family are susceptible to clubroot. Most rutabaga varieties and many turnip varieties are resistant. Weeds in this family, such as mustard, pennycress, and shepherds purse, can also harbor the disease.

SOLUTION: Once a plant is infected, it cannot be cured. To reduce the severity of the disease next year, do not grow susceptible plants where any members of the cabbage family have grown for the past 7 years. If you must plant in infected soil, pour ¾ cup of a solution of 3 tablespoons of *PCNB 75 WP* fungicide per gallon of water in the soil around the roots of each transplant. To discourage infection, lime the soil to a pH of 7.2. For liming instructions, see page 1002.

CARROTS

CARROTS

ADAPTATION: Throughout the United States.

PLANTING TIME: See page 1009.

PLANTING METHOD: Sow carrot seeds ¼ inch deep. When they have 2 or 3 leaves, thin them to stand 1 to 3 inches apart. Thinning is very important for good shape.

SOIL: Light, friable, and free from rocks and clods. For heavy soil, see page 719. pH 6.0 to 8.0

FERTILIZER: At planting time, use 2 pounds of ORTHO Vegetable Garden Food 5–10–10 per 100 square feet, or ¾ pound per 25-foot row. Side-dress every 3 to 4 weeks with ¾ pound per 25-foot row.

WATER:
How much: Apply enough water at each irrigation to wet the soil 12 to 15 inches deep.
How often: Water when the soil 1 inch deep is barely moist. Do not let the soil dry out.

HARVEST: Pull carrots any time from finger-size until they reach the size stated on the seed packet. When pulling carrots, select the largest first, so that those remaining have room to enlarge. Carrots can be left in the ground and harvested over the winter.

Green root top.

PROBLEM: Carrot root tops are green and have a strong flavor. Leaves are healthy.

ANALYSIS: Green root tops
Tops of carrot roots turn green when exposed to sunlight. The root tops may become exposed when heavy rains or irrigation water wash away the soil. Soil may also be moved away during cultivation. The green portions of the root have a strong flavor. The orange part of the root is edible.

SOLUTION: Cut away the green portion of the carrot before eating. Protect the carrot root tops in the ground by covering with a 1 to 2-inch layer of soil whenever exposed. Or mulch the plants with a 4 to 6-inch layer of straw or several sheets of newspaper to prevent water from washing away the soil. Do not cultivate closer than 6 to 8 inches to the plants.

Carrots stunted from growing in heavy soil.

PROBLEM: Roots are forked, twisted, or abnormally shaped.

ANALYSIS: Misshapen roots
Carrot roots may be misshapen for any of several reasons.
1. *Overcrowding:* Crowded seedlings do not have room to develop properly.
2. *Soil debris:* Stones or clods of soil prevent even expansion of the root.
3. *Fresh manure:* Fresh, undecomposed manure stimulates root branching.
4. *Heavy soil:* Carrot roots have difficulty expanding in heavy, tight soil. Soil-inhabiting rot fungi that may cause forking are also prevalent in these wet soils.
5. *Nematodes:* These microscopic worms live in the soil and feed on plant roots.

SOLUTION: Follow these suggestions for smooth, elongated carrots.
1. Plant carrot seeds ¼ to ½ inch deep and ½ inch apart. When the seedlings are 1 inch tall, thin them to stand ½ to 2 inches apart, depending on the variety planted.
2. Before planting, rake out and discard stones ½ inch and larger in diameter. Break up soil clods.
3. If you add manure, use only decomposed manure. Or fertilize with a balanced fertilizer such as ORTHO Vegetable Garden Food 5–10–10 or ORTHO Tomato Food 5–10–10.
4. Incorporate organic matter such as peat moss or humus into heavy soil. Short, blunt varieties of carrots that do well in heavy soil include Short 'n Sweet, Oxhart, and the Nantes and Chantenay types.
5. For information on nematodes, see page 720.

CARROTS

Misshapen carrots.

Carrot weevil larvae damage (3 times life size).

Carrot rust fly damage.

PROBLEM: Plants are stunted and yellow. The main root may be forked, and numerous side roots are produced, or tiny beads or knots are attached to the roots.

ANALYSIS: Nematodes
Nematodes are microscopic worms that live in the soil. They are not related to earthworms. Nematodes feed on plant roots, damaging and stunting them. The damaged roots can't supply sufficient water and nutrients to the above-ground plant parts, and the plant is stunted or slowly dies. Nematodes are found throughout the United States, but are most severe in the South. They prefer moist, sandy loam soils. Nematodes can move only a few inches each year on their own, but they may be carried long distances by soil, water, tools, or infested plants. Testing roots and soil is the only positive method for confirming the presence of nematodes. Contact your local Cooperative Extension Office (see page 1011) for sampling instructions and addresses of testing laboratories. Soil and root problems such as poor soil structure, drought stress, nutrient deficiency, and root rots can also produce symptoms of decline similar to those caused by nematodes. These problems should be eliminated as causes before sending soil and root samples for testing. For information on soil problems and root rots, see pages 901 and 856.

SOLUTION: There are no chemicals available to homeowners to kill nematodes in planted soil. However, they can be controlled before planting by soil fumigation. For information on fumigating soil, see page 919.

PROBLEM: The upper part of the root is scarred with zigzag tunnels. White, curved, legless grubs, about ⅓ inch long, may be found in the root and soil.

ANALYSIS: Carrot weevil
(*Listronotus oregonensis*)
This insect feeds on carrots, dill, celery, parsley, and parsnips. The adult is a dark brown beetle that lays eggs in the carrot tops. In May and June the eggs hatch into white grubs, which travel down to the developing root. Here the grub tunnels into and feeds on the upper tissue, scarring the root. After a short resting period in the soil, the pest emerges as an adult and lays eggs that hatch into a second generation in August. The adults of this second generation spend the winter in debris in and around the garden. The following spring, the cycle repeats itself.

SOLUTION: There are no insecticides currently registered for use on this insect pest. Some control may be obtained when spraying for leafhoppers (see page 880). Clean up garden debris in the fall to eliminate overwintering spots for the adults. Do not add infested debris to the compost pile.

PROBLEM: Burrows with rust-red sawdustlike material inside wind through the carrot root. Scars also mar the surface. Plant tops may look healthy, or they may be stunted, turn yellow, and die.

ANALYSIS: Carrot rust fly
(*Psila rosae*)
This insect pest attacks carrots, celery, parsnips, and parsley. It damages the plants by eating small roots and tunneling into larger roots. The rust-red excrement in the tunnels gives the insect its name. The adult fly, which causes no damage, lays eggs on the soil surface in late spring and early summer. The eggs hatch into yellowish white maggots, ⅓ inch long. The maggots feed on and in the roots until they pupate and emerge as adults in late summer. These adults lay eggs that hatch into a second generation of maggots in August and September. It is this second generation that does the most damage. The maggots may also feed in stored carrots. Disease-causing organisms often enter carrot roots through wounds made by the rust fly maggot. These diseases cause the roots to rot before they are ready to be harvested, and also in storage. Roots with only a few tunnels are still edible; cut out the damaged part.

SOLUTION: Destroy badly damaged plants to reduce the source of next year's population. Next year at planting time, work ORTHO Diazinon Soil & Turf Insect Control into the top 4 inches of soil.

CELERY

Alternaria leaf blight.

Aster yellows. *Insert:* Infected root.

PROBLEM: Tan, gray-brown, or black spots with pale centers appear on the leaves. The spots enlarge, forming blotches that may eventually kill the leaves. Similar spots also occur on the leaf stems. Infected leaf stems shrivel and die. Severely infected plants look as if they've been burned by fire.

ANALYSIS: Leaf blights
Leaf blights on carrots are caused by two different fungi (*Alternaria dauci* and *Cercospora carotae*) that produce similar symptoms. They also attack parsley. The diseases spread rapidly in humid weather with frequent rains and heavy dews. The leaves and stems must remain wet for several hours for the spores to infect them. The spores are spread from plant to plant by wind and splashing water. Plants under stress from poor nutrition are the most susceptible to attack. Although these fungi don't attack the carrot root directly, if enough leaves die to reduce the amount of food manufactured, the root size and flavor may be reduced.

SOLUTION: Pick off infected leaves. Treat the plants with ORTHO Vegetable Disease Control at the first sign of the disease. Continue the treatments at intervals of 10 to 14 days until the leaf blights are no longer present. Water the garden by midafternoon so the foliage is dry at night. Do not work among wet plants. Clean all plant debris from the garden after the harvest to reduce next year's infection. Plant blight-resistant carrot varieties.

Carrot varieties resistant to leaf blight: Ace, Denver 126, Imperator 58, Imperator 408, and Spartan Bonus.

PROBLEM: Inner leaves are yellow, stunted, and grow in tight bunches. Outer leaves turn rusty red to reddish purple. The roots are stunted, deformed, and have a bitter taste. Tiny hairlike roots grow in great profusion out of the main root. Numerous tiny leaves grow from the top of the root.

ANALYSIS: Aster yellows
This plant disease is caused by myco-plasmas, microscopic organisms similar to bacteria. The mycoplasmas are transmitted from plant to plant primarily by leafhoppers. (For information about leafhoppers, see page 880.) The symptoms of aster yellows are more severe and appear more quickly in warm weather. Even when the disease is present in the plant, aster yellows may not manifest its symptoms in temperatures of 55°F or less. The disease also infects many other vegetables, ornamental plants, and weeds. For a list of plants susceptible to aster yellows, see page 994.

SOLUTION: Aster yellows cannot be eliminated entirely, but can be kept under control. Move and destroy infected plants. To remove sources of infection, eradicate nearby weeds that may harbor aster yellows and leafhopper eggs. Treat leafhopper-infested plants with ORTHO Sevin Garden Dust or ORTHO Malathion 50 Insect Spray. Repeat the treatment whenever leafhoppers are seen. For more information about controlling disease-carrying insects, see page 880.

CELERY

ADAPTATION: Zones 4 through 10. To determine your zone, see the map on page 1004.

PLANTING TIME: See page 1009.

PLANTING METHOD: Set transplants so that the top of their rootball is even with the garden soil. Space 6 to 10 inches apart. Or, sow seeds indoors 8 to 10 weeks before planting outside. Soak the seeds in warm water overnight, and plant 1/8 inch deep. Thin to stand 1½ to 2½ inches apart when the seedlings have 2 or 3 leaves. At the recommended time, set outdoors as stated above.

SOIL: Any good garden soil that is high in organic matter. pH 6.0 to 8.0

FERTILIZER: At planting time, apply 5 pounds of ORTHO Vegetable Garden Food 5–10–10 per 100 square feet, or 2 pounds per 25-foot row. Side-dress every 3 to 4 weeks with 2 pounds per 25-foot row.

WATER:
How much: Apply enough water at each irrigation to wet the soil 8 to 10 inches deep.
How often: Keep the soil evenly moist, never allowing it to dry out.

HARVEST: Cut the plants at the base of the stalks with a sharp knife when they are 10 to 12 inches tall, and before they become tough and stringy. Outside stalks may also be harvested as needed. For white celery, blanch the stalks when they are 6 to 8 inches tall by wrapping with paper or shading with boards. Store in the refrigerator.

CELERY

Overmature plant.

Leaf webbed together by celery leaftier.

Late blight.

PROBLEM: Celery stalks are tough, stringy, and off-flavor. There are no signs of insects or disease. A tall stalk may emerge from the plant.

ANALYSIS: Tough, stringy, and bitter stalks
Celery stalks become tough, stringy, and off-flavor for any of several different reasons.
1. *High temperatures when maturing:* Celery is a cool season crop that grows poorly in temperatures over 70°F.
2. *Lack of water:* Celery requires a constant and abundant supply of moisture. Without this moisture, the stalks are not tender. Celery plants have shallow roots and are very subject to drought damage.
3. *Low fertility:* Celery plants are heavy feeders and must be adequately fertilized at planting time and throughout the season.
4. *Overmaturity:* The tenderness and flavor of celery deteriorate rapidly when it becomes overmature.
5. *Seedstalk formation:* Celery plants form seedstalks prematurely when exposed to cool temperatures when young. Temperatures between 40° and 50°F for 2 weeks, or between 50° and 60°F for 1 to 2 months initiate seedstalk formation. When plant growth is later stimulated by fertilizing, the stalk elongates.

SOLUTION: Celery grows best when the night temperatures are around 50°F and daytime temperatures range between 60° and 70°F. It requires a long growing season of 120 to 140 days. To help reduce tough, stringy, and bitter stalks, follow the feeding, watering, and harvesting instructions on page 721.

PROBLEM: Leaves are webbed together with white silken threads. Inside the webs are pale green to yellow caterpillars, ½ to ¾ inch long, with a white and green stripe down the back. They wriggle when disturbed.

ANALYSIS: Celery leaftier
(*Udea rubigalis*)
This moth larva attacks many garden and greenhouse plants, especially celery, aster, beets, dahlias, sweetpeas, and spinach. The brown moth lays its eggs on the underside of the celery leaf. The pale green caterpillars that hatch from these eggs feed on celery foliage and leaf stalks, mining into the soft stems and hearts of the plants and webbing the foliage together. As they mature, the caterpillars turn yellow, pupate in the webs, then emerge as adult moths to continue the cycle. There are several generations each year, and leaftiers may be active all year in warm areas of the country.

SOLUTION: Spray with an insecticide containing *malathion* as soon as webbing appears. Clean up garden debris to reduce overwintering spots.

PROBLEM: Small yellow spots appear on older leaves in cool, moist weather in the fall, winter, and spring. Spots turn dark brownish gray and are speckled with tiny black dots. Seriously affected leaves die. Stalks may also be affected.

ANALYSIS: Late blight
This plant disease is caused by a destructive fungus (*Septoria apiicola*) that is prevalent in cool, rainy weather. It attacks celery in the fall, winter, and early spring. Only wet leaves are infected. The tiny black dots in the leaf spots contain spores that live in infected celery debris and are spread by splashing raindrops, people, animals, and tools. The spores may also survive on the seeds for many months. Severely infected leaves die, and if weather conditions that are favorable for the disease continue, eventually the whole plant may die.

SOLUTION: Spray the plants with ORTHO Vegetable Disease Control as soon as the disease appears. Repeat at intervals of 7 to 10 days. Remove and destroy plant debris after harvest. In the future, use treated seed, or soak seed in hot water (118°F) for 30 minutes, then dry at room temperature. Grow late blight tolerant varieties.

Celery variety tolerant to late blight: Emerson Pascal.

Early blight.

Black heart.

Aster yellows.

PROBLEM: In summer and early fall small yellow spots appear on both sides of the leaves. These spots enlarge, turning ash gray in color. Elongated tan spots appear on stalks just before harvest. During warm, humid weather, a velvety growth covers the affected spots.

ANALYSIS: Early blight
This plant disease is caused by a fungus (*Cercospora apii*) that usually attacks celery in the summer and early fall. It is most prevalent when days are warm and night temperatures are in the 60s. Only wet leaves are infected. Heavy dews and light rains provide enough moisture for infection. The fungus attacks the entire plant and, when severe, all the foliage may be killed. The spores survive from one crop to the next in celery debris left in the garden.

SOLUTION: Spray the plants with ORTHO Vegetable Disease Control as soon as the disease appears. Repeat at intervals of 7 to 10 days. Remove and destroy plant debris after harvest. Next spring, purchase treated or resistant seeds, or soak the seeds in hot water (118°F) for 30 minutes, then dry at room temperature.

Celery varieties that are tolerant to early blight: Early Belle, Emerson Pascal, and June Belle.

PROBLEM: Early maturing leaves turn pale yellow and the heart of the plant turns black and dies. A slimy decay may follow.

ANALYSIS: Black heart
This disorder is caused by a calcium deficiency in the growing tip. It occurs most frequently in crops where the soil moisture fluctuates from very dry to very wet, rather than remaining constant. Heavy watering after a long dry period frequently induces black heart. High temperatures, excess soil salts, and rapid growth from excess nitrogen may also promote the condition. A bacterial soft rot often enters the dying heart, resulting in slimy, watery, rotting tissue.

SOLUTION: Discard affected plants. Keep the soil constantly moist, and use a complete fertilizer such as ORTHO Vegetable Garden Food 5–10–10. Avoid fertilizers that are extremely high in nitrogen. Test your soil pH as outlined on page 903 and correct if necessary. Celery grows best at a pH of 6.5 to 8.0.

PROBLEM: Plants are stunted and light yellow. Stems become curled, twisted, and brittle. Leaves thicken and become brittle.

ANALYSIS: Aster yellows
This plant disease is caused by mycoplasmas, microscopic organisms similar to bacteria. The mycoplasmas are transmitted from plant to plant primarily by leafhoppers. (For more information on leafhoppers, see page 880.) Green celeries and some self-blanching varieties are resistant to aster yellows. The symptoms of aster yellows are more severe and appear more quickly in warm weather. Even when the disease is present in the plant, aster yellows may not manifest its symptoms in temperatures of 55°F or less. The disease also infects many other vegetable plants, ornamentals, and weeds. For a list of plants susceptible to aster yellows, see page 994.

SOLUTION: Aster yellows cannot be eliminated entirely, but can be kept under control. Remove and destroy infected plants. To remove sources of infection, eradicate nearby weeds that may harbor aster yellows and leafhopper eggs. Spray leafhopper-infested plants with an insecticide containing *malathion*. Repeat the spray whenever leafhoppers are seen. For more information on controlling disease-carrying insects, see page 880. Grow resistant varieties.

Self-blanching varieties resistant to aster yellows: Florida Golden, Forbes Golden Plume, and Michigan Golden.

CORN

PROBLEMS WITH THE EAR

CORN

ADAPTATION: Throughout the United States.

PLANTING TIME: See page 1009.

PLANTING METHOD: Sow seeds 1 to 2 inches deep and 12 to 16 inches apart. Or, set transplants so that the top of their rootball is even with the garden soil. Space 12 to 16 inches apart.

SOIL: Any good garden soil that is high in organic matter. pH 6.0 to 8.0

FERTILIZER: At planting time, use 3 pounds of ORTHO Vegetable Garden Food 5–10–10 per 100-foot row. Side-dress with the same amount when the plants are 8 inches tall, and again when they are 18 inches tall.

WATER:
How much: Apply enough water at each irrigation to wet the soil 8 to 10 inches deep.
How often: Keep the soil moist, never allowing it to dry out. Corn needs constant moisture all season, but especially from tasseling to picking time.

HARVEST: Corn is generally ready to be picked 3 weeks after the silks appear. When ready, the silks become dark brown and dry. The best method for testing ripeness is to press a kernel with your finger. If it spurts milky juice, it is ready. To pick, grab the ear at its base, bend it downward, and twist. Do not damage the main stalk. Pick corn just before cooking, as its flavor deteriorates rapidly when stored.

Corn earworm (¾ life size).

PROBLEM: Striped yellow, brown, or green worms are feeding on the tip of the ear inside the husk. The worms range in size from ¼ to 2 inches long. Leaves may be chewed and ragged.

ANALYSIS: Corn earworm
(*Heliothis zea*)
This is the most serious pest of corn. It also attacks many other garden vegetables and flowers, and is also known as the *tomato fruitworm* and the *cotton bollworm*. The worm is the larva of a light gray-brown moth with dark lines on its wings. In the spring, the moth lays yellow eggs singly on corn silks and the undersides of leaves. The worms that hatch from these eggs feed on the new leaves in the whorls. This feeding doesn't reduce the corn yield, but the leaves that develop are ragged and the plant may be stunted. More serious damage is caused when the worms feed on the silks, causing poor pollination, and when they feed on the developing kernels. Worms enter the ear at the silk end, or they may bore through the husk. There are several generations a year. In the South, where these pests survive the winter, early and late plantings suffer the most damage. Adult moths migrate into northern areas, where late plantings are severely damaged. Uneaten parts of infested ears are still edible.

SOLUTION: Once the worms are in the ears, sprays are ineffective. In the future, spray plants with ORTHO Sevin Garden Dust when 10 percent of the ears show silk. For best control, spray until the silks are thoroughly wet. Repeat the treatment 3 to 4 times at intervals of 3 days. If the infestation continues, repeat as necessary until harvest.

Armyworm (¾ life size).

PROBLEM: Leaf edges are chewed and some leaves may be completely eaten. Light tan to dark brown caterpillars 1½ to 2 inches long, with yellow, orange, or dark brown stripes, are feeding on the leaves and may be boring into the ears.

ANALYSIS: Armyworm
Armyworms attack corn, grains, grasses, and other garden crops. These pests do not overwinter in cold winter areas, but the moths migrate great distances in the spring in search of places to lay their eggs. The tan to gray adult moths lay eggs on the blades of grasses and grains. The caterpillars that hatch from these eggs feed on corn leaves, ears, and ear stalks. They get their name from their feeding habits. After they have eaten everything in one area, they crawl in droves to another area in search of more food. After several weeks of feeding they pupate in the soil, then emerge as adult moths to repeat the cycle. There are several generations each year, beginning in mid-May. These pests are most numerous after cold, wet spring weather that slows the development of the natural parasites and diseases that help keep the population in check.

SOLUTION: When the worms are first seen, spray with ORTHO Fruit & Vegetable Insect Control, or dust with ORTHO Sevin Garden Dust. It may be 4 or 5 days before results are seen. Repeat at weekly intervals if the plants become reinfested. To control worms that bore into the ears, spray when 10 percent of the ears show silk, and repeat 3 or 4 more times at intervals of 3 days.

Poor pollination.

Bird damage.

Corn smut.

PROBLEM: Corn ears are not completely filled with kernels. Plants are healthy.

ANALYSIS: Poor pollination
Poorly filled ears result from ineffective or incomplete pollination. Pollen grains produced on the tassels must fall on the sticky silks for complete pollination. Each strand of silk is attached to a kernel, so for each silk that is pollinated, one kernel will develop on the ear. Corn pollen is spread by the wind; if the wind is blowing across a single row of corn, the pollen on the tassels will be carried away from the silks, resulting in poorly filled ears. Poor pollination can also result from dry soil during pollination and from hot, dry winds. Prolonged periods of rain reduce the amount of pollen shed from the tassels. Damage to the silks from corn earworms, (see page 724), rootworm adults (see page 728), armyworms (see page 724), and grasshoppers (see page 728) may also result in incomplete ears.

SOLUTION: To help ensure pollination, grow corn in blocks of at least 3 or 4 short rows rather than in 1 long row. Plant seeds 12 to 16 inches apart in rows 30 to 36 inches apart. Keep the soil moist, letting the surface dry slightly between waterings. Control corn insect pests. Corn can be hand-pollinated by shaking the tassels onto the silks.

PROBLEM: Holes are pecked in the ears through the husk. Some kernels are missing from the ears. Birds are active in the corn.

ANALYSIS: Birds
Birds are attracted to certain grains, including corn. Blackbirds, grackles, cowbirds, starlings, and crows frequently feed on corn seed and developing ears. The developing ears are particularly inviting to birds from the milk stage to harvest. Blackbirds and grackles pierce the husk and puncture the soft kernels. Cowbirds feed on ears where the husk has been removed by other birds.

SOLUTION: To protect developing ears, put a paper bag over each ear after it has been pollinated — when the silk begins to turn brown. Bird netting placed over the rows also protects the ears. These nets are available at garden centers and through mail order garden supply companies. For more information on birds in the garden, see page 893.

PROBLEM: Puffballs or galls appear on the stalk, leaves, ears, or tassels. Galls are white and may be smooth, or they may be covered with a black greasy or powdery material. They range from peasize to 5 inches in diameter.

ANALYSIS: Corn smut
This plant disease is caused by a fungus (*Ustilago maydis*) that attacks any aboveground part of corn. Germinating seedlings are not affected. Galls are full of black powdery spores that survive the winter on or in soil, corn debris, and manure. They are spread from plant to plant by wind, water, and manure. A gall forms only where a spore lands. The disease does not spread throughout the plant. Younger plants are more susceptible; most plants are infected when they are from 1 to 3 feet tall. Corn is less susceptible after the ears have formed. Corn smut is most prevalent in warm (80° to 95°F) temperatures, and when dry weather early in the season is followed by moderate rainfall as the corn matures. Stem and leaf smut don't reduce the corn yield directly, but rather sap the plant's energy, reducing ear development.

SOLUTION: There are no chemical controls for this disease. Cut off smuts before they break open and release the black powdery spores. Grow varieties tolerant to corn smut. Clean all plant debris from the garden after harvest. Avoid using manure in the soil if corn smut is a problem in your garden.

Varieties of corn tolerant to smut: Aztec, Calumet, Comanche, Deep Gold, Golden Beauty, Gusto, Merit, Midway, Tender Sweet, and Victory Golden.

CORN — EAR PROBLEMS

Fusarium ear rot.

PROBLEM: Dark brown lesions spot the corn stalks near their joints. The stalks are rotted inside, are often pink, and break easily. Kernels are moldy, and pink to reddish brown. Plants die.

ANALYSIS: Root, stalk, and ear rot
This plant disease is caused by a soil-inhabiting fungus (*Fusarium moniliforme*) that attacks roots, stalks, and ears. It is prevalent during warm, dry weather, and can attack corn plants any time during their life. The fungi are prevalent in nutrient-deficient soils. The rot often originates in the roots and crown of the plant, and spreads upward into the stalk. Stalks injured by insects, disease, or hail are very susceptible. The fungal spores survive the winter on or in seeds and dead stalks left in the garden. Infected seeds don't sprout, or the seedlings die soon after emerging. The spores are spread from plant to plant by the wind, splashing water, insects, and infected tools. Spores that land on the stalks are washed into the leaf sheaths where they germinate and infect the stalk, resulting in lesions at the stalk joints.

SOLUTION: There is no chemical control for this disease. Destroy infected plants and ears. Maintain balanced nutrition by fertilizing with ORTHO Vegetable Garden Food 5–10–10. Clean all plant debris from the garden after harvest.

DISCOLORED LEAVES

Small yellow plants.

PROBLEM: Corn plants are short and produce few or no ears. Leaves may be pale green to yellow.

ANALYSIS: Poor yield
Sweet corn is exacting in its growth requirements and, if these requirements are not met, can be a disappointment in the garden. Corn plants may be small, yellow, and yield poorly for any of several reasons.
1. *Planted too close:* Corn plants have extensive root systems and are very competitive.
2. *Nutrient deficiency:* Plants are heavy feeders and require abundant supplies of nutrients, especially nitrogen, throughout the season.
3. *Poor irrigation:* Corn needs abundant water throughout the season, but especially from tasseling to picking time.
4. *Poorly drained soil:* Shallow, weak roots develop in poorly drained soil. Corn plants are vigorous and need deep healthy roots.
5. *Nematodes:* These soil-inhabiting, microscopic worms damage corn roots, reducing the plant's vigor. For more information on nematodes, see page 685.

SOLUTION: Follow the cultural guidelines on page 724 for healthy and productive sweet corn. Plant seeds 12 to 16 inches apart, in rows 30 to 36 inches apart. Improve soil drainage as described on page 901.

Bacterial wilt.

PROBLEM: Long irregular streaks up to 1 inch wide appear on leaves. The streaks turn brown and dry. Plants may be stunted and produce few ears, or wilt rapidly and die. Seedlings rapidly wilt and die. Brown cavities occur inside the stalks near the soil line.

ANALYSIS: Bacterial wilt
This plant disease, also called *Stewart's wilt,* is caused by a bacterium (*Erwinia stewartii*). The bacteria spend the winter in the bodies of corn flea beetles and then infect healthy plants as the flea beetles feed on the corn leaves. (For more information on the corn flea beetle, see page 691.) The bacteria then move through and infect the entire plant. The severity of the wilt disease depends on the number of flea beetles that survive the winter. Bacterial wilt is most severe after mild winters when numerous beetles survive. Plants growing in rich soil are the most susceptible to attack, as are early yellow varieties. Spotted cucumber beetles (see page 690) also spread the bacteria during the growing season.

SOLUTION: There are no chemical controls for this disease. Remove and destroy all infected plants. Control flea beetles and cucumber beetles with ORTHO Fruit & Vegetable Insect Control. Plant varieties tolerant of this disease.

Corn varieties tolerant of bacterial wilt: Apache, Bi-Queen, Calumet, Cherokee, Comanche, Merit, NK 199, Seneca Chief, Seneca Sentry, and Silverqueen.

Northern corn leaf blight.

Maize dwarf mosaic.

Flea beetle (12 times life size).

PROBLEM: Greenish yellow to grayish tan elliptical spots appear on the lower leaves first and on the upper leaves later. The spots may be surrounded by a reddish brown or yellow margin, and range in size from very small to 1 to 5 inches long and 1 inch wide. In humid weather, the spots may be covered with tiny black specks on a velvety growth.

ANALYSIS: Leaf blights
Northern and southern leaf blights are caused by fungi (*Helminthosporium* species) that usually attack corn plants when they are about 15 inches tall. The fungi thrive in warm (70° to 85°F), wet weather. The spores can infect leaves only when the leaves remain wet for 6 to 18 hours. Leaf blights are seldom a problem in hot, dry weather. The spores spend the winter on diseased plant parts left in the garden, and are spread to new crops in the early summer by the wind. Leaf blights seldom kill the corn plants, but may weaken them and make them more susceptible to root and stalk rots.

SOLUTION: Spray the plants with ORTHO Vegetable Disease Control when spotting first appears. Continue spraying every 4 to 7 days until dry weather resumes. Grow corn varieties that are tolerant of leaf blight. Clean all corn debris from the garden after harvest.

Corn varieties that are resistant to leaf blight: Apache, Bi-Queen, Capitan, Comanche, Comet, Commander, Silver Dollar, and Spring Calico.

PROBLEM: The upper part of the plant is dwarfed, causing the plant to look like a feather duster. Leaves are striped with yellow and green in a mosaic pattern. As the plant matures the mosaic disappears, and late in the season the leaves turn yellow-green with red blotches or streaks.

ANALYSIS: Maize dwarf mosaic
This plant disease is caused by a virus that is transmitted primarily by aphids, and occasionally by equipment and man. It also infects wild and cultivated grasses, especially Johnsongrass, in which it survives the winter. The symptoms are most obvious in plants that are infected before silking. If infected after silking or later, the symptoms may not show, and the plants appear to be healthy.

SOLUTION: There are no chemical controls for virus diseases. Destroy all infected plants. Do not touch a healthy plant after touching an infected one. Prevent the spread of the disease by controlling aphids when they appear with ORTHO Fruit & Vegetable Insect Control. (For information on aphids, see page 877.) Grow varieties of corn tolerant of MDM. Kill Johnsongrass growing nearby with ORTHO Kleenup Systemic Weed & Grass Killer. For more information on virus diseases, see page 861.

Maize dwarf mosaic tolerant varieties: Apache, Bellringer, Calumet, Capitan, Guardian, Merit, Quicksilver, Seneca, Sentry, White Lightning, and Wintergreen.

PROBLEM: Leaves are riddled with shotholes about 1/8 inch in diameter. Tiny (1/16 inch) black beetles jump like fleas when disturbed. Leaves of seedlings and eventually whole plants may wilt and die.

ANALYSIS: Flea beetles
These beetles jump like fleas, but are not related to them. Both adult and immature flea beetles feed on a wide variety of garden vegetables. Some flea beetles are responsible for spreading the bacterial wilt that kills corn plants. For more information on these wilts, see page 726. The immature beetle, a legless gray grub, injures plants by feeding on the roots and the lower surfaces of leaves. Adults chew holes in leaves. Flea beetles are most damaging to seedlings and young plants. Leaves of seedlings riddled with holes dry out quickly and die. Adult beetles survive the winter in soil and garden debris. They emerge in early spring to feed on weeds until vegetables sprout or plants are set in the garden. Grubs hatch from eggs laid in the soil and feed for 2 to 3 weeks. After pupating in the soil, they emerge as adults to repeat the cycle. There are 1 to 4 generations a year. Adults may feed for up to 2 months.

SOLUTION: Control flea beetles on corn with ORTHO Fruit & Vegetable Insect Control, ORTHO Sevin Garden Dust, or ORTHO Tomato & Vegetable Insect Spray when the leaves first show damage. Watch new growth for evidence of further damage, and repeat the treatment at weekly intervals as needed. Remove all plant debris from the garden after harvest to eliminate overwintering spots for adult beetles.

Adult corn rootworm (3 times life size).

Grasshoppers (1/10 life size).

European corn borer (twice life size).

PROBLEM: Yellow, pale green, or brownish red beetles with very long antennae crawl on the plants. Some may have black spots or stripes. The ears are malformed, with undeveloped or partially developed kernels; leaves may be chewed.

ANALYSIS: Corn rootworm
(*Diabrotica* species)
Both adult beetles and young worms of this pest attack corn. For information on the larva, see page 730. The adult beetles feed on the pollen, silks, and tassels, resulting in malformed ears and undeveloped kernels from improper or incomplete pollination. Some beetles may also feed on the leaves. The adults lay yellow-orange eggs in the soil at the base of the corn plants. The young worms that hatch from these eggs feed on the corn roots for several weeks, then pupate in the soil to emerge as beetles in late July and August. These pests are most common where corn has grown consecutively for 2 or more years. Late-planted corn and corn under drought stress are the most susceptible.

SOLUTION: Dust the plants with ORTHO Sevin Garden Dust when the beetles first appear on the plants. Repeat at weekly intervals if the plants become reinfested. Control the rootworm larvae as suggested on page 730.

PROBLEM: Large holes are chewed in the margins of the leaves. Greenish yellow to brown jumping insects, 1/2 to 1 1/2 inches long, with long hind legs infest corn plants. Kernels on ears may be chewed or undeveloped.

ANALYSIS: Grasshoppers
Grasshoppers attack a wide variety of plants including corn, grains, and grasses. They eat corn leaves and silk, migrating as they mature and as they deplete their food sources. They are most numerous in the rows adjacent to weedy areas. In the late summer, adult grasshoppers lay eggs in pods in the soil. The adults continue feeding until cold weather kills them. The eggs hatch the following spring. Grasshopper populations are most severe during hot, dry weather. They migrate into green gardens and yards as surrounding areas dry up in the summer heat. Periods of cool, wet weather help keep their numbers under control. The loss of a small amount of leaf tissue by a small population of grasshoppers doesn't reduce the corn yield significantly.

SOLUTION: Treat the plants with ORTHO Fruit & Vegetable Insect Control as soon as grasshoppers appear. Repeat at weekly intervals if the plants become reinfested. Clean up weedy areas near the garden and remove all plant debris from the garden after harvest.

PROBLEM: Leaves are riddled with tiny shotholes. Tassels may be broken and ear stalks bent. Holes filled with sawdust are bored into the main stalks. Pinkish caterpillars with dark brown heads and 2 rows of brown dots are found inside the stalks.

ANALYSIS: European corn borer
(*Ostrinia nubilalis*)
The European corn borer is one of the most destructive pests of corn. It also feeds on tomatoes, potatoes, and peppers. Early plantings are the most severely affected. The borer survives the winter in corn plants, pupates in the spring, and emerges as an adult moth in early summer. The moth, which is tan with dark wavy lines on the wings, lays clusters of about 20 white eggs on the undersides of the lower corn leaves. The borers that hatch from these eggs feed first in the whorl of leaves, riddling the leaves with shotholes. Later they bore into stalks and the bases of ears. This feeding results in broken stalks and tassels, poor ear development, and dropped ears. The borers continue feeding for a month, pupate, and emerge as moths to repeat the cycle. Cool, rainy weather in the early summer inhibits egg laying and washes the hatching larvae from the plants, reducing borer populations. Very dry summers and cold winters also reduce borer populations.

SOLUTION: Treat ear shoots and centers of leaf whorls at the first sign of borers or when 10 percent of the ears show silk with ORTHO Sevin Garden Dust or ORTHO Rotenone Dust or Spray. Repeat at weekly intervals until borers are no longer seen. Destroy the plants at the end of the season. Avoid early planting.

Stalk borer damage. *Insert:* Larva (life size).

Lesser corn stalk borer (half life size).

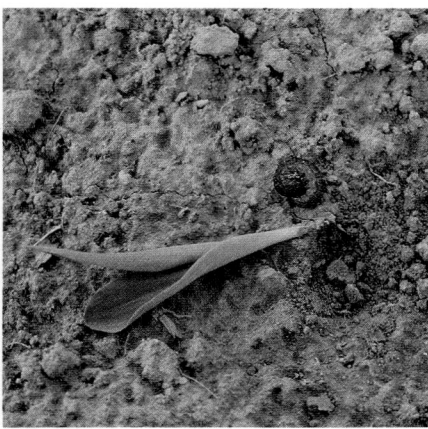

Black cutworm (⅓ life size).

PROBLEM: Leaves are chewed and ragged. Stalks don't produce ears and may be distorted and curled. Dark brown to purple caterpillars, 1 inch long, with white stripes and bands may be found inside the stalks.

ANALYSIS: Common stalk borer
(*Papaipema nebris*)
The common stalk borer is a serious pest of corn east of the Rocky Mountains. These borers feed on a variety of plants, but prefer corn. They spend the winter as eggs on grasses and weeds, especially giant ragweed. After hatching in the early spring, the worms feed in the leaf whorls and then bore into the side of the stalks and burrow upward. After pupating in the soil, the adult moths emerge in late summer and early fall. These grayish brown moths lay eggs on grasses for next year's generation. There is only one generation per year.

SOLUTION: Once the damage is noticed, it is too late for any controls. Destroy all infested plants. Clean all plant debris from the garden after harvest. Eliminate nearby grasses and weeds, especially giant ragweed. If stalk borers were serious this year, next year treat the plants with an insecticide containing *diazinon* or *carbaryl* in early to midspring.

PROBLEM: Leaves are chewed and ragged. Stalks are distorted and curled, with few or no ears. A hole appears in the corn stalk about 2 inches above the soil surface. A ¾ inch bluish-green caterpillar with brown stripes may be found in the soil near the plants.

ANALYSIS: Lesser corn stalk borer
(*Elasmopalpus lignosellus*)
These worms damage plants by boring and tunneling into the stalks. One larva may injure or kill several plants. In the spring a brownish yellow moth with black spots lays eggs on corn leaves and stalks. The borers that hatch from these eggs feed on the leaves and burrow into the lower 2 inches of the stalk, causing curled and distorted plants. After feeding for about 3 weeks the borers pupate in the soil and emerge as adults to repeat the cycle. There are 2 or more generations a year. The lesser corn stalk borer feeds on a variety of plants, and is often found on Johnsongrass.

SOLUTION: Once the damage is noticed, it is too late for any controls. Destroy all infested plants, and clean all plant debris from the garden after harvest. Pull out surrounding weeds and grasses, especially Johnsongrass, where the borers may breed and spend the winter. Next year at planting time, apply an insecticide containing *diazinon* granules to the soil.

PROBLEM: Young plants are chewed or cut off near the ground. Gray, brown, or black worms, 1½ to 2 inches long, may be found about 2 inches deep in the soil near the base of the damaged plants. The worms coil when disturbed.

ANALYSIS: Cutworms
Several species of cutworms attack plants in the vegetable garden. The most likely pests of corn seedlings are the surface-feeding cutworms. The two most common on corn are the black cutworm (*Agrotis ipsilon*) and the dingy cutworm (*Feltia ducens*). For information on the climbing cutworms, see page 689. A single surface-feeding cutworm can sever the stems of many young plants in one night. Cutworms hide in the soil during the day, and feed only at night. All adult cutworms are dark night-flying moths with bands or stripes on their forewings.

SOLUTION: Apply ORTHO Diazinon Soil & Turf Insect Control or ORTHO Diazinon Soil & Foliage Dust around the base of undamaged plants when stem cutting is observed. Since cutworms are difficult to control, it may be necessary to repeat dusting at weekly intervals. Before planting more corn in the same area, apply a preventive treatment of ORTHO Diazinon Soil & Turf Insect Control and work it into the soil. Cultivate the soil thoroughly in late summer and fall to expose and destroy eggs, larvae, and pupae. Further reduce damage with "cutworm collars" around the stem of each plant or group of plants. These collars can be made of stiff paper or aluminum foil. They should be at least 2 inches high, and pressed firmly into the soil.

CORN — SOIL INSECTS

Corn rootworm larvae (life size).

Seed corn maggot damage.

Wireworm feeding on corn seed (3 times life size).

PROBLEM: Corn plants are dwarfed, yellow, and fall over easily. The base of the stalks may have a crook-necked shape. White worms, from ½ to ¾ inch long, with brown heads are eating the roots.

ANALYSIS: Corn rootworm larvae (*Diabrotica* species)
Several species of this pest attack corn. The beetle larva, or worm, feeds on corn roots, completely devouring small ones and tunneling into larger ones. The worms hatch from eggs in early summer to midsummer and migrate through the soil, feeding on corn roots. This feeding damage can be so serious to young plants that some gardens may need to be replanted. When populations are large, all the roots may be destroyed. The worms pupate in the soil and emerge as greenish yellow or light brown beetles, some with black spots or stripes, to repeat the cycle. There are 1 to 3 generations per year. Adult beetles feed on larvae and silks. For information on adult corn rootworms, see page 728. Corn plants are affected most severely when they are growing in dry soil, where root regrowth is minimal. Rot diseases may enter the damaged roots, injuring them further. Several parasitic insects and diseases help keep beetle populations under control most years.

SOLUTION: Discard damaged plants and clean up weedy areas where the insects lay eggs and spend the winter. Apply ORTHO Diazinon Soil & Turf Insect Control to the soil at planting time. Don't grow corn in the same soil for more than two consecutive years.

PROBLEM: Seeds don't sprout, or the seedlings are weak and don't develop leaves. Pearly white worms, ¼ inch long, are feeding in the seeds. The seeds are hollow.

ANALYSIS: Seed corn maggot (*Hylemya platura*)
Seed corn maggots feed on seeds and seedlings. They are attracted to large-seeded vegetables such as peas, beans, and corn. The maggots are most numerous in cool periods in the spring and fall, and in cold soil that is high in organic matter. The black, hairy adult flies are attracted to the organic matter, and lay eggs in the soil. The maggots that hatch from these eggs burrow into the seeds and eat the inner tissue, leaving a hollow shell. Rot fungi may enter a damaged seed and further destroy it. After 1 to 2 weeks, the maggots burrow deep into the soil and pupate. The adult flies that emerge feed on nectar and plant juices before laying more eggs. There are several generations a year. In warm winter areas, these pests are active all year. In cold winter areas, they survive the winter as pupae, emerging as adults in the early spring.

SOLUTION: Treat seed with an insecticide powder that contains 50 percent *diazinon*. Mix ¼ teaspoon of insecticide with each packet of seed. Shake off the excess, and plant the seeds 1 to 2 inches deep. Since adult flies are attracted to organic matter, don't add manure to the soil in the spring when planting beans, peas, or corn.

PROBLEM: Plants are stunted and grow slowly. Holes are drilled into the base of the plants. Shiny, hard, jointed, cream to yellow worms up to ⅝ inch long are found in the soil or on plant roots. Seeds don't sprout. Unsprouted seeds are hollow.

ANALYSIS: Wireworms
Wireworms are found throughout the United States. They feed on corn, carrots, potatoes, beets, peas, and many other plants. Wireworms feed entirely on underground plant parts, devouring seeds, underground stems, tubers, and roots. Infestations are most extensive in soil where lawn grass was previously grown, in poorly drained soil, and in soil that is high in organic matter. The adult form is known as the *click beetle* because it makes a clicking sound when turning from its back to its feet. Click beetles lay eggs in the spring. The eggs hatch into wireworms, which feed for 2 to 6 years before maturing into adult beetles. All sizes and ages of wireworms may be in the soil at the same time. Infestations may be scattered throughout a planting. Sometimes damaged plants resprout from the base, resulting in a bushy, stunted plant.

SOLUTION: Destroy damaged plants, since they won't produce ears. Replant unsprouted rows. At planting time, incorporate ORTHO Diazinon Soil & Turf Insect Control or ORTHO Diazinon Soil & Foliage Dust into the top 4 to 6 inches of soil.

CUCURBITS

CUCURBITS

ADAPTATION: Throughout the United States.

PLANTING TIME: See page 1009.

PLANTING METHOD: Start seeds indoors or directly in the garden. Plant cucumber, muskmelon, and watermelon seeds 1 to 2 inches deep. Plant squash and pumpkins 2 to 3 inches deep. Set transplants in the garden so that the top of their rootball is even with the surrounding garden soil. Space transplants or thin seedlings as follows: Cucumbers and muskmelons — 12 inches apart, or 24 to 36 inches apart if planted in hills. Pumpkins and vining squash — 36 to 40 inches apart. Bush squash and watermelon — 24 to 36 inches apart.

SOIL: Any good garden soil high in organic matter. pH 5.5 to 8.0.

FERTILIZER: At planting time, use 2 pounds of ORTHO Vegetable Garden Food 5–10–10 per 50-foot row, or 1 to 2 tablespoons per plant. Side-dress when the runners are 12 to 18 inches long and again when the first fruit have set.

WATER:
How much: Apply enough water at each irrigation to wet the soil 1 to 1½ feet deep.
How often: Water when the soil 2 inches deep is barely moist.

HARVEST:
Cucumbers: Slicing: 8 to 10 inches long. Pickles: 2 to 4 inches. Dill and larger pickles: 6 to 8 inches.
Muskmelons: When netting becomes pronounced and skin color turns yellow-tan; stem should separate or slip easily from the fruit.
Pumpkins and gourds: After the vines die in the fall but before a hard frost.
Summer squash: Continuous picking insures a steady supply. Zucchini and crook-neck: 1½ to 2 inches in diameter. Bush scallop: 3 to 4 inches.
Watermelon: When the spot where the melon touches the ground turns from white to creamy yellow. Green skin is dull, not shiny; the melon makes a dull thud when hit with the palm of the hand.
Winter squash: After the vines die in the fall, but before a hard frost; when your fingernail doesn't scratch the hardened skin.

STORING: Most cucurbits are used soon after harvesting. Cool in refrigerator until use. Winter squash and pumpkins can be stored over the winter. Pick only mature fruit, and cure them at temperatures between 80° and 85°F for 10 days. Then move the squash or pumpkins to a well-ventilated place with temperatures between 50° and 60°F. Store in a single layer; they rot easily if stored in piles.

PROBLEMS WITH THE FRUIT

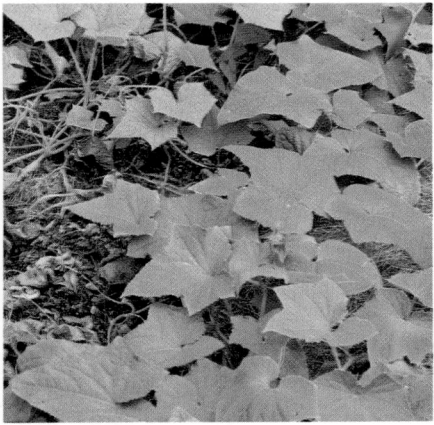

Healthy plants with no fruit.

PROBLEM: Few or no fruit are produced on melon, squash, or cucumber plants. Plants are healthy, with no signs of insect or disease problems.

ANALYSIS: Few fruit
Few or no fruit are produced on cucurbit plants because of poor pollination. Members of this family produce two kinds of flowers, male and female. For fruit production, pollen produced on male flowers must be carried by insects, especially honeybees, to the female flowers. The male flower, on the end of a long stalk, is the first to bloom. The female flowers bloom shortly thereafter. The female flower is not on a stalk, but is attached to a swelling resembling a miniature fruit. Once pollination is complete, the small swelling at the base of the female flower grows into a full-size edible fruit. Anything that interferes with pollination reduces fruit set and yield. Cold, rainy weather reduces bee activity. Improper use of insecticides may kill bees. Sometimes male and female flowers do not bloom at the same time.

SOLUTION: Male and female flowers are produced all season, so be patient. To aid pollination, hand pollinate by transferring pollen from the male flowers to the female flowers with a small paintbrush. Spray insecticides in the late afternoon when bees are not flying.

CUCURBITS — PROBLEMS WITH THE FRUIT

Misshapen and tough cucumbers.

Bitter cucumbers.

Blossom-end rot on squash.

PROBLEM: Fruit are misshapen or tough with large seeds inside. Plants may be wilted or growing slowly.

ANALYSIS: Misshapen and tough fruit

Cucumbers are misshapen when the flowers are improperly pollinated. This can result from reduced honeybee activity or from hot temperatures that kill the pollen. For more information on cucurbit pollination, see page 731. Squash and cucumber plants growing in dry soil with low fertility frequently produce misshapen fruit. Overmature fruit are tough with large seeds inside. They lack a sweet flavor.

SOLUTION: Discard all misshapen fruit. To keep your plants healthy and productive, follow the cultural and harvesting guidelines on page 731.

For a tasty treat, dip fading squash flowers in batter and pan fry in butter, or deep fry in vegetable oil. Serve hot.

PROBLEM: Cucumbers taste bitter.

ANALYSIS: Bitterness

Bitter cucumbers are usually produced on unhealthy plants late in the season. A bitter taste results from adverse growing conditions that stress the plant. These conditions include hot temperatures, dry soil, and low fertility. Plants with diseased foliage may also produce bitter fruit. Usually only the stem end is affected, but sometimes the entire fruit is bitter. Some older varieties produce fruit that is more bitter than newer varieties. Bitter fruit does not result from cross pollination between cucumbers and squash or melons. These plants do not cross pollinate. Different varieties of cucumbers will cross pollinate with each other, but they will not cross pollinate with melons or squash.

SOLUTION: As long as hot weather continues or the plant is stressed, it will continue to produce bitter fruit. This is especially true late in the season. For healthy, productive plants, follow the cultural guidelines on page 731.

PROBLEM: A water-soaked, sunken spot develops on the blossom end (opposite the stem end) of squash and watermelons. The spot enlarges and turns brown to black. Mold may grow on the spot.

ANALYSIS: Blossom-end rot

This disorder of squash, watermelons, tomatoes, and peppers is caused by a lack of calcium in the developing fruit. This lack of calcium is the result of slowed growth and damaged roots caused by any of the following factors:
1. Extreme fluctuations in soil moisture, either very wet or very dry.
2. Rapid plant growth early in the season followed by extended dry weather.
3. Excessive rains that smother root hairs.
4. Excess soil salts.
The first fruit are the most severely affected. As the name implies, the disorder always starts at the blossom end, and may enlarge to affect half of the fruit. Moldy growths on the rotted area are caused by fungi or bacteria that frequently invade the damaged tissue. The rotted area is unsightly, but the rest of the ripened fruit is edible.

SOLUTION: The numbers below correspond to numbers in the analysis.
1. Maintain uniform soil moisture by mulching (see page 918), and by following the watering guidelines on page 731.
2. Avoid high-nitrogen fertilizers and large quantities of fresh manure.
3. Plant in well-drained soil, as outlined on page 901.
4. If your soil or water is salty, provide more water at each watering to help leach salts through the soil.

_____ **INSECTS** _____

Feeding pickleworms (half life size).

Scab on squash.

Beet leafhopper damage to zucchini.

PROBLEM: Light green worms about ⅝ inch long, with black dots and dark brown heads, feed on blossoms and vines and tunnel into the fruit.

ANALYSIS: Pickleworm
(*Diaphania nitidalis*)
This moth larva favors summer squash, but also attacks cucumbers and muskmelons. Pickleworms can be a serious problem in some areas of the South. They damage plants by feeding on the vines, and reduce the fruit yield by feeding on the blossoms. Their tunneling into the fruit makes it unappetizing and often inedible. The adult moth lays clusters of eggs on the plant in late spring. The worms that hatch from these eggs feed on blossoms, buds, vines, and fruit for 2 to 3 weeks, then pupate in silken tubes on the leaves. In several days, adults emerge to repeat the cycle. The worms are active throughout the growing season. In southern Florida they are active all year.

SOLUTION: Apply ORTHO Tomato Vegetable Dust, ORTHO Sevin Garden Spray, or ORTHO Liquid Sevin at the first sign of worms in buds or blossoms. Repeat at weekly intervals as long as the pickleworms are present. Clean up plant debris and pupae to reduce the infestation.

PROBLEM: Dry corky spots up to ½ inch in diameter appear on the fruit. A sticky substance may ooze from the spots. In moist weather, a dark green velvety growth covers the spots. Fruit may be cracked and decay. White or gray spots appear on leaves. The dead tissue falls out of these spots, leaving ragged holes.

ANALYSIS: Scab
This plant disease is caused by a fungus (*Cladosporium cucumerinum*) that attacks cucumbers, squash, and muskmelons. All aboveground parts are affected. Fruit is attacked at all stages of growth, but young fruit are the most susceptible. The disease is most prevalent in foggy, cool (60° to 65°F) weather, and when night temperatures fall below 60°F for several nights in a row. The fungal spores spend the winter in diseased plant debris left in the garden and on seeds.

SOLUTION: Treat the plants with ORTHO Vegetable Disease Control at the first sign of the disease. Repeat at weekly intervals until harvest. Next year, begin spraying when the runners are 6 inches long. Clean all plant debris from the garden after harvest. Rotate your cucurbit planting site every year.

_____

Cucumber varieties resistant to scab:
Early Set, Gemini Hybrid, Marketmore 70, 76, and 80, Pacer, Poinsett 76, Slicemaster, Sweet Slice, and Victory.
Pickles: Calico, Calypso, Carolina, Commander, Frontier, and SMR 15 and 18. There are no resistant muskmelon varieties.

_____

PROBLEM: Spotted, pale green, winged insects up to ⅛ inch long hop and fly away quickly when a plant is touched. The leaves are stippled, and may be curled, puckered, and brittle.

ANALYSIS: Beet leafhopper
(*Circulifer tenellus*)
The beet leafhopper is a western insect that is found only as far east as Missouri and Illinois. It attacks all members of the cucurbit family and frequently infects them with the virus that causes curly top. Plants infected with curly top are stunted, brittle, and sometimes die. (For more information on curly top, see page 861.) The beet leafhopper feeds from early May through June. It sucks the sap and virus from the infected leaves, and then injects the virus into healthy plants at its next feeding stop.

SOLUTION: Treat infested plants with ORTHO Fruit & Vegetable Insect Control, ORTHO Sevin Garden Dust, or ORTHO Tomato Vegetable Dust. Be sure to cover the lower surfaces of the leaves. Repeat the treatment at intervals of 7 to 10 days if the plants become reinfested. For more information on controlling disease-carrying insects, see page 880.

CUCURBITS — INSECTS

Striped cucumber beetle (4 times life size).

Squash bugs (⅓ life size).

Spider mite damage on melons.

PROBLEM: Holes are chewed in the leaves, leaf stalks, and stems by yellow-green beetles with black stripes or spots. Plants may wilt and die.

ANALYSIS: Cucumber beetles
Cucumber beetles, both *striped* (*Acalymma* species) and *spotted* (*Diabrotica* species), are common pests of cucumbers, melons, squash, and pumpkins. It is important to control these beetles because they carry two serious diseases that damage and may kill cucurbits: mosaic (page 736) and bacterial wilt (page 735). The adults survive the winter in plant debris and weeds. They emerge in the early spring and feed on a variety of plants. As soon as cucurbits are planted in the garden, the beetles attack the leaves and stems, and may totally destroy the plant. They lay their yellow-orange eggs in the soil at the base of the plants. The grubs that hatch from these eggs eat the roots and the stems below the soil line, causing the plant to be stunted or to wilt. The slender white grubs feed for several weeks, pupate in the soil, and emerge as adults to repeat the cycle. There is one generation a year in the North and two or more in the South. The adults and larvae of the spotted cucumber beetle also attack corn, as described on pages 728 and 730.

SOLUTION: Treat the plants with ORTHO Fruit & Vegetable Insect Spray, ORTHO Sevin Garden Dust, or ORTHO Tomato & Vegetable Insect Spray at the first sign of the beetles. Repeat at weekly intervals as the plants become reinfested. Control early in the season helps prevent susceptible young seedlings and plants from becoming infected with bacterial wilt.

PROBLEM: Squash and pumpkin leaves wilt and may become black and crisp. Bright green to dark gray or brown flat-backed bugs, about ½ inch long, cluster on the plants.

ANALYSIS: Squash bug (*Anasa tristis*)
Both the young (nymphs) and adult squash bugs attack cucurbits, but they are most serious on squash and pumpkins. They injure and kill the plants by sucking the sap from the leaves and stems. The dark brown adults, which are sometimes incorrectly called stink bugs, emit a disagreeable odor when crushed. They lay brick-red egg clusters on the leaves in the spring. Although there is only one generation each year, all stages are found throughout the summer.

SOLUTION: Squash bugs are elusive and difficult to control. Treat the plants and the soil around the plants with ORTHO Sevin Garden Dust or ORTHO Tomato Vegetable Dust when the bugs first appear. Repeat the treatment every 7 days until the bugs are controlled. Plant varieties that are resistant to attack by squash bugs.

Squash varieties resistant to squash bugs: Butternut, Royal Acorn, and Sweet Cheese.

PROBLEM: Leaves are stippled, yellowing, and dirty. Leaves may dry out and drop. There may be webbing over flower buds, between leaves, or on the lower surfaces of the leaves. To determine if the plant is infested with mites, hold a sheet of white paper underneath an affected leaf and tap the leaf sharply. Minute green, red, or yellow specks the size of pepper grains will drop to the paper and begin to crawl around. The pests are easily seen against the white background.

ANALYSIS: Two-spotted spider mite (*Tetranychus urticae*)
These mites, related to spiders, are major pests of many garden and greenhouse plants. They cause damage by sucking sap from the underside of the leaves. As a result of feeding, the green leaf pigment disappears, producing the stippled appearance. Mites are active throughout the growing season, but are favored by hot, dry weather (70°F and up). By midsummer, they build up to tremendous numbers. In mild winter areas, mites can be a problem throughout the winter.

SOLUTION: Spray infested plants with ORTHO Fruit & Vegetable Insect Control when damage is first noticed. Spray the foliage thoroughly, being sure to cover both the upper and lower surfaces of the leaves. Repeat applications 3 more times at intervals of 7 days. Hose plants frequently to knock off webs and mites.

DISCOLORED OR SPOTTED LEAVES

Borer in stem (¾ life size).

Bacterial wilt. *Insert:* Bacterial ooze.

Alternaria leaf spot on muskmelon.

PROBLEM: Squash vines suddenly wilt. Holes in the stems are filled with a tan sawdustlike material. Fat white worms up to 1 inch long are found in the affected vines when the stems are slit open lengthwise with a knife.

ANALYSIS: Squash vine borer
(*Melittia satyriniformis*)
This insect pest primarily attacks squash and gourds, and only rarely attacks cucumbers and melons. Hubbard squash is especially susceptible. The larvae damage and kill the plants by tunneling in the stems, preventing the rest of the vine from receiving the water and nutrients it needs. The metallic green adult moth lays eggs on the vines in early summer. Egg laying occurs in April and May in the South, and June and July in the North. When the eggs hatch, the white larvae bore into the stems and feed for 4 to 5 weeks. They then crawl out of the stem and into the soil to pupate.

SOLUTION: Insecticides applied after the borer is inside the stem are not effective. Instead, slit the affected stems with a knife and destroy the borer. If the plant has not died, cover the damaged portion of the stem with soil. Keep the soil moist to encourage new roots to grow. The vine may recover. Next year, dust the plant with ORTHO Tomato Vegetable Dust during the egg-laying period.

PROBLEM: A few leaves wilt and dry and may be chewed. Wilted leaves often recover at night, but wilt again on sunny days and finally die. Fruit shrivels. To test for bacteria, cut a wilted stem near the base of the plant and squeeze out the sap, looking for a milky white substance. Touch a knife to the sap and withdraw it slowly. Look for a white ooze that strings out in a fine thread as you withdraw the knife.

ANALYSIS: Bacterial wilt
This plant disease is caused by a bacterium (*Erwinia tracheiphila*) and is more prevalent on cucumbers and muskmelons than on pumpkins and squash. Watermelons are not affected. The bacteria spend the winter in striped or spotted cucumber beetles, and are spread to plants when the beetles feed. (For more information on cucumber beetles, see page 734.) An entire plant may become infected within 12 to 15 days. The disease is most prevalent in cool (45° to 75°F) weather in areas with moderate rainfall.

SOLUTION: There are no chemical controls for bacterial wilt. Remove and discard all infected plants promptly. Control cucumber beetles with ORTHO Fruit & Vegetable Insect Control, ORTHO Sevin Garden Dust, or ORTHO Diazinon Insect Spray. Repeat the treatments every 7 days if the plants become reinfected. For more information about controlling disease-carrying insects, see page 880. Grow varieties resistant to this disease.

Cucumber variety resistant to bacterial wilt: Saladin. There are no resistant muskmelon varieties.

PROBLEM: Circular water-soaked spots up to ½ inch in diameter appear on the leaves. Dark concentric circles appear in the spots. Spots eventually enlarge into dry blotches and the leaves drop. Center or older leaves are affected first, progressing to those at the tips of the vines.

ANALYSIS: Alternaria leaf spot
This plant disease, which is caused by a fungus (*Alternaria cucumerina*), is severe on muskmelons, and also occurs on cucumbers and other cucurbits. The fungus defoliates the vines, reducing fruit yields. Weak plants, especially those bearing heavily, and those suffering from poor fertility, are most susceptible to attack. Vigorous, healthy vines are rarely attacked. The fungal spores survive the winter in plant debris left in the garden, and in and on seeds. They infect plants at temperatures between 60° and 90°F, causing the most damage from 80° to 90°F.

SOLUTION: Treat plants at the first sign of the disease with a fungicide containing *maneb, chlorothalonil,* or *anilazine.* Repeat every 7 to 10 days. Keep the plants healthy with adequate water and fertilizer and the correct soil pH (6.0 to 7.0). For more information on soil pH, see page 902.

CUCURBITS — DISCOLORED OR SPOTTED LEAVES

Anthracnose on melon.

Angular leaf spot.

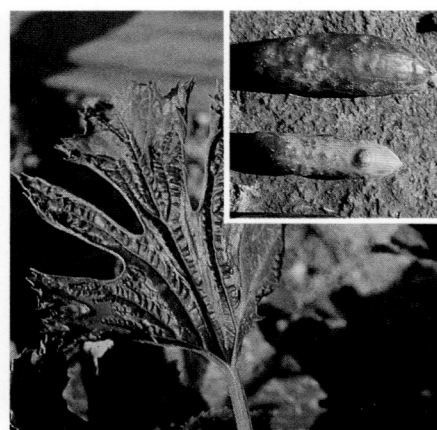

Mosaic on squash. *Insert:* Mosaic on cucumbers.

PROBLEM: Yellow, water-soaked areas spot melon and cucumber leaves, enlarge rapidly, and turn brown and dry. These spots then shatter, leaving a ragged hole in the spot. On watermelon leaves, the spots turn black. Elongated dark spots with light centers may appear on the stems. Whole leaves and vines die. Large fruit are spotted with sunken, dark brown, circular spots. Pinkish ooze may emerge from the spots. Young fruit darkens, shrivels, and dies.

ANALYSIS: Anthracnose
This plant disease is caused by a fungus (*Colletotrichum lagenarium*) and is the most destructive disease of melons and cucumbers in the East. It rarely attacks squash and pumpkin. The disease affects all aboveground parts of the plant, and is most prevalent in warm (70° to 80°F), humid weather with frequent rains. The spores overwinter in seeds and plant debris not removed from the garden. They are spread by splashing water, cucumber beetles, and tools.

SOLUTION: Treat plants with ORTHO Vegetable Disease Control at the first appearance of the disease. Repeat every 7 days, or more frequently if warm, humid weather occurs. Grow varieties resistant to this disease.

Cucumbers resistant to anthracnose: Gemini 7 Hybrid, Poinsett 76 Liberty Hybrid, Slicemaster, and Sweet Slice Hybrid.
   Muskmelons: Saticoy Hybrid and Samson Hybrid.
   Watermelons: Charleston Gray, Sweet Favorite Hybrid, and You Sweet Thing Hybrid.

PROBLEM: Water-soaked, angular spots appear on the leaves. Tearlike droplets may ooze from the spots and dry into a white residue. Spots turn gray or tan, then drop out, leaving ragged holes. Fruit may be covered with cracked white spots.

ANALYSIS: Angular leaf spot
This plant disease is caused by a bacterium (*Pseudomonas lachrymans*) that attacks the leaves, stems, and fruits of cucurbits. The bacteria survive the winter on seed and plant debris not removed from the garden. The bacteria are spread from the soil to the plants by splashing rain, cucumber beetles, and hands and clothing, and infect the leaves and stems when they are wet with dew, rain, or irrigation water. The disease is most active between 75° and 80°F.

SOLUTION: Treat the plants with a pesticide containing *basic copper sulfate* at the first sign of the disease. Repeat every 7 to 10 days as long as the disease is a problem. To reduce the spread of the bacteria, don't work among wet plants. Avoid overhead watering by using drop or furrow irrigation. Clean all plant debris from the garden after harvest to reduce the amount of overwintering bacteria. Purchase seeds and plants from a reputable company. Grow varieties resistant to this disease.

Cucumbers resistant to angular leaf spot: Cherokee 7, Dasher, Frontier, Gemini 7 Hybrid, Liberty Hybrid, Pioneer Hybrid, Poinsett 76, Slicemaster, Sweet Slice, and Victory. There are no melon, squash, or pumpkin varieties resistant to this leaf spot.

PROBLEM: Leaves are mottled yellow and green, and are distorted, stunted, and curled. Cucumber fruits are mottled with dark green and pale green to white blotches and covered with warts. Sometimes the skin is smooth and completely white. Summer squash fruit may be also covered with warts.

ANALYSIS: Mosaic virus
This plant disease is caused by several viruses that attack cucumbers, muskmelons, and summer squash. The viruses overwinter in perennial plants, and weeds, including catnip, pokeweed, wild cucumber, motherwort, and milkweed. The viruses are spread from plant to plant by aphids and cucumber beetles, and can infect plants at any time from the seedling stage to maturity. Infection early in the season is more damaging. Affected fruits taste bitter. Fruits that are more than half grown at the time of infection are immune to attack. Roots are not affected.

SOLUTION: There are no chemical controls for virus diseases. Remove and destroy all infected plants immediately. Control aphids and cucumber beetles with ORTHO Fruit & Vegetable Insect Control. Repeat at intervals of 7 to 10 days if the plants become reinfested. For more information on controlling disease-carrying insects, see page 880. Remove weeds in and near the garden. Grow resistant cucumber varieties. For a list of these varieties, see page 1009. There are not yet any resistant varieties of summer squash or muskmelon.

Powdery mildew on pumpkin.

Downy mildew.

PROBLEM: The upper surfaces of the leaves are covered with a white powdery growth. Areas of the leaves and stems turn brown, wither, and dry. Fruit may be covered with the white powdery growth.

ANALYSIS: Powdery mildew
This common plant disease is caused by either of two fungi (*Erysiphe cichoracearum* and *Sphaerotheca fuliginea*) that thrive in both humid and dry weather. The powdery patches consist of fungal strands and spores. The spores are spread by the wind to healthy plants. The fungus saps the plant nutrients, causing yellowing and sometimes death of the leaf. A severe infection may kill the plant. Since these powdery mildews attack several different kinds of plants, the fungus from a diseased plant may infect other types of plants in the garden. For a list of powdery mildews and the plants which they attack, see page 995. Under favorable conditions, powdery mildew can spread through a closely spaced planting in a matter of days or weeks.

SOLUTION: Treat the plants with ORTHO Vegetable Disease Control at the first sign of the disease. Continue treatments at intervals of 7 days as long as the disease is a problem. Grow varieties resistant to powdery mildew.

_____

Cucumber varieties resistant to powdery mildew: Burpless, Cherokee, Gemini 7 Hybrid, Marketmore 76, Slicemaster, and Sweet Slice.
Cantaloupes: Ambrosia, Classic, Delicious 51, Early Dawn, Edisto, PRM #45, Saticoy, and Summet.

PROBLEM: Areas between the leaf veins turn yellow and then brown. In humid weather, the lower surfaces of the leaves are covered with a white, purple, or black hairy growth. Leaves die quickly. The older leaves are attacked first, progressing outward until the entire vine dies. Fruit is small and has a poor taste.

ANALYSIS: Downy mildew
This plant disease is caused by a fungus (*Pseudoperonospora cubensis*). The disease is severe on cucumbers and muskmelons, and less severe on pumpkins and squash. Watermelons are rarely attacked. The downy growth on the undersides of the leaves consists of fungus spores that break off and are spread by splashing water, tools, and clothing to other plants and leaves. The disease develops most rapidly in warm (60° to 85°F), wet weather.

SOLUTION: Treat the plants with ORTHO Vegetable Disease Control at the first sign of the disease. Repeat at intervals of 7 days as long as the disease continues. Those leaves already infected will not be cured. However, the sprays will protect healthy leaves from becoming infected. Clean all plant debris from the garden after harvest. Grow varieties resistant to this disease.

_____

Cucumbers resistant to downy mildew: Bounty, Burpless, Comanche, Early Surecrop, Gemini, Liberty Hybrid, Marketmore 76, Pioneer, Poinsett 76, Slicemaster, and Sweet Slice.
Muskmelons: Ambrosia, Dixie Jumbo, Early Dawn, Summet, Topmark, and Topset.

CURRANTS AND GOOSEBERRIES _____

ADAPTATION: Northern United States.

PLANTING TIME: Early spring and fall.

PLANTING METHOD: Select 1 to 2-year-old plants that are 12 to 24 inches tall. Set the plants 3 to 4 feet apart, and deep enough so that the top of their rootball is 1 inch deeper than the surrounding garden soil.

SOIL: Any good garden soil that is high in organic matter. pH 5.5 to 7.5

FERTILIZER: At planting time, incorporate a 1 to 2-inch layer of partially decomposed manure. In early spring before new growth begins, add 1 pound of ORTHO General Purpose Plant Food 8-8-8 per 100 square feet, or 1 tablespoon per plant. Side-dress with the same amount in midspring and midsummer.

WATER:
How much: Apply enough water at each irrigation to wet the soil 1½ to 2 feet deep.
How often: Water when the soil 2 inches deep is dry.

HARVEST: Gently pull fruit from the stem when evenly colored, plump, and slightly soft. Use currants right after picking. Nearly ripe currants can be left on the bush for a week or more before picking. Immature gooseberries make tasty pies.

CURRANTS AND GOOSEBERRIES

Powdery mildew on gooseberries.

White pine blister rust on currant.

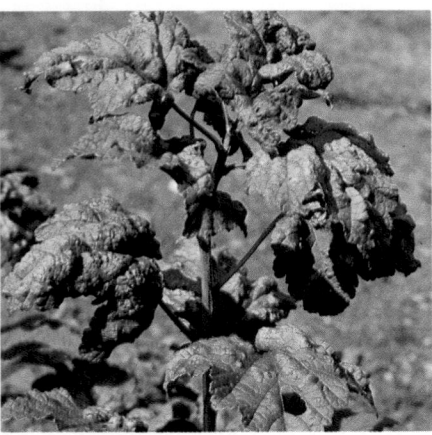

Aphid damage on currant.

PROBLEM: White powdery material covers leaves and stems. Fruit is covered with a white or brown powdery growth.

ANALYSIS: Powdery mildew
This common plant disease is caused by a fungus (*Sphaerotheca mors-uvae*) that thrives in both humid and dry weather. The powdery patches consist of fungal strands and spores. The spores are spread by the wind to healthy plants. The fungus saps plant nutrients, causing yellowing and sometimes death of the leaf. A severe infection may kill the plant. The white or brown growth on the fruit makes them unpalatable. Under favorable conditions, powdery mildew can spread through a closely spaced planting or a dense bush in a matter of days or weeks.

SOLUTION: Treat the plants with a *lime sulfur* fungicide when the tips of the new leaves show green through the bud. Use a *wettable sulfur* for the following additional three sprays: as the blossoms open, at full bloom, and 2 weeks later. Prune the bushes for good air circulation.

PROBLEM: In midsummer, orange-brown blisters appear on the undersides of older leaves. A yellow material may ooze from the blisters. Leaves turn yellow.

ANALYSIS: White pine blister rust
This plant disease is caused by a fungus (*Cronartium ribicola*) that requires both white pines and currants or gooseberries (*Ribes* species) to complete its life cycle. If either one is not present, the disease does not occur. Wild gooseberries, and black, skunk, stink, and red-flowering currants are all highly susceptible. Cultivated red currants are somewhat resistant. Currants and gooseberries are not severely affected by this disease. However, white pine trees are often killed. Federal and state quarantine laws prohibit planting currants or gooseberries closer than 300 to 900 feet to white pine plantings. In midsummer, yellow spores are produced in blisters on currant or gooseberry leaves, and then blown to pine trees. White blisters form on pine bark and rupture to release another type of spore. These orange-yellow spores are then blown back to currants or gooseberries, where the cycle begins again. For information on this disease on white pine, see page 559.

SOLUTION: Quarantine regulations require elimination of all black currant bushes within 1 mile of white pine plantings. Remove red currant and gooseberry bushes closer than 300 feet to pines.

Red currant varieties resistant to blister rust: Viking and Red Dutch.

PROBLEM: Leaves are cupped and distorted, and may turn red. Small yellow soft-bodied insects cluster on the undersides of the leaves. A shiny, sticky substance often covers the leaves and fruit.

ANALYSIS: Aphids
Aphids do little damage in small numbers. However, they are extremely prolific and populations can rapidly build up to damaging numbers during the growing season. Damage occurs when the aphid sucks the juices from the currant or gooseberry leaves and flower buds. The aphid is unable to digest fully all the sugar in the plant sap and excretes the excess in a fluid called honeydew. The honeydew is unsightly and makes the fruit undesirable. Ants feed on this sticky substance and are often present where there is an aphid infestation.

SOLUTION: Spray the plants with an insecticide containing *malathion* as soon as the insects appear. Repeat the spray at intervals of 10 days if the plant becomes reinfested.

EGGPLANT

Currant borer (4 times life size).

PROBLEM: Leaves turn yellow and wilt in the summer and fall. Canes produce fewer fruits and eventually die. Pale yellow caterpillars, ½ inch long, are found inside the canes.

ANALYSIS: Currant borer (*Synanthedon tipuliformis*)
This insect pest attacks currants and gooseberries, but red currants are the most susceptible. The borer feeds on the inner cane tissue and weakens the canes, thereby reducing the fruit yield. Weakened canes eventually die. The immature borer hibernates for the winter in the canes and pupates in the spring. In June and July, the adult black and yellow moth emerges and lays eggs on the bark of the canes. The larvae that hatch from these eggs bore into the canes. They feed in the canes all summer and hibernate there for the winter. There is one generation each year.

SOLUTION: The chemical used to control this pest is not available to home gardeners. Contact a pest control operator. Prune out and destroy all infested canes as soon as the borers are noticed. Keep the plants healthy with regular maintenance as outlined on page 737.

EGGPLANT

ADAPTATION: Throughout the United States.

PLANTING TIME: See page 1009.

PLANTING METHOD: Sow eggplant seeds ¼ to ½ inch deep. Thin seedlings or plant transplants to stand 18 to 24 inches apart.

SOIL: Any good garden soil high in organic matter. pH 5.5 to 8.0

FERTILIZER: At planting time, use 3 to 4 pounds of ORTHO Vegetable Garden Food 5–10–10 per 100 square feet, or 1 pound per 25-foot row. Side dress every 3 to 4 weeks with 1 pound per 25-foot row, or 1 to 2 tablespoons per plant.
 Containers: Water thoroughly every 2 to 4 weeks with a solution of ORTHO Tomato & Vegetable Food 6–18–6.

WATER:
 How much: Apply enough water at each irrigation to wet the soil 10 to 12 inches deep.
 How often: Water when the soil 2 inches deep is barely moist.

HARVEST: Fruit is usually mature 80 to 90 days after transplanting. Pick it while the skin is glossy, before it turns dull. When you press the skin with your thumb, a slight indentation should remain. Seeds inside should not be brown or hardened. Cut the stem with sharp knife, leaving ½ to 1 inch attached to the fruit. Store in the refrigerator until use.

Flea beetle (twice life size).

PROBLEM: Leaves are riddled with shotholes about ⅛ inch in diameter. Tiny (¹⁄₁₆ inch) black beetles jump like fleas when disturbed. Leaves of seedlings and eventually whole plants may wilt and die.

ANALYSIS: Flea beetles
These beetles jump like fleas, but are not related to them. Both adult and immature flea beetles feed on a wide variety of garden vegetables, including eggplants. The immature beetle, a legless gray grub, injures plants by feeding on the roots and the lower surface of leaves. Adults chew holes in leaves. Flea beetles are most damaging to seedlings and young plants. Leaves of seedlings riddled with holes dry out quickly and die. Adult beetles survive the winter in soil and garden debris. They emerge in early spring to feed on weeds until vegetable seeds sprout or plants are set in the garden. Grubs hatch from eggs laid in the soil and feed for 2 to 3 weeks. After pupating in the soil, they emerge as adults to repeat the cycle. There are 1 to 4 generations a year. Adults may feed for up to 2 months.

SOLUTION: Control flea beetles on eggplants with ORTHO Sevin Garden Dust, ORTHO Tomato & Vegetable Insect Spray, or ORTHO Tomato Vegetable Dust when the leaves first show damage. Watch new growth for evidence of further damage, and repeat the treatment at weekly intervals as needed. Clean all plant debris from the garden after harvest to eliminate overwintering spots for adult beetles.

EGGPLANT

Colorado potato beetle (life size).

Blister beetles (life size).

Tomato hornworm (⅓ life size).

PROBLEM: Yellow beetles ⅜ inch long with black stripes are chewing holes in the leaves. Fat, red, humpbacked grubs with two rows of black dots also feed on the leaves.

ANALYSIS: Colorado potato beetle (*Leptinotarsa decemlineata*)
This insect pest, also known as the *potato bug*, often devastates eggplant, potato, tomato, and pepper plantings. Both the adults and the larvae damage plants by eating leaves and stems. Small plants are most severely affected. The beetle was originally native to the Rocky Mountains, and spread eastward in the late 1800s as potato plantings increased. Now they are found in all states except California, Nevada, and parts of Florida. In some areas of the country the beetle population may reach epidemic proportions. Adult beetles overwinter in the soil and emerge in the spring as eggplants are set in the garden. They lay orange-yellow eggs on the undersides of the leaves. The larvae that hatch from the eggs are dark red. They feed for 2 to 3 weeks, pupate in the soil, and emerge 1 to 2 weeks later as adults. One generation is completed in a month. There are 1 to 3 generations a year, depending on the part of the country.

SOLUTION: Control Colorado potato beetles with ORTHO Sevin Garden Dust or ORTHO Tomato Vegetable Dust. Treat when the insects are first noticed, and repeat every 7 days as long as the infestation continues.

PROBLEM: Leaves are chewed. Black, gray, brown, or yellow beetles cluster on the leaves. These slender beetles range from ½ to ¾ inch long, and are sometimes striped.

ANALYSIS: Blister beetle (*Epicauta* species)
These insect pests feed on a wide variety of vegetables and flowers. The adult beetles damage plants by chewing the leaves, often defoliating an entire plant. The larvae, however, feed on grasshopper egg masses, and help to reduce the grasshopper population. Adult beetles emerge from hibernation in swarms in June and July. They feed voraciously, and after stripping one plant they move on to another. They lay yellow egg clusters in the soil. The grubs that hatch from these eggs migrate through the soil, feeding on grasshopper eggs. There is only one generation each year. Be careful when handling these beetles; the juices from crushed beetles cause blisters.

SOLUTION: Treat the plants with ORTHO Tomato Vegetable Dust or ORTHO Tomato & Vegetable Insect Spray as soon as the beetles appear in June or July. Repeat the treatments if the plants become reinfested.

PROBLEM: Fat green or brown worms, up to 5 inches long, with white diagonal side stripes, chew on the leaves. A red or black "horn" projects from the rear end. Black droppings soil the leaves.

ANALYSIS: Tomato hornworm (*Manduca quinquemaculata*) and tobacco hornworm (*M. sexta*)
Hornworms feed on the fruit and foliage of eggplants, peppers, and tomatoes. Although there may be only a few worms present, each worm consumes large quantities of foliage and causes extensive damage. The large gray or brown adult moth with yellow and white markings emerges from hibernation in late spring, and drinks nectar from petunias and other garden flowers. The worms hatch from eggs laid on the undersides of the leaves, and feed for 3 to 4 weeks. Then they crawl into the soil, pupate, and later emerge as adults to repeat the cycle. There is 1 generation a year in the North and 2 to 4 in the South. Some worms may have white sacs that look like puffed rice on their bodies. These sacs are the cocoons of parasitic wasps that feed on and eventually kill the hornworm.

SOLUTION: Treat the plants with ORTHO Sevin Garden Dust or ORTHO Tomato & Vegetable Insect Spray. Don't destroy worms covered with white sacs. Let the wasps inside the worms mature, emerge, and infest other hornworms. If practical, handpick unaffected worms.

Whiteflies (half life size).

Aphids (life size).

Verticillium wilt.

PROBLEM: Tiny, winged insects $\frac{1}{12}$ inch long feed on the undersides of the leaves. The insects are covered with white waxy powder. When the plant is touched, insects flutter rapidly around it. Leaves may be mottled and yellowing. In warm winter areas, black mold may cover the leaves.

ANALYSIS: Greenhouse whitefly
(*Trialeurodes vaporariorum*)
This insect is a common pest of many garden and greenhouse plants. The four-winged adult lays eggs on the undersides of leaves. The larvae are the size of a pinhead, flat, oval-shaped, and semitransparent, with white waxy filaments radiating from the body. They feed for about a month before changing to the adult form. Both the larval and adult forms suck sap from the leaves. The larvae are more damaging because they feed more heavily. Adults and larvae cannot fully digest all the sugar in the plant sap, and excrete the excess in a fluid called honeydew, which often drops onto the leaves below. A sooty mold fungus may develop on the honeydew, causing the eggplant leaves to appear black and dirty. In warm winter areas the insect can be active year-round, with eggs, larvae, and adults present at the same time. The whitefly is unable to live through freezing winters. Spring reinfestations in freezing winter areas come from migrating whiteflies and from infested greenhouse-grown plants placed in the garden.

SOLUTION: Control whiteflies by spraying with ORTHO Tomato & Vegetable Insect Spray every 7 to 10 days as necessary. Spray the foliage thoroughly, being sure to cover both the upper and lower surfaces of the leaves.

PROBLEM: Leaves are yellow, curled, and often distorted. Soft-bodied insects cluster on the undersides of the leaves and new growth. They are about $\frac{1}{8}$ inch long, and may be green, black, or purple. A shiny, sticky substance may coat some of the leaves and fruit.

ANALYSIS: Aphids
Aphids do little damage in small numbers. However, they are extremely prolific and populations can rapidly build up to damaging numbers during the growing season. Damage occurs when the aphid sucks the juices from the eggplant leaves, flower buds, and fruit. The aphid is unable to digest fully all the sugar in the plant sap and excretes the excess in a fluid called honeydew. The honeydew often drops onto the leaves below. Ants feed on this sticky substance, and are often present where there is an aphid infestation.

SOLUTION: Spray with ORTHO Tomato Vegetable Dust or ORTHO Tomato & Vegetable Insect Spray as soon as the aphids appear. Repeat the treatment if the plants become reinfested. Occasionally hose down the plants with a strong stream of water to wash the aphids off.

PROBLEM: Plants are stunted. The lower leaves turn yellow. Finally the entire plant wilts and dies. The inside of the stem, near the surface, is discolored brown.

ANALYSIS: Verticillium wilt
This wilt disease affects many ornamental plants. It is caused by a soil-inhabiting fungus (*Verticillium albo-atrum*) that persists indefinitely on plant debris or in the soil. The disease is spread by contaminated seeds, plants, soil, and equipment. The fungus enters the plant through the roots and spreads up into the stems and leaves through the water-conducting vessels in the stems. The vessels become discolored and plugged. This plugging cuts off the flow of water and nutrients to the leaves, causing leaf yellowing and wilting.

SOLUTION: No chemical control is available. It is best to destroy infected plants. Verticillium can be removed from the soil only by fumigation techniques. (For more information about soil fumigation, see page 919.) There are no eggplant varieties resistant to this wilt disease. Do not plant members of the tomato family (tomato, pepper, eggplant, potato) or okra in the same area of the garden more frequently than once every 3 years.

EGGPLANT

Phomopsis leaf spot. *Insert:* Infected fruit.

PROBLEM: Circular gray to brown spots with light centers appear on the lower leaves. The spots may be covered with tiny black specks and affected leaves may turn yellow and die. The base of the stem darkens, and the plant falls over easily. Fruit is speckled with pale sunken spots that often spread to include the whole fruit. Fruit then rots and shrivels.

ANALYSIS: Leaf spot and fruit rot
This plant disease is caused by a fungus (*Phomopsis vexans*) that attacks every aboveground part of the plant, and can infect the plant at any stage in its life. It causes the death of seedlings, lesions on the main stem, leaf blight, and fruit rot. The disease is most prevalent in very warm (70° to 90°F), wet weather. The fungal spores spend the winter in and on diseased seeds, plant debris, and soil. They are spread from plant to plant by splashing rain, tools, and insects.

SOLUTION: Treat the plants with ORTHO Tomato Vegetable Dust at the first sign of the disease. Repeat the treatment every 10 to 14 days until harvest. Discard affected fruit and plants immediately. Clean the garden at the end of the season. If the disease develops in your garden, wait 3 years before planting eggplant in that area again.

Eggplant varieties resistant to leaf spot and fruit rot: Florida Beauty, Florida High Bush, and Florida Market.

Spider mite damage.

PROBLEM: Leaves are stippled, yellowing, and dirty. Leaves may dry out and drop. There may be webbing over flower buds, between leaves, or on the lower surfaces of the leaves. To determine if the plant is infested with mites, hold a sheet of white paper underneath an affected leaf and tap the leaf sharply. Minute green red or yellow specks the size of pepper grains will drop to the paper and begin to crawl around. The pests are easily seen against the white background.

ANALYSIS: Two-spotted spider mite
(*Tetranychus urticae*)
These mites, related to spiders, are major pests of many garden and greenhouse plants. They cause damage by sucking sap from the underside of the leaves. As a result of feeding, the green leaf pigment disappears, producing the stippled appearance. Mites are active throughout the growing season, but are favored by hot, dry weather (70°F and up). By midsummer, they build up to tremendous numbers.

SOLUTION: Treat the infested plants with ORTHO Fruit & Vegetable Insect Control, or an insecticide containing *malathion*, as soon as the damage appears. Repeat the treatment 3 more times at intervals of 7 to 10 days.

GRAPES

GRAPES

ADAPTATION: Throughout the United States; for regional recommendations, see page 1007.

PLANTING TIME: Spring.

PLANTING METHOD: Purchase 1-year-old rooted vines, either bare-root or in containers. Plant them 6 to 10 feet apart and so that the top of their rootball is even with the surrounding soil. Cut the tops back, leaving only 2 or 3 buds.

SOIL: Any good garden soil that is high in organic matter. pH 6.0 to 8.0

FERTILIZER: At planting time, use 1 pound of ORTHO General Purpose Plant Food 8–8–8 per 100 square feet, or 1 tablespoon per plant. For the first year, side-dress with the same amount in midspring and midsummer. In subsequent years, fertilize each spring before new growth begins with ½ to 1 pound of fertilizer per plant.

WATER:
How much: Apply enough water at each irrigation to wet the soil 1½ to 3 feet deep.
How often: Water when the soil 6 to 12 inches deep is almost dry.

HARVEST: Table grapes should taste sweet and be plump with even color. Wine grapes may be slightly tart, but plump and slightly soft with even color.

GRAPES — PROBLEMS WITH THE FRUIT _____ **INSECTS** _____

Black rot.

Grapes damaged by grape berry moth larvae.

Leafroller on damaged leaf (¼ life size).

PROBLEM: Light brown spots surrounded by a dark brown line appear on the grapes. The grapes turn black, shrivel, and dry up like raisins. They remain attached to the stems. Reddish brown circular spots appear on the leaves. Sunken purple to black elongated lesions spot the canes, leaf stems, and tendrils.

ANALYSIS: Black rot
This plant disease is caused by a fungus (_Guignardia bidwelli_). It is the most destructive disease that attacks grapes, often destroying all the fruit. The fungus spends the winter in infected dormant canes, tendrils on the support wires, and mummified fruit. In warm, moist spring weather, spores infect new shoots, leaves, tendrils, and eventually the developing fruit. The fruit is affected in all stages of development, but most severely when it is half to two-thirds grown. Spores for future infections are produced on infected leaves, canes, and fruit. The severity of the disease depends on the amount of diseased material that survives the winter, and on the spring and early summer weather.

SOLUTION: Discard all infected fruit and prune out infected canes and tendrils. Once the fruit has begun to shrivel, fungicide sprays are ineffective. Next year, spray the plants with ORTHO Home Orchard Spray. It is important to spray early in the season to keep the spread of the disease to a minimum. Treat when new shoots are 6 to 10 inches long; just before and immediately after bloom; and continue at intervals of 10 to 14 days until the grapes are full size. Treat more frequently if leaf symptoms develop, or if the season is wet. For a list of grapes resistant to this disease, see page 1007.

PROBLEM: Grapes are webbed together and to leaves. Dark green to purple worms, up to ⅜ inch long, with dark brown heads are inside the grapes. White cocoons cling to the leaves between flaps of leaf tissue.

ANALYSIS: Grape berry moth
(_Endopiza viteana_)
The grape berry moth is the most serious insect pest of grapes in the East. The worms damage both green and ripening fruit by feeding on the inner pulp and seeds. They web the grapes together and to leaves with silken threads as they feed and move from cluster to cluster of grapes. One worm can injure several berries. The worms spend the winters as pupae on leaves and on the ground. The brown moths emerge in early June, and lay eggs on blossom stems and small fruit. The larvae that hatch from these eggs feed on the buds, blossoms, and fruit. After 3 to 4 weeks of feeding, they cut a small bit of leaf, fold it over, and make a cocoon inside, where they pupate. Within a few weeks, adult moths emerge to repeat the cycle, this time laying eggs on ripening fruit. This second generation feeds for 3 to 4 weeks, then pupates for the winter.

SOLUTION: Discard infested grapes. At the end of the season, clean up all fallen grape leaves to reduce the number of overwintering pupae. Next year, treat the plants immediately after bloom with ORTHO Fruit & Vegetable Insect Control or ORTHO Home Orchard Spray. Repeat the application 7 to 10 days later. To control the second generation, spray again in late July to early August.

PROBLEM: Leaves are rolled up in a curl. A white webbing covers grape clusters and leaves. Inside the webbing are pale green to yellow caterpillars, up to ¾ inch long, with brown heads. Holes are chewed in leaves and fruit.

ANALYSIS: Redbanded leafroller
(_Argyrotaenia velutinana_)
and omnivorous leafroller
(_Platynota stultana_)
These caterpillars feed on buds, fruit, and leaves in the protection of rolled and webbed leaves and fruit. They feed on the surface of the berry, not inside. They also chew into the cluster stem, so the grape clusters dangle from the plants by a slender thread, causing the fruit to shrivel and drop. Leafrollers spend the winter as larvae and pupae on vines and fruit clusters lying on the ground. As the weather warms in the spring, they emerge and begin feeding on the young foliage. They later pupate and emerge as brown adult moths to lay light green eggs on bark, leaves, and fruit. There are 2 to 3 generations a year, so damage may continue from April until October or November.

SOLUTION: Sprays are ineffective once the caterpillars are rolled in the leaves. Pinch rolled leaves or webbing around grapes and leaves to kill the leafrollers inside. Destroy all mummified fruit. Control future generations with ORTHO Home Orchard Spray or ORTHO Malathion 50 Insect Spray. Next year, treat when the shoots are 6 to 8 inches long; when they are 18 inches long; at petal fall; when the fruit is ⅛ inch in diameter; and when the fruit just touch each other in the cluster.

GRAPES — INSECTS

Grape leaf skeletonizers (life size).

Grape flea beetle larvae (life size).

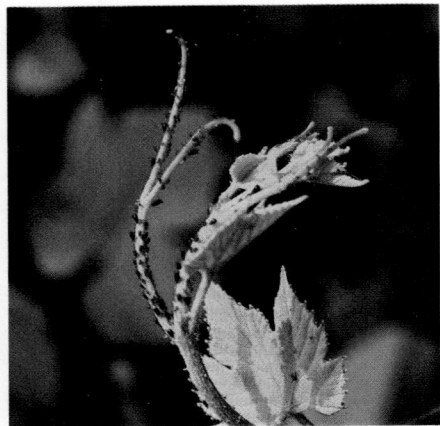

Aphids (life size).

PROBLEM: Yellow caterpillars with purple or black stripes feed in rows on the leaves. The caterpillars may be covered with black spines. They chew on the upper and lower surfaces of the leaves, eating everything but the leaf veins.

ANALYSIS: Grape leaf skeletonizer (*Harrisina* species)
These pests frequently attack grapes in home gardens and abandoned vineyards. The young caterpillars characteristically feed side by side in a row on the leaves. They feed heartily, and may defoliate a vine in several days. The loss of leaf tissue slows the growth of the vine and fruit, and reduces production. These pests survive the winter as pupae in cocoons on leaves and in debris on the ground. In late spring the metallic green or smoky black adult moths emerge, and lay their eggs on the lower surfaces of the leaves. The yellow caterpillars that hatch from those eggs feed on the leaves, usually chewing on the upper or lower surfaces; but sometimes as they mature, they eat all the tissue between the veins. There are 2 to 3 generations each year, so damage continues from mid-May to August. The black spines on the western grape skeletonizer may cause welts on your fingers if you touch them.

SOLUTION: Treat the infested plants with an insecticide containing *carbaryl* as soon as the caterpillars appear. Spray both the upper and lower surfaces of the leaves. Repeat the treatment if the plants become reinfested.

PROBLEM: Metallic, blue-green beetles, 1/5 inch long, feed on buds and unfolding leaves. Brown grubs with black spots damage the foliage by feeding on the upper surfaces of the leaves, causing the lower surfaces to turn brown.

ANALYSIS: Grape flea beetle (*Altica chalybea*)
Both the adults and larvae of the grape flea beetle damage grape plants. In the early spring, as the leaf buds swell, the adult beetles migrate to the plants from wild grapes and abandoned plantings. They feed on the tender buds, chewing out the centers and destroying future canes. One adult beetle damages several buds; if the beetles are numerous, crop yield and cane growth may be reduced. The adults lay yellow eggs on the buds, bark, and leaves. From June to mid-July the eggs hatch and the larvae feed for 3 to 4 weeks on the leaves. They then pupate in the soil for 1 to 2 weeks, and emerge as adults. The adults feed on new growth through the summer and hibernate for the winter under leaves and other garden debris. There is only one generation each year. Grape flea beetles are most prevalent on neglected plants.

SOLUTION: Treat infested plants with ORTHO Diazinon Insect Spray or ORTHO Home Orchard Spray as soon as these pests appear. Repeat applications 10 to 14 days apart if the beetles reappear.

PROBLEM: Leaves are curled, puckered, and distorted. Soft-bodied purple, brown, or green insects cluster under the leaves and on stems and new growth. They may disappear after a heavy rain. Some grapes may drop from the clusters. A shiny, sticky substance may coat the leaves and discolor the fruit. A black sooty fungus may cover affected leaves and fruit.

ANALYSIS: Aphids
Aphids do little damage in small numbers. However, they are extremely prolific and populations can rapidly build up to damaging numbers during the growing season. Damage occurs when the aphid sucks the juices from the grape leaves. The aphid is unable to digest fully all the sugar in the plant sap and excretes the excess in a fluid called honeydew, which often drops onto the leaves below. Ants feed on this sticky substance and are often present where there is an aphid infestation.

SOLUTION: Treat the infested plants with ORTHO Home Orchard Spray, ORTHO Malathion 50 Insect Spray, or ORTHO Diazinon Insect Spray as soon as the aphids appear. Repeat at intervals of 10 to 14 days if the plants become reinfested.

DISCOLORED LEAVES

Grape leafhopper (15 times life size).

PROBLEM: Areas on the leaves are stippled and turn pale yellow, white, then brown. Some of the leaves may fall. On the undersides of the leaves are found pale yellow or white, ⅛ inch, flying or jumping insects, with red or yellow body markings.

ANALYSIS: Grape leafhoppers
(*Erthroneura* species)
Both the young and adult grape leafhoppers suck the juices from grape leaves, causing white spots that later turn brown. This damage reduces normal vine growth, resulting in delayed maturity of fruit and poor vine growth the following year. Their black droppings may also mar the fruit, making it unappetizing. Leafhoppers survive the winter as adults in protected places. When new growth begins in the spring, these adults emerge and begin feeding. The adults lay their eggs in the leaves, causing blisterlike swellings. There are 2 or 3 overlapping generations each season, so leafhoppers of all stages of maturity can be found feeding from the time of new growth in the spring until the leaves drop in the fall.

SOLUTION: Treat infested grape vines with ORTHO Fruit & Vegetable Insect Control, ORTHO Home Orchard Spray, or ORTHO Malathion 50 Insect Spray as soon as leafhoppers are noticed. Spray both the upper and lower surfaces of the leaves. Repeat the treatment at intervals of 10 to 14 days if the plants become reinfested. Clean all plant debris from the planting after harvest to reduce the number of overwintering leafhoppers.

Spider mite damage.

PROBLEM: Leaves are stippled, yellowing, and dirty. Leaves may dry out and drop. There may be webbing between leaves or on the lower surfaces of the leaves. To determine if the plant is infested with mites, hold a sheet of white paper underneath an affected leaf and tap the leaf sharply. Minute green, red, or yellow specks the size of pepper grains will drop to the paper and begin to crawl around. The pests are easily seen against the white background.

ANALYSIS: Spider mites
These mites, related to spiders, are major pests of many garden and greenhouse plants. They cause damage by sucking sap from the undersides of the grape leaves. As a result of feeding, leaf pigment disappears, producing the stippled appearance. Mites are active throughout the growing season, but are favored by hot, dry weather (70°F and up). By midsummer, they build up to tremendous numbers.

SOLUTION: Treat the infested grape vines with ORTHO Home Orchard Spray, ORTHO Malathion 50 Insect Spray, or ORTHO Fruit & Vegetable Insect Control as soon as damage appears. Repeat 3 more times at intervals of 7 to 10 days.

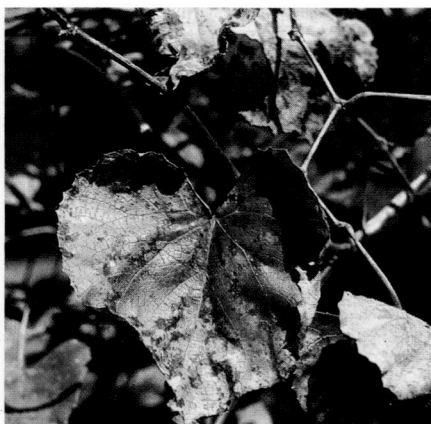

Anthracnose.

PROBLEM: Circular, sunken spots with light gray centers and dark borders appear on shoots, fruit, tendrils, and leaf stalks. The fruit remains firm. The leaves may curl downward, and the brown areas drop out.

ANALYSIS: Anthracnose
This plant disease is caused by a fungus (*Elsinoe ampelina*) that may do considerable damage a few years in a row, and then disappear. It is often called *birdseye rot* because of the similarity of the spots on the fruit to a bird's eye. It is seldom severe on Concord or muscadine grape vines. The disease first attacks the new growth. The spots on the stems often merge, girdling the stem and killing the vine tips. Anthracnose is prevalent during wet periods in the spring and in poorly maintained vineyards. The fungus survives the winter on old lesions on the canes. Although this disease doesn't kill the grape vines, the infected fruit are often misshapen and unappetizing. Several years of attack from anthracnose sufficiently weakens the vines to make them more susceptible to other problems.

SOLUTION: Discard infected fruit, and prune out diseased canes. Sprays applied after spotting occurs are ineffective. Next spring, before the buds open, spray the vines with a fungicide containing *lime sulfur*. Treat the plants with a fungicide containing *ferbam* when the shoots are 1 to 2 inches long, when they are 6 to 10 inches long, just before bloom, just after the blossoms fall, and 2 to 3 more times at intervals of 2 weeks. Spray all canes and leaves thoroughly.

GRAPES — DISCOLORED LEAVES

Armillaria root rot.

Twig and branch borer (3 times life size).

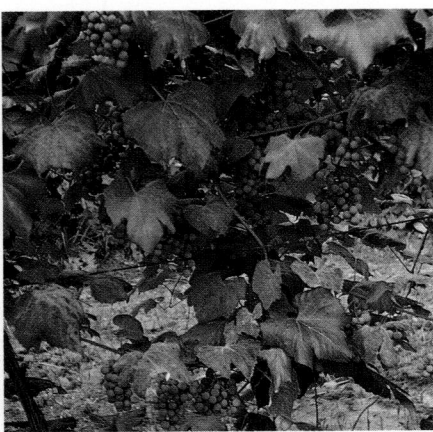

Powdery mildew.

PROBLEM: Leaves are reddened or yellow. Shoot growth is stunted. Few grapes are produced. Plants decline, produce no new growth, and die. In the fall and winter, honey-colored mushrooms 2 to 5 inches in diameter may develop singly or in clusters on the lower trunks or on the soil. Black rootlike strands somewhat smaller than the diameter of a pencil lead grow in the soil out of larger roots. A white, fan-shaped growth occurs between the bark and the wood of large roots and on the main stem just below the soil line.

ANALYSIS: Armillaria root rot
This plant disease, also called *oak root fungus* and *shoestring root rot*, is caused by a fungus (*Armillaria mellea*) that attacks the roots of many woody and nonwoody plants. Plants under stress from severe drought, overwatering, physical injury, insects, or disease are the most susceptible to attack. Once the fungus enters the plant, it produces the white fungal strands under the bark that invade and decay the roots and lower trunk. Water and nutrient uptake are inhibited, causing the foliage and branches to die. In the fall and winter, mushrooms appear at the base of the plant. For more information on this disease, see page 858.

SOLUTION: No chemical controls are available that are suitable for the home gardener. Remove and destroy infected plants, including the stump and root. Check the roots and stems of surrounding plants, and remove if infected. Avoid planting grapes in recently cleared forest land, especially where old oak trees existed.

PROBLEM: Grape shoots wilt and die. Holes about ⅛ inch in diameter appear in the year-old wood below the shoots. A white flaky material is exuded from the hole. Inside the shoots are ½-inch white grubs.

ANALYSIS: Twig and branch borer (*Polycaon confertus*)
This insect pest is common in grape plantings neighboring brushy or wooded areas, or in plantings adjacent to piles of year-old prunings or dead vines. The borers damage grape vines by boring into the base of succulent new shoots. Infested shoots are weak and frequently break during wind storms. Sap flows freely from damaged branches. A few broken or dead shoots will not severely damage grape plants, but when borers are numerous many of the leaves may drop, weakening the vine. The brownish black adult beetles emerge from hibernation in mid to late spring, chew holes about ⅛ inch in diameter in the base of the tender shoots, and lay their eggs. The larvae that hatch from these eggs feed inside the branch, mining downward through the pith. The borers pupate and spend the winter in the dormant canes. There is only one generation a year.

SOLUTION: No chemical controls are available. Prune out and destroy any shoots infested with the borers. Remove and destroy all dead vines. Destroy all pruned brush from adjacent orchards, vineyards, and shade trees before the grape vines start growth each spring. Keep the plants healthy with regular maintenance as outlined on page 742.

PROBLEM: The upper surfaces of the leaves, the fruit, and cluster stems are covered with a white powdery growth. Leaves turn brown and fall. Fruit may be rusty or scaly.

ANALYSIS: Powdery mildew
This common plant disease is caused by a fungus (*Uncinula necator*) that thrives in both humid and dry weather. It is encouraged by warm days and cool nights. The powdery patches consist of fungal strands and spores. The spores are spread by the wind to healthy leaves. The fungus saps the plant nutrients, causing yellowing and sometimes the death of the leaf. Seriously affected leaves retard fruit ripening. The vine's overall vigor may be reduced, resulting in poor wood maturity and increased susceptibility to winter damage. Fruit may also be attacked. Powdery mildew is a major problem in the West. Under favorable conditions, powdery mildew can spread through a closely spaced planting in a matter of days or weeks.

SOLUTION: Treat infected grape plants with ORTHO Flotox Garden Sulfur or a spray containing *folpet* at the first sign of the disease. Clean up and discard any debris around the plants at the end of the season. Next year, begin spraying the plants when the shoot growth is 4 to 6 inches long, and repeat at intervals of 2 weeks for 4 to 6 applications. Sulfur sprays may burn leaves when temperatures are above 85°F. *Folpet* is safe above 85°F.

GRAPES — BIRDS

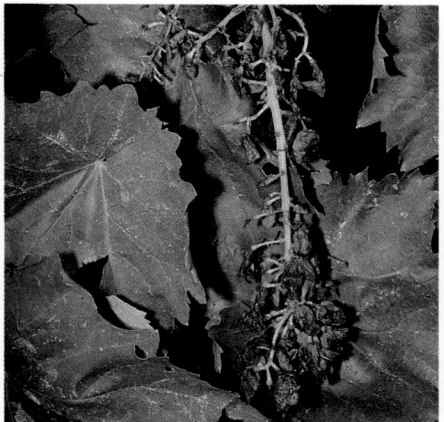

Bird damage.

PROBLEM: Ripening grapes disappear. Some may be broken, with holes pecked in them. Birds are active in the grape planting.

ANALYSIS: Birds
Starlings, robins, finches, grackles, and blackbirds like the sweetness of ripe grapes. Entire bunches of grapes may disappear within a few hours. Birds are hearty eaters, and if not discouraged from the vineyard, may devour all the grapes in a planting. The sugar level in grapes increases during the ripening process. As the grapes approach maturity, birds keep a watchful eye on their progress. Birds seem to be more attracted to the wine or vinifera type grapes than to the American bunch types. Early-ripening varieties and those with red or black fruit are most often attacked. However, when they are hungry, birds are not choosy.

SOLUTION: To protect ripening grapes, put a brown paper bag or cheesecloth over each cluster as it begins to ripen. Do not use plastic bags, because moisture will build up inside. Pick grapes promptly as they ripen. Bird netting placed over the plants and secured at the base with rocks or logs also protects the bunches. Nets are available at garden centers. For more information on birds in the garden, see page 893.

GROWTHS ON LEAVES

Grapevine tomato gall.

PROBLEM: Green to deep red round or slender swellings appear on grape leaves, canes, or tendrils. Greenish yellow to red grubs may be found inside.

ANALYSIS: Galls
Tiny insects, called gall wasps or gall midges cause different types of galls to develop on grapes. The growths may be round, slender, or pear-shaped. Each species of insect (midge, nonstinging wasp, or weevil) causes its own type of gall to form. The galls are caused by a chemical that the insect injects into the plant tissue. The mature female lays her eggs on various parts of the plant. The eggs hatch into legless grubs that cause galls to form around themselves. The insects feed and develop inside the galls, mature, and either spend the winter there or emerge to produce another generation. Young, tender growth is the most susceptible to attack. Most galls do not harm the vines. However, one gall maker, the grape phylloxera, attacks the roots and leaves and interrupts the flow of nutrients in the vines, killing the plants.

SOLUTION: Chemical controls are not necessary for galls. Prune out and destroy severely infested leaves and canes before the grubs inside emerge.

Galls. *Insert:* Grape phylloxeras (3 times life size).

PROBLEM: Vines grow slowly and produce few clusters of grapes. Very often plants die. Tubers or swellings are found on the roots. Pea-shaped galls that are open on the underside may appear on the leaves.

ANALYSIS: Grape phylloxera
(*Phylloxera vitifoliae*)
The grape phylloxera is a serious pest of grape vines in California and Europe. In the late 1800s it killed almost a third of the vineyards in France before it was discovered that American-type grapes were resistant, and that European varieties could be grafted onto these rootstocks and then be planted in phylloxera-infested soil. This orange to yellow aphidlike pest is native to the eastern United States, where cultivated grapes have become resistant to its attack, and only wild grapes are affected. There are two forms of this pest. One form, found only in the East, attacks the leaves and roots. The other form, found only in California, attacks only the roots. The grape phylloxera sucks the juices from the roots, causing galls to form. These galls interrupt the nutrient flow in the roots, and the vines become stunted and unproductive, and often die. American-type varieties that are commonly grown in the East are resistant to this pest, but the European types or vinifera varieties grown in California are very susceptible. French hybrid types are only mildly affected.

SOLUTION: There are no chemical controls for the grape phylloxera for home gardeners. Select resistant American grape varieties, or plant European varieties with phylloxera-resistant rootstocks.

GRAPES

Downy mildew.

PROBLEM: Small yellow spots appear on the upper surfaces of the leaves. The surfaces are covered with a white cottony growth. Older leaves are affected first. Leaves, shoots, and tendrils turn brown and brittle, and are often distorted. Grapes may be covered with the white growth, or they may be shriveled and brown, yellow, or red.

ANALYSIS: Downy mildew
This plant disease is caused by a fungus (*Plasmopara viticola*) that attacks grape foliage and fruit from before bloom to the end of harvest. Downy mildew causes leaf defoliation, which exposes the fruit to sunscald and prevents proper ripening. When the disease is severe, entire grape clusters may be killed. Reduced vine vigor results in poor growth the following season. This disease is more prevalent in cool, moist weather, and is always more serious in rainy growing seasons. The most damage occurs during August and September. The fungus survives the winter in diseased leaves on the ground.

SOLUTION: Discard severely infected leaves and fruit. At the first sign of the disease, spray the vines with a fungicide containing *captan* or *folpet*. Repeat every 10 days until 7 days before harvest. Remove all plant debris from the vineyard at the end of the season to reduce the number of overwintering spores. Next year, spray just before bloom, just after bloom fall, when the grapes are about the size of peas, and every 10 days thereafter until 7 days before harvest.

HERBS

ADAPTATION: Throughout the United States.

PLANTING TIME: See page 1009.

PLANTING METHOD: Transplants or seeds.

SOIL: Any good garden soil. pH 6.0 to 8.0.

FERTILIZER: At planting time, use 1 to 2 pounds of ORTHO Vegetable Garden Food 5–10–10 per 100 square feet, or ½ pound per 25-foot row. Side dress every 6 to 8 weeks with ½ pound per 25-foot row, or ½ teaspoon per plant.
  Containers: Water thoroughly every 4 to 6 weeks with a solution of ORTHO Tomato & Vegetable Food 6–18–6.

WATER:
  How much: Apply enough water at each irrigation to wet the soil 10 to 12 inches deep.
  How often: Water when the soil 1 inch deep is dry.

HARVEST: Pick young leaves for use any time. Flavor is best just before blooming. After the dew dries in the morning, snip leaves or sprigs with sharp scissors. Wash and use or hang to dry. After herbs are thoroughly dry, store in an airtight container. Never harvest more than a third of the plant at a time.

HERBS

Caterpillars feeding on dill (life size).

PROBLEM: Holes appear in the leaves and buds. Leaves, buds, and flowers may be entirely chewed off. Worms or caterpillars are feeding on the plants.

ANALYSIS: Caterpillars
Many species of these moth or butterfly larvae feed on herbs and many other garden plants. Some common caterpillars include budworms, hornworms, and loopers. As a rule, the adult moths or butterflies begin to lay their eggs on garden plants with the onset of warm weather in the spring. The larvae that emerge from these eggs feed on the leaves, flowers, and buds for 2 to 6 weeks, depending on weather conditions and species. Mature caterpillars pupate in cocoons attached to leaves or structures, or buried in the soil. There may be one to several overlapping generations during the growing season. The last generation of caterpillars in the fall survives the winter as pupae. The adult moths and butterflies emerge the following spring.

SOLUTION: If practical, handpick caterpillars as they appear. Or spray with the bacterial insecticide *Bacillus thuringiensis*.

LETTUCE

ADAPTATION: Throughout the United States.

PLANTING TIME: See page 1009.

PLANTING METHOD: Sow seeds ¼ inch deep. Thin seedlings or set transplants 4 to 6 inches apart. For a continuous harvest, plant some seeds or plants every 2 weeks.

SOIL: Any good garden soil. pH 6.0 to 8.0

FERTILIZER: At planting time, use 3 to 4 pounds of ORTHO Vegetable Garden Food 5–10–10 per 100 square feet, or 1 pound per 25-foot row. Side-dress every 3 to 4 weeks with 1 pound per 25-foot row, or 1 to 2 tablespoons per plant; or fertilize with a solution of ORTHO Tomato & Vegetable Food 6–18–6.

WATER:
How much: Apply enough water at each irrigation to wet the soil 8 to 10 inches deep.
How often: Water when the soil 1 inch deep is barely moist. Do not allow the soil to dry out.

HARVEST: Cut plants with a sharp knife in the early morning.
Head types: Head should be full and firm. Cut just above the soil line.
Looseleaf types: The entire plant may be cut when it is the size of your hand; or pick the outer leaves as you need them, leaving a few center leaves for future picking.

Bibb lettuce bolting.

PROBLEM: A seed stalk emerges from the center of the lettuce plant. The lettuce tastes bitter.

ANALYSIS: Bolting
Lettuce is a cool-weather crop, and grows best between 55° and 60°F. When temperatures rise above 60°F for several days in a row, the plants will form a flower stock if they are mature enough. As the stalk grows, sugars and nutrients are withdrawn from the leaves for the growth of the stalk, making the leaves bitter and tough. The formation of a flower stalk in vegetables that are grown for their leaves is known as "bolting." Once bolting begins, it cannot be stopped; cutting off the stalk does not help.

SOLUTION: If it is harvested as soon as bolting begins, the lettuce may still be edible, but quality deteriorates rapidly as the stalk forms. In the future, plant lettuce so that it matures during cool weather, or grow varieties that are slow to bolt.

Lettuce varieties that are resistant to bolting:
Head — Great Lakes 659.
Loose Leaf — Oak Leaf, Royal Oak Leaf, Salad Bowl, and Slo-Bolt.
Butterhead — Augusta, Buttercrunch, Butter King, Green Lake, and Hot Weather.

Potato aphid (5 times life size).

PROBLEM: Leaves turn yellow and may be distorted, curled, and puckered. Pale green, yellow, or purple insects, some with 3 dark lines on the back, cluster on the undersides of the leaves.

ANALYSIS: Aphids
Aphids do little damage in small numbers. However, they are extremely prolific and populations can rapidly build up to damaging numbers during the growing season. Damage occurs when the aphid sucks the juices from the lettuce leaves. The green peach aphid (*Myzus persicae*) may also spread lettuce mosaic virus, which dwarfs lettuce plants, rendering them unproductive. (For more information on lettuce mosaic virus, see page 752.) The green peach aphid is pale green with 3 dark lines on the back. Its shiny black eggs spend the winter on the bark of fruit trees. About the time peach trees bloom, the eggs hatch and the aphids begin feeding, first on the tree, then migrating to vegetable and flower plants.

SOLUTION: Control aphids on lettuce with ORTHO Fruit & Vegetable Insect Control or ORTHO Malathion 50 Insect Spray as soon as the aphids appear. Repeat the spray if the plant becomes reinfested.

To rid lettuce of aphids at harvest time, swish the head or leaves in a solution of ½ cup salt in a bucket of water. The aphids and other insects will drop off the lettuce. Rinse the lettuce thoroughly afterwards.

LETTUCE

Cabbage looper damage and droppings.

Cutworm (⅓ life size).

Leafhopper (8 times life size).

PROBLEM: Leaves have round or irregular holes. Green worms up to 1½ inches long, with light stripes down their backs, feed on the leaves or heads. Masses of green or brown pellets may be found between the leaves.

ANALYSIS: Cabbage looper
(*Trichoplusia ni*)
Several worms attack lettuce, the most damaging of which is the cabbage looper. The looper attacks all varieties of lettuce, as well as members of the cabbage family. Adults lay eggs throughout the growing season. The brownish cabbage looper moth lays pale green eggs on the upper sides of the leaves in the evening. The worms eat lettuce leaves and heads. Their greenish brown excrement makes the plants unappetizing. Worms may be present from early spring until late fall. In the South, they may be present all year. Worms spend the winter as pupae attached to a plant or nearby object.

SOLUTION: Control cabbage loopers with ORTHO Fruit & Vegetable Insect Control, ORTHO Sevin Garden Dust, or ORTHO Diazinon Soil & Foliage Dust as soon as damage is seen, or with the bacterial spray *Bacillus thuringiensis*. *Bacillus thuringiensis* is effective only while the caterpillars are small. Repeat treatments at weekly intervals if the plants become reinfested. Clean all plant debris from the garden to reduce the number of overwintering pupae.

PROBLEM: Young plants are chewed or cut off near the ground. Gray, brown, or black worms, 1½ to 2 inches long, may be found about 2 inches deep in the soil near the base of the damaged plants. The worms coil when disturbed.

ANALYSIS: Cutworms
Several species of cutworms attack plants in the vegetable garden. The most likely pests of lettuce plants in the spring are the surface-feeding cutworms. A single surface-feeding cutworm can sever the stems of many young plants in one night. Cutworms hide in the soil during the day, and feed only at night. Adult cutworms are dark, night-flying moths with bands or stripes on their forewings. In the South, cutworms may also attack fall-planted lettuce.

SOLUTION: Apply ORTHO Diazinon Soil & Turf Insect Control or ORTHO Diazinon Soil & Foliage Dust around the base of undamaged plants when stem cutting is observed. Since cutworms are difficult to control, it may be necessary to repeat the dusting at weekly intervals. Before transplanting into the area, apply a preventive treatment of ORTHO Diazinon Soil & Turf Insect Control and work it into the soil. Cultivate the soil thoroughly in late summer and fall to expose and destroy eggs, larvae, and pupae. Further reduce damage with "cutworm collars" around the stem of each plant. These collars can be made of stiff paper or aluminum foil. They should be at least 2 inches high, and pressed firmly into the soil.

PROBLEM: Spotted, pale green insects up to ⅛ inch long hop or fly away quickly when a plant is touched. The leaves are stippled and may turn brown.

ANALYSIS: Aster leafhopper
(*Macrosteles fascifrons*)
This insect, also known as the *six-spotted leafhopper*, feeds on many vegetable and ornamental plants. It generally feeds on the undersides of leaves, sucking the sap, which causes stippling. This leafhopper transmits *aster yellows*, a plant disease that can be quite damaging. (For further details, see page 752.) Leafhoppers at all stages of maturity are active during the growing season. They hatch in the spring from eggs laid on perennial weeds and ornamental plants. Even areas where the winters are so cold that the eggs cannot survive are not free from infestation because leafhoppers migrate in the spring from warmer regions.

SOLUTION: It is important to keep leafhoppers under control because, in addition to their feeding damage, they can infect plants with aster yellows. Spray infested plants with ORTHO Fruit & Vegetable Insect Control, ORTHO Malathion 50 Insect Spray, or ORTHO Sevin Garden Dust at the first sign of infestation, being sure to cover the lower surfaces of the leaves. Repeat the spray as often as necessary to keep the insects under control, leaving at least 10 days between applications. Eradicate nearby weeds, especially thistles, plantains, and dandelions, which may harbor leafhopper eggs and aster yellows. For more information about controlling disease-carrying insects, see page 880.

Tip burn.

Bottom rot.

Watery soft rot. *Insert:* Close-up.

PROBLEM: Small, dark brown spots appear ¼ inch from the margins of outer and inner leaves. Spots enlarge and the entire margins die and turn brown. Leaves may become slimy and black.

ANALYSIS: Tip burn
This problem on lettuce is caused by a lack of calcium in the leaves. There is probably enough calcium in the soil, but it is not being transported to the leaf tips. Tip burn is most severe when lettuce is grown under conditions of fluctuating soil moisture. The disease frequently occurs when bright, warm days follow damp or foggy weather. Overmature heads and rapidly growing succulent plants are particularly susceptible to injury. Leaf lettuce varieties are seldom affected. Head varieties are affected after the plants have begun to develop solid heads. Soft rot organisms often invade the dead tissue and turn the plants slimy and black.

SOLUTION: Clip off the brown tissue and use the rest of the head. Keep the soil evenly moist, letting the surface dry out slightly between waterings. Pick the heads when they are mature. Grow loose-leaf types or resistant head varieties.

Head lettuce varieties that are resistant to tip burn: Great Lakes 659, Ithaca, and Mesa 659.

PROBLEM: Rust-colored sunken spots appear on the lower leaf stems and midribs, especially on leaves touching the ground. The entire leaf then turns brown and slimy. The infection spreads to adjacent leaves until the entire head is infected. The head may dry and shrivel into a mummylike form.

ANALYSIS: Bottom rot
This plant disease is caused by a fungus (*Rhizoctonia solani*) that is widespread on lettuce grown in soil high in organic matter, or after a period of excessive rainfall. Head lettuce is more commonly affected than loose-leaf types. The fungus lives in the soil and on diseased plant debris. The spores infect the head whenever the plant is large enough to retain dampness between itself and the moist soil. This is usually after the head has developed and is approaching maturity. The lower leaves or those touching the soil are the first infected.

SOLUTION: There are no chemical controls for this disease. Harvest infected heads immediately, discarding the infected leaves. Store the healthy portion in the refrigerator. Pick healthy heads as soon as possible so they don't become infected. Harvest every other head to improve air circulation and reduce the chances of infection. Plant lettuce in well-drained soil or raised beds, spacing the plants 5 to 8 inches apart in rows 12 to 14 inches apart. Or grow lettuce in containers. Plant lettuce in the same area only once every 4 years. Other years plant nonsusceptible crops such as sweet corn and onions. Tomatoes, celery, and cabbage are also susceptible to bottom rot.

PROBLEM: A water-soaked area develops on the stem near the soil line. As it extends upward the outer leaves die, wither, and droop to the ground. The head becomes wet and slimy. In moist weather a thick white cottony mold covers the head. White, gray, or black pellets about the size of a pea are found in the mold and between dead leaves.

ANALYSIS: Watery soft rot
This plant disease, also called *white mold*, is caused by a fungus (*Sclerotinia sclerotiorum*) that attacks many vegetables in the garden, including lettuce. All parts of the plant may be infected. The infection starts on the stem and spreads downward, rotting the roots. As it spreads upward, the outer leaves die and the head rots. This fungus is most active in moderate (55° to 75°F), wet weather. Moisture on the leaves from rain, fog, dew, or irrigation provides the water necessary for infection. The spores survive the winter inside pellets in the soil and plant debris. They are generally spread by diseased plant parts and the wind.

SOLUTION: There are no chemical controls for this disease. Remove and destroy all infected plants at the first sign of the disease. Avoid overhead watering by using drip or furrow irrigation. Clean all plant debris from the garden after harvest to reduce the amount of overwintering spores. Rotate your lettuce planting site every year into an area where the disease has not yet occurred.

Lettuce

Mosaic virus.

PROBLEM: Leaves turn yellow or are mottled light green and yellow. The veins are pale, and the leaf edges may curl inward or be ruffled. The plants are stunted, and heading varieties don't produce heads.

ANALYSIS: Mosaic virus
This plant disease is caused by at least two viruses that attack all varieties of lettuce. It is most evident in cool, cloudy weather, usually disappearing in midsummer. The viruses usually enter the garden in infected seed, but they may also live in weeds, including wild lettuce, pokeweed, wild cucumber, and groundsel. Once the infection is present in the garden, aphids, primarily the green peach aphid, spread the viruses from plant to plant. The viruses can also be transmitted mechanically as diseased and healthy plants rub together. Symptoms appear 8 to 14 days after infection. Occasionally a plant will show symptoms and then recover and grow to normal size.

SOLUTION: Once the symptoms occur, there are no practical controls. Discard severely infected plants; they will produce very little. If the plants are infected just before harvest, they are still edible. There are no resistant varieties. Buy lettuce seed from a reputable company. Do not save seed from infected plants. Control aphids with ORTHO Fruit & Vegetable Insect Control or ORTHO Malathion 50 Insect Spray, repeating at intervals of 7 to 10 days if the plants become reinfested. For information on controlling disease-carrying insects, see page 880. For information about aphids, see page 749.

Aster yellows.

PROBLEM: Heart leaves turn pale yellow to white. They may be short, thick stubs. Pink to tan latex deposits occur on leaf midribs and deep in the heart of mature plants. Plants are stunted and fail to head.

ANALYSIS: Aster yellows
This plant disease is caused by mycoplasmas, microscopic organisms similar to bacteria. The mycoplasmas are transmitted from plant to plant primarily by leafhoppers. (For information about leafhoppers, see page 750.) The symptoms of aster yellows are more severe and appear more quickly in warm weather. Even when the disease is present in the plant, aster yellows may not manifest its symptoms in temperatures of 55°F or less. Infected lettuce heads are often bitter. The disease also infects celery, onion, potato, and several ornamentals and weeds. For a list of plants susceptible to aster yellows, see page 994.

SOLUTION: Aster yellows cannot be eliminated entirely, but can be kept under control. Remove and destroy infected plants. To remove sources of infection, eradicate nearby weeds that may harbor aster yellows and leafhopper eggs. Spray leafhopper-infested plants with ORTHO Fruit & Vegetable Insect Control or ORTHO Malathion 50 Insect Spray. Repeat the spray whenever leafhoppers are seen. For more information about controlling disease-carrying insects, see page 880.

Okra

Okra

ADAPTATION: Throughout the warmer areas of the United States.

PLANTING TIME: See page 1009.

PLANTING METHOD: Soak seeds overnight in warm water for better germination. Plant them ½ to 1 inch deep. When they have 2 or 3 leaves, thin to stand 1 to 2 feet apart.

SOIL: Any good garden soil high in organic matter. pH 6.0 to 8.0.

FERTILIZER: At planting time, use 1 to 1½ pounds of ORTHO Vegetable Garden Food 5–10–10 per 25-foot row. Side-dress every 4 to 6 weeks with ½ to 1 pound per 25-foot row.

WATER:
How much: Apply enough water at each irrigation to wet the soil 12 to 14 inches deep.
Containers: 10 percent of the water should drain from the bottom of the container.
How often: Water when the soil 1 inch deep is dry.

HARVEST: Cut pods close to the stem with a sharp knife or shears when they are about 4 inches long, and before they become fibrous. A knife should pass easily through a mature, edible pod. Harvest every 2 or 3 days so the plants will continue to produce. Handle pods carefully to avoid bruising them. Store in the refrigerator.

Corn earworm (life size).

Stink bug (twice life size).

Nematode damage.

PROBLEM: Holes are chewed into the okra pods. Inside the pods are striped yellow, green, or brown worms ¼ to 2 inches long. These worms may also be feeding on the leaves.

ANALYSIS: Corn earworm
(*Heliothis zea*)
The corn earworm, also known as the *tomato fruitworm* or *cotton bollworm*, attacks many vegetables and flowers. The worms feed on the foliage, and also chew holes in the fruit, making them worthless. The worm is the larva of a light gray-brown moth with dark lines on its wings. In the spring, the moth lays yellow eggs on leaves and stems. The worms that hatch from these eggs feed on the new leaves. When they are about ½ inch long, the worms move to the pods and bore inside. After feeding for 2 to 4 weeks, they drop to the ground, pupate, and emerge in several weeks as adults. There are several generations a year. In the South, where these pests survive the winter, early and late plantings suffer the most damage.

SOLUTION: Once the worms are inside the pods, sprays are ineffective. Hand-pick and destroy infested pods. Clean all plant debris from the garden after harvest to reduce the number of overwintering adults. Next year treat your plants with ORTHO Sevin Garden Dust when the worms are feeding on the foliage, or when the pods are about ½ to 1 inch long. Repeat in 2 to 4 weeks if the plants become reinfested.

PROBLEM: Fruit is distorted and spotted with hard calluses. Some fruit may drop. Green, blue, or red insects, ⅝ inch long and shaped like a shield, are found on the plants.

ANALYSIS: Stink bugs
Stink bugs attack a wide variety of vegetables including okra, squash, beans, peas, and tomatoes. They get their name because they emit a strong odor when crushed. Both the adults and nymphs damage okra plants by sucking the sap from buds, blossoms, and fruit. This feeding causes the fruit to become distorted and dimpled. Hard calluses form around the spot where the stink bug inserted its mouthparts to feed. Young tender growth is the most susceptible to attack. In the spring, stink bugs lay clusters of eggs on the undersides of the leaves. Young stink bugs look like smaller versions of the adult. There are several generations each year, so damage occurs throughout the growing season.

SOLUTION: Treat infested okra plants with ORTHO Sevin Garden Dust as soon as stink bugs or their damage are noticed. Repeat at intervals of 5 to 7 days if the plants become reinfested.

PROBLEM: Plants are stunted and yellow, and wilt in hot, dry weather. Few pods are produced. Round or elongated nodules occur on the roots.

ANALYSIS: Nematodes
Nematodes are microscopic worms that live in the soil. They are not related to earthworms. Nematodes feed on plant roots, damaging and stunting them. The damaged roots can't supply sufficient water and nutrients to the aboveground plant parts, and the plant is stunted or slowly dies. Nematodes are found throughout the United States, but are most severe in the South. They prefer moist, sandy loam soils. Nematodes can move only a few inches each year on their own, but they may be carried long distances by soil, water, tools, or infested plants. Testing roots and soil is the only positive method for confirming the presence of nematodes. Contact your local Cooperative Extension Office (see page 1011) for sampling instructions and addresses of testing laboratories. Soil and root problems such as poor soil structure, drought stress, nutrient deficiency, and root rots can also produce symptoms of decline similar to those caused by nematodes. These problems should be eliminated as causes before sending soil and root samples for testing. For information on soil problems and root rots, see pages 901 and 857.

SOLUTION: There are no chemicals available to homeowners to kill nematodes in planted soil. However, they can be controlled before planting by soil fumigation. For information on fumigating soil, see page 919.

ONION FAMILY _____

ONION FAMILY _____

ADAPTATION: Throughout the United States.

PLANTING TIME: See page 1009.

PLANTING METHOD:
Onions: Sow onion seeds ½ inch deep and thin to stand ¼ to 3 inches apart. Plant sets 1 to 2 inches deep, side by side or up to 3 inches apart. Set transplants 2 to 3 inches deep and 3 to 5 inches apart. When growing for green onions, plant bulbs closer than when growing for dry onions. For a continuous harvest, plant every couple of weeks.
Garlic: Plant individual cloves 1 to 2 inches deep and 5 to 6 inches apart.
Shallots: Plant individual sections 1 to 1½ inches apart and 3 to 5 inches apart.
Chives: Sow seeds ½ inch deep. Thin seedlings or set transplants to grow 8 inches apart. Plant transplants so that the top of their rootball is even with the surrounding garden soil.
Leeks: Plant as for onion transplants or seeds.

SOIL: Loose, crumbly soil that is rich in organic matter. pH 6.0 to 8.0

FERTILIZER: At planting time, use 2 pounds of ORTHO General Purpose Plant Food 8–8–8 per 100 square feet, or 1½ pounds per 50-foot row. Side-dress every 3 to 4 weeks with 1 pound per 25-foot row.

WATER:
How much: Apply enough water at each watering to wet the soil 8 to 10 inches deep.
How often: Water when the soil 2 inches deep is barely moist.

HARVEST:
Green onions: Pull the largest as needed, when about pencil size.
Dry onions: Harvest when half or more of the tops have turned yellow and fallen over. Dry in a warm, airy spot for 4 to 5 days. Shake off loose soil and skins. Place bulbs in a slatted crate or mesh bag, and continue drying in a well-ventilated, dry area for 2 to 4 weeks. After drying, store in a dry area between 35° and 40°F.
Garlic: Harvest when the tops dry; cure as for dry onions.
Shallots: Treat like dry onions.
Chives: Snip with sharp shears any time there are young, fresh leaves. Use fresh, or dry or freeze for later use.
Leeks: For white stems, gradually hill soil around the plants through the growing season. Pick when the stems are ¾ to 1 inch in diameter. Store in a root cellar or in the refrigerator until use.

Onion seedstalk.

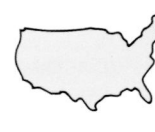

PROBLEM: A tall seedstalk emerges from the onion bulb. Purple or white flowers bloom on top.

ANALYSIS: Seedstalk formation
Onions prefer cool temperatures in their early growth, and warm temperatures near maturity. When temperatures fluctuate between cool and warm, the plants may become dormant. Dormancy then initiates seedstalk formation. Plants from larger bulbs or sets form seedstalks more readily than do those from smaller bulbs. As the seedstalk grows, sugars and nutrients are withdrawn from the bulb for the growth of the stalk, inhibiting future bulb enlargement. Once the seedstalk begins growing, it cannot be stopped; cutting off the stalk does not help.

SOLUTION: Onion bulbs with seedstalks are still edible, but should not be stored. Harvest and use bulbs as soon as possible. In the future, plant onions recommended for your area at the proper time. See page 1009 for a list of regional onion recommendations, and page 1009 for planting times.

Onion maggot damage.

PROBLEM: Plants grow slowly, turn yellow, wilt, and die. Bulbs may rot in storage. White legless maggots, up to 1/3 inch long, burrow inside the bulb.

ANALYSIS: Onion maggot
(*Hylemya antiqua*)
This fly larva is the most serious pest of onions. The larvae burrow into the onion bulb, causing the plant to wilt and die. Once the bulb is damaged by the maggot's feeding, it is susceptible to attack by bacterial soft rot. Early plantings are the most severely injured. When the onions are young and growing close together, the maggots move easily from one bulb to another, destroying several plants. Cool, wet weather favors serious infestations. Maggots spend the winter as pupae in plant debris or in the soil. The brownish gray adult fly emerges in the spring to lay clusters of white eggs at the base of plants. The maggots that hatch from these eggs burrow into the soil and bulbs. After feeding, they pupate in the soil and emerge as adults to repeat the cycle. There are 2 or 3 generations a year, the last one attacking onions shortly before they are harvested. When maggot-infested bulbs are placed in storage, the maggots continue to feed and damage the bulbs.

SOLUTION: Discard and destroy maggot-infested onions. Clean all debris from the garden at the end of the season to reduce the number of overwintering pupae. At planting time, treat the soil in the row with ORTHO Diazinon Soil & Foliage Dust or ORTHO Diazinon Soil & Turf Insect Control. Repeat the treatment 7 to 10 days after plants emerge through the soil.

Fusarium basal rot.

PROBLEM: Leaf tips wilt and die back. The neck of the bulb is soft. A white fungal growth may appear on the base of the bulb. The bulb is soft and brown inside. Bulbs may also be affected in storage.

ANALYSIS: Fusarium basal rot
This plant disease is caused by a soil-inhabiting fungus (*Fusarium* species) that attacks onions, shallots, garlic, and chives. It persists indefinitely in the soil. The disease is spread by contaminated bulbs, soil, and equipment. The fungus enters the bulb through wounds from maggots and old root scars, and spreads up into the leaves, resulting in leaf yellowing and dieback. Bulbs approaching maturity are the most susceptible to attack. If infection occurs during or after harvest, the rot may not show until the bulbs are in storage. Fusarium basal rot is most serious when bulbs are stored in a moist area at temperatures above 70°F.

SOLUTION: No chemical controls are available. Destroy infected plants and bulbs. Harvest healthy bulbs promptly at maturity. Dry according to the instructions on page 754. Fusarium can be removed from the soil only by fumigation techniques. For information on soil fumigation, see page 919. Grow varieties that are tolerant of this disease. Control onion maggots to reduce chances of infection. Store bulbs in a cool (35° to 40°F), dry area. Rotate the planting site if possible.

Onion varieties that are tolerant of basal rot: Elba Globe, Exporter, Gambler, Harvestmore, Sentinel, Spartan Banner, and Stuttgarten.

Pink root.

PROBLEM: Plants grow slowly and their tops may be stunted. Roots turn light pink, shrivel, then a darker pink, and die. Leaves may turn yellow or white and die.

ANALYSIS: Pink root
This plant disease is caused by a fungus (*Pyrenochaeta terrestris*) that attacks onions, garlic, shallots, leeks, and chives. It persists indefinitely in the soil, and infects plants at all stages of growth. Mature and weakened bulbs are the most susceptible to attack. Plants infected early in their life seldom produce large bulbs. Pink root is favored by warm (60° to 85°F) weather.

SOLUTION: No chemical control is available. Discard all infected plants. Pink root fungus can be removed from the soil only by fumigation techniques. (For information on soil fumigation, see page 919.) Weak plants are the most susceptible to attack, so keep the plants healthy with adequate water and nutrition, as discussed on page 754. Grow varieties that are resistant to pink root.

Onion varieties that are resistant to pink root: Danvers, El Capitan, Fiesta, Yellow Bermuda, and Yellow Globe.
Shallots that are resistant: Evergreen.

ONION FAMILY

Smut on green onions.

PROBLEM: Black elongated streaks or blisters appear on seedling leaves, break open, and emit a black powdery substance. Seedlings may die.

ANALYSIS: Smut
This plant disease is caused by a fungus (*Urocystis cepulae*) that attacks onions, leeks, and shallots. Garlic is not affected. The disease persists in the soil for several years, attacking only seedlings. The seedlings are susceptible to attack only from the second day of seed germination until the seedling has one leaf — a period of approximately 10 to 15 days. Many seedlings may die from smut, requiring replacement. If the seedling does survive, the bulb is often distorted, with dark streaks and lesions. Smut is prevalent in cool summer areas with soil temperatures between 60° and 75°F. The black fungal spores live in the soil. They often enter a garden initially on diseased sets or plants.

SOLUTION: Sprays are not effective on infected seedlings. Discard all diseased plants. Since only seedlings are attacked, grow onions from sets or transplants, rather than from seeds. Select clean sets and transplants free of black streaking or stripes. If using seeds, dust the soil at planting time with a fungicide containing *thiram* or *captan*.

Purple blotch.

PROBLEM: Pale yellow, slightly sunken spots with purple centers and yellow margins appear on the leaves. The spots enlarge rapidly, covering the entire leaf. In moist weather, the spots may be covered with a brown to black powdery growth. Bulbs in storage may be rotted around the neck, and yellow to wine-red inside.

ANALYSIS: Purple blotch
This plant disease is caused by a fungus (*Alternaria porri*) that attacks onions, garlic, and shallots. Infection often occurs following injury from other fungi or insects. Plants are seldom killed, but bulbs infected in storage are inedible. The fungal spores pass the winter in infected bulbs and plant debris left in the garden. Infection occurs and spreads rapidly in warm (75° to 80°F), rainy weather or heavy dew.

SOLUTION: Spray infected plants with a fungicide containing *maneb* or *zineb* as soon as blotches appear on the leaves. Repeat at weekly intervals until dry weather resumes. Discard infected bulbs in storage. To prevent infection in storage, dry harvested bulbs properly as outlined on page 754. Clean all debris from the garden at the end of the season.

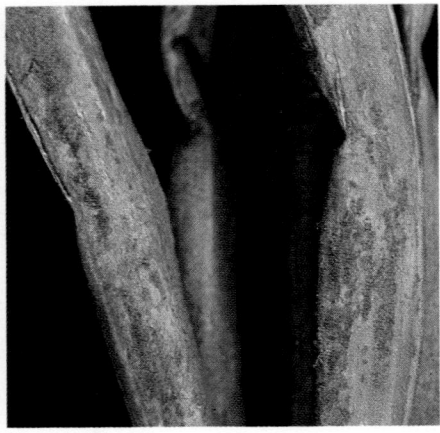

Downy mildew.

PROBLEM: Pale green to yellow spots appear on the outer, older leaves. In humid weather, a fuzzy purple growth may cover these spots. The entire leaf eventually yellows, drops over, and dies. Young leaves may be twisted and distorted. The bulb is soft and small.

ANALYSIS: Downy mildew
This plant disease is caused by a fungus (*Peronospora destructor*) that attacks onions and shallots primarily, although garlic, leeks, and chives are also susceptible. The occurrence of downy mildew may be sporadic — appearing one year and disappearing the next — or it may continue for several consecutive years. It is most prevalent during cool, moist nights and warm, cloudy days. Most infections occur when the temperature is between 50° and 65°F. Downy mildew is especially troublesome, and many plants are killed, during periods of heavy dew or high humidity. If dry weather resumes before the plant dies, new growth may emerge. The spores are spread from plant to plant by the wind, and die rapidly when exposed to the sun and low humidity.

SOLUTION: Treat infected plants with a fungicide containing *zineb* or *maneb* at the first sign of the disease. Repeat at intervals of 7 to 10 days as long as weather conditions continue that are favorable for the spread of the disease. For best results, add a spreader-sticker to the spray. (For instructions on using spreader-stickers, see page 915.) The recommended fungicides will not cure infected leaves, but will protect healthy ones from infection. Avoid overhead watering by using drip irrigation.

Onion thrips damage (life size).

PROBLEM: White streaks or blotches appear on onion leaves. Tips may be distorted. Plants may wilt, wither, turn brown, and die. Bulbs may be distorted and small.

ANALYSIS: Onion thrips
(*Thrips tabaci*)
Onion thrips attack many vegetables, including onions, peas, and cabbages. Thrips are barely visible insects, less than 1/25 inch long, dark brown to black. They reduce the quality and yield of onion bulbs by rasping holes in the leaves and sucking out the plant sap. This rasping causes the white streaks. Plants often die when thrips populations are high. Damage is most severe in the leaf sheath at the base of the plant. Thrips favor this protected area where the elements and pesticides have difficulty reaching them. Onion thrips survive the winter in grass stems, plant debris, and bulbs in storage. Thrips are active throughout the growing season; in warm climates they are active all year.

SOLUTION: Treat infested onion plants with ORTHO Fruit & Vegetable Insect Control or ORTHO Diazinon Soil & Foliage Dust at the first sign of thrips damage. Repeat at weekly intervals until the new growth is no longer damaged.

PARSLEY

ADAPTATION: Throughout the United States.

PLANTING TIME: See page 1009.

PLANTING METHOD: For best germination, soak seeds in warm water overnight. Then plant 1/4 to 1/2 inch deep. Thin seedlings or set transplants to grow 3 to 6 inches apart. Plant transplants so the top of their rootball is even with the surrounding garden soil.

SOIL: Any good garden soil that is rich in organic matter. pH 5.5 to 7.5

FERTILIZER: At planting time, use 2 tablespoons of ORTHO Vegetable Garden Food 5-10-10 for each plant, or 1 pound per 25-foot row. Side-dress every 3 to 4 weeks with 1 to 2 tablespoons per plant, or 1 pound per 25-foot row.

WATER:
How much: Apply enough water at each irrigation to wet the soil 8 to 10 inches deep.
How often: Water when the soil 2 inches deep is moist but not wet.

HARVEST: Snip or pinch parsley stems after the plants are at least 6 inches tall. Store in the refrigerator until use. Parsley can also be frozen or dried. To dry, place sprigs on a screen in a shady, well-ventilated area. To freeze, wash and dry parsley sprigs and immediately freeze in plastic bags or containers.

Parsleyworm (life size).

PROBLEM: Parsley leaves are eaten. Green worms, 2 inches long, with a black band on each body segment, feed on the leaves. When disturbed, these worms emit a sickly sweet odor, and two orange horns project behind the head.

ANALYSIS: Parsleyworm
(*Papilio polyxenes asterius*)
This insect pest is the larva of the *black swallowtail butterfly*. It is also called the *celeryworm*. As its names suggest, it feeds on parsley and celery, as well as on dill and parsnips. Although seldom a serious pest, these worms may strip plants of foliage. In the North, they spend the winter in tan cocoons hanging from host plants. The adult butterfly overwinters in the South. The butterfly has black wings spotted with yellow, orange, and blue dots, and a wingspan of 3 to 4 inches. The worms that hatch from eggs laid on the leaves feed on the foliage for several weeks, pupate in suspended cocoons, and emerge as adults to repeat the cycle. There are 2 to 4 generations a year.

SOLUTION: Handpick as the worms appear. They are seldom serious enough to warrant sprays. However, if they are numerous, treat with an insecticidal spray containing *malathion* or the bacteria *Bacillus thuringiensis*. *Bacillus thuringiensis* is effective only while the caterpillars are small.

Poor germination.

PARSNIPS

ADAPTATION: Throughout the United States.

PLANTING TIME: See page 1009.

PLANTING METHOD: Sow seeds ½ inch deep directly in the garden. Thin to stand 3 to 4 inches apart. Parsnip seeds germinate slowly (up to 30 days) and poorly, so plant twice as many seeds as the number of plants you need.

SOIL: Light, crumbly, and free from rocks and clods. pH 6.0 to 8.0

FERTILIZER: At planting time, use 2 pounds of ORTHO Vegetable Garden Food 5–10–10 per 100 square feet, or ¾ pound per 25-foot row. Side dress every 3 to 4 weeks with ¾ pound per 25-foot row.

WATER:
How much: Apply enough water at each irrigation to wet the soil 15 to 18 inches deep.
How often: Water when the soil 1 inch deep is barely moist. Do not let the soil dry out.

HARVEST: For best flavor, parsnips should be exposed to a frost or continuous cold weather. They can remain in the garden through the winter, or be stored in moist sand in a cool garage or root cellar. Dig carefully, being careful not to damage the foot-long root.

PROBLEM: Seeds germinate slowly, or not at all.

ANALYSIS: Poor germination
Parsnip seeds take longer to germinate than most other vegetables, requiring 21 to 25 days to sprout. Be sure the soil is well drained and loose, or the seedlings may have difficulty pushing up through the heavy soil. Loose soil also gives the root room to expand and makes harvesting easier. Parsnip seeds are seldom attacked by insects or diseases.

SOLUTION: The percentage of seeds that germinate is usually low, so increase your chances of success by soaking the seeds in warm water for 24 hours before planting. Sow the seed heavily. Plant seeds ½ inch deep in rows 15 to 18 inches apart. Thin the seedlings to stand 3 to 4 inches apart when they are 1 inch tall. Radish seeds planted along with parsnip seeds will break the soil and loosen any crust before parsnip seedlings emerge. Or keep the soil from crusting by covering the seed row with burlap strips, sand, or vermiculite. Parsnip seeds are short-lived, so buy fresh seed every year.

PEAS

ADAPTATION: Throughout the United States.

PLANTING TIME: See page 1009.

PLANTING METHOD: Plant peas 1 to 2 inches deep and 1 to 4 inches apart directly in the soil outdoors. Do not thin.

SOIL: Any good garden soil. pH 5.5 to 8.0

FERTILIZER: At planting time, use 3 pounds of ORTHO Vegetable Garden Food 5–10–10 per 100 square feet, or 1 pound per 25-foot row. Side-dress every 3 to 4 weeks with 1 pound per 25-foot row.

WATER:
How much: Apply enough water to wet the soil 8 to 10 inches deep.
How often: Water when the soil 1 inch deep is barely moist.

HARVEST:
Garden peas: Pick as soon as the peas fill the pods. Pods should be tender and bright green. Faded pods are overmature, and peas inside will be tough and starchy.
Edible podded peas: Harvest pods when peas inside just begin to form and pods are tender and bright green.
Southern or blackeye peas: Pick when the pods change from deep green to light yellow, silver, red, or purple, depending on the variety. Seeds inside should be fully developed but not hard.

Hot weather damage.

Powdery mildew.

Ascochyta blight.

PROBLEM: Pea plants stop producing pods. Leaves turn yellow, then brown, wither, and die.

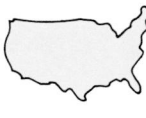

ANALYSIS: Hot weather
The garden pea is a cool season vegetable. It grows best with daytime temperatures below 80°F and nighttime temperatures below 65°F. When temperatures are hotter than this, the plants stop producing and gradually die. In the South, garden peas grow best in the fall, winter, and spring. In the North, grow them as a spring and fall crop.

SOLUTION: Plant peas early enough in the season so they mature in cool weather. Follow the cultural guidelines on page 758 so the plants grow quickly with high yields. Grow varieties that are tolerant of hot weather.

Pea varieties that are heat tolerant: Freezer 692, Sugar Snap, and Wando.

PROBLEM: A white powdery coating develops first on the upper surfaces of the lower leaves. Stems, pods, and other leaves may then become infected. Leaves may turn yellow and be malformed. Pods may be distorted, with dark streaks or spots.

ANALYSIS: Powdery mildew
This common plant disease is caused by a fungus (*Erysiphe polygoni*) that thrives in both humid and dry weather. The powdery coating consists of fungal strands and spores. The spores are spread by the wind to healthy plants. The fungus saps plant nutrients, causing yellowing and sometimes death of the leaf. A severe infection reduces pea yield considerably, and may kill the plant. Fall crops are most susceptible to serious damage; spring crops are attacked late in the season. Since this powdery mildew attacks many vegetables, the fungus from a diseased plant may infect other plants in the garden. (For a list of susceptible plants, see page 995.) Under favorable conditions, powdery mildew can spread through a planting in a matter of days or weeks.

SOLUTION: Treat plants with ORTHO Flotox Garden Sulfur. Repeat at intervals of 7 to 10 days as needed. This fungicide does not cure infected leaves, but does protect healthy ones from infection.

PROBLEM: Small, light brown to purple spots appear on leaves, stems, and pods. Spots enlarge, turning brown to black, and may have gray centers and purple margins. Concentric rings may appear in the spots. Lower leaves shrivel and drop off. The stem may darken at the soil line, and the plant may die.

ANALYSIS: Ascochyta blight
This plant disease is caused by several fungi that attack both garden peas and sweet peas. All parts of the plant are affected. Ascochyta blight is favored by warm (65° to 80°F), wet weather. The fungal spores overwinter in plant debris left in the garden, and are spread to susceptible plants by splashing water and moist winds. The disease is also spread through infected seeds. When infected seeds are planted, they either don't sprout or sprout into weak seedlings that soon die. Although slightly blemished pods and peas are unattractive, they are still edible.

SOLUTION: No chemical controls are available. Discard infected plants and clean the garden thoroughly at the end of the season. Buy pea seeds from a reputable dealer, and plant in well-drained soil.

Pea aphids (twice life size).

Pea weevil (5 times life size).

PROBLEM: Plants turn yellow and wilt. Pods may not be completely filled with peas. Clustered on the leaves, especially the young, tender ones, are tiny, soft-bodied, light to deep green insects with red eyes. Leaves may be covered with a sticky material or black powder.

ANALYSIS: Pea aphid
(*Acyrthosiphon pisum*)
Several species of aphids attack peas, but the most common and damaging is the pea aphid. Aphids generally do little damage in small numbers. However, they are extremely prolific and populations can build up to damaging numbers during the growing season. Damage occurs when the aphid sucks the juices from the pea leaves, stems, blossoms, and pods. This feeding results in stunted plants and fewer and smaller pods that may be only partially filled with peas. The aphid is unable to digest fully all the sugar in the plant sap and excretes the excess in a fluid called honeydew. The honeydew often drops onto the leaves below. Ants feed on this sticky substance, and are often present where there is an aphid infestation. Some aphids also transmit viruses, plant diseases which can be quite damaging. Infected pea plants and pods are distorted, and plants sometimes die. For more information on viruses, see page 861.

SOLUTION: Spray infested plants with ORTHO Fruit & Vegetable Insect Control or ORTHO Malathion 50 Insect Spray as soon as the aphids appear. Repeat the spray if the plants become reinfested.

PROBLEM: Peas have small round holes. The peas are partially or completely hollow, and fat white grubs with brown heads may be found inside. When the pea plants are blooming, $\frac{1}{5}$-inch-long dark brown beetles with light markings may be seen crawling or flying about the plants.

ANALYSIS: Pea weevil
(*Bruchus pisorum*)
This insect pest attacks all varieties of edible peas. Weevils emerge from hibernation as peas are beginning to bloom. The adults feed on pea nectar and pollen. This feeding does not harm the plant. Adults can migrate up to 3 miles in search of food. They lay orange to white eggs on the developing pods. The white grubs that hatch from these eggs eat through the pod and into the pea. They continue feeding for 6 to 8 weeks, then pupate inside the hollow pea. The adult weevil emerges in 1 to 3 weeks, and hibernates to repeat the cycle the following year. There is only one generation each year. Infested peas are inedible.

SOLUTION: Insecticides must be applied to kill the adults before they lay eggs. Once the eggs are laid on the pods it is too late to prevent injury. Treat the plants with ORTHO Rotenone Dust or Spray soon after the first blooms appear, and before pods start to form. Additional sprays may be needed to control migrating weevils.

PEANUTS _____

ADAPTATION: Southeast and Southwest.

PLANTING TIME: See page 1009.

PLANTING METHOD: Plant peanuts 1 to 2 inches deep. For Spanish types, allow 4 to 6 inches between plants; between Virginia types, allow 6 to 8 inches.

SOIL: Loose and crumbly soil. pH 5.5 to 6.5

FERTILIZER: At planting time, use 2 to 3 pounds of ORTHO Vegetable Garden Food 5–10–10 per 100 square feet, or 2 pounds per 100-foot row. Peanuts need adequate calcium. To avoid empty pods, dust the plants with gypsum (calcium sulfate) when flowering. Use 2½ pounds per 100-foot row.

WATER:
How much: Apply enough water at each irrigation to wet the soil 10 to 12 inches deep.
How often: Water when the soil 1 inch deep is barely moist. Stop watering before harvest, as the leaves just begin to yellow.

HARVEST: When the leaves have turned yellow and veins in the pods have darkened, dig the plants and shake off soil. Hang upside down in a warm airy place for 2 to 3 weeks. Then strip the peanuts and use. Discard any rotted or moldy pods.
To roast: Preheat the oven to 500°F. Put nuts in a wire basket or colander. Place them in the oven and turn it off. When the peanuts are cool enough to touch, they are finished roasting.

Spider mite damage.

Leaf spot.

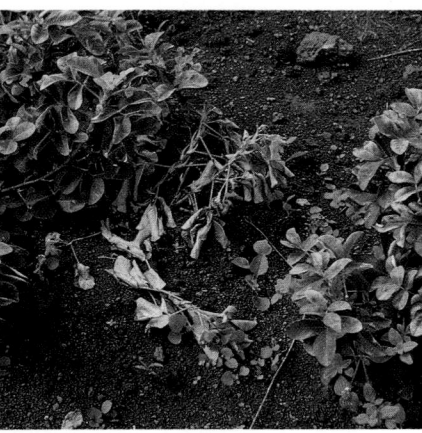

Stem rot.

PROBLEM: Leaves are stippled, yellowing, and dirty. Leaves may dry out and drop. There may be webbing over flower buds, between leaves, or on the lower surfaces of the leaves. To determine if the plant is infested with mites, hold a sheet of white paper underneath an affected leaf and tap the leaf sharply. Minute green, red, or yellow specks the size of pepper grains will drop to the paper and begin to crawl around. The mites are easily seen against the white background.

ANALYSIS: Two-spotted spider mite (*Tetranychus urticae*)
These mites, related to spiders, are major pests of many garden and greenhouse plants. They cause damage by sucking sap from the underside of the peanut leaves. As a result of feeding, the green leaf pigment disappears, producing the stippled appearance. Mites are active throughout the growing season, but are favored by hot, dry weather (70°F and up). By midsummer, they build up to tremendous numbers.

SOLUTION: There are no chemical controls for use by homeowners to control spider mites. Hose plants frequently to knock off webbing and spider mites.

PROBLEM: Pale green to brownish black spots occur on the lower leaves first, then spread to the upper leaves. A pale green to yellow "halo" may surround the spots. The spots range in size from barely visible to ¼ inch in diameter. Several spots may join to form blotches. Leaf spotting is most severe in warm, humid weather. Infected leaves drop off.

ANALYSIS: Leaf spot
There are a number of different fungi that cause leaf spot on peanuts. Some of these fungi may eventually kill the plant, or weaken it so that it is susceptible to other organisms. Although peanut leaves are susceptible to attack by leaf spot throughout the growing season, the problem is most severe in hot (75° to 95°F), humid weather. Plants affected by leaf spot have low yields of poor quality peanuts. Leaf spot spores survive the winter in plant debris in the garden.

SOLUTION: Treat infected plants with a *copper sulfur* fungicide or one containing *mancozeb*. Repeat every 7 to 10 days while warm, humid weather persists. Discard severely infected and fallen leaves. Thoroughly clean the garden at the end of the season to reduce the number of overwintering spores.

PROBLEM: Plants suddenly wilt. Leaves turn pale green, then brown and dry. A brown rot occurs at the base of the stems. During humid weather a white, cottony growth covers the soil and infected plant. White to dark brown pellets may form a crust on the soil around the infected plant.

ANALYSIS: Stem rot
This plant disease, also called *Southern blight* or *Southern stem rot*, is caused by a fungus (*Sclerotium rolfsii*). It attacks and kills a wide variety of vegetables and flowers. Peanut roots, stems, pegs, and pods are attacked. The fungus invades the plant through the stems at the soil line, then progresses into the pegs, pods, and roots. Affected pegs are weakened, so pods break off easily during harvest. Infection occurs in hot (85° to 95°F), dry weather. The fungus persists from one crop to the next in plant debris.

SOLUTION: Remove and destroy plants at the first sign of infection. Clean all debris from the garden at the end of the season. Rotate peanuts with a nonsusceptible crop every year. For a list of resistant plants, see page 996. Before planting peanuts or any crop in an area where stem rot has been a problem, incorporate a fungicide containing *PCNB* into the top 6 inches of soil.

PEPPERS

Blossom drop.

Sunscald.

PEPPERS

ADAPTATION: Throughout the United States.

PLANTING TIME: See page 1009.

PLANTING METHOD: Sow seeds ¼ inch deep. Thin seedlings or set transplants to grow 18 to 24 inches apart. Plant transplants so the top of their rootball is even with the surrounding garden soil.

SOIL: Any good garden soil that is rich in organic matter. pH 5.5 to 8.0

FERTILIZER: At planting time, use 3 to 4 pounds of ORTHO Vegetable Garden Food 5–10–10 per 100 square feet, or 1 pound per 25-foot row. Side-dress every 3 to 4 weeks with 1 pound per 25-foot row, or 1 to 2 tablespoons per plant.

WATER:
How much: Apply enough water at each irrigation to wet the soil 10 to 12 inches deep.
Containers: 10 per cent of the applied water should drain out the bottom.
How often: Water when the soil 2 inches deep is barely moist.

HARVEST:
Green or yellow peppers: Pick when of usable size with a rich color. Fruit should be slightly soft.
Red peppers: Red peppers are green peppers that have remained on the plants and matured. Pick when they have a rich red color. Cut peppers from the plant with pruning shears or a sharp knife, leaving ½ to 1 inch of the stem attached. Cool in the refrigerator.

PROBLEM: Few or no fruit develop. Those that do develop may have rough skin or be misshapen. Plants remain vigorous, with lush foliage.

ANALYSIS: Blossom drop
Pepper blossoms are sensitive to temperature fluctuations during pollination. Normal pollination and fruit set don't occur when night temperatures fall below 58°F and daytime temperatures rise above 85°F. Under these temperature conditions, the blossoms fall off, often before pollination. If pollination has occurred and the fruit has begun to set, but isn't completely fertilized at the time the blossoms drop, rough and misshapen fruit result.

SOLUTION: Blossom drop only causes a delay in fruit production. When the temperatures are less extreme, a full crop of fruit will set, and the plants will be productive the rest of the season. Discard rough or misshapen fruit; they will never develop fully. Irrigation for cooling during hot periods can help to reduce losses.

PROBLEM: An area on the pepper fruit becomes soft, wrinkled, and light in color. Later, this area dries and becomes slightly sunken, with a white, paperlike appearance. An entire side of the fruit may be affected. Black mold may grow in the affected areas.

ANALYSIS: Sunscald
Pepper fruit exposed directly to sunlight may be burned by the heat of the sun. The fruit may be exposed to the sun as a result of leaf diseases that cause leaf drop. Early fruits on small plants without enough protective foliage may be burned. Also, some varieties do not produce enough foliage to shade the fruit. Rot organisms sometimes enter the fruit through the damaged area, making the fruit unappetizing or inedible. Sunscalded fruit without these molds is still edible if the discolored tissue is removed.

SOLUTION: Control leaf diseases that may defoliate the plants. (See pages 763 and 765.) Fertilize according to the guidelines on this page to keep plants healthy with lush foliage. Select pepper varieties that form a protective canopy of leaves.

Blossom-end rot.

Anthracnose.

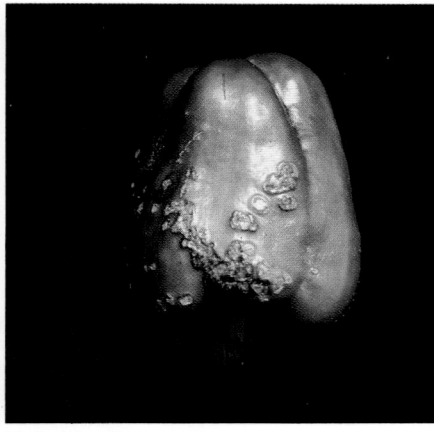

Bacterial spot.

PROBLEM: A round, sunken, water-soaked spot develops on the bottom of the fruit. The spot enlarges, turns brown to black, and feels leathery. Mold may grow on the rotted surface.

ANALYSIS: Blossom-end rot
Blossom-end rot occurs on peppers, tomatoes, squash, and watermelons from a lack of calcium in the developing fruit. This lack results from slowed growth and damaged roots caused by the following factors:
1. Extreme fluctuations in soil moisture, either very wet or very dry.
2. Rapid plant growth early in the season, followed by extended dry periods.
3. Excessive rains that smother root hairs.
4. Excess soil salts.
5. Cultivating too close to the plant. The first fruit are the most severely affected. As the name implies, the disorder always starts at the blossom end, the end farthest from the stem, and may enlarge to affect up to half of the fruit. Moldy growths on the rotted area are from fungi or bacteria that frequently invade the damaged tissue. This rotted area is unsightly, but the rest of the fruit is edible.

SOLUTION: Blossom-end rot is difficult to eliminate, but it can be controlled by following these guidelines.
1. Maintain uniform soil moisture by mulching and proper watering.
2. Avoid overuse of high nitrogen fertilizers and large quantities of fresh manure.
3. Plant in well-drained soil.
4. If your soil or water is salty, provide more water at each watering to help leach salts through the soil.
5. Do not cultivate deeper than 1 inch within 1 foot of the plant.

PROBLEM: Dark brown to black sunken spots appear on both green and ripe fruit. The centers of the spots are darker, with concentric rings. The spots may enlarge, covering a large part of the fruit. Small dark spots may appear on leaves and stems.

ANALYSIS: Anthracnose
This plant disease is caused by a fungus (*Gloesoporium piperatum*) that is a common rot of peppers. Both green and ripe fruit are attacked, and become worthless. Occasionally spots may occur on leaves and stems. The fungus is most active in warm (70° to 80°F), wet weather. When it is severe, many fruits become infected in a short period. Heavy dew, overhead watering, fog, and drizzling rain provide the water necessary for infection. The fungal spores are carried on and in seed. Young plants can become infected through the diseased seed, although the disease is not evident until the fruits form. Spores are spread to healthy plants by splashing water, people, and tools.

SOLUTION: Remove and discard infected fruit. Treat plants with ORTHO Tomato Vegetable Dust at the first sign of the disease. Repeat the treatment at intervals of 1 to 2 weeks as long as weather continues that is favorable to the spread of the disease. Avoid overhead watering by using drip or furrow irrigation. Do not work among wet plants. Clean all plant debris from the garden after harvest. Purchase seeds or transplants from a reputable garden company.

PROBLEM: Tan to dark brown spots, 1/8 to 1/4 inch in diameter, occur on the lower leaves. Spotted leaves turn yellow and drop. Brown, corky, wartlike, raised spots appear on the fruit.

ANALYSIS: Bacterial spot
This plant disease is caused by a bacterium (*Xanthomonas vesicatoria*) that also attacks tomatoes. It affects all aboveground parts of the plant at any stage of growth. When the disease is serious, many blossoms may drop, reducing the fruit yield. The bacteria are most prevalent after heavy rains and in very warm (75° to 85°F) weather. In damp weather, with frequent splashing rains, they spread very rapidly, often resulting in complete leaf drop. Fruit are unsightly, but edible if the blemishes are removed. Molds and decay organisms may enter the fruit through the corky spots and rot the fruit. The bacteria are carried on seed, and persist from one crop to the next in the soil and on diseased plant parts left in the garden.

SOLUTION: Clean all infected plant debris from the garden. Spray the plants with *basic copper sulfate* when the fruit first forms or at the first sign of the disease. Continue the sprays every 10 to 14 days as long as weather conditions are favorable for the spread of the disease. Fertilize plants (see page 762) to help them to replace any leaves lost to bacterial spot. Plant pepper and tomato plants in the same area only once every 3 or 4 years. Purchase healthy transplants. Avoid overhead watering by using drip or furrow irrigation.

PEPPERS

Corn earworm (half life size).

European corn borers (half life size).

Tomato hornworm (⅓ life size).

PROBLEM: Holes are chewed in the fruit. Inside the fruit are striped yellow, green, or brown worms from ½ to 2 inches long. These worms may also be feeding on the leaves.

ANALYSIS: Corn earworm
(*Heliothis zea*)
The corn earworm attacks many vegetables and flowers. It is also known as the *tomato fruitworm* and *cotton bollworm*. The worms feed on the foliage, and also chew holes in the fruit, making them worthless. The worm is the larva of a light gray-brown moth with dark lines on its wings. In the spring, the moth lays yellow eggs on the leaves and stems. The worms that hatch from these eggs feed on the new leaves. When they are about ½ inch long, the worms move to the fruit and bore inside. After feeding for 2 to 4 weeks, they drop to the ground and pupate 2 to 6 inches deep in the soil. After several weeks they emerge as adults to repeat the cycle. There are several generations a year. In the South, where earworms survive the winter, early and late plantings suffer the most damage. Adult moths migrate into northern areas, where they do not survive the winter.

SOLUTION: Once the worms are inside the fruit, sprays are ineffective. Pick and destroy infested fruit. Clean all plant debris from the garden after harvest to reduce the number of overwintering adults. Next year, treat the plants with ORTHO Sevin Garden Dust or ORTHO Sevin Garden Spray when the worms are feeding on the foliage, or when the fruit are about 1 to 2 inches in diameter. Repeat the treatment at intervals of 10 to 14 days if the plants become reinfested.

PROBLEM: Pink or tan worms, up to 1 inch long, with dark brown heads and two rows of brown dots, are feeding inside the pepper. The fruit is decayed inside.

ANALYSIS: European corn borer
(*Ostrinia nubilalis*)
This moth larva is a destructive pest of peppers, corn, tomatoes, beans, and eggplant. The worms feed and promote decay inside the fruit. The borers spend the winter in plant debris, pupate in the spring, and emerge as adults in early summer. The adults are tan moths with dark wavy lines on their wings. The moths lay clusters of 15 to 30 white eggs on the undersides of the leaves. In midsummer, the eggs hatch and young borers enter the fruit where it attaches to the cap. After feeding for 1 month inside the fruit, they pupate and later emerge as adults to repeat the cycle. There are 2 to 3 generations a year. Cool, rainy weather in early summer inhibits egg laying and washes the hatching larvae from the plants, reducing borer populations. Very dry summers and cold winters also reduce borer populations. Peppers are edible if the damaged part is cut away.

SOLUTION: Remove infested fruit. Treat the plants with ORTHO Liquid Sevin or ORTHO Sevin Garden Dust when the fruits are 1 to 1½ inches in diameter. Repeat the treatment 2 more times, 7 days apart. Clean all debris from the garden after harvest to reduce overwintering sites for the larvae.

PROBLEM: Fat green or brown worms, up to 5 inches long, with white diagonal side stripes, chew on the leaves. A red or black "horn" projects from the rear end. Black droppings soil the leaves.

ANALYSIS: Tomato hornworm
(*Manduca quinquemaculata*)
or tobacco hornworm (*M. sexta*)
Hornworms feed on the fruit and foliage of peppers, eggplants, and tomatoes. Although there may be only a few worms present, each worm consumes large quantities of foliage and causes extensive damage. The large gray or brown adult moth with yellow and white markings emerges from hibernation in late spring, and drinks nectar from petunias and other garden flowers. The worms hatch from eggs laid on the undersides of the leaves, and feed for 3 to 4 weeks. Then they crawl into the soil, pupate, and later emerge as adults to repeat the cycle. There is 1 generation a year in the North, and 2 to 4 in the South. Some worms may have white sacs that look like puffed rice on their bodies. These sacs are the cocoons of parasitic wasps that feed on and eventually kill the hornworm.

SOLUTION: Treat the plants with ORTHO Sevin Garden Dust or ORTHO Tomato & Vegetable Insect Spray. Don't destroy worms covered with white sacs. Let the wasps inside the worms mature, emerge, and infest other hornworms. If practical, handpick unaffected worms.

Cutworm (⅓ life size).

Cercospora leaf spot.

Mosaic.

PROBLEM: Young plants are chewed or cut off near the ground. Gray, brown, or black worms, 1½ to 2 inches long, may be found about 2 inches deep in the soil near the base of the damaged plants. The worms coil when disturbed.

ANALYSIS: Cutworms
Several species of cutworms attack plants in the vegetable garden. The most likely pests of young pepper plants are the surface-feeding cutworms. For information on the climbing cutworms, see page 689. A single surface-feeding cutworm can sever the stems of many young plants in one night. Cutworms hide in the soil during the day and feed only at night. Adult cutworms are dark, night-flying moths with bands of stripes on their forewings.

SOLUTION: Apply ORTHO Diazinon Soil & Turf Insect Control or ORTHO Diazinon Soil & Foliage Dust around the base of undamaged plants when stem cutting is observed. Since cutworms are difficult to control, it may be necessary to repeat the dusting at weekly intervals. Destroy any cutworms found hiding in the soil. Before transplanting into the area, apply a preventive treatment of ORTHO Diazinon Soil & Turf Insect Control and work it into the soil. Cultivate the soil thoroughly in late summer and fall to expose and destroy eggs, larvae, and pupae. Further reduce damage with "cutworm collars" around the stem of each plant. These collars can be made of stiff paper or aluminum foil. They should be at least 2 inches high, and pressed firmly into the soil.

PROBLEM: Circular or oblong spots, up to ½ inch in diameter, develop on the leaves and stems. The spots have light gray centers and dark margins. Leaves may yellow and drop.

ANALYSIS: Cercospora leaf spot
This plant disease is caused by a fungus (*Cercospora capsici*). It is also known as *frog-eye leaf spot* because of the resemblance of the spots to frog's eyes. The disease is most prevalent during hot (75° to 85°F), wet weather. Under these conditions, complete leaf defoliation may occur within 2 to 3 weeks. This leaf drop not only reduces fruit yield, but also exposes the fruit to sunscald. For information on sunscald, see page 762. The fungal spores persist from crop to crop in plant debris, and also survive in the soil for at least one year. Spores are spread by the wind, and may also be carried in the seed.

SOLUTION: Treat the plants with ORTHO Tomato & Vegetable Dust at the first sign of the disease. Repeat the treatment at intervals of 7 to 10 days until no new infections occur. Destroy severely infected plants. Discard all plant debris at the end of the season. Purchase disease-free seeds or plants from a reputable company.

PROBLEM: Leaves are curled and mottled yellow and green. Fruit is misshapen, with rough skin and brown streaks, rings, or yellow, green, and red mottling. Plants are stunted.

ANALYSIS: Mosaic
This plant disease may be caused by any of several different viruses. One common virus that infects peppers is *tobacco mosaic virus* (*TMV*). Young plants infected with viruses seldom produce fruit. Plants infected at maturity are less severely affected, and produce misshapen but edible fruit. Seed is one source of infection, but viruses more commonly are transmitted from weeds, including pokeweed, plantain, catnip, and motherwort. Aphids spread viruses from plant to plant while feeding. Viruses are also transmitted mechanically when diseased and healthy leaves rub together.

SOLUTION: Discard infected plants at the first sign of infection. Control aphids with ORTHO Fruit & Vegetable Insect Control or ORTHO Tomato & Vegetable Insect Spray. Repeat the treatment at intervals of 7 to 10 days if the plants become reinfested. For more information on controlling disease-carrying insects, see page 880. Because some viruses are present in tobacco products, wash your hands thoroughly with soap and water after smoking and before working in the garden. Plant varieties resistant to mosaic.

Pepper varieties resistant to mosaic: Ace, Keystone Resistant Giant, Lady Bell, Liberty Bell, New Ace, Rutgers World Beater No. 13, and Yolo Wonder.

POTATOES

PROBLEMS WITH THE TUBER

Green potato tuber.

Scab.

POTATOES

ADAPTATION: Throughout the United States.

PLANTING TIME: See page 1009.

PLANTING METHOD: Plant 1½ to 2-ounce seed pieces (about the size of a medium egg) in trenches 3 to 4 inches deep. Allow 12 to 18 inches between pieces. Plant pieces whole or cut, with at least one eye on each piece. Certified potato seed pieces are certified by the State Department of Agriculture to be free of viruses. Purchase new seed pieces each year.

SOIL: Any good garden soil that is rich in organic matter. pH 4.8 to 6.8

FERTILIZER: At planting time, use 1 to 2 pounds of ORTHO Vegetable Garden Food 5–10–10 per 100 square feet, or ½ pound per 25-foot row. Side-dress when the plants are 4 to 6 inches tall.

WATER:
How much: Apply enough water at each irrigation to wet the soil 8 to 12 inches deep.
How often: Water when the soil 2 inches deep is barely moist.

HARVEST: Dig and use potatoes as needed about 2 to 3 weeks after flowering. Dig those to be stored after the tops naturally turn yellow and die. Carefully dig with a spade or pitchfork, being careful not to puncture or wound the tubers. Discard any diseased tubers.
To store: Cure in the dark for 1 week at 70°F and high humidity. Then store in a humid area at between 40° and 45°F until use. Check stored tubers periodically for storage rot.

PROBLEM: Potato tubers turn green while in the ground or in storage.

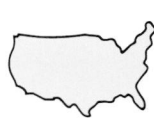

ANALYSIS: Green tubers
Potato tubers turn green when exposed to light. Tubers are modified stems, and produce the green pigment chlorophyll when they receive light. Tubers may be exposed to light when the plants are not properly hilled, or when they are stored in a light place. Excessively green tubers are bitter and inedible. If only slightly green, the tubers are still edible if the green tissue is peeled off.

SOLUTION: Discard tubers, or peel them before eating. Protect tubers in the ground from sunlight by mounding loose soil around the plants when they are 5 to 6 inches tall to completely cover developing tubers. Replace the soil if it is washed away by rain or irrigation water. Store potatoes in a dark, humid place at temperatures between 35° and 45°F.

PROBLEM: Brown corky scabs or pits occur on potato tubers. Spots enlarge and merge together, sometimes covering most of the tuber. Leaves and stems are not affected.

ANALYSIS: Common scab
This plant disease is caused by a fungus (*Streptomyces scabies*) that persists in the soil for long periods of time. Besides potatoes, scab also infects beets, carrots, and parsnips. Scab affects only the tubers, not the leaves and stems. The fungus spends the winter in the soil and in infected tubers left in the garden. Infection occurs through wounds and through the breathing pores in the tuber skins when the tubers are young and growing rapidly. Scab is most severe in warm (75° to 85°F) dry soil with a pH of 5.7 to 8.0. The severity of scab often increases when the pH is raised with lime or wood ashes. Scab is not a problem in acid soils with a pH of 5.5 or less. Poorly fertilized soil also encourages scab. The fungal spores withstand temperature and moisture extremes. Because the spores pass intact through the digestive tracts of animals, manure can spread the disease. Tubers infected with scab are edible, but much may be wasted as the blemishes are removed.

SOLUTION: No chemical control is available. Test your soil pH, and if necessary correct it to 5.0 to 5.5 with *aluminum sulfate*. (For information on soil testing, see page 903.) Avoid alkaline materials such as wood ashes and lime. Do not use manure on potatoes. Plant potatoes in the same area only once every 3 to 4 years. Use certified seed pieces that are resistant to scab.

Wireworms (twice life size).

Root knot nematode damage.

Internal discolorations.

PROBLEM: Plants are stunted and grow slowly. Tunnels wind through stems, roots, and in and on the surface of tubers. Shiny, hard, jointed, cream to yellow worms up to ⅝ inch long are found in the tuber and in the soil.

ANALYSIS: Wireworms
Wireworms feed on potatoes, corn, carrots, beets, peas, beans, lettuce, and many other plants. Wireworms feed entirely on underground plant parts, devouring seed potatoes, underground stems, tubers, and roots. Infestations are most extensive in soil where lawn grass was recently grown. Adults are known as "click" beetles because they make a clicking sound when turning from their back to their feet. Wireworm larvae feed for 2 to 6 years before maturing into adult beetles, so all sizes and ages of wireworms may be found in the soil at the same time. Undamaged portions of the tubers are edible.

SOLUTION: Control wireworms with ORTHO Diazinon Soil & Foliage Dust at the first sign of damage. Incorporate into the top 6 to 8 inches of soil. Do not store damaged tubers. Repeat the soil treatment next year just before planting.

PROBLEM: The leaves turn bronze to yellow. They may wilt on hot, dry days, then recover at night. Plants are stunted. Tubers may have a roughened and pebbly skin.

ANALYSIS: Nematodes
Nematodes are microscopic worms that live in the soil. They are not related to earthworms. Nematodes feed on plant roots, damaging and stunting them. The damaged roots can't supply sufficient water and nutrients to the above-ground plant parts, and the plant is stunted or slowly dies. Infested tubers are unsightly, but edible if peeled. Nematodes are found throughout the United States, but are most severe in the South. They prefer moist, sandy loam soils. Nematodes can move only a few inches each year on their own, but they may be carried long distances by soil, water, tools, or infested plants. Testing roots and soil is the only positive method for confirming the presence of nematodes. Contact your local Cooperative Extension Office (see page 1011) for sampling instructions and addresses of testing laboratories. Soil and root problems such as poor soil structure, drought stress, nutrient deficiency, and root rots can also produce symptoms of decline similar to those caused by nematodes. These problems should be eliminated as causes before sending soil and root samples for testing. For information on soil problems and root rots, see pages 901 and 857.

SOLUTION: There are no chemicals available to homeowners to kill nematodes in planted soil. However, they can be controlled before planting by soil fumigation. For information on fumigating soil, see page 919.

PROBLEM: The inside of a tuber is streaked or spotted with brown to black discolorations. The discolorations may extend throughout the tuber, or occur in just a few small spots.

ANALYSIS: Internal discoloration
Discoloration inside potato tubers results from unfavorable growing and harvesting conditions. It can be caused by an early frost, by alternating periods of very wet and very dry soil, or by drought conditions at harvest time. Plants infected with leaf roll or mosaic virus also produce discolored tubers. For information on these diseases, see page 771. Discolored tubers are inedible.

SOLUTION: Provide good growing conditions, as outlined on page 766. Control aphids, which spread virus diseases, with ORTHO Malathion 50 Insect Spray. Plant only certified seed pieces.

POTATOES — PROBLEMS WITH THE TUBER   **INSECTS**

Bacterial ring rot.

Hollow heart.

Adult (half life size). *Insert:* Larva (life size).

PROBLEM: Shoot tips are stunted, forming rosettes. Leaves turn yellow, then brown between the veins. Leaf margins curl upward, and stems may wilt. Stems cut at the ground level exude a creamy white ooze. Only a few stems on a plant may show symptoms. Tubers may be cracked and, when cut near the stem end, reveal a yellow to light brown ring of crumbly decay.

ANALYSIS: Ring rot
This disease is caused by a bacterium (*Corynebacterium sepedonicum*) that attacks both tubers and stems. Infected tubers are inedible. Tuber decay may be evident at harvest, or it may not develop until after several months in storage. Other rot organisms frequently invade and completely rot the tubers. Ring rot bacteria enter plants through wounds, especially those caused by cutting seed pieces before planting. They do not spread from plant to plant in the field. The bacteria survive between seasons in infected tubers and storage containers.

SOLUTION: Discard all infected tubers and plants at the first sign of the disease. Next year, use only certified potato seed pieces for plants. Plant whole; or if you cut them, disinfect the knife between cuts by dipping it in rubbing alcohol. Disinfect storage containers with a chlorine bleach. Wash storage bags in hot water.

PROBLEM: Tubers develop irregular white to brown cavities. Tubers are generally very large.

ANALYSIS: Hollow heart
Discolored cavities result when potato tubers develop too rapidly during the growing season. This rapid growth may be encouraged by excessive soil fertility and moisture. Plants spaced too far apart may also develop hollow heart. These cavities occur mainly on very large or oversized tubers. Tubers are still edible if the discolored cavities are cut away. The cavities do not decay unless bacterial or fungal rot organisms enter the tuber from the outside.

SOLUTION: Follow the planting and maintenance guidelines outlined on page 766.

If you're short of space, grow potatoes in bushel baskets, buckets, or large plastic garbage bags.

PROBLEM: Yellow-orange beetles with black stripes, about ⅜ inch long, are eating the leaves. Fat, red, humpbacked larvae with 2 rows of black dots may also be present.

ANALYSIS: Colorado potato beetle
(*Leptinotarsa decemlineata*)
This insect pest, also known as the *potato bug,* often devastates potato, tomato, and pepper plantings. Both the adults and the larvae damage plants by devouring leaves and stems. Small plants are most severely damaged. The beetle was originally native to the Rocky Mountains, and spread eastward in the late 1800s as potato plantings increased. In some areas of the country, the beetle population may reach epidemic proportions. The beetles lay their yellow-orange eggs on the undersides of the leaves as the first potatoes emerge from the ground in the spring. The larvae that hatch from these eggs feed for 2 to 3 weeks, pupate in the soil, and emerge 1 to 2 weeks later as adults, which lay more eggs. One generation is completed in a month. There are 1 to 3 generations a year, depending on the area of the country.

SOLUTION: Control Colorado potato beetles with ORTHO Fruit & Vegetable Insect Control, ORTHO Sevin Garden Dust, or ORTHO Tomato Vegetable Dust. Treat when the insects are first noticed, and repeat every 7 days as long as the infestation continues.

Blister beetle (twice life size).

Flea beetle damage.

Potato leafhopper (4 times life size).

PROBLEM: Black or gray slender beetles feed in clusters on the leaves. They are ½ to ¾ inch long, and may be striped.

ANALYSIS: Blister beetle
(*Epicauta* species)
This insect pest feeds on a wide variety of vegetables and flowers. The adult beetles eat plant leaves, and can defoliate entire plants. The larvae, however, eat grasshopper eggs, and help to reduce the grasshopper population. Adult beetles emerge from hibernation in swarms in June and July. They feed voraciously, and after stripping one plant move on to another. They lay yellow egg clusters in the soil. The grubs that hatch from these eggs migrate through the soil, feeding on grasshopper eggs. There is only one generation each year. Be careful when handling these beetles; the juice from crushed beetles causes blisters.

SOLUTION: Treat the plants with ORTHO Tomato Vegetable Dust or ORTHO Tomato & Vegetable Insect Spray as soon as the beetles appear in June or July. Repeat the treatments at intervals of 7 to 10 days if the plants become reinfested.

PROBLEM: Leaves are riddled with shotholes about ⅛ inch in diameter. Tiny (1/16 inch) black beetles jump like fleas when disturbed. Leaves of seedlings and eventually whole plants may wilt and die.

ANALYSIS: Flea beetles
These beetles jump like fleas, but are not related to them. Both adult and immature flea beetles feed on a wide variety of garden vegetables, including potatoes. The immature beetle, a legless gray grub, injures plants by feeding on the roots and the lower surfaces of leaves. Adults chew holes in leaves. Flea beetles are most damaging to young plants. Adult beetles survive the winter in soil and garden debris. They emerge in early spring to feed on weeds until potatoes sprout. Grubs hatch from eggs laid in the soil and feed for 2 to 3 weeks, damaging the tubers. After pupating in the soil, they emerge as adults to repeat the cycle. There are 1 to 4 generations a year. Adults may feed for up to 2 months.

SOLUTION: Control flea beetles on potatoes with ORTHO Fruit & Vegetable Insect Control, ORTHO Sevin Garden Dust, ORTHO Diazinon Soil & Foliage Dust, or ORTHO Tomato Vegetable Dust when the leaves first show damage. Spray or dust carefully at the base of stems. Watch new growth for evidence of further damage, and repeat the treatment at weekly intervals as needed. Clean all plant debris from the garden after harvesting to eliminate overwintering spots for adult beetles.

PROBLEM: Spotted, pale green insects up to ⅛ inch long hop, run sideways, or fly away quickly when a plant is touched. The leaves are stippled or appear scorched, with a green midrib and brown edges curled under.

ANALYSIS: Potato leafhopper
(*Empoasca fabae*)
This insect feeds on potatoes, and beans, and on some fruit and ornamental trees. It sucks plant sap from the undersides of the leaves, causing leaf stippling. This leafhopper is responsible for *hopperburn*, and the browning and curling of the edges of potato leaves. The leafhopper injects toxic saliva into the nutrient-conducting tissue, interrupting the flow of food within the plant. Potato yields may be reduced drastically by hopperburn. Leafhoppers at all stages of maturity are active during the growing season. Both early and late varieties of potatoes are infested. Leafhoppers live year-round in the Gulf States, and migrate northward on warm spring winds, so even areas that have winters so cold that the eggs cannot survive are not free from infestation.

SOLUTION: Spray infested plants with ORTHO Tomato & Vegetable Insect Spray, ORTHO Malathion 50 Insect Spray, or ORTHO Sevin Garden Dust. Be sure to cover the lower surfaces of the leaves. Repeat the spray as often as necessary to keep the insects under control. Allow at least 10 days between applications. Eradicate nearby weeds that may harbor leafhopper eggs, especially thistles, plantains, and dandelions.

POTATOES — LEAVES DISCOLORED OR DYING

Early blight.

Late blight.

Black leg.

PROBLEM: Irregular dark brown to black spots, ⅛ to ½ inch in diameter, appear on the lower leaves. Concentric rings develop in the spots. Spots may enlarge, causing the leaf to die and fall off. Tubers may be infected with brown, corky, dry spots.

ANALYSIS: Early blight
This plant disease is caused by a fungus (*Alternaria solani*) that attacks both vines and tubers. It is most severe toward the end of the growing season when the vines approach maturity and after tubers are formed. Many leaves may be killed. The potato yield is reduced, but the plant seldom dies. Tubers are frequently infected through wounds inflicted during harvest. Early blight is favored by warm (75° to 85°F) weather and moisture. The fungal spores spend the winter in plant debris left in the garden. Infected tubers are inedible.

SOLUTION: Spray plants with ORTHO Vegetable Disease Control as soon as leaf spotting occurs. Repeat the treatment every 7 to 10 days until the leaves die back naturally. Clean all plant debris from the garden after harvest. Do not store infected tubers. Next year, begin spraying the plants when they are 6 inches tall, and continue at intervals of 7 to 10 days until the tops die back. Avoid overhead watering by using drip or furrow irrigation. Maintain adequate fertility as outlined on page 766. Use seed potatoes certified by State Departments of Agriculture to be free of diseases.

PROBLEM: Brownish water-soaked spots appear on the leaves. Spots enlarge rapidly, turn black and kill leaves, then leaf stems and stems. In moist weather, a gray mildew grows on the lower surfaces of the leaves. Tuber skins are infected in the ground or in storage with brownish purple spots that become a wet or dry rot.

ANALYSIS: Late blight
This plant disease is caused by a fungus (*Phytophthora infestans*) that seriously injures potatoes and tomatoes. This disease was responsible for the great famine in Ireland from 1845 to 1850. The fungus spreads very rapidly, killing an entire planting in a few days. Infected tubers are inedible. The tubers are infected when the spores wash off the leaves and into the soil. Tubers may also be attacked during harvest and rot in storage. A soft rot often invades the damaged tubers. (For information on soft rot, see page 771.) Late blight is prevalent in moist humid weather with cool nights and warm days. Foggy, misty weather and heavy dews provide enough moisture for infection. The spores survive the winter in infected tubers in the garden or compost pile.

SOLUTION: Sprays are ineffective once the disease appears. Discard infected tubers and vines. Next year, spray plants with ORTHO Vegetable Disease Control when the plants are 6 inches tall. Continue at intervals of 7 to 10 days until the plants naturally turn yellow and die. Avoid overhead watering; use a drip or furrow irrigation. Wait at least a week after plants die naturally before digging the tubers. This allows time for the spores to die.

PROBLEM: Leaves roll, turn yellow, and wilt. The lower stem becomes black, slimy, and smelly from the soil line to 3 or 4 inches up the stem. Aerial tubers may form along the stems.

ANALYSIS: Black leg
This plant disease is caused by a bacterium (*Erwinia carotovora var. atroseptica*) that is spread in seed potatoes and sometimes persists in the soil. Bacteria in the soil may infect the plants through wounds in the stem or through the seed piece. If infected seed is planted, it rots after it sprouts. The rot spreads from the seed piece into the stem of the potato plant. As the tuber rots, toxic substances are released that cause the plant to wilt, collapse, and often die. The lower stem turns black and rots. If the plant does not die, it yields poorly, and the tubers may rot in storage. Plants growing in wet soil are very susceptible.

SOLUTION: No chemical controls are available. Avoid overwatering and damaging the plants in any way. Use certified seed potatoes that are resistant to black leg. Plant small whole tubers 2 to 3 inches deep in well-drained soil.

Potato varieties that are resistant to black leg: Atlantic, Katahdin, Kennebec, La Rouge, Red LaSoda, Red Norland, Red Pontiac, and Superior.

Bacterial soft rot.

Virus.

Potato leaf roll.

PROBLEM: A slimy, smelly decay infects potatoes either in the ground or in storage. Small, soft, circular discolored spots may occur on tubers.

ANALYSIS: Bacterial soft rot
This plant disease is caused by a bacterium (*Erwinia carotovora var. aroideae*) that attacks potatoes, tomatoes, peppers, parsnips, carrots, and many other vegetables. The bacteria rarely attack potato leaves, but severely infect the tubers, rendering them inedible. The tubers may be infected either in the ground or in storage. Bacteria can rot tubers completely in 3 to 10 days. Tubers bruised during harvest are likely to become infected and rot in storage. The bacteria that cause soft rot are almost always present in the soil, but they infect only potatoes that have been wounded, or are growing in wet soil.

SOLUTION: No chemical controls are available. Keep potato plants healthy and control insect and disease problems. Wait until vines turn yellow and die before digging potatoes. Dig carefully to avoid bruising them. If you want to store the tubers, cure them in the dark for one week at 70°F to heal any bruises and to condition them. Then store them in a humid area between 35° and 45°F. Do not store blemished tubers. Next year, plant in well-drained soil, and ridge or hill the plants to encourage excess water to flow away from them.

PROBLEM: Leaves are small, mottled light and dark green, and may be wrinkled or curled. Plants are stunted and may die prematurely. Tubers may be elongated, cracked, or discolored inside.

ANALYSIS: Viruses
Several viruses infect potatoes, causing distortion, slow growth, a reduction in the size, quality, and number of tubers, and sometimes death of the plant. Infected tubers are inedible. Viruses may be introduced into the garden in infected seed pieces; or they may live in weeds, including pokeweed, plantain, horsenettle, catnip, and motherwort. Once the infection is present in or near the garden, aphids spread the viruses from plant to plant while feeding.

SOLUTION: There are no chemical controls for viruses. Discard infected plants and tubers promptly. At the first sign of aphids, treat the potato plants with ORTHO Malathion 50 Insect Spray or ORTHO Fruit & Vegetable Insect Control. Repeat the treatment at intervals of 7 to 10 days if the plants become reinfested. (For more information about controlling disease-carrying insects, see page 880.) Plant only pieces certified by State Departments of Agriculture to be free of disease. Do not save your own tubers for replanting. Do not plant tubers from the grocery store.

PROBLEM: Leaves roll upward, turn light green to yellow, and feel leathery. Lower leaves are affected first, then upper leaves. Plants may be stunted and produce few tubers. Tubers may be discolored inside. Pale green or yellow insects may cluster on the leaves and stems.

ANALYSIS: Leaf roll
This plant disease is caused by a virus that is carried in infected tubers and spread by aphids. As a result of the widespread distribution and severity of leaf roll virus by infected tubers, the seed potato certification program was started. Potato tubers are tested for the virus, and if clean, are certified by State Departments of Agriculture. Several species of aphids transmit this virus, the most common being the green peach aphid. This is a pale green aphid with 3 dark lines on its back. The aphid injects the virus into the plant while sucking the sap from the leaves and stems. Leaf roll virus affects potatoes in two ways: by reducing the yield, and by discoloring the tuber. Discolored tubers are inedible.

SOLUTION: No chemical control is available for leaf roll, although controlling aphids with ORTHO Fruit & Vegetable Insect Control or ORTHO Malathion 50 Insect Spray will help. Repeat at intervals of 7 to 10 days if the plants become reinfested. For more information on controlling disease-carrying insects, see page 880. Discard all infected plants and tubers. Plant only certified seed potatoes.

RADISHES

RADISHES

ADAPTATION: Throughout the United States.

PLANTING TIME: See page 1009.

PLANTING METHOD: Sow seeds ½ inch deep and thin to grow 1 inch apart. Do not transplant. For a continuous harvest, plant seeds every 2 weeks.

SOIL: Any good garden soil. pH 5.5 to 7.0

FERTILIZER: At planting time, add 3 to 4 pounds of ORTHO Vegetable Garden Food 5–10–10 per 100 square feet, or 1 pound per 25-foot row.
   Containers: Water thoroughly 1 to 2 weeks after seeds sprout with a solution of ORTHO Tomato & Vegetable Food 6–18–6.

WATER:
   How much: Apply enough water at each irrigation to wet the soil 6 to 8 inches deep.
   Containers: 10 per cent of the applied water should drain out the bottom.
   How often: Water when the soil 2 inches deep is barely moist.

HARVEST: Pull radishes and use as needed. They are usually ready for eating 25 to 30 days after sprouting. Large radishes may be tougher and more stringy than smaller ones. Dig winter radishes or daikon when the roots attain the length stated on the seed packet. Pull one or two to check. Store radishes in the refrigerator.

Flea beetle damage.

PROBLEM: Leaves are riddled with shotholes about ⅛ inch in diameter. Tiny (1/16 inch) black beetles jump like fleas when disturbed.

ANALYSIS: Flea beetles
These beetles jump like fleas, but are not related to them. Both adult and immature flea beetles feed on a wide variety of garden vegetables. The immature beetle, a legless gray grub, injures plants by feeding on the roots and the lower surfaces of leaves. Adults chew holes in leaves. Adult beetles survive the winter in soil and garden debris. They emerge in early spring to feed on weeds until vegetable seeds sprout. Grubs hatch from eggs laid in the soil and feed for 2 to 3 weeks. After pupating in the soil, they emerge as adults to repeat the cycle. There are 1 to 4 generations a year. Adults may feed for up to 2 months.

SOLUTION: Control flea beetles on radishes with an insecticide containing *carbaryl* or *methoxychlor* when the plants first emerge through the soil or at the first sign of damage. Watch new growth for evidence of further damage, and repeat the treatment at weekly intervals as needed. Clean all plant debris from the garden after harvest to eliminate overwintering spots for adult beetles.

Root maggot (twice life size).

PROBLEM: Young plants wilt in the heat of the day. They may later turn yellow and die. Soft-bodied, yellow-white maggots, about ¼ inch long, are feeding in the roots. The roots are honeycombed with slimy channels and scarred by brown grooves.

ANALYSIS: Root maggots
(*Hylemya* species)
Root maggots are most numerous during cool, wet weather in spring, early summer, and fall. Early maggots attack the roots, stems, and seeds of radishes, cabbage, broccoli, and turnips in the spring and early summer. Later insects damage fall crops. The adult is a gray fly slightly smaller than a housefly, with black stripes and bristles down its back. It lays eggs on stems and nearby soil. The maggots hatch in 2 to 5 days and tunnel into radish roots, making them inedible.

SOLUTION: Once the growing plant wilts and turns yellow, nothing can be done. To control maggots in the next planting of radishes, mix ORTHO Diazinon Soil & Turf Insect Control 4 to 6 inches into the soil before seeding. Control lasts about one month. To prevent egg laying, screen adult flies from the seedbed with a cheesecloth cover.

RHUBARB

Black root rot.

PROBLEM: Bluish black spots develop on the roots of white radishes. The spots enlarge, infecting the entire root. The infected tissue remains firm. A black discoloration extends into the root in radial streaks.

ANALYSIS: Black root rot
This plant disease is caused by a fungus (*Aphanomyces raphani*) that is especially severe on long-rooted white radish varieties. The variety White Icicle is the most susceptible. Colored and late-maturing varieties are also affected, but less severely. Plants may be infected at any time from the seedling stage to maturity. The fungus is most active in warm (68° to 80°F), wet soils, and the spores may live in the soil for several years. Abundant water is necessary for infection, and spores are spread by splashing and running water.

SOLUTION: Discard all infected roots. Clean all plant debris from the garden after harvest. Plant radishes in the same area only once every 3 or 4 years. Because this fungus requires abundant water for infection, grow radishes in well-drained soil and avoid overwatering. The soil should remain moist, but not soggy. Before planting, dust seeds with a fungicide containing *captan* or *thiram*.

The variety White Spike is less susceptible to black root rot than White Icicle. Red Prince is more resistant than other red globe varieties.

RHUBARB

ADAPTATION: Northern United States.

PLANTING TIME: See page 1009.

PLANTING METHOD: Plant root divisions or crowns so the buds are no deeper than 2 inches. Allow 2½ to 3 feet between plants.

SOIL: Any well-drained soil that is rich in organic matter. pH 5.0 to 7.0

FERTILIZER: At planting time, use 2 to 3 pounds of ORTHO General Purpose Plant Food 8-8-8 per 100 square feet, or 1½ pounds per 50-foot row. Following years, fertilize with 1½ to 2 pounds of ORTHO General Purpose Plant Food 8-8-8 each spring before the new leaves begin to grow. After harvest, side-dress with ORTHO Dried Blood Meal 12-0-0 using 1½ pounds per 50-foot row.

WATER:
  How much: Apply enough water at each irrigation to wet the soil 15 to 18 inches deep.
  How often: Water when the soil 2 inches deep is barely moist.

HARVEST: Do not pick stalks the first year after planting. The second year, pick for about 2 weeks. The third and following years, pick for about 6 to 8 weeks, or until the stalks become small. Pull only large stalks, leaving smaller ones to grow. Never pick more than two-thirds of the stalks present on the plant. To pick, hold the stalk near its base and pull toward one side until it breaks. Do not cut. Discard the leaf blade, which is not edible.

Crown rot.

PROBLEM: Leaves wilt. Brown, sunken, water-soaked spots appear on the base of the leaf stalks. Leaves yellow and stalks collapse and die. The whole plant eventually dies.

ANALYSIS: Crown rot
This plant disease, also called *foot rot* or *root rot*, is caused by a fungus (*Phytophthora* species) that lives in the soil. It thrives in waterlogged, heavy soils, and attacks the crown and base of the stems. The stems and eventually the roots rot, resulting in wilting and finally the death of the plant. The fungus is most active in warm (60° to 75°F), moist soils in the late spring and early summer. The spores are spread to healthy plants in running or splashing water, or by contaminated soil or infected plants brought into the garden.

SOLUTION: Remove and destroy dying leaves and plants. Apply a drench of a fungicide containing *captan* or *basic copper sulfate* to the crown or base of the plant and to the surrounding soil. When replanting, purchase disease-free plants from a reputable company, and plant in well-drained soil. (For information on improving soil drainage, see page 901.) Avoid overwatering.

RHUBARB ─────────────────

Damaged rhubarb and curculio (twice life size).

PROBLEM: Small black spots occur on the stalks. Slow-moving, ½ inch, black weevils covered with rusty-yellow powder are found on the stalks. They have long curved snouts.

ANALYSIS: Rhubarb curculio (*Lixus concavus*)
The rhubarb curculio is one of the largest snout-nosed beetles in the United States. It does not feed on rhubarb at all, but injures the plants by boring into or puncturing the stalks, roots, and crown to lay eggs. This causes black spots on the stalks. After laying eggs, the adult curculio travels to nearby large-stemmed weeds, usually curly dock, and feeds on the foliage. (For information about curly dock, see page 842.) When the eggs in the rhubarb hatch, the larvae also leave the rhubarb plants to feed on curly dock roots. Rhubarb stalks marred with puncture holes are edible if the discolored area is cut away.

SOLUTION: There are no chemical controls currently available for curculio. Control grassy and large-stemmed weeds, especially curly dock, in the vicinity of your garden. Handpick adult beetles when you see them.

SPINACH ─────────────────

SPINACH ─────────────────

ADAPTATION: Throughout the United States.

PLANTING TIME: See page 1009.

PLANTING METHOD: Sow seeds ½ inch deep and 1 inch apart. When the plants have 2 to 3 leaves, thin to stand 4 to 8 inches apart.

SOIL: Any good garden soil that is rich in organic matter. pH 6.0 to 8.0

FERTILIZER: At planting time, use 2 pounds of ORTHO General Purpose Plant Food 8–8–8 per 100 square feet, or 1½ pounds per 50-foot row. Side-dress in 2 weeks with 1 to 2 pounds per 50-foot row.
  Containers: Water thoroughly every 2 weeks with a solution of ORTHO Tomato & Vegetable Food 6–18–6.

WATER:
  How much: Apply enough water at each irrigation to wet the soil 8 to 10 inches deep.
  Containers: 10 per cent of the applied water should drain out the bottom.
  How often: Water when the soil 2 inches deep is barely moist.

HARVEST: Pick individual leaves as needed. Just before seed stalks emerge, use a sharp knife to cut the entire plant just above the soil line.

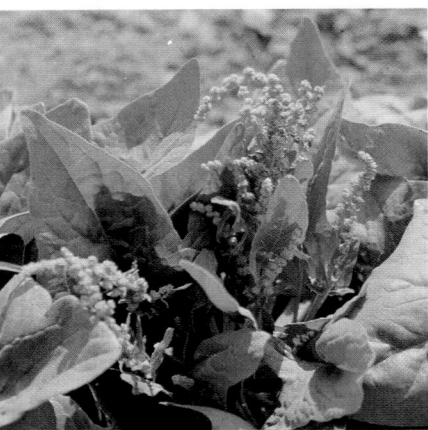

Bolting spinach.

PROBLEM: Flower stalks grow from the center of spinach plants in late spring and summer.

ANALYSIS: Bolting
Spinach makes seed stalks (bolts) in late spring and summer as temperatures rise and the length of the day increases. Some varieties bolt more easily than others. Once the flower stalk forms, leaves may become bitter, and edible foliage is no longer produced. Fall-planted spinach seldom bolts.

SOLUTION: Plant spinach as soon as possible in the late winter or early spring. Plant approximately 4 to 6 weeks before the last spring frost, and no later than 6 to 8 weeks before the daytime temperatures remain over 75°F. Use bolt-resistant or long-standing varieties for spring planting. For a summer crop, plant New Zealand spinach, a spinach substitute that thrives in summer heat. Although it is not a true spinach, the taste is similar.

─────────────────

Bolt-resistant spinach varieties: America, Bloomsdale, Long Standing, and Melody.

Downy mildew.

White rust.

Leafminers (life size).

PROBLEM: During cool, humid weather, pale yellow spots appear on the upper surfaces of the lower leaves. These spots enlarge and spread to the upper leaves. A gray-purple mold grows on the undersides of the leaves. Leaves may turn black, and the whole plant may die.

ANALYSIS: Downy mildew
This plant disease, also called *blue mold*, is caused by a fungus (*Peronospora effusa*) that attacks only spinach. Bloomsdale variety is particularly susceptible. During prolonged cool (45° to 65°F), humid weather, the fungus spreads rapidly, often destroying the entire planting. The fungus can invade a healthy leaf only if the leaf remains wet for extended periods. Spores are produced on the undersides of the leaves.

SOLUTION: Fungicidal sprays for the control of this disease are seldom practical in home gardens. It is difficult to spray the lower surfaces of the spinach leaves. If downy mildew is severe, and your planting is large, you may treat with a fungicide containing *maneb* or *zineb*. Repeat the treatment at weekly intervals until the disease is no longer seen, or until the weather becomes less favorable for the disease. Remove all plant debris from the garden after harvest. Plant disease-resistant varieties. Water early in the day, so that the plants dry before nightfall.

Varieties resistant to downy mildew: Badger Savoy, Bouquet, Dixie Market, Duet, Early Smooth, Grand Stand, Melody, Nares, No. 8 Hybrid, No. 424 Hybrid, and Savoy Supreme.

PROBLEM: White, blisterlike spots with a yellow border appear on the undersides of leaves. The upper surfaces of the leaves are pale green to yellow, and may also have blisterlike spots.

ANALYSIS: White rust
This plant disease is caused by a fungus (*Albugo occidentalis*) that attacks all varieties of spinach. Infected plants are weakened and collapse quickly. White rust is most active during prolonged periods of cool, humid nights and mild days, with temperatures between 55° and 80°F. The leaves must be wet for infection to take place. The fungal spores survive the winter in plant debris in the garden, and are spread to healthy plants by the wind, or by splashing or running water.

SOLUTION: Fungicidal sprays are seldom practical in home gardens for this disease. The spinach usually matures before enough applications can be made to control the disease. If white rust is severe in your area, or if your planting is large, treat the plants with a fungicide containing *maneb* or *zineb* when the first 3 to 4 leaves are three-quarters grown. Controls are effective only if started early. Repeat at weekly intervals until 10 days before harvest. To help reduce infections, water early in the day so the plants dry before nightfall. Remove all plant debris from the garden after harvest. Don't plant spinach in the same spot more often than once every 3 years.

PROBLEM: Irregular tan blotches, blisters, or tunnels appear in the leaves. The tan areas peel apart like facial tissue. Tiny black specks and white or yellow maggots are found inside the tunnels.

ANALYSIS: Leafminers
These insect pests belong to a family of leaf-mining flies. The tiny black or yellow adult fly lays her white eggs on the undersides of leaves. The maggots that hatch from these eggs bore into the leaf and tunnel between the upper and lower surfaces, feeding on the inner tissue. The tunnels and blotches are called *mines*. The black specks inside are the maggots' droppings. Several overlapping generations occur during the growing season, so larvae are present continually from spring until fall. Infested leaves are not edible.

SOLUTION: Control leafminers on spinach with ORTHO Fruit & Vegetable Insect Control when the white egg clusters are first seen under the leaves. Repeat 2 more times at weekly intervals to control succeeding generations. Once the leafminers enter the leaves, the sprays are ineffective. Spraying after the mines first appear will control only those leafminers that attack after the application. Clean all plant debris from the garden after harvest to reduce overwintering spots for the pupae.

STRAWBERRIES

STRAWBERRIES

ADAPTATION: Throughout the United States.

PLANTING TIME: See page 1009.

PLANTING METHOD: Select dormant or growing plants. Pick off all but two or three of the healthiest leaves. Prune away a third of the roots. Set the plants 18 inches apart and so that the roots fan outward. The crown should be just above the soil level. As runners develop, maintain the rows no wider than 18 to 24 inches.

SOIL: Any good garden soil that is high in organic matter. pH 5.5 to 8.0

FERTILIZER: At planting time, add 1 to 2 pounds of ORTHO Vegetable Garden Food 5–10–10 per 100 square feet, or ½ pound per 25-foot row. Side-dress after harvest each year with ½ to 1 pound of fertilizer per 25-foot row.
  Containers: Water thoroughly every 3 to 4 weeks with a solution of ORTHO Tomato & Vegetable Food 6–18–6.

WATER:
How much: Apply enough water at each irrigation to wet the soil 8 to 10 inches deep.
How often: Water when the soil 1 inch deep is barely moist.

HARVEST: For maximum production the second year, remove blossoms and runners the first year. Pick berries, with the stem and cap attached, when they are completely red. Pinch the stem between your fingers, being careful not to jerk or uproot the plants. Store berries in the refrigerator until use.

Slug (3 times life size).

PROBLEM: Stems and leaves may be sheared off and eaten. Silvery trails wind around on the plants and soil nearby. Snails or slugs may be seen moving around or feeding on the plants, especially at night. Inspect the garden for them at night by flashlight.

ANALYSIS: Snails and slugs
These pests are mollusks, and are related to clams, oysters, and other shellfish. They feed on a wide variety of garden plants. Like other mollusks, snails and slugs need to be moist all the time. For this reason, they avoid direct sun and dry places, and hide during the day in damp places, such as under flower pots or in thick groundcover. The emerge at night or on cloudy days to feed. Snails and slugs are similar except that the snail has a hard shell, into which it withdraws when disturbed. Slugs lay masses of white eggs encased in a slimy mass in protected places. Snails bury their eggs in the soil, also in a slimy mass. The young look like miniature versions of their parents.

SOLUTION: Scatter ORTHO Bug-Geta Snail & Slug Pellets around the areas you wish to protect. Also scatter the pellets in areas where snails or slugs might be hiding, such as in dense groundcover, weedy areas, compost piles, or pot storage areas. Before spreading the pellets, wet down the areas to be treated to encourage snail and slug activity that night. Repeat the application every 2 weeks as long as snails and slugs are active. Do not apply pellets to leaves.

Meadow spittlebug (half life size).

PROBLEM: White, frothy masses of bubbles, ½ inch long, appear on leaves, stems, and flowers. Hidden in this froth is a small, smooth, tan to green insect.

ANALYSIS: Meadow spittlebug (*Philaenus spumarius*)
Spittlebugs are related to leafhoppers (see page 880). Both the adults and the nymphs damage plants by sucking the sap from the leaves and stems. When populations are high, this results in stunted plants that are low in vigor and produce few berries. Small numbers of spittlebugs do little damage to strawberry plants. Spittlebug eggs survive the winter in plant debris, and hatch in the early spring. The nymphs produce the frothy "spittle," which protects them from the sun and from other insects. The nymphs remain in the spittle until they emerge in early summer as hopping, tan to black adults. The adults feed until frost, laying eggs in August and September. Spittlebugs are most numerous in areas with high humidity. There is one generation a year.

SOLUTION: Once the nymphs are protected inside the froth, insecticides are ineffective. Hose off the frothy masses with a strong stream of water. If spittlebugs are numerous in your area and your plants are suffering, control the adults in the summer and fall with ORTHO Home Orchard Spray or ORTHO Malathion 50 Insect Spray. Clean all plant debris from the garden at the end of the season to reduce the number of overwintering eggs.

Gray mold.

Strawberry leafroller (life size).

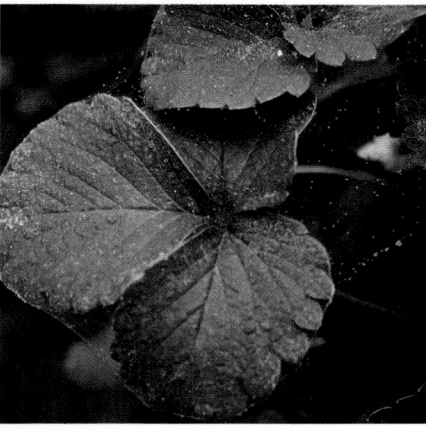

Spider mite webbing.

PROBLEM: A light tan spot appears on berries. Some berries are soft, mushy, and rotting. A fluffy gray mold may cover rotting berries.

ANALYSIS: Gray mold
Gray mold is caused by a fungus (*Botrytis cinerea*). It is the most damaging rot of strawberries, and greatly reduces the amount of edible fruit. Both flowers and berries are attacked. The flowers are infected when in bloom, and may not produce berries. Berries are attacked at all stages of development. They are infected directly when a healthy berry touches a decaying one, the ground, or a dead leaf. Infected berries are inedible. The fuzzy gray mold on the berries is composed of fungal strands and millions of microscopic spores. The fungus is most active in cool, humid weather, and is spread by splashing water, people, or infected fruit. Crowded plantings, rain, and overhead watering enhance the spread of the fungus.

SOLUTION: Discard infected fruit. To reduce the spread of the fungus to uncontaminated fruit, treat with ORTHO Home Orchard Spray, ORTHO Orthocide Garden Fungicide, or ORTHO Tomato Vegetable Dust at the first sign of the disease. Continue treating every 8 to 10 days. Pick berries as they ripen. Avoid overhead watering by using soaker or drip hoses. Mulch with straw, pine needles, or other material to keep fruit off the ground. To prevent infection next year, treat the plants when in bloom, and repeat every 8 to 10 days. When setting out new plants, provide enough space between plants to allow for good air circulation and rapid drying after rain and irrigation.

PROBLEM: Leaves are rolled, folded, or webbed together. Some leaves may turn brown and die. Inside the rolled leaves are 1/2-inch brown or green worms that wriggle when disturbed.

ANALYSIS: Strawberry leafroller
(*Ancylis comptana fragariae*)
This moth larva damages plants by feeding from inside the rolled leaves. This feeding weakens the plant, causing leaves to die and fruit to be deformed. Leafrollers hibernate for the winter as larvae and pupae in plant debris and folded leaves. In May, the adult moths, rusty red with brown and white markings, lay their eggs on the undersides of the leaves. The worms that hatch from these eggs roll the leaves and feed inside. After feeding for 4 to 7 weeks, the worms pupate in the rolled leaves, and emerge as adults to repeat the cycle. There are 2 or 3 generations a year.

SOLUTION: Treat with ORTHO Fruit & Vegetable Insect Control or ORTHO Diazinon Insect Spray as soon as the worms or rolled leaves are noticed. Repeat the treatments at intervals of 10 to 14 days if leaf rolling continues. If practical, pick the worms off by hand.

PROBLEM: Leaves are stippled, yellowing, and dirty. Leaves may dry out and drop. There may be webbing between leaves, or on the lower surfaces of the leaves. Few berries are produced. To determine if the plant is infested with mites, hold a sheet of white paper underneath an affected leaf and tap the leaf sharply. Minute green, red, or yellow specks the size of pepper grains will drop to the paper and begin to crawl around. These pests are easily seen against the white background.

ANALYSIS: Spider mites
Spider mites, related to spiders, are major pests of many garden and greenhouse plants. Spider mites are larger than cyclamen mites, which also attack strawberries. Spider mites attack the older leaves, while cyclamen mites attack the younger leaves. For more information on cyclamen mites, see page 778. Spider mites cause damage by sucking sap from the undersides of the leaves. As a result of feeding, the green leaf pigment disappears, producing the stippled appearance. Berry production is also reduced. Mites are active throughout the growing season, but are favored by hot, dry weather (70°F and up). By midsummer, they build up to tremendous numbers.

SOLUTION: Treat infested strawberry plants with ORTHO Fruit & Vegetable Insect Control or a miticide containing *dicofol* when the damage first appears. Repeat the treatment at intervals of 7 to 10 days until harvest, or until damage no longer occurs. Be sure the pesticide contacts the lower surfaces of the leaves where the mites live.

STRAWBERRIES

Cyclamen mite damage.

Virus disease.

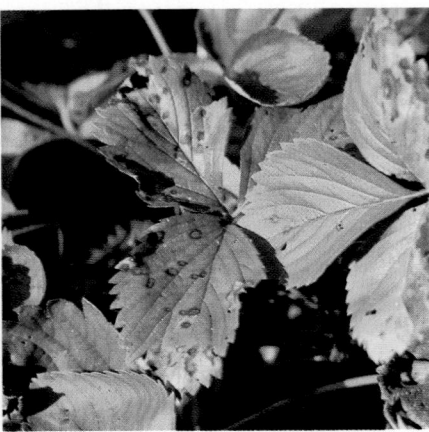

Fungal leaf spot.

PROBLEM: Leaves are curled, distorted, and stunted. Leaves in the center of the plant grow in tight bunches. Flower buds fall prematurely. Berries are distorted and shriveled.

ANALYSIS: Cyclamen mites
(*Steneotarsonemus pallidus*)
These pests of strawberries, also called *strawberry crown mites*, attack many garden and greenhouse plants including delphiniums, dahlias, African violets, and snapdragons. They attack the young leaves and damage them by sucking sap from the midvein on the undersides of the folded leaves. This causes the leaves to remain curled and tight in the center of the plant. Berry production is also reduced. Cyclamen mites are very tiny ($\frac{1}{100}$th of an inch) and can be seen only with a microscope or high-power hand lens. The mites survive the winter in the crowns of the strawberry plants. They feed in cool weather, and are seldom found in hot weather.

SOLUTION: Treat infested plants and those nearby with ORTHO Diazinon Soil & Foliage Dust, or with a miticide containing *dicofol*. Be sure the pesticide contacts the lower surfaces of the leaves where the mites live. Repeat at intervals of 7 to 10 days until the new leaves grow normally and are no longer curled or distorted. Avoid touching healthy plants after handling infested ones.

PROBLEM: Strawberry leaves are crinkled, yellowed, or distorted. Plants may be stunted with cupped leaves, or may grow in a tight rosette. Small, dull fruits or no fruits are produced. Plants grow few runners.

ANALYSIS: Viruses
Two types of viruses attack strawberries: killer viruses and latent viruses. Killer viruses have obvious symptoms, and kill individual mother plants and daughter plants attached to the ends of runners. Latent viruses show few or no symptoms. A single latent virus may merely reduce the number of runners and fruit produced. However, plants infected with more than one kind of latent virus are so weakened that they are frequently attacked and killed by other diseases. Viruses are transmitted by aphids and through runners from mother to daughter plants. Aphids are most numerous in cool spring and fall weather.

SOLUTION: Remove and discard all infected plants. If aphids are present, control them with ORTHO Diazinon Insect Spray, ORTHO Home Orchard Spray, or ORTHO Malathion 50 Insect Spray. (For more information about controlling disease-carrying insects, see page 880.) When replanting, buy certified plants from a reputable company. Certified plants are grown in special isolated conditions, and are essentially virus-free. Or choose virus-tolerant varieties.

PROBLEM: Purple spots, $\frac{1}{8}$ to $\frac{1}{4}$ inch in diameter, with tan to white centers occur on young leaves, fruitstalks, runners, and berry caps. Black spots may appear on unripe berries.

ANALYSIS: Leaf spot
A number of fungi cause leaf spots on strawberries. One of the most prevalent (*Mycosphaerella fragariae*) may kill many leaves. The most serious injury, however, occurs from spotting on fruitstalks and caps. This spotting reduces the size of the fruit, or kills the entire cluster. Berries attacked before they ripen never fully ripen and are inedible. Infected caps are discolored and killed, making the fruit unappetizing. Plantlets growing at the end of infected runners are weak and produce poorly. Leaf spot is most prevalent in cool, damp, humid weather in spring and fall, but occurs through the summer as long as moist weather continues.

SOLUTION: Treat plants with a fungicidal spray containing *benomyl* or *basic copper sulfate* at the first sign of leaf spotting. Repeat at intervals of 7 to 10 days until 3 days before harvest. Be sure to spray both the upper and lower surfaces of the leaves. Treat the plants in the fall if spotting occurs. Repeat as long as weather favorable for the spread of the disease continues. Clean all plant debris from the garden at the end of the season. Grow resistant varieties.

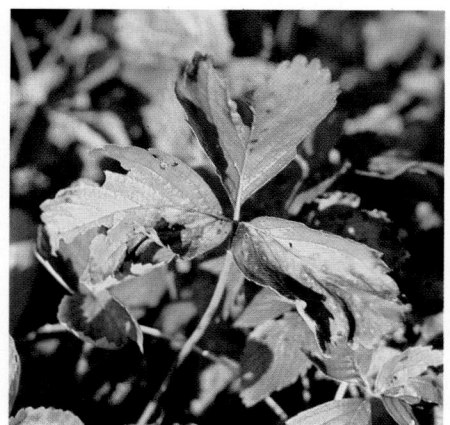

Leaf scorch.

PROBLEM: Purple to brown spots, up to ¼ inch in diameter, occur on the leaves, fruitstalks, and runners. The spots enlarge into blotches that may cover the entire leaf. Leaves become dry as if scorched. Berry caps may be black.

ANALYSIS: Leaf scorch
This plant disease is caused by a fungus (*Diplocarpon earliana*) that attacks strawberry leaves, fruitstalks, runners, and berry caps. Both older and younger leaves are attacked. When severe, the disease may destroy many leaves, weakening and killing plants. Spots on fruitstalks reduce berry size and cause flowers and young fruit to die. Infected berry caps turn black, making the fruit unattractive. Leaf scorch is most prevalent in cool, damp, humid weather in the spring and fall, but may occur throughout the summer as long as moist weather continues.

SOLUTION: Treat plants with a fungicidal spray containing *benomyl* or *basic copper sulfate* at the first sign of leaf spotting. Repeat at intervals of 7 to 10 days before harvest. Be sure to spray both the upper and lower surfaces of the leaves. Treat the plants in the fall if spotting occurs. Repeat as long as weather favorable to the spread of the disease continues. Clean all plant debris from the garden at the end of the season. Grow resistant varieties.

Verticillium wilt.

PROBLEM: Outer leaves wilt and turn dark brown along the margins and between the veins. Few new leaves are formed. Plants are flattened and few berries are produced. Brown spots or streaking may appear on leafstalks and runners and in crown tissue.

ANALYSIS: Verticillium wilt
This wilt disease affects many ornamental plants. It is caused by a soil-inhabiting fungus (*Verticillium dahliae*) that persists indefinitely on plant debris or in the soil. The disease is spread by contaminated seeds, plants, soil, and equipment. The fungus enters the plant through the roots and speads up into the crown and leaves through water-conducting vessels, which become discolored and plugged. This plugging cuts off the flow of water and nutrients to the leaves, causing leaf yellowing and wilting. Affected plants may or may not recover and yield fruit the following year. Sometimes the disease appears in mother plants, but not in rooted daughter plants.

SOLUTION: No chemical control is available. It is best to destroy infected plants. Verticillium can be removed from the soil only by fumigation techniques. (For more information about soil fumigation, see page 919.) However, the best solution is usually to plant varieties that are tolerant of verticillium wilt.

Black root rot.

PROBLEM: Plants grow poorly, wilt, and produce very few berries. Leaves turn yellow, then red and finally brown, and die. Dark brown to black spots occur on roots. The outer tissue layer of the main roots blackens, while the center core remains a normal pale yellow.

ANALYSIS: Black root rot
Black root rot is caused by any of several soil-inhabiting fungi. These fungi thrive in waterlogged, heavy soils. The fungi attack the plant roots, causing them to decay. This results in wilting, then yellowing leaves, and eventually the death of the plant. Plants weakened by frost injury, drought stress, nematodes, buried crowns, or wet soil are more susceptible to these fungi.

SOLUTION: Remove and discard all infected plants. Avoid future black root rot problems by planting in well-drained soil. For information on improving soil drainage, see page 901. Buy healthy plants from a reputable company. Do not purchase any plants with black or darkened roots.

STRAWBERRIES

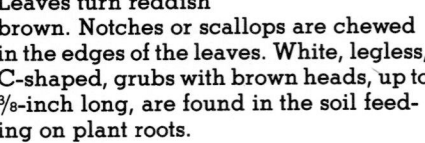

Damaged roots. *Insert:* Root weevil (half life size).

Red stele.

Armillaria root rot.

PROBLEM: Plants grow slowly and are stunted. Leaves turn reddish brown. Notches or scallops are chewed in the edges of the leaves. White, legless, C-shaped, grubs with brown heads, up to ³/₈-inch long, are found in the soil feeding on plant roots.

ANALYSIS: Root weevils
Several weevils attack strawberries. The brown to black, hard shelled, ¼-inch-long adult beetles with long snouts feed on the leaves at night. They hide during the day under leaves and clods of soil. Their feeding causes little damage, but is a warning sign that grubs may be present. Adults are present from spring through summer, and lay their eggs in the crowns of plants in early summer. The grubs that hatch from these eggs burrow into the soil and feed on the roots until late fall, then resume feeding in the spring. Their feeding reduces berry production and sometimes kills the plant. There is only one generation a year. The adult weevils occasionally become a nuisance in the house. As they migrate in search of more food, they enter homes through open doors and windows and cracks in the foundation. Although they may feed on some houseplants, they do not eat food or clothing.

SOLUTION: There are no chemicals available to home gardeners to control root weevils on strawberries. Destroy infested plants and any grubs found in the soil. Do not plant in infested soil.

PROBLEM: Plants grow poorly, are stunted, and frequenty wilt. The young leaves turn bluish-green. Older leaves turn yellow and red. In the spring, the center of the root is discolored reddish brown instead of the normal pale yellow color. Black tips or patches may appear on feeder roots. Few berries are produced, and the plants eventually die.

ANALYSIS: Red stele
This root rot disease of strawberries is caused by a fungus (*Phytophthora fragariae*) that persists in the soil for many years. It is the most damaging disease that attacks strawberries. The small feeder roots are attacked first. Then the fungus invades the center core — the stele — of the roots. The reddish brown discoloration is most visible in the spring. In the summer the rotted roots are replaced by new healthy roots, so the symptoms often disappear. Red stele is most destructive in cool spring and fall weather in poorly drained, heavy soil or low spots in the garden. Plants growing in well-drained soil are less frequently attacked.

SOLUTION: There is no chemical control available for red stele on strawberry. The most practical method of control is to plant tolerant varieties in well-drained soil. For instructions on improving drainage, see page 901.

PROBLEM: Leaves are stunted and yellow. Few berries are produced. Plants decline, produce no new growth, and die. In the fall, honey-colored mushrooms, 2 to 5 inches in diameter, may develop singly or in clusters on the base of the plant or in the soil. Black, rootlike strands about the diameter of a pencil lead grow out of the roots into the soil.

ANALYSIS: Armillaria root rot
This plant disease, also called *oak root fungus* and *shoestring root rot*, is caused by a fungus (*Armillaria mellea*) that rots the roots of many woody and nonwoody plants. Plants under stress from severe drought, overwatering, physical injuries, insects, or diseases are the most susceptible to attack. The fungus is spread long distances by spores from the mushrooms, or short distances through the soil by the rootlike fungal strands. Once the fungus enters the plant, the roots decay, and water and nutrient uptake are inhibited, causing the plant to die. In the fall, mushrooms appear at the base of the plant.

SOLUTION: No chemical controls are available. Remove and destroy infected plants, including the roots. Check surrounding plants and remove if infected. Keep strawberry plants healthy with regular maintenance as outlined on page 776. Avoid planting strawberries in recently cleared forest lands or old orchards, where armillaria root rot is common.

SWEET POTATOES

Symphylan damaged plants.

PROBLEM: Slender, white pests about ¼ inch long with 6 to 12 pairs of legs and long antennae are present in the soil. Plants may be stunted.

ANALYSIS: Garden symphylans (*Scutigerella immaculata*)
These soil-inhabiting pests, also called *garden centipedes*, are a problem in both outdoor plantings and greenhouses. They live in damp soil that is high in organic matter, and avoid sunlight. Symphylans feed on the fine roots and root hairs of many different plants, and tunnel through crowns, stunting and sometimes killing plants. They may also invade fruit close to the ground. Symphylans are most active in the spring, but egg laying occurs from spring through summer. They lay white eggs in clusters 1 foot deep in the soil. The young have 6 pairs of legs and short antennae, but these develop to 12 pairs and long antennae as they mature into adults. Symphylans may live 4 to 5 years, so symphylans of all ages are found in the soil at one time.

SOLUTION: Treat the soil around strawberry plants with an insecticide containing *diazinon* at the first sign of symphylans. Repeat the treatment as needed to control these pests. Mulch plants with straw or leaf mold to keep the fruit off the ground. For more information on these pests, see page 885.

SWEET POTATOES

ADAPTATION: Southern United States.

PLANTING TIME: See page 1009.

PLANTING METHOD: Plant slips or sprouts 2 to 3 inches deep and 12 to 16 inches apart. In poorly drained soil, plant in ridges or hills so the roots do not rot in the ground.

SOIL: Loose, crumbly soil high in organic matter. pH 5.0 to 6.5

FERTILIZER: At planting time, use 1½ to 2 pounds of ORTHO Vegetable Garden Food 5–10–10 per 50-foot row. Side-dress 3 to 4 weeks after planting with the same amount as at planting time.

WATER:
How much: Apply enough water at each irrigation to wet the soil 8 to 10 inches deep.
How often: Water when the soil 2 inches deep is dry. Sweet potatoes are drought-hardy, and grow well under dry conditions.

HARVEST: Sweet potatoes are usually ready for eating about 110 to 120 days after planting. With a shovel, dig around a few plants to check tuber size. When ready, dig carefully to avoid bruising, and use as needed.
To store: Brush off all soil and discard infected or damaged roots. Cure at 85°F with high humidity for 6 to 8 days. After curing, store the roots at 55° to 60°F with high humidity until use.

Growth cracks.

PROBLEM: Sweet potato roots are cracked when harvested. Some may also crack in storage.

ANALYSIS: Growth cracks
Cracking of sweet potato roots is a disorder that results from prolonged dry periods followed by excessive moisture. In some varieties, it seems to be an inherited characteristic. The cracks heal over by harvest time, with no loss in eating or storage quality. Roots may also crack in storage if the temperature and humidity fluctuate greatly.

SOLUTION: Avoid excessively wet or dry soil. For best yields, sweet potatoes require adequate water throughout the growing season, especially when they are older and growing vigorously in hot weather in sandy soil. Store roots in a cool (55° to 60°F) place with high humidity (85 percent).

Sweet potato varieties less susceptible to cracking: Jewel and Porto Rico 198.

SWEET POTATOES

Black rot.

Sweet potato weevil larvae (half life size).

Scurf.

PROBLEM: Black spots occur on roots in the ground and in storage. Tiny black specks appear in the center of blackened areas. Black lesions occur on stems at the soil line. Leaves are yellow and dwarfed.

ANALYSIS: Black rot
This plant disease is caused by a fungus (*Ceratocystis fimbriata*) that attacks all underground parts of sweet potato plants. The fungi usually enter the plants through injuries, but healthy parts may also be attacked under favorable conditions. Infections occur between 75° and 85°F during periods of high humidity. Infected roots may not show symptoms when dug up, but once in storage they develop blackened areas. Both discolored tissue and the surrounding healthy tissue taste bitter. The fungus survives in sweet potato debris, manure, and weeds for at least 2 years. Spores are spread by wind, water, and insects, including the sweet potato weevil. For information on the sweet potato weevil, see page 782.

SOLUTION: There are no chemical controls for this disease. Remove and discard all infected plants and roots. Disinfect the storage area thoroughly with a solution of 1 part household bleach to 9 parts water. Purchase certified slips or seed potatoes. Do not plant sweet potatoes in the same soil two years in a row.

PROBLEM: Tunnels are bored into sweet potato vines and roots. Inside the tunnels are white, ⅜ inch legless grubs with pale brown heads. Reddish antlike weevils with bluish black heads and long snouts may be seen feeding on leaves. Roots in storage may also be tunneled by grubs.

ANALYSIS: Sweet potato weevil
(*Cylas formicarius elegantulus*)
This weevil, also called the *sweet potato borer*, attacks roots both in the ground and in storage. Both adults and larvae damage the plants. Adult weevils feed on leaves, vines, and roots, and lay their eggs on the plant near the soil surface. The grubs that hatch from these eggs burrow into the vines and through the roots. This feeding kills the plants and makes the roots unappetizing. Roots are edible if the damaged parts are removed. The grubs pupate inside the roots and adults emerge in one week. There may be as many as 8 generations a year. The sweet potato weevil does not hibernate for the winter, but feeds on weeds, especially wild morning glory, through the winter. The weevil also feeds and breeds in stored sweet potatoes.

SOLUTION: There are no chemical controls available for this pest. Carefully select and store only clean tubers. Purchase only certified, weevil-free sweet potato slips or seed potatoes. Mound the soil slightly around the stems to make it difficult for the grubs to reach the roots. Clean all plant debris and weeds, especially wild morning glory, from the garden to reduce the amount of food available to adults for the winter.

PROBLEM: Dark brown to black spots or irregular patches stain sweet potato skins. Discoloration affects only the skin, not the inside of the root.

ANALYSIS: Scurf
This disease, also called *soil stain*, is caused by a fungus (*Monilochaetes infuscans*) that attacks only the roots. Although their appearance is somewhat unappetizing, the flavor of the tubers is not affected and they are still edible. Scurf is most severe in wet, poorly drained soils and those high in organic matter. It is more prevalent in soils with a high pH and at temperatures betwen 70° and 80°F. It also appears more frequently when heavy rains occur just before harvest. The spots may enlarge in storage. Injury to the root surface allows rapid water loss, causing roots to shrivel. The fungus is introduced into the garden on infected roots and slips. The spores persist from one crop to the next in infected vines rotting in the garden, and in humus or partially decomposed organic matter.

SOLUTION: Use scurf-infected roots promptly, without storing them. Avoid planting in heavy soil. Improve soil drainage as instructed on page 901. If you add organic matter, till it into the soil a year before planting so it will decompose. Test the soil pH according to the directions on page 903 and make it more acid (see page 1002) if necessary. Purchase disease-free slips from a reputable company. If possible, rotate the sweet potato planting site every 3 or 4 years.

--------- SWISS CHARD ---------

Flea beetle larva (half life size).

PROBLEM: Yellow irregular channels are chewed in the surface of the leaves. Tiny (1/16 inch) black beetles jump like fleas when disturbed. Shallow, dark tunnels scar the surface of the root.

ANALYSIS: Sweet potato flea beetle (*Chaetocnema confinis*)
These beetles jump like fleas, but are not related to them. Both adults and immature flea beetles feed on sweet potatoes. The immature beetle, a legless white grub, feeds on the surface tissue of the roots, making them unattractive but still edible. Adults chew channels in leaves. Flea beetles are present nearly everywhere sweet potatoes are grown. They are most damaging to young plants. Adult beetles survive the winter in soil and garden debris. They emerge in early spring to feed on weeds until slips are set in the garden. Grubs hatch from eggs laid in the soil and feed for 2 to 3 weeks. After pupating in the soil, they emerge as adults to repeat the cycle. There are several generations a year.

SOLUTION: Control flea beetles on sweet potatoes with an insecticidal spray containing *methoxychlor* when the leaves first show damage. Watch new growth for evidence of further damage, and repeat the treatment at weekly intervals as needed. Clean all plant debris from the garden after harvest to eliminate overwintering spots for the adult beetles.

SWISS CHARD

ADAPTATION: Throughout the United States.

PLANTING TIME: See page 1009.

PLANTING METHOD: Sow seeds 1/2 inch deep and 1 to 2 inches apart. Thin seedlings when they have 2 to 3 leaves, and set transplants to grow 12 inches apart. Use the thinnings as greens. Plant transplants so the top of their rootball is even with the surrounding garden soil.

SOIL: Any good garden soil high in organic matter. pH 6.0 to 8.0

FERTILIZER: At planting time, use 2 pounds of ORTHO General Purpose Plant Food 8–8–8 per 100 square feet, or 1 1/2 pounds per 50-foot row. Side-dress every 3 to 4 weeks with 1 to 2 pounds per 50-foot row.
Containers: Water every 2 to 3 weeks with a solution of ORTHO Tomato & Vegetable Food 6–18–6.

WATER:
How much: Apply enough water at each irrigation to wet the soil 10 to 12 inches deep.
Containers: 10 per cent of the applied water should drain out the bottom.
How often: Water when the soil 2 inches deep is barely moist.

HARVEST: Harvest leaves about 50 to 60 days after planting. Using a sharp knife, cut the outer leaves about 1 inch above the soil level. Be careful not to damage young leaves and center buds. Store in the refrigerator.

Aphids (twice life size).

PROBLEM: Leaves turn yellow and may be curled, distorted, and puckered. Pale green, yellow, or purple soft-bodied insects cluster on the undersides of the leaves.

ANALYSIS: Aphids
Aphids do little damage in small numbers. However, they are extremely prolific and populations can rapidly build up to damaging numbers during the growing season. Damage occurs when the aphid sucks the juices from the Swiss chard leaves. Aphids feed on nearly every plant in the garden, and are spread from plant to plant by wind, water, and people.

SOLUTION: Spray infested plants with an insecticide containing *diazinon* or *malathion* as soon as the insects appear. Repeat the spray if the plant becomes reinfested. If aphids are present during harvest, hose them off with a strong stream of water.

SUNFLOWER

Leafminer damage.

PROBLEM: Light-colored irregular blotches, blisters, or tunnels appear in the leaves. The tan areas peel apart like cleansing tissue. Tiny black specks are inside the tunnels.

ANALYSIS: Spinach leafminer (*Pegomyahyoscyami*)
This insect belongs to a family of leaf-mining flies. The tiny, black adult fly lays its white eggs on the undersides of the leaves. The maggots that hatch from these eggs bore into the leaves. Once inside a leaf, the maggot tunnels between the upper and lower surfaces of the leaves, feeding on the inner tissue. The tunnels and blotches are called "mines." The black specks inside the mines are the maggots' droppings. Several overlapping generations occur during the growing season, so the white larvae are present continually from spring until fall. Leaves are edible if the damaged portions are cut away.

SOLUTION: Once the leafminers enter the leaves, sprays are ineffective. Squash the miners inside the leaves when you first notice the mines. Spraying after the mines first appear will control only those leafminers that attack after the application. To control succeeding generations of leafminers, treat with an insecticidal spray containing *malathion*. Repeat 2 more times at weekly intervals. Clean all plant debris from the garden after harvest to reduce the number of overwintering pupae.

SUNFLOWER

ADAPTATION: Throughout the United States.

PLANTING TIME: See page 1009.

PLANTING METHOD: Sow seeds 1 inch deep and 5 to 6 inches apart. When the seedlings have 2 or 3 leaves, thin to stand 16 to 24 inches apart.

SOIL: Any good garden soil. pH 6.0 to 8.0

FERTILIZER: At planting time, use 2 to 3 pounds of ORTHO Vegetable Garden Food 5–10–10 per 100 square feet, or 1 pound per 25-foot row. Side-dress every 3 to 4 weeks with 1 pound per 25-foot row, or 1 to 2 tablespoons per plant.

WATER:
How much: Apply enough water at each irrigation to wet the soil 12 to 15 inches deep.
How often: Water when the soil 1 inch deep is dry.

HARVEST: Sunflower seeds begin to mature when the seeds along the outside of the head fatten. Protect the seeds from birds by covering the head with cheesecloth, tying it securely with string. When the back of the head becomes tough, leathery, and dries out, cut the entire head with a sharp knife and shake or scrape out the seeds, collecting them on newspaper or a sheet. Wash thoroughly, and dry at room temperature. Store in an air-tight container.

Powdery mildew.

PROBLEM: A grayish white, powdery growth appears on the upper surfaces of the leaves. Infected leaves shrivel and die.

ANALYSIS: Powdery mildew
This common plant disease is caused by a fungus (*Erysiphe cichoracearum*) that thrives in both humid and dry weather. The powdery patches consist of fungal strands and spores. The spores are spread by the wind to healthy plants. The fungus saps the plant nutrients, causing yellowing and sometimes death of the leaf. A severe infection may kill the plant. Since this powdery mildew attacks many different kinds of plants, the fungus from a diseased plant may infect other types of plants in the garden. (For a list of susceptible plants see page 995.) Under favorable conditions, powdery mildew can spread though a closely spaced planting in a matter of days or weeks.

SOLUTION: Treat infected plants with a fungicidal spray containing *benomyl* or *wettable sulfur* at the first sign of the disease. Repeat at weekly intervals as long as new growth is attacked. Do not use sulfur when temperatures are above 90°F. Clean all debris from the garden at the end of the season to eliminate overwintering spores.

Rust.

Poor fruit set.

TOMATOES

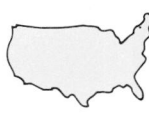

Rust

PROBLEM: Yellow-white specks spot the upper surfaces of the leaves. Rust-colored pustules form on the lower surfaces of the leaves and often on the stem. Infected leaves may wither and drop. Plants are stunted and sometimes die.

ANALYSIS: Rust
This plant disease is caused by a fungus (*Puccinia helianthi*) that attacks sunflower relatives, including Jerusalem artichokes and ornamental sunflowers. The spores are spread by splashing water and wind. The disease is favored by moist conditions with cool nights and warm days. Temperatures above 90°F kill the spores. Plants must remain wet for 6 to 8 hours before the fungus can infect the leaf. Rust spores spend the winter on infected plant debris that has been left in the garden. Rust seldom affects the flavor of the sunflower seeds.

SOLUTION: Rust is not easy to control. Pick off and destroy infected leaves. Apply a fungicide containing *zineb, maneb,* or *wettable sulfur* as soon as the disease is noticed. Since rust needs water on the leaves in order to infect them, water in the morning rather than the evening to allow wet foliage time to dry. Avoid overhead watering; if possible, use drip or furrow irrigation. Thin seedlings and space plants far enough apart to allow air to circulate freely. Remove all plant debris at the end of the season to reduce the number of overwintering spores.

TOMATOES (center column)

ADAPTATION: Throughout the United States.

PLANTING TIME: See page 1009.

PLANTING METHOD: Sow seeds ½ inch deep. Thin seedlings when they have 2 or 3 leaves, or set transplants to grow 18 to 36 inches apart. Set transplants horizontally with only the top third of the plant above the soil.

SOIL: Any good garden soil that is high in organic matter. pH 5.5 to 8.0

FERTILIZER: At planting time, use 3 to 4 pounds of ORTHO Vegetable Garden Food 5–10–10 per 100 square feet, or 1 pound per 25-foot row. In hot summer areas, side-dress every 3 to 4 weeks with 1 pound per 25-foot row, or 1 to 2 tablespoons per plant. In cool summer areas, side-dressing may produce excess foliage and green fruit that don't ripen.
   Containers: Water thoroughly every 2 to 4 weeks with a solution of ORTHO Tomato & Vegetable Food 6–18–6.

WATER:
   How much: Apply enough water at each irrigation to wet the soil 18 to 20 inches deep.
   How often: Water when the soil 2 inches deep is barely moist.

HARVEST: Harvest tomatoes when they have a deep, rich color. Store at room temperature until use. If your plants still have many green fruit at the first frost, the fruit can be ripened in either of two ways. Hang the plants upside down in the garage until the fruit ripen; or pick the green fruit and store in boxes at room temperature until they ripen.

Problems with the fruit (right column)

PROBLEM: Few or no fruit develop. The plants are healthy, and may even be extremely vigorous.

ANALYSIS: Poor fruit set
Poor fruit set occurs on tomatoes for any of several reasons:
1. *Extreme temperatures:* The blossoms drop off without setting fruit when night temperatures fall below 55°F or day temperatures rise above 90°F.
2. *Dry soil:* Blossoms dry and fall when the plants don't receive enough water.
3. *Shading:* Few blossoms are produced when the plants receive less than 6 hours of sunlight a day.
4. *Excessive nitrogen:* High levels of nitrogen in the soil promote leaf growth at the expense of blossom and fruit formation.

SOLUTION: Follow these guidelines to reduce the chances of poor fruit set.
1. Plant early, mid, and late-season varieties at the appropriate time of year. For a list of these varieties, see page 1010.
2. Water tomatoes regularly, never allowing the soil to dry out. Mulch with straw or black plastic, as discussed on page 918, to reduce the need for watering.
3. Plant tomatoes in an area that receives at least 6 hours of sunlight a day. If your yard is shady, grow tomatoes in containers on your porch or patio.
4. Correct the nitrogen imbalance with ORTHO Superphosphate 0–20–0 or ORTHO Bloom Builder 0–10–10. To prevent future problems, follow the fertilizing recommendations on this page.

TOMATOES — PROBLEMS WITH THE FRUIT

Growth cracks.

Sunscald on tomatoes.

Blossom-end rot.

PROBLEM: Circular or radial cracks mar the stem end (top) of ripening fruit. Cracks may extend deep into the fruit, causing it to rot.

ANALYSIS: Growth cracks
Tomatoes crack when certain environmental conditions encourage rapid growth during ripening. The rapid growth is frequently promoted by heavy rains or watering following a drought period. Tomatoes are most susceptible to cracking after they have reached full size and begin to change color. Some varieties crack more easily than others. Cracking is more severe in hot weather. Some cracks may be deep, allowing decay organisms to enter the fruit and rot it. Shallow cracks frequently heal over, but may rupture if the fruit is roughly handled when picked. Cracked tomatoes are still edible.

SOLUTION: Maintain even soil moisture with regular watering according to the instructions on page 785. Grow crack-tolerant varieties.

Tomato varieties that are crack tolerant: Avalanche, Bragger, Early Girl, Glamor, Heinz 1350, Heinz 1439, Jet Star, Marglobe Supreme F, Red Glow, Roma, and Willamette.

PROBLEM: On green and ripening fruit, a light patch develops on the side facing the sun. These areas blister, and finally become slightly sunken and grayish white, with a paperlike surface. A black mold may grow on the affected area, causing the fruit to rot.

ANALYSIS: Sunscald
Sunscald occurs on tomatoes when they are exposed to the direct rays of the sun during hot weather. It is most common on green fruit, but ripening fruit is also susceptible. It is most prevalent on staked plants that have lost their foliage due to leaf diseases such as early or late blight (see pages 793 and 792), septoria leaf spot (see page 793), fusarium and verticillium wilt (see pages 791 and 792), or leaf roll (see page 793). Fruit on plants that have been pruned to hasten ripening are also subject to sunscald. Tomatoes need warm temperatures — not direct sun — to ripen. Tomatoes are still edible if the sunscalded area is removed. Rot fungi frequently invade the damaged tissue, resulting in moldy and inedible fruit.

SOLUTION: Cover exposed fruit with straw or other light material to protect them from the sun's rays. Do not prune leaves to hasten ripening. Control leaf diseases. Grow verticillium and fusarium wilt-resistant plants. For a list of these varieties, see page 1010.

PROBLEM: A round, sunken, water-soaked spot develops on the bottom of the fruit. The spot enlarges, turns brown to black, and feels leathery. Mold may grow on the rotted surface.

ANALYSIS: Blossom-end rot
Blossom-end rot occurs on tomatoes, peppers, squash, and watermelons from a lack of calcium in the developing fruit. This results from slowed growth and damaged roots caused by any of several factors:
1. Extreme fluctuations in soil moisture, from very wet to very dry.
2. Rapid plant growth early in the season, followed by extended dry weather.
3. Excessive rains that smother root hairs.
4. Excess soil salts.
5. Cultivating too close to the plant.
The first fruit are the most severely affected. As the name implies, the disorder always starts at the blossom end, and may enlarge to affect ¼ to ½ of the fruit. Moldy growths on the rotted area are from fungi or bacteria that invade the damaged tissue. The rotted area is unsightly but the rest of the fruit is edible.

SOLUTION: To prevent future blossom-end rot, follow these guidelines:
1. Maintain uniform soil moisture by mulching (see page 918), and by following the watering guidelines on page 785.
2. Avoid using high-nitrogen fertilizers or large quantities of fresh manure.
3. Plant in well-drained soil, as outlined on page 901.
4. If your soil or water is salty, provide more water at each watering to help leach salts through the soil.
5. Do not cultivate deeper than 1 inch within 1 foot of the plant.

Anthracnose.

Bacterial spot.

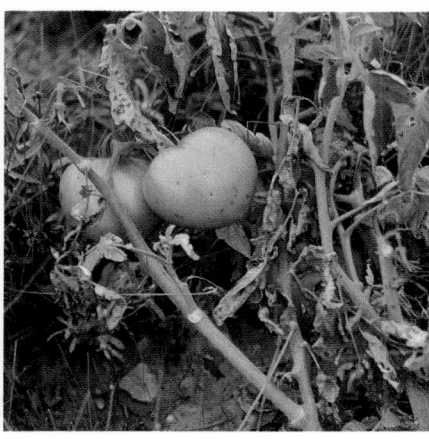

Bacterial speck.

PROBLEM: Sunken spots up to 1/2 inch in diameter occur on ripe tomatoes. The centers of the spots darken and form concentric rings. Spots may merge, covering a large part of the tomato.

ANALYSIS: Anthracnose
This plant disease is caused by a fungus (*Colletotrichum coccodes*) that rots ripe tomatoes. Green tomato fruit are also attacked, but the spots don't appear until the fruit ripen. Infected fruit are inedible. Anthracnose is most common on overripe fruit and those close to the ground. Fruit on plants partially defoliated by leaf spot diseases are also prone to infection. The leaves may be infected, but are usually not severely damaged. The fungus is most active in warm (60° to 90°F), wet weather and when infection is severe many fruit are damaged in a short period of time. Infections frequently become epidemic in hot, rainy weather. Water from heavy dews, overhead watering, and frequent abundant rains provides the moisture necessary for infection.

SOLUTION: Spray tomato plants at the first sign of the disease with ORTHO Vegetable Disease Control. Repeat at intervals of 7 to 10 days until harvest. Discard all infected fruit. Pick tomatoes as they mature and use promptly. To reduce the spread of the disease, do not work among wet plants. Remove all plant debris from the garden after harvest.

PROBLEM: Dark, raised, scablike spots, 1/8 to 1/4 inch in diameter, appear on green tomatoes. The centers of the spots are slightly sunken. Dark, greasy, 1/8 inch spots occur on the older leaves, causing them to drop.

ANALYSIS: Bacterial spot
This plant disease is caused by a bacterium (*Xanthomonas vesicatoria*) that attacks green but not red tomatoes. Peppers are also attacked. The bacteria infect all aboveground parts of the plant at any stage of growth. Infected blossoms drop, reducing the fruit yield. Fruit are infected through skin wounds caused by insects, blowing sand, and mechanical injuries. Infected fruit do not ripen properly, and are frequently invaded by rot organisms. The bacteria are most active after heavy rains and in very warm (75° to 85°F) weather. They spread rapidly in the rain, often resulting in severe defoliation, which weakens the plant and exposes the fruit to sunscald. The bacteria spend the winter in the soil, and are carried on tomato seeds.

SOLUTION: Pick and discard all infected green fruit. If the infection is severe, spray with a fungicide containing both *maneb* and *basic copper sulfate* at the first sign of the disease. Repeat at intervals of 7 to 10 days as long as weather conditions continue that are favorable to the spread of bacterial spot. To reduce the spread of the disease, do not work among wet plants. Avoid overhead watering by using drip or furrow irrigation. Purchase disease-free plants or seeds from a reputable dealer.

PROBLEM: Many tiny (1/16 inch), slightly raised, dark brown specks appear on the green fruit. A white border surrounds each speck. Dark brown to black spots 1/16 inch in diameter occur on the leaves. The surrounding tissue turns yellow.

ANALYSIS: Bacterial speck
This plant disease is caused by a bacterium (*Pseudomona syringae*) that attacks young tomatoes. This disease is commonly confused with bacterial spot. Bacterial speck attacks tomatoes only; peppers are not infected. The specks on the fruit mar the skin but do not extend into the inner tissue. The fruit appear unappetizing, but are still edible when they ripen. The bacteria are most active in warm (65° to 75°F) weather following heavy rains when the bacteria are splashed from plant to plant. The bacteria spend the winter in the soil. They may also be carried on tomato seeds.

SOLUTION: If the infection is severe, spray the plants with a fungicide containing *maneb* or *basic copper sulfate* at the first sign of the disease. Repeat at intervals of 7 to 10 days as long as weather conditions continue that are favorable to the spread of bacterial speck. To reduce the chances of spreading the bacteria, do not work among wet plants. Avoid overhead watering by using drip or furrow irrigation. Do not save seeds from infected fruit.

TOMATOES — PROBLEMS WITH THE FRUIT

Blotchy ripening.

Catface.

Tomato fruitworm damage.

PROBLEM: Irregular grayish brown or yellow blotches appear on green tomatoes. When the tomato is cut open crosswise, the tissue just inside the skin may be brown, sometimes with pits and cavities. Fruits feel hard and are sometimes ridged.

ANALYSIS: Blotchy ripening and internal browning
Blotchy ripening results from any of a variety of environmental factors:
1. Tomatoes ripen poorly and irregularly at temperatures below 60°F.
2. Compacted soil and overly wet soil inhibit the root system, which restricts fruit ripening.
3. Low levels of potassium in the soil inhibit proper fruit growth and maturity.

Brown wall tissue, called *internal browning*, results when the plant is infected with tobacco mosaic virus (TMV) as the fruit begin to ripen. For information on TMV, see page 794. Usually only the first and sometimes the second pickings are affected by blotchy ripening and internal browning. Later fruit ripen normally.

SOLUTION: Plant tomatoes according to the planting chart on page 1009. Improve soil drainage as instructed on page 901. Water and fertilize according to the guidelines on page 785. Give your plants a boost of potassium with ORTHO Bloom Builder 0–10–10. To prevent internal browning, see page 794 for ways to prevent tobacco mosaic virus.

PROBLEM: Green and red tomatoes are malformed, scarred, and puckered. Greenish tan streaks and bands of scar tissue mar the blossom end (bottom) of the fruit.

ANALYSIS: Catface
Certain conditions that occur during bloom disturb the normal growth of the tomato flower, resulting in catfaced fruit. These conditions include extreme heat (above 85°F) or cold (below 55°F), drought, and 2,4-D herbicide sprays. Usually only the first fruits to form are affected. These fruits are of poor quality and ripen unevenly. Although some varieties seem to be more susceptible to this disorder, many of the modern varieties are seldom affected.

SOLUTION: Water tomatoes regularly according to the instructions on page 785. Avoid exposing tomato plants to herbicides by washing sprayers thoroughly after herbicide use, or by keeping separate sprayers for herbicides and other sprays. Select varieties that seldom catface.

Tomato varieties that seldom catface:
Avalanche, Bonus, Floramerica, and Floridol.

PROBLEM: Deep holes are chewed in the fruit. Striped yellow, green, or brown worms from ¼ to 2 inches long are feeding in them. Worms may also be feeding on the leaves.

ANALYSIS: Tomato fruitworm
(*Heliothis zea*)
Tomato fruitworms, also known as *corn earworms* and *cotton bollworms*, attack many plants, including tomatoes, corn, and cotton. The worms feed on the foliage, and also chew deep holes in the fruit and feed inside. Damaged fruit is inedible. The adult tomato fruitworm is a light grayish brown moth with dark lines on the wings. In the spring, the adults lay white eggs on the leaves and stems. The worms that hatch from these eggs feed on the leaves until they are about ½ inch long. Then they move to the fruit and bore inside. After feeding for 2 to 4 weeks, they drop to the ground, burrow 2 to 6 inches deep, pupate, and emerge in several weeks as adults. There are several generations of worms a year, so damage can continue until fall.

SOLUTION: Once the fruitworms are inside the tomatoes, there is nothing you can do. Destroy infested fruit. Clean all plant debris from the garden after harvest to reduce the number of overwintering adults. If fruitworms were numerous this year, next year treat your plants with ORTHO Liquid Sevin, ORTHO Sevin Garden Dust, or ORTHO Tomato Vegetable Dust when the worms are feeding on the foliage, and fruit are about ½ inch in diameter. Repeat in 2 and 4 weeks if the plants become reinfested.

INSECTS

Tobacco (top) and tomato hornworms (life size).

Flea beetle damage.

Stink bug (twice life size).

PROBLEM: Fat green or brown worms, up to 5 inches long, with white diagonal stripes chew on the leaves. A red or black "horn" projects from the rear end. Black droppings soil the leaves.

ANALYSIS: Tomato hornworm (*Manduca quinquemaculata*) **and tobacco hornworm** (*M. sexta*)
Hornworms feed on the fruit and foliage of tomatoes, peppers, and eggplants. Although only a few worms may be present, each worm consumes large quantities of foliage and causes extensive damage. The large gray or brown adult moth with yellow and white markings emerges from hibernation in late spring, and drinks nectar from petunias and other garden flowers. The worms that hatch from eggs laid on the undersides of the leaves feed for 3 to 4 weeks. Then they crawl into the soil, pupate, and later emerge as adults to repeat the cycle. There is 1 generation a year in the North and 2 to 4 in the South. Some worms may have white sacs that look like puffed rice on their bodies. These sacs are the cocoons of parasitic wasps that feed on and eventually kill the hornworm.

SOLUTION: Treat the plants with ORTHO Sevin Garden Dust or ORTHO Fruit & Vegetable Insect Control. But don't destroy worms covered with white sacs. Let the wasps inside the worms mature, emerge, and infest other hornworms. If practical, handpick and destroy unaffected worms.

PROBLEM: Leaves are riddled with shotholes about ⅛ inch in diameter. Tiny 1/16 inch black beetles jump like fleas when disturbed. Leaves of seedlings may wilt and die.

ANALYSIS: Flea beetles
These beetles jump like fleas, but are not related to them. Both adult and immature flea beetles feed on a wide variety of garden vegetables, including tomatoes. The immature beetle, a legless gray grub, injures plants by feeding on the roots and the lower surfaces of the leaves. Adults chew holes in leaves. Flea beetles are most damaging to seedlings and young plants. Leaves of seedlings riddled with holes dry out quickly and die. Adult beetles survive the winter in soil and garden debris. They emerge in early spring to feed on weeds until vegetables sprout or plants are set in the garden. Grubs hatch from eggs laid in the soil and feed for 2 to 3 weeks. After pupating in the soil, they emerge as adults to repeat the cycle. There are 1 to 4 generations a year. Adults may feed for up to 2 months.

SOLUTION: Control flea beetles on tomatoes with ORTHO Fruit & Vegetable Insect Control, ORTHO Sevin Garden Dust, or ORTHO Tomato Vegetable Dust. Treat when the leaves first show damage. Watch new growth for evidence of further damage, and repeat the treatment at weekly intervals as needed. Clean all plant debris from the garden after harvest to eliminate overwintering spots for adult beetles.

PROBLEM: Light yellow to white, cloudy spots occur on the tomato fruit. The tissue under these spots is pithy and corky. Young fruits are deformed and may drop. Bright green, gray, blue, or red insects, ⅝ inch long and shaped like a shield are present on the plants.

ANALYSIS: Stink bugs
Stink bugs attack a wide variety of vegetables, including tomatoes, okra, squash, and beans. They emit a strong odor when crushed. Both the adults and nymphs damage tomato plants by sucking sap from buds, blossoms, and fruit. This feeding causes the fruit to become distorted and dimpled with corky inner tissue. Hard calluses form around the spots where the stink bugs feed. Damaged tomatoes are edible, but unappetizing. Young tender growth is the most susceptible to attack. Stink bugs spend the winter as adults in sheltered areas. In the spring, they lay clusters of eggs on the undersides of leaves. The young that hatch from these eggs mature into adults in 6 weeks. There are several generations each year, so damage occurs throughout the season.

SOLUTION: Treat infested tomato plants with ORTHO Tomato & Vegetable Insect Spray or an insecticide containing *carbaryl* as soon as stink bugs and their damage are noticed. Repeat the treatment at intervals of 7 to 10 days if the plants become reinfested.

TOMATOES — INSECTS

Potato aphids (life size).

Whiteflies (life size).

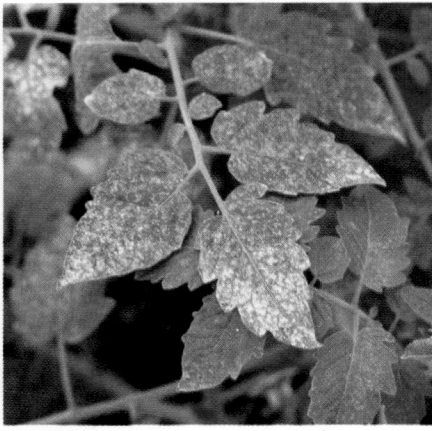

Mite damage.

PROBLEM: Leaves turn yellow, and may be curled, distorted, and puckered. Pale green, yellow, or purple soft-bodied insects cluster on the stems and the undersides of the leaves.

ANALYSIS: Aphids
Aphids do little damage in small numbers. However, they are extremely prolific and populations can rapidly build up to damaging numbers during the growing season. Damage occurs when the aphid sucks the juices from the tomato leaves. Aphids feed on nearly every plant in the garden and are spread from plant to plant by wind, water, and people.

SOLUTION: Control aphids on tomatoes with ORTHO Fruit & Vegetable Insect Control, ORTHO Malathion 50 Insect Spray, or ORTHO Tomato Vegetable Dust. Treat at the first sign of infestation, and repeat at intervals of 7 to 10 days if the plants become reinfested.

PROBLEM: Tiny, winged insects 1/12 inch long feed on the undersides of the leaves. The insects are covered with white waxy powder. When the plant is touched, insects flutter rapidly around it. Leaves may be mottled and yellowing. A black mold may cover the leaves.

ANALYSIS: Greenhouse whitefly (*Trialeurodes vaporariorum*)
This insect is a common pest of many garden and greenhouse plants. The 4-winged adult lays eggs on the undersides of leaves. The larvae are the size of a pinhead, flat, oval-shaped, and semi-transparent, with white waxy filaments radiating from the body. They feed for about a month before changing to the adult form. Both the larvae and adult forms suck sap from the leaves. The larvae are more damaging because they feed more heavily. Adults and larvae cannot fully digest all the sugar in the plant sap, and excrete the excess in a fluid called honeydew, which often drops onto the leaves or plants below. A sooty mold fungus may develop on the honeydew, causing the tomato leaves to appear black and dirty. In warm winter areas, these insects can be active year-round, with eggs, larvae, and adults present at the same time. Whiteflies are unable to live through freezing winters. Spring reinfestations in freezing winter areas come from migrating whiteflies and infested greenhouse-grown plants placed in the garden.

SOLUTION: Control whiteflies by spraying with ORTHO Malathion 50 Insect Spray or ORTHO Fruit & Vegetable Insect Control every 7 to 10 days as necessary. Spray thoroughly, being sure to cover both the upper and lower surfaces of the leaves.

PROBLEM: Leaves may be stippled, yellowing, and dirty. There may be webbing over flower buds, between leaves, or on the lower surfaces of the leaves. Lower stems and leaves may be bronzed, with cracks in the main stem. Leaves dry out and drop. To determine if the plant is infested with mites, hold a sheet of white paper underneath an affected leaf and tap the leaf sharply. Minute green, red, or yellow specks the size of a pepper grain or smaller will drop to the paper and begin to crawl around. The pests are easily seen against the white background.

ANALYSIS: Two-spotted spider mite (*Tetranychus urticae*) **and tomato russet mite** (*Aculops lycopersici*)
These mites, related to spiders, are major pests of many garden and greenhouse plants. Tomato russet mites, which bronze the stems and leaves, are a problem mainly in the Southwest and California. Mites cause damage by sucking sap from the undersides of the leaves and stems. As a result of feeding, the green leaf pigment disappears, producing the stippled or bronze appearance. Fruit are seldom attacked. When populations are high and not controlled, many leaves may drop, weakening the plant and exposing the fruit to sunscald. Mites are active throughout the growing season, but are favored by hot, dry weather (70°F and up). By midsummer, they build up to tremendous numbers.

SOLUTION: Treat infested plants with ORTHO Malathion 50 Insect Spray or ORTHO Flotox Garden Sulfur when the first fruit begin to set or at the first sign of damage. Repeat at intervals of 7 to 10 days if plants become reinfested.

WILTING

Wilting caused by nearby walnut tree.

Fusarium wilt.

Bacterial canker.

PROBLEM: Tomato plants suddenly wilt and die. Inner stem tissue is dark brown. A black walnut tree is growing nearby.

ANALYSIS: Walnut wilt
Some plants growing within 50 feet of black walnut trees are killed by a toxic substance called juglone that is released from the tree roots. Tomato plants are very sensitive to juglone, which is emitted from both living and dead tree roots. Juglone remains active in the soil and root debris for at least 3 years after a black walnut tree is removed. The substance kills the tomato roots, causing the inner tissue to darken and the plant to suddenly wilt and die.

SOLUTION: Plant tomato plants at least 50 feet from black walnut trees. Wait at least 3 years before planting tomatoes in an area where black walnut trees once grew.

PROBLEM: Lower leaves turn yellow, wilt, and die. Then upper shoots wilt, and eventually the whole plant dies. Wilting usually occurs first on one side of the leaf or plant, then the other. When the stem is sliced lengthwise near the soil line, the tissue 1/8 inch under the bark is found to be dark brown.

ANALYSIS: Fusarium wilt
This wilt disease is caused by a soil-inhabiting fungus (*Fusarium oxysporum f. lycopersici*) that infects only tomatoes. The fungus persists indefinitely on plant debris or in the soil. Fusarium is more prevalent in warm-weather areas. The disease is spread by contaminated soil, seeds, plants, and equipment. The fungus enters the plant through the roots and spreads up into the stems and leaves through the water-conducting vessels in the stems. These vessels become discolored and plugged. This plugging cuts off the flow of water and nutrients to the leaves, causing leaf yellowing and wilting. Affected plants may or may not produce fruit. Fruit that is produced is usually deformed and tasteless. Many plants will die.

SOLUTION: No chemical control is available. Destroy infected plants promptly. Fusarium can be removed from the soil only by fumigation techniques. (For more information on soil fumigation, see page 919.) However, the best solution is usually to use plants that are resistant to fusarium wilt. This is denoted by the letter "F" after the tomato variety name. For a list of wilt-resistant varieties, see page 1010.

PROBLEM: Margins of the lower leaves wilt, dry, and then curl upward. One side of the plant may be affected first, then the other. Yellow-white streaks develop on the stem, break open, and may ooze. When the stem is split lengthwise, the center tissue appears pale yellow and mealy, and separates easily from the outer woody tissue. Plants may die. Raised tan spots with flattened white margins mar the fruit. Dark cavities may occur inside the fruit.

ANALYSIS: Bacterial canker
This destructive disease of tomatoes is caused by a bacterium (*Corynebacterium michiganense*) that also attacks peppers, potatoes, and eggplants. The bacteria are carried on seeds and are most frequently introduced into the garden on infected transplants. The bacteria can survive in the soil for 2 to 3 years. Plants may be infected at any stage of growth. Some infected plants die, but others survive weakly until harvest. If fruit is produced, it is deformed or spotted. The fruit is infected in either of two ways: the bacteria pass from the stem into the fruit, resulting in dark inner cavities; or the bacteria are washed by the rain onto the fruit skin, resulting in skin spotting.

SOLUTION: There are no chemical controls for this disease. Remove and destroy infected plants and fruit at the first sign of infection. Don't plant tomatoes in the same spot every year. Purchase healthy plants from a reputable company. Do not save seeds from infected fruit.

TOMATOES — LEAVES DISCOLORED OR DISTORTED

Nematode-infested roots.

Verticillium wilt.

Late blight. *Insert:* Close-up.

PROBLEM: Plants are stunted, yellow, and wilt in hot, dry weather. Round and elongated nodules occur on roots.

ANALYSIS: Nematodes
Nematodes are microscopic worms that live in the soil. They are not related to earthworms. Nematodes feed on plant roots, damaging and stunting them. The damaged roots can't supply sufficient water and nutrients to the aboveground plant parts, and the plant is stunted or slowly dies. Nematodes are found throughout the United States, but are most severe in the South. They prefer moist, sandy loam soils. Nematodes can move only a few inches each year on their own, but they may be carried long distances by soil, water, tools, or infested plants. Testing roots and soil is the only positive method for confirming the presence of nematodes. Contact your local Cooperative Extension Office (see page 1011) for sampling instructions and addresses of testing laboratories. Soil and root problems such as poor soil structure, drought stress, nutrient deficiency, and root rots can also produce symptoms of decline similar to those caused by nematodes. These problems should be eliminated as causes before sending soil and root samples for testing. For information on soil problems and root rots, see pages 901 and 856.

SOLUTION: No chemicals are available to homeowners to kill nematodes in planted soil. However, they can be controlled before planting by soil fumigation (see page 919). Some varieties are resistant to nematodes. Resistance is indicated by an "N" after the variety name. For a list of resistant varieties, see page 1010.

PROBLEM: Older lower leaves turn yellow, dry, and fall. Tip leaves curl upward at the margins, but remain green. When the stem is sliced lengthwise near the soil line, the tissue ⅛ inch below the bark is seen to be tan in color.

ANALYSIS: Verticillium wilt
This wilt disease affects many plants in the garden, including potatoes, eggplants, peppers, strawberries, and raspberries. It is caused by a soil-inhabiting fungus (*Verticillium albo-atrum*) that persists indefinitely on plant debris or in the soil. It is more prevalent in cool-weather areas. The disease is spread by contaminated seeds, soil, plants, and equipment. The fungus enters the plant through the roots and spreads into the stems and leaves through the water-conducting vessels in the stems. The vessels become discolored and plugged. This plugging cuts off the flow of water and nutrients to the leaves, causing leaf yellowing and death. Affected plants may or may not produce fruit. Fruit that is produced is usually small, deformed, and tasteless. The plant is not usually killed.

SOLUTION: No chemical control is available. Destroy infected plants promptly. Verticillium can be removed from the soil only by fumigation techniques. (For more information about soil fumigation, see page 919.) However, the best solution is usually to use plants that are resistant to this wilt disease. This is denoted by the letter "V" after the tomato variety name. For a list of wilt-resistant tomato varieties, see page 1010.

PROBLEM: Bluish gray water-soaked patches appear on the leaves. During humid weather, a white downy mold grows on the lower surfaces of the leaves. Leaves dry, shrivel, and turn brown. Water-soaked spots also occur on the stems. Grayish green water-soaked spots appear on the fruit. The spots turn dark brown, become wrinkled and corklike, and may enlarge to cover the entire fruit. Dying plants have an offensive odor.

ANALYSIS: Late blight
This plant disease is caused by a fungus (*Phytophthora infestans*) that attacks both tomatoes and potatoes. Late blight does not attack tomatoes every year, but is very destructive when it does occur. The fungus attacks leaves, stems, and fruit, causing severe defoliation and rotted fruit. Infected fruit is inedible. Plants can be infected at all stages of growth. Late blight frequently enters the garden on infected transplants or infected potato seed pieces. The fungus is most active in wet weather with cool (45° to 60°F) nights and warm (70° to 85°F) days. Spores spend the winter in infected potato tubers in the garden or compost pile.

SOLUTION: Treat infected plants promptly with ORTHO Vegetable Disease Control at the first sign of the disease. Repeat the treatments at intervals of 7 to 10 days as long as weather conditions continue that are favorable to the spread of the disease. Remove all potato and tomato debris from the garden after harvest. Do not compost infected tubers.

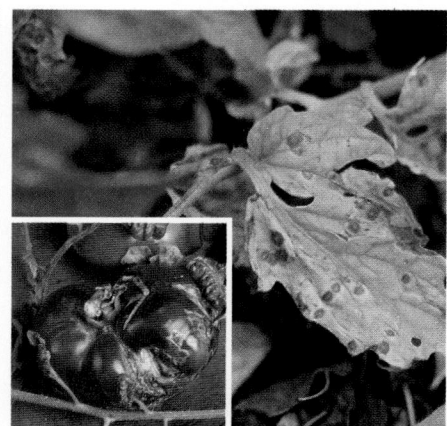

Early blight. *Insert:* Infected fruit.

Septoria leaf spot.

Tomato leaf roll.

PROBLEM: Irregular brown spots, 1/4 to 1/2 inch in diameter, with concentric rings in their centers appear on the lower leaves. A yellow margin may outline the spot. When many spots appear, the entire leaf turns yellow and drops. Dark spots with light centers and concentric rings may occur on the stems. Dark, leathery, sunken spots with concentric rings mar the fruit where it joins the stem. The discoloration extends into the fruit.

ANALYSIS: Early blight
This plant disease is caused by a fungus (*Alteraria solani*) that attacks tomatoes at any stage of growth. Some leaf spotting appears early in the season, but most occurs as the fruit matures. Plants heavily loaded with fruit and those that are poorly fertilized are the most susceptible to attack. Severe early blight causes partial to complete defoliation, which weakens the plant, reduces the size and quality of fruit, and exposes the fruit to sunscald. Infected fruit should not be canned, but can be eaten fresh if the diseased portion is removed. The spores survive in plant debris in the soil for at least a year. The fungus is most active in warm (75° to 85°F), humid weather.

SOLUTION: Treat infected plants with ORTHO Orthocide Garden Fungicide or ORTHO Vegetable Disease Control at the first sign of the disease. Repeat at intervals of 7 to 10 days as long as weather conditions continue that are favorable to the spread of the disease. Remove all plant debris from the garden after harvest to reduce the amount of overwintering spores. Fertilize according to the guidelines on page 785.

PROBLEM: Numerous brown spots, 1/8 inch in diameter, with dark borders appear on the older lower leaves. A few tiny black specks appear in the center of the spots. Severely spotted leaves turn yellow, dry, and fall. In warm, wet weather, all the leaves may become spotted and drop except for a few at the top of the plant.

ANALYSIS: Septoria leaf spot
This tomato plant disease is caused by a fungus (*Septoria lycopersici*) that is most severe in warm (60° to 80°F) wet weather. Tomato plants are attacked at any stage of growth, but most commonly after the first fruit are set. Fruit are rarely infected. Severe infection causes extensive leaf yellowing and defoliation. This weakens the plant, reduces the size and quality of the fruit, and exposes the fruit to sunscald. Spores are formed in the tiny black specks in the leaf spots, and are spread by splashing rain and by people and animals brushing against wet foliage. Foggy, misty weather and heavy dews provide enough moisture for infection. The fungus survives on tomato plant debris for at least 3 years.

SOLUTION: Treat infected plants with ORTHO Orthocide Garden Fungicide or ORTHO Tomato Vegetable Dust at the first sign of the disease. Repeat treatment at intervals of 7 to 10 days as long as weather conditions continue that are favorable to the spread of the disease. To help prevent the spread of the disease, do not work among wet plants. Remove all plant debris from the garden after harvest to reduce the amount of overwintering spores. Avoid overhead watering by using drip or furrow irrigation.

PROBLEM: Older lower leaves roll upward until the margins touch or overlap each other. Eventually most of the leaves may be rolled. Leaves feel leathery and remain green. No other symptoms develop.

ANALYSIS: Leaf roll
Leaf roll on tomatoes is a temporary disorder resulting from excessively wet soil, especially after heavy rains. It occurs most commonly during wet springs on staked tomatoes, although unstaked tomatoes may also be affected. Leaf roll does not slow the plant's growth, and a normal crop of fruit is produced. Within a few days, as the soil dries, the symptoms disappear and the plants return to normal. The varieties Big Boy, Floramerica, and Beefsteak are affected more often than are other varieties.

SOLUTION: Plant tomatoes in well-drained soil, where this problem is least likely to occur. Water regularly, following the guidelines on page 785, so that the soil is neither excessively wet nor dry.

TOMATOES — LEAVES DISCOLORED OR DISTORTED

PROBLEMS WITH SEEDLINGS

Curly top. *Insert:* Close-up.

Mosaic.

Cutworm (life size).

PROBLEM: Leaflets roll upward, twist, and feel tough and leathery. Veins turn purple, and the whole plant is dull yellow and stunted. Young plants die.

ANALYSIS: Curly top
This virus disease affects many vegetables including tomatoes, beets, peppers, beans, and squash. The virus is transmitted from plant to plant by the beet leafhopper (*Circulifer tenellus*), and is common only where this insect lives, west of the Mississippi River. The beet leafhopper is a pale greenish yellow insect about 1/8 inch long that feeds from early May through June. It sucks the sap and virus from the infected leaves, and then injects the virus into healthy plants at its next feeding stop. (For more information on leafhoppers, see page 880.) Curly top symptoms vary in their severity depending on the variety and age of the plant. Young infected plants usually die. Older plants may turn yellow and die. Little if any fruit is produced.

SOLUTION: There is no direct control for curly top. To reduce the chances of infection, control the beet leafhopper with an insecticidal spray containing *malathion,* beginning when insect swarms first appear. (For information about controlling disease-carrying insects, see page 880.) Destroy infected plants. Keep leafhoppers away from tomato plants with a screen of cheesecloth stretched on a frame. Where possible, plant tolerant varieties from the list on page 1010. But if the leafhopper population is large, even resistant varieties may become infected.

PROBLEM: Leaves are mottled light and dark green, curled, and deformed. Plants are stunted. Fruit is mottled and deformed, with a rough texture and poor flavor.

ANALYSIS: Mosaic
Mosaic is caused by a plant virus. The two most common virus diseases that infect tomatoes are *tobacco mosaic virus* and *cucumber mosaic virus.* Viruses weaken the plants, reducing fruit quality and yield. Plants infected when young do not produce fruit. Viruses may be introduced into the garden on infected transplants, but most viruses live in weeds, including pokeweed, Jimson weed, catnip, plantain, horsenettle, and motherwort. Once the viruses are present in or near the garden, aphids spread them from plant to plant while feeding. Viruses are also transmitted when diseased and healthy leaves rub together, especially during weeding and transplanting. Tobacco mosaic virus is sometimes present in cigar, pipe, and cigarette tobacco, and smokers may carry the virus on their hands.

SOLUTION: There are no chemical controls for viruses. Discard infected plants promptly. Control aphids with ORTHO Fruit & Vegetable Insect Control or ORTHO Malathion 50 Insect Spray. Repeat the treatment at intervals of 7 to 10 days if the plants become reinfested. (For more information about controlling disease-carrying insects, see page 880.) Wash your hands thoroughly with soap and water after smoking and before working in the garden. Remove host weeds around the garden.

PROBLEM: Young plants are chewed or cut off near the ground. Gray, brown, or black worms, 1 1/2 to 2 inches long, may be found about 2 inches deep in the soil near the base of the damaged plants. The worms coil when disturbed.

ANALYSIS: Cutworms
Several species of cutworms attack plants in the vegetable garden. The most likely pests of young tomato plants set out early in the season are the surface-feeding cutworms. For information on climbing cutworms, see page 689. A single surface-feeding cutworm can sever the stems of many young plants in one night. Cutworms hide in the soil during the day, and feed only at night. Adult cutworms are dark, night-flying moths with bands or stripes on their forewings.

SOLUTION: Apply ORTHO Diazinon Soil & Turf Insect Control or ORTHO Diazinon Soil & Foliage Dust around the base of undamaged plants when stem cutting is observed. Since cutworms are difficult to control, it may be necessary to repeat the dusting at weekly intervals. Before transplanting into the area, apply a preventive treatment of ORTHO Diazinon Soil & Turf Insect Control and work it into the soil. Cultivate the soil thoroughly in late summer and fall to expose and destroy eggs, larvae, and pupae. Further reduce damage with "cutworm collars" around the stem of each plant. These collars can be made of stiff paper or aluminum foil. They should be at least 2 inches high, and pressed firmly into the soil.

TURNIPS

Damping-off.

PROBLEM: Seeds don't
sprout, or seedlings fall
over soon after they
emerge. The stem at the soil line is water-
soaked and discolored. The base of the
stem is soft and thin.

ANALYSIS: Damping-off
Damping-off is a common problem in wet
soil with a high nitrogen level. Wet, rich
soil promotes damping-off in two ways:
the fungi are more active under these
conditions, and the seedlings are more
succulent and susceptible to attack.
Damping-off is often a problem with
crops that are planted too early in the
spring, before the soil has had a chance
to dry and warm sufficiently for quick
seed germination. Damping-off can also
be a problem when the weather remains
cloudy and wet while seeds are germinating, or if seedlings are too heavily
shaded.

SOLUTION: To prevent damping-off, take
these precautions:
1. Allow the surface of the soil to dry
slightly between waterings.
2. Do not start seeds in soil that has a
high nitrogen level. Add nitrogen fertilizers after the seedlings have produced
their first true leaves.
3. Plant seeds after the soil has reached
at least 70°F or start seeds indoors in
sterilized potting mix.
4. Protect seeds during germination by
coating them with a fungicide containing
captan, *thiram*, or *chloroneb*. Add a
pinch of fungicide to a packet of seeds
and shake well to coat the seeds with the
fungicide. For more information on starting seeds, see page 917.

TURNIPS

ADAPTATION: Throughout the United
States.

PLANTING TIME: See page 1009.

PLANTING METHOD: Sow seeds ½
inch deep. When the seedlings have 2
or 3 leaves, thin to stand 2 to 6 inches
apart.

SOIL: Any good garden soil. pH 5.5 to
7.0

FERTILIZER: At planting time, use 3 to 4
pounds of ORTHO Vegetable Garden
Food 5–10–10 per 100 square feet, or 1
pound per 25-foot row. Side dress every 3 to 4 weeks with 1 pound per 25-
foot row.
  Containers: Water thoroughly every
2 to 3 weeks with a solution of ORTHO
Tomato & Vegetable Food 6–18–6.

WATER:
  How much: Apply enough water at
each irrigation to wet the soil 8 to 10
inches deep.
  Containers: 10 per cent of the applied water should drain out the
bottom.
  How often: Water when the soil 2
inches deep is barely moist.

HARVEST: Pull turnips when the root is
about 2 to 4 inches in diameter. Use
both greens and roots.

Root maggots (half life size).

PROBLEM: Young plants
wilt in the heat of the day.
They may later turn yel-
low and die. Soft-bodied, yellow-white
maggots, ¼ to ⅓ inch long, are feeding
in the roots and on seeds. The roots are
honeycombed with slimy channels and
scarred by brown grooves.

ANALYSIS: Root maggots
(*Hylemya* species)
Root maggots are a damaging pest of turnips in the northern United States. They
are most numerous during cool, wet
weather in the spring, early summer, and
fall. Early maggots attack the roots,
stems, and seeds of turnips, cabbage,
broccoli, and radishes in the spring and
early summer. Later insects damage
crops in the fall. The adult is a gray fly
somewhat smaller than a housefly, with
black stripes and bristles down its back.
It lays eggs on stems and in nearby soil.
The maggots hatch in 2 to 5 days to feed
and tunnel into the roots, rendering them
inedible.

SOLUTION: Once the maggots are in the
roots, nothing can be done. To control
maggots in the planting of turnips, mix
an insecticide containing *diazinon* into
the top 4 to 6 inches of soil before seeding. Control lasts about a month. To prevent egg laying, screen adult flies from
the seedbed with a cheesecloth cover.

Turnips

Cabbage looper (life size).

PROBLEM: Leaves have ragged, irregular, or round holes. Green caterpillars, up to 1½ inches long, are feeding on the leaves. Masses of greenish brown pellets may be found when the outer leaves are parted.

ANALYSIS: Cabbage caterpillars
These destructive caterpillars are either the *cabbage looper* (*Trichoplusia ni*), native to the United States, or the *imported cabbageworm* (*Pieris rapae*), introduced into North America from Europe around 1860. Both species attack all members of the cabbage family, including turnips. Adults lay their eggs singly on leaves in the spring. The white cabbage butterfly attaches its tiny, yellow, bullet-shaped eggs to the underside of leaves; the brownish cabbage looper moth lays its pale green eggs at night on the upper surfaces of leaves. The larvae that hatch from these eggs feed on leaves. The cabbageworm also causes damage by contaminating plants with its greenish brown excrement. There are as many as 5 generations in a season, so caterpillar damage can occur from early spring through late fall. The caterpillars spend the winter as pupae attached to a plant or nearby object.

SOLUTION: Treat the turnip leaves with ORTHO Fruit & Vegetable Insect Control when the caterpillars first appear. Or, if practical, handpick and destroy caterpillars on the leaves. Clean all plant debris from the garden to reduce the number of overwintering pupae.

Flea beetles (life size).

PROBLEM: Leaves are riddled with shotholes about ⅛ inch in diameter. Tiny (¹⁄₁₆ inch) black beetles jump like fleas when disturbed. Leaves of seedlings and eventually whole plants may wilt and die.

ANALYSIS: Flea beetles
These beetles jump like fleas, but are not related to them. Both adult and immature flea beetles feed on a wide variety of garden vegetables, including turnips. The immature beetle, a legless gray grub, injures plants by feeding on the roots and the lower surfaces of leaves. Adults chew holes in leaves. Flea beetles are most damaging to seedlings and young plants. Leaves of seedlings riddled with holes dry out quickly and die. Adult beetles survive the winter in soil and garden debris. They emerge in early spring to feed on weeds until vegetables sprout or plants are set in the garden. Grubs hatch from eggs laid in the soil and feed for 2 to 3 weeks. After pupating in the soil, they emerge as adults to repeat the cycle. There are 1 to 4 generations a year. Adults may feed for up to 2 months.

SOLUTION: Control flea beetles in turnips with ORTHO Fruit & Vegetable Insect Control when the leaves first show damage, or when the plants first emerge through the ground. Watch new growth for evidence of further damage, and repeat the treatment at weekly intervals as needed. Clean all plant debris from the garden after harvest to eliminate overwintering spots for adult beetles.

HOUSEHOLD PESTS

If you don't know the name of a household pest, look through the photographs in the next 18 pages, and read the descriptions of the pests and the damage they cause. This section is grouped into these categories:

HOUSEHOLD PESTS

Finding cockroaches, mice, or ants in the home can be a shocking experience — as if your privacy was being invaded. But it happens to everybody occasionally, and to some people frequently. Some of these pests are only nuisances, such as boxelder bugs or clover mites, which often invade our homes in the fall looking for a warm place to spend the winter. They do no direct harm, but their presence is distasteful. But other pests spoil our food, weaken our homes, or even feed on us!

The two most effective ways to control pests in the house are to remove their reason for invading the house, and to make the house so tight that they can't get in. Many of these pests enter our homes because they find food more easily there than outside. The way to avoid them is to keep food locked up tight. This means practicing careful sanitation in the kitchen, and keeping attractive foods in glass jars or other tight containers. It may also mean sealing woolen clothes in plastic bags, or washing a pet's bedding frequently.

We think of the walls of our houses as barriers but, to an insect, they may have open portals. Many insect problems can be solved by making a careful inspection of the house, then patching holes and caulking cracks.

Also included in this section are some of the biting and stinging pests that annoy or alarm us outside. Although it is usually not possible to erect barriers against outside pests, sanitation helps to limit their numbers. Some dangerous pests such as black widow spiders and scorpions can most easily be eliminated by ridding the yard of the places they like to hide. Honeybees will stay away from the yard if you don't plant their favorite flowers.

As with many of the garden pests, household pests are most easily controlled by avoiding the conditions that attract them.

Above: Ants around a drop of bait. See page 803.
Left: A pest-free patio makes outdoor living more pleasant.

_____ PESTS IN THE HOME _____

INDEX TO HOUSEHOLD PESTS

Housefly (4 times life size).

PROBLEM: Flies are present in the home and other living areas.

ANALYSIS: Houseflies
(*Musca domestica*)
These insect pests are common throughout the world. In addition to their annoying presence, they can spread a number of serious human diseases and parasites such as diarrhea, dysentery, typhoid, cholera, intestinal worms, and *Salmonella* bacteria. In addition to houseflies, several other fly species may infest the home, including face flies (*M. autumnalis*) and little houseflies (*Fannia canicularis*).
Flies feed on and lay their eggs in decaying organic materials. The eggs hatch within several days, and even within 12 hours if conditions are ideal. The creamy-white maggots (about ⅓ inch long) burrow into and feed on the decaying material for several days, pupate, and then emerge as adult flies. Under warm conditions, the entire life cycle may be completed within 14 days. However, cooler conditions will greatly extend this period. The adults usually live for 15 to 25 days.

SOLUTION: To reduce the fly population, maintain sanitary conditions in the home and garden. Keep garbage tightly covered, and dispose of it regularly. Maintain door and window screens in good condition. Kill flies indoors with Flying & Crawling Insect Killer, ORTHO Hi-Power Household Insect Fogger, or ORTHO Home Pest Killer. Kill flies outdoors with ORTHO Malathion 50 Insect Spray or ORTHO Outdoor Insect Fogger. Apply according to label directions.

Vinegar fly (10 times life size).

PROBLEM: Tiny (up to ⅙ inch), yellowish brown, clear-winged insects fly around rotting fruits and vegetables, garbage cans, and other wet, fermenting, or rotting materials. These insects fly in a slow, hovering manner.

ANALYSIS: Vinegar flies
(*Drosophila* species)
These insects, also known as *fruit flies*, do not constitute a serious health menace, but can be annoying in locations where fruit, vegetables, or garbage are allowed to rot and ferment. The adult flies lay their eggs in the decaying fruits or vegetables. The eggs hatch in a few days, and the tiny maggots feed on yeasts growing in the decaying food. The maggots pupate and become adults; the entire life cycle takes only 10 to 12 days.

SOLUTION: To reduce the fly population, maintain sanitary conditions. Keep garbage tightly covered, and dispose of it regularly. Kill flies with ORTHO Flying & Crawling Insect Killer or ORTHO Hi-Power Household Insect Fogger. Apply according to label directions.

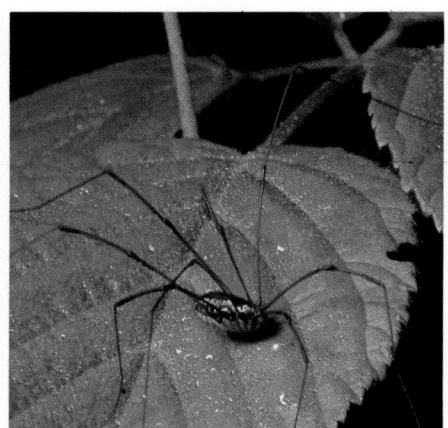

Daddy longlegs (life size).

PROBLEM: Garages, attics, ceilings, basements, and other rarely disturbed areas are infested with spiders and their silken webs. Daddy longlegs, spiderlike creatures with long, delicate legs, may be seen crawling on walls and ceilings.

ANALYSIS: Spiders and daddy longlegs

With only a few exceptions, these familiar animals are harmless and often beneficial. Spiders feed mainly on insects, including such household pests as flies and moths. Most spiders spin silken webs that trap insect prey. Although all spiders are capable of injecting venom when they bite, only a few, such as the black widow and brown recluse spiders, are dangerous to people. (For more information about these spiders, see page 815.) Most spiders are nocturnal, shy, and will not bite unless crushed or held. Daddy longlegs, also known as *harvestmen*, are not true spiders, but are closely related. Daddy longlegs are commonly found near a source of water. They are completely harmless and, unlike spiders, do not spin webs.

SOLUTION: Remove loose wood, trash, or debris from living areas where spiders might hide. Knock down webs with brooms, sticks, or dusters. Kill spiders by spraying infested areas with ORTHO Ant, Roach & Spider Killer, ORTHO Outdoor Insect Fogger, or ORTHO Home Pest Killer. In heavily infested areas, fog the room with ORTHO Hi-Power Household Insect Fogger. To reduce the numbers of spiders entering the home, spray outdoor living areas, and clean up debris outside the home that may harbor spiders.

Cricket (life size).

PROBLEM: Crickets are chirping in the home. These insects, which look like grasshoppers, are light to dark brown, 1/2 to 3/4 inch long, and have long antennae that curve back along the sides of the body. Holes may be chewed in clothing, curtains, carpets, and upholstery in severely infested homes.

ANALYSIS: Crickets (*Gryllus assimilis* and *Acheta domesticus*)

The two types of crickets that may invade the home are field crickets and house crickets. Field crickets usually live outdoors, feeding on vegetation and plant debris. In the fall, when their natural food supply fails, or during periods of heavy rainfall, they may invade buildings in search of food. Field crickets cannot reproduce in the home, and usually die by winter. House crickets, however, can survive and reproduce indoors. During the day, both types of crickets hide in dark, warm locations such as behind baseboards, in closets, and in attics. Male crickets make a chirping sound by rubbing their legs together. Crickets may feed on fabrics and paper items, and large numbers of them may cause serious problems.

SOLUTION: To control crickets outdoors, spray with ORTHO Outdoor Insect Fogger, or apply ORTHO Earwig, Roach & Sowbug Bait or ORTHO Pest-B-Gon Roach Bait according to label directions. To control crickets indoors, spray with ORTHO Ant, Roach & Spider Killer or ORTHO Home Pest Killer according to label directions. Remove dense vegetation and debris around the building foundation where crickets may hide. Seal openings around doors and windows.

Earwig (twice life size).

PROBLEM: Reddish brown, flat, elongated insects up to an inch long with straight or curved pincers projecting from the rear of the body are present in the home. They are often found in dark, secluded places such as in pantries, closets, and drawers, and even in bedding. They may be seen scurrying along baseboards, or moving from room to room.

ANALYSIS: Earwigs

Several species of these nocturnal insects may infest the home, including the European earwig (*Forficula auricularia*), the ringlegged earwig (*Euborellia annulipes*), and the striped earwig (*Labidura riparia*). Earwigs are usually found in the garden, where they feed on mosses, decaying organic matter, vegetation, and other insects. However, large numbers of earwigs may invade homes through cracks or openings in the foundation, doors, and window screens, especially during hot, dry spells. Although they do not damage household furnishings, their presence is annoying, and they may feed on stored food items, or hide in areas where food is kept. They inflict painful pinches when provoked.

SOLUTION: Store food in sealed containers. Repair cracks or openings in window screens, doors, and the building foundation. Control earwigs indoors by baiting with ORTHO Earwig, Roach & Sowbug Bait or ORTHO Pest-B-Gon Roach Bait, or by spraying with ORTHO Home Pest Killer or ORTHO Flying & Crawling Insect Killer. Use according to label directions. To prevent reinfestations, control earwigs outdoors. For more information about controlling earwigs outdoors, see page 884.

PESTS IN THE HOME

Silverfish (3 times life size).

Carpet beetles and larvae (3 times life size).

Clothes moths (life size).

PROBLEM: Paper and fabric products, especially those made with glue, paste, or sizing, are stained yellow, chewed, or notched, and may be covered with excrement and silver or gray scales. When infested products are moved, flattened, slender, wingless insects up to ½ inch long may scurry away. These insects have long, thin antennae, and may be silvery and shiny, or dull and mottled gray.

ANALYSIS: Silverfish and firebrats
(*Lepisma* and *Thermobia* species)
These common household pests are similar in size, shape, and feeding habits except for their coloration and hiding places. Silverfish are silvery, and prefer damp, cool to warm (70° to 80°F) locations such as basements and wall voids. Firebrats are mottled gray, and prefer damp, hot (90° to 105°F) locations such as hot-water pipes and areas near the oven or furnace. These pests are active at night, and hide during the day. They feed on a wide range of foods, especially products high in starches, including human food, paper, paste, and linen and other fabrics. Silverfish damage books by feeding on the bindings. These pests crawl throughout the house along pipes and through holes or crevices in the walls or floor. The adult females lay eggs in cracks or openings behind baseboards and other protected areas. The young look like miniature versions of their parents.

SOLUTION: Spray with ORTHO Home Pest Killer or ORTHO Ant, Roach & Spider Killer according to label directions. Where practical, seal all cracks and crevices in the infested areas. Store valued papers and clothes in tightly sealed plastic bags.

PROBLEM: Irregular holes are chewed in carpets, blankets, clothing, and other articles made of animal fur, hair, feathers, or hides. Light brown to black grubs up to ¼ inch long may be seen crawling on both damaged and undamaged items. The grubs are distinctly segmented, and covered with circular rows of stiff, dark hairs.

ANALYSIS: Carpet beetles
The larvae of these beetles damage carpets, clothes, upholstery, and other products of animal origin. Some species also feed on stored foods. The adult beetles are about ⅛ inch long, and may be black or mottled gray, brown, and white. They usually live outdoors, feeding on pollen and nectar. The beetles fly into homes during the late spring or early summer and lay their eggs in cracks or crevices, or on clothes, carpets, or other materials. The emerging larvae seek out dark, undisturbed locations in which to feed. They shed their skins a number of times during their development. Most of the larvae hibernate during the winter, and pupate in the spring.

SOLUTION: Shake out, brush, and air infested clothes and blankets. To kill remaining grubs, dry clean infested items. Pack clean clothes with *paradichlorobenzene* crystals in closets or containers. Vacuum or sweep infested rooms, and destroy the sweepings immediately. Kill remaining insects by treating rooms with ORTHO Hi-Power Household Insect Fogger or ORTHO Home Pest Killer. Seek professional help to protect carpets and furs.

PROBLEM: Holes are chewed in clothing, blankets, carpets, pillows, upholstery, and other items. Infested articles may be covered with a webbing of silken tubes, cases, and strands. Shiny white worms up to ½ inch long may be seen crawling on damaged items.

ANALYSIS: Clothes moths
Two closely related species of clothes moths are common in the United States. The larvae of these small, yellowish to tan moths damage clothes and other items made of fur, wool, feathers, and leather. The female moths attach their eggs to the fabric. Soon after the larvae emerge they spin silken tubes, mats, or cases. The larvae usually feed from within these protective casings, but may crawl out to feed unprotected. The larvae pupate in cocoons attached by silken threads to the infested item, and emerge as adult moths. New infestations occur when moths lay eggs on clothing, carpets, and other articles, and when moth, larva, and egg-ridden items are stored with uninfested articles.

SOLUTION: Shake out, brush, and air infested clothes and blankets in a sunny location. To kill remaining moths, dry clean infested items. Pack clean clothes with *paradichlorobenzene* crystals in closets or containers. Vacuum or sweep infested rooms, and destroy the sweepings immediately. Seek professional help to protect carpets and furs.

Black ants (twice life size).

Boxelder bug (4 times life size).

Clover mite (30 times life size).

PROBLEM: Ants are present in the house. Trails of ants may be seen crawling on floors, walls, baseboards, counters, and in cupboards. They are generally most troublesome in the kitchen or pantry.

ANALYSIS: Ants
A number of closely related species of ants invade households. Most ants are strongly attracted to sweets, starches, fats, and grains, and invade households in order to carry these foods back to their nests. Adverse outdoor conditions, such as flooding or drought, may cause ants to move their nests or colonies into buildings. Ant colonies are often built underground in the garden, but may also be found in building foundations, under flooring, between wall partitions, in attics, and in other protected locations. The colonies may contain from several hundred to several thousand individuals. Ant colonies may be located by following the established ant trails to their source.

SOLUTION: Destroy ant colonies by spraying the nests and ant trails with ORTHO Home & Garden Insect Killer, ORTHO Home Pest Killer, or ORTHO Ant, Roach & Spider Killer, as directed on the label. Eliminate ant colonies from the garden by treating the anthills with ORTHO Diazinon Granules or spraying the nest and surrounding soil with ORTHO Diazinon Insect Spray. Store food in sealed containers, and keep kitchens and pantries free of exposed foods.

PROBLEM: During the fall, hordes of brownish black bugs ½ inch long with red stripes on their wings swarm into the home and outdoor living areas. They congregate on walls, walks, furniture, drapes, and other objects. When crushed, they emit a strong, unpleasant odor.

ANALYSIS: Boxelder bugs
(*Leptocoris* species)
These insects are common in all parts of the United States. They are most numerous in areas where boxelder trees (*Acer negundo*) grow. In the spring, the female bugs lay their eggs in the bark of boxelders, or sometimes of maples, ash, and fruit trees. The young feed on tender twigs, foliage, and seeds through the spring and summer. During the fall, especially on bright, sunny days, the bugs migrate in large numbers into tree trunks, homes, buildings, or other dry, protected locations to hibernate for the winter. Boxelder bugs do not feed on fabric or furniture, but may stain household items with their excrement. Occasionally, boxelder bugs will bite, and they may feed on houseplants.

SOLUTION: Vacuum boxelder bugs with a tank-type vacuum cleaner, and then destroy the bag. Or spray the bugs with an insecticide containing *malathion, diazinon,* or *pyrethrum*. Spray outdoor areas with insecticides containing *malathion* or *diazinon*. Keep the doors and windows screened and the cracks around them well sealed.

PROBLEM: Reddish brown mites smaller than a pinhead, with long front legs, are present in the home in the fall. They may be found on walls, window sills, floors, and furniture and even in bedding and clothes. When crushed, these mites leave a blood-red stain. They are often so numerous that they give infested surfaces a reddish appearance.

ANALYSIS: Clover mites (*Bryobia praetiosa*)
These pests, related to spiders, are found throughout the United States. Clover mites feed and reproduce on clover, grasses, and other plants. They are most active in the spring and fall, and on warm winter days. The mites lay eggs during the summer and fall. The young that hatch from these eggs feed on vegetation, and then migrate into homes and other protected areas during the early fall. Mites enter homes through cracks or openings in the foundation and around doors and windows. Mite activity usually decreases when temperatures rise above 85°F or fall below 40°F.

SOLUTION: Remove mites from household furnishings by vacuuming them from infested surfaces. Kill mites indoors by spraying them directly with household insecticides containing *pyrethrum, allethrin,* or *malathion*. Treat window sills and other areas where clover mites may enter with insecticides containing *malathion, propoxur,* or *resmethrin*. Treat outdoor areas with ORTHO Home Pest Killer, ORTHO Hornet & Wasp Killer, or ORTHO Malathion 50 Insect Spray as directed on the label. Keep a strip of soil 18 to 24 inches wide around the foundation of the building free of vegetation and debris to reduce mite movement into homes.

PESTS IN THE HOME

Pigeon.

House mouse.

House mouse.

PROBLEM: Birds are roosting or nesting in wall voids, under eaves, and in other areas around the home.

ANALYSIS: Birds
Most birds are harmless and pleasant, but a few species, especially pigeons, starlings, and sparrows, may become a nuisance around the home. These birds are adapted to urban and suburban environments. They roost and build nests on chimneys, ledges, rafters, eaves, drainpipes, and similar locations, and often return to the same nesting site year after year. In addition to their messy droppings and irritating chirping, birds may transmit to humans such diseases as pigeon ornithosis, aspergillosis, encephalitis, and histoplasmosis.

SOLUTION: Where possible, exclude birds with screens. Apply a bird repellent adhesive or jelly to roosting and nesting areas. Clean up possible food or nest-building materials (such as dried weeds or vegetation) to discourage bird activity in the vicinity. Place flashings of wood, plastic, or metal at a 45 degree angle on nesting or roosting areas. Birds may also be trapped or poisoned. If you are considering poison, contact a licensed pest control operator or your county agricultural commissioner's office for regulations pertaining to your city.

PROBLEM: Mice are seen in the garage or home. Or signs of mouse infestation are found, including droppings and tracks, or gnawed doors, baseboards, or kitchen cabinets. Books, fabrics, furniture, and other objects may be chewed or shredded, and packages of food may be gnawed open and the contents eaten.

ANALYSIS: House mice (*Mus musculus*)
These familiar pests often go unnoticed if only a few are present, but may cause significant damage when their numbers are large. In addition to gnawing on clothing, furniture, and other items, mice contaminate food with their urine and droppings, and may spread parasites and diseases. Mice are generally active at night. Under ideal conditions, the females produce up to 50 young in a year. Mice are very agile, and can jump to 12 inches off the ground, run up almost any rough vertical surface, swim, and squeeze through openings slightly larger than $1/4$ inch. House mice feed primarily on cereal grains, but will eat many other kinds of food including butter, fat, meat, sweets, and nuts.

SOLUTION: The best way to eliminate mice in the home is to trap them. Mice are more likely to seek bait in traps if their normal source of food is scarce. Remove food from areas where mice can get to it, and store grains in sealed metal, glass, or heavy plastic containers. Place traps where mouse droppings, gnawings, and damage indicate their presence such as behind refrigerators and other protective objects, in dark corners, along baseboards, and in cupboards. Bait the traps with pieces of bacon, nutmeats, raisins, or peanut butter. Tie the bait to the trigger so the mouse won't be able to remove the bait without springing the trap. Check the traps daily to dispose of trapped mice. Wear gloves when handling dead mice, or use tongs to pick them up to avoid bites from mouse parasites. Poisoned baits are also effective in controlling mice. If you are unable to eliminate all the mice, contact a professional pest control operator. After the mice have been eliminated, prevent them from returning by sealing holes or cracks larger than $1/4$ inch in the walls, floors, windows, doors, and foundation that open to the outside. For details on mouse-proofing your home, contact your local Cooperative Extension Office. For a list of extension offices, see page 1011.

Roof rat.

Norway rat.

Raccoon.

PROBLEM: Rats are seen or heard in the attic, garage, basement, wall voids, or other areas of the home. Or signs of rat infestation are found, including droppings, tracks, and loosely constructed nests made of rags, paper, and other scraps. Pipes, beams, and wiring may be gnawed. Books, fabrics, furniture, and other objects may be chewed or shredded, and packages of food may be gnawed open and the contents eaten.

ANALYSIS: Rats (*Rattus* species)
Rats are distributed world-wide, and infest well-maintained suburban residences as well as run-down urban houses and apartments. The species that most frequently infest houses are the Norway rat (also known as the brown, house, wharf, or sewer rat) and the roof rat. Rats enter buildings through any opening, including toilets, pipes, chimneys, and garbage chutes. Young rats can squeeze through openings as small as 1/2 inch wide. These animals make their nests and breed in wall voids, attics, crawl spaces, basements, and other secluded locations. They also breed in heavy vegetation near the home, such as ivy or juniper groundcovers. Their long front teeth grow constantly. To keep them worn down, rats gnaw on almost anything, including clothing, furniture, and electrical wires. They can also gnaw through gas lines, causing gas leaks. Rats are notorious for contaminating food with their urine, droppings, and hair, spreading parasites and diseases. They occasionally bite people, especially sleeping infants. The bites are dangerous, and should be treated by a doctor.

SOLUTION: Control rats in the home by trapping them. Rats are more likely to seek bait in traps if their normal source of food is scarce. Remove food from areas where rats can get to it easily. Store food in glass or tin containers with screw-on or otherwise tightly sealed lids. Place traps along rat runways, anchoring the trap securely to a nearby object so the animal won't drag it away. Bait traps with pieces of beef, bacon, fish, nutmeats, or carrots. Tie the bait to the trigger so the rat won't remove the bait without springing the trap. Check the traps daily to dispose of captured rats. Wear gloves when handling dead rats, or use tongs to pick them up to avoid bites from rat parasites such as fleas and mites. Poisoned baits may also be used. If you are unable to eliminate the rats, contact a professional pest control operator. Keep rats out by rat-proofing the building. Rat-proofing may involve much expense and work because it involves sealing all openings larger than 1/2 inch leading into the building from the outside. For details, contact your Cooperative Extension Office. For a list of extension offices, see page 1011.

PROBLEM: Raccoons are present around the home. They overturn garbage cans at night, scattering and feeding on the contents and causing a great commotion. They occasionally invade attics, crawl spaces under buildings, and other secluded locations.

ANALYSIS: Raccoons (*Procyon lotor*)
Raccoons are a nuisance mainly in rural and suburban areas. They generally live near a source of natural water such as a stream, marsh, or pond. Raccoons are very dextrous and inquisitive animals. They frequently turn over garbage cans in their search for food. They sometimes take up residence in attics, basements, barns, or similar locations. Although these animals carry fleas and ticks, they are not a serious health threat. Raccoons can be dangerous if cornered.

SOLUTION: Keep garbage cans securely anchored in racks or immovable frames. Lids should be tightly secured to the can. Screen or seal openings into buildings. Consult your Department of Fish and Game regional office to find out about local raccoon control restrictions and regulations. Live traps baited with pieces of melon, prunes, honey-coated bread, or smoked fish are usually effective in controlling raccoons. Attach traps to a tree, stake, or fence post. If possible, push the trap back and forth in the ground until the soil covers the wire mesh on the bottom of the trap. Wait a few days before setting the trap; this allows the animal a chance to become accustomed to it. Transport the trapped animal to a wooded area at least several miles away.

PESTS IN THE HOME

Gray squirrel.

Fleas.

Fleabites.

PROBLEM: Squirrels are seen or heard in the building. Or nuts or other food remnants, droppings, gnawed holes, and nesting materials in the attic, garage, wall voids, and other areas indicate their presence.

ANALYSIS: Tree squirrels
Several species of tree squirrels invade houses, including the fox squirrel (*Sciurus niger*), eastern gray squirrel (*S. carolinensis*), and flying squirrels (*Glaucomys* species). Squirrels enter buildings through vents, broken windows, construction gaps under eaves and gables, and occasionally chimneys and fireplaces. They may build nests or store food in attics, wall voids, garages, and similar locations, and damage items stored in attics or garages.

SOLUTION: Contact your State Department of Fish and Game regional office for regulations governing the control of tree squirrels in your area. Eliminate animals inside the building by placing traps in the areas they are inhabiting. Bait the traps with nutmeats, chunk-style peanut butter, sunflower seeds, or raisins. If tree squirrels are entering the building via trees or power lines, secure traps to tree limbs or the roof top to intercept them. For more information about traps, see page 891. Once squirrels have been eliminated from the building, seal entry routes into the home with sheet metal or hardware cloth. Prune off tree limbs at least 6 feet away from the roof or any other part of the building.

PROBLEM: Fleas infest pets, pet quarters, rooms, carpets, upholstered furniture, or the garden.

ANALYSIS: Fleas
These pests of humans, dogs, cats, and many other warm-blooded animals are found throughout the world. In addition to causing annoying bites, they can transmit several serious diseases such as bubonic plague, murine typhus, and tapeworms. The cat flea (*Ctenocephalides felis*), the dog flea (*C. canis*), and the human flea (*Pulex irritans*) are the most common species found around the home. These fleas have a wide host range, attacking humans, dogs and cats, and a number of other animals. The female fleas lay eggs shortly after feeding upon animal blood. The eggs are usually laid on the host's body, or the host's bedding. The eggs often fall off of the host's body into floor crevices, dog and cat boxes, carpets, and other areas where the infested animals spend time. Within 10 days, the eggs hatch into tiny, wormlike larvae that feed on dried blood, lint, excrement, and other organic debris. Pupation occurs after one week to several months. The adult fleas may emerge after only a week if conditions are favorable, or emergence may be delayed up to a year. The adults often remain in their pupal cocoons until a host is present. A flea's life cycle may vary from two weeks up to two years. Because fleas have the ability to survive for many months without a blood meal, they can remain in vacated residences for long periods of time, ready to bite returning pets and humans. Fleas are mainly spread by infested animals. Uninfested animals can easily pick up fleas when visiting flea-ridden premises. Fleas may also be spread by infested articles of clothing or furniture.

SOLUTION: Treat infested pets. Dust them with ORTHO Sevin Garden Dust, or spray them with ORTHO Flea-B-Gon Flea Killer. Spray infested animal quarters with ORTHO Flea-B-Gon Flea Killer, ORTHO Malathion 50 Insect Spray, or ORTHO Flying & Crawling Insect Killer; or dust with ORTHO Sevin Garden Dust. Read and follow label directions carefully. Flea-repellent collars may help to control fleas on animals. Destroy infested pet bedding, or wash it thoroughly in hot, soapy water. Vacuum carpeting, chairs, sofas, and other areas or objects that may contain eggs and larvae-ridden lint or debris, and then dispose of the vacuum bag. Kill remaining fleas with ORTHO Flea-B-Gon Flea Killer, ORTHO Hi-Power Household Insect Fogger, or ORTHO Home & Garden Insect Killer, used according to label directions. Kill fleas in the yard by spraying with ORTHO Liquid Sevin, ORTHO Malathion 50 Insect Spray, or ORTHO Diazinon Insect Spray, used according to label directions. To prevent reinfestations, do not allow infested animals to enter the house and yard, and keep pets away from infested areas.

Skunk in a live trap.

Pajaroello tick (twice life size).

Pacific coast tick (4 times life size).

PROBLEM: Skunks are observed living beneath the building, or their tracks and strong scent are present around the home.

ANALYSIS: Skunks

Skunks become household pests when they take up residence under a house. They are most likely to make a den under a house when natural burrows or dens are not readily available. The strong scent they spray when threatened may cause nausea and even temporary blindness. Skunks can eject this potent fluid as far as 10 feet. Skunks carry a variety of diseases, including rabies. They may transmit rabies to humans and pets. Rabid skunks often show abnormal behavior such as listlessness, unprovoked aggressiveness, or a tendency to wander around during the day. Such animals will bite if handled.

SOLUTION: Contact your local Department of Fish and Game office for skunk control regulations. Eliminate skunks by placing moth balls or open pans of household ammonia under the building, or place several floodlights under the building to drive them out. Live-catch box-type traps may also be used. For more information about traps, see page 891. When handling skunks, wear old clothing and goggles. After the animals have been eliminated, screen off or seal openings into the building. Skunk bites should be treated immediately by a physician or veterinarian. Skunk scent may be neutralized with *neutroleum alpha*, a compound that may be obtained through a hospital supply outlet. For information about controlling skunks in the garden, see page 895.

PROBLEM: Oval, leathery, reddish brown to dark brown ticks are attached to a person or pet. These pests, which range in size from $\frac{1}{16}$ to $\frac{1}{8}$ inch before feeding, are usually found on the pet's ears and neck, and between the toes. Engorged ticks are round, $\frac{1}{2}$ inch in diameter, and blue to olive-gray.

ANALYSIS: Ticks

These blood-sucking pests, which are related to spiders, attack humans, dogs, cats, and other animals. Most ticks are found in grassy or brushy areas. In addition, the *brown dog tick* may drop off infested dogs in households, and establish itself in the home. Ticks attach themselves to passing people and pets, and sink their "heads" and mouthparts into the flesh. If left undisturbed, they may continue to suck blood for 5 to 50 days before dropping off. Tick-infested dogs become restless and often lose their vitality because of the irritating bites and loss of blood. Ticks can live for up to 18 months without food or water.

SOLUTION: When ticks are sharply pulled or brushed off the skin, their mouthparts usually break off, remaining embedded in the flesh. This may cause small ulcers or infections to develop in the wounded areas. There are no foolproof methods to make a tick withdraw its mouthparts, but the following techniques may be tried.
1. Touch the tick with the lit end of a cigarette, a hot needle, or a lit match. The heat may cause it to remove its mouthparts.
2. Suffocate the tick by covering it with petroleum jelly, fingernail polish, or butter. After several minutes to half an hour, the tick will withdraw its mouthparts.
3. Slowly and steadily pull the tick from the skin.

If the wound becomes infected, or illness ensues, contact a doctor or veterinarian. Dust infested pets lightly with ORTHO Sevin Garden Dust according to label directions. If the animal is severely infested, contact a veterinarian. Spray grassy or brushy areas around the home with ORTHO Ant, Roach & Spider Killer or ORTHO Home Pest Killer according to label directions. Kill ticks in the home by fogging with ORTHO Hi-Power Household Insect Fogger. Destroy infested animal bedding, and spray animal quarters and other infested indoor areas with ORTHO Ant, Roach & Spider Killer according to label directions.

PET AND BODY PESTS

Chigger-infested field.

STRUCTURAL PESTS

Subterranean termites (twice life size).　　Termite-damaged book.

PROBLEM: Welts and hard, raised bumps (papules) appear on the skin, particularly on parts of the body where clothing is binding or where body parts come in contact, such as the belt line, the armpits, the backs of the knees, and under cuffs and collars. Itching is severe and may last as long as 2 weeks. Welts and itching often develop within several hours to a day after the affected person has been in a scrubby, thicket-covered, or otherwise heavily vegetated area.

ANALYSIS: Chiggers
(*Trombicula* species)
These parasites, also known as *red bugs*, are the larval forms of several closely related microscopic mites. Only the larvae are harmful. They hatch from eggs laid in the soil of uncultivated, scrubby woodland or marshy areas, and attach themselves to people and other hosts passing by. Chiggers insert their mouthparts into the skin and feed on blood for several days until they become engorged and drop off. Chiggers are sometimes a problem in lawns around new home developments.

SOLUTION: To remove chiggers from the skin, bathe thoroughly in hot, soapy water. Contact your druggist for compounds to relieve itching. When walking through chigger-infested areas, wear protective clothing, and tightly button or tape sleeves, pant cuffs, and collars. Apply repellents such as *diethyl toluamide* or *ethyl hexanediol* to the skin and clothing, especially around the ankles, armpits, waist, sleeves, and cuffs. If vegetated areas around your home are infested, spray with ORTHO Home Pest Killer according to label directions.

PROBLEM: On warm, sunny spring or fall days, brown to brownish black winged insects, about ⅜ inch long, swarm in and around the building. These insects resemble flying ants, but have thick rather than constricted waists. Their discarded wings may be found around the building. Earthen tubes extend from the soil up along the building foundation and any other termite-proof surface to the infested wooden structures. These tubes are commonly found in basements and crawlspaces under the building. When broken off, they are rebuilt within several days. Dark or blistered areas may develop in the flooring.

ANALYSIS: Subterranean termites
These wood-feeding insects cause more structural damage to buildings than any other insect. Subterranean termites live in colonies as deep as 5 feet in the ground, and move up to infest wooden structures through tubes of soil they build over masonry or metal to bridge the gap from soil to wood. Except for the dark, winged swarmers, these termites are white, wingless, and very sensitive to moisture loss. They always remain within the nest, soil tubes, or infested wood, protected from desiccation and insect predators. Termites maintain a complicated caste system within their colony that includes sterile workers and soldiers, winged reproducers, and an egg-laying queen. Colonies are formed when a pair of winged reproducers leaves the parent colony and excavates a nest in a piece of wood that is on top of or buried in the ground. As the new colony develops, galleries are formed deep in the soil. Termite colonies develop slowly; 3 or 4 years usually pass before the reproductive swarmers develop, and structural damage may not be noticed for several more years. However, when buildings are erected over established termite colonies, serious damage may occur within a year. Termites hollow out the inside of a wooden structure, leaving only an outer shell. Damage is most severe when they infest main supporting wooden beams and girders.

SOLUTION: Termite infestations can be treated most effectively only after a thorough and accurate diagnosis of the damage is made. Accurate diagnosis is usually very difficult and requires the aid of a professional termite or pest control operator. Once the termite colony has been located, and the damage has been revealed, a physical or chemical barrier is placed between the soil and the building to prevent the termites from reaching the building. An insecticide containing *chlordane, dieldrin,* or *aldrin* is applied to the soil around and underneath the building. If infestations are small and localized, you may control them by applying ORTHO Ortho-Klor 44 Chlordane Spray to the soil according to label directions. Discourage additional infestations by keeping the area under and around the house free of wood debris above and below the ground. If the soil around the foundation remains moist due to faulty plumbing or improper grade, repair the plumbing and alter the grade; termites prefer moist soil. A number of preventive measures should be followed when building new structures. For details on termite-resistant construction methods, contact a reliable building contractor or your local Cooperative Extension Office (see page 1011).

Bedbugs (6 times life size).

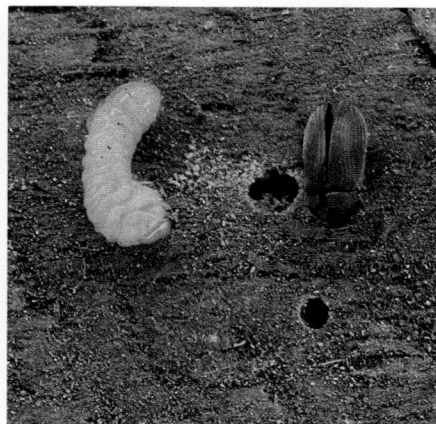

Powderpost beetle and larva (3 times life size).

Emergence holes.

PROBLEM: Painful swellings develop on the body. Dark brown to black spotted stains appear on pillows, sheets, and other bedding. When the lights are turned on at night, reddish brown, oval-shaped bugs about ¼ inch long may be seen crawling on the skin and bedding.

ANALYSIS: Bedbugs
(*Cimex lectularius*)
These distasteful bugs have become an infrequent problem in the United States. However, they still infest homes where living conditions are unsanitary, and may be transported to well-maintained residences on infested clothing and furniture. Bedbugs hide during the day behind baseboards, in mattresses and upholstered furniture, in cracks and crevices in the floor, bedframes, and similar locations. These pests are nocturnal, and become very active at night. They crawl onto a sleeping person, pierce their skin, and suck their blood for several minutes. Bedbugs usually deposit telltale masses of dark excrement on bedding after they feed. They are very active, and may crawl from room to room or even from house to house during the night.

SOLUTION: Spray baseboards, wall crevices, and floor cracks with a 2 percent solution of *malathion* or *ronnel*. Spray bed frames and springs with a 1 percent solution of *malathion* or *ronnel*. Mist mattresses with a 1 percent solution of *malathion*, but do not soak them. Be sure to spray mattress seams and tufts. Let mattresses dry completely before reusing. Do not spray infant cribs and bedding. If bedbugs reinfest the home, treat again after an interval of 2 weeks. Launder all bedding thoroughly. Keep the house clean.

PROBLEM: Wood flooring, structural timbers, cabinets, furniture, and other items are riddled with round holes that range in size from ¹⁄₁₆ to ³⁄₈ inch. Wood powder or tiny pellets may be piled around the holes or on the floor below. When the infested item is tapped, additional pellets or wood powder are expelled from the holes. Tiny red, brown, or black beetles ranging in size from ¹⁄₁₂ to ⅓ inch may be seen crawling around the infested wood, or flying around windows and electric lights in the evening. When the damaged wood is cut open, the inside is found to be riddled with sawdust-filled tunnels; or it may be pulverized into a mass of wood powder or pellets.

ANALYSIS: Powderpost beetles
These wood-feeding beetles, including the *powderpost, false powderpost,* and *deathwatch* beetles, damage wood houses and household furnishings throughout the United States. Powderpost beetles feed only on dead wood. They are brought into the home in infested timber or furnishings; or they may fly from infested lumber or wood piles in the yard. The female beetles deposit their eggs in unfinished wood. The grubs that hatch from the eggs tunnel through the wood, leaving masses of wood powder or pellets behind them. They pupate just under the surface of the wood, and emerge as adult beetles through the round holes they chew in the wood. Beetle eggs or larvae present in wood before it has been coated with paint, varnish, shellac, or other finishings can chew through the finished surface when they have matured, leaving round emergence holes. However, they do not lay eggs in coated wood surfaces, and reinfestation cannot occur.

SOLUTION: If the infestation is localized, remove and destroy badly infested timbers. Replace them with kiln-dried or insecticide-treated wood. Or treat unfinished wood yourself by painting or spraying it with *lindane* dissolved in deodorized kerosene. Wherever possible, apply paint, shellac, varnish, paraffin wax, or other wood coatings to unfinished wood around the home to prevent further infestation. Inspect wood piles periodically for signs of powderpost beetle infestation. Burn infested wood. If the infestation is widespread, contact a professional pest control operator to fumigate the building. Individual pieces of furniture may also be fumigated to kill beetle eggs and larvae. Many pest control operators maintain fumigation chambers for movable items. Eggs and larvae in small wooden items may be killed by placing them in the freezer for 4 days.

STRUCTURAL PESTS _____

Drywood termites (twice life size).

Old house borer damage.

Old house borer (twice life size).

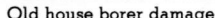

PROBLEM: On warm, sunny days, ½-inch winged insects with reddish brown heads may be seen flying in and around a building. These insects resemble flying ants, but have thick rather than constricted waists. Their discarded wings may be found around the building. Tiny elongated brown fecal pellets are piled below cracks or chinks in infested rafters, window frames and sills, door and window jambs, and other wooden structures.

ANALYSIS: Drywood termites
These wood-feeding insects cause structural damage to buildings in the warmer areas of the United States. Drywood termites live in colonies within wooden structures, including furniture. Except for the dark, winged swarmers, drywood termites are white and wingless. They can withstand desiccation for long periods of time. Infestations start when a pair of winged reproductive termites leaves the main colony and burrows into a wood structure. As the colony grows, the wood is slowly hollowed out. Piles of termite pellets are pushed out through cracks in the weakened wood. Drywood termite infestations develop slowly and are usually small. These pests may be spread long distances in infested pieces of wood.

SOLUTION: Drywood termites are most effectively controlled by fumigation, which must be done by a professional pest control operator. Several preventive measures should be followed when building new structures to prevent future infestation. For details on termite-resistant construction methods, contact your local County Extension Office (see page 1011) or a reliable building contractor.

PROBLEM: Oval holes ¼ to ⅓ inch wide appear in walls and flooring. Or holes appear in wallpaper, plaster, linoleum, and other types of wood coverings. Sawdustlike borings may be piled around the holes. In some cases, rasping or ticking sounds may be heard before the holes appear, and the wood may be blistered or rippled. Grayish brown to black beetles 1 inch long with antennae may be seen around the house.

ANALYSIS: Roundheaded borers
The larvae of these beetles, including the new house borer (*Arhopalus productus*) and the old house borer (*Hylotrupes bajulus*), cause damage to softwood (fir, pine) structural timbers. New house borers mainly infest fir subflooring. They do not cause structural damage; the holes they make in wood or covered wood surfaces are of cosmetic concern only. The adults lay their eggs in the bark of weak and dying forest trees. The yellow grubs tunnel into wood that is later incorporated into a building before the adult beetles emerge. New house borers continue to emerge through holes in wood and wood coverings for up to a year after construction. They cannot reinfest the building. Old house borer beetles do not emerge from timbers until 3 to 5 years after the building has been constructed. They continue to reinfest the damaged wood, and may cause serious structural damage. Sometimes the grubs make rasping or clicking noises while they feed. If they are tunneling close to the surface, wood blistering or rippling may result.

SOLUTION: New house borers are the problem if damage occurs within a year after construction. To repair new house borer damage, seal or fill emergence holes. The only thing you can do to prevent beetles from emerging is to hire a professional pest control operator to fumigate the building. Because damage is only cosmetic and will stop within a year, this expensive procedure is seldom justified. Old house borers are the problem if damage occurs at least 3 years after construction. Buildings infested with old house borers must be fumigated. Contact a professional pest control operator to fumigate the building. To prevent future infestations of old house borers when building new structures, purchase pressure-treated wood.

Carpenter ants (twice life size).

Galleries. *Insert:* Adult carpenter bee (life size).

Woodwasp (life size).

PROBLEM: Black or reddish black winged or wingless ants up to ½ inch long are seen around the home. Piles of sawdust may be found in basements or attics, under porches, or near supporting girders or joists. Slitlike holes are often present in woodwork. On warm spring days, swarms of winged ants may cluster around windows. Unlike termites, these pests have constricted waists.

ANALYSIS: Carpenter ants
(*Camponotus* species)
Many closely related species of these wood-damaging ants are found throughout the United States. Carpenter ants bore into moist, decaying wood, forming extensive galleries in which they make nests. They do not eat their sawdustlike wood borings, but feed on other insects, plant sap, pollen, and seeds. When ant colonies grow too large, part of the colony will migrate, often invading nearby homes through windows, foundation openings, or similar entry points. They will either colonize undisturbed hollow spaces such as wall voids and hollow doors, or bore into structural timbers, ceilings, and floor and subfloor areas. They prefer damp and rotted wood. In addition to weakening wood, carpenter ants may infest pantries, and often inflict painful bites when disturbed.

SOLUTION: Spray baseboards, window sills, door frames, and other surfaces where ants crawl with ORTHO Ant, Roach & Spider Killer or ORTHO Home Pest Killer. Spray into nests if possible. Remove nearby logs, stumps, and woodpiles. Seal openings in the foundation, windows, and other access areas into the home.

PROBLEM: Metallic blue or black buzzing bees fly around the home and yard. They may be seen entering and leaving holes about 1 inch wide in decks, posts, beams, rafters, and other wooden structures. When damaged wood is sliced open, partitioned galleries may be seen. The partitions may contain immature bees.

ANALYSIS: Carpenter bees
(*Xylocopa virginica*)
These insects do not usually cause serious damage; however, continued burrowing and gallery formation year after year will eventually weaken wooden structures. These insects burrow into wood to make their nests. The female bees partition the galleries into small cells in which the carpenter bee larvae mature. When bee nests are approached, the males hover around the head of the intruder. Although they are frightening because of their loud buzzing and large size, the male bees do not sting, and the females sting only when handled.

SOLUTION: Paint wood surfaces once a year to discourage bee tunneling. Flood galleries in exposed wood with an insecticide containing *carbaryl*. Close the holes with putty, caulking compound, dowel pins, or plastic wood to prevent bees from returning to the nest.

PROBLEM: Round holes about ¼ inch in diameter appear in wood floors, walls, doors, and other surfaces. Or holes appear in wallpaper, linoleum, carpeting, and other types of covering over wood. Metallic blue, black, or multicolored wasplike insects may be seen flying around the home. These buzzing insects are 1 to 2 inches long, and have hornlike "tails."

ANALYSIS: Woodwasps
These insects, also known as *horntails*, do not cause structural damage; the holes they make in wood or covered wood surfaces are of cosmetic concern only. Woodwasps lay their eggs in weak and dying forest trees. The adult insects emerge from the wood 3 to 5 years later, often long after the tree has been used for construction. Woodwasp holes may continue to appear for up to 5 years after the cut wood has been used. These insects lay their eggs only in forest trees; they do not reinfest buildings.

SOLUTION: Seal or fill emergence holes. There is nothing you can do to prevent the woodwasps from emerging. For future construction, purchase lumber that has been kiln-dried or vacuum fumigated. These processes kill woodwasp larvae embedded in the wood.

STRUCTURAL PESTS

Dry rot.

BITING AND STINGING PESTS

Yellowjackets (twice life size).

Yellowjacket (twice life size).

PROBLEM: Foundation timbers, paneling, flooring, and other wooden structures are damp and soft, or dry, cracked, brown, and crumbling. Often the wood is broken into small, cubical pieces. Thin mats of white fungal strands may be seen on the rotted wood. Thick white, brown, or black fungal cords up to 2 inches wide may extend across the rotted area. These cords often extend over impenetrable surfaces such as brick and concrete to reach wood surfaces beyond.

ANALYSIS: Dry rot
Dry rot is caused by fungi that live in the soil, and grow into wood that is in direct contact with damp soil. The white fungal strands penetrate and decay the wood fibers, causing a soft rot. In some cases, the fungus draws water from the soil up through the thick fungal cords that extend across the rotted area. The water is used to moisten dry wood, providing the damp condition in which the fungus thrives. After the fungus dies, badly rotted wood cracks and crumbles into chunks when handled.

SOLUTION: Remove any water-conducting fungal cords from the wood. Eliminate moist soil conditions around wood structures as much as possible by improving ventilation, changing soil grade and drainage, or fixing leaky plumbing. As soon as the soil and wood dry out, the fungus will die. Replace badly rotted wood with wood that has been pressure-treated with preservatives. Remove all wood scraps around the building foundation. When building new structures, use pressure-treated wood in all areas where wood and soil make contact.

PROBLEM: Yellowjackets are present around the home. They hover around patios, picnic areas, garbage cans, and other areas where food or garbage is exposed. Yellowjackets may be seen flying into underground nests. Yellowjackets inflict painful stings when threatened or harmed, or when their nests are approached.

ANALYSIS: Yellowjackets (*Vespa* and *Vespula* species)
Unlike most other species of wasps, yellowjackets live in large colonies, often numbering in the thousands. Some species of yellowjackets feed on insects and spiders, while others scavenge scraps of meat from recreational areas or dumpsites. These pests may also feed on nectar, sap, and other sugary fluids, and may be seen hovering around soft drinks and cut fruit. Yellowjackets can inflict painful stings, and are capable of repeated stings. The venom injected along with the sting causes reddening, swelling, and itching of the affected area. Some people who are very sensitive to the stings experience extreme swelling, dizziness, difficulty in breathing, and even death. Yellowjackets are very protective of their nests, and large numbers may emerge to sting intruders. Yellowjacket nests are difficult to find because they are built underground. The only evidence of the nest is a raised mound of dirt surrounding a depression several inches deep. Almost all yellowjackets die in the late fall, and new nests are started the following spring in a different location.

SOLUTION: Keep food and garbage covered, and empty garbage frequently. To kill yellowjackets before picnicking, spray with ORTHO Outdoor Insect Fogger according to label directions. To remove yellowjackets from the vicinity, you must eliminate the nests. After locating the nests, spray them at dusk or during the night with ORTHO Hornet & Wasp Killer. Stay 8 feet away from the nest, and spray directly into the entrance hole. If you need to illuminate the area, use a flashlight covered with red cellophane. Use it for only short periods of time. Stop spraying when the yellowjackets begin to emerge; leave the nest area quickly by walking, not running away. Repeat the spraying every evening until the insects fail to emerge, then quickly cover the hole with moistened soil. Contact a professional pest control operator to remove yellowjacket nests in difficult locations. If you are stung, apply a cold compress or ice pack to the affected area. If a severe reaction develops, call your doctor.

Swarm (1/10 life size). *Insert:* Honeybee.

Paper wasps (life size).

Mud dauber nest.

PROBLEM: Bees are hovering around flowering plants in the garden, and may inflict stings when threatened or harmed. Large numbers of bees may cluster on shrubs or trees. Hives may be located in attics, chimneys, and wall voids.

ANALYSIS: Honeybees
(*Apis mellifera*)
These familiar and often feared insects provide honey and wax, and are very important as pollinators. On warm, sunny days, bees forage for nectar among flowering garden plants, then return to their hives in the evening. When an established hive gets too crowded, thousands of bees leave in a swarm. Swarms fly for a mile or so before settling in a new location. En route, they often rest in a tight cluster on a tree branch or other object. Some people are allergic to bee stings, and experience extreme swelling, dizziness, difficulty in breathing, and possibly death. A bee does not sting more than once because the stinger and venom sac rip out of its body when it flies away. The injured bee soon dies.

SOLUTION: When stung, scrape the stinger off the skin with a knife or fingernail. Avoid squeezing it; this forces more venom into the wound. Apply cold compresses or ice packs to the swollen area. If a severe reaction develops, call a doctor immediately. Avoid using plants that are attractive to bees, especially around pools, patios, and other recreational areas. For a list of plants that are attractive to bees, see page 996. Do not try to remove hives or swarms yourself. Contact a professional beekeeper or pest control operator if bees are nesting in your home or garden.

PROBLEM: Single-layered paper nests are suspended from eaves, ceilings, or branches. These nests are composed of exposed, open cells, and have a honeycomb appearance. They are often umbrella-shaped. Black or brown wasps with yellow or red stripes may be seen hovering around or crawling on the nests.

ANALYSIS: Paper wasps
(*Polistes* species)
Most paper wasps live in small colonies, usually consisting of 20 to 30 wasps. They build paper nests in which they raise their young. Paper wasps feed on insects, nectar, and pollen. They are not as aggressive and protective of their nests as are yellowjackets. (For more information about yellowjackets, see page 812.) However, they will sting if threatened, causing swelling, itching, and more generalized symptoms in sensitive individuals.

SOLUTION: To remove paper wasps from the vicinity, you must eliminate their nests. Spray the nests at dusk or during the night with ORTHO Hornet & Wasp Killer or ORTHO Outdoor Insect Fogger. Spray the nest from a distance of 8 feet. Stop spraying when wasps begin to emerge; leave the nest area quickly by walking, not running away. Repeat the spraying every evening until the insects fail to emerge. Remove the nest and dispose of it. If you are stung, apply a cold compress or ice pack to the swollen area. If a severe reaction develops, call your doctor.

PROBLEM: Wasps are flying around the garden. Some of these insects are black with yellow, red, or white markings. Others are black, brown, blue, red, or yellow. Many wasps have very thin elongated waists. Their mud nests may be found under eaves and on plants or rocks.

ANALYSIS: Solitary wasps
Unlike the social yellowjackets, many species of wasps, including the potter and mason wasps, mud daubers, and spider wasps, live alone. Most of them build nests of mud and sand in which they raise their young. Many of these wasps feed on insects; a few feed on pollen and nectar. These wasps are not as aggressive and protective of their nests as are yellowjackets, and will not sting as readily. (For more information about yellowjackets, see page 812.) If highly provoked, however, they can sting, causing swelling, itching, and more generalized symptoms in sensitive individuals.

SOLUTION: Eliminate mud nests by hosing or knocking them down. Kill wasps by spraying them with ORTHO Hornet & Wasp Killer or ORTHO Outdoor Insect Fogger according to label directions. Even though many of the solitary wasps are docile, they may be confused with yellowjackets; it is best to avoid threatening or provoking them. If you are stung, apply a cold compress or ice pack to the swollen area. If a severe reaction develops, call your doctor.

BITING AND STINGING PESTS

Horsefly (3 times life size).

Blackflies (3 times life size).

Biting midge (15 times life size).

PROBLEM: Black, brown, or black and white biting flies about ½ to 1 inch long are present around the home. They are especially bothersome in areas where horses and domestic animals are common.

ANALYSIS: Biting flies
These flies, including several species of *horseflies* and *deerflies*, attack humans and domestic animals in rural and suburban areas. The female flies deposit their eggs in still pools of water, in moist soil, or on vegetation. The larvae feed on other insects or decaying vegetation, and pupate in damp plant debris. The adult flies inflict painful bites that often continue to bleed after the fly has left. The victim may suffer from fever and general illness.

SOLUTION: Keep doors and windows tightly screened. Spray outdoor living areas with ORTHO Outdoor Insect Fogger or ORTHO Home & Garden Insect Killer. Kill biting flies indoors by spraying with ORTHO Household Insect Killer, ORTHO Home & Garden Insect Killer, or ORTHO Hi-Power Household Insect Fogger. Apply insect repellents to the skin. Such repellents may be purchased at drugstores. Remove fly breeding areas by cleaning up stagnant pools of water and wet, decaying vegetation around the yard.

PROBLEM: During the late spring and summer, many black or gray humpbacked flies ½₅ to ⅛ inch long are present around the home. They inflict painful bites.

ANALYSIS: Black flies
These annoying flies, also known as *buffalo gnats* or *turkey gnats*, attack humans and domestic animals in rural and suburban areas throughout the United States. The female flies deposit their eggs in swiftly running water, including streams and irrigation ditches. The larvae develop in the water, and emerge as adult flies during the spring and summer. Black flies may be blown many miles from their breeding areas. They bite any exposed part of the body and may also bite under clothing, especially where clothes are binding, such as around belts and collars. These irritating bites often swell and itch for several days. The victim may suffer headaches, fever, and nausea.

SOLUTION: Keep windows and doors tightly screened. Spray outdoor living areas with ORTHO Outdoor Insect Fogger or ORTHO Home & Garden Insect Killer. Kill black flies indoors by spraying with ORTHO Household Insect Killer or ORTHO Home & Garden Insect Killer. Apply insect repellents to the skin. Repellents may be purchased at drugstores.

PROBLEM: During the spring and summer, tiny black biting midges ½₅ to ⅛ inch long infest the yard. They are most common in coastal areas and near lakes, streams, marshlands, and swamps.

ANALYSIS: Biting midges
These annoying insects are also known as *no-see-ums*, *sand flies*, or *black gnats*. They feed on humans, many warm-blooded animals, and birds. Biting midges breed in wet sand or mud, damp, rotting vegetation, very shallow stagnant or brackish water, and similar locations. They rarely infest the home, but are bothersome outdoors, inflicting bites around the feet, legs, ears, and eyes, and under clothes, especially in cuff, collar, and belt areas where clothing binds. The bites are not usually painful, but produce tiny swellings or blisters that continue to itch for several days.

SOLUTION: Spray infested areas of the yard with ORTHO Outdoor Insect Fogger according to label directions. Apply insect repellents to the skin. Such repellents may be purchased at drugstores.

Mosquito (8 times life size).

Black widow spider (life size).

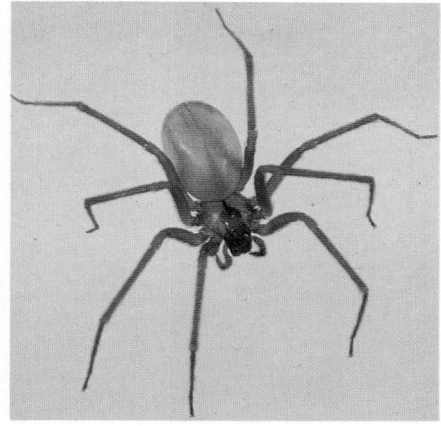

Brown recluse spider (twice life size).

PROBLEM: Biting mosquitoes are present in the home and yard. They are most bothersome at dusk and during the night.

ANALYSIS: Mosquitoes
Many different species of this insect pest occur throughout the world. In addition to their annoying bites, they transmit encephalitis within the United States, and other serious diseases such as yellow fever and malaria in other parts of the world. Adults emerge from hibernation with warm spring weather. The males feed on nectar, honeydew, and plant sap; the females require a blood meal in order to produce their eggs. Larval development takes place exclusively in water. Typically, eggs are laid in shallow accumulations of fresh, stagnant, or salty water. The larvae may mature within 5 days, or may take many months to mature.

SOLUTION: Maintain door and window screens in good repair. Kill mosquitoes indoors by fogging with ORTHO Hi-Power Household Insect Fogger or spraying with ORTHO Home & Garden Insect Killer. Kill mosquitoes outdoors by spraying with ORTHO Lawn Insect Spray or ORTHO Malathion 50 Insect Spray around the lawn and foundation of the house. Spray resting areas under eaves with ORTHO Home & Garden Insect Killer or ORTHO Outdoor Insect Fogger. Apply insect repellents to the skin. Drain unnecessary accumulations of water. Stock ornamental ponds with mosquitofish (*Gambusia affinis*), which eat mosquito larvae. Goldfish also eat mosquito larvae, but are not as effective as mosquitofish.

PROBLEM: Black widow spiders are shiny, black, about the size of a quarter, and have a red hourglass marking on the underside of the abdomen. Outdoors, they live under rocks or clods of dirt, or in wood and rubbish piles. Indoors, they are found in garages, attics, cellars, and other dark secluded places such as under boards or cluttered debris, in old clothing, or in crevices. Black widow webs are coarse and irregular, about 1 foot wide.

ANALYSIS: Black widow spiders
(*Latrodectus* species)
Several species of these poisonous spiders are found throughout the United States. Black widows live in secluded locations and feed on insects trapped in their webs. If the spiders are accidentally touched, or their webs are disturbed, they will bite the intruder. The venom may cause serious illness and possibly death. The females produce spherical egg sacs that contain hundreds of eggs. The tiny spiderlings that emerge from the sac are also capable of inflicting poisonous bites. They may be carried long distances by the wind, eventually dropping down to infest new areas.

SOLUTION: Kill spiders by fogging with ORTHO Hi-Power Household Insect Fogger or spraying webs and infested areas with ORTHO Ant, Roach & Spider Killer or ORTHO Outdoor Insect Fogger. Remove loose wood, trash, and clutter from areas where spiders might hide. Wear gloves and protective clothing when cleaning up infested areas. Vacuum infested areas to remove eggs sacs, and destroy the contents of the vacuum cleaner bag. Put ice on spider bites, and call a doctor immediately.

PROBLEM: Brown recluse spiders are light to dark brown, 1/3 to 1/2 inch in length, with a violin-shaped marking behind the head. Outdoors, they are found under rocks. Indoors, they are found in old boxes, among papers and old clothes, behind baseboards, underneath tables and chairs, and in other secluded places. Grayish, irregular, sticky webs and round white egg sacs 3/4 inch wide may be found in the infested areas.

ANALYSIS: Brown recluse spiders
(*Loxosceles reclusa*)
These poisonous spiders are found in the Midwest and Southeast. Other related but less poisonous spiders (*Loxosceles* species) are found throughout most of the United States. Brown recluse spiders live in secluded places and are very shy, moving away quickly when disturbed. If they are touched or trapped in shoes, clothing, or bedding, they may bite. Their venom is rarely fatal, but causes a severe sore that is slow to heal, and sometimes causes illness.

SOLUTION: Kill spiders by fogging with ORTHO Hi-Power Household Insect Fogger or spraying webs and infested areas with ORTHO Ant, Roach & Spider Killer, ORTHO Home Pest Killer, or ORTHO Outdoor Insect Fogger. Remove loose wood, trash, or clutter from areas where spiders might hide. Wear gloves and protective clothing when cleaning up infested areas. Spray outdoor living areas, and clean up debris around the home that may harbor spiders. Vacuum infested areas to remove egg sacs, and destroy the contents of the vacuum bag. Put ice on spider bites and call a doctor immediately.

Scorpion (twice life size).

German cockroaches (life size).

Oriental cockroaches (twice life size).

PROBLEM: Scorpions are usually found in the garden under rocks, boards, and protective debris. Indoors, they may inhabit attics or crawl spaces under the home. They may move down into living areas such as kitchens and bathrooms when attic temperatures rise above 100°F.

ANALYSIS: Scorpions
All scorpions are capable of inflicting stings; however, only a few species found in the South are dangerous. Scorpions are nocturnal creatures, feeding at night on insects and small animals. During the day, they hide in dark, protected locations. They are shy, and sting only when touched, trapped, or otherwise provoked. Except for a few fatally poisonous scorpions (*Centuroides* species), most scorpions deliver stings that are no more serious than a bee sting. The venom varies in potency from season to season, however, and like many insect stings may cause severe illness in a sensitive individual. Although they live mostly in the garden, scorpions may crawl into the home through open or loose doors and windows.

SOLUTION: Remove loose boards, rocks, clutter, and other debris around the yard and in the home to eliminate scorpion hiding places. Wear gloves and protective clothing when cleaning up infested areas. Spray or dust locations where scorpions might hide in the yard and home with ORTHO Diazinon Insect Spray. Maintain window and door screens and weather stripping in good repair. Call a doctor if you are stung by a scorpion.

PROBLEM: Cockroaches infest the kitchen, bathroom, and other areas of the home. These flat, shiny insects range in size from ½ to 1¾ inches long. They may be light brown, golden tan, reddish brown, or black. In large numbers, they emit a fetid odor.

ANALYSIS: Cockroaches
These insect pests thrive in human habitations throughout the world. The most important household species in the United States are the *German cockroach* (*Blattella germanica*), the *brown-banded cockroach* (*Supella longipalpa*), the *oriental cockroach* (*Blatta orientalis*), and the *American cockroach* (*Periplaneta americana*). In addition to their annoying presence, cockroaches spread diseases such as salmonella poisoning and parasitic toxoplasmosis by contaminating food with their infected droppings. These pests proliferate in areas where food and water are available. Cockroaches prefer starchy foods, but will feed on any human food scraps, garbage, paper, or fabrics soiled with food. Unless infestations are heavy, or their hiding places are disturbed, they are rarely seen in exposed locations during the day. These nocturnal insects seek out dark, protected areas in which to live and breed. Usually they congregate in kitchens and bathrooms. They may be found behind or under sinks, refrigerators, and water heaters, within the walls of household appliances, behind baseboards and molding, in wall voids, around pipes, in garbage cans, and in piles of cluttered paper or grocery bags. They may be present in cracks or crevices in cupboards, cabinets, desks, dressers, and closets. They may infest basements, crawl spaces, and sewers. Cockroaches move from one room to another through wall voids or through cracks in walls, floors, and ceilings, and along pipes and conduits. If their living conditions become too crowded, they may migrate. Infestations usually begin when stray insects or egg cases are brought into the home with shipped items, second-hand furniture or appliances, grocery bags, or debris. They may also move into homes from sewers.

SOLUTION: Eliminate cockroach food sources by keeping the kitchen and other areas of the home free of food scraps. Clean up the kitchen after each meal and store food in tightly sealed metal, glass, or heavy plastic containers. Empty household garbage and pet litter regularly. Do not leave pet food out overnight. Fix leaking faucets and pipes. Clean up water puddles or moist areas around the kitchen, basement, and other infested areas. Plug cracks around baseboards, shelves, cupboards, sinks, and pipes with a filling material, such as putty or caulk. Remove food and utensils, then spray ORTHO Home Pest Killer or ORTHO Ant, Roach & Spider Killer in cracks in cupboards, surfaces underneath sinks, along molding, behind appliances, and in other areas where insects are likely to congregate. Allow the spray to dry and then reline the shelves with fresh paper before replacing food and utensils. Bait with ORTHO Pest-B-Gon Roach Bait under sinks and refrigerators and in other hiding places according to label directions. Boric acid dust may also be used. Avoid inhaling or ingesting boric acid dust when applying. If infestations remain severe or persistent, contact a professional pest control operator.

Angoumois grain moth (6 times life size).

Mealworms (life size).

Red flour beetle (6 times life size).

PROBLEM: Pinkish or greenish caterpillars up to ⅝ inch long are feeding inside silken webbing in stored grain, flour, cereals, and other grain products. Beige, gray, and coppery-winged moths ⅓ inch long may be seen flying around lights in the home.

ANALYSIS: Flour moths
The larvae of *Indian meal moths* (*Plodia interpunctella*) and *Mediterranean flour moths* (*Anagasta kuehniella*) damage ground or broken grain products, dried fruits, powdered milk, and other pantry items. The larvae of *angoumois grain moths* infest whole wheat and corn kernels. The adult moths lay eggs in stored grain products. The larvae that emerge spin silken webs, under which they feed. When mature, they usually leave the infested food to pupate in a corner or crack in the cupboard. The adult moths fly to nearby sources of food in which they lay their eggs.

SOLUTION: Discard all infested food. Clean out cupboards thoroughly before restocking. If infestation is widespread, remove all food and utensils, and fog the infested area with ORTHO Hi-Power Household Insect Fogger; or spray shelves and cracks in the pantry with an insecticide containing *pyrethrin* or *methoxychlor*. Do not spray countertops or other food work areas. Reline shelves with paper and replace food after the spray has dried. If you suspect that food is infested, kill the eggs, larvae, and pupae by deep-freezing food for 4 days or heating it in a shallow pan at 150°F for half an hour. Keep foods in airtight glass, plastic, or metal containers. Keep the pantry clean, and avoid buying broken packages; they are more likely to be infested.

PROBLEM: Shiny, yellow to brown grubs up to 1¼ inches long are feeding in damp or moldy flour, grain, or cereal products. Flat, shiny, brown to black beetles ¼ to ¾ inch long may also be found.

ANALYSIS: Mealworms
(*Tenebrio* and *Alphitobius* species)
These insects prefer to feed on damp or moldy grain products stored in dark, rarely disturbed, dusty locations such as warehouses. However, if infested food items are brought into the pantry, the mealworms and beetles may migrate to infest and reproduce in poorly sealed bags of flour, bran, crackers, and other grain products.

SOLUTION: Chemical control is not necessary. Discard infested food items. Clean out cupboards thoroughly. Keep grain products in dry, tightly sealed glass, plastic, or metal containers.

PROBLEM: Reddish to dark brown, elongated beetles ⅒ to ⅐ inch long, and yellowish white, wiry grubs ⅕ inch long are feeding in flour, cereals, cake mix, macaroni, and other flour and grain products.

ANALYSIS: Flour beetles
(*Tribolium* and *Oryzaephilus* species)
Several species of beetles infest grain products in the pantry, grocery store, and packing plant, including the *sawtoothed grain beetle*, the *red flour beetle*, and the *confused flour beetle*. These pests feed on and reproduce in stored flour products. They can migrate to and infest nearby broken or poorly sealed containers, and can also chew through and infest flimsy paper and cellophane packages. Even when infested packages are removed, the beetles can live on flour and cereals that sift into cracks in the cupboard.

SOLUTION: Discard all infested food. Clean out cupboards thoroughly before restocking. If infestation is widespread, remove all food items and spray shelves and cracks in the pantry with an insecticide containing *malathion*; or fog the infested area with ORTHO Hi-Power Household Insect Fogger. Let the spray dry before replacing food. Keep foods in air-tight glass, plastic, or metal containers. If you suspect food is contaminated, kill the beetles, grubs, and eggs by deep-freezing for 4 days; or heat the food in a shallow pan at 130°F for half an hour. Keep the pantry clean, and avoid buying broken packages; they are more likely to be infested.

PANTRY PESTS

Rice weevils (4 times life size).

Cigarette beetle, larva, and pupa (twice life size).

PROBLEM: Reddish brown to black beetles ⅛ to ⅙ inch long with elongated snouts are feeding in stored whole grain rice, corn, wheat, and beans. The beetles may be seen crawling around the pantry. Yellow-white grubs may be found inside infested kernels.

ANALYSIS: Grain weevils
(*Sitophilus* species)
These pantry pests include the *granary weevil* and the *rice weevil*. They usually damage whole grains, but occasionally infest flour and other broken or processed grain products. The adult weevils lay eggs inside grain kernels. Larvae that hatch from the eggs mature inside the kernels, pupate, and emerge as adult weevils. The adults wander about, and are often seen far from the site of infestation.

SOLUTION: Discard all infested food. Clean out cupboards thoroughly before restocking. If the infestation is widespread, remove all food items and fog the kitchen with ORTHO Hi-Power Household Insect Fogger according to label directions; or spray shelves and cracks in pantry cupboards with an insecticide containing *malathion* or *propoxur*. Do not spray countertops or other food preparation areas. Reline shelves with paper and replace food after the spray has dried. Keep foods in air-tight glass, plastic, or metal containers, and avoid buying broken packages; they are more likely to be infested.

PROBLEM: Reddish or reddish brown, oval-shaped beetles, ⅛ inch long, or yellowish white, curved grubs are feeding in stored tobacco, cigars, or cigarettes. They may also be found in spices, such as red pepper and paprika, coffee beans, and other stored foods derived from plants.

ANALYSIS: Cigarette and drugstore beetles (*Lasioderma serricorne* and *Stegobium paniceum*)
These beetles are native to tropical parts of the world and can survive in the United States only in warm buildings (65°F and up). These pests feed on and reproduce in foods and spices. They may also feed on wool, leather, paper, drugs, and other household items. When infested products are brought into the home, the beetles can invade nearby uncontaminated foods that are kept in unsealed, broken, or flimsy containers. They may also chew through sealed paper containers.

SOLUTION: Remove and destroy all infested foods. Clean out cupboards thoroughly before restocking. If the infestation is widespread, remove all food items and spray shelves and cracks with an insecticide containing *malathion* or *rotenone*. Let the spray dry before replacing food. Keep foods and spices in air-tight glass, metal, or plastic containers. Refrigerate food kept in paper packages. Do not purchase items in broken or unsealed packages; they are more likely to be infested.

A GALLERY
OF PROBLEMS
AND SOLUTIONS

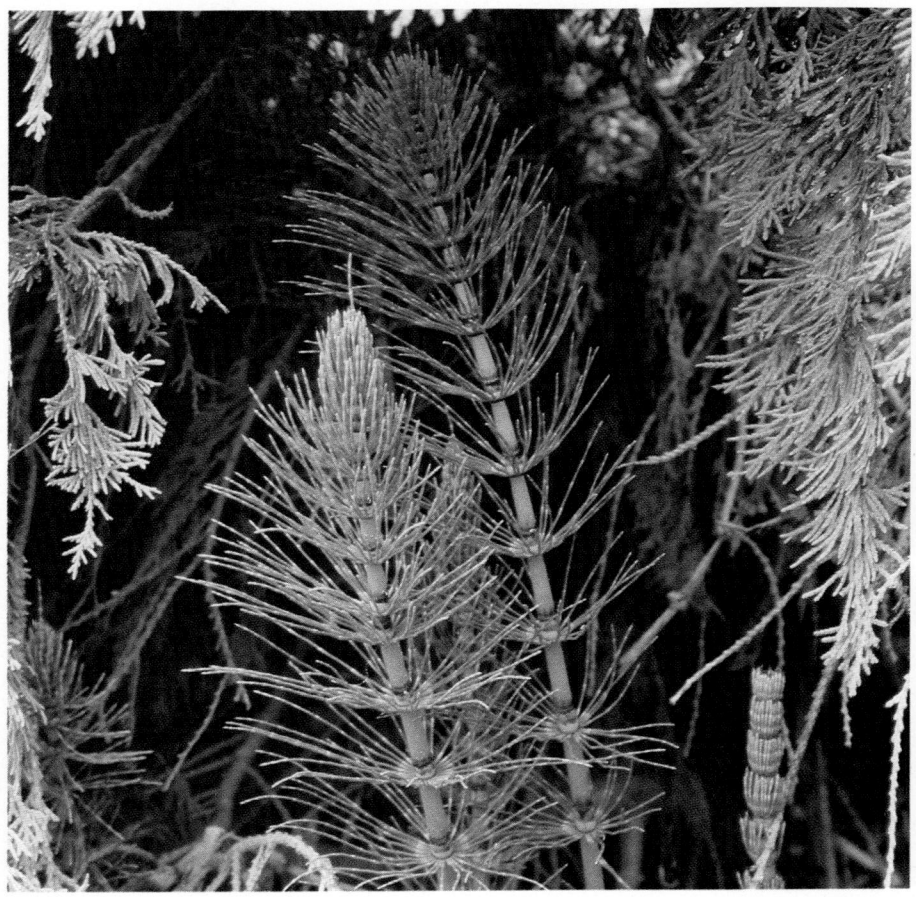

A GALLERY OF WEEDS

Most gardeners would agree that weeds are the most time-consuming and persistent garden problem. Yet, for most gardeners, they don't need to be. Weed control can be reduced to a minimum by spending one or two growing seasons diligently removing every weed before it makes seeds. This year or two of extra effort will pay off with many years of reduced work in the garden.

Weeds can be divided into two categories. Weeds in the first category produce a copious amount of seed, and begin producing it early in life. These weeds often are easy to kill, either with herbicides or with a hoe, but new ones keep appearing. Weeds in the second category are hard to kill, often because they have persistent underground parts

that can sprout into new plants. And a few weeds, such as dandelions, have both of these characteristics.

The first category of weeds is most easily controlled by keeping its seeds from sprouting. Begin the battle in the spring, or whenever seeds germinate, by applying a pre-emergence herbicide — an herbicide that kills seeds as they germinate — or a mulch wherever the weed has been a problem. Then, once a week throughout the growing season, remove every weed that appears in your yard, either with a hoe, or by spot-treating with an herbicide.

The second category of weeds is best controlled with a translocated herbicide — one that is carried to every part of the plant. *Glyphosate*, the active ingredient

in ORTHO Kleenup Systemic Weed & Grass Killer, has been a real help to gardeners (but it can't be used in the vegetable garden). It controls most of the difficult weeds, then breaks down in the soil, so it has no lasting effect on garden plants. Or cover the area with a black plastic mulch for a growing season. This treatment kills all plants under the mulch by excluding light.

Then, as with weeds in the first category, inspect the entire garden once a week and kill every weed seen. If this routine is followed carefully for a year, all the weeds in your garden will be eliminated, and only a few that blow in from outside will bother you in future years. Weed control will have been reduced to a routine chore.

Above: Horsetail. See page 832. Left: Dandelions in a lawn. These common weeds are a nuisance in many lawns. See page 845.

INDEX TO WEEDS

WEED CONTROL

Effective weed control on right.

Weed-free annual bed.

WEED CONTROL IN LAWNS

The best way to control weeds in a lawn is to keep the lawn thick and vigorous by following the guidelines beginning on page 294. A vigorous lawn is a strong competitor, and will crowd out most weeds.

Broadleaf weeds: Kill broadleaf weeds in lawns with ORTHO Weed-B-Gon Lawn Weed Killer or ORTHO Weed-B-Gon For Southern Grasses.

Weed grasses: Kill crabgrass and dallisgrass in lawns with ORTHO Crab Grass Killer. Other weed grasses can be spot treated with ORTHO Kleenup Systemic Weed & Grass Killer or ORTHO Kleenup Ready-To-Use Weed & Grass Killer. You can reseed or resod the dead spots one week after treatment. For instructions on lawn repair, see page 908.

Reestablishing the lawn: If the lawn is in disrepair, and is mostly weeds rather than turfgrass, the best solution might be to kill it all, then reseed or resod a new lawn. For instructions on establishing a new lawn, see page 295.

Preventive care: Pre-emergence herbicides kill seedlings as they germinate, but do not harm existing plants. ORTHO Garden Weed Preventer is a pre-emergence herbicide for lawns and gardens. One application in early spring will prevent most lawn weeds from emerging from the soil.

WEED CONTROL IN ANNUAL BEDS

Annuals have a short life, growing quickly from seeds to bloom. Any weeds that compete with the annuals for water and nutrients slow their growth and bloom. Before tilling and planting an annual bed, kill the existing weeds or lawn grass. Annual weeds can be killed by an herbicide or by cultivation. If the area is being reclaimed from a lawn, or if perennial weeds are present, use ORTHO Kleenup Systemic Weed & Grass Killer. For small gardens or to spot treat individual weeds, use ORTHO Kleenup Ready-To-Use Weed & Grass Killer, the same product in a premixed formulation. Kleenup will not affect the roots of untreated annual flowers, since it is inactivated on contact with soil. Once the flower bed is weed-free, prevent weed seeds from germinating with a pre-emergence herbicide such as ORTHO Garden Weed Preventer. Established weeds and plants are not affected, so use only on weed-free soil. Don't use in an area where you have planted annual flower seeds. Pre-emergence herbicides form a barrier to emerging seedlings. If the barrier is disturbed by cultivating or hoeing, the herbicide's effectiveness is reduced, so don't disturb the soil until you reapply the herbicide. For more information on the products mentioned, see the gallery of ORTHO products beginning on page 920.

Weed control in vegetable garden.

Weed-free perennial bed.

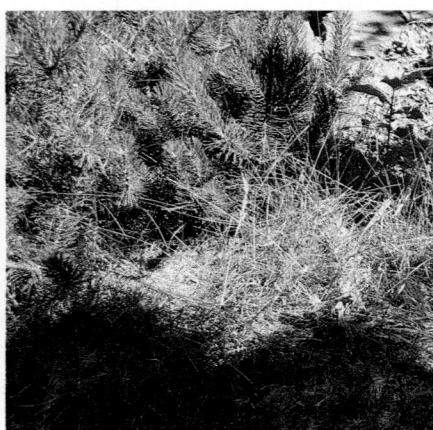

Poor weed control.

WEED CONTROL IN VEGETABLE GARDENS

It is important to remove weeds in the vegetable garden because they compete with vegetables, reducing their growth and yield. However, control measures are complicated by the fact that the vegetable garden offers an ideal environment for plant growth, with lots of water and fertilizer. Also, because vegetables are eaten, the use of herbicides around them must be limited. Remove existing weeds by cultivating with a sharp hoe. Cut off the weeds just below the soil line, rather than trying to dig them from the ground. Most vegetable garden weeds are killed by this treatment, and the roots of the vegetables are not disturbed. To remove small weeds close to seedlings, pinch them off, or cut them at the ground line with a pair of scissors. Prevent weeds from returning with ORTHO Garden Weed Preventer. This pre-emergence herbicide kills weed seedlings as they germinate, but does not harm existing plants. Or smother weeds with a mulch. Black plastic stops all weed growth, and 2 to 4 inches of sawdust, straw, or other loose material discourages most weeds. Be careful in choosing an organic mulch. It should be free of weed seeds, and must not have been treated with herbicides before being cut. A mulch of organic materials can be turned under in the fall to improve the tilth of the soil. To save yourself much weeding next year, be diligent about weeding this year. Only a few weed seeds blow in from outside the garden; most of this year's weeds are the progeny of last year's weeds.

WEED CONTROL IN PERENNIAL BEDS

Weeds are usually more numerous, vigorous, and difficult to control in flower beds growing in full sun. Before establishing a perennial bed in an area that was once lawn or a neglected plot, kill all the present weeds or they will be a continuous maintenance problem. Kill the existing weeds with ORTHO Kleenup Systemic Weed & Grass Killer or ORTHO Contax Weed & Grass Killer. These herbicides are also effective in cleaning up an established but neglected bed. In small flower beds or to spot treat individual weeds, use ORTHO Kleenup Ready-To-Use Weed & Grass Killer, a premixed formulation. Kleenup is inactivated on contact with the soil, so it won't harm the roots of established perennials. Once the flower bed is established, use a pre-emergence herbicide to keep the area weed-free. Pre-emergence herbicides such as ORTHO Garden Weed Preventer kill seedlings as they emerge. They don't affect established plants or weeds, so use only on weed-free soil. Pre-emergence herbicides form a barrier to emerging seedlings. If the barrier is disturbed by cultivating or hoeing, the herbicide's effectiveness is reduced, so don't disturb the soil until you are ready to reapply the herbicide. For more information on the products mentioned, see the gallery of ORTHO products beginning on page 920.

WEED CONTROL UNDER TREES AND SHRUBS

Weed control under trees and shrubs is usually simpler and easier than weed control in other areas because the trees and shrubs shade the bed, reducing the vigor of the weeds. If the area has been neglected for some time, and is full of perennial weeds, kill them with ORTHO Kleenup Systemic Weed & Grass Killer. If the area is small, or to spot treat individual weeds, use ORTHO Kleenup Ready-To-Use Weed & Grass Killer. If the weeds are young and soft, kill them with ORTHO Contax Weed & Grass Killer. It will probably not be necessary to remove the dead weeds, since small weeds dry up and disappear. Kleenup and Contax are inactivated on contact with soil so they won't harm the roots of nearby plants. To prevent weed seeds from germinating after you have cleared an area, apply ORTHO Casoron Granules or ORTHO Garden Weed Preventer. These pre-emergence herbicides kill young seedlings as the seeds germinate. They won't kill existing weeds, so apply them only to weed-free soil. The herbicide forms a barrier that kills emerging seedlings. If the barrier is disturbed by hoeing or cultivating, the protection is dispersed. Once the herbicide is applied and watered in, don't disturb the soil until you reapply the herbicide. (For more information on these products, see the gallery of ORTHO products beginning on page 920.) Light, shallow cultivation and mulching (see page 918) under trees are also effective in controlling weeds.

Weeds growing in patio.

Weeds growing in unimproved area.

Annual bluegrass.

WEED CONTROL IN DRIVEWAYS, WALKWAYS, AND PATIOS

Weeds growing in the cracks and crevices of walkways, brick patios, and driveways are often difficult to hand-pull. Most perennial weeds have deep roots that become anchored underneath the permanent surface. To eliminate weeds in these situations, use an herbicide that won't harm surrounding lawn grasses, trees, and shrubs if it is washed from the treated area by rain or irrigation water. Treat existing weeds with an herbicide such as ORTHO Liquid Fence & Grass Edger, ORTHO Contax Weed & Grass Killer, or ORTHO Kleenup Ready-To-Use Weed & Grass Killer. For scattered or few weeds, treat with ORTHO Spot Weed & Grass Control. All of these herbicides are inactivated on contact with the soil, so they won't harm the roots of surrounding desirable plants. For longer-term control where desirable plants are not present nearby, kill existing weeds with ORTHO Triox Liquid Vegetation Killer. This residual herbicide prevents weed growth for up to a year. For more information on the products mentioned, see the gallery of ORTHO products beginning on page 920.

WEED CONTROL IN UNIMPROVED AREAS

One reason to keep weeds to a minimum in vacant lots and fields is that these weeds produce the seeds that germinate in your garden. If you prevent them from setting seeds, you can often nip your garden weed problems in the bud.

Mowing: One way to control weeds in unused places is to mow them regularly. While this method keeps the area neat, and keeps some of the weeds from setting seed, many weed varieties set seed in only a few days, and others have flower heads close to the ground, so that a mower misses them.

Killing weeds: If you wish to kill all the weeds in an empty lot, use a nonselective herbicide — an herbicide that kills just about any plant it touches. If you wish to replant the area soon, choose ORTHO Kleenup Systemic Weed & Grass Killer, which becomes inactive on contact with the soil. If most of the weeds are woody, such as shrubs or vines, use ORTHO Brush Killer A.

Keeping the weeds out: If you wish to keep the area clear of all vegetation, apply ORTHO Triox Liquid Vegetation Killer. Triox not only kills the weeds it contacts, but remains in the soil for up to a year to prevent further weed growth. For more information about these products, see the gallery of ORTHO products beginning on page 920.

ANNUAL BLUEGRASS
Poa annua

Annual bluegrass, also called *annual speargrass, dwarf speargrass,* or *walkgrass,* is a troublesome weed in all areas of the yard. In lawns it is not easily noticed because it resembles Kentucky bluegrass. Annual bluegrass prefers areas with moist, rich, or compacted soil. This pale green grass reproduces by seeds and lives for only one year, although in some areas there are perennial strains. Annual bluegrass grows most rapidly in cool spring weather. In mid to late spring, white seed heads appear on the plants. The seeds fall to the soil, and germinate in the cooler weather of late summer to midfall. Annual bluegrass is not heat or drought tolerant, and dies in the summer.

CONTROL: For information on controlling annual bluegrass in lawns, see page 311. Around trees and shrubs, and in flower and vegetable gardens, prevent annual bluegrass with ORTHO Garden Weed Preventer. Apply to the soil in late summer to midfall. While the weeds are actively growing around trees and shrubs, flower beds, and in nonplanted areas, use ORTHO Kleenup Ready-To-Use Weed & Grass Killer or ORTHO Spot Weed & Grass Control. Prevent annual bluegrass around trees and shrubs with ORTHO Casoron Granules. If your soil is compacted, correct as outlined on page 900. Reduce the chances of invasion by allowing the soil to become moderately dry between waterings when the seeds are germinating in the fall.

Quackgrass.

Velvetgrass.

Bermudagrass.

QUACKGRASS
Agropyron repens

Quackgrass, also called *couchgrass* or *witchgrass*, is one of the most troublesome perennial grasses in the northern United States. Its extensive fibrous system consists of long, yellow-white roots that may grow 5 feet or more in one growing season. The narrow, bluish green blades grow on stalks 1 to 3 feet tall. Wheatlike spikes produce seeds from May to September. These seeds may survive in the soil for up to 4 years, but most germinate in the spring within 2 years. The underground creeping rootstocks also send up new shoots, increasing the infestation. Quackgrass tolerates any type of soil. Its roots are very competitive, and crowd out desirable plants.

CONTROL: Hand-digging is not a practical solution, since any rootstock pieces left behind will generate new plants. Kill existing weeds in lawns, around trees and shrubs, and in nonplanted areas with ORTHO Kleenup Systemic Weed & Grass Killer or ORTHO Kleenup Ready-To-Use Weed & Grass Killer. Use an herbicide containing *eptam* or *trifluralin* to prevent quackgrass seedlings from becoming established in flower beds and landscaped areas. Apply in early spring 2 weeks before the last expected frost, or about the time the forsythia bloom. Patches of quackgrass can be killed by covering with black plastic sheeting for one year.

GERMAN VELVETGRASS
Holcus mollis

German velvetgrass is a perennial grassy weed. In unmowed areas, the stems grow 2 to 4 feet tall. In mowed areas, they grow flat, and root wherever their joints touch the soil. The 4 to 8-inch leaves are velvety and bright green. Seeds are produced from July to August on seedheads 2 to 4 inches long. They lie dormant in the soil over the winter, and germinate in the spring. Plants grow from vigorous, slender underground rootstocks. Velvetgrass thrives in damp areas with rich soil. Although mostly a problem in fields and along roadways and walkways, it can become established and unsightly in lawns.

CONTROL: Kill existing velvetgrass in walkways and lawns and around trees, shrubs, and flower beds with an herbicide containing *glyphosate*. Treat any time the plants are actively growing, but preferably before the seeds appear.

BERMUDAGRASS
Cynodon dactylon

This perennial grass is also called *devilgrass*, *wiregrass*, or *dog's tooth grass*. It is adapted to areas where the ground does not freeze. Its vigorous creeping habit makes it a weed that invades lawns, flower and landscaped beds, and nonplanted areas where it crowds out desirable plants. The leaf blades are ⅛ inch wide and attached to slightly hairy, gray-green stems. The leaves are not cold tolerant, and turn brown when the temperature falls below 50°F. Seeds are formed on 3 to 7 short, fingerlike segments that are about 3 inches across and grow taller than the stems. The vigorous roots may grow several feet deep making the plants drought and heat tolerant, and also difficult to eliminate. Bermudagrass reproduces by seeds, stems, and underground stems. It prefers sandy soil, and will not grow in dense shade.

CONTROL: To control Bermudagrass in non-Bermudagrass lawns, see page 311. To control Bermudagrass around trees and shrubs, flower beds, and nonplanted areas, use ORTHO Kleenup Systemic Weed & Grass Killer or ORTHO Kleenup Ready-To-Use Weed & Grass Killer. Apply any time the plants are actively growing. A treatment in the early fall about 2 to 3 weeks before the first killing frost is very effective. Treat again in the spring as soon as plants are noticed. Repeated treatments are usually necessary because of the tough, extensive rhizomes. Hand-digging is not effective; any pieces left behind will sprout into new plants.

Crabgrass.

Nimblewill.

Dallisgrass.

CRABGRASS
Digitaria species

Crabgrass is one of the most troublesome weeds in yards throughout the country. Although it is known to most gardeners as a lawn weed, it is frequently found in flower and vegetable gardens and growing in cracks in sidewalks and driveways. In some areas of the country crabgrass is called *fingergrass* or *crowfootgrass*. This annual grassy weed grows in most soils, but prefers light, sandy areas. Crabgrass is most troublesome in hot, dry weather. The pale, bluish green blades are 2 to 5 inches long and 1/3 inch wide. They may be slightly hairy. Stems root at the lower joints. Seed heads 4 to 5 inches across grow from the center of the plant from July to October. The seeds remain dormant over the winter, then sprout in the spring. The tops of the plants are killed by the first frost in the fall. Plants grow in broad, flat clumps that crowd out desirable plants.

CONTROL: To control crabgrass in lawns, see page 312. Around trees and shrubs, and in flower beds and nonplanted areas, kill existing weeds with ORTHO Kleenup Systemic Weed & Grass Killer or ORTHO Spot Weed & Grass Control. Prevent crabgrass from sprouting around trees and shrubs with ORTHO Casoron Granules. In flower and vegetable gardens and around trees and shrubs, prevent crabgrass with ORTHO Garden Weed Preventer. Apply the preventive measures in the early spring about 2 weeks before the last expected frost, or about the time the forsythia bloom. The many fibrous roots make this weed difficult to remove by digging.

NIMBLEWILL
Muhlenbergia schreberi

The leaves of this perennial grass are flat, smooth, bluish green, and 1/2 to 2 inches long. The wiry stems grow up to 10 inches tall, first outward, then upward from the central crown. The stems root at the lower nodes, increasing the size of the plant. Seeds are produced on inconspicuous spikes from August to October. The seeds lie dormant in the soil for the winter, and sprout in late spring. Plants develop a shallow root system. Plant tops turn whitish tan and become dormant with the first killing frost in the fall. They begin growth again late the following spring. This warm-season grass invades moist lawns, gardens, and nonplanted areas with rich, gravelly soil.

CONTROL: Eliminate nimblewill in lawns with an herbicide containing *DSMA*. Around trees and shrubs and in flower beds and nonplanted areas, kill existing weeds with ORTHO Kleenup Systemic Weed & Grass Killer, ORTHO Kleenup Ready-To-Use Weed & Grass Killer, or ORTHO Spot Weed & Grass Control. Nimblewill is easiest to kill when it is a seedling, from late spring to early summer. In vegetable gardens, remove the weeds by hand-digging.

DALLISGRASS
Paspalum dilatatum

The coarse leaves of this perennial grass are 1/2 inch wide and 4 to 10 inches long. Stems 2 to 6 inches long radiate from the center of the plant in a star pattern. Plants grow in spreading clumps with deep roots. Seeds are produced on 3 to 5 fingerlike segments that grow from May to October from the top of the stems. Silken hairs cover the seeds, which lie dormant over the winter, and sprout very early in the spring. Dallisgrass also reproduces by underground stems. Dallisgrass grows across the southern states in lawns, gardens, and fields. It prefers moist soil, but will tolerate any type of soil. It grows most vigorously in warm summer weather.

CONTROL: Treat actively growing clumps of dallisgrass with ORTHO Crab Grass Killer in spring or summer. Repeated treatments are often necessary, since dallisgrass has deep roots. In landscaped beds and nonplanted areas, treat with an herbicide containing *glyphosate*. Patches of dallisgrass can also be killed by covering with black plastic sheeting for one year.

Goosegrass.

GOOSEGRASS
Eleusine indica

This annual grassy weed is also called *silver crabgrass* or *yardgrass*. Goosegrass is frequently confused with crabgrass, but it is darker green, does not root at the stem joints, and germinates later in the spring. (For more information on crabgrass, see page 827.) Goosegrass stems are smooth and flat, forming a rosette that resembles the spokes of a wheel. The leaf blades are 1/8 inch wide and 2 to 10 inches long. Seeds are produced on stalks 2 to 6 inches tall from July to October. The seeds fall to the soil, remain dormant over the winter, and sprout in the spring. The plants are killed in the fall by the first frost. Goosegrass has an extensive root system, and grows in lawns, gardens, and cracks in walkways where the soil is compacted and low in fertility.

CONTROL: Eliminate existing goosegrass in lawns by spot treating with ORTHO Kleenup Ready-To-Use Weed & Grass Killer. Around trees and shrubs and in nonplanted areas, kill existing weeds with ORTHO Spot Weed & Grass Control or ORTHO Kleenup Ready-To-Use Weed & Grass Killer. Prevent goosegrass in vegetable and flower gardens and lawns and around trees and shrubs with ORTHO Garden Weed Preventer. Apply to the soil before the plants sprout in early spring. Where appropriate, reduce the soil compaction as outlined on page 900. Improve soil fertility with regular fertilization.

Fall panicum.

FALL PANICUM
Panicum dichotomiflorum

This grassy annual is also known as *spreading* or *smooth witchgrass*. The rough leaves, 4 to 8 inches long, have a prominent midrib. The stems grow 1 to 4 feet tall, and root wherever the nodes touch the soil. Seeds are produced from June to October on gray-brown panicles that grow 4 to 10 inches long on the tips of the stems. When mature, the panicles break off and tumble about, scattering the seeds. The seeds do not sprout until the following spring. Fall panicum thrives in moist soil in fields and waste places and along roadways and stream banks.

CONTROL: Kill existing weeds with an herbicide containing *glyphosate*. Prevent the seeds from germinating throughout the yard with ORTHO Garden Weed Preventer. Apply in early spring about 2 weeks before the last expected frost, or when the forsythia bloom. Fall panicum has shallow roots and can be hand-pulled or hoed.

Johnsongrass.

JOHNSONGRASS
Sorghum halepense

Also called *Egyptiangrass*, this persistent perennial plant is a serious problem in the South. The roots may penetrate 3 to 6 feet into loose, rich soil. The stems grow 1 to 6 feet tall, and frequently root at their lower nodes, forming dense clusters that crowd out desirable plants. The leaves grow 1 to 2 feet long and up to 1 inch wide, with a conspicuous greenish white midvein. Hairy purple seedheads, from 4 to 16 inches long, appear on the ends of the stems from June to October. The reddish brown seeds germinate in the spring. New plants also sprout from creeping rootstocks. Johnsongrass is commonly found in areas with rich, moist soil along roadways and in fields, lawns, landscaped beds, and nonplanted areas.

CONTROL: Johnsongrass is difficult to control because of its extensive rootstocks. To eliminate the weeds in landscaped beds and nonplanted areas and to spot treat in lawns, use ORTHO Kleenup Systemic Weed & Grass Killer. Repeated treatments may be necessary if new growth appears. To prevent seeds from sprouting, use ORTHO Garden Weed Preventer. Apply to the soil in the spring about the time of the last frost, or 2 weeks after the forsythia bloom. Hand-pulling is not a practical solution, since new plants will sprout from any rootstocks left in the soil.

Barnyardgrass.

BARNYARDGRASS

Echinochloa crus-galli

Also called *cockspurgrass* or *watergrass*, this annual has upright, reddish purple stems that grow 1 to 4 feet tall. When mowed in lawns, the stems grow close to the ground. The large, smooth leaves are ¼ to ½ inch wide with a prominent midvein. Plants develop deep, fibrous root systems. Seeds are produced on 6 to 8 segments on the stems from July to September. One plant may produce as many as 40,000 seeds. The seeds fall to the soil, remain dormant over the winter, and sprout the following year in early summer. Barnyardgrass is a troublesome weed from midsummer to midfall. It thrives in lawns, gardens, and nonplanted areas with rich, moist soil.

CONTROL: To control barnyardgrass in lawns, see page 313. Kill existing weeds around trees and shrubs and in nonplanted areas with an herbicide containing *glyphosate*. Plants can also be handpulled. To prevent barnyardgrass from becoming established, treat the soil with ORTHO Garden Weed Preventer. Apply in early spring before the plants sprout.

Sandbur.

SANDBUR

Cenchrus species

Sandbur, also called *burgrass* or *sandburgrass*, is an annual grass that grows 6 inches to 2 feet tall. The narrow, yellow-green leaf blades are ¼ inch wide and 2 to 5 inches long. They may be rough on the upper surface. The blades are attached to flattened stems that may grow upright or spread along the soil. Plants have shallow, fibrous roots, and when growing in mowed lawns, they form low mats. From July to September, seeds are produced inside the spiny, ½-inch, straw-colored burs that are formed on the stems. Each bur contains only 2 seeds, but one plant may produce as many as 1000 seeds. Seeds are spread to new areas when the burs cling to clothing and animals. The seeds germinate in the spring. Sandbur is most troublesome in orchards, vineyards, fields, and lawns with light, sandy, well-drained soils.

CONTROL: In lawns, kill sandbur by spot treating with ORTHO Kleenup Systemic Weed & Grass Killer. Also use around trees and shrubs and in flower beds and nonplanted areas. For best results, treat in early to midsummer before burs and seeds are produced. Prevent sandbur from returning to these areas by applying a pre-emergence herbicide containing *trifluralin* or *eptam* in early spring. Plants can be removed by hand if handled carefully with gloves.

Foxtails.

FOXTAILS

Setaria species

Foxtails, sometimes called *bristlegrass* or *pigeongrass*, are summer annual grasses that grow 1 to 2 feet tall. In a mowed lawn, they will form low mats. The leaves are flat, sometimes twisted, ¼ to ½ inch wide, and 2 to 6 inches long. Spikelets consisting of 5 to 20 bristles, 2 to 4 inches long, appear from July to September. The bristle resembles a fox's tail, hence the name. The bristles contain seeds that sprout from midspring to early summer. Foxtails grow in clumps and are often mistaken for crabgrass, but form smaller clumps than crabgrass. (For information on crabgrass, see page 827.) Foxtails are found in yards with rich soil bordering fields, roadways, and other unmaintained areas.

CONTROL: Spot treat in lawns with ORTHO Kleenup Ready-To-Use Weed & Grass Killer. Around trees and shrubs and in flower beds and nonplanted areas, use ORTHO Kleenup Ready-To-Use Weed & Grass Killer or ORTHO Spot Weed & Grass Control to kill existing weeds. To prevent foxtails in lawns and flower and vegetable gardens and around trees and shrubs, apply ORTHO Garden Weed Preventer in early spring 2 weeks before the last expected frost, or about the time the forsythia bloom. Plants can also be successfully removed by hand.

GRASSLIKE WEEDS

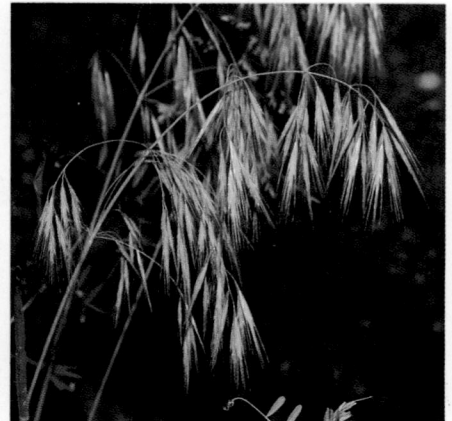

Downy brome.

DOWNY BROME
Bromus tectorum

This annual grass is also known as *bromegrass*, *cheatgrass*, or *military grass*. The smooth stems grow ½ to 2 feet tall with fibrous, shallow roots. The light green leaves are 2 to 6 inches long and covered with soft hairs. Drooping purple panicles appear from April to May. The seeds they produce mature in May and June, and germinate in the fall or early spring. They may remain viable in the soil for more than 2 years. The plants turn purplish tan when mature. When dry, they are a fire hazard, burning very rapidly and creating intense heat. Downy brome is most troublesome in areas with dry, sandy, or gravelly soil.

CONTROL: Kill existing weeds with ORTHO Kleenup Systemic Weed & Grass Killer. Apply any time the plants are actively growing, but preferably right after they sprout in the fall or early spring. To keep downy brome from returning, apply an herbicide containing *trifluralin*, *eptam*, or *DCPA* to the soil before the seeds sprout. Downy brome can also be removed by hand-pulling.

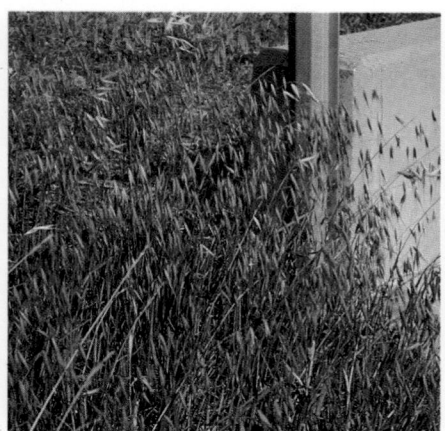

Wild oats.

WILD OATS
Avena fatua

Also called *wheat oats* or *oatgrass*, this annual grassy weed has smooth stems that grow 1 to 4 feet tall. The leaves are ¼ inch wide and 3 to 8 inches long, with hairs along the margins. The extensive, fibrous roots make the plants somewhat drought tolerant. Seeds are produced from June to October on 1-inch spikelets in 6 to 10-inch panicles. The seeds may lie dormant in the soil for several years before sprouting in the fall or spring. Plants are very conspicuous when they turn yellow in early or midsummer, while surrounding plants remain green. This weed tolerates many types of soil. It is found most frequently in fields and along roadsides, occasionally invading neighboring yards.

CONTROL: Kill existing plants around trees and shrubs and in flower beds and nonplanted areas with ORTHO Spot Weed & Grass Control or ORTHO Contax Weed & Grass Killer. Prevent seeds from germinating in lawns, flower beds, and around trees and shrubs with an herbicide containing *eptam* or *simazine*. Apply in the fall or early spring.

Wild iris.

WILD IRIS
Iris species

Wild irises closely resemble the cultivated irises grown in home gardens. They grow slowly in clumps from underground, tightly gnarled rootstocks. The plants grow ½ to 1½ feet tall with sword-like bright green leaves. Yellow to purple flowers bloom from spring through summer. The petals are marked with very conspicuous veins. Wild irises are most notable for gracing meadows, hillsides, and woodlands with their delicate flowers. However, in some situations they may become noxious. Wild irises that grow along the edges of ponds and lakes may gradually creep into the water, reducing water flow and flora and fauna habitats. The dense clumps of wild iris may be a nuisance when an uncultivated area is being reclaimed for cultivated gardens or lawns.

CONTROL: Spot treat individual plants or clumps of wild iris with an herbicide containing *dalapon* or *2,4-D*. Apply when the plants just begin to bloom. Cover all the foliage thoroughly. Avoid contaminating any nearby bodies of water. Clumps of wild iris may be hand-dug, although new plants will sprout from any rootstocks left in the soil. Because the rootstocks grow in tight groups, the entire clump can be removed with some effort.

RUSHES

Wild onion.

Nutsedge.

Bulrush.

WILD GARLIC AND WILD ONION
Allium vineale and *A. canadense*

These perennial weeds grow from underground bulbs. They are easily recognized by the garlic or onion odor of their crushed leaves. The slender, hollow leaves grow 10 to 15 inches tall. Greenish purple or white flowers bloom from May to July. Although they produce seeds in the spring that germinate in the fall, they reproduce mostly by bulbs and bulblets formed in the summer. In addition to the bulbs that are formed underground, tiny bulblets that look like leaves are formed at the tips of the flower stalks. Some of the new bulbs germinate in the fall; others can remain dormant in the soil for a year or two before germination. Wild garlic and onion thrive in heavy soil, and tolerate wet soil. They are hardy to both cold and drought. They spread rapidly and are difficult to control.

CONTROL: In the lawn, control these weeds with ORTHO Weed-B-Gon Lawn Weed Killer or ORTHO Chickweed, Spurge & Oxalis Killer D. Around trees and shrubs and in flower beds, spot treat with ORTHO Weed-B-Gon Jet Weeder. Treat as soon as the leaves emerge in the spring, or any time the plants are actively growing. Because dormant bulbs sprout at different times of the year, it will probably be necessary to repeat the treatments for the next 2 or 3 years. Hand-digging is impractical, since any bulbs left behind will sprout into new plants.

NUTSEDGES
Cyperus species

The two most common nutsedges troublesome as weeds are *yellow nutsedge* (*Cyperus esculentus*) and *purple nutsedge* (*C. rotundus*). Purple nutsedge is primarily a problem in the southeastern United States and in coastal California. Yellow nutsedge is found throughout the United States. These perennials are also called *nutgrass*, *cocosedge*, or *cocograss*. There are also some annual nutsedges that are troublesome in the southeastern United States. Nutsedges prefer poorly drained, rich soil. They thrive in frequently watered garden areas. Nutsedges are particularly noticeable in lawns in the summer, when they grow more quickly than the mowed grass and stand above it. The grasslike, yellow-green leaves grow on erect triangular stems. Seed heads are purple or yellow, appearing from July to October. Nutsedges reproduce by seeds, underground stems, and nutlike tubers. The tubers store food and are drought tolerant.

CONTROL: To control nutsedges in lawns, see page 314. To control existing plants around trees and shrubs and in flower beds and nonplanted areas, use ORTHO Kleenup Ready-To-Use Weed & Grass Killer. Treat as soon as the plants are noticed, preferably before seed heads appear. Nutsedges are difficult to control, so repeated treatments may be necessary. To control nutsedge seeds as they germinate around trees and shrubs and in flower beds, use an herbicide containing *eptam* in the mid to late spring. Hand-pulling is not practical, since any tubers left behind will sprout into new plants.

BULRUSH
Scirpus species

These perennials, also called *tule* or *meadow rush*, grow from thick tubers, underground rhizomes, or seeds. Olive green, round stems grow 3 to 9 feet tall. Clusters of reddish brown spikelets grow on the tips of the stems from June to October. Seeds produced on these spikelets germinate in the spring and rapidly grow into mature plants. There are several different kinds of bulrush, but all grow in moist, marshy ground in swamps and shallow water and along shores. They are troublesome in cranberry bogs, rice fields, and ornamental ponds. Many cultures use bulrush stems to build small boats and to weave mats.

CONTROL: Treat established plants with an herbicide containing *2,4-D* in the spring before the spikelets appear. Spot treat the stems of individual plants, being careful not to contaminate any surrounding water. Repeated treatments, 3 to 4 weeks apart, are necessary because of the thick rootstocks. Hand-dig young bulrushes before the fleshy tubers or rhizomes form. Or if possible, dry out the area and cultivate to expose and dry the tubers.

Cattails.

Horsetail.

Bracken.

COMMON CATTAIL
Typha latifolia

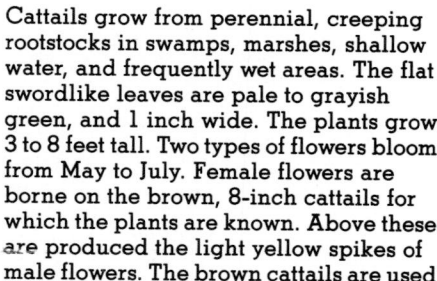

Cattails grow from perennial, creeping rootstocks in swamps, marshes, shallow water, and frequently wet areas. The flat swordlike leaves are pale to grayish green, and 1 inch wide. The plants grow 3 to 8 feet tall. Two types of flowers bloom from May to July. Female flowers are borne on the brown, 8-inch cattails for which the plants are known. Above these are produced the light yellow spikes of male flowers. The brown cattails are used in dried flower arrangements, and by the redwing blackbird in making its nest. Before using freshly picked cattails in flower arrangements, dry in a well-ventilated area to avoid odors.

CONTROL: Cattails are difficult to control because of their vigorous creeping roots. Hand-pulling is not practical because any pieces of root left behind will sprout into new plants. For top kill, use an herbicide containing *diquat*. Apply before the cattails are fully developed. Repeated treatments are necessary to kill the regrowth. For complete elimination of cattails, treat the plants with an herbicide containing *aminotriazole* or *dalapon*, from after the cattails are formed until frost. Do not use around water used for drinking, swimming, irrigation, or washing, or if fish are present. Repeated treatments may be necessary if the plants are firmly established and re-growth occurs.

HORSETAIL
Equisetum species

Horsetail is a perennial that grows in wooded areas, roadsides, and stream banks with wet, sandy, or gravelly soil. Two types of stalks — branched and unbranched — grow from the deep, thick rootstocks. The unbranched stalks, topped by cones, appear from April to May. The cones, 1 to 4 inches long, are filled with pale green to yellowish spores. Horsetail reproduces from these spores, as well as from the rootstocks. After the spores mature, these stalks die. From late spring until fall, jointed hollow stalks grow 1 to 3 feet tall. Branches 4 to 6 inches long grow in whorls at the joints on the stalks. These stems are killed by the first frost in the fall. Food is stored in the thick roots to enable the plant to survive under adverse growing conditions.

CONTROL: There are no chemicals that are effective against existing horsetail plants. Dig out the roots, being careful to get them all; any pieces of root or rootstock left in the ground will resprout. Or, if possible, cover the area with a sheet of black plastic for a full year. This will starve the horsetail by preventing light from reaching it. Prevent the spores from germinating in landscaped beds by applying ORTHO Casoron Granules or an herbicide containing *dichlobenil* in the late spring as the unbranched stalks die.

BRACKEN
Pteridium species

Bracken, also known as *brake fern*, is a nonbunching fern that grows from rootstocks that may extend up to 20 feet in the soil. The fronds grow 1 to 4 feet tall directly from the roots. Plants are usually found in clusters or colonies since new plants sprout from the creeping rootstocks. Light brown spores are produced along the margin on the undersides of the fronds. The spores mature in late summer, lie dormant over the winter, and sprout the following spring. Bracken prefers dry, sandy, acid soils in woodlands, pastures, and fields. It sometimes creeps into home gardens from these surrounding areas.

CONTROL: Kill existing bracken with an herbicide containing *glyphosate* any time the plants are actively growing. Hand-pull young bracken. Be sure to get all the rootstocks, as any pieces left behind will sprout into new plants.

BROADLEAF WEEDS

Moss and liverworts.

Virginia peppergrass.

Klamath weed.

MOSSES AND LIVERWORTS

Most mosses grow only an inch or two tall. A mat of moss actually consists of thousands of minute plants with stems and leaves. They attach themselves to the soil and absorb nutrients through thread-like *rhizoids*. They reproduce by spores instead of by seeds. The best-known of the mosses may be *sphagnum moss*, which grows in bogs in the northern United States and southern Canada, and is used as a soil amendment. *Liverworts* grow in thin, lobed sheets along the ground. Each is only 1 to 2 inches long. They fork at the base, and grow in several different directions. Liverworts are sometimes added to aquariums as hiding places for young fish. Both mosses and liverworts are exacting in their growing conditions. They need moist, shady areas with acid soil. In cultivated gardens and lawns, they are an indication of poor fertility and drainage.

CONTROL: Remove mosses and liverworts by hand-raking. Reduce shade by pruning nearby trees. Improve soil fertility with regular fertilization, and follow the guidelines on page 901 to improve soil drainage. Correct pH if necessary (see page 902). Large patches of moss not easily removed by raking may be removed by ''burning'' with *ferrous ammonium sulfate*. Apply to damp moss in early spring. Surrounding lawn grass may darken for about a week.

VIRGINIA PEPPERGRASS
Lepidium virginicum

This annual grass, also known as *bird's pepper* or *tonguegrass*, grows 1 to 2 feet tall with slightly hairy, branched stems. The blades are toothed and 1 to 3 inches long. Very small white flowers with greenish petals bloom from May to November. They produce seeds in ½-inch reddish yellow pods. Seedpods and flowers are usually present on the plant at the same time. Peppergrass is usually found along roadsides and in waste places and fields. It grows in most soils, but is more troublesome in dry areas. In home gardens, it frequently sprouts in landscaped beds, lawns, and cracks in walkways.

CONTROL: Eliminate peppergrass in lawns with ORTHO Chickweed, Spurge & Oxalis Killer D. Treat when the plants are actively growing in the spring or early summer, preferably before the flowers and seedpods appear. To prevent peppergrass seeds from germinating in landscaped beds, use a pre-emergence herbicide containing *diphenamid*. Apply to the soil in early spring about the time of the last expected frost, or when the forsythia bloom. In nonplanted areas, kill existing weeds with an herbicide containing *aminotriazole* and *linuron*. Treat in the spring when the plants are actively growing. Peppergrass plants have shallow roots and can be hand-pulled.

KLAMATH WEED
Hypericum perforatum

Klamath weed, also known as *St. Johns-wort*, is a perennial that produces by seeds and short runners. These horizontal stems grow from the crown of the plant out along the soil or just below it. The roots grow deep in the soil. The main upright stems are branched, and grow 1 to 2 feet tall. The ½ to 1-inch-long, oblong leaves are marked with clear dots. From June to September, flowers ¾ inch in diameter bloom and produce seeds. The flowers are orange-yellow with black dots along the edges of the petals. Black fruit capsules are evident from late summer into the fall. Each contains several seeds that lie dormant over the winter, and sprout in the spring. The tops of the plants die back to the ground in cold weather. Klamath weed is poisonous to livestock that graze on it. It prefers dry, sandy, or gravelly soil in fields and pastures and along roadways. In home gardens, it may become established in landscaped beds and unmaintained areas.

CONTROL: Around trees and shrubs and in flower beds, nonplanted areas, and lawns, kill existing weeds with an herbicide containing *glyphosate*. Repeated applications are often necessary because of this plant's deep root system.

BROADLEAF WEEDS

Wild mustard.

Russian thistle.

Spanishneedles.

WILD MUSTARD
Brassica kaber

Wild mustard is an annual also known as *field mustard* or *charlock*. The erect stems grow 1 to 3 feet tall, and have bristly hairs at their base. The upper portion is branched. The lower leaves are irregularly lobed or toothed, and the upper leaves are oval. From May to August, yellow clusters of flowers bloom and produce seeds. Severely infested fields appear completely yellow. Seeds lie dormant in the soil for 1 or more years, germinating in the spring or fall. Although primarily troublesome in grain fields in the Midwest, wild mustard may also occur in home gardens throughout the country.

CONTROL: In lawns, kill existing weeds with ORTHO Chickweed & Clover Control or ORTHO Chickweed, Spurge & Oxalis Killer D. Treat any time the plants are actively growing, but preferably before they bloom and produce seeds. Around trees and shrubs, prevent the seeds from sprouting with ORTHO Casoron Granules. Apply in early fall or in early spring before the seeds germinate. Wild mustard has a shallow root system, and can be removed by hand-pulling or hoeing.

RUSSIAN THISTLE
Salsola kali var. tenuifolia

A native of eastern Europe, this annual is also known as *tumbleweed*. The plants grow ½ to 3 feet tall with reddish, spreading, or erect stems. The leaves on seedlings and younger plants are fleshy and cylindrical. As the leaves mature they drop, and stiff, narrow leaves ending in a spike appear. From July to October, greenish flowers bloom and produce seeds throughout the plant. Each plant produces thousands of seeds. When the plants mature in early fall, they break off at the soil line and tumble about, distributing the seeds. Russian thistle prefers areas with dry soil along roadways, fields, and unmaintained areas. It is a host to the beet leafhopper, which spreads *curly top*, a plant disease.

CONTROL: Eliminate Russian thistle in lawns with ORTHO Weed-B-Gon Lawn Weed Killer. Spot treat in nonplanted areas with ORTHO Contax Weed & Grass Killer. To prevent seeds from germinating around trees and shrubs and in flower beds, use a pre-emergence weed killer containing *trifluralin*. Apply to the soil in the spring about the time of the last frost, or 2 weeks after the forsythia bloom.

SPANISHNEEDLES
Bidens bipinnata

Spanishneedles, also known as *cuckold*, is a summer annual. The stems grow erect 1 to 5 feet tall, with the upper portion branched. Leaves are smooth, segmented, and 4 to 8 inches long. From July to October, flowers with yellow centers and white petals bloom on the ends of leafless branches. They produce ½-inch long, brown to black seeds with spines and bristles. These seeds lie dormant in the soil over the winter, sprouting in the spring. The plants are killed with the first frost in the fall. Spanishneedles grows in moist or wet places and in areas with sandy soil. Although native to fields and woodlots, it is occasionally found in yards and gardens.

CONTROL: Plants have somewhat shallow roots, and can be hand-pulled. Around trees and shrubs and in lawns, prevent Spanishneedles with a pre-emergence herbicide containing *simazine*. Apply to the soil 2 weeks before the last expected frost, or about the time the forsythia bloom.

Puncturevine.

Redstem filaree.

Wild carrot.

PUNCTUREVINE
Tribulus terrestris

Puncturevine, also called *caltrop* or *ground burnut*, is an annual weed found in dry sandy areas. The prostrate stems branch from the crown of the plant, forming dense mats that crowd out desirable plants. The stems grow 6 to 8 feet long, and may twine up buildings and fences. Oblong leaves, 1 to 2 inches long, consist of 5 to 8 pairs of oval leaflets. Both the stems and the leaves are covered with silken hairs, giving the plants a silvery appearance. Small yellow flowers bloom in the leaf axils from June to September. They open only in the morning on clear days. They are followed by pods consisting of five ¼-inch spiny burs. When the burs mature, they separate and fall to the soil, where they may lie for several years before germinating. The burs are able to puncture shoe leather and bicycle and automobile tires. They not only injure animals by sticking in their feet, but also adhere to their fur, and are spread from place to place. The plant develops from a short taproot that branches into many fine rootlets, enabling it to survive periods of drought.

CONTROL: Treat puncturevine plants around trees, shrubs, and buildings and in nonplanted areas with ORTHO Kleenup Systemic Weed & Grass Killer. (For best results, treat before burs are produced.) To prevent seedlings from becoming established, apply a pre-emergence herbicide containing *trifluralin* or *dichlobenil* to the soil before seedlings emerge.

REDSTEM FILAREE
Erodium cicutarium

Redstem filaree is a low-growing spreading annual or biennial with stems 3 to 12 inches long and fernlike, dark green leaves, ½ to 4 inches long. Both the stems and leaves are hairy. Plants form a rosette, especially when young. Rose-purple clusters of flowers bloom and produce seeds from April to June. Because the seeds are inside capsules with one long pointed end, resembling a crane's beak, this plant is also known as *cranesbill* or *storksbill*. When mature, the capsules fall to the soil. In alternately moist and dry weather, the beaks coil and uncoil, gradually planting themselves. Seeds sprout in the fall, or remain dormant until the following spring. Redstem filaree thrives in dry soil. It is most commonly found in lawns, but also occurs in landscaped beds and cracks in walkways.

CONTROL: To kill existing weeds around trees and shrubs and in flower beds and nonplanted areas, use ORTHO Kleenup Systemic Weed & Grass Killer. In lawns, use an herbicide containing *2,4-D.* For best results, treat in the spring before the flowers appear and produce seeds. Prevent redstem filaree from returning by using a pre-emergence herbicide containing *trifluralin* or *DCPA.* Apply to the soil in early fall or spring before seeds sprout. Keep redstem filaree from returning to the lawn by increasing the lawn's fertility. Follow the fertilization guidelines on page 295. Redstem filaree can be hand-pulled or hoed when small.

WILD CARROT
Daucus carota

Wild carrot, also called *Queen Anne's lace* or *bird's nest plant*, is a biennial that grows in a rosette the first year. The second year, hollow, branching stems grow 2 to 3 feet high. The fleshy, carrot-shaped root is not edible. The finely dissected leaves give the plant a lacy appearance. Flat-tipped clusters of white or pinkish flowers bloom and produce seeds from May to October. The seeds lie dormant in the soil over the winter, and sprout in early spring. At the end of the second year, the entire plant is killed by the first frost in the fall. Wild carrot prefers dry soil in fields and meadows and along roadways. It is occasionally found in landscaped beds and lawns.

CONTROL: Kill existing weeds in landscaped beds and in nonplanted and unmaintained areas with ORTHO Kleenup Ready-To-Use Weed & Grass Killer. Treat any time the plants are actively growing, but preferably before they bloom. In lawns, treat wild carrot with ORTHO Weed-B-Gon Lawn Weed Killer in the spring and fall. Young plants can be hand-pulled or hoed.

BROADLEAF WEEDS

Common yarrow.

Cudweed.

Pineappleweed.

COMMON YARROW
Achillea millefolium

Common yarrow, also called *milfoil*, is a perennial that grows 1 to 3 feet tall. If it occurs in mowed lawns, it forms a rosette. The fernlike leaves are covered with fine gray hairs, and are aromatic when crushed. The flattened flower heads are white or yellow, and bloom and produce seeds from June to November. It reproduces by creeping underground rootstocks as well as by seeds. Yarrow flowers are sometimes dried and used in flower arrangements. Some other species of *Achillea* are valued as ornamental perennials. Yarrow is most common in gardens bordering roadways, fields, and vacant lots, and thrives in poor, dry soil where few plants can survive.

CONTROL: Eliminate yarrow in lawns with ORTHO Weed-B-Gon Lawn Weed Killer or ORTHO Chickweed, Spurge & Oxalis Killer D. Treat any time the plants are actively growing, from spring to fall. In flower beds and vegetable gardens and around trees and shrubs, dig the plants while still young before flowers bloom and seeds form.

CUDWEED
Gnaphalium species

Cudweed, also called *fragrant everlasting* or *cotton batting plant*, is an annual or biennial. The stems branch at their base and grow ½ to 2 feet tall. They are woolly-white, and fragrant when rubbed. The lance-shaped leaves are also fragrant and woolly on the underside. The top is smooth and dark green. Tubular white, tan, or purple flowers bloom and produce seeds in August and September. They appear at the ends of the branches and in the axils of the upper leaves. Seeds lie dormant in the soil over the winter, sprouting in the cool, moist spring weather. They grow slowly in the summer heat, resuming normal growth in late summer until the first killing frost in the fall. Cudweed grows in moist or dry soil. It is most commonly found along roadways and in fields and wooded lots, but may appear in lawns and landscaped beds.

CONTROL: Use ORTHO Kleenup Ready-To-Use Weed & Grass Killer to control existing cudweed around trees and shrubs in flower beds and nonplanted areas, and for spot treating in lawns. Treat any time the plants are actively growing, but preferably in the spring before they bloom and produce seeds. For overall lawn treatment, use ORTHO Weed-B-Gon For Southern Grasses or an herbicide containing *2,4-D* and *dicamba*. Treat in the spring when the plants are growing most rapidly.

PINEAPPLEWEED
Matricaria matricarioides

The stems and leaves of this annual have a pleasant pineapple fragrance when crushed. Many stems, 6 to 18 inches tall, grow from the base of the plant. The finely dissected leaves grow 1 to 4 inches long. Greenish yellow, ¼-inch flowers bloom at the ends of the branches from May to September. The seeds they produce do not sprout until early the following spring. Pineappleweed grows along roadsides, in fields, waste places, and sometimes in landscaped beds. It tolerates many types of soil, and frequently grows where other plants do not survive.

CONTROL: Treat young plants (1 to 3 inches tall) with ORTHO Contax Weed & Grass Killer. To kill established plants around trees and shrubs, in flower beds and unplanted areas, and to spot treat in lawns, use an herbicide containing *glyphosate*. Use ORTHO Casoron Granules to prevent pineappleweed seeds from sprouting around trees and shrubs. Apply in the early spring about 2 weeks before the last expected frost, or when the forsythia bloom. Regular mowing will help control pineappleweed in lawns. The plants have shallow roots, and can be hand-pulled or hoed, especially when young.

Mayweed.

Prostrate knotweed.

Common chickweed.

MAYWEED
Anthemis cotula

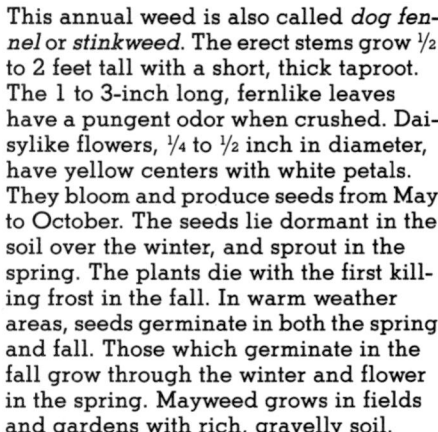

This annual weed is also called *dog fennel* or *stinkweed*. The erect stems grow ½ to 2 feet tall with a short, thick taproot. The 1 to 3-inch long, fernlike leaves have a pungent odor when crushed. Daisylike flowers, ¼ to ½ inch in diameter, have yellow centers with white petals. They bloom and produce seeds from May to October. The seeds lie dormant in the soil over the winter, and sprout in the spring. The plants die with the first killing frost in the fall. In warm weather areas, seeds germinate in both the spring and fall. Those which germinate in the fall grow through the winter and flower in the spring. Mayweed grows in fields and gardens with rich, gravelly soil.

CONTROL: Eliminate mayweed by spot treating around trees and shrubs in lawns, around trees and flower beds, and nonplanted areas with ORTHO Kleenup Systemic Weed & Grass Killer. Treat any time the plants are actively growing, but preferably before they flower and produce seeds. Plants can be hoed or hand-pulled.

PROSTRATE KNOTWEED
Polygonum aviculare

This annual weed is also called *knotgrass*, *doorweed*, and *matgrass*. It grows in areas with compacted, infertile soil, such as driveways, dirt walkways, and recreation areas where the soil and grass are heavily trampled. Oval, bluish green leaves, 1 inch long and ¼ inch wide, are attached to the stems at swollen joints. Very tiny greenish white flowers bloom and produce seeds at the leaf and stem joints from June to November. The seeds produced by these flowers remain dormant over the winter and germinate in the spring as the soil warms. Prostrate knotweed grows low to the ground, forming dense wiry mats up to 2 feet in diameter that crowd out desirable plants.

CONTROL: For overall treatment in lawns, use ORTHO Weed-B-Gon Lawn Weed Killer. Spot treat with ORTHO Weed-B-Gon Jet Weeder. To help prevent knotweed in the lawn, maintain a vigorous turf by following the guidelines beginning on page 294. Around trees and shrubs kill existing weeds with ORTHO Kleenup Systemic Weed & Grass Killer. Or prevent the weeds in the early spring with ORTHO Casoron Granules. Cultivating is also helpful. In driveways, walkways, and other nonplanted areas, use ORTHO Kleenup Systemic Weed & Grass Killer. Prevent knotweed in flower and vegetable gardens with an herbicide containing *trifluralin*, applied in the spring before the weeds germinate. Knotweed may also be hand-pulled or hoed.

COMMON CHICKWEED
Stellaria media

This weed, also called *starwort*, *satin flower*, or *starweed*, prefers damp, shady areas with rich cultivated soil. Common chickweed is a winter annual that grows from seeds that sprout in the fall. It grows vigorously in cool wet weather, forming a dense mat that crowds out desirable plants. The ½ to 2-inch heart-shaped leaves are attached to the stems by a slightly hairy stalk. Fine white hairs grow in a single line on one side of the stem. The creeping stems root at their joints wherever they touch the soil. Small, white, starlike flowers bloom in clusters on the ends of the stems from March to December. In mild winter areas they bloom and produce seeds throughout the winter. Seeds are carried by birds and by the wind.

CONTROL: In lawns, control chickweed with ORTHO Weed-B-Gon Lawn Weed Killer, ORTHO Chickweed & Clover Control, or ORTHO Chickweed, Spurge & Oxalis Killer D. To help prevent chickweed in lawns, maintain a vigorous turf by following the guidelines beginning on page 294. Around trees and shrubs, and in nonplanted areas, kill existing weeds with ORTHO Kleenup Systemic Weed & Grass Killer. Apply these herbicides to actively growing plants in the early spring or late fall just after they have sprouted. Cultivating is also helpful. Prevent weeds from returning around trees and shrubs with ORTHO Casoron Granules. Prevent chickweed in vegetable gardens and flower gardens with ORTHO Garden Weed Preventer. Apply in the fall before the seeds sprout.

BROADLEAF WEEDS

Creeping veronica.

Florida pusley.

Purslane.

CREEPING VERONICA
Veronica filiformis

Creeping veronica, also called *speed-well*, is a perennial weed that prefers acid soil in moist, shady garden areas. It is found in sunny areas if the soil remains moist. Areas that are well fertilized, well drained, and get lots of sunlight are not invaded by this weed. Creeping veronica was originally used as a rock garden plant, but over the years has become a nuisance by invading lawns and flower beds. Oval bright green leaves with scalloped edges are paired opposite each other on low-growing creeping stems. Tiny white flowers with blue or lavender edges bloom from May to July. Seeds are produced in heart-shaped pods. The seeds seldom mature, so the plant does not reproduce from them. The creeping stems, however, root easily wherever the stem joints touch the soil. Pieces of stem cut and distributed by lawn mowers also root to start new plants. If uncontrolled, veronica can cover an entire lawn or flower bed within a few years. However, it does not completely crowd out other plants.

CONTROL: Creeping veronica is difficult to control. In lawns, treat with ORTHO Chickweed, Spurge & Oxalis Killer D or ORTHO Weed-B-Gon Lawn Weed Killer. In landscaped beds and flower beds, treat in the spring or early fall with an herbicide containing *DCPA*. Veronica dies slowly, so repeated applications may be necessary. Veronica can also be hand-pulled, removing all parts of the plant so new plants do not emerge.

FLORIDA PUSLEY
Richardia scabra

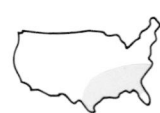

This annual is also known as *Florida purslane* or *Mexican clover*. The hairy stems grow 4 to 12 inches tall, and are tinged with red. The leaves are oblong, 1 to 3 inches long, and are also hairy. Star-like white flowers bloom in the leaf axils at the ends of the branches from May to September. The seeds produced by these flowers do not germinate until the following spring. Florida pusley thrives in sandy soils in the warm southern states. This weed hugs the ground, forming dense patches that crowd out desirable plants, especially lawn grasses. It also grows in landscaped beds and cracks in walkways.

CONTROL: In lawns, eliminate Florida pusley with ORTHO Weed-B-Gon Lawn Weed Killer or ORTHO Weed-B-Gon For Southern Grasses. Use ORTHO Kleenup Systemic Weed & Grass Killer to kill existing weeds around trees and shrubs, in nonplanted areas, and to spot treat in lawns. Treat when the weeds are actively growing. For best results, apply before the plants flower and produce seeds for the following year. To prevent Florida pusley seeds from germinating throughout the yard, apply ORTHO Garden Weed Preventer to the soil in early spring, 2 weeks before the last expected frost, or when the forsythia bloom. Florida pusley has shallow roots and can be hand-pulled or hoed.

PURSLANE
Portulaca oleracea

Purslane, also called *wild portulaca* or *pusley*, is a particularly troublesome weed in vegetable and flower gardens. This summer annual thrives in hot, dry weather and is seldom found in the spring when gardeners are controlling other weeds. Leaves are ½ to 1½ inches long, rubbery, and wedge-shaped. Small yellow flowers open only in full sunlight from midsummer to frost. The seeds may remain viable in the soil for many years, and will sprout in warm weather when brought to the surface during plowing or cultivating. The thick reddish brown stems grow vigorously, forming a thick mat and rooting wherever they touch the soil. The stems and leaves store water that enables purslane to survive drought periods, and to grow in cracks in sidewalks and driveways. Plants pulled and allowed to lie on the soil will reroot. Plants are killed by the first frost in the fall.

CONTROL: In lawns, control purslane with ORTHO Weed-B-Gon Lawn Weed Killer, ORTHO Weed-B-Gon For Southern Grasses, or spot treat with ORTHO Weed-B-Gon Jet Weeder. To help prevent purslane in the lawn, maintain a vigorous turf by following the guidelines beginning on page 294. Kill existing weeds around trees and shrubs and in driveways and flower beds with ORTHO Kleenup Systemic Weed & Grass Killer. Keep weeds from returning around trees and shrubs with ORTHO Casoron Granules. Prevent weeds from sprouting in vegetable and flower gardens with ORTHO Garden Weed Preventer. Purslane may also be hand-pulled. Remove the plants from the garden.

Spotted spurge.

Mouseear chickweed.

Lippia.

SPOTTED SPURGE

Euphorbia maculata

This annual weed, also called *milk purslane*, thrives in infertile soil and in sandy, poorly maintained areas. It is often found in lawns and shrub beds, and in cracks in walkways and driveways. Spurge is a low-growing plant that may form dense mats up to 2 feet in diameter. Leaves are oval, ¼ to ¾ inch long, and pale to dark green with a purple smudge. The slender reddish stems ooze a milky white sap when broken. The sap may irritate the skin. Pinkish white flowers bloom and produce seeds from May to October. Many of the seeds remain dormant over the winter and sprout the following spring. Some sprout immediately. Plants may complete one generation within 2 weeks. They die with the first frost in the fall.

CONTROL: For overall lawn treatment, use ORTHO Weed-B-Gon Lawn Weed Killer or ORTHO Chickweed, Spurge & Oxalis Killer D. Kill existing weeds around trees and shrubs and in walkways and driveways with ORTHO Kleenup Systemic Weed & Grass Killer. Treat any time the plants are actively growing in the spring and summer. Do not treat in the fall, since the plants will be killed anyway by the first frost. Prevent seeds from germinating in lawns, flower beds, and landscaped beds with an herbicide containing *DCPA*. ORTHO Casoron Granules can also be used to prevent the seeds from sprouting around trees and shrubs. These shallow-rooted plants can also be hand-pulled or hoed. Because spotted spurge forms seeds when only 2 weeks old, it is especially important to follow a regular control program.

MOUSEEAR CHICKWEED

Cerastium vulgatum

This perennial weed is troublesome throughout the United States in lawns, vegetable and flower gardens, around trees and shrubs, and in nonplanted areas. It thrives in full sunlight on wet, infertile soil. The hairy leaves are ½ inch long and lance-shaped. Starlike white flowers bloom and produce seeds from April to October. These low-growing plants root easily wherever their stem joints touch the soil, starting new plants. Seeds germinate throughout the growing season, rapidly increasing the number of plants. Dense mats of mouseear chickweed crowd out desirable plants.

CONTROL: For overall lawn treatment use ORTHO Weed-B-Gon Lawn Weed Killer when plants are actively growing in the early spring and fall. Or spot treat with ORTHO Weed-B-Gon Jet Weeder. Around trees and shrubs, and in flower beds, kill existing weeds with ORTHO Kleenup Systemic Weed & Grass Killer or ORTHO Spot Weed & Grass Control. To prevent mouseear chickweed seeds from germinating around trees and shrubs, use ORTHO Casoron Granules. Mouseear chickweed is difficult to control, so repeated treatments may be necessary. These shallow-rooted plants can also be hand-pulled or hoed, but be sure to remove all parts of the plants so they do not resprout.

LIPPIA
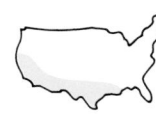
Phyla nodiflora

This perennial, also known as *matchweed* or *matgrass*, is used in hot, dry areas as a groundcover or lawn substitute. The creeping stems grow 1 to 3 feet long, and root wherever their nodes touch the soil, forming dense mats that crowd out desirable plants. Lippia has wedge-shaped, slightly hairy leaves up to 1¾ inches long. The edges are toothed. Bees are attracted to the white or pink flowers that bloom on oblong heads from late spring through early summer. In the sun, lippia grows 1 to 2 inches tall; in the shade, it grows up to 6 inches tall. Lippia grows vigorously, creeping from its planted areas into surrounding non-lippia areas.

CONTROL: In lawns, eliminate lippia with ORTHO Weed-B-Gon Lawn Weed Killer. In landscaped beds and noncrop areas, treat with an herbicide containing *glyphosate*. Apply in the spring or fall. The plants have shallow roots, and can also be hand-pulled.

Dichondra.

Oxalis.

Black medic.

DICHONDRA
Dichondra repens

This popular grass substitute in the South and West sometimes becomes a weed when it creeps into nondichondra lawns and landscaped beds. Dichondra is a broadleafed perennial with heart-shaped, rounded leaves ¼ to ½ inch in diameter. The leaves are attached to the stems opposite each other. The creeping stems root wherever the nodes touch the soil. Inconspicuous flowers produce seeds that may remain in the soil for many years before sprouting. Dichondra will not grow where temperatures fall below 25°F. It grows in both sun and shade, but prefers fertile soil in areas that are watered frequently. Dichondra seldom grows in areas that are not maintained.

CONTROL: Eliminate dichondra in nondichondra lawns with ORTHO Weed-B-Gon Lawn Weed Killer or ORTHO Weed-B-Gon For Southern Grasses. Treat any time the plants are actively growing. Dichondra has shallow roots, and can be removed by hand in landscaped beds and other areas.

OXALIS
Oxalis species

Some oxalis are grown for ornamental purposes, but two, *Oxalis stricta* and *O. corniculata*, are common weeds throughout the yard and in greenhouses. Also called *yellow woodsorrel* or *sourgrass*, these perennials grow most commonly in well-maintained areas. The pale green or purple leaves are divided into 3 heart-shaped leaflets, like clover leaves. The leaflets usually close up at night. Small, bright yellow flowers, ½ inch long with 5 petals, bloom from May to September. Cucumber-shaped light green seed pods develop from the fading flowers. When the pods dry, a light touch causes them to explode, shooting their seeds several feet in all directions. The seeds germinate throughout the growing season. Plants grow 4 to 12 inches tall. Although the stems root wherever they touch the soil, new plants do not form at these spots. Oxalis leaves contain oxalic acid, which gives them a sour taste.

CONTROL: In lawns, treat oxalis with ORTHO Chickweed, Spurge & Oxalis Killer D or ORTHO Weed-B-Gon Lawn Weed Killer. Around trees and shrubs, flower beds, driveways, and other non-planted areas, kill the weeds with ORTHO Kleenup Systemic Weed & Grass Killer or ORTHO Spot Weed & Grass Control. Treat weeds when they are actively growing in the spring or late summer to fall. The late summer to fall application is the most effective. Oxalis is not easy to kill, so several treatments may be necessary. Oxalis can also be hand-pulled or hoed if it is done before rooting occurs on stems.

BLACK MEDIC
Medicago lupulina

Black medic, sometimes called *black clover* or *trefoil*, is frequently confused with clover. The low-growing, hairy, trailing stems of this summer or winter annual form dense mats that crowd out desirable plants. The stems do not root where they touch the soil. Cloverlike leaves grow in threes on the stems. Small bright yellow flowers bloom and produce seeds in black, kidney-shaped pods from May to September. In warm-weather areas, blooming may last until December. Seeds lie dormant in the soil, sprouting in the spring, and, in warm-weather areas, also in the fall. Black medic grows in lawns with low nitrogen fertility, in gardens, and in cracks in sidewalks and driveways.

CONTROL: Eliminate black medic in lawns with ORTHO Chickweed, Spurge & Oxalis Killer D, ORTHO Weed-B-Gon Lawn Weed Killer, or ORTHO Weed-B-Gon For Southern Grasses. Treat from late spring to early summer or midfall when the weeds are actively growing, and preferably before seeds form. In landscaped beds and nonplanted areas, kill existing weeds with ORTHO Kleenup Systemic Weed & Grass Killer. Prevent black medic from becoming established by mulching landscaped beds as discussed on page 918. Where appropriate, improve the nitrogen fertility with regular fertilization, thus reducing black medic invasion. Black medic can also be hand-pulled.

Ground ivy.

Lawn pennywort.

Mallow.

GROUND IVY
Glechoma hederacea

Ground ivy, a perennial, is also called *creeping ivy, creeping charlie,* and *gill-over-the-ground.* It was originally planted in many areas as a shade tolerant ground cover, but has since become a nuisance, invading lawns and landscaped areas. Rounded, scalloped leaves, about the size of a nickel or quarter, grow opposite each other on creeping stems. Light blue to purple flowers, ½ to ¾ inch long, bloom and produce seeds from April to July. These seeds germinate as soon as they ripen. Ground ivy also reproduces by the creeping stems that root wherever they touch the soil. It has shallow roots and forms a dense mat, crowding out desirable plants. Ground ivy prefers damp, shady areas with rich soil, but may also grow in the sun.

CONTROL: Control ground ivy in the lawn with ORTHO Weed-B-Gon Lawn Weed Killer or spot treat with ORTHO Weed-B-Gon Jet Weeder. Around trees and shrubs and nonplanted areas, use an herbicide containing *glyphosate.* Treat any time the plants are actively growing, but preferably in the spring when the leaves are still tender. If ground ivy has grown into a dense mat, annual treatments may be necessary for the next 2 to 3 years. Although ground ivy has shallow roots, hand-pulling is not a practical solution. Any pieces of stem left behind in the soil will sprout into new plants.

LAWN PENNYWORT
Hydrocotyle sibthorpioides

Lawn pennywort is a member of the parsley family. It is a perennial that has bright green, ½ inch, rounded leaves with wavy margins. Small white flowers bloom from July to August. The creeping stems root wherever their nodes touch the soil, increasing the number of plants. If not controlled, pennywort can form dense mats that crowd out desirable plants. Pennywort grows in moist, shady lawns, gardens, and nonplanted areas. It is frequently mistaken for ground ivy (previous column). Some gardeners prefer to allow pennywort to grow as a shade-tolerant groundcover rather than try to eliminate it.

CONTROL: In lawns, control pennywort with ORTHO Weed-B-Gon Lawn Weed Killer or spot treat with ORTHO Weed-B-Gon Jet Weeder. Around trees and shrubs and in flower beds and nonplanted areas, kill existing weeds with ORTHO Kleenup Systemic Weed & Grass Killer. Treat weeds any time they are actively growing, from late spring to fall. In vegetable gardens, remove weeds by hand-digging. Be careful to remove all the stem pieces so they do not resprout into new plants.

MALLOW
Malva species

These weeds, also called *cheeseweed, cheeses,* or *musk plant,* are found in lawns, fields, vacant lots, and landscaped beds throughout the country. They are annuals, or — in warmer climates — biennials. Although mallow tolerates all types of soil, it prefers infertile, poorly maintained areas. The hairy stems grow from several inches to a foot or more in length. They may grow from close to the soil to 3 to 6 feet tall. The taproot is straight and deep. The hairy, round, heart-shaped leaves are ½ to 5 inches wide. The edges are slightly lobed. From April to October, flowers with 5 white to lavender petals bloom at the leaf and stem joints. Mallow reproduces by seeds that remain dormant in the soil over the winter and germinate in the spring. The plants are killed by the first frost in the fall. In warmer climates, the plant survives the winter and grows and flowers a second year.

CONTROL: In lawns, eliminate mallow with ORTHO Weed-B-Gon Lawn Weed Killer or ORTHO Chickweed, Spurge & Oxalis Killer D. Or spot treat individual plants with ORTHO Kleenup Systemic Weed & Grass Killer. Around trees and shrubs and in flower beds and nonplanted areas, treat existing weeds with ORTHO Kleenup Systemic Weed & Grass Killer. Treat with these herbicides from midspring to early summer when the plants are still young, and before they produce flowers and seeds for next year's generation. Follow the lawn maintenance guidelines beginning on page 294 to help prevent mallow from becoming established in the lawn.

WEEDS

BROADLEAF WEEDS ────────────────────────────────

Prickly lettuce.

Curly dock.

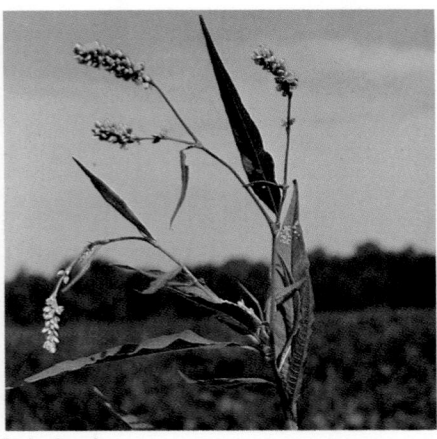

Ladysthumb.

PRICKLY LETTUCE
Lactuca serriola

Prickly lettuce, also known as *wild lettuce*, is an annual or biennial. Pale green or straw-colored stems grow 1½ to 6 feet tall. The lower part is covered with prickly spines. The lower leaves are 2 to 12 inches long and lobed, with prickly edges. The upper leaves are short, elongated, and lobed or prickly toothed. Both kinds of leaves are bluish green with prickles on the midrib. A milky sap oozes from the leaves and taproot when they are broken. Prickly lettuce reproduces by seeds that are formed on flowers that bloom from July to September. These yellow flowers are ⅓ inch in diameter and bloom at the ends of the lateral stems. When the seeds are mature, they fall to the soil and either sprout in the fall or, in colder areas, the following spring. Prickly lettuce prefers areas with dry or light soil, and is troublesome along roadways and in fields, walkways, and unmaintained areas.

CONTROL: Control this weed in lawns with ORTHO Chickweed, Spurge & Oxalis Killer D. Around trees and shrubs, in flower beds and nonplanted areas, and to spot treat in lawns, use ORTHO Kleenup Ready-To-Use Weed & Grass Killer. Apply either herbicide when the plants are actively growing, preferably before they bloom and produce seeds.

CURLY DOCK
Rumex crispus

Curly dock, a persistent perennial, is also called *sour dock* or *yellow dock*. Plants may be found anywhere in the yard, except in the shade. Curly dock prefers wet, low areas with heavy soil. The curly leaves, which form a rosette, are 6 to 12 inches long and reddish green. A 2 to 3-foot stalk with green to brown flowers grows from June to September. The flowers turn dark brown and dry and cling to the stalk. Seeds produced by these flowers fall to the soil and remain dormant over the winter, sprouting in the spring and summer. The plant tops are killed in the fall by the first frost. The thick, yellow taproot is drought resistant and very difficult to dig from the soil. It remains dormant over the winter and resprouts in the spring. Once curly dock is established, it is very difficult to eliminate.

CONTROL: To control curly dock in the lawn, use ORTHO Weed-B-Gon Lawn Weed Killer. Or spot treat individual plants with ORTHO Kleenup Systemic Weed & Grass Killer. Around trees and shrubs and in flower gardens and nonplanted areas, kill existing weeds with ORTHO Kleenup Systemic Weed & Grass Killer. Hand-digging is not practical, since any root pieces left behind will resprout into new plants.

LADYSTHUMB
Polygonum persicaria

Ladysthumb, also known as *spotted smartweed*, prefers moist soil. It is usually found growing in waste places and fields, and along roadways. It may occur in lawns, as well as in landscaped beds and cracks in walkways. The smooth stems grow 6 inches to 3 feet tall. The narrow leaves are pointed at both ends, and have a peppery taste. They are marked in the middle with a triangular purple spot. Tiny pink flowers bloom on 1-inch spikes from July to October. The seeds they produce lie dormant in the soil over the winter, sprouting in the spring.

CONTROL: Eliminate ladysthumb in lawns with ORTHO Weed-B-Gon Lawn Weed Killer. Around trees and shrubs, in flower beds and nonplanted areas, and to spot treat in lawns, use ORTHO Kleenup Ready-To-Use Weed & Grass Killer. Treat any time the plants are actively growing, but preferably before they flower and produce seeds for next year. To prevent seeds from germinating around trees and shrubs, apply ORTHO Casoron Granules to the soil just after the last expected frost in the spring, or 2 weeks after the forsythia bloom. This weed has shallow roots, and can be hand-pulled or hoed.

Broadleaf plantain.

Ragweed.

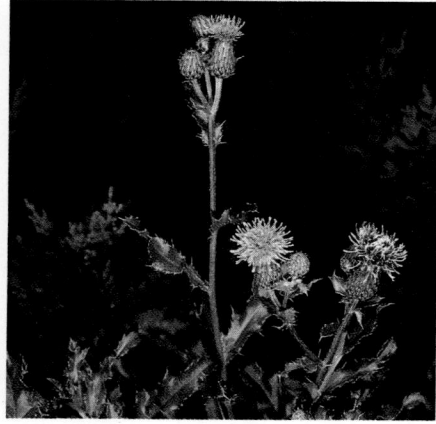

Canada thistle.

PLANTAINS
Plantago species

The two most common plantains that invade landscaped areas are *buckhorn plantain* (P. *lanceolata*) and *broadleaf plantain* (P. *major*). These are perennial weeds that grow in all kinds of soil, but prefer rich, moderately moist areas. The lance-shaped leaves of buckhorn plantain are 4 to 12 inches long, with 3 to 5 prominent veins in each leaf. White flower spikes 4 to 12 inches tall appear from May to October. Broadleaf plantain has oval leaves, 2 to 10 inches long, with 5 to 7 veins per leaf. Greenish white flower spikes, 2 to 10 inches tall, appear from May to September. The plantains reproduce from seeds formed on the flower spikes through the summer and fall. Seeds remain dormant over the winter and germinate the following spring. New plants also sprout from the perennial roots throughout the growing season. These ground-hugging, rosette-shaped plants suffocate desirable plants as they increase in size.

CONTROL: Control plantains in lawns with ORTHO Weed-B-Gon Lawn Weed Killer or ORTHO Weed-B-Gon For Southern Grasses. Spot treat lawns with ORTHO Weed-B-Gon Jet Weeder. Around trees and shrubs and in flower beds, driveways, and nonplanted areas, use ORTHO Kleenup Systemic Weed & Grass Killer or ORTHO Spot Weed & Grass Control. Treat in the spring or fall when the plants are actively growing. Repeated applications are often necessary.

RAGWEED
Ambrosia species

This group of both annual and perennial plants is responsible for the agony of hay fever sufferers in late summer and fall. Ragweeds may also be called *wild tansy* or *hogweed*. The hairy stems grow 1 to 6 feet tall with shallow roots. The fernlike smooth leaves are 2 to 4 inches long. Two kinds of flowers bloom from August to September. The greenish male flowers appear at the tips of the stems and produce vast quantities of pollen. The female flowers are less noticeable, since they bloom in the axils of the leaves. The seeds produced by the female flowers lie dormant for the winter, to sprout in the spring. Ragweed tolerates many types of soil, and is found most commonly in fields and vacant lots and along roadways.

CONTROL: Eliminate ragweed in lawns with ORTHO Weed-B-Gon Lawn Weed Killer, ORTHO Chickweed & Clover Control, or ORTHO Chickweed, Spurge & Oxalis Killer D. Around trees and shrubs and in flower beds and nonplanted areas, kill existing weeds with ORTHO Kleenup Systemic Weed & Grass Control. Treat ragweed any time it is actively growing. For best results, treat by midsummer, before the flowers open and produce seeds. Plants have shallow roots, and can be hand-pulled.

CANADA THISTLE
Cirsium arvense

Also known as *creeping thistle*, this perennial is adapted only to cool climates. The slender, prickly stems grow 1 to 4 feet tall. The prickly leaves have smooth upper surfaces, with woolly undersides. They are lobed and 4 to 8 inches long. Small purple, rose, or white flowers bloom from June to October. The seeds they produce are attached to a tuft of hairs that makes them readily windborne. Seeds germinate throughout the growing season, usually within 2 weeks from the time they mature and fall from the flower. The tops of the plants are killed in the fall by the first frost. The rootstocks grow horizontally through the soil, often up to 15 feet from the plant. New plants that sprout from the rootstocks grow rapidly, blooming in 7 to 8 weeks. Food stored in the roots enables the plants to survive extended droughts and other adverse growing conditions for several years. Canada thistle tolerates many types of soil, but is most troublesome in moist areas with rich, heavy soil. It is very competitive in fields and pastures.

CONTROL: Treat Canada thistle in lawns with ORTHO Weed-B-Gon Lawn Weed Killer in the spring and fall. Around trees and shrubs, in flower beds and nonplanted areas, and for spot treating in lawns, use ORTHO Kleenup Systemic Weed & Grass Killer. For best results, treat in the spring when the food reserves in the roots are low. Repeated treatments are necessary. Repetitive mowing or weekly hand-pulling gradually weakens the roots, eventually killing the plant.

Yellow starthistle.

Common groundsel.

Chicory.

YELLOW STARTHISTLE
Centaurea solstitialis

Yellow starthistle, also known as *Barnaby's thistle*, is an annual, or sometimes a biennial. The stems grow 1 to 3 feet tall, and branch at the base. Both the stems and the leaves are covered with a white, cottony fleece. The deeply lobed basal leaves are 2 to 3 inches long, and form a rosette. The upper leaves are narrow and ½ to 1 inch long. Small yellow tubular flowers grow at the ends of the branches. They bloom and produce seeds from May to the first killing frost in the fall. The seeds germinate readily throughout the growing season, and are spread by the wind. The sharp, ¼ to 1-inch spines at the base of the flowers make this plant injurious to livestock and people. Yellow starthistle is found in fields and vacant lots and along roadways.

CONTROL: In lawns, treat young plants with ORTHO Weed-B-Gon Lawn Weed Killer before spines form. Prevent weeds from becoming established in landscaped beds with a pre-emergence herbicide containing *dichlobenil*. Apply to the soil before any seedlings emerge. Hand-pull or hoe the plants when small, before they develop a long taproot.

COMMON GROUNDSEL
Senecio vulgaris

This annual, also known as *grimsel*, grows ½ to 1½ feet tall with hollow stems that may root at the lower nodes. The toothed leaves are 4 inches long. The lower leaves are attached to the stems by a short leafstalk, and the upper ones cling directly to the stems. From April to October, yellow flowers up to 1 inch in diameter bloom on the ends of the branches. The seeds they produce germinate in cool, moist weather. Common groundsel is most troublesome in the fall and spring. It prefers areas with moist, rich soil, and is found in fields, along roadways, and throughout home gardens.

CONTROL: To control this weed around trees and shrubs, in flower beds and non-planted areas, and to spot treat in lawns, use ORTHO Kleenup Systemic Weed & Grass Killer. Treat any time the plants are actively growing, but preferably soon after they germinate. To prevent the seeds from sprouting around trees and shrubs, apply ORTHO Casoron Granules to the soil in early fall and again in early spring. Hand-pull groundsel plants before they produce seeds.

CHICORY
Cichorium intybus

Chicory, also called *succory* or *blue daisy*, is a perennial weed along roadways, in fields, and occasionally in lawns. Although it tolerates most types of soil, it is most troublesome in areas with neutral or alkaline soil. Chicory reproduces by seeds and by a deep, fleshy taproot. Hollow stems grow erect 1 to 3 feet tall. In lawns, the leaves grow in a tight rosette. Stems and roots ooze a white milky juice when broken. The 3 to 8-inch basal leaves spread outward into a rosette. The oval upper leaves have toothed or smooth edges. Flowers bloom and produce seeds on the ends of the branches or in the axils of the upper leaves. Flowers appear from March to August, and are usually sky blue, but sometimes white, or rarely, pink. They open in the early morning, and close by midday. Roasted chicory root is used as a coffee substitute. Young leaves may be eaten fresh in salads or cooked as greens if they haven't been sprayed.

CONTROL: In lawns, control chicory with ORTHO Chickweed, Spurge & Oxalis Killer D. Treat in the spring or early fall. In nonplanted areas, kill existing weeds with ORTHO Contax Weed & Grass Killer. Repeated treatments may be necessary because of the deep taproot.

Red sorrel.

Dandelion.

Sowthistle.

RED SORREL
Rumex acetosella

This perennial weed is also called *sheep sorrel*, *field sorrel*, and *sour grass*. It prefers cool, moist weather, but thrives in dry, sandy soil in lawns and landscaped beds. It is frequently an indication of low nitrogen fertility and acid soil, but will survive in neutral or slightly alkaline soil. (For more information on soil acidity, see page 902.) The stems on this rosette-shaped plant grow 4 to 14 inches tall. The leaves are 1 to 4 inches long and arrow-shaped, with 2 lobes at the base of each leaf. Flowers bloom from May to September. The yellow male flowers are on separate plants from the red female flowers. Plant tops are killed by the first frost in the fall. The rootstocks and seeds remain dormant until spring. Red sorrel has a shallow but extensive root system. The plants reproduce by seeds and red underground rootstalks.

CONTROL: In lawns, treat red sorrel with ORTHO Weed-B-Gon Lawn Weed Killer in the spring or fall. To help prevent it in lawns, maintain a vigorous turf by following the guidelines beginning on page 294. There are no herbicides to kill existing weeds around trees, shrubs, and flower beds. To prevent seeds from sprouting in these areas, apply an herbicide containing *dichlobenil* in early spring before the seeds sprout. Red sorrel can be removed by cultivating or hand-pulling. Remove all the rootstocks, since any left behind will resprout. Test the soil pH (see page 903), and correct if necessary.

DANDELION
Taraxacum officinale

Dandelions are the most common and easily identified weed in the United States. They grow anywhere there is bare soil and full sunlight. They do, however, prefer wet soil, and may indicate overwatering or poor drainage. These rosette-shaped, perennial plants grow from thick fleshy taproots that may grow 2 to 3 feet deep in the soil. A white milky sap oozes from broken flower stems and leaves. The yellow flowers bloom from mid-spring until frost. In warm weather areas they bloom all year. As the flowers mature and ripen, they form white "puff-balls" containing seeds. The wind carries the seeds for miles to other lawns and bare spots of soil. The seeds sprout the following spring. The tops of the plants are killed in the fall by the first frost, but the taproot survives even the severest winters to resprout in the spring.

CONTROL: In lawns, control dandelions with ORTHO Weed-B-Gon Lawn Weed Killer, or spot treat with ORTHO Weed-B-Gon Jet Weeder. To help prevent dandelions in the lawn, maintain a vigorous turf by following the guidelines beginning on page 294. Around trees and shrubs and in flower beds and nonplanted areas, treat with ORTHO Kleenup Systemic Weed & Grass Killer or ORTHO Kleenup Ready-To-Use Weed & Grass Killer. Apply to actively growing plants, preferably before the seeds ripen. Hand-digging is impractical, since pieces of root that are broken off and left in the soil will sprout new plants.

SOWTHISTLE
Sonchus species

These annual weeds are found throughout the United States, but are most common in the South and along the West Coast. The reddish stems arise from a short taproot and grow upright 1 to 6 feet. In mowed lawns they form tight rosettes. A milky sap oozes from the stems when broken. The upper branches may be covered with hairs. From July to September, yellow flowers, 1/2 to 1 inch in diameter, bloom on branches at the top of the plants. In Florida, Texas, and California, the plants may germinate or bloom year round. The seeds these flowers produce are contained in brownish seedheads. They germinate either that fall, or the following spring. Sowthistles prefer rich soil along roadways and in fields, lawns, and landscaped beds.

CONTROL: Treat lawns with ORTHO Weed-B-Gon Lawn Weed Killer. To spot treat, use ORTHO Weed-B-Gon Jet Weeder. Or frequently mow off the flower stalks before they produce seeds. The plants will then be killed in the fall by frost. Around trees and shrubs and in nonplanted areas, use ORTHO Kleenup Systemic Weed & Grass Killer. Prevent sowthistle seedlings from becoming established in landscaped beds by applying a pre-emergence herbicide containing *dichlobenil* to the soil in early fall or early spring. Sowthistle can be hand-pulled, but wear gloves. The fine hairs are irritating.

Horseweed.

Shepherds purse.

Tansy ragwort.

HORSEWEED
Conyza canadensis

Horseweed is an annual plant that grows in dry soil in fields, along roadways, in lawns and landscaped beds, and in non-planted areas. It is also known as *flea-bane*, *mare's tail*, and *bitterweed*. The erect, bristly stems grow 1 to 4 feet tall, branching in the upper portion. In lawns, the stems form a rosette. The narrow, dark green leaves are covered with white bristles. Clusters of small yellow to white flowers bloom on the upper stems from July to October. The seeds they produce may blow long distances in the wind, then lie dormant in the soil over the winter, germinating in the early spring. The plants are killed by the first frost in the fall. Horseweed grows from a short taproot that can be hand-pulled or hoed.

CONTROL: Eliminate horseweed in lawns with ORTHO Weed-B-Gon Lawn Weed Killer. Apply in the spring and early summer. For best results, treat before the plants bloom and produce seed for next year. In nonplanted areas, treat existing weeds with ORTHO Contax Weed & Grass Killer. Hand-pull or hoe any plants growing in landscaped beds.

SHEPHERDS PURSE
Capsella bursa-pastoris

Shepherds purse, also called *lady's purse* or *shepherds bag*, is a common summer or winter annual. It grows in lawns, landscaped beds, nonplanted areas, and fields throughout the United States. It tolerates most types of soil, but will not grow in the shade. Lobed or toothed leaves form a rosette at the base of the plant. Arrow-shaped leaves and tiny white flowers grow on stems 3 to 18 inches tall. Flowers bloom and produce seeds in triangular pods from March to December. The seeds fall to the soil and may remain dormant for several years before germinating in the spring. The plants are killed in the fall by the first frost. In warm winter areas, seeds may germinate in the fall. The plants then grow through the winter until the fall. The triangular seed pods resemble purses once carried by shepherds; hence the name shepherds purse.

CONTROL: Eliminate shepherds purse in lawns with ORTHO Weed-B-Gon Lawn Weed Killer or ORTHO Chick-weed & Clover Control. Follow the lawn maintenance guidelines beginning on page 294. Treat when the weeds are actively growing. Around trees and shrubs, flower beds, and nonplanted areas, kill existing weeds with ORTHO Kleenup Ready-To-Use Weed & Grass Killer. Prevent this weed around trees and shrubs with ORTHO Casoron Granules. Apply in the early spring, or in warm winter areas in the early fall, before the weeds sprout. Shepherds purse can also be hand-pulled or hoed.

TANSY RAGWORT
Senecio jacobaea

Tansy ragwort is a prolific biennial or perennial that grows 1 to 4 feet tall and is most noticeable when the daisylike golden flowers bloom in late summer. The leaves are 5 to 9 inches long, and lobed with a full blade at the tip. Seeds produced by the flowers germinate in the fall into rosette-shaped plants. The first year, the plants remain rosettes. The second year, most plants blossom, produce seeds, and die. Sometimes the plants survive a third year, blossom again, and produce more seeds. Each plant may produce as many as 150,000 seeds, which remain viable in the soil for 3 or 4 years. Tansy ragwort survives most soil conditions. It is troublesome in fields and pastures and along roadways and unmaintained areas. It may be introduced into home gardens by windblown seeds or when straw contaminated by tansy ragwort is used for mulching. Several insects — including the cinnabar moth larvae — eat this weed, helping keep it under control.

CONTROL: Hand-pull tansy ragwort. If it is in bloom, cover with a plastic bag before you pull to keep the seeds from spreading. Or spray with an herbicide containing *2,4-D* and *dicamba*. Treat in early spring or midfall when the plants are rosettes. Plants in bloom are much more difficult to control, and repeated treatments are often necessary.

Milkweed.

Pigweed.

Mugwort.

MILKWEED
Asclepias syriaca

This perennial is also known as *silkweed* or *cottonweed*. The hairy, erect stems grow 2 to 5 feet tall. A milky sap oozes from the stems when broken. The 4 to 8-inch elliptical leaves are smooth on the upper surface; the lower surface is covered with white hairs. Young milkweed shoots resemble asparagus shoots. Plants reproduce from their thick creeping rootstocks, as well as from seeds. Clusters of fragrant, pinkish white flowers bloom from June to August. The milkweed plant is best known for its gray pods, 2 to 4 inches long, covered with soft spines. Evident in late summer and fall, the pods contain brown seeds with white silken hairs attached. When mature, they split open, releasing the seeds. The seeds lie dormant over the winter, sprouting in the spring. Milkweed usually grows in patches in rich, sandy, or gravelly loam soils in fields and along roadways. Because the seeds are windborne, it is occasionally found in flower and vegetable gardens.

CONTROL: Spot treat milkweed plants with an herbicide containing *aminotriazole*. Or pull plants while young before they develop extensive rootstocks. Plants will resprout from pieces of rootstock left behind.

PIGWEEDS
Amaranthus species

Members of the pigweed group are annuals that grow upright, except in mowed lawns, where they form mats. Leaves are oval to egg-shaped, and may be hairy. Flower spikes bloom and produce seeds from July to October. In one season, each plant may produce thousands of seeds, which sprout in the spring. Pigweeds prefer hot, dry weather and dry soil. They are found in fields and vacant lots, along roadways, and in lawns and gardens.

CONTROL: Control pigweeds in lawns with ORTHO Weed-B-Gon Lawn Weed Killer any time they are actively growing. In other areas, use ORTHO Kleenup Ready-To-Use Weed & Grass Killer. For best results, and to reduce the number of plants the following year, treat before flowers and seeds are produced. Prevent pigweeds around trees and shrubs, in flower and vegetable gardens, and in lawns with ORTHO Garden Weed Preventer. Apply to the soil 2 weeks before the last expected frost, or about the time the forsythia bloom. Pigweeds have shallow roots and can be removed by hand.

MUGWORT
Artemisia vulgaris

Mugwort, also called *chrysanthemum weed* or *wormwood*, is a perennial with underground creeping rootstocks and upright stems 3 to 6 feet high. The segmented leaves, green on the upper surface, and woolly-white on the lower surface, are 2 to 6 inches long and aromatic when crushed. From July to September, greenish yellow flower spikes bloom and produce seeds. Mugwort reproduces by these seeds, which germinate in the spring, and by the extensive rootstocks. It prefers limey soil and grows primarily in moist areas near streams, highways, and fields. In yards, mugwort often creeps from lawns into landscaped beds and sprouts in cracks in walkways.

CONTROL: Mugwort is difficult to control. Spot treat with an herbicide containing *aminotriazole*. To prevent seeds from germinating around trees and shrubs and in flower beds, use a pre-emergence herbicide containing *eptam*. Apply to the soil in the spring, 2 weeks before the last expected frost, or about the time the forsythia bloom. Hand-pulling is not effective, since any rootstock pieces left behind will sprout into new plants.

BROADLEAF WEEDS

Common lamb's-quarters.

Horsenettle.

Stinging nettle.

COMMON LAMB'S-QUARTERS
Chenopodium album

This annual is also known as *white pig-weed* or *white goosefoot*. The ridged stems are frequently lined with red or light green stripes. They grow 1 to 4 feet tall from a short, branched taproot. The wedge-shaped leaves are 1 to 3 inches long with toothed edges. The undersides of the leaves are covered with a white, mealy coating. At the ends of the branches and in the leaf axils, small green flowers bloom and produce seeds from June to October. The pollen from these flowers irritates hay fever sufferers. The seeds remain dormant over the winter, and sprout in the spring. The entire plant is killed by the first frost in the fall. Common lamb's-quarters is a trouble-some weed in cultivated fields and gardens. It is a major host for the beet leafhopper, which transmits *curly top*, a virus disease.

CONTROL: In lawns, eliminate lamb's-quarters with ORTHO Weed-B-Gon Lawn Weed Killer. Treat in the spring when the plants are young. Kill existing weeds around trees and shrubs and in flower beds and nonplanted areas with ORTHO Kleenup Systemic Weed & Grass Killer. Treat any time the plants are actively growing, but preferably before they bloom and produce seeds. Prevent the seeds from germinating in these areas as well as in vegetable gardens with ORTHO Garden Weed Preventer. Apply in the spring 2 weeks before the last expected frost, or about the time the forsythia bloom. Lamb's-quarters can also be hand-pulled or hoed.

HORSENETTLE
Solanum carolinense

Also called *bull nettle* or *Carolina nettle*, this perennial grows 1 to 3 feet tall. The stems, petioles, midribs, and veins of the leaves are prickled with yellow spines. Oval, 2 to 6-inch leaves with lobed or wavy margins are covered with fine hairs. Clusters of white to purple flowers that look like tomato flowers bloom from the sides of the stems from May to October. They are followed by ½ inch yellow-orange berries that are first smooth and later become wrinkled. New plants sprout from the seeds contained in these berries, as well as from the rootstocks. The berries and leaves are poisonous to humans and animals. Horsenettle thrives in areas with sandy, well-drained soil. It spreads 5 or more feet across, crowding out desirable plants.

CONTROL: Horsenettle has deep roots and is difficult to control. To kill existing weeds around trees and shrubs, in flower beds and nonplanted areas, and to spot treat lawns, use an herbicide containing *glyphosate*. Regular mowing will also control horsenettle in lawns. Hand-pulling is not practical, as any root pieces left behind will sprout into new plants. Contact your doctor or veterinarian if horsenettle berries or leaves are eaten.

STINGING NETTLE
Urtica dioica

Tiny hairs on stinging nettle cause welts or inflammations on the skin when touched. The 3 to 8-foot-tall stems and the leaves are covered with these sting-ing hairs. The irritation caused by contact with nettles usually heals in a day or so. The egg-shaped leaves are 5 inches long and 3 inches wide, with saw-toothed margins. Small greenish flowers bloom on clusters of spikes in the leaf axils from June to September. Stinging nettle grows in damp, rich soil. It is found along creeks, in waste places, on the edges of wooded lots, and occasionally in lawns, nonplanted areas, and landscaped beds. It reproduces by seeds and underground creeping rootstocks. A greenish yellow dye can be made from the upper part of the plant.

CONTROL: Spray nonplanted areas with ORTHO Contax Weed & Grass Killer. Repeated applications may be necessary to kill all the roots. Treat the plants any time they are growing actively, but pref-erably before they bloom. Prevent seeds from germinating in vegetable gardens with a pre-emergent herbicide contain-ing *trifluralin*. Apply to the soil in the early spring, about 2 weeks before the last expected frost, or when the forsythia are in bloom.

Field dodder.

Morning glory.

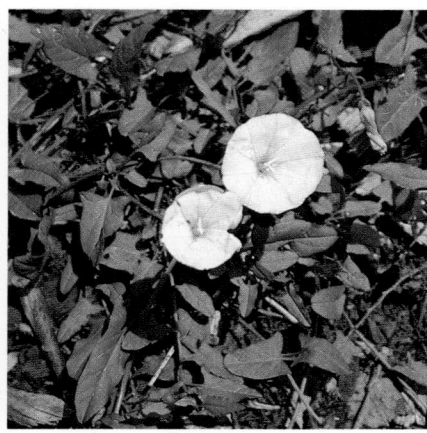

Field bindweed.

FIELD DODDER
Cuscuta campestris

This leafless, parasitic annual is also known as *strangleweed* or *devil's hair*. The threadlike, golden yellow stems twine and coil on other plants. Short suction-cup-like suckers then sprout along the undersides of the dodder stems, penetrating the stems of the host plant. Dodder obtains its nourishment through these suckers. The stems branch repeatedly, attacking additional host plants. White or creamy flowers, ¼ inch in diameter, bloom and produce seeds from April to October. The seeds may germinate that year, or lie dormant in the soil for many years before sprouting in the spring. The seeds germinate in the soil, but the roots die as soon as the dodder is attached to a host plant. Once attached, the dodder lives completely off its host plant. Dodder is killed in the fall by the first frost. It is found most commonly in pastures and fields where alfalfa has been grown. Occasionally it may be found living on herbaceous plants in the home garden.

CONTROL: Once dodder has attached itself to another plant, there is no way to remove it. Destroy infested host plants. Do not pull dodder off the plants, since any stem pieces left behind will continue to grow. Prevent the seeds from germinating with a pre-emergence herbicide containing *DCPA*. For best results, apply in early spring, about the time of the last expected frost, when the majority of dodder seeds sprout. Repeat the application in 6 to 8 weeks.

MORNING GLORY
Ipomoea species

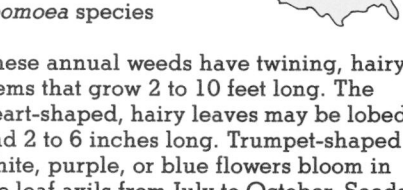

These annual weeds have twining, hairy stems that grow 2 to 10 feet long. The heart-shaped, hairy leaves may be lobed and 2 to 6 inches long. Trumpet-shaped white, purple, or blue flowers bloom in the leaf axils from July to October. Seeds are formed within bristly, brown, egg-shaped pods that adhere to clothing or animal fur and are carried to other areas. The seeds lie dormant in the soil over the winter, and germinate in the spring. The plants are killed in the fall by the first frost. Morning glories are found in fields and along roadsides. They may sprout anywhere in the yard, and frequently creep into yards from neighboring areas. They tolerate any type of soil, but are most troublesome in areas with sandy soil.

CONTROL: In lawns, control morning glories with ORTHO Weed-B-Gon Lawn Weed Killer. Treat in the spring and early summer when the plants are growing most actively. Kill existing weeds around trees and shrubs and in noncrop areas with ORTHO Kleenup Systemic Weed & Grass Killer. To prevent morning glory seeds from sprouting around trees and shrubs, use a pre-emergent herbicide containing *simazine* or *eptam*. Apply to the soil in the spring about the time of the last expected frost. Young plants can be hand-pulled or hoed.

FIELD BINDWEED
Convolvulus arvensis

Field bindweed, a troublesome perennial, is also called *wild morning glory* or *cornbind*. It grows in lawns and flower and vegetable gardens, and around trees and shrubs. The creeping, twining stems frequently invade yards from nearby roadways, fields, and vacant lots. Field bindweed thrives in rich, heavy soil. The stems may be 3 to 9 feet long with arrow-shaped leaves 1 to 2 inches long. White to pink funnel-shaped flowers, the size of a nickel, bloom and produce seed from May to September. Field bindweed is difficult to control because the roots may grow 15 to 20 feet deep in the soil. The roots store food and water so the plant can survive under adverse growing conditions. It reproduces by seeds and pieces of the root. The seeds may remain dormant in the soil for many years before sprouting. Any root pieces left behind after hand-pulling will sprout into new plants.

CONTROL: In lawns, control field bindweed with ORTHO Weed-B-Gon Lawn Weed Killer. Apply from late spring through early summer, or early to late fall. Around trees and shrubs and in flower beds and nonplanted areas, kill existing weeds with ORTHO Kleenup Systemic Weed & Grass Killer. Repeat the treatments as new growth emerges. In vegetable gardens, control this weed with an herbicide containing *trifluralin*. Apply in the spring before the plants emerge. Bindweed cannot be controlled by hand-pulling or hoeing.

BROADLEAF WEEDS

Japanese honeysuckle.

JAPANESE HONEYSUCKLE
Lonicera japonica

Japanese honeysuckle, a perennial woody vine, is best known for its fragrant flowers, which are used to scent soaps, perfumes, and bath oils. They are white, tinged with pink or yellow, and bloom in pairs in the upper leaf axils from April to November. The twining, climbing stems grow on valuable plants, strangling them. As the stems creep along the ground, they root wherever the nodes touch the soil. The oval leaves, 1 to 3 inches long, smooth on the upper surface and hairy below, frequently remain on the plant through the winter. Honeysuckle fruit, evident from September to November, are ¼-inch black berries that contain 2 or 3 seeds. The seeds sprout the following spring. New plants also sprout from underground rootstocks.

CONTROL: Control honeysuckle in lawns with an herbicide containing *2,4-D*, *dicamba*, and *mecoprop*. In landscaped beds and nonplanted areas, spot treat with an herbicide containing *glyphosate* or *aminotriazole*. Apply in mid to late summer when the plants will readily absorb the herbicide. Hand-pulling is not a practical solution, since any underground rootstocks left behind will sprout into new plants.

Nightshade.

NIGHTSHADES
Solanum species

This group of annual and perennial weeds includes *bitter nightshade* (*S. dulcamara*), *black nightshade* (*S. nigrum*), and *hairy nightshade* (*S. sarachoides*). Nightshades belong to the same family as tomatoes, potatoes, and eggplant. They grow in rich, moist soil and frequently creep into home gardens from surrounding fields, hedgerows, and unmaintained areas. The stems may grow up to 9 feet long, creeping along the ground or twining on fences and plants. The stems frequently root where they touch the soil. Dark green to purple leaves, 1 to 4 inches long, have varying shapes. They may be mitten-shaped, heart-shaped, or lobed at the base. Blue, violet, or white flowers with yellow centers resemble tomato flowers. They bloom from May to November. The flowers are followed by green berries, which turn red or black when ripe. The berries are very attractive to children and small pets, and are poisonous if eaten in quantity. The leaves are also poisonous. Yellow seeds inside the berries are often spread by birds, and sprout into new plants in the spring.

CONTROL: Spot treat around trees and shrubs and in noncrop areas with ORTHO Contax Weed & Grass Killer. Repeated treatments are often necessary because of the long, woody stems. Or hand-pull the vines, being careful not to drop any berries. Any pieces of stem left behind will sprout into new plants. If berries or leaves are eaten by children or pets, call your doctor or veterinarian promptly.

Florida betony.

FLORIDA BETONY
Stachys floridana

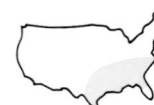

Also known as *rattlesnakeweed*, this perennial sprouts from white tubers that resemble the rattles on a rattlesnake. The 4-sided stems grow 6 to 20 inches tall. The elliptical leaves have saw-toothed edges. Trumpet-shaped white to lavender flowers bloom in the leaf axils from late spring to early summer. The seeds lie dormant through the summer, and sprout in the fall. New plants emerge from seeds and tubers in cool, moist fall weather. The plants grow and spread rapidly through the winter and spring until the heat of the summer, when the tops die. Florida betony is a nuisance in lawns and landscaped beds. If not controlled, it rapidly takes over large areas.

CONTROL: In lawns, use ORTHO Weed-B-Gon For Southern Grasses in the spring when the plants are rapidly growing. Kill existing weeds in landscaped beds and nonplanted areas with an herbicide containing *glyphosate*. To prevent seedlings from becoming established, apply a pre-emergence herbicide containing *dichlobenil* or *eptam* to the soil in September. Individual plants may be hand-dug before the tubers become large.

Carpetweed.

CARPETWEED
Mollugo verticillata

Also known as *Indian chickweed* or *whorled chickweed*, this annual weed's smooth, prostrate stems form circular mats up to 20 inches in diameter, crowding out desirable plants. Whorls of 5 to 6 leaves grow at each stem joint. Small white flowers bloom in the leaf axils from June to November. They produce orange-red, kidney-shaped seeds that lie dormant in the soil over the winter and sprout slowly in the spring. The plants develop a short taproot and grow rapidly in the summer heat. Carpetweed prefers fertile, dry sandy or gravelly soil in lawns and gardens and along walkways.

CONTROL: In lawns, treat with ORTHO Weed-B-Gon Lawn Weed Killer. Apply in early to midsummer when the plants are actively growing. Prevent seeds from germinating throughout the yard with ORTHO Garden Weed Preventer. Apply to the soil in midspring about the time of the last expected frost, or 2 weeks after the forsythia bloom. Carpetweed can be hand-pulled or hoed.

Douglas fiddleneck.

DOUGLAS FIDDLENECK
Amsinckia douglasiana

Douglas fiddleneck is also called *burweed* or *buckthorn*. The erect stems grow 1 to 4 feet tall and are covered with stiff white hairs. The lance-shaped leaves are also covered with white hairs. From May to July, 5 to 10-inch-long, orange to yellow flower spikes resembling a fiddle's neck bloom and produce seeds. The seeds germinate in the winter, and the plants mature in the summer. Douglas fiddleneck is common in fields and pastures and along roadways. It is occasionally found in yards bordering these areas.

CONTROL: Use ORTHO Kleenup Systemic Weed & Grass Killer to spot treat around trees and shrubs and in lawns, flower beds, and nonplanted areas. Apply any time the plants are actively growing. Plants have shallow roots and can be hand-pulled. Wear gloves so the spiny hairs don't prick the skin.

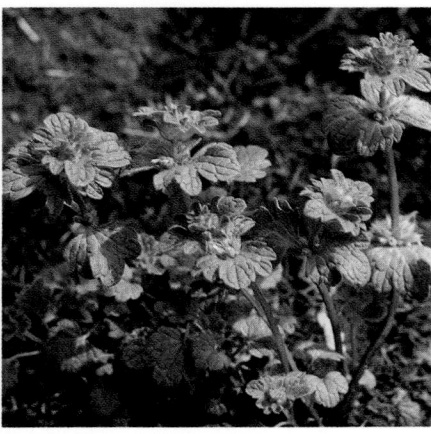

Henbit.

HENBIT
Lamium amplexicaule

This winter annual or biennial is also called *dead nettle* or *bee nettle*. It grows rapidly in early spring, fall, and winter in lawns and in landscaped beds with rich soil. Rounded, toothed leaves up to ¾ inch wide grow on creeping square stems. Lavender flowers, ½ inch in diameter, bloom and produce seeds from April to June and again in September. Seeds sprout in the fall. Henbit also reproduces by the creeping stems that root wherever they touch the soil.

CONTROL: In lawns, eliminate henbit with ORTHO Chickweed, Spurge & Oxalis Killer D. Or spot treat individual plants with ORTHO Weed-B-Gon Jet Weeder. Treat in the spring when henbit is actively growing. Around trees and shrubs and in flower beds, kill existing weeds with ORTHO Kleenup Ready-To-Use Weed & Grass Killer, or ORTHO Spot Weed & Grass Control. Around trees and shrubs, prevent henbit with ORTHO Casoron Granules. Apply it in the fall before the plants sprout. Follow the lawn maintenance guidelines beginning on page 294 to help keep henbit out of your lawn.

MUSHROOMS

Mushrooms.

WOODY WEEDS

Poison ivy berries.

Poison ivy.

MUSHROOMS

The folklore surrounding mushrooms has given them the additional name of *toadstool*. Some types are also known as *puffballs*. The mushroom is the aboveground fruiting or reproducing structure, the "flower," of a fungus that lives on and helps to decay organic matter in the soil. In wooded areas, some mushrooms live on the leaves that accumulate each year on the ground. Others may grow on the roots of trees and benefit both the trees and the mushrooms. Mushrooms thrive in warm, damp areas. They are seldom found in cool, dry spots. In cold winter areas, they disappear with the first frost, and return with wet spring weather. Spores are produced on the underside of the mushroom cap, and are spread by the wind. Some mushrooms are poisonous; identify them carefully before eating. Mushrooms growing in circles in lawns are called fairy rings. For more information on fairy rings, see page 309.

CONTROL: There is no practical way to eliminate mushrooms. When the buried organic matter is completely decayed, the mushrooms will disappear. For temporary control, break the mushrooms with a rake, or mow the lawn. For information on suppressing mushrooms in lawns, see page 321.

POISON IVY
Rhus radicans

This woody perennial may grow as a small shrub in full sunlight. The stems often grow up to 8 feet long, and may be 5 inches in diameter. The leaves have 3 leaflets, 2 to 4 inches long, with margins that may be toothed, smooth, or lobed. All three forms may occur on the same plant. The terminal leaflet is attached by an elongated leafstalk. In the spring, the small new leaves are red, turning a glossy or dull green as they enlarge. In the fall, they turn bright red or reddish yellow. Poison ivy is sometimes confused with Virginia creeper (*Parthenisisus quinquefolia*), which has 5 leaflets and blue berries. Clusters of greenish white flowers bloom on poison ivy from late spring to early summer. They produce white, waxy, 1/4-inch berries with seeds. The fruit first appear in the late summer, and remain on the plant through the winter. They are a way of identifying the plant in the winter, when there are no leaves. Some plants produce only male flowers, so fruit will not be present on all poison ivy plants. Poison ivy reproduces by seeds, which birds distribute, and by underground creeping stems and roots. It is frequently found climbing buildings, trees, fences, and along the ground. An oil present in all parts of poison ivy plants causes skin irritations. Poisoning can occur throughout the year, and from live or dead plants. These irritations develop after contact with the plant, or with contaminated clothing, tools, pet hair, or smoke from burning plants.

CONTROL: Hand-pulling and burning are not practical solutions. Any pieces of root left behind will sprout into new plants. The irritating oil in poison ivy vaporizes when burned, and the smoke causes lung, eye, and skin irritations. Control poison ivy around trees, on fences and buildings, and in noncrop areas with ORTHO Poison Ivy Control, ORTHO Poison Oak & Poison Ivy Killer, or ORTHO Kleenup Systemic Weed & Grass Killer. Treat any time the plants are actively growing, but at least 2 weeks before the first killing frost in the fall. Spray the leaves thoroughly. Plants turn white or brown in 10 days to 2 weeks. The vigorous roots are difficult to kill, so repeated treatments may be necessary if new growth appears. Handle dead plants with rubber gloves, since they may still be toxic. Dispose of plants and rubber gloves in tightly sealed garbage bags. If you come in contact with poison ivy, wash as soon as possible with a drying agent such as rubbing alcohol or a solution of baking soda and water.

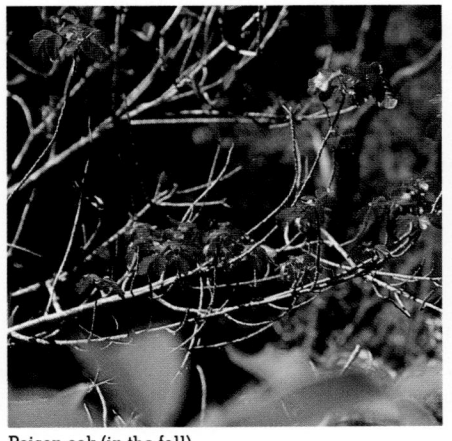

Poison oak (in the fall).

Poison oak (in the summer).

Wild blackberry.

POISON OAK AND PACIFIC POISON OAK
Rhus toxicodendron and *R. diversiloba*

This perennial grows as an upright shrub as well as a twining vine. The leaves, 1½ to 4 inches long with 3 to 7 shallow lobes, are composed of 3 elliptical or oval leaflets. The terminal leaflet is attached with an elongated petiole. The lower surfaces of the leaves and the petiole are velvety; the upper surfaces are hairy. The leaflets resemble white oak leaves, except that oak leaves are smooth. Poison oak leaves turn a brilliant orange to red color in the fall. In May and June, clusters of greenish flowers bloom from the centers of the leaves. They are followed by round, green to tan fruit containing seeds. New plants sprout from these seeds, as well as from the creeping underground stems. Poison oak prefers dry areas with poor, sandy soil. It is frequently found in wooded lots, along roadways, and in yards and noncrop areas. It is well known for the irritating rash caused by the oily sap. The oil is found in all parts of the plant. The greatest irritations occur in the spring and summer when the sap is flowing freely. However, rashes can develop if the plant is contacted any time of year. Irritations develop after contact with the plant directly, or with contaminated clothing, tools, pet hair, or smoke from burning plants.

CONTROL: Do not hand-pull or burn poison oak plants. Any pieces of root left behind will sprout into new plants. The oil also remains potent on clothing for up to 2 years. When burned, the oil vaporizes and the smoke causes skin, eye, and lung irritations. Herbicides are the safest way to rid an area of this weed. Around homes, buildings, fences, noncrop areas, and trees, treat the plants with ORTHO Poison Oak & Poison Ivy Killer, ORTHO Poison Ivy Control, or ORTHO Kleenup Systemic Weed & Grass Killer. Treat any time the plants are actively growing, but at least 2 weeks before the first killing frost in the fall. Spray the leaves thoroughly. Plants begin to turn white or brown in 10 days to 2 weeks. The vigorous roots are difficult to kill, so repeated treatments may be necessary if new growth appears. Handle dead plants with rubber gloves, since they may still be toxic. Place dead plants in plastic bags and tie securely. Discard bags and rubber gloves. If you come in contact with poison oak, wash as soon as possible with a drying agent such as rubbing alcohol or a solution of baking soda and water.

WILD BLACKBERRY
Rubus species

Wild blackberries are perennial shrubs with thorny, arching stems that grow 3 to 8 feet tall and live for only 2 years. The first year only leaves are produced. They have 3 to 5 leaflets that are hairy with toothed edges, green on the upper surface, and silver on the lower surface. Spines grow on the midrib on the underside of the leaflets. The second year, clusters of 12 to 30 white or pink flowers bloom in May and June. Red to black edible fruit then appear in July. New plants may sprout from underground runners or from seeds that are spread by birds that eat the fruit. Wild blackberry plants have deep roots, making them difficult to control. They prefer dry gravelly or sandy soil along roadways, fences, and unmaintained areas.

CONTROL: Treat existing plants with ORTHO Kleenup Systemic Weed & Grass Killer any time the plants are actively growing. Repeated treatments are often necessary to kill the deep roots. Hand-pulling is not effective against blackberries; any pieces of rootstock left behind will sprout into new plants. If feasible, control blackberries by allowing the soil to dry out in the summer.

This section was included for the person who wants to learn more about plant diseases than was presented in the first part of the book. It contains additional information about some of the most common plant diseases, especially those that attack a wide variety of plants. Locate the disease you are looking for in the index on the next page.

A GALLERY OF PLANT DISEASES

Most plant diseases are caused by either fungi or bacteria. A key to understanding plant diseases and their prevention lies in the fact that both fungi and bacteria need wet conditions.

Plant diseases can be divided into two broad categories: those that are spread by wind or splashing water, and those that live in the soil.

Most diseases in the first category are spread as spores by wind or splashing raindrops to plant leaves or flowers. The spores sprout — usually within a drop of water on the leaf surface — and enter the leaf. Infection from this type of disease can be prevented by protecting the leaf with a fungicide, and by keeping the leaf as dry as possible. Most fungicides provide a protective barrier on the leaf sur-

face, preventing the spore from germinating or killing it before it can enter the leaf. To be effective, the protective barrier must be in place before the spore lands on the leaf, so timing is important with fungicidal sprays. The fungicide must also be renewed periodically as it wears off.

If you live in an area where summer rainfalls are frequent, there isn't much you can do to keep the leaves dry. But if you must irrigate during the summer, chose irrigation methods that don't wet the leaves. Or water in the morning, so the leaves will dry as rapidly as possible.

The second category of plant diseases includes those diseases that live in the soil. These diseases usually attack plants through their roots or the base of the stem

or trunk. Some of these organisms — such as the water molds — are present in most soils, but are not a problem if the soil is allowed to dry out periodically. This can be accomplished by improving the drainage so that water can escape from the soil, and by watering thoroughly but infrequently, so that the soil has a chance to dry out between waterings.

Other disease organisms are only present in some soils. They are usually transferred to a garden on the roots of infected plants. It's a good idea to buy plants only from reputable nurseries, most of which pasteurize their planting mixes or use soilless mixes. Or keep new plants in "quarantine" for a few weeks before planting them in your garden, to make sure they are healthy.

Above: Gray mold spots on a calceolaria blossom.
See page 857. Left: Disease-free impatiens and
begonias brighten a garden corner.

INDEX TO PLANT DISEASES

Fungal leaf spot on rhubarb.

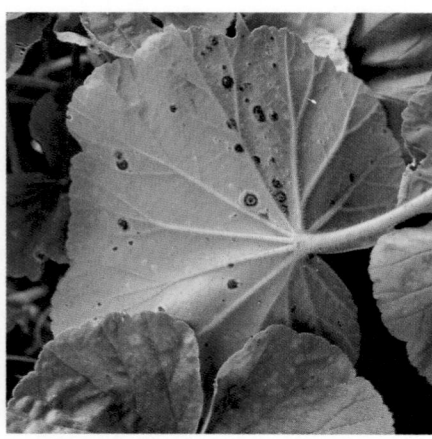

Rust on geranium.

FUNGUS DISEASES

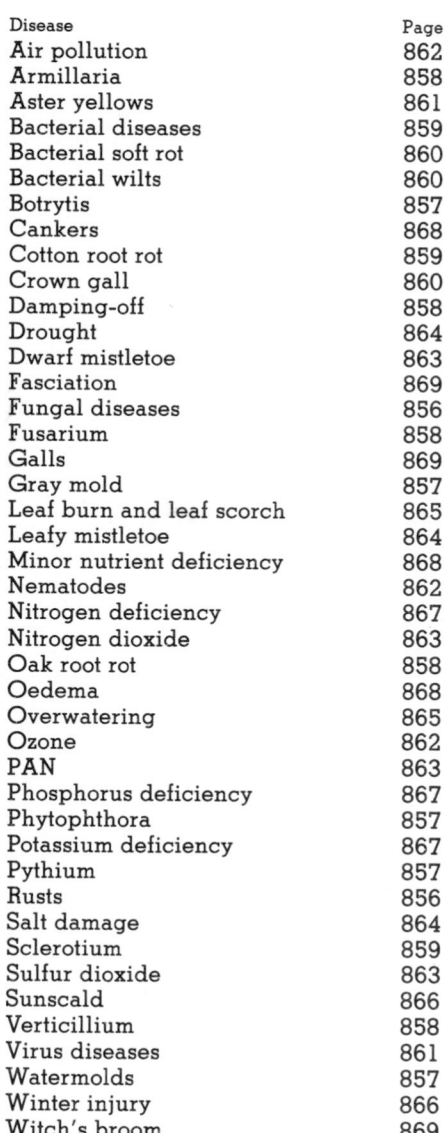

Fungi are plants that lack chlorophyll, the green pigment that enables plants to make their own food in the presence of light. Most fungi live on decaying organic matter, but about 8000 species infect live plants. In fact, most plant diseases are caused by fungi. Some of these fungi require a live host plant to survive. Others continue to live and grow in the soil or plant debris after their host plant has died. Although individual fungal filaments are microscopic, some species form dense mats of visible growth on the plant surface. Most fungi cannot grow without water or in temperatures colder than 25°F or hotter than 110°F. When their plant hosts die, or during periods of temperature extremes or drought, fungi produce resistant dormant strands or pellets that can survive for long periods until the environment is favorable for growth again. Fungi reproduce by means of spores, which are microscopic equivalents of seeds. In some cases, the fruiting bodies that produce spores are very noticeable. These are the familiar mushrooms and conks. Other fungi, such as gray mold, powdery mildew, and rust, produce spores on the surface of leaves they infect. Spores are usually spread to new host plants by wind or water. Most spores must be in a drop of water for 6 to 8 hours in order to germinate and infect the leaf. Powdery mildew is the exception to this rule.

CONTROL: Many fungus diseases may be controlled or prevented by applying fungicides, keeping plant leaves dry, and growing disease-resistant plants.

RUSTS

These fungi are aptly named: most rusts produce rust-colored or brown powdery pustules on the leaves and stems of their host plants. Rusts infect all kinds of plants, but most rust fungi infect only 1 or 2 plant species, or only certain varieties of a species. Some rusts, such as cedar-apple rust (see page 630), must alternate between two specific host plants. Diseased plants are usually weak and stunted, and severely infected plants may die. Spores may be blown hundreds of miles to infect healthy plants. Some rust fungi cannot infect their host unless the foliage remains wet for at least 6 hours. Most rusts require a living host to survive the winter; others can survive on plant debris.

CONTROL: Many methods can be used to control or prevent rust infections. Spray infected plants with a fungicide containing *folpet, triforine, mancozeb,* or *zineb.* Make sure your plant is listed on the product label. Pick off badly infected plant leaves as long as the practice doesn't damage the overall beauty of the plant. Keep the foliage as dry as possible. One way to do this is to water in the morning, which gives the plant a chance to dry out quickly, reducing the chance of infection. The best way to avoid rust infections is to plant resistant varieties of grasses, flowers, vegetables, and woody ornamentals, which may be found in local nurseries or through seed companies.

Botrytis blight on calceolaria.

Phytophthora rot of rhododendron.

Pythium stem and root rot of geranium.

BOTRYTIS BLIGHT

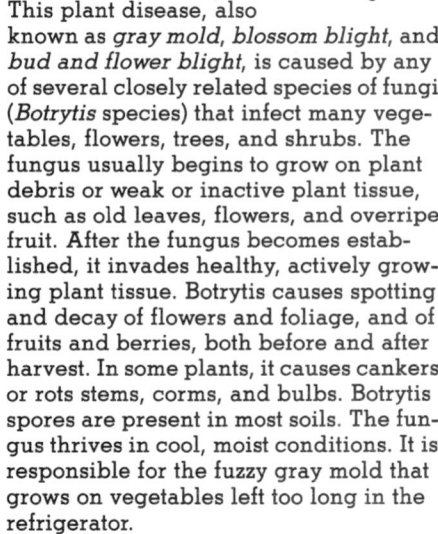

This plant disease, also known as *gray mold*, *blossom blight*, and *bud and flower blight*, is caused by any of several closely related species of fungi (*Botrytis* species) that infect many vegetables, flowers, trees, and shrubs. The fungus usually begins to grow on plant debris or weak or inactive plant tissue, such as old leaves, flowers, and overripe fruit. After the fungus becomes established, it invades healthy, actively growing plant tissue. Botrytis causes spotting and decay of flowers and foliage, and of fruits and berries, both before and after harvest. In some plants, it causes cankers or rots stems, corms, and bulbs. Botrytis spores are present in most soils. The fungus thrives in cool, moist conditions. It is responsible for the fuzzy gray mold that grows on vegetables left too long in the refrigerator.

CONTROL: The key to avoiding problems is good sanitation. Keep dead leaves and flowers picked up so the fungus will not have a chance to produce the thousands of spores necessary to mount an assault on healthy plants. Keep the foliage as dry as possible. Water the plants at the soil level, instead of overhead, and space them far enough apart so that air can circulate between plants. Fungicides can also be helpful. Spray with *maneb* or *mancozeb* every 10 to 14 days as long as the mold is visible. Check to make sure that your plant is listed on the product label.

WATER MOLDS

Water molds are fungi (*Pythium* species and *Phytophthora* species) that thrive in wet, poorly drained soils. They produce motile spores that swim through soil water to attack the roots of susceptible plants. Water molds are most active in warm (55° to 80°F) soils, but they survive as spores when the soil is cold or dry. Water molds are especially troublesome in frequently watered areas such as lawns or flower beds. They cause *damping-off* of seedlings and young plants (see page 858). Both fungi cause root rots of many plants. In addition, phytophthora causes crown rots and collar rots of many herbaceous and woody plants. The fungus attacks stems or trunks just at or below the soil surface. Reddish to brown lesions usually form on the infected tissue, and sunken, girdling cankers may develop. In some cases, phytophthora attacks the roots, and then spreads to the trunk. The foliage of infected plants dulls, and individual branches or the entire plant wilts, turns yellow, and eventually dies. Gardeners frequently mistake this wilting for drought stress and water more heavily, speeding the demise of the plant.

CONTROL: If the plant is so severely infected that most or all of the branches are dying, remove it. You may be able to save plants that are mildly infected by water molds by letting the soil dry out. If the plant is a tree or large shrub, remove the soil from around the rotted parts of the trunk and roots. Exposure to air will slow down or stop further decay.

The drying-out technique: This process involves careful observation in order to let the soil dry out as much as possible without placing plants under too much drought stress. Stop watering infected plants. To dry the soil as quickly as possible, place container plants in a well-ventilated, even breezy location. If they can tolerate direct sun, put them in a sunny spot. But if the roots are damaged badly enough that plants wilt or drop leaves, don't put them in the sun. Eventually the soil will dry out to the point where the plants would normally need another watering. Allow the soil to become drier yet to stop the fungi from continuing their decay. Take steps to minimize the water needs of the plants. Place container plants in a shaded location to reduce evaporation from the foliage. Provide shade for plants in the ground. Spray trees and shrubs that are growing in the shade with an antitranspirant, which reduces the amount of water that evaporates from the leaves. (Antitranspirants are available in many nurseries.) Further relieve drought stress by placing clear plastic tents over the plants. The tents maintain high humidity, reducing the plants' water loss. Use tents only in the shade; if used in the sun, they can heat up enough to kill plants. Begin watering again when the plant shows signs of drought stress, such as heavy wilting or yellowing and dropping of leaves.

Prevention: To help prevent future root rot problems, allow the soil to dry slightly between waterings, and provide good drainage. (For details about proper watering techniques and improving soil drainage, see pages 906 and 901.) Phytophthora-resistant plants may be used in wet areas that are hard to drain. For a list, see page 1000.

FUNGUS DISEASES

Damping-off of beet seedlings.

Fusarium wilt of cabbage.

Armillaria root rot on sour cherry.

DAMPING·OFF

This plant disease is caused by any of several species of fungi (including *Pythium*, *Rhizoctonia*, *Fusarium*, *Phytophthora*, and *Sclerotium* species). These fungi, common in soils throughout the world, are one of the major causes of poor germination. They infect seeds and seedlings at several stages. Seeds are often attacked before they germinate. Or seeds germinate, but the growing tips are infected and killed before they emerge from the soil. Seedlings are susceptible even after they emerge. The fungi can attack the stems and roots just at or below the soil level, causing the seedlings to fall over. Although older seedlings are more resistant, damping-off fungi may still infect them, producing dark lesions on the lower stems and roots that stunt and weaken their growth. Damping-off is most severe in soil with lots of nitrogen and soil that is constantly wet. Seedlings growing in soils that are too warm or cold for rapid germination and growth are also more susceptible to infection.

CONTROL: Incorporate lots of sand or perlite into the soil mix to increase drainage. Don't add fertilizers that are high in nitrogen until your seedlings have produced at least one pair of true leaves. Encourage rapid growth by planting seeds in soils that are the proper temperature for rapid germination (see page 1009). Also, coating seeds with recommended fungicides will help discourage damping-off. For more information on starting seeds, see page 917.

VERTICILLIUM OR FUSARIUM WILT

These fungi (*Verticillium* species and *Fusarium* species) cause wilting, stem and leaf discoloration, and the death of many plants. Both types of fungi live in the soil for years, even after the host plants have died. Fusarium thrives in warm soils, and is most severe in the southern states. Verticillium is more of a problem in the cooler soils of the northern states. They both infect annual vegetables, flowers, and herbaceous perennials. Verticillium also infects many woody shrubs, and ornamental, fruit, and nut trees. Infection begins when fungal strands penetrate the roots of a susceptible plant. The fungus spreads up into the water-conducting vessels in the stems and leaves and breaks down some of the plant cells, producing gels and gums. The accumulation of gels, gums, cell debris, and fungal strands and spores in the vessels reduces the water flow up into the leaves. The clogging results in wilting, leaf and stem discoloration, and eventually the death of the plant. The fungus also produces toxins that move up into uninfected leaves. These toxins interfere with photosynthesis and the production of chlorophyll, the green pigment necessary for plant health and growth.

CONTROL: Once these fungi have infected the plant, you cannot save it. Diseased flowers and vegetables often last through the season if they are cared for properly. Replace infected plants with varieties resistant to these wilt diseases (see pages 994 and 995). If you want to use susceptible plants, remove the fungus from the soil by fumigation. For information on soil fumigation, see page 919.

ARMILLARIA ROOT ROT

This plant disease, also known as *mushroom root rot*, *honey mushroom*, *oak root fungus*, and *shoestring fungus*, is caused by a soil-borne fungus (*Armillaria mellea*) that rots the roots of a wide range of plants. Many diseased ornamental and fruit trees die slowly over a period of years. However, these plants may die suddenly, especially if they are under stress. The fungus spreads short distances (under a foot) through the soil by thick fungal strands (rhizomorphs) that penetrate the roots of nearby susceptible plants. Infection is most severe in heavy, poorly drained soil. Once the fungus enters the plant, it produces a white, fan-shaped mat between the bark and the wood that decays the roots and lower trunk. As the roots die, the top of the plant slowly starves. If the crown is girdled by the fungus, the top wilts and dies quickly. In the fall, mushrooms — the spore-producing fruiting bodies of the fungus — often appear around the base of the infected plant. A different fungus (*Clitocybe tabescens*) also known as *mushroom root rot*, causes similar and often identical damage to woody trees and shrubs in the Southeast.

CONTROL: Remove badly infected trees, including the stumps and, if possible, the roots. You can usually save mildly infected plants, or at least prolong their lives. Remove the soil from around the rotted parts of the roots and trunk. Cut out the diseased tissue and allow the healthy wood to air through the summer. When temperatures drop toward freezing, cover the exposed roots with loose soil. Replace dying plants with armillaria-resistant plants. For a list, see page 1001.

Sclerotium rot of carrot.

Cotton root rot on pecan.

Bacterial crown rot on orchid.

SCLEROTIUM ROOT ROT

This plant disease, also known as *southern wilt*, *southern blight*, and *crown rot*, is caused by a soil-borne fungus (*Sclerotium rolfsii*) that occurs primarily in the southern states. The fungus infects many flowers and vegetables, and a few woody shrubs. *Sclerotium* causes root and crown rots, stem cankers, and bulb and tuber rots. It usually attacks plant stems at or just below the soil level. Infected plants wilt, turn yellow, and decay as the fungus spreads throughout the roots and stems. White fungal threads that surround or cover infected plants produce oxalic acid, which kills healthy plant cells, allowing the fungus to gain entrance. *Sclerotium* forms yellow or tan pellets that resemble mustard seeds. Under adverse conditions, these pellets and fungal strands survive in the soil and plant debris to reinfect healthy plants when conditions become favorable. This disease is most severe in warm (80°F and up), moist, sandy soils that are low in nitrogen.

CONTROL: Once plants become infected, there is no way to save them. It's best to pull out and destroy infected plants and remove the soil in the diseased area and 6 inches beyond. You can discourage rapid reinfection by making the soil unfavorable for fungal growth. Add a fertilizer, such as ORTHO General Purpose Plant Food 8–8–8, and liberal quantities of compost, leaf mold, or other organic matter. Clean up plant debris to eliminate fungal pellets.

COTTON ROOT ROT

This plant disease, also known as *Texas root rot*, is caused by a fungus (*Phymatotrichum omnivorum*) that lives in soils throughout much of the Southwest. This fungus infects more than 1700 species of plants, eventually killing them by rotting their roots. Infected plants wilt and may die within a few days if they are suffering from drought or heat stress. When pulled out of the ground, the roots are covered with yellow or tan fungal growth. The fungus thrives in warm, poorly aerated, alkaline (pH 8.0 and up) soils that are low in organic matter. In many areas, the fungal strands and spores are concentrated 1 to 3 feet below the soil surface. Cotton root rot can survive in the soil for 5 years after plants have died. It is spread from plant to plant by brown fungal strands that grow through the soil, and by the movement of contaminated soil and transplants. Cotton root rot is most active from midsummer to frost.

CONTROL: Creating a soil environment unfavorable to its development can reduce the severity of cotton root rot. Improve soil aeration by digging or tilling your soil. To improve the drainage and increase the number of competing beneficial microorganisms, incorporate lots of mulch, compost, or other organic matter into the soil. Reducing the alkalinity of the soil also helps. Fumigating the soil will kill the fungus (see page 919). For a list of plants resistant to cotton root rot that may be used to replace infected plants, see page 994.

BACTERIAL DISEASES

Bacteria are microscopic organisms that are neither plant nor animal; they do not have an organized, well-defined cell nucleus like plant and animal cells. Most bacteria live on decaying organic matter. About 200 species of bacteria cause plant diseases. Bacteria vary in their ability to survive in the soil without a host; some can live and multiply in the soil, while others die off. They damage plants by causing leaf spots, soft rots, blights, wilts, cankers, and galls. Bacteria often live within a protective ooze that they produce on infected plant parts. When conditions are warm and moist, this ooze, containing millions of bacteria, is exuded by infected plants. Infection spreads when the ooze is splashed to healthy plant parts or other plants, and when bacteria are transferred from diseased plants to healthy plants by contaminated hands, tools, and insects.

CONTROL: Bacterial diseases are more difficult to control than fungal diseases. The available chemicals, such as *streptomycin* or *basic copper sulfate*, are not very effective, but when used in combination with good sanitation, can usually keep infection to a minimum. When possible, use resistant plant varieties.

BACTERIAL DISEASES

Bacterial wilt on cucumber.

Bacterial soft rot of cabbage.

Crown gall on euonymus.

BACTERIAL WILTS

Several kinds of bacteria can cause bacterial wilt in vegetables, flowers, tropical plants, and other herbaceous plants. Infection begins when bacteria in the soil or on contaminated tools and hands penetrate wounds in the roots, leaves, or stems, or when infected seed is planted. In some cases, infection begins when insects transmit the bacteria to healthy plants. The bacteria enter the water-conducting vessels of the plant, where they break down plant cells, producing gums and gels. The bacteria also move out of these vessels to attack and dissolve the walls of adjacent cells. Sometimes bacterial ooze emerges from cracks in the leaf and stem tissue. The accumulation of gels, gums, cell debris, and bacteria in the vessels clogs the water flow throughout the plant. This clogging and the destruction of cell walls causes the plant to discolor, wilt, and finally die.

CONTROL: Once the bacteria infect the plant, there is no way to stop them. It's best to throw out the plants to avoid spreading the infection. Keep the garden clean; destroy plant debris. If you want to replant in infested soil, use resistant varieties. Because bacteria may remain in the seed, do not plant seed obtained from infected plants. If infection is widespread and severe, you can kill the bacteria in the soil by using fumigation techniques. For information on soil fumigation, see page 919.

BACTERIAL SOFT ROT

Bacterial soft rot occurs on succulent fruits, vegetables, bulbs, and tubers. Any diseased, weak, or overripe fruit, vegetables, or flowers are susceptible. However, a few kinds of bacteria can infect and decay actively growing plants. These bacteria penetrate the plant through wounds made by insect feeding or damage from tools or handling. The bacteria produce enzymes that break down plant cells, causing the infected tissue to turn soft, mushy, and watery. Masses of bacteria and cell debris may ooze through growth cracks in the plant tissue. This sticky ooze dries and turns tan, gray, or brown. Bacterial soft rot is most severe in warm (80° to 85°F), moist conditions. The bacteria survive from season to season in infected plant debris and soil. Infection is spread by diseased plants or plant parts, water, and contaminated tools, soil, and plant debris.

CONTROL: Chemicals aren't effective in controlling this disease; once your plants are infected, there is nothing you can do. The key to control is good sanitation. Help prevent bacterial soft rot by cleaning up plant debris around the garden. When working in the yard, be careful not to injure plants with hoes, cultivators, or other garden tools. You can further reduce infection by leaving enough space between plants so they get a chance to dry out after they are watered. Plant in well-drained soil. For more information about improving soil drainage, see page 901.

CROWN GALL

Crown gall is caused by soil-inhabiting bacteria (*Agrobacterium tumefaciens*) that infect the plant through wounds in the roots, crown, or stems. After infection, they produce a substance that stimulates plant cells to enlarge and divide rapidly and continuously, independent of the normal hormonal control of the host plant. This uncontrolled growth is similar in several respects to tumors in animals and humans. As the galls enlarge, they become woody and hard, and the outer layers die, turning brown and corky. Growing galls may exert pressure on the underlying normal plant tissues. The galls interfere with the plant's circulation, slowing the flow of water and nutrients through the galled area to the top of the plant. Infected plants are often weak, stunted, and more susceptible to other sources of plant stress, such as drought and winter injury. The bacteria are spread by infested soil, transplants, and contaminated tools, and through soil water.

CONTROL: Even though infected plants cannot be cured, they usually survive for many years. The plants look better if stems with galls are pruned off. It's much more difficult to properly remove galls on tree roots and trunks. Professional horticulturists or landscape contractors can remove large galls. When you replant in infested soil, choose plants that are resistant to crown gall. For a list, see page 998.

VIRUS DISEASES

Squash mosaic.

Virus infection of mint.

Aster yellows. Infected marigold bud on left.

VIRUS DISEASES

Viruses are complex, submicroscopic particles composed of proteins and nucleic acids. They are much smaller than fungi or bacteria, and are not made of cells. A few virus diseases of plants are serious or fatal. These are usually transmitted by insects or spread by hands or equipment. Most viruses only slightly impair the growth of the plant, and manifest symptoms only under certain conditions. They are usually transmitted when diseased stock is propagated by cuttings or grafting. Viruses may spread slowly from cell to cell, eventually infecting all of the plant tissue. Or they may spread quickly through the nutrient-conducting vessels to specific parts of the plant. Infection usually decreases the plant's ability to manufacture food. Less chlorophyll (green plant pigment) is produced, and the amounts of nitrogen and stored foods in the plant are reduced. Some of the common types of viruses, such as *mosaics, ring spots*, and *stunts*, produce specific symptoms. *Mosaic* viruses cause the foliage to become mottled or streaked. *Ring-spot* viruses cause pale rings to form on the leaves. *Stunts* viruses cause stunting of plant foliage. Often the symptoms overlap. In some hosts, these viruses cause leaf thickening, curling, and distortion; slow growth; and reduced yields of fruit, flowers, and vegetables. The severity of virus infections varies, depending on the host plant and strain of virus. Sometimes viruses infect certain host plants without showing symptoms of disease. In other cases, symptoms appear with changes in the environment, such as a rise or drop in temperature.

CONTROL: There are no chemical cures for virus infections. Aphids, leafhoppers, and certain other insects transmit viruses while feeding, so you can control infection by keeping the insect population down. For more information about controlling virus-carrying insects, see page 880. Pulling out infected plants will also help reduce the spread of virus diseases. Because seed, bulbs, corms, and cuttings taken from infected plants are likely to be infected, it's best to purchase healthy plants and seed from a reputable nursery and discard seeds and cuttings from diseased plants.

ASTER YELLOWS

Aster yellows is a plant disease that is caused by *mycoplasmas*, microscopic organisms similar to bacteria. Many vegetables, ornamentals, and weeds are susceptible to this disease. Infected plants are usually stunted and yellowing. They produce many spindly stems and flower stalks. The flowers are often green, and don't produce seeds or fruit. Mycoplasmas are spread from plant to plant by leafhoppers. (For more information about leafhoppers, see page 880.) When a leafhopper feeds on a diseased plant, mycoplasmas are transferred into its body along with the plant sap. The mycoplasmas multiply in the insect's body. After an incubation period of 10 days, the leafhopper infects healthy plants when it feeds.

CONTROL: Once the plant is infected, there is no way to cure it. Keep aster yellows under control by destroying infected plants and keeping the garden free of weeds, especially those weeds that are likely to be infected. It's also a good idea to spray for leafhoppers early in the season to keep populations from soaring later. Spray leafhopper-infested plants with ORTHO Diazinon Insect Spray, or ORTHO Isotox Insect Killer according to label directions. Make sure your plant is listed on the product label.

Weeds commonly infected with aster yellows: Black-eyed Susan, dandelion, field daisy, thistle, wideleafed plantain, wild carrot, and wild chicory.

NEMATODES

AIR POLLUTION

Root knot nematode damage to snap bean.

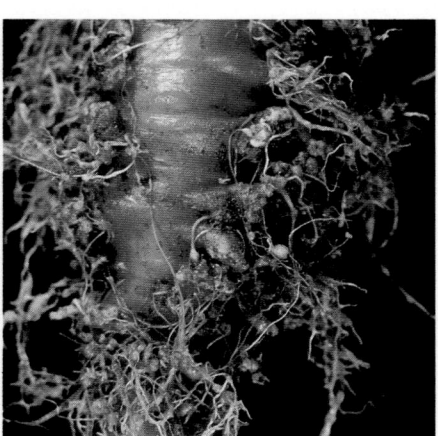

Root knot nematode damage to carrot.

Ozone damage to bean.

NEMATODES

Nematodes are also known as *eelworms, nemas,* or *round worms.* They include some well-known parasites of humans, such as pinworms. Nematodes are found throughout the world in soil, fresh and salt water, and plants and animals. The several hundred species of nematodes that parasitize plants are microscopic. Most of them live in the soil and feed on plant roots; a few (foliar nematodes) feed on aboveground plant parts. Nematodes are found throughout the United States, but they are most severe in the Southeast. They prefer moist, sandy soils.

Root nematodes: Root-feeding nematodes are attracted to substances exuded by plant roots. Some of them remain on the outside of the root while feeding; others penetrate the root tissue, and live inside the root. Roots may be damaged from the punctures made during feeding, but the most significant damage occurs when nematodes inject "saliva" into the roots. This saliva contains a toxin that causes cells to collapse or disintegrate, resulting in dark lesions and dead areas along the roots. In some cases, the toxin stimulates rapid cell growth or enlargement, resulting in numerous dark, bushy roots, or galls or swellings on roots. Nematode damage limits the ability of the root system to supply the aboveground plant parts with water and nutrients, causing plant wilting, discoloration, stunting, and in severe cases death. Some nematodes indirectly injure plants by rendering them more susceptible to root-rot fungi. Although the nematodes do not directly transmit fungi, they can transmit certain virus diseases while feeding. Nematodes can move through the soil by themselves, but they move slowly, traveling at most 3 feet during a season. They are spread more rapidly by infested soil and transplants, contaminated equipment, and irrigation water.

Foliar nematodes: Foliar nematodes live and feed mainly inside plant stems and leaves. They spread through the plant by swimming through moisture on wet leaves. The foliage of infested plants is stunted and distorted, and brownish black blotches develop on the leaves.

CONTROL: Nematode damage is difficult to distinguish from other soil and root problems. Test the plants and a soil sample to confirm nematode damage. (For more information about soil testing, see page 903.) There are no chemicals that can be used to kill nematodes in planted soil. Remove and destroy infested plants, and fumigate the soil to control nematodes. (For more information on soil fumigation, see page 919.) Many varieties of plants are resistant to nematodes. If you have a serious problem with nematodes, plant resistant varieties. For a list of nematode-resistant plants adapted to your area, check with your local Cooperative Extension Office (see page 1011). Avoid moving infested soil and transplants to clean soil.

OZONE

Ozone forms when gases produced by combustion engines and other industrial processes interact in the presence of sunlight with materials given off by automobiles, solvents, and vegetation. Ozone is common throughout the United States, and is the primary air pollutant on the East Coast. All types of plants are affected. Ozone causes small white to tan flecks to appear on the upper surfaces of the leaves. On some plants the flecks are visible on both the upper and lower surfaces. Conifers display mottled needles, or the needle tips turn reddish brown to gray. Repeated exposure to ozone reduces growth, causes blossom, fruit, and needle drop, and may eventually kill the plant. Ozone injury usually occurs when the air is still; concentrations are highest in the early afternoon from mid to late summer. Ozone is absorbed through the leaf pores. Once inside the leaf, it disrupts the cell membranes. This causes the cells to collapse, resulting in the white flecks. Environmental factors influence the susceptibility of plants to injury. Plants growing in light, moist soil with optimum nutrient levels are more sensitive to injury, as are those growing in warm temperatures (80° to 90°F) and high light levels at the time of exposure. Once plants are damaged, regular watering and fertilizing will speed recovery. In smoggy areas, select plants that are tolerant of ozone from the list on page 996.

PAN damage to lettuce.

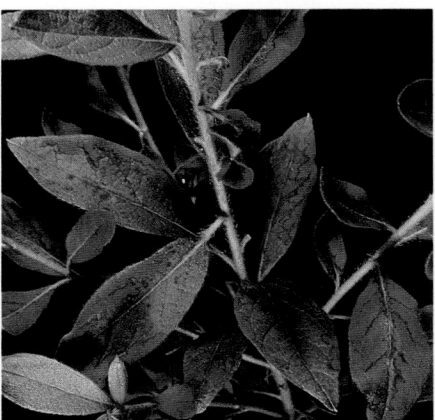

Sulfur dioxide damage to azalea.

Dwarf mistletoe.

PAN

PAN (*peroxyacetyl nitrate*), an ingredient of smog, damages herbaceous plants mainly on the West Coast. Trees are seldom affected by this pollutant. PAN enters the leaves through microscopic breathing pores causing a characteristic silvering or glazing on the lower surfaces of the leaves. When damage is severe, the injured tissue dies and turns whitish tan. Young, rapidly growing leaves and plants are especially sensitive to PAN exposure. Injury may also occur in bands across the leaf, with each band corresponding to a different exposure. Healthy green tissue separates each band. Plants repeatedly exposed to PAN grow slowly and drop their leaves. Sunscald, frost injury, and damage by mites, thrips, and leafhoppers resemble PAN injury. The most severe injury occurs at midday on sunny days. Plants growing in moist soil in very warm weather (80° to 95°F) are highly sensitive. Water and fertilize injured plants regularly to help speed recovery. In smoggy areas, select PAN-tolerant plants from the list on page 996.

SULFUR DIOXIDE AND NITROGEN DIOXIDE

Sulfur dioxide is an industrial pollutant resulting from burning sulfur-containing fuels such as coal and refining oil, and from smelting ores. Full grown and nearly grown leaves are the most susceptible to injury. All types of plants are affected. Injured areas first become water-soaked and then turn yellowish; or they dry up, turning ivory or brown. Injured areas may appear along the margins and between the veins on both surfaces of the leaves. On conifers, the young needles turn orange-red. Severely injured plants drop their leaves or needles and eventually die. Plants are most sensitive to sulfur dioxide from late spring to late summer. Sensitive plants are more likely to be injured at midday than in the early morning or evening. Plants are more sensitive at temperatures above 60°F, and when they are growing in moist soil. *Nitrogen dioxide* causes symptoms very similar to those caused by sulfur dioxide. It can be a problem in areas near factories that manufacture munitions or nitric acid, or that do electroplating, engraving, or welding. The greatest concentrations of this pollutant occur in midsummer. Nitrogen dioxide damage occurs mainly during the night. Plants growing in moist soil are especially sensitive to injury. Nitrogen dioxide frequently interacts with other pollutants, causing extensive injury. Help injured plants to recover by watering and fertilizing them regularly. In industrial areas, select plants tolerant to sulfur dioxide and nitrogen dioxide from the list on page 996.

DWARF MISTLETOE

Dwarf mistletoes (*Arceuthobium* species) are parasitic plants that grow only on conifers. The grayish green to brownish green scaly shoots of this parasite rarely grow longer than 8 inches; they are usually 4 inches or shorter. Unlike leafy mistletoes, dwarf mistletoes are true parasites, obtaining all their food from the host plant. Their rootlike attachment organs (haustoria) penetrate the host's food-conducting vessels. As the haustoria continue to spread through a limb, they form buds that sprout tufts of dwarf mistletoe along the infected branch. This parasite disrupts the normal functioning and hormonal balance of infected branches, often starving the branch growth beyond the point of infection. Limbs usually swell around the infected area, and cankers and witch's brooms (many small tufted branches) may form. Infected trees are stunted, weakened, and sometimes killed by this parasite.

CONTROL: The only effective way to get rid of dwarf mistletoe is to prune off the limbs on which it is growing. The haustoria spread several feet inside the branch from the site of the mistletoe tufts, so cut the branch off at the trunk to make sure that you've eliminated all of the haustoria. Be on the lookout for additional resprouting of the mistletoe; prune it out as soon as you see it. If a tree is severely infected (more than half of the branches are parasitized), consider removing the entire tree. The tree is bound to decline in health if it hasn't already, and will be a source of infection for other trees.

Leafy mistletoe.

Drought.

Salt damage.

LEAFY MISTLETOE

Leafy mistletoes (*Phoradendron* species) are plants that grow on broadleafed trees throughout the United States; they rarely attack conifers. Leafy mistletoes have chlorophyll (green plant pigment) and can manufacture their own food. To obtain water and minerals, their rootlike attachment organs (haustoria) penetrate the host plant's water-conducting vessels. These haustoria can grow through the branch, sending up more leafy tufts several feet from the original site of attachment. Branches usually swell around the infected area, and branch growth is sometimes sparse beyond the mistletoe site. Leafy mistletoes are spread to other areas of the tree when their sticky seeds drop to branches below. Also, the seeds may be eaten or accidentally carried by birds and tree-dwelling animals and deposited on other trees. Trees infested with leafy mistletoe usually continue to survive for many years, but their overall growth and vigor may be reduced.

CONTROL: The most effective way to get rid of leafy mistletoe is to prune off the branch on which it is growing. To be sure that the haustoria have been removed, prune off the branch at least 3 feet below the point of mistletoe attachment. The haustoria are visible as green streaks or dots in the wood. For more information about controlling leafy mistletoe, see page 447.

DROUGHT

Plants suffer from drought stress any time they receive less water than they need. Water is essential to the normal maintenance and growth of all plants. It moves into plant roots from the soil and is transported up through the water-conducting vessels in the branches, stems, and foliage to all the plant cells. The pressure exerted by water in the cells keeps them turgid. Eventually it evaporates from the plant through tiny breathing pores in the leaves. When plants don't receive enough water, the water pressure in the cells drops, the cells lose their turgidity, and the plant wilts. If drought continues, normal metabolic functions are disrupted. Plants grown in mild drought conditions are usually stunted and slow growing. They are also hardier and better able to withstand stress. Plants grown in more severe drought conditions stop growing, discolor, drop their leaves and fruit, and eventually starve and die. Plants wilt permanently when deprived of water for long periods, or when grown in soil so dry that the roots cannot extract water at all.

CONTROL: Growth will be more rapid and luxuriant if you give plants enough water. For more information about proper watering techniques, see page 906. If drought is a common problem in your area because of low rainfall, plant drought tolerant plants. For a list, see page 997.

SALT DAMAGE

Salts in the soil come from natural minerals in the soil or dissolved in the irrigation water; from improperly applied manure, lime, or fertilizer; or from deicing salts. If the concentration of salts dissolved in the soil water is too high, plants can't get enough water for healthy growth. As a result, growth slows and the leaves turn yellow. Salt also enters the plant, where it is deposited in the leaf tips or edges as the water in which it was dissolved evaporates. When enough salt accumulates, the tissue at the edge of the leaf turns yellow, then dies. As water evaporates from the soil, the salts become more concentrated, and more damaging. Salt damage and drought damage often occur together, compounding the problem. Salt accumulation in the soil is often caused by poor drainage, which keeps the salts from being leached through the soil. For information on inexpensive laboratory tests for salts, see page 903.

CONTROL: Leach salts from the soil with periodic heavy irrigations. Enough water should be applied to wash the salts below the plant roots. If the soil does not drain well, improve drainage according to the instructions on page 901. Keep the soil moist enough so that the plants are never under stress. Follow label instructions when using fertilizer. Apply the fertilizer to moist soil, and water it in thoroughly. If you are applying lime to soil already high in salts, use ground limestone rather than agricultural lime or quicklime; it is less soluble, and less likely to cause problems. If you have salt problems, do not use bagged steer manure (feedlot manure), which contains high levels of salts.

Root rot of succulent caused by overwatering.

Leaf burn on fuchsia.

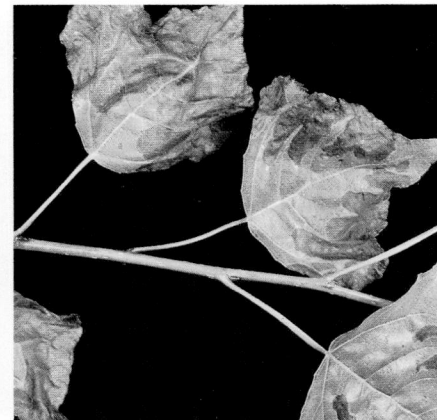
Leaf scorch on poplar.

OVERWATERING

Overwatering is one of the most common plant problems, especially in areas where the soil is heavy and poorly drained. Plant roots require oxygen to function normally. They obtain oxygen from tiny air spaces (pores) in the soil. When the soil is irrigated, air is pushed out of the soil pores and replaced with water. Pores refill with air when water drains through the soil, as plant roots absorb water, and as water evaporates up through the soil surface. If water is constantly reapplied, the soil pores will remain filled with water. Roots growing in such soil die because they cannot absorb the oxygen they need. The dying roots decay and are unable to supply the plant with water and nutrients. This results in plant stunting, weakening, and eventually death. Sometimes plants respond to wet soil conditions by growing roots just under the soil surface where the soil dries out more rapidly and oxygen is more available. These plants are often stunted and slow growing. They may wilt and die quickly if the soil is allowed to dry out past their shallow root zone. Overwatering frequently causes root rot diseases. For more information about root rot, see page 857.

CONTROL: Allow the soil to dry out somewhat between waterings. (For information on watering, see page 906.) If your soil is heavy and poorly drained, improve the soil drainage. (For more information on improving drainage, see page 901.) Some plants can tolerate wet soil; for a list, see page 997.

LEAF BURN AND LEAF SCORCH

Leaf burn and *leaf scorch* occur when leaf cells overheat. Although the two terms are often used interchangeably, leaf scorch usually refers to browning and tissue death around leaf margins and between veins, while leaf burn usually refers to dead patches in the middle of the leaf. Normally, leaves are cooled by the evaporation of water from their surfaces. When leaves dry out, the amount of water that evaporates is reduced and they overheat, then burn or scorch. Sometimes entire leaves or shoots are damaged. Several different conditions may cause leaf burn or leaf scorch. Many of these factors are interrelated; when they occur in combination, damage may be severe.

Lack of water: Leaf burn and leaf scorch often occur when plant roots can't get enough water. Many soil conditions may cause dehydration. Plants growing in dry, salty, frozen, or restricted soil areas may not get as much water as they need.

Too much water: Overwatered or heavy, poorly drained soils can cause burn or scorch. Roots require oxygen to function properly. Wet soils are often low in oxygen, causing root death. As the roots start to die, they absorb less water.

Wind and heat: Hot, windy conditions cause burn and scorch in some plants, even when the soil is moist. Wind and heat cause water to evaporate more quickly from the leaves than it can be replaced.

Freezing damage: Leaf burn or leaf scorch may result when foliage freezes. Frozen leaf cells rupture or dry out and die.

Other factors: Roots that are diseased or mechanically damaged often cannot supply as much water as the plant needs, resulting in leaf burn or leaf scorch. Burn and scorch can also be caused by an accumulation of salt in the leaf tissue. For more information, see page 864.

CONTROL: Leaves damaged by leaf scorch or leaf burn will not recover. Keep plants properly watered to help reduce further damage. For more information about proper watering, see page 906. If possible, shade plants during very hot weather, and hose down foliage a couple of times a day. (For more information about heat protection, see page 912.) Make sure the soil is moist when it freezes, and reduce chances of dehydration resulting from frozen soils by applying a mulch around the base of the plant. (For more information about mulching, see page 918.) Inspect damaged plants for root rot or mechanical damage. (For more information on root rots, see page 857.) Protect shade-loving plants by providing adequate shade.

TEMPERATURE-RELATED DISEASES _____

Sunscald on maple.

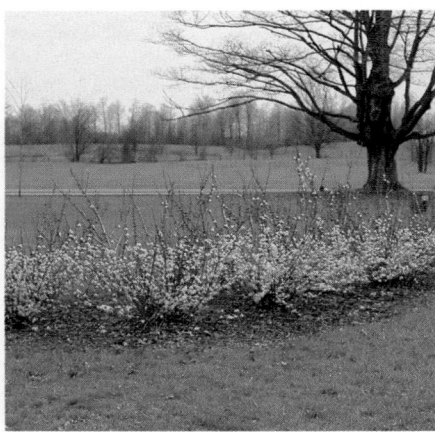

Upper flower buds killed by winter cold.

Frost cracks.

SUNSCALD

Sunscald occurs when bark is killed by overexposure to the sun. Trees that have been recently transplanted or pruned are most susceptible to sunscald. When a tree is shaded by other trees, buildings, or dense foliage, the bark on the trunk and branches remains thin and tender. If exposed to intense sunlight, the bark cells heat up rapidly. Because they are not adapted to such high temperatures, the cells are easily injured or killed. Dark brown or black barks are particularly susceptible to sunscald because they absorb more heat than lighter barks. Sunscald may also occur during cold, sunny winter days. The killed bark turns dark and splits open, forming long cracks or cankers, usually on the southwest side of the tree. Decay organisms may invade the damaged bark and wood. Sunscald is most severe when the tree is suffering from drought stress.

CONTROL: Unless the tree is very young or extremely damaged, it will usually recover with proper care. Water and fertilize the tree to stimulate new growth. As the tree adapts to its sunnier location, its bark will thicken; new growth will also shade the bark, protecting it from sunscald. To prevent damage, wrap the trunks and main branches of recently pruned or newly transplanted trees with burlap or tree-wrapping paper. Or paint the exposed bark with whitewash or white interior latex paint. If possible, transplant in overcast, cool weather, and water trees as soon as they've been transplanted. For more information about watering, see page 906.

COLD DAMAGE

Low temperatures damage plants in several ways.

Freezing: Leaves, stems, and sometimes the entire plant may be killed by freezing. Foliage damaged by freezing temperatures looks water-soaked and wilts. In a few hours or days, it darkens and turns black.

Tender plants: Tender plants are most likely to suffer from freezing temperatures in the fall and spring. Seedlings or plants that have been raised in the house or greenhouse are very susceptible to freezing damage if they are planted outdoors too early in the spring or left out too late in the fall.

Early or late cold snaps: Plants that are hardened off (adjusted to outdoor conditions) and adapted to the area in which they are growing do not usually suffer from freezing damage unless the temperature drops much lower than normal. However, during mild fall weather hardening off is delayed, and unexpected cold snaps in early fall may freeze tender leaves and stems. When premature warm spells during the spring stimulate the production of new growth, cold snaps can be very damaging to this tender foliage.

Chilling injury: Cold-sensitive, tender plants growing in warm winter areas, and greenhouse-grown or house-raised plants, may be susceptible to chilling temperatures (50°F and lower). Chilling injury usually occurs when these plants are set outdoors when night temperatures drop below 50°F. Even though the leaf tissue doesn't freeze, these tender plants cannot tolerate cool conditions. Their foliage may discolor and die.

Winter sunscald and frost cracks: For information about cold damage to woody plants, see page 457.

CONTROL: There is not much you can do about unanticipated freezing or chilling temperatures during cold snaps. If you anticipate damagingly low temperatures, cover plants with burlap, cardboard, or heavy paper during the night. It's usually a good idea to wait until spring before pruning out dead twigs and branches. Often the full amount of dieback caused by cold damage isn't obvious until the tree or shrub begins to grow again in the spring. However, it's best to prune or pinch off frozen leaves, flowers, and stems of herbaceous flowers and vegetables as soon as damage is noticed. Use only plants adapted to your area, or be prepared to shelter or protect tender plants when temperatures drop below 50°F. Harden off house-raised plants before setting them outside by gradually exposing them to cool temperatures over a period of a week.

Nitrogen-deficient Swedish ivy.

NITROGEN DEFICIENCY

Nitrogen is the most commonly deficient plant nutrient. Nitrogen-starved plants grow slowly. New leaves are small and pale green. The older leaves turn yellow and fall off or die and remain hanging on the plant.

Nitrogen in the plant: Nitrogen is taken up by plant roots from the soil, and is used in the formation of many plant tissues and compounds such as proteins, chlorophyll (green plant pigment), enzymes, and nucleic acids. Because plants use nitrogen whenever they form new tissue this nutrient is used in large quantities whenever growth is rapid; plants that are dormant or growing slowly use less nitrogen.

Soil deficient in nitrogen: If the soil is deficient in nitrogen, plants break down the compounds in older leaves to recycle the nitrogen to new growth. This is why the older leaves of plants suffering from nitrogen deficiency turn yellow and die.

High nitrogen levels: High nitrogen levels stimulate leaf growth, often at the expense of root growth or flower production.

CONTROL: Most plants need to be fertilized regularly with nitrogen fertilizers. While nitrogen is needed all the time a plant is not dormant, it is needed in the greatest amounts when leaves are growing most rapidly. For most plants, this is from spring through early summer. Use fertilizers such as ORTHO General Purpose Plant Food 8–8–8, ORTHO Evergreen, Tree & Shrub Food 12–6–6, or ORTHO Dried Blood Meal 12–0–0. For more information about fertilization, see page 904.

Phosphorus-deficient tomato seedling.

PHOSPHORUS DEFICIENCY

Plants that are starved for phosphorus are stunted, and darker than usual. The leaves are dull and gray-green, and may be tinged with magenta. Some plants develop magenta coloring under the leaves, especially on the veins or around the edge of the leaf. Flowering and fruiting are usually poor. Plants that are only slightly deficient in phosphorus grow more slowly than normal, and produce fewer flowers and fruit, but often have no specific symptoms.

Phosphorus in the plant: Phosphorus is used in the enzyme systems that produce new cells and supply energy to the plant tissues. It promotes healthy root growth and the production of flowers and fruit.

Seedlings: Seedlings and other plants with limited root systems need more phosphorus than plants with more developed root systems. Even in areas where phosphorus seldom needs to be applied to growing plants, seedlings may be deficient. If this is the case, their growth is slowed for a few weeks until the root system develops enough to supply the plant with phosphorus. Trees seldom need added phosphorus.

CONTROL: For a quick response, spray the leaves with Ra-Pid-Gro Plant Food. Add ORTHO Superphosphate 0–20–0 to the soil, placing it within the root zone, either by cultivation or by dropping it into holes dug into the root zone. Water transplants with ORTHO Up-Start Plant Starter 5–15–5. In the future, use a fertilizer that contains at least 5 percent phosphate, such as ORTHO General Purpose Plant Food 8–8–8 or ORTHO Rose & Flower Food 8–12–4.

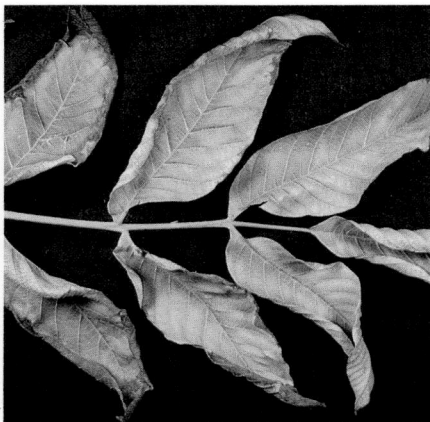

Potassium-deficient walnut leaf.

POTASSIUM DEFICIENCY

Plants that are deficient in potassium grow slowly. The older leaves are mottled with yellow or pale green smudges. The edges of the leaves scorch and die. The dead area may extend inward between the leaf veins. Badly scorched leaves usually drop. Slightly deficient plants grow more slowly than usual and have low yields of flowers and fruit. They are especially susceptible to disease.

Potassium in the plant: Potassium is essential to the normal functioning of many plant enzymes, and facilitates the production of chlorophyll (green plant pigment), proteins, carbohydrates, and other plant tissues. Potassium is used in the production of new cells, and is necessary for the proper opening and closing of the tiny breathing pores (stomata) in leaves. This nutrient is used most heavily in rapidly growing plant parts.

Lack of potassium: When potassium is in short supply, plants break down potassium-containing compounds in their older leaves, and recycle the potassium to the new growth. That is why the symptoms develop first on older leaves.

CONTROL: Spray the leaves with Ra-Pid-Gro Plant Food. Fertilize the plant with ORTHO Bloom Builder 0–10–10. In the future, use a fertilizer that contains at least 5 percent potassium, such as ORTHO General Purpose Plant Food 8–8–8, ORTHO Evergreen, Tree & Shrub Food 12–6–6, or ORTHO Azalea, Camellia & Rhododendron Food 5–10–10.

NUTRIENT DEFICIENCIES

SPOTS AND GROWTHS

Iron-deficient oak.

Oedema on cabbage.

Cankers on chestnut.

MINOR NUTRIENT

The leaves of plants deficient in minor nutrients are pale green or yellow between the veins; the veins remain bright green. In extreme cases, the entire leaf is bright yellow or almost white, and small, so that the new growth looks like a flower. Older leaves usually remain green.

Minor nutrients in the plant: Iron and several other elements (including manganese and zinc) are essential plant nutrients. They are called "minor" only because they are needed by the plant in small quantities. Minor nutrients are required for the production of chlorophyll (green plant pigment), and are essential to the proper functioning of many plant enzymes.

Minor nutrients in the soil: These nutrients are present in most soils. However, alkaline soil or wet soil often cause them to form compounds that cannot be used by the plant. Minor nutrients are not mobile throughout the plant. Once they have been incorporated into leaf tissue, the plant cannot reuse them for new growth. Therefore minor nutrient deficiencies show up in the newest growth first.

CONTROL: Spray the foliage with ORTHO Greenol Liquid Iron 6.13%, and apply it to the soil around the plants to correct the deficiency of minor nutrients. Check the soil pH. (For information on pH, see page 902; for information on soil testing, see page 903.) If your soil is too alkaline, correct the pH by treating with ORTHO Orthorix Spray. Maintain an acid pH by fertilizing with ORTHO Azalea, Camellia & Rhododendron Food 5–10–10.

OEDEMA

Oedema, also known as *edema*, affects houseplants and some outdoor herbaceous plants. This condition is not caused by an insect or disease, but by a buildup of water in the plant. Oedema usually develops in plants that are overwatered and growing in a cool, humid atmosphere. Under these conditions, water is absorbed rapidly from the soil, and lost slowly through the leaves. The excess water that builds up in the plant causes cells to burst. Water-soaked spots or pale green blisters or bumps form on the leaves and stems. Eventually these bumps and spots develop into reddish brown corky ridges and spots. Some of the badly affected leaves may turn yellow and drop off.

CONTROL: Oedema is not a serious condition in itself, but often indicates an overwatering problem. Eliminate oedema by planting in well-drained soil and watering properly. For information on proper watering, see page 906. For information on improving soil drainage, see page 901.

CANKERS

Most cankers are dark, sunken areas on trunks or branches. The bark over these areas cracks, then usually dies and falls off, revealing the wood beneath. Many trees produce a sticky sap that oozes from cankers. Cankers are caused by fungi and bacteria that infect the soft tissue just under the bark. Bark that has been damaged by sunscald, cold injury, pruning or insect wounds, or mechanical injury is especially susceptible. As the infection spreads, the infected bark and wood tissues darken and die. The water and nutrient-conducting vessels that pass through the cankered area are cut off. If the canker girdles a branch, the branch dies; if the trunk is girdled, the whole tree dies. Sometimes the plant walls off and stops canker growth by surrounding the canker with corky, barklike cells. Trees and shrubs are not usually killed by cankers, but are weakened and become more vulnerable to insects, diseases, and winter injury.

CONTROL: Remove badly infected branches, and cut out cankers. For details about canker removal and treatment, see page 911. Keep tree wounds to a minimum to cut down on canker formation. When pruning or working around plants, use the proper equipment and work carefully. Steer carefully around trunks when mowing the lawn. Infected trees will heal more quickly if they are watered and fertilized properly. For information about fertilizers, see page 904; for information about watering, see page 906.

Oak gall.

Fasciation on willow.

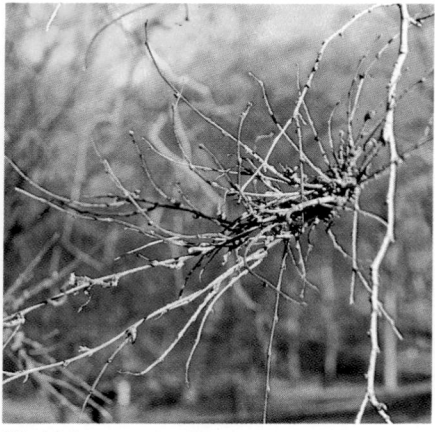

Witch's broom on hackberry.

GALLS

Galls are growths on plants. They may be simple lumps, or they may have a complicated structure. Some galls are brightly colored. Galls form on leaves, twigs, and branches. In most cases they are unsightly but not damaging to the plant, although small plants may be stunted. The water and nutrient circulatory system of a small plant may be disrupted by the galls. Some galls form when insects (certain wasps, midges, and aphids) or mites feed on or lay eggs in leaves, stems, and twigs. While feeding or laying eggs, these insects inject a toxin that stimulates rapid and abnormal cell growth. Galls may also develop as a response to infection by any of several kinds of fungi, bacteria, and viruses. Galls caused by fungi and bacteria are usually most numerous in wet years. A soil-inhabiting bacterium (*Agrobacterium tumefaciens*) causes a common plant disease called *crown gall*. For more information about crown gall, see page 860.

CONTROL: Pruning off gall-infested growth usually takes care of the problem. If galls are especially unsightly and numerous, you can control the insects or diseases that are causing them. Look up your plant in the index to determine which pests may be causing the galls.

FASCIATION

Fasciation is an abnormal growth that affects many different kinds of plants. In nonwoody plants, fasciation often occurs at or just above the soil line, where many short, thick stems arise. A bacterium (*Corynebacteriuim fascians*) is often responsible. Seeds or cuttings from affected plants will usually produce fasciated growth. In woody plants, a branch or stem grows in a thick, flattened curl. Many stunted leaves are often bunched together on the fasciated stem. Growth above and below the area may be normal, and a plant that develops a fasciated stem may never produce another one. It is not known what produces fasciation in woody plants.

CONTROL: Fasciation does not harm trees and shrubs, although it may be unsightly. Prune off fasciated growth. It's best to discard fasciated nonwoody plants. Replace them with healthy plants.

WITCH'S BROOM

Witch's brooms are dense tufts of weak, twiggy growth that develop on the branches of woody trees and shrubs. The foliage that grows on a witch's broom is usually smaller and paler than normal. Witch's brooms are not a disease in themselves; they grow when a hormonal imbalance develops in the plant, usually as the result of disease. Some mites or an infestation of dwarf mistletoe can also cause witch's brooms. (For more information about dwarf mistletoe, see page 863.) Sometimes environmental factors or chemicals (such as herbicides) stimulate the growth of witch's brooms. Certain kinds of plants are more likely to develop these growths. Although witch's brooms weaken the affected branch, they do not seriously damage the plant. However, the disease or mite that caused the witch's broom may kill the plant.

CONTROL: If a plant has many witch's brooms it is probably diseased or infested. You can improve the appearance of the tree or shrub by pruning off the witch's brooms, but unless you can control the disease or mite that is causing these growths, witch's brooms will continue to develop. Look up your plant in the index to determine what may be causing these growths. Contact a professional horticulturist or your local Cooperative Extension Office (see page 1011) for additional help.

Only a few of the thousands of insects are represented here, but these few are the insects that are most likely to be problems in the garden. Locate your insect in the index on the next page.

A GALLERY OF INSECTS

Insects and plants have evolved together. Insects exist in vast numbers; they will always be present in our gardens. Our goal should not be to eradicate all insects, or even the harmful ones, but to control their numbers so the damage they do is held in check.

Entomologists — scientists who study insects — place a great deal of importance on developing *life histories* of insects they study. A life history tells when the eggs hatch, what the larvae eat, how they survive the winter, where they lay eggs, and other information about an insect's growth and development.

Life histories help us to locate weaknesses — times of year or stages of growth when the insect is most amenable to control measures. Scale insects, for in-stance, are covered with a waxy shell for most of their life. This shell protects them from predators and insecticides. But when they first hatch out they are soft-bodied and easily killed by insecticides. A well-timed spray or two can control a whole generation of scales.

Timing is particularly important with insects that have a single generation each year. All the eggs of single-generation insects hatch at once, and they go through the life stages at once. But other insects, such as aphids, have multiple generations a year. All life stages are apt to be present at once. Control of multiple-generation insects usually depends on a series of treatments over a period of time to kill new generations as they hatch from eggs.

Winter is a particularly vulnerable time for many insects. Being cold-blooded, they must spend the winter in an inactive state, often as eggs or pupae. Sanitation measures — such as removing dead plants from the garden, picking up trash, and tilling — remove, kill, or expose to the cold many insect pests. Dormant oil sprays suffocate eggs and insects on trees. Although we don't often think of insect control in the winter, this may be the best time to reduce next summer's insect population.

Also, many plants are now being bred that are resistant to their most damaging pests. Ask your Cooperative Extension agent about insect-resistant varieties for your area.

Above: Tent caterpillar. See page 874. Left: This tomato hornworm is feeding on a pepper plant. The ''horn'' is harmless.

INDEX TO INSECTS

Elm leaf beetles (4 times life size).

BEETLES

Beetles are members of the order *Coleoptera*, which is the largest insect order, containing 40 percent of all insects. The shiny or dull insects are easily recognized by their tough, leathery wing covers, called *elytra*. The wing covers meet in the middle of the back, forming a straight line down the insect's body. Some beetles, distinguished by their long snouts, are also called *weevils* or *curculios*. When beetles are at rest, the elytra hide a pair of clear, membranous wings. Some beetles don't have wings, and can't fly. The larvae of beetles are sometimes called *grubs*. Those grubs that have legs usually have three pairs. The larvae of weevils and curculios are legless. Both the larvae and adults may be harmful to plants. They have chewing mouthparts, and feed on plant tissue, other insects, or as scavengers. Plant feeders may devour any part of the plant. Some beetles feed inside the leaf tissue as leafminers (page 874), borers (page 873), or bark beetles (page 468). Others feed outside the plant or on the roots.

CONTROL: There are many methods of controlling beetles, depending on the part of the plant they infest. Control measures are often aimed at the adults, because grubs may be hidden or protected from chemicals inside plants or in the ground.

Japanese beetle (life size).

Flat-headed borer (half life size).

Damaged rose. *Insert:* Rose curculio (life size).

JAPANESE BEETLES

Japanese beetles are beautiful little (½ inch) metallic green insects with bronze wing covers. They were accidentally introduced into this country, and first noticed in New Jersey in 1916. From there they have spread throughout the eastern half of the country. The adults feed during the day on a wide variety of plants. They devour flowers, ripening fruit, and tender leaves with small veins, but eat only the tissue between the veins on tree leaves. The beetles are often seen in clusters of a hundred or more hanging from fruit or flowers. When the beetles emerge in June, they begin feeding on low-growing plants and then later fly to tree leaves. The adults live for 30 to 45 days, and are most abundant in July. Just before they die, the females lay their eggs in lawns or other grassy areas under the soil surface. The grubs that hatch from these eggs are grayish white with brown heads. They feed on grass roots until cold weather drives them further down into the soil below the frost line. When the soil warms in the spring, the grubs move back up and resume feeding on grass roots. The grubs pupate in the soil and then emerge as adults to feed above ground.

CONTROL: Adult beetles can be controlled on ornamentals with ORTHO Malathion 50 Insect Spray, ORTHO Liquid Sevin, ORTHO Gypsy Moth & Japanese Beetle Killer, or ORTHO Isotox Insect Killer. Spray food crops with ORTHO Malathion 50 Insect Spray. To control grubs in the soil, follow the instructions on page 299. Before spraying, make sure your plant is listed on the product label.

BORERS

Most borers are the larvae of beetles or moths that tunnel in wood or soft stems. Their presence is usually indicated by the sap or sawdust that surrounds holes in the tissue, and by wilting and drying foliage on the affected stems or branches. Hundreds of different kinds of borers infest trees, shrubs, and herbaceous plants. Borers that infest trees and shrubs usually favor weak, wounded, or recently set plants. However, borers commonly attack healthy flowers and vegetables as well. Vigorous trees and shrubs are often able to resist borer infestations. When the larvae try to burrow into such plants, they are overcome by oozing plant sap. Weak plants, such as those that have damaged roots or are suffering from drought, have reduced sap flow, making it easier for borers to enter them and develop inside.

CONTROL: The best control for borers in many herbaceous plants is sanitation, cutting out and destroying infested stems and removing dying plants. To control with chemicals, sprays must be applied before they burrow into the plant. The time varies with different species. For timing of sprays, look under your plant in the index, or contact your local Cooperative Extension Office (see page 1011). Many woody plants can be sprayed with ORTHO Lindane Borer & Leaf Miner Spray. Spray herbaceous plants with an insecticide containing *carbaryl*. Make sure your plant is listed on the product label. Keep plants in vigorous growing condition by fertilizing and watering regularly, and by controlling diseases and other insects. Avoid wounding plants.

WEEVILS

Weevils, also known as *snout beetles*, are beetles that have long snouts with chewing mouthparts at the end. Some weevils are called *curculios*. Curculios usually have snouts that are longer and more curved than those of weevils. Weevil adults are hard-bodied, usually dark-colored insects that play dead when disturbed. They feed on many different types of plants, often chewing holes in leaves, buds, and flowers. The larvae are white, fleshy, legless grubs that usually live inside plant tissue. Grubs may feed inside seeds, fruit, buds, leaves, or stems. Some weevil grubs live in the soil and feed on plant roots. These *root weevils* are very damaging to their host plants. For more information about root weevils, see page 874.

CONTROL: Control is most often aimed at the adults, since the larvae are usually protected inside plant tissue. To control weevils on fruit and nut trees, spray with ORTHO Home Orchard Spray. Several different insecticides, including *malathion*, *lindane*, and *carbaryl*, are used to control weevils on vegetables and ornamentals. Look under the entry for your specific plant.

BEETLE FAMILY

Black vine weevil larvae (life size).

ROOT WEEVILS

Root weevils are serious pests of berries, ornamentals, and grasses. Both adults and larvae cause damage. The adults are snout beetles, with chewing mouthparts at the end of their long snouts. They have light brown to black hard-shelled bodies, with rows of tiny round depressions on their backs. In most species the adults cannot fly because their elytra (wing covers) are fused down the middle of the back. The adult weevils feed at night, notching the edges of leaves. In the summer, each female lays hundreds of eggs on the soil at the base of plants. The emerging larvae are white, C-shaped, legless grubs with brown heads. The grubs sometimes feed on the base of plant stems before burrowing down into the soil to feed on roots. They spend the winter in the soil and resume feeding in the spring. Larval feeding is most severe in spring and often results in severe weakening or death of the plant.

CONTROL: Since the grubs are protected by soil, there are no effective controls for them. Control of root weevils must be aimed at the adults. The best time to spray is in May or June as the adults emerge from the soil. Check your plants periodically for notched leaves; or contact your local Cooperative Extension Office (see page 1011) for the time of weevil emergence. Spray the foliage and the ground under the plant thoroughly with ORTHO Orthene Systemic Insect Control or ORTHO Isotox Insect Killer on ornamentals. Make sure your plant is listed on the product label. Repeat the spray 2 more times at intervals of 3 weeks.

BUTTERFLY FAMILY

Tent caterpillar (life size).

CATERPILLARS

Caterpillars, the larvae of moths and butterflies, are serious pests of garden plants. Moths and butterflies do not feed on tissue or harm plants, but drink nectar from flowers. They may also help to pollinate flowers. Caterpillars are smooth, hairy, or spiny wormlike creatures with 3 pairs of legs near their heads and several pairs of prolegs (false legs) in the middle and rear of the abdomen. Their mouthparts are adapted for chewing plant tissue. They generally confine themselves to tissue that is soft and succulent. After hatching, caterpillars go through as many as 11 stages of development (instars). At the end of each instar, caterpillars must molt (shed their skin) to make room for their larger body size. During the first instars, caterpillars may feed as leafminers between the upper and lower surfaces of leaves; or as skeletonizers, eating only one leaf surface. As the caterpillars increase in size in later stages, they require more food, devouring entire leaves. Caterpillar populations often fluctuate greatly from year to year due to unfavorable environmental conditions and to control by natural enemies such as birds, rodents, diseases, and other insects.

CONTROL: Inspect garden plants periodically for signs of caterpillar infestation. Control caterpillars on ornamentals with ORTHO Orthene Systemic Insect Control, ORTHO Isotox Insect Killer, or ORTHO Liquid Sevin. Spray food crops with ORTHO Fruit & Vegetable Insect Control, ORTHO Liquid Sevin, or ORTHO Malathion 50 Insect Spray. Make sure your plant is listed on the label.

LEAFMINERS

Leafminer trails.

Leafminers are insect larvae that feed inside a leaf, between the upper and lower surfaces. They may be the larvae of flies, moths, sawflies, or beetles. Females lay their eggs on or in the leaves, and the larvae that hatch from these eggs burrow into the leaves. Leafminers must be able to survive in a small living space, so they are tiny and somewhat flattened. The thinner the leaf the flatter and smaller the leafminer. As the larvae mine the leaf tissue, there is more room for them to expand, but their heads always remain somewhat flattened. Leafminer feeding produces blisters, blotches, or tunnels in the leaf, which turns yellow or brown as the tissue dies. If more than one larva is mining the tissue, the tunnels often run together, forming large blotches that cover much of the leaf. Infested plants may have a scorched appearance.

CONTROL: Leafminers are protected inside leaves for most of their lives, which makes control difficult. If the spray used for control is not a systemic insecticide, then sprays must be applied when the adults emerge to lay their eggs. Most ornamentals can be sprayed with the systemic insecticides ORTHO Orthene Systemic Insect Control or ORTHO Isotox Insect Killer. Food crops can also be treated with ORTHO Diazinon Insect Spray or ORTHO Fruit & Vegetable Insect Control if the spray is carefully timed. Check with your local Cooperative Extension Office (see page 1011) for the best time to spray for the insect in your area. Make sure your plant is listed on the spray label.

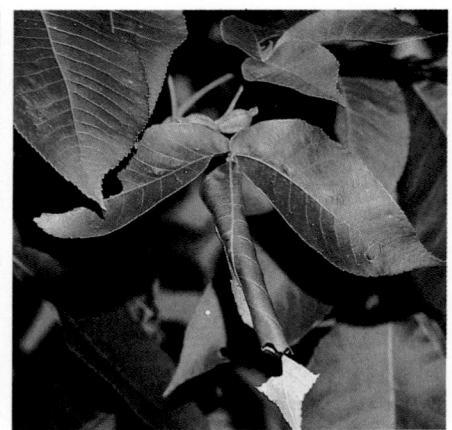

Leafroller feeding on hickory leaf.

Climbing cutworms (half life size).

Surface cutworm (twice life size).

LEAFROLLERS AND LEAFTIERS

Leafrollers and leaftiers are small caterpillars that feed inside leaves, which they roll or tie together. They are similar in their habits, but leafrollers roll leaves around themselves, and leaftiers tie leaves together with silk threads. This feeding habit gives the insects some protection from unfavorable weather, predators, and chemical sprays. Leafrollers and leaftiers may be serious pests in the garden, feeding on many fruits, vegetables, and ornamentals. Their feeding habits vary, depending on their age. Only part of their life may be spent feeding inside the rolled or tied leaves. At other times they may feed inside buds, flowers, or fruit. The species of leafrollers and leaftiers that feed on flowers and fruits are usually much more damaging than the species that feed exclusively on the leaves.

CONTROL: Insecticides are most effective if they are applied before the larvae are protected inside the leaves. Check your plants periodically in the spring for the first sign of infestation. Spray ornamentals with ORTHO Isotox Insect Killer, ORTHO Orthene Systemic Insect Control, or ORTHO Liquid Sevin. Spray fruits with ORTHO Liquid Sevin or ORTHO Malathion 50 Insect Spray. Control insects on food crops with ORTHO Fruit & Vegetable Insect Control or with an insecticide containing *carbaryl* or *malathion*. Make sure your plant is listed on the product label.

CUTWORMS

Cutworms are large (up to 2 inches), fleshy, hairless caterpillars that curl up when disturbed. They are serious pests of vegetables and flowers, and sometimes infest vines and trees. There are many species of cutworms in the United States. They are grouped according to their feeding habits.

Surface cutworms are pests of early season vegetables and flowers, feeding on the succulent tissue of newly transplanted or emerging plants. A single surface-feeding cutworm may destroy many plants in one night. They chew or cut off the plant at or below the soil surface, and then hide under dirt clods or in the soil during the day. They do not eat much of the plant, but take only a few bites from the stem, often causing the plant to topple over.

Climbing cutworms feed aboveground on any part of the plant. Their favorite foods are the tender young leaves, buds, and flowers of vegetables and herbaceous plants. Sometimes they infest vines or climb up into the tops of fruit trees to feed on leaves or buds. In one night, climbing cutworms may devour all but the stem of a young plant and then move to another plant to feed.

Subterranean cutworms spend their lives in the soil. They feed day and night on the roots and underground stems of vegetables, sod, and grains, causing plants to wilt and die. Many other insects and diseases cause similar symptoms. Dig in the soil around the dying plant for cutworms to confirm that they are the cause of the problem.

The adults of all cutworms are dark, night-flying moths with bands or stripes on their forewings and lighter-colored hindwings. They feed at dusk on the nectar from flowers, and may be seen fluttering around lights at night.

CONTROL: Since cutworms feed in the soil or hide there during the day, insecticides are most effective if they are applied around the base of plants. Use ORTHO Diazinon Soil & Foliage Dust or ORTHO Diazinon Soil & Turf Insect Control on vegetables and lawns when stem cutting or leaf chewing is observed. To control subterranean cutworms, water the soil lightly after applying the insecticide. Control cutworms on flowers with ORTHO Diazinon Insect Spray. Make sure your plant is listed on the product label. Since cutworms are difficult to control, it may be necessary to repeat the dusting or spraying at weekly intervals. Before transplanting in the area, apply a preventive treatment of ORTHO Diazinon Soil & Turf Insect Control and work it into the soil. Cultivate the soil thoroughly in late summer and fall to expose and destroy larvae and pupae. Further reduce damage with "cutworm collars" around the stem of each plant or group of plants. These collars can be made of stiff paper, milk cartons, tin cans, or aluminum foil. They should be at least 2 inches high and pressed firmly into the soil. To reduce injury from climbing cutworms, inspect your plants at night with a flashlight and pick off and destroy any cutworms you find.

BUTTERFLY FAMILY

Gypsy moth larvae (half life size).

Gypsy moth adult and pupae (half life size).

BUG FAMILY

Harlequin bugs (life size).

GYPSY MOTH

Gypsy moth (*Porthetria dispar*) larvae are large (up to 2½ inches),
hairy, blackish caterpillars, with two rows of longitudinal red and blue spots on their
backs. They are the most serious shade tree pest in this country. When their numbers
are small, the caterpillars prefer to feed on oak leaves. As population levels increase,
entire forests may be defoliated and then the insects spread to other types of trees and
shrubs. The gypsy moth was introduced into this country in the mid-1800s from Europe, where it is a native pest. It was brought in by an entomologist searching for a
hardy silk moth. Some of the larvae escaped and became established on plants. The
East Coast has large forests of the insects' preferred food (oak) that can support huge
populations of gypsy moths. This allowed the moths to increase in numbers rapidly.
Besides defoliating and weakening plants, the insects are a nuisance. In mid to late
summer, the female moths attach masses of eggs covered with yellow hairs to almost
any outdoor object. The larvae that hatch from these eggs from April to June may completely cover the sides of houses or other objects during the day when they're not feeding. Some people are allergic to the hairs of the larvae, which blow about in the wind.
Where insects are feeding, large amounts of excrement accumulate beneath the plant.
There is only one generation of gypsy moths a year.

CONTROL: It may not be necessary to spray your tree if it is healthy and vigorous.
Hardwood trees can generally withstand 2 to 5 successive years of defoliation before
dying (although a single season's defoliation can stress a tree so badly that it may take
many years to recover fully). Evergreen trees may die after one complete defoliation
since they cannot totally replace their foliage. If the insects are bothersome, or if trees
are weak or unhealthy either from last year's gypsy moth feeding or from drought, mechanical damage, or other insects and diseases, treatment with insecticides should be
considered. Insecticides should be applied in the spring or early summer before the
larvae are 1 inch long; the tree must be covered thoroughly. It is best to contact a professional arborist for spraying large trees. Spray smaller trees with ORTHO Gypsy
Moth & Japanese Beetle Killer, ORTHO Liquid Sevin, ORTHO Orthene Systemic Insect Control, or ORTHO Isotox Insect Killer. Repeat the sprays at weekly intervals if
damage continues. Homeowners can reduce infestations by destroying egg masses
found on walls, wood piles, buildings, trees, and other objects when they are noticed
during the winter months. During the spring when larvae are feeding, place burlap
bands on trees, leaving the bottom edge unattached. Larvae will crawl under these
flaps to hide during the daylight hours. Collect and destroy them. This is most effective when infestations are light to moderate. Keep trees in a healthy growing condition; avoid damaging the roots or injuring the tree. Fertilize and water trees during
periods of drought. When planting trees in the yard, choose species that are less favored by the gypsy moth. (For a list of these plants, see page 1000.) Trees less favored
by the insects are damaged only slightly by larval feeding. In addition, they may reduce the mortality of more favored hosts when interplanted, by preventing a large
buildup of insects in the area.

PLANT BUGS

Plant bugs are a large
group of insects that infest many plants in
the garden. This group includes many
species of *plant bugs*, *leaf bugs*, *lygus
bugs*, and *garden fleahoppers*. These insects are true bugs, of the order *Hemiptera*. They have long legs and antennae,
large eyes, and the adults hold their
wings flat over their bodies. Immature
plant bugs have no wings. Both the immature and mature bugs feed on succulent plant tissue. They pierce the tissue
and remove the cell contents, resulting in
tan or bleached spots and distortion. Infested fruits and flowers often drop off
the plant. The mature females may also
damage plants by laying eggs inside the
leaves or stems. Many plant bugs have
two or more generations a year, so late-season populations can be very large and
damaging.

CONTROL: It is important to control
plant bugs before they build up to damaging numbers. Watch for signs of infestation during the growing season. If
damage is noticed, spray or dust plants
with ORTHO Malathion 50 Insect Spray
or ORTHO Sevin Garden Dust. Make
sure your plant is listed on the product
label. If migrating plant bugs reinfest the
plant, repeat the spray.

APHID FAMILY

Lacebug (10 times life size).

Aphids on ivy (life size).

Woolly hemlock aphids (twice life size).

LACEBUGS

Lacebugs are small (⅛ inch) insects of the family *Tingidae*, which means "ornamented." The adults have delicate clear wings that they hold flat over their bodies. The wings have many veins, giving them a lacy appearance. Immature lacebugs are dark and wingless, with spines radiating from the edges of their bodies. Lacebugs are pests primarily of ornamental trees and shrubs, although several species infest a few vegetables. Most lacebugs feed on only one type of plant. They damage plants by sucking the sap and cell contents from the undersides of the leaves, producing a mottling or speckling on the upper surfaces. Lacebug damage often resembles leafhopper or spider mite damage. However, lacebugs excrete drops of shiny, varnishlike excrement, which accumulates around them as they feed. Several generations of lacebugs occur each year. Certain lacebugs may build up to such tremendous numbers on their host plant that very little green tissue remains to produce food for the plant.

CONTROL: Lacebugs should be controlled early, before they cause much damage. This is especially important on broadleaved evergreen plants because they retain the unproductive leaves for several years. Spray ornamentals with ORTHO Orthene Systemic Insect Control or ORTHO Isotox Insect Killer. Control lacebugs on food crops with ORTHO Fruit & Vegetable Insect Control. Make sure your plant is listed on the product label. Reinfestations may come from infested plants in nearby gardens. Check your plant periodically for insects. Repeat the spray if the plant becomes reinfested.

APHIDS

Aphids, also called *plant lice* or *aphis*, are small (up to ¼ inch), soft-bodied insects that infest most garden plants. Some aphids spend their entire life on one type of plant; others infest several different plant species. Aphids have a complicated life history because they produce an additional form besides male and female aphids. Aphids that hatch from overwintering eggs are wingless females, called *stem mothers*. They give live birth without fertilization by a male. Many generations of females may be produced throughout the summer. Some of these aphids are born with wings so they can fly to less densely populated plants, or to another species of plant. In the fall, stem mothers give birth to males and females that mate and produce the fertilized eggs that survive the winter. In warm climates there may be continuous production of living young, with no development of sexual males and females. Large numbers of aphids may cause little damage to a plant; or just a few aphids on a plant may cause severe distortion and stunting. Certain aphids are also vectors of plant diseases (see page 880).

CONTROL: Aphids are usually easy to control if they are not protected by tightly curled leaves, galls, or cottony material. Use ORTHO Fruit & Vegetable Insect Control or ORTHO Malathion 50 Insect Spray to quickly knock out existing aphids on food crops. Use ORTHO Isotox Insect Killer or ORTHO Orthene Systemic Insect Control on ornamentals, to protect them for a couple of weeks from new infestations. Make sure your plant is listed on the product label. Aphids may continually reinfest the garden from other plants nearby. Inspect your plants regularly for aphids.

WOOLLY APHIDS

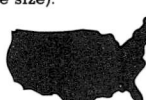

Aphids that cover themselves with white or gray waxy threads that look like wool or cotton are called woolly aphids. If the threads are removed, small (⅛ inch), dark, soft-bodied insects will be found clustered beneath. Woolly aphids infest only woody plants. Some species infest leaves, often causing them to curl inward. The damage is unsightly but rarely fatal to the plant. Other types of woolly aphids cover the trunk, branches, and roots. Galls may develop where they feed, and infested roots may be heavily branched. Young plants severely infested with woolly aphids are often stunted and may die. Older plants with galls on the roots may be weak and produce few fruits. Most of these aphids have a summer and a winter host. They spend the summer on one type of plant and then, in the fall, produce a generation that migrates to another plant species. Sometimes, especially in warmer climates, woolly aphids spend their entire life on the summer host.

CONTROL: Woolly aphids protected inside curled leaves are best controlled with a systemic insecticide such as ORTHO Isotox Insect Killer or ORTHO Orthene Systemic Insect Control. Use these sprays or ORTHO Malathion 50 Insect Spray on woolly aphids infesting branches or trunks, which are more exposed. Make sure your plant is listed on the product label. Repeat the spray if the plant becomes reinfested.

APHID FAMILY

Mealybugs on oleander (life size).

Cottony cushion scale (twice life size).

Japanese wax scale on holly (twice life size).

MEALYBUGS

Mealybugs are soft-bodied insects that are close relatives of scales. Their name derives from the white or gray threads of wax with which they cover themselves. Plant parts heavily infested with mealybugs often appear to be covered with cotton. Mealybugs may damage any part of the plant by sucking out the sap, which may cause leaf distortion, yellowing, stunting, galls, and the death of the plant. They also coat the plant with large quantities of undigested sap, called *honeydew*. Most species of mealybugs are garden pests only in the subtropical areas of the country, infesting house plants and greenhouse plants in the colder northern states. However, several species that infest woody plants can survive through the extreme cold of northern winters. Mealybugs are very active when young, crawling all over the plant until they find a suitable place to settle. As the young mealybugs mature, they become sluggish. Mature females move around very little, but males develop into winged insects that look like minute flies. Adult males do not feed, but die after mating.

CONTROL: Mealybugs are often difficult to control because they are protected by their waxy threads. Spray ornamentals thoroughly with ORTHO Isotox Insect Killer or ORTHO Malathion 50 Insect Spray. Spray food crops with ORTHO Fruit & Vegetable Insect Control or ORTHO Malathion 50 Insect Spray. Check to make sure your plant is listed on the product label. Repeat the spray if the plant becomes reinfested.

COTTONY SCALES

Cottony scales are a type of soft scale (see page 879). Like other soft scales, they have a crusty skeleton on the outside of their bodies. However, it is rarely seen because the mature female scales lay hundreds of eggs in white, waxy egg sacs that are attached to their bodies, giving them a cottony appearance. The females die and shrivel after they lay their eggs. The young scales, called *crawlers*, emerge from the egg sacs and migrate to leaves and young twigs. They insert their mouthparts into the plant and suck sap throughout the summer. Trees and shrubs infested with cottony scales may be coated with large quantities of a sticky substance called *honeydew*, undigested sap excreted by the insects. Male cottony scales are tiny winged insects, which mature before females. They mate with immature females and die. Many species of cottony scales remain mobile throughout their life. Before the leaves drop, scales migrate to bark to spend the winter.

CONTROL: Cottony scales may be difficult to control because they are protected by the waxy egg sacs. Control is often aimed at the crawler stage, whose time of appearance varies with the species. Spray crawlers on ornamentals with ORTHO Orthene Systemic Insect Control or ORTHO Isotox Insect Killer. Crawlers on fruit trees can be controlled with ORTHO Fruit & Vegetable Insect Control or ORTHO Diazinon Insect Spray. Contact your local Cooperative Extension Office (see page 1011) to determine the best time to spray for scales in your area. ORTHO Volck Oil Spray is very effective against the eggs and often against the crawlers.

WAX SCALES

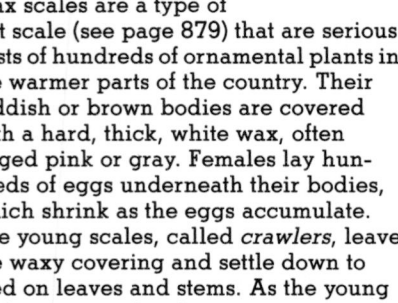

Wax scales are a type of soft scale (see page 879) that are serious pests of hundreds of ornamental plants in the warmer parts of the country. Their reddish or brown bodies are covered with a hard, thick, white wax, often tinged pink or gray. Females lay hundreds of eggs underneath their bodies, which shrink as the eggs accumulate. The young scales, called *crawlers*, leave the waxy covering and settle down to feed on leaves and stems. As the young scales mature, they begin excreting cones of wax on top of their bodies. The wax gives the scales a different appearance when they are in various stages of development (instars). When the immature insects have reached their second instar, they have a "cameo" appearance. The wax is secreted rapidly during the third instar, producing a cone — the "dunce-cap" stage. By the time the insects mature, the wax is very thick, and convex or globular.

CONTROL: Mature female wax scales are difficult to control because they are protected by the thick wax covering. Control is often aimed at the crawler stage, whose seasonal appearance varies with each species. Spray crawlers with ORTHO Orthene Systemic Insect Control or ORTHO Isotox Insect Killer. Contact your local Cooperative Extension Office (see page 1011) to determine the best time to spray for scales in your area. ORTHO Volck Oil Spray is very effective against the eggs and often against the crawlers.

Oystershell scale (3 times life size).

Hemispherical scale (3 times life size).

Whiteflies (life size).

ARMORED SCALES

Armored scales appear as somewhat flattened bumps, either round or very elongated, and are often clustered together on leaves, stems, or bark. Small, immobile, soft-bodied insects live beneath these shells, which are made of wax and cast skins. The shells are not attached to the insect; if the shells are picked off, the insect remains attached to the plant. Females lay their eggs underneath the shells. The young scales, called *crawlers*, are active, usually moving from beneath their mothers' shells to find suitable feeding sites. The crawlers eventually settle down in one spot, where they remain for the rest of their lives, feeding on plant sap. Some armored scales produce a toxin that causes discolored or dead spots on leaves or fruit. Armored scales do not produce honeydew, as other scales do.

CONTROL: Mature scales are difficult to control because they are protected by their shell. Control is usually aimed at the crawlers, whose seasonal appearance varies with species. Spray crawlers with ORTHO Orthene Systemic Insect Control or ORTHO Isotox Insect Killer. Contact your local Cooperative Extension Office (see page 1011) to determine the best time to spray for scales in your area. ORTHO Volck Oil Spray may be used very effectively to smother scales during the dormant season and during the growing season. Before spraying, check to make sure your plant is listed on the product label.

SOFT SCALES

Soft scales are serious pests of hundreds of woody plants, appearing as crusty bumps on bark and leaves. This scale group contains some of the largest species of scales found in the United States. Soft scales (also see page 878) are related to both mealybugs (see page 878) and armored scale (see page 879). Many soft scales look like mealybugs; they are covered with a white, powdery wax during part of their life. Like mealybugs, soft scales excrete large quantities of undigested sap, called *honeydew*, as they feed on plant tissue. Soft scales develop an external skeleton that looks like the armored scales' shell-like covering. This skeleton can't be removed without killing the insect. Depending on the species, female scales lay eggs or produce living young beneath their bodies. The egg-laying females die and shrivel, and the skeletons protect the eggs until they hatch. The young scales, called *crawlers*, move away from their protected sites to find a suitable spot to feed. This stage of the insect, when it is not protected by a skeleton, is most susceptible to insecticides.

CONTROL: Control is often aimed at the susceptible crawler stage, whose seasonal appearance varies with each species. Spray crawlers on ornamentals with ORTHO Orthene Systemic Insect Control or ORTHO Isotox Insect Killer. Contact your local Cooperative Extension Office (see page 1011) for the best time to spray for scales in your area. Control scales on fruit trees with ORTHO Fruit & Vegetable Insect Control or ORTHO Malathion 50 Insect Spray. ORTHO Volck Oil Spray is very effective against the eggs and often against the crawlers.

WHITEFLIES

Whiteflies are tiny ($\frac{1}{12}$ inch), winged insects that are found mainly on the undersides of leaves. When the plant is touched, insects flutter rapidly around it. Whiteflies belong to a family of insects called *Aleyrodidae*, which means "flourlike." The wings of the adults are covered with a white, powdery substance. Whiteflies are mostly tropical insects that are able to survive outdoors only in the southern parts of the country. Their population may build up to tremendous numbers during the growing season. Whiteflies may also infest outdoor plants in colder climates. Infestations come from migrating whiteflies and infested greenhouse-grown plants placed in the garden.

CONTROL: Whiteflies have five stages of development, and each stage has a different tolerance to insecticides. The minute eggs are resistant to most insecticides. The crawlers that hatch from the eggs can be controlled by contact insecticides, such as ORTHO Malathion 50 Insect Spray. The crawlers settle to feed, inserting their mouthparts into plant tissue. They soon lose their legs and take on the appearance of a scale insect. The "scale" stage is resistant to contact insecticides, but can be controlled on ornamentals by insecticides — such as ORTHO Isotox Insect Killer or ORTHO Orthene Systemic Insect Control — that act systemically. On vegetables, the adults can be controlled with ORTHO Fruit & Vegetable Insect Control. All life stages may be present at the same time, but a single application of insecticides affects only susceptible stages, leaving other stages to survive and reproduce. Sprays must be applied at least 3 times at intervals of 4 to 6 days to achieve control.

APHID FAMILY

Blue sharpshooter leafhopper (10 times life size).

Apple sucker psyllid (4 times life size).

Grape leafhoppers (3 times life size).

LEAFHOPPERS

Leafhoppers are small
(under ½ inch), wedge-shaped insects
that hop or fly away quickly when disturbed. Some can run backwards and
sideways as rapidly as they move forward. The adults have wings that are
held over their bodies in a rooflike position. Immature leafhoppers are wingless.
All stages have large eyes on the sides of
their heads and piercing-sucking mouthparts for feeding on plant sap. Leafhoppers feed on many garden plants, causing leaf stippling, stunting, and distortion of the leaves and stems. As they
feed, most leafhoppers excrete large
quantities of a sticky substance called
honeydew, undigested sap that coats the
plants. Many of these pests are also vectors of plant diseases that can damage
plants severely. In addition, certain leafhoppers cause a condition called *hopperburn*. Infested leaves turn brown on
the edges and curl upward. Leafhopper
saliva kills leaf tissue as it is injected into
the conducting vessels.

CONTROL: Leaves that are severely
damaged by leafhoppers are unsightly
and lose much of their ability to produce
food. Insects should be controlled early
before damage is serious. Spray ornamentals with ORTHO Isotox Insect Killer
or ORTHO Diazinon Insect Spray. Spray
food crops with ORTHO Fruit & Vegetable Insect Control or ORTHO Malathion
50 Insect Spray. Cover the lower surfaces
of the leaves thoroughly. Make sure your
plant is listed on the product label.

PSYLLIDS

Psyllids are related to
aphids, and are often called *jumping
plant lice*. The winged adults are small
(up to ⅙ inch) brownish or green insects
that can spring from leaves into flight
with their large hind legs. The wingless
immature psyllids are often covered with
white, waxy threads, or with drops of
honeydew. Psyllids damage plants by
sucking the plant sap. They feed on
shoots and leaves, causing distortion,
stunted growth, and sometimes tip dieback. They may also cover the plant with
honeydew, undigested plant sap that is
excreted as they feed. Some psyllids
transmit plant diseases; others cause leaf
galls to form. Infested leaves curl around
one or more insects and enlarge to form a
gall that completely surrounds them; or
blisterlike galls develop in the center of
leaves (for more information about galls,
see page 869). The insects feed inside
the galls, mature, and the galls split open
to release the adult psyllids. When
plants are heavily infested, thousands of
adults may swarm around and invade
homes.

CONTROL: Psyllids should be controlled early before they are protected inside curled leaves and galls. In mid-May,
spray ornamentals with ORTHO Isotox
Insect Killer or ORTHO Orthene Systemic Insect Control; spray fruits and
vegetables with an insecticide containing *malathion*. Make sure your plant is
listed on the product label. Repeat the
spray in 10 to 14 days.

VECTORS OF
PLANT DISEASES

Many different insects transmit plant diseases, but the most common and widespread carriers are aphids and leafhoppers. Aphids transmit most plant
diseases, especially those caused by
viruses. A single species of aphid may
transmit up to 50 different viruses.
Aphids and leafhoppers are small insects with sucking mouthparts. Their
needlelike "mouths" pierce plant tissue
and suck out the sap. Aphids and leafhoppers may acquire disease organisms
as they feed on an infected plant. Disease
organisms may also be transmitted to offspring through the eggs laid by the infective mother. When the infective insects feed on healthy, susceptible plants,
they inject the disease organisms into the
tissue, infecting the plant. Less common
disease vectors are treehoppers, whiteflies, mealybugs, grasshoppers, beetles,
earwigs, and mites.

CONTROL: Controlling insect vectors is
especially difficult because it takes only
one insect to infect a plant. If you are
troubled by a vector-borne disease, you
can reduce future damage by taking
these precautions:
1. Begin a spray program before the
insect is expected in the spring. To determine when the insect is expected, contact your local Cooperative Extension Office (see page 1011). Spray the plants
you wish to protect and any nearby plants
that the insect may feed on.
2. Destroy any diseased plants and any
weeds that may harbor the disease.
3. If possible, construct a cage of
cheesecloth around the plants you wish
to protect to keep the insect vector from
reaching them.

GRASSHOPPER FAMILY

Spittlebugs on rosemary.

Grasshopper (life size).

Camel cricket (life size).

SPITTLEBUGS

Immature spittlebugs
(nymphs) are small, green, soft-bodied
insects that have an unusual and distinctive characteristic that distinguishes
them from other insects. The nymphs,
clustered in between leaves and stems,
surround themselves with a frothy, white
mass that looks like spittle, which protects them from sun and preying insects.
Adult spittlebugs are small (¼ inch),
winged insects that hop or fly away
quickly when disturbed. They feed on
plant sap and lay their eggs inside stems
or between the leaf blades and stems of
many garden plants and forage crops.
The greenish nymphs that hatch from the
eggs suck sap from the plant. The insect
excretes drops of undigested sap mixed
with air. Its tail moves up and down as if
working a bellows, forcing out bubbles
of sap. The bug then reaches back and
covers itself with the frothy spittle. Spittlebugs are most noticeable in the spring
when the nymphs are feeding, but adults
may be found on the plants throughout
the summer.

CONTROL: A few spittlebugs on a plant
do little harm. However, if the insects appear to be weakening the plant, control
them on ornamentals with ORTHO Isotox
Insect Killer, and on food crops with an
insecticide containing *malathion*. Make
sure your plant is listed on the product
label.

GRASSHOPPERS

Grasshoppers, also
called *locusts*, are large (up to 2½
inches), light and dark-mottled insects
with hind legs enlarged for jumping.
There are hundreds of different species
throughout the United States, but only a
few of these are damaging to garden
plants. Grasshoppers are not a serious
pest every year. Seasonal conditions
must be ideal for them to build up to
large numbers. They are found primarily
in areas that receive only 10 to 30 inches
of rain annually. When winter temperatures are mild and other conditions are
optimum, grasshopper populations increase to tremendous numbers and food
becomes scarce. Under these conditions,
many types of grasshoppers become nonselective in their food preference. Millions of migratory grasshoppers have
been known to form swarms hundreds of
miles across, devouring every green
plant in their path. When infestations
build up to such tremendous numbers,
these grasshoppers pollute water, invade
homes, destroy fabric, and become a
hazard to motorists.

CONTROL: Handpicking eliminates
small populations of grasshoppers. In order to minimize damage, controls should
be applied while the grasshoppers are
young. (Young grasshoppers are distinguished from the adults by their lack of
fully developed wings.) As grasshoppers
mature and increase in size, they require
larger quantities of food. They will migrate, usually from mature and drying
crops and weeds, to the garden to find
food. Spray with ORTHO Fruit & Vegetable Insect Control or with an insecticide
containing *carbaryl* or *malathion*. Repeat
at weekly intervals if the plants become
reinfested.

CRICKETS

Crickets are black,
brown, or green insects, up to 1½ inches
long, that are closely related to grasshoppers (see page 881). Outdoors they feed
on many plants; indoors they feed on
clothes or other materials that have food
or perspiration on them. Some crickets
are beneficial, feeding on aphids and
other small pests. Crickets fly or jump
with their long legs, and have long antennae that reach down their backs. The
males produce a loud chirping sound by
rubbing together parts of their front
wings. Females have long, spear-shaped
ovipositors (egg-laying organs). Depending on the species, females insert eggs
either in the soil or in plant tissue, which
may kill the tissue. Crickets have chewing mouthparts and feed at night on foliage, flowers, seeds, and seedlings, or
on other insects. They hide during the
day in trash, around plants, along walkways, at the foot of walls or fences, or in
the ground. The ground species are
called mole crickets. (For more information about mole crickets, see page 303.)
Crickets also invade homes, especially
in the fall when their natural food supply
disappears. For more information about
crickets as household pests, see
page 801.

CONTROL: If crickets become a problem in the garden, spray with ORTHO
Diazinon Insect Spray or scatter ORTHO
Pest-B-Gon Roach Bait or ORTHO Earwig, Roach & Sowbug Bait in a 2 to 4-foot
band around ornamental plants or other
areas where they congregate. Do not use
around food crops.

GRASSHOPPER FAMILY

FLY FAMILY

Cicada (twice life size).

Mediterranean fruit fly larvae (¾ life size).

Mediterranean fruit fly (4 times life size).

CICADAS

Cicadas are large (up to 1½ inches long), dark-bodied insects, with transparent wings held over their bodies in a rooflike position. The males have special vibratory organs that produce loud, strident sounds. Immature cicadas suck sap from roots (large numbers on the roots of fruit trees may severely reduce flowers and fruit), and adults may suck sap from young twigs. However, the main damage to plants is from egg-laying. Females use their sawlike egg-laying organ to cut the bark and sapwood of twigs. Rows of 24 to 48 eggs are deposited in the sapwood, up to 20 times per female, causing the leaves on damaged twigs to turn brown. Damaged twigs may eventually break and fall to the ground. The young insects that hatch from the eggs enter the soil, where they burrow down to the roots. There are many species of cicadas in the United States. The periodical cicada (*Magicicada septendecim*), found only in the eastern United States, is the longest-lived insect in North America. The southern race has a 13-year life cycle; the northern race, called the *17 year locust*, occurs every 17 years. The various broods (populations) are numbered, so their appearance can be accurately predicted. On the thirteenth or seventeenth spring, as many as 40,000 cicadas may appear from beneath a single tree.

CONTROL: Mature cicadas can be controlled by spraying with an insecticide containing *carbaryl* when their singing is first heard and then repeating the spray after 6 or 7 days. Cut off and destroy injured twigs as soon as possible. Young trees can be protected with mosquito netting. Do not plant new trees in the spring when periodical cicada emergence is predicted.

MEDITERRANEAN FRUIT FLY

The Mediterranean fruit fly, commonly known as the *medfly*, is a tropical insect that infests over 250 species of plants, including many fruits, nuts, and vegetables. (For a list, see page 1002.) Because of its rapid development and wide host range, the medfly is one of the most serious agricultural problems in warm parts of the world. The adult is a little smaller than a house fly, with drooping wings that are banded with yellow, brown, and black.

The spread of the medfly: The medfly is a native of tropical West Africa. Since the mid-1800s it has been spreading to many of the warmer parts of the world, including Hawaii, Southern Europe, and Central and South America. It has been found in the United States off and on since 1929, when it was first discovered in central Florida. Since that time, outbreaks in Florida, Texas, and Southern California have been eradicated. In 1980, a small infestation in Southern California and a larger one in Florida were wiped out. But an infestation in San Jose spread throughout much of the San Francisco Bay Area and developed into a serious threat to California agriculture. The medfly is usually transported into the country as a larva in infested fruit. Most new infestations are the result of travelers bringing home infested fruit and vegetables.

The life cycle: Egg laying begins in the spring after the weather has remained warm (over 75°F) for a week. Male and female flies congregate on fruit, where they mate. The female then finds a fruit that is beginning to ripen. She drills a hole through the skin with her ovipositor (egg-laying organ) and inserts up to 10 white eggs in a cavity. One female can produce up to 1000 eggs during her lifetime. The larvae feed on the ripening fruit, which may rot on the inside. The fruit may appear normal, but fall off the plant prematurely. The mature larvae bore an exit hole and drop to the ground. They pupate in the soil or under objects on the ground. The adults feed on honeydew (see page 454) that is excreted by aphids, mealybugs, and scale insects. Medflies can fly over a mile, but usually remain near the plants in which they developed as larvae. There may be as many as 14 generations during the growing season.

CONTROL: The Mediterranean fruit fly is under quarantine laws and its spread is constantly monitored by detection traps operated by state and federal departments of agriculture. Fruit shipped from countries with medfly infestations must be fumigated or otherwise treated before it is accepted by countries in which the medfly is likely to survive. Despite these precautions, the insect sometimes gains entry and spreads. Summer and fall (May to October) are the most likely times to detect the fly. If you live in an infested area, you should learn to identify the medfly, and notify your local Co-operative Extension Office (see page 1011) if you suspect an outbreak in your neighborhood. In California, spray the ground under host plants with ORTHO Fruit & Vegetable Insect Control or ORTHO Diazinon Insect Spray.

THRIPS FAMILY ———————————————————————————————— SOIL PESTS ——————————————

Flower thrips damage to pansy.

Leaf thrips damage to viburnum.

Ants (twice life size).

FLOWER THRIPS

Flower thrips (*Frankliniella* species) are tiny (¹⁄₂₀ inch long) insects that infest the flowers, flower buds, and growing points of many plants. They are able to distinguish different colors of flowers, usually preferring those that are yellow or light-colored. The amber-colored adults and lemon-yellow nymphs (immature thrips) feed by rasping the plant tissue and then sucking the released plant sap. The injured tissue dies, producing dead spots, distorted blossoms and new leaves, and balled flowers (flower buds that turn brown and never open). Flower thrips are most abundant between late spring and midsummer. They reproduce mainly on the flowers of trees, grasses, and weeds, and then migrate to gardens nearby. In the western states, thrips are most damaging when uncultivated plants dry up in summer, forcing the insects to migrate to gardens where plants are still green.

CONTROL: Flower thrips are difficult to control because they are usually protected in plant tissue, and they constantly reinfest garden flowers from nearby plants. Spraying ornamentals with a systemic insecticide (one that moves through the plant) will protect flowers for up to 10 days. Use ORTHO Orthene Systemic Insect Control or ORTHO Isotox Insect Killer at the first sign of damage. Control thrips on food crops with ORTHO Malathion 50 Insect Spray or ORTHO Fruit & Vegetable Insect Control. Make sure your plant is listed on the label. Repeat the spray 2 more times at intervals of 7 to 10 days to control thrips as they hatch.

THRIPS

Thrips are tiny (less than ¹⁄₁₆ inch), slender insects of the order *Thysanoptera*, which means "bristle wings" or "fringe wings." Adults are tan to dark brown or black with two pairs of featherlike wings. The immature insects (nymphs) are wingless, and usually lighter in color. Thrips are serious pests of hundreds of plants in the garden. Nymphs and adults feed by scraping or rasping the plant tissue and then sucking the released plant sap. Blossoms, fruit, foliage, and shoots become flecked, streaked, or distorted. Females lay fertilized or unfertilized eggs in plant tissue. The unfertilized eggs develop only into males. Most species of thrips complete a life cycle in 2 to 3 weeks, so populations can rapidly build up to tremendous numbers. In warm winter areas, reproduction may continue throughout the year.

CONTROL: Exposed thrips (those that feed unprotected on foliage) are easier to control than flower thrips, which are protected from chemicals inside the flowers or growing points of the plant. Remove infested buds and blooms. Spray flowers with a systemic insecticide such as ORTHO Isotox Insect Killer or ORTHO Orthene Systemic Insect Control. Spray ornamentals for exposed thrips with ORTHO Isotox Insect Killer, ORTHO Malathion 50 Insect Spray, or ORTHO Liquid Sevin. Control thrips on food crops with ORTHO Fruit & Vegetable Insect Control or ORTHO Malathion 50 Insect Spray. Apply sprays 2 more times at intervals of 7 to 10 days to control thrips as they hatch. Because most types of thrips migrate long distances on wind currents, they can quickly reinfest plants. Check your plants periodically for new damage.

ANTS

Ants are social insects, relatives of bees and wasps, and live in colonies or nests. Each colony has large egg-laying queens, larvae, pupae, and wingless, sterile workers, which are all females. In the spring or early summer, the queen produces winged males and females that may leave the nest to start new colonies or enter established colonies. After mating, the males die, and the queens shed their wings and begin laying eggs. Many different types of ants are found throughout the United States. All ants have a constricted abdomen, and they range in color from yellow to black. Some ants invade homes looking for food (see page 803). Others find their food outside, where they feed on insects, seeds, vegetable roots, flower nectar, or honeydew, a sweet, sticky excretion from sucking insects, including aphids, soft scales, mealybugs, leafhoppers, and whiteflies. Certain ants caress aphids to increase their production of honeydew, or carry them to uninfested plants to supply them with ample food. Ant colonies or mounds located in the garden, lawn, or cultivated fields disturb plant roots and interfere with the use of equipment. The mounds are often more of a nuisance than the ants themselves.

CONTROL: Ant mounds in the garden can be treated with ORTHO Diazinon Granules or sprayed with ORTHO Diazinon Insect Spray. Control aphids (page 877), scales (page 879), mealybugs (page 878), leafhoppers (page 880) and whiteflies (page 879) to eliminate the production of honeydew, which attracts ants.

SOIL PESTS

Fire ant mound.

Earwig (twice life size).

Centipede (life size).

FIRE ANTS

Fire ants (*Solenopsis* species) are small (up to ¼ inch) red or black ants that build large, hard nests in the ground, 15 inches to 3 feet high. Mounds or nests are found in lawns and gardens, or in houses, when ants are driven inside by rain or drought. They are especially numerous in pasture lands, where there may be up to 60 mounds per acre. Damage from fire ants is due mainly to their mounds, which interfere with mowing or cultivating in the garden, and with harvest operations in commercial vegetable production. The large mounds ruin garden equipment and machinery. Fire ants may also damage plants. Some species feed on young succulent vegetables, bark, and insects, while others eat almost anything, including seeds, plants, insects, nesting birds, household foods, and clothes. The ants may attack and kill young animals and ground birds, such as quail; they also sting people, usually on the feet or legs, who accidentally disturb their nests. Depending on the degree of allergy, people react differently to the sting, which may be very painful and serious. The ant first bites the skin, raising it slightly, and then inserts its stinger, leaving it there for up to 25 seconds. It may repeat this procedure 2 or 3 more times, causing a cluster of stings. Within 24 hours, pustules develop that are up to ⅛ inch in diameter.

CONTROL: Fire ants can be controlled in the lawn by treating their mounds as they appear with ORTHO Fire Ant Control, ORTHO Lawn Insect Spray, or ORTHO Diazinon Insect Spray. Break up the hard surfaces and then wet them thoroughly with the insecticide, including a circle 4 feet in diameter around the mounds. If you have a severe reaction to fire ant stings, call your doctor.

EARWIGS

Earwigs are hard, flattened, reddish brown insects, up to 1 inch long with forcepslike pincers that extend from the back end. The pincers on the females are almost straight, with a sharp inward curve on the end. On the males, the pincers are longer and have a wide curve. The pincers are used as offensive and defensive weapons, and sometimes to catch insects, on which they feed. However, their main source of food is from plants, ripe fruit, and decaying organic matter. Young earwigs eat ragged holes in the leaves of many vegetables and flowers in spring or early summer. Older earwigs feed on blossoms and corn silk, causing poor kernel development on the cobs. The insects may even climb into large fruit trees, such as apricot and peach trees, and feed on ripening fruit. Earwigs are nocturnal insects, feeding at night and hiding during the day. In daylight hours they hide in damp, dark places, such as in wood piles or plant refuse, under flower pots, or in homes, where they become household pests. For more information about earwigs as household pests, see page 801.

CONTROL: If you think earwigs are eating your plants, inspect the plants at night with a flashlight. Spray with ORTHO Diazinon Insect Spray or scatter ORTHO Pest-B-Gon Roach Bait or ORTHO Earwig, Roach & Sowbug Bait lightly in a 2 to 4-foot band around plants, flower pots, house and porch foundations, woodpiles, or anywhere else you think earwigs may be hiding. Do not use on food crops. To keep earwigs out of fruit trees growing in lawn areas, sprinkle ORTHO Diazinon Soil & Turf Insect Control around the base of the trees about a month before the fruit ripens.

CENTIPEDES

Centipedes, often called *hundred-legged worms*, are not true insects, but they are closely related. They have no wings; only two main body parts instead of three; and instead of three pairs of legs like true insects, they have one pair on each segment of their body. Most centipedes have at least 15 pairs of legs. Their bodies are long in relation to width and somewhat flattened, which make it possible for them to squeeze into cracks and crevices of foundations and around windows. Most centipedes are about 1 inch long, but some of the tropical species reach 18 inches in length. Centipedes look like millipedes (see page 885), but are more active. Centipedes scurry rapidly away when disturbed; millipedes usually curl into a tight spiral. Centipedes do not injure plants. They are beneficial, preying on snails, insects, and earthworms. Centipedes hide in damp areas under logs and stones, and in plant debris. They can move swiftly to catch their prey, which they paralyze by injecting poison from claws located behind the head. Some of the larger species of centipedes may inflict a painful bite if they are handled by humans.

CONTROL: It is usually unnecessary to control centipedes unless they start infesting your home. Sealing cracks in the foundation or holes in window frames will help prevent centipedes from entering the house. Clear wood, stones, and dead vegetation away from the base of the house. Scatter ORTHO Pest-B-Gon Roach Bait or ORTHO Earwig, Roach & Sowbug Bait around areas where centipedes hide. Do not use on food crops. Inside the home, use ORTHO Flying & Crawling Insect Killer.

Millipede (twice life size).

Damaged root. *Insert:* Symphylan (4 times life size).

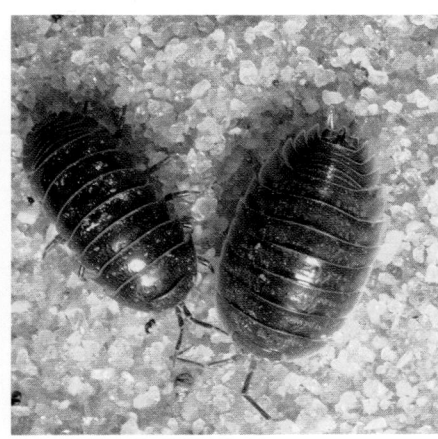

Sowbugs (twice life size).

MILLIPEDES

Millipedes, also called *thousand-legged worms*, are distant relatives of centipedes (see page 884). Millipedes are one to several inches long, hard-bodied, cylindrical, and wormlike, usually brown, pinkish brown, or grayish. They have two very short legs on each body segment, numbering from 30 to 400 legs. Young millipedes look like the adults, but initially have only 3 pairs of legs. Millipedes curl up in a coil when they are touched or picked up. They hide in damp, dark places, such as under stones or boards, or in plant debris. Large numbers of them may crawl into houses during heavy rains or during dry periods in summer and fall. Millipedes normally feed on decaying matter. But when they become numerous, they may feed on small roots, seedlings, or vegetable seeds. Root crops, decaying flower bulbs, and overripe fruit that touch damp ground, especially muskmelons, tomatoes, and strawberries, may attract millipedes.

CONTROL: If millipedes are a problem in your garden, scatter ORTHO Pest-B-Gon Roach Bait, ORTHO Slug-Geta Snail & Slug Bait, or ORTHO Earwig, Roach & Sowbug Bait lightly in a 2 to 4-foot band around plants and other areas where millipedes hide. Do not use around food crops. Protect ripening fruits on the ground with straw or other mulch. To reduce the number of millipedes that enter your home, remove vegetation and plant debris from around your house foundation and spray around the foundation with ORTHO Diazinon Insect Spray. Millipedes move slowly, which makes them simple to remove from inside the house. Pick them up by hand or with a vacuum cleaner, or sweep them up with a broom.

SYMPHYLANS

Symphylans are small (up to ¼ inch), pure white, soft-bodied animals with 12 pairs of legs. They are often called *garden centipedes* because of their similarity to centipedes (see page 884). The tiny animals are very active in damp soil, outside in warm climates or in greenhouses everywhere. They feed on many vegetables, fruits, and flowers, attacking germinating seeds, plant root systems, and aboveground parts in contact with the soil. Small plants may die or be severely stunted. Larger, more mature plants can usually withstand a symphylan infestation. When the weather warms in the spring, symphylans migrate up to the top 6 inches of soil where they usually remain feeding throughout the summer. In late fall, they move deeper in the soil to more protected sites. Symphylans are often found in large numbers in localized areas, marked by a group of stunted plants. Sifting through a shovelful of soil from the site will confirm their presence.

CONTROL: Drenching the soil with an insecticide containing *malathion* may reduce injury to plants. An insecticide containing *diazinon* granules mixed into the top 4 to 8 inches of soil before planting may allow vegetable plants to establish a good root system and become resistant to damage by symphylans. Seeds and plants must be set immediately after treatment. An insecticide containing *lindane* can be used for nonfood crops. Thorough discing or tilling of the soil before planting will scatter and destroy many symphylans, which gives plants time to grow before the symphylan population builds up again.

SOWBUGS AND PILLBUGS

Sowbugs and pillbugs are crustaceans, and are related to lobsters and shrimp. They are dark gray, with hard, flattened, segmented bodies, about ½ inch long, and have many legs. Pillbugs roll up into a ball when disturbed. Sowbugs and pillbugs are nocturnal insects. They feed at night on decaying vegetable matter, and are destructive to plants only when their populations build up to very large numbers. When this happens, they feed on the fine roots of seedlings in the garden or greenhouse. They also feed on fruit and leaves that are in contact with the ground. During the day, sowbugs and pillbugs hide in damp, dark places, such as under boards, rocks, or flower pots, or in plant debris. Sometimes they invade homes through cracks or windows, and hide in dark places like basements. They do no damage inside, but they can be a nuisance.

CONTROL: If you notice large numbers of sowbugs or pillbugs under your flower pots or in the garden, scatter ORTHO Slug-Geta Snail & Slug Bait, ORTHO Pest-B-Gon Roach Bait, or ORTHO Earwig, Roach & Sowbug Bait lightly in a 2 to 4-foot band around plants, flower pots, boards, plant debris, and other areas where sowbugs and pillbugs congregate. Do not use around food crops. Where possible, eliminate moist, dark breeding sites (rocks, boards, leaves). Spray around house foundations with ORTHO Diazinon Insect Spray.

MITES

BENEFICIAL INSECTS

Mite damage on hollyhock.

Lady beetle (twice life size).

Praying mantid (¾ life size).

MITES

Mites are minute pests that infest many garden plants. There are many injurious species, some of which are commonly called *spider mites*. Some mites may injure humans or animals; others are beneficial predators of plant pests. Mites are not insects, but belong to the animal class *Arachnida*, along with spiders, ticks, and several other groups. They have 4 pairs of legs instead of 3, and lack antennae and true jaws. Each mite has a pair of needlelike stylets that pierce plant tissue. The sap and cell contents are sucked out, resulting in leaf stippling. Most mites have many generations each year, often completing a life cycle in 7 to 10 days. Mites, cast skins, egg shells, and webbing may cover the surfaces of leaves or other plant parts. Heavy rains usually limit spider mite populations by washing them off the plant.

CONTROL: Mites can be difficult to control because the egg stage is resistant to most chemical sprays. Chemicals are effective against other stages, however. They must be applied at least 3 times at intervals of 7 to 10 days for effective control. Spray ornamentals with ORTHO Isotox Insect Killer or ORTHO Orthene Insect Spray. Control mites on fruits and vegetables with ORTHO Fruit & Vegetable Insect Control, ORTHO Diazinon Insect Spray, or ORTHO Malathion 50 Insect Spray.

LADY BEETLES

Lady beetles, also called *ladybugs* and *ladybird beetles*, are beneficial insects that prey mostly on aphids, but also eat scales, mealybugs, and mites. They belong to the large insect family *Coccinellidae*, which means "scarlet red." People often think of lady beetles as red with black spots, but there are many different species that range in color from gray and black to bright orange. The larvae are flat, orange or gray, alligator-shaped insects, with legs on the front half of the body. Unlike the adults, they have no wings or wing covers. The cigar-shaped eggs are usually orange, and stand upright in clusters of a dozen or more. A single lady beetle may lay up to 1500 eggs during her life. The larvae that hatch from the eggs feed on aphids or other insects, devouring up to 25 aphids a day. Because lady beetles are such voracious eaters, they require high populations of aphids to maintain themselves. Adults may eat 50 or more aphids a day. If the prey population is reduced to such low numbers that there are not enough aphids on which to feed, the lady beetles will migrate or starve to death. The aphid population will gradually rebuild, possibly followed by a return of the lady beetle population. These population fluctuations are very common between predators and their prey. Lady beetles can be purchased at garden stores or through mail-order houses. These insects have been collected from huge masses in areas where they hibernate. When they are placed out in the garden, there is no guarantee they will stay. Even when there is food available, lady beetles often have an urge to migrate. Some may remain in the garden, but most will move to your neighbors' yards.

PRAYING MANTIDS

Praying mantids are considered beneficial insects because they prey on many insect pests. However, they are just as likely to prey on a harmless insect or even another beneficial insect, such as a honeybee, as they are on a pest species. Their name comes from the position in which they wait for their prey — a position of prayer. They are large (up to 5 inches), slender, green or straw-colored insects with wings and long legs. The front legs are larger than the hind legs and have spines that are used to grasp and hold their prey. The immature mantids look just like the adults but are smaller and do not have wings. In the fall, the females lay 100 or more eggs in foamlike, straw-colored masses attached to any type of plant in the garden. After mating, the female often devours the male mantid. The following May or June the emerging young begin feeding on aphids or other small, slow-moving prey. They may also feed on one another. As they increase in size, they feed on larger insects. The mantids kill their prey by biting the back of the neck, which severs the main nerves and renders the animal helpless. Praying mantid eggs can be purchased or gathered from roadside borders, around fields, or from shrubs. Leave them attached to a section of the plant and place them in your garden off the ground where they won't be soaked by rain. Because they are not heavy feeders, mantids are relatively ineffective as insect controls. But they are interesting.

Larva (6 times life size). Adult (twice life size).

LACEWINGS

Lacewings are beneficial
insects that belong to a group called
nerve-winged insects. The adults are up
to ¾ inch long, have long antennae, and
transparent green or brown lacy wings
held over the body in a rooflike position.
The green species has iridescent red-
gold eyes and, in its adult form, is one of
the most beautiful insects. The larvae are
small (up to ½ inch), flat, spindle-shaped
insects resembling miniature alligators.
They are yellow to gray with reddish
brown markings and sickle-shaped jaws
for capturing their prey. The larvae suck
the body fluids from aphids, mealybugs,
scales, and other small insects. Some
species carry the remains of their victims
on their backs. The larvae are such voracious eaters that they are commonly
called *aphid lions*. The female lacewings
lay their eggs singly on top of a delicate,
hairlike stalk projecting from the surface of a leaf or twig. This prevents the
hatching larvae from devouring other
unhatched eggs. At night, the adult lacewings are attracted to bright lights,
and may cling to screen doors. Lacewings can be purchased from insectar-
ies, companies that raise insect predators
and parasites. Because they don't survive
the winter well, they should be reintro-
duced each spring.

A GALLERY OF ANIMAL PESTS

Animals in the garden can be the worst problem the gardener has. Their presence influences the way he gardens and often which plants he selects. Control of animals in the garden is difficult for a couple of reasons.

One reason is that animals are more intelligent than insects or plant diseases, and can overcome the obstacles we place in their path. The other reason is that we often can't kill them as we can insects or disease-causing organisms. The sight of a deer and her fawn browsing in our back yard in the morning may give us as much pleasure as the roses she is eating. Or the culprit may be our neighbor's cat — or even our own!

Over the centuries, gardeners have developed a multitude of ways to repel animals. Most of these methods work for some and not for others, or work one year and fail the next. Repellents are not very reliable because animals and birds learn from experience. A radio in the orchard may frighten off the deer one year, or for a few months, but eventually the deer learn that the radio is harmless and will browse next to it. Deer in populated areas even learn which dogs to fear and which are harmless nuisances.

Usually the most effective way to control animal pests is to fence them out. This may mean a fence around the garden, or a sheet of hardware cloth laid over the bulb bed to keep mice from digging up the bulbs.

When animal pests need to be removed, traps are usually more effective than poisons, although in some cases poison baits work well. Traps let you see that you have caught the animal, for one thing. And if the animal is one you don't want to kill, you can catch it in a live trap (see page 891) and release it in a nearby wilderness area. But there are local regulations governing this — ask your county agricultural commissioner about the rules in your area.

Above: Tree squirrel. See page 893. Left: A doe browsing at the edge of a yard. See page 891.

Meadow mouse runway. *Insert:* Meadow mouse.

Mole tunnels.

Gopher mound.

MICE

Several kinds of mice invade gardens throughout the United States. Mice live in grassy or brushy areas, nesting underground in shallow burrows, or aboveground in densely vegetated, protected spots. They may also establish nests in thick hay or leaf mulches in the garden. Mice usually move along narrow runways from their nesting areas to their source of food. They are active throughout the year, digging up and feeding on seeds and nuts. They also feed on bulbs and tender vegetables and flowers, and may severely damage young trees by gnawing on the bark and roots. Mice are nocturnal, and do most of their damage at night.

CONTROL: You can keep mice out of the garden by putting up a fence. Surround the area you wish to protect with a woven wire fence (¼-inch mesh) at least 12 inches high. To prevent mice from tunneling underneath, extend the fence 12 inches below the soil surface. Or bend 12 inches of the wire mesh outward before burying it a few inches deep. Protect young tree trunks by placing hardware cloth cylinders 12 inches high around the tree, burying several inches of the cylinder in the soil. You may also protect the trunk by wrapping tree-wrapping plastic, available in nurseries, around the bottom of the trunk. Keep your garden free of grassy areas and hay or leaf mulches to reduce possible hiding and breeding areas for mice. Protect bulbs by covering the planted areas with hardware mesh, burying the edges in the ground. Traps or poisoned baits placed along mouse runways may be used. For more information about traps, see page 891. A few active cats will help reduce the mouse population.

MOLES

Moles are small (up to 9 inches), gray to black mammals with fine velvety fur. They have slender hairless snouts and inconspicuous eyes and ears. Their eyesight is poor but they have superior senses of smell, touch, and hearing. The front feet are much larger than the hind feet and have long trowellike claws used for tunneling in the ground. Moles live in burrows made up of many interconnecting runways that are usually about 6 to 8 inches underground. Some species also dig many shallow feeding runways only a few inches below ground, which produces ridges on the soil surface. These ridges are especially noticeable in lawns. Moles dig lateral tunnels to the surface, where they deposit surplus soil in volcano shaped mounds. Occasionally they leave their tunnels to search for food or to move to new areas. Moles seldom feed on plants. They eat slugs, earthworms, grubs, and other small insects. Damage to plants is caused by their tunneling, which uproots plants or loosens the soil around roots so they dry out and die.

CONTROL: The best way to rid your lawn of moles is to control the insects that they feed on. (For more information, see page 309.) Traps are generally used for the rest of the garden, and can also be used in lawns. Before placing traps on shallow tunnels, you must determine which tunnels are still active. Roll or tamp down the ridges. Those that are raised the following day are still active. Trapping in main runways is usually more productive. To detect these deeper runways, probe between mounds with a rod. Poison baits, fumigants, and repellents are generally ineffective.

POCKET GOPHERS

These burrowing rodents live and feed almost entirely underground. Pocket gophers eat roots and bulbs, and plants that they pull down into their burrows. They can kill shrubs by eating most of the roots and girdling the underground part of the trunk or stems. Damaged plants wilt, sometimes on only one side. Pocket gophers are solitary and fiercely territorial, so only one gopher inhabits a run system at a time. They are also quite active, and seem to be constantly digging new tunnels. The crescent-shaped mounds of soil they leave on the surface are excavated from new runs. Their tunnels sometimes drain irrigation ditches or basins, so the water does not soak into the soil.

CONTROL: Gophers are best controlled by trapping. Find the main runway by probing with a sharp rod about a foot deep near a fresh mound or an eaten plant. Dig a hole to intersect the run, and insert 2 wire or box traps in the run, one facing in each direction. Tie the traps together or to a stake above ground. To keep soil from falling on the traps, cover the hole with sod or a board, and sprinkle with soil to block out all light. Check and move the traps daily. Although only one gopher occupies a burrow system at a time, migrating gophers will move into an abandoned burrow. Level all the mounds, and watch for signs that the burrow has been reoccupied. Gophers can also be controlled by an active cat.

Deer.

Snap beans damaged by deer.

Live-catch traps.

DEER

Deer can be very damaging to gardens in rural and suburban areas.
They feed on many vegetables and flowers, stripping off new growth and often eating the entire plant. Deer may also browse on the tender bark, leaves, and twigs of shrubs and trees. Usually they feed on tree buds and bark during the winter or when other sources of food are scarce. The males may damage trees by rubbing their antlers on the trunks and branches. While feeding, they may trample on plants.

CONTROL: The best way to prevent deer damage is to fence them out. Deer are strong and agile jumpers; to be effective, a vertical fence must be at least 8 feet high. Enclose all areas of the garden that are accessible to deer. The fencing material should be a woven wire mesh. Stretch it between wooden or steel posts placed 10 to 12 feet apart. The wire mesh should fit tightly along the ground to prevent deer from forcing their way under the fence. A strand of barbed wire stretched along the ground will discourage deer from attempting to go under the fence. If the ground is uneven, secure the mesh to depressions in the ground, or fill in the depressions with soil, rocks, or other material.

Slanted fences: A slanted fence may also be used. Although deer are good high jumpers, they will not jump a barricade that is both high and wide. You can keep deer out with a fence that is only 4 feet high if it is also 4 feet wide. Anchor 6-foot steel posts in the ground 30 to 40 feet apart, burying the bottom third of the post. Attach a heavy guy wire along the top. Stretch 6-foot-wide wire mesh fencing at a 45° angle along the posts, securing the mesh with stakes at the bottom, and attaching it to the guy wires at the top. Build the fence so that the deer will approach it from the side where the posts are anchored. If you live in an area where snowfall is heavy, wire mesh is likely to be crushed by settling snow pack. Instead, use smooth wire stretched horizontally 4 inches apart.

Other methods: Electric fences are also effective. After deer have been shocked a few times, they will learn to avoid the fence. Individual trees or small areas can be protected with individual wire mesh cages (1 or 2-inch mesh). You can also spray repellents such as *tetramethylthiuram disulfide* or *zinc dithiocarbamate amine* on trees to prevent browsing damage. Deer may also be repelled by nylon stockings filled with human hair or small sacks of blood meal hung on trees you wish to protect. Kerosene or creosote-soaked rags, or perforated cans of mothballs hung from trees, may also repel deer. Sometimes all deer control measures fail, and killing certain problem deer may be the only solution. Because deer are protected by law, contact your agricultural commissioner or State Department of Fish and Game regional office for regulations.

ABOUT TRAPS

Traps are used to control many animal pests, either in combination with other methods or when other methods fail. The two most commonly used types are live-catch traps and snap traps. Before purchasing a trap, check with your agricultural commissioner or regional Department of Fish and Game to determine what regulations govern the type of animal you are trying to control. Some states prohibit trapping or killing certain animal species. Purchase the appropriate size trap for the animal you are trapping. Live-catch traps are the most humane. They are rectangular boxes with trap doors at both ends that shut when the animal touches a trigger in the box. The animal may be safely carried in the trap to your local humane society, or released in an acceptable area. Snap traps close on the leg or body of the animal when it touches the trigger. Some types, such as mousetraps, kill or severely injure the animal. Others, such as leghold traps, hold on to the animal until the trapper disposes of it. When using snap traps, fasten them to a stake or tree to prevent the animal from dragging the trap away. Snap traps should not be used in areas where pets can be trapped accidentally. If possible, tie the bait to the trigger with a piece of string or wire to prevent the animal from stealing the food. Most animals are fearful of new objects. If allowed to explore the unset trap and feed on the bait for a few days, they'll become accustomed to the trap, and will be easier to capture after you set it. Check traps daily.

Dog digging in garden.

Cat.

Earthworm (life size).

DOGS

Dogs can devastate a garden, especially when allowed to play or romp freely in a small yard. They cause damage by trampling or lying on plants, digging up the soil, and depositing droppings and urine around the yard.

CONTROL: Discourage dogs from digging around or urinating on plants by spraying the affected area with ORTHO Scram Dog & Cat Repellent according to label directions. Further dog-proof these spots by putting up a fence. The sturdiness of the fence will depend on the size, strength, and determination of your pet. A flimsy fence made of wire strung between stakes may be adequate for a small, well-behaved animal. Larger, more rambunctious dogs will require sturdier fences. Eventually the animal will adjust to the new boundaries, and will be less likely to damage planted areas when the fence is removed. Proper discipline and the provision of an alternate location in which the animal can play will reduce damage to garden plants.

CATS

Cats are usually beneficial to a home garden; they help keep mice, rats, and other rodents under control, and frighten away nuisance birds. But cats can be damaging in newly planted areas. They dig up soft, loose soil where they bury their droppings and urine. They unearth seeds and transplants while digging, and may continue to damage these areas until the soil becomes compacted or plants fill in the area.

CONTROL: You can discourage cats from digging in newly planted areas by spraying the soil with ORTHO Scram Dog & Cat Repellent according to label directions. Protect seedbeds by laying chicken wire on the soil; remove the wire before the plants are too large to slip through the mesh. If plants are already present, set up cages made of 1-inch chicken wire over newly planted spots. You can take away protective devices after the soil packs down, or when vegetation covers bare areas.

EARTHWORMS

Earthworms are beneficial soil-dwelling animals. They surface in large numbers during a heavy rain or other times when the soil is saturated with water. As they tunnel through the ground earthworms ingest soil, digesting any organic matter in it. They may deposit the soil that passes through their bodies as crumbly mounds (castings) on the soil surface. A large population of earthworms can sometimes be a nuisance in a lawn when many castings accumulate. Earthworm tunnels help to aerate and loosen the soil, improving soil drainage and tilth and facilitating root growth. Although they are most numerous in the top 6 inches of soil, earthworms may tunnel 6 feet down into the ground, bringing up deep layers of soil to the surface. Sometimes earthworms enter the drainage holes of containers sitting on the soil, or sunken into the ground. As their castings accumulate in the container, the drainage becomes clogged.

CONTROL: For the most part, earthworm activity in the ground is beneficial, and should be encouraged. If you are having trouble with castings on your lawn, see page 310 for information on how to treat this problem. To prevent earthworms from getting into containers in or on the ground, place a piece of screen over the drainage hole. Or set the container on a layer of gravel or cinders; earthworms will not move through such a coarse layer.

Starling.

Yellow-bellied sapsucker damage.

Tree squirrel.

BIRDS

Many types of birds feed on seeds, seedlings, fruit, and berries in the garden. Birds scratch away at soft soil to unearth newly planted seeds. They peck at seedlings and young, tender leaves. Birds are especially damaging to berries, grapes, and soft fruit.

CONTROL: Once birds develop the habit of feeding in your garden, you will probably have to exclude them with wire or fabric cages. Make wire cages out of 1-inch chicken wire. Cages that are about 10"x10"x24" are self-supporting. Larger cages may need to be reinforced with heavy wire. You can also make cages or protective coverings with cheesecloth or plastic bird netting supported by stakes or stretched over a wooden frame. If birds have not yet developed the habit of feeding in your garden, you may be able to repel them without having to construct cages. Set up stakes around the plantings you wish to protect and tie criss-crossing strings between the stakes. Attach strips of aluminum foil to the strings. Birds will not readily fly through the crossing strings, and will avoid the shiny aluminum. Scarecrows are usually not effective for long. You can remove protective devices once plants have produced several sets of mature leaves, or in the case of berries, after you've harvested all of the fruit. To prevent birds from digging up seeds, lay hardware cloth (¼-inch mesh) over the seed bed. It must be removed before the plants are too large to slip through the mesh. For information on controlling bird damage on tree fruit, see page 616.

SAPSUCKERS

Sapsuckers are members of the woodpecker family that feed on tree bark and sap. The red-breasted sapsucker (*Sphyrapicus varius ruber*) is found in the Pacific Northwest and British Columbia. The yellow-breasted sapsucker (*S. varius varius*) is common throughout much of the United States. Sapsuckers peck into many trees before finding a suitable one that has sap with a high sugar content. Once the birds find a favorite tree, they visit it many times a day and feed on it year after year. Sapsucker damage to the tree is very distinctive. They drill uniform round or rectangular holes in the bark, ¼ inch in diameter, arranged in horizontal rings around the trunk. Sap often oozes from the holes, and portions of the tree bark may fall off after sapsuckers have drilled many holes. The tree trunk may eventually be girdled by sapsucker drilling, causing the tree above the damaged area to die. Sometimes the birds' beaks are contaminated with fungus spores, or the spores are blown or splashed into the holes. Once inside the tree, the disease organisms may damage or kill the tree.

CONTROL: It is difficult to prevent sapsucker damage to trees. Wrapping the damaged trunk with burlap or smearing a sticky material (such as the latex used for ant control) above and below the holes may inhibit new pecking damage. For a list of trees most commonly attacked by sapsuckers, see page 999.

TREE SQUIRRELS

Tree squirrels are mainly a problem in forested or lightly wooded rural or suburban areas. These animals establish nests in tree hollows, or build nests of leaves, twigs, and bark in trees. They are omnivorous, feeding on fruit, seeds, nuts, insects, and bark. Tree squirrels are agile climbers and jumpers; they can easily jump 6 feet from the ground to a branch or structure, or between branches. These animals damage gardens by digging up newly planted seeds and bulbs, and sometimes entire plants. They may strip the bark or leaves from trees and shrubs, and feed on fruits and nuts.

CONTROL: Keep tree squirrels out of newly planted seed and bulb beds by placing chicken wire over the planted area. Bury the edges of the mesh in the soil, or weight them down with bricks. Remove the wire before the plants are too large to fit through the mesh. Prevent tree squirrels from climbing up fruit and nut trees by snugly placing 2-foot-wide bands of metal (made from material such as aluminum roof flashing) around tree trunks at least 6 feet above the ground. Prune branches so that they are at least 6 feet above the ground, and 6 feet away from structures or the branches of other trees. If permissible in your area, you can also trap tree squirrels. Contact your Department of Fish and Game to determine local regulations. Place or tie traps near tree squirrel trails or nests. Bait the traps with nuts, sunflowers seeds, peanut butter, or raisins. For more information about trapping, see page 891.

Lined ground squirrel.

Rabbit damage to dwarf apples.

Raccoon.

GROUND SQUIRRELS

Several types of ground squirrels are found throughout the United States, but these animals are mainly a problem west of the Rocky Mountains. Ground squirrels live in underground burrows located in open, sunny areas. Many species are social, forming large underground colonies that may extend over an acre. Sometimes ground squirrels excavate burrows under buildings, causing stress cracking of the foundation. In certain areas, ground squirrels and some of their parasites may transmit serious diseases to humans. These animals can be very damaging to gardens. In the late winter and spring, they emerge from hibernation to invade gardens, feeding on tender green growth. Later in the season they feed on seeds, grains, vegetables, fruits, and nuts.

CONTROL: Ground squirrels are agile climbers; they can climb over most fences. If there are only a few ground squirrels causing damage, trap them. Set the traps near burrow entrances or along pathways used by the animals. Use baits such as peanut butter, nuts, raisins, or cereals. Because ground squirrels may carry diseases, always wear gloves and protective clothing when handling them. For more information about traps, see page 891. Contact the Humane Society for information on how to get rid of the trapped animals. If large colonies (more than a dozen ground squirrels) are present, contact a pest control operator, who will eliminate the colony using fumigants or poisoned baits.

RABBITS

Rabbits are cute little animals but they may be very annoying and damaging pests in the garden. Their reproductive rate is high. They produce several litters a year, with 4 to 7 babies in each litter. Rabbits are active all year long, mainly during the day. In the summer, they feed on any tender young plants, especially garden vegetables. During the winter, they gnaw on bark, twigs, and buds. They are especially destructive to young fruit trees in the winter. Much of the bark on small trees may be eaten, and young branches are often clipped off. Clipped twigs are removed cleanly, without ragged edges. Rabbits can also clip off twigs on older trees up to 2 feet above snow or ground level.

CONTROL: The best way to keep rabbits out of a vegetable garden or small orchard is to enclose it with a 1½-inch mesh chicken wire fence. The fence should be 2 feet high in areas with little snow, or 2 feet above the snow level in areas where snow accumulates. The bottom must be tight to the ground. Or build portable cages to place over small garden plots. Single trees can be protected by building a cylindrical chicken wire fence 2 feet high around the trunk. Several other methods of control may help prevent rabbit damage. Sprinkling dried blood meal near plants may repel rabbits, and it is also beneficial to the soil. It must be reapplied every few days during wet weather. Chemical repellents, cats, dogs, or live traps may also be used to protect the garden from rabbits.

RACCOONS

Raccoons are a nuisance mainly in wooded rural or lightly populated suburban areas. They usually establish their dens in hollow logs, trees, or other natural shelters near a source of water. Raccoons are omnivorous, feeding on insects, small mammals, fish, fruit, nuts, grains, and vegetables; they are especially fond of corn. Raccoons are nocturnal animals, foraging at night and returning to their dens during the day. They are agile climbers, and climb trees to feed on fruit or nuts, often knocking many to the ground. Sometimes they invade attics and basements.

CONTROL: Raccoons are intelligent, inquisitive animals that can be very difficult to exclude. You can discourage raccoons from invading your vegetable garden by erecting a 4-foot-high chicken wire fence, with its top extending 18 inches above the fence post. As the raccoon climbs up onto the unattached portion of the fence, his weight will pull him down to the ground. Low-voltage electric fences are also effective in excluding raccoons from the garden. To keep raccoons from climbing between trees or from a building to a tree, keep the limbs pruned so that they do not touch each other or make contact with the roof. Prevent raccoons from climbing up trees by wrapping metal guards at least 18 inches wide around the trunk. Place the guards at least 3 feet above the ground. For information about controlling raccoons as household pests, see page 805.

Skunk.

Woodchuck.

SKUNKS

Skunks are mainly a problem in rural and outlying suburban areas. They invade gardens at night, then return to their dens during the day. They are omnivorous, feeding on insects, small rodents, fruits, berries, corn and other garden vegetables, and garbage. They do not usually cause much damage in the garden, but are unacceptable to many people because of the strong scent they spray when threatened or provoked. In addition, skunks may carry rabies. Skunks that are rabid often show abnormal behavior such as listlessness, unprovoked aggressiveness, or a tendency to wander around during the day. Such animals will bite when handled.

CONTROL: The best way to keep skunks out of the garden is to fence them out. Enclose the area you want to protect with a 3-foot-high fence made of chicken wire. Extend 12 inches of the bottom outward below the soil surface to discourage animals from digging beneath it. You may also trap skunks, placing traps near their dens or trails. Bait traps with sardines or cat food. When handling skunks, wear protective goggles and old clothing in case you are sprayed. Before attempting to trap or kill skunks, contact your agricultural commissioner's office or local Department of Fish and Game to find out if these animals are protected in your area. For more information about trapping, see page 891. If you or your pets are sprayed, neutralize the scent with *neutroleum alpha*, a compound that is available through pest control operators or hospital supply outlets. Contact a doctor or veterinarian if you or a pet are bitten by a skunk.

WOODCHUCKS

Woodchucks are also known as *groundhogs*. They are a problem in rural and suburban areas throughout most of the United States. Woodchucks live in underground burrows, from which they emerge in the early morning and late afternoon to feed. Woodchucks prefer tender vegetables, flowers, and other succulent greenery, but they may occasionally gnaw on tree bark. These animals seldom invade gardens in large numbers. They do not tunnel to their food source, but feed aboveground. Woodchucks occasionally contract diseases that they may transmit to humans.

CONTROL: The best way to eliminate damage is to fence the woodchucks out. Surround the area you wish to protect with a woven wire fence about 3 feet high. To prevent woodchucks from burrowing under the fence, bend the bottom 12 inches of the wire mesh outward before burying it a few inches deep in the soil. To prevent woodchucks from climbing over the top, leave the upper 18 inches of mesh unattached to the supporting stakes. Bend this upper portion outward. As the animal climbs the fence, the weight of its body will pull the upper portion down toward the ground. Traps may also be used. For more information about traps, see page 891. In some states, these animals are protected by law. Before attempting to trap or kill woodchucks, contact your agricultural commissioner's office or local Department of Fish and Game to determine the regulations for your area. Always wear gloves and protective clothing when handling woodchucks; they may be diseased.

SOIL, CULTURAL, AND CLIMATE PROBLEMS

This section contains garden problems that aren't related to a particular plant, or even to a particular section of the garden. It also contains some cultural guidelines.

Most of the soil problems a gardener might experience are in this section. Some soils are more difficult to work with than others, but any garden soil that will grow weeds will grow garden plants, too. The difference between good garden soil and difficult garden soil is the amount of latitude the gardener has in his cultural practices. If your soil drains well, you don't have to worry about overwatering. If, in addition, it holds ample water, you are also less likely to underwater. But if you have a heavy clay or a droughty sand, proper watering takes skill and

attention. These soils can still raise good garden plants, though; they just take more careful handling.

There are two basic approaches to both soil and climate problems. One — and by far the simplest one — is to grow plants that are adapted to the soil and climate of your garden. This requires no extra work on your part, and little skill or garden knowledge beyond that needed to select adapted plants.

The limitation of this system is that you may not like the plants available to you, or you may want plants not adapted to your area. For instance, lawns are not adapted to much of the arid West. In some areas, it takes almost heroic measures to keep a lawn healthy. But garden-

ers are so fond of lawns that the majority of homes in these areas have them.

The second method is to adapt your garden to the plants. This may involve installing irrigation systems, or building structures to shelter garden plants from the sun, wind, or cold.

You will also find some garden practices in this section. These are practices that are solutions to garden problems in general, but not to any one problem. For instance, you will find directions for patching a lawn, which may have been damaged by a fungus disease or an insect. After you have dealt with the fungus or insect, you can use these guidelines to clear up the secondary problem of dead patches in the lawn.

Above: Deep-watering of pumpkin seedlings. The slow flow from this punctured can allows water to penetrate deep into the soil. Left: Turning organic amendments into soil. These materials improve almost any soil. See page 918.

INDEX TO SOIL, CULTURAL, AND CLIMATE PROBLEMS

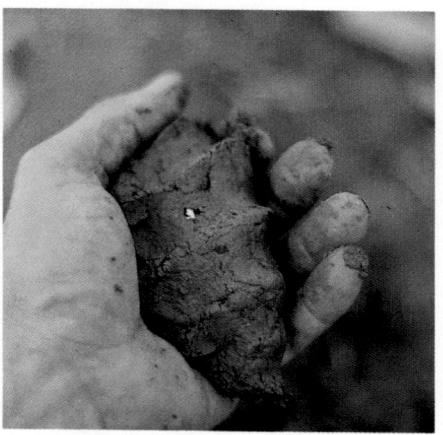

Heavy soil.

HEAVY SOIL

When used to describe soil, the word "heavy" does not mean weight, but the sensation of working the soil. Heavy soils can be difficult to work. Heaviness comes from a high proportion of clay in the soil. If the soil does not have a crumbly texture, the pores in clay soil are very small. It is these pores that let air and water into the soil.

Difficulties with heavy soil: Heavy soil may be sticky when wet and hard when dry, and may go rapidly from one to the other. Water passes through its small pores very slowly. If the soil is not managed properly, it is easy to overwater, keeping the soil pores full of water and excluding air.

Advantages of heavy soil: When heavy soil has a crumbly structure it drains well, yet still retains much water. Heavy soils also hold onto nutrients well, and are fertile. Because they need feeding and watering less often than other soils, they are easier to manage.

Managing heavy soil: Be careful not to overwater. Water slowly and deeply, but infrequently. The heavier your soil, the more important it is to work it when the water content is just right. There is a point between too wet and too dry when it works easily. Gypsum will sometimes improve the structure of clay soils. Work a cup of gypsum into the soil in a watering basin to see if drainage is improved. Organic matter, such as manure, compost, or ammoniated sawdust, always improves heavy soil. Spread from 1 to 4 inches of organic matter on the surface and turn it in every time you work the soil. In 2 or 3 years, the soil will be vastly improved.

Sandy soil.

Shallow soil.

Erosion.

SANDY SOIL

Sandy soil contains a high proportion of sand. It can be identified by the characteristic grittiness when the soil is rubbed between the thumb and fingers. Sandy soil has large pore spaces, so water and air enter it easily; however, the soil dries out rapidly and it does not retain nutrients well. Sandy soil cultivates easily either dry or wet. It seldom puddles or becomes muddy or sticky, and seldom has erosion problems because water enters it immediately, so there is none to run off on the surface.

Managing sandy soil: Sandy soil must have both water and fertilizer applied lightly and frequently. Because it retains very little water, plants wilt quickly. This type of soil is often called "droughty." A simple way to feed the garden is to use liquid fertilizers, such as ORTHO Ortho-Gro Liquid Plant Food 12–6–6 or ORTHO Tomato & Vegetable Food 6–18–6. These can be added to the irrigation water with an ORTHO Lawn Sprayer or a siphoning fertilizer injector. Fertilize once a month during the growing season. Improve sandy soil by adding organic matter, such as peat moss, compost, or manure. Spread from 1 to 4 inches of organic material on the surface and turn it in every time you till the soil. The organic matter acts like a sponge, retaining water and nutrients. (For more information about organic amendments, see page 918.) Drip irrigation systems are especially effective and useful in sandy soils.

SHALLOW SOIL

Depth of soil is important for the growth of plants. Shallow soil does not provide enough root space and has less water storage capacity than deep soil. It dries out rapidly, but since, on flat land, the water has no place to drain, it is also easy to overwater. Soil depth can be determined by digging a hole. A lawn can be grown in 6 inches of soil, but trees need from 1½ feet to 4 feet. Sometimes the underlayment is not bedrock but a rocklike layer called *hardpan*, which can be penetrated. For more information about hardpan, see page 900.

Living with shallow soil: If your garden is already planted, watch the amount of water you apply. You may need to water more frequently than if the soil were deeper, but apply less at each watering. Guy trees to keep them from blowing over.

Improving shallow soil: In areas that are not yet planted, you have two options. One is to choose shallow-rooted plants, such as lawns and annuals. A second option is to deepen the soil in raised planting beds. But avoid planting large trees, even in raised beds. Also resist the temptation to deepen the soil by digging into the underlayment. Drainage would be nonexistent in these holes, so maintenance would be very difficult.

EROSION

Erosion occurs on bare ground when soil is worn away by wind and water. Eroding winds can carry away dry soil, but water erosion is more common and more severe. When raindrops fall on bare soil, their impact loosens soil particles. On a slope, water starts to flow over the surface as soon as the ground stops absorbing it. The force of the moving water and the scouring action of the soil particles carried in the water erode the bare ground further down the slope. Erosion is most severe on long, steep slopes.

Stop erosion by covering the soil. If the slope is not too steep, cover it with a heavy mulch, such as gravel or fir bark. Cover steep slopes with burlap or coarse netting sold for this purpose. Plant a groundcover through holes in the fabric. By the time the fabric rots, the groundcover will be established. The most effective plantings for erosion control are low, dense groundcovers or turfgrasses. The roots help to hold soil particles in place, and the leaves and stems break the impact of water drops and reduce the momentum of runoff. If slopes are already deeply eroded, it may be necessary to construct retaining walls or check dams to prevent further erosion.

Rocky soil.

Compacted soil.

Turf over hardpan killed by drought.

ROCKY SOILS

Rocky soils do not usually affect plant growth. Water drainage is not impaired in rocky soil, and plant roots easily grow around rocks. The major problem with rocky soil is that planting and cultivating are difficult, especially in vegetable and flower beds where plants are replaced frequently and the soil is intensely cultivated. If your garden is not yet planted, hire a contractor with a stone-picker attachment on a tractor to clear it of surface rocks. If this is not practical, hand-pick rocks in vegetable gardens and other areas where cultivation is intense, or plant in raised beds. If rocks are so numerous throughout your garden that there is very little soil, add topsoil.

COMPACTION

Soil compaction is the result of foot or vehicle traffic. The pressure packs the soil tightly, squeezing the pores closed. Compacted soil contains little air, restricting root growth to the surface levels. Also, roots have difficulty in penetrating the dense soil. Water penetrates the soil slowly, making irrigation difficult. Some soils, especially clay soils and some loamy sands, are more susceptible to compaction than others, and dry soil has more resistance to compaction than wet soil. Soil compaction should be corrected before planting in the area. Different techniques are needed in planted and unplanted areas.

Before planting: Till the soil to loosen the compaction. Large areas that are badly compacted require the use of a rotary tiller. Organic matter should be mixed in as the soil is tilled. (For information about adding organic matter to the soil, see page 918.) If the compaction was caused by heavy construction equipment, it may be necessary to have the soil loosened to a depth of 2 feet with a chisel plow. Foot traffic compacts only a couple of inches of surface soil.

In planted areas: Relieve compaction in planted areas by aeration (see pages 305 and 467).

Preventing compaction: The most effective way to prevent compaction is to keep traffic off the soil. Make paths, or place fences or shrubs to act as barriers. If heavy equipment must be driven across the soil, make sure the soil is as dry as possible at the time. If foot traffic can't be kept off an area, mulch it with 4 inches of gravel or rocks.

HARDPAN

Hardpan is a cementlike layer of soil that impedes the downward flow of water and restricts root growth. Soil particles in the hardpan layer are cemented together by minerals, usually iron compounds, that have accumulated there. Hardpan is usually within a foot or so of the surface, and is only a few inches thick. Or it may be very close to the soil surface if erosion has washed away the topsoil. The hardpan has two effects on plants growing above it. Since roots cannot grow through hardpan, they are restricted to the shallow soil layer above it. Trees grow slowly, and may be blown over in a wind storm. Also, since water does not penetrate it, the hardpan impedes drainage. To determine if your soil has a hardpan layer, dig a hole 2 to 3 feet deep. The rocklike layer can, with persistence, be penetrated. It's not necessary to remove hardpan, but only to provide a hole or channel through it for water flow and root growth. Around established plants, break holes in the hardpan with a crowbar or jackhammer. Depending on the depth of the soil, the holes should be 4 to 6 feet apart. When establishing a new planting area, break up hardpan with a chisel plow or backhoe. Hardpan reforms very slowly, so any holes made in it will last for many years. Or install drain pipes on top of the hardpan to drain water away from the plant roots. Another possibility is to grow vegetables and flowers in raised beds. For information on raised beds, see ORTHO's book *All About Fertilizers, Soils & Water.*

DRAINAGE PROBLEMS

Drainage problems due to heavy soil.

Poor drainage due to layered soil.

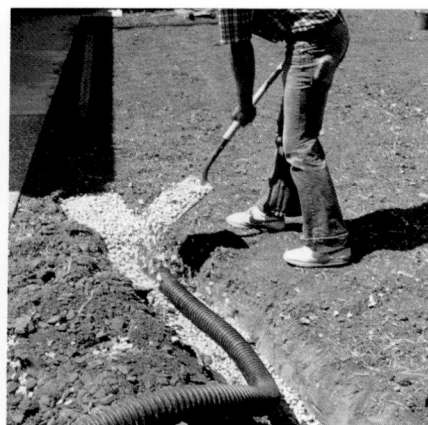

Drain line.

SOIL TYPE

Certain types of soil naturally have drainage problems.

Soils that crust: Some types of soil form a thin (1/8 to 1/4 inch) crust on the soil surface. The crust can be broken with the fingers, and flakes when handled. Even though the soil below the crust drains well, water does not penetrate quickly and tends to puddle or run off. Prevent crusting by cultivating organic matter into the soil, or by mulching. For more information about organic matter and mulching, see page 918.

Sodic soil: Sodic soils are high in certain forms of sodium. They are impermeable to water; puddling and runoff are common. Sodium hydroxide (caustic soda) in sodic soils dissolves organic matter, which becomes suspended in puddled water, turning it brown or black. For more information about sodic soils, see page 903.

Heavy soil: Heavy soils are those with a large proportion of clay. They crack and are very hard when dry, and are sticky and difficult to mix or turn over when wet. To determine if your soil is heavy, dig a hole 2 feet deep in a poorly drained area. Fill the hole with water. If the water level drops more slowly than 1/10 inch per hour, heavy soil is probably causing your problem. Runoff and puddling may be reduced on heavy soils (and other poorly drained soils) by applying water more slowly. Use sprinkler heads with a lower water output, or oscillating or impulse hose-end sprinklers. Or cycle sprinklers by pausing for half an hour when runoff begins. For more information about heavy soil, see page 898.

SOIL STRUCTURE

The soil structure may be altered by natural processes or by human activities, causing poor drainage.

Compacted soil: Compacted soils are hard, dense, and impermeable to water. Compacted areas are usually on the surface, and only 2 to 4 inches deep. Compaction is usually caused by foot traffic, but construction equipment can compact the soil 2 feet deep. Dig a hole through the compacted layer in the poorly drained area when the soil is moist but not wet. Fill the hole with water. Compaction is the problem if the water level drops faster than 1/10 inch per hour. For more information about compacted soil, see page 900.

Layered soil: Layered soils are those in which soils of different textures are layered like a cake. If the layers are very different in texture, drainage problems may result. This kind of problem is most often caused when soil of a different texture than the native soil is added as fill material. Even a thin layer of added soil can slow drainage. Dig a hole to see if your soil has distinctly different layers. If this is what is causing your drainage problem, stir the layers together by tilling or, if the layers are deep, chisel-plowing. If the area is planted, dig holes or a trench through the layers. Fill the holes to the surface with gravel or wood chips. Water will drain quickly through these holes.

Hardpan: Hardpan is a cementlike layer of soil that forms a foot or two below the surface. Water does not drain through this layer. When struck with a shovel or pick, hardpan feels like rock. For more information about hardpan, see page 900.

GROUNDWATER

Poor drainage occurs in soils where the water table is high.

High water table: The water table is usually tens or hundreds of feet below the surface, but in some areas it is close enough to the surface to keep the soil wet. The water table rises and falls during the year, and is most likely to be high in the spring. If a hole, such as a well, is dug into the water table, it will spontaneously fill with water. The water level in the hole is the same as that in the water table. A high water table must be drained with underground drain lines or deep ditches. See a contractor.

Springs: Springs may surface in the garden, especially on a hillside. Even though free-flowing water is not produced, springs may produce soggy areas that never dry out. Drain away the excess water by installing an interception drain. To do this, dig a ditch several feet up the slope from the wet area, and parallel to it. The ditch should be dug straight down until it fills with water, intercepting the spring. Install a drain line in the ditch to carry away the water. Or, better yet, dig into the spring and use its water in the garden.

Soil pH test kit.

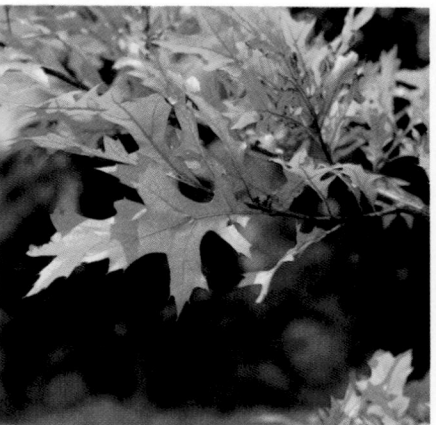

Pin oak in alkaline soil.

Magnesium deficiency caused by acid soil.

pH

pH is a measure of acidity and alkalinity, on a scale from 0 to 14. The lower the number, the more acid the soil. pH of 7.0 is neutral, neither acid or alkaline. (For a list of common substances and their pH, see the chart below.) Many of the chemical reactions that occur in all soils depend on the pH. The soil pH often determines what nutrients are available for plant use. Soils are rarely more acidic than 4.0 or more alkaline than 9.0. Most plants will grow in soils with a pH of 5.5 to 8.0. Some plants need acid soil (4.0 to 5.5). Others will tolerate alkaline conditions (8.0 to 9.0). (For a list, see page 1002.) To determine your soil pH, have your soil tested. For more information about soil testing, see page 903.

The pH Scale

Some common substances	Acid	Soils
Grapefruit	3	Peat moss
Grapes	4	Best for rhododendrons, azaleas, and other acid-loving plants
Bread	5	
Milk	6	Average Eastern soils
Pure water Neutral	7	
Baking soda	8	Average Western soils
Soap	9	
Milk of magnesia	10	Alkali Soils
	11	

Alkaline

ALKALINE SOILS

Alkaline soils are those with a pH of more than 7.0, the neutral point. The soil is usually alkaline in regions that receive less than 20 inches of rain a year.

Effect on plants: Most plants grow well in slightly alkaline soil (pH 7.0 to 8.0). However, in soils that are more alkaline than 8.0 some plant nutrients, including iron and manganese, become insoluble and are not available to plants even though they are present in the soil. Plants growing in soil that is too alkaline for them develop yellow areas between the veins on their newest leaves. Older leaves usually remain green, unless the plant has been growing for some time in soil that is too alkaline.

Acid-loving plants: Plants that are adapted to acid soil, such as azaleas and rhododendrons, may show symptoms of iron deficiency even when the soil is slightly acid.

Over-limed soils: If soil that is naturally acid has so much lime added to it that the pH rises above about 7.2, plants may show iron deficiency symptoms.

Decreasing soil alkalinity: Make soils more acid by adding ORTHO Aluminum Sulfate, *ferrous sulfate*, or *soil sulfur*. Add 5 pounds per 100 square feet, wait 2 weeks, then test the soil pH. Reapply these acidifying amendments until the desired pH has been attained. Amounts will vary depending upon the soil type. Maintain acidity by using a fertilizer that has an acid reaction in the soil, such as ORTHO Azalea, Camellia & Rhododendron Food 5–10–10. Or select plants that are tolerant of alkaline soil from the list on page 1003.

ACID SOILS

Strictly speaking, any soil with a pH below 7.0 — the neutral point — is acid. However, the term *acid soils* usually refers to soils that are too acid for good plant growth, those with a pH below about 5.5. As the pH decreases, the soil becomes increasingly acidic. Acidity develops naturally in soils that are heavily leached by rainfall. Most plants grow well in slightly acid soils (pH 6.0 to 7.0).

Effect on plant nutrients: As acidity increases, chemical changes occur in the soil that reduce the overall growth and health of most plants, except for acid-loving plants such as rhododendrons, azaleas, and blueberries. Many plant nutrients, especially phosphorous, calcium, and magnesium, become less available for plant use in acid soils. Other elements, such as aluminum and manganese, become available in quantities toxic to plants. The beneficial soil organisms that decompose organic matter are less active in acid soils, so the nitrogen obtained from the breakdown of organic matter is reduced.

Effect on plants: Plants growing in acid soils are often stunted and off-color. Their roots are sparse and small.

Decreasing soil acidity: To decrease soil acidity, add ground dolomitic limestone according to the chart on page 1002. In addition to raising the soil pH, dolomitic limestone supplies magnesium and calcium, nutrients in which acidic soils are usually deficient. Do not over-lime acid soils, because when the soil pH is too high the availability of some nutrients may be decreased.

Leaf scorch on oleander caused by salty soil.

Salt damage to white pine.

Soil sampling tube.

SALTY SOIL

Soil salts are soluble minerals. They include table salt (sodium chloride) as well as salts of calcium, magnesium, and potassium. Salty soil occurs mainly in arid regions where there is not enough rainfall to wash the salts from the soil. Soil salts originate from several sources. As soil minerals weather, they slowly break down into salts that dissolve in the soil water. Irrigation water that contains dissolved salts contributes to soil salinity, and so do fertilizers. As water evaporates from the surface it moves up through the soil, bringing dissolved salts up into the topsoil. Salts may accumulate in poorly drained soils because rainfall and irrigation water cannot drain through and leach the soil. Roadside soil may become very saline in areas where deicing salts are used in the winter. Salty soil may develop a white crust of salt deposits on the surface. Most garden plants will not tolerate much salt in the soil. For more information about plant reactions to salt, see page 864.

Removing salts: Leach salty soils periodically by watering them deeply. About 12 inches of water are needed to remove most of the salts in a foot of soil. If soil salinity is a result of poor drainage, improve the soil drainage. (For information on drainage, see page 901.) The use of mulches in arid regions helps reduce the evaporation of soil water and the subsequent salt accumulation in the topsoil. For a list of plants that are tolerant of salty soils, see page 999.

Sodic soils: Soils with a high concentration of free sodium are called *sodic* or *alkali* soils. Sodium destroys the soil structure and causes clay particles to become lodged in soil pores, making the soil impermeable to water. Water puddles on sodic soils, and usually evaporates before it enters the soil. Some of the sodium forms caustic soda (sodium hydroxide), which dissolves organic matter. The organic substances in solution are dark brown or black. A black crust often forms on sodic soils. Sodic soils are often very alkaline, and usually do not support plant growth. To improve sodic soils, add gypsum at a rate of 5 pounds to every 100 square feet. Cultivate the gypsum into the soil, then water it well to leach the sodium from the soil. If drainage is only slightly improved, add more gypsum.

SOIL TESTING

Every few years, test the acidity of your soil. If you live in an area that gets less than 25 inches of rain a year, test also for soluble salts. In most states, the Cooperative Extension Offices will test your soil. (For a list of Cooperative Extension Offices, see page 1011.) Commercial soil laboratories, listed under *Soil* in the yellow pages, also test soil. Or test soil acidity yourself with a test kit, available in most garden centers. It is not practical for home gardeners to test for nutrient levels because the cost of the test is usually more than might be saved in fertilizers. Take a soil sample like this:

1. Use a clean bucket and trowel, as any traces of fertilizer or lime will offset the test.

2. Select the areas that you wish to test separately. Different soil types should be tested separately, as should areas you put to different uses.

3. Dig a hole 6 inches deep, or deeper when testing for soil around tree roots.

4. With a trowel, cut a thin slice from the side of the hole. Scrape the top ½ inch of soil from the slice.

5. Place the slice in a bucket. Take more samples from the same area.

6. Mix the soil in the bucket thoroughly. Measure out 2 cups for testing.

7. If someone other than yourself is testing the soil, be sure to note what type of plants are growing, or will be planted, in the area.

8. Repeat the sampling procedure for each area you wish to test. Rinse the trowel and bucket between areas.

Nitrogen-deficient euonymus.

Nitrogen-deficient tomato.

Phosphorus-deficient corn.

NITROGEN

Nitrogen is one of the three primary nutrients necessary for plant growth. It is used by plants to form proteins that are required for the development of new shoots and leaves, and to make chlorophyll, the green pigment in leaves. Most soils require additional nitrogen to produce healthy plants. (For information about nitrogen deficiency in plants, see page 867.) There are three major forms of nitrogen.

Ammoniacal nitrogen: Ammoniacal nitrogen includes ammonium, ammonia, and urea, all of which quickly become ammonium in the soil. Ammonium is not readily leached from the soil. It binds to the surfaces of the soil particles, which keeps it from washing away. Although many plants use ammonium, the availability of ammoniacal nitrogen is slow to most plants, because it must be changed to nitrate by soil micro-organisms before it can be washed to the plant roots. The activity of these microbes depends on soil moisture, aeration, and temperature. In warm, well-aerated soils, the nitrogen is changed to nitrate and is available to plants for a couple of weeks. The process is much slower in cold, wet soils, and will not take place at all when the soil temperature is below 30° to 40°F. If a plant growing in cold soil is in immediate need of nitrogen, a fertilizer should be applied that also contains *nitrate nitrogen* (see below). Ammoniacal nitrogen fertilizers have an acidifying effect on the soil. In areas of high rainfall, where soils are already acidic, it may be necessary to add lime.

Nitrate nitrogen: Fertilizers containing nitrate nitrogen are fast acting. They are very useful for plants in immediate need of nitrogen. The nitrogen is in a form that is readily available to plants. Microorganisms are not needed to break down the nitrogen, so the fertilizers are effective in cold or warm soils. Nitrate nitrogen does not become attached to soil particles, but floats freely in the soil water. With heavy rains or deep watering, the nitrogen may be washed below the root zone. Nitrate fertilizers are most effective if applied in frequent, light feedings, or in combination with a long-lasting ammoniacal or organic nitrogen.

Organic nitrogen: Organic nitrogen is in the form of protein or other insoluble compounds. It is found in plant and animal derivatives such as blood meal, manure, and sewage sludge. In uncomposted organic material, the nitrogen is not available to plants. The protein must be decomposed by soil microorganisms to ammonium, and then to nitrate, before the plant can use it. As with ammoniacal nitrogen, the rate of decomposition depends on soil temperature and moisture. Organic nitrogen usually lasts for a few months in the soil.

PHOSPHORUS

Phosphorus is one of the three primary plant nutrients. It is used in all phases of plant growth, and in all parts of the plant. In the soil, phosphorus is taken up by plants in the form of phosphate. Phosphate compounds have two qualities that govern phosphate use by the plant. One of these qualities is that only a tiny amount of phosphate dissolves at any time in the soil water. Because the part that does not dissolve cannot be washed from the soil, phosphorus lasts for a long time in the soil. One application lasts for months or years. This also means that plants must have an extensive root system to get enough phosphate from this dilute soil solution. The other quality of phosphate is that it is very active chemically, and quickly forms compounds with many chemicals. Because of this quality, phosphate does not move through the soil. Therefore phosphorus fertilizers should be placed in the root zone of the plant. Southern and eastern soils are often deficient in phosphorus.

Rock phosphate: Most phosphorus fertilizers begin as phosphate rock. This material is almost insoluble, and only slightly available to plants.

Superphosphate: Superphosphate is phosphate rock that has been treated with acid to make it soluble. In this form, the phosphate remains soluble for a few weeks or months in the soil.

Bone meal: This organic form of phosphate is made of ground bones. Chemically, it is similar to rock phosphate, and is almost insoluble.

Potassium-deficient soybeans.

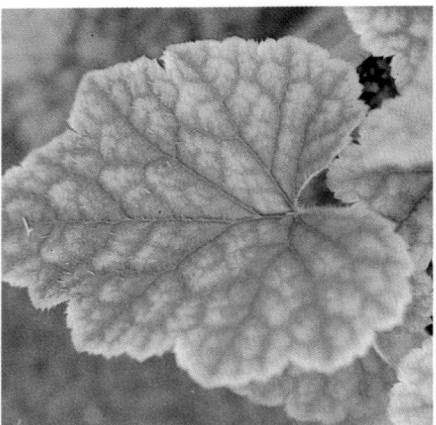
Iron-deficient piggyback.

Fertilizer label.

POTASSIUM

Potassium is the third primary nutrient contained in complete fertilizers. Plants use potassium to maintain their salt balance, and in many other ways. (For information about potassium deficiency in plants, see page 867.) All potassium fertilizers are mined from the ground, either as potassium sulfate or as potassium chloride. They can be bought in these forms, but are most commonly purchased as part of a complete fertilizer. Potassium is soluble, and usually remains in solution in the soil water, but it adheres to clay particles and humus in the soil, so it is not as readily leached from the soil as nitrogen. Potassium is about midway between nitrogen and phosphorus in persistence in the soil. In soils that are rich in clay or humus, one application a year is often enough. But in sandy soils or in containers, potassium should be applied more frequently. Eastern and southern soils, which receive abundant rainfall, are usually deficient in potassium, and need regular applications. Western soils usually need added potassium only for heavily cropped areas, such as vegetable gardens or annual beds, and on lawns and container plants.

MINOR NUTRIENTS

Minor nutrients, also called *trace elements* or *micronutrients*, are nutrients that are needed in small amounts by plants. They include boron, iron, manganese, copper, zinc, molybdenum, and chlorine. Yearly applications of minor nutrients are not necessary; they need to be added only when deficiency symptoms appear in the plant. (For more information about deficiency symptoms, see page 868.)

Minor nutrient deficiencies in the soil: When deficiencies develop in soils, they are usually in localized areas. The most commonly deficient minor nutrient is iron, which is tied up in insoluble forms in alkaline or poorly aerated soils. Alkaline soils may also be deficient in manganese and zinc. (For more information about minor nutrient deficiencies in alkaline soil, see page 902.) Zinc deficiency is much more common than manganese deficiency, especially in citrus and other tree and vegetable crops.

Correcting minor nutrient deficiencies: Minor nutrient deficiencies are corrected in the plant by applying fertilizers to the soil or spraying the foliage. Minor nutrients may be contained in complete fertilizers, and are often contained in specialty fertilizers, such as ORTHO Evergreen, Tree & Shrub Food 12–6–6, ORTHO Rose Food 8–12–4, and ORTHO Vegetable Garden Food 5–10–10. For immediate results, minor nutrients can be applied in a foliar spray using a liquid fertilizer such as ORTHO Greenol Liquid Iron 6.13%.

HOW TO READ A FERTILIZER LABEL

The law requires that fertilizer labels inform the consumer of the minimum guaranteed contents of the product. Information on labels is fairly standardized. Manufacturers give the percentages of nitrogen, phosphate, and potash, and the sources of the nutrients. Some manufacturers also include secondary nutrients (calcium, magnesium, and sulfur) or minor nutrients in their fertilizers, which may or may not be listed. The brand name of the product is listed first, followed by the formula or analysis of the fertilizer. The analysis always gives the percentages of nitrogen, phosphate, and potash that the fertilizer contains, listed in that order. For example, a fertilizer with an analysis of 12–8–16 contains 12 percent nitrogen, 8 percent phosphate, and 16 percent potash. The guaranteed analysis is the manufacturer's warranty of the minimum nutrient content of the fertilizer. The analysis may also list some secondary nutrients or minor nutrients. The source of the primary nutrients — the chemicals from which they were derived — is stated next. The derivation determines their availability to plants. Some fertilizers have an acid reaction in the soil. If this potential exists, the label will indicate the number of pounds of lime it would take to neutralize the acidity of the fertilizer once it is in the soil. On the labels of some specialty fertilizers, the words "chelating agent" appear. A chelating agent is a substance that is added to fertilizers containing nutrients derived from metals.

Measuring sprinkler output.

Sprinkler irrigation.

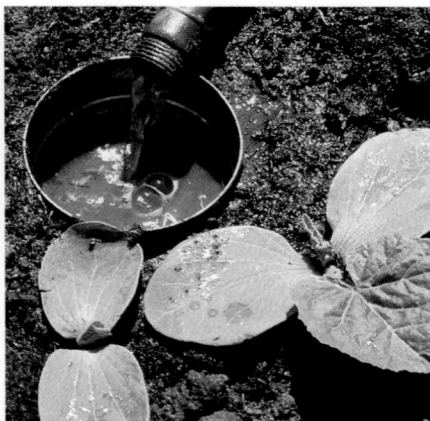
Punctured can for deep-watering.

HOW MUCH WATER TO APPLY

Each time you water, apply enough water to wet the soil to the bottom of the root zone. Water is measured in inches. If a tin can is placed on a lawn when the sprinklers are turned on, the soil has received an inch of water when the water in the container is an inch deep. If a watering basin is 3 inches deep, 3 inches of water is applied to the soil when the basin is filled with water. Because sandy soils do not hold as much water as clay soils, it takes less water to wet them to the same depth. To wet one foot of a sandy loam that has dried out to the point where average plants need water (just barely moist), apply about 1 inch of water. To wet 1 foot of a loam or clay loam that is just barely moist, apply about 1½ inches of water. Soils vary greatly in their ability to hold water, so these figures are only guidelines. To see how much water your soil needs to wet it a foot deep, measure the amount of water you apply at an irrigation. The next day, after the wetting front has moved down as far as it will go (clay soils may take 2 or 3 days), dig a hole to see where the wetting front is. You will be able to calculate from this how much water you need to apply to wet the soil to the bottom of the root zone. Then, by measuring the time it takes your sprinkler system to apply an inch of water, you can calculate how long you need to leave the system on to apply enough water.

ABOUT WATERING

Plants suffer more from improper watering than from any other cause. Watering is more difficult to master than other gardening techniques because it depends on many variables. The amount of water a plant needs varies with the kind of plant, the soil, the location, and all of the continually changing components of the weather including temperature, humidity, and wind, so it is easy to overwater or underwater. Several methods are commonly used to irrigate plants.

Hand watering: This method involves watering the garden with a hand-held hose, usually with a spray head on the end. Hand watering is the simplest method of irrigation. It involves no previous soil preparation or equipment installation. But it is time-consuming, and leads to underwatering because most gardeners do not have the patience to water for many hours at a time.

Furrow irrigation: Furrow irrigation works best when you are watering rows of plants; it is often used in vegetable gardens. Furrows are dug beside plant rows and filled with water. The water is left in the furrows for several hours. Plant foliage stays dry when furrow irrigation is used; only the roots receive water.

Basin irrigation: Watering basins are used mainly around shrubs and trees. A ridge of soil is built to contain the water, then the basin formed by this ridge is filled with water, either from a hand-held hose or a bubbler head on a permanent sprinkler system. A few basins can be filled quickly with water, but if many plants are irrigated by hand in this manner, watering may be time-consuming. Plant foliage stays dry when water basins are used.

Sprinklers: Both hose-end sprinklers and underground installed sprinklers irrigate a large area at once. They are most effective when used to water heavily planted areas. Sprinklers are wasteful if they are used to irrigate sparsely planted areas. They are also hard to control in windy areas, and they get plant leaves wet, which may lead to disease problems. But they are effective for delivering water evenly over a large area, and require less time than most other systems.

Drip irrigation: Drip irrigation systems apply the water very slowly, allowing it to seep into the soil. They are left on for many hours at a time, often for 4 to 16 hours a day. Many types of delivery systems are available. If they are properly operated, drip systems do the best watering job because they keep the soil at a relatively constant state of moisture, without the wet-to-dry fluctuations of other methods. Drip systems work best in light soils, and are a perfect solution to watering plants on steep slopes. They do not wet the leaves.

Some methods, including hand watering and some sprinklers, make water puddle or run off long before the soil receives as much water as it needs. Many gardeners stop watering when the soil surface becomes soggy, or when water starts to puddle or run off. This practice wets only the top few inches of the soil. Because the rate of water absorption into the soil is slow, it may take several hours to several days to wet some types of soil 3 to 4 feet deep. To water deeply and prevent runoff, apply water at the same rate at which it enters the soil. If your irrigation system cannot be adjusted to apply water that slowly, use another system, or water until runoff begins, stop watering for an hour, then water again, until the soil has been wetted as deeply as necessary.

Irrigating vegetable seedlings.

Furrow irrigation.

Watering annual bed.

How Water Moves in Soil

Water enters soil by moving into the pores between the soil particles. As water fills the pores, the soil becomes saturated, and water can move farther down into deeper air-filled pores. This wetting front cannot move down in the soil unless the soil above it is saturated. The rate at which the wetting front moves through the soil varies, depending on the texture of the soil. Water moves quickly through soil with large pores, such as sandy soil, and much more slowly in soil with tiny pores, such as compacted or clay soil. It is important to remember that each layer of soil must get very wet before the wetting front moves deeper into the soil. After the wetting front stops moving downward, the soil below it remains dry. There is no such thing as "keeping the soil slightly moist." Some of the soil always gets very wet. The more water you put on, the deeper you are watering. At each rainfall or irrigation, the soil gets as wet as possible, then it dries slowly until the next wetting. Soil moisture is in a constant state of flux.

Soil drainage: If you place a sponge in water and lift it out, water runs freely from it, pulled by gravity. Soil drains in the same way. Eventually the sponge will stop dripping. Gravity has pulled out all the water it can; the rest of the water in the sponge is held by capillary forces, the forces that make water stick to some surfaces instead of beading. When soil has finished draining, it is holding all the water it can against the pull of gravity. The amount of water in the soil at this point varies greatly from one type of soil to another. As water drains from the soil, air is drawn into it, so the amount of air in the soil also depends on the soil type. Sandy soils hold the least water and the most air; clay soils hold the most water.

Plants and soil water: If you squeeze a sponge that has quit draining, more water will drip from it. As you squeeze the sponge, it requires more and more effort to get it to drip, until you can't squeeze out more water, no matter how hard you try. But the sponge is not yet dry. In the same way, a plant can get water easily from very moist soil, but as the soil dries out, the water moves less and less freely into the plant, until finally the plant can't extract any more water at all. But even at this point, the soil still contains some water. Healthy plant growth requires free movement of water into the plant. When the soil is so dry that the plant cannot get enough water for its needs, the plant is under drought stress. The best time to water is when the plant has used about half the water available to it, before the plant is under any stress.

When to Water

There are two primary skills involved in watering plants: knowing how much water to apply at each irrigation (see page 906), and knowing when to water. There are many methods for knowing when to water, some of them very sophisticated. The method described here is one of the simplest and easiest to learn, and it always works. The first step is to dig a hole into the root zone of the plant, from 2 to 6 inches deep. In loose soil you can dig a hole with a finger. Otherwise use a trowel or a shovel. Then feel the soil in the hole. Dig a new hole each time you check. In this book, plants are divided into 3 watering categories: those that can't tolerate drought, average plants, and those that can't tolerate wet soil. When the soil reaches a certain level of dryness, it is time to water again.

Plants that can't tolerate drought: The soil in the root zone is moist but not wet. When you touch it, it makes your finger damp but not muddy. If you squeeze a ball of this soil, water will not run out.

Average plants: The soil in the root zone is just barely moist. When you touch it, it feels cool and moist, but does not dampen your finger. Most soils are crumbly at this stage, but not dusty.

Plants that can't tolerate wet soil: When it is time to water, the soil in the root zone feels completely dry. It is not cool to the touch, and it is probably dusty. It is important to water these plants as soon as the soil reaches this state. Although they can usually withstand long periods of drought, they grow much better if they are watered regularly.

Lawn renovation.

Patching.

Drip emitter.

LAWN REPAIR

Lawn repair is necessary when dead or bare spots develop, or when a neglected lawn needs to be renovated.

Patching dead spots: With a sharp spade, outline a triangle or a rectangle around the dead spot. With the spade held horizontally, cut the sod free, removing about 1 inch of soil. If the patch is large, roll up the sod as you cut it. Using the removed piece as a pattern, cut a replacement piece of sod from an inconspicuous part of the lawn. Loosen the surface of the soil in the bare spot, and lay the new piece. Press it firmly into place, and water thoroughly. Keep the soil moist until the new piece mends. For more information about laying sod, see page 295.

Sod nursery: Establish your own sod nursery so that matching sod will always be available for patching dead spots. Plant the nursery in an out-of-the-way part of the yard, or use an edge of the lawn. Plant either seed or sod of the same kind as the lawn. Maintain the turf nursery as you do the rest of the lawn. Use as needed.

Spot seeding: Do not plant seeds on top of dead grass or crusted soil. Remove all debris and dead grass. Scratch the surface of the soil ¼ to ½ inch deep. Sow seeds, and top dress lightly with fine soil. Press the soil down firmly. If the weather is dry, mulch lightly (⅛ inch) with sawdust or leaf mold. Water thoroughly and keep the surface of the soil moist until the seedlings are established. For more information about sowing grass seeds, see page 295.

Edging: For a neat, straight edge of grass, use a board as a cutting guide. Trim the edge with a sharp spade or half-moon edging tool. Slice through the turf at an outward angle. Cutting inward will remove the roots of the grass plants growing along the edge. Throughout the season, trim any overhanging grass with grass shears or a trimmer.

Leveling: To level bumps, cut an "H" across the bump. Roll the two flaps of sod back like a carpet. Scrape off enough soil to level the bump. Roll back the cut turf, making sure it is level. Press into place and water thoroughly. Keep the sod moist until it mends. To raise depressions, follow the instructions above, but bring the exposed soil to level by filling and tamping. Or without cutting the sod, sift ¼ inch of soil into the depression at each mowing until the lawn is level. Use soil that is similar to the soil in the lawn.

Renovating the lawn: You can renovate a neglected lawn without beginning over. First kill any weeds. Carry out the renovation just before a period of rapid growth — early summer for southern grasses, spring or fall for northern grasses. (To determine which type you have, see page 991.) Relieve any compaction as described on page 305. Remove thatch as described on page 304. Mow the lawn as short as possible. Loosen the soil surface with a rake in bare or thin spots. Reseed with matching grass seed. Top dress lightly with fine soil. Water thoroughly, and keep the surface moist until the seedlings are established.

TROUBLESHOOTING DRIP IRRIGATION SYSTEMS

The most common problems with drip irrigation systems are uneven watering, clogging, and breaking.

Uneven watering: In drip systems installed on slopes, the emitters at the base of the slope may apply more water than those at the top. Install pressure-compensating emitters on the circuit. Or split up the circuit into several circuits, so that the emitters on each circuit are on approximately the same level. This will require installation of a new valve and line for each circuit.

Clogged lines or emitters: Once a month, turn the system on and check each emitter. Remove clogged emitters from the line and blow through them, or insert a small wire through the orifice. Make sure that a filter is installed at the valve, and keep it clean.

Surface flooding caused by broken or separated lines: Remove the damaged piece of line or the broken fitting. Cut the line ends cleanly with a pocket knife, insert new line or fittings, and slip it together. Use digging tools with care around drip systems, since the polyethylene plastic is easily cut. If a particular fitting frequently pulls out of the line, check the pressure reducer to make sure the setting is correct (20 to 25 pounds per square inch for most drip systems). Attach the fitting to the line with metal screw clamps if necessary.

Malfunctioning sprinklers.

Electronic sprinkler system.

Shrub sprinkler.

TROUBLESHOOTING SPRINKLER SYSTEMS

Three types of problems are common with sprinkler systems: dry spots, flooding, and stuck electric valves.

Dry spots: First check the sprinkler heads (the parts that spray water). Clean them if they are clogged. Next check the sprinkler circuit (the group of heads that operate from the same valve). A complete sprinkler system often has many circuits. If the circuit is new and the heads clog repeatedly, flush the circuit by removing the heads. Unscrew the nozzles first, and turn on the valve for a moment to flush out the sprinkler heads. Then remove the sprinkler heads and flush out the entire circuit. Working from the valve outward, toward the end sprinklers, replace the heads one by one while the water is running. This will remove debris from the lines. If the circuit is over 10 years old, and the pipes are galvanized iron, consider replacing them with plastic lines, since they are probably clogged with pipe scale or corrosion. If the heads are covered by foliage, reset them at a greater height by substituting longer risers (the upright pipes that run from the buried lines to the heads above ground). Pruning the plants may also help. If you have done all this and you still have dry patches between the sprinkler heads or

at the corners of the planted areas, you may need to replace the heads with others that cover a larger area. Another possible reason for dry spots is inadequate pressure for the number of heads on each circuit. Replace the existing heads with heads that will give full coverage of the area with the lower available pressure. Many manufacturers make low-pressure heads. If none of these steps solves the problem, you may have to rebuild the circuit. Sometimes several heads can be moved a few inches each to fill in gaps in coverage, or a head can be added to an existing circuit, if the water pressure will permit it. This is usually a matter for professional determination. The last possible step involes splitting a circuit that has too many heads into two or more circuits. Install a new valve for each new circuit, and new pipe from the valve to the sprinkler heads.

Flooding: When water is delivered more rapidly than the soil can absorb it, flooding results. This problem is most common on slopes. Improve the drainage of the soil by one of the methods described on page 901, or replace the heads with a type that delivers water more slowly. Or turn the circuit on until

flooding begins, then turn it off until the water has been absorbed. Repeat this cycle until enough water has been applied, allowing the water to soak in each time. Flooding in one spot is probably caused by a break in the pipe or fittings, especially on PVC plastic or polyethylene systems. Dig up the line, cut out the damaged part cleanly, refit and glue in the new piece of pipe or fitting. Compression couplings can be useful in difficult places, eliminating the need for glue. Pipe breaks at the base of risers are common. Replace the broken fitting and replace the riser with a flexible type to prevent future breakage.

Stuck electric valves on automatic sprinkler systems: If the valve fails to shut off automatically, check the screws holding the valve together. If they are loose, they can allow a pressure leak and activate the valve. If the valve fails to turn on automatically, check the wiring at the clock and the valve. Look for loose or corroded electrical connections, and be sure that all outdoor connections are thoroughly waterproofed. If these steps do not solve your problem, you may need professional help to detect and repair defects in the clock or valve.

Broken apple branches.

Cabling.

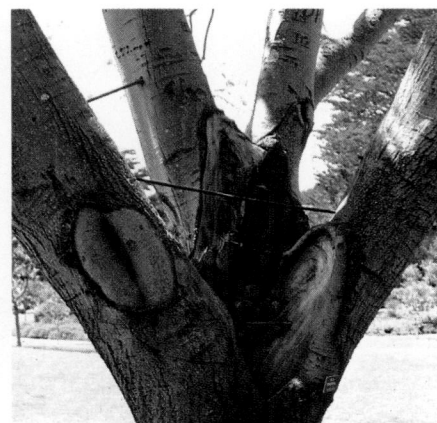

Rod bracing.

BROKEN BRANCHES

Broken branches that are not removed or repaired properly are a potential threat to the life of the tree.

Removing broken branches: If the branch is broken beyond repair (the branch is split so that the bark is intact over less than a third of the circumference of the branch, or only a stub remains), remove it with a pruning saw. First, prune off the dangling part of the broken branch. Next, remove any attached stubs. If a stub is less than a foot long, remove it by making one cut almost flush against the trunk or branch where it is attached. To remove a larger stub, make three cuts in the wood to prevent the bark from tearing as the stub falls off. Make the first cut on the bottom of the branch one foot out from where the stub is attached and at least a third of the way through the wood. A second cut on top of the branch, an inch beyond the first cut, will sever the branch. Remove the remaining small stub as described above.

Repairing branches: If broken branches are still attached to the tree they can sometimes be repaired by splinting. Do not attempt to repair large branches, because they never regain their full strength, and may be hazardous. Lift it back into position, matching the wood as carefully as possible. Prune off loose bark and ragged edges, but do not remove any more bark than necessary. Spray a thin film of ORTHO Pruning Sealer on the bark edges. Support the branch by nailing a board to it to serve as a splint. If additional support is needed, prop it in place as described on page 618, or cable it as described on this page.

CABLING AND BRACING

Cables and braces are used to support weak tree branches or crotches, or to repair split crotches. Cables and braces are often used to support heavy branches overhanging homes and other buildings. Weak branches (with narrow, creased or wrinkled crotches), and branches or trunks that are partially hollowed-out or rotted may also require the support of cables and braces.

Rigid bracing (rods): Rods are used to repair or prevent a split crotch. If the crotch is already split, repairs should be made within 3 weeks. Rods are always used in horizontal pairs. If the wood is sound, threaded rods (obtained from an arboriculture supply house) can be used. Drill a hole slightly smaller than the rod, and screw the rod into the hole with a pipe wrench. Cut off the rod flush with the trunk and paint the end with ORTHO Pruning Seal. If the tree is hollow, drill a hole all the way through and insert a length of all-thread rod. Fasten the ends with large washers and nuts, countersinking the holes through the bark so the washers are pressing against the wood. To reinforce a sound crotch, insert one or two pairs of rods above the crotch. If the crotch has already split, close the split with a block and tackle, and insert the rods right through the split.

Cabling: Wire rope or cables are used to provide a flexible brace for tree branches. Cables must be galvanized, and are attached to screw hooks or lag-screw hooks that are screwed into the branches. The hooks should be in line with the cable for the greatest strength. The best place to attach a cable is $\frac{2}{3}$ of the way from the crotch to the branch tip. For maximum strength, cable three branches together in a triangular pattern. Branches may also be cabled to buildings or other structures. To provide support, the cable must be taut. Tighten it with a turnbuckle, or attach the cable while the branches are pulled together slightly with a block and tackle.

Caution: Tree work is dangerous. If your tree is tall or very large, have the job done by a professional arborist.

Canker removal.

Bark wound caused by lawn mower.

Staked tree.

CANKER REMOVAL

Cankers are caused by any of a number of different fungi and bacteria. They usually appear as discolored, sunken areas on a branch or on the main trunk, and often have sap oozing from them. As the organisms spread through the tissue, the cankers increase in size. If the cankers girdle the wood, the portion of the tree above the canker dies. Remove cankered branches by pruning off the branch at the trunk, or at least 6 inches below the canker. When the canker appears on the main trunk or a large branch, the tree or branch can sometimes be saved by surgical removal of the canker. Using a chisel and a sharp knife, excise all discolored bark and wood from the wound. All tools should be sterilized with rubbing alcohol after each cut to prevent spreading the disease organisms to healthy tissue. Spray the wound lightly with ORTHO Pruning Sealer. To hasten the healing process and promote vigorous growth, fertilize and water the tree regularly. For more information about fertilizers and watering, see pages 904 and 906.

BARK WOUNDS

The bark is a protective layer that serves many of the same functions as our skin. When this layer is breached, disease organisms and insects may invade the plant through the break. Directly under the bark is the conductive tissue of the plant — the circulatory system that carries water and minerals to the leaves, and sugar and protein to the roots. If the break in the bark does not heal quickly, this tissue dries out and dies, stopping circulation through that part of the trunk or branch. Bark wounds that encircle more than a quarter of the circumference of a trunk or branch slow the growth of the plant past that point. Small breaks in a healthy tree — those less than 1/2 inch wide — usually heal within a couple of weeks during the growing season. Larger breaks heal more slowly, as the tree grows a layer of tissue across them. If the break remains open for too long, heartrot fungi often invade the wound, rotting the wood and beginning the process that leads to hollow trees.

If the edges of a wound are ragged, trim the bark with a sharp knife to make a clean edge, but don't remove any more bark than is necessary. Smooth the underlying wood with a chisel. On wounds over 1/2 inch across, spray the exposed wood lightly with ORTHO Pruning Sealer. If the wound has begun to heal, a roll of new tissue can be seen at the edge of the wound. Do not cut into this tissue.

STAKING AND GUYING

Many newly transplanted trees require temporary support until the roots grow into the surrounding soil and the tree establishes itself. This is especially true of shade trees, which just after transplanting have much larger crowns (branch systems at the top of the tree) than root systems, making them top heavy. Most trees are able to support themselves after 1 to 2 years. To avoid girdling the tree, stakes and ties should be checked annually and either readjusted or removed. Staked trees that are held rigidly in place develop weaker trunks than unstaked trees, so support should allow some natural sway.

Trees with trunks less than 3 inches in diameter: Support the tree with two directly opposed stakes (8 feet long by 3 inches in diameter), driven at least 2 feet into the ground. The stakes should not interfere with the roots. Loop two strands of plastic tape or rubber ties (available in garden centers) around the tree trunk, and tie them around each stake. Leave enough slack in the tie to allow the trunk to sway slightly.

Trees with trunks greater than 3 inches in diameter: Space three stakes (3 feet by 2 inches by 4 inches), or 18-inch screw-type ground anchors, around the tree and drive them into the soil at an angle away from the tree. Place the stakes or anchors at a distance from the tree equal to 2/3 of the height of attachment to the tree. Loop three strands of thick tape or rubber ties around the tree trunk and over a branch or nail, and tie one to each of the stakes. Tighten the ties as in the method above. Flag the ties so that people don't trip over them.

Protecting tomato transplant from the sun.

Fir branches used as protective mulch.

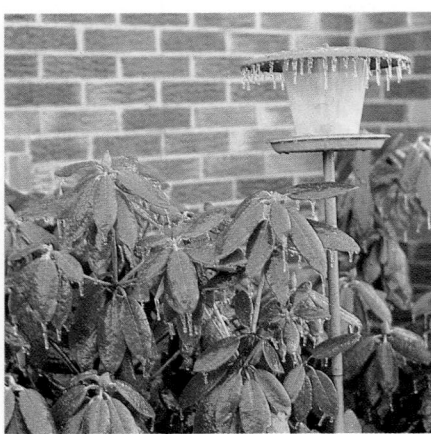

Frozen rhododendron.

HEAT PROTECTION

Plants cool their leaves by evaporation. If the soil dries out during hot weather, leaf temperatures rise rapidly to killing levels. To prevent heat injury to plants, keep them well watered during hot weather, never letting the soil around them dry out. For small plants such as annuals and vegetables, and plants growing in containers, this may mean watering as often as twice a day during heat waves. The lawn grasses that are used in the northern states are especially susceptible to heat. Keep the soil moist during hot weather. The lawn — and most other plants in the garden — benefits by being wet down during the hottest part of the day. To further protect sensitive plants, erect temporary shade structures. Shade larger plants with burlap or cheesecloth stretched on a wooden frame. Shade small plants with shingles or pieces of cardboard, set at an angle in the soil beside the plant.

PROTECTING PLANTS FROM THE COLD

Low temperatures can cause severe damage in the home garden. Take these precautions against winter cold:

1. Protect tender plants from light frost with newspapers or sheets of fabric or plastic. When night temperatures below 32°F are predicted, cover the plants loosely. Remove the covers in the morning. In the South, protect tender or half-hardy plants during especially cold weather by covering them, or by providing heat sources throughout the garden. Many small heat sources are more effective than a few large ones. Use electric lights, piles of charcoal, cans of jellied alcohol, or other slow-burning material.

2. In the North, continue watering the garden until the ground freezes in the winter. Plants need water in the soil to replace any lost through their leaves to the winter winds.

3. After the ground freezes, mulch perennials and trees and shrubs with chopped leaves, wood chips, straw, evergreen boughs, or pine needles. A 4 to 6-inch layer will help maintain even soil temperatures and prevent alternate freezing and thawing, which can heave plants out of the soil, tearing their roots. If plants are heaved, replant them as soon as the soil can be worked. Meanwhile, mulch the disrupted roots. For more information on mulching, see page 918.

4. Wrap the trunks of newly planted trees with burlap or tree-wrap paper to prevent sunscald or cracks in the trunk caused by fluctuating day and night temperatures.

5. Shield evergreens from drying winds and sun with burlap stretched over wooden frames, or with snow fencing.

CHILLING INJURY

Plants that have been grown in a house or greenhouse may be damaged if they are planted in the garden while night temperatures are still below 50°F. The growth of damaged plants may be temporarily halted, or parts of the leaves may die and turn black. To prevent this damage, accustom your plants to cool weather by hardening them off. A week or two before planting them outdoors, place them outside in a sunny spot for one to three hours. Each day, increase the time they are outside until they are being left outside for a full day by the end of the one to two week period. If frost is predicted, bring them indoors. Water wilted plants promptly. Plants can also be hardened off in a cold frame. Gradually open the sash more each day to expose the plants to cooler temperatures. Remove any shading gradually to allow in more sunlight. If it is impractical to take plants outside, they may be hardened off by gradually increasing the length of time between waterings. Repeated drought stress has the same effect as cold.

Watering containerized shrub.

Potting.

Filling container with potting mix.

WATERING CONTAINER PLANTS

Apply enough water to container plants so that some water drains from the bottom. Drainage water should flow freely away from the container so that water doesn't collect around the base. If the container is sitting in a saucer, wait for all of the water to drain through (10 to 15 minutes is adequate for most plants), then empty the water from the saucer. Sometimes the drainage hole becomes blocked and water accumulates inside the container rather than flowing out. Make sure the container drains after you've watered. If it doesn't, poke a stick up into the drainage hole to loosen compacted soil. Water again when the soil just below the surface is barely moist. In large containers (more than 10 inches wide and 10 inches high), water when the soil 1 to 2 inches below the surface is barely moist. Plants in containers without drainage holes are difficult to water properly. Water accumulates in the bottom of the container, causing root rot. If the soil in a container is allowed to become too dry, it may be difficult to rewet. Instead of penetrating the soil, the water runs down the inside edge of the container and immediately drains out the bottom. To wet the soil, soak the container in a tub or sink full of water for a few hours. The rim of the container should be submerged. Or add a soil penetrant (available in garden centers) to the irrigation water.

PLANTING IN CONTAINERS

Potting soils: Potting soils may be purchased or made. The best potting mixes provide good drainage, yet retain enough water so that the soil doesn't dry out too frequently. Any of the following recipes will provide 1 cubic foot of good potting mix, enough to fill ten to twelve 1-gallon containers.

Mix thoroughly and store in a closed container until use:

1. 4 gallons of medium or coarse sand
4 gallons of moistened peat moss
4 gallons of composted bark or sawdust
¼ cup dolomitic limestone
3 tablespoons of ORTHO Superphosphate 0–20–0
1 tablespoon ORTHO General Purpose Plant Food 8–8–8

2. 6 gallons of moistened peat moss
6 gallons of perlite
¼ cup dolomitic limestone
3 tablespoons of ORTHO Superphosphate 0–20–0
1 tablespoon ORTHO General Purpose Plant Food 8–8–8

3. 4 gallons of pasteurized garden soil
4 gallons of medium or coarse sand
4 gallons of leaf mold
3 tablespoons of ORTHO Superphosphate 0–20–0
1 tablespoon of ORTHO General Purpose Plant Food 8–8–8

Pasteurizing soil: To pasteurize garden soil, moisten it and spread it about two inches deep on a cookie sheet. Place a thermometer so that the bulb is about in the center of the soil, but not touching the metal sheet. Put the pan of soil in the oven and turn it on. Heat the soil to 140°F, and keep it at that temperature for 30 minutes. If your oven thermostat can't be set as low as 140°F, heat the soil to that temperature, then turn off the oven and crack the door slightly. Do not heat the soil higher than 140°F or for longer than 30 minutes. This temperature is high enough to kill all disease producing organisms and insect pests, and will even kill some weed seeds. However, many of the beneficial soil organisms will survive. Clean clay pots can be pasteurized at the same time as the soil.

Planting in containers: When potting, do not put a layer of gravel in the bottom of the container. A gravel layer does not improve drainage, and it reduces the amount of soil that can be used by the roots. If necessary, keep soil from spilling out of the drain holes by placing a piece of screen or broken crockery over the hole before planting. Do not fill the container to the rim with soil. The space between the surface of the soil and the container rim is a watering reservoir. The reservoir should be deep enough after settling so that one filling provides enough water to wet the mix to the bottom.

Supplemental light.

Rooting a dieffenbachia cutting.

Examining plant roots.

SUPPLEMENTARY LIGHTING

In many homes, it is hard to find enough bright locations for all the plants. It is particularly important that plants grown for their flowers or colorful foliage have bright light.

Lengthening the day: Giving some extra light after nightfall is often enough to keep a plant vigorous. This is especially true in the winter, when the days are short. These extra hours of light can be achieved by placing the plant near a reading light in the evening, but not so near that the heat burns the leaves.

Making extra light: If the plant cannot be moved, bring more light to the plant by training a decorator spotlight on it in its present location. This light can be used to extend the day or, if the location is dim, it can be left on all day to brighten the location.

Growing under lights: You can make plants independent of natural light by supplying all their light needs with artificial lighting. Fluorescent fixtures with cool-white bulbs are most practical. Use a reflector to focus the light on the plants. About 15 to 20 watts are needed for each square foot you wish to illuminate. Fix the lights one to two feet above the tops of the plants, and leave them on for 12 hours a day for foliage plants, and 16 hours a day for flowering plants. Most houseplants can be grown under fluorescent fixtures, but a few that need full sun, such as miniature roses, may not get enough light to bloom.

ROOTING CUTTINGS

Many houseplants root easily. If a houseplant has lost many of its lower leaves, or is suffering from root rot, the top can often be saved by following these guidelines:

Preparing the rooting mix: Fill flower pots with equal parts of perlite and peat moss. Add 1 teaspoon of lime per quart of mix, and blend it in thoroughly. Wet the mix thoroughly and let it drain.

Making the frame: Bend 1 or 2 wire coathangers or sturdy wire into a U shape and insert the ends of the wire into the rooting mix.

Preparing the cuttings: Cut off the top of the plant you wish to save. Take the part that will be the new plant, plus 2 to 4 inches of stem. Strip off all of the leaves on the extra stem portion. Dip the bottom of the stem in a rooting powder. Insert the stem into the rooting mix. Press the mix gently around the stem, then slip a clear plastic bag over the wire frame. Secure the bag around the pot with rubber bands. The bag acts as a miniature greenhouse by maintaining high moisture levels in the soil and air. Keep the cuttings in a warm place where they receive bright, indirect light, but not direct sunlight. Remove the plastic cover once a week to make sure the rooting mix has not dried out; water if necessary.

Checking for roots: Check for roots after 3 weeks by gently tugging the cutting. If the cutting is firmly bound to the mix by the new roots, it is ready to transplant into potting soil. If the cutting has not rooted adequately, check weekly until it is well rooted.

EXAMINING PLANT ROOTS

Rootballs can be inspected without harming the plant. However, the plant must be established in the container — that is, roots must have grown all through the potting mix — or else much of the rootball will fall apart when the plant is removed from the pot. It is easier to remove the plant from the container when the soil is moist. If your plant is small enough to hold in one hand, put your hand on the soil surface, with the plant stems between your fingers. Invert the container and gently knock the rim on the edge of a table or other firm surface. The rootball will dislodge from the inside of the pot and fall into your hand. To inspect the rootball of a plant that is too large to hold, lay the container on its side, and place a piece of 2×4 or 4×4 lumber across the rim of the container as close to the stem of the plant as possible. Strike the board with a hammer to dislodge the rootball. Slide the plant gently out of the container. Roots will be visible on the outside of the rootball. Healthy roots have many white or tan threadlike tips. These tips are the part of the root system that most actively absorbs water and nutrients. Unhealthy roots have fewer white tips, and the larger roots may be dark and rotting. Dead roots have no white tips.

GARDENING PRACTICES

Spraying coleus plant.

Using a hose-end sprayer.

Thistle treated with herbicide.

SPRAYING HOUSEPLANTS

Some houseplant sprays, such as ORTHO House Plant Insect Spray and ORTHO Whitefly & Mealybug Killer, are designed to be used inside the house. But if the label does not say the product can be used indoors, take the plants outside to a shady spot to spray them. In cold weather, spray in a heated garage or basement. Don't spray in front of air intakes for heating units. Let the plants dry thoroughly before taking them back into the living quarters.

Applying the spray: Read the label and follow the directions exactly. Be sure the plant you wish to spray is listed on the label. The chemical may damage the leaves if it is applied in too high a concentration, or if the plants are sprayed more frequently than recommended. Leaves may also be burned if aerosol cans are held too close to them when spraying. Do not spray in the sun, or when the temperature is higher than 85°F.

Applying insecticides: Spray both sides of the leaves, all around the stems, the surface of the soil, and the outside of the pot. Unless a product is specially formulated for mealybugs, adding a few drops of a spreader-sticker — a wetting agent available in most garden centers — will help the insecticide penetrate this insect's waxy coating and increase its effectiveness. A spreader-sticker will also help to keep the spray from beading on waxy leaves.

SPRAYING AND DUSTING

In order for pesticides to be most effective, they must be properly applied. Choose a calm day when the temperature is under 85°F and no rain is expected for at least 12 hours. Early morning is often the best time.

Spraying: It is important that the plant be thoroughly covered. If the label instructions say "wet thoroughly" or "to the drip point," apply as much spray as possible, until the plant begins to drip. To get thorough coverage, spray the plant from two or three directions, and from underneath as well as from above. If there is any breeze, spray downwind to avoid having the mist drift back to you.

Dusting: Since dust is carried by air currents, it is especially important that dusting be done when the air is still. Apply a thin coat of dust, not a heavy layer. Work the duster vigorously, so that the air currents carry the dust onto the foliage and cover all the surfaces of the leaves. Dust from the bottom of the plant as well as from the top.

Spreader-stickers: These additives perform two functions: they break the surface tension of the spray droplets, preventing them from beading on waxy leaves and helping them to penetrate wax-covered insects, such as mealybugs and scales. They also make pesticides adhere better in rainy weather. Spreader-stickers are available in garden centers. ORTHO products are formulated to wet foliage quickly, so additional spreader-stickers are usually not needed.

APPLYING HERBICIDES

There are two categories of herbicides: *pre-emergence* herbicides, which are applied to the soil before weed seeds germinate, and *post-emergence* herbicides, which are applied to actively growing weeds.

Pre-emergence herbicides: These herbicides do not kill growing weeds. They should be applied to weed-free soil, either before weed seeds sprout in the spring, or after weeds have been removed. Pre-emergence herbicides attach to soil particles in the top inch of soil, where most seed germination takes place, and kill weed seeds as they germinate. If the soil is cultivated after application, the herbicide will be diluted and its effectiveness diminished.

Post-emergence herbicides: These herbicides control weeds that are actively growing. When spraying them, be careful not to allow the material to touch desirable plants. This can be most easily done by following these guidelines:
1. Spray on a windless day.
2. Use low pressures when spraying.
3. Keep the nozzle as close to the weeds as possible.
4. Use a shield of cardboard, plywood, or sheet metal to protect garden plants when working near them.
Clean sprayers carefully before using them for fungicides or insecticides. Some gardeners keep separate sprayers for herbicides.

Choosing plants.

Planting a tomato.

Planting a balled and burlapped shrub.

CHOOSING PLANTS

Plants are available in several different forms. Inspect all plants for visible insects and diseases. Here are some standards for choosing plants.

Balled and burlapped (B&B): The leaves are large, of good color, and free from spots or dead areas. The stems do not show signs of recent heavy pruning. Stem diameter is in good proportion to the size of the plant. The roots do not encircle the base of the trunk, and the rootball inside the burlap is not broken or very dry.

Bare root: The trunk is a good diameter for the size of the plant. The stem is flexible and the bark is not broken or dried. The roots are symmetrical and flexible. The buds and roots are still dormant, with no new growth evident.

Containerized: The leaves are large, of good color, and free from spots or dead areas. The stems do not show signs of recent heavy pruning. The stem diameter is in proportion with the size of the plant. The roots do not encircle the base of the trunk, and the plant is firmly rooted. When the plant is removed from the container, many roots are visible on the outside of the rootball, but they are not thick or woody.

Flats or small pots: Plants are young and stocky, without dead or discolored leaves. No plants should be missing from the flat.

Sod: The grass is a good green color without yellow blades. The soil is about ¾ inch thick, and moist. The sod holds together when handled.

Bulbs: The bulbs are firm without wounds, or soft or deep blemishes. They are not moldy or dried, and the basal plate is firm and not cracked. The skins may be loose.

PLANTING AND TRANSPLANTING

Survival of a plant after transplanting often depends on how much care was taken during planting. This includes selection of the plant, site selection, preparation of the planting site, and the actual setting of the plant. To avoid problems after transplanting, all of these factors must be considered. Choose a plant that will survive in your climate. Do not transplant at a time when the plant will be damaged by unfavorable weather (extreme heat or cold).

Storing the plant: Before planting, protect the plant from heat, cold, or drying. It is best to plant soon after purchase. Bare root plants and balled and burlapped plants are extremely susceptible to drying. If planting is to be delayed more than a few days, cover the roots of a balled and burlapped plant with moist mulch or loose soil. To store a bare root plant, dig a trench in a shady location, place the plant in the trench, and cover the roots with mulch or soil.

The planting site: Select a planting site in an area where the plant will have room for spread and height, and receive the right light for its needs. Choose a site that has good drainage. If the area has poor drainage, improve it, following the directions on page 901. If planting in a lawn, keep the lawn away from the root area of the plant to avoid competition.

Planting: Prepare the planting hole by digging a hole approximately twice as wide as the root system and deep enough so that the plant will be at the same level as it was in the nursery. Leave the sides of the hole rough, so the roots can penetrate the soil. Use topsoil for backfill. Break up dirt clods and remove rocks. If the soil is very sandy or heavy clay, improve it by adding organic matter (see page 918). Carefully remove the container from potted plants. Make 3 vertical cuts down the sides of the rootball. This pruning prevents circling roots that may later constrict the trunk, and stimulates new root growth into the surrounding soil. Inspect bare root plants for broken or damaged roots, and prune off any that are damaged. Do not remove the burlap from balled and burlapped plants before setting them in the planting hole. Spread out the roots on bare root plants. Fill in the hole with soil until it is ¾ full, settling the soil around the roots to prevent large air pockets from forming. Cut the twine on balled and burlapped plants and fold back the burlap so it is below the soil surface. Fill the hole with water, then cover the rest of the roots with soil. Do not tamp the soil down.

Care of the plant: Proper care after transplanting is essential for the survival of the plant. Prune off broken branches, and if necessary prune to shape the plant. On bare root plants, prune off about a third of the branches to compensate for root loss. Newly transplanted trees with tops that are large in proportion to their roots should be staked (see page 911). To prevent sunscald, wrap trunks of trees (especially those with smooth, thin bark) with tree-wrap paper or burlap. Build a basin around the plant and water the plant by filling the basin whenever the rootball is barely moist. Water in the basin until the roots grow into the surrounding soil. For more information about watering, see page 906.

Starting seeds indoors.

Starting seeds outdoors.

Storing bulbs.

STARTING SEEDS INDOORS

Growing transplants requires bright light and moderate temperatures.

1. Wash containers (milk or egg cartons, cans, flower pots) to remove soil and debris. Disinfect in a solution of 1 part household bleach to 9 parts water.

2. Fill the containers to within ½ inch of the top with vermiculite, or a mix of 1 part peat moss and 10 parts perlite.

3. Wet and drain the mix.

4. Sprinkle the seeds over the surface.

5. Cover lightly with soil mix or peat moss.

6. Place the containers in clear plastic bags and seal, to provide humidity and prevent the soil from drying out. Place the container in a location in which the temperature is suitable for seed germination (see page 1009).

7. As soon as the seedlings emerge, remove the bag and move the containers to a warm area with bright light, either a windowsill or under fluorescent lights.

8. As soon as the seedlings are large enough to handle, transplant them into disinfected flats or peat pots containing a mix of equal parts peat moss and perlite, and ½ teaspoon limestone per quart of mix.

9. Place the flats in a warm area with bright light.

10. Feed the seedlings weekly with ORTHO Tomato & Vegetable Food 6–18–6 mixed at half strength.

11. One week before planting outdoors, harden off the plants by placing them outdoors a few hours a day, until they are outside a full day by the end of the week. Transplant into the garden according to the spacing recommended on the seed packet.

STARTING SEEDS OUTDOORS

Some plants should be seeded directly in the garden.

1. Till the soil, incorporating a fertilizer that is high in phosphate such as ORTHO Vegetable Garden Food 5–10–10. Rake to level and remove stones and clods larger than ½ inch. Water well 1 or 2 days before planting.

2. If you have been troubled with damping-off fungi in the past, treat the seeds with a fungicide containing *captan* or *thiram*. Add a pinch to a packet of seeds, or ½ teaspoon per pound. For more information on damping-off, see page 858.

3. Using a board or a string stretched between two stakes as a guide, make a furrow as deep as the planting depth suggested on the seed packet, or 4 times as deep as the seed is wide.

4. Drop the seeds into the furrow, spacing them about twice as close together as you wish the mature plants to stand.

5. Fill the furrow with sand, compost, or light soil.

6. Press firmly to settle the seeds and soil.

7. Water gently, sprinkling the soil. Be careful not to wash away the newly planted seeds. Allow the soil surface to dry slightly between waterings.

8. In hot, dry weather, mulch the seed row lightly with straw, sawdust, or leaf mold. Or place a board or a strip of burlap on the row. Remove the latter promptly as soon as the seeds begin to germinate.

9. When the seedlings are large enough to handle, thin according to the recommended spacings on the seed packet. To avoid disturbing the roots of the remaining seedlings, pinch the thinnings off at the ground level, or cut them with a pair of scissors.

STORING BULBS

In areas where bulbs are not winter hardy, they must be dug up and stored for the winter.

1. After the foliage has yellowed or been killed by a frost in the fall, carefully dig up the bulbs with a spading fork.

2. Discard any wounded, diseased, or deformed bulbs.

3. Cut off the foliage close to the bulb, and shake off any loose soil. Dry the bulbs in a well-ventilated area out of direct sunlight for about a week.

4. Carefully brush off any soil. To protect the bulbs from storage rots, dust them with a fungicide containing *captan*.

5. Bulbs are live plants, and continue to breathe. Store them in shallow trays or plastic buckets, covered with dry sand, peat moss, perlite, or vermiculite.

6. Store the bulbs at temperatures between 35° and 45°F. They must not be allowed to freeze.

7. Store until the proper planting time for your plant.

Precooling: In mild winter areas where the bulbs' chilling requirements are not satisfied, purchase precooled bulbs, or precool them yourself. To do this, place the uncovered bulbs in a shallow pan. Store in the refrigerator or any area where the temperature remains just above freezing for 6 weeks. Plant outdoors or in pots. Blooms will appear in 2 to 4 months, depending on the plant variety.

Measuring organic matter.

Compost bin.

Pine cone mulch.

ORGANIC MATTER

The organic matter that is added to soil is derived from plants or animals. Any soil will benefit from the addition of organic material, but heavy or sandy soils are especially helped.

How organic matter improves the soil: Organic matter incorporated into clay or compacted soils opens up the soil, giving it a crumbly structure. This reduces stickiness, improves drainage, and allows air to move more easily into the soil. In sandy soils, organic matter acts like a sponge, holding moisture and nutrients in the root zone. The quantity of organic matter added to the soil must be large enough to change the soil structure. Spread from 1 to 4 inches over the soil and then till or mix it in. As organic matter decomposes into humus, it continues to improve the soil. For best results, add organic matter whenever the soil is worked. Many different types of organic matter can be used as soil amendments. The amendments should be free of weed seeds, toxic materials, and disease organisms. When buying organic matter, especially in bulk, it is best to buy from a well-established, reputable dealer. The most commonly used types of organic matter are compost, peat moss, manure, ground bark, and sawdust, but other materials may be available locally.

Compost: Compost can be purchased or made at home. (For instructions on making compost, see ORTHO's book *All About Fertilizers, Soils & Water.*) Besides improving soil structure, compost also provides some of the essential nutrients for plant growth, depending on what originally went into it.

Peat moss: Peat moss is one of the most commonly used soil conditioners. Since peat moss is acid (pH 3.5 to 4.5), it is especially good for acid-loving plants, and as much as 50 percent may be added to the soil before planting. If peat moss is allowed to dry out, it will shed water. It can be remoistened by loosening the peat moss, spreading it under a sprinkler, and then mixing it several times while it is absorbing water. If the peat moss is already mixed into the soil and it does not moisten, add a wetting agent, which can be purchased from your local nursery, to the water.

Manure: Manure is a very common and widely available soil amendment. It is a good conditioner, but has several drawbacks. Fresh manure may burn tender roots, so it should be partially decomposed before it is used. Some manure, especially bagged steer manure, has a high salt content, and should be used in moderation if you already have salt problems or alkaline soil. (For more information about salt damage, see page 864.)

Ground bark and sawdust: Ground bark and sawdust are byproducts of the lumber industry. Unless they have been fortified with nitrogen (if they are purchased in bags it will say so on the bag) or are well composted, the bacteria that decompose them will rob the soil of nitrogen. To prevent a nitrogen deficiency, add ½ pound of nitrogen to every cubic yard of bark or sawdust. For example, 10 pounds of ORTHO Tomato & Vegetable Food 6–18–6 or 6¼ pounds of ORTHO General Purpose Plant Food 8–8–8 should be added to the bark or sawdust during tillage.

MULCHING

A mulch is an insulating layer of material that is spread over the ground. The most important types of mulches are:

Organic material: A wide variety of organic materials are used for mulching. Some of the most common are straw, leaves, lawn clippings, wood chips, shredded bark, and ground corncobs. All organic mulches conserve soil moisture and modify the soil temperature near the surface. As these materials decompose, they improve the tilth of the soil. Choose a mulching material that is free of weed seeds, and that has not been recently sprayed with an herbicide. Apply organic mulches 3 to 6 inches thick. A thick mulch also controls weeds.

Inorganic material: These materials do not decompose, so they are more permanent than organic mulches. Inorganic mulches include rocks, gravel, and coarse sand. These materials are more expensive but longer lasting than organic mulches. There is also less danger of bringing weed seeds or diseases into your garden.

Impervious films: The most popular impervious film mulch is black polyethylene. Clear plastic and builder's paper are also used. Black plastic gives excellent control of weeds. It can even be placed over existing weeds to kill them. Films also control water loss and warm the soil slightly. Clear plastic does not control weeds, but warms the soil quickly, and can even be used to pasteurize the soil with heat (see page 919). Because plastic films reduce the amount of oxygen that penetrates the soil, do not use them over large areas around trees and shrubs.

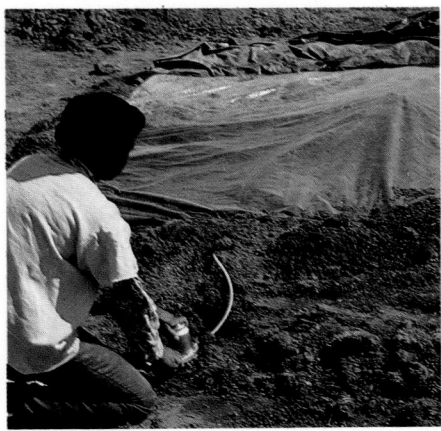

Soil fumigation with methyl bromide.

Fumigation with VPM.

Pinching.

SOIL FUMIGATION

Soil fumigants kill all living matter present in the soil, including plants, weed seeds, nematodes, insects, and disease organisms. Soil fumigation is used to kill organisms for which there is no other control. For best results, treat when the soil temperature is between 60° and 85°F. Do not use around desirable plants where the roots growing into the treated soil may be killed. The only soil fumigant available to home gardeners is VPM, a liquid. More potent fumigants are available to commercial pest control operators, the most common of which is *methyl bromide*.

Using VPM:
1. Till the soil 6 inches deep. Remove all debris larger than 2 inches.
2. Water thoroughly and let the soil sit for 1 to 3 days.
3. Divide the area to be treated into sections 5 feet by 10 feet (50 square feet).
4. Add 1 pint (2 cups) of VPM to a watering can full of water.
5. Sprinkle the solution on the first 50 square foot section. Water immediately.
6. Repeat the same procedure for each section.
7. When the entire area is treated, water with a sprinkler, applying 1 or 2 inches of water.
8. Break up the soil crust with a rake in 7 to 10 days. Otherwise, do not disturb the area for 2 to 3 weeks following the treatment.
9. After this time, loosen the soil with a rake. To be sure the fumigant has completely dissipated, test by planting some radish seeds. If the seeds germinate, then the soil is ready for planting. If they don't germinate, wait a week and plant again. Repeat this procedure until the seeds sprout.

Pasteurizing the soil with clear plastic: This method of soil pasteurization has only recently been developed, and is still being tested, but initial results look promising for controlling fungus diseases. Shallow tree roots may be killed by soil pasteurization.
1. This method uses the heat of the sun to sterilize the soil. It must be applied during the hottest part of the summer.
2. Till and water the soil as described in steps 1 and 2 above.
3. Cover the soil with clear polyethylene, sealing the edges and all seams with soil.
4. Leave the plastic in place for 6 weeks. During this period, the heat of the sun will warm the surface of the soil to 120°F or more, enough to kill many disease organisms.

PINCHING

The technique of pinching plants is used to produce dense, stocky plants and more (but smaller) blossoms. When the growing tip of the stem is removed, the plant's energy is channeled into the side branches and buds, forcing them to grow. Although annuals, perennials, and houseplants are the plants most commonly pinched, woody ornamentals — especially azaleas and rhododendrons — may also be pinched. With your thumbnail and finger, gently squeeze the stem just above a set of leaves until it breaks. Most annuals and perennials are pinched when they are 2 to 4 inches tall, with several sets of leaves. Usually only the growing tip with one set of leaves is removed, but for tall, spindly plants up to a third of the height of the plant may be pinched. Herbaceous plants are usually pinched when they are transplanted into the garden, and any time throughout the season if they become leggy. Pinch off old flowers to encourage more blossoms. Pinch houseplants whenever they become leggy. Pinching woody ornamentals periodically will help save on pruning later. Pinch out the growing tip of any erratically growing branches when the tip is still tender, before it becomes woody. Pinching is also an easy way to harvest sprigs of herbs.

To find out more about an ORTHO product, locate the product in the index on the next page. This section is arranged into these broad categories:

A GALLERY OF ORTHO PRODUCTS

Each ORTHO product in this section solves a garden or household problem. Some of them, such as ORTHO Mole Cricket Bait, solve a very specific problem; others, such as ORTHO General Purpose Plant Food 8–8–8, are solutions to a wide range of plant problems.

This section presents information about each of these products as an aid to the reader in selecting a solution to a garden problem. Most of the problems discussed in this book have a number of possible solutions. Where several products have been offered as solutions to a problem, any of them may be chosen, depending on availability in your region.

Aside from some of the obvious considerations, such as whether you already have a bottle of one of the recommended products in your garage, there are a few

major product differences to take into account when making your selection.

One difference is the way a product is formulated. For instance, a dust can be used right from the package without mixing or measuring, and may be applied with a dust applicator. Liquids or wettable powders must be mixed with water so that they can be applied. The choice depends on your preference.

Another consideration in choosing a product is the size of the job it is meant to do. ORTHO Weed-B-Gon Jet Weeder, for instance, is quick and convenient for spot-treating a few weeds in a lawn, but is not suitable for killing many weeds in a large lawn area. ORTHO Weed-B-Gon Lawn Weed Killer can be applied over the entire lawn and is more suitable for large jobs.

Perhaps the most important consideration, though, is the plant or the part of the garden on which a product is to be used. A product intended for use on trees and shrubs may not be registered for use in the vegetable garden, and a product intended for the vegetable garden may not be effective on lawn problems.

You should always read a product label twice: once when you buy it, to decide if it is the right product for the job you need done, and a second time before you use it, to get specific instructions for applying it. Always use chemical products exactly as the label directions say; these directions have been carefully worked out by the manufacturer (and approved by the government) to give you the maximum satisfaction from the use of the product.

Above: Broadcast Spreader. See page 979.
Left: Lawn and Garden Sprayer. See page 980.

INDEX TO ORTHO PRODUCTS

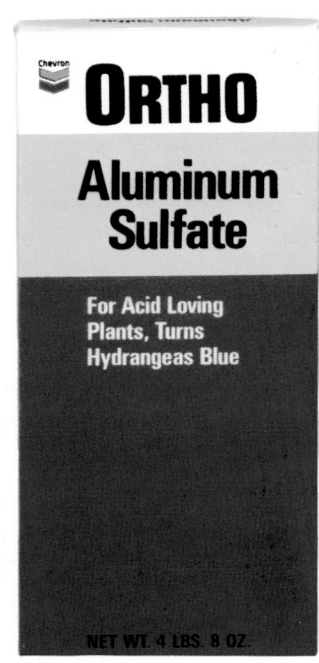

ALUMINUM SULFATE

GENERAL DESCRIPTION:
A granular soil amendment for making soils more acid. It is especially useful in changing the color of hydrangeas to a deep blue. It is beneficial to acid-loving plants (azaleas, camellias, gardenias, rhododendrons, hydrangeas, orchids, ixora, hibiscus, etc.) by helping to keep the soil acid.

AREAS SOLD:
National

GUARANTEED ANALYSIS:
100% Hydrated aluminum sulfate

BENEFITS THESE PLANTS:
Azaleas
Camellias
Hydrangeas
Rhododendrons

FOR USE IN THESE AREAS:
Acid-loving plants

AZALEA & CAMELLIA FOOD 10–8–7

GENERAL DESCRIPTION:
A liquid fertilizer specially formulated for acid-loving plants. As a liquid, it is readily available to the roots and foliage, giving quick and lasting response. It also aids in correcting iron chlorosis (yellowing leaves), and can be applied with an ORTHO Lawn Sprayer or sprinkling can. It contains the 3 major plant nutrients — nitrogen, phosphate, and potash as well as additional important nutrients — boron, iron, manganese, molybdenum, and zinc. Treats 15 to 30 plants.

AREAS SOLD:
South

GUARANTEED ANALYSIS:
10% Nitrogen
8% Phosphate
7% Potash
Traces of these nutrients:
  Boron
  Iron
  Manganese
  Molybdenum
  Zinc

BENEFITS THESE PLANTS:
Aucuba
Azaleas
Caladiums
Camellias
Clevera
Crotons
Gardenias
Hibiscus
Ixora
Ligustrum
Magnolia
Pyracantha
Rhododendron
Rubber Plants
Viburnum

FOR USE IN THESE AREAS:
Acid-loving plants

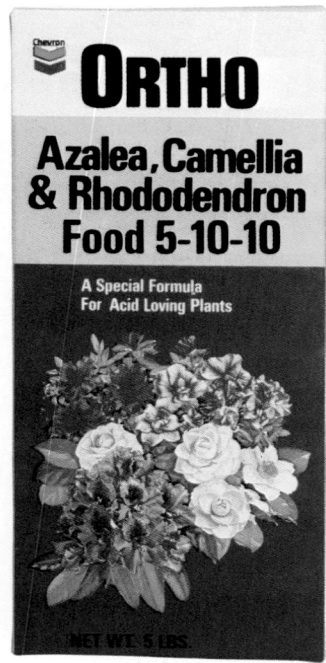

AZALEA, CAMELLIA & RHODODENDRON FOOD 5-10-10

GENERAL DESCRIPTION:

A granular fertilizer specially designed for acid-loving plants. It contains the 3 major plant nutrients — nitrogen, phosphate, and potash, as well as other important nutrients including calcium, magnesium, sulfur, iron, manganese and zinc — to provide a balanced food for plants. The label lists over 35 acid-loving plants that respond well to this formula, along with rates of application for established plants and potted plants.

AREAS SOLD:
National

GUARANTEED ANALYSIS:
5% Nitrogen
10% Phosphate
10% Potash
Traces of these nutrients:
   Calcium
   Magnesium
   Sulfur
   Iron
   Manganese
   Zinc

BENEFITS THESE PLANTS:
Aucuba
Azalea
Caladium
Calla Lilly
Camellia
Clevera
Columbine
Crape Myrtle
Croton
Cyclamen
Delphinium
Dogwood
Easter Lily
Fern
Fir
Gardenia
Heather
Hibiscus
Holly
Hydrangea
Ixora
Japanese Maple
Juniper
Laurel
Ligustrum
Magnolia
Mahonia
Pine
Pyracantha
Rhododendron
Spruce
Star Jasmine
Tuberous Begonia
Viburnum
White Cedar
Yew

FOR USE IN THESE AREAS:
Acid-loving plants

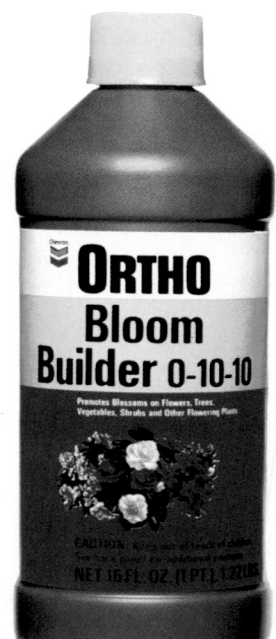

BLOOM BUILDER 0-10-10

GENERAL DESCRIPTION:
A liquid fertilizer specially formulated to increase the size, color, and quality of fruit, strengthen the branches of fruit and shade trees, and promote beautiful blossoms on annual and perennial flowers, flowering shrubs and trees, azaleas, camellias, rhododendrons, and other acid-loving plants, potted or container-grown flowering plants, and fruits and vegetables. It contains equal amounts of phosphate and potash and should be used before the plant's blooming period when a flush of foliar growth is not desired. It mixes readily with water to be applied with a sprinkling can or an ORTHO hose-end sprayer.

AREAS SOLD:
South
West

GUARANTEED ANALYSIS:
10% Phosphoric Acid
10% Potash

BENEFITS THESE PLANTS:
Acid-loving Plants
Azaleas
Camellias
Flowers
Fruit Trees
Rhododendrons
Shade Trees
Shrubs
Vegetables

FOR USE IN THESE AREAS:
Trees and shrubs
Fruits and vegetables
Flowers
Container plants

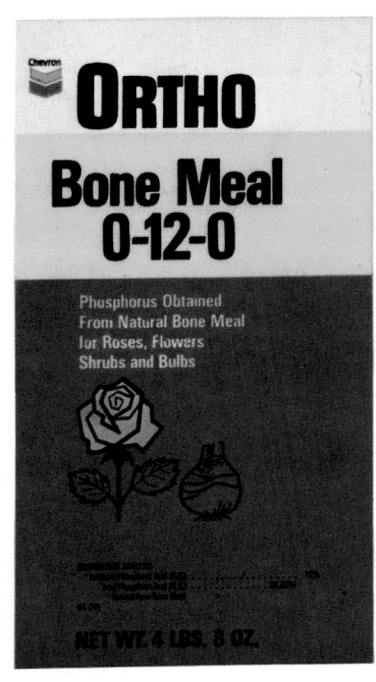

BENEFITS THESE PLANTS:
Bulbs
Container Plants
Flowers
Roses
Shrubs
Trees
Vegetables

FOR USE IN THESE AREAS:
Roses and flowers
Trees and shrubs
Bulbs and vegetables

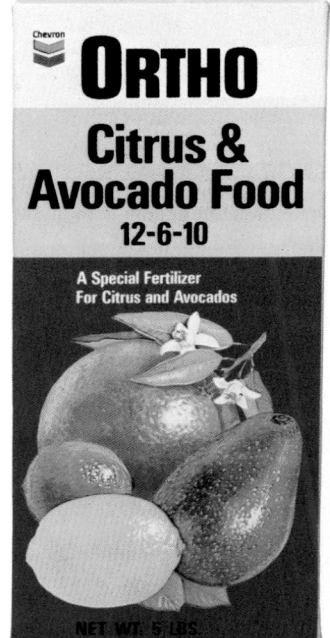

BENEFITS THESE PLANTS:
Avocados
Grapefruit
Lemons
Limes
Oranges
Other citrus trees
Tangerines

FOR USE IN THESE AREAS:
Citrus and avocados

BONE MEAL 0-12-0

GENERAL DESCRIPTION:
A granular phosphorus obtained from bone meal for use as a natural organic supplemental source of phosphorus, one of the important plant nutrients. Since phosphorus does not move much once placed in the soil, it is important to incorporate it into the soil to a depth of 6 to 8 inches. Bulbs respond especially well to bone meal placed in the bottom of the planting hole. Do not use ORTHO Bone Meal 0-12-0 for acid-loving plants such as azaleas, rhododendrons, and blueberries.

AREAS SOLD:
National

GUARANTEED ANALYSIS:
12% Phosphate

CITRUS & AVOCADO FOOD 12-6-10

GENERAL DESCRIPTION:
A granular fertilizer specially designed for citrus and avocados. It is clean and odorless, and contains the essential primary plant nutrients of nitrogen phosphate, and potash, plus the other essential nutrients calcium, magnesium, sulfur, iron, manganese, and zinc for good plant growth and fruit production.

AREAS SOLD:
South
West

GUARANTEED ANALYSIS:
12% Nitrogen
6% Phosphoric Acid
10% Potash
Traces of these nutrients:
   Calcium
   Magnesium
   Sulfur
   Iron
   Manganese
   Zinc

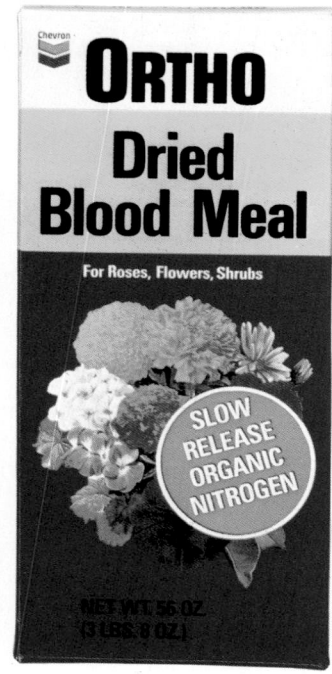

ORTHO
Dried
Blood Meal

For Roses, Flowers, Shrubs

SLOW
RELEASE
ORGANIC
NITROGEN

NET WT 56 OZ
(3 LBS 8 OZ)

BENEFITS THESE PLANTS:
Bedding Plants
Flowers
Roses
Shrubs
Vegetables

FOR USE IN THESE AREAS:
Roses and flowers
Vegetables
Shrubs

DRIED BLOOD MEAL 12-0-0

GENERAL DESCRIPTION:
This granular fertilizer is a natural, organic source of long-lasting, slow-release nitrogen. Nitrogen is the most important element for vigorous plant growth and greenness. The fertilizer is easy to use as a supplement to a regular feeding program on flowers, vegetables, bedding plants, shrubs, and roses. For best results, scatter the recommended amount evenly on the soil surface, rake into the top 1 or 2 inches, and water thoroughly.

AREAS SOLD:
National

GUARANTEED ANALYSIS:
12% Nitrogen

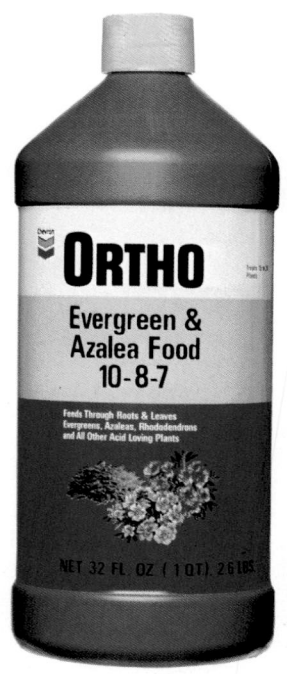

ORTHO

Evergreen &
Azalea Food
10-8-7

Feeds Through Roots & Leaves
Evergreens, Azaleas, Rhododendrons
and All Other Acid Loving Plants

NET 32 FL. OZ. (1 QT). 2.6 LBS.

EVERGREEN & AZALEA FOOD 10-8-7

GENERAL DESCRIPTION:
A special acid-forming fertilizer that contains a chelating agent, the three major plant nutrients — nitrogen, phosphate, and potash — and numerous minor elements. It promotes vigorous green growth and helps correct iron chlorosis (yellowing leaves) on evergreens, azaleas, rhododendrons, and all other acid-loving plants. As a liquid, it is readily available to the roots and foliage, giving a quick and lasting response. The label contains complete dilution instructions and recommended amounts for plants of various sizes. For best results, apply with an ORTHO Spray-ette, ORTHO Lawn Sprayer, or sprinkling can.

AREAS SOLD:
Northeast
Northwest
West

GUARANTEED ANALYSIS:
10% Nitrogen
8% Phosphoric acid
7% Potash
Traces of these nutrients:
  Boron
  Iron
  Manganese
  Molybdenum
  Zinc

BENEFITS THESE PLANTS:
Arborvitae
Azaleas
Douglas Fir
Euonymus
Gardenias
Hemlock
Holly
Juniper
Larch
Magnolias
Privet
Pyracantha
Rhododendrons
Spirea
Spruce
Taxus
Wax Leaf Ligustrum
  and all other
  acid-loving
  plants

FOR USE IN THESE AREAS:
Acid-loving trees and
  shrubs

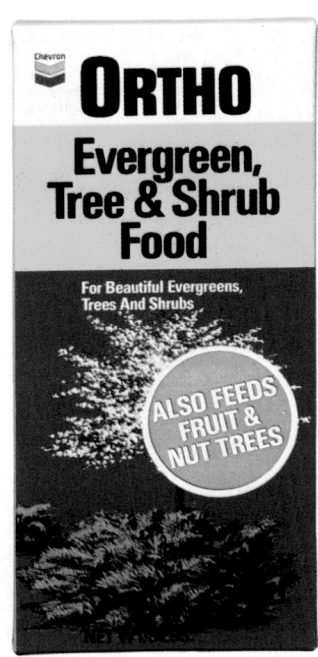

EVERGREEN, TREE & SHRUB FOOD 12-6-6

GENERAL DESCRIPTION:
A pelleted fertilizer made with a balance of nutrients to promote hardy, sturdy plants. It is formulated for use on evergreens, shrubs, shade trees, citrus, and fruit and nut trees. It supplies plants with the three major plant nutrients, nitrogen, phosphate, and potash, plus numerous minor elements. This fertilizer is clean, odorless, and easy to use on new plantings and established trees and shrubs. For best results, apply evenly beneath the outer ends of the branches and away from the trunk. Water thoroughly afterward to dissolve the pellets and carry the nutrients down into the root zone.

AREAS SOLD:
Midwest
Northeast
West

GUARANTEED ANALYSIS:
12% Nitrogen
6% Phosphoric acid
6% Potash
Traces of these nutrients:
  Calcium
  Magnesium
  Sulfur
  Iron
  Manganese
  Zinc

BENEFITS THESE PLANTS:
Arborvitae
Almond
Apple
Apricot
Ash
Beech
Birch
Cherry
Citrus
Elm
Euonymus
Fir
Hazelnut
Hemlock
Hickory
Ligustrum
Maple
Mulberry
Oak
Palm
Peach
Pear
Pecan
Pine
Plum
Poplar
Spirea
Spruce
Sycamore
Walnut and many other trees and shrubs

FOR USE IN THESE AREAS:
Trees and shrubs
Fruit and citrus

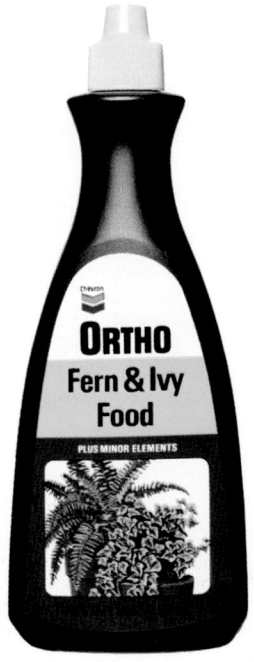

FERN & IVY FOOD 10-8-7

GENERAL DESCRIPTION:
A ready-to-use fertilizer solution specially formulated for ferns and ivy houseplants. It helps promote vigorous green growth and healthy root systems by supplying plants with the three major plant nutrients, nitrogen, phosphate, and potash, plus several minor elements. For easy, no-mess fertilization, simply add the recommended number of drops directly to the soil and then water in the usual way. Or dilute 1 capful in 1 quart of water and water plants with this solution.

AREAS SOLD:
National

GUARANTEED ANALYSIS:
10% Nitrogen
8% Phosphoric acid
7% Potash
Traces of these nutrients:
  Iron
  Manganese
  Zinc

BENEFITS THESE PLANTS:
Ferns
Ivy

FOR USE IN THESE AREAS:
Fern and ivy houseplants

FISH EMULSION FERTILIZER 5-1-1

GENERAL DESCRIPTION:

A liquid organic fertilizer made entirely of seagoing fish and designed for general indoor and outdoor use. It is absorbed by plants through their roots and leaves. When used as directed, it is nonburning. It promotes overall strong, healthy growth by supplying plants with the three major plant nutrients, nitrogen, phosphate, and potash. Because it does not burn, it is a very popular houseplant fertilizer. The label gives detailed dilution directions for use on various plants.

AREAS SOLD:

National

GUARANTEED ANALYSIS:

5% Nitrogen
1% Phosphoric acid
1% Potash

BENEFITS THESE PLANTS:

African Violets
Azaleas
Beans
Berries
Cabbage
Camellias
Carrots
Ferns
Fuchsias
Lettuce
Orchids
Peas
Philodendrons
Rhododendrons
Roses
Tuberous Begonias
and many other
    plants

FOR USE IN THESE AREAS:

Fruits and vegetables
Roses and flowers
Trees and shrubs

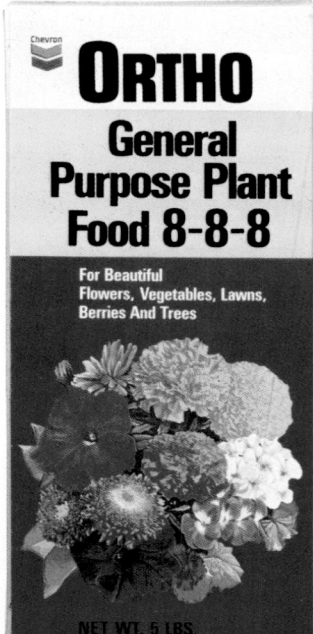

GENERAL PURPOSE PLANT FOOD 8-8-8

GENERAL DESCRIPTION:

A pelleted fertilizer designed for use on listed flowers, roses, shrubs, trees, and lawns. It is clean, odorless, and easy to use on new plantings as well as on established plants. It supplies equal amounts of the three major plant nutrients, nitrogen, phosphate, and potash, plus numerous minor elements. It helps promote strong healthy growth with abundant flowering and high fruit yields. For best results, water immediately after application to dissolve the pellets and carry the nutrients down into the root zone. Detailed instructions on fertilization timing and amount for each area of the garden are included on the box.

AREAS SOLD:

National

GUARANTEED ANALYSIS:

8% Nitrogen
8% Phosphoric acid
8% Potash
Traces of these nutrients:
    Calcium
    Magnesium
    Sulfur
    Iron
    Manganese
    Zinc

BENEFITS THESE PLANTS:

Bush Berries
Evergreens
Flowers
Lawns
Roses
Shrubs
Strawberries
Trees
Vegetables

FOR USE IN THESE AREAS:

Fruits and vegetables
Trees and shrubs
Roses and flowers
Lawns

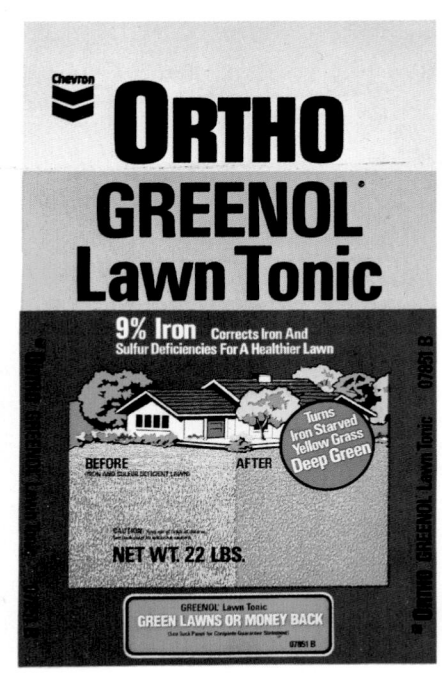

BENEFITS THESE PLANTS:
Lawns

FOR USE IN THESE AREAS:
Lawns

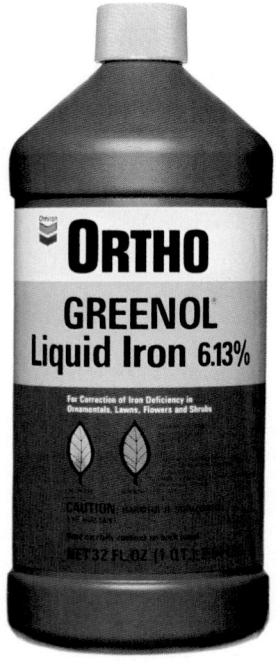

BENEFITS THESE PLANTS:
Azalea
Camellia
Carnation
Chrysanthemum
Gardenia
Gladiola
Golf Course Greens
Hibiscus
Holly
Ixora
Lawns
Ligustrum
Petunia
Rhododendron
Rose
Snapdragon
Turf and other
    annuals,
    perennials, and
    shrubs

FOR USE IN THESE AREAS:
Flowers and shrubs
Lawns

GREENOL® LAWN TONIC 13-0-0

GENERAL DESCRIPTION:
A pelleted fertilizer designed to correct and prevent chlorosis (yellowing) caused by iron and sulfur deficiencies and to give a prolonged greening response. It also provides the necessary nitrogen to help build thick green grass. For fast results, water the lawn thoroughly after the application to dissolve the pellets and carry the nutrients down into the root zone. Twenty-two pounds of fertilizer covers 5,000 square feet, and is easily applied with an ORTHO Drop or Broadcast Spreader or ORTHO Whirly Bird Spreader. Complete instructions are given on the bag for applying the fertilizer with these spreaders. Greenol Lawn Tonic 13-0-0 will stain cement if not swept off immediately after application.

AREAS SOLD:
West
South
Midwest (Kansas, Missouri, Nebraska)

GUARANTEED ANALYSIS:
13% Nitrogen
20% Sulfur
9% Iron

GREENOL® LIQUID IRON 6.13%

GENERAL DESCRIPTION:
A liquid concentrate containing the specific trace elements necessary to correct iron deficiency and to produce vigorous, green growth of lawns, flowers, and ornamentals. It is a supplemental fertilizer, and should be used in conjunction with a regular fertilization program. Dilute the concentrate according to the label directions and apply to either the soil or the foliage. Water thoroughly following soil treatments. To treat lawns, use an ORTHO Lawn Sprayer, diluting so that 32 ounces of concentrate treats 1,000 square feet of turf.

AREAS SOLD:
National

GUARANTEED ANALYSIS:
3.64% Sulfur
0.13% Copper
6.13% Iron
0.10% Zinc

BENEFITS
THESE PLANTS:
All Houseplants

**FOR USE IN
THESE AREAS:**
Houseplants

HOUSE PLANT FOOD
5-10-5

GENERAL DESCRIPTION:

A liquid fertilizer designed for all house-plants to promote overall strong, healthy growth. It provides plants with the three major plant nutrients, nitrogen, phosphate, and potash plus numerous minor elements. For quick, no-mess weekly fertilizing, just add the required number of drops directly to the soil. Then immediately water the plant in the usual way. Or dilute 1 capful in 1 quart of water and fertilize every 2 weeks. Water immediately afterward. Slow-growing plants need less frequent feeding.

AREAS SOLD:
National

GUARANTEED ANALYSIS:
5% Nitrogen
10% Phosphoric acid
5% Potash
Traces of these nutrients:
  Iron
  Manganese
  Zinc

BENEFITS
THESE PLANTS:
Dichondra Lawns
Grass Lawns

**FOR USE IN
THESE AREAS:**
Lawns

LAWN GREEN
17-0-0

GENERAL DESCRIPTION:

A liquid lawn fertilizer designed for use on both grass and dichondra lawns. It fertilizes with two forms of nitrogen to promote greenness and rapid growth. It also contains soluble calcium for the improvement of soil tilth, increased water penetration, more efficient water utilization, and plant growth. One gallon of this fertilizer dilutes readily in water to cover 2,000 square feet of lawn. The label contains detailed instructions for applying Lawn Green with an ORTHO Lawn Sprayer or other applicator. For a quicker response, water heavily afterward to wash the spray off the grass and into the soil.

AREAS SOLD:
West

GUARANTEED ANALYSIS:
17% Nitrogen
Traces of this nutrient:
  Calcium

**BENEFITS
THESE PLANTS:**
African Violets

**FOR USE IN
THESE AREAS:**
African Violets

LIQUID AFRICAN VIOLET FOOD 6-9-5

GENERAL DESCRIPTION:
A liquid fertilizer designed for growing African violets. It helps promote vigorous green growth and numerous full-size blossoms by supplying plants with the three major plant nutrients, nitrogen, phosphate, and potash, plus several minor elements. For easy, no-mess fertilization, simply add the recommended number of drops directly to the soil and then water in the usual way. Or dilute 1 capful in 1 quart of water and water plants with this solution.

AREAS SOLD:
National

GUARANTEED ANALYSIS:
6% Nitrogen
9% Phosphoric acid
5% Potash
Traces of these nutrients:
  Manganese
  Zinc

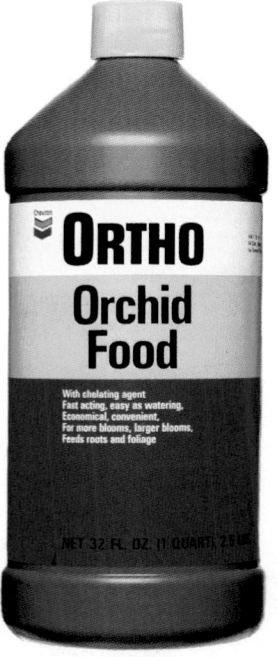

**BENEFITS
THESE PLANTS:**
Anthuriums
Orchids
Other Ornamentals

**FOR USE IN
THESE AREAS:**
Orchids and
  ornamentals

ORCHID FOOD 8-12-4

GENERAL DESCRIPTION:
A liquid fertilizer designed to provide good growth and larger blooms on orchids and certain other garden plants. The added chelating agent keeps the nutrients available in the soil until they are used by plants. As a liquid, it is available to the roots and foliage for a quick and lasting response. It supplies plants with the three major plant nutrients, nitrogen, phosphate, and potash. One quart mixes readily with water to make 64 gallons of fertilizer. Follow the dilution rates on the label and apply with an ORTHO Lawn Sprayer, other sprayer, or sprinkling can to thoroughly wet the plant, roots, and rooting medium.

AREAS SOLD:
Hawaii

GUARANTEED ANALYSIS:
8% Nitrogen
12% Phosphoric acid
4% Potash

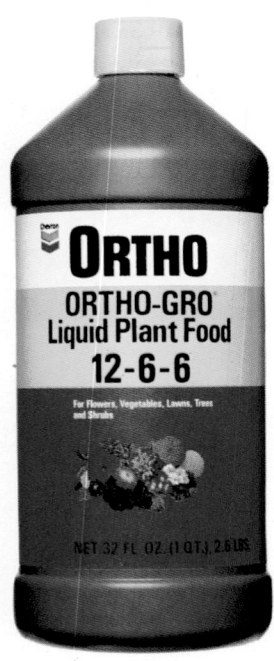

ORTHO·GRO® LIQUID PLANT FOOD 12-6-6

GENERAL DESCRIPTION:
A liquid fertilizer formulated for general garden use. As a liquid, it is readily available to the roots and foliage. This fertilizer dilutes readily in water and is easy to use on established plants and also when transplanting. It promotes vigorous overall growth by supplying plants with the three major plant nutrients, nitrogen, phosphate, and potash, plus several minor elements. For fertilizing flowers, vegetables, and shrubs, dilute the concentrate in a bucket or sprinkling can and apply from 1 quart to 1 gallon of liquid to the foliage and soil, depending on the size of the plant. For fertilizing houseplants, apply the diluted material to the soil or in the trays when watering.

AREAS SOLD:
National

GUARANTEED ANALYSIS:
12% Nitrogen
6% Phosphoric acid
6% Potash
Traces of these nutrients:
  Iron
  Zinc

BENEFITS THESE PLANTS:
African Violets
Azaleas
Beans
Berries
Camellias
Carrots
Fuchsias
Lawns
Peas
Philodendrons
Primroses
Radishes
Roses
Tomatoes
Trees
Tuberous Begonias
Other flowers and
  vegetables
Other houseplants
  and potted plants

FOR USE IN THESE AREAS:
Houseplants
Lawns and flowers
Trees and shrubs
Vegetables and
  berries

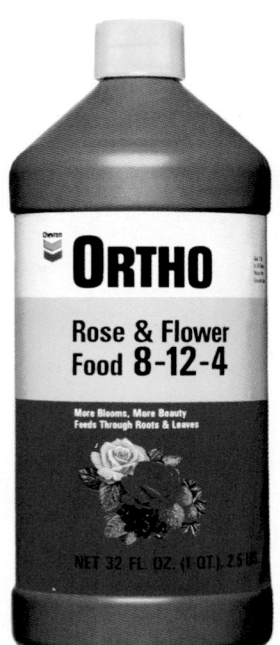

ROSE & FLOWER FOOD 8-12-4

GENERAL DESCRIPTION:
This liquid fertilizer is designed to provide good growth of blooms on roses and certain other garden plants. As a liquid, it provides nutrients to the roots and foliage for a quick response. It provides plants with the three major plant nutrients, nitrogen, phosphate, and potash. It mixes easily with water to be applied with an ORTHO Lawn Sprayer or a sprinkling can. One quart of concentrate makes 60 gallons of fertilizer for general use. The label contains complete dilution instructions for soil and foliage feeding.

AREAS SOLD:
National

GUARANTEED ANALYSIS:
8% Nitrogen
12% Phosphoric acid
4% Potash

BENEFITS THESE PLANTS:
Ornamentals
Roses

FOR USE IN THESE AREAS:
Roses and
  ornamentals

BENEFITS THESE PLANTS:
Roses

FOR USE IN THESE AREAS:
Roses

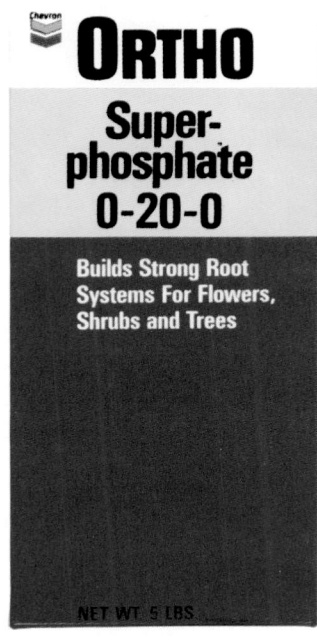

BENEFITS THESE PLANTS:
Bulbs
Flowers
Roses
Shrubs
Vegetables

FOR USE IN THESE AREAS:
Vegetables and flowers
Roses and shrubs
Compost piles

ROSE FOOD
8–12–4

GENERAL DESCRIPTION:
A granular plant food specially formulated for roses. It is clean, odorless, and easy to apply. The formula provides nitrogen, phosphate, and potash and the essential secondary and trace elements calcium, magnesium, sulfur, iron, manganese, and zinc. These plant nutrients help produce healthy, productive plants with beautiful blooms. The label contains complete directions for using this fertilizer on new plantings and on established plants.

AREAS SOLD:
National

GUARANTEED ANALYSIS:
8% Nitrogen
12% Phosphoric acid
4% Potash
Traces of these nutrients:
  Calcium
  Magnesium
  Sulfur
  Iron
  Manganese
  Zinc

SUPERPHOSPHATE
0–20–0

GENERAL DESCRIPTION:
This granular fertilizer is a rich source of phosphorus. Phosphorus is one of the three primary plant nutrients, and is used by plants to build sturdy root systems, to develop new tissues, and to aid in the formation of blooms and fruit. Since phosphorus moves very little in the soil, it is necessary to place it where the roots can obtain a good supply. Superphosphate is often used as a supplement to a regular fertilizer program where additional phosphorus is needed. In the home garden use Superphosphate when planting vegetables, shrubs, bulbs, roses, and other flowers. It can also be used around established roses and shrubs if carefully worked into the soil. Also add this material to compost piles to improve their phosphorus content.

AREAS SOLD:
National

GUARANTEED ANALYSIS:
20% Phosphoric acid

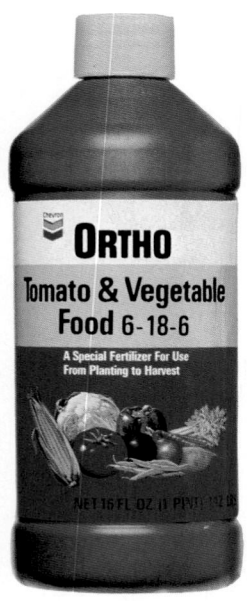

TOMATO & VEGETABLE FOOD 6–18–6

GENERAL DESCRIPTION:
A liquid fertilizer specially formulated for use on tomatoes and other vegetables including carrots, eggplants, peas, and strawberries. It promotes healthy green growth, abundant flowering, and high yields by supplying the three major plant nutrients, nitrogen, phosphate, and potash. It mixes readily with water and is easy to use when transplanting and seeding, and to maintain healthy plants. It can also be used on container vegetable plants. The label lists dilution rates for foliar and soil feedings. For best results, apply this fertilizer with an ORTHO hose-end sprayer.

AREAS SOLD:
National

GUARANTEED ANALYSIS:
6% Nitrogen
18% Phosphoric acid
6% Potash

BENEFITS THESE PLANTS:
Asparagus
Beans
Beets
Broccoli
Brussels Sprouts
Cabbage
Carrots
Cauliflower
Celery
Corn
Cucumbers
Eggplant
Endive
Lettuce
Melons
Onions
Peas
Peppers
Potatoes
Pumpkins
Radishes
Spinach
Squash
Strawberries
Swiss Chard
Turnips

FOR USE IN THESE AREAS:
Vegetables

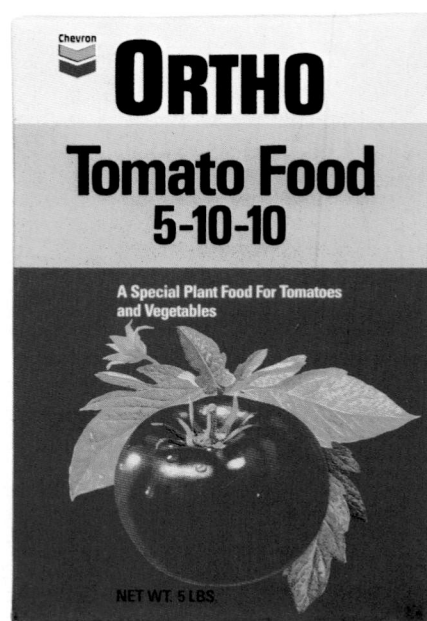

TOMATO FOOD 5–10–10

GENERAL DESCRIPTION:
A granular fertilizer specially formulated for use on tomatoes. It is designed to produce sturdy plants with many top-quality tomatoes. This product can also be used on other vegetable crops. It supplies plants with the nutrients they need most, nitrogen, phosphate, and potash, plus several minor elements. It can be worked into the soil before planting, and also used later to side-dress plantings.

AREAS SOLD:
National

GUARANTEED ANALYSIS:
5% Nitrogen
10% Phosphoric acid
10% Potash
Traces of these nutrients:
   Calcium
   Magnesium
   Sulfur
   Iron
   Manganese
   Zinc

BENEFITS THESE PLANTS:
Beans
Beets
Broccoli
Cabbage
Carrots
Cauliflower
Collards
Corn
Cucumbers
Eggplant
Lettuce
Onions
Peas
Peppers
Radishes
Spinach
Squash
Tomatoes
Turnips and other
   vegetables

FOR USE IN THESE AREAS:
Tomatoes and
   vegetables

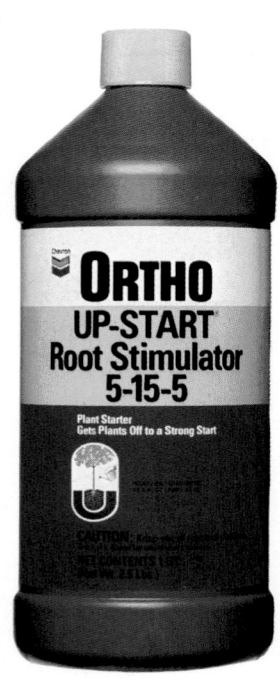

UP·START® ROOT STIMULATOR 5–15–5

GENERAL DESCRIPTION:
This liquid starter solution is a combination of a fertilizer and a hormonelike root stimulator. When it is diluted with water, this solution stimulates early root formation and stronger root development. It helps reduce transplant shock and promotes a greener, more vigorous plant by supplying it with the three major nutrients, nitrogen, phosphate, and potash. Simply pour the diluted solution into the planting hole and over the soil as the roots are being covered.

AREAS SOLD:
National

GUARANTEED ANALYSIS:
5% Nitrogen
15% Phosphoric acid
5% Potash
Root stimulator:
    0.003% Indole-3-butyric acid

UP·START® VITAMIN B·1 PLANT STARTER 3–10–3

GENERAL DESCRIPTION:
This liquid starter solution is a combination of a fertilizer and a hormonelike root stimulator. When it is diluted with water, this solution stimulates early root formation and stronger root development. It also reduces transplant shock and promotes a greener, more vigorous plant. Simply pour the diluted solution into the planting hole and over the soil as the roots are being covered. It supplies plants with the three major nutrients, nitrogen, phosphate, and potash. For use in California only.

AREAS SOLD:
California

GUARANTEED ANALYSIS:
3% Nitrogen
10% Phosphoric acid
3% Potash
Root stimulator:
    0.015% Alpha naphthalene acetic acid
0.01% Thiamine hydrochloride (Vitamin B-1)

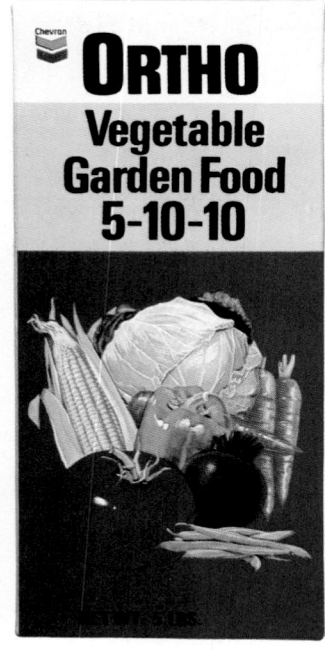

VEGETABLE GARDEN FOOD 5–10–10

GENERAL DESCRIPTION:
A granular fertilizer specially formulated for vegetables and strawberries. It is designed to produce sturdy plants with vigorous root systems, healthy green leaves, abundant flowers, and high-quality produce. It is clean and easy to use. Work it into the soil at planting time and also use it later in the season to side-dress plantings. Around established plants, water thoroughly after applying to dissolve the pellets and wash the nutrients down into the root zone. This fertilizer provides vegetable plants with the three major plant nutrients, nitrogen, phosphate, and potash, plus numerous minor elements.

AREAS SOLD:
National

GUARANTEED ANALYSIS:
5% Nitrogen
10% Phosphoric acid
10% Potash
Traces of these nutrients:
 Calcium
 Magnesium
 Sulfur
 Iron
 Manganese
 Zinc

BENEFITS THESE PLANTS:
Asparagus
Beans
Beets
Broccoli
Brussels Sprouts
Cabbage
Carrots
Cauliflower
Celery
Corn
Cucumbers
Eggplant
Endive
Melons
Onions
Peas
Peppers
Potatoes
Pumpkins
Radishes
Spinach
Squash
Strawberries
Swiss Chard
Tomatoes
Turnips

FOR USE IN THESE AREAS:
Vegetables

ACID-GRO FERTILIZER 30–12–11

GENERAL DESCRIPTION:
This water-soluble fertilizer is especially designed for use on acid-loving plants. It is readily available to plants through foliar and root feeding, and gives a quick response. It contains the primary nutrients nitrogen, phosphate, and potash, together with the trace elements iron, zinc, copper, manganese, and boron. Acid-Gro helps correct chlorosis (yellowing leaves) and other mineral deficiencies. It will not discolor or stain blooms or burn plants when used as directed. Apply this fertilizer with a sprinkling can, hose-end sprayer, or tank-type sprayer at planting time or around established plants. The label contains complete dilution and application directions.

AREAS SOLD:
National

GUARANTEED ANALYSIS:
30% Nitrogen
12% Phosphoric acid
11% Potash
Traces of these nutrients:
 Boron
 Copper
 Iron
 Manganese
 Zinc

BENEFITS THESE PLANTS:
Arborvitae
Avocados
Azaleas
Blueberries
Camellias
Citrus
Dogwood
Douglas Fir
Euonymus
Ferns
Gardenias
Hawthorn
Hemlock
Hibiscus
Holly
Houseplants
Hydrangeas
Ixora
Juniper
Larch
Laurel
Ligustrum
Magnolia
Mountain Ash
Oak
Orchids
Pine
Privet
Pyracantha
Rhododendrons
Spirea
Spruce
Taxus and other
 acid-loving
 plants

FOR USE IN THESE AREAS:
Acid-loving plants
Trees and shrubs
Fruits
Houseplants

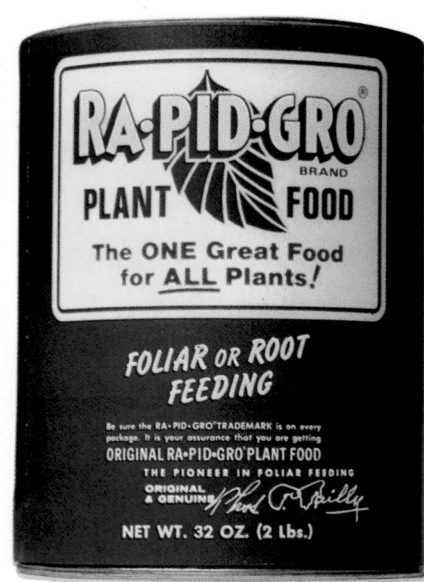

**BENEFITS
THESE PLANTS:**
Bedding Plants
Berries
Bulbs
Evergreens
Flowers
Fruit Trees
Houseplants
Lawns
Roses
Shade Trees
Shrubs
Tomatoes
Vegetables

**FOR USE IN
THESE AREAS:**
Roses and flowers
Fruits and vegetables
Trees and shrubs
Lawns
Houseplants

RA·PID·GRO
PLANT FOOD

GENERAL DESCRIPTION:
This water-soluble fertilizer is designed
for use on a wide variety of plants including shrubs, vegetables, and flowers. The
Ra-Pid-Gro method of regular, continuing applications gives plants a steady,
even supply of nutrients for uniform
growth. Because it is a liquid, it is
readily available to the plant through the
roots, leaves, stems, and buds. Fertilize
small areas and individual plants with a
sprinkling can. Large areas can be fed
quickly and easily with a hose-end
sprayer. Combine the fertilizer with insecticides and fungicides to help
strengthen pest-damaged plants as you
kill the pests. The label contains complete directions for diluting and applying this fertilizer.

AREAS SOLD:
National

GUARANTEED ANALYSIS:
23% Nitrogen
19% Phosphoric acid
17% Potash

Ants
Brown Dog Ticks
Crickets
Earwigs
Roaches
Silverfish
Sowbugs
Spiders

**FOR USE IN
THESE AREAS:**
Indoors
Outdoors
Not for use on plants

ANT, ROACH &
SPIDER KILLER

GENERAL DESCRIPTION:
An aerosol that gives rapid contact kill of
crawling pests as listed, including those
resistant to certain chlorinated hydrocarbon and phosphate insecticides. In addition to rapid initial kill, it also provides
residual insect killing power after the
spray deposit has dried.

AREAS SOLD:
National

ACTIVE INGREDIENT:
1% Propoxur *2-(1-Methylethoxy)phenyl
methylcarbamate*

HINTS FOR USE:
To enhance performance, use this spray
in conjunction with an ORTHO Hi-Power
Household Insect Fogger. The fogger
flushes the insects out of hiding
into the treated area.

**KILLS THESE
PESTS:**
Snails
Slugs

**FOR USE ON
THESE PLANTS:**
Fruits:
Apples
Avocados
Blackberries
Cherries
Citrus
Grapes
Peaches
Plums
Strawberries

Vegetables:
Asparagus
Beans
Beets
Cabbage
Carrots
Corn
Cucumbers
Eggplant
Lettuce
Melons
Onions
Peas
Peppers
Potatoes
Radishes
Spinach
Squash
Tomatoes
Turnips

**FOR USE IN
THESE AREAS:**
Fruits and vegetables
Greenhouse and lath
  houses

BUG·GETA®
SNAIL & SLUG PELLETS

GENERAL DESCRIPTION:
A pellet bait specially formulated to attract and kill snails and slugs. The highly
compressed pellets are easy to use, clean
to handle, and economical. Two pounds
of pellets will bait approximately 2,000
square feet. The presence of snails and
slugs can be detected by their shiny mu-
couslike trail. They are night feeders and
prefer damp, cool places. Do not apply
the bait to the foliage or place in piles,
but scatter pellets on the soil surface
around plants. Repeated treatments every 2 weeks are usually sufficient to protect plants. This bait can be used around
fruit and vegetable plantings.

AREAS SOLD:
National

ACTIVE INGREDIENT:
3.25% Metaldehyde

HINTS FOR USE:
To encourage snail and slug movement
and feeding, sprinkle the soil lightly
after application.

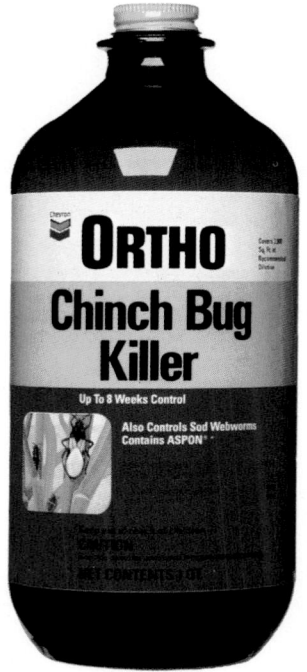

CHINCH BUG & SOD WEBWORM CONTROL

GENERAL DESCRIPTION:
This granular material controls chinch bugs and sod webworms for up to 8 weeks, and can be applied with a fertilizer drop spreader. St. Augustine and zoysia lawns in particular are often attacked by chinch bugs. As a preventive treatment, apply every 2 months starting in early summer. The entire lawn should be treated if either of these pests is found.

AREAS SOLD:
Midwest
Northeast
South

ACTIVE INGREDIENT:
3.2% Aspon® *0,0,0,0-Tetrapropyl dithiopyrophosphate*

KILLS THESE INSECTS:
Chinch Bugs
Sod Webworms

CHINCH BUG KILLER

GENERAL DESCRIPTION:
This liquid concentrate mixes readily with water and may be applied with an ORTHO Lawn Sprayer, ORTHO Lawn & Garden Sprayer, or tank-type sprayer. It controls chinch bugs and sod webworms (lawn moth larvae) for up to 8 weeks. St. Augustine and zoysia lawns in particular are often attacked by chinch bugs. The entire lawn should be treated if either of these insects is found.

AREAS SOLD:
Midwest
Northeast
South

ACTIVE INGREDIENT:
13% Aspon® *0,0,0,0-Tetrapropyl dithiopyrophosphate*

HINTS FOR USE:
Since these insects feed on the grass stems and blades, do not water heavily for 2 or 3 days following treatment. If lawn is dry, water well before treatment.

Aspon® is a registered trademark of Stauffer Chemical Co.

KILLS THESE INSECTS:
Aphids
Black Scales
Chaff Scales
Citrus Red Mites
Citrus Rust Mites
Florida Red Scales
Glover Scales
Purple Scales
Snow Scales
Texas Citrus Mites
Yellow Scales
Whiteflies

FOR USE IN THESE AREAS:
Citrus

CITRUS INSECT SPRAY

GENERAL DESCRIPTION:
A liquid concentraté containing *ethion* — a proven and widely recommended organic phosphate insecticide — and petroleum oil for excellent control of scales, mites, aphids, and whiteflies on oranges, grapefruit, tangerines, tangelos, lemons, and limes. This product helps protect citrus plantings with only one or two sprayings per season. Apply with an ORTHO Spray-ette for good coverage of all foliage and branches wherever these insects are found. In addition to controlling insects and mites, this product improves the appearance of the plant by giving a bright, shiny finish to the leaves, and helps eliminate the sooty mold fungus that grows on the honeydew excreted by the insects listed above.

AREAS SOLD:
South

ACTIVE INGREDIENT:
10% Ethion *0,0,0',0'-Tetraethyl S,S'-methylene bisphosphorodithioate*
75% Petroleum oil

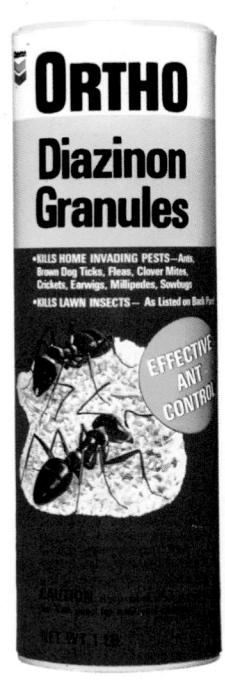

KILLS THESE INSECTS:
Ants
Armyworms
Bermudagrass
Billbugs
Brown Dog Ticks
Clover Mites
Crickets
Cutworms
Digger Wasps
Earwigs
Fleas
Leafhoppers
Millipedes
Sod Webworms
  (Lawn Moths)
Sowbugs
Springtails
  (Collembola)
White Grubs

FOR USE IN THESE AREAS:
Lawns
Building foundations

DIAZINON GRANULES

GENERAL DESCRIPTION:
These granules kill home-invading pests including ticks, ants, crickets, fleas, and sowbugs. Apply the granules to individual nesting areas, or in a band around the house. The granules also control sod webworms, Bermuda mites, grubs, and other lawn pests in both grasses and dichondra lawns. They can be easily sprinkled directly from the canister without any additional equipment. One canister treats an area of up to 200 square feet.

AREAS SOLD:
National

ACTIVE INGREDIENT:
2% Diazinon *0,0-Diethyl 0-(2-isopropyl-6-methyl-4-pyrimidinyl) phosphoro-thioate*

HINTS FOR USE:
This product is an effective replacement for chlordane dust for ant control.

DIAZINON
INSECT SPRAY

GENERAL DESCRIPTION:
This liquid concentrate kills many outdoor insects that can destroy lawns, roses, flowers, trees, and shrubs, or annoy people and pets. It controls white grubs, sod webworms, armyworms, and other listed pests in lawns for up to 8 weeks. When diluted, one quart treats up to 4,000 square feet of lawn. It also controls vegetable pests including aphids, whiteflies, and flea beetles. Use it on tomatoes to within one day of harvest. On ornamental trees and shrubs, control such pests as leafhoppers, leafminers, and mealybugs. Treat around patios, windows, and foundations to control home-invading pests. The label contains complete dilution directions and lists days to harvest for fruits and vegetables.

AREAS SOLD:
National

ACTIVE INGREDIENT:
25% Diazinon *0,0-Diethyl 0-(2-isopropyl-6-methyl-4-pyrimidinyl) phosphorothioate*

KILLS THESE INSECTS:
Ants
Aphids
Armyworms
Bagworms
Bean Beetles
Bermuda Mites
Box Elder Bugs
Brown Dog Ticks
Cabbageworms
Chiggers
Chinch Bugs
Clover Mites
Cockroaches
Codling Moths
Crickets
Cucumber Beetles
Cutworms
Dichondra Flea
    Beetles
Earwigs
Fire Ants
Flea Beetles
Fleas
Flies
Holly Bud Moths
Lawn Billbugs
Lawn Moths
Leafhoppers
Leafminers
Leafrollers
Mealybugs
Millipedes
Mites
Scorpions
Sod Webworms
Sowbugs (Pillbugs)
Spiders
Thrips
Whiteflies
White Grubs

FOR USE IN THESE AREAS:
Lawns
Fruits and vegetables
Roses and flowers

DIAZINON
SOIL & FOLIAGE DUST

GENERAL DESCRIPTION:
This insecticide controls both soil-inhabiting and foliage-feeding pests. It dusts easily from the container onto the soil to control cutworms and wireworms; 2 pounds covers up to 900 square feet. When treating plants, use ORTHO Whirly Duster or similar applicator to avoid over-application. It may be applied to tomatoes and melons up to 3 days before harvest.

AREAS SOLD:
National

ACTIVE INGREDIENT:
4% Diazinon *0,0-Diethyl 0-(2-isopropyl-6-methyl-4-pyrimidinyl) phosphorothioate*

HINTS FOR USE:
For cutworm and wireworm control, dust the soil before planting and work into the top 6 to 8 inches of soil.

KILLS THESE INSECTS:
Aphids
Cucumber Beetles
Cutworms
Diamondback Moth
    Larvae
Flea Beetles
Imported Cabbage
    Worms
Lacebugs
Leafhoppers
Leafminers
Mealybugs
Mites
Root Maggots
Scale Crawlers
Spittlebugs
Thrips
Wireworms

FOR USE IN THESE AREAS:
Fruits and vegetables
Roses and flowers
Shrubs

DIAZINON SOIL & INSECT CONTROL

GENERAL DESCRIPTION:
These granules are formulated to control ants, chinch bugs, grubs, and other listed insect pests on both grass and dichondra lawns. Apply the material with a fertilizer spreader according to the spreader settings listed on the bag. Also use the granules at planting time to control root maggots, cutworms, wireworms, and other listed pests on most vegetables including broccoli, melons, onions, and tomatoes. Foliage-feeding pests on sweet corn are also controlled. When applied in a band along foundations, it helps to control and prevent clover mites, earwigs, fleas, and other pests from entering homes.

AREAS SOLD:
National

ACTIVE INGREDIENT:
5% Diazinon *0,0-Diethyl 0-(2-isopropyl-6-methyl-4-pyrimidinyl) phosphorothioate*

KILLS THESE INSECTS:
Ants
Armyworms
Bermuda Mites
Billbugs
Brown Dog Ticks
Carrot Rust Flies
Chiggers
Chinch Bugs
Clover Mites
Corn Rootworms
Crickets
Cutworms
Digger Wasps
Earwigs
European Corn
  Borers
Fleas
Hyperodes Weevils
Lawn Moths (Sod
  Webworms)
Leafhoppers
Millipedes
Mole Crickets
Root Maggots
Southwestern Corn
  Borers
Sowbugs (Pillbugs)
Springtails
  (Collembola)
Vinegar Flies
White Grubs
Wireworms

FOR USE IN THESE AREAS:
Lawns
Vegetables
Building foundations

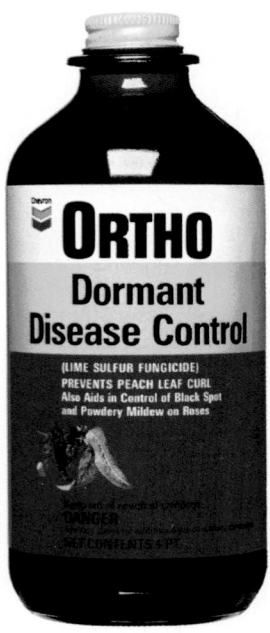

DORMANT DISEASE CONTROL

GENERAL DESCRIPTION:
A liquid spray designed for use on listed fruits, berries, and roses to prevent foliage diseases during the growing season. When applied in late fall, winter, and spring, it kills disease-causing spores that overwinter on buds, twigs, and bark. It also forms a protective coating over buds before they open in the spring, to give control of peach leaf curl. It mixes readily with water, and can be applied with an ORTHO Spray-ette, or a tank-type or power sprayer.

AREAS SOLD:
West

ACTIVE INGREDIENT:
26% Lime sulfur *Calcium polysulfide*

HINTS FOR USE:
It is important that sprays be applied before the buds open. If the buds have begun to open, it is too late to obtain satisfactory control of peach leaf curl disease, since infection has already occurred.

CONTROLS THESE DISEASES AND PESTS:
Black Spot
Blister Mites
Cane Blight
Powdery Mildew
Peach Blight
Peach Leaf Curl
Powdery Mildew
Rust

FOR USE IN THESE AREAS:
Fruits
Roses

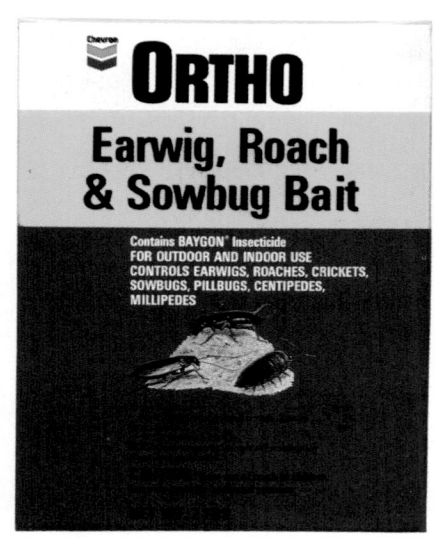

KILLS THESE INSECTS:
Centipedes
Cockroaches
Crickets
Earwigs
Pillbugs
Millipedes
Sowbugs

FOR USE IN THESE AREAS:
Indoors
Outdoors

EARWIG, ROACH & SOWBUG BAIT

GENERAL DESCRIPTION:
A granular, ready-to-use formulation for use indoors and outdoors to control the listed pests that feed upon it or come in contact with it. It rapidly kills both resistant and nonresistant cockroaches. Use the bait any time insects are noticed. Since most of the listed outdoors pests are night feeders, distribute the bait in late afternoon or early morning wherever pests congregate, and along foundations to prevent them from entering buildings. Indoors, sprinkle lightly under sinks and refrigerators and in areas where the pests hide, but which are inaccessible to children and pets. Do not place in piles or use on food crops.

AREAS SOLD:
West

ACTIVE INGREDIENT:
2% Propoxur *2-(1-Methylethoxy)phenyl methylcarbamate*

KILLS THESE INSECTS:
Ants
Armyworms
Brown Dog Ticks
Chiggers
Chinch Bugs
Clover Mites
Crickets
Earwigs
Fire Ants
Fleas
Grasshoppers
Lawn Moth Larvae
  (Sod Webworms)
Millipedes
Sowbugs (Pillbugs)

FOR USE IN THESE AREAS:
Lawns
Building foundations

FIRE ANT CONTROL

GENERAL DESCRIPTION:
This liquid concentrate controls fire ants, numerous lawn pests, and home-invading pests outside buildings. Treat the entire fire ant mound or lawn when the pests first appear. For best results, apply Fire Ant Control to the lawn 2 hours before dark, when lawn insects become active. Use a sprinkling can to treat fire ant mounds and surrounding areas, and an ORTHO Lawn Sprayer for treating lawns and building foundations for general pest control. Mosquitoes coming to rest on treated lawns and foundations will also be killed.

AREAS SOLD:
South

ACTIVE INGREDIENT:
5.3% Chloropyrifos *0,0-Diethyl 0-(3,5,6-trichloro-2-pyridyl) phosphorothioate*

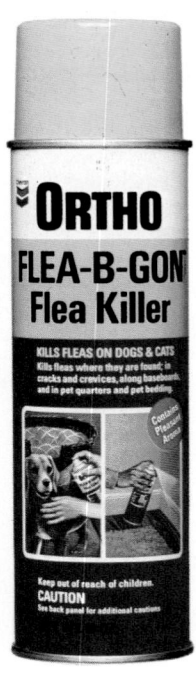

Ants
Centipedes
Earwigs
Fleas
Roaches
Sowbugs
Spiders

**FOR USE IN
THESE AREAS:**
Pets
Indoors

FLEA·B·GON™
FLEA KILLER

GENERAL DESCRIPTION:
This aerosol controls fleas on dogs and
cats, in their bedding, and inside doghouses. It can also be sprayed on carpets
and in cracks and crevices where fleas
hide. To ensure good coverage when
treating pets, part the animal's fur so that
the spray contacts the skin. This spray is
also effective against cockroaches, spiders, and other listed indoor pests
throughout the home.

AREAS SOLD:
National

ACTIVE INGREDIENT:
.250% Resmethrin [5-(Phenylmethyl)-3-
furanyl] methyl 2,2-dimethyl-3-(2-meth-
yl-1-propenyl) cyclopropanecarboxylate

HINTS FOR USE:
The aerosol's hissing sound and cool
sensation may startle nervous pets, so
hold them securely. They will soon become accustomed to the spray.

**KILLS THESE
PESTS:**
Aphids
Leafhoppers
Red Spider Mites
Russet Mites
Thrips

**CONTROLS
THESE
DISEASES:**
Black Spot
Brown Rot
Powdery Mildew
Scab

**FOR USE IN
THESE AREAS:**
Fruits and vegetables
Roses and flowers
Shrubs and lawns

FLOTOX®
GARDEN SULFUR

GENERAL DESCRIPTION:
A wettable powder designed for use as a
dust or spray to control powdery mildew,
brown rot, black spot, and certain other
pests on listed fruits and ornamentals. It
also controls russet and red spider mites
on tomatoes. For lasting disease and mite
protection, repeat the applications
throughout the season. Use around acid-
loving plants, including camellias,
azaleas, rhododendrons, and heather,
and in new lawn soil to make the soil
more acidic. It may cause foliage injury
if the temperature is over 90°F. When it
is used as a spray, continue to agitate the
solution during application to keep it
dissolved.

AREAS SOLD:
National

ACTIVE INGREDIENT:
90% Sulfur

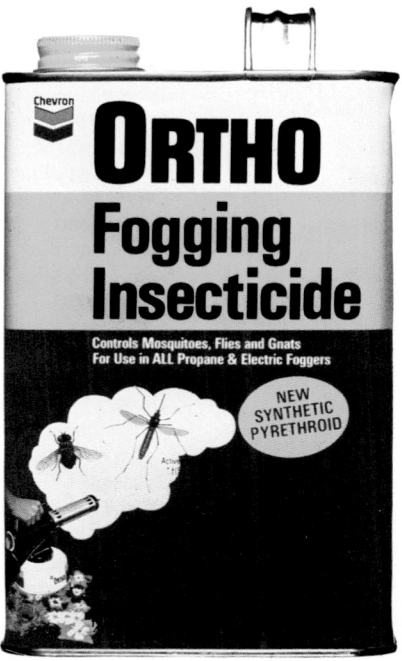

FLYING & CRAWLING INSECT KILLER

GENERAL DESCRIPTION:

An aerosol contact insecticide that kills both flying and crawling insects. Used as a room spray, it controls flies, mosquitoes, and gnats. It also kills cockroaches, spiders, and other listed pests when sprayed on the pests and along baseboards, cabinets, and areas where these crawling insects are found. It controls fleas on dogs and in their bedding, and also kills wasps when sprayed into their nests.

AREAS SOLD:

National

ACTIVE INGREDIENT:

0.250% Resmethrin *[5-(Phenylmethyl)-3-furanyl] methyl 2,2-dimethyl-3-(2-methyl-1-propenyl) cyclopropane-carboxylate*

FOGGING INSECTICIDE

GENERAL DESCRIPTION:

Contains the synthetic pyrethroid *resmethrin*, which controls mosquitoes, flies, and gnats in listed *outdoor* areas. It is specially formulated to be used undiluted in portable electric, propane, or gas-powered thermo-foggers that produce spray particles in the aerosol size range. Use at dusk when the wind dies down and the ground and air temperatures are approximately the same. The fog will then linger longer in the treated area. Do not re-enter the treated area until after the fog dissipates.

AREAS SOLD:

Northeast
Midwest

ACTIVE INGREDIENT:

0.200% Resmethrin *(5-Benzyl-3-furyl) methyl 2,2-dimethyl-3-(2-methyl-propenyl) cyclopropanecarboxylate*

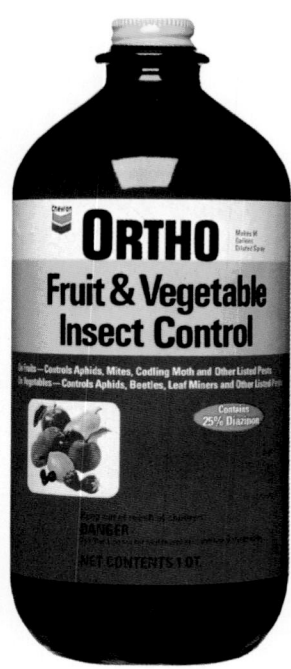

FRUIT & VEGETABLE INSECT CONTROL

GENERAL DESCRIPTION:
A liquid concentrate used to control codling moths, leafrollers, mites, beetles, and other listed pests on fruits, nuts, and vegetables. One quart mixes readily with water to make 96 gallons of diluted spray, and it may be used in all types of sprayers. It can be used on tomatoes and peas up to 1 day before harvest. For a combination spray on fruits, combine with ORTHO Orthocide® Garden Fungicide; for vegetables, combine with ORTHO Vegetable Disease Control.

AREAS SOLD:
National

ACTIVE INGREDIENT:
25% Diazinon *0,0-Diethyl 0-(2-isopropyl-6-methyl-4-pyrimidinyl) phosphorothioate*

KILLS THESE INSECTS:
Aphids
Apple Maggots
Armyworms
Blueberry Maggots
Cherry Fruit Flies
Cherry Fruitworms
  (Maggots)
Citrus Thrips
Codling Moths
Colorado Potato
  Beetles
Cranberry
  Fruitworms
Cucumber Beetles
Diamondback Moths
  (Larvae)
Dipterous Leafminers
Dried Fruit Beetles
Flea Beetles
Fruit Tree Leafrollers
Grape Berry Moths
Grape Leaf-folders
Grasshoppers
Imported Cabbage
  Worms
Leafhoppers
Mealybugs
Mexican Bean Beetles
Mites
Pecan Nut
  Casebearers
Pear Psyllas
Raspberry Sawflies
Raspberry
  Fruitworms
Scale Crawlers
Strawberry
  Leafrollers
Tentiform Leafminers
Thrips
Vinegar Flies
Walnut Caterpillars
Whiteflies

FOR USE IN THESE AREAS:
Fruits and nuts
Vegetables

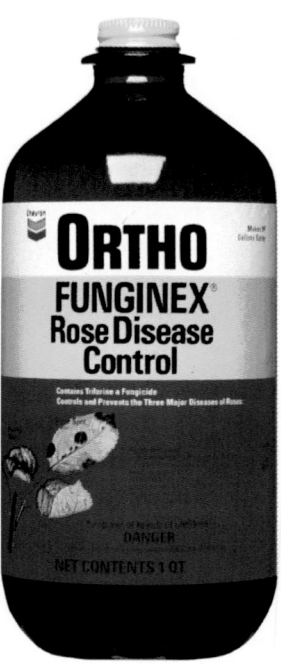

FUNGINEX® ROSE DISEASE CONTROL

GENERAL DESCRIPTION:
A quick-wetting liquid spray, containing the systemic fungicide *triforine*, designed to control or prevent the three most important diseases of roses — black spot, powdery mildew, and rust. It also controls powdery mildew and rust on other listed flowers. When used as directed, it gives uniform coverage and does not leave an unsightly residue on foliage or flowers. Disease-spotted leaves will not clear up, but unaffected leaves will be protected if a regular spray program is followed. One quart of concentrate makes up to 64 gallons of spray.

AREAS SOLD:
National

ACTIVE INGREDIENT:
6.5% Triforine *N,N'(1,4-piperazinediyl-bis[2,2,2-trichloroethylidene])bis(formamide)*

HINTS FOR USE:
A systemic fungicide is absorbed into the plant roots, leaves, or stems and moves with the sap throughout the plant, providing protection against invading fungi.

CONTROLS THESE DISEASES:
Black Spot
Powdery Mildew
Rust

FOR USE ON THESE PLANTS:
Aster
Calendula
Carnation
Crapemyrtle
Dahlia
Euonymus
Jerusalem Thorn
Lilac
Phlox
Photinia
Poplar
Rose
Snapdragon
Zinnia

FOR USE IN THESE AREAS:
Roses and flowers

Funginex is a registered trademark of Celamerck GmbH & Co.

KILLS THESE INSECTS:

Aphids
Apple Maggots
Blister Beetles
Codling Moths
Corn Borers
Elm Leaf Beetles
Fall Armyworms
Fruitworms
Gypsy Moths
Hornworms
Japanese Beetles
Leafminers
Leafrollers
Melonworms
Oriental Fruit Moths
Peachtree Borers
Periodical Cicadas
Pickleworms
Plum Curculios
Rose Slugs
Scale Insects
Tent Caterpillars
Thrips

FOR USE IN THESE AREAS:

Trees and shrubs
Roses and flowers
Fruits and vegetables

GYPSY MOTH & JAPANESE BEETLE KILLER

GENERAL DESCRIPTION:

A liquid concentrate designed to control gypsy moth larvae, Japanese beetles, and a broad range of pests that damage vegetables, fruits, roses, flowers, and other ornamentals. It dilutes readily with water to be applied with all types of sprayers. It can be applied to tomatoes, peppers, and other listed vegetables up to the day of harvest.

AREAS SOLD:

Northeast
Midwest
South

ACTIVE INGREDIENT:

27% Carbaryl 1-Naphthyl N-methylcarbamate

HINTS FOR USE:

Thoroughly spray both the upper and the lower surfaces of the leaves so that any Japanese beetles that may fly to your plants from surrounding areas will be controlled. For rapid control of gypsy moth larvae, spray when they are young, up to 1 inch long. Thoroughly spray the entire plant, including the trunk, where the larvae frequently congregate.

KILLS THESE INSECTS:

Black Carpet Beetles
Centipedes
Cockroaches
Crickets
Fleas
Flies
Mosquitoes
Sowbugs (Pillbugs)
Rice Weevils
Sawtoothed Grain Beetles
Silverfish
Small Flying Moths
Spiders
Ticks
Wasps

FOR USE IN THESE AREAS:

Indoors

HI-POWER HOUSEHOLD INSECT FOGGER

GENERAL DESCRIPTION:

This fogger rapidly knocks down many flying and crawling pests including flies, fleas, silverfish, and assorted pantry pests. The easy-to-use formulation treats up to 5,000 cubic feet (25' x 25' room). When activated, the aerosol can automatically releases its entire contents, filling the room with a penetrating fog that flushes pests out of hiding. Keep the treated area closed for 4 hours, and then air out for 30 minutes before re-entering.

AREAS SOLD:

National

ACTIVE INGREDIENTS:

.300% Allethrin (Allyl homolog of Cinerin D)
.191% Phenothrin 3-Phenoxybenzyl d-cis and trans 2,2-dimethyl-3-(2-methypropenyl)

HINTS FOR USE:

For long-lasting residual control of crawling pests, use ORTHO Ant, Roach, & Spider Killer before activating the fogger.

HOME & GARDEN INSECT KILLER

GENERAL DESCRIPTION:
An aerosol household and garden contact insecticide. Indoors, use it as a room and surface spray for flying and crawling pests including cockroaches, flies, and earwigs. It also controls whiteflies, aphids, and other pests on African violets, philodendrons, coleus, begonias, and geraniums. Outdoors, use it as an area spray against flying insects and as a plant spray to control the listed foliage-feeding pests.

AREAS SOLD:
National

ACTIVE INGREDIENT:
0.250 % Resmethrin [5-(Phenylmethyl)-3-furanyl] methyl 2,2-dimethyl-3-(2-methyl-1-propenyl) cyclopropanecarboxylate

KILLS THESE INSECTS:
Ants
Aphids
Biting Flies
Centipedes
Earwigs
Fleas
Gnats
House Flies
Japanese Beetles
Leafhoppers
Mosquitoes
Plant Bugs
Roaches
Sowbugs
Spiders
Spittlebugs
Thrips
Wasps
Whiteflies

FOR USE ON THESE PLANTS:
African Violet
Ageratum
Azalea
Begonia
Camellia
Ceanothus
Chrysanthemum
Coleus
Cotoneaster
Daisy
Daphne
Dogwood
Euonymus
Fatshedera
Forsythia
Geranium
Iris
Ivy
Juniper
Marigold
Nasturtium
Ornamental Quince
Peony
Philodendron
Pyracantha
Rhododendron
Rose
Snapdragon
Spirea
Viburnum
Zinnia

FOR USE IN THESE AREAS:
Indoors
Outdoors
Flowers and shrubs
Houseplants
Pets

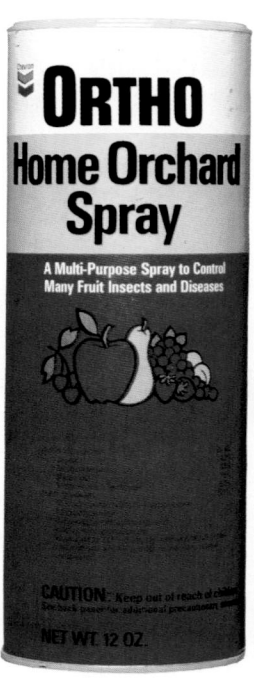

HOME ORCHARD SPRAY

GENERAL DESCRIPTION:
A multipurpose formulation designed to be used as a dust or spray. It is formulated to control a broad range of insects and diseases on many fruits including apples, cherries, peaches, grapes, and strawberries. The fungicide *captan* kills fungal infections as listed on the label. The insecticides *malathion* and *methoxychlor* kill both sucking and chewing insects. The label contains detailed application instructions and days to harvest for each fruit and berry.

AREAS SOLD:
National

ACTIVE INGREDIENTS:
14.2 % Captan N-([Trichloromethyl] thio)-4-cyclohexene-1,2-dicarboximide
7.5 % Malathion 0,0-Dimethyl dithiophosphate of diethyl mercaptosuccinate
15 % Methoxychlor 2,2-Bis (p-methoxyphenyl)-1,1,1-trichloroethane

KILLS THESE INSECTS:
Aphids
Apple Maggots
Cankerworms
Codling Moths
Curculios
Flea Beetles
Grape Berry Moths
Japanese Beetles
Leafhoppers
Leafrollers
Oriental Fruit Moths
Peachtree Borers
Peach Twig Borers
Pear Slugs
Plant Bugs
Red Spider Mites
Rose Chafers
Spittlebugs
Strawberry Leaf
    Beetles
Strawberry Weevils
Tent Caterpillars
Thrips

CONTROLS THESE DISEASES:
Bitter Rot
Black Pox
Black Rot
Botryosphaeria
Botrytis Rot
Brooks Fruit Spot
Brown Rot
Dead Arm
Fly Speck
Scab

FOR USE IN THESE AREAS:
Fruits

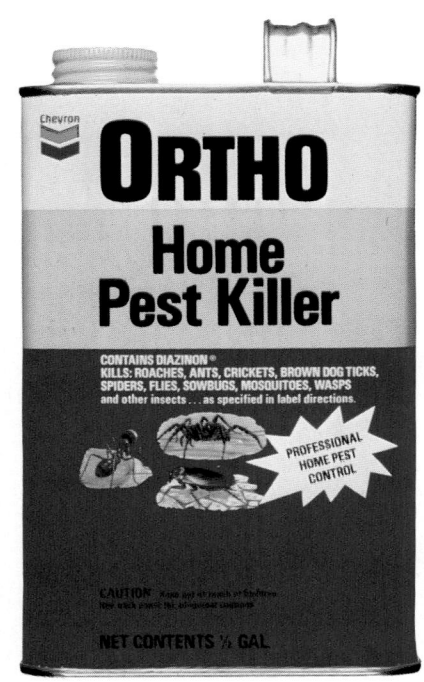

KILLS THESE INSECTS:
Ants
Brown Dog Ticks
Carpet Beetles
Chiggers
Clover Mites
Cockroaches
Crickets
Earwigs
Firebrats
Flies
Flying Moths
Mosquitoes
Silverfish
Sowbugs (Pillbugs)
Spiders
Springtails
Wasps

FOR USE IN THESE AREAS:
Indoors
Outdoors
Not for use on plants

HOME PEST KILLER

GENERAL DESCRIPTION:
A ready-to-use liquid with no unpleasant odor that controls indoor pests including cockroaches, silverfish, spiders, ants, ticks, crickets, and carpet beetles. Also use it outdoors around foundations, garbage cans, and patios to reduce annoyance from flies, mosquitoes, wasps, and flying moths, and to prevent them from entering homes. The easy-to-use trigger sprayer has a two-way nozzle for spray or stream, and is helpful for treating inaccessible areas and places insects walk or hide.

AREAS SOLD:
National

ACTIVE INGREDIENT:
0.50% Diazinon *0,0-Diethyl 0-(2-isopropyl-6-methyl-4n-pyrimidinyl) phosphorothioate*

KILLS THESE INSECTS:
Ants
Brown Dog Ticks
Clover Mites
Crickets
Earwigs
Fleas
Hornets
Millipedes
Sowbugs
Spiders
Wasps

FOR USE IN THESE AREAS:
Outdoors
Not for use on plants

HORNET & WASP KILLER

GENERAL DESCRIPTION:
An aerosol that shoots a jet of spray up to 10 feet to eliminate hornets and wasps from a safe distance. For best results, treat the nest after dark when all the insects are inside. Soak the entire nest, inside and out. The spray also controls clover mites, fleas, crickets, earwigs, and other listed pests outdoors to prevent them from entering homes.

AREAS SOLD:
National

ACTIVE INGREDIENT:
0.50% Propoxur *2-(1-Methylethoxy)phenylmethylcarbamate*

KILLS THESE INSECTS:
Ants
Centipedes
Earwigs
Fleas
Flies
Gnats
Mosquitoes
Roaches
Sowbugs
Spiders
Wasps

FOR USE IN THESE AREAS:
Indoors
Outdoors
Pets

KILLS THESE INSECTS:
Aphids
Red Spider Mites
Thrips
Whiteflies

FOR USE IN THESE AREAS:
Houseplants

HOUSEHOLD INSECT KILLER

GENERAL DESCRIPTION:
An easy-to-use aerosol that kills both flying and crawling pests. Use it as a room spray to control flying pests, such as mosquitoes, flies, and gnats, and as a surface spray for crawling pests, including cockroaches, earwigs, and sowbugs. Keep the room closed for at least 15 minutes after treatment; air out thoroughly before re-entering. It also kills fleas on dogs, and reduces reinfestations when bedding and doghouses are sprayed. It effectively eliminates wasps when sprayed into their nests after dark.

AREAS SOLD:
National

ACTIVE INGREDIENT:
0.250% Resmethrin *[5-(Phenylmethyl) 3-furanyl] methyl 2,2-dimethyl-3-(2-methyl-1-propenyl) cyclopropanecarboxylate*

HOUSE PLANT INSECT SPRAY

GENERAL DESCRIPTION:
A ready-to-use liquid with a convenient pump sprayer designed to control common pests, including red spider mites and whiteflies, on houseplants. The pump sprayer makes it easy to contact both upper and lower surfaces of the leaves where pests feed and hide. Gently pump for an effective, insect-killing, light mist.

AREAS SOLD:
National

ACTIVE INGREDIENTS:
0.020% Pyrethrins
0.080% Resmethrin *(5-Benzyl-3-furyl) methyl 2,2-dimethyl-3-(2-methylpropenyl) cyclopropane carboxylate*

HOUSE PLANT INSECT CONTROL

GENERAL DESCRIPTION:
An aerosol designed for use in interior and exterior plantscapes. It kills chewing and sucking pests that attack house-plants, roses, flowers, and ornamentals. It kills both on contact and by systemic action. Provides residual control of aphids for up to 3 weeks. This spray is particularly effective on hard-to-control pests such as mites, whiteflies, scale crawlers, and thrips. For best results, apply a light spray at the first sign of the pests, and repeat at intervals of 7 to 10 days.

AREAS SOLD:
National

ACTIVE INGREDIENTS:
.25% Acephate *0,S-dimethyl acetyl-phosphoramidothioate*
.10% Resmethrin *5-(phenylmethyl)-3-furanyl methyl 2,2-dimethyl-3-(2-methyl-1-propenyl) cyclopropanecarboxylate*

KILLS THESE INSECTS:
Aphids
Armyworms
Bagworms
Catalpa Sphinx Moth (Larvae)
Cuban Laurel Thrips
Diabrotica Beetles
Eastern Tent Caterpillars
Fall Webworms
Flower Thrips
Lace Bugs
Leafbeetles
Leafhoppers
Leafminers
Maple Shoot Moths (Larvae)
Mealybugs
Oleander Caterpillars
Orange-striped Oakworms
Poplar Tentmakers
Psyllids
Rose Midges
Salt Marsh Caterpillars
Sawflies
Scale Crawlers
Southern Red Mites
Spittlebugs
Two-spotted Spider Mites

FOR USE IN THESE AREAS:
Roses and flowers
Houseplants
Trees and shrubs

ISOTOX® INSECT KILLER

GENERAL DESCRIPTION:
This liquid concentrate contains Orthene®, a systemic insecticide, and *dicofol*, a miticide. It controls chewing and sucking pests, including hard-to-control scales, flower thrips, whiteflies, and mites on the many ornamentals specified on the label. It gives both contact and residual control; Orthene's systemic killing action remains effective for up to 3 weeks. For best results, treat at the first sign of insects, before populations become large. Apply with any ORTHO hose-end sprayer or any tank-type or power sprayer. Not for use on food crops.

AREAS SOLD:
National

ACTIVE INGREDIENTS:
8.0% Orthene (Acephate) *(0,S-Dimethyl-acetylphosphoramidothioate)*
3.0% Dicofol *1,1-Bis (p-chlorophenyl)-2,2,2-trichloroethanol*

KILLS THESE INSECTS:
Aphids
Ash Plant Bugs
Bagworms
Beet Armyworms
Birch Leafminers
Black Vine Weevils
Budworms
Cabbage Loopers
Catalpa Sphinx Moths (Larvae)
Cottonwood Leaf Beetle
Cuban Laurel Thrips
Elm Leaf Beetles
Fall Cankerworms
Fall Webworms
Gypsy Moths (Larvae)
Holly Leafminers
Japanese Beetles
Lacebugs
Leafhoppers
Leafrollers
Lilac Leafminers
Maple Shoot Moths (Larvae)
Mealybugs
Mimosa Webworms
Nantucket Pine Tip Moths (Larvae)
Oak Webworms
Obscure Root Weevils
Orange-striped Oakworms
Poplar Tentmakers
Psyllids
Saddled Prominent Caterpillars
Sawflies (Dusky Birch, Blackheaded Ash, Redheaded Pine, European Pine)
Scales (Crawlers)
Spittlebugs
Spruce Mites
Stinkbugs
Tent Caterpillars
Thrips
Two-spotted Spider Mites
Whiteflies
Willow Leaf Beetles

FOR USE IN THESE AREAS:
Roses and flowers
Trees and shrubs

LAWN INSECT SPRAY

GENERAL DESCRIPTION:
A liquid concentrate used to control common lawn pests, home-invading pests, and imported fire ants. It is effective on both grass and dichondra lawns, and also prevents ants, ticks, and other listed pests from invading buildings when applied around and on foundations. When diluted, one quart of concentrate treats up to 4,000 square feet. Apply with an ORTHO Lawn Sprayer. For best results, treat the entire lawn rather than spot spraying.

AREAS SOLD:
National

ACTIVE INGREDIENT:
5.3% Chlorpyrifos [0,0-Diethyl 0-(3,5,6-trichloro-2-pyridyl) phosphorothioate]

KILLS THESE INSECTS:
Ants
Armyworms
Brown Dog Ticks
Chinch Bugs
Crickets
Cutworms
Dichondra Flea Beetles
Earwigs
Fiery Skipper Larvae (California and Hawaii only)
Fire Ants
Grasshoppers
Lawn Moth Larvae (Sod Webworms)
Sowbugs (Pillbugs)
Tropical Grass Webworms (Hawaii only)
White Grubs

FOR USE IN THESE AREAS:
Lawns
Building foundations

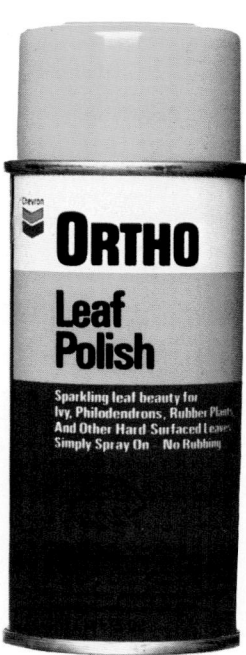

LEAF POLISH (AEROSOL)

GENERAL DESCRIPTION:
An easy-to-use aerosol spray that forms a lasting dust-resistant natural glow on all houseplants with hard-surfaced leaves, including philodendrons, pothos, and dieffenbachias. Clean all leaves with a damp clean cloth before using this spray. When the leaves dry, hold the can 10 to 12 inches away from the plant and evenly spray the leaves. Protect furniture and floors from the spray with newspaper or cloth. The spray dries in 5 to 10 minutes. For a higher gloss, gently rub the leaves after the spray dries. Do not apply to succulents.

AREAS SOLD:
National

POLISHES THESE PLANTS:
Anthuriums
Dieffenbachias
Gardenias
Ivy
Philodendrons
Pothos
Rubber Plants
Snake Plants
And all other houseplants with hard-surfaced leaves

FOR USE IN THESE AREAS:
Houseplants

Dieffenbachias
Gardenias
Ivy
Philodendrons
Rubber Plants
Scheffleras
Wax Plants
And all other
houseplants with
hard-surfaced
leaves

**FOR USE IN
THESE AREAS:**
Houseplants

LEAF POLISH
(PUMP)

GENERAL DESCRIPTION:
A liquid designed to give hard-surfaced
leaves a lasting natural glow. When used
as directed, it will not injure plants. The
hand pump makes application quick and
easy. Before using, wipe dusty leaves
clean with a damp cloth, and dry. Direct
the nozzle at the leaves and gently pump,
covering the leaves evenly. Protect furniture and floors from the spray with newspaper or cloth. Do not use on succulents
such as jade plants, or on plants with soft
or hairy foliage. Do not apply more often
than every 3 to 4 weeks.

AREAS SOLD:
National

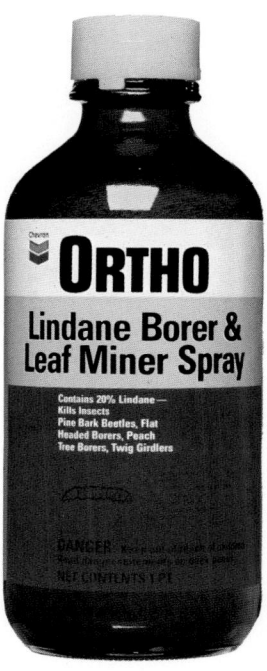

**KILLS THESE
INSECTS:**
Bark Beetles
Dogwood Borers
Flat-headed Borers
Fruit Tree Bark
   Beetles
Iris Borers
Leafminers
Lilac Borers
Peach Tree Borers
Pine Bark Beetles
Rhododendron Borers
Round-headed Borers
Taxus Weevils
Twig Girdlers
White Pine Weevils
Wood-Boring Beetles

**FOR USE IN
THESE AREAS:**
Flowers and fruits
Trees and shrubs

LINDANE BORER &
LEAF MINER SPRAY

GENERAL DESCRIPTION:
A liquid that is applied as a foliage
spray, trunk paint, and soil drench. It
controls wood-boring beetles, weevils,
and leafminers that are not easily contacted by insecticides. It kills borers inside trees as the vapor penetrates into
their feeding tunnels. To prevent new infestations, drench tree trunks to form a
protective coating. Invading borers ingest the chemical as they chew into the
trunk.

AREAS SOLD:
National

ACTIVE INGREDIENT:
20% Lindane *Gamma isomer of benzene
hexachloride*

HINTS FOR USE:
Some borers, including peachtree borers, pupate in the soil below infested
trees. Soak the soil to kill the adults as
they emerge.

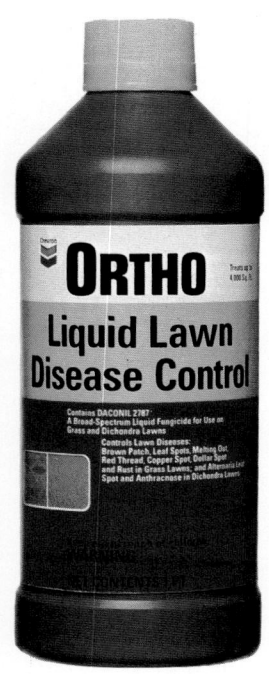

CONTROLS THESE DISEASES:
Alternaria Leaf Spot
Anthracnose
Copper Spot
Curvularia Leaf Spot
Dollar Spot
Gray Leaf Spot
Large Brown Patch
Leaf Spot (Melting Out)
Red Thread
Stem Rust of Bluegrass

FOR USE IN THESE AREAS:
Lawns

LIQUID LAWN DISEASE CONTROL

GENERAL DESCRIPTION:
A broad-spectrum, liquid fungicide for use on all grass and dichondra lawns. It controls brown patch, dollar spot, leaf spot, anthracnose, and other listed diseases. It contains the proven fungicide *chlorothalonil* to kill existing infections, and also provides protection against additional infections. For best results, spray wherever weather conditions favor disease development, or before the problem becomes extensive. The label lists weather conditions that favor various diseases and the appropriate dilution rates for control. One quart of concentrate mixes readily with water to treat up to 8,000 square feet. Mow and water the lawn prior to use. Apply with an ORTHO Sprayette, ORTHO Lawn & Garden Sprayer (foliage setting), or a tank-type or power sprayer.

AREAS SOLD:
National

ACTIVE INGREDIENT:
29.6% Chlorothalonil *Tetrachloroisophthalonitrile*

KILLS THESE INSECTS:
Ants
Aphids
Apple Aphids
Apple Maggots
Bagworms
Blister Beetles
Codling Moths
Corn Borers
Earwigs
Elm Leaf Beetles
Fall Armyworms
Fleas
Fruitworms
Grasshoppers
Gypsy Moths
Hornworms
Japanese Beetles
Leafminers
Leafrollers
Melon Worms
Oriental Fruit Moths
Peachtree Borers
Periodical Cicadas
Pickleworms
Plum Curculios
Rose Slugs
Scale Insects
Sod Webworms
Tent Caterpillars
Thrips

FOR USE IN THESE AREAS:
Fruits and vegetables
Trees and shrubs
Roses and flowers
Lawns

LIQUID SEVIN®

GENERAL DESCRIPTION:
A liquid concentrate designed to control a broad range of insects on contact and as they feed on roses, ornamentals, lawns, and food crops. It mixes readily with water to be used in all types of sprayers. For best results, apply when the insects first appear. Treat all exposed parts of plants, especially the upper and lower surfaces of the leaves. Liquid Sevin may be applied to specified vegetables up to the day of harvest. Combine with ORTHO Funginex® Rose Disease Control for a combination spray on roses.

AREAS SOLD:
National

ACTIVE INGREDIENT:
27% Carbaryl *1-Naphthyl N-methylcarbamate*

MALATHION 50 INSECT SPRAY

GENERAL DESCRIPTION:
A multipurpose liquid that kills on contact a broad range of chewing and sucking insects on lawns, ornamentals, and food crops. Thorough coverage of branches and the upper and lower surfaces of the leaves is necessary to control insects. *Malathion* may be applied to broccoli and peas within 3 days of harvest, and to citrus within 7 days of harvest. Use around building foundations to control fleas, clover mites, and mosquitoes. One quart of concentrate readily mixes with water to make 96 gallons of diluted spray. *Malathion* is one of the least toxic insecticides used in home gardens, and has been used successfully for many years.

AREAS SOLD:
National

ACTIVE INGREDIENT:
50% Malathion *0,0-Dimethyl dithiophosphate of diethyl mercaptosuccinate*

KILLS THESE INSECTS:
Aphids
Bagworms
Box Elder Bugs
Clover Mites
Codling Moths
Fleas
Fourlined Leaf Bugs
Grape Leafhoppers
Houseflies
Japanese Beetle Adults
Mealybugs
Mosquitoes
Pear Psyllids
Potato Leafhoppers
Red-Banded Leafrollers
Rose Leafhoppers
Spittlebugs
Red Spider Mites
Tarnished Plant Bugs
Tent Caterpillars
Thrips
Whiteflies
Woolly Aphids

FOR USE IN THESE AREAS:
Trees and shrubs
Roses and flowers
Fruits and vegetables
Outdoors
Around dwellings
Lawns

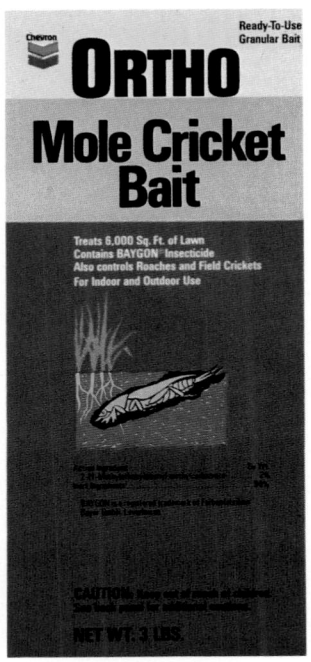

MOLE CRICKET BAIT

GENERAL DESCRIPTION:
A ready-to-use granular bait for controlling mole crickets, field crickets, and cockroaches. It rapidly kills these insects, including cockroaches resistant to certain chlorinated hydrocarbon and phosphate insecticides. Three pounds of granules treats up to 6,000 square feet of lawn. For fast, easy application outdoors, use an ORTHO Whirlybird Spreader. Indoors, lightly sprinkle in cracks and crevices and other areas where pests may hide, but which are inaccessible to children and pets. Do not place in piles or use on food crops.

AREAS SOLD:
South

ACTIVE INGREDIENT:
2% Propoxur *2-(1-Methylethoxy) phenyl methylcarbamate*

KILLS THESE INSECTS:
Cockroaches
Field Crickets
Mole Crickets

FOR USE IN THESE AREAS:
Indoors
Outdoors

ORTHENE® SYSTEMIC INSECT CONTROL

GENERAL DESCRIPTION:

A liquid that effectively controls on contact and with residual systemic action many of the chewing and sucking pests that attack roses, flowers, ornamentals, and lawns. It is absorbed systemically by plants, so it controls present insects and future infestations for up to 3 weeks. It is particularly effective on hard-to-control insects such as scales, thrips, mealybugs, and black vine weevils. It controls imported fire ants and listed lawn pests, including fall armyworms and sod webworms. It may be applied with an ORTHO Spray-ette, ORTHO Lawn & Garden Sprayer, or a tank-type or power sprayer.

AREAS SOLD:
National

ACTIVE INGREDIENT:
9.4% Orthene (Acephate) *0,S-Dimethyl acetylphosphoramidothioate*

KILLS THESE INSECTS:

Aphids
Armyworms
Ash Hornworms
Bagworms
Black Vine Weevils
Budworms
Cabbage Loopers
Casebearers
Catalpa Sphinx
  Moths
Cherry Laurel
  Leaftiers
Cuban Laurel Thrips
Elm Leafbeetles
Fall Cankerworms
Fall Webworms
Flower Thrips
Gladiolus Thrips
Grasshoppers
Greenbugs
Green Striped
  Mapleworms
Gypsy Moths
Hornworms
Imported Fire Ants
Japanese Beetles
Lacebugs
Leafhoppers
Leafminers
Oblique-banded
  Leafrollers
Omnivorous Leaftiers
Maple Shoot Moths
Mealybugs
Mimosa Webworms
Nantucket Pine Tip
  Moths
Oak Webworm
Obscure Root
  Weevils (Adults)
Oleander
  Caterpillars
Orange-striped
  Oakworms
Poplar Tentmakers
Psyllids
Rose Midges
Sawflies
Scales (Crawlers)
Spittlebugs
Sunflower Moths
Tent Caterpillars
Whiteflies
White-marked
  Tussock Moths
Willow Leafbeetles
Yellow-necked
  Caterpillars

FOR USE IN THESE AREAS:
Roses and flowers
Trees and shrubs
Lawns

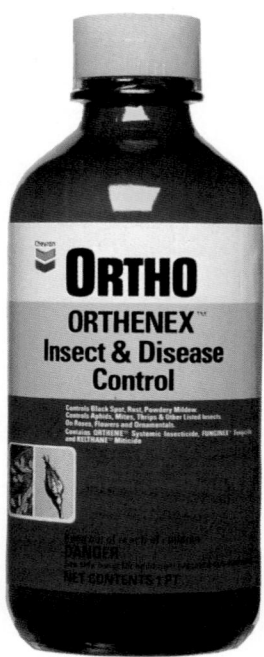

ORTHENEX™ INSECT & DISEASE CONTROL

GENERAL DESCRIPTION:

A liquid combination of three highly effective pesticides, Orthene® for insects, *dicofol* for mites, and *triforine* for disease control on roses, flowers, and ornamentals. The systemic action of the ingredients Orthene and *triforine* enables them to be absorbed into plants through the leaves and stems, resulting in longer, more effective protection with no unsightly residue on the foliage. Insects and mites are killed on contact. For best results, use as a preventive spray, applying before or at the first sign of insects and diseases. One quart of concentrate dilutes easily with water to make 32 gallons of diluted spray. Apply with an ORTHO Spray-ette, ORTHO Lawn & Garden Sprayer, or a tank-type or power sprayer.

AREAS SOLD:
National

ACTIVE INGREDIENTS:
4.00% Orthene (Acephate) *O,S-Dimethyl acetylphosphoramidothioate*
3.25% Triforine *N,N'-(1,4-Piperazinediylbis [2,2,2-trichloroethylidene])bis (formamide)*
3.00% Dicofol *1,1-Bis(p-chlorophenyl)-2,2,2-trichloroethanol*

KILLS THESE INSECTS:

Aphids
Budworms
Flower Thrips
Lacebugs
Leafhoppers
Leafminers
Spittlebugs
Two-spotted Mites

CONTROLS THESE DISEASES:
Black Spot
Powdery Mildew
Rust

FOR USE IN THESE AREAS:
Roses and flowers
Trees and shrubs

ORTHOCIDE®
GARDEN FUNGICIDE

GENERAL DESCRIPTION:
A wettable powder used to control many garden plant diseases on roses, flowers, lawns, vegetables, and fruits as listed on the label. It contains the fungicide *captan* to kill existing fungal infections, and provides protection against additional infections for 1 to 2 weeks. It is also used on cuttings, bulbs, and seeds before planting to prevent damping-off. For best results, apply with an ORTHO Spray-ette garden hose sprayer or power sprayer; continue to agitate during application to keep the powder dissolved. It is compatible with most commonly used insecticides and fungicides except for highly alkaline materials such as hydrated lime.

AREAS SOLD:
National

ACTIVE INGREDIENTS:
47.3% Captan *N-([Trichloromethyl] thio)-4-cyclohexene-1,2-dicarboximide*
2.7% Related derivatives

HINTS FOR USE:
An eradicant fungicide kills fungi that are present on, and sometimes in, infected plant parts. For best disease control, apply the fungicide at the first sign of the disease.

CONTROLS THESE DISEASES:
Alternaria (Leaf Spot)
Angular Leaf Spot
Anthracnose
Bitter Rot
Black Spot
Botrytis Flower Blight
Botrytis Rot
Brown Patch
Brown Rot
Cercospora Spot or Blotch
Cherry Leaf Spot
Damping-off
Downy Mildew
Early Blight
Fruit Spot
Gray Leaf Spot
Helminthosporium (Melting Out)
Late Blight
Leaf Spot
Peach Scab
Powdery Mildew
Root Rot
Rust
Scab
Seed Rot
Septoria Leaf Spot

FOR USE IN THESE AREAS:
Roses and flowers
Fruits and vegetables
Lawns

ORTHO-KLOR® 44
CHLORDANE SPRAY

GENERAL DESCRIPTION:
A liquid insecticide with extended residual properties that effectively controls termites. Termites regularly travel from soil to buildings. To prevent termite entry, establish a barrier of *chlordane* in the soil around buildings. Detailed instructions are given on the label for treating foundations, raised porches, terraces, and entranceways. It mixes readily with water to be used in an ORTHO Lawn Sprayer or ORTHO Lawn & Garden Sprayer.

AREAS SOLD:
National

ACTIVE INGREDIENT:
44% Chlordane *Octachloro-4,-7-methanotetrahydroindane* and related compounds

KILLS THESE INSECTS:
Termites

FOR USE IN THESE AREAS:
Around buildings

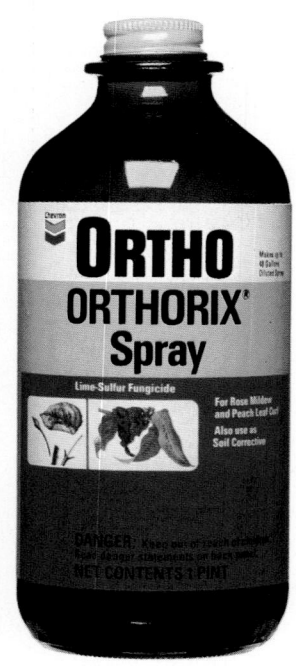

CONTROLS THESE DISEASES AND PESTS:

Blackspot
Blister Mites
Cane Blight
Leaf Spot
Peach Blight
Peach Leaf Curl
Powdery Mildew
Red Berry Trouble
Red Spider Mites
Rust
Rust Mites
Scab

FOR USE IN THESE AREAS:

Trees and shrubs
Roses and flowers
Fruits

KILLS THESE INSECTS:

Ants
Centipedes
Crickets
Flies
Flying Moths
Gnats
Hornets
Mosquitoes
Sowbugs
Spiders
Wasps

FOR USE IN THESE AREAS:

Outdoors

ORTHORIX® SPRAY

GENERAL DESCRIPTION:

A liquid formulated for use in both dormant and growing seasons to kill overwintering fungal spores and existing infections on roses and listed ornamentals, fruits, and berries. It also controls rust mites on citrus, and can be used as a soil correction for acid-loving plants including rhododendrons, azaleas, and camellias. It can also be used as a lawn and soil treatment to condition soils and to improve water penetration and moisture retention in heavy soils. One pint of concentrate makes up to 48 gallons of diluted spray. Depending on use, apply the solution with an ORTHO Spray-ette, ORTHO Lawn Sprayer or watering can. Combine it with ORTHO Isotox® Insect Killer for a combination spray on roses and many ornamentals. It can also be combined with ORTHO Volck® Oil Spray or ORTHO Volck® Supreme Oil Spray for a combination winter spray on dormant deciduous fruits, ornamentals and roses.

AREAS SOLD:

National

ACTIVE INGREDIENT:

26% Lime sulfur *Calcium polysulfides*

OUTDOOR INSECT FOGGER

GENERAL DESCRIPTION:

This insecticide is specially formulated for use in backyards, patios, and picnic areas to control flying and crawling insects in a wide area, as far as 21 feet away. When sprayed, it blankets the area with a penetrating insect-killing fog that contains both an insecticide and a repellent. It is very effective against mosquitoes, gnats, flies, ants, spiders, and other outdoor pests. For best results, spray in the direction of a slight breeze that will carry the fog into the infested areas. Do not reenter the area until after the spray dissipates.

AREAS SOLD:

National

ACTIVE INGREDIENTS:

0.250% Resmethrin *(5-[Phenylmethyl]-3-furanyl)methyl 2,2-dimethyl-3-(2-methyl-1-propenyl) cyclopropane-carboxylate*
0.950% MGK Repellent 874 *2-Hydroxyethyl-n-octyl sulfide*

HINTS FOR USE:

For pest-free outdoor parties, spray into shrubs around the perimeter of gardens and lawns one hour before using outdoor patio areas.

Centipedes
Cockroaches
Crickets
Earwigs
Millipedes
Sowbugs

FOR USE IN THESE AREAS:
Indoors
Outdoors

CONTROLS THESE DISEASES:
Anthracnose
Black Spot
Citrus Scab
Corm Rot
Damping-off
   (Cylindrocladium)
Leaf Spot (Alternaria)
Leaf Spot
   (Didymellina)
Leaf Spot (Septoria)
Melanose
Powdery Mildew
Root Rot (Pythium)
Rust

FOR USE IN THESE AREAS:
Roses and flowers
Citrus

PEST-B-GON® ROACH BAIT

GENERAL DESCRIPTION:
A ready-to-use granular bait for indoor and outdoor control of the listed pests that feed upon it or come in contact with it. It rapidly kills both resistant and non-resistant cockroaches. For best results outdoors, distribute the granules where pests congregate late afternoon or the early morning, when they are most active; also sprinkle around foundations to prevent pests from entering buildings. Indoors, treat in cracks and crevices and in other areas where pests hide. Do not apply directly to foliage of ornamentals — apply the bait to the soil around the plants.

AREAS SOLD:
South

ACTIVE INGREDIENT:
2% Propoxur *2-(1-Methylethoxy)phenyl methylcarbamate*

PHALTAN® ROSE & GARDEN FUNGICIDE

GENERAL DESCRIPTION:
A wettable powder used to control black spot, powdery mildew, leaf spot, and other listed diseases on roses, flowers, and citrus. When applied as a preventive spray at the intervals specified on the label, it provides lasting protection against future infections. It is also used as a dip solution prior to planting to prevent corm rot on gladiolus. Mix it with any rooting medium to prevent damping-off on azalea cuttings. It may be combined with most common insecticides and fungicides, except for such strongly alkaline materials as hydrated lime.

AREAS SOLD:
National

ACTIVE INGREDIENT:
75% Phaltan (Folpet) *N-([Trichloromethyl]thio)phthalimide*

HINTS FOR USE:
A protective fungicide protects healthy plant parts from infection by forming a chemical barrier between the fungi and the plant tissues, killing the spores before they germinate. This type of fungicide cannot kill fungi that are already growing on or in plant tissue.

PRUNING SEAL

GENERAL DESCRIPTION:

A ready-to-use liquid designed as a fast, effective dressing to aid in the healing of pruning cuts, grafts, abrasions, and wounds on woody plants, and fruit and shade trees. The material provides a protective coating that prevents the entry of moisture into the exposed cut and also prevents excessive sap flow. The built-in applicator makes the application fast and easy, and requires no additional equipment. Remove spills from clothing with turpentine. Wash spills from skin with white mineral oil.

AREAS SOLD:

National

ACTIVE INGREDIENT:

Petroleum naphtha

HINTS FOR USE:

Trim and clean tree wounds before applying ORTHO Pruning Seal. Using a sharp knife, trim away all splinters and dead wood, making a smooth wound. Then shape the wound into a vertical ellipse, pointed at the top and bottom. This shape hastens healing and callusing. Then apply the pruning seal evenly over the entire wound.

PRUNING SEALER

GENERAL DESCRIPTION:

An aerosol spray formulated as a fast, easy, effective dressing to aid in the healing of pruning cuts, grafts, abrasions, and wounds on woody plants and trees. It provides a protective coating against moisture, and helps prevent excessive sap flow. It can also be used to waterproof planting pots and wooden tubs. The ready-to-use aerosol makes application clean and easy. Remove any stains on clothing or skin with white mineral oil.

AREAS SOLD:

National

ACTIVE INGREDIENT:

Liquid asphalt

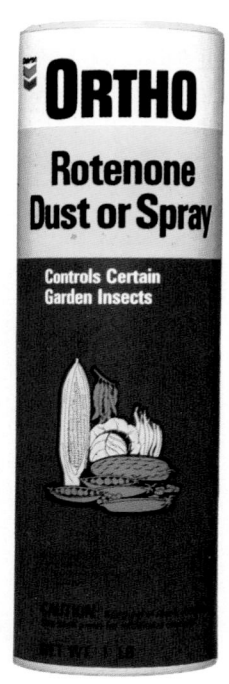

KILLS THESE INSECTS:
Asparagus Beetles
Cabbage Worms
Cucumber Beetles
European Corn
    Borers
Flea Beetles
Pea Weevils
Thrips
Twelve-spotted
    Beetles

FOR USE IN THESE AREAS:
Vegetables

ROTENONE DUST OR SPRAY

GENERAL DESCRIPTION:
A wettable powder insecticide designed to be used as either a dust or a spray to control certain garden pests on the vegetables listed on the label. *Rotenone*, the active ingredient, is a botanical insecticide derived from the roots of leguminous plants. One application provides protection for about a week. Repeated treatments are necessary for continuous insect control. When used as a dust, 1 pound will treat 1,000 square feet. It may be used on vegetables to within 1 day of harvest.

AREAS SOLD:
National

ACTIVE INGREDIENT:
1% Rotenone

HINTS FOR USE:
A contact insecticide kills insects by direct contact when absorbed through the insect's body. For best results, the plant must be thoroughly sprayed so that all insects are contacted.

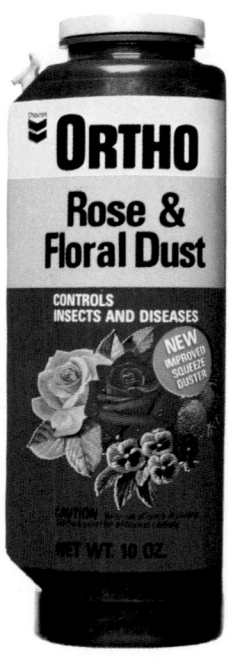

KILLS THESE INSECTS:
Aphids
Bagworms
Boxwood Leafminers
Japanese Beetles
Lacebugs
Leafrollers
Rose Chafers
Rose Leafhoppers
Rose Slugs
Scale Crawlers
Spider Mites

CONTROLS THESE DISEASES:
Black Spot
Leaf Spot
Powdery Mildew

FOR USE IN THESE AREAS:
Roses and flowers

ROSE & FLORAL DUST

GENERAL DESCRIPTION:
A dust specially formulated to control insects and major diseases on roses and other flowers. The insecticides kill both sucking and chewing pests that feed on leaves and blossoms. The fungicide protects the foliage from fungal infections, but does not kill existing infections. So for best results, begin applying as new growth appears in the spring. Repeated applications are necessary through the growing season for good insect and disease control. The unique patented squeeze duster easily treats all parts of the plants, including the upper and lower surfaces of the leaves, without clumping or clogging. Apply in early morning or late evening when the temperature is low and the air is still.

AREAS SOLD:
National

ACTIVE INGREDIENTS:
3.0% Carbaryl *1-Naphthyl N-methylcarbamate*
4.0% Malathion *0,0-Dimethyl dithiophosphate of diethyl mercaptosuccinate*
5.0% Phaltan (Folpet) *N-([Trichloromethyl]thio)phthalimide*
1.5% Dicofol *1,1-Bis (p-chlorophenyl)-2,2,2-trichloroethanol*

ROSE & FLOWER JET DUSTER

GENERAL DESCRIPTION:

A dust containing insecticides, a miticide, and a fungicide designed to control insects and major diseases on roses and other listed flowers. This ready-to-use formulation makes treating all plant parts easy without any mixing or additional equipment. Seven ounces of dust thoroughly treats up to 33 average-size (3 feet in diameter) rose bushes. The fungicide protects the foliage from infections. So for best results, begin applying early in the season as soon as the foliage appears. The insecticides control both sucking and chewing insects. Treat at the first sign of damage or insects.

AREAS SOLD:

National

ACTIVE INGREDIENTS:

2.4% Carbaryl *1-Naphthyl N-methylcarbamate*
3.2% Malathion *0,0-Dimethyl dithiophosphate of diethyl mercaptosuccinate*
4.0% Phaltan (Folpet) *N-([Trichloromethyl]thio)phthalimide*
1.2% Dicofol *1,1-Bis (p-chlorophenyl)-2,2,2-trichloroethanol*

SCRAM® DOG & CAT REPELLENT

GENERAL DESCRIPTION:

An aerosol spray designed to repel dogs and cats from forbidden areas of the home such as furniture and rugs. Outdoors it prevents pets or stray animals from damaging garden areas, including ornamentals beds and lawns. However, do not apply the spray directly to the foliage of shrubs or to ornamental soft-bodied plants. When applied daily, this repellent is effective for 12 to 24 hours. The spray may stain or soften some fabrics or plastics, so test first by treating a small inconspicuous area. The label contains complete instructions for indoor and outdoor use.

AREAS SOLD:

National

ACTIVE INGREDIENT:

1.9% MGK 1770 Repellent *Methyl nonyl ketone*

HINTS FOR USE:

This product works best in conjunction with voice commands to pets. Read the label completely and follow directions for best results.

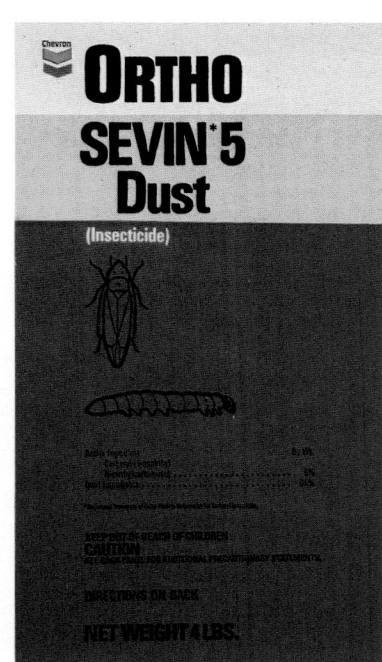

KILLS THESE INSECTS:

Armyworms
Bean Leaf Beetles
Bedbugs
Chicken Mites
Colorado Potato
   Beetles
Corn Earworms
Corn Rootworm
   Adults
Cucumber Beetles
European Corn
   Borers
Flea Beetles
Fleas
Harlequin Bugs
Imported
   Cabbageworms
Japanese Beetles
Lace Bugs
Leafhoppers
Lice
Lygus Bugs
Melonworms
Mexican Bean Beetles
Northern Fowl Mites
Pickleworms
Salt Marsh
   Caterpillars
Sap Beetles
Six-spotted
   Leafhoppers
Spittlebugs
Squash Bugs
Stink Bugs
Strawberry
   Leafrollers
Strawberry Weevils
Tarnished Plant Bugs
Ticks
Tomato Fruitworms
Tomato Hornworms
Velvetbean
   Caterpillars
Western Bean
   Cutworms

FOR USE IN THESE AREAS:

Vegetables and fruits
Pets and poultry

SEVIN® 5 DUST

GENERAL DESCRIPTION:

A 5 percent dust designed to control chewing and sucking insects including beetles, leafhoppers, and fruitworms on the vegetables listed on the label. It can be applied to beans, corn, carrots, cucumbers, melons, and squash up to the day of harvest. It also kills ticks and fleas on dogs and cats when lightly dusted on their fur. Treat poultry and in and around their houses to control lice, fleas, chicken mites, and northern fowl mites. Apply at the first sign of insects or damage, and repeat at intervals of 7 days unless the label specifies otherwise. For easy application in evenly covering both the upper and lower surfaces of the leaves, and in treating cracks and crevices in poultry houses and doghouses, apply with an ORTHO Whirly Duster.
Note: Do not use inside the home.

AREAS SOLD:

Northeast
South
Midwest (Kansas)

ACTIVE INGREDIENT:

5% Carbaryl *1-Naphthyl N-methylcarbamate*

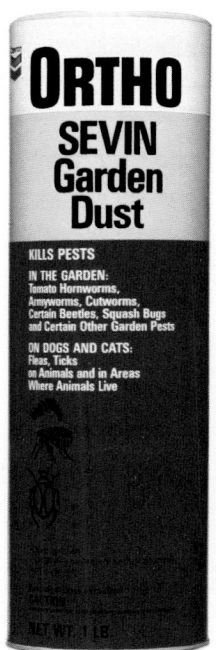

SEVIN® GARDEN DUST

GENERAL DESCRIPTION:

A dust formulated to kill vegetable garden pests including hornworms, cutworms, beetles, and squash bugs on the listed vegetables. It can be applied to many vegetables up to harvest, including tomatoes, peppers, and beans. The label gives full instructions, with days to harvest for all listed vegetables. It also controls ticks and fleas on dogs and cats and in and around their homes. Ruffle their fur while treating to ensure contact with the skin. For even application to plants and in and around doghouses and kennels, apply the dust with an ORTHO Whirly Duster. Not for use inside the home.

AREAS SOLD:

National

ACTIVE INGREDIENT:

5% Carbaryl *1-Naphthyl N-methylcarbamate*

KILLS THESE INSECTS:

Armyworms
Bean Leaf Beetles
Cabbage Caterpillars
Colorado Potato
   Beetles
Corn Earworms
Corn Rootworm
   Adults
Cucumber Beetles
European Corn
   Borers
Flea Beetles
Harlequin Bugs
Japanese Beetles
Lace Bugs
Leafhoppers
Lygus Bugs
Melonworms
Mexican Bean Beetles
Pickleworms
Sap Beetles
Spittlebugs
Squash Bugs
Stink Bugs
Strawberry
   Leafrollers
Strawberry Weevils
Tarnished Plant Bugs
Tomato Fruitworms
Tomato Hornworms
Velvetbean
   Caterpillars
Western Bean
   Cutworms

FOR USE IN THESE AREAS:

Fruits and vegetables
Pets

Sevin is a registered trademark of Union Carbide Corp.

SEVIN®
GARDEN SPRAY

GENERAL DESCRIPTION:
A wettable powder containing *carbaryl*, designed to control a wide range of chewing and sucking pests that damage and reduce yields of vegetables, fruits, flowers, ornamentals, and lawns. It is especially effective on hard-to-control apple maggots, gypsy moths, Japanese beetles, and cicadas. For best results and even coverage, apply the solution with an ORTHO Spray-ette or ORTHO Lawn Sprayer at the first sign of insects or damage. Repeat the treatment weekly, or as noted on the label. Sevin Garden Spray may be used on the listed vegetables up to harvest. Six ounces of concentrate makes up to 15 gallons of diluted spray.

AREAS SOLD:
Midwest
Northeast
South

ACTIVE INGREDIENT:
50% Carbaryl *1-Naphthyl N-methylcarbamate*

HINTS FOR USE:
To dilute easily, mix the measured amount of powder with a little water to form a paste, then add the required amount of water.

KILLS THESE INSECTS:
Ants
Aphids
Apple Aphids
Apple Maggots
Bagworms
Blister Beetles
Codling Moths
Corn Borers
Earwigs
Elm Leaf Beetles
Fall Armyworms
Fleas
Fruitworms
Grasshoppers
Gypsy Moths
Hornworms
Japanese Beetles
Leafminers
Leafrollers
Melon Worms
Oriental Fruit Moths
Peachtree Borers
Periodical Cicadas
    (17-Year Locusts)
Plum Curculio
Pickleworms
Rose Slugs
Scale Insects
Sod Webworms
Tent Caterpillars
Thrips

FOR USE IN THESE AREAS:
Fruits and vegetables
Roses and flowers
Trees and shrubs

Sevin is a registered trademark of Union Carbide Corp.

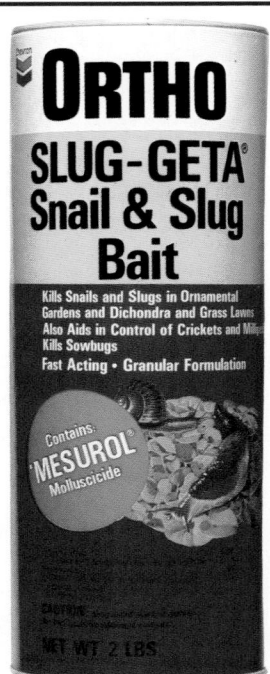

SLUG-GETA®
SNAIL & SLUG BAIT

GENERAL DESCRIPTION:
A granular, easy-to-use formulation that effectively controls snails and slugs and other listed pests in ornamental gardens, dichondra and grass lawns, and turf. Simply scatter the granules directly from the canister, or apply them with an ORTHO Whirlybird Spreader. One pound of granules covers up to 1,000 square feet. Do not put granules in piles. Snails and slugs prefer damp, protected areas, so lightly sprinkle the area to be treated before application. This encourages movement and increases feeding on the bait. Do not use on or around food crops.

AREAS SOLD:
National

ACTIVE INGREDIENT:
2% Methiocarb *3.5-Dimethyl-4-(methylthio) phenyl methylcarbamate*

KILLS THESE INSECTS:
Crickets
Millipedes
Slugs
Snails
Sowbugs

FOR USE IN THESE AREAS:
Lawns and
    groundcovers
Ornamental gardens
Noncrop areas

SOD WEBWORM CONTROL

GENERAL DESCRIPTION:
A liquid designed for the control of sod webworms and chinch bugs in lawns. Sod webworms chew on grass blades at night. Chinch bugs suck the juice from the base of grass blades. When either or both are present, treat the entire lawn. Aspon kills these pests on contact, and remains effective for up to 8 weeks against additional infestations.

AREAS SOLD:
Midwest
Northeast
South

ACTIVE INGREDIENT:
13.0% Aspon® *0,0,0,0-Tetrapropyl dithiopyrophosphate*

HINTS FOR USE:
To verify the presence of chinch bugs in a lawn, drive a coffee can from which both ends have been removed into the lawn at the edge of a damaged area and fill it with water. If chinch bugs are present they will float to the surface. For sod webworm detection, apply 1 gallon of soapy water over any damaged area suspected of harboring pests. If present, small tan caterpillars ¼ to ¾ inch long will begin to emerge.

KILLS THESE INSECTS:
Chinch Bugs
Sod Webworms

FOR USE IN THESE AREAS:
Lawns

Aspon is a registered trademark of Stauffer Chemical Co.

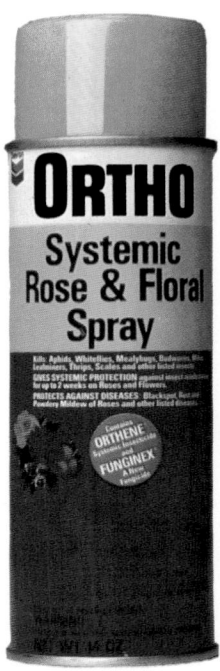

SYSTEMIC ROSE & FLORAL SPRAY

GENERAL DESCRIPTION:
An aerosol containing the insecticide Orthene® and *resmethrin* and the systemic fungicide *triforine* to control a broad range of both insects and diseases on plants listed on the label. The insecticides kill both on contact and by systemic action to provide protection of all plant parts against insect reinfestations for up to 2 weeks. The fungicide kills present fungal infections and systemically protects against additional infections for 1 to 2 weeks. Systemic action is internal, and cannot be washed off by rain or sprinkling. The 14-ounce size is especially convenient for gardeners with only a few rosebushes or plants, or for spot treatment in large gardens when only a few plants are infested.

AREAS SOLD:
National

ACTIVE INGREDIENTS:
0.250% Orthene (Acephate) *O,S-Dimethyl acetylphosphoramidothioate*
0.100% Resmethrin *(5-[Phenylmethyl]-3-furanyl)methyl 2,2-dimethyl-3-(2-methyl-1-propenyl) cyclopropane-carboxylate*
0.100% Triforine *N,N'-(1,4-piperazine-diylbis [2,2,2-trichloroethylidene])bis (formamide)*

KILLS THESE INSECTS:
Aphids
Armyworms
Bagworms
Budworms
Cuban Laurel Thrips
Diabrotica Beetles
Flower Thrips
Lacebugs
Leafhoppers
Leafminers
Leaftiers
Mealybugs
Oleander
    Caterpillars
Rose Midges
Salt Marsh
    Caterpillars
Scales (Crawlers)
Southern Red Mites
Spittlebugs
Two-spotted Spider
    Mites
Whiteflies

CONTROLS THESE DISEASES:
Blackspot
Powdery Mildew
Rust

FOR USE IN THESE AREAS:
Roses and flowers
Trees and shrubs
Not for use on
    houseplants
    indoors

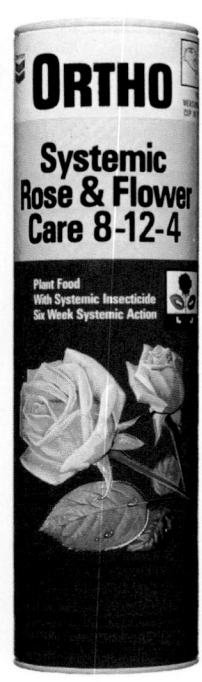

KILLS THESE INSECTS:
Aphids
Birch Leafminers
Holly Leafminers
Lacebugs
Leafhoppers
Mimosa Webworms
Pine Tip Moths
Spider Mites

SYSTEMIC ROSE & FLOWER CARE 8-12-4

GENERAL DESCRIPTION:
This granular formulation is an effective systemic insecticide combined with a fertilizer containing the three essential plant food elements, nitrogen, phosphate, and potash. It provides the proper amount of plant food and systemic insecticide necessary for strong, vigorous plants free of damage from sucking and certain chewing insects. The insecticide is absorbed through the roots and moves to all parts of the plant. The protection is internal and cannot be washed off by rain or sprinkling. All parts of the plant, including new growth, are protected for up to 6 weeks. Do not use near food crops.

AREAS SOLD:
National

ACTIVE INGREDIENT:
1% Disulfoton *0,0-Diethyl S-(2-[ethylthio]ethyl) phosphorodithioate*

GUARANTEED ANALYSIS:
8% Nitrogen
12% Phosphoric Acid
4% Potash

3-WAY ROSE AND FLOWER CARE

GENERAL DESCRIPTION:
A granular formulation that kills sucking and chewing insects, prevents weeds, and feeds plants. It contains *disulfoton*, a systemic insecticide that is absorbed into plants through the roots and then moves internally into the branches, leaves, and blossoms. The pre-emergence herbicide *trifluralin* kills annual grasses and broadleaf weeds as they germinate. The fertilizer supplies plants with nitrogen, phosphate, and potash, plus minor elements. Do not use near the roots of food crops.

AREAS SOLD:
Midwest
Northeast
West

ACTIVE INGREDIENTS:
1.000% Disulfoton *0,0-Diethyl S-(2-[ethylthio]ethyl) phosphorodithioate*
0.174% Trifluralin *a,a,a-trifluoro-2,6-dinitro-N,N-dipropyl-p-toluidine*

GUARANTEED ANALYSIS:
8% Nitrogen
12% Phosphoric Acid
4% Potash
10% Calcium
1% Magnesium
9.5% Sulfur

KILLS THESE INSECTS:
Aphids
Birch Leafminers
Holly Leafminers
Lacebugs
Leafhoppers
Mimosa Webworms
Pine Tip Moths
Spider Mites
Whiteflies

CONTROLS THESE WEEDS:
Annual Bluegrass
Barnyardgrass
Bromegrass
Carelessweed
Carpetweed
Cheat
Chickweed
Crabgrass
Florida Pusley
Foxtail
Goosefoot
Goosegrass
Johnsongrass
Jungle Rice
Knotweed
Kochia
Lamb's Quarters
Pigweed (Spiny and Redfoot)
Puncturevine
Purslane
Russian Thistle
Sandbur
Sprangeletop
Stinging Nettle
Stinkgrass
Texas Panicum

FOR USE IN THESE AREAS:
Roses and flowers

TOMATO & VEGETABLE INSECT SPRAY

GENERAL DESCRIPTION:
An aerosol spray designed for rapid control of flea beetles, hornworms, stinkbugs, and other listed insects on vegetables. This formulation contains two insecticides that are derived from plants and have quick contact-killing power. For best results, repeat the treatments to prevent a buildup of insect populations. The ready-to-use can makes treating both the upper and lower surfaces of the leaves an easy task. Food crops may be treated to within 1 day of harvest.

AREAS SOLD:
National

ACTIVE INGREDIENTS:
0.030% Pyrethrins
0.128% Rotenone

HINTS FOR USE:
A stomach insecticide kills insects when it is ingested as the insect feeds on treated plant tissue. Treat the entire plant thoroughly, so that insects do not survive on untreated tissue.

KILLS THESE INSECTS:
Aphids (Green Peach)
Blister Beetles
Colorado Potato Beetles
Flea Beetles
Hornworms
Japanese Beetles
Leafhoppers
Mexican Bean Beetles
Stinkbugs
Striped Cucumber Beetles
Twelve-spotted Cucumber Beetles
Whiteflies

FOR USE IN THESE AREAS:
Vegetables

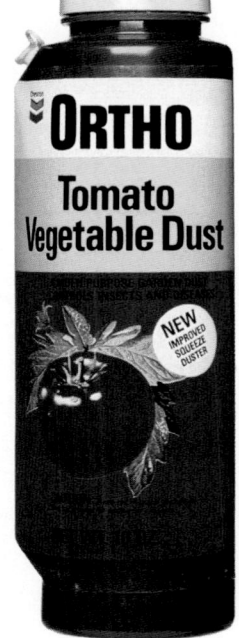

TOMATO VEGETABLE DUST

GENERAL DESCRIPTION:
A multipurpose garden dust that contains the insecticides *methoxychlor* and *rotenone* and the fungicide *captan* for insect and disease control on listed vegetables and berries including tomatoes, melons, squash, potatoes, and strawberries. When applied according to the label directions, it kills fungal infections and protects the foliage from additional infections for up to 2 weeks. It kills insects both on contact and as they feed on the leaves. Repeated treatments are necessary for good insect and disease control. It can be used on most vegetables and berries up to 7 days before harvest.

AREAS SOLD:
National

ACTIVE INGREDIENTS:
4.7% Captan *N-([trichloromethyl]thio)-4-cyclohexene-1,2-dicarboximide*
5.00% Methoxychlor *2,2-bis (p-methoxyphenyl)-1,1,1-trichloroethane* and related compounds
0.75% Rotenone

KILLS THESE INSECTS:
Aphids
Blister Beetles
Colorado Potato Beetles
Cucumber Beetles
Flea Beetles
Fleahoppers
Japanese Beetles
Leafhoppers
Melonworms
Mexican Bean Beetles
Omnivorous Leaftiers
Pickleworms
Raspberry Fruitworms
Spittlebugs
Squash Bugs (Nymphs)
Squash Vine Borers
Thrips
Tomato Fruitworms

CONTROLS THESE DISEASES:
Alternaria
Anthracnose
Botrytis Rot
Cercospora
Early Blight
Fruit Rot
Late Blight
Phomopsis
Septoria Leaf Spot
Spur Blight

FOR USE IN THESE AREAS:
Vegetables

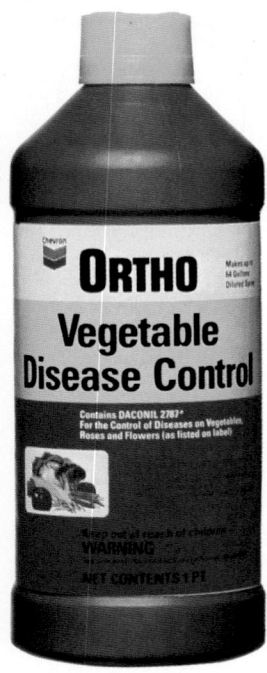

VEGETABLE DISEASE CONTROL

GENERAL DESCRIPTION:
A liquid spray used to control diseases on vegetables, roses, and flowers as listed on the label. When applied according to the label directions and repeated at specified intervals, it provides protection against fungal infections. One pint of concentrate makes up to 64 gallons of diluted spray. It dilutes easily in water to be applied with an ORTHO Spray-ette or ORTHO Lawn & Garden Sprayer, or a tank-type or power sprayer. Use up to the day of harvest on tomatoes, cucumbers, broccoli, and carrots. The label lists days to harvest for other vegetables.

AREAS SOLD:
National

ACTIVE INGREDIENT:
29.6% Chlorothalonil *Tetrachloroisophthalonitrile*

FOR USE IN THESE AREAS:
Roses and flowers
Vegetables

CONTROLS THESE DISEASES:
Alternaria Fruit Rot or Black Mold on Tomatoes
Alternaria Leaf Spot on Broccoli, Brussels Sprouts, Cabbage, and Cauliflower
Anthracnose on Cucumbers, Melons, Pumpkins, Squash, and Tomatoes
Ascochyta Ray Blight on Chrysanthemums
Basal Stalk Rot on Celery
Blackspot on Roses
Blossom Blight on Roses
Botrytis Blight on Geraniums and Iris
Botrytis Vine Rot on Potatoes
Cercospora Leaf Spot on Melons, Pumpkins, and Squash
Downy Mildew on Broccoli, Brussels Sprouts, Cabbage, and Cauliflower
Early Blight on Carrots, Celery, Potatoes, and Tomatoes
Fruit Rot (Rhizoctonia) on Cucumbers and Tomatoes
Gray Leaf Spot on Tomatoes
Gray Mold (Botrytis) on Tomatoes and Chrysanthemums
Gummy Stem Blight on Cucumbers, Melons, Pumpkins, Squash, and Tomatoes
Helminthosporium Leaf Blight on Sweet Corn
Late Blight on Carrots, Celery, Potatoes, and Tomatoes
Leaf Blight on Cucumbers, Melons, Pumpkins, Squash, and Tomatoes
Leaf Spot on Iris
Powdery Mildew (*Erysiphe*) on Cucumbers, Melons, and Zinnias
Ring Spot on Brussels Sprouts
Rust on Beans

VOLCK® OIL SPRAY

GENERAL DESCRIPTION:
A liquid dormant and growing season insect spray that controls scale insects, mealybugs, and red spider mites on ornamentals, citrus, fruits, and palms, and in greenhouses. It also acts as a leaf polish to brighten the leaves of hardy houseplants, and helps to suffocate listed insect eggs. It can be combined with ORTHO Orthorix® Spray for a winter spray on dormant deciduous fruits, roses, and ornamentals. Or combine it with ORTHO Malathion 50 Insect Spray for improved insect control on citrus, avocados, mangos, gardenias, and ixora. It is also effective in removing sooty mold fungus by controlling whitefly larvae.

AREAS SOLD:
Midwest
Northeast
South

ACTIVE INGREDIENT:
97% Petroleum Oil

KILLS THESE INSECTS:
Codling Moth Eggs
Lacebug Larvae
Mealybugs
Oak Moth Eggs
Red Spider Mites
Red Spider Mite Eggs
Scales
Whitefly Larvae

FOR USE IN THESE AREAS:
Trees and shrubs
Fruits
Greenhouses

VOLCK® SUPREME OIL SPRAY

GENERAL DESCRIPTION:
A liquid dormant and growing season spray used to control scale insects, mealybugs, and red spider mites on ornamentals, citrus, fruits, and palms, and in greenhouses. It also removes sooty mold fungus by controlling whitefly larvae. It can also be used as a spreader-sticker in other insecticidal and fungicidal sprays to increase the effectiveness of the spray. It is easily applied with an ORTHO Spray-ette garden hose sprayer or any tank-type or power sprayer. Mix with ORTHO Orthorix® Spray for a combination winter spray on deciduous fruits, roses, and ornamentals. It can also be mixed with ORTHO Isotox® Insect Killer for additional effectiveness on ornamental shrubs.

AREAS SOLD:
West

ACTIVE INGREDIENT:
98% Petroleum Oil

KILLS THESE INSECTS:
Mealybugs
Red Spider Mites
Scales
Whiteflies

FOR USE IN THESE AREAS:
Trees and shrubs
Fruits and citrus
Greenhouses

WHITEFLY & MEALYBUG KILLER

GENERAL DESCRIPTION:
A liquid designed to control all the major houseplant pests, including hard-to-kill mealybugs, whiteflies, and two-spotted spider mites. It kills on contact, so pests must be sprayed directly. This spray can be used on the listed plants indoors or out. The ready-to-use container with hand-pump nozzle makes treating both the upper and lower surfaces of the leaves a quick and easy task. Repeat the treatment if needed, but not more frequently than every 7 days.

AREAS SOLD:
National

ACTIVE INGREDIENT:
0.050% Resmethrin (5-[Phenyl-methyl]-3-furanyl) methyl 2,2-dimethyl-3-(2-methyl-1-propenyl) cyclopropane-carboxylate

KILLS THESE INSECTS:
Aphids
Mealybugs
Scales (Crawlers)
Two-spotted Spider Mites
Whiteflies

FOR USE ON THESE PLANTS:
Aluminum Plant
Asparagus Fern
African Violet
Angelwing Begonia
Bird's-nest Fern
Bird's-nest Sansevieria
Bloodleaf
Boston Fern
Coleus
Coral Berry
Dieffenbachia
Dracaena
English Ivy
False Aralia
Fiddle Leaf Philodendron
Fluffy Ruffles
Fuchsia
Geranium
Holly Fern
Ivy Geranium
Jade Plant
Japanese Aralia
Kalanchoe
Lace Fern
Marigold
Neanthe Bella Palm
Needle Point Ivy
Nephthytis
Parlor Palm
Peperomia
Philodendron
Piggyback Plant
Polka Dot Plant
Pothos
Prayer Plant
Purple Passion
Ribbon Plant
Rubber Plant
St. Katherine's Ivy
Salvia
Schefflera
Shasta Daisy
Silver Tree
Spider Plant
Sprengeri Fern
Strawberry Begonia
Swedish Ivy
Table Fern
Variegated Spider Plant
Variegated Vanilla
Wandering Jew
Wax Plant
Weeping Fig
Zebra Plant

FOR USE IN THESE AREAS:
Houseplants

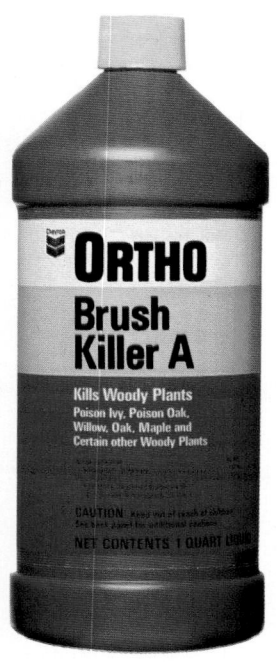

KILLS THESE PLANTS:
Ash
Beech
Hickory
Oak
Poison Ivy
Poison Oak
Sweet Gum
Willow
and other woody
    perennial plants

FOR USE IN THESE AREAS:
Noncrop areas

BRUSH KILLER A

GENERAL DESCRIPTION:
A liquid concentrate containing the proven ingredient *AMS*, formulated for the control of a broad range of woody perennial plants, vines, and trees, including poison ivy and poison oak. It mixes with water and can be applied to the leaves and stems with a tank-type sprayer, or used undiluted directly on stumps to prevent resprouting.
Important: nonselective — do not apply on desirable plants.

AREAS SOLD:
National

ACTIVE INGREDIENT:
43% AMS *Ammonium sulfamate*

HINTS FOR USE:
For killing trees too large to spray, or 6 inches or more in diameter, the frill method is recommended. Make a frill by using an ax to cut overlapping notches in a continuous ring around the tree trunk near its base. Cut through the bark but do not remove the chips. Pour in as much undiluted material as the frill will hold.

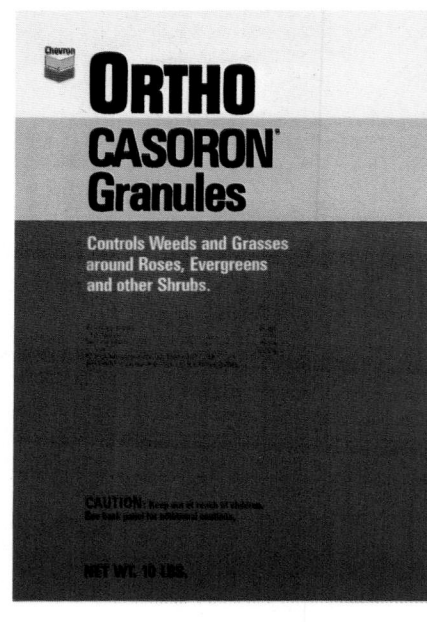

KILLS THESE PLANTS:
Annual Bluegrass
Carpetweed
Chickweed
Crabgrass
Foxtail
Groundsel
Henbit
Horsetail
Knotweed
Lamb's-quarters
Pigweed
Pineapple Weed
Purslane
Mustard
Shepherds Purse
Smartweed

FOR USE IN THESE AREAS:
Trees and shrubs
Roses

CASORON® GRANULES

GENERAL DESCRIPTION:
A granular pre-emergence weed killer designed to control annual and perennial weeds and grasses around roses, evergreens, and other shrubs and trees. Before applying, existing weeds should be removed and the soil worked and smoothed. Sprinkle the granules uniformly over the soil and water in lightly. Do not disturb soil in a treated area as long as the weed control program is being maintained.

AREAS SOLD:
West (Oregon, Washington, and Idaho)

ACTIVE INGREDIENT:
2.0% Dichlobenil *2,6-Dichlorobenzonitrile*

Casoron is a registered trademark of Thompson-Hayward Chemical Co.

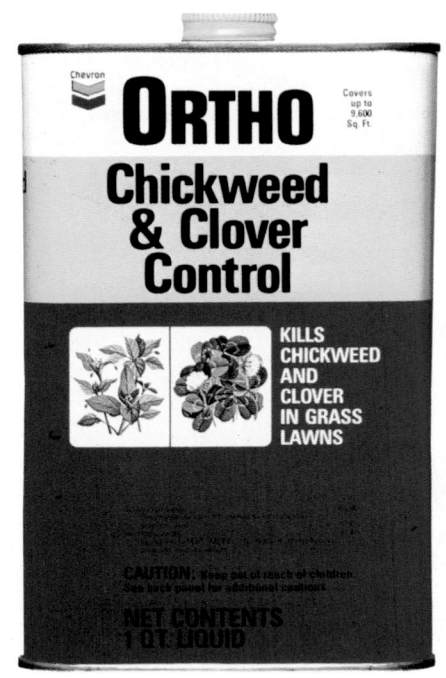

CHICKWEED & CLOVER CONTROL

GENERAL DESCRIPTION:
A liquid broadleaf weed killer concentrate to be mixed with water and applied with any ORTHO hose-end sprayer to control chickweed, clover, and a number of broadleaf weeds in grass lawns as listed. It can be used any time that weeds are actively growing; however, applications are most effective in the spring and fall when the weeds are small and temperatures are mild. For best results, apply when the air is calm in the morning (after the leaves are dry) on a sunny day when no rain is expected and the temperatures will not exceed 85°F for 24 hours. Water the lawn thoroughly 2 or 3 days before spraying, and do not water for 48 hours after application. When diluted, one quart of concentrate covers up to 9,600 square feet.

AREAS SOLD:
Midwest
Northeast
South

ACTIVE INGREDIENT:
14.6% MCPP *Dimethylamine salt of 2-(methyl-4-chlorophenoxy) propionic acid*

KILLS THESE PLANTS:
Clover
Common Chickweed
Dandelion
Dichondra
Ground Ivy
Knotweed
Lamb's-quarters
Mouseear Chickweed
Mustard
Pigweed
Plantain
Ragweed
Shepherds Purse

FOR USE IN THESE AREAS:
Lawns

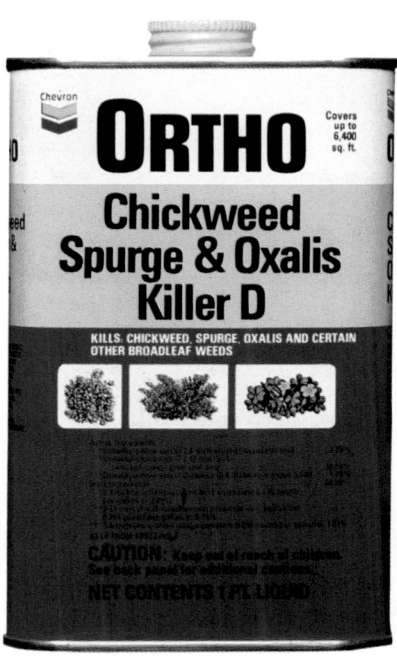

CHICKWEED, SPURGE & OXALIS KILLER D

GENERAL DESCRIPTION:
A liquid broadleaf weed killer concentrate that mixes with water; for best results, apply when weeds are small and tender. If weeds are older and harder to kill, use the higher rates listed on the label. This product is especially effective against the troublesome lawn weeds — spotted spurge, oxalis, chickweed, knotweed, sheep sorrel, and henbit. In addition to these, it kills virtually all broadleaf weeds. For best results, apply when the air is calm in the morning (after the leaves are dry) on a sunny day when no rain is expected for 24 hours. Water the lawn thoroughly 2 or 3 days before spraying. When diluted, one pint covers up to 6,400 square feet.

AREAS SOLD:
West

ACTIVE INGREDIENTS:
3.05% 2,4-D *Dimethylamine salt of 2,4-dichlorophenoxyacetic acid*
10.60% MCPP *Dimethylamine salt of 2-(2-methyl-4-chlorophenoxy) propionic acid*
1.30% Dicamba *Dimethylamine salt of Dicamba (3,6-dichloro-o-anisic acid)*

KILLS THESE PLANTS:
Bedstraw
Black Medic
Buckhorn
Bull Thistle
Burdock
Buttercup
Chicory
Chickweed
Clover
Cocklebur
Dandelion
Dock
Galinsoga
Ground Ivy
Hawkweed
Heal-all
Henbit
Knotweed
Lambsquarters
Lespedeza
Mallow
Morning Glory
Mustard
Oxalis
Peppergrass
Pigweed
Plantain
Poison Ivy
Poison Oak
Purslane
Ragweed
Sheep Sorrel
Shepherdspurse
Speedwell
Spurge
Tansy Mustard
Thistle
Velvet Leaf
Wild Carrot
Wild Garlic
Wild Lettuce
Wild Onion
Yarrow
and many other
    broadleaf weeds

FOR USE IN THESE AREAS:
Lawns

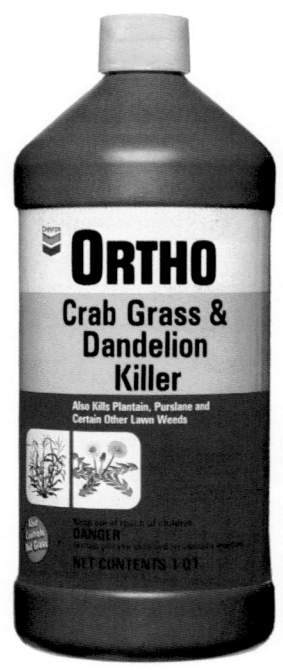

CONTAX®
WEED & GRASS KILLER

GENERAL DESCRIPTION:
A liquid, nonselective herbicide that top-kills weeds and grasses on contact. It becomes quickly inactivated on contact with the soil. It is designed for use around trees and shrubs, and in non-planted areas. It can also be used to control grasses and weeds before reseeding lawns. It is also used to kill winter weeds on dormant Bermudagrass lawns. Apply with an ORTHO Spray-ette, tank-type or power sprayer, or sprinkling can, depending on the area being treated. When the weather is sunny and warm, treated plants wilt in 1 to 3 days, with complete browning in 5 to 7 days. The herbicide will not stain gravel or paved areas.

AREAS SOLD:
National

ACTIVE INGREDIENTS:
10.40% Sodium cacodylate (*Sodium dimethylarsinate*)
1.77% Dimethylarsinic acid

CRAB GRASS &
DANDELION KILLER

GENERAL DESCRIPTION:
A liquid post-emergence herbicide that controls established crabgrass, dandelions, nutgrass, and other listed weeds in major turf grasses. It mixes readily with water as directed, to be applied with an ORTHO Spray-ette or tank-type sprayer with a coarse spray. For best results, apply when weeds are 1 to 2 inches tall and temperatures are below 90°F. Reseed bare spots 3 weeks after treatment. Do not apply to newly seeded lawns until after 3 mowings. Do not use on dichondra, St. Augustine, carpet, centipede, bahia, or bentgrass lawns. Avoid spray or drift onto nearby desirable plants.

AREAS SOLD:
Midwest
Northeast

ACTIVE INGREDIENTS:
8.0% Dodecylammonium methanearsonate
8.0% Octylammonium methanearsonate
7.67% 2,4-D *Octylammonium salt of 2,4-dichlorophenoxyacetic acid*

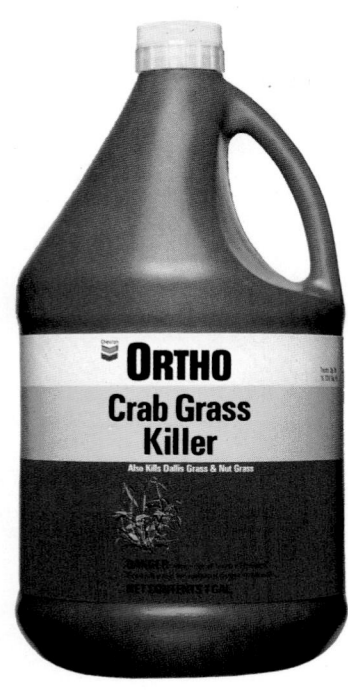

KILLS THESE WEEDS:
Crabgrass
Dallisgrass
Nutgrass

FOR USE IN THESE AREAS:
Lawns

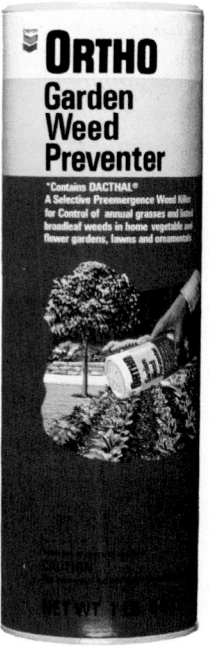

KILLS THESE PLANTS:
Annual Bluegrass
Barnyardgrass
Carpetweed
Common Chickweed
Crabgrass (Both Smooth and Large)
Florida Pusley
Goosegrass
Green and Yellow Foxtail
Johnsongrass (From Seed)
Lamb's-quarters
Lovegrass
Nodding Spurge
Pigweed
Purslane
Witchgrass

FOR USE IN THESE AREAS:
Lawns
Trees and shrubs
Vegetables and flowers

CRAB GRASS KILLER

GENERAL DESCRIPTION:
A liquid, selective post-emergence weed killer used to control crabgrass, dallisgrass, and nutgrass on all major turf grasses including dichondra, bent, and fescue grasses. One quart of concentrate mixes readily with water to treat up to 4,000 square feet. Apply it with an ORTHO Spray-ette or tank-type sprayer. For best results, treat when weeds are 1 to 2 inches tall. Control older weeds with repeated applications. This herbicide may be used on newly seeded lawns after 2 mowings. When the weeds are dead, remove and reseed bare spots. Do not use on St. Augustine, carpet, or centipede-grass lawns.

AREAS SOLD:
National

ACTIVE INGREDIENTS:
8% Octylammonium methanearsonate
8% Dodecylammonium methane-arsonate

GARDEN WEED PREVENTER

GENERAL DESCRIPTION:
A granular pre-emergence herbicide used to prevent annual grasses and broadleafed weeds from becoming established in lawns and flower gardens and around trees, shrubs, and vegetables as listed on the label. Use this herbicide at seeding or transplanting time and around established plants as directed. When applied according to label directions, it keeps treated areas free of listed weeds for up to 4 months.

AREAS SOLD:
National

ACTIVE INGREDIENT:
5% DCPA
Dimethyltetrachloroterephthalate

HINTS FOR USE:
Pre-emergence herbicides kill only germinating seedlings, not existing weeds. So for best results clean all weeds from the area to be treated, and cultivate. Then spread the herbicide immediately and rake it into the top 1 or 2 inches of soil, or water lightly. The herbicide forms a barrier on the soil that kills seedlings. Disturbing the soil after application reduces the herbicide's effectiveness.

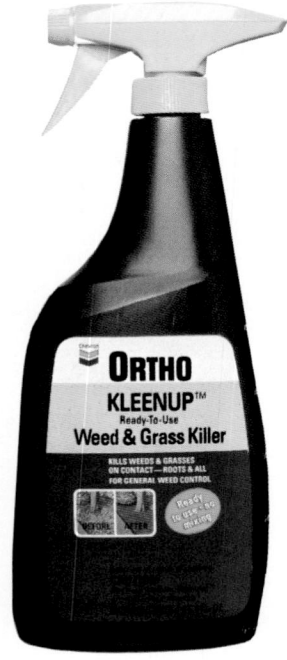

KLEENUP™ READY-TO-USE WEED & GRASS KILLER

GENERAL DESCRIPTION:
A premixed liquid formulation for spot application to individual weeds around trees and shrubs, in flowerbeds, lawns, walks, driveways, gravel, or bark mulches. It contains the nonselective herbicide *glyphosate* in a ready-to-use container with a hand-trigger sprayer. The weed killer moves systemically through the plant, killing tops and roots. Its killing action is inactivated on contact with soil to prevent harming the roots of surrounding trees and shrubs. Treated lawn areas can be reseeded 7 days after application. Most weeds begin to show symptoms within a week, with complete kill in 2 to 4 weeks. The container can be refilled with ORTHO Kleenup® Systemic Weed & Grass Killer.

AREAS SOLD:
National

ACTIVE INGREDIENT:
0.50 % Glyphosate *N-(phosphono-methyl)glycine*

FOR USE IN THESE AREAS:
Flower beds and lawns
Trees and shrubs
Noncrop areas

KILLS THESE WEEDS:
Annuals:
Annual Bluegrass
Chickweed
Common Fiddleneck
Common Ragweed
Cudweed
Evening Primrose
Florida Pusley
Garden Spurge
Goosegrass
Green Foxtail
Hairy Crabgrass
Henbit
Lamb's-quarters
Large Crabgrass
London Rocket
Mayweed
Oxalis
Prickly Lettuce
Prostrate Knotweed
Prostrate Pigweed
Puncture Vine
Purslane
Red Dead Nettle
Redroot Pigweed
Sandspur
Shepherds Purse
Smartweed
Smooth Crabgrass
Sowthistle
Velvetweed
Wild Geranium
Biennials and Perennials:
Bahiagrass
Bentgrass
Bermudagrass
Blackseed Plantain
Brownseed Paspalum
Buckhorn Plantain
Bull Thistle
Canada Thistle
Centipedegrass
Clover
Common Mullein
Common Plantain
Creeping Beggarweed
Creeping Charlie
Creeping Lantana
Dandelion
Dogfennel
False Dandelion
Field Bindweed (Wild Morning Glory)
Hypericum
Johnsongrass
Kentucky Bluegrass
Nimblewill
Nutgrass (Nutsedge)
Orchardgrass
Poison Ivy
Poison Oak
Quackgrass
Ragweed
St. Augustinegrass
Sour Dock
Spurge
Tall Fescue
Tall Thistle (Field Thistle)
Torpedograss
Virginia Creeper
Wild Blackberry
Wild Carrot
Yellow Oxalis
Zoysiagrass

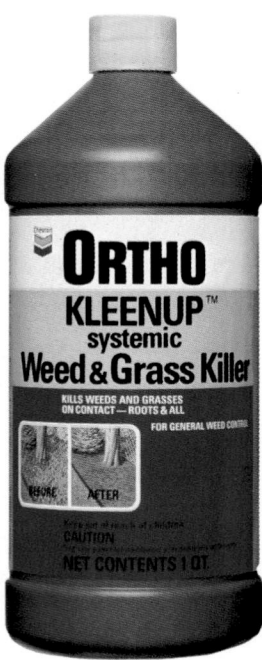

KLEENUP™ SYSTEMIC WEED & GRASS KILLER

GENERAL DESCRIPTION:
A liquid, nonselective herbicide that controls annual and perennial grasses, weeds, and other unwanted vegetation. Also use it for spot treatment in lawns. It contains the proven herbicide *glyphosate*, which moves systemically through the plant, killing tops and roots. Its killing power is inactivated on contact with soil, so the roots of surrounding trees and shrubs are not harmed. Treated lawn areas can be tilled and seeded after 7 days. Treated plants generally begin to show symptoms within a week, with complete kill in 2 to 4 weeks. All use as a refill for ORTHO Kleenup® Ready-To-Use Weed & Grass Killer.

AREAS SOLD:
National

ACTIVE INGREDIENT:
5.00 % Glyphosate *N-(phosphono-methyl) glycine*

FOR USE IN THESE AREAS:
Trees and shrubs
Flower beds and lawns
Noncrop areas

KILLS THESE WEEDS:
Bahiagrass
Bentgrass
Bermudagrass
Bindweed (Wild Morning Glory)
Blackberries
Black Medic
Bluegrass
Blue Toadflax
Brassbuttons
Broadleaf Plantain
Bromegrass
Burclover
Canada Thistle
Chickweed
Common Groundsel
Common Plantain
Crabgrasses
Creeping Beggarweed
Creeping Bentgrass
Creeping Charlie
Curly Dock
Dandelion
Diffuse Lovegrass
Dog Fennel
Evening Primrose
False Dandelion
Fennel
Fescue
Fiddleneck
Filaree
Florida Pusley
Garden Spurge
Henbit
Johnsongrass
Knotweed
Lamb's-quarters
Little Bittercress
London Rocket
Maiden Cane
Mallow
Mayweed
Mouseear Chickweed
Nimblewill
Oldenlandia
Orchardgrass
Oxalis
Pennsylvania Smartweed
Pennywort
Perennial Ryegrass
Poison Ivy
Poison Oak
Primrose
Prostrate Spurge
Puncture Vine
Quackgrass
Ragweed
Sandspur
Shepherds Purse
Smooth Cat's Ear
Sowthistle
Spotted Spurge
St. Augustinegrass
Tall Fescue
Torpedograss
White Clover
Whitetop
Wild Barley
Yellow Nutgrass
Zoysia

KILLS THESE WEEDS:
All weeds and grasses

FOR USE IN THESE AREAS:
Trees and shrubs
Noncrop areas

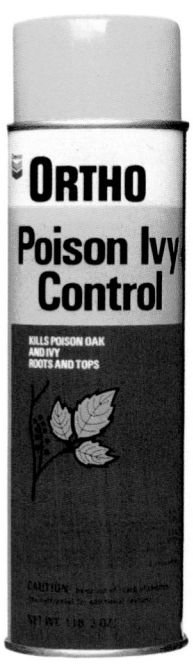

KILLS THESE PLANTS:
Poison Ivy
Poison Oak

FOR USE IN THESE AREAS:
Noncrop areas

LIQUID FENCE & GRASS EDGER

GENERAL DESCRIPTION:
A liquid, nonselective, ready-to-use contact herbicide that top-kills weeds and grasses. Its killing action is quickly inactivated on contact with soil so it won't sterilize the soil or harm the roots of nearby shrubs and trees. It controls unwanted plants around trees, shrubs, and buildings, in brick and gravel walks, in patios, and along fences, sidewalks, driveways, curbs, and gutters. To apply, simply attach the applicator cap and invert the jug. One gallon of liquid covers up to 200 square feet. It does not stain gravel or paved areas. In warm (above 80°F), sunny weather, wilting occurs in 1 to 3 days, with complete browning in 5 to 7 days.

AREAS SOLD:
National

ACTIVE INGREDIENTS:
2.27% Sodium cacodylate *Sodium dimethylarsinate*
0.39% Dimethylarsinic Acid

HINTS FOR USE:
A contact herbicide kills only the top growth of weeds. The roots remain alive, and in time new shoots will emerge, requiring additional treatments.

POISON IVY CONTROL

GENERAL DESCRIPTION:
An easy-to-use aerosol for controlling poison ivy and poison oak around homes and buildings, along fence rows, in vacant lots, and on tree trunks. It contains two proven selective herbicides, 2,4-D and MCPP, that are translocated throughout the entire plant, killing roots and tops. An added foam marker helps ensure complete coverage of all leaves. In warm, sunny summer weather, the treated leaves turn brown in 10 days to 2 weeks after spraying. Discard dead plants in sealed plastic bags. Wear rubber gloves whenever handling poison ivy or poison oak, whether it is alive or dead. Discard the gloves after use, since irritating oils may remain potent for months.

AREAS SOLD:
Midwest
Northeast

ACTIVE INGREDIENTS:
0.70% 2,4-D *Diethanolamine salt of 2,4-Dichlorophenoxyacetic acid*
0.75% MCPP *Diethanolamine salt of 2-(2-Methyl-4-chlorophenoxy) propionic acid*

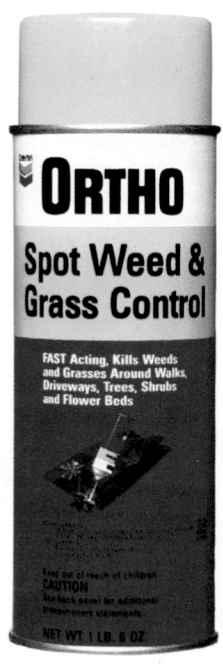

KILLS THESE PLANTS:
Poison Ivy
Poison Oak

FOR USE IN THESE AREAS:
Noncrop areas

KILLS THESE WEEDS:
Annual Bluegrass
Bermudagrass
Bullgrass
Chickweed
Clover
Crabgrass
Dandelions
Docks
Florida Pusley
Foxtail
Goosegrass
Henbit
Lamb's-quarters
Nimblewill
Nutgrass
Orchardgrass
Oxalis
Plantains
Poison Ivy
Ragweed
Spurge
Tall Fescue
Velvetgrass
Wild Oats

POISON OAK & POISON IVY KILLER

GENERAL DESCRIPTION:
An easy-to-use aerosol for controlling poison ivy and poison oak around homes and buildings, along fence rows, in vacant lots, and on tree trunks. It contains two proven selective herbicides, 2,4-D and MCPP, that are translocated throughout the entire plant, killing roots and tops. An added foam marker helps ensure complete coverage of all leaves. In warm and sunny summer weather, the treated leaves turn brown in 10 days to 2 weeks after spraying. Discard dead plants in sealed plastic bags. Wear rubber gloves whenever handling poison ivy or poison oak, whether it is alive or dead. Discard the gloves after use, since irritating oils may remain potent for months.

AREAS SOLD:
South
West

ACTIVE INGREDIENT:
0.70% 2,4-D *Diethanolamine salt of 2,4-Dichlorophenoxyacetic acid*
0.75% MCPP *Diethanolamine salt of 2-(2-Methyl-4-chlorophenoxy) propionic acid*

SPOT WEED & GRASS CONTROL

GENERAL DESCRIPTION:
An aerosol specially formulated for spot application on individual weeds in lawns, foundation plantings, walks, driveways, and for edging grass around flowerbeds, trees, posts, and shrubs. It contains *paraquat*, a fast-acting contact herbicide that becomes inactivated on contact with soil. It kills annual broadleaf weeds and grasses and top-kills and suppresses perennial weeds including dandelions, nutgrass, and poison ivy. It is effective whenever weeds and grasses are green, but for best results, apply when they are small.

AREAS SOLD:
National

ACTIVE INGREDIENT:
0.276% Paraquat dichloride *1,1' Dimethyl-4,4'-bipyridinum dichloride*

HINTS FOR USE:
Nonselective herbicides kill any vegetation they contact. To avoid serious damage on nearby desirable plants, spray on a nonwindy day, or in the late evening or early morning when the air is still. Protect surrounding plants from the spray with cardboard, plastic, or tarpaper shields.

FOR USE IN THESE AREAS:
Trees and shrubs
Flower beds and lawns
Noncrop areas

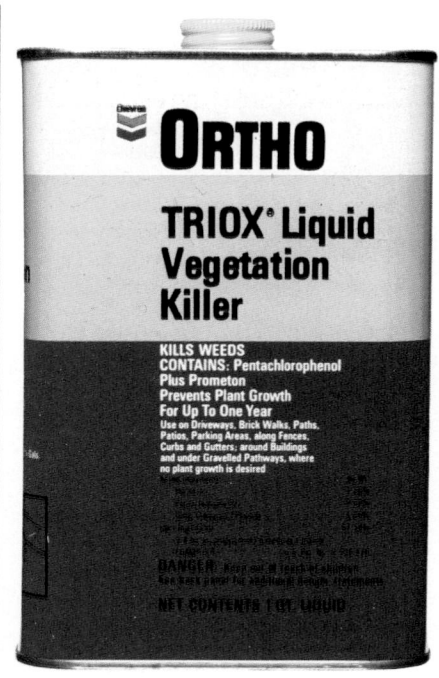

KILLS THESE PLANTS:

Wild Morning Glory
Bermudagrass
Johnsongrass
And all other
    vegetation

FOR USE IN THESE AREAS:

Noncrop areas

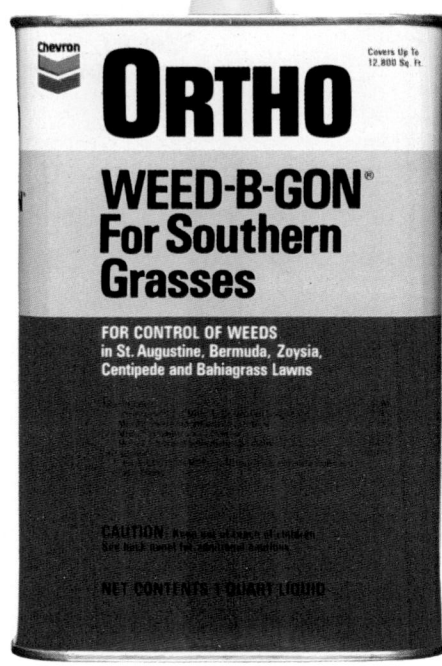

KILLS THESE WEEDS:

Black Medic
Bracted Plantain
Chickweed
Clover
Cudweed
Dichondra
Evening Primrose
Florida Betony
Florida Pusley
Oxalis
Pigweed
Purslane
Sensitive Mimosa
Shepherds Purse
Sow Thistle
Spurge
Toadflax
Wild Geranium

FOR USE IN THESE AREAS:

Lawns

TRIOX® LIQUID VEGETATION KILLER

GENERAL DESCRIPTION:

A liquid semi-soil-sterilant containing *prometon*, designed to kill existing vegetation and prevent plant growth for up to a year after treatment. Use it only in areas where plant growth is unwanted, such as driveways, brick walks, gravel pathways, patios, parking areas, along fences, curbs and gutters, and in cracks in sidewalks. Do not apply over root systems of desirable plants. Treat any time, but for best results apply to bare soil or just as new growth emerges in the spring. See label for detailed instructions.

AREAS SOLD:

National

ACTIVE INGREDIENT:

1.86% Prometon *2-Methoxy-4,6-bix(iso-propylamino)-s-triazine*

HINTS FOR USE:

If the weeds are taller than 5 inches, cut them down and remove before application. If no rain has fallen after 2 to 3 days, water thoroughly to help move the herbicide into the soil. Do not apply to slopes or where desired vegetation is to be grown in the future.

WEED-B-GON® FOR SOUTHERN GRASSES

GENERAL DESCRIPTION:

A liquid herbicide containing MCPP and designed for control of broadleaf weeds in St. Augustine, Bermuda, zoysia, centipede, and bahiagrass lawns. When used as directed, it does not injure the lawn grass, and controls a wide range of broadleaf weeds including hard-to-kill oxalis, spurge, and wild geranium. One quart of concentrate diluted as directed covers up to 12,800 square feet. For best results, apply with an ORTHO Spray-ette or tank-type sprayer. Treated weeds may remain green for 2 to 3 weeks following the application. Complete kill may take 4 to 6 weeks. Do not use on dichondra, lippia, clover, bluegrass, or fescue lawns, or around desirable plants.

AREAS SOLD:

South

ACTIVE INGREDIENTS:

17.74% MCPP *Isooctyl ester of 2-(2-Methyl-4-chlorophenoxy) propionic acid*
2.70% *Methyl 2-chloro-9-hydroxyfluorene-9-carboxylate*
0.65% *Methyl 9-hydroxyfluorene-9-carboxylate*
0.49% *Methyl 2,7 dichloro-9-hydroxyfluorene-9-carboxylate*

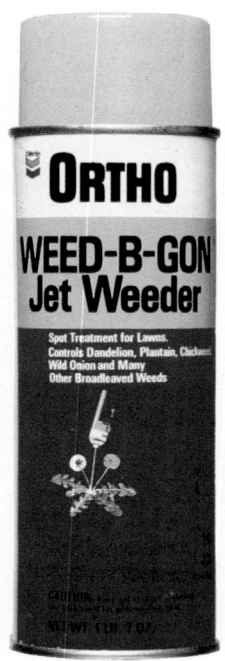

KILLS THESE WEEDS:

Annual Morning
  Glory
Chickweed
Cinquefoil
Clovers
Dandelions
Ground Ivy
Henbit
Knotweed
Pennywort
Plantain
Poison Ivy
Poison Oak
Purslane
Spotted Spurge
Thistles
Wild Onion

FOR USE IN THESE AREAS:

Lawns

WEED·B·GON® JET WEEDER

GENERAL DESCRIPTION:

A clean, easy-to-use aerosol for spot treating individual broadleaf weeds in most grass lawns. It produces a foamy white lather for direct weed contact and to avoid drift. The foam also serves as a marker to prevent repeated applications. This herbicide is effective on persistent broadleaf weeds including chickweed, thistles, annual morningglory, and dandelions. It contains 2,4-D and MCPP, hormonal weed killers that cause susceptible weeds to shrivel up and disappear. One application kills most weeds listed.

AREAS SOLD:

National

ACTIVE INGREDIENTS:

0.70% 2,4-D *Diethanolamine salt of 2,4-Dichlorophenoxyacetic acid*
0.75% MCPP *Diethanolamine salt of 2-(2-Methyl-4-chlorophenoxy) propionic acid*

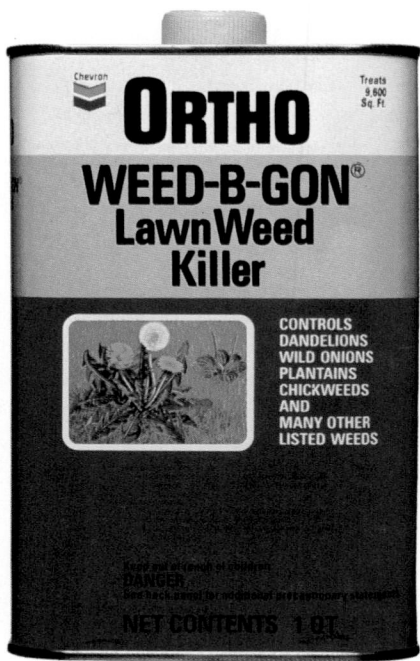

KILLS THESE WEEDS:

Annuals:
Black Medic
Carpetweed
Clover
Common Chickweed
Creeping
  Beggarweed
Fennel
Fleabane
Florida Pusley
Hawkweed
Lamb's-quarters
Mallow
Mouseear Chickweed
Oxalis
Pigweed
Purslane
Ragweed
Shepherds Purse
Smartweed
Sow Thistle
Speedwell
Spurge
Wild Geranium
*Biennials and
  Perennials:*
Buckhorn Plantain
Canada Thistle
Common Burdock
Common Plantain
Curly Dock
Dandelion
Dichondra
Ground Ivy
Lawn Pennywort
Lippia
Morningglory
Oxalis
Sheep Sorrel
Thistles
Wild Carrot
Wild Garlic
Wild Onion
Yarrow

FOR USE IN THESE AREAS:

Lawns

WEED·B·GON® LAWN WEED KILLER

GENERAL DESCRIPTION:

A liquid formulation containing 2,4-D and MCPP that effectively controls broadleaf weeds in most grass lawns. It singles out broadleaf weeds growing among grasses and, without injuring the grasses, kills the weeds from the tops right down to the roots. Susceptible weeds shrivel up and disappear completely. One quart of concentrate mixes readily with water to treat up to 9,600 square feet. Apply this herbicide with an ORTHO hose-end sprayer. It can be used on newly seeded lawns after three mowings. Reseed bare treated spots 3 to 4 weeks after the treatment. Do not apply to dichondra, lippia, St. Augustine, or clover lawns.

AREAS SOLD:

National

ACTIVE INGREDIENTS:

10.8% 2,4-D *Dimethylamine salt of 2,4-dichlorophenoxyacetic acid*
11.6% MCPP *Dimethylamine salt of 2-(2-methyl-4-chlorophenoxy) propionic acid*

BROADCAST SPREADER

The broadcast spreader distributes granular materials and grass seed in a wide arc in all directions across the lawn and garden. Designed for use on large areas, it covers a larger area more efficiently than does a drop spreader. It is useful on nonlevel surfaces for fertilizing landscaped beds, vegetable gardens, and other large areas. The broadcast spreader consists of a hopper, agitator, and spinning disc. The sturdy plastic hopper holds up to 55 pounds of fertilizer, and won't rust or corrode. The shape of the hopper allows the fertilizer bag to be tipped, package and all, into the hopper, preventing blowing, spilling, and extra handling of the material. As you begin walking with the spreader, the material moves down the hopper to the agitator, which ensures that the material flows evenly onto the spinning disc. The spinning disc broadcasts the material in a uniform pattern from 6 to 16 feet in diameter. Fertilizers are usually broadcast about 10 to 12 feet. The micrometer setting for the disc is easily adjusted for dispensing almost any kind of fertilizer, pesticide, or seed. The on-off control is located on the T-bar handle. To keep the spreader clean, hose off the hopper after each use. Occasionally lubricate the wheel bearings and rotor shaft lightly. The drive gear unit is self-lubricating and needs no servicing. The ORTHO Broadcast Spreader is covered by a limited 4-year parts guarantee.

DROP SPREADER

The drop spreader is designed to apply granular fertilizers, insecticides, and grass seed on small to medium-sized lawns and gardens. It distributes the material in a path as wide as the spreader itself. The spreader consists of a hopper, agitator bar, and shutoff blade. The sturdy plastic hopper holds up to 55 pounds of fertilizer. As you begin walking with the hopper open, the fertilizer or other material falls down the hopper onto the agitator bar. This bar ensures that the material flows evenly through the hopper opening onto the ground. The shutoff blade that opens and closes the hopper is made of nonrusting stainless steel; the on-off control for this blade is located on the T-bar handle. The micrometer setting that regulates the size of the hopper opening can be adjusted easily for dispensing many different kinds of fertilizers, pesticides, and grass seed. The plastic wheels provide good traction on both grass and dichondra lawns, and will not deteriorate from weather or fertilizers. Keep the hopper clean by washing with tap water after each use. Lubricate the wheel bearings and shutoff blade with a light oil. The ORTHO Drop Spreader is covered by a limited 4-year parts guarantee.

Using a drop spreader:
1. Fill the spreader off the lawn.
2. Open the hopper only after you have begun walking.
3. Make two passes at each end of the lawn first, as a turn-around space, and then go back and forth the long way.
4. Close the hopper on the turns.
5. Overlap the wheel marks on adjacent passes.
6. Calibrate the spreader occasionally to make sure it is dropping the correct amount of fertilizer. To calibrate, mark out an area of 100 square feet (10' × 10') on the driveway or patio. Spread the fertilizer over the marked area with the spreader adjusted to the proper setting. Sweep up and weigh the fertilizer in the measured area. It should be within 10 percent of what the bag says should be spread per 100 square feet. If it is too much or too little, try another setting and test again.

INSECT FOGGER

This device is designed to fog outdoor areas with insecticides to control flies, gnats, mosquitoes, and other pests. The main components of the fogger are an insecticide jar, pressurized propane cylinder, coil, and trigger. A recommended insecticide such as ORTHO Fogging Insecticide is poured into the jar, which is then attached to the bottom of the fogger. The propane cylinder attaches to the rear of the fogger and serves as the fuel source to vaporize the liquid insecticide into a fog. When the propane valve is opened, propane flows from the cylinder into the shroud where a burner unit heats the coil. The fogger is ignited by holding a lighted match under the tip of the coil. Pressure on the trigger activates the pump inside the insecticide jar, causing the material to flow up to and through the heated coil. The insecticide then emerges as a fog from the nozzle. For the most effective fog, pump the fogger once every 3 or 4 seconds. Safety features on this fogger include a safety button and an "on-off" fuel valve. The safety button engages the trigger lock to prevent accidental pumping of insecticide into the coil.

Reading a pesticide label:
Federal law requires that the following information be stated on a pesticide label.
1. Product name
2. Kind of formulation
3. Active ingredients
4. A statement of hazard to people and wildlife
   Caution — relatively safe
   Warning — intermediately toxic
   Danger — toxic
5. Environmental Protection Agency registration number
6. The manufacturer or formulator
7. The type of pesticide (insecticide, fungicide, herbicide, etc.) or its purpose
8. Net contents
9. General information and directions for use

LAWN AND GARDEN SPRAYER

This hose-end sprayer is designed to apply pesticides and fertilizers to plants throughout the garden. It is actually two sprayers in one, with two separate proportioners or dilution ratios. One solution (soil setting) allows for a maximum amount of water, to carry the sprayed material into the soil. This setting has a 15 gallon capacity and a dilution ratio of 60:1. The other proportion (foliage setting) allows for a minimum amount of water, to prevent washing the spray off the leaves during application. This setting has a capacity of 6 gallons and a dilution ratio of 24:1. The jar sprayer is made of shatterproof, noncorrodible plastic, and works on water pressure as low as 25 pounds. The jar has a wide mouth and a broad flat base for easy filling. An automatic "fill" button on the side of the lid allows you to add water to the concentrate in the jar while the sprayer is connected to the hose.

Mixing pesticides and fertilizers:
Dilute the product according to the label directions. Measure accurately and level, using the measuring spoons and cups for these chemicals only. Wearing rubber gloves is suggested.
  Wettable powders: Make a thin paste first by mixing the measured amount of powder with a small amount of water. Then add this paste to the required amount of water in the sprayer. Always handle wettable powders upwind to help avoid inhaling any dust. Keep the solution agitated while spraying to prevent the powder from coming out of solution. If your sprayer doesn't have an agitator, shake the mixture occasionally.
  Emulsifiable concentrates and oils: Measure the specified amount into the sprayer. Then slowly add the required amount of water, being careful not to splash or spill any of the mixture. Although these materials do not need as frequent agitation as do wettable powders, shake periodically to keep them from separating.
  Water-soluble fertilizers: Measure the specified amount into the sprayer, bucket, or watering can. Add the required amount of water and shake or stir to mix.

LAWN SPRAYER

This hose-end sprayer is designed to spray fungicides, insecticides, and herbicides on lawns, and to foliar-feed ornamentals and lawns. The garden hose provides the pressure to suction material from the jar through the siphon tube, into the mixing jets, and then through the nozzle and onto the plant. The sprayer is designed with a 60:1 dilution ratio to accurately dilute the product with the large volume of water necessary to carry liquid fertilizers down to the root zone, or to apply other garden chemicals that must be carried into the soil with sufficient water. It operates on all water pressures from 20 to 90 pounds. The wide-mouthed plastic jar is easy to fill, and has a spray capacity of 15 gallons. The thumb-controlled valve shuts off the water supply, and in the "on" position sprays a mixture of water and spray material. A swivel hose-nut connector with an antisiphoning device enables you to connect the hose to a filled jar without spilling any material or twisting the hose.

Cleaning a clogged sprayer:
Sprayers fail to work when they are clogged by undissolved pesticides, soil, or garden debris. To unclog the sprayer, insert the cleaning wire provided in the sprayer jet with a small amount of water running. Move the cleaner straight in and out a few times to scrape loose the material that has caked or dried in the spray jet hole. Finish cleaning with a final back flush. Poke out any material that may be clogging the breather hole on the sprayer lid. To prevent getting soil and garden debris in the sprayer, do not place the sprayer on the bare ground, and clean the end of the hose before each connection.

SPRAY-ETTE 4

This hose-end sprayer applies up to 4 gallons of diluted spray to trees and shrubs, lawns, flowers, or vegetables. Your garden hose provides the pressure that develops the suction to force the spray material from the jar, to the mixing jets, and out the nozzle onto the plant. The sprayer mixes water with the spray material in a ratio of 24:1, and operates on all water pressures from 20 to 90 pounds. The thumb-controlled valve on the lid shuts off the water supply, and in the "on" position sprays a mixture of water and spray material. The deflector on the end of the nozzle can be pushed in or out of the spray stream for a fan-shaped or straight spray pattern. It can also be turned 360° to spray up, down, or sideways to treat all plant surfaces. The hose connector rotates so that a full sprayer can be attached to the hose without spilling any material or twisting the hose. The antisiphoning device in the connector prevents any spray material from being sucked back down the hose in case of a sudden drop in water pressure.

When to spray:
To control the army of insects and diseases that destroy your garden, spray thoroughly at the first signs of damage and repeat as necessary. For best results, spray when the insects are most active so that the insecticide will kill them more rapidly. Avoid spraying in the heat of the day during hot summer months because of the possibility of injury to the foliage. Irrigate plants the day before you spray during summer weather because thirsty plants will absorb spray material, which could burn the leaves and damage the plant.

SUPER SIX SPRAY·ETTE

This hose-end sprayer is especially designed with an elongated nozzle shaft for spraying the tops of trees and inside shrubs and hedges. It has a 6-gallon spray capacity, and operates on all water pressures from 25 to 90 pounds. The wide-mouth jar and sprayer lid are made of shatterproof plastic that won't corrode. With the pressure of the garden hose, the sprayer automatically mixes water with the material in a ratio of 24:1. The "on-off" valve that controls the water supply is easily controlled by thumb. The deflector on the nozzle tip is adjustable for a fan-shaped or straight spray. It also turns 360° to spray up, down, and sideways to cover all plant surfaces. The hose-nut connector with an antisiphoning device swivels so a full sprayer can be attached to the hose without spilling any material or twisting the hose. The antisiphoning device prevents any spray from being sucked back down the hose in case of a sudden drop in water pressure.

How to spray trees and shrubs:
Using as much pressure as possible, spray the plant until the excess spray begins to drip off. The spray that drips off isn't wasted, since it wets the leaves, grass, and soil under the plant where insects often live. It is important to get thorough coverage of the plant when you spray. The sucking insects that are not actually hit by the spray, and the chewing insects that feed on untreated areas of leaves, are still alive. Insects not killed can spread new infestations. Spray more than just the outside foliage. Spray the trunks, branches, and leaves. Get into the main trunk area of densely-leaved shrubs and hedges. Be sure to spray both sides of the leaves, because many insects are found on the undersides. Adjust the nozzle so the spray is directed upward.

TRACTOR PULL SPREADER

This broadcast spreader attaches easily to the back of any size riding lawn mower or tractor for easy application of granular material including fertilizers, insecticides, and grass seed to large lawns and gardens. The spreader consists of a hopper, agitator, and spinning disc. The plastic hopper holds up to 55 pounds of fertilizer, and is easy to fill with no spilling and no tipping. When the spreader is moving and the spinning disc is rotating, the material flows down the hopper to the agitator. The agitation ensures that the material flows evenly from the hopper onto the spinning disc. The spinning disc then throws the material in a 6 to 16-foot-wide arc in all directions across the lawn or garden. Fertilizers are usually broadcast 10 to 12 feet. The micrometer setting that regulates the disc movement adjusts easily for dispensing many different kinds of granular material and grass seed. Hose off the spreader after each use to keep it clean. Occasionally lubricate the wheel bearings and the rotor shaft lightly. The drive gear is self-lubricating and needs no servicing. The ORTHO Tractor Pull Spreader is covered by a limited 4-year guarantee.

Here is a way to determine the area of your lawn or garden with about 5 percent accuracy:
Measure a long axis of the area. At every 10 feet on the length line measure the width at right angles to the length line. Total all widths and multiply by 10.

$$\text{Area} = (A_1A_2 + B_1B_2 + C_1C_2) \times 10$$
$$\text{Area} = (40' + 60' + 32') \times 10$$
$$\text{Area} = 132' \times 10'$$
$$\text{Area} = 1{,}320 \text{ square feet}$$

WHIRLYBIRD SPREADER

This hand-held broadcast spreader is designed for fertilizing lawns, groundcovers, landscaped beds, and vegetable gardens, and for seeding lawns. It consists of a hopper, crank handle, and broadcast wheel. The polypropylene hopper won't rust or corrode. As you turn the crank handle, the material flows from the hopper down onto the broadcast wheel. This rotating wheel throws the material outward in an 8 to 12-foot arc. For uniform coverage, walk at a comfortable, even pace, turning the handle one complete turn for each step forward with your right foot. There are four adjustable settings on the pistol-grip handle for dispensing different kinds of fertilizers and grass seed. The trigger control that opens and closes the hopper is also located on the handle for quick, easy use. The bearings are self-lubricating, and require no additional servicing. Keep the spreader clean and in good working order by washing it with tap water after each use. A 4-year guarantee accompanies this spreader.

Using a broadcast spreader:
1. Fill the spreader off the lawn, measuring the amount of fertilizer that is put into the hopper.
2. Spread that much fertilizer across the area listed on the bag. For example, if the bag says to apply 20 pounds of fertilizer per 1,000 square feet, and the hopper holds 10 pounds, measure off 500 square feet and spread the fertilizer evenly across it.
3. Overlap the patterns about a third of their width.
4. Open the hopper only when you are walking and the disc or plate is spinning.

WHIRLY DUSTER

This hand-held duster is designed for applying insecticide and fungicide dusts to vegetables, flowers, roses, shrubs, and small trees. It consists of a polypropylene hopper, crank handle, blower, and extension tubes. The nonrusting, noncorroding hopper holds up to 8 ounces of dust. The lid helps reduce contact with the material during use. As the crank handle is turned, the dust is propelled by the blower from the hopper down the elongated extension tubes and onto the plant. The deflector at the end of the tubes helps direct the material to avoid creating a cloud of dust. The tubes enable you to dust the undersides of the leaves and to reach inside and around shrubs. Dust is expelled only when the handle is turned. The pistol-grip handle ensures a firm, steady hold. The gears are nylon-fiberglass reinforced and require no special servicing. After dusting, wash the duster with tap water, turning the crank handle to clean the blower and the tubes.

Storing pesticides and equipment:
Store pesticides in their original containers. Do not put them in other containers, especially containers that are commonly used to store food or drink. Do not store any diluted solutions; make a new mixture for each use. Place the tightly sealed containers in a locked cabinet, room, or shed out of reach of children and pets. A dry, well-ventilated area where the temperature remains above freezing is best. Date the container when purchased, so outdated materials can be disposed of promptly. Store weedkillers containing *2,4-D* away from other pesticides, as the vapor may contaminate other materials. Thoroughly clean and dry all equipment at the end of the season. Lubricate any moving parts as specified in your instruction manual.

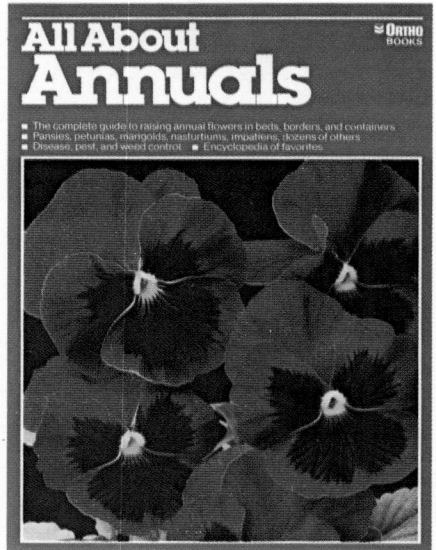

ORTHO's complete guide to raising favorite annuals in beds, borders, and containers. Disease, pest, and weed control. Encyclopedia of favorite annuals. Full color, 96 pages.

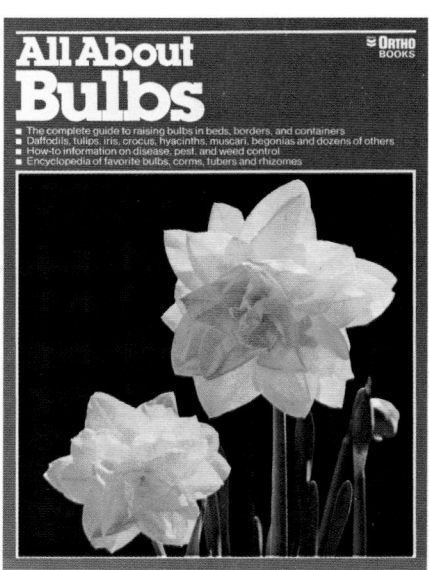

Learn how to design, plant, and care for a spectacular bulb garden that will please you every year. Complete encyclopedia of favorites. Full color, 96 pages.

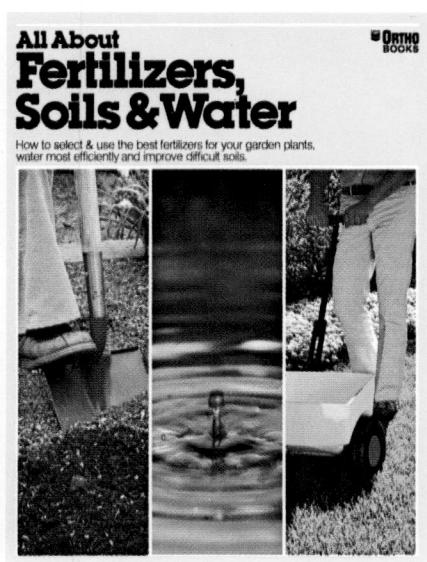

Learn how to select and apply fertilizers, improve your soil, and water effectively. Full color, 112 pages.

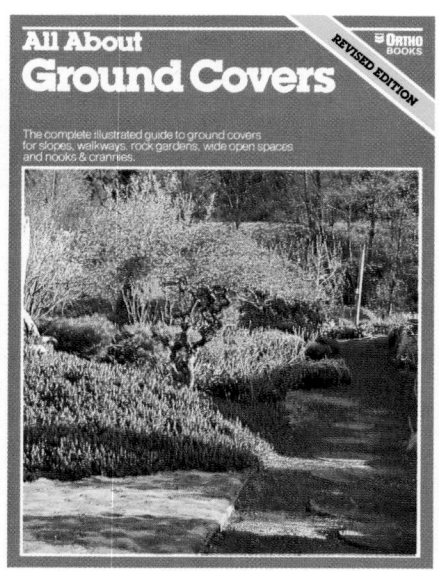

How to select and successfully grow plants that creep, mat, vine, or spread to cover the ground. Full color, 96 pages.

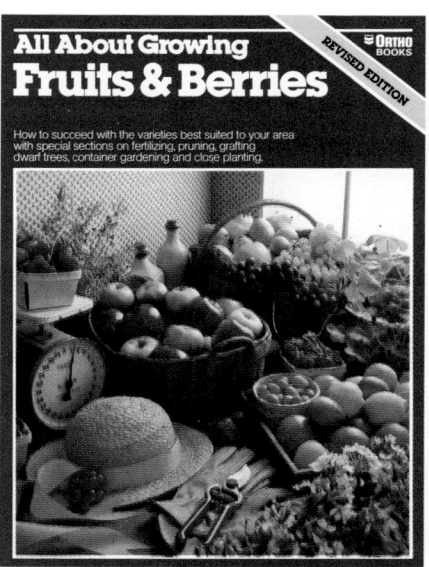

A guide to growing more than 25 different kinds of fruits and berries, with climate maps and pest and disease charts. Full color, 112 pages.

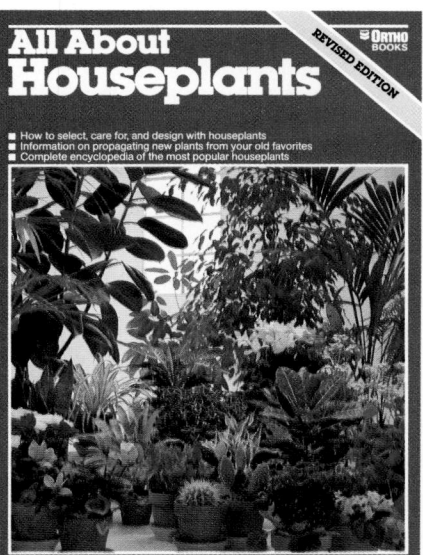

Revised. This up-to-date edition is full of practical, useful information for selecting, propagating, and designing with houseplants. Encyclopedia of favorite houseplants. New ideas for terrariums, bottle gardens, and hanging gardens. Complete cultivation guide. Full color, 96 pages.

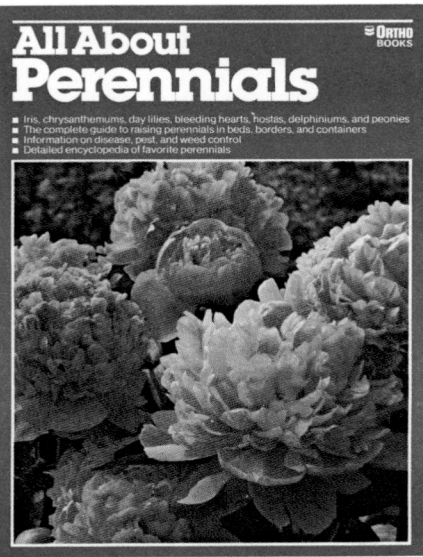

The techniques, tools, and insights you need to create a landscape that is uniquely your own. Covers all aspects, from design through construction. Full color, 96 pages.

Clearly and completely outlines the way to a beautiful lawn with a climatized guide to seeding, sodding, fertilizing, and watering. Full color, 96 pages.

How to select and grow perennials that are just right for you. Fresh ideas on how to mix and coordinate your flowers for every season. Encyclopedia of favorite perennials. Full color, 96 pages.

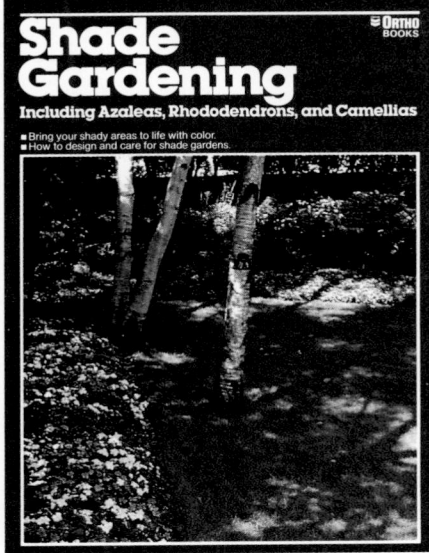

When, why, and how to prune everything, from trees and shrubs to vines and perennials. Includes tools, techniques, and tricks of the trade. Full color, 96 pages.

Revised. This up-to-date edition features sections on pruning, propagating, selecting, cutting, and preserving roses. Complete charts and descriptions of all types of roses, including the latest varieties. Full color, 96 pages.

Complete information on designing, maintaining, and understanding shade gardening. Traditional and innovative landscaping ideas for different climates. Photos and descriptions of more than 100 plant varieties. Full color, 96 pages.

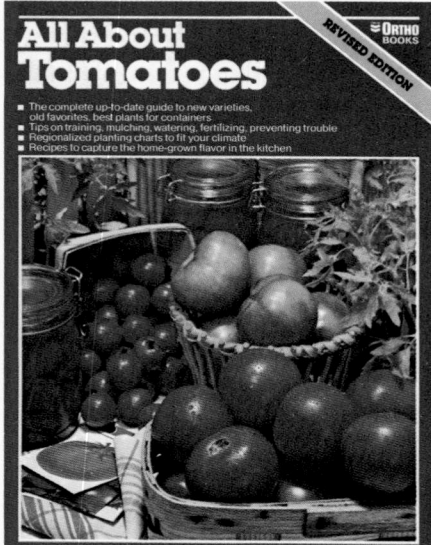

Revised. This up-to-date guide features new varieties, old favorites, and the best plants for containers. How to select, plant, grow, and harvest tomatoes especially suited to your climate. Recipes that capture that home-grown flavor in the kitchen. Full color, 96 pages.

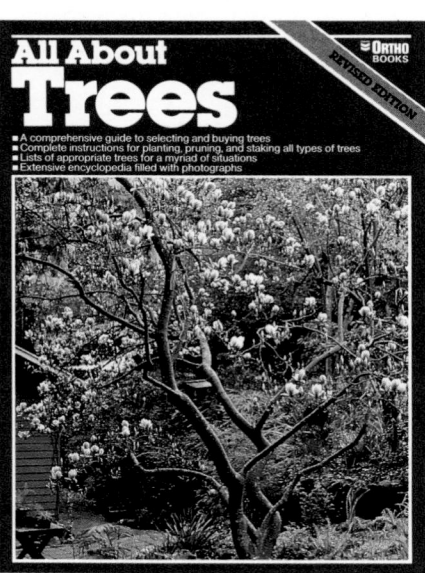

Revised. This up-to-date edition features the latest information on planting, staking, watering, fertilizing, and pruning. Complete selection guide. Full color, 112 pages.

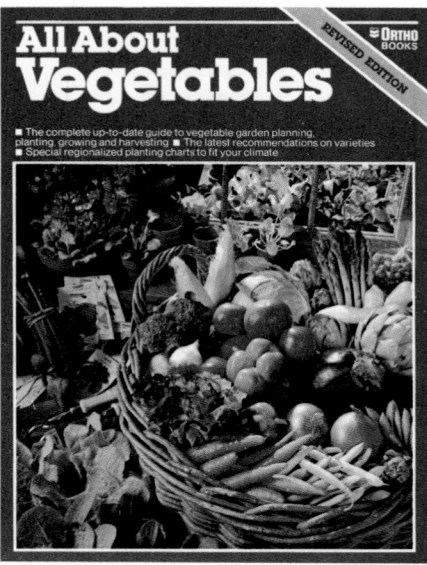

Revised, up-to-date edition of the complete guide to planting, growing, and harvesting vegetables. Special regionalized planting charts. Latest recommendation on varieties. Full color, 112 pages.

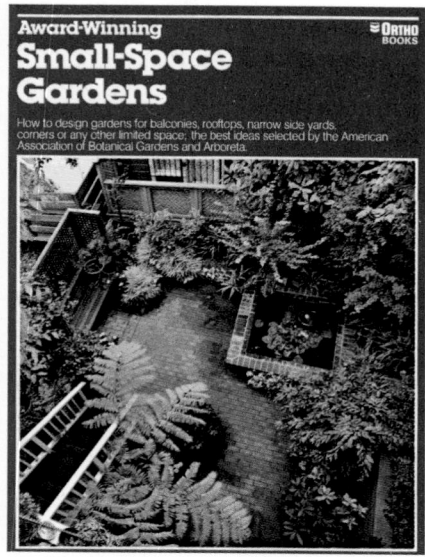

Learn to design both flower and food gardens for balconies, rooftops, narrow side yards, or any limited space. Full color, 112 pages.

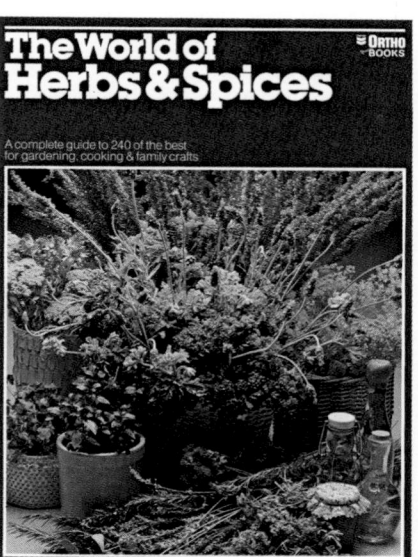

Covers 240 herbs and spices, including how to select and grow them indoors or out. Ideas for landscaping, and creative recipes for foods, cosmetics, dyes, and crafts. Full color, 96 pages.

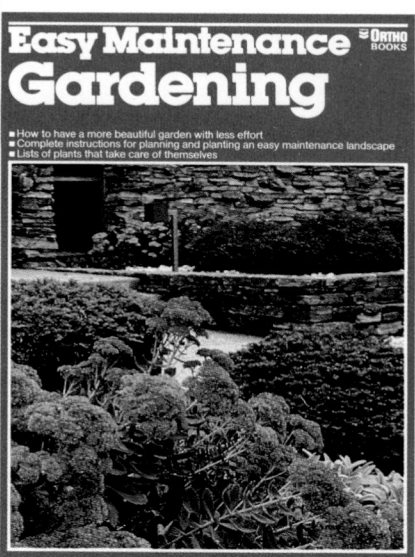

Learn the latest time-saving gardening techniques including labor-saving tools, equipment, construction details, and weeds and pest control. Sample gardens from landscape architects around the country. Detailed information on mulching. Special regionalized selection guide to low maintenance plants. Full color, 96 pages.

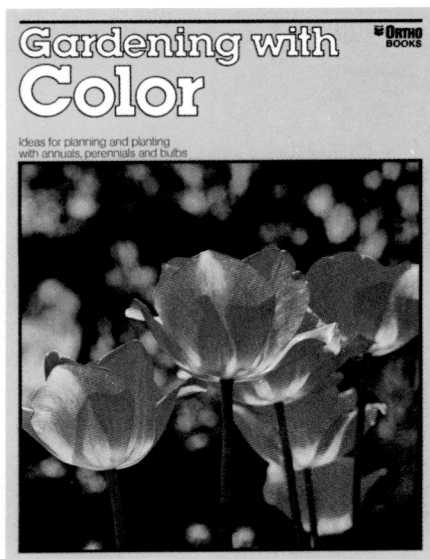

Teaches principles of color combination
in your garden, using nature's colors
as your gardening palette. Full color, 96
pages.

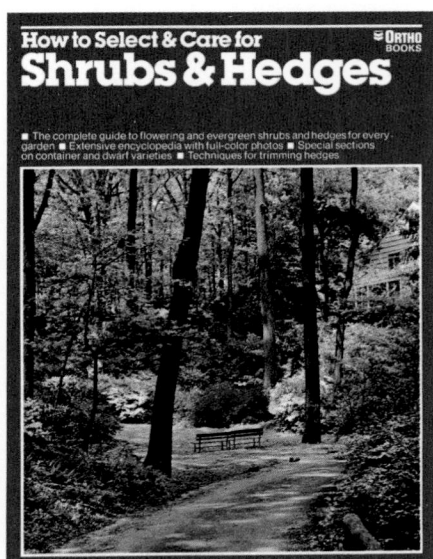

The complete guide to flowering and
evergreen shrubs and hedges. Extensive
encyclopedia of types. Special sections on container and dwarf varieties.
Full color, 96 pages.

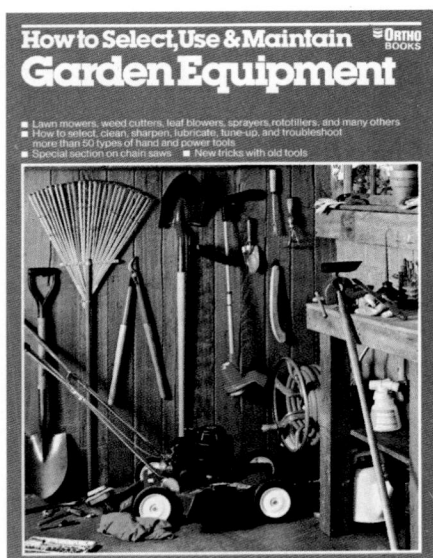

The authoritative guide to all types
of garden equipment. Professional tips
on how to select, use, clean, sharp-
en, and tune up more than 50 hand and
power tools. Full color, 96 pages.

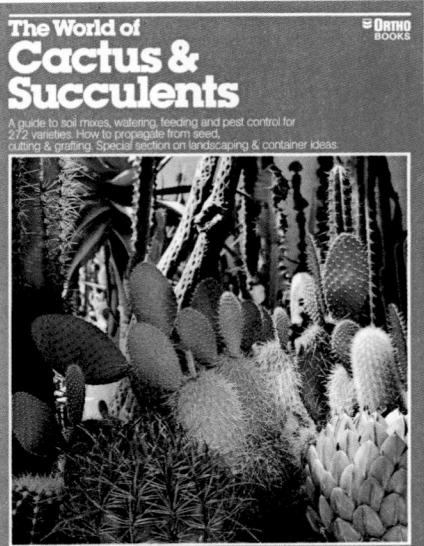

How to select and grow cacti and
other succulents indoors and outdoors,
with an explanation of botanical no-
menclature. Full color, 96 pages.

APPENDIX

Some houseplants that tolerate low light:

Botanical name	Common name
Aglaonema	Chinese evergreen
Aspidistra	Cast iron plant
Dieffenbachia	Dumb cane
Dracaena	
Ficus elastica	Rubber plant
Ficus lyrata	Fiddle leaf fig
Peperomia	
Philodendron	
Scindapsus	Pothos
Spathiphyllum	White flag

Some houseplants that are sensitive to salts in the soil:

Botanical name	Common name
Aphelandra	
Aspidistra	Cast iron plant
Asplenium	Bird's-nest fern
Avocado	
Calathea	Zebra plant
Chamaedorea	Parlor palm
Chlorophytum	Spider plant
Cissus	Grape ivy
Citrus	
Coffea	Coffee tree
Cordyline	Ti plant
Cycas	Sago palm
Dracaena	
Fatshedera	
Fatsia	Japanese aralia
Ferns	
Ficus	Ornamental fig, rubber plant
Haworthia	
Hedera	English ivy
Howea	Kentia palm
Maranta	Prayer plant
Monstera	Split-leaf philodendron
Palms	
Pandanus	Screw pine
Philodendron	
Saxifraga	Strawberry geranium
Spathiphyllum	White flag
Tolmiea	Piggy-back plant

Turfgrass varieties resistant to dollar spot:

BLUEGRASS
A-20
Adelphi
Bonnieblue
Bristol
Majestic
Parade
Park
Touchdown
Vantage
Victa

FESCUE
Jamestown chewings
Pennlawn creeping

BENTGRASS
Arlington
Pennpar

Bluegrass resistance to fusarium blight:

RESISTANT
A-20
Adelphi
Bonnieblue
Enmundi
Glade
Parade
Rugby
Sydsport
Trenton
Vantage
Windsor

MODERATELY RESISTANT
Majestic
Merit
Ram #2

SUSCEPTIBLE
Arboretum
Belturf
Brunswick
Campus
Cougar
Delft
Enita
Fylking
Geronimo
Merion
Modena
Newport
Nugget
Park
Pennstar
Pio-Cebaco
Plush
Ram #1
South Dakota Certified

Bluegrass varieties resistant to fusarium patch:

Adelphi
Birka
Bonnieblue
Touchdown

Bluegrass resistance to helminthosporium leaf spot:

RESISTANT
A-20
Adelphi
Birka
Bonnieblue
Bristol
Brunswick
Majestic
Merion
Newport
Nugget
Parade
Pennstar
Rugby
Sydsport
Touchdown
Vantage
Victa

MODERATELY RESISTANT
Baron
Cheri
Enmundi
Glade

SUSCEPTIBLE
Delta
Geary
Kenblue
Newport
Park

Bluegrass varieties resistant to red thread:

A-34
Adelphi
Birka
Bonnieblue
Touchdown

Bluegrass varieties resistant to rust:

A-20
A-34
Bonnieblue
Fylking
Glade
Majestic
Park
Pennstar
Rugby

Bluegrass varieties resistant to stripe smut:

A-20
A-34
Adelphi
Aquila
Birka
Bonnieblue
Brunswick
Enmundi
Glade
Newport
Plush
Ram #1
Sydsport
Touchdown
Vantage

Turfgrass climate zones:

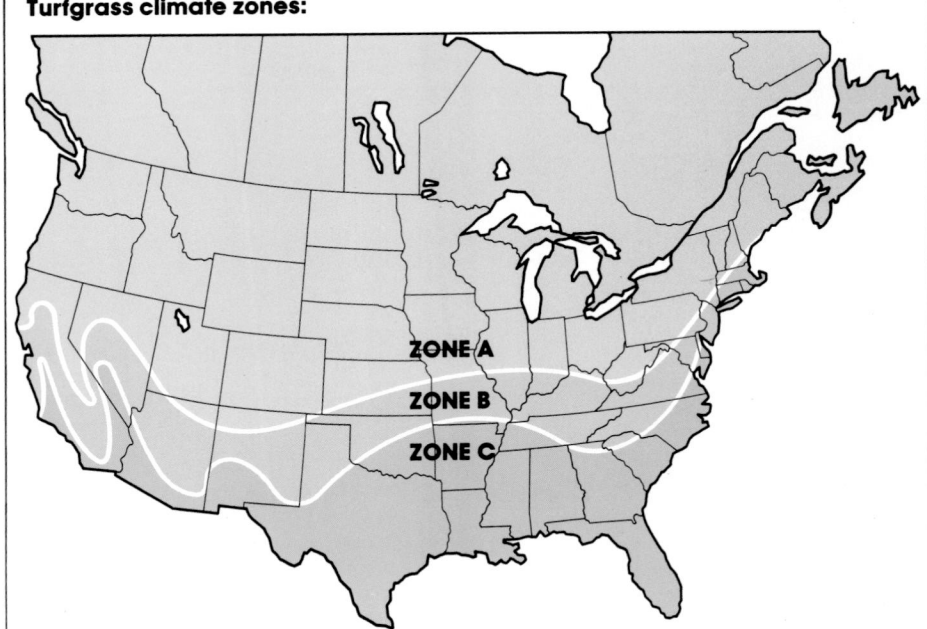

ZONE A
ZONE B
ZONE C

Zone A Cool-season grasses.

Zone C Warm-season grasses.

Zone B This is a transition zone, where the climate zones overlap. Both warm-season and cool-season grasses are grown here. Because warm-season grasses have long dormant periods in this zone, cool-season grasses are usually preferred. Tall fescue does particularly well in this zone.

From *Turf Managers Handbook*, W.H. Daniel and R.P. Freeborg.

Characteristics of some turfgrasses:

Grass	Zone	Drought Resistant	Shade Tolerant	Days to Germinate	Low* Maintenance
Bahiagrass	C			21-28	•
Bentgrass	A		•	5-12	
Bermudagrass, Common	C	•		14-20	•
Bermudagrass, Improved	C	•		Sprigs	•
Carpetgrass	C			21	•
Centipedegrass	C			14-20	•
Fescue, Red	A	•	•	5-12	•
Fescue, Tall	A	•	•	5-12	•
Kentucky Bluegrass	A			20-30	
St. Augustine grass	C		•	Sprigs	
Zoysiagrass	C	•	•	Sprigs	

*Low maintenance turfgrasses are those that tolerate irregular fertilizing, watering, and mowing.

Some drought resistant groundcovers:

Botanical name	Common name
Arctostaphylos uva-ursi	Bearberry
Baccharis pilularis	Coyote bush
Carpobrotus, Lampranthus, Mesembryan-themum	Ice plant
Cotoneaster	
Hypericum	St. John's wort
Rosmarinus officinalis 'Prostratus'	Dwarf rosemary
Santolina	Lavender cotton
Sedum	Stonecrop
Thymus	Creeping thyme

Some groundcovers for shady areas:

Botanical name	Common name
Ajuga	Carpet bugle
Duchesnea	Mock strawberry
Epimedium	
Euonymus fortunei	Winter creeper
Fragaria chiloensis	Wild strawberry
Hedera	Ivy
Hypericum	St. John's wort
Pachysandra	Japanese spurge
Soleirolia soleirolii	Baby's tears
Vinca	Periwinkle

Some groundcovers for sunny areas:

Botanical name	Common name
Carpobrotus, Lampranthus, Mesembry-anthemum	Ice plant
Cotoneaster	
Gazania	
Hypericum	St. John's wort
Juniperus horizontalis	Creeping juniper
Rosmarinus officinalis 'Prostatus'	Dwarf rosemary
Santolina	Lavender cotton
Sedum	Stone crop
Thymus	Creeping thyme

Planting and blooming of some common flowers:

Flower	Plant	Planting season	Blooming season	Ideal soil temperature for germination	Days to germination
Achillea	P	Sp	Su-F	70°F	5-15
Ageratum	A	Sp*	Sp-Su	60-65	10
Alcea	Bi	Sp-Su	Sp-Su	68	7-21
Allium	B	Sp or F	Sp-Su	**	**
Amaranthus	A	Sp	Sp-Su	60-70	12
Anemone	Tu	F or Sp	Sp	**	**
Antirrhinum	A	Sp*	Sp-Su	70	15
Aquilegia	P	F or Sp	Sp-Su	70-85	21-28
Aster	A, P	Sp	Sp-Su-F	70	12-14
Astilbe	P	Sp	Sp-Su	60-70	14-21
Begonia	Tp	Sp	Sp-Su	70-75	15-20
Browallia	A	Sp	Su	75	14-21
Calendula	A	Sp*	W-Sp	70-85	7-14
Callistephus	A	Sp	Su	70	15-20
Campanula	P	Sp	Sp-F	68-86	10-14
Canna	Tu	Sp	Su-F	**	**
Capsicum	A	Sp	Su	70	15-20
Celosia	A	Sp	Su	70-85	7-14
Chrysanthemum	A, P	Sp	Su-F	70	7-10
Cineraria	A	Sp*	W-Sp	45-60	20
Cleome	A	Sp*	Su	55-85	10-14
Coleus	Tp	Sp	Sp-Su	70-85	15-20
Convallaria	P	F (from pips)	Sp	**	**
Coreopsis	A, P	F or Sp	Su-F	70	15-20
Cosmos	A	Sp	Su-F	70-85	10-15
Crocus	Corm	F	Sp	**	**
Dahlia	Tu	Sp	Su-F	70-85 (seed)	15-20
Delphinium	A, P	Sp*	Su	55-60	15-30
Dianthus	A, P	Sp*	Sp-Su	70	15-30
Digitalis	Bi, P	Su	Sp-Su	70-85	15-20
Dimorphotheca	A	Sp	Su	70-85	15-20
Freesia	Corm	Sp	Sp	**	**
Gaillardia	A, P	Sp*	Su-F	70	15-20
Gerbera	Tp	Sp	Su	70	15
Gladiolus	Corm	Sp	Su-F	**	**
Helianthemum	P	F or Sp	Su	70	15-20
Helianthus	A, P	Sp	Su	70-85	15-20
Helleborus	P	F	Sp	30 days (freeze seed to break dormancy)	70-75

Florida gardeners may find differences in planting times and soil temperatures. Check with your local extension agent.

* Planted in the fall in zones 9 and 10. See page 1004 for USDA zone map.

** Not usually planted from seed.

KEY: A – Annual; Bu – Bulb; Bi – Biennial; P – Perennial; Rh – Rhizome; Tp – Tender perennial, grown as annual in all but zones 9 and 10; Tu – Tuber; Sp – Spring; Su – Summer; F – Fall; W – Winter.

Planting and blooming of some common flowers (continued):

Flower	Plant	Planting season	Blooming season	Ideal soil temperature for germination	Days to germination
Hemerocallis	Tu	Sp*	Su	**	**
Heuchera	P	F or Sp	Sp-Su	70-85	5-20
Hosta	P	Sp	Su-F	70	15-20
Hyacinthus	Bu	F	Sp	**	**
Iberis	A, P	Sp*	Sp-Su	70-85	7-15
Impatiens	A, P	Tp	Su	70	15-20
Iris	Rh	F	Sp-Su	**	**
Lantana	Tp	Sp	Sp-F	70	40-50
Lathyrus	A	W-Sp	Sp	70	15
Lilium	Bu	Sp	Su	**	**
Lobelia	A	Sp*	Su-F	70-85	15-20
Lobularia	A, P	Sp	Sp-Su-F	70	7-15
Matthiola	A	Sp	Sp-Su	55-90	15
Pelargonium	P	Sp	Sp-Su-F	68-86	5-15
Phlox	A, P	Sp*	Su-F	55-65	8-20
Primula	A, P	Sp	Sp	55-65	20
Ranunculus	Tu	F	Su	**	**
Rudbeckia	A, P	Sp	Su-F	70-75	5-10
Salpiglossis	A	Sp	Su	70-75	15-20
Salvia	A, P	Sp	Su	70	12-15
Sedum	P	Sp	Su	70-80	15-30
Solanum	A, P	Sp	Su-F	70	15-30
Tagetes	A	Sp	Su-F	70-75	5-7

Florida gardeners may find differences in planting times and soil temperatures. Check with your local extension agent.

* Planted in the fall in zones 9 and 10. See page 1004 for USDA zone map.

** Not usually planted from seed.

KEY: A – Annual; Bu – Bulb; Bi – Biennial; P – Perennial; Rh – Rhizome; Tp – Tender perennial, grown as annual in all but zones 9 and 10; Tu – Tuber; Sp – Spring; Su – Summer; F – Fall; W – Winter.

Some lily species resistant and susceptible to lily mosaic:

RESISTANT TO MODERATELY RESISTANT
Lilium amabile
L. brownii
L. davidii
L. hansonii
L. henryi
L. martagon
L. monadelphum
L. paradalinum
L. pumilum
L. regale

SUSCEPTIBLE
L. auratum
L. canadense
L. concolor
L. formosanum
L. lancifolium
L. maculatum
L. pennsylvanicum
L. superbum
L. tigrinum is easily infected, but is not apparently injured. This species can become a carrier to other susceptible species.

Some rose varieties tolerant of powdery mildew (PM), black spot (BS), or rust (R):

HYBRID TEAS
Carousel — PM
Charlotte Armstrong — BS
Chrysler Imperial — BS
Command Performance — BS, R
Garden Party — BS, R
John F. Kennedy — BS, R
Lowell Thomas — PM
Miss All American Beauty — PM
Sutter's Gold — PM
Tiffany — BS
Tropicana — BS

CLIMBERS
Blaze — BS, PM
Cecil Brunner — PM
Paul's Scarlet — BS, PM

FLORIBUNDAS
Red Gold — BS, R
Sarabande — BS, R

Some flowers susceptible to various fusarium wilts:

Botanical name	Common name
Antirrhinum	Snapdragon
Astilbe	
Browallia	
Callistephus	China aster
Campanula	Bellflower
Centaurea	Bachelor's button
Chrysanthemum	
Cineraria	
Cosmos	
Cyclamen	
Dahlia	
Delphinium	
Dianthus	Carnation, pink, sweet William
Digitalis	Foxglove
Dimorphotheca	Cape marigold
Lantana	
Lilium	Lily
Matthiola	Stock
Narcissus	Daffodil
Paeonia	Peony
Salpiglossis	Painted tongue
Tagetes	Marigold
Tulipa	Tulip

Some plants susceptible to aster yellows:

FLOWERS

Botanical name	Common name
Anemone	
Antirrhinum	Snapdragon
Aster	
Calendula	Pot marigold
Callistephus	China aster
Celosia	Cockscomb
Centaurea	Bachelor's buttons
Chrysanthemum	
Coreopsis	
Cosmos	
Delphinium	
Dianthus	Sweet William, carnation, pinks
Dimorphotheca	Cape marigold
Gaillardia	Blanket flower
Gladiolus	
Helichrysum	Straw flower
Lobelia	
Petunia	
Phlox	
Scabiosa	Pincushion flower
Tagetes	Marigold

VEGETABLES
Broccoli
Cabbage
Carrot
Cauliflower
Celery
Endive
Lettuce
New Zealand spinach
Onion
Parsley
Parsnip
Potato
Pumpkin
Radish
Spinach
Squash
Tomato

WEEDS

Botanical name	Common name
Ambrosia	Ragweed
Cirsium	Thistle
Conyza	Horseweed
Daucus	Wild carrot
Erigeron	Fleabane
Plantago	Plantain
Taraxacum	Dandelion

Some plants resistant to cotton root rot (*Phymatotrichum*):

TREES AND SHRUBS

Botanical name	Common name
Celtis	Hackberry
Deutzia	
Morus alba 'Pendula'	Weeping mulberry
Palmae	Palm family
Polypodiaceae	Ferns
Punica	Pomegranate
Quercus	Oak

FLOWERS

Botanical name	Common name
Amaranthus	Amaranth
Antirrhinum	Snapdragon
Calceolaria	
Canna	
Cyclamen	
Digitalis	Foxglove
Eschscholzia	California poppy
Freesia	
Gypsophila	Baby's breath
Hyacinthus	
Iberis	Candytuft
Iris	
Lobularia	Sweet alyssum
Matthiola	Stock
Narcissus	Daffodil
Nasturtium	
Papaver	Poppy
Petunia	
Phlox	
Portulaca	Moss rose
Primula	Primrose
Zantedeschia	Calla
Zinnia	

VEGETABLES AND BERRIES
Asparagus
Cabbage family
Cantaloupe
Celery
Cranberry
Cucumber
Currant
Dewberry
Garlic
Grape
Leek
Onion
Pumpkin
Spinach
Squash
Strawberry
Watermelon

Some plants that are resistant to verticillium wilt:

PLANT GROUPINGS
Ferns
Conifers (Cypress, fir, larch, juniper, pine, sequoia, spruce, and others.)
Monocots (Bamboo, bulbs, corn, gladiolus, grasses, iris, onion, orchids, palm, and others.)
Cacti

TREES AND SHRUBS

Botanical name	Common name
Arctostaphylos	Manzanita
Betula	Birch
Buxus	Boxwood
Carpinus	Hornbeam
Ceanothus	
Cornus	Dogwood
Crataegus	Hawthorn
Eucalyptus	
Fagus	Beech
Gleditsia	Locust
Ilex	Holly
Juglans	Walnut
Liquidambar	Sweet gum
Malus	Apple, crabapple
Morus	Mulberry
Nerium	Oleander
Platanus	Plane tree, sycamore
Pyracantha	Firethorn
Quercus	Oak
Salix	Willow
Tilia	Linden

FLOWERS

Botanical name	Common name
Ageratum	Lily of the Nile
Alcea	Hollyhock
Alyssum	
Anemone	
Aquilegia	Columbine
Begonia	
Calendula	Pot marigold
Dianthus	Carnation, pink, sweet William
Gaillardia	
Gypsophila	Baby's breath
Helianthemum	Sun rose
Helianthus	Sunflower
Helleborus	Christmas rose
Heuchera	Coral bells
Iberis	Candytuft
Impatiens	
Lantana	
Mimulus	Monkey flower
Nemesia	
Nemophila	Baby-blue-eyes
Penstemon	
Platycodon	Balloon flower
Portulaca	Moss rose
Potentilla	
Primula	Primrose
Ranunculus	
Scabiosa	
Tropaeolum	Nasturtium
Verbena	
Vinca	Periwinkle
Viola	Pansy, viola, violet
Zinnia	

VEGETABLES

Asparagus	Lettuce
Beans	Peas
Carrot	Sweet potato
Celery	

Adapted from *Plants Resistant or Susceptible to Verticillium Wilt*, University of California Cooperative Extension Leaflet 2703.

Powdery mildews and some of the plants they infect:

ERYSIPHE CICHORACEARUM:

Botanical name	Common name
Achillea	Yarrow
Ajuga	Carpet bugle
Alcea	Hollyhock
Antirrhinum	Snapdragon
Aster	
Baccharis	Coyote bush
Begonia	
Calendula	Pot marigold
Centaurea	Bachelor's button
Chrysanthemum	
Cineraria	
Citrullus	Watermelon
Cosmos	
Cotinus	Smoke tree
Dahlia	
Eucalyptus	
Gerbera	Transvaal daisy
Hebe	
Helianthus	Sunflower
Lactuca	Lettuce
Myosotis	Forget-me-not
Papaver	Poppy
Ranunculus	
Rhus	Sumac
Rudbeckia	Black-eyed Susan
Salpiglossis	Painted tongue
Salvia	
Spiraea	
Verbena	
Zinnia	

ERYSIPHE POLYGONI:

Botanical name	Common name
Amaranthus	Amaranth
Aquilegia	Columbine
Begonia	
Beta	Beet
Brassica	Cabbage family
Delphinium	
Eschscholzia	California poppy
Iberis	Candytuft
Lathyrus	Sweet pea
Lobularia	Sweet alyssum
Phaseolus	Beans
Pisum	Peas
Raphanus	Radish
Vinca	Periwinkle
Viola	Pansy, viola

MICROSPHAERA ALNI:

Botanical name	Common name
Alnus	Alder
Corylus	Hazelnut
Lonicera	Honeysuckle
Platanus	Plane tree
Quercus	Oak
Symphoricarpos	Snowberry
Syringa	Lilac

Adapted from, "A List of Powdery Mildews of California," California Cooperative Extension Service. Leaflet 217.

MICROSPHAERA SPECIES:

Botanical name	Common name
Acacia	
Catalpa	
Ceanothus	
Erica	Heath
Euonymus	
Hydrangea	
Juglans	Walnut
Lagerstroemia	Crapemyrtle
Ligustrum	Privet
Liriodendron	Tuliptree
Lonicera	Honeysuckle
Magnolia	
Passiflora	Passion flower
Platanus	Plane tree
Populus	Poplar
Raphiolepis	India hawthorn
Rhododendron	Rhododendron, azalea
Robinia	Locust
Vaccinium	Blueberry
Viburnum	

PHYLLACTINIA CORYLEA:

Botanical name	Common name
Aesculus	Horse chestnut
Cornus	Dogwood
Philadelphus	Mock orange
Quercus	Oak
Rubus	Brambles

PODOSPHAERA SPECIES:

Botanical name	Common name
Acer	Maple
Fraxinus	Ash
Malus	Apple, crabapple
Photinia	
Prunus	Peach, plum, etc.
Pyracantha	Firethorn
Pyrus	Pear
Spiraea	

SPHAEROTHECA FULIGINEA:

Cantaloupe
Cucumber
Winter squash

SPHAEROTHECA SPECIES:

Botanical name	Common name
Cotoneaster	
Crataegus	Hawthorn
Dianthus	Sweet William, carnation, pink
Erica	Heath
Fragaria	Strawberry
Gaillardia	Blanket flower
Heuchera	Coral bells
Kalanchoe	
Nicotiana	
Petunia	
Phlox	
Potentilla	Cinquefoil
Ribes	Currant, gooseberry
Rosa	Rose
Tolmiea	

Some plants tolerant of smog (ozone and PAN):

TREES AND SHRUBS

Botanical name	Common name
Acer platanoides	Norway maple
Acer saccharum	Sugar maple
Betula pendula	European white birch
Cornus florida	White dogwood
Euonymus alata	Winged euonymus
Picea abies	Norway spruce
Picea pungens	Colorado blue spruce
Pinus resinosa	Red pine
Pseudotsuga menziesii	Douglas fir
Quercus rubra	Red oak
Thuja occidentalis	Arborvitae
Tsuga canadensis	Eastern hemlock

FLOWERS

Botanical name	Common name
Agapanthus	Lily of the Nile
Aquilegia	Columbine
Eschscholzia california	California poppy
Heuchera sanguinea	Coral bells
Iris	
Liliaceae	Lily family
Narcissus	Daffodil, narcissus
Viola tricolor	Pansy

GROUNDCOVERS

Botanical name	Common name
Hedera helix	English ivy
Helxine	Baby tears
Vinca minor	Periwinkle

FRUITS AND VEGETABLES

Beet	Strawberry
Squash	Sweet potato

Some plants tolerant of industrial pollution (SO₂):

TREES AND SHRUBS

Botanical name	Common name
Acer	Maple
Cedrus	Cedar
Ligustrum	Privet
Syringa	Lilac
Tilia	Linden

FRUITS AND VEGETABLES

Cabbage	Onion
Celery	Potato
Corn	

Some plants susceptible to southern blight (Sclerotium rolfsii):

SHRUBS

Botanical name	Common name
Daphne	
Hydrangea	
Pittosporum	
Rosa	Rose

FLOWERS

Botanical name	Common name
Anemone	
Alcea	Hollyhock
Calendula	Pot marigold
Callistephus	China aster
Campanula	Bell flower
Canna	
Chrysanthemum	Mum, daisy, marguerite
Cosmos	
Dahlia	
Delphinium	
Dianthus	Sweet William, carnation, pinks
Gladiolus	
Iris	
Lathyrus	Sweet pea
Lilium	Lily
Lupinus	Lupine
Narcissus	Daffodil, narcissus
Phlox	
Rudbeckia	Black-eyed Susan
Scabiosa	Pincushion flower
Sedum	
Tagetes	Marigold
Tulipa	Tulip
Viola	Pansy, viola
Zinnia	

VEGETABLES AND FRUITS

Apple
Artichoke
Avocado
Bean
Beet
Cabbage
Cantaloupe
Carrot
Cucumber
Eggplant
Lettuce
Okra
Onion
Pea
Peanut
Pepper
Potato
Rhubarb
Squash
Strawberry
Tomato
Turnip
Watermelon

*Southern blight has been reported on hundreds of plants. This is a partial list of plants that are frequently infected by this disease.

Some plants attractive to bees:

TREES AND SHRUBS

Botanical name	Common name
Abelia	
Acacia	
Arctostaphylos	Bearberry
Berberis	Barberry
Callistemon	Bottlebrush
Calluna	Heather
Ceanothus	Wild lilac
Cotoneaster	
Cytisus	Broom
Erica	Heath
Eriobotrya	Loquat
Escallonia	
Gleditsia	Honeylocust
Lantana	
Ligustrum	Privet
Lonicera	Honeysuckle
Myrtus	Myrtle
Nerium	Oleander
Pittosporum	Mock orange
Pyracantha	Firethorn
Raphiolepis	India hawthorn
Rosmarinus	Rosemary
Thymus	Thyme
Trachelospermum	Star jasmine
Wisteria	

FLOWERS

Botanical name	Common name
Achillea	Yarrow
Campanula	Bell flower
Helianthus	Sunflower
Lavandula	Lavender
Lobularia	Sweet alyssum
Myosotis	Forget-me-not
Nicotiana	Flowering tobacco
Salvia	

A few small trees for areas with restricted root space:

Botanical name	Common name
Acer campestre	Hedge maple
Acer ginnala	Amur maple
Acer palmatum	Japanese maple
Albizia julibrissin	Silk tree
Carpinus	Hornbeam
Cercis	Redbud
Cornus	Dogwood
Crataegus	Hawthorn
Elaeagnus angustifolia	Russian olive
Ilex	Holly
Koelreuteria	Golden-rain tree
Magnolia soulangiana	Saucer magnolia
Magnolia stellata	Star magnolia
Malus	Crabapple
Pistacia chinensis	Chinese pistache
Prunus	Flowering peach, plum, cherry
Styrax	Snowbell
Viburnum prunifolium	Black haw
Viburnum rufidulum	Southern black haw
Viburnum sieboldii	Siebold viburnum

Plants rarely fed upon by adult Japanese beetles:

TREES AND SHRUBS

Botanical name	Common name
Abies	Fir
Acer negundo	Boxelder
Acer rubrum	Red maple
Acer saccharinum	Silver maple
Cercis	Redbud
Celastrus	Bittersweet
Clematis	
Cornus	Dogwood
Forsythia	
Fraxinus	Ash
Ginkgo	
Hydrangea	
Ilex	Holly
Juniperus	Juniper
Kalmia	Mountain laurel
Ligustrum	Privet
Liquidambar	Sweet gum
Lonicera	Honeysuckle
Magnolia	
Morus	Mulberry
Picea	Spruce
Pinus	Pine
Quercus alba	White oak
Q. coccinea	Scarlet oak
Q. rubra	Red oak
Q. stellata	Post oak
Q. velutina	Black oak
Rhododendron	Rhododendron, azalea
Robinia	Locust
Symphoricarpos	Snowberry
Syringa	Lilac
Thuja occidentalis	Arborvitae
Tsuga	Hemlock

Adapted from "Japanese Beetle," Cooperative Extension Service, West Virginia University, Pest Information Series 68.

FLOWERS

Botanical name	Common name
Aquilegia	Columbine
Aster	
Celosia	Cock's comb
Chrysanthemum	Mum, daisy
Dianthus	Sweet William, carnation, pink
Digitalis	Foxglove
Iberis	Candytuft
Iris	
Lathyrus	Sweet pea
Papaver	Poppy
Petunia	
Phlox	
Portulaca	
Viola	Pansy, viola

GROUNDCOVERS

Botanical name	Common name
Hedera	Ivy
Pachysandra	

VEGETABLES

Brussels sprout
Cabbage
Cantaloupe
Carrot
Cauliflower
Cucumber
Eggplant
Lettuce
Onion
Pea
Pumpkin
Radish
Spinach
Squash
Sweet potato
Turnip
Watermelon

FRUIT TREES

Pear

Some trees and shrubs for wet soil:

Botanical name	Common name
Acer rubrum	Red maple
Alnus	Alder
Amelanchier	Serviceberry
Betula nigra	River birch
Calycanthus	Sweet shrub
Lindera	Spicebush
Liquidambar	Sweet gum
Myrica	Bayberry
Nyssa	Black gum
Platanus	Sycamore
Populus	Poplar
Quercus bicolor	Swamp white oak
Quercus palustris	Pin oak
Salix	Willow
Sambucus	Elderberry
Taxodium	Bald cypress
Thuja	Arborvitae

Some drought tolerant plants suitable for growing in areas with restricted root space:

Botanical name	Common name
Albizia julibrissin	Silk tree
Arbutus unedo	Strawberry tree
Carpinus	Hornbeam
Cercis	Redbud
Cercocarpus	Mountain mahogany
Cotoneaster	
Crataegus	Hawthorn
Elaeagnus	
Ginkgo	Maidenhair tree
Juniperus	Juniper
Koelreuteria	Golden-rain tree
Pinus edulis	Pinon pine
Pinus mugo mugo	Mugho pine
Potentilla fruticosa	Cinquefoil
Rosmarinus	Rosemary

Some trees and shrubs for shady areas:

Botanical name	Common name
Acer circinatum	Vine maple
Acer palmatum	Japanese maple
Amelanchier	Serviceberry
Aucuba	
Buxus	Boxwood
Calycanthus	Sweet shrub
Camellia	
Cercis	Redbud
Chamaecyparis	False cypress
Cornus	Dogwood
Daphne	
Halesia	Silver-bell
Hamamelis	Witch hazel
Hydrangea	
Ilex	Holly
Kalmia	Mountain laurel
Laurus nobilis	Laurel

Botanical name	Common name
Leucothoe	
Ligustrum	Privet
Mahonia	Oregon grape, holly grape
Nandina	Heavenly bamboo
Pieris	Andromeda
Pittosporum	
Podocarpus	
Rhododendron	Azalea, rhododendron
Sarcococca	
Taxus	Yew
Thuja	Arborvitae
Tsuga	Hemlock
Viburnum davidii	David viburnum
Viburnum tinus	Laurestinus

A few trees that tolerate competition from lawn grasses:

Botanical name	Common name
Acer campestre	Hedge maple
Acer ginnala	Amur maple
Acer palmatum	Japanese maple
Albizia	Silk tree
Cornus	Dogwood
Cotinus	Smoke tree
Crataegus	Hawthorn
Fraxinus velutina glabra	Modesto ash
Koelreuteria	Golden-rain
Lagerstroemia	Crapemyrtle
Magnolia soulangiana	Saucer magnolia
Magnolia stellata	Star magnolia
Prunus	Flowering cherry, peach, plum

Low-growing trees suitable for planting under wires along streets:

Botanical name	Common name
Acer campestre	Hedge maple
Acer ginnala	Amur maple
Acer palmatum	Japanese maple
Acer spicatum	Mountain maple
Acer tataricum	Tatarian maple
Cercis	Redbud
Cotinus	Smoketree
Koelreuteria paniculata	Golden-rain tree
Lagerstroemia indica	Crapemyrtle
Malus	Crabapple
Prunus	Flowering cherry, peach, plum
Styrax japonicus	Snowbell

Some oaks that need no water after the first two seasons in the ground:

Botanical name	Common name
Quercus agrifolia	Coast live oak
Q. chrysolepis	Canyon live oak
Q. douglasii	Blue oak
Q. dumosa	California scrub oak
Q. engelmannii	Mesa oak
Q. garryana	Oregon white oak
Q. ilex	Holly oak
Q. kelloggii	California black oak
Q. lobata	Valley oak
Q. suber	Cork oak
Q. wislizenii	Interior live oak

Some oaks that need added water during periods of drought:

Botanical name	Common name
Quercus alba	White oak
Q. bicolor*	Swamp white oak
Q. coccinea	Scarlet oak
Q. macrocarpa	Bur oak
Q. palustris*	Pin oak
Q. phellos	Willow oak
Q. robur	English oak
Q. rubra	Red oak

*Will tolerate wet soil.

Pines susceptible to diplodia tip blight:*

Botanical name	Common name
Pinus mugo mugo	Mugho pine
Pinus nigra	Austrian pine
Pinus ponderosa	Ponderosa pine
Pinus resinosa	Red pine
Pinus strobus	White pine
Pinus sylvestris	Scotch pine
Pinus virginiana	Scrub pine

*Susceptibility may vary according to region.

Trees and shrubs that are relatively free of insects and diseases:

Botanical name	Common name
Ailanthus	Tree-of-heaven
Brachychiton	Bottletree
Carpinus	Hornbeam
Cedrus	Cedar
Celtis australis	European hackberry
Ceratonia siliqua	Carob
Cercidiphyllum japonicum	Katsura tree
Clematis	
Cornus mas	Cornelian cherry
Cornus officinalis	Japanese cornelian cherry
Corylus colurna	Turkish filbert
Cotinus	Smoke tree
Cytisus	Broom
Eucommia ulmoides	Hardy rubber tree
Ficus	Fig
Franklinia	Franklin tree
Gingko	Maidenhair tree
Grevillea robusta	Silk oak
Gymnocladus dioica	Kentucky coffeetree
Kalopanax pictus	Castor-aralia
Kerria	Japanese rose
Koelreuteria paniculata	Varnish tree
Laburnum	Bean tree
Libocedrus decurrens	Incense cedar
Ligustrum lucidum	Glossy privet
Magnolia acuminata	
M. Kobus borealis	
M. salicifolia	Anise magnolia
M. stellata	Star magnolia
Metasequoia	Dawn redwood
Myrica	Bayberry
Myrtus	Myrtle
Nyssa	
Ostrya	Hop hornbeam
Parrotia persica	Persian parrotia
Phellodendron	Cork tree
Pistacia chinensis	Chinese pistache
Podocarpus	
Potentilla	Cinquefoil
Rhamnus	Buckthorn
Sciadopitys verticillata	Umbrella pine
Sophora japonica	Japanese pagoda tree
Stewartia	
Styrax	Snowbell
Tamarix	Tamarisk
Taxodium	Bald cypress
Viburnum sieboldii	Siebold viburnum
Xylosma congestum	Shiny xylosma

Some trees and shrubs with shallow root systems:

Botanical name	Common name
Acacia	
Acer saccharinum	Silver maple
Ailanthus altissima	Tree-of-heaven
Alnus	Alder
Cornus nuttallii	Pacific dogwood
Eucalyptus	
Ficus	Fig
Fraxinus uhdei	Evergreen ash
Gleditsia	Honeylocust
Morus	Mulberry
Platanus	Sycamore
Populus	Poplar
Rhus	Sumac
Robinia	Black locust
Salix	Willow
Ulmus	Elm

Some trees and shrubs that are resistant to crown gall:

Botanical name	Common name
Abelia	
Ailanthus	Tree-of-heaven
Albizia	Mimosa
Amelanchier	Serviceberry
Berberis	Barberry
Betula	Birch
Buxus	Boxwood
Calluna	Heather
Carpinus	Hornbeam
Catalpa	
Cedrus	Cedar
Cercis	Redbud
Cladrastis	Yellowwood
Cotinus	Smoke tree
Cryptomeria	
Deutzia	
Fagus	Beech
Ginkgo	Maidenhair tree
Gymnocladus	Coffee tree
Ilex	Holly
Kalmia	Mountain laurel
Koelreuteria	Golden-rain tree
Laburnum	Golden-chain tree
Larix	Larch
Leucothoe	
Liquidambar	Sweet gum
Liriodendron	Tuliptree
Magnolia	
Mahonia	Oregon grape
Nyssa	Black gum
Picea	Spruce
Pieris	Andromeda
Pyracantha	Firethorn
Rhus	Sumac
Sambucus	Elderberry
Sassafras	
Tsuga	Hemlock
Zelkova	

Adapted from *Crown Gall*, W.A. Sinclair and W.T. Johnson. Cornell Tree Pest Leaflet A-5.

Some trees with weak forks and brittle wood:

Botanical name	Common name
Acacia	
Acer saccharinum	Silver maple
Aesculus	Horse chestnut
Ailanthus	Tree-of-heaven
Callistemon citrinus	Bottlebrush
Casuarina stricta	She-oak
Eucalyptus	
Fraxinus velutina glabra	Modesto ash
Liriodendron	Tuliptree
Magnolia grandiflora	Southern magnolia
Melaleuca	
Melia azedarach	Chinaberry
Morus alba	White mulberry
Populus	Poplar
Quercus prinus	Chestnut oak
Robinia	Locust
Salix	Willow
Sassafras	
Sequoia sempervirens	Coast redwood
Ulmus pumila	Siberian elm

Susceptibility of some trees to injury from fill:

MOST SUSCEPTIBLE

Botanical name	Common name
Acer saccharum	Sugar maple
Cornus	Dogwood
Fagus	Beech
Liriodendron	Tuliptree
Picea	Spruce
Pinus	Pine
Quercus	Oak

MODERATELY SUSCEPTIBLE

Botanical name	Common name
Betula	Birch
Carya	Hickory
Tsuga	Hemlock

LEAST SUSCEPTIBLE

Botanical name	Common name
Platanus	Sycamore
Populus	Poplar
Quercus palustris	Pin oak
Robinia	Locust
Salix	Willow
Ulmus	Elm

From *Tree Maintenance*, P.P. Pirone. Copyright © 1978 Oxford University Press, Inc. Reprinted by permission.

Some trees that are commonly damaged by sapsuckers:

Botanical name	Common name
Abies	Fir
Acacia	
Acer rubrum	Red maple
Acer saccharum	Sugar maple
Betula	Birch
Casuarina	Beefwood
Eriobotrya	Loquat
Fagus	Beech
Grevillea	Silk oak
Larix	Larch
Magnolia	
Malus	Apple
Palmae	Palms
Picea rubens	Red spruce
Pinus	Pine
Populus tremuloides	Quaking aspen
Pseudotsuga menziesii	Douglas fir
Salix	Willow
Tsuga	Hemlock

Some trees susceptible to lightning injury:

SUSCEPTIBLE

Botanical name	Common name
Fraxinus	Ash
Liriodendron	Tuliptree
Picea	Spruce
Pinus	Pine
Populus	Poplar
Quercus	Oak
Ulmus	Elm

LESS SUSCEPTIBLE*

Botanical name	Common name
Aesculus	Horse chestnut
Betula	Birch
Fagus	Beech

*No species is totally immune, and location and size of the tree are also factors influencing susceptibility.

From *Tree Maintenance*, P.P. Pirone. Copyright © 1978 Oxford University Press, Inc. Reprinted by permission.

Palms most frequently attacked by the palm leaf skeletonizer (Homaledra sabalella):

Botanical name	Common name
Acoelorrhaphe wrightii	Paurotis palm
Butia capitata	Pindo palm
Cocos nucifera	Coconut palm
Livistona chinensis	Chinese fan palm
Phoenix	Date palms
Sabal palmetto	Cabbage palm
Washingtonia	Washington palms

Susceptibility of palm species to lethal yellows disease in Florida:

HIGHLY SUSCEPTIBLE

Botanical name	Common name
Cocos nucifera L. 'Jamaica Tall'	Coconut palm
Pritchardia species	

MODERATELY SUSCEPTIBLE

Botanical name	Common name
Arenga engleri	Englers palm
Caryota mitis	Fishtail palm
Corypha elata	Buri palm
Dictyosperma album	Hurricane palm
Latania species	Latan palm
Phoenix canariensis	Canary Island date palm
Phoenix dactylifera	Date palm
Trachycarpus fortunei	Chinese windmill palm
Veitchia merrillii	Christmas (adonidia) palm

SLIGHTLY SUSCEPTIBLE

Botanical name	Common name
Arikuryroba schizophylla	Arikury palm
Borassus flabellifer	Palmyra palm
Chrysalidocarpus cabadae	Cadaba palm
Hyophorbe vershaffeltii	Spindle palm
Livistona chinensis	Chinese fan palm
Phoenix reclinata	Senegal date palm
Phoenix sylvestris	Wild date palm
Veitchia montgomeryana	Montgomery's palm

Some plants tolerant of saline soil:

Botanical name	Common name
Araucaria heterophylla	Norfolk Island pine
Arctotheca calendula	Arctotheca
Baccharis pilularis	Coyote bush
Bougainvillea	
Callistemon viminalis	Weeping bottlebrush
Carissa grandiflora	Natal plum
Chamaerops humilis	European fan palm
Coprosma repens	Mirror plant
Cordyline indivisa	Blue dracaena
Cortaderia selloana	Pampas grass
Delosperma 'Alba'	White ice plant
Drosanthemum	Rosea ice plant
Euonymus japonica	
Gazania	
Lampranthus	Trailing ice plant
Nerium oleander	Oleander
Phyla nodiflora	Lippia
Pinus halepensis	Alleppo pine
Pittosporum crassifolium	Evergreen pittosporum
Pyracantha	Firethorn
Rosmarinus lockwoodii	Rosemary
Syzygium paniculatum	Brush cherry

Gypsy moth food plant preferences:

MOST PREFERRED

Botanical name	Common name
Amelanchier	Serviceberry
Betula alleghaniensis	Gray birch
Betula papyrifera	Paper birch
Crataegus species	Hawthorn
Hamamelis	Witch hazel
Malus	Apple, crabapple
Populus tremuloides	Quaking aspen
Quercus	Oak
Rosa	Rose
Salix	Willow
Sorbus	Mountain ash
Tamarix	Tamarisk
Tilia	Linden

INTERMEDIATE

Botanical name	Common name
Acer	Maple
Carya	Hickory
Celtis	Hackberry
Cercis	Redbud
Fagus	Beech
Liquidambar	Sweet gum
Magnolia	
Nyssa	Tupelo
Pinus	Pine
Populus deltoides	Cottonwood
Prunus avium	Cherry
Sassafras	
Tsuga	Hemlock
Ulmus	Elm

LEAST PREFERRED

Botanical name	Common name
Abies	Fir
Aesculus	Horse chestnut
Catalpa	
Cornus	Dogwood
Fraxinus	Ash
Ilex	Holly
Juglans nigra	Black walnut
Kalmia	Mountain laurel
Liriodendron	Tuliptree
Morus	Mulberry
Platanus	Sycamore, plane tree
Robinia	Locust

Some plants susceptible to bacterial blight (Pseudomonas syringae):

Almond	Citrus	Oleander
Apple	Lilac	Plum
Avocado	Pea	Rose
Bean	Peach	Stock
Cherry	Pear	

Some plants susceptible and resistant to Phytophthora cinnamoni and P. lateralis:

SUSCEPTIBLE TREES AND SHRUBS

Botanical name	Common name
Abelia	
Abies	Fir
Acacia	
Arctostaphylos	Manzanita
Calluna	Heather
Camellia japonica	
Castanea	Chestnut
Casuarina	Beefwood
Ceanothus	
Cedrus	Cedar
Chamaecyparis	False cypress
Cinnamomum	Camphor tree
Cornus	Dogwood
Cupressus	Cypress
Daphne	
Erica	Heath
Eucalyptus	
Fatsia	Aralia
Hibiscus	
Hypericum	St. John's wort
Juglans	Walnut
Juniperus	Juniper
Larix	Larch
Laurus	Sweet bay
Libocedrus	Incense cedar
Myrtus	Myrtle
Olea	Olive
Picea	Spruce
Pieris	Andromeda
Pinus	Pine
Pittosporum	Mock orange
Platanus	Sycamore
Pseudotsuga	Douglas fir
Quercus	Oak
Rhododendron	Rhododendron, azalea
Salix	Willow
Sequoia sempervirens	Coast redwood
Taxodium	Bald cypress
Taxus	Yew
Thuja	Arborvitae
Viburnum	

Some plants that are susceptible to quince rust (Gymnosporangium clavipes or G. libocedri):

Botanical name	Common name
Amelanchier	Serviceberry
Aronia	Chokeberry
Crataegus	Hawthorn
Juniperus communis and its varieties	Common juniper
Juniperus virginiana	Red cedar
Libocedrus decurrens	Incense cedar
Sorbus	Mountain ash

SUSCEPTIBLE FRUITS AND BERRIES

Apricot
Avocado
Blueberry (highbush)
Cherry
Citrus
Peach
Pear
Rhubarb

RESISTANT TREES AND SHRUBS

Botanical name	Common name
Camellia sasangua	
Chamaecyparis nootkatensis	Alaska cypress
Chamaecyparis pisifera var. filifera	Sawara
Chamaecyparis thyoides	White cedar
Daphne cneorum	Rock daphne
Juniperus chinensis 'Pfitzerana'	Pfitzer's juniper
Juniperus sabina	Savin juniper
Juniperus squamata 'Meyeri'	Meyer juniper
Pinus mugo 'Mughus'	Mugho pine
Rhododendron obtusum	Hiryu azalea
Thuja occidentalis	Arborvitae

RESISTANT BERRY

Blueberry (rabbiteye)

Some plants that are susceptible to cedar-apple rust (Gymnosporangium juniperi-virginianae):

Botanical name	Common name
Juniperius scopulorum and its varieties	Rocky Mountain juniper
Juniperus virginiana	Red cedar
Malus	Apples

PARTICULARLY SUSCEPTIBLE APPLE VARIETIES:

Jonathan
Rome
Wealthy
York Imperial
Bechtel crabapple
Parkman flowering crabapple

Most cultivars of Juniperus chinensis and Juniperus horizontalis are resistant to cedar-apple rust.

Some plants that are resistant to armillaria root rot:

TREES AND SHRUBS

Botanical name	Common name
Abies concolor	White fir
Acacia longifolia	Bush acacia
Acacia mearnsii	Black wattle
Acacia verticillata	Star acacia
Acer macrophyllum	Bigleaf maple
Acer palmatum	Japanese maple
Ailanthus altissima	Tree-of-heaven
Arbutus menziesii	Madrone
Berberis polyantha	Barberry
Betula pumila	Swamp birch
Buxus sempervirens	Boxwood
Calocedrus decurrens	Incense cedar
Catalpa bignonioides	Common catalpa
Celtis species	Hackberry
Ceratonia siliqua	Carob
Cercis occidentalis	California redbud
Cercis siliquastrum	Judas tree
Chaenomeles lagenaria	Japanese quince
Chamaecyparis lawsoniana 'Ellwoodii'	Elwood cypress
Cotinus coggygria	Smoke tree
Cryptomeria japonica	Japanese cedar
Cupaniopsis anacardioides	Carrotwood
Cupressocyparis leylandii	Leyland cypress
Cupressus arizonica var. glabra	Smooth Arizona cypress
Elaeagnus angustifolia	Russian olive
Erica arborea	Tree heath
Eucalyptus camaldulensis	Red gum
Eucalyptus cinerea	Silver-dollar tree
Eugenia species	Eugenia
Fraxinus uhdei	Evergreen ash
Fraxinus velutina var. glabra 'Modesto'	Modesto ash
Ginkgo biloba	Ginkgo
Gleditsia triacanthos 'Shademaster'	Shademaster locust
Hibiscus syriacus	Rose-of-Sharon
Hypericum patulum	St. John's wort
Ilex aquifolium	English holly
Jacaranda acutifolia	Jacaranda
Liquidambar orientalis	Oriental sweet gum
Liquidambar styraciflua	Sweet gum
Liriodendron tulipifera	Tuliptree
Lonicera nitida	Box honeysuckle
Magnolia grandiflora	Southern magnolia
Mahonia aquifolium	Oregon grape
Malus floribunda	Japanese flowering crab
Maytenus boaria	Mayten tree
Metasequoia glyptostroboides	Dawn redwood
Morus species	Mulberry
Myrica pensylvanica	Bayberry
Nandina domestica	Heavenly bamboo
Palms	
Pinus canariensis	Canary Island pine
Pinus nigra	Austrian pine
Pinus radiata	Monterey pine
Pinus sylvestris	Scotch pine
Pinus torreyana	Torrey pine
Pistacia chinensis	Chinese pistache
Pittosporum rhombifolium	Queensland pittosporum
Platanus species	Sycamore
Prunus caroliniana	Cherry laurel
Prunus ilicifolia	Holly-leaved cherry
Prunus lyonii	Catalina cherry
Quercus ilex	Holly oak
Quercus lobata	Valley oak
Raphiolepis umbellata	Yedda hawthorn
Rhus aromatica	Fragrant sumac
Sambucus canadensis	American elder
Sequoia sempervirens	Coast redwood
Sophora japonica	Japanese pagoda tree
Taxodium distichum	Bald cypress
Ternstroemia species	Ternstroemia
Ulmus parvifolia	Chinese elm
Vitex agnus-castus	Chaste tree
Wisteria sinensis	Chinese wisteria

FRUITS, NUTS, AND BERRIES

Botanical name	Common name
Carya illinoinensis	Pecan
Castanea dentata	American chestnut
Diospyros kaki	Japanese persimmon
Diospyros virginiana	Common persimmon
Ficus carica 'Kadota'	Kadota fig
Ficus carica 'Mission'	Mission fig
Juglans hindsii	Black walnut
Malus pumila	Common apple
Malus species	Crabapple
Persea americana	Avocado
Prunus cerasifera	Cherry plum
Prunus serotina salicifolia	Black cherry
Pyrus calleryana	Callery pear
Pyrus communis	Pear
Rubus ursinus loganobaccus	Loganberry
Rubus ursinus	Ollalie

Some plants that are susceptible to fireblight:

TREES AND SHRUBS

Botanical name	Common name
Amelanchier	Serviceberry
Chaenomeles	Flowering quince
Cotoneaster	
Crataegus	Hawthorn
Eriobotrya	Loquat
Malus	Apple, crabapple
Photinia	
Prunus	Flowering almond, plum, and cherry
Rosa	Rose
Sorbus	Mountain ash
Spiraea	

FRUIT TREES AND BERRIES

Apple
Pear
Quince
Raspberry

Varieties of crabapple, pyracantha, and hawthorn that are tolerant of fireblight.

These varieties are not immune to fireblight, but are not damaged by it as severely as are other varieties.

CRABAPPLES

Albright*
Callaway
David
Dolgo*
Liset*
Makamit
Profusion*
Selkirk

PYRACANTHA

Botanical name	Common name
P. coccinea 'lalandii'	Laland's firethorn
P. fortuneana	

HAWTHORN

Botanical name	Common name
Crataegus phaenopyrum	Washington hawthorn

*These varieties are also resistant to scab.

Some varieties of pyracantha resistant to scab:

Mohave
Orange glow
Rogersiana
Shawnee
Watereri

Some avocado varieties for California and Florida, from most hardy to least hardy:

For California	For Florida
Bacon	Brogdon
Zutano	Tonnage
Fuerte	Choquette
Hass	Pollock

Some plants susceptible to *Botryosphaeria ribis*:

TREES AND SHRUBS

Botanical name	Common name
Acer	Maple
Castanea	Chestnut
Cercis	Redbud
Cornus	Dogwood
Forsythia	
Ilex	Holly
Liquidambar	Sweet gum
Nyssa	Tupelo, sour gum
Populus	Poplar
Pyracantha	Firethorn
Rhododendron	Rhododendron, azalea
Rosa	Rose
Salix	Willow

FRUIT AND NUT TREES AND SMALL FRUITS

Apple
Avocado
Citrus
Currant
Fig
Hickory
Pear
Pecan

Some plants that may be infested by the Mediterranean fruit fly:

Apple
Apricot
Avocado
Cantaloupe
Cherry
Citrus
Cucumber
Fig
Grape
Guava
Loquat
Olive
Peach
Pear
Pepper
Persimmon
Plum
Pumpkin
Pyracantha
Quince
Squash (Hubbard)
Strawberry
Tomato
Walnut

Adapted from "California Agriculture," March-April 1981.

The pH Scale

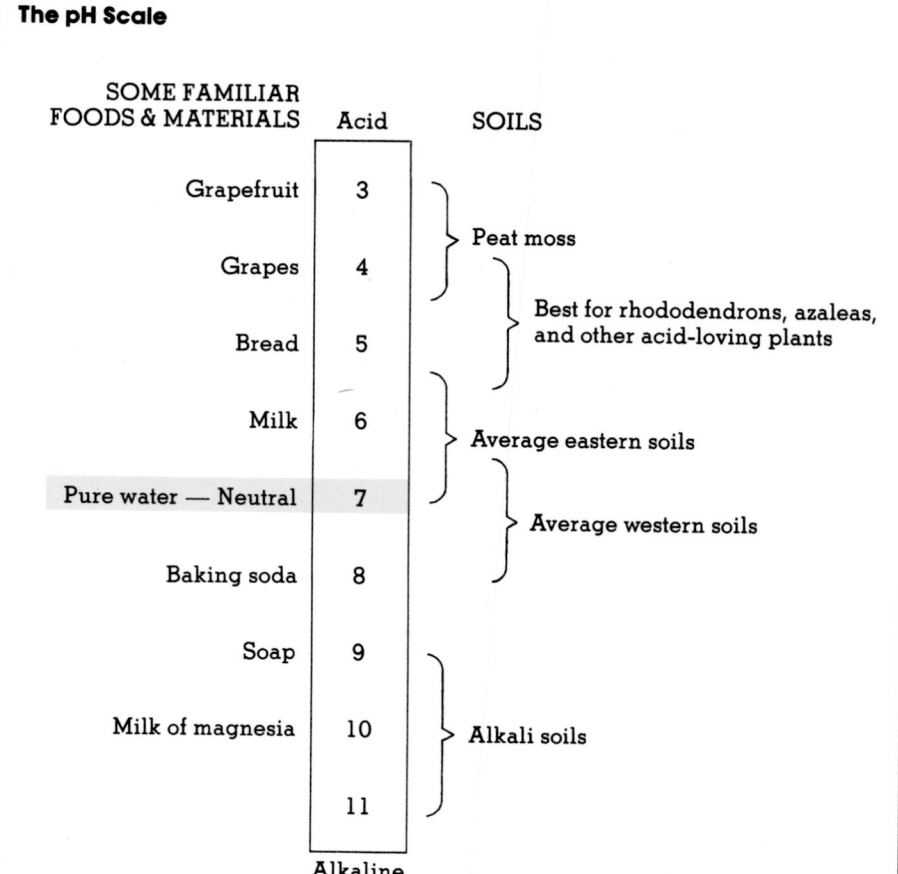

Apply limestone to raise pH

Pounds of ground limestone needed per 100 square feet to raise pH to 6.5:

Present pH of soil	Pounds needed to raise sandy loam to pH 6.5	Pounds needed to raise loam to pH 6.5	Pounds needed to raise clay loam to pH 6.5
4.0	11.5	16	23
4.5	9.5	13.5	19.5
5.0	8	10.5	15
5.5	6	8	10.5
6.0	3	4	5.5

Dolomitic limestone is recommended because it adds magnesium as well as calcium to the soil. The limestone should be cultivated into the soil.

Adapted from "Soil acidity needs of plants," New York Cooperative Extension Service, publication D-2-25.

Some pecan varieties — regional adaptation, pollination requirements, and disease resistance:

Variety	Regional Adaptation	Pollination Requirements	Disease Resistance
Cape Fear	I, II	A	
Cheyenne	II	B	S
Colby	III	D	
Elliot	II	B	S+
Mahan	II	A	
Major	III	D	
Missouri Hardy	III	C	
Schley	I, II	A	
Stuart's Paper Shell	I, II	A	S+
Success	II	A	
Western Schley	II	B	

REGIONAL ADAPTATION
I Louisiana to Florida.
II Areas of Texas, Arizona, New Mexico, and California within USDA Plant Hardiness Zones 7 through 9. See page 1004.
III Oklahoma, Kansas, Missouri, Iowa, Illinois, Indiana, Kentucky, and Tennessee.

POLLINATION REQUIREMENTS
Pecans are self-fruitful, but crops will be improved by use of a pollinator.
A Use another A.
B Use another B.
C Plant two of this variety.
D Use another D.

DISEASE RESISTANCE
S+ Resistant to scab.
S Moderately resistant to scab.

Some fig varieties, with special regional adaptations:

Variety	South*	California interior valleys	California coastal areas	Northwest coastal areas
Brown Turkey		•	•	
Celeste	•			
Eastern Brown Turkey**	•			
Green Ischia	•			
Kadota		•		
King ('Desert King')				•
Latterula				•
Magnolia	•			
Mission		•	•	

* Southern areas suitable for growing figs are Florida, Georgia, South Carolina, North Carolina, Alabama, Mississippi, Louisiana, southern Arkansas, and Texas.
** Also called Lee's Perpetual, Brunswick, Ramsey, Harrison, and Everbearing.

Some plants that will grow in acid soil (pH 4.5 to 5.5):

TREES AND SHRUBS

Botanical name	Common name
Amelanchier	Serviceberry
Arctostaphylos	Manzanita, kinnikinick
Calluna	Heather
Camellia	
Cytisus	Broom
Erica	Heath
Gardenia	
Hydrangea	
Ilex	Holly
Kalmia	Mountain laurel
Lagerstroemia indica	Crapemyrtle
Leucothoe	
Magnolia	
Picea	Spruce
Pieris	Andromeda
Pinus	Pine
Populus tremuloides	Quaking aspen
Quercus palustris	Pin oak
Rhododendron	Azalea, rhododendron
Salix babylonica	Weeping willow
Sorbus	Mountain ash
Tsuga	Hemlock

FLOWERS

Botanical name	Common name
Convallaria	Lily-of-the-valley
Coreopsis	
Gypsophila	Baby's-breath
Lupinus	Lupine

Cold hardiness of citrus, from most hardy to least hardy:

Kumquat
Meyer lemon
Mandarin orange
Orange
Grapefruit
Lemon
Lime

Home gardeners in Florida and California can plant a wide variety of citrus in the milder areas of their states. In the warmest areas, you will have success with the more tender citrus such as grapefruit, lemons, and limes. South Texas gardeners can plant Meyer lemon, Satsuma mandarin, and Marr's Early Orange.

Regional adaptations of some blueberry varieties:

FOR THE SOUTH AND SOUTHERN CALIFORNIA:

Rabbiteye (*Vaccinium ashei*)

Bluebelle	Tifblue
Bluegem	Woodward
Climax	

Highbush (*Vaccinium* species)

Avonblue	Sharpblue
Flordablue	

FOR THE VERY COLDEST REGIONS:

Meader	Northland

WIDELY ADAPTED:

Berkeley	Collins
Bluecrop	Jersey
Blueray	Patriot
Bluetta	

Some plants that will grow in alkaline soil (pH 7.5 to 8.4):

TREES AND SHRUBS

Botanical name	Common name
Acer negundo	Box elder
Albizia	Silk tree
Berberis thunbergii	Japanese barberry
Casuarina	Beefwood
Celtis	Hackberry
Cercocarpus	Mountain mahogany
Deutzia	
Elaeagnus angustifolia	Russian olive
Forsythia	
Fraxinus velutina	Velvet ash
Hibiscus syriacus	Rose-of-Sharon
Kerria	
Lonicera fragrantissima	Fragrant honeysuckle
Malus sargentii	Sargent crabapple
Philadelphus	Mock orange
Phoenix dactylifera	Date palm
Populus fremontii	Fremont cottonwood
Potentilla fruticosa	Bush cinquefoil
Robinia	Black locust
Sophora japonica	Japanese pagoda
Spiraea vanhouttei	Vanhoutte spirea
Viburnum dentatum	Arrowwood
Viburnum dilatatum	Linden viburnum
Washingtonia	Washington palm
Ziziphus jujuba	Common Jujube

Plant Climate Zone Map

These zones are based on mean minimum temperatures, and represent only an *average* for areas within the zone. Your location might be a zone or two warmer than the map shows if you live near a large body of water, or a zone or two colder if you live at a high elevation or on a north-facing slope. Adapted from the USDA Plant Climate Zone Map.

Range of average minimum temperatures for each zone:

Zone 1	Below −50°F		**Zone 6**	−10° to 0°
Zone 2	−50° to −40°		**Zone 7**	0° to 10°
Zone 3	−40° to −30°		**Zone 8**	10° to 20°
Zone 4	−30° to −20°		**Zone 9**	20° to 30°
Zone 5	−20° to −10°		**Zone 10**	30° to 40°

Apples

Variety	Pollination	Disease Resistance	2	3	4	5	6	7	8	9	10[2]
Anna	D								•	•	•
Baldwin	A	FB	•	•	•	•					
Cortland	B	*PM*		•	•	•	•				
Dorsett Golden	D							•	•	•	•
Ein Shemer	D							•	•	•	
Empire	B	FB				•	•	•			
Golden Delicious	A					•	•	•	•		
Granny Smith	B								•	•	
Gravenstein	E	*PM*					•	•	•	•	
Idared	E	*FB, PM*			•	•	•				
Jonathan	B	*CAR, FB, PM*			•	•	•	•	•		
McIntosh	B				•	•	•				
Newton Pippin	B					•	•	•	•		
Northern Spy	B			•	•	•	•	•			
Prima	C	PM, S+, FB				•	•	•	•		
Priscilla	C	CAR+, S+, FB				•	•	•	•		
Red Delicious	Spur B	BR, *CAR*				•	•	•	•		
Red Rome Beauty	A	*FB, PM*				•	•	•	•		
Rhode Island Greening	E	*FB*			•	•	•				
Sir Prize	C	S+, PM				•	•	•	•		
Stayman Winesap	E	BR, FB				•	•	•			
Winesap	E					•	•	•	•		
Winter Banana	B					•	•	•	•		
Yellow Transparent	B	*FB*			•	•	•	•	•		

[1]Based on USDA Plant Hardiness Zone Map. See page 1004.
[2]Florida only.

POLLINATION KEY
A Self-fruitful, but crop is improved with a pollinator.
B Pollinate with any A or B.
C Prima and Priscilla cross-pollinate well. Sir Prize needs either Prima or Priscilla for pollination, but will not pollinate them.
D Pollinate with another D.
E Not a pollinator. Pollinate with an A or a B.

DISEASE KEY
BR Fairly resistant to bitter rot.
CAR Highly susceptible to cedar-apple rust.
CAR+ Resistant to cedar-apple rust.
FB Fairly resistant to fireblight.
FB Highly susceptible to fireblight.
PM Fairly resistant to powdery mildew.
PM Highly susceptible to powdery mildew.
S+ Resistant to scab.

Apricots

Variety	Pollination	Disease Resistance	2	3	4	5	6	7	8	9[2]	10
Blenheim	A	*BR*					•	•	•	•	
Goldcot	A					•	•	•	•		
Perfection	B						•	•	•		
Royal	A	*BR*					•	•	•		
Tilton	A	BR					•	•	•	•	
Stella	A					•	•	•	•		

[1]Based on USDA Plant Hardiness Map. See page 1004.
[2]California only.

POLLINATION KEY
A Self-fruitful. Needs no pollinator.
B Not self-fruitful. Pollinate with Blenheim or Royal.

DISEASE KEY
BR Fairly resistant to brown rot.
BR Highly susceptible to brown rot.

Peaches

Variety	Pollination	Disease Resistance	2	3	4	5	6	7	8	9	10
Belle of Georgia	A	BLS+				•	•	•	•		
Desertgold	A								•	•	•
Early-Red-Fre	A	BLS+				•	•	•	•		
Elberta	A	*BLS*				•	•	•	•		
Flordasun	A									•	•[3]
J.H. Hale	B					•	•	•	•		
Madison[2]	A	BLS				•	•	•	•		
Redhaven	A	BLS				•	•	•	•		
Redskin	A	BLS				•	•	•	•		
Reliance[2]	A					•	•	•			
Rio-oso-gem	A	*BLS*				•	•	•	•		
Sunhaven	A	BLS				•	•	•	•		

[1] Based on USDA Plant Hardiness Zone Map. See page 1004.
[2] Does well in colder areas of Zone 5.
[3] Florida only.

POLLINATION KEY
A Self-fruitful. Requires no pollinator.
B Requires pollinator. Use an A.

DISEASE KEY
BLS+ Resistant to bacterial leaf spot.
BLS Fairly resistant to bacterial leaf spot.
BLS Susceptible to bacterial leaf spot.

Pears

Variety	Pollination	Disease Resistance	2	3	4	5	6	7	8	9[2]	10
Bartlett	B	*FB*				•	•	•		•	
Bosc	B	*FB*				•	•	•		•	
Clapp's favorite	B	*FB*				•	•	•			
Comice	B	(FB)				•	•	•		•	
D'Anjou	B	*FB*				•	•	•			
Kieffer[3]	A	FB			•	•	•	•	•	•	
Moonglow	A	FB+				•	•	•	•		
Orient[3]	A	FB+				•	•	•	•	•	
Seckel	C	FB				•	•	•			

[1] Based on USDA Plant Hardiness Zone Map. See page 1004.
[2] California only.
[3] Grown in Florida.

POLLINATION KEY
A Pollinate with another A.
B Pollinate with any B.
C Pollinate with any B except Bartlett.

DISEASE KEY
FB+ Resistant to fireblight.
FB Fairly resistant to fireblight.
(FB) Moderately susceptible to fireblight.
FB Highly susceptible to fireblight.

Plums

Variety	Type	Pollination	Disease Resistance	4	5	6	7	8	9[2]	10
Blue Damson	E	B	*BK*		•	•	•			
Burbank	J	D			•	•	•	•	•	
Ember	J	E		•	•	•	•	•		
Green Gage	E	B				•	•	•		
Italian Prune (Fellenberg)	EPP	F				•	•	•		
Methley	J	C	BK		•	•	•	•	•	
Ozark Premier	J	D			•	•	•	•	•	
President	E	A	BK+		•	•	•	•	•	
Santa Rosa	J	C	BK		•	•	•	•	•	
Shiro	J	D	BK			•	•	•	•	•
Stanley	EPP	F	*BK*	•	•	•	•	•		
Underwood	J	E				•	•	•	•	•

[1] Based on USDA Plant Hardiness Map. See page 1004.
[2] California only.

TYPES
E European blue plum
EPP European prune plum
J Japanese red plum

POLLINATION KEY
A Not self-fruitful, pollinate with a B.
B Self-fruitful, no pollinator necessary.
C Self-fruitful, but crop is improved by a pollinator; use a D.
D Not self-fruitful, pollinate with another D.
E Ember and Underwood cross-pollinate well.
F Self-fruitful, but crop improved by a pollinator; use an F.

DISEASE RESISTANCE
BK+ Resistant to black knot.
BK Fairly resistant to black knot.
BK Highly susceptible to black knot.

Some strawberry varieties — regional adaptation and disease resistance:

Variety	Disease Resistance	Widely Adapted	South	North	California	Northwest
Blakemore	S+, LS, VW+	•				
Catskill	S+, VW+			•		
Darrow	LS, PM, S, RS+, VW	•				
Delite	RS+, VW+	•				
Earlibelle	LS, S		•			
Empire	VW+			•		
Fletcher	S+, VW+			•		
Florida 90*	V		•			
Guardian	RS+, VW+	•				
Hood	RS+, VW+, LS					•
Midway	RS			•		
Northwest	V, LS+					•
Ogallala	LS+	•				
Pocahontas	LS+		•			
Redchief	RS+, S+, VW	•				
Salinas	VW+				•	•
Sequoia					•	
Sparkle	RS+			•		
Surecrop	VW+, RS+	•				
Tioga	V				•	•

*Adapted to extreme southern regions.

DISEASE RESISTANCE KEY
LS   Moderately resistant to leaf spot.
LS+ Resistant to leaf spot.
PM   Moderately resistant to powdery mildew.
RS   Moderately resistant to one or more races of red stele.
RS+ Resistant to one or more races of red stele.
S   Moderately resistant to scorch
S+   Resistant to scorch
V   Moderately resistant to virus.
VW   Moderately resistant to verticillium wilt.
VW+ Resistant to verticillium wilt.

Some grape varieties, with disease resistance and regional adaptation:

Variety	Disease Resistance	Northeast	Midwest	Pacific Northwest	Southeast	California Arizona
Aurore	DM	•		•		
Beta	BR+	•	•	•		
Campbell's Early	BR+	•		•		
Concord	DM	•	•	•		•
Delaware	PM	•	•	•		
Fredonia	BR+	•		•		
Magnolia					•	
Missouri Reisling	BR+	•				
Niagara	PM	•	•	•		•
Scuppernong*					•	
Thompson Seedless						•
Tokay						•
Worden	BR+	•	•	•		

*Needs pollinator; use Magnolia.

DISEASE RESISTANCE KEY
BR+ Resistant to black rot.
DM   Moderately resistant to downy mildew.
PM   Moderately resistant to powdery mildew.

Some bramble varieties, with special regional adaptation and/or disease resistance:

BLACKBERRIES	Disease Resistance	Widely Adapted	North	South	Pacific Coast	California
Black Satin				•		
Darrow		•	•			
Ebony King	OR	•				
Eldorado	OR	•				
Flordagrand*	LS			•		
Lawton	OR, V					
Oklawaha*				•		

RED RASPBERRIES						
August Red			•			
Latham		•	•			
Meeker	PM	•			•	
Southland	LS, A, PM			•		
Sumner	PM	•			•	
Willamette	PM	•			•	

TRAILING BLACKBERRIES						
Boysenberry					•	•
Loganberry					•	
Ollaliberry	V,M					•
Youngberry					•	•

*Need cross-pollination.

DISEASE RESISTANCE KEY
A — Resistant to anthracnose.
LS — Resistant to leaf spot.
M — Resistant to mosaic.
OR — Resistant to orange rust.
PM — Resistant to powdery mildew.
V — Resistant to verticillium wilt.

Sweet cherries

Variety	Pollination	Disease Resistance	2	3	4	5	6	7	8	9²	10
Bing	A	*BC*				•	•	•	•	•	
Black Tartarian	B					•	•	•	•	•	
Corum	C	BC				•	•	•			
Early Burlat	C	BC+				•	•	•	•	•	
Lambert	A	*BC*				•	•	•			
Royal Ann	A	*BC*				•	•	•			
Sam	C	BC				•	•	•			
Sue	C	BC				•	•	•			
Van	B	*BC*				•	•	•	•	•	

(Zone Adaptation¹)

¹Based on USDA Plant Hardiness Zone Map. See page 1004.
²California only.

POLLINATION KEY
A Pollinate with a B.
B Pollinate with an A.
C Pollinate with an A or a B.
D Self-fruitful, needs no pollinator.

DISEASE KEY
BC+ Resistant to bacterial canker.
BC Fairly resistant to bacterial canker.
BC Susceptible to bacterial canker.
CLS Fairly resistant to cherry leafspot.

Sour cherries

Variety	Pollination	Disease Resistance	2	3	4	5	6	7	8	9	10
Meteor	D	CLS		•	•	•	•				
Montmorency	D				•	•	•				
North Star	D	CLS		•	•	•	•	•			

Earliest dates for safe spring planting of vegetables:

To find the average date of the last freeze, ask at your local nursery or Cooperative Extension office (see page 1011).

Planting dates for localities in which average date of last freeze is:

Crop	Feb. 1	Feb. 15	Mar. 1	Mar. 15	Apr. 1	Apr. 15	May 1	May 15	June 1
Asparagus	—	—	—	2/1	2/15	3/15	3/15	4/15	5/1
Bean, lima	2/1	3/1	3/15	4/1	4/15	5/1	5/15	6/1	—
Bean, snap	2/1	3/1	3/15	3/15	4/1	4/15	5/1	5/15	6/1
Beet	1/1	1/15	2/15	2/15	3/1	3/15	4/1	4/15	5/1
Broccoli*	1/1	1/15	2/1	2/15	3/1	3/15	4/1	4/15	5/15
Brussels sprout*	1/1	1/15	2/1	2/15	3/1	3/15	4/1	4/15	5/15
Cabbage*	1/1	1/1	1/15	2/1	2/15	3/1	3/15	4/15	5/15
Carrot	1/1	1/15	2/1	2/15	3/1	3/15	4/1	5/1	5/15
Cauliflower*	1/1	1/15	1/15	2/1	2/15	3/1	4/1	4/15	5/15
Cucumber	2/15	2/15	3/1	4/1	4/15	5/1	5/15	6/1	—
Eggplant*	2/1	2/15	3/15	4/1	4/15	5/1	5/15	6/1	—
Lettuce	1/1	1/1	1/1	2/1	2/15	3/15	4/1	4/15	5/15
Muskmelon	2/15	2/15	3/1	4/1	4/15	5/1	6/1	—	—
Onion	1/1	1/1	1/1	2/1	2/15	3/1	3/15	4/15	5/1
Parsley	1/1	1/1	1/15	2/1	2/15	3/15	4/1	4/15	5/15
Pea	1/1	1/1	1/15	2/1	2/15	3/15	4/1	4/15	5/1
Pepper*	2/1	3/1	3/15	4/1	4/15	5/1	5/15	6/1	6/1
Potato	1/1	1/15	1/15	2/1	3/1	3/15	4/1	4/15	5/1
Radish	1/1	2/2	1/1	1/15	2/15	3/1	3/15	4/1	5/1
Spinach	1/1	1/1	1/1	1/15	2/1	2/15	3/15	4/1	4/15
Squash	2/1	3/1	3/15	4/1	4/15	5/1	5/1	5/15	6/1
Tomato*	2/1	3/1	3/15	4/1	4/15	5/1	5/15	5/15	6/1
Turnip	1/1	1/15	2/1	2/1	2/15	3/1	3/15	4/1	5/1
Watermelon	2/15	2/15	3/1	3/15	4/15	5/1	5/15	6/1	—

* Seeds may be started indoors 4 to 6 weeks before planting date.

Vegetable seed information:

	Optimum germination temperatures	Days to germination
Asparagus	70-75°F	14-21
Bean, lima	70	7-10
Bean, snap	70	6-10
Beet	50-85	10-14
Broccoli	70-75	10-14
Brussels sprout	70-75	10-14
Cabbage	70-75	10-14
Carrot	50-85	14-21
Cauliflower	70-75	8-10
Cucumber	70	7-10
Eggplant	70	10-15
Lettuce	65-70	7-10
Melon	75	5-7
Onion	70-75	10-14
Parsley	70-75	14-21
Pea, garden	40-75	7-10
Pepper	75-80	10
Radish	45-85	4-6
Spinach	70	8-10
Squash	70-75	7-10
Sweet corn	70	5-7
Tomato	70-75	5-8
Turnip	60-85	7-10

Some vegetables that are susceptible to verticillium wilt:

Artichoke
Beet
Brussels sprout
Cabbage
Eggplant
Melon[1]
New Zealand spinach
Okra
Peanut
Pepper
Potato
Pumpkin
Radish
Rhubarb
Spinach
Strawberry[2]
Tomato

[1]Watermelon, cantaloupe, and honeydew become infected, but are not seriously damaged. Persian, casaba, and crenshaw melons are very susceptible.

[2]See page 1007 for strawberry varieties that are resistant to verticillium.

Adapted from "Plants resistant or susceptible to verticillium wilt," University of California Cooperative Extension leaflet 2703.

Some cucumber varieties that are resistant to mosaic virus:

Bounty
Burpless
Early Surecrop
Gemini 7
Liberty hybrid
Marketmore 70, 76, 80
Saladin hybrid
Slicemaster
Sweet Slice
Victory

Regional adaptation of some onion varieties:

FOR THE SOUTH
Excel
Granex
Texas Grano
Tropicana Red
White Granex

FOR THE WEST
California Early Red
Early Yellow Globe
Southport Yellow Globe
Yellow Bermuda

FOR THE NORTH
Downing Yellow Globe
Early Yellow Globe
Empire
Nutmeg
Spartan lines

Some vegetables that are susceptible to fusarium wilt caused by various forms of Fusarium oxysporum:

Asparagus
Beans
Brussels sprout
Cabbage
Cauliflower
Celery
Cucumber
Melons
Okra
Onion
Pea
Pepper
Radish
Spinach
Sweet potato
Tomato
Turnip

Some tomato varieties — adaptation and disease resistance:

EARLY SEASON

	Disease Resistance	Widely Adapted	For the South	For the North	For the West
Early Cascade	V, F	•			
Jetfire	V, F				•
New Yorker	V			•	
Porter Improved					•
Small Fry	V, F, N	•			
Spring Set	V, F	•			

MIDSEASON

	Disease Resistance	Widely Adapted	For the South	For the North	For the West
Ace 55	V, F				•
Atkinson	F, N		•		
Better Boy	V, F, N	•			
Big Girl Hybrid	V, F	•			
Big Set	V, F, N	•			
Bonus	V, F, N	•			
Burpee's VF	V, F	•			
Columbia	V, F, Ct	•			
Floradel	F		•		
Floramerica	V, F	•			
Heinz 1350	V, F	•			
Jet Star	V, F			•	
Marglobe	F	•			
Park's Whopper	V, F, N, T	•			
Roma VF	V, F	•			
Rowpac	V, F, Ct				•
Roza	V, F, Ct				•
Salad Master	V, F, Ct				•
Supersonic	V, F			•	•
Terrific	V, F, N	•			
Tropi-Red	V, F		•		

LATE SEASON

	Disease Resistance	Widely Adapted	For the South	For the North	For the West
Beefeater	V, F, N	•			
Beefmaster	V, F, N	•			
Manalucie	F		•		
Ramapo	V, F			•	
Tropic	V, F, T		•		
Wonder Boy	V, F	•			
Vineripe	V, F, N	•			

DISEASE KEY
V   Resistant to verticillium wilt.
F   Resistant to fusarium wilt.
N   Resistant to nematodes.
T   Resistant to tobacco mosaic virus.
Ct   Resistant to curly top.

Bean varieties resistant to bean mosaic:

BUSH BEANS
Contender
Harvester
Provider
Tender Crop
Top Crop

WAX BUSH BEANS
Cherokee
Gold Crop
Sungold

POLE BEANS
McClasan

COUNTY EXTENSION AGENTS

ALABAMA
Autauga	205-365-2243
Baldwin	205-937-7176
Barbour	205-775-3284
Bibb	205-926-4818
Blount	205-274-2129
Bullock	205-738-2580
Butler	205-382-5111
Calhoun	205-237-1621
Chambers	205-864-9373
Cherokee	205-927-3250
Chilton	205-755-3240
Choctaw	205-459-2133
Clarke	205-275-3121
Clay	205-354-2183
Cleburne	205-463-2620
Coffee	205-894-5596
Colbert	205-383-1363
Conecuh	205-578-1311
Coosa	205-377-4713
Covington	205-222-1125
Crenshaw	205-335-6551
Cullman	205-739-3530
Dale	501-774-2329
Dallas	205-875-3200
DeKalb	205-845-3323
Elmore	205-567-6301
Escambia	205-867-6038
Etowah	205-546-2821
Fayette	205-932-5248
Franklin	205-332-2101
Geneva	205-684-2484
Greene	205-372-3401
Hale	205-624-8710
Henry	205-585-2349
Houston	205-794-4108
Jackson	205-574-2143
Jefferson	205-325-5342
Lamar	205-695-7139
Lauderdale	205-766-5180
Lawrence	205-974-1177
Lee	205-749-3353
Limestone	205-232-5510
Lowndes	205-548-2315
Macon	205-727-0340
Madison	205-536-5911
Marengo	205-295-5959
Marion	205-921-3551
Marshall	205-582-2000
Mobile	205-690-8445
Monroe	205-575-3477
Montgomery	205-832-4950
Morgan	205-773-2549
Perry	205-683-6888
Pickens	205-367-8148
Pike	205-566-1656
Randolph	205-357-2841
Russell	205-298-6845
St. Clair	205-338-9416
Shelby	205-669-6763
Sumter	205-652-9501
Talladega	205-362-6187
Tallapoosa	205-825-4228
Tuscaloosa	205-349-3870
Walker	205-221-3392
Washington	205-847-2295
Wilcox	205-682-4289
Winston	205-489-5376

ARIZONA
Apache	602-337-2267
Cochise	602-384-3594
Coconino	602-774-5011
Gila	602-425-7179
Graham	602-428-2611
Greenlee	602-359-2261
Maricopa	602-255-4456
Mohave	602-753-3788
Navajo	602-524-6271
Pima	602-882-5161
Pinal	602-836-5221
Santa Cruz	602-287-4689
Yavapai	602-445-6597
Yuma	602-783-4451

ARKANSAS
Arkansas	501-946-3231
Ashley	501-853-8391
Baxter	501-425-2335
Benton	501-273-3346
Boone	501-741-6168
Bradley	501-226-5813
Calhoun	501-798-2231
Carroll	501-423-2958
Chicot	501-265-5883
Clark	501-246-2281
Clay	501-598-2246
Cleburne	501-362-2524
Cleveland	501-325-6321
Columbia	501-234-1390
Conway	501-354-2494
Craighead	501-932-3621
Crawford	501-474-5286
Crittenden	501-739-3239
Cross	501-238-2335
Dallas	501-352-3505
Desha	501-222-3972
Drew	501-367-3128
Faulkner	501-329-8344
Franklin	501-667-3720
Fulton	501-895-3301
Garland	501-623-6841
Grant	501-942-2231
Greene	501-236-6921
Hempstead	501-777-5771
Hot Spring	501-332-5267
Howard	501-845-2375
Independence	501-793-6826
Izard	501-368-4323
Jackson	501-523-6594
Jefferson	501-534-1033
Johnson	501-754-2240
Lafayette	501-921-4744
Lawrence	501-886-3741
Lee	501-295-5202
Lincoln	501-628-4247
Little River	501-898-3394
Logan	501-963-2360
Lonoke	501-676-3124
Madison	501-738-6826
Marion	501-449-6349
Miller	501-773-4666

Mississippi	501-762-2075
Monroe	501-747-3397
Montgomery	501-867-2311
Nevada	501-887-2818
Newton	501-446-2240
Quachita	501-836-6858
Perry	501-889-2661
Phillips	501-338-7447
Pike	501-285-2161
Poinsett	501-578-5496
Polk	501-394-2323
Pope	501-968-7098
Prairie	501-998-2614
Pulaski	501-661-4676
Randolph	501-892-4504
St. Francis	501-633-3034
Saline	501-778-2483
Scott	501-637-2173
Searcy	501-448-3981
Sebastian	501-782-4947
Sevier	501-584-3013
Sharp	501-994-7363
Stone	501-269-3336
Union	501-862-4226
Van Buren	501-745-7117
Washington	501-442-9821
White	501-268-5394
Woodruff	501-347-2556
Yell	501-495-2216

CALIFORNIA
Alameda	415-881-6341
Amador	209-223-3151
Butte	916-534-4201
Calaveras	209-754-4160
Colusa	916-458-2105
Contra Costa	415-439-4398
El Dorado	916-626-2468
Fresno	209-453-5931
Glenn	916-865-4487
Humboldt-Del Norte	707-443-0896
Imperial	714-352-3610
Inyo-Mono	714-873-5891
Kern	805-861-2631
Kings	209-582-3211
Lake	707-263-2281
Lassen	916-257-5505
Los Angeles	213-744-4851
Madera	209-674-4641
Marin	415-499-6352
Mariposa	209-966-2417
Mendocino	707-468-4495
Merced	209-726-7404
Modoc	916-233-2123
Monterey	408-758-4637
Napa	707-253-4221
Orange	714-774-7050
Placer-Nevada	916-823-4581
Plumas-Sierra	916-283-0250
Riverside	714-683-6491
Sacramento	916-366-2013
San Benito	408-637-5346
San Bernardino	714-383-3871
San Diego	714-565-5376
San Joaquin	209-944-2665

San Luis Obispo	805-549-5940
San Mateo-San Francisco	415-726-9059
Santa Barbara	805-964-9869
	805-961-3689
Santa Clara	408-299-2635
Santa Cruz	408-724-4734
Shasta	916-246-5621
Siskiyou	916-842-2711
Solano	707-429-6381
Sonoma	707-527-2621
Stanislaus	209-526-6654
Sutter-Yuba	916-673-9645
Tehama	916-527-3101
Trinity	916-623-2361
Tulare	209-733-6363
Tuolumne	209-533-5695
Ventura	805-654-2924
Yolo	916-666-8435

COLORADO
Adams	303-659-4150
Arapahoe	303-795-4670
Archuleta	303-264-5931
Boulder	303-776-4865
Chaffee	303-539-6447
Custer	303-783-2514
Denver	303-355-4416
Dolores	303-677-2283
Douglas	303-688-3096
Eagle	303-328-7311
Elbert	303-541-2361
El Paso	303-471-5764
Fremont	303-275-1514
Garfield	303-945-7437
Grand	303-724-3436
Gunnison	303-641-4100
Huerfano	303-738-2170
Jackson	303-723-4298
Jefferson	303-277-8980
La Plata	303-247-4355
Larimer	303-221-7580
Las Animas	303-846-6881
Lincoln	303-743-2542
Logan	303-522-3200
Moffat	303-824-6673
Montezuma	303-565-3123
Morgan	303-867-2493
Park	303-836-2771
Pitkin	303-925-5185
Pueblo	303-543-3550
Rio Blanco	303-878-5682
Routt	303-879-0825
San Miguel	303-327-4393
Sedgwick	303-474-3479
Summit	303-668-3595
Teller	303-689-2552
Weld	303-356-4000

CONNECTICUT
Fairfield	203-797-4176
Hartford	203-236-6151
Litchfield	203-567-9447
Middlesex	203-345-4511
New Haven	203-269-7788

COUNTY EXTENSION AGENTS

New London	203-887-1608	Putnam	904-328-5181	Elbert	404-283-3001	Rabun	404-782-3113
Tolland	203-875-3331	St. Johns	904-824-8131	Emanuel	912-237-9933	Randolph	912-732-2311
Windham	203-774-9600	St. Lucie	305-464-2900	Evans	912-739-1292	Richmond	404-828-6812
		Santa Rosa	904-623-3868	Fannin	404-632-5722	Rockdale	404-922-7750
DELAWARE		Sarasota	813-955-6239	Fayette	404-461-4580	Schley	912-937-2601
Kent	302-736-1448	Seminole	305-323-2500	Floyd	404-295-6210	Screven	912-564-2064
New Castle	302-738-2506	Sumter	904-793-2728	Forsyth	404-887-2418	Seminole	912-524-2326
Sussex	302-856-5250	Suwannee	904-362-2771	Franklin	404-384-2843	Spalding	404-228-9900
		Taylor	904-584-4345	Fulton	404-572-3261	Stephens	404-886-4046
DISTRICT OF COLUMBIA		Union	904-496-2321	Gilmer	404-635-4426	Stewart	912-838-4908
	202-727-2016	Volusia	904-736-0624	Glascock	404-598-2811	Sumter	912-924-4476
		Wakulla	904-926-3931	Glynn	912-265-0610	Talbot	404-665-3230
FLORIDA		Walton	904-892-5415	Gordon	404-629-8685	Tattnall	912-654-2593
Alachua	904-377-0400	Washington	904-638-0740	Grady	912-377-1312	Taylor	912-862-5496
Baker	904-259-3520			Greene	404-453-2083	Telfair	912-868-6489
Bay	904-763-5456	**GEORGIA**		Gwinnett	404-962-1480	Terrell	912-995-2165
Bradford	904-964-6280	Appling	912-367-2372	Habersham	404-754-2318	Thomas	912-226-3954
Brevard	305-632-9505	Atkinson	912-422-3277	Hall	404-536-6681	Tift	912-382-3600
Broward	305-475-8010	Bacon	912-632-5601	Hancock	404-444-6596	Toombs	912-526-3101
Calhoun	904-674-8323	Baker	912-734-5252	Haralson	404-646-5288	Towns	404-896-2024
Charlotte	813-639-6255	Baldwin	912-453-4394	Harris	404-628-4824	Treutlen	912-529-4913
Citrus	904-726-2141	Banks	404-677-2245	Hart	404-376-3134	Troup	404-884-6686
Clay	904-284-9951	Barrow	404-867-7581	Heard	404-675-3513	Turner	912-567-3448
Collier	813-774-8370	Bartow	404-382-2324	Henry	404-957-9131	Twiggs	912-945-3391
Columbia	904-752-5247	Ben Hill	912-423-2360	Houston	912-987-2028	Union	404-745-2524
Dade	305-248-3311	Berrien	912-686-5431	Irwin	912-468-7409	Upson	404-647-8989
Desoto	813-494-0303	Bibb	912-744-6338	Jackson	404-367-8789	Walker	404-638-2548
Dixie	904-498-3330	Bleckley	912-934-6917	Jasper	404-468-6479	Walton	404-267-3101
Duval	904-384-2062	Brantley	912-462-5724	Jeff Davis	912-375-2631	Ware	912-283-6223
Escambia	904-438-1020	Brooks	912-263-4103	Jefferson	912-625-3046	Warren	404-465-2136
Flagler	904-437-3122	Bryan	912-653-2231	Jenkins	912-982-4408	Washington	912-552-2011
Franklin	904-653-9337	Bulloch	912-764-6101	Johnson	912-864-3373	Wayne	912-427-6865
Gadsden	904-627-6315	Burke	404-554-2119	Jones	912-986-3948	Webster	912-828-2325
Gilchrist	904-463-2022	Butts	404-775-2601	Lamar	404-358-0281	Wheeler	912-568-3081
Glades	813-946-0244	Calhoun	912-849-2685	Lanier	912-482-3895	White	404-865-2832
Gulf	904-229-6123	Camden	912-576-5465	Laurens	912-272-2277	Whitfield	404-278-8207
Hamilton	904-792-1312	Candler	912-685-2408	Lee	912-759-6426	Wilcox	912-365-2323
Hardee	813-773-2164	Carroll	404-834-1490	Liberty	912-876-2133	Wilkes	404-678-2332
Hendry	813-675-2361	Catoosa	404-935-4211	Lincoln	404-359-3233	Wilkinson	912-946-2367
Hernando	904-796-9421	Charlton	912-496-2040	Long	912-545-9549	Worth	912-776-2011
Highlands	813-385-5158	Chatham	912-944-2291	Lowndes	912-242-1858		
Hillsborough	813-621-5605	Chattooga	404-857-1410	Lumpkin	404-864-2275		
Holmes	904-547-2584	Cherokee	404-479-1966	Macon	912-472-7588	**IDAHO**	
Indian River	305-562-0350	Clarke	404-546-8330	Madison	404-795-2281	Ada	208-384-8780
Jackson	904-482-2064	Clay	912-768-2247	Marion	912-649-2625	Adams	208-253-4279
Jefferson	904-997-3573	Clayton	404-478-9911	McDuffie	404-595-1815	Bannock	208-236-7310
Lafayette	904-294-1279	Clinch	912-487-2169	McIntosh	912-437-6651	Bear Lake	208-945-2266
Lake	904-343-4101	Cobb	404-422-3330	Meriwether	404-672-4235	Benewah	208-245-2422
Lee	813-335-2421	Coffee	912-384-1402	Miller	912-758-3416	Bingham	208-785-5005
Leon	904-877-3815	Colquitt	912-985-1321	Mitchell	912-336-8464	Blaine	208-788-3451
Levy	904-486-2165	Columbia	404-541-0557	Monroe	912-994-1118	Bonner	208-263-8511
Liberty	904-643-2478	Cook	912-896-4040	Montgomery	912-583-2240	Bonneville	208-529-1390
Madison	904-973-4138	Coweta	404-253-2450	Morgan	404-342-2214	Boundary	208-267-3235
Manatee	813-747-3007	Crawford	912-836-3121	Murray	404-695-3031	Butte	208-527-8587
Marion	904-629-8067	Crisp	912-273-1217	Muscogee	404-324-7711	Camas	208-764-2230
Martin	305-283-6760	Dade	404-657-4116	Newton	404-786-2574	Canyon	208-459-1654
Monroe	305-294-4641	Dawson	404-265-2442	Oconee	404-769-5207	Caribou	208-547-3205
Nassau	904-845-2121	Decatur	912-246-4528	Oglethorpe	404-743-8341	Cassia	208-678-9461
Okaloosa	904-682-2711	Dekalb	404-371-2821	Paulding	404-445-3885	Clark	208-374-5405
Okeechobee	813-763-6469	Dodge	912-374-4702	Peach	912-825-6466	Clearwater	208-476-4434
Orange	305-420-3265	Dooly	912-268-4171	Pickens	404-692-2531	Custer	208-879-2344
Osceola	305-846-4181	Dougherty	912-436-7216	Pierce	912-449-4733	Elmore	208-587-4826
Palm Beach	305-683-1777	Douglas	404-949-2000	Pike	404-567-8948	Fort Hall Indian Reservation	
Pasco	904-567-5167	Early	912-723-3072	Polk	404-748-3051		208-237-0600
Pinellas	813-448-3771	Echols	912-559-5562	Pulaski	912-783-1171	Franklin	208-852-1097
Polk	813-533-0765	Effingham	912-754-6665	Putnam	404-485-4151	Fremont	208-624-3102
				Quitman	912-334-4303	Gem	208-365-6363

Gooding	208-934-4401	Kane	312-584-6166	Carroll	317-564-3169	Starke	219-772-3553
Idaho	208-983-2390	Kankakee	815-939-3626	Cass	219-722-5050	Steuben	219-665-2189
Jefferson	208-745-6685	Kendall	312-553-5823	Clark	812-283-4451	Sullivan	812-268-4332
Jerome	208-324-8811	Knox	309-342-5108	Clay	812-446-2413	Switzerland	812-427-3152
Kootenai	208-667-6426	Lake	312-223-8627	Clinton	317-654-8721	Tippecanoe	317-423-9378
Latah	208-882-8580	La Salle	815-433-0707	Crawford	812-338-2352	Tipton	317-675-2694
Lemhi	208-756-2824	Lawrence	618-943-5018	Daviess	812-254-2188	Union	317-458-5055
Lewis	208-937-2311	Lee	815-857-3525	Dearborn	812-926-1189	Vanderburgh	812-426-5287
Lincoln	208-886-2406	Livingston	815-844-3622	Decatur	812-663-8388	Vermillion	317-492-3394
Madison	208-356-3191	Logan	217-732-8289	De Kalb	219-925-2562	Vigo	812-238-8371
Minidoka	208-436-9331	McDonough	309-837-3939	Delaware	317-747-7732	Wabash	219-563-8311
Nez Perce	208-799-3096	McHenry	815-338-3737	Dubois	812-482-1782	Warren	317-762-3231
North Idaho Agency		McLean	309-663-8306	Elkhart	219-533-0554	Warrick	812-897-2500
	208-843-2267	Macon	217-877-6042	Fayette	317-825-8502	Washington	812-883-4601
Oneida	208-766-2243	Macoupin	217-854-9604	Floyd	812-948-1141	Wayne	317-966-7541
Owyhee	208-896-4104	Madison	618-656-8400	Fountain	317-793-2297	Wells	219-824-0116
Payette	208-642-9397	Marion	618-548-1446	Franklin	317-647-6261	White	219-583-7442
Power	208-226-2077	Marshall-Putnam	309-364-2356	Fulton	219-223-3397	Whitley	219-244-7615
Teton	208-354-2961	Mason	309-543-3308	Gibson	812-385-3491		
Twin Falls	208-734-3300	Massac	618-524-2270	Grant	317-668-8871		
Valley	208-325-8566	Menard	217-632-7491	Greene	812-659-2122		
Washington	208-549-0415	Mercer	309-582-5106	Hamilton	317-773-6110	**IOWA**	
		Monroe	618-939-6617	Hancock	317-462-1113	Adair	515-743-8412
		Montgomery	217-532-5763	Harrison	812-738-4236	Adams	515-322-3184
		Morgan	217-243-7424	Hendricks	317-745-5533	Allamakee	319-568-3327
ILLINOIS		Moultrie	217-728-4318	Henry	317-529-5002	Appanoose	515-856-3885
Adams	217-223-8380	Ogle	815-732-2191	Howard	317-459-8031	Audubon	712-563-3261
Bond	618-664-3665	Peoria	309-686-6033	Huntington	219-356-1728	Benton	319-472-4739
Boone	815-544-3710	Perry	618-357-2126	Jackson	812-358-3110	Black Hawk	319-234-6811
Brown	217-773-3013	Piatt	217-762-2655	Jasper	219-866-5741	Boone	515-432-3882
Bureau	815-875-2878	Pike	217-285-5543	Jay	219-726-4707	Bremer	319-882-4275
Calhoun	618-576-2293	Pope-Hardin	618-695-2441	Jefferson	812-265-3418	Buchanan	319-334-7161
Carroll	815-244-9444	Pulaski-Alexander	618-745-6310	Jennings	812-346-5209	Buena Vista	712-732-5056
Cass	217-452-7255	Randolph	618-443-4364	Johnson	317-738-3211	Butler	319-267-2707
Champaign	217-352-3312	Richland	618-395-2191	Knox	812-882-6368	Calhoun	712-297-8611
Christian	217-287-7246	Rock Island	309-796-1233	Kosciusko	219-267-4444	Carroll	712-792-2364
Clark	217-826-5422	St. Clair	618-233-1047	La Grange	219-463-3512	Cass	712-243-1132
Clay	618-665-3328	Saline	618-252-8391	Lake	219-738-2020	Cedar	319-886-2252
Clinton	618-526-4551	Sangamon	217-782-4617	La Porte	219-326-6808	Cerro Gordo	515-423-0844
Coles	217-345-7034	Schuyler	217-322-6033	Lawrence	812-275-4623	Cherokee	712-225-6196
Cook	312-996-2620	Scott	217-742-3172	Madison	317-646-9231	Chickasaw	515-394-2174
Crawford	618-546-1549	Shelby	217-774-4321	Marion	317-253-0871	Clarke	515-342-3316
Cumberland	217-849-3931	Stark	309-286-5421	Marshall	219-936-3141	Clay	712-262-2264
De Kalb	815-758-8194	Stephenson	815-235-4125	Martin	812-247-3041	Clayton	319-235-1451
De Witt	217-935-5764	Tazewell	309-347-6614	Miami	317-472-1921	Clinton	319-659-5125
Douglas	217-253-2713	Union	618-833-5341	Monroe	812-332-2366	Crawford	712-263-4697
Du Page	312-682-7485	Vermilion	217-442-8615	Montgomery	317-362-5940	Dallas	515-993-4281
Edgar	217-465-8585	Wabash	618-262-5725	Morgan	317-342-6679	Davis	515-664-2730
Edwards	618-445-2934	Warren	309-734-5161	Newton	219-474-5187	Decatur	515-446-4723
Effingham	217-347-7773	Washington	618-327-8881	Noble	219-636-2111	Delaware	319-927-4201
Fayette	618-283-2753	Wayne	618-842-3702	Ohio	812-438-3656	Des Moines	319-754-7556
Ford	217-388-7791	White	618-382-2276	Orange	812-723-2439	Dickinson	712-336-3488
Franklin	618-439-3178	Whiteside	815-772-4075	Owen	312-829-2258	Dubuque	319-583-6496
Fulton	309-547-3711	Will	815-727-9296	Parke	317-569-3176	Emmet	712-362-3434
Gallatin	618-272-4561	Williamson	618-993-3304	Perry	812-547-7084	Fayette	319-425-3331
Greene	217-942-6996	Winnebago	815-987-7379	Pike	812-354-6838	Floyd	515-228-1453
Grundy	815-942-2725	Woodford	309-467-3789	Porter	219-464-8661	Franklin	515-456-4811
Hamilton	618-643-3416			Posey	812-838-4449	Fremont	712-374-2351
Hancock	217-357-2150			Pulaski	219-946-3412	Greene	515-386-2138
Henderson	309-924-1471			Putnam	317-653-8411	Grundy	319-824-6315
Henry	309-937-2424	**INDIANA**		Randolph	317-584-2271	Guthrie	515-747-2276
Iroquois	815-432-5416	Adams	219-724-3000	Ripley	812-689-6511	Hamilton	515-832-5278
Jackson	618-687-1727	Allen	219-482-5401	Rush	317-932-2761	Hancock	515-923-2856
Jasper	618-783-2521	Bartholomew	812-376-9337	St. Joseph	219-284-9604	Hardin	515-858-5425
Jefferson	618-242-0780	Benton	317-884-0140	Scott	812-752-2841	Harrison	712-644-2105
Jersey	618-498-4821	Blackford	317-348-3213	Shelby	317-398-4489	Henry	319-385-8126
Jo Daviess	815-858-2273	Boone	317-482-0750	Spencer	812-649-2236	Howard	319-547-3001
Johnson	618-658-5322	Brown	812-988-4386			Humboldt	515-332-2201

COUNTY EXTENSION AGENTS

Ida	712-364-2820	Cherokee	316-429-3849
Iowa	319-642-5504	Cheyenne	913-332-3171
Jackson	319-652-4923	Clark	316-635-2811
Jasper	515-792-6433	Clay	913-632-5335
Jefferson	515-472-4166	Cloud	913-243-4549
Johnson	319-337-2145	Coffey	316-364-5313
Jones	319-462-2791	Comanche	316-582-2411
Keokuk	515-622-2680	Cowley	316-221-4066
Kossuth	515-295-2469	Crawford	316-724-8233
Lee	319-835-5116	Decatur	913-475-3142
Linn	319-377-9839	Dickinson	913-263-2001
Louisa	319-523-2371	Doniphan	913-985-3623
Lucas	515-774-2016	Douglas	913-843-7058
Lyon	712-472-2146	Edwards	316-659-3241
Madison	515-462-1001	Elk	316-374-2320
Mahaska	515-673-5841	Ellis	913-625-6571
Marion	515-842-2014	Ellsworth	913-472-3233
Marshall	515-752-1551	Finney	316-276-3205
Mills	712-624-8253	Ford	316-227-3159
Mitchell	515-732-4903	Franklin	913-242-3166
Monona	712-423-2175	Geary	913-238-4161
Monroe	515-932-5612	Gove	913-938-4480
Montgomery	712-623-3820	Graham	913-674-3411
Muscatine	319-263-5701	Grant	316-356-1721
O'Brien	712-757-5045	Gray	316-855-3821
Osceola	712-754-3648	Greeley	316-376-4284
Page	712-542-5171	Greenwood	316-583-6151
Palo Alto	712-852-2865	Hamilton	316-384-5225
Plymouth	712-546-7835	Harper	316-842-5445
Pocahontas	712-335-3103	Harvey	316-283-7232
Polk	515-284-4158	Haskell	316-675-2261
East Pottawattamie	712-482-6449	Hodgeman	316-357-6234
West Pottawattamie	712-325-5551	Jackson	913-364-4125
Poweshiek	515-623-5188	Jefferson	913-863-2212
Ringgold	515-464-3333	Jewell	913-378-3174
Sac	712-662-7131	Johnson	913-764-6300
Scott	319-359-7577	Kearny	316-355-6551
Shelby	712-755-3104	Kingman	316-532-3721
Sioux	712-737-4230	Kiowa	316-723-2156
Story	515-382-6551	Labette	316-784-5337
Tama	515-484-2703	Lane	316-397-5811
Taylor	712-523-2137	Leavenworth	913-682-6872
Union	515-782-8426	Lincoln	913-524-4548
Van Buren	319-293-3039	Linn	913-795-2829
Wapello	515-682-9892	Logan	913-672-3580
Warren	515-961-6237	Lyon	316-342-2437
Washington	319-653-4811	Marion	316-382-2325
Wayne	515-872-1755	Marshall	913-562-3531
Webster	515-576-2119	McPherson	316-241-1523
Winnebago	515-584-2261	Meade	316-873-2021
Winneshiek	319-382-2949	Miami	913-294-4306
Woodbury	712-276-2157	Mitchell	913-738-3597
Worth	515-324-1531	Montgomery	316-331-2690
Wright	515-532-3453	Morris	316-767-5611
		Morton	316-697-2558
		Nemaha	913-336-2184
KANSAS		Neosho	316-244-3251
Allen	316-365-2242	Ness	913-798-3193
Anderson	913-448-6826	Norton	913-877-2173
Atchison	913-883-5450	Osage	913-828-4438
Barber	316-886-3313	Osborne	913-346-2521
Barton	316-793-3549	Ottawa	913-392-3096
Bourbon	316-223-3720	Pawnee	316-285-6901
Brown	913-742-2971	Phillips	913-543-2722
Butler	316-321-9660	Pottawatomie	913-457-3319
Chase	316-273-6491	Pratt	316-672-6121
Chautauqua	316-725-3675	Rawlins	913-626-3192

Reno	316-662-2371	Franklin	502-223-7616
Republic	913-527-5084	Fulton	502-236-2351
Rice	316-257-5131	Gallatin	502-567-5481
Riley	913-776-4781	Garrard	606-792-2571
Rooks	913-425-6851	Grant	606-824-3355
Rush	913-222-2710	Graves	502-247-2334
Russell	913-483-3157	Grayson	502-259-3492
Saline	913-827-3651	Green	502-932-5311
Scott	316-872-2930	Greenup	606-473-9881
Sedgwick	316-722-7721	Hancock	502-927-6618
Seward	316-624-5604	Hardin	502-765-4121
Shawnee	913-295-4120	Harlan	606-573-4464
Sheridan	913-675-3722	Harrison	606-234-5510
Sherman	913-899-7110	Hart	502-524-2451
Smith	913-282-6151	Henderson	502-826-8387
Stafford	316-549-3502	Henry	502-845-2811
Stanton	316-492-2240	Hickman	502-653-2231
Stevens	316-544-4359	Hopkins	502-821-3650
Sumner	316-326-7477	Jackson	606-287-7693
Thomas	913-462-2491	Jefferson	502-425-4482
Trego	913-743-6361	Jessamine	606-885-4811
Wabaunsee	913-765-3821	Johnson	606-789-8108
Wallace	913-852-4285	Kenton	606-356-3155
Washington	913-325-2121	Knott	606-785-5329
Wichita	316-375-2724	Knox	606-546-3447
Wilson	316-378-2167	Larue	502-358-3401
Woodson	316-625-3113	Laurel	606-864-4167
Wyandotte	913-299-9300	Lawrence	606-638-9495
		Lee	606-464-2759
		Leslie	606-672-2154
KENTUCKY		Letcher	606-633-2362
Adair	502-384-2317	Lewis	606-796-2732
Allen	502-237-3146	Lincoln	606-365-2459
Anderson	502-839-7271	Livingston	502-928-2168
Ballard	502-665-9118	Logan	502-726-6323
Barren	502-651-3818	Lyon	502-388-2341
Bath	606-674-6121	Madison	606-623-4072
Bell	606-337-2376	Magoffin	606-349-3216
Boone	606-586-6101	Marion	606-692-2421
Bourbon	606-987-1895	Marshall	502-527-3285
Boyd	606-739-5184	Martin	606-298-7742
Boyle	606-236-4484	Mason	606-564-6808
Bracken	606-735-3150	McCracken	502-442-2718
Breathitt	606-666-8812	McCreary	606-376-2524
Breckenridge	502-756-2182	McLean	502-273-3690
Bullitt	502-543-2257	Meade	502-422-4958
Butler	502-526-3767	Menifee	606-768-3866
Caldwell	502-365-2787	Mercer	606-734-4378
Calloway	502-753-1452	Metcalfe	502-432-3561
Campbell	606-635-2116	Monroe	502-487-5504
Carlisle	502-628-5447	Montgomery	606-498-5856
Carroll	502-732-4209	Morgan	606-743-3292
Carter	606-474-6686	Muhlenberg	502-338-3124
Casey	606-787-7384	Nelson	502-348-9204
Christian	502-886-6328	Nicholas	606-289-2312
Clark	606-744-4682	Ohio	502-298-7441
Clay	606-598-2789	Oldham	502-222-9543
Clinton	606-387-5404	Owen	502-484-2237
Crittenden	502-965-5236	Owsley	606-593-5109
Cumberland	502-864-2681	Pendleton	606-654-3354
Daviess	502-684-5228	Perry	606-436-2044
Edmonson	502-597-2954	Pike	606-432-2553
Elliott	606-738-6440	Powell	606-663-2252
Estill	606-723-4557	Pulaski	606-679-6361
Fayette	606-255-5582	Robertson	606-724-5796
Fleming	606-845-4641	Rockcastle	606-256-2403
Floyd	606-886-2668	Rowan	606-784-5457

Russell	502-343-2161	St. John	504-497-3261	Bristol	617-669-6744	Menominee	906-753-2209
Scott	502-863-0984	St. Landry	318-942-5761	Dukes	617-693-0694	Midland	517-832-8838
Shelby	502-633-4593	St. Martin	318-332-2181	Essex	617-774-0050	Missaukee	616-839-4667
Simpson	502-586-4788	St. Mary	318-828-4100	Franklin	413-774-2902	Monroe	313-243-7113
Spencer	502-477-2217	St. Tammany	504-892-2208	Hampden	413-736-7204	Montcalm	517-831-5226
Taylor	502-465-2497	Tangipahoa	504-748-9381	Hampshire	413-584-2556	Muskegon	616-724-6361
Todd	502-265-5659	Tensas	318-766-3222	Middlesex	617-369-4845	Newaygo	616-924-0500
Trigg	502-522-3269	Terrebonne	504-868-3000	Norfolk	617-668-0268	Oakland	313-858-0880
Trimble	502-255-7188	Union	318-368-9935	Plymouth	617-293-3541	Oceana	616-873-2129
Union	502-389-1400	Vermillion	318-893-1356	Suffolk	617-482-0395	Ogemaw	517-345-0692
Warren	502-781-3600	Vernon	318-239-3231	Worcester	617-753-5477	Ontanagon	906-884-4386
Washington	606-336-7741	Washington	504-839-4695			Osceola	616-832-9011
Wayne	606-348-5686	Webster	318-371-1371			Oscoda	517-826-3280
Webster	502-639-9011	West Baton Rouge	504-387-1448	**MICHIGAN**		Otsego-Montmorency	
Whitley	606-549-1130	West Caroll	318-428-3571	Alcona	517-724-6478		517-732-5445
Wolfe	606-668-3712	West Feliciana	504-635-3614	Alger	906-387-2530	Ottawa	616-846-8250
Woodford	606-873-4601	Winn	318-628-4528	Allegan	616-673-8471	Presque Isle	517-734-2168
				Alpena	517-354-3636	Roscommon-Crawford	
LOUISIANA		**MAINE**		Antrim	616-533-8607		517-275-5043
Acadia	318-783-4772	Androscoggin-Sagadahoc		Arenac	517-846-4111	St. Clair	313-985-7169
Allen	318-639-4376		207-783-8301	Baraga	906-524-6300	St. Joseph	616-467-6361
Ascension	504-644-8429	Aroostock	207-834-3905	Barry	616-948-8039	Saginaw	517-790-5291
Assumption	504-369-6386	Cumberland	207-780-4205	Bay	517-893-3523	Sanilac	313-648-2515
Avoyelles	318-253-7526	Franklin	207-778-4650	Benzie	616-882-9931	Schoolcraft	906-341-5050
Beauregard	318-463-7006	Hancock	207-667-8212	Berrien	616-983-7111	Shiawassee	517-743-3421
Bienville	318-263-2321	Kennebec	207-622-7546	Branch	517-279-8411	Tuscola	517-673-3161
Bossier	318-965-2326	Knox-Lincoln	207-594-2104	Calhoun	616-781-9811	Van Buren	616-657-5564
Caddo	318-226-6805	Oxford	207-743-6329	Cass	616-445-8661	Washtenaw	313-973-9510
Calcasieu	318-433-4671	Penobscot	207-942-7396	Charlevoix	616-582-6232	Wayne	313-721-6550
Caldwell	318-649-2663	Piscataquis	207-564-3301	Cheboygan	616-627-4501	Wexford	616-775-7241
Cameron	318-775-5516	Somerset	207-474-9622	Chippewa	906-632-2871		
Catahoula	318-744-5442	Waldo	207-338-1650	Clare	517-539-7805		
Claiborne	318-927-3110	Washington	207-255-3345	Clinton	517-224-3288	**MINNESOTA**	
Concordia	318-336-5315	York	207-324-2814	Delta	906-786-3032	Aitkin	218-927-2102
Desoto	318-872-0533			Dickinson	906-774-0363	Anoka	612-755-1281
East Baton Rouge	504-389-3056			Eaton	517-543-2310	Becker	218-847-7195
East Carroll	318-559-1459	**MARYLAND**		Emmet	616-347-0330	Beltrami	218-751-7300
East Felciana	504-683-5456	Allegany	302-724-3320	Genesee	313-732-1474	Benton	612-968-7213
Evangeline	318-363-5646	Anne Arundel	301-224-7111	Gladwin	517-426-7741	Big Stone	612-839-6151
Franklin	318-435-7551	Baltimore City	301-528-6990	Gogebic	906-932-1420	Blue Earth	507-625-3031
Grant	318-627-3675	Baltimore	301-666-0445	Grand Traverse	616-941-2256	Brown	507-794-7993
Iberia	318-367-7768	Calvert	301-535-3662	Gratiot	517-875-4125	Carlton	218-384-4281
Iberville	504-687-3540	Caroline	301-479-0990	Hillsdale	517-439-9301	Carver	612-448-3435
Jackson	318-259-2452	Carroll	301-848-4611	Houghton-Keweenaw		Cass	218-547-3300
Jefferson	504-341-7271	Cecil	301-398-0200		906-482-5830	Chippewa	612-269-6521
Jefferson Davis	318-824-1773	Charles	301-645-3903	Huron	517-269-9949	Chisago	612-674-4417
Lafayette	318-233-1770	Dorchester	301-228-8800	Ingham	517-676-5222	Clay	218-299-5020
Lafourche	504-446-1316	Frederick	301-694-1599	Ionia	616-527-1400	Clearwater	218-694-6151
Lasalle	318-992-2205	Garrett	301-334-2145	Iosco	517-362-3449	Cook	218-387-2015
Lincoln	318-255-3402	Harford	301-838-6000	Iron	906-875-6642	Cottonwood	507-831-4022
Livingston	504-686-2593	Howard	301-997-7878	Isabella	517-772-0911	Crow Wing	218-829-1497
Madison	318-574-2465	Kent	301-778-1661	Jackson	517-788-4292	Dakota	612-463-3302
Morehouse	318-281-5741	Montgomery	301-948-9070	Kalamazoo	616-383-8830	Dodge	507-374-6435
Natchitoches	318-352-4421	Prince George's	301-952-3312	Kalkaska	616-258-5074	Douglas	612-763-6077
Orleans	504-527-6950	Queen Anne's	301-758-0166	Kent	616-774-3265	Faribault	507-526-2138
Ouachita	318-323-2251	St. Mary's	301-475-5621	Lake	616-745-3759	Fillmore	507-765-3896
Plaquemines	504-682-0081	Somerset	301-651-1351	Lapeer	313-667-0343	Freeborn	507-373-1475
Pointe Coupee	504-638-7115	Talbot	301-822-1244	Leelanau	616-256-9888	Goodhue	612-388-8261
Rapides	318-445-9313	Washington	301-791-1304	Lenawee	517-263-8831	Grant	218-685-4820
Red River	318-932-4342	Wicomico	301-749-6141	Livingston	517-546-3950	Hennepin	612-559-4321
Richland	318-728-3216	Worcester	301-632-1972	Luce	906-293-5091	Hennepin	612-872-9441
Sabine	318-256-3662			Mackinac	906-643-9570	Houston	507-724-5211
St. Bernard	504-279-9402			Macomb	313-469-5180	Hubbard	218-732-3391
St. Charles	504-783-6231	**MASSACHUSETTS**		Manistee	616-889-4277	Isanti	612-689-1810
St. Helena	504-222-4414	Barnstable	617-362-2511	Marquette	906-228-8500	Itasca	218-326-9466
St. James	504-562-7431	Berkshire	413-448-8285	Mason	616-757-4789	Jackson	507-662-5293
				Mecosta	616-796-7637	Kanabec	612-679-3010

COUNTY EXTENSION AGENTS

Kandiyohi	612-235-1485	Bolivar	601-843-8361	Union	601-534-4146
Kittson	218-843-3674	Calhoun	601-628-6671	Walthall	601-876-4021
Koochiching	218-283-2581	Carroll	601-237-4413	Warren	601-636-5442
Lac Qui Parle	612-598-3325	Chickasaw	601-456-4269	Washington	601-332-0524
Lake	218-834-4395	Choctaw	601-285-6337	Wayne	601-735-2243
Lake of the Woods	218-634-1511	Claiborne	601-437-5011	Webster	601-258-3971
Le Sueur	612-445-7543	Clarke	601-776-3951	Wilkinson	601-888-3211
Lincoln	507-694-1470	Clay	601-494-5371	Winston	601-773-3091
Lyon	507-532-5230	Coahoma	601-627-5204	Yalobusha	601-675-2730
Mahnomen	218-935-2226	Copiah	601-894-4081	Yazoo	601-746-2453
Marshall	218-745-5232	Covington	601-765-8252		
Martin	507-235-3341	Desoto	601-368-4401		
McLeod	612-864-5551	Forrest	601-545-2412	**MISSOURI**	
Meeker	612-693-2801	Franklin	601-384-2349	Adair	816-665-9866
Mille Lacs	612-983-2561	George	601-947-4223	Andrew	816-324-3147
Morrison	612-632-2941	Greene	601-394-2702	Atchison	816-744-2490
Mower	507-437-6616	Grenada	601-226-2061	Audrain	314-581-3231
Murray	507-836-8551	Hancock	601-467-5456	Barry	417-847-3161
Nicollet	507-931-6800	Harrison	601-863-6941	Barton	417-682-3570
Nobles	507-372-7711	Hinds	601-372-4651	Bates	816-679-4167
Norman	218-784-7183	Holmes	601-834-2795	Benton	816-438-5012
Olmsted	507-285-8250	Humphreys	601-247-2915	Bollinger	314-238-2420
E. Otter Tail	218-346-5750	Issaquena	601-873-2322	Boone	314-449-2541
W. Otter Tail	218-739-2271	Itawamba	601-862-3201	Buchanan	816-279-1691
Pennington	218-681-2116	Jackson	601-762-1303	Butler	314-785-3634
Pine	612-384-6156	Jasper	601-764-2314	Caldwell	816-586-2761
Pipestone	507-825-5416	Jefferson	601-786-3131	Callaway	314-642-5924
E. Polk	218-563-2465	Jefferson Davis	601-792-5121	Camden	314-346-7214
W. Polk	218-281-1751	Jones	601-428-5201	Cape Girardeau	314-334-5219
Pope	612-634-5115	Kemper	601-743-2837	Carroll	816-542-1788
Ramsey	612-777-1327	Lafayette	601-234-4451	Carter	314-323-4418
Red Lake	218-253-2897	Lamar	601-794-8504	Cass	816-884-5100
Red Lake Indian Reservation		Lauderdale	601-693-6851	Cedar	417-276-3313
	218-679-3366	Lawrence	601-587-2271	Chariton	816-288-3239
Redwood	507-637-8323	Leake	601-267-7301	Christian	417-485-2466
Renville	612-523-2522	Lee	601-842-7461	Clark	816-727-3330
Rice	507-334-2281	Leflore	601-453-6803	Clay	816-781-0360
Rock	507-283-2648	Lincoln	601-833-5711	Clinton	816-539-2156
Roseau	218-463-1052	Lowndes	601-328-2111	Cole	314-634-2824
Northern St. Louis	218-749-7120	Madison	601-859-3842	Cooper	816-882-5661
South St. Louis	218-726-7512	Marion	601-736-8251	Crawford	314-775-2135
Scott	612-492-2370	Marshall	601-252-3541	Dade	417-637-2112
Sherburne	612-441-1441	Monroe	601-369-4951	Dallas	417-345-7551
Sibley	612-237-2344	Montgomery	601-283-4133	Daviess	816-663-3232
Stearns	612-252-2132	Neshoba	601-656-4602	DeKalb	816-449-5811
Steele	507-451-8040	Newton	601-635-2267	Delta Center	314-379-5431
Stevens	612-589-4884	Noxubee	601-726-4326	Dent	314-729-3196
Swift	612-842-4761	Oktibbeha	601-323-5916	Douglas	417-683-4409
Todd	612-732-6181	Panola	601-487-1725	Dunklin	314-888-4722
Traverse	612-563-4515	Pearl River	601-795-4224	Franklin	314-583-5141
Wabasha	612-565-4509	Perry	601-964-3668	Gasconade	314-437-2165
Wadena	218-631-2332	Pike	601-783-5321	Gentry	816-726-5610
Waseca	507-835-3610	Pontotoc	601-489-4631	Greene	417-862-9284
Washington	612-777-4411	Prentiss	601-728-5631	Grundy	816-359-5643
Watonwan	507-375-3341	Quitman	601-326-8939	Harrison	816-425-6434
Wilkin	218-643-5481	Rankin	601-825-2217	Henry	816-885-5556
Winona	507-454-5101	Scott	601-469-4241	Hickory	417-745-6767
Wright	612-339-6881	Sharkey	601-873-4246	Holt	816-446-3724
Yellow Medicine	612-669-4825	Simpson	601-847-1335	Howard	816-248-2272
		Smith	601-782-4454	Howell	417-256-2391
		Stone	601-928-5286	Iron	314-546-7515
MISSISSIPPI		Sunflower	601-887-4601	Jackson	816-373-5500
Adams	601-445-8201	Tallahatchie	601-647-8746	Jasper	417-358-2158
Alcorn	601-286-5731	Tate	601-562-4274	Jefferson	314-789-2691
Amite	601-657-8902	Tippah	601-837-8184	Johnson	816-747-3193
Attala	601-289-5431	Tishomingo	601-423-3616	Knox	816-397-2179
Benton	601-224-6722	Tunica	601-363-2911	Laclede	417-532-7126

LaFayette	816-584-3658
Lawrence	417-466-3102
Lewis	314-767-5273
Lincoln	314-528-4613
Linn	816-895-5123
Livingston	816-646-0811
Macon	816-385-2173
Madison	314-783-2735
Maries	314-422-3359
Marion	314-769-2177
McDonald	417-223-4775
Mercer	816-748-3315
Miller	314-369-2394
Mississippi	314-683-6129
Moniteau	314-796-3154
Monroe	816-327-4158
Montgomery	314-564-3733
Morgan	314-378-5358
New Madrid	314-748-5531
Newton	417-451-1616
Nodaway	816-582-8101
Oregon	417-778-7490
Osage	314-897-3648
Ozark	417-679-3525
Pemiscot	314-333-0258
Perry	314-547-4504
Pettis	816-827-0591
Phelps	314-364-3147
Pike	314-324-5464
Platte	816-431-2165
Polk	417-326-4916
Pulaski	314-774-2111
Putnam	816-947-2705
Ralls	314-985-3911
Randolph	816-263-3534
Ray	816-776-6961
Reynolds	314-663-2251
Ripley	314-996-2921
St. Charles	314-623-4513
St. Clair	417-646-2419
St. Francois	314-756-4539
St. Genevieve	314-883-3548
St. Louis	314-553-5184
Saline	816-886-6908
Schuyler	816-457-8569
Scotland	816-465-8569
Scott	314-545-3516
Shannon	314-226-3715
Shelby	314-633-2640
Stoddard	314-568-3344
Stone	417-357-6812
Sullivan	816-265-4541
Taney	417-546-2371
Texas	417-967-3862
Vernon	417-667-7203
Warren	314-456-3444
Washington	314-438-2671
Wayne	314-224-3322
Webster	417-468-2044
Worth	816-564-3610
Wright	417-741-6465

MONTANA

Beaverhead	406-683-2842
Big Horn	406-665-1405
Blaine	406-357-3200

APPENDIX

Broadwater	406-266-3419	Custer	308-872-6831	**NEVADA**	
Carbon	406-962-3545	Dakota	402-987-3541	Carson City, Storey	702-887-2252
Cascade	406-761-6700	Dawes	308-432-3373	Churchill	702-423-5121
Chouteau	406-622-3751	Dawson	308-324-5501	Clark	702-731-3130
Custer	406-232-4781	Deuel	308-874-2705	Douglas	702-782-5176
Daniels	406-487-2861	Dixon	402-584-2261	Or From Reno	883-1670,
Dawson	406-365-4277	Dodge	402-721-2081		Ext. 278 or 279
Deer Lodge-Powell	406-846-1852	Douglas	402-444-7804	Elko	702-738-7291
Fallon-Carter	406-778-2424	Dundy	308-423-2021	Eureka/Lander North	
Fergus	406-538-3919	Fillmore	402-759-3712		702-635-5565
Flathead	406-755-5300	Franklin	308-425-6277	Eureka/Lander South	
Gallatin	406-587-5271	Frontier	308-367-4424		702-237-5326
Garfield	406-557-2770	Furnas	308-268-3105	Humboldt	702-623-5081,
Glacier	406-873-2382	Gage	402-228-3315		Ext. 295 or 296
Granite	406-859-3292	Garden	308-772-3311	Lincoln	702-726-3101
Hill	406-265-5481	Garfield, Loup, Wheeler		Lyon	702-463-3341, Ext. 236
Judith Basin	406-566-2210		308-346-4200	Nye & Esmeralda	702-482-6794
Lake	406-676-4271	Greeley	308-428-2835	Pershing	702-273-2922
Lewis & Clark	406-443-1010	Hall	308-381-5088	Washoe	702-784-4848
Liberty	406-759-5625	Hamilton	402-694-6174	White Pine	702-289-4459
Lincoln	406-293-7781	Harlan	308-928-2119		
Madison-Jefferson	406-287-3282	Hayes	308-286-3312	**NEW HAMPSHIRE**	
McCone	406-485-2605	Hitchcock	308-334-5666	Belknap	603-524-1737
Mineral	406-822-4561	Holt	402-336-2760	Carroll	603-447-5922
Missoula	406-721-5700	Howard	308-754-5422	Cheshire	603-352-4550
Musselshell-Golden Valley		Jefferson	402-729-3487	Coos	603-788-4961
	406-323-2704	Johnson	402-335-3669	Grafton	603-787-6944
Park	406-222-1273	Kearney	308-832-0430	Hillsboro	603-673-2510
Phillips	406-654-2543	Keith-Arthur	308-284-6051	Merrimack	603-225-5505
Pondera	406-278-3121	Kimball-Banner	308-235-3122	Rockingham	603-679-5616
Powder River	406-436-2424	Knox	402-288-4224	Strafford	603-749-4555
Prairie	406-637-5786	Lancaster	402-423-3806	Sullivan	603-543-3181
Ravalli	406-363-2044	Lincoln	308-532-2683		
Richland	406-482-1206	Logan, McPherson	308-636-2332	**NEW JERSEY**	
Roosevelt	406-787-5312	Madison	402-675-2785	Atlantic	609-625-7000
Rosebud-Treasure	406-356-7320	Merrick	308-946-3843	Bergen	201-646-2979
Sanders	406-827-3532	Morrill	308-262-1022	Burlington	609-267-3300
Sheridan	406-765-1020	Nemaha	402-274-4959	Camden	609-784-1001
Silver Bow	406-723-8262	Nukolls	402-225-2381	Cape May	609-465-5115
Stillwater	406-322-5334	Otoe	402-269-2301	Cumberland	609-451-2800
Sweet Grass	406-932-2445	Pawnee	402-852-2970	Essex	201-239-5213
Teton	406-466-2491	Perkins	308-352-4340	Gloucester	609-881-1200
Toole	406-434-5351	Phelps-Gosper	308-995-4222	Hunterdon	201-788-1340
Valley	406-228-2456	Pierce	402-329-4615	Jersey City	201-432-0574
Wibaux	406-795-2432	Platte	402-564-1311	Mercer	609-989-6830
Yellowstone	406-252-5181	Polk	402-747-2321	Middlesex	201-745-3442
		Red Willow	308-345-3390	Monmouth	201-431-7260
		Richardson	402-245-4324	Morris	201-285-6141
NEBRASKA		Saline	402-821-2151	Ocean	201-349-1227
Adams	402-463-2491	Sarpy	402-339-3225	Passaic	201-881-4537
Antelope	402-887-4122	Saunders	402-443-3522	Salem	609-935-7510
Boone-Nance	402-395-2158	Scotts Bluff	308-436-6622	Somerset	201-725-4700
Box Butte	308-762-5616	Seward	402-643-2981	Sussex	201-383-3800
Boyd	402-775-2491	Sheridan	308-327-2312	Union	201-233-9366
Brown, Rock, Keya Paha		Sherman	308-745-1518	Warren	201-475-5361
	402-387-2213	Sioux	308-668-2428		
Buffalo	308-237-5966	Stanton	402-439-2231	**NEW MEXICO**	
Burt	402-374-2693	Thayer	402-768-7212	Bernalillo	505-243-1386
Butler	402-367-3091	Thomas, Blaine, Grant, Hooker		Catron	505-533-6430
Cass	402-267-2205		308-546-2247	Chaves	505-622-3210
Cedar	402-254-6821	Thurston	402-846-5656	Colfax	505-445-8071
Chase	308-882-4731	Valley	308-728-5071	Curry	505-763-6505
Cherry	402-376-1850	Washington	402-426-9455	De Baca	505-355-2381
Cheyenne	308-254-4455	Wayne	402-375-3310	Dona Ana	505-523-5618
Clay	402-762-3644	Webster	402-746-3417	Eddy	505-887-6595
Colfax	402-352-3821	York	402-362-5508	Grant	505-388-1559
Cuming	402-372-5356				

Guadalupe	505-472-3652
Harding	505-673-2341
Hidalgo	505-542-9291
Lea	505-396-3613
Lincoln	505-648-2311
Los Alamos	505-662-2656
Luna	505-546-6501
McKinley	505-863-3432
Mora	505-387-2856
Otero	505-437-0231
Quay	505-461-0562
Rio Arriba	505-753-3405
Roosevelt	505-356-4417
Sandoval	505-867-2582
San Juan	505-334-9496
San Miguel	505-425-6721
Santa Fe	505-471-4711
Sierra	505-894-2375
Socorro	505-835-0610
Taos	505-758-3982
Torrance	505-384-2372
Union	505-374-9361
Valencia	505-865-9561

NEW YORK	
Albany	518-765-3635
Allegany	716-268-7644
Broome	607-722-8953
Cattaraugus	716-699-2377
Cayuga	315-255-1183
Chautauqua	716-664-9502
Chemung	607-739-0347
Chenango	607-334-5841
Clinton	518-561-7450
Columbia	518-828-3346
Cortland	607-756-7587
Delaware	607-865-6531
Dutchess	914-677-3489
Erie	716-652-3370
Essex	518-962-4810
Franklin	518-483-6767
Fulton	518-725-6441
Genesee	716-343-3040
Greene	518-622-9820
Hamilton	518-548-6191
Herkimer	315-866-7920
Jefferson	315-788-8450
Lewis	315-376-6551
Livingston	716-658-3250
Madison	315-684-3001
Monroe	716-461-1000
Montgomery	518-853-3471
Nassau	516-454-0900
Niagara	716-433-8839
Oneida	315-732-7131
Onondaga	315-424-9485
Ontario	716-394-4110
Orange	914-343-1105
Orleans	716-589-5561
Oswego	315-963-7286
Otsego	607-547-2536
Putnam	914-628-0454
Rensselaer	518-270-5376
Rockland	914-425-5500
St. Lawrence	315-379-2311
Saratoga	518-885-8995

1017

COUNTY EXTENSION AGENTS

Schenectady	518-382-3374	Hoke	919-875-3461	Dickey	701-349-3211	Delaware	614-369-8761
Schoharie	518-234-4303	Hyde	919-926-3201	Divide	701-965-6501	Erie	419-627-7631
Schuyler	607-535-7466	Iredell	704-873-0507	Dunn	701-764-5593	Fairfield	614-654-6530
Seneca	315-539-9252	Jackson	704-586-4009	Eddy	701-947-2454	Fayette	614-335-1150
Steuben	607-776-2127	Johnston	919-934-5003	Emmons	701-254-4811	Franklin	614-469-5595
Suffolk	516-727-7850	Jones	919-448-9621	Fort Berthold	701-627-3446	Fulton	419-337-5515
Sullivan	914-292-6180	Lee	919-775-5624	Foster	701-652-2581	Gallia	614-446-4612
Tioga	607-687-4020	Lenoir	919-527-2191	Golden Valley	701-872-4332	Geauga	216-834-4656
Tompkins	607-272-2292	Lincoln	704-732-3361	Grand Forks	701-775-2571	Greene	513-372-9971
Ulster	914-331-1680	McDowell	704-652-7030	Grant	701-622-3470	Guernsey	614-432-2959
Warren	518-623-3291	Macon	704-524-6421	Griggs	701-797-3312	Hamilton	513-825-6000
Washington	518-747-2861	Madison	704-649-2411	Hettinger	701-824-2095	Hancock	419-422-3851
Wayne	315-483-6918	Martin	919-792-1621	Kidder	701-475-2672	Hardin	419-675-6262
Westchester	914-682-3340	Mecklenburg	704-374-2561	LaMoure	701-883-5388	Harrison	614-942-8823
Wyoming	716-786-2251	Mitchell	704-688-4811	Logan	701-754-2504	Henry	419-592-0806
Yates	315-536-3381	Montgomery	919-576-6011	McHenry	701-537-5405	Highland	513-393-1918
		Moore	919-947-5371	McIntosh	701-288-3465	Hocking	614-385-3222
NORTH CAROLINA		Nash	919-459-4117	McKenzie	701-842-3451	Holmes	216-674-3015
Alamance	919-227-1482	New Hanover	919-762-1848	McLean	701-462-3535	Huron	419-668-8219
Alexander	704-632-4451	Northampton	919-534-2711	Mercer	701-873-5195	Jackson	614-286-5044
Alleghany	919-372-5597	Onslow	919-455-5873	Morton	701-663-4235	Jefferson	614-283-3757
Anson	704-694-2415	Orange	919-732-9361	Mountrail	701-628-2835	Knox	614-397-0401
Ashe	919-246-3021	Pamlico	919-745-4121	Nelson	701-247-2521	Lake	216-354-3554
Avery	704-733-2415	Pasquotank	919-338-3954	Oliver	701-794-8748	Lawrence	614-532-7982
Beaufort	919-946-0111	Pender	919-259-2330	Pembina	701-265-8411	Licking	614-345-6631
Bertie	919-794-3194	Perquimans	919-426-5428	Pierce	701-776-6234	Logan	513-599-4227
Bladen	919-862-4591	Person	919-599-1195	Ramsey	701-662-5354	Lorain	216-322-0127
Brunswick	919-253-4425	Pitt	919-758-1196	Ransom	701-683-4175	Lucas	419-259-6364
Buncombe	704-255-5522	Polk	704-894-8218	Renville	701-756-6392	Madison	614-852-0975
Burke	704-433-4050	Randolph	919-629-2131	Richland	701-642-8481	Mahoning	216-533-5538
Cabarrus	704-782-0212	Richmond	919-997-6251	Rolette	701-477-5671	Marion	614-387-2260
Caldwell	704-758-8451	Robeson	919-738-8111	Sargent	701-724-3355	Medina	216-725-4911
Camden	919-338-0171	Rockingham	919-349-3371	Sheridan	701-363-2242	Meigs	614-992-6696
Carteret	919-728-3870	Rowan	704-633-0571	Sioux	701-854-3412	Mercer	419-586-2179
Caswell	919-694-4158	Rutherford	704-287-2211	Slope	701-879-6270	Miami	513-335-8341
Catawba	704-464-7880	Sampson	919-592-7161	Stark	701-225-6006	Monroe	614-472-0810
Chatham	919-542-3974	Scotland	919-276-2411	Steele	701-524-2253	Montgomery	513-224-9654
Cherokee	704-837-2210	Stanly	704-983-2123	Sutsman	701-252-9030	Morgan	614-962-4854
Cherokee Reservation		Stokes	919-593-8179	Towner	701-968-3433	Morrow	419-947-1070
	704-497-3521	Surry	919-386-8773	Traill	701-436-5665	Muskingum	614-454-0144
Chowan	919-482-8431	Swain	704-488-2193	Walsh	701-284-6248	Noble	614-732-5681
Clay	704-389-6301	Transylvania	704-884-2112	Ward	701-839-2412	Ottawa	419-894-1618
Cleveland	704-482-4365	Tyrrell	919-796-1581	Wells	701-547-3341	Paulding	419-399-3731
Columbus	919-642-2788	Union	704-289-5511, Ext. 335	Williams	701-572-6373	Perry	614-743-1602
Craven	919-633-1477	Vance	919-438-8188			Pickaway	614-474-7534
Cumberland	919-484-7156	Wake	919-755-6100			Pike	614-947-2121
Currituck	919-232-2261	Warren	919-257-3640	**OHIO**		Portage	216-296-6432
Dare	919-473-2143	Washington	919-793-2223	Adams	513-544-2339	Preble	513-456-3828
Davidson	704-246-5233	Watauga	704-264-3061	Allen	419-222-9946	Putnam	419-523-6294
Davie	704-634-6297	Wayne	919-735-4331	Ashland	419-289-0000	Richland	419-589-2919
Duplin	919-296-1996	Wilkes	919-667-5111	Ashtabula	216-576-3866	Ross	614-775-3200
Durham	919-688-2240	Wilson	919-237-0111	Athens	614-593-8555	Sandusky	419-332-5581
Edgecombe	919-823-8131	Yadkin	919-679-2061	Auglaize	419-738-2219	Scioto	614-353-5111
Forsyth	919-767-8213	Yancey	704-682-6187	Belmont	614-695-1455	Seneca	419-447-9722
Franklin	919-496-3344			Brown	513-378-6716	Shelby	513-492-9195
Gaston	704-866-3002			Butler	513-867-5925	Stark	216-489-4488
Gates	919-357-1400	**NORTH DAKOTA**		Carroll	216-627-4310	Summit	216-929-7391
Graham	704-479-3320	Adams	701-567-2735	Champaign	513-652-2204	Trumbull	216-394-9246
Granville	919-693-8806	Barnes	701-845-9031	Clark	513-324-5791	Tuscarawas	216-364-8811
Greene	919-747-5831	Benson	701-473-5363	Clermont	513-732-7195	Union	513-642-1926
Guilford	919-375-5876	Billings	701-225-6006	Clinton	513-382-0901	Van Wert	419-238-1214
Halifax	919-583-5161	Bottineau	701-228-2253	Columbiana	216-424-7291	Vinton	614-596-5961
Harnett	919-893-3339	Bowman	701-523-5271	Coshocton	614-622-2265	Warren	513-932-1891
Haywood	704-456-3575	Burke	701-377-2927	Crawford	419-562-8731	Washington	614-373-6623
Henderson	704-692-0216	Burleigh	701-255-4011	Cuyahoga	216-631-1890	Wayne	216-264-8722
Hertford	919-358-1591	Cass	701-232-7455	Darke	513-548-5215	Williams	419-636-5608
		Cavalier	701-256-2955	Defiance	419-782-4771	Wood	419-352-6531

Wyandot	419-294-4931	Pottawatomie	405-273-7683	Cambria	814-472-7986	Aiken	803-649-6671
		Pushmataha	405-298-5563	Cameron	814-483-3350	Allendale	803-584-4231
		Roger Mills	405-497-3339	Carbon	717-325-2788	Anderson	803-226-1581

OKLAHOMA

		Rogers	918-341-2736	Centre	814-355-4897	Bamberg	803-245-2661
Adair	918-774-2253	Seminole	405-257-5433	Chester	215-696-3500	Barnwell	803-259-7141
Alfalfa	405-596-3131	Sequoyah	918-775-4838	Clarion	814-226-8230	Beaufort	803-524-4444
Atoka	405-889-2376	Stephens	405-255-0510	Clearfield	814-765-7878	Berkeley	803-899-3431
Beaver	405-625-3464	Texas	405-338-7300	Clinton	717-748-3110	Calhoun	803-874-2354
Beckham	405-928-2139	Tillman	405-335-2515	Columbia	717-784-6660	Charleston	803-724-4226
Blaine	405-623-5195	Tulsa	918-939-6635	Crawford	814-336-1151	Cherokee	803-489-3141
Bryan	405-924-5312	Wagoner	918-485-2412	Cumberland	717-249-7220	Chester	803-385-6181
Caddo	405-247-3376	Washington	918-534-2216	Dauphin	717-652-8460	Chesterfield	803-623-2134
Canadian	405-262-0155	Washita	405-832-3460	Delaware	215-566-0142	Clarendon	803-435-8429
Carter	405-223-6570	Woods	405-327-2786	Elk	814-776-1161	Colleton	803-549-2596
Cherokee	918-456-6163	Woodward	405-254-3391	Erie	814-825-0900	Darlington	803-393-0481
Chocktaw	405-326-3359			Fayette	412-438-0111	Dillon	803-774-8218
Cimarron	405-544-2562			Forest	814-755-3544	Dorchester	803-563-3441
Cleveland	405-321-4774	**OREGON**		Franklin	717-263-9226	Edgefield	803-637-3161
Coal	405-927-2262	Baker	503-523-6414	Fulton	717-485-4111	Fairfield	803-635-4722
Comanche	405-355-1176	Benton	503-757-6750	Greene	412-627-3745	Florence	803-662-8719
Cotton	405-875-3136	Clackamas	503-655-8631	Huntingdon	814-643-1660	Georgetown	803-546-4481
Craig	918-256-7569	Clatsop	503-325-8625	Indiana	412-465-2661	Greenville	803-232-4431
Creek	912-224-2192	Columbia	503-397-3462	Jefferson	814-849-7361	Greenwood	803-229-6681
Custer	405-323-2291	Coos	503-396-3121	Juniata	717-436-8991	Hampton	803-943-3427
Delaware	918-253-4332	Crook	503-447-6228	Lackawanna	717-961-4761	Horry	803-248-2267
Dewey	405-328-5351	Curry	503-247-7011	Lancaster	717-394-6851	Jasper	803-726-3470
Ellis	405-885-4021	Deschutes	503-548-6088	Lawrence	412-658-2541	Kershaw	803-432-9071
Garfield	405-237-1229	Douglas	503-672-4461	Lebanon	717-274-2801	Lancaster	803-283-3302
Garvin	405-239-6681	Gilliam	503-384-2271	Lehigh	215-820-3085	Laurens	803-984-2514
Grady	405-224-5371	Grant	503-575-1911	Luzerne	717-825-1701	Lee	803-484-5416
Grant	405-395-2134	Harney	503-575-2506	Lycoming	717-327-2350	Lexington	803-359-4265
Greer	405-782-2688	Hood River	503-386-3343	McKean	814-887-5571	McCormick	803-465-2112
Harmon	405-688-3584	Jackson	503-776-7371	Mercer	412-622-3800	Marion	803-423-0891
Harper	405-735-2252	Jefferson	503-475-3808	Mifflin	717-248-9618	Marlboro	803-479-6851
Haskell	918-967-4330	Josephine	503-476-6613	Monroe	717-421-6430	Newberry	803-276-1091
Hughes	405-379-5470	Klamath	503-883-7131	Montgomery	215-277-0574	Oconee	803-638-5889
Jackson	405-482-0823	Lake	503-947-2279	Montour	717-275-3731	Orangeburg	803-534-6280
Jefferson	405-228-2332	Lane	503-687-4243	Northampton	215-759-6120	Pickens	803-868-2810
Johnston	405-371-3053	Lincoln	503-265-6111	Northumberland	717-286-4569	Richland	803-256-1678
Kay	405-362-3104	Linn	503-967-3871	Perry	717-582-2131	Saluda	803-445-8117
Kingfisher	405-375-3822	Malheur	503-881-1417	Philadelphia	215-424-0650	Spartanburg	803-582-6779
Kiowa	405-726-3217	Marion	503-588-5301	Pike	717-296-8566	Sumter	803-773-5561
Latimer	918-465-3349	Morrow	503-676-9642	Potter	814-274-8540	Union	803-427-6259
LeFlore	918-647-2314	Multnomah	503-229-4830	Schuylkill	717-385-3431	Williamsburg	803-354-6106
Lincoln	405-258-0560	Polk	503-623-8171	Snyder	717-837-0691	York	803-684-9919
Logan	405-282-3331	Sherman	503-565-3230	Somerset	814-445-8911		
Love	405-276-2110	Tillamook	503-842-5511	Sullivan	717-928-9264		
Major	405-227-3786	Umatilla	503-276-7111	Susquehanna	717-278-1158	**SOUTH DAKOTA**	
Marshall	405-795-3563	Union	503-963-8686	Tioga	717-724-1906	Aurora	605-942-6411
Mayes	918-825-3241	Wallowa	503-426-3143	Union	717-524-4461	Beadle	605-352-8559
McClain	405-527-2174	Wasco	503-296-5494	Venango	814-437-7607	Bennett/Shannon	605-685-6972
McCurtain	405-286-7558	Washington	503-648-8771	Warren	814-723-7550	Bon Homme	605-589-3531
McIntosh	918-689-2341	Wheeler	503-763-4115	Washington	412-228-6881	Brookings	605-692-6268
Murray	405-622-3016	Yamhill	503-472-9371	Wayne	717-253-5970	Brown	605-225-2500
Muskogee	918-687-2458			Westmoreland	412-837-1402	Brule	605-734-6589
Noble	405-336-4621			Wyoming	717-836-3196	Butte	605-892-3371
Nowata	918-273-3345	**PENNSYLVANIA**		York	717-757-9657	Campbell	605-995-3305
Okfuskee	918-623-0641	Adams	717-334-6271			Charles Mix	605-487-7666
Oklahoma		Allegheny	412-355-4275			Cheyenne	605-964-4955
	405-236-2727, Ext. 256	Armstrong	412-543-2500	**RHODE ISLAND**		Clark	605-532-3681
Okmulgee	918-756-1958	Beaver	412-728-5700	Eastern RI	401-847-0287	Clay	605-624-2005
Osage	918-287-4170	Bedford	814-623-5148	Northern RI	401-949-0670	Codington	605-886-7100
Ottawa	918-542-1688	Berks	215-378-1327	Southern RI	401-277-3982	Corson	605-273-4368
Pawnee	918-762-2735	Blair	814-695-5541			Crow Creek/Lower Brule	
Payne	405-372-3163	Bradford	717-265-2896				605-473-5491
Pittsburgh	918-423-4120	Bucks	215-343-2800	**SOUTH CAROLINA**		Custer	605-673-2372
Pontotoc	405-332-2153	Butler	412-287-4761	Abbeville	803-459-4106	Davison	605-996-7536

COUNTY EXTENSION AGENTS

Day	605-345-4641	Crockett	901-696-2412	Tipton	901-476-8616
Deuel	605-874-2681	Cumberland	615-484-6743	Trousdale	615-374-2421
Dewey	605-865-3652	Davidson	615-259-6467	Unicoi	615-743-9584
Douglas	605-724-2719	Decatur	901-852-2831	Union	615-992-8038
Edmunds	605-426-6971	DeKalb	615-597-4945	Van Buren	615-946-2435
Fall River	605-745-5133	Dickson	615-446-2788	Warren	615-473-8484
Faulk	605-598-6221	Dyer	901-285-4781	Washington	615-753-3138
Grant	605-432-9221	Fayette	901-465-3302	Wayne	615-722-3229
Gregory	605-775-2581	Fentress	615-879-9117	Weakley	901-364-2269
Haakon-Jackson	605-859-2840	Franklin	615-967-2741	White	615-836-3348
Hamlin	605-783-3656	Gibson	901-855-2061	Williamson	615-794-8476
Hand	605-853-3643	Giles	615-363-3523	Wilson	615-444-9584
Hanson	605-239-4542	Grainger	615-828-3411		
Harding	605-375-3412	Greene	615-638-4196		
Hughes	605-224-6217	Grundy	615-592-3971	**TEXAS**	
Hutchinson	605-387-2836	Hamblen	615-586-6111	Anderson	214-729-5864
Hyde	605-852-2515	Hamilton	615-757-2533	Andrews	915-523-2182
Jerauld	605-539-9471	Hancock	615-733-2526	Angelina	713-634-3916
Jones	605-669-2512	Hardeman	901-658-2421	Aransas	See San Patricio
Kingsbury	605-854-3851	Hardin	901-925-3441	Archer	817-574-4914
Lake	605-256-3596	Hawkins	615-272-7241	Armstrong	806-226-3021
Lawrence	605-642-2941	Haywood	901-772-2861	Atascosa	512-769-3066
Lincoln	605-987-2756	Henderson	901-968-2751	Austin	713-865-2301
Lyman	605-869-2226	Henry	901-642-2941	Bailey	806-272-4559
McCook	605-425-2242	Hickman	615-729-2404	Bandera	512-796-3840
McPherson	605-439-3331	Houston	615-289-3242	Bastrop	512-321-2184
Marshall	605-448-5171	Humphreys	615-296-2543	Baylor	817-888-5581
Meade	605-347-2436	Jackson	615-268-9437	Bee	512-358-4717
Mellette	605-259-3385	Jefferson	615-397-2969	Bell	817-939-3521
Miner	605-772-4661	Johnson	615-727-8161	Bexar	512-220-2774
Minnehaha	605-334-7700	Knox	615-521-2340	Blanco	512-868-7256
Moody	605-997-2469	Lake	901-253-6528	Borden	915-856-4201
Pennington	605-394-2188	Lauderdale	901-635-9551	Bosque	817-435-2791
Perkins	605-244-5622	Lawrence	615-762-5506	Bowie	214-628-2571
Potter	605-765-9414	Lewis	615-796-3091	Brazoria	713-849-5711
Roberts	605-698-7627	Lincoln	615-433-1582	Brazos	713-822-7373
Sanborn	605-796-4380	Loudon	615-458-5612	Brewster-Jeff Davis	915-837-2265
Spink	605-472-2023	Macon	615-666-3341	Briscoe	806-823-2343
Standing Rock	605-845-2118	Madison	901-668-8543	Brooks	512-325-3681
Stanley	605-223-2812	Marion	615-942-2656	Brown	915-646-0386
Sully	605-258-2334	Marshall	615-359-1929	Burleson	713-567-3255
Todd	605-856-4468	Maury	615-388-9557	Burnet	512-756-4641
Tripp	605-842-2858	McMinn	615-745-2852	Caldwell	512-398-3122
Turner	605-297-3112	McNairy	901-645-3598	Calhoun	512-552-9747
Union	605-356-2321	Meigs	615-334-5781	Callahan	915-854-1518
Walworth	605-649-7607	Monroe	615-442-2433	Cameron	512-399-2448
Yankton	605-665-3387	Montgomery	615-647-6514	Carson	806-537-3882
Ziebach	605-365-5161	Moore	615-759-7163	Camp	214-856-5005
		Morgan	615-346-3000	Cass	214-756-5391
		Obion	901-885-3742	Castro	806-647-4115
TENNESSEE		Overton	615-823-2735	Chambers	713-267-3185
Anderson	615-457-5400	Perry	615-589-2331	Cherokee	214-683-4613
Bedford	615-684-5971	Pickett	615-864-3310	Childress	817-937-2351
Benton	901-584-4601	Polk	615-338-2841	Clay	817-538-5042
Bledsoe	615-447-2451	Putnam	615-526-4561	Cochran	806-266-5215
Blount	615-982-6430	Rhea	615-775-9222	Coke	915-453-2461
Bradley	615-476-4552	Roane	615-376-5558	Coleman	915-625-4519
Campbell	615-562-9474	Robertson	615-384-7936	Collin	214-542-4413
Cannon	615-563-2554	Rutherford	615-893-5010	Collingsworth	806-447-2313
Carroll	901-986-3062	Scott	615-663-2003	Colorado	713-732-2082
Carter	615-542-2641	Sequatchie	615-949-2611	Comal	512-625-9178
Cheatham	615-792-4420	Sevier	615-453-3695	Comanche	915-356-2424
Chester	901-989-2461	Shelby	901-521-2946	Concho	915-732-4351
Claiborne	615-626-3742	Smith	615-735-2900	Cooke	817-665-4931
Clay	615-243-2311	Stewart	615-232-5682	Coryell	817-865-2414
Cocke	615-623-7531	Sullivan	615-323-7173	Cottle	806-492-3151
Coffee	615-728-2612	Sumner	615-452-1423	Crane	915-558-3522

Crockett	915-392-2721
Crosby	806-675-2003
Culberson	915-283-2057
Dallam	806-249-4434
Dallas	214-749-8401
Dawson	806-872-3444
Deaf Smith	806-364-3573
Delta	214-395-4417
Denton	817-566-3607
Dewitt	512-275-5132
Dickens	806-623-5243
Dimmit	512-876-2133
Donley	806-874-2141
Duval and Jim Hogg	512-256-3651
Eastland	817-629-1093
Ector	915-332-3321
Edwards	512-683-4310
El Paso	915-543-7419
Ellis	214-937-4461
Erath	817-965-3510
Falls	817-883-5311
Fannin	214-583-2929
Fayette	713-968-5831
Fisher	915-776-2171
Floyd	806-983-2806
Foard	817-684-1919
Fort Bend	713-342-3034
Franklin	214-537-4017
Freestone	214-389-3436
Frio	512-334-2372
Gaines	915-758-2241
Galveston	713-534-3413
Garza	806-495-2050
Gillespie	512-997-3452
Glasscock	915-354-2381
Goliad	512-645-3353
Gonzales	512-672-3149
Grayson	214-892-6541
Gray	806-669-7429
Gregg	214-758-6181
Grimes	713-825-3495
Guadalupe	512-379-1972
Hale	806-293-8481
Hall	806-259-3015
Hansford	806-659-2030
Hardeman	817-663-2312
Hardin	713-246-3484
Hamilton	817-386-3919
Harris	713-221-5020
Harrison	214-935-5278
Hartley	806-235-3122
Haskell	817-864-2658
Hays	512-392-4525
Hamphill	806-323-6891
Henderson	214-675-9161
Hill	817-582-5222
Hidalgo	512-383-2751
Hockley	806-894-3159
Hood	817-573-2438
Hopkins	214-885-3443
Houston	713-544-2358
Howard	915-267-6671
Hudspeth	915-369-2291
Hunt	214-455-4203
Hutchinson	806-878-2884
Irion	915-835-2711

Jack	817-567-2132	Polk	713-327-8811	Zapata	512-765-4663	Brunswick	804-848-2151
Jackson	512-782-3312	Potter	806-372-3829	Zavala	512-374-2883	Buchanan	703-935-2567
Jasper	713-384-3721	Presidio	915-729-3261			Buckingham	804-969-4241
Jeff Davis	See Brewster	Rains	214-473-2412			Campbell	804-332-5161
Jefferson	713-835-8461	Randall	806-655-3371	**UTAH**		Caroline	804-633-6550
Jim Hogg-Duval	512-527-4748	Reagan	915-884-2335	Beaver	801-438-2252	Carroll	703-728-7611
Jim Wells	512-664-3461	Real	512-232-6673	Box Elder	801-734-2031	Charles City	804-829-2401
Johnson	817-645-6695	Red River	214-427-2493	Cache	801-752-6263	Charlotte	804-542-5884
Jones	915-823-3801	Reeves-Loving	915-445-2438	Carbon	801-637-4700	Charlottesville, City of	
Karnes	512-780-3380	Refugio	512-526-2825	Davis	801-451-3402		804-296-7104
Kaufman	214-932-2217	Roberts	806-868-3191	Duchesne	801-722-2296	Chesapeake, City of	
Kendall	512-249-2661	Robertson	713-828-4270	Emery	801-748-2381		804-547-6348
Kenedy	See Kleberg	Rockwall	214-722-5747	Garfield	801-676-2201	Chesterfield	804-271-8989
Kent	806-237-3751	Runnels	915-365-2219	Grand	801-259-7213	Clarke	703-955-1131
Kerr	512-257-6568	Rusk	214-657-9546	Iron	801-586-8132	Craig	703-864-5812
Kimble	915-446-2620	Sabine	713-787-3752	Juab	801-623-1791	Culpeper	703-825-2233
King	806-596-4451	San Augustine	713-275-3644	Kane	801-644-2460	Cumberland	804-492-4390
Kinney	512-563-2442	San Jacinto	713-653-2396	Millard	801-743-5412	Danville, City of	
Kleberg-Kenedy	512-592-3316	San Patricio-Aransas		Morgan	801-829-3472		804-799-6558
Knox	817-454-2651		512-364-2334	Piute	801-577-2901	Dickenson	703-926-4605
Lamb	806-385-4004	San Saba	915-372-5416	Rich	801-793-2435	Dinwiddie	804-469-3713
Lampasas	512-556-3191	Schleicher	915-853-2610	Salt Lake	801-533-7757	Essex	804-443-3551
La Salle	512-879-2213	Scurry	915-573-5423	San Juan	801-587-2234	Fairfax	703-691-3350
Lavaca	512-798-2221	Shackelford	915-762-2233	Sanpete	801-835-2151	Fauquier	703-347-8650
Lee	713-542-2753	Shelby	713-598-3223	Sevier	801-896-4609	Floyd	703-745-4135
Leon	214-536-2531	Sherman	806-396-2081	Summit	801-336-5921	Fluvanna	804-589-8122
Liberty	713-336-6532	Smith	214-595-4861	Tooele	801-882-5550	Franklin	703-483-5161
Limestone	817-729-5314	Somervell	817-897-2289	Uintah	801-789-1542	Franklin, City of	
Limpscomb	806-862-4601	Starr	512-487-2306	Utah	801-377-2797		804-562-4111
Live Oak	512-449-1014	Stephens	817-559-2313	Wasatch	801-654-3211	Frederick	703-662-8745
Loving	See Reeves	Sterling	915-378-3181	Washington	801-673-9647	Giles	703-921-3455
Lamar	214-785-4513	Stonewall	817-989-3510	Wayne	801-836-2662	Gloucester	804-693-2602
Llano	915-247-5159	Sutton	915-387-3604	Weber	801-399-5501	Goochland	804-556-3361
Lubbock	806-741-8084	Swisher	806-995-3726			Grayson	703-773-2491
Lynn	806-998-4650	Tarrant	817-334-1293			Greene	804-985-2510
Madison	713-348-2234	Taylor	915-677-1711	**VERMONT**		Greensville	804-634-6563
Marion	214-665-2421	Terrell	915-345-2291	Addison	802-388-4969	Halifax	804-476-2147
Martin	915-756-3316	Terry	806-637-4060	Bennington	802-447-7582	Hampton	804-772-3791
Mason	915-347-6459	Throckmorton	817-849-3321	Caledonia	802-748-8177	Hampton, City of	
Matagorda	713-245-8415	Titus	214-572-5201	Chittenden	802-656-4420		804-727-6403
Maverick	512-773-3450	Tom Green	915-653-2385	Essex	802-676-3900	Hanover	804-798-6081
Medina	512-426-2233	Travis	512-478-5608	Franklin	802-524-6501	Henrico	804-747-4637
Menard	915-396-4787	Trinity	713-642-1421	Lamoille	802-888-4972	Henry	703-638-5311
McCulloch	915-597-2371	Tyler	713-283-2482	Orange	802-685-4540	Highland	703-468-2225
McLennan	817-756-7171	Upshur	214-843-2511	Orleans	802-334-7325	Holiday Lake	804-248-5444
McMullen	512-274-3323	Upton	915-693-2313	Rutland	802-773-3349	Isle of Wight	804-357-4391
Midland	915-682-9481	Uvalde	512-278-3114	Washington	802-223-2380	James City	804-564-3379
Milam	817-697-3382	Val Verde	512-774-3621	Windham	802-257-7967	Jamestown	804-229-2571
Mills	915-648-2650	Van Zandt	214-567-4149	Windsor	802-457-2664	King George	703-775-3062
Mitchell	915-728-3111	Victoria	512-575-4581			King & Queen	804-785-2962
Montague	817-894-2833	Walker	713-295-5481			King William	804-769-2884
Montgomery	713-756-0571	Waller	713-826-3357	**VIRGINIA**		Lancaster	804-462-5780
Moore	806-935-2594	Ward	915-943-4112	Abingdon	703-628-6033	Lee	703-346-1522
Morris	214-645-3531	Washington	713-836-6128	Accomack	804-787-1361	Loudon	703-777-0373
Motley	806-347-2733	Webb	512-723-8412	Albemarle	804-296-2191	Louisa	703-967-1222
Nacagdoches	713-564-0427	Wharton	713-532-3371	Alexandria, City of		Lunenburg	804-676-2497
Newton	713-379-4831	Wheeler	806-826-5243		703-750-6393	Lynchburg, City of	
Navarro	214-874-4778	Wichita	817-766-0131	Alleghany	703-962-0276		804-847-9096
Nolan	915-235-3184	Wilbarger	817-552-2841	Amelia	804-561-2481	Madison	703-948-6881
Nueces	512-387-2051	Willacy	512-689-2031	Amherst	804-946-5445	Mathews	804-725-7196
Ochiltree	806-435-4501	Williamson	512-863-2318	Appomattox	804-352-8244	Mecklenburg	804-738-6133
Oldham	806-267-2692	Wilson	512-393-2850	Arlington	703-558-2475	Middlesex	804-758-4355
Orange	713-883-7740	Winkler	915-586-2593	Augusta	703-885-8931	Montgomery	703-382-4919
Palo Pinto	817-659-3651	Wise	817-627-3341	Bath	703-839-2661	Nelson	804-263-4035
Parker	817-594-6143	Wood	214-763-2924	Bedford	703-586-1053	New Kent	804-730-9550
Parmer	806-481-3619	Yoakum	806-456-2263	Bland	703-688-3542	Newport News, City of	
Pecos	915-336-2541	Young	817-549-0737	Botetourt	703-473-8260		804-595-7206

APPENDIX

COUNTY EXTENSION AGENTS

County	Phone
Norfolk, City of	804-441-5147
Northhampton	804-678-5134
Northern Virginia 4-H Ctr	703-636-1777
Northumberland	804-580-5694
Nottoway	804-645-9315
Orange	703-672-1361
Page	703-743-5794
Patrick	703-694-3341
Petersburg, City of	804-732-2775
Pittsylvania	804-432-2041
Powhatan	804-598-4271
Prince Edward	804-392-4246
Prince George	804-733-4189
Prince William	703-368-8989
Pulaski	703-980-8888
Radford	703-639-9313
Rappahannock	703-675-3619
Richmond	804-333-3420
Richmond, City of	804-786-4150
Richmond-NE	804-257-0027
Roanoke	703-387-6113
Roanoke, City of	703-982-7915
Rockbridge	703-463-4734
Rockingham	703-434-4455
Russell	703-889-1198
Scott	703-386-7574
Shenandoah	703-459-3739
Smyth	703-783-5175
Southampton	804-653-2572
Southeast 4-H Educ Ctr	804-242-6195
Southwest Virginia 4-H Educ Ctr	703-628-7231
Spotsylvania	703-582-6361
Stafford	703-899-4020
Suffolk, City of	804-539-2381
Surry	804-294-3650
Sussex	804-246-5511
Tazewell	703-988-2588
Virginia Beach, City of	804-427-4769
Warren	703-635-4549
Washington	703-628-2161
West Central 4-H Educ Ctr	703-721-2759
Westmoreland	804-493-8911
Windsor	804-242-6195
Wise	703-328-3699
Wythe	703-228-2148
York	804-898-0050

WASHINGTON

County	Phone
Adams	509-659-0090
Asotin	509-243-4118
Benton	509-786-1912
Chelan	509-663-1121
Clallam	206-452-7831
Clark	206-699-2385
Columbia	509-382-4741
Cowlitz	206-577-3014
Douglas	509-745-3001
Ferry	509-775-3161
Franklin	509-545-3511
Garfield	509-843-3701
Grant	509-754-2011
Grays Harbor	206-249-4332
Island	206-678-5111
Jefferson	206-385-3581
King	206-344-2686
Kitsap	206-876-7157
Kittitas	509-925-3157
Klickitat	509-773-5817
Lewis	206-748-9121
Lincoln	509-725-4171
Mason	206-426-4732
Okanogan	509-422-3670
Pacific	206-875-6541
Pend Oreille	509-447-3325
Pierce	206-593-4190
San Juan	206-378-4414
Skagit	206-336-9322
Skamania	509-427-5141
Snohomish	206-259-9422
Spokane	509-456-3651
Stevens	509-684-2588
Thurston	206-753-8056
Wahkiakum	206-795-3278
Walla Walla	509-525-7930
Whatcom	206-676-6736
Whitman	509-397-3401
Yakima	509-575-4218

WEST VIRGINIA

County	Phone
Barbour	304-457-3254
Berkeley	304-263-4901
Boone	304-369-3925
Braxton	304-765-2881
Brooke	304-737-3666
Cabell	304-522-8301
Calhoun	304-354-6332
Clay	304-587-4267
Doddridge	304-873-1801
Fayette	304-574-1200
Gilmer	304-462-7061
Grant	304-257-4688
Greenbrier	304-645-1525
Hampshire	304-822-5013
Hancock	304-564-3311
Hardy	304-538-2373
Harrison	304-624-7431
Jackson	304-372-2011
Jefferson	304-725-9766
Kanawha	304-348-7176
Lewis	304-269-4660
Lincoln	304-824-7472
Logan	304-752-2000
McDowell	304-585-7237
Marion	304-366-3331
Marshall	304-843-1170
Mason	304-675-3710
Mercer	304-487-1439
Mineral	304-788-3621
Mingo	304-235-2175
Monongalia	304-296-6621
Monroe	304-772-3003
Morgan	304-258-1431
Nicholas	304-872-3630
Ohio	304-234-3673
Pendleton	304-358-2286
Pleasants	304-684-3119
Pocahontas	304-799-4852
Preston	304-329-1391
Putnam	304-586-2321
Raleigh	304-255-1401
Randolph	304-636-2455
Ritchie	304-643-2162
Roane	304-927-1930
Summers	304-466-3711
Taylor	304-265-3303
Tucker	304-478-2949
Tyler	304-758-2101
Upshur	304-472-2660
Wayne	304-272-5101
Webster	304-847-2727
Wetzel	304-455-1601
Wirt	304-275-3101
Wood	304-422-6461
Wyoming	304-732-6711

WISCONSIN

County	Phone
Adams	608-339-7811
Ashland	715-682-8137
Barron	715-537-3124
Bayfield	715-373-2221
Brown	414-497-3216
Buffalo	608-685-4560
Burnett	715-866-4201
Calumet	414-849-2361
Chippewa	715-723-9195
Clark	715-743-3118
Columbia	608-742-2191
Crawford	608-326-6431
Dane	608-266-4271
Dodge	414-386-4411
Door	414-743-5511
Douglas	715-394-0363
Dunn	715-232-1636
Eau Claire	715-839-4712
Florence	715-528-4480
Fond Du Lac-UW Ctr	414-921-5600
Forest	715-478-2212
Grant	608-723-2125
Green	608-325-5181
Green Lake	414-294-6573
Iowa	608-935-3354
Iron	715-561-2695
Jackson	715-284-7441
Jefferson	414-674-2500
Juneau	608-843-1341
Kenosha	414-656-6793
Kewaunee	414-388-2542
LaCrosse	608-785-9593
Lafayette	608-776-4494
Langlade	715-623-4156
Lincoln	715-536-7151
Manitowoc	414-682-8877
Marathon	715-842-0471
Marinette	715-735-3371
Marquette	414-297-2141
Menominee	715-799-3641
Milwaukee	414-257-5351
Monroe	608-269-6718
Oconto	414-834-5322
Oneida	715-362-6314
Outagamie	414-735-5119
Ozaukee	414-284-9411
Pepin	715-672-5214
Pierce	715-273-4376
Polk	715-485-3136
Portage	715-346-3573
Price	715-339-2555
Racine	414-886-2744
Richland	608-647-6148
Rock	608-755-2196
Rusk	715-532-5539
St. Croix	715-684-3301
Sauk	608-356-5581
Sawyer	715-634-4839
Shawano	715-526-6136
Sheboygan	414-459-3141
Taylor	715-748-3327
Trempealeau	715-538-2311
Vernon	608-637-2165
Vilas	715-479-4797
Walworth	414-723-3838
Washburn	715-635-3192
Washington	414-338-4479
Waukesha	414-544-8080
Waupaca	715-258-7681
Waushara	414-787-4631
Winnebago	414-424-0050
Wood	715-423-3000

WYOMING

County	Phone
Albany	307-742-3749
Big Horn	307-568-2281
Campbell	307-682-7282
Carbon	307-324-4751
Converse	307-358-2417
Crook	307-283-1192
Fremont	307-332-5673
Goshen	307-532-2436
Hot Springs	307-864-3421
Johnson	307-684-7522
Laramie	307-634-4415
Lincoln	307-886-3132
Natrona	307-234-8811
Niobrara	307-334-3534
Park	307-587-2204
Platte	307-322-3667
Sheridan	307-672-2733
Sublette	307-367-4380
Sweetwater	307-362-3461
Teton	307-733-3087
Uinta	307-789-3277
Washakie	307-347-3431
Weston	307-746-4550

Reprinted from the *County Agents Directory* with permission from Century Communications Inc.